SOCIAL SECURITY LEGISLATION 2024/25

VOLUME III: ADMINISTRATION, ADJUDICATION AND THE EUROPEAN DIMENSION

SOCIAL SECURITY LEGISLATION 2024/25

General Editor
Nick Wikeley, M.A. (Cantab)

VOLUME III: ADMINISTRATION, ADJUDICATION AND THE EUROPEAN DIMENSION

Commentary by

Will Rolt, LL.B.
Judge of the First-tier Tribunal

Christopher Ward, M.A. (Cantab)
Judge of the Upper Tribunal

Consultant Editor
Child Poverty Action Group

Sweet & Maxwell

Published in 2024 by
Thomson Reuters, Sweet & Maxwell.
Thomson Reuters is registered in England & Wales,
Company No. 1679046.
Registered office and address for service:
5 Canada Square, Canary Wharf, London E14 5AQ.

For further information on our products and services,
visit *www.sweetandmaxwell.co.uk*

Typeset by Cheshire Typesetting Ltd, Cuddington, Cheshire
Printed and bound by CPI Group (UK) Ltd, Croydon, CR0 4YY

A CIP catalogue record for this book is available from the British Library

ISBN (print): 978-0-414-12153-9
ISBN (e-book): 978-0-414-12157-7
ISBN (print and e-book): 978-0-414-12155-3

CHILD POVERTY ACTION GROUP

The Child Poverty Action Group (CPAG) is a charity, founded in 1965, which campaigns for the relief of poverty in the United Kingdom. It has a particular reputation in the field of welfare benefits law derived from its legal work, publications, training and parliamentary and policy work, and is widely recognised as the leading organisation for taking test cases on social security law.

CPAG is therefore ideally placed to act as Consultant Editor to this 5-volume work—**Social Security Legislation**. CPAG is not responsible for the detail of what is contained in each volume, and the authors' views are not necessarily those of CPAG. The Consultant Editor's role is to act in an advisory capacity on the overall structure, focus and direction of the work.

For more information about CPAG, its rights and policy publications or training courses, its address is 30 Micawber Street, London, N1 7TB (telephone: 020 7837 7979—website: *http://www.cpag.org.uk*).

FOREWORD

These volumes of *Social Security Legislation* are an indispensable resource for the judiciary of the First-tier Tribunal (Social Entitlement Chamber) and all those involved in social security proceedings. Along with expert commentaries, they provide comprehensive, up-to-date and learned coverage of this vast and complex field of law. Given the scale and complexity of the legislation and the continuing development of the jurisprudence by the Upper Tribunal and appellate courts, the subject matter would be practically inaccessible without these books. As ever, I am grateful to the authors and to Sweet and Maxwell for their continued commitment to producing them each year.

Judge Kate Markus KC
Chamber President of the First-tier Tribunal,
Social Entitlement Chamber

PREFACE

Administration, Adjudication and the European Dimension is Volume III of Social Security Legislation 2024/25. The companion volumes are Volume I: *Non-Means Tested Benefits*; Volume II: *Universal Credit, State Pension Credit and the Social Fund*; Volume IV: *HMRC-administered Social Security Benefits and Scotland.*

Volume V: *Income Support and the Legacy Benefits* was last published in 2021/22 and readers needing to refer to legislation concerning those benefits and to the commentary upon it should keep a copy of that edition, to which there is an up-dating supplement within Volume II of this year's edition.

Also, readers who need to refer to European Union legislation as it was before the United Kingdom's withdrawal and to the commentary upon it (which continues to have relevance under some parts of the post-Brexit law), should continue to retain the 2020/21 edition of this volume and read it with the up-to-date material within Part V of this edition.

Each of the volumes in the series provides the text of legislation clearly showing the form and date of amendments, and is up to date to April 10, 2024 although the commentary in this volume includes references to some later case law.

The 2023/24 main edition of Vol.III was the last for which Mark Rowland had a direct responsibility, although much of what he has written will undoubtedly continue to feature in the book for many editions to come. All of the current editors of the series would like to take this opportunity to pay tribute to Mark's tremendous contribution to the series since 1993, when he first produced the volume on Medical and Disability Appeal Tribunals that went into three editions before the restructuring of the series in 2000. In that restructuring, he took on joint responsibility with Robin White for Vol.III, Administration, Adjudication and the European Dimension. Thus, for more than 20 years Mark has brought his formidable knowledge and experience of social security law and adjudication, from his work as an advocate, as a part-time chair of appeal tribunals and then as a Social Security Commissioner and later Upper Tribunal Judge to bear on the often opaque legislative material on administration, decision-making and appeals. As readers will know, his gift for clarity of exposition enabled his commentary both to bring out matters of principle and to provide practical guidance to tribunals and users with an appreciation of the way problems actually arise. More behind the scenes, Mark's contribution to the way in which the series as a whole has developed, from wise advice about the needs of readers to knowledge of why choices were or were not made over the years, cannot be overstated. The current editors will greatly miss having that wisdom and experience on tap.

This year, as did the last few, has seen a variety of legislative changes, most—perhaps with the exception of the Retained EU Law (Revocation and Reform) Act 2023—making relatively minor amendments, although some of them affect a lot of people, and also a large variety of judicial decisions on both substantive issues and procedural ones. These are all reflected in the up-dated legislative text and commentary.

The decision has been taken to drop information-sharing from this year's volume, as it is an area which rarely seems to arise in tribunals and to do it justice requires expanding into areas of law far removed from social security.

Revising and updating the legislative text and commentary has, as always, required considerable flexibility on the part of the publisher and a great deal of help from colleagues and a number of other sources, including CPAG as advisory editor to the series. We remain grateful for this assistance in our task of providing an authoritative reflection on the current state of the law.

Users of the series and its predecessor works have over the years contributed to their effectiveness by providing valuable comments on our commentary, as well as pointing out where the text of some provision has been omitted in error, become garbled, or not been brought fully up to date. In some cases, this has drawn attention to an error which might otherwise have gone unnoticed. In providing such feedback, users of the work have helped to shape the content and ensure the accuracy of our material, and for that we continue to be grateful. We hope that users will continue to provide such helpful input and feedback. Please write to, or email, the General Editor of the series: Emeritus Professor Nick Wikeley, c/o School of Law, University of Southampton, Highfield, Southampton SO17 1BJ, (njw@soton.ac.uk); and he will pass on any comments received to the appropriate commentator. We are also grateful to the Chamber President of the Social Entitlement Chamber of the First-tier Tribunal and her colleagues there for continuing to follow the now long tradition of help and encouragement in our endeavours.

July 2024

Christopher Ward
Will Rolt

CONTENTS

PART I
SOCIAL SECURITY STATUTES

PART II
SOCIAL SECURITY REGULATIONS

SECTION A — DWP-ADMINISTERED BENEFITS

Section B — HMRC-Administered Benefits

PART III
TRIBUNALS

Paras

PART IV
HUMAN RIGHTS LAW

PART V
THE EUROPEAN DIMENSION

USING THIS BOOK: AN INTRODUCTION TO LEGISLATION AND CASE LAW

Introduction

This book is not a general introduction to, or general textbook on, the law relating to social security but it is nonetheless concerned with both of the principal sources of social security law—*legislation* (both primary and secondary) and *case law*. It sets out the text of the most important legislation, as currently in force, and then there is added commentary that refers to the relevant case law. Lawyers will be familiar with this style of publication, which inevitably follows the structure of the legislation.

This note is designed primarily to assist readers who are not lawyers to find their way around the legislation and to understand the references to case law, but information it contains about how to find social security case law is intended to be of assistance to lawyers too.

Primary legislation

Primary legislation of the United Kingdom Parliament consists of *Acts of Parliament* (also known as *Statutes*). They will have been introduced to Parliament as *Bills*. There are opportunities for Members of Parliament and peers to debate individual clauses and to vote on amendments before a Bill is passed and becomes an Act (at which point the clauses become sections). No tribunal or court has the power to disapply, or hold to be invalid, an Act of Parliament, although, until December 31, 2020, that could be done if it was inconsistent with European Union law.

An Act is known by its "short title", which incorporates the year in which it was passed (e.g. the Social Security Contributions and Benefits Act 1992), and is given a chapter number (abbreviated as, for instance, "c.4" indicating that the Act was the fourth passed in that year). It is seldom necessary to refer to the chapter number but it appears in the running headers in this book.

Each *section* (abbreviated as "s." or, in the plural, "ss.") of an Act is numbered and may be divided into *subsections* (abbreviated as "subs." and represented by a number in brackets), which in turn may be divided into *paragraphs* (abbreviated as "para." and represented by a lower case letter in brackets) and *subparagraphs* (abbreviated as "subpara." and represented by a small roman numeral in brackets). Subparagraph (ii) of para.(a) of subs.(1) of s.72 will usually be referred to simply as "s.72(1)(a)(ii)". Upper case letters may be used where additional sections or subsections are inserted by amendment and additional lower case letters may be used where new paragraphs and subparagraphs are inserted. This accounts for the rather ungainly s.109B(2A)(aa) of the Social Security Administration Act 1992.

Sections of a large Act may be grouped into a numbered *Part*, which may even be divided into *Chapters*. It is not usual to refer to a Part or a Chapter unless referring to the whole Part or Chapter.

Where a section would otherwise become unwieldy because it is necessary to include a list or complicated technical provisions, the section may simply refer to a *Schedule* at the end of the Act. A Schedule (abbreviated as "Sch.") may be divided into paragraphs and subparagraphs and further divided into heads and subheads. Again, it is usual to refer simply to, say, "para.23(3)(b)(ii) of Sch.3". Whereas it is conventional to speak of a section *of* an Act, it is usual to speak of a Schedule *to* an Act.

Secondary legislation

Secondary legislation (also known as *subordinate legislation* or *delegated legislation*) is made by *statutory instrument* in the form of a set of *Regulations* or a set of *Rules* or an *Order*. The power to make such legislation is conferred on ministers and other persons or bodies by Acts of Parliament. To the extent that a statutory instrument is made beyond the powers (in Latin, *ultra vires*) conferred by primary legislation, it may be held by a tribunal or court to be invalid and ineffective. Secondary legislation must be laid before Parliament. However, most secondary legislation is not debated in Parliament and, even when it is, it cannot be amended although an entire statutory instrument may be rejected.

A set of Regulations or Rules or an Order has a name indicating its scope and the year it was made and also a number, as in the Social Security (Disability Living Allowance) Regulations 1991 (SI 1991/2890) (the 2890th statutory instrument issued in 1991). Because there are over a thousand statutory instruments each year, the number of a particular statutory instrument is important as a means of identification and it should usually be cited the first time reference is made to that statutory instrument.

Sets of Regulations or Rules are made up of individual *regulations* (abbreviated as "reg.") or *rules* (abbreviated as "r." or, in the plural, "rr."). An Order is made up of *articles* (abbreviated as "art."). Regulations, rules and articles may be divided into paragraphs, subparagraphs and heads. As in Acts, a set of Regulations or Rules or an Order may have one or more Schedules attached to it. The style of numbering used in statutory instruments is the same as in sections of, and Schedules to, Acts of Parliament. As in Acts, a large statutory instrument may have regulations or rules grouped into Parts and, occasionally, Chapters. Statutory instruments may be amended in the same sort of way as Acts.

Scottish legislation

Most of the social security legislation passed by the United Kingdom Parliament applies throughout Great Britain, i.e. in England, Wales and Scotland, but a separate Scottish social security system is gradually being developed and relevant legislation is included in Volume IV in this series. Acts of the Scottish Parliament are similar to Acts of the United Kingdom Parliament and Scottish Statutory Instruments are also similar to their United Kingdom counterparts. One minor difference is that "schedule" usually has a lower case "s" and references are to a schedule *of* an Act, rather than *to* an Act.

Northern Ireland legislation

Most of the legislation set out in this series applies only in Great Britain, social security not generally being an excepted or reserved matter in relation to Northern Ireland. However, Northern Irish legislation—both primary legislation, most relevantly in the form of *Orders in Council* (which, although statutory instruments, had the effect of primary legislation in Northern Ireland while there was direct rule from Westminster and still do when made under the Northern Ireland (Welfare Reform) Act 2015) and *Acts of the Northern Ireland Assembly*, and subordinate legislation, in the form of *statutory rules*—largely replicates legislation in Great Britain so that much of the commentary in this book will be applicable to equivalent provisions in Northern Ireland legislation. Although there has latterly been a greater reluctance in Northern Ireland to maintain parity with Great Britain, one example of which led to some delay in enacting legislation equivalent to the Welfare Reform Act 2012, this is usually resolved politically by, for instance, the allocation of funds to allow the effects of some of the changes to be mitigated in Northern Ireland while the broad legislative structure remains similar.

European Union legislation

European Union primary legislation is in the form of the *Treaties* agreed by the Member States. Relevant subordinate legislation is in the form of *Regulations*, adopted to give effect to the provisions of the Treaties, and *Directives*, addressed to Member States and requiring them to incorporate certain provisions into their domestic laws. Directives are relevant because, where a person brings proceedings against an organ of the State, as is invariably the case where social security is concerned, that person may rely on the Directive as having direct effect if the Member State has failed to comply with it. Treaties, Regulations and Directives are divided into *Articles* (abbreviated as "Art.").

While the United Kingdom was a Member State of the European Union, United Kingdom legislation that was inconsistent with European Union legislation had to be disapplied. The United Kingdom ceased to be a Member State on January 31, 2020, but the effect of the European Union (Withdrawal Act) 2018, as amended in 2020, is that, with very limited exceptions, European Union law continued to apply in the United Kingdom during the implementation period ending on December 31, 2020. After that date, European Union law remains relevant only to the extent that United Kingdom legislation so provides. For instance, the 2018 Act, as amended, provides for the enforcement of the Withdrawal Agreement, under which rights acquired by individuals before the end of the implementation period may be retained.

Finding legislation in this book

If you know the name of the piece of legislation for which you are looking, use the list of contents at the beginning of each volume of this series which lists the pieces of legislation contained in the volume. That will give you the paragraph reference to enable you to find the beginning of the piece of legislation. Then, it is easy to find the relevant section, regulation, rule, article or Schedule by using the running headers on the right-hand pages. If you do not know the name of the piece of legislation, you will probably need to use the index at the end of the volume in order to find the relevant paragraph number but will then be taken straight to a particular provision.

The legislation is set out as amended, the amendments being indicated by numbered sets of square brackets. The numbers refer to the numbered entries under the heading "AMENDMENTS" at the end of the relevant section, regulation, rule, article or Schedule, which identify the amending statute or statutory instrument. Where an Act has been consolidated, there is a list of "DERIVATIONS" identifying the provisions of earlier legislation from which the section or Schedule has been derived.

As regards the European Union, United Kingdom legislation concerned with the consequences of the United Kingdom's withdrawal is set out in Part V of this volume, together with relevant extracts from the Withdrawal Agreement and the Social Security Protocol to the Trade and Cooperation Agreement. Following the extracts from the Withdrawal Agreement is up-dating commentary on the European Union legislation that is set out in Part III of the 2020-21 edition of this volume. Readers are encouraged to retain that volume so as to be able to find the main text of relevant European Union legislation there.

Finding other legislation

United Kingdom legislation and legislation made by the legislatures in Scotland, Wales and Northern Ireland may now be found on *http://www.legislation.gov.uk* in both its original form and (usually) its amended form. Northern Ireland social security legislation may also be found at *https://www.communities-ni.gov.uk/services/law-relating-social-security-northern-ireland-blue-volumes*. European Union legislation may be found at *https://eur-lex.europa.eu/homepage.html.*

Interpreting legislation

Legislation is written in English (or, at least, there is an official English version) and generally means what it says. However, languages being complicated, more than one interpretation is often possible. Most legislation itself contains definitions. Sometimes these are in the particular provision in which a word occurs but, where a word is used in more than one place, any definition will appear with others. In an Act, an interpretation section is usually to be found towards the end of the Act or of the relevant Part of the Act. In a statutory instrument, an interpretation provision usually appears near the beginning of the statutory instrument or the relevant Part of it. In the more important pieces of legislation in this series, there is included after every section, regulation, rule, article or Schedule a list of "DEFINITIONS", showing where definitions of words used in the provision are to be found.

However, not all words are statutorily defined and there is in any event more to interpreting legislation than merely defining its terms (see the note to s.3(1) of the Tribunals, Courts and Enforcement Act 2007 in Part III of this volume). Decision-makers and tribunals need to know how to apply the law in different types of situations. That is where case law comes in.

Case law and the commentary in this book

In deciding individual cases, courts and tribunals interpret the relevant law and incidentally establish legal principles. Decisions on questions of legal principle of the superior courts and appellate tribunals are said to be binding on decision-makers and the First-tier Tribunal, which means that decision-makers and the First-tier Tribunal must apply those principles. Thus the judicial decisions of the superior courts and appellate tribunals form part of the law. The commentary to the legislation in this series, under the heading "GENERAL NOTE" after a section, regulation, rule, article or Schedule, refers to this *case law*.

Most case law regarding social security benefits is in the form of decisions of the Upper Tribunal (Administrative Appeals Chamber), to which the functions of the former Social Security Commissioners and Child Support Commissioners in Great Britain were transferred on November 3, 2008. However, decisions of those Commissioners remain relevant, as are decisions of the Commissioners who still sit in Northern Ireland.

The commentary in this series is not itself binding on any decision-maker or tribunal because it is merely the opinion of the author. It is what is actually said in the legislation or in the judicial decision that is important. The legislation is set out in this series, but it will generally be necessary to look elsewhere for the precise words used in judicial decisions. The way that decisions are cited in the commentary enables that to be done.

The reporting of decisions of the Upper Tribunal and Commissioners

A few of the most important decisions of the Administrative Appeals Chamber of the Upper Tribunal are selected to be "reported" each year in the Administrative Appeals Chamber Reports (AACR), using the same criteria as were formerly used for reporting Commissioners' decisions in Great Britain. The selection is made by an editorial board of judges and decisions are selected for reporting only if they are of general importance and command the assent of at least a majority of the relevant judges. The term "reported" simply means that they are published in printed form as well as on the Internet (see *Finding case law*, below) with headnotes (i.e. summaries) and indexes, but reported decisions also have a greater precedential status than ordinary decisions (see *Judicial precedent* below).

A handful of Northern Ireland Commissioners' decisions are also selected for reporting in the Administrative Appeals Chamber Reports each year, the selection being made by the Chief Social Security Commissioner in Northern Ireland.

Citing case law

As has been mentioned, much social security case law is still to be found in decisions of Social Security Commissioners and Child Support Commissioners, even though the Commissioners have now effectively been abolished in Great Britain.

Reported decisions of Commissioners were known merely by a number or, more accurately, a series of letters and numbers beginning with an "R". The type of benefit in issue was indicated by letters in brackets (e.g. "IS" was income support, "P" was retirement pension, and so on) and the year in which the decision was selected for reporting or, from 2000, the year in which it was published as a reported decision, was indicated by the last two digits, as in *R(IS) 2/08*. In Northern Ireland there was a similar system until 2009, save that the type of benefit was identified by letters in brackets after the number, as in *R 1/07 (DLA)*.

Unreported decisions of the Commissioners in Great Britain were known simply by their file numbers, which began with a "C", as in *CIS/2287/2008*. The letters following the "C" indicated the type of benefit in issue in the case. Scottish and, at one time, Welsh cases were indicated by a "S" or "W" immediately after the "C", as in *CSIS/467/2007*. The last four digits indicated the calendar year in which the case was registered, rather than the year it was decided. A similar system operated in Northern Ireland until 2009, save that the letters indicating the type of benefit appeared in brackets after the numbers and, from April 1999, the financial year rather than the calendar year was identified, as in *C 10/06-07 (IS)*.

Decisions of the Upper Tribunal, of courts and, since 2010, of the Northern Ireland Commissioners are generally known by the names of the parties (or just two of them in multi-party cases). In social security and some other types of cases, individuals are anonymised through the use of initials in the names of decisions of the Upper Tribunal and the Northern Ireland Commissioners. Anonymity is much rarer in the names of decisions of courts. In this series, the names of official bodies are also abbreviated in the names of decisions of the Upper Tribunal and the Northern Ireland Commissioners (e.g. "SSWP" for the Secretary of State for Work and Pensions, "HMRC" for Her/His Majesty's Revenue and Customs, "CMEC" for the Child Maintenance and Enforcement Commission, "DSD" for the Department for Social Development in Northern Ireland and "DC" for the Department for Communities in Northern Ireland). Since 2010, such decisions have also been given a "flag" in brackets to indicate the subject matter of the decision, which in social security cases indicates the principal benefit in issue in the case. Thus, the name of one universal credit case is *SSWP v AJ (UC)*.

Any decision of the Upper Tribunal, of a court since 2001 or of a Northern Ireland Commissioner since 2010 that has been intended for publication has also given a neutral citation number which enables the decision to be more precisely identified. This indicates, in square brackets, the year the decision was made (although in relation to decisions of the courts it sometimes merely indicates the year the number was issued) and also indicates the court or tribunal that made the decision (e.g. "UKUT" for the Upper Tribunal (which sits in Great Britain for social security purposes but throughout the United Kingdom for some others), "UT" for the separate Upper Tribunal for Scotland, "NICom" for a Northern Ireland Commissioner, "EWCA Civ" for the Civil Division of the Court of Appeal in England and Wales, "NICA" for the Court of Appeal in Northern Ireland, "CSIH" for the Inner House of the Court of Session (in Scotland), "UKSC" for the Supreme Court and so on). A number is added so that the reference is unique and finally, in the case of the Upper Tribunal or the High Court in England and Wales, the relevant chamber of the Upper Tribunal or the relevant division or other part of the High Court is identified (e.g. "(AAC)" for the Administrative Appeals Chamber, "(Admin)" for the Administrative Court and so on). Examples of decisions of the Upper Tribunal and a Northern Ireland Commissioner with their neutral citation numbers are *SSWP v AJ (UC)* [2020] UKUT 48 (AAC) and *AR v DSD (IB)* [2010] NICom 6.

If the case is reported in the Administrative Appeals Chamber Reports or another series of law reports, a reference to the report usually follows the neutral citation number. Conventionally, this includes either the year the case was decided (in round brackets) or the year in which it was reported (in square brackets), followed by the volume number (if any), the name of the series of reports (in abbreviated form, so see the Table of Abbreviations at the beginning of each volume of this series) and either the page number or the case number. However, before 2010, cases reported in the Administrative Appeals Chamber Reports or with Commissioners' decisions were numbered in the same way as reported Commissioners' decisions. *Abdirahman v Secretary of State for Work and Pensions* [2007] EWCA Civ 657; [2008] 1 W.L.R. 254 (also reported as *R(IS) 8/07*) is a Court of Appeal decision, decided in 2007 but reported in 2008 in volume 1 of the Weekly Law Reports at page 254 and also in the 2007 volume of reported Commissioners' decisions. *NT v SSWP* [2009] UKUT 37 (AAC); *R(DLA) 1/09* is an Upper Tribunal case decided in 2009 and reported in the Administrative Appeals Chamber Reports in the same year. *Martin v Secretary of State for Work and Pensions* [2009] EWCA Civ 1289; [2010] AACR 9 is a decision of the Court of Appeal that was decided in 2009 and was the ninth decision reported in the Administrative Appeals Chamber Reports in 2010.

It is usually necessary to include the neutral citation number or a reference to a series of reports only the first time a decision is cited in any document. After that, the name of the case is usually sufficient.

All decisions of the Upper Tribunal that are on their website have neutral citation numbers. If you wish to refer a tribunal or decision-maker to a decision of the Upper Tribunal that does not have a neutral citation number, contact the office of the Administrative Appeals Chamber (*adminappeals@justice.gov.uk*) who will provide a number and add the decision to the website.

Decision-makers and claimants are entitled to assume that judges of both the First-tier Tribunal and the Upper Tribunal have immediate access to reported decisions of Commissioners or the Upper Tribunal and they need not provide copies, although it may sometimes be helpful to do so. However, where either a decision-maker or a claimant intends to rely on an unreported decision, it will be necessary to provide a copy of the decision to the judge and other members of the tribunal. A copy of the decision should also be provided to the other party before the hearing because otherwise it may be necessary for there to be an adjournment to enable that party to take advice on the significance of the decision.

Finding case law

The extensive references described above are used so as to enable people easily to find the full text of a decision. Most decisions of any significance since the late 1990s can be found on the Internet.

Decisions of the Upper Tribunal may be found at *https://www.gov.uk/administrative-appeals-tribunal-decisions*. The link from that page to "decisions made in 2015 or earlier" leads also to decisions of the Commissioners in Great Britain. This includes reported decisions since 1991 and other decisions considered likely to be of interest to tribunals and tribunal users since about 2000, together with a few older decisions. Decisions of Commissioners in Northern Ireland may be found on *https://iaccess.communities-ni.gov.uk/NIDOC*.

The Administrative Appeals Chamber Reports are also published by the Stationery Office in bound volumes which follow on from the bound volumes of Commissioners' decisions published from 1948.

Copies of decisions of the Administrative Appeals Chamber of the Upper Tribunal or of Commissioners that are otherwise unavailable may be obtained from the offices of the Upper Tribunal (Administrative Appeals Chamber) or, in Northern Ireland, from the Office of the Social Security and Child Support Commissioners.

Decisions of a wide variety of courts and tribunals in the United Kingdom may be found on the free website of the British and Irish Legal Information Institute, *http://www.bailii.org*. It includes all decisions of the Supreme Court and provides fairly comprehensive coverage of decisions given since about 1996 by the House of Lords and Privy Council and most of the higher courts in England and Wales, decisions given since 1998 by the Court of Session and decisions given since 2000 by the Court of Appeal and High Court in Northern Ireland. Some earlier decisions have been included, so it is always worth looking and, indeed, those decisions dating from 1873 or earlier and reported in the English Reports may be found through a link to *http://www.commonlii.org/uk/cases/EngR/*. Since 2022, decisions of the Upper Tribunal, the Employment Appeal Tribunal and most courts that sit in England and Wales are also to be found on The National Archives' website at *https://caselaw.nationalarchives.gov.uk/structured_search*. However, courts and tribunals that sit only in Wales, Scotland or Northern Ireland are not included there. Decisions of the Upper Tribunal for Scotland and of Scottish courts can be found at *https://www.scotcourts.gov.uk*.

Decisions of the Court of Justice of the European Union are all to be found at *https://curia.europa.eu*.

Decisions of the European Court of Human Rights are available at *https://www.echr.coe.int*.

Most decisions of the courts in social security cases, including decisions of the Court of Justice of the European Union on cases referred by United Kingdom courts and tribunals, are reported in the Administrative Appeals Chamber Reports or with the reported decisions of Commissioners and may therefore be found on the same websites and in the same printed series of reported decisions. So, for example, *R(I)1/00* contains Commissioner's decision *CSI/12/1998*, the decision of the Court of Session upholding the Commissioner's decision and the decision of the House of Lords in *Chief Adjudication Officer v Faulds*, reversing the decision of the Court of Session. The most important decisions of the courts can also be found in the various series of law reports familiar to lawyers (in particular, in the *Law Reports*, the *Weekly Law Reports*, the *All England Law Reports*, the *Public and Third Sector Law Reports*, the *Industrial Cases Reports* and the *Family Law Reports*) but these are not widely available outside academic or other law libraries, or subscription-based websites. See the Table of Cases at the beginning of each volume of this series for all the places where a decision mentioned in that volume is reported.

If you know the name or number of a decision and wish to know where in a volume of this series there is a reference to it, use the Table of Cases or the Table of Commissioners' Decisions 1948–2009 in the relevant volume to find the paragraph(s) where the decision is mentioned.

Judicial precedent

As already mentioned, decisions of the Upper Tribunal, the Commissioners and the higher courts in Great Britain become case law because they set binding precedents which must be followed by decision-makers and the First-tier Tribunal in Great Britain. This means that, where the Upper

Tribunal, Commissioner or court has decided a point of legal principle, decision-makers and appeal tribunals must make their decisions in conformity with the decision of the Upper Tribunal, Commissioner or court, applying the same principle and accepting the interpretation of the law contained in the decision. So a decision of the Upper Tribunal, a Commissioner or a superior court explaining what a term in a particular regulation means, lays down the definition of that term in much the same way as if the term had been defined in the regulations themselves. The decision may also help in deciding what the same term means when it is used in a different set of regulations, provided that the term appears to have been used in a similar context.

Only decisions on points of law set precedents that are binding and, strictly speaking, only decisions on points of law that were necessary to the overall conclusion reached by the Upper Tribunal, Commissioner or court are binding. Other parts of a decision (which used to be known as obiter dicta) may be regarded as helpful guidance but need not be followed if a decision-maker or the First-tier Tribunal is persuaded that there is a better approach. It is particularly important to bear this in mind in relation to older decisions of Social Security Commissioners because, until 1987, most rights of appeal to a Commissioner were not confined to points of law.

Where there is a conflict between precedents, a decision-maker or the First-tier Tribunal is generally free to choose between decisions of equal status. For these purposes, most decisions of the Upper Tribunal and decisions of Commissioners are of equal status. However, a decision-maker or First-tier Tribunal should generally prefer a reported decision to an unreported one unless the unreported decision was the later decision and the Commissioner or Upper Tribunal expressly decided not to follow the earlier reported decision. This is simply because the fact that a decision has been reported shows that at least half of the relevant judges of the Upper Tribunal or the Commissioners agreed with it at the time. A decision of a Tribunal of Commissioners (i.e. three Commissioners sitting together) or a decision of a three-judge panel of the Upper Tribunal must be preferred to a decision of a single Commissioner or a single judge of the Upper Tribunal.

A single judge of the Upper Tribunal will normally follow a decision of a single Commissioner or another judge of the Upper Tribunal, but is not bound to do so. A three-judge panel of the Upper Tribunal will generally follow a decision of another such panel or of a Tribunal of Commissioners, but similarly is not bound to do so, whereas a single judge of the Upper Tribunal will always follow such a decision.

Strictly speaking, the Northern Ireland Commissioners do not set binding precedent that must be followed in Great Britain but their decisions are relevant, due to the similarity of the legislation in Northern Ireland, and are usually regarded as highly persuasive with the result that, in practice, they are generally given as much weight as decisions of the Great Britain Commissioners. The same approach is taken in Northern Ireland to decisions of the Upper Tribunal on social security matters and to decisions of the Great Britain Commissioners. Similarly, the Upper Tribunal and the Upper Tribunal for Scotland are likely to find each other's decisions persuasive where the issues are the same, or similar.

Decisions of the superior courts in Great Britain and Northern Ireland on questions of legal principle are almost invariably followed by decision-makers, tribunals and the Upper Tribunal, even when they are not strictly binding because the relevant court was in a different part of the United Kingdom or exercised a parallel – but not superior – jurisdiction.

Decisions of the Court of Justice of the European Union come in two parts: the Opinion of the Advocate General and the decision of the Court. It is the decision of the Court which is binding. The Court is assisted by hearing the Opinion of the Advocate General before itself coming to a conclusion on the issue before it. The Court does not always follow its Advocate General. Where it does, the Opinion of the Advocate General often elaborates the arguments in greater detail than the single collegiate judgment of the Court. Within the European Union, courts and tribunals must apply decisions of the Court of Justice of the European Union, where relevant to cases before them, in preference to other authorities binding on them. This is no longer so in the United Kingdom, but it will still be necessary for courts and tribunals in the United Kingdom to take account of such decisions when issues of European Union law are relevant, and they are arguably bound by a decision of the Court of Justice on the interpretation of the Citizens' Rights provisions of the Withdrawal Agreement.

The European Court of Human Rights in Strasbourg is quite separate from the Court of Justice of the European Union in Luxembourg and serves a different purpose: interpreting and applying the European Convention on Human Rights, which is incorporated into United Kingdom law by the Human Rights Act 1998. Since October 2, 2000, public authorities in the United Kingdom, including courts, Commissioners, tribunals and decision-makers have been required to act in accordance with the incorporated provisions of the Convention, unless statute prevents this. They must take into account the Strasbourg case law and are required to interpret domestic legislation, so far as it is possible to do so, to give effect to the incorporated Convention rights. Any court or tribunal may declare secondary legislation incompatible with those rights and, in certain circumstances, invalidate it. Only the higher courts can declare a provision of primary legislation to be incompatible with those rights, but no court, tribunal or Upper Tribunal can invalidate primary legislation. The work of the Strasbourg Court and the impact of the Human Rights Act 1998 on social security are discussed in the commentary in Part IV of this volume of this series.

See the note to s.3(2) of the Tribunals, Courts and Enforcement Act 2007 in Part III of this volume for a more detailed and technical consideration of the rules of precedent.

Other sources of information and commentary on social security law

For a comprehensive overview of the social security system in Great Britain, CPAG's *Welfare Benefits and Tax Credits Handbook*, published annually each spring, is unrivalled as a practical introduction from the claimant's viewpoint.

From a different perspective, the Department for Work and Pensions publishes the 14-volume *Decision Makers' Guide* and the newer *Advice for Decision Making*, which covers personal independence payment, universal credit and the "new" versions of Jobseeker's Allowance and Employment and Support Allowance (search for the relevant guide by name at *https://www.gov.uk* under the topic "Welfare"). Similarly, His Majesty's Revenue and Customs publish manuals relating to tax credits, child benefit and guardian's allowance, which they administer, see *https://www.gov.uk/government/collections/hmrc-manuals*. (Note that the *Child Benefit Technical Manual* also covers guardian's allowance.) These guides and manuals are extremely useful but their interpretation of the law is not binding on tribunals and the courts, being merely internal guidance for the use of decision-makers.

There are a number of other sources of valuable information or commentary on social security case law: see in particular publications such as the *Journal of Social Security Law*, CPAG's *Welfare Rights Bulletin*, *Legal Action* and the *Adviser*. As far as online resources go there is little to beat *Rightsnet* (*https://www.rightsnet.org.uk*). This site contains a wealth of resources for people working in the welfare benefits field but of special relevance in this context are Commissioners'/Upper Tribunal Decisions section of the "Toolkit" area and also the "Briefcase" area which contains summaries of the decisions (with links to the full decisions). Sweet and Maxwell's online subscription service *Westlaw* is another valuable source (*https://legalsolutions.thomsonreuters.co.uk/en/products-services/westlaw-uk.html*), as is LexisNexis *Lexis* (*https://www.lexisnexis.co.uk*).

Conclusion

The internet provides a vast resource but a search needs to be focused. Social security schemes are essentially statutory and so in Great Britain the legislation which is set out in this series forms the basic structure of social security law. However, the case law shows how the legislation should be interpreted and applied. The commentary in this series should point the way to the case law relevant to each provision and the Internet can then be used to find it where that is necessary.

CHANGE OF NAME FROM DEPARTMENT OF SOCIAL SECURITY TO DEPARTMENT FOR WORK AND PENSIONS

The Secretaries of State for Education and Skills and for Work and Pensions Order 2002 (SI 2002/1397) makes provision for the change of name from the Department of Social Security to Department for Work and Pensions. Article 9(5) provides:

"(5) Subject to article 12 [which makes specific amendments], any enactment or instrument passed or made before the coming into force of this Order shall have effect, so far as may be necessary for the purposes of or in consequence of the entrusting to the Secretary of State for Work and Pensions of the social security functions, as if any reference to the Secretary of State for Social Security, to the Department of Social Security or to an officer of the Secretary of State for Social Security (including any reference which is to be construed as such as reference) were a reference to the Secretary of State for Work and Pensions, to the Department for Work and Pensions or, as the case may be, to an officer of the Secretary of State for Work and Pensions."

CHANGES IN TERMINOLOGY CONSEQUENT UPON THE ENTRY INTO FORCE OF THE TREATY OF LISBON

The Treaty of Lisbon (Changes in Terminology) Order 2011 (SI 2011/1043) (which came into force on April 22, 2011) makes a number of changes to terminology used in primary and secondary legislation as a consequence of the entry into force of the Treaty of Lisbon on December 1, 2009. The Order accomplishes this by requiring certain terms in primary and secondary legislation to be read in accordance with the requirements of the Order. No substantive changes to the law are involved.

The changes are somewhat complex because of the different ways in which the term "Community" is used, and the abbreviations "EC" or "EEC" are used. References to the "European Community", "European Communities", "European Coal and Steel Communities", "the Community", "the EC", and "the EEC" are generally to be read as references to the "European Union".

The following table shows the more common usages involving the word "Community" in the first column which are now to be read in the form set out in the second column:

Original term	**To be read as**
Community treaties	EU treaties
Community institution	EU institution
Community instrument	EU instrument
Community obligation	EU obligation
Enforceable Community right	Enforceable EU right
Community law, or European Community law	EU law
Community legislation, or European Community legislation	EU legislation
Community provision, or European Community provision	EU provision

Provision is also made for changes to certain legislation relating to Wales in the Welsh language.

THE MARRIAGE (SAME SEX COUPLES) ACT 2013

The Marriage (Same Sex Couples) Act 2013 (c.30) provides in s.3 and Schs 3 and 4 that the terms "marriage", "married couple" and being "married" in existing and future legislation in England and Wales are to be read as references to a marriage between persons of the same sex. The same approach is taken to any legislation about couples living together as if married. This is subject to certain specified exclusions contained in Sch.4 and in any Order providing for a contrary approach to be taken.

Schedule 2 to The Marriage (Same Sex Couples) Act 2013 (Consequential and Contrary provisions and Scotland) Order 2014 (SI 2014/560) contains a substantial list of contrary provisions to s.11(1) and (2) and paras 1 to 3 of Sch.3 to the 2013 Act. Most of these relate to specific enactments, but note that Pt 2 of the Schedule provides that s.11(1) and (2) do not apply to "EU instruments". This term is defined in Sch.1 to the European Communities Act 1972 (as amended) as "any instrument issued by an EU institution". It refers mainly to Regulations, Directives, Decisions, recommendations and opinions issued by the institutions.

TABLE OF CASES

TABLE OF SOCIAL SECURITY COMMISSIONERS' DECISIONS 1948–2009

Northern Ireland Commissioners' Decisions from 2010 and all Upper Tribunal decisions will be found in the Table of Cases above.

TABLE OF ABBREVIATIONS USED IN THIS SERIES

1975 Act	Social Security Act 1975
1977 Act	Marriage (Scotland) Act 1977
1979 Act	Pneumoconiosis (Workers' Compensation) Act 1979
1986 Act	Social Security Act 1986
1996 Act	Employment Rights Act 1996
1998 Act	Social Security Act 1998
2002 Act	Tax Credits Act 2002
2004 Act	Gender Recognition Act 2004
2006 Act	Armed Forces Act 2006
2008 Act	Child Maintenance and Other Payments Act 2008
2013 Act	Marriage (Same Sex Couples) Act 2013
2014 Act	Marriage and Civil Partnership (Scotland) Act 2014
A1P1	Art.1 of Protocol 1 to the European Convention on Human Rights
AA	Attendance Allowance
AA 1992	Attendance Allowance Act 1992
AAC	Administrative Appeals Chamber
AACR	Administrative Appeals Chamber Reports
A.C.	Law Reports, Appeal Cases
A.C.D.	Administrative Court Digest
Admin	Administrative Court
Admin L.R.	Administrative Law Reports
Administration Act	Social Security Administration Act 1992
Administration Regulations	Statutory Paternity Pay and Statutory Adoption Pay (Administration) Regulations 2002
AIP	assessed income period
All E.R.	All England Reports
All E.R. (E.C.)	All England Reports (European Cases)
AMA	Adjudicating Medical Authorities
AO	Adjudication Officer
AOG	Adjudication Officers Guide
art.	article
Art.	Article
ASD	Autistic Spectrum Disorder
ASPP	Additional Statutory Paternity Pay
ASVG	Allgemeines Sozialversicherungsgesetz (General Social Security Act)

A.T.C.	Annotated Tax Cases
Attendance Allowance Regulations	Social Security (Attendance Allowance) Regulations 1991
AWT	All Work Test
BA	Benefits Agency
Benefits Act	Social Security Contributions and Benefits Act 1992
B.H.R.C.	Butterworths Human Rights Cases
B.L.G.R.	Butterworths Local Government Reports
Blue Books	The Law Relating to Social Security, Vols 1–11
B.P.I.R.	Bankruptcy and Personal Insolvency Reports
BSVG	Bauern-Sozialversicherungsgesetz (Social Security Act for Farmers)
B.T.C.	British Tax Cases
BTEC	Business and Technology Education Council
B.V.C.	British Value Added Tax Reporter
B.W.C.C.	Butterworths Workmen's Compensation Cases
c.	chapter
C	Commissioner's decision
C&BA 1992	Social Security Contributions and Benefits Act 1992
CAA 2001	Capital Allowances Act 2001
CAB	Citizens Advice Bureau
CAO	Chief Adjudication Officer
CB	Child Benefit
CBA 1975	Child Benefit Act 1975
CBJSA	Contribution-Based Jobseeker's Allowance
C.C.L. Rep.	Community Care Law Reports
CCM	HMRC New Tax Credits Claimant Compliance Manual
C.E.C.	European Community Cases
CERA	cortical evoked response audiogram
CESA	Contribution-based Employment and Support Allowance
CFS	chronic fatigue syndrome
Ch.	Chancery Division Law Reports; Chapter
Citizenship Directive	Directive 2004/38/EC of the European Parliament and of the Council of April 29, 2004
CJEC	Court of Justice of the European Communities
CJEU	Court of Justice of the European Union
Claims and Payments Regulations	Social Security (Claims and Payments) Regulations 1987
Claims and Payments Regulations 1979	Social Security (Claims and Payments) Regulations 1979
Claims and Payments Regulations 2013	Universal Credit, Personal Independence Payment, Jobseeker's Allowance and Employment and Support Allowance (Claims and Payments) Regulations 2013

CM	Case Manager
CMA	Chief Medical Adviser
CMEC	Child Maintenance and Enforcement Commission
C.M.L.R.	Common Market Law Reports
C.O.D.	Crown Office Digest
COLL	Collective Investment Schemes Sourcebook
Community, The	European Community
Computation of Earnings Regulations	Social Security Benefit (Computation of Earnings) Regulations 1978
Computation of Earnings Regulations 1996	Social Security Benefit (Computation of Earnings) Regulations 1996
Consequential Provisions Act	Social Security (Consequential Provisions) Act 1992
Contributions and Benefits Act	Social Security Contributions and Benefits Act 1992
Contributions Regulations	Social Security (Contributions) Regulations 2001
COPD	chronic obstructive pulmonary disease
CP	Carer Premium; Chamber President
CPAG	Child Poverty Action Group
CPR	Civil Procedure Rules
Cr. App. R.	Criminal Appeal Reports
CRCA 2005	Commissioners for Revenue and Customs Act 2005
Credits Regulations 1974	Social Security (Credits) Regulations 1974
Credits Regulations 1975	Social Security (Credits) Regulations 1975
Crim. L.R.	Criminal Law Review
CRU	Compensation Recovery Unit
CSA 1995	Children (Scotland) Act 1995
CSIH	Inner House of the Court of Session (Scotland)
CSM	Child Support Maintenance
CS(NI)O 1995	Child Support (Northern Ireland) Order 1995
CSOH	Outer House of the Court of Session (Scotland)
CSPSSA 2000	Child Support, Pensions and Social Security Act 2000
CTA	Common Travel Area
CTA 2009	Corporation Tax Act 2009
CTA 2010	Corporation Tax Act 2010
CTB	Council Tax Benefit
CTC	Child Tax Credit
CTC Regulations	Child Tax Credit Regulations 2002
CTF	child trust fund
CTS	Carpal Tunnel Syndrome
DAC	Directive 2011/16/ EU (Directive on administrative co-operation in the field of taxation)
DAT	Disability Appeal Tribunal

dB	decibels
DCA	Department for Constitutional Affairs
DCP	Disabled Child Premium
Decisions and Appeals Regulations 1999	Social Security Contributions (Decisions and Appeals) Regulations 1999
Dependency Regulations	Social Security Benefit (Dependency) Regulations 1977
DfEE	Department for Education and Employment
DHSS	Department of Health and Social Security
Disability Living Allowance Regulations	Social Security (Disability Living Allowance) Regulations
DIY	do it yourself
DLA	Disability Living Allowance
DLA Regs 1991	Social Security (Disability Living Allowance) Regulations 1991
DLAAB	Disability Living Allowance Advisory Board
DLADWAA 1991	Disability Living Allowance and Disability Working Allowance Act 1991
DM	Decision Maker
DMA	Decision-making and Appeals
DMG	Decision Makers' Guide
DMP	Delegated Medical Practitioner
DP	Disability Premium
DPP	Director of Public Prosecutions
DPT	diffuse pleural thickening
DPTC	Disabled Person's Tax Credit
DRO	Debt Relief Order
DSD	Department for Social Development (Northern Ireland)
DSM IV; DSM-5	Diagnostic and Statistical Manual of Mental Disorders of the American Psychiatric Association
DSS	Department of Social Security
DTI	Department of Trade and Industry
DWA	Disability Working Allowance
DWP	Department for Work and Pensions
DWPMS	Department for Work and Pensions Medical Service
EAA	Extrinsic Allergic Alveolitis
EAT	Employment Appeal Tribunal
EC	European Community
ECHR	European Convention on Human Rights
ECJ	European Court of Justice
E.C.R.	European Court Reports
ECSC	European Coal and Steel Community
ECSMA	European Convention on Social and Medical Assistance
EEA	European Economic Area

EEC	European Economic Community
EESSI	Electronic Exchange of Social Security Information
E.G.	Estates Gazette
E.G.L.R.	Estates Gazette Law Reports
EHC plan	education, health and care plan
EHIC	European Health Insurance Card
EHRC	European Human Rights Commission
E.H.R.R.	European Human Rights Reports
EL	employers' liability
E.L.R	Education Law Reports
EMA	Education Maintenance Allowance
EMP	Examining Medical Practitioner
Employment and Support Allowance Regulations	Employment and Support Allowance Regulations 2008
EPS	extended period of sickness
Eq. L.R.	Equality Law Reports
ERA	evoked response audiometry
ERA scheme	Employment, Retention and Advancement scheme
ES	Employment Service
ESA	Employment and Support Allowance
ESA Regs 2013	Employment and Support Allowance Regulations 2013
ESA Regulations	Employment and Support Allowance Regulations 2008
ESA WCAt	Employment and Support Allowance Work Capability Assessment
ESC	employer supported childcare
ESE Scheme	Employment, Skills and Enterprise Scheme
ESE Regulations	Jobseeker's Allowance (Employment, Skills and Enterprise Scheme) Regulations 2011
ESES Regulations	Jobseeker's Allowance (Employment, Skills and Enterprise Scheme) Regulations 2011
ETA 1973	Employment and Training Act 1973
ETA(NI) 1950	Employment and Training Act (Northern Ireland) 1950
ETS	European Treaty Series
EU	European Union
Eu.L.R.	European Law Reports
EWCA Civ	Civil Division of the Court of Appeal (England and Wales)
EWHC Admin	Administrative Court Division of the High Court (England and Wales)
FA 1993	Finance Act 1993
FA 1996	Finance Act 1996
FA 2004	Finance Act 2004

Fam. Law	Family Law
FAS	Financial Assistance Scheme
FCDO	Foreign, Commonwealth and Development Office
F.C.R.	Family Court Reporter
FEV	forced expiratory volume
FIS	Family Income Supplement
FISMA 2000	Financial Services and Markets Act 2000
F.L.R.	Family Law Reports
FME	further medical evidence
F(No.2)A 2005	Finance (No.2) Act 2005
FOTRA	Free of Tax to Residents Abroad
FRAA	flat rate accrual amount
FRS Act 2004	Fire and Rescue Services Act 2004
FSCS	Financial Services Compensation Scheme
FTT	First-tier Tribunal
General Benefit Regulations 1982	Social Security (General Benefit) Regulations 1982
General Regulations	Statutory Shared Parental Pay (General) Regulations 2014
GMC	Group Medical Coverage
GMCA	Greater Manchester Combined Authority
GMFRA	Greater Manchester Fire and Rescue Authority
GMP	Guaranteed Minimum Pension
GMWDA	Greater Manchester Waste Disposal Authority
GNVQ	General National Vocational Qualification
GP	General Practitioner
GRA	Gender Recognition Act 2004
GRB	Graduated Retirement Benefit
GRP	Graduated Retirement Pension
GSVG	Gewerbliches Sozialversicherungsgesetz (Federal Act on Social Insurance for Persons engaged in Trade and Commerce)
HB	Housing Benefit
HB (WSP) R (NI) 2017	Housing Benefit (Welfare Social Payment) Regulations (Northern Ireland) 2017
HBRB	Housing Benefit Review Board
HCA	Homes and Communities Agency
HCD	House of Commons Debates
HCP	healthcare professional
HCV	Hepatitis C virus
Health Service Act	National Health Service Act 2006
Health Service (Wales) Act	National Health Service (Wales) Act 2006
HIV	Human Immunodeficiency Virus
HL	House of Lords
H.L.R.	Housing Law Reports

HMIT	His Majesty's Inspector of Taxes
HMRC	His Majesty's Revenue and Customs
HMSO	His Majesty's Stationery Office
Hospital In-Patients Regulations 1975	Social Security (Hospital In-Patients) Regulations 1975
HP	Health Professional
HPP	Higher Pensioner Premium
HRA 1998	Human Rights Act 1998
H.R.L.R.	Human Rights Law Reports
HRP	Home Responsibilities Protection
HSE	Health and Safety Executive
IAC	Immigration and Asylum Chamber
IAP	Intensive Activity Period
IB	Incapacity Benefit
IB PCA	Incapacity Benefit Personal Capability Assessment
IB Regs	Social Security (Incapacity Benefit) Regulations 1994
IB Regulations	Social Security (Incapacity Benefit) Regulations 1994
IB/IS/SDA	Incapacity Benefits Regime
IBJSA	Income-Based Jobseeker's Allowance
IBS	Irritable Bowel Syndrome
ICA	Invalid Care Allowance
I.C.R.	Industrial Cases Reports
ICTA 1988	Income and Corporation Taxes Act 1988
IFW Regulations	Incapacity for Work (General) Regulations 1995
IH	Inner House of the Court of Session
I.I.	Industrial Injuries
IIAC	Industrial Injuries Advisory Council
IIDB	Industrial Injuries Disablement Benefit
ILO	International Labour Organization
Imm. A.R.	Immigration Appeal Reports
Incapacity for Work Regulations	Social Security (Incapacity for Work) (General) Regulations 1995
Income Support General Regulations	Income Support (General) Regulations 1987
IND	Immigration and Nationality Directorate of the Home Office
I.N.L.R.	Immigration and Nationality Law Reports
I.O.	Insurance Officer
IPPR	Institute of Public Policy Research
IRESA	Income-Related Employment and Support Allowance
I.R.L.R.	Industrial Relations Law Reports
IS	Income Support
IS Regs	Income Support Regulations

IS Regulations	Income Support (General) Regulations 1987
ISA	Individual Savings Account
ISBN	International Standard Book Number
ITA 2007	Income Tax Act 2007
ITEPA 2003	Income Tax, Earnings and Pensions Act 2003
I.T.L. Rep.	International Tax Law Reports
I.T.R.	Industrial Tribunals Reports
ITS	Independent Tribunal Service
ITTOIA 2005	Income Tax (Trading and Other Income) Act 2005
IVB	Invalidity Benefit
IW (General) Regs	Social Security (Incapacity for Work) (General) Regulations 1995
IW (Transitional) Regs	Incapacity for Work (Transitional) Regulations
Jobseeker's Allowance Regulations	Jobseeker's Allowance Regulations 1996
Jobseeker's Regulations 1996	Jobseeker's Allowance Regulations 1996
JSA	Jobseeker's Allowance
JSA 1995	Jobseekers Act 1995
JSA (NI) Regulations	Jobseeker's Allowance (Northern Ireland) Regulations 1996
JSA (Transitional) Regulations	Jobseeker's Allowance (Transitional) Regulations 1996
JSA Regs 1996	Jobseeker's Allowance Regulations 1996
JSA Regs 2013	Jobseeker's Allowance Regulations 2013
JS(NI)O 1995	Jobseekers (Northern Ireland) Order 1995
J.S.S.L.	Journal of Social Security Law
J.S.W.L.	Journal of Social Welfare Law
K.B.	Law Reports, King's Bench
L.& T.R.	Landlord and Tenant Reports
LCW	limited capability for work
LCWA	Limited Capability for Work Assessment
LCWRA	limited capability for work-related activity
LDEDC Act 2009	Local Democracy, Economic Development and Construction Act 2009
LEA	local education authority
LEL	Lower Earnings Limit
LET	low earnings threshold
L.G. Rev.	Local Government Review
L.G.L.R.	Local Government Reports
L.J.R.	Law Journal Reports
LRP	liable relative payment
L.S.G.	Law Society Gazette
Luxembourg Court	Court of Justice of the European Union (also referred to as CJEC and ECJ)
MA	Maternity Allowance
MAF	Medical Assessment Framework

Maternity Allowance Regulations	Social Security (Maternity Allowance) Regulations 1987
MDC	Mayoral development corporation
ME	myalgic encephalomyelitis
Medical Evidence Regulations	Social Security (Medical Evidence) Regulations 1976
MEN	Mandatory Employment Notification
Mesher and Wood	Income Support, the Social Fund and Family Credit: the Legislation (1996)
M.H.L.R.	Mental Health Law Reports
MHP	mental health problems
MIF	minimum income floor
MIG	minimum income guarantee
Migration Regulations	Employment and Support Allowance (Transitional Provisions, Housing Benefit and Council Tax Benefit (Existing Awards) (No.2) Regulations 2010
MP	Member of Parliament
MRSA	methicillin-resistant Staphylococcus aureus
MS	Medical Services
MWA Regulations	Jobseeker's Allowance (Mandatory Work Activity Scheme) Regulations 2011
MWAS Regulations	Jobseeker's Allowance (Mandatory Work Activity Scheme) Regulations 2011
NCB	National Coal Board
NDPD	Notes on the Diagnosis of Prescribed Diseases
NHS	National Health Service
NI	National Insurance
N.I..	Northern Ireland Law Reports
NICA	Northern Ireland Court of Appeal
NICom	Northern Ireland Commissioner
NICs	National Insurance Contributions
NINO	National Insurance Number
NIRS 2	National Insurance Recording System
N.L.J.	New Law Journal
NMC	Nursing and Midwifery Council
Northern Ireland Contributions and	Social Security Contributions and Benefits
Benefits Act	(Northern Ireland) Act 1992
N.P.C.	New Property Cases
NRCGT	non-resident capital gains tax
NTC Manual	Clerical procedures manual on tax credits
NUM	National Union of Mineworkers
NUS	National Union of Students
OCD	obsessive compulsive disorder
Ogus, Barendt and Wikeley	A. Ogus, E. Barendt and N. Wikeley, The Law of Social Security (1995)

Old Cases Act	Industrial Injuries and Diseases (Old Cases) Act 1975
OPB	One Parent Benefit
O.P.L.R.	Occupational Pensions Law Reports
OPSSAT	Office of the President of Social Security Appeal Tribunals
Overlapping Benefits Regulations	Social Security (Overlapping Benefits) Regulations 1975
P	retirement pension case
P. & C.R.	Property and Compensation Reports
para.	paragraph
Pay Regulations	Statutory Paternity Pay and Statutory Adoption Pay (General) Regulations 2002; Statutory Shared Parental Pay (General) Regulations 2014
PAYE	Pay As You Earn
PC	Privy Council
PCA	Personal Capability Assessment
PCC	Police and Crime Commissioner
PD	Practice Direction; prescribed disease
Pens. L.R.	Pensions Law Reports
Pensions Act	Pension Schemes Act 1993
PEP	Personal Equity Plan
Persons Abroad Regulations	Social Security Benefit (Persons Abroad) Regulations 1975
Persons Residing Together Regulations	Social Security Benefit (Persons Residing Together) Regulations 1977
PIE	Period of Interruption of Employment
PILON	pay in lieu of notice
Pilot Scheme Regulations	Universal Credit (Work-Related Requirements) In Work Pilot Scheme and Amendment Regulations 2015
PIP	Personal Independence Payment
P.I.Q.R.	Personal Injuries and Quantum Reports
Polygamous Marriages Regulations	Social Security and Family Allowances (Polygamous Marriages) Regulations 1975
PPF	Pension Protection Fund
Prescribed Diseases Regulations	Social Security (Industrial Injuries) (Prescribed Diseases) Regulations 1985
PSCS	Pension Service Computer System
Pt	Part
PTA	pure tone audiometry
P.T.S.R.	Public and Third Sector Law Reports
PTWR 2000	Part-time Workers (Prevention of Less Favourable Treatment) Regulations 2000
PVS	private and voluntary sectors
Q.B.	Queen's Bench Law Reports
QBD	Queen's Bench Division

QCS Board	Quality Contract Scheme Board
QEF	qualifying earnings factor
QYP	qualifying young person
r.	rule
R	Reported Decision
R.C.	Rules of the Court of Session
REA	Reduced Earnings Allowance
reg.	regulation
REULRRA	Retained EU Law (Revocation and Reform) Act 2023
RIPA	Regulation of Investigatory Powers Act 2000
RMO	Responsible Medical Officer
rr.	rules
RR	reference rate
RSI	repetitive strain injury
RTI	Real Time Information
R.V.R.	Rating & Valuation Reporter
s.	section
S	Scottish Decision
SAP	Statutory Adoption Pay
SAPOE Regulations	Jobseeker's Allowance (Schemes for Assisting Persons to Obtain Employment) Regulations 2013
SAWS	Seasonal Agricultural Work Scheme
SAYE	Save As You Earn
SB	Supplementary Benefit
SBAT	Supplementary Benefit Appeal Tribunal
SBC	Supplementary Benefits Commission
S.C.	Session Cases
S.C. (H.L.)	Session Cases (House of Lords)
S.C. (P.C.)	Session Cases (Privy Council)
S.C.C.R.	Scottish Criminal Case Reports
S.C.L.R.	Scottish Civil Law Reports
Sch.	Schedule
SDA	Severe Disablement Allowance
SDP	Severe Disability Premium
SEC	Social Entitlement Chamber
SEN	special educational needs
SERPS	State Earnings Related Pension Scheme
ShPP	statutory shared parental pay
ShPP Regulations	Statutory Shared Parental Pay (General) Regulations 2014
SI	Statutory Instrument
SIP	Share Incentive Plan
S.J.	Solicitors Journal

S.J.L.B.	Solicitors Journal Law Brief
SLAN	statement like an award notice
S.L.T.	Scots Law Times
SMP	Statutory Maternity Pay
SMP (General) Regulations 1986	Statutory Maternity Pay (General) Regulations 1986
SPC	State Pension Credit
SPC Regulations	State Pension Credit Regulations 2002
SPCA 2002	State Pension Credit Act 2002
SPL Regulations	Shared Parental Leave Regulations 2014
SPP	Statutory Paternity Pay
ss.	sections
SS (No.2) A 1980	Social Security (No.2) Act 1980
SSA 1975	Social Security Act 1975
SSA 1977	Social Security Act 1977
SSA 1978	Social Security Act 1978
SSA 1979	Social Security Act 1979
SSA 1981	Social Security Act 1981
SSA 1986	Social Security Act 1986
SSA 1988	Social Security Act 1988
SSA 1989	Social Security Act 1989
SSA 1990	Social Security Act 1990
SSA 1998	Social Security Act 1998
SSAA 1992	Social Security Administration Act 1992
SSAC	Social Security Advisory Committee
SSAT	Social Security Appeal Tribunal
SSCBA 1992	Social Security Contributions and Benefits Act 1992
SSCB(NI)A 1992	Social Security Contributions and Benefits (Northern Ireland) Act 1992
SSCPA 1992	Social Security (Consequential Provisions) Act 1992
SSD	Secretary of State for Defence
SSHBA 1982	Social Security and Housing Benefits Act 1982
SSHD	Secretary of State for the Home Department
SSI	Scottish Statutory Instrument
SS(MP)A 1977	Social Security (Miscellaneous Provisions) Act 1977
SSP	Statutory Sick Pay
SSP (General) Regulations	Statutory Sick Pay (General) Regulations 1982
SSPA 1975	Social Security Pensions Act 1975
SSPP	statutory shared parental pay
SSWP	Secretary of State for Work and Pensions
State Pension Credit Regulations	State Pension Credit Regulations 2002
S.T.C.	Simon's Tax Cases

S.T.C. (S.C.D.)	Simon's Tax Cases: Special Commissioners' Decisions
S.T.I.	Simon's Tax Intelligence
STIB	Short-Term Incapacity Benefit
subpara.	subparagraph
subs.	subsection
T	Tribunal of Commissioners' Decision
T.C.	Tax Cases
TCA 1999	Tax Credits Act 1999
TCA 2002	Tax Credits Act 2002
TCC	Technology and Construction Court
TCEA 2007	Tribunals, Courts and Enforcement Act 2007
TCGA 1992	Taxation of Chargeable Gains Act 2002
TCTM	Tax Credits Technical Manual
TEC	Treaty Establishing the European Community
TENS	transcutaneous electrical nerve stimulation
TEU	Treaty on European Union
TFC	tax-free childcare
TFEU	Treaty on the Functioning of the European Union
TIOPA 2010	Taxation (International and Other Provisions) Act 2010
TMA 1970	Taxes Management Act 1970
T.R.	Taxation Reports
Transfer of Functions Act	Social Security Contributions (Transfer of Functions etc.) Act 1999
Tribunal Procedure Rules	Tribunal Procedure (First-tier Tribunal)(Social Entitlement Chamber) Rules 2008
UB	Unemployment Benefit
UC	Universal Credit
UC Regs 2013	Universal Credit Regulations 2013
UCITS	Undertakings for Collective Investments in Transferable Securities
UKAIT	UK Asylum and Immigration Tribunal
UKBA	UK Border Agency of the Home Office
UKCC	United Kingdom Central Council for Nursing, Midwifery and Health Visiting
UKFTT	United Kingdom First-tier Tribunal Tax Chamber
UKHL	United Kingdom House of Lords
U.K.H.R.R.	United Kingdom Human Rights Reports
UKSC	United Kingdom Supreme Court
UKUT	United Kingdom Upper Tribunal
UN	United Nations
Universal Credit Regulations	Universal Credit Regulations 2013
URL	uniform resource locator

USI Regs	Social Security (Unemployment, Sickness and Invalidity Benefit) Regulations 1983
USI Regulations	Social Security (Unemployment, Sickness and Invalidity Benefit) Regulations 1983
UT	Upper Tribunal
VAT	Value Added Tax
VCM	vinyl chloride monomer
Vol.	Volume
VWF	Vibration White Finger
W	Welsh Decision
WCA	Work Capability Assessment
WCAt	limited capability for work assessment
WFHRAt	Work-Focused Health-Related Assessment
WFI	work-focused interview
WFTC	Working Families Tax Credit
Wikeley, Annotations	N. Wikeley, "Annotations to Jobseekers Act 1995 (c.18)" in Current Law Statutes Annotated (1995)
Wikeley, Ogus and Barendt	Wikeley, Ogus and Barendt, The Law of Social Security (2002)
W.L.R.	Weekly Law Reports
WLUK	Westlaw UK
Workmen's Compensation Acts	Workmen's Compensation Acts 1925 to 1945
WP	Widow's Pension
WPS	War Pensions Scheme
WRA 2007	Welfare Reform Act 2007
WRA 2009	Welfare Reform Act 2009
WRA 2012	Welfare Reform Act 2012
W-RA Regulations	Employment and Support Allowance (Work-Related Activity) Regulations 2011
WRAAt	Work-Related Activity Assessment
WRPA 1999	Welfare Reform and Pensions Act 1999
WRP(NI)O 1999	Welfare Reform and Pensions (Northern Ireland) Order 1999
WRWA 2016	Welfare Reform and Work Act 2016
WSP (LCP) R (NI) 2016	Welfare Supplementary Payment (Loss of Carer Payments) Regulations (Northern Ireland) 2016
WSP (LDRP) R (NI) 2016	Welfare Supplementary Payment (Loss of Disability-Related Premiums) Regulations (Northern Ireland) 2016
WSPR (NI) 2016	Welfare Supplementary Payment Regulations (Northern Ireland) 2016
WTC	Working Tax Credit
WTC Regulations	Working Tax Credit (Entitlement and Maximum Rate) Regulations 2002

PART I

SOCIAL SECURITY STATUTES

Forfeiture Act 1982

(1982 c.34)

Arrangement of Sections

An Act to provide for relief for persons guilty of unlawful killing from forfeiture of inheritance and other rights; to enable such persons to apply for financial provision out of the deceased's estate; to provide for the question whether pension and social security benefits have been forfeited to be determined by the Social Security Commissioners; and for connected purposes.
[13th July 1982]

1.—(1) In this Act, the "forfeiture rule" means the rule of public policy which in certain circumstances precludes a person who has unlawfully killed another from acquiring a benefit in consequence of the killing. 1.2

(2) References in this Act to a person who has unlawfully killed another include a reference to a person who has unlawfully aided, abetted, counselled or procured the death of that other and references in this Act to unlawful killing shall be interpreted accordingly.

General Note

There is a general rule of English law that a person should not benefit from his or her wrongdoing. More specifically, the forfeiture rule has the effect that, generally, a person who has unlawfully killed another forfeits his or her right to any benefit that might otherwise have been acquired as a result of the death, e.g. an inheritance under a will or an indemnity under an insurance policy. In *R. v National Insurance Commissioner, Ex p. Connor* [1981] Q.B. 758 (also reported as an appendix to *R(G) 2/79*), the forfeiture rule was applied to prevent a woman convicted of the manslaughter of her husband from obtaining entitlement to widow's benefit. A Tribunal of Commissioners subsequently held that it also applied to entitlement to a Category B retirement pension based on a victim's contribution record (*R(P) 1/88*). The same rule applies in Scotland (*Burns v Secretary of State for Social Services* 1985 S.L.T. 351 (also reported as an appendix to *R(G) 1/83*)). 1.3

This Act was passed following *Connor*, the purpose being to mitigate the effect of the forfeiture rule where its operation could be harsh. Thus s.2 permits courts to modify the effect of the rule where it would otherwise prevent a person from obtaining certain interests in property and s.3 provides that the rule shall not preclude a person from applying to a court for certain types of financial provision. Section 4 deals with the rule's application to social security benefits. Section 5 provides that there may be no modification in a case of murder.

The leading modern case on the forfeiture rule is *Dunbar v Plant* [1998] Ch. 412, in which it was held that, since the coming into force of this Act, a strict approach should be taken to the question of whether death has been caused by criminal conduct and any mitigation should be achieved through a modification of the effect of the rule, so that some of the earlier cases, in which regard was had to the degree of culpability in deciding whether the rule applied at all, should no longer be followed. The rule applies where a court or the Upper Tribunal finds that a crime causing death has been committed, even if the relevant person has not been convicted of any crime or the criminal conduct was not the most immediate cause of death. Thus, in *Dunbar v Plant*, the rule was held to apply in the case of a woman who had survived a suicide pact, where she had not been prosecuted but her actions amounted to aiding and abetting suicide (which was a crime under the Suicide Act 1961 even though suicide itself is not). It follows from this strict approach that the forfeiture rule applies in any case where a person has been convicted of manslaughter, including manslaughter on the ground of diminished responsibility (*R(FP) 1/05*), and it seems likely that it would now also be found to apply in a case of causing death by dangerous, or careless or inconsiderate, driving. The rule can apply even where the person concerned has been prosecuted and acquitted of murder or manslaughter, provided that the court or Upper Tribunal is nonetheless satisfied that the offence has been committed (*Gray v Barr* [1970] 2 Q.B. 626, upheld on appeal [1971] 2 Q.B. 554), although the Upper Tribunal is unlikely to go behind an acquittal unless satisfied that there is material evidence that was not available to the criminal court (*R(G) 2/90*) and may not consider it proportionate to direct that there be further investigation if such evidence is not supplied by the Secretary of State when the reference is made (*SSWP v LK (RP)* [2019] UKUT 421 (AAC) at [46] to [48]). The rule also applies if the action bringing about the death occurred abroad, provided it would have amounted to a crime in Great Britain (*R(G) 1/88*). Subsection (2) recognises that acting as an accessory to a crime may be enough to cause the forfeiture rule to apply and, in *R(FG) 1/04*, it was held that a person convicted under s.4 of the Offences against the Person Act 1861 of soliciting to murder was likely to have "counselled . . . the death of [the victim]" for the purposes of the subsection.

The forfeiture rule does not apply where a person is of unsound mind to the extent of being incapable of committing a crime (*Re Houghton, Houghton v Houghton* [1915] 2 Ch. 173). In *Reference under the Forfeiture Act 1982 in respect of W (GRB)* [2020] UKUT 155 (AAC), it was held that the rule also does not apply where the person who did the act was subsequently found, under s.4 of the Criminal Procedure (Insanity) Act 1964, to be unfit to be tried. However, it is arguable that that is not necessarily so, since a finding under s.4 of the 1964 Act depends on the defendant's mental state at the time of the trial, rather than at the time of the commission of the act. On the other hand, it may not be proportionate to try to investigate a case in which a claimant was found unfit to be tried in order to reach a conclusion as to his or her responsibility for causing the death, given the likelihood of the claimant's mental health having been a relevant factor when the death was caused, unless there is clear evidence to the contrary.

1.4 **2.** *Omitted.*

1.5 **3.** *Omitted.*

[6Upper Tribunal] to decide whether rule applies to social security benefits

1.6 **4.**—(1) Where a question arises as to whether, if a person were otherwise entitled to or eligible for any benefit or advantage under a relevant enactment, he would be precluded by virtue of the forfeiture rule from receiving the whole or part of the benefit or advantage, that question shall (notwithstanding anything in any relevant enactment) be determined by [6the Upper Tribunal].

[1(1A) Where [6the Upper Tribunal] determines that the forfeiture rule has precluded a person (in this section referred to as "the offender") who has unlawfully killed another from receiving the whole or part of any such benefit or advantage, [6the Upper Tribunal] may make a decision under this subsection modifying the effect of that rule and may do so whether the unlawful killing occurred before or after the coming into force of this subsection.

(1B) [6The Upper Tribunal] shall not make a decision under subsection (1A) above modifying the effect of the forfeiture rule in any case unless [6it] is satisfied that having regard to the conduct of the offender and of the deceased and to such other circumstances as appear to [6the Upper Tribunal] to be material, the justice of the case requires the effect of the rule to be so modified in that case.

(1C) Subject to subsection (1D) below, a decision under subsection (1A) above may modify the effect of the forfeiture rule in either or both of the following ways—

(a) so that it applies only in respect of a specified proportion of the benefit or advantage;

(b) so that it applies in respect of the benefit or advantage only for a specified period of time.

(1D) Such a decision may not modify the effect of the forfeiture rule so as to allow any person to receive the whole or any part of a benefit or advantage in respect of any period before the commencement of this subsection.

(1E) If [6the Upper Tribunal] thinks it expedient to do so, [6the Upper Tribunal may direct that its] decision shall apply to any future claim for a benefit or advantage under a relevant enactment, on which a question such as is mentioned in subsection (1) above arises by reason of the same unlawful killing.

(1F) It is immaterial for the purposes of subsection (1E) above whether the claim is in respect of the same or a different benefit or advantage.

(1G) For the purposes of obtaining a decision whether the forfeiture rule should be modified the Secretary of State may refer to [6the Upper Tribunal] for review any determination of a question such as is mentioned in subsection (1) above that was made before the commencement of subsections (1A) to (1F) above (whether by [6the Upper Tribunal] or not) and shall do so if the offender requests him to refer such a determination.

(1H) Subsections (1A) to (1F) above shall have effect on a reference under subsection (1G) above as if in subsection (1A) the words "it has been determined" were substituted for the words "[6the Upper Tribunal] determines".]

(2) [6Tribunal Procedure Rules may make provision] for carrying this section into effect; and (without prejudice to the generality of that) the rules may, in relation to the question mentioned in subsection (1) above or any determination under that subsection [2 or any decision under subsection (1A) above]—

(a) apply any provision of any relevant enactment, with or without modifications, or exclude or contain provisions corresponding to any such provisions; [6. . .]

(b) [6. . .]

(3) [6. . .]

(4) [6. . .]

(5) In this section—

[6. . .]; and

"relevant enactment" means any provision of the following and any instrument made by virtue of such a provision:

the Personal Injuries (Emergency Provisions) Act 1939,
the Pensions (Navy, Army, Air Force and Mercantile Marine) Act 1939,
the Polish Resettlement Act 1947,
[3 . . .],
[2 the Social Security Acts 1975 to 1991],
[3 the Social Security Contributions and Benefits Act 1992],
[5 section 1 of the Armed Forces (Pensions and Compensation) Act 2004],
[4 the Pension Schemes Act 1993],
[7 Part 1 of the Pensions Act 2014],
[8 section 30 of that Act],

and any other enactment relating to pensions or social security prescribed by regulations under this section.

AMENDMENTS

1. Social Security Act 1986 s.76 (July 25, 1986).
2. Statutory Sick Pay Act 1991 s.3(1)(c) (February 12, 1991).
3. Social Security (Consequential Provisions) Act 1992 ss.3 and 4 and Sch.2 para.63.
4. Pension Schemes Act 1993 Sch.8 para.15 (February 7, 1994).
5. Armed Forces (Pensions and Compensation) Act 2004 s.7(1) (April 6, 2005).
6. Transfer of Tribunal Functions Order 2008 (SI 2008/2833) Sch.3 para.38 (November 3, 2008).
7. Pensions Act 2014 Sch.12 para.1 (April 6, 2016).
8. Pensions Act 2014 Sch.16 para.1 (April 6, 2017).

DEFINITIONS

"forfeiture rule"—see s.1(1).
"offender"—see subs.(1A).
"relevant enactment—see subs.(5).

GENERAL NOTE

Subsection (1)

1.7 Until November 3, 2008, the powers provided for in this section were exercised by Social Security Commissioners.

Whenever a claimant's entitlement to a social security benefit under a "relevant enactment" (see subs.(5)) arises at least partly in consequence of the death of someone the claimant has killed, there may arise the question whether the killing was unlawful and the forfeiture rule applies (see the note to s.1). The Secretary of State or other authority responsible for determining entitlement to benefit is then bound to refer the case to the Upper Tribunal so that it can decide whether the forfeiture rule does apply and, if so, whether it should be modified under subs.(1A).

The duty to refer in any such case where the claimant would be entitled to a Category B retirement pension, state pension or graduated retirement benefit on the basis of his or her spouse's contributions will arise even if the claimant has claimed only a Category A retirement pension, state pension or graduated retirement pension on the basis of his or her own contributions, because there is no requirement to make a separate claim for a pension or graduated retirement benefit based on a spouse's contributions.

Arguably, the forfeiture question does not arise if a competent authority, such as a coroner, has decided that the death was accidental or due to misadventure, but it is likely to arise if the claimant was prosecuted, even if he or she was acquitted (*SSWP v LK (RP)* [2019] UKUT 421 (AAC)). However, where there has been an acquittal, the Upper Tribunal is unlikely to go behind it and so will usually decide that the forfeiture rule does not apply and may indeed do so without carrying out a detailed investigation (*R(G) 1/90*; *SSWP v LK (RP)* [2019] UKUT 421 (AAC)).

Subsections (1A)—(1H)

These subsections were added after a Tribunal of Commissioners held that subs.(1) gave Commissioners power only to decide whether the forfeiture rule applied and did not give them any power to modify it (*R/G) 1/84*, *R(G) 2/84*, *R(P) 1/84*). Whenever a claimant's entitlement to a social security benefit under a "relevant enactment" (see subs.(5)) arises at least partly in consequence of the death of someone the claimant has killed, there is likely to arise the question whether the killing was unlawful and the forfeiture rule applies. The Secretary of State or other authority responsible for determining entitlement to benefit is then bound to refer the case to the Upper Tribunal so that it can decide under subs.(1) whether the forfeiture rule does apply (see the note to s.1) and, if so, whether it should be modified under subs.(1A). **1.8**

The forfeiture rule cannot be modified in a case of murder (see s.5). However, the Act recognises that in other cases the forfeiture rule is capable of being unduly harsh and so the Upper Tribunal may modify the effect of the rule. The paramount consideration when considering modification is the culpability of the claimant (*Dunbar v Plant* [1998] Ch. 412). The Upper Tribunal has a broad discretion and may even decide that the forfeiture rule should have no effect at all, although that will be rare (*R(G) 1/98*, holding *R(G) 3/90* to have been implicitly overruled). Equally, though, the Upper Tribunal may decline to modify the effect of the forfeiture rule. In *R(G) 1/91*, a Commissioner refused to modify the rule where the Court of Appeal had quashed a conviction for murder and substituted a verdict of manslaughter on the ground of diminished responsibility because the trial judge had failed adequately to address the jury in relation to two written medical reports put to a defence witness in cross-examination when the prosecution had failed to call the authors of the reports to give evidence. The Commissioner, who was not bound by the same rules of evidence, held that the weight of evidence was against a finding of diminished responsibility and pointed to a finding of murder, although he acknowledged that s.5 did not apply because the claimant did not actually stand convicted of murder. In *Henderson v Wilcox* [2015] EWHC 3469 (Ch), the High Court decided not to modify the forfeiture rule in a case where there had been a conviction for manslaughter on the basis of an absence of intention to kill or cause serious injury, rather than on the ground of diminished responsibility, although a hospital order had been made under s.37 of the Mental Health Act 2013. The assault had been a serious one and the culmination of a series of attacks for at least several months and, although the assailant had had a low IQ and had been frustrated by having to assume the role of carer of his mother in circumstances where he did not have the necessary life skills, he had had a good understanding of what he was doing and that it was wrong. The judge said: "Sympathy for the applicant is not . . . the guiding factor for the court, as Patten J made clear in *Dalton v Latham* [2003] EWHC 796 (Ch). I must be satisfied that justice requires modification of the forfeiture rule." On the other hand, in *In re Land, decd.* [2006] EWHC 2069 (Ch); [2007] 1 W.L.R. 1009, where the claimant was too late to apply for modification of the forfeiture rule under s.2 of this Act so as to be able to inherit under his mother's will, s.3 was applied instead and it was held that the court was not precluded from making reasonable financial provision for the claimant under the Inheritance (Provision for Family and Dependants Act) 1975. The claimant, who had again been his mother's carer, had been sentenced to four years' imprisonment for manslaughter on the basis, it appeared, of gross negligence. The judge said: "the picture that presents itself to me is one of the inadequacy to meet the challenges presented by the deceased's condition, an inability to recognise that inadequacy, and a hesitancy in turning to outside help. The claimant must be and has been punished for the wrong that he did; he has also been punished by being deprived of the provision which the Deceased intended for him. But he should not be further punished by being deprived of the reasonable provision that he might otherwise expect under the 1975 Act." However, the amount at stake may be relevant. In *R(FP) 1/05*, where the claimant's plea of guilty to manslaughter on the ground of diminished responsibility had been accepted, a Commissioner considered the claimant's culpability to be low but he still refused to modify the forfeiture rule because only 47p pw was at stake and he considered that the effect of the forfeiture rule was not harsh but was just. More recently, the forfeiture rule was disapplied (under s.2) in *Re Challen, decd* [2020] EWHC 1330 (Ch); [2020] Ch. 692, where a woman had pleaded guilty to manslaughter on the grounds of diminished responsibility. She had beaten her husband to death with a hammer after she had endured his coercive control throughout a 40-year relationship. The judgment of the High Court includes a useful survey of the case law. In *In the estate of ES (deceased) (FRP)* [2022] UKUT 48 (AAC), another case of a wife killing her husband and being convicted of manslaughter on the ground of diminished responsibility, the rule was modified so that only one quarter of the part of the wife's retirement pension based on her husband's contributions was forfeited. In that case, the claimant had been sentenced to three years' imprisonment and the Secretary of State had failed to refer the forfeiture question to the Social Security Commissioner when she was released in 1989 and potentially became entitled to receive the payments. It appears that he had failed altogether to consider whether she was entitled to any extra retirement pension based on her husband's contributions and it was only when she died in 2018 and there arose the question of paying the arrears to her estate that the reference was made. The Upper Tribunal held that the failure to make the reference earlier was irrelevant when it came to deciding the extent to which the rule should be modified, save that the judge had to consider what decision would have been made by a Commissioner had the reference been made in 1989.

Modification under this section is usually in the form of an order directing that the forfeiture rule will have effect only for a certain period or that it will have effect only to reduce benefit by a certain proportion or both (subs.(1C)).

Subsection (2)

1.9 See the Tribunal Procedure (Upper Tribunal) Rules 2008 and, in particular, rr. 26 and 47.

Subsection (5)

1.10 Although the term "relevant enactment" includes war pensions schemes made under the first three statutes mentioned in the definition, it does not include the main war pensions scheme covering former members of the Armed Forces injured or killed due to service before April 6, 2005, which is not made under those enactments. This is presumably because that scheme contains its own, rather broader, forfeiture provision in respect of which decisions are made by the Secretary of State for Defence with a right of appeal to the First-tier Tribunal (War Pensions and Armed Forces Compensation Chamber) in England and Wales or a Pensions Appeal Tribunal in Scotland or Northern Ireland. The war pensions schemes to which this Act applies are the scheme covering civilians injured by enemy action in the Second World War, various schemes covering merchant seaman and other civilians who served afloat in that conflict and subsequent conflicts and the scheme covering members of the Polish Armed Forces who served under British command, none of which schemes has a forfeiture provision. On the other hand, the Armed Forces Compensation Scheme that applies in respect of members of the Armed Forces injured or killed due to service since April 6, 2005 is a "relevant enactment" for the purposes of this Act, being made under s.1 of the Armed Forces (Pensions and Compensation) Act 2004.

In addition to the statutes listed in this definition, the Social Security Act 1998 is prescribed as a relevant enactment by reg.14(1) of the Forfeiture Regulations

1999 (SI 1999/1495). Those Regulations started life as the Social Security Commissioners (Procedure) Regulations 1999 but, with effect from November 3, 2008, paras 130–136 of Sch.1 to the Tribunals, Courts and Enforcement Act 2007 (Transitional and Consequential Provisions) Order 2008 (SI 2008/2683) renamed them, amended regs 1 and 4(1) and deleted all the rest of the regulations except regulation 14(1), subject to a saving in respect of Scotland (see the note to ss.5–7 of the Social Security Act 1998). What is left reads—

1. These Regulations may be cited as the Forfeiture Regulations 1999 and shall come into force on June 1, 1999.

4.—(1) In these Regulations, unless the context otherwise requires—"the 1998 Act" means the Social Security Act 1998.

14.—(1) For the purposes of section 4(5) of the Forfeiture Act 1982, the 1998 Act shall be prescribed as a relevant enactment.

This appears to be an unnecessary provision but arguably reg.14(1) could not be deleted as an amendment consequential on the coming into force of the Tribunals, Courts and Enforcement Act 2007. Presumably the 1998 Act was originally prescribed with subs.(2)(a) in mind rather than any other part of s.4 because, unlike the Acts mentioned in subs.(5) itself, the 1998 Act is entirely procedural.

Exclusion of murderers

5.—Nothing in this Act or in any order made under section 2 or referred **1.11**
to in section 3(1) of the Act [[1] or in any decision made under section 4(1A) of this Act] shall affect the application of the forfeiture rule in the case of a person who stands convicted of murder.

AMENDMENT

1. Social Security Act 1986 s.76(4) (July 25, 1986).

DEFINITION

"forfeiture rule"—see s.1(1).

GENERAL NOTE

This section applies only if the claimant has actually been convicted of murder, **1.12**
although if the Upper Tribunal is satisfied that the actions of the claimant amounted to murder notwithstanding the lack of a conviction, it would be likely to refuse to exercise the power of modification conferred by s.4(1A) anyway (see, for instance, *R(G) 1/91*). In *R(G) 1/88*, the claimant was convicted of homicide in Germany where the killing took place and a Commissioner held that it was necessary to consider whether the claimant's actions would have amounted to murder had the killing taken place in Great Britain. A conviction for soliciting to murder, contrary to s.4 of the Offences against the Person Act 1861, does not amount to a conviction for murder, even though it may be tantamount to finding the claimant was an accessory to murder which, in many cases, would mean that he or she could in fact have been convicted of murder (*R(FG) 1/04*).

6. *Omitted.* **1.13**

7. *Omitted.* **1.14**

Child Support Act 1991

(1991 c.48)

Arrangement of Sections

Special cases

An Act to make provision for the assessment, calculation, collection and enforcement of periodical maintenance payable by certain parents with respect to children of theirs who are not in their care; for the collection and enforcement of certain other kinds of maintenance; and for connected purposes.

[25th July 1991]

Special cases

[1 Recovery of child support maintenance by deduction from benefit]

1.16 **43.**—[2 (1) The power of the Secretary of State to make regulations under section 5 of the Social Security Administration Act 1992 by virtue of subsection (1)(p) of that section may be exercised with a view to securing the making of payments in respect of child support maintenance by a non-resident parent.

(2) The reference in subsection (1) to the making of payments in respect of child support maintenance includes the recovery of—

(a) arrears of child support maintenance, and

(b) fees payable under section 6 of the Child Maintenance and Other Payments Act 2008.]

(3) For the purposes of this section, the benefits to which section 5 of the 1992 Act applies are to be taken as including war disablement pensions and war widows' pensions (within the meaning of section 150 of the Social Security Contributions and Benefits Act 1992 (interpretation)).

Amendments

1. Child Support, Pensions and Social Security Act 2000 s.21 (March 3, 2003).
2. Welfare Reform Act 2012 s.139 (February 4, 2014).

Definitions

"child support maintenance": see Child Support Act 1991 s.54
"non-resident parent": see Child Support Act 1991 s.54

General Note

1.17 For the background to this provision (which was formerly included in Vol.II), see the annotations in editions of Vol.II prior to 2021–2022.

See also Sch.9B to the Social Security (Claims and Payments) Regulations 1987 (SI 1987/1968) as amended, and Sch.7 to the Universal Credit, Personal Independence Payment, Jobseeker's Allowance and Employment and Support Allowance (Claims and Payments) Regulations 2013 (SI 2013/380) as amended.

Social Security Administration Act 1992

(1992 c.5)

Note that a number of sections not included in Vol.III may be found in Vol.IV: ss.13A, 14, 15, 113A, 113B, 122AA, 129–132.

ARRANGEMENT OF SECTIONS

PART I

CLAIMS FOR AND PAYMENTS AND GENERAL ADMINISTRATION OF BENEFIT

SECTION

Necessity of Claim

1. Entitlement to benefit dependent on claim. **1.18**
2. Retrospective effect of provisions making entitlement to benefit dependent on claim.

Work-focused interviews and work-related activity

2A. Claim or full entitlement to certain benefits conditional on work-focused interview.
2AA. Full entitlement to certain benefits conditional on work-focused interview for partner.
2B. Supplementary provisions relating to work-focused interviews.
2C. Optional work-focused interviews.
2D. Work-related activity.
2E. Action plans in connection with work-focused interviews.
2F. Directions about work-related activity.
2G. Contracting-out.
2H. Good cause for failure to comply with regulations.

Bereavement benefits

3. Late claims for widowhood benefit where death is difficult to establish.
4. Treatment of payments of benefit to certain widows.

Claims and payments regulations

5. Regulations about claims for and payments of benefit.

Community charge benefits etc.†

6. Regulations about community charge benefits administration.
7. Relationship between community charge benefits and other benefits.
7A. Sharing of functions as regards certain claims and information.
7B. Use of social security information.
8. Notification of accidents, etc.
9. Medical examination and treatment of claimants.
10. Obligations of claimants.

†Unreliable heading. (Council tax benefit replaced community charge benefits w.e.f. 1.4.93.)

Industrial injuries benefit

Disabled person's tax credit

11. Initial claims and repeat claims.

The social fund

12. *Repealed.*

Health in pregnancy grant

12A. Necessity of application for health in pregnancy grant.

Child benefit

13. Necessity of application for child benefit.
13A. *Omitted.*

Statutory sick pay

14. *Omitted.*

Statutory maternity pay

15. *Omitted.*

Payments in respect of mortgage interest etc.

15A. *Payment out of benefit of sums in respect of mortgage interest etc.*

Expenses of paying sums in respect of vehicle hire etc.

15B. *Omitted.*

Emergency payments

16. Emergency payments by local authorities and other bodies.

PART II

ADJUDICATION

17.–70. *Repealed.*

PART III

OVERPAYMENTS AND ADJUSTMENTS OF BENEFIT

Misrepresentation etc.

71. Overpayments—general.
71ZA. Overpayments out of social fund.

Recovery of benefit payments

71ZB. Recovery of overpayments of certain benefits.
71ZC. Deduction from benefit.
71ZD. Deduction from earnings.
71ZE. Court action etc.
71ZF. Adjustment of benefit.
71ZG. Recovery of payments on account.
71ZH. Recovery of hardship payments etc.

Jobseeker's allowance

71A. Recovery of jobseeker's allowance: severe hardship cases.

Misrepresentation etc. (continued)

72. *Repealed.*

Adjustments of benefits

73. Overlapping benefits—general.
74. Income support and other payments.
74A. Payment of benefit where maintenance payments collected by Secretary of State.

Housing benefit

75. *Omitted.*

Community charge benefits†

76. *Omitted.*
77. *Omitted.*

†Unreliable heading. (Council tax benefit replaced community charge benefits w.e.f. 1.4.93.)

Social fund awards

78. Recovery of social fund awards.

Northern Ireland payments

79. Recovery of Northern Ireland payments.

Adjustment of child benefit

80. Child benefit—overlap with benefits under legislation of other member States.

PART IV

RECOVERY FROM COMPENSATION PAYMENTS

81–104. *Repealed.*

Personal representatives—income support and supplementary benefit

126. Personal representatives to give information about the estate of a deceased person who was in receipt of income support or supplementary benefit.
126A. *Omitted.*

Housing benefit

127. *Repealed.*

Community charge benefits

128. *Repealed.*

Expedited claims for housing and council tax benefit

128A. *Repealed.*

Statutory sick pay and other benefits

129. *Omitted.*
130. *Omitted.*

Statutory maternity pay and other benefits

131. *Omitted.*
132. *Omitted.*

Maintenance proceedings

133. Furnishing of addresses for maintenance proceedings, etc.

Universal Credit Information

133A. Supply of universal credit information.

Part VIII

Arrangements for Housing Benefit and Community Charge Benefits† and Related Subsidies

134.–140. *Omitted.*

Part IX

Alteration of Contributions etc.

141.–149. *Omitted.*

Part X

Review and Alteration of Benefits

Part XI

Computation of Benefits

Part XII

Finance

Part XIII

Advisory Bodies and Consultation

The Social Security Advisory Committee and the Industrial Injuries Advisory Council

PART I

CLAIMS FOR AND PAYMENTS AND GENERAL ADMINISTRATION OF BENEFIT

Necessity of claim

Entitlement to benefit dependent on claim

1.19 **1.**—(1) Except in such cases as may be prescribed, and subject to the following provisions of this section and to section 3 below, no person shall be entitled to any benefit unless, in addition to any other conditions relating to that benefit being satisfied—

(a) he makes a claim for it in the manner, and within the time, prescribed in relation to that benefit by regulations under this Part of this Act; or

(b) he is treated by virtue of such regulations as making a claim for it.

[[2](1A) No person whose entitlement to any benefit depends on his making a claim shall be entitled to the benefit unless subsection (1B) below is satisfied in relation both to the person making the claim and to any other person in respect of whom he is claiming benefit.

(1B) This subsection is satisfied in relation to a person if—

(a) the claim is accompanied by—

(i) a statement of the person's national insurance number and information or evidence establishing that that number has been allocated to the person; or

(ii) information or evidence enabling the national insurance number that has been allocated to the person to be ascertained; or

(b) the person makes an application for a national insurance number to be allocated to him which is accompanied by information or evidence enabling such a number to be so allocated.

(1C) Regulations may make provision disapplying subsection (1A) above in the case of—

(a) prescribed benefits;

(b) prescribed descriptions of persons making claims; or

(c) prescribed descriptions of persons in respect of whom benefit is claimed,

or in other prescribed circumstances.]

[[10] (2) Where under subsection (1) a person is required to make a claim or to be treated as making a claim for a benefit in order to be entitled to it, the person is not entitled to it in respect of any period more than 12 months before the date on which the claim is made or treated as made.

(2A) But subsection (2) does not apply—

(a) to a disablement benefit or reduced earnings allowance, or

(b) in a case where a claim for the benefit is made or treated as made by virtue of section 3(2).]

(3) Where a person purports to make a claim for benefit on behalf of another—

[[7] (za) for personal independence payment by virtue of section 82 of the Welfare Reform Act 2012; or]

(a) for an attendance allowance by virtue of section 66(1) of the Contributions and Benefits Act; [[7] . . .]

that other shall be regarded for the purposes of this section as making the claim, notwithstanding that it is made without his knowledge or authority.

(4) In this section and section 2 below "benefit" means—

[[8] (za) universal credit;]

[[9] (zb) state pension or a lump sum under Part 1 of the Pensions Act 2014;]

[[10] (zc) bereavement support payment under section 30 of the Pensions Act 2014;]

(a) benefit as defined in section 122 of the Contributions and Benefits Act;

[[1] (aa) a jobseeker's allowance;]

[[4] (ab) state pension credit;]

[[5] (ac) an employment and support allowance,]

[[7] (ad) personal independence payment.]

(b) any income-related benefit.

(5) This section (which corresponds to section 165A of the 1975 Act, as it had effect immediately before this Act came into force) applies to claims made on or after 1st October 1990 or treated by virtue of regulations under that section or this section as having been made on or after that date.

(6) Schedule 1 to this Act shall have effect in relation to other claims.

Amendments

1. Jobseekers Act 1995 Sch.2 para.38 (October 7, 1996).
2. Social Security Administration (Fraud) Act 1997 s.19 (December 1, 1997).
3. Welfare Reform and Pensions Act 1999 Sch.8 para.16 (April 24, 2000).
4. State Pension Credit Act 2002 s.11 and Sch.1 paras 1–2 (April 7, 2003).
5. Welfare Reform Act 2007 s.28 and Sch.3, para.10 (October 27, 2008).
6. Welfare Reform Act 2012 s.31 and Sch.2 para.3 (February 25, 2013).
7. Welfare Reform Act 2012 Sch.9 para.8 (April 8, 2013).
8. Welfare Reform Act 2012 Sch.2 para.4 (February 25, 2013 for regulation making purposes April 29, 2013 otherwise).
9. Pensions Act 2014 s.56(4), s.23 and Sch.12, para.9 (April 6, 2016).
10. Pensions Act 2014 s.31 and Sch.16 para.21 (April 6, 2017).

DERIVATION

1.20 Social Security Act 1975 s.165A.

DEFINITIONS

"the 1975 Act"—see s.191.
"claim"—*ibid.*
"disablement benefit"—*ibid.*
"the Contributions and Benefits Act"—*ibid.*
"income-related benefit"—*ibid.*
"prescribe"—*ibid.*

GENERAL NOTE

Subsection (1)

1.21 The general rule is that there cannot be entitlement to benefit unless a claim is made for it. But note that this is a general rule, not a universal one. The general rule is subject to special cases for which special provision is made, and to the provisions of this section. "Benefit" for the purposes of this section is defined in para.(4). Section 1 applies to claims made on or after October 1, 1990. Schedule 1 deals with earlier claims.

The introduction of the predecessor of s.1 was precipitated by the decision of the House of Lords in *Insurance Officer v McCaffrey* [1984] 1 W.L.R. 1353 that (subject to an express provision to the contrary) a person was entitled to benefit if he met the conditions of entitlement even though he had not made a claim for that benefit. Claiming went to payability, not entitlement. This was contrary to the long-standing assumption of the Department and was corrected with effect from September 2, 1985.

Section 3, which is excluded from the operation of s.1, deals with late claims for bereavement benefit where the death of the spouse is difficult to establish.

Secretary of State for Work and Pensions v Nelligan, R(P) 2/03 [2003] EWCA Civ 555, Judgment of April 15, 2003, is the Court of Appeal's decision on the appeal against the Commissioner's decision in *CP/3643/2001*. The Commissioner had concluded that s.43(5) of the Contributions and Benefits Act 1992 contained an exception to the general rule that there must always be a claim for benefit. He decided that a married woman does not need to claim *both* a Category A *and* a Category B pension in order to obtain payment of the latter. The Court of Appeal allowed the appeal. It concluded that s.43(5) only applied where there had been a claim for *both* a Category A *and* a Category B retirement pension. There was no derogation from the general principle in s.1 of the Administration Act 1992. The Court of Appeal considered that s.43 was about making a choice between two competing entitlements rather than about establishing entitlement to benefit.

For a decision exploring the impact of subss.(1), (1A) and (1B) where a person had used a wholly fictitious identity to obtain—unmeritoriously—Indefinite Leave to Remain (ILR) and subsequently to claim benefit, see *ED v SSWP* [2020] UKUT 352 (AAC). The judge is at pains however to make clear that the decision should not necessarily be applied in all circumstances where a claim is made in a false name, giving as an example at [84] a person with a good claim for ILR who is required to use a false name for reasons linked to their claim for refugee status.

The Court of Appeal's decision in *SSWP v Abdul Miah (by Mashuq Miah)* [2024] EWCA Civ 186 is discussed more fully at **2.310**. In relation to s.1, Underhill L.J. observed that the effect of s.1(1) is that if a person claims outside the prescribed time, they will not be entitled to benefit. However, it did not follow that the issue of whether a claim had in fact been made in time fell outside normal procedures for determining claims, including those of revision and appeal.

Subsections (1A)–(1C)

These provisions were inserted by s.19 of the Social Security Administration (Fraud) Act 1997 and came into force on December 1, 1997. The effect of subss. (1A) and (1B) is to impose an additional condition of entitlement to benefit where subs.(1)(a) applies (i.e. in the normal case). Claimants will not be entitled to benefit unless when making a claim they provide a national insurance (NI) number, together with information or evidence to show that it is theirs, or provide evidence or information to enable their NI number to be traced, or apply for a NI number and provided sufficient information or evidence for one to be allocated to them. This requirement for an NI number applies to both claimants and any person for whom they are claiming, except in prescribed circumstances (subs.(1C)). See reg.2A of the Income Support Regulations, and the Jobseeker's Allowance Regulations, for who is exempt and note the different dates from which this requirement bites for these benefits. 1.22

The operation of s.1(1B)(b), previously considered by a three-judge panel in *R(Bui) v SSWP* and *R(Onekoya) v SSWP* [2022] UKUT 189 (AAC) was examined by the Court of Appeal in *SSWP v Bui and Onekoya* [2023] EWCA Civ 566; [2023] AACR 9. Nugee LJ, giving the judgment of the Court, held (at [55]) that:

> "Evidence that enables a NINo to be allocated seems to me plainly to refer to evidence that does in fact justify the allocation of a NINo, not evidence that merely purports to but in fact does not."

This view was reinforced by the fact that the amendment introducing these subsections had been made by an anti-fraud measure, the Social Security Administration (Fraud) Act 1997.

As to the issue of whether SSWP could refuse to make an interim payment unless a claimant had been allocated a NINo, the Court, taking a different view from the Upper Tribunal, said:

> "79. ... I do not think we can properly say that in every case where a claimant applies for UC and does not have a NINo, it necessarily follows that the Secretary of State will be unable to determine whether it is likely that the claimant will satisfy the requirements of s. 1(1B)(b) so as to be entitled to benefit. It does not seem self-evident that this will always be impossible; nor do I think that the evidence expressly deals with this question. The scheme of the provisions contemplates that in a case where a claimant's claim has not yet been determined and the claimant is in need the Secretary of State will consider whether it appears likely that the conditions of entitlement are met; and it seems to me that this is just as much so in a case where the claimant does not have a NINo as in the case when they do. In my judgment therefore the Secretary of State's practice in never considering whether this is likely in a case where the claimant does not have a NINo is flawed.
> 80. ... All that I mean to decide is that the Secretary of State's position that it is never possible to pay an advance payment to a claimant without a NINo (because it is not possible to assess whether it is likely that the claimant meets the conditions of entitlement until their application for a NINo has been verified) is not one that is warranted by the language of the regulation. Pending such verification it seems to me to be possible in principle for the Secretary of State to consider whether it is likely that such a claimant meets the conditions of entitlement or not. How that can be done in practice is not I think something we can rule on."

However, on this aspect, the effect of the Court of Appeal's decision has now been reversed by reg.6 of the Social Security and Universal Credit (Migration of Tax Credit Claimants and Miscellaneous Amendments) Regulations 2024 (SI 2024/341) which has amended reg.5 of the Social Security (Payments on Account of Benefit) Regulations 2013.

A rationality challenge by the claimants to the practice whereby the process of allocating a NINo does not begin until every other aspect of a claimant's eligibility to universal credit has been determined failed, the Court holding at [69]:

"It is not suggested in those circumstances that there is anything irrational in the Secretary of State making use of a limited number of specialist, security-cleared officers to carry out the verification checks involved in the NINo allocation process, something which the ordinary UC agents are not in a position to do. And it seems to me that [counsel for SSWP] is right that once this position is accepted, it is also rational for this necessarily resource-intensive process to be reserved for those cases which have been shown to need it."

Notwithstanding the difficulties which the lack of a NI number may cause a prospective benefit claimant, the administrative process by which NI numbers are allocated does not fall within the ambit of either art.8 or art.1 of Protocol 1 to the European Convention on Human Rights: *R(BK) v SSWP* [2023] EWHC 378 (Admin).

Subsection (2)

1.23 This provision imposes an overall limit of 12 months to the entitlement to benefit before the date of claim. Not all benefits are caught by subs.(1) and there is a further exclusion in para.(b). Regulation 19 of and Sch.4 to the Claims and Payments Regulations impose the ordinary time-limits for claiming and since April 1997 allow the limits in the cases of income support, JSA, family credit and disability working allowance (and their successor benefits) to be extended for a maximum of three months only in tightly defined circumstances. The test of good cause has been abandoned. Where there is such an extension, the claim is then treated as made on the first day of the period for which the claim is allowed to relate (reg.6(3)). Although the drafting is not at all clear, the reference in subs.(2) to the 12-month limit from the date on which the claim is made or is treated as made seems to make the limit start from the date fixed by reg.6(3). However, reg.19(4) prevents an extension of the time-limit for the benefits covered by reg.6(3) leading to entitlement earlier than three months before the actual date of claim. But the restriction seems to stem from that regulation and not from s.1(2), or the earlier forms set out in Sch.1.

Note that from April 1997 the time limit for claiming social fund maternity and funeral payments is three months (Claims and Payments Regulations, reg.19(1) and Sch.4, paras 8 and 9).

Subsection (3)

1.24 Subsection (3) deals with a particular situation which may arise in connection with claims to attendance allowance and disability living allowance. In general, there is no objection to claims being made by someone on behalf of another person, though the Department will require a clear indication that the agent is acting with the express authority of the person claiming.

Subsection (4)

1.25 This subsection contains the definition of "benefit" for the purposes of the section.

The starting point is the definition of benefit in s.122 of the Contributions and Benefits Act, which (so far as current benefits are concerned) refers to benefits under Pts II–V of the Contributions and Benefits Act. Specific provisions of para.(4) add most other benefits.

Though fairly comprehensive, this list does not include child benefit and winter fuel payments. On the latter see *CIS/2337/2004*, para.9. This does not mean that claims are not required for those benefits (indeed provision is made for claims elsewhere in the social security legislation), but it does mean that s.1 does not apply in relation to entitlement to benefit being dependent upon a claim.

It can be argued that the form of decision will differ depending upon whether a claim is a condition of entitlement. It is at least arguable that, if a claim is not a condition of entitlement and no claim has been made but a person claims to be entitled to the benefit, any decision should be in the form that there is a nil award. By contrast, if an adverse decision is made because no claim has been made where a claim is a condition of entitlement, then the form of the decision should be that there is no entitlement. This fine distinction is unlikely to impress those seeking a benefit, but may assist in drawing a distinction between the majority of cases where s.1 makes a claim a condition of entitlement, and the much smaller class of cases where s.1 does not apply.

Subsection (5)

There were a number of different versions of the section from which this section is derived and subs.(5) indicates that this section is limited to claims made on or after October 1, 1990. Schedule 1 sets out the earlier variations of the section. 1.26

Retrospective effect of provisions making entitlement to benefit dependent on claim

2.—(1) This section applies where a claim for benefit is made or treated as made at any time on or after 2nd September 1985 (the date on which section 165A of the 1975 Act (general provision as to necessity of claim for entitlement to benefit), as originally enacted, came into force) in respect of a period the whole or any part of which falls on or after that date. 1.27

(2) Where this section applies, any question arising as to—

(a) whether the claimant is or was at any time (whether before, on or after 2nd September 1985) entitled to the benefit in question, or to any other benefit on which his entitlement to that benefit depends; or

(b) in a case where the claimant's entitlement to the benefit depends on the entitlement of another person to a benefit, whether that other person is or was so entitled,

shall be determined as if the relevant claim enactment and any regulations made under or referred to in that enactment had also been in force, with any necessary modifications, at all times relevant for the purpose of determining the entitlement of the claimant, and, where applicable, of the other person, to the benefit or benefits in question (including the entitlement of any person to any benefit on which that entitlement depends, and so on).

(3) In this section "the relevant claim enactment" means section 1 above as it has effect in relation to the claim referred to in subsection (1) above.

(4) In any case where—

(a) a claim for benefit was made or treated as made (whether before, on or after 2nd September 1985, and whether by the same claimant as the claim referred to in subsection (1) above or not), and benefit was awarded on that claim, in respect of a period falling wholly or partly before that date; but

(b) that award would not have been made had the current requirements applied in relation to claims for benefit, whenever made, in respect of periods before that date; and

(c) entitlement to the benefit claimed as mentioned in subsection (1) above depends on whether the claimant or some other person was previously entitled or treated as entitled to that or some other benefit,

then, in determining whether the conditions of entitlement to the benefit so claimed are satisfied, the person to whom benefit was awarded as mentioned in paragraphs (a) and (b) above shall be taken to have been entitled to the benefit so awarded, notwithstanding anything in subsection (2) above.

(5) In subsection (4) above "the current requirements" means—

(a) the relevant claim enactment, and any regulations made or treated as made under that enactment, or referred to in it, as in force at the time of the claim referred to in subsection (1) above, with any necessary modifications; and

(b) subsection (1) (with the omission of the words following "at any time") and subsections (2) and (3) above.

DERIVATION

1.28 Social Security Act 1975 s.165B.

DEFINITIONS

"the 1975 Act"—s.191.
"benefit"—see s.1(1).
"claim"—see s.191.
"claimant"—*ibid.*

GENERAL NOTE

1.29 There are a number of benefits where entitlement can depend on whether a person was entitled to a benefit at some earlier date (e.g. on reaching pensionable age). While the predecessor of s.1 clearly governed such questions from September 2, 1985, onwards, it was arguable that in relation to earlier dates the *McCaffrey* principle (see note to s.1(1) above) had to be applied. *R(S) 2/91* decided that that argument was correct. The predecessor of s.2 was inserted by the Social Security Act 1990 to reverse the effect of that decision and to do so retrospectively back to September 2, 1985.

The form of s.2 is complex and the retrospective effects are difficult to work out. It only applies to claims made or treated as made on or after September 2, 1985 (subs.(1)). Thus very late appeals or very long good causes for late claim might not be affected. Then on any such claim if a question of entitlement at any other date arises (including dates before September 2, 1985) that question is to be decided according to the principle of s.1 as it was in force at the relevant time (subs.(2)). The only exception to this is that if for any period benefit has been awarded following a claim, that beneficiary is to be treated as entitled to that benefit even though under the current requirements he would not be (subs.(4)).

Work-focused interviews and work-related activity

[1 Claim or full entitlement to certain benefits conditional on work-focused interview.

1.30 **2A.**—(1) Regulations may make provision for or in connection with—

(a) imposing, as a condition falling to be satisfied by a person who—
   (i) makes a claim for a benefit to which this section applies, and
   [4 (ii) has not attained pensionable age at the time of making the claim (but see subsection (1A)),]

   a requirement to take part in [4 one or more work-focused interviews];

(b) imposing at a time when—
   (i) a person [4 has not attained pensionable age and is] entitled to such a benefit, and
   (ii) any prescribed circumstances exist,

   a requirement to take part in [4 one or more work-focused interviews] as a condition of that person continuing to be entitled to the full amount which is payable to him in respect of the benefit apart from the regulations.

[4 (1A) For the purposes of subsection (1) a man born before [8 6 December 1953] is treated as attaining pensionable age when a woman born on the same day as the man would attain pensionable age.]

(2) The benefits to which this section applies are—

(a) income support;

(b) housing benefit;

(c) council tax benefit;

(d) widow's and bereavement benefits falling within section 20(1)(e) and (ea) of the Contributions and Benefits Act [9 . . .];

(e) incapacity benefit;

(f) severe disablement allowance; and

(g) [2 carer's allowance].

[6 (2A) No requirement may be imposed by virtue of this section on a person who—

(a) is not a member of a couple, and

(b) is responsible for, and a member of the same household as, a child under the age of one.

(2B) For the purposes of subsection (2A)(b) regulations may make provision—

(a) as to circumstances in which one person is to be treated as responsible or not responsible for another;

(b) as to circumstances in which persons are to be treated as being or not being members of the same household.]

(3) Regulations under this section may, in particular, make provision—

(a) for securing, where a person would otherwise be required to take part in interviews relating to two or more benefits—

  (i) that he is only required to take part in one interview, and

  (ii) that any such interview is capable of counting for the purposes of all those benefits;

(b) for determining the person by whom interviews are to be conducted;

(c) conferring power on such persons or the designated authority to determine when and where interviews are to take place (including power in prescribed circumstances to determine that they are to take place in the homes of those being interviewed);

(d) prescribing the circumstances in which persons attending interviews are to be regarded as having or not having taken part in them;

(e) for securing that the appropriate consequences mentioned in subsection (4)(a) or (b) below ensue if a person who has been notified that he is required to take part in an interview—

  (i) fails to take part in the interview, and

  (ii) does not show, within the prescribed period, that he had good cause for that failure;

(f) prescribing—

  (i) matters which are or are not to be taken into account in determining whether a person does or does not have good cause for any failure to comply with the regulations, or

  (ii) circumstances in which a person is or is not to be regarded as having or not having good cause for any such failure.

(4) For the purposes of subsection (3)(e) above the appropriate consequence of a failure falling within that provision are—

(a) where the requirement to take part in an interview applied by virtue of subsection (1)(a) above, that as regards any relevant benefit either—

(i) the person in question is to be regarded as not having made a claim for the benefit, or

(ii) if (in the cases of an interview postponed in accordance with subsection (7)) that person has already been awarded the benefit, his entitlement to the benefit is to terminate immediately;

(b) where the requirement to take part in an interview applied by virtue of subsection (1)(b) above, that the amount payable to the person in question in respect of any relevant benefit is to be reduced by the specified amount until the specified time.

(5) Regulations under this section may, in relation to any such reduction, provide—

(a) for the amount of the reduction to be calculated in the first instance by reference to such amount as may be prescribed;

(b) for the amount as so calculated to be restricted, in prescribed circumstances, to the prescribed extent;

(c) where the person in question is entitled to two or more relevant benefits, for determining the extent, and the order, in which those benefits are to be reduced in order to give effect to the reduction required in his case.

(6) Regulations under this section may provide that any requirement to take part in an interview that would otherwise apply to a person by virtue of such regulations—

(a) is, in any prescribed circumstances, either not to apply or not to apply until such time as is specified;

(b) is not to apply if the designated authority determines that an interview—

(i) would not be of assistance to that person, or

(ii) would not be appropriate in the circumstances,

(c) is not to apply until such time as the designated authority determines, if that authority determines that an interview—

(i) would not be of assistance to that person, or

(ii) would not be appropriate in the circumstances,

until that time;

and the regulations may make provision for treating a person in relation to whom any such requirement does not apply, or does not apply until a particular time, as having complied with that requirement to such extent and for such purposes as are specified.

(7) Where—

(a) a person is required to take part in an interview by virtue of subsection (1)(a), and

(b) the interview is postponed by or under regulations made in pursuance of subsection (6)(a) or (c),

the time to which it is postponed may be a time falling after an award of the relevant benefit to that person.

[[7] (7A) Information supplied in pursuance of regulations under this section shall be taken for all purposes to be information relating to social security.]

(8) In this section—

[[6] "couple" has the meaning given by section 137(1) of the Contributions and Benefits Act;]

"the designated authority" means such of the following as may be specified, namely—

(a) the Secretary of State,
(b) a person providing services to the Secretary of State,
(c) a local authority,
[3 (ca) subject to subsection (9), a county council in England,]
(d) [3 subject to subsection (9),] a person providing services to, or authorised to exercise any function of, [3 any authority mentioned in paragraph (c) or (ca)];

"interview" (in subsections (3) to (7)) means a work-focused interview;

"relevant benefit", in relation to any person required to take part in a work-focused interview, means any benefit in relation to which that requirement applied by virtue of subsection (1)(a) or (b) above;

"specified" means prescribed by or determined in accordance with regulations;

"work-focused interview", in relation to a person, means an interview conducted for such purposes connected with employment or training in the case of that person as may be specified;

and the purposes which may be specified include purposes connected with a person's existing or future employment or training prospects or needs, and (in particular) assisting or encouraging a person to enhance his employment prospects.]

[3 (9) A county council in England or a person providing services to, or authorised to exercise any function of, such a council may be specified as the designated authority only in relation to interviews with persons to whom the council is required to make support services available under section 68(1) of the Education and Skills Act 2008 (support services: provisions by [5 local authorities]).]

AMENDMENTS

1. This section was added by the Welfare Reform and Pensions Act 1999 ss.57–58 with effect from November 11, 1999.

2. The Regulatory Reform (Carer's Allowance) Order 2002 (SI 2002/1457) art.1 (September 1, 2002 for the purpose of making regulations; April 1, 2003 for all other purposes).

3. Education and Skills Act 2008 Sch.1 para.45 (January 26, 2009).

4. Welfare Reform Act 2009 s.35(2) (February 10, 2010).

5. Education and Skills Act 2008 Sch.1 para.45 (May 5, 2010; commenced by an amendment).

6. Welfare Reform Act 2009 s.3(2) (October 6, 2011 for the purpose of making regulations) (October 31, 2011 for all other purposes).

7. Welfare Reform Act 2009 s.34(1) (January 12, 2010).

8. Pensions Act 2011 Sch.1 para.3 (January 3, 2012).

9. Pensions Act 2014 s.31 and Sch.16 para.22 (April 6, 2017).

[1 Full entitlement to certain benefits conditional on work-focused interview for partner

2AA.—(1) Regulations may make provision for or in connection with imposing, at a time when— 1.31
(a) a person ("the claimant") who—
[6 (i) has not attained pensionable age (but see subsection (1A)), and
(ii) has a partner who has also not attained pensionable age,]
is entitled to a benefit to which this section applies at a higher rate referable to his partner, and
(b) prescribed circumstances exist,

a requirement for the partner to take part in [6 one or more work-focused interviews] as a condition of the benefit continuing to be payable to the claimant at that rate.

[6 (1A) For the purposes of subsection (1) a man born before 6 December 1953 is treated as attaining pensionable age when a woman born on the same day as the man would attain pensionable age.]

(2) The benefits to which this section applies are—

(a) income support;

(b) an income-based jobseeker's allowance other than a joint-claim jobseeker's allowance;

(c) incapacity benefit;

(d) severe disablement allowance; [6 . . .]

(e) [3 carer's allowance] [6; and]

[4 (f) an employment and support allowance.]

(3) For the purposes of this section a benefit is payable to a person at a higher rate referable to his partner if the amount that is payable in his case—

(a) is more than it would be if the person concerned was not a member of a couple; or

(b) includes an increase of benefit for his partner as an adult dependant of his.

(4) Regulations under this section may, in particular, make provision—

(a) for securing, where the partner of the claimant would otherwise be required to take part in work-focused interviews relating to two or more benefits—

(i) that the partner is required instead to take part in only one such interview; and

(ii) that the interview is capable of counting for the purposes of all those benefits;

(b) in a case where the claimant has more than one partner, for determining which of those partners is required to take part in the work-focused interview or requiring each of them to take part in such an interview;

(c) for determining the persons by whom work-focused interviews are to be conducted;

(d) conferring power on such persons or the designated authority to determine when and where work-focused interviews are to take place (including power in prescribed circumstances to determine that they are to take place in the homes of those being interviewed);

(e) prescribing the circumstances in which partners attending work-focused interviews are to be regarded as having or not having taken part in them;

(f) for securing that if—

(i) a partner who has been notified of a requirement to take part in a work-focused interview fails to take part in it, and

(ii) it is not shown (by him or by the claimant), within the prescribed period, that he had good cause for that failure,

the amount payable to the claimant in respect of the benefit in relation to which the requirement applied is to be reduced by the specified amount until the specified time;

(g) prescribing—

(i) matters which are or are not to be taken into account in determining whether a partner does or does not have good cause for any failure to comply with the regulations; or

(ii) circumstances in which a partner is or is not to be regarded as having or not having good cause for any such failure.

(5) Regulations under this section may, in relation to a reduction under subsection (4)(f), provide—

(a) for the amount of the reduction to be calculated in the first instance by reference to such amount as may be prescribed;

(b) for the amount as so calculated to be restricted, in prescribed circumstances, to the prescribed extent;

(c) where the claimant is entitled to two or more benefits in relation to each of which a requirement to take part in a work-focused interview applied, for determining the extent to, and the order in, which those benefits are to be reduced in order to give effect to the reduction required in his case.

(6) Regulations under this section may provide that any requirement to take part in a work-focused interview that would otherwise apply to a partner by virtue of the regulations—

(a) is, in any prescribed circumstances, either not to apply or not to apply until the specified time;

(b) is not to apply if the designated authority determines that such an interview would not be of assistance to him or appropriate in the circumstances;

(c) is not to apply until such time as the designated authority determines (if that authority determines that such an interview would not be of assistance to him or appropriate in the circumstances until that time);

and the regulations may make provision for treating a partner to whom any such requirement does not apply, or does not apply until a particular time, as having complied with that requirement to such extent and for such purposes as are specified.

[[7] (6A) Information supplied in pursuance of regulations under this section shall be taken for all purposes to be information relating to social security.]

(7) In this section—

[[2] "couple" has the meaning given by s.137(1) of the Contributions and Benefits Act;]

"designated authority" means such of the following as may be specified, namely—

(a) the Secretary of State,

(b) a person providing services to the Secretary of State,

(c) a local authority, [[5]. . .]

[[5] (ca) subject to subsection (8), a county council in England, and]

(d) [[5] subject to subsection (8),] a person providing services to, or authorised to exercise any function of, [[5] any authority mentioned in paragraph (c) or (ca)];

"partner" means a person who is a member of the same couple as the claimant;

"specified" means prescribed by or determined in accordance with regulations; and

"work-focused interview" has the same meaning as in section 2A above.]

[[5] (8) A county council in England or a person providing services to, or authorised to exercise any function of, such a council may be specified as the designated authority only in relation to interviews with persons to whom the council is required to make support services available under section 68(1) of the Education and Skills Act 2008 (support services: provisions by [8 local authorities]).]

Amendments

1. Inserted by the Employment Act 2002 s.49 (July 5, 2003).
2. Civil Partnership Act 2004 s.254 and Sch.24 para.55 (December 5, 2005).
3. Welfare Reform Act 2007 Sch.7(3) (July 3, 2007).
4. Welfare Reform Act 2007 s.28 and Sch.3 para.10 (October 27, 2008).
5. Education and Skills Act 2008 Sch.1 para.46 (January 26, 2009).
6. Welfare Reform Act 2009 s.35 (February 10, 2010).
7. Welfare Reform Act 2009 s.34 (January 12, 2010).
8. Education and Skills Act 2008 Sch.1 para.45 (May 5, 2010; commenced by an amendment).

[1 Supplementary provisions relating to work-focused interviews

1.32 **2B.**—(1) Chapter II of Part I of the Social Security Act 1998 (social security decisions and appeals) shall have effect in relation to relevant decisions subject to and in accordance with subsections (3) to (8) below (and in those subsections "the 1998 Act" means that Act).

(2) For the purposes of this section a "relevant decision" is a decision made under regulations under section 2A above that a person—

(a) has failed to comply with a requirement to take part in an interview which applied to him by virtue of the regulations, or

(b) has not shown, within the prescribed period mentioned in section 2A(3)(e)(ii) above, that he had good cause for such a failure.

[3 (2A) For the purposes of this section a "relevant decision", in relation to regulations under section 2AA above, is a decision that—

(a) the partner of a person entitled to a benefit has failed to comply with a requirement to take part in an interview which applied to the partner by virtue of the regulations, or

(b) it has not been shown within the prescribed period mentioned in section 2AA(4)(f)(ii) above that the partner had good cause for such a failure.]

(3) Section 8(1)(c) of the 1998 Act (decisions falling to be made under or by virtue of certain enactments are to be made by the Secretary of State) shall have effect subject to any provisions of regulations under section 2A [4 or 2AA] above by virtue of which relevant decisions fall to be made otherwise than by the Secretary of State.

(4) For the purposes of each of sections 9 and 10 of the 1998 Act (revision and supersession of decisions of Secretary of State) any relevant decision made otherwise than by the Secretary of State shall be treated as if it were such a decision made by the Secretary of State (and accordingly may be revised by him under section 9 or superseded by a decision made by him under section 10).

(5) Subject to any provisions of regulations under either section 9 or 10 of the 1998 Act, any relevant decision made, or (by virtue of subsection (4) above) treated as made, by the Secretary of State may be—

(a) revised under section 9 by a person or authority exercising functions under regulations under section 2A [4 or 2AA] above other than the Secretary of State, or

(b) superseded under section 10 by a decision made by such a person or authority,

as if that person or authority were the Secretary of State.

(6) Regulations shall make provision for conferring (except in any prescribed circumstances) a right of appeal under section 12 of the 1998 Act (appeal to [5First-tier Tribunal]) against—

(a) any relevant decision, and

(b) any decision under section 10 of that Act superseding any such decision, whether made by the Secretary of State or otherwise.

(7) Subsections (4) to (6) above apply whether—

(a) the relevant decision, or

(b) (in the case of subsection (6)(b)) the decision under section 10 of the 1998 Act,

is as originally made or has been revised (by the Secretary of State or otherwise) under section 9 of that Act; and regulations under subsection (6) above may make provision for treating, for the purposes of section 12 of that Act, any decision made or revised otherwise than by the Secretary of State as if it were a decision made or revised by him.

(8) Section 12 of the 1998 Act shall not apply to any decision falling within subsection (6) above except in accordance with regulations under that subsection.

(9) In [2. . .]

(b) section 72(6) of the Welfare Reform and Pensions Act 1999 (supply of information),

any reference to information relating to social security includes any information supplied by a person for the purposes of an interview which he is required to take part in by virtue of section 2A [4 or 2AA] above.

(10) In this section "interview" means a work-focused interview within the meaning of section 2A above.]

AMENDMENTS

1. Welfare Reform and Pensions Act 1999 s.57 (November 11, 1999).
2. Employment Act 2002 s.54 and Sch.8 (November 24, 2002).
3. Employment Act 2002 s.54 and Sch.7 (July 5, 2003).
4. Employment Act 2002 s.53 and Sch.7 (July 5, 2003).
5. The Transfer of Tribunal Functions Order 2008 (SI 2008/2833) art.102 (November 3, 2008).

[1 Optional work-focused interviews

2C.—(1) Regulations may make provision for conferring on local authorities functions in connection with conducting work-focused interviews in cases where such interviews are requested or consented to by persons to whom this section applies. 1.33

(2) This section applies to[3 . . .] [3 —

(a) persons making claims for or entitled to any of the benefits listed in section 2A(2) above or any prescribed benefit; and

(b) partners of persons entitled to any of the benefits listed in section 2AA(2) above or any prescribed benefit;]

and it so applies regardless of whether such persons have, in accordance with regulations under section 2A [3 or 2AA] above, already taken part in interviews conducted under such regulations.

(3) The function which may be conferred on a local authority [4 or on a county council in England] by regulations under this section include functions relating to—

(a) the obtaining and receiving of information for the purposes of work-focused interviews conducted under the regulations;
(b) the recording and forwarding of information supplied at, or for the purposes of, such interviews;
(c) the taking of steps to identify potential employment or training opportunities for persons taking part in such interviews.

[4(3A) Regulations under this section may confer functions on a county council in England only in relation to interviews with persons to whom the council is required to make support services available under section 68(1) of the Education and Skills Act 2008 (support services: provision by [5 local authorities]).]

(4) Regulations under this section may make different provision for different areas or different authorities.

(5) In this section "work-focused interviews", in relation to a person to whom this section applies, means an interview conducted for such purposes connected with employment or training in the case of such a person as may be prescribed; and the purposes which may be so prescribed include—

(a) purposes connected with the existing or future employment prospects or needs of such a person, and
(b) (in particular) assisting or encouraging such a person to enhance his employment prospects.]

AMENDMENTS

1. This section was added by the Welfare Reform and Pensions Act 1999 ss.57–58 with effect from November 11, 1999.

2. Employment Act 2002 s.54 and Sch.8 (November 24, 2002).

3. Employment Act 2002 s.53 and Sch.7 (July 5, 2003).

4. Education and Skills Act 2008 Sch.1 para.47 (January 26, 2009).

5. Education and Skills Act 2008 Sch.1 para.45 (May 5, 2010; commenced by an amendment).

[1 2D. Work-related activity

1.34 (1) Regulations may make provision for or in connection with imposing on a person who—

(a) is entitled to income support, and
(b) is not a lone parent of a child under the age of 3,

a requirement to undertake work-related activity in accordance with regulations as a condition of continuing to be entitled to the full amount of income support payable apart from the regulations.

(2) Regulations may make provision for or in connection with imposing on a person ("P") who—

(a) is under pensionable age, and
(b) is a member of a couple the other member of which ("C") is entitled to a benefit to which subsection (3) applies at a higher rate referable to P,

a requirement to undertake work-related activity in accordance with regulations as a condition of the benefit continuing to be payable to C at that rate.

(3) The benefits to which this subsection applies are—

(a) income support;

(b) an income-based jobseeker's allowance other than a joint-claim jobseeker's allowance; and
(c) an income-related employment and support allowance.

(4) Regulations under this section may, in particular, make provision—

(a) prescribing circumstances in which a person is to be subject to any requirement imposed by the regulations (a "relevant requirement");
(b) for notifying a person of a relevant requirement;
(c) prescribing the time or times at which a person who is subject to a relevant requirement is required to undertake work-related activity and the amount of work-related activity the person is required at any time to undertake;
(d) prescribing circumstances in which a person who is subject to a relevant requirement is, or is not, to be regarded as undertaking work-related activity;
(e) in a case where C is a member of more than one couple, for determining which of the members of the couples is to be subject to a relevant requirement or requiring each of them to be subject to a relevant requirement;
(f) for securing that the appropriate consequence follows if—
    (i) a person who is subject to a relevant requirement has failed to comply with the requirement, and
    (ii) it is not shown, within a prescribed period, that the person had good cause for that failure;
(g) prescribing the evidence which a person who is subject to a relevant requirement needs to provide in order to show compliance with the requirement;
(h) prescribing matters which are, or are not, to be taken into account in determining whether a person had good cause for any failure to comply with a relevant requirement;
(i) prescribing circumstances in which a person is, or is not, to be regarded as having good cause for any such failure.

(5) For the purposes of subsection (4)(f) the appropriate consequence is that the amount of the benefit payable is to be reduced by the prescribed amount until the prescribed time.

(6) Regulations under subsection (5) may, in relation to any such reduction, provide—

(a) for the amount of the reduction to be calculated in the first instance by reference to such amount as may be prescribed;
(b) for the amount as so calculated to be restricted, in prescribed circumstances, to the prescribed extent.

(7) Regulations under this section may include provision that in such circumstances as the regulations may provide a person's obligation under the regulations to undertake work-related activity at a particular time is not to apply, or is to be treated as not having applied.

(8) Regulations under this section must include provision for securing that lone parents are entitled (subject to meeting any prescribed conditions) to restrict the times at which they are required to undertake work-related activity.

(9) For the purposes of this section and sections 2E and 2F—

(a) "couple" has the meaning given by section 137(1) of the Contributions and Benefits Act;
(b) "lone parent" means a person who—

(i) is not a member of a couple, and
(ii) is responsible for, and a member of the same household as, a child;
(c) "prescribed" means specified in, or determined in accordance with, regulations;
(d) "work-related activity", in relation to a person, means activity which makes it more likely that the person will obtain or remain in work or be able to do so;
(e) any reference to a person attaining pensionable age is, in the case of a man born before [2 6 December 1953] a reference to the time when a woman born on the same day as the man would attain pensionable age;
(f) any reference to a benefit payable to C at a higher rate referable to P is a reference to any case where the amount payable is more than it would be if C and P were not members of the same couple.

(10) For the purposes of this section regulations may make provision—
(a) as to circumstances in which one person is to be treated as responsible or not responsible for another;
(b) as to circumstances in which persons are to be treated as being or not being members of the same household.

(11) Information supplied in pursuance of regulations under this section is to be taken for all purposes to be information relating to social security.]

AMENDMENTS

1. Inserted by the Welfare Reform Act 2009 s.2 (November 12, 2009).
2. Pensions Act 2011 Sch.1 para.5 (January 3, 2012).

[1 2E. Action plans in connection with work-focused interviews

1.35 (1) The Secretary of State must in prescribed circumstances provide a document (referred to in this section as an "action plan") prepared for such purposes as may be prescribed to a person who is subject to a requirement imposed under section 2A or 2AA in relation to any of the following benefits.

(2) The benefits are—
(a) income support;
(b) an income-based jobseeker's allowance other than a joint-claim jobseeker's allowance; and
(c) an income-related employment and support allowance.

(3) Regulations may make provision about—
(a) the form of action plans;
(b) the content of action plans;
(c) the review and updating of action plans.

(4) Regulations under this section may, in particular, make provision for action plans which are provided to a person who is subject under section 2D to a requirement to undertake work-related activity to contain particulars of activity which, if undertaken, would enable the requirement to be met.

(5) Regulations may make provision for reconsideration of an action plan at the request of the person to whom it is provided and may, in particular, make provision about—
(a) the circumstances in which reconsideration may be requested;
(b) the period within which any reconsideration must take place;

(c) the matters to which regard must be had when deciding on reconsideration whether the plan should be changed;
(d) notification of the decision on reconsideration;
(e) the giving of directions for the purpose of giving effect to the decision on reconsideration.

(6) In preparing any action plan, the Secretary of State must have regard (so far as practicable) to its impact on the well-being of any person under the age of 16 who may be affected by it.]

AMENDMENT

1. Inserted by the Welfare Reform Act 2009 s.2 (November 12, 2009).

[[1] 2F. Directions about work-related activity

(1) In prescribed circumstances, the Secretary of State may by direction given to a person subject to a requirement imposed under section 2D provide that the activity specified in the direction is— **1.36**

(a) to be the only activity which, in the person's case, is to be regarded as being work-related activity; or
(b) to be regarded, in the person's case, as not being work-related activity.

(2) But a direction under subsection (1) may not specify medical or surgical treatment as the only activity which, in any person's case, is to be regarded as being work-related activity.

(3) A direction under subsection (1) given to any person—

(a) must be reasonable, having regard to the person's circumstances;
(b) must be given to the person by being included in an action plan provided to the person under section 2E; and
(c) may be varied or revoked by a subsequent direction under subsection (1).

(4) Where a direction under subsection (1) varies or revokes a previous direction, it may provide for the variation or revocation to have effect from a time before the giving of the direction.]

AMENDMENT

1. Inserted by the Welfare Reform Act 2009 s.2 (November 12, 2009).

[[1] 2G. Contracting-out

(1) The following functions of the Secretary of State may be exercised by, or by employees of, such person (if any) as the Secretary of State may authorise for the purpose, namely— **1.37**

(a) conducting interviews under section 2A or 2AA;
(b) providing documents under section 2E;
(c) giving, varying or revoking directions under section 2F.

(2) Regulations may provide for any of the following functions of the Secretary of State to be exercisable by, or by employees of, such person (if any) as the Secretary of State may authorise for the purpose—

(a) any function under regulations under any of sections 2A to 2F, except the making of an excluded decision (see subsection (3));
(b) the function under section 9(1) of the 1998 Act (revision of decisions) so far as relating to decisions (other than excluded decisions) that relate to any matter arising under regulations under any of sections 2A to 2F;
(c) the function under section 10(1) of the 1998 Act (superseding of decisions) so far as relating to decisions (other than excluded

decisions) of the Secretary of State that relate to any matter arising under regulations under any of sections 2A to 2F;

(d) any function under Chapter 2 of Part 1 of the 1998 Act (social security decisions), except section 25(2) and (3) (decisions involving issues arising on appeal in other cases), which relates to the exercise of any of the functions within paragraphs (a) to (c).

(3) Each of the following is an "excluded decision" for the purposes of subsection (2)—

(a) a decision about whether a person has failed to comply with a requirement imposed by regulations under section 2A, 2AA or 2D;

(b) a decision about whether a person had good cause for failure to comply with such a requirement;

(c) a decision about the reduction of a benefit in consequence of a failure to comply with such a requirement.

(4) Regulations under subsection (2) may provide that a function to which that subsection applies may be exercised—

(a) either wholly or to such extent as the regulations may provide,

(b) either generally or in such cases as the regulations may provide, and

(c) either unconditionally or subject to the fulfilment of such conditions as the regulations may provide.

(5) An authorisation given by virtue of any provision made by or under this section may authorise the exercise of the function concerned—

(a) either wholly or to such extent as may be specified in the authorisation,

(b) either generally or in such cases as may be so specified, and

(c) either unconditionally or subject to the fulfilment of such conditions as may be so specified;

but, in the case of an authorisation given by virtue of regulations under subsection (2), this subsection is subject to the regulations.

(6) An authorisation given by virtue of any provision made by or under this section—

(a) may specify its duration,

(b) may be revoked at any time by the Secretary of State, and

(c) does not prevent the Secretary of State or any other person from exercising the function to which the authorisation relates.

(7) Anything done or omitted to be done by or in relation to an authorised person (or an employee of that person) in, or in connection with, the exercise or purported exercise of the function concerned is to be treated for all purposes as done or omitted to be done by or in relation to the Secretary of State.

(8) But subsection (7) does not apply—

(a) for the purposes of so much of any contract made between the authorised person and the Secretary of State as relates to the exercise of the function, or

(b) for the purposes of any criminal proceedings brought in respect of anything done by the authorised person (or an employee of that person).

(9) Any decision which an authorised person makes in exercise of the function concerned has effect as a decision of the Secretary of State under section 8 of the 1998 Act.

(10) Where—

(a) the authorisation of an authorised person is revoked at any time, and

(b) at the time of the revocation so much of any contract made between the authorised person and the Secretary of State as relates to the exercise of the function is subsisting, the authorised person is entitled to treat the contract as repudiated by the Secretary of State (and not as frustrated by reason of the revocation).

(11) In this section—

(a) "the 1998 Act" means the Social Security Act 1998;

(b) "authorised person" means a person authorised to exercise any function by virtue of any provision made by or under this section;

(c) references to functions of the Secretary of State under any enactment (including one comprised in regulations) include functions which the Secretary of State has by virtue of the application of section 8(1)(c) of the 1998 Act in relation to the enactment.]

AMENDMENT

1. Inserted by the Welfare Reform Act 2009 s.2 (November 12, 2009).

[1 2H. Good cause for failure to comply with regulations

(1) This section applies to any regulations made under section 2A, 2AA or 2D that prescribe matters to be taken into account in determining whether a person has good cause for any failure to comply with the regulations. 1.38

(2) The provision made by the regulations prescribing those matters must include provision relating to—

(a) the person's physical or mental health or condition;

(b) the availability of childcare.]

AMENDMENT

1. Inserted by the Welfare Reform Act 2009 s.2 (November 12, 2009).

[1Bereavement benefits

Late claims for bereavement benefit where death is difficult to establish

3.—(1) This section applies were a person's spouse [2 or civil partner] has died or may be presumed to have died on or after the appointed day and the circumstances are such that— 1.39

(a) more than 12 months have elapsed since the date of death; and

(b) either—

(i) the spouse's [2 or civil partner's] body has not been discovered or identified or, if it has been discovered and identified, the surviving spouse [2 or civil partner] does not know that fact; or

(ii) less than 12 months have elapsed since the surviving spouse [2 or civil partner] first knew of the discovery and identification of the body.

(2) Where this section applies, notwithstanding that any time prescribed for making a claim for a bereavement benefit in respect of the death has elapsed, then—

(a) in any case falling within paragraph (b)(i) of subsection (1) above where it has been decided under section 8 of the Social Security Act 1998 that the spouse [3 or civil partner] has died or is presumed to have died, or

(b) in any case falling within paragraph (b)(ii) of subsection (1) above where the identification was made not more than 12 months before the surviving spouse [2 or civil partner] first knew of the discovery and identification of the body,

such a claim may be made or treated as made at any time before the expiration of the period of 12 months beginning with the date on which that decision was made or, as the case may be, the date on which the surviving spouse [2 or civil partner] first knew of the discovery and identification.

(3) [3 . . .]

(4) In subsection (1) above "the appointed day" means the day appointed for the coming into force of sections 54 to 56 of the Welfare Reform and Pensions Act 1999.]

[3 (5) In subsection (2) "bereavement benefit" means—

(a) bereavement support payment, or

(b) widowed parent's allowance.]]

AMENDMENTS

1. Substituted by Welfare Reform and Pensions Act 1999, Sch.8 para.17 and SI 2000/1047 (April 9, 2001).

2. Civil Partnership Act 2004 s.254 and Sch.24 para.56 (December 5, 2005).

3. Pensions Act 2014 s.31 and Sch.16 para.23 (April 6, 2017).

GENERAL NOTE

1.40 For the disapplication from the normal 12 months arrears rule in cases within s.3(2), see s.1(2A)(b).

Subsection (4)

1.41 The appointed day referred to in this subsection is April 9, 2001.

Treatment of payments of benefit to certain widows

1.42 **4.** In any case where—

(a) a claim for widow's pension or a widowed mother's allowance is made, or treated as made, before 13th July 1990 (the date of the passing of the Social Security Act 1990); and

(b) the Secretary of State has made a payment to or for the claimant on the ground that if the claim had been received immediately after the passing of that Act she would have been entitled to that pension or allowance, or entitled to it at a higher rate, for the period in respect of which the payment is made,

the payment so made shall be treated as a payment of that pension or allowance, and, if and to the extent that an award of the pension or allowance, or an award at a higher rate, is made for the period in respect of which the payment was made, the payment shall be treated as made in accordance with that award.

DERIVATION

1.43 SSA 1990 s.21(1) and Sch.6 para.27(2).

Claims and payments regulations

Regulations about claims for and payments of benefit

5.—(1) Regulations may provide— 1.44

(a) for requiring a claim for a benefit to which this section applies to be made by such person, in such manner and within such time as may be prescribed;

(b) for treating such a claim made in such circumstances as may be prescribed as having been made at such date earlier or later than that at which it is made as may be prescribed;

(c) for permitting such a claim to be made, or treated as if made, for a period wholly or partly after the date on which it is made;

(d) for permitting an award on such a claim to be made for such a period subject to

[15 (i) the condition that the requirements for entitlement are satisfied at a prescribed time after the making of the award, or

(ii) other prescribed conditions;

(e) [3 for any such award to be revised under section 9 of the Social Security Act 1998, or superseded under section 10 of that Act, if any of [15 the conditions referred to in paragraph (d)] are found not to have been satisfied;]

(f) for the disallowance on any ground of a person's claim for a benefit to which this section applies to be treated as a disallowance of any further claim by that person for that benefit until the grounds of the original disallowance have ceased to exist;

(g) for enabling one person to act for another in relation to a claim for a benefit to which this section applies [15 (including in particular, in the case of a benefit to be claimed by persons jointly, enabling one person to claim for such persons jointly)] and for enabling such a claim to be made and proceeded with in the name of a person who has died;

(h) [16. . .]

(hh) [16. . .]

(i) for the person to whom, time when and manner in which a benefit to which this section applies is to be paid and for the information and evidence to be furnished in connection with the payment of such a benefit;

(j) for notice to be given of any change of circumstances affecting the continuance of entitlement to such a benefit or payment of such a benefit [15 or of any other change of circumstances of a prescribed description];

(k) for the day on which entitlement to such a benefit is to begin or end;

(l) for calculating the amounts of such a benefit according to a prescribed scale or otherwise adjusting them so as to avoid fractional amounts or facilitate computation;

(m) for extinguishing the right to payment of such a benefit if payment is not obtained within such period, not being less than 12 months, as may be prescribed from the date on which the right is treated under the regulations as having arisen;

(n) [3. . .]

(nn) [2. . .]
(o) [3. . .]
(p) for the circumstances and manner in which payments of such a benefit may be made to another person on behalf of the beneficiary for any purpose, which may be to discharge, in whole or in part, an obligation of the beneficiary or any other person;
(q) for the payment or distribution of such a benefit to or among persons claiming to be entitled on the death of any person and for dispensing withstrict proof of their title;
[18 (r) for the making of a payment on account of such a benefit—
(i) in cases where it is impracticable for a claim to be made or determined immediately, or for an award to be determined or paid in full immediately,
(ii) in cases of need, or
(iii) in cases where the Secretary of State considers in accordance with prescribed criteria that the payment can reasonably be expected to be recovered;]

[16 (1A) Regulations may make provision for requiring a person of a prescribed description to supply any information or evidence which is, or could be, relevant to—
(a) a claim or award relating to a benefit to which this section applies, or
(b) potential claims or awards relating to such a benefit.]

(2) This section applies to the following benefits—
[19(za) universal credit;]
[21(zb) state pension of a lump sum under Part 1 of the Pensions Act 2014;]
[24 (zc) bereavement support payment under section 30 of the Pensions Act 2014;]
(a) benefits as defined in section 122 of the Contributions and Benefits Act;
[1(aa) a jobseeker's allowance;]
[6(ab) state pension credit;]
[11(ac) an employment and support allowance;]
[20(ad) personal independence payment]
(b) income support;
(c) [9 . . .];
(d) [9 . . .];
(e) housing benefit;
(f) any social fund payments such as are mentioned in section 138(1)(a) or (2) of the Contributions and Benefits Act;
[13(fa) health in pregnancy grant;]
(g) child benefit; and
(h) Christmas bonus.

[10 . . .]

[12 (2A) The regulations may also require such persons as are prescribed to provide a rent officer with information or evidence of such descriptions as is prescribed.

(2B) For the purposes of subsection (2A), the Secretary of State may prescribe any description of information or evidence which he thinks is necessary or expedient to enable rent officers to carry out their functions under section 122 of the Housing Act 1996.

(2C) Information or evidence required to be provided by virtue of subsection (2A) may relate to an individual claim or award or to any description of claims or awards.]

(3A) [16 . . .]

[17 (3B) The power in subsection (1)(i) above to make provision for the person to whom a benefit is to be paid includes, in the case of a benefit awarded to persons jointly, power to make provision for the Secretary of State to determine to which of them all or any part of a payment should be made, and in particular for the Secretary of State—

(a) to determine that payment should be made to whichever of those persons they themselves nominate, or

(b) to determine that payment should be made to one of them irrespective of any nomination by them.]

(4) Subsection (1)(n) above shall have effect in relation to housing benefit as if the reference to the Secretary of State were a reference to the authority paying the benefit.

(5) Subsection (1)(g), (i), (l), (p) and (q) above shall have effect as if statutory sick pay [8,] statutory maternity pay [22 statutory paternity pay] and statutory adoption pay] [24, statutory shared parental pay or statutory parental bereavement pay] were benefits to which this section applies.

[5(6) As it has effect in relation to [19 universal credit or] housing benefit subsection (1)(p) above authorises provision requiring the making of payments of benefit to another person, on behalf of the beneficiary, in such circumstances as may be prescribed.]

AMENDMENTS

1. Jobseekers Act 1995 Sch.2 para.39 (October 7, 1996).

2. Social Security Act 1998 Sch.6 para.5(1) (May 21, 1998). This amendment applies from May 21, 1998 until s.21(2)(d) of the 1998 Act comes into force.

3. Social Security Act 1998 Sch.8 (July 5, 1999).

4. Social Security Act 1998 s.74 (March 4, 1999).

5. Housing Act 1996 s.120 (with unlimited retrospective effect, so with effect from July 1, 1992).

6. State Pension Credit Act 2002 s.11 and Sch.1 (July 2, 2002 for the purpose of making regulations only).

7. State Pension Credit Act 2002 s.11 and Sch.1 (July 2, 2002 for the purpose of making regulations only).

8. Employment Act 2002 s.53 and Sch.7 (December 8, 2002).

9. Tax Credits Act 2002 s.60 and Sch.6 (April 8, 2003).

10. Welfare Reform Act 2007 s.67 and Sch.8 (April 7, 2008).

11. Welfare Reform Act 2007 s.28 and Sch.3 para.10 (October 27, 2008).

12. Welfare Reform Act 2007 s.35 (April 7, 2008).

13. Health and Social Care Act 2008 s.132(1) (July 21, 2008 in relation to enabling the exercise on or after July 21, 2008 of any power to make orders or regulations and defining expressions relevant to the exercise of any such power; January 1, 2009 in relation to England and Wales; not yet in force otherwise).

14. Work and Families Act 2006, Sch.1, para.24 (March 3, 2010).

15. Welfare Reform Act 2012 s.98 (February 25, 2013).

16. Welfare Reform Act 2012 s.99 (February 25, 2013).

17. Welfare Reform Act 2012 s.100 (February 25, 2013).

18. Welfare Reform Act 2012 s.101 (February 25, 2013).

19. Welfare Reform Act 2012 s.31 and Sch. 2, para.5 (February 25, 2013).

20. Welfare Reform Act 2012 s.91 and Sch.9 para.9 (February 25, 2013).

21. Pensions Act 2014, s.56(4), s.23 and Sch.12, para.10 (April 6, 2016).
22. Children and Families Act 2014 Sch.7 para.24(a) (April 5, 2015).
23. Pensions Act 2014 s.31 and Sch.16 para.24 (April 6, 2017).
24. Parental Bereavement (Leave and Pay) Act 2018 s.1 and Sch. para.15 (January 18, 2020).

Derivation

1.45 Subsections (1) and (2): Social Security Act 1986 s.51(1) and (2).

Definitions

"the Contributions and Benefits Act"—see s.191.
"prescribed"—*ibid.*

General Note

1.46 In *AM v SSWP (UC)* [2022] UKUT 242 (AAC) a three-judge panel held that the regulation-making power in s.5 was concerned with the manner and time of a claim rather than with its content. In dismissing SSWP's appeal (*SSWP v Abdul Miah (by Mashuq Miah)* [2024] EWCA Civ 186) the Court of Appeal did not express itself in that way, although its decision is consistent with it. Underhill LJ relied on the terms of s.5(1)(b) in order to give a purposive interpretation of the problematic (now superseded) version of reg.26 of the Universal Credit [etc.] Claims and Payments Regulations: the case is discussed more fully in the note to that regulation at **2.310**.

1.47 An argument was put in *R(DLA) 4/05* concerning the relationship of reg.13C of the Claims and Payments Regulations (further claim for and award of disability living allowance—the provision which permits a continuation claim for a disability living allowance to be made during the last six months of the current award) with s.5. The Tribunal of Commissioners responded:

> "Although at first sight regulation 13C(2)(b) may appear to provide a power to make an award, that is not so. Regulation 13C can best be understood by looking at the enabling provisions in section 5 of the 1992 Act. Section 5(1)(c) authorises the making of a regulation that permits a claim to be made in advance. Section 5(1)(d) authorises the making of a regulation that permits an award on such a claim to be made subject to a condition. It does not authorise the making of a regulation that permits an award to be made in advance because it is unnecessary to do so. The power to make an award follows from the duty to determine a claim, imposed on the Secretary of State by sections 1 and 8(1) of the 1998 Act. One can see that regulation 13C(1) is made under section 5(1)(c), regulation 13C(2)(a) is made under section 5(1)(b), regulation 13C(2)(b) is made under section 5(1)(d) and regulation 13C(3) is made under section 5(1)(e). Thus, what regulation 13C(2)(b) permits is not the making of an award in the light of the prospective claim but the imposition of a condition on the award that is required to be made by the 1998 Act. The word 'accordingly' [in reg.13C(2)(b)] therefore means no more than 'on that claim' and its only significance is that it links paragraph (2)(b) with paragraphs (1) and (2)(a) so that, in conformity with the enabling provision (giving effect to the word "such" in both places where it occurs in section 5(1)(d)), the condition may be imposed only on an award made on a renewal claim made in advance and treated as made on the renewal date." (para.16)

Community charge benefits etc.

Regulations about community charge benefits administration

6. [1 . . .] 1.48

AMENDMENT

1. Welfare Reform Act 2012 Sch.14(1) para.1 and the Welfare Reform Act 2012 (Commencement No.8 and Savings and Transitional Provisions) Order 2013 (SI 2013/358), subject to savings and transitional provisions (April 1, 2013).

GENERAL NOTE

In relation to the abolition of council tax benefit (which was all the section was expressed to concern), s.6 was repealed as noted above. 1.49

Relationship between [1 . . .] benefits

7.—(1) Regulations may provide for a claim for one relevant benefit to be treated, either in the alternative or in addition, as a claim for any other relevant benefit that may be prescribed. 1.50

[1 . . .]

(3) For the purposes of subsections (1) and (2) above relevant benefits are—

(a) any benefit to which section 5 above applies; [1 . . .]

AMENDMENT

1. Welfare Reform Act 2012 Sch.14 para.1 (April 1, 2013).

DERIVATION

Social Security Act 1986 s.51B. 1.51

DEFINITIONS

"claim"—see s.191.
"prescribed"—*ibid.*

[1 Sharing of functions as regards certain claims and information

7A.—(1)Regulations may, for the purpose of supplementing the persons or bodies to whom claims for relevant benefits may be made, make provision— 1.52

(a) as regards housing benefit or council tax benefit, for claims for that benefit to be made to—
  (i) a Minister of the Crown, or
  (ii) a person providing services to a Minister of the Crown;
(b) as regards any other relevant benefit for claims for that benefit to be made to—
  (i) a local authority,
  (ii) a person providing services to a local authority, or
  (iii) a person authorised to exercise any function of a local authority relating to housing benefit or council tax benefit.

[4 (c) as regards any relevant benefit, for claims for that benefit to be made to—

(i) a county council in England,
(ii) a person providing services to a county council in England, or
(iii) a person authorised to exercise any function a county council in England has under this section.]

(2) Regulations may make provision for or in connection with—

(a) the forwarding by a relevant authority of—
(i) claims received by virtue of any provision authorised by subsection (1) above, and
(ii) information or evidence supplied in connection with making such claims (whether supplied by persons making the claims or by other persons);

(b) the receiving and forwarding by a relevant authority of information or evidence relating to social security [3 or work] matters supplied by, or the obtaining by a relevant authority of such information or evidence from—
(i) persons making, or who have made, claims for a relevant benefit, or
(ii) other persons in connection with such claims, including information or evidence not relating to the claim or benefit in question;

(c) the recording by a relevant authority of information or evidence relating to social security [3 or work] matters supplied to, or obtained by, the authority and the holding by the authority of such information or evidence (whether as supplied or obtained or recorded);

(d) the giving of information or advice with respect to social security matters by a relevant authority to persons making, or who have made, claims for a relevant benefit.

[4 (e) the verification by a relevant authority of information or evidence supplied to or obtained by the authority in connection with a claim for or an award of a relevant benefit.]

(3) In paragraphs (b), [4 (d) and (e)] of subsection (2) above—

(a) references to claims for a relevant benefit are to such claims whether made as mentioned in subsection [4 (1)(a), (b) or (c)] above or not; and

(b) references to persons who have made such claims include persons to who awards of benefit have been made on the claims.

(4) Regulations under this section may make different provision for different areas.

(5) Regulations under any other enactment may make such different provision for different areas as appears to the Secretary of State expedient on connection with any exercise by regulations under this section of the power conferred by subsection (4) above.

(6) In this section—

(a) "benefit" includes child support or a war pension (any reference to a claim being read, in relation to child support, as a reference to an application [2 (or an application treated as having been made)] under the Child Support Act 1991 for a [2 maintenance calculation]);

(b) "local authority" means an authority administering housing benefit or council tax benefit;

[4 (c) "relevant authority" means—
(i) a Minister of the Crown;
(ii) a local authority;

(iii) a county council in England;
(iv) a person providing services to a person mentioned in sub-paragraphs (i) to (iii);
(v) a person authorised to exercise any function of a local authority relating to housing benefit or council tax benefit;
(vi) a person authorised to exercise any function a county council in England has under this section;]

(d) "relevant benefit" means housing benefit, council tax benefit or any other benefit prescribed for the purposes of this section;

[3 (e) "social security or work matters" means matters relating to—
(i) social security, child support or war pensions, or
(ii) employment or training;]

and in this subsection "war pension" means a war pension within the meaning of section 25 of the Social Security Act 1989 (establishment and functions of war pensions committees).]

AMENDMENTS

1. Welfare Reform and Pensions Act 1999 s.71 (November 11, 1999).
2. Child Support, Pensions and Social Security Act 2000 s.26 and Sch.3 para.12 (March 3, 2003 for certain purposes only: see SI 2003/192).
3. Employment Act 2002 s.53 and Sch.7 (November 24, 2002).
4. Welfare Reform Act 2007 s.41 (July 3, 2007).

[1 7B. Use of social security information

(1) A relevant authority may use for a relevant purpose any social security information which it holds. 1.53

(2) Regulations may make provision as to the procedure to be followed by a relevant authority for the purposes of any function it has relating to the administration of a specified benefit if the authority holds social security information which—

(a) is relevant for the purposes of anything which may or must be done by the authority in connection with a claim for or an award of the benefit, and
(b) was used by another relevant authority in connection with a claim for or an award of a different specified benefit or was verified by that other authority in accordance with regulations under section 7A(2)(e) above.

(3) A relevant purpose is anything which is done in relation to a claim which is made or which could be made for a specified benefit if it is done for the purpose of—

(a) identifying persons who may be entitled to such a benefit;
(b) encouraging or assisting a person to make such a claim;
(c) advising a person in relation to such a claim.

(4) Social security information means—

(a) information relating to social security, child support or war pensions;
(b) evidence obtained in connection with a claim for or an award of a specified benefit.

(5) A specified benefit is a benefit which is specified in regulations for the purposes of this section.

(6) Expressions used in this section and in section 7A have the same meaning in this section as in that section.

(7) This section does not affect any power which exists apart from this section to use for one purpose social security information obtained in connection with another purpose.]

AMENDMENT

1. Welfare Reform Act 2007 s.41 (October 1, 2007).

Industrial injuries benefit

Notification of accidents, etc.

1.54 **8.** Regulations may provide—

(a) for requiring the prescribed notice of an accident in respect of which industrial injuries benefit may be payable to be given within the prescribed time by the employed earner to the earner's employer or other prescribed person;

(b) for requiring employers—

(i) to make reports, to such person and in such form and within such time as may be prescribed, of accidents in respect of which industrial injuries benefit may be payable;

(ii) to furnish to the prescribed person any information required for the determination of claims, or of questions arising in connection with claims or awards;

(iii) to take such other steps as may be prescribed to facilitate the giving notice of accidents, the making of claims and the determination of claims and of questions so arising.

DERIVATION

1.55 SSA 1975 s.88.

GENERAL NOTE

1.56 The regulations made under this section are the Claims and Payment Regulations 1979 regs 24 and 25. The provisions of the regulations are, of course, significant in trying to ensure that the adjudicating authorities have access to a record of the circumstances surrounding an industrial accident, and the opportunity to put questions to the employer. Entries in the accident book are not always illuminating, but it is in the interests of the employees that they give the fullest possible contemporaneous account of the accident, particularly where its effects may be slow to emerge (as, sometimes, in head or back injuries).

Medical examination and treatment of claimants

1.57 **9.**—(1) Regulations may provide for requiring claimants for disablement benefit—

(a) to submit themselves from time to time to medical examination for the purpose of determining the effect of the relevant accident, or the treatment appropriate to the relevant injury or loss of faculty;

(b) to submit themselves from time to time to appropriate medical treatment for the injury or loss of faculty.

(2) Regulations under subsection (1) above requiring persons to submit themselves to medical examination or treatment may—

(a) require those persons to attend at such places and at such times as may be required; and

(b) with the consent of the Treasury provide for the payment by the Secretary of State to those persons of travelling and other allowances (including compensation for loss of remunerative time).

DERIVATION

SSA 1975 s.89. 1.58

DEFINITION

"medical examinations," "medical treatment"—see s.191.

GENERAL NOTE

The regulations referred to are the Claims and Payments Regulations 1979 reg.26. 1.59

Obligations of claimants

10.—(1) Subject to subsection (3) below, regulations may provide for disqualifying a claimant for the receipt of industrial injuries benefit— 1.60

(a) for failure without good cause to comply with any requirement of regulations to which this subsection applies (including in the case of a claim for industrial death benefit, a failure on the part of some other person to give the prescribed notice of the relevant accident);

(b) for wilful obstruction of, or other misconduct in connection with, any examination or treatment to which he is required under regulations to which this subsection applies to submit himself, or in proceedings under this Act for the determination of his right to benefit or to its receipt,

or for suspending proceedings on the claim or payment of benefit as the case may be, in the case of any such failure, obstruction or misconduct.

(2) The regulations to which subsection (1) above applies are—

(a) any regulations made by virtue of section 5(1)(h), (i) or (l) above, so far as relating to industrial injuries benefit; and

(b) regulations made by virtue of section 8 or 9 above.

(3) Regulations under subsection (1) above providing for disqualification of the receipt of benefit for any of the following matters, that is to say—

(a) for failure to comply with the requirements of regulations under section 9(1) or (2) above;

(b) for obstruction of, or misconduct in connection with, medical examination or treatment, shall not be made so as to disentitle a claimant to benefit for a period exceeding 6 weeks on any disqualification.

DERIVATION

SSA 1975 s.90(2)–(4) as amended. 1.61

GENERAL NOTE

In *R(S)9/51* it was held that a deeply held personal conviction that a claimant's religious beliefs require him or her to refuse to have a medical examination amounted to good cause for refusal to do so. Mere prejudice or distaste for the 1.62

process will not alone suffice. But the decision did go on to point out the possible consequential difficulties of meeting the burden of proof for entitlement to benefit if the refusal to submit to a medical examination resulted in their being no, or little, medical evidence available. Much would depend on the cogency of the other evidence available which might be sufficient to establish incapacity without full medical evidence. See also *CSIS/065/1991* discussed in the annotations to reg.2 of the Medical Evidence Regulations.

1.63 *Section 11 repealed.*
1.64 *Section 12 repealed.*

[1 Health in pregnancy grant

12A. Necessity of application for health in pregnancy grant

1.65 (1) No person is entitled to health in pregnancy grant unless she claims it in the manner, and within the time, prescribed in relation to health in pregnancy grant by regulations under section 5.

(2) No person is entitled to health in pregnancy grant unless subsection (3) or (4) is satisfied in relation to her.

(3) This subsection is satisfied in relation to a person if her claim for health in pregnancy grant is accompanied by—

(a) a statement of her national insurance number and information or evidence establishing that that number has been allocated to her; or
(b) information or evidence enabling the national insurance number that has been allocated to her to be ascertained.

(4) This subsection is satisfied in relation to a person if she makes an application for a national insurance number to be allocated to her which is accompanied by information or evidence enabling a national insurance number to be allocated to her.

(5) The Commissioners for Her Majesty's Revenue and Customs may by regulations make provision disapplying subsection (2) in the case of prescribed descriptions of persons making a claim.]

AMENDMENT

1. Added by Health and Social Care Act 2008 s.132(3) (July 21, 2008 in relation to enabling the exercise on or after July 21, 2008 of any power to make orders or regulations and defining expressions relevant to the exercise of any such power; January 1, 2009 in relation to England and Wales; not yet in force otherwise).

GENERAL NOTE

1.66 Health in pregnancy grant was a short-lived benefit. It was only made available to those who had reached the 25th week of their pregnancy by January 1, 2011: see s.3 of the Savings Accounts and Health in Pregnancy Grants Act 2010.

Child benefit

Necessity of application for child benefit

1.67 **13.**—(1) Subject to the provisions of this Act, no person shall be entitled to child benefit unless he claims it in the manner, and within the time, prescribed in relation to child benefit by regulations under section 5 above.

[1 (1A) No person shall be entitled to child benefit unless subsection (1B) below is satisfied in relation to him.

(1B) This subsection is satisfied in relation to a person if—

(a) his claim for child benefit is accompanied by—

(i) a statement of his national insurance number and information or evidence establishing that that number has been allocated to him; or

(ii) information or evidence enabling the national insurance number that has been allocated to him to be ascertained; or

(b) he make an application for a national insurance number to be allocated to him which is accompanied by information or evidence enabling such a number to be so allocated.

(1C) Regulations may make provision disapplying subsection (1A) above in the case of—

(a) prescribed descriptions of persons making claims, or

(b) prescribed descriptions of children [2 or qualifying young persons] in respect of whom child benefit is claimed,

or in other prescribed circumstances.]

(2) Except where regulations otherwise provide, no person shall be entitled to child benefit for any week on a claim made by him after that week if child benefit in respect of the same child [2 or qualifying young person] has already been paid for that week to another person, whether or not that other person was entitled to it.

AMENDMENTS

1. Welfare Reform and Pensions Act 1999 s.69 (May 15, 2000).
2. Child Benefit Act 2005 Sch.1 Pt 1 para.20 (April 10, 2006).

DERIVATION

CBA 1975 s.6. **1.68**

GENERAL NOTE

There is a general bar on receiving child benefit if it has already been paid to someone else in respect of the same child even though that other person was not entitled to it. **1.69**

The rules relating to claims for and payments of child benefit are now to be found in the Claims and Payments Regulations 1987.

See reg.38 of the Child Benefit (General) Regulations 2006 in Vol.IV for an escape route from the application of the rule in subs.(2).

Section 13A Omitted. **1.70**

Statutory sick pay

Section 14 Omitted. **1.71**

Statutory maternity pay

Section 15 Omitted. **1.72**

[[1]Payments in respect of mortgage interest etc.

1.73 *Section 15A Repealed.*

GENERAL NOTE

Repeal with transitional provisions

1.74 Section 15A was repealed by s.20 of the Welfare Reform and Work Act 2016 from April 6, 2018, subject to transitional provisions.

1.75 *Section 15B Omitted.*

Emergency payments

Emergency payments by local authorities and other bodies

1.76 **16.**—(1) The Secretary of State may make arrangements—

(a) with a local authority to which this section applies; or

(b) with any other body,

for the making on his behalf by members of the staff of any such authority or body of payments on account of benefits to which section 5 above applies in circumstances corresponding to those in which the Secretary of State himself has the power to make such payments under subsection (1)(r) of that section; and a local authority to which this section applies shall have power to enter into any such arrangements.

(2) A payment under any such arrangements shall be treated for the purposes of any Act of Parliament or instrument made under an Act of Parliament as if it had been made by the Secretary of State.

(3) The Secretary of State shall repay a local authority or other body such amount as he determines to be the reasonable administrative expenses incurred by the authority or body in making payments in accordance with arrangements under this subsection.

(4) The local authorities to which this section applies are—

(a) a local authority as defined in section 270(1) of the Local Government Act 1972, other than a parish or community council;

(b) the Common Council of the City of London; and

(c) a local authority as defined in section 235(1) of the Local Government (Scotland) Act 1973.

DERIVATION

1.77 Social Security Act 1988 s.8.

PART II

ADJUDICATION

1.78 *Repealed.*

PART III

OVERPAYMENTS AND ADJUSTMENTS OF BENEFIT

GENERAL NOTE

Overview of overpayments

The overpayments landscape has changed. There are now two distinct systems for recovering benefit which has been overpaid, though there remain some similarities between the two systems. While not a matter within the jurisdiction of tribunals, SSWP's policy on exercising her discretion not to recover overpaid sums becomes, in particular in relation to the newer system, of considerable importance. This aspect is discussed in the General Note to s.71B below. **1.79**

Overpayments that are automatically recoverable

Provision has been made by the Welfare Reform Act 2012 for the recovery of overpaid benefit whatever the circumstances in which the overpayment has arisen. Overpayments under this new system, which might conveniently be thought of as recovery under the 2013 rules, are automatically recoverable. The relevant provisions are to be found in ss.71ZB–71ZF, and the Social Security (Overpayments and Recovery) Regulations 2013 (paras 2.869–2.914 below). The benefits subject to this new regime are: **1.80**

- Universal credit;
- New-style Contributory Jobseeker's Allowance where the claim was made on or after April 29, 2013;
- New-style Contributory Employment and Support Allowance where the claim was made on or after April 29, 2013; and
- (when the relevant regulation is brought into force) the housing credit element of state pension credit.

In addition there are three further situations in which an overpayment is always recoverable:

- where the late payment of income has resulted in a person being paid more income support, income-based jobseeker's allowance, income-based employment and support allowance, or pension credit: s.74 of the SSAA 1992;
- where too much mortgage interest has been paid to the beneficiary's lender where the beneficiary is in receipt of income support, income-based jobseeker's allowance, income-based employment and support allowance, or pension credit: Sch.9A para.11 of the Claims and Payments Regulations; and
- where too much benefit has been credited to a beneficiary's bank account: s.71(4) of the SSAA 1992.

Appeals are available against decisions that an overpayment is automatically recoverable but the grounds for a successful appeal will relate to the formalities rather than what might be called the merits of recovery, though it may be possible to appeal against any decision changing entitlement if something has gone wrong in that respect.

Overpayments which are sometimes recoverable

This is the traditional territory of overpayment recovery and applies to all benefits other than those mentioned above and overpayments of housing benefit. The relevant rules are to be found in s.71 of the SSAA 1992 and the Social Security (Payments on Account, Overpayments and Recovery) Regulations 1988 (paras 2.915–2.955 below). Under this system, the overpayment can only be recovered if: **1.81**

- the decision awarding benefit has been changed; and
- there has been a failure to disclose a material fact or misrepresentation of a material fact; and
- the overpayment was caused by the failure to disclose or the misrepresentation.

Misrepresentation etc.

Overpayments—general

1.82 **71.**—(1) Where it is determined that, whether fraudulently or otherwise, any person has misrepresented, or failed to disclose, any material fact and in consequence of the misrepresentation or failure—

(a) a payment has been made in respect of a benefit to which this section applies; or

(b) any sum recoverable by or on behalf of the Secretary of State in connection with any such payment has not been recovered,

the Secretary of State shall be entitled to recover the amount of any payment which he would not have made or any sum which he would have received but for the misrepresentation or failure to disclose.

[[1](2) Where any such determination as is referred to in subsection (1) above is made, the person making the determination shall [[2] in the case of the Secretary of State or a [[12] First-tier Tribunal], and may in the case of [[12] the Upper Tribunal] or court]—

(a) determine whether any, and if so what, amount is recoverable under that subsection by the Secretary of State, and

(b) specify the period during which that amount was paid to the person concerned.]

(3) An amount recoverable under subsection (1) above is in all cases recoverable from the person who misrepresented the fact or failed to disclose it.

(4) In relation to cases where payments of benefit to which this section applies have been credited to a bank account or other account under arrangements made with the agreement of the beneficiary or a person acting for him, circumstances may be prescribed in which the Secretary of State is to be entitled to recover any amount paid in excess of entitlement; but any such regulations shall not apply in relation to any payment unless before he agreed to the arrangements such notice of the effect of the regulations as may be prescribed was given in such manner as may be prescribed to the beneficiary or to a person acting for him.

(5) [[10] . . .]

[[3] (5A) Except where regulations otherwise provide, an amount shall not be recoverable [[10] under subsection (1) or under regulations under subsection (4)] unless the determination in pursuance of which it was paid has been reversed or varied on an appeal or [[2] has been revised under section 9 or superseded under section 10 of the Social Security Act 1998]].

(6) Regulations may provide—

(a) that amounts recoverable under subsection (1) above or regulations under subsection (4) above shall be calculated or estimated in such manner and on such basis as may be prescribed;

(b) for treating any amount paid to any person under an award which is subsequently determined was not payable—

(i) as properly paid; or
(ii) as paid on account of a payment which it is determined should be or should have been made,

and for reducing or withholding any arrears payable by virtue of the subsequent determination;

(c) for treating any amount paid to one person in respect of another as properly paid for any period for which it is not payable in cases where in consequence of the subsequent determination—
(i) the other person is himself entitled to a payment for that period; or
(ii) a third person is entitled in priority to the payee to a payment for that period in respect of the other person,

and for reducing or withholding any arrears payable for that period by virtue of the subsequent determination.

(7) [[16] . . .]

(8) Where any amount paid [[14] . . .] is recoverable under—
(a) subsection (1) above;
(b) regulations under subsection (4) [[16] . . .] above; or
(c) section 74 below,

it may, without prejudice to any other method of recovery, be recovered by deduction from prescribed benefits.

(9) Where any amount paid in respect of a [[9] couple] is recoverable as mentioned in subsection (8) above, it may, without prejudice to any other method of recovery, be recovered, in such circumstances as may be prescribed, by deduction from prescribed benefits payable to either of them.

[[15] (9A) Regulations may provide for amounts recoverable under the provisions mentioned in subsection (8) above to be recovered by deductions from earnings.

(9B) In subsection (9A) above "earnings" has such meaning as may be prescribed.

(9C) Regulations under subsection (9A) above may include provision—
(a) requiring the person from whom an amount is recoverable ("the beneficiary") to disclose details of their employer, and any change of employer, to the Secretary of State;
(b) requiring the employer, on being served with a notice by the Secretary of State, to make deductions from the earnings of the beneficiary and to pay corresponding amounts to the Secretary of State;
(c) as to the matters to be contained in such a notice and the period for which a notice is to have effect;
(d) as to how payment is to be made to the Secretary of State;
(e) as to a level of earnings below which earnings must not be reduced;
(f) allowing the employer, where the employer makes deductions, to deduct a prescribed sum from the beneficiary's earnings in respect of the employer's administrative costs;
(g) requiring the employer to keep records of deductions;
(h) requiring the employer to notify the Secretary of State if the beneficiary is not, or ceases to be, employed by the employer;
(i) creating a criminal offence for non-compliance with the regulations, punishable on summary conviction by a fine not exceeding level 3 on the standard scale;

(j) with respect to the priority as between a requirement to deduct from earnings under this section and—
(i) any other such requirement;
(ii) an order under any other enactment relating to England and Wales which requires deduction from the beneficiary's earnings;
(iii) any diligence against earnings.]

(10) Any amount recoverable under the provisions mentioned in subsection (8) above—
(a) if the person from whom it is recoverable resides in England and Wales and the county court so orders, shall be recoverable [19 under section 85 of the County Courts Act 1984] or otherwise as if it were payable under an order of that court; and
(b) if he resides in Scotland, shall be enforced in like manner as an extract registered decree arbitral bearing a warrant for execution issued by the sheriff court of any sheriffdom in Scotland.

[4(10A) [17 . . .]

(10B) [17 . . .]

(11) This section applies to the following benefits—
[18 (za) state pension or a lump sum under Part 1 of the Pensions Act 2014;]
(a) benefits as defined in section 122 of the Contributions and Benefits Act;
[5(aa) [17 . . .]
[7(ab) state pension credit;]
[11(ac) [17 . . .]
[20(ad) personal independence payment;]
[21 (ae) bereavement support payment under section 30 of the Pensions Act 2014;]
(b) [6 . . .] income support;
(c) [8 . . .]
(d) [8 . . .]
(e) any social fund payments such as are mentioned in section 138(1)(a) or (2) of the Contributions and Benefits Act; and
[13 (ea) health in pregnancy grant; and]
(f) child benefit."

[9 (12) In this section, "couple" has the meaning given by section 137(1) of the Contributions and Benefits Act.]

AMENDMENTS

1. Social Security (Overpayments) Act 1996 s.1(2) (for determination made after July 24, 1996).
2. Social Security Act 1998 Sch.7 (July 5, 1999).
3. Social Security (Overpayments) Act 1996 s.1(4) (for determinations made after July 24, 1996).
4. Jobseekers Act 1995 s.32(1) (October 7, 1996).
5. Jobseekers Act 1995 Sch.2 (October 7, 1996).
6. Jobseekers Act 1995 Sch.3 (October 7, 1996).
7. State Pension Credit Act 2002 s.14 and Sch.2 (July 2, 2002 for the purposes of making regulations only; fully in force October 6, 2003).
8. Tax Credits Act 2002 s.60 and Sch.6 (April 8, 2003).
9. Civil Partnership Act 2004 s.254 and Sch.24 para.58 (December 5, 2005).
10. Welfare Reform Act 2007 s.44 (July 3, 2007).

11. Welfare Reform Act 2007 s.28 and Sch.3 para.10 (October 27, 2008).
12. The Transfer of Tribunal Functions Order 2008 (SI 2008/2833) art.103 (November 3, 2008).
13. Health and Social Care Act 2008 s.132(4) (January 1, 2009 in relation to England and Wales; not yet in force otherwise).
14. Welfare Reform Act 2012 s.150(2) (May 9, 2012).
15. Welfare Reform Act 2012 s.106 (July 1, 2012).
16. Welfare Reform Act 2012 s.147 and Sch.14 Pt 11 (April 1, 2013).
17. The Welfare Reform Act 2012 (Commencement No.8 and Savings and Transitional Provisions) Order 2013 (SI 2013/358) art.5(4) brings into force provisions of the Welfare Reform Act 2012 repealing subs.(10A) and (10B), as well as subs.(11)(aa) (jobseeker's allowance), and 11(ac) (employment and support allowance). However, art.5(6) provides that jobseeker's allowance and employment and support allowance "remain benefits to which section 71 of the 1992 Act applies to the extent that those benefits have been claimed before 29th April 2013." (April 29, 2013).
18. Pensions Act 2014, s.56(4), s.23 and Sch.12, para. 11 (April 6, 2016).
19. Tribunals, Courts and Enforcement Act 2007, Sch.13, para.102 (April 6, 2014).
20. Welfare Reform Act 2012, Sch.9, para.10 (June 10, 2013).
21. Pensions Act 2014 s.31 and Sch.16 para.25 (April 6, 2017).

General Note

The structure of the following commentary is as follows: **1.83**

Introduction

A complex body of case-law has built up on the proper application of s.71, which has included some significant changes of approach over time. What follows is a commentary on the current state of the case-law as it applies to typical benefit arrangements today without the detail of its historical development. For that, readers are referred to the more lengthy annotations in earlier editions of this work. **1.84**

The regulations to which this section makes reference are the Social Security (Payments on Account, Overpayments and Recovery) Regulations 1988 (paras 2.915–2.955 below).

For an overview of the new landscape for overpayments, see the general note appended to the heading to Pt III of this Act (paras 1.79–1.81 above).

The basic requirements

1.85 A decision maker dealing with an overpayment question must:

- make an "entitlement decision" by revising or superseding all relevant decisions awarding benefit during the period for which the overpayment is sought;
- where necessary offset the benefit paid against any residual amount of benefit under the entitlement decision;
- determine the period during which the overpayment occurred;
- calculate the amount of the recoverable overpayment;
- make an "overpayment decision" specifying the amount that is recoverable, the period of the overpayment, and the person from whom it is recoverable, and set out the basis for recovery; and
- give a decision on whether and on whom to apply a civil penalty ("a penalty decision").

On civil penalties, see the annotations to ss.115C and 115D of the SSAA 1992.

Before addressing these requirements in more detail, one or two general points about the application of s.71 need to be made.

Limitation periods

1.86 Arguments that overpayments are not recoverable because of the application of limitation periods applicable to the recovery of debts in actions before the courts have long been held to be destined to fail: *R(SB) 5/91*. The matter has been put completely beyond doubt by the amendment made to s.38 of the Limitation Act 1980 by s.108 of the Welfare Reform Act 2012. The amendment is to have effect as if it came into force at the same time as s.38 of the Limitation Act 1980, except for the purposes of proceedings brought before the coming into force of the section, that is, on March 8, 2012 (which was the date s.108 entered into force).

Recovery at common law not possible

1.87 The Supreme Court has confirmed that s.71 is the only route to recovery of overpayments of social security benefits to the exclusion of any common law entitlement to recover the money: *CPAG v SSWP* [2010] UKSC 54.

Recovery of overpayments and bankruptcy

1.88 A number of cases have considered the interrelationship between s.71 and the bankruptcy provisions of the Insolvency Act 1986. It seems that the timing of determinations under s.71 will be relevant in deciding whether a discharged bankrupt is freed from liability for deductions from benefit in repayment of an overpayment of benefit.

R (Steele) v Birmingham CC [2005] EWCA Civ 1824 concerned an overpayment of jobseeker's allowance. The claimant was awarded the benefit in December 1999. In September 2001, he was adjudged bankrupt on his own petition. In March 2002 an overpayment decision was made by the Secretary of State. Recovery of the overpayment was by means of deductions from benefit. The deductions were suspended during the period of bankruptcy, but were started again when the claimant was discharged from his bankruptcy. The claimant argued that the payments were a contingent liability within the meaning of the Insolvency Act 1986 and therefore he was released from this debt following his discharge from bankruptcy. In judicial review proceedings at first instance, the claimant was successful. However, the decision was successfully appealed by the Secretary of State. The Court of Appeal ruled that the claimant was under no obligation or liability to repay the overpaid benefit until a determination was made under s.71. No such determination had been made before the date of his bankruptcy. It followed that the overpaid amount was not a bankruptcy debt for the purposes of a release on discharge from bankruptcy under s.281(1) of the Insolvency Act 1986.

Different timings applied in *R (Balding) v Secretary of State for Work and Pensions* [2007] EWCA Civ 1327. The claimant was in receipt of income support. An overpayment determination was made in July 1994. In June 1995 the claimant, on his own petition, was adjudged to be bankrupt. The claimant was discharged from bankruptcy in June 1998. The Secretary of State sought to recover the overpayment by deductions from the claimant's benefit, arguing that such deductions were outside the scope of the bankruptcy legislation. The Court of Appeal upheld the decision of the Administrative Court: [2007] EWCA 759 (Admin) and praised the judgment of Davis J. in the court below for its depth of analysis of the issues involved. Regardless of the method of recovery chosen by the Secretary of State (deductions from benefit or recovery in debt proceedings in the courts), there was a liability to repay money under an enactment. Discharge from bankruptcy wiped out the liability to repay the sum under the insolvency legislation.

In *SSWP v Payne* [2011] UKSC 60 the Supreme Court brought the law in relation to bankruptcy and debt relief orders into line, ruling that *Balding* was correctly decided, and raising a question mark over the correctness of aspects of a House of Lords decision in the Scottish case of *Mulvey v Secretary of State for Social Security* [1997] UKHL 10. The decision of the administrative court in *R v Secretary of State for Social Security, ex p. Taylor and Chapman* was wrongly decided. The effect of the decision in *Payne* is that the Secretary of State loses the power to recoup overpayments on the making of a bankruptcy order just as he does on the making of a debt relief order (at [23]).

From whom can recovery be sought

Section 71 refers to the possibility of recovery from "any person" and the provision has been interpreted as widely as these sweeping words suggest. Therefore, recovery can be sought from claimants, their appointees, their spouses or partners, their children, their solicitors, and their personal representatives. However, where recovery is sought other than from the claimant, special considerations will apply where recovery can only be triggered by a misrepresentation or a failure to disclose a material fact. In particular, careful consideration will need to be given to the question of whether the party against whom recovery is sought was under an obligation to disclose facts to the Secretary of State. **1.89**

Appointees: the term "appointee" means a person who has been appointed by the Secretary of State under reg.33 of the Claims and Payments Regulations to administer a particular benefit on behalf of a person unable to act. It does not include a person holding a Power of Attorney for a claimant who has not been made an appointee under reg.33: see *CA/1014/1999*, discussed in *CSDLA/1282/2001* and *CIS/242/2003*. **1.90**

The leading authority is the decision of a Tribunal of Commissioners in *R(IS) 5/03*, which was set up to resolve a difference between the decisions in *CIS/332/1993* and *R(IS) 5/00*. *CIS/332/1993* had ruled that the acts of the appointee, when acting as such, are treated as acts of the claimant and so recovery is only available from the claimant (or the claimant's estate) and not the appointee. *R(IS) 5/00* had ruled that recovery was available from the appointee, the claimant's mother, who had not disclosed an increase in the claimant's savings. *R(IS) 5/03* concerned an overpayment which had arisen when income support continued in payment at the previous rate when the costs of the claimant's accommodation in a nursing home were met wholly by the health authority. The claimant's mother was her appointee under an appointment made by the Secretary of State for all benefit purposes. The appointee had failed to inform the Department that the costs of her daughter's accommodation in a nursing home were fully met by the health authority.

The Tribunal of Commissioners draws on the common law relating to agency but recognises that the social security context requires certain modifications to the common law rules applicable in a contractual situation. This is justified, in particular, because normal agency principles come into play where the principal has delegated authority to an agent. In the social security context, no such delegation exists, since it is the payer (the Secretary of State) who authorises another to act on behalf of persons unable to act for themselves. The benefit recipient, where reg.33 of the Claims and Payments Regulations applies, is not a party to the delegation of powers. It had been argued by the appellant and CPAG that to render the appointee personally liable would produce a situation in which, for example, social workers might be unwilling to undertake responsibilities as appointees to the disadvantage of benefit recipients. The Tribunal of Commissioners in preferring the principles set out in *R(IS) 5/00*, and concluding that *CIS/332/1993* is wrongly decided, mollified the impact of their decision by finding that there are exceptions to the liability of an appointee. Generally, both the claimant and the appointee will be liable for overpayments resulting from misrepresentations or failure to disclose. There are two exceptions to this rule. The first is that only the appointee will be liable for the overpayment if the appointee has retained the benefit instead of paying it to or applying it for the benefit of the claimant. The second exception is that the appointee will not be liable if the appointee has acted with "due care and diligence". This will avoid an appointee becoming personally liable where they make a wholly innocent representation, because some change in the claimant's affairs has not been made known to the appointee, and the appointee has not failed to exercise the powers of appointee in such a manner that they could be held to be at fault.

Despite the inevitable intricacies which always seem to arise in the manifold scenarios in which overpayments of benefits arise, this decision now makes it clear that the starting point is that both the claimant and any appointee are liable for overpayments of benefit subject to the two qualifications set out in *R(IS) 5/03*.

1.91 **Personal representatives:** it had been made clear in *Secretary of State for Social Services v Solly* [1974] 3 All E.R. 922 that recovery from the estate of a deceased person was possible. *R(SB) 28/83* is an example of recovery from the claimant's personal representative. However, tribunals are not the place in which objections to liability by the executor on the grounds, for example, that the estate has already been distributed are to be resolved. Those are matters concerning a decision to pursue recovery (which were reserved under the old adjudication system for the Secretary of State) rather than liability for the overpayment and may need adjudication in court: *R(SB) 1/96*.

In *R(IS) 6/01* the Commissioner held that the Secretary of State has no power under s.71 to seek recovery from the estate of a deceased claimant where there are no duly constituted personal representatives. The Secretary of State is not, however, without any powers in such circumstances, since "he could have made application to the High Court for a limited grant of administration under s.116 of the Supreme Court Act 1981. The court can apparently make a limited grant of that kind for a variety of purposes." (At para.38.)

1.92 **Spouses and partners:** special considerations arise where recovery is sought from spouses or partners. In *CIS/619/1997* the Commissioner follows *CIS/13742/1996* in holding that s.71 requires a review of the claims of both husband and wife before reg.13 of the Payments on Account Regulations can be used to offset benefit payable to one spouse against an overpayment that is recoverable from the other spouse. Tribunals faced with such cases should have regard to these two decisions in dealing with an appeal before them. The Commissioner also questions the propriety of inclusion in papers relating to the wife's appeal of details concerning the husband where she had maintained throughout that she was living separately from him. He suggests that there might be breach of confidentiality in relation to the husband's affairs, and appears to urge that such cases may be ones in which consideration would need to be given to disclosure of the husband's affairs to the tribunal as distinct from disclosure to the claimant. He recognises that this in turn gives rise to issues touching on the requirement to provide a fair hearing for the claimant and of natural justice.

Agents: in *Tkachuk v SSWP,* reported as *R(IS) 3/07*, the Court of Appeal agreed with the Commissioner that a number of provisions in social security legislation supplement or modify the common law of agency. It would accordingly not always be the case that knowledge of an agent is attributed to the principal. In *VB v SSWP* [2008] UKUT 15 (AAC) which concerned the attribution of knowledge by a financial advisor who was not the claimant's appointee, the judge said: **1.93**

> "79. In my view it would be a quite unwarranted extension of the scope of section 71 to hold that where a claimant's advisor is aware of a material fact, the claimant herself is necessarily fixed with knowledge of that same fact by means of importing the common law rules of agency."

Evidence required to sustain a decision that an overpayment is recoverable

It is for the Secretary of State to show on the balance of probabilities all the facts which are needed to justify the recovery of any overpayment: *R(SB) 6/85*, at para.5 and *DG v SSWP (DLA)* [2011] UKUT 14 (AAC), at [75]. This means that the Secretary of State should adduce evidence to support all elements required for a proper overpayment decision. This will include documentary evidence which is reasonably available: see *C1/06-07 (IS)* and *CIS/1462/2006*. Tribunals need to be alert to whether a paper submission adduces adequate evidence to show that all of the requirements are met where, as is commonplace, there is no representative of the Secretary of State before the tribunal. Where the Secretary of State has been given every opportunity to prove the statutory conditions but has manifestly failed to do so, and does not appear before a First-tier Tribunal (in this case after an adjournment with directions), then it is entirely appropriate to find against the Secretary of State: *FW v SSWP (IS)* [2010] UKUT 374 (AAC). **1.94**

Where the Secretary of State seeks to adduce surveillance evidence, questions can arise as to the legitimacy of the surveillance. In such cases the existence of authorisation under the Regulation of Investigatory Powers Act 2000 will be relevant. How the system operates and its compatibility with art.8 ECHR is discussed in *DG v SSWP (DLA)* [2011] UKUT 14 (AAC), [43]–[47] and see annotations to art.8 ECHR.

In *JF v SSWP (DLA)* [2015] UKUT 267 (AAC) and *AF v SSWP (DLA)* [2015] UKUT 266, Judge Wikeley sets out the due process requirements that apply in overpayment cases where the claimant's credibility is in issue. Care must be taken to consider all the evidence, to show why a discretion to consider an issue not raised in this appeal was exercised, to make clear findings of fact which reflect all the evidence before it, and to be very careful about considering even part of the evidence in the absence of the claimant (part of a DVD was viewed by the tribunal while the claimant was not in the room).

Missing documents: There is no presumption that missing documents contain material favourable to a claimant: *R(IS) 11/92*. Where a key document (for example, a claim form as in *CG/3049/2002*) has gone missing, a tribunal should seek to reconstruct the form from the best evidence available. However, a tribunal should not engage in guesswork, nor make any assumptions about who is most likely to have made a mistake: *CG/3049/2002*, at para.14. **1.95**

Evidence of a criminal conviction: In *R(S) 2/80*, the Commissioner ruled that the fact of a conviction should not be ignored and should have a bearing on any appeal relating to benefit. The initial burden must lie on the insurance officer, now Secretary of State, to show that a conviction is related to the benefit in issue in the appeal and covered the same period, although the onus of proof then shifts to the claimant to show that, notwithstanding the conviction, the claimant is entitled to the benefit in issue. **1.96**

This and other authorities have been considered in *AM v SSWP (DLA)* [2013] UKUT 94 (AAC). The case concerned the recovery of an overpayment against both the claimant and her appointee, who was her husband. The appointee was prosecuted and convicted of an offence under s.112(1D) SSAA 1992. The judge held that the criminal conviction against the appointee was not conclusive in any way against the claimant herself and was only of very limited effect as against the appointee.

After reviewing the earlier authorities, the judge considered that *R(S) 2/80* was wrongly decided in so far as it finds that a conviction leads to the legal burden of proof being shifted. The judge held that:

(a) the fact that the strict rules of evidence do not apply in social security cases does not mean that a tribunal can take into account matters that are not probative;

(b) on the basis of the decision of the Court of Appeal in *Hollington v Hewthorn* [1943] K.B. 587, a conviction has no probative value as it represents only the opinion of the relevant judge or jury;

(c) applying *Hunter v Chief Constable of the West Midlands Police* [1982] A.C. 529 there is a general rule of public policy that the use of a civil action to initiate a collateral attack on the decision of a criminal court is an abuse of process in the absence of fresh evidence which entirely changes an aspect of the case;

(d) this applies in social security cases to a limited extent only, as entitlement to benefits is required by statute to be determined by a specialist tribunal with a superior knowledge of social security law and, where appropriate, with members with medical expertise and a disability qualification; and

(e) in any event it is necessary for tribunals to examine very carefully the factual and legal basis of any conviction, looking at the charges, the evidence, and the findings of fact of the court, and also, where there is a guilty plea, at the facts admitted by the guilty plea, which may not be everything included in the charges.

Finally, the judge found that although the conviction was subsequent to the decision under appeal it could still be taken into account notwithstanding s.12(8)(b) of the Social Security Act 1998.

In *Newcastle CC v LW* [2013] UKUT 123, the same judge applied these principles in a case concerning an overpayment of housing benefit in which the claimant had pleaded guilty to a criminal charge relating to her failure to disclose that she was living together with a man as husband and wife. She argued that she had pleaded guilty to the offence to avoid facing more serious charges relating to mortgage fraud. The judge ruled that, on public policy grounds, the claimant could not resile from her guilty plea on appealing to the tribunal against the overpayment decision. However, the tribunal must look carefully at the conviction and the plea in order to be clear what it was that she had admitted, as well as the extent to which she should, as a consequence, be precluded from challenging the basis of the overpayment decision.

See also *JCW v SSWP (IS)* [2015] UKUT 283 (AAC).

The requirement for revision or supersession of all decisions in the overpayment period

1.97 Section 71(5A) requires, with only limited exceptions, that the decision awarding benefit must be revised under s.9 SSA 1998 or superseded under s.10 SSA 1998 (or reversed or varied on an appeal). Such a decision is commonly referred to as "the entitlement decision". This requirement is fundamental to recovery under s.71(1) and the absence of an entitlement decision renders any overpayment decision of no effect. A tribunal will err in law if it fails to consider whether there are grounds for a revision or supersession: *RH v SSWP (DLA)* [2015] UKUT 453 (AAC). However, there is nothing to preclude the Secretary of State from starting the whole process afresh if it transpires that there is no proper entitlement decision: *R(IS) 13/05* and *AG v SSWP (IS)* [2010] UKUT 291 (AAC).

An entitlement decision determines just that: entitlement to benefit. So, a decision that a couple are living together as husband and wife is *not* an entitlement decision since it is merely a precursor to an entitlement decision: *SSWP v AM* [2010] UKUT 428 (AAC).

The exceptions to the requirement for a prior entitlement decision are:

(a) Where the facts and circumstances of the misrepresentation or failure to disclose do not provide the basis for revising or superseding the decision: Payments on Account Regulations 1988 reg.12. The DMG gives as examples of such cases the correction of accidental errors and irregular encashments: para.09032.

(b) Certain JSA overpayments to 16 and 17 year olds: SSAA 1992 s.71A.

The Secretary of State should ensure that evidence is provided that an entitlement decision has been made prior to the overpayment decision, which has been sent to the claimant. The best evidence is a copy of the decision accompanied by a copy of the letter sent to the claimant communicating that decision. Computer printouts are commonly presented as evidence, although these are only acceptable if they are comprehensible and are explained.

Often entitlement decisions and overpayment decisions are made at the same time or within a short period of each other. However, sometimes the time lag is much longer. Plainly an entitlement decision attracts its own appeal if the claimant takes issue with its correctness. An appeal against an overpayment decision after the expiry of the time for an appeal against the entitlement decision does not constitute an appeal against the entitlement decision and this can cause difficulties for the person from whom recovery is sought since the Secretary of State argues that the underlying factual basis has been established by either the initial decision or a failed appeal against the entitlement decision. That is, however, not correct. The judge in *SSWP v AM (IS)* [2010] UKUT 428 (AAC) ruled that, when making findings of fact, the effect of s.17(2) SSA 1998 on the finality of decisions is that neither the Secretary of State nor a tribunal is bound by findings of fact made in the course of dealing with an entitlement decision when dealing with an overpayment decision. The same conclusion was reached in *KJ v SSWP (DLA)* [2010] UKUT 452 (AAC), where the judge said: **1.98**

> "16. This demonstrates, yet again, the unsatisfactory consequences which can ensue if entitlement and overpayment appeals are not heard together. In effect, the decision of the First Tribunal in this case was a complete waste of time. The Claimant was entitled to reargue in the overpayment appeal the issues of fact decided by the First Tribunal."

The decision of a Tribunal of Commissioners in *R(IB) 2/04* is the lead authority on the extent to which a tribunal can cure a defect in an entitlement decision so that the overpayment decision will not fail. This ruled that tribunals have power to remedy defects in decisions where they were not so serious as to render the decision in issue wholly incoherent. In general a Secretary of State's decision which altered the original decision with effect from the date of the original decision should be treated as a revision under s.9 and a Secretary of State's decision which altered the decision from a later date should be treated as a supersession under s.10. However, there must be something which can properly be regarded as a decision; a document which has so little coherence or connection to the legal powers of the decision maker cannot properly be regarded as a decision.

SS v SSWP (JSA) [2013] UKUT 233 (AAC) contains some useful observations of dealing with cases where the Secretary of State's decision-making is arguably incoherent in that there is inconsistency of decision-making resulting in considerable lack of clarity as to whether there has been a proper revision or supersession of the entitlement decision.

To be effective, a decision must not only be made but must also be communicated to its recipient. As long ago as 2003, in *R v SSHD, ex p. Anufrijeva* [2003] UKHL 36, the House of Lords had ruled, in the context of an asylum decision, that where a statutory scheme contemplated notification of some decision affecting a person, the **1.99** affected person is entitled to notification of the decision if it is to have legal effect. Lord Steyn said:

> "Notice of a decision is required before it can have the character of a determination with legal effect because the individual concerned must be in a position to challenge the decision in the courts if he or she wishes to do so. This is not a technical rule. It is simply an application of the right of access to justice. That is a fundamental and constitutional principle of our legal system . . . ." (At [26].)

In the social security context, an issue can arise in relation to the timing of the making of the decision, its effective date, and the notification of the decision to the claimant. What is clear is that there must be an entitlement decision prior to or at the latest contemporaneous with the overpayment decision. A decision of the Northern Ireland Court of Appeal in *Hamilton v Department for Social Development* [2010] NICA 46 ruled that failure to notify one of the two entitlement decisions in issue was corrected when it was incorporated by reference in the notification of the overpayment decision. Her appeal rights had not been compromised.

In *SSWP v Deane* [2010] EWCA Civ 699, the Court of Appeal ruled that there was no obligation on the English Court of Appeal to follow decisions of the Northern Ireland Court of Appeal but that where the decision of the Northern Ireland court relates to a statutory provision which is the same as that applicable in England and Wales, then it should be followed in order to avoid "the wholly undesirable situation arising of identically worded legislation . . . being applied in inconsistent ways." (Per Ward L.J. at [26].)

The decision in the *Hamilton* case is considered in *DK v SSWP (IS)* [2011] UKUT 230 (AAC): see [10]–[17]. Difficulties do seem to arise, as explained in *DK v SSWP*, because the DWP's computerised system is only able to handle supersession decisions taking effect no more than 14 months before the date of the decision. Rather than making the whole decision by hand, the DWP appears to engage in a double act: using the computer for the maximum period the programme will permit, and making a manual decision in relation to any earlier period. This has resulted in some cases in the computer-generated decision being sent to the claimant but not the one based on a manual record. A question then arises as to whether the decision based on the manual record has been properly notified to the claimant.

1.100 *SSWP v AD (IS)* [2011] UKUT 184 is just such a case. It contains a useful analysis of the effect of the *Hamilton* case, and raises some doubts about the circumstances in which communication of an overpayment decision can properly encompass a notification of an entitlement decision. These doubts arise from the decision in *CPC/3743/2006*, followed in *CIS/527/2010*, requiring that there are proper decisions altering entitlement for all parts of the period of the claimed overpayment as at the date on which the recoverability decision is made.

Both the *Hamilton* decision and *SSWP v AD* are the subject of analysis in *LL v SSWP (IS)* [2013] UKUT 208. The judge describes the making of an entitlement decision as the internal aspect of the rule in s.71(5A) and its notification as the external aspect of the rule. He confirms that both steps must have been taken before a recoverability decision is made. In general supersession decisions take effect on the day on which they are made, although certain non-advantageous decisions based on a change of circumstances may take effect from an earlier date. Some cases will accordingly require clear recognition of both the internal aspects of the requirements of s.71(5A), as well as the date from which the entitlement decision takes effect. These three temporal aspects of an entitlement decision should not be confused. The judge also indicates that his view of the *Hamilton* decision is that it decides only that simultaneous notification of an entitlement decision and a recoverability decision is legally permissible where the notification was sufficiently clear to enable its recipient to appreciate that it served the dual function of notifying both an entitlement decision and an overpayment decision in terms which ensured a right of appeal in respect of both decisions. Like the judge in *SSWP v AD*, the judge in *LL v SSWP* has some reservations about whether simultaneous notification of the entitlement decision and the overpayment decision is compatible with s.71(5A). This is because an entitlement decision had not been perfected by notification at the time the recoverability decision was made. In such cases, the requirements of s.71(5A) have not been met at the time when the recoverability decision is made. Furthermore, s.12(8)(b) of the SSA 1998 means that facts obtained after the date of the decision (that is, the communication of a relevant entitlement decision) under appeal cannot be taken into account.

Intention

The use of the words "whether fraudulently or otherwise" show that there is no need to prove any fraudulent intent. Wholly innocent mistakes by claimants can result in recoverable overpayments: *R(SB) 28/83*; *R(SB) 9/85*; and *R(SB) 18/85*. Innocent misrepresentations are easy to imagine. However, it may be better to think of non-fraudulent failures to disclose rather than innocent failures, since non-disclosures involve some breach of a duty to disclose. In *R(SB) 28/83* it was suggested that the duty to disclose extends to matters relevant to the claim to benefit which a person with reasonable diligence would have been aware. **1.101**

This interpretation of the section is confirmed by the Court of Appeal in *Page and Davis v Chief Adjudication Officer*, published as a supplement to *R(SB) 2/92*, where Dillon L.J. said:

> "The whole burden of the phrase 'whether fraudulently or otherwise' must be . . . that it is to apply even if the misrepresentation is not fraudulent, in other words, if it is innocent. No other construction makes any sense, in my view, of this particular subsection."

Misrepresentation

A misrepresentation can arise by a positive or deliberate act or as a result of omission: *R(SB) 9/85*; and may be a written statement, an oral statement, or even in some cases the result of silence (as when part of a claim form is left blank): *R(SB) 18/85*. Innocent misrepresentations are caught as well as deliberate misrepresentations; what is relevant is that there is some statement which is untrue for whatever reason: *Page v CAO (CA)* reported as appendix to *R(SB) 2/92* and *CSIS/0345/2004*. **1.102**

However, it is essential in every case to identify with some accuracy exactly what the misrepresentation is on which the Secretary of State relies in making the recoverability decision: see, for example, *NS v SSWP (CA)* [2014] UKUT 7 (AAC). It will not be enough simply to indicate that the claimant must have got something wrong. This can involve careful analysis of all the evidence in cases involving overpayments of benefit over significant periods of time. It is not enough for a decision maker or tribunal simply to assert that a claimant must have misrepresented something in a claim form or claim forms. It will not suffice to argue that there must have been misrepresentations because the claimant received benefit to which subsequent findings suggest that they were not entitled. There must be some evidence of the misrepresentation or misrepresentations on which the award of benefit was founded: *MK v SSWP (DLA)* [2011] UKUT 12 (AAC).

In providing information, claimants are not expected to be aware of the technicalities of social security legislation: *CTC/4025/2003*. In *KW v SSWP* [2009] UKUT 143 (AAC), the judge said:

> ". . . people are not to be accused or made liable for misrepresentation when they truthfully answer the questions they are actually asked, understanding the language used in its ordinary simple sense, instead of the different and more elaborate questions they *might* have been asked if the focus had been on some more artificial and restricted meaning." (At [41].)

The need to take a reasonable approach to responses to questions put to claimants is illustrated in *EL v SSWP* [2008] UKUT 4 (AAC). The Secretary of State sought to argue that a claimant had misrepresented his circumstances by not **1.103** providing a response to the question, "Please use this space to tell anything else you think we might need to know" on the claim form. The claimant was a Mexican national who had been given limited leave to remain in the United Kingdom on the condition that he have no recourse to public funds. His employment had come to an end and he had claimed and been awarded income-based jobseeker's allowance. The judge concluded that failure to respond to so open-ended a question cannot constitute a misrepresentation. Failure to reply to a specific question would generally constitute a misrepresentation, although failure to respond to a question couched in such general terms would not. The claimant had been asked no question about his immigration status. The overpayment was accordingly not recoverable.

It has long been accepted that a written statement may be qualified by an oral statement; it is often asserted by claimants that a form does not accurately reflect everything that was said. While generally claimants bear responsibility for the contents of forms, if it is accepted that an oral qualification has not been properly noted, this may preclude the written representation from being a misrepresentation: *R(SB) 18/85*.

A written misrepresentation may also be qualified or modified when that written communication is read in conjunction with other written communications which should be before the decision-maker in making the decision which resulted in the overpayment of benefit: *R(SB) 2/91*, at paras 10–13. In such cases, it goes without saying that careful findings of fact are vital. Tribunals should call for originals (or clear copies) of statements signed by persons which are claimed to be the misrepresentation on which an overpayment decision is founded.

1.104 In *R(SB) 3/90* the Commissioner holds that there can still be a misrepresentation of a material fact even where there has been an earlier disclosure of that fact (at para.11). Although disclosure prevents any recovery of an overpayment based on the failure to disclose head, a misrepresentation by declaration on a claim form that a claimant had no money coming in when superannuation payments from a former employer were in payment, receipt of which had previously been disclosed, overrides that disclosure. The Commissioner specifically states that the Department is entitled to rely on statements in the current claim form and is under no duty to check back to see whether those statements are consistent with earlier disclosures. So it remains incumbent on claimants to be meticulous in their completion of claim forms even after a course of dealing with the Department. The reasoning of the Commissioner in *R(SB) 3/90* is implicitly approved by the Court of Appeal in *Morrell v SSWP* [2003] EWCA Civ 526; *R(IS) 6/03*, [38]–[48].

CSU/03/1991 adds a gloss to *R(SB) 3/90. CSU/03/1991* was a case in which two forms had been submitted by the claimant containing conflicting information about the claimant's pension position. When he initially claimed unemployment benefit, he disclosed on Form UB461 the correct amount of his pension expressed as a weekly amount. However, a few days later he erred in recording on Form UB81(PEN) the pension as £293.75 per *year* rather than per *month*. The claimant's argument was that in considering his claim the adjudication officer should have had regard to both documents and that this would have indicated the error and no overpayment would have resulted. The adjudication officer sought to argue that there was no obligation to check back to see whether any inconsistent information was given in earlier documents. The Commissioner held that something had clearly gone wrong in the Department; both documents should have been before the adjudication officer in determining this claim and the adjudication officer could not rely on *R(SB) 3/90* as the basis for recovering the overpayment of benefit which resulted from the adjudication officer's reliance on the incorrect figure on the Form UB81(PEN).

ED v SSWP [2009] UKUT 161 (AAC), adds a further gloss on *R(SB) 3/90*. The Upper Tribunal judge observed:

> "... *R(SB) 3/90* and *Morrell* are not to be interpreted as meaning that whenever a misrepresentation of material fact has been made nothing that has gone before can ever be relevant to the question of whether a subsequent overpayment of benefit was in consequence of the misrepresentation. In *R(SB) 3/90*

the question was of linking back into previous claims whose administration had been completed. In *Morrell,* the provision of income by the claimant's mother was something that in its nature was capable of stopping or being interrupted at any time, so that there was no necessary inconsistency between the information given earlier by the local authority and a 'no' answer on the review form. Those decisions do not exclude the consideration of all the circumstances of particular cases and the fundamental test must in accordance with *Duggan* be that of causation, whether the misrepresentation or failure to disclose was *a* cause, possibly amongst other causes, of the subsequent overpayment." (At [27].)

In *CIS/5117/1998,* the Commissioner addresses the question of the extent to which silence can constitute a misrepresentation. The claim form for income support had been completed by an officer of the Department and read back to him. The form indicated that the claimant was married and living with his wife. None of the questions about his wife, particularly about her earnings or other income, had been answered. The tribunal found as a fact that the claimant had not been asked questions about his wife's earnings or other income by the Department's officer. An overpayment decision went on appeal to the tribunal which found that there had been no misrepresentation or failure to disclose in the circumstances of this case. The adjudication officer appealed. The Commissioner upheld the tribunal; the only substantial issue was whether or not the claimant made a misrepresentation by his silence when he made the claim on which the award of income support was based. 1.105

The Commissioner concludes that *R(SB) 18/85* applied to this case. The claimant had answered all of the questions put to him by the officer of the Department and the form was not read over to the claimant in its entirety. In these circumstances, says the Commissioner, the claimant's "misrepresentation" that the information on the form was complete "was qualified by the fact that he had supplied all the information for which he had been asked" in circumstances where the officer had given him no opportunity to answer the relevant questions about his wife's earnings, gave no indication that such matters might be material to benefit entitlement and did not read back the entries on the claim form to confirm their correctness. The facts of this case are unusual and appear to represent a failure by the Department to follow its own recommended procedures. However, where such unusual circumstances are established, the claimant's silence does not amount to a misrepresentation. In so far as *CIS/645/1993* suggests that silence as to material facts known to the claimant amounts to a misrepresentation, that decision must be read as referring to a deliberate decision to say nothing on a matter known to be material.

Now that most benefit payments are paid direct into a bank account, there are fewer cases involving the signing of declarations, yet there are still declarations at the end of claim forms, and on Jobcentre Plus coupons (Form ES25JP). The key to good decision making is to consider carefully the terms of the declaration. Many older postal claims forms were in terms that the information on the form is true and complete *as far as the claimant was aware.* These qualifying words protected a claimant against an innocent misrepresentation arising as a result of something they did not know at the time. More modern declarations are not qualified in this way but are a simple declaration that the information on the form is true and complete. A declaration in these terms does not protect a claimant from an innocent misrepresentation arising because of things they do not know when completing the form: *Jones & Sharples v CAO)* [1994] 1 All E.R. 225 (CA), reported as *R(IS) 7/94,* and *CIS/674/1994*; see also *Franklin v CAO* (CA), reported as *R(IS) 16/96.*

Mental capacity and misrepresentation

CSB/1093/1989 explores in some detail issues concerning mental capacity in overpayment cases. The particular question addressed was the extent to which claimants are entitled to escape the normal consequences of material misrepresentations by contending that they were mentally incapacitated at the time 1.106

when they signed the relevant document. The case concerned an overpayment of supplementary benefit which had arisen when, over a period of six months, the claimant misrepresented that her son was still a member of the family for benefit purposes when he had left school and had undertaken a Youth Training Scheme. It was argued on behalf of the claimant that her mental condition, combined with effects of anti-depressant drugs, was such that she could not be held responsible for putting her signature to the declarations in connection with the benefit claim. There is a discussion of the possibility of pleading *non est factum* (that the mind did not go with the pen with the result that the signature is to be treated as not having been made). The Commissioner stresses the narrow nature of the defence of *non est factum* and the difficulty of applying the doctrine to the realities of a modern social security system. As established in *Saunders v Anglia Building Society* [1971] A.C. 1004, three conditions must be met for a plea of *non est factum* to succeed:

(a) The claimant was under a disability, which might include being illiterate.

(b) The document signed was fundamentally, radically or totally different from that which the person thought they were signing.

(c) The person signing the document was not careless in doing so, and took such precautions as ought to have been taken in all the circumstances to ascertain the content and significance of the document.

In the *Saunders* case, Purchas L.J. had stressed the need for satisfying each of the three conditions set out above, particularly the third one. The overall effect is that the plea is unlikely to be available where the claimant has made a claim. A claimant who has the capacity to make a claim also has the capacity to make a representation affecting it: *CG/4494/1999 (T)*, [18].

The Commissioner in *CSB/1093/1989* indicates at paras 17 and 18 that he believes that the case of *Re Beaney, deceased* [1978] 1 W.L.R. 770, which was not concerned with social security at all, might be of assistance to tribunals. Mrs Beaney was an old lady whose health had been deteriorating for some time. She executed a transfer of a house to her eldest daughter in circumstances where all parties present at the signing of the document, including a solicitor who was an old friend of Mrs Beaney's late husband, thought that she understood what she was doing. Medical evidence, however, was that she had advanced senile dementia and her mental state was such that she could not have understood what she was doing. The two younger children sought a declaration that the transfer was void for want of capacity. The judge stated in his judgment that the degree or extent of understanding required in respect of any instrument is relative to the particular transaction which it is to effect. The more trivial the transaction, the lower the requisite degree of understanding. The Commissioner indicates that regard must be had to this test and that the key question is whether a claimant at the time of signing realised that they were signing a document in connection with a claim to benefit which could result in the payment of benefit. If the answer is negative, then s.71 cannot be applied to that claimant.

1.107 In difficult cases all the evidence will need to be considered over the period under review. So lucid letters written by the claimant about benefit in the relevant period will be relevant evidence of capacity. The most important evidence will be that of expert medical witnesses, whose views are to be preferred, as in *Re Beaney*, to the views of witnesses who are without medical qualifications.

In *CAO v Sheriff* (CA) reported as *R(IS) 14/96*, the Court of Appeal concluded that, even where a receiver has been appointed by the Court of Protection, a claimant who signs a claim form for benefit is capable of making a misrepresentation as to the facts upon which payment of benefit is based. Nor can such a person defeat a claim to repayment of overpaid benefit by arguing that they lacked capacity to make a representation. Nourse L.J. said:

> "If the representor need not know of the material fact misrepresented, I cannot see why it should make any difference if she does not know that she is making a

representation. That no doubt would make the misrepresentation more innocent. But it would not take it outside s.53(1) [now s.71(1)]. So that can be no ground for saying that the misrepresentation was not made by the claimant."

Millett L.J. put it even more bluntly:

"... it does not avail a recipient of benefit from whom the Secretary of State seeks repayment of benefit on the ground that he misrepresented a material fact to deny that he had mental capacity to make the representation."

R(IS) 4/06 places formidable hurdles in the path of a claimant seeking to rely on an argument that a claimant did not know what they were doing when completing a claim form. The decision is authority for three key propositions. First, even if the doctrine of *non est factum* applied to social security, which was doubtful, there was no evidence that the form was fundamentally different from the form the claimant thought he was signing and he could reasonably have taken precautions to ascertain its contents and significance (*Lloyds Bank Plc v Waterhouse* [1993] 2 F.L.R. 97 followed, at [9]–[23]). Secondly, there is a difference between acting deliberately and acting dishonestly or fraudulently and it is possible for a claimant to make an innocent misrepresentation by omission (see [30] and [31]). Thirdly, the language of the declaration signed by the claimant could not be read other than as a guarantee that the form had been completed in a way that accurately set out all details that might affect entitlement to the benefit claimed and hence was a misrepresentation and not a failure to disclose (*CAO v Sherriff*, reported as *R(IS) 14/96*, followed, at para.39).

Failure to disclose

Note that where something is not disclosed on a *claim* for benefit which results in an overpayment, the basis of recovery under s.71(1) can only be misrepresentation. This is because the duties which give rise to a failure to disclose relate to beneficiaries. At the point of claim, a person is a claimant and not yet a beneficiary: *CPC/196/2012*. **1.108**

However, in *R(SB) 40/84*, at para.12, the Commissioner ruled that a tribunal may switch from failure to disclose to misrepresentation as the basis for the recovery provided that the following conditions are met:

(a) the tribunal has told the appellant that they have such a course of action under consideration;

(b) the misrepresentation relied upon has been clearly identified; and

(c) the appellant has been afforded an adequate opportunity to address the changed basis of recovery without being disadvantaged by surprise.

An adjournment may be necessary to enable an appellant to give full consideration to the implications of the changed basis upon which recovery is to be considered.

Failure to disclose is now much more closely linked to specific instructions given to beneficiaries by the Secretary of State than it once was. Except in the case of jobseeker's allowance, the Secretary of State may require beneficiaries to provide information or evidence in relation to their continuing entitlement to benefit: reg.32(1) of the Claims and Payments Regulations.

Beneficiaries have a duty to provide such information or evidence as the Secretary of State may require in connection with payment of a benefit awarded: reg.32(1A) of the Claims and Payments Regulations.

Except in the case of jobseeker's allowance, beneficiaries have a duty to notify the Secretary of State of any change of circumstances which they might reasonably be expected to know might affect continuing entitlement to benefit.

There are specific duties in relation to jobseeker's allowance to be found in reg.24 of the JSA Regulations. This is why jobseeker's allowance is omitted from the application of reg.32(1) and (1B) but not reg.32(1A).

1.109 The decision of the Tribunal of Commissioners in *CIS/4348/2003,* affirmed on appeal to the Court of Appeal as *B v SSWP* [2005] EWCA Civ 929 reported as *R(IS) 9/06* (leave to appeal to the House of Lords was refused—the claimant made an application to the Court of Human Rights which ruled on February 14, 2012, that there had been no violation of art.14 when read with art.1 of Protocol 1), overturns some leading authorities of long standing in ruling, in essence, that there is no overriding requirement applying in every case that disclosure must be reasonably expected of the claimant before an overpayment of benefit can be recovered on the grounds of the failure to disclose. The duty to disclose flows from the statutory provisions quoted above. Then following propositions were common ground:

(a) There can be a wholly innocent failure to disclose, exemplified by those who do not disclose some material fact because they do not appreciate that it is a material fact.

(b) Persons cannot fail to disclose for the purposes of s.71 a matter unless it is known to them. Whether a matter is known to someone is determined by applying a subjective test.

(c) A material fact for the purposes of s.71 is a fact which is objectively material to the decision to award benefit.

(d) Failure to disclose is not the same as mere non-disclosure. "It imports a breach of some obligation to disclose" (see [13]).

The duty of disclosure flowing from reg.32(1A) is almost always unqualified, but see *LH v SSWP (RP)* [2017] UKUT 249 (AAC) below. It relates to specific matters which a claimant or other beneficiary has been instructed to disclose. In meeting this obligation no question arises concerning the mental capacity of the person required to furnish the information. It is not open to claimants to argue that they were unable to respond to an unambiguous request because, as a result of mental incapacity, they did not understand the request. The Tribunal of Commissioners considers what protection there is for claimants whose capacity may affect their ability to handle their affairs. Two protections are identified. First, there is the possibility that an appointee is appointed to act on their behalf. The Tribunal of Commissioners notes that, where no appointment has been made, "the higher courts have in the past taken a fairly robust approach to submissions based on a lack of capacity" (at para.64). Secondly, there is the possibility that the Secretary of State will exercise the discretion not to recover the overpayment in the particular circumstances of any given case, though the Tribunal comments that it is not "aware of any published guidelines on the exercise of this discretion." (See para.65.)

Decision makers and other adjudicating authorities will need to determine whether a failure to disclose arises in the context of the duty in reg.32(1A) or 32(1B) of the Claims and Payments Regulations. Where reg.32(1A) is in issue, the focus should be on the specific instructions given to the claimant or other person: were there clear and unambiguous instructions of the need to disclose specific facts which have not been disclosed? The relevant instructions may be found in claim forms, notes accompanying claim forms, award notifications and leaflets accompanying these, as well as specific instructions addressed to a person. Such forms and leaflets change from time to time and a copy of the instructions at the relevant time should be provided for tribunals where a person appeals.

1.110 In *R(IB) 4/05* the Commissioner follows the decision in *CIB/3925/2003* to the effect that the advice given to recipients of incapacity benefit about exempt work are couched in terms which do not *require* notification to the DWP before undertaking such work, though it was accepted that undertaking the work without giving the required notice had the result that entitlement to incapacity benefit ceased. The advice to benefit recipients could not be said to be "unambiguous" such that non-disclosure of undertaking such work could ground recovery of any overpayment of incapacity benefit.

This approach is confirmed in the decision of the Court of Appeal in *Hooper v SSWP* [2007] EWCA Civ 495, reported as *R(IB) 4/07*, which concerned an overpayment that had arisen when a recipient of incapacity benefit had started work without notifying the Secretary of State. The Commissioner had taken the view that a direction in a factsheet given to the claimant that "you should tell the office ... before you start work" constituted a requirement because it was a "polite way of wording an instruction". The Court of Appeal disagreed. There was no reason why the language used could not be clearer in indicating a formal requirement to notify by using the word "must" rather than "should". Dyson L.J. said, "The context is not one which demanded politeness at the expense of clarity." (At [57].) In the course of his judgment, Dyson L.J. expressly approves the reasoning of Commissioners Mesher and Howell in *CIB/3925/2003* and *R(IB) 4/05*.

In order to determine whether a claimant has complied with instructions given (and so discharged the duty under reg.32(1A)), close attention may need to be given to the terms of those instructions. In *SSWP v NS (ESA)* [2024] UKUT 5 (AAC), the claimant had told the DWP that he was about to retire, that he would be getting a pension (but not how much, or when) and who the provider would be. Judge Church held that the instructions in leaflet ESA40, which required the claimant to notify SSWP if he started to "get a pension" or "start[ed] getting any pension income" was not fulfilled by such disclosure, the judge observing that

> "The claimant must give the information that the Secretary of State has required, not some other information which the claimant might consider to be equivalent."

As to why the disclosure made was insufficient to fulfil the duty under the regulation:

> "The word "get" is, clearly and unambiguously, the language of receipt. You "get" something when you receive it. You "start to get it" when you first receive it. You are "getting" something for as long as you continue to receive it. .... It is instructive to take a step back to look at the issue in the context of the purpose of requiring benefit claimants to disclose information, which is to allow the Secretary of State to calculate any changes to benefit entitlement that might result from changes in a claimant's income. It is the receipt of income that is relevant to such a calculation, not the accrual of benefits under a scheme. To calculate a claimant's entitlement to benefit the Secretary of State needs to know about receipts, not entitlements."

Only once a claimant has complied with the duty might the co-operative nature of the investigation described in *Kerr v Department for Social Development (Northern Ireland)* [2004] UKHL 23; [2004] 1 W.L.R. 1372 require SSWP to follow up by way of making further enquiries of the claimant or of third parties, thus arguments that he could have obtained the information from HMRC or from the pension provider failed.

In *WS v SSWP (ESA)* [2023] UKUT 81, the facts similarly involved whether disclosure of a forthcoming pension, but not subsequently that it had come into payment, was sufficient. Judge Church held that the availability of information regarding the latter to SSWP from HMRC via the "Real Time Information" system was insufficient either to create a duty of further enquiry on SSWP or to mean that SSWP already had the information and so a submission based on *LH v SSWP (RP)* (see next paragraph) that the claimant could not "disclose" (and so fail to disclose) what the Secretary of State already knew failed.

Even if there is a duty to notify under reg.32(1A) or reg.32(1B), failure to comply with it may not amount to a failure to "disclose": *LH v SSWP (RP)* [2017] UKUT 249 (AAC), disagreeing with *GK v SSWP* [2009] UKUT 98 (AAC). The claimant was in receipt of a state retirement pension, and claimed a dependency increase for his wife. The wife subsequently became entitled to a state retirement pension on her own right. An overpayment arose because the dependency increase was not adjusted to take account of the wife's own retirement pension. The Secretary of State initially argued that the claimant had failed to disclose the receipt by his wife of her own state retirement pension. However, on closer enquiry it was accepted that the claimant had been in contact with the Department about the effect of an award of a state retirement pension for his wife. The Secretary of State then changed his argument: the claimant could reasonably be expected to disclose the annual uprating of his benefit and had failed to do so. Judge Wright resurrects aspects of *R(SB)15/87* to hold that the word "disclose" is not synonymous with, or limited to, breach of the reg.32 duties and thus that there was no failure to disclose an annual uprating, of which the Department was already aware.

1.111 In *SS v SSWP* [2009] UKUT 260 (AAC), the judge ruled that the standard letter advising incapacity benefit claimants that their entitlement to incapacity credits had ended because, as a result of a personal capability assessment, they were to be treated as available for work, "implied very strongly that, if the effect of the decision about incapacity credits was that the Claimant ceased to be entitled to income support, Jobcentre Plus would take steps to terminate the income support award." (See [11].) It followed that there was no breach of the obligation to disclose under reg.32(1B) of the Claims and Payments Regulations and that any overpayment of income support which arose in those circumstances would not be recoverable.

A common ground of appeal against an overpayment decision based on failure to disclose a change in entitlement to one benefit which affects another benefit is that the Secretary of State must be aware of the change and this means there has been no failure to disclose. However, *Hinchy v SSWP* [2005] UKHL 16, reported as *R(IS) 7/05*, established that claimants are not entitled to make assumptions about the administrative arrangements for communications between parts of the DWP, and are certainly not entitled to assume the existence of effective channels of communication between one office and another. Lord Hoffmann, giving the lead opinion in the House of Lords, considered that the line of authority established in the relevant Commissioners' decisions reflected the realities of benefit administration and went on to say:

> "32. . . . The claimant is not concerned or entitled to make any assumptions about the internal administrative arrangements of the department. In particular, she is not entitled to assume the existence of infallible channels of communication between one office and another. Her duty is to comply with what the Tribunal called the 'simple instruction' in the order book. . . . For my part, I would approve the principles stated by the Commissioners in *R(SB) 15/87* and *CG/4494/99*. The duty of the claimant is the duty imposed by regulation 32 or implied by section 71 to make disclosure to the person or office identified to the claimant as the decision maker. The latter is not deemed to know anything which he did not actually know."

Lady Hale agreed, noting that there was nothing intrinsically wrong in requiring disclosure from the claimant of information known to one part of the DWP which may or may not be known to another part of the DWP. Lady Hale has some reservations about whether the requirement to disclose the termination of the disability living allowance was made sufficiently clear in this case but concedes that this goes to findings of fact rather than a question of law.

The Northern Ireland Social Security Commissioners, with the benefit of unusually detailed evidence, considered the extent to which *Hinchy* may be applicable given the move from paper-based to computerised systems in the period since 1993–98 (which *Hinchy* concerned), see *SK v Department for Communities (ESA)* [2020] NiCom 73 and *PMcL v Department for Communities* (ESA) [2020] NiCom 20. However, the administrative arrangements in Northern Ireland on one hand and Great Britain on the other are different.

In *MW v SSWP (ESA)* [2023] UKUT 50 (AAC), Judge West rejected an attempt to apply *SK* in Great Britain, concluding following close attention to the First-tier Tribunal's careful findings of fact that *SK* could be distinguished. The judge went on to observe:

"35. At some point the Upper Tribunal will have to grapple with the decision in *Hinchy* in the light of 21st century developments in computer technology. That was very much an analogue decision relating to a paper-based system and the question which will fall for decision is how it now translates into the computerised and digital age. This case, however, is not an appropriate vehicle for essaying that decision.

36. There is nevertheless force in Mr Commissioner Stockman's comment that

> 'There is a vast difference between the manual administrative systems that pertained in the days before computerisation and the technology available to the Department today. *Hinchy* addressed a disjointed Departmental administration in the period from 1993 to 1998 passing information about DLA awards around on pieces of card, where one branch did not know what the other was doing. The evidence in this case indicates that that system has been consigned to the past.'

37. It is plainly time that the factual circumstances underpinning the decision in *Hinchy* are considered afresh in order to reflect the reasonably expected standards of 21st century benefits administration. In that context in the appropriate case it will have to be determined, on the appropriate facts, whether and to what extent a social entitlement claimant in 2023 is, or is not, entitled to make any assumptions about the internal administrative arrangements of the Department and in particular whether (a) a claimant is, or is not, entitled to assume the existence of efficacious (if not infallible) channels of communication between one office and another and (b) a claimant is, or is not, entitled to assume that when a decision is received in relation to one benefit, the Department's modern computerised systems will not just have communicated that decision to the individual claimant, but also to any other branches of the departmental administration where that decision has an impact."

The case law in this area, in any event, is not entirely clear. In *CIS/1887/2002*, the Commissioner ruled that there can be no failure to disclose where both benefits in question were being handled by the same local office, even where the benefits were being handled by different sections of that local office. The claimant submitted a claim for both income support and incapacity benefit to the same office. Income support was awarded and an award of incapacity benefit was subsequently made. The claimant did not tell the local office of this award and his income support continued to be paid resulting in a substantial overpayment of that benefit. The Commissioner, following *CSB/0677/1986*, concluded:

"21. It is also in my judgment a principle established beyond question that for the purposes of section 71 there is no 'failure to disclose' where the material fact in question is already known to the person or office to whom, under the principle laid down by the House of Lords in *Hinchy,* notification would otherwise have to be made. This too I take to be axiomatic and not called in question by anything said in the recent decision of their Lordships. It may be the kind of point Lord Hoffmann had in mind when he said 'a disclosure which would be thought necessary only by a literal-minded pedant . . . need not be made', though perhaps a true pedant would be the least likely to think disclosure necessary in such circumstances, taking the (accurate) view that there can be no question of 'disclosure' to a person or entity of something that he or it knows already.

22. In my judgment the question of liability under section 71 is concluded in favour of the claimant, and against the Department's view as accepted by the tribunal, by the fact that all questions affecting both of the interconnected benefits involved in this case were being dealt with by the single local benefits office at the same address; and there was nothing in any of the correspondence, literature or other evidence put before the tribunal to show that the staff from time to time dealing with the relevant incapacity benefit and income support questions were

separately identified to the claimant or any else as different 'offices'; or that the need to track down and notify any separate individual or section of individuals within that same office at the same address was either reasonably to be expected mf the claimant or in any way brought to his attention. On the contrary, all the material before the tribunal pointed to the opposite conclusion, and that has been reinforced by the further submissions and explanations of the system in such an office provided for me for the purposes of this appeal."

In *KI v HMRC (TC)* [2023] UKUT 212 (AAC) the lack of a legal duty to share information between the DWP and HMRC meant that there was no "official error" for the purposes of tax credit overpayment legislation when information was not shared.

ME v SSWP (SPC) [2016] UKUT 12 (AAC) illustrates the need for careful enquiry. The appellant was the subject of an overpayment decision in relation to an award of pension credit on the basis that he had failed to disclose receipt of an occupational pension. The appellant had made disclosures to Jobcentre Plus by telephone. On close enquiry and from a telephone number on a letter (other than the relevant award letter which was no longer available) from the Pension Service sent to the appellant, it appeared that the telephone numbers on letters he had received from both Jobcentre Plus and the Pension Service may well have been identical, which could have resulted in his having made the disclosure required of him by the Pension Service. Since the Secretary of State could not produce the original award letter, the Secretary of State accepted that he could not show, on the balance of probabilities, that there had been a failure to disclose.

1.112 In cases where different benefits are being handled by different parts of the DWP, and notification from one of them to the other does take place, the arguments now focus on the question of causation: whether the failure to disclose resulted in the overpayment. These issues are discussed in the section of this commentary headed "Causation" at paras 1.115–1.116 below.

In *CIS/1996/2006* and *CIS/2125/2006* the Commissioner alludes to the negative consequences of the decision in *B v SSWP* in noting that there can be no obligation on a claimant's partner to disclose, and so, if the partner was the only person who knew the material fact, there can be no failure to disclose. The pertinent paragraph of the decision reads:

"As the submissions . . . on behalf of the Secretary of State in each of these appeals are right to concede, the tribunal's findings of facts and reasons were insufficient to show how the duty of disclosure it placed on the appellant arose. Moreover in my judgment the tribunal misdirected itself in holding that the facts could bring him within regulation 32(1B) of the Claims and Payments Regulations at all. That provision, as the decision rightly said, imposes a duty; but a person in this appellant's position is not one of the people on whom that duty is expressed to be imposed. An income support claimant's partner, whose details have to be included in the claim, does not thereby become another claimant; is not a 'beneficiary' (an expression which is undefined, but in this context must mean a person with some entitlement to the relevant benefit); or a person 'by whom' the benefit awarded, not to the partner but to the claimant in his or her own right, is receivable. Nor is the income support under such an award receivable by the claimant in any sense as agent for or 'on behalf of' a partner merely because that partner's existence and resources are disclosed in the claim and taken into account in calculating the applicable amount, and thus the net overall level of benefit, appropriate to the *claimant* on the claim and any resulting award." (See [14].)

JM v SSWP (DLA) [2010] UKUT 135 (AAC) illustrates the need to analyse carefully what is in issue in an overpayment recoverability decision. The claimant had been in receipt of the lowest rate of the care component on the grounds that she could not cook a main meal for herself. She subsequently asked for the mobility component to be added but raised no issue relating to the care component. The mobility component was added. It was then established that she was working as a cleaning supervisor and that her mobility was, in fact, far in excess of the description of her walking ability on which the award had been based. Those circumstances also called into question her entitlement to the care component. An entitlement decision was made removing entitlement to both components from their initial award and an overpayment decision was made seeking recovery. A First-tier tribunal confirmed the entitlement decision and the Upper Tribunal judge on appeal found no fault with it. However, the First-tier tribunal had not sufficiently examined the basis for recovery of the overpaid benefit. It was accepted that there had been a serious misrepresentation of her walking ability by the claimant, which was "simply and obviously far beyond any genuine margin of error or imprecise description" (see [22]). Regardless, the appellant had not made any representations beyond statements made at the time of the original award of just the care component and that had been based on her claim supported only by her GP. The First-tier tribunal had, in the opinion of the Upper Tribunal judge, been right to conclude that an overpayment of the care component could only arise if the Secretary of State could establish that there had been a failure to disclose a material fact. The Upper Tribunal judge observes:

> "What the evidence showed was that in making her application in early November 2004 to have the mobility component added to her existing disability living allowance award, the claimant simply said nothing about her care needs because she was not asked to. On her own admission and the tribunal's findings, she knew she could in fact cook a main meal for herself all along, and knew the basis for her existing award of care component was a mistaken assumption that she could not reasonably do so. What she did then was simply to keep mum, and not volunteer any information to the department from which they could see they had made a mistake." (See [27].)

The Upper Tribunal judge notes that prior to *R(IS) 9/06 B v SSWP* disclosure **1.113**
by the appellant would have been regarded as being reasonably to be expected, but following that decision, the proper enquiry was to ask whether she had been required to disclose her knowledge that she had been awarded the care component on a mistaken basis. The judge concludes that none of the requirements imposed on the appellant required her to disclose information concerning her care needs or specifically on her ability to cook a main meal for herself. In all the circumstances the Secretary of State had not shown a required basis for recovery of the overpaid care component of the disability living allowance.

One of the issues which arose in *AS v SSWP (CA)* [2015] UKUT 592 (AAC); [2016] AACR 22, concerned the burden of proof which falls on the Secretary of State where claimants state that they have made disclosure by way of telephone communication with the Department. The issue arose in an overpayment case involving a claimed failure to disclose earnings on making a claim for carer's allowance where the existence of those earnings only came to light some years later. On the first question, the claimant's representative argued, relying on *CSB/347/1983* and *R(SB) 10/85,* that, in the face of the claimant's evidence that he had disclosed his earnings in a telephone call to the Department, the Secretary of State was required as a matter of law to adduce evidence as to the procedures in place at the relevant office of the Department at the relevant time, and could not merely adduce evidence that no record of the telephone conversation could be found. Judge Wright does not consider that *R(SB) 10/85* supports the proposition to be found in *CSB/347/1983*. Furthermore, even if *CSB/347/1983* constituted a principle of law in December 1983 when it was decided, it did not survive the approach advocated in *Kerr v Department for Social Development* [2004] UKHL 23; *R 1/04(SF)* which explained that the inquisitorial approach adopted in tribunals meant that "it will rarely be necessary to resort to concepts taken from adversarial litigation such as the burden of proof" (para.63). Under s.12(8)(a) of the Social Security Act 1998 what evidence is or is not needed in any case will depend on the facts of the case. The circumstances of the case before Judge Wright did not put in issue the procedures for recording telephone conversations. Judge Wright concludes:

"43. Accordingly, in so far as the comments in *CSB/347/1983* about telephone recording systems was laying down a rule of law, in my judgment it should no longer be followed."

In *R(A) 2/06*, the Commissioner considered the extent to which oral representations by an officer of the DWP can have an impact on the statutory duty to disclose. The case concerned a claimant with an appointee who was in a care home. When the local authority took over the payment of the care home fees, no disclosure was made and attendance allowance continued to be paid resulting in an overpayment of that benefit. In the run-up to the change of legislation which resulted in the local authority payment of the care home fees, the daughter (who was the appointee) was visited by a Customer Liaison Manager. In evidence, the appointee said that the Customer Liaison Manager "told me that the visit . . . would initiate any action required with regard to my mother's benefit changes when council funding started and there was no need for me to take any further action." (See [6] of the Decision.) The Commissioner accepts that a particular duty to provide information is capable of being modified by an oral representation made by an officer of the DWP, though it will be vital that careful findings of fact are made about such representations and their context. Finally, the Secretary of State must present evidence to show any duty to disclose; such a duty will not be implied and any assumption made by the Secretary of State that there is a duty to disclose is likely to be challenged in overpayment cases.

It follows from *Hinchy* that disclosure must be made to the local office handling the benefit claim in question. The disclosure may be in writing, though it need not be. In practice any disclosure not in writing will be reduced to writing by someone in the DWP. All disclosures must be made as soon as is practicable after the event which triggers the need for them.

A decision by Commissioner Stockman in Northern Ireland could well have implications for analogous cases elsewhere in the United Kingdom: *RM v Department for Communities C8/16-17 (JSA)*. The appeal concerned an overpayment of jobseeker's allowance. The obligations corresponding to those found in reg.32 of the Claims and Payments Regulations are in reg.24 of the JSA Regulations. In Northern Ireland, the instruction given to claimants is to notify either the Department for Social Development or his or her employment adviser (who was at the time an employee of the Department for Employment and Learning—the two departments have since been unified as the Department for Communities). The claimant told his employment adviser that his partner was working. The employment adviser told the claimant to notify someone in the Department for Social Development, but the claimant (a Lithuanian national) did not do so and said he had not understood the instruction to do so.

Commissioner Stockman rules that disclosure was complete when notice was given to the employment adviser, and it was not open to the employment adviser to vary the statutory requirement by oral instruction.

A further question was whether there was a continuing duty to disclose. Commissioner Stockman distinguished *R(SB) 15/87* and *R(SB) 54/83* because communication in those cases was not to an officer in the section handling the benefit in respect of which the overpayment arose. Here the claimant had complied with the directions he had received by giving notice to his employment adviser.

1.114 A continuing duty to disclose will arise where disclosure is made by someone other than the claimant. However, it should be noted that *R(SB) 15/87* establishes that where disclosure is made by a third party (other than an appointee, personal representatives, guardians and both members of joint claim couples), such notification is sufficient only if all the following conditions are met:

(a) the information is given in connection with the claimant's benefit entitlement and in compliance with any instructions from the Secretary of State;

(b) the claimant is aware that the information has been provided; and

(c) in the circumstances it is reasonable for the claimant to believe that it is unnecessary that further action is taken.

MW v SSWP (ESA) [2023] UKUT 50 (AAC) demonstrated the continuing need to meet the conditions in *R(SB) 15/87* before disclosure by a third party could be valid disclosure on behalf of a claimant, holding that they failed on the evidence.

CIS/14025/1996 establishes that such third party disclosures must be adequate to alert an officer of the DWP that it is a disclosure on behalf of another in respect of their benefit entitlement. Mere casual or incidental disclosure will not suffice.

If, following a disclosure by a third party, nothing changes, the claimant may well be under a continuing duty to disclose. This is illustrated by *WW v HMRC (CHB)* [2011] UKUT 11 (AAC). The claimant was in receipt of child benefit but her entitlement ceased when the child was taken into care. The claimant did not disclose the change in the child's circumstances to HMRC but it was found that she had certain dealings with officers of the DWP. The judge found that, in the course of one of those dealings, the officer of the DWP had indicated that the change of circumstances would be reported to HMRC with the result that payment of child benefit would cease. That did not happen. The judge ruled that an officer of the DWP has ostensible authority to make oral representations to pass on information to HMRC. This was based in part on the absence of any complete separation of the administration of child benefits between the DWP and HMRC. However, when the promised onward transmission of information did not take place, the claimant should have noticed that child benefit was still in payment and done something about this. She could only escape liability to repay three months worth of child benefit.

TM v SSWP (ESA) [2015] UKUT 109 (AAC) concerned an overpayment which arose on a conversion decision from entitlement to income support to entitlement to income-related ESA. The conversion decision was made in ignorance of the fact that the claimant had capital exceeding £16,000. It was eventually conceded that this could only be recovered on the grounds of a failure to disclose. The claimant's representative raised a number of arguments in support of his client's appeal. He argued that, as the alleged failures to disclose occurred while the claimant was entitled to income support, it could not be the basis for recovery in relation to ESA. Judge Rowland rejected that argument:

> "As long as there was a duty to make disclosure and the failure to disclose the material facts has caused the overpayment, it does not matter that the duty to disclose arose in respect of a different benefit from the one in respect of which it is submitted that the overpayment is recoverable." (para.7).

A further argument was that, as at the date of the award, the Secretary of State was fully aware of the claimant's capital but made a mistake for which the Secretary of State was wholly responsible. Judge Rowland said:

> "… it is difficult to see how any overpayment arising under the award … can be said to have been in consequence of the claimant's failure to disclose his capital if the Secretary of State already knew about the capital then and the decision was based on a mistake for which only he was responsible, unless, perhaps, the claimant was aware that the award was wrongly made."

Since this issue had not been fully explored by the First-tier Tribunal, the appeal was remitted for a rehearing.

Duty to disclose and JSA: As with other benefits, the Secretary of State may give specific instructions to those claiming or awarded jobseeker's allowance: reg.24 JSA Regulations. Regulation 24(7), however, goes further and requires claimants to notify the Secretary of State of any change of circumstances which has occurred or they are aware is likely to occur which they might reasonably be expected to know might affect their entitlement to JSA. Such disclosure must take place as soon as reasonably practicable after the change occurs, or after they become aware that it is likely to occur. 1.115

What is a material fact?

1.116 Both misrepresentation and failure to disclose involve the misrepresentation of, or the failure to disclose, a "material fact". What constitutes a material fact? *Jones & Sharples v CA* [1994] 1 All E.R. 225 (CA), reported as *R(IS) 7/94*, establishes that a material fact is any fact, which if had been known to, and acted upon by, the Secretary of State would have prevented the overpayment in question. It is some fact which is objectively material to the Secretary of State in determining entitlement to benefit: *R(IS) 9/06*. There is no requirement that the claimant is aware of the significance of the material fact, unless there has been an instruction to report facts which a claimant might reasonably realise would affect benefit entitlement: see above at paras 1.107-1.109.

Causation

1.117 Under s.71(1) the overpayment must be "in consequence of the misrepresentation or failure to disclose" and so there must be a clear causal connection between the misrepresentation or failure to disclose and the overpayment: *R(SB) 3/81*; *R(SB) 21/82*; and *R(SB) 15/87*. The onus is on the Secretary of State to show that each relevant payment of benefit would not have been made if the material fact had been either disclosed or not misrepresented. It is not sufficient to show that it might not have been made.

AH, VH and MH v SSWP (DLA) [2015] UKUT 108 (AAC); [2015] AACR 40; issues a reminder that, where a claimant continues to misrepresent a factual position up to and beyond an interview under caution, there is not necessarily a break in the chain of causation between the misrepresentation and the continuing payments. But Judge Gray also observes that the issue of causation is one of fact, which "precludes there being a legal principle that an interview under caution will itself break the chain of causation."

It seems that an error by the DWP (or HMRC) will only break the chain of causation where it is the sole cause of the overpayment. Arguments that a breakdown of internal communication between parts of the DWP have caused the overpayment, have been met with the consistent riposte that the test of causation is whether, if the claimant had disclosed or not misrepresented the material fact, the Secretary of State would have made payment of the benefit. If the answer is that he would not, then the necessary causal connection is made: *R(SB)3/90* and *Duggan v Chief Adjudication Officer*, appendix to *R(SB)13/89*. However, if it can be shown that the inter-office communication system did operate (that is, that there was actual rather than deemed knowledge) but was not then used to initiate any reviews, there maybe a break in the chain of causation: *R(SB)15/87*; *CIS/159/1990*; *CSIS/7/1994*; and *GJ v SSWP (IS)* [2010] UKUT 107 (AAC).

The scope of *Duggan* where there has been an error or neglect by an adjudication officer was discussed in *CIS/2447/1997*. The claimant stated on her income support claim form in November 1993 that her partner was not working. In October 1995 it came to light that he had always been in full-time work. The claimant's income support award had been reviewed in March 1994 following the birth of her son. It was argued that any overpayment after that review resulted not from the misrepresentation on the claim form but from the adjudication officer's negligence. This was because the adjudication officer had failed to identify any basis for the claimant's continued entitlement to income support after that time. She was no longer exempted from the condition of being available for work on the ground of pregnancy and she was not a single parent. The tribunal rejected this argument, holding that the circumstances were not distinguishable from those in *Duggan*. The Court of Appeal's decision in that case was closely related to its particular facts. It had not laid down a general rule that, whatever the extent or nature of the error by an adjudication officer, it did not remove the causative effect of some earlier failure to disclose or misrepresentation by a claimant. All the circumstances of the case had to be looked at. For example, if in the present case, the claimant had later told the income support office that she had won £10,000 and the adjudication officer had mistakenly determined that that did not affect entitlement to income support, the continued payment of benefit could not be said to have as even one of its causes the initial misrepresentation that her partner was not in full-time work. However, the actual facts of this case did not fall into that category. The information that her baby had been born would not on its own have inevitably led to the conclusion that entitlement to income support would cease. Even though the claimant might have become a person required to be available for work, her entitlement to income support would only have ceased if she had, for example, refused to make herself available for work. The adjudication officer's failure to investigate such issues was an *additional* but not the *sole* cause of overpayment and, as such, did not break the chain of causation between the initial misrepresentation and the overpayment.

An example of an error by the adjudication officer which did exonerate the claimant can be found in *CIS/222/1991*. The Commissioner holds that if the claimant's answers on the claim form were plainly inconsistent and ambiguous, this put the adjudication officer on notice to investigate the position. If this was not done, any overpayment was not recoverable as it was due to error on the part of the Department rather than a misrepresentation by the claimant. Here the information *on the claim form* should have triggered investigation by the adjudication officer but the adjudication officer chose not to resolve those conflicts before awarding benefit. 1.118

In *R(IS) 4/06* the overpayment arose because the appellant's wife's pension was not taken into account in relation to a claim for income support. The appellant himself was illiterate and the form was completed on his behalf by his wife. The appellant signed the form and this was said to constitute a misrepresentation on his part. Some questions on the claim form were unanswered. It was argued that this was a case of a failure by the DWP to investigate the claim fully and this had caused the overpayment. The Commissioner rejected that argument on the grounds that the claim form was incomplete rather than ambiguous and contained sufficient information to enable a decision to be made. He distinguished *CIS/222/1991* as a case in which a proper decision could not be made without further investigations. Even if the decision maker in *R(IS) 4/06* was partly responsible for the incorrect decision, the appellant was also to blame for not giving correct answer's about his wife's pension.

The failure or absence of communication between the various parts of the DWP handling different types of benefit continues to be a source of argument that the chain of causation has been broken. The authorities still maintain the position that the chain of causation is only broken where it can be shown that some failure within the DWP is the sole cause of the overpayment: *GK v SSWP (IS)* [2009] UKUT 98 (AAC), at [34]. However, there are cases where it can be shown that there was actual knowledge in the relevant office which should have been acted upon. This is illustrated in *GJ v SSWP (IS)* [2010] UKUT 107 (AAC), which also includes at [27]–[48] a useful recapitulation of the law on causation. The judge in this case stresses the need for evidence of office practice:

> "44. . . . it would normally be relevant to have evidence as to why the information was not acted on, and as to the procedures in place at the time for dealing with the receipt from the claimant of the relevant information. It is for the Secretary of State to produce evidence (as opposed to submissions) as to why the error occurred if the information was available in the office, and even more so when it was clearly available on the relevant file. The evidence should also deal with the standard procedures in place to review an award in a case such as the present, where there may have been a case control or a reminder at the relevant time in 2005, and as to what happened in relation to those procedures."

SSWP v SS (SPC) [2013] UKUT 272 (AAC) considers when the chain of causation is broken and how a tribunal should proceed when an argument on this issue arises in the course of the hearing. The judge rules that it will be a breach of natural justice to fail to adjourn a hearing to enable the Secretary of State to respond to arguments that the chain of causation has been broken (at [6]). Whether and when the chain of causation is broken is a question of fact but a failure to respond immediately to information arising from a Generalised Matching Service Scan will not necessarily result in a break in the chain of causation (see especially [15]). The case includes a review of some earlier case-law.

1.119 *BD v SSWP (PC)* [2016] UKUT 162 (AAC) contains a detailed account (at paras 8-9) of arrangements for computerised communications between various parts of the Department and the expectations as to action that would be taken on those communications. The case also considers the application of the principles set out in *GJ v SSWP (IS)* and *SSWP v SS (SPC)*.

For decisions by the Northern Ireland Social Security Commissioners, with the benefit of unusually detailed evidence, on the extent to which *Hinchy* may be applicable given the move from paper-based to computerised systems in the period since 1993-98 (which *Hinchy* concerned) and the impact on issues of causation, see *SK v Department for Communities (ESA)* [2020] NiCom 73 and *PMcL v Department for Communities (ESA)* [2020] NiCom 21. However, the administrative arrangements in Northern Ireland on one hand and Great Britain on the other are different and the case was distinguished in Great Britain in *MW v SSWP (ESA)* [2023] UKUT 50.

The evidential base regarding the DWP's working practices is important. Thus, in *WS v SSWP (ESA)* [2023] UKUT 81, evidence was provided (albeit only at Upper Tribunal level) regarding how a particular information feed from HMRC to the DWP operated, as a result of which the judge, on that evidence, held:

> "38. Although the information sharing between HMRC and the Department for Work and Pensions is described as "RTI" or "real time information", that doesn't mean that the First-tier Tribunal was obliged to find that the Secretary of State had knowledge of the information shared with HMRC on a "real time" basis. Even if the information is transmitted electronically on a "real time" basis, when that information becomes "known" to the Secretary of State depends on how the systems work and how they are operated.
>
> 39. While it does not appear that the First-tier Tribunal had a great deal of evidence on these topics (the explanation summarised in paragraph 38 above having been provided in the Secretary of State's submissions on this appeal rather than the appeal before the First-tier Tribunal), the fact remains that the Secretary of State reaches decisions on benefit matters through human decision makers, and not by having his computer system simply apply an algorithm to a data feed and "push" a decision outcome to a decision maker, or indeed a claimant. Information in the RTI data feed being available to the Secretary of State (or to a relevant officer at an appropriate office) is not the same thing as it being known to them. To be "known" the data must not be merely available, but must have been accessed and, to some degree, analysed, by a human being, who then decides what to do with the information so gleaned."

The calculation of the overpayment

1.120 *KP v RB of Kensington and Chelsea (HB)* [2014] UKUT 393 (AAC) determines that a compensation order made by the Crown Court does not act as a cap on the amount of overpaid housing benefit and excess council tax benefit which is recoverable.

There are two linked aspects of the calculation of the overpayment: the period of the overpayment and the amount of the overpayment. Both must be specified in the overpayment decision. It is not at all uncommon to see variations both in dates and amounts where there is an appeal against an overpayment decision. It is for the Secretary of State to determine both the period and the amount of the overpayment. Tribunals may be called upon to check the accuracy of the determination. A failure by the tribunal to do something about the local authority's failure in a housing benefit case to explain the calculation of an alleged overpayment was held to be an error of law in *KH v LB Wandsworth (HB)* [2019] UKUT 45 (AAC).

In *CS/366/1993* the Commissioner gives advice on the level of proof of payment of a benefit recovery of which is being sought. This is an issue which can come up in overpayment appeals, when a claimant either directly or indirectly puts in issue whether they have ever received the money which the adjudication officer, or now decision-maker, says is recoverable. The Commissioner reminds tribunals that the burden of proof is on the balance of probabilities. Where there is evidence of entitlement to and payment of benefit that may be sufficient to show that the benefit was paid. It certainly is in the absence of any challenge by the claimant. Equally, no higher burden will lie with the adjudication officer if the claimant does not adduce evidence that they did not receive the benefit but simply asked the adjudication officer to prove that the benefit was paid.

In *R(SB) 11/86* it was held that underpayments of benefit during the relevant period could be taken into account. The sums to be deducted in calculating recoverable amounts are governed by reg.13 of the Payments on Account Regulations.

A schedule showing how the overpayment is calculated is normally included in the appeal papers, although great care must be taken in simply adopting these, especially if there is any variation of the decision under appeal. The tribunal may, for example, find that an overpayment is recoverable for a different period. This will affect the amount recoverable. The need for tribunals to state expressly the sum which is recoverable and how it is calculated was stressed in *R(SB) 9/85*. This advice was repeated in *R(SB) 11/86* where the Commissioner helpfully approves the practice of leaving a difficult recalculation to the adjudication officer *provided that* it is made clear that the claimant or the adjudication officer may refer the matter back to the tribunal in the event of any particular difficulty or disagreement arising. The approach tribunals should adopt is to recalculate benefit in the light of the facts as found by them to determine the amount of the overpayment: *R(SB) 20/84* and *R(SB) 10/85(T)*. **1.121**

In *CIS/442/1992* the Commissioner reminds tribunals of the proper procedure to follow when the calculation of the amount of the overpayment is initially left for determination by the parties. Where reference back to the tribunal is necessary, then that reference should be to the same tribunal which dealt with the issue of liability (at para.5). Should it prove necessary to refer the case back to a differently constituted tribunal, then both the issue of liability and the issue of calculation will need to be considered at the adjourned hearing (at para.7). A different tribunal should only hear the case if satisfied that it is not practicable to reconvene the original tribunal (at para.7).

Where capital is in issue, then the rules on diminishing capital are likely to come into play. This is governed by reg.14 of the Payments on Account Regulations. This provides for the reduction of the figure of capital resources at quarterly intervals from the beginning of the period of the overpayment period by the amount overpaid in respect of the listed benefits in the previous quarter. No other reduction of the actual amount of capital resources is allowed: reg.14(2).

For the proper approach to whether arrears in respect of a period of suspension may be set off against an overpayment in respect of an earlier period, see *MR v SSWP (IS)* [2013] UKUT 588 (AAC).

In *LB v SSWP* (ESA) [2019] UKUT 178 (AAC), Upper Tribunal Judge Poole QC rejected a submission by the claimant that the amount recoverable by the SSWP should be limited to the particular "material fact" that was not properly disclosed.

The method of recovery

Whether a recoverable overpayment is actually recovered, and if so, how, are matters for the Secretary of State, and do not concern tribunals. Nevertheless, it is worth noting the judgment of the Supreme Court in *SSWP v Payne* [2011] UKSC 60, in which the court ruled that the DWP cannot recover overpayments of benefit or Social Fund loans by deductions from benefit where that overpayment or loan has been included in a Debt Relief Order (DRO) in insolvency proceedings. The Supreme Court went on to consider the position following the making of **1.122** a bankruptcy order and decided that it should be the same for bankruptcy as for DROs. In other words, there is no power to make deductions from benefits following the making of a bankruptcy order, just as after a DRO.

Direct payments to bank accounts

1.123 Section 71(4) provides for the automatic recovery of overpaid benefit arising from incorrect payments into bank accounts. Subsection (4) provides an independent ground for recovering overpayments resulting from the use of payments to a bank account or other similar account. Recovery will only be available if the claimant received, before agreeing to such method of payment, notice in the form specified in reg.11 of the Payments on Account Regulations. If the conditions in reg.11 are not satisfied, an overpayment may still be recoverable under s.71(1).

Tax credits: substitution of subs(8)–(9)

1.124 Section 71(8)–(9) is, with effect from October 5, 1999, by virtue of s.2 and Pt. IV para.10 of Sch.2 to the Tax Credits Act 1999, to be read as follows in any case where the overpayment was made in respect of tax credits:

"(8) An amount recoverable under subsection (1) above in any year of assessment—

(a) shall be treated for the purposes of Part VI of the Taxes Management Act 1970 (collection and recovery) as if it were tax charged in an assessment and due and payable;

(b) shall be treated for the purposes of section 203(2)(a) of the Income and Corporation Taxes Act 1988 (PAYE) as if it were an underpayment of tax for a previous year of assessment.

(8A) Where—

(a) an amount paid in respect of a claim is recoverable under subsection (1) above; and

(b) a penalty has been imposed under section 9(1) of the Tax Credits Act 1999 (penalties for fraud etc.) on the ground that a person fraudulently or negligently made an incorrect statement or declaration in connection with that claim,

the amount shall carry interest at the rate applicable from the date on which it becomes recoverable until payment.

(9) The rate applicable for the purposes of subsection (8A) above shall be the rate from time to time prescribed under section 178 of the Finance Act 1989 for those purposes."

1.125 See *Larusai v SSWP* [2003] EWHC 371 (Admin), discussed in the annotations to reg.13 of the Payments on Account Regulations, for the relationship between working families tax credit and benefits administered by the DWP in relation to recovery of overpayments of benefits administered by the DWP.

[1 Overpayments out of social fund

1.126 **71ZA.**—(1) Subject to subsection (2) below, section 71 above shall apply in relation to social fund payments to which this section applies as it applies in relation to payments made in respect of benefits to which that section applies.

(2) Section 71 above as it so applies shall have effect as if

(a) in [2subsection (5A)], for the words "reversed or varied on an appeal or has been revised under section 9 or superseded under section 10 there were substituted the words "revised on a review under section 38";[2 and]

[2. . .]

(c) subsections (7), (10A) and (10B) were omitted.

[3 (2A) Subsection (9A) of section 71 above as it so applies shall have effect as if the reference to amounts recoverable under the provisions mentioned in subsection (8) of that section were to amounts recoverable under subsections (1) and (4) of that section by virtue of subsection (1) above.]

(3) This section applies to social fund payments such as are mentioned in section 138(1)(b) of the Contributions and Benefits Act.]

Amendments

1. Social Security Act 1998 s.75(1) (October 5, 1998).
2. Welfare Reform Act 2007 Sch.8 (July 3, 2007).
3. Welfare Reform Act 2012 s.106 (July 1, 2012).

General Note

Section 75(2) of the Social Security Act 1998 provides that s.71ZA applies to social fund overpayment decisions made on or after October 5, 1998. 1.127

[1 *Recovery of benefit payments*

Recovery of overpayments of certain benefits

71ZB.—(1) The Secretary of State may recover any amount of the following paid in excess of entitlement— 1.128

(a) universal credit,
(b) jobseeker's allowance,
(c) employment and support allowance,
(d) *except in prescribed circumstances, housing credit (within the meaning of the State Pension Credit Act 2002).*

(2) An amount recoverable under this section is recoverable from—

(a) the person to whom it was paid, or
(b) such other person (in addition to or instead of the person to whom it was paid) as may be prescribed.

(3) An amount paid in pursuance of a determination is not recoverable under this section unless the determination has been—

(a) reversed or varied on an appeal, or
(b) revised or superseded under section 9 or section 10 of the Social Security Act 1998,

except where regulations otherwise provide.

(4) Regulations may provide that amounts recoverable under this section are to be calculated or estimated in a prescribed manner.

(5) Where an amount of universal credit is paid for the sole reason that a payment by way of prescribed income is made after the date which is the prescribed date for payment of that income, that amount is for the purposes of this section paid in excess of entitlement.

(6) In the case of a benefit referred to in subsection (1) which is awarded to persons jointly, an amount paid to one of those persons may for the purposes of this section be regarded as paid to the other.

(7) An amount recoverable under this section may (without prejudice to any other means of recovery) be recovered—

(a) by deduction from benefit (section 71ZC);
(b) by deduction from earnings (section 71ZD);
(c) through the courts etc (section 71ZE);
(d) by adjustment of benefit (section 71ZF).]

AMENDMENT

1. The Welfare Reform Act 2012 s.105 and the Welfare Reform Act 2012 (Commencement No. 8 and Savings and Transitional Provisions) Order 2013 (SI 2013/358) art.5(2) (April 29, 2013).

GENERAL NOTE

1.129 Sections 71ZB to 71ZF contain the "new style" provisions on the recovery of overpayments and should be read together with the Social Security (Overpayments and Recovery) Regulations 2013 (paras 2.869–2.914 below).

This section effects a fundamental shift in the law relating to the recovery of overpayments of benefit. It deals (at present only) with the recovery of overpaid universal credit, JSA and ESA and will address the housing credit element of state pension credit (it is not yet fully in force—see further below). Furthermore, so far as ESA and JSA are concerned, the present effect of the commencement provisions is that the new test applies only to overpayments of the "new-style" contributory versions of ESA and JSA, introduced as part of the universal credit regime.

In view of the fundamental shift effected by this group of sections, permitting the Secretary of State to recover even when the fault was that of his Department, how the power conferred by s.71ZB is exercised becomes of critical importance. The decision in *R(K) v SSWP* [2023] EWHC 233 (Admin) on facts described by the judge as "remarkable" shows some of the challenges faced by a claimant and the relevance of public law concepts in challenging the DWP's repeated refusals to grant a waiver.

In summary, the claimant, on universal credit, had two disabled sons, at least one of whom, and sometimes both, lived with her. When one son started an apprenticeship, this should have resulted in a reduction in her universal credit. The claimant reported it and on a number of occasions was told that the change made no difference. Although she was assiduous in checking the position with the DWP, the response remained the same and she continued to be paid the same amount. When the DWP realised the error, £8623.20 had been overpaid, which it sought to recover.

The claimant's circumstances, as a carer for two disabled young adults, were extremely difficult, including poor health, an inability to work any more hours than she already was and a need to resort to food banks. In all, three applications were made for a waiver, all were refused. (As the decision illustrates, anyone contemplating applying for a waiver should be under no illusions as to the breadth and detail of the evidence that is likely to be required in support, nor as to the limited number of cases in which over the few years before the case a waiver had been granted.)

Some aspects of the case concern the policy framework then in force which included both the published Benefit Overpayment Recovery Guide and an unpublished Decision Makers' Guide to Waiver, the lack of publication of the latter being held to be unlawful in itself. The latter has been withdrawn and at the time of writing (4 May 2023), the policy is to be found in Ch.8 of the Benefit Overpayment Recovery Guide, last updated in February 2023 and accessible at *https://www.gov.uk/government/publications/benefit-overpayment-recovery-staff-guide/benefit-overpayment-recovery-guide*.

The refusal to waive recovery was also held to be unlawful for other reasons. The dealings between the claimant and the DWP, on which she had relied to her detriment by spending the money and by not pursuing alternative ways to arrange her finances, were held to give rise to a legitimate expectation that the DWP would not recover the money, from which it would not be permitted to resile. Furthermore, the decision had failed to take into account material considerations, including that the claimant acted in good faith; the claimant timeously provided all the information required to the DWP; and she took all reasonable steps both to clarify her entitlement and to prevent any overpayment by actively querying her entitlement on at least four occasions.

The Secretary of State is given the power to recover any amount of Universal Credit, JSA and ESA, which has been paid in excess of entitlement (subs.(1)(a)–(c)).

The same principle will apply also to housing credit which has been paid in excess of entitlement, except in circumstances that will be prescribed in regulations once subs.(1)(d) has been brought into force. There is no requirement on the Secretary of State to establish either a misrepresentation or failure to disclose as a precondition for recovery. It follows that any payment of one of the relevant benefits in excess of the claimant's appropriate entitlement will be a recoverable overpayment, including those overpayments which arise purely as a result of official error. The underlying philosophy is that even the need for the Department to take responsibility for its own mistakes "does not give people the right to keep tax-payers' money that they are not entitled to" (Explanatory Memorandum to the Social Security (Overpayments and Recovery) Regulations 2013 para.7.2).

The overpaid benefit can be recovered from the person to whom it was paid or such other person as is prescribed (subs.(2); see further the Social Security (Overpayments and Recovery) Regulations 2013 (SI 2013/384) reg.4). There must have been a relevant revision, supersession or appellate decision (subs.(3)). This requirement is broadly equivalent to the existing s.71(5A) of the SSAA 1992. However, note that the Social Security (Overpayments and Recovery) Regulations 2013 reg.5 provides that "Section 71ZB(3) of the Act (recoverability of an overpayment dependent on reversal, variation, revision or supersession) does not apply where the circumstances of the overpayment do not provide a basis for the decision pursuant to which the payment was made to be revised under section 9 of the Social Security Act 1998 or superseded under section 10 of that Act."

Subsection (5) has the effect that where another income or benefit that would affect the award of universal credit is paid late, any amount of universal credit, which would not have been paid had the other income or benefit been paid on time, is treated as an overpayment and is recoverable from the universal credit recipient.

Where an award of benefit is made to persons jointly, an amount paid to one member of the couple may be treated as paid to the other and so recovered (subs (6)).

The various methods of recovery are set out in subs.(7), namely deduction from benefit (s.71ZC), by deduction from earnings (s.71ZD) (a new method akin to attachment of earnings), through the courts (s.71ZE) or by adjustment of subsequent benefit payments (s.71ZF).

Note that this section is not fully in force. Article 5(3)(a) of the Welfare Reform Act 2012 (Commencement No.8 and Savings and Transitional Provisions) Order 2013 (SI 2013/358) provided for the amending s.105(1) of the WRA 2012 to have effect in so far as it was not already in force "except in so far as it inserts section 71ZB(1)(d) of the 1992 Act and the word 'and' immediately preceding it" (the italicised text above). The Commencement No.8 Order was then modified by art.23(3) of the Welfare Reform Act 2012 (Commencement No.9 and Transitional and Transitory Provisions and Commencement No. 8 and Savings and Transitional Provisions (Amendment)) Order 2013 (SI 2013/983), which provides that new s.71ZB(1)(b) and (c) "come into force on 29th April 2013 only in so far as they relate respectively to a new style JSA award and a new style ESA award".

[1 71ZC. Deduction from benefit

(1) An amount recoverable from a person under section 71ZB may be recovered by deducting the amount from payments of prescribed benefit. 1.130

(2) Where an amount recoverable from a person under section 71ZB was paid to the person on behalf of another, subsection (1) authorises its recovery from the person by deduction—

(a) from prescribed benefits to which the person is entitled,

(b) from prescribed benefits paid to the person to discharge (in whole or in part) an obligation owed to that person by the person on whose behalf the recoverable amount was paid, or

(c) from prescribed benefits paid to the person to discharge (in whole or in part) an obligation owed to that person by any other person.

(3) Where an amount is recovered as mentioned in paragraph (b) of subsection (2), the obligation specified in that paragraph shall in prescribed circumstances be taken to be discharged by the amount of the deduction.

(4) Where an amount is recovered as mentioned in paragraph (c) of subsection (2), the obligation specified in that paragraph shall in all cases be taken to be so discharged.]

Amendment

1. Welfare Reform Act 2012 s.105(1) (July 1, 2012 for the purpose only of prescribing under s.71ZC(1) the benefits from which deductions may be made in order to recover penalties, October 1, 2012 to the extent that it inserts s.71ZC(1) for the purpose only of enabling recovery of the penalties to take place by these methods; and April 29, 2013 for remaining purposes).

General Note

1.131 This section provides for the recovery of overpayments under s.71ZB by deduction from benefit. Thus overpayments of universal credit, JSA and ESA can be recovered by making deductions from payments of prescribed benefits (subs.(1)). Where a relevant benefit is paid to a third party (e.g. a landlord) on the claimant's behalf, overpayments of those benefits may be recovered from prescribed benefits to which the third party is entitled; ongoing payments of prescribed benefits to the third party being made on the benefit claimant's behalf; or ongoing payments of prescribed benefits paid to the third party on other benefit claimants' behalf (e.g. if a landlord has other tenants who are in receipt of universal credit) (subs.(2)). Furthermore, in circumstances to be prescribed by regulations, where deductions are made from payments of prescribed benefits to the third party on the claimant's behalf, then the claimant's obligations to the third party will be discharged, e.g. the landlord would not be able to put the claimant into arrears with their rent (subs.(3)). Similarly, in all cases where deductions are made from payments of prescribed benefits to the third party on behalf of other benefit claimants, the other claimants' obligations to the third party will likewise be discharged (and so the landlord would not be able to hold those other claimants as being in arrears with their rent) (subs.(4)). See further Social Security (Overpayments and Recovery) Regulations 2013 (SI 2013/384) Pt 5 (regs 10–16) and especially reg.15.

[1 71ZD. Deduction from earnings

1.132 (1) Regulations may provide for amounts recoverable under section 71ZB to be recovered by deductions from earnings.

(2) In this section "earnings" has such meaning as may be prescribed.

(3) Regulations under subsection (1) may include provision—

(a) requiring the person from whom an amount is recoverable ("the beneficiary") to disclose details of their employer, and any change of employer, to the Secretary of State;

(b) requiring the employer, on being served with a notice by the Secretary of State, to make deductions from the earnings of the beneficiary and to pay corresponding amounts to the Secretary of State;

(c) as to the matters to be contained in such a notice and the period or which a notice is to have effect;

(d) as to how payment is to be made to the Secretary of State;

(e) as to a level of earnings below which earnings must not be reduced;

(f) allowing the employer, where the employer makes deductions, to deduct a prescribed sum from the beneficiary's earnings in respect of the employer's administrative costs;
(g) requiring the employer to keep records of deductions;
(h) requiring the employer to notify the Secretary of State if the beneficiary is not, or ceases to be, employed by the employer;
(i) creating a criminal offence for non-compliance with the regulations, punishable on summary conviction by a fine not exceeding level 3 on the standard scale;
(j) with respect to the priority as between a requirement to deduct from earnings under this section and—
  (i) any other such requirement;
  (ii) an order under any other enactment relating to England and Wales which requires deduction from the beneficiary's earnings;
  (iii) any diligence against earnings.]

AMENDMENT

1. Welfare Reform Act 2012 s.105(1) and the Welfare Reform Act 2012 (Commencement No.2) Order 2012 (SI 2012/1246) (July 1, 2012).

GENERAL NOTE

Under the previous arrangements, the Secretary of State typically recovered overpayment debts through deductions from ongoing benefit entitlement. However, once a claimant subject to an overpayment liability stopped receiving benefit, further recovery relied heavily on the debtor's compliance with repayment. If a former claimant chose not to pay the money owed, then the Department's option to take court action was not always cost effective. In principle, however, the Department has always been able to apply to the magistrates' court for an attachment of earnings order as a means of recovering outstanding overpayments. 1.133

This section for the first time empowers both the Department and local authorities to recover debt by attachment of earnings without the need for an application to court. Direct Earnings Attachments (DEA) are thus designed to act as an incentive to those liable for overpayments to make arrangements to repay their debts and, if they still refuse to repay, to provide the Department (or local authority) with a simpler alternative means to secure recovery. See further Social Security (Overpayments and Recovery) Regulations 2013 (SI 2013/384) especially Pt 6 (regs 17–30). These Regulations set out the circumstances in which a DEA can be issued, the type of earnings from which a deduction can be taken, the responsibilities of employers and the relevant rates of deduction where a DEA is in place.

[1 71ZE. Court action etc.

(1) Where an amount is recoverable under section 71ZB from a person residing in England and Wales, the amount is, if [2 the county court] so orders, recoverable— 1.134
(a) under section 85 of the County Courts Act 1984, or
(b) otherwise as if it were payable under an order of the court.

(2) Where an amount is recoverable under section 71ZB from a person residing in Scotland, the amount recoverable may be enforced as if it were payable under an extract registered decree arbitral bearing a warrant for execution issued by the sheriff court of any sheriffdom in Scotland.

(3) Any costs of the Secretary of State in recovering an amount of benefit under this section may be recovered by him as if they were amounts recoverable under section 71ZB.

(4) In any period after the coming into force of this section and before the coming into force of section 62 of the Tribunals, Courts and Enforcement Act 2007, subsection (1)(a) has effect as if it read "by execution issued from the county court".]

AMENDMENTS

1. Welfare Reform Act 2012 s.105(1) (October 1, 2012, for the purpose only of enabling recovery of the penalties to take place by these methods (SI 2012/1246) and April 29, 2013 for other purposes (SI 2013/358)).

2. Crime and Courts Act 2013 s.17(5) and Sch.9(3) para.52(1)(b) (April 22, 2014).

GENERAL NOTE

1.135 This section provides for the recovery of overpayments under new s.71ZB through the courts. Thus overpayments are recoverable through the county courts for claimants residing in England and Wales (subs.(1)) and through the sheriff courts for those residing in Scotland (subs.(2)). The Secretary of State's normal practice is to try and recover court costs when there is a court judgment in his favour. However, under the previous law there was no mechanism for the Secretary of State to recover such associated costs in the same way as if they formed part of the overpayment debt (e.g. by deduction from benefit or by adjustment of subsequent payments of benefit). Accordingly, subs.(3) allows the Secretary of State to recover costs by the same method as the overpayment itself is recovered.

[[1] Adjustment of benefit

1.136 **71ZF.** Regulations may for the purpose of the recovery of the amounts recoverable under section 71ZB make provision—

(a) for treating any amount paid to a person under an award which it is subsequently determined was not payable—

(i) as properly paid, or

(ii) as paid on account of a payment which it is determined should be or should have been made,

and for reducing or withholding arrears payable by virtue of the subsequent determination;

(b) for treating any amount paid to one person in respect of another as properly paid for any period for which it is not payable in cases where in consequence of a subsequent determination—

(i) the other person is entitled to a payment for that period, or

(ii) a third person is entitled in priority to the payee to a payment for that period in respect of the other person,

and by reducing or withholding any arrears payable for that period by virtue of the subsequent determination.]

AMENDMENT

1. The Welfare Reform Act 2012 s.105(1) and Welfare Reform Act 2012 (Commencement No. 8 and Savings and Transitional Provisions) Order 2013 (SI 2013/358) art.5(2) (April 29, 2013).

GENERAL NOTE

1.137 This section concerns the recovery of overpayments under s.71ZB using the method of adjusting subsequent benefit payments. It provides that the Secretary of State may prescribe in regulations that in certain circumstances, amounts paid but subsequently determined as not payable, can be treated as properly paid and be set against future payments of benefit or against certain payments to third parties.

[1 Recovery of payments on account

71ZG.—(1) The Secretary of State may recover any amount paid under section 5(1)(r) (payments on account). 1.138

(2) An amount recoverable under this section is recoverable from—

(a) the person to whom it was paid, or

(b) such other person (in addition to or instead of the person to whom it was paid) as may be prescribed.

(3) Regulations may provide that amounts recoverable under this section are to be calculated or estimated in a prescribed manner.

(4) in the case of a payment on account of a benefit which is awarded to persons jointly, an amount paid to one of those persons may for then purposes of this section be regarded as paid to the other.

(5) section 71ZC, 71ZD and 71ZE apply in relation to amounts recoverable under this section as to amounts recoverable under section 71ZB.]

AMENDMENT

1. The Welfare Reform Act 2012 s.105(1) and Welfare Reform Act 2012 (Commencement No. 8 and Savings and Transitional Provisions) Order 2013 (SI 2013/358) art.5(2) (April 29, 2013).

[1 Recovery of hardship payments etc

71ZH.—(1) The Secretary of State may recover any amount paid by way of— 1.139

(a) a payment under section 28 of the Welfare Reform Act 2012 (universal credit hardship payments) which is recoverable under that section,

(b) *payment under section 19C of the Jobseeker's Act 1995 (jobseeker's allowance hardship payments) which is recoverable under that section,*

(c) a payment of a jobseeker's allowance under paragraph 8 or 8A of Schedule 1 to that Act (exemptions), where the allowance is payable at a prescribed rate under paragraph 9 of that Schedule and is recoverable under that paragraph,

(d) a payment of a jobseeker's allowance under paragraph 10 of that Schedule (claims yet to be determined etc) which is recoverable under that paragraph, or

(e) a payment which is recoverable under section 6B(5A)(d) or (7)(d), 7(2A)(d) or (4)(d), 8(3)(aa), (4)(d) or 9(2A)(d) of the Social Security Fraud Act 2001.

(2) An amount recoverable under this section is recoverable from—

(a) the person to whom it was paid, or

(b) such other person (in addition to or instead of the person to whom it was paid) as may be prescribed.

(3) Regulations may provide that amount recoverable under this section are to be calculated or estimated in a prescribed manner.

(4) Where universal credit or a jobseeker's allowance is claimed by persons jointly, an amount paid to one claimant may for the purposes of this section be regarded as paid to the other.

(5) Sections 71ZC to 71ZF apply in relation to amounts recoverable under this section as to amounts recoverable under section 71ZB.]

AMENDMENT

1. The Welfare Reform Act 2012 (Commencement No. 8 and Savings and Transitional Provisions) Order 2013 (SI 2013/358) art.5(2) (April 29, 2013).

GENERAL NOTE

1.140 The significance of the words in italics in s.71ZH(1)(b) is that this paragraph is repealed with effect from April 29, 2013 but is maintained in force for certain purposes: see the Welfare Reform Act 2012 Sch.14(4) para.1 and the Welfare Reform Act 2012 (Commencement No. 9 and Transitional and Transitory Provisions and Commencement No. 8 and Savings and Transitional Provisions (Amendment)) Order 2013 (SI 2013/983) art.7(1)(e).

See further reg.119 of the Universal Credit Regulations.

Recovery of jobseeker's allowance: severe hardship cases

1.141 **71A.**—(1) Where—

(a) a severe hardship direction is revoked; and
(b) it is determined by [2 the Secretary of State] that—
 (i) whether fraudulently or otherwise, any person has misrepresented, or failed to disclose, any material fact; and
 (ii) in consequence of the failure or misrepresentation, payment of a jobseeker's allowance has been made during the relevant period to the person to whom the direction related,

[2 the Secretary of State] may determine that [2 he] is entitled to recover the amount of the payment.

(2) In this section—

"severe hardship direction" means a direction given under section 16 of the Jobseekers Act 1995; and

"the relevant period" means—

(a) if the revocation is under section 16(3)(a) of that Act, the period begining with the date of the change of circumstances and ending with the date of the revocation; and
(b) if the revocation is under section 16(3)(b) or (c) of that Act, the period during which the direction was in force.

(3) Where a severe hardship direction is revoked, the Secretary of State may certify whether there has been misrepresentation of a material fact or failure to disclose a material fact.

(4) If the Secretary of State certifies that there has been such misrepresentation or failure to disclose, he may certify—

(a) who made the misrepresentation or failed to make the disclosure; and
(b) whether or not a payment of jobseeker's allowance has been made in consequence of the misrepresentation or failure.

(5) If the Secretary of State certifies that a payment has been made, he may certify the period during which a jobseeker's allowance would not have been paid but for the misrepresentation or failure to disclose.

(6) A certificate under this section shall be conclusive as to any matter certified.

(7) Subsections (3) and (6) to (10) of section 71 above apply to a jobseeker's allowance recoverable under subsection (1) above as they apply to a jobseeker's allowance recoverable under section 71(1) above.

(8) The other provisions of section 71 above do not apply to a jobseeker's allowance recoverable under subsection (1) above.]

AMENDMENTS

1. Jobseekers Act 1995 s.18 (October 7, 1996).
2. Social Security Act 1998 Sch.7 para.82 (October 18, 1999).

GENERAL NOTE

Section 16 of the Jobseekers Act 1995 enables the Secretary of State to direct that a person under the age of 18 is to qualify for JSA in order to avoid severe hardship. The direction may be revoked on the ground of change of circumstances (s.16(3)(a)) or on the ground that the young person has failed to pursue an opportunity, or rejected an offer, of training without good cause (s.16(3)(b)) or on the ground that mistake as to or ignorance of a material fact led to the determination that severe hardship would result if JSA was not paid (s.16(3)(c)). A special provision is needed for recovery in cases of misrepresentation or failure to disclose because the revocation of the direction is not a review which can found action under s.71 and it appears that it does not enable the decision on entitlement to JSA to be reviewed for any period before the date of the revocation. Note that the Secretary of State's certificate is conclusive on almost every issue (subs.(3)–(6)). The provisions of s.71 about the mechanics of recovery apply. 1.142

Special provision as to recovery of income support

72. [1. . .] 1.143

AMENDMENT

1. Repealed by Jobseekers Act 1995 Sch.3 (October 7, 1996).

Adjustments of benefits

Overlapping benefits—general

73.—(1) Regulations may provide for adjusting [8 state pension under Part 1 of the Pensions Act 2014 or] benefit as defined in section 122 of the Contributions and Benefits Act [1, or a contribution-based jobseeker's allowance] [6 or a contributory employment and support allowance] which is payable to or in respect of any person, or the conditions for [2 receipt of that benefit] where— 1.144

(a) there is payable in his case any such pension or allowance as is described in subsection (2) below; or
(b) the person is, or is treated under the regulations as, undergoing medical or other treatment as an in-patient in a hospital or similar institution.

(2) Subsection (1)(a) above applies to any pension, allowance or benefit payable out of public funds (including any other benefit as so defined, whether it is of the same or a different description) which is payable to or in respect of—

(a) the person referred to in subsection (1);
(b) that person's [4 wife, husband or civil partner];
(c) any [5 . . .] dependant of that person; or
(d) the [4 wife, husband or civil partner] of any adult dependant of that person.

(3) Where but for regulations made by virtue of subsection (1)(a) above two persons would both be entitled to an increase of benefit in respect of a third person, regulations may make provision as to their priority.

[3(4) Regulations may provide for adjusting—

[8 (za) state pension under Part 1 of the Pensions Act 2014;]

(a) benefit as defined in section 122 of the Contributions and Benefits Act;

(b) a contribution-based jobseeker's allowance, or

[6(c) a contributory employment and support allowance,]

payable to or in respect of any person where there is payable in his case any such benefit as is described in subsection (5) below.]

(5) Subsection (4) above applies to any benefit payable under the legislation of any [9 member State] which is payable to or in respect of—

(a) the person referred to in that subsection;

(b) that person's [4 wife, husband or civil partner];

(c) any [4 . . .] dependant of that person; or

(d) the [4 wife, husband or civil partner] of any adult dependant of that person.

[7 (6) Personal independence payment is to be treated for the purposes of this section as if it were benefit as defined in section 122 of the Contributions and Benefits Act.]

Amendments

1. Jobseekers Act 1995 Sch.2 para.49(2)(a) (June 11, 1996).
2. Jobseekers Act 1995 Sch.2 para.49(2)(b) (June 11, 1996).
3. Jobseekers Act 1995 Sch.2 para.49(3) (June 11, 1996).
4. Civil Partnership Act 2004 s.254 and Sch.24 para.59 (December 5, 2005).
5. Child Benefit Act 2005 Sch.1 Pt 1 para.21 (April 10, 2006).
6. Welfare Reform Act 2007 s.28 and Sch.3 para.10 (October 27, 2008).
7. Welfare Reform Act 2012, Sch.9, para.11 (April 8, 2013).
8. Pensions Act 2014, s.56(4), s.23 and Sch.12, para.12 (April 6, 2016).
9. Social Security (Amendment) (EU Exit) Regulations 2019 (SI 2019/128), reg.3(2) (as applied by European Union (Withdrawal Agreement) Act 2020 Sch.5 para.1(1)) (December 31, 2020).

Derivation

1.145 SSA 1975 s.85 as amended.

General Note

1.146 See the Hospital In-Patients Regulations and Overlapping Benefits Regulations.

Income support and other payments

1.147 **74.**—(1) Where—

(a) a payment by way of prescribed income is made after the date which is the prescribed date in relation to the payment; and

(b) it is determined that an amount which has been paid by way of income support [2 . . .] [2, an income-based jobseeker's allowance [3, state pension credit or an income-related employment and support allowance]] would not have been paid if the payment had been made on the prescribed date,

the Secretary of State shall be entitled to recover that amount from the person to whom it was paid.

(2) Where—

(a) a prescribed payment which apart from this subsection falls to be made from public funds in the United Kingdom or under the law of any [6 member State] is not made on or before the date which is the prescribed date in relation to the payment; and

(b) it is determined that an amount ("the relevant amount") has been paid by way of [5 universal credit or] income support [2 . . .] [2, an income-based jobseeker's allowance [3, state pension credit or an income-related employment and support allowance]] that would not have been paid if the payment mentioned in paragraph (a) above had been made on the prescribed date,

then—

(i) in the case of a payment from public funds in the United Kingdom, the authority responsible for making it may abate it by the relevant amount; and

(ii) in the case of any other payment, the Secretary of State shall be entitled to receive the relevant amount out of the payment.

(3) Where—

(a) a person (in this subsection referred to as A) is entitled to any prescribed benefit for any period in respect of another person (in this subsection referred to as B); and

(b) either—

(i) B has received income support [1 or an income-based jobseeker's allowance] for that period; or

(ii) B was, during that period, a member of the same family as some person other than A who received income support [1 or an income-based jobseeker's allowance] for that period; and

(c) the amount of the income support [4 an income-based jobseeker's allowance or an income-based employment and support allowance] has been determined on the basis that A has not made payments for the maintenance of B at a rate equal to or exceeding the amount of the prescribed benefit,

the amount of the prescribed benefit may, at the discretion of the authority administering it, be abated by the amount by which the amounts paid by way of income support . . . [4, an income-based jobseeker's allowance or an income-related employment and support allowance] exceed what it is determined that they would have been had A, at the time the amount of the income support [1or an income-based jobseeker's allowance] was determined, been making payments for the maintenance of B at a rate equal to the amount of the prescribed benefit.

(4) Where an amount could have been recovered by abatement by virtue of subsection (2) or (3) above but has not been so recovered, the Secretary of State may recover it otherwise than by way of abatement—

(a) in the case of an amount which could have been recovered by virtue of subsection (2) above, from the person to whom it was paid; and

(b) in the case of an amount which could have been recovered by virtue of subsection (3) above, from the person to whom the prescribed benefit in question was paid.

(5) Where a payment is made in a currency other than sterling, its value in sterling shall be determined for the purposes of this section in accordance with regulations.

AMENDMENTS

1. Jobseekers Act 1995 Sch.2 para.50 (October 7, 1996).
2. State Pension Credit Act 2002 s.14 and Sch.2 (July 2, 2002 for the purposes of making regulations only; fully in force October 6, 2003).
3. Welfare Reform Act 2007 s.28 and Sch.3 para.10 (October 27, 2008).
4. The Employment and Support Allowance (Miscellaneous Amendments) Regulations 2008, (SI 2008/2428) reg.23 (October 27, 2008).
5. Welfare Reform Act 2012 s.31 and Sch.2 para.7 (February 25, 2013).
6. Social Security (Amendment) (EU Exit) Regulations 2019 (SI 2019/128), reg.3(3) (as applied by European Union (Withdrawal Agreement) Act 2020 Sch.5 para.1(1)) (December 31, 2020).

DERIVATION

1.148 Social Security Act 1986 s.27.

DEFINITION

"prescribed"—see s.191.

GENERAL NOTE

1.149 This is an important provision, which is often overlooked. In *R(IS) 14/04* the Commissioner confirms that there is an appeal against a determination that there is a recoverable overpayment under this section to an appeal tribunal under the Social Security Act 1998 in the following terms:

> ". . . a determination made by the Secretary of State under section 74(1) that a particular amount of income support has been paid to the claim but would not have been so paid had he received his prescribed income payments at the prescribed date, and in consequence is legally recoverable from him under the terms of section 74(1), is an appealable decision within the jurisdiction of the tribunal under section 12 Social Security Act 1998. The appeal does not however extend to any subsequent question of whether or how to enforce any liability so established, which is an administrative or discretionary matter for the Secretary of State." (para.21)

The question which arises under this section is whether there has been a payment of a prescribed benefit which would not have been made had prescribed income been paid to the claimant on the prescribed date.

CIS/5048/2002 illustrates the limitations of this section. The claimant had been receiving income support for herself and her husband. The claimant's husband had applied for, and was awarded, incapacity benefit for himself which he had not disclosed to his wife. The result was an overpayment of income support, which the Secretary of State sought to recover under s.74. The Commissioner ruled on the appeal:

> "10. Two subsections of section 74 were invoked in the submission to the tribunal, subsections (2) and (4). Subsection (2) allows, on the facts of this case, an abatement of the incapacity benefit paid to the husband. It does not authorise any deduction from the claimant. There is nothing in the subsection that allows recovery from 'the other' member of a married or unmarried couple (other than joint claimants). For the record, I indicated in a direction that I do not see how section 74(3) could be applied here either, and the secretary of state's representaive has not disputed this. As I noted in those directions, there is in any event no mention of subsection (3) anywhere in the papers. Subsection (4) applies where an abatement could have been made under subsection (2) or subsection (3) but has not been made. As applied with subsection (2) it allows recovery from the person from whom the abatement could have been retained the husband, not the claimant. So neither of the preconditions for subsection (4) to be applicable

to the claimant are present. The decision of the tribunal therefore cannot stand. Equally, neither can the decision of the Secretary of State.

11. I have not considered whether section 74(1) could apply to the claimant because it has not been put in issue. The secretary of state's representative makes the suggestion, which I agree is the best way forward in this case, that the appropriate action is for me to set aside the decision of the Secretary of State and refer the matter back to the Secretary of State. That I do. The Secretary of State can make further decisions about overpayment if he so decides, and those decisions will have their own rights of appeal. He will note the comments of the solicitors about the inapplicability of section 71 to the claimant."

Subsection (1)

Prescribed income is defined in reg.7(1) of the Social Security (Payments on account, Overpayments and Recovery) Regulations 1988 ("the Overpayments Regulations"). The prescribed date under reg.7(2) is, in general, the first day of the period to which that income relates. If as a result of that income being paid after the prescribed date, more benefit is paid than would have been paid if the income had been paid on the prescribed date, the excess may be recovered. Note that the right to recover is absolute and does not depend on lack of care on the claimant's part, or on the effect of this section having been pointed out. That approach is confirmed in *CIS/625/1991*, where the Commissioner rejected the argument that there had to be an investigation of what an adjudication officer would in practice have done if the income had been paid on time. An example would be where a claimant has not been paid part-time earnings when they were due and as a result has been paid income support on the basis of having no earnings. Once the arrears of wages are received, the excess benefit would be recoverable. Late payment of most social security benefits is covered in subss.(2) and (4), but can also come within subs.(1). For instance, if a claim is made for child benefit and while a decision is awaited income support is paid without any deduction for the amount of the expected child benefit, then if arrears of child benefit are eventually paid in full (i.e. the abatement procedure of subs.(2) does not work) the "excess" income support for the period covered by the arrears is recoverable under subs.(1) or (4). **1.150**

It is essential that the dates on which prescribed income was due to be paid and on what dates due payments would have affected income support entitlement should be determined: *R(SB) 28/85* and *CIS/625/1991*.

Subsection (2)

Prescribed payments are listed in reg.8(1) of the Overpayments Regulations and include most social security benefits, training allowances and social security benefits from other EC countries. As under the excess income support or JSA, if the abatement mechanism breaks down, the Secretary of State may recover the excess under subs.(4). **1.151**

In *CIS/12082/1996* and *CIS/4316/1999* the same Commissioner ruled that art.111 of EC Reg.574/72 does not preclude the application of s.74(2). *CIS/4316/1999* illustrates the application of s.74(2) in the context of the complex rules for determining entitlement to retirement pension where contributions have been made in more than one Member State of the European Union.

In *CIS/764/2002* the Commissioner says,

"I conclude in the present case (although the issue may need eventually to be argued out in some other case) that when there has been an abatement under section 74(2) of the Social Security Administration Act 1992, the relevant amount of income support is to be treated as if had not been paid as income support. Therefore it cannot be touched by a subsequent decision about the recoverability of an overpayment of income support under section 71. I rest that on the overall context of sections 71 and 74, if the conclusion is not required by regulations 5 and 13(a) of the Payments Regulations." (para.22)

The Commissioner had concluded that the requirements of regs 5 and 13(a) of the Payments on Account Regulations required the same result: see para.20 of the decision.

In *PT v SSWP (JSA)* [2013] UKUT 372 (AAC), the judge explained that s.74(2) "is concerned with cases where a claimant in receipt of an income-related benefit is entitled to arrears of another benefit (or other payment from public funds) that would have fallen to be taken into account as income and so would have reduced entitlement to the income-related benefit had it been paid at the correct time." (At [10].) It does not cover the situation of a person where an error in the Department has resulted in a failure to recoup overpaid jobseeker's allowance from arrears of an employment and support allowance. The only way such a sum could be recouped was through the operation of reg.5 of the Social Security (Payments on account etc) Regulations 1988. As s.74(2) did not apply, s.74(4) could not apply to justify recovery under s.74.

Subsection (5)

1.152 *R(SB) 28/85* had revealed problems in valuing a payment of arrears in a foreign currency which might cover quite a long period during which exchange rates varied. This provision authorises regulations to be made to deal with the conversion. See reg.10 of the Payments Regulations, which appears to require the actual net amount received to be taken into account, reversing the effect of *R(SB) 28/85*.

[1 Payment of benefit where maintenance payments collected by Secretary of State

1.153 **74A.**—(1) This section applies where—

(a) a person ("the claimant") is entitled to a benefit to which this section applies;

(b) the Secretary of State is collecting periodical payments of child or spousal maintenance made in respect of the claimant or a member of the claimant's family; and

(c) the inclusion of any such periodical payment in the claimant's relevant income would, apart from this section, have the effect of reducing the amount of the benefit to which the claimant is entitled.

(2) The Secretary of State may, to such extent as he considers appropriate, treat any such periodical payment as not being relevant income for the purposes of calculating the amount of benefit to which the claimant is entitled.

(3) The Secretary of State may, to the extent that any periodical payment collected by him is treated as not being relevant income for those purposes, retain the whole or any part of that payment.

(4) Any sum retained by the Secretary of State under subsection (3) shall be paid by him into the Consolidated Fund.

(5) In this section—

"child" means a person under the age of 16;

"child maintenance", "spousal maintenance" and "relevant income" have such meaning as may be prescribed;

[2 "couple" has the meaning given by section 137(1) of the Contributions and Benefits Act;]

"family" means—

(a) [2 couple];

(b) a [2 couple] and a member of the same household for whom one of them is, or both are, responsible and who is a child or a person of a prescribed description;

(c) except in prescribed circumstances, a person who is not a member of a [2 couple] and a member of the same household for whom that person is responsible and who is a child or a person of a prescribed description;

[2 . . .]

(6) For the purposes of this section, the Secretary of State may by regulations make provision as to the circumstances in which—

(a) persons are to be treated as being or not being members of the same household;

(b) one person is to be treated as responsible or not responsible for another.

(7) The benefits to which this section applies are [4 universal credit,] income support, an income-based jobseeker's allowance [3, an income-related employment and support allowance] and such other benefits (if any) as may be prescribed.]

Amendments

1. Child Support Act 1995 s.25 (October 1, 1995).
2. Civil Partnership Act 2004 s.254 and Sch.24 para.60 (December 5, 2005).
3. Welfare Reform Act 2007 s.28 and Sch.3 para.10 (October 27, 2008).
4. The Welfare Reform Act 2012 (Commencement No. 9 and Transitional and Transitory Provisions and Commencement No. 8 and Savings and Transitional Provisions (Amendment)) Order 2013 (SI 2013/983) art. 3(1)(b) (April 29, 2013).

General Note

See reg.2 of the Social Security Benefits (Maintenance Payments and Consequential Amendments) Regulations 1996 (SI 1996/940) for definitions of "child maintenance", "spousal maintenance" and "relevant income" and regs 3–5 for other points of interpretation. 1.154

75.–77. *Omitted.* 1.155

Social fund awards

Recovery of social fund awards

78.—(1) A social fund award which is repayable shall be recoverable by the Secretary of State. 1.156

(2) Without prejudice to any other method of recovery, the Secretary of State may recover an award by deduction from prescribed benefits.

(3) The Secretary of State may recover an award—

(a) from the person to or for the benefit of whom it was made;

(b) where that person is a member of a [3 couple], from the other member of the couple;

(c) from a person who is liable to maintain the person by or on behalf of whom the application for the award was made or any person in relation to whose needs the award was made.

[1 (3A) Where—

(a) a jobseeker's allowance is payable to a person from whom an award is recoverable under subsection (3) above; and

(b) that person is subject to a bankruptcy order,

a sum deducted from that benefit under subsection (2) above shall not be treated as income of his for the purposes of the Insolvency Act 1986.

(3B) Where—

(a) a jobseeker's allowance is payable to a person from whom an award is recoverable under subsection (3) above; and

(b) the estate of that person is sequestrated,

a sum deducted from that benefit under subsection (2) above shall not be treated as income of his for the purposes of the Bankruptcy (Scotland) Act [6 2016].]

(4) Payments [4 out of the social fund] to meet funeral expenses may in all cases be recovered, as if they were funeral expenses, out of the estate of the deceased, and (subject to section 71 above) by no other means.

[3 (5) In this section "couple" has the meaning given by section 137(1) of the Contributions and Benefits Act.]

(6) For the purposes of this section—

(a) a man shall be liable to maintain his wife [3 or civil partner] and any children of whom he is the father; and

(b) a woman shall be liable to maintain her husband [3 or civil partner] and any children of whom she is the mother;

(c) a person shall be liable to maintain another person throughout any period in respect of which the first-mentioned person has, on or after 23rd May 1980 (the date of the passing of the Social Security Act 1980) and either alone or jointly with a further person, given an undertaking in writing in pursuance of immigration rules within the meaning of the Immigration Act 1971 to be responsible for the maintenance and accommodation of the other person; and

(d) "child" includes a person who has attained the age of 16 but not the age of 19 and in respect of whom either parent, or some person acting in place of either parent, is receiving [5 universal credit,] income support [2 or an income-based jobseeker's allowance].

(7) Any reference in subsection (6) above to children of whom the man or the woman is the father or mother shall be construed in accordance with section 1 of the Family Law Reform Act 1987.

(8) Subsection (7) above does not apply in Scotland, and in the application of subsection (6) above to Scotland any reference to children of whom the man or the woman is the father or the mother shall be construed as a reference to any such children whether or not their parents have ever been married to one another.

(9) A document bearing a certificate which—

(a) is signed by a person authorised in that behalf by the Secretary of State; and

(b) states that the document apart from the certificate is, or is a copy of, such an undertaking as is mentioned in subsection (6)(c) above,

shall be conclusive of the undertaking in question for the purposes of this section; and a certificate purporting to be so signed shall be deemed to be so signed until the contrary is proved.

AMENDMENTS

1. Jobseekers Act 1995 s.32(2) (October 7, 1996).

2. Jobseekers Act 1995 Sch.2 para.51 (October 7, 1996).

3. Civil Partnership Act 2004 s.254 and Sch.24, para.61 (December 5, 2005).

4. Welfare Reform Act 2012 s.70 and Sch.8, para.2 (April 1, 2013).

5. The Welfare Reform Act 2012 (Commencement No. 8 and Savings and Transitional Provisions) Order 2013 (SI 2013/358) art.5(5) (April 29, 2013).

6. Bankruptcy (Scotland) Act 2016 (Consequential Provisions and Modifications) Order 2016 (SI 2016/1034) art.7 and Sch.1 para.9 (November 30, 2016).

DERIVATIONS

Subss.(1)–(3): Social Security Act 1986 s.33(5)–(7). **1.157**
Subs.(4): 1986 Act s.32(4).
Subs.(5): 1986 Act s.33(12).
Subss.(6)–(9): 1986 Act ss.26(3)–(6) and 33(8).

DEFINITION

"prescribed"—see s.191.

GENERAL NOTE

Subsections (1)–(3)

These provisions give the framework for recovery of social fund loans. See the Social Fund (Recovery by Deductions from Benefits) Regulations 1988. **1.158**

Income support and JSA are prescribed benefits for the purposes of subs.(2) (reg.3(a) and (c) of the Social Fund (Recovery by Deductions from Benefits) Regulations). In *Mulvey v Secretary of State for Social Security*, *The Times*, March 20, 1997, the House of Lords on March 13, 1997 held that where deductions were being made from benefit under subs.(2) when the claimant was sequestrated (the Scottish equivalent of a declaration of bankruptcy), the Secretary of State was entitled to continue to make the deductions. If that were not so, the gross benefit would become payable to the claimant, who would thus gain an immediate financial advantage from sequestration, a result which Parliament could not have intended.

> "Prior to sequestration the [claimant] had no right to receive by way of income support more than her gross entitlement under deduction of such sum as had been notified to her by the [Secretary of State] prior to payment of the award by the [Secretary of State]. This was the result of the statutory scheme and she could not have demanded more. The [Secretary of State's] continued exercise of a statutory power of deduction after sequestration was unrelated thereto and was not calculated to obtain a benefit for him at the expense of other creditors. The only person who had any realistic interest in the deductions was the [claimant] from which it follows that the [Secretary of State] was not seeking to exercise any right against the permanent trustee." (Lord Jauncey)

The view of the Inner House of the Court of Session was thus approved. See the notes in the 1996 edition for the earlier decisions in *Mulvey*.

English bankruptcy law is not the same as Scottish sequestration law. However, in *R. v Secretary of State for Social Security, Ex p. Taylor and Chapman*, *The Times*, February 5, 1996, Keene J. reached the same conclusion as the Inner House in *Mulvey* in relation to the effect of s.285(3) of the Insolvency Act 1986 in these circumstances. The deductions in *Chapman* were not being made under subs.(2) but from the claimant's retirement pension under s.71(8) in order to recover an overpayment of income support, but it was accepted that the position was the same in both cases. Keene J. rejected a submission by the Secretary of State that the operation of s.285(3) was precluded in this situation, but held that it did not prevent the deductions under subs.(2) and s.71(8) being made. The Secretary of State was not seeking to go against "the property of the bankrupt" within the terms of s.285(3) as the claimants' entitlement under the 1992 Act was to the net amount of benefit. In *Mulvey* (above) Lord Jauncey said this about the contrary argument:

> "Even more bizarre would be the situation where overpayments obtained by fraud were being recovered by deduction from benefits. On sequestration the fraudster would immediately receive the gross benefit. It is difficult to believe that Parliament can have intended such a result."

Note that s.32 of the Jobseekers Act 1995 amends both ss.78 and 71 to provide that amounts deducted under subs.(2) or s.71(8) from JSA payable to a bankrupt person are not to be treated as income for the purposes of the Insolvency Act 1986 and the Bankruptcy (Scotland) Act 1985 (in effect giving preference to the DSS over other creditors, although the House of Lords in *Mulvey* rejected such a comparison).

These decisions now need to be read in the light of the judgment of the Supreme Court in *SSWP v Payne* [2011] UKSC 60, which took the view that *Taylor and Chapman* was wrongly decided. The Supreme Court decided that the Secretary of State lost the power to seek recovery of social fund loans on the making of either a bankruptcy order, or a debt relief order in insolvency proceedings.

Subsection (4)

1.159 Subsection (4) contains an important provision for the recovery of any payment for funeral expenses out of the estate of the deceased. Regulation 8 of the Social Fund Maternity and Funeral Expenses (General) Regulations lists sums to be deducted in calculating the amount of a funeral payment. These include assets of the deceased which are available before probate or letters of administration have been granted. The old reg.8(3)(a) of the Single Payments Regulations required the deduction of the value of the deceased's estate, but since it might take some time for the estate to become available, the provision in subs.(4) is preferable.

The funeral payment is to be recovered as if it was funeral expenses. Funeral expenses are a first charge on the estate, in priority to anything else (see *R(SB) 18/84*, paras 8 and 10, for the law in England and Scotland). *CIS/616/1990* decides that the right to recover is given to the Secretary of State. The adjudication officer (and the tribunal) has no role in subs.(4).

The only other method of recovery is under s.71, which applies generally where there has been misrepresentation or a failure to disclose and does depend on a review of entitlement by an adjudication officer followed by a determination of an overpayment.

Subsections (6)–(9)

1.160 See the notes to s.105.

Northern Ireland payments

Recovery of Northern Ireland payments

1.161 **79.** Without prejudice to any other method of recovery—

(a) amounts recoverable under any enactment or instrument having effect in Northern Ireland and corresponding to an enactment or instrument mentioned in section 71(8) above shall be recoverable by deduction from benefits prescribed under that subsection;

(b) amounts recoverable under any enactment having effect in Northern Ireland and corresponding to section 75 above shall be recoverable by deduction from benefits prescribed under subsection (4) of that section; and

(c) awards recoverable under Part III of the Northern Ireland Administration Act shall be recoverable by deduction from benefits prescribed [1 under section 71(8).]

DERIVATIONS

1.162 Paragraph (a): Social Security Act 1986 s.53(7A).
Paragraph (b): 1986 Act s.29(8).
Paragraph (c): 1986 Act s.33(8A).

AMENDMENT

1. Welfare Reform Act 2012 s.70 and Sch.8 para.3 (April 1, 2013).

DEFINITIONS

"the Northern Ireland Administration Act"—see s.191.
"prescribed"—*ibid.*

Adjustment of child benefit

Child benefit—overlap with benefits under legislation of [2 . . .] member States

80. Regulations may provide for adjusting child benefit payable in respect of any child [1 or qualifying young person] in respect of whom any benefit is payable under the legislation of any [2 member State]. **1.163**

DERIVATION

CBA 1975 s.4A. **1.164**

AMENDMENTS

1. Child Benefit Act 2005 Sch.1 Pt 1 para.22 (April 10, 2006).
2. Social Security (Amendment) (EU Exit) Regulations 2019 (SI 2019/128), reg.3(4) (as applied by European Union (Withdrawal Agreement) Act 2020 Sch.5 para.1(1)) (December 31, 2020).

PART IV

RECOVERY FROM COMPENSATION PAYMENTS

Repealed. **1.165**

PART V

INCOME SUPPORT AND THE DUTY TO MAINTAIN

Failure to maintain—general

105.—(1) If— **1.166**
(a) any person persistently refuses or neglects to maintain himself or any person whom he is liable to maintain; and
(b) in consequence of his refusal or neglect [5 universal credit,] income support [1 . . .] [3 , an income-based jobseeker's allowance or an income-related employment and support allowance] is paid to or in respect of him or such a person,

he shall be guilty of an offence and liable on summary conviction to imprisonment for a term not exceeding 3 months or to a fine of an amount not exceeding level 4 on the standard scale or to both.

(2) For the purposes of subsection (1) above a person shall not be taken to refuse or neglect to maintain himself or any other person by reason only of anything done or omitted in furtherance of a trade dispute.

[4 (3) Subject to subsection (4), for the purposes of this Part, a person shall be liable to maintain another person if that other person is—

(a) his or her spouse or civil partner, or

(b) a person whom he or she would be liable to maintain if sections 78(6)(c) and (9) had effect for the purposes of this Part.]

[1(4) For the purposes of this section, in its application to an income-based jobseeker's allowance [3or an income-related employment and support allowance], [4 subsection (3)(b) shall not apply.]]

AMENDMENTS

1. Jobseekers Act 1995 Sch.2 para.53 (October 7, 1996).
2. Civil Partnership Act 2004 s.254 and Sch.24, para.62 (December 5, 2005).
3. Welfare Reform Act 2007 s.28 and Sch.3 para.10 (October 27, 2008).
4. Child Maintenance and Other Payments Act 2008 s.45 (July 14, 2008).
5. The Welfare Reform Act 2012 (Commencement No. 9 and Transitional and Transitory Provisions and Commencement No. 8 and Savings and Transitional Provisions (Amendment)) Order 2013 (SI 2013/983) art.3(1)(b) (April 29, 2013).

Recovery of expenditure on benefit from person liable for maintenance

1.167 **106.**—(1) Subject to the following provisions of this section, if income support [2 or universal credit] is claimed by or in respect of a person whom another person is liable to maintain or paid to or in respect of such a person, the Secretary of State may make [3 an application] against the liable person to [3 the family court] for an order under this section.

(2) On the hearing of [3 an application] under this section the court shall have regard to all the circumstances and, in particular, to the income of the liable person, and may order him to pay such sum, weekly or otherwise, as it may consider appropriate, except that in a case falling within section 78(6)(c) above that sum shall not include any amount which is not attributable to income support [2 or universal credit] (whether paid before or after the making of the order).

(3) In determining whether to order any payments to be made in respect of income support [2 or universal credit] for any period before the [3 application]was made, or the amount of any such payments, the court shall disregard any amount by which the liable person's income exceeds the income which was his during that period.

(4) Any payments ordered to be made under this section shall be made—

(a) to the Secretary of State in so far as they are attributable to any income support [2 or universal credit] (whether paid before or after the making of the order);

(b) to the person claiming income support [2 or universal credit] or (if different) the dependant; or

(c) to such other person as appears to the court expedient in the interests of the dependant.

(5) [3 . . .]

(6) In the application of this section to Scotland, [3 for the references to the family court there shall be substituted references to the sheriff.]

(7) [1 . . .]

DERIVATION

Social Security Act 1986 s.24. 1.168

AMENDMENTS

1. Child Maintenance and Other Payments Act 2008 Sch.8 para.1 (July 14, 2008).
2. The Welfare Reform Act 2012 (Commencement No. 9 and Transitional and Transitory Provisions and Commencement No. 8 and Savings and Transitional Provisions (Amendment)) Order 2013 (SI 2013/983) art.3(1)(b) (April 29, 2013).
3. Crime and Courts Act 2013 Sch.11(1) para.128(1) (April 22, 2014).

DEFINITION

"child"—see ss.105(3) and 78(b).

Recovery of expenditure on income support: additional amounts and transfer of orders

107.[[1] . . .] 1.169

AMENDMENT

1. Repealed by Child Maintenance and Other Payments Act 2008 Sch.8 para.1 (October 27, 2008).

Reduction of expenditure on income support: certain maintenance orders to be enforceable by the Secretary of State

108.—(1) This section applies where— 1.170
(a) a person ("the claimant") who is the parent of one or more children is in receipt of income support [[4] or universal credit] either in respect of those children or in respect of both himself and those children; and
(b) there is in force a maintenance order made against the other parent ("the liable person")—
(i) in favour of the claimant or one or more of the children, or
(ii) in favour of some other person for the benefit of the claimant or one or more of the children,

and in this section "the primary recipient" means the person in whose favour that maintenance order was made.

(2) If, in a case where this section applies, the liable person fails to comply with any of the terms of the maintenance order—
(a) the Secretary of State may bring any proceedings or take any other steps to enforce the order that could have been brought or taken by or on behalf of the primary recipient; and
(b) any court before which proceedings are brought by the Secretary of State by virtue of paragraph (a) above shall have the same powers in connection with those proceedings as it would have had if they had been brought by the primary recipient.

(3) The Secretary of State's powers under this section are exercisable at his discretion and whether or not the primary recipient or any other person consents to their exercise; but any sums recovered by virtue of this section shall be payable to or for the primary recipient, as if the proceedings or steps in question had been brought or taken by him or on his behalf.

(4) The powers conferred on the Secretary of State by subsection (2)(a) above include power—

(a) to apply for the registration of the maintenance order under—

(i) section 17 of the Maintenance Orders Act 1950; [2or]

(ii) section 2 of the Maintenance Orders Act 1958;

[7...] [8...]

[7...] [9...]

[10...]

[11(ab) to apply for recognition and enforcement of the maintenance order under the Convention on the International Recovery of Child Support and other forms of Family Maintenance done at The Hague on 23rd November 2007, to the extent permitted by Article 36 of that Convention; and]

(b) to make an application under section 2 of the Maintenance Orders (Reciprocal Enforcement) Act 1972 (application for enforcement in reciprocating country).

(5) Where this section applies, the prescribed person shall in prescribed circumstances give the Secretary of State notice of any application—

(a) to alter, vary, suspend, discharge, revoke, revive, or enforce the maintenance order in question; or

(b) to remit arrears under that maintenance order;

and the Secretary of State shall be entitled to appear and be heard on the application.

(6) Where, by virtue of this section, the Secretary of State commences any proceedings to enforce a maintenance order, he shall, in relation to those proceedings, be treated for the purposes of any enactment or instrument relating to maintenance orders as if he were a person entitled to payment under the maintenance order in question (but shall not thereby become entitled to any such payment).

(7) Where, in any proceedings under this section in England and Wales, the court makes an order for the whole or any part of the arrears due under the maintenance order in question to be paid as a lump sum, the Secretary of State shall inform [4 the Lord Chancellor] of the amount of that lump sum if he knows—

(a) that the primary recipient either—

(i) received legal aid under the Legal Aid Act 1974 in connection with the proceedings in which the maintenance order was made, or

(ii) was an assisted party, within the meaning of the Legal Aid Act 1988, in those proceedings, or

[1(iii) received services funded by the Legal Services Commission as part of the Community Legal Service; and]

[5 (iv) was provided with civil legal services (within the meaning of Part 1 of the Legal Aid, Sentencing and Punishment of Offenders Act 2012) under arrangements made for the purposes of that Part of that Act; and]

(b) that a sum remains unpaid on account of the contribution required of the primary recipient—

(i) under section 9 of the Legal Aid Act 1974 in respect of those proceedings, or

(ii) under section 16 of the Legal Aid Act 1988 in respect of the costs of his being represented under Part IV of that Act in those proceedings, [1 or

(iii) by virtue of section 10 of the Access to Justice Act 1999 in respect of services funded by the Legal Services Commission as part of the Community Legal Service.]

[5 (iv) under regulations under sections 23 or 24 of the Legal Aid, Sentencing and Punishment of Offenders Act 2012 in respect of civil legal services (within the meaning of Part 1 of that Act) provided under arrangements made for the purposes of that Part of that Act,]

as the case may be.

[3 (8) In this section "maintenance order"—

(a) in England and Wales, means—

(i) any order for the making of periodical payments which is, or has at any time been, a maintenance order within the meaning of the Attachment of Earnings Act 1971;

(ii) any order under Part 3 of the Matrimonial and Family Proceedings Act 1984 (overseas divorce) for the making of periodical payments;

(iii) any order under Schedule 7 to the Civil Partnership Act 2004 for the making of periodical payments;

(b) Scotland, means any order, except an order for the payment of a lump sum, falling within the definition of "maintenance order" in section 106 of the Debtors (Scotland) Act 1987, but disregarding paragraph (h) (alimentary bond or agreement).]

AMENDMENTS

1. Access to Justice Act 1999 Sch.4 para.48 (April 1, 2000).
2. Civil Jurisdiction and Judgments (Amendment) (EU Exit) Regulations 2019 (SI 2019/479) Pt 2 reg.66(a) (December 31, 2020).
3. Child Maintenance and Other Payments Act 2008 Sch.7 para.2(2) (October 27, 2008).
4. Welfare Reform Act 2012 (Commencement No.9 and Transitional and Transitory Provisions and Commencement No.8 and Savings and Transitional Provisions (Amendment)) Order 2013 (SI 2013/983) art.3(1)(b) (April 29, 2013).
5. Legal Aid, Sentencing and Punishment of Offenders Act 2012 Sch.5(1) para.41 (April 1, 2013).
6. Civil Jurisdiction and Judgments Order 2011 (SI 2011/1484) Sch.7 para.14 (June 18, 2011).
7. Civil Jurisdiction and Judgments (Amendment) (EU Exit) Regulations 2019 (SI 2019/479) Pt 2 reg.66(b) (December 31, 2020).
8. Civil Jurisdiction and Judgments Order 2001 (SI 2001/3929) Sch.3 para.24(a) (March 1, 2002).
9. Civil Jurisdiction and Judgments (Maintenance) Regulations 2011 (SI 2011/1484) Sch.7 para.14(a)(ii) (June 18, 2011).
10. Jurisdiction and Judgments (Family) (Amendment etc.) (EU Exit) Regulations 2019 (SI 2019/519) Sch. para.21 (December 31, 2020).
11. International Recovery of Maintenance (Hague Convention 2007 etc.) Regulations 2012 (SI 2012/2814) Sch.4 para.6(b) (August 1, 2014).

DERIVATION

Social Security Act 1986 s.24B. **1.171**

Diversion of arrested earnings to Secretary of State—Scotland

1.172 **109.**—(1) Where in Scotland a creditor who is enforcing a maintenance order or alimentary bond or agreement by a current maintenance arrestment or a conjoined arrestment order is in receipt of [2 universal credit,] income support [1 or an income-related employment and support allowance] the creditor may in writing authorise the Secretary of State to receive any sums payable under the arrestment or order until the creditor ceases to be in receipt of [2 universal credit,] income support [1 or an income-related employment and support allowance] or in writing withdraws the authorisation, whichever occurs first.

(2) On intimation by the Secretary of State—

(a) to the employer operating the current maintenance arrestment; or

(b) to the sheriff clerk operating the conjoined arrestment order;

of an authorisation under subsection (1) above, the employer or sheriff clerk shall, until notified by the Secretary of State that the authorisation has ceased to have effect, pay to the Secretary of State any sums which would otherwise be payable under the arrestment or order to the creditor.

AMENDMENTS

1. Welfare Reform Act 2007 s.28 and Sch.3 para.10 (October 27, 2008).

2. The Welfare Reform Act 2012 (Commencement No. 9 and Transitional and Transitory Provisions and Commencement No. 8 and Savings and Transitional Provisions (Amendment)) Order 2013 (SI 2013/983) art.3(1)(b) (April 29, 2013).

DERIVATION

1.173 Social Security Act 1986 s.25A.

PART VI

ENFORCEMENT

Inspection and offences

[1 Authorisations for investigators.

1.174 **109A.**—(1) An individual who for the time being has the Secretary of State's authorisation for the purposes of this Part shall be entitled, for any one or more of the purposes mentioned in subsection (2) below, to exercise any of the powers which are conferred on an authorised officer by sections 109B and 109C below.

(2) Those purposes are—

(a) ascertaining in relation to any case whether a benefit is or was payable in that case in accordance with any provision of the relevant social security legislation;

(b) investigating the circumstances in which any accident, injury or disease which has given rise, or may give rise, to a claim for—

(i) industrial injuries benefit, or

(ii) any benefit under any provision of the relevant social security legislation, occurred or may have occurred, or was or may have been received or contracted;

(c) ascertaining whether provisions of the relevant social security legislation are being, have been or are likely to be contravened (whether by particular persons or more generally);

(d) preventing, detecting and securing evidence of the commission (whether by particular persons or more generally) of benefit offences.

(3) An individual has the Secretary of State's authorisation for the purposes of this Part if, and only if, the Secretary of State has granted him an authorisation for those purposes and he is—

(a) an official of a Government department;

(b) an individual employed by an authority administering housing benefit or council tax benefit;

(c) an individual employed by an authority or joint committee that carries out functions relating to housing benefit or council tax benefit on behalf of the authority administering that benefit; or

(d) an individual employed by a person authorised by or on behalf of any such authority or joint committee as is mentioned in paragraph (b) or (c) above to carry out functions relating to housing benefit or council tax benefit for that authority or committee.

(4) An authorisation granted for the purposes of this Part to an individual of any of the descriptions mentioned in subsection (3) above–

(a) must be contained in a certificate provided to that individual as evidence of his entitlement to exercise powers conferred by this Part;

(b) may contain provision as to the period for which the authorisation is to have effect; and

(c) may restrict the powers exercisable by virtue of the authorisation so as to prohibit their exercise except for particular purposes, in particular circumstances or in relation to particular benefits or particular provisions of the relevant social security legislation.

(5) An authorisation granted under this section may be withdrawn at any time by the Secretary of State.

(6) Where the Secretary of State grants an authorisation for the purposes of this Part to an individual employed by a local authority, or to an individual employed by a person who carries out functions relating to housing benefit or council tax benefit on behalf of a local authority—

(a) the Secretary of State and the local authority shall enter into such arrangements (if any) as they consider appropriate with respect to the carrying out of functions conferred on that individual by or in connection with the authorisation granted to him; and

(b) the Secretary of State may make to the local authority such payments (if any) as he thinks fit in respect of the carrying out by that individual of any such functions.

(7) The matters on which a person may be authorised to consider and report to the Secretary of State under section 129A below shall be taken to include the carrying out by any such individual as is mentioned in subsection (3)(b) to (d) above of any functions conferred on that individual by virtue of any grant by the Secretary of State of an authorisation for the purposes of this Part.

(8) The powers conferred by sections 109B and 109C below shall be exercisable in relation to persons holding office under the Crown and persons in the service of the Crown, and in relation to premises owned or

occupied by the Crown, as they are exercisable in relation to other persons and premises.

[2 (9) This section and sections 109B to 109C below apply as if—

(a) the Tax Credits Act 2002 were relevant social security legislation, and

(b) accordingly, child tax credit and working tax credit were relevant social security benefits for the purposes of the definition of "benefit offence".]]

AMENDMENTS

1. Inserted by the Child Support, Pensions and Social Security Act 2000 c.19, Sch.6 para.2 (April 2, 2001).

2. Welfare Reform Act 2012 s.122 (June 6, 2012).

[1 Power to require information.

1.175 **109B.**—(1) An authorised officer who has reasonable grounds for suspecting that a person—

(a) is a person falling within subsection (2) [2 or (2A)] below, and

(b) has or may have possession of or access to any information about any matter that is relevant for any one or more of the purposes mentioned in section 109A(2) above,

may, by written notice, require that person to provide all such information described in the notice as is information of which he has possession, or to which he has access, and which it is reasonable for the authorised officer to require for a purpose so mentioned.

(2) The persons who fall within this subsection are—

(a) any person who is or has been an employer or employee within the meaning of any provision made by or under the Contributions and Benefits Act;

(b) any person who is or has been a self-employed earner within the meaning of any such provision;

(c) any person who by virtue of any provision made by or under that Act falls, or has fallen, to be treated for the purposes of any such provision as a person within paragraph (a) or (b) above;

(d) any person who is carrying on, or has carried on, any business involving the supply of goods for sale to the ultimate consumers by individuals not carrying on retail business from retail premises;

(e) any person who is carrying on, or has carried on, any business involving the supply of goods or services by the use of work done or services performed by persons other than employees of his;

(f) any person who is carrying on, or has carried on, an agency or other business for the introduction or supply, to persons requiring them, of persons available to do work or to perform services;

(g) any local authority acting in their capacity as an authority responsible for the granting of any licence;

(h) any person who is or has been a trustee or manager of a personal or occupational pension scheme;

(i) any person who is or has been liable to make a compensation payment or a payment to the Secretary of State under section 6 of the Social Security (Recovery of Benefits) Act 1997 (payments in respect of recoverable benefits); [16 . . .]

[16 (ia) a person of a prescribed description; and]

(j) the servants and agents of any such person as is specified in any of paragraphs (a) to [16 (ia)] above.

[3 (2A) The persons who fall within this subsection are—

(a) any bank;

[4 (aa) the Director of National Savings;]

(b) any person carrying on a business the whole or a significant part of which consists in the provision of credit (whether secured or unsecured) to members of the public;

[5 (c) any insurer;]

(d) any credit reference agency (within the meaning given by section 145(8) of the Consumer Credit Act 1974 (c. 39));

(e) any body the principal activity of which is to facilitate the exchange of information for the purpose of preventing or detecting fraud;

(f) any person carrying on a business the whole or a significant part of which consists in the provision to members of the public of a service for transferring money from place to place;

(g) any water undertaker or sewerage undertaker, [6 Scottish Water or any local authority which is to collect charges by virtue of an order under section 37 of the Water Industry (Scotland) Act 2002 (asp 3);]

[7 (h) any person who—

(i) is the holder of a licence under section 7 of the Gas Act 1986 (c. 44) to convey gas through pipes, or

(ii) is the holder of a licence under section 7A(1) of that Act to supply gas through pipes;]

[8 (i) any person who (within the meaning of the Electricity Act 1989 (c. 29)) distributes or supplies electricity;]

[17 . . .]

(k) any person conducting any educational establishment or institution;

(l) any body the principal activity of which is to provide services in connection with admissions to educational establishments or institutions;

(m) the Student Loans Company;

(n) any servant or agent of any person mentioned in any of the preceding paragraphs.

(2B) Subject to the following provisions of this section, the powers conferred by this section on an authorised officer to require information from any person by virtue of his falling within subsection (2A) above shall be exercisable for the purpose only of obtaining information relating to a particular person identified (by name or description) by the officer.

(2C) An authorised officer shall not, in exercise of those powers, require any information from any person by virtue of his falling within subsection (2A) above unless it appears to that officer that there are reasonable grounds for believing that the identified person to whom it relates is–

(a) a person who has committed, is committing or intends to commit a benefit offence; or

(b) a person who (within the meaning of Part 7 of the Contributions and Benefits Act) is a member of the family of a person falling within paragraph (a) above.

(2D) Nothing in subsection (2B) or (2C) above shall prevent an authorised officer who is an official of a Government department and whose authorisation states that his authorisation applies for the purposes of this subsection from exercising the powers conferred by this section for obtaining from–

(a) a water undertaker or [9 Scottish Water,]

(b) any person who (within the meaning the Gas Act 1986) supplies gas conveyed through pipes,

(c) any person who (within the meaning of the Electricity Act 1989) supplies electricity conveyed by distribution systems, or

(d) any servant or agent of a person mentioned in any of the preceding paragraphs,

any information which relates exclusively to whether and in what quantities water, gas or electricity are being or have been supplied to residential premises specified or described in the notice by which the information is required.

(2E) The powers conferred by this section shall not be exercisable [[17]so as to secure the disclosure by a telecommunications operator or postal operator of communications data without the consent of the operator.]

[[17] . . .]

(3) The obligation of a person to provide information in accordance with a notice under this section shall be discharged only by the provision of that information, at such reasonable time and in such form as may be specified in the notice, to the authorised officer who—

(a) is identified by or in accordance with the terms of the notice; or

(b) has been identified, since the giving of the notice, by a further written notice given by the authorised officer who imposed the original requirement or another authorised officer.

(4) The power of an authorised officer under this section to require the provision of information shall include a power to require the production and delivery up and (if necessary) creation of, or of copies of or extracts from, any such documents containing the information as may be specified or described in the notice imposing the requirement.

[[10] (5) No one shall be required under this section to provide—

(a) any information that tends to incriminate either himself or, in the case of a person who is [[11] married or is a civil partner, his spouse or civil partner]; or

(b) any information in respect of which a claim to legal professional privilege or, in Scotland, confidentiality as between client and professional legal adviser, would be successful in any proceedings;

and for the purposes of this subsection it is immaterial whether the information is in documentary form or not.]

[[13] (6) Provision may be made by order—

(a) adding any person to the list of persons falling within subsection (2A) above;

(b) removing any person from the list of persons falling within that subsection;

(c) modifying that subsection for the purpose of taking account of any change to the name of any person for the time being falling within that subsection.

(7) In this section—

[[13] "bank" means—

(a) a person who has permission under Part of the Financial Services and Markets Act 2000 (c. 8) to accept deposits;

[[18] . . .] or

(c) a person who does not require permission under that Act to accept deposits, in the course of his business in the United Kingdom;]

"credit" includes a cash loan or any form of financial accommodation, including the cashing of a cheque;

[14 "insurer" means—

(a) a person who has permission under Part [19 4A] of the Financial Services and Markets Act 2000 to effect or carry out contracts of insurance; [18 . . .]

[18 . . .]

[17 "postal operator" has the same meaning as in the Investigatory Powers Act 2016 (see s.262 of that Act);]

"residential premises", in relation to a supply of water, gas or electricity, means any premises which–

(a) at the time of the supply were premises occupied wholly or partly for residential purposes, or

(b) are premises to which that supply was provided as if they were so occupied; and

[17 "telecommunications operator" has the same meaning as in the Investigatory Powers Act 2016 (see s.261 of that Act).]

[15 (7A) The definitions of "bank" and "insurer" in subsection (7) must be read with—

(a) section 22 of the Financial Services and Markets Act 2000;

(b) any relevant order under that section; and

(c) Schedule 2 to that Act.]]

AMENDMENTS

1. Inserted by the Child Support, Pensions and Social Security Act 2000 Sch.6 para.2 (April 2, 2001).

2. Social Security Fraud Act 2001 s.1(2) (April 30, 2002).

3. Social Security Fraud Act 2001 s.1(2) (April 30, 2002).

4. Social Security Administration Act 1992 (Amendment) Order 2002 (SI 2002/817) art.2(a) (April 30, 2002).

5. Social Security Administration Act 1992 (Amendment) Order 2002 (SI 2002/817) art.2(b) (April 30, 2002).

6. Water Industry (Scotland) Act 2002 (Consequential Modifications) Order 2004 (SI 2004/1822) Sch.1(1) para.16(a) (July 14, 2004).

7. Social Security Administration Act 1992 (Amendment) Order 2002 (SI 2002/817) art.2(c) (April 30, 2002).

8. Social Security Administration Act 1992 (Amendment) Order 2002 (SI 2002/817) art.2(d) (April 30, 2002).

9. Water Industry (Scotland) Act 2002 (Consequential Modifications) Order 2004 (SI 2004/1822) Sch.1(1) para.16(b) (July 14, 2004).

10. Social Security Fraud Act 2001 s.1(3) (April 30, 2002).

11. Civil Partnership Act 2004 Sch.24(4), para.64 (December 5, 2005).

12. Social Security Fraud Act 2001 s.1(4) (February 26, 2002).

13. Social Security Administration Act 1992 (Amendment) Order 2002 (SI 2002/817) art.3(a)(i) (April 1, 2002).

14. Social Security Administration Act 1992 (Amendment) Order 2002 (SI 2002/817) art.3(a)(ii) (April 1, 2002).

15. Social Security Administration Act 1992 (Amendment) Order 2002 (SI 2002/817) art.3(b) (April 1, 2002).

16. The Welfare Reform Act 2012 (Commencement No. 10) Order 2013 (SI 2013/1250) art.3 (June 17, 2013).

17. Investigatory Powers Act 2016 Sch.2 para.5 (July 22, 2020).

18. EEA Passport Rights (Amendment, etc., and Transitional Provisions) (EU Exit) Regulations 2018 (SI 2018/1149) Sch.1(2) para.32(a) (December 31, 2020).

19. Financial Services Act 2012 Sch.18(2) para.74(3) (April 1, 2013).

[1 Power of Secretary of State to require electronic access to information

1.176 **109BA.**—(1) Subject to subsection (2) below, where it appears to the Secretary of State—

(a) that a person falling within section 109B(2A) keeps any electronic records,
(b) that the records contain or are likely, from time to time, to contain information about any matter that is relevant for any one or more of the purposes mentioned in section 109A(2) above, and
(c) that facilities exist under which electronic access to those records is being provided, or is capable of being provided, by that person to other persons,

the Secretary of State may require that person to enter into arrangements under which authorised officers are allowed such access to those records.

(2) An authorised officer—

(a) shall be entitled to obtain information in accordance with arrangements entered into under subsection (1) above only if his authorisation states that his authorisation applies for the purposes of that subsection; and
(b) shall not seek to obtain any information in accordance with any such arrangements other than information which relates to a particular person and could be the subject of a requirement under section 109B above.

(3) The matters that may be included in the arrangements that a person is required to enter into under subsection (1) above may include—

(a) requirements as to the electronic access to records that is to be made available to authorised officers;
(b) requirements as to the keeping of records of the use that is made of the arrangements;
(c) requirements restricting the disclosure of information about the use that is made of the arrangements; and
(d) such other incidental requirements as the Secretary of State considers appropriate in connection with allowing access to records to authorised officers.

(4) An authorised officer who is allowed access in accordance with any arrangements entered into under subsection (1) above shall be entitled to make copies of, and to take extracts from, any records containing information which he is entitled to require under section 109B.]

AMENDMENT

1. Inserted by the Social Security Fraud Act 2001, s.2(1) (April 30, 2002).

[1 Powers of entry

1.177 **109C.**—(1) An authorised officer shall be entitled, at any reasonable time and either alone or accompanied by such other persons as he thinks fit, to enter any premises which—

(a) are liable to inspection under this section; and
(b) are premises to which it is reasonable for him to require entry in order to exercise the powers conferred by this section.

(2) An authorised officer who has entered any premises liable to inspection under this section may—

(a) make such an examination of those premises, and
(b) conduct any such inquiry there,

as appears to him appropriate for any one or more of the purposes mentioned in section 109A(2) above.

(3) An authorised officer who has entered any premises liable to inspection under this section may—

(a) question any person whom he finds there;
(b) require any person whom he finds there to do any one or more of the following—
   (i) to provide him with such information,
   (ii) to produce and deliver up and (if necessary) create such documents or such copies of, or extracts from, documents,

   as he may reasonably require for any one or more of the purposes mentioned in section 109A(2) above; and
(c) take possession of and either remove or make his own copies of any such documents as appear to him to contain information that is relevant for any of those purposes.

(4) The premises liable to inspection under this section are any premises (including premises consisting in the whole or a part of a dwelling house) which an authorised officer has reasonable grounds for suspecting are—

(a) premises which are a person's place of employment;
(b) premises from which a trade or business is being carried on or where documents relating to a trade or business are kept by the person carrying it on or by another person on his behalf;
(c) premises from which a personal or occupational pension scheme is being administered or where documents relating to the administration of such a scheme are kept by the person administering the scheme or by another person on his behalf;
(d) premises where a person who is the compensator in relation to any such accident, injury or disease as is referred to in section 109A(2)(b) above is to be found;
(e) premises where a person on whose behalf any such compensator has made, may have made or may make a compensation payment is to be found.

(5) An authorised officer applying for admission to any premises in accordance with this section shall, if required to do so, produce the certificate containing his authorisation for the purposes of this Part.

[[2](6) Subsections (2E) and (5) of section 109B apply for the purposes of this section as they apply for the purposes of that section.]

AMENDMENT

1. Inserted by the Child Support, Pensions and Social Security Act 2000 Sch.6 para.2 (April 2, 2001).
2. Investigatory Powers Act 2016 Sch.2 para.6 (July 22, 2020).

[[1] Class 1, 1A, 1B or 2 contributions: powers to call for documents etc. 1.178

[[2] **110ZA.**—(1) Schedule 36 to the Finance Act 2008 (information and inspection powers) applies for the purpose of checking a person's position as regards relevant contributions as it applies for the purpose of checking a person's tax position, subject to the modifications in subsection (2).

(2) That Schedule applies as if—
(a) references to any provision of the Taxes Acts were to any provision of this Act or the Contributions and Benefits Act [3 or the National Insurance Contributions Act 2014] relating to relevant contributions,
(b) references to prejudice to the assessment or collection of tax were to prejudice to the assessment of liability for, and payment of, relevant contributions,
(c) the reference to information relating to the conduct of a pending appeal relating to tax were a reference to information relating to the conduct of a pending appeal relating to relevant contributions, and
(d) [4 paragraphs 21, 21A, 35(4A)(c), 36, 37(2) and (2A), 37A and 37B] of that Schedule (restrictions on giving taxpayer notice where taxpayer has made tax return) were omitted.]

[5 (2A) Part 3 of Schedule 38 to the Finance Act 2012 (power to obtain tax agent's files etc.) applies in relation to relevant contributions as in relation to tax and, accordingly—
(a) the cases described in paragraph 7 of that Schedule (case A and case B) include cases involving conduct or an offence relating to relevant contributions,
(b) (whether the case involves conduct or an offence relating to tax or relevant contributions) the papers and other documents that may be sought under that Part include ones relating to relevant contributions, and
(c) the other Parts of that Schedule apply so far as necessary to give effect to the application of Part 3 by virtue of this subsection.]

(3) In this section "relevant contributions" means Class 1, Class 1A, Class 1B or Class 2 contributions.]

AMENDMENTS

1. National Insurance Contributions and Statutory Payments Act 2004 s.7 (April 6, 2005).
2. Finance Act 2008 Sch.36(10) para.84 (April 1, 2009: substitution has effect subject to savings provision specified in SI 2009/404 art.9).
3. National Insurance Contributions Act 2014 s.7(5) (April 6, 2014).
4. Finance Act 2009, s.96 and Sch.48 (Appointed Day, Savings and Consequential Amendments) Order 2009 (SI 2009/3054) Sch.1 para.3(b) (April 1, 2010).
5. Finance Act 2012 Sch.38(7) para.56 (April 1, 2013).

1.179 *Section 110A–111 omitted.*

[1Dishonest representations for obtaining benefit etc.

1.180 **111A.** (1) If a person dishonestly—
(a) makes a false statement or representation; [2 or]
(b) produces or furnishes, or causes or allows to be produced or furnished, any document or information which is false in a material particular;

[2...] with a view to obtaining any benefit or other payment or advantage under the [3relevant] social security legislation (whether for himself or for some other person), he shall be guilty of an offence.

[4(1A) A person shall be guilty of an offence if—

(a) there has been a change of circumstances affecting any entitlement of his to any benefit or other payment or advantage under any provision of the relevant social security legislation;

(b) the change is not a change that is excluded by regulations from the changes that are required to be notified;

(c) he knows that the change affects an entitlement of his to such a benefit or other payment or advantage; and

(d) he dishonestly fails to give a prompt notification of that change in the prescribed manner to the prescribed person.

(1B) A person shall be guilty of an offence if—

(a) there has been a change of circumstances affecting any entitlement of another person to any benefit or other payment or advantage under any provision of the relevant social security legislation;

(b) the change is not a change that is excluded by regulations from the changes that are required to be notified;

(c) he knows that the change affects an entitlement of that other person to such a benefit or other payment or advantage; and

(d) he dishonestly causes or allows that other person to fail to give a prompt notification of that change in the prescribed manner to the prescribed person.

(1C) This subsection applies where—

(a) there has been a change of circumstances affecting any entitlement of a person ("the claimant") to any benefit or other payment or advantage under any provision of the relevant social security legislation;

(b) the benefit, payment or advantage is one in respect of which there is another person ("the recipient") who for the time being has a right to receive payments to which the claimant has, or (but for the arrangements under which they are payable to the recipient) would have, an entitlement; and

(c) the change is not a change that is excluded by regulations from the changes that are required to be notified.

(1D) In a case where subsection (1C) above applies, the recipient is guilty of an offence if—

(a) he knows that the change affects an entitlement of the claimant to a benefit or other payment or advantage under a provision of the relevant social security legislation;

(b) the entitlement is one in respect of which he has a right to receive payments to which the claimant has, or (but for the arrangements under which they are payable to the recipient) would have, an entitlement; and

(c) he dishonestly fails to give a prompt notification of that change in the prescribed manner to the prescribed person.

(1E) In a case where that subsection applies, a person other than the recipient is guilty of an offence if—

(a) he knows that the change affects an entitlement of the claimant to a benefit or other payment or advantage under a provision of the relevant social security legislation;

(b) the entitlement is one in respect of which the recipient has a right to receive payments to which the claimant has, or (but for the arrangements under which they are payable to the recipient) would have, an entitlement; and

(c) he dishonestly causes or allows the recipient to fail to give a prompt notification of that change in the prescribed manner to the prescribed person.

(1F) In any case where subsection (1C) above applies but the right of the recipient is confined to a right, by reason of his being a person to whom the claimant is required to make payments in respect of a dwelling, to receive payments of housing benefit—

(a) a person shall not be guilty of an offence under subsection (1D) or (1E) above unless the change is one relating to one or both of the following—
   (i) the claimant's occupation of that dwelling;
   (ii) the claimant's liability to make payments in respect of that dwelling;

but

(b) subsections (1D)(a) and (1E)(a) above shall each have effect as if after "knows" there were inserted "or could reasonably be expected to know".

(1G) For the purposes of subsections (1A) to (1E) above a notification of a change is prompt if, and only if, it is given as soon as reasonably practicable after the change occurs.]

[5...]

(3) A person guilty of an offence under this section shall be liable—

(a) on summary conviction, to imprisonment for a term not exceeding six months, or to a fine not exceeding the statutory maximum, or to both; or

(b) on conviction on indictment, to imprisonment for a term not exceeding seven years, or to a fine, or to both.

(4) In the application of this section to Scotland, in [6subsections (1) to (1E)] for "dishonestly" substitute "knowingly".]

AMENDMENTS

1. Social Security Administration (Fraud) Act 1997 s.13 (July 1, 1997).
2. Social Security Fraud Act 2001 s.16(1)(a) (October 18, 2001).
3. Child Support, Pensions and Social Security Act 2000 Sch.6 para.5 (April 2, 2001).
4. Social Security Fraud Act 2001 s.16(2) (October 18, 2001).
5. Child Support, Pensions and Social Security Act 2000 Sch.9(VI) para.1 (April 2, 2001).
6. Social Security Fraud Act 2001 s.16(1)(c) (October 18, 2001).

False representations for obtaining benefit etc.

1.181 **112.** (1) If a person for the purpose of obtaining any benefit or other payment under the [1relevant] [2social security legislation] whether for himself or some other person, or for any other purpose connected with that legislation—

(a) makes a statement or representation which he knows to be false; or

(b) produces or furnishes, or knowingly causes or knowingly allows to be produced or furnished, any document or information which he knows to be false in a material particular,

he shall be guilty of an offence.

[3(1A) A person shall be guilty of an offence if—

(a) there has been a change of circumstances affecting any entitlement of his to any benefit or other payment or advantage under any provision of the relevant social security legislation;

(b) the change is not a change that is excluded by regulations from the changes that are required to be notified;

(c) he knows that the change affects an entitlement of his to such a benefit or other payment or advantage; and

(d) he fails to give a prompt notification of that change in the prescribed manner to the prescribed person.

(1B) A person is guilty of an offence under this section if—

(a) there has been a change of circumstances affecting any entitlement of another person to any benefit or other payment or advantage under any provision of the relevant social security legislation;

(b) the change is not a change that is excluded by regulations from the changes that are required to be notified;

(c) he knows that the change affects an entitlement of that other person to such a benefit or other payment or advantage; and

(d) he causes or allows that other person to fail to give a prompt notification of that change in the prescribed manner to the prescribed person.

(1C) In a case where subsection (1C) of section 111A above applies, the recipient is guilty of an offence if—

(a) he knows that the change affects an entitlement of the claimant to a benefit or other payment or advantage under a provision of the relevant social security legislation;

(b) the entitlement is one in respect of which he has a right to receive payments to which the claimant has, or (but for the arrangements under which they are payable to the recipient) would have, an entitlement; and

(c) he fails to give a prompt notification of that change in the prescribed manner to the prescribed person.

(1D) In a case where that subsection applies, a person other than the recipient is guilty of an offence if—

(a) he knows that the change affects an entitlement of the claimant to a benefit or other payment or advantage under a provision of the relevant social security legislation;

(b) the entitlement is one in respect of which the recipient has a right to receive payments to which the claimant has, or (but for the arrangements under which they are payable to the recipient) would have, an entitlement; and

(c) he causes or allows the recipient to fail to give a prompt notification of that change in the prescribed manner to the prescribed person.

(1E) Subsection (1F) of section 111A above applies in relation to subsections (1C) and (1D) above as it applies in relation to subsections (1D) and (1E) of that section.

(1F) For the purposes of subsections (1A) to (1D) above a notification of a change is prompt if, and only if, it is given as soon as reasonably practicable after the change occurs.]

(2) A person guilty of an offence under [[4]this section] shall be liable on summary conviction to a fine not exceeding level 5 on the standard scale, or to imprisonment for a term not exceeding 3 months, or to both.

[[5]...]

AMENDMENTS

1. Child Support, Pensions and Social Security Act 2000 Sch.6 para.6 (April 2, 2001).
2. Social Security Administration (Fraud) Act 1997 Sch.1 para.4(2) (July 1, 1997).
3. Social Security Fraud Act 2001 s.16(3) (October 18, 2001).
4. Social Security Administration (Fraud) Act 1997 Sch.1 para.4(3) (July 1, 1997).
5. Child Support, Pensions and Social Security Act 2000 Sch.9(VI) para.1 (April 2, 2001).

[1 Breach of regulations

1.182 **113.**—(1) Regulations and schemes under any of the [2 legislation to which this section applies] may provide that any person who contravenes, or fails to comply with, any provision contained in regulations made under [2 that legislation]—

(a) in the case of a provision relating to contributions, shall be liable to a penalty;
(b) in any other case, shall be guilty of an offence under [2 any enactment contained in the legislation in question].

[3 (1A) The legislation to which this section applies is—

(a) the relevant social security legislation; and
(b) the enactments specified in section 121DA(1) so far as relating to contributions, [4 . . .].]

(2) Any regulations or scheme making such provision as is mentioned in subsection (1)(a) above shall—

(a) prescribe the amount or rate of penalty, or provide for how it is to be ascertained;
(b) provide for the penalty to be imposed by the [5 Inland Revenue]—
   (i) within six years after the date on which the penalty is incurred; or
   (ii) where the amount of the penalty is to be ascertained by reference to the amount of any contributions payable, at any later time within three years after the final determination of the amount of those contributions;
(c) provide for determining the date on which, for the purposes of paragraph (b) above, the penalty is incurred;
(d) prescribe the means by which the penalty is to be enforced; and
(e) provide for enabling the [1Inland Revenue], in [1their] discretion, to mitigate or to remit any such penalty, or to stay or to compound any proceedings for a penalty.

(3) *Omitted*

(4) Any provision contained in regulations which authorises statutory sick pay or statutory maternity pay to be set off against secondary Class 1 contributions is not a provision relating to contributions for the purposes of this section.]

AMENDMENTS

1. This section substituted by the Social Security Act 1998 s.60 (March 4, 1999).
2. The Child Support, Pensions and Social Security Act 2000 s.67 (November 1, 2000).
3. Transfer of Functions Act 1999 Sch.5 para.5 (April 6, 1999).
4. National Insurance and Statutory Payments Act 2004 s.9 (April 6, 2005).

5. Social Security Contributions (Transfer of Functions etc) Act 1999 Sch.5 para.5 (April 6, 1999).

Sections 113A–115 omitted. **1.183**

[1 Penalty as an alternative to prosecution

115A.—(1) This section applies where an overpayment is recoverable from a person by, or due from a person to, the Secretary of State [2 . . .] under or by virtue of section 71, [3 71ZB] [2 . . .] above and it appears to the Secretary of State [2 . . .] that **1.184**

(a) the making of the overpayment was attributable to an act or omission on the part of that person; and

(b) there are grounds for instituting against him proceedings for an offence (under this Act or any other enactment) relating to the overpayment.

[4 (1A) This section also applies where—

(a) it appears to the Secretary of State [2 . . .] that there are grounds for instituting proceedings against a person for an offence (under this Act of any other enactment) relating to an act or omission on the part of that person in relation to any benefit, and

(b) if an overpayment attributable to that act or omission had been made, the overpayment would have been recoverable from the person by, or due from the person to, the Secretary of State [2 . . .] under or by virtue of section 71, 71ZB, [2 . . .] above.]

(2) The Secretary of State [2 . . .] may give the person a written notice—

(a) stating that he may be invited to agree to pay a penalty and that, if he does so in the manner specified by the Secretary of State [2 . . .], no [4 proceedings referred to in subsection (1) or (1A) above] will be instituted against him; and

(b) containing such information relating to the operation of this section as may be prescribed.

[5 (3) The amount of the penalty in a case falling within subsection (1) is 50% of the amount of the overpayment (rounded down to the nearest whole penny), subject to—

(a) a minimum amount of £350, and

(b) a maximum amount of [5 £5000].

(3A) The amount of the penalty in the case falling within subsection (1A) is £350.

(3B) The Secretary of State may by order amend—

(a) the percentage for the time being specified in subsection (3);

(b) any figure for the time being specified in subsection (3)(a) or (b) of (3A).]

(4) If the person agrees in the specified manner to pay the penalty—

(a) the amount of the penalty shall be recoverable by the same methods as those by which the overpayment is [4 or would have been] recoverable; and

(b) no proceedings will be instituted against him for an offence (under this Act or any other enactment) relating to the overpayment [4 or to the act or omission referred to in subsection (1A)(a).]

(5) The person may withdraw his agreement to pay the penalty by notifying the Secretary of State [2 . . .] in the manner specified by the Secretary of State [2 . . .], at any time during the period of [4 14] days beginning with the day on which he agrees to pay it; and if he does so—

(a) so much of the penalty as has already been recovered shall be repaid; and

(b) subsection (4)(b) above shall not apply.

(6) [5 In a case referred to in subsection (1A)(a)] where, after the person has agreed to pay the penalty, the amount of the overpayment is revised on a review or appeal or in accordance with regulations—

(a) so much of the penalty as has already been recovered shall be repaid; and

(b) subsection (4)(b) above shall no longer apply by reason of the agreement;

but if a new agreement is made under this section in relation to the revised overpayment, the amount already recovered by way of penalty, to the extent that it does not exceed the amount of the new penalty, may be treated as recovered under the new agreement instead of being repaid.

(7A) [2 . . .]

(8) In this section "overpayment" means—

(a) a payment which should not have been made;

(b) a sum which the Secretary of State should have received;

(c) an amount of benefit paid in excess of entitlement; or

(d) an amount equal to an excess of benefit allowed;

and the reference in subsection (1)(a) [4 or (1A)(b)] above to the making of the overpayment is to the making of the payment, the failure to receive the sum, the payment of benefit in excess of entitlement or the allowing of an excess of benefit.

AMENDMENTS

1. This section inserted by the Social Security Administration (Fraud) Act 1997 (December 18, 1997).

2. Welfare Reform Act 2012 Sch.14 (April 1, 2013).

3. Welfare Reform Act 2012 s.105(3) (April 29, 2013).

4. Welfare Reform Act 2012 ss.113–115 (May 8, 2012).

5. The Social Security (Penalty as Alternative to Prosecution) (Maximum Amount) Order 2015 (SI 2015/202) reg.2 (April 1, 2015).

1.185 *Section 115B Omitted.*

[1 Civil penalties

Incorrect statements

1.186 **115C.**—(1) This section applies where—

(a) a person negligently makes an incorrect statement or representation, or negligently gives incorrect information or evidence—

(i) in or in connection with a claim for a relevant social security benefit, or

(ii) in connection with an award of a relevant social security benefit,

(b) the person fails to take reasonable steps to correct the error,

(c) the error results in the making of an overpayment, and

(d) the person has not been charged with an offence or cautioned, or been given a notice under section 115A, in respect of the overpayment.

(2) A penalty of a prescribed amount may be imposed by the appropriate authority—

(a) in any case, on the person,

(b) in a case where the person ("A") is making, or has made, a claim for the benefit for a period jointly with another ("B"), on B instead of A.

(c) The error results in the making of an overpayment, and

(d) the person has not been charged with an offence or cautioned, or been given a notice under section 115A, in respect of the overpayment.

(3) Subsection (2)(b) does not apply if B was not, and could not reasonably be expected to have been, aware that A had negligently made the incorrect statement or representation or given the incorrect information or evidence.

(4) A penalty imposed under subsection (2) is recoverable by the appropriate authority from the person on whom it is imposed.

(5) Sections 71ZC, 71ZD and 71ZE apply in relation to amounts recoverable by the appropriate authority under subsection (4) as to amounts recoverable by the Secretary of State under section 71ZB (and, where the appropriate authority is not the Secretary of State, those sections so apply as if references to the Secretary of State were to that authority).

(6) In this section and section 115D—"appropriate authority" means—

(a) the Secretary of State, or

(b) an authority which administers housing benefit or council tax benefit;

"overpayment" has the meaning given in section 115A(8), and the reference to the making of an overpayment is to be construed in accordance with that provision;

"relevant social security benefit" has the meaning given in section 121DA(7).]

Amendment

1. This provision inserted by Welfare Reform Act 2012 s.116 (May 10, 2012 for the purpose of making regulations; October 1, 2012 for all other purposes).

General Note

Civil penalties were introduced with effect from October 1, 2012 as part of the strategy to reduce both fraud and error in the benefit system. However, civil penalties can only be imposed where no benefit fraud is involved. They cannot be applied where an overpayment arises solely from official error within the DWP or HMRC. DMG 09420 indicates that there must be a recoverable overpayment of £65.01 or more before a civil penalty can be imposed. This would appear to be DWP policy since no minimum amount is specified in primary or secondary legislation. 1.187

Penalty decisions will be added to overpayment decisions; overpayments are defined broadly in s.115A(8). This means that where a civil penalty is imposed, there will be three relevant decisions in cases under s.71(1): the entitlement decision revising or superseding decisions on entitlement; the overpayment decision determining that there is a recoverable overpayment; and the penalty decision imposing a civil penalty. For overpayment decisions under the 2013 rules (see annotations immediately under the heading to Pt.III SSAA 1992 above at paras 1.77–1.79).

The prescribed amount of the penalty under this section is £50: Social Security (Civil Penalties) Regulations 2012 reg.2. Civil penalties are only available where the overpayment period began on, or falls wholly after October 1, 2012.

1.188 There are four conditions required before the discretion to impose a civil penalty arises:

(a) the overpayment does not involve fraud: subs.(1)(d);
(b) there has been an incorrect statement, representation, information or evidence made or given negligently by the person upon whom the penalty is imposed in connection with a claim or an award of benefit (which is defined broadly in s.121DA(7)): subs.(1)(a);
(c) the person has failed to take reasonable steps to correct the error: (subs.(1)(b); and
(d) the error has resulted in the overpayment: subs.(1)(c).

Some of the issues these conditions raise—such as causation under subs.(1)(c)—may well be resolved in determining whether there is a recoverable overpayment under s.71(1), although others will involve additional findings of fact. Since negligence is required before a penalty can be imposed, the wholly innocent misrepresentation will not attract a civil penalty, even though it may ground an overpayment decision. Negligence is a question of fact but will include consideration of whether the person acted carelessly without paying sufficient intention to the importance of making correct statements in relation to benefit matters. Findings of fact will also be needed on whether reasonable steps have been taken to correct the error and as to matters going to the exercise of discretion. See further the General Note to s.115D.

Subsections (2) and (3) make provision for a civil penalty to be imposed on the other half of a joint claim couple. However, this is only the case if that other party could reasonably be expected to have been aware that the first party had negligently made an incorrect statement or representation or given incorrect information or evidence.

[[1] Failure to disclose information

1.189 **115D.**—(1) A penalty of a prescribed amount may be imposed on a person by the appropriate authority where—

(a) the person, without reasonable excuse, fails to provide information or evidence in accordance with requirements imposed on the person by the appropriate authority in connection with a claim for, or an award of, a relevant social security benefit,
(b) the failure results in the making of an overpayment, and
(c) the person has not been charged with an offence or cautioned, or been given a notice under section 115A, in respect of the overpayment.

(2) A penalty of a prescribed amount may be imposed on a person by the appropriate authority where—

(a) the person, without reasonable excuse, fails to notify the appropriate authority of a relevant change of circumstances in accordance with requirements imposed on the person under relevant social security legislation,
(b) the failure results in the making of an overpayment, and
(c) the person has not been charged with an offence or cautioned, or been given a notice under section 115A, in respect of the overpayment.

(3) Where a person is making, or has made, a claim for a benefit for a period jointly with another, and both of them fail as mentioned in

subsection (1) or (2), only one penalty may be imposed in respect of the same overpayment.

(4) A penalty imposed under subsection (1) or (2) is recoverable by the appropriate authority from the person on whom it is imposed.

(5) Sections 71ZC, 71ZD and 71ZE apply in relation to amounts recoverable by the appropriate authority under subsection (4) as to amounts recoverable by the Secretary of State under section 71ZB (and, where the appropriate authority is not the Secretary of State, those sections so apply as if references to the Secretary of State were to that authority).

(6) In this section "relevant change of circumstances, in relation to a person, means a change of circumstances which affects any entitlement of the person to any benefit or other payment or advantage under any provision of the relevant social security legislation.]

AMENDMENT

1. This provision inserted by Welfare Reform Act 2012 s.116 (May 10, 2012 for the purpose of making regulations; October 1, 2012 for all other purposes).

GENERAL NOTE

While s.115C deals with civil penalties imposed where there have been incorrect statements, s.115D deals with civil penalties imposed where there has been a failure to disclose or provide information or evidence. There are separate provisions dealing with a failure to provide required information or evidence (subs.(1)); and with a failure to notify a relevant change of circumstances (subs.(2)). 1.190

There are three conditions required for the imposition of a penalty under subs.(1):

(a) the overpayment does not involve fraud: subs.(1)(c);
(b) there has been a failure by the person upon whom the penalty is imposed, without reasonable excuse, to provide information of evidence required by the Secretary of State in connection with a claim or an award of benefit (which is defined broadly in s.121DA(7)): subs.(1)(a); and
(c) the failure has resulted in the overpayment: subs.(1)(b).

There are three conditions required for the imposition of a penalty under subs.(2):

(a) the overpayment does not involve fraud: subs.(2)(c);
(b) there has been a failure by the person upon whom the penalty is imposed, without reasonable excuse, to notify a relevant change of circumstances in connection with a claim or an award of benefit (which is defined broadly in s.121DA(7)): subs.(2)(a); and
(c) the failure has resulted in the overpayment: subs.(2)(b).

Relevant change of circumstances is defined in subs.(6).

Findings of fact will be needed on whether any circumstances put forward by the person upon whom the penalty has been imposed constitute a reasonable excuse for the failure issue. This is likely to include consideration of the timing of any action where late notification has been given.

In joint claims, where there has been a failure by both parties to provide information or evidence, or to notify a relevant change of circumstances, a penalty can only be imposed on one of them: subs.(3).

In *VT v SSWP (IS)* [2016] UKUT 178 (AAC), [2016] AACR 42, Judge Rowland makes several important points. 1.191

The first is that there is both an objective and a subjective aspect to the concept of what amounts to a "reasonable excuse":

"11. The Secretary of State submits that the First-tier Tribunal did err in law because it overlooked the words "without reasonable excuse", which appear in both subsection (1)(a) and subsection (2)(a). He further submits, and I agree, that whether a person has a reasonable excuse raises the question whether what

> he or she did (or did not do) was a reasonable thing for a responsible person, conscious of, and intending to comply with, his or her obligations regarding benefit but having the experience and other relevant attributes of the person in question and placed in the situation in which that person found himself or herself at the relevant time, to do (or not to do)."

Secondly, even if all the conditions for the imposition of a civil penalty are met, including claimants' lacking a reasonable excuse for a failure to disclose material facts, the imposition of a civil penalty (though not its amount) is still a matter of discretion.

Thirdly, Judge Rowland confirms, accepting the Secretary of State's submission, that there is a right of appeal in respect of the imposition of a penalty. The Secretary of State shifted his ground during the course of the appeal, and Judge Rowland notes that the present state of the legislation is "unsatisfactory".

In *CT v SSWP (ESA)* [2021] UKUT 6 Judge Wikeley applies *VT*, firmly rejecting SSWP's position that

> "there is only one mitigating factor that falls to be considered, and that is the amount of the overpayment. What is more, the Secretary of State considers that the question of whether the amount of an overpayment warrants a civil penalty must be determined by strict reference to DWP's 'small overpayment' (or 'SMOP') threshold. This is amount below which the Secretary of State does not consider it economic to recover overpayments. It currently stands at £65.01. In effect, then, the Secretary of State considers that where section 115D is met, a civil penalty is appropriate for all overpayments that it is viable for DWP to recover."

1.192 *Section 116–121D omitted.*

[Interpretation of Part VI

1.193 [1] **121DA.**— (1) In this Part "the relevant social security legislation" means the provisions of any of the following, except so far as relating to contributions, [[2] . . .] statutory sick pay or statutory maternity pay, that is to say—

(a) the Contributions and Benefits Act;
(b) this Act;
(c) the Pensions Act, except Part III;
(d) section 4 of the Social Security (Incapacity for Work) Act 1994;
(e) the Jobseekers Act 1995;
(f) the Social Security (Recovery of Benefits) Act 1997;
(g) Parts I and IV of the Social Security Act 1998;
(h) Part V of the Welfare Reform and Pensions Act 1999;
[[3] (hh) the State Pension Credit Act 2002;]
[[4] (hi) Part 1 of the Welfare Reform Act 2007;]
[[5] (hj) Part 1 of the Welfare Reform Act 2012;]
[[6] (hk) Part 4 of that Act;]
[[10] (hl) Part 1 of the Pensions Act 2014;]
[[11] (hm) Part 5 of the Pensions Act 2014;]
(i) the Social Security Pensions Act 1975;
(j) the Social Security Act 1973;
(k) any subordinate legislation made, or having effect as if made, under any enactment specified in paragraphs (a) to (j) above.

(2) In this Part "authorised officer" means a person acting in accordance

with any authorisation for the purposes of this Part which is for the time being in force in relation to him.

(3) For the purposes of this Part—

(a) references to a document include references to anything in which information is recorded in electronic or any other form;

(b) the requirement that a notice given by an authorised officer be in writing shall be taken to be satisfied in any case where the contents of the notice—

(i) are transmitted to the recipient of the notice by electronic means; and

(ii) are received by him in a form that is legible and capable of being recorded for future reference.

(4) In this Part "premises" includes—

(a) moveable structures and vehicles, vessels, aircraft and hovercraft;

(b) installations that are offshore installations for the purposes of the Mineral Workings (Offshore Installations) Act 1971;

(c) places of all other descriptions whether or not occupied as land or otherwise;

and references in this Part to the occupier of any premises shall be construed, in relation to premises that are not occupied as land, as references to any person for the time being present at the place in question.

(5) In this Part—

"benefit" includes any allowance, payment, credit or loan;

[[7] "benefit offence" means—

(a) any criminal offence in connection with a claim for a relevant social security benefit;

(b) any criminal offence in connection with the receipt or payment of any amount by way of such a benefit;

(c) any criminal offence committed for the purpose of facilitating the commission (whether or not by the same person) of a benefit offence;

(d) any attempt or conspiracy to commit a benefit offence;] and

"compensation payment" has the same meaning as in the Social Security (Recovery of Benefits) Act 1997.

(6) [[8] . . .]

(7) In this section [[9] "relevant social security benefit" means a benefit under any provision of the relevant social security legislation; and] "subordinate legislation" has the same meaning as in the Interpretation Act 1978.]

AMENDMENTS

1. Child Support, Pensions and Social Security Act 2000 s.67 (April 2, 2001).
2. Tax Credits Act 2002 Sch.6 (April 8, 2003).
3. State Pension Credit Act 2002 Sch.2 para.12 (July 2, 2002).
4. Welfare Reform Act 2007 Sch.3 para.10(12) (October 27, 2008).
5. Welfare Reform Act 2012 Sch.9 (April 29, 2013).
6. Welfare Reform Act 2012 Sch.9 para.12 (April 8, 2013).
7. Social Security Fraud Act 2001 s.1(7) (April 30, 2002).
8. Welfare Reform Act 2012 Sch.14 (April 1, 2013).
9. Social Security Fraud Act 2001 s.1(8) (April 30, 2002).
10. Pensions Act 2014 s.56(4), s.23 and Sch.12, para.13 (April 6, 2016).
11. Pensions Act 2014 Sch.16 para.26 (April 6, 2017).

Part VII

Information

1.194 **121E.–123.** *Omitted.*

The Registration Service

Provisions relating to age, death and marriage

1.195 **124.**—(1) Regulations made by the Registrar General under section 20 of the Registration Service Act 1953 or section 54 of the Registration of Births, Deaths and Marriages (Scotland) Act 1965 may provide for the furnishing by superintendent registrars and registrars, subject to the payment of such fee as may be prescribed by the regulations, of such information for the purposes—

(a) of the provisions of the Contributions and Benefits Act to which this section applies;

[[1] (aa) of the provisions of Parts I and II of the Jobseekers Act 1995;]

[[3] (ab) of the provisions of the State Pension Credit Act 2002;]

[[6] (ac) of the provisions of Part 1 of the Welfare Reform Act 2007;]

[[8] (ad) of the provisions of Part 1 of the Welfare Reform Act 2012;]

[[9] (ae) of the provisions of Part 4 of that Act;]

[[11] (af) of the provisions of Part 1 of the Pensions Act 2014; and]

[[12] (ag) of section 30 of the Pensions Act 2014; and]

(b) of the provisions of this Act so far as they have effect in relation to matters arising under those provisions,

including copies or extracts from the registers in their custody, [[10] (or in the case of marriages converted from civil partnerships, copies or extracts from the register of conversions)] as may be so prescribed.

(2) This section applies to the following provisions of the Contributions and Benefits Act—

(a) Parts I to VI except section 108;

(b) Part VII, so far as it relates to income support and [[5] . . .];

(c) Part VIII, so far as it relates to any social fund payment such as is mentioned in section 138(1)(a) or (2);

(d) Part IX;

(e) Part XI; and

(f) Part XII.

(3) Where the age, marriage or death of a person is required to be ascertained or proved for the purposes mentioned in subsection (1) above, any person—

(a) on presenting to the custodian of the register under the enactments relating to the registration of births, marriages and deaths, in which particulars of the birth, marriage or death (as the case may be) of the first-mentioned person are entered, a duly completed requisition in writing in that behalf; and

(b) on payment of [[11]the appropriate fee in England and Wales and a fee of] [[7] £10.00] in Scotland,

shall be entitled to obtain a copy, certified under the hand of the custodian, of the entry of those particulars.

[[10] (3A) Where it is required to be ascertained or proved for the purposes mentioned in subsection (1) above, that a civil partnership has been converted into a marriage, any person—

(a) on presenting to the superintendent registrar in whose district the conversion took place, a duly completed requisition in writing in that behalf; and

[11 (b) on payment of the appropriate fee;]

is entitled to obtain a copy, certified under the hand of the superintendent registrar, of the entry relating to that marriage in the register of conversions.]

(4) Requisitions for the purposes of [10 subsections (3) and (3A)] above shall be in such form and contain such particulars as may from time to time be specified by the Registrar General, and suitable forms of requisition shall, on request, be supplied without charge by superintendent registrars and registrars.

(5) In this section—

[11"the appropriate fee" means the fee payable to the registrar or superintendent registrar for a certified copy of an entry in the register concerned by virtue of section 38A of the Births and Deaths Registration Act 1953, section 71A of the Marriage Act 1949 or section 9 of the Marriage (Same Sex Couples) Act 2013.]

[10 "register of conversions" means the register of conversions of civil partnerships into marriages kept by the Registrar General in accordance with section 9 of the Marriage (Same Sex Couples) Act 2013 and regulations made under that section.]

(a) as it applies to England and Wales—

"Registrar General" means the Registrar General for England and Wales; and

"superintendent registrar" and "registrar" mean a superintendent registrar or, as the case may be, registrar for the purposes of the enactments relating to the registration of births, deaths and marriages; and

(b) as it applies to Scotland—

"Registrar General" means the Registrar General of Births, Deaths and Marriages for Scotland;

"registrar" means a district registrar, senior registrar or assistant registrar for the purposes of the enactment relating to the registration of births, deaths and marriages in Scotland.

AMENDMENTS

1. Jobseekers Act 1995 Sch.2 para.59 (October 7, 1996).

2. The Registration of Births, Deaths and Marriages (Fees) Order 2002 (SI 2002/3076) art.1 (April 1, 2003; this Order specifies a fee of £7 where the certificate is issued by a superintendent registrar or any other custodian of the register).

3. State Pension Credit Act 2002 s.14 and Sch.2 (July 2, 2002 for the purpose of making regulations only; fully in force October 6, 2003).

4. The Registration of Births, Deaths and Marriages (Fees) (Scotland) Order 2009 (SSI 2009/65) (April 1, 2009).

5. Tax Credits Act 2002 s.60 and Sch.6 (April 8, 2003).

6. Welfare Reform Act 2007 s.28 and Sch.3 para.10 (October 27, 2008).

7. The Registration of Birth, Deaths and Marriages (Fees) (Scotland) Order 2010 (Scottish SI 2010/428) Sch.1 para.1 (January 1, 2011).

8. Welfare Reform Act 2012 Sch.2 para.17 (April 29, 2013).

9. Welfare Reform Act 2012 Sch.9 para.15 (April 8, 2013).

10. The Marriage (Same Sex Couples) Act 2013 (Consequential and Contrary Provisions and Scotland) and Marriage and Civil Partnership (Scotland) Act

(Consequential Provisions) Order 2014 (SI 2014/3168), art.12 (December 10, 2014).

11. Immigration Act 2016 Sch.15 para.36 (July 12, 2016).

Derivation

1.196 Social Security Act 1975 s.160.

Definitions

"the Contributions and Benefits Act"—see s.191.
"prescribed"—*ibid.*

[1 Provisions relating to civil partnership: England and Wales

1.197 **124A.**—(1) Regulations made by the Registrar General under section 36 of the Civil Partnership Act 2004 may provide for the furnishing by registration authorities, subject to the payment of the prescribed fee, of such information for the purposes mentioned in section 124(1) above as may be so prescribed.

(2) Where the civil partnership of a person is required to be ascertained or proved for those purposes, any person—

(a) on presenting to the registration authority for the area in which the civil partnership was formed a request in the prescribed manner in that behalf, and

(b) on payment of the prescribed fee,

shall be entitled to obtain a certified copy of such entries in the register as are prescribed by regulations made under section 36 of the 2004 Act.

(3) "The prescribed fee" means any fee prescribed under section 34(1) of the 2004 Act.

(4) "The prescribed manner" means—

(a) in accordance with any regulations made under section 36 of the 2004 Act, and

(b) in such form as is approved by the Registrar General for England and Wales,

and forms for making a request under subsection (2) shall, on request, be supplied without charge by registration authorities.]

Amendment

1. Civil Partnership Act 2004 (Overseas Relationships and Consequential etc. Amendments) Order 2005 (SI 2005/3129) Sch.1 para.4 (December 5, 2005).

[1 Provisions relating to civil partnership: Scotland

1.198 **124B.**—(1) Where the civil partnership of a person is required to be ascertained or proved for the purposes mentioned in section 124(1) above, any person, on presenting to a district registrar a request in the approved manner in that behalf, [2 and on payment of the sum of [3 £10.00]] shall be entitled to obtain a copy, certified by the registrar, of the entry in the civil partnership register of the particulars of the civil partnership.

(2) "The approved manner" means in such form and containing such particulars as may be approved by the Registrar General for Scotland.

(3) Forms for making a request under subsection (1) shall, on request, be supplied without charge by district registrars.

(4) "Civil partnership register" has the same meaning as in Part 3 of the Civil Partnership Act 2004.]

AMENDMENTS

1. Civil Partnership Act 2004 (Overseas Relationships and Consequential etc. Amendments) Order 2005 (SI 2005/3129) Sch.1 para.4 (December 5, 2005).

2. Local Electoral Administration and Registration Services (Scotland) Act 2006 asp 14 (Scottish Act) Pt 2 s.53(2) (October 1, 2006).

3. Registration of Births, Deaths and Marriages (Fees) (Scotland) Order (Scottish SI 2010/428) Sch.1 para.1 (January 1, 2011).

Regulations as to notifications of deaths

125.—(1) Regulations [[3]made with the concurrence of the Inland Revenue] may provide that it shall be the duty of any of the following persons— 1.199

(a) the Registrar General for England and Wales;

(b) the Registrar General of Births, Deaths and Marriages for Scotland;

(c) each registrar of births and deaths,

to furnish the Secretary of State, [[3]or the Inland Revenue, for the purposes of their respective functions] under the Contributions and Benefits Act [[1], the Jobseekers Act 1995] [[2]the Social Security (Recovery of Benefits) Act 1997] [[4], the Social Security Act 1998] [[5], the State Pension Credit Act 2002] [[6] , Part 1 of the Welfare Reform Act 2007] [[7] , Part 1 of the Welfare Reform Act 2012] [[8], Part 4 of that Act] [[9] , Part 1 of the Pensions Act 2014] [[10], section 30 of that Act] and this Act and the functions of the Northern Ireland Department under any Northern Ireland legislation corresponding to [[1]any of those Acts], with the prescribed particulars of such deaths as may be prescribed.

(2) The regulations may make provision as to the manner in which and the times at which the particulars are to be furnished.

AMENDMENTS

1. Jobseekers Act 1995 Sch.2 para.60 (October 7, 1996).

2. Social Security (Recovery of Benefits) Act 1997 s.33 and Sch.3 para.5 (October 6, 1997).

3. Social Security Contributions (Transfer of Functions, etc.) Act 1999 s.1(1) and Sch.1 para.25 (April 1, 1999).

4. Social Security Act 1998 s.86 and Sch.7 (dates as for implementation of SSA 1998 for various benefits as set out on para.1.88 of this volume).

5. State Pension Credit Act 2002 s.14 and Sch.2 (July 2, 2002 for the purpose of making regulations only; fully in force October 6, 2003).

6. Welfare Reform Act 2007 s.28 and Sch.3 para.10 (October 27, 2008).

7. The Welfare Reform Act 2012 (Commencement No. 9 and Transitional and Transitory Provisions and Commencement No. 8 and Savings and Transitional Provisions (Amendment)) Order 2013 (SI 2013/983) art.3(1)(b) (April 29, 2013).

8. Welfare Reform Act 2012 Sch.9 para.16 (June 10, 2013).

9. Pensions Act 2014 s.56(4), s.23 and Sch.12, para.16 (April 6, 2016).

10. Pensions Act 2014 s.31 and Sch.16 para.29 (April 6, 2017).

DERIVATION

1.200 Social Security Act 1986 s.60.

DEFINITIONS

"the Contributions and Benefits Act"—see s.191.
"the Northern Ireland Department"—*ibid.*
"prescribed"—*ibid.*

Personal representatives—income support and supplementary benefit

Personal representatives to give information about the estate of a deceased person who was in receipt of income support or supplementary benefit

1.201 **126.**—(1) The personal representatives of a person who was in receipt of [4 universal credit,] income support [1, an income-based jobseeker's allowance] [2, state pension credit] [3, an income-related employment and support allowance] or supplementary benefit at any time before his death shall provide the Secretary of State with such information as he may require relating to the assets and liabilities of that person's estate.

(2) If the personal representatives fail to supply any information within 28 days of being required to do so under subsection (1) above, then—

(a) the appropriate court may, on the application of the Secretary of State, make an order directing them to supply that information within such time as may be specified in the order; and
(b) any such order may provide that all costs (or, in Scotland, expenses) of and incidental to the application shall be borne personally by any of the personal representatives.

(3) In this section "the appropriate court" means—

(a) in England and Wales, [5 the county court];
(b) in Scotland, the sheriff;

and any application to the sheriff under this section shall be made by summary application.

AMENDMENTS

1. Jobseekers Act 1995 Sch.2 para.61 (October 7, 1996).
2. State Pension Credit Act 2002 s.14 and Sch.2 (July 2, 2002 for the purpose of making regulations only; fully in force October 6, 2003).
3. Welfare Reform Act 2007 s.28 and Sch.3 para.10 (October 27, 2008).
4. The Welfare Reform Act 2012 (Commencement No. 9 and Transitional and Transitory Provisions and Commencement No. 8 and Savings and Transitional Provisions (Amendment)) Order 2013 (SI 2013/983) art.3(1)(b) (April 29, 2013).
5. Crime and Courts Act 2013 s.175(5) and Sch.9 para.52 (April 22, 2014).

DERIVATION

1.202 Social Security Act 1986 s.27A.

GENERAL NOTE

1.203 Under s.71(3) an overpayment which would have been recoverable from a person may be recoverable from that person's estate (*Secretary of State for Social Services v Solly* [1974] 3 All E.R. 922, *CSSB 6/1995*). Section 126 provides a specific obligation for the estate to provide information about the assets in it. However, s.126 only applies to the estates of income support, income-based JSA or supplementary benefit claimants. It does not apply to all benefits. Nor does it apply to anyone other than a recipient of income support, JSA or supplementary benefit. Sometimes a person other than a recipient may become liable to recovery by making a misrepresentation or failing to disclose a material fact: *R(SB) 21/82* and *R(SB) 28/83*. See the note to s.71(3).

126A. *Omitted.* **1.204**

127.–128A. *Repealed by Sch.2 to the Social Security Administration (Fraud) Act 1997 (July 1, 1997).* **1.205**

Statutory sick pay and other benefits

Section 129 Omitted. **1.206**

Section 130 Omitted. **1.207**

Section 131 Omitted. **1.208**

Section 132 Omitted. **1.209**

Section 132A Omitted. **1.210**

Maintenance proceedings

Furnishing of addresses for maintenance proceedings, etc.

133. The Secretary of State may incur expenses for the purpose of furnishing the address at which a [1person] is recorded by him as residing, where the address is required for the purpose of taking or carrying on legal proceedings to obtain or enforce an order for the making by the [1person] of payments— **1.211**

(a) for the maintenance of the [1 person's spouse, former spouse, civil partner or former civil partner]; or

[1 (b) for the maintenance or education of any child of the person, or of any child of the person's spouse, former spouse, civil partner or former civil partner.]

DERIVATION

SSA 1975 s.161. **1.212**

AMENDMENT

1. Civil Partnership (Pensions and Benefit Payments) (Consequential, etc. Provisions) Order 2005 (SI 2005/2053) Sch.1(2) para.6(2) (December 5, 2005).

[1 *Universal Credit Information*

Supply of universal credit information

133A.—(1) This section applies to information that is held by— **1.213**

(a) the Secretary of State; or

(b) a person providing services to the Secretary of State, in connection with the provision of those services,

that relates to an award of universal credit.

(2) Information to which this section applies may be supplied to—

(a) a local housing authority;

(b) a licensing authority; or

(c) a person authorised to exercise any function of a local housing authority or a licensing authority,

for use in connection with obtaining a rent repayment order in respect of an award of universal credit or recovering an amount payable under such an order.

(3) For the purposes of this section—

"licensing authority" means a person designated by order under section 3 of the Housing (Wales) Act 2014(1);

"local housing authority" has the meaning given by section 261 of the Housing Act 2004(2); and

"rent repayment order" means a rent repayment order as referred to in section 73 or 96 of the Housing Act 2004 or section 32 of the Housing (Wales) Act 2014.]

AMENDMENT

1. Inserted by The Universal Credit and Miscellaneous Amendments (No.2) Regulations 2014 (SI 2014/2888), reg.9(1) (November 26, 2014).

1.214 **134.–149.** *Omitted.*

PART X

REVIEW AND ALTERATION OF BENEFITS

GENERAL NOTE

1.215 Sections 150-154 concern the review and alteration of benefits, and are principally concerned with the annual up-rating of benefits. They are not reproduced here to save space.

PART XI

COMPUTATION OF BENEFITS

Effect of alteration of rates of benefit under Parts II to V of Contributions and Benefits Act

1.216 **155.**—(1) This section has effect where the rate of any benefit to which this section applies is altered—

(a) by an Act subsequent to this Act;

(b) by an order under [4 section 150, 150A or 152] above; or

(c) in consequence of any such Act or order altering any maximum rate of benefit;

and in this section "the commencing date" means the date fixed for payment of benefit at an altered rate to commence.

(2) This section applies to benefit under Part II, III, IV or V of the Contributions and Benefits Act.

(3) Subject to such exceptions or conditions as may be prescribed, where—

(a) the weekly rate of a benefit to which this section applies is altered to a fixed amount higher or lower than the previous amount; and

(b) before the commencing date an award of that benefit has been made (whether before or after the passing of the relevant Act or the making of the relevant order),

except as respects any period falling before the commencing date, the benefit shall become payable at the altered rate without any claim being made for it in the case of an increase in the rate of benefit or any review of the award in the case of a decrease, and the award shall have effect accordingly.

(4) Where—

(a) the weekly rate of a benefit to which this section applies is altered; and

(b) before the commencing date (but after that date is fixed) an award is made of the benefit,

the award either may provide for the benefit to be paid as from the commencing date at the altered rate or may be expressed in terms of the rate appropriate at the date of the award.

(5) Where in consequence of the passing of an Act, or the making of an order, altering the rate of disablement pension, regulations are made varying the scale of disablement gratuities, the regulations may provide that the scale as varied shall apply only in cases where the period taken into account by the assessment of the extent of the disablement in respect of which the gratuity is awarded begins or began after such day as may be prescribed.

(6) Subject to such exceptions or conditions as may be prescribed, where—

(a) for any purpose of any Act or regulations the weekly rate at which a person contributes to the cost of providing for a child [[2] or qualifying young person], or to the maintenance of an adult dependant, is to be calculated for a period beginning on or after the commencing date for an increase in the weekly rate of benefit; but

(b) account is to be taken of amounts referable to the period before the commencing date,

those amounts shall be treated as increased in proportion to the increase in the weekly rate of benefit.

(7) So long as sections 36 and 37 of the National Insurance Act 1965 (graduated retirement benefit) continue in force by virtue of regulations made under Schedule 3 of the Social Security (Consequential Provisions) Act 1975 or under Schedule 3 to the Consequential Provisions Act, regulation may make provision for applying the provisions of this section—

[[1](a) to the amount of graduate retirement benefit payable for each unit of graduated contributions,

(b) To increased of such benefit under any provisions made by virtue of section 24(1)(b) of the Social Security Pensions Act 1975 or section 62(1)(a) of the Contributions and Benefits Act, and

(c) to any addition under section 37(1) of the National Insurance Act 1965 (addition to weekly rate of retirement pension for [[3] widows, widowers and surviving civil partners]) to the amount of such benefit].

AMENDMENTS

1. Pensions Act 1995 s.131(3) (July 19, 1995).
2. Child Benefit Act 2005 Sch.1 Pt 1 para.23 (April 10, 2006).
3. Civil Partnership (Pensions and Benefit Payments) (Consequential, etc. Provisions) Order 2005 (SI 2005/2053) Sch.1(2) para.9 (December 5, 2005).
4. Pensions Act 2007 Sch.1(5) para.23 (July 26, 2007: insertion has effect as specified in 2007 c.22 s.5(3) and (7)).

DERIVATION

1.217 SSA 1986 s.64.

GENERAL NOTE

1.218 The effect of s.155(3) is frequently modified or disapplied by the various annual up-rating regulations.

[1Power to anticipate pensions up-rating order

1.219 **155A.**—(1) This section applies where a statement is made in the House of Commons by or on behalf of the Secretary of State which specifies—

(a) the amounts by which he proposes, by an order under [4 [5 150, 150A or 151A] above (as the case may be)] above, to increase—
 (i) the weekly sums that are payable by way of [5 a state pension under Part 1 of the Pensions Act 2014,] retirement pension [2 or shared additional pension]; or
 (ii) the amount of graduated retirement benefit payable for each unit of graduated contributions; and
(b) the date of which he proposes to bring the increases into force ("the commencing date").

(2) Where before the commencing date and after the date on which the statement is made, an award is made of [5 a state pension,] a retirement pension [3, a shared additional pension] or a graduated retirement benefit, the award may provide for the pension or benefit to be paid as from the commencing date at the increased rate or may be expressed in terms of the rate appropriate at the date of the award.]

AMENDMENTS

1. Social Security Act 1998 s.76 (November 16, 1998).
2. Welfare Reform and Pensions Act 1999 Sch.12 para.25(3) (December 1, 2000).
3. Welfare Reform and Pensions Act 1999 Sch.12 para.25(3) (December 1, 2000).
4. Pensions Act 2007 Sch.1(5) para.24 (July 26, 2007: substitution has effect as specified in 2007 c.22 s.5(3) and (7)).
5. Pensions Act 2014, s.56(4), s.23 and Sch.12, para.22 (April 6, 2016).

Up-rating under sections 150 above of pensions increased under section 52(3) of the Contributions and Benefits Act

1.220 [1**156.**—(1) This section applies in any case where a person is entitled to a Category A retirement pension with an increase, under section 52(3) of the Contributions and Benefits Act, in the additional pension on account of the contributions of a spouse [2 or civil partner] who had died.

(2) Where in the case of any up-rating order under section 150 above—

(a) The spouse's [2 or civil partner's] final relevant year is the tax year preceding the tax year in which the up-rating order comes into force, but

(b) The person's final relevant year was an earlier tax year,

then the up-rating order shall not have effect in relation to that part of the additional pension which is attributable to the spouse's [2 or civil partner] contributions.

(3) Where in the case of any up-rating order under section 150 above—

(a) The person's final relevant year is the tax year preceding the tax year in which the up-rating order comes into force, but

(b) The spouse's [2 or civil partner's] final relevant year was an earlier tax year,

Then the up-rating order shall not have effect in relation to that part of the additional pension which is attributable to the person's contributions.]

AMENDMENTS

1. Pensions Act 1995 s.130(1) (July 19, 1995).
2. Civil Partnership Act 2004 s.254 and Sch.24 para.66 (December 5, 2005).

DERIVATION

SSPA 1975 s.23(2A). 1.221

Effect of alteration of rates of child benefit

157.—(1) Subsections (3) and (4) of section 155 above shall have effect where there is an increase in the rate or any of the rates of child benefit as they have effect in relation to the rate of benefit to which that section applies. 1.222

(2) Where in connection with child benefit—

(a) any question arises in respect of a period after the date fixed for the commencement of payment of child benefit at an increased rate—
   (i) as to the weekly rate at which a person is contributing to the cost of providing for a child [1 or qualifying young person]; or
   (ii) as to the expenditure that a person is incurring in respect of a child [1 or qualifying young person]; and

(b) in determining that question account falls to be taken of contributions made or expenditure incurred for a period before that date,

the contributions made or expenditure incurred before that date shall be treated as increased in proportion to the increase in the rate of benefit.

DERIVATION

CBA 1975 s.5(6). 1.223

AMENDMENT

1. Child Benefit Act 2005 Sch.1 Pt 1 para.24 (April 10, 2006).

Treatment of excess benefit as paid on account of child benefit

158.—(1) In any case where— 1.224

(a) any benefit as defined in section 122 of the Contributions and Benefits Act or any increase of such benefit ("the relevant benefit or increase") has been paid to a person for a period in respect of a child [1 or qualifying young person]; and

(b) subsequently child benefit for that period in respect of the child [1 or qualifying young person] becomes payable at a rate which is such that, had the relevant benefit or increase been awarded after the child benefit became payable, the rate of the relevant benefit or increase would have been reduced,

then, except in so far as regulations otherwise provide, the excess shall be treated as paid on account of child benefit for that period in respect of the child [1 or qualifying young person].

(2) In subsection (1) above "the excess" means so much of the relevant benefit or increase as is equal to the difference between—

(a) the amount of it which was paid for the period referred to in that subsection; and

(b) the amount of it which would have been paid for that period if it had been paid at the reduced rate referred to in paragraph (b) of that subsection.

Derivation

1.225 SS(MP)A 1977 s.17(4).

Amendment

1. Child Benefit Act 2005 Sch.1 Pt 1 para.25 (April 10, 2006).

General Note

1.226 This provision avoids increases of benefits overlapping with, in particular, increase of child benefit.

Effect of alteration in the component rates of income support

1.227 **159.**—(1) Subject to such exceptions and conditions as may be prescribed, where—

(a) an award of income support is in force in favour of any person ("the recipient"); and

(b) there is an alteration in any of the relevant amounts, that is to say—

(i) any of the component rates of income support;

(ii) any of the other sums specified in regulations under Part VII of the Contributions and Benefits Act; or

(iii) the recipient's benefit income; and

(c) the alteration affects the computation of the amount of income support to which the recipient is entitled,

then subsection (2) or (3) below (as the case may be) shall have effect.

(2) Where, in consequence of the alteration in question, the recipient becomes entitled to an increased or reduced amount of income support ("the new amount"), then, as from the commencing date, the amount of income support payable to or for the recipient under the award shall be the new amount, without any further decision of [1the Secretary of State], and the award shall have effect accordingly.

(3) Where, notwithstanding the alteration in question, the recipient continues on and after the commencing date to be entitled to the same

amount of income support as before, the award shall continue in force accordingly.

(4) In any case where—

(a) there is an alteration in any of the relevant amounts; and

(b) before the commencing date (but after that date is fixed) an award of income support is made in favour of a person,

the award either may provide for income support to be paid as from the commencing date, in which case the amount shall be determined by reference to the relevant amounts which will be in force on that date, or may provide for an amount determined by reference to the amounts in force at the date of the award.

(5) In this section—

"alteration" means—

(a) in relation to—

(i) the component rates of income support; or

(ii) any other sums specified in regulations under Part VII of the Contributions and Benefits Act,

their alteration by or under any enactment whether or not contained in that Part; and

(b) in relation to a person's benefit income, the alteration of any of the sums referred to in [4 section 150, 150A or 151A] above—

(i) by any enactment; or

(ii) by an order under [2 section 150, 150A [4, 151A] or 152] above,

to the extent that any such alteration affects the amount of his benefit income;

"benefit income", in relation to any person, means so much of his income as consists of—

(a) benefit under the Contributions and Benefits Act, other than income support; [3 . . .]

[4 (za) state pension under Part 1 of the Pensions Act 2014;]

[3 (aa) personal independence payment; or]

(b) a war disablement pension or war widow's pension;

"the commencing date" in relation to an alteration, means the date on which the alteration comes into force in the case of the person in question;

"component rate", in relation to income support, means the amount of—

(a) the sum referred to in section 126(5)(b)(i) and (ii) of the Contributions and Benefits Act; or

(b) any of the sums specified in regulations under section 135(1) of that Act; and

"relevant amounts" has the meaning given by subsection (1)(b) above.

AMENDMENTS

1. Social Security Act 1998 Sch.7 para.95 (November 29, 1999 for purposes specified in SI 1999/3178 art.2(1) and Sch.1; not yet in force otherwise).

2. Pensions Act 2007 Sch.1(5) para.25 (July 26, 2007: insertion has effect as specified in 2007 c.22 s.5(3) and (7)).

3. Welfare Reform Act 2012 Sch.9 para.18 (April 8, 2013).
4. Pensions Act 2014 (Consequential Amendments) Order 2016 (SI 2016/931) art.2(2) (September 16, 2016).

DERIVATION

1.228 Social Security Act 1986 s.64A.

DEFINITIONS

"the Contributions and Benefits Act"—see s.191.
"war disablement pension"—*ibid.*
"war widow's pension"—*ibid.*

GENERAL NOTE

1.229 The general rule under s.159 is that if there is an alteration in the prescribed figures for personal allowances, premiums, the relevant sum (i.e. assumed "strike pay" in trade dispute cases), or any social security benefits which count as income for income support purposes (subss.(1) and (5)), then any consequent change in the amount of income support which is payable takes effect automatically without the need for a decision (subs.(2)).

[1 Effect of alteration of rates of a jobseeker's allowance

1.230 **159A.**—(1) This section applies where—

(a) an award of a jobseeker's allowance is in force in favour of any person ("the recipient"); and
(b) an alteration—
  (i) in any component of the allowance, or
  (ii) in the recipient's benefit income,
affects the amount of the jobseeker's allowance to which he is entitled.

(2) Subsection (3) applies where, as a result of the alteration, the amount of the jobseeker's allowance to which the recipient is entitled is increased or reduced.

(3) As from the commencing date, the amount of the jobseeker's allowance payable to or for the recipient under the award shall be the increased or reduced amount, without any further decision of [2 the Secretary of State]; and the award shall have effect accordingly.

(4) In any case where—

(a) there is an alteration of a kind mentioned in subsection (1)(b); and
(b) before the commencing date (but after that date is fixed) an award of a jobseeker's allowance is made in favour of a person,

the award may provide for the jobseeker's allowance to be paid as from the commencing date, in which case the amount of the jobseeker's allowance shall be determined by reference to the components applicable on that date, or may provide for an amount determined by reference to the components applicable at the date of the award.

(5) In this section—

"alteration" means—

(a) in relation to any component of a jobseeker's allowance, its alteration by or under any enactment; and
(b) in relation to a person's benefit income, the alteration of any of the sums referred to in [3 section [5 150, 150A or 151A]] above by any

enactment or by an order under section [5 150, 150A or 151A] above, to the extent that any such alteration affects the amount of the recipient's benefit income;

"benefit income", in relation to a recipient, means so much of his income as consists of—

(a) benefit under the Contributions and Benefits Act; or

[4 (ab) personal independence payment; or]

[5 (za) state pension under Part 1 of the Pensions Act 2014;]

(b) a war disablement pension or war widow's pension;

"the commencing date" in relation to an alteration, means the date on which the alteration comes into force in relation to the recipient;

"component", in relation to a jobseeker's allowance, means any of the sums specified in regulations under the Jobseekers Act 1995 which are relevant in calculating the amount payable by way of a jobseeker's allowance.]

AMENDMENTS

1. Jobseekers Act 1995 s.24 (October 7, 1996).
2. Social Security Act 1998 Sch.7 para.96 (October 18, 1999).
3. Pensions Act 2007 Sch.1(5) para.26 (July 26, 2007: insertion has effect as specified in 2007 c.22 s.5(3) and (7)).
4. Welfare Reform Act 2012 Sch.9 para.19 (April 8, 2013).
5. Pensions Act 2014 (Consequential Amendments) Order 2016 (SI 2016/931) art.2(3) (September 16, 2016).

DEFINITIONS

"the Contributions and Benefit Act"—see s.191.
"war disablement pension"—*ibid.*
"war widow's pension—*ibid.*

GENERAL NOTE

This section has the same effect for income-based JSA as s.159 does for income support. 1.231

[1 Effect of alterations affecting state pension credit]

159B.—(1) Subject to such exceptions and conditions as may be prescribed, subsection (2) or (3) below shall have effect where— 1.232

(a) an award of state pension credit is in force in favour of any person ("the recipient"); and

(b) an alteration—

(i) in any component of state pension credit,

(ii) in the recipient's benefit income,

(iii) in any component of a contribution-based jobseeker's allowance,

[3 (iiia) in any component of a contributory employment and support allowance,] or

(iv) in the recipient's war disablement pension or war widow's or widower's pension,

affects the computation of the amount of state pension credit to which he is entitled.

(2) Where, as a result of the alteration, the amount of state pension credit to which the recipient is entitled is increased or reduced, then, as from the commencing date, the amount of state pension credit payable in the case of the recipient under the award shall be the increased or reduced amount, without any further decision of the Secretary of State; and the award shall have effect accordingly.

(3) Where, notwithstanding the alteration, the recipient continues on and after the commencing date to be entitled to the same amount of state pension credit as before, the award shall continue in force accordingly.

(4) Subsection (5) below applies where a statement is made in the House of Commons by or on behalf of the Secretary of State which specifies—

(a) in relation to any of the items referred to in subsection (1)(b)(i) to (iv) above, the amount of the alteration which he proposes to make by an order under [4 section 150,150A [6, 151A] or 152] above or by or under any other enactment; and

(b) the date on which he proposes to bring the alteration into force ("the proposed commencing date").

(5) If, in a case where this subsection applies, an award of state pension credit is made in favour of a person before the proposed commencing date and after the date on which the statement is made, the award—

(a) may provide for state pension credit to be paid as from the proposed commencing date at a rate determined by reference to the amounts of the items specified in subsection (1)(b)(i) to (iv) above which will be in force on that date; or

(b) may be expressed in terms of the amounts of those items in force at the date of the award.

(6) In this section—

"alteration" means—

(a) in relation to any component of state pension credit, its alteration by or under any enactment;

(b) in relation to a person's benefit income, the alteration of any of the sums referred to in [6 section 150, 150A or 151A] above by any enactment or by an order under [6 section 150, 150A or 151A] or 152 above to the extent that any such alteration affects the amount of his benefit income;

(c) in relation to any component of a contribution-based jobseeker's allowance, its alteration by or under any enactment; and

(d) in relation to a person's war disablement pension or war widow's or widower's pension, its alteration by or under any enactment;

"benefit income", in relation to a person, means so much of his income as consists of benefit under the Contributions and Benefits Act [6, state pension under Part 1 of the Pensions Act 2014] [7 or personal independence payment];

"the commencing date", in relation to an alteration, means the date on which the alteration comes into force in relation to the recipient;

"component"—

(a) in relation to contribution-based jobseeker's allowance, means any of the sums specified in regulations under the Jobseekers Act 1995 (c 18) which are relevant in calculating the amount payable by way of a jobseeker's allowance;

(b) in relation to state pension credit, means any of the sums specified in regulations under section 2, 3 or 12 of the State Pension Credit Act 2002;

[3 (c) in relation to a contributory employment and support allowance, means any of the sums specified in regulations under Part 1 of the Welfare Reform Act 2007 which are relevant in calculating the amount payable by way of a contributory employment and support allowance;]

"war disablement pension" means—

(a) any retired pay, pension or allowance granted in respect of disablement under powers conferred by or under—

(i) the Air Force (Constitution) Act 1917 (c 51);

(ii) the Personal Injuries (Emergency Provisions) Act 1939 (c 82);

(iii) the Pensions (Navy, Army, Air Force and Mercantile Marine) Act 1939 (c 83);

(iv) the Polish Resettlement Act 1947 (c 19); or

(v) Part 7 or section 151 of the Reserve Forces Act 1980 (c 9); or

(b) without prejudice to paragraph (a), any retired pay or pension to which [2 any of paragraphs (a) to (f) of that section 641(1) of the Income Tax (Earnings and Pensions) Act 2003] applies;

"war widow's or widower's pension" means—

(a) [5 any widow's widower's or surviving civil partner's] pension or allowance granted in respect of a death due to service or war injury and payable by virtue of any enactment mentioned in paragraph (a) of the definition of "war disablement pension"; or

(b) a pension or allowance for a [5 widow, widower or surviving civil partner] granted under any scheme mentioned in [2 section 641(1)(e) or (f) of the Income Tax (Earnings and Pensions) Act 2003.]

AMENDMENTS

1. Inserted by State Pensions Credit Act 2002 s.14 and Sch.2 (July 2, 2002 for the purpose of making regulations only; fully in force October 6, 2003).

2. Income Tax (Earnings and Pensions) Act 2003 s.722 Sch.6 Pt 2 paras 186, 188(1), (3). (Income Tax (Earnings and Pensions) Act 2003 s.722 Sch.6 Pt.2 paras 186, 188(1), (3).

3. Welfare Reform Act 2007 s.28 and Sch.3 para.10 (October 27, 2008).

4. Pensions Act 2007 Sch.1(5) para.27 (July 26, 2007: insertion has effect as specified in 2007 c.22 s.5(3) and (7)).

5. Civil Partnership (Pensions and Benefit Payments) (Consequential, etc. Provisions) Order 2005 (SI 2005/2053) Sch.1(2) para.10 (December 5, 2005).

6. Pensions Act 2014 (Consequential Amendments) Order 2016 (SI 2016/931) art.2(4) (September 16, 2016).

7. Welfare Reform Act 2012 Sch.9 para.20 (June 10, 2013).

[1 159C. Effect of alteration of rates of an employment and support allowance

(1) Subject to such exceptions and conditions as may be prescribed, subsection (2) or (3) shall have effect where— 1.233

(a) an award of an employment and support allowance is in force in favour of any person ("the recipient"), and
(b) an alteration—
  (i) in any component of the allowance,
  (ii) in the recipient's benefit income, or
  (iii) in the recipient's war disablement or war widow's or widower's pension,

affects the computation of the amount of the employment and support allowance to which he is entitled.

(2) Where, as a result of the alteration, the amount of the employment and support allowance to which the recipient is entitled is increased or reduced, then, as from the commencing date, the amount of the employment and support allowance payable in the case of the recipient under the award shall be the increased or reduced amount, without any further decision of the Secretary of State; and the award shall have effect accordingly.

(3) Where, notwithstanding the alteration, the recipient continues on and after the commencing date to be entitled to the same amount by way of an employment and support allowance as before, the award shall continue in force accordingly.

(4) Subsection (5) applies where a statement is made in the House of Commons by or on behalf of the Secretary of State which specifies—
(a) in relation to any of the items referred to in subsection (1)(b)(i) to (iii), the amount of the alteration which he proposes to make by an order under [2 section 150, 150A [4, 151A] or 152] or by or under any other enactment, and
(b) the date on which he proposes to bring the alteration into force ("the proposed commencing date").

(5) If, in a case where this subsection applies, an award of an employment and support allowance is made in favour of a person before the proposed commencing date and after the date on which the statement is made, the award—
(a) may provide for the employment and support allowance to be paid as from the proposed commencing date at a rate determined by reference to the amounts of the items referred to in subsection (1)(b)(i) to (iii) which will be in force on that date, or
(b) may be expressed in terms of the amounts of those items in force at the date of the award.

(6) In this section—

"alteration" means—
(a) in relation to any component of an employment and support allowance, its alteration by or under any enactment;
(b) in relation to a person's benefit income, the alteration of any of the sums referred to in [4 section 150, 150A or 151A] by any enactment or by an order under [2 [4 section 150, 150A, 151A] or 152] to the extent that any such alteration affects the amount of his benefit income;
(c) in relation to a person's war disablement pension or war widow's or widower's pension, its alteration by or under any enactment;

"benefit income", in relation to a person, means so much of his income as consists of benefit under the Contributions and Benefits Act [4, state pension under Part 1 of the Pensions Act 2014] [2 or personal independence payment];

"the commencing date", in relation to an alteration, means the date on which the alteration comes into force in relation to the recipient;

"component", in relation to an employment and support allowance, means any of the sums specified in regulations under Part 1 of the Welfare Reform Act 2007 which are relevant in calculating the amount payable by way of an employment and support allowance;

"war disablement pension" and "war widow's or widower's pension" have the same meaning as in section 159B.]

AMENDMENTS

1. Welfare Reform Act 2007 s.28 and Sch.3 para.10 (October 27, 2008).

2. Pensions Act 2007 Sch.1(5) para.28 (October 27, 2008: insertions came into force on July 26, 2007 but could not take effect until the commencement of the Welfare Reform Act 2007 Sch.3 para.10(23) on October 27, 2008 and has effect as specified in 2007 c.22 s.5(3) and (7)).

3. Welfare Reform Act 2012 Sch.9 para.21 (April 8, 2013).

4. Pensions Act 2014 (Consequential Amendments) Order 2016 (SI 2016/931) art.2(5) (September 16, 2016.)

[1 Effect of alterations affecting universal credit

159D.—(1) Subject to such exceptions and conditions as may be prescribed, subsection (2) or (3) shall have effect where— 1.234

(a) an award of universal credit is in force in favour of any person ("the recipient"), and

(b) an alteration—

(i) in any element of universal credit,

(ii) in the recipient's benefit income,

(iii) in any amount to be deducted in respect of earned income under section 8(3)(a) of the Welfare Reform Act 2012,

(iv) in any component of a contribution-based jobseeker's allowance,

(v) in any component of a contributory employment and support allowance, or

(vi) in such other matters as may be prescribed, affects the computation of the amount of universal credit to which he is entitled.

(2) Where, as a result of the alteration, the amount of universal credit to which the recipient is entitled is increased or reduced, then, as from the commencing date, the amount of universal credit payable in the case of the recipient under the award shall be the increased or reduced amount, without any further decision of the Secretary of State; and the award shall have effect accordingly.

(3) Where, notwithstanding the alteration, the recipient continues on and after the commencing date to be entitled to the same amount by way of universal credit as before, the award shall continue in force accordingly.

(4) Subsection (5) applies where a statement is made in the House of Commons by or on behalf of the Secretary of State which specifies—

(a) in relation to any of the items referred to in subsection (1)(b)(i) to (vi), the amount of the alteration which he proposes to make by an order under section 150, 150A [2, 151A] or 152 or by or under any other enactment, and

(b) the date on which he proposes to bring the alteration in force ("the proposed commencing date").

(5) If, in a case where this subsection applies, an award of universal credit is made in favour of a person before the proposed commencing date and after the date on which the statement is made,

the award—

(a) may provide for the universal credit to be paid as from the proposed commencing date at a rate determined by reference to the amounts of the items referred to in subsection (1)(b)(i) to (vi) which will be in force on that date, or

(b) may be expressed in terms of the amounts of those items in force at the date of the award.

(6) In this section—

"alteration"—

(a) in relation to any element of universal credit, means its alteration by or under any enactment;

(b) in relation to a person's benefit income, means the alteration of any of the sums referred to in [2 section 150, 150A or 151A] by any enactment or by an order under [2 section 150, 150A, 151A] or 152 to the extent that any such alteration affects the amount of his benefit income;

(c) in relation to any component of a contribution-based jobseeker's allowance or a contributory employment and support allowance, means its alteration by or under any enactment;

(d) in relation to any other matter, has such meaning as may be prescribed;

"benefit income", in relation to a person, means so much of his income as consists of benefit under the Contributions and Benefits Act [2, state pension under the Pensions Act 2014] [1 or personal independence payment];

"the commencing date", in relation to an alteration, means the date on which the alteration comes into force in relation to the recipient;

"component"—

(a) in relation to contribution-based jobseeker's allowance, means any of the sums specified in regulations under the Jobseekers Act 1995 which are relevant in calculating the amount payable by way of a jobseeker's allowance;

(b) in relation to a contributory employment and support allowance, means any of the sums specified in regulations under Part 1 of the Welfare Reform Act 2007 which are relevant in calculating the amount payable by way of such an allowance;

"element", in relation to universal credit, means any of the amounts specified in regulations under sections 9 to 12 of the Welfare Reform Act 2012 which are included in the calculation of an award of universal credit.]

AMENDMENTS

1. Inserted by Welfare Reform Act 2012 s.31 and Sch.2 para.23 (February 25, 2013).

2. Pensions Act 2014 (Consequential Amendments) Order 2016 (SI 2016/931) art.2(6) (September 16, 2016).

GENERAL NOTE

1.235 The scope of this section is problematic when considered together with para.6(b)(v) of Sch.2 to the Social Security Act 1998. That Schedule stipulates decisions against which no appeal lies, including decisions where the amount of benefit is determined by an alteration of a kind referred to in s.159D(1)(b). For further discussion of the issues, see the notes to Sch.2 of the 1998 Act and to reg.41(3) of the Universal Credit, Personal Independence Payment, Jobseeker's Allowance and Employment and Support Allowance (Decisions and Appeals) Regulations 2013 (the latter makes express provision where a person disputes the figure used to calculate earnings for the purposes of universal credit).

[1 Effect of alteration of rates of personal independence payment

159E.—(1) Subject to such exceptions and conditions as may be prescribed, subsection (2) or (3) shall have effect where— 1.236

(a) an award of personal independence payment is in force in favour of any person ("the recipient"); and

(b) an alteration in the rate of any component of personal independence payment affects the amount of personal independence payment to which he is entitled.

(2) Where, as a result of the alteration, the amount of personal independence payment to which the recipient is entitled is increased or reduced, then, as from the commencing date, the amount of personal independence payment in the case of the recipient under the award shall be the increased or reduced amount, without any further decision of the Secretary of State; and the award shall have effect accordingly.

(3) Where, notwithstanding the alteration, the recipient continues on and after the commencing date to be entitled to the same amount by way of personal independence payment as before, the award shall continue in force accordingly.

(4) Subsection (5) applies where a statement is made in the House of Commons by or on behalf of the Secretary of State which specifies—

(a) the amount of the alteration in the rate of any component of personal independence payment which he proposes to make by an order under section 150 or 152 or by or under any other enactment, and

(b) the date on which he proposes to bring the alteration in force ("the proposed commencing date").

(5) If, in a case where this subsection applies, an award of personal independence payment is made in favour of a person before the proposed commencing date and after the date on which the statement is made, the award—

(a) may provide for personal independence payment to be paid as from the proposed commencing date by reference to the rates of the component of personal independence payment which will be in force on that date, or

(b) may be expressed in terms of the rates of those components in force at the date of the award.

(6) In this section—

"alteration" means alteration by or under any enactment;

"the commencing date", in relation to an alteration, means the date on which the alteration comes into force in relation to the recipient;

"component", in relation to personal independence payment, means the daily living component or mobility component (see sections 78 and 79 of the Welfare Reform Act 2012).]

Amendment

1. Inserted by The Personal Independence Payments (Supplementary Provisions and Consequential Amendments) Regulations 2013 (SI 2013/388) reg.8 and Sch. para.6 (April 8, 2013).

Implementation of increases in income support due to attainment of particular ages

1.237 **160.**—(1) This section applies where—

(a) an award of income support is in force in favour of a person ("the recipient"); and

(b) there is a component which becomes applicable, or applicable at a particular rate, in his case if he or some other person attains a particular age.

(2) If, in a case where this section applies, the recipient or other person attains the particular age referred to in paragraph (b) of subsection (1) above and, in consequence—

(a) the component in question becomes applicable, or applicable at a particular rate, in the recipient's case (whether or not some other component ceases, for the same reason, to be applicable, or applicable at a particular rate, in his case; and

(b) after taking account of any such cessation, the recipient becomes entitled to an increased amount of income support,

then, except as provided by subsection (3) below, as from the day on which he becomes so entitled, the amount of income support payable to or for him under the award shall be that increased amount, without any further decision of [1 the Secretary of State], and the award shall have effect accordingly.

(3) Subsection (2) above does not apply in any case where, in consequence of the recipient or other person attaining the age in question, some question arises in relation to the recipient's entitlement to [1 personal independence payment, or] any benefit under the Contributions and Benefits Act, other than—

(a) the question whether the component concerned, or any other component, becomes or ceases to be applicable, or applicable at a particular rate, in his case; and

(b) the question whether, in consequence, the amount of his income support falls to be varied.

(4) In this section "component", in relation to a person and his income support, means any of the sums specified in regulations under section 135(1) of the Contributions and Benefits Act.

Amendments

1. Social Security Act 1998 Sch.7 para.97 (November 29, 1999).
2. Welfare Reform Act 2012 Sch.9 para.22 (April 8, 2013).

Derivation

1.238 Social Security Act 1986 s.64B.

Definition

"the Contributions and Benefits Act"—see s.191.

GENERAL NOTE

Section 160 extends the process begun by s.159 of taking routine adjustments in the amount of income support out of the ordinary mechanism of review. 1.239

[1Implementation of increases in income-based jobseeker's allowance due to attainment of particular ages

160A.—(1) This section applies where— 1.240

(a) an award of an income-based jobseeker's allowance is in force in favour of a person ("the recipient"); and

(b) a component has become applicable, or applicable at a particular rate, because he or some other person has reached a particular age ("the qualifying age")

(2) If, as a result of the recipient or other person reaching the qualifying age, the recipient becomes entitled to an income-based jobseeker's allowance of an increased amount, the amount payable to or for him under the award shall, as from the day on which he becomes so entitled, be that increased amount, without any further decision of [2 the Secretary of State]; and the award shall have effect accordingly.

(3) Subsection (2) above does not apply where, in consequence of the recipient or other person reaching the qualifying age, a question arises in relation to the recipient's entitlement to—

(a) a benefit under the Contributions and Benefits Act; [3. . .]

[3 (aa) personal independence payment; or]

(b) a jobseeker's allowance.

(4) Subsection (3)(b) above does not apply to the question—

(a) whether the component concerned, or any other component, becomes or ceases to be applicable, or applicable at a particular rate, in the recipient's case; and

(b) whether, in consequence, the amount of his income-based jobseeker's allowance falls to be varied.

(5) In this section "component", in relation to a recipient and his jobseeker's allowance, means any of the amounts determined in accordance with regulations made under section 4(5) of the Jobseekers Act 1995.]

AMENDMENTS

1. Jobseekers Act 1995 s.25 (October 7, 1996).
2. Social Security Act 1998 Sch.7 para.98 (October 18, 1999).
3. Welfare Reform Act 2012 Sch.9 para.23 (April 8, 2013).

DEFINITION

"the Contributions and Benefits Act"—see s.191.

GENERAL NOTE

See s.160. 1.241

[1 160B. Implementation of increases in employment and support allowance due to attainment of particular ages

(1) This section applies where— 1.242

(a) an award of an employment and support allowance is in force in favour of a person ("the recipient"), and

(b) a component has become applicable, or applicable at a particular rate, because he or some other person has reached a particular age ("the qualifying age").

(2) If, as a result of the recipient or other person reaching the qualifying age, the recipient becomes entitled to an employment and support allowance of an increased amount, the amount payable to or for him under the award shall, as from the day on which he becomes so entitled, be that increased amount, without any further decision of the Secretary of State; and the award shall have effect accordingly.

(3) Subsection (2) does not apply where, in consequence of the recipient or other person reaching the qualifying age, a question arises in relation to the recipient's entitlement to

[[2] (a) a benefit under the Contributions and Benefits Act; or

(b) personal independence payment.]

(4) Subsection (2) does not apply where, in consequence of the recipient or other person reaching the qualifying age, a question arises in relation to the recipient's entitlement to an employment and support allowance, other than—

(a) the question whether the component concerned, or any other component, becomes or ceases to be applicable, or applicable at a particular rate, in the recipient's case, and

(b) the question whether, in consequence, the amount of his employment and support allowance falls to be varied.

(5) In this section, "component", in relation to a recipient and his employment and support allowance, means any of the amounts determined in accordance with regulations made under section 2(1)(a) or 4(2)(a) of the Welfare Reform Act 2007.]

AMENDMENTS

1. Welfare Reform Act 2007 s.28 and Sch.3 para.10 (October 27, 2008).
2. Welfare Reform Act 2012 Sch.9 para.24 (April 8, 2013).

PART XII

FINANCE

1.243 **161.–166.** *Omitted.*

The social fund

1.244 **167.**—(1) The fund known as the social fund shall continue in being by that name.

(2) The social fund shall continue to be maintained under the control and management of the Secretary of State and payments out of it shall be made by him.

(3) The Secretary of State shall make payments into the social fund of such amounts, at such times and in such manner as he may with the approval of the Treasury determine.

(4) Accounts of the social fund shall be prepared in such form, and in such manner and at such times, as the Treasury may direct, and the Comptroller

and Auditor General shall examine and certify every such account and shall lay copies of it, together with his report, before Parliament.

(5) The Secretary of State shall prepare an annual report on the social fund.

(6) A copy of every such report shall be laid before each House of Parliament.

DERIVATIONS

Subs.(1): Social Security Act 1986 s.32(1). **1.245**
Subss.(2)–(6): 1986 Act s.32(5)–(7B).

Allocations from social fund

s.168. Repealed.

Adjustments between social fund and other sources of finance

169.—(1) There shall be made— **1.246**

(a) out of the social fund into the Consolidated Fund or the National Insurance Fund;

(b) into the social fund out of money provided by Parliament or the National Insurance Fund, **1.247**

such payments by way of adjustment as the Secretary of State determines (in accordance with any directions of the Treasury) to be appropriate in consequence of any enactment or regulations relating to the repayment or offsetting of a benefit or other payment under the Contributions and Benefits Act [[1] or the State Pension Credit Act 2002].

(2) Where in any other circumstances payments fall to be made by way of adjustment—

(a) out of the social fund into the Consolidated Fund or the National Insurance Fund; or

(b) into the social fund out of money provided by Parliament or the National Insurance Fund,

then, in such cases or classes of cases as may be specified by the Secretary of State by order, the amount of the payments to be made shall be taken to be such, and payments on account of it shall be be made at such times and in such manner, as may be determined by the Secretary of State in accordance with any direction given by the Treasury.

AMENDMENT

1. State Pension Credit Act 2002 s.14 and Sch.2 (July 2, 2002 for the purpose of making regulations only; fully in force October 6, 2003).

DERIVATION

Social Security Act 1986 s.85(11) and (12). **1.248**

DEFINITION

"the Contributions and Benefits Act"—see s.191.

Part XIII

Advisory Bodies and Consultation

The Social Security Advisory Committee and the Industrial Injuries Advisory Council

The Social Security Advisory Committee

1.249 **170.**—(1) The Social Security Advisory Committee (in this Act referred to as "the Committee") constituted under section 9 of the Social Security Act 1980 shall continue in being by that name—

(a) to give (whether in pursuance of a reference under this Act or otherwise) advice and assistance to the Secretary of State in connection with the discharge of his functions under the relevant enactments;

(b) to give (whether in pursuance of a reference under this Act or otherwise) advice and assistance to the Northern Ireland Department in connection with the discharge of its functions under the relevant Northern Ireland enactments; and

(c) to perform such other duties as may be assigned to the Committee under any enactment.

(2) Schedule 5 to this Act shall have effect with respect to the constitution of the Committee and the other matters there mentioned.

(3) The Secretary of State may from time to time refer to the Committee for consideration and advice such questions relating to the operation of any of the relevant enactments as he thinks fit (including questions as to the advisability of amending any of them).

(4) The Secretary of State shall furnish the Committee with such information as the Committee may reasonably require for the proper discharge of its functions.

(5) In this Act—

"the relevant enactments" means—

(a) the provisions of the Contributions and Benefits Act [1, this Act and the Social Security (Incapacity for Work) Act 1994], except as they apply to industrial injuries benefit and Old Cases payments;

[2 (aa) the provisions of the Jobseekers Act 1995;]

[19 ...]

[4 (ac) the provisions of the Social Security (Recovery of Benefits) Act 1997; and]

[5 (ad) the provisions of Chapter II of Part I of the Social Security Act 1998 and section 72 of that Act;]

[6 (ae) sections 60, 72 and 79 of the Welfare Reform and Pensions Act 1999;]

[7 (af) section 42 [21...] and [14 sections 69 and 70 of the Child Support Pensions and Social Security Act 2000;]

[8 (ag) sections [22 6A] to 11 of the Social Security Fraud Act 2001;]

[9 (ah) the provisions of the State Pension Credit Act 2002;]

[11 (ai) section 7 of the Age-Related Payments Act 2004;]

[12 (aia) the provisions of Part 1 of the Welfare Reform Act 2007;]

[13 (aj) sections 32 and 33 of the Welfare Reform Act 2007;]

[14 (ak) the provisions of Part I of the Welfare Reform Act 2012;]
[15 (al) Part 4 of that Act;]
[23(ala) sections 96 to 97 of that Act;]
[16 (am) the provisions of Part 1 of the Pensions Act 2014;]
[17 (an) section 30 of the Pensions Act 2014;]
[18 (ao) sections 18, 19 and 21 of the Welfare Reform and Work Act 2016;]
(b) the provisions of Part II of Schedule 3 to the Consequential Provisions Act, except as they apply to industrial injuries benefit; and

"the relevant Northern Ireland enactments" means—

(a) the provisions of the Northern Ireland Contributions and Benefits Act and the Northern Ireland Administration Act, except as they apply to Northern Ireland industrial injuries benefit and payments under Part I of Schedule 8 to the Northern Ireland Contributions and Benefits Act; and
[2 (aa) any provisions in Northern Ireland which correspond to provisions of the Jobseekers Act 1995; and]
[20 ...]
[4 (ac) any provisions in Northern Ireland which correspond to provisions of the Social Security (Recovery of Benefits) Act 1997; and]
[5 (ad) any provisions in Northern Ireland which correspond to provisions of Chapter II of Part I of the Social Security Act 1998 and section 72 of that Act;]
[6 (ae) any provisions in Northern Ireland which correspond to sections 60, 72 and 79 of the Welfare Reform and Pensions Act 1999;]
[7 (af) any provisions in Northern Ireland which correspond to section 42, [21...] and [14 sections 69 and 70 of the Child Support Pensions and Social Security Act 2000;]; and]
[8 (ag) any provisions in Northern Ireland which correspond to sections [22 6A] to 11 of the Social Security Fraud Act 2001, and]
[9 (ah) any provisions in Northern Ireland which correspond to provisions of the State Pension Credit Act 2002; and]
[24 (ai) Article 9 of the Age-Related Payments (Northern Ireland) Order 2004;]
[12 (aia) any provisions in Northern Ireland which correspond to Part 1 of the Welfare Reform Act 2007;]
[13 (aj) any provisions in Northern Ireland which correspond to sections 32 and 33 of the Welfare Reform Act 2007;]
[14 (ak) any provisions in Northern Ireland which correspond to the provisions of Part I of the Welfare Reform Act 2012;]
[15 (al) any provisions in Northern Ireland which correspond to Part 4 of that Act;]
[23 (ala) any provisions in Northern Ireland which correspond to sections 96 to 97 of that Act;]
[16 (am) any provisions in Northern Ireland which correspond to the provisions of Part 1 of the Pensions Act 2014;]
[17 (an) any provisions in Northern Ireland which correspond to section 30 of the Pensions Act 2014;]
[18 (ao) any provisions in Northern Ireland which correspond to sections 18, 19 and 21 of the Welfare Reform and Work Act 2016;]
(b) the provisions of Part II of Schedule 3 to the Social Security (Consequential Provisions) (Northern Ireland) Act 1992, except as they apply to Northern Ireland industrial injuries benefit;

[25 ...]

and in this definition—

(i) "Northern Ireland Contributions and Benefits Act" means the Social Security Contributions and Benefits (Northern Ireland) Act 1992;

(ii) "Northern Ireland industrial injuries benefit" means benefit under Part V of the Northern Ireland Contributions and Benefits Act other than under Schedule 8 to that Act.

AMENDMENTS

1. Social Security (Incapacity for Work) Act 1994 Sch.1 para.51 (April 13, 1995).
2. Jobseekers Act 1995 Sch.2 para.67 (April 22, 1996).
3. Child Support Act 1995 Sch.3 para.20 (October 6, 1997).
4. Social Security (Recovery of Benefits) Act 1997 Sch.3 para.8 (October 6, 1997).
5. Social Security Act 1998 Sch.7 para.104 (March 4, 1999).
6. Welfare Reform and Pensions Act 1999 Sch.12 para.81 (November 11, 1999).
7. Child Support, Pensions and Social Security Act 2000 s.73 (December 1, 2000).
8. Social Security Fraud Act 2001 s.12 (April 1, 2002).
9. State Pension Credit Act 2002 Sch.2 para.20 (July 2, 2002 for the purpose of making regulations only; fully in force October 6, 2003).
10. Pension Schemes (Northern Ireland) Act 1993 Sch.7 para.26 (February 7, 1994).
11. Age-Related Payments Act 2004 s.7(5) (July 8, 2004).
12. Welfare Reform Act 2007 s.28 and Sch.3 para.10 (October 27, 2008).
13. Welfare Reform Act 2007 s.33(7)(a) (October 6, 2008).
14. Welfare Reform Act 2012 s.31 and Sch.2 para.26 (February 25, 2013).
15. Welfare Reform Act 2012 s.91 and Sch.9 para.26 (February 25, 2013).
16. Pensions Act 2014 s.56(4), s.23 and Sch.12, para.24 (April 6, 2016).
17. Pensions Act 2014 s.31 and Sch.16 para.32 (April 6, 2017).
18. Welfare Reform and Work Act 2016 s.20(2) (July 27, 2017).
19. Child Support, Pensions and Social Security Act 2000 Sch.9 Pt 1 (April 2, 2001).
20. Child Support, Pensions and Social Security (Northern Ireland) Act 2000 Sch.9 Pt 1 (April 2, 2001).
21. Welfare Reform Act 2009 Sch.7 Pt 3 (March 22, 2010).
22. Welfare Reform Act 2009 Sch.4 para.9 (January 12, 2010).
23. Welfare Reform and Work Act 2016 s.10 (June 9, 2016).
24. Age-Related Payments (Northern Ireland) Order 2001 (NISR 2004/1987) art.9(6) (August 3, 2004).
25. Pensions (Northern Ireland) Order 1995 (NISR 1995/3213) Sch.5 (April 6, 1996).

GENERAL NOTE

1.250 In *Howker v Secretary of State for Work and Pensions* [2002] EWCA Civ. 1623, *R(IB)3/03* the Court of Appeal (hearing the appeal against the decision in *CIB/4563/1998*, confirmed the jurisdiction of Commissioners (and presumably also tribunals) to invalidate subordinate legislation. The circumstances of this case involved the Secretary of State through his official misleading the Social Security Advisory Committee by presenting information which was obviously incorrect which resulted in the securing of the agreement of the Committee to the proposed changes. The Court of Appeal concluded that it was manifest that the procedure intended by Parliament for the making of regulations had not been observed and so the regulations as made were invalid for failure to comply with the requirements of s.172.

The Industrial Injuries Advisory Council

171.—(1) The Industrial Injuries Advisory Council (in this Act referred to as "the Council") constituted under section 62 of the National Insurance (Industrial Injuries) Act 1965 shall continue in being by that name. 1.251

(2) Schedule 6 to this Act shall have effect with respect to the constitution of the Council and the other matters there mentioned.

(3) The Secretary of State may from time to time refer to the Council for consideration and advice such questions as he thinks fit relating to industrial injuries benefit or its administration.

(4) The Council may also give advice to the Secretary of State on any other matter relating to such benefit or its administration.

Functions of Committee and Council in relation to regulations

172.—(1) Subject— 1.252

(a) to subsection (3) below; and

(b) to section 173 below,

where the Secretary of State proposes to make regulations under any of the relevant enactments, he shall refer the proposals, in the form of draft regulations or otherwise, to the Committee.

(2) Subject—

(a) to subsection (4) below; and

(b) to section 173 below, where the Secretary of State proposes to make regulations relating only to industrial injuries benefit or its administration, he shall refer the proposals, in the form of draft regulations or otherwise, to the Council for consideration and advice.

(3) Subsection (1) above does not apply to the regulations specified in Part I of Schedule 7 to this Act.

(4) Subsection (2) above does not apply to the regulations specified in Part II of that Schedule.

(5) In relation to regulations required or authorised to be made by the Secretary of State in conjunction with the Treasury, the reference in subsection (1) above to the Secretary of State shall be construed as a reference to the Secretary of State and the Treasury.

Cases in which consultation is not required

173.—(1) Nothing in any enactment shall require any proposals in respect of regulations to be referred to the Committee or the Council if— 1.253

(a) it appears to the Secretary of State that by reason of the urgency of the matter it is inexpedient so to refer them; or

(b) the relevant advisory body have agreed that they shall not be referred.

(2) Where by virtue only of subsection (1)(a) above the Secretary of State makes regulations without proposals in respect of them having been referred, then, unless the relevant advisory body agrees that this subsection shall not apply, he shall refer the regulations to that body as soon as practicable after making them.

(3) Where the Secretary of State has referred proposals to the Committee or the Council, he may make the proposed regulations before the Committee have made their report or, as the case may be the Council have given their advice, only if after the reference it appears to him that by reason of the urgency of the matter it is expedient to do so.

(4) Where by virtue of this section regulations are made before a report of the Committee has been made, the Committee shall consider them and make a report to the Secretary of State containing such recommendations with regard to the regulations as the Committee thinks appropriate; and a copy of any report made to the Secretary of State on the regulations shall be laid by him before each House of Parliament together, if the report contains recommendations, with a statement—

(a) of the extent (if any) to which the Secretary of State proposes to give effect to the recommendations; and

(b) in so far as he does not propose to give effect to them, of his reasons why not.

(5) Except to the extent that this subsection is excluded by an enactment passed after 25th July 1986, nothing in any enactment shall require the reference to the Committee or the Council of any regulations contained in either—

(a) a statutory instrument made before the end of the period of 6 months beginning with the coming into force of the enactment under which those regulations are made; or

(b) a statutory instrument—

(i) which states that it contains only regulations made by virtue of, or consequential upon, a specified enactment; and

(ii) which is made before the end of the period of 6 months beginning with the coming into force of that specified enactment.

(6) In relation to regulations required or authorised to be made by the Secretary of State in conjunction with the Treasury, any reference in this section to the Secretary of State shall be construed as a reference to the Secretary of State and the Treasury.

(7) In this section "regulations" means regulations under any enactment, whenever passed.

1.254 **174.–176.** *Omitted.*

PART XIV

SOCIAL SECURITY SYSTEMS OUTSIDE GREAT BRITAIN

Co-ordination

1.255 **Section 177:** *repealed by the Northern Ireland Act 1998, Sch.15 (December 2, 1999).*

1.256 **Section 178:** *repealed by the Northern Ireland Act 1998, Sch.15 (December 2, 1999).*

Reciprocal agreements with countries outside the United Kingdom

1.257 **179.**—(1) For the purpose of giving effect—

(a) to any agreement with the government of a country outside the United Kingdom [13 or an international organisation] providing for reciprocity in matters relating to payments for purposes similar or comparable to the purposes of legislation to which this section applies, or

(b) to any such agreement as it would be if it were altered in accordance with proposals to alter it which, in consequence of any change in the law of Great Britain, the government of the United Kingdom has made to the other government [13 or international organisation] in question,

Her Majesty may by Order in Council make provision for modifying or adapting such legislation in its application to cases affected by the agreement or proposed alterations.

(2) An Order made by virtue of subsection (1) above may, instead of or in addition to making specific modifications or adaptions, provide generally that legislation to which this section applies shall be modified to such extent as may be required to give effect to the provisions contained in the agreement or, as the case may be, alterations in question.

(3) The modifications which may be made by virtue of subsection (1) above include provisions—

(a) for securing that acts, omissions and events having any effect for the purposes of the [13 law in force in the country] in respect of which the agreement is made [13 or has effect] have a corresponding effect for the purposes of this Act, [1 the Jobseeker's Act 1995], [2 Chapter II of Part I of the Social Security Act 1998] [3 Part II of the Social Security Contributions (Transfer of Functions, etc.) Act 1999] [5, Part III of the Social Security Contributions (Transfer of Functions etc.) (Northern Ireland) Order 1999] [6, the State Pension Credit Act 2002] [7, Part 1 of the Welfare Reform Act 2007] [9 , Part 1 of the Welfare Reform Act 2012] [, Part 4 of that Act] [11 , Part 1 of the Pensions Act 2014] [12, Part 5 of that Act] and the Contributions and Benefits Act (but not so as to confer a right to double benefit);

(b) for determining, in cases where rights accrue under such legislation and under the [13 law in force in that country], which of those rights is to be available to the person concerned;

(c) for making any necessary financial adjustments.

(4) This section applies—

(a) to the Contributions and Benefits Act;

(aa) [1 to the Jobseeker's Act 1995];

(ab) [2 to Chapter II of Part I of the Social Security Act 1998];

(ac) [3 to Part II of the Social Security Contributions (Transfers of Functions, etc.) Act 1999]; and

[4(ad) to Part III of the Social Security Contributions (Transfer of Functions etc.) (Northern Ireland) Order 1999;]

[5(ae) to the State Pension Credit Act 2002; and]

[7(af) to part 1 of the Welfare Reform Act 2007;]

[9 (ag) to Part 1 of the Welfare Reform Act 2012; and]

[10 (ah) to Part 4 of that Act;]

[11 (ai) to Part 1 of the Pensions Act 2014;]

[12 (aj) to Part 5 of the Pensions Act 2014;]

[13(ak) to Regulation (EC) No 883/2004 of the European Parliament and of the Council of 29 April 2004 on the coordination of social security systems, as it forms part of domestic law by virtue of section 3 of the European Union (Withdrawal) Act 2018;

(al) to Regulation (EC) No 987/2009 of the European Parliament and of the Council of 16 September 2009 laying down the procedure for implementing Regulation (EC) No 883/2004, as it forms part of domestic law by virtue of section 3 of the European Union (Withdrawal) Act 2018;

(am) to Council Regulation (EEC) No 1408/71 of 14 June 1971 on the application of social security schemes to employed persons, to self-employed persons and to members of their families moving within the Community, as it forms part of domestic law by virtue of section 3 of the European Union (Withdrawal) Act 2018;

(an) to Council Regulation (EEC) No 574/72 of 21 March 1972 laying down the procedure for implementing Regulation (EEC) No 1408/71 on the application of social security schemes to employed persons, to self-employed persons and to members of their families moving within the Community, as it forms part of domestic law by virtue of section 3 of the European Union (Withdrawal) Act 2018;

(ao) to Council Regulation (EC) No 859/2003 of 14 May 2003 extending the provisions of Regulation (EEC) No 1408/71 and Regulation (EEC) No 574/72 to nationals of third countries who are not already covered by those provisions solely on the ground of their nationality, as it forms part of domestic law by virtue of section 3 of the European Union (Withdrawal) Act 2018.]

(b) to this Act,

except in relation to the following benefits—

(i) community charge benefits;

(ii) payments out of the social fund;

(iii) Christmas bonus;

(iv) statutory sick pay; and

(v) statutory maternity pay.

(5) The power conferred by subsection (1) above shall also be exercisable in relation to regulations made under the Contributions and Benefits Act [[8], this Act or Part I of the Welfare Reform Act 2007] [[11] or Part 1 of the Pensions Act 2014] [[12] or section 30 of that Act] and concerning—

[[9] (za) universal credit;]

(a) income support;

[[1](aa) jobseeker's allowance];

[[5](ab) state pension credit];

[[7](ac) employment and support allowance;]

[[11] (ad) state pension under Part 1 of the Pensions Act 2014;]

[[12] (ae) bereavement support payment;]

(b) [[6] . . .];

(c) [[6] . . .];

(d) housing benefit; or

(e) child benefit.

[[13] (6) In this section, "international organisation" means an organisation of which—

(a) two or more sovereign powers are members, or

(b) the governments of two or more sovereign powers are members.]

AMENDMENTS

1. Jobseekers Act 1995 Sch.2 (April 22, 1996).
2. Social Security Act 1998 Sch.7 (July 5, 1999).
3. Transfer of Functions Act 1999 Sch.7 (April 1, 1999).
4. Social Security Contributions (Transfer of Functions etc.) (Northern Ireland) Order 1999 (April 1, 1999).
5. State Pension Credit Act 2002 s.14 and Sch.2 (July 2, 2002 for the purpose of making regulations only; fully in force October 6, 2003).
6. Tax Credits Act 2002 s.60 and Sch.6 (April 8, 2003).
7. Welfare Reform Act 2007 s.28 and Sch.3 para.10 (October 27, 2008).
8. The Social Security (Miscellaneous Amendments) (No.3) Regulations 2011 (SI 2011/2425) reg.3 (October 31, 2011).
9. The Welfare Reform Act 2012 (Commencement No. 9 and Transitional and Transitory Provisions and Commencement No. 8 and Savings and Transitional Provisions (Amendment)) Order 2013 (SI 2013/983) art.3(1)(b) (April 29, 2013).
10. Welfare Reform Act 2012 Sch.9 para.27(3) (April 8, 2013).
11. Pensions Act 2014 s.23 and Sch.12 para.25 (July 7, 2015).
12. Pensions Act 2014 s.31 and Sch.16 para.33 (February 8, 2017).
13. The Social Security Co-ordination (Revocation of Retained Direct EU Legislation and Related Amendments) (EU Exit) Regulations 2020 (SI 2020/1508) reg.10 and Schedule (December 16, 2020).

DERIVATION

SSA 1975 s.143 as amended and CBA 1975 s.15 as amended. **1.258**

GENERAL NOTE

For further information concerning reciprocal arrangements, see annotations to s.113 of the Contributions and Benefits Act 1992. **1.259**

For a discussion on how s.179 acts to modify other social security provisions, see *Campbell v Secretary of State for Work and Pensions* [2005] EWCA Civ 989.

[1 Exchange of information with overseas authorities]

179A.—(1) This section applies where it appears to the Secretary of State— **1.260**

(a) that there are arrangements in force for the exchange of relevant information between him and any authorities in a country outside the United Kingdom ("the overseas country"); and
(b) that the arrangements and the law in force in the overseas country are such as to ensure that there are adequate safeguards in place against any improper use of information disclosed by the Secretary of State under this section.

(2) For the purpose of facilitating the carrying out by authorities in the overseas country of any function relating to anything corresponding to, or in the nature of, a social security benefit, the Secretary of State may make any such disclosure of relevant information to authorities in the overseas country as he considers necessary to give effect to the arrangements.

(3) It shall be the duty of the Secretary of State to take all such steps as may be reasonable for securing that relevant information disclosed to him in accordance with the arrangements is not used for any purpose for which its use is not expressly or impliedly authorised by or under the arrangements.

(4) This section does not apply where provision is in force under section 179 above for giving effect to the arrangements in question.

(5) The purposes for which information may be required to be disclosed to the Secretary of State under section 122D above or section 116D of the Northern Ireland Administration Act (information required from authorities administering housing benefit or council tax benefit) shall be deemed to include the further disclosure of that information in accordance withthis section.

(6) In this section "relevant information" means any information held by the Secretary of State or any authorities in a country outside the United Kingdom for the purposes of any functions relating to, or to anything corresponding to or in the nature of, a social security benefit.]

AMENDMENT

1. Inserted by the Social Security Fraud Act 2001 ss.1 and 5 (February 14, 2003).

PART XV

MISCELLANEOUS

1.261 **180.–182B.** *Omitted.*

National insurance numbers

[1 Requirement to apply for national insurance number

1.262 **182C.**—(1) Regulations may make provision requiring a person to apply for a national insurance number to be allocated to him.

[2(1A) Regulations under subsection (1) above may require the application to be made to the Secretary of State or to the Inland Revenue.]

(2) An application required by regulations under subsection (1) above shall be accompanied by information or evidence enabling such a number to be allocated.]

AMENDMENTS

1. Social Security Administration (Fraud) Act 1997 Sch.1 para.9 (July 1, 1997).
2. Social Security Contributions (Transfer of Functions, etc.) Act 1999 s.1(1) and Sch.1 para.31 (April 1, 1999).

GENERAL NOTE

1.263 See subss.(1A)–(1C) of s.1, inserted by s.19 of the Social Security Administration (Fraud) Act, which make having, or applying for, a national insurance number a condition of entitlement to benefit in most cases.

1.264 **183.** *Omitted.*

Control of pneumoconiosis

1.265 **184.** As respects pneumoconiosis, regulations may provide—

(a) for requiring persons to be medically examined before, or within a prescribed period after, becoming employed in any occupation in relation to which pneumoconiosis is prescribed, and to be medically examined periodically while so employed, and to furnish information required for the purposes of any such examination;

(b) for suspending from employment in any such occupation, and in such other occupations as may be prescribed, persons found on such an examination—
   (i) to be suffering from pneumoconiosis or tuberculosis, or
   (ii) o be unsuitable for such employment, having regard to the risk of pneumoconiosis and such other matters affecting their susceptibility to pneumoconiosis as may be prescribed;

(c) for the disqualification for the receipt [1 personal independence payment, or benefit as defined in section 122 of the Contributions and Benefits Act,] in respect of pneumoconiosis of any person who fails without good cause to submit himself to any such examination or to furnish information required by the regulations or who engages in any employment from which he has been suspended as mentioned in paragraph (b) above;

(d) for requiring employers—
   (i) to provide facilities for such examinations,
   (ii) not to employ in any occupation a person who has been suspended as mentioned in paragraph (b) above from employment in that occupation or who has failed without good cause to submit himself to such an examination,
   (iii) to give to such officer as may be prescribed the prescribed notice of the commencement of any prescribed industry or process;

(e) for the recovery on summary conviction of monetary penalties in respect of any contravention of or failure to comply with any such requirement as is mentioned in paragraph (d) above, so, however, that such penalties shall not exceed £5.00 for every day on which the contravention or failure occurs or continues;

(f) for such matters as appear to the Secretary of State to be incidental to or consequential on provisions included in the regulations by virtue of paragraphs (a) to (d) above or section 110(1) of the Contributions and Benefits Act.

AMENDMENT

1. Welfare Reform Act 2012 Sch.9 para.30 (April 8, 2013).

185. *Omitted.* 1.266

Supplementary benefit etc.

186. *Omitted.* 1.267

Miscellaneous

Certain benefit to be inalienable

187.—(1) Subject to the provisions of this Act, every assignment of or charge on— 1.268

[5 (za) universal credit;]

[6 (zb) state pension under Part 1 of the Pensions Act 2014;]

(a) benefit as defined in section 122 of the Contributions and Benefits Act;

[1(aa) a jobseeker's allowance;]
[2(ab) state pension credit;]
[3(ac) an employment and support allowance;]
[4(ad) personal independence payment]
[7 (ae) bereavement support payment under section 30 of the Pensions Act 2014;]
(b) any income-related benefit; or
(c) child benefit,

and every agreement to assign or charge such benefit shall be void; and, on the bankruptcy of a beneficiary, such benefit shall not pass to any trustee or other person acting on behalf of his creditors.

(2) In the application of subsection (1) above to Scotland—

(a) the reference to assignment of benefit shall be read as a reference to assignation, "assign" being construed accordingly;
(b) the reference to a beneficiary's bankruptcy shall be read as a reference to the sequestration of his estate or the appointment on his estate of a judicial factor under section 41 of the Solicitors (Scotland) Act 1980.

(3) In calculating for the purposes of section 5 of the Debtors Act 1869 or section 4 of the Civil Imprisonment (Scotland) Act 1882 the means of any beneficiary, no account shall be taken of any increase of disablement benefit in respect of a child or of industrial death benefit.

Amendments

1. Jobseekers Act 1995 Sch.2 para.72 (October 7, 1996).
2. State Pension Credit Act 2002 s.14 and Sch.2 (July 2, 2002 for the purposes of making regulations only; fully in force October 6, 2003).
3. Welfare Reform Act 2007 s.28 and Sch.3 para.10 (October 27, 2008).
4. Welfare Reform Act 2012 Sch.9 para.31 (April 8, 2013).
5. The Welfare Reform Act 2012 (Commencement No. 9 and Transitional and Transitory Provisions and Commencement No. 8 and Savings and Transitional Provisions (Amendment)) Order 2013 (SI 2013/983) art.3(1)(b) (April 29, 2013).
6. Pensions Act 2014, s.56(4), s.23 and Sch.12, para.26 (April 6, 2016).
7. Pensions Act 2014 s.31 and Sch.16 para.34 (April 6, 2017).

Derivations

1.269 Social Security Act 1975 s.87.
"the Contributions and Benefits Act"—see s.191.
"income-related benefit"—*ibid.*

General Note

1.270 The House of Lords in *Mulvey v Secretary of State for Social Security*, *The Times*, March 20, 1997 dealt with the part of s.187(1) providing that, on bankruptcy or sequestration of a beneficiary, benefit does not pass to the trustee in bankruptcy. It held that the purpose was "to make clear beyond peradventure that the permanent trustee [the Scottish equivalent of the trustee in bankruptcy] could have no interest in any entitlement of a debtor to receive any of the social security benefits to which it applied" (Lord Jauncey). The Secretary of State's obligation to make payment of benefit is owed to the beneficiary and cannot be owed to the trustee in bankruptcy or permanent trustee. See the notes to s.78(2) for the situation where deductions are being made from benefit for the repayment of social fund loans or the recovery of overpayments.

In *McKenzie v Edinburgh City Council* [2023] SLT (Sh Ct) 127; [2023] 7 WLUK 332, the Sherriff Court held that benefits, even once paid into a claimant's bank account, remained protected under s.187 (and under the Social Security (Scotland) Act 2018, s.83 which has a similar effect). Confusion had resulted because a successful appeal against an earlier decision to contrary effect in another case (*North Lanarkshire Council v Crossan*) had not previously been published.

188. *Omitted.* 1.271

PART XVI

GENERAL

Subordinate legislation

Regulations and Orders - General

189.—(1) Subject to [. . .[1]] [[2]any provision proving for an order or regulations to be made by the Treasury or the Inland Revenue and to] any [[8] . . .] express provision of this Act, regulations and orders under this Act shall be made by the Secretary of State. 1.272

(2) [. . .[1]]

(3) Powers under this Act to make regulations or orders are exercisable by statutory instrument.

(4) Except in the case of regulations under section [. . .[1]] 175 above and in so far as this Act otherwise provides, any power conferred by this Act to make an Order in Council, regulations or an order may be exercised—

- (a) either in relation to all cases to which the power extends, or in relation to those cases subject to specified exceptions, or in relation to any specified cases or classes of case;
- (b) so as to make, as respects the cases in relation to which it is exercised—
  - (i) the full provision to which the power extends or any less provision (whether by way of exception or otherwise);
  - (ii) the same provision for all cases in relation to which the power is exercised, or different provision for different cases or different classes of case or different provision as respects the same case or class of case for different purposes of this Act;
  - (iii) any such provision either unconditionally or subject to any specified condition;

and where such a power is expressed to be exercisable for alternative purposes it may be exercised in relation to the same case for any or all of those purposes; and powers to make an Order in Council, regulations or an order for the purposes of any one provision of this Act are without prejudice to powers to make regulations or an order for the purposes of any other provision.

(5) Without prejudice to any specific provision in this Act, a power conferred by this Act to make an Order in Council, regulations or an order [. . .[1]] includes power to make thereby such incidental, supplementary, consequential or transitional provision as appears to Her Majesty, or the authority making the regulations or order, as the case may be, to be expedient for the purposes of the Order in Council, regulations or order.

[[11] (5A) The provision referred to in subsection (5) includes, in a case where regulations under this Act require or authorise the use of electronic communications, provision referred to in section 8(4) and (5) and 9(5) of the Electronic Communications Act 2000.

(5B) For the purposes of subsection (5A), references in section 8(4) and (5) and 9(5) of the Electronic Communications Act 2000 to an order under section 8 of that Act are to be read as references to regulations under this Act; and references to anything authorised by such an order are to be read as references to anything required or authorised by such regulations.]

(6) Without prejudice to any specific provisions in this Act, a power conferred by any provision of this Act, except section 14, [. . .[1]], 130 and 175, to make an Order in Council, regulations or an order includes power to provide for a person to exercise a discretion in dealing with any matter.

(7) [[12]. . .]

[[7] (7A) [[12]. . .]

(8) An order under [[9] section [[12]. . .] 150, 150A, 152, 165(4)(a) or 169] above [. . .[7]] shall not be made [[8] by the Secretary of State] without the consent of the Treasury.

(9) Any powers of the Secretary of State under any provision of this Act, except under [sections 80, 154 and 175] to make any regulations or order, where the power is not expressed to be exercisable with the consent of the Treasury, shall if the Treasury so direct be exercisable only in conjunction with them.

(10) Where the Lord Chancellor proposes to make regulations under this Act, other than under section 24 above, it shall be his duty to consult the Secretary of State with respect to the proposal.

(11) A power under any of section 179 above to make provision by regulations or Order in Council for modifications or adaptations of the Contributions and Benefits Act or this Act shall be exercisable in relation to any enactment passed after this Act which is directed to be construed as one withthem, except in so far as any such enactment relates to a benefit in relation to which the power is not exercisable; but this subsection applies only so far as a contrary intention is not expressed in the enactment so passed, and is without prejudice to the generality of any such direction.

(12) Any reference in this section or section 190 below to an Order in Council, or an order or regulations, under this Act includes a reference to an Order in Council, an order or regulations made under any provision of an enactment passed after this Act and directed to be construed as one with this Act; but this subsection applies only so far as a contrary intention is not expressed in the enactment so passed, and without prejudice to the generality of any such direction.

AMENDMENTS

1. Social Security Act 1998 Sch.7 (September 6, 1999).

2. Transfer of Functions Act 1999 Sch.3 (April 1, 1999).

3. Local Government Finance Act 1992 Sch.9 (April 1, 1993).

4. Social Security Administration (Fraud) Act 1997 Sch.1 (July 1, 1997).

5. Housing Act 1996 Sch.13 (April 1, 1997).

6. Social Security (Recovery of Benefits) Act 1997, Sch.3 (October 6, 1997).

7. Welfare Reform and Pensions Act 1999 Sch.12 paras 79 and 82 (November 11, 1999).

8. Tax Credits Act 2002 s.60 and Sch.6 (February 26, 2003 for the purpose of making regulations in relation to child benefit and guardian's allowance; April 1, 2003 for remaining purposes).

9. Pensions Act 2007 Sch.1(5) para.29 (July 26, 2007: insertion has effect as specified in 2007 c.22 s.5(3) and (7)).

10. Welfare Reform Act 2009 s.2(4) (November 12, 2009).

11. Welfare Reform Act 2012 s.104(1) (February 25, 2013).
12. Welfare Reform Act 2012 s.147 and Sch.14 Pt 1; and SI 2013/358 art.8(c) (April 1, 2013).

GENERAL NOTE

In accordance with s.2(1) of the Tax Credits Act 1999, this section is to be read, in relation to tax credit, as if references to the Secretary of State were references to the Treasury or, as the case may be, the Board. **1.273**

For Directions under the authority of s.189(5A), see the Social Security (Electronic Communications) Consolidation and Amendment Directions 2011 (as amended), set out in the General Note to Sch.2 to the Universal Credit, Personal Independence Payment, Jobseeker's Allowance and Employment and Support Allowance (Claims and Payments) Regulations 2013.

DERIVATIONS

SSA 1975 ss.113, 133, 166 and 168 as amended. **1.274**

Parliamentary control of orders and regulations

190.—(1) Subject to the provisions of this section, a statutory instrument containing (whether alone or with other provisions)— **1.275**

[11 (zza) an order under section 115A(3B);]
[12 (zzb) regulations under section 115C(2) or 115D(1) or (2);]
[13 (za) regulations under section 132A(4);]
(a) an order under [10 section 141, 143, 145, 150, 150A, [14 151A,] or 162(7)] above; or
[7(aza) any order containing provision adding any person to the list of persons falling within section 109B(2A) above; or]
[8(aa) the first regulations to be made under section 2A;]
[9 (ab) the first regulations to be made under section 2AA;]
(b) regulations under [3section 154] above,

shall not be made unless a draft of the instrument has been laid before Parliament and been approved by a resolution of each House of Parliament.

(2) Subsection (1) above does not apply to a statutory instrument by reason only that it contains regulations under section 154 above which are to be made for the purpose of consolidating regulations to be revoked in the instrument.

(3) A statutory instrument—

(a) which contains (whether alone or with other provisions) orders or regulations made under this Act by the Secretary of State [5, the Treasury or the Inland Revenue]; and
(b) which is not subject to any requirement that a draft of the instrument be laid before and approved by a resolution of each House of Parliament,

shall be subject to annulment in pursuance of a resolution of either House of Parliament.

(4) [1 . . .]

AMENDMENTS

1. Social Security Act 1998 Sch.7 (November 29, 1998).
2. Social Security Act 1998 Sch.7 (April 6, 1999).
3. Social Security (Recovery of Benefits) Act 1997 Sch.3 (October 6, 1997).
4. Social Security Administration (Fraud) Act 1997 Sch.1 (July 1, 1997).
5. Transfer of Functions Act 1999 Sch.3 (April 1, 1999).

6. Welfare Reform and Pensions Act 1999 Sch.13 (April 6, 2000).
7. Social Security Fraud Act 2001 s.20 (February 26, 2002).
8. Welfare Reform and Pensions Act 1999 Sch.12 paras 79 and 83 (November 11, 1999).
9. Employment Act 2002 s.53 and Sch.7 (July 5, 2003).
10. Pensions Act 2007 Sch.1(5) para.30 (July 26, 2007: insertion has effect as specified in 2007 c.22 s.5(3) and (7)).
11. Welfare Reform Act 2012 s.114(2) (May 8, 2012).
12. Welfare Reform Act 2012 s.116(2) (May 10, 2012).
13. National Insurance Contributions Act 2006 s.7(3) (March 30, 2006).
14. Pensions Act 2014 s.56(4), s.23 and Sch.12, para.27 (April 6, 2016).

GENERAL NOTE

1.276 In accordance with s.2(1) of the Tax Credits Act 1999, this section is to be read, in relation to tax credit, as if references to the Secretary of State were references to the Treasury or, as the case may be, the Board.

DERIVATION

1.277 SSA 1975 s.167 as amended and CBA 1975 s.22.

Supplementary

Interpretation—general

1.278 **191.** In this Act, unless the context otherwise requires—

"the 1975 Act" means the Social Security Act 1975;

"the 1986 Act" means the Social Security Act 1986;

"benefit" means benefit under the Contributions and Benefits Act [[1] and includes [[27] universal credit,] [[30] state pension under Part 1 of the Pensions Act 2014,] a jobseeker's allowance] [[20] . . .] , [[28] state pension credit, an employment and support allowance [[33], personal independence payment and bereavement support payment under section 30 of the Pensions Act 2014]];

[[9] "billing authority" has the same meaning as in Part 1 of the Local Government Finance Act 1992;]

"Christmas bonus" means a payment under Part X of the Contributions and Benefits Act;

"claim" is to be construed in accordance with "claimant";

"claimant" (in relation to contributions under Part I and to benefit under Parts II to IV of the Contributions and Benefits Act) means—

(a) a person whose right to be excepted from liability to pay, or to have his liability deferred for, or to be credited with, a contribution, is in question;

(b) a person who has claimed benefit;

and includes, in relation to an award or decision a beneficiary under the award or affected by the decision;

"claimant" (in relation to industrial injuries benefit) means a person who has claimed such a benefit and includes—

(a) an applicant for a declaration under [[3] section 29 of the Social Security Act 1998] that an accident was or was not an industrial accident; and

(b) in relation to an award or decision, a beneficiary under the award or affected by the decision;

[. . .]

[. . .[4]]
"the Consequential Provisions Act" means the Social Security (Consequential Provisions) Act 1992;
[[5]"contribution" means a contribution under Part I of the Contributions and Benefit Act;]
[[6]"contribution-based jobseeker's allowance" has the same meaning as in the Jobseekers Act 1995;]
"contributions card" has the meaning assigned to it by section 114(6) above;
"the Contributions and Benefits Act" means the Social Security Contributions and Benefits Act 1992;
[[22] "contributory employment and support allowance" means a contributory allowance under Part 1 of the Welfare Reform Act 2007 (employment and support allowance);]
[[29] . . .]
"disablement benefit" is to be construed in accordance with section 94(2)(a) of the Contributions and Benefits Act;
[[19] . . .]
"dwelling" means any residential accommodation, whether or not consisting of the whole or part of a building and whether or not comprising separate and self-contained premises;
[[9]"financial year" has the same meaning as in the Local Government Finance Act 1992;]
[[19] . . .]
"housing authority" means a local authority [[34] or a new town corporation];
"housing benefit scheme" is to be construed in accordance with section 134(1) above;
[[1]"income-based jobseeker's allowance" has the same meaning as in the Jobseekers Act 1995;]
"income-related benefit" means—
(a) income support;
[[35]...]
(d) housing benefit; and
[[2](e) council tax benefit];
[[22] "income-related employment and support allowance" means an income-related allowance under Part 1 of the Welfare Reform Act 2007 (employment and support allowance);]
"industrial injuries benefit" means benefit under Part V of the Contributions and Benefits Act, other than under Schedule 8;
[[10]"Inland Revenue" means the Commissioners of Inland Revenue]
. . .[10];
. . .[11];
"local authority" means—
(a) in relation to England . . .[12], the council of a district or London borough, the Common Council of the City of London or the Council of the Isles of Scilly;
[[11](aa) in relation to Wales, the council of a county or county borough;] and
(b) in relation to Scotland [[12]a council constituted under section 2 of the Local Government etc. (Scotland) Act 1994];
"medical examination" includes bacteriological and radiographical tests and similar investigations, and "medically examined" has a corresponding meaning;

"medical practitioner" means—

(a) a registered medical practitioner; or

(b) a person outside the United Kingdom who is not a registered medical practitioner, but has qualifications corresponding (in the Secretary of State's opinion) to those of a registered medical practitioner;

"medical treatment" means medical, surgical or rehabilitative treatment (including any course of diet or other regimen), and references to a person receiving or submitting himself to medical treatment are to be construed accordingly;

[[25] "money purchase contracted-out scheme" is to be construed in accordance with [[31] section 7B] of the Pensions Act"]

"new town corporation" means—

[[23] (a) in relation to England—

(i) a development corporation established under the New Towns Act 1981; or

(ii) the Homes and Communities Agency so far as exercising functions in relation to anything transferred (or to be transferred) to it as mentioned in section 52(1)(A) to (d) of the Housing and Regeneration Act 2008;

[[26] (iii) the Greater London Authority so far as exercising its new towns and urban development functions;]

(ab) in relation to Wales—

(i) a development corporation established under the New Towns Act 1981; and

(ii) the Welsh Ministers so far as exercising functions in relation to anything transferred (or to be transferred) to them as mentioned in section 36(1)(A)(i) to (iii) of that Act; and]

(b) in relation to Scotland, a development corporation established under the New Towns (Scotland) Act 1968;]

[[21] "the Northern Ireland Department" means the Department for Social Development but—

(a) in section 122 and sections 122B to 122E also includes the Department of Finance and Personnel; and

(b) in sections 121E, 121F, 122, 122ZA, 122C and 122D also includes the Department for Employment and Learning;]

"the Northern Ireland Administration Act" means the Social Security (Northern Ireland) Administration Act 1992;

"occupational pension scheme" has the same meaning as in [[15]section 1] of the Pensions Act;

"the Old Cases Act" means the Industrial Injuries and Diseases (Old Cases) Act 1975;

"Old Cases payments" means payments under Part I of Schedule 8 to the Contributions and Benefits Act;

[[17]"pensionable age" has the meaning given by the rules in paragraph 1 of Schedule 4 to the Pensions Act 1995];

"the Pensions Act" means the [[15]Pension Schemes Act 1993];

"personal pension scheme" has the meaning assigned to it by [[15]section 1 of the Pensions Act] [[15]and "appropriate", in relation to such a scheme, shall be construed in accordance with [[31] section 7B(6)], of that Act]

"prescribe" means prescribe by regulations; [[24] and "prescribed" must be construed accordingly;]

[[19] . . .]

"rent rebate", [. . .[18]] and "rent allowance" shall be construed in accordance with section 134 above;

[. . .[18]]

[[20] "state pension credit" means state pension credit under the State Pension Credit Act 2002;]

"tax year" means the 12 months beginning with 6th April in any year;

[[19] . . .]

[[32] "universal credit assessment period" means an assessment period for the purposes of Part 1 of the Welfare Reform Act 2012;]

"widow's benefit" has the meaning assigned to it by section 20(1)(e) of the Contributions and Benefits Act.

AMENDMENTS

1. Jobseekers Act 1995 Sch.2 (April 22, 1996).
2. Local Government Finance Act 1992 Sch.9 (March 6, 1992).
3. Social Security Act 1998 Sch.7 (July 7, 1999).
4. Social Security (Recovery of Benefits) Act 1997 Sch.3 (October 6, 1997).
5. Social Security Administration (Fraud) Act 1997 Sch.1 (July 1, 1997).
6. Jobseekers Act 1995 Sch.2 (April 22, 1996).
7. Housing Benefit Act 1996 Sch.13 (April 1, 1997).
8. Tax Credits Act 1999 Sch.1 (October 5, 1999).
9. Local Government Finance Act 1992 Sch.9 (March 6, 1992).
10. Transfer of Functions Act 1999 Sch.1 (April 1, 1999).
11. Social Security (Incapacity for Work) Act 1994 Sch.1 (April 13, 1995).
12. Local Government etc. (Scotland) Act 1994 Sch.14 (April 1, 1996).
13. Local Government (Wales) Act 1994 Sch.16 (April 1, 1996).
14. Local Government etc. (Scotland) Act 1994 Sch.13 (April 1, 1996).
15. Pension Schemes Act 1993 Sch.8 (February 7, 1994).
16. Social Security Administration (Fraud) Act Sch.1 (July 1, 1997).
17. Pensions Act 1995 Sch.4 (July 19, 1995).
18. Housing Act 1996 Sch.13 (April 1, 1997).
19. Social Security Act 1998 Sch.8 para.1 (November 29, 1999).
20. State Pension Credit Act 2002 s.14 and Sch.2 (July 2, 2002 for the purpose of making regulations only; fully in force October 6, 2003).
21. Employment Act 2002 s.53 and Sch.7 (September 9, 2002).
22. Welfare Reform Act 2007 s.28 and Sch.3 para.10 (October 27, 2008).
23. Housing and Regeneration Act 2008 Sch.8 para.61 (December 1, 2008).
24. Welfare Reform Act 2007 Sch.5 para.10 (July 3, 2007).
25. The Pensions Act 2007, (Abolition of Contracting-out for Defined Contribution Pensions Schemes) (Consequential Amendments) (No.2) Regulations 2011 (SI 2011/1724) reg.2 (April 6, 2012).
26. Localism Act 2011 Sch.19 para.31 (April 1, 2012).
27. Welfare Reform Act 2012 s.31 and Sch.2 para.31 (February 25, 2013).
28. Welfare Reform Act 2012 s.91 and Sch.9 para.32 (February 25, 2013).
29. Welfare Reform Act 2012 s.147 and Sch.14 Pt 1; and SI 2013/358 art.8(c) (April 1, 2013).
30. Pensions Act 2014, s.56(4), s.23 and Sch.12 para.28 (April 6, 2016).
31. Pensions Act 2014, s.56(4), s.23 and Sch.13 para.57 (April 6, 2016).
32. The Universal Credit and Miscellaneous Amendments (No.2) Regulations 2014 (SI 2014/2888) reg.7(1)(c) (November 26, 2014).
33. Pensions Act 2014 s.31 and Sch.16 para.35 (April 6, 2017).
34. Housing (Scotland) Act 2001 Sch.10 para.17 (April 1, 2002).
35. Tax Credits Act 2002 Sch.6 (April 8, 2002).

DERIVATIONS

1.279 SSA 1975 s.168 and Sch.20.

GENERAL NOTE

1.280 The definition of "the Northern Ireland Department" is stated in accordance with the legislation but is obsolete. The Department for Social Development and the Department of Finance and Personnel were renamed by the Departments Act (Northern Ireland) 2016 (as, respectively, the Department for Communities and the Department of Finance). The Department for Employment and Learning was abolished altogether.

Short title, commencement and extent

1.281 **192.**—(1) This Act may be cited as the Social Security Administration Act 1992.

(2) This Act is to be read, where appropriate, with the Contributions and Benefits Act and the Consequential Provisions Act.

(3) The enactments consolidated by this Act are repealed, in consequence of the consolidation, by the Consequential Provisions Act.

(4) Except as provided in Schedule 4 to the Consequential Provisions Act, this Act shall come into force on 1st July 1992.

(5) The following provisions extend to Northern Ireland—
[. . .[1]];
[[2]]
section 170 (with Schedule 5);
[[3] section 171(with schedule 6);]
section 177 (with Schedule 8);
and this section.

(6) Except as provided by this section, this Act does not extend to Northern Ireland.

AMENDMENTS

1. Social Security Act 1998 Sch.7 (October 5, 1999).
2. Social Security (Recovery of Benefits) Act 1997 Sch.3 (October 6, 1997).
3. Northern Ireland Act 1998 Pt VIII s.89(9) (December 2, 1999).

SCHEDULES

SCHEDULE 1

CLAIMS FOR BENEFIT MADE OR TREATED AS MADE BEFORE 1ST OCTOBER 1990

Claims made or treated as made on or after 2nd September 1985 and before 1st October 1986

1.282 **1.** Section 1 above shall have effect in relation to a claim made or treated as made on or after 2nd September 1985 and before 1st October 1986 as if the following subsections were substituted for subsections (1) to (3)—

"(1) Except in such cases as may be prescribed, no person shall be entitled to any benefit unless, in addition to any other conditions relating to that benefit being satisfied—

(a) he makes a claim for it—
 (i) in the prescribed manner; and
 (ii) subject to subsection (2) below, within the prescribed time; or
(b) by virtue of a provision of Chapter VI of Part II of the 1975 Act or of regulations made under such a provision he would have been treated as making a claim for it."

"(2) Regulations shall provide for extending, subject to any prescribed conditions, the time within which a claim may be made in cases where it is not made within the prescribed time but good cause is shown for the delay.

(3) Notwithstanding any regulations made under this section, no person shall be entitled to any benefit (except disablement benefit or industrial death benefit) in respect of any period more than 12 months before the date on which the claim is made."

Claims made or treated as made on or after 1st October 1986 and before 6th April 1987

2. Section 1 above shall have effect in relation to a claim made or treated as made on or after 1986 and before 6th April 1987 as if the subsections set out in paragraph 1 above were substituted for subsections (1) to (3) but with the insertion in subsection (3) of the words "reduced earnings allowance" after the words "disablement benefit".

Claims made or treated as made on or after 6th April 1987 and before 21st July 1989

3. Section 1 above shall have effect in relation to a claim made or treated as made on or after 6th April 1987 and before 21st July 1989, as if—

(a) the following subsection were substituted for subsection (1)—

"(1) Except in such cases as may be prescribed, no person shall be entitled to any benefit unless, in addition to any other conditions relating to that benefit being satisfied—

(a) he makes a claim for it in the prescribed manner and within the prescribed time; or
(b) by virtue of regulations made under section 51 of the 1986 Act he would have been treated as making a claim for it."; and
(c) there were omitted—
    (i) from subsection (2), the words "except as provided by section 3 below"; and
    (ii) subsection (3).

Claims made or treated as made on or after 21st July 1989 and before 13th July 1990

4. Section 1 above shall have effect in relation to a claim made or treated as made on or after 21st July 1989 and before 13th July 1990 as if there were omitted—

(a) from subsection (1), the words "and subject to the following provisions of this section and to section 3 below";
(b) from subsection (2), the words "except as provided by section 3 below"; and
(c) subsection (3).

Claims made or treated as made on or after 13th July 1990 and before 1st October 1990

5. Section 1 above shall have effect in relation to a claim made or treated as made on or after 13th July 1990 and before 1st October 1990 as if there were omitted—

(a) from subsection (1), the words "the following provisions of this section and to"; and
(b) subsection (3)

GENERAL NOTE

See annotations to s.1 **1.283**

Pension Schemes Act 1993

(1993 C.48)

ARRANGEMENT OF SECTIONS

 1.284

An Act to consolidate certain enactments relating to pension schemes with-amendments to give effect to recommendations of the Law Commission and the Scottish Law Commission

[5th November 1993]

[1 Decisions and appeals

1.285 **170.**—(1) Section 2 (use of computers) of the Social Security Act 1998 ("the 1998 Act") applies as if, for the purposes of subsection (1) of that section, this Act were a relevant enactment.

[2(2) It shall be for an officer of the Inland Revenue—

(a) to make any decision that falls to be made under or by virtue of Part III of this Act, other than a decision which under or by virtue of that Part falls to be made by the Secretary of State;

(b) to decide any issue arising in connection with payments under section 7 of the Social Security Act 1986 (occupational pension schemes becoming contracted out between 1986 and 1993); and

(c) to decide any issue arising by virtue of regulations made under paragraph 15 of Schedule 3 to the Social Security (Consequential Provisions) Act 1992 (continuing in force of certain enactments repealed by the Social Security Act 1973).

(3) In the following provisions of this section a "relevant decision" means any decision which under subsection (2) falls to be made by an officer of the Inland Revenue, other than a decision under section 53 [5 . . .]

(4) Sections 9 and 10 of the 1998 Act (revisions of decisions and decisions superseding earlier decisions) apply as if—

(a) any reference in those sections to a decision of the Secretary of State under section 8 of that Act included a reference to a relevant decision; and

(b) any other reference in those sections to the Secretary of State were, in relation to a relevant decision, a reference to an officer of the Inland Revenue.

(5) Regulations may make provision—

[3(a) generally with respect to the making of relevant decisions;

(b) with respect to the procedure to be adopted on any application made under section 9 or 10 of the 1998 Act by virtue of subsection (4); and

(c) generally withrespect to such applications, revisions under section 9 and decisions under section 10;]

but may not prevent [3 a revision under section 9 or decision under section 10] being made without such an application.

(6) Section 12 of the 1998 Act (appeal to [4First-tier Tribunal] applies as if, for the purposes of subsection (1)(b) of that section, a relevant decision were a decision of the Secretary of State falling within Schedule 3 to the 1998 Act.

(7) The following provisions of the 1998 Act (which relate to decisions and appeals)—

sections 13 to 18,
sections 25 and 26,
section 28, and
Schedules 4 and 5,

shall apply in relation to any appeal under section 12 of the 1998 Act by virtue of subsection (6) above as if any reference to the Secretary of State were a reference to an officer of the Inland Revenue.]]

AMENDMENTS

1. Social Security Act 1998 s.86(1) and Sch.7 para.131 (March 4, 1999).

2. Social Security Contributions (Transfer of Functions, etc.) Act 1999 s.16 (April 1, 1999).

3. Welfare Reform and Pensions Act 1999 Sch.11 para.22.

4. Transfer of Tribunal Functions Order 2008 (SI 2008/2833) Sch.3 paras 111 and 112 (November 3, 2008).

5. Pensions Act 2008 (Abolition of Protected Rights) (Consequential Amendments) (No.2) Order 2011 (SI 2011/1730) art.5(1) and (19) (April 6, 2012).

GENERAL NOTE

A former employee may be entitled to both a state pension and one or more private pensions. The Social Security Contributions and Benefits Act 1992 provides for a Category A retirement pension, the old state pension, consisting of a basic pension and an additional pension under either the former State Earnings-Related Pension Scheme or, from 2002, the new "second state pension" scheme. However, until April 15, 2016, employees were able to "contract out" of the liability to make contributions for an additional pension provided they were making contributions to an approved occupational or personal pension scheme. The Pensions Schemes Act 1993, provides for guaranteed minimum pensions from contracted-out occupational pension schemes. See Vol.I of this work for both Acts. **1.286**

Over a working life, a person may have contributed both to an additional pension under one or both of the state schemes and to one or more occupational or personal pension schemes. Where a guaranteed minimum pension is payable under an occupational scheme to a person entitled to an additional pension under the State Earnings-Related Pension Scheme, overlap is avoided by s.46 of the 1993 Act which provides for an adjustment to the Category A retirement pension. This involves the determination of a number of questions, some of which are to be determined by the Secretary of State and some of which are allocated to HMRC (to whom the functions of the Commissioners for Inland Revenue have been transferred by the Commissioners for Revenue and Customs Act 2005 s.5(2)) by this section. In *R(P) 1/04*, the Commissioner held that it was for the Secretary of State to determine entitlement to a Category A retirement pension and to identify the occupational pension schemes relevant to that entitlement, for the Inland Revenue to determine entitlement to a guaranteed minimum pension in respect of each occupational pension scheme and for the Secretary of State to aggregate the guaranteed minimum pensions and decide on the amount of any reduction of the Category A retirement pension under s.46 of the 1993 Act.

Section 170(6) and (7) provides for appeals against decisions of HMRC relating to guaranteed minimum pensions to be heard by the First-tier Tribunal as though it were a social security case rather than a tax case. However, it was pointed out in *R(P) 1/04* that there can be no appeal until a formal decision is issued and that the Inland Revenue did not always issue a formal decision unless a calculation was disputed. In those circumstances, as any dispute was likely to be raised first in a challenge to the final decision issued by the Secretary of State, it was suggested that it might be necessary for the Secretary of State or an appeal tribunal to refer a question to the Inland Revenue for formal determination even though regs 11A and 38A of the Social Security and Child Support (Decisions and Appeals) Regulations 1999 did not strictly apply.

Perhaps surprisingly, an appeal against a refusal to issue a contracting-out certificate is one type of case that falls, by virtue of this section, to be treated as a social security case. However, where a question arises as to whether a particular claimant was in contracted-in or contracted-out employment for the purpose of ascertaining his entitlement to a pension, it arises as part of a question as to his liability to pay contributions or as to what contributions have been paid and so is a question falling within the jurisdiction of the tax authorities by virtue of s.8(1)(c) or (e) of the Social Security Contributions (Transfer of Functions, etc.) Act 1999 (*CP/3833/2003*).

Employment Tribunals Act 1996

(1996 c.17)

Arrangement of Sections

An Act to consolidate enactments relating to industrial tribunals and the Employment Appeal Tribunal.

[22nd May 1996]

General Note

1.288 This Act started life as the Industrial Tribunals Act 1996 but was given its new short title by s.1(2) of the Employment Rights (Dispute Resolution) Act 1998, which also renamed the tribunals themselves, with effect from August 1, 1998.

Power to provide for recoupment of benefits

1.289 **16.**—(1) This section applies to payments which are the subject of proceedings before [1 employment tribunals] and which are—

(a) payments of wages or compensation for loss of wages,

(b) payments by employers to employees under sections 146 to 151, sections 168 to 173 or section 192 of the Trade Union and Labour Relations (Consolidation) Act 1992,

(c) payments by employers to employees under —

  (i) Part III, V, VI or VII,

  (ii) section 93, or

  (iii) Part X,

  of the Employment Rights Act 1996, [5. . .]

(d) payments by employers to employees of a nature similar to, or for a purpose corresponding to the purpose of, payments within paragraph (b) or (c), [5 [7 . . .]

(e) payments by employers to employees under regulation 5, 6 or 9 of the Employment Relations Act 1999 (Blacklists) Regulations 2010,] [7 or

(f) payments by NHS employers to applicants under regulation 6 of the Employment Rights Act 1996 (NHS Recruitment—Protected Disclosure) Regulations 2018 (remedies),]

and to payments of remuneration under a protective award under section 189 of the Trade Union and Labour Relations (Consolidation) Act 1992.

(2) The Secretary of State may by regulations make with respect to payments to which this section applies provision for any or all of the purposes specified in subsection (3).

(3) The purposes referred to in subsection (2) are—

(a) enabling the Secretary of State to recover from an employer, by way of total or partial recoupment of [6 universal credit,] jobseeker's allowance [3 , income support or income-related employment and support allowance]—

(i) a sum not exceeding the amount of the prescribed element of the monetary award, or

(ii) in the case of a protective award, the amount of the remuneration,

(b) requiring or authorising an [1employment tribunal] to order the payment of such a sum, by way of total or partial recoupment of [6 universal credit,] [3 jobseeker's allowance, income support or income-related employment and support allowance], to the Secretary of State instead of to an employee, and

(c) requiring an [1employment tribunal] to order the payment to an employee of only the excess of the prescribed element of the monetary award over the amount of any [6 universal credit,] jobseeker's allowance [3 , income support or income-related employment and support allowance] shown to the tribunal to have been paid to the employee and enabling the Secretary of State to recover from the employer, by way of total or partial recoupment of the benefit, a sum not exceeding that amount.

(4) Regulations under this section may be framed—

(a) so as to apply to all payments to which this section applies or to one or more classes of those payments, and

[3 (b) so as to apply to all or any of the benefits mentioned in subsection (3).]

(5) Regulations under this section may—

(a) confer powers and impose duties on [1 employment tribunals] or [2 . . .] other persons,

(b) impose on an employer to whom a monetary award or protective award relates a duty—

(i) to furnish particulars connected with the award, and

(ii) to suspend payments in pursuance of the award during any period prescribed by the regulations,

(c) provide for an employer who pays a sum to the Secretary of State in pursuance of this section to be relieved from any liability to pay the sum to another person,

[2(cc) provide for the determination by the Secretary of State of any issue arising as to the total or partial recoupment in pursuance of the regulations of [6 universal credit,] a jobseeker's allowance, unemployment benefit [3 , income support or income-related employment and support allowance],

(d) confer on an employee a right of appeal to [4the First-tier Tribunal] against any decision of the Secretary of State on any such issue, and]

(e) provide for the proof in proceedings before [1 employment tribunals] (whether by certificate or in any other manner) of any amount of [6 universal credit,] jobseeker's allowance [3 , income support or income-related employment and support allowance] paid to an employee.

(6) Regulations under this section may make different provision for different cases.

AMENDMENTS

1. Employment Rights (Dispute Resolution) Act 1998 s.1(2) (August 1, 1998).
2. Social Security Act 1998 Sch.7 para.147 (October 18, 1999).
3. Welfare Reform Act 2007 s.28(1) and Sch.3 para.15(1) and (2) (October 27, 2008).
4. Transfer of Tribunal Functions Order 2008 (SI 2008/2833) Sch.3 para.137 (November 3, 2008).
5. Employment Relations Act 1999 (Blacklists) Regulations 2010 (SI 2010/493) reg.17(3) (March 2, 2010).
6. Universal Credit (Consequential, Supplementary, Incidental and Miscellaneous Provisions) Regulations 2013 (SI 2013/630) reg.11(1) to (3) (April 29, 2013).
7. Employment Rights Act 1996 (NHS Recruitment—Protected Disclosure) Regulations 2018 (SI 2018/579) reg.10(3) (May 23, 2018).

DEFINITIONS

"income-based jobseeker's allowance"—see s.17(4).
"income-related employment and support allowance"—see s.17(5).
"monetary award"—see s.17(3).
"the prescribed element"—*ibid.*

GENERAL NOTE

1.290 See the Employment Protection (Recoupment of Benifits) Regulations 1996.

Recoupment: further provisions

1.291 **17.**—(1) Where in pursuance of any regulations under section 16 a sum has been recovered by or paid to the Secretary of State by way of total or partial recoupment of [2 universal credit,] jobseeker's allowance [1 , income support or income-related employment and support allowance]—

(a) no sum shall be recoverable under Part III or V of the Social Security Administration Act 1992, and
(b) no abatement, payment or reduction shall be made by reference to the [2 universal credit,] jobseeker's allowance [1 , income support or income-related employment and support allowance] recouped.

(2) Any amount found to have been duly recovered by or paid to the Secretary of State in pursuance of regulations under section 16 by way of total or partial recoupment of jobseeker's allowance shall be paid into the National Insurance Fund.

(3) In section 16—

"monetary award" means the amount which is awarded, or ordered to be paid, to the employee by the tribunal or would be so awarded or ordered apart from any provision of regulations under that section, and

"the prescribed element", in relation to any monetary award, means so much of that award as is attributable to such matters as may be prescribed by regulations under that section.

(4) In section 16 "income-based jobseeker's allowance" has the same meaning as in the Jobseekers Act 1995.

[1 (5) In this section and section 16 "income-related employment and support allowance" means an income-related allowance under Part 1 of the Welfare Reform Act 2007 (employment and support allowance).]

AMENDMENTS

1. Welfare Reform Act 2007 s.28(1) and Sch.3 para.15(1), (3) and (4) (October 27, 2008).

2. Universal Credit (Consequential, Supplementary, Incidental and Miscellaneous Provisions) Regulations 2013 (SI 2013/630) reg.11(1) and (4) (April 29, 2013).

Social Security (Recovery of Benefits) Act 1997

(1997 c.27)

ARRANGEMENT OF SECTIONS

Introductory

Certificates of recoverable benefits

Liability of person paying compensation

Reduction of compensation payment

Reviews and appeals

Courts

An Act to re-state, with amendments, Part IV of the Social Security Administration Act 1992.

[19th March 1997]

GENERAL NOTE

1.293 This Act provides for the recovery by the Secretary of State from those liable to pay compensation for an injury or disease (or from schemes making equivalent payments where the person who would otherwise be liable to pay compensation was uninsured) of an amount equal to the amount of social security benefits he has paid to the victims. As the long title says, the Act is to "re-state, with amendments," Pt IV of the Social Security Act 1992, which was a true consolidation measure and re-enacted s.22 of, and Sch.4 to, the Social Security Act 1989 which first introduced a scheme like this for recovering benefits. This Act is not a consolidation measure because, while a number of the provisions are the same as under the old schemes, the amendments make some fundamental changes.

The Compensation Recovery Unit of the Department for Work and Pensions is in Sunderland, Tyne and Wear. It administers this legislation and similar legislation, outside the scope of this book, relating to the recovery of certain costs to the health service. A fairly detailed guide to its procedures is obtainable from its webpage: *https://www.gov.uk/government/collections/cru.*

A person making a compensation payment in consequence of an accident injury or disease (whether voluntarily or pursuant to a court order or agreement or otherwise—see s.1(3)—unless the payment is exempt—see s.1(2) and Sch.1) *must* apply under s.4 to the Compensation Recovery Unit for a "certificate of recoverable benefits" *before* making the payment. Under s.5, that certificate should specify the amount of relevant benefits (listed in col.2 of Sch.2) paid, or expected to be paid within the "relevant period" (which will end when the compensation payment is made if the maximum period of five years has not already elapsed—see s.3), *in respect of* the accident, injury or disease (see the definition of "recoverable benefit" in s.1(4)(c) which refers back to s.1(1)(b)). The compensator must then pay to the Secretary of State a sum equal to the total amount of those recoverable benefits (s.6) and pay to the victim the compensation payment. Certain parts of the compensation payment may be reduced to reflect the benefits received by the victim during the "relevant period" (s.8), but benefits paid after that period must be ignored in the assessment of damages (s.17).

Sections 10–14 provide for reviews of, and appeals against, certificates of recoverable benefits.

Introductory

Cases in which this Act applies

1.—(1) This Act applies in cases where— 1.294

(a) a person makes a payment (whether on his own behalf or not) to or in respect of any other person in consequence of any accident, injury or disease suffered by the other, and

(b) any listed benefits have been, or are likely to be, paid to or for the other during the relevant period in respect of the accident, injury or disease.

(2) The reference above to a payment in consequence of any accident, injury or disease is to a payment made—

(a) by or on behalf of a person who is, or is alleged to be, liable to any extent in respect of the accident, injury or disease, [1. . .]

(b) in pursuance of a compensation scheme for motor accidents[1 , or

(c) under the Diffuse Mesothelioma Payment Scheme (established under the Mesothelioma Act 2014);]

but does not include a payment mentioned in Part I of Schedule 1.

(3) Subsection (1)(a) applies to a payment made—

(a) voluntarily, or in pursuance of a court order or an agreement, or otherwise, and

(b) in the United Kingdom or elsewhere.

(4) In a case where this Act applies—

(a) the "injured person" is the person who suffered the accident, injury or disease,

(b) the "compensation payment" is the payment within subsection (1)(a), and

(c) "recoverable benefit" is listed benefit which has been or is likely to be paid as mentioned in the subsection (1)(b).

AMENDMENT

1. Mesothelioma Act 2014 s.11 and Sch.1 paras. 1 and 2 (March 31, 2014).

DEFINITIONS

"compensation scheme for motor accidents"—see s.29.
"listed benefit"—*ibid.*
"payment"—*ibid.*
"the relevant period"—see s.3.

GENERAL NOTE

1.295 The principle behind this legislation is that, where a person is liable under the law to compensate a victim of any accident, injury or disease, that person should also compensate the Secretary of State for the social security benefits paid to the victim in respect of that accident, injury or disease during the "relevant period" as defined in s.3. In practice, the scheme is operated with the co-operation of insurance companies and subs.(2) provides that relevant payments include those made through certain schemes set up to ensure payments are made to victims where the person liable was not insured. The key questions are therefore those posed by subs.(1): whether the payment is made "in consequence of any accident, injury or disease" and whether benefits have been paid "in respect of" that particular accident, injury or disease.

Subsection (1)(a)

1.296 In *Rand v East Dorset Health Authority* [2001] P.I.Q.R. Q1, this Act was held not to apply where parents of a child were awarded damages in respect of the defendants' negligence in failing to inform them before the child's birth that the child would be suffering from Down's Syndrome. It had been claimed that the child would have been aborted had the parents received the information but it was held that the damages had been awarded purely for economic loss resulting from negligent mis-statement and so were not awarded "in consequence of any accident, injury or disease suffered by the [parents]". That decision was distinguished in *R(CR) 4/03*, which was also a case of medical negligence. There, a doctor was alleged to have failed to recognise symptoms of diabetes in a woman in an advanced stage of pregnancy. It was claimed that, had the symptoms been detected, the condition would have been confirmed and an emergency Caesarean section could have been performed with a high chance of the child being born alive. As it was, the child died in utero and labour had to be induced and the mother suffered a major depressive episode. Compensation was claimed not only under the Fatal Accidents Act 1976 (which compensation is exempt under reg.2 of the Social Security (Recovery of Benefits) Regulations 1997) but also for the mother's psychiatric injury. The case was settled. The Commissioner held that compensation was paid in consequence of an accident, injury or disease suffered by the mother. The Commissioner also commented that the phrase "accident, injury or disease" was an "odd one" because it was not clear how benefits might be paid in respect of an accident if there was neither injury nor disease. He suggested that there might be little difference between an "accident" and an "injury" in this context.

Subsection (1)(b)

1.297 The crucial question in most cases arising under this Act is whether listed benefits have been paid "in respect of" the accident, injury or disease within the meaning that phrase has in subs.(1)(b), so as to fall within the scope of the term "recoverable benefit" as defined in subs.(4)(c).

For a benefit to be paid "in respect of " an accident, injury or disease, the accident, injury or disease must be an effective cause of the payment of benefit and an accident may cease to be an effective cause of disablement if its effects have worn off and been replaced by the effects of a worsening pre-accident condition (*R(CR) 1/01*). In *R(CR) 3/03*, it was held that only benefits the payment of which was caused by the relevant disease were paid "in respect of" the disease and that ordinary principles of causation applied, having regard to the conditions of entitlement to each benefit. A relevant accident, injury or disease could therefore cease to be an effective cause of the payment of benefit even if its effects had not worn off. It was enough merely for it to be shown that the benefit would have been paid due to a pre-existing condition even if the relevant disease had not been developed. In that case, the claimant was paid compensation in respect of asbestos–induced disease but the evidence was that the claimant was suffering from other, longer-standing, conditions that contributed to his disablement and were getting worse. The Commissioner found the claimant would have become incapable of work from a certain date even if he had not suffered from the asbestos-induced disease and therefore that the asbestos-induced disease ceased to be a cause of the payment of benefits paid in respect of incapacity from that date, although it had accelerated the onset of incapacity. In relation to disability living allowance, he found that the asbestos-related disease had been a contributory factor in the claimant's entitlement to the mobility component throughout that part of the "relevant period" for which it had been paid but that it had never been a contributory factor in the claimant's entitlement to the care component. Thus, part of the incapacity benefits listed in the original certificate of recoverable benefits and all of the care component of disability living allowance were not recoverable but the rest of the incapacity benefits and all of the mobility component were recoverable.

Conversely, where the other cause of disablement arises *after* the relevant accident, benefit that would have been paid as a result of the relevant accident if the other cause had not arisen is attributable to the relevant accident, whereas benefit that would not have been paid but for the other cause of disablement is attributable to that other cause. In *R(CR) 2/04*, the claimant had returned to work for another employer after the relevant accident, even though he was still suffering from some minor disablement, and then suffered a second industrial accident, following which he was incapable of work again. The Commissioner found that the incapacity was initially attributable to the second accident because the claimant would have been able to continue working but for that accident. However, the effects of that accident then wore off and the effects of the relevant accident worsened and the Commissioner found that there came a time when the claimant would have been incapable of work due to the relevant accident even if the second accident had not occurred so that the payment of benefits became attributable to the relevant accident again. **1.298**

In these sorts of cases, it may be necessary to pay careful attention to the precise statutory bases upon which a benefit may be awarded. Moreover, when considering whether a claimant would have been entitled to a benefit due to a pre-existing condition, it may be necessary to consider the basis upon which that benefit was, or probably was, in fact awarded. For example, in *TC v SSWP (CR)* [2018] UKUT 272 (AAC), where the claimant had been entitled to incapacity benefit before the relevant accident occurred and there arose the question whether her award would have qualified for conversion to an award of contributory employment and support allowance even if the relevant accident had not occurred, it was relevant that the findings of the examining medical practitioner suggested that she had been awarded incapacity benefit only because she had very high blood pressure and so had been treated as being incapable of work under reg.27(2)(a) of Social Security (Incapacity for Work) (General) Regulations 1995 (SI 1995/311), rather than because she had scored any points under the Schedule to those Regulations. Consequently, although the First-tier Tribunal was entitled to find that the claimant would not have satisfied any of the descriptors under Sch.2 or 3 to the Employment and Support Regulations 2008 (see Vol.V of this work) had the relevant accident not occurred, it had erred in not also considering whether the conditions of reg.29(2) or 35(2) would have been satisfied.

Where a claimant undergoes a medical operation as a result of an accident, injury or disease and the operation causes further disablement, benefits paid in consequence of that further disablement will have been paid "in respect of" the accident (*CCR/2046/2002*). The same applied where the claimant suffered a psychological reaction due to stress caused by a misdiagnosis due to the misreading of an X-ray that was required by the relevant accident, although it was suggested that the result might have been different if it had been proved that the misdiagnosis had been due to negligence (*CCR/4307/2000* – there had been no suggestion of negligence in *CCR/2046/2002* either).

Where there has been medical negligence, compensation may be paid in respect of any injury or disease caused by the negligence. In *CCR/1022/2006*, it was pointed out that it was important to distinguish between the effects of the accident, injury or disease that led to the claimant being admitted to hospital and the effects of the medical negligence that occurred while he was a patient there. "The question for the tribunal was whether, had there not been the delay in arranging the MRI scan and therefore a delay in surgery, the appellant would have qualified for disability living allowance at the rate at which it was awarded or at a lower rate. If the answer was 'yes', the benefit was to that extent not recoverable."

1.299 A similar approach was taken in *AW v SSWP (CR)* [2011] UKUT 223 (AAC), despite the parties not having drawn the judge's attention to any of the Commissioners' decision in this area and the Secretary of State having inappropriately relied upon *Hassall v Secretary of State for Social Security* [1995] 1 W.L.R. 812 (also reported as *R(CR) 1/95*) (see below). The claimant, who was already suffering from some disablement as a result of earlier injures sustained while he was in the army, suffered serious injuries in a motor cycle accident and during the course of treatment was infected with MRSA as a result of negligence by the hospital. That infection, rather than his injuries, required the amputation of his left leg. The Secretary of State sought to recover disability living allowance from compensation received by the claimant from the hospital and the claimant's appeal was dismissed by the First-tier Tribunal. The Upper Tribunal approved the First-tier Tribunal's approach to the case, in which it had considered that the issue was whether the claimant would have been entitled to disability living allowance if the amputation had not occurred, although it allowed the claimant's appeal on the ground that the First-tier Tribunal had not adequately considered the effects of the injuries sustained by the claimant while in the army.

However, where a claimant had accepted £50,000 in respect of a claim that injuries from a particular date were due solely to medical negligence, it was necessary to adopt a consistent approach and the claimant was not entitled to argue that the injuries he had suffered after that date were entirely due to the accident that had led him to be hospitalised rather than to the medical negligence (*CCR/2232/2006*).

The need for consistency between the approach taken by a party to court proceedings and the approach taken by the same party in proceedings under this Act is not confined to medical negligence cases and such consistency is expected from compensators as well as from claimants. In *R(CR) 1/07*, where a compensator settled a claim made on the basis that psychiatric injury was due to a particular cause, the compensator was not entitled to argue that the injury was due to only a cause not covered by the claim and that the compensator was therefore not in fact liable in respect of the injury in consequence of which the compensation was paid. Attention was drawn to the word "alleged" in s.1(2)(a). Compensators must therefore pay careful attention to the certificate of recoverable benefits when deciding whether to compromise a case that could be defended.

1.300 Benefits that ought not to have been paid at all—because they were paid under a mistake of fact or medical opinion or law, whether deliberately induced by the claimant or not—cannot be said to have been paid "in respect of " an accident, injury or disease (*R(CR) 1/02*, a decision of a Tribunal of Commissioners, and *Eagle Star Insurance v Department for Social Development*, a decision of the Court of

Appeal in Northern Ireland reported as *R1/01(CRS)*). It follows that, if it is shown that benefit was paid at too high a rate, only that part of the benefit properly paid was paid "in respect of" the accident, injury or disease (*R(CR) 1/03*). See further the note to s.11.

However, in *R1/05(CRS)*, it was held that benefits paid as a result of bureaucratic delay between the date of a medical examination and a consequent supersession decision do not necessarily cease to be recoverable.

Again, it may be necessary to pay careful attention to the precise statutory bases upon which a benefit may be awarded. As already indicated, it is a gross over-simplification to believe that employment and support allowance is paid because a person is actually incapable of work. Indeed, until an initial assessment is carried out, a claimant is usually treated as having a limited capability for work on the basis of the mere submission of medical certificates provided by a doctor. Similar provision was formerly made in respect of incapacity benefit. In *R(CR) 2/02*, it was suggested by the Tribunal of Commissioners that, as long as a claimant was providing medical certificates referring to the relevant disease, incapacity benefit was properly awarded in respect of that disease whether or not the claimant was actually incapable of work or would actually have satisfied a personal capability assessment. Doubtless, there would be exceptions where, for instance, a claimant was working and so was required to be treated as capable of work or as not having limited capability for work. It may also be arguable that, where a claimant had obtained the medical certificate by misleading his doctor as to the severity of his or her condition or, perhaps, where the doctor plainly ought not to have given a certificate, benefit can be said not to have been properly paid in respect of the relevant accident, injury or disease but, given that a medical certificate merely certifies that the claimant was advised not to work and is not actually a certificate that the person is incapable of work (see Sch.1 to the Social Security (Medical Evidence) Regulations 1976), it will not be easy to demonstrate that a certificate was inappropriate. In any event, *R(CR) 2/02* was distinguished in *R(CR) 1/04*. In the latter case, incapacity benefit had been awarded pending the carrying out of a personal capability assessment on the basis of medical certificates supplied by the claimant's doctor, which referred to an eye injury sustained when a fire extinguisher had gone off accidentally. That was obviously the injury in consequence of which the compensation payment had been made but the Commissioner found that the eye injury caused by the fire extinguisher had in fact had no disabling effect on the claimant after a week and that the disablement was the result of a pre-existing condition in the claimant's eye and, later, from both that cause and a depressive illness. In those circumstances, he held that the incapacity benefit had not been paid "in respect of" the relevant accident, notwithstanding that the claimant had been deemed to be incapable of work on the strength of the medical certificates.

There is no provision for reducing the amount of recoverable benefit because some other benefit would have been paid to the claimant if the relevant accident or injury had not occurred or the relevant disease had not been developed. Furthermore, income support was paid "in respect of" an accident if it was paid on the basis of the claimant being incapable of work due to the accident, even if the claimant would have been paid income support on some other basis if the accident had not happened (*Hassall v Secretary of State for Social Security* [1995] 1 W.L.R. 812 (also reported as *R(CR) 1/95*)). Where a claimant might be at risk of having compensation reduced under s.8 in respect of post-accident benefits paid in place of pre-accident benefits, he or she may need to include a claim for the loss of the pre-accident benefits in the claim for compensation (*ibid.*, and *Neal v Bingle* [1998] Q.B. 466), although this is less of a problem under this Act than it was under the legislation it replaced. In *R1/06 (CRS)*, the Commissioner followed *Hassall* when deciding that the whole of income support awarded during the relevant period on the grounds of incapacity caused by the accident was recoverable notwithstanding that part of it was attributable to dependants acquired by the claimant after the relevant accident. It would not have been necessary for benefit to be paid in respect of the dependants if the accident had not occurred. In *R(CR) 1/96*, the claimant was a hairdresser injured in a road accident. She was awarded income support on the basis of incapacity for work and later, after she became capable of light work, on the basis that she was available for work, although she was still unfit for work as a hairdresser. The Commissioner held that the income support paid on the basis of the claimant's availability for work was paid "otherwise than in consequence of the accident". It is suggested that this part of the decision is based on a misreading of *Hassall* and would probably not be followed by the Upper Tribunal if the issue were to arise again. *Hassall* was concerned with income support paid on the basis of availability for work *before* the accident but there seems no reason why such a benefit should not be recoverable when a claimant has lost employment as the result of an accident, particularly as jobseeker's allowance, which has replaced income support when a claimant is capable of, and available for, work is clearly listed in Sch.2. However, the issue may not arise for determination because, in practice, the Secretary of State seldom seeks recovery of jobseeker's allowance (see *R(CR) 2/04*, at para.19).

There may be a question as to whether benefit paid in consequence of a disease for a period before the beginning of the "relevant period" is recoverable (see the note to s.3).

[[1] Lump sum payments: regulation-making power

1.301 **1A.**—(1) The Secretary of State may by regulations make provision about the recovery of the amount of a payment to which subsection (2) applies (a "lump sum payment") where—

(a) a compensation payment in consequence of a disease is made to or in respect of a person ("P") to whom, or in respect of whom, a lump sum payment has been, or is likely to be, made, and

(b) the compensation payment is made in consequence of the same disease as the lump sum payment.

(2) This subsection applies to—

(a) a payment made in accordance with the Pneumoconiosis etc. (Workers' Compensation) Act 1979 ("the 1979 Act"),

(b) a payment made in accordance with Part 4 of the Child Maintenance and Other Payments Act 2008, [[2]. . .]

(c) an extra-statutory payment (within the meaning given by subsection (5)(d) below) [[2] , and

(d) a payment under the Diffuse Mesothelioma Payment Scheme (established under the Mesothelioma Act 2014),

(but this subsection does not apply to a payment within paragraph (d) in a case where the compensation payment is itself such a payment).]

(3) Regulations under this section may, in particular—

(a) make provision about the recovery of the amount of a lump sum payment made to or in respect of a dependant of P;

(b) make provision enabling the recovery of the amount of a lump sum payment from a compensation payment (including provision enabling the recovery of an amount which reduces the compensation payment to nil);

(c) enable the amount of a lump sum payment made before commencement to be recovered from a compensation payment made after commencement;

(d) make provision about certificates in respect of lump sum payments;

(e) apply any provision of this Act, with or without modifications.

(4) References in subsection (1) to a payment made in consequence of a disease—

(a) are references to a payment made [2 as specified in section 1(2)(a) or (c)] in respect of the disease, but
(b) do not include references to a payment mentioned in Part 1 of Schedule 1.
(5) In this section—
(a) "commencement" means the date on which this section comes into force,
(b) "compensation payment" means a payment within section 1(1)(a) above,
(c) "dependant" has the meaning given by section 3 of the 1979 Act, and
(d) "extra-statutory payment" means a payment made by the Secretary of State to or in respect of a person following the rejection by the Secretary of State of a claim under the 1979 Act.]

Amendments

1. Child Maintenance and Other Payments Act 2008 s.54 (June 10, 2008 for the purpose only of making regulations and October 1, 2008 for other purposes).
2. Mesothelioma Act 2014 s.11 and Sch.1 paras 1 and 17 (March 31, 2014).

Definitions

"commencement"—see subs.(5).
"compensation payment"—*ibid.*
"dependant"—*ibid.*
"extra-statutory payment"—*ibid.*
"lump sum payment"—see subs.(1).
"payment"—see s.29.
"regulations"—*ibid.*

General Note

The Social Security (Recovery of Benefits) (Lump Sum Payments) Regulations 2008 are made under this section (and other provisions of this Act). They provide a scheme for the recovery of payments within the scope of subs.(2) that have been made by the Secretary of State in respect of death or disablement due to pneumoconiosis or mesothelioma from a person making a compensation payment on or after October 1, 2008 in respect of the relevant disease. The main differences between the scheme created by the Regulations and the scheme under the Act are that there is no five-year "relevant period" as there is under s.3 of the Act and that the Regulations also apply where the lump sum payment and compensation payment have been made to a dependant of the person who was suffering from the disease. Regulations 4 and 5 define the scope of the scheme, and s.1(3) of the Act applies with "Section 1A(1)(a)" substituted for "Subsection (1)(a)". Regulations 8–13 are broadly equivalent to ss.4–9 of the Act and reg.2 applies ss.10–34 (except ss.16, 24, 25, 32 and 34(2)) of, and Sch.1 to the Act, with modifications. Most of the modifications are minor, but s.15 is completely substituted. Regulations 7 and 14–19 make provision equivalent to regs 2, 9, 3, 4, 6, 10 and 11, respectively, of the Social Security (Recovery of Benefits) Regulations 1997. 1.302

Compensation payments to which this Act applies

2. This Act applies in relation to compensation payments made on or after the day on which this section comes into force, unless they are made in pursuance of a court order or agreement made before that day. 1.303

DEFINITION

"compensation payment"—see s.1(4)(b).

GENERAL NOTE

1.304 By virtue of the Social Security (Recovery of Benefits) Act 1997 (Commencement Order) 1997 (SI 1997/2085), this section came into force on October 6, 1997. Where a court order or agreement was made before that date, the recovery provisions of Pt IV of the Social Security Administration Act 1992 continued to apply, unless the accident or injury occurred before January 1, 1989 (or, in the case of a disease, benefit was claimed before January 1, 1989), in which case benefits were not recoverable by the Secretary of State at all (see s.81(7) of the 1992 Act). Regulation 12 of the Social Security (Recovery of Benefits) Regulations 1997 makes transitional provision for cases arising under the 1992 Act.

Lump sum payments within the scope of s.1A(2) may be recovered only where the compensation payment was made on or after October 1, 2008 (see reg.6 of the Social Security (Recovery of Benefits) (Lump Sum Payments) Regulations 2008).

"The relevant period"

1.305 **3.**—(1) In relation to a person ("the claimant") who has suffered any accident, injury or disease, "the relevant period" has the meaning given by the following subsections.

(2) Subject to subsection (4), if it is a case of accident or injury, the relevant period is the period of five years immediately following the day on which the accident or injury in question occurred.

(3) Subject to subsection (4), if it is a case of disease, the relevant period is the period of five years beginning with the date on which the claimant first claims a listed benefit in consequence of the disease.

(4) If at any time before the end of the period referred to in subsection (2) or (3)—

(a) a person makes a compensation payment in final discharge of any claim made by or in respect of the claimant and arising out of the accident, injury or disease, or

(b) an agreement is made under which an earlier compensation payment is treated as having been made in final discharge of any such claim,

the relevant period ends at that time.

DEFINITIONS

"claimant"—see subs.(1).
"compensation payment"—see s.1(4)(b).
"listed benefit"—see s.29.

GENERAL NOTE

1.306 Subsection (2) identifies the beginning of the "relevant period" if the compensation is paid in consequence of an accident or injury and subs.(3) identifies the beginning of the "relevant period" if compensation is paid in consequence of a disease.

It was observed in *R(CR) 4/03* that this section implies that "accident" and "injury" are indistinguishable in this Act in cases where the injury is due to an accident, because subs.(2) clearly envisages them occurring on the same specific date, rather than contemplating the injury being the, possibly long-standing and possibly delayed, result of an accident. It was also observed that this section requires a distinction to be drawn between an "injury" and a "disease" and that that might not always be straightforward. It may be noted that the Social Security (Industrial Injuries) (Prescribed Diseases) Regulations 1985 in fact include prescribed injuries as well as diseases (see also s.108(1)(b) of the Social Security Contributions and Benefits Act 1992). It is unclear when the "relevant period" begins if a disease is caused by an accident and benefit in respect of the disease is not claimed until some time after the date of the accident.

If s.1(1)(b) and (4)(c) and subs.(3) of this section are all read literally, it appears that there is a possibility of more than five years' worth of benefit being recovered where compensation is paid in consequence of a disease. That is because the "relevant period" appears to run from the date of claim, rather than the date from which benefit is awarded. Typically, arrears of disablement benefit in respect of a prescribed disease are paid in respect of a period of three months before the date of claim, although the payment of those arrears is obviously made after that date and within the "relevant period". It may be arguable that one or more of the provisions should not be read literally on the basis that it is unlikely that it was intended that more than five years' worth of benefit should be recoverable, although the counter-argument is that the possibility of arrears being caught should have been obvious to the draftsman and could easily have been avoided if it was unintended.

Subsections (2) and (3) provide for a "relevant period" of five years but subs. (4) shortens it if compensation is paid sooner. As benefits payable after the "relevant period" are not recoverable (s.1(1)(b) and (4)(c)) and are ignored in the calculation of damages (s.17), it is likely to be in the interests of a compensator and, usually, a claimant to settle a claim for compensation as soon as possible.

Certificates of recoverable benefits

Applications for certificates of recoverable benefits

4.—(1) Before a person ("the compensator") makes a compensation payment he must apply to the Secretary of State for a certificate of recoverable benefits. **1.307**

(2) Where the compensator applies for a certificate of recoverable benefits, the Secretary of State must—

(a) send to him a written acknowledgement of receipt of his application, and

(b) subject to subsection (7), issue the certificate before the end of the following period

(3) The period is—

(a) the prescribed period, or

(b) if there is no prescribed period, the period of four weeks,

which begins with the day following the day on which the application is received.

(4) The certificate is to remain in force until the date specified in it for that purpose.

(5) The compensator may apply for fresh certificates from time to time.

(6) Where a certificate of recoverable benefits ceases to be in force, the Secretary of State may issue a fresh certificate without an application for one being made.

(7) Where the compensator applies for a fresh certificate while a certificate ("the existing certificate") remains in force, the Secretary of State must issue the fresh certificate before the end of the following period.

(8) The period is—

(a) the prescribed period, or

(b) if there is no prescribed period, the period of four weeks,

which begins with the day following the day on which the existing certificate ceases to be in force.

(9) For the purposes of this Act, regulations may provide for the day on which an application for a certificate of recoverable benefits is to be treated as received.

DEFINITIONS

"compensator—see subs.(1).
"compensation payment"—see s.1(4)(b).
"existing certificate"—see subs.(7).
"prescribed—see s.29.
"recoverable benefit"—see s.1(4)(c).
"regulations"—see s.29.

GENERAL NOTE

1.308 No period has yet been prescribed for the purposes of subss.(3)(a) or (8)(a). By virtue of s.21, the consequence of the Secretary of State failing to issue a certificate of recoverable benefits within the specified period is that no benefits are recoverable and the victim is entitled to the full compensation without deduction. However, for s.21 to apply, the application for the certificate of recoverable benefits must have been accurate and it must have been acknowledged. The Compensation Recovery Unit asks compensators to tell them if an acknowledgement has not been received within 14 days.

Potential compensators must notify the Compensation Recovery Unit of any claim within 14 days of the claim being received (see s.23 and regulations made under it). This is usually done by completing form CRU1 (obtainable from the Unit's webpage: *https://www.gov.uk/government/collections/cru*) and it enables the Unit to start collecting the relevant information from the offices responsible for the payment of benefits. The Unit sends to the potential compensator a form CRU4 which is the form the compensator must use to obtain the certificate of recoverable benefits. A copy of the certificate is sent to both the compensator and the injured person (or other person expected to receive the compensation), thus ensuring compliance with s.5(5).

A fresh certificate, issued under subs.(5) after a previous certificate has expired, may include benefits not included in the previous certificate (*SSWP v Lanarkshire Health Board (CR)* [2014] UKUT 177 (AAC).

This section does not apply in respect of the recovery of lump sum payments within the scope of s.1A(2). See, instead, reg.8 of the Social Security (Recovery of Benefits) (Lump Sum Payments) Regulations 2008.

Subsection (9)

1.309 See reg.7(2) of the Social Security (Recovery of Benefits) Regulations 1997.

Information contained in certificates

1.310 **5.**—(1) A certificate of recoverable benefits must specify, for each recoverable benefit—

(a) the amount which has been or is likely to have been paid on or before a specified date, and
(b) if the benefit is paid or likely to be paid after the specified date, the rate and period for which, and the intervals at which, it is or is likely to be paid.

(2) In a case where the relevant period has ended before the day on which the Secretary of State receives the application for the certificate, the date specified in the certificate for the purposes of subsection (1) must be the day on which the relevant period ended.

(3) In any other case, the date specified for those purposes must not be earlier than the day on which the Secretary of State received the application.

(4) The Secretary of State may estimate, in such manner as he thinks fit, any of the amounts, rates or periods specified in the certificate.

(5) Where the Secretary of State issues a certificate of recoverable benefits, he must provide the information contained in the certificate to—

(a) the person who appears to him to be the injured person, or

(b) any person who he thinks will receive a compensation payment in respect of the injured person.

(6) A person to whom a certificate of recoverable benefits is issued or who is provided with information under subsection (5) is entitled to particulars of the manner in which any amount, rate or period specified in the certificate has been determined, if he applies to the Secretary of State for those particulars.

DEFINITIONS

"benefit"—see s.29.
"compensation payment"—see s.1(4)(b).
"injured person"—see s.1(4)(a).
"recoverable benefit"—see s.1(4)(c).
"the relevant period"—see s.3.

GENERAL NOTE

Note that only "recoverable" benefits should be specified on the certificate and, by virtue of s.1(1)(b) and (4)(c), that means benefits listed in col.2 of Sch.2 that have been, or are likely to be, paid to or for the victim during the relevant period *in respect of* the accident, injury or disease. Thus, not all benefits paid, or to be paid, during the relevant period should be specified in the certificate; only those that are attributable to the accident, injury or disease are recoverable. See the note to s.1. 1.311

For reviews of, and appeals against, certificates of recoverable benefits, see ss.10–14.

This section does not apply in respect of the recovery of lump sum payments within the scope of s.1A(2). See, instead, reg.9 of the Social Security (Recovery of Benefits) (Lump Sum Payments) Regulations 2008.

Liability of person paying compensation

Liability to pay Secretary of State amount of benefits

6.—(1) A person who makes a compensation payment in any case is liable to pay to the Secretary of State an amount equal to the total amount of the recoverable benefits. 1.312

(2) The liability referred to in subsection (1) arises immediately before the compensation payment or, if there is more than one, the first of them is made.

(3) No amount becomes payable under this section before the end of the period of 14 days following the day on which the liability arises.

(4) Subject to subsection (3), an amount becomes payable under this section at the end of the period of 14 days beginning with the day on which a certificate of recoverable benefits is first issued showing that the amount of recoverable benefit to which it relates has been or is likely to have been paid before a specified date.

DEFINITIONS

"amount of the recoverable benefits"—see s.9(4)(b).
"compensation payment"—see s.1(4)(b).
"recoverable benefit"—see s.1(4)(c).

GENERAL NOTE

1.313 The compensator may recoup some of the payment by reducing under s.8 the amount of compensation paid to the victim. However, the additional cost of benefits paid to the victim during the relevant period falls on the compensator. The compensator may not appeal against the certificate of recoverable benefits until the compensation has been paid (s.11(3)).

This section does not apply in respect of the recovery of lump sum payments within the scope of s.1A(2). See, instead, reg.10 of the Social Security (Recovery of Benefits) Lump Sum Payments) Regulations 2008.

In *R. (on the application of Aviva Insurance Ltd) v Secretary of State for Work and Pensions* [2022] EWCA Civ 15; [2022] 1 W.L.R. 2753, insurance companies argued that the 1997 Act was incompatible with the European Convention on Human Rights because, combined with other developments in the law concerned with liability to pay compensation to those suffering from certain industrial diseases, it had the effect of requiring insurers under policies underwritten before the Act was enacted to pay to the Secretary of State amounts that did not correspond to any damage caused by their insured where either the insured was guilty of contributory negligence or the insured was only one of two or more employers liable for such damage and the insured's contribution to the victim's exposure was limited. The High Court had largely accepted the argument, but the Court of Appeal rejected it and allowed the Secretary of State's appeal.

Recovery of payments due under section 6

1.314 **7.**—(1) This section applies where a person has made a compensation payment but—

(a) has not applied for a certificate of recoverable benefits, or
(b) has not made a payment to the Secretary of State under section 6 before the end of the period allowed under that section.

(2) The Secretary of State may—

(a) issue the person who made the compensation payment with a certificate of recoverable benefits, if none has been issued, or
(b) issue him with a copy of the certificate of recoverable benefits or (if more than one has been issued) the most recent one,

and (in either case) issue him with a demand that payment of any amount due under section 6 be made immediately.

(3) The Secretary of State may, in accordance with subsections (4) and (5), recover the amount for which a demand for payment is made under subsection (2) from the person who made the compensation payment.

(4) If the person who made the compensation payment resides or carries on business in England and Wales and [2 the county court] so orders, any amount recoverable under subsection (3) is recoverable [1 under section 85 of the County Courts Act 1984] or otherwise as if it were payable under an order of that court.

(5) If the person who made the payment resides or carries on business in Scotland, any amount recoverable under subsection (3) may be enforced in like manner as an extract registered decree arbitral bearing a warrant for execution issued by the sheriff court of any sheriffdom in Scotland.

(6) A document bearing a certificate which—

(a) is signed by a person authorised to do so by the Secretary of State, and

(b) states that the document, apart from the certificate, is a record of the amount recoverable under subsection (3),

is conclusive evidence that that amount is so recoverable.

(7) A certificate under subsection (6) purporting to be signed by a person authorised to do so by the Secretary of State is to be treated as so signed unless the contrary is proved.

AMENDMENTS

1. Tribunals, Courts and Enforcement Act 2007 s.62(3) and Sch.13 para.127 (April 6, 2014).

2. Crime and Courts Act 2013 s.17(5) and Sch.9 para.52 (April 22, 2014).

DEFINITIONS

"compensation payment"—see s.1(4)(b).
"payment"—see s.29.
"recoverable benefit"—see s.1(4)(c).

GENERAL NOTE

This section provides a simple way of recovering not only sums due under s.6 from compensators who have followed the proper procedures but also sums due from those who have failed to apply for a certificate of recoverable benefits at all. For reviews of, and appeals against, certificates issued under s.7(2)(a), see ss.10–14. **1.315**

This section does not apply in respect of the recovery of lump sum payments within the scope of s.1A(2). See, instead, reg.11 of the Social Security (Recovery of Benefits) (Lump Sum Payments) Regulations 2008.

Reduction of compensation payment

Reduction of compensation payment

8.—(1) This section applies in a case where, in relation to any head of compensation listed in column 1 of Schedule 2— **1.316**

(a) any of the compensation payment is attributable to that head, and

(b) any recoverable benefit is shown against that head in column 2 of the Schedule.

(2) In such a case, any claim of a person to receive the compensation payment is to be treated for all purposes as discharged if—

(a) he is paid the amount (if any) of the compensation payment calculated in accordance with this section, and
(b) if the amount of the compensation payment so calculated is nil, he is given a statement saying so by the person who (apart from this section) would have paid the gross amount of the compensation payment.

(3) For each head of compensation listed in column 1 of the Schedule for which paragraphs (a) and (b) of subsection (1) are met, so much of the gross amount of the compensation payment as is attributable to that head is to be reduced (to nil, if necessary) by deducting the amount of the recoverable benefit or, as the case may be, the aggregate amount of the recoverable benefits shown against it.

(4) Subsection (3) is to have effect as if a requirement to reduce a payment by deducting an amount which exceeds that payment were a requirement to reduce that payment to nil.

(5) The amount of the compensation payment calculated in accordance with this section is—
(a) the gross amount of the compensation payment, and
(b) the sum of the reductions made under subsection (3),
(and, accordingly, the amount may be nil).

Definitions

"amount of the recoverable benefit"—see s.9(4)(b).
"compensation payment"—see s.1(4)(b).
"gross amount of the compensation payment"—see s.9(4)(a).
"payment"—see s.29.
"recoverable benefit"—see s.1(4)(c).

General Note

1.317 Under the scheme replaced by this Act, the compensation payment was reduced by the whole amount of benefits paid within the relevant period in respect of the accident, injury or disease, even if the compensation had been awarded solely in respect of pain and suffering (*CSS/36/1992*). The effect was that the compensator almost always passed the entire cost of thc recovery of benefits on to the injured person. This could produce unfair results, because the claimant's compensation for pain and suffering was eroded, particularly in two types of cases. The first was where the benefits were paid in respect of, say, a need for personal care (i.e. where the care component of disability living allowance was paid) for which the claimant had not claimed compensation because, say, the care was provided by a spouse free of charge. To some extent this could be avoided by claimants inventing new and cumbersome claims for loss based on the effects of the legislation for recovery of benefits. The second was a less tractable problem, which arose because most claims for compensation are settled and there is likely to be an element of compromise. If a claim for loss of earnings was settled on the basis that was inconsistent with the basis of a claim for benefits, the recovery of benefits from the claimant could appear disproportionate (*CCR/8023/1995*). Whether that was unfair or not depended on whether or not the basis of settlement more accurately reflected the truth than the basis of the claim for benefit, but there could obviously be unfairness where there was a genuine compromise of the claim for compensation but the real burden of repaying the Secretary of State fell wholly on the claimant, rather than being shared by the compensator.

Under the new scheme, the compensator bears the cost of the alleged wrongdoing, being able to pass the cost on to the claimant only to the extent that he has paid relevant compensation to the claimant. Schedule 2 sets out three relevant heads of compensation (lost earnings, cost of care and loss of mobility) and sets out beside each of them the benefits in respect of which a deduction may be made under this section. Where a court makes an award of damages, it must quantify the amount allowed in respect of each of the heads of compensation set out in Sch.2 (s.15(2)). It is then for the compensator to make the appropriate deduction under s.8. Disputes as to the proper amount to be deducted under s.8 are not unusual. The legislation does not make explicit provision for the resolution of such disputes. Presumably, if the parties have become aware in the course of pre-trial negotiations that there is an issue as to the operation of s.8, the court can be asked to deal with that issue at the same time as assessing damages. What is quite clear is that the issue is to be determined by a court and not on an appeal to a tribunal under s.11. See *R(CR) 2/03* and *R(CR) 2/04*. In those decisions it was suggested that the issue could be determined in enforcement proceedings if it had not been dealt with by the judge at trial. Most cases, of course, are settled. Amendments to the Civil Procedure Rules have since made it clearer that the question whether a deduction is being properly made needs to be considered *before* a defendant's offer of settlement is accepted (see the note to s.16).

Where a payment into court is made, the compensator must state whether any deduction has been made under this section (see the note to s.16). Where a case is settled without there being a payment into court, the parties will no doubt have had regard to the operation of this section in reaching the settlement but it will usually be presumed that there was no reduction under this section unless the agreement expressly records such a reduction. It is important for the parties to record such a reduction if it is intended that the claimant should bring an appeal before a tribunal challenging the recoverability of benefits, because a claimant has a right of appeal only if there has been a reduction (see s.11(2)(b)). Otherwise only the compensator has a right of appeal. The question of who should bear the cost or risk of such an appeal can be a matter to be taken into account in negotiating a settlement but the settlement must be worded appropriately if it is to have the intended effect. Section 11(3) provides that an appeal may be brought only after the claim giving rise to the compensation payment has been disposed of, so that the Secretary of State does not get caught up in arguments between the claimant and the compensator as to the amount of compensation and the proper application of s.8. Where an application for review or an appeal by either party is successful in a case where there was a reduction of the compensation payment under this section, the refund is made to the compensator who must make a new calculation under this section (reg.11(4) and (5) of the Social Security (Recovery of Benefits) Regulations 1997). This has the effect that a compensator has no practical interest in appealing where the compensation payment has been reduced by the whole amount of recoverable benefits (*R(CR) 2/03*). The compensator has an interest only to the extent to which the amount of recoverable benefits *has not* been reflected in a reduction under this section, just as a claimant has an interest only to the extent to which the amount of recoverable benefits *has* been reflected in a reduction. The fact that a compensator clearly had no right to make a reduction under s.8 in respect of employment and support allowance because the injured person had not claimed compensation in respect of lost earnings does not preclude the injured person from appealing when a reduction has in fact been made, but the illegality of the reduction is not a relevant issue on the appeal (*TC v SSWP (CR)* [2018] UKUT 272 (AAC)).

Where, following a review or appeal, a compensator is obliged to make a further payment to the Secretary of State in a case where there was a reduction under this section, there are limited circumstances in which the reduction may be recalculated and the claimant may be required to make a refund to the compensator (*ibid.*, reg.11(6) and (7)).

Although neither s.8 nor Sch.2 refers to the period in respect of which recoverable **1.318**
benefits may be taken into account, it was suggested in *R(CR) 2/04* that benefits

should be deducted under s.8 only in so far as they are payable in respect of the period for which compensation in respect of the relevant head of damages has been paid. The Commissioner also suggested that the calculation under s.8 should be made *before* the amount of compensation is reduced to take account of contributory negligence. However, as he also held that the proper operation of s.8 was a matter for the courts and not for tribunals or Commissioners, those suggestions are obiter dicta.

This section does not apply in respect of the recovery of lump sum payments within the scope of s.1A(2). See, instead, reg.12 of the Social Security (Recovery of Benefits) Lump Sum Payments) Regulations 2008. Nor does it apply in respect of the recovery of payments under the Diffuse Mesothelioma Payment Scheme established under the Mesothelioma Act 2014. See instead s.8A, below.

[1 Reduction of payment under Diffuse Mesothelioma Payment Scheme

1.319 **8A.—**(1) This section applies instead of section 8 in a case where the compensation payment is a payment under the Diffuse Mesothelioma Payment Scheme.

(2) The gross amount of the compensation payment—

(a) is to be reduced by the amount of the recoverable benefit, and

(b) accordingly, is to be reduced to nil in any case where the amount of the recoverable benefit is equal to or greater than the gross amount of the compensation payment.

(3) Any claim of a person to receive the compensation payment is to be treated for all purposes as discharged if—

(a) the person is paid the gross amount of the compensation payment less the amount of the recoverable benefit, or

(b) the amount of the recoverable benefit is equal to or greater than the gross amount of the compensation payment and the person is given a statement by the scheme administrator saying that the compensation payment has been reduced to nil.]

AMENDMENT

1. Mesothelioma Act 2014 s.11 and Sch.1 paras. 1 and 3 (March 31, 2014).

DEFINITIONS

"compensation payment"—see s.1(4)(b).
"gross amount of the compensation payment"—see s.8(4)(a).
"payment"—see s.29.
"recoverable benefit"—see s.1(4)(c).
"scheme administrator"—see s.29.

GENERAL NOTE

1.320 The Diffuse Mesothelioma Payment Scheme is established under the Mesothelioma Act 2014 (see Vol.I).

Section 8: supplementary

1.321 **9.**—(1) A person who makes a compensation payment calculated in accordance with section 8 [1 or 8A] must inform the person to whom the payment is made—

(a) that the payment has been so calculated, and

(b) of the date for payment by reference to which the calculation has been made.

(2) If the amount of a compensation payment calculated in accordance with section 8 [1 or 8A] is nil, a person giving a statement saying so is to be treated for the purposes of this Act as making a payment within section 1(1)(a) on the day on which he gives the statement.

(3) Where a person—

(a) makes a compensation payment calculated in accordance with section 8 [1 or 8A], and

(b) if the amount of the compensation payment so calculated is nil, gives a statement saying so,

he is to be treated, for the purpose of determining any rights and liabilities in respect of contribution or indemnity, as having paid the gross amount of the compensation payment.

(4) For the purposes of this Act—

(a) the gross amount of the compensation payment is the amount of the compensation payment apart from section 8 [1 or 8A], and

(b) the amount of any recoverable benefit is the amount determined in accordance with the certificate of recoverable benefits.

AMENDMENT

1. Mesothelioma Act 2014 s.11 and Sch.1 paras. 1 and 8 (March 31, 2014).

DEFINITIONS

"compensation payment"—see s.1(4)(b).
"gross amount of the compensation payment"—see subs.(4)(a).
"payment"—see s.29.
"recoverable benefit"—see s.1(4)(c).

GENERAL NOTE

This section does not apply in respect of the recovery of lump sum payments within the scope of s.1A(2). See, instead, reg.13 of the Social Security (Recovery of Benefits) (Lump Sum Payments) Regulations 2008. Presumably it is intended that the heading of the section should be read since the 2014 amendments as referring to s.8A as well as s.8. 1.322

Reviews and appeals

Review of certificates of recoverable benefits

10.—[1(1) Any certificate of recoverable benefits may be reviewed by the Secretary of State— 1.323

(a) either within the prescribed period or in prescribed circumstances; and

(b) either on an application made for the purpose or on his own initiative.]

(2) On a review under this section the Secretary of State may either—

(a) confirm the certificate, or

(b) (subject to subsection (3)) issue a fresh certificate containing such variations as he considers appropriate[1 or

(c) revoke the certificate.]

(3) The Secretary of State may not vary the certificate so as to increase the total amount of the recoverable benefits unless it appears to him that the variation is required as a result of the person who applied for the certificate supplying him with incorrect or insufficient information.

[2 (4) The scheme administrator of the Diffuse Mesothelioma Payment Scheme may not apply for a review under this section.]

AMENDMENTS

1. Social Security Act 1998 Sch.7 para.149 (March 4, 1999 for the making of regulations, November 29, 1999 for other purposes).
2. Mesothelioma Act 2014 s.11 and Sch.1 paras 1 and 4 (March 31, 2014).

DEFINITIONS

"amount of the recoverable benefits"—see s.9(4)(b).
"prescribed"—see s.29.
"recoverable benefit"—see s.1(4)(c).
"regulations"—see s.29.
"scheme administrator"–*ibid.*

GENERAL NOTE

1.324 This section is applied with modifications to cases concerned with the recovery of payments within the scope of s.1A(2) (see the Social Security (Recovery of Benefits) (Lump Sum Payments) Regulations 2008 reg.2 and Sch.1 para.3).

Subsection (1)

1.325 Note that the Social Security Act 1998 does not abolish the concept of review in this context. No period has been prescribed, so an application for review may be made at any time. The circumstances in which a decision may be reviewed are prescribed by regs 9 and 9ZA of the Social Security and Child Support (Decisions and Appeals) Regulations 1999 and are very broad.

Generally, a certificate of recoverable benefits is accompanied by a notice to the effect that there is a right of appeal in relation to the certificate only if the Secretary of State has considered an application for review of the certificate, in which case an application for review is a necessary precursor to an appeal (see reg.9ZB of the Social Security and Child Support (Decisions and Appeals) Regulations 1999). Note that subs.(3) provides protection on a review that is lacking on an appeal. There does not seem to be any reason why there should not be a further review after an appeal has been brought. In *CCR/3391/2005*, it was said that the Secretary of State should always consider reviewing a decision against which an appeal has been brought, so as to prevent unnecessary appeals reaching tribunals. "In effect, a submission to a tribunal should be an explanation for the Secretary of State not reviewing the decision in the light of the grounds of appeal." That approach is still necessary where the appellant has provided on the appeal evidence that was not before the Secretary of State either when the certificate of recoverable benefits was issued or when the benefits concerned were awarded so that there is a factual issue upon which the Secretary of State has not previously made a decision.

Subsection (3)

1.326 This is an important provision. Once a certificate has been issued, it cannot be varied on review so as to increase the amount of recoverable benefits unless the person who applied for the certificate (the compensator) caused the error. Where the compensator has provided incorrect or insufficient information as a result of being given incorrect or insufficient information by a claimant who knew it to be incorrect or insufficient and who provided it with intent to limit the amount of a reduction under s.8, the compensator may be able to recover from the claimant some or all of the additional money due to the Secretary of State (reg.11(6) and (7) of the Social Security (Recovery of Benefits) Regulations 1997). As the Secretary of State has only four weeks in which to issue the certificate (s.4(3)(b) and (8)(b)), it may occasionally be impossible to obtain accurate information and resort may be had to estimation (s.5(4)). If lack of information or an inaccurate estimate results in a calculation that turns out to be unfavourable to the Secretary of State, he is nevertheless bound by it until the certificate expires under s.4(4). However, any new certificate issued in respect of a later period may list the benefit omitted from the earlier one (*SSWP v Lanarkshire Health Board (CR)* [2014] UKUT 177 (AAC), in which this statement was expressly approved). Furthermore, subs.(3) does not prevent the amount of recoverable benefits from being increased on an appeal (*CSCR/1/1995*).

Appeals against certificates of recoverable benefits

11.—(1) An appeal against a certificate of recoverable benefits may be made on the ground— **1.327**

(a) that any amount, rate or period specified in the certificate is incorrect, or

(b) that listed benefits which have been, or are likely to be, paid otherwise than in respect of the accident, injury or disease in question have been brought into account [1 or

(c) that listed benefits which have not been, and are not likely to be, paid to the injured person during the relevant period have been brought into account, or

(d) that the payment on the basis of which the certificate was issued is not a payment within section 1(1)(a)].

(2) An appeal under this section may be made by—

(a) the person who applied for the certificate of recoverable benefits, or

[1(aa) (in a case where the certificate was issued under section 7(2)(a)) the person to whom it was so issued, or]

(b) (in a case where the amount of the compensation payment has been calculated under section 8 [5 or 8A]) the injured person or other person to whom the payment is made

[5 but the scheme administrator of the Diffuse Mesothelioma Payment Scheme may not appeal under this section.]

[4 (2A) Regulations may provide that, in such cases or circumstances as may be prescribed, an appeal may be made under this section only if the Secretary of State has reviewed the certificate under section 10.

(2B) The regulations may in particular provide that that condition is met only where—

(a) the review by the Secretary of State was on an application,

(b) the Secretary of State considered issues of a specified description, or

(c) the review by the Secretary of State satisfied any other condition specified in the regulations.]

(3) No appeal may be made under this section until—

(a) the claim giving rise to the compensation payment has been finally disposed of, and

(b) the liability under section 6 has been discharged.

(4) For the purposes of subsection (3)(a), if an award of damages in respect of a claim has been made under or by virtue of—

(a) section 32A(2)(a) of the [3 Senior Courts Act 1981],

(b) section 12(2)(a) of the Administration of Justice Act 1982, or

(c) section 51(2)(a) of the County Courts Act 1984,

(orders for provisional damages in personal injury cases), the claim is to be treated as having been finally disposed of.

(5) Regulations may make provision—

(a) as to the manner in which, and the time within which, appeals under this section may be made,

(b) [2 . . .] and

(c) for the purpose of enabling any such appeal [4 (or, where in accordance with regulations under subsection (2A) there is no right of appeal, any purported appeal)] to be treated as an application for review under section 10.

(6) [1 . . .]

AMENDMENTS

1. Social Security Act 1998 Sch.7 para.150 and Sch.8 (November 29, 1999).
2. Transfer of Tribunal Functions Order 2008 (SI 2008/2833) Sch.3 paras 138 and 139 (November 3, 2008).
3. Constitutional Reform Act 2005 s.59(5) and Sch.11 para.1(2) (October 1, 2009).
4. Welfare Reform Act 2012 s.102(6) and Sch.11 paras 9 and 10 (February 25, 2013 for regulation-making purposes and April 29, 2013 for all other purposes).
5. Mesothelioma Act 2014 s.11 and Sch.1 paras 1, 5 and 8 (March 31, 2014).

DEFINITIONS

"compensation payment"—see s.1(4)(b).
"injured person"—see s.1(4)(a).
"listed benefit"—see s.29.
"payment"—*ibid.*
"recoverable benefit"—see s.1(4)(c).
"regulations"—see s.29.
"scheme administrator"—*ibid.*

GENERAL NOTE

1.328 This section is applied with modifications to cases concerned with the recovery of payments within the scope of s.1A(2) (see the Social Security (Recovery of Benefits) (Lump Sum Payments) Regulations 2008 reg.2 and Sch.1 para.4).

Subsection (1)

1.329 Any appeal is heard by the First-tier Tribunal (see s.12).

It is not easy to see the distinction between paras (a) and (c), save perhaps that para.(a) more clearly allows a challenge to the Secretary of State's view as to the appropriate "relevant period". Both paragraphs appear to permit an appeal based on a dispute as to the amount of benefit actually paid to the claimant.

Paragraph (b) permits an appeal where there is a dispute as to whether benefit was paid "in respect of" the relevant accident, injury or disease (see the note to s.1). This is the ground on which most appeals are brought. The burden of proving that benefit was paid otherwise than in respect of the relevant accident, injury or disease is placed on the appellant but the Secretary of State can be expected to provide a prima facie justification for the inclusion of the benefits in the certificate in the first place (*CCR/4307/2000*) and an adverse inference may be drawn if he fails to do so. A tribunal considering an appeal under this section is entitled to reach a decision that is inconsistent with the decision awarding benefit because benefit that ought not to have been awarded cannot be said to have been awarded "in respect of" the relevant accident, injury or disease (*R(CR) 1/02*, a decision of a Tribunal of Commissioners, and *Eagle Star Insurance v Department for Social Development* [2001] NICA 4 (reported as *R1/01 (CRS)*), a decision of the Court of Appeal in Northern Ireland). It follows that, on an appeal brought under this section as modified and applied to the recovery under the Social Security (Recovery of Benefits) (Lump Sum Payments) Regulations 2008 of lump sum payments made under the Pneumoconiosis etc. (Workers' Compensation) Act

1979, the compensator is in principle entitled to argue that the payment made to the claimant under the 1979 Act ought not to have been made (*Aviva Insurance Ltd v SSWP* [2015] UKUT 613 (AAC); [2016] AACR 29). Similarly, a tribunal is entitled to find that benefit was paid at too high a rate (*R(CR) 1/03*). In *C2/01–02(CRS)*, a Commissioner in Northern Ireland held that it was not the tribunal's function to substitute their judgment for the authority who awarded benefit and that the question was whether benefit had reasonably been awarded. Thus, if the awarding authority could properly have awarded benefit in respect of the relevant accident, injury or disease on the evidence before them and there is no new evidence, it will be impossible to show that benefit was awarded otherwise than in respect of the accident, injury or disease. However, in many cases a tribunal considering an appeal under s.11 will have before them evidence that was not before the authority awarding benefit and in those circumstances the tribunal's judgment will be the only one that can be applied. Moreover, some claimants are not required to be assessed in the usual way and are treated as being incapable of work or having limited capability for work under various deeming provisions. Again, a submission that benefit was not properly paid would have to focus on the terms of those regulations. In particular, before such an initial assessment is actually carried out, a claimant is usually treated as incapable of work on the basis of medical certificates provided by a doctor. In *R(CR) 2/02*, it was suggested by the Tribunal of Commissioners that as long as a claimant was providing such certificates referring to the relevant disease, benefit was properly awarded in respect of that disease whether or not the claimant was actually incapable of work or would actually have satisfied a personal capability assessment. Doubtless, there would be exceptions where, for instance, a claimant was working and so was required to be treated as capable of work or as not having limited capability for work. It may also be arguable that, where a claimant had obtained the medical certificate by misleading his doctor as to the severity of his or her condition or, perhaps, where the doctor plainly ought not to have given a certificate, benefit can be said not to have been properly paid in respect of the relevant accident, injury or disease but, given that a medical certificate merely certifies that the claimant was advised not to work and is not actually a certificate that the person is incapable of work (see Sch.1 to the Social Security (Medical Evidence) Regulations 1976), it will not be easy to demonstrate that a certificate was inappropriate. In any event, *R(CR) 2/02* was distinguished in *R(CR) 1/04*. In the latter case, incapacity benefit had been awarded pending the carrying out of a personal capability assessment on the basis of medical certificates supplied by the claimant's doctor, which referred to an eye injury sustained when a fire extinguisher had gone off accidentally. The Commissioner found that the eye injury caused by the fire extinguisher had in fact had no disabling effect on the claimant after a week and that the disablement was the result of a pre-existing condition in the claimant's eye and, later, from both that cause and a depressive illness. In those circumstances, he held that the incapacity benefit had not been paid "in respect of" the relevant accident, notwithstanding that the claimant had been deemed to be incapable of work on the strength of the medical certificates.

Paragraph (d) permits an appeal where there is a dispute as to whether the Act applies at all because it is claimed that compensation was not paid "in consequence of any accident, injury or disease". Insofar as it might also permit an appeal where there is a dispute as to whether the payment of compensation was made in respect of a particular accident, injury or disease, it is not clear that, in practice, it adds anything to para.(b), given the words "in question" in that paragraph (see *CCR/2232/2006* and *R(CR) 1/07*). **1.330**

Note that no appeal lies under this section against a compensator's decision to make a reduction under s.8. Any dispute about such a reduction must be determined by the court seised of the claim for compensation, either when compensation is assessed or in enforcement proceedings. A claimant should not accept a payment into court or an offer of settlement if he or she is not prepared to accept that s.8 has been applied reasonably or at least that the net award of compensation is adequate (see *R(CR) 2/03* and *R(CR) 2/04*).

Subsection (2)

1.331 A compensator always has a right of appeal but in fact has no interest in appealing insofar as the amount of compensation was reduced under s.8, due to the effect of reg.11(5) of the Social Security (Recovery of Benefits) Regulations 1997 which requires the recalculation of the s.8 reduction if the appeal is successful (*R(CR) 2/03*). An injured person has a right of appeal only if there has been a s.8 reduction and, indeed, may appeal even if the compensator plainly had no right to make the reduction, although the illegality of the reduction is not a relevant issue in such a case (*TC v SSWP (CR)* [2018] UKUT 272 (AAC)). In any appeal under this section, any other person who could have appealed is made a party to the proceedings (see the definition of "respondent" in the Tribunal Procedure (First-tier Tribunal) (Social Entitlement Chamber) Rules 2008). In *CCR/3425/2003*, the Commissioner said that, as a claimant was entitled to be a party to a compensator's appeal only where there had been a deduction under s.8, it was to be inferred that the right to respond arose because the claimant might be entitled to a refund from the compensator under reg.11(5) of the 1997 Regulations, rather than because the Secretary of State might decide to revise or supersede an award of benefit, if the compensator was successful. Accordingly, as the claimant did not support the compensator's appeal and did not seek a refund, he had suffered no material loss when he had been misled by a letter from the Department suggesting that he need not attend the hearing.

If both the claimant and the compensator appeal, the Compensation Recovery Unit should inform the tribunal and ask for the appeals to be heard together (*CCR/2231/2003*).

Subssections (2A) and (2B)

1.332 See regs 9ZB and 29(6) of the Social Security and Child Support (Decisions and Appeals) Regulations 1999, which generally require a person to seek a review of a decision before lodging an appeal but enable the Secretary of State to treat a purported appeal as an application for a review.

Subsection (3)

1.333 An appeal cannot be brought until after the compensation claim has been fully disposed of and the s.6 payment has been paid to the Secretary of State. A claim is not finally disposed of until any appeal against a court's order or judgment is determined (*Williams v Devon CC* [2003] EWCA Civ. 365 (*The Times*, March 26, 2003)) and so presumably the reference to the s.6 payment having been made must include any further payments required under reg.9 of the Social Security (Recovery of Benefits) Regulations 1997 in the event of a claimant's appeal being successful and requiring a further payment of compensation to be made. Generally, payment of compensation is made following the settlement of a claim, which implies agreement by the claimant as to the net amount of compensation to be paid after any reduction under s.8. However, where a court assesses compensation, it is not obliged at that stage to assess the appropriate amount of any reduction under s.8. That is left to the compensator. It was suggested in *R(CR) 2/04* that if the claimant wishes to challenge the amount of a s.8 reduction, he or she can do so in enforcement proceedings brought on the basis that the compensator has not fully satisfied the court's judgment.

See r.22(2)(d) of the Tribunal Procedure (First-tier Tribunal) (Social Entitlement Chamber) Rules 2008 for the time within which an appeal to a tribunal must be brought.

Subsection (5)

1.334 Regulations made under this subsection have all been revoked except for reg.29(6) of the Social Security and Child Support (Decisions and Appeals) Regulations 1999, made under subs.(5)(c). Note that a tribunal considering an appeal under this section has no express power either to refer the victim for examination or to examine him themselves because the primary legislation contains no power equivalent to s.20 of the Social Security Act 1998 under which r.25 of the Tribunal Procedure (First-tier Tribunal) (Social Entitlement Chamber) Rules 2008 is made. However, the Secretary of State may be directed to arrange for an examination and report.

Reference of questions to [2 the First-tier Tribunal]

12.—[1(1) The Secretary of State must refer an appeal under section 11 to an [2 the First-tier Tribunal].] 1.335

(2) [1. . .]

(3) In determining [1 any appeal under section 11], the tribunal must take into account any decision of a court relating to the same, or any similar, issue arising in connection with the accident, injury or disease in question.

(4) On [1 an appeal under section 11 [2 the First-tier Tribunal]] may either—

(a) confirm the amounts, rates and periods specified in the certificate of recoverable benefits, or

(b) specify any variations which are to be made on the issue of a fresh certificate under subsection (5) [1 or

(c) declare that the certificate of recoverable benefits is to be revoked.]

(5) When the Secretary of State has received [1the decision of the tribunal on the appeal under section 11, he must in accordance with that decision] either—

(a) confirm the certificate against which the appeal was brought, or

(b) issue a fresh certificate [1 or

(c) revoke the certificate.]

(6) [1 . . .]

(7) Regulations [1 . . .] may (among other things) provide for the nondisclosure of medical advice or medical evidence given or submitted following a reference under subsection (1).

(8) [1 . . .]

AMENDMENTS

1. Social Security Act 1998 Sch.7 para.151 and Sch.8 (November 29, 1999).

2. Transfer of Tribunal Functions Order 2008 (SI 2008/2833) Sch.3 paras 138 and 140 (November 3, 2008).

DEFINITIONS

"recoverable benefit"—see s.1(4)(c).

"regulations"—see s.29.

GENERAL NOTE

This section is applied with modifications to cases concerned with the recovery of payments within the scope of s.1A(2) (see the Social Security (Recovery of Benefits) (Lump Sum Payments) Regulations 2008 reg.2 and Sch.1 para.5). 1.336

Subsection (1)

The primary legislation includes no provision equivalent to s.20 of the Social Security Act 1998. Therefore, even when the tribunal includes a medically qualified panel member, the tribunal has no express power to examine the victim, although there is also no express prohibition on such an examination. Presumably the victim 1.337

could consent to an examination. There is not even any express power to refer a victim for examination but it is difficult to see any objection to there being such a reference, provided the victim were to consent and some arrangement could be made for the payment of an examining doctor.

Subsection (3)

1.338 Note that the tribunal need only "take into account" any decision of a court; it is not bound by such a decision. This is partly because it would be unfair on the Secretary of State to be bound by a decision in proceedings to which he was not a party (*R(CR) 1/02*). Most proceedings before courts are settled and do not result in reasoned decisions but claimants and compensators are expected to act before a tribunal in a manner that is consistent with the way they have settled a case or, in the case of a claimant, have claimed benefits. Thus a tribunal should be slow to accept an argument advanced by a compensator that is inconsistent with a section 8 deduction that it has made, unless the claimant agrees that the deduction should not have been made, and, equally, a tribunal should be slow to accept an argument advanced by a claimant that is inconsistent with the basis on which compensation was obtained or benefits were claimed (*R(CR) 2/03*). Where a claimant had accepted £50,000 in respect of a claim that injury in respect of which benefits had been paid was due solely to medical negligence, he was not entitled to argue that the benefits were paid otherwise than in respect of that injury (*CCR/2232/2006*).

Similarly, where a compensator had settled a claim made on the basis that psychiatric injury was due to a particular cause, the compensator was not entitled to argue that the injury was due wholly to a cause not covered by the claim for compensation (*R(CR) 1/07*).

Subsection (4)

1.339 In *CCR/4/1993* and *CSCR/1/1995*, Commissioners held that, on appeals, the Secretary of State was entitled to refer to the tribunal questions which related to benefits that were not on the original "certificates of total benefit" (the forerunners of certificates of recoverable benefits). In the first case the Commissioner held that, on an appeal, all matters were at large. In the second case, the Commissioner took a narrower approach and held that a tribunal was strictly confined to the issues referred to it by the Secretary of State but that, in that case, the new benefits were within the scope of the reference. The Commissioner noted the contrast between the position on appeal and the limitation, now contained in s.10(3), with respect to reviews and warned of the perils of appealing.

Under the new legislation as amended, what are before the tribunal by virtue of subs.(1) are the "appeal" under s.11 and all matters that can fairly be said to arise within that appeal—and within the jurisdiction of the tribunal bearing in mind its constitution (see the note to subs.(1) above). There is no provision in this Act equivalent to s.12(8)(a) of the Social Security Act 1998, but it is suggested that the approach should be the same: the tribunal may deal with issues not expressly raised by the notice of appeal but is not bound to do so, provided it exercises that discretion judicially.

Subsection (7)

1.340 Since Tribunal Procedure Rules have replaced regulations made by the Secretary of State, this provision has fallen into disuse. See now r.14(2)–(6) of the Tribunal Procedure (First-tier Tribunal) (Social Entitlement Chamber) Rules 2008.

Appeal to [2Upper Tribunal]

1.341 **13.**—(1) [2. . .]

(2) An appeal [2 to the Upper Tribunal under section 11 of the Tribunals, Courts and Enforcement Act 2007 which arises from any

decision of the First-tier Tribunal under section 12 of this Act] may be made by—

(a) the Secretary of State,

(b) the person who applied for the certificate of recoverable benefits,

[1(bb) (in a case where that certificate was issued under section 7(2)(a)) the person to whom it was issued, or]

(c) (in a case where the amount of the compensation payment has been calculated in accordance with section 8 [3 or 8A]) the injured person or other person to whom the payment is made

[3 but the scheme administrator of the Diffuse Mesothelioma Payment Scheme may not appeal under this section.]

(3) [2. . .]

(4) [1. . .]

AMENDMENTS

1. Social Security Act 1998 Sch.7 para.152 and Sch.8 (November 29, 1999).

2. Transfer of Tribunal Functions Order 2008 (SI 2008/2833) Sch.3 paras 138 and 141 (November 3, 2008).

3. Mesothelioma Act 2014 s.11 and Sch.1 paras 1, 6 and 8 (March 31, 2014).

DEFINITIONS

"compensation payment"—see s.1(4)(b).
"injured person"—see s.1(4)(a).
"scheme administrator"—see s.29.

GENERAL NOTE

This section is applied with modifications to cases concerned with the recovery of payments within the scope of s.1A(2) (see the Social Security (Recovery of Benefits) (Lump Sum Payments) Regulations 2008 reg.2 and Sch.1 para.6). It does not add anything to s.11(2) of the 2007 Act. **1.342**

Reviews and appeals: supplementary

14.—(1) This section applies in cases where a fresh certificate of recoverable benefits is issued as a result of a review under section 10 or an appeal under section 11. **1.343**

(2) If—

(a) a person has made one or more payments to the Secretary of State under section 6, and

(b) in consequence of the review or appeal, it appears that the total amount paid is more than the amount that ought to have been paid,

regulations may provide for the Secretary of State to pay the difference to that person, or to the person to whom the compensation payment is made, or partly to one and partly to the other.

(3) If—

(a) a person has made one or more payments to the Secretary of State under section 6, and

(b) in consequence of the review or appeal, it appears that the total amount paid is less than the amount that ought to have been paid,

regulations may provide for that person to pay the difference to the Secretary of State.

(4) Regulations under this section may provide—

(a) for the re-calculation in accordance with section 8 [1 or 8A] of the amount of any compensation payment,
(b) for giving credit for amounts already paid, and
(c) for the payment by any person of any balance or the recovery from any person of any excess,

and may provide for any matter by modifying this Act.

AMENDMENT

1. Mesothelioma Act 2014 s.11 and Sch.1 paras 1 and 8 (March 31, 2014).

DEFINITIONS

"compensation payment"—see s.1(4)(b).
"payment"—see s.29.
"recoverable benefit"—see s.1(4)(c).
"regulations"—see s.29.

GENERAL NOTE

1.344 See reg.11 of the Social Security (Recovery of Benefits) Regulations 1997.

This section is applied with modifications to cases concerned with the recovery of payments within the scope of s.1A(2) (see the Social Security (Recovery of Benefits) (Lump Sum Payments) Regulations 2008 reg.2 and Sch.1 para.7). Regulation 19 of the 2008 Regulations makes provision equivalent to reg.11 of the 1997 Regulations.

Courts

Court orders

1.345 **15.**—(1) This section applies where a court makes an order for a compensation payment to be made in any case, unless the order is made with the consent of the injured person and the person by whom the payment is to be made.

(2) The court must, in the case of each head of compensation listed in column 1 of Schedule 2 to which any of the compensation payment is attributable, specify in the order the amount of the compensation payment which is attributable to that head.

DEFINITIONS

"compensation payment"—see s.1(4)(b).
"injured person"—see s.1(4)(a).

GENERAL NOTE

1.346 A substituted version of this section is applied to cases concerned with the recovery of payments within the scope of s.1A(2) (see the Social Security (Recovery of Benefits) (Lump Sum Payments) Regulations 2008 reg.2 and Sch.1 para.8).

Subsection (2)

1.347 A court hearing a case within five years of a relevant accident must specify the amount of the compensation awarded that was attributable to any particular head in col.1 of Sch.2 in respect of the whole five-year period, because the court cannot know when payment of the sum awarded will actually be made (*Mitchell v Laing*,

1998 S.C. 342). Nonetheless, the compensator was to deduct only those benefits that had been paid or were due to be paid up until the date of the payment of the sum awarded by the court.

The court's view must be taken into account by any tribunal considering an appeal against a certificate of recoverable benefits (see s.12(3)) and, presumably, also by the Secretary of State considering a review (see reg.9(d) of the Social Security and Child Support (Decisions and Appeals) Regulations 1999). However, the principal purpose of s.15(2) is to enable s.8 to be operated properly. There is no express requirement to state the period in respect of which each head of the compensation is paid (which, it has been suggested in *R(CR) 2/04*, is a material fact limiting the amount of any deduction under s.8) but that information will usually be clear from the court's reasoning.

Payments into court

16.—(1) Regulations may make provision (including provision modifying this Act) for any case in which a payment into court is made. **1.348**

(2) The regulations may (among other things) provide—

(a) for the making of a payment into court to be treated in prescribed circumstances as the making of a compensation payment,

(b) for application for, and issue of, certificates of recoverable benefits, and

(c) for the relevant period to be treated as ending on a date determined in accordance with the regulations.

(3) Rules of court may make provision governing practice and procedure in such cases.

(4) This section does not extend to Scotland.

DEFINITIONS

"compensation payment"—see s.1(4)(b).
"recoverable benefit"—see s.1(4)(c).
"payment"—see s.29.
"prescribed"—*ibid.*
"regulations"—*ibid.*
"relevant period"—see s.3.

GENERAL NOTE

Subssections (1) and (2)

Regulation 8 of the Social Security (Recovery of Benefits) Regulations 1997 provides that a payment into court is treated as a compensation payment under the Social Security (Recovery of Benefits) Act 1997 and a current certificate of recoverable benefits must be lodged with it (reg.8(1)). However, the liability of the compensator under s.6 of the Act to pay the Secretary of State the recoverable benefits does not arise until notice has been given that all or part of the payment into court has been paid to the victim (reg.8(2)). If the payment into court is accepted by the victim within 21 days, the "relevant period" under s.3 is taken to have ended on the date the money, or the last part of it, was paid into court (reg.8(3)). If, however, the case is settled after that 21 days have expired and the money is paid to the victim by consent in satisfaction of the claim, the "relevant period" is taken to have ended on the date on which the application to the court for the payment is made (reg.8(4)). If all or part of the money in court is paid to the victim following an order of the court, the "relevant period" is taken to have ended on the date of the order (reg.8(5)). If the whole of the payment into court is returned to the defendant, the making of the payment into court ceases to be treated as the making of a compensation payment and there is no liability to pay anything to the Secretary of State (reg.8(7)). **1.349**

Subsection (3)

1.350 Part 36 of the Civil Procedure Rules deals with offers to settle cases in England and Wales. Rule 36.22 (which is to be renumbered as r.36.20 with effect from October 1, 2023) provides—

"(1) In this rule and rule 36.11—

(a) "the 1997 Act" means the Social Security (Recovery of Benefits) Act 1997;
(b) "the 2008 Regulations" means the Social Security (Recovery of Benefits) (Lump Sum Payments) Regulations 2008;
(c) "recoverable amount" means—
  (i) "recoverable benefits" as defined in section 1(4)(c) of the 1997 Act; and
  (ii) "recoverable lump sum payments" as defined in regulation 4 of the 2008 Regulations;
(d) "deductible amount" means—
  (i) any benefits by the amount of which damages are to be reduced in accordance with section 8 of, and Schedule 2 to, the 1997 Act ("deductible benefits"); and
  (ii) any lump sum payment by the amount of which damages are to be reduced in accordance with regulation 12 of the 2008 Regulations ("deductible lump sum payments"); and
(e) "certificate"—
  (i) in relation to recoverable benefits is construed in accordance with the provisions of the 1997 Act; and
  (ii) in relation to recoverable lump sum payments has the meaning given in section 29 of the 1997 Act as applied by regulation 2 of, and modified by Schedule 1 to, the 2008 Regulations.

(2) This rule applies where a payment to a claimant following acceptance of a Part 36 offer would be a compensation payment as defined in section 1(4)(b) or 1A(5)(b) of the 1997 Act.

(3) A defendant who makes a Part 36 offer should state either—

(a) that the offer is made without regard to any liability for recoverable amounts; or
(b) that it is intended to include any deductible amounts.

(4) Where paragraph (3)(b) applies, paragraphs (5) to (9) of this rule will apply to the Part 36 offer.

(5) Before making the Part 36 offer, the offeror must apply for a certificate.

(6) Subject to paragraph (7), the Part 36 offer must state—

(a) the gross amount of compensation;
(b) the name and amount of any deductible amount by which the gross amount is reduced; and
(c) the net amount of compensation.

(7) If at the time the offeror makes the Part 36 offer, the offeror has applied for, but has not received, a certificate, the offeror must clarify the offer by stating the matters referred to in paragraphs (6)(b) and (6)(c) not more than 7 days after receipt of the certificate.

(8) For the purposes of rule 36.17(1)(a), a claimant fails to recover more than any sum offered (including a lump sum offered under rule 36.6) if the claimant fails upon judgment being entered to recover a sum, once deductible amounts identified in the judgment have been deducted, greater than the net amount stated under paragraph (6)(c).

(Section 15(2) of the 1997 Act provides that the court must specify the compensation payment attributable to each head of damage. Schedule 1 to the 2008 Regulations modifies section 15 of the 1997 Act in relation to lump sum payments and provides that the court must specify the compensation payment attributable to each or any dependant who has received a lump sum payment.)

(9) Where—

(a) further deductible amounts have accrued since the Part 36 offer was made; and

(b) the court gives permission to accept the Part 36 offer,

the court may direct that the amount of the offer payable to the offeree shall be reduced by a sum equivalent to the deductible amounts paid to the claimant since the date of the offer.

(Rule 36.11(3)(b) states that permission is required to accept an offer where the relevant period has expired and further deductible amounts have been paid to the claimant)"

The effect of CPR r.36.17 is that a failure to recover a sum greater than the amount offered under Pt.36 is usually that the claimant has to pay any costs incurred by the defendant after the latest date the offer could have been accepted without the permission of the court. Rule 36.22(8), which makes it clear that the relevant sum for the purposes of the comparison is the net amount after deductions have been made under s.8. CPR r.36.17 is modified by r.36.21 in cases started under the pre-action protocols for "Low Value Personal Injuries Claims" arising out of road traffic accidents or employers' liability or public liability claims but no longer proceeding under those protocols, but r.36.21(3)(c) has the same effect in such cases as r.36.22(8) does in other cases. Rule 36.21 will be replaced by new provisions with effect from October 1, 2023.

Benefits irrelevant to assessment of damages

17. In assessing damages in respect of any accident, injury or disease, the amount of any listed benefits paid or likely to be paid is to be disregarded. 1.351

DEFINITION

"listed benefit"—see s.29.

GENERAL NOTE

This section is applied with modifications to cases concerned with the recovery of payments within the scope of s.1A(2) (see the Social Security (Recovery of Benefits) (Lump Sum Payments) Regulations 2008 reg.2 and Sch.1 para.9). 1.352

Benefits are disregarded not only when assessing damages but also when calculating interest on the damages, so that recoverable benefits are not to be deducted from damages for loss of earnings before calculating the interest due (*Wisely v John Fulton (Plumbers) Ltd, Wadey v Surrey CC* [2000] 1 W.L.R. 820 (HL)).

This section is not an overriding mandatory provision within the scope of Art.16 of Regulation (EC) No.864/2007 so that, in *Syred v Powszechny Zaklad Ubezpreczen (PZU) SA* [2016] EWHC 254 (QB); [2016] 1 W.L.R. 3211 where the claimant was severely injured in a road accident in Poland and the Regulation had the effect that quantum fell to be determined by Polish law subject to any overriding mandatory provision of English law, Polish law was applied and required credit to be given for benefits when assessing damages. A "nil" certificate had been issued in that case but, even if recoverable benefits had been paid during the "relevant period", the ruling would probably have made a difference only in respect of benefits that had been received, or were likely to be received, after the "relevant period" had ended. That is because applying the compensatory principle of Polish law would presumably have had the same effect as is achieved by s.8 in respect of the "relevant period" and the compensator could not have expected to be entitled to reduce the amount of damages twice in respect of the same benefits.

Reduction of compensation: complex cases

Lump sum and periodical payments

1.353 **18.**—(1) Regulations may make provision (including provision modifying this Act) for any case in which two or more compensation payments in the form of lump sums are made by the same person to or in respect of the injured person in consequence of the same accident, injury or disease.

(2) The regulations may (among other things) provide—

(a) for the re-calculation in accordance with section 8 of the amount of any compensation payment,

(b) for giving credit for amounts already paid, and

(c) for the payment by any person of any balance or the recovery from any person of any excess.

(3) For the purposes of subsection (2), the regulations may provide for the gross amounts of the compensation payments to be aggregated and for—

(a) the aggregate amount to be taken to be the gross amount of the compensation payment for the purposes of section 8,

(b) so much of the aggregate amount as is attributable to a head of compensation listed in column 1 of Schedule 2 to be taken to be the part of the gross amount which is attributable to that head;

and for the amount of any recoverable benefit shown against any head in column 2 of that Schedule to be taken to be the amount determined in accordance with the most recent certificate of recoverable benefits.

(4) Regulations may make provision (including provision modifying this Act) for any case in which, in final settlement of the injured person's claim, an agreement is entered into for the making of—

(a) periodical compensation payments (whether of an income or capital nature), or

(b) periodical compensation payments and lump sum compensation payments.

(5) Regulations made by virtue of subsection (4) may (among other things) provide—

(a) for the relevant period to be treated as ending at a prescribed time,

(b) for the person who is to make the payments under the agreement to be treated for the purposes of this Act as if he had made a single compensation payment on a prescribed date.

(6) A periodical payment may be a compensation payment for the purposes of this section even though it is a small payment (as defined in Part II of Schedule 1).

DEFINITIONS

"amount of any recoverable benefit"—see s.9(4)(b).
"compensation payment"—see s.1(4)(b).
"gross amount of the compensation payment"—see s.9(4)(a).
"injured person"—see s.29.
"recoverable benefit"—see s.1(4)(c).
"payment"—see s.29.
"prescribed"—*ibid.*

"regulations"—*ibid.*
"the relevant period"—see s.3.

General Note

Regulation 9 of the Social Security (Recovery of Benefits) Regulations 1997 is made under subss.(1) to (3) and reg.10 is made under subss.(4) and (5). 1.354

This section is applied with modifications to cases concerned with the recovery of payments within the scope of s.1A(2) (see the Social Security (Recovery of Benefits) (Lump Sum Payments) Regulations 2008 reg.2 and Sch.1 para.10). Regulations 14 and 18 of the 2008 Regulations make provision equivalent to regs 9 and 10 of the 1997 Regulations.

Payments by more than one person

19.—(1) Regulations may make provision (including provision modifying this Act) for any case in which two or more persons ("the compensators") make compensation payments to or in respect of the same injured person in consequence of the same accident, injury or disease. 1.355

(2) In such a case, the sum of the liabilities of the compensators under section 6 is not to exceed the total amount of the recoverable benefits, and the regulations may provide for determining the respective liabilities under that section of each of the compensators.

(3) The regulations may (among other things) provide in the case of each compensator—

(a) for determining or re-determining the part of the recoverable benefits which may be taken into account in his case,
(b) for calculating or re-calculating in accordance with section 8 [[1] or 8A] the amount of any compensation payment,
(c) for giving credit for amounts already paid, and
(d) for the payment by any person of any balance or the recovery from any person of any excess.

Amendment

1. Mesothelioma Act 2014 s.11 and Sch.1 paras 1 and 8 (March 31, 2014).

Definitions

"amount of any recoverable benefit"—see s.9(4)(b).
"compensation payment"—see s.1(4)(b).
"compensator"—see subs.(1).
"injured person"—see s.1(4)(a).
"recoverable benefit"—see s.1(4)(c).
"payment"—see s.29.
"regulations"—*ibid.*
"the relevant period"—see s.3.

General Note

See reg.9 of the Social Security (Recovery of Benefits) Regulations 1997. Note that the liability for benefits paid before the making of the first compensation payment generally falls on the compensator who makes that payment and there is no provision for apportionment as such. Compensators therefore need to co-operate among themselves to ensure that the burden of making payments to the Secretary of State is shared appropriately. Note also that no provision can be made for cases where a claimant's disablement is attributable to two successive accidents caused by 1.356

the negligence or breach of statutory duty of different compensators. The payment of benefits in consequence of the disablement must therefore be attributed solely to one accident or the other so that only one of the compensators is liable to make payments to the Secretary of State (*R(CR) 2/04* and see the note to s.1 for how the attribution is to be made).

This section is applied with modifications to cases concerned with the recovery of payments within the scope of s.1A(2) (see the Social Security (Recovery of Benefits) (Lump Sum Payments) Regulations 2008 reg.2 and Sch.1 para.11). Regulation 14 of the 2008 Regulations makes provision equivalent to reg.9 of the 1997 Regulations.

Miscellaneous

Amounts overpaid under section 6

1.357 **20.**—(1) Regulations may make provision (including provision modifying this Act) for cases where a person has paid to the Secretary of State under section 6 any amount ("the amount of the overpayment") which he was not liable to pay.

(2) The regulations may provide—

(a) for the Secretary of State to pay the amount of the overpayment to that person, or to the person to whom the compensation payment is made, or partly to one and partly to the other, or

(b) for the receipt by the Secretary of State of the amount of the overpayment to be treated as the recovery of that amount.

(3) Regulations made by virtue of subsection (2)(b) are to have effect in spite of anything in section 71 of the Social Security Administration Act 1992 (overpayments—general).

(4) The regulations may also (among other things) provide—

(a) for the re-calculation in accordance with section 8 [[1] or 8A] of the amount of any compensation payment,

(b) for giving credit for amounts already paid, and

(c) for the payment by any person of any balance or the recovery from any person of any excess.

(5) This section does not apply in a case where section 14 applies.

AMENDMENT

1. Mesothelioma Act 2014 s.11 and Sch.1 paras 1 and 8 (March 31, 2014).

DEFINITIONS

"compensation payment"—see s.1(4)(b).
"payment"—see s.29.
"regulations"—*ibid.*
"the amount of the overpayment"—see subs.(1).

GENERAL NOTE

No regulations have been made under this section.

The section is nonetheless applied with modifications to cases concerned with the recovery of payments within the scope of s.1A(2) (see the Social Security (Recovery of Benefits) (Lump Sum Payments) Regulations 2008 reg.2 and Sch.1 para.12).

1.358

Compensation payments to be disregarded

21.—(1) If, when a compensation payment is made, the first and second conditions are met, the payment is to be disregarded for the purposes of sections 6 and 8 [1 or 8A]. 1.359

(2) The first condition is that the person making the payment—

(a) has made an application for a certificate of recoverable benefits which complies with subsection (3), and

(b) has in his possession a written acknowledgement of the receipt of his application.

(3) An application complies with this subsection if it—

(a) accurately states the prescribed particulars relating to the injured person and the accident, injury or disease in question, and

(b) specifies the name and address of the person to whom the certificate is to be sent.

(4) The second condition is that the Secretary of State has not sent the certificate to the person, at the address, specified in the application, before the end of the period allowed under section 4.

(5) In any case where—

(a) by virtue of subsection (1), a compensation payment is disregarded for the purposes of sections 6 and 8 [1 or 8A], but

(b) the person who made the compensation payment nevertheless makes a payment to the Secretary of State for which (but for subsection (1)) he would be liable under section 6,

subsection (1) is to cease to apply in relation to the compensation payment.

(6) If, in the opinion of the Secretary of State, circumstances have arisen which adversely affect normal methods of communication—

(a) he may by order provide that subsection (1) is not to apply during a specified period not exceeding three months, and

(b) he may continue any such order in force for further periods not exceeding three months at a time.

AMENDMENT

1. Mesothelioma Act 2014 s.11 and Sch.1 paras 1 and 8 (March 31, 2014).

DEFINITIONS

"compensation payment"—see s.1(4)(b).
"injured person"—see s.29.
"payment"—see s.29.
"prescribed—*ibid.*
"recoverable benefit"—see s.1(4)(c).

GENERAL NOTE

If a certificate of recoverable benefits is not issued within four weeks (subject to subs.(6)) following receipt and acknowledgement of a full and accurate application, the Secretary of State loses his right of recovery. It is clear from subs.(4) that the late issue of a certificate will not do. However, if the compensator makes a payment to the Secretary of State in error—perhaps in reliance on an expired certificate—the Secretary of State is not obliged to pay it back because the dispensation under this section ceases to apply (subs.(5)). For the date on which an application is treated as 1.360

received, see reg.7(2) of the Social Security (Recovery of Benefits) Regulations 1997 which is made under s.4(9).

This section is applied with modifications to cases concerned with the recovery of payments within the scope of s.1A(2) (see the Social Security (Recovery of Benefits) (Lump Sum Payments) Regulations 2008 reg.2 and Sch.1 para.13).

Subsection (3)

1.361 For the prescribed particulars, see reg.7(1) of the Social Security (Recovery of Benefits) Regulations 1997.

Subsection (4)

1.362 The period allowed under s.4(3) and (8) is four weeks, but see s.21(6).

Subsection (5)

1.363 It is not clear whether the Secretary of State can, by issuing an out of time certificate, insist on obtaining more than the payment made by the compensator or whether he is confined to accepting what has been sent, which is likely to have been based on an earlier certificate.

1.364 **22.** *Omitted.*

Provision of information

1.365 **23.**—(1) Where compensation is sought in respect of any accident, injury or disease suffered by any person ("the injured person"), the following persons must give the Secretary of State the prescribed information about the injured person—

(a) anyone who is, or is alleged to be, liable in respect of the accident, injury or disease, and

(b) anyone acting on behalf of such a person.

(2) A person who receives or claims a listed benefit which is or is likely to be paid in respect of an accident, injury or disease suffered by him, must give the Secretary of State the prescribed information about the accident, injury or disease.

(3) Where a person who has received a listed benefit dies, the duty in subsection (2) is imposed on his personal representative.

(4) Any person who makes a payment (whether on his own behalf or not)—

(a) in consequence of, or

(b) which is referable to any costs (in Scotland, expenses) incurred by reason of,

any accident, injury or disease, or any damage to property, must, if the Secretary of State requests him in writing to do so, give the Secretary of State such particulars relating to the size and composition of the payment as are specified in the request.

(5) The employer of a person who suffers or has suffered an accident, injury or disease, and anyone who has been the employer of such a person at any time during the relevant period, must give the Secretary of State the prescribed information about the payment of statutory sick pay in respect of that person.

(6) In subsection (5) "employer" has the same meaning as it has in Part XI of the Social Security Contributions and Benefits Act 1992.

[1 (6A) The following persons must give the Secretary of State the prescribed information for the purposes of this Act—

(a) the scheme administrator of the Diffuse Mesothelioma Payment Scheme, and

(b) any person providing services to the scheme administrator.]

(7) A person who is required to give information under this section must do so in the prescribed manner, at the prescribed place and within the prescribed time.

(8) Section 1 does not apply in relation to this section.

AMENDMENT

1. Mesothelioma Act 2014 s.11 and Sch.1 para.19 (March 31, 2014).

DEFINITIONS

"employer"—see subs.(6).
"injured person"—see subs.(1) (and subs.(8), disapplying s.1).
"listed benefit"—see s.29.
"payment"—*ibid.*
"prescribed"—*ibid.*
"the relevant period"—see s.3.
"scheme administrator"—see s.29.

GENERAL NOTE

Regulations 3, 4, 5 and 6 of the Social Security (Recovery of Benefits) Regulations 1997 are made under subss (1), (2), (5) and (7) respectively. **1.366**

This section is applied with modifications (which, among other things, disapply subss.(5), (6) and (8)) to cases concerned with the recovery of payments within the scope of s.1A(2). See the Social Security (Recovery of Benefits) (Lump Sum Payments) Regulations 2008 reg.2 and Sch.1 para.15. Regulations 15, 16 and 17 of the 2008 Regulations respectively make provision equivalent to regs 3, 4 and 6 of the 1997 Regulations.

Power to amend Schedule 2

24.—(1) The Secretary of State may by regulations amend Schedule 2. **1.367**

(2) A statutory instrument which contains such regulations shall not be made unless a draft of the instrument has been laid before and approved by resolution of each House of Parliament.

DEFINITION

"regulations"—see s.29.

Provisions relating to Northern Ireland

25.–27. *Omitted.* **1.368**

General

The Crown

28. This Act applies to the Crown. **1.369**

General Note

1.370 This is effectively a new provision because s.104 of the Social Security Administration Act 1992 was never brought into force (see Social Security (Consequential Provisions) Act 1992 Sch.4 para.3). It is applied to cases concerned with the recovery of payments within the scope of s.1A(2) (see the Social Security (Recovery of Benefits) (Lump Sum Payments) Regulations 2008 reg.2).

General interpretation

1.371 **29.** In this Act—

[2. . .]

"benefit" means [4 universal credit] any benefit under the Social Security Contributions and Benefits Act 1992, a jobseeker's allowance [1, an employment and support allowance] [3, personal independence payment] or mobility allowance,

[2. . .]

"compensation scheme for motor accidents" means any scheme or arrangement under which funds are available for the payment of compensation in respect of motor accidents caused, or alleged to have been caused, by uninsured or unidentified persons,

"listed benefit" means a benefit listed in column 2 of Schedule 2,

"payment" means payment in money or money's worth, and related expressions are to be interpreted accordingly,

"prescribed" means prescribed by regulations, and

"regulations" means regulations made by the Secretary of State.

[5 "scheme administrator", in relation to the Diffuse Mesothelioma Payment Scheme, has the meaning given by section 18 of the Mesothelioma Act 2014.]

Amendments

1. Employment and Support Allowance (Consequential Provisions) (No.2) Regulations 2008 (SI 2008/1554) reg.50(1) and (2) (October 27, 2008).
2. Transfer of Tribunal Functions Order (SI 2008/2833) Sch.3 paras 138 and 142 (November 3, 2008).
3. Welfare Reform Act 2012 s.91 and Sch.9 paras 34 and 35 (April 8, 2013).
4. Welfare Reform Act 2012 s.31 and Sch.2 paras 40 and 41 (April 29, 2013).
5. Mesothelioma Act 2014 s.11 and Sch.1 para.7 (March 31, 2014).

General Note

1.372 This section is applied with modifications to cases concerned with the recovery of payments within the scope of s.1A(2) (see the Social Security (Recovery of Benefits) (Lump Sum Payments) Regulations 2008 reg.2 and Sch.1 para.18). In particular, "certificate" is defined as meaning "a certificate which includes amounts in respect of recoverable benefits and of recoverable lump sum payments, including where any of those amounts are nil".

Regulations and orders

1.373 **30.**—(1) Any power under this Act to make regulations or an order is exercisable by statutory instrument.

(2) A statutory instrument containing regulations or an order under this Act (other than regulations under section [1 11(2A) or] 24 or an order

under section 34) shall be subject to annulment in pursuance of a resolution of either House of Parliament.

[[1] (2A) A statutory instrument containing regulations under section 11(2A) may not be made unless a draft of the instrument has been laid before and approved by a resolution of each House of Parliament.]

(3) Regulations under section 20, under section 24 amending the list of benefits in column 2 of Schedule 2 or under paragraph 9 of Schedule 1 may not be made without the consent of the Treasury.

(4) Subsections (4), (5), (6) and (9) of section 189 of the Social Security Administration Act 1992 (regulations and orders—general) apply for the purposes of this Act as they apply for the purposes of that.

DEFINITIONS

"benefit"—see s.29.
"regulations"—*ibid.*

AMENDMENT

1. Welfare Reform Act 2012 s.102(6) and Sch.11 paras 9 and 11 (February 25, 2013 for regulation-making purposes and April 29, 2013 for all other purposes).

GENERAL NOTE

This section is applied to cases concerned with the recovery of payments within the scope of s.1A(2) (see the Social Security (Recovery of Benefits) (Lump Sum Payments) Regulations 2008 reg.2). **1.374**

31. *Omitted.* **1.375**

Power to make transitional, consequential etc. provisions

32.—(1) Regulations may make such transitional and consequential provisions, and such savings, as the Secretary of State considers necessary or expedient in preparation for, in connection with, or in consequence of— **1.376**

(a) the coming into force of any provision of this Act, or
(b) the operation of any enactment repealed or amended by a provision of this Act during any period when the repeal or amendment is not wholly in force.

(2) Regulations under this section may (among other things) provide—

(a) for compensation payments in relation to which, by virtue of section 2, this Act does not apply to be treated as payments in relation to which this Act applies,
(b) for compensation payments in relation to which, by virtue of section 2, this Act applies to be treated as payments in relation to which this Act does not apply, and
(c) for the modification of any enactment contained in this Act or referred to in subsection (1)(b) in its application to any compensation payment.

DEFINITIONS

"compensation payment"—see s.1(4)(b).
"payment"—see s.29.
"regulations"—*ibid.*

GENERAL NOTE

1.377 See reg.12 of the Social Security (Recovery of Benefits) Regulations 1997.

1.378 **33.** *Omitted.*

Short title, commencement and extent

1.379 **34.**—(1) This Act may be cited as the Social Security (Recovery of Benefits) Act 1997.

(2) Sections 1 to 24, 26 to 28 and 33 are to come into force on such day as the Secretary of State may by order appoint, and different days may be appointed for different purposes.

(3) Apart from sections 25 to 27, section 33 so far as it relates to any enactment which extends to Northern Ireland, and this section this Act does not extend to Northern Ireland.

GENERAL NOTE

1.380 Some regulation-making powers were brought into force on September 3, 1997 but the main provisions of the Act came into force on October 6, 1997 (see the Social Security (Recovery of Benefits) Act 1997 (Commencement Order) 1997 (SI 1997/2085)).

Subss.(1) and (3) are applied to cases concerned with the recovery of payments within the scope of s.1A(2) (see the Social Security (Recovery of Benefits) (Lump Sum Payments) Regulations 2008 reg.2).

SCHEDULES

SCHEDULE 1

COMPENSATION PAYMENTS

PART I

Exempted payments

1.381 **1.** Any small payment (defined in Part II of this Schedule).

2. Any payment made to or for the injured person under [1 section 130 of the Powers of Criminal Courts (Sentencing) Act] [5 2000, [6 or Chapter 2 of Part 7 of the Sentencing Code,] section 8 of the Modern Slavery Act 2015,] [3 section 175 of the Armed Forces Act 2006] or section 249 of the Criminal Procedure (Scotland) Act 1995 (compensation orders against convicted persons).

3. Any payment made in the exercise of a discretion out of property held subject to a trust in a case where no more than 50 per cent. by value of the capital contributed to the trust was directly or indirectly provided by persons who are, or are alleged to be, liable in respect of—

(a) the accident, injury or disease suffered by the injured person, or
(b) the same or any connected accident, injury or disease suffered by another.

4. Any payment made out of property held for the purposes of any prescribed trust (whether the payment also falls within paragraph 3 or not).

5. [2 —(1)] Any payment made to the injured person by an [2 insurer] under the terms of any contract of insurance entered into between the injured person and [2 the insurer] before—

(a) the date on which the injured person first claims a listed benefit in consequence of the disease in question, or
(b) the occurrence of the accident or injury in question.

[2 (2) "Insurer" means—

(a) a person who has permission under [4 Part 4A] of the Financial Services and Markets Act 2000 to effect or carry out contracts of insurance; [7 . . .]

(b) [7 . . .]

(3) Sub-paragraph (2) must be read with—

(a) section 22 of the Financial Services and Markets Act 2000;

(b) any relevant order under that section; and

(c) Schedule 2 to that Act.]

6. Any redundancy payment falling to be taken into account in the assessment of damages in respect of an accident, injury or disease.

7. So much of any payment as is referable to costs.

8. Any prescribed payment.

Part II

Power to disregard small payments

9.—(1) Regulations may make provision for compensation payments to be disregarded for the purposes of sections 6 and 8 in prescribed cases where the amount of the compensation payment, or the aggregate amount of two or more connected compensation payments, does not exceed the prescribed sum. **1.382**

(2) A compensation payment disregarded by virtue of this paragraph is referred to in paragraph 1 as a "small payment".

(3) For the purposes of this paragraph—

(a) two or more compensation payments are "connected" if each is made to or in respect of the same injured person and in respect of the same accident, injury or disease, and

(b) any reference to a compensation payment is a reference to a payment which would be such a payment apart from paragraph 1.

Amendments

1. Powers of Criminal Courts (Sentencing) Act 2000 s.165(1) and Sch.9 para.181 (August 25, 2000).
2. Financial Services and Markets Act 2000 (Consequential Amendments and Repeals) Order 2001 (SI 2001/3649) art.358 (December 1, 2001).
3. Armed Forces Act 2006 s378(1) and Sch.16 para.140 (March 28, 2009 for specified purposes and October 31, 2009 for all other purposes).
4. Financial Services Act 2012 s.114(1) and Sch.18 para.84 (April 1, 2013).
5. Modern Slavery Act 2015 s.57(1) and Sch.5 para.13 (July 31, 2015).
6. Sentencing Act 2020 s.410 and Sch.24 para.143 (December 1, 2020).
7. EEA Passport Rights (Amendment, etc., and Transitional Provisions) (EU Exit) Regulations 2018 (SI 2018/1149) reg.3(b) and Sch para.34 (December 31, 2020).

Definitions

"compensation payment"—see s.1(4)(b) and para.9(3)(b).
"connected"—see para.9(3)(a).
"injured person"—see s.1(4)(a).
"insurer"—see para.5(2).
"listed benefit"—see s.29.
"payment"—*ibid.*
"prescribed"—*ibid.*
"regulations"—*ibid.*
"small payment"—see para.9.

General Note

For exempted trusts and payments prescribed for the purposes of paras 4 and 8, see reg.2 of the Social Security (Recovery of Benefits) Regulations 1997. **1.383**

No regulations have been made under para.9. Under the former legislation, payments not exceeding £2,500 were disregarded. Now, general damages for pain and suffering are protected, because benefits can be recovered only from compensation for loss of earnings, care or loss of mobility, and so there is not considered to be a need for a general exemption for small claims.

This Schedule is applied with modifications to cases concerned with the recovery of payments within the scope of s.1A(2). See the Social Security (Recovery of Benefits) (Lump Sum Payments) Regulations 2008 reg.2 and Sch.1 paras 19 and 20. Regulation 7 of the 2008 Regulations makes provision equivalent to reg.2 of the 1997 Regulations.

SCHEDULE 2

Calculation of Compensation Payment

1.384

(1) Head of compensation	(2) Benefit
1. Compensation for earnings lost during the relevant period	[3 Universal credit] Disability working allowance Disablement pension payable under section 103 of the 1992 Act [1Employment and support allowance] Incapacity benefit Income support Invalidity pension and allowance Jobseeker's allowance Reduced earnings allowance Severe disablement allowance Sickness benefit Statutory sick pay Unemployability supplement Unemployment benefit
2. Compensation for cost of care incurred during the relevant period	Attendance allowance [2 Daily living component of personal independence payment] Care component of disability living allowance Disablement pension increase payable under section 104 or 105 of the 1992 Act
3. Compensation for loss of mobility during the relevant period.	Mobility allowance [2 Mobility component of personal independence payment] Mobility component of disability living allowance

Notes

1.385 **1.**—(1) References to incapacity benefit, invalidity pension and allowance, severe disablement allowance, sickness benefit and unemployment benefit also include any income support paid with each of those benefits on the same instrument of payment or paid concurrently with each of those benefits by means of an instrument for benefit payment.

(2) For the purpose of this Note, income support includes personal expenses addition, special transitional additions and transitional addition as defined in the Income Support (Transitional) Regulations 1987.

2. Any reference to statutory sick pay—

(a) includes only 80 per cent. of payments made between 6th April 1991 and 5th April 1994, and

(b) does not include payments made on or after 6th April 1994.

3. In this Schedule "the 1992 Act" means the Social Security Contributions and Benefits Act 1992.

AMENDMENTS

1. Employment and Support Allowance (Consequential Provisions) (No.2) Regulations 2008 (SI 2008/1554) reg.50(1) and (3) (October 27, 2008).
2. Welfare Reform Act 2012 s.91 and Sch.9 paras 34 and 36 (April 8, 2013).
3. Welfare Reform Act 2012 s.31 and Sch.2 paras 40 and 42 (April 29, 2013).

DEFINITIONS

"compensation payment"—see s.1(4)(b).
"payment"—*ibid.*
"the relevant period"—see s.3.

GENERAL NOTE

In *R(CR) 2/04*, the Commissioner commented that disablement pension was not, strictly speaking, paid in respect of loss of earnings but, in *AL v SSD (WP)* [2014] UKUT 524 (AAC) at [38], he pointed out that, although basic disablement pension is more akin to general damages, the legislation "has the effect of protecting awards of general damages and ensuring that the basic disablement pension is recoverable only if compensation is calculated on the basis that the claimant has lost earnings". 1.386

In *Lowther v Chatwin* [2003] EWCA Civ 729, the claimant had to close her business due to injuries sustained in an accident. She had been trading at a loss but had been able to pay 5/7ths of her business rent from the income of the business. She claimed damages in respect of her continuing liability to her landlord. The judge awarded her 5/7ths of the rent settlement and he held that that compensation was not for loss of earnings but for the destruction of the business. The Court of Appeal held that it was "compensation for earnings lost" and that the compensator was therefore entitled to deduct from that compensation the amount of relevant benefits paid to the claimant.

By reg.16 of the Employment and Support Allowance (Transitional Provisions, Housing Benefit and Council Tax Benefit) (Existing Awards) (No.2) Regulations 2010 (SI 2010/1907), this Act is applied with effect from October 1, 2010 for the purposes of enabling the Secretary of State to recover employment and support allowance paid in consequence of a "conversion decision" if a compensation payment is made. This is achieved by treating a conversion decision as though it were a decision as to a person's entitlement to an employment and support allowance which had been made on a claim. Whether it was really necessary to include this Act within the scope of reg.16 seems doubtful.

"Compensation for earnings lost" includes interest on damages for loss of earnings (*Griffiths v British Coal Corp* [2001] EWCA Civ 336; [2001] 1 W.L.R. 1493). 1.387

Given the way that ss.6 and 8 operate together, compensation for lost earnings presumably includes compensation for loss of *potential* earnings in the case of a person who was not employed at the time of a relevant accident or who was in temporary employment only. A benefit is recoverable only if it was paid "in respect of" the relevant accident, injury or disease (see the note to s.1).

"Compensation for cost of care" includes damages for services in the nature of care and domestic assistance given gratuitously, because the object of the legislation is to avoid double recovery as well as avoiding loss to the Secretary of State who had become liable to pay the benefits (*Griffiths v British Coal Corp* [2001] EWCA Civ 336; [2001] 1 W.L.R. 1493).

"Compensation for loss of mobility" in para.3, col.1 refers only to compensation for patrimonial (i.e. financial) loss, such as the cost of fares for journeys by bus or taxi, and does not refer to any element of solatium (i.e. compensation for pain and suffering or loss of amenity) (*Mitchell v Laing*, 1998 S.C. 342).

Schedules 3 and 4: *Omitted.* 1.388

Social Security Act 1998

(1998 c.14)

ARRANGEMENT OF SECTIONS

PART I

DECISIONS AND APPEALS

CHAPTER I

GENERAL

Decisions

Appeals

CHAPTER II

SOCIAL SECURITY DECISIONS AND APPEALS

Decisions

Appeals

Procedure etc.

Medical examinations

19. Medical examination required by Secretary of State.
20. Medical examination required by appeal tribunal.

Suspension and termination of benefit

21. Suspension in prescribed circumstances.
22. Suspension for failure to furnish information etc.
23. Termination in cases of failure to furnish information.
24. Suspension and termination for failure to submit to medical examination.

Appeals dependent on issues falling to be decided by Inland Revenue

24A. Appeals dependent on issues falling to be decided by Inland Revenue.

Decisions and appeals dependent on other cases

25. Decisions involving issues that arise on appeal in other cases.
26. Appeals involving issues that arise on appeal in other cases.

Cases of error

27. Restrictions on entitlement to benefit in certain cases of error.
28. Correction of errors and setting aside of decisions.

Industrial accidents

29. Decision that accident is an industrial accident.
30. Effect of decision.

Other special cases

31. Incapacity for work.
32. Industrial diseases.
33. Christmas bonus.

Housing benefit and council tax benefit

34. and 35. *Omitted.*

Social fund payment

36. to 38. *Repealed.*

Supplemental

39. Interpretation etc. of Chapter II.

An Act to make provision as to the making of decisions and the determination of appeals under enactments relating to social security, child support, vaccine damage payments and war pensions; to make further provision with respect to social security; and for connected purposes.

[21st May 1998]

PART I

DECISIONS AND APPEALS

CHAPTER I

GENERAL

Decisions

Transfer of functions to Secretary of State

1. *Omitted.* 1.390

Use of computers

2.—(1) Any decision, determination or assessment falling to be made or certificate falling to be issued by the Secretary of State under or by virtue of a relevant enactment, or in relation to a war pension, may be made or issued not only by an officer of his acting under his authority but also— 1.391

(a) by a computer for whose operation such an officer is responsible; and
(b) in the case of a decision, determination or assessment that may be made or a certificate that may be issued by a person providing services to the Secretary of State, by a computer for whose operation such a person is responsible.

(2) In this section "relevant enactment" means any enactment contained in—
(a) Chapter II of this Part;
(b) the Social Security Contributions and Benefits Act 1992 ("the Contributions and Benefits Act");
(c) the Administration Act;
(d) the Child Support Act;
(e) the Social Security (Incapacity for Work) Act 1994;
(f) the Jobseekers Act 1995 ("the Jobseekers Act");
(g) the Child Support Act 1995; [1 . . .]
(h) the Social Security (Recovery of Benefits) Act 1997 [2 . . .]
[1 (i) the State Pension Credit Act 2002;]
[2(j) Part 1 of the Welfare Reform Act 2007;] [4 . . .]
[4 (k) Part 1 of the Welfare Reform Act 2012;] [5 . . .]
[3 (l) Part 4 of that Act;]
[5 (m) Part 1 of the Pensions Act 2014;] [7 . . .]
[6 (n) section 30 of the Pensions Act 2014] [7 or
(o) sections 18 to 21 of the Welfare Reform and Work Act 2016.]

(3) In this section and section 3 below "war pension" has the same meaning as in section 25 of the Social Security Act 1989 (establishment and functions of war pensions committees).

AMENDMENTS

1. State Pension Credit Act 2002 Sch.1 para.5 and Sch.3 (July 2, 2002 for the purpose of exercising any power to make regulations or orders and April 7, 2003 for other purposes).

2. Welfare Reform Act 2007 Sch.3 para.17(1) and (2) (July 27, 2008).
3. Welfare Reform Act 2012 s.91 and Sch.9 paras 37 and 38 (April 8, 2013).
4. Welfare Reform Act 2012 s.31 and Sch.2 paras 43 and 44 (April 29, 2013).
5. Pensions Act 2014 s.23 and Sch.12 paras 31 and 32 (April 6, 2016).
6. Pensions Act 2014 s.31(5) and Sch.16 paras 37 and 38 (April 6, 2017).
7. Welfare Reform and Work Act 2016 s.20(3) (July 27, 2017).

DEFINITIONS

"the Administration Act"—see s.84.
"the Child Support Act"—*ibid.*
"relevant enactment"—see subs.(2).
"war pension"—see subs.(3).

GENERAL NOTE

1.392 This section applies as though the Pension Schemes Act 1993 were a relevant enactment (Pension Schemes Act 1993 s.170(1)).

In *C3/07-08(IS)*, a Deputy Commissioner in Northern Ireland was highly critical of the failure of computer-generated letters issued in Northern Ireland to reflect the statutory provisions for decision-making in the Northern Ireland equivalent to this Act. He held a decision that failed adequately to inform the recipient of her rights to seek reasons or to appeal to be so defective as to be invalid.

Use of information

1.393 **3.**—(1) Subsection (2) below applies to information relating to [2 any of the matters specified in subsection (1A) below] which is held—
(a) by the Secretary of State or the Northern Ireland Department; or
(b) by a person providing services to the Secretary of State or the Northern Ireland Department in connection with the provision of those services.

[2 (1A) The matters are—
(a) social security [3 . . .] or war pensions;
[3 (aa) child support [5 . . .];]
(b) employment or training;
(c) private pensions policy;
(d) retirement planning:]
[4 (e) the investigation or prosecution of offences relating to tax credits.]
[6 (f) the Diffuse Mesothelioma Payment Scheme.]]

(2) Information to which this subsection applies—
(a) may be used for the purposes of, or for any purposes connected with, the exercise of functions in relation to [2 any of the matters specified in subsection (1A) above]; and
(b) may be supplied to, or to a person providing services to, the Secretary of State or the Northern Ireland Department for use for those purposes.

(3) [1 . . .]

(4) In this section "the Northern Ireland Department" means the Department of Health and Social Services for Northern Ireland [1 or the Department for Employment and Learning in Northern Ireland].

[2 (5) In this section—
"private pensions policy" means policy relating to—
[7(a) occupational pension schemes or personal pension schemes (within the meaning given by section 1 of the Pension Schemes Act 1993);] [or

(b) occupational pension schemes or private pension schemes within the meaning of Part 1 of the Pensions Act 2008, if they do not fall within paragraph (a);]

"retirement planning" means promoting financial planning for retirement.]

AMENDMENTS

1. Employment Act 2002 Sch.6 paras 1 and 4 (September 9, 2002).
2. Pensions Act 2004 Sch.10 para.1 (November 18, 2004).
3. Child Maintenance and Other Payments Act 2008 s.57(1) and Sch.7 para.3(1) and (2) (April 6, 2010).
4. Welfare Reform Act 2012 s.127(10) (May 8, 2012).
5. Public Bodies (Child Maintenance and Enforcement Commission: Abolition and Transfer of Functions) Order 2012 (SI 2012/2007) art.3(2) and Sch. para.64(a) (August 1, 2012).
6. Mesothelioma Act 2014 s.11 and Sch.1 paras 1 and 21 (March 31, 2014).
7. Pensions Act 2008 s. 63(6)(a) and (b) (SI 2009/82) art. 2(1)(a) (January 26, 2009).

DEFINITIONS

"the Administration Act"—see s.84.
"the Northern Ireland Department"—see subs.(4).
"private pensions policy"—see subs.(5).
"retirement planning"—*ibid.*
"war pension"—see s.2(3).

GENERAL NOTE

This section provides for the sharing of what would otherwise be confidential information between the Department for Work and Pensions in Great Britain and departments in Northern Ireland. See also the Social Security Investigation Powers (Arrangements with Northern Ireland) Regulations 2007 (SI 2007/271). Most, if not all, of those functions of the Department of Health and Social Services (which is now the Department of Health) that are relevant to this section were transferred to a new Department for Social Development in 1999. The functions of both the Department for Social Development and the Department for Employment and Learning were then transferred to the Department for Communities in 2016. **1.394**

Provision is made for functions under this section to be exercised on behalf of the Secretary of State by the Scottish Ministers (see s.93(1) of the Scotland Act 1998 and art.2(1)(b) of the Scotland Act 1998 (Agency Arrangements) (Specification) Order 2014 (SI 2014/1892)), because the Scottish Ministers exercise relevant functions relating to employment and training.

Appeals

4. [1 . . .] **1.395**

AMENDMENT

1. Transfer of Tribunal Functions Order 2008 (SI 2008/2833) Sch.3 paras 143 and 144 (November 3, 2008).

5.–7. [1 . . .] **1.396**

AMENDMENT

1. Transfer of Tribunal Functions Order 2008 (SI 2008/2833) Sch.3 paras 143 and 145–147 (November 3, 2008), subject to a saving under art.1(5).

General Note

1.397 These sections made provision for appeal tribunals, to whom appeals lay under s.12 and from whom appeals lay to Social Security Commissioners under s.14. Both the appeal tribunals and Commissioners also had functions under other legislation. Subject to one exception, the functions of appeal tribunals constituted under this Act and Commissioners have been transferred respectively to the First-tier Tribunal and the Upper Tribunal.

The exception is the determination by appeal tribunals of appeals referred by Scottish Ministers under s.158 of the Health and Social Care (Community Health and Standards) Act 2003 and the determination by Commissioners of appeals against such determinations under s.159. Those functions relate to the recovery of National Health Service charges in Scotland and could not be transferred because health is a devolved function in Scotland. Therefore, although ss.5–7 are repealed for all other purposes, art.1(5) of the Transfer of Tribunal Functions Order 2008 has the effect that those provisions, and a number of other provisions relating to the appointment of appeal tribunals and Commissioners and their procedural rules, remain in force in Scotland for the purposes of the 2003 Act. The Personal Injuries (NHS Charges) (Reviews and Appeals) (Scotland) Regulations 2006 (SSI 2006/593) make procedural provision for these appeals and reg.8(2) applies a number of otherwise revoked regulations in Pts IV and V of the Social Security and Child Support (Decisions and Appeals) Regulations 1999 Regulations for those purposes.

If there were in fact any such appeals in Scotland, the Scottish Parliament might perhaps legislate to redirect the appeals to another tribunal or court. In England and Wales, s.158 of the 2003 Act has been amended by the 2008 Order and now provides for the Secretary of State to refer appeals to the First-tier Tribunal. See the Personal Injuries (NHS Charges) (Reviews and Appeals) and Road Traffic (NHS Charges) (Reviews and Appeals) (Amendment) Regulations 2006 (SI 2006/3398), as amended, for procedural provisions. However, these appeals are beyond the scope of this work.

Chapter II

Social Security Decisions and Appeals

Decisions

Decisions by Secretary of State

1.398 **8.**—(1) Subject to the provisions of this Chapter, it shall be for the Secretary of State—

(a) to decide any claim for a relevant benefit;
(b) [[6] . . .] [[1]and]
(c) subject to subsection (5) below, to make any decision that falls to be made under or by virtue of a relevant enactment; [[1] . . .]
(d) [[1] . . .]

(2) Where at any time a claim for a relevant benefit is decided by the Secretary of State—

(a) the claim shall not be regarded as subsisting after that time; and
(b) accordingly, the claimant shall not (without making a further claim) be entitled to the benefit on the basis of circumstances not obtaining at that time.

(3) In this Chapter "relevant benefit" [2 . . .] means any of the following, namely—

(a) benefit under Parts II to V of the Contributions and Benefits Act;

[8 (aa) universal credit;]

[9 (ab) state pension or a lump sum under Part 1 of the Pensions Act 2014;]

[10 (ac) bereavement support payment under section 30 of the Pensions Act 2014;].

(b) a jobseeker's allowance;

[5(ba) an employment and support allowance]

[7(baa) personal independence payment;]

[3(bb) state pension credit;]

[11(bc) a loan under section 18 of the Welfare Reform and Work Act 2016;]

(c) income support;

(d) [4 . . .];

(e) [4 . . .];

(f) a social fund payment mentioned in section 138(1)(a) or (2) of the Contributions and Benefits Act;

(g) child benefit;

(h) such other benefit as may be prescribed.

(4) In this section "relevant enactment" means any enactment contained in this Chapter, the Contributions and Benefits Act, the Administration Act, the Social Security (Consequential Provisions) Act 1992 [3, the Jobseekers Act [5, the State Pension Credit Act 2002 [8, Part 1 of the Welfare Reform Act 2007, Part 1 of the Welfare Reform Act 2012] [7 [9, Part 4 of that Act or Part 1 of the Pensions Act 2014]]] [10 [11, section 30 of that Act or sections 18 to 21 of the Welfare Reform and Work Act 2016]], other than one contained in—

(a) Part VII of the Contributions and Benefits Act so far as relating to housing benefit and council tax benefit;

(b) Part VIII of the Administration Act (arrangements for housing benefit and council tax benefit and related subsidies).

(5) [1 Subsection (1)(c) above does not include any decision which under section 8 of the Social Security Contributions (Transfer of Functions, etc.) Act 1999 falls to be made by an officer of the Inland Revenue.]

AMENDMENTS

1. Social Security Contributions (Transfer of Functions, etc.) Act 1999 Sch.7, para.22 (April 1, 1999).

2. Welfare Reform and Pensions Act 1999 s.88 and Sch.13 (April 6, 2000).

3. State Pension Credit Act 2002 Sch.1 para.6 (July 2, 2002 for regulation-making and order-making purposes and April 7, 2003 for other purposes).

4. Tax Credits Act 2002 Sch.6 (April 8, 2003, subject to a saving in respect of outstanding questions concerning work families' tax credit and disabled person's tax credit—see Tax Credits Act 2002 (Commencement No.4, Transitional Provisions and Savings) Order 2003 (SI 2003/962) art.3(1)–(3)).

5. Welfare Reform Act 2007 Sch.3 para.17(1) and (3) of and July 27, 2008 for other purposes (March 18, 2008 for regulation-making purposes).

6. Welfare Reform Act 2012 s.147 and Sch.14 Pt.8 (April 1, 2013).

7. Welfare Reform Act 2012 s.91 and Sch.9 paras 37 and 39 (February 25, 2013 for regulation-making purposes and April 8, 2013 for other purposes).

8. Welfare Reform Act 2012 s.31 and Sch.2 paras 43 and 45 (February 25, 2013 for regulation-making purposes and April 29, 2013 for other purposes).

9. Pensions Act 2014 s.23 and Sch.12 paras 31 and 33 (April 6, 2016).

10. Pensions Act 2014 s.31(5) and Sch.16 paras 37 and 39 (April 6, 2017).
11. Welfare Reform and Work Act 2016 s.20(4) (July 27, 2017).

DEFINITIONS

"the Administration Act"—see s.84.

"claim"—by virtue of s.39(2), see s.191 of the Social Security Administration Act 1992.

"claimant"—see s.39(1) and, by virtue of s.39(2), see s.191 of the Social Security Administration Act 1992.

"the Contributions and Benefits Act"—see s.84.

"Inland Revenue"—by virtue of s.39(2), see s.191 of the Social Security Administration Act 1992 but note that the Inland Revenue was merged into Her Majesty's Revenue and Customs by the Commissioners for Revenue and Customs Act 2005.

"the Jobseekers Act"—see s.84.

"prescribed"—*ibid.*

"relevant benefit"—see subs.(3).

"relevant enactment"—see subs.(4).

GENERAL NOTE

1.399 This section makes general provision for initial decisions by the Secretary of State. However, by Tax Credits Act 1999 s.2(1)(b) and Sch.2 para.5(b)(i), the functions of making initial decisions in respect of working families' tax credit and disabled person's tax credit (both now abolished) were transferred to officers of the Inland Revenue. By s.50(2)(e) of the Tax Credits Act 2002, the Secretary of State's functions under this Act relating to child benefit and guardian's allowance were transferred to the Board of Inland Revenue with effect from April 7, 2003. The Inland Revenue has now been merged into HMRC, by the Commissioners for Revenue and Customs Act 2005.

By regs 6 and 16 of the Employment and Support Allowance (Transitional Provisions, Housing Benefit and Council Tax Benefit) (Existing Awards) (No.2) Regulations 2010 (SI 2010/1907), the whole of Ch.II of Pt I of the 1998 Act was applied to a "conversion decision", made when employment and support allowance was first introduced, by treating it as though it were a decision as to a person's entitlement to an employment and support allowance which had been made on a claim.

Section 6 of the Social Security (Additional Payments) Act 2022 provides that, for all purposes relating to the administration of an additional payment, any provision applying in relation to a benefit or tax credit by reference to which that additional payment is made is to apply in relation to that payment as if it were a payment or award of the benefit or tax credit in question, subject to any necessary modifications. This would appear to have the effect that, among other provisions, ss.8, 9, 10 and 12 of the 1998 Act apply to at least some extent where the additional payment is paid by reference to a benefit to which they apply. However, s.6(2)(a) of the 2022 Act provides that the legislation that may be applied includes "provision relating to overpayments and recovery, and appeals relating to overpayments and recovery (but not provision relating to appeals or reviews about entitlement to the social security benefit, tax credit or disability benefit in question)".

Subsection (1)

1.400 The Secretary of State must investigate any claim to a relevant benefit (which includes an application for a loan under s.18 of the Welfare Reform and Work Act 2016 – see s.39(1A)(b) of this Act) and ensure that the claimant is asked the appropriate questions so that he or she has a reasonable opportunity to produce material evidence. See under the heading *The inquisitorial role of the tribunal and the burden of proof* in the note to s.3(1) of the Tribunals, Courts and Enforcement Act 2007 in Part III below. Much of what is said in that note under the heading *Evidence* is also relevant to the Secretary of State's consideration of a claim, as is what is said under the heading *Relying on decisions of other bodies*. Thus, where another body has made a decision on a question relevant to a claim for benefit, it is not necessary for the Secretary of State to consider that question from scratch as though the other decision did not exist, provided the other body made a considered decision on the point. He is entitled, in the absence of anything to compel a contrary conclusion, to regard the existence of that decision as satisfactory evidence (*R(H) 9/04*) of the facts found by that body. However, he is not bound to reach the same conclusion as the other body and must take account of any new evidence or any contrary submission made by the claimant.

In *C v Secretary of State for Work and Pensions (Zacchaeus 2000 intervening)* [2015] EWHC 1607 (Admin), it was held that delays of thirteen and ten months in making decisions on claims for personal independence payment were unlawful because the Secretary of State must act reasonably in allocating resources for adjudication in the light of the volume of applications, the resources available and the need to ensure fairness and consistency (see *R v Secretary of State for Social Services, ex parte CPAG* [1990] 2 QB 540 and *R.(S) v Secretary of State for the Home Department* [2007] EWCA Civ 546; [2007] Imm AR 781 at [51]). However, they did not breach the European Convention on Human Rights. Accordingly, declarations of illegality were made but the claimants were not entitled to compensation.

In *MH v SSWP (II)* [2020] UKUT 297 (AAC), the judge raised the question whether a claim for disablement pension made in respect of one prescribed industrial disease may, before it is determined, be treated as having been made, additionally or alternatively, in respect of another prescribed disease without a further, formal, claim having been submitted. In the event, he left that question open, but he accepted that the Secretary of State was entitled, although perhaps not required, to issue a separate decision as regards entitlement to disablement pension in respect of each prescribed disease that she had considered.

Regulation 30 of the Employment and Support Allowance Regulations 2008 **1.401**
makes provision for a claimant to be treated as having limited capability for work between the date of claim and the date it is determined whether he does have limited capability for work or may be treated as doing so by virtue of some other provision. However, this does not apply if there has been a previous finding that the claimant does not have limited capability for work unless, inter alia, the claimant is suffering from a new condition or his or her previous condition has "significantly worsened". In *EI v SSWP (ESA)* [2016] UKUT 397 (AAC), detailed consideration was given to whether a decision of the Secretary of State to the effect that the claimant did not satisfy either of those conditions and that he was therefore not entitled to employment and support allowance under reg.30 was a decision made under s.8(1)(c) so that the claimant would have a right of appeal under s.12. However, the Upper Tribunal reached no firm conclusion because the question had turned out to be academic as it had subsequently been decided that the claimant did have limited capability for work and so benefit had been awarded from the date of claim anyway. The same judge revisited the issue in *CM v SSWP (ESA)* [2019] UKUT 284 (AAC) and there held that the claimant was entitled to benefit under reg.30 of the 2008 Regulations although he again considered it to be unnecessary to decide whether the Secretary of State's decision under reg.30 had been made under s.8(1) and therefore whether the claimant had had an independent right of appeal against that decision. He noted that the question whether a claimant's condition was the same or had worsened was likely to be relevant in practical terms not only to a decision under reg.30 but also to the related decision made under reg.19 of the 2008 Regulations as to whether the claimant actually had limited capability for work. A decision under reg.19 is undoubtably appealable and he referred to the Tribunal of Commissioners' decision in *R(IB) 2/04*, where it was held that a tribunal had the power to make any decision that the Secretary of State could have made, and decided (apparently with the agreement of both parties) that, because the claimant had appealed against the reg.19 decision, the First-tier Tribunal had jurisdiction to

consider the reg.30 issue. However, he did not refer to the warning in *R(IS) 15/04* against permitting "by the back door what is not permitted by the front door" (see the note to s.12(2) under the heading *Can supersession decisions be substituted for revision decisions and vice versa?*). Arguably, the Upper Tribunal had jurisdiction to make the award it did only if the decision of the Secretary of State under reg.30 had, like the decision under reg.19, been made under s.8(1).

It is not easy to see why decisions under reg.30 (and the equivalent provision in reg.26 of the Employment and Support Allowance Regulations 2013) should not have been found to be made under s.8(1) and therefore appealable. They are arguably akin to decisions to make payments on account and it has been regarded as necessary to provide for appeals relating to those decisions expressly to be excluded from the right of appeal under s.12 (see paras 20 and 20A of Sch.2 to the Social Security and Child Support (Decisions and Appeals) Regulations 1999 and para.14 of Sch.3 to the Universal Credit, Personal Independence Payment, Jobseeker's Allowance and Employment and Support Allowance (Decisions and Appeals) Regulations 2013). It may be true that, if a decision of the Secretary of State under reg.30 was in principle appealable, any such appeal would probably be completely academic if the related challenge to the reg.19 decision was successful (as in *EI*) and would usually be of relatively limited value if the related challenge was unsuccessful because the period in issue under reg.30 would often be fairly short simply because an adverse decision under reg.30 would generally be related to an adverse decision under reg.19 made summarily without the claimant being referred for another medical examination (as in *CM*). There would, on the other hand, have been no other way for a claimant who was, say, suffering from a new condition (contrary to the Secretary of State's view) but who did not actually have limited capability for work to recover benefit for that short period before he or she was alerted to the need to claim jobseeker's allowance.

Subsection (2)

1.402 This subsection is disapplied in industrial disease cases where there has been recrudescence (see reg.12A of the Social Security and Child Support (Decisions and Appeals) Regulations 1999).

Paragraph (a) refers to a "claim" but in this context that is not to be read as being in contradistinction to, say, a supersession. The purpose of para.(a), read with s.12(8)(b) is to reverse the effect of *R(S) 1/83* and *R(S) 2/98*, in which it was held that a tribunal was entitled to take account of changes of circumstances occurring after the decision under appeal, on the basis that the claim made by the claimant subsisted until finally disposed of by the decision of the tribunal.

Paragraph (b) is not well drafted. The point being made in para.(a) is that a claim is effective only until it is decided *by the Secretary of State* (although benefit may then be awarded indefinitely or for a specified period in the future) and para.(b) is intended to make it clear that the consequence is that a change of circumstances taking place after the date of decision cannot give rise to entitlement under the original claim. This means that if a claimant appeals against the Secretary of State's decision, the tribunal cannot award benefit on the basis of a change of circumstances that has taken place between the Secretary of State's decision and its own decision. If no benefit was awarded on the initial claim, a new claim must, as para.(b) makes clear, be made if the claimant wishes to take advantage of the change of circumstances. That a decision refusing benefit cannot be superseded on the ground of a change of circumstances has been confirmed by a Tribunal of Commissioners in *R(I) 5/02*.

1.403 An assessment of disablement is a freestanding decision made under s.8(1)(c) and is appealable by virtue of reg.26 of the Social Security (Decisions and Appeals) Regulations 1999. In *R(I) 5/02*, the Tribunal of Commissioners held that a final assessment of disablement that had originally been made under s.47 of the Social Security Administration Act 1992 for a period that had come to an end could be superseded (having regard to para.4(1) of Sch.12 to the Social Security Act 1998 (Commencement No.8 and Savings and Consequential and Transitional Provisions)

Order 1999) because it had continuing effect. However, they expressly declined to say whether the same approach would apply to an assessment originally made under s.8(1)(c). It is suggested that it would not, because such an assessment has no effect after the period for which it has been made comes to an end. What is required is an entirely new assessment made on a new claim for disablement benefit.

However, para.(b) overlooks the possibility that a claim may be decided some while after the date of claim and may be made in respect of a period beginning before the date of claim. In some cases a claimant will have been entitled to benefit in respect of the early part of the period for which it is claimed but, by reason of a change of circumstances, will have ceased to be entitled to benefit by the time the Secretary of State gives his decision. Read literally, para.(b) would require the claimant to be refused benefit altogether in such a case because, on the basis of circumstances obtaining at the date of decision, he or she would not qualify. However, it is suggested that the word "accordingly" shows that para.(b) merely makes provision for the natural consequence of para.(a) and should be read to the effect that the claimant shall not be entitled to the benefit on the basis of circumstances not obtaining at *or before* the date of decision. This approach is consistent with that taken in *CIS/2428/1999* in the context of s.12(8)(b). In that case, it was pointed out that a literal interpretation of s.12(8)(b) would prevent a tribunal from taking account of a cause for a late claim which existed before the claim was made and had ceased to exist before the Secretary of State's decision on the claim. The Commissioner considered that that would be absurd and would prevent adjudication on a case falling within reg.19(5) of the Social Security (Claims and Payments) Regulations 1987. He held that a circumstance "obtains" at the date of decision if it is a circumstance, whenever it occurred, that is relied on by a claimant in justifying a late claim.

Equally, of course, a person may not have been entitled to benefit at the date of claim but may, due to a change of circumstances, have become entitled by the time the Secretary of State makes her decision. In such a case, the claimant is not required to make a new claim in order to be entitled to an award, even if a considerable period of time has elapsed (*SSWP v KK (JSA)* [2019] UKUT 313 (AAC)).

In *R(DLA) 4/05*, a Tribunal of Commissioners held that para.(b) precluded the Secretary of State from taking account of an anticipated change of circumstances, even on a claim made in advance. However, they held that it did not preclude the Secretary of State from having regard to the effect on entitlement to benefit on the mere passage of time. Therefore, he can make an advance decision on a renewal claim taking into account the fact that by the renewal date the qualifying period for a particular rate of benefit will have elapsed or the claimant will have attained a certain age. Prediction is also permitted where entitlement to benefit at the date of decision depends on what is "likely" to happen in the future (*R(DLA) 3/01*). Otherwise, where the Secretary of State anticipates a change of circumstances, he must either defer making a decision or make a decision ignoring the expected change but possibly marking the case for future consideration of revision or supersession. *R(DLA) 4/05* has been followed by a Tribunal of Commissioners in Northern Ireland (*R 2/05 (DLA)*). In *Secretary of State for Work and Pensions v Bhakta* [2006] EWCA Civ 65 (reported as *R(IS) 7/06*), the Court of Appeal approved *R(DLA) 4/05*. *Bhakta* was a case where the claimant intended to reside in the United Kingdom but had not become habitually resident in the United Kingdom at the date of the Secretary of State's decision only because a sufficient period of residence had not yet elapsed. The Court held that the Secretary of State could, under reg.13 of the Social Security (Claims and Payments) Regulations 1987, have made an advance award of income support from the date on which habitual residence had been likely to be established on the assumption that there would be no change in the claimant's circumstances. Regulation 13 has been amended with effect from May 23, 2007 so as to exclude that class of case (and all claims by "persons from abroad") from the scope of the regulation (see reg.2(2)(c) of the Social Security, Housing Benefit and Council Tax Benefit (Miscellaneous Amendments) Regulations 2007 (SI 2007/1331)), but the principle confirmed in *Bhakta* remains good in other contexts.

Subsection (3)

1.404 It having been pointed out that the lack of any reference in subs.(3) to mobility allowance meant that there was no power to revise or supersede a decision relating to mobility allowance so as to be able to recover an overpayment (*CDLA/2999/2004*), the Social Security Act 1998 (Prescribed Benefits) Regulations 2006 prescribe a number of benefits payable under the Social Security Act 1995 and the Supplementary Benefits Act 1976. The benefits prescribed were all abolished before the 1998 Act came into force and are unemployment benefit, sickness benefit, invalidity benefit, attendance allowance (as paid to those under 65), mobility allowance and supplementary benefit.

The provisions of Ch.II of Pt I of the 1998 Act are applied to decisions under ss.2 and 3 of the Age-Related Payments Act 2004, not by virtue of regulations made under this subsection but by s.5(5) of the 2004 Act.

Subsection (5)

1.405 Under s.8(1)(e) of the Social Security Contributions (Transfer of Functions, etc.) Act 1999 and the Commissioners for Revenue and Customs Act 2005, it is for HMRC to determine whether contributions of a particular class have been paid in respect of any period. Thus, it is for HMRC to determine the amount of contributions paid but it is for the Secretary of State to decide any question about the interpretation or application of the Social Security (Earnings Factor) Regulations 1979 (*R(IB) 1/09*).

However, any question as to the amount of contributions paid for graduated retirement benefit remains a matter for the Secretary of State (*R(P) 1/08*) as are the questions whether a person is entitled to "credits" (Sch.3 para.17 to the Social Security Act 1998, *CIB/2338/2000*) or is entitled to home responsibilities protection (Sch.3 para.16). It also appears that any dispute as to which is the relevant contribution year in respect of any claim is a matter for the Secretary of State, so that the effect of *Secretary of State for Social Security v Scully* [1992] 1 W.L.R. 927 (reported also as *R(S) 5/93*) is reversed and the effect of *R(G) 1/82* is restored. The Secretary of State's decisions are appealable under s.12.

Revision of decisions

1.406 **9.**—(1) [1 . . .] Any decision of the Secretary of State under section 8 above or section 10 below may be revised by the Secretary of State—

(a) either within the prescribed period or in prescribed cases or circumstances; and

(b) either on an application made for the purpose or on his own initiative;

and regulations may prescribe the procedure by which a decision of the Secretary of State may be so revised.

(2) In making a decision under subsection (1) above, the Secretary of State need not consider any issue that is not raised by the application or, as the case may be, did not cause him to act on his own initiative.

(3) Subject to subsections (4) and (5) and section 27 below, a revision under this section shall take effect as from the date on which the original decision took (or was to take) effect.

(4) Regulations may provide that, in prescribed cases or circumstances, a revision under this section shall take effect as from such other date as may be prescribed.

(5) Where a decision is revised under this section, for the purpose of any rule as to the time allowed for bringing an appeal, the decision shall be regarded as made on the date on which it is so revised.

(6) Except in prescribed circumstances, an appeal against a decision of the Secretary of State shall lapse if the decision is revised under this section before the appeal is determined.

AMENDMENT

1. Welfare Reform Act 2012 s.147 and Sch.14 Pt.8 (April 1, 2013).

DEFINITION

"prescribed"—see s.84.

GENERAL NOTE

This section applies to decisions under ss.2 and 3 of the Age-Related Payments Act 2004 (see s.5(5) of the 2004 Act). In relation to child benefit and guardian's allowance, the functions of the Secretary of State under this section were transferred with effect from April 7, 2003 to the Board of Inland Revenue (Tax Credits Act 2002 s.50(2)(e)). The functions of the Secretary of State in relation to the former working families' tax credit and disabled person's tax credit were similarly transferred to officers of the Inland Revenue from October 5, 1999 (Tax Credit Act 1999 s.2(1)(b) and Sch.2). The Inland Revenue has now been merged into HMRC, by the Commissioners for Revenue and Customs Act 2005. **1.407**

This section also applies to most decisions of HMRC made under s.170(2) of the Pensions Schemes Act 1993, by virtue of s.170(4).

See also regs 6 and 16 of the Employment and Support Allowance (Transitional Provisions, Housing Benefit and Council Tax Benefit) (Existing Awards) (No.2) Regulations 2010 (SI 2010/1907) under which this section was applied to a "conversion decision", made when employment and support allowance was first introduced, by treating it as though it were a decision as to entitlement to an employment and support allowance which had been made on a claim.

Section 6 of the Social Security (Additional Payments) Act 2022 provides that, for all purposes relating to the administration of an additional payment, any provision applying in relation to a benefit or tax credit by reference to which that additional payment is made is to apply in relation to that payment as if it were a payment or award of the benefit or tax credit in question, subject to any necessary modifications. This appears to have the effect that, among other provisions, s.9 of the 1998 Act applies to at least some extent where the additional payment is paid by reference to a benefit to which it applies. However, s.6(2)(a) of the 2022 Act provides that the legislation that may be applied includes "provision relating to overpayments and recovery, and appeals relating to overpayments and recovery (but not provision relating to appeals or reviews about entitlement to the social security benefit, tax credit or disability benefit in question)". This raises two questions. The first is whether revision and supersession fall within the scope of "review". It is certainly arguable that the legislation is to be read literally and that review is excluded in tax credit cases, but revision and supersession are not excluded in ordinary social security cases. The second question is whether the words in parenthesis are intended to prevent a person from challenging an overpayment or recovery decision on the ground that he or she was entitled to the additional payment or whether they are merely intended to emphasise that there is no right of appeal save in the context of an overpayment or recovery. Given the nature of the payments, it seems unlikely that there will in fact be many disputes, save where it is alleged that the related benefit was wrongly paid.

Subsection (1)

Under the Social Security Administration Act 1992, provision was made for the "review" of decisions. Such reviews are replaced by "revisions" under s.9 and **1.408** "supersessions" under s.10. Note that only a decision of the Secretary of State may be revised whereas a decision of the Secretary of State *or* of a tribunal or a Commissioner may be superseded. Apart from that, there is little that can be gleaned from the primary legislation as to the difference between revision and supersession. The most obvious distinction between the two concepts probably lies in the date from which the new decision takes effect. Where a decision is revised, the revised decision has effect from the effective date (or what should have been the effective date) of the original decision (see s.9(3)). On a supersession, the new decision takes effect from the date on which it is made and does not affect any past period, subject to limited provision for backdating in some cases (s.10(5)). A related distinction is that there is no appeal under s.12 against a refusal to revise under s.9. Formally, there is only a right of appeal against the original decision but s.9(5) extends the time for appealing against the original decision if it is revised, although not always if there is a refusal to revise (see the annotation to subs.(5)). By contrast, an appeal may be brought under s.12 against any decision under s.10. Beyond all that, no indication is given by the primary legislation as to the circumstances in which a revision of a decision is more appropriate than a supersession or vice versa. For that information, one must look at regs 3 and 4 of the Social Security and Child Support (Decisions and Appeals) Regulations 1999, regs 5–11 of the Child Benefit and Guardian's Allowance (Decisions and Appeals) Regulations 2003 and regs 5, 6 and 8–19 of the Universal Credit, Personal Independence Payment, Jobseeker's Allowance and Employment and Support Allowance (Decisions and Appeals) Regulations 2013 relating to revisions and at reg.6 of the 1999 Regulations, reg.13 of the 2003 Regulations and regs 22–31 of the 2013 Regulations relating to supersession. There would still be some overlap between the two procedures if it were not for reg.6(3) of the 1999 Regulations, reg.15 of the 2003 Regulations, and reg.32 of the 2013 Regulations which provide that a decision that may be revised cannot be superseded (save in limited circumstances where the revision could not take into account a further ground of supersession).

Happily, an application for supersession may be treated as an application for revision and vice versa (regs 3(10) and 6(5) of the 1999 Regulations regs 7(1)(a) and 14(1)(a) of the 2003 Regulations and regs 20(1) and 33(1) of the 2013 Regulations), so that it is not fatal if claimants or their advisors do not fully understand the difference when making the application.

Despite, or perhaps because of, this flexibility, experience shows that decisions are not always issued in the correct form. Indeed, it is often Departmental practice to issue decisions that state the outcome without stating whether the decision is a revision or supersession. It has been suggested that that is not necessarily improper when the decision is first issued to the claimant but that the decision ought nonetheless to have been made in the appropriate form so that, if there is a request for reasons or an appeal, the true basis of the decision can be explained (*CIB/313/2002*). However, strong criticisms have been made of the Secretary of State's failure in many circumstances to record any decision at all in the proper form (see *CPC/3891/2004* and *R(IS) 13/05*). Even where a decision is made in terms of a revision or supersession, there are occasions when the wrong type of decision is issued. This is unfortunate because the distinction between revision and supersession is very important when an appeal is lodged. While an appeal following a revision or refusal to revise lies against the original decision, an appeal following a supersession or refusal to supersede lies against the later decision. It is particularly important for a decision terminating an award to be issued in the correct form if the Secretary of State or HMRC intends subsequently to make a decision to the effect that there has been a recoverable overpayment, because s.71(5A) of the Social Security Administration Act 1992 generally requires there to have been a revision or supersession before an overpayment can be recovered (*CIS/3228/2003*, *R(IS) 13/05*). Section 71(5A) recognises that, unless an award is either revised or else superseded on a ground that makes the supersession retrospective by virtue of reg.7 of the 1999 Regulations, reg.16 of the 2003

Regulations, or regs 34–37 of the 2013 Regulations, the original award still governs entitlement in respect of the period before the decision terminating it was made and it cannot be shown that any benefit was overpaid.

For the circumstances in which a tribunal may give a decision in terms of supersession on an appeal following a revision or refusal to revise and vice versa, see the note to s.12(2), where it is suggested that many of the difficulties identified would be removed if some grounds for revision were instead grounds for supersession. In deciding whether revision or supersession was the more appropriate remedy, the draftsmen of the Regulations appear to have placed too much emphasis on the date from which a decision is effective and too little on the lack of an appropriate right of appeal against a decision given in terms of revision and the lack of any express provision for correcting on appeal a decision-maker's mistaken choice as to the appropriate procedure for making a change to an earlier decision. **1.409**

Section 9(1) provides that "any decision . . . under section 8 above or section 10 below" may be revised. However, in s.12(1) there is reference to "any decision . . . under section 8 or 10 above (whether as originally made or as revised under section 9 above)" and similar words referring to section 9 are to be found in s.10(1)(a). Do those references to s.9 in ss.10 and 12 suggest that references to decisions under ss 8 and 10 normally include decisions that have been revised? Or does the fact that there are references to s.9 in ss.10 and 12 but none in s.9 itself suggest that a decision that has already been revised cannot be revised again? In *CIS/3535/2003*, the Deputy Commissioner preferred the former approach and said, obiter, that a decision that has already been revised may be revised again and that the time for bringing an application under reg.3(1) of the Social Security and Child Support (Decisions and Appeals) Regulations 1999 starts again from the date the revision is notified.

Subsection (2)

Note that the Secretary of State "need not", but nonetheless may, consider additional issues. On an appeal following a revision or refusal to revise, the decision under appeal is the original decision (see subs.(5) read with s.12(1)). The tribunal's duty to consider issues is determined by the issues raised by the appeal (see s.12(8)(a)) rather than by the issues raised by the earlier application for revision because it is not obliged to consider independently the merits of the revision or refusal to revise, save to the extent that it must be satisfied that the Secretary of State had the power to revise the decision on the date on which the decision was revised (see *R(IB) 2/04* at [39]) or not revised (see the note to subs.(5)). **1.410**

Subsection (4)

See reg.5 of the Social Security and Child Support (Decisions and Appeals) Regulations 1999, reg.12 of the Child Benefit and Guardian's Allowance (Decisions and Appeals) Regulations 2003 and reg.21 of the Universal Credit, Personal Independence Payment, Jobseeker's Allowance and Employment and Support Allowance (Decisions and Appeals) Regulations 2013 which provide that the principal exception to the general rule is where a ground for the revision is that the original decision was made effective from the wrong date in the first place. **1.411**

Subsection (5)

Although s.12(1) does not confer a right of appeal against a decision made under this section either to revise or not to revise an earlier decision, it does confer a right of appeal against that earlier decision "whether as originally made or as revised". Therefore, if a person disagrees with a decision made under this section either to revise or not to revise an earlier decision, the remedy provided by this Act is to appeal against the earlier decision. **1.412**

This subsection facilitates such an appeal in a case where the earlier decision has been revised. It does so by providing, in effect, that the time for appealing re-starts from the date on which the decision is revised under this section. Otherwise, any appeal would be liable to be out of time.

However, it does not apply where the decision under this section is a refusal to revise. It appears never to have been argued that this subsection should be read as including a refusal to revise in the same way that s.12(9) must be read as including a refusal to supersede, but the argument is probably no longer open in the light of *R(IS) 15/04* and *Beltekian v Westminster CC* [2004] EWCA Civ 1784 (reported as *R(H) 8/05*) and anyway the context is different. It has certainly always been assumed that it is necessary to make provision in subordinate legislation for any extension of time for appealing where there has been a refusal to revise.

Currently, such provision is made in the Tribunal Procedure (First-tier Tribunal) (Social Entitlement Chamber) Rules 2008: by r.22(2)(d)(i) where notice of the refusal to revise is "notice of the result of mandatory reconsideration" and by r.22(2)(d)(ii) and para.5(c) of Sch.1 in certain other cases. In *PH v SSWP (DLA)* [2018] UKUT 404 (AAC); [2019] AACR 14, it was held that, because reg.3ZA(2) of the Social Security and Child Support (Decisions and Appeals) Regulations 1999 did not refer only to applications for revision within the scope of reg.3(1) or (3) of those Regulations, a refusal to revise on the ground of "official error" could (depending on the procedural history of the case and provided that the application for revision on that ground was not spurious) be "the result of mandatory reconsideration" and so have the effect of extending the time for appealing under r.22(2)(d)(i), with the result that the constraints imposed by the limited terms of para.5(c) of Sch.1 to the Rules in the light of *R(IS) 15/04* and *Beltekian* do not apply. Although it was held that it had to be shown by an appellant that the application for revision was not "spurious" in order to establish that the First-tier Tribunal had jurisdiction, it is suggested that it is necessary for the First-tier Tribunal in fact to be satisfied that there was an official error (or that some other ground of revision is made out), rather than merely that the point was arguable, in order for jurisdiction to be established. Otherwise, as was suggested in *CCS/5515/2002* at [36] and appears to have been conceded by leading counsel for the claimant in *R(IS) 15/04* (as recorded in *R(IB) 2/04* at [39]), the time limit for appealing and the restrictions on revisions would be subverted.

Where the time for appealing against a decision is not extended by a refusal to revise it and it is too late for an appeal to be brought, any challenge to the refusal to revise must be by way of an application for judicial review. It follows that, although a refusal to revise a decision may include a refusal to supersede the decision and an appeal might be brought against the refusal to supersede, it is not permissible for the First-tier Tribunal when deciding such an appeal to substitute a decision in terms of revision, at least where the refusal to revise is explicit (*R(IS) 15/04*, applied in *AW v SSWP (IB)* [2013] UKUT 20 (AAC)). Attention was drawn in *JA v SSWP (DLA)* [2014] UKUT 44 (AAC) to anomalies that can flow from this approach, given some of the circumstances in which decisions must be revised rather than superseded.

Subsection (6)

1.413 Regulations made under this subsection are reg.30 of the Social Security and Child Support (Decisions and Appeals) Regulations 1999, reg.27 of the Child Benefit and Guardian's Allowance (Decisions and Appeals) Regulations 2003 and reg.52 of the Universal Credit, Personal Independence Payment, Jobseeker's Allowance and Employment and Support Allowance (Decisions and Appeals) Regulations 2013.

Lapsing under this subsection is automatic and therefore, where the Secretary of State was minded to revise a decision to the advantage of the claimant but not to the fullest extent possible, she developed a practice of telling the claimant that she considered that she could revise the decision but inviting the claimant to say whether he or she agreed with the proposed decision. If the claimant replied in the affirmative, the decision was duly revised and the appeal lapsed. Otherwise, the decision was not revised but the Secretary of State informed the First-tier Tribunal of the proposed decision, effectively submitting that the appeal should be allowed to that extent. This procedure had the advantage of avoiding the Appellant having to initiate a new appeal if not satisfied with the proposed decision. It was considered in *DO v SSWP (PIP)* [2021] UKUT 161 (AAC), where the Secretary of State had omitted to tell the claimant that, if the decision were revised, he would have a fresh right of appeal against the decision as revised and where the First-tier Tribunal had, as the Upper Tribunal held at [47], failed to give the claimant an adequate warning that it was contemplating not accepting the Secretary of State's concession. In the course of its decision, the Upper Tribunal referred to judicial review proceedings then pending in another case, in which it was being argued that the Secretary of State was bound to revise a decision that was under appeal, if she was satisfied that it was wrong, with the result that the appeal would necessarily lapse. Those judicial review proceedings were subsequently withdrawn in the light of assurances given by the Secretary of State as to amendments to be given to guidance for decision-makers. In particular, it has been made clear that, where the Secretary of State considers that a decision should be revised to the advantage of the claimant, it will not be revised only "if the claimant indicates that they wish their appeal to continue, having been made aware of their right to appeal any revised decision".

Although lapsing under this subsection is automatic, any dispute as to whether an appeal has properly lapsed is a question as to the First-tier Tribunal's jurisdiction, upon which the First-tier Tribunal should rule (*GM v SSWP (JSA)* [2014] UKUT 57 (AAC)), either on the Appellant's application for directions for the determination of the case or on the Respondent's application that the case be stuck out. As pointed out in *AI v SSWP (PIP)* [2019] UKUT 103 (AAC), it is a breach of r.8(4) of the Tribunal Procedure (First-tier Tribunal) (Social Entitlement Chamber) Rules 2008 for a case to be struck out on the ground that it has lapsed without the appellant being given an opportunity to object.

In practice, where the Secretary of State has informed the Upper Tribunal that he has revised a decision under appeal and considers the appeal to have lapsed, the appellant is usually informed that the appeal has lapsed and the First-tier Tribunal's file is closed administratively without a judicial ruling, although it is reopened if the claimant objects, in which case the matter is put before a judge. Whether or not this is a strictly permissible practice, it is not necessarily unfair provided that the appellant has been told that the appeal has lapsed because a more favourable decision has been made in the case and that he or she may appeal against the new decision if he or she wishes, since, if the appellant is not satisfied that a more favourable decision has been made, he or she is still enabled to get the issue before the First-tier Tribunal one way or another and it is then for that Tribunal to make the appropriate ruling in the light of the true procedural history.

The procedural history in *KB v SSWP (UC)* [2019] UKUT 408 (AAC) shows that, where the First-tier Tribunal informs a claimant that an appeal has lapsed without there being a judicial decision to that effect, it will equally reinstate the appeal without a judicial decision if it considers that, due to a clerical error by the DWP, it was wrongly informed that the decision under appeal had been revised to the appellant's advantage. It is not clear whether the question whether the appeal had lapsed was raised at the subsequent hearing before the First-tier Tribunal in that case, but it was raised on the claimant's further appeal to the Upper Tribunal. The claimant argued that the Secretary of State had in fact revised the decision that had been appealed to the First-tier Tribunal so that the First-tier Tribunal had not had jurisdiction to determine her appeal and make the decision it did, but the Upper Tribunal found as a fact that there had been no relevant revision in the claimant's favour and accordingly rejected the claimant's argument.

In *AI* (mentioned above), it was held that, where a claim for personal independence payment is disallowed because a claimant has failed to attend a consultation with a health care professional and, after the claimant has appealed, the Secretary of State accepts that the claimant had good cause for the non-attendance and accordingly "puts the claimant back on the PIP journey" by arranging another medical consultation, the appeal does not lapse by virtue of that new decision alone as the decision is not "more advantageous" to the claimant for the purposes of reg.52 of the Universal Credit, Personal Independence Payment, Jobseeker's Allowance and Employment and Support Allowance (Decisions and Appeals) Regulations 2013 (which is similar terms to reg.30 of the Social Security and Child Support (Decisions and Appeals) Regulations 1999). What the First-tier Tribunal should clearly do in such circumstances is simply stay the appeal until the Secretary of State makes his or her determination following receipt of the health care professional's report. There is arguably an anomaly because, if the First-tier Tribunal, rather than the Secretary of State, had decided that the claimant had good cause for the non-attendance, it would have had a choice between adjourning or, in effect, remitting the case to the Secretary of State (*R(IS) 2/08* (see the annotation to s.12(2) under the heading *The powers of the First-tier Tribunal*), but that is the effect of the terms of reg.52 of the 2013 Regulations. It would, however, arguably be different in an employment and support allowance case if, as well as arranging a new consultation, the Secretary of State decided that employment and support allowance should be paid to the claimant under reg.30 of the Employment and Support Allowance Regulations 2008 or reg.26 of the Employment and Support Allowance Regulations 2013 pending her determination of the question whether the claimant had limited capability for work, because that would presumably involve a revision of the disallowance of employment and support allowance and would be advantageous to the claimant. *AI* was considered in *JW v SSWP (PIP)* [2019] UKUT 279 (AAC). The facts in the latter case were similar in that the claimant had appealed against a disallowance of a claim for failure to attend a consultation with a health care professional and the Secretary of State then accepted that she had had good cause for the non-attendance and arranged a new consultation. However, this time there appears to have been no suggestion that the appeal had lapsed. Instead, the Secretary of State sent a copy of the health care professional's report to the First-tier Tribunal, although without making either a formal decision or a response to the appeal in the light of it, and the First-tier Tribunal decided that the claimant did not have limited capability for work and so dismissed the appeal. Possibly due in part to the lack of an appropriate response to the appeal, the First-tier Tribunal made inadequate findings of fact and the Upper Tribunal set the decision on that ground. Save for the lack of a response to the appeal addressing the question whether the claimant had limited capability for work, the procedure adopted by the Secretary of State seems to have been entirely in accordance with *AI*. The Upper Tribunal therefore rejected a suggestion that it should, in effect, remit the case to the Secretary of State to make a decision on the question whether the claimant had limited capability for work and instead remitted the case to the First-tier Tribunal. It always had been, and remained, open to the Secretary of State to revise the disallowance and award employment and support allowance if she was satisfied that the claimant had limited capability for work, in which case the appeal would have lapsed, and in the absence of any indication that she wished to do so in a way that the claimant would accept, there was no point in remitting the case to the Secretary of State with the likelihood that the claimant would be forced to make another appeal, even if it were technically permissible to do so.

Decisions superseding earlier decisions

1.414 **10.**—(1) Subject to [1 subsection (3)] [4 . . .] below, the following, namely—

(a) any decision of the Secretary of State under section 8 above or this section, whether as originally made or as revised under section 9 above; [3 ...]

[3(aa) any decision under this Chapter of an appeal tribunal or a Commissioner; and]

(b) any decision under this Chapter [2 of the First-tier Tribunal or any decision of the Upper Tribunal which relates to any such decision] may be superseded by a decision made by the Secretary of State, either on an application made for the purpose or on his own initiative.

(2) In making a decision under subsection (1) above, the Secretary of State need not consider any issue that is not raised by the application or, as the case may be, did not cause him to act on his own initiative.

(3) Regulations may prescribe the cases and circumstances in which, and the procedure by which, a decision may be made under this section.

(4) [[1] . . .]

(5) Subject to subsection (6) and section 27 below, a decision under this section shall take effect as from the date on which it is made or, where applicable, the date on which the application was made.

(6) Regulations may provide that, in prescribed cases or circumstances, a decision under this section shall take effect as from such other date as may be prescribed.

[[3] (7) In this section—

"appeal tribunal" means an appeal tribunal constituted under Chapter 1 of this Part (the functions of which have been transferred to the First-tier Tribunal);

"Commissioner" means a person appointed as a Social Security Commissioner under Schedule 4 (the functions of whom have been transferred to the Upper Tribunal), and includes a tribunal of such persons.]

AMENDMENTS

1. Social Security Contributions (Transfer of Functions, etc.) Act 1999 Sch.7 para.23 (April 1, 1999).

2. Transfer of Tribunal Functions Order 2008 (SI 2008/2833) Sch.3 paras 143 and 148 (November 3, 2008).

3. Welfare Reform Act 2012 s.103 and Sch.12 para.4 (November 3, 2008).

4. Welfare Reform Act 2012 s.147 and Sch.14 Pt.8 (April 1, 2013).

DEFINITIONS

"appeal tribunal" –see subs.(7).
"Commissioner"—*ibid.*
"prescribed"—see s.84.

GENERAL NOTE

Transitional provisions in the various commencement orders bringing this Act into force (see the note to s.87), provide for the supersession under this section of decisions made by the various adjudicating authorities that existed under earlier legislation and, in *CI/1800/01*, the Commissioner construed a reference to adjudicating medical authorities as including medical appeal tribunals so as to enable a claimant to apply for supersession of a decision of a medical appeal tribunal that had continuing effect. However, in *CDLA/2999/2004*, the Commissioner declined to find any power to supersede an award of mobility allowance (which was a benefit that was replaced by the mobility component of disability living allowance in April 1992) made by an adjudication officer in 1986. **1.415**

The practical effect of *CDLA/2999/2004* has now substantially been reversed by the Social Security Act 1998 (Prescribed Benefits) Regulations 2006, which prescribes mobility allowance (and certain other benefits) for the purposes of s.8(3)(h) of this Act, and by the Social Security Act 1998 (Commencement Nos.9 and 11) (Amendment) Order 2006 (SI 2006/2540), which amends transitional provisions relating to the replacement of sickness and invalidity benefit by incapacity benefit and to the replacement of attendance allowance for people under 65 and mobility allowance by disability living allowance.

The insertion of subs.(1)(aa) retrospectively makes transitional provision (previously assumed to be unnecessary) expressly enabling decisions of appeal tribunals and Commissioners made before November 3, 2008 to be superseded.

1.416 This section applies to decisions under ss.2 and 3 of the Age-Related Payments Act 2004 (see s.5(5) of the 2004 Act).

In relation to child benefit and guardian's allowance, the functions of the Secretary of State under this section were transferred with effect from April 7, 2003 to the Board of Inland Revenue (Tax Credits Act 2002 s.50(2)(e)). The functions of the Secretary of State in relation to the former working families' tax credit and disabled person's tax credit were similarly transferred to officers of the Inland Revenue from October 5, 1999 (Tax Credit Act 1999 s.2(1)(b) and Sch.2). The Inland Revenue has now been merged into HMRC, by the Commissioners for Revenue and Customs Act 2005.

This section also applies to most decisions of HMRC made under s.170(2) of the Pensions Schemes Act 1993, by virtue of s.170(4).

See also regs 6 and 16 of the Employment and Support Allowance (Transitional Provisions, Housing Benefit and Council Tax Benefit) (Existing Awards) (No.2) Regulations 2010 (SI 2010/1907) under which this section was applied to a "conversion decision", made when employment and support allowance was first introduced, by treating it as though it were a decision as to a person's entitlement to an employment and support allowance which had been made on a claim.

Section 6 of the Social Security (Additional Payments) Act 2022 provides that, for all purposes relating to the administration of an additional payment, any provision applying in relation to a benefit or tax credit by reference to which that additional payment is made is to apply in relation to that payment as if it were a payment or award of the benefit or tax credit in question, subject to any necessary modifications. This appears to have the effect that, among other provisions, s.10 of the 1998 Act applies to at least some extent where the additional payment is paid by reference to a benefit to which it applies. However, s.6(2)(a) of the 2022 Act provides that the legislation that may be applied includes "provision relating to overpayments and recovery, and appeals relating to overpayments and recovery (but not provision relating to appeals or reviews about entitlement to the social security benefit, tax credit or disability benefit in question)". This raises two questions. The first is whether revision and supersession fall within the scope of "review". It is certainly arguable that the legislation is to be read literally and that review is excluded in tax credit cases, but revision and supersession are not excluded in ordinary social security cases. The second question is whether the words in parenthesis are intended to prevent a person from challenging an overpayment or recovery decision on the ground that he or she was entitled to the additional payment or whether they are merely intended to emphasise that there is no right of appeal save in the context of an overpayment or recovery. Given the nature of the payments, it seems unlikely that there will in fact be many disputes, save where it is alleged that the related benefit was wrongly paid.

Subsection (1)

1.417 For the distinction between revision and supersession, see the note to s.9(1). Note that an application for supersession may be treated as an application for revision and vice versa (regs 3(10) and 6(5) of the Social Security and Child Support (Decisions and Appeals) Regulations 1999 regs 7(1)(a) and 14(1)(a) of the Child Benefit and Guardian's Allowance (Decisions and Appeals) Regulations 2003 and regs 20(1) and 33(1) of the Universal Credit, Personal Independence Payment, Jobseeker's Allowance and Employment and Support Allowance (Decisions and Appeals) Regulations 2013).

Also, under reg.6(5) of the 1999 Regulations or reg.33(1) of the 2013 Regulations, the provision of information to the Secretary of State may be treated as an application for supersession. There are no other provisions specifying what constitutes an application for supersession. In *CI/954/2006*, the Commissioner doubted that giving information to a medical adviser during an examination was to be treated as an application for supersession, although the Secretary of State could have superseded on his own motion in the light of the information.

Sometimes departmental procedures require a claimant to complete a claim form for what is really an application for supersession rather than a claim. This can lead to confusion. One example was the practice of requiring claimants of income support who moved to a new address to complete a new claim. If this was not done promptly, a claimant might find that there was a gap in benefit payments that was not subsequently made up. The grounds upon which benefit was withheld in those circumstances were somewhat dubious.

In *CI/954/2006*, it was pointed out that where a claimant is in receipt of disablement benefit and suffers another industrial accident, a claim in respect of the subsequent accident may have to be treated in the alternative as an application for supersession of the original award, because, following *R(I) 4/03*, aggregation of assessments of disablement is an alternative to the making of two separate awards. One practical difference is that claims may be backdated but supersessions in those circumstances cannot, which the Commissioner suggested is anomalous. The Commissioner also pointed out that an application for supersession of an assessment of disablement needed to be treated also as an application for supersession of the underlying award if proper effect was to be given to any supersession of the assessment of disablement (see the annotations to regs 6 and 26 of the 1999 Regulations, below). Similarly, in *ED v SSWP* [2009] UKUT 206 (AAC) it was held that a claimant was applying for supersession of an earlier tribunal's decision, rather than making a new claim, when he had an existing award of disablement benefit in respect of one injury and was seeking to reopen the question whether he was suffering from a loss of faculty in respect of another condition following the earlier tribunal's decision that he was not.

That case differed from *R(I) 4/03*, which concerned a new claim that a claimant had suffered an industrial injury, because, in *ED v SSWP*, it had been accepted that the claimant had suffered an industrial injury. *DD v SSWP (II)* [2020] UKUT 302 (AAC), was a case indistinguishable from *ED* save that it concerned a prescribed disease rather than an injury arising from an industrial accident. In some cases, there may be a question whether a disease of the same type as one from which the claimant had previously suffered has been contracted afresh or whether the condition has merely lain dormant for a while, but that issue was not specifically raised in *DD*.

It was held in *PH v SSWP (DLA)* [2013] UKUT 268 (AAC) that the Secretary of State is entitled to extend the period of an award of disability living allowance by way of supersession. It is unlikely that he would often wish to do so, rather than requiring the claimant to make a renewal claim, but the point was important in that case because the question that arose was whether the First-tier Tribunal, standing in the shoes of the Secretary of State, had the power to extend the period of an award when allowing an appeal against a supersession decision that had prematurely ended an award with the result that the claimant had not made a renewal claim.

A supersession decision that is to the effect that the claimant has ceased to be entitled to a benefit brings the award to an end so that, if it is not challenged, it is necessary for the claimant to make another claim in order to regain entitlement. However, if the award was subsisting until the date of the supersession decision, that is only true if it is decided that the claimant is not entitled to the benefit at that date. Thus, in *SSWP v NC (ESA)* [2023] UKUT 124 (AAC), where the Secretary of State superseded a decision awarding contributory employment and support allowance and decided that the claimant had not been entitled to that benefit while in prison, but made that decision only after the claimant had been released, she erred in stating that the claimant was not entitled to employment and support allowance after his release merely because he had not made a new claim. The judge said at [27]:

> "A person who has a current award of a benefit cannot be expected to, and is neither obliged nor entitled to, make a new claim for the same benefit, even if payments

have been suspended. A supersession decision must therefore determine entitlement up to the date of the decision itself without a new claim having been made."

Subsection (2)

1.418 A person may appeal against aspects of a decision superseding an earlier decision notwithstanding that the decision maker did not address his or her mind to those aspects of the decision on the supersession, having done so only when making the earlier decision (*MF v Redcar and Cleveland BC (HB)* [2015] UKUT 634 (AAC)). Thus, although, when superseding and terminating an award of contributory employment and support allowance on the ground that 365 days had elapsed without the claimant having been in the support group, the Secretary of State was entitled to rely on his previous decision that the claimant did not have a limited capability for work-related activity, the claimant was entitled to raise on an appeal against the supersession decision the question whether she did have a limited capability for work-related activity at the date of the supersession decision (*MC v SSWP (ESA)* [2014] UKUT 125 (AAC); [2014] AACR 35). However, where an issue is not raised by an appeal, the fact that it was not raised before the Secretary of State either may be a factor the tribunal should take into account when deciding whether to consider the issue on the appeal (see s.12(8)(a)).

Subsection (3)

1.419 See regs 6 and 8 of the Social Security and Child Support (Decisions and Appeals) Regulations 1999, regs 13 and 14 of the Child Benefit and Guardian's Allowance (Decisions and Appeals) Regulations 2003 and regs 22–31 and 33 of the Universal Credit, Personal Independence Payment, Jobseeker's Allowance and Employment and Support Allowance (Decisions and Appeals) Regulations 2013.

Where a person applies for supersession and the Secretary of State decides that the case and circumstances are not among those prescribed by reg.6 of the 1999 Regulations (or, equally, reg.13 of the 2003 Regulations or any of regs 23 to 31 of the 2013 regulations), it has now been established that the Secretary of State may issue a decision refusing to supersede the original decision, rather than superseding it but without making any change (see *Wood v Secretary of State for Work and Pensions* [2003] EWCA Civ 53 (reported as *R(DLA) 1/03*)). It is not entirely clear whether he may still, as an alternative approach, supersede the original decision without making any change, but the distinction is of little practical importance. See the note to reg.6 of the 1999 Regulations.

Subsection (5)

1.420 In *R(IB)2/04*, the Tribunal of Commissioners decided that where a claimant has applied for supersession in order to obtain an increase of benefit but the Secretary of State supersedes the award so as to reduce entitlement, the supersession is made on the Secretary of State's own initiative and not on the claimant's application. Therefore, subject to the effect of any regulations made under subs.(6), it is effective from the date of the decision and not the date of the claimant's application. Similarly, where the Secretary of State's supersession decision is not less favourable than the original decision but the claimant appeals and the tribunal not only does not allow the appeal but also makes a decision even less favourable than the original decision, the tribunal's decision is usually effective from the date of the Secretary of State's supersession decision. See paras 95–97 of the Tribunal's decision.

Where a decision has been made that one benefit is no longer payable because another benefit has become payable and reg.4 of the Social Security (Overlapping Benefits) Regulations 1977 precludes the payment of both benefits, a decision to resume payment of the first benefit after payment of the second benefit has ceased is a decision under s.8 and not a supersession under s.10 (*Secretary of State for Work and Pensions v Adams* [2003] EWCA Civ 796 (reported as *R(G) 1/03*)). This means that, where there is a delay in making a decision to reinstate payment of the first benefit, the decision is nonetheless automatically effective from the date when payment of the second benefit ceased, rather than from a later date determined by s.10(5).

Subsection (6)

See reg.7 of, and Schs 3A to 3C to, the Social Security and Child Support (Decisions and Appeals) Regulations 1999 reg.16 of the Child Benefit and Guardian's Allowance (Decisions and Appeals) Regulations 2003 and regs 34–37 of the Universal Credit, Personal Independence Payment, Jobseeker's Allowance and Employment and Support Allowance (Decisions and Appeals) Regulations 2013. **1.421**

[1 *Reference of issues by Secretary of State to Inland Revenue*

References of issues by Secretary of State to Inland Revenue

10A.—(1) Regulations may make provision requiring the Secretary of State, where on consideration of any claim or other matter he is of the opinion that there arises any issue which under section 8 of the Social Security Contributions (Transfer of Functions, etc.) Act 1999 falls to be decided by an officer of the Inland Revenue, to refer the issue to the Inland Revenue. **1.422**

(2) Regulations under this section may—

(a) provide for the Inland Revenue to give the Secretary of State a preliminary opinion on any issue referred to them,

(b) specify the circumstances in which an officer of the Inland Revenue is to make a decision under section 8 of the Social Security Contributions (Transfer of Functions, etc.) Act 1999 on a reference by the Secretary of State,

(c) enable or require the Secretary of State, in specified circumstances to deal withany other issue arising on consideration of the claim or other matter pending the decision of the referred issue, and

(d) require the Secretary of State to decide the claim or other matter in accordance with the decision of an officer of the Inland Revenue on the issue referred to them, or in accordance with any determination of the [2 First-tier Tribunal or Upper Tribunal] made on appeal from [2 the tribunal's decision].]

AMENDMENTS

1. Social Security Contributions (Transfer of Functions, etc.) Act 1999 Sch.7 para.24 (July 5, 1999).

2. Transfer of Tribunal Functions and Revenue and Customs Appeals Order 2009 (SI 2009/56) Sch.1 paras 247 and 248 (April 1, 2009).

DEFINITIONS

"claim"—by virtue of s.39(2), see s.191 of the Social Security Administration Act 1992.

"Inland Revenue"—*ibid*, but note that the Inland Revenue was merged into Her Majesty's Revenue and Customs by the Commissioners for Revenue and Customs Act 2005.

"prescribed"—see s.84.

"tax appeal Commissioners"—see s.39(1).

GENERAL NOTE

See reg.11A of the Social Security and Child Support (Decisions and Appeals) Regulations 1999 and reg.42 of the Universal Credit, Personal Independence Payment, Jobseeker's Allowance and Employment and Support Allowance (Decisions and Appeals) Regulations 2013. **1.423**

Some decisions fall to be made by HMRC by virtue of s.170 of the Pensions Schemes Act 1993 (rather than by virtue of s.8 of the Social Security Contributions

(Transfer of Functions, etc.) Act 1999) but the Secretary of State may nevertheless refer to HMRC issues for determination under the 1993 Act notwithstanding that regulations under this section do not apply (*R(P) 1/04*).

The substitution of "the tribunal's decision" for "their decision" in subs.(2)(d) seems to have been an error, because "their decision" clearly originally referred to the decision of the officer of the Inland Revenue.

Regulations with respect to decisions

1.424 **11.**—(1) Subject to the provisions of this Chapter and the Administration Act, provision may be made by regulations for the making of any decision by the Secretary of State under or in connection with the current legislation, or the former legislation, including a decision on a claim for benefit.

(2) Where it appears to the Secretary of State that a matter before him involves a question of fact requiring special expertise, he may direct that in dealing with that matter he shall have the assistance of one or more experts.

(3) In this section—

"the current legislation" means the Contributions and Benefits Act, the Jobseekers Act [[1], the Social Security (Recovery of Benefits) Act 1997 [[2] , the State Pension Credit Act 2002 [[3], Part 1 of the Welfare Reform Act 2007, Part 1 of the Welfare Reform Act 2012 [[4] , Part 4 of that Act and Part 1 of the Pensions Act 2014]]]] [[5] [[6], section 30 of that Act and sections 18 to 21 of the Welfare Reform and Work Act 2016]];

"expert" means a person appearing to the Secretary of State to have knowledge or experience which would be relevant in determining the question of fact requiring special expertise;

"the former legislation" means the National Insurance Acts 1965 to 1974, the National Insurance (Industrial Injuries) Acts 1965 to 1974, the Social Security Act 1975 and Part II of the Social Security Act 1986.

AMENDMENTS

1. State Pension Credit Act 2002 ss.11 and 21 and Sch.1 para.7 and Sch.3 (July 2, 2002 for the purpose of exercising any power to make regulations or orders and April 7, 2003 for other purposes).

2. Welfare Reform Act 2007 Sch.3 para.17(1) and (4) (October 27, 2008).

3. Welfare Reform Act 2012 ss.31 and 91 Sch.2 para.46 and Sch.9 para.40 (February 25, 2013).

4. Pensions Act 2014 s.23 and Sch.12 paras 31 and 34 (April 6, 2016).

5. Pensions Act 2014 s.31(5) and Sch.16 paras 37 and 40 (April 6, 2017).

6. Welfare Reform and Work Act 2016 s.20(5) (July 27, 2017).

DEFINITIONS

"the Administration Act"—see s.84.

"benefit"—by virtue of s.39(2), see s.191 of the Social Security Administration Act 1992.

"claim"—*ibid.*

"Contributions and Benefits Act"—see s.84.

"the current legislation"—see subs.(3).

"expert"—*ibid.*

"the former legislation"—*ibid.*

"the Jobseeker's Act"—see s.84.

GENERAL NOTE

1.425 In relation to the former working families' tax credit and disabled person's tax credit, the power to make regulations was transferred to the Commissioners of

Inland Revenue and the other functions of the Secretary of State were transferred to officers of the Inland Revenue, with effect from October 5, 1999 (Tax Credits Act 1999, s.2(1)(b) and Sch.2, paras 5(b)(iii) and 8(a)). In relation to child benefit and guardian's allowance, powers and functions were similarly transferred to the Inland Revenue by the Tax Credits Act 2002 (see s.50(2)(e)). The Inland Revenue was merged into Her Majesty's Revenue and Customs, by the Commissioners for Revenue and Customs Act 2005.

Subsection (1)

See in particular reg.28 of the Social Security and Child Support (Decisions and Appeals) Regulations 1999 and reg.51 of the Universal Credit, Personal Independence Payment, Jobseeker's Allowance and Employment and Support Allowance (Decisions and Appeals) Regulations 2013. 1.426

Appeals

Appeal to [2 First-tier Tribunal]

12.—(1) This section applies to any decision of the Secretary of State under section 8 or 10 above (whether as originally made or as revised under section 9 above) which— 1.427

(a) is made on a claim for, or on an award of, a relevant benefit, and does not fall within Schedule 2 to this Act; [1 or]

(b) is made otherwise than on such a claim or award, and falls within Schedule 3 to this Act; [1 . . .]

(c) [1 . . .]

[1 (2) In the case of a decision to which this section applies, the claimant and such other person as may be prescribed shall have a right to appeal to [2 the First-tier Tribunal], but nothing in this subsection shall confer a right of appeal –

[3(a) in relation to a prescribed decision, or a prescribed determination embodied in or necessary to a decision;

(b) where regulations under subsection (3A) so provide.]]

(3) Regulations under subsection (2) above shall not prescribe any decision or determination that relates to the conditions of entitlement to a relevant benefit for which a claim has been validly made or for which no claim is required.

[3(3A) Regulations may provide that, in such cases or circumstances as may be prescribed, there is a right of appeal under subsection (2) in relation to a decision only if the Secretary of State has considered whether to revise the decision under section 9.

(3B) The regulations may in particular provide that that condition is met only where—

(a) the consideration by the Secretary of State was on an application,

(b) the Secretary of State considered issues of a specified description, or

(c) the consideration by the Secretary of State satisfied any other condition specified in the regulations.

(3C) The references in subsections (3A) and (3B) to regulations and to the Secretary of State are subject to any enactment under or by virtue of which the functions under this Chapter are transferred to or otherwise made exercisable by a person other than the Secretary of State.]

[5 (3D) In the case of a decision relating to child benefit or guardian's allowance, the making of any appeal under this section against the decision as originally made must follow the Commissioners for Her Majesty's Revenue and Customs first deciding, on an application made for revision of that decision under section 9, not to revise the decision.]

(4) Where the Secretary of State has determined that any amount is recoverable under or by virtue of section 71 [4 , 71ZB, 71ZG, 71ZH,] or 74 of the Administration Act, any person from whom he has determined that it is recoverable shall have the same right of appeal to [2 the First-tier Tribunal] as a claimant.

(5) In any case where—

(a) the Secretary of State has made a decision in relation to a claim under Part V of the Contributions and Benefits Act; and

(b) the entitlement to benefit under that Part of that Act of any person other than the claimant is or may be, under Part VI of Schedule 7 to that Act, affected by that decision,

that other person shall have the same right of appeal to [2 the First-tier Tribunal] as the claimant.

(6) A person with a right of appeal under this section shall be given such notice of a decision to which this section applies and of that right as may be prescribed.

(7) Regulations may –

[3(a) make provision as to the manner in which, and the time within which, appeals are to be brought;

(b) provide that, where in accordance with regulations under subsection (3A) there is no right of appeal against a decision, any purported appeal may be treated as an application for revision under section 9.]

(8) In deciding an appeal under this section, [2 the First-tier Tribunal]—

(a) need not consider any issue that is not raised by the appeal; and

(b) shall not take into account any circumstances not obtaining at the time when the decision appealed against was made.

(9) The reference in subsection (1) above to a decision under section 10 above is a reference to a decision superseding any such decision as is mentioned in paragraph (a) or (b) of subsection (1) of that section.

AMENDMENTS

1. Social Security Contributions (Transfer of Functions, etc.) Act 1999 Sch.7 para.25 (April 1, 1999).

2. Transfer of Tribunal Functions Order 2008 (SI 2008/2833) Sch.3 paras 143 and 149 (November 3, 2008).

3. Welfare Reform Act 2012 s.102(1)–(4) (February 25, 2013).

4. Welfare Reform Act 2012 s.105(6) (April 29, 2013).

5. Tax Credits, Child Benefit and Guardian's Allowance Reviews and Appeals Order 2014 SI 2014/886 art.4(1) (April 6, 2014).

DEFINITIONS

"the Administration Act"—see s.84.

"claim"—by virtue of s.39(2), see s.191 of the Social Security Administration Act 1992.

"claimant"—see s.39(1) and, by virtue of s.39(2), see s.191 of the Social Security Administration Act 1992.

"the Contributions and Benefits Act"—see s.84.

"prescribed"—*ibid.*

"relevant benefit"—see s.8(3).

General Note

This section provides only for appeals against decisions made by the Secretary of State under ss.8 and 10 of this Act. However, it applies to decisions under ss.2 and 3 of the Age-Related Payments Act 2004 by virtue of s.5(5) of the 2004 Act) and is also applied to other decisions of the Secretary of State by reg.9 of the Social Security (Work-focused Interviews for Lone Parents) and Miscellaneous Amendments Regulations 2000 reg.15 of the Social Security (Jobcentre Plus Interviews) Regulations 2002 and reg.14 of the Social Security (Jobcentre Plus Interviews for Partners) Regulations 2003, all of which are concerned with decisions that claimants have failed without good cause to attend interviews. **1.428**

It also applies—with only the modification that references to the Secretary of State are to be construed as references to the Board of Inland Revenue or to an officer of the Inland Revenue—so as to provide for appeals against decisions relating to child benefit and guardian's allowance (by virtue of the Tax Credits Act 2002 Sch. para.50), against decisions relating to the former working families' tax credit and disabled person's tax credit (by virtue of the Tax Credits Act 1999 Sch.2 para.21), against penalties imposed under s.9(1), (3)(a) or (5)(a) of the 1999 Act (by virtue of Sch.4 para.3(2) of the 1999 Act) and against decisions given under s.170 of the Pension Schemes Act 1993 in respect of retirement pensions (by virtue of s.170(6) of the 1993 Act). The Inland Revenue was merged into Her Majesty's Revenue and Customs, by the Commissioners for Revenue and Customs Act 2005.

Quite separate rights of appeal to the First-tier Tribunal are given under s.4 of the Vaccine Damage Payments Act 1979 (in respect of vaccine damage payments—see Vol.I of this work), under ss.11 and 12 of the Social Security (Recovery of Benefits) Act 1997 (in respect of the recovery of benefits from those making compensation payments in respect of personal injury), under reg.10(2B) of the Employment Protection (Recoupment of Jobseeker's Allowance and Income Support) Regulations 1996 (in respect of the recovery of benefits from those making compensation payments in employment tribunal proceedings), under s.38 of the Tax Credits Act 2002 (in respect of tax credits),under s.50 of the Child Maintenance and Other Payments Act 2008 (in respect of mesothelioma lump sum payments), under reg.25 of the Diffuse Mesothelioma Payment Scheme Regulations 2014, under s.56 of the Childcare Payments Act 2014 and under reg.39 of the Childcare (Free of Charge for Working Parents) (England) Regulations 2022. For the 2008 Act and 2014 Regulations, see Vol.I of this work and, for the 2002 and 2014 Acts and the 2022 Regulations, see Vol.IV.

Section 6 of the Social Security (Additional Payments) Act 2022 provides that, for all purposes relating to the administration of an additional payment, any provision applying in relation to a benefit or tax credit by reference to which that additional payment is made is to apply in relation to that payment as if it were a payment or award of the benefit or tax credit in question, subject to any necessary modifications. This appears to have the effect that, among other provisions, s.12 of the 1998 Act applies where the additional payment is paid by reference to a benefit to which it applies. However, s.6(2)(a) of the 2022 Act provides that the legislation that may be applied includes "provision relating to overpayments and recovery, and appeals relating to overpayments and recovery (but not provision relating to appeals or reviews about entitlement to the social security benefit, tax credit or disability benefit in question)". It is not entirely clear whether the words in parenthesis are intended to prevent a person from challenging an overpayment or recovery decision on the ground that he or she was entitled to the additional payment or whether they are merely intended to emphasise that there is no right of appeal save in the context of an overpayment or recovery. Given the nature of the payments, it seems unlikely that there will in fact be many disputes, save where it is alleged that the related benefit was wrongly paid.

Separate rights of appeal to the First-tier Tribunal are also conferred by ss.21(9) and 22 of the Child Trust Funds Act 2004, but subss.(7) and (8)(b) of this section are applied in modified form to such appeals by reg.6 of the Child Trust Funds **1.429**

(Non-tax Appeals) Regulations 2005 (SI 2005/191) (which were originally made under s.24(5) of the 2004 Act and remain valid under the new s.23(6)). See Vol. IV for the 2004 Act and the Child Trust Funds (Appeals) Regulations 2005, made under subs.(7) as so applied.

Until April 1, 2009, a version of subs.(1) of this section, substituted for subs (1) and (2), and modified versions of subss.(7) and (8)(b) were applied to appeals under the Tax Credits Act 2002 by reg.4 of the Tax Credits (Appeals) Regulations 2002 (SI 2002/2926). However, those Regulations then lapsed insofar as they applied in Great Britain for reasons explained in *JI v HMRC (TC)* [2013] UKUT 199 (AAC) and alternative provision has now been made (see Vol.IV).

Numerous statutes and regulations outside the scope of this work also provide rights of appeal to the First-tier Tribunal in classes of case allocated to the Social Entitlement Chamber.

Subsection (1)

1.430 This section provides only for appeals against decisions under ss.8 and 10 of this Act (but see the note above). Challenges to decisions under s.9 are brought by appealing against the original decision rather than the s.9 decision. The phrase "decision . . . under section . . . 10" includes a decision to refuse to supersede (*Wood v Secretary of State for Work and Pensions* [2003] EWCA Civ 53 (reported as *R(DLA) 1/03*)), notwithstanding the terms of subs.(9).

There cannot be an appeal unless there has been a decision under s.8 or s.10 and so the First-tier Tribunal had no jurisdiction to consider a challenge to a refusal to make such a decision (*MM v SSWP (IS)* [2020] UKUT 220 (AAC)). If the First-tier Tribunal thought there might be merit in such an argument, it could say so and seek observations from the Secretary of State, but any formal judicial remedy would have to be sought by the claimant through judicial review proceedings in the High Court or, in Scotland, the Court of Session. Similarly, a tribunal had no jurisdiction to consider a challenge to the Secretary of State's failure to exercise his power to make a winter fuel payment without a claim (*R(IS) 12/05*). In *CIS/4088/2004*, the Commissioner considered that there must have been a decision refusing to make a payment in circumstances where the claimant had previously received a winter fuel payment and it was erroneously believed within the Department for Work and Pensions that no further payment could be made in the absence of a claim after the claimant had ceased to be entitled to incapacity benefit, but that decision was doubted in *CIS/840/2005*.

A lacuna in subs.(1) was explored in *R(IS)14/04*, where the claimant had purported to appeal to an appeal tribunal against a decision to the effect that benefit was recoverable from him under s.74 of the Social Security Administration Act 1992. The Commissioner agreed with the tribunal that a right of appeal could not arise under subs.(1)(b) because there was no reference in Sch.3 to decisions under s.74 of the 1992 Act, although paras 5 and 6 of the Schedule refer to recoverability decisions made under s.71 of the 1992 Act and subs.(4) shows that it is intended that claimants should be entitled to appeal against decisions under either s.71 or s.74. He concluded that the right of appeal arose under subs.(1)(a) because the decision under s.74 "is sufficiently related to the award of income support on which the excess payment has been made". The same reasoning was applied in *VT v SSWP (IS)* [2016] UKUT 178 (AAC); [2016] AACR 42, where it was held that there was a right of appeal against the imposition of a civil penalty under s.115D of the Social Security Administration Act 1992.

The scope of an appeal

1.431 The scope of the First-tier Tribunal's jurisdiction must depend on the scope of the decision which is the subject of the appeal. Paragraph (a) provides for an appeal against any decision made *on* a claim or award. Section 20(1)(a) and (b) of the Social Security Administration Act 1992 drew a distinction between a "claim" and a "question" and s.36 expressly enabled a tribunal to deal with any question first arising before them and not previously considered by an adjudication officer. The new legislation does not use the terms "claim" and "question" and there is no provision similar to the old s.36.

However, this may not make much difference. In *CIB/2338/2000*, the Commissioner held that the only type of "decision" that could be appealed was an "outcome" decision which is "a useful expression to refer to decisions that have, in crude terms, an impact on a claimant's pocket". He pointed out that an appeal lay only against decisions under ss.8 and 10. Section 8(1)(a) provides only that the Secretary of State shall "decide any claim". Section 8(1)(c) provides for the making of "any decision that falls to be made under or by virtue of any enactment" but the Commissioner did not construe that as referring to the individual determinations that are the building blocks of a decision on a claim for benefit. He understood it to refer to the making of decisions in relation to, say, crediting of earnings for contributions purposes. Section 10 refers to the supersession of decisions under s.8 or decisions of tribunals or Commissioners on appeal against from s.8 decisions. Therefore, there is no appeal against a decision on what used to be called a "question". In *CIB/2338/2000*, that meant that there was no appeal solely against the determination that the claimant was incapable of work; the appeal was against the consequential decision that he was not entitled to a "credit". This approach, which was endorsed by a Tribunal of Commissioners in *R(IB) 2/04*, makes it unnecessary for there to be a provision equivalent to the old s.36 expressly providing for a tribunal to deal with an issue that has not been considered by a decision-maker, because it is implicit that, if a tribunal has rejected a ground upon which the decision-maker has made an "outcome decision", it is necessary (subject to s.12(8)(a)) for the tribunal to consider such other issues as are necessary in order to substitute its own "outcome decision" for the decision-maker's. However, this is all subject to two qualifications. First, Sch.3 to the Act and reg.26 of the Social Security and Child Support (Decisions and Appeals) Regulations 1999 make provision for appeals to be brought against certain freestanding decisions that are not "outcome decisions". Secondly, there are circumstances in which a tribunal is not obliged to substitute an "outcome decision" for one under appeal but may, in effect, remit the case to the Secretary of State or HMRC (*R(IS) 2/08*, discussed in more detail in the annotation to subs.(2) below).

Accurately identifying the scope of the appeal may be very important in some cases although, in an appeal against a supersession decision, this does not necessarily involve being able to identify the precise details of all the decisions being superseded if adequate inferences can be drawn from, for instance, a record of payments of benefit (*AR v SSWP (ESA)* [2013] UKUT 358 (AAC); *JG v SSWP (ESA)* [2019] UKUT 25 (AAC)).

By virtue of s.12(1)(b) there is a right of appeal against an assessment of disablement for industrial disablement benefit, as a freestanding decision (see para.9 of Sch.3 to the Act and reg.26 of the Social Security and Child Support (Decisions and Appeals) Regulations 1999). In *R(I) 5/02*, the Tribunal of Commissioners held that a tribunal considering such an appeal had no jurisdiction to consider a refusal of benefit consequent upon the assessment of disablement. It is not clear how the two decisions were notified to the claimant in that case but it has been suggested that an appeal against an assessment of disablement should be treated as being also an appeal against the refusal of benefit, unless the Secretary of State is prepared to treat it as an application for revision of the refusal of benefit (*CI/1547/2001*). This is because, if there is no appeal against the refusal of benefit, it would have to be revised or superseded to give effect to a successful appeal in respect of the assessment of disablement. It does not appear that any such revision or supersession could be effective from the beginning of the period of assessment if action for revision or supersession is taken only after the tribunal's decision.

There are other circumstances where an appeal against one decision should be taken to be also an appeal against another decision, even where the other decision is implicit and has not actually been recorded. Thus, in *R(JSA) 2/04*, it was held that, where a claimant seeks benefit for the period between the end of one award and a new claim, an appeal against a refusal to backdate the new claim must sometimes be treated as being also an appeal against the termination of that previous award, because the latter may be the decision that is really being challenged. Similarly, in *CS v SSWP (DLA)* [2011] UKUT 509 (AAC), an appeal against a decision in respect of entitlement was held also to have been an appeal against a separate decision that an overpayment was recoverable. In *Abbas v Secretary of State for Work and Pensions* [2005] EWCA Civ 652, where the claimant had made a continuation claim for disability living allowance and the Secretary of State's response was to supersede the existing award and terminate it before it had originally been due to end, it was necessary for the appeal against the supersession decision to be treated also as an appeal against a disallowance of the continuation claim because otherwise, even if the claimant showed that she satisfied the conditions for entitlement to disability living allowance, benefit could not be awarded in respect of any period after the original renewal date.

Subsection (2)

1.432 Note that s.39(1) has the effect that, in relation to a joint-claim couple, "claimant" means the couple or either of them. If the appeal is not brought by both members of the couple, the other member is a "respondent" by virtue of r.1(3) of the Tribunal Procedure (First-tier Tribunal) Social Entitlement) Rules 2008. This may not be of much practical effect if the couple are still living together, but it may be if they are not, because, in principle, both members should be provided with documents and given notice of any hearing (*PD v HMRC (TC)* [2010] UKUT 159 (AAC); *SSWP v WV (UC)* [2023] UKUT 112 (AAC) at [76]).

For regulations made under this subsection, see regs 25 and 27 of the Social Security and Child Support (Decisions and Appeals) Regulations 1999, regs 24 and 25 of the Child Benefit and Guardian's Allowance (Decisions and Appeal) Regulations 2003 and regs 49 and 50(2) of the Universal Credit, Personal Independence Payment, Jobseeker's Allowance and Employment and Support Allowance (Decisions and Appeals) Regulations 2013.

Even where an appeal to the First-tier Tribunal must be lodged with a decision-maker, the decision-maker is not entitled to refuse to refer the case to a tribunal if he considers that the tribunal has no jurisdiction to hear it. It is for the tribunal to determine whether it has jurisdiction to hear a case (*R(I) 7/94*) and, if the decision-maker were to refuse to refer an appeal to the tribunal, it would be open to the tribunal to consider whether it had jurisdiction and, if it had, to determine the appeal without the appeal having been passed to it (*R(H) 1/07*).

The nature of an appeal to the First-tier Tribunal

1.433 For the investigatory approach of the First-tier Tribunal and its approach to evidence, see the note to s.3(1) of the Tribunals, Courts and Enforcement Act 2007.

An appeal to the First-tier Tribunal is a rehearing (*R(F) 1/72*); it is not just a review of the decision under appeal. The tribunal stands in the shoes of the decision-maker and has the power to consider any issue and make any decision the decision-maker could have made (*R(IB) 2/04*). Thus, when considering an appeal against a decision that a claimant of employment and support allowance does not have limited capability for work-related activity, the First-tier Tribunal may consider whether the claimant had a limited capability for work (*AE v SSWP (ESA)* [2014] UKUT 5 (AAC); [2014] AACR 23). A person may appeal against aspects of a decision superseding an earlier decision notwithstanding that the decision-maker did not address his or her mind to those aspects of the decision on the supersession, having done so only when making the earlier decision (*MF v Redcar and Cleveland BC (HB)* [2015] UKUT 634 (AAC)). Thus, on an appeal against a decision superseding and terminating an award of contributory employment and support allowance on the ground that 365 days have elapsed without the claimant having been in the support group, the claimant is entitled to raise the question whether they did have a limited capability for work-related activity at the date of the supersession decision (*MC v SSWP (ESA)* [2014] UKUT 125 (AAC); [2014] AACR 35). Moreover, where the Secretary of State has a broad discretion, e.g. as to the period of disqualification for jobseeker's allowance to be imposed when a person leaves his employment voluntarily without just cause, the tribunal has to substitute its own judgment for that of the Secretary of State, rather than merely considering whether the Secretary of State has acted reasonably (*CJSA/1703/2006*).

The same approach applies in contexts other than social security law (see *R(AF) 3/07*, *MC v SSD* [2009] UKUT 173 (AAC), *Ofsted v GM* [2009] UKUT 89 (AAC); [2010] AACR 21 and *Vesco v IC* [2019] UKUT 247 (AAC). However, not only does the First-tier Tribunal have no less power than the Secretary of State, it also has no greater power and so is equally unable to supersede an earlier decision of a tribunal on the ground of mistake of law (*NH v CMEC* [2009] UKUT 183 (AAC)).

In *AC v SSWP (Credits)* [2019] UKUT 267 (AAC), the First-tier Tribunal had dismissed an appeal from a decision of the Secretary of State refusing to extend time for claiming national insurance contribution "credits" under reg.12(b) of the Social Security (Contributions Credits for Parents and Carers) Regulations 2010 and the judge had said in [13] of his decision that "... I was of the view that the respondent in considering the exercise of that discretion was entitled to make the decision that it did". The Upper Tribunal judge considered that that paragraph was "more consistent with the tribunal having exercised a reviewing function rather than an appellate one, by which I mean that it did not consider afresh the judgment required by regulation 12(b), but merely asked whether the decision-maker had been entitled to decide as they did". He nevertheless read the decision as a whole and looked at the substance of the judge's reasons as well as the language used before deciding that the First-tier Tribunal had not shown that it had taken the correct approach.

In *R(H) 6/06*, it was said that "a right of appeal against an exercise of discretion that is non-justiciable because the relevant considerations cannot be discerned must be limited to points of law". Arguably, it would have been more accurate to say that the appeal would be by way of a review (as opposed to a rehearing), rather than that the appeal would be only on a point of law, but the practical difference may be limited in such a case. A discretion is non-justiciable only if the relevant considerations are policy matters requiring "essentially non-legal judgments" (*R(H) 3/04*) and legislation does not normally confer a right of appeal to a tribunal against such a decision unless it expressly limits the right to points of law. If legislation appears to confer such a right in respect of a non-justiciable decsion, there may arise questions as to the construction or validity of the legislation, as in *R(H) 6/06*. In *R(H) 1/08*, the Commissioner pointed out that the mere fact that different people might legitimately exercise their judgment differently on the same facts does not make the judgment a discretion and, if there is a discretion, does not make it non-justiciable. It has not been suggested that any appeal under s.12 is capable of raising a non-justiciable issue.

The powers of the First-tier Tribunal

There is nothing in s.12 to indicate what powers a tribunal has when it allows an **1.434** appeal, and, although it stands in the shoes of the decision-maker and can make any decision the decision-maker could have made, it is therefore also open to a tribunal to set aside a decision and, in effect, to remit the case to the original decision-maker where that appears to be more appropriate than substituting its own decision. Examples of cases where that might be done are where a recoverability decision should have been made against a person who is not a party to the appeal *(R(H) 6/06)* or where issues first arise in the course of an appeal (*R(IS) 2/08*, where it was made clear that the tribunal must nonetheless deal with the issues originally raised in the appeal). Thus, although an appeal to a tribunal normally lies only against an "outcome decision" (*R(IB) 2/04*), a tribunal hearing an appeal against an "outcome decision" is not always obliged to substitute another such decision. The Tribunal of Commissioners said, at para.48 of *R(IS) 2/08*—

> "When an appeal against an outcome decision raises one issue on which the appeal is allowed but it is necessary to deal with a further issue before another outcome decision is substituted, a tribunal may set aside the original outcome decision without substituting another outcome decision, provided it deals with the original issue raised by the appeal and substitutes a decision on that issue. The Secretary of State must then consider the new issue and decide what outcome decision to give. In that outcome decision, he must give effect to the tribunal's decision on the

original issue unless, at the time he makes the outcome decision, he is satisfied that there are grounds on which to supersede the tribunal's decision so as, for instance, to take account of any changes of circumstances that have occurred since he made the decision that was the subject of the appeal to the tribunal. Because his decision is an outcome decision, the claimant will have a right of appeal against it."

The Tribunal of Commissioners gave the following additional guidance at [55(2)]—

"Where a tribunal, having dealt with the issues originally raised in an appeal, is not able immediately to give an outcome decision, it must decide whether to adjourn or whether to remit the question of entitlement to the Secretary of State. The technical difficulty of the outstanding issues and the likelihood of a further appeal if the entitlement question is remitted will be relevant considerations. The tribunal should consider whether the Secretary of State would be in a better position to decide the issue and to seek further information from the claimant. It may have to balance the desirability of a decision being made as quickly as possible against the desirability of it being made as accurately as possible, given that an appeal on a point of fact will not lie against a decision of the tribunal on any fresh issue. The wishes of the parties should be taken into account."

However, what the First-tier Tribunal cannot do is provide a remedy that the decision-maker could not provide in a decision under s.8 or 10. Thus, if delay in deciding a case is such as to breach an appellant's rights under art.6 of the European Convention on Human Rights, the First-tier Tribunal cannot, on an appeal under this section, provide any remedy for that breach (*AS v SSWP (CA)* [2015] UKUT 592 (AAC); [2016] AACR 22).

There is an important distinction between the First-tier Tribunal remitting a case to the Secretary of State to make an "outcome decision", where the First-tier Tribunal has dealt with the issue arising on the appeal and the consequence is that other issues that have not previously been considered need to be determined (as in *R(IS) 2/08*), and the First-tier Tribunal making an "outcome decision" but leaving to the Secretary of State a precise assessment or calculation necessary to implement the decision (which was held in *R(SB) 11/86* also to be an acceptable procedure). In the former, the Secretary of State is left to make the "outcome decision" and any challenge to it can be brought before the First-tier Tribunal only by way of a fresh appeal (after "mandatory reconsideration"). In the latter, the First-tier Tribunal has made an "outcome decision" but it is incomplete if there is no agreement as to the assessment or calculation and so the First-tier Tribunal remains seised of the case. It was therefore stated in *R(SB) 11/86* that "it is essential, when such a course is adopted, that the appeal tribunal should make it clear that, in the event that the issue cannot be disposed of by agreement between the parties, the matter must be restored before the appeal tribunal so that it—and it alone—may discharge its duty of finally determining the claimant's appeal thereto". Thus, the parties have what lawyers call "liberty to apply" (although it may not be helpful to use that term when the parties do not have legal representation). In *MQ v SSWP (CSM)* [2017] UKUT 392 (AAC), it was held that a request to the First-tier Tribunal to resolve such a disagreement about an assessment or calculation was a form of post-hearing application that might be considered by the judge sitting alone even though the main decision had been given by a panel consisting of the judge and another member.

Correcting procedural errors by the Secretary of State

1.435 In *R(IB)2/04*, a Tribunal of Commissioners considered in depth the jurisdiction of tribunals and the extent to which tribunals are limited, or not limited, by the terms of the decision against which an appeal has been brought. They noted that s.12 makes no positive provision at all as to a tribunal's powers so that those powers must be found by a process of implication. They therefore considered the case law on adjudication before the 1998 Act came into force (in particular, *R(F) 1/72*, *R(P) 1/55*, *R(SB) 1/82* and *R(SB) 42/83*). That led to the conclusion that an appeal to an appeal tribunal under s.12 is by way of rehearing. At para.24, the Tribunal said:

"As a matter of principle, on such an appeal the tribunal may make any decision which the officer below could have made on the legal questions before that officer. That principle encompasses dealing with new questions so as to reach the right result on an appeal, within the limit that the appeal tribunal has no jurisdiction (in the absence of express legislation to that effect) to determine questions which fall outside the scope of that which the officer below could have done on the proper legal view of the issues before him, by way of a claim or an application or otherwise."

They pointed out, at para.31, that s.12(8)(a) reinforces that approach because it is implicit in that provision that an appeal tribunal is not limited to considering issues actually raised by the parties.

Against that background, the Tribunal considered three issues concerning the powers of tribunals: whether supersession decisions can be substituted for revision decisions and vice versa, whether defects in supersession decisions can be remedied, and whether a tribunal can make a decision less favourable to a claimant than the decision under appeal. (Other issues considered by the Tribunal are noted in the annotations to regs 3 and 6 of the Social Security and Child Support (Decisions and Appeals) Regulations 1999).

Can supersession decisions be substituted for revision decisions and vice versa?

The Tribunal's decision in *R(IB) 2/04* on this issue is based on their view of the nature of appeals following supersession decisions under s.10 and revision decisions under s.9. In the former case, the appeal is, both in form and in substance, an appeal against the decision to supersede or not to supersede. Where there has been a revision or a refusal to revise, any appeal is, in form, against the original decision because s.12(1) does not provide for an appeal against the decision under s.9 but, the Tribunal held at para.40, in substance, an appeal against the decision under s.9. 1.436

The parties had argued that the legislation did not allow a tribunal to give a supersession decision on appeal from a revision decision and vice versa, although counsel for the claimants submitted that it should readily be implied that a revision decision included a refusal to supersede and that a supersession decision included a refusal to revise. However, the Tribunal considered that the result of taking the approach advocated by the parties had too often been absurd. At para.50, they said:

"The meaning of a statutory provision which is so clear that it admits only one possible construction cannot be altered or departed from by reference to the consequences, however inconvenient or anomalous. However, in our judgement the statutory provisions relevant to this issue fail by some margin to reach the degree of clarity which would bring that principle into play. In these circumstances, in ascertaining the legislature's intention, it is quite proper to have regard to the potential consequences of possible alternative constructions, in the context of the statutory scheme as a whole. In the field of benefit decisions and appeals procedure, we consider it proper, in construing the relevant provisions, to assume that the legislature did not intend to create a scheme which would be likely to lead to impracticable or indeed absurd results in a significant number of cases. On the contrary, we proceed on the basis that the legislature intended the provisions relating to decisions and appeals (and in particular those relating to provisions changing the effect of a previous decision) to form at least a reasonably workable scheme."

Having given examples of some of the more absurd consequences of the parties' submissions, the Tribunal held, at para.55:

"In our judgment, if an appeal tribunal decides that the Secretary of State's decision under Section 9 or Section 10 changing or refusing to change a previous decision was wrong then (subject to the restriction in Section 12(8)(b), if relevant) it has jurisdiction to make the revision or supersession decision which it considers the Secretary of State ought to have made, even if that means making a decision under Section 9 when the Secretary of State acted only under Section 10, and vice versa."

1.437 They rejected the need to resort to the theory of implied decisions on the ground that "the 1998 legislation could not have been intended to involve consideration of such arid technicalities and complications" (at para.59).

However, in *R(IS) 15/04*, the same Tribunal, sitting a few weeks later, resiled somewhat from what they had said in both [55] and [59] of *R(IB) 2/04*. In *R(IS) 15/04* (subsequently approved by the Court of Appeal in *Beltekian v Westminster CC* [2004] EWCA Civ 1784 (reported as *R(H) 8/05*)), the Secretary of State had expressly both superseded and refused to revise a decision. The claimant appealed but was out of time for appealing against the original decision and so was unable to challenge the refusal to revise although he could challenge the supersession. The Tribunal of Commissioners held that the appeal tribunal had had no jurisdiction to substitute a revision for the supersession, saying, at para.78:

> "It seems to us, in those circumstances, if an appeal tribunal were permitted to substitute a revision decision for the supersession decision, that would in effect be to permit by the back door what is not permitted by the front door, namely an appeal against the refusal to revise."

Obscurely, they added that "[i]t would have been a different matter if the Secretary of State had not made a decision (whether express or implied) on the issue of revision for official error". It is not clear why they took that view, which, strictly speaking, is obiter, particularly as it is not clear what they meant by an implied decision, given their rejection of the theory in *R(IB) 2/04*. It is suggested that the theory of implied decisions would always treat a decision in terms of supersession as an implied refusal to revise, even if the issue of official error had not expressly been considered, because it is a precondition of any supersession decision that there are no grounds for revision (see reg.6(3) of the Social Security and Child Support (Decisions and Appeals) Regulations 1999, which allows only a technical exception to that general rule). However, in *CDLA/1707/2005*, the Deputy Commissioner applied the approach of the Tribunal of Commissioners and substituted for a refusal to supersede an award of benefit a decision revising the award on the ground of "official error". In *JS v SSWP (DLA)* [2014] UKUT 44 (AAC), the judge suggested that, had the issue been central to the case, he would have given the Chamber President an opportunity to direct that a three-judge panel should consider again the question whether a revision could properly be substituted for a supersession. He drew attention to further anomalies that can arise if there is no such power (see the note to reg.3(5) of the 1999 Regulations).

1.438 Although s.9(5) of this Act has the effect that the time for appealing against a decision that has been revised runs from the date of the revision, a similar approach is not always taken to refusals to revise and, at the time that *R(IB) 2/04* and *R(IS) 15/04* were decided, it was only where a claimant had applied for revision under reg.3(1) or (3) of the 1999 Regulations that time ran from a refusal to revise (under, then, reg.31(2)). Where the decision on the application for revision is not the result of mandatory reconsideration (because, for instance, the decision that was not revised was itself made on mandatory reconsideration but was not appealed at the time) it remains the case that only refusals to revise under reg.3(1) and (3) of the 1999 Regulations and the equivalent reg.5 of the Universal Credit, Personal Independence Payment, Jobseeker's Allowance and Employment and Support Allowance (Decisions and Appeals) Regulations 2013 start the time for appealing running again (see reg.22(2)(d)(ii) of, and para.5(c) of Sch.1 to, the Tribunal Procedure (First-tier Tribunal) (Social Entitlement Chamber) Rules 2008).

However, in *PH v SSWP (DLA)* [2018] UKUT 404 (AAC); [2019] AACR 14, it was held that, because reg.3ZA(2) of those Regulations did not refer only to applications for revision within the scope of reg.3(1) or (3), a refusal to revise on the ground of "official error" could (depending on the procedural history of the case and provided that the application for revision on that ground was not spurious) be "the result of mandatory reconsideration" and so have the effect of restarting the time for appealing under r.22(2)(d)(i) of the 2008 Rules. Although it was held in that case that it had to be shown by an appellant that the application for revision was not "spurious" in order to establish that the First-tier Tribunal had jurisdiction, it is suggested that it is in fact necessary for the First-tier Tribunal ultimately to be satisfied that there was in fact a material official error (or that some other material ground for an "anytime" ground of revision is made out) if an appeal is to succeed. Otherwise, as was suggested in *CCS/5515/2002*, the time limit for appealing and the restrictions on revisions would be subverted. This was effectively the approach taken in *DB v SSWP (PIP)* [2023] UKUT 95 (AAC), where there was an admitted official error in the Secretary of State's approach to the claimant's case and so the Upper Tribunal had no difficulty in finding at [73] to [75] that an apparently very late application for mandatory reconsideration made by the claimant had been an application for revision based on official error with the result that there had in fact been no time limit for that application and the claimant's subsequent appeal against the original decision had been in time. The First-tier Tribunal had accordingly erred in holding that it had no jurisdiction, and the case was remitted to the First-tier Tribunal for it to consider whether the official error had caused the Secretary of State to reach the wrong conclusion on the facts and, if so, to give the correct decision (at [76] to [80]).

The decision in *PH* does not affect the argument that, because there is a right of appeal against a supersession or refusal to supersede, but not against a revision or refusal to revise, the First-tier Tribunal cannot replace a supersession decision with a revision. On the other hand, if an appeal against a supersession decision is submitted within the absolute 13-month time limit for appealing against the original decision that was, or was not, superseded, it may be appropriate to treat the appeal as also being an appeal against that original decision and, if necessary, to extend time. That would achieve the same effect as substituting a revision "on any ground". Moreover, in considering whether the appeal was in time, it would arguably be necessary to treat the application for supersession as an application for revision "on any ground" if such an application for revision would itself have been in time, since supersession is only permissible if there are no grounds for revision (see reg.6(3) of the 1999 Regulations, reg.15 of the Child Benefit and Guardian's Allowance (Decisions and Appeals) Regulations 2003 or reg.32 of the Universal Credit, Personal Independence Payment, Jobseeker's Allowance and Employment and Support Allowance (Decisions and Appeals) Regulations 2013) and, as stated above, a refusal of revision "on any ground" has the effect of extending the time for appeal. These issues did not arise in *R(IS) 15/04* because both the application for supersession and the appeal in that case had been lodged more than 13 months after the original decision. It is arguable that they also did not arise in *CDLA/1707/2005* because, although the application for supersession in that case was made within 13 months of the original decision, it was made more than 3 months after the original decision and any extension of time would have been a matter for the Secretary of State under reg.4 of the 1999 Regulations in respect of which there was no right of appeal.

However, this raises the question whether, on an appeal against a decision under s.10 where the appellant is out of time for appealing against the decision that was or was not superseded, it might be arguable that, if the First-tier Tribunal were to consider that the original decision ought to have been revised (perhaps on the ground of "official error") rather than superseded, it would be bound to refuse to decide that the original decision should be superseded even though it did not itself have the power to revise that decision. Arguably, the implication of such a decision of the First-tier Tribunal could not be ignored and its effect would be to oblige the Secretary of State or HMRC to revise the original decision unless the First-tier Tribunal's decision were overturned by the Upper Tribunal. But, would the effect of that approach be to "permit by the back door" an appeal against a refusal to revise, which is what the Tribunal of Commissioners refused to countenance in *R(IB) 2/04*?

See also the discussion of *CM v SSWP (ESA)* [2019] UKUT 284 (AAC) in the note to s.8(1).

Can defects in supersession decisions be remedied?

1.439 The Tribunal of Commissioners in *R(IB)2/04* held that an appeal tribunal can remedy defects in a decision such as failing to acknowledge that an existing decision needed superseding, failing to state the grounds of supersession or relying on the wrong grounds of supersession.

"72. . . . there may be some decisions made by the Secretary of State which have so little coherence or connection to legal powers that they do not amount to decisions under Section 10 at all. . . .
73. If, however, the Secretary of State's decision was made under Section 10 (as to which, see paragraph 76 below), . . . the appeal tribunal has jurisdiction, on appeal, to decide whether the outcome arrived at by that decision (i.e. either to change or not to change the original decision) was correct. . . .
76. In our judgment a decision should generally be regarded as having been made under Section 10, regardless of the form in which it may be expressed, if it has the effect of terminating an existing entitlement from the date of the decision (or from some later date than the effective date of the original decision). . . . Similarly, a decision should generally be regarded as having been made under Section 9 if it changes the original decision with effect from the effective date of that decision."

The implication of the Tribunal's decision appears to be that an appeal tribunal should limit its decision to holding that the Secretary of State's decision was invalid only in cases where the Secretary of State's decision is completely incoherent and the nature of the decision cannot be implied or where the Secretary of State had no power to make any decision at all. Another implication of a tribunal being entitled to correct defects in decisions of the Secretary of State is that it will often be unnecessary for a tribunal to consider the exact nature of the decision of the Secretary of State that is under appeal; it will usually be enough to consider what he *should* have decided (*R(IS) 2/08*). Indeed, in *SSWP v AM (IS)* [2010] UKUT 428, it was noted that there is no statutory requirement to record a decision in writing and, in *SSWP v JM (SPC)* [2013] UKUT 72 (AAC), it was said that the implication was that notice of a decision need not necessarily record the precise wording of the decision although it was also said that there were good reasons why it should. In the latter case, the judge was satisfied that a decision was a supersession because it had obviously "involved the mental processes required for a supersession" (since it was the correct decision on the Secretary of State's understanding of the substantive law and the facts) and the First-tier Tribunal was held to have erred in law in finding the decision to be inchoate. See also *DB v SSWP (SPC)* [2013] UKUT 74 (AAC).

The Tribunal of Commissioners in *R(IB) 2/04* went on to say, at para.82, that it is necessary for an appeal tribunal chairman to "perfect" or "recast" a defective decision in the tribunal's decision notice only "if either (i) the decision as expressed is wrong in some material respect (e.g. states an incorrect ground of appeal) or (ii) there is likely to be some particular practical benefit to the claimant or to the adjudication process in future in reformulating the decision". However, if a statement of reasons is requested, giving reasons for the tribunal's decision is likely to involve explaining how any defects in the Secretary of State's decision were approached.

1.440 The ability of a tribunal to correct defects in a decision of the Secretary of State means that, where the Secretary of State wrongly applied the personal capability assessment as amended by regulations that had been held to be ultra vires, the tribunal was entitled to substitute a decision by applying the unamended test (*R(IB)5/05*).

The approach taken in *R(IB)* 2/04 has been followed by a Tribunal of Commissioners in Northern Ireland (*BMcD v DSD (DLA)* [2011] NICom 175; [2013] AACR 29) but they suggested a degree of caution: "principally in order to ensure that the perception of the independence of the appeal tribunal is not damaged" and also "to ensure that the appellant is aware of the effect that the exercise of the power to remedy defects may have on the issues of the case".

Where the First-tier Tribunal considers that an award has been wrongly superseded, it may be particularly important that, rather than simply substituting a decision not to supersede the award, it considers whether the award should be superseded on a different ground and to a different effect. In *SC v SSWP (PIP)* [2019] UKUT 165 (AAC), the claimant had been awarded the enhanced rate of the mobility component of personal independence payment until December 2017 but the Secretary of State then superseded the award with effect from April 2017 and awarded only the standard rate of the mobility component until March 2021. The ground of supersession was the receipt of a new report from a health care professional. The First-tier Tribunal, sitting in February 2018, considered that the reasons given for the supersession were inadequate and, on that basis and without finding that there were no grounds for supersession, reinstated the original award which had by then expired, leaving the claimant worse off overall, notwithstanding that it had observed that the health care professional's report might be said to have supported an award of the standard rate of the daily living component. The Upper Tribunal pointed out that the First-tier Tribunal's role was not just to consider the merits of the Secretary of State's reasoning but to make the correct decision. It had failed to consider whether the evidence suggested a decision superseding the original award in favour of the claimant and, given that the period of the original award had expired (and no renewal claim had been invited in view of the supersession decision), it had been particularly important to consider whether the evidence showed that, at the date of the Secretary of State's supersession decision, the claimant might have been expected to continue to be entitled to personal independence payment after the expiry of the original award, which would have justified a supersession to alter the end date of the award even if the amount of benefit was not altered.

Can a tribunal make a decision less favourable to a claimant than a supersession decision under appeal?

The Tribunal held that an appeal tribunal could make a decision less favourable to a claimant than a supersession decision under appeal. This followed both from the Tribunal's view as to the nature of an appeal to an appeal tribunal and from the terms of s.12(8)(a), implicitly providing that a tribunal may consider issues not raised by the parties. However, the Tribunal made two important comments at paras 94 and 97 of their decision. **1.441**

First, a tribunal must consciously exercise the discretion in s.12(8)(a) to consider a point not raised by the parties and, if a statement of reasons is requested, must explain in that statement why the discretion was exercised in the manner it was. For the points to be taken into account when exercising the discretion, see the annotation to s.12(8)(a) below.

Secondly, where the tribunal's decision is even less favourable to the claimant than the original decision that was the subject of the supersession decision under appeal, the tribunal's decision is "effectively the exercise by the tribunal of the Secretary of State's power to supersede 'on his own initiative" and so, by virtue of s.10(5), the decision is usually effective from the date of the Secretary of State's decision under appeal rather than from the date of the claimant's application for supersession.

Although the First-tier Tribunal is therefore entitled to make a decision less favourable to a claimant than the one under appeal, a Commissioner discouraged tribunals from doing so in borderline cases. In *CDLA/2738/2007*, it was said— **1.442**

"The tribunal was entitled to take the view that the claimant was not virtually unable to walk but the Secretary of State was equally entitled to take the opposite view. Where a tribunal's findings are not materially different from the Secretary of State's and the Secretary of State's conclusion in favour of the claimant is not perverse, a tribunal should be slow to interfere and must, in accordance with R(IB) 2/04, give reasons for considering it necessary to do so."

In *CDLA/884/2008*, he said —

"8. An increasing number of appeals before Commissioners seem to be cases where a tribunal has made a decision less favourable to the claimant than the one the claimant was challenging before the tribunal. It is not surprising that appeals should be brought before Commissioners in such cases, particularly as the consequence of any such decision is that there will have been an overpayment, the recoverability of which will have been left undetermined by the tribunal. Tribunals need to be aware of the dangers of being both prosecutor and judge, one of which is the risk of making errors unprompted by the parties. Such errors are too common and are contributing significantly to the caseload of Commissioners. It is particularly unfortunate that two of the several errors made by the tribunal in the present case were on points in respect of which a Tribunal of Commissioners had relatively recently given clear guidance.

9. There are other risks in being both prosecutor and judge. The most obvious is that there can be a perception that the tribunal has prejudged the case. Of course a tribunal has an inquisitorial or investigative role but here it is noteworthy that the tribunal, having apparently formed the (not unreasonable) view on the papers that the claimant's entitlement to any disability living allowance was doubtful, started the proceedings by warning the claimant that his existing award was at risk and advising him that he could withdraw his appeal. The claimant having declined to withdraw his appeal, the tribunal then launched straight into the question of the claimant's entitlement to the mobility component, by questioning him about how he had got to the hearing, without first listening to what the claimant had to say about his needs for care which was the issue upon which he had brought his appeal. It is little wonder that the claimant says, in effect, that he formed an early view that the tribunal was more interested in its own agenda than in what he had to say."

He pointed out that it was not necessarily enough to give a claimant an opportunity to withdraw his appeal; it had been said in *R(IB) 2/04* that the claimant had to be given sufficient notice to enable him to prepare his case on the new issue, which meant being given notice of the case against him where that would not be obvious to him.

"10. . . . A tribunal is in a difficult position. If it gives the claimant too robust a warning at the beginning of a hearing, it runs the risk of giving the impression of having prejudged the case. If it does not give such a robust warning, the warning may not adequately convey to the claimant the case he or she needs to consider resisting with the consequence that a decision not to withdraw the appeal, or not to ask for an adjournment, is not fully informed. This is a powerful reason for tribunals refraining from making decisions less favourable to claimants than the decisions being challenged, except in the most obvious cases (e.g., where the evidence is overwhelming or the facts are not in dispute and no element of judgment is involved or where the law has been misapplied by the Secretary of State) or after an appropriate adjournment. In such obvious cases, a failure expressly to state why a tribunal has considered a point not in issue between the parties will not necessarily render the tribunal's decision erroneous in point of law; in less obvious cases, the absence of a reason for considering the point may suggest that the discretion to do so has not been exercised properly.

11. If a tribunal does not consider the correctness of an award that is not directly in issue before it, it does not follow that it should do nothing if it has doubts about the award. The chairman is at liberty to draw the doubts to the Secretary of State's attention in the decision notice and can arrange for the parties to be sent a copy of the record of proceedings (including his or her note of evidence) without them having to request it. That would enable the Secretary of State to consider a supersession or revision and, in disability living allowance cases, would often avoid the possibility of there having been an overpayment, which is often a consequence of a tribunal considering the issue and which often worries claimants more than the mere cessation of entitlement."

In both cases, the Commissioner restored the Secretary of State's decision. In practice, cases often turn on the claimant's own oral evidence which, if unfavourable to the claimant, is unlikely to be in dispute and, provided the findings of fact are such as to make it clear why the claimant could not be entitled to benefit in the light of that evidence, a tribunal is unlikely then to be found to have erred in not expressly stating why it took the point on its own initiative. An adjournment is also unlikely to be necessary where a case can be determined on the basis of the claimant's own oral evidence and where it could not reasonably be argued that the claimant was entitled to benefit in the light of that evidence. The cases where most care is needed are those truly on a borderline and those where a claimant might be able to provide further evidence if given an opportunity to do so.

In *BK v SSWP* [2009] UKUT 258 (AAC), the Upper Tribunal judge rejected an argument that the First-tier Tribunal had failed to act impartially when, after a represented claimant had declined an opportunity to ask for an adjournment, it made a decision less favourable to the claimant than the one being challenged. She said that the First-tier Tribunal's inquisitorial role meant that it ought to investigate an unappealed element of an award if it had a "real doubt" about it. This is not necessarily inconsistent with the approach taken in *CDLA/884/2008* because "real doubt" is a ground for investigating a case rather than a ground for reaching a different conclusion from that reached by the Secretary of State, particularly where grounds for supersession would be required. The comments in *CDLA/884/2008* were concerned mainly with the position after such investigation as is possible at a hearing—which in practice usually consists simply of asking the claimant a few questions—has been concluded. **1.443**

In *C15/08-09(DLA)*, a Northern Ireland Commissioner has expressed a more fundamental disagreement with the approach taken in *CDLA/884/2008*, stating that, "[w]here the appeal tribunal has any doubt concerning the validity of the decision under appeal, where that decision incorporates an existing award, it is under a duty to undertake a full investigation of the legitimacy of the existing award and determine whether that award is correct".

However, in *AP-H v SSWP (DLA)* [2010] UKUT 183 (AAC), the judge disagreed with both *BK v SSWP* and *C15/08-09(DLA)* insofar as they suggested that there was a duty to consider issues not raised by the appeal. He emphasised that *R(IS) 2/04* made it plain there was a discretion, albeit one that had to be exercised judicially. Nonetheless, he rejected an argument, based on *CDLA/884/2008*, to the effect that the First-tier Tribunal had erred in considering an undisputed award that was not "clearly wrong". He said that the First-tier Tribunal was entitled to consider any issue and that *CDLA/884/2008* was concerned with the question whether it was clear why it had done so in a case where no reason had been given. Looking at the evidence in the case before him, he was satisfied that it *was* clear why the First-tier Tribunal had considered an award that was not in dispute.

The point made in *CDLA/884/2008* about the need to give a claimant an adequate opportunity to put his or her case was repeated in *BTC v SSWP (PIP)* [2015] UKUT 155 (AAC), where it was pointed out that, in any case where the First-tier Tribunal takes a new point, "the claimant will not have had advance notice of the issue, as would be the case if the Secretary of State had been required to give grounds for opposing the appeal under Rule 24(2)(e) of the Tribunal Procedure (First-tier Tribunal) (SEC) Rules 2008" and it was held that "the tribunal's decision to consider on its own initiative whether to remove mobility component led to precisely the kind of unprompted error envisaged in *CDLA/884/2008*. The tribunal's failure to invite the claimant to put her case with regard to the distance from her home to her G.P.'s surgery and with regard to what she did while on holiday, when she could not possibly know that those matters would be crucial to the tribunal's decision, deprived the claimant of the opportunity to correct any errors by the tribunal and amounted to serious breaches of the requirement of fairness."

In *MS v SSWP (DLA and PIP)* [2021] UKUT 41 (AAC), the First-tier Tribunal was held to have erred in law, not because it decided to make a less favourable decision—there were grounds for doing so—but because it did not adjourn for that issue to be considered on another day. It had offered to adjourn so that the claimant could seek advice, but the claimant had declined the offer. However, the claimant had been unrepresented and the First-tier Tribunal's decision, not only had the effect of increasing the amount of the relevant overpayment that was recoverable by about

£20,000, but also involved the consideration of additional questions of law about which the claimant would have been ignorant because they had not been addressed in the Secretary of State's submission to the First-tier Tribunal. Indeed, the claimant's appeal to the Upper Tribunal was supported by the Secretary of State on that ground.

Even where the Secretary of State has not awarded personal independence payment because a claimant has not scored a sufficient number of points, a claimant may assume that descriptors found by the Secretary of State to have been satisfied are not in issue and so the duty to act fairly may require the First-tier Tribunal to indicate that it is minded to make a contrary finding before doing so. It may make no difference that the claimant is represented by an experienced representative (*LJ v SSWP (PIP)* [2017] UKUT 455 (AAC)).

Litigants who lack capacity

1.444 Although having litigation capacity—i.e. the mental capacity to conduct proceedings in a court or tribunal—is not necessarily the same as having the mental capacity to make other types of decision, it is unlikely that a person who lacks the capacity to make a claim for benefit can be said to have the capacity to conduct proceedings in an appeal in respect of the claim (*Sheffield City Council v E* [2004] EWHC 2808 (Fam); [2005] Fam. 326 at [49]; *An NHS Trust v P (by her litigation friend, the Official Solicitor* [2021] EWCOP 27 at [33]). Moreover, because the First-tier Tribunal has an inquisitorial or investigatory role in social security cases and its procedures and processes are designed to make representation of any sort unnecessary in proceedings before it (see the annotation to the Tribunals, Courts and Enforcement Act 2007 s.3, below), it is arguable that anyone who does have the capacity to claim a benefit (in the sense of being capable of understanding instructions on a claim form and instructions to report changes of circumstances) must be taken also to have the capacity to conduct an appeal before the First-tier Tribunal against a decision made on the claim. For these reasons, a claimant who lacks capacity to bring or conduct tribunal proceedings is, in practice, likely also to lack capacity to claim benefit and so someone is likely to have been appointed to act on his or her behalf as regards the claim. Such appointees are prescribed for the purpose of s.12(2) as persons with an independent right of appeal (see reg.25(a) of the Social Security and Child Support (Decisions and Appeals) Regulations 1999, reg.24(a) of the Child Benefit and Guardian's Allowance (Decisions and Appeals) Regulations 2003 and reg.49(b) of the Universal Credit, Personal Independence Payment, Jobseeker's Allowance and Employment and Support Allowance (Decisions and Appeals) Regulations 2013). However, that does not preclude a claimant from also bringing an appeal or participating in one if he or she wishes to do so because, for instance, he or she wishes to raise an issue that the appointee does not or because the claimant considers that he or she does not in fact lack capacity. If the claimant does lack capacity, the First-tier Tribunal has the power to appoint a litigation friend where that is necessary in order to avoid unfairness (*AM (Afghanistan) v Secretary of State for the Home Department* [2017] EWCA Civ 1123), although a formal appointment requiring a determination of the question whether the claimant has capacity may not always be required where that issue is a matter of dispute (*RH v SSWP (DLA)* [2018] UKUT 48 (AAC); [2018] AACR 33).

In *SB v SSWP (PIP)* [2020] UKUT 198 (AAC), the claimant's appointee appeared at the hearing before the First-tier Tribunal but the tribunal was not satisfied that she was in fact the appointee and proceeded to determine the appeal without discussing its concerns about the medical evidence with her, apparently on grounds of confidentiality. Allowing the claimant's appeal, the Upper Tribunal said that the First-tier Tribunal should have adjourned to allow the appointee's status to be clarified, rather than proceeding in the way that it did which gave rise to unfairness.

It has been held that a person may have capacity to bring an appeal even if he or she does not have capacity to conduct proceedings – all that appears to be required is that the claimant understands that he or she is in dispute with a decision-maker and that the First-tier Tribunal is a body that will be able to resolve the dispute (*VS v St Andrew's Healthcare* [2018] UKUT 250 (AAC); [2019] AACR 4, approved by a three-judge panel in *SM v Livewell Southwest CIC* [2020] UKUT 191 (AAC); [2020] 1 W.L.R. 5171) – so that it is unlikely to matter that a claimant lacking capacity to conduct proceedings brought an appeal before the appointment of an appointee or litigation friend. In any event, such an appointment probably has the effect of validating an earlier appeal that would otherwise be invalid due to a lack of capacity on the part of the claimant who brought it, provided that the appointee or litigation friend wishes to pursue it (*R(SB) 8/88, R(SB) 5/90*).

Vexatious litigants

The courts have power to make orders barring litigants who persistently bring inappropriate proceedings from bringing further proceedings without permission. This raises the question of the extent to which such orders apply so as to bar a person from exercising a right of appeal to a tribunal. **1.445**

An extended civil restraint order made against a vexatious litigant in the County Court does not prevent the litigant from appealing to the First-tier Tribunal and participating fully in the proceedings (*JW v SSWP* [2009] UKUT 198 (AAC)). Indeed, even when made by the Court of Appeal, an "extended civil restraint order" or "general civil restraint order" can extend only to civil proceedings in the County Court, the High Court or the Court of Appeal, because such orders are made under Practice Direction 3C to supplement r.3.11 of the Civil Procedure Rules which apply only in those courts.

On the other hand, differing views have been expressed by the Upper Tribunal as to whether a "civil proceedings order" or an "all proceedings order" made under s.42 of the Senior Courts Act 1981 prevents a person from appealing to the First-tier Tribunal without the permission of the High Court. It is well established that the word "courts" in s.42 has a wide meaning that includes tribunals. In *IB v IC* [2011] UKUT 370 (AAC), the Upper Tribunal decided that both the First-tier Tribunal and the Upper Tribunal were courts for the purposes of s.42. However, in *AO v Shepway DC (HB)* [2013] UKUT 9 (AAC), the judge disagreed and held that a civil proceedings order did not preclude a claimant from bringing an appeal before the First-tier Tribunal without the permission of the High Court, at least in a social security case. Considerations which led him to his conclusion included the fact that such cases can be concerned with entitlement to income-related benefits of last resort, that a vexatious litigant cannot bring a case before the First-tier Tribunal without there being a decision against which to appeal, that the First-tier Tribunal has ample powers to deal with hopeless appeals, and that in practice it is impossible to administer a bar because every case would have to be checked against the list of vexatious litigants. Nonetheless, he held that the claimant was not entitled to apply to the Upper Tribunal for permission to appeal without first obtaining the permission of a High Court judge.

However in *Att-Gen v Vaidya* [2017] EWHC 2152 (Admin), the High Court made an order to prevent Mr Vaidya "without leave of the court from instituting or making applications in cases in the civil courts and tribunals, in particular the employment tribunal and the Employment Appeal Tribunal" or from acting as a representative or McKenzie friend in any court or tribunal. That makes it difficult to argue that the First-tier Tribunal is in a different position from the Upper Tribunal and even more difficult to argue that, while some types of proceedings in the First-tier Tribunal fall within the scope of such an order, others do not. Moreover, although the law in Scotland is different, it is to similar effect and, in *PA v HMRC (TC)* [2020] UKUT 324 (AAC), the judge disagreed with the reasoning in *AO v Shepway DC (HB)* [2013] UKUT 9 (AAC) and held that the First-tier Tribunal was a "court" within s.1 of the Vexatious Actions (Scotland) Act 1898. In appealing to the First-tier Tribunal, the Appellant had "instituted" "legal proceedings" contrary to an order made under that provision, because he had not obtained the leave of a Lord Ordinary, and so the First-tier Tribunal had not had jurisdiction to consider his appeal and ought to have struck it out.

In addition to the powers of courts to make civil restraint orders and orders under s.42 of the Senior Courts Act 1981, the High Court has the power to issue an injunction restraining a person from bringing proceedings in a tribunal without the permission of the Court (*Law Society of England and Wales v Sheikh* [2018] EWHC 1644 (QB)). However, it seems unlikely that such an injunction would ever be sought in terms that would restrict a person's right to appeal in social security cases.

Subsection (3)

1.446 See the note to Sch.2 to the Social Security and Child Support (Decisions and Appeals) Regulations 1999 in which it is suggested that either much of that schedule is ultra vires or else this subsection is of no practical effect.

Subsections (3A)–(3C)

1.447 Regulations under subs.(3A) may effectively require would-be appellants to apply for a revision of the decision being challenged before appealing. See reg.3ZA of the Social Security and Child Support (Decisions and Appeals) Regulations 1999 and reg.7 of the Universal Credit, Personal Independence Payment, Jobseeker's Allowance and Employment and Support Allowance (Decisions and Appeals) Regulations 2013. This is known as "mandatory reconsideration". Previously, there was a practice of considering revising a decision (under reg.3(4A) of the 1999 Regulations) on the papers after an appeal has been lodged. The intention was to reduce the number of appeals by introducing a more intensive revision process *before* an appeal is lodged in which claimants are telephoned so that they can discuss their cases.

The Social Security Advisory Committee considered the impact of "mandatory reconsideration" in a study published in July 2016 (Occasional Paper No.18), which may be found at *https://www.gov.uk/government/publications/government-response-ssac-report-on-decision-making-and-mandatory-reconsideration* (accessed August 2023), together with the Government's responses.

Subsection (3D)

1.448 This subsection is plainly intended to have the same sort of effect as regulations made under subs.(3A). However, if read literally, it not only requires a person to apply for a revision before appealing but if the revision is only partially successful, requires them to apply for further revisions until HMRC makes a decision refusing to revise the decision at all. It may, perhaps, be arguable that a revision includes a decision "not to revise" to the extent that it gives the claimant less than had been sought in the application for revision.

Subsection (4)

1.449 Although this subsection assumes that a claimant has a right of appeal against a decision under s.74 of the 1992 Act, such decisions are not mentioned in Sch.3. However, in *R(IS) 14/04*, the Commissioner held that a claimant was entitled to appeal against a decision under s.74 by virtue of subs.(1)(a) of this section, rather than subs.(1)(b).

Subsection (7)

1.450 Provision for the time and manner in which appeals are to be brought is now made in Tribunal Procedure Rules and so regulations made under subs.(7)(a) have all been revoked except for regs 29A and 30 of the Child Benefit and Guardian's Allowance (Decisions and Appeals) Regulations 2003. Regulation 3ZA(5) of the Social Security and Child Support (Decisions and Appeals) Regulations 1999 and reg.7(5) of the Universal Credit, Personal Independence Payment, Jobseeker's Allowance and Employment and Support Allowance (Decisions and Appeals) Regulations 2013 have been made under subs.(7)(b).

Subsection (8)(a)

1.451 In *CDLA/1000/2001*, it was held that the question whether an issue is "raised by the appeal" is to be determined by reference to the substance of the appeal and not just the wording of the letter of appeal. The claimant was in receipt of the mobility component of disability living allowance and was seeking the care component.

The Commissioner decided that, as the claimant had attributed some of his care needs to the arthritis that caused his mobility difficulties, it was impossible for the tribunal to consider the care component without also considering the basis of the award of the mobility component. Therefore, the claimant's entitlement to the mobility component was raised by his appeal in respect of the care component. The Commissioner also held that the claimant had no preserved right to the protection formerly accorded to life awards of one component when a claimant had sought the other. That protection had been swept away when Pt II of the Social Security Administration Act 1992 was repealed by the Social Security Act 1998.

Paragraph (a) confers a discretion. However, there can be jurisdictional difficulties in relation to prescribed industrial diseases. In *MH v SSWP (II)* [2020] UKUT 297 (AAC) at [20], the judge left open the question whether, on an appeal against a decision relating to one prescribed disease, the First-tier Tribunal could consider whether the claimant had been suffering from another prescribed disease that had never been considered by the Secretary of State. In *CI/531/2000*, the Commissioner considered a standard submission by the Secretary of State in appeals relating to the diagnosis of industrial diseases in which it was said that the only issue before the tribunal was the diagnosis question and that, if the tribunal decided that question in the claimant's favour, it was not possible for them to go on and consider whether to award benefit. The Commissioner held the submission to be wrong in law but that the discretion to consider other issues must be exercised judicially. He pointed out that it was often desirable to deal with disablement at the same time as diagnosis but he said that natural justice required that the claimant (and, it can be added, the Secretary of State) be warned that disablement would also be considered and that when a tribunal dealt with a factual issue that had not previously been considered, the result was that the claimant was deprived of any appeal on the facts (and, it may be added, any application for revision under reg.3(1)(b) of the Social Security and Child Support (Decisions and Appeals) Regulations 1999). However, as already noted in relation to subs.(1), it was held in *CIB/2338/2000* that appeals lie only against "outcome decisions" and not against determinations of mere "questions". It follows that, in any case where a claimant has claimed disablement benefit, a determination that he or she is not suffering from a prescribed disease will be a determination made for the purpose of deciding that disablement benefit is not payable and any challenge to the determination will be made in an appeal against the refusal of benefit. If, on such an appeal, a tribunal decides that the claimant *was* suffering from the prescribed disease at the date the Secretary of State's decision was given, can the tribunal refuse to go on and determine all the other issues that must be determined if a decision is to be made as to whether or not to award benefit? In the light of *R(IS) 2/08*, the answer is now clearly "yes" and, in situations like that arising in *CI/531/2000*, it is often very much easier for everyone if the tribunal leaves the Secretary of State to make a new "outcome decision" than it would be if it does so itself. Thus, it may be that the only error in the Secretary of State's submission in *CI/531/2000* was that it was written in terms of what the tribunal could legally do rather than in terms of what it could do as a matter of practicality without obtaining further submissions.

The approach taken in *R(IS) 2/08* gives greater effect to subs.(8)(a) than the alternative approach would, but the provision would in any event apply where a tribunal could give an "outcome decision" without considering any new issue. In some instances considering a new issue may be to the considerable disadvantage of the claimant who has appealed to the tribunal.

In *R(IB) 2/04* at paras 93 and 94, the Tribunal of Commissioners held that, where **1.452**
an appeal tribunal is minded to make a decision less favourable to the claimant than the one under appeal and the respondent has not invited them to make such a decision, a tribunal must address its mind to the power conferred by subs.(8)(a) not to consider the issue. The discretion is one to be exercised judicially, taking into account all the circumstances of the particular case. Furthermore, the tribunal's decision is likely to be held to be erroneous in point of law if the statement of reasons does not show that there has been a conscious exercise of the discretion.

"In exercising the discretion, the appeal tribunal must of course have in mind, in particular, two factors. First, it must bear in mind the need to comply with Article 6 of the Convention and the rules of natural justice. This will involve, at the very least, ensuring that the claimant has had sufficient notice of the tribunal's intention to consider superseding adversely to him to enable him properly to prepare his case. The fact that the claimant is entitled to withdraw his appeal any time before the appeal tribunal's decision may also be material to what Article 6 and the rules of natural justice demand. Second, the appeal tribunal may consider it more appropriate to leave the question whether the original decision should be superseded adversely to the claimant to be decided subsequently by the Secretary of State. This might be so if, for example, deciding that question would involve factual issues which do not overlap those raised by the appeal, or if it would necessitate an adjournment of the hearing."

See also *BMcD v DSD (DLA)* [2011] NICom 175; [2013] AACR 29, a decision of a Tribunal of Commissioners in Northern Ireland.

The same approach is required where a tribunal takes a new point against the Secretary of State. In *CH/3009/2002*, a decision had been made on a claim that could have been treated also as an application for the revision of a decision terminating an earlier award. The Commissioner held that, although it followed from *R(IB) 2/04* that the tribunal had the power to give a decision in terms of revision, the question of revision could be left to the Secretary of State. Thus, subs.(8)(a) can be seen as providing an alternative course of action to the adjournment that will sometimes be required where a new point is taken, although the Commissioner deciding *CH/3009/2002* did comment that, depending on the terms of the Secretary of State's decision, it might not be possible for a claimant to get the case back before a tribunal given the decision of the Tribunal of Commissioners in *R(IS) 15/04* (subsequently approved by the Court of Appeal in *Beltekian v Westminster CC* [2004] EWCA Civ 1784 (reported as *R(H) 8/05*)). It is suggested that the position might be no different if there were an adjournment because the Secretary of State could presumably make a decision before the tribunal was reconvened.

1.453 In considering how the discretion conferred by para.(a) should be exercised, a tribunal ought to have regard (among other things) to the adequacy of any alternative action that the claimant or Secretary of State might take to have the new issue taken into account and, if it is not obvious, ought to draw attention to that alternative action (*CDLA/15961/1996*). If an entirely new point is being taken at a hearing, it is necessary for the parties to have the opportunity of dealing with it but that does not necessarily mean there must be an adjournment because it ought to be possible for most points to be adequately considered immediately. If a party has deliberately chosen not to attend, the question whether there should be an adjournment so that he or she may consider the new point may be more complicated. There are three options: to refuse to consider the new point, to consider it immediately or to adjourn. A lot will depend on the nature of the issue and whether any advance notice was given of it, as well as the possibility of applying for a revision or supersession on the new ground. A wise appellant who wishes to raise a new point will give both the tribunal and the Secretary of State notice as soon as possible. However, if the Secretary of State chooses not to be represented at a hearing, it may be thought that he can hardly complain about not being allowed to comment on any evidence the claimant may give.

Subsection (8)(a) implies a power to consider new issues but makes it clear that there are limits to the extent to which the inquisitorial role of a tribunal imposes a duty to consider such issues. As was said by a Tribunal of Commissioners in *R(SB) 2/83*,

"Everything will depend on the circumstances in any given instance. We would be slow to convict a tribunal of failure to identify an uncanvassed factual point in favour of the claimant in the absence of the most obvious and clear cut circumstances."

In particular, where a claimant has an apparently competent representative, it is not always necessary for a tribunal to explore matters not raised by the representative (see *CSDLA/336/2000*, in which the Commissioner reviews the authorities and emphasises the summary nature of proceedings before tribunals). Thus, in *CSIB/160/2000*, the representative identified the descriptors in issue on the all work test and the tribunal were entitled to assume that the representative knew the claimant's case and so therefore the tribunal did not err in not considering other descriptors. In *CH/2484/2006*, the Deputy Commissioner said that "it would be unrealistic—especially in a case like this where both parties were represented—to expect tribunals to read every clause of a tenancy agreement in case a representative fails to rely on a clause which might be helpful to his case". He also said—

> "To the extent that the local authority is dissatisfied with the outcome of this case, that perhaps highlights the need for thorough preparation of a local authority's factual case in advance of tribunal hearings, so that all the points can be raised there. Even the most thoroughly prepared appeal to a Commissioner is not an adequate substitute for doing so, for the reason that, however strongly a Commissioner might doubt the factual correctness of a tribunal decision . . ., the Commissioner's doubts are irrelevant in the absence of an error of law. And it will seldom be an error of law for a tribunal to fail to deal with a point that a local authority representative has not raised before it."

Even less is a tribunal required to investigate issues when a representative has declined to make submissions on them having been given a specific opportunity to do so (*CSIB/588/1998*).

However, sometimes issues raised by the evidence but overlooked by otherwise **1.454**
competent professional representatives are so fundamental that a tribunal will err in not dealing with them. That was the case in *R4/01(IS)*, a decision of a Tribunal of Commissioners in Northern Ireland. The claimant's executor had appealed to a tribunal against a decision that £63,735.31 had been overpaid to the claimant and was recoverable from her estate because the claimant had failed to disclose capital assets in the form of land. The executor was represented by counsel. The case was argued on the basis that there had been disclosure but it was stated that, although the legal interest in the land was vested in the claimant, the land had been regarded as belonging to her brother. The Tribunal of Commissioners held that that clearly raised the question whether the claimant had any beneficial interest in the land and that the appeal tribunal had erred in failing to consider that issue notwithstanding that it had not been raised by counsel representing the executor. The issue had been fundamental to the appeal. However, the Tribunal of Commissioners also said that an appeal tribunal must have a reasonable expectation that important and fundamental issues will be brought to its attention by professional representatives. Given the professional representation, if the issue of the property being regarded as belonging to the brother had not been mentioned by a witness at the hearing itself, the appeal tribunal would have been entitled to conclude it had been dropped.

The Court of Appeal in Northern Ireland has, in *Mongan v Department for Social Development* [2005] NICA 16 (reported as *R3/05 (DLA)*), taken a similar approach to that taken by Commissioners and the approach taken in *Mongan* has been expressly endorsed by the Court of Appeal in England and Wales (*Secretary of State for Work and Pensions v Hooper* [2007] EWCA Civ 495 (reported as *R(IB) 4/07*). In *Mongan*, the Court held that the identical wording of the Northern Ireland equivalent of s.12(8)(a) suggests "that the tribunal would not be absolved of the duty to consider relevant issues simply because they have been neglected by the appellant or her legal representatives and that it has a role to identify what issues are at stake on the appeal even if they have not been clearly or expressly articulated by the appellant." There is no duty "to exhaustively trawl the evidence to see if there is any remote possibility of an issue being raised by it" but issues "clearly apparent from the evidence" must be considered.

> "[17] Whether an issue is sufficiently apparent from the evidence will depend on the particular circumstances of each case. Likewise, the question of how far

the tribunal must go in exploring such an issue will depend on the specific facts of the case. The more obviously relevant an issue, the greater will be the need to investigate it. An extensive enquiry into an issue will not invariably be required. Indeed, a perfunctory examination of the issue may often suffice. It appears to us, however, that where a higher rate of benefit is claimed and the facts presented to the tribunal suggest that an appellant might well be entitled to a lower rate, it will normally be necessary to examine the issue, whether or not it has been raised by the appellant or her legal representatives.

[18] In carrying out their inquisitorial function, the tribunal should have regard to whether the party has the benefit of legal representation. It need hardly be said that close attention should be paid to the possibility that relevant issues might be overlooked where the appellant does not have legal representation. Where an appellant is legally represented the tribunal is entitled to look to the legal representative for elucidation of the issues that arise. But this does not relieve them of the obligation to enquire into potentially relevant matters. A poorly represented party should not be placed at any greater disadvantage than an unrepresented party."

In that case, the claimant had sought the higher rate of the mobility component of disability living allowance but the Court held that the arguments and evidence presented to the tribunal were such that it should have been alert to the need to investigate entitlement to the lower rate of the mobility component, whether or not that question was raised by the claimant's solicitor.

1.455 In *KN v SSWP (ESA)* [2021] UKUT 155 (AAC), the Upper Tribunal said that, in the light of *Mongan, CSIB/588/1998, CSDLA/336/2000* and *CSIB/160/2000* (mentioned above) have no continuing relevance beyond cases where the First-tier Tribunal is seeking to establish whether an issue is "clearly apparent from the evidence". It emphasised that, if an issue is clearly raised by the evidence, the failure of an experienced representative to argue the point cannot alter that fact. But, presumably, the reason why it was accepted that the old cases do still have some relevance is that they were all cases where it could reasonably have been implied from the representative not taking the relevant point that the representative was conceding it, which is different from simply overlooking it.

In *C37/09-10 (DLA)*, a Northern Ireland Commissioner has held that, in the light of *Mongan*, a concession made by a representative should not be accepted without the tribunal first looking behind it to see whether it was properly made, but that goes much further than the approach to concessions taken in most cases and, it is suggested, a tribunal is entitled to have regard to an explicit, or clearly implicit, concession when considering whether an issues arises that is "clearly apparent from the evidence". Indeed, it is striking that the appellant claimant in that case did not resile from the concession even on the appeal to the Commissioner.

On the other hand, in *KN*, the issue that had not been argued by the representative was clearly raised in the documents and had been considered by the Secretary of State and the appeal before the Upper Tribunal proceeded on the basis that the First-tier Tribunal had not mentioned the issue during the hearing so as to check that the point really was being conceded. Moreover, even explicit concessions are sometimes questionable and there may be reasons for doubting whether they have been rightly made, particularly if they are not questions of pure fact and may be based on a misapprehension as to the law. Thus, it is suggested, whether a tribunal errs in law in accepting a concession without investigating it must depend to a substantial extent on the nature of the concession and the particular facts of the case.

Moreover, in *CDLA/4099/2004*, the Commissioner held that a tribunal had not erred in law in failing to deal with an issue when the claimant had an adequate alternative remedy. The claimant had applied for supersession of an award of disability living allowance. The application was treated as effective from the date it was received and, on appeal, the case was argued before the tribunal on that basis because the claimant's representative wrongly considered that an award of benefit for a period before the application could be considered on a subsequent application for revision. In fact, the tribunal could, by virtue of s.12(8)(a), have considered entitlement to benefit during that earlier period (because reg.7(6) of the Social Security and Child Support (Decisions and Appeals) Regulations 1999 would have applied if the claimant's proposed argument in respect of that earlier period had been accepted). However, the Commissioner held that the tribunal had not been *bound* to consider entitlement during that earlier period because the claimant still had an adequate alternative remedy in a further application for supersession.

If the First-tier Tribunal does *not* accept a concession, its reasons must show not only why it reached the opposite conclusion but also that it had been aware that the concession had been made and so had *consciously* decided not to accept it (*LH v SSWP (PIP)* [2022] UKUT 32 (AAC) at [33], where the Secretary of State had effectively conceded in her written submission that the appellant had been entitled to the standard rate of the mobility component of personal independence payment but the First-tier Tribunal nonetheless dismissed the appellant's appeal against her decision awarding only the daily living component and did so without mentioning the concession).

It follows from the power under s.12(8)(a) to deal with issues not raised in an appeal that it is open to the First-tier Tribunal to deal with issues raised by a respondent to a multi-party case without it being necessary for the respondent to cross-appeal or submit a respondent's notice. However, in *John v IC* [2014] UKUT 444 (AAC) where the Upper Tribunal reached a similar conclusion in relation to appeals under the Freedom of Information Act 2000, it referred to *Birkett v Department for the Environment, Food and Rural Affairs* [2011] EWCA Civ 1606 and held that the First-tier Tribunal could exercise its case-management powers to prevent unfairness to an appellant as a result of a new point being raised at a late stage. This can apply both ways, by way of enforcement of the time limits in the Tribunal Procedure (First-tier Tribunal) (Social Entitlement Chamber) Rules 2008 for appeals, responses and replies, in which parties are expected to include their grounds for challenging or defending the decision under appeal (see rr.22–24).

Subsection (8)(b)

By contrast with para.(a), para.(b) confers no discretion. In the light of reg.3(9) of the Social Security and Child Support (Decisions and Appeals) Regulations 1999 and s.9(5) of the Act, when a decision has been revised under s.9, "the time when the decision appealed against was made" must refer to the date on which the original decision was made. Paragraph (b) is therefore consistent with the approach that any change of circumstances requires a new claim or a supersession under s.10 and it reverses the effect of *R(S)2/98*. Paragraph (b) did not apply where the appeal was brought before May 21, 1998 when this Act received the Royal Assent and Sch.6, para.3 (which made transitory provision preventing social security appeal tribunals and disability appeal tribunals from taking account of circumstances not obtaining at the date of the decision under appeal) came into force. In such a case, a tribunal had still to consider the claimant's entitlement to benefit throughout the period to the date of its decision or down to the date from which another decision was effective (*CIB/213/1999*). **1.456**

In *NC v SSWP (ESA)* [2015] UKUT 147 (AAC), it was pointed out that the draftsman of s.12(8)(b) may not have foreseen that, in the absence of an equivalent provision in s.10, regulations under s.10(3) might enable a supersession to take account of circumstances not obtaining at the time of the Secretary of State's decision. It is not easy to see how a decision of the Secretary of State to supersede a decision on the ground of an anticipated change of circumstances (see reg.6(2)(a)(ii) of the Social Security and Child Support (Decisions and Appeals) Regulations 1999) can be upheld by the First-tier Tribunal.

However, it is important to note that para.(b) does not prevent a tribunal having regard to evidence that was not before the Secretary of State and came into existence after the decision was made or to evidence of events after the decision under appeal was made for the purpose of drawing inferences as to the circumstances obtaining when, or before, the decision was made (*R(DLA) 2/01*, *R(DLA) 3/01* and *BMcD v DSD (DLA)* [2011] NICom 175; [2013] AACR 29, a decision of a Tribunal of Commissioners in Northern Ireland).

This creates particular difficulties where entitlement to benefit depends on a prognosis. Thus, in *R(DLA) 3/01*, the claimant would be entitled to disability living allowance only if she was likely to satisfy the relevant conditions for six months. She was recovering from an operation. The Commissioner held that, in such a case, a tribunal was entitled to take account of the actual rate of recovery, even though the evidence of that arose after the date of the decision under appeal, provided that the fact that the claimant had not recovered as quickly as originally expected merely reflected the natural vagaries of an uncertain recovery process. Untoward circumstances arising after the date of the decision had to be disregarded, whether that operated to the claimant's advantage or to her disadvantage. Thus the fact that a claimant recovering from a heart attack developed pneumonia after the Secretary of State's decision was made would have to be ignored. So too would a dramatic improvement in a claimant's condition due to the use of a new drug. A similar case came before a Commissioner in *CDLA/2878/2000*. The claimant was a nurse who became incapacitated due to a slipped disc. She claimed disability living allowance on August 31, 1999, had a successful operation on December 17, 1999 and was able to return to work on February 14, 2000. The tribunal said simply that disability living allowance could not be awarded because there was no evidence that the claimant could have satisfied the conditions of entitlement from February 14, 2000, which was less than six months from the date of claim. The Commissioner set aside the tribunal's decision on the ground that the tribunal had not considered whether, at the date of claim, it had been likely that she would cease to satisfy the conditions of entitlement within six months. He directed the new tribunal to determine that likelihood on the basis of what was known at the date of claim.

1.457 A contention that subs.(8)(b) did not apply to changes of circumstances occurring between the date of a decision made in advance and the date from which the decision was effective was rejected by a Tribunal of Commissioners in *R(DLA) 4/05* who pointed out that s.8(2)(b) precluded the Secretary of State from taking account of any such change of circumstances that he might anticipate. However, they stressed that they were not disagreeing with the approach taken in *R(DLA) 3/01* and also that the Secretary of State (when making an advance award) could take account of the effects of the mere passage of time, such as the claimant attaining a certain age or the qualifying period for a benefit being completed. Consequently, a tribunal may take account of the effect of the mere passage of time after the date of the Secretary of State's decision in any case where the Secretary of State could have made an advance award of disability allowance under reg.13A of the Social Security (Claims and Payments) Regulations 1987. In *Secretary of State for Work and Pensions v Bhakta* [2006] EWCA Civ 65 (reported as *R(IS) 7/06*), the Court of Appeal approved *R(DLA) 4/05* and applied it to an income support case where an advance award could have been made under reg.13. The case was one where the only reason that the claimant had not been found by the Commissioner to be habitually resident at the date of the Secretary of State's decision was that a sufficient period of residence had not elapsed by that date. Regulation 13 has been amended with effect from May 23, 2007 so as to exclude that class of case (and all claims by "persons from abroad") from the scope of the regulation, but the principle confirmed in *Bhakta* remains good in other contexts. *R(DLA) 4/05* has also been followed by a Tribunal of Commissioners in Northern Ireland (*R3/05 (DLA)*).

In *CDLA/3293/2000*, a case where the claimant had appealed against a decision of the Secretary of State to make no award of disability living allowance, the Commissioner held that s.12(8)(b) did not preclude a tribunal from using hindsight to fix the length of an award that they considered should be made. Similarly, in *PH v SSWP (DLA)* [2013] UKUT 268 (AAC), it was held that the First-tier Tribunal is entitled to extend the original period of an award of disability living allowance when allowing an appeal against a supersession decision that had prematurely ended the award (which had had the result that the claimant had not made a renewal claim before the original award would have ended). The judge suggested that, in that case, the First-tier Tribunal should have extended the award for long enough to enable the claimant to make an effective renewal claim. Since by the time he decided the appeal to the Upper Tribunal the claimant had made a new claim, the judge substituted for the First-tier Tribunal's decision an award terminating on the day before the day from which the new claim was effective. He said:

> "Section 12(8)(b) is clearly intended to prevent the First-tier Tribunal from having regard to such changes of circumstances as a change in a claimant's condition but I do not think that the legislature contemplated that the First-tier Tribunal should ignore administrative events such as the making of a new claim if that would force it to make a potentially overlapping award that might require unscrambling through a further supersession decision."

However, in *CDLA/3722/2000*, an appeal tribunal was held not to be entitled to use hindsight to reduce the period of a claimant's award to less than the minimum period of six months. At the time of the Secretary of State's decision she was likely to satisfy the conditions for disability living allowance for six months. In fact, she had a course of treatment and got better much earlier than had been expected. The Commissioner held that the tribunal were obliged to turn a blind eye to the improvement and the Secretary of State would not be able to supersede the decision so as to prevent benefit being paid for longer than the claimant's condition merited.

The Commissioner deciding *R(DLA) 3/01* observed that s.12(8)(b) required tri- **1.458**
bunals to indulge in the sort of artificial exercise that is frowned upon in modern courts where judges are not expected to close their eyes to reality and he referred to *Charles v Hugh James Jones and Jenkins (a firm)* [2000] 1 All E.R. 289, 299–301. Section 12(8)(b) is of particular importance in disablement benefit cases where tribunals can usually themselves examine the claimant (see reg.52 of the Social Security and Child Support (Decisions and Appeals) Regulations 1999) and must be careful to distinguish between those of their findings that are relevant to circumstances obtaining at the time of the decision under appeal and those that are not.

Section 12(8)(b) applies to changes of legal circumstances as well as changes of factual circumstances so that, as one might expect, the First-tier Tribunal usually has to apply the law as it was in force when the Secretary of State made his decision. However, the First-tier Tribunal may be obliged to give effect to retrospective legislation passed after the date of the Secretary of State's decision. Although the passing of a retrospective Act of Parliament is itself a change of circumstances (*Chief Adjudication Officer v McKiernon* (reported as *R(I) 2/94*)), a retrospective Act passed after the Secretary of State has made a decision can alter the legal circumstances obtaining at the time of his decision. Thus it was held in *Secretary of State for Work and Pensions v Reilly* [2016] EWCA Civ 413; [2017] Q.B. 257; [2017] AACR 14 at [137] that, where the Secretary of State has made a decision on the basis of regulations that have been subsequently held to be ultra vires and the regulations are then retrospectively validated by Act of Parliament, the Secretary of State is entitled to rely on the effect of that Act in responding to an appeal against his decision. Similarly, where entitlement to one benefit depends on the claimant being entitled to another benefit, it is not the decision of the Secretary of State or tribunal to the effect that the claimant was "entitled" to that other benefit that is the material change of circumstances; it is the beginning of the period of entitlement that is material (*MW v SSWP (IS)* [2022] UKUT 59 (AAC) at [26] and [27], it being pointed out at [28] that being "entitled" to benefit is not necessarily the same as being "in receipt of" it).

In *CIS/2428/1999*, it was pointed out that a literal interpretation of s.12(8)(b) would prevent a tribunal from taking account of a cause for a late claim which existed before the claim was made and had ceased to exist before the Secretary of

State's decision on the claim. The Commissioner considered that that would be absurd and would prevent adjudication on a case falling within reg.19(5) of the Social Security (Claims and Payments) Regulations 1987. He extended the principle behind *R(DLA) 3/01* and held that a circumstance "obtains" at the date of decision if it is a circumstance, whenever it occurred, that is relied on by a claimant in justifying a late claim. The principle has been further extended in *CJSA/2375/00*. In that case, the claimant had failed to attend two courses and had been disqualified from jobseeker's allowance for two weeks in respect of the first failure and four weeks in respect of the second failure. The disqualification for four weeks was permitted only because there had been a previous disqualification. The claimant appealed against both disqualifications and the appeals came before two different tribunals. The appeal against the first disqualification was allowed. The second appeal was dismissed and the claimant appealed to the Commissioner. The Commissioner said that, following the decision of the first tribunal, the Secretary of State should have revised the second disqualification under reg.3(6) of the Social Security and Child Support (Decisions and Appeals) Regulations 1999, so as to reduce the period to two weeks. However, as the Secretary of State had not done so, the second tribunal should have reduced the period, notwithstanding that the decision of the first tribunal had been given after the Secretary of State's decision on the second disqualification. The Commissioner said:

> "In a case like this, an appeal tribunal is entitled to take account of any factor known to it that relates to a past period or past event that was relevant to the decision under appeal, even if the position at the date of the hearing is different from that at the date of the decision. This gives section 12(8)(b) a sensible operation. It allows an appeal tribunal to substitute a decision on factors relevant to the period the Secretary of State had considered. But it prevents the tribunal from trespassing into the period after that date by taking account of factors that are only relevant to that later period.
>
> I repeat that I have not defined the words used in section 12(8)(b). I have simply tried to give them a sensible operation in circumstances like those involved in this case. I emphasise that I have been concerned in this decision with past periods or events. I have not been concerned with cases where the Secretary of State has had to speculate on the likely future course of events, such as the qualifying period for a disability living allowance, which I considered in [*R(DLA) 3/01*]".

Similar contortions were required in *CJSA/2472/2005*. In this case, entitlement to jobseeker's allowance had been terminated on the ground that the claimant had to be treated as not being available for work because the restrictions he had put on his availability were more restrictive than those recorded in his jobseeker's agreement. He had already, before the termination of his entitlement to benefit, applied for a variation of his jobseeker's agreement. That application had been only partially successful and the claimant had appealed against both the variation of his jobseeker's agreement and the termination of his entitlement to jobseeker's allowance. The Commissioner held that the Secretary of State, a tribunal or a Commissioner may direct that a varied jobseeker's agreement be given retrospective effect so that it has effect from the date of the application for variation. The consequence of the Commissioner allowing the claimant's appeal in respect of the jobseeker's agreement and making such a direction in that case was that, if the claimant signed the varied agreement, the circumstances obtaining at the date of the decision in respect of entitlement to jobseeker's allowance would be changed, affecting the operation of s.12(8)(b). He therefore adjourned the appeal in respect of entitlement to jobseeker's allowance in order to give the claimant the opportunity to sign the varied jobseeker's agreement, pointing out that the Secretary of State would be able to revise the termination of entitlement if the agreement were signed.

Section 12(8)(b) would be unobjectionable if, like s.12(8)(a), it said "need not" instead of "shall not". As it is, it introduces an unwelcome element of technicality into appeals to tribunals that are generally supposed to be user-friendly. As the cases demonstrate, this is particularly so where "outcome decisions" in respect of entitlement are dependent on other decisions. In less complex cases, the remedy for a claimant is to make a new claim, or application for supersession, whenever there is an event that might be regarded as a new circumstance. There may be some cases where the wise claimant will make such claims or applications at regular intervals while an appeal is pending. The Secretary of State would then be obliged to make separate decisions on each claim or application (because the power to refer claims or applications to a tribunal so that they can be considered with a pending appeal has been abolished) and there would be a separate right of appeal against each decision. However, experience suggests that claimants do not consider new claims or applications to be necessary while an appeal is pending, even though some of the literature provided to them makes the suggestion, and so the reality may be that claimants lose benefit that they would undoubtedly have been entitled to but for s.12(8)(b). 1.459

Note that where a claimant does make a new claim or application for supersession pending an appeal, the Secretary of State is now empowered to revise the decision made on that claim or application in the light of the decision given on appeal (reg.3(5A) of the Social Security and Child Support (Decisions and Appeals) Regulations 1999). This makes it unnecessary for claimants to lodge repeated appeals based on the same grounds, but it remains necessary to lodge a further appeal if the point in issue arises out of a change of circumstances since the decision that was the subject of the original appeal.

Of course, s.12(8)(b) can work in a claimant's favour if there has been a new circumstance since the decision under appeal that would have reduced his or her entitlement to benefit. It may well be that the Secretary of State could not supersede the tribunal's decision (see the note to reg.6(2)(a) of the Social Security and Child Support (Decisions and Appeals) Regulations 1999). See *CDLA/3722/2000*, mentioned above. Giving effect to the tribunal's decision in the claimant's favour might, in some cases, give rise to an overpayment that was recoverable under s.71 of the Social Security Administration Act 1992 on the basis that the change of circumstances should have been disclosed to the Secretary of State so that the decision under appeal could have been superseded before the appeal was heard. However, in a case where the Secretary of State had refused benefit altogether in the decision under appeal and benefit had then been awarded by the tribunal on the basis of their findings as to the circumstances obtaining at the date of the Secretary of State's decision, it seems unlikely that there would have been any duty on the claimant to disclose any changes of circumstances while the appeal was pending. Even if the Secretary of State does have power to supersede a tribunal's decision in the light of a change of circumstances arising before the decision was given, another problem facing the Secretary of State may be continued ignorance of the new circumstance. He does not always send a representative to tribunal hearings and he does not usually ask for a copy of the record of proceedings or a full statement of the tribunal's findings and reasoning. Unless a tribunal refers in the short decision notice, recorded under r.33(2)(a) of the Tribunal Procedure (First-tier Tribunal) (Social Entitlement Chamber) Rules 2008, to a change of circumstances mentioned at the hearing, the Secretary of State may remain ignorant of it for ever and, of course, the tribunal will have been obliged by s.12(8)(b) to ignore the change when awarding benefit.

Although an element of discretion in s.12(8)(b) might make it much easier to do justice, a provision similar to s.12(8)(b) has been held not to be incompatible with the European Convention on Human Rights even in the context of asylum claims (*AS (Somalia) v Secretary of State for the Home Department* [2009] UKHL 32; [2009] 1 W.L.R. 1385).

Subsection (9)

1.460 In *Wood v Secretary of State for Work and Pensions* [2003] EWCA Civ 53 (reported as *R(DLA) 1/03*), the Court of Appeal overruled *R(DLA) 6/02* and held that the phrase "a decision superseding" should be read as "a decision taken pursuant to the power to supersede", so as to permit an appeal against a refusal to supersede. Rix L.J. conceded that that left this subsection as "a fairly redundant provision".

Redetermination etc. of appeals by tribunal

1.461 **13.**—(1) This section applies where an application is made [2 to the First-tier Tribunal for permission to appeal to the Upper Tribunal from any decision of the First-tier Tribunal under section 12 or this section].

(2) [2 . . .]

(3) If each of the principal parties to the case expresses the view that the decision was erroneous in point of law, [2the First-tier Tribunal] shall set aside the decision and refer the case for determination by a differently constituted [2the First-tier Tribunal].

[1(4) In this section and section 14 below "the principal parties" means—

(a) the persons mentioned in subsection (3)(a) and (b) of that section, and

(b) where applicable, the person mentioned in subsection (3)(d) and such a person as is first mentioned in subsection (4) of that section.]

AMENDMENTS

1. Social Security Contributions (Transfer of Functions, etc.) Act 1999 Sch.7 para.26 (April 1, 1999).

2. Transfer of Tribunal Functions Order 2008 (SI 2008/2833) Sch.3 paras 143 and 150 (November 3, 2008), subject to a saving under art.1(5).

DEFINITION

"the principal parties"—see subs.(4).

GENERAL NOTE

1.462 By reg.7 of the Child Trust Funds (Non-tax Appeals) Regulations 2005 (SI 2005/191), this section is applied in a modified form to appeals under ss.21(9) and 22 of the Child Trust Funds Act 2004 (see Vol.IV) but, as the modifications involve the omission of subs.(3), which is now the only operative part of the section, and as the only reference to "principal parties" in s.14 has been repealed, the continued application of this section to those cases seems entirely pointless. Until April 1, 2009, this section was also applied in a similarly modified form to appeals under the Tax Credits Act 2002 but, as explained in the note to s.12, the regulation applying it has lapsed in relation to cases in Great Britain.

Indeed, it is not easy to see why this section has not been completely repealed for ordinary social security cases as well. Subsection (2) provided a power to set aside a decision where a tribunal chairman considering an application for leave to appeal against a decision of the tribunal considered that the decision was erroneous in point of law. That was obviously a useful power, enabling unnecessary appeals to be avoided, and it has been extended to all decisions of the First-tier Tribunal against which there is a right of appeal by s.9 of the Tribunals, Courts and Enforcement Act 2007. Subsection (2) has been repealed (subject to a saving for reasons explained in the note to ss.5–7) because it would add nothing to s.9 of the 2007 Act.

Now, subs.(3) is the only operative part of the section. It is a strange provision that was described in *AF v SSWP (DLA) (No.2)* [2017] UKUT 366 (AAC) as "less than helpful", *requiring* a judge to set aside a decision of the First-tier Tribunal if the principal parties express the view that it was erroneous in point of law, whether or not he or she agrees. It would be unobjectionable if it conferred a *power* to set aside a decision with which all the parties were dissatisfied but it is the duty to do so that creates the difficulty. The First-tier Tribunal will always have included a judge, whereas it is very rare for any party to be represented by a lawyer. Yet, if the parties express the view, no matter how unreasonably, that the decision is erroneous in point of law, their view prevails and the judge must set the decision aside. It is not even necessary for the parties to agree on the error of law. It might, perhaps, be arguable that, in some cases, different parts of a decision of a tribunal are different decisions for the purposes of this section but that will not always be possible. The First-tier Tribunal may have steered carefully between two extreme views advanced by the parties, all to no avail. If re-determining tribunals took the same approach and the parties remained stubborn, the litigation could go on for ever unless action were taken to avoid subs.(3) coming into play. There is no scope for a judge to take the view that the case would be better determined by the Upper Tribunal than by the First-tier Tribunal differently constituted.

Happily, the necessity of applying subs.(3) seldom arises because it is comparatively rare for all parties to assert that there is an error of law in a tribunal's decision. This is largely because it is unnecessary to ascertain the views of a respondent to an application for permission to appeal, since granting permission is not a final determination of the parties' rights and refusing permission is a decision in favour of the respondent. Most applications for permission are made by claimants. However, for some reason that may owe more to history rather than principle, where the Secretary of State applies for permission to appeal, it is the practice of the Social Entitlement Chamber of the First-tier Tribunal always to seek the view of the claimant before determining the application. That might be necessary if the judge were contemplating reviewing the decision instead of granting permission but is unnecessary otherwise. If, in those circumstances, the claimant asserts that the tribunal's decision is erroneous in point of law the judge will be bound to set the decision aside. **1.463**

The other circumstance where this section may be brought into play is where both parties seek permission to appeal against a decision. However, a decision may not be set aside under this section once one such application for permission to appeal has been determined and permission has been either granted or refused (*CF/6923/1999*, but see *CIB/2949/2005*, where the Commissioner suggested that this might have been too broadly expressed).

It seems unlikely that this section will be found to apply where the First-tier Tribunal has refused to admit an application for permission because it was late (see r.38(5)(b) of the Tribunal Procedure (First-tier Tribunal) (Social Entitlement Chamber) Rules 2008).

Note that, where a decision is set aside, the case must be referred to a differently constituted tribunal. It is usual for the decision that has been set aside to be included in the papers before the new tribunal. **1.464**

That is not inappropriate. Even if their findings of fact cannot be relied upon, issues identified by the first tribunal may well be of assistance to the new tribunal, although it must be careful not to be influenced by the discredited findings (*Swash v Secretary of State for the Home Department* [2006] EWCA Civ 1093; [2007] 1 W.L.R. 1264). There may, however, be special circumstances in which the legally qualified panel member setting the first decision aside considers that the interests of justice require the case to be heard by a tribunal that has not seen that decision and he or she will be able to issue appropriate directions to ensure that that happens (*ibid.*).

In *CIB/4193/2003*, a decision made on a consideration of the papers was set aside and a new paper consideration was arranged without that being made clear to the claimant who had decided that she wanted to attend a hearing. The Commissioner set aside the second decision and suggested that claimants should be given an opportunity to ask for a hearing when a decision is set aside under this section.

In *CIS/4533/2001*, it was held that there was no appeal against a setting aside under this section but that was because a decision under this section was then made by a legally qualified panel member whereas the right of appeal was expressed as being against a decision of an appeal tribunal. Since the coming into force of the Tribunals, Courts and Enforcement Act 2007, different considerations would apply.

Appeal from [2First-tier Tribunal to Upper Tribunal]

1.465 **14.**—(1) [2. . .]

(2) [1 . . .]

(3) [1 . . .] An appeal [2 to the Upper Tribunal under section 11 of the Tribunals, Courts and Enforcement Act 2007 from any decision of the First-tier Tribunal under section 12 or 13 above lies] at the instance of any of the following—

(a) the Secretary of State;
(b) the claimant and such other person as may be prescribed;
(c) in any of the cases mentioned in subsection (5) below, a trade union; and
(d) a person from whom it is determined that any amount is recoverable under or by virtue of section 71 or 74 of the Administration Act.

(4) In a case relating to industrial injuries benefit an appeal [2 to the Upper Tribunal under section 11 of the Tribunals, Courts and Enforcement Act 2007 from any decision of the First-tier Tribunal under section 12 or 13 above lies] at the instance of a person whose entitlement to benefit is, or may be, under Part VI of Schedule 7 to the Contributions and Benefits Act, affected by the decision appealed against, as well as at the instance of any person or body such as is mentioned in subsection (3) above.

(5) The following are the cases in which an appeal lies at the instance of a trade union—

(a) where the claimant is a member of the union at the time of the appeal and was so immediately before the matter in question arose;
(b) where that matter in any way relates to a deceased person who was a member of the union at the time of his death;
(c) where the case relates to industrial injuries benefit and the claimant or, in relation to industrial death benefit, the deceased, was a member of the union at the time of the relevant accident.

(6) Subsections [1. . .] (3) and (5) above, as they apply to a trade union, apply also to any other association which exists to promote the interests and welfare of its members.

(7) [2 . . .]
(8) [2 . . .]
(9) [2 . . .]
(10) [2 . . .]
(11) [2 . . .]
(12) [2 . . .]

AMENDMENTS

1. Social Security Contributions (Transfer of Functions, etc.) Act 1999 Sch.7 para.27 (April 1, 1999).

2. Transfer of Tribunal Functions Order 2008 (SI 2008/2833) Sch.3 paras 143 and 151 (November 3, 2008), subject to a saving under art.1(5).

DEFINITIONS

"the Administration Act"—see s.84.

"claimant"—see s.39(1) and, by virtue of s.39(2), see s.191 of the Social Security Administration Act 1992.

"the Contributions and Benefits Act"—*ibid.*

"industrial injuries benefit"—by virtue of s.39(2), see s.191 of the Social Security Administration Act 1992.

"prescribed"—see s.84.

GENERAL NOTE

Originally, this section provided for a right of appeal to a Social Security Commissioner from a decision of an appeal tribunal and it also introduced Sch.4, providing for the appointment of Commissioners. The right of appeal has now been replaced by the right of appeal to the Upper Tribunal under s.11 of the Tribunals, Courts and Enforcement Act 2007. However, the repeals of subsections (7)–(12) are subject to a saving for the reason given in the note to ss.5–7. **1.466**

Now this section merely makes provision as to who may appeal in social security cases. Subsections (3) and (4) probably add little to s.11(2) of the 2007 Act, which provides that "any party" has a right of appeal. Section 11(2) certainly means that the failure to exercise the power to make regulations under subs.(3)(b) to the same extent as the equivalent power in s.12(2) of this Act no longer creates any substantial difficulty. Subsections (5) and (6) reproduce provisions in earlier legislation which fell into disuse in the 1970s or 1980s. The modern approach of trade unions and other organisations is to act as a representative of a member rather than appealing in their own right.

In relation to cases where the original decision was made by HMRC (i.e. cases under s.170 of the Pension Schemes Act 1993 or cases concerning the former working families' tax credit or disabled person's tax credit or, now child benefit or guardian's allowance), this section applies with the modification that the reference to the Secretary of State are to be read as a reference to HMRC (Pensions Schemes Act 1993 s.170(7), Tax Credits Act 1999 Sch.2 para.21 and Sch.4 para.3(2), Tax Credits Act 2002 Sch.4, para.15 and Commissioners for Revenue and Customs Act 2005 s.4(1)).

By reg.8 of the Child Trust Funds (Non-tax Appeals) Regulations 2005 (SI 2005/191), this section is applied in a rather more modified form to appeals under ss.21(9) and 22 of the Child Trust Funds Act 2004 (see Vol.IV). Until April 1, 2009, this section was also applied, with similar modifications, to appeals under the Tax Credits Act 2002 but, as explained in the note to s.12, the regulation applying it has lapsed in relation to cases in Great Britain.

Application for permission to appeal against a decision of the Upper Tribunal

15.—(1) [1 . . .] **1.467**

(2) [1 . . .]

(3) [1 An application for permission to appeal from a decision of the Upper Tribunal in respect of a decision of the First-tier Tribunal under section 12 or 13] may only be made by—

(a) a person who, before the proceedings before the [1 Upper Tribunal] were begun, was entitled to appeal to the [1 Upper Tribunal] from the decision to which the [1 Upper Tribunal's] decision relates;

(b) any other person who was a party to the proceedings in which the first decision mentioned in paragraph (a) above was given;

(c) any other person who is authorised by regulations to apply for [1 permission];

[1 . . .]

(4) [1 . . .]

(5) [1 . . .]

AMENDMENT

1. Transfer of Tribunal Functions Order 2008 (SI 2008/2833) Sch.3 paras 143 and 152 (November 3, 2008), subject to a saving under art.1(5).

GENERAL NOTE

1.468 Originally, this section provided for a right of appeal to an appellate court from a decision of a Social Security Commissioner. The equivalent right of appeal from a decision of the Upper Tribunal is now provided by s.13 of the Tribunals, Courts and Enforcement Act 2007. Now this section merely makes provision as to who may appeal in social security cases. It will seldom be necessary for a person to rely on this section rather than s.13(2) of the 2007 Act, which provides that "any party" has a right of appeal, and therefore the continued application of this section to appeals under ss.21(9) and 22 of the Child Trust Funds Act 2004, by reg.10 of the Child Trust Funds (Non-tax Appeals) Regulations 2005 (SI 2005/191), seems unnecessary. Until April 1, 2009, this section was also applied to appeals under the Tax Credits Act 2002 but, as explained in the note to s.12, the regulation applying it has lapsed in relation to cases in Great Britain. The repeal of most of this section and the amendments to subs.(3) are subject to a saving so as to enable a person to appeal to the Court of Session against a decision of a Social Security Commissioner under s.159 of the Health and Social Care (Community Health and Standards) Act 2003 (see the note to ss.5–7).

[1 Functions of Senior President of Tribunals

1.469 **15A.**—(1) The Senior President of Tribunals shall ensure that appropriate steps are taken by the First-tier Tribunal to secure the confidentiality, in such circumstances as may be prescribed, of any prescribed material, or any prescribed classes or categories of material.

(2) [2 . . .]

(3) [2 . . .]]

AMENDMENTS

1. Transfer of Tribunal Functions Order 2008 (SI 2008/2833) Sch.3 paras 143 and 153 (November 3, 2008).

2. Deregulation Act 2015, s.79 (May 26, 2015).

GENERAL NOTE

1.470 This section replaced paras 7 and 10 of Sch.1 when that Schedule was repealed in 2008, but the duty under subs.(2) to make an annual report to the Secretary of State on the standards achieved by him or her in the making of decisions against which an appeal lay to the First-tier Tribunal was abolished in 2015. The Senior President may delegate his functions under this section to another judge, e.g. the President of the Social Entitlement Chamber of the First-tier Tribunal (see s.8 of the Tribunals, Courts and Enforcement Act 2008).

Procedure etc.

Procedure

1.471 **16.**—(1) Regulations ("procedure regulations") may make any such provision as is specified in Schedule 5 to this Act.

(2) [1 . . .]

(3) It is hereby declared—

(a) [1 . . .]

(b) that the power to provide for the procedure to be followed in connection with the making of decisions by the Secretary of State includes power to make provision with respect to the formulation of the matters to be decided, whether on a reference under section 117 of the Administration Act or otherwise.

(4) *Omitted.*

(5) *Omitted.*

(6) [[1] . . .]

(7) [[1] . . .]

(8) [. . .]

(9) [. . .]

AMENDMENT

1. Transfer of Tribunal Functions Order 2008 (SI 2008/2833) Sch.3 paras 143 and 154 (November 3, 2008), subject to a saving under art.1(5).

DEFINITIONS

"the Administration Act"—see s.84.
"procedure regulations"—see subs.(1).

GENERAL NOTE

The repeal of most of this section is subject to a saving for reasons explained in the note to ss.5–7. 1.472

Subsection (1)

See the Social Security and Child Support (Decisions and Appeals) Regulations 1999, the Child Benefit and Guardian's Allowance (Decisions and Appeals) Regulations 2003 and the Universal Credit, Personal Independence Payment, Jobseeker's Allowance and Employment and Support Allowance (Decisions and Appeals) Regulations 2013. By reg.11 of the Child Trust Funds (Non-tax Appeals) Regulations 2005 (SI 2005/191), this subsection is applied to appeals under ss. 21(9) and 22 of the Child Trust Funds Act 2004. See Vol.IV for that Act and the Child Trust Funds (Appeals) Regulations 2005 which are made under this subsection as so applied. Until April 1, 2009, it was also applied to appeals under the Tax Credits Act 2002 but, as explained in the note to s.12, the regulation applying it has lapsed in relation to cases in Great Britain. 1.473

Subssections (4) and (5)

These subsections are to be repealed by the Social Security Contributions (Transfer of Functions, etc.) Act 1999 Sch.7 para.28, presumably at the same time as the only provisions that would have given them practical effect and which have never been brought into force. 1.474

Finality of decisions

17.—(1) Subject to the provisions of this Chapter [[1] and to any provision made by or under Chapter 2 of Part 1 of the Tribunals, Courts and Enforcement Act 2007], any decision made in accordance with the foregoing provisions of this Chapter shall be final; and subject to the provisions of any regulations under section 11 above, any decision made in accordance with those regulations shall be final. 1.475

(2) If and to the extent that regulations so provide, any finding of fact or other determination embodied in or necessary to such a decision, or on which such a decision is based, shall be conclusive for the purposes of—

(a) further such decisions;

(b) decisions made under the Child Support Act; and

(c) decisions made under the Vaccine Damage Payments Act.

Amendment

1. Transfer of Tribunal Functions Order 2008 (SI 2008/2833) Sch.3 paras 143 and 155 (November 3, 2008).

Definitions

"the Child Support Act"—see s.84.
"the Vaccine Damage Payments Act"—see s.84.

General Note

1.476 By reg.12 of the Child Trust Funds (Non-tax Appeals) Regulations 2005 (SI 2005/191), this section is applied with substantial modifications to appeals under ss.21(9) and 22 of the Child Trust Funds Act 2004 (see Vol.IV). Similarly, reg.3 of the Childcare Payments (Appeals) Regulations 2016 (SI 2016/1078) applies this section to appeals under the Childcare Payments Act 2014, with substantial modifications the precise effects of which are not entirely clear (see Vol.IV).Until April 1, 2009, it was also applied in modified form to appeals under the Tax Credits Act 2002 but, as explained in the note to s.12, the regulation applying it has lapsed in relation to cases in Great Britain (and the implication of *HO v HMRC (TC)* [2018] UKUT 105 (AAC) is that it was unnecessary anyway).

Subsection (1)

1.477 This re-enacts s.60(1) of the Social Security Administration Act 1992. Decisions are "final" subject to appeals and revisions or supersesssions.

The principal effect of this subsection is to prevent there being two decisions in respect of the same benefit for the same period. Thus, where a claimant appeals against a decision of the Secretary of State refusing a benefit and, before the appeal is determined, the Secretary of State makes a determination on a new claim for that benefit from a later date, the First-tier Tribunal has jurisdiction in respect only of a period ending on the day before the period covered by the Secretary of State's determination on the new claim begins (*GG v SSWP (PIP)* [2019] UKUT 318 (AAC)), save to the extent that the Secretary of State's second determination might have been based on the lack of a valid claim or perhaps in some similar circumstances. The claimant's remedy if he or she is dissatisfied with the Secretary of State's second decision is usually to apply for "mandatory reconisideration" and, if necessary, appeal against that decision too, in which case consideration can be given to hearing the two appeals together. There may be cases where it would be appropriate for the First-tier Tribunal to suggest that such an appeal be brought.

On the other hand, in *CDLA/3323/2003*, where a decision awarding one component of disability living allowance on a renewal claim had been made before an appeal to a Commissioner in respect of the previous award had been allowed and the Commissioner had awarded both components, the Commissioner extended the period of the previous award to cover the period for which the renewal claim had been allowed. He acknowledged that the award on the renewal claim could have been revised under reg.3(5A) of the Social Security and Child Support (Decisions and Appeals) Regulation 1999 to achieve the same effect but commented that, in the light of *R(IS) 15/04*, the claimant might not have had any way of challenging a refusal to revise short of an application for judicial review, and he said:

> "I do not consider that a determination on a renewal claim necessarily prevents a tribunal or Commissioner from extending the period of the award under appeal to them, where it is necessary to do so to do justice. However, as there cannot be two awards in respect of one period, the Secretary of State's [renewal] decision must be treated as having lapsed (on the basis that the renewal claim has become unnecessary) and the payment under that decision must be treated as having been paid on account of the decision of the tribunal or Commissioner."

Where an interim assessment of disablement is made on a claim for disablement benefit, it is made in respect of a specific period and the decision is final only for that period. Thus, the decision that must be made in respect of the following period does not involve any revision or supersession of the interim decision in respect of the earlier period; it is simply a further decision on the claim (*DW v SSWP (II)* [2022] UKUT 183 (AAC) at [11] and [23]).

Another consequence of this subsection is that it is not possible to sue the Secretary of State in negligence in respect of a decision (*Jones v Department of Employment* [1989] Q.B. 1) although an action could lie in misfeasance. That does not prevent the Department for Work and Pensions being sued in respect of bad advice.

However, the finality of decisions does not prevent decisions being challenged by way of judicial review (*R. v Medical Appeal Tribunal, Ex p. Gilmore* [1957] 1 Q.B. 574, a decision made before there was a right of appeal from a medical appeal tribunal to a Commissioner) although the reluctance of the High Court to allow such challenges when there is a statutory right of appeal means that they are confined to exceptional cases.

Subsection (2)

See reg.10 of the Social Security and Child Support (Decisions and Appeals) Regulations 1999 and reg.40(1) and (2) of the Universal Credit, Personal Independence Payment, Jobseeker's Allowance and Employment and Support Allowance (Decisions and Appeals) Regulations 2013 (in relation to decisions as to whether or not a person has, or is to be treated as having, limited capability for work) and regs 5(2) and 6(1) of the Social Security (Industrial Diseases) (Prescribed Diseases) Regulations 1985 (in relation to whether or not a person has been suffering from a prescribed disease). **1.478**

Note that there is no express provision re-enacting s.60(2) of the 1992 Act which provided that, as a general rule, a finding in one decision was *not* conclusive for the purpose of any other decision. However, it is suggested that such an express provision is not necessary and that, in the absence of any rule of evidence to the contrary, a person or body making a decision is entitled to rely on an earlier finding but is not bound to do so. If that were not the approach to be taken in the absence of any express provision, subs.(2) would be unnecessary. Thus, as was pointed out in *CIB/3327/2004*, although a decision as to whether or not a person was incapable of work that was made on a claim for incapacity benefit was conclusive for the purposes of credits in respect of incapacity for work (by virtue of reg.10 of the 1999 Regulations), a decision as to whether or not a person was engaged in remunerative work made on a claim for jobseeker's allowance was not conclusive for the purposes of credits in respect of involuntary unemployment.

There is no power to make decisions under this Act conclusive for the purpose of decisions under the Social Security (Recovery of Benefits) Act 1997. Therefore, a tribunal considering an appeal under s.11 of that Act is entitled to find that benefit was not paid in respect of an accident, even if that conclusion is inconsistent with the benefit having been awarded at all (*R(CR) 1/02*). Similarly, *CIS/1330/2002* holds that a finding of fact within a decision as to a claimant's entitlement to benefit is not conclusive for the purposes of a decision as to whether an overpayment has been made and is recoverable. In *SSWP v AM (IS)* [2010] UKUT 428 (AAC), the judge took a subtly different approach from that taken in *CIS/1330/2002* and held that "an entitlement decision necessarily establishes that there has been an overpayment, because it proves that the amount paid during a particular period was more than the claimant was entitled to" although he also held, consistently with *CIS/1330/2002*, that "when making findings of fact, the effect of section 17(2) of the 1992 Act is that the decision maker or tribunal dealing with the overpayment recoverability decision cannot be bound by the findings in relation to those facts made in the course of dealing with the entitlement decision". The difference in approach is therefore of little, if any, practical importance. Again, it was held in *CIS/3605/2005* that an erroneous decision on entitlement was a valid revision or supersession decision for the purposes of s.71(5A) of the Social Security Administration Act 1992, so as to enable the Secretary of State to recover an overpayment, but was not conclusive as to the amount of the overpayment, with the result that only the amount actually overpaid was recoverable. This approach was applied in *CA/2650/2006*, where a tribunal had found a claimant not to be ordinarily resident in Great Britain from October 27, 2003, when she had moved abroad, and had upheld a decision superseding her award of attendance allowance from that date. On an appeal against a second tribunal decision to the effect that an overpayment from October 27, 2003 to January 4, 2004 was recoverable from the claimant, the Commissioner found that she had ceased to be ordinarily resident in Great Britain only from January 4, 2004 (even though she was also resident abroad) and so she had not been overpaid benefit as a result of any failure to disclose a material fact. Accordingly, he allowed her appeal. However, under the law as it then stood, the first tribunal ought to have superseded her award only from the date of supersession in February 2004. The Commissioner pointed out that, even if the claimant had in fact ceased to be ordinarily resident in Great Britain on October 27, 2003, the first tribunal would have wrongly decided that she had not been entitled to attendance allowance from then until January 4, 2004, but that decision was final by virtue of s.17(1) of the Social Security Act 1998. Moreover, if she had ceased to be ordinarily resident, she would have actually been overpaid during that period because, had she reported the fact that she had moved overseas straightaway, her award would have been terminated immediately. He considered that, in those circumstances, he would have been bound to find that there had been an overpayment and that it was recoverable, despite the first tribunal's error. That suggestion is, strictly speaking, obiter dicta. However, the same Commissioner returned to the point in *CIB/2762/2007* in circumstances where a supersession had been made effective from a date before it was made, when, under the defective legislation then in force, that was not permissible even though the claimant had been overpaid and it was arguable that she had failed to disclose a material fact. The claimant had appealed against a later decision that the overpayment was recoverable and the Commissioner held that the tribunal considering the appeal against the recoverability was bound to find that there had been an overpayment but he said that the appropriate course of action would have been to adjourn and allow the Secretary of State to revise the supersession decision on the ground of official error and then revise the overpayment decision in the claimant's favour, causing the appeal to lapse.

Note that s.29(4) makes an industrial accident declaration conclusive for the purposes of any claim for industrial injuries benefit in respect of that accident. That provision is not applied in respect of the onset of industrial diseases. However, in *Secretary of State for Work and Pensions v Whalley* [2002] EWCA Civ 166 (reported as *R(I) 2/03*), the Court of Appeal held that a finding as to the date of onset of an industrial disease made in the context of a claim for disablement benefit was binding in respect of a later claim for reduced earnings allowance. The Court appears to have accepted an argument advanced by the Secretary of State that s.60(1) of the 1992 Act made the finding binding and that s.60(2) was concerned only with "preliminary matters such as the precise symptoms displayed at any particular time". This is, in effect, an argument that was rejected by the Tribunal of Commissioners in *R(CR) 1/02*. *Whalley* was considered in *R(I) 2/04*, in which it was held that the reason that a finding as to a date of onset of an industrial disease is conclusive lies in reg.6(1) of the Social Security (Industrial Injuries) (Prescribed Diseases) Regulations 1985 rather than in s.17. It was pointed out that in *Whalley* the issue had been whether a finding that the claimant was *not* suffering from a prescribed disease so that there was *no* date of onset was conclusive and that that had turned on the finality of a decision on a diagnosis question under the pre-1998 Act system of adjudication, which in turn had precluded a finding in a later claim for disablement pension that there had been an earlier date of onset. In *R(I) 5/04*, it was held that, while a finding that a claimant had suffered from a prescribed disease from a particular date was conclusive as to the date of onset by virtue of reg.6(1) of the 1985 Regulations, a finding that the claimant had *not* been suffering from a prescribed disease was not conclusive under the new system of adjudication in the context of the legislation then in force, but was merely final in respect of the period up to the date of the decision of the Secretary of State in which the finding was made. However, reg.5(2) of the 1985 Regulations was introduced with effect from March 18, 2005 to reverse *R(I) 5/04* by providing that a negative finding is now also conclusive.

In *LS v Lambeth LBC (HB)* [2010] UKUT 461 (AAC); [2011] AACR 27, the three-judge panel was invited to consider whether the First-tier Tribunal had been bound by a decision of a legally qualified panel member of an appeal tribunal to admit an appeal that it considered ought not to have been admitted because the legally qualified panel member had had no power to admit it. The majority held that it was unnecessary to decide whether the First-tier Tribunal had had a discretion to reconsider the legally qualified panel member's decision because it found the First-tier Tribunal's decision to be erroneous in point of law on another ground and substituted a decision that the legally qualified panel member's decision would not be reconsidered. The implication is that the First-tier Tribunal was at least not bound to reconsider the legally qualified panel member's decision. The issue arose because, in *Watt v Ahsan* [2007] UKHL 51; [2008] A.C. 696, the House of Lords held that an employment tribunal had been bound by a decision of the Employment Appeal Tribunal, dismissing an appeal from the employment tribunal's ruling made in the same proceedings to the effect that it had jurisdiction to consider the case before it, notwithstanding that a subsequent decision of the Court of Appeal in different proceedings had overruled the Employment Appeal Tribunal's decision. It might just have been arguable that the legally qualified panel member's determination would have been a "determination embodied in or necessary to such a decision" so as to have brought s.17(2) of the Social Security Act 1998 into play had the issue arisen in the context of an ordinary social security decision, but there is no equivalent to s.17(2) in para.11 of Sch.7 to the Child Support, Pensions and Social Security Act 2000, which provides for the finality of decisions in housing benefit cases, and so the point did not arise in *LS v Lambeth LBC (HB)*. On the other hand, the First-tier Tribunal's power under r.5(3)(e) of the Tribunal Procedure (First-tier Tribunal) (Social Entitlement Chamber) Rules 2008 to deal with an issue as a preliminary issue would be undermined if a decision on a preliminary issue were not binding in the same proceedings. Section 17 appears more concerned with whether a decision made in one set of proceedings is binding on a decision-maker or tribunal concerned with another set of proceedings than with whether a decision of a tribunal binds it for the purposes of further steps in the same proceedings. 1.479

In *MW v Leeds CC (HB)* [2018] UKUT 319 (AAC), the claimant made a claim on a factual basis that was entirely different from the one she had advanced on earlier claims that had been rejected both by the local authority and by the First-tier Tribunal. The Upper Tribunal said

> "[7] ... Decision-making in relation to social security is generally fairly summary. Revision and supersession provide ways of correcting errors and there is no reason why errors should not equally easily be corrected in new claims. As was pointed out in *CH/1210/2003*, decisions are final for the period to which they relate, but a new decision made in respect of a different period, whether on supersession or a new claim, need not perpetuate any error made in an earlier decision in respect of an earlier period.
>
> [8]. That is not to say that earlier decisions in respect of claims made by the same claimant are irrelevant; it may be difficult for a claimant to persuade a local authority or a tribunal to take a different view from that previously taken, particularly when the claimant has admitted lying and, as it would seem in this case, committing criminal offences by making false statements for the purpose of obtaining benefits. However, as the Secretary of State submits, the possibility that the claimant is 'an untruthful person, telling the truth on this issue' (*Onassis v Vergottis* [1968] 2 Lloyds Rep 403 at p.431, per Lord Pearce) must be recognised and so, in this case, the First-tier Tribunal ought to have considered

whether the claimant was now telling the truth and, if so, what the legal implications were."

In *CM v HMRC (TC)* [2014] UKUT 272 (AAC), the Upper Tribunal suggested that, where there were competing claims for child tax credit, the second claimant could be added as a party to an appeal brought by the first claimant, on the basis that the decision would then be binding on both claimants. If a person is added as a party to proceedings and has all the rights of a party to make representations and is made properly aware of the issues, there is no reason in principle (absent s.17(2)) why findings of fact made in any proceedings to which he or she is a party should not be binding on him or her. This section does not now apply in tax credits cases (see above).

However, a similar approach was taken in a child benefit case, *GC v HMRC (CHB)* [2018] UKUT 223 (AAC), without any mention being made of s.17(2) (see the note to r.9 of the Tribunal Procedure (First-tier Tribunal) (Social Entitlement Chamber) Rules 2008). In any event, presumably a separate decision would have subsequently to be made in respect of the second claimant's award and the implication of s.17(2) cannot be ignored. On the other hand, even if the decision to which both claimants were parties was not formally binding, it would obviously carry practical weight and arguably sufficient weight to justify any appeal that required the issue to be reargued being struck out under r.8(3)(c) of the 2008 Rules on the ground of a lack of any reasonable prospect of success in the absence of compelling new evidence or some other compelling reason.

Matters arising as respects decisions

1.480 **18.**—(1) Regulations may make provision as respects matters arising—

(a) pending any decision under this Chapter of the Secretary of State, [3 or the First-tier Tribunal or any decision of the Upper Tribunal which relates to any decision of this Chapter of the First-tier Tribunal] which relates to—

  (i) any claim for a relevant benefit; [1 or]

  (ii) any person's entitlement to such a benefit or its receipt; [1 or]

  (iii) [1 . . .]

  (iv) [1 . . .]

(b) out of the revision under section 9 above or on appeal of any such decision.

(2) Regulations under subsection (1) above as it applies to child benefit may include provision as to the date from which child benefit is to be payable to a person in respect of a child [2 or qualifying young person] in a case where, before the benefit was awarded to that person, child benefit in respect of the child [2 or qualifying young person] was awarded to another person.

Amendments

1. Social Security Contributions (Transfer of Functions, etc.) Act 1999 Sch.7 para.29 (April 1, 1999).

2. Child Benefit Act 2005, Sch.1, para.26 (April 10, 2006).

3. Transfer of Tribunal Functions Order 2008 (SI 2008/2833) Sch.3 paras 143 and 156 (November 3, 2008).

Definitions

"claim"—by virtue of s.39(2), see s.191 of the Social Security Administration Act 1992.

"relevant benefit"—see s.8(3).

Medical examinations

Medical examination required by Secretary of State

19.—(1) Before making a decision on a claim for a relevant benefit, or as to a person's entitlement to such a benefit [1 . . .], the Secretary of State may refer the person— 1.481

(a) in respect of whom the claim is made; or

(b) whose entitlement is at issue,

to a [2 health care professional approved by the Secretary of State] for such examination and report as appears to the Secretary of State to be necessary for the purpose of providing him with information for use in making the decision.

(2) Subsection (3) below applies where—

(a) the Secretary of State has exercised the power conferred on him by subsection (1) above; and

(b) the [2 health care professional approved by the Secretary of State] requests the person referred to him to attend for or submit himself to medical examination.

(3) If the person fails without good cause to comply with the request, the Secretary of State shall make the decision against him.

AMENDMENTS

1. Social Security Contributions (Transfer of Functions, etc.) Act 1999 Sch.7 para.30 (April 1, 1999).

2. Welfare Reform Act 2007 s.62(1) and (2) (July 3, 2007).

DEFINITIONS

"claim"—by virtue of s.39(2), see s.191 of the Social Security Administration Act 1992.

"health care professional"—see s.39(1).

"medical examination"—by virtue of s.39(2), see s.191 of the Social Security Administration Act 1992.

"relevant benefit"—see s.8(3).

GENERAL NOTE

Subsections (1) and (2)

This section must be distinguished from reg.19 of the Social Security and Child Support (Decisions and Appeals) Regulations 1999. Under this section, the Secretary of State refers the claimant for examination and report but it is the *health care professional* who *requests* attendance for, or submission to, a medical examination. The penalty imposed by subs.(3) is imposed for failing to comply with that person's request. Under reg.19, it is the *Secretary of State* who *requires* the claimant to attend the examination and the penalty for failure to do so is different. These distinctions reflect the different purposes of the two provisions. Section 19 makes provision for the obtaining of a report for the purpose of determining a claim whereas reg.19 makes provision for obtaining a report for the purpose of determining whether an award should be revised or superseded. 1.482

Whereas both reg.19 of the 1999 Regulations and reg.9(1) of the Social Security (Personal Independence Payment) Regulations 2013 provide that a claimant may be "required" to attend for and participate in an examination, s.19(2) and (3) of the 1998 Act contemplate a mere "request" and regs 23 and 38 of the Employment and Support Allowance Regulations 2008 provide that a claimant "may be called ...

to attend for a medical examination" as do regs 19 and 35 of the Employment and Support Allowance Regulations 2013 and reg.44 of the Universal Credit Regulations 2013. The distinction in the wording may not be important. On one hand, it has been held in *IR v SSWP (PIP)* [2019] UKUT 374 (AAC) that, in the light of *OM v SSWP (PIP)* [2017] UKUT 458 (AAC) and *MB v SSWP (PIP)* [2018] UKUT 213 (AAC), where the legislation permits a person to "require" a claimant to attend and participate in a medical consultation, it is not enough to make it clear in the text of the letter sent to the claimant that he or she may lose benefit if he or she does not attend if the letter does not also, on a literal interpretation, impose a mandatory requirement, rather than merely telling the claimant that "[i]t is important that you attend this appointment". On the other hand, it has now been held in *PPE v SSWP (ESA)* [2020] UKUT 59 (AAC) that a person does not "fail" to attend an appointment for the purposes of the 2008 Regulations (and therefore, presumably, for the purpose of this section) unless there was a legal obligation to attend it—reference being made to the cases on failing to disclose material facts for the purposes of s.71 of the Social Security Administration Act 1992—and that to impose a legal obligation notice of the appointment must use "the language of clear and unambiguous mandatory requirement". Those decisions are binding on the First-tier Tribunal. It might perhaps be arguable in the Upper Tribunal that an over-strict approach has been adopted, particularly in *PPE*, but, whether or not that is so, a person is likely to be able to show good cause for failing to comply with a request made under s.19(2)(b) that was not made in terms that indicated the likely consequence of failing to attend and so the terms in which the request was made may be highly relevant to the question whether there was good cause for a failure to attend. Therefore a copy of the request should be provided with the Secretary of State's response to an appeal, even if the claimant has not expressly put its terms in issue, although a failure to do so will not necessarily justify the First-tier Tribunal drawing inferences against the Secretary of State (*SSWP v DC (JSA)* [2017] UKUT 464 (AAC); [2018] AACR 16, where the question was whether the claimant had had good cause for failing to participate in a back-to-work scheme). This need to include a copy of the request in a response to an appeal does not depend on there being any technical necessity to prove that the request was put in terms of a "requirement".

There is no general rule that a report has no probative value if the claimant's condition is not within the health care professional's obvious area of expertise, partly because assessments for benefit purposes usually focus the functional effects of an already diagnosed condition rather than on diagnosis. Thus, the weight to be given to a physiotherapist's opinion in relation to mental health issues in a particular case is a matter for the decision-maker or First-tier Tribunal—see *ST v SSWP (ESA)* [2014] UKUT 547 (AAC) in which the three-judge panel recorded evidence given to it about the recruitment, training and assessment of health care professionals. In order to consider how much weight to put on a health care professional's opinion, it will generally be necessary for the First-tier Tribunal to know the professional qualification and areas of expertise of the health care professional providing the opinion (*CDLA/2466/2007*) although not having that information does not necessarily require the First-tier Tribunal to reject the opinion (*JM v SSWP (ESA)* [2013] UKUT 234 (AAC); [2014] AACR 5, at 76).

1.483 A claimant is entitled to know the name of the health care professional (subject to security considerations in any particular case) and to make a reasonable request for proof that a purported health care professional is in fact a health care professional (*RO v SSWP (ESA)* [2016] UKUT 402 (AAC) and see the annotation to s.39) but is not entitled to further information about the health care professional's qualifications and experience. Demanding such further information and refusing to be examined unless it is provided is likely to be considered a failure to submit to the examination without good cause (*JW v SSWP (ESA)* [2016] UKUT 208 (AAC)). So too is behaviour which is intimidating to the extent that it is reasonable for a health care professional not to proceed with the examination (*ibid.*). However, once an examination has been cancelled, there cannot be a failure to submit to it. Thus, where a claimant was asked to sign an audio-recording agreement but, due to a combination of mental health problems and the unexpected situation in which he found himself, was apparently unable to take it in so that he was told to take the agreement away to read and that a new examination would be booked, his subsequent behaviour when an attempt was made at the reception desk to book the new date could not amount to a failure to submit to the original examination (*PH v SSWP (ESA)* [2016] UKUT 119 (AAC)). On the other hand, a clear refusal to attend any future examination probably would amount to a failure to comply with a request to "submit himself to medical examination" (*R(IB) 1/01*).

In *CDLA/4127/2003*, the Secretary of State conceded that a full-time medical practitioner had gone too far in not only drawing the attention of a part-time examining medical practitioner to apparent contradictions and other failings in his report, which was originally favourable to the claimant in certain respects, but also in suggesting alterations that made the report unfavourable. The Commissioner further observed that difficulties were created by the fact that the examining medical practitioner had declared his original findings and opinions to be correct to the best of his knowledge but he had not made any such declaration in respect of his amendments or explained why the particular amendments made were justified despite the original declaration. On the claimant's appeal, the tribunal relied on the corrected report on the ground that it was "objective", without making any comment on the significance of the amendments. It was held that they had erred in law in exercising their inquisitorial role selectively, asking probing question of the claimant but not, even rhetorically, of the Secretary of State.

Subsection (1) is in permissive terms and does not require that a person be referred to a health care professional for examination and report. Therefore, the Secretary of State is entitled to, and should, consider whether an examination is really necessary in a case where a claimant has contended that (e.g. for mental health reasons) he or she has good cause for not attending any examination. On the other hand, it is not unlawful for the Secretary of State generally to approach cases where claimants have severe mental health difficulties on the basis that, while obtaining evidence other sources will be considered, ultimately the burden of proving "good cause" lies on the claimant (*R. (Turner) v Secretary of State for Work and Pensions* [2021] EWHC 465 (Admin)). If the Secretary of State is satisfied that the claimant cannot reasonably be expected to attend for an examination but also considers that there is insufficient evidence upon which to make a decision awarding benefit, it may be appropriate for him to make a decision not to award the benefit. However, there may be adequate written evidence to justify an award. See *CG v SSWP (II)* [2015] UKUT 400 (AAC).

A health care professional is entitled to decline to examine a person in the **1.484** absence of a chaperon and a claimant's unreasonable refusal to allow a chaperon to be present may constitute failing without good cause to submit to an examination (*CIB/2011/2001*). However, it may still be possible for a report to be completed on the basis of informal observations and a lengthy conversation with the claimant, without there having been an examination within the terms of this section, and the health care professional's opinion may be taken into account as evidence, provided the decision-maker or tribunal can identify the factual basis on which the opinion was given (*CDLA/2466/2007*), although, in *CDLA/4208/2004*, the Commissioner criticised a tribunal for referring to opinions formed by a doctor in those circumstances as "clinical findings".

A health care professional's report may be altered on an audit forming part of his or her employer's internal quality assurance procedures, but, if there is then an appeal, the claimant and tribunal ought to be made aware of the changes made (see *MP v Department for Communities (PIP)* [2019) NICom 55, in which the nature of such audits is explained in detail).

For the recovery of expenses incurred in attending an examination, see s.20A.

Subsection (3)

1.485 What the decision is, depends on what the question was. It may be a decision to reject a whole claim but it may be a decision to award benefit but on a basis less favourable to the claimant than would otherwise have been the case. The claimant will usually be able to appeal against the decision (and apply for revision under s.9) and will be entitled to argue that he did have good cause for failing to comply with the request. He or she would also be entitled to argue that the decision was less favourable than was required by subs.(3), having regard to what was really in issue. The other remedy open to a claimant is to make a new claim (if benefit was not awarded) or make a new application for a supersession (if there is some continuing entitlement). The consequence will be to raise the question again and the Secretary of State will be obliged to make a new decision, which he will not be able to make under subs.(3) unless the claimant has failed without good cause to comply with a new request to attend for, or submit to, a medical examination.

Where the First-tier Tribunal allows an appeal against a decision made under subs.(3), it has the power to give a substantive decision on the claimant's entitlement to benefit but it will rarely be able to do so without adjourning either for an examination or to give the Secretary of State an opportunity to make further submissions (*CG v SSWP (II)* [2015] UKUT 400 (AAC)). It cannot direct the health care professional to carry out a domiciliary visit for the purpose of a medical examination under this section, but it can make a suggestion to that effect. (It can only direct a domiciliary visit when exercising its own power to refer a case to a health care professional under s.20(2).)

It is suggested that what amounts to "good cause" under this provision is the same as under all similar provisions where benefit claimants are required to attend medical examinations. A number of decisions on the meaning of "good cause" were considered in *AF v SSWP* [2009] UKUT 56 (AAC) in the context of reg.8(2) of the Social Security (Incapacity for Work) (General) Regulations 1995. It was emphasised that the integrity of the social security scheme depends on there being appropriate tests in place, so that, in the absence of "good cause" a person who decides as a matter of principle not to attend an examination must be taken to accept the consequence that benefit is likely to be refused. On the other hand, reference was made to *R(S) 9/51* where the claimant was a Christian Scientist and the Commissioner accepted that an objection based on a firm religious conviction, rather than mere prejudice or distaste for the process, would amount to "good cause". See, further, the annotation to subss.(1) and (2), above.

Medical examination required by appeal tribunal

1.486 **20.**—(1) This section applies where an appeal has been brought under section 12 above against a decision on a claim for a relevant benefit, or as to a person's entitlement to such a benefit [1 . . .].

(2) [3 The First-tier Tribunal may, if conditions prescribed by Tribunal Procedure Rules] are satisfied, refer the person—

(a) in respect of whom the claim is made; or

(b) whose entitlement is at issue,

to a [2 health care professional approved by the Secretary of State] for such examination and report as appears to [3 the First-tier Tribunal] to be necessary for the purpose of providing [3 it] with information for use in determining the appeal.

[3 . . .]

[2 (2A) The power under subsection (2) to refer a person to a healthcare professional approved by the Secretary of State includes power to specify the description of health care professional to whom the person is to be referred.]

(3) At a hearing before [3 the First-tier Tribunal, except in cases or circumstances prescribed by Tribunal Procedure Rules,] the tribunal—

(a) may not carry out a physical examination of the person mentioned in subsection (2) above; and

(b) may not require that person to undergo any physical test for the purpose of determining whether he satisfies the condition mentioned in section 73(1)(a) of the Contributions and Benefits Act.

AMENDMENTS

1. Social Security Contributions (Transfer of Functions, etc.) Act 1999 Sch.7 para.31 (April 1, 1999).

2. Welfare Reform Act 2007 s.62(1), (3) and (4) (July 3, 2007).

3. Transfer of Tribunal Functions Order 2008 (SI 2008/2833) Sch.3 paras 143 and 157 (November 3, 2008).

DEFINITIONS

"claim"—by virtue of s.39(2), see s.191 of the Social Security Administration Act 1992.

"the Contributions and Benefits Act"—see s.84.

"health care professional"—see s.39(1).

"medical examination"—by virtue of s.39(2), see s.191 of the Social Security Administration Act 1992.

"relevant benefit"—see s.8(3).

GENERAL NOTE

Subssections (2) and (2A)

A reference may be made only if there arises one or more of the issues listed in Sch.2 to the Tribunal Procedure (First-tier Tribunal (Social Entitlement Chamber) Rules 2008 (see r.25(3)). For the recovery of expenses incurred in attending an examination, see s.20A. Note that this section and the rules made under it apply only to cases under s.12 of this Act and not to other cases before the First-tier Tribunal. Note also, that the examination may not require a person to undergo a physical test for the purpose of determining whether that person is unable to walk or virtually unable to do so (see r.25(4)).There is no statutory penalty for failing to attend for, or submit to, a medical examination required by an "eligible person" or requested by a health care professional making a report under this section. Such a penalty is unnecessary as it is open to the tribunal to draw such inferences from the failure as appear proper when deciding the medical issues arising before them. 1.487

It is not the practice for the First-Tier Tribunal to obtain reports from the claimant's own doctors as a matter of course. However, claimants sometimes expect that that will be done. In *R(M) 2/80*, the claimant's consultant wrote suggesting that the Mobility Allowance Unit obtain medical evidence from his department. They did not do so. The Commissioner held that the claimant should have been told that her consultant's suggestion would not be followed up and that it would be up to her to obtain any further evidence if she so wished. Similar approaches were taken in *CI/13/1986* and *CA/133/1988*. These decisions were applied in *CIB/16604/1996* where the claimant wrote in his letter of appeal that "you are quite free to check my hospital and [doctor's] records". Neither the claimant nor the adjudication officer attended the hearing before the tribunal. The Commissioner held that there had been a breach of the rules of natural justice because the claimant reasonably believed that the tribunal would have before them his medical records and he was therefore prevented from providing relevant evidence in the sense that he could not reasonably be expected to produce evidence he thought the tribunal already had.

That case was distinguished in *CIB/5030/1998* because there was evidence before the Commissioner that the Independent Tribunal Service issued a leaflet making it clear that claimants' doctors would not automatically be approached by the Benefits Agency, the Department of Social Security or the tribunal. The Commissioner held that it was not reasonable for the claimant to believe that the tribunal would have before them evidence from his doctors. That was so even though the claimant said that he had misunderstood the leaflet and thought he had only to give his consent. The Commissioner considered that there was no basis for that misunderstanding.

Subsection (3)

1.488 See r.25(2) and (4) of the Tribunal Procedure (First-tier Tribunal (Social Entitlement Chamber) Rules 2008. In *CDLA/433/1999*, it was held that carrying out a physical examination in breach of the forerunner of this subsection was not an error of law rendering a decision liable to be set aside but relying on evidence from the examination would have been. Observing a claimant during a hearing is not a physical examination or test (*R(DLA) 1/95*). In *R4/99(IB)*, the Commissioner in Northern Ireland said that a tribunal were entitled to use all their senses, including sight, in assessing evidence before them. In *R1/01(IB)*, a Tribunal of Commissioners in Northern Ireland adopted both those views. They held that the phrase "may not carry out a physical examination" suggests some formal process beyond mere observing and that a tribunal is not prohibited from looking at an injury if it is either readily visible or if the claimant wishes them to see it. They said that the tribunal had erred in simply rejecting the claimant's request to look at his knee. The tribunal should either have acceded to the request or else they should have given the claimant the opportunity of obtaining alternative evidence. A tribunal should not simply refuse such a request, unless they consider the evidence unnecessary or irrelevant. The Tribunal of Commissioners said that the legislation prohibits a tribunal from asking to see a part of the claimant's body but it does not prevent the claimant from asking the tribunal to look. Nor does it prevent the tribunal from looking at what they can see without making any request. However, they are not entitled to do more than observe and, except in a case within the scope of r.25(2), a tribunal member ought not to accede to a request to feel a lump or manipulate a limb. If such evidence is necessary, the tribunal should adjourn in order to obtain a report. That decision was followed in *MA v SSWP (ESA)* [2015] UKUT 290 (AAC), where the First-tier Tribunal had invited the claimant to lift his trouser legs so that the medically qualified member could determine whether or not there was muscle wasting. Nonetheless, in the circumstances of that case, the Upper Tribunal held that the error was not material and it upheld the First-tier Tribunal's decision that the claimant was not entitled to employment and support allowance. However, in *R(DLA) 5/03*, the Commissioner noted the distinction between a "physical examination" and a "physical test" and held that the prohibition on tests for the purpose of determining whether a claimant is unable, or virtually unable, to walk did not prevent a tribunal from asking a claimant to demonstrate activities for other purposes. He further said that a tribunal might be entitled to draw inferences from a refusal to comply with such a request, depending on the reasonableness of the request and any reasons given by the claimant for not complying. In *GL v SSWP* [2008] UKUT 36 (AAC), it was suggested that testing a claimant's ability to estimate time by asking him for how long he had been sitting in the tribunal hearing was "approaching, if not crossing," the line between observing a claimant and conducting a physical examination, but that seems inconsistent with *R(DLA) 5/03* and to overlook the word "physical" used in both subparagraphs. In *R(IB) 2/06*, it was held that examining x-rays is not a "physical examination" but that a tribunal was entitled to decline to look at x-rays on the ground that it did not have the expertise to analyse them. However, in such a case, the tribunal was obliged to consider whether to adjourn to obtain a report, which would involve considering whether it was likely that such a report would assist the tribunal in determining the point in issue before it.

[1 Travelling and other allowances

20A.—(1) The Lord Chancellor may pay to any person required under this Part (whether for the purposes of this Part or otherwise) to attend for or to submit to medical or other examination or treatment such travelling and other allowances as the Lord Chancellor may determine. **1.489**

(2) In subsection (1) the reference to travelling and other allowances includes compensation for loss of remunerative time but such compensation shall not be paid to any person in respect of any time during which the person is in receipt of remuneration under section 28 of, or paragraph 5 of Schedule 2 to, the Tribunals, Courts and Enforcement Act 2007 (assessors and judges of First-Tier Tribunal).]

Amendment

1. Transfer of Tribunal Functions Order 2008 (SI 2008/2833) Sch.3 paras 143 and 158 (November 3, 2008).

General Note

This section replaces para.4(1)(b) (and para.4(2) so far as relevant) of Sch.1 of this Act, which has been repealed. **1.490**

Suspension and termination of benefit

Suspension in prescribed circumstances

21.—(1) Regulations may provide for— **1.491**

(a) Suspending payments of a relevant benefit, in whole or in part, in prescribed circumstances;

(b) the subsequent making in prescribed circumstances of any or all of the payments so suspended.

(2) Regulations made under subsection (1) above may, in particular, make provision for any case where—

(a) it appears to the Secretary of State that an issue arises whether the conditions for entitlement to a relevant benefit are or were fulfilled;

(b) it appears to the Secretary of State that an issue arises whether a decision as to an award of a relevant benefit should be revised (under section 9 above) or superseded (under section 10 above);

(c) an appeal is pending against a decision of [2 the First-tier Tribunal, the Upper Tribunal] or a court; or

(d) an appeal is pending against the decision given in a different case by a [2 the Upper Tribunal] or a court, and it appears to the Secretary of State that if the appeal were to be determined in a particular way an issue would arise whether the award of a relevant benefit (whether the same benefit or not) in the case itself ought to be revised or superseded.

(3) For the purposes of subsection (2) above, an appeal against a decision is pending if—

(a) an appeal against the decision has been brought but not determined;

(b) an application for [2 permission] to appeal against the decision has been made but not determined; or

(c) in such circumstances as may be prescribed, an appeal against the decision has not been brought (or, as the case may be, an application for [2 permission] to appeal against the decision has not been made) but the time for doing so has not yet expired.

(4) [1 . . .]

AMENDMENTS

1. Social Security Contributions (Transfer of Functions, etc.) Act 1999 Sch.7 para.32 (April 1, 1999).

2. Transfer of Tribunal Functions Order 2008 (SI 2008/2833) Sch.3 paras 143 and 159 (November 3, 2008).

DEFINITIONS

"prescribed"—s.84.
"relevant benefit"—see s.8(3).

GENERAL NOTE

1.492 See regs 16 and 20 of the Social Security and Child Support (Decisions and Appeals) Regulations 1999 regs 18 and 21 of the Child Benefit and Guardian's Allowance (Decisions and Appeals) Regulations 2003 and regs 44 and 46 of the Universal Credit, Personal Independence Payment, Jobseeker's Allowance and Employment and Support Allowance (Decisions and Appeals) Regulations 2013.

Suspension for failure to furnish information etc.

1.493 **22.**—(1) The powers conferred by this section are exercisable in relation to persons who fail to comply with information requirements.

(2) Regulations may provide for—

(a) suspending payments of a relevant benefit, in whole or in part;

(b) the subsequent making in prescribed circumstances of any or all of the payments so suspended.

(3) In this section and section 23 below "information requirement" means a requirement, made in pursuance of regulations under [2 section 5(1A)] of the Administration Act, to furnish information or evidence needed for a determination whether a decision on an award of benefit to which that section applies should be revised under section 9 or superseded under section 10 above.

[1 (4) Subsection (3A) of section 5 of the Administration Act (which glosses paragraph (hh) in the case of state pension credit) shall apply in relation to subsection (3) above as it applies in relation to paragraph (hh) of subsection (1) of that section.]

AMENDMENTS

1. State Pension Credit Act 2002 Sch.1 para.8 (July 2, 2002 for the purpose of exercising any power to make regulations or orders and October 6, 2003 for other purposes).

2. Welfare Reform Act 2012 s.99(5) (February 25, 2013).

DEFINITIONS

"the Administration Act"—see s.84.
"information requirement"—see subs.(3).
"prescribed"—see s.84.
"relevant benefit"—see s.8(3).

General Note

See reg.17 of the Social Security and Child Support (Decisions and Appeals) Regulations 1999, reg.19 of the Child Benefit and Guardian's Allowance (Decisions and Appeals) Regulations 2003 and reg.45 of the Universal Credit, Personal Independence Payment, Jobseeker's Allowance and Employment and Support Allowance (Decisions and Appeals) Regulations 2013. 1.494

Termination in cases of failure to furnish information

23. Regulations may provide that, except in prescribed cases or circumstances, a person— 1.495

(a) whose benefit has been suspended in accordance with regulations under section 21 above and who subsequently fails to comply withan information requirement; or

(b) whose benefit has been suspended in accordance with regulations under section 22 above for failing to comply with such a requirement,

shall cease to be entitled to the benefit from a date not earlier than the date on which payments were suspended.

Definitions

"information requirement"—see s.22(3).
"prescribed"—see s.84.

General Note

See reg.18 of the Social Security and Child Support (Decisions and Appeals) Regulations 1999, reg.20 of the Child Benefit and Guardian's Allowance (Decisions and Appeals) Regulations 2003 and reg.47 of the Universal Credit, Personal Independence Payment, Jobseeker's Allowance and Employment and Support Allowance (Decisions and Appeals) Regulations 2013. 1.496

Suspension and termination for failure to submit to medical examination

24. Regulations may make provision— 1.497

(a) enabling the Secretary of State to require a person to whom a relevant benefit has been awarded to submit to medical examination;

(b) for suspending payments of benefit, in whole or in part, in a case of a person who fails to submit himself to a medical examination to which he is required to submit in accordance with regulations under paragraph(a) above;

(c) for the subsequent making in prescribed circumstances of any or all of the payments so suspended;

(d) for entitlement to the benefit to cease, except in prescribed cases or circumstances, from a date not earlier than the date on which payments were suspended.

Definitions

"medical examination"—by virtue of s.39(2), see s.191 of the Social Security Administration Act 1992.
"prescribed"—see s.84.
"relevant benefit"—see s.8(3).

General Note

1.498 See reg.19 of the Social Security and Child Support (Decisions and Appeals) Regulations 1999.

[1 Appeals dependent on issues falling to be decided by Inland Revenue

Appeals dependent on issues falling to be decided by Inland Revenue

1.499 **24A.**—(1) Regulations may make provision for [2 the First-tier Tribunal or Upper Tribunal], where on any appeal there arises any issue which under section 8 of the Social Security Contributions (Transfer of Functions, etc.) Act 1999 falls to be decided by an officer of the Inland Revenue, to require the Secretary of State to refer the issue to the Inland Revenue.

(2) Regulations under this section may—

(a) provide for the appeal to be referred to the Secretary of State pending the decision of the Inland Revenue,

(b) enable or require the Secretary of State, in specified circumstances, to deal with any other issue arising on the appeal pending the decision on the referred issue, and

(c) enable the Secretary of State, on receiving the decision of an officer of the Inland Revenue, or any determination of the [3 First-tier Tribunal or Upper Tribunal] made on appeal from his decision—

(i) to revise his decision,

(ii) to make a decision superseding his decision, or

(iii) to refer the appeal to the [2 First-tier Tribunal or Upper Tribunal] for determination.]

Amendments

1. Social Security Contributions (Transfer of Functions, etc.) Act 1999 Sch.7 para.33 (July 5, 1999).

2. Transfer of Tribunal Functions Order 2008 (SI 2008/2833) Sch.3 paras 143 and 160 (November 3, 2008).

3. Transfer of Tribunal Functions and Revenue and Customs Appeals Order 2009 (SI 2009/56) Sch.1 paras 247 and 249 (April 1, 2009).

Definition

"Inland Revenue"—by virtue of s.39(2), see s.191 of the Social Security Administration Act 1992 but note that the Inland Revenue was merged into Her Majesty's Revenue and Customs by the Commissioners for Revenue and Customs Act 2005.

General Note

1.500 See reg.38A of the Social Security and Child Support (Decisions and Appeals) Regulations 1999 and reg.43 of the Universal Credit, Personal Independence Payment, Jobseeker's Allowance and Employment and Support Allowance (Decisions and Appeals) Regulations 2013.

Decisions and appeals dependent on other cases

Decisions involving issues that arise on appeal in other cases

25.—(1) This section applies where— 1.501

(a) a decision by the Secretary of State falls to be made under section 8, 9 or 10 above in relation to a particular case; and

(b) an appeal is pending against the decision given in another case by [[1]the Upper Tribunal] or a court (whether or not the two cases concern the same benefit).

(2) In a case relating to a relevant benefit, the Secretary of State need not make the decision while the appeal is pending if he considers it possible that the result of the appeal will be such that, if it were already determined, there would be no entitlement to benefit.

(3) If the Secretary of State considers it possible that the result of the appeal will be such that, if it were already determined, it would affect the decision in some other way—

(a) he need not, except in such cases or circumstances as may be prescribed, make the decision while the appeal is pending;

(b) he may, in such cases or circumstances as may be prescribed, make the decision on such basis as may be prescribed.

(4) Where the Secretary of State acts in accordance with subsection (3)(b) above, following the determination of the appeal he shall if appropriate revise his decision (under section 9 above) in accordance with that determination.

(5) For the purposes of this section, an appeal against a decision is pending if—

(a) an appeal against the decision has been brought but not determined;

(b) an application for leave to appeal against the decision has been made but not determined; or

(c) in such circumstances as may be prescribed, an appeal against the decision has not been brought (or, as the case may be, an application for leave to appeal against the decision has not been made) but the time for doing so has not yet expired.

(6) In paragraphs (a), (b) and (c) of subsection (5) above, any reference to an appeal, or an application for leave to appeal, against a decision includes a reference to—

(a) an application for, or for leave to apply for judicial review of the decision under section 31 of the [[2] Senior Courts Act 1981]; or

(b) an application to the supervisory jurisdiction of the Court of Session in respect of the decision.

AMENDMENTS

1. Transfer of Tribunal Functions Order 2008 (SI 2008/2833) Sch.3 paras 143 and 161 (November 3, 2008).

2. Constitutional Reform Act 2005 s.59(5) and para.1(2) of Sch.11 (October 1, 2009).

DEFINITIONS

"prescribed"—see s.84.
"relevant benefit"—see s.8(3).

GENERAL NOTE

Subsection (1)

1.502 This section applies only where a decision falls to be made by the Secretary of State (or, in relation to decisions under s.170 of the Pension Schemes Act 1993 or in respect of child benefit or guardian's allowance, HMRC—see s.170(7) of the 1993 Act (if it is not construed too literally) and ss.50(2)(e) and 51 of, and Sch.4 para.15 to, the Tax Credits Act 2002). See s.26 where a decision falls to be made by a tribunal. No appeal lies against a decision under this section (see Social Security and Child Support (Decisions and Appeals) Regulations 1999 Sch.2 para.7, Child Benefit and Guardian's Allowance (Decisions and Appeals) Regulations 2003 Sch.2 para.4 and Universal Credit, Personal Independence Payment, Jobseeker's Allowance and Employment and Support Allowance (Decisions and Appeals) Regulations 2013 Sch.3 para.8).

"Court" is not defined for the purposes of this section (compare s.27(7)) but the context in which the word appears limits its scope. There must be an appeal pending against a decision "in another case" of the Upper Tribunal or a court. This includes an application for judicial review of a tribunal decision (see subs. (6)) but not an application for judicial review of a decision of the Secretary of State or HMRC or, in a housing benefit case, a local authority. However, an appeal to the Court of Appeal against a decision of the High Court, or to the Inner House of the Court of Session from a decision of the Outer House, on judicial review of the Secretary of State, HMRC or a local authority would appear to be caught. The words in parenthesis tend to suggest that the court must be concerned with some sort of social security benefit as does the general context of the provision and the need to have some sort of practical boundary. Otherwise, it might be suggested that, say, an appeal to the Supreme Court from a decision of the Court of Appeal dealing with the meaning of the word "misrepresentation" in a marine insurance policy was a relevant appeal (because it might possibly assist with the understanding of that word in s.71 of the Social Security Administration Act 1992).

Subssections (2) and (3)

1.503 The Secretary of State (or HMRC) must consider two separate issues. The first is whether a possible result of the appeal would affect the decision before him. The Secretary of State would be a party to most such appeals and it is to be hoped that he does not indulge in too much wishful thinking. The word "possible" is broad. And what is the meaning of "result of the appeal"? Is it confined to the ratio decidendi or is it sufficient that the Secretary of State considers that there might be some useful obiter dicta? The second issue the Secretary of State (or HMRC) must consider is whether he should not make the decision or should decide it in accordance with subs.(3)(b) or whether he should ignore the fact that there is an appeal pending. He has a broad discretion and much will depend on such circumstances as the number of cases, the amount of money at stake, hardship to the claimants and the degree of probability that the court's decision will provide significant assistance with the determination of the cases before him.

For regulations under subs.(3)(b), see reg.21(1)–(3) of the Social Security and Child Support (Decisions and Appeals) Regulations 1999, reg.22(1)–(3) of the Child Benefit and Guardian's Allowance (Decisions and Appeals) Regulations 2003 and reg.53(1) of the Universal Credit, Personal Independence Payment, Jobseeker's Allowance and Employment and Support Allowance (Decisions and Appeals) Regulations 2013.

Subsection (4)

1.504 The revision usually has effect from the same date as the original decision (see s.9(3)).

Subsection (5)

See reg.21(4) of the Social Security and Child Support (Decisions and Appeals) Regulations 1999, reg.22(4) of the Child Benefit and Guardian's Allowance (Decisions and Appeals) Regulations 2003 and reg.53(2) of the Universal Credit, Personal Independence Payment, Jobseeker's Allowance and Employment and Support Allowance (Decisions and Appeals) Regulations 2013. 1.505

Appeals involving issues that arise on appeal in other cases

26.—(1) This section applies where— 1.506

(a) an appeal ("appeal A") in relation to a decision under section 8, 9 or 10 above is made to [1 the First-tier Tribunal, or from the First-tier Tribunal to the Upper Tribunal] and

(b) an appeal ("appeal B") is pending against a decision given in a different case by [1 the Upper Tribunal] or a court (whether or not the two appeals concern the same benefit).

(2) If the Secretary of State considers it possible that the result of appeal B will be such that, if it were already determined, it would affect the determination of appeal A, he may serve notice requiring [1 First-tier Tribunal or Upper Tribunal]—

(a) not to determine appeal A but to refer it to him; or

(b) to deal withthe appeal in accordance with subsection (4) below.

(3) Where appeal A is referred to the Secretary of State under subsection (2)(a) above, following the determination of appeal B and in accordance with that determination, he shall if appropriate—

(a) in a case where appeal A has not been determined by the [1 First-tier Tribunal], revise (under section 9 above) his decision which gave rise to that appeal; or

(b) in a case where appeal A has been determined by the [1 First-tier Tribunal], make a decision (under section 10 above) superseding the tribunal's decision.

(4) Where appeal A is to be dealt with in accordance with this subsection, the [1 First-tier Tribunal or Upper Tribunal] shall either—

(a) stay appeal A until appeal B is determined; or

(b) if the [1 First-tier Tribunal or Upper Tribunal] considers it to be in the interests of the appellant to do so, determine appeal A as if—

(i) appeal B had already been determined; and

(ii) the issues arising on appeal B had been decided in the way that was most unfavourable to the appellant.

In this subsection "the appellant" means the person who appealed or, as the case may be, first appealed against the decision mentioned in subsection (1)(a) above.

(5) Where the [1 First-tier Tribunal or Upper Tribunal] acts in accordance with subsection (4)(b) above, following the determination of appeal B the Secretary of State shall, if appropriate, make a decision (under section 10 above) superseding the decision of the [1 First-tier Tribunal or Upper Tribunal] in accordance withthat determination.

(6) For the purposes of this section, an appeal against a decision is pending if—

(a) an appeal against the decision has been brought but not determined;

(b) an application for leave to appeal against the decision has been made but not determined; or

(c) in such circumstances as may be prescribed, an appeal against the decision has not been brought (or, as the case may be, an application for leave to appeal against the decision has not been made) but the time for doing so has not yet expired.

(7) In this section—

(a) the reference in subsection (1)(a) above to an appeal to [1 the Upper Tribunal] includes a reference to an application for leave to appeal to [1 the Upper Tribunal]; and

(b) any reference in paragraph (a), (b) or (c) of subsection (6) above to an appeal, or to an application for leave to appeal, against a decision includes a reference to—

(i) an application for, or for leave to apply for, judicial review of the decision under section 31 of the [2 Senior Courts Act 1981]; or

(ii) an application to the supervisory jurisdiction of the Court of Session in respect of the decision.

(8) Regulations may make provision supplementing that made by this section.

AMENDMENTS

1. Transfer of Tribunal Functions Order 2008 (SI 2008/2833) Sch.3 paras 143 and 162 (November 3, 2008).

2. Constitutional Reform Act 2005 s.59(5) and para.1(2) of Sch.11 (October 1, 2009).

DEFINITION

"prescribed"—see s.84.

GENERAL NOTE

Subsection (1)

1.507 See the note to s.25(1) for the meaning of "court". See also subss.(6) and (7).

Subsection (2)

1.508 It is for the Secretary of State (or, in relation to decisions under s.170 of the Pension Schemes Act 1993 or in respect of child benefit or guardian's allowance, HMRC—see s.170(7) of the 1993 Act (if it is not construed too literally) and ss.50(2)(e) and 51 of, and Sch.4, para.15 to, the Tax Credits Act 2002) to identify both appeal B and appeal A although there is no reason why one notice may not be issued in respect of several appeals A. As in s.25(2) and (3), the Secretary of State (or HMRC) must first make a judgment as to the possible effects of the decision in appeal B and must then consider whether to serve notice under this subsection. It will not always be appropriate to do so. If the Secretary of State does decide to issue the notice, he must go on to decide whether the tribunal should be required to refer appeal A to him under para.(a) or to deal with the appeal in accordance with subs.(4) under para.(b). Which option is appropriate will depend on the circumstances of the case.

It may be thought to be unobjectionable that there be specific provision as to the way appeals should be handled while the decision in a "test case" is awaited, but to be highly objectionable that the decision as to the appropriate procedure should lie wholly in the hands of the Secretary of State who is a party in appeal A and is usually a party in appeal B. The perception that this provision was desirable appears to have arisen out of an occasion when the then President of social security appeal tribunals directed tribunals to determine a vast number of appeals notwithstanding the fact that an appeal against a Social Security Commissioner's decision was pending in the courts. This resulted in some thousands of extra appeals being brought before the Commissioners. It may be thought that this is unlikely to be repeated. In practice the Secretary of State is very often content to allow tribunals to manage blocks of "lookalike" cases without resorting to serving a notice under this section and where a notice is served it is usually after consultation with the relevant Chamber President. There can be an advantage to a claimant in having a notice served under this section where a tribunal might award some benefit on appeal A even if that appeal is determined on the basis that appeal B is determined adversely to the claimant. The claimant is then not deprived of that benefit while appeal B is awaiting final determination. It might be better if the legislation merely allowed the Secretary of State to seek a general direction in respect of a block of similar cases from the relevant Chamber President. As it is, any challenge to the Secretary of State's judgment must be by way of an application for judicial review.

Subsection (3)

Presumably para.(b) exists in case appeal A was decided in ignorance of the notice requiring it not to be determined. The decision is not rendered ineffective and so operates until it is superseded. It is not clear what happens if either party appeals against it. **1.509**

Subsection (4)

It is for the tribunal to decide whether para.(a) or para.(b) should apply in any particular case. Paragraph (b) is unlikely to be used a great deal unless either the claimant asks for it to be used or else the tribunal is fairly sure that the decision on appeal B is unlikely to assist the claimant. A judgment as to what is the most unfavourable way in which the issues arising on appeal B might be decided requires that the tribunal be given considerable information about the appeal, including pleadings, so that it can be established what the issues really are. **1.510**

Subsection (5)

The supersession is effective from the date from which the tribunals decision would have been effective had it been decided in accordance with the decision in "Appeal B", the test case (reg.7(33) of the Social Security and Child Support (Decisions and Appeals) Regulations 1999 reg.16(8) of the Child Benefit and Guardian's Allowance (Decisions and Appeals) Regulations 2003 and reg.27(4) of the Universal Credit, Personal Independence Payment, Jobseeker's Allowance and Employment and Support Allowance (Decisions and Appeals) Regulations 2013). **1.511**

Subsection (6)

See reg.22 of the Social Security and Child Support (Decisions and Appeals) Regulations 1999 reg.23 of the Child Benefit and Guardian's Allowance (Decisions and Appeals) Regulations 2003 and reg.54 of the Universal Credit, Personal Independence Payment, Jobseeker's Allowance and Employment and Support Allowance (Decisions and Appeals) Regulations 2013. **1.512**

Cases of error

Restrictions on entitlement to benefit in certain cases of error

27.—(1) Subject to subsection (2) below, this section applies where— **1.513**

(a) the effect of the determination, whenever made, of an appeal to [3the Upper Tribunal] or the court ("the relevant determination") is that the adjudicating authority's decision out of which the appeal arose was erroneous in point of law; and

(b) after the date of the relevant determination a decision falls to be made by the Secretary of State in accordance with that determination (or would, apart from this section, fall to be so made)—

(i) in relation to a claim for benefit;

(ii) as to whether to revise, under section 9 above, a decision as to a person's entitlement to benefit; or

(iii) on an application made under section 10 above for a decision as to a person's entitlement to benefit to be superseded.

(2) This section does not apply where the decision of the Secretary of State mentioned in subsection (1)(b) above—

(a) is one which, but for section 25(2) or (3)(a) above, would have been made before the date of the relevant determination; or

(b) is one made in pursuance of section 26(3) or (5) above.

(3) In so far as the decision relates to a person's entitlement to a benefit in respect of—

(a) a period before the date of the relevant determination; or

(b) in the case of a widow's payment, a death occurring before that date,

it shall be made as if the adjudicating authority's decision had been found by [3the Upper Tribunal] or court not to have been erroneous in point of law.

(4) In deciding whether a person is entitled to benefit in a case where his entitlement depends on his having been entitled to the same or some other benefit before attaining a particular age, subsection (3) above shall be disregarded for the purpose only of deciding whether he was so entitled before attaining that age.

(5) Subsection (1)(a) above shall be read as including a case where—

(a) the effect of the relevant determination is that part or all of a purported regulation or order is invalid; and

(b) the error of law made by the adjudicating authority was to act on the basis that the purported regulation or order (or the part held to be invalid) was valid.

(6) It is immaterial for the purposes of subsection (1) above—

(a) where such a decision as is mentioned in paragraph (b)(i) falls to be made, whether the claim was made before or after the date of the relevant determination;

(b) where such a decision as is mentioned in paragraph (b)(ii) or (iii) falls to be made on an application under section 9 or (as the case may be) 10 above, whether the application was made before or after that date.

(7) In this section—

"adjudicating authority" means—

(a) the Secretary of State;

(b) any former officer, tribunal or body; or

(c) any officer, tribunal or body in Northern Ireland corresponding to a former officer, tribunal or body;

"benefit" means—

(a) benefit under Parts II to V of the Contributions and Benefits Act, other than Old Cases payments;

(b) benefit under Part II of the Social Security Act 1975 (in respect of a period before July 1, 1992 but not before April 6, 1975);

(c) benefit under the National Insurance Act 1946 or 1965, or the National Insurance (Industrial Injuries) Act 1946 or 1965 (in respect of a period before April 6, 1975);

(d) a jobseeker's allowance;
[1 (dd) state pension credit;]
[2 (de) an employment and support allowance;]
[5 (df) personal independence payment;]
[8 (dg) bereavement support payment under section 30 of the Pensions Act 2014;]
(e) any benefit corresponding to a benefit mentioned in [1 paragraphs (a) [8 to (dg)] above]; and
(f) any income-related benefit [6 *universal credit*];
[7 (g) state pension or a lump sum under Part 1 of the Pensions Act 2014;]

"the court" means the High Court, the Court of Appeal, the Court of Session, the High Court or Court of Appeal in Northern Ireland, the [4 Supreme Court] or the Court of Justice in the European Community;

"former officer, tribunal or body" means any of the following, that is to say—

(a) an adjudication officer or, in the case of a decision given on a reference under section 21(2) or 25(1) of the Administration Act, a social security appeal tribunal, a disability appeal tribunal or a medical appeal tribunal;
(b) an adjudicating medical practitioner appointed under section 49 of that Act or a specially qualified adjudicating medical practitioner appointed in accordance with regulations under section 62(2) of that Act; or
(c) the National Assistance Board, the Supplementary Benefits Commission, the Attendance Allowance Board, a benefit officer, an insurance officer or a supplement officer.

(8) For the purposes of this section, any reference to entitlement to benefit includes a reference to entitlement—

(a) to any increase in the rate of a benefit; or
(b) to a benefit, or increase of benefit, at a particular rate.

(9) The date of the relevant determination shall, in prescribed cases, be determined for the purposes of this section in accordance with any regulations made for that purpose.

(10) Regulations made under subsection (9) above may include provision—

(a) for a determination of a higher court to be treated as if it had been made on the date of a determination of a lower court or [3 the Upper Tribunal]; or
(b) for a determination of a lower court or [3 the Upper Tribunal] to be treated as if it had been made on the date of a determination of a higher court.

AMENDMENTS

1. State Pension Credit Act 2002 Sch.1 para.9 (July 2, 2002 for the purposes of exercising any power to make regulations or orders and October 6, 2003 for other purposes).

2. Welfare Reform Act 2007 Sch.3 para.17(1) and (5) (October 27, 2008).

3. Transfer of Tribunal Functions Order 2008 (SI 2008/2833) Sch.3 paras 143 and 163 (November 3, 2008).

4. Constitutional Reform Act 2005 s.40(4)(c) and Sch.9 para.64 (October 1, 2009).

5. Welfare Reform Act 2012 s.91 and Sch.9 paras 37 and 41 (February 25, 2013 for regulation-making purposes and April 8, 2013 for other purposes).

6. Welfare Reform Act 2012 s.31 and Sch.2 paras 43 and 47 (February 25, 2013 for regulation-making purposes and April 29, 2013 for other purposes).

7. Pensions Act 2014 s.23 and Sch.12 paras 31 and 35 (April 6, 2016).

8. Pensions Act 2014 s.31(5) and Sch.16 paras 37 and 41 (April 6, 2017).

DEFINITIONS

"adjudicating authority"—see subs.(7).
"the Administration Act"—see s.84.
"benefit"—see subs.(7).
"claim"—by virtue of s.39(2), see s.191 of the Social Security Administration Act 1992.
"the Contributions and Benefits Act"—see s.84.
"the court"—see subs.(7).
"former officer, tribunal or body"—*ibid.*
"income-related benefit"—by virtue of s.39(2), see s.191 of the Social Security Administration Act 1992.
"Old Cases payments"—*ibid.*
"prescribed"—see s.84.
"the relevant determination"—see subs.(1).

GENERAL NOTE

1.514 In so far as they apply to child benefit and guardian's allowance, the Secretary of State's functions under this section were transferred to the Board of Inland Revenue (Tax Credit Act 2002 s.50(2)(e)) and are now exercised by HMRC (Commissioners for Revenue and Customs Act 2005).

Subsection (1)

1.515 The Secretary of State is an adjudicating authority but an appeal tribunal is not (see subs.(7)). As the question for the Upper Tribunal or court is whether the *First-tier Tribunal* has erred in law, it may not always be easy to tell whether the effect of the Upper Tribunal's or court's determination is that the Secretary of State's decision was erroneous in point of law. See also subss.(5) and (6).

It was held in *JK v SSWP (DLA)* [2013] UKUT 218 (AAC) that, since proceedings before the Court of Justice of the European Union were not appeals, they were not within the scope of para.(a), although that would have rendered the reference to the Court in the definition of "the court" in subs.(7) otiose. The section would nonetheless have applied in cases where the reference to the Court had been made by the Upper Tribunal or an appellate court within the definition of "the court", although the "relevant determination" would then have been the decision of that court following the reference, but the section appears not to have had effect where a question was referred by the European Commission or a court of another Member State. A similar point might be made of decisions of the High Court or Upper Tribunal on judicial review.

The effect of s.27, of which subss.(1) and (3) are the key elements, was described by Underhill L.J. in para.103 of *Secretary of State for Work and Pensions v Reilly* [2016] EWCA Civ 413; [2017] QB 657; [2017] AACR 14 at [103]:

> "In bare outline, and at the risk of some oversimplification, its effect is that, where the Upper Tribunal or a court considering an appeal relating to a claim under social security legislation holds that a provision of such legislation has a different effect from that on the basis of which the DWP had proceeded previously, the law as thereby established will for most purposes take effect only from the date of that decision: in other words, the usual rule that the decision of the court establishes what the law has always been does not apply."

That is plainly the purpose of the legislation and so it is clear that a decision falls to be made "in accordance with" a determination of the Upper Tribunal or a court only if the Upper Tribunal or court has interpreted the law in a way not previously understood. It is therefore unlikely that a decision will fall to be made in accordance with a determination of the Upper Tribunal or a court where the words of legislation are so clear that no interpretation was required (see *BD v SSWP (DLA)* [2013] UKUT 216 (AAC), decided in the context of the definition of "official error" in reg.1(3) of the Social Security and Child Support (Decisions and Appeals) Regulations 1999, which excludes any error shown to have been such by a decision of the Upper Tribunal or a court) and, where successive Commissioners' decisions had held a departmental practice to be wrong, it was the first such decision that was "the relevant determination", even where the Commissioners had differed as to their reasoning (*R(I) 1/03*, a decision of a Tribunal of Commissioners).

However, where the Secretary of State has previously misinterpreted the law and has realised his error before a ruling is made by the Upper Tribunal or a court to that effect, decisions made subsequently to correct the error in other cases fall to be made by way of revision on the ground of "official error" rather than by way of supersession on the ground of error of law (because the exclusion in the definition of "official error" does not apply and a decision may be superseded only if it cannot be revised) and s.27 cannot apply because the revision does not fall to be made "in accordance with" a decision of the Upper Tribunal or a court. This was the basis of concessions made by the Secretary of State and accepted by the Upper Tribunal in a consent order made in *R. (DS) v Secretary of State for Work and Pensions* [2018] UKUT 270 (AAC). It was recorded in that order that *SK v SSWP (ESA)* [2018] UKUT 267 (AAC) should no longer been followed insofar as it held to the contrary and the claimant's appeal against the decision in *SK* was subsequently allowed by an unpublished interlocutor in the Court of Session in the light of the Secretary of State's concessions. *SK* had been wrongly decided, not because the Upper Tribunal's analysis of s.27 was wrong, but because it had proceeded on the basis that the relevant error of law had been "established" by an earlier decision of the Upper Tribunal, whereas, not only had the error been obvious on the face of the legislation, but the Secretary of State had accepted as much before the Upper Tribunal had made the earlier decision and indeed he had conceded the point in that earlier case.

Subsection (3)

As noted by Underhill L.J. in *Reilly*, (see above), this subsection has the effect **1.516** that any decision of the Upper Tribunal or a court that is unfavourable to the Secretary of State is only prospective in its effect in other cases. Such a provision is not necessarily unreasonable to the extent that it does not require existing decisions in respect of earlier periods to be reversed but this one takes the principle to extremes by requiring the Secretary of State to continue giving erroneous decisions in respect of the period before the Upper Tribunal's or court's decision after the error has been discovered. This is done so that all claimants are treated equally unfavourably in respect of that period. The perceived need for the provision appears to have arisen from previous versions of the general power to revise at any time a decision arising from an official error (reg.3(5)(a) of the Social Security and Child Support (Decisions and Appeals) Regulations 1999, reg.10(1)(a) and (2)(a) of the Child Benefit and Guardian's Allowance (Decisions and Appeals) Regulations 2003 and reg.9(a) of the Universal Credit, Personal Independence Payment, Jobseeker's Allowance and Employment and Support Allowance (Decisions and Appeals) Regulations 2013) which, until 2000, applied even where an error was shown to have been an error by a decision of the Upper Tribunal or court. Now that revision for official error is not a live issue where s.27 might apply, due to way that "official error" is defined (see above), it might be thought that s.27 is unnecessary because the conventional time limits (much more restrictive than when the forerunner of s.27 was first introduced in 1990) adequately limit the extent to which an unexpected decision could apply retrospectively and to be objectionable to the extent that it acts to the disadvantage of claimants who complied with the time limits.

On the other hand, the corollary of para.(3) is that any supersession as a result of the Upper Tribunal's or court's determination – supersession for error of law generally being appropriate because there can be no revision for official error – is effective from the date of that determination (reg.7(6) of the 1999 Regulations, reg.16(9) of the 2003 Regulations and reg.37(6) of the 2013 Regulations), which operates to the advantage of claimants who would not satisfy the conventional time limits just as s.27(3) operates to the disadvantage of those who would. Presumably, this is because claimants cannot be expected to know what decisions the Upper Tribunal and courts are making and it is considered that the Secretary of State should be under a duty to rectify errors revealed by such decisions, from the date of the decisions, without claimants asking him or her to do so.

Subsection (5)

1.517 This is logical but may be thought to reinforce the view that subs.(3) is objectionable. Parliament has here not only ratified in advance decisions made, presumably in good faith, in excess of powers; it has also enabled (and required) the Secretary of State to continue making decisions (in respect of past periods) in excess of those powers once he knows the limits of the powers. This is despite the fact that Parliament could not have known the extent to which the powers would be exceeded. Henry VIII could hardly have asked for more.

Subsection (7)

1.518 Note that the First-tier Tribunal is not an "adjudicating authority". Quite why a social security appeal tribunal giving a decision on a reference should have been included as a "former tribunal" is unclear because there was no reason to suppose that their view of the law would necessarily be consistent with that held by the Department of Social Security. Perhaps the draftsman had a particular case in mind. The inclusion of disability appeal tribunals and medical appeal tribunals is even more obscure as there was no power to refer cases to them under the provisions cited. The inclusion of the Court of Appeal in Northern Ireland in the definition of "court" is interesting as a decision of that court is not, strictly speaking, binding in Great Britain. Such a decision is, however, highly persuasive and should usually be followed. The implication is that, if the Secretary of State does decide to follow a decision of the Court of Appeal in Northern Ireland, the decision before him "falls to be made . . . in accordance with" the decision of the court for the purpose of subs.(1).

Subssections (9) and (10)

1.519 No regulations have yet been made under these powers.

Correction of errors and setting aside of decisions

1.520 **28.**—(1) Regulations may make provision with respect to—

(a) the correction of accidental errors in any decision [4 of the Secretary of State] or record of a decision [4 of the Secretary of State] made under any relevant enactment;

(b) [4. . .]

[4. . .]

[1 (1A) In subsection (1) "decision" does not include [4 any decision of the First-tier Tribunal or] any decision made by an officer of the Inland Revenue, other than a decision under or by virtue of Part III of the Pensions Schemes Act 1993.]

(2) Nothing in subsection (1) above shall be construed as derogating from any power to correct errors [4. . .] which is exercisable apart from regulations made by virtue of that subsection.

(3) In this section "relevant enactment" means any enactment contained in—

(a) this Chapter;
(b) the Contributions and Benefits Act;
(c) the Pension Schemes Act 1993;
(d) the Jobseekers Act; [[2] . . .]
(e) the Social Security (Recovery of Benefits) Act 1997; [[2] [[3] . . .]]
[[2] (f) the State Pension Credit Act 2002;] [[3][[5] . . .]]
[[3] (g) Part 1 of the Welfare Reform Act 2007;]
[[5] (h) Part 1 of the Welfare Reform Act 2012; [[6] . . .]
(i) Part 4 of that Act;] [[6] [[8] . . .]]
[[6] (j) Part 1 of the Pensions Act 2014 [[7] or section 30 of that Act]]; [[8] or
(k) sections 18 to 21 of the Welfare Reform and Work Act 2016.]

AMENDMENTS

1. Social Security Contributions (Transfer of Functions, etc.) Act 1999 Sch.7 para.34 (July 5, 1999).
2. State Pension Credit Act 2002 Sch.1 para.10 and Sch.3 (July 2, 2002 for regulation-making purposes and April 7, 2003 for other purposes).
3. Welfare Reform Act 2007 Sch.3 para.17(1) and (6) (March 18, 2008 for regulation-making purposes and July 27, 2008 for other purposes).
4. Transfer of Tribunal Functions Order 2008 (SI 2008/2833) Sch.3 paras 143 and 164 (November 3, 2008).
5. Welfare Reform Act 2012 ss.31 and 91 Sch.2 paras 43 and 48 and Sch.9 paras 37 and 42 (February 25, 2013).
6. Pensions Act 2014 s.23 and Sch.12 paras 31 and 36 (April 6, 2016).
7. Pensions Act 2014 s.31(5) and Sch.16 paras 37 and 42 (April 6, 2017).
8. Welfare Reform and Work Act 2016 s.20(5) (July 27, 2017).

DEFINITIONS

"Contributions and Benefits Act"—see s.84.

"Inland Revenue"—by virtue of s.39(2), see s.191 of the Social Security Administration Act 1992 but note that the Inland Revenue was merged into Her Majesty's Revenue and Customs by the Commissioners for Revenue and Customs Act 2005.

"the Jobseekers Act"—see s.84.

"prescribed"—see s.84.

"relevant enactment"—see subs.(3).

GENERAL NOTE

See reg.9A of the Social Security and Child Support (Decisions and Appeals) Regulations 1999 and reg.38 of the Universal Credit, Personal Independence Payment, Jobseeker's Allowance and Employment and Support Allowance (Decisions and Appeals) Regulations 2013. This section is no longer concerned with the correction and setting aside of tribunal decisions, for which see now para.15 of Sch.5 to the Tribunals, Courts and Enforcement Act 2007. 1.521

Industrial accidents

Decision that accident is an industrial accident

1.522 **29.**—(1) Where, in connection with any claim for industrial injuries benefit, it is decided that the relevant accident was or was not an industrial accident—

(a) an express declaration of that fact shall be made and recorded; and

(b) subject to subsection (3) below, a claimant shall be entitled to have the issue whether the relevant accident was an industrial accident decided, notwithstanding that his claim is disallowed on other grounds.

(2) [[2] . . .]

(3) The Secretary of State, [[1]the First-tier Tribunal or the Upper Tribunal] (as the case may be) may refuse to decide the issue whether an accident was an industrial accident, if satisfied that it is unlikely to be necessary to decide the issue for the purposes of any claim for benefit and this Chapter shall apply as if any such refusal were a decision on the issue.

(4) Subject to sections 9 to 15 above, any declaration under this section that an accident was or was not an industrial accident shall be conclusive for the purposes of any claim for industrial injuries benefit in respect of that accident.

(5) Where subsection (4) above applies—

(a) in relation to a death occurring before April 11, 1988; or

(b) for the purposes of section 60(2) of the Contributions and Benefits Act,

it shall have effect as if at the end there were added the words "whether or not the claimant is the person at whose instance the declaration was made".

(6) For the purposes of this section (but subject to section 30 below), an accident whereby a person suffers personal injury shall be deemed, in relation to him, to be an industrial accident if—

(a) it arises out of and in the course of his employment;

(b) that employment is employed earner's employment for the purposes of Part V of the Contributions and Benefits Act; and

(c) payment of benefit is not under section 94(5) of that Act precluded because the accident happened while he was outside Great Britain.

(7) A decision under this section shall be final except that sections 9 and 10 above apply to a decision under this section that an accident was or was not an industrial accident as they apply to a decision under section 8 above if, but only if, the Secretary of State is satisfied that the decision under this section was given in consequence of any wilful non-disclosure or misrepresentation of a material fact.

AMENDMENTS

1. Transfer of Tribunal Functions Order 2008 (SI 2008/2833) Sch.3 paras 143 and 165 (November 3, 2008).

2. Welfare Reform Act 2012, s.68(1) (December 5, 2012).

DEFINITIONS

"benefit—by virtue of s.39(2), see s.191 of the Social Security Administration Act 1992.

"claim"—*ibid.*

"claimant"—see s.39(1) and, by virtue of s.39(2), see s.191 of the Social Security Administration Act 1992.

"Contributions and Benefits Act"—see s.84.

"industrial injuries benefit"—by virtue of s.39(2), see s.191 of the Social Security Administration Act 1992.

General Note

This section re-enacts s.44 of the Social Security Administration Act 1992 with only minor changes. It provides for the Secretary of State to make a declaration that a person has suffered an industrial accident, whether or not the claim has any prospects of success on other grounds, although, under subs.(3), the Secretary of State (or a tribunal) may refuse to determine that question if it is unlikely there will ever be a claim for benefit. 1.523

Subsection (2) used to provide that a declaration could be made even if there was no claim for benefit. Since a declaration must be made if there is a claim for benefit and a future claim might succeed even if the present one does not, the repeal does not prevent a person from seeking a declaration if minded to do so but it does make it unnecessary to advertise the existence of a right to seek a declaration without a claim, and it has the effect that a claimant cannot be criticised for not seeking a declaration when suffering no relevant symptoms.

A determination that there was or was not an industrial accident is conclusive for the purposes of later claims for benefit (unless it is set aside on appeal or is revised or superseded). However, it is important to note that this section is expressed to be subject to s.30, so that a decision under this section which implies that a person has suffered personal injury as a result of an accident does not require anyone to find that the claimant has suffered disablement as a result of the injury even though the two decisions may appear, in the circumstances of the case, to contradict one another.

The usual rights of appeal apply to declarations under this section, but the power to revise or supersede such decisions is strictly limited, by subs.(7), to cases of *wilful* non-disclosure or misrepresentation of a material fact. 1.524

Where the Secretary of State has decided that a claimant has not suffered an industrial accident and the claimant appeals against that decision, a tribunal may exercise the power conferred by subs.(3) to refuse to decide the issue on the ground that it is unlikely to be relevant to any claim to benefit (*CI/1297/2002*). That refusal to decide the issue must replace the Secretary of State's decision, and will make an important difference if the tribunal is wrong and there ever is a claim for benefit, because the Secretary of State's decision would have been conclusive by virtue of subs.(4) and the scope for revision or supersession would have been limited by virtue of subs.(7). In *CI/732/2007*, the Commissioner accepted a submission by the Secretary of State to the effect that it was also open to a tribunal to refuse to make a declaration where a claimant had suffered a vaccination reaction as the result of a vaccination in the course of her employment. A vaccination reaction is normal and so the claimant had not suffered an industrial accident, because there had been no unexpected or untoward event. The Secretary of State's submission was in the claimant's favour because its acceptance meant the claimant was not precluded from advancing new medical evidence in the future to show that other ill health was attributable to the vaccination, which would lead to a finding that she had suffered an industrial accident.

Effect of decision

30.—(1) A decision [1 . . .] that an accident was an industrial accident is to be taken as determining only that paragraphs (a), (b) and (c) of subsection (6) of that section are satisfied in relation to the accident. 1.525

(2) Subject to subsections (3) and (4) below, no such decision is to be taken as importing a decision as to the origin of any injury or disability suffered by the claimant, whether or not there is an event identifiable as an accident apart from any injury that may have been received.

(3) A decision that, on a particular occasion when there was no event so identifiable, a person had an industrial accident by reason of an injury shall be treated as a decision that, if the injury was suffered by accident on that occasion, the accident was an industrial accident.

(4) A decision that an accident was an industrial accident may be given, and a declaration to that effect be made and recorded in accordance with section 29 above, without its having been found that personal injury resulted from the accident.

(5) Subsection (4) above has effect, subject to the discretion under section 29(3) above, to refuse to decide the issue if it is unlikely to be necessary for the purposes of a claim for benefit.

AMENDMENT

1. Welfare Reform Act 2012 s.68(2) (December 5, 2012).

DEFINITIONS

"benefit"—by virtue of s.39(2), see s.191 of the Social Security Administration Act 1992.

"claim"—*ibid.*

"claimant"—see s.39(1) and, by virtue of s.39(2), see s.191 of the Social Security Administration Act 1992.

GENERAL NOTE

1.526 This section replaces s.60(3) of the Social Security Administration Act 1992. The drafting of the new provision is a great improvement (or was until subs.(1) was amended – the repealed words showed that the reference to "that section" is to s.29). The overall effect is the same. A finding that there has been an industrial accident does not prevent it from being found that there has been no loss of faculty resulting from the accident even if the two decisions appear to be inconsistent. This is so even in a case where a person suffers a heart attack and the only "accident" found was the heart attack itself. Another decision-maker is still entitled to hold that the heart attack was not the result of an accident. This provision was first introduced by the National Insurance Act 1972 to reverse the effect of *Jones v Secretary of State for Social Services* [1972] A.C. 944 (also reported as an appendix to *R(I) 3/69*). It is less important than it used to be now that all material decisions are made by the Secretary of State and there is no longer the old division of jurisdiction between adjudication officers and adjudicating medical authorities. However, it still has significance where different decision-makers deal with the question whether there was an industrial accident and the question whether the claimant suffers a loss of faculty as a result of the accident (e.g. where a tribunal reverses a decision to the effect that there was no industrial accident but does not go on and deal with the other questions arising on the claim). In *CI/105/1998*, it was pointed out that, quite apart from cases where the accident is indistinguishable from the injury suffered, there are cases where an indication that an accident was one giving rise to personal injury is a necessary part of a decision-maker's reasoning because it may help to explain why a declaration is made in respect of that alleged cause of the injury rather than another. However, it was also made clear that the effect of the forerunner of this section was that any view as to causation expressed when making the decision that an accident was an industrial accident could be only provisional.

Other special cases

Incapacity for work

31.—(1) Regulations may provide that a determination that a person is disqualified for any period in accordance with regulations under section 171E of the Contributions and Benefits Act shall have effect for such purposes as may be prescribed as a determination that he is to be treated as capable of work for that period, and vice versa. 1.527

[1 (1A) Regulations may provide that a determination that a person is disqualified for any period in accordance with regulations under section 18(1) to (3) of the Welfare Reform Act 2007 shall have effect for such purposes as may be prescribed as a determination that he is to be treated as not having limited capability for work for that period, and vice versa.]

(2) Provision may be made by regulations for matters of such descriptions as may be prescribed to be determined by the Secretary of State, notwithstanding that other matters fall to be determined by another authority.

(3) Nothing in this section shall be taken to prejudice the generality of the power conferred by section 17(2) above.

Amendment

1. Welfare Reform Act 2007 Sch.3 para.17(1) and (7) (March 18, 2008 for regulation-making purposes and October 27, 2008 for other purposes).

Definitions

"Contributions and Benefits Act"—see s.84.
"prescribed"—*ibid.*

General Note

Subsections (1) and (1A)

See reg.10 of the Social Security and Child Support (Decisions and Appeals) Regulations 1999 and reg.40(1) of the Universal Credit, Personal Independence Payment, Jobseeker's Allowance and Employment and Support Allowance (Decisions and Appeals) Regulations 2013. 1.528

Subsection (2)

See reg.11 of the 1999 Regulations and reg.40(3) of the 2013 Regulations. 1.529

Industrial diseases

32. Regulations shall provide for applying the provisions of this Chapter, subject to any prescribed additions or modifications, in relation to decisions made or falling to be made under sections 108 to 110 of the Contributions and Benefits Act. 1.530

Definitions

"Contributions and Benefits Act"—see s.84.
"prescribed"—*ibid.*

General Note

See the Social Security (Industrial Injuries) (Prescribed Diseases) Regulations 1985, as amended by art.4(8) of and Sch.8 to the Social Security Act 1998 1.531

(Commencement No.8 and Savings and Consequential and Transitional Provisions) Order 1999, (in Vol.I) and reg.12A of the Social Security and Child Support (Decisions and Appeals) Regulations 1999.

Christmas bonus

1.532 **33.**—(1) A decision by the Secretary of State that a person is entitled or not entitled to payment of a qualifying benefit in respect of a period which includes a day in the relevant week shall be conclusive for the purposes of section 148 of the Contributions and Benefits Act.

(2) In this section, expressions to which a meaning is assigned by section 150 of that Act have that meaning.

DEFINITIONS

"Contributions and Benefits Act"—see s.84.

"qualifying benefit"—by virtue of subs.(2), see s.150 of the Social Security Contributions and Benefits Act 1992.

"relevant week"—*ibid.*

GENERAL NOTE

1.533 This replaces s.67 of the Social Security Administration Act 1992.

Housing benefit and council tax benefit

1.534 **34.–35.** *Omitted.*

Social fund payments

1.535 **36.–38**. *Repealed.*

Supplemental

[1 Certificates

1.536 **39ZA.** A document bearing a certificate which—

(a) is signed by a person authorised in that behalf by the Secretary of State, and

(b) states that the document, apart from the certificate, is a record of a decision of an officer of the Secretary of State,

shall be conclusive evidence of the decision; and a certificate purporting to be so signed shall be deemed to be so signed unless the contrary is proved.]

AMENDMENT

1. Transfer of Tribunal Functions Order 2008 (SI 2008/2833) Sch.3 paras 143 and 166 (November 3, 2008).

GENERAL NOTE

1.537 This section partially replaces para.13 of Sch.1 to this Act, which has been repealed. However, there is no longer any provision for certifying decisions of tribunals.

Computer records often need some interpretation in order to make them intelligible. However, a certificate is conclusive only to the extent that it authenticates the record of the decision. This section does not make the certificate conclusive to the extent that the certificate purports also to interpret the record of the decision.

It does not follow from the fact that a certified copy of a decision is conclusive evidence of the decision that other evidence cannot be relied upon, although such other evidence would not be conclusive (*JM v SSWP (ESA)* [2013] UKUT 234 (AAC); [2014] AACR 5 at [74]).

Interpretation etc. of Chapter II

39.—(1) In this Chapter— 1.538

[4. . .]

[2 "claimant", in relation to a joint-claim couple claiming a joint-claim jobseeker's allowance (within the meaning of the Jobseekers Act 1995), means the couple or either member of the couple;]

[6 "claimant", in relation to a couple jointly claiming universal credit, means the couple or either member of the couple;]

[4. . .]

[3 "health care professional" means—

(a) a registered medical practitioner,

(b) a registered nurse,

(c) an occupational therapist or physiotherapist registered with a regulatory body established by an Order in Council under section 60 of the Health Act 1999, or

(d) a member of such other profession regulated by a body mentioned in section 25(3) of the National Health Service Reform and Health Care Professions Act 2002 as the Secretary of State may prescribe;]

"relevant benefit" has the meaning given by section 8(3) above;

[5. . .]

[7 (1A) In this Chapter—

(a) a reference to a benefit includes a reference to a loan under section 18 of the Welfare Reform and Work Act 2016;

(b) a reference to a claim for a benefit includes a reference to an application for a loan under section 18 of the Welfare Reform and Work Act 2016;

(c) a reference to a claimant includes a reference to an applicant for a loan under section 18 of the Welfare Reform and Work Act 2016 or, in relation to a couple jointly applying for a loan under that section, a reference to the couple or either member of the couple;

(d) a reference to an award of a benefit to a person includes a reference to a decision that a person is eligible for a loan under section 18 of the Welfare Reform and Work Act 2016;

(e) a reference to entitlement to a benefit includes a reference to eligibility for a loan under section 18 of the Welfare Reform and Work Act 2016.]

(2) Expressions used in this Chapter to which a meaning is assigned by section 191 of the Administration Act have that meaning in this Chapter.

(3) Part II of the Administration Act, which is superseded by the foregoing provisions of this Chapter, shall cease to have effect.

AMENDMENTS

1. Social Security Contributions (Transfer of Functions, etc.) Act 1999 Sch.7 para.35 (April 1, 1999).

2. Welfare Reform and Pensions Act 1999 Sch.7 para.17 (March 19, 2001).

3. Welfare Reform Act 2007 s.62(1) and (5) (July 3, 2007).

4. Transfer of Tribunal Functions Order 2008 (SI 2008/2833) Sch.3 paras 143 and 167 (November 3, 2008), subject to a saving under art.1(5).

5. Transfer of Tribunal Functions and Revenue and Customs Appeals Order 2009 (SI 2009/56), Sch.1, paras 247 and 250 (April 1, 2009).

6. Welfare Reform Act 2012, s.31 and 91, Sch.2, paras 43 and 49 (February 25, 2013 for regulation-making purposes and April 29, 2013 for other purposes).

7. Welfare Reform and Work Act 2016 s.20(7) (July 27, 2017).

DEFINITION

"the Administration Act"—see s.84.

GENERAL NOTE

1.539 By reg.14 of the Child Trust Funds (Non-tax Appeals) Regulations 2005 (SI 2005/191), this subsection is applied with some modifications to appeals under ss.21(9) and 22 of the Child Trust Funds Act 2004 (see Vol.IV). Until April 1, 2009, it was also applied in modified form to appeals under the Tax Credits Act 2002 but, as explained in the note to s.12, the regulation applying it appears to have lapsed in relation to cases in Great Britain.

Definitions omitted by virtue of the Transfer of Tribunal Functions Order 2008 remain in force for the purpose explained in the note to ss.5–7.

"health care professional"

1.540 Until 2007, all medical examinations were carried out by registered medical practitioners. However, as the focus on examinations for social security purposes is usually the functional effects of a medical condition, the expertise of nurses, occupational therapists and physiotherapists may be as relevant and so provision is now made for many medical examinations to be carried out by a health care professional falling within this definition. This may result in a physiotherapist making an assessment in respect of a person suffering from a mental disorder. In *ST v SSWP (ESA)* [2014] UKUT 547 (AAC); [2015] AACR 23, the three-judge panel recorded evidence given to it about the recruitment, training and assessment of health care professionals and it held that the weight to be given to a physiotherapist's opinion in relation to mental health issues is a matter for the decision-maker or tribunal. The professional qualification of a health care professional is usually recorded in the relevant report but not having that information or not knowing the precise areas of expertise of the health care professional does not necessarily require the First-tier Tribunal to reject opinions expressed in the report (*JM v SSWP (ESA)* [2013] UKUT 234 (AAC); [2014] AACR 5, at [76]).

From June 29, 2010, reg.3 of the Social Security (Disability Living Allowance) (Amendment) Regulations 2010 (SI 2010/1651), made under this section, provides—

"Health care professionals

3. For the purposes of section 39(1) of the Social Security Act 1998 (meaning of health care professional), in relation to a claim for disability living allowance under section 73(1AB) of the Social Security Contributions and Benefits Act 1992, the following persons are health care professionals –

(a) an optometrist registered with the General Optical Council;
(b) an orthoptist registered with the Health Professions Council."

Note, therefore, that optometrists and orthoptists are health care professionals only for the purposes of claims to the mobility component of disability living allowance made on the ground of severe visual impairment.

The effect of s.39 and the 2010 Regulations made under it is that all health care professionals must be "registered" members of their professions. In relation to doctors and nurses, this is because s.39 must be read with s.5 of, and Sch.1 to, the Interpretation Act 1978 which provide that, unless the contrary intention appears—

"Registered" in relation to nurses and midwives, means registered in the register maintained under article 5 of the Nursing and Midwifery Order 2001 by virtue of qualifications in nursing or midwifery, as the case may be.

"Registered medical practitioner" means a fully registered person within the meaning of the Medical Act 1983 who holds a licence to practise under that Act.

It was held in *RO v SSWP (ESA)* [2016] UKUT 402 (AAC) that a claimant required to attend for, or submit to, a medical examination by a health care professional is entitled to make a reasonable request for proof that a purported healthcare professional is in fact a health care professional. However, the First-tier Tribunal did not err in finding that an offer extended to the claimant at the assessment centre to check the assessor's credentials on the Nursing and Midwifery Council website was sufficient. It did not matter that the website did not contain photographs so that the identity of the health care professional could not also be checked. **1.541**

In *MH v SSWP (II)* [2020] UKUT 297 (AAC), a health care professional was required to advise the Secretary of State whether a disease suffered by the claimant had been caused by his exposure to chemical agents in the course of his employment. The judge said—

> "53. . . .the lack of evidence in the documentation did not entitle the health care professional simply to say that the claimant had not proved his case, given that the Secretary of State had accepted that the claimant had been exposed to chemical agents known to cause the prescribed disease. It was, as I understand her role, her function to use her expertise to give her own opinion and, unless there was an adverse inference to be drawn from the lack of evidence, the lack of documentary evidence on that particular issue required her to obtain evidence either by taking a history from the claimant or examining him or obtaining (or suggesting that someone else obtain) the results of tests or the opinion of a specialist or whatever else might be required."

This is because the Secretary of State's role, and therefore that of a health care professional upon whose advice the Secretary of State will rely and who in practice has the role formerly exercised by adjudicating medical authorities, is inquisitorial or at least investigatory (see *Kerr v Department for Social Development* [2004] UKHL 23; [2004] 1 W.L.R. 1372 (also reported as an appendix to *R1/04(SF)*).

CHAPTER III

OTHER DECISIONS AND APPEALS

40.–47. *Omitted.* **1.542**

PART II

CONTRIBUTIONS

48.–66. *Omitted.* **1.543**

Part III

Benefits

1.544 **67.–76.** *Omitted.*

Part IV

Miscellaneous and Supplemental

Pilot schemes

1.545 77.—(1) Any regulations to which this subsection applies may be made so as to have effect for a specified period not exceeding 12 months.

(2) Any regulations which, by virtue of subsection (1) above, are to have effect for a limited period are referred to in this section as "a pilot scheme".

(3) A pilot scheme may provide that its provisions are to apply only in relation to—

(a) one or more specified areas of localities;
(b) one or more specified classes of person;
(c) persons selected—
  (i) by reference to prescribed criteria; or
  (ii) on a sampling basis,

(4) A pilot scheme may make consequential or transitional provision with respect to the cessation of the scheme on the expiry of the specified period.

(5) A pilot scheme ("the previous scheme") may be replaced by a further pilot scheme making the same, or similar, provision (apart from the specified period) to that made by the previous scheme.

(6) In so far as a pilot scheme would, apart from this subsection, have the effect of—

(a) treating as capable of work any person who would not otherwise be so treated; or
(b) reducing the total amount of benefit that would otherwise be payable to any person,

it shall not apply in relation to that person.

(7) Subsection (1) above applies to—

(a) regulations made under section 171D of the Contributions and Benefits Act (incapacity for work: persons treated as incapable of work); and
(b) in so far as they are consequential on or supplementary to any such regulations, regulations made under any of the provisions mentioned in subsection (8) below.

(8) The provisions are—

(a) subsection (5)(a) of section 22 of the Contributions and Benefits Act (earnings factors);
(b) section 30C of that Act (incapacity benefit);
(c) [1 . . .];
(d) subsection (1)(e) of section 124 of that Act (income support) and, so far as relating to income support, subsection (1) of section 135 of that Act (the applicable amount);
(e) Part XIIA of that Act (incapacity for work);

(f) section 61A of the Administration Act and section 31 above (incapacity for work).

(9) A statutory instrument containing (whether alone or with other provisions) a pilot scheme shall not be made unless a draft of the instrument has been laid before Parliament and approved by a resolution of each House of Parliament.

AMENDMENT

1. Welfare Reform and Pensions Act 1999 Sch.13 Pt IV (April 6, 2001).

DEFINITIONS

"the Administration Act"—see s.84.
"the Contributions and Benefits Act"—*ibid.*
"prescribed"—*ibid.*

78. *Omitted.* **1.546**

Regulations and orders

79.—(1) [2Subject to subsection 2A below] regulations under this Act shall be made by the Secretary of State. **1.547**

(2) [2. . .]

[1 (2A) Subsection (1) has effect subject to any provision providing for regulations to be made by the Treasury or the Commissioners of Inland Revenue.]

(3) Powers under this Act to make regulations or orders are exercisable by statutory instrument.

(4) Any power conferred by this Act to make regulations or orders may be exercised—

(a) either in relation to all cases to which the power extends, or in relation to those cases subject to specified exceptions, or in relation to any specified cases or classes of case;

(b) so as to make, as respects the cases in relation to which it is exercised—

(i) the full provision to which the power extends or any less provision (whether by way of exception or otherwise);

(ii) the same provision for all cases in relation to which the power is exercised, or different provision for different cases or different classes of case or different provision as respects the same case or class of case for different purposes of this Act;

(iii) any such provision either unconditionally or subject to any specified condition;

and where such a power is expressed to be exercisable for alternative purposes it may be exercised in relation to the same case for any or all of those purposes.

(5) Powers to make regulations for the purposes of any one provision of this Act are without prejudice to powers to make regulations for the purposes of any other provision.

(6) Without prejudice to any specific provision in this Act, a power conferred by this Act to make regulations includes power to make thereby such incidental, supplementary, consequential or transitional provision as appears to the authority making the regulations to be expedient for the purposes of those regulations.

[3 (6A) The provision referred to in subsection (6) includes, in a case where regulations under this Act require or authorise the use of electronic communications, provision referred to in section 8(4) and (5) and 9(5) of the Electronic Communications Act 2000.]

[3 (6B) For the purposes of subsection (6A), references in section 8(4) and (5) and 9(5) of the Electronic Communications Act 2000 to an order under section 8 of that Act are to be read as references to regulations under this Act; and references to anything authorised by such an order are to be read as references to anything required or authorised by such regulations."]

(7) Without prejudice to any specific provisions in this Act, a power conferred by any provision of this Act to make regulations includes power to provide for a person to exercise a discretion in dealing with any matter.

(8) Any power conferred by this Act to make regulations relating to housing benefit or council tax benefit shall include power to make different provision for different areas or different authorities.

(9) [2. . .]

AMENDMENTS

1. Tax Credits Act 2002 Sch.4 para.13 (February 26, 2003).

2. Transfer of Tribunal Functions Order 2008 (SI 2008/2833) Sch.3 paras 143 and 168 (November 3, 2008), subject to a saving under art.1(5).

3. Section 104(2) of the Welfare Reform Act 2012 (February 2, 2013).

GENERAL NOTE

1.548 Subsections (2) and (9) remain in force for the purpose explained in the note to ss.5–7. In so far as it relates to council tax benefit, subs.(8) has been repealed with effect from April 1, 2013, subject to a saving (Welfare Reform Act 2012 s.147 and Pt 1 of Sch.14; Welfare Reform Act 2012 (Commencement No.8 and Savings and Transitional Provisions) Order 2013 (SI 2013/358) arts 8(c) and 9 and Sch.4).

Subsection (2A)

1.549 The functions of the Commissioners of Inland Revenue have been transferred to HMRC (Commissioners for Revenue and Customs Act 2005 s.5(2)(a)).

Parliamentary control of regulations

1.550 **80.**—(1) Subject to the provisions of this section, a statutory instrument containing (whether alone or with other provisions) regulations under—

(a) section [3. . .] 12(2) [4 or (3A)] or 72 above; or
(b) [3. . .] paragraph 9 of Schedule 2 [3. . .]

shall not be made unless a draft of the instrument has been laid before Parliament and been approved by a resolution of each House of Parliament.

(2) A statutory instrument—

(a) which contains (whether alone or with other provisions) regulations made under this Act by the Secretary of State [1, the Treasury or the Commissioners of Inland Revenue]; and
(b) which is not subject to any requirement that a draft of the instrument be laid before and approved by a resolution of each House of Parliament,

shall be subject to annulment in pursuance of a resolution of either House of Parliament.

(3) [3. . .]

[2(4) [3. . .]]

AMENDMENTS

1. Tax Credits Act 2002 Sch.4 para.14 (February 26, 2003).
2. Tribunals, Courts and Enforcement Act 2007 Sch.10 para.29(5) (July 21, 2008).
3. Transfer of Tribunal Functions Order 2008 (SI 2008/2833) Sch.3 paras 143 and 169 (November 3, 2008), subject to a saving under art.1(5).
4. Welfare Reform Act 2012 s.102(1) and (5) (February 25, 2013).

GENERAL NOTE

The omitted provisions remain in force for the purpose explained in the note to ss.5–7. **1.551**

Reports by Secretary of State

81. [[1] . . .] **1.552**

AMENDMENT

1. Welfare Reform Act 2012 s.143 (May 8, 2012).

82. *Omitted.* **1.553**

83. *Omitted.* **1.554**

Interpretation: general

84. In this Act— **1.555**

"the Administration Act" means the Social Security Administration Act 1992;
"the Child Support Act" means the Child Support Act 1991;
"the Contributions and Benefits Act" means the Social Security Contributions and Benefits Act 1992;
"the Jobseekers Act" means the Jobseekers Act 1995;
"the Vaccine Damage Payments Act" means the Vaccine Damage Payments Act 1979;
"prescribe" means prescribe by regulations.

85. *Omitted.* **1.556**

86. *Omitted.* **1.557**

Short title, commencement and extent

87.—(1) This Act may be cited as the Social Security Act 1998. **1.558**

(2) This Act, except—

(a) sections 66, 69, 72 and 77 to 85, this section and Schedule 6 to this Act; and
(b) subsection (1) of section 50 so far as relating to a sum which is chargeable to tax by virtue of section 313 of the Income and Corporation Taxes Act 1988, and subsections (2) to (4) of that section,

shall come into force on such day as may be appointed by order made by the Secretary of State; and different days may be appointed for different provisions and for different purposes.

(3) An order under subsection (2) above may make such savings, or such transitional or consequential provision, as the Secretary of State considers necessary or expedient—

(a) in preparation for or in connection with the coming into force of any provision of this Act; or
(b) in connection with the operation of any enactment repealed or amended by a provision of this Act during any period when the repeal or amendment is not wholly in force.

(4) This Act, except—
(a) section 2 so far as relating to war pensions;
(b) sections 3, 15, 45 to 47, 59, 78 and 85 and this section; and
(c) section 86 and Schedules 7 and 8 so far as relating to enactments which extend to Northern Ireland,

does not extend to Northern Ireland.

(5) The following provisions of this Act extend to the Isle of Man, namely—
(a) in section 4, subsections (1)(c) and (2)(c);
(b) sections 6 and 7 and Schedule 1 so far as relating to appeals under the Vaccine Damage Payments Act;
(c) sections 45 to 47 and this section;
(d) paragraphs 5 to 10 of Schedule 7 and section 86(1) so far as relating to those paragraphs; and
(e) section 86(2) and Schedule 8 so far as relating to the Vaccine Damage Payments Act.

DEFINITION

"Vaccine Damage Payments Act"—see s.84.

GENERAL NOTE

Subsections (2) and (3)

1.559 The following commencement orders have been made: SI 1998/2209, SI 1998/2708, SI 1999/418, SI 1999/526, SI 1999/528, SI 1999/1055, SI 1999/1510, SI 1999/1958, SI 1999/2422, SI 1999/2739, SI 1999/2860, and SI 1999/3178. The main provisions relating to social security adjudication were brought into effect at different times, depending on the benefit in issue, according to the following time-table:

Industrial injuries benefit; Guardian's allowance; Child benefit; Pension Schemes Act 1993—July 5, 1999 (see, primarily, SI 1999/1958).

Retirement pension; Widow's benefit; Incapacity benefit; Severe disablement allowance; Maternity allowance—September 6, 1999 (see, primarily, SI 1999/2422).

Working families' tax credit; Disabled person's tax credit—October 5, 1999 (see, primarily, SI 1999/2739).

Attendance allowance; Disability living allowance; Invalid care allowance; Jobseeker's allowance; Credits of contributions or earnings; Home responsibilities protection; Vaccine damage payments—October 18, 1999 (see, primarily, SI 1999/2860).

All other purposes (including income support)—November 29, 1999 (see, primarily, SI 1999/3178).

SCHEDULES

SCHEDULE 1

1.560 [1. . .]

AMENDMENT

1. Transfer of Tribunal Functions Order 2008 (SI 2008/2833) Sch.3 paras 143 and 171 (November 3, 2008), subject to a saving under art.1(5).

General Note

This Schedule remains in force for the limited purpose explained in the note to ss.5–7. 1.561

Schedule 2

Decisions Against Which No Appeal Lies

Jobseeker's allowance for persons under 18

1. In relation to a person who has reached the age of 16 but not the age of 18, a decision— 1.562
(a) whether section 16 of the Jobseekers Act is to apply to him; or
(b) whether to issue a certificate under section 17(4) of that Act.

Christmas bonus

2. A decision whether a person is entitled to payment under section 148 of the Contributions and Benefits Act. 1.563

Priority between persons entitled to [3 carer's allowance] [8, carer support payment and the carer element of universal credit]

3. [8 A decision as to whether a person has entitlement under section 70 (7ZA), (7ZC) or (7ZE) of the Contributions and Benefits Act.] 1.564

Priority between persons entitled to child benefit

4. A decision as to the exercise of the discretion under paragraph 5 of Schedule 10 to the Contributions and Benefits Act. 1.565

Persons treated as if present in Great Britain

5. A decision whether to certify, in accordance with regulations made under section 64(1), 71(6), 113(1) or 119 of the Contributions and Benefits Act, that it is consistent with the proper administration of that Act to treat a person as though he were present in Great Britain. 1.566

[1 *Work-focused interviews*

5A. A decision terminating or reducing the amount of a person's benefit made in consequence of any decision made under regulations under section 2A [4 or 2AA] of the Administration Act (work-focused interviews).] 1.567

Alteration of rates of benefit

6. A decision as to the amount of benefit to which a person is entitled, where it appears to the Secretary of State that the amount is determined by— 1.568
(a) the rate of benefit provided for by law; or
(b) an alteration of a kind referred to in—
  (i) section 159(1)(b) of the Administration Act (income support); [2 . . .]
  (ii) section 159A(1)(b) of that Act (jobseeker's allowance) [2 or
  (iii) section 129B(1)(b) of that Act (state pension credit)]][5 , or
  (iv) section 159C(1)(b) of that Act (employment and support allowance).] [7 or
  (v) section 159D(1)(b) of that Act (universal credit).]

Increases in income support due to attainment of particular ages

7. A decision as to the amount of benefit to which a person is entitled, where it appears to the Secretary of State that the amount is determined by the recipient's entitlement to an increased amount of income support or income-based jobseeker's allowance in the circumstances referred to in section 160(2) or 160A(2) of the Administration Act. 1.569

Reduction in accordance with reduced benefit direction

1.570 **8.** A decision to reduce the amount of a person's benefit in accordance with a reduced benefit direction (within the meaning of section 46 of the Child Support Act).

[6 Reduction on application of benefit cap

1.571 **8A.** A decision to apply the benefit cap in accordance with regulations under section 96 of the Welfare Reform Act 2012.]

Power to prescribe other decisions

1.572 **9.** Such other decisions as may be prescribed.

AMENDMENTS

1. Welfare Reform and Pensions Act 1999 s.81 and Sch.11 para.87 (November 11, 1999).
2. State Pension Credit Act 2002 ss.11 and 21 and Sch.1 para.11 and Sch.3 (October 6, 2003).
3. Regulatory Reform (Carer's Allowance) Order 2002 (SI 2002/1457) art.2(1) and Sch. para.3(b) September 2002 for the purposes of exercising powers to make subordinate legislation and October 28, 2002 for all other purposes).
4. Employment Act 2002. s.53 and Sch.7 para.51 (July 5, 2003).
5. Welfare Reform Act 2007 Sch.3 para.17(1) and (8) (October 27, 2008).
6. Welfare Reform Act 2012 s.97(6) (April 15, 2013).
7. Welfare Reform Act 2012 s.31 and Sch.2 paras 50(1) and (2) (April 29, 2013).
8. The Carer's Assistance (Carer Support Payment) (Scotland) Regulations 2023 (Consequential Modifications) Order 2023 (SI 2023/1214) art.6 (November 16, 2023).

DEFINITIONS

"the Administration Act"—see s.84.
"benefit"—by virtue of reg.39(2), see s.191 of the Social Security Administration Act 1992.
"the Child Support Act"—see s.84.
"the Contributions and benefits Act"—*ibid.*
"the Jobseekers Act"—*ibid.*
"prescribed"—*ibid.*

GENERAL NOTE

Paragraphs 3 and 4

1.573 In *TD v SSWP (CSM)* [2013] UKUT 282 (AAC); [2014] AACR 7, the Upper Tribunal held that para.4 did not involve a breach of art.6 of the European Convention on Human Rights because, there being no guidance in the legislation or regulations as to how the discretion to award child benefit to one parent rather than the other in a case where they shared care equally, the issue was non-justiciable in the sense in which that term was used in *R(H) 3/04* and *R(H) 6/06* so that an appeal to the First-tier Tribunal would effectively be confined to points of law and judicial review provided an adequate alternative remedy. That decision was followed in *SSWP v AK (CA)* [2014] UKUT 415 (AAC) insofar as it was held that para.3 was also not inconsistent with the European Convention on Human Rights. However, it was held that, while para.3 precluded an appeal against a decision as to which of two people caring for the relevant disabled person and otherwise entitled to carer's allowance should receive the allowance, it did not preclude an appeal brought on the ground that the other potential claimant was not in fact caring for the disabled person.

Paragraph 6

1.574 A decision under reg.22A of the Income Support (General) Regulations 1987, reducing the amount of income support payable to a person while an appeal against a decision that the claimant is capable of work is pending, is not a decision on the "rate of benefit" within para.6(a). (*Re Smyth's Application* [2001] NIQB 29; [2001] N.I. 393, in which Kerr J. considered the equivalent provision in the Social Security (Northern Ireland) Order 1998). Similarly, it was held in *MM v SSWP (ESA)* [2012] UKUT 443 (AAC) that para.6(a) did not prohibit an appeal against a decision that a prisoner was entitled to employment and support allowance at the rate of nil, it being arguable that he was entitled to it at a higher rate. In both cases, the appeal was not about the rate of benefit prescribed in relation to a class of person but about whether the claimant fell within that class. In *DC v Bromley LBC (HB)* [2018] UKUT 416 (AAC), it was said that, in the equivalent provision in the Child Support, Pensions and Social Security Act 2000, "[t]he term 'the rate of benefit provided for by law' is to be construed narrowly so that it only applies to specific rates of benefit set out in legislation" and that that was "apparent when consideration is given to . . . paragraph 6(a) of Schedule 2 to the Social Security Act 1998, which clearly takes its flavour from paragraph 6(b)". In *MM*, the judge commented that para.6(a) seemed unnecessary and "owes more to history than anything else".

It is not entirely clear that para.6(b) is necessary either. The various provisions of the Social Security Administration Act 1992 mentioned in it provide that, where the amount of a statutory rate of an income-related benefit or some other benefit alters and that alteration affects the amount of the income related-benefit in question, the amount of the income-related benefit "shall be" the increased or reduced amount "without any further decision of the Secretary of State". It is therefore not obvious that, at least as regards heads (i) to (iv), the amount of benefit to which a person is entitled by virtue of a decision of the Secretary of State can ever be "determined by . . . an alteration of a kind referred to in [those provisions]" and so a right of appeal may have been excluded only out of an abundance of caution. Section 159D(1), relating to universal credit and mentioned in head (v), goes further than the other provisions in that, by para.(b)(iii), an alteration "in any amount to be deducted in respect of earned income under section 8(3)(a) of the Welfare Reform Act 2012" may also result in the amount of universal credit being increased or reduced without a decision of the Secretary of State. That, however, is subject to "such exceptions and conditions as may be prescribed" and reg.41(3) of the Universal Credit, Personal Independence Payment, Jobseeker's Allowance and Employment and Support Allowance (Decisions and Appeals) Regulations 2013 provides that, if a person "disputes the figure" used for employed earnings, he or she must be offered an opportunity to request a Secretary of State's decision as to the amount of universal credit payable. The question then arises whether para.6(b)(v) of Sch.2 to the 1998 Act excludes any right of appeal against such a decision on the ground that it is determined by an alteration of a kind referred to in s.159D(1)(b)(iii). It is suggested that it does not and that, for the purposes of para.6(b), an alteration ceases to be "of a kind referred to in s.159D(1)(b)" when a prescribed exclusion of s.159D(1) applies or a prescribed condition does not. Otherwise, the most likely purpose of an exclusion or condition, which it is suggested will be precisely to ensure that a decision is made in a form that is appealable, would be liable to be undermined.

It appears not to have been thought necessary to add a further head to para.6(b) in the light of s.159E of the 1992 Act.

Paragraph 7

No equivalent provision has been made in respect of employment and support allowance following the insertion of s.160B into the 1992 Act. **1.575**

Paragraph 9

See Sch.2 to the Social Security and Child Support (Decisions and Appeals) Regulations 1999 Sch.2 to the Child Benefit and Guardian's Allowance (Decisions and Appeals) Regulations 2003. and Sch.3 to the Universal Credit, Personal **1.576**

Independence Payment, Jobseeker's Allowance and Employment and Support Allowance (Decisions and Appeals) Regulations 2013.

SCHEDULE 3

DECISIONS AGAINST WHICH AN APPEAL LIES

PART I

BENEFIT DECISIONS

Entitlement to benefit without a claim

1.577 **1.** In such cases or circumstances as may be prescribed, a decision whether a person is entitled to a relevant benefit for which no claim is required.

2. If so, a decision as to the amount to which he is entitled.

Payability of benefit

1.578 **3.** A decision whether a relevant benefit (or a component of a relevant benefit) to which a person is entitled is not payable by reason of—

(a) any provision of the Contributions and Benefits Act by which the person is disqualified for receiving benefit;
(b) regulations made under section 72(8) of that Act (disability living allowance);
(c) regulations made under section 113(2) of that Act (suspension of payment); [1 . . .]
(d) [8 . . .]
[5 (da) [8 . . .]]
[1 (e) [6 . . .]] [2 or
(f) section [7 6B,] 7, 8 or 9 of the Social Security Fraud Act 2001] [4 ; [10 . . ..]
(g) section 18 of the Welfare Reform Act 2007];
[10 (h) regulations made under section 85(1) or 86(1) of the Welfare Reform Act 2012;
(i) section 87 of that Act.]

[9 **3A.** A decision as to the amount of a relevant benefit that is payable to a person by virtue of regulations under section 6B, 7, 8 or 9 of the Social Security Fraud Act 2001.]

Payments to third parties

1.579 **4.** Except in such cases or circumstances as may be prescribed, a decision whether the whole or part of a benefit to which a person is entitled is, by virtue of regulations, to be paid to a person other than him.

Recovery of benefits

1.580 **5.** A decision whether payment is recoverable under section 71 or 71A of the Administration Act.

6. If so, a decision as to the amount of payment recoverable.

6A. *Not yet in force.*

[11 **6B.** A decision as to the amount of payment recoverable under section 71ZB, 71ZG or 71ZH of the Administration Act.]

[12 *State pension: prisoners and overseas residents*

1.581 **6C.** A decision that a state pension under Part 1 of the Pensions Act 2014 is not payable by reason of regulations under section 19 of that Act (prisoners).

6D. A decision that a person is not entitled to increases in the rate of a state pension under Part 1 of the Pensions Act 2014 by reason of regulations under section 20 of that Act (overseas residents).]

Industrial injuries benefit

1.582 **7.** A decision whether an accident was an industrial accident for the purposes of industrial injuries benefit.

Jobseekers' agreements

8. A decision in relation to a jobseeker's agreement as proposed to be made under section 9 of the Jobseekers Act, or as proposed to be varied under section 10 of that Act. **1.583**

[3 *State pension credit*

8A. A decision whether to specify a period as an assessed income period under section 6 of the State Pension Credit Act 2002. **1.584**

8B. If so, a decision as to the period to be so specified.

8C. A decision whether an assessed income period comes to an end by virtue of section 9(4) or (5) of that Act.

8D. If so, a decision as to when the assessed income period so ends.]

Power to prescribe other decisions

9. Such other decisions relating to a relevant benefit as may be prescribed. **1.585**

PART II

CONTRIBUTIONS DECISIONS

10.–15. *Omitted.* **1.586**

16. A decision whether a person was (within the meaning of regulations) precluded from regular employment by responsibilities at home.

17. A decision whether a person is entitled to be credited with earnings or contributions in accordance with regulations made under section 22(5) [13 or (5ZA)] of the Contributions and Benefits Act.

18.–29. *Omitted.* **1.587**

AMENDMENTS

1. Child Support, Pensions and Social Security Act 2000 s.66 and Sch.9 Pt V (October 15, 2001).
2. Social Security Fraud Act 2001 s.12(2) (April 1 2002).
3. State Pension Credit Act 2002 Sch.1 para.12 (July 2, 2002 for the purpose of exercising any power to make regulations or orders and October 6, 2003 for other purposes).
4. Welfare Reform Act 2007 Sch.3 para.17(1) and (9) (October 27, 2008).
5. Welfare Reform Act 2009 s.1(4) and Sch.3 para.4 (November 12, 2009).
6. Welfare Reform Act 2009 Sch.7 (March 22, 2010).
7. Welfare Reform Act 2009 Sch.4 para.10 (April 1, 2010).
8. Welfare Reform Act 2012 s.46(4) (October 22, 2012).
9. Welfare Reform Act 2012 s.31 and Sch.2 paras 43 and 51 (April 1, 2013).
10. Welfare Reform Act 2012 s.91 and Sch.9 paras 37 and 43 (April 8, 2013).
11. Welfare Reform Act 2012 s.105(7) (April 29, 2013).
12. Pensions Act 2014 s.23 and Sch.12 paras 31 and 37 (April 6, 2016).
13. Pensions Act 2014 (Consequential Amendments) Order 2016 (SI 2016/931) art.3 (September 15, 2016).

DEFINITIONS

"the Administration Act"—see s.84.

"benefit"—by virtue of reg.39(2), see s.191 of the Social Security Administration Act 1992.

"claim"—*ibid.*

"the Child Support Act"—see s.84.

"the Contributions and Benefits Act"—*ibid.*

"industrial injuries benefit"—by virtue of s.39(2), see s.191 of the Social Security Administration Act 1992.

"the Jobseekers Act"—s.84.
"prescribed"—*ibid.*
"relevant benefit"—see s.8(3).

GENERAL NOTE

1.588 By reg.16 of, and para.5 of Sch.2 to the Employment and Support Allowance (Transitional Provisions, Housing Benefit and Council Tax Benefit) (Existing Awards) (No.2) Regulations 2010 (SI 2010/1907), (as amended by reg.15 of the Employment and Support Allowance (Transitional Provisions, Housing Benefit and Council Tax Benefit) (Existing Awards) (No.2) (Amendment) Regulations 2010 (SI 2010/2430)), this Schedule is modified with effect from October 1, 2010 for the purpose of migrating claimants from incapacity benefit to employment and support allowance. It is to be read as though there were inserted—

"Conversion of certain existing awards into awards of an employment and support allowance

8E. A conversion decision within the meaning of the Employment and Support Allowance (Transitional Provisions, Housing Benefit and Council Tax Benefit) (Existing Awards) (No.2) Regulations 2010."

Paragraph 3

1.589 A decision under art.13(2) of the Convention on Social Security between Great Britain and Jamaica that a person is not permanently incapacitated for work is not a decision under s.113 of the Social Security Contributions and Benefits Act 1992 disqualifying a person from benefit, even though it may lead to such a decision, and therefore it does not fall within para.3(a) (*Campbell v Secretary of State for Work and Pensions* [2005] EWCA Civ 989).

Paragraphs 5 to 6B

1.590 It was suggested in *VT v SSWP (IS)* [2016] UKUT 178 (AAC); [2016] AACR 42 that these paragraphs may be otiose because, in *R(IS) 14/04* and that decision respectively, it has been held that decisions as to the recoverability of benefits under s.74 of the Social Security Administration Act 1992 and the imposition of civil penalties under s.115D of that Act fall within the scope of s.12(1)(a) of this Act (and so are appealable), with the implication that the decisions covered by these paragraphs as to the recoverability of other payments also do so, rather than falling within s.12(1)(b).

Paragraph 6A is to be inserted by s.105(7) of the Welfare Reform Act 2012 when housing credit is introduced for claimants of state pension credit.

Paragraph 9

1.591 Regulation 26 of the Social Security and Child Support (Decisions and Appeals) Regulations 1999 is made under para.9 and so too are reg.50(1) of, and Sch.3 to, the Universal Credit, Personal Independence Payment, Jobseeker's Allowance and Employment and Support Allowance (Decisions and Appeals) Regulations 2013.

Parasgraphs 10 – 29

1.592 Paragraphs 10–15 and 18–29 have never been brought into force and are all to be repealed by the Social Security Contributions (Transfer of Functions, etc.,) Act 1999 Sch.7 para.36 but so far the repealing provision has been brought into effect only in respect of para.23 (twice! See SI 1999/527 and SI 1999/1662). The jurisdictions which would have been conferred on appeal tribunals were instead transferred to the tax commissioners. Paragraphs 16 and 17, on the other hand, introduce new rights of appeal to tribunals where none existed before 1999. In *CIB/3327/2004*, the Commissioner commented on the lack of arrangements within the Department for Work and Pensions for proper decisions to be made in respect of the crediting of earnings or contributions. In particular, it appeared that such decisions as were made did not include information about the new right of appeal conferred by para.17. Arrangements have been made under s.17 of the Social Security Contributions (Transfer of Functions, etc.) Act 1999 for HMRC to make decisions on behalf of the Secretary of State in respect of matters falling within the scope of para.16 (mentioned in *SF v SSWP (HRP)* [2013] UKUT 175 AAC), in which it was pointed out that, notwithstanding that HMRC makes the decisions, appeals lie within the jurisdiction of the Social Entitlement Chamber of the First-tier Tribunal rather than the Tax Chamber) and in respect of some matters falling within the scope of para.17. These arrangements appear not to cover decisions relating to the crediting of earnings or contributions in respect of unemployment or incapacity for work, although *CIB/3327/2004* revealed some confusion among staff as to the division of responsibility between the Department for Work and Pensions and HMRC. Further criticism of the handling of credits cases was voiced in *CIB/1602/2006*. In particular, the Commissioner criticised instructions to staff causing them to make undisclosed assumptions about contributions and credits issues instead of issuing decisions in respect of such issues informing claimants of their rights of appeal.

The function of making decisions in respect of Class 3 credits to those entitled to them by virtue of being entitled to child benefit has been transferred to HMRC who administer child benefit itself (National Insurance Contribution Credits (Transfer of Functions) Order 2009 (SI 2009/1377) with effect from April 6, 2010. However, nearly all the provisions of this Act continue to apply to such decisions, as though references to the Secretary of State were references to HMRC.

Schedule 4

[1. . .] **1.593**

Amendment

1. Transfer of Tribunal Functions Order 2008 (SI 2008/2833) Sch.3 paras 143 and 172 (November 3, 2008), subject to a saving under art.1(5).

General Note

This Schedule remains in force for the limited purpose explained in the note to ss.5–7. **1.594**

Schedule 5

Regulations as to Procedure: Provision Which may be Made

1. Provision prescribing the procedure to be followed in connection with— **1.595**
- (a) the making of decisions or determinations by the Secretary of State, [1. . .] and
- (b) the withdrawal of claims, applications, appeals or references falling to be decided or determined by the Secretary of State, [1. . .].

2. [1. . .]

3. Provision as to the form which is to be used for any document, the evidence which is to be required and the circumstances in which any official record or certificate is to be sufficient or conclusive evidence.

4. Provision as to the time within which, or the manner in which—
- (a) any evidence is to be produced; or
- (b) any application, reference or appeal is to be made.

5. [1. . .]
6. [1. . .]
7. [1. . .]
8. [1. . .]

9. Provision for the non-disclosure to a person of the particulars of any medical advice or medical evidence given or submitted for the purposes of a determination.

Amendment

1. Transfer of Tribunal Functions Order 2008 (SI 2008/2833) Sch.3 paras 143 and 173 (November 3, 2008), subject to a saving under art.1(5).

General Note

1.596 This Schedule no longer enables regulations to be made in respect of the procedure before tribunals, having been replaced by Sch.5 to the Tribunals, Courts and Enforcement Act 2007, but the omitted provisions remain in force for the purpose explained in the note to ss.5–7. By reg.11(5) of the Child Trust Funds (Non-tax Appeals) Regulations 2005 (SI 2005/191), this Schedule is applied to appeals under ss.21(9) and 22 of the Child Trust Funds Act 2004 with the modification that "the Secretary of State" is omitted from both places where it occurs in para.1, which makes that paragraph redundant. Until April 1, 2009, it was also applied in similarly modified form to appeals under the Tax Credits Act 2002 but, for reasons explained in the note to s.12, the regulation applying it has lapsed in relation to cases in Great Britain. It is still applied, with references to the Board substituted for references to the Secretary of State, to child benefit and guardian's allowance decisions and appeals (Tax Credits Act 2002 Sch.4 para.15).

See the Social Security and Child Support (Decisions and Appeals) Regulations 1999, the Universal Credit, Personal Independence Payment, Jobseeker's Allowance and Employment and Support Allowance (Decisions and Appeals) Regulations 2013, the Child Benefit and Guardian's Allowance (Decisions and Appeals) Regulations 2003 and, in Vol.IV, the Child Trust Funds (Appeals) Regulations 2005.

Schedules 6 To 8

1.597 *Omitted.*

Social Security Contributions (Transfer of Functions, etc.) Act 1999

(1999 c.2)

Arrangement of Sections

Part I

General

1.598 1.–7. *Omitted.*

Part II

Decisions and Appeals

PART III

MISCELLANEOUS AND SUPPLEMENTAL

SCHEDULES

Omitted.

An Act to transfer from the Secretary of State to the Commissioners of Inland Revenue or the Treasury certain functions relating to national insurance contributions, the National Insurance Fund, statutory sick pay, statutory maternity pay or person schemes and certain associated functions relating to benefits; to enable functions relating to any of those matters in respect of Northern Ireland to be transferred to the Secretary of State, the Commissioners of Inland Revenue or the Treasury; to make further provision, in connection with the functions transferred, as to the powers of the Commissioners of Inland Revenue, the making of decisions and appeals; to provide that rebates payable in respect of members of money purchase contracted-out pension schemes are to be payable out of the National Insurance Fund; and for connected purposes.

[25th February 1999]

PART I

GENERAL

1.–7. *Omitted.* **1.599**

PART II

DECISIONS AND APPEALS

Decisions by officers of Board

8.—(1) Subject to the provisions of the Part, it shall be for an officer of the Board— **1.600**

(a) to decide whether for the purposes of Parts I to V of the Social Security Contributions and Benefits Act 1992 a person is or was an earner and, if so, the category of earners in which he is or was to be included,
(b) to decide whether a person is or was employed in employed earner's employment for the purposes of Part V of the Social Security Contributions and Benefits Act 1992 (industrial injuries),
(c) to decide whether a person is or was liable to pay contributions of any particular class and, if so, the amount that he is or was liable to pay,
(d) to decide whether a person is or was entitled to pay contributions of any particular class that he is or was not liable to pay and, if so, the amount that he is or was entitled to pay,

(e) to decide whether contributions of a particular class have been paid in respect of any period,

[5 (ea) to decide whether a person is or was entitled to make a deduction under section 4 of the National Insurance Contributions Act 2014 (deductions etc. of employment allowance) and, if so, the amount the person is or was entitled to deduct,

(eb) to decide whether a person is or was entitled to a repayment under that section and, if so, the amount of the repayment,]

(f) subject to and in accordance with regulations made for the purposes of this paragraph by the Secretary of State with the concurrence of the Board, to decide any issue arising as to, or in connection with, entitlement to statutory sick pay [3, statutory maternity pay, [4 [7 statutory paternity pay,]] [7 . . .] statutory adoption pay] [6 [9, statutory shared parental pay or statutory parental bereavement pay]],

(g) to make any other decision that falls to be made [3 under Parts 11 to [6 [9 12ZD]] of the Social Security Contributions and Benefits Act 1992 (statutory sick pay, statutory maternity pay, [4 [7 statutory paternity pay,]] [7 . . .] statutory adoption pay] [6 [9 , statutory shared parental pay and statutory parental bereavement pay]],

[3 (ga) to make any decision that falls to be made under regulations under section 7 of the Employment Act 2002 (funding of employers' liabilities to make payments of [4 [7 statutory paternity pay,]] [7 . . .] statutory adoption pay] [6 [9 , statutory shared parental pay or statutory parental bereavement pay]]),]

(i) to decide any issue arising under section 27 of the Jobseekers Act 1995 (employment of long-term unemployed; deductions by employers), or under any provision of regulations under that section, as to—

(i) whether a person is or was an employee or employer of another,

(ii) whether an employer is or was entitled to make any deduction from his contributions payments in accordance with regulations under section 27 of that Act,

(iii) whether a payment falls to be made to an employer in accordance with those regulations,

(iv) the amount that falls to be so deducted or paid, or

(v) whether two or more employers are, by virtue of regulations under section 27 of that Act, to be treated as one,

[2 (ia) to decide whether to give or withdraw an approval for the purposes of paragraph 3B(1)(b) of Schedule 1 to the Social Security Contributions and Benefits Act 1992,]

(j) [2 . . .],

(k) to decide whether a person is liable to a penalty under—

(i) paragraph 7A(2) or 7B(2)(h) of Schedule 1 to the Social Security Contributions and Benefits Act 1992, or

(ii) section 113(1)(a) of the Social Security Administration Act 1992,

(l) to decide the [2 . . .] penalty payable under any of the provisions mentioned in [2 paragraph k] above, and

(m) to decide such issues relating to contributions, other than the issues specified in paragraphs (a) to (l) above or in paragraphs 16 and 17 of Schedule 3 to the Social Security Act 1998, as may be prescribed by regulations made by the Board.

[8 (1A) No decision in respect of Class 2 contributions under section 11(2) of the Social Security Contributions and Benefits Act 1992 may be made under subsection (1) in relation to an issue specified in paragraph (c) or (e) of that subsection if the person to whom the decision would relate—

(a) has appealed under Part 5 of the Taxes Management Act 1970 in relation to that issue,

(b) can appeal under that Part in relation to that issue, or

(c) might in the future, without the agreement of Her Majesty's Revenue and Customs or permission of the tribunal, be able to appeal under that Part in relation to that issue.]

(2) Subsection (1)(c) and (e) above do not include any decision relating to Class 4 contributions other than a decision falling to be made—

(a) under sub section (1) of section 17 of the Social Security Contributions and Benefits Act 1992 as to whether by regulations under that subsection a person is or was excepted from liability for Class 4 contributions, or his liability is or was deferred; or

(b) under regulations made by virtue of sub section (3) or (4) of that section or section 18 of that Act.

(3) Subsection (1)(g) above does not include—

(a) any decision as to the making of subordinate legislation; or

(b) any decision as to whether the liability to pay statutory sick pay [3, statutory maternity pay, [4 [7 statutory paternity pay,]] [7 . . .] statutory adoption pay] [6 [9 , statutory shared parental pay or statutory parental bereavement pay]] is a liability of the Board rather than the employer.

(4) [1 . . .]

Amendments

1. Welfare Reform and Pensions Act 1999 s.88 and Sch.13 Pt.VI (April 6, 2000).
2. Child Support, Pensions and Social Security Act 2000 ss. 76(6), 77(5) and 85 and Sch.9 Pt. VIII (July 28, 2000).
3. Employment Act 2002 s.9(2) and (3) (December 8, 2002).
4. Work and Families Act 2006 s.11 and Sch.1 para.46 (March 3, 2010).
5. National Insurance Contributions Act 2014 s.6(1) (April 6, 2014).
6. Children and Families Act 2014 s.126(1) and Sch.7 paras. 44 and 45(1), (2)(b), (c), (e) and (g) and (3)(b) (December 1, 2014).
7. Children and Families Act 2014 s.126(1) and Sch.7 paras. 44 and 45(1), (2)(a), (d) and (f) and (3)(a) (April 5, 2015).
8. National Insurance Contributions Act 2015 s.2 and Sch.1 para.25 (April 6, 2015).
9. Parental Bereavement (Leave and Pay) Act 2018 s.2(2) and Sch. para.30 (January 18, 2020).

Definitions

"the Board"—see s.27, but note that the functions of the Board were transferred to Her Majesty's Revenue and Customs by the Commissioners for Revenue and Customs Act 2005.

"contributions"—see s.27.

GENERAL NOTE

1.601 This section provides for a number of matters previously determined by the Secretary of State for Social Security to be determined by the Board of Inland Revenue (see s.27), whose functions have now been transferred to the HMRC by s.5(2) of the Commissioners for Revenue and Customs Act 2005. They are mainly concerned with contributions and employment status (which is important for entitlement to industrial injuries benefits (see para.(b)), but also include statutory sick pay and statutory maternity pay (see paras (f) and (g)). Entitlement to statutory sick pay and statutory maternity pay had been determined by adjudication officers, until the Social Security Act 1998 transferred that function to the Secretary of State by provisions that never came fully into force because they were overtaken by this Act. Sections 9–14 of this Act make provision for decisions by HMRC and appeals to the Tax Chamber of the First-tier Tribunal which are beyond the scope of this volume, but see Vol.IV.

The questions listed in s.8(1) are *not* to be decided by the Secretary of State (see s.8(5) of the Social Security Act 1998) and do not fall within the jurisdiction of the Social Entitlement Chamber of the First-tier Tribunal. However, although it was for the Inland Revenue to consider whether a person is or was in employed earner's employment, the Commissioner in *CI/7507/1999* accepted a submission by the Secretary of State that the question whether a person was to be *treated* as having been an employed earner for the purposes of the industrial injuries scheme was a matter for the Secretary of State and, on appeal, for an appeal tribunal. If that is the construction to be given to s.8(1)(b), presumably the same approach must be taken to s.8(1)(a), although questions relating to the payment of contributions will be matters for HMRC by virtue of s.8(1)(c)–(e) and regulations made under s.8(1)(m). *CI/7507/1999* was distinguished in *R(JSA)8/02*, where the Commissioner held that the question whether a person was to be *treated* as having paid contributions (where contributions had been deducted from her salary but not passed on to the Inland Revenue) was a question to be determined by the Inland Revenue. Where, following a claim for retirement pension, there is a dispute between the Secretary of State and a claimant as to whether employment he had been in was contracted-out or contracted-in employment, it arises as part of a question as to his liability to pay contributions or as to what contributions have been paid and so is a question falling within the jurisdiction of HMRC by virtue of s.8(1)(c) or (e) (*CP/3833/2003*). Therefore any appeal lies to the Tax Chamber of the First-tier Tribunal and not to the Social Entitlement Chamber, notwithstanding that appeals against refusals of contracting-out certificates lie to the Social Entitlement Chamber by vir tue of s.170 of the Pension Schemes Act 1993 (see the note to art.3 of the First-tier Tribunal and Upper Tribunal (Chambers) Order 2008). On the other hand, while HMRC are responsible for determining the amount of contributions paid, it is for the Secretary of State to determine any question as to which contribution year is relevant to a claim for benefit (because it would appear from the language of s.8(1)(e) that the effect of *Secretary of State for Social Security v Scully* [1992] 1 W.L.R. 927 (reported as *R(S) 5/93*) has been reversed and the effect of *R(G) 1/82* has been restored) and also any question as to the application of the Social Security (Earnings Factor) Regulations 1979 (*R(IB) 1/09*).

1.602 Regulation 155A of the Social Security (Contributions) Regulations 2001 (SI 2001/1004) prescribes issues upon which decisions are to be taken by HMRC for the purposes of s.8(1)(m) of this Act. Such issues include disputes as to the appropriate "earnings period" for calculating contributions and a variety of decisions relating to late applications for refunds or repayments of overpaid contributions and the late payment of contributions, such as whether "the reason for the non-payment is the contributor's ignorance or error, and, if so, whether that ignorance or error was due to his failure to exercise due care and diligence" or whether an employer's failure to pay contributions was "neither with the consent or connivance of the primary contributor nor attributable to any negligence on the part of the [employee]". The consequence of such decisions may be that late-paid contributions should be treated as having been paid earlier than they were actually paid, so that entitlement to benefit can be derived from them. In *NJ v SSWP (RP)* [2021] UKUT 21 (AAC), the First-tier Tribunal was misled by an inadequate submission by the Secretary of State and consequently erred in failing to refer to the Secretary of State, for onward reference to HMRC under reg.38A of the Social Security and Child Support (Decisions and Appeals) Regulations 1999), a question relating to late-paid contributions.

Questions relating to "home responsibilities protection" and the crediting of contributions or earnings remain matters for the Secretary of State by virtue of the combined effect of s.8(1)(m) of this Act and s.8(1)(c) of the Social Security Act 1998. So too do matters relating to the payment of contributions for graduated retirement benefit, which were not contributions of a "class" and so do not fall within the scope of s.8(1)(c) of this Act with the result that they remain within the scope of s.8(1)(c) of the 1998 Act (*R(P) 1/08*). Note, however, that s.17 permits the Secretary of State to make arrangements for HMRC to discharge his decision-making functions in relation to those matters.

Moreover, s.23 of this Act permits the functions listed in s.8 to be transferred back to the Secretary of State and also permits other functions of the Secretary of State relating to contributions to be transferred to HMRC. Under these powers, the function of making decisions in respect of Class 3 "credits" to those entitled to them by virtue of being entitled to child benefit has been transferred to HMRC (who administer child benefit itself) with effect from April 6, 2010. However, nearly all the provisions of the Social Security Act 1998 continue to apply to such decisions, as though references to the Secretary of State were references to HMRC (National Insurance Contribution Credits (Transfer of Functions) Order 2009 (SI 2009/1377)).

9.–16. *Omitted.* 1.603

Arrangements for discharge of decision-making functions

17.—(1) The Secretary of State may make arrangements with the Board for any his functions under Chapter II of Part I of the Social Security Act 1998 in relation to— 1.604

(a) a decision whether a person was (within the meaning of regulations) precluded from regular employment by responsibilities at home, or

(b) a decision whether a person is entitled to be credited with earnings or contributions in accordance with regulations made under section 22(5) [[1] or (5ZA)] of the Social Security Contributions and Benefits Act 1992,

to be discharged by the Board or by officers of the Board.

(2) No such arrangements shall effect the responsibility of the Secretary of State or the application of Chapter II of Part I of the Social Security Act 1998 in relation to any decision.

(3) *Omitted.*

AMENDMENT

1. Pensions Act 2014 (Consequential and Supplementary Amendments) Order 2016 (SI 2016/224) art.5 (April 6, 2016).

DEFINITIONS

"the Board"—see s.27, but note that the functions of the Board were transferred to Her Majesty's Revenue and Customs by the Commissioners for Revenue and Customs Act 2005.

"contributions"—see s.27.

GENERAL NOTE

1.605 Questions about home responsibilities protection and the crediting of earnings or contributions are questions that are relevant to a person's contributions record, but they are nonetheless decisions within the jurisdiction of the Secretary of State and there are rights of appeal to the Social Entitlement Chamber of the First-tier Tribunal (see the Social Security Act 1998 Sch.3 paras 16 and 17). Despite this, decisions about home responsibilities protection are made by HMRC under an arrangement under this section. So too are most decisions about "credits" other than those related to incapacity for work or availability for work, which are made by the Secretary of State because a person claiming benefit on the ground of incapacity for work or availability for work is usually treated also as claiming "credits". It appears that there is also an arrangement under this section in respect of questions concerning records of payment of contributions for graduated retirement benefit (*R(P)1/08*). However, notwithstanding that HMRC makes decisions where there are such arrangements, appeals still lie within the jurisdiction of the Social Entitlement Chamber of the First-tier Tribunal rather than the Tax Chamber. As explained in *SF v SSWP (HRP)* [2013] UKUT 175 AAC), this is because the decisions are not made under s.8 and so the right of appeal is still conferred by para.16 of Sch.3 to the Social Security Act 1998 and not by s.11 of this Act with the consequence that appeals do not fall within exception (i) of art.6(c) of the First-tier Tribunal and Upper Tribunal (Chambers) Order 2010 (SI 2010/2655), set out in the note to s.7 of the Tribunals, Courts and Enforcement Act 2007, below).

1.606 **18.–19.** *Omitted.*

PART III

MISCELLANEOUS AND SUPPLEMENTAL

1.607 **20.–26.** *Omitted.*

Interpretation

1.608 **27.** In this Act, unless a contrary intention appears—

"the Board" means the Commissioners of Inland Revenue;

"contributions" means contributions under Part I of the Social Security Contributions and Benefits Act 1992.

GENERAL NOTE

"the Board"

1.609 The functions of the Commissioners of Inland Revenue were transferred to the Commissioners for Her Majesty's Revenue and Customs by s.5(2) of the Commissioners for Revenue and Customs Act 2005.

Short title, commencement and extent

28.—(1) This Act may be cited as the Social Security Contributions (Transfer of Functions, etc.) Act 1999. **1.610**

(2) *Omitted.*

(3) *Omitted.*

Welfare Reform and Pensions Act 1999

(1999 c.30)

Arrangement of Sections

Parts I to IV (*omitted*)

Part V

Welfare

Chapter I

Social Security Benefits

Miscellaneous

Supplementary

Certain overpayments of benefit not to be recoverable

68.—(1) An overpayment to which this section applies shall not be recoverable from the payee, whether by the Secretary of State or a local authority, under any provision made by or under Part III of the Administration Act (overpayments and adjustments of benefit). **1.612**

(2) This section applies to an overpayment if—

(a) it is in respect of a qualifying benefit;

(b) it is referable to a decision given on a review that there has been an alteration in the relevant person's condition, being a decision to which effect is required to be given as from a date earlier than that on which it was given;

(c) the decision was given before June 1, 1999; and

(d) the overpayment is not excluded by virtue subsection (6).

(3) In subsection (2)(b) the reference to a decision on a review that there has been an alteration in the relevant person's condition is a reference to

a decision so given that that person's physical or mental condition either was at the time when the original decision was given, or has subsequently become, different from that on which that decision was based, with the result—

(a) that he did not at that time, or (as the case may be) has subsequently ceased to, meet any of the conditions contained in the following provisions of the Contributions and Benefits Act, namely—

(i) section 64 (attendance allowance),

(ii) section 72(1) or (2) (care component of disability living allowance), and

(iii) section 73(1) or (2) (mobility component of that allowance); or

(b) that he was at that time, or (as the case may be) has subsequently become, capable of work in accordance with regulations made under section 171C(2) of that Act (the all work test).

(4) For the purposes of this section "qualifying benefit" means—

(a) attendance allowance;

(b) disability living allowance;

(c) any benefit awarded wholly or partly by reason of a person being (or being treated as being) in receipt of a component of disability living allowance or in receipt of attendance allowance;

(d) incapacity benefit;

(e) any benefit (other than incapacity benefit) awarded wholly or partly by reason of a person being (or being treated as being) in receipt of any benefit falling within paragraph (c), (d) or (e).

(5) For the purposes of this section—

(a) "review" means a review taking place by virtue of section 25(1)(a) or (b), 30(2)(a) or (b) or 35(1)(a) or (b) of the Administration Act;

(b) "the relevant person", in relation to a review, means the person to whose entitlement to a qualifying benefit or to whose incapacity for work the review related; and

(c) "the original decision", in relation to a review, means the decision as to any such entitlement or incapacity to which the review related.

(6) An overpayment is excluded by virtue of this subsection if (before or after the passing of this Act)—

(a) the payee has agreed to pay a penalty in respect of the overpayment under section 115A of the Administration Act,

(b) the payee has been convicted of any offence (under section 111A or 112(1) or (1A) of that Act or otherwise) in connection with the overpayment, or

(c) proceedings have been instituted against the payee for such an offence and the proceedings have not been determined or abandoned.

(7) Nothing in this section applies to an overpayment to the extent that it was recovered from the payee (by any means) before February 26, 1999.

(8) In this section—

"benefit" includes any amount included in—

(a) the applicable amount in relation to an income-related benefit (as defined by section 135(1) of the Contributions and Benefits Act), or

(b) the applicable amount in relation to a jobseeker's allowance (as defined by section 4(5) of the Jobseekers Act 1995);

"income-related benefit" has the meaning given by section 123(1) of the Contributions and Benefits Act;

"overpayment" means an amount of benefit paid in excess of entitlement;

"the payee", in relation to an overpayment, means the person to whom that amount was paid.

COMMENCEMENT

November 11, 1999. **1.613**

GENERAL NOTE

The purpose of this provision is to give an amnesty to certain benefit holders held to have been overpaid benefit in the circumstances set out in subs.(2). The section is replete with difficulty. Subsection (1) says that the overpayment is not to be recoverable; quite what this means in the context of the section is not clear. Subsection (6) refers to circumstances which take the overpayment out of the scope of subs.(2). There are both issues of timing and of culpability in the section which it is difficult to understand. Clearly subs.(6) is intended to exempt culpable overpayments from the amnesty, but the drafting is obscure. **1.614**

Supply of information for certain purposes

72. —(1) The Secretary of State may by regulations make such provision for or in connection with any of the following matters, namely— **1.615**

(a) the use by a person within subsection (2) of social security information [1 , or information relating to employment or training,] held by that person,

(b) the supply (whether to a person within subsection (2) or otherwise) of social security information [1 , or information relating to employment or training,] held by a person within that subsection,

(c) the relevant purposes for which a person to whom such information is supplied under the regulations may use it, and

(d) the circumstances and extent (if any) in and to which a person to whom such information is supplied under the regulations may supply it to any other person (whether within subsection (2) or not),

as the Secretary of State considers appropriate in connection with any provision to which subsection (3) applies or in connection with any scheme or arrangements to which subsection (4) applies.

(2) The persons within this subsection are—

(a) a Minister of the Crown;

(b) a person providing services to, or designated [2 (specifically or by description)] for the purposes of this section by an order of, a Minister of the Crown;

(c) a local authority (within the meaning of the Administration Act); [3 . . .]

[4 (ca) a county council in England; and]

(d) a person providing services to, or authorised to exercise any function of, [5 any authority mentioned in paragraph (c) or (ca)].

(3) This subsection applies to any provision made by or under—

[7 (a) any of sections 2A to 2F and 7A of the Administration Act,]
(b) section 60 of this Act, [8 . . .]
(c) the Jobseekers Act 1995 [9 , [10 . . .]]
[9 (d) Part 1 of the Welfare Reform Act 2007, or]
[6 (e) Part 1 of the Welfare Reform Act 2012.]

(4) This subsection applies to—

(a) any scheme designated by regulations under subsection (1), being a scheme operated by the Secretary of State (whether under arrangements with any other person or not) for any purposes connected with employment or training in the case of persons of a particular category or description;
(b) any arrangements of a description specified in such regulations, being arrangement made by the Secretary of State for any such purposes [14;
(c) any arrangements made by the Scottish Ministers under section 2 of the Employment and Training Act 1973 by virtue of article 2(1) of the Scotland Act 1998 (Transfer of Functions to the Scottish Ministers etc.) Order 2020.]

(5) Regulations under subsection (1) may, in particular, authorise information supplied to a person under the regulations—

(a) to be used for the purpose of amending or supplementing other information held by that person; and
(b) if it is so used, to be supplied to any other person, and used for any purpose, to whom or for which that other information could be supplied or used.

(6) In this section—

"relevant purposes" means purposes connected with—
(a) social security, child support or war pensions, or
(b) employment or training;

"social security information" [11 . . .] means information relating to social security, child support or war pensions and in this subsection "war pensions" means war pensions within the meaning of section 25 of the Social Security Act 1989 (establishment and functions of war pensions committees).

(6A) [12 . . .]

(7) Any reference in this section to [13 information relating to, or purposes connected with, employment or training includes information relating to, or purposes connected with,] the existing or future employment or training prospects or needs of persons, and (in particular) assisting or encouraging persons to enhance their employment prospects.

AMENDMENTS

1. Welfare Reform Act 2009 s.34(4)(a) (January 12, 2010).
2. Welfare Reform Act 2012 s.134(2) (May 8, 2012).
3. Education and Skills Act 2008 Sch.2 para.1 (January 26, 2009).
4. Education and Skills Act 2008 Sch.1(2) para.74(2)(a) (March 30, 2010).
5. Education and Skills Act 2008 Sch.1(2) para.74(2)(b) (March 30, 2010).
6. Universal Credit (Consequential, Supplementary, Incidental and Miscellaneous Provisions) Regulations 2013 (SI 2013/630) reg.15(b) (April 29, 2013).
7. Welfare Reform Act 2009 s.2(5) (November 12, 2009).
8. Welfare Reform Act 2007 Sch.8 para.1 (October 27, 2008).
9. Welfare Reform Act 2007 Sch.3 para.18 (October 27, 2008).

10. Universal Credit (Consequential, Supplementary, Incidental and Miscellaneous Provisions) Regulations 2013 (SI 2013/630) reg.15(a) (April 29, 2013).
11. Welfare Reform Act 2012 s.134(3)(a) (May 8, 2012).
12. Welfare Reform Act 2012 s.134(3)(b) (May 8, 2012).
13. Welfare Reform Act 2009 s.34(4)(b) (January 12, 2010).
14. Scotland Act 1998 (Transfer of Functions to the Scottish Ministers etc.) Order 2020 (SI 2020/276) art.4(1) (March 12, 2020).

Social Security Fraud Act 2001

(2001 c.11)

Arrangement of Sections

Loss of benefit provisions

Loss of benefit provisions

[1 Meaning of "disqualifying benefit" and "sanctionable benefit" for purposes of sections 6B and 7

6A.—(1) In this section and sections 6B and 7— 1.617

"disqualifying benefit" means (subject to any regulations under section 10(1))—

[2 (za) any benefit under Part 1 of the Welfare Reform Act 2012 (universal credit) or under any provision having effect in Northern Ireland corresponding to that Part;]

[5 (zb) state pension or a lump sum under Part 1 of the Pensions Act 2014 or under any provision in Northern Ireland which corresponds to that Part;]

(a) any benefit under the Jobseekers Act 1995 or the Jobseekers (Northern Ireland) Order 1995;

(b) any benefit under the State Pension Credit Act 2002 or the State Pension Credit Act (Northern Ireland) 2002;

(c) any benefit under Part 1 of the Welfare Reform Act 2007 or Part 1 of the Welfare Reform Act (Northern Ireland) 2007 (employment and support allowance);

[4 (ca) any benefit under Part 4 of the Welfare Reform Act 2012 (personal independence payment) or under any provision in Northern Ireland which corresponds to that Part;]

[6 (cb) bereavement support payment under section 30 of the Pensions Act 2014 or under any provision in Northern Ireland which corresponds to that section;]

(d) any benefit under the Social Security Contributions and Benefit Act 1992 or the Social Security Contributions and Benefits (Northern Ireland) Act 1992 other than—

(i) maternity allowance;

(ii) statutory sick pay and statutory maternity pay;

(e) any war pension;

[2 (f) child tax credit;

(g) working tax credit.]

"sanctionable benefit" means (subject to subsection (2) and to any regulations under section 10(1)) any disqualifying benefit other than—

(a) joint-claim jobseeker's allowance;

[5 (aa) state pension or a lump sum under Part 1 of the Pensions Act 2014;]

(b) any retirement pension;

(c) graduated retirement benefit;

[4 (ca) personal independence payment;]

(d) disability living allowance;

(e) attendance allowance;

(f) child benefit;

[3 (fa) child tax credit;

(fb) working tax credit;]

(g) guardian's allowance;

(h) a payment out of the social fund in accordance with Part 8 of the Social Security Contributions and Benefits Act 1992;

(i) a payment under Part 10 of that Act (Christmas bonuses).

(2) In their application to Northern Ireland sections 6B and 7 shall have effect as if references to a sanctionable benefit were references only to a war pension.]

AMENDMENTS

1. Welfare Reform Act 2009 s.24(1) (January 12, 2010 for regulation-making purposes and April 1, 2010 for all other purposes).

2. Welfare Reform Act 2012 ss.31 and 117(1) and (2) and Sch.2 paras 56 and 57 (April 1, 2013).

3. Welfare Reform Act 2012 s.117(1) and (3) (April 6, 2013).

4. Welfare Reform Act 2012 s.91 and Sch.9 paras 45 and 46 (April 8, 2013).

5. Pensions Act 2014 s.23 and Sch.12 paras 39 and 40 (April 6, 2016).

6. Pensions Act 2014 s.31(5) and Sch.16 paras 43 and 44 (April 6, 2017).

DEFINITIONS

"benefit"—see s.13.

"joint-claim jobseeker's allowance—*ibid.*

"war pension"—*ibid.*

GENERAL NOTE

1.618 These definitions were formerly in s.7(8). An offence in connection with a claim for a "disqualifying benefit" is a benefit offence (see s.6B(13)(a)) liable to result in the loss under s.6B or 7 of all or part of a "sanctionable benefit". However, although working tax credit is not a sanctionable benefit for the purposes of this Act, an offence in connection with a claim for a disqualifying benefit will result in a loss of working tax credit under ss.36A–36D of the Tax Credits Act 2002 (see Vol.IV).

Note that regs 19 and 19A of the Social Security (Loss of Benefit) Regulations 2001 supplement this section. Regulation 19 provides that, although they are disqualifying benefits, a bereavement support payment and certain increases of industrial disablement benefit and war pensions for the severely disabled are not sanctionable benefits. Regulation 19A provides that statutory adoption pay, statutory paternity pay and the abolished health in pregnancy grant are neither disqualifying benefits nor sanctionable benefits.

[1 Loss of benefit in case of conviction, penalty or caution for benefit offence

6B.—(1) Subsection (4) applies where a person ("the offender")— 1.619

(a) is convicted of one or more benefit offences in any proceedings,

(b) after being given a notice under subsection (2) of the appropriate penalty provision by an appropriate authority, agrees in the manner specified by the appropriate authority to pay a penalty under the appropriate penalty provision to the appropriate authority [2 . . .], in a case where [2 the offence to which the notice relates] is a benefit offence, or

(c) is cautioned in respect of one or more benefit offences.

(2) In subsection (1)(b)—

(a) "the appropriate penalty provision" means section 115A of the Administration Act (penalty as alternative to prosecution) or section 109A of the Social Security Administration (Northern Ireland) 1992 (the corresponding provision for Northern Ireland);

(b) "appropriate authority" means—

(i) in relation to section 115A of the Administration Act, the Secretary of State or an authority which administers housing benefit or council tax benefit, and

(ii) in relation to section 109A of the Social Security Administration (Northern Ireland) Act 1992, the Department (within the meaning of that Act) or the Northern Ireland Housing Executive.

(3) Subsection (4) does not apply by virtue of subsection (1)(a) if, because the proceedings in which the offender was convicted constitute the [4 current] set of proceedings for the purposes of section 7, the restriction in subsection (2) of that section applies in the offender's case.

(4) If this subsection applies and the offender is a person with respect to whom the conditions for an entitlement to a sanctionable benefit are or become satisfied at any time within the disqualification period, then, even though those conditions are satisfied, the following restrictions shall apply in relation to the payment of that benefit in the offender's case.

(5) Subject to subsections [4 (5A)] to (10), the sanctionable benefit shall not be payable in the offender's case for any period comprised in the disqualification period.

[3 (5A) The Secretary of State may by regulations provide that, where the sanctionable benefit is universal credit, the benefit shall be payable, during the whole or a part of any period comprised in the disqualification period, as if one or more of the following applied—

(a) the amount payable were reduced in such manner as may be prescribed;

(b) the benefit were payable only if there is compliance by the offender with such obligations with respect to the provision of information as may be imposed by the regulations;

(c) the benefit were payable only if the circumstances are otherwise such as may be prescribed;

(d) any amount of the benefit payable in prescribed circumstances were recoverable by the Secretary of State.]

(6) Where the sanctionable benefit is income support, the benefit shall be payable in the offender's case for any period comprised in the disqualification period as if the applicable amount used for the determination under section 124(4) of the Social Security Contributions and Benefits Act 1992 of the amount of the offender's entitlement for that period were reduced in such manner as may be prescribed.

(7) The Secretary of State may by regulations provide that, where the sanctionable benefit is jobseeker's allowance, any income-based jobseeker's allowance shall be payable, during the whole or a part of any period comprised in the disqualification period, as if one or more of the following applied—

(a) the rate of the allowance were such reduced rate as may be prescribed;

(b) the allowance were payable only if there is compliance by the offender with such obligations with respect to the provision of information as may be imposed by the regulations;

(c) the allowance were payable only if the circumstances are otherwise such as may be prescribed.

(8) The Secretary of State may by regulations provide that, where the sanctionable benefit is state pension credit, the benefit shall be payable in the offender's case for any period comprised in the disqualification period as if the rate of the benefit were reduced in such manner as may be prescribed.

(9) The Secretary of State may by regulations provide that, where the sanctionable benefit is employment and support allowance, any income-related allowance shall be payable, during the whole or a part of any period comprised in the disqualification period, as if one or more of the following applied—

(a) the rate of the allowance were such reduced rate as may be prescribed;

(b) the allowance were payable only if there is compliance by the offender with such obligations with respect to the provision of information as may be imposed by the regulations;

(c) the allowance were payable only if the circumstances are otherwise such as may be prescribed.

(10) The Secretary of State may by regulations provide that, where the sanctionable benefit is housing benefit or council tax benefit, the benefit shall be payable, during the whole or a part of any period comprised in the disqualification period, as if one or more of the following applied—

(a) the rate of the benefit were reduced in such manner as may be prescribed;

(b) the benefit were payable only if the circumstances are such as may be prescribed.

(11) For the purposes of this section the disqualification period, in relation to any disqualifying event, means [5 the relevant period] beginning with such date, falling after the date of the disqualifying event, as may be determined by or in accordance with regulations made by the Secretary of State.

[5 (11A) For the purposes of subsection (11) the relevant period is—

(a) in a case falling within subsection (1)(a) where the benefit offence, or one of them, is a relevant offence, the period of three years,

(b) in a case falling within subsection (1)(a) (but not within paragraph (a) above), the period of 13 weeks, or

(c) in a case falling within subsection (1)(b) or (c), the period of four weeks.]

(12) This section has effect subject to section 6C.

(13) In this section and section 6C—

"benefit offence" means—

(a) any post-commencement offence in connection with a claim for a disqualifying benefit;

(b) any post-commencement offence in connection with the receipt or payment of any amount by way of such a benefit;

(c) any post-commencement offence committed for the purpose of facilitating the commission (whether or not by the same person) of a benefit offence;

(d) any post-commencement offence consisting in an attempt or conspiracy to commit a benefit offence;

"disqualifying event" means the conviction falling within subsection (1)(a), the agreement falling within subsection (1)(b) or the caution falling within subsection (1)(c);

"post-commencement offence" means any criminal offence committed after the commencement of this section.]

[4 (14) In this section and section 7 "relevant offence" means—

(a) in England and Wales, the common law offence of conspiracy to defraud, or

(b) a prescribed offence which, in the offender's case, is committed in such circumstances as may be prescribed, and which, on conviction—

  (i) is found by the court to relate to an overpayment (as defined in section 115A(8) of the Administration Act) of at least £50,000,

  (ii) is punished by a custodial sentence of at least one year (including a suspended sentence as defined in [6 section 286(6) of the Sentencing Code], or

  (iii) is found by the court to have been committed over a period of at least two years.]

[5 (15) The Secretary of State may by order amend subsection (11A) (a), (b) or (c), or (14)(b)(i), (ii) or (iii) to substitute a different period or amount for that for the time being specified there.]

AMENDMENTS

1. Welfare Reform Act 2009 s.24(1) (January 12, 2010 for regulation-making purposes and April 1 2010 for all other purposes).

2. Welfare Reform Act 2012 s.113(8)(a) (May 8, 2012).

3. Welfare Reform Act 2012 s.31 Sch.2 paras 56 and 58(1) and (3) (February 25, 2013).

4. Welfare Reform Act 2012 s.118(1), (2) and (5) (February 25, 2013 for regulation-making purposes and April 1, 2013 for other purposes).

5. Welfare Reform Act 2012 ss.31 and 118(1)–(6), and 119(1) and (2) and Sch.2 paras 56, 58(1) and (2) (April 1, 2013).

6. Sentencing Act 2000 s.410 and Sch.24 para.177 (December 1, 2020).

DEFINITIONS

"appropriate penalty provision"—see subs.(2)
"appropriate authority—*ibid.*
"benefit"—see s.13.
"benefit offence"—see subs.(13).
"caution"—see s.13.
"disqualification period"—see subs.(11).
"disqualifying benefit"—see s.6A(1).
"disqualifying event"—see subs.(13).
"income-based jobseeker's allowance—by virtue of s.13, see s.1(4) of the Jobseeker's Act 1995.
"income-related allowance" – *ibid.*
"post-commencement offence" – see subs.(13).
"prescribed" – see s.11(1).
"relevant offence"–see subs.(14).
"sanctionable benefit" – see s.6A.
"state pension credit" – see s.13.

GENERAL NOTE

1.620 This section was introduced in 2010 to extend the loss-of-benefit provisions, which already applied to second convictions by virtue of s.7, to first convictions and, like the amended s.7, to offences in respect of which a penalty has been imposed or the offender has been cautioned. Under subs.(11) as originally enacted, the loss of benefit for an offence not falling within the five-year period following a previous conviction that leads to a loss of benefit under s.7 was for only four weeks, whereas the loss of benefit under s.7 was for 13 weeks. Since April 1, 2013, the loss of benefit has been three years if the offence is sufficiently serious to fall within subs.(14) (whether or not the offence is a first offence) and 13 weeks for other benefit offences of which the claimant is actually convicted but to which s.7 does not apply. Four weeks remains the period only for benefit offences that are not within the scope of s.7 and in respect of which the claimant accepts an alternative penalty (see subs.(2)) or has been cautioned. (DWP policy is no longer to give cautions and s.121 of the Welfare Reform Act 2012 will remove all references to cautions in this Act if and when it is brought into force.) Income-related benefits are paid at a reduced rate during the relevant period (see subss.(6)–(10)). Other benefits are not paid at all (see subs.(5)).

Subsection (3) prevents an offence being taken into account twice.

For regulations made under this section, see the Social Security (Loss of Benefit) Regulations 2001.

Section 6C makes provision for cases where a conviction is quashed or a penalty is withdrawn and makes it clear that convictions include certain cases where a defendant is absolutely of conditionally discharged. It also makes it clear that the date of conviction is the date on which a person is found guilty, even if he or she is sentenced later.

The words "or an authority which administers housing benefit or council tax benefit" in subs.(2)(b)(i) and the whole of subss.(6), (7), (9) and (10) have formally been repealed with effect from April 1, 2013 in so far as they apply to council tax benefit, subject to a saving (Welfare Reform Act 2012 s.147 and Pt 1 of Sch.14; Welfare Reform Act 2012 (Commencement No.8 and Savings and Transitional Provisions) Order 2013 (SI 2013/358), arts. 8(c) and 9 and Sch.4).

[1 Section 6B: supplementary provisions

6C.—(1) Where— 1.621

(a) the conviction of any person of any offence is taken into account for the purposes of the application of section 6B in relation to that person, and

(b) that conviction is subsequently quashed,

all such payments and other adjustments shall be made as would be necessary if no restriction had been imposed by or under section 6B that could not have been imposed if the conviction had not taken place.

(2) Where, after the agreement of any person ("P") to pay a penalty under the appropriate penalty provision is taken into account for the purposes of the application of section 6B in relation to that person—

(a) P's agreement to pay the penalty is withdrawn under subsection (5) of the appropriate penalty provision, or

(b) it is decided on an appeal or in accordance with regulations under the Social Security Act 1998 or the Social Security (Northern Ireland) Order 1998 that [3 any overpayment made] to which the agreement relates is not recoverable or due,

all such payments and other adjustments shall be made as would be necessary if no restriction had been imposed by or under section 6B that could not have been imposed if P had not agreed to pay the penalty.

(3) Where, after the agreement ("the old agreement") of any person ("P") to pay a penalty under the appropriate penalty provision is taken into account for the purposes of the application of section 6B in relation to P, the amount of [3 any overpayment made] to which the penalty relates is revised on an appeal or in accordance with regulations under the Social Security Act 1998 or the Social Security (Northern Ireland) Order 1998—

(a) section 6B shall cease to apply by virtue of the old agreement, and

(b) subsection (4) shall apply.

(4) Where this subsection applies—

(a) if there is a new disqualifying event consisting of—

(i) P's agreement to pay a penalty under the appropriate penalty provision in relation to the revised overpayment, or

(ii) P being cautioned in relation to the offence to which the old agreement relates,

the disqualification period relating to the new disqualifying event shall be reduced by the number of days in so much of the disqualification period relating to the old agreement as had expired when section 6B ceased to apply by virtue of the old agreement, and

(b) in any other case, all such payments and other adjustments shall be made as would be necessary if no restriction had been imposed by or under section 6B that could not have been imposed if P had not agreed to pay the penalty.

(5) For the purposes of section 6B—

(a) the date of a person's conviction in any proceedings of a benefit offence shall be taken to be the date on which the person was found guilty of that offence in those proceedings (whenever the person was sentenced) or in the case mentioned in paragraph (b)(ii) the date of the order for absolute discharge; and

(b) references to a conviction include references to—

(i) a conviction in relation to which the court makes an order for absolute or conditional discharge [2 ...],
(ii) an order for absolute discharge made by a court of summary jurisdiction in Scotland under section 246(3) of the Criminal Procedure (Scotland) Act 1995 without proceeding to a conviction, and
(iii) a conviction in Northern Ireland.

(6) In this section "the appropriate penalty provision" has the meaning given by section 6B(2)(a).]

AMENDMENTS

1. Welfare Reform Act 2009 s.24(1) (January 12, 2010 for regulation-making purposes and April 1, 2010 for all other purposes).

2. Criminal Justice and Licensing (Scotland) Act 2010 (asp 13) Sch.2 para.45(1) and (2) (February 1, 2011, in relation to Scotland); Criminal Justice and Licensing (Scotland) Act 2010 (Consequential Provisions and Modifications) Order 2011 (SI 2011/2298) Sch.4 para.13(1) and (2) (September 16, 2011, in relation to England and Wales).

3. Welfare Reform Act 2012 s.113(8)(b) (May 8, 2012).

GENERAL NOTE

1.622 Subsection (1) makes provision for cases where a conviction has been quashed, subss.(2)–(4) make provision for cases where a penalty is withdrawn, including cases where a new penalty or caution is put in its place, and subs.(5) clarifies the scope of the term "conviction".

Loss of benefit for [4 [7 repeated benefit fraud]]

1.623 7.—(1) If—

[7(a) a person ("the offender") is convicted of one or more benefit offences in a set of proceedings ("the current set of proceedings"),
(b) within the period of five years ending on the date on which the benefit offence was, or any of them were, committed, one or more disqualifying events occurred in relation to the offender (the event, or the most recent of them, being referred to in this section as "the earlier disqualifying event"),
(c) the current set of proceedings has not been taken into account for the purposes of any previous application of this section or section 8 or 9 in relation to the offender or any person who was then a member of his family,
(d) the earlier disqualifying event has not been taken into account as an earlier disqualifying event for the purposes of any previous application of this section or either of those sections in relation to the offender or any person who was then a member of his family, and
(e) the offender is a person with respect to whom the conditions for an entitlement to a sanctionable benefit are or become satisfied at any time within the disqualification period,]

then, even though those conditions are satisfied, the following restrictions shall apply in relation to the payment of that benefit in the offender's case.

[7 (1A) The following restrictions do not apply if the benefit offence referred to in subsection (1)(a), or any of them, is a relevant offence.]

(2) Subject to subsections [7 (2A)] to (5), the sanctionable benefit shall not be payable in the offender's case for any period comprised in the disqualification period.

[6 (2A)The Secretary of State may by regulations provide that, where the sanctionable benefit is universal credit, the benefit shall be payable, during the whole or a part of any period comprised in the disqualification period, as if one or more of the following applied—

(a) the amount payable were reduced in such manner as may be prescribed;

(b) the benefit were payable only if there is compliance by the offender with such obligations with respect to the provision of information as may be imposed by the regulations;

(c) the benefit were payable only if the circumstances are otherwise such as may be prescribed;

(d) any amount of the benefit payable in prescribed circumstances were recoverable by the Secretary of State.]

(3) Where the sanctionable benefit is income support, the benefit shall be payable in the offender's case for any period comprised in the disqualification period as if the applicable amount used for the determination under section 124(4) of the Social Security Contributions and Benefits Act 1992 of the amount of the offender's entitlement for that period were reduced in such a manner as may be prescribed.

(4) The Secretary of State may by regulations provide that, where the sanctionable benefit is jobseeker's allowance, any income-based jobseeker's allowance shall be payable, during the whole or a part of any period comprised in the disqualification period, as if one or more of the following applied—

(a) the rate of the allowance were such reduced rate as may be prescribed;

(b) the allowance were payable only if there is compliance by the offender with such obligations with respect to the provision of information as may be imposed by the regulations;

(c) the allowance were payable only if the circumstances are otherwise such as may be prescribed.

[1 (4A) The Secretary of State may be regulations provide that, where the sanctionable benefit is state pension credit, the benefit shall be payable in the offender's case for any period comprised in the disqualification period as if the rate of benefit were reduced in such manner as may be prescribed.]

[3 (4B) The Secretary of State may by regulations provide that, where the sanctionable benefit is employment and support allowance, any income-related allowance shall be payable, during the whole or a part of any period comprised in the disqualification period, as if one or more of the following applied—

(a) the rate of the allowance were such reduced rate as may be prescribed;

(b) the allowance were payable only if there is compliance by the offender with such obligations with respect to the provision of information as may be imposed by the regulations;

(c) the allowance were payable only if the circumstances are otherwise such as may be prescribed.]

(5) The Secretary of State may by regulations provide that, where the sanctionable benefit is housing benefit or council tax benefit, the benefit shall be payable, during the whole or a part of any period comprised in the disqualification period, as if one or both of the following applied—

(a) the rate of the benefit were reduced in such manner as may be prescribed;
(b) the benefit were payable only if the circumstances are such as may be prescribed.

(6) For the purposes of this section the disqualification period, [7 in an offender's case, means the relevant period beginning with a prescribed date falling after the date of the conviction in the current set of proceedings.]

[7 (6A) For the purposes of subsection (6) the relevant period is—
(a) in a case where, within the period of five years ending on the date on which the earlier disqualifying event occurred, a previous disqualifying event occurred in relation to the offender, the period of three years;
(b) in any other case, 26 weeks.]

(7) Where—
(a) the conviction of any person of any offence is taken into account for the purposes of the application of this section in relation to that person, and
(b) that conviction is subsequently quashed,

all such payments and other adjustments shall be made as would be necessary if no restriction had been imposed by or under this section that could not have been imposed if the conviction had not taken place.

[7 (7A) Subsection (7B) applies where, after the agreement of any person ("P") to pay a penalty under the appropriate penalty provision is taken into account for the purposes of the application of this section in relation to that person—
(a) P's agreement to pay the penalty is withdrawn under subsection (5) of the appropriate penalty provision,
(b) it is decided on an appeal or in accordance with regulations under the Social Security Act 1998 or the Social Security (Northern Ireland) Order 1998 (S.I. 1998/1506 (N.I. 10)) that any overpayment to which the agreement relates is not recoverable or due, or
(c) the amount of any overpayment to which the penalty relates is revised on an appeal or in accordance with regulations under the Social Security Act 1998 or the Social Security (Northern Ireland) Order 1998 and there is no new agreement by P to pay a penalty under the appropriate penalty provision in relation to the revised overpayment.

(7B) In those circumstances, all such payments and other adjustments shall be made as would be necessary if no restriction had been imposed by or under this section that could not have been imposed if P had not agreed to pay the penalty.]

(8) In this section—

[7 "appropriate penalty provision" has the meaning given in section 6B(2)(a);]

"benefit offence" means—
(a) any post-commencement offence in connection with a claim for a disqualifying benefit;
(b) any post-commencement offence in connection with the receipt or payment of any amount by way of such a benefit;
(c) any post-commencement offence committed for the purpose of facilitating the commission (whether or not by the same person) of a benefit offence;

(d) any post-commencement offence consisting in an attempt or conspiracy to commit a benefit offence;

[4 . . .]

[7 "disqualifying event" has the meaning given in section 6B(13);]

[4 "post-commencement offence" means an offence committed on or after 1 April 2002 (the day on which this section came into force).]

[4 . . .]

[7 (8A)Where a person is convicted of more than one benefit offence in the same set of proceedings, there is to be only one disqualifying event in respect of that set of proceedings for the purposes of this section and—

(a) subsection (1)(b) is satisfied if any of the convictions take place in the five year periods mentioned there;

(b) the event is taken into account for the purposes of subsection (1)(d) if any of the convictions have been taken into account as mentioned there;

(c) in the case of the earlier disqualifying event mentioned in subsection (6A)(a), the reference there to the date on which the earlier disqualifying event occurred is a reference to the date on which any of the convictions take place;

(d) in the case of the previous disqualifying event mentioned in subsection (6A)(a), that provision is satisfied if any of the convictions take place in the five year period mentioned there.]

(9) For the purposes of this section—

(a) the date of a person's conviction in any proceedings of a benefit offence shall be taken to be the date on which he was found guility of that offence in those proceedings (whenever he was sentenced [4 or in the case mentioned in paragraph (b)(ii) the date of the order for absolute discharge]); and

(b) [4 references to a conviction include references to—

(i) a conviction in relation to which the court makes an order for absolute or conditional discharge [5 . . .],

(ii) an order for absolute discharge made by a court of summary jurisdiction in Scotland under section 246(3) of the Criminal Procedure (Scotland) Act 1995 without proceeding to a conviction, and

(iii) a conviction in Northern Ireland.]

(10) In this section references to any previous application of this section or section 8 or 9—

(a) include references to any previous application of a provision having an effect in Northern Ireland corresponding to provision made by this section, or either of those sections; but

(b) do not include references to any previous application of this section, or of either of those sections, the effect of which was to impose a restriction for a period comprised in the same disqualification period.

[7 (10A)The Secretary of State may by order amend subsection (6A) to substitute different periods for those for the time being specified there.

(10B) An order under subsection (10A) may provide for different periods to apply according to the type of earlier disqualifying event or events occurring in any case.]

(11) [4 . . .].

AMENDMENTS

1. State Pension Credit Act 2002 Sch.2 para.45 (July 2, 2002 for the purpose of exercising any power to make regulations or orders and October 6, 2003 for other purposes).

2. Welfare Reform Act 2007 s.49(1), (April 1, 2008, subject to a saving (see note below)).

3. Welfare Reform Act 2007 Sch. para.23(1)–(3) (March 18, 2008 for regulation-making purposes and October 27, 2008 for other purposes).

4. Welfare Reform Act 2009 Sch.4 para.2 (January 12, 2010 for regulation-making purposes and April 1, 2010 for all other purposes).

5. Criminal Justice and Licensing (Scotland) Act 2010 (asp 13) Sch.2 para.45(1) and (3) (February 1, 2011, in relation to Scotland); Criminal Justice and Licensing (Scotland) Act 2010 (Consequential Provisions and Modifications) Order 2011 (SI 2011/2298) Sch.4 para.13(1) and (3) (September 16, 2011, in relation to England and Wales).

6. Welfare Reform Act 2012 s.31 Sch.2 paras.56 and 59(1) and (3) (February 25, 2013).

7. Welfare Reform Act 2012 ss.31 and 118(1) and (7), and 119(3)–(11) and Sch.2 paras 56, 59(1) and (2) (April 1, 2013).

DEFINITIONS

"appropriate penalty provision"–see subs.(8).
"benefit"—see s.13.
"benefit offence"—see subs.(8).
"disqualification period"—see subs.(6).
"disqualifying benefit"—see s.6A(1).
"disqualifying event"–see subs.(8).
"family"—by virtue of s.13, see s.137(1) of the Social Security Contributions and Benefits Act 1992.
"income-based jobseeker's allowance"—by virtue of s.13, see s.1(4) of the Jobseekers Act 1995.
"joint-claim jobseeker's allowance"—*ibid.*
"offender"—see subs.(1).
"post-commencement offence"—see subs.(8).
"prescribed"—see s.11(1).
"relevant offence"–see s.6B(14).
"sanctionable benefit"—see s.6A.
"state pension credit"—see s.13.
"war pension"—by virtue of s.13, see s.25 of the Social Security Act 1989.

GENERAL NOTE

1.624 As originally enacted, this Act provided for the loss of a "sanctionable benefit" for 13 weeks if the claimant, having been convicted of a benefit offence, was subsequently convicted of another benefit offence committed within three years of the date of the earlier conviction. There was no loss of benefit for first offences or offences more than three years after a previous conviction for a benefit offence. Since then, these provisions have steadily become more draconian. A period of five years was substituted for the period of three years in 2008. Section 6B, providing for a loss of benefit for four weeks for first offences and other benefit offences not within the scope of this section was introduced in 2010. From April 1, 2013, the amount of loss of benefit is substantially increased. Section 6B now makes provision for the loss of three years' benefit in respect of offences sufficiently serious to be a "relevant offence" within s.6B(14), whether or not they are first or subsequent offences (since s.7 does not apply by virtue of subs.(1A)). It also continues to make provision for the loss of benefit following other benefit offences that do not fall within the scope of s.7, but the loss where a person has been convicted—as opposed to having accepted an alternative penalty or caution—has been increased to 13 weeks.

Section 7 continues to provide for the loss of benefit where a claimant commits a further benefit offence (other than a serious "relevant offence") within five years of having been convicted of another benefit offence—the date of conviction being the date on which the claimant was found guilty even if sentence was passed later (see subs.(9)(a)). The loss of benefit is now ordinarily for 26 weeks but it is for three years if the benefit offence is committed within five years of a conviction for a previous benefit offence which was itself committed within five years of yet an earlier benefit offence (see subs.(6A)). For these purposes, absolute or conditional discharges count as convictions (subs.(9)(b)) and acceptance of an alternative penalty or a caution has the same effect as a conviction because they are all "disqualifying events" within the scope of s.6B(13). However, several convictions in one set of proceedings count only as a single disqualifying event (subs.(8A)). Subsection (1)(c) and (d) are intended to prevent double-counting and subs.(7)–(7B) make provision for adjustments following the quashing of convictions or the cancelling of penalties.

Income-related benefits are paid at a reduced rate during the relevant period (under regulations made under subss.(2A–(5)) and other benefits are withheld altogether (subs.(2)).

For regulations made under this section, see the Social Security (Loss of Benefit) Regulations 2001.

The words "8 or" in subs.(10) and the whole of subss.(3), (4), (4B) and (5) have formally been repealed with effect from April 1, 2013 in so far as they apply to council tax benefit, subject to a saving (Welfare Reform Act 2012 s.147 and Pt 1 of Sch.14; Welfare Reform Act 2012 (Commencement No.8 and Savings and Transitional Provisions) Order 2013 (SI 2013/358) arts 8(c) and 9 and Sch.4).

Effect of offence on joint-claim jobseeker's allowance

8.—(1) Subsections (2) and (3) shall have effect, subject to the other provisions of this section, where— **1.625**

(a) the conditions for the entitlement of any joint-claim couple to a joint-claim jobseeker's allowance are or become satisfied at any time; and

(b) [3 an offence-related restriction] would apply in the case of at least one of the members of the couple if the entitlement were an entitlement of that member to a sanctionable benefit.

[3 (1A) In this section—

(a) "an offence-related restriction" means the restriction in subsection (5) of section 6B or the restriction in subsection (2) of section 7, and

(b) in relation to an offence-related restriction, any reference to the relevant period is a reference to a period which is the disqualification period for the purposes of section 6B or section 7, as the case requires.]

(2) [5 Except in prescribed circumstances] the allowance shall not be payable in the couple's case for so much of any period comprised in [3 the relevant period] as is a period for which—

(a) in the case of each of the members of the couple, [1 an offence-related restriction] would apply if the entitlement were an entitlement of that member to a sanctionable benefit; [2 ...]

(b) [3 an offence-related restriction] would so apply in the case of one of the members of the couple and the other member of the couple—

(i) [5 is a person whose failure sanctionable under section 19, 19A or 19B of the Jobseekers Act 1995 has given rise to a reduction under that section; or]; [2 ...]

(ii) [2 ...]

(3) For any part of any period comprised in [3 the relevant period] for which subsection (2) does not apply, the allowance—

(a) shall be payable in the couple's case as if the amount of the allowance were reduced to an amount calculated using the method prescribed for the purposes of this subsection; but

(b) shall be payable only to the member of the couple who is not the person by reference to whose [3 conduct section 6B or 7] would apply.

(4) The Secretary of State may by regulations provide in relation to cases to which subsection (2) would otherwise apply that joint-claim jobseeker's allowance shall be payable in a couple's case, during the whole or a part of so much of any period comprised in [3 the relevant period] as falls within paragraph (a) or (b) of that subsection, as if one or more of the following applied—

(a) the rate of the allowance were such reduced rate as may be prescribed;

(b) the allowance were payable only if there is compliance by each of the members of the couple with such obligations with respect to the provision of information as may be imposed by the regulations;

(c) the allowance were payable only if the circumstances were otherwise such as may be prescribed.

(5) [5 . . .]

(6) Where—

(a) the conviction of any member of a couple for any offence is taken into account for the purposes of the application of this section in relation to that couple, and

(b) that conviction is subsequently quashed,

all such payments and other adjustments shall be made as would be necessary if no restriction had been imposed by or under this section that could not have been imposed had the conviction not taken place.

[3 (7) Where, after the agreement of any member of a couple ("M") to pay a penalty under the appropriate penalty provision is taken into account for the purposes of any restriction imposed by virtue of any regulations under this section—

(a) M's agreement to pay the penalty is withdrawn under subsection (5) of the appropriate penalty provision, or

(b) it is decided on an appeal or in accordance with regulations under the Social Security Act 1998 or the Social Security (Northern Ireland) Order 1998 that [4 any overpayment made] to which the agreement relates is not recoverable or due,

all such payments and other adjustments shall be made as would be necessary if no restriction had been imposed by or under this section that could not have been imposed had M not agreed to pay the penalty.

(8) Where, after the agreement ("the old agreement") of any member of a couple ("M") to pay a penalty under the appropriate penalty provision is taken into account for the purposes of any restriction imposed by virtue of any regulations under this section, the amount of [4 any overpayment made] to which the penalty relates is revised on an appeal or in accordance

with regulations under the Social Security Act 1998 or the Social Security (Northern Ireland) Order 1998—

(a) if there is a new disqualifying event for the purposes of section 6B consisting of M's agreement to pay a penalty under the appropriate penalty provision in relation to the revised overpayment or M being cautioned in relation to the offence to which the old agreement relates, the new disqualification period for the purposes of section 6B falls to be determined in accordance with section 6C(4)(a), and

(b) in any other case, all such payments and other adjustments shall be made as would be necessary if no restriction had been imposed by or under this section that could not have been imposed had M not agreed to pay the penalty.

(9) In this section "the appropriate penalty provision" has the meaning given by section 6B(2)(a).]

AMENDMENTS

1. Welfare Reform Act 2009 s.1(5) (November 12, 2009).
2. Welfare Reform Act 2009 Sch.7 (March 22, 2010).
3. Welfare Reform Act 2009 Sch.4 para.3 (January 12, 2010 for regulation-making purposes and April 1, 2010 for all other purposes).
4. Welfare Reform Act 2012 s.113(8)(b) (May 8, 2012).
5. Welfare Reform Act 2012 s.48 and Sch.7 para.12 (October 22, 2102).

DEFINITIONS

"joint-claim couple"—by virtue of s.13, see s.1(4) of the Jobseekers Act 1995.
"joint-claim jobseeker's allowance"—*ibid.*
"prescribed"—see s.11(1).
"sanctionable benefit"—see s.6A.
"the appropriate penalty provision"—see subs.(9).

Effect of offence on benefits for members of offender's family

9.—(1) This section applies to— 1.626

[5 (za) universal credit;]
(a) income support;
(b) jobseeker's allowance;
[1 (bb) state pension credit;]
[2(bc) employment and support allowance]
(c) housing benefit; and
(d) council tax benefit.

(2) The Secretary of State may by regulations make provision in accordance with the following provisions of this section in relation to any case in which—

(a) the conditions for entitlement to any benefit to which this section applies are or become satisfied in the case of any person ("the offender's family member");

(b) that benefit falls to be paid in that person's case for the whole or any part of a period comprised in a period ("the relevant period") which is the disqualification period in relation to restrictions imposed under [3 section 6B or 7] in the case of a member of that person's family; [5 and]

(c) that member of that family ("the offender") is a person by reference to whom—
   (i) the conditions for the entitlement of the offender's family member to the benefit in question are satisfied; or
   (ii) the amount of benefit payable in the case of the offender's family member would fall (apart from any provision made under this section) to be determined.

[[5] (2A) In relation to cases in which the benefit is universal credit, the provision that may be made by virtue of subsection (2) is provision that, in the case of the offender's family member, any universal credit shall be payable, during the whole or a part of any period comprised in the relevant period, as if one or more of the following applied—

(a) the amount payable were reduced in such manner as may be prescribed;

(b) the benefit were payable only if there is compliance by the offender or the offender's family member, or both of them, with such obligations with respect to the provision of information as may be imposed by the regulations;

(c) the benefit were payable only if the circumstances are otherwise such as may be prescribed;

(d) any amount of the benefit payable in prescribed circumstances were recoverable by the Secretary of State.]

(3) In relation to cases in which the benefit is income support, the provision that may be made by virtue of subsection (2) is provision that, in the case of the offender's family member, the benefit shall be payable for the whole or any part of any period comprised in the relevant period as if the applicable amount used for the determination under section 124(4) of the Social Security Contributions and Benefits Act 1992 of the amount of the offender's entitlement for that period were reduced in such manner as may be prescribed.

(4) In relation to cases in which the benefit is jobseeker's allowance, the provision that may be made by virtue of subsection (2) is provision that, in the case of the offender's family member, any income-based jobseeker's allowance shall be payable, during the whole or a part of any period comprised in the relevant period, as if one or more of the following applied—

(a) the rate of the allowance were such reduced rate as may be prescribed;

(b) the allowance were payable only if there is compliance by the offender or the offender's family member, or both of them, with such obligations with respect to the provision of information as may be imposed by the regulations;

(c) the allowance were payable only if the circumstances are otherwise such as may be prescribed.

[[1] (4A) In relation to cases in which the benefit is state pension credit, the provision that may be made by virtue of subsection (2) is provision that, in the case of the offender's family member, the benefit shall be payable for the whole or any part of any period comprised in the relevant period as if the rate of the benefit were reduced in such manner as may be prescribed.]

[[2] (4B) In relation to cases in which the benefit is employment and support allowance, the provision that may be made by virtue of subsection

(2) is provision that, in the case of the offender's family member, any income-related allowance shall be payable, during the whole or a part of any period comprised in the relevant period, as if one or more of the following applied—

(a) the rate of the allowance were such reduced rate as may be prescribed;

(b) the allowance were payable only if there is compliance by the offender or the offender's family member, or both of them, with such obligations with respect to the provision of information as may be imposed by the regulations;

(c) the allowance were payable only if circumstances are otherwise such as may be prescribed.]

(5) In relation to cases in which the benefit is housing benefit or council tax benefit, the provision that may be made by virtue of subsection (2) is provision that, in the case of the offender's family member, the benefit shall be payable, during the whole or a part of any period comprised in the relevant period, as if one or both of the following applied—

(a) the rate of the benefit were reduced in such manner as may be prescribed;

(b) the benefit were payable only if the circumstances are such as may be prescribed.

(6) Where—

(a) the conviction of any member of a person's family for any offence is taken into account for the purposes of any restriction imposed by virtue of any regulations under this section, and

(b) that conviction is subsequently quashed,

all such payments and other adjustments shall be made in that person's case as would be necessary if no restriction had been imposed that could not have been imposed had the conviction not taken place.

[[3] (7) Where, after the agreement of any member of a person's family ("M") to pay a penalty under the appropriate penalty provision is taken into account for the purposes of any restriction imposed by virtue of any regulations under this section—

(a) M's agreement to pay the penalty is withdrawn under subsection (5) of the appropriate penalty provision, or

(b) it is decided on an appeal or in accordance with regulations under the Social Security Act 1998 or the Social Security (Northern Ireland) Order 1998 that [[4] any overpayment made] to which the agreement relates is not recoverable or due,

all such payments and other adjustments shall be made as would be necessary if no restriction had been imposed that could not have been imposed had M not agreed to pay the penalty.

(8) Where, after the agreement ("the old agreement") of any member of a person's family ("M") to pay a penalty under the appropriate penalty provision is taken into account for the purposes of any restriction imposed by virtue of any regulations under this section, the amount of [[4] any overpayment made] to which the penalty relates is revised on an appeal or in accordance with regulations under the Social Security Act 1998 or the Social Security (Northern Ireland) Order 1998—

(a) if there is a new disqualifying event for the purposes of section 6B consisting of M's agreement to pay a penalty under the appropriate penalty provision in relation to the revised overpayment or

M being cautioned in relation to the offence to which the old agreement relates, the new disqualification period for the purposes of section 6B falls to be determined in accordance with section 6C(4)(a), and

(b) in any other case, all such payments and other adjustments shall be made as would be necessary if no restriction had been imposed by or under this section that could not have been imposed had M not agreed to pay the penalty.

(9) In this section "the appropriate penalty provision" has the meaning given by section 6B(2)(a).]

AMENDMENTS

1. State Pension Credit Act 2002 Sch.2 para.46 (July 2, 2002 for the purpose of exercising any power to make regulations or orders and October 6, 2003 for other purposes).

2. Welfare Reform Act 2007 Sch.3 para.23(1), (4) and (5) (March 18, 2008 for regulation-making purposes and October 27, 2008 for other purposes).

3. Welfare Reform Act 2009 Sch.4 para.4 (January 12, 2010 for regulation-making purposes and April 1, 2010 for all other purposes).

4. Welfare Reform Act 2012 s.113(8)(b) (May 8, 2012).

5. Welfare Reform Act 2012 s.31 Sch.2 paras 56 and 61(1)–(4) (February 25, 2013).

DEFINITIONS

"benefit"—see s.13.

"disqualifying benefit"—see s.6A(1).

"family"—by virtue of s.13, see s.137(1) of the Social Security Contributions and Benefits Act 1992.

"income-based jobseeker's allowance"—by virtue of s.13, see s.1(4) of the Jobseekers Act 1995.

"the offender"—see subs.(2)(c).

"the offender's family member"—see subs.(2)(a).

"prescribed"—see s.11(1).

"the appropriate penalty provision"–see subs.(9).

"the relevant period"—see subs.(2)(b).

"state pension credit"—see s.13.

GENERAL NOTE

1.627 This section allows the loss of benefit to be incurred by another member of the offender's family where that other person is claiming an income-related benefit that takes account of the offender's membership of the family.

Subsections (1)(a), (b), (bc), (c) and (d), (3), (4), (4B) and (5) have formally been repealed with effect from April 1, 2013 in so far as they apply to council tax benefit, subject to a saving (Welfare Reform Act 2012 s.147 and Pt 1 of Sch.14; Welfare Reform Act 2012 (Commencement No.8 and Savings and Transitional Provisions) Order 2013 (SI 2013/358) arts 8(c) and 9 and Sch.4).

Power to supplement and mitigate loss of benefit provisions

1.628 **10.**—(1) The Secretary of State may by regulations provide for any social security benefit to be treated for the purposes of [3 sections 6A to 9] —

(a) as a disqualifying benefit but not a sanctionable benefit; or

(b) as neither a sanctionable benefit nor a disqualifying benefit.

(2) The Secretary of State may by regulations provide for any restriction in section [[3]6B,] 7, 8 or 9 not to apply in relation to payments of benefit to the extent of any deduction that (if any payment were made) would fall, in pursuance of provision made by or under any enactment, to be made from the payments and paid to a person other than the offender or, as the case may be, a member of his family.

(3) In this section "social security benefit" means—

(a) any benefit under the Social Security Contributions and Benefits Act 1992 or the Social Security Contributions and Benefits (Northern Ireland) Act 1992; [[1] . . .]

(b) any benefit under the Jobseekers Act 1995 or the Jobseekers (Northern Ireland) Order 1995 (S.I. 1995/2705 (N.I. 15));

[[1] (bb) any benefit under the State Pension Credit Act 2002 or under any provision having effect in Northern Ireland corresponding to that Act; or]

[[2] (bc) any benefit under Part 1 of the Welfare Reform Act 2007 (employment and support allowance) or under any provision having effect in Northern Ireland corresponding to that Part;]

[[4] (bd) any benefit under Part 1 of the Welfare Reform Act 2012 (universal credit) or under any provision having effect in Northern Ireland corresponding to that Part;]

[[5] (be) any benefit under Part 4 of the Welfare Reform Act 2012 (personal independence payment) or under any provision in Northern Ireland which corresponds to that Part;]

[[6] (bf) state pension or a lump sum under Part 1 of the Pensions Act 2014 or under any provision in Northern Ireland which corresponds to that Part;]

[[7] (bg) bereavement support payment under section 30 of the Pensions Act 2014 or under any provision in Northern Ireland which corresponds to that section;]

(c) any war pension.

AMENDMENTS

1. State Pension Credit Act 2002 Sch.2 para.47 and Sch.3 (July 2, 2002 for the purpose of exercising any power to make regulations or orders and October 6, 2003 for other purposes).

2. Welfare Reform Act 2007 Sch. para.23(1) and (6) (March 18, 2008 for regulation-making purposes and October 27, 2008 for other purposes).

3. Welfare Reform Act 2009 Sch.4 para.5 (January 12, 2010 for regulation-making purposes and April 1, 2010 for all other purposes).

4. Welfare Reform Act 2012 ss.31 and Sch.2 paras 56 and 62 (April 1, 2013).

5. Welfare Reform Act 2012 s.91 and Sch.9 paras 45 and 47 (April 8, 2013).

6. Pensions Act 2014 s.23 and Sch.12 paras 39 and 41 (April 6, 2016).

7. Pensions Act 2014 s.31(5) and Sch.16 paras 43 and 45 (April 6, 2017).

DEFINITIONS

"benefit"—see s.13.

"disqualifying benefit"—see s.6A.

"family"—by virtue of s.13, see s.137(1) of the Social Security Contributions and Benefits Act 1992.

"sanctionable benefit"—see s.6A.

"social security benefit"—see subs.(3).
"war pension"—by virtue of s.13, see s.25 of the Social Security Act 1989.

Loss of benefit [6 orders and] regulations

1.629 **11.**—(1) In [3 sections 6B to 10] "prescribed" means prescribed by or determined in accordance with regulations made by the Secretary of State.

(2) Regulations under any of the provisions of [3 sections 6B to 10] small be made by statutory instrument which (except in the case of regulations to which subsection (3) applies) shall be subject to annulment in pursuance of a resolution of either House of Parliament.

(3) A statutory instrument containing (whether alone or with other provisions)—

(a) a provision by virtue of which anything is to be treated for the purposes of section [36B or] 7 as a disqualifying benefit but not a sanctionable benefit,

(b) a provision prescribing the manner in which the applicable amount is to be reduced for the purposes of section [36B (6),] 7(3) or 9(3),

(c) a provision the making of which is authorised by section [3[4 6B(5A), (7)], (8), (9) or (10)] [4 7(2A), (4)] [1, (4A)][2,(4B)] or (5), 8(4) or [4 9(2A), (4)] [1, (4A)] [2,(4B)] or (5), or

(d) a provision prescribing the manner in which the amount of joint-claim jobseeker's allowance is to be reduced for the purposes of section 8(3)(a),

[5 (e) regulations under section 6B(14) or an order under section 6B(15), or]

[6 (f) an order under section 7(10A),"...]

shall not be made unless a draft of the instrument has been laid before, and approved by a resolution of, each House of Parliament.

(5) The provision that may be made in exercise of the powers to make regulations that are conferred by [3 sections 6B to 10] shall include different provision for different areas.

AMENDMENTS

1. State Pension Credit Act 2002 Sch.2 para.48 (July 2, 2002 for the purpose of exercising any power to make regulations or orders and October 6, 2003 for other purposes).

2. Welfare Reform Act 2007 Sch. para.23(1) and (7) (March 18, 2008 for regulation-making purposes and October 27, 2008 for other purposes).

3. Welfare Reform Act 2009 Sch.4 para.6 (January 12, 2010 for regulation-making purposes and April 1, 2010 for all other purposes).

4. Welfare Reform Act 2012 s.31 Sch.2 paras 56 and 63(1) and (2) (February 25, 2013).

5. Welfare Reform Act 2012 s.118(1) and (8)(b) (February 25, 2013 for regulation-making purposes and April 1, 2013 for other purposes).

6. Welfare Reform Act 2012 ss.118(1) and (8)(a) and (c), and 119(1)–(12) (April 1, 2013).

DEFINITION

"the Administration Act", by virtue of s.18, means the Social Security Administration Act 1992.

Consequential amendments

12. *Omitted.* 1.630

Interpretation of [3 sections 6A to 12]

13.—In this section and [3 sections 6A to 12]— 1.631

"benefit" includes any allowance, payment, credit or loan;

[3 "cautioned", in relation to any person and any offence, means cautioned after the person concerned has admitted the offence; and caution is to be interpreted accordingly;]

[3 . . .]

"family" has the same meaning as in Part 7 of the Social Security Contributions and Benefits Act 1992;

"income-based jobseeker's allowance", "joint-claim jobseeker's allowance" and "joint-claim couple" have the same meanings as in the Jobseekers Act 1995;

[2 "income-related allowance" has the same meaning as in Part 1 of the Welfare Reform Act 2007 (employment and support allowance);]

[3 . . .]

"sanctionable benefit" has the meaning given by [3 section 6A(1)];

[1 "state pension credit" means state pension credit under the State Pension Credit Act 2002;]

"war pension" has the same meaning as in section 25 of the Social Security Act 1989 (establishment and functions of war pensions committees).

AMENDMENTS

1. State Pension Credit Act 2002 Sch.2 para.49 (July 2, 2002 for the purpose of exercising any power to make regulations or orders and October 6, 2003 for other purposes).

2. Welfare Reform Act 2007 Sch. para.23(1) and (8) (March 18, 2008 for regulation-making purposes and October 27, 2008 for other purposes).

3. Welfare Reform Act 2009 Sch.4 para.7 (January 12, 2010 for regulation-making purposes and April 1, 2010 for all other purposes).

Tax Credits Act 2002

(2002 C. 21)

ARRANGEMENT OF SECTIONS

PART 1

TAX CREDITS

1.–48. *Omitted.* 1.632

PART 2

CHILD BENEFIT AND GUARDIAN'S ALLOWANCE

Transfer of functions etc.

PART 3

SUPPLEMENTARY

Information etc.

Other supplementary provisions

An Act to make provision for tax credits; to amend the law about child benefit and guardian's allowance; and for connected purposes.

[8th July 2002]

GENERAL NOTE

1.633 Part 1 of the Act provides for child tax credit and working tax credit which are dealt with within Vol.IV of this work.

Part 2 of the Act transfers functions relating to child benefit and guardian's allowance from the Department for Work and Pensions to the Treasury and the Board of Inland Revenue which has now been merged into HMRC. Those benefits remain social security benefits despite the change in responsibility for them and administration and adjudication remain under the Social Security Administration Act 1992 and the Social Security Act 1998, although new secondary legislation has been made.

1.634 **1.–48.** *Omitted.*

Part 2

Child Benefit and Guardian's Allowance

Transfer of functions etc.

Functions transferred to Treasury

49.—(1) The functions of the Secretary of State under— 1.635

(a) section 77 of the Social Security Contributions and Benefits Act 1992 (c.4) (guardian's allowance: Great Britain),

(b) Part 9 of that Act (child benefit: Great Britain), except [1 . . .] paragraphs 5 and 6(1) of Schedule 10,

(c) section 80 of the Social Security Administration Act 1992 (c.5) (overlap with benefits under legislation of other member States: Great Britain), and

(d) section 72 of the Social Security Act 1998 (c.14) (power to reduce child benefit for lone parents: Great Britain),

are transferred to the Treasury.

(2) The functions of the Northern Ireland Department under—

(a) section 77 of the Social Security Contributions and Benefits (Northern Ireland) Act 1992 (c.7) (guardian's allowance: Northern Ireland),

(b) Part 9 of that Act (child benefit: Northern Ireland), except [1 . . .] paragraphs 5 and 6(1) of Schedule 10,

(c) section 76 of the Social Security Administration (Northern Ireland) Act 1992 (c.8) (overlap with benefits under legislation of other member States: Northern Ireland), and

(d) Article 68 of the Social Security (Northern Ireland) Order 1998 (1998/1506 (N.I. 10)) (power to reduce child benefit for lone parents: Northern Ireland),

are transferred to the Treasury.

(3) The functions of the Secretary of State under Part 10 of the Social Security Administration Act 1992 (c.5) (review and alteration of benefits: Great Britain) so far as relating to child benefit and guardian's allowance are transferred to the Treasury.

(4) The functions of the Northern Ireland Department under sections 132 to 134 of the Social Security Administration (Northern Ireland) Act 1992 (c. 8) (review and alteration of benefits: Northern Ireland) so far as relating to child benefit and guardian's allowance are transferred to the Treasury.

Amendment

1. Child Benefit Act 2005 s.3 and Sch.2 (April 10, 2006).

Definition

"the Northern Ireland Department": see s.67.

GENERAL NOTE

1.636 This section transfers policy responsibility for child benefit and guardian's allowance (i.e. making the regulations as to entitlement and fixing the rates) from the Secretary of State for Work and Pensions to the Treasury.

Functions transferred to Board

1.637 **50.**—(1) The functions of the Secretary of State and the Northern Ireland Department under the provisions specified in subsection (2), so far as relating to child benefit and guardian's allowance, are transferred to the Board.

(2) The provisions referred to in subsection (1) are—

(a) the Social Security Contributions and Benefits Act 1992 (c.4),

(b) the Social Security Administration Act 1992, except Part 13 (advisory bodies and consultation: Great Britain),

(c) the Social Security Contributions and Benefits (Northern Ireland) Act 1992 (c. 7),

(d) the Social Security Administration (Northern Ireland) Act 1992, except Part 12 (advisory bodies and consultation: Northern Ireland),

(e) Chapter 2 of Part 1 of the Social Security Act 1998 (c.14) (social security decisions and appeals: Great Britain),

(f) Chapter 2 of Part 2 of the Social Security (Northern Ireland) Order 1998 (1998/1506 (N.I. 10)) (social security decisions and appeals: Northern Ireland), and

(g) any subordinate legislation made under any of the provisions specified in section 49 or any of the preceding provisions of this subsection.

(3) This section has effect subject to section 49.

DEFINITIONS

"the Board"—see s.67, but note that the functions of the Board were transferred to Her Majesty's Revenue and Customs by the Commissioners for Revenue and Customs Act 2005.

"the Northern Ireland Department"—*ibid.*

GENERAL NOTE

1.638 While s.49 transfers policy responsibility for child benefit and guardian's allowance to the Treasury, this section transfers operational responsibility (i.e. administration and adjudication) from the Secretary of State for Work and Pensions to the Board of Inland Revenue, whose functions have now been transferred to HMRC by the Commissioners for Revenue and Customs Act 2005. The primary legislation governing administration and adjudication remains the same (subject to consequential amendments made by s.51 and Sch.4 and repeals under s.60 and Sch.6) but the Board made new subordinate legislation (see the Child Benefit and Guardian's Allowance (Administrative Arrangements) Regulations 2003, the Child Benefit and Guardian's Allowance (Administration) Regulations 2003 and the Child Benefit and Guardian's Allowance (Decisions and Appeals) Regulations 2003).

Consequential amendments

1.639 **51.** *Omitted.*

1.640 **52.** *Omitted.*

[1 General functions of Commissioners for Revenue and Customs

53.—The Commissioners for Her Majesty's Revenue and Customs shall be responsible for the payment and management of child benefit and guardian's allowance.] 1.641

AMENDMENT

1. Commissioners for Revenue and Customs Act 2005 s.50 and para.90 of Sch.4 (April 18, 2005).

Transitional provisions

54.—(1) Any function covered by section 49 which is a function of making subordinate legislation may be exercised by the Treasury at any time after the passing of this Act if the subordinate legislation made in the exercise of the function comes into force after the commencement of that section. 1.642

(2) Any function covered by section 50 which is a function of making subordinate legislation may be exercised by the Board at any time after the passing of this Act if the subordinate legislation made in the exercise of the function comes into force after the commencement of that section.

(3) Nothing in section 49 or 50 affects the validity of anything done by or in relation to the Secretary of State or the Northern Ireland Department before its commencement.

(4) Anything (including legal proceedings) relating to any functions transferred by section 49, or any property, rights or liabilities transferred by section 52(1), which is in the course of being done or carried on by or in relation to the Secretary of State or the Northern Ireland Department immediately before the transfer may be continued by or in relation to the Treasury.

(5) Anything (including legal proceedings) relating to any functions transferred by section 50, or any property, rights or liabilities transferred by section 52(2), which is in the course of being done or carried on by or in relation to the Secretary of State or the Northern Ireland Department immediately before the transfer may be continued by or in relation to the Board.

(6) Anything done by the Secretary of State or the Northern Ireland Department for the purposes of or in connection with any functions transferred by section 49, or any property, rights or liabilities transferred by section 52(1), which is in effect immediately before the transfer has effect afterwards as if done by the Treasury.

(7) Anything done by the Secretary of State or the Northern Ireland Department for the purposes of or in connection with any functions transferred by section 50, or any property, rights or liabilities transferred by section 52(2), which is in effect immediately before the transfer has effect afterwards as if done by the Board.

(8) The Treasury is substituted for the Secretary of State or the Northern Ireland Department in any subordinate legislation, any contracts or other documents and any legal proceedings relating to any functions transferred by section 49, or any property, rights or liabilities transferred by section 52(1), made or commenced before the transfer.

(9) The Board are substituted for the Secretary of State or the Northern Ireland Department in any subordinate legislation, any contracts or other documents and any legal proceedings relating to any functions transferred by section 50, or any property, rights or liabilities transferred by section 52(2), made or commenced before the transfer.

(10) Any order made under section 8 of the Electronic Communications Act 2000 (c.7) which—

(a) modifies provisions relating to child benefit or guardian's allowance, and

(b) is in force immediately before the commencement of this subsection,

is to continue to have effect for the purposes of child benefit and guardian's allowance, despite subsection (7) of that section, until regulations made by the Board under section 132 of the Finance Act 1999 (c.16) which are expressed to supersede that order come into force.

Definitions

"the Board"—see s.67, but note that the functions of the Board were transferred to Her Majesty's Revenue and Customs by the Commissioners for Revenue and Customs Act 2005.

"the Northern Ireland Department"—*ibid.*

General Note

1.643 Subsections (1) and (2) came into force on the passing of the Act (s.61), but the remaining provisions of this Part came into force for the purpose of making subordinate legislation on February 26, 2003, for the purpose of the transfer of functions on April 1, 2003 and for the purpose of entitlement to payment of child benefit and guardian's allowance on April 7, 2003 (Tax Credits Act 2002 (Commencement No.2) Order 2003).

Subsection 10

1.644 The Social Security (Electronic Communications) (Child Benefit) Order 2002 remains in force.

1.645 **55.–57.** *Omitted.*

Part 3

Supplementary

Information etc.

Administrative arrangements

1.646 **58.**—(1) This section applies where regulations under—

(a) section 4 or 6 of this Act,

(b) section 5 of the Social Security Administration Act 1992 (c.5), or

(c) section 5 of the Social Security Administration (Northern Ireland) Act 1992 (c.8),

permit or require a claim or notification relating to a tax credit, child benefit or guardian's allowance to be made or given to a relevant authority.

(2) Where this section applies, regulations may make provision—

(a) for information or evidence relating to tax credits, child benefit or guardian's allowance to be provided to the relevant authority (whether by persons by whom such claims and notifications are or have been made or given, by the Board or by other persons),

(b) for the giving of information or advice by a relevant authority to persons by whom such claims or notifications are or have been made or given, and

(c) for the recording, verification and holding, and the forwarding to the Board or a person providing services to the Board, of claims and notifications received by virtue of the regulations referred to in subsection (1) and information or evidence received by virtue of paragraph (a),

(3) "Relevant authority" means—

(a) the Secretary of State,

(b) the Northern Ireland Department, or

(c) a person providing services to the Secretary of State or the Northern Ireland Department.

DEFINITIONS

"the Board"—see s.67, but note that the functions of the Board were transferred to Her Majesty's Revenue and Customs by the Commissioners for Revenue and Customs Act 2005.

"relevant authority"—see subs.(3).

"tax credit"—by virtue of s.67, see s.1(2).

GENERAL NOTE

See the Child Benefit and Guardian's Allowance (Administrative Arrangements) Regulations 2003. **1.647**

59. *Omitted.* **1.648**

Other supplementary provisions

60.–64. *Omitted.* **1.649**

Regulations, orders and schemes

65.—(1) Any power to make regulations under sections 3, 7 to 13, 42 and 43, and any power to make regulations under this Act prescribing a rate of interest, is exercisable by the Treasury. **1.650**

(2) Any other power to make regulations under this Act is exercisable by the Board.

(3) Subject to subsection (4), any power to make regulations, orders or schemes under this Act is exercisable by statutory instrument.

(4) The power—

(a) of the Department of Health, Social Services and Public Safety to make schemes under section 12(5), and

(b) of the Northern Ireland Department to make orders under section 62(1),

is exercisable by statutory rule for the purposes of the Statutory Rules (Northern Ireland) Order 1979 (S.I. 1979/1573 (N.I. 12)).

(5) Regulations may not be made under section 25 or 26 in relation to appeals in Scotland without the consent of the Scottish Ministers.

(6) Regulations may not be made under section 39(6) or 63(8) without the consent of the Lord Chancellor [[1], the Department of Justice in Northern Ireland] and the Scottish Ministers.

(7) Any power to make regulations under this Act may be exercised—

(a) in relation to all cases to which it extends, to all those cases with prescribed exceptions or to prescribed cases or classes of case,

(b) so as to make as respects the cases in relation to which it is exercised the full provision to which it extends or any less provision (whether by way of exception or otherwise),

(c) so as to make the same provision for all cases in relation to which it is exercised or different provision for different cases or classes of case or different provision as respects the same case or class of case for different purposes,

(d) so as to make provision unconditionally or subject to any prescribed condition,

(e) so as to provide for a person to exercise a discretion in dealing with any matter.

(8) Any regulations made under a power under this Act to prescribe a rate of interest may—

(a) either themselves specify a rate of interest or make provision for any such rate to be determined by reference to such rate or the average of such rates as may be referred to in the regulations,

(b) provide for rates to be reduced below, or increased above, what they otherwise would be by specified amounts or by reference to specified formulae,

(c) provide for rates arrived at by reference to averages to be rounded up or down,

(d) provide for circumstances in which alteration of a rate of interest is or is not to take place, and

(e) provide that alterations of rates are to have effect for periods beginning on or after a day determined in accordance with the regulations in relation to interest running from before that day as well as from or from after that day.

(9) Any power to make regulations or a scheme under this Act includes power to make any incidental, supplementary, consequential or transitional provision which appears appropriate for the purposes of, or in connection with, the regulations or scheme.

AMENDMENT

1. Northern Ireland Act 1998 (Devolution of Policing and Justice Functions) Order 2010 (S.I. 2010/976), Sch.18 paras 59 and 60 (April 12, 2010).

DEFINITIONS

"the Board"—see s.67, but note that the functions of the Board were transferred to Her Majesty's Revenue and Customs by the Commissioners for Revenue and Customs Act 2005.

"prescribe"—see s.67.

Parliamentary etc. control of instruments

66.—(1) No [1 order or] regulations to which this subsection applies may be made unless a draft of the instrument containing [1 the order or regulations] (whether or not together with other provisions) has been laid before, and approved by a resolution of, each House of Parliament. 1.651

(2) Subsection (1) applies to—

[1 (za) an order made by the Treasury under section 36A(8) or 36C(9),

(zb) regulations made under section 36A(5) or 36C(4),]

(a) regulations prescribing monetary amounts that are required to be reviewed under section 41,

(b) regulations made by virtue of subsection (2) of section 12 prescribing the amount in excess of which charges are not taken into account for the purposes of that subsection, and

(c) the first regulations made under sections 7(8) and (9), 9, 11, 12 and 13(2).

(3) A statutory instrument containing—

(a) [1 an order or] regulations under this Act,

(b) a scheme made by the Secretary of State under section 12(5),or

(c) an Order in Council under section 52(7),

is (unless a draft of the instrument has been laid before, and approved by a resolution of, each House of Parliament) subject to annulment in pursuance of a resolution of either House of Parliament.

(4) A statutory instrument containing a scheme made by the Scottish Ministers under section 12(5) is subject to annulment in pursuance of a resolution of the Scottish Parliament.

(5) A statutory rule containing a scheme made by the Department of Health, Social Services and Public Safety under section 12(5) is subject to negative resolution within the meaning of section 41(6) of the Interpretation Act (Northern Ireland) 1954 (c. 33 (N.I.)).

AMENDMENT

1. Welfare Reform Act 2012 s.120(4) (February 1, 2013).

Interpretation

67.—In this Act— 1.652

"the Board" means the Commissioners of Inland Revenue,

[1 "cautioned", in relation to any person and any offence, means cautioned after the person concerned has admitted the offence; and "caution" is to be interpreted accordingly;]

"modifications" includes alterations, additions and omissions, and "modifies" is to be construed accordingly,

"the Northern Ireland Department" means the Department for Social Development in Northern Ireland,

"prescribed" means prescribed by regulations, and

"tax credit" and "tax credits" have the meanings given by section 1(2).

AMENDMENT

1. Welfare Reform Act 2012 s.120(5) (April 6, 2013).

GENERAL NOTE

1.653 "the Board"

The functions of the Commissioners of Inland Revenue were transferred to the Commissioners for Her Majesty's Revenue and Customs by s.5(2) of the Commissioners for Revenue and Customs Act 2005.

1.654 **68.–70.** *Omitted.*

1.655 **Schedules 1.–6.** *Omitted.*

PART II

SOCIAL SECURITY REGULATIONS

SECTION A

DWP-ADMINISTERED BENEFITS

NOTE

References to 1992 Acts in pre-1992 Regulations

Some regulations made before the consolidation of social security legislation in 1992 still refer to provisions in the earlier legislation even though they have been replaced by provisions of the Social Security Contributions and Benefits Act 1992 or Social Security Administration Act 1992. This is technically acceptable because those references are deemed to be references to that have replaced them but is apt to be confusing.

In order to be as helpful as possible to users of this volume, the authors have, wherever practicable, inserted in square brackets reference to the relevant provisions of the 1992 legislation.

However, some of the older regulations contain many references to legislation which has either been repealed or is only of significance to those able to retain an entitlement to a defunct benefit. In these cases, reference has generally been left to the earlier legislation. Equally, in some regulations, it was considered that it might mislead if the interpretation regulation was amended.

Readers should therefore note that the material appearing in square brackets is the authors' amendment to include reference to the 1992 legislation. Such amendments have no official standing. All other references to legislation are as they appear in the current version of the regulations printed in this volume.

The Social Security (Civil Penalties) Regulations 2012

(SI 2012/1990)

IN FORCE OCTOBER 1, 2012

ARRANGEMENT OF REGULATIONS

The Secretary of State for Work and Pensions makes the following Regulations in exercise of the powers conferred by sections 115C(2), 115D(1) and (2), 189(1) and 191 of the Social Security Administration Act 1992.

In accordance with section 190(1) of that Act, a draft of this instrument was laid before Parliament and approved by a resolution of each House of Parliament

This instrument contains only regulations made by virtue of section 116(1) of the Welfare Reform Act 2012 and is made before the end of the period of 6 months beginning with the coming into force of that section.

In so far as these Regulations relate to housing benefit and council tax benefit, in accordance with section 176(1) of the Social Security Administration Act 1992(5), consultation has taken place with organisations appearing to the Secretary of State to be representative of the authorities concerned.

Citation, commencement and interpretation 2.2

1. (1) These Regulations may be cited as the Social Security (Civil Penalties) Regulations 2012 and come into force on 1st October 2012.

(2) In these Regulations, "the Act" means the Social Security Administration Act 1992.

Prescribed amount of penalty: section 115C of the Act 2.3

2. The prescribed amount of the penalty for the purpose of section 115C(2) of the Act (incorrect statements etc.) is £50.

Prescribed amount of penalty: section 115D(1) of the Act 2.4

3. The prescribed amount of the penalty for the purpose of section 115D(1) of the Act (failure to provide information) is £50.

Prescribed amount of penalty: section 115D(2) of the Act 2.5

4. The prescribed amount of the penalty for the purpose of section 115D(2) of the Act (failure to notify appropriate authority of a relevant change of circumstances) is £50.

The Social Security (Claims and Information) Regulations 1999

(SI 1999/3108)

ARRANGEMENT OF REGULATIONS

The Secretary of State for Social Security, in exercise of the powers conferred upon him by sections 2C, 7A, 189(1), (4) and (5) and 1919 of the Social Security Administration Act 1992 and sections 72 and 83(1) and (4) to (8) of the Welfare Reform and Pensions Act 1999 and of all other powers enabling him in that behalf, after consultation in respect of provisions in these Regulations relating to housing benefit and council tax benefit with organisations appearing to him to be representative of the authorities concerned, by this instrument, which contains only regulations made by virtue of or consequential upon sections 58, 71 and 72 of the Welfare Reform and Pensions Act 1999 and which is made before the end of a period of 6 months beginning with the coming into force of those provisions, hereby makes the following Regulations:

Citation and commencement

2.7 **1.** These Regulations may be cited as the Social Security (Claims and Information) Regulations 1999 and shall come into force on 29th November 1999.

Interpretation

2.8 **2.** In these Regulations,—

"the Act" means the Welfare Reform and Pensions Act 1999;

"the Child Support Acts" means the Child Support Act 1991 and the Child Support Act 1995;

[4 . . .]

"relevant authority" means a person within section 72(2) of the Act.

Work-focused interview

3. A work-focused interview is an interview conducted for any or all of the following purposes— 2.9

(a) assessing a person's prospects for existing or future employment (whether paid or voluntary);
(b) assisting or encouraging a person to enhance his prospects of such employment;
(c) identifying activities which the person may undertake to strengthen his existing or future prospects of such employment;
(d) identifying current or future employment or training opportunities suitable to the person's needs; and
(e) identifying educational opportunities connected with the existing or future employment prospects or needs of the person.

Additional functions of local authorities

4.—(1) A local authority to whom Part I of Schedule I to these Regulations applies may conduct a work-focused interview with, or provide assistance to, a person to whom paragraphs (2) and (3) apply, where the interview or assistance is requested or consented to by that person. 2.10

(2) This paragraph applies to a person who resides in a postcode district identified in Part I of Schedule 2 to these Regulations.

(3) This paragraph applies to any person making a claim for, or entitled to, any benefit specified in paragraph (4) and applies whether or not a person has had an interview in accordance with regulations made under section 2A of the Administration Act.

(4) The benefits specified in this paragraph are—

(a) income support;
(b) housing benefit;
(c) council tax benefit;
(d) widow's benefit;
(e) bereavement benefits;
[3 (ea) bereavement support payment under section 30 of the Pensions Act 2014;]
(f) incapacity benefit;
(g) severe disablement allowance;
(h) [2 carer's allowance];
(i) a jobseeker's allowance;
(j) disability living allowance.

(5) For the purposes of paragraph (1), the request or consent may be made or given to—

(a) the local authority conducting the interview or giving the assistance;
(b) any person who, or authority which, may be specified as a designated authority for the purposes of section 2A(8) of the Administration Act; or
(c) a person designated an employment officer for the purposes of section 9 of the Jobseekers Act 1995.

(6) For the purposes of carrying out functions under paragraph (1), a local authority may in particular—

(a) obtain and receive information or evidence for the purpose of any work-focused interview to be conducted with that person;

(b) arrange for the work-focused interview to be conducted by one of the following—
 (i) the Secretary of State;
 (ii) a person providing services to the Secretary of State; or
 (iii) a person providing services to, or authorised to exercise any function of, the local authority;
(c) forward information supplied for the purpose of a work-focused interview to any person or authority conducting that interview;
(d) take steps to identify potential employment or training opportunities for persons taking part in work-focused interviews;
(e) [1 . . .];
(f) take steps to identify—
 (i) obstacles which may hinder a person in taking up employment or training opportunities;
 (ii) educational opportunities which may assist in reducing or removing such obstacles; and
(g) record information supplied at a work-focused interview.

AMENDMENTS

1. The Social Security (Work-focused Interviews for Lone Parents) and Miscellaneous Amendments Regulations 2000 (SI 2000/1926) Sch.2 (August 14, 2000).
2. The Social Security Amendment (Carer's Allowance) Regulations 2002 (SI 2002/2497) Sch.2 (October 28, 2002).
3. The Pensions Act 2014 (Consequential, Supplementary and Incidental Amendments) Order 2017 (SI 2017/422) art.16 (April 6, 2017).
4. Housing Benefit and Council Tax Benefit (Consequential Provisions) Regulations 2006 (SI 2006/217) Sch.1 para.1 (March 6, 2006).

Further provisions as to claims

2.11 *Regulation 5 amends the Claims and Payments Regulations 1987; the changes are incorporated in those regulations.*

War Pensions and Child Support

2.12 **6.**—(1) Where a person resides in the area of an authority to which [2 paragraph (3)] refers, he may make a claim for a war pension, or submit an application under the Child Support Acts to any office [1 of a relevant authority] displaying the **one** logo (whether or not that office is situated within the area of the local authority in which the person resides).

(2) Any change of circumstances arising since a claim or application was made in accordance with paragraph (1) may be reported to the office to which that claim or application was made.

(3) The areas to which this paragraph refers are those areas which are within both—
(a) the area of a local authority identified in Part I or II of Schedule1 to these Regulations, and
(b) a postcode area identified in Part I or II of Schedule 2 to these Regulations.

(4) A person making a claim or application to a participating authority in accordance with paragraph (1) shall comply with any requirements for the time being in force in relation to—
(a) claims for war pensions or applications under the Child Support Acts;

(b) the provision of information and evidence in support of such claims or applications,

as if those requirements also applied to the participating authority.

(5) A participating authority shall forward to the Secretary of State—

(a) any claim for a war pension or application under the Child Support Acts made in accordance with this regulation;

(b) details of changes of circumstances reported to the authority in accordance with this regulation; and

(c) any information or evidence—

(i) given to the authority by the person making a claim or application or reporting the change of circumstances; or

(ii) which is relevant to the claim or application or the change reported and which is held by the authority.

(6) For the purpose of this regulation, a "participating authority" means any authority or person to whom a claim or application may be made or change of circumstances reported in accordance with paragraphs (1) and (2).

AMENDMENTS

1. The Social Security (Work-focused Interviews for Lone Parents) and Miscellaneous Amendments Regulations 2000 (SI 2000/1926) Sch.2 (August 14, 2000).

2. Social Security (Work-focused Interviews) Regulations 2000 (SI 2000/897) Pt II reg.17(2) (April 3, 2000).

Holding information

7. A relevant authority to whom information or evidence relating to social security matters [1, or information relating to employment or training] is supplied or by whom such information or evidence is obtained, including information obtained under regulation 8(2), may— **2.13**

(a) make a record of that information or evidence; and

(b) hold the information or evidence, whether as supplied or as recorded.

AMENDMENT

1. The Social Security (Claims and Information) (Amendment) Regulations 2010 (SI 2010/508) reg.2(2) (April 6, 2010).

Provision of information

8.—(1) A relevant authority may give information or advice to any person, or to a person acting on his behalf, concerning— **2.14**

(a) a claim he made, or a decision given on a claim he made, for a social security benefit or a war pension;

(b) an application he made, or a decision given on an application he made, under the Child Support Acts.

(2) For the purpose of giving information or advice in accordance with paragraph (1), a relevant authority may obtain information held by any other relevant authority.

9.–12. *Repealed.* **2.15**

Information

2.16 **13.**—(1) A relevant authority which holds social security information may—

(a) use that information—

(i) in connection with arrangements [1 . . .] made under section 2 of the Employment and Training Act 1973;

(ii) for any purpose to which regulations 3, 4 and 6 of these Regulations, or any regulations inserted by these Regulations, apply; or

(iii) for purposes connected with the employment or training of the persons to whom it relates;

(b) supply the information—

(i) to any other relevant authority to enable that authority to carry out a work-focused interview or any function conferred upon it by these Regulations or by regulations inserted by these Regulations;

(ii) in so far as relevant for the purpose for which it is being provided, to any person in respect of whom the person undertaking the work-focused interview is notified has a vacancy or is about to have a vacancy in his employment or at his place of employment;

(iii) to any person (an "employment zone provider") to whom payments are made by the Secretary of State in accordance with section 60(5)(c)(i) of the Act (special schemes for claimants for jobseeker's allowance);

(iv) to any other relevant authority in connection with any scheme operated by, or any arrangements made by, the authority for purposes connected with employment or training;

[1 (v) to any other relevant authority in connection with arrangements made under section 2 of the Employment and Training Act 1973, in particular for use by that authority in connection with the provision of advice, support and assistance which persons may need in order to acquire or enhance their skills and qualifications with a view to improving their prospects of finding and retaining employment.]

[1 (1A) A relevant authority which holds employment or training information about a person ("P") may supply that information to another relevant authority for use by that second authority in connection with the provision to P (pursuant to arrangements made by the Secretary of State) of advice, support and assistance which P may need in order to acquire or enhance P's skills and qualifications with a view to improving P's prospects of finding and retaining employment.]

(2) An employment zone provider may supply to any other relevant authority information relating to any person participating in a scheme for which he receives a payment under section 60(5)(c)(i) of the Act where the information may be relevant to the person's benefit entitlement.

(3) Where the work-focused interview is undertaken by a relevant authority other than the authority which obtained the information, then the authority supplying the information shall, for the purposes of that interview, supply any other social security information held by them.

(4) A relevant authority which holds social security information [1 or information relating to employment or training] may supply that information to any other relevant authority for the purposes of research, monitoring or evaluation in so far as it relates to [1 any of the purposes] specified in paragraph (5).

(5) The purposes [1 . . .] are—

(a) work-focused interviews;

(b) any purpose for which regulations 3, 4 and 6 of these Regulations, or any regulations inserted by these Regulations, applies;

(c) any scheme or arrangements made by the Secretary of State connected with employment or training; [1 . . .]

(d) section 60 of the Act.

[1 (e) any arrangements made by the Secretary of State of the nature referred to in paragraph (1)(b)(v) or (1A); and

(f) monitoring the retention of employment.]

AMENDMENT

1. The Social Security (Claims and Information) (Amendment) Regulations 2010 (SI 2010/508) reg.2(3) (April 6, 2010).

Purposes for which information may be used

14.—(1) The purposes for which information supplied in connection with matters referred to in paragraph (2) may be used are for— 2.17

(a) the processing of any claim for a social security benefit or a war pension or for an application for a maintenance assessment under the Child Support Act 1991;

(b) the consideration of any application for employment by a person to whom information is supplied in connection with any employment opportunity;

(c) the consideration of the training needs of the person who supplied the information;

(d) any purpose for which a work-focused interview may be conducted;

(e) the prevention, detection, investigation or prosecution of offences relating to social security matters.

[1 (f) assessing the employment or training needs of the person to whom the information relates;

(g) evaluating the effectiveness of training, advice, support and assistance provided;

(h) monitoring the retention of employment.]

(2) The matters referred to in this paragraph are—

(a) work-focused interviews; or

(b) any other provision in or introduced by these Regulations.

AMENDMENT

1. The Social Security (Claims and Information) (Amendment) Regulations 2010 (SI 2010/508) reg.2(4) (April 6, 2010).

Information supplied

15. Information supplied to a person or authority under these Regulations— 2.18

(a) may be used for the purposes of amending or supplementing information held by the person or authority to whom it is supplied; and
(b) if it is so used, may be supplied to another person or authority, and used by him or it for any purpose, to whom or for which that other information could be supplied or used.

Partners of claimants on jobseeker's allowance

2.19 **16.**—(1) The social security information specified in paragraph (2) may be supplied by a relevant authority to the partner of a claimant for a jobseeker's allowance where—
(a) the allowance has been in payment to the claimant, or would have been in payment to him but for section 19 of the Jobseekers Act 1995 (circumstances in which jobseeker's allowance is not payable) for a period of six months or more;
(b) the allowance remains in payment or would be in payment but for that section; and
(c) the partner is being invited to attend the office of the relevant authority for purposes connected with employment or training.

(2) The information which may be supplied is—
(a) that jobseeker's allowance is in payment to the claimant or would be in payment to him but for section 19 of the Jobseekers Act; and
(b) that payment has been made to the claimant or would have been so made but for section 19, for a period of at least six months.

(3) In this regulation, "partner" has the same meaning as in the Jobseeker's Allowance Regulations 1996 by virtue of section 1(3) of those Regulations.

Partners of claimants

2.20 **17.**—(1) The social security information specified in paragraph (4) may be supplied by a relevant authority to the partner of a claimant for a qualifying benefit where [1 . . .] [1 one or more of the qualifying benefits has been payable to the claimant for at least six months.]

(2) The qualifying benefits are—
(a) a jobseeker's allowance;
(b) income support;
(c) incapacity benefit;
(d) severe disablement allowance;
(e) [2 carer's allowance]

(3) [1 . . .]

(4) The information which may be supplied is—
(a) that a qualifying benefit is or has been payable to the claimant;
(b) the period for which the qualifying benefit has been payable.

(5) In this regulation, [3 "partner"] means one member of [3 a couple] of which the claimant is also a member [3, and "couple" has the same meaning as in regulation 1(3) of the Jobseeker's Allowance Regulations 1996"].

AMENDMENTS

1. The Social Security (Claims and Information and Work-focused Interviews for Lone Parents) Amendment Regulations 2001 (SI 2001/1189) reg.2 (April 23, 2001).

2. The Social Security Amendment (Carer's Allowance) Regulations 2002 (SI 2002/2497) Sch.2 (October 28, 2002).

3. The Civil Partnership (Pensions, Social Security and Child Support) (Consequential etc. Provisions) Order 2005 (SI 2005/2877) (December 5, 2005).

Consequentials

18. *Omitted.* 2.21

The Social Security (Claims and Information) Regulations 2007

(SI 2007/2911)

IN FORCE OCTOBER 31, 2007

ARRANGEMENT OF REGULATIONS

The Secretary of State for Work and Pensions makes the following Regulations in exercise of the powers conferred by sections 5(1)(a), 7A(1), (2) and (6)(d), 7B(2) and (5), 189(1) and (4) to (6) and 191 of the Social Security Administration Act 1992.

In accordance with section 176(1)(a) of that Act, as regards provisions in the Regulations relating to housing benefit and council tax benefit, he has consulted organisations appearing to him to be representative of the authorities concerned.

The Social Security Advisory Committee has agreed that proposals in respect of these Regulations should not be referred to it.

Citation, commencement and interpretation

1.—(1) These Regulations may be cited as the Social Security (Claims and Information) Regulations 2007 and shall come into force on 31st October 2007. 2.23

(2) In regulations 4 and 5 "the Administration Act" means the Social Security Administration Act 1992.

(3) In regulations 2 to 4—

"specified benefit" means one or more of the following benefits—

(a) attendance allowance;

[[2] (b) bereavement support payment under section 30 of the Pensions Act 2014;]

(c) [[2] . . .];

(d) carer's allowance;

(e) disability living allowance;

[1](ee) employment and support allowance;]

(f) incapacity benefit;

(g) income support;

(h) jobseeker's allowance;
(i) retirement pension;
(j) state pension credit;
(k) widowed parent's allowance;
(l) winter fuel payment;

"the Secretary of State" includes persons providing services to the Secretary of State;

"local authority" includes persons providing services to a local authority and persons authorised to exercise any function of a local authority relating to housing benefit or council tax benefit.

AMENDMENTS

1. Social Security (Miscellaneous Amendments) (No.3) Regulations 2010 (SI 2010/840) reg.8 (June 28, 2010).

2. The Pensions Act 2014 (Consequential, Supplementary and Incidental Amendments) Order 2017 (SI 2017/422) art.30 (April 6, 2017).

Use of social security information: local authorities

2.24 **2.**—(1) This regulation applies where social security information held by a local authority was supplied by the Secretary of State to the local authority and this information—

(a) was used by the Secretary of State in connection with a person's claim for, or award of, a specified benefit; and
(b) is relevant to that person's claim for, or award of, council tax benefit or housing benefit.

(2) The local authority must, for the purposes of the person's claim for, or award of, council tax benefit or housing benefit, use that information without verifying its accuracy.

(3) Paragraph (2) does not apply where—

(a) the information is supplied more than twelve months after it was used by the Secretary of State in connection with a claim for, or an award of, a specified benefit; or

(b) the information is supplied within twelve months of its use by the Secretary of State but the local authority has reasonable grounds for believing the information has changed in the period between its use by the Secretary of State and its supply to the local authority; or
(c) the date on which the information was used by the Secretary of State cannot be determined.

Use of social security information: Secretary of State

2.25 **3.**—(1) This regulation applies where social security information held by the Secretary of State was supplied by a local authority to the Secretary of State and this information—

(a) was used by the local authority in connection with a person's claim for, or award of, council tax benefit or housing benefit; and
(b) is relevant to that person's claim for, or award of, a specified benefit.

(2) The Secretary of State must, for the purposes of the person's claim for, or award of, a specified benefit, use that information without verifying its accuracy.

(3) Paragraph (2) does not apply where—
(a) the information is supplied more than twelve months after it was used by a local authority in connection with a claim for, or an award of, council tax benefit or housing benefit; or
(b) the information is supplied within twelve months of its use by the local authority but the Secretary of State has reasonable grounds for believing the information has changed in the period between its use by the local authority and its supply to the Secretary of State; or
(c) the date on which the information was used by the local authority cannot be determined.

Social security information verified by local authorities

4.—(1) This regulation applies where social security information is verified by a local authority by virtue of regulations made under section 7A(2)(e) of the Administration Act and forwarded by that local authority to the Secretary of State. **2.26**

(2) The Secretary of State must, for the purposes of a person's claim for, or award of, a specified benefit, use this information without verifying its accuracy.

(3) Paragraph (2) does not apply where—
(a) the Secretary of State has reasonable grounds for believing the social security information received from the local authority is inaccurate; or
(b) the Secretary of State receives the information more than four weeks after it was verified by the local authority.

Specified benefits for the purpose of section 7B(3) of the Administration Act

5. The benefits specified for the purpose of section 7B(3) of the Administration Act are— **2.27**
(a) a "specified benefit" within the meaning given in regulation 1(3);
(b) housing benefit; and
(c) council tax benefit.

Regs 6–10 amend other legislation and the amendments are incorporated in the relevant regulations.

The Social Security (Claims and Payments) Regulations 1987

(SI 1987/1968)

ARRANGEMENTS OF REGULATIONS

PART I

General

PART II

Claims

PART III

Payments

PART IV

Third Parties

PART V

Extinguishment

PART VI

Mobility Component of Disability Living Allowance and Disability Living Allowance for Children

PART VII

Miscellaneous

SCHEDULES

Whereas a draft of this instrument was laid before Parliament and approved by resolution of each House of Parliament:

Now therefore, the Secretary of State for Social Services, in exercise of the powers conferred by sections 165A and 166(2) of the Social Security Act 1975, section 6(1) of the Child Benefit Act 1975, sections 21(7), 51(1)(a) to (s), 54(1) and 84(1) of the Social Security Act 1986 and, as regards the revocations set out in Schedule 10 to this instrument, the powers specified in that Schedule, and all other powers enabling him in that behalf by this instrument which contains only regulations made under the sections of the Social Security Act 1986 specified above and provisions consequential on those sections and which is made before the end of a period of 12 months from the commencement of those sections, makes the following Regulations:

PART I

GENERAL

Citation [1 , commencement and application]

1.—[1 (1)] These Regulations may be cited as the Social Security (Claims and Payments) Regulations 1987 and shall come into operation on 11th April 1988. 2.29

[1(2) In so far as these Regulations apply to—

(a) an employment and support allowance, they apply to that allowance under Part 1 of the Welfare Reform Act as it has effect apart from the amendments made by Schedule 3 and Part 1 of Schedule 14 to the Welfare Reform Act 2012 that remove references to an income-related allowance;

(b) a jobseeker's allowance, they apply to that allowance under the Jobseekers Act as it has effect apart from the amendments made by Part 1 of Schedule 14 to the Welfare Reform Act 2012 that remove references to an income-based allowance.

(3) These Regulations do not apply to universal credit (within the meaning of Part 1 of the Welfare Reform Act 2012) or personal independence payment (within the meaning of Part 4 of that Act).]

AMENDMENT

1. The Universal Credit, Personal Independence Payment, Jobseeker's Allowance and Employment and Support Allowance (Claims and Payments) Regulations 2013 (SI 2013/380), reg.4 and Sch.3, para.(2) (April 8, 2013).

GENERAL NOTE

The Universal Credit, Personal Independence Payment, Jobseeker's Allowance and Employment and Support Allowance (Claims and Payments) Regulations 2013 (SI 2013/380) govern claims and payments for a personal independence payment. Those regulations are extended to cover claims for universal credit and to the contribution-based forms of jobseeker's allowance and employment and support allowance with effect from April 29, 2013. 2.30

Interpretation

2.—(1) In these Regulations, unless the context otherwise requires— 2.31

[20 . . .];

[27 "the 1992 Act" means the Social Security Administration Act 1992;]

[23 "the 2000 Act" means the Electronic Communications Act 2000;]

[22 "the 2002 Act" means the State Pension Credit Act 2002;]

[33 "the 2013 Regulations" means the Universal Credit, Personal Independence Payment, Jobseeker's Allowance and Employment and Support Allowance (Claims and Payments) Regulations 2013;]

[22 "advance period" means the period specified in regulation 4E(2);]

[40 "the 2018 Scotland Act" means the Social Security (Scotland) Act 2018;]

[30 "appropriate office" means an office of the Department for Work and Pensions and where any provision in these Regulations relates to a claim, notice or other information, evidence or document being received by or sent, delivered or otherwise furnished in writing to an appropriate office, include a postal address specified by the Secretary of State for that purpose.]

[[36] "bereavement benefit" means—

(a) a bereavement payment referred to in section 36 of the Contributions and Benefits Act as in force immediately before it was repealed by paragraph 8 of Schedule 16 to the Pensions Act 2014;

(b) a bereavement allowance referred to in section 39B of the Contributions and Benefits Act as in force immediately before it was repealed by paragraph 13 of Schedule 16 to the Pensions Act 2014;

(c) widowed parent's allowance;

"bereavement support payment" means bereavement support payment under section 30 of the Pensions Act 2014;]

[[21] "the Board" means the Commissioners of Inland Revenue; and references to "the Board" in these regulations have effect only with respect to working families tax credit;]

[[11] "claim for asylum" has the same meaning as in the Asylum and Immigration Appeals Act 1993;]

"claim for benefit" includes—

(a) an application for a declaration that an accident was an industrial accident;

(b) [[3]. . .]

(c) an application for [[14]a revision under section 9 of the Social Security Act 1998 or a supersession under section 10 of that Act of] a decision for the purpose of obtaining any increase of benefit [[6]in respect of a child or adult dependant under the Social Security Act 1975 or an increase in disablement benefit under section 60 (special hardship), 61 (constant attendance), 62 (hospital treatment allowance) or 63 (exceptionally severe disablement) of the Social Security Act 1975], but does not include any other application for [[14] a revision or supersession of] a decision;

[[15] "Contributions and Benefits Act" means the Social Security Contributions and Benefits Act 1992;]

[[34] "couple" means

(a) two people who are married to, or civil partners of, each other and are members of the same household; or

(b) two people who are not married to, or civil partners of, each other but are living together [[38] as if they were a married couple or civil partners;]]

[[17] "Crown servant posted overseas" means a person performing the duties of any office or employment under the Crown in right of the United Kingdom who is, or was prior to his posting, ordinarily resident in the United Kingdom;]

[[13] "disabled person's tax credit and working families tax credit" shall be construed in accordance with section 1(1) of the Tax Credits Act 1999];

[[23] "electronic communication" has the same meaning as in section 15(1) of the 2000 Act];

[[29] "the Employment and Support Allowance Regulations" means the Employment and Support Allowance Regulations 2008;]

[22 "guarantee credit" is to be construed in accordance with sections 1 and 2 of the 2002 Act;]

[26 . . .]

[10 "the Jobseekers Act" means the Jobseekers Act 1995;

"jobseeker's allowance" means an allowance payable under Part I of the Jobseekers Act;

"the Jobseeker's Allowance Regulations" means the Jobseeker's Allowance Regulations 1996;]

[16 "joint-claim couple" and "joint-claim jobseeker's allowance" have the same meaning in these Regulations as they have in the Jobseekers Act by virtue of section 1(4) of that Act;]

[29 "'limited capability for work'" has the same meaning as in section 1(4) of the Welfare Reform Act";]

"long-term benefits" means any retirement pension, [24 a shared additional pension] a widowed mother's allowance, a widow's pension, [15widowed parent's allowance, [36 . . .]] attendance allowance, [5disability living allowance], [19 carer's allowance], [12. . .], any pension or allowance for industrial injury or disease and any increase in any such benefit;

[25 . . .];

"partner" means one of a [25 couple]; [4. . .]

[9 "pension fund holder" means with respect to a personal pension scheme or retirement annuity contract, the trustees, managers or scheme administrators, as the case may be, of the scheme or contract concerned;]

[9 "personal pension scheme" has the same meaning as in section 1 of the Pension Schemes Act 1993 in respect of employed earners and in the case of self-employed earners, includes a scheme approved by the Board of Inland Revenue under Chapter IV of Part XIV of the Income and Corporation Taxes Act 1988;]

[22 "qualifying age" has the same meaning as in the 2002 Act by virtue of section 1(6) of that Act;]

[11 "refugee" means a person recorded by the Secretary of State as a refugee within the definition in Article 1 of the Convention relating to the Status of Refugees done at Geneva on 28th July 1951 as extended by Article 1(2) of the Protocol relating to the Status of Refugees done at New York on 31st January 1967;]

[20 "relevant authority" means a person within section 72(2) of the Welfare Reform and Pensions Act 1999;]

[9 "retirement annuity contract" means a contract or trust scheme approved under Chapter III of Part XIV of the Income and Corporation Taxes Act 1988;]

[24 "shared additional pension" means a shared additional pension under section 55A [35 or 55AA] of the Contributions and Benefits Act;]

[37 "social fund funeral payment" means a funeral payment within the meaning of regulation 7(1) of the Social Fund Maternity and Funeral Expenses (General) Regulations 2005] [39, including social fund payments made under the Social Fund (Children's Funeral Fund for England) Regulations 2019];

[22 "state pension credit" means state pension credit under the 2002 Act;]

[32 "universal credit" means universal credit under Part 1 of the Welfare Reform Act 2012;]

[25 . . .]

"week" means a period of 7 days beginning with midnight between Saturday and Sunday.

[[29] "the Welfare Reform Act" means the Welfare Reform Act 2007;]

[[15] "widowed parent's allowance" means an allowance referred to in section 39A of the Contributions and Benefits Act;]

[[31] "working age benefit" means any of the following—

(a) [[36] . . .];

(b) an employment and support allowance;

(c) incapacity benefit;

(d) income support;

(e) a jobseeker's allowance;

(f) widowed mother's allowance;

(g) widowed parent's allowance;

(h) widow's pension.]

(2) Unless the context otherwise requires, any reference in these Regulations to—

(a) a numbered regulation, Part or Schedule is a reference to the regulation, Part or Schedule bearing that number in these Regulations and any reference in a regulation to a numbered paragraph is a reference to the paragraph of that regulation having that number;

(b) a benefit includes any benefit under the Social Security Act 1975 [SSCBA], child benefit under Part I of the Child Benefit Act 1975, income support [[22] state pension credit] [[7], family credit and disability working allowance under the Social Security Act 1986 [SSCBA] and any social fund payments such as are mentioned in section 32(2)(a) [[1]and section 32(2A)] of that Act [SSCBA, s.138(1)(a) and (2)] [[35] , state pension under Part 1 of the Pensions Act 2014] [[10]and a jobseeker's allowance under Part I of the Jobseekers Act] [[29], a shared additional pension] [[36], bereavement support payment] or an employment and support allowance under Part 1 of the Welfare Reform Act.

[[10](2A) References in regulations 20, 21 (except paragraphs (3) and (3A)), 29, 30, 32 to 34, 37 (except paragraph (1A)), 37A, 37AA (except paragraph (3)), 37AB, 37B, 38 and 47 to "benefit", "income support" or "a jobseeker's allowance", include a reference to a back to work bonus which, by virtue of regulation 25 of the Social Security (Back to Work Bonus) Regulations 1996, is to be treated as payable as income support or, as the case may be, as a jobseeker's allowance [[24] . . .] [[29] , a shared additional pension or an employment and support allowance under Part 1 of the Welfare Reform Act].]

(3) For the purposes of the provisions of these Regulations relating to the making of claims every increase of benefit under the Social Security Act 1975 [SSCBA] shall be treated as a separate benefit [[12]. . .].

[[22] (4) In these Regulations references to "beneficiaries" include any person entitled to state pension credit.]

Amendments

1. The Social Security (Common Provisions) Miscellaneous Amendments Regulations 1988 (SI 1988/1725) reg.3 (November 7, 1988).

2. Transfer of Functions (Health and Social Security) Order 1988 (SI 1988/1843) art.3(4) (November 28, 1988).

3. The Social Security (Medical Evidence, Claims and Payments) Amendment Regulations 1989 (SI 1989/1686) reg.3 (October 9, 1989).

4. The Social Security (Miscellaneous Provisions) Amendment Regulations 1991 (SI 1991/2284) reg.5 (November 1, 1991).

5. The Social Security (Claims and Payments) Amendment Regulations 1991 (SI 1991/2741) reg.2(a) (February 3, 1992).

6. The Social Security (Miscellaneous Provisions) Amendment Regulations 1992 (SI 1992/247) reg.9 (March 9, 1992).

7. The Social Security (Claims and Payments) Amendment Regulations 1991 (SI 1991/2741) reg.2(b) (March 10, 1992).

8. The Social Security (Claims and Payments) Amendment (No.4) Regulations 1994 (SI 1994/3196) reg.2 (January 10, 1995).

9. Income-related Benefit Schemes and Social Security (Claims and Payments) (Miscellaneous Amendments) Regulations 1995 (SI 1995/2303) reg.10(2) (October 2, 1995).

10. The Social Security (Claims and Payments) (Jobseeker's Allowance Consequential Amendments) Regulations 1996 (SI 1996/1460) reg.2(2) (October 7, 1996).

11. The Income Support and Social Security (Claims and Payments) (Miscellaneous Amendments) Regulations 1996 (SI 1996/2431) reg.7(a) (October 15, 1996).

12. The Social Security (Claims and Payments) Amendment Regulations 1999 (SI 1999/2358) reg.2 (September 20, 1999) and The Child Benefit, Child Support and Social Security (Miscellaneous Amendments) Regulations 1996 (SI 1996/1803) reg.18 (April 7, 1997).

13. The Tax Credits (Claims and Payments) (Amendment) Regulations 1999 (SI 1999/2572) reg.3 (October 5, 1999).

14. The Social Security Act 1998 (Commencement No.12 and Savings and Consequential and Transitional Provisions) Order 1999 (SI 1999/3178) Sch.6 (November 29, 1999).

15. The Social Security (Benefits for Widows and Widowers) (Consequential Amendments) Regulations 2000 reg.9 (SI 2000/1483) (April 9, 2001).

16. The Social Security (Joint Claims: Consequential Amendments) Regulations 2000 (SI 2000/1982) reg.2(2) (March 19, 2001).

17. Tax Credits (Miscellaneous Amendments No.4) Regulations 2002 (SI 2002/696) reg.2 (July 23, 2002).

18. Social Security (Electronic Communications) (Child Benefit) Order 2002 (SI 2002/1789) art.2 (October 28, 2002); revoked with effect from December 1, 2003.

19. The Social Security Amendment (Carer's Allowance) Regulations 2002 (SI 2002/2497) Sch.2 (October 28, 2002).

20. Social Security Act 1998 Sch.6 (November 29, 1999).

21. Tax Credits (Claims and Payments) (Amendment) Regulations 1999 (SI 1999/2572) reg.3 (October 5, 1999).

22. State Pension Credit (Consequential, Transitional and Miscellaneous Provisions) Regulations 2002 SI 2002/3019 reg.3 (April 7, 2003).

23. The Social Security (Electronic Communications) (Carer's Allowance) Order 2003 (SI 2003/2800) reg.2 (December 1, 2003).

24. The Social Security (Shared Additional Pension) (Miscellaneous Amendments) Regulations 2005 (SI 2005/1551) (July 6, 2005).

25. The Civil Partnership (Pensions, Social Security and Child Support) (Consequential etc. Provisions) Order 2005 (SI 2005/2887) (December 5, 2005).

26. The Social Security (Miscellaneous Amendments) (No.2) Regulations 2006 (SI 2006/832) reg.2 (April 10, 2006).

27. The Social Security (Claims and Payments) Amendment (No.2) Regulations 2006 (SI 2006/3188) (December 27, 2006).

28. The Social Security (Miscellaneous Amendments) (No.2) Regulations 2007 (SI 2007/1626) (July 3, 2007).

29. The Employment and Support Allowance (Consequential Provisions) (No.2) Regulations 2008 (SI 2008/1554) reg.10 (October 27, 2008).

30. The Social Security (Miscellaneous Amendments) (No.2) Regulations 2009 (SI 2009/1490) reg.2 (July 13, 2009).

31. The Social Security (Miscellaneous Amendments) (No.6) Regulations 2009 (SI 2009/3229) reg.2 (April 6, 2010).

32. The Universal Credit (Consequential Supplementary, Incidental and Miscellaneous Provisions) Regulations 2013 (SI 2013/630) reg.29(2) (April 29, 2013).

33. The Social Security (Miscellaneous Amendments) (No.2) Regulations 2013 (SI 2013/1508) reg.2(2) amends reg.2(1) (July 29, 2013).

34. The Marriage (Same Sex Couples) Act 2013 (Consequential Provisions) Order 2014 (SI 2014/107) reg.10 (March 13, 2014).

35. The Pensions Act 2014 (Consequential, Supplementary and Incidental Amendments) Order 2015 (SI 2015/1985) art.9(2) (April 6, 2016).

36. The Pensions Act 2014 (Consequential, Supplementary and Incidental Amendments) Order 2017 (SI 2017/422) art.10 (April 6, 2017).

37. The Social Fund Funeral Expenses Amendment Regulations 2018 (SI 2018/61) reg.2 (April 2, 2018).

38. The Civil Partnership (Opposite-sex Couples) Regulations 2019 (SI 2019/1458) Sch.3 para.41 (December 2, 2019).

39. The Social Fund (Children's Funeral Fund for England) Regulations 2019 (SI 2019/1064) reg.8 (July 23, 2019).

40. The Scotland Act 2016 (Social Security) (Consequential Provision) (Miscellaneous Amendment) Regulations 2021 (SI 2021/804) reg.9 (July 26, 2021).

GENERAL NOTE

2.32 Section 15(1) of the Electronic Communications Act 2000 defines "electronic communication" as follows:

> "'electronic communication' means a communication transmitted (whether from one person to another, from one device to another or from a person to a device or vice versa)—
> (a) by means of a telecommunication system (within the meaning of the Telecommunications Act 1984); or
> (b) by other means but while in an electronic form;"

With effect from December 16, 2014, art.29 and Sch.6 para.6 of the Marriage and Civil Partnership (Scotland) Act 2014 and Civil Partnership Act 2004 (Consequential Provisions and Modifications Order 2001 (SI 2014/3229) amended the definition of "couple" by substituting a definition in the same terms as the existing definition. However, the existing definition applied only to England and Wales; the new definition applies to England, Wales, Scotland and Northern Ireland.

PART II

CLAIMS

Claims not required for entitlement to benefit in certain cases

2.33 **3.**—[17—(1)] It shall not be a condition of entitlement to benefit that a claim be made for it in the following cases—

[15 (za) in the case of a Category A or B retirement pension, where the beneficiary is a person to whom regulation 3A applies;]

- (a) in the case of a Category C retirement pension where the beneficiary is in receipt of—
  - (i) another retirement pension under the Social Security Act 1975; or
  - (ii) widow's benefit under Chapter 1 of Part II of that Act; or
  - (iii) benefit by virtue of section 39(4) of that Act corresponding to a widow's pension or a widowed mother's allowance;

[19 (iv) widowed parent's allowance;]]
(b) in the case of a Category D retirement pension where the beneficiary—
(i) was ordinarily resident in Great Britain on the day on which he attained 80 years of age; and
(ii) is in receipt of another retirement pension under the Social Security Act 1975;
(c) age addition in any case;
[10 (ca) in the case of a Category A retirement pension where the beneficiary—
(i) is entitled to any category of retirement pension other than a Category A retirement pension; and
(ii) becomes divorced or the beneficiary's civil partnership is dissolved;]
[11 (cb) in the case of a Category B retirement pension where the beneficiary is entitled to either a Category A retirement pension or to a graduated retirement benefit or to both and
(i) the spouse or civil partner of the beneficiary becomes entitled to a Category A retirement pension [18 or a state pension under section 4 of the Pensions Act 2014]; or
(ii) the beneficiary marries or enters into a civil partnership with a person who is entitled to a Category A retirement pension [18 or a state pension under section 4 of the Pensions Act 2014];] [14 or
(iii) the spouse or civil partner of the beneficiary dies having been entitled to a Category A retirement pension [18 or a state pension under section 4 of the Pensions Act 2014] at the date of death;]
(d) in the case of a Category A or B retirement pension [18 or a state pension under Part 1 of the Pensions Act 2014]—
(i) where the beneficiary is a woman [6 who has reached pensionable age and is] entitled to a widowed mother's allowance [6 . . .], on her ceasing to be so entitled; [6 . . .]

[6 . . .]
[10 . . .]
[19 . . .]
(e) [1in the case of retirement allowance;]
(f) [2. . .]
(g) [3 in the case of a jobseeker's allowance where—
(i) payment of benefit has been suspended in the circumstances described in regulation 16(2) of the Social Security and Child Support (Decisions and Appeals) Regulations 1999; and
(ii) the claimant whose benefit has been suspended satisfies the conditions of entitlement (apart from the requirement to claim) to that benefit immediately before the suspension ends;]
(h) [5 in the case of income support where the beneficiary—
(i) is a person to whom regulation [8 . . .] [7 6(5)] of the Income Support (General) Regulations 1987 (persons not treated as engaged in remunerative work) applies;
(ii) was in receipt of an income-based jobseeker's allowance [12 or an income-related employment and support allowance] on the day before the day on which he was first engaged in the work referred to in sub-paragraph (a) of [7 those paragraphs] and

(iii) would satisfy the conditions of entitlement to income support (apart from the condition of making a claim would apply in the absence of this paragraph) only by virtue of regulation [8 . . . [7 . . .] regulation 6(6)] of those regulations;]

[9 (i) in the case of a shared additional pension where the beneficiary is in receipt of a retirement pension of any category;]

[17 (j) in the case of an employment and support allowance where—

(i) the beneficiary has made and is pursuing an appeal against a relevant decision of the Secretary of State, and

(ii) that appeal relates to a decision to terminate or not to award a benefit for which a claim was made;]

[18 (ja) in the case of a state pension under any section of Part 1 of the Pensions Act 2014 where the beneficiary is entitled to—

(i) a state pension under a different section of Part 1 of that Act; or

(ii) another state pension under the same section of Part 1 of that Act;]

[17 (2) In this regulation—

"appellate authority" means the First-tier Tribunal, the Upper Tribunal, the Court of Appeal, the Court of Session, or the Supreme Court; and

"relevant decision" means—

(a) a decision that embodies the first determination by the Secretary of State that the claimant does not have limited capability for work; or

(b) a decision that embodies the first determination by the Secretary of State that the claimant does not have limited capability for work since a previous determination by the Secretary of State or appellate authority that the claimant does have limited capability for work.]

AMENDMENTS

1. The Social Security (Claims and Payments on Account, Overpayments and Recovery) Amendment Regulations 1989 (SI 1989/136) reg.3 (April 10, 1989).

2. The Social Security (Claims and Payments) Amendment (No.2) Regulations 1994 (SI 1994/2943) reg.2 (April 13, 1995).

3. The Social Security Act 1998 (Commencement No.12 and Consequential and Transitional Provisions) Order 1999 (SI 1999/3178) Sch.6 para.3 (November 29, 1999).

4. The Social Security Act 1998 (Commencement No.11 and Transitional Provisions) Order 1989 (SI 1999/2860) Sch.3 (October 18, 1999).

5. The Social Security (Miscellaneous Amendments) (No.2) Regulations 1999 (SI 1999/2556) reg.7 (October 4, 1999).

6. The Social Security (Miscellaneous Amendments No.4) Regulations 2017 (SI 2017/1015) reg.5(2) (December 6, 2018).

7. The Social Security (Miscellaneous Amendments) Regulations 2001 (SI 2001/488) reg.11 (April 9, 2001).

8. Social Security (Back to Work Bonus and Lone Parent Run-on) (Amendment and Revocation) Regulations 2003 (SI 2003/1589) reg.5 (October 25, 2004).

9. The Social Security (Shared Additional Pension) (Miscellaneous Amendments) Regulations 2005 (SI 2005/1551) (July 6, 2005).

10. The Social Security (Miscellaneous Amendments) (No.4) Regulations 2007 (SI 2007/2470) (September 24, 2007).

11. The Social Security (Claims and Payments) Amendment Regulations 2008 (SI 2008/441) reg.2 (March 17, 2008).

12. The Employment and Support Allowance (Consequential Provisions) (No.2) Regulations 2008 (SI 2008/1554) reg.11 (October 27, 2008).

13. The Social Security (Miscellaneous Amendments) (No.5) Regulations 2008 (SI 2008/2667) reg.2 (October 30, 2008).
14. The Social Security (Miscellaneous Amendments) (No.2) Regulations 2009 (SI 2009/1490) reg.2 (July 13, 2009).
15. Social Security (Exemption from Claiming Retirement Pension) Regulations 2010 (SI 2010/1794) reg.2 (November 2, 2010).
16. Social Security (Miscellaneous Amendments) (No.3) Regulations 2010 (SI 2010/840) reg.2 (June 28, 2010).
17. The Employment and Support Allowance (Repeat Assessments and Pending Appeal Awards) (Amendment) Regulations 2015 (SI 2015/437) reg.5 (March 30, 2015).
18. The Pensions Act 2014 (Consequential, Supplementary and Incidental Amendments) Order 2015 (SI 2015/1985) art.9(3) (April 6, 2016).
19. The Pensions Act 2014 (Consequential, Supplementary and Incidental Amendments) Order 2017 (SI 2017/422) art.10 (April 6, 2017).

General Note

On the meaning of "ordinarily resident" see annotation to reg.5 of the Persons Abroad Regulations in Vol.I. 2.34

In *CSP/005/2013* the judge ruled, departing from his earlier decision in *CP/345/2011* that reg.3(1)(cb) did not permit the backdating of a Category B pension beyond the date the amendment contained in reg.3(1)(cb) came into effect, namely March 17, 2008. In *GM v SSWP (RP)* [2022] UKUT 85 (AAC);[2023] AACR 2 a different judge approached the matter afresh, holding that the amendment made in 2008 by which reg.3(1)(cb) was introduced:

> "must be recognised for what it was—a further incremental change to the carefully and narrowly-defined list of exceptions in regulation 3 of the 1987 Regulations to the general principle enshrined in section 1 of SSAA 1992" i.e. that "making a claim is a condition of entitlement to a social security benefit in the same way any one of the substantive qualifying criteria is."

The judge reached his conclusion with the benefit of detailed evidence showing that the amendment had been introduced at a point when the DWP's computer systems could cope without the need for a separate claim from the cohort of claimants concerned. Further, a detailed examination of the ordinary meaning of the words and a comparison with other sub-paragraphs indicated that the words "becomes entitled" referred to when a claimant's spouse gained entitlement to a Category A pension *after* the regulation introducing the sub-paragraph came into force. Consequently Mrs GM, whose husband had become entitled to a category A pension before that point, could not rely on it to avoid the need to make a claim and when she did make one, it could only be backdated to the extent of the much shorter period contemplated by reg.19. A human rights challenge also failed: see 4.166.

[1 Notification that claim not required for entitlement to a Category A or B retirement pension

3A.—(1) Subject to paragraph (4), this regulation applies to a beneficiary who has received, on or before the day provided for in paragraph (2), a written notification from the Secretary of State that no claim is required for a Category A or B retirement pension. 2.35

(2) The day referred to in paragraph (1) is—

(a) the day which falls 2 weeks before the day on which the beneficiary reaches pensionable age; or

(b) such later day as the Secretary of State may consider reasonable in any particular case or class of case.

(3) The Secretary of State may give a notification under paragraph (1) only in a case where, on the day which falls 8 weeks before the day on which the beneficiary reaches pensionable age, the beneficiary—

(a) is in receipt of an exempt benefit, or would be in receipt of it but for that benefit not being payable as a result of the application of any of the legislation listed in paragraph (7); and

(b) is neither entitled to, nor awaiting the determination of a claim for, a non-exempt benefit.

(4) Receipt of a written notification under paragraph (1) does not affect the requirement that a beneficiary who—

(a) before reaching pensionable age, informs the Secretary of State that they want their entitlement to a Category A or B retirement pension to be deferred in accordance with section 55(3)(a) of the Contributions and Benefits Act(a); or

(b) after reaching pensionable age, elects to be treated as not having become entitled to either a Category A or B retirement pension in accordance with regulation 2 of the Social Security (Widow's Benefit and Retirement Pensions) Regulations 1979(b),

must make a claim in order subsequently to be entitled to a Category A or B retirement pension.

(5) For the purposes of paragraph (3)(a), a beneficiary who is in receipt of an exempt benefit includes a beneficiary who—

(a) has been awarded such a benefit on or before the day which falls 8 weeks before the day on which the beneficiary reaches pensionable age; and

(b) has not yet received the first payment of that benefit.

(6) For the purposes of this regulation—

"exempt benefit" means any of the following—

(a) an employment and support allowance;

(b) income support;

(c) a jobseeker's allowance;

(d) long-term incapacity benefit;

(e) state pension credit; and

"non-exempt benefit" means any of the following—

(a) carer's allowance;

[[3](ab) carer support payment under the Carer's Assistance (Carer Support Payment) (Scotland) Regulations 2023;]

(b) short-term incapacity benefit;

(c) severe disablement allowance;

(d) widowed mother's allowance;

(e) widow's pension.

(7) The legislation referred to in paragraph (3)(a) is—

(a) section 19 of the Jobseekers Act(a)(circumstances in which a jobseeker's allowance is not payable);

(b) section 20A of that Act(b)(denial or reduction of joint-claim jobseeker's allowance);

(c) regulations made by virtue of any of the following provisions of the Jobseekers Act—

(i) section 8(2)(a)(c)(attendance, information and evidence);

(ii) section 17A(5)(d)(d)(schemes for assisting persons to obtain employment: "work for your benefit" schemes etc.);

(iii) paragraph 7(1)(a) of Schedule A1(e)(persons dependent on drugs etc.);

[2 (ca) any provision of the Social Security Fraud Act 2001 and regulations made by virtue of any such provision.]

(d) regulation 18 of the Social Security (Incapacity for Work) (General) Regulations 1995(f) (disqualification for misconduct etc.); and

(e) regulation 157 of the Employment and Support Allowance Regulations (disqualification for misconduct etc.).]

AMENDMENTS

1. Social Security (Exemption from Claiming Retirement Pension) Regulations 2010 (SI 2010/1794) reg.2 (November 2, 2010).

2. The Social Security (Exemption from Claiming Retirement Pension) Regulations 2011 (SI 2011/1554) reg.3A (October 11, 2011).

3. The Carer's Assistance (Carer Support Payment) (Scotland) Regulations 2023 (Consequential Amendments) Order 2023, art.6 (SI 2023/1218) (November 19, 2023).

Making a claim for benefit

4.—(1) [13 Subject to [21 paragraphs (10) to (11B)], every] claim for benefit [7other than a claim for income support or jobseeker's allowance] shall be made in writing on a form approved by the Secretary of State [3for the purpose of the benefit for which the claim is made], or in such other manner, being in writing, as the Secretary of State [8 or the Board] may accept as sufficient in the circumstances of any particular case. 2.36

[7 (1A) [21 Subject to paragraph (11A), in the case of] a claim for income support or jobseeker's allowance, the claim shall—

(a) be made in writing on a form approved by the Secretary of State for the purpose of the benefit for which the claim is made;

(b) unless any of the reasons specified in paragraph (1B) applies, be made in accordance with the instructions on the form; and

(c) unless any of the reasons specified in paragraph (1B) applies, include such information and evidence as the form may require in connection with the claim.

(1B) The reasons referred to in paragraph (1A) are—

(a) [10 subject to paragraph (1BA)—

(i) the person making the claim is unable to complete the form in accordance with the instructions or to obtain the information or evidence it requires because he has a physical, learning, mental or communication difficulty; and

(ii) it is not reasonably practicable for the claimant to obtain assistance from another person to complete the form or obtain the information or evidence; or

(b) the information or evidence required by the form does not exist; or

(c) the information or evidence required by the form can only be obtained at serious risk of physical or mental harm to the claimant, and it is not reasonably practicable for the claimant to obtain the information or evidence by other means; or

(d) the information or evidence required by the form can only be obtained from a third party, and it is not reasonably practicable for the claimant to obtain such information or evidence from such third party; or

(e) the Secretary of State is of the opinion that the person making the claim [[10]or, in the case of claim for a jobseeker's allowance by a joint-claim couple, either member of that couple,] has provided sufficient information or evidence to show that he is not entitled to the benefit for which the claim is made, and that it would be inappropriate to require the form to be completed or further information or evidence to be supplied.

[[10] (1BA) In the case of a joint-claim couple claiming a jobseeker's allowance jointly, paragraph (1B)(a) shall not apply to the extent that it is reasonably practicable for a member of a joint-claim couple to whom that sub-paragraph applies to obtain assistance from the other member of that couple.]

(1C) If a person making a claim is unable to complete the claim form or supply the evidence or information it requires because one of the reasons specified in sub-paragraphs (a) to (d) of paragraph (1B) applies, he may so notify an appropriate office by whatever means.]

[[18] (1D) In calculating any period of one month for the purposes of paragraph (7) and regulation 6(1A)(b), there shall be disregarded any period commencing on a day on which a person is first notified of a decision that he failed to take part in a work-focused interview and ending on a day on which he was notified that that decision has been revised so that the decision as revised is that he did take part.]

(2) [[8]In the case of a claim for working families' tax credit, where a married or unmarried couple is included in the family, the claim shall be made by whichever partner they agree should so claim.

(2A) Where, in a case to which paragraph (2) applies, the partners are unable to agree which of them should make the claim, the Board may in their discretion determine that the claim shall be made by the partner who, on the information available to the Board at the time of their determination, is in their opinion mainly caring for the children.]

(3) [[5]*Subject to paragraph (3C),*] in the case of a [[16] couple], a claim for income support shall be made by whichever partner they agree should so claim or, in default of agreement, by such one of them as the Secretary of State shall in his discretion determine.

[[2](3A) In the case of a married or unmarried couple where both partners satisfy the conditions set out in [[8] section 129(1) of the Social Security Contributions and Benefits Act 1992], a claim for [[8] disabled persons tax credit] shall be made by whichever partner they agree should so claim, or in default of agreement, by such one of them as [[8] the Board] shall determine.]

[[4](3B) For the purposes of income-based jobseeker's allowance—

(a) in the case of a [[16] couple], a claim shall be made by whichever partner they agree should so claim or, in default of agreement, by such one of them as the Secretary of State shall in his discretion determine;

(b) [[10] (b) where there is no entitlement to a contribution-based jobseeker's allowance on a claim made—

(i) by a member of a joint-claim couple, he subsequently claims a joint-claim jobseeker's allowance with the other member of that couple, the claim made by the couple shall be treated as having been made on the date on which the member of that couple made the claim for a jobseeker's allowance in respect of which there was no entitlement to contribution-based jobseeker's allowance;

(ii) by one partner and the other partner wishes to claim incomebased jobseeker's allowance, the claim made by that other partner shall be treated as having been made on the date on which the first partner made his claim;]

(c) where entitlement to income-based jobseeker's allowance arises on the expiry of entitlement to contribution-based jobseeker's allowance consequent on a claim made by one partner and the other partner then makes a claim—

(i) the claim of the first partner shall be terminated; and

(ii) the claim of the second partner shall be treated as having been made on the day after the entitlement to contribution-based jobseeker's allowance expired.]

[[9] . . .]

(4) Where one of a [[16] couple] is entitled to income support under an award and, with his agreement, his partner claims income support that entitlement shall terminate on the day before that claim is made or treated as made.

[[6](5) Where a person who wishes to make a claim for benefit and who has not been supplied with an approved form of claim notifies an appropriate office (by whatever means) of his intention to make a claim, he [[10]or if he is a member of a joint-claim couple, either member of that couple] shall be supplied, without charge, with such form of claim by such person as the Secretary of State [[8] or the Board] may appoint or authorise for that purpose.]

[[4](6) [[12] Subject to paragraphs (6A) to (6D),] a person wishing to make a claim for benefit shall—

(a) if it is a claim for a jobseeker's allowance, unless the Secretary of State otherwise directs, attend in person at an appropriate office or such other place, and at such time, as the Secretary of State may specify in his case in a [[10]notification under regulation 23 or 23A] of the Jobseeker's Allowance Regulations;

(b) if it is a claim for any other benefit, deliver or send the claim to an appropriate office.]

[[12] (6A) [[19]This paragraph applies to a person]—

(a) who has attained the qualifying age and makes a claim for—

(i) an attendance allowance, [[29] widowed parent's allowance] a carer's allowance, a disability living allowance or incapacity benefit; or

(ii) a retirement pension of any category [[27] , a state pension under Part 1 of the Pensions Act 2014] [[15] or a shared additional pension] for which a claim is required or a winter fuel payment for which a claim is required under regulation 3(1)(b) of the Social Fund Winter Fuel Payment Regulations 2000;

(b) who has not yet attained the qualifying age and makes a claim for a retirement pension [[27] , a state pension under Part 1 of the Pensions Act 2014] [[15] or a shared additional pension] in advance in accordance with regulation 15(1); [[17] . . .]

[[19] (c) who makes a claim for income support; or

(d) who has not attained the qualifying age and who makes a claim for a carer's allowance, disability living allowance [[22], incapacity benefit or an employment and support allowance.]]

(6B) A person to whom paragraph (6A) applies may make a claim by sending or delivering it to, or by making it in person at—

(a) an office designated by the Secretary of State for accepting such claims; [[17] . . .]

[[19] (b) the offices of—

(i) a local authority administering housing benefit [[25] . . .]

(ii) a county council in England,
(iii) a person providing services to a person mentioned in head (i) or (ii),
(iv) a person authorised to exercise any function of a local authority relating to housing benefit [25 . . .], or
(v) a person authorised to exercise any function a county council in England has under section 7A of the Social Security Administration Act 1992,

if the Secretary of State has arranged with the local authority, county council or other person for them to receive claims in accordance with this sub-paragraph.]

(6C) Where a person to whom paragraph (6A) applies makes a claim in accordance with paragraph (6B)(b), on receipt of the claim the local authority or other person specified in that sub-paragraph—

(a) shall forward the claim to the Secretary of State as soon as reasonably practicable;
(b) may receive information or evidence relating to the claim supplied by—
 (i) the person making, or who has made, the claim; or
 (ii) other persons in connection with the claim,
 and shall forward it to the Secretary of State as soon as reasonably practicable;
(c) may obtain information or evidence relating to the claim from the person who has made the claim, but not any medical information or evidence except for that which the claimant must provide in accordance with instructions on the form, and shall forward the information or evidence to the Secretary of State as soon as reasonably practicable;
[19(cc) may verify any non-medical information or evidence supplied or obtained in accordance with sub-paragraph (b) or (c) and shall forward it to the Secretary of State as soon as reasonably practicable;]
(d) may record information or evidence relating to the claim supplied or obtained in accordance with sub-paragraphs (b) or (c) and may hold the information or evidence (whether as supplied or obtained or as recorded) for the purpose of forwarding it to the Secretary of State; and
(e) may give information and advice with respect to the claim to the person who makes, or who has made, the claim.

[14 (6CC) Paragraphs (6C)(b) to (e) apply in respect of information, evidence and advice relating to any claim by a person to whom paragraph (6A) applies, whether the claim is made in accordance with paragraph (6B)(b) or otherwise.]

(6D) The benefits specified in paragraph (6A) are relevant benefits for the purposes of section 7A of the Social Security Administration Act 1992.]

[22 (7) If a claim, other than a claim for income support or jobseeker's allowance, is defective at the date it is received in an appropriate office or office specified in paragraph (6B) where that paragraph applies—

(a) the Secretary of State shall advise the claimant of the defect; and
(b) if a properly completed claim is received within one month, or such longer period as the Secretary of State may consider reasonable, from the date on which the claimant is [23 first] advised of the defect, the Secretary of State shall treat the claim as properly made in the first instance.

(7ZA) If a claim, other than a claim for income support or jobseeker's allowance, has been made in writing but not on the form approved for the time being—

(a) the Secretary of State may supply the claimant with the approved form; and

(b) if the form is received properly completed within one month, or such longer period as the Secretary of State may consider reasonable, from the date on which the claimant is supplied with the approved form, the Secretary of State shall treat the claim as properly made in the first instance.]

[[10] (7A) In the case of a claim for income support, if a defective claim is received, the Secretary of State shall advise the person making the claim of the defect and of the relevant provisions of regulation 6(1A) relating to the date of claim.

(7B) In the case of a claim for a jobseeker's allowance, if a defective claim is received, the Secretary of State shall advise—

(a) in the case of a claim made by a joint-claim couple, each member of the couple of the defect and of the relevant provisions of regulation 6(4ZA) relating to the date of that claim;

(b) in any other case, the person making the claim of the defect and of the relevant provisions of regulation 6(4A) relating to the date of claim.]

(8) A claim, other than a claim for income support or jobseeker's allowance, which is made on the form approved for the time being is, for the purposes of these Regulations, properly completed if completed in accordance with the instructions on the form and defective if not so completed.

[[8](8A) Where—

(a) the Board determine under paragraph (2A) that a claim for working families' tax credit shall be made by the partner who in their opinion is mainly caring for the children,

(b) a claim for working families' tax credit is made by that partner on the form approved for the time being, and

(c) the claim is not completed in accordance with the instructions on the form by reason only that, in consequence of the other partner not agreeing which of them should make the claim, it has not been signed by the other partner

the Board may in their discretion treat that claim as completed in accordance with the instructions on the form for the purposes of paragraph (8), notwithstanding that it has not been signed by the other partner in accordance with those instructions.]

(9) In the case of a claim for income support or jobseeker's allowance, a properly completed claim is a claim which meets the requirements of paragraph (1A) and a defective claim is a claim which does not meet those requirements.]

[[11] (10) This regulation shall not apply to a claim for state pension credit [[22], subject to regulation 6(1G)], [[20] or an employment and support allowance.]

[[28] (11) A claim for the following benefits may be made by telephone call to a telephone number specified by the Secretary of State for the purpose of the benefit for which the claim is made, unless the Secretary of State directs, in any particular case, that the claim must be made in writing—

(a) graduated retirement benefit;

(b) a shared additional pension;

(c) a retirement pension;
(d) a state pension under Part 1 of the Pensions Act 2014;
[[29] (e) widowed parent's allowance;
(ea) bereavement support payment;]
(f) a social fund payment for funeral expenses or winter fuel payment;
(g) industrial injuries benefit.]

[[21] (11A) A claim for income support or jobseeker's allowance may be made by telephone call to the telephone number specified by the Secretary of State where such a claim falls within a category of case [[22] for which the Secretary of State accepts telephone claims, or in any other case where the Secretary of State is willing to do so]

(11B) Paragraph (11A) shall apply unless in any particular case the Secretary of State directs that the claim must be made in writing.]

[[22] (12) A claim made by telephone in accordance with paragraph (11) or (11A) is properly completed if the Secretary of State is provided with all the information required to determine the claim and the claim is defective if not so completed.

(13) Where a claim made by telephone is defective—
(a) in the case of a claim other than a claim for income support or jobseeker's allowance, paragraph (7) applies;
(b) in the case of a claim for income support, paragraph (7A) applies; and
(c) in the case of a claim for jobseeker's allowance, paragraph (7B) applies,

except that references to a defective claim being received or received in an appropriate office or office specified in paragraph (6B) where that paragraph applies are to be read as references to a defective claim being made by telephone and the reference in paragraph (7)(b) to a properly completed claim being received is to be read as a reference to a claim made by telephone being properly completed.]

[[22] . . .]

AMENDMENTS

1. The Social Security (Miscellaneous Provisions) Amendment Regulations 1990 (SI 1990/2208) reg.8 (December 5, 1990).

2. The Social Security (Claims and Payments) Amendment Regulations 1991 (SI 1991/2741) reg.3 (February 3, 1992).

3. The Social Security (Miscellaneous Provisions) Amendment Regulations 1992 (SI 1992/247) reg.10 (March 9, 1992).

4. The Social Security (Claims and Payments) (Jobseeker's Allowance Consequential Amendments) Regulations 1996 (SI 1996/1460) reg.2(4) (October 7, 1996).

5. The Income Support and Social Security (Claims and Payments) (Miscellaneous Amendments) Regulations 1996 (SI 1996/2431) reg.7(b) (October 15, 1996).

6. The Social Security (Miscellaneous Amendments) (No.2) Regulations 1997 (SI 1997/793) reg.2(4) (April 7, 1997).

7. The Social Security (Miscellaneous Amendments) (No.2) Regulations 1997 (SI 1997/793) reg.2 (October 6, 1997).

8. The Tax Credits (Claims and Payments) (Amendment) Regulations 1999 (SI 1999/2572) reg.4 (October 5, 1999).

9. "Lapsed" by the Asylum and Immigration (Treatment of Claimants etc.) Act 2004 s.12(2) (June 14, 2007).

10. The Social Security (Joint Claims: Consequential Amendments) Regulations 2000 (SI 2000/1982) reg.2(3) (March 19, 2001).

11. State Pension Credit (Consequential, Transitional and Miscellaneous Provisions) Regulations 2002 (SI 2002/3019) reg.4 (April 7, 2003).

12. The Social Security (Claims and Payments and Miscellaneous Amendments) Regulations 2003 (SI 2003/1632) reg.2(2) (July 21, 2003).

13. The Social Security (Claims and Payments and Payments on account, Overpayments and Recovery) Amendment Regulations 2005 (SI 2005/34) reg.2 (May 2, 2005).

14. The Social Security, Child Support and Tax Credits (Miscellaneous Amendments) Regulations 2005 (SI 2005/337) reg.7 (March 18, 2005).

15. The Social Security (Shared Additional Pension) (Miscellaneous Amendments) Regulations 2005 (SI 2005/1551) (July 6, 2005).

16. The Civil Partnership (Pensions, Social Security and Child Support) (Consequential etc. Provisions) Order 2005 (SI 2005/2887) (December 5, 2005).

17. The Social Security (Miscellaneous Amendments) (No.2) Regulations 2006 (SI 2006/832) (April 10, 2006).

18. The Social Security (Work-focused Interviews) Regulations 2000 (SI 2000/897) (April 3, 2000).

19. The Social Security (Claims and Information) Regulations 2007 (SI 2007/2911) (October 31, 2007).

20. The Employment and Support Allowance (Consequential Provisions) (No.2) Regulations 2008 (SI 2008/1554) reg.12 (October 27, 2008).

21. The Social Security (Miscellaneous Amendments) (No.5) Regulations 2008 (SI 2008/2667) reg.2 (October 30, 2008).

22. The Social Security (Miscellaneous Amendments) (No.2) Regulations 2009 (SI 2009/1490) reg.2 (July 13, 2009).

23. The Social Security (Miscellaneous Amendments) (No.4) Regulations 2009 (SI 2009/2655) reg.3 (October 26, 2009).

24. Social Security (Claims and Payments) Amendment (No.3) Regulations 2010 (SI 2010/1676) reg.2 (July 29, 2010).

25. The Council Tax Benefit Abolition (Consequential Provision) Regulations 2013 (SI 2013/458) reg.3 (April 1, 2013).

26. The Social Security (Miscellaneous Amendments) Regulations 2014 (SI 2014/591) reg.3 (April 28, 2014).

27. The Pensions Act 2014 (Consequential, Supplementary and Incidental Amendments) Order 2015 (SI 2015/1985) art.9(4) (April 6, 2016).

28. Social Security (Claims and Payments) Amendment Regulations 2016 (SI 2016/544) reg.2 (June 15, 2016).

29. The Pensions Act 2014 (Consequential, Supplementary and Incidental Amendments) Order 2017 (SI 2017/422) art.10 (April 6, 2017).

DEFINITIONS

"appropriate office"—see reg.2(1).
"benefit"—see reg.2(2).
"claim for benefit"—see reg.2(1).
"jobseeker's allowance"—*ibid.*
"married couple"—*ibid.*
"partner"—*ibid.*
"refugee"—*ibid.*
"unmarried couple"—*ibid.*

GENERAL NOTE

Introduction

Note that this regulation does not apply to claims for state pension credit, or for an employment and support allowance: para.(10). **2.37**

Section 1 of the Administration Act requires a claim to be submitted for any benefit to which the section applies except where regulations otherwise prescribe (see reg.3), as a condition of entitlement to benefit. This largely removes the effect of the decision of the House of Lords in *Insurance Officer v McCaffrey* [1984] 1 W.L.R. 1353, though some doubt remained in relation to entitlement prior to September 2, 1985, when the first version of s.1 was implemented. This is now resolved by s.2 of the Administrative Act.

The claims system is largely predicated on a system of written claims, but recent amendments now make provision for telephone claims.

2.38 A fine line used to be drawn between the responsibilities of the Secretary of State and the adjudicating authorities under this regulation. It has been consistently held that it is for the Secretary of State to say whether a document (not in the prescribed form) is acceptable as "sufficient in the circumstances of the particular case," but the duty lies on the adjudicating authorities to decide whether such a document is a claim for benefit: *R(U)9/60* and *R(S)1/63*. It may be significant that in both these cases the Commissioner concluded that a document accepted by the Secretary of State did not constitute a claim for benefit. It is sometimes argued that the Secretary of State's authority under para.(1) extends to determining the date of the claim. This is not so. The sole issue reserved for the Secretary of State under para.(1) is whether the *form* of the claim (if not on a prescribed form) is acceptable as a claim. It is left for decision makers and tribunals to determine the date of the claim and what has been claimed once the Secretary of State has determined that it is in acceptable form: *R(SB)5/89* confirmed in *CU/94/1994*. This distinction now largely disappears with the abolition of adjudication officers.

Novitskaya v London Borough of Brent (SSWP intervening) [2009] EWCA Civ 1260; [2010] AACR 6, is a judgment on a housing benefit claim, but the propositions stated by the Court of Appeal must relate to the general concept of a claim for benefit. The Court of Appeal ruled that a claim did not need to be in any particular form, nor did it need to name a benefit, but it must raise the possibility of its being a claim for benefit. Referring to *R(S) 1/63*, Arden L.J. said:

> "19. While this is a very helpful decision, excessive reliance should not be placed on the Commissioner's statement that the intention to claim benefit should appear on the face of the document alleged to constitute a claim. Claims are no different from any other document requiring interpretation and it is now well-established that the meaning of documents should be ascertained in the light of the relevant surrounding facts (*Investors Compensation Scheme Ltd v West Bromwich Building Society* [1998] 1 WLR 896). Thus, it may be possible to infer that a claim is being made from some other document. The Commissioner refers to the possibility that an accompanying letter might be enough to make it clear that another document was making a claim. In my view this is certainly legally possible."

A claim not in the prescribed form would be a defective claim, but that defect would be capable of being corrected, and would not necessarily defeat the claim altogether. In response to the judgment the Department has three principles for determining guidance in Memo DMG 3/10, which suggests the application of three principles of determining whether a claim not on an official claim form is a claim for benefit (albeit defective):

(1) The contested document should be able to be read as a claim for benefit and not simply as a request for information.

(2) A particular benefit does not necessarily have to be named; but there is a clear inference that the vaguer the document the less likely it will be that decision maker will conclude that it is a defective claim for benefit rather than some other communication.

(3) The contested document should not be considered in isolation, but should be read in the context of any accompanying documents or statements made to the Department by the author of the document.

2.39 The issue of whether tribunals have jurisdiction to consider the decision of the Secretary of State as to when a claim was validly made where it is initially defective has been considered in cases *R(IS) 6/04* and *CIS/758/2002*. The Commissioner, in *R(IS) 6/04,* ruled that the absence of a right of appeal was incompatible with art.6 of the European Convention, and so disapplied the provision in Sch.2 to the Decisions and Appeals Regulations in so far as it was necessary to do so in order to ensure that the claimant was entitled to appeal against a decision as to whether or when a claim had been validly made in accordance with this regulation. This has restored the position to that which previously applied before the SSA 1998 entered into force: see *R(U) 9/60.*

On the substance of what is required for a valid claim, the Commissioner has this to say:

> "I do not think an over-literal approach should be taken in this context: if, for example, all the figures required to determine entitlement are supplied and identified sufficiently clearly when the claimant submits his claim, either in answers recorded on the claim form itself or in annexed documents to which those answers expressly or impliedly refer, then it would in my judgment be open to a tribunal to hold on the facts that there has been no *material* failure such as to render the claim and the information supplied with it incomplete, even if admittedly the claimant has not complied with the instructions to the letter by repeating the actual figures in the boxes on the form itself. In addition, it seems to have been regarded as a defect fatal to the *claim* that he only gave details of his bank, and not of a Post Office, in the part of the form that asked him about the method of *payment* he preferred if benefit was in due course awarded." (para.54)

and:

> "I direct the tribunal that for this purpose they should concern themselves only with the matters and information necessary to determine entitlement to the benefit claimed. It seems to me that both sides are right in saying, as Mr Wright submits and Mr Spencer very fairly agrees in the most recent written submissions, that the requirements in regulation 4(1A)(b)–(c) strictly concern the information and evidence required in connection with the *claim* so as to enable it to be determined; not such things as the administrative arrangements for payment of any benefit that may subsequently be awarded on that claim. Thus even though it is of course convenient and sensible for the claimant to be asked about these at the same time and to put them on the same form, the omission of such additional details as the Post Office, needed (if at all) only for payment purposes (and as Mr Spencer points out, not in any event crucial or binding so far as the Secretary of State is concerned, under regulation 20 of the Claims and Payments regulations) does not render an otherwise complete claim defective." (para.56)

CIS/758/2002 added a gloss on this case in relation to defective claims for income support or a jobseeker's allowance, namely that the mandatory four week time limit for correcting defects on the claim form is not contrary to Convention rights protected by the Human Rights Act 1998 when compared with the longer discretionary time limit allowed for correcting defects in claims for other benefits. This is said to be because income support and income-based jobseeker's allowance are not possessions for the purposes of the protection of property rights under art.1 of Protocol 1 of the European Convention, although that proposition is almost certainly no longer good law following the decision of the Grand Chamber in the *Stec* case: see annotations to art.1 of Protocol 1 at para.4.180.

Once a claim has been made, it may only be withdrawn before it has been adjudicated upon by an adjudication officer (now decision maker): *R(U) 2/79* and *R(U) 7/83* and see reg.5(2).

Paragraph (1)

Unless provision is made for telephone claims, para.(1) provides that claims must be made in writing, normally on an official form, although the Secretary of State may accept some other kind of written claim. In such a case, under para.(7), the **2.40**

Secretary of State may require the claimant to fill in the proper form. If this is done in the proper time the claim is treated as duly made in the first instance. It no longer seems possible for an oral claim to be accepted, but see below on telephone claims. However, see reg.6(1)(aa) for the position when a claimant contacts an office with a view to making a claim.

Note also *R(SB) 9/84* where a Tribunal of Commissioners holds that where a claim has been determined, the Secretary of State must be deemed, in the absence of any challenge at the time, to have accepted that the claim was made in sufficient manner. See the notes to reg.33. See also *CDLA/1596/1996* in which the Commissioner set aside the tribunal's decision because they had failed to consider whether they should refer to the Secretary of State the question whether the claimant's application for review should be treated as a claim under para.(1).

MS v SSWP (JSA) [2016] UKUT 206 (AAC) establishes that the defective claim rule in reg.4(1) is limited to information or evidence required by the claim form and not that required at a later interview. Judge Wright said:

> "10. It is thus apparent from the wording of regulation 4(9) that the statutory 'defective claim' is limited to a claim which does not meet the requirements of regulation 4(1A) alone. Moreover, and most importantly for the purposes of this appeal, the information or evidence (the lack of which, or failure to provide which may render a claim defective) has to be information or evidence that has been required <u>by the claim form</u> as the . . . words ['as the form may require'] in regulation 4(1A)(c) and the 'required by the form' language in regulation 4(1B) in my judgment make evident. Information or evidence required other than by the claim form, at a follow-up interview for example, cannot therefore make the claim 'defective' if not provided."

2.41 In *SSWP v BM (RP)* [2016] UKUT 419 (AAC), the claimant had deferred his entitlement to a retirement pension for some years. He sent in a letter on March 6, 2015 claiming his retirement pension and stating that he would "like to receive any back-dated payments from my 65th birthday onwards to which I am entitled." The claimant died on 11 March. The administrator of the claimant's estate subsequently completed a formal claim form, but the Secretary of State only awarded retirement pension including three months' arrears prior to the date of claim. The letter setting out the decision said that the administrator did not have the option of choosing a lump sum payment on behalf of the claimant's estate because the claimant had not made the claim before he died. The First-tier Tribunal found as a fact that the letter had been received by the Department on March 9, that it was a valid claim, and that the claimant had made clear that he wanted a lump sum payment. But, in the alternative, if he had not, he was deemed to have chosen a lump sum because of para. A1(2) of Sch.5 to the Contributions and Benefits Act.

Two issues were before the Upper Tribunal: (1) whether the First-tier Tribunal had erred in law in concluding that the Department received the letter on March 9; and (2) whether the claim was procedurally effective. Judge Markus QC analyses the case law on posting and its receipt, and rejects the argument that the First-tier Tribunal had erred in applying s.7 of the Interpretation Act 1978; the tribunal had rather made a finding of fact that was open to it in the light of the all the circumstances. There was, just to mention one factor, no date stamp on the claimant's letter. Judge Markus QC says, in a context in which the Department admitted receipt of the letter but asserted that it was not received until March 12:

> "The tribunal was entitled to take judicial notice of Royal Mail practice and to find, in the absence of any evidence to the contrary, that it was likely that collection and delivery occurred accordingly." (para.21)

Judge Markus QC also upholds the First-tier Tribunal's finding that the letter constituted a claim. The Secretary of State argued that the administrator was not able to perfect the claim by providing the information missing from the initial letter. Judge Markus disagreed; *R(IS) 3/04* did not apply; the Claims and Payments Regulations make different provision for claims to income support and claims to retirement pension. In this case, the administrator must have been acting under an appointment covered by reg.30(1)—and not reg.30(6)—and this enabled the administrator to perfect the claim. Finally, Judge Markus sees no error of law in the First-tier Tribunal's concluding that the import of the claimant's letter of 6 March was that he wanted a lump sum payment.

Paragraphs (1A)–(1C)

These provisions, together with reg.6(1A) and (4A)–(4AB), introduce the so-called "onus of proof" changes for claims for income support and JSA from October 6, 1997. The aim is to place more responsibility on claimants for these benefits to provide information and evidence to support their claim (see the DSS's Memorandum to the Social Security Advisory Committee (SSAC) annexed to the Committee's report (Cmnd. 3586) on the proposals). SSAC supported this principle but considered that it was "premature to introduce penalties for failure to provide information when it is more likely that the current problems lie more with the forms and procedures than with dilatory or obstructive claimants". As the Committee pointed out, the current claim forms are lengthy, complex and difficult for many people to understand, and moreover in the past told claimants not to delay sending in the claim form even if they had not got all the required information. Furthermore, since income support and income-based JSA are basic subsistence benefits, claimants have every incentive to cooperate in providing all the information needed to get an early payment. Thus SSAC's main recommendation was that the claim forms and guidance to claimants should first be revised and tested "before introducing new penalties, which together with the proposed changes to backdating rules [see reg.19], will only serve to complicate the social security system and penalise the most disadvantaged claimants". But this recommendation was rejected by the Government, although the final form of the regulations did take limited account of some of SSAC's other recommendations. 2.42

Under the rules, in order for a claim for income support or JSA to be validly made, it must be in writing (unless telephone claims are permitted) on a properly completed approved form (there is no longer any provision for the Secretary of State to accept any other kind of written claim) and all the information and evidence required by the form must have been provided (para.(1A)). However, the requirement to complete the form fully or to provide the required evidence does not apply in the circumstances set out in para.(1B). The list in para.(1B) is exhaustive and there is no category of analogous circumstances. If any of sub-paras (a)–(d) of para.(1B) do apply, the person can inform an appropriate office (defined in reg.2(1)) "by whatever means" (e.g. verbally or through a third party) (para.(1C)). Note that the obligation to provide information and evidence only relates to that required by the claim form; if a claim is accepted as validly made it will still be open to the Department to seek further information if this is required in order to decide the claim, but this will not alter the date of claim.

See reg.6(1A) for the date of claim for an income support claim and reg.6(4A)–(4AB) for the date of claim for JSA claims (and note the differences).

Thus the major effect of these rules is that there is a requirement to produce the specified information and evidence *before* a claim is treated as having been made (although see reg.6(1A) and (4A)–(4AB) for the date of claim). Whether the necessary evidence has been produced or whether a claimant is exempt under para.(1B) will, however, now be subject to appeal to a tribunal, on the application, by analogy, of the principle established in *R(IS) 6/04*. The contrary position which has been set out in earlier editions and was approved by the Commissioner in *CJSA/69/2001* would seem to be inconsistent with the approach adopted in *R(IS) 6/04*. 2.43

For a decision addressing the proper approach to a case in which a person seeks to resurrect a claim for income support some considerable time after sending in a letter indicating an intention to claim income support, see *IJ v SSWP (IS)* [2013] UKUT 302 (AAC).

For a decision exploring issues which can arise when an electronic claim for a jobseeker's allowance goes wrong, see *CW v SSWP (JSA)* [2016] UKUT 114 (AAC).

Note also s.1(1A) of the Administration Act, under which claimants will not be entitled to benefit unless they satisfy requirements relating to the provision of national insurance numbers.

Paragraphs (2) and (2A)

2.44 In working families' tax credit cases, if a couple is involved, the claim may be made by either partner.

Paragraph (3)

2.45 In income support cases, where a couple is involved, either partner can be the claimant, except in the case of a refugee under para.(3C). There is a free choice. If the couple cannot jointly agree who should claim, the Secretary of State is to break the tie. There are still some differences in entitlement according to which partner is the claimant, particularly since only the claimant is required to be available for work. In addition, head (b) of para.12(1) of Sch.2 to the Income Support Regulations (disability and higher pensioner premium) can only be satisfied by the claimant. But there is now no long-term rate and the full-time employment of either partner excludes entitlement to income support. See reg.7(2). Under the Income Support (Transitional) Regulations transitional protection is lost if the claimant for the couple changes. *CIS 8/1990* and *CIS 375/1990* challenged this rule on the grounds that it was indirectly discriminatory against women (since in 98 per cent of couples (at that time) the man was the claimant). Following the European Court of Justice's decision in the *Cresswell* case that income support is not covered by EC Directive 79/7 on equal treatment for men and women in social security (see the notes to reg.36 of the Income Support Regulations), the claimants could not rely on European law. The Commissioner also rejects a submission that the Sex Discrimination Act 1975 prevented the discriminatory effect of regs 2 and 10 of the Transitional Regulations. Paragraph (4) below deals with changes of partner.

Paragraph (3C) has been "lapsed" (see Amendments) but the italicised words remain.

Paragraph (3A)

2.46 Under para.(3A), if both partners in a couple satisfy the conditions of entitlement for a disabled person's tax credit, they may choose which one of them is to claim. If they cannot choose, the Secretary of State makes the decision.

Paragraph (3B)

2.47 Sub-paragraph (a) applies the normal income support rule for couples to income-based JSA. Sub-paragraphs (b) and (c) make provision about the deemed date of the claim for income-based JSA by one partner when a claim for contribution-based JSA by the other partner fails or entitlement comes to an end.

[. . .]

Paragraph (4)

2.48 If there is a change of claimant within a couple in the middle of a continuing income support claim, the claims are not to overlap. The change is a matter of a new claim for benefit, not review as it was for supplementary benefit (*R(SB) 1/93*). In *CSIS 66/1992* the Commissioner rejects the argument that para.(4) combined with s.20(9) of the Social Security Act 1986 (SSCBA s.134(2)) meant that a change of claimant could not be backdated. If the claimant could show good cause for her delay in claiming, regs 19(2) and 6(3) enabled her claim to be backdated to the date from which she had good cause (subject to the then what was then a 12-month limit in reg.19(4)). Duplication of payment could be avoided by the AO reviewing the claimant's husband's entitlement for any past period in respect of which the claimant was held to be entitled to benefit and applying reg.5(1) and (2),

Case 1, of the Payments Regulations. By becoming the claimant the wife qualified for a disability premium. There is a specific provision in para.19 of Sch.7 to the Income Support Regulations for arrears of a disability premium in these circumstances.

Paragraph (5)

Regulation 4(5) imposes a duty on the Department to provide a claim form in the circumstances set out there. The effect of a failure by the Department to comply with that duty is considered in *R (IS) 4/07*, which also reviews the earlier authorities on the point. The specific issue raised was whether a breach of reg.4(5) results in suspension of the operation of the time limits for claiming. The Commissioner concludes that it does not. However, the provisions of reg.19 on backdating would be available to a claimant who sought to have a claim backdated in such circumstances. **2.49**

Paragraph (6)

The claim must be delivered or sent to the appropriate office, though increasing provision is now being made for telephone or electronic claims. **2.50**

For a discussion of some evidential and practical issues in relation to the making of a claim and the timing of it, see *SSWP v LM (IS)* [2015] UKUT 202 (AAC).

For JSA, a claimant wishing to make an initial claim must normally go in person to the nearest Job Centre to obtain a claim pack from the new jobseeker receptionist. An appointment will then be made for the claimant to return, usually within five days, for a new jobseeker interview. This is all part of the concept of "active signing". The claim will be treated as made on the date of the first attendance, if it is received properly completed within a month (reg.6(1)(aa) and (4A)).

For a decision exploring issues which can arise when an electronic claim for a jobseeker's allowance goes wrong, see *CW v SSWP (JSA)* [2016] UKUT 114 (AAC).

Paragraphs (6A)–(6D)

Note the rules in these paragraphs which relate to claims for the named benefits by those who have attained "the qualifying age". This is defined in reg.2 by reference to s.1(6) of the State Pension Credit Act 2002, which provides: **2.51**

In this Act "'the qualifying age'" means—

(a) in the case of a woman, pensionable age; or
(b) in the case of a man, the age which is rising: pensionable age in the case of a woman born on the same day as the man.

Pensionable age for women is see s.126 and Sch.4 to the Pensions Act 1995 for the detail.

Paragraphs (7) and (8)

Paragraph (7), which does not apply to claims for income support or JSA (for which see para.(7A)), deals with written claims not made on the proper form (for which, see para.(1)), and situations where the proper form is not completed according to the instructions (see para.8)). The Secretary of State may simply treat this as an ineffective attempt to claim, but also has power to refer the form back to the claimant. Then there is one month (extendable by the Secretary of State) to complete the form properly, in which case the claim is treated as made on the date of the original attempt to claim (see reg.6(1)(b)). Note also *R(SB) 9/84*; see the note to para.(1). **2.52**

CP/3447/2003 concerned a claim for an adult dependency increase to a retirement pension for the claimant's wife. The claimant had made his claim for retirement pension at the proper time in advance of his 65th birthday indicating on the claim form that he wished to claim the increase for his wife. Adult dependency increase is, by virtue of reg.2(3) of the Claims and Payments Regulations, treated as a separate benefit requiring a separate claim. The Department failed to pick up the statement in the retirement pension claim form and did not send the claimant a further form **2.53** to complete. In the following year, the claimant wrote to ask whether he was getting the increase after a query on his tax return. The required form was then issued to him. He completed it and it was clear that he should have been receiving the increase all along. The Secretary of State refused to pay it back to the start of the retirement pension on the grounds that the claim was received following the enquiry and could only be backdated three months from that date. By the time the appeal came before the tribunal, the Secretary of State accepted that the decision was wrong. The issue turned on the proper interpretation of reg.4(7). In particular, what was the date on which the claim was made 'in the first instance' in this case. Was it the date on which the claimant wrote his letter asking about his entitlement to the increase of his wife, or was it the indication in his original claim form for retirement pension indicating that he wanted the increase for his wife?

The Commissioner concluded,

> "In those circumstances, given that (a) a claim in writing for the increase is now accepted as having been made in the first instance by the claimant in early 1999 as part of the original claim for his pension, and (b) the Secretary of State did in fact exercise his powers in regulation 4(7) to supply the claimant with the approved form which was returned duly completed well within the month stipulated, the conditions under which the Secretary of State is bound to treat the claim as if it had been duly made "in the first instance" are in my judgment satisfied in reference to the *original* date of claim in 1999, not just the enquiry letter the following year. Since the requirement to treat the claim as duly made "in the first instance" is mandatory once the conditions are met, there is no further exercise of discretionary or administrative judgment for the Secretary of State to make under regulation 4(7) before the effect in terms of entitlement to benefit can be properly determined. Although it was only in response to the further enquiry that the form was eventually supplied the Secretary of State could not in my judgment possibly rely on that as an argument for saying that the existence of the first claim should be ignored, when the failure to supply the form in the first instance was admittedly an administrative error by his own local officials and should never have happened at all." (para.15)

The Commissioner does, however, note that in so finding in the particular circumstances of this case, he is not to be taken as pronouncing as a matter of general principle that ticking boxes on a form in the expectation of receiving a further form ought in every case to constitute making a claim in writing for the benefit in question. (para.14)

Paragraph (7A)

2.54 There are special rules in reg.4 where the benefit claimed is income support. In *CIS/3173/2003*, the claimant had contacted an office of the Department with a view to making a claim for income support on October 14, 2002, and she had subsequently completed an income support claim form on October 24, 2002, but did not include payslips with that form. These were required since she declared that she was doing "therapeutic work" (actually work accepted as permitted for the purposes of incapacity benefit). The Department contacted the claimant on December 18, 2002 regarding the missing payslips. These were provided on December 19, 2002. The decision maker awarded income support only from December 19, 2002. The tribunal upheld that decision. The Commissioner also concludes that there was no entitlement until December 19, 2002. He concludes that the claim form sent in without the accompanying payslips was a defective claim under sub-para.(7A) with the consequences stated there, but that reg.6(1A) makes provision only for one month's leeway in providing the information or evidence required to cure the defect. More than one month had passed here, and accordingly no claim which complied with the requirement of reg.4(1A) was made until December 19, 2002. It did not matter that the Department had not requested the payslips earlier. The Commissioner has granted leave to appeal in this case.

Paragraphs (7A), (7B) and (9)

If a claim for income support or JSA is defective (on which see para.(9)), the 2.55
Secretary of State will simply advise the claimant of the defect and of the rules in reg.6(1A) (for income support claims) or reg.6(4A) (for JSA claims) as appropriate. It will then be up to the claimant to comply with those provisions if he is in a position to do so.

Paragraphs (11)–(14)

These paragraphs make provision, in a system which has previously been based 2.56
upon a requirement for written claims, for telephone claims for retirement pension and graduated retirement pension. Telephone claims will take the form of an interview between an officer of the Department and the claimant whose answers will be input directly into the Department's computer system. A decision on the claim may be made on the spot, since entitlement to pensions can very often be determined easily by reference to information already held in Departmental records. These paragraphs make provision for telephone claims, but reserve the Secretary of State's power to insist upon a written claim. Provision is also made for treating a telephone claim as a defective claim and allowing a period for the defect to be remedied.

[[1] Further provisions as to claims

4A.—(1) Where a claimant resides in both— 2.57
(a) the area of a local authority specified in Part I or II of Schedule 1 to the Social Security (Claims and Information) Regulations 1999; and
(b) a postcode district identified in Part I or II of Schedule 2 to the Social Security (Claims and Information) Regulations 1999,

any claim for a benefit to which paragraph (2) applies may be made to any office displaying the **one** logo (whether or not that office is situated within the area of the local authority in which the claimant resides).

(2) The benefits to which this paragraph applies are—
(a) a jobseeker's allowance;
(b) income support;
(c) incapacity benefit;
(d) [[2] carer's allowance];
(e) severe disablement allowance;
(f) widow's benefit;
(g) bereavement benefits;
(h) disability living allowance.

(3) A claim made in accordance with paragraph (1), other than a claim for income support or a jobseeker's allowance, shall be made in writing on a form approved by the Secretary of State for the purpose of the benefit to which the claim is made, or in such other manner, being in writing, as the person to whom the claim is made may accept as sufficient in the circumstances of the particular case.

(4) In the case of a claim for income support or a jobseeker's allowance, the provisions of regulation 4(1A) to (1C) shall apply.

(5) In its application to the area of any authority specified in Part I or II of Schedule 1 to the Social Security (Claims and Information) Regulations 1999, the "appropriate office" in these Regulations includes also an office of an authority or person to whom claims may be made in accordance with paragraph (1).

(6) In these Regulations, a "participating authority" means any local authority or person to whom claims may be made in accordance with paragraph (1).

AMENDMENTS

1. This regulation inserted by The Social Security (Claims and Information) Regulations 1999 (SI 1999/3108) reg.5 (November 29, 1999).

2. The Social Security Amendment (Carer's Allowance) Regulations 2002 (SI 2002/2497) Sch.2 (October 23, 2002).

Forwarding claims and information

2.58 **4B.**—(1) A participating authority may—

(a) record information or evidence relating to any social security matter supplied by or obtained from a person at an office displaying the **one** logo, whether or not the information or evidence is supplied or obtained in connection with the making of a claim for benefit;

(b) give information or advice with respect to any social security matter to persons who are making, or have made, claims for any benefit to which regulation 4A(2) applies [2 or for state pension credit.]

(2) A participating authority shall forward to the Secretary of State—

(a) any claim for benefit, other than a claim for housing benefit [3 . . .], together with any information or evidence supplied to the authority in connection with that claim; and

(b) any information or evidence relating to any other social security matter, except where the information or evidence relates solely to housing benefit [3 . . .] given to the authority by a person making a claim for, or who has claimed, a benefit to which regulation 4A(2) applies.]

AMENDMENTS

1. This regulation inserted by The Social Security (Claims and Information) Regulations 1999 (SI 1999/3108) reg.5 (November 29, 1999).

2. State Pension Credit (Consequential, Transitional and Miscellaneous) Regulations 2002 (SI 2002/3019) reg.4 (April 7, 2003).

3. The Council Tax Benefit Abolition (Consequential Provision) Regulations 2013 (SI 2013/458) reg.3 (April 1, 2013).

[1 Electronic claims for benefit

2.59 **4ZC.**—(1) Any claim for benefit in relation to which this regulation applies, and any certificate, notice, information or evidence given in connection with that claim, may be made or given by means of an electronic communication, in accordance with the provisions set out in Schedule 9ZC.

[5 "(2) This regulation applies to the following benefits—

(a) carer's allowance;

(b) attendance allowance;

[6 (ba) bereavement support payment;]

(c) disability living allowance;

(d) graduated retirement benefit;

(e) a jobseeker's allowance;

(f) a retirement pension;

(g) state pension under Part 1 of the Pensions Act 2014;

(h) shared additional pension;

(i) industrial injuries benefit;
(j) an employment and support allowance;]
[7 (k) state pension credit.]
[8(l) a social fund funeral payment;
(m) a social fund payment in respect of maternity expenses;
(n) maternity allowance.]

AMENDMENTS

1. The Social Security (Electronic Communications) (Carer's Allowance) Order 2003 (SI 2003/2800) reg.2 (December 1, 2003).
2. The Social Security (Electronic Communications) (Miscellaneous Benefits) Order 2005 (SI 2005/3321) (January 30, 2006).
3. The Social Security (Electronic Communications) Order 2011 (SI 2011/1498) (February 1, 2012).
4. The Pensions Act 2014 (Consequential, Supplementary and Incidental Amendments) Order 2015 (SI 2015/1985) art.9(5) (April 6, 2016).
5. Social Security (Claims and Payments) Amendment Regulations 2016 (SI 2016/544) reg.2 (June 15, 2016).
6. The Pensions Act 2014 (Consequential, Supplementary and Incidental Amendments) Order 2017 (SI 2017/422) art.10 (April 6, 2017).
7. The State Pension Credit (Coronavirus) (Electronic Claims) (Amendment) Regulations 2020 (SI 2020/456) reg.2 (May 4, 2020).
8. The Social Fund and Social Security (Claims and Payments) (Amendment) Regulations 2020 (SI 2020/600) reg.4 (July 9, 2020).

GENERAL NOTE

CW v SSWP (JSA) [2016] UKUT 114 concerned an attempt to claim jobseeker's allowance online which went wrong. The claimant attempted to make a claim online, but received no acknowledgement of it. She subsequently wrote to her local Jobcentre about the failed attempt to claim online. The response was that there was no record of an online claim and that the claimant should make a claim. The claimant then (well over a month after her initial attempt) made an online claim which was recorded, and she subsequently attended an interview at her local Jobcentre. She sought an award back-dated to her initial attempt to make an online claim, but this was refused. Judge Mitchell notes that the electronic date of claims rules are to be found in Schedule 9ZC, which requires that "information shall not be taken to have been delivered to an official computer system by means of an electronic communication unless it is accepted by the system to which it is delivered" para.4(3) of Sch.9ZC). Furthermore, paragraph 6 contains a presumption that an electronic claim has not been received if it has not been recorded on an official computer system. He then concludes that the backdating provisions in regulation 19 of the Claims and Payments Regulations could not assist the claimant, since it would be distorting language to apply the provisions about the use of the post and the telephone to online communications. However, the tribunal had not fully enquired as to when the claimant had first enquired about benefit after the failure of the online claim—the evidence suggested that she had written a letter about this earlier than the first letter in the tribunal documents. He accordingly remitted to appeal for a fresh hearing at which this issue could be explored. 2.60

Electronic claims for benefit

4C.—*Repealed subject to transitional provisions by the Child Benefit and Guardian's Allowance (Administration) Regulations 2003 (SI 2003/492) Sch.3(1) para.1 (April 7, 2003).* 2.61

[1 Making a claim for state pension credit

2.62 **4D.**—(1) A claim for state pension credit need only be made in writing if the Secretary of State so directs in any particular case.

(2) A claim is made in writing either—

(a) by completing and returning in accordance with the instructions printed on it a form approved or provided by the Secretary of State for the purpose; or

(b) in such other written form as the Secretary of State accepts as sufficient in the circumstances of the case.

(3) A claim for state pension credit may be made in writing whether or not a direction is issued under paragraph (1) and may also be made [5 . . .] in person at an appropriate office [3 . . .].

[3 (3A) A claim made in writing may also be made at an office designated by the Secretary of State for accepting claims for state pension credit.]

[7 (4) A claim made in writing may also be made at the offices of—

(a) a local authority administering housing benefit [3 . . .];

(b) a county council in England;

(c) a person providing services to a person mentioned in sub-paragraph (a) or (b);

(d) a person authorised to exercise any functions of a local authority relating to housing benefit [3 . . .]; or

(e) a person authorised to exercise any function a county council in England has under section 7A of the Social Security Administration Act 1992,

if the Secretary of State has arranged with the local authority, county council or other person for them to receive claims in accordance with this paragraph.]

[3 (5) Where a claim is made in accordance with paragraph (4), the local authority or other specified person—

(a) shall forward the claim to the Secretary of State as soon as reasonably practicable;

(b) may receive information or evidence relating to the claim supplied by the person making, or who has made, the claim to another person, and shall forward it to the Secretary of State as soon as reasonably practicable;

(c) may obtain information or evidence relating to the claim from the person who has made the claim and shall forward it to the Secretary of State as soon as reasonably practicable;

[7(cc) may verify any non-medical information or evidence supplied or obtained in accordance with sub-paragraph (b) or (c) and shall forward it to the Secretary of State as soon as reasonably practicable;]

(d) may record information or evidence relating to the claim supplied or obtained in accordance with sub-paragraph (b) or (c) and may hold the information or evidence (whether as supplied or obtained or as recorded) for the purpose of forwarding it to the Secretary of State; and

(e) may give information and advice with respect to the claim to the person who makes, or has made, the claim.]

[3 (5A) Paragraph (5)(b) to (e) applies in respect of information, evidence and advice relating to any claim for state pension credit, whether it is made in accordance with paragraph (4) or otherwise.]

(6) A claim for state pension credit made in person [5 . . .] is not a valid claim unless a written statement of the claimant's circumstances, provided for the purpose by the Secretary of State, is approved by the person making the claim.

[5 (6A) A claim for state pension credit may be made by telephone call to the telephone number specified by the Secretary of State.

(6B) Where the Secretary of State, in any particular case, directs that the person making the claim approves a written statement of his circumstances, provided for the purpose by the Secretary of State, a claim made by telephone is not a valid claim unless the person complies with the direction.

(6C) A claim made by telephone in accordance with paragraph (6A) is defective unless the Secretary of State is provided, during that telephone call, with all the information he requires to determine the claim.

(6D) Where a claim made by telephone in accordance with paragraph (6A) is defective, the Secretary of State is to provide the person making it with an opportunity to correct the defect.

(6E) If the person corrects the defect within one month, or such longer period as the Secretary of State considers reasonable, of the date the Secretary of State [8 first] drew attention to the defect, the Secretary of State shall treat the claim as if it had been duly made in the first instance.]

(7) A [4 couple] may agree between them as to which partner is to make a claim for state pension credit, but in the absence of an agreement, the Secretary of State shall decide which of them is to make the claim.

(8) Where one member of a [4 couple] ("the former claimant") is entitled to state pension credit under an award but a claim for state pension credit is made by the other member of the couple, then, if both members of the couple confirm in writing that they wish the claimant to be the other member, the former claimant's entitlement shall terminate on the last day of the benefit week specified in paragraph (9).

(9) That benefit week is the benefit week of the former claimant which includes the day immediately preceding the day the partner's claim is actually made or, if earlier, is treated as made.

(10) If a claim for state pension credit is defective when first received, the Secretary of State is to provide the person making it with an opportunity to correct the defect.

(11) If that person corrects the defect so that the claim then satisfies the requirements of paragraph (2) and does so within 1 month [6 or such longer period as the Secretary of State considers reasonable] of the date the Secretary of State [8 first] drew attention to the defect, the claim shall be treated as having been properly made on the date—

(a) the defective claim was first received by the Secretary of State or the person acting on his behalf; or

(b) if regulation 4F(3) applies, the person informed an appropriate office [1 or other office specified in regulation 4F(3)] of his intention to claim state pension credit.

(12) [5 Paragraph (6E) and (11) do] not apply in a case to which regulation 4E(3) applies.

(13) State pension credit is a relevant benefit for the purposes of section 7A of the Social Security Administration Act 1992.]

AMENDMENTS

1. Inserted by The State Pension Credit (Consequential, Transitional and Miscellaneous) Regulations 2002 (SI 2002/3019) reg.4 (April 7, 2003).

2. The Social Security (Claims and Payments and Miscellaneous Amendments) Regulations 2003 (SI 2003/1632) reg.2 (July 21, 2003).

3. The Social Security, Child Support and Tax Credits (Miscellaneous Amendments) Regulations 2005 (SI 2005/337) reg.7 (March 18, 2005).

4. The Civil Partnership (Pensions, Social Security and Child Support) (Consequential etc. Provisions) Order 2005 (SI 2005/2887) (December 5, 2005).

5. The Social Security (Miscellaneous Amendments) (No.2) Regulations 2006 (SI 2006/832) (July 24, 2006).

6. The Social Security (Miscellaneous Amendments) (No.3) Regulations 2006 (SI 2006/2377) (October 2, 2006).

7. The Social Security (Claims and Information) Regulations 2007 (SI 2007/2911) (October 31, 2007).

8. The Social Security (Miscellaneous Amendments) (No.4) Regulations 2009 (SI 2009/2655) reg.3 (October 26, 2009).

9. The Council Tax Benefit Abolition (Consequential Provision) Regulations 2013 (SI 2013/458) reg.3 (April 1, 2013).

[[1] Making a claim before attaining the qualifying age

2.63 **4E.**—(1) A claim for state pension credit may be made, and any claim made may be determined, at any time within the advance period.

(2) The advance period begins on the date which falls 4 months before the day on which the claimant attains the qualifying age and ends on the day before he attains that age.

(3) A person who makes a claim within the advance period which is defective may correct the defect at any time before the end of the advance period.]

AMENDMENT

1. Inserted by the State Pension Credit (Consequential, Transitional and Miscellaneous) Regulations 2002 (SI 2002/3019) reg.4 (April 7, 2003).

[[1] Making a claim after attaining the qualifying age: date of claim

2.64 **4F.**—(1) This regulation applies in the case of a person who claims state pension credit on or after attaining the qualifying age.

(2) The date on which a claim is made shall, subject to paragraph (3), be—

(a) where the claim is made in writing and is not defective, the date on which the claim is first received—

(i) by the Secretary of State or the person acting on his behalf; or

(ii) in a case to which regulation 4D(4) relates, in the office of a person specified therein;

(b) where the claim is not made in writing but is otherwise made in accordance with regulation 4D(3) [[4] or (6A)] and is not defective, the date the claimant provides details of his circumstances by telephone to, or in person at, the appropriate office or other office designated by the Secretary of State to accept claims for state pension credit; or

(c) where a claim is initially defective but the defect is corrected under regulation [[4] 4D(6E) or (11)], the date the claim is treated as having been made under that regulation.

(3) If a [3 person wishing to make a claim]—

(a) informs [3 (by whatever means) an appropriate office [2, or other office designated by the Secretary of State for accepting claims for state pension credit or the office of the person specified in regulation 4(D)] of his intention to claim state pension credit; and

(b) subsequently makes the claim in accordance with regulation 4D within 1 month of complying with sub-paragraph (a), or within such longer period as the Secretary of State may allow,

the claim may, where in the circumstances of the particular case it is appropriate to do so, be treated as made on the day the claimant first informed [2 an office specified in subparagraph (a)] of his intention to claim the credit.]

AMENDMENTS

1. Inserted by the State Pension Credit (Consequential, Transitional and Miscellaneous) Regulations 2002 (SI 2002/3019) reg.4 (April 7, 2003).

2. The Social Security (Claims and Payments and Miscellaneous Amendments) Regulations 2003 (SI 2003/1632) reg.2 (July 21, 2003).

3. Social Security (Housing Benefit, Council Tax Benefit, State Pension Credit and Miscellaneous Amendments) Regulations 2004 (SI 2004/2327) reg.8 (October 6, 2004).

4. The Social Security (Miscellaneous Amendments) (No.2) Regulations 2006 (SI 2006/832) (July 24, 2006).

GENERAL NOTE

The amendments to reg.4 of the Claims and Payments Regulations are significant in that they may provision for much greater co-operation between the Department and local authorities in relation to the receipt of claims for benefits administered by these agencies. **2.65**

Claims under these provisions may be directed to an office designated by the Secretary of State for accepting such claims. In relation to benefits administered by the Department, the party receiving the claim is under a duty to forward the claim to the Department as soon as reasonably practicable.

[1 Making a claim for employment and support allowance by telephone

4G.—(1) A claim ("a telephone claim") for an employment and support allowance may be made by telephone call to the telephone number specified by the Secretary of State. **2.66**

(2) Where the Secretary of State, in any particular case, directs that the person making the claim approves a written statement of his circumstances, provided for the purpose by the Secretary of State, a telephone claim is not a valid claim unless the person complies with the direction.

(3) A telephone claim is defective unless the Secretary of State is provided, during that telephone call, with all the information he requires to determine the claim.

(4) Where a telephone claim is defective, the Secretary of State is to advise the person making it of the defect and of the relevant provisions of regulation 6(1F) relating to the date of claim.

(5) If the person corrects the defect within one month, or such longer period as the Secretary of State considers reasonable, of the date the

Secretary of State [2 first] drew attention to the defect, the Secretary of State must treat the claim as if it had been properly made in the first instance.]

AMENDMENTS

1. The Employment and Support Allowance (Consequential Provisions) (No.2) Regulations 2008, (SI 2008/1554) reg.13 (October 27, 2008).

2. The Social Security (Miscellaneous Amendments) (No.4) Regulations 2009 (SI 2009/2655) reg.3 (October 26, 2009).

GENERAL NOTE

2.67 In *TR v SSWP (ESA)* [2013] UKUT 555 (AAC) the judge draws attention to the distinction between the provision of information (as required by this and similar regulations) and the provision of information *and evidence,* which is required elsewhere in the regulations. The judge says that information "comprises facts" whereas evidence requires some documentary evidence to support those facts (see [7]).

[1 Making a claim for employment and support allowance in writing

2.68 **4H.**—(1) A claim ("a written claim") for employment and support allowance need only be made in writing if the Secretary of State so directs in any particular case but a written claim may be made whether or not a direction is issued.

(2) A written claim must be made on a form approved for the purpose by the Secretary of State and be made in accordance with the instructions on the form.

(3) A claim in writing may also be made at the offices of—

(a) a local authority administering housing benefit [3 . . .];
(b) a person providing to such an authority services relating to housing benefit [3 . . .]; or
(c) a person authorised to exercise the function of a local authority relating to housing benefit [3 . . .],

if the Secretary of State has arranged with the local authority or person specified in sub-paragraph (b) or (c) for them to receive claims in accordance with this paragraph.

(4) Where a written claim is made in accordance with paragraph (3), on receipt of that claim the local authority or other person specified in that paragraph—

(a) must forward the claim to the Secretary of State as soon as reasonably practicable;
(b) may receive information or evidence relating to the claim supplied by—
  (i) the person making, or who has made, the claim; or
  (ii) other persons in connection with the claim,

  and shall forward it to the Secretary of State as soon as reasonably practicable;
(c) may obtain information or evidence relating to the claim from the person who has made the claim, but not any medical information or evidence except for that which the claimant must provide in accordance with instructions on the form, and must forward the information or evidence to the Secretary of State as soon as reasonably practicable;
(d) may record information or evidence relating to the claim supplied or obtained in accordance with sub-paragraph (b) or (c) and may hold

the information or evidence (whether as supplied or obtained or as recorded) for the purpose of forwarding it to the Secretary of State; and

(e) may give information and advice with respect to the claim to the person who makes, or who has made, the claim.

(5) Paragraphs (4)(b) to (e) apply in respect of information, evidence and advice relating to any claim whether the claim is made in accordance with paragraph (3) or otherwise.

(6) If a written claim is defective when first received, the Secretary of State is to advise the person making it of the defect and of the provisions of regulation 6(1F) relating to the date of claim.

(7) If that person corrects the defect so that the claim then satisfies the requirements of paragraph (2) and does so within one month, or such longer period as the Secretary of State considers reasonable, of the date the Secretary of State [2 first] drew attention to the defect, the claim must be treated as having been properly made in the first instance.]

AMENDMENTS

1. The Employment and Support Allowance (Consequential Provisions) (No.2) Regulations 2008 (SI 2008/1554) reg.13 (October 27, 2008).

2. The Social Security (Miscellaneous Amendments) (No.4) Regulations 2009 (SI 2009/2655) reg.3 (October 26, 2009).

3. The Council Tax Benefit Abolition (Consequential Provision) Regulations 2013 (SI 2013/458) reg.3 (April 1, 2013).

[1 Claims for employment and support allowance: supplemental

4I.—(1) Where a person who is a member of a couple may be entitled to an income-related employment and support allowance the claim for an employment and support allowance must be made by whichever member of the couple they agree should claim or, in default of agreement, by such one of them as the Secretary of State may choose. 2.69

(2) Where one member of a couple ("'the former claimant'") is entitled to an income-related employment and support allowance under an award but a claim for an employment and support allowance is made by the other member of the couple and the Secretary of State considers that the other member is entitled to an income-related employment and support allowance, then, if both members of the couple confirm in writing that they wish the claimant to be the other member, the former claimant's entitlement terminates on the day the partner's claim is actually made or, if earlier, is treated as made.

(3) In calculating any period of one month for the purposes of regulations 4G and 4H, any period commencing on a day on which a person is first notified of a decision in connection with his failure to take part in a work-focused interview and ending on a day on which he was notified that that decision has been revised so that the decision as revised is that he did take part is to be disregarded.

(4) Employment and support allowance is a relevant benefit for the purposes of section 7A of the 1992 Act.]

AMENDMENT

1. The Employment and Support Allowance (Consequential Provisions) (No.2) Regulations 2008 (SI 2008/1554) reg.13 (October 27, 2008).

Amendment and withdrawal of claim

2.70 **5.** [[3] (1) A person who has made a claim for benefit may amend it at any time before a determination has been made on the claim by notice in writing received at an appropriate office, by telephone call to a telephone number specified by the Secretary of State or in such other manner as the Secretary of State may decide or accept.

(1A) Any claim amended in accordance with paragraph (1) may be treated as if it had been so amended in the first instance.]

(2) A person who has made a claim may withdraw it at any time before a determination has been made on it, by notice to an appropriate office, and any such notice of withdrawal shall have effect when it is received.

AMENDMENTS

1. The Social Security (Claims and Payments and Payments on account, Overpayments and Recovery) Amendment Regulations 2005 (SI 2005/34) reg.2 (May 2, 2005).

2. The Social Security (Miscellaneous Amendments) (No.2) Regulations 2009 (SI 2009/1490) reg.2 (July 13, 2009).

3. The Social Security (Miscellaneous Amendments) (No.3) Regulations 2013 (SI 2013/2536) reg.5(2) (October 29, 2013).

DEFINITION

"appropriate office"—see reg.2(1).

GENERAL NOTE

Paragraphs (1) and (1A)

2.71 An issue arose in *CTC/1061/2001* on the meaning of reg.5. The claimant had claimed a disabled person's tax credit, reporting that he worked as a private hire driver. He answered a question about the amount of usage of the car for private purpose and responded that he used it 50 per cent for private purposes; he later said he had intended to indicate that he used the car for 50 per cent of the time and five per cent or less was for private purposes. The Secretary of State argued that this was irrelevant since a claim could not be altered after it had been determined. The tribunal accepted the argument. The Commissioner notes that there is nothing in reg.5 which prevents a claimant from seeking to explain an answer in a way which is different from how the decision-maker interpreted it. He goes on to raise the question whether there might be a difference for the purpose of reg.5(1) between a claim and evidence on a claim, but does not seek to answer the question.

Regulation 5(1) would appear to be drafted sufficiently widely that it would encompass an amendment not only to the claim, but also to the evidence on which the claim is based. The underlying purpose of the regulation appears to be to ensure that the decision is based on full circumstances obtaining when the claim is determined. So, for example, a claimant might wish to include new members of his family to the claim, or correct an error on the claim form which has just been noticed. Both would appear to be within reg.5(1).

Paragraph (2)

2.72 In *CJSA/3979/1999* the Commissioner explored the possibility of a claimant's being able to withdraw a claim where there has been an award of benefit for an indefinite period. The Commissioner concluded,

> "that even where there is a current award of benefit, a claimant may withdraw a claim on a prospective basis." (para.24)

However, the Commissioner's decision was given under the adjudication regime which pre-dated the Social Security Act 1998 and should no longer be regarded as good law: see CDLA/1589/2005 (in which the judge did, however confirm that it remained open to a claimant to surrender an award of benefit.)

In *JL v Calderdale MBC and SSWP* [2022] UKUT 9 (AAC), the claimant (who had been in receipt of housing benefit) claimed universal credit, which resulted in the DWP's computer immediately recognising that the legislative triggers had been met for his transfer to universal credit from legacy benefits (such as housing benefit). Within a very short time thereafter, the claimant sought to withdraw his universal credit claim, which at that point had not been the subject of a (final) decision. Judge Jacobs considered the Universal Credit [etc.] (Claims and Payments) Regulations 2013 (SI 2013/380) reg.31, which is in the same form as reg.5 of the present Regulations. He concluded, applying *Carpenter v Secretary of State for Work and Pensions* (reported as *R(IB) 6/03*) and relying on the legislative history of reg.5, that "determination" in the regulation referred to an earlier stage than that of the final decision, so that in the present case, as it had already been decided by the time of the attempted withdrawal that the triggers for transfer to universal credit had been met, it was no longer open to the claimant to withdraw. The judge added that even if he was wrong on the "determination" point, reg.31(2) (the equivalent for universal credit of reg.5(2) of the present Regulations) could not authorise a retrospective withdrawal to treat the claim as if it had never existed.

R(H) 2/06 concerned the interpretation of a provision of the Housing Benefit (General) Regulations 1987 (SI 1987/1971) in identical terms to reg.5(2). The Commissioner ruled that, although in some cases it may be possible to make a fresh claim which can be backdated to cover the period of a claim which has been withdrawn, the consequence of a genuine and effective withdrawal is, in the absence of any provision permitting reinstatement, to prevent any award from being made on the claim after the withdrawal took effect. Although different considerations might apply to claimants who are not fully able to manage their affairs or to understand the consequences of their actions, claimants who are not subject to any such disability would normally have to establish that the withdrawal of the claim was induced by some factor such as threatening or overbearing behaviour, deception or similar improper conduct in order to show that the notice of withdrawal of a claim was not a genuine expression of the claimant's intention at the time when the notice was given.

Date of claim

6.—(1) [[3]Subject to the following provisions of this regulation] [[29] or regulation 6A (claims by persons subject to work-focused interviews)] the date on which a claim is made shall be— 2.73

(a) in the case of a claim which meets the requirements of regulation 4(1), the date on which it is received in an appropriate office;

[[12](aa) in the case of a claim for—

[[30] . . .]

[[30] . . .]

jobseeker's allowance if first notification is received before 6th October 1997; or

income support if first notification is received before 6th October 1997;

which meets the requirements of regulation 4(1) and which is received in an appropriate office within one month of first notification in accordance with regulation 4(5), whichever is the later of—

(i) the date on which that notification is received; and

(ii) the first date on which that claim could have been made in accordance with these Regulations;]

(b) in the case of a claim which does not meet the requirements of regulation 4(1) but which is treated, under regulation 4(7) as having been [36 properly] made, the date on which the claim was received in an appropriate office in the first instance.

[23 (c) in the case of a claim made by telephone in accordance with [34 regulation 4(11) or (11A), the date [36 the claim is properly completed;]

(d) in the case of a claim made by telephone which is defective but which is treated, under regulation [36 4(13)(a) as having been properly] made, the date of that telephone call.]

[21 (1ZA) In the case of a claim made in accordance with regulation 4(6B)—

(a) paragraph (1) shall apply in relation to a claim received at an office specified in that regulation as it applies in relation to a claim received at an appropriate office; and

(b) paragraph (1A) shall apply in relation to an office specified in that regulation as it applies in relation to an appropriate office.]

[13 (1A) In the case of claim for income support—

(a) subject to the following sub-paragraphs, the date on which a claim is made shall be the date on which a properly completed claim is received in an appropriate office [36 or a claim made by telephone is properly completed] or the first day in respect of which the claim is made if later;

(b) where a properly completed claim is received in an appropriate office [36 or a claim made by telephone is properly completed] within one month of first notification of intention to make that claim, the date of claim shall be the date on which that notification is [36 made or is] deemed to be made or the first day in respect of which the claim is made if later;

(c) a notification of intention to make a claim will be deemed to be made on the date when an appropriate office receives—

(i) a notification in accordance with regulation 4(5); or

(ii) a defective claim.]

[18a (1B) Subject to paragraph (1C), in the case of a claim for working families' tax credit or disabled person's tax credit which meets the requirements of regulation 4(1) and which is received in an appropriate office within one month of first notification in accordance with regulation 4(5)—

(a) where the claimant is entitled to that credit on the date on which that notification is received ("the notification date") and the first day of the period in respect of which that claim is made is on or before the notification date, the date on which a claim is made shall be the notification date; or

(b) where the claimant is not entitled to that credit on the notification date but becomes so entitled before the date on which the claim is received, the date on which the claim is received, the date on which a claim is made shall be—

(i) the date on which the claimant becomes so entitled, or

(ii) if later, the first day of the period in respect of which the claim is made provided that it is not later than the date on which the claim is received.

(1C) Paragraph (1B) shall not apply in the case of a claim which is received in an appropriate office—

(a) in the case of working families' tax credit, within the period specified opposite that credit at paragraphs (a) or (aa) in column (2) of Schedule 4(a); or

(b) in the case of disabled person's tax credit, within the period specified opposite that credit in paragraphs (a) or (b) in column (2) of Schedule 4.]

[18b unless the previous award of working families' tax credit or disabled person's tax credit was terminated by virtue of regulation 49ZA of the Family Credit (General) Regulations 1987 or regulation 54A of the Disability Working Allowance (General) Regulations 1991.]

[27 (1D) Subject to paragraph (1E) and without prejudice to the generality of paragraph (1), where a properly completed claim for incapacity benefit is received in an appropriate office within one month of the claimant first notifying such an office, by whatever means, of his intention to make that claim, the date of claim shall be the date on which that notification is made or the first day in respect of which the claim is made if later.

(1E) For the purposes of paragraph (1D), a person [32 . . .] may notify his intention and may send or deliver his claim to an office specified in regulation 4(6B)]

[36 (1F) In the case of a claim for an employment and support allowance, the date on which the claim is made or treated as made shall be the first date on which—

(a) a claim made by telephone is properly completed, or a properly completed claim is received in an appropriate office, or office mentioned in regulation 4H(3);
(b) a defective claim is received or made but is treated as properly made in the first instance in accordance with regulation 4G(5) in the case of a telephone claim, or 4H(7) in the case of a written claim; or
(c) the Secretary of State is notified of an intention to claim and within one month or such longer period as the Secretary of State considers reasonable of first notification, a claim made by telephone is properly completed, or a properly completed claim is received in an appropriate office, or office mentioned in regulation 4H(3),

or the first day in respect of which the claim is made, if later.

(1G) In paragraph (1F) "properly completed" has the meaning assigned by regulation 4(8) in the case of a written claim and 4(12) in the case of a telephone claim.]

(2) [1. . .]

[1(3) In the case of a claim for income support, [14 working families' tax credit, disabled person's tax credit] [12or jobseeker's allowance] [5. . .], where the time for claiming is extended under regulation 19 the claim shall be treated as made on the first day of the period in respect of which the claim is, by reason of the operation of that regulation, timeously made.

(4) Paragraph (3) shall not apply when the time for claiming income support [14 working families' tax credit, disabled person's tax credit] or jobseeker's allowance]] has been extended under regulation 19 and the failure to claim within the prescribed time for the purposes of that regulation is for the reason only that the claim has been sent by post.]

[18 (4ZA)Where a member of a joint-claim couple notifies the employment officer (by whatever means) that he wishes to claim a jobseeker's allowance jointly with the other member of that couple, the claim shall be treated as made on the relevant date specified in accordance with paragraphs (4ZB) to (4ZD).

(4ZB) Where each member of a joint-claim couple is required to attend under regulation 4(6)(a)—

(a) if each member subsequently attends for the purpose of jointly claiming a jobseeker's allowance at the time and place specified by the employment officer and complies with the requirements of paragraph (4AA)(a), the claim shall be treated as made on whichever is the later of the first notification of intention to make that claim and the first day in respect of which the claim is made;

(b) if, without good cause, either member fails to attend for the purpose of jointly claiming a jobseeker's allowance at either the time or the place so specified or does not comply with the requirements of paragraph (4AA)(a), the claim shall be treated as made on the first day on which a member of the couple attends at the specified place and complies with the requirements of paragraph (4AA)(a).

(4ZC) Where only one member of the couple is required to attend under regulation 4(6)(a)—

(a) subject to the following paragraphs, the date on which the claim is made shall be the sate on which a properly completed claim is received in an appropriate office [36 or a claim made by telephone is properly completed] or the first day in respect of which the claim is made, if later, provided that the member of the couple who is required to attend under regulation 4(6)a) does so attend;

(b) where a properly completed form is received in an appropriate office [36 or a claim made by telephone is properly completed] within one month of first notification of intention to make that claim, the date of claim shall be the date of that notification;

(c) if, without good cause, the member of the couple who is required to attend under regulation 4(6)(a) fails to attend for the purpose of making a claim at either the time or place so specified or does not comply with the requirements of paragraph (4AA), the claim shall be treated as made on the first day on which that member does attend at that place and does provide a properly completed claim.

(4ZD) Where, as at the day on which a member of a joint-claim couple ("the first member") notifies the employment officer in accordance with paragraph (4ZA), the other member of that couple is temporarily absent from Great Britain in the circumstances specified in regulation 50(6B) of the Jobseeker's Allowance Regulations, the date on which the claim is made shall be the relevant date specified in paragraph (4ZB) or (4ZC) but nothing in this paragraph shall treat the claim as having been made on a day which is more than three months after the day on which the first member notified the employment officer in accordance with paragraph (4ZA).

[13(4A) Where a person [18who is not a member of a joint-claim couple] notifies the Secretary of State (by whatever means) that he wishes to claim a jobseeker's allowance—

(a) if he is required to attend under regulation 4(6)(a)—

(i) if he subsequently attends for the purpose of making a claim for that benefit at the time and place specified by the Secretary of State and complies with the requirements of paragraph (4AA) [18(b)], the claim shall be treated as made on whichever is the later of first notification of intention to make that claim and the first day in respect of which the claim is made;

(ii) if, without good cause, he fails to attend for the purpose of making a claim for that benefit at either the time or place so specified, or does not comply with the requirements of paragraph (4AA) [[18](b)], the claim shall be treated as made on the first day on which he does attend at that place and does provide a properly completed claim;

(b) if under regulation 4(6)(a) the Secretary of State directs that he is not required to attend—

(i) subject to the following sub-paragraph, the date on which the claim is made shall be the date on which a properly completed claim is received in an appropriate office [[36] or a claim made by telephone is properly completed] or the first day in respect of which the claim is made if later;

(ii) where a properly completed claim is received in an appropriate office [[36] or a claim made by telephone is properly completed] within one month of first notification of intention to make that claim, the date of claim shall be the date of that notification.

[[18] (4AA) Unless the Secretary of State otherwise directs, a properly completed claim for shall be provided [[36] or made]—

(a) in a case to which paragraph (4ZA) applies, at or before the time when a member of the joint-claim couple is first required to attend for the purpose of making a claim for a jobseeker's allowance;

(b) in any other case, at or before the time when the person making the claim for a jobseeker's allowance is required to attend for the purpose of making a claim.]

(4AB) The Secretary of State may direct that the time for providing [[36] or making] a properly completed claim may be extended to a date no later than the date one month after the date of first notification of intention to make that claim.]

(4B) Where a person's entitlement to a jobseeker's allowance has ceased in any of the circumstances specified in regulation 25(1)(a), (b) or (c) of the Jobseeker's Allowance Regulations (entitlement ceasing on a failure to comply) and—

(a) where he had normally been required to attend in person, he shows that the failure to comply which caused the cessation of his previous entitlement was due to any of the circumstances mentioned in regulation 30(c) or (d) of those Regulations, and no later than the day immediately following the date when those circumstances cease to apply he makes a further claim for jobseeker's allowance; or

(b) where he had not normally been required to attend in person, he shows that he did not receive the notice to attend and he immediately makes a further claim for jobseeker's allowance,

that further claim shall be treated as having been made on the day following that cessation of entitlement.

(4C) Where a person's entitlement to a jobseeker's allowance ceases in the circumstances specified in regulation 25(1)(b) of the Jobseeker's Allowance Regulations (failure to attend at time specified) and that person makes a further claim for that allowance on the day on which he failed to attend at the time specified, that claim shall be treated as having been made on the following day.]

[[11] . . .]

[[2](5) Where a person submits a claim for attendance allowance [[6]or disability living allowance or a request under paragraph (8)] by post and the arrival of that [[6]claim or request] at an appropriate office is delayed by postal disruption caused by industrial action, whether within the postal service or elsewhere, the [6claim or request] shall be treated as received on the day on which it would have been received if it had been delivered in the ordinary course of post.]

[3(6) Where—

(a) on or after 9th April 1990 a person satisfies the capital condition in section 22(6) of the Social Security Act 1986 [SSCBA, s.134(1)] for income support and he would not have satisfied that condition had the amount prescribed under regulation 45 of the Income Support (General) Regulation 1987 been £6,000; and

(b) a claim for that benefit is received from him in an appropriate office not later than 27th May 1990;

the claim shall be treated as made on the date [4not later than 5th December 1990] determined in accordance with paragraph (7).

(7) For the purpose of paragraph (6), where—

(a) the claimant satisfies the other conditions of entitlement to income support on the date on which he satisfies the capital condition, the date shall be the date on which he satisfies that condition;

(b) the claimant does not satisfy the other conditions of entitlement to income support on the date on which he satisfies the capital condition, the date shall be the date on which he satisfies the conditions of entitlement to that benefit.]

[6(8) [8Subject to paragraph (8A [21 and (8B)]),] where—

(a) a request is received in an appropriate office for a claim form for disability living allowance or attendance allowance; and

(b) in response to the request a claim form for disability living allowance or attendance allowance is issued from an appropriate office; and

(c) within the time specified the claim form properly completed is received in an appropriate office,

the date on which the claim is made shall be the date on which the request was received in the appropriate office.

[8(8A) Where, in a case which would otherwise fall within paragraph (8), it is not possible to determine the date when the request for a claim form was received in an appropriate office because of a failure to record that date, the claim shall be treated as having been made on the date 6 weeks before the date on which the properly completed claim form is received in an appropriate office.]

[21 (8B) In the case of a claim for disability living allowance or attendance allowance made in accordance with regulation 4(6B), paragraphs (8) and (8A) shall apply in relation to an office specified in that regulation as they apply in relation to an appropriate office.]

(9) [9In paragraph (8) and (8A)]—

"a claim form" means a form approved by the Secretary of State under regulation 4(1); "properly completed" has the meaning assigned by regulation 4(8);

"the time specified" means 6 weeks from the date on which the request was received or such longer period as the Secretary of State may consider reasonable.]

[7(10) Where a person starts a job on a Monday or Tuesday in any week and he makes a claim for [14 disabled person's tax credit] in that week the claim shall be treated as made on the Tuesday of that week.

(11) [14 . . .]

[12 (12) [14 . . .] Where a person has claimed [14 disabled person's tax credit] and that claim ("the original claim") has been refused, and a further claim is made in the circumstances specified in paragraph (13), that further claim shall be treated as made—

(a) on the date of the original claim; or

(b) on the first date in respect of which the qualifying benefit was payable, whichever is the later.

(13) The circumstances referred to in paragraph (12) are that—

(a) the original claim was refused on the ground that the claimant did not qualify under section 129(2) of the Contributions and Benefits Act;

(b) at the date of the original claim the claimant had made a claim for a qualifying benefit and that claim had not been determined;

(c) after the original claim had been determined, the claim for the qualifying benefit was determined in the claimant's favour; and

(d) the further claim for [14 disabled person's tax credit] was made within three months of the date that the claim for the qualifying benefit was determined.

(14) [14 . . .]

(15) In paragraphs (12) and (13) "qualifying benefit" means any of the benefits referred to in section 129(2) of the Contributions and Benefits Act.

[31 (15A) Paragraphs (16) to (34) shall not apply in any case where it would be advantageous to the claimant to apply the provisions of regulation 19 (time for claiming benefit.)]

[16 (16) Where a person has claimed a relevant benefit and that claim ("the original claim") has been refused in the circumstances specified in paragraph (17), and a further claim is made in the additional circumstances specified in paragraph (18), that further claim shall be treated as made—

(a) on the date of the original claim; or

(b) on the first date in respect of which the qualifying benefit was [19 awarded],

whichever is the later.

(17) The circumstances referred to in paragraph (16) are that the ground for refusal was—

(a) in the case of severe disablement allowance, that the claimant's disablement was less than 80 per cent;

(b) [27 . . .];

(c) in any case, that the claimant [19, a member of his family or the disabled person] had not been awarded a qualifying benefit.

(18) The additional circumstances referred to in paragraph (16) are that—

[19(a) a claim for the qualifying benefit was made not later than 10 working days after the date of the original claim and the claim for the qualifying benefit had not been decided;

(b) after the original claim had been decided the claim for the qualifying benefit had been decided in favour of the claimant, a member or his family or the disabled person; and]

(c) the further claim was made within three months of the date on which the claim for the qualifying benefit was decided.

(19) Where a person has been awarded a relevant benefit and that award ("the [31 "original award") has been terminated or reduced or payment under that award ceases in the circumstances] specified in paragraph (20), and a further claim is made in the additional circumstances specified in paragraph (21), that further claim shall be treated as made—

(a) on the date of termination of the original award; or

(b) on the first date in respect of which the qualifying benefit [[19] is [[28] awarded or] [[31] re-awarded or becomes payable again]],

whichever is the later.

[[28] (20) The circumstances referred to in paragraph (19) are—

(a) that the award of the qualifying benefit has itself been terminated or reduced by means of a revision, supersession, appeal [[39] , determination of entitlement] or termination of an award for a fixed period in such a way as to affect the original award; [[31] . . .]

(b) at the date the original award was terminated the claimant's claim for a qualifying benefit had not been decided] [[31] or]

[[31] (c) that the qualifying benefit has ceased to be payable in accordance with—

(i) regulation 6(1) of the Social Security (Attendance Allowance) Regulations 1991 or regulation 8(1) of the Social Security (Disability Living Allowance) Regulations 1991 because the claimant is undergoing treatment as an in-patient in a hospital or similar institution, *or*

(ii) regulation 7 of the Social Security (Attendance Allowance) Regulations 1991 or regulation 9 of the Social Security (Disability Living Allowance) Regulations 1991 because the claimant is resident in certain accommodation other than a hospital.]

[[39](iii) regulation 17 (effect of admission to a care home on ongoing entitlement to care component) of the Disability Assistance for Children and Young People (Scotland) Regulations 2021 because the claimant is resident in a care home, or

(iv) regulation 27 (effect of admission to a care home on ongoing entitlement to daily living component), or as the case may be, regulation 28 (effect of admission to hospital on ongoing entitlement to Adult Disability Payment) of the Disability Assistance for Working Age People (Scotland) Regulations 2022 because the claimant is, respectively, a resident of a care home or undergoing treatment in a hospital.]

(21) [[31] Subject to paragraph (21A), the additional] circumstances referred to in paragraph (19) are that—

(a) after the original award has been terminated the claim for the qualifying benefit is decided in [[19] favour of the claimant, a member of his family or the disabled person]; [[31] or]

[[31] (b) the qualifying benefit is re-awarded following revision, supersession [[39] , determination of entitlement] or appeal; or

(c) the qualifying benefit is re-awarded on a renewal claim when an award for a fixed period expires; or

(d) the cessation of payment ends when the claimant leaves the hospital or similar institution or accommodation referred to in paragraph(20)(c); and

the further claim [[34] for a relevant benefit] referred to in paragraph (19), is made within three months of the date [[34] of the decision to award, re-award, or recommence payment of the qualifying benefit on the grounds that sub-paragraph (a), (b), (c) or (d) was satisfied.]]

[[31] (21A) Paragraph (21) applies whether the benefit is re-awarded [[39] or the subject of a determination of entitlement] when the further claim is decided or following a revision of, or an appeal against, such a decision.]

(22) In paragraphs (16) to (21) [19 . . .] [27, (30) and (33)]—

"relevant benefit" means any of the following, namely—

(a) benefits under Parts II to V of the Contributions and Benefits Act except incapacity benefit;

(b) income support;

(c) a jobseeker's allowance;

(d) a social fund payment mentioned in section 138(1)(a) or (2) of the Contributions and Benefits Act;

(e) child benefit;

[24 (f) state pension credit]

"qualifying benefit" means—

(a) in relation to severe disablement allowance, the highest rate of the care component of disability living allowance;

(b) in relation to invalid care allowance, any benefit referred to in section 70(2) of the Contributions and Benefits Act;

(c) in relation to a social fund payment in respect of maternity or funeral expenses, any benefit referred to in [37 regulation 5(1)(a) or 7(4)(a) of the Social Fund Maternity and Funeral Expenses (General) Regulations 2005];

(d) any other relevant benefit [39 or Scottish disability benefit] which [19, when it is awarded or reawarded,] has the effect of making another relevant benefit payable or payable at an increased rate;

"the disabled person" means the person for whom the invalid care allowanced claimant is caring in accordance with section 70(1)(a) of the Contributions and Benefits Act.

[19 "family" has the same meaning as in section 137(1) of the Contributions and Benefits Act or, as the case may be, section 35(1) of the Jobseekers Act [24, and in the case of state pension credit "member of his family" means the other member of a couple where the claimant is a member of a [25 . . .] couple].]

(23) Where a person has ceased to be entitled to incapacity benefit, and a further claim for that benefit is made in the circumstances specified in paragraph (24), that further claim shall be treated as made—

(a) on the date on which entitlement to incapacity benefit ceased; or

(b) on the first date in respect of which the qualifying benefit was payable,

whichever is the later.

(24) The circumstances referred to in paragraph (23) are that—

(a) entitlement to incapacity benefit ceased on the ground that the claimant was not incapable of work;

(b) at the date that entitlement ceased the claimant had made a claim for a qualifying benefit and that claim had not been decided;

(c) after entitlement had ceased, the claim for the qualifying benefit was decided in the claimant's favour; and

(d) the further claim for incapacity benefit was made within three months of the date on which the claim for the qualifying benefit was decided.

(25) In paragraphs (23) and (24) "qualifying benefit" means any of the payments referred to in regulation 10(2)(a) of the Social Security (Incapacity for Work) (General) Regulations 1995.

(26) In paragraph [27 (18)(a) and (c), 21(a), (24) and (30) and in paragraph (18)(b)] where the word appears for the second time, "decided" includes [39 a determination of entitlement and] the making of a decision

following a revision, supersession or an appeal, whether by the Secretary of State, [35 the First-tier Tribunal, the Upper Tribunal] or the court.]

(27) Where a claim is made for [14 working families' tax credit or disabled person's tax credit], and—

(a) the claimant had previously made a claim for income support or jobseeker's allowance ("the original claim");
(b) the original claim was refused on the ground that the claimant or his partner was in remunerative work; and
(c) the claim for [14 working families' tax credit or disabled person's tax credit] was made within 14 days of the date that the original claim was determined,

that claim shall be treated as made on the date of the original claim, or, if the claimant so requests, on a later date specified by the claimant.

(28) Where a claim is made for income support or jobseeker's allowance, and—

(a) the claimant had previously made a claim for [20 working tax credit] ("the original claim");
(b) the original claim was refused on the ground that the claimant or his partner was not in remunerative work [20 for the purposes of that tax credit]; and
(c) the claim for income support or jobseeker's allowance was made within 14 days of the date that the original claim was determined,

that claim shall be treated as made on the date of the original claim, or, if the claimant so requests, on a later date specified by the claimant.]

(29) In the case of a claim for an increase of severe disablement allowance or of invalid care allowance in respect of a child or adult dependant, [17 paragraph (16) and (19)] shall apply to the claim as if it were a claim for severe disablement allowance or, as the case may be, invalid care allowance.

[19 (30) Where—

(a) a claimant was awarded income support or income-based jobseeker's allowance ("the original award");
(b) the original award was termination and [31 . . .], the claimant, a member of his family or the disabled person claimed a qualifying benefit; and
(c) the claimant makes a further claim for income support or income-based jobseeker's allowance within 3 months of the date on which the claim for the qualifying benefit was decided,

the further claim shall be treated as made on the date of termination of the original award or the first date in respect of which the qualifying benefit is awarded, whichever is the later.]

[22 (31) Subject to paragraph (32), where—

(a) a person—
    (i) has attained pensionable age, but for the time being makes no claim for a Category A retirement pension; or
    (ii) has attained pensionable age and has a spouse [26 or civil partner] who has attained pensionable age, but for the time being makes no claim for a Category B retirement pension;
(b) in accordance with regulation 50A of the Social Security (Contributions) Regulations 2001, (Class 3 contributions: tax years 1996–97 to 2001–02) the Commissioners of Inland Revenue subsequently accept Class 3 contributions paid after the due date by

the person or, in the case of a Category B retirement pension, the spouse [26 or civil partner];

(c) in accordance with regulation 6A of the Social Security (Crediting and Treatment of Contributions, and National Insurance Numbers) Regulations 2001 the contributions are treated as paid on a date earlier than the date on which they were paid; and

(d) the person claims a Category A or, as the case may be, a Category B retirement pension,

the claim shall be treated as made on—

(i) 1st October 1998; or

(ii) the date on which the person attained pensionable age in the case of a Category A retirement pension, or, in the case of a Category B retirement pension, the date on which the person's spouse [26 or civil partner] attained pensionable age,

whichever is later.

(32) Paragraph (31) shall not apply where—

(a) the person's entitlement to a Category A or B retirement pension has been deferred by virtue of section 55(2)(a) of the Contributions and Benefits Act (increase of retirement pension where entitlement is deferred); or

(b) the person's nominal entitlement to a Category A or B retirement pension is deferred in pursuance of section 36(4) and (7) of the National Insurance Act 1965 (increase of graduated retirement benefit where entitlement is deferred),

nor where sub-paragraph (a) and (b) both apply.]

[27 (33) [31 Subject to paragraph 34, where] a person makes a claim for a carer's allowance [34 or for an increase in carer's allowance in respect of an adult or child dependent] within 3 months of a decision made—

(a) on a claim;

(b) on revision [39 , determination of entitlement] or supersession; or

(c) on appeal whether by [35 the First-tier Tribunal, the Upper Tribunal] or the court,

awarding a qualifying benefit to the disabled person, the date of claim [34 shall be treated as the first day of the benefit week in which the award of the qualifying benefit became payable.]

[31. . . .]

[34 (34) Where the decision awarding a qualifying benefit is made in respect of a renewal claim where a fixed period award of that benefit has expired, or is due to expire, the date of claim for carer's allowance shall be treated as the first day of the benefit week in which the renewal award of qualifying benefit became payable.]

[38 (35) A claim for attendance allowance or the care component of disability living allowance which is in respect of a period beginning on or before 18th October 2007 but which is made after that date, is to be treated as made on 18th October 2007 where—

(a) on or after 8th March 2001, the claimant had an award of that benefit;

(b) the Secretary of State made a superseding decision to end that award on the ground that there had been, or it was anticipated that there would be, a relevant change of circumstances as a result of the claimant's moving, or planning to move, from Great Britain to an EEA state or Switzerland;

(c) that superseding decision was confirmed on appeal; and
(d) the claimant has not received an extra-statutory payment in respect of the benefit being claimed.

(36) A claim for carer's allowance which is in respect of a period beginning on or before 18th October 2007 but which is made after that date, is to be treated as made on 18th October 2007 where—

(a) on or after 8th March 2001, the claimant had an award of that benefit;
(b) the Secretary of State made a superseding decision to end that award on the ground that there had been, or it was anticipated that there would be, a relevant change of circumstances as a result of—
  (i) the claimant's moving from Great Britain to an EEA state or Switzerland; or
  (ii) the claimant no longer caring for a severely disabled person, as defined in section 70(2) of the Contributions and Benefits Act, because that person's award of attendance allowance or the care component of disability living allowance had ended, or would end, by virtue of a superseding decision made on the ground of that person's moving from Great Britain to an EEA state or Switzerland; and
(c) the claimant has not received an extra-statutory payment in respect of that allowance.

(37) In paragraphs (35)(d) and (36)(c), "extra-statutory payment" means a payment made by the Secretary of State, in respect of attendance allowance, the care component of disability living allowance or carer's allowance which, but for the superseding decision referred to in paragraph (35)(b) or, as the case may be, (36)(b), would have been payable from 18th October 2007.]

[[39](38) In this regulation—

(a) "determination of entitlement" has the meaning given in section 25 of the Social Security (Scotland) Act 2018;
(b) "Scottish disability benefit" means, as the context requires, either of the following benefits—
  (i) adult disability payment within the meaning of regulation 2 of the Disability Assistance for Working Age People (Scotland) Regulations 2022; and
  (ii) child disability payment within the meaning of regulation 2 of the Disability Assistance for Children and Young People (Scotland) Regulations 2021.]

AMENDMENTS

1. The Social Security (Claims and Payments) Amendment Regulations 1988 (SI 1988/522) reg.2 (April 11, 1988).

2. The Social Security (Medical Evidence, Claims and Payments) Amendment Regulations 1989 (SI 1989/1686), reg.4 (October 9, 1989).

3. The Social Security (Claims and Payments) Amendment Regulations 1990 (SI 1990/725) reg.2 (April 9, 1990).

4. The Social Security (Miscellaneous Provisions) Amendment Regulations 1990 (SI 1990/2208) reg.9 (December 5, 1990).

5. The Social Security (Miscellaneous Provisions) Amendment Regulations 1991 (SI 1991/2284) reg.6 (November 1, 1991).

6. The Social Security (Claims and Payments) Amendment Regulations 1991 (SI 1991/2741) reg.4 (February 3, 1992).

7. The Social Security (Claims and Payments) Amendment Regulations 1991 (SI 1991/2741) reg.4 (March 10, 1992).

8. The Social Security (Claims and Payments) Amendment (No.3) Regulations 1993 (SI 1993/2113) reg.3 (September 27, 1993).

9. The Social Security (Claims and Payments) Amendment Regulations 1994 (SI 1994/2319) reg.2 (October 3, 1994).

10. The Social Security (Claims and Payments) (Jobseeker's Allowance Consequential Amendments) Regulations 1996 (SI 1996/1460) reg.2(5) (October 7, 1996).

11. "Lapsed" by the Asylum and Immigration (Treatment of Claimants etc.) Act 2004 s.12(2) (June 14, 2007).

12. The Social Security (Miscellaneous Amendments) (No.2) Regulations 1997 (SI 1997/793) reg.3 (April 7, 1997).

13. The Social Security (Miscellaneous Amendments) (No.2) Regulations 1997 (SI 1997/793) reg.3(3) and (5) (October 6, 1997).

14. The Tax Credits (Claims and Payments) (Amendment) Regulations 1999 (SI 1999/2572) reg.5 (October 5, 1999).

15. The Social Security (Immigration and Asylum) Consequential Amendments Regulations 2000 (SI 2000/636) reg.5 (April 3, 2000).

16. The Social Security and Child Support (Miscellaneous Amendments) Regulations 2000 (SI 2000/1596) reg.3(a) (June 19, 2000).

17. The Social Security and Child Support (Miscellaneous Amendments) Regulations 2000 (SI 2000/1596) reg.3(b) (June 19, 2000).

18. The Social Security (Joint Claims: Consequential Amendments) Regulations 2000 (SI 2000/1982) reg.2(4) (March 19, 2001).

18a. The Tax Credits (Claims and Payments) (Amendment) Regulations 2001 (SI 2001/567) (April 10, 2001).

18b. The Tax Credits (Claims and Payments) Amendment (No.3) Regulations 2001 (SI 2001/892) (April 10, 2001).

19. The Social Security (Claims and Payments and Miscellaneous Amendments) Regulations 2002 (SI 2002/428) reg.2 (April 2, 2002).

20. The Social Security (Working Tax Credit and Child Tax Credit) (Consequential Amendments) Regulations 2003 (SI 2003/455) Sch.4 (April 1, 2003).

21. The Social Security (Claims and Payments and Miscellaneous Amendments) Regulations 2003 (SI 2003/1632) reg.2 (July 21, 2003).

22. Social Security (Retirement Pensions) Amendment Regulations 2004 (SI 2004/2283) reg.2 (September 27, 2004).

23. The Social Security (Claims and Payments and Payments on account, Overpayments and Recovery) Amendment Regulations 2005 (SI 2005/34) reg.2 (May 2, 2005).

24. The Social Security, Child Support and Tax Credits (Miscellaneous Amendments) Regulations 2005 (SI 2005/337) reg.7 (March 19, 2005).

25. The Social Security (Civil Partnerships) (Consequential Amendments) Regulations 2005 (SI 2005/2878) (December 5, 2005).

26. The Civil Partnership (Pensions, Social Security and Child Support) (Consequential etc. Provisions) Order 2005 (SI 2005/2877) (December 5, 2005).

27. The Social Security (Miscellaneous Amendments) (No.2) Regulations 2006 (SI 2006/832) (April 10, 2006).

28. The Social Security (Miscellaneous Amendments) (No.3) Regulations 2006 (SI 2006/2377) (October 2, 2006).

29. The Social Security (Work-focused Interviews) Regulations 2000 (SI 2000/897) (April 3, 2000).

30. The Tax Credits (Claims and Payments) (Amendment) Regulations 2001 (SI 2001/567) (April 10, 2001).

31. The Social Security (Miscellaneous Amendments) (No.4) Regulations 2007 (SI 2007/2470) (September 24, 2007).

32. The Social Security (Claims and Information) Regulations 2007 (SI 2007/2911) (October 31, 2007).

33. The Employment and Support Allowance (Consequential Provisions) (No.2) Regulations 2008 (SI 2008/1554) reg.13 (October 27, 2008).

34. The Social Security (Miscellaneous Amendments) (No.5) Regulations 2008 (SI 2008/2667) reg.2 (October 30, 2008).

35. The Tribunals, Courts and Enforcement Act 2007 (Transitional and Consequential Provisions) Order 2008 (SI 2008/2683) reg.43 (November 3, 2008).

36. The Social Security (Miscellaneous Amendments) (No.2) Regulations 2009 (SI 2009/1490) reg.2 (July 13, 2009).

37. The Social Security (Miscellaneous Amendments) Regulations 2010 (SI 2010/510) reg.3(2) (April 6, 2010).

38. The Social Security (Disability Living Allowance, Attendance Allowance and Carer's Allowance) (Miscellaneous Amendments) Regulations 2011 (SI 2011/2426) reg.3 (October 31, 2011).

39. The Social Security (Disability for Working Age People) (Consequential Amendments) Order 2022 (SI 2022/177) reg.3 (March 21, 2022).

DEFINITIONS

"appropriate office"—see reg.2(1).
"claim for asylum"—*ibid.*
"claim for benefit"—*ibid.*
"jobseeker's allowance"—*ibid.*

GENERAL NOTE

Introduction

2.74 Claims are generally not made until received in any appropriate office.

R(SB) 8/89 concerns the date of a claim for a single payment of supplementary benefit, but, since the date of claims for most benefits is also the date of receipt in the office of the Department, the decision is directly in point in relation to these benefits. The Commissioner's comments are worth quoting at length since the determination of the date of claim is often an issue arising on appeals:

> "In order for the claim to be made it is not alone necessary for the claimant to despatch the form but it is also necessary for the office of the Department to receive it. In my judgment if the office of the Department puts it out of its power to receive the claim by closing its offices and also arranging with the Post Office not to deliver mail on the days upon which the office is closed, then it put it out of its power to receive the claim. It may be that the claim can be received by the office of the Department whether such office is open or closed, but it cannot be received in circumstances where the Department arranges that mail should not be delivered. In her submission to me the adjudication officer now concerned refers to no deliveries being made by the Post Office on days upon which the office of the Department are [*sic*] closed. It will be a question of fact for the new tribunal to find whether such is by arrangement between the Department and Post Office and then to consider whether the Department has put it out of its power to receive claims on a Saturday. If they come to the conclusion that it did and find that in the normal course of delivery on that day then such is the date of claim." (At para.7.)

Where claim packs are sent out for disability living allowance and attendance allowance, it is not the practice of the Department (in contrast to the position where enquiries are made about other benefits) to follow the matter up if no completed claim is returned. The Claims and Payments Regulations clearly do not require such action, but it is understood that a number of welfare rights units are concerned that the variation in practice may operate to the disadvantage of claimants. It is, of course, the receipt of a completed claim (or at least some document which can be regarded as a claim under reg.4) which constitutes a claim under the regulations.

Establishing whether a person has claimed, and, if so, the date of a claim can arise with some frequency before tribunals. In *CP/4104/2004* the Commissioner reminds tribunals of the need to check on both departmental policies of destruction of documents and available computer records in assessing whether a claimant has made a claim. It may be necessary to receive evidence as to what a computer printout actually means. The core advice is not to accept unquestioningly assertions by the Department that it has no record of a claim or enquiry. In the case before the Commissioner that assertion was made to the tribunal, but on further enquiry turned out not to be the correct position.

Regulation 6 is one of the longest social security regulations, and is full of twists and turns. Great care should be taken in reading the regulation in any case raising questions concerning the date of claim.

Paragraph (1)

A properly completed claim on the proper form is made on the date that it is received in a benefit office. For a decision on the proper approach where the Department contends that a claim form has not been received, see *SSWP v ZVR (CA)* [2013] UKUT 515 (AAC). **2.75**

There are many complications around this basic rule following the introduction of JSA and the severe restriction on the backdating of claims under reg.19 from April 1997.

R(SB) 8/89 holds that if the Department puts it out of its power to receive a claim, as by closing its office and arranging with the Post Office not to deliver mail, e.g. on a Saturday, then if that day is the day on which the claim would have been delivered, it is the date of claim. It can be said that by making the arrangement with the Post Office the Department constitute the Post Office bailees of the mail (see *Hodgson v Armstrong* [1967] Q.B. 299 and *Lang v Devon General Ltd* [1987] I.C.R. 4). The Commissioner does not deal expressly with the situation where the office is closed, but there is no arrangement about the mail, e.g. if an office is closed on a Saturday and the Saturday and Monday mail is all stamped with the Monday date in the office. Here, principle would suggest that if it can be shown that in the normal course of the post delivery would have been on the Saturday, then the Saturday is the date of receipt and the date of claim. If a claimant proves a delivery by hand when the office is closed, the date of delivery is the date of receipt.

Note also *CIS/4901/2002* relating to arrangements between the Department and the Post Office for the handling of mail, which is reported in more detail in the annotations to reg.19. **2.76**

Levy v Secretary of State for Work and Pensions [2006] EWCA Civ 890, reported as *R(G) 2/06* considered the applicability to social security claims of the rebuttable presumption in s.7 of the Interpretation Act 1978 that a letter put in the post is delivered to its addressee. The Court of Appeal ruled that reg.6(1) was not ultra vires. The next question was whether s.7 of the Interpretation Act 1978 applied. Dyson L.J. (with whom Hallett and Pill L.JJ. agreed) concluded that the provision has no application in this context. Even if s.7 did apply, its application would appear to be excluded by the words "unless the contrary intention appears" in s.7 of the Interpretation Act. The Court of Appeal concludes that "It is plain that regulation 6(1) requires that the claim be received in fact and not merely that it be sent." (para. 32 of the judgment). It follows that *CIS/306/2003* and *CG/2973/2004* correctly analyse the legal position and that *CSIS/48/1992* and *CIS/759/1992* are wrong in so far as they suggest otherwise.

Paragraph (1A)

This provides that the date of claim for an income support claim will be the date a properly completed claim (i.e. one that complies with reg.4(1A)) is received (or the first day claimed for, if later). But if such a claim is received within one month of the date that the person first contacted the Department with a view to making a claim, or a previous defective claim (i.e. one that does not comply with reg.4(1A)), the date **2.77** of claim will be the date of that initial contact or defective claim (or the first day claimed for, if later). Thus if more than a month elapses before the claimant complies with the requirements of reg.4(1A), the date of claim will be the date of that compliance (unless the rules on backdating apply: see reg.19(4)–(7)). See further the note to reg.4(1A)–(1C).

In *R(IS) 10/06* the Commissioner considers whether there is any priority in the claims covered by reg.6(1A)(c). He concludes:

> "16. On further consideration, I now realise that I was wrong to be concerned about the absence of any specified priority between the two heads of reg.6(1A)(c).
> 17. This only appears puzzling if the heads in that provisions are read in isolation from subparagraph (b). Subparagraph (c) is expressed as a deeming provision. Its function, though, is more akin to a definition. It sets out the circumstances in which a person is tread as notifying an intention to make a claim. If heads (i) and (ii) are read into paragraph (b), it reads:
>
> > 'where a properly completed claim is received in an appropriate office within one month of first notification of intention to make that clauim, *which may be shown by (i) a notification in accordance with regulation 4(5) or (ii) a defective claim*, the date of claim shall be the date on which that notification is deemed to be made or the first day in respect of which the claim is made if later.'
>
> Set out like that, no issue of priority arises. The claimant is given a choice to rely on one month from the date of notification or from the date of defective claim."

It is worth noting that the view of the Department is that this decision conflicts with *R(IS)14/04* (which, the Department contends, holds that the one-month period runs from the *first* point of contact; that is, the request for the claim form or the submission of the defective claim form), and argues that the *R(IS)14/04* should be followed in preference to *R(IS) 10/06*.

In *R(IS) 3/04* the Commissioner rules that it is not possible for a valid claim to income support to be made where a claimant dies having given notification of intention to make a claim but not having perfected the claim before his death by completing and submitting a claim form. The case concerned a situation in which the claim was completed and submitted by the executor of the claimant's will.

Paragraph (3)

2.78 For these benefits, if the time for claiming is extended under reg.19, the claim is treated as made at the beginning of the period for which the claim is deemed to be in time. Initial claims for working families tax credit and disabled person's tax credit and claims for income support and JSA have to be made on the first day of the period claimed for (Sch.4, paras 6, 7 and 11).

Paragraph (4)

2.79 The interaction of this provision with others is far from clear. It does not look as though it can apply directly in a case where the decision maker has extended the time for claiming by up to a month under reg.19(6). If the claim is not actually made (i.e. received: para.(1)) within the extended period, the claim is not timeously made and para.(3) above does not apply anyway. Postal delay is not a circumstance listed in reg.19(5) (replacing the old good cause rule), but may be relevant to the reasonableness of the delay in claiming. See also reg.19(7).

Paragraphs (4A)–(4AB)

2.80 In the case of JSA, if the person attends the Job Centre for the purpose of making a claim when required to do so and provides a properly completed claim (i.e. with all the necessary information: see reg.4(1A) and (9)), the date of claim will be the date the person first contacted the Job Centre (or the first day claimed for, if later) (para.(4)(a)(i) and (4AA)). Note the *discretion* to extend the time for delivery of a properly completed claim form under para.(4AB); unlike income support (and JSA postal signers) the month's allowance to return the fully completed claim form is not automatic. Note also para.(4A)(a)(ii) which provides that if the person fails to comply with these requirements without good cause the date of claim will be the date that he does comply. Thus if the person does have good cause for not so complying, presumably para.(4A)(a)(i) will apply when he does attend and does provide a fully completed claim form (and note the discretion in relation to the claim form under para.(4AB)). For claimants who are not required to attend the Job Centre in person (i.e. who are allowed to apply by post), their claim will be treated as made on the day they first contacted the Job Centre with a view to making a claim (or on the first day claimed for, if later) if a properly completed claim is received within one month, or the date the properly completed claim is received if more than one month has elapsed (para.(4A)(b)). See further the note to reg.4(1A)–(1C)).

In *CG/4060/2005* the Commissioner decided that reg.6(4AB) applied only to claims for a jobseeker's allowance, and so was of no assistance to persons claiming carer's allowance.

Paragraphs (4B) and (4C)

These paragraphs deal with certain cases where entitlement to JSA has ceased because of a failure to attend the Job Centre or to provide a signed declaration of availability and active search for employment, so that a new claim is necessary. **2.81**

Paragraphs (6) and (7)

These provisions create a special rule on the increase of the capital limit for income support to £8,000. Where, from April 9, 1990, a claimant has capital of more than £6,000 but not more than £8,000, a claim made before May 28, 1990, can be back-dated to the date on which all the conditions of entitlement are satisfied. **2.82**

Paragraph (10)

Where a claimant starts work on a Monday or Tuesday and makes a claim for disability working allowance at any time in that week (i.e. Sunday to Saturday), the claim is treated as made on the Tuesday. **2.83**

Paragraphs (12)–(15)

Where a claim for disabled persons tax credit is disallowed on the ground that a qualifying benefit is not payable, although a claim for that benefit has been made, and later the qualifying benefit is awarded, a fresh claim for the tax credit made within three months of the award of the qualifying benefit is to be treated as made on the date of the original claim (or the date from which the qualifying benefit is awarded, if later). This rule is made necessary by the restrictions from April 1997 on the backdating of claims under reg.19 and on the effect of reviews. **2.84**

Paragraph (20)

The word "or" at the end of reg.6(20)(c)(i), which has been italicised in the present volume, was doubtless intended to be removed by SI 2022/177. However, the Queen's Printer's copy of that SI refers to sub-para.(20)(c)(ii)—not (i). **2.85**

Paragraph (22)

The definition of "relevant benefit" does not include personal independence payment, and so does not count as a "qualifying benefit" for the purpose of the backdating provisions in reg.6(16)–(21). The Department has advised CPAG the omission is an oversight and will be remedied by regulations in 2015, and that, in the meantime, the Department will treat personal independence payment as if it were a "relevant benefit." The Department has, however, subsequently advised that it now has no current plans to amend the regulations to this effect. **2.86**

Paragraphs (31) and (32)

2.87 These provisions "get around" the 12-month limitation on back-dating set out in s.1(2) of the Administration Act in relation to claims for retirement pension. They enable claimants to go back as far as October 1, 1998 in certain circumstances. The Explanatory Memorandum to the regulations indicates that the intended beneficiaries of the provisions are those who did not receive notice that their contribution records were deficient for the tax years 1996/97 to 2002/02 because the annual Deficiency Notice procedure which identifies such cases and advises customers of the need to consider making voluntary contributions to make good the shortfall did not take place in those years.

Paragraphs (35) and (36)

2.88 These paragraphs accommodate the consequences of the judgment of the Court of Justice in *Commission v European Parliament and Council* (C-299/05) [2007] E.C.R. I-8730, which determined that attendance allowance, carer's allowance, and the care component of a disability living allowance constitute sickness benefits within Regulation 1408/71 (which are exportable by the beneficiary), and not special non-contributory benefits (which are not exportable).

Claims by persons subject to work-focused interviews

2.89 [1**6A.**—[2 (1) This regulation applies to any person who is required to take part in a work-focused interview in accordance with regulations made under section 2A(1)(a) of the Social Security Administration Act 1992.]

(2) Subject to the following provisions of this regulation, where a person takes part in a work-focused interview, the date on which the claim is made shall be—

(a) in a case where—

(i) the claim made by the claimant meets the requirements of regulation 4(1), or

(ii) the claim made by the claimant is for income support and meets the requirements of regulation 4(1A),

the date on which the claim is received in the appropriate office.

(b) in a case where a claim does not meet the requirements of regulation 4(a) but is treated, under regulation 4(7), as having been duly made, the date on which the claim was treated as received in the appropriate office in the first instance;

(c) in a case where—

(i) first notification of intention to claim income support is made to an appropriate office, or

(ii) a claim for income support is received in an appropriate office which does not meet the requirements of regulation 4(1A),

[5 (d) without prejudice to sub-paragraphs (a) and (b), where a properly completed claim for incapacity benefit is received in an appropriate office within one month of the claimant first notifying such an office, by whatever means, of his intention to make that claim, the date of claim shall be the date on which that notification is made or the first day in respect of which the claim is made if later.]

the date of notification of, as the case may be, the date the claim is first received where the properly complete claim form is received within 1 month of notification or the date the claim is first received, or the day on which a properly completed claim form is received where these requirements are not met.

(3) In a case where a decision is made that a person is regarded as not having made a claim for any benefit because he failed to take part in a work-focused interview but subsequently claims such a benefit, in applying paragraph (2) to that claim no regard shall be had to any claim regarded as not having been made in consequence of that decision.

(4) Paragraph (2) shall not apply in any case where a decision has been made that the claimant has failed to take part in a work-focused interview.

[4 (5) In regulation 4 and this regulation, "work-focused interview" means an interview which [. . .] [is conducted for such purposes connected with employment or training as are specified under section 2A of the Social Security Administration Act 1992.]

AMENDMENTS

1. Regulation inserted by The Social Security (Work-focused Interviews) Regulations 2000 (SI 2000/897) (April 3, 2000).

2. The Social Security (Jobcentre Plus Interviews) Regulations 2001 (SI 2001/3210) (October 22, 2001).

3. Social Security (Jobcentre Plus Interviews) Regulations 2002 (SI 2002/1703) Sch.2 (September 30, 2002).

4. Social Security (Working Neighbourhoods) Regulations 2004 (SI 2004/959) reg.22 (April 26, 2004).

5. The Social Security (Miscellaneous Amendments) (No.2) Regulations 2006 (SI 2006/832) (April 10, 2006).

Evidence and information

7.—(1) [3Subject to paragraph (7),] every person who makes a claim for benefit shall furnish such certificates, documents, information and evidence in connection with the claim, or any question arising out of it, as may be required by the Secretary of State [4 or the Board] and shall do so within one month of being required to do so or such longer period as the Secretary of State [5Board] may consider reasonable. 2.90

[6 (1A) A claimant shall furnish such information and evidence as the Secretary of State may require as to the likelihood of future changes in his circumstances which is needed to determine—

(a) whether a period should be specified as an assessed income period under section 6 of the 2002 Act in relation to any decision; and

(b) if so, the length of the period to be so specified.

(1B) The information and evidence required under paragraph (1A) shall be furnished within 1 month of the Secretary of State notifying the claimant of the requirement, or within such longer period as the Secretary of State considers reasonable in the claimant's case.

(1C) In the case of a claimant making a claim for state pension credit in the advance period, time begins to run for the purposes of paragraphs (1) and (1B) on the day following the end of that period.]

(2) [3Subject to paragraph (7),] where a benefit may be claimed by either of two partners or where entitlement to or the amount of any benefit is or may be affected by the circumstances of a partner, the Secretary of State may require the partner other than the [5claimant to do either or both of the following, within one month of being required to do so or such longer period as the Board may consider reasonable—

(a) to certify in writing whether he agrees to the claimant making or, as the case may be, that he confirms the information given about his circumstances;

(b) to furnish such certificates, documents, information and evidence in connection with the claim, or any question arising out of it, as the Board may require.]

claimant to certify in writing whether he agrees to the claimant making the claim or, as the case may be, that he confirms the information given about his circumstances [[4]working families tax credit or disabled persons tax credit].

(3) In the case of a claim for [[4]working families' tax credit] or [[4]disabled person's tax credit], the employer of the claimant or, as the case may be, of the partner shall [[4]within one month of being required to do so or such longer period as the Board may consider reasonable] furnish such certificates, documents, information and evidence in connection with the claim or any question arising out of it as may be required by the Secretary of State [[4]Board].

[[2] (4) In the case of a person who is claiming [[4] disabled person's tax credit, working families' tax credit], [[3] income support] [[6] jobseeker's allowance [[7] state pension credit or employment and support allowance.] where that person or any partner is aged not less than 60 and is a member of, or a person deriving entitlement to a pension under, a personal pension scheme, or is a party to, or a person deriving entitlement to a pension under, a retirement annuity contract, he shall where the [[5] Board so require, within one month of being required to do so or such longer period as the Board may consider reasonable] Secretary of State so requires furnish the following information—

(a) the name and address of the pension fund holder;

(b) such other information including any reference or policy number as is needed to enable the personal pension scheme or retirement annuity contract to be identified.

(5) Where the pension fund holder receives from the Secretary of State [[5]Board] a request for details concerning the personal pension scheme or retirement annuity contract relating to a person or any partner to whom paragraph (4) refers, the pension fund holder shall [[5], within one month of the request or such longer period as the Board may consider reasonable] provide the Secretary of State [[5]Board] with any information to which paragraph (6) refers.

(6) The information to which this paragraph refers is—

(a) where the purchase of an annuity under a personal pension scheme has been deferred, the amount of any income which is being withdrawn from the personal pension scheme;

(b) in the case of—

(i) a personal pension scheme where income withdrawal is available, the [[8] rate of annuity which may have been purchased with the funds held under the scheme]; or

(ii) a personal pension scheme where income withdrawal is not available, or a retirement annuity contract, the [[8] rate of annuity which might have been purchased with the fund] if the fund were held under a personal pension scheme where income withdrawal was available,

calculated by or on behalf of the pension fund holder by means of tables prepared from time to time by the Government Actuary which are appropriate for this purpose.]

[3(7) Paragraphs (1) and (2) do not apply in the case of jobseeker's allowance.]

[4(8) Every person providing childcare in respect of which a claimant to whom regulation 46A of the Family Credit (General) Regulations 1987 applies is incurring relevant childcare charges, including a person providing childcare on behalf of a school, local authority, childcare scheme or establishment within paragraph (2)(b), (c) or (d) of that regulation, shall furnish such certificates, documents, information and evidence in connection with the claim made by the claimant, or any question arising out of it, as may required by the Board, and shall do so within one month of being required to do so or such longer period as the Board may consider reasonable.

(9) In paragraph (8) "relevant childcare charges" has the meaning given by regulation 46A(2) of the Family Credit (General) Regulations 1987.]

AMENDMENTS

1. The Social Security (Claims and Payments) Amendment Regulations 1991 (SI 1991/2741) reg.5 (March 10, 1992).

2. Income-related Benefit Schemes and Social Security (Claims and Payments) (Miscellaneous Amendments) Regulations 1995 (SI 1995/2303) reg.10(3) (October 2, 1995).

3. The Social Security (Claims and Payments) (Jobseeker's Allowance Consequential Amendments) Regulations 1996 (SI 1996/1460) reg.2(6) (October 7, 1996).

4. The Tax Credits (Claims and Payments) (Amendment) Regulations 1999 (SI 1999/2572) reg.6 (October 5, 1999).

5. For tax credits purposes only: The Tax Credits (Claims and Payments) (Amendment) Regulations 1999 (SI 1999/2572) reg.6 (October 5, 1999).

6. State Pension Credit (Consequential, Transitional and Miscellaneous) Regulations 2002 (SI 2002/3019) reg.4 (April 7, 2003).

7. The Employment and Support Allowance (Consequential Provisions) (No.2) Regulations 2008 (SI 2008/1554) reg.15 (October 27, 2008).

8. Social Security (Miscellaneous Amendments No.4) Regulations 2017 (SI 2017/1015) reg.5(3) (November 16, 2017).

DEFINITIONS

"benefit"—see reg.2(2).
"claim for benefit"—see reg.2(1).
"jobseeker's allowance"—*ibid.*
"partner"—*ibid.*
"pension fund holder"—*ibid.*
"personal pension scheme"—*ibid.*
"retirement annuity contract"—*ibid.*

GENERAL NOTE

From time to time, decision makers have suggested that a person is not entitled to benefit because they have failed to furnish the Secretary of State with information within the one month referred to in reg.7(1). *R(IS)4/93* was just such a case. The adjudication officer decided that the claimant was not entitled to income support because the claimant had failed—inter alia to provide sufficient evidence as to the amount of capital held. The tribunal confirmed the adjudication officer's decision and the claimant appealed to the Commissioner. 2.91

Deputy Commissioner Mesher (as he then was) concluded that both the adjudication officer and the tribunal had misunderstood the operation of reg.7(1). Drawing on the reasoning of the Court of Appeal in *R. v Secretary of State for Social Services Ex p. Child Poverty Action Group* [1990] 2 Q.B. 540, the Deputy Commissioner explains that reg.7(1) is concerned with the responsibilities of the Secretary of State to collect information so that the Secretary of State can submit a claim to an adjudication officer for determination:

> "Once such a submission is made, it is simply irrelevant whether or not the claimant has satisfied the Secretary of State under reg.7(1) of the Claims and Payments Regulations or whether or not the claimant has furnished sufficient information for the Secretary of State to refer the claim to the adjudication officer. Those matters are entirely for the Secretary of State [see para.11 of *R(SB)29/83*]. Once the claim is submitted to him under section 98(1) [now s.20(1) of the Administration Act], the adjudication officer's duty is to take it into consideration and, so far as practicable, dispose of it within 14 days of its submission (Social Security Act 1975, s.99(1)) [now s.21(1) of the Administration Act]. As decided by the Court of Appeal in the passage quoted above, the adjudication officer has the power to make further investigations or call for further evidence before determining the claim. Or he may determine the claim on the evidence currently available, especially if he considers that the claimant has already had a reasonable opportunity of producing the required information or evidence." (At [13].)

The Deputy Commissioner goes on to advise that adjudication officers and tribunals when presented with a claim for determination (whether initially or on appeal) must focus on the "essential elements of entitlement directly" in the light of the evidence available. Since claimants generally have the burden of showing on the balance of probabilities that they meet the conditions of entitlement, the absence of information from the claimant will often result in a finding against them.

2.92 The Deputy Commissioner does not spell out how tribunals should proceed if the absence of information means that the tribunal cannot make any findings of fact. There will be cases where there is insufficient information to find positively some fact which results in there being no entitlement. In these rare cases where a claimant's reluctance to participate defeats the inquisitorial jurisdiction of tribunals, it is open to the tribunal to decide the matter purely on the burden of proof. In such cases the proper approach is for the tribunal:

- to record no findings of fact, or perhaps only those that are proved, *avoiding* the inclusion of reference to those issues on which facts cannot be found;
- to record in the decision that the claimant is not entitled to the benefit on the claim made on such and such a day because they have not proved on the balance of probabilities that they meet the conditions of entitlement for the benefit; and
- to explain fully in the reasons for the decision what the relevant conditions of entitlement are and why the tribunal is unable to make findings of fact on all the material issues.

R(IS)4/93 has been referred to and disapproved by the Court of Appeal in Northern Ireland in *Kerr v Department for Social Development* [2002] NICA 32, Judgment of July 4, 2002. That decision went an appeal to the House of Lords. The decision of the House of Lords in *Kerr v Department for Social Development*, [2004] UKHL 23; [2004] 1 W.L.R. 1372 (appendix to *R1/04(SF)*) was handed down on May 6, 2004. The discussion in the House of Lords broadened from the considerations which had taken place in the courts below. The comments, in particular of Baroness Hale, on the decision-making process are discussed in detail in the annotations to s.3(1) of the Tribunals, Courts and Enforcement Act 2007. The House of Lords dismissed the appeal. In their opinions, no mention is made of *R(IS) 4/93* which had been disapproved in the reasons of the Court of Appeal. Notwithstanding the absence of any comment, its authority must be considerably weakened by the dismissal of the appeal. However, it is suggested that it will still provide some useful guidance in those cases where, despite the best endeavours of the adjudicating authorities to collect all the evidence needed to determine a claim for benefit, they remain short of evidence on key matters. For a discussion of the similar provisions in relation to the adjudication of housing benefit and council tax benefit claims see the decision of the Tribunal of Commissioners in *R(H) 3/05*.

In *CIS/51/2007* and *CIB/52/2007* the Commissioner comments on the relationship between regs 4–6A, and reg.7. The context was a claim which left some uncertainty about the claimant's identity (the national insurance number provided did not correspond to the identity of the claimant) and the correctness of his address (enquiries to the address given had resulted in denials that the claimant had ever lived there). The Commissioner notes that there are requirements for making a claim under the regulations, which are a matter of form and procedure, and that these should be distinguished from "the obvious and universal necessity for any person making such a claim to substantiate it by showing he meets the qualifying conditions for entitlement". This is a matter of fact and evidence (para. 8). The provisions of reg.7(1) apply only to those who have made something that can be identified as a procedurally effective claim. That is determined by applying the rules in reg.4 to 6A. A claim which raises questions about the identity of the claimant may be a claim. Establishing identity is a matter of fact and evidence. If claimants cannot establish these matters, then they have failed to comply with the reasonable evidence requirements, and it will be appropriate to determine that they have not met the conditions of entitlement.

Attendance in person

8.—(1) [1. . .] 2.93

(2) Every person who makes a claim for benefit [1 (other than a jobseeker's allowance)] shall attend at such office or place and on such days and at such times as the Secretary of State [2 or the Board] may direct, for the purpose of furnishing certificates, documents, information and evidence under regulation 7, if reasonably so required by the Secretary of State [2 or the Board].

AMENDMENTS

1. The Social Security (Claims and Payments) (Jobseeker's Allowance Consequential Amendments) Regulations 1996 (SI 1996/1460) reg.2(7) (October 7, 1996).

2. The Tax Credits (Claims and Payments) (Amendment) Regulations 1999 (SI 1999/2572) reg.20 (October 5, 1999).

DEFINITIONS

"benefit"—see reg.2(2).
"claim for benefit"—see reg.2(1).

GENERAL NOTE

There seems now to be no direct sanction for a failure to comply with reg.8(2) in relation to benefits other than JSA. For JSA obligations, see reg.23 of the Jobseeker's Allowance Regulations. 2.94

Interchange with claims for other benefits

9.—(1) Where it appears that a person who has made a claim for benefit specified in column (1) of Part I of Schedule 1 may be entitled to the benefit specified opposite to it in column (2) of that Part, any such claim may be treated by the Secretary of State [1 or the Board] as a claim alternatively, or in addition, to the benefit specified opposite to it in that column. 2.95

(2) Where it appears that a person who has claimed any benefit specified in Part II of Schedule 1 in respect of a child may be entitled to child benefit in respect of the same child, the Secretary of State may treat the claim alternatively, or in addition, for the benefit in question as a claim by that person for child benefit.

(3) Where it appears that a person who has claimed child benefit in respect of a child may be entitled to any benefit specified in Part II of Schedule 1 [2. . .] in respect of the same child, the Secretary of State may treat the claim for child benefit as a claim alternatively, or in addition, by that person for the benefit in question specified in that Part.

(4) Where it appears that a person who has made a claim for benefit other than child benefit is not entitled to it, but that some other person may be entitled to an increase of benefit in respect of him, the Secretary of State may treat the claim as if it were a claim by such other person for an increase of benefit in respect of the claimant.

(5) Where it appears that a person who has made a claim for an increase of benefit other than child benefit in respect of a child or adult dependant is not entitled to it but that some other person may be entitled to such an increase of benefit in respect of that child or adult dependant, the Secretary of State may treat the claim as if it were a claim by that other person for such an increase.

(6) Where it appears that a person who has made a claim for a guardian's allowance in respect of any child is not entitled to it, but that the claimant or the wife or husband of the claimant, may be entitled to an increase of benefit for that child, the Secretary of State may treat the claim as if it were a claim by the claimant or the wife or husband of the claimant for an increase of benefit for that child.

[3 (7) In determining whether he [1 or they] should treat a claim alternatively or in addition to another claim (the original claim) under this regulation the Secretary of State shall treat the alternative or additional claim, whenever made, as having been made at the same time as the original claim.]

AMENDMENTS

1. The Tax Credits (Claims and Payments) (Amendment) Regulations 1999 (SI 1999/2572) regs 20 and 22 (October 5, 1999).

2. The Child Benefit, Child Support and Social Security (Miscellaneous Amendments) Regulations 1996 (SI 1996/1803) reg.19 (April 7, 1997).

3. The Social Security (Miscellaneous Provisions) Amendment Regulations 1992 (SI 1992/247) reg.12 (March 9, 1992).

GENERAL NOTE

2.96 This invaluable provision removes some of the rigour of ensuring that a claimant chooses the right benefit to claim and is not prejudiced by making a mistaken choice. The regulation now also covers interchange of claims for child benefit with claims for other benefits. There was originally some doubt over whether a decision to treat a claim as one in the alternative was for the adjudicating authorities or the Secretary of State.

In *R. v Secretary of State for Social Security Ex p. Cullen and Nelson* (*The Times*, May 16, 1997 reported as *R(A) 1/97*), the Court of Appeal confirmed the decision of Harrison J. in *Cullen* (November 16, 1996) and reversed the decision of the Commissioner in *Nelson* (*CA 171/1993*). In both cases, unsuccessful claims for supplementary benefit had been made prior to April 11, 1988. At that time, the 1979 Claims and Payments Regulations allowed the Secretary of State to treat a claim for supplementary benefit as in the alternative a claim for attendance allowance. The Claims and Payments Regulations 1987, which came into effect on April 11, 1988, contained no such power. In 1991 (*Cullen*) and 1993 (*Nelson*) claims for attendance allowance were made and it was sought to have the supplementary benefit claims treated as claims for attendance allowance. The Court of Appeal held that the Secretary of State had no power to do so, so that the Commissioner in *CA/171/1993* was wrong to refer the question to the Secretary of State for determination. Once the 1979 Regulations were revoked, the Secretary of State could no longer exercise a power which no longer existed. As the Secretary of State had only had a discretion under the 1979 Regulations whether or not to treat a supplementary benefit claim as in the alternative a claim for attendance allowance, the claimants had no accrued rights which were preserved on the revocation of the 1979 Regulations under s.16 of the Interpretation Act 1978.

[[1] Claim for incapacity benefit [[3], severe disablement allowance or employment and support allowance] where no entitlement to statutory sick pay or statutory maternity pay]

10.—(1) Paragraph (2) applies to a claim for incapacity benefit or severe] disablement allowance for a period of incapacity for work of which the claimant gave his employer a notice of incapacity under regulation 7 of the Statutory Sick Pay (General) Regulations 1982, and for which he has been informed in writing by his employer that there is no entitlement to statutory sick pay. 2.97

[[3] (1A) Paragraph (2) also applies to a claim for an employment and support allowance for a period of limited capability for work in relation to which the claimant gave his employer a notice of incapacity under regulation 7 of the Statutory Sick Pay (General) Regulations 1982, and for which he has been informed in writing by his employer that there is no entitlement to statutory sick pay.]

(2) A claim to which this paragraph applies shall be treated as made on the date accepted by the claimant's employer as the first day of incapacity, provided that he makes the claim—

(a) within the appropriate time specified in paragraph 2 of Schedule 4 beginning with the day on which he is informed in writing that he was not entitled to statutory sick pay; or

(b) [[2] . . .]

(3) Paragraph (4) applies to a claim for maternity allowance for a pregnancy or confinement by reason of which the claimant gave her employer notice of absence from work under [section 164(4) of the Social Security Contributions and Benefits Act 1992] and regulation 23 of the Statutory Maternity Pay (General) Regulations 1986 and in respect of which she has been informed in writing by her employer that there is no entitlement to statutory maternity pay.

(4) A claim to which this paragraph applies shall be treated as made on the date when the claimant gave her employer notice of absence from work or at the beginning of the 14th week before the expected week of confinement, whichever is later, provided that she makes the claim—

(a) within three months of being informed in writing that she was not entitled to statutory maternity pay; or

(b) [[2] . . .]

AMENDMENTS

1. The Social Security (Claims and Payments) Amendment (No.2) Regulations 1994 (SI 1994/2943) reg.3 (April 13, 1995).

2. The Social Security (Miscellaneous Amendments) (No.2) Regulations 1997 (SI 1997/793) reg.4 (April 7, 1997).

3. The Employment and Support Allowance (Consequential Provisions) (No.2) Regulations 2008 (SI 2008/1554) reg.16 (October 27, 2008).

Special provisions where it is certified that a woman is expected to be confined or where she has been confined

2.98 **11.**—(1) Where in a certificate issued or having effect as issued under the Social Security (Medical Evidence) Regulations 1976 it has been certified that it is to be expected that a woman will be confined, and she makes a claim for maternity allowance in expectation of that confinement any such claim may, unless the Secretary of State otherwise directs, be treated as a claim for [1 incapacity benefit] [3, severe disablement allowance or employment and support allowance] made in respect of any days in the period beginning with either—

(a) the beginning of the 6th week before the expected week of confinement; or

(b) the actual date of confinement, whichever is the earlier, and ending in either case on the 14th day after the actual date of confinement.

(2) Where, in a certificate issued under the Social Security (Medical Evidence) Regulations 1976 it has been certified that a woman has been confined and she claims maternity allowance within [2 three months] of that date, her claim may be treated in the alternative or in addition as a claim for incapacity benefit [3, severe disablement allowance or employment and support allowance] for the period beginning with the date of her confinement and ending 14 days after that date.

AMENDMENTS

1. The Social Security (Claims and Payments) Amendment (No.2) Regulations 1994 (SI 1994/2943) reg.4 (April 13, 1995).

2. The Social Security (Miscellaneous Amendments) (No.2) Regulations 1997 (SI 1997/793) reg.5 (April 7, 1997).

3. The Employment and Support Allowance (Consequential Provisions) (No.2) Regulations 2008, (SI 2008/1554) reg.17 (October 27, 2008).

GENERAL NOTE

2.99 In *R(S)1/74* the Commissioner held that a similarly worded predecessor to this regulation which made similar, though not identical, provision neither confers title to sickness benefit nor restricts the right to it. The regulation does no more than define the period for which, having made an unsuccessful claim to maternity allowance, a woman may be treated as having made a claim to incapacity benefit. There is nothing to prevent her seeking to prove incapacity for some period or periods additional to that to which her claim is taken to relate.

2.100 *Regulation 12 revoked by The Social Security (Claims and Payments on account, Overpayments and Recovery) Amendment Regulations 1989 (SI 1989/136) (February 27, 1989).*

Advance claims and awards

13.—(1) Where, although a person does not satisfy the requirements of entitlement to benefit on the date on which a claim is made, the [3 Secretary of State] is of the opinion that unless there is a change of circumstances he will satisfy those requirements for a period beginning on a day (the relevant day") not more than 3 months after the date on which the claim is made, then [3 the Secretary of State] may— 2.101

(a) treat the claim as if made for a period beginning with the relevant day; and

(b) award benefit accordingly, subject to the condition that the person satisfies the requirements for entitlement when benefit becomes payable under the award.

(2) [3 A decision pursuant to paragraph (1)(b) to award benefit may be revised under section 9 of the Social Security Act 1998] if the requirements for entitlement are found not to have been satisfied on the relevant day.

(3) [2][6. . .][Paragraphs (1) and (2) do not] apply to any claim for maternity allowance, attendance allowance, [1 disability living allowance], retirement pension or increase, [8 state pension under Part 1 of the Pensions Act 2014,] [5 a shared additional pension,] [6. . .] [4 state pension credit] or any claim within regulation 11(1)(a) or (b).

(4)–(8) [6. . .]

[6 (9) Paragraphs (1) and (2) do not apply to—

(a) a claim for income support made by a person from abroad as defined in regulation 21AA of the Income Support (General) Regulations 1987 (special cases: supplemental—persons from abroad); [7 . . .]

(b) a claim for a jobseeker's allowance made by a person from abroad as defined in regulation 85A of the Jobseeker's Allowance Regulations (special cases: supplemental—persons from abroad).] [7 and

(c) a claim for an employment and support allowance made by a person from abroad as defined in regulation 70 of the Employment and Support Allowance Regulations (special cases: supplemental—persons from abroad).]

Amendments

1. The Social Security (Claims and Payments) Amendments Regulations 1991 (SI 1991/2741) reg.13 (March 9, 1992).

2. The Social Security (Claims and Payments) Amendment Regulations 1994 (SI 1994/2319) reg.3 (October 3, 1994).

3. The Social Security Act 1998 (Commencement No 9, and Savings and Consequential and Transitional Provisions) Order 1999 (SI 1999/2422) Sch.7 (September 6, 1999).

4. State Pension Credit (Consequential, Transitional and Miscellaneous) Regulations 2002 (SI 2002/3019) reg.6 (April 7, 2003).

5. The Social Security (Shared Additional Pension) (Miscellaneous Amendments) Regulations 2005 (SI 2005/1551) reg.2 (July 6, 2005).

6. The Social Security, Housing Benefit and Council Tax Benefit (Miscellaneous Amendments) Regulations 2007 (SI 2007/1331) (May 23, 2007).

7. The Employment and Support Allowance (Consequential Provisions) (No.2) Regulations 2008 (SI 2008/1554) reg.18 (October 27, 2008).

8. The Pensions Act 2014 (Consequential, Supplementary and Incidental Amendments) Order 2015 (SI 2015/1985) art.9(6) (April 6, 2016).

GENERAL NOTE

2.102 This regulation contains a useful power in the case of the specified benefits to make awards in advance, subject to revision if the conditions of entitlement are found not to be satisfied as at the date the award takes effect. But amendments following the Court of Appeal's decision in *Secretary of State for Work and Pensions* v. *Bhakta,* [2006] EWCA Civ. 65 exclude advance awards for persons from abroad in relation to the habitual residence test.

The weight of authority on the proper interpretation of reg.13(1) is that a claim is to be treated as continuously made until it is determined: see *AW v SSWP (IB)* [2013] UKUT 20 (AAC), [15]–[19], and the authorities cited there.

Advance award of disability living allowance

2.103 [1 **13A.**—(1) Where, although a person does not satisfy the requirements for entitlement to disability living allowance on the date on which the claim is made, the [2 Secretary of State] is of the opinion that unless there is a change of circumstances he will satisfy those requirements for a period beginning on a day ("the relevant day") not more than 3 months after the date on which the claim is made, then [2 the Secretary of State] may award disability living allowance from the relevant day subject to the condition that the person satisfies the requirements for entitlement on the relevant day.

(2) Where a person makes a claim for disability living allowance on or after 3rd February 1992 and before 6th April 1992 the adjudicating authority may award benefit for a period beginning on or after 5th April 1992 being a day not more than three months after the date on which the claim was made, subject to the condition that the person satisfies the requirements for entitlement when disability living allowance becomes payable under the award.

(3) [2 A decision pursuant to paragraph (1) or (2) to award benefit may be revised under section 9 of the Social Security Act 1998] if the requirements for entitlement are found not to have been satisfied when disability living allowance becomes payable under the award.]

AMENDMENTS

1. The Social Security (Claims and Payments) Amendment Regulations 1991 (SI 1991/2741) reg.7 (February 3, 1992).

2. The Social Security Act 1998 (Commencement No.11 and Transitional Provisions) Order 1999 (SI 1999/2860) Sch.3 (October 18, 1999).

GENERAL NOTE

2.104 In *CSDLA/852/2002,* and repeated in *CSDLA/553/2005* the Commissioner explains:

> "4. Regulation 13A thus permits an award of DLA where a claim is made no more than three months before the date from which the award takes effect, if the DM considers that by that date the claimant will satisfy the three months qualifying period for DLA and is then likely so to satisfy the qualifying conditions for a further six-month period. The claim subsists until the matter is determined by the DM (s.8(2)(a) of the Social Security Act 1998).
>
> 5. A claim is to be treated as being continuously made until it is determined. Therefore, although Regulation 13A only benefits the claimant if the claim is made within the relevant three-month period, it applies provided that the DLA conditions in question are satisfied by the date of the Secretary of State's decision under appeal and seemed likely to continue for both the three-month qualifying

period and the six-month prospective period, so that the Secretary of State could then have made an advance award.

6. The issue for the tribunal was, therefore, whether . . . when the claim was decided by the Secretary of State (and beyond which circumstances could not be taken because of section 12(8)(b) of the Social Security Act 1998), circumstances existed, (even if proved by later evidence not available to the DM at the time) which justified an award under regulation 13A."

A different Commissioner had come to the same conclusion in *CDLA/3971/2008*. In *KH v SSWP* [2009] UKUT 54 (AAC), the judge also came to the same conclusion by slightly different reasoning. Regulation 6(8) of the Claims and Payments Regulations did not require the date of claim to be regarded as the date a claim form was requested (provided that it was returned within six weeks or such longer period as the Secretary of State chooses to accept), since this would deprive Regulation 13A of much of its significance. The judge says:

"12. As I have said, there is no reason to give effect to regulation 6(8) beyond its context and purpose. Regulation 13A, in contrast to regulation 6(8), is concerned with the future, not the past. There is no need or reason to allow that provision to control the power to make an advance award. The natural meaning of 'the date on which the claim is made' in the context of regulation 13A is the date on which it is received. If the Secretary of State's argument is correct, the effectiveness of regulation 13A is significantly reduced. Potentially six weeks (or longer at the Secretary of State's discretion) may have past before the claim is even received and further weeks may pass while the Secretary of State obtains medical evidence and decides the claim. In that context, there may be little or no scope for an advance award if the 3 months begins on the date the claimant asked for a claim pack."

See also the review of the authorities on this regulation in *TS and EK v SSWP (DLA)* [2020] UKUT 284 (AAC) at paras.185–196.

[1 Advance claim for and award of disability working allowance

13B.—(1) Where a person makes a claim for disability working allowance on or after 10th March 1992 and before 7th April 1992 the adjudicating authority may— 2.105

(a) treat the claim as if it were made for a period beginning on 7th April 1992; and

(b) An award benefit accordingly, subject to the condition that the person satisfies the requirements for entitlement on 7th April 1992.

(2) An award under paragraph (1)(b) shall be reviewed by the adjudicating authority if the requirements for entitlement are found not to have been satisfied on 7th April 1992.]

AMENDMENT

1. The Social Security (Claims and Payments) Amendment Regulations 1991 (SI 1991/2741) reg.7(2) (March 10, 1992).

DEFINITION

"adjudicating authority"—see reg.2(1).

GENERAL NOTE

This allowed an advance claim in the few weeks immediately before the start of the scheme on April 7, 1992. 2.106

[1 [2 Further claim for and award of disability living allowance or attendance allowance

2.107 **13C.**—(1) A person entitled to an award of disability living allowance or attendance allowance may make a further claim for disability living allowance or attendance allowance, as the case may be, during the period of 6 months immediately before the existing award expires.]

(2) Where a person makes a claim in accordance with paragraph (1) the [3 Secretary of State] may—

(a) treat the claim as if made on the first day after the expiry of the existing award ("the renewal date"); and

(b) award benefit accordingly, subject to the condition that the person satisfies the requirements for entitlement on the renewal date.

(3) [4 A decision pursuant to paragraph (2)(b) to award benefit may be revised under section 9 of the Social Security Act 1998] if the requirements for entitlement are found not to have been satisfied on the renewal date.]

Amendments

1. The Social Security (Claims and Payments) Amendment Regulations 1991 (SI 1991/2741) reg.8 (February 3, 1992).

2. The Social Security, Child Support and Tax Credits (Miscellaneous Amendments) Regulations 2005 (SI 2005/337) reg.7 (March 18, 2005).

3. The Social Security Act 1998 (Commencement No.11, and Savings and Consequential and Transitional Provisions) Order 1999 (SI 1999/2860) Sch.3 para.2 (October 18, 1999).

General Note

2.108 This permits a continuation claim for disability living allowance to be made during the last six months of an existing award.

In *CDLA/14895/1996*, it was held that reg.13C(2) should not be applied until it has been considered whether, if the claim were treated as an application for review under s.30(13) of the Social Security Administration Act 1992, there would be grounds for review. If there are grounds for review, the existing award should be reviewed. Otherwise, the claim should be treated as a renewal claim, effective only from the end of the existing award.

The relationship of this regulation and the prohibition on tribunals of considering circumstances obtaining after the date of claim under s.12(8)(b) of the Social Security Act 1998 was considered in *CDLA/3848/2001*, where the Commissioner said,

> "In my judgment it is implicit in Reg.13C of the 1987 Regulations that circumstances occurring between the date of a decision on a renewal claim and the renewal date can (and therefore must) be taken into account by an appeal tribunal.
>
> . . .
>
> Regulation 13C(2), having stated that the Secretary of State may treat the claim as if made on the renewal date, goes on to provide that he may 'award benefit accordingly.' That means that the task of a decision maker (and appeal tribunal on appeal) is to determine whether the conditions for disability living allowance will be (or were) satisfied *on the renewal date*. It is in my view implicit that circumstances which occur between the date of the decision maker's decision and the renewal date can be taken into account by an appeal tribunal. It cannot have been the intention of s.12(8)(b) and Reg.13C, read together, that an appeal tribunal is prevented from taking into account changes in circumstances relevant to the

very issue which it has to decide. If it were to ignore such changes, the effect of its decision would not be to 'award benefit accordingly' (i.e. on the basis of a claim treated as made on the renewal date)."

A Scottish Commissioner agreed with this reasoning in deciding an appeal relating to a claim for an attendance allowance, where there is no corresponding provision. Though disability living allowance and attendance allowance are separate benefits, there is no logical reason why there should not be similar provision in relation to renewal claims. However, there is not. The Commissioner in *CSA/248/2002* had to decide the effect of a tribunal's only deciding matters down to the date of the decision, and whether this had constituted an error of law. The Commissioner concluded that the renewal claim could be competently made in advance of the expiry of the existing award (at paras 12 and 13). But the Commissioner found himself compelled to conclude that s.12(8)(b) did apply to the renewal of an attendance allowance claim (at para.19).

In *CDLA/4331/2002,* it was held that, when hearing an appeal from a decision on a renewal claim effective from the claimant's 16th birthday, a tribunal is required to determine the appeal on the basis that that the claimant was 16, even if she was only 15 at the date of the Secretary of State's decision. The approach taken was different from that in *CDLA/3848/2001,* but the result was the same on the facts of the case. In *C12/2003–04 (DLA),* a Commissioner in Northern Ireland expressly disagreed with *CDLA/3848/2001* and concluded that the Secretary of State was not entitled to refuse benefit at all until the date from which the renewal claim would have been effective. A tribunal, faced with an appeal against a disallowance of a renewal claim made before the date from which a new award would have been effective, therefore had no power to do more than set aside the Secretary of State's decision as having been made without jurisdiction, leaving the Secretary of State to make a new decision. 2.109

This conflict of authority was resolved in a decision of a Tribunal of Commissioners in *R(DLA)4/05.* The Tribunal of Commissioners departs from the reasoning in both *CDLA/3848/2001* and *C12/2003–04 (DLA). CDLA/3848/2001* had failed to take into account that effect had to be given to the provisions of ss.8(2)(b) and 12(8)(b) of the Social Security Act 1998 in the context of renewal claims. This precluded the Secretary of State from taking into account any circumstances not obtaining at the date of the decision. This meant that the Secretary of State had to determine the renewal claim on the basis of circumstances existing at the time the decision was made. In so doing they dissent from paras 106–107 of another decision of a Tribunal of Commissioners in *R(IB)2/04* (see below) which had indicated that renewal claims required prediction. The later Tribunal of Commissioners concludes that this part of the earlier decision was made without full argument and consideration of the implications of s.8(2)(b). They consider that, if a change of circumstances before the renewal date is anticipated, best practice would be to defer the making of the decision until closer to the renewal date in order to know whether the anticipated change had indeed materialised. The Tribunal's disagreement with the Northern Ireland decision in that reg.13C(2)(b) only permits the imposition of a condition in the case of an advance award that all the conditions of entitlement exist as at the renewal date. So the Secretary of State did have power to disallow a renewal claim before the renewal date.

The earlier decision of the Tribunal of Commissioners in *R(IB)2/04* had, in its third issue, addressed the question of whether the power to revise in reg.13C(3) is a free-standing one, or whether reg.3 of the Decisions and Appeals Regulations needs to be established before a decision on a renewal claim can be altered under reg.13C(3). The Tribunal of Commissioners concludes that there is no need for a ground for revision under reg.3 of the Decisions and Appeals Regulations to exist to trigger a reg.13C(3) revision. However, in the usual case where the issue concerns the condition of the claimant at the renewal date, "it can be exercised only on the ground that the claimant's condition has either improved between the date of decision and the renewal date to a greater extent than anticipated by the decision maker or has not deteriorated during that period to the extent anticipated by the decision maker." (para.13 of the summary of conclusions on issues of law.' This conclusion must, however, now be read in the light of the decision of the Tribunal of Commissioners in the later decision referred to above.

[1 Advance claims for an award of state pension credit

2.110 **13D.**—(1) Paragraph (2) applies if—

(a) a person does not satisfy the requirements for entitlement to state pension credit on the date on which the claim is made; and

(b) the Secretary of State is of the opinion that unless there is a change of circumstances he will satisfy those requirements—

(i) where the claim is made in the advance period, when he attains the qualifying age; or

(ii) in any other case, within 4 months of the date on which the claim is made.

(2) Where this paragraph applies, the Secretary of State may—

(a) treat the claim as made for a period beginning on the day ("the relevant day") the claimant—

(i) attains the qualifying age, where the claim is made in the advance period; or

(ii) is likely to satisfy the requirements for entitlement in any other case; and

(b) if appropriate, award state pension credit accordingly, subject to the condition that the person satisfies the requirements for entitlement on the relevant day.

(3) An award under paragraph (2) may be revised under section 9 of the Social Security Act 1998 if the claimant fails to satisfy the conditions for entitlement to state pension credit on the relevant day.]

[2 (4) This regulation does not apply to a claim made by a person not in Great Britain as defined in regulation 2 of the State Pension Credit Regulations (persons not in Great Britain).]

AMENDMENTS

1. Inserted by the State Pension Credit (Consequential, Transitional and Miscellaneous Provisions) Regulations 2002 (SI 2002/3019) reg.6 (April 7, 2003).

2. The Social Security, Housing Benefit and Council Tax Benefit (Miscellaneous Amendments) Regulations 2007 (SI 2007/1331) (May 23, 2007).

Advance claim for and award of maternity allowance

2.111 **14.**—(1) Subject to the following provisions of this regulation, a claim for maternity allowance in expectation of confinement, or for an increase in such an allowance in respect of an adult dependent, and an award on such a claim, may be made not earlier than 14 weeks before the beginning of the expected week of confinement.

(2) A claim for an increase of maternity allowance in respect of an adult dependant may not be made in advance unless, on the date when made, the circumstances relating to the adult dependant concerned are such as would qualify the claimant for such an increase if they occurred in a period for which she was entitled to a maternity allowance.

Advance notice of retirement and claim for and award of pension

15.—(1) A claim for a retirement pension of any category, and for any increase in any such pension, [8 or a state pension under Part 1 of the Pensions Act 2014] [6 or a shared additional pension] and an award on such a claim, may be made at any time not more than 4 months before the date on which the claimant will, subject to the fulfilment of the necessary conditions, become entitled to such a pension. 2.112

(2) [1. . .]

(3) [1. . .]

(4) [1. . .]

[2 (5) Where a person claims a Category A or Category B retirement pension and is, or but for that claim would be, in receipt of [3 incapacity benefit] [4. . .] for a period which includes the first day to which the claim relates, then if that day is not the appropriate day for the payment of retirement pension in his case, the claim shall be treated as if the first day of the claim was instead the next following such pay day.

(6) Where the spouse of such a person as is mentioned in paragraph (5) above claims a Category A or Category B retirement pension and the first day of that claim is the same as the first day of the claim made by that person, the provisions of that paragraph shall apply also to the claim made by the spouse [7 or civil partner].]

(7) For the purposes of facilitating the determination of a subsequent claim for a Category A, B or C retirement pension [8 or a state pension under Part 1 of the Pensions Act 2014], a person may at any time not more than 4 months before the date on which he will attain pensionable age, and notwithstanding that he [5 intends to defer his entitlement to a Category A or Category B retirement pension] [8 or a state pension under Part 1 of the Pensions Act 2014] at that date, submit particulars in writing to the Secretary of State in a form approved by him for that purpose with a view to the determination (in advance of the claim) of any question under the Act [8 or the Pensions Act 2014] relating to that person's title to such a [8 pension] [5. . .] and subject to the necessary modifications, the provisions of these regulations shall apply to any such particulars.

AMENDMENTS

1. Social Security Act 1986 (October 1, 1989).

2. The Social Security (Abolition of Earnings Rule) (Consequential) Regulations 1989 (SI 1989/1642) reg.2(2) (October 1, 1989).

3. The Social Security (Claims and Payments) Amendment (No.2) Regulations 1994 (SI 1994/2943) reg.5 (April 13, 1995).

4. The Social Security (Claims and Payments) (Jobseeker's Allowance Consequential Amendments) Regulations 1996 (SI 1996/1460) reg.2 (October 7, 1996).

5. The Social Security (Abolition of Earnings Rule) (Consequential) Regulations 1989 (SI 1989/1642) reg.2(3) (October 1, 1989).

6. The Social Security (Shared Additional Pension) (Miscellaneous Amendments) Regulations 2005 (SI 2005/1551) (July 6, 2005).

7. The Civil Partnership (Pensions, Social Security and Child Support) (Consequential etc. Provisions) Order 2005 (SI 2005/2877) (December 5, 2005).

8. The Pensions Act 2014 (Consequential, Supplementary and Incidental Amendments) Order 2015 (SI 2015/1985) art.9(7) (April 6, 2016).

General Note

2.113 In *CP/1074/1997* a Commissioner had to consider the proper approach to be taken to the determination of a date of birth in relation to a claim for retirement pension. The claimant had been born in the Punjab, and his year of birth had been consistently stated on a number of documents as 1931, but there was no clear evidence of the day he was born in that year. On September 13, 1995 he made a claim for retirement pension, but the adjudication officer treated his date of birth as December 31, 1931 and concluded that the claim made on September 13, 1995 could not be accepted. This would have required the claimant to have been born no later than January 13, 1931 in order to be within the four months provided for in reg.15(1). The claimant adduced evidence that he had been born on December 18, 1930, but his was not accepted by the tribunal. In dealing with the appeal the Commissioner addresses a number of arguments put forward on behalf of the claimant. The Commissioner accepted that the claimant did not need to prove a particular date of birth, merely that he had reached retirement age by a particular date. He did not, however, accept a second argument which was based on the application of a mathematical approach to the evidential test of the balance of probabilities. The claimant argued that as each day passed in the year in which it was accepted that a person was born, it became more probable that the person had been born by that day in the year. By the beginning of July it could therefore be said that it was more probable than not that the claimant had been born by that date. In such circumstances, the practice of the adjudication officer in using the last day of the year as the date of birth was an error of law. The Commissioner rejects this argument, citing *Re JS (a minor)* [1980] 1 All E.R. 1061, for the proposition that the concept of evidential probability is not the same as the mathematical concept. The Commissioner approves the proposition in that case that the civil burden of proof requires the party on whom the burden falls to "satisfy the court that it is reasonably safe in all the circumstances of the case to act on the evidence before the court, bearing in mind the consequences which will follow". The Commissioner finally notes that this may not, in every case where a date of birth in the year is not known, result in the choice of the last day in the year. Regard must be had to all the evidence available at the time the decision is made in determining which date in the year is to be selected as the date by which the person was born.

In *CP/3017/2004* the Commissioner held, applying *R(DLA) 4/05* by analogy, that there is a power to disallow an advance claim made under reg.15(1) for an increase of retirement pension for a wife up to four months before a claimant might become entitled to the pension (see para.7). However, the Commissioner considers,

> " . . . in some cases where there was likely to be a significant change of circumstances before the start date of the period covered by a claim, it might well be good practice to defer making a decision until it was known whether that change had actually materialised. It seems to me that the present case is one where that course should have been taken. It was plain from the evidence provided that the claimant's wife's earnings fluctuated a great deal from one pay period to another. And the nature of the case is different from that of a person suffering some potentially disabling or incapacitating condition, where in most cases there can be a sensible prediction about how the condition might progress in the future. It was simply unknown on 3 March 2004 what the claimant's wife's earnings might be in the week prior to 31 May 2004. Quite apart from the doubts that I explain below about the averaging process carried out by the officer, it would have been better to have waited until close to 28 May 2004 and then considered the current evidence about the wife's earnings. I do not think that there would have been any difficulty in making an advance decision on the claimant's own retirement pension entitlement, but deferring the decision on the increase. However, that did not happen."

Cold weather payments

15A. [[1]. . .] 2.114

AMENDMENT

1. Social Security (Miscellaneous Provisions) Amendment Regulations 1991 (SI 1991/2284) reg.8 (November 1, 1991).

GENERAL NOTE

Claims for cold weather payments are no longer necessary or possible. 2.115

[[1] [[2]Advance claim for pension following deferment

15B. [[3] (1)] Where a person's entitlement to a Category A or Category B retirement pension or a shared additional pension is deferred in accordance with section 55(3) of the Contributions and Benefits Act (pension increase or lump sum where entitlement to retirement pension is deferred) or section 55C(3) (pension increase or lump sum where entitlement to shared additional pension is deferred) thereof (as the case may be) a claim for— 2.116

(a) a Category A or Category B retirement pension;
(b) any increase in that pension;
(c) a shared additional pension,

may be made at any time not more than 4 months before the day on which the period of deferment, within the meaning of section 55(3) or section 55C(3) (as the case may be), ends.]]

[[3] (2) Where a person's entitlement to a state pension under Part 1 of the Pensions Act 2014 is deferred in accordance with sections 16 and 17 of that Act (option to defer and effect of deferring a state pension), a claim for such a state pension may be made at any time not more than 4 months before the date on which the period during which the person's entitlement to a state pension was deferred ends.]

AMENDMENTS

1. Orginally inserted by the Social Security (Claims and Payments) Amendment Regulations 2005 (SI 2005/455) reg.2 (April 6, 2005).
2. The Social Security (Shared Additional Pension) (Miscellaneous Amendments) Regulations 2005 (SI 2005/1551) (July 6, 2005).
3. The Pensions Act 2014 (Consequential, Supplementary and Incidental Amendments) Order 2015 (SI 2015/1985) art.9(8) (April 6, 2016).

GENERAL NOTE

This additional regulation regularises what had been operational practice in allowing those who claim a deferred retirement pension to do so four months in advance of the date on which they wish to claim their pension. The purpose of the advance claims provisions is to ensure that the retirement pension is put into payment on the due date without any delays. 2.117

Date of entitlement under an award for the purpose of payability of benefit and effective date of change of rate

16.—(1) For the purpose only of determining the day from which benefit is to become payable, where a benefit other than one of those specified in paragraph (4) is awarded for a period of a week, or weeks, and the earliest date on which entitlement would otherwise commence is not the first day 2.118

of a benefit week entitlement shall begin on the first day of the benefit week next following.

[1 (1A) Where a claim for [6 working families' tax credit] is made in accordance with paragraph 7(a) [2 or (aa)] of Schedule 4 for a period following the expiration of an existing award of family credit [6 or disabled person's tax credit], entitlement shall begin on the day after the expiration of that award.

(1B) Where a claim for [6 working families' tax credit or disabled person's tax credit] is made on or after the date when an up-rating order is made under [6 section 150 of the Social Security Administration Act 1992], but before the date when that order comes into force, and—

(a) an award cannot be made on that claim as at the date it is made but could have been made if that order were then in force, and
(b) the period beginning with the date of claim and ending immediately before the date when the order came into force does not exceed 28 days,

entitlement shall begin from the date the up-rating order comes into force.]

[2 (1C) Where a claim for [6 disabled person's tax credit] is made in accordance with paragraph 11(a) or (b) of Schedule 4 for a period following the expiration of an existing award of [6 disabled person's tax credit or working families' tax credit], entitlement shall begin on the day after the expiration of that award.]

[10 (1D) Except in a case where regulation 22D(1) or (2) applies, for the purpose only of determining the day from which retirement pension payable in arrears under regulation 22C is to become payable, where entitlement would otherwise begin on a day which is not the first day of the benefit week, entitlement shall begin on the first day of the benefit week next following.]

[11 (1E) Except in a case where regulation 22DA applies, for the purpose only of determining the day from which state pension under Part 1 of the Pensions Act 2014 payable in arrears under regulation 22CA is to become payable, where entitlement would otherwise begin on a day which is not the first day of the benefit week, entitlement shall begin on the first day of the benefit week next following.]

(2) Where there is a change in the rate of any benefit to which paragraph (1) applies [8 (other than widowed mother's allowance and widow's pension)] the change, if it would otherwise take effect on a day which is not the [8 first day of the benefit week] for that benefit, shall take effect from the [8 first day of the benefit week] next following.

[8 (2A) Subject to paragraph (2B), where there is a change in the rate of [12 . . .], widowed mother's allowance, widowed parent's allowance or widow's pension, the change, if it would otherwise take effect on a day which is not the first day of the benefit week, shall take effect from the first day of the benefit week next following.

(2B) Paragraph (2A) shall not apply in a case where an award of benefit is terminated and benefit is paid in arrears.

(2C) Where a benefit specified in paragraph (2A) is paid in advance and the award is terminated, the termination, if it would otherwise take effect on a day which is not the first day of a benefit week, shall take effect on the first day of the benefit week next following.]

[9 (2D) [10 Where an award of retirement pension] is terminated due to the death of the beneficiary, the termination shall take effect on the first day of the benefit week next following the date of death.

(2E) Except in a case where [10 paragraph (2F) or] regulation 22D(2) applies, where a retirement pension is paid in arrears under regulation 22C and there is a change in the rate of that benefit, the change, if it would otherwise take effect on a day which is not the first day of the benefit week, shall take effect from the start of the benefit week in which the change occurs.]

[10 (2F) Except in a case where regulation 22D(2) applies, where a retirement pension is paid in arrears under regulation 22C and a change in the rate of that benefit takes effect under an order made under section 150 or 150A of the 1992 Act (annual up-rating of benefits, basic pension etc.) the change, if it would otherwise take effect on a day which is not the first day of the benefit week, shall take effect on the first day of the benefit week next following.]

[11 (2G) Except in a case where paragraph (2H) applies, where—

(a) a state pension under Part 1 of the Pensions Act 2014 is paid in arrears under regulation 22CA; and

(b) there is a change in the rate of that benefit,

the change, if it would otherwise take effect on a day which is not the first day of the benefit week, shall take effect from the start of the benefit week in which the change occurs.

(2H) Where—

(a) a state pension under Part 1 of the Pensions Act 2014 is paid in arrears under regulation 22CA; and

(b) a change in the rate of that benefit takes effect under an Order made under section 150, 150A or 151A of the 1992 Act,

the change, if it would otherwise take effect on a day which is not the first day of the benefit week, shall take effect on the first day of the benefit week next following.]

[1 (3) For the purposes of this regulation the first day of the benefit week—

(a) in the case of child benefit [5 and guardian's allowance] is Monday,

(b) in the case of [6 disabled person's tax credit or working families' tax credit] is Tuesday, and

[8 (c) in any other case is—

(i) when paid in advance, the day of the week on which the benefit is payable in accordance with regulation 22 (long-term benefits) or 22A ([12 bereavement support payment], widowed mother's allowance, widowed parent's allowance and widow's pension;

(ii) when paid in arrears, the first day of the period of 7 days which ends on the day on which the benefit is payable in accordance with [9 regulation 22, 22A or [11 , 22C or 22CA]]].

(4) The benefits specified for exclusion from the scope of paragraph (1) are [4 jobseeker's allowance], [3 incapacity benefit], [7,employment and support allowance] maternity allowance, [1. . .], severe disablement allowance, income support [6, state pension credit] [8 , [12 bereavement support payment], widowed parent's allowance] [9 , retirement pension payable in arrears under regulation 22C] [11 , state pension under Part 1 of the Pensions Act 2014 payable in arrears under regulation 22CA] [1. . .] and any increase of those benefits.

AMENDMENTS

1. The Social Security (Claims and Payments) Amendment Regulations 1988 (SI 1988/522) reg.3 (April 11, 1988).

2. The Social Security (Claims and Payments) Amendment Regulations 1991 (SI 1991/2741) reg.9 (March 10, 1992).

3. The Social Security (Claims and Payments) Amendment (No.2) Regulations 1994 (SI 1994/2943) reg.6 (April 13, 1995).

4. The Social Security (Claims and Payments) (Jobseeker's Allowance Consequential Amendments) Regulations 1996 (SI 1996/1460) reg.2(9) (October 7, 1996).

5. The Social Security (Claims and Payments) Amendment Regulations 1999 (SI 1999, No.2358) reg.2 (September 20, 1999).

6. State Pension Credit (Consequential, Transitional and Miscellaneous Provisions) Regulations 2002, (SI 2002/3019) reg.7 (April 7, 2003).

7. The Employment and Support Allowance (Consequential Provisions) (No.2) Regulations 2008 (SI 2008/1554) reg.19 (October 27, 2008).

8. The Social Security (Claims and Payments) Amendment Regulations 2009 (SI 2009/604) reg.2 (April 6, 2009).

9. The Social Security (Miscellaneous Amendments) (No.6) Regulations 2009 (SI 2009/3229) reg.2(3) (April 6, 2010).

10. The Social Security (Miscellaneous Amendments) Regulations 2010 (SI 2010/510) reg.3(3) (April 6, 2010).

11. The Pensions Act 2014 (Consequential, Supplementary and Incidental Amendments) Order 2015 (SI 2015/1985) art.9(9) (April 6, 2016).

12. The Pensions Act 2014 (Consequential, Supplementary and Incidental Amendments) Order 2017 (SI 2017/422) art.10 (April 6, 2017).

DEFINITIONS

"benefit"—see reg.2(2).
"jobseeker's allowance"—see reg.2(1).
"week"—*ibid.*

GENERAL NOTE

2.119 This regulation restates in part the rules formerly contained in reg.16(10) of the Claims and Payments Regulations 1979. In *R(P)2/73* it was held that the effect of a similarly worded predecessor to reg.16(10) was not just to make benefit payable from the next pay day but to make it begin on that day. The Commissioner made clear, though, that the regulation was concerned with "payability not title". The new wording does not appear wholly to resolve the difficulty, since para.(1) is prefaced by the intention only to concern itself with payability, though later the word "entitlement" is used. Presumably that means "entitlement to payment of benefit" and not title to the benefit itself. There are occasions where title to the benefit arising on an earlier date than the first date of payment has significant consequences.

[1 Date of entitlement under an award of state pension credit for the purpose of payability and effective date of change of rate

2.120 **16A.**—(1) For the purpose only of determining the day from which state pension credit is to become payable, where the credit is awarded from a day which is not the first day of the claimant's benefit week, entitlement shall begin on the first day of the benefit week next following.

(2) In the case of a claimant who—

(a) immediately before attaining the qualifying age was entitled to income support [4 or universal credit] [2, income-based jobseekers allowance or income-related employment and support allowance] and is awarded state pension credit from the day on which he attains the qualifying age; or

(b) was entitled to an income-based jobseeker's allowance [4 or universal credit] after attaining the qualifying age and is awarded state pension credit from the day which falls after the date that entitlement ends,

entitlement to the guarantee credit shall, notwithstanding paragraph (1), begin on the first day of the award.

(3) Where a change in the rate of state pension credit would otherwise take effect on a day which is not the first day of the claimant's benefit week, the change shall take effect from the first day of the benefit week next following.

[3 (4) For the purpose of this regulation, "benefit week" means—

(a) where state pension credit is paid in advance, the period of 7 days beginning on the day on which, in the claimant's case, that benefit is payable;

(b) where state pension credit is paid in arrears, the period of 7 days ending on the day on which, in the claimant's case, that benefit is payable.]

AMENDMENTS

1. State Pension Credit (Consequential, Transitional and Miscellaneous Provisions) Regulations 2002 (SI 2002/3019) reg.7 (April 7, 2003).

2. The Employment and Support Allowance (Consequential Provisions) (No.2) Regulations 2008 (SI 2008/1554) reg.20 (October 27, 2008).

3. The Social Security (Miscellaneous Amendments) Regulations 2010 (SI 2010/510) reg.3(4) (April 6, 2010).

4. The Universal Credit (Consequential Supplementary, Incidental and Miscellaneous Provisions) Regulations 2013 (SI 2013/630) reg.29(3) (April 29, 2013).

Duration of awards

17.—(1) Subject to the provisions of this regulation and of section [137ZA(3) of the Social Security Act 1975 (disability living allowance) and section] 20(6) [2 and (6F)] of the Social Security Act 1986 [4 working families' tax credit and disabled person's tax credit] [SSCBA, ss.71(3), 128(3) and 129(6)] a claim for benefit shall be treated as made for an indefinite period and any award of benefit on that claim shall be made for an indefinite period. 2.121

[3 (1A) Where an award of income support or an income-based jobseeker's allowance is made in respect of [7 a couple] and one member of the couple is, at the date of claim, a person to whom section 126 of the Contributions and Benefits Act or, as the case may be, section 14 of the Jobseekers Act applies, the award of benefit shall cease when the person to whom section 126 or, as the case may be, section 14 applies returns to work with the same employer.]

(2) [3. . .]

(3) [6 Except in the case of claims for and awards of state pension credit,] if [3. . .] it would be inappropriate to treat a claim as made and to make an award for an indefinite period (for example where a relevant change of circumstances is reasonably to be expected in the near future) the claim shall be treated as made and the award shall be for a definite period which is appropriate in the circumstances.

(4) In any case where benefit is awarded in respect of days subsequent to the date of claim the award shall be subject to the condition that the claimant satisfies the requirements for entitlement [5. . .]

(5) The provisions of Schedule 2 shall have effect in relation to claims for [3a jobseeker's allowance] made during periods connected with public holidays.

AMENDMENTS

1. The Social Security (Claims and Payments) Amendment Regulations 1991 (SI 1991/2741) reg.10 (February 3, 1992).

2. The Social Security (Claims and Payments) Amendment Regulations 1991 (SI 1991/2741) reg.10 (March 10, 1992).

3. The Social Security (Claims and Payments) (Jobseeker's Allowance Consequential Amendments) Regulations 1996 (SI 1996/1460) reg.2(10) (October 7, 1996).

4. The Tax Credits (Claims and Payments) (Amendment) Regulations 1999 (SI 1999/2572) regs 24 and 25 (October 5, 1999).

5. The Social Security Act 1998 (Commencement No.12 and Consequential and Transitional Provisions) Order 1999 (SI 1999/3178) Sch.6 (November 29, 1999).

6. State Pension Credit (Consequential, Transitional and Miscellaneous Provisions) Regulations 2002 (SI 2002/3019) reg.8 (April 7, 2003).

7. The Civil Partnership (Pensions, Social Security and Child Support) (Consequential etc. Provisions) Order 2005 (SI 2005/2877) (December 5, 2005).

DEFINITIONS

"benefit"—see reg.2(2).
"claim for benefit"—see reg.2(1).
"jobseeker's allowance"—*ibid.*
"the Jobseekers Act"—*ibid.*

GENERAL NOTE

2.122 In general awards are to be made for an indefinite period (para.1), subject to revision or supersession where the claimant's circumstances change such that the entitlement is reduced or removed. An award of benefit can only be terminated by supersession. In *CIS/4167/2003* the Commissioner queries whether terminations of indefinite awards have always been accompanied by the required supersession decision. In the case before him an award had been closed without the making of a supersession decision in circumstances where this suggested possible standard practice.

Paragraph (3) deals with short-term situations and allows awards for a fixed period, except in the case of state pension credit.

R(S) 1/92 held at [8] that:

> "It is to be noted that the word 'inappropriate', which is wide in scope, is in no way cut down by any limitation, and the reference to 'a relevant change of circumstances' being 'reasonably to be expected in the near future' was expressly stated to be only by way of example. Accordingly, I consider that the words of regulation 17(3) are wide in their effect [. . .]."

As to the interaction with s.12(8)(b) in determining whether subsequent developments may be taken into account in deciding whether a fixed-term award is "appropriate", contrast *CDLA/3293/2000* at [22] and *CDLA/3722/2000* at [9].

The effect of para.(1) is that awards of most benefits are now made for an indefinite period. Entitlement only ceases where there has been a revision or supersession which establishes that the conditions of entitlement are no longer met. In earlier times, there was a distinct tendency on reviews for adjudication officers to argue that it was for the claimant to establish continuing entitlement to the benefit, whereas the true position was that, where an indefinite award had been made, it was for the decision maker to show that there were good grounds to revise or supersede the award: see generally *R(S) 3/90.*

2.123 In *CIS/620/1990,* the Commissioner stressed that the requirements of reg.17 were not a mere technicality. An indefinite award of benefit can only be terminated on review if it its shown on review (under the earlier legislation) that the conditions of entitlement cease to be met. In any other circumstances the original award continues. Any purported subsequent award of benefit cannot overlap with the earlier award. Indeed there would be no jurisdiction to make a subsequent award since the matter is res judicata: see paras 8 and 11 of *CIS/620/1990*.

The power to review or supersede an award of benefit will arise under s.9 (revision, which takes effect from the operative date of the decision being revised) or s.10 (supersession, which takes effect from the date of the supersession decision) of the Social Security Act 1998. There must be grounds on which the decision maker can determine that the conditions of entitlement have ceased to exist. Some are specific to certain benefits while others are more general in application. Reference should be made to the annotations to ss.9 and 10 of the 1998 Act, as well as to Pt II of the Decisions and Appeals Regulations and the commentary on these regulations, if any issue under reg.17 arises.

Regulation 18 revoked by The Social Security (Claims and Payments) (Jobseeker's Allowance Consequential Amendments) Regulations 1996 (SI 1996/1460) (October 7, 1996). 2.124

[1 Time for claiming benefit

19.—(1) Subject to the following provisions of this regulation, the prescribed time for claiming any benefit specified in column (1) of Schedule 4 is the appropriate time specified opposite that benefit in column (2) of that Schedule. 2.125

(2) The prescribed time for claiming the benefits specified in paragraph (3) is three months beginning with any day on which, apart from satisfying the condition of making a claim, the claimant is entitled to the benefit concerned.

(3) The benefits to which paragraph (2) applies are—

(a) child benefit;

(b) guardian's allowance;

(c) [13 . . .];

(d) invalid care allowance or carer's allowance;

(e) maternity allowance;

(f) [13 . . .];

[10 (ff) . . .]

(g) widow's benefit;

[17 (ga) subject to paragraph (3B), widowed parent's allowance;

(gb) subject to paragraph (3BA), bereavement support payment;]

(h) [11 . . .] any increase in any benefit (other than income support or jobseeker's allowance) in respect of a child or adult dependant.

[16 (i) state pension credit]

[17 . . .]

[11 (3B) The time prescribed for claiming [17 widowed parent's allowance] in respect of the day on which the claimant's spouse [12 or civil partner] has died or may be presumed to have died where—

(a) less than 12 months have elapsed since the day of the death; and

(b) the circumstances are as specified in section 3(1)(b) of the Social Security Administration Act 1992 (death is difficult to establish),

is that day and the period of 12 months immediately following that day if the other conditions of entitlement are satisfied.]

[17 (3BA) The prescribed time for claiming bereavement support allowance in respect of—

(a) the rate set out in regulation 3(2) or (5) of the Bereavement Support Payment Regulations 2017 (rate of bereavement support payment); and

(b) the date on which the claimant's spouse or civil partner died,

is 12 months beginning with the date of that death.]

[15 (3C) In any case where the application of paragraphs (16) to (34) of regulation 6 would be advantageous to the claimant, this regulation shall apply subject to those provisions.]

(4) Subject to paragraph (8), in the case of a claim for income support, jobseeker's allowance, [3 working families' tax credit or disabled persons' tax credit], where the claim is not made within the time specified for that benefit in Schedule 4, the prescribed time for claiming the benefit shall be extended, subject to a maximum extension of three months, to the date on which the claim is made, where—

(a) any [7 one or more] of the circumstances specified in paragraph (5) applies or has applied to the claimant; and

(b) as a result of that circumstance or those circumstances the claimant could not reasonably have been expected to make the claim earlier.

(5) The circumstances referred to in paragraph (4) are—

(a) the claimant has difficulty communicating because—

(i) he has learning, language or literacy difficulties; or

(ii) he is deaf or blind,

and it was not reasonably practicable for the claimant to obtain assistance from another person to make his claim;

(b) except in the case of a claim for jobseeker's allowance, the claimant was ill or disabled, and it was not reasonably practicable for the claimant to obtain assistance from another person to make his claim;

(c) the claimant was caring for a person who is ill or disabled, and it was not reasonably practicable for the claimant to obtain assistance from another person to make his claim;

(d) the claimant was given information by an officer of the [3 Department for Work and Pensions] [or in a case to which regulation 4A applies, a representative of a relevant authority] or the Board which led the claimant to believe that a claim for benefit would not succeed;

(e) the claimant was given written advice by a solicitor or other professional adviser, a medical practitioner, a local authority, or a person working in a Citizens Advice Bureau or a similar advice agency, which led the claimant to believe that a claim for benefit would not succeed;

(f) the claimant or his partner was given written information about his income or capital by his employer or former employer, or by a bank or building society, which led the claimant to believe that a claim for benefit would not succeed;

(g) the claimant was required to deal with a domestic emergency affecting him and it was not reasonably practicable for him to obtain assistance from another person to make his claim; or

(h) the claimant was prevented by adverse weather conditions from attending the appropriate office.

(6) In the case of a claim for income support, jobseeker's allowance, [3working families' tax credit or disabled person's tax credit] [7 where the claim is not made within the time specified for that benefit in Schedule 4,

the prescribed time for claiming the benefit shall be extended, subject to a maximum extension of one month, to the date on which the claim is made, where—

(a) any one or more of the circumstances specified in paragraph (7) applies or has applied to the claimant; and

(b) as a result of that circumstance or those circumstances the claimant could not reasonably have been expected to make the claim earlier.]

(7) The circumstances referred to in paragraph (6) are—

(a) the appropriate office where the claimant would be expected to make a claim was closed and alternative arrangements were not available;

(b) the claimant was unable to attend the appropriate office due to difficulties with his normal mode of transport and there was no reasonable alternative available;

(c) there were adverse postal conditions;

(d) the claimant [7 or, in the case of income support or jobseeker's allowance, the claimant or his partner] was previously in receipt of another benefit, and notification of expiry of entitlement to that benefit was not sent to the claimant [7 or his partner, as the case may be,] before the date that his entitlement expired;

[9 (e) in the case of a claim for working families' tax credit, the claimant had previously been entitled, or the partner of the claimant had previously been entitled in relation to the claimant, to income support or jobseeker's allowance and the claim for working families' tax credit was made within one month of—

(i) the expiry of entitlement to income support ignoring any period in which entitlement resulted from the person entitled not being treated as engaged in remunerative work by virtue of regulation 6(2) and (3), or paragraphs (5) and (6) of regulation 6 of the Income Support (General) Regulations 1987; or

(ii) the expiry of entitlement to jobseeker's allowance;]

(f) except in the case of a claim for working families' tax credit or disabled persons' tax credit, the claimant had ceased to be a member of a married or unmarried couple within the period of one month before the claim was made; [2 . . .]

(g) during the period of one month before the claim was made a close relative of the claimant had died, and for this purpose "close relative" means partner, parent, son, daughter, brother or [2 sister; or]

[9 (h) in the case of a claim for disabled person's tax credit, the claimant had previously been entitled to income support, jobseeker's allowance, incapacity benefit or severe disablement allowance and the claim for disabled person's tax credit was made within one month of—

(i) the expiry of entitlement to income support ignoring any period in which entitlement resulted from the claimant being treated as engaged in remunerative work by virtue of paragraphs (2) and (3) or paragraph (5) and (6) of the Income Support (General) Regulations 1987; or

(ii) the expiry of entitlement to jobseeker's allowance, incapacity benefit or severe disablement allowance;

(ha) in the case of a claim for disabled person's tax credit, the partner of the claimant had previously been entitled in relation to the claimant to income support or jobseeker's allowance, and the claim for disabled person's tax credit was made within one month of—

(i) the expiry of entitlement to income support ignoring any period in which entitlement resulted from the partner of the claimant not being treated as engaged in remunerative work by virtue of paragraphs (2) and (3) or paragraph (5) and (6) of the Income Support (General) Regulations 1987; or

(ii) the expiry of entitlement to jobseeker's allowance;]

[[6] (i) in the case of a claim for a jobseeker's allowance by a member of a joint-claim couple where the other member of that couple failed to attend at the time and place specified by the Secretary of State for the purposes of regulation 6.]

[[14] (j) the claimant was unable to make telephone contact with the appropriate office where he would be expected to notify his intention of making a claim because the telephone lines to that office were busy or inoperative.]

[[8] . . .]

[[19](7A) Where—

(a) a claim for a social fund payment in respect of maternity expenses (a "relevant social fund payment") is made by a person to whom paragraph (7B) or (7C) applies; and

(b) both of the conditions in paragraph (7D) are met, sub-paragraphs (a) to (f) of the entry in column (2) of Schedule 4 relating to the relevant social fund payment each have effect as if at the end there were added "or, if later, 8th December 2023".

(7B) This paragraph applies to a person who—

(a) is granted leave in accordance with the immigration rules made under section 3(2) of the Immigration Act 1971 ("the 1971 Act") where such leave is granted by virtue of—

(i) Appendix Afghan Relocations and Assistance Policy of those rules; or

(ii) the previous scheme for locally-employed staff in Afghanistan (sometimes referred to as the ex-gratia scheme); or

(b) does not come within sub-paragraph (a) and who left Afghanistan in connection with the collapse of the Afghan government that took place on 15th August 2021.

(7C) This paragraph applies to a person who was residing in Ukraine immediately before 1st January 2022, who left Ukraine in connection with the Russian invasion which took place on 24th February 2022 and who—

(a) has a right of abode in the United Kingdom within the meaning given in section 2 of the 1971 Act;

(b) has been granted leave in accordance with immigration rules made under section 3(2) of the 1971 Act;

(c) has been granted, or is deemed to have been granted, leave outside those rules; or

(d) does not require leave to enter or remain in the United Kingdom in accordance with section 3ZA of the 1971 Act.

(7D) The conditions for the purposes of paragraph (7A)(b) are that—

(a) at the date of the claim for a relevant social fund payment, there is an existing member of the family (within the meaning given in regulation 5A of the Social Fund Maternity and Funeral Expenses (General) Regulations 2005); and

(b) that existing member of the family is under the age of 16 on that date.]

AMENDMENTS

1. The Social Security (Miscellaneous Amendments) (No.2) Regulations 1997 (SI 1997/793) reg.6 (April 7, 1997).
2. The Social Security (Claims and Payments and Adjudication) Amendment (No.2) Regulations 1997 (SI 1997/2290) reg.6 (October 13, 1997).
3. Tax Credits (Claims and Payments) (Amendment) Regulations 1999 (SI 1999/2572) Sch.1 (October 5, 1999).
4. The Social Security (Immigration and Asylum) Consequential Amendments Regulations 2000 (SI 2000/636) reg 5 (April 3, 2000).
5. The Social Security (Benefits for Widows and Widowers) (Consequential Amendments) Regulations 2000 (SI 2000/1483) reg.9 (April 9, 2001).
6. The Social Security (Joint Claims: Consequential Amendments) Regulations 2000 (SI 2000/1982) reg.2(5) (March 19, 2001).
7. The Social Security (Claims and Payments and Miscellaneous Amendments) Regulations 2002 (SI 2002/428) reg.3 (April 2, 2002).
8. The Social Security (Claims and Payments and Miscellaneous Amendments) (No.3) Regulations 2002 (SI 2002/2660) reg.2 (April 1, 2003).
9. The Tax Credits Schemes (Miscellaneous Amendments No.4) Regulations 2000 (SI 2000/2978) reg.10 (November 28, 2000).
10. Social Security (Claims and Payments) Amendment (No.2) Regulations 2004 (SI 2004/1821) reg.2(a) (October 6, 2004).
11. Social Security (Claims and Payments) Amendment (No.2) Regulations 2005 (SI 2005/777) reg.2 (April 11, 2005).
12. The Social Security (Civil Partnerships) (Consequential Amendments) Regulations 2005 (SI 2005/2878) (December 5, 2005).
13. The Social Security (Claims and Payment) Regulations 2005 (SI 2005/455) reg.3 (April 6, 2006).
14. The Social Security (Miscellaneous Amendments) (No.3) Regulations 2006 (SI 2006/2377) (October 2, 2006).
15. The Social Security (Miscellaneous Amendments) (No.4) Regulations 2007 (SI 2007/2470) (September 24, 2007).
16. The Social Security (Miscellaneous Amendments) (No.4) Regulations 2008 (SI 2008/2424) reg.2 (October 6, 2008).
17. The Pensions Act 2014 (Consequential, Supplementary and Incidental Amendments) Order 2017 (SI 2017/422) art.10 (April 6, 2017).
18. "Lapsed" by the Asylum and Immigration (Treatment of Claimants etc.) Act 2004 s.12(2) (June 14, 2007).
19. The Social Fund Maternity and Funeral Expenses (General) and Social Security (Claims and Payments) (Amendment) Regulations 2023 (SI 2023/545) reg.2 (June 8, 2023).

DEFINITIONS

"appropriate office"—see reg.2(1).
"jobseeker's allowance"—*ibid.*
"married couple"—*ibid.*
"partner"—*ibid.*
"unmarried couple"—*ibid.*

GENERAL NOTE

Introduction

There are broadly two groups of benefits: those which must be claimed on the day in respect of which the situation giving rise to the claim first occurs, and those **2.126** where a three months time limit is allowed for claiming. There are also two groups of benefits where issues of backdating arise.

The first group of benefits is income support, jobseeker's allowance whether income-based or contribution-based, working families' tax credit, and disabled person's tax credit. For this first group, there are two possible extensions available. They may be backdated for up to three months if the conditions set out in paras (4) and (5) are met. If the conditions are met, the backdating is mandatory. There is also the possibility of an extension of the time limit for claiming for up to one month if a different set of conditions set out in paras (6) and (7) are met.

The second group of benefits is child benefit, guardian's allowance, carer's allowance, maternity allowance, certain widowhood benefits (see para.(3)(h)), and increases of benefit (other than income support and jobseeker's allowance) in respect of a child or adult dependent. Those benefits listed in Sch. 4 for which the time limit is three months can also be included in this second group: incapacity benefit; disablement benefit and increases; reduced earnings allowance; and social fund payment for funeral expenses. For these benefits there is a three month time limit for claiming, which means that whatever the reasons for any delay in claiming, they can be backdated for up to three months.

2.127 The regulation does not apply to claims within reg.21ZB of the Income Support General Regulations. These set out special rules for claims for income support for a person who has submitted a claim for asylum on or after April 3, 2000 and is treated as a refugee. See commentary on the regulation in Vol.II.

Regulation 19 can only apply where there is a claim which is properly constituted for the purposes of reg.4: *CIS/157/2001*.

Note that reg.19 does not apply to claims for winter fuel payments: *CIS/2337/2004*, para.19.

RR v SSWP (JSA) [2017] UKUT 50 (AAC) concerned an online claim for jobseeker's allowance which the claimant asked to be back-dated for two years. There was some dispute as to whether there was an undetermined claim from the earlier date, though the First-tier Tribunal found that there was not. Judge Poynter makes the important point that the effect of a decision covering a two-year period was that such a decision would determine all and any claims that may have been extant in relation to that period. There can only be one outcome decision for any given period. (paras 30-31).

Paragraph (1): the time limits

2.128 Paragraph (1) sets out the time limits for those benefits listed in Sch.4 to the regulations. These include income support.

If a claimant signs an ordinary income support claim form which contains no question asking from what date benefit is claimed, the claim will be interpreted as a claim for an indefinite period from the date on which the claim is made. If claimants wish to claim for a past period, that must be expressly stated: *R(SB)9/84*, at para.11. But note that in *CIS/2057/1998* the Commissioner accepted that a claimant who had put on her claim form "disabled—aged 16" had indicated an intention to claim income support from her 16th birthday. If, before a decision is made on an ordinary claim, a claimant indicates a wish to claim for a past period, that can operate as an amendment of the original claim taking effect on the original date. But if, after there has been a decision on the claim, the claimant indicates such a wish (as often happens when the original claim has been successful), it is generally assumed that such a claim can only be treated as a fresh claim on the date on which it is made, and that any question of back-dating under reg.19(4) has to be assessed according to that date of claim.

Paragraphs (2) and (3): benefits for which the time limit for claiming is three months

2.129 The prescribed time for claiming the benefits listed in para.(3) is three months beginning the any day of potential entitlement. The contrast between this formulation of backdating and the technique adopted for income-related benefits may be important. If the claimant was entitled to the benefit (apart from the requirement to make a claim for the benefit) where the three-month time limit applies, the payment of benefit can be backdated for three months without any reason being shown for the delay in claiming.

Note that reg.19(2) is to be read as if "three months" read "12 months" in the case of claims by those who, as a result of the Bereavement Benefits (Remedial) Order 2023 (SI 2023/134) have become eligible for widowed parent's allowance for any part of the period from August 30, 2018 to February 9, 2023: Remedial Order, art.3(2). In relation to bereavement support payment, Art.3(5) of the Remedial Order provides that in reg.19(2), the words from "three months" to the end of paragraph (2) are to be read as "21 months beginning with the day after the day the Bereavement Benefits (Remedial) Order 2023 comes into force."

Paragraph (3BA): claims for bereavement support payment

In addition to the modification to reg.19(2) set out above, art.3(5) of the Remedial Order further provides that in paragraph (3BA): **2.130**

(i) sub-paragraph (b) is to be read as though the following was substituted for it:

"(b) the date on which the claimant's cohabiting partner (within the meaning in section 30(6B) of the Pensions Act 2014) died,"; and

(ii) "that date of death" is to be read as "the day the Bereavement Benefits (Remedial) Order 2023 comes into force".

Paragraphs (4) and (5): claims for income support and jobseeker's allowance

(1) Introduction: Although it is common to speak of the backdating of claims, it should be appreciated that the technique adopted in para.(4) is to extend the time for claiming for a past period forward from the first day of that period. There is an immediate problem in the working of the three month time limit. If, on May 31 in any year, a claim is made for income support for the period from February 1 to May 30 in that year, it appears that the time for claiming for the whole period cannot be extended under para.(4) because to do so would go beyond the maximum period of three months permitted under the regulation. It does not matter that one of the listed circumstances has made it reasonable for the claim not to have been made earlier. The claim could be amended before a decision is made on it so as to make it a claim from March 1 to May 30, that is, the maximum permitted period of backdating. **2.131**

It follows that it would be good practice for decision-makers in dealing with a claim which inevitably breaks the maximum period of backdating not to decide the claim, but to invite the claimant to amend the period claimed for.

An alternative approach would be for a decision-maker to treat a claim for an extension of the time limit for claiming beyond three months as being a claim for the maximum permitted period. It seems likely that most claimants, if asked, would say that they would prefer this approach if the alternative was the total rejection of the claim for an extension of the time limit for claiming.

Although reg.5(1) only provides for a claim to be amended before a determination of it, it does not explicitly state that a claim may not be amended after a determination has been made. Thus if an amendment is made before, or even at, an appeal hearing, it is suggested that a tribunal would be able to deal with the claim for an extension, as amended. Since the tribunal is conducting a complete rehearing of all the issues under appeal, it may also wish to consider whether to treat the claim as simply being a claim for the maximum period allowed for an extension whatever period was initially requested by the claimant. It certainly seems doubtful that the intention was that only claims for extensions of up to three months could be considered under para.(4). This view is supported by *CJSA/3994/1998* where the Deputy Commissioner held that a claimant who had asked for his claim to be backdated for nearly a year should be treated as asking for the time for his making his claim to be extended to the maximum permitted by the regulations.

In *R(IS) 16/04*, the Commissioner follows the approach adopted in *CIS/849/1998* and *CJSA/3994/1998* (the correctness of which was conceded by the Secretary of

State) to the effect that a claim can be taken as including a claim for a period starting with the earliest date which would make the claim in time.

Note too that *R(IS) 3/01* holds that the maximum period of extension should be calculated backwards from the date of actual claim, not forwards from the first day of the period expressly claimed for.

2.132 In *R(IS) 16/04*, the Commissioner rules that the question of reasonableness under regs 19(4)(b) and 19(6)(b) can only be asked in relation to each particular period of claim, and not the totality of any delay. The Commissioner gives as an example the position of a claimant who delays making a claim for income support for several months, but who then makes a claim. Just after he posts the claim form, there is a strike by postal workers which holds up delivery of the claim for some weeks. The fact that the claimant could have claimed earlier than he did should not defeat his reliance on adverse postal conditions in relation to the claim he actually made.

For an interesting case concerning the position of jurors and benefits, see *CIS/1010/2003.*

2.133 *(2) The test to be satisfied under paras (4) and (5):* There are two questions which must be answered before there can be an extension of the time for claiming. The first is that one of the circumstances listed in para.(5) has applied to the claimant. There is no condition that the circumstances must have applied *throughout* the period claimed for or continues to apply at the date of claim. Such considerations may come in under the second question, which is whether as a result of the circumstances or a combination of them, the claimant could not reasonably have been expected to make the claim earlier. This approach is explicitly set out in the reported Northern Ireland decision *R2/01(IS)*. Thus, if a claimant who has been affected, for example, by illness delays unreasonably after recovery from the illness in making the claim, the request for an extension of the time limit for claiming will fail on the second ground. Such a claim could also fail if there has been unreasonable delay at some earlier stage before one of the listed circumstances applies.

Just as careful findings of fact were the secret of good decision-making under the old good cause rules, so too similar attention to detail will be required under the rules introduced in 1997. This will include findings of fact on key dates, and precision in making findings about what a claimant has been told and by whom.

Note that the list of circumstances set out in para.(5) is exhaustive, and there is no category of analogous circumstances to deal with meritorious cases which were not foreseen by the draftsman: *CJSA/3121/1998*, para.9. Ignorance of one's rights or of the procedure for claiming, whether reasonable or otherwise, does not feature in the circumstances listed in para.(5).

Finally, since the maximum period of backdating is now three months (previously it was 12 months), will this change the qualitative nature of the decision-making? Perhaps not, when the restrictive grounds on which the Secretary of State can extend the period to one month as set out in paras (6) and (7) are considered.

2.134 *(3) Paragraphs (5)(a), (b), (c) and (g): reasonable practicability of obtaining assistance:* Several of the paragraphs provide, in addition to a primary set of circumstances, a further requirement, namely that "it was not reasonably practicable for the claimant to obtain assistance from another person to make his claim". In *CIS/2057/1998*, the Commissioner points out that the question is whether it is reasonable practicable for the claimant to seek assistance from another person to make the claim, not whether it is reasonable practicable for another person to take the initiative in offering assistance.

The corresponding words of the Northern Ireland regulations have been considered by the Chief Commissioner in Northern Ireland. In *C12/98 (IS)* the Chief Commissioner notes, having regard to the two-stage test set out in para.(4), that:

> "'reasonably practicable for him to obtain assistance' . . . must mean something other than 'can reasonably have been expected to make the claim earlier',

otherwise there would be no need for the two sub-paragraphs to consist of different terminology in qualifying reasonableness." (See para.11.)

The Chief Commissioner adds:

> "... I accept that [the adjudication officer] is correct in submitting that regulation 19(5)(b) places an obligation on a sick or disabled person to seek assistance with his or her claim unless it is not practicable for him to obtain it; but while it might be more likely that someone who suffers a mental health problem could satisfy the provisions of regulation 19(4) and (5), it is necessary for the Adjudicating Authorities to look at the circumstances of each case and they are not entitled to make an assumption that a person suffering from a mental health problem would automatically be unable to seek assistance from another person to make a claim."

The circumstances in which it will and will not be reasonably practicable to obtain assistance from another person are so varied that, once again, full and careful findings or fact are the key to good decision making in all claims involving consideration of this issue.

(4) Paragraph (5)(a): difficulty communicating: This sub-para. concerns difficulties of communication arising because a person has learning, language or literacy difficulties, or because a person is deaf or blind. The words "deaf" or "blind" are not defined and so should be given their ordinary meaning, namely and respectively a person without hearing and a person without sight. Those who are hearing impaired or visually impaired may not be properly described as deaf or blind, but might well fall within the scope of someone who has difficulty communicating because of learning, language or literacy difficulties. Note that those who are deaf and blind must have difficulty communicating as a result of that disability and, additionally, must show that it was not reasonably practicable to obtain assistance from another person to make the claim. This is certainly an area where the qualification of *reasonable* practicability will be important. 2.135

In *CIS/2057/1998* the claimant had learning difficulties. She made a claim for income support which was awarded. Later her mother requested on her behalf that benefit be backdated to her sixteenth birthday (no-one had been appointed to act on behalf of the claimant). The tribunal erred in taking the view that the claimant had a supportive family who should have taken the initiative in finding out about her benefit entitlement. The proper approach was to determine (and the Commissioner so found) whether the claimant came within sub-para.(a)(i) and then to ask whether it was reasonably practicable for her to obtain assistance, not whether it was reasonably practicable for her family to provide it.

(5) Paragraph (5)(b): illness and disability: This sub-paragraph does not apply to claims for jobseeker's allowance. It deals with those many situations in which a person's delay is caused by illness or disability. In *CIS/610/1998* (discussed below in relation to sub-para.(d)) the Commissioner noted that the tribunal should have investigated the nature of the claimant's illness and whether this prevented him from queuing. 2.136

The first determination is the nature and dates of the person's illness or disability. The illness or disability must be compounded by its not being reasonably practicable for the claimant to obtain assistance from another person to make the claim.

(6) Paragraph (5)(c): caring responsibilities: This sub-para. offers an escape route for those with caring responsibilities. The situation in which the sub-para. applies are likely to be (but not expressed exclusively to be) situations where a period of intensive caring arises, or perhaps where another carer becomes unavailable and the claimant has stepped in to help. It is easy to think of circumstances where the circumstances will be satisfied, but also easy to think of rather more marginal cases. The sub-para. also requires the claimant to show that it was not reasonably practicable to obtain assistance from another person to make the claim. 2.137

2.138 *(7) Paragraph (5)(d): information from an officer of the Department leading a claimant to believe that a claim for benefit would not succeed:* This has proved to be a troublesome provision which the Department sought to argue was much narrower in its scope than its interpretation by the Commissioners. Note that there is no requirement that the claimant's belief that a claim would not succeed was reasonable in all the circumstances. But an unreasonably held belief might result in the claimant's failing the test in para.(4)(b).

Note that in [13] and [14] of *R(IS) 4/07* the Commissioner ruled that a breach of reg. 4(5) of the Claims and Payments Regulations (duty to provide a claim form) does not suspend time limits for making a claim.

A very common problem is the gap in benefit which often occurs when claimants transfer from jobseeker's allowance to income support because they have become incapable of work. It was thus perhaps predictable that the first Commissioners' decisions on the 1997 backdating rules would stem from this issue.

In *CIS/610/1998* the claimant, who had been claiming a jobseeker's allowance, took a Form Med. 3 issued by his GP to the Benefits Agency. There was a queue so he approached a security guard. The guard advised him that he did not need to fill in any forms, took his medical certificate, and wrote his national insurance number in a logging-in book. A week later the claimant received an incapacity benefit claim form through the post. He completed it and took it to the Benefits Agency. While in the queue, he was advised by another claimant that he needed to complete an income support claim form with his incapacity benefit claim form. He checked this advice when he reached the counter and then submitted claims for both benefits. The adjudication officer refused to backdate the claim for income support. The matter came before the Commissioner for consideration.

2.139 The Commissioner concluded on the facts of this case that the security guard was an "officer of the Department". The information supplied by the guard to the claimant could have left the claimant with the impression that he did not need to make another claim in connection with his transfer from a jobseeker's allowance to income support, and that in that sense any new claim would not succeed.

However, in *S K-G v SSWP (JSA)* [2014] UKUT 430 (AAC) Judge Wikeley decided that reg.19(5)(d) does not apply either to information in a standard DWP letter or to information on the direct.gov website to claims being made online or by telephone. Regulation 19(5)(d) is directed to "the situation where a claimant is given information by a DWP officer as part of some specific interchange or transaction relevant to their personal circumstances" (para.17). Furthermore, reg.19(5)(d) is not directed to official information about the process or method of claiming (para.21).

In *SSWP v PG (JSA)* [2015] UKUT 616 (AAC), Judge Wright disagrees with Judge Wikeley's conclusions in *SK-G v SSWP (JSA)* [2014] UKUT 430 that information on the Department's website does not constitute information given by an officer of the Department within reg.19(5)(d). Judge Wright had the benefit of argument in an oral hearing and provides detailed consideration of the process by which information finds its way onto the Department's website (paras 18-20)—in this case the *DirectGov* website. Judge Wright concludes that information on the website is capable of falling within the scope of reg.19(5)(d).

In *CIS/1721/1998* the claimant was given an incapacity benefit claim form when she went to the Job Centre with a medical certificate after fracturing her wrist. Two weeks later her claim for incapacity benefit was refused and she was advised to claim income support. The adjudication officer refused to backdate the claim.

2.140 The Commissioner accepts that the implication of the advice to claim incapacity benefit was that the claimant would be entitled to that benefit and not to income support. He considered that this was a reasonable belief on her part (incapacity benefit, if payable, would have exceeded her income support applicable amount). The Commissioner also took account of reg.4(5). The official to whom she produced the medical certificate should have supplied her with an income support claim form. A failure to supply this form would also have led her to believe that there was no entitlement to income support.

CIS/3749/1998 expands on this point. The Commissioner states that claimants were entitled by reason of reg.4(5) to assume that they had been given the right forms for the benefits they requested, and, if they were not, sub-para.(d) should clearly be considered. The claimant in this case had been receiving an income-based jobseeker's allowance, so there was at least a reasonable possibility that a claim for incapacity benefit would fail for lack of contributions. The Commissioner also drew attention to the fact that a failure to provide the right form brought reg.4(7A) into effect which would give the Secretary of State a discretion at accept a late claim.

In *CIS/3994/1998* (followed in *CSIS/815/2004*) the claimant had received advice that he was not entitled to income support on making two enquiries of the Department. That advice seemed to be correct in the light of the evidence of what the claimant had told the Department when he telephoned. The tribunal had ruled that this was not enough to bring the claimant within sub-para.(5)(d) in that the information he had received was reasonable. The Deputy Commissioner could find no such qualification in the sub-para.; the claimant had made an enquiry and had received information which caused him not to make a claim for income support sooner than he did. He was entitled to have the time limit for claiming extended.

In a Northern Ireland decision of a Tribunal of Commissioners in *R1/01(IS)(T)* 2.141 (unreported reference *C3/00–01 (IS)(T))*, the tribunal had to decide whether a New Deal adviser was an "officer of the Department". The claimant was a 59-year-old married man who had been claiming income-based JSA for a number of years, when he was told he was being sent on the New Deal scheme. The claimant obtained a medical certificate that he was incapable of work. He presented this at the Jobseekers Section, his claim to JSA was terminated, but he was not advised to claim income support. The claimant later claimed income support and sought to have the claim back-dated. The tribunal notes that the Northern Ireland legislation refers to "an officer of the Department" whereas the Great Britain legislation refers to "an officer of the Department of Social Security or of the Department for Education and Employment". In Northern Ireland New Deal advisers are not officers of the Department of Social Development. Thus, they are covered by the legislation applicable in Great Britain, but not that in Northern Ireland. The tribunal doubted whether this distinction was intended.

The second question was whether a failure to give advice can be said to come within these provisions. The tribunal concluded that the giving of information required "the transfer of factual data from an officer to a claimant" (at para.35). The regulation requires the giving of information to lead the claimant to believe that a claim for benefit will not succeed; it is not enough that the information left the claimant in ignorance of the possibility of claiming a different benefit. The tribunal says it must actually have led him to believe that a claim would not succeed.

The tribunal goes on to find that the information referred to in sub-para.(d) does not need to relate in some way to the benefit that is claimed late. Information about one claim or benefit could lead a claimant to believe that a claim for another benefit would not succeed.

The fourth issue addressed by the tribunal was whether the test is an objective 2.142 or subjective one. The tribunal agreed with the conclusions of a Great Britain Commissioner in *R(IS)3/01* (the report of *CIS/4354/1999*) that adjudicating authorities,

> "may legitimately test whether or not it believes a claimant's evidence about what he was led to believe by what reason a person in the claimant's circumstances might have been led to believe." (See [18]).

In *R(IS)3/01* the Commissioner had held that the words of reg.19(5)(d) "are not to be given any artificially restricted meaning" (See [14]). The information to which the regulation refers is not limited to information given in respect of the claim in question, but could include information concerning the ending of entitlement to some other benefit (See [13]–[18]).

In *CIS/4884/2002* the Commissioner was considering a tribunal's decision following a paper hearing in which they had concluded that the claimant, who had been told to apply for incapacity benefit which had delayed his claim for income support to which he was actually entitled, had not received "advice that a claim for income support would not succeed." In concluding that the tribunal had erred in law, the Commissioner warns of the need to take care to avoid looseness of language, since the receipt of advice is different from the receipt of information. Indeed the Commissioner doubts the correctness of the Northern Ireland Commissioners as expressed in this regard in *C3/00–01 (IS)* The Commissioner goes on to advise,

> "In my judgment the correct approach to regulation 19(5)(d) is that adopted by the Commissioner in report decision *R(IS)3/01.* The wording that 'the claimant was given information . . . which led the claimant to believe' needs to be given a practical, not an artificially restricted meaning, and it is not necessary for this purpose that what the claim was told by a departmental official should have referred *expressly* to the benefit afterwards sought to be claimed, if for example the information was that some different benefit was available which, if correct, would have made such a claim beside the point. Whether the claimant was given such information, and what he was or was not actually led to believe about the possibility of putting in a concurrent claim just in case, are matters of fact that need to be determined by the tribunal on the actual evidence; tested if necessary by cross-examination to resolve any doubt or dispute about what actually took place, or what the claimant afterwards says he believed at the time. Only when those facts have been clearly identified can a tribunal say if the condition in regulation 19(5)(d) has been met, and (if it has) then go on to assess as a matter of objective reasonableness whether the claimant also meets the further condition in regulation 19(4)(b) that he could not reasonably have been expected to make the claim earlier (not even one day earlier) than the date he did." (See para.7).

The Commissioner in *CJSA/580/2003* also followed the approach which had been adopted by Commissioners in Great Britain.

A rather unusual set of circumstances arose in *CJSA/3084/2004*. The claimant attended at an office of the Department to claim a jobseeker's allowance. He completed a form. This transpired to be not a claim form but a locally-used preliminary questionnaire (whose format frequently changed) which the Secretary of State conceded before the Commissioner gave the impression that a claim was being made. In allowing the backdating of a claim for a jobseeker's allowance, the Commissioner says:

> "9. The point of law that emerged during the hearing before me of the application for leave to appeal, and which the tribunal did not consider is as follows. Regulation 19(5)(d) refers, not to advice, but to information. Reference was made to decisions by Commissioners in *R(IS) 3/01* and *CIS/4884/2002*. If a claimant has been led to believe that he has made a claim, but he has not in fact made a claim, and because no decision has been received therefore believes that the claim has not succeeded, that seems to me to amount to having been given information which led him to believe that a subsequent real or effective claim would also not succeed."

2.143 *(8) Paragraph (5)(e) and (f): written advice or information leading the claimant to believe that a claim to benefit would not succeed:* Sub-paragraph (e) is concerned with written advice given by knowledgeable advisers other than officers of the Department which also leads that claimant to believe that a claim for benefit would not succeed, while sub-para.(f) is concerned with written information from an employer or former employer, or a bank or a building society about income or capital which leads claimant to believe that a claim for benefit would not succeed. The additional requirement here is that the claimant must have received "written advice" or "written information". There may be significance in the use of the words "advice" and "information"; sub-para.(e) requires the advice to have led the claimant to believe that a claim for benefit would not succeed, whereas sub-para.(f) simply requires "information". So in the latter case, a bank statement may suffice. Quite what the limits of written advice and information are remains to be tested. Would oral advice backed up by a written file note setting out the advice be sufficient? That would appear to be a forced interpretation of the sub-para., which appears to suggest that the advice has been reduced to writing and given to the claimant. But it is suggested that a claimant should be able to rely on the sub-para. if they were given a document which they have lost. Here the issue will be whether the decision-maker accepts their account of the contents of the written advice. That is a matter of the claimant's credibility rather than substance. Not every advice agency keeps file copies of written advice to their clients.

CJSA/1136/1998 considers the requirement that the advice must be in writing. The claimant had been dismissed and was advised by his trade union official not to claim any benefit until the reasons for his dismissal had been investigated through his employer's appeal procedures. This advice was confirmed in writing in a letter produced by the tribunal hearing in January 1998. The Commissioner states that the reason the sub-para. required the advice to be in writing was to avoid any doubt or argument as to the contents of that advice. If before the decision made by the decision-maker or tribunal, the advice was confirmed in writing, these difficulties were avoided and the advice amounted to written advice for the purposes of the sub-para. The reasoning is questionable since the wording of the provision appears to require the written advice to be what leads the claimant to believe that a claim will not succeed. The Commissioners' approach could also raise difficulties now that tribunals cannot take account of any circumstances not obtaining at the time when the decision appealed against was made: s.12(8)(b) of SSA 1998.

The group of advisers within the sub-paragraph is drawn widely, and covers a wide range of agencies.

In *CIS/1107/2008* the Commissioner ruled that reg.19(5)(e) was broad enough to include advice given by officials in the visa section of the British Embassy in Addis Ababa. The appellant had, incorrectly, been issued with a two year visa with a restriction on recourse to public funds. This resulted in his not claiming income support until he had received the correct visa which was for indefinite leave to remain with no restriction in relation to recourse to public funds.

As with sub-para.(5)(d), there is no requirement that the claimant's belief that a claim would not succeed was reasonable in all the circumstances. But an unreasonably held belief might result in the claimant's failing the test in para.(4)(b).

(9) Paragraph (5)(g): domestic emergencies: These circumstances are rather surprisingly included in para.(5) when they might more appropriately be included within the Secretary of State's discretion, since it is difficult to think of circumstances which would meet the requirements of the sub-para. which would last more than a month. Perhaps the distinction originally lay in the mandatory nature of the extension where para.(5) is satisfied compared with the discretionary nature of the extension in para.(7), but if that is the distinction, there are circumstances listed in para.(7) which should also be in para.(5). The extension in para.(6) is mandatory following the April 2002 amendment. **2.144**

(10) Paragraph (5)(h): adverse weather conditions: Again these circumstances will usually be of very limited duration save in the more remote parts of the country, and the circumstances seem more appropriate for determination under the Secretary of State's decision-making under para.(6). **2.145**

2.146 *(11) Paragraphs (6) and (7): the decision-maker's one-month decision:* As originally drafted, this was the Secretary of State's discretion to extend the time limit for claiming up to one month and applies to claims for income support, jobseeker's allowance, working families' tax credit and disabled person's tax credit. The Secretary of State could extend the time limit for claiming for any period up to a maximum of one month,

- if the Secretary of State considered that to do so would be consistent with the proper administration of benefit, and
- any of the circumstances in para.(7) applied.

The April 2002 amendment makes this a mandatory list of special circumstances which justify a one month extension to the time limit for claiming. The reference to consistency with the proper administration of benefit happily disappears. Once again the list is exhaustive and has no category of analogous circumstances.

In *CJSA/3659/2001* the Commissioner notes that decisions under reg.19(6) and (7), which contain the requirement that the Secretary of State in the circumstances set out in these paragraphs extend the time limit for claiming to one month, are within the jurisdiction of tribunals. This flows from the provision in para.5(a) of Sch.2 to the Decisions and Appeals Regulations which excludes from the list of Secretary of State's decisions against which no appeal lies a decision under reg.19 as to the time for claiming benefit. This is drafted widely enough to bring within the tribunal's jurisdiction not only the matters in reg.19(4) and (5), but also those in reg.19(6) and (7). It follows that tribunals must consider both sets of rules relating to extension of the time limit for claiming.

2.147 Note in relation to these provisions, reg.6(1)(aa) and (1A) for the automatic allowance of one month to return the claim forms in the cases mentioned there, and note the discretionary rule in reg.6(4B) in relation to claims for a jobseeker's allowance.

It would seem that the principle of *CSIS/61/1992* still applies that in every case where a claim is made outside the time limit specified in Sch.4, the Secretary of State should consider the use of the operation of the extension under para.(6) before the claim is referred to a decision-maker for decision. If this has not been done, a tribunal may decide to adjourn for the matter to be considered. There may also be cases where information comes to light in the hearing which makes it appropriate to adjourn to enable the decision maker to re-consider the matter.

It is sometimes argued that the circumstances envisaged in sub-para.(7)(a) are exceptional, as when an office closes unexpectedly due to flooding or industrial action. It is submitted that this is to apply too narrow an interpretation to the words. The sub-para. surely covers situations where a claim would need to be made on a Saturday, but the office is closed and the claim is submitted on the following Monday.

2.148 There has been a decision on reg.19(7)(b), which may be limited to some rather special facts: *CSJSA/0811/2006*. It concerned a claimant's lack of funds to pay the ferry fare from Islay to the mainland. He argued that this meant that he was unable to attend the appropriate office due to difficulties with his normal mode of transport and there was no reasonable alternative available. The Deputy Commissioner, in remitting the appeal for determination a new tribunal, considered that "difficulties" in this context could include an inability to pay. He then addressed the issue of whether there was any reasonable alternative, and interpreted the regulation here as referring to reasonable alternative transport. Finally, it was necessary to consider whether the claimant could reasonably have been expected to make the claim earlier than he did. Here the issue was whether earlier claim by telephone was a reasonable course of action for the claimant to have taken. This would require consideration of any enquiry made by the claimant about telephone claims, and whether the claimant did as much as could reasonably be expected of him. If, having done that, he remained ignorant of the possibility of a telephone claim, then he would not fall foul of the provision in reg.19(6)(b).

In *CIS/4901/2002* the Commissioner considered what is meant by the term "adverse postal conditions" as used in reg.19(7)(c), but ultimately decided the case on different grounds. The circumstances of the case were that the claimant had received some claim forms in the post but no reply paid envelope had been provided. The forms were completed and mailed to the Department in an envelope provided by the claimant to which he affixed a single first class stamp. However, the correct postage was more than this. It was not received by the Department. A second claim was made and benefit paid from a later date; the claimant sought to have this claim backdated to the date of an enquiry made of the Jobcentre about his benefit entitlement which had resulted in his being advised to claim income support or incapacity benefit, and in his being sent the first set of forms. Eventually, the first set of forms was returned to the claimant by the Post Office endorsed by the Revenue Protection Section indicating that insufficient postage had been attached to the letter. Some £0.77 needed to be paid for the forms to be delivered. A second endorsement was to the effect that the package had "not [been] called for." It was established that there was, in relation to the Benefit Office to which the claimant had sent the first set of forms, an arrangement under which the Post Office adopted a different policy from that which normally applies in relation to under-stamped mail. The normal practice is to advise the addressee that mail awaits them and is available on payment of the amount of the underpayment plus handling fee. The practice which it was accepted should have been adopted in this case was for the forms to have been delivered and for the amount of the underpayment to be included in a bulk surcharge arrangement with the Department. It would seem to flow from the detailed reasoning of the Commissioner in the case that he would accept that there might be an argument to bring the failure of such arrangements within the ambit of the phrase "adverse postal conditions." However, he decided the case on the basis that the Post Office in holding the first set of claim forms was the bailee for the Department and so the original forms are to be treated as being in the hands of the Department between the date of its receipt until they were returned to the claimant. This was sufficient to ground entitlement to the benefit from the earlier date.

In *R(IS) 16/04*, the Commissioner accepts that delays in post arriving over the Christmas period constitute adverse postal conditions within para.(7)(c).

In *CJSA/3960/2006*, the Deputy Commissioner ruled that a delay of two working days beyond the maximum period within which a letter should have been delivered constituted "adverse postal conditions". The mere fact of the delay established that there were adverse postal conditions. A second issue arose in the case on the interpretation of the words "before the date that his entitlement expired" in reg.19(7)(d). The Deputy Commissioner ruled that a decision that a person was not entitled to income support from February 4, 2006 meant that the claimant's entitlement ended on February 3, 2006, since "her entitlement expired on the very last moment of the Friday but before the very first moment of the Saturday." (See para.20.) 2.149

In *CJSA/0743/2006* the Commissioner ruled that the words "another benefit" in reg.19(7)(d) referred to a different benefit. He said, "I consider that the natural meaning of the work in that context is 'different'" (See para.9.)

Part III

Payments

[1 Time of payment: general provision

20. Subject to regulations 21 to 26B, benefit shall be paid in accordance with an award as soon as is reasonably practicable after the award has been made.] 2.150

AMENDMENT

1. Inserted by The Social Security (Miscellaneous Amendments) (No.2) Regulations 2006 (SI 2006/832) reg.2 (April 10, 2006).

DEFINITION

"benefit"—see reg.2(2).

2.151 **20A.**—[1 . . .]

AMENDMENT

1. The Social Security (Miscellaneous Amendments) (No.2) Regulations 2006 (SI 2006/832) reg.2 (April 10, 2006).

Direct credit transfer

2.152 **21.**—[12 (1) The Secretary of State may arrange for benefit to be paid by way of direct credit transfer into a bank or other account nominated by the person entitled to benefit or a person acting on their behalf.]

(2) [9 . . .]

(3) [2Subject to paragraph (3A)] benefit shall be paid in accordance with paragraph (1) within seven days of the last day of each successive period of entitlement [9 . . .] [7or, so far as concerns working familiar tax credit, within such time as the Board may direct]

[2(3A) Income Support shall be paid in accordance with paragraph (1) within 7 days of the time determined for the payment of income support in accordance with Schedule 7.]

[6(3B) Where child benefit is payable in accordance with paragraph (1), [9 an arrangement under that paragraph] shall also have effect for any guardian's allowance to which the claimant is entitled and that allowance shall be paid in the same manner as the child benefit due in his case.

(3C) Where guardian's allowance is payable in accordance with paragraph (1), [9 an arrangement under that paragraph] shall also have effect for the child benefit to which the claimant is entitled and that child benefit shall be paid in the same manner as the guardian's allowance which is due in his case.]

(4) In respect of benefit which is the subject of an arrangement for payment under this regulation, the Secretary of State [7or the Board] may make a particular payment by credit transfer otherwise than is provided by paragraph (3) [2or (3A)] if it appears to him [7or them] appropriate to do so for the purpose of—

(a) paying any arrears of benefit, or
(b) making a payment in respect of a terminal period of an award or for any similar purpose.

(5) [11 . . .]

[8 (5A) In relation to payment of a joint-claim jobseeker's allowance, references in this regulation to the person entitled to benefit shall be construed as references to the member of the joint-claim couple who is the nominated member for the purposes of section 3B of the Jobseekers Act.]

(6) [5. . .]

AMENDMENTS

1. The Social Security (Miscellaneous Provisions) Amendment Regulations 1992 (SI 1992/247) reg.15 (March 9, 1992).
2. The Social Security (Claims and Payments) Amendment (No.2) Regulations 1993 (SI 1993/1113) reg.2 (May 12, 1993).
3. The Social Security (Claims and Payments) Amendment Regulations 1994 (SI 1994/2319) reg.4 (October 3, 1994).
4. The Social Security (Claims and Payments) Amendment Regulations 1994 (SI 1994/2319) reg.8 (April 13, 1995).
5. The Social Security (Claims and Payments) Amendment Regulations 1996 (SI 1996/672) reg.2(3) (April 4, 1996).
6. The Social Security (Claims and Payments) Amendment Regulations 1999 (SI 1999/2358) reg.2 (September 20, 1999).
7. The Tax Credits (Claims and Payments) (Amendment) Regulations 1999 (SI 1999/2572) regs 20, 23 and 24 (October 5, 1999).
8. The Social Security (Joint Claims: Consequential Amendments) Regulations 2000 (SI 2000/1982) reg.2(6) (March 19, 2001).
9. The Social Security (Claims and Payments and Miscellaneous Amendments) (No.2) Regulations 2002 (SI 2002/2441) reg.2 (April 6, 2003).
10. The Social Security (Miscellaneous Amendments) (No.2) Regulations 2006 (SI 2006/832) reg.2 (April 10, 2006).
11. The Social Security (Miscellaneous Amendments) Regulations 2012 (SI 2012/757) reg.15(2) (April 1, 2012).
12. The Universal Credit and Miscellaneous Amendments (No.2) Regulations 2014 (SI 2014/2888), reg.5(2) (November 26, 2014).

DEFINITIONS

"appropriate office"—see reg.2(1).
"partner"—*ibid.*

[1Payment of arrears of benefit by instalments

21ZA. Except where regulation 23 applies, the Secretary of State may pay arrears of benefit in instalments where— 2.153
(a) the Secretary of State considers it is necessary for protecting the interests of the beneficiary; and
(b) the beneficiary agrees that those arrears may be paid in instalments.]

AMENDMENT

1. The Social Security Benefits (Claims and Payments) (Amendment) Regulations 2021 (SI 2021/1065) (October 18, 2021).

GENERAL NOTE

Regulation 2 of SI 2021/1065, making the amendment, extends, so far as England and Wales are concerned, to all benefits to which the 1987 Regulations apply. In relation to such of those benefits as fall within the competence of the Scottish Ministers, see reg.21ZB below; otherwise, reg.2 applies. 2.154

[1Payment of arrears of benefit by instalments

21ZB. (1) In relation to payments made under provisions related to devolved social security matters, the Scottish Ministers may pay arrears of benefit in instalments where— 2.155

(a) the Scottish Ministers consider it is necessary for protecting the interests of the beneficiary, and
(b) the beneficiary agrees that those arrears may be paid in instalments.

(2) For the purpose of paragraph (1), "devolved social security matters" means matters which are within the legislative competence of the Scottish Parliament by virtue of exceptions 1 to 10 in Section F1 of Part 2 of schedule 5 of the Scotland Act 1998.]

AMENDMENT

1. The Social Security (Claims and Payments) (Miscellaneous Amendments) (Scotland) Regulations 2021 (SSI 2021/305) reg.3 (October 18, 2021).

[1 Delayed payment of lump sum

2.156 **21A.**—(1) The regulation applies where—
(a) a person ("P") is entitled to a lump sum under, as the case may be—
(i) Schedule 5 to the Contributions and Benefits Act (pensions increase or lump sum where entitlement to retirement pension is deferred);
(ii) Schedule 5A to that Act (pension increase or lump sum where entitlement to share additional pension is deferred); or
(iii) Schedule 1 to the Social Security (Graduated Retirement Benefit) Regulations 2005 (further provisions replacing section 36(4) of the National Insurance Act 1965: increases of graduated retirement benefit and lump sums);
[2 (iv) section 8 of the Pensions Act 2014 (choice of lump sum or survivor's pension in certain cases); or
(v) Regulations under section 10 of the Pensions Act 2014 (inheritance of graduated retirement benefit) which makes provision corresponding or similar to section 8 of that Act;]

or
(b) the Secretary of State decides to make a payment on account of such a lump sum.

(2) Subject to paragraph (3), for the purposes of section 7 of the Finance (No. 2) Act 2005 (charge to income tax of lump sum), P may elect to be paid the lump sum in the tax year ("the later year of assessment") next following the tax year which would otherwise be the applicable year of assessment by virtue of section 8 of that Act (meaning of "applicable year of assessment" in section 7).

(3) P may not elect in accordance with paragraph (2) ("a tax election") unless he elects on the same day as he chooses a lump sum in accordance with, as the case may be—
(a) paragraph A1 or 3C of Schedule 5 to the Contributions and Benefits Act;
(b) paragraph 1 of Schedule 5A to that Act;
(c) paragraph 12 or 17 of Schedule 1 to the Social Security (Graduated Retirement Benefit) Regulations 2005;
[2 (d) section 8 of the Pensions Act 2014;
(e) Regulations under section 10 of the Pensions Act 2014 which make provision corresponding or similar to section 8 of that Act,]

or within a month of that day.

(4) A tax election may be made in writing to an office specified by the Secretary of state for accepting such elections or, except where in any particular case the Secretary of State directs that the election must be made in writing, it may be made by telephone call to the number specified by the Secretary of State.

(5) If P makes a tax election, payment of the lump sum, or any payment on account of the lump sum, shall be made in the first month of the later year of assessment or as soon as reasonably practicable after that month, unless P revokes the tax election before the payment is made.

(6) If P makes no tax elections in accordance with paragraph (2) and (3), or revokes a tax election, payment of the lump sum or any payment on account of the lump sum shall be made as soon as reasonably practicable after P—

(a) elected for a lump sum, or was treated as having so elected; or
(b) revoked a tax election.

(7) If P dies before the beginning of the later year of assessment—

(a) any tax election in respect of P's lump sum shall cease to have effect; and
(b) no person appointed under regulation 30 to act on P's behalf may make a tax election.

(8) In this regulation "the later year of assessment" has the meaning given by section 8(5) of the Finance (No. 2) Act 2005.]

AMENDMENTS

1. The Social Security (Deferral of Retirement Pensions, Shared Additional Pension and Graduated Retirement Benefit) (Miscellaneous Provisions) Regulations 2005 (SI 2005/2677) (April 6, 2006).

2. The Pensions Act 2014 (Consequential, Supplementary and Incidental Amendments) Order 2015 (SI 2015/1985) art.9(10) (April 6, 2016).

Long term benefits

22.—[5 (1) Subject to the provisions of this regulation and [8 regulations 22A, 22C and 25(1)], long term benefits may be paid at intervals of [6 four weekly in arrears, weekly in advance or, where the beneficiary agrees, at intervals not exceeding 13 weeks in arrears.] 2.157

(1A) [9 Subject to paragraph (1B), disability] living allowance shall be paid at intervals of four weeks.]

[9 (1B) The Secretary of State may, in any particular case or class of case, arrange that attendance allowance or disability living allowance shall be paid at such other intervals not exceeding four weeks as may be specified.]

(2) Where the amount of long-term benefit payable is less than[4]£5.00] a week the Secretary of State may direct that it shall be paid (whether in advance or in arrears) at such intervals as may be specified not exceeding 12 months.

(3) Schedule 6 specifies the days of the week on which the various long term benefits are payable.

AMENDMENTS

1. The Social Security (Claims and Payments) Amendment Regulations 1991 (SI 1991/2741) reg.12(a) (February 3, 1992).

2. The Social Security (Claims and Payments) Amendment Regulations 1991 (SI 1991/2741) reg.12(b) (February 3, 1992).

3. The Social Security (Claims and Payments) Amendment (No.4) Regulations 1994 (SI 1994/3196) reg.5 (January 10, 1995).
4. The Social Security (Claims and Payments and Adjudication) Amendment Regulations 1996 (SI 1996/2306) reg.22(2) (October 7, 1996).
5. The Social Security (Claims and Payments and Miscellaneous Amendments) (No.2) Regulations 2002 (SI 2002/2441) reg.2 (April 6, 2003).
6. The Social Security (Miscellaneous Amendments) (No.5) Regulations 2008 (SI 2008/2667) reg.2 (October 30, 2008).
7. The Social Security (Claims and Payments) Amendment Regulations 2009 (SI 2009/604) reg.2 (April 6, 2009).
8. The Social Security (Miscellaneous Amendments) (No.6) Regulations 2009 (SI 2009/3229) reg.2(4) (April 6, 2010).
9. The Social Security (Miscellaneous Amendments) Regulations 2010 (SI 2010/510) reg.3(5) (April 6, 2010).

[1 [2 . . .] Widowed mother's allowance, widowed parent's allowance and widow's pension

2.158 **22A.**—(1) Subject to paragraphs (2) and (4), [2 . . .] widowed mother's allowance, widowed parent's allowance and widow's pension shall be paid fortnightly in arrears on the day of the week specified in paragraph (3).

(2) The Secretary of State may, in any particular case or class of case, arrange that a benefit specified in paragraph (1) be paid on any other day of the week.

(3) The day specified for the purposes of paragraph (1) is the day in column (2) which corresponds to the series of numbers in column (1) which includes the last 2 digits of the person's national insurance number—

(1)	*(2)*
00 to 19	Monday
20 to 39	Tuesday
40 to 59	Wednesday
60 to 79	Thursday
80 to 99	Friday.

(4) The Secretary of State may, in any particular case or class of case, arrange that the beneficiary be paid weekly in advance or in arrears or, where the beneficiary agrees to be paid in such manner, at intervals of four or 13 weeks in arrears.]

AMENDMENTS

1. Inserted by The Social Security (Claims and Payments) Amendment Regulations 2009 (SI 2009/604) reg.2 (April 6, 2009).
2. The Pensions Act 2014 (Consequential, Supplementary and Incidental Amendments) Order 2017 (SI 2017/422) art.10 (April 6, 2017).

[1 Payment of [2 . . .] widowed mother's allowance, widowed parent's allowance and widow's pension at a daily rate

2.159 **22B.**—(1) Where entitlement to a [2 . . .] widowed parent's allowance begins on a day which is not the first day of the benefit week, it shall be paid at a daily rate in respect of the period beginning with the day on which entitlement begins and ending on the day before the first day of the following benefit week.

(2) Where the Secretary of State changes the day on which a benefit mentioned in paragraph (5) is payable, the benefit shall be paid at a daily rate in respect of any day for which payment would have been made but for that change.

(3) An award of benefit mentioned in paragraph (5) shall be paid at a daily rate where—

(a) the award is terminated;

(b) entitlement ends on a day other than the last day of the benefit week; and

(c) the benefit is paid in arrears.

(4) Where benefit is paid at a daily rate in the circumstances mentioned in paragraph (3), it shall be so paid in respect of the period beginning with the first day of the final benefit week and ending on the last day for which there is an entitlement to the benefit.

[2 . . .]

(6) Where benefit is payable at a daily rate in the circumstances mentioned in this regulation, the daily rate shall be 1/7th of the weekly rate.]

AMENDMENTS

1. Inserted by The Social Security (Claims and Payments) Amendment Regulations 2009 (SI 2009/604) reg.2 (April 6, 2009).

2. The Pensions Act 2014 (Consequential, Supplementary and Incidental Amendments) Order 2017 (SI 2017/422) art.10 (April 6, 2017).

GENERAL NOTE

The Social Security (Transitional Payments) Regulations 2009 (SI 2009/609) make provision for the payment of a one-off transitional payment and an adjusting payment of benefit when payment of certain benefits was changed from payment in advance to payment in arrears. **2.160**

[1 Retirement pension

22C.—(1) This regulation applies in relation to payment of a retirement pension to persons who reach pensionable age on or after April 6, 2010, other than to a person to whom paragraph (7) applies. **2.161**

(2) Subject to paragraphs (4) to (6), a retirement pension shall be paid weekly, fortnightly or four weekly (as the Secretary of State may in any case determine) in arrears on the day of the week specified in paragraph (3).

(3) The day specified for the purposes of paragraph (2) is the day in column (2) which corresponds to the series of numbers in column (1) which includes the last 2 digits of the person's national insurance number—

(1)	(2)
00 to 19	Monday
20 to 39	Tuesday
40 to 59	Wednesday
60 to 79	Thursday
80 to 99	Friday

(4) The Secretary of State may, in any particular case or class of case, arrange that retirement pension be paid on any other day of the week.

(5) The Secretary of State may, in any particular case or class of case, arrange that the beneficiary be paid in arrears at intervals of 13 weeks where the beneficiary agrees.

(6) Where the amount of a retirement pension payable is less than £5.00 per week the Secretary of State may direct that it shall be paid in arrears at such intervals, not exceeding 12 months, as may be specified in the direction.

(7) This paragraph applies to a man who—

(a) was in receipt of state pension credit in respect of any day in the period beginning with the day 4 months and 4 days before the day on which he reaches pensionable age and ending on April 5, 2010; or

(b) was in continuous receipt of state pension credit from April 5, 2010 until a day no earlier than the day 4 months and 4 days before the day on which he reaches pensionable age.]

AMENDMENT

1. Inserted by The Social Security (Miscellaneous Amendments) (No.6) Regulations 2009 (SI 2009/3229) reg.2(5) (April 6, 2010).

[1 State pension under Part 1 of the Pensions Act 2014

2.162 **22CA.**—(1) This regulation applies in relation to payment of a state pension under Part 1 of the Pensions Act 2014.

(2) State pension is to be paid in arrears.

(3) The Secretary of State may arrange to pay state pension at intervals of—

(a) one week;

(b) two weeks, if the beneficiary was in receipt of a working age benefit immediately before becoming entitled to the state pension which was paid fortnightly;

(c) four weeks;

(d) 13 weeks, if the beneficiary agrees; or

(e) such length not exceeding 12 months as the Secretary of State may choose, if—

(i) the Secretary of State makes a direction specifying that length; and

(ii) the amount of the state pension payable is less than £5.00 per week.

(4) State pension is to be paid—

(a) on the day in column (2) which corresponds to the series of numbers in column (1) which includes the last 2 digits of the person's national insurance number; or

(b) In any particular case or class of case, on any other day of the week that the Secretary of State may choose.

(1) Last 2 digits national insurance number	*(2) Day to be paid state pension*
00 to 19	Monday
20 to 39	Tuesday
40 to 59	Wednesday
60 to 79	Thursday
80 to 99	Friday]

AMENDMENT

1. Added by The Pensions Act 2014 (Consequential, Supplementary and Incidental Amendments) Order 2015 (SI 2015/1985) art.9(11) (April 6, 2016).

[1 Payment of retirement pension at a daily rate

22D.—(1) Where the entitlement of a person (B) to a retirement pension begins on a day which is not the first day of the benefit week in the circumstances specified in paragraph (3), it shall be paid at a daily rate in respect of the period beginning with the day on which entitlement begins and ending on the day before the first day of the following benefit week. 2.163

(2) Where in respect of a retirement pension—

(a) the circumstances specified in paragraph (3) apply,

(b) B's entitlement to that benefit begins on a day which is not the first day of the benefit week, and

(c) a change in the rate of that benefit takes effect under an order made under [2 section 150 or 150A] of the 1992 Act (annual up-rating of basic pension etc.) on a day, in the same benefit week, subsequent to the day on which B's entitlement arose,

it shall be paid at a daily rate in respect of the period beginning with the day on which entitlement begins and ending on the day before the first day of the following benefit week.

(3) The circumstances referred to in paragraphs (1) and (2) are where—

(a) the retirement pension is paid in arrears,

(b) B has not opted to defer entitlement to a retirement pension under section 55 of the Contributions and Benefits Act(13), and

(c) B—

(i) was in receipt of a working age benefit in respect of any day in the period beginning with the day 8 weeks and a day before B reaches pensionable age and ending immediately before the day B reaches such age, or

(ii) has reached pensionable age and is a dependent spouse of a person who is in receipt of an increase for an adult dependant under section 83 or 84 of the Contributions and Benefits Act.

(4) Where benefit is payable at a daily rate in the circumstances mentioned in this regulation, the daily rate which shall apply in respect of a particular day in the relevant period shall be 1/7th of the weekly rate which, if entitlement had begun on the first day of the benefit week, would have had effect on that particular day.

(5) In this regulation, "benefit week" means the period of 7 days which ends on the day on which, in B's case, the benefit is payable in accordance with regulation 22C.]

AMENDMENTS

1. Inserted by The Social Security (Miscellaneous Amendments) (No.6) Regulations 2009 (SI 2009/3229) reg.2(5) (April 6, 2010).

2. The Social Security (Miscellaneous Amendments) Regulations 2010 (SI 2010/510) reg.3(6) (April 6, 2010).

[1 Payment of state pension under Part 1 of the Pensions Act 2014 at a daily rate

2.164 **22DA.**—(1) State pension under Part 1 of the Pensions Act 2014 is to be paid at a daily rate where—

(a) the day on which a person's first benefit week begins is after—

(i) the day on which the person reaches pensionable age; or

(ii) where the person has deferred their state pension under sections 16 and 17 of the Pensions Act 2014, the first day in respect of which the person makes a claim for their state pension; or

(b) the day on which a person's last benefit week begins is before the day on which the person dies.

(2) The period for which a daily rate is to be paid is—

(a) where paragraph (1)(a) applies, the period—

(i) beginning on the day on which the person reaches pensionable age or the first day in respect of which the person makes a claim for their state pension; and

(ii) ending on the day before the day on which the person's first benefit week begins; or

(b) where paragraph (1)(b) applies, the period beginning on the day on which the person's last benefit week begins and ending on the day on which the person dies.

(3) The daily rate at which state pension is payable under this regulation is 1/7th of the weekly rate which would have had effect on the day if a weekly rate had been payable.

(4) In this regulation, "benefit week" means the period of 7 days ending on the day on which the person's state pension is payable in accordance with regulation 22CA(4).]

AMENDMENT

1. Added by The Pensions Act 2014 (Consequential, Supplementary and Incidental Amendments) Order 2015 (SI 2015/1985) art.9(12) (April 6, 2016).

[1 Child benefit and guardian's allowance.]

2.165 **23.**—(1) Subject to the provisions of this regulation [3 . . .], child benefit shall be payable as follows:—

(a) in a case where a person entitled to child benefit elects to receive payment weekly in accordance with the provisions of Schedule 8, child benefit shall be payable weekly from the first convenient date after the election has been made;

(b) in any other case child benefit shall be payable in the last week of each successive period of four weeks of the period of entitlement.

(2) Subject to paragraph (3) and regulation 21, child benefit payable weekly or four-weekly shall be payable on Mondays or Tuesdays (as the Secretary of State may in any case determine) [2 by means of serial orders or on presentation of an instrument for benefit payment]

(3) In such cases as the Secretary of State may determine, child benefit shall be payable otherwise than—

(a) by means of serial order [2or on presentation of an instrument for benefit payment,]

(b) on Mondays or Tuesdays, or
(c) at weekly or four-weekly intervals,

and where child benefit is paid at four-weekly intervals in accordance with paragraph (1)(b) the Secretary of State shall arrange for it to be paid weekly if satisfied that payment at intervals of four weeks is causing hardship.

[1 (3A) Where a claimant for child benefit is also entitled to guardian's allowance, that allowance shall be payable in the same manner and at the same intervals as the claimant's child benefit under this regulation.]

(4) The Secretary of State shall take steps to notify persons to whom child benefit is payable of the arrangements he has made for payment so far as those arrangements affect such persons.

AMENDMENTS

1. The Social Security (Claims and Payments) Amendment Regulations 1999 (SI 1999/2358) reg.2(5) (September 20, 1999).

2. The Social Security (Claims and Payments) Amendment (No.4) Regulations 1994 (SI 1994/3196) reg.6 (January 10, 1995).

3. The Social Security (Claims and Payments and Miscellaneous Amendments) (No.2) Regulations 2002 (SI 2002/2441) reg.2 (April 1, 2003).

[1 Incapacity benefit, maternity allowance and severe disablement allowance

24.—(1) Subject to [3 . . .] [4 paragraphs (3) and (3A)], incapacity benefit [4 , maternity allowance] and severe disablement allowance shall be paid fortnightly in arrears unless [4 in any particular case or class of case], the Secretary of State arranges otherwise. 2.166

[4 "(1A) Subject to paragraph (1B), the benefits specified in paragraph (1) shall be paid on the day of the week specified in paragraph (1C).

(1B) The Secretary of State may, in any particular case or class of case, arrange that a benefit specified in paragraph (1) be paid on any other day of the week.

(1C) The day specified for the purposes of paragraph (1A) is the day in column (2) which corresponds to the series of numbers in column (1) which includes the last 2 digits of the person's national insurance number—

(1)	(2)
00 to 19	Monday
20 to 39	Tuesday
40 to 59	Wednesday
60 to 79	Thursday
80 to 99	Friday.

]

(2) [4 . . .]

(3) If the weekly amount of incapacity benefit or severe disablement allowance is less than £1.00 it may be paid in arrears at intervals of 4 weeks.

[2 (3A) Where the amount of incapacity benefit payable after reduction for pension payments under section 30DD of the Social Security Contributions and Benefits Act 1992 (including any reduction for other purposes) is less than £5.00 per week, the Secretary of State may direct that it shall be paid [4 in arrears] at such intervals as may be specified not exceeding 12 months.]

(4) [4 . . .]]

AMENDMENTS

1. Regulation.24 substituted by The Social Security (Claims and Payments) Amendment (No.2) Regulations 1994 (SI 1994/2943) reg.9 (April 13, 1995); words in heading to, and certain words in, regulation deleted by The Social Security (Claims and Payments) (Jobseeker's Allowance Consequential Amendments) Regulations 1996 (SI 1996/1460) reg.2(13) (October 7, 1996).

2. The Social Security (Incapacity Benefit) Miscellaneous Amendments Regulations 2000 (SI 2000/3210) reg.3 (April 6, 2001).

3. The Social Security (Claims and Payments and Miscellaneous Amendments) (No.2) Regulations 2002 (SI 2002/2441) reg.2 (April 8, 2003).

4. The Social Security (Claims and Payments) Amendments Regulations 2009 (SI 2009/604) reg.2 (April 6, 2009).

Payment of attendance allowance and constant attendance allowance at a daily rate

2.167 **25.**—(1) Attendance allowance [[1]or disability living allowance] [[2]. . .] shall be paid in respect of any person, for any day falling within a period to which paragraph (2) applies, at the daily rate (which shall be equal to ⅐th of the weekly rate) and attendance allowance [[1] or disability living allowance] [[2]. . .] payable in pursuance of this regulation shall be paid weekly or as the Secretary of State may direct in any case.

(2) This paragraph applies to any period which—

(a) begins on the day immediately following the last day of the period during which a person was living in [[3] a hospital specified in or other accommodation provided as specified in regulations made under [section 72(8) of the Social Security Contributions and Benefits Act 1992] ("specified hospital or other accommodation")]; and

(b) ends—

(i) if the first day of the period was a day of payment, at midnight on the day preceding the [[3] 4th] following day of payment, or

(ii) if that day was not a day of payment, at midnight on the day preceding the [[3] 5th] following day of payment, or

(iii) if earlier, on the day immediately preceding the day on which [[3] he next lives in specified hospital or other accommodation],

if on the first day of the period it is expected that, before the expiry of the period of [[3] 28 days] beginning with that day, he will return to [[3] specified hospital or other accommodation].

(3) An increase of disablement pension under [section 104 of the Social Security Contributions and Benefits Act 1992] where constant attendance is needed ("constant attendance allowance") shall be paid at a daily rate of 1/7th of the weekly rate in any case where it becomes payable for a period of less than a week which is immediately preceded and immediately succeeded by periods during which the constant attendance allowance was not payable because regulation 21(1) of the Social Security (General Benefit) Regulations 1982 applied.

AMENDMENTS

1. The Social Security (Claims and Payments) Amendment Regulations 1991 (SI 1991/2741) reg.13(a) (April 6, 1992).

2. The Social Security (Disability Living Allowance and Claims and Payments) Amendment Regulations 1996 (SI 1996/1436) reg.3 (July 31, 1996).

3. The Social Security (Claims and Payments) Amendment Regulations 1991 (SI 1991/2741) reg.13(b)–(f) (April 6, 1992).

Income support

26.—(1) [3 Subject to regulation 21 (direct credit transfer), Schedule 7] shall have effect for determining the [6 . . .] time at which income support is to be paid, [. . .5] and the day when entitlement to income support is to begin. 2.168

(2) [6 . . .]

[2 (3) [6 . . .].]

(4) Where the entitlement to income support is less than 10 pence or, in the case of a beneficiary to whom [1 section 23(a)] of the Social Security Act 1986 [SSCBA, s.126] applies, £5, that amount shall not be payable unless the claimant is also entitled to payment of any other benefit with which income support [2may be paid] under arrangements made by the Secretary of State.

Amendments

1. The Social Security (Claims and Payments) Amendment Regulations 1988 (SI 1988/522) reg.6 (April 11, 1988).

2. The Social Security (Claims and Payments and Payments on account, Overpayments and Recovery) Amendment Regulations 1989 (SI 1989/136) reg.2 (February 27, 1989).

3. The Social Security (Claims and Payments) Amendment (No.2) Regulations 1993 (SI 1993/1113) reg.3 (May 12, 1993).

4. The Social Security Act 1998 (Commencment No.12 and Consequential and Transitional Provisions) Order 1999 (SI 1999/3178) Sch.6 (November 29, 1999).

5. The Social Security and Child Support (Miscellaneous Amendments) Regulations 2000 (SI 2000/1596) reg.4(1) (June 19, 2000).

6. The Social Security (Miscellaneous Amendments) (No.2) Regulations 2006 (SI 2006/832) reg.2 (April 10, 2006).

[1 Jobseeker's allowance

26A.—(1) Subject to the following provisions of this regulation, jobseeker's allowance shall be paid fortnightly in arrears unless in any particular case or class of case the Secretary of State arranges otherwise. 2.169

(2) The provisions of paragraph 2A of Schedule 7 (payment of income support at times of office closure) shall apply for the purposes of payment of a jobseeker's allowance as they apply for the purposes of payment of income support [5 . . .]

(3) Where the amount of a jobseeker's allowance is less than £1.00 a week the Secretary of State may direct that it shall be paid at such intervals, not exceeding 13 weeks, as may be specified in the direction.

(4)–(8) [. . .4].

Amendments

1. The Social Security (Claims and Payments) (Jobseeker's Allowance Consequential Amendments) Regulations 1996 (SI 1996/1460) reg.2(14) (October 7, 1996).

2. The Social Security (Miscellaneous Amendments) (No.4) Regulations 1998 (SI 1998/1174) reg.8(3)(a) (June 1, 1998).

3. The Social Security Act 1998 (Commencement No.12 and Consequential and Transitional Provisions) Order 1999 (SI 1999/3178) Sch.6 (November 29, 1999).

4. The Social Security and Child Support (Miscellaneous Amendments) Regulations 2000 (SI 2000/1596) reg.4(2) (June 19, 2000).

5. The Secretaries of State for Education and Skills and for Work and Pensions Order 2002 (SI 2002/1397) art.18 (June 27, 2002).

DEFINITIONS

"jobseeker's allowance"—see reg.2(1).
"the Jobseeker's Allowance Regulations"—*ibid.*
"partner"—*ibid.*
"week"—*ibid.*

[1 State pension credit

2.170 **26B.**—(1) Except where [3 paragraph (2) or regulation 26BA] applies, state pension credit shall be payable on Mondays, but subject [2 to regulation 21 where payment is by direct credit transfer].

(2) State pension credit shall be payable—

[4 (a) on the same day as any—

(i) state pension under Part 1 of the Pensions Act 2014; or

(ii) retirement pension,

is payable to the claimant; or]

(b) on such other day of the week as the Secretary of State may, in the particular circumstances of the case, determine.

(3) [2 . . .]

(4) [3 Subject to regulation 26BA, state pension credit] paid [2 otherwise than in accordance with regulation 21] shall be paid weekly in advance.

(5) Where the amount of state pension credit payable is less than £1.00 per week, the Secretary of State may direct that it shall be paid at such intervals, not exceeding 13 weeks, as may be specified in the direction.

(6) [2 . . .]

(7) [2 . . .].]

AMENDMENTS

1. Inserted by State Pension Credit (Consequential, Transitional and Miscellaneous Provisions) Regulations 2002 (SI 2002/3019) reg.9 (April 7, 2003).

2. The Social Security (Miscellaneous Amendments) (No.2) Regulations 2006 (SI 2006/832) reg.2 (April 10, 2006).

3. The Social Security (Miscellaneous Amendments) (No.6) Regulations 2009 (SI 2009/3229) reg.2(6) (April 6, 2010.

4. The Pensions Act 2014 (Consequential, Supplementary and Incidental Amendments) Order 2015 (SI 2015/1985) art.9(13) (April 6, 2016).

[1 Intervals for payment of state pension credit

2.171 **26BA.**—(1) Where state pension credit is payable to a person who reaches pensionable age on or after 6th April 2010, other than a person to whom regulation 22C(7) applies, it shall be paid weekly, fortnightly or four weekly (as the Secretary of State may in any case determine) in arrears on the day of the week specified in paragraph (2).

(2) The day specified for the purposes of paragraph (1) is the day in column (2) which corresponds to the series of numbers in column

(1) which includes the last 2 digits of the person's national insurance number—

(1)	(2)
00 to 19	Monday
20 to 39	Tuesday
40 to 59	Wednesday
60 to 79	Thursday
80 to 99	Friday

(3) The Secretary of State may, in any particular case or class of case, arrange that state pension credit be paid on any other day of the week.

(4) Where the amount of state pension credit payable is less than £1.00 per week the Secretary of State may direct that it shall be paid in arrears at such intervals, not exceeding 13 weeks, as may be specified in the direction.]

AMENDMENT

1. Inserted by The Social Security (Miscellaneous Amendments) (No.6) Regulations 2009 (SI 2009/3229) reg.2(7) (April 6, 2010).

[1 Employment and support allowance

26C.—(1) Subject to paragraphs (3) to (7), employment and support allowance is to be paid fortnightly in arrears on the day of the week determined in accordance with paragraph (2). 2.172

(2) The day specified for the purposes of paragraph (1) is the day in column (2) which corresponds to the series of numbers in column (1) which includes the last 2 digits of the claimant's national insurance number—

(1)	(2)
00 to 19	Monday
20 to 39	Tuesday
40 to 59	Wednesday
60 to 79	Thursday
80 to 99	Friday

(3) The Secretary of State may, in any particular case or class of case, arrange that the claimant be paid otherwise than fortnightly.

(4) The Secretary of State may, in any particular case or class of case, arrange that employment and support allowance be paid on any day of the week and where it is in payment to any person and the day on which it is payable is changed, it must be paid at a daily rate of 1/7th of the weekly rate in respect of any of the days for which payment would have been made but for that change.

(5) Where the weekly amount of employment and support allowance is less than £1.00 it may be paid in arrears at intervals of not more than 13 weeks.

(6) Where the weekly amount of an employment and support allowance is less than 10 pence that allowance is not payable.

(7) The provisions of paragraph 2A of Schedule 7 (payment of income support at time of office closure) apply for the purposes of payment of employment and support allowance as they apply for the purposes of payment of income support.]

AMENDMENT

1. The Employment and Support Allowance (Consequential Provisions) (No.2) Regulations 2008 (SI 2008/1554) reg.21 (October 27, 2008).

GENERAL NOTE

2.173 Note that Pt 4 of Sch.2 to the Employment and Support Allowance (Transitional Provisions, Housing Benefit and Council Tax Benefit) (Existing Awards) (No.2) Regulations 2010 (SI 2010/1907) (as amended) contains modifications of reg.26C for the purposes of the transition to employment and support allowance.

[[1] [[2] Working families' tax credit and disabled persons' tax credit]]

2.174 **27.**—(1) Subject to regulation 21 [[3]and paragraph (1A)] [[2]working families' tax credit] and [[2]disabled persons' tax credit] shall be payable in respect of any benefit week on the Tuesday next following the end of that week by means of a book of serial orders [[3]or on presentation of an instrument for benefit payment] unless in any case the Secretary of State arranges [[4] Board arrange] otherwise.

[[5] (1A) Subject to paragraph (2), where an amount of [[2] working families' tax credit] and [[2] disabled persons' tax credit] becomes payable which is at a weekly rate of note more than £4.00, that amount shall, if the Secretary of State so directs [[4] Board so direct], be payable as soon as practicable by means of a single payment; except that if that amount represents an increase in the amount of either of those benefits which has previously been paid in respect of the same period, this paragraph shall apply only if that previous payment was made by means of a single payment.]

(2) Where the entitlement to [[2]working families' tax credit] and [[2] disabled persons' tax credit] is less than 50 pence a week that amount shall not be payable.]

AMENDMENTS

1. Reg.27 substituted by The Social Security (Claims and Payments) Amendment Regulations 1991 (SI 1991/2741) reg.14 (April 6, 1992).

2. The Tax Credits (Claims and Payments) (Amendment) Regulations 1999 (SI 1999/2752) regs 24 and 25 (October 5, 1999).

3. The Social Security (Claims and Payments) Amendment (No.3) Regulations 1993 (SI 1993/2113) reg.3(4) (October 25, 1993).

4. For tax credits purposes only, these words are substituted for the words "Secretary of State arranges" or "directs" (as the case may be): The Tax Credits (Claims and Payments) (Amendment) Regulations 1999 (SI 1999/2572) reg.12(a) (October 5, 1999).

5. The Social Security (Claims and Payments) Amendment (No.3) Regulations 1993 (SI 1993/2113) reg.3(4) (October 25, 1993).

Fractional amounts of benefit

2.175 [[1] **28.**—(1) Subject to paragraph (2),] where the amount of any benefit payable would, but for this regulation, include a fraction of a penny, that fraction shall be disregarded if it is less than half a penny and shall otherwise be treated as a penny.

[[1] (2) Where the amount of any maternity allowance payable would, but for this regulation, include a fraction of a penny, that fraction shall be treated as a penny.]

AMENDMENT

1. Social Security (Claims and Payments) Amendment (No.2) Regulations 2002 (SI 2002/1950) reg.2 (September 2, 2002).

DEFINITION

"benefit"—see reg.2(2).

[1 Payments to persons under age 18

29.—Where benefit is paid to a person under the age of 18 (whether on his own behalf or on behalf of another) [2 . . .] [2 a direct credit transfer under regulation 21 into any such person's account, or the receipt by him of a payment made by some other means] shall be sufficient discharge to the Secretary of State [3 or the Board].] 2.176

AMENDMENTS

1. The Social Security (Claims and Payments etc.) Amendment Regulations 1996 (SI 1996/672) reg.2(4) (April 4, 1996).
2. Social Security (Claims and Payments and Miscellaneous Amendments) (No.2) Regulations 2002 (SI 2002/2441) reg.6 (October 23, 2002).
3. The Tax Credits (Claims and Payments) (Amendment) Regulations 1999 (SI 1999/2572) reg.30 (October 5, 1999).

DEFINITION

"benefit"—see reg.2(2).

Payments on death

30.—(1) On the death of a person who has made a claim for benefit, the Secretary of State [1or the Board] may appoint such person as he [1or they] may think fit to proceed with the claim [15 and any related issue of revision, supersession or appeal]. 2.177

(2) Subject to [12 paragraphs (4) and (4A)], any sum payable by way of benefit which is payable under an award on a claim proceeded with under paragraph (1) may be paid or distributed by the Secretary of State to or amongst persons over the age of 16 claiming as personal representatives, legatees, next of kin, or creditors of the deceased (or, where the deceased was illegitimate, to or amongst other persons over the age of 16), and the provisions of regulation 38 (extinguishment of right) shall apply to any such payment or distribution; and—

(a) [13 a direct credit transfer under regulation 21 into any such person's account, or the receipt by him of a payment made by some other means,] shall be a good discharge to the Secretary of State [1or the Board] for any sum so paid; and
(b) where the Secretary of State is satisfied [1or the Board is satisfied] that any such sum or part thereof is needed for the benefit of any person under the age of 16, he [1or they] may obtain a good discharge therefor by paying the sum or part thereof to a person over that age who satisfies the Secretary of State [1or the Board] that he will apply the sum so paid for the benefit of the person under the age of 16.

(3) Subject to paragraph (2), any sum payable by way of benefit to the deceased, payment of which he had not obtained at the date of his death,

may, unless the right thereto was already extinguished at that date, be paid or distributed to or amongst such persons as are mentioned in paragraph (2), and regulation 38 shall apply to any such payment or distribution, except that, for the purpose of that regulation, the period of 12 months shall be calculated from the date on which the right to payment of any sum is treated as having arisen in relation to any such person and not from the date on which that right is treated as having arisen in relation to the deceased.

(4) [[19] Subject to paragraph (4B), paragraphs] (2) and (3) shall not apply in any case unless written application for the payment of any such sum is made to the Secretary of State [[1]or the Board] within 12 months from the date of the deceased's death or within such longer period as the Secretary of State [[1]or the Board] may allow in any particular case.

[[12] (4A) In a case where a joint-claim jobseeker's allowance has been awarded to a joint-claim couple and one member of the couple dies, the amount payable under that award shall be payable to the other member of that couple.]

[[19] (4B) A written application is not required where—

(a) an executor or administrator has not been appointed; [[21] and]

(b) the deceased was in receipt of a retirement pension [[20] , a state pension under Part 1 of the Pensions Act 2014] of any category or state pension credit including where any other benefit was combined for payment purposes with either of those benefits at the time of death.

[[21] . . .]

(5) [[16] Subject to paragraphs (5A) to [[20] (5H),] where the conditions specified in paragraph (6) are satisfied, a claim may be made on behalf of the deceased to any benefit other than [[2]jobseeker's allowance,] income support, [[14], state pension credit] [[3]working families' tax credit or disabled person's tax credit] or a social fund payment such as is mentioned in section 32(2)(a) [[4]and section 32(2A)] of the Social Security Act 1986 [[5], or reduced earnings allowance or disablement benefit], to which he would have been entitled if he had claimed it in the prescribed manner and within the prescribed time.

[[18] (5A) Subject to paragraphs (5B) to (5G), a claim may be made in accordance with paragraph (5) on behalf of the deceased for a Category A or Category B retirement pension or graduated retirement benefit provided that the deceased was not married or in a civil partnership on the date of his death.

(5B) But, subject to paragraphs (5C) to (5G), a claim may be made in accordance with paragraph (5) on behalf of the deceased for a Category A or Category B retirement pension or graduated retirement benefit where the deceased was a married woman or a civil partner on the date of death if the deceased's widower or surviving civil partner was under pensionable age on that date and due to attain pensionable age before 6th April 2010.

(5C) Where a claim is made for a shared additional pension [[20] or a state pension under Part 1 of the Pensions Act 2014] under paragraph (5) or for a retirement pension or graduated retirement benefit under paragraphs (5) and (5A) or (5B), in determining the benefit to which the deceased would have been entitled if he had claimed within the prescribed time, the prescribed time shall be the period of three months ending on the date of his death and beginning with any day on which, apart from satisfying the condition of making a claim, he would have been entitled to the pension or benefit.

(5D) Paragraph (5E) applies where, throughout the period of 12 months ending with the day before the death of the deceased person, his entitlement to a Category A or a Category B retirement pension, shared additional pension or graduated retirement benefit was deferred in accordance with, as the case may be—

(a) section 55 of the Contributions and Benefits Act (pension increase or lump sum where entitlement to retirement pension is deferred);

(b) section 55C of that Act (pension increase or lump sum where entitlement to shared additional pension is deferred); or

(c) section 36(4A) of the National Insurance Act 1965 (deferment of graduated retirement benefit).

(5E) Where a person claims under paragraph (5) or under paragraphs (5) and (5A) or (5B) the deceased shall be treated as having made an election in accordance with, as the case may be—

(a) paragraph A1(1)(a) of Schedule 5 to the Contributions and Benefits Act (electing to have an increase of pension), where paragraph (5D)(a) applies;

(b) paragraph 1(1)(a) of Schedule 5A to that Act (electing to have an increase of a shared additional pension) where paragraph (5D)(b) applies; or

(c) paragraph 12(1)(a) of Schedule 1 to the Social Security (Graduated Retirement Benefit) Regulations 2005 (electing to have an increase of benefit), where paragraph (5D)(c) applies.

(5F) [20 Paragraphs (5G) and (5H) apply]

(a) the deceased person was a widow, widower or surviving civil partner ("W") who was married to, or in a civil partnership with, the other party of the marriage or civil partnership ("S") when S died;

(b) throughout the period of 12 months ending with the day before S's death, S's entitlement to a Category A or a Category B retirement pension or graduated retirement benefit was deferred in accordance with, as the case may be, paragraph (5D)(a) or (c); and

(c) W made no statutory election [20 , or choice under section 8(2) of the Pensions Act 2014 or Regulations under section 10 of that Act which make provision corresponding or similar to section 8(2),] in consequence of the deferral.

(5G) Where a person claims under paragraphs (5) and (5A) the deceased [20 (referred to as W in paragraph (5F))] shall be treated as having made an election in accordance with, as the case may be—

(a) paragraph 3C(2)(a) of Schedule 5 to the Contributions and Benefits Act (electing to have an increase of pension), where paragraph (5D)(a) applies; or

(b) paragraph 17(2)(a) of Schedule 1 to the Social Security (Graduated Retirement Benefit) Regulations 2005 (electing to have an increase in benefit), where paragraph (5D)(c) applies.]

[20 (5H) Where a person makes a claim under paragraph (5) for a state pension under Part 1 of the Pensions Act 2014, the deceased (referred to as W in paragraph (5F)) shall be treated as having made a choice to be paid a state pension under—

(a) section 9 of the Pensions Act 2014 (survivor's pension based on inheritance of deferred old state pension) in accordance with section 8(2)(b) of that Act; or

(b) Regulations under section 10 of the Pensions Act 2014 which make provision corresponding or similar to section 9 of that Act in accordance with Regulations under section 10 which make provision corresponding or similar to section 8(2)(b).]

(6) [[6]Subject to the following provisions of this regulation,] the following conditions are specified for the purposes of paragraph (5)—

(a) Within six months of the death an application must have been made in writing to the Secretary of State for a person, whom the Secretary of State thinks fit to be appointed to make the claim, to be so appointed;

(b) a person must have been appointed by the Secretary of State to make the claim;

(c) there must have been no longer period than six months between the appointment and the making of the claim.

[[7](6A) Where the conditions specified in paragraph (6B) are satisfied, a person may make a claim for reduced earnings or disablement benefit, including any increase under [section 104 or 105 of the Social Security Contributions and Benefits Act 1992], in the name of a person who had died.

(6B) [[8]Subject to the following provisions of this regulation,] the conditions specified for the purposes of paragraph (6A) are—

(a) that the person who had died would have been entitled to the benefit claimed if he had made a claim for it in the prescribed manner and within the prescribed time;

(b) that within 6 months of a death certificate being issued in respect of the person who has died, the person making the claim has applied to the Secretary of State to be made an appointee of the person who has died

[[9](ba) that person has been appointed by the Secretary of State to make the claim]

(c) the claim is made within six months of the appointment.]

[[10](6C) Subject to paragraph (6D), where the Secretary of State certifies that to do so would be consistent with the proper administration of the Social Security Contributions and Benefits Act 1992 the period specified in paragraphs (6)(a) and (c) and (6B)(b) and (c) shall be extended to such period, not exceeding 6 months, as may be specified in the certificate.

(6D)(a) Where a certificate is given under paragraph (6C) extending the period specified in paragraph (6)(a) or (6B)(b), the period specified in paragraph (6)(c) or (6B)(c) shall be shortened by a period corresponding to the period specified in the certificate;

(b) no certificate shall be given under paragraph (6C) which would enable a claim to be made more than 12 months after the date of death (in a case falling within paragraph (6)) or the date of a death certificate being issued in respect of the person who has died (in a case falling within paragraph (6B)); and

(c) in the application of sub-paragraph (b) any period between the date when an application for a person to be appointed to make a claim is made and the date when that appointment is made shall be disregarded.]

(7) A claim made in accordance with paragraph (5) [[11]or paragraph (6A)] shall be treated, for the purposes of these regulations, as if made by the deceased on the date of his death.

(8) The Secretary of State [[1]or the Board] may dispense with strict proof of the title of any person claiming in accordance with the provisions of this regulation.

(9) In paragraph (2) "next of kin" means—

(a) in England and Wales, the persons who would take beneficially on an intestacy; and

(b) in Scotland, the persons entitled to the moveable estate of the deceased on intestacy.

AMENDMENTS

1. The Tax Credits (Claims and Payments) (Amendment) Regulations 1999 (SI 1999/2572) regs 13, 20 and 22 (October 5, 1999).

2. The Social Security (Claims and Payments) (Jobseeker's Allowance Consequential Amendments) Regulations 1996 (SI 1996/1460) reg.2(15) (October 7, 1996).

3. The Tax Credits (Claims and Payments) (Amendments) Regulations 1999 (SI 1999/2572) regs 24 and 25 (October 5, 1999).

4. The Social Security (Claims and Payments) Amendment Regulations 1991 (SI 1991/2741) reg.15 (March 10, 1992).

5. The Social Security (Common Provisions) Miscellaneous Amendments Regulations 1988 (SI 1988/1725) reg.3(6) (November 7, 1988).

6. The Social Security (Claims and Payments) Amendment (No.3) Regulations 1993 (SI 1993/2113) reg.3(5)(a) (September 27, 1993).

7. Paragraphs (6A) and (6B) inserted by The Social Security (Miscellaneous Provisions) Amendment Regulations 1990 (SI 1990/2208) reg.11(3) (December 5, 1990).

8. The Social Security (Claims and Payments) Amendment (No.3) Regulations 1993 (SI 1993/2113) reg.3(5)(a) (September 29, 1993).

9. The Social Security (Claims and Payments) Amendment Regulations 1994 (SI 1994/2319) reg.5 (October 3, 1994).

10. Paragraphs (6C) and (6D) inserted by The Social Security (Claims and Payments) Amendment (No.3) Regulations 1993 (SI 1993/2113) reg.3(5)(b) (September 27, 1993).

11. The Social Security (Miscellaneous Provisions) Amendment Regulations 1990 (SI 1990/2208) reg.11(4) (December 5, 1990).

12. The Social Security (Joint Claims: Consequential Amendments) Regulations 2000 (SI 2000/1982) reg.2(7) (March 19, 2001).

13. Social Security (Claims and Payments and Miscellaneous Amendments) (No.2) Regulations 2002 (SI 2002/2441) reg.7 (October 23, 2002).

14. State Pension Credit (Consequential, Transitional and Miscellaneous Provisions) Regulations 2002 (SI 2002/3019) reg.10 (April 7, 2003).

15. The Social Security, Child Support and Tax Credits (Miscellaneous Amendments) Regulations 2005 (SI 2005/337) reg.7 (March 18, 2005).

16. The Social Security (Claims and Payments) Amendment Regulations 2005 (SI 2005/455) reg.4 (April 6, 2006).

17. The Social Security (Shared Additional Pension) (Miscellaneous Amendments) Regulations 2005 (SI 2005/1551) reg.3 (April 6, 2006).

18. The Social Security (Retirement Pensions and Graduated Retirement Benefit) (Widowers and Civil Partnership) Regulations 2005 (SI 2005/3078) reg.4 (April 6, 2006).

19. The Social Security (Miscellaneous Amendments) (No.4) Regulations 2007 (SI 2007/2470) (September 24, 2007).

20. The Pensions Act 2014 (Consequential, Supplementary and Incidental Amendments) Order 2015 (SI 2015/1985) art.9(14) (April 6, 2016).

21. The Social Fund and Social Security (Claims and Payments) (Amendment) Regulations 2020 (SI 2020/600) reg.4 (July 9, 2020).

GENERAL NOTE

2.178 Note the decisions referred to in the annotations to reg.33.

It would seem that the power of appointment in reg.30(1) on the death of the claimant is a separate appointment from that under reg.33. It would follow that where a claimant has an appointee under reg.33 and dies, there should at least be confirmation of continuation of the appointment under reg.33 to enable the appointee to act under reg.30. The better course, since there are specific requirements in the regulation, would be for a separate appointment to be made.

In *CIS/1423/1997* the Commissioner holds, at para.21 of his decision, that the plain words of reg.30 do not allow the Secretary of State to appoint a person to represent the claimant or their estate in the context of a decision for the recoverability of an overpayment from the claimant's estate.

Note that paras (4)–(7) contain a special power of appointment to enable *a claim* to be made after a person's death.

R(IS)3/04 discusses aspects of reg.30 at paras 14–17 of the decision. The Commissioner notes that reg.30(5) is the only provision permitting claims to be made in respect of deceased persons, and reg.30(5) expressly does not apply to income support.

Death of claimant pending appeal to the Commissioner

2.179 It sometimes happens that the claimant dies while the appeal is pending before the Commissioner. In such cases the surviving partner may not wish to take on an appointment enabling the matter to continue, and there may be no personal representatives because there is no estate. The result is that, where there is a claimant's appeal, there is no one who can withdraw the appeal. In such circumstances, the practice of the Commissioners is to treat the appeal as abated: see *R(S)7/56*, *R(I)2/83* and *R(SB)25/84*. For all practical purposes the matter is then closed, though the possibility remains that the matter could be revived on application. This could happen if, for example, the Secretary of State chose to appoint someone to act for the deceased claimant. The most likely appointee would be the Official Solicitor, but is difficult to imagine circumstances in which it would be appropriate to take such action. In overpayment cases, care should be taken to ensure that the Benefits Agency has given an assurance that it will not seek recovery from the estate before treating an appeal as abated, since abatement of a claimant's appeal without such an assurance would not preclude recovery against the estate.

The use of the abatement procedure is not appropriate where the appellant is the adjudication officer. In such cases, the proper course of action is for the adjudication officer to withdraw the appeal: *R(I)2/83*, at para.6.

In *CIS/1340/1999* the Commissioner was considering an appeal involving a substantial overpayment of benefit in which the claimant had died since filing the appeal. No executors or administrators were appointed, and the claimant's husband did not respond to an invitation by the Department to consider applying to be the claimant's appointee. The Commissioner comments on the reference in these annotations that care should be taken to obtain an assurance that the Benefits Agency will not seek to recover the overpayment from the estate before treating the appeal as abated. He states that he does not consider that proposition to flow from the cases, and that *R(I)2/83* is merely authority for the proposition that, where such an assurance is available in an overpayment case, it may be appropriate to dismiss the appeal rather than merely declare it abated. At para.20, he says,

> "But I see no reason why, before declaring the appeal abated or indeed striking it out, I should require an assurance to be sought from the Secretary of State that

recovery of the overpayment will not be pursued. So long as the original decision of the adjudication officer stands the Secretary of State should be entitled to recover the overpayment. If he does so and there is anyone who has an interest in ensuring that it is not recovered, that person will be able to take steps to have the appeal reinstated."

The appeal was declared abated.

[1 Payment of arrears of joint-claim jobseeker's allowance where the nominated person can no longer be traced

30A. Where— 2.180

(a) an award of joint-claim jobseeker's allowance has been awarded to a joint-claim couple;
(b) that couple ceases to be a joint-claim couple; and
(c) the member of the joint-claim couple nominated for the purposes of section 3B of the Jobseekers Act cannot be traced,

arrears on the award of joint-claim jobseeker's allowance shall be paid to the other member of the former joint-claim couple.]

AMENDMENT

1. The Social Security Amendment (Joint Claims) Regulations 2001 (SI 2001/518) reg.5 (March 19, 2001).

Time and manner of payments of industrial injuries gratuities

31.—(1) This regulation applies to any gratuity payable under [Part V of the Social Security Contributions and Benefits Act 1992]. 2.181

[2 (1A) In the case of a person who made a claim for benefit in accordance with regulation 4A(1), a change of circumstances may be notified to a relevant authority at any office to which the claim for benefit could be made in accordance with that provision.]

(2) Subject to the following provisions of this regulation, every gratuity shall be payable in one sum.

(3) A gratuity may be payable by instalments of such amounts and at such times as appear reasonable in the circumstances of the case to the adjudicating authority awarding the gratuity if—

(a) the beneficiary to whom the gratuity has been awarded is, at the date of the award, under the age of 18 years, or
(b) in any other case, the amount of the gratuity so awarded (not being a gratuity payable to the widow of a deceased person on her remarriage) exceeds £52 and the beneficiary requests that payments should be made by instalments.

(4) An appeal shall not be brought against any decision that a gratuity should be payable by instalments or as to the amounts of any such instalments or the time of payment.

(5) Subject to the provisions of regulation 37 (suspension), a gratuity shall—

(a) if it is payable by equal weekly instalments, be paid in accordance with the provisions of regulation 22 insofar as they are applicable; or
(b) in any case, be paid by such means as may appear to the Secretary of State to be appropriate in the circumstances.

AMENDMENTS

1. The Social Security Act 1998 (Commencement No.12 and Consequential and Transitional Provisions) Order 1999 (SI 1999/3178) Sch.6 (November 29, 1999).

2. The Social Security (Claims and Information) Regulations 1999 (SI 1999/3108) (November 29, 1999).

[5 Information to be given and changes to be notified

2.182 **32.**—(1) Except in the case of a jobseeker's allowance, every beneficiary and every person by whom or on whose behalf, sums by way of benefit are receivable shall furnish in such manner [12 . . .] as the Secretary of State may determine [12 and within the period applicable under regulation 17(4) of the Decisions and Appeals Regulations] such information or evidence as the Secretary of State may require for determining whether a decision on the award of benefit should be revised under section 9 of the Social Security Act 1998 or superseded under section 10 of that Act.

(1A) Every beneficiary and every person by whom, or on whose behalf, sums by way of benefit are receivable shall furnish in such manner and at such times as the Secretary of State may determine such information or evidence as the Secretary of State may require in connection with payment of the benefit claimed or awarded.

(1B) Except in the case of a jobseeker's allowance, every beneficiary and every person by whom or on whose behalf sums by way of benefit are receivable shall notify the Secretary of State of any change of circumstances which he might reasonably be expected to know might affect—

(a) the continuance of entitlement to benefit; or

(b) the payment of benefit

as soon as reasonably practicable after the change occurs by giving notice [8 of the change to the appropriate office—

(i) in writing or by telephone (unless the Secretary of State determines in any particular case that notice must be in writing or may be given otherwise than in writing or by telephone; or

(ii) in writing if in any class of case he requires written notice (unless he determines in any particular case to accept notice given otherwise than in writing)]]

[7 (1C) In the case of a person who made a claim for benefit in accordance with regulation 4A(1), a change of circumstances may be notified to a relevant authority at any office to which the claim for benefit could be made in accordance with that provision.]

(2) Where any sum is receivable on account of an increase of benefit in respect of an adult dependant, the Secretary of State may require the beneficiary to furnish a declaration signed by such dependant confirming the particulars respecting him, which have been given by the claimant.

[2(3) In the case of a person who is claiming income support, state pension credit . . . [11, a jobseekers allowance or an employment and support allowance], where that person or any partner is aged not less than 60 and is a member of, or a person deriving entitlement to a pension under, a personal pension scheme, or is a party to, or a person deriving entitlement to a pension under, a retirement annuity contract, he shall where the Secretary of State so requires furnish the following information—

(a) the name and address of the pension fund holder;
(b) such other information including any reference or policy number as is needed to enable the personal pension scheme or retirement annuity contract to be identified.

(4) Where the pension fund holder receives from the Secretary of State a request for details concerning a personal pension scheme or retirement annuity contract relating to a person or any partner to whom paragraph (3) refers, the pension fund holder shall provide the Secretary of State with any information to which paragraph (5) refers.

(5) The information to which this paragraph refers is—
(a) where the purchase of an annuity under a personal pension scheme has been deferred, the amount of any income which is being withdrawn from the personal pension scheme;
(b) in the case of—
(i) a personal pension scheme where income withdrawal is available, the [13 rate of annuity which may have been purchased with the funds held under the scheme]; or
(ii) a personal pension scheme where income withdrawal is not available, or a retirement annuity contract, the [13 rate of annuity which might have been purchased with the fund] if the fund were held under a personal pension scheme where income withdrawal was available,

calculated by or on behalf of the pension fund holder by means of tables prepared from time to time by the Government Actuary which are appropriate for this purpose.]

[6 (6) This regulation shall apply in the case of state pension credit subject to the following modifications—
(a) [10 in connection with the setting of a new assessed income period], the information and evidence [10 which the Secretary of State may require] to be notified in accordance with this regulation includes information and evidence as to the likelihood of future changes in the claimant's circumstances needed to determine—
(i) whether a period should be specified as an assessed income period under section 6 of the 2002 Act in relation to any decision; and
(ii) if so, the length of the period to be so specified; and

[9 (b) except to the extent that sub-paragraph (a) applies, changes to an element of the claimant's retirement provision need not be notified if—
(i) an assessed income period is current in his case; [12 or]
[12 (ii) the period applicable under regulation 17(4) of the Decisions and Appeals Regulations has not expired;

. . .

(7) In this regulation, "the Decisions and Appeals Regulations" means the Social Security and Child Support (Decisions and Appeals) Regulations 1999.]

AMENDMENTS

1. The Social Security (Miscellaneous Provisions) Amendment (No.2) Regulations 1992 (SI 1992/2595) reg.4 (November 16, 1992).

2. Income-related benefit Schemes and Social Security (Claims and Payments) (Miscellaneous Amendments) Regulations 1995 (SI 1995/2303) reg.10(4) (October 2, 1995).

3. The Social Security (Claims and Payments) (Jobseeker's Allowance Consequential Amendments) Regulations 1996 (SI 1996/1460) reg.2(16) (October 7, 1996).
4. The Tax Credits (Claims and Payments) (Amendment) Regulations 1999 (SI 1999/2572) reg.14 (October 5, 1999).
5. The Social Security and Child Support (Miscellaneous Amendments) Regulations 2003 (SI 2003/1050) reg.2 (May 5, 2003).
6. State Pension Credit (Consequential, Transitional and Miscellaneous Provisions) Regulations 2002 (SI 2002/3019) reg.11 (April 7, 2003).
7. The Social Security (Claims and Payments and Miscellaneous Amendments) Regulations 2003 (SI 2003/1632) reg.2 (July 21, 2003).
8. The Social Security (Notification of Change of Circumstances) Regulations 2003, SI 2003/3209 reg.2 (January 6, 2004).
9. The State Pension Credit (Transitional and Miscellaneous Provisions) Amendment Regulations 2003 (SI 2003/2274) (October 6, 2003).
10. The Social Security (Students and Miscellaneous Amendments) Regulations 2008 (SI 2008/1599) reg.3 (August 25, 2008).
11. The Employment and Support Allowance (Consequential provisions) (No.2) Regulations 2008 (SI 2008/1554) reg.22 (October 27, 2008).
12. The Social Security (Suspension of Payment of Benefits and Miscellaneous Amendments) Regulations 2012 (SI 2012/824) (April 17, 2012).
13. Social Security (Miscellaneous Amendments No.4) Regulations 2017 (SI 2017/1015) reg.5(3) (November 16, 2017).

DEFINITIONS

"appropriate office"—see reg.2(1).
"beneficiary"—see SSCBA s.122.
"benefit"—see reg.2(2).
"jobseeker's allowance"—see reg.2(1).
"pension fund holder"—*ibid.*
"personal pension scheme"—*ibid.*
"retirement annuity contract"—*ibid.*

GENERAL NOTE

2.183 A Tribunal of Commissioners in *CIS/4348/2003* (subsequently upheld by the Court of Appeal in *B v SSWP* [2005] EWCA Civ 929) ruled that the duty to disclose under s.71 of the Administration Act flowed from the provisions of reg.32. Note that the duty applies to beneficiaries and "every person by whom or on whose behalf, sums by way of benefit are receivable". The latter group includes appointees under reg.33. In *IL v SSWP (JSA)* [2019] UKUT 200 (AAC), Judge Hemingway followed CPC/196/2012 in holding that because of the definition of "beneficiary", the duty to disclose could not apply at the stage of filling in the claim form and recovery would have to be based on misrepresentation.

The Tribunal of Commissioners draws a clear distinction between the two duties set out in reg.32. There is a duty in regs 32(1) and (1A) to notify the Secretary of State or Board of Inland Revenue of any matter where the Secretary of State or the Board has given unambiguous directions for the disclosure of the matter. There is no question of deciding in such cases whether disclosure was reasonably to be expected to the claimant. Any failure to disclose such information will render any overpayment of benefit resulting from the failure to disclose recoverable.

By contrast the duty in reg.32(1B) is to notify changes of circumstances which a benefit recipient might reasonably be expected to know might affect the continuance of entitlement to benefit or the payment of benefit. In *DG v SSWP* [2009] UKUT 120 (AAC), Judge Lane suggests that the logic of *R(IS) 9/06* (a case under what is now reg.32(1A)) in excluding any room for consideration of whether disclosure was reasonably to be expected applies equally to cases under reg.32(1B). To hold otherwise, she suggests, "would, in effect, impose a double hurdle on the Secretary of State, who would first have to establish what the claimant might reasonably be expected to know might affect his benefit, and then whether he could reasonably be expected to make disclosure."

While the two may on occasion overlap, they will not always do so.

The distinction may be easier to make in theory than in practice, but, given the different consequences of failure to disclose under the two separate duties, it will be necessary to consider very carefully the source of any obligation to provide the Secretary of State or Her Majesty's Revenue and Customs with information and the specificity of that information. So, a requirement to disclose that children are no longer living with the claimant but had been taken into care (as was the case in *CIS/4348/2003*) which is clearly set out in documentation given to the claimant, will give rise to the duty to disclose under the first duty. Arguments about the claimant's capacity are not relevant. By contrast, failure to disclose some unspecified set of circumstances which might affect benefit entitlement will fall under the second duty.

In *CDLA/2328/2006* the Commissioner said:

"... There is nothing wrong in a tribunal relying on one paragraph rather than the other. The duties under paragraphs (1A) and (1B) are cumulative. The tribunal was entitled to rely on either duty. A finding that a claimant was in breach of paragraph (1B) is not rendered wrong in law just because the claimant was also in breach of paragraph (1A). What the tribunal must do is to rely on one or the other and make clear which." (See para.20.)

In interpreting the duty under paragraph (1A), the Commissioner stresses the distinction between information gathering and decision making. The claimant is required to report facts which might show that entitlement is affected. It is then for the decision maker to decide whether to investigate further, if necessary, and to make a decision on whether entitlement is in fact affected by the change in circumstances. The Commissioner says:

"23. The interpretation of the duties must reflect their nature and purpose. So the duty to report 'if things get easier for you' is not a duty to report 'if you believe that you are no longer virtually unable to walk'. Nor does this duty necessarily require a comparison between the claimant's abilities and disabilities at the time of the original award and those current at the time when the Secretary of State says a change should have been reported. That comparison does not arise until the later decision-making stage. The notes deal only with the earlier information-gathering stage. It is important not to confuse the issue whether the claimant failed to report a change of circumstances (an information-gathering question) and the issue whether that change was material to his entitlement (a decision-making question).
24. The duty does not set the focus of comparison on the time of the original award. If it did, it would become increasingly burdensome as time passes. In this case it would require the claimant to remember precisely how disabled he had been 18 years previously. The duty, like all the duties, is continuously speaking. It is to report if at any time things are easier for the claimant. That means easier by reference to the preceding period. Obviously that has to be applied in a reasonable time frame. It would not be necessary to report if a claimant were feeling a bit better today than yesterday. The test has to be applied over a period that is sufficient to show overall a sustained improvement or deterioration, taking account of any usual variation. This is not precise, but that is because it is a matter of judgment for each case."

On the interpretation of para.(1B) the Commissioner says:

"28. ... If the Secretary of State has issued an instruction to the claimant or to claimants generally, that will found a duty under paragraph (1A) and there should be no need to rely on paragraph (1B). There may be circumstances in which the Secretary of State could not rely on paragraph (1A) and could only rely on the instructions under paragraph (1B), but I have not been able to imagine one. But, assuming that this is possible, I accept that the notes issued by the Secretary of State are relevant under paragraph (1B). The instructions they contain may inform what is reasonable to expect a claimant to know. It would usually be reasonable for a claimant to know the contents of those instructions. (I do not exclude the possibility that it may not be reasonable for the claimant to know everything that is in the Secretary of State's notes. For example, this may, perhaps, not be reasonable on account of the claimant's mental state.) And the notes may be so comprehensive that, in a particular case, there is no need to consider anything else. But the duty under paragraph (1B) is defined by the terms of that paragraph. The instructions given to claimants do not define that duty. They are merely evidence of what it was reasonable to expect the claimant to know. And the duty to report may be wider than any instructions given by the Secretary of State. For example, it may be reasonable for the claimant to realise from questions in a claim pack that a particular matter is relevant to entitlement, even if the notes issued by the Secretary of State do not specifically refer to them.

29. For completeness, I will mention that the focus under paragraph (1B) is different from that under paragraph (1A). There the duty refers to entitlement, but only whether the claimant might reasonably be expected to know a change of circumstances *might* affect entitlement. It is not necessary for the claimant to understand the actual impact that a change will have, but the focus is different from that appropriate to the duty imposed under paragraph (1A). A comparison with his disablement at the time of the award may be justified. But it is also possible to envisage cases in which a claimant ought reasonably to realise that a change of circumstances might affect entitlement without undertaking a comparison with the time of the award. For example, a claimant's mobility may improve to such an extent that no reasonable person would consider that the claimant was virtually unable to walk."

In *GJ v SSWP (IS)* [2010] UKUT 107 (AAC), the Judge rules (at [18]–[21]) that reg.32 does not require a claimant to notify the local office with information which the local office handling the claim has provided. This would be pointless and such a requirement would not be lawful in regulations made under s.5 of the Administration Act. For consideration of the notion of "disclosing" what the Department already knows, see the discussion of *LH v SSWP (RP)* [2017] UKUT 249 (AAC) at 1.108.

Note that there is no general requirement that the form of disclosure must be in writing, though any disclosure will often be reduced to writing and signed by the claimant.

2.184 In *CSDLA/1282/2001* the Deputy Commissioner held that, where there was no appointment by the Secretary of State under reg.33, but there was a Power of Attorney, then benefit was not receivable by the person holding the Power of Attorney, and accordingly that person was under no duty to provide information under reg.32.

Note that Pt 3 of Sch.1 and Pt 4 of Sch.2 to the Employment and Support Allowance (Transitional Provisions, Housing Benefit and Council Tax Benefit) (Existing Awards) (No.2) Regulations 2010 (SI 2010/1907) (as amended) contains modifications of reg.32 for the purposes of the transition to employment and support allowance.

[1 Alternative means of notifying changes of circumstances

2.185 **32ZZA.—**(1) In such cases and subject to such conditions as the Secretary of State may specify, the duty in regulation 32(1B) to notify a change of circumstances may be discharged by notifying the Secretary of State as soon as reasonably practicable—

(a) where the change of circumstances is a birth or death, through a relevant authority, or a county council in England, by personal attendance at an office specified by that authority or county council, provided the Secretary of State has agreed with that authority or county council for it to facilitate such notification; or

(b) where the change of circumstances is a death, by telephone to a telephone number specified for that purpose by the Secretary of State.

(2) In this regulation "relevant authority" has the same meaning as in the Housing Benefit Regulations 2006. [3 . . .]]

AMENDMENTS

1. Inserted by The Social Security (Notification of Changes of Circumstances) Regulations 2010 (SI 2010/444) reg.2 (April 5, 2010).
2. The Council Tax Benefit Abolition (Consequential Provision) Regulations 2013 (SI 2013/458) reg.3 (April 1, 2013).

[1 Information given electronically

32ZA.—(1) Where this regulation applies a person may give any certificate, notice, information or evidence required to be given and in particular may give notice or any change of circumstances required to be notified under regulation 32 by means of an electronic communication, in accordance with the provisions set out in Schedule 9ZC. **2.186**

[2 (2) This regulation applies in relation to an award of—

(a) attendance allowance;
[6 (aa) bereavement support payment;]
(b) carer's allowance;
(c) disability living allowance;
(d) an employment and support allowance;
[3 (da) incapacity benefit;]
(e) income support;
(f) a jobseeker's allowance];
[3 (g) retirement pension;
(h) state pension credit;]
[4 (i) state pension under Part 1 of the Pensions Act 2014;]
[5 (j) industrial injuries benefit;]
[7(k) a social fund funeral payment.]
[8 (l) a social fund payment in respect of maternity expenses;
(m) maternity allowance.]

AMENDMENTS

1. The Social Security (Electronic Communications) (Carer's Allowance) Order 2003 SI 2003/2800 reg.2 (December 1, 2003).
2. The Social Security (Electronic Communications) Order 2011 (SI 2011/1498) reg.4(3) (June 20, 2011).
3. The Social Security (Electronic Communications) (No.2) Order 2011 (SI 2011/2943) (January 23, 2012).
4. The Pensions Act 2014 (Consequential, Supplementary and Incidental Amendments) Order 2015 (SI 2015/1985) art.9(15) (April 6, 2016).
5. Social Security (Claims and Payments) Amendment Regulations 2016 (SI 2016/544) reg.2 (June 15, 2016).
6. The Pensions Act 2014 (Consequential, Supplementary and Incidental Amendments) Order 2017 (SI 2017/422) art.10 (April 6, 2017).

7. The Social Fund Funeral Expenses Amendment Regulations 2018 (SI 2018/61) reg.2 (April 2, 2018).
8. The Social Fund and Social Security (Claims and Payments) (Amendment) Regulations 2020 (SI 2020/600) reg.4 (July 9, 2020).

Information given electronically

2.187 **32A.**—*Repealed subject to transitional provisions by the Child Benefit and Guardian's Allowance (Administration) Regulations 2003 (SI 2003/492) Sch.3(1) para.1 (April 7, 2003).*

[1 Information relating to awards of benefit

2.188 **32B.** —(1) Where an authority or person to whom paragraph (2) applies has arranged with the Secretary of State for the authority or person to receive claims for a specified benefit or obtain information or evidence relating to claims for a specified benefit in accordance with regulation 4 or 4D, the authority or person may—

(a) receive information or evidence which relates to an award of that benefit and which is supplied by—
  (i) the person to whom the award has been made; or
  (ii) other persons in connection with the award,
  and shall forward it to the Secretary of State as soon as reasonably practicable;
(b) verify any information or evidence supplied; and
(c) record the information or evidence supplied and hold it (whether as supplied or recorded) for the purpose of forwarding it to the Secretary of State.

(2) This paragraph applies to—
(a) a local authority administering housing benefit [3 . . .];
(b) a county council in England;
(c) a person providing services to a person mentioned in sub-paragraph (a) or (b);
(d) a person authorised to exercise any function of a local authority relating to housing benefit [3 . . .];
(e) a person authorised to exercise any function a county council in England has under section 7A of the Social Security Administration Act 1992.

(3) In paragraph (1), "specified benefit" means one or more of the following benefits—
(a) attendance allowance;
(b) [5 . . .]
(c) [5 . . .]
(d) carer's allowance;
(e) disability living allowance;
[1 (ee) employment and support allowance;]
(f) incapacity benefit;
(g) income support;
(h) jobseeker's allowance;
(i) retirement pension;
(j) state pension credit;
(k) widowed parent's allowance;
(l) winter fuel payment.]
[4 (m) state pension under Part 1 of the Pensions Act 2014.]

AMENDMENTS

1. The Social Security (Claims and Information) Regulations 2007 (SI 2007/2911) (October 31, 2007).

2. The Social Security (Miscellaneous Amendments) (No.2) Regulations 2009 (SI 2009/1490) reg.2 (July 13, 2009).

3. The Council Tax Benefit Abolition (Consequential Provision) Regulations 2013 (SI 2013/458) reg.3 (April 1, 2013).

4. The Pensions Act 2014 (Consequential, Supplementary and Incidental Amendments) Order 2015 (SI 2015/1985) art.9(16) (April 6, 2016).

5. The Pensions Act 2014 (Consequential, Supplementary and Incidental Amendments) Order 2017 (SI 2017/422) art.10 (April 6, 2017).

PART IV

THIRD PARTIES

Persons unable to act

33.—(1) Where— 2.189

(a) a person is, or is alleged to be, entitled to benefit, whether or not a claim for benefit has been made by him or on his behalf; and

(b) that person is unable for the time being to act; and either

(c) no [6 deputy] has been appointed by the Court of Protection [6 under Part 1 of the Mental Capacity Act 2005 or receiver appointed under Part 7 of the Mental Health Act 1983 but treated as a deputy by virtue of the Mental Capacity Act 2005] with power to claim, or as the case may be, receive benefit on his behalf; or

(d) in Scotland, his estate is not being administered by [4 a judicial factor or any guardian acting or appointed under the Adults with Incapacity (Scotland) Act 2004 who has power to claim or, as the case may be, receive benefit on his behalf],

the Secretary of State [2 or the Board] may, upon written application made to him by a person who, if a natural person, is over the age of 18, appoint that person to exercise, on behalf of the person who is unable to act, any right to which that person may be entitled and to receive and deal on his behalf with any sums payable to him.

[7 (1A) Where a person has been appointed under regulation 82(3) of the Housing Benefit Regulations 2006 or regulation 63(3) of the Housing Benefit (Persons who have attained the qualifying age for state pension credit) Regulations 2006 by a relevant authority within the meaning of those Regulations to act on behalf of another in relation to a benefit claim or award, the Secretary of State may, if the person agrees, treat him as if he had appointed him under paragraph (1).]

[8 (1B) Where a natural person over the age of 18 has been appointed by the Scottish Ministers under a qualifying appointment pursuant to the 2018 Scotland Act in connection with the determination of assistance under section 24 of that Act (whether or not including an appointment to receive assistance on behalf of the individual), the Secretary of State may, if the person agrees, treat that person as if she had appointed them under paragraph (1).

(1C) In paragraph (1B), a qualifying appointment means—

(a) an appointment made under section 58(1) of the 2018 Scotland Act in a case where section 58(4) of that Act applies, or

(b) an appointment made under section 85B(1)(4) of the 2018 Scotland Act in a case where section 85B(7) of that Act applies.]

(2) Where the Secretary of State has made [2 or the Board have made] an appointment [4, or treated an appointment as made,] under paragraph (1)—

(a) he [2 or they] may at any time revoke it;

(b) the person appointed may resign his office after having given one month's notice in writing to the Secretary of State [2 or the Board] of his intention to do so;

(c) any such appointment shall terminate when the Secretary of State is notified [2 or the Board are notified] that a receiver or other person to whom paragraph (1)(c) or (d) applies has been appointed.

(3) Anything required by these regulations to be done by or to any person who is for the time being unable to act may be done by or to the receiver, [4 judicial factor or] guardian, if any, or by or to the person appointed under this regulation or regulation 43 [1(disability living allowance for a child)] and [3 . . .] [3 a direct credit transfer under regulation 21 into the account of any person so appointed, or the receipt by him of a payment made by some other means] shall be a good discharge to the Secretary of State [2 or the Board] for any sum paid.

AMENDMENTS

1. The Social Security (Claims and Payments) Amendment Regulations 1991 (SI 1991/2741) reg.16 (February 3, 1992).

2. The Tax Credits (Claims and Payments) (Amendment) Regulations 1999 (SI 1999/2572) regs 15, 20, 22 and 23 (October 5, 1999).

3. Social Security (Claims and Payments and Miscellaneous Amendments) (No.2) Regulations 2002 (SI 2002/2441) reg.8 (October 23, 2002).

4. The Social Security, Child Support and Tax Credits (Miscellaneous Amendments) Regulations 2005 (SI 2005/337) reg.7 (March 18, 2005).

5. The Housing Benefit and Council Tax Benefit (Consequential Provisions) Regulations 2006 (SI 2006/217) Sch.2 para.2 (March 6, 2006).

6. The Social Security (Miscellaneous Amendments) (No.4) Regulations 2007 (SI 2007/2470) (September 24, 2007).

7. The Council Tax Benefit Abolition (Consequential Provision) Regulations 2013 (SI 2013/458) reg.4 (April 1, 2013).

8. The Scotland Act 2016 (Social Security) (Consequential Provision) (Miscellaneous Amendment) Regulations 2021 (SI 2021/804).

DEFINITIONS

"benefit"—see reg.2(2).
"claim for benefit"—see reg.2(1).

GENERAL NOTE

2.190 Appointment under the powers contained in reg.33 should be carefully distinguished from situations in which a person is appointed under a private arrangement as an adviser to a claimant: see *Tkachuk v Secretary of State for Work and Pensions*, reported as *R(IS) 3/07*, and *VB v SSWP* [2008] UKUT 15 (AAC).

Even if no appointment has been made, a claim made by a person unable to act, or by an "unauthorised person" on their behalf, is still valid (*CIS/812/1992*, applying para.8

of *R(SB) 9/84* where a Tribunal of Commissioners holds that in the absence of any challenge at the time the Secretary of State must be deemed to have accepted that the claim was made in sufficient manner). In *Walsh v CAO* (Consent Order, January 19, 1995) the Court of Appeal also applied *R(SB)9/84* when setting aside *CIS/638/1991* in which the Commissioner had held that a claim made on behalf of a person unable to act by a person who had not been formally appointed was a nullity.

Note that any subsequent appointment has retrospective effect (*R(SB)5/90*).

In *CIS/642/1994* the claimant's husband was her appointee under reg.33. She died before the tribunal hearing. The Commissioner holds that the tribunal decision was a nullity because there had been no appointment under reg.30 (deceased persons). Appointments under reg.30 were a distinct and different form of appointment from reg.33 appointments. He dissents from para.8 of *R(SB)9/84* and repeats his view (see *CIS/638/1991*) that it is open to adjudication officers and tribunals (and Commissioners) to determine that a claim is a nullity in cases where a person is unable to act and there has been no valid appointment. This is out of step with the current weight of authority. **2.191**

CIS/812/1992 also confirms that, in relation to the pre-April 1997 form of the rules for backdating claims, if there has been no appointment it is only necessary to decide whether the claimant has good cause for a late claim; it is not necessary to consider the reasonableness of the failure to claim of a person who has been acting informally on his behalf. The Commissioner declines to follow paras 12 and 13 of *R(IS)5/91* since this could not be reconciled with paras 9 and 10 of *R(SB)9/84* (which was a Tribunal of Commissioners' decision). See also *CSB/168/1993* which takes a similar view and contains a useful summary of the authorities on this issue.

Under the current form of reg.19(5) the test is also of the claimant's personal circumstances, if there is no appointee, but those circumstances sometimes expressly include whether there is anyone who could help the claimant.

The Secretary of State's normal practice in making appointments is not to make an appointment generally but to limit it to a specific benefit: see *R(IS)5/91*. *R(IS)5/91* concerned the effect of an appointment for supplementary benefit purposes on a subsequent income support claim following the 1988 changes. There is some doubt whether such a limited appointment has survived the changes brought about then. There is now a single regulation governing appointments, and some argue that, at a consequence appointments are for all benefits. Tribunals do, however, continue to see appointments limited to certain benefits. The message is that the scope of the appointment needs to be considered in every case where it is relevant, though in the absence of any limiting conditions, there is a strong case for considering that it applies to all benefits. **2.192**

Where a claimant has died, the Secretary of State may appoint a person to act: *R(SB)8/88*. Unless the Secretary of State does so, the tribunal has no jurisdiction to proceed in the absence of action by a personal representative under a grant of probate or letters of administration.

In *CSDLA/1282/2001*, the Deputy Commissioner concludes, following *CA/1014/1999*, that a person holding a Power of Attorney is not a person made an appointee under reg.33: see para.18.

In *R(SB)5/90*, Commissioner Goodman clarifies the decision in *R(SB)8/88* in holding that the appointment of a person to act by the Secretary of State operates retrospectively. Thus, so far as tribunals are concerned, an appointment after the date of the appeal but before the date of the hearing will be sufficient to ground jurisdiction. The power of appointment is to be found in reg.30(1). **2.193**

Note that the power of appointment under this regulation is a separate power of appointment from that under reg.30 which arises on the death of the claimant, or where a claim is made after death, a potential claimant.

On the liability of appointees in respect of overpayments of benefit, see the discussion in the notes to s.71 of the Administration Act.

The practice of the Secretary of State in making appointments under reg.33 appears to vary. Since April 1988 there has been a single regulation governing appointments and the regulation is drafted in sufficiently wide terms to encompass a single appointment to cover all social security benefits; it covers "any sums payable to him". Previously there were separate sets of regulations covering means-tested and non-means-tested benefits, and it was the interaction of the sets of regulations which was primarily in issue in *R(IS)5/91*. The experience of tribunals appears to be that in some cases the appointment is for all benefits, and in other cases it is limited to particular benefits. Indeed, in some cases it is not clear what the scope of the appointment is, as when a claimant asks for an appointment in relation to a particular benefit and the appointment is made in general terms. The nature of the appointment seldom seems to be an issue upon which the appeal turns.

See also annotation to reg.30.

Payment to another person on the beneficiary's behalf

2.194 **34.**—[3 (1) Except in a case to which paragraph (2) applies,] the Secretary of State [2 or the Board] may direct that benefit may be paid, wholly or in part, to [1 another natural person] on the beneficiary's behalf if such a direction as to payment appears to the Secretary of State [2 or the Board] to be necessary for protecting the interests of the beneficiary, or any child or dependant in respect of whom benefit is payable.

[3 (2) The Secretary of State may direct that a joint-claim jobseeker's allowance shall be paid wholly or in part to a natural person who is not a member of the joint-claim couple who is the nominated member for the purposes of section 3B of the Jobseekers Act if such a direction as to payment appears to the Secretary of State to be necessary for protecting the interests of the other member of that couple or, as the case may be, both members of that couple.]

AMENDMENTS

1. The Social Security (Miscellaneous Provisions) Amendment (No.2) Regulations 1992 (SI 1992/2595) reg.5 (January 4, 1993).

2. The Tax Credits (Claims and Payments) (Amendment) Regulations 1999 (SI 1999/2572) reg.20 (October 5, 1999).

3. The Social Security (Joint Claims: Consequential Amendments) Regulations 2000 (SI 2000/1982) reg.2(8) (March 19, 2001).

DEFINITIONS

"beneficiary"—see Social Security Act 1975 Sch.20.

"benefit"—see reg.2(2).

"child"—see 1986 Act s.20(11).

Deductions of mortgage interest which shall be made from benefit and paid to qualifying lenders

2.195 ***34A.**—Revoked by the Loans for Mortgage Interest Regulations 2017 (SI 2017/725), Sch.5(1), para.7(2) from April 6, 2018, subject to transitional provisions specified in regs 19, 19A and 20 of those Regulations (as amended).*

Deductions of mortgage interest which may be made from benefits and paid to qualifying lenders in other cases

2.196 ***34B.**—Revoked by the Loans for Mortgage Interest Regulations 2017 (SI 2017/725), Sch.5(1), para.7(2) from April 6, 2018, subject to transitional provisions specified in regs 19, 19A and 20 of those Regulations (as amended).*

[1 [3Deductions which may be made from benefit and paid to third parties

35.—(1) [6. . .] Deductions may be made from benefit and direct payments may be made to third parties on behalf of a beneficiary in accordance with the provisions of Schedule 9 [4 and Schedule 9B]. 2.197

(2) Where a social fund payment for maternity or funeral expenses [2or expenses for heating which appear to the Secretary of State to have been or to be likely to be incurred in cold weather] is made, wholly or in part, in respect of a debt which is, or will be, due to a third person, [5 . . .] [5 payment may be, and in the case of funeral expenses shall be, made to that person and where an instrument of payment is made to that person it may be sent to the beneficiary].

AMENDMENTS

1. The Social Security (Claims and Payments) Amendment Regulations 1988 (SI 1988/522) reg.7 (April 11, 1988).

2. The Social Security (Common Provisions) Miscellaneous Amendments Regulations 1988 (SI 1988/1725) reg.3 (November 7, 1988).

3. The Social Security (Claims and Payments) Amendment Regulations 1992 (SI 1992/1026) reg.4 (May 25, 1992).

4. The Social Security (Claims and Payments) Amendment Regulations 2001 (SI 2001/18) reg.2 (January 31, 2001).

5. Social Security (Claims and Payments and Miscellaneous Amendments) (No.2) Regulations 2002 (SI 2002/2441) reg.9 (April 8, 2003).

6. Loans for Mortgage Interest Regulations 2017 (SI 2017/725), Sch.5(1), para.7(3) (April 6, 2018), subject to transitional provisions specified in regs 19, 19A and 20 of those Regulations (as amended).

DEFINITIONS

"beneficiary"—see Social Security Act 1975 Sch.20.
"benefit"—see reg.2(2).

GENERAL NOTE

Child support payments

Regulation 35 and Sch.9 make provision for various deductions from benefit to be paid to third parties. These include payments in lieu of child support payments, which are at the bottom of the list of priorities. A new Sch.9B was introduced dealing specifically with child support maintenance and payments to persons with care. But the relationship between Sch.9B deductions and those arising under Sch.9 is not spelled out, so that it is unclear whether flat rate child support liabilities take precedence over other deductions from benefit under Sch.9. 2.198

The policy response appears to be that child support deductions from a range of benefits will set apart from the rest of the direct payments scheme rather than take precedence over them. So child support deductions will, as a matter of policy rather than law, be taken without regard to other Sch.9 deductions. Administrative arrangements were to ensure that where only one of a child support deduction and another deduction can be taken, priority will be given to the child support deduction.

This is all a most unsatisfactory way of sorting out deficiencies in the clarity of the legislative scheme.

In *R(Timson) v SSWP and another* [2022] EWHC 2392 (Admin), Cavanagh J conducted a lengthy examination of law, policy and practice relating to third party deductions in the context of a challenge to SSWP's guidance to decision-makers on common law and human rights grounds. The claim for judicial review succeeded only on the aspect that SSWP's written guidance to decision-makers in relation to third party deductions was unlawful because, by implication and omission, it had the effect that, read as a whole, it presented a misleading picture of the true legal position to decision-makers, in that it did not make clear that claimants should be offered the opportunity to make representations and/or provide relevant information to the decision-maker before the decision whether to make a third party deduction was taken. The claims in relation to the ECHR were dismissed. The Court of Appeal dismissed SSWP's challenges in *SSWP v Timson* [2023] EWCA Civ 656. So far as the construction of the Regulations was concerned

> "The terms of the provisions ...require that the Secretary of State must either form an "opinion" or be "satisfied" that the TPD would be "in the interests of the family". This makes it clear that the TPD is only available following a consideration of the interests of the claimant and, if there are any, other members of the claimant's family. I find it impossible to see how such a consideration can take place fairly without the claimant and other members of the family being able to say what they think is in their interests, and why. It may include matters which are uniquely within the knowledge of the claimant."

Thus (at [66]) the Guidance, which did not require such an opportunity to be given, was "obviously unfair".

The view based on construction of the Regulations was consistent with the close analysis at paras 50–64 of the judgment as to when a duty of prior consultation can be implied as a matter of public law.

2.199 *Regulation 35A revoked by The Social Security (Care Homes and Independent Hospitals) Regulations 2005 (SI 2005/2687) (October 24, 2005).*

Payment to a partner as alternative payee

2.200 **36.**—[3(1)] [1 Except where a wife has elected in accordance with regulation 6A of the Social Security (Guardian's Allowances) Regulation 1975 (prescribed manner of making an election under section 77(9) of the Social Security Contributions and Benefits Act 1992) that guardian's allowance is not to be paid to her husband,] where one of a married or unmarried couple residing together is entitled to child benefit [2 working families' tax credit, disabled person's tax credit] [1 or guardian's allowance] the Secretary of State [2 or the Board] may make arrangements whereby that benefit as well as being payable to the person entitled to it, may, in the alternative, be paid to that person's partner on behalf of the person entitled.

[3 (2) Where a person is entitled to a winter fuel payment within the meaning of the Social Fund Winter Fuel Payment Regulations 2000 and—

(a) that person is one [4 member of a] couple of a member of a polygamous marriage;

(b) the other member of that couple or another member of that marriage ("the other person") is in receipt of income support [5 , an income-based jobseeker's allowance or an income-related employment and support allowance] and

(c) both members of the couple or marriage are living together within the meaning of regulation 1(3)(b) of those Regulations,

the Secretary of State may pay the winter fuel payment to the other person on behalf of the person entitled notwithstanding that [6 in the qualifying week the other person has not yet attained the qualifying age].]

AMENDMENTS

1. The Social Security (Claims and Payments) Amendment Regulations 1999 (SI 1999/2358) reg.2(6) (September 20, 1999).

2. The Tax Credits (Claims and Payments) (Amendment) Regulations 1999(SI 1999/2752) regs 20, 24 and 25 (October 5, 1999).

3. The Social Security (Claims and Payments and Miscellaneous Amendments) (No.3) Regulations 2002 (SI 2002/2660) reg.2 (November 2, 2002).

4. The Civil Partnership (Pensions, Social Security and Child Support) (Consequential etc. Provisions) Order 2005 (SI 2005/2877) (December 5, 2005).

5. The Employment and Support Allowance (Consequential Provisions) (No.2) Regulations 2008 (SI 2008/1554) reg.23 (October 27, 2008).

6. The Social Security (Equalisation of State Pension Age) Regulation 2009 (SI 2009/1488) reg.6 (April 6, 2010).

Regulation 36A revoked by The Social Security (Claims and Payments) Amendment Regulations 1991 (SI 1991/2741) reg.18 (April 6, 1992). 2.201

PART V

[1 . . .] EXTINGUISHMENT

AMENDMENT

1. Words in heading omitted by The Social Security Act 1998 (Commencement No.8, and Savings and Consequential and Transitional Provisions) Order 1999 (SI 1999/1958) Sch.9 (July 5, 1999).

Regulations 37–37B revoked by The Social Security Act 1998 (Commencement No.8, and Savings and Consequential and Transitional Provisions) Order 1999 (SI1999/1958), Sch.9 (July 5, 1999). 2.202

Extinguishment of right to payment of sums by way of benefit where payment is not obtained within the prescribed period

38.—(1) [1Subject to paragraph (2A), the right to payment of any sum by way of benefit shall be extinguished] where payment of that sum is not obtained within the period of 12 months from the date on which the right is to be treated as having arisen; and for the purposes of this regulation the right shall be treated as having arisen— 2.203

(a) in relation to any such sum contained in an instrument of payment which has been given or sent to the person to whom it is payable, or to a place approved by the Secretary of State [4 or the Board] for collection by him (whether or not received or collected as the case may be)—

(i) on the date of the said instrument of payment, or

(ii) if a further instrument of payment has been so given or sent as a replacement, on the date of the last such instrument of payment;

[3(aa) [8 . . .];]

(b) in relation to any such sum to which sub-paragraph (a) does not apply, where notice is given (whether orally or in writing) or is sent that the sum contained in the notice is ready for collection on the date of the notice or, if more than one such notice is given or sent, the date of the first such notice;

[7 (bb) in relation to any such sum which [9 the Secretary of State has] arranged to be paid by means of direct credit transfer into a bank or other account, on the due date for payment of the sum;]

(c) in relation to any such sum to which [3 none of (a), [8 . . .] or [7 (b) or (bb) apply], on such date as the Secretary of State determines [4 or the Board determine].

(2) The giving or sending of an instrument of payment under paragraph (1)(a), or of a notice under paragraph (1)(b), shall be effective for the purposes of that paragraph, even where the sum contained in that instrument, or notice, is more or less than the sum which the person concerned has the right to receive.

[1(2A) Where a question arises whether the right to payment of any sum by way of benefit has been extinguished by the operation of this regulation and the [5 Secretary of State] is satisfied that—

(a) [5 he] first received [4 or the Board first received] written notice requesting payment of that sum after the expiration of 12 months; and

(b) from a day within that period of 12 months and continuing until the day the written notice was given, there was good cause for not giving the notice; and

[2(c) [5. . .] either—

(i) [5. . .] no instrument of payment has been given or sent to the person to whom it is payable and [5. . .] no payment has been made under the provisions of regulation 21 ([6 direct] credit transfer); or

(ii) that such instrument has been produced to [5 the Secretary of State] and [5. . .] no further instrument has been issued as a replacement,]

the period of 12 months shall be extended to the date on which the [5 Secretary of State] decides that question, and this regulation shall accordingly apply as though the right to payment had arisen on that date.]

(3) For the purposes of paragraph (1) the date of an instrument of payment is the date of issue of that instrument or, if the instrument specifies a date which is the earliest date on which payment can be obtained on the instrument and which is later than the date of issue, that date.(4) This regulation shall apply to a person authorised or appointed to act on behalf of a beneficiary as it applies to a beneficiary.(5) This regulation shall not apply to the right to a single payment of any industrial injuries gratuity or in satisfaction of a person's right to graduated retirement benefit.

AMENDMENTS

1. The Social Security (Medical Evidence, Claims and Payments) Amendment Regulations 1989 (SI 1989/1686) reg.7 (October 9, 1989).

2. Social Security (Claims and Payments) Amendment (No.3) Regulations 1993 (SI 1993/2113) reg.3(8) (September 27, 1993).

3. Social Security (Claims and Payments Etc.) Amendment Regulations 1996 (SI 1996/672) reg.2(5) (April 4, 1996).

4. The Tax Credits (Claims and Payments) (Amendment) Regulations 1999(SI 1999/2572) reg.20 (October 5, 1999).

5. The Social Security Act 1998 (Commencement No.9, and Savings and Consequential and Transitional Provisions) Order 1999 (SI 1999/2422) Sch.7 (September 6, 1999).

6. Social Security (Claims and Payments and Miscellaneous Amendments) (No.2) Regulations 2002 (SI 2002/2441) reg.10 (April 8, 2003).

7. The Social Security, Child Support and Tax Credits (Miscellaneous Amendments) Regulations 2005 (SI 2005/337) reg.7 (March 18, 2005).

8. The Social Security (Miscellaneous Amendments) (No.2) Regulations 2006 (SI 2006/832) reg.2 (April 10, 2006).
9. The Social Security (Miscellaneous Amendments) Regulations 2012 (SI 2012/757) reg.15(3) (April 1, 2012).

DEFINITIONS

"beneficiary"—see Social Security Act 1975 Sch.20.
"benefit"—see reg.2(2).
"instrument for benefit payment"—see reg.2(1).

GENERAL NOTE

In *CDLA/2807/2003* the Commissioner said, **2.204**

"It seems to me quite impossible to say in circumstances where the operative decision is that no benefit is payable that any right to payment, let alone a right to payment of any amount that has been quantified, is in existence. There could be no right to payment until that decision has been altered in some way. Regulation 38 simply cannot have any operation in such circumstances."

In *CU/2604/1999*, the Commissioner said, **2.205**

"The subject of regulation 38 is the 'right to payment of any sum'. The regulation sets out various rules for ascertaining the date on which that right is to be treated as having arisen. This includes the rule in regulation 38(1)(c). However, there must *first* be a right to payment of a *sum*. The word 'sum' means something otherwise it could have been omitted and left the provision meaning something slightly different. . . . In my view, if the amount has not been quantified, there is no 'sum', even if there has been identified a basis for quantifying it. Contrary to what has been argued on behalf of the Secretary of State, the fact that the tribunal later quantified the amount does not affect the fact it had not bee quantified at the time when the adjudication officer sought to extinguish the right to payment. If there is no sum, then the right to payment of it cannot arise, and cannot be extinguished under regulation 38." (See para.17.)

In *CDLA/2609/2002,* the Commissioner offers a helpful overview of reg.38: **2.206**

"15. I start with the overall scheme of regulation 38 of the Claims and Payments Regulations. It is concerned not with payment of benefit in a general sense, but with the extinguishment of a 'right to payment of any sum by way of benefit' (regulation 38(1)). The basic condition for such extinguishment is that 'payment of that sum is not obtained within the period of 12 months from the date on which the right is to be treated as having arisen'. Mr Commissioner Levenson has in decision *CU/2604/1999* (in the papers under that reference, but now reported as *R(U) 1/02*) stressed that some meaning must be given to the word 'sum'. So he held there that where a Commissioner had decided that unemployment benefit was payable to a claimant for a specified period, without quantifying the amount of benefit, there was no sum identified to which a right of payment attached which could be extinguished. Likewise, it seems to me that some weight must be attached to the use of the term 'any sum by way of benefit' and to the test being in terms of 'obtaining' payment of such a sum. The use of language does not point towards a situation where benefit of a sufficiently ascertainable amount has been merely been awarded by a decision on entitlement and payability, so that the Secretary of State is under an obligation to pay the benefit as soon as reasonably practicable (Claims and Payments Regulations, regulation 20). It points towards a situation where a particular sum has been allocated to the claimant and some steps along the administrative process of making payment have been taken, leaving the claimant with some relatively mechanical steps to take to 'obtain' payment.

16. That view is also consistent with the provisions of subparagraphs (a) to (b) of regulation 38(1), which define the dates on which the right to payment of a sum by way of benefit is to be treated as having arisen in certain circumstances. The rules are that: where the claimant has been given or sent an instrument of payment or an instrument has been made available for collection, the right arises on the date of the instrument or any replacement instrument (subparagraph (a)); where a sum is payable by means of an instrument for benefit payment (see regulation 20A), the right arises on the first date on which payment could be obtained by that means (subparagraph (aa)); and, where subparagraph (a) does not apply and notice is given or sent that the sum is available for collection, the right arises on the date that the notice is sent (subparagraph (b)). It makes perfect sense to say in all those situations that a right to payment of the particular sum by way of benefit had arisen and that, if the claimant does not take the other necessary steps to get paid (even in a situation, for instance, where a letter gets lost in the post), payment has not been obtained. The final provision in regulation 38(1), the crucial provision in this case, is subparagraph (c), under which the right to payment is to be treated as having arisen:

> '(c) in relation to any such sum to which none of (a), (aa) or (b) apply, on such date as the Secretary of State determines or the [Board of Inland Revenue] determine.'

17. It is plainly arguable that subparagraph (c) does not give the Secretary of State an unfettered discretion to choose any date whatsoever, but must be interpreted in accordance with the overall scheme and scope of regulation 38(1) and by reference to the circumstances of subparagraphs (a) to (b). It is true that regulation 38(2A) on good cause is drafted on the assumption that regulation 38(1) can apply in a case where no instrument of payment was given or sent to the claimant, but I do not think that that undermines what I have said above. Miss Topping submitted that, although subparagraph (c) might exclude irrational or completely unreasonable choices, it certainly allowed the Secretary of State to determine that a right to payment of a sum by way of benefit arose on the date on which a weekly payment of benefit would have been made in the ordinary course of things, even though no administrative steps at all had actually been taken towards making payment."

2.207 It is a common feature of social security benefit that the right to payment of benefit does not survive a delay of more than 12 months in obtaining payment of it. The determination of the date on which the right to payment is treated as arising may be crucial and is a matter for the Secretary of State (or Board of the Inland Revenue as appropriate).

Only where reg.38(2A) applies does any issue for the adjudicating authorities arise. Then it is only whether the right to payment has been extinguished, but it will still be for the Secretary of State to determine "whether there should be a replacement instrument." (See [7]).

Cases in which the claimant says that no giro was received are governed by *R(IS) 7/91* under which questions of payment were held not to be questions relating to the award of benefit.

Good cause

2.208 The classic definition of good cause is that found in *R(S)2/63:*

> "In Decision *CS371/49* the Commissioner said 'Good cause' means, in my opinion, some fact which, having regard to all the circumstances (including the claimant's state of health and the information which he had received and that which he might have obtained) would probably have caused a reasonable person of his age and experience to act (or fail to act) as the claimant did.' This description of good cause has been quoted in countless cases. It has stood

the test of time. In our judgment it is correct. The word 'fact' of course includes a combination of events happening either simultaneously or in succession."

PART VI

[[1]MOBILITY COMPONENT OF DISABILITY LIVING ALLOWANCE AND DISABILITY LIVING ALLOWANCE FOR CHILDREN]

AMENDMENT

1. The Social Security (Claims and Payments) Amendment Regulations 1991 (SI 1991/2741) reg.19(a) (February 3, 1992).

Regulations 39–41 revoked by The Social Security (Claims and Payments) Amendment Regulations 1991 (SI 1991/2741), reg.19(b) (February 3, 1992). 2.209

Cases where allowance not to be payable

42.—(1) Subject to the provisions of this regulation, [[1]disability living allowance by virtue of entitlement to the mobility component] shall not be payable to any person who would otherwise be entitled to it in respect of any period— 2.210

(a) during which that person has the use of an invalid carriage or other vehicle provided by the Secretary of State under section 5(2) of and Schedule 2 to the National Health Service Act 1977 or section 46 of the National Health Service (Scotland) Act 1978 which is a vehicle propelled by petrol engine or by electric power supplied for use on the road and to be controlled by the occupant; or

(b) in respect of which that person has received, or is receiving, any payment—

(i) by way of grant under the said section 5(2) and Schedule 2 or section 46 towards the costs of running a private car, or

(ii) of mobility supplement under the Naval, Military and Air Forces etc., (Disablement and Death) Service Pensions Order 1983 or the Personal Injuries (Civilians) Scheme 1983 or under the said Order by virtue of the War Pensions (Naval Auxiliary Personnel) Scheme 1964, the Pensions (Polish Forces) Scheme 1964, the War Pensions (Mercantile Marine) Scheme 1964 or an Order of Her Majesty in relation to the Home Guard dated 21st December, 1964 or 22nd December, 1964 or in relation to the Ulster Defence Regiment dated 4th January, 1971,

or any payment out of public funds which the Secretary of State is satisfied is analogous thereto.

(2) A person who has notified the Secretary of State that he no longer wishes to use such an invalid carriage or other vehicle as if referred to in paragraph (1)(a) and has signed an undertaking that he will not use it while it remains in his possession awaiting collection, shall be treated, for the purposes of this regulation, as not having the use of that invalid carriage or other vehicle.

(3) Where a person in respect of whom [[1]disability living allowance] is claimed for any period has received any such payment as referred to in paragraph (1)(b) for a period which, in whole or in part, covers the period for which the allowance is claimed, such payment shall be treated as an aggregate of

equal weekly amounts in respect of each week in the period for which it is made and, where in respect of any such week a person is treated as having a weekly amount so calculated which is less than the weekly rate of [1 mobility component of disability living allowance to which, apart from paragraph (1), he would be entitled], any allowance to which that person may be entitled for that week shall be payable at a weekly rate reduced by the weekly amount so calculated.

(4) In a case where the Secretary of State has issued a certificate to the effect that he is satisfied—

(a) that the person in question either—

(i) has purchased or taken on hire or hire-purchase; or

(ii) intends to purchase or take on hire or hire-purchase a private car or similar vehicle ("the car") for a consideration which is more than nominal, on or about a date (not being earlier than 13th January, 1982) specified in the certificate ("the said date");

(b) that that person intends to retain possession of the car at least during, and to learn to drive it within, the period of 6 months or greater or lesser length of time as may be specified in the certificate ("the said period") beginning on the said date; and

(c) that the person will use [1 disability living allowance by virtue of entitlement to the mobility component] in whole or in part during the said period towards meeting the expense of acquiring the car, paragraph (1)(a) shall not apply, and shall be treated as having never applied, during a period beginning on the said date and ending at the end of the said period or (if earlier) the date on which the Secretary of State cancels the certificate because that person has parted with possession of the car or for any other reason.

AMENDMENT

1. The Social Security (Claims and Payments) Amendment Regulations 1991 (SI 1991/2741) reg.20 (February 3, 1992).

Children

2.211 **43.**—(1) In any case where a claim for [1disability living allowance] for a child is received by the Secretary of State, he shall, in accordance with the following provisions of this regulation, appoint a person to exercise, on behalf of the child, any right to which he may be entitled under the Social Security Act 1975 in connection with [1disability living allowance] and to receive and deal on his behalf with any sums payable by way of [1that allowance].

[6 (1A) Subject to paragraph (1B), where a person has been appointed by the Scottish Ministers under section 85A(1) of the 2018 Scotland Act in connection with the determination of assistance under section 24 of that Act (whether or not including an appointment to receive assistance on behalf of the child), the Secretary of State may, if the person agrees, treat that person as if she had appointed them under paragraph (1).

(1B) Paragraph (1A) does not apply if the person appointed by the Scottish Ministers does not satisfy the conditions in paragraph (2).]

(2) Subject to the following provisions of this regulation, a person appointed by the Secretary of State under this regulation to act on behalf of the child shall—

(a) be a person with whom the child is living; and

(b) be over the age of 18 [2 or, if the person is a parent of the child and living with him, be over the age of 16]; and

(c) be either the father or mother of the child, or, if the child is not living with either parent, be such other person as the Secretary of State may determine; and

(d) have given such undertaking as may be required by the Secretary of State as to the use, for the child's benefit, of any allowance paid.

(3) For the purpose of paragraph (2)(a), a person with whom a child has been living shall, subject to paragraph (4) and to the power of the Secretary of State to determine in any case that the provisions of this paragraph should not apply, be treated as continuing to live with that child during any period—

(a) during which that person and the child are separated but such separation has not lasted for a continuous period exceeding [[1]12 weeks]; or

(b) during which the child is absent by reason only of the fact that he is receiving full-time education at a school; or

(c) during which the child is absent and undergoing medical or other treatment as an in-patient in a hospital or similar institution; or

(d) during such other period as the Secretary of State may in any particular case determine:

Provided that where the absence of the child under (b) has lasted for a continuous period of 26 weeks or the child is absent under (c), that person shall only be treated as continuing to live with that child if he satisfies the Secretary of State that he has incurred, or has undertaken to incur, expenditure for the benefit of the child of an amount not less than the allowance payable in respect of such period of absence.

(4) Where a child in respect of whom an allowance is payable, is, by virtue of any provision of an Act of Parliament—

(a) committed to, or received into the care of, a local authority; or

(b) subject to a supervision requirement and residing in a residential establishment under arrangements made by a local authority in Scotland;

any appointment made under the foregoing provisions of this regulation shall terminate forthwith:

Provided that, when a child is committed to, or received into, care or is made subject to a supervision requirement for a period which is, and when it began was, not intended to last for more than [[1]12 weeks] the appointment shall not terminate by virtue of this paragraph until such period has lasted for 8 weeks.

(5) In any case where an appointment on behalf of any child in the care of, or subject to a supervision requirement under arrangements made by, a local authority is terminated in accordance with paragraph (4), the Secretary of State may, upon application made to him by that local authority or by an officer of such authority nominated for the purpose by that authority, appoint the local authority or nominated officer thereof or appoint such other person as he may, after consultation with the local authority, determine, to exercise on behalf of the child any right to which that child may be entitled under the Act in connection with the allowance and to receive and deal on his behalf with any sums payable to him by way of [[1]disability living allowance] for any period during which he is in the care of, or, as the case may be, subject to a supervision requirement under arrangements made by, that authority.

(6) Where a child is undergoing medical or other treatment as an inpatient in a hospital or similar institution and there is no other person to whom [[1]disability living allowance] may be payable by virtue of an

appointment under this regulation, the Secretary of State may, upon application made to him by the [4 health authority] [1 National Health Service Trust] [3 NHS Foundation Trust] or, as the case may be, social services authority, controlling the hospital or similar institution in which the child is an in-patient, or by an officer of that authority [1 or Trust] nominated for the purpose by the authority, appoint that authority [1 or Trust] or the nominated officer thereof or such other person as the Secretary of State may, after consultation with that authority [1 or Trust], determine, to exercise on behalf of the child any right to which that child may be entitled in connection with the allowance and to receive and deal on his behalf with any sums payable to him by way of [1 disability living allowance] for any period during which he is an in-patient in a hospital or similar institution under the control of that authority [1 or Trust].

(7) For the purposes of this regulation—

[4 . . .]

[2 "child" means a person under the age of 16;]

"child's father" and "child's mother" include a person who is the child's father or mother by adoption or would be such a relative if an illegitimate child had been born legitimate;

[4 "health authority" means—

(a) [5 . . .]

(b) in relation to Wales, a Health Authority established under section 8 of that Act; and

(c) in relation to Scotland, a Health Board within the meaning of the National Health Service (Scotland) Act 1978;]

"hospital or similar institution" means any premises for the reception of and treatment of persons suffering from any illness, including any mental disorder, or of persons suffering from physical disability, and any premises used for providing treatment during convalescence or for medical rehabilitation;

"local authority" means, in relation to England and Wales, a local authority as defined in the Local Government Act 1972 and, in relation to Scotland, a local authority as defined in the Local Government (Scotland) Act 1973;

"social services authority" means—

(a) in relation to England and Wales, the social services committee established by a local authority under section 2 of the Local Authority Social Services Act 1970; and

(b) in relation to Scotland, the social work committee established by a local authority under section 2 of the Social work (Scotland) Act 1968.

AMENDMENTS

1. The Social Security (Claims and Payments) Amendment Regulations 1991 (SI 1991/2741) reg.21 (February 3, 1992).

2. The Social Security, Child Support and Tax Credits (Miscellaneous Amendments) Regulations 2005 (SI 2005/337) reg.7 (March 18, 2005).

3. The Health and Social Care (Community Health and Standards) Act 2003 (Supplementary and Consequential Provisions) (NHS Foundation Trusts) Order 2004 (SI 2004/696) art.3 and Sch.3 (March 11, 2004).

4. The National Health Service Reform and Health Care Professions Act 2002 (Supplementary, Consequential etc. Provisions) Regulations 2002 (SI 2001/2469) Sch.1 Pt.2 (October 1, 2002).

5. National Treatment Agency (Abolition) and the Health and Social Care Act 2012 (Consequential, Transitional and Saving Provisions) Order (SI 2013/235) art.11 and Sch.2 Pt.1 para.11 (April 1, 2013).

6. The Scotland Act 2016 (Social Security) (Consequential Provision) (Miscellaneous Amendment) Regulations 2021 (SI 2021/804) reg.9(4) (July 26, 2021).

General Note

A child claimant of DLA will have had to have an appointee under this regulation. On conversion to PIP, however, an appointee can only be appointed under reg.57 of the Universal Credit etc. (Claims and Payments) Regulations 2013 – there is no automatic conversion of the appointee who has acted for the child for DLA purposes: see *P v SSWP (PIP)* [2018] UKUT 359 (AAC). 2.212

Payment of [1 disability living allowance] on behalf of a beneficiary

44.—(1) Where, under arrangements made or negotiated by Motability, an agreement has been entered into by or on behalf of a beneficiary in respect of whom [1 disability living allowance is payable by virtue of entitlement to the mobility component at the higher rate] for the hire or hire-purchase of a vehicle, the Secretary of State may arrange that any [1 disability living allowance by virtue of entitlement to the mobility component at the higher rate payable] to the beneficiary shall be paid in whole or in part on behalf of the beneficiary in settlement of liability for payments due under that agreement. 2.213

(2) Subject to regulations 45 and 46 an arrangement made by the Secretary of State under paragraph (1) shall terminate at the end of whichever is the relevant period specified in paragraph (3), in the case of hire, or paragraph (4), in the case of a hire-purchase agreement.

(3) In the case of hire the relevant period shall be—

(a) where the vehicle is returned to the owner at or before the expiration of the [3 . . .] term of hire, the period of the [3 . . .] term; or

(b) where the vehicle is retained by or on behalf of the beneficiary with the owner's consent after the expiration of the original term of hire [3, other than where sub-paragraph (d) applies,], the period of the original term; or

(c) where the vehicle is retained by or on behalf of the beneficiary otherwise than with the owner's consent after the expiration of the original term of hire or its earlier termination, whichever is the longer of the following periods—

(i) the period ending with the return of the vehicle to the owner; or

(ii) the period of the original term of hire.

[3; or

(d) where the original term of hire is extended by an agreed variation of the agreement, the period of the extended term.]

(4) In the case of a hire-purchase agreement, the relevant period shall be—

(a) the period ending with the purchase of the vehicle; or

(b) where the vehicle is returned to the owner or is repossessed by the owner under the terms of the agreement before the completion of the purchase, the original period of the agreement.

[2(5) In this regulation "Motability" means the company, set up under that name as a charity and originally incorporated under the Companies Act 1985 and subsequently incorporated by Royal Charter].

AMENDMENTS

1. The Social Security (Claims and Payments) Amendment Regulations 1991 (SI 1991/2741) reg.22 (February 3, 1992).

2. The Social Security (Miscellaneous Provisions) Amendment Regulations 1990 (SI 1990/2208) reg.13 (December 5, 1990).

3. The Social Security, Child Support and Tax Credits (Miscellaneous Amendments) Regulations 2005 (SI 2005/337) reg.7 (March 18, 2005).

[1 Recovery of expenses

2.214 **44A.**—(1) Paragraph (2) applies where—

(a) an agreement referred to in regulation 44(1) has been entered into; and

(b) a relevant provider is receiving payments of disability living allowance in settlement of liability for payments due under that agreement.

(2) The Secretary of State may require the relevant provider to make payments to meet the reasonable expenses of the Secretary of State in administering the making of the payments of disability living allowance to the relevant provider.

(3) The method by which the expenses under paragraph (2) are to be met is for the Secretary of State to issue an invoice to the relevant provider setting out the expenses that have been incurred and for the relevant provider to pay the sum stated to the Secretary of State.

(4) The first invoice issued by the Secretary of State may recover expenses incurred between 21st July 2016 and the date of the invoice.

(5) Subsequently the Secretary of State may issue invoices no more frequently than annually and only in respect of expenses incurred since the period covered by the previous invoice.

(6) The expenses that the Secretary of State may take into account for the purposes of paragraph (2) include—

(a) the salaries and other costs relating to the employment of staff wholly engaged in the administering of the payments of disability living allowance and where staff have other responsibilities, an apportioned amount of those costs; and

(b) overheads, including rent and other shared costs, relating to those staff.

(7) In determining what expenses were reasonably incurred in administering the making of payments of disability living allowance to a relevant provider, the Secretary of State must have regard to any agreement between the Secretary of State and the relevant provider concerning the level of service to be provided by the Secretary of State in the making of such payments to that relevant provider.]

AMENDMENT

1. Inserted by the Social Security (Expenses of Paying Sums in Relation to Vehicle Hire) Regulations 2016 (SI 2016/674) reg.3 (July 21, 2016).

Power for the Secretary of State to terminate an arrangement

2.215 **45.** The Secretary of State may terminate an arrangement for the payment of [1disability living allowance by virtue of entitlement to the mobility component at the higher rate] on behalf of a beneficiary under regulation 44 on such date as he shall decide—

(a) if requested to do so by the owner of the vehicle to which the arrangement relates, or

(b) where it appears to him that the arrangement is causing undue hardship to the beneficiary and that it should be terminated before the end of any of the periods specified in regulation 44(3) or 44(4).

Amendment

1. The Social Security (Claims and Payments) Amendment Regulations 1991 (SI 1991/2741) reg.23 (February 3, 1992).

Restriction on duration of arrangements by the Secretary of State

46. The Secretary of State shall end an arrangement for the payment of [1 disability living allowance by virtue of entitlement to the mobility component at the higher rate] on behalf of a beneficiary made under regulation 44, where he is satisfied that the vehicle to which the arrangement relates has been returned to the owner, and that the expenses of the owner arising out of the hire or hire-purchase agreement have been recovered following the return of the vehicle. 2.216

Part VII

Miscellaneous

[1 Instruments of payment

47.—(1) Instruments of payment issued by the Secretary of State shall remain his property. 2.217

(2) Any person having an instrument of payment shall, on ceasing to be entitled to the benefit to which the instrument relates, or when so required by the Secretary of State, deliver it to the Secretary of State or such other person as he may direct.]

Amendment

1. Inserted by The Social Security (Miscellaneous Amendments) (No.2) Regulations 2006 (SI 2006/832) reg.2 (April 10, 2006).

Revocations

48. The regulations specified in column (1) of Schedule 10 to these regulations are hereby revoked to the extent mentioned in column (2) of that Schedule, in exercise of the powers specified in column (3). 2.218

Savings

49. [1. . .] 2.219

Amendment

1. The Social Security (Miscellaneous Provisions) Amendment (No.2) Regulations 1992 (SI 1992/2595) reg.6 (November 16, 1992).

General Note

Regulation 49 maintained in force regulations about claims and reviews relating to supplementary benefit and family income support. See *CIS/465/1991*. Because its terms led to the mistaken impression that the substantive terms of the schemes 2.220

survived the repeal of the Supplementary Benefits Act 1976 and the Family Income Supplements Act 1970 by the Social Security Act 1986, reg.49 has been revoked from November 16, 1992. See *R(SB) 1/94*. It is not immediately apparent that reg.49 was necessary in order to allow claims to be made for supplementary benefit for periods prior to April 11, 1988, and reviews of entitlement for such periods to be carried out. Therefore its revocation may have no effect on such matters. See Sch.10 to the Administration Act. However, *CSB 168/1993* is to the contrary.

In *CIS/12016/1996* a Commissioner, after a detailed review of the legal issues, concluded that from November 16, 1992, it has been impossible for an effective claim to be made for supplementary benefit. This was in spite of the powerful argument that an underlying entitlement to supplementary benefit for a period before April 11, 1988, and the right to pursue a remedy in respect of that entitlement could be preserved by s.16(1) of the Interpretation Act 1978 on the revocation of the supplementary benefit legislation. The reason was that any remedy protected would be under reg.3(1) of the Supplementary Benefit (Claims and Payments) Regulations 1981, which required a claim for weekly supplementary benefit to be made in writing on a form approved by the Secretary of State or in such other manner as the Secretary of State accepted as sufficient. In *CIS/12016/1996* the claim was made in a letter in July 1993. By that date, the Secretary of State had no power to accept the manner of claim as sufficient, because the 1981 Regulations no longer existed. Since the Secretary of State's power was discretionary, the claimant had no accrued right which could be preserved by s.16(1). It had been held in *R. v Secretary of State for Social Security Ex p. Cullen* (November 21, 1996), now confirmed by the Court of Appeal (*The Times*, May 16, 1997, and see the notes to reg.9) that the hope of having a discretion to treat a claim for supplementary benefit as in the alternative a claim for attendance allowance was not preserved by s.16(1) as an accrued right. The same had to apply to the power to accept claims as made in sufficient manner.

Note also *CIS/7009/1995* which confirms that it was not possible to make a late claim for National Assistance after the start of the supplementary benefit scheme on November 24, 1966. There were no savings provisions to enable claims for National Assistance to succeed after that date (see *CSB 61/1995*).

SCHEDULE 1

PART I

BENEFIT CLAIMED AND OTHER BENEFIT WHICH MAY BE TREATED AS IF CLAIMED IN ADDITION OR IN THE ALTERNATIVE

2.221

Benefit claimed (1)	Alternative benefit (2)
[1 Incapacity benefit]	[1 Severe disablement allowance]
[2 . . .]	[2 . . .]
Severe disablement allowance	[1 Incapacity benefit]
[2 . . .]	[2 . . .]
[1 Incapacity benefit for a woman]	[1 Maternity allowance]
Severe disablement allowance for a woman	Maternity allowance
[11 Employment and support allowance for a women]	[11 Maternity allowance]
Maternity allowance	[1 Incapacity benefit [11, severe disablement allowance or employment and support allowance]
A retirement pension of any category	Widow's benefit [9 or bereavement benefit]

A retirement pension of any category	A retirement pension of any other category a shared additional pension [3 or graduated retirement benefit]
[1 An increase of incapacity benefit]	An increase of severe disablement allowance
Attendance allowance	An increase of disablement pension where constant attendance is needed
An increase of disablement pension where constant attendance is needed	Attendance allowance [4 or disability living allowance]
An increase of severe disablement allowance	[1 An increase of incapacity benefit]
Income support	[5 . . .] [4 . . .] or [10 carer's allowance]
[6 Widow's benefit [9 or bereavement benefit]]	[6 A retirement pension of any category or graduated retirement benefit]
[4 Disability living allowance]	[4 Attendance allowance or an increase of disablement pension where constant attendance is needed]
[4 Attendance allowance or an increase of disablement pension where constant attendance is needed]	[4 Disability living allowance]
[7 Disabled person's tax credit]	[7 Working families' tax credit]
[7 Working families' tax credit]	[7 Disabled person's tax credit]
[13 Bereavement benefit	Bereavement support payment
Bereavement support payment	Bereavement benefit]
[12 A state pension under any section of Part 1 of the Pensions Act 2014]	[12 A state pension under any other section of Part 1 of the Pensions Act 2014 or bereavement benefit]
[12 Bereavement benefit]	[12 A state pension under Part 1 of the Pensions Act 2014]

In this part of this Schedule—

(a) Reference to an increase of any benefit (other than an increase of disablement pension where constant attendance is needed) are to an increase of that benefit in respect of a child or adult dependant;

(b) "widow's benefit" means widow's benefit under [Part II of the Social Security Contributions and Benefits Act 1992] and benefit by virtue of section [78(9)] of that Act corresponding to a widow's pension or a widowed mother's allowance.

PART II

INTERCHANGE OF CLAIMS FOR CHILD BENEFIT WITH CLAIMS FOR OTHER BENEFITS

[8 . . .] 2.222

Guardian's allowance

Maternity allowance claimed after confinement

Increase of child dependant by virtue of [sections 80 and 90 of the Social Security Contributions and Benefits Act 1992], or regulations made under [section 78(9)] of that Act.

AMENDMENTS

1. The Social Security (Claims and Payments) Amendment (No.2) Regulations 1994 (SI 1994/2943) reg.10 (April 13, 1995).

2. The Social Security (Claims and Payments) (Jobseeker's Allowance Consequential Amendments) Regulations 1996 (SI 1996/1460) reg.2 (October 7, 1996).

3. The Social Security (Claims and Payments) Amendment Regulations 1988 (SI 1988/522) reg.8 (April 11, 1988).

4. The Social Security (Claims and Payments) Amendment Regulations 1991 (SI 1991/2741) reg.25 (February 3, 1992).

5. The Social Security (Miscellaneous Provisions) Amendment (No.2) Regulations 1992 (SI 1992/2595) reg.7 (November 16, 1992).

6. The Social Security (Miscellaneous Provisions) Amendment Regulations 1990 (SI 1990/2208) reg.14 (December 5, 1990).

7. The Tax Credits (Claims and Payments) (Amendment) Regulations 1999 (SI 1999/2572) regs 24 and 25 (October 5, 1999).

8. The Child Benefit, Child Support and Social Security (Miscellaneous Amendments) Regulations 1996 (SI 1996/1803) reg.20 (April 7, 1997).

9. The Social Security (Benefits for Widows and Widowers) (Consequential Amendments) Regulations 2000 (SI 2000/1483) reg.9 (April 9, 2001).

10. The Social Security Amendment (Carer's Allowance) Regulations 2002 (SI 2002/2497) Sch.2 (October 28, 2002).

11. The Employment and Support Allowance (Consequential provisions) (No.2) Regulations 2008 (SI 2008/1554) reg.24 (October 27, 2008).

12. The Pensions Act 2014 (Consequential, Supplementary and Incidental Amendments) Order 2015 (SI 2015/1985) art.9(17) (April 6, 2016).

13. The Pensions Act 2014 (Consequential, Supplementary and Incidental Amendments) Order 2017 (SI 2017/422) art.10 (April 6, 2017).

SCHEDULE 2 **Regulation 17(5)**

Special Provisions Relating to Claims for [1Jobseeker's Allowance] During Periods Connected with Public Holidays

2.223 **1.**—(1) In this Schedule—

(a) "public holiday" means, as the case may be, Christmas Day, Good Friday or a Bank Holiday under the Banking and Financial Dealings Act 1971 or in Scotland local holidays; and "Christmas and New Year holidays" and "Good Friday and Easter Monday" shall be construed accordingly and shall in each case be treated as one period;

(b) "office closure" means a period during which an [1 office of the Department for Education an Employment] or associated office is closed in connection with a public holiday;

(c) in computing any period of time Sundays shall not be disregarded.

(2) Where any claim for [1a jobseeker's allowance] is made during one of the periods set out in paragraph (3), the following provisions shall apply—

(a) a claim for [1a jobseeker's allowance] may be treated by [2 the Secretary of State as a claim for that benefit for period, to be specified in his decision, not exceeding 35 days after the date of the claim where that claim is made during the period specified in sub-paragraph (a) of paragraph (3), or 21 days after the date of claim where the claim is made during the period specified in either sub-paragraph (b) or (c) of paragraph (3);

(b) on any claim so treated, benefit may be awarded as if the provisions of paragraph (4) of regulation 17 applied.

(3) For the purposes of paragraph (2) the periods are—

(a) in the case of Christmas and New Year holidays, a period beginning with the start of the 35th day before the first day of office closure and ending at midnight between the last day of office closure and the following day;

(b) in the case of Good Friday and Easter Monday, a period beginning with the start of the 16th day before the first day of the office closure and ending at midnight between the last day of office closure and the following day;

(c) in the case of any public holiday, a period beginning with the start of the 14th day before the first day of office closure and ending at midnight between the last day of office closure and the following day.

Amendments

1. The Social Security (Claims and Payments) (Jobseeker's Allowance Consequential Amendments) Regulations 1996 (SI 1996/1460) reg.2 (October 7, 1996).

2. The Social Security Act 1998 (Commencement No.11 and Transitional Provisions) Order 1999 (SI 1999/2860) Sch.3 (October 18, 1999).

Schedule 3 revoked by The Social Security (Claims and Payments) (Jobseeker's Allowance Consequential Amendments) Regulations 1996 (SI 1996/1460) reg.2 (October 7, 1996). 2.224

SCHEDULE 4

Prescribed Time For Claiming Benefit

2.225

Description of benefit (1)	Prescribed time for claiming benefit (2)
1. [1 Jobseeker's allowance]	[1 The first day of the period in respect of which the claim is made]
[2 **2.** Incapacity benefit or severe disablement allowance]	[2 The day in respect of which the claim is made and period of [3 3 months] immediately following it.]
3. Disablement benefit (not being an increase of benefit)	As regards any day on which, apart from satisfying the condition of making a claim, the claimant is entitled to benefit, that day and the period of 3 months immediately following it.
4. Increase of disablement benefit under section 61 (constant attendance), or 63 (exceptionally severe disablement) of the Social Security Act 1975.	As regards any day which apart form satisfying the conditions that there is a current award of disablement benefit and the making of a claim, the claimant is entitled to benefit, that day and the period of 3 months immediately following it.
5. Reduced earnings allowance	As regards any day on which apart from satisfying the conditions that there is an assessment of disablement of not less than one percent. and the making of a claim, the claim is entitled to the allowance, that day and the period of 3 months immediately following it.
6. Income support	The first day of the period in respect of which the claim is made.
7. [4 Working families' tax credit]	(a) Where [4 working families' tax credit] has previously been claimed and awarded the period beginning 28 days before and ending 14 days after the last day of that award; [5 (aa) where [4 disabled person's tax credit] has previously been claimed and awarded the period beginning 42 days before and ending 14 days after the last day of that award of [4 disabled person's tax credit]] (b) Subject to [5 (a) and (aa)], the first day of the period in respect of which the claim is made; (c) where a claim for [4 working families' tax credit] is treated as if made for a period beginning with the relevant day by virtue of regulation 13 of these Regulations, the period beginning on 10th March 1992 and ending on 6th April 1992]
8. Social fund payment in respect of maternity expenses	[17 (a) In a case where regulation 5(3)(a) of maternity expenses the Social Fund Maternity and Funeral Expenses (General) Regulations 2005 applies ("the 2005 Regulations"), the period beginning 11 weeks before the first day of the expected week of confinement and ending [21 6] months after the actual date of confinement.

	[18 (b) In a case where regulation 5(3)(b) of the 2005 Regulations applies, the period beginning with the date on which the claimant becomes responsible for the child and ending [21 6] months after that date.] (c) In a case where regulation 5(3)(c) of the 2005 Regulations applies, the period beginning with the date on which an order referred to in that sub-paragraph is made and ending [21 6] months after that date. (d) In a case where regulation 5(3)(d) of the 2005 Regulations applies, the period beginning with the date on which the guardianship takes effect and ending [21 6] months after that date. (e) In a case where regulation 5(3)(e) of the 2005 Regulations applies, the period beginning with the date on which the child is placed with the claimant or the claimant's partner for adoption and ending [21 6] months after that date. (f) In a case where regulation 5(3)(f) of the 2005 Regulations applies, the period beginning with the date on which the adoption— (i) takes effect in respect of an adoption mentioned in section 66(1)(c) or (d), or (ii) is recognised under section 66(1)(e), of the Adoption and Children Act 2002, and ending [21 6] months after that date.]
9. Social fund payment in respect of funeral expenses	[8 The period beginning with the date of death and ending [20 6] months after the date of the funeral.]
9A. [9 . . .]	
10. Increase of disablement benefit under [10 section 60 of the Social Security Act 1975 on grounds of special hardship or] section 62 of the Social Security Act 1975 on the grounds of receipt of hospital treatment.	A regards any day on which, apart form satisfying the conditions that there is a current award of disablement benefit and the making of a claim, the claimant is entitled to benefit, that day and the period 3 months immediately following it.
[11 **11.** [12 Disabled person's tax credit]	(a) Where [12 disabled person's tax credit] has previously been claimed and awarded the period beginning 42 days before and ending 14 days after the last day of that award; (b) where [12 working families' tax credit] has previously been claimed and awarded the period beginning 28 days before and ending 14 days after the last day of that award of [12 working families' tax credit]; (c) subject to (a) and (b), the first day of the period in respect of which the claim is made; (d) where a claim for [12 disabled person's tax credit] is made by virtue of regulation 13B(1), the period beginning on 10th March 1992 and ending on 6th April 1992.]
[13 **12.** . . .]	
[14 **13.** Retirement pension of any category	As regards any day on which apart from

[19 or state pension under Part 1 of the Pensions Act 2014]	satisfying the condition of making a claim, the claimant is entitled to the pension, that day and the period of 12 months immediately following it.]
[14 **14.** Graduated retirement benefit	As regards any day on which, apart from satisfying the condition of making a claim, the claimant is entitled to benefit, that day and the period of 12 months immediately following it.]
[15 **15.** Shared additional pension	As regards any day on which, apart from satisfying the condition of making a claim, the claimant is entitled to the pension, that day and the period of 12 months immediately following it.]
[16 **16.** Employment and support allowance	The day in respect of which the claim is made and the period of three months immediately following it.]

For the purposes of this Schedule—

"actual date of confinement" means the date of the [17 birth] of the child or, if the woman is confined of twins or a greater number of children, the date of the [17 birth] of the last of them; and

"confinement" means labour resulting in the [17 birth] of a living child, or labour after [17 24] weeks of pregnancy resulting in the [17 birth] of a child whether alive or dead.

AMENDMENTS

1. The Social Security (Claims and Payments) (Jobseeker's Allowance Consequential Amendments) Regulations 1996 (SI 1996/460) reg.2 (October 7, 1996).
2. The Social Security (Claims and Payments) Amendment (No.2) Regulations 1994 (SI 1994/2943) reg.12 (April 13, 1995).
3. The Social Security (Miscellaneous Provisions) (No.2) Regulations 1997 (SI 1997/793) reg.7 (April 7, 1997).
4. The Tax Credits (Claims and Payments) (Amendment) Regulations 1999 (SI 1999/2572) regs 24 and 25 (October 5, 1999).
5. The Social Security (Claims and Payments) Amendment Regulations 1991 (SI 1991/2741) reg.26 (March 10, 1992).
6. The Social Security (Miscellaneous Provisions) Amendment Regulations 1991 (SI 1991/2284) reg.10 (November 1, 1991).
7. The Social Security (Social Fund and Claims and Payments) (Miscellaneous Amendments) Regulations 1997 (SI 1997/792) reg.8 (April 7, 1997).
8. The Social Security (Claims and Payments and Adjudication) Amendment Regulations 1996 (SI 1996/2306) reg.6 (October 7, 1996).
9. The Social Security (Miscellaneous Provisions) Amendment Regulations 1991 (SI 1991/2284) reg.11 (November 1, 1991).
10. The Social Security (Claims and Payments) Amendment Regulations 1988 (SI 1988/522) reg.9 (April 11, 1988).
11. The Social Security (Claims and Payments) Amendment Regulations 1991 (SI 1991/2741) reg.26(b) (March 10, 1992).
12. The Tax Credits (Claims and Payments) (Amendment) Regulations 1999 (SI 1999/2572) regs 24 and 25 (October 5, 1999).
13. The Social Security (Miscellaneous Amendments) (No.4) Regulations 2008 (SI 2008/2424) reg.2(3) (October 6, 2008).
14. The Social Security (Claims and Payments) Amendment Regulations 2005 (SI 2005/455) reg.5 (April 6, 2006).
15. The Social Security (Shared Additional Pension) (Miscellaneous Amendments) Regulations 2005 (SI 2005/1551) reg.3 (April 6, 2006).
16. The Employment and Support Allowance (Consequential Provisions) (No.2) Regulations 2008 (SI 2008/1554) reg.24 (October 27, 2008).

17. The Social Fund Maternity Grant Amendment Regulations 2010 (SI 2010/2760) reg.3 (December 13, 2010).
18. The Social Fund Maternity Grant Amendment Regulations 2011 (SI 2011/100) reg.4 (January 24, 2011).
19. The Pensions Act 2014 (Consequential, Supplementary and Incidental Amendments) Order 2015 (SI 2015/1985) art.9(18) (April 6, 2016).
20. The Social Fund Funeral Expenses Amendment Regulations 2018 (SI 2018/61) reg.2 (April 2, 2018).
21. The Social Security (Claims and Payments) (Social Fund Maternity Grant) (Amendment) Regulations 2018 (SI 2018/989) reg.2 (October 18, 2018).

General Note

2.226 Sometimes there is a need to be very precise about dates. *CIB/2805/2003* was just such a case. The Deputy Commissioner notes that the formulation used in relation to incapacity benefit (and, it should be noted, in relation to several other benefits) is to specify the time limit by reference to the day of claim and a period of three months immediately following it. The Deputy Commissioner rules that this means that the claimant gets the day of claim and a full three months immediately following the date in respect of which the claim is made. This gave the claimant two more days than the Secretary of State had calculated.

2.227 *Schedule 5 revoked by The Social Security (Claims and Payments and Adjudication) Amendment Regulations 1996 (SI 1996/2306) reg.7 (October 7, 1996).*

SCHEDULE 6 **Regulation 22(3)**

Days for Payment of Long Term Benefits

[1 Attendance allowance and disability living allowance

2.228 **1.** Subject to the provisions of regulation 25 (payment of attendance allowance, constant attendance allowance and the care component of a disability living allowance at a daily rate) attendance allowance shall be payable on Mondays and disability living allowance shall be payable on Wednesdays, except that the Secretary of State may in a particular case arrange for either allowance to be payable on any other day of the week and where it is in payment to any person and the day on which it is payable is changed, it shall be paid at a daily rate of 1/7th of the weekly rate in respect of any of the days for which payment would have been made but for that change.]
2. [2. . .]

Industrial injuries benefit

2.229 **3.** Any pension or allowance under [Part V of the Social Security Contributions and Benefits Act 1992], including any increase, shall be payable on Wednesdays.

[5Carer's allowance]

2.230 **4.** [5Carer's allowance] shall be payable on Mondays, except that where a person is entitled to that allowance in respect of a severely disabled person by virtue of regulation 3 of the Social Security (Invalid Care Allowance) Regulations 1976 the [5carer's allowance] shall be payable on Wednesdays.

Retirement pension

2.231 **5.** [8 Subject to regulation 22C, retirement pension] shall be payable on Mondays, except that—
(a) where a person became entitled to a retirement pension before September 28, 1984, that pension shall be payable on Thursdays;
[3(b) where—
(i) a woman was entitled to a widow's benefit, or
(ii) a man or a woman was entitled to a bereavement benefit,
immediately before becoming entitled to a retirement pension, that pension shall be payable on [4 . . .] [4 the day of the week which has become the appropriate day for payment of such a benefit to him in accordance with paragraph 6];]

(c) where a woman becomes entitled to a retirement pension immediately following the payment to her husband of an increase of retirement pension in respect of her, the retirement pension to which she becomes entitled shall be payable on the same days as those upon which the retirement pension of the husband is payable;

(d) the Secretary of State may, notwithstanding anything contained in the foregoing provisions of this paragraph, arrange for retirement pension to be payable on such other day of the week as he may [4 . . .] [4 where payment is by credit transfer, or in the circumstances of any particular case, determine];

(e) where, in relation to any person, any particular day of the week has become the appropriate day of the week for the payment of retirement pension, that day shall thereafter remain the appropriate day in his case for such payment.

Shared additional pension

[6 **5A.** Shared additional pension shall be payable on Mondays, except that— **2.232**

(a) where a retirement pension is payable to the claimant, it shall be payable on the same day as the retirement pension; or

(b) the Secretary of State may, notwithstanding the provisions of sub-paragraph (a), arrange for a shared additional pension to be payable on such other day of the week as he may, in the circumstances of any particular case, determine.]

Widowed mother's allowance and widow's pension

6. Widowed mother's allowance [7 . . .] **2.233**

7. [1. . .]

AMENDMENTS

1. The Social Security (Claims and Payments) Amendment Regulations 1991 (SI 1991/2741) reg.27 (April 6, 1992).

2. The Social Security (Claims and Payments) Amendment Regulations 1999 (SI 1999/2358) reg.2 (September 20, 1999).

3. The Social Security (Benefits for Widows and Widowers) (Consequential Amendments) Regulations 2000 (SI 2000/1483) reg.9 (April 9, 2001).

4. Social Security (Claims and Payments and Miscellaneous Amendments) (No.2) Regulations 2002 (SI 2002/2441) reg.11 (October 23, 2002).

5. The Social Security Amendment (Carer's Allowance) Regulations 2002 (SI 2002/2497) Sch.2 (October 28, 2002).

6. The Social Security (Shared Additional Pension) (Miscellaneous Amendments) Regulations 2005 (SI 2005/1551) (July 6, 2005).

7. The Social Security (Claims and Payments) Amendments Regulations 2009 (SI 2009/604) reg.2 (April 6, 2009).

8. The Social Security (Miscellaneous Amendments) (No.6) Regulations 2009 (SI 2009/3229) reg.2(8) (April 6, 2010).

SCHEDULE 7

Regulation 26

[15 TIME OF PAYMENT AND COMMENCEMENT OF ENTITLEMENT IN INCOME SUPPORT CASES]

Manner of payment

1. Except as otherwise provided in these Regulations income support shall be paid in arrears in accordance with the award.] **2.234**

Time of payment

2. Income support shall be paid in advance where the claimant is— **2.235**

(a) in receipt of retirement pension; or

(b) over pensionable age and not in receipt of [9. . .] [7incapacity benefit or severe disablement allowance and is not a person to whom section 126 of the Social Security

Contributions and Benefits Act 1992 (trade disputes) applies] unless he was in receipt of income support immediately before the trade dispute began; or

(c) [16 subject to paragraph 2ZA] in receipt of widow's benefit [13or [17 widowed parent's allowance]] and is not [14 . . .] providing or required to provide medical evidence of incapacity for work; or

(d) a person to whom [1section 23(a)] of the Social Security Act 1986 [SSCBA, s.127] applies, but only for the period of 15 days mentioned in that subsection.

[16 2ZA. Paragraph 2(c) shall only apply where a widow's benefit or a [17 widowed parent's allowance] is paid in advance.]

[2**2A.**—(1) For the purposes of this paragraph—

(a) "public holiday" means, as the case may be, Christmas Day, Good Friday or a Bank Holiday under the Banking and Financial Dealings Act 1971 or in Scotland local holidays, and

(b) "office closure" means a period during which an office of the Department of Social Security or associated office is closed in connection with a public holiday.

(2) Where income support is normally paid in arrears and the day on which the benefit is payable by reason of paragraph 3 is affected by office closure it may for that benefit week be paid wholly in advance or partly in advance and partly in arrears and on such a day as the Secretary of State may direct.

(3) Where under this paragraph income support is paid either in advance or partly in advance and partly in arrears it shall for any other purposes be treated as if it was paid in arrears.]

[3**3.** (1) Subject to [7sub-paragraph (1A) and to] any direction given by the Secretary of State in accordance with sub-paragraph (2), income support in respect of any benefit week shall, if the beneficiary is entitled to a relevant social security benefit or would be so entitled but for failure to satisfy the contribution conditions or had not exhausted his entitlement, be paid on the day and at the intervals appropriate to payment of that benefit.

[7(1A) Subject to sub-paragraph (2), where income support is paid to a person on the grounds of incapacity for work, that entitlement commenced on or after 13th April 1995, and no relevant social security benefit is paid to that person, the income support shall be paid fortnightly in arrears.]

(2) The Secretary of State may direct that income support in respect of any benefit week shall be paid at such intervals and on such days as he may in any particular case or class of case determine.

3A.—(1) Income support for any part-week shall be paid in accordance with an award on such day as the Secretary of State may in any particular case direct.

(2) In this paragraph, "part-week" has the same meaning as it has in Part VII of the Income Support (General) Regulations 1987.]

4. [1In this Schedule]—

"benefit week" means, if the beneficiary is entitled to a relevant social security benefit or would be so entitled but for failure to satisfy the contribution conditions or had not exhausted his entitlement, the week corresponding to the week in respect of which that benefit is paid, and in any other case a period of 7 days beginning or ending with such day as the Secretary of State may direct;

[1"Income Support Regulations" means the Income Support (General) Regulations 1987;] and

"relevant social security benefit" means [9. . .] [7incapacity benefit], severe disablement allowance, retirement pension [12 [17 widowed parent's allowance]] or widow's benefit.

Payment of small amounts of income support

2.236 **5.** Where the amount of income support is less than £1.00 a week the Secretary of State may direct that it shall be paid at such intervals as may be specified not exceeding 13 weeks.

Commencement of entitlement to income support

2.237 **6.**—(1) Subject to sub-paragraphs (3) and (4), in a case where income support is payable in arrears entitlement shall commence on the date of claim.

(2) [1Subject to sub-paragraphs (2A) and (3)], in a case where, under paragraph 2, income support is payable in advance entitlement shall commence on the date of claim if that day is a day for payment of income support as determined under paragraph 3 but otherwise on the first such day after the date of claim.

[1(2A) Where income support is awarded under regulation 17(3) for a definite period which is not a benefit week or a multiple of such a week entitlement shall commence on the date of claim.

(3) In a case where regulation 13 applies, entitlement shall commence on the day which is the relevant day for the purposes of that regulation [[5] except where income support is paid in advance, when entitlement shall commence on the relevant day, if that day is a day for payment as determined under paragraph 3 but otherwise on the first day for payment after the relevant day].]

(4) [[1]. . .]

[[9](5) If a claim is made by a claimant within 3 days of the date on which he became resident in a resettlement place provided pursuant to section 30 of the Jobseekers Act or at a centre providing facilities for the rehabilitation of alcoholics or drug addicts, and the claimant is so resident for the purposes of that rehabilitation, then the claim shall be treated as having been made on the day the claimant became so resident.]

(6) Where, in consequence of a further claim for income support such as is mentioned in sub-paragraph 4(7) of Schedule 3 to the Income Support (General) Regulations 1987, a claimant is treated as occupying a dwelling as his home for a period before moving in, that further claim shall be treated as having been made on the date from which he is treated as so occupying the dwelling or the date of the claim made before he moved in to the dwelling and referred to in that sub-paragraph, whichever is the later.

7. [. . .[12]].

AMENDMENTS

1. The Social Security (Claims and Payments) Amendment Regulations 1988 (SI 1988/522) reg.10 (April 11, 1988).

2. Transfer of Functions (Health and Social Security) Order 1988 (SI 1988/1843); The Social Security (Claims and Payments and Payments on account, Overpayments and Recovery) Amendment Regulations 1989 (SI 1989/136) reg.2(b) (February 27, 1989).

3. The Social Security (Medical Evidence, Claims and Payments) Amendment Regulations 1989 (SI 1989/1686) reg.8 (October 9, 1989).

4. The Social Security (Miscellaneous Provisions) Amendment Regulations 1990 (SI 1990/2208) reg.15 (December 5, 1990).

5. The Enterprise (Scotland) Consequential Amendments Order 1991 (SI 1991/387) art.2 and Sch.(April 1, 1991).

6. The Social Security (Miscellaneous Provisions) Amendment Regulations 1992 (SI 1992/247) reg.17 (March 9, 1992).

7. The Social Security (Claims and Payments) Amendment (No.2) Regulations 1994 (SI 1994/2943) reg.14 (April 13, 1995).

8. The Social Security (Claims and Payments etc.) Amendment Regulations 1996 (SI 1996/672) reg.2(6) (April 4, 1996).

9. The Social Security (Claims and Payments) (Jobseeker's Allowance Consequential Amendments) Regulations 1996 (SI 1996/1460) reg.2(24) (October 7, 1996).

10. The Social Security (Miscellaneous) Amendment (No.4) Regulations 1998 (SI 1998/1174) reg.8(3)(b) (June 1, 1998).

11. The Social Security Act 1998 (Commencement No.12 and Consequential and Transitional Provisions) Order 1999 (SI 1999/3178) Sch.6 (November 29, 1999).

12. The Social Security and Child Support (Miscellaneous Amendments) Regulations 2000 (SI 2000/1596) reg.5 (June 19, 2000).

13. The Social Security (Benefits for Widows and Widowers) (Consequential Amendments) Regulations 2000 (SI 2000/1483) reg.9 (April 9, 2001).

14. The Social Security, Child Support and Tax Credits (Miscellaneous Amendments) Regulations 2005 (SI 2005/337) reg.7 (March 18, 2005).

15. The Social Security (Miscellaneous Amendments) (No.2) Regulations 2006 (SI 2006/832) reg.2 (April 10, 2006).

16. The Social Security (Claims and Payments) Amendments Regulations 2009 (SI 2009/604) reg.2 (April 6, 2009).

17. The Pensions Act 2014 (Consequential, Supplementary and Incidental Amendments) Order 2017 (SI 2017/422) art.10 (April 6, 2017).

General Note

Paragraph 2

2.238 These categories of claimant are paid income support in advance. Apart from pensioners and most widows, those returning to work after a trade dispute are covered.

Paragraphs 3 and 4

2.239 Where a claimant meets the conditions of entitlement for one of the benefits listed as a "relevant social security benefit," the income support benefit week, pay-day and interval of payment is the same as for that benefit. Thus, those incapable of work are paid fortnightly in arrears (reg.24(1)), although under reg.24 the Secretary of State can arrange payment of incapacity benefit at other intervals (e.g. weekly), in which case income support follows suit. Otherwise the benefit week is to be defined by the Secretary of State. Income support paid for a definite period under reg.17(3) need not be in terms of benefit weeks. Paragraph 3A provides that payments for part-weeks may be made as the Secretary of State directs.

Paragraph 6

2.240 The general rule for income support paid in arrears is that entitlement begins on the date of claim. The first payment on the pay day at the end of the first benefit week (or the second benefit week in the case of the unemployed) can thus be precisely calculated to include the right number of days. Payments can then continue on a weekly basis.

If income support is paid in advance, then, as for supplementary benefit, entitlement begins on the next pay day following the claim or coinciding with the date of claim.

Where the award is for a definite period under reg.17(3) entitlement begins with the date of claim (sub-para.(2A)). Sub-paragraph (3) deals with the special case of advance awards. Sub-paragraphs (5) and (6) cover other special cases.

SCHEDULE 8 — **Regulation 23(1)(a)**

Election to Have Child Benefit Paid Weekly

2.241 **1.** A person to whom benefit is payable for an uninterrupted period beginning before and ending after March 15, 1982 may make an election, in accordance with paragraph 3, that benefit be payable weekly after that date, if either—

(a) he makes the election before the end of the 26th week from the day on which benefit was payable for the first four weeks in respect of which the Secretary of State made arrangements for four-weekly payment to the person entitled in accordance with regulation 21 or regulation 23(1)(b); or

(b) he was absent from Great Britain on the March 15, 1982 for one of the reasons specified in paragraph 4 and he makes the election before the end of the 26th week of the period beginning with the first week in respect of which benefit became payable to him in Great Britain on his return.

2. Subject to paragraph 5, a person entitled to benefit may make an election, in accordance with paragraph 3, that benefit be paid weekly if he satisfies either of the following conditions—

(a) he is a lone parent within the meaning set out in regulation 2(2) of the Child Benefit and Social Security (Fixing and Adjustment of Rates) Regulations 1976, or]

(b) he, or his spouse residing with him or the person with whom he is living as husband and wife, is receiving income support, [[2]an incomed-based jobseeker's allowance], [[3] or payment in accordance with an award of family credit or disability working allowance which was awarded with effect for a date falling before 5th October 1999.]

3. An election for benefit to be payable weekly under paragraphs 1 or 2 shall be effected by giving notice in writing to the Secretary of State delivered or sent to the appropriate office and shall be made when it is received.

4. An election may not be made under paragraph 1(b) unless the person's absence abroad on the March 15, 1982 was by reason of his being—

(a) a serving member of the forces, as defined by regulation 1(2) of the Social Security (Contributions) Regulations 1979, or
(b) the spouse of such a member, or
(c) a person living with such a member as husband and wife.

5. Every person making an election for benefit to be paid weekly under paragraph 2 shall furnish such certificates, documents and such other information of facts as the Secretary of State may, in his discretion, require, affecting his right to receive payment of benefit weekly and in particular shall notify the Secretary of State in writing of any change of circumstances which he might reasonably be expected to know might affect the right to receive payment of benefit weekly, as soon as reasonably practicable after the occurrence thereof.

6. Where a person makes an election, in accordance with this regulation, for benefit to be paid weekly, it shall continue to be so payable—

(a) in the case of an election under paragraph 1, so long as that person remains continually entitled to benefit, or
(b) in the case of an election under paragraph 2, so long as that person remains continually entitled to benefit and the conditions specified in that paragraph continue to be satisfied.

7. A person who has made an election that benefit be payable weekly may cancel it at any time by a notice in writing delivered or sent to the appropriate office; and effect shall be given to such a notice as soon as is convenient.

AMENDMENTS

1. The Child Benefit, Child Support and Social Security (Miscellaneous Amendments) Regulations 1996 (SI 1996/1803) reg.21 (April 7, 1997).

2. The Social Security (Claims and Payments) (Jobseeker's Allowance Consequential Amendments) Regulations 1996 (SI 1996/1460) reg.2 (October 7, 1996).

3. The Social Security and Child Support (Tax Credits) Consequential Amendments Regulations 1999 (SI 1999/2566) Sch.8 (September 5, 1999).

SCHEDULE 9 **Regulation 35**

DEDUCTIONS FROM BENEFIT AND DIRECT PAYMENT TO THIRD PARTIES

Interpretation

1. [18—(1)] In this Schedule— 2.242

[11"the Community Charges Regulations" means the Community Charges (Deductions from Income Support (No.2) Regulations 1990;

"the Community Charges (Scotland) Regulations" means the Community Charges (Deductions from Income Support) (Scotland) Regulations 1989;]

[19"contribution-based jobseeker's allowance" [49 (except where used in sub-paragraph (2)(b)] means any contribution-based jobseeker's allowance which does not fall within the definition of "specified benefit";]

[40 "contributory employment and support allowance" [49 (except where used in sub-paragraph (3)(b)] means any contributory employment and support allowance which does not fall within the definition of "specified benefit"]

[11"the Council Tax Regulations" mean the Council Tax (Deductions from Income Support) Regulations 1993;]

"family" in the case of a claimant who is not a member of a family means that claimant [28 and for the purposes of state pension credit "a family" comprises the claimant, his partner, any additional partner to whom section 12(1)(c) of the 2002 Act applies and any person who has not attained the age of 19, is treated as a child for the purposes of section 142 of the Contributions and Benefits Act and lives with the claimant or the claimant's partner;];

[11"the Fines Regulations" means the Fines (Deductions from Income Support) Regulations 1992;]

[6"5 per cent of the personal allowance for the single claimant aged not less than 25" means where the percentage is not a multiple of 5 pence the sum obtained by rounding that 5 per cent to the next higher such multiple;

[32 "hostel" means a building—

(a) in which there is provided for persons generally, or for a class of persons, accommodation, otherwise than in separate and self-contained premises, and either board or facilities of a kind set out in paragraph 4A(1)(d) below adequate to the needs of those persons and—

(b) which is—

(i) managed by or owned by a housing association registered with [45 the Regulator of Social Housing of the Welsh Ministers]

[41 (ii) managed or owned by a registered social landlord which is registered in accordance with [50 Part 2 of the Housing (Scotland) Act 2010]]

(iii) operated other than on a commercial basis and in respect of which funds are provided wholly or in part by a government department or a local authority; or

(iv) managed by a voluntary organisation or charity and provides care, support or supervision with a view to assisting those persons to be rehabilitated or resettled within the community, and

(c) which is not—

(i) a care home;

(ii) an independent hospital; or

(iii) an establishment run by the Abbeyfield Society including all bodies corporate or incorporated which are affiliated to that Society, and

(d) in sub-paragraph (b)(iv) above, "voluntary organisation" shall mean a body the activities of which are carried out otherwise than for profit, but shall not include any public or local authority;]

"housing authority" means a local authority, a new town corporation, [41. . .] or the Rural Development Board for Rural Wales;]

[33 "the Housing Benefit Regulations" mean the Housing Benefit Regulations 2006;

"the Housing Benefit (State Pension Credit) Regulations" mean the Housing Benefit (Persons who have attained the qualifying age for state pension credit) Regulations 2006;]

[18"housing costs" means any housing costs met under—

(a) Schedule 3 to the Income Support Regulations but—

(i) excludes costs under paragraph 17(1)(f) of that Schedule (tents and tent sites); and

(ii) includes costs under paragraphs 17(1)(a) (ground rent [31 . . .]) and 17(1)(c) (rentcharges) of that Schedule but only when they are paid with costs under paragraph 17(1)(b) of that Schedule (service charges); or

(b) Schedule 2 to the Jobseeker's Allowance Regulations but—

(i) excludes costs under paragraph 16(1)(f) of that Schedule (tents and tent sites); and

(ii) includes costs under paragraphs 16(1)(a) (ground rent and feu duty) and 16(1)(c) (rentcharges) of that Schedule but only when they are paid with costs under paragraph 16(1)(b) of that Schedule (service charges);]

[28 (c) Schedule II to the State Pension Credit Regulations but—

(i) excludes costs under paragraph 13(1)(f) of that Schedule (tents and sites); and

(ii) includes costs under paragraphs 13(1)(a) (ground rent and feu duty) and 13(1)(c) (rent charges) of that Schedule but only when they are paid with costs under paragraph 13(1)(b) of that Schedule (service charges);] [40 or

(d) Schedule 6 to the Employment and Support Allowance Regulations but—

(i) excludes costs under paragraph 18(1)(f) of that Schedule (tents and tent sites); and

(ii) includes costs under paragraph 18(1)(a) (ground rent) and 18(1)(c) (rent charges) of that Schedule but only where they are paid with costs under paragraph 18(1)(b) of that Schedule (service charges);]

[31 . . .]

"the Income Support Regulations" means the Income Support (General) Regulations 1987;

[38 "integration loan which is recoverable by deductions" means an integration loan which is made under the Integration Loans for Refugees and Others Regulations 2007 and which is recoverable from the recipient by deductions from a specified benefit under regulation 9 of those Regulations;]

"miscellaneous accommodation costs" has the meaning assigned by paragraph 4(1);

[59 "moratorium debt" has the same meaning as in regulation 6 of the Debt Respite Scheme (Breathing Space Moratorium and Mental Health Crisis Moratorium) (England and Wales) Regulations 2020;

[56. . .]

"personal allowance for a single claimant aged not less than 25 years" means the amount specified [28 in connection with income support and state pension credit] in [6paragraph 1(1)(e)] of column 2 of Schedule 2 to the Income Support Regulations [18or, [28 in connection with jobseeker's allowance], paragraph 1(1)(e) of Schedule 1 to the Jobseeker's Allowance Regulations]; [40 or, in connection with employment and support allowance, paragraph 1(1)(b) of Schedule 4 to the Employment and Support Allowance Regulations]

[2. . .]

"rent" has the meaning assigned to it in the Housing Benefit Regulations and, for the purposes of this Schedule

(a) includes any water charges which are paid with or as part of the rent;

(b) where in any particular case a claimant's rent includes elements which would not otherwise fall to be treated as rent, references to rent shall include those elements; and

(c) references to "rent" include references to part only of the rent; and

[16"specified benefit" means—

[31 (a) income support or, where in respect of any period it is paid together with any incapacity benefit or severe disablement allowance—

(i) in a combined payment;

(ii) in part to the beneficiary and in part to another person in accordance with regulation 34; or

(iii) by means of two or more instruments of payment,

income support and incapacity benefit or severe disablement allowance if the income support alone is insufficient for the purposes of this Schedule;]

(b) [27 . . ..]

(c) subject to sub-paragraph (2), jobseeker's allowance;]

[31 (d) state pension credit or, where in respect of any period it is paid together with any retirement pension, [34 , state pension under Part 1 of the Pensions Act 2014] incapacity benefit or severe disablement allowance—

(i) in a combined payment; or

(ii) in part to the beneficiary and in part to another persion in accordance with regulation 34; or

(iii) by means of two or more instruments of payment,

state pension credit and retirement pension, [34 , state pension under Part 1 of the Pensions Act 2014] incapacity benefit or severe disablement allowance if the state pension credit alone is insufficient for the purposes of this Schedule;] [40 (e) subject to sub-paragraph (3), employment and support allowance;]

[48 . . .]]

[51 "water charges" means—

(a) as respects England and Wales, any water and sewerage charges under Chapter 1 of Part 5 of the Water Industry Act 1992;

(b) as respects Scotland, any water and sewerage charges established by Scottish Water under a charges scheme made under section 29A of the Water Industry (Scotland) Act 2002;

[6"water undertaker" means a company which has been appointed under section 11(1) of the Water Act 1989 to be the water or sewerage undertaker for any area in England and Wales] [51 or in respect of any area in Scotland, Scottish Water].

[18(2) For the purposes of the definition of "specified benefit" in sub-paragraph (1), "jobseeker's allowance" means—

(a) income-based jobseeker's allowance; and

[49 (b) contribution-based jobseeker's allowance where—

(i) both income-based jobseeker's allowance and contribution-based jobseeker's allowance are in payment and the income-based jobseeker's allowance alone is insufficient for the purposes of this Schedule; or

(ii) if there was no entitlement to contribution-based jobseeker's allowance, there would be entitlement to income-based jobseeker's allowance at the same rate.]

[40 (3) For the purposes of the definition of "specified benefit" in sub-paragraph (1) "employment and support allowance" means—

(a) income-related employment and support allowance; and

[49 (b) contributory employment and support allowance where—

(i) both income-related employment and support allowance and contributory employment and support allowance are in payment and the income-related employment and support allowance alone is insufficient for the purposes of this Schedule; or

(ii) if there was no entitlement to a contributory employment and support allowance, there would be entitlement to income-related employment and support allowance at the same rate.]

General

2.243 **2.**—(1) The specified benefit may be paid direct to a third party in accordance with the following provisions of this Schedule in discharge of a liability of the beneficiary or his partner to that third party in respect of—

(a) housing costs;

(b) miscellaneous accommodation costs;

[6(bb) hostel payments;]

(c) service charges for fuel, and rent not falling within head (a) above;

(d) fuel costs; [10. . .]

(e) water charges; [10 and

(f) payments in place of payments of child support maintenance under section 43(1) of the Child Support Act 1991 and regulation 28 of the Child Support (Maintenance Assessments and Special Cases) Regulations 1992.]

(2) No payment to a third party may be made under this Schedule unless the amount of the beneficiary's award of the specified benefit is not less than the total of the amount otherwise authorised to be so paid under this Schedule plus 10 pence.

(3) A payment to be made to a third party under this Schedule shall be made, at such intervals as the Secretary of State may direct, on behalf of and in discharge (in whole or in part) of the obligation of the beneficiary or, as the case may be, of his partner, in respect of which the payment is made.

Housing costs

2.244 **3.**—(1) Subject to [7sub-paragraphs (4) to (6)] and paragraph 8, where a beneficiary who has been awarded the specified benefit or his partner is in debt for any item of housing costs which continues to be applicable to the beneficiary in the determination of his applicable amount [28 or appropriate minimum guarantee], the [23Secretary of State] may, if in [24 his] opinion it would be in the interests of the family to do so, determine that the amount of the award of the specified benefit ("the amount deductible") calculated in accordance with the following sub-paragraphs shall be paid in accordance with sub-paragraph 2(3).

(2) [7Subject to sub-paragraphs (2A) and (3)], the amount deductible shall be such weekly aggregate of the following as is appropriate:—

(a) in respect of any debt to which sub-paragraph (1) applies, or where the debt owed is in respect of an amount which includes more than one item of housing costs, a weekly amount equal to 5 per cent. of the personal allowance for a single claimant aged not less than 25 [1. . .] for such period as it is necessary to discharge the debt, so however that in aggregate the weekly amount calculated under this sub-paragraph shall not exceed 3 times that 5 per cent;

(b) for each such debt—

[56. . .]

(ii) for any [56. . .] housing item, the actual weekly cost necessary in respect of continuing needs for the relevant items,

and the [23Secretary of State] may direct that, when the debt is discharged [59 or is a moratorium debt], the amount determined under sub-paragraph (b) shall be the amount deductible.

[7(2A) Where a payment falls to be made to a third party in accordance with this Schedule, and—

(a) more than one item of housing costs falls to be taken into account in determining the beneficiary's applicable amount; and

(b) in accordance with [56. . .] [14paragraph 18] of Schedule 3 to the Income Support Regulations [20or, as the case may be, [59 *paragraph 4(8) or (11) or*] paragraph 17 of Schedule 2 to the Jobseeker's Allowance Regulations] [40 *or [56. . .]* paragraph 19 of

Schedule 6 to the Employment and Support Allowance Regulations] [28 or [56. . .] paragraph 14 of Schedule II to the State Pension Credit Regulations] an amount is not allowed or a deduction falls to be made from the amount to be met by way of housing costs,

then in calculating the amount deductible, the weekly aggregate amount ascertained in accordance with sub-paragraph (2) shall be reduced by an amount determined by applying the formula—

$$C \times \frac{B}{A}$$

where—

A = housing costs;

B = the item of housing costs which falls to be paid to a third party under this Schedule;

C = the sum which is not allowed or falls to be deducted in accordance with [14paragraph 4(8) or (11) or paragraph 18] of Schedule 3 to the Income Support Regulations. [18or, as the case may be, paragraph 4(8) or (11) or paragraph 17 of Schedule 2 to the Jobseeker's Allowance Regulations][28 or paragraph 5(9) or (12) or paragraph 14 of Schedule II to the State Pension Credit Regulations]] [40 or paragraph 6(10) or (13) or paragraph 19 of Schedule 6 to the Employment and Support Allowance Regulations]

(3) Where the aggregate amount calculated under sub-paragraph (2) is such that paragraph 2(2) would operate to prevent any payment under this paragraph being made that aggregate amount shall be adjusted so that 10 pence of the award is payable to the beneficiary.

[57 (4) Sub-paragraph (1) shall not apply to any debt which is for any item of housing costs and is less than half the annual amount due to be paid by the beneficiary or his partner in respect of that item, unless, in the opinion of the Secretary of State it is in the overriding interests of the family that paragraph (1) should apply.]

[56. . .]

Miscellaneous accommodation costs

[9**4.**—(1) Where an award of income support [29, jobseeker's allowance or [40, state pension credit or employment and support allowance]]— 2.245

(a) [29 in the case of income support] is made to a person [32 residing in a care home, an Abbeyfield Home or an independent hospital] as defined in regulation [25 2(1)] of the Income Support Regulations [19 or [29 in the case of jobseeker's allowance], regulation 1(3) of the Jobseeker's Allowance Regulations], [40 or in the case of employment and support allowance, regulation 2(1) of the Employment and Support Allowance Regulations] or]

[54 (b) in the case of income support, jobseeker's allowance or employment and support allowance, is made to person who is in accommodation provided under section 3(1) of, and Part 2 of the Schedule to, the Polish Resettlement Act 1947(2) (provision by the Secretary of State of accommodation in camps); or

(c) in the case of state pension credit, is made to a person residing in—

(i) a care home as defined in regulation 1(2) of the State Pension Credit Regulations;

(ii) an independent hospital as defined in regulation 1(2) of those Regulations;

(iii) an establishment run by the Abbeyfield Society (including all bodies corporate or incorporate which are affiliated to the Society); or

(iv) accommodation provided under section 3(1) of, and Part 2 of the Schedule to, the Polish Resettlement Act 1947 where the person requires personal care,]

[29 or to a person who is only temporarily absent from such accommodation] the [23 Secretary of State] may determine that an amount of the specified benefit shall be paid direct to the person or body to whom the charges in respect of that accommodation are payable, [29 hereafter in this paragraph referred to as "miscellaneous accommodation costs"] but, [25 except in a case where accommodation is provided under section 3(1) of, and Part II of the Schedule to, the Polish Resettlement Act 1947] or where the accommodation is [2run by a voluntary organisation either for purposes similar to the purposes for which resettlement units are provided] or which provides facilities for alcoholics or drug addicts, only if the adjudicating authority is satisfied that the beneficiary has failed to budget for the charges and that it is in the interests of the family.

[29 (2) Subject to sub-paragraphs (3) and (3A), the amount of any payment of income support, jobseeker's allowance [40, state pension credit or employment and support allowance] to a third party determined under sub-paragraph (1) shall be—

(a) in a case where the beneficiary is not in accommodation [32 . . .] as specified in [54 sub-paragraph (1)(c)(ii)], an amount equal to the award of income support, jobseeker's allowance, [40 , guarantee credit or employment and support allowance] payable to the claimant but excluding an amount, if any, which when added to any other income of the beneficiary as determined in accordance with regulation 28 of the Income Support Regulations, regulation 93 of the Jobseeker's Allowance Regulations [40 , regulation 90 of the Employment and Support Allowance Regulations] or regulation 17 of the State Pension Credit Regulations will equal the amount prescribed in respect of personal expenses in sub-paragraph (2A); and

(b) in any other case, the amount of the award of income support, jobseeker's allowance [40 , guarantee credit or employment and support allowance], excluding the amount allowed by sub-paragraph (2A) in respect of personal expenses.

(2A) The amount in respect of personal expenses where a beneficiary is in accommodation referred to in paragraphs 4(1)(a) [54 (b) or (c)]shall be—

(a) for a single person the sum of [55 £31.75];

(b) for a couple where both members of the couple are in such accommodation, [55 £31.75] for each member;

(c) for a member of a polygamous marriage where more than one member is in such accommodation, [55 £31.75] for each member in such accommodation.

(3) This sub-paragraph shall apply where an award is made of—

(a) income support calculated in accordance with Part VII of the Income Support Regulations (calculation of income support for part-weeks); or

(b) jobseeker's allowance calculated in accordance with Part XI of the Jobseeker's Allowance Regulations (part-weeks);

(c) state pension credit for a period of less than a week calculated under regulation 13A of the State Pension Credit Regulations (part-weeks), or a part week payment of state pension credit calculated otherwise. [40 or

(d) employment and support allowance for a period of less than a week calculated in accordance with Part 14 of the Employment and Support Allowance Regulations (periods of less than a week).]

(3A) Where sub-paragraph (3) applies then the amount of any payment to a third party determined under sub-paragraph (1) shall be an amount calculated in accordance with sub-paragraph (2)(a) or (b) as appropriate except that in respect of—

(a) the income of the beneficiary, if any; and

(b) the amount allowed for personal expenses by sub-paragraph (2A) above,

the amount shall be the amount used in the calculation under the provisions listed in sub-paragraph (3)(a), (b) or (c), divided by 7 and multiplied by the number of days in the part-week and no payment shall be made to a third party where the Secretary of State certifies it would be impracticable to do so in that particular case.]

(4) Where the amount calculated under sub-paragraph [29 (2) or (3A) is such that paragraph 2(2) would operate to prevent any payment under this paragraph being made the amount shall be adjusted so that 10 pence of the award is payable to the beneficiary.]

[6Hostel payments

2.246 **4A.**—(1) This paragraph applies to a beneficiary if—

(a) [42 the beneficiary] has been awarded specified benefit; and

[42 (b) either the beneficiary or the beneficiary's partner—

(i) is resident in a hostel and has claimed housing benefit in the form of a rent rebate or rent allowance; or

(ii) is resident in approved premises under section 13 of the Offender Management Act 2007; and]

(c) [42 . . .]

(d) the charge for [42 the hostel or approved premises, as the case may be,] includes a payment, whether direct or indirect, for one or more of the following services—

(i) water;

(ii) a service charge for fuel;

(iii) meals;

(iv) laundry;

(v) cleaning (other than communal areas).

(2) Subject to sub-paragraph (3) below, where a beneficiary [8 . . .] has been awarded specified benefit the [23 Secretary of State] may determine that an amount of specified benefit shall be paid to the person or body to whom the charges referred to in subparagraph (1)(d) above are or would be payable.

(3) The amount of any payment to a third party under this paragraph shall be either—

(a) the aggregate of the amounts determined by a housing authority in accordance with the provisions specified in sub-paragraph (4); or

(b) if no amount has been determined under paragraph (a) of this sub-paragraph, an amount which the adjudicating authority estimates to be the amount which is likely to be so determined.

[33 (4) The provisions referred to in sub-paragraph (3)(a) above are regulation 12(6) of, and paragraphs 1(a)(ii) and (iv), 2, 3, 4 and either 6(1)(b) or 6(2) or 6(3) or 6(4) of Schedule 1 to, the Housing Benefit Regulations or, as the case may be, the Housing Benefit (State Pension Credit) Regulations;]

(5) [33 . . .]

[18(6) Where—

(a) an award of income support is calculated in accordance with regulation 73(1) of the Income Support Regulations (calculation of income support for part-weeks);

(b) an award of jobseeker's allowance is calculated in accordance with regulation 150(1) of the Jobseeker's Allowance Regulations (amount of a jobseeker's allowance payable), [40 or

(c) an award of employment and support allowance is calculated in accordance with regulation 165 of the Employment and Support Allowance Regulations (entitlement of less than a week etc.),]

the amount of any payment of income support or, as the case may be, jobseeker's allowance [40 or employment and support allowance] payable to a third party determined under sub-paragraph (2) above shall be an amount calculated in accordance with sub-paragraph (3)(a) or (b) above divided by 7 and multiplied by the number of days in the part-week, and no payment shall be made to a third party under this sub-paragraph where the Secretary of State certifies that it would be impracticable to do so in that particular case.]]

Service charges for fuel, and rent not falling within paragraph 2(1)(a)

5.—(1) Subject to paragraph 8, this paragraph applies to a beneficiary if— 2.247

(a) he has been awarded the specified benefit; and

(b) he or his partner is entitled to housing benefit in the form of a rent rebate or rent allowance [43 or is resident in approved premises under section 13 of the Offender Management Act 2007]; and

(c) [unless sub-paragraph (1A) applies] he or his partner has arrears of rent which equal or exceed four times the full weekly rent payable and—

(i) there are arrears of rent in respect of at least 8 weeks and the landlord has requested the Secretary of State to make payments in accordance with this paragraph; or

(ii) there are arrears of rent in respect of less than 8 weeks and in the opinion of the [23 Secretary of State] it is in the overriding interests of the family that payments shall be made in accordance with this paragraph.

[39 (1A) This sub-paragraph applies where the rent includes charges for services included under paragraph 4A(1)(d) and the arrears for these services exceeds £100.00.]

[43 (1B) For the purposes of sub-paragraphs (1) and (1A), references to "rent" include charges incurred in respect of accommodation in approved premises under section 13 of the Offender Management Act 2007.]

[48 (2) For the purposes of sub-paragraph (1) arrears of rent do not include any amount which falls to be deducted under regulation 74 of the Housing Benefit Regulations (non-dependant deductions) or, as the case may be, regulation 55 of the Housing Benefit (State Pension Credit) Regulations (non-dependant deductions) when assessing a person's housing benefit.

(3) [43 The adjudicating authority shall determine that a weekly amount of the specified benefit awarded to the beneficiary shall be paid to his or his partner's landlord if—

(a) he or his partner is entitled to housing benefit and in calculating that benefit a deduction is made under [33 regulation 12(3) of the Housing Benefit Regulations or, as the case may be, the Housing Benefit (State Pension Credit) Regulations] in respect of either or both of water charges or service charges for fuel; and

(b) the amount of the beneficiary's award is not less than the amount of the deduction, and the amount to be paid shall be equal to the amount of the deduction.

(4) [33. . .].

[18(5) A determination under this paragraph shall not be made without the consent of the beneficiary if the aggregate amount calculated in accordance with sub-paragraphs (3) and (6) exceeds [35 a sum calculated in accordance with paragraph 8(4);]

[28 (5A) [35 . . .]]

(6) In a case to which sub-paragraph (1) [39 or (1A)] applies the adjudicating authority may determine that a weekly amount of the specified benefit awarded to that beneficiary equal to 5 per cent. of the personal allowance for a single claimant aged not less than 25 [6 . . .] shall be paid to his landlord [43 , or the person or body to whom charges are payable in respect of the residence of the beneficiary or the beneficiary's partner in approved premises under section 13 of the Offender Management Act 2007,] until the debt is discharged.

[8(7) Immediately after the discharge of any arrears of rent to which sub-paragraph (1) [39 or (1A)] applies and in respect of which a determination has been made under sub-paragraph (6) the adjudicating authority may, if satisfied that it would be in the interests of the family to do so, direct that an amount, equal to the amount by which the eligible rent is to be reduced by virtue of [33 regulation 12(3) of the Housing Benefit Regulations or, as the case may be, the Housing Benefit (State Pension Credit) Regulations] in respect of charges for water or service charges for fuel or both, shall be deductible.]

Fuel costs

2.248 **6.**—(1) [28 Subject to sub-paragraphs [60(3A), (6) and (6A)]] and paragraph 8, where a beneficiary who has been awarded the specified benefit or his partner is in debt for any [52 fuel item] to an amount not less than the rate of personal allowance for a single claimant aged not less than 25 and continues to require [52 the fuel in respect of which the debt arose ("the relevant fuel")] the [5 Secretary of State], if in its opinion it would be in the interests of the family to do so, may determine that the amount of the award of the specified benefit ("the amount deductible") calculated in accordance with the following paragraphs shall be paid to the person or body to whom payment is due in accordance with paragraph 2(3).

(2) The amount deductible shall, in respect of any fuel item, be such weekly aggregate of the following as is appropriate:—

[6(a) in respect of each debt to which sub-paragraph (1) applies ("the original debt"), a weekly amount equal to 5 per cent of the personal allowance for a person aged not less than 25 for such period as is necessary to discharge the original debt, but the aggregate of the amounts, calculated under this paragraph shall not exceed twice 5 per cent of the personal allowance for a single claimant aged not less than 25;]

(b) except where current consumption is paid for by other means (for example pre-payment meter), an amount [60 not more than] the estimated average weekly cost necessary to meet the continuing needs for [52 the relevant fuel], varied, where appropriate, in accordance with sub-paragraph (4)(a)[52 ", plus such weekly amount as is required to meet any payments required to be made under a green deal plan within the meaning of section 1 of the Energy Act 2011 ("the 2011 Act").]

[60(3A) The Secretary of State may only include an amount under sub-paragraph (2)(b) in the amount deductible if—

(a) an application for a determination under sub-paragraphs (1) or (4)(a) is made by the person or body to whom payment is due; and

(b) except where the application is for a reduction in the amount deductible, the beneficiary consents to the application.]

(3) [6 . . .]

(4) Where an amount is being paid direct to a person or body on behalf of the beneficiary or his partner in accordance with a determination under sub-paragraph (1) and [24 a decision which enbodies that determination falls to be reviewed]—

(a) where since the date of that determination the average weekly cost estimated for the purpose of sub-paragraph (2)(b) has either exceeded or proved insufficient to meet the actual cost of continuing consumption so that in respect of the continuing needs for [52 the relevant fuel] the beneficiary or his partner is in credit or, as the case may be, a further debt has accrued, the adjudicating authority may determine that the weekly amount calculated under that paragraph shall, for a period of 26 weeks [8or such longer period as may be reasonable in the circumstances of the case], be adjusted so as to take account of that credit or further debt;

(b) where an original debt in respect of any fuel item has been discharged [59 or is a moratorium debt] the adjudicating authority may determine that the amount deductible in respect of that fuel item shall be the amount determined under sub-paragraph (2)(b).

(5) [6 . . .]

[18(6) Subject to paragraph 8, a determination under this paragraph shall not be made without the consent of the beneficiary if the aggregate amount calculated in accordance with sub-paragraph (2) exceeds [35 a sum calculated in accordance with paragraph 8(4).]

[28 [35 . . .]]
(7) [6 . . .]
[52 (8) In this paragraph, "fuel item" means—
(a) any charge for mains gas, including for the reconnection of mains gas; and
(b) any charge for mains electricity, including any charge for the disconnection or reconnection of mains electricity and including any payments required to be made under a green deal plan within the meaning of section 1 of the 2011 Act.]

[6 Water charges

7.—(1) This paragraph does not apply where water charges are paid with rent; and in this paragraph "original debt" means the debt to which sub-paragraph (2) applies, [12 including any disconnection or reconnection charges and any other costs (including legal costs) arising out of that debt]. 2.249

(2) Where a beneficiary or his partner is liable, whether directly or indirectly, for water charges and is in debt for those charges, the [23 Secretary of State] may determine, subject to paragraph 8, that a weekly amount of the specified benefit shall be paid either to a water undertaker to whom that debt is owed, or to the person or body authorised to collect water charges for that undertaker, [8 but only if [24 the Secretary of State] is satisfied that the beneficiary or his partner has failed to budget for those charges, and that it would be in the interests of the family to make the determination.]

(3) Where water charges are determined by means of a water meter, the weekly amount to be paid under sub-paragraph (2) shall be the aggregate of—
(a) in respect of the original debt, an amount equal to 5 per cent of the personal allowance for a single claimant aged not less than 25 years; and
(b) the amount which the [23 Secretary of State] estimates to be the average weekly cost necessary to meet the continuing need for water consumption.

(4) Where the sum estimated in accordance with sub-paragraph (3)(b) proves to be greater or less than the average weekly cost necessary to meet continuing need for water consumption so that a beneficiary or his partner accrues a credit, or as the case may be a further debt, the adjudicating authority may determine that the sum so estimated shall be adjusted for a period of 26 weeks [8 or such longer period as may be reasonable in the circumstances of the case] to take account of that credit or further debt.

(5) Where water charges are determined other than by means of a water meter the weekly amount to be paid under sub-paragraph (2) shall be the aggregate of—
(a) the amount referred to in sub-paragraph (3)(a); and
(b) an amount equal to the weekly cost necessary to meet the continuing need for water consumption.

(6) Where the original debt in respect of water charges is discharged [59 or is a moratorium debt], the [23 Secretary of State] may direct that the amount deductible shall be—
(a) where water charges are determined by means of a water meter, the amount determined under sub-paragraph (3)(b) taking into account any adjustment that may have been made in accordance with sub-paragraph (4); an
(b) in any other case, the amount determined under sub-paragraph (5)(b).

(7) Where the beneficiary or his partner is in debt to two water undertakers—
(a) only one weekly amount under sub-paragraph (3)(a) or (5)(a) shall be deducted; and
(b) a deduction in respect of an original debt for sewerage shall only be made after the whole debt in respect of an original debt for water has been paid; and
(c) deductions in respect of continuing charges for both water and for sewerage may be made at the same time.

[18 (8) Subject to paragraph 8 (maximum amount of payments to third parties), a determination under this paragraph shall not be made without the consent of the beneficiary if the aggregate amount calculated in accordance with sub-paragraphs (3), (4), (5) and (6) exceeds [35 a sum calculated in accordance with paragraph 8(4).]
[28 [35 . . .]]
[58 7A. ...]
[58 7B. ...]

[36 Eligible loans

7C. —(1) In this paragraph— 2.250
"borrower" means a person who has, either solely or jointly, entered into a loan agreement with an eligible lender in respect of an eligible loan and who is, for the time being, entitled to an eligible benefit;
"eligible lender" means—

(a) a body registered under section 1 of the Industrial and Provident Societies Act 1965 (societies which may be registered);
(b) a credit union within the meaning of section 1 of the Credit Unions Act 1979 (registration under the Industrial and Provident Societies Act 1965);
(c) a charitable institution within the meaning of section 58(1) of the Charities Act 1992 (interpretation of Part II);
(d) a body entered on the Scottish Charity Register under section 3 of the Charities and Trustee Investment (Scotland) Act 2005 (Scottish Charities Register);
[39 (e) a community interest company within the meaning of Part 2 of the Companies (Audit, Investigations and Community Enterprise) Act 2004,]

which, except for a credit union, is licensed under the Consumer Credit Act 1974 and which may be determined by the Secretary of State as an appropriate body to which payments on behalf of the borrower may be made in respect of loans made by that body;

"eligible loan" means a loan made by a lender, who is at that time an eligible lender, to a borrower except a loan—
(a) which is secured by a charge or pledge;
(b) which is for the purpose of business or self-employment; or
(c) which was made by means of a credit card;

"loan agreement" means an agreement between the eligible lender and the borrower in respect of an eligible loan.

(2) In this paragraph "eligible benefit" means—
(a) carer's allowance;
(b) the following contributory benefits—
(i) incapacity benefit;
(ii) retirement pension; [34. . .]
[34 (iii) state pension under Part 1 of the Pensions Act 2014; or]
(c) the following benefits—
(i) income support;
(ii) jobseeker's allowance;
(iii) state pension credit.
[40 (iv) employment and support allowance.]

(3) Where the conditions set out in sub-paragraph (4) are met the Secretary of State may deduct a sum from an eligible benefit to which the borrower is entitled equal to 5 per cent. of the personal allowance for a single [39 claimant] aged not less than 25 and pay that sum to the eligible lender towards discharge of the sum owing under the loan agreement at the date of the application.

(4) The conditions referred to in sub-paragraph (3) are—
(a) the borrower has failed to make payments as agreed with the eligible lender for a period of 13 weeks before the date of the application and has not resumed making payments;
(b) the borrower has given his written permission to the eligible lender to provide to the Secretary of State personal data within the meaning of section 1 of the Data Protection Act 1998 (basic interpretive provisions);
(c) the eligible lender has agreed that no interest or other charge will be added to the amount owed at the date of the application;
(d) no sum is being deducted under this paragraph;
(e) no sum is being deducted from the borrower's eligible benefit under section 71(8) of the 1992 Act (overpayments-general) at the date of the application; and
(f) no sum is being deducted from the borrower's eligible benefit under section 78 of the 1992 Act (recovery of social fund awards) at the date of the application.

(5) The Secretary of State shall notify the borrower and the eligible lender in writing of a decision to make a deduction under this paragraph.

(6) The Secretary of State may make deductions under this paragraph only if the borrower is entitled to an eligible benefit throughout any benefit week.

[53 (6A) The Secretary of State shall not make deductions from a benefit mentioned in sub-paragraph (2) where the borrower is in receipt of any benefit within the meaning of "eligible benefit" in paragraph 11(8) (eligible loans) of Schedule 6 (deductions from benefit and direct payment to third parties) to the 2013 Regulations unless the amount of benefit mentioned in that definition is insufficient to meet the deduction.]

(7) The Secretary of State shall not make deductions from a benefit mentioned in sub-paragraph (2)(a) where the borrower is in receipt of another eligible benefit unless that benefit is one mentioned in sub-paragraph (2)(b) and is insufficient to enable the deduction to be

made or is a benefit mentioned in sub-paragraph (2)(c) and the amount is insufficient to meet the deduction plus 10 pence.

(8) The Secretary of State shall not make deductions from a benefit mentioned in sub-paragraph (2)(b) where the borrower is in receipt of a benefit mentioned in sub-paragraph (2)(c) unless the amount of that benefit is insufficient to meet the deduction plus 10 pence.

(9) The Secretary of State shall cease making deductions from an eligible benefit [[46] under this paragraph] if—

(a) there is no longer sufficient entitlement to an eligible benefit to enable him to make the deduction;
(b) entitlement to all eligible benefits has ceased;
(c) a sum is deducted from the borrower's eligible benefit under section 71(8) of the 1992 Act;
(d) an eligible lender notifies the Secretary of State that he no longer wishes to accept payments by deductions;
(e) the borrower's liability to make payment in respect of the eligible loan has ceased;
(f) the lender has ceased to be an eligible lender; or
(g) the borrower no longer resides in Great Britain.

(10) The sums deducted from an eligible benefit by the Secretary of State under this paragraph shall be paid to the eligible lender.

(11) The Secretary of State shall notify the borrower in writing of the total of sums deducted by him under any application—

(a) on receipt of a written request for such information from the borrower; or
(b) on the termination of deductions.

(12) Where a deduction is made under this paragraph from a specified benefit, paragraph 8 (maximum amount of payment to third parties) is to have effect as if—

(a) in sub-paragraph (1) for "and 7A" there were substituted ", 7A and 7C"; and
(b) in sub-paragraph (2) for "and 7" there were substituted ", 7 and 7C".]

[[38] **Integration loans**

7D. Subject to paragraphs 2(2), 8 and 9, where a person has an integration loan which is recoverable by deductions, any weekly amount payable shall be equal to 5 per cent of the personal allowance of a single claimant aged not less than 25 years, including where the loan is a joint loan.] **2.251**

[[46] **Tax credits overpayment debts and self-assessment debts**

7E.—(1) In this paragraph— **2.252**

"self-assessment debt" means any debt which—

(a) has arisen from submission of a self-assessment to Her Majesty's Revenue and Customs under section 9 of the Taxes Management Act 1970 (returns to include self-assessment); and
(b) is recoverable under Part 6 of that Act;

"tax credits overpayment debt" means any debt which is recoverable under section 29 of the Tax Credits Act 2002 (recovery of overpayments).

(2) Where the conditions set out in sub-paragraph (3) are met, the Secretary of State may deduct from a specified benefit to which the beneficiary is entitled a sum which is up to a maximum of 3 times 5 per cent of the personal allowance for a single claimant aged not less than 25 and pay that sum to Her Majesty's Revenue and Customs towards discharge of any outstanding tax credits overpayment debt or self-assessment debt owed by the beneficiary to Her Majesty's Revenue and Customs.

(3) The conditions mentioned in sub-paragraph (2) are—

(a) that the beneficiary has given written consent to Her Majesty's Revenue and Customs for deductions to be made from a specified benefit towards discharge of any outstanding tax credits overpayment debt or self-assessment debt owed by the beneficiary to Her Majesty's Revenue and Customs; and
(b) no sum is being deducted under this paragraph.

(4) The Secretary of State shall cease making deductions from a specified benefit under this paragraph if—

(a) there is no longer sufficient entitlement to a specified benefit to enable deductions to be made;
(b) entitlement to all specified benefits has ceased;

(c) the beneficiary withdraws consent for the Secretary of State to make deductions from a specified benefit; or

(d) the beneficiary is no longer liable to repay any tax credits overpayment debt or self-assessment debt.

(5) The Secretary of State shall notify the beneficiary in writing of the total sums deducted under this paragraph—

(a) on receipt of a written request for such information from the beneficiary; or

(b) on the termination of deductions.

(6) Where a deduction is made under this paragraph from a specified benefit, paragraph 8 (maximum amount of payment to third parties) is to have effect as if—

(a) in sub-paragraph (1) for "and 7A" there were substituted ", 7A and 7E"; and

(b) in sub-paragraph (2) for "and 7D" there were substituted ", 7D and 7E".

Maximum amount of payments to third parties

2.253 **8.**—(1) The maximum aggregate amount payable under [17paragraphs] 3(2)(a), 5(6), 6(2)(a)[6, 7(3)(a)[11, 7(5)(a) and 7A]] [20. . .] [11, and [31 regulation 5 of the Council Tax Regulations and regulation 4 of the Fines Regulations] [38, and in respect of an integration loan which is recoverable by deductions] shall not exceed an amount equal to 3 times 5 per cent of the personal allowance for a single claimant aged not less than 25 years.

(2) The maximum [5aggregate] amount payable under [6 paragraphs 3(2)(a), 5, 6 [38, 7 and 7D]] shall not without the consent of the beneficiary, exceed [35 a sum calculated in accordance with sub-paragraph (4).]

[28 (2A) In the case of state pension credit, the maximum aggregate amount payable under paragraphs 3(2)(a), 5, 6, and 7 shall not, without the consent of the beneficiary, exceed a sum equal to 25 per cent. of the appropriate minimum guarantee less any housing costs under Schedule II to the State Pension Credit Regulations which may be applicable in the particular case.]

(3) [20. . .]

[35 (4) The sum referred to in sub-paragraph (2) is—

(a) where the claimant or partner does not receive child tax credit, 25 per cent of—

(i) in the case of income support, the applicable amount for the family as is awarded under sub-paragraphs (a) to (d) of regulation 17(1) (applicable amounts) or sub-paragraphs (a) to (e) of regulation 18(1) (polygamous marriages) of the Income Support Regulations;

(ii) in the case of jobseeker's allowance, the applicable amount for the family as is awarded under paragraphs (a) to (e) of regulation 83 (applicable amounts) or sub-paragraphs (a) to (f) of regulation 84(1) (polygamous marriages) of the Jobseeker's Allowance Regulations; or

(iii) in the case of state pension credit, the appropriate minimum guarantee less any housing costs under Schedule 2 to the State Pension Credit Regulations 2002 which may be applicable in the particular case;

[47 (iv) in the case of an employment and support allowance, the applicable amount for the family as is awarded under paragraph (1)(a) and (b) of regulation 67 (prescribed amounts) or paragraph (1)(a) to (c) of regulation 68 (polygamous marriages) of the Employment and Support Allowance Regulations; or]

(b) where the claimant or his partner receives child tax credit, 25 per cent of the sum of—

(i) the amount mentioned in [51 sub-paragraphs (a)(i) to (iv)], which applies to the claimant;

(ii) the amount of child benefit awarded to him or his partner by the Board under Part 2 of the Tax Credits Act 2002; and

(iii) the amount of child tax credit awarded to him or his partner by the Board under section 8 of that Act.]

Priority as between certain debts

2.254 [11**9.**—(1A) Where in any one week—

(a) more than one of the paragraphs 3 to [46 7A, 7C or 7E] are applicable to the beneficiary; or

(b) one or more of those paragraphs are applicable to the beneficiary and one or more of the following provisions, namely, [20. . .] [31 regulation 3 of the Community Charges Regulations, regulation 3 of the Community Charges (Scotland) Regulations, regulation 4 of the Fines Regulations [38, regulation 5 of the Council Tax Regulations and regulation 9 of the Integration Loans for Refugees and Others Regulations 2007] also applies; and

(c) the amount of the specified benefit which may be made to third parties is insufficient to meet the whole of the liabilities for which provision is made;

the order of priorities specified in sub-paragraph (1)(B) shall apply.

(1B) The order of priorities which shall apply in sub-paragraph (1)(A) is—

(za) [[20]. . .]

(a) any liability mentioned in paragraph 3 (housing costs) [[41] paragraph 4 (accomodation costs) or paragraph 4A (hostel payments)];

(b) any liability mentioned in paragraph 5 (service charges for fuel and rent not falling within paragraph 2(1)(a));

(c) any liability mentioned in paragraph 6 (fuel costs);

(d) any liability mentioned in paragraph 7 (water charges);

(e) any liability mentioned in [[31] regulation 3 of the Community Charges Regulations (deductions from income support etc.), regulation 3 of the Community Charges (Scotland) Regulations (deductions from income support etc.) or any liability mentioned in regulation 5 of the Council Tax Regulations (deduction from debtor's income support etc.)];

(f) any liability mentioned in [[31] regulation 4 of the Fines Regulations (deductions from offender's income support etc.)];

(g) any liability mentioned in paragraph 7A (payments in place of payments of child support maintenance).]

[[38] (ga) any liability to repay an integration loan which is recoverable by deductions.]

[[36] (h) any liability mentioned in paragraph 7C (liability in respect of loans).]

[[46] (i) any liability mention in paragraph 7E (tax credits overpayment debts and self-assessment debts.).]

[[56] *(2) As between liability for items of housing costs liabilities in respect of mortgage payments shall have priority over all other items.*]

(3) As between liabilities for items of gas or electricity the [[23] Secretary of State] shall give priority to whichever liability it considers it would, having regard to the circumstances and to any requests of the beneficiary, be appropriate to discharge.

(4) [[6]. . .]

AMENDMENTS

1. The Social Security (Claims and Payments) Amendment Regulations 1988 (SI 1988/522) reg.11 (April 11, 1988).

2. The Social Security (Claims and Payments and Payments on account, Overpayments and Recovery) Amendment Regulations 1989 (SI 1989/136) reg.2(7) (February 27, 1989).

3. The Social Security (Claims and Payments and Payments on account, Overpayments and Recovery) Amendment Regulations 1989 (SI 1989/136) reg.2(7) (April 10, 1989).

4. The Social Security (Medical Evidence, Claims and Payments) Amendment Regulations 1989 (SI 1989/1686) reg.9 (October 9, 1989).

5. The Social Security (Miscellaneous Provisions) Amendment Regulations 1990 (SI 1990/2208) reg.16 (December 5, 1990).

6. The Social Security (Miscellaneous Provisions) Amendment Regulations 1991 (SI 1991/2284) regs 12–20 (November 1, 1991).

7. The Social Security (Claims and Payments) Amendment Regulations 1992 (SI 1992/1026) reg.5 (May 25, 1992).

8. The Social Security (Miscellaneous Provisions) Amendment (No.2) Regulations 1992 (SI 1992/2595) reg.8 (November 16, 1992).

9. The Social Security (Miscellaneous Provisions) Amendment (No.2) Regulations 1992 (SI 1992/2595) Sch.1 para.8 (April 1, 1993).

10. The Social Security (Claims and Payments) Amendment Regulations 1993 (SI 1993/478) reg.2 (April 1, 1993).

11. The Deductions from Income Support (Miscellaneous Amendments) Regulations 1993 (SI 1993/495) reg.2 (April 1, 1993).

12. The Social Security (Claims and Payments) Amendment Regulations 1994 (SI 1994/2319) reg.7 (October 3, 1994).

13. The Social Security (Claims and Payments) Amendment (No.2) Regulations 1994 (SI 1994/2943) reg.15 (April 13, 1995).

14. The Social Security (Income Support and Claims and Payments) Amendment Regulations 1995 (SI 1995/1613) reg.3 and Sch.2 (October 2, 1995).

15. The Social Security (Income Support, Claims and Payments and Adjudication) Amendment Regulations 1995 (SI 1995/2927) reg.3 (December 12, 1995).

16. The Social Security (Claims and Payments etc.) Amendment Regulations 1996 (SI 1996/672) reg.2(7) (April 4, 1996).

17. The Child Support (Maintenance Assessments and Special Cases) and Social Security (Claims and Payments) Amendment Regulations 1996 (SI 1996/481) reg.6 (April 8, 1996).

18. The Social Security (Claims and Payments) (Jobseeker's Allowance Consequential Amendments) Regulations 1996 (SI 1996/1460) reg.2(26) (October 7, 1996).

19. The Social Security (Jobseeker's Allowance Consequential Amendments) (Deductions) Regulations 1996 (SI 1996/2344) reg.25 (October 7, 1996).

20. The Social Security and Child Support (Miscellaneous Amendments) Regulations 1997 (SI 1997/827) reg.7(2) (April 7, 1997).

21. The Social Security (Child Maintenance Bonus) Regulations 1996 (SI 1996/3195) reg.16(2) (April 7, 1997).

22. The Social Security (Miscellaneous Amendments) Regulations 1997 (SI 1997/454) reg.8(10) (April 6, 1997).

23. The Social Security Act 1998 (Commencement No.11 and Transitional Provisions) Order 1999 (SI 1999/2860) Sch.3 (October 18, 1999).

24. The Social Security Act 1998 (Commencement No.12 and Consequential and Transitional Provisions) Order 1999 (SI 1999/3178) Sch.6 (November 29, 1999).

25. The Social Security Amendment (Residential Care and Nursing Homes) Regulations 2002 (SI 2002/398) reg.2(2) (April 8, 2002).

26. The Social Security Amendment (Residential Care and Nursing Homes) Regulations 2002 (SI 2002/398) reg.2(3) (April 8, 2002).

27. Social Security (Claims and Payments and Miscellaneous Amendments) (No.2) Regulations 2002 (SI 2002/2441) reg.12 (October 23, 2002).

28. State Pension Credit (Consequential, Transitional and Miscellaneous Provisions) Regulations 2002 (SI 2002/3019) reg.14 (April 7, 2003).

29. The Social Security (Third Party Deductions and Miscellaneous Amendments) Regulations 2003 (SI 2003/2325) reg.2 (October 6, 2003).

30. The Social Security (Claims and Payments) Amendment Regulations 2004 (SI 2004/576) (April 12, 2004 or first benefit pay day thereafter).

31. Social Security (Claims and Payments) Amendment (No.2) Regulations 2005 (SI 2005/777) reg.3 (April 11, 2005).

32. The Social Security (Care Homes and Independent Hospitals) Regulations 2005 (SI 2005/2687) (October 24, 2005).

33. The Housing Benefit and Council Tax Benefit (Consequential Provisions) Regulations 2006 (SI 2006/217) Sch.2 para.2 (March 6, 2006).

34. The Social Security (Miscellaneous Amendments) (No.2) Regulations 2006 (SI 2006/832) reg.2 (April 10, 2006).

35. The Social Security (Miscellaneous Amendments) (No.3) Regulations 2006 (SI 2006/2377) (October 2, 2006).

36. The Social Security (Claims and Payments) Amendment (No.2) Regulations 2006 (SI 2006/3188) (December 27, 2006).

37. The Social Security Benefits Up-rating Regulations 2009 (SI 2009/607) (April 6, 2009).

38. The Social Security (Claims and Payments) Amendment (No.2) Regulations 2007 (SI 2007/1866) (July 31, 2007).

39. The Social Security (Miscellaneous Amendments) Regulations 2008 (SI 2008/698) reg.3 (April 14, 2008).

40. The Employment and Support Allowance (Consequential provisions) (No.2) Regulations 2008 (SI 2008/1554) reg.26 (October 27, 2008).

41. The Social Security (Miscellaneous Amendments) (No.6) Regulations 2008 (SI 2008/2767) reg.3 (November 17, 2008).

42. The Social Security (Miscellaneous Amendments) (No.2) Regulations 2009 (SI 2009/1490) reg.2 (July 13, 2009).

43. The Social Security (Miscellaneous Amendments) Regulations 2010 (SI 2010/510) reg.3(7) (April 6, 2010).

44. The Social Security Benefits Up-rating Regulations 2013 (SI 2013/599) reg.4 (April 8, 2013).

45. Housing and Regeneration Act 2008 (Consequential Provisions) (No.2) Order (SI 2010/671) art.4 and Sch.1 (April 1, 2010).

46. Social Security (Claims and Payments) Amendments (No.2) Regulations 2010 (SI 2010/870) reg.2 (April 30, 2010).

47. Employment and Support Allowance (Transitional Provisions, Housing Benefit and Council Tax Benefit (Existing Awards) (No.2) Regulations 2010 (SI 2010/1907) reg.26 (October 1, 2010).

48. The Social Security (Miscellaneous Amendments) Regulations 2011 (SI 2011/674) reg.4 (April 1 *or* April 4, 2011).

49. The Social Security (Miscellaneous Amendments) (No.3) Regulations 2011 (SI 2011/2425) reg.8 (October 31, 2011).

50. The Housing (Scotland) Act 2010 (Consequential Provisions and Modifications) Order 2012 (SI 2012/700) art.4 and Sch. para.10 (April 1, 2012).

51. The Social Security (Miscellaneous Amendments) Regulations 2012 (SI 2012/757) reg.12(4) (April 1, 2012).

52. The Social Security (Miscellaneous Amendments) Regulations 2013 (SI 2013/443) reg.3 (April 2, 2013).

53. The Social Security (Miscellaneous Amendments) (No.2) Regulations 2013 (SI 2013/1508) reg.2(3) (July 29, 2013).

54. The Social Security (Miscellaneous Amendments) (No.3) Regulations 2013 (SI 2013/2536) reg.5(3) (October 29, 2013).

55. The Social Security Benefits Up-rating Regulations 2024 (SI 2024/386) reg.5 (April 8, 2024).

56. The Loans for Mortgage Interest Regulations 2017 (SI 2017/725), Sch.5(1), para.7(4) from April 6, 2018, subject to transitional provisions specified in regs 19, 19A and 20 of those Regulations (as amended).

57. Words substituted by the Loans for Mortgage Interest Regulations 2017 (SI 2017/725), Sch.5(1), para.7(4) from April 6, 2018, subject to transitional provisions specified in regs 19, 19A and 20 of those Regulations (as amended).

58. The Child Support (Miscellaneous Amendments) Regulations 2019 (SI 2019/1084) reg.4 (July 4, 2019).

59. The Social Security (Claims and Payments) (Amendment) Regulations 2021 (SI 2021/456) (May 4, 2021).

60. The Social Security Benefits (Claims and Payments) (Amendment) Regulations 2023 (SI 2023/232) reg.2 (April 1, 2023, in relation to applications for a deduction for a fuel item, or for supersession in relation to a deduction for a fuel item, made on or after that date: reg.1).

DEFINITIONS

"adjudicating authority"—see reg.2(1).
"beneficiary"—see Social Security Act 1975 Sch.20.
"family"—see 1986 Act, s.20(11) (SSCBA s.137(1)).
"instrument for benefit payment"—see reg.2(1).
"jobseeker's allowance"—*ibid.*
"partner"—*ibid.*
"qualifying lender"—see Administration Act s.15A(3).

Note that these references are only to phrases defined outside Sch.9 itself. See para.1 for definitions special to Sch.9.

GENERAL NOTE

2.255 The provisions for part of weekly benefit to be diverted direct to a third party are of great importance in determining the actual weekly incomes of claimants.

On deductions in respect of rent arrears under para.5(6), *R(IS) 14/95* holds that the arrears must be proved, at least where these are disputed. In addition, the existence of an arguable counterclaim in possession proceedings is a matter that an adjudicating authority might properly take into account in deciding whether to exercise the discretionary power to make deductions under para.5(6).

See annotations to reg.35 for comment on the precedence to be accorded to child support payments and the relationship between Sch.9 and Sch.9B.

[1 SCHEDULE 9A

DEDUCTIONS OF MORTGAGE INTEREST FROM BENEFIT AND PAYMENT TO QUALIFYING LENDERS

2.256 *Schedule 9A is omitted by the Loans for Mortgage Interest Regulations 2017 (SI 2017/725), Sch.5(1), para.7(5) from April 6, 2018, subject to transitional provisions specified in regs 19, 19A and 20 of those Regulations (as amended).*

SCHEDULE 9B

DEDUCTIONS FROM BENEFIT IN RESPECT OF CHILD SUPPORT MAINTENANCE AND PAYMENT TO PERSONS WITH CARE

Interpretation

2.257 **1.** In this Schedule—

"the Act" means the Child Support Act 1991,

"beneficiary" means a person who has been awarded a specified benefit and includes each member of a joint-claim couple awarded joint-claim jobseeker's allowance,

[7 "fee" means any collection fee under Part 3 of the Child Support Fees Regulations 2014 which is payable by the non-resident parent,]

"maintenance" [2, except in [8 paragraph 3(1),]] means maintenance which a non-resident parent is liable to pay under the Act at a flat rate of child support maintenance (or would be so liable but for a variation having been agreed to), and that rate applies (or would have applied) because he falls within paragraph 4(1)(b) or (c) or 4(2) of Schedule 1 to the Act, and includes such maintenance payable at a transitional rate in accordance with Regulations made under section 29(3)(a) of the Child Support, Pensions and Social Security Act 2000,

"specified benefit" means either a benefit, pension or allowance mentioned in section 5(2) of the Social Security Administration Act 1992 and which is prescribed for the purpose of paragraph 4(1)(b) or (c) of Schedule 1 to the Act or a war disablement pension or a war widow's pension within the meaning of section 150(2) of the Social Security Contributions and Benefits Act 1992.

Deductions

2.258 **2.**—(1) Subject to paragraphs 5 and 6, the Secretary of State may deduct from a specified benefit awarded to a beneficiary, an amount equal to the amount of maintenance [7 and any fee] which is payable by the beneficiary (or in the case of income support [3, state pension credit [4, income-based jobseekers allowance or income-related employment and support allowance] payable either by the beneficiary or his partner) and pay the amount deducted to or among the person or persons with care in discharge (in whole or in part) of the liability to pay maintenance. [7, and retain any amount deducted in discharge of any liability to pay a fee.]

(2) A deduction [7 for maintenance and fees] may only be made from one of the specified benefits in any one week.

[5 (2A) Where paragraph 5 (flat rate maintenance) of Schedule 7 (deductions from benefit in respect of child support maintenance and payment to persons with care) to the 2013 Regulations applies, the Secretary of State shall not make deductions under paragraphs 5 and 6 of this Schedule, unless the amount of "specified benefit" within the meaning of paragraph 1 of Schedule 7 to the 2013 Regulations is insufficient to meet the deduction under paragraph 5 of that Schedule.]

(3) No deduction may be made unless the amount of the relevant specified benefit is not less than the total of the amounts to be deducted under this Schedule plus 10 pence.

Arrears

3.—(1) [8 . . .] The Secretary of State may deduct the sum of [8 £8.40] per week from a specified benefit which the beneficiary has been awarded and [8 . . .] pay the amount deducted to or among the person or persons with care in discharge (in whole or in part) of the beneficiary's liability to pay arrears of maintenance [7, and retain any amount deducted in discharge of any liability to pay a fee.]. 2.259

[8(1A) No deduction may be made under sub-paragraph (1) if the beneficiary is liable to pay maintenance.]

(2) [8 . . .]

[2 (3) In sub-paragraph (1) "maintenance" means child support maintenance as defined by section 3(6) of the Act—

(a) before the amendment of the definition of such maintenance by section 1(2)(a) of the Child Support, Pensions and Social Security Act 2000;

(b) after the amendment of the definition; or

(c) both before and after the amendment of the definition,

and includes maintenance payable at a transitional rate in accordance with regulations made under section 29(3)(a) of that Act.]

Apportionment

4. Where maintenance is payable to more than one person with care, the amount deducted [7 in respect of maintenance] shall be apportioned between the persons with care in accordance with paragraphs 6, 7 and 8 of Schedule 1 to the Act. 2.260

Flat rate maintenance

5.—(1) This sub-paragraph applies where the beneficiary and his partner are each liable to pay maintenance at a flat rate in accordance with paragraph 4(2) of Schedule 1 to the Act and either of them has been awarded income support [3, state pension credit] [4, income-based jobseekers allowance or income-related employment and support allowance]. 2.261

(2) Where sub-paragraph (1) applies, an amount not exceeding [6 the flat rate of maintenance] [7 and any fee] may be deducted in respect of the sum of both partners' liability to pay maintenance [7 and any fee], in the proportions described in regulation 4(3) of the Child Support (Maintenance Calculations and Special Cases) Regulations 2000 [6 or regulation 44(3) of the Child Support Maitenance Calculation Regulation 2012] and shall be paid in discharge (in whole or in part) of the respective liabilities to pay maintenance [7 or retained in discharge of any liability to pay a fee.].

Flat rate maintenance (polygamous marriage)

6.—(1) This sub-paragraph applies where two or more members of a polygamous marriage are each liable to pay maintenance at a flat rate in accordance with paragraph 4(2) of Schedule 1 to the Act and any member of the polygamous marriage has been awarded income support [3, state pension credit] [4, income-based jobseekers allowance or income-related employment and support allowance]. 2.262

(2) Where sub-paragraph (1) applies, an amount not exceeding [6 the flat rate of maintenance] [7 and any fee] may be deducted in respect of the sum of all the members' liability to pay maintenance [7, and any fee], in the proportions described in regulation 4(3) of

the Child Support (Maintenance Calculations and Special Cases) Regulations 2000 [6 or regulation 44(3) of the Child Support Maintenance Calculation Regulation 2012] and shall be paid in discharge (in whole or in part) of the respective liabilities to pay maintenance [7 or retained in discharge of any liability to pay a fee.].

(3) In this paragraph "polygamous marriage" means any marriage during the subsistence of which a party to it is married to more than one person and the ceremony of marriage took place under the law of a country which permits polygamy.

Notice

2.263 **7.** When the Secretary of State commences making deductions, he shall notify the beneficiary in writing of the amount and frequency of the deduction and the benefit from which the deduction is made and shall give further such notice when there is a change to any of the particulars specified in the notice.

General

2.264 **8.** A deduction made in accordance with this Schedule is a deduction by way of recovery for the purposes of regulation 40(3) of the Income Support (General) Regulations 1987 [4, regulation 104 of the Employment and Support Allowance Regulation] and regulation 103(3) of the Jobseeker's Allowance Regulations 1996."

Amendments

1. The Social Security (Claims and Payments) Amendment Regulations 2001 (SI 2001/18) reg.2 (January 31, 2001).

2. Social Security (Claims and Payments) Amendment (No.2) Regulations 2002 (SI 2002/1950) reg.3 (entry into force tied to entry into force of s.43 of the Child Support Act 1991 as substituted by s.21 of the Child Support, Pensions and Social Security Act 2000: March 3, 2003 in relation to certain cases, see SI 2003/192; date to be appointed for remaining cases: see Child Support, Pensions and Social Security Act 2000 s.86(2)).

3. State Pension Credit (Consequential, Transitional and Miscellaneous Provisions) Regulations 2002, SI 2002/3019 reg.14 (April 7, 2003).

4. The Employment and Support Allowance (Consequential provisions) (No.2) Regulations 2008 (SI 2008/1554) reg.28 (October 27, 2008).

5. The Social Security (Miscellaneous Amendments) (No.2) Regulations 2013 (SI 2013/1508) reg.2(4) (July 29, 2013).

6. The Child Support and Claims and Payments (Miscellaneous amendments and Change to the Minimum Amount of Liability) Regulations 2013 (SI 2013/1654) reg.3 (July 29, 2013).

7. The Child Support Fees Regulations 2014 (SI 2014/612) reg.14 (August 11, 2014).

8. The Child Support (Miscellaneous Amendments) Regulations 2019 (SI 2019/1084) reg.5 (July 4, 2019).

General Note

2.265 This schedule empowers the Secretary of State to deduct an amount in respect of certain child support maintenance liabilities from certain social security benefits where the person in receipt of the benefit is a non-resident parent. That sum is than paid to the person with the care of the child.

Regulation 3 of the amending regulations (SI 2001/18) contain a transitional provision as follows:

> "No deductions shall be made under paragraph 7A or 7B of Schedule 9 to the Claims and Payments Regulations in respect of maintenance to which Schedule 9B applies."

See annotations to reg.35 for comment on the precedence to be accorded to child support payments and the relationship between Sch.9 and Sch.9B.

[1 SCHEDULE 9ZC **Regulations 4ZC and 32ZA**

ELECTRONIC COMMUNICATION

PART 1

INTRODUCTION

Interpretation

1. In this Schedule "official computer system" means a computer system maintained by or on behalf of the Secretary of State for the sending, receiving, processing or storing of any claim, certificate, notice, information or evidence. **2.266**

PART 2

ELECTRONIC COMMUNICATION—GENERAL PROVISIONS

Conditions for the use of electronic communication

[6 **2.** (1) The Secretary of State may use an electronic communication in connection with claims for, and awards of— **2.267**

(a) carer's allowance;
(b) attendance allowance;
[7 (ba) bereavement support payment;]
(c) disability living allowance;
(d) graduated retirement benefit;
(e) a jobseeker's allowance;
(f) a retirement pension;
(g) state pension under Part 1 of the Pensions Act 2014;
(h) shared additional pension;
(i) industrial injuries benefit;
(j) an employment and support allowance;
[8 (k) a social fund funeral payment;]
[9 (l) state pension credit.]
[10 (m) a social fund payment in respect of maternity expenses;
(n) maternity allowance.]

(1A) The Secretary of State may use an electronic communication in connection with awards of—

(a) incapacity benefit;
(b) income support.
(c) [9...]

(2) A person other than the Secretary of State may use an electronic communication in connection with the matters referred to in [6 sub-paragraphs (1) and (1A)] if the conditions specified in sub-paragraphs (3) to (6) are satisfied.

(3) The first condition is that the person is for the time being permitted to use an electronic communication by an authorisation given by means of a direction of the Secretary of State.

(4) The second condition is that the person uses an approved method of—

(a) authenticating the identity of the sender of the communication;
(b) electronic communication;
(c) authenticating any claim, certificate, notice, information or evidence delivered by means of an electronic communication; and
(d) subject to sub-paragraph (7), submitting to the Secretary of State any claim, certificate, notice, information or evidence.

(5) The third condition is that any claim, certificate, notice, information or evidence sent by means of an electronic communication is in a form approved for the purpose of this Schedule.

(6) The fourth condition is that the person maintains such records in written or electronic form as may be specified in a direction given by the Secretary of State.

(7) Where the person uses any method other than the method approved by the Secretary of State, of submitting any claim, certificate, notice, information or evidence, that claim, certificate, notice, information or evidence shall be treated as not having been submitted.

(8) In this paragraph "approved" means approved by means of a direction given by the Secretary of State for the purposes of this Schedule.

Use of intermediaries

2.268 **3.** The Secretary of State may use intermediaries in connection with—

(a) the delivery of any claim, certificate, notice, information or evidence by means of an electronic communication; and

(b) the authentication or security of anything transmitted by such means,

and may require other persons to use intermediaries in connection with those matters.

PART 3

ELECTRONIC COMMUNICATION—EVIDENTIAL PROVISIONS

Effect of delivering information by means of electronic communication

2.269 **4.**—(1) Any claim, certificate, notice, information or evidence which is delivered by means of an electronic communication shall be treated as having been delivered, in the manner or form required by any provision of these Regulations, on the day the conditions imposed—

(a) by this Schedule; and

(b) by or under an applicable enactment,

are satisfied.

(2) The Secretary of State may, by a direction, determine that any claim, certificate, notice, information or evidence is to be treated as delivered on a different day (whether earlier or later) from the day provided for in sub-paragraph (1).

(3) Information shall not be taken to have been delivered to an official computer system by means of an electronic communication unless it is accepted by the system to which it is delivered.

Proof of identity of sender or recipient of information

2.270 **5.** If it is necessary to prove, for the purpose of any legal proceedings, the identity of—

(a) the sender of any claim, certificate, notice, information or evidence delivered by means of an electronic communication to an official computer system; or

(b) the recipient of any such claim, certificate, notice, information or evidence delivered by means of an electronic communication from an official computer system,

the sender or recipient, as the case may be, shall be presumed to be the person whose name is recorded as such on that official computer system.

Proof of delivery of information

2.271 **6.**—(1) If it is necessary to prove, for the purpose of any legal proceedings, that the use of an electronic communication has resulted in the delivery of any claim, certificate, notice, information or evidence this shall be presumed to have been the case where—

(a) any such claim, certificate, notice, information or evidence has been delivered to the Secretary of State, if the delivery of that claim, certificate, notice, information or evidence has been recorded on an official computer system; or

(b) any such certificate, notice, information or evidence has been delivered by the Secretary of State, if the delivery of that certificate, notice, information or evidence has been recorded on an official computer system.

(2) If it is necessary to prove, for the purpose of any legal proceedings, that the use of an electronic communication has resulted in the delivery of any such claim, certificate, notice, information or evidence, this shall be presumed not to be the case, if that claim, certificate, notice, information or evidence delivered to the Secretary of State has not been recorded on an official computer system.

(3) If it is necessary to prove, for the purpose of any legal proceedings, when any such claim, certificate, notice, information or evidence sent by means of an electronic communication has been received, the time and date of receipt shall be presumed to be that recorded on an official computer system.

Proof of content of information

7. If it is necessary to prove, for the purpose of any legal proceedings, the content of any claim, certificate, notice, information or evidence sent by means of an electronic communication, the content shall be presumed to be that recorded on an official computer system.] 2.272

AMENDMENTS

1. The Social Security (Electronic Communications) (Carer's Allowance) Order 2003 (SI 2003/2800) reg.2 (December 1, 2003).

2. The Social Security (Electronic Communications) (Miscellaneous Benefits) Order 2005 (SI 2005/3321) (January 30, 2006).

3. The Social Security (Electronic Communications) Order 2011 (SI 2011/1498) reg.4(4) (June 20, 2011).

4. The Social Security (Electronic Communications) (No.2) Order 2011 (SI 2011/2943) (January 23, 2012).

5. The Pensions Act 2014 (Consequential, Supplementary and Incidental Amendments) Order 2015 (SI 2015/1985) art.9(20) (April 6, 2016).

6. Social Security (Claims and Payments) Amendment Regulations 2016 (SI 2016/544) reg.2 (June 15, 2016).

7. The Pensions Act 2014 (Consequential, Supplementary and Incidental Amendments) Order 2017 (SI 2017/422) art.10 (April 6, 2017).

8. The Social Fund Funeral Expenses Amendment Regulations 2018 (SI 2018/61) reg.2 (April 2, 2018).

9. The State Pension Credit (Coronavirus) (Electronic Claims) (Amendment) Regulations 2020 (SI 2020/456) reg.2 (May 4, 2020).

10. The Social Fund and Social Security (Claims and Payments) (Amendment) Regulations 2020 (SI 2020/600) reg.4 (July 9, 2020).

GENERAL NOTE

Details of what is authorised to be done by way of electronic communication, what information may be given in that way and the approved methods of doing so and of associated issues such as authentication are set out in the Social Security (Electronic Communications) Consolidation and Amendment Directions 2011 (as amended). They are at para.2.377 below. 2.273

For a case exploring the issues when an electronic claim goes wrong, see *CW v SSWP (JSA)* [2016] UKUT 114 discussed in the annotations to reg.4ZC at para.2.59 above.

A number of issues relating to the making of a claim online—albeit in the context of a claim for universal credit to which the Universal Credit, Personal Independence Payment, Jobseeker's Allowance and Employment and Support Allowance (Claims and Payments) Regulations 2013 (SI 2014/380) rather than the present Regulations apply—were canvassed by Judge Wikeley in *GDC v SSWP (UC)* [2020] UKUT 108 (AAC), including the legal basis for, and the interpretation of, the 2011 Directions mentioned above.

SCHEDULE 9C

ELECTRONIC COMMUNICATION

Revoked subject to transitional provisions by the Child Benefit and Guardian's Allowance (Administration) Regulations 2003 (SI 2003/492) Sch.3(1) para.1 (April 7, 2003). 2.274

The Universal Credit, Personal Independence Payment, Jobseeker's Allowance and Employment and Support Allowance (Claims and Payments) Regulations 2013

(SI 2013/380)

COMMENCEMENT: APRIL 8, 2013—FOR THE PURPOSE OF PERSONAL INDEPENDENCE PAYMENT

COMMENCEMENT: APRIL 29, 2013—FOR THE PURPOSES OF UNIVERSAL CREDIT, JOBSEEKER'S ALLOWANCE AND EMPLOYMENT AND SUPPORT ALLOWANCE

PART 1

GENERAL

PART 2

CLAIMS

PART 3

EVIDENCE, INFORMATION AND NOTIFICATION OF CHANGES OF CIRCUMSTANCES

PART 4

PAYMENTS

PART 5

THIRD PARTIES

PART 6

MOBILITY COMPONENT OF PERSONAL INDEPENDENCE PAYMENT

SCHEDULES

The Secretary of State, in exercise of the powers conferred upon him by the provisions set out in Schedule 1 to these Regulations, makes the following Regulations.

In accordance with section 172(1) of the Social Security Administration Act 1992, the Secretary of State has referred the proposals for these Regulations to the Social Security Advisory Committee.

The Secretary of State has consulted with organisations representing qualifying lenders likely to be affected by the fee specified in paragraph 9(2) of Schedule 5 to the Regulations (direct payment to lender of deductions in respect of interest on secured loans)(**2**).

In accordance with section 176(2)(b) of the Social Security Administration Act 1992 and in so far as these Regulations relate to housing benefit, the Secretary of State has obtained the agreement of organisations appearing to him to be representative of the authorities concerned that proposals in respect of these Regulations should not be referred to them.

PART 1

GENERAL

Citation and commencement

1.—(1) These Regulations may be cited as the Universal Credit, Personal Independence Payment, Jobseeker's Allowance and Employment and Support Allowance (Claims and Payments) Regulations 2013. **2.276**

(2) For the purpose of personal independence payment these Regulations come into force on 8th April 2013.

(3) For the purposes of universal credit, jobseeker's allowance and employment and support allowance these Regulations come into force on 29th April 2013.

GENERAL NOTE

Note the commencement provisions in relation to the matters covered by these regulations, especially when considering benefits other than universal credit. The provisions affecting a personal independence payment entered into force on April 8, 2013, while those relating to universal credit and new-style employment and support allowance and jobseeker's allowance entered into force on April 29, 2013. Care must be taken to apply the right regulations to old-style and new-style employment and support allowance and jobseeker's allowance. **2.277**

In particular, the new regulations signal the move to online claiming of benefit as the primary channel of communication between the Department and a claimant.

Interpretation

2. In these Regulations— **2.278**

"the 1991 Act" means the Child Support Act 1991;

"the 2012 Act" means the Welfare Reform Act 2012;

"the Administration Act" means the Social Security Administration Act 1992;

"the Contributions and Benefits Act" means the Social Security Contributions and Benefits Act 1992;

"the Jobseeker's Allowance Regulations" means the Jobseeker's Allowance Regulations 2013;

"the Personal Independence Payment Regulations" means the Social Security (Personal Independence Payment) Regulations 2013;

"the Universal Credit Regulations" means the Universal Credit Regulations 2013;

"appropriate office" means—

(a) an office of the Department for Work and Pensions or any other place designated by the Secretary of State in relation to any case or class of case as a place to, or at which, any claim, notice, document, evidence or other information may be sent, delivered or received for the purposes of these Regulations and includes a postal address specified by the Secretary of State for that purpose; or

(b) in the case of a person who is authorised or required by these Regulations to use an electronic communication for any purpose, an address to which such communications may be sent in accordance with Schedule 2;

"assessment period" has the meaning given by regulation 21 of the Universal Credit Regulations;

"attendance allowance" means an allowance payable by virtue of section 64 of the Contributions and Benefits Act;

"benefit", except in regulation 60 and Schedules 5 and 6, means universal credit, personal independence payment, a jobseeker's allowance or an employment and support allowance;

"child" has the meaning given by section 40 of the 2012 Act;

"claimant" in relation to—

(a) universal credit, has the meaning given by section 40 of the 2012 Act;

(b) personal independence payment, means any person who is a claimant for the purposes of regulations made under Part 4 (personal independence payment) of that Act;

(c) a jobseeker's allowance, has the meaning given by section 35(1) of the Jobseekers Act 1995; and

(d) an employment and support allowance, has the meaning given by section 24(1) of the Welfare Reform 2007 Act;

"couple" has the meaning given by section 39 of the 2012 Act;

"disability living allowance" means an allowance payable by virtue of section 71 of the Contributions and Benefits Act;

"earned income" has the meaning given by regulation 52 of the Universal Credit Regulations;

"electronic communication" has the meaning given by section 15(1) of the Electronic Communications Act 2000;

"employment and support allowance" means an allowance under Part 1 of the Welfare Reform Act 2007 as amended by the provisions of Schedule 3, and Part 1 of Schedule 14, to the 2012 Act that remove references to an income-related allowance;

"jobseeker's allowance" means an allowance under the Jobseekers Act 1995 as amended by the provisions of Part 1 of Schedule 14 to the 2012 Act that remove references to an income-based allowance;

"limited capability for work" has the meaning given by section 1(4) of the Welfare Reform Act 2007;

"local authority" has the meaning given by section 191 of the Administration Act;

"maternity allowance" means an allowance payable by virtue of section 35 of the Contributions and Benefits Act;

"official computer system" means a computer system maintained by or on behalf of the Secretary of State to—

(a) send or receive any claim or information; or

(b) process or store any claim or information;

"partner" means one of a couple;

"personal independence payment" means the allowance under Part 4 of the 2012 Act;

"qualifying young person" has the meaning given by regulation 5 of the Universal Credit Regulations;

"regular and substantial caring responsibilities for a severely disabled person" has the meaning given by regulation 30 of the Universal Credit Regulations;

"universal credit" means the benefit under Part 1 of the 2012 Act;

"writing" includes writing produced by means of electronic communications used in accordance with Schedule 2.

General Note

Section 15 of the Electronic Communications Act 2000 (as amended) provides that: 2.279

"electronic communication" means a communication transmitted (whether from one person to another, from one device to another or from a person to a device or vice versa)—

(a) by means of an electronic communications network; or
(b) by other means but while in an electronic form.

Use of electronic communications

3.—Schedule 2 makes provision as to the use of electronic communications 2.280

Definition

"electronic communication"—see reg.2 and its General Note.

Consequential amendments

4.—Schedule 3 makes amendments to other regulations which are consequential upon these Regulations. 2.281

Disapplication of section 1(1A) of the Administration Act

5. Section 1(1A) of the Administration Act (requirements in respect of a national insurance number) is not to apply to a child or a qualifying young person in respect of whom universal credit is claimed. 2.282

Definitions

"the Administration Act"—see reg.2.
"universal credit"—*ibid.*

PART 2

Claims

Claims not required for entitlement to universal credit in certain cases

6. [1 . . .] 2.283

Amendment

1. Revoked by the Universal Credit (Digital Service) Amendment Regulations 2014 (SI 2014/2887) reg.3(2)(a) (November 26, 2014). The revocation is subject to a saving provision in reg.5 of SI 2014/2887.

General Note

SSAA 1992 s.1(1) provides that except in such cases as may be prescribed, no person shall be entitled to any benefit unless, in addition to satisfying any other conditions of entitlement, he or she "makes a claim for it in the manner, and within the time, prescribed in relation to that benefit by regulations" under SSAA Pt 1. 2.284

From April 29, 2014, reg.6 set out the exceptions to that general rule, in which a former entitlement to universal credit could revive without a claim being made, if not more than six months had elapsed since the previous entitlement ended. The only such exceptions relate to people who cease to be—or become—members of a couple and are to be found in reg.9(6) and (7). Claimants who were formerly entitled to universal credit and become so entitled again must now make a new claim. However, more favourable rules apply if the claim is made within six months of the old entitlement ending and (if applicable) within seven days of any claimant ceasing paid work: see UC Regulations regs 21(3C) and 22A.

Claims not required for entitlement to an employment and support allowance in certain cases

2.285 [1 **7.**—(1) It is not to be a condition of entitlement to an employment and support allowance that a claim be made for it where—

(a) the claimant has made and is pursuing an appeal against a relevant decision of the Secretary of State, and

(b) the appeal relates to a decision to terminate or not to award an employment and support allowance for which a claim was made.

(2) In this regulation—

"appellate authority" means the First-tier Tribunal, the Upper Tribunal, the Court of Appeal, the Court of Session, or the Supreme Court; and

"relevant decision" means—

(a) a decision that embodies the first determination by the Secretary of State that the claimant does not have limited capability for work; or

(b) a decision that embodies the first determination by the Secretary of State that the claimant does not have limited capability for work since a previous determination by the Secretary of State or appellate authority that the claimant does have limited capability for work.]

AMENDMENT

1. The Employment and Support Allowance (Repeat Assessments and Pending Appeal Awards) (Amendment) Regulations 2015 (SI 2015/437) reg.6 (March 30, 2015).

DEFINITIONS

"claimant"—see reg.2.

"employment and support allowance"—*ibid.*

Making a claim for universal credit

2.286 **8.**—(1) Except as provided in paragraph (2), a claim for universal credit must be made by means of an electronic communication in accordance with the provisions set out in Schedule 2 and completed in accordance with any instructions given by the Secretary of State for that purpose.

(2) A claim for universal credit may be made by telephone call to the telephone number specified by the Secretary of State if the claim falls within a class of case for which the Secretary of State accepts telephone claims or where, in any other case, the Secretary of State is willing to do so.

(3) A claim for universal credit made by means of an electronic communication in accordance with the provisions set out in Schedule 2 is defective if it is not completed in accordance with any instructions of the Secretary of State.

(4) A claim made by telephone in accordance with paragraph (2) is properly completed if the Secretary of State is provided during that call with all the information required to determine the claim and the claim is defective if not so completed.

(5) If a claim for universal credit is defective the Secretary of State must inform the claimant of the defect and of the relevant provisions of regulation 10 relating to the date of claim.

(6) The Secretary of State must treat the claim as properly made in the first instance if—

(a) in the case of a claim made by telephone, the person corrects the defect; or

(b) in the case of a claim made by means of an electronic communication, a claim completed in accordance with any instructions of the Secretary of State is received at an appropriate office,

within one month, or such longer period as the Secretary of State considers reasonable, from the date on which the claimant is first informed of the defect.

General Note

In *GDC v SSWP (UC)* [2020] UKUT 108 (AAC), Judge Wikeley had to consider whether a claim (albeit a defective claim) for universal credit was made when a person began populating the online claim form with data and saving it to the official computer system, or only at the end of the process, potentially some days later, when the claimant clicked on the "Submit claim" button. The decision notes that telephone claims under reg.8(2) are, in reality, online claims made through an intermediary and thus that universal credit, unlike the legacy benefits, is "digital by default". Regulation 8(1) requires that to be valid an electronic claim must be both in accordance with the provisions of Sch.2 and completed in accordance with any instructions given by SSWP for that purpose, although the judge considered it hard to see what the latter category might add. In order to be capable of constituting a defective claim (and so potentially having the benefit of reg.8(5) and (6)), it is a precondition that the electronic claim should have been made in accordance with Sch.2, thus a failure to meet the requirements of the Schedule results in a claim that has not yet been made, rather than a defective one. The housing benefit decision in *Novitskaya v Brent LBC* [2009] EWCA Civ 1260 could be distinguished and wider dicta in it "must be applied with some caution in the very different digital environment of online claims for universal credit" (at [65]). In practical terms, the decision means that a claimant who logs out of the universal credit claim site, for instance in order to get information or just to have a rest, will not have made a claim at that point and will only have done so when they return to it and submit it subsequently. 2.287

Claims for universal credit by members of a couple

9.—(1) Where a person is a member of a couple and may make a claim as a single person by virtue of regulation 3(3) (couples) of the Universal Credit Regulations, but instead makes a claim for universal credit jointly, that claim is to be treated as a claim made by that person as a single person. 2.288

(2) Where a claim for universal credit is made jointly by a member ("M1") of a polygamous marriage with another member of the polygamous marriage ("M2"), that claim is to be treated as a claim made by M1 as a single person where—

(a) M1 is not a party to an earlier marriage in the polygamous marriage, and

(b) any party to an earlier marriage is living in the same household as M1 and M2.

(3) In paragraph (2) "polygamous marriage" means a marriage during which a party to it is married to more than one person and which took place under the laws of a country which permits polygamy.

(4) The Secretary of State may treat a claim made by members of a couple as single persons as a claim made jointly by the couple where it is determined by the Secretary of State that they are a couple.

(5) Where the Secretary of State considers that one member of a couple is unable to make a joint claim with the other member of that couple, the other member of the couple may make a claim jointly for both of them.

[[2] (6) Where an award of universal credit to joint claimants is terminated because they cease to be a couple an award may be made, without a claim, to either or each one of them—

(a) as a single person; or

(b) if either of them has formed a new couple with a person who is already entitled to universal credit, jointly with that person.]

(7) Where awards of universal credit to two single claimants are terminated because they form a couple who are joint claimants, it is not to be a condition of entitlement to universal credit that the couple make a claim for it and universal credit may be awarded to them jointly.

(8) A couple who are joint claimants are to be treated as making a claim for universal credit where—

[[2] (a) one of them ceased to be entitled to an award of universal credit (whether as a single person or as a member of a different couple) on the formation of that couple;] and

(b) the other member of the couple did not have an award of universal credit as a single person before formation of the couple,

[[1] and the claim is to be treated as made on the day after the member of the couple mentioned in sub-paragraph (a) ceased to be entitled to universal credit.]

(9) In relation to an award which may be made by virtue of paragraph (6) or (7) without a claim being required, a claimant and every person by whom or on whose behalf, sums by way of universal credit are receivable must supply in such manner and at such times as the Secretary of State may determine such information or evidence as the Secretary of State may require in connection with the formation or dissolution of a couple.

(10) Where an award of universal credit to joint claimants is terminated because one of them has died it is not to be a condition of entitlement to universal credit that the surviving partner makes a claim for it.

AMENDMENTS

1. The Social Security (Miscellaneous Amendments) No.2) Regulations 2013 (SI 2013/1508) reg.6 (July 29, 2013).

2. The Universal Credit (Digital Service) Amendment Regulations 2014 (SI 2014/2887) reg.3 (November 26, 2014). There are savings provisions in reg.5 of SI 2014/2887.

DEFINITIONS

"couple"—see reg.2 and WRA 2012 s.39.

"universal credit"—see reg.2.

2.289 GENERAL NOTE

See the commentary to reg.3 of the Universal Credit Regulations (in Vol.II).

Date of claim for universal credit

10.—(1) Where a claim for universal credit is made, the date on which the claim is made is— 2.290

(a) subject to sub-paragraph (b), in the case of a claim made by means of an electronic communication in accordance with regulation 8(1), the date on which the claim is received at an appropriate office;

(b) in the case of a claim made by means of an electronic communication in accordance with regulation 8(1), where the claimant receives assistance at home or at an appropriate office from the Secretary of State, or a person providing services to the Secretary of State, which is provided for the purpose of enabling that person to make a claim, the date of first notification of a need for such assistance;

(c) subject to sub-paragraph (d), in the case of a claim made by telephone in accordance with 8(2), the date on which that claim is properly completed in accordance with regulation 8(4); or

(d) where the Secretary of State is unable to accept a claim made by telephone in accordance with regulation 8(2) on the date of first notification of intention to make the claim, the date of first notification, provided a claim properly completed in accordance with regulation 8(4) is made within one month of that date,

or the first day in respect of which the claim is made if later than the above.

(2) In the case of a claim which is defective by virtue of regulation 8, the date of claim is to be the first date on which the defective claim is received or made but is treated as properly made in the first instance in accordance with regulation 8(6).

DEFINITIONS

"appropriate office"—see reg.2.
"claimant"—*ibid.*
"electronic communication"—*ibid.*
"universal credit"—*ibid.*

GENERAL NOTE

Regulation 10 identifies the date on which a claim for universal credit is made. Online claims are made when received by the DWP (para.(1)(a)), unless the person received assistance to complete the form from an officer of the Department (or a contractor providing services to the Secretary of State) in which case the date of claim is the date on which the Secretary of State was told that assistance was needed (para.(1)(b)). A telephone claim is made on the day reg.8(4) is satisfied (i.e., when the Secretary of State is provided with all the information required to determine the claim) (para.(1)(c)). But if the Department cannot accept a telephone claim on the same day as the claimant first notifies it that it would like to make one, then the claim is made on that day as long as a properly completed telephone claim is made within a month of that day (para.(1)(d)). 2.291

Paragraph (2) applies where a defective claim is treated as properly made in the first instance under reg.8(6). Such a claim is made on the first date the defective claim was received.

See *GDC v SSWP (UC)* [2020] UKUT 108, considered under reg.8 above.

Making a claim for personal independence payment

2.292 **11.**—(1) A claim for personal independence payment must be made—

(a) in writing on a form authorised by the Secretary of State for that purpose and completed in accordance with the instructions on the form;

(b) by telephone call to the telephone number specified by the Secretary of State; or

(c) by receipt by the claimant of a telephone call from the Secretary of State made for the purpose of enabling a claim for personal independence payment to be made,

unless in any case or class of case the Secretary of State decides only to accept a claim made in one of the ways specified in paragraph (a), (b) or (c).

(2) In the case of a claim made in writing the claim must be sent to or received at the appropriate office.

(3) A claim for personal independence payment made in writing is defective if it is not completed in accordance with any instructions of the Secretary of State.

(4) A claim made by telephone in accordance with paragraph (1) is properly completed if the Secretary of State is provided during that call with all the information required to determine the claim and the claim is defective if not so completed.

(5) If a claim for personal independence payment is defective the Secretary of State must inform the claimant of the defect and of the relevant provisions of regulation 12 relating to the date of claim.

(6) The Secretary of State must treat the claim as properly made in the first instance if a claim completed in accordance with any instructions of the Secretary of State is received within one month, or such longer period as the Secretary of State may consider reasonable, from the date on which the claimant is first informed of the defect.

(7) Paragraph (8) applies where—

(a) a person ("P1") makes a claim for personal independence payment on behalf of another person ("P2") whom P1 asserts to be a person unable for the time being to act; and

(b) the Secretary of State makes a decision not to appoint P1 under regulation 57.

(8) The Secretary of State must treat the claim made by P1 as properly made by P2 in the first instance if a further claim made by P2 is received within one month, or such longer period as the Secretary of State may consider reasonable, from the date the Secretary of State notified the decision not to appoint P1 under regulation 57.

DEFINITIONS

"claimant"—see reg.2.
"personal independence payment"—*ibid.*
"writing"—*ibid.*

GENERAL NOTE

2.293 Claims for personal independence payment are generally initiated by telephone in the first instance. Although the Explanatory Memorandum indicated that an online service was planned for introduction in 2014, it is not currently possible to claim PIP online. This regulation provides also for paper claims until such time as the Secretary of State decides to accept claims made only through a particular medium.

In *GG v SSWP (PIP)* [2019] UKUT 318 (AAC), Judge Hemingway, obiter, explores some of the difficulties in reg.11(4) and records a pragmatic submission on behalf of SSWP which he found helpful:

> "[I]t is odd, as the claimant picks up on, that regulation 11 of the PIP C and P Regs 2013 states that a claim made by telephone is properly completed if the Secretary of State is provided during that call with all the information required to determine the claim and that, otherwise, the claim is defective. But it is really very difficult to envisage a telephone conversation in which all of the information which might conceivably be required before a fair and informed decision can be made might be provided. That would certainly mean, in effect, the person receiving the call going through each and every question with the claimant which would be asked on the claimant questionnaire. Even then, very probably, there would need to be further medical information and opinion obtained from a health professional via a paper based report or (I think much more commonly) a face-to-face assessment with a report following that. That medical input cannot, of course, be obtained by way of a telephone conversation between the claimant and the call handler. Further, the contention put forward by the claimant would mean, in effect, that a claim had not been properly completed until the point at which it was ready to be actually determined. The better way of looking at it, it seems to me, is to say, as the Secretary of State's representative suggests, that notwithstanding the rather loose, misleading or unclear wording of regulation 11(4), the claim if made by telephone is actually made once the various questions concerning the 'lay conditions' have been answered to the satisfaction of the Secretary of State such that she accepts the claim as having been made and as not being defective. What then follows is really the gathering of evidence relevant to the question of whether the claim, as made, should be allowed and if so on what terms. The phrase "all the information required to determine the claim" is not to be taken to mean all the information a diligent decision-maker might wish to have before making a fully informed decision but, rather, enough information to enable the making of a coherent decision on the claim in light of whatever evidence might or might not then be obtained in the process of considering that claim. There might though be some merit in consideration being given to rewording the regulation in order to aid clarity of understanding."

Date of claim for personal independence payment

12.—(1) Subject to paragraph (4), where a claim for personal independence payment is made in accordance with regulation 11 the date on which the claim is made is— 2.294

(a) in the case of a claim in writing made by means of an electronic communication in accordance with the provisions set out in Schedule 2, the date on which the claim is received at the appropriate office;

(b) in the case of a claim made by telephone, the date on which a claim made by telephone is properly completed; or

(c) where a person first notifies an intention to make a claim and provided that a claim made in writing produced other than by means of an electronic communication is properly completed and received at the appropriate office designated by the Secretary of State in that claimant's case within one month or such longer period as the Secretary of State considers reasonable of the date of first notification, the date of first notification,

or the first day in respect of which the claim is made if later than the above.

(2) In the case of a claim which is defective by virtue of regulation 11(3) or (4)—

(a) subject to sub-paragraph (b) and paragraph (4), the date of claim is to be the first date on which the defective claim is received or made but is treated as properly made in the first instance in accordance with regulation 11(6);
(b) the date of claim is to be the date of first notification of an intention to make a claim where a claim made by a person to whom paragraph (1)(c) applies is defective but is treated as properly made in the first instance in accordance with regulation 11(6).

(3) In the case of a claim which is treated as properly made by the claimant in accordance with regulation 11(8), the date on which the claim is made is the date on which it was received in the first instance.

(4) Where a further claim made by a person ("P2") in the circumstances set out in regulation 11(8) is defective and that further claim is treated as properly made in the first instance in accordance with regulation 11(6), the date of claim is to be the date on which the claim made by the person ("P1") whom the Secretary of State decided not to appoint under regulation 57 was received in the first instance.

(5) In a case where the Secretary of State decides not to award personal independence payment following a claim for it being made on behalf of another expressly on the ground of terminal illness (which has the meaning given by section 82(4) of the 2012 Act), the date of claim is to be—
(a) the date that claim was made if a further claim, made in accordance with regulation 11, is received within one month, or such longer period as the Secretary of State may consider reasonable, from the date the Secretary of State notified the decision not to award personal independence payment on the ground of terminal illness; or
(b) the date that claim was made where the further claim is defective but is treated as properly made in the first instance in accordance with regulation 11(6).

DEFINITIONS

"appropriate office"—see reg.2.
"claimant"—*ibid.*
"electronic communication"—*ibid.*
"personal independence payment"—*ibid.*
"writing"—*ibid.*

Making a claim for an employment and support allowance by telephone

2.295 **13.**—(1) Except where the Secretary of State directs in any case or class of case that a claim must be made in writing, a claim for an employment and support allowance may be made by telephone call to the telephone number specified by the Secretary of State.

(2) Where the Secretary of State, in any particular case, directs that the person making the claim approves a written statement of the person's circumstances provided for the purpose by the Secretary of State, a telephone claim is not a valid claim unless the person complies with the direction.

(3) A claim made by telephone in accordance with paragraph (1) is properly completed if the Secretary of State is provided during that call with all the information required to determine the claim and the claim is defective if not so completed.

(4) Where a telephone claim is defective, the Secretary of State must advise the person making it of the defect and of the effect on the date of claim of the provisions of regulation 14.

(5) If the person corrects the defect so that the claim then satisfies the requirements of paragraph (3) and does so within one month, or such longer period as the Secretary of State considers reasonable, of the date the Secretary of State first drew attention to the defect, the Secretary of State must treat the claim as if it had been properly made in the first instance.

DEFINITION

"employment and support allowance"—see reg.2.

Date of claim for an employment and support allowance where claim made by telephone

14. In the case of a telephone claim, the date on which the claim is made is to be the first date on which— 2.296

(a) a claim made by telephone is properly completed;
(b) a person first notifies the Secretary of State of an intention to make a claim, provided that a claim made by telephone is properly completed within one month or such longer period as the Secretary of State considers reasonable of first notification; or
(c) a defective claim is received but is treated as properly made in the first instance in accordance with regulation 13(5),

or the first day in respect of which the claim is made if later than the above.

Making a claim for an employment and support allowance in writing

15.—(1) A claim for an employment and support allowance may be made to the Secretary of State in writing on a form authorised by the Secretary of State for that purpose and must be completed in accordance with the instructions on the form. 2.297

(2) A written claim for an employment and support allowance, which is made on the form approved for the time being, is properly completed if completed in accordance with the instructions on the form and defective if not so completed.

(3) If a written claim is defective when first received, the Secretary of State must advise the person making it of the defect and of the effect on the date of claim of the provisions of regulation 16.

(4) If the person corrects the defect so that the claim then satisfies the requirements of paragraph (2) and does so within one month, or such longer period as the Secretary of State considers reasonable, of the date the Secretary of State first drew attention to the defect, the Secretary of State must treat the claim as if it had been properly made in the first instance.

DEFINITIONS

"employment and support allowance"—see reg.2.
"writing"—*ibid.*

Date of claim for an employment and support allowance where claim made in writing

16. In the case of a written claim for an employment and support allowance, the date on which the claim is made is to be the first date on which— 2.298

(a) a properly completed claim is received in an appropriate office;
(b) a person first notifies an intention to make a claim, provided that a properly completed claim form is received in an appropriate office within one month, or such longer period as the Secretary of State considers reasonable, of first notification; or
(c) a defective claim is received but is treated as properly made in the first instance in accordance with regulation 15(4),

or the first day in respect of which the claim is made if later than the above.

DEFINITIONS

"appropriate office"—see reg.2.
"employment and support allowance"—*ibid.*

Claims for an employment and support allowance where no entitlement to statutory sick pay

2.299 **17.**—(1) Paragraph (2) applies to a claim for an employment and support allowance for a period of limited capability for work in relation to which the claimant gave the claimant's employer a notice of incapacity under regulation 7 of the Statutory Sick Pay (General) Regulations 1982 and for which the claimant has been informed in writing by the employer that there is no entitlement to statutory sick pay.

(2) A claim to which this paragraph applies is to be treated as made on the date accepted by the claimant's employer as the first day of incapacity, provided that the claimant makes the claim within the period of 3 months beginning with the day on which the claimant is informed in writing by the employer that the claimant was not entitled to statutory sick pay.

DEFINITIONS

"claimant"—see reg.2.
"employment and support allowance"—*ibid.*
"limited capability for work"—*ibid.*
"writing"—*ibid.*

Special provisions where it is certified that a woman is expected to be confined or where she has been confined

2.300 **18.** Where, in a certificate issued or having effect as issued under the Social Security (Medical Evidence) Regulations 1976, it has been certified that it is to be expected that a woman will be confined and she makes a claim for maternity allowance in expectation of that confinement, any such claim may, unless the Secretary of State otherwise directs, be treated as a claim for an employment and support allowance, made in respect of any days in the period beginning with either—

(a) the beginning of the sixth week before the expected week of confinement; or
(b) the actual date of confinement,

whichever is the earlier, and ending in either case on the 14th day after the actual date of confinement.

(2) Where, in a certificate issued under the Social Security (Medical Evidence) Regulations 1976 it has been certified that a woman has been

confined and she claims maternity allowance within three months of the date of her confinement, her claim may be treated in the alternative or in addition as a claim for an employment and support allowance for the period beginning with the date of her confinement and ending 14 days after that date.

DEFINITIONS

"employment and support allowance"—see reg.2.
"maternity allowance"—*ibid.*

Making a claim for a jobseeker's allowance: attendance at an appropriate office

19. A person wishing to make a claim for a jobseeker's allowance, unless the Secretary of State otherwise directs, is required to attend for the purpose of making a claim for that allowance, in person at an appropriate office or such other place, and at such time, as the Secretary of State may specify in that person's case. 2.301

DEFINITIONS

"appropriate office"—see reg.2.
"jobseeker's allowance"—*ibid.*

Date of claim where a person claiming a jobseeker's allowance is required to attend at an appropriate office

20.—(1) Subject to regulation 29(6), where a person is required to attend in accordance with regulation 19, if the person subsequently attends for the purpose of making a claim for a jobseeker's allowance at the place and time specified by the Secretary of State and, if so requested, provides a properly completed claim form at or before the time when the person is required to attend, the claim is to be treated as made on whichever is the later of the date of first notification of intention to make that claim or the first day in respect of which the claim is made. 2.302

(2) Where a person who is required to attend in accordance with regulation 19 without good cause fails to attend at either the place or time specified in that person's case, or does not, if so requested, provide a properly completed claim form at or before the time when the person is required to attend, the claim is to be treated as made on the first day on which the person does attend at the specified place or time or does provide a properly completed claim form, or if later the first day in respect of which the claim is made.

(3) The Secretary of State may direct that the time for providing a properly completed claim form may be extended to a date no later than the date one month after the date of first notification of intention to make that claim.

DEFINITION

"jobseeker's allowance"—see reg.2.

Making a claim for a jobseeker's allowance in writing

21.—(1) Except where a person is required to attend in accordance with regulation 19, a claim for a jobseeker's allowance may be made in writing 2.303

on a form authorised by the Secretary of State for that purpose and may be delivered or sent to the Secretary of State at an appropriate office.

(2) A claim made in accordance with paragraph (1) must be completed in accordance with the instructions on the form.

(3) A written claim for a jobseeker's allowance made under this regulation or regulation 20, which is made on the form approved for the time being, is properly completed if completed in accordance with the instructions on the form and defective if not so completed.

(4) If a written claim made under this regulation is defective when first received, the Secretary of State must advise the person making it of the defect and of the effect on the date of claim of the provisions of regulation 22.

(5) If that person corrects the defect so that the claim then satisfies the requirements of paragraph (3) and does so within one month, or such longer period as the Secretary of State considers reasonable, from the date the Secretary of State first drew attention to the defect, the claim must be treated as having been properly made in the first instance.

DEFINITIONS

"appropriate office"—see reg.2.
"jobseeker's allowance"—*ibid.*
"writing"—*ibid.*

Date of claim for a jobseeker's allowance where claim made in writing

2.304 **22.** Subject to regulation 29(6), in the case of a written claim for a jobseeker's allowance made under regulation 21, the date on which the claim is made or treated as made is to be the first date on which—

(a) a properly completed claim is received in an appropriate office;
(b) a person first notifies an intention to make a claim, provided that a properly completed claim form is received in an appropriate office within one month or such longer period as the Secretary of State considers reasonable of first notification; or
(c) a defective claim is received but is treated as properly made in the first instance in accordance with regulation 21(5),

or the first day in respect of which the claim is made if later than the above.

DEFINITIONS

"appropriate office"—see reg.2.
"jobseeker's allowance"—*ibid.*

Making a claim for a jobseeker's allowance by telephone

2.305 **23.**—(1) Except where a person is required to attend in accordance with regulation 19, or where the Secretary of State in any case directs that the claim must be made in writing in accordance with regulation 21, a claim for a jobseeker's allowance may be made by telephone call to the telephone number specified by the Secretary of State where such a claim falls within a class of case for which the Secretary of State accepts telephone claims or in any other case where the Secretary of State is willing to do so.

(2) A claim made by telephone in accordance with paragraph (1) is properly completed if the Secretary of State is provided during that call with all

the information required to determine the claim and the claim is defective if not so completed.

(3) Where a telephone claim is defective, the Secretary of State must advise the person making it of the defect and of the effect on the date of claim of the provisions of regulation 24.

(4) If the person corrects the defect so that the claim then satisfies the requirements of paragraph (2) and does so within one month, or such longer period as the Secretary of State considers reasonable, of the date the Secretary of State first drew attention to the defect, the Secretary of State must treat the claim as if it had been properly made in the first instance.

DEFINITIONS

"jobseeker's allowance"—see reg.2.
"writing"—*ibid.*

Date of claim for a jobseeker's allowance where claim made by telephone

24. Subject to regulation 29(6), in the case of a telephone claim made under regulation 23, the date on which the claim is made or treated as made is to be the first date on which— **2.306**

(a) a claim made by telephone is properly completed;
(b) a person first notifies an intention to make a claim, provided that a claim made by telephone is properly completed within one month or such longer period as the Secretary of State considers reasonable of first notification; or
(c) a defective claim is received but is treated as properly made in the first instance in accordance with regulation 23(4),

or the first day in respect of which the claim is made if later than the above.

Interchange with claims for other benefits

25.—(1) The Secretary of State may treat a claim for an employment and support allowance by a woman in addition or in the alternative as a claim for maternity allowance. **2.307**

(2) The Secretary of State may treat a claim for a maternity allowance in addition or in the alternative as a claim for an employment and support allowance.

(3) Where it appears that a person who has made a claim for personal independence payment is not entitled to it but may be entitled to disability living allowance or attendance allowance, the Secretary of State may treat any such claim alternatively, or in addition, as a claim for either disability living allowance or attendance allowance as the case may be.

(4) Where it appears that a person who has made a claim for disability living allowance or attendance allowance is not entitled to it but may be entitled to personal independence payment, the Secretary of State may treat any such claim alternatively, or in addition, as a claim for personal independence payment.

(5) In determining whether the Secretary of State should treat a claim as made alternatively or in addition to another claim ("the original claim") under this regulation the Secretary of State must treat the alternative or additional claim, whenever made, as having been made at the same time as the original claim.

DEFINITIONS

"attendance allowance"—see reg.2.
"disability living allowance"—*ibid.*
"employment and support allowance"—*ibid.*
"maternity allowance"—*ibid.*
"personal independence payment"—*ibid.*

Time within which a claim for universal credit is to be made

2.308 **26.**—(1) Subject to the following provisions of this regulation, a claim for universal credit must be made on the first day of the period in respect of which the claim is made.

(2) Where the claim for universal credit is not made within the time specified in paragraph (1), the Secretary of State is to extend the time for claiming it, [[3]up to and including the day that would be the last day of the first assessment period for an award beginning on the first day in respect of] which the claim is made, if—

(a) any one or more of the circumstances specified in paragraph (3) applies or has applied to the claimant; and
(b) as a result of that circumstance or those circumstances the claimant could not reasonably have been expected to make the claim earlier.

(3) The circumstances referred to in paragraph (2) are—

(a) the claimant was previously in receipt of a jobseeker's allowance or an employment and support allowance and notification of expiry of entitlement to that benefit was not sent to the claimant before the date that the claimant's entitlement expired;
[[1] (aa) the claimant was previously in receipt of an existing benefit (as defined in the Universal Credit (Transitional Provisions) Regulations 2014) and notification of expiry of entitlement to that benefit was not sent to the claimant before the date that the claimant's entitlement expired;]
(b) the claimant has a disability;
(c) the claimant has supplied the Secretary of State with medical evidence that satisfies the Secretary of State that the claimant had an illness that prevented the claimant from making a claim;
(d) the claimant was unable to make a claim in writing by means of an electronic communication used in accordance with Schedule 2 because the official computer system was inoperative;
(e) [[2] . . .]
(f) where—
 (i) the Secretary of State decides not to award universal credit to members of a couple cause one of the couple does not meet the basic condition in section 4(1)(e) of the 2012 Act;
 (ii) they cease to be a couple; and
 (iii) the person who did meet the basic condition in section 4(1)(e) makes a further claim as a single person;
(g) where—
 (i) an award of universal credit to joint claimants has been terminated because one of the couple does not meet the basic condition in section 4(1)(e) of the 2012 Act;
 (ii) they cease to be a couple; and
 (iii) the person who did meet the basic condition in section 4(1)(e) makes a further claim as a single person.

(4) In the case of a claim for universal credit made by each of joint claimants, the prescribed time for claiming is not to be extended under paragraph (2) unless both claimants satisfy that paragraph.

[[2] (5) In the case of a claim for universal credit referred to in regulation 21(3C) of the Universal Credit Regulations (assessment period applied from a previous award within the last 6 months) the claim for universal credit must be made before the end of the assessment period in respect of which it is made.]

AMENDMENTS

1. The Universal Credit (Transitional Provisions) Regulations 2014 (SI 2014/1230) reg.15 (June 16, 2014).

2. The Universal Credit (Digital Service) Amendment Regulations 2014 (SI 2014/2887) reg.3 (November 26, 2014). There are savings provisions in reg.5 of SI 2014/2887.

3. The Social Security and Universal Credit (Miscellaneous Amendments) Regulations 2023 (SI 2023/543) reg.5 (June 29, 2023).

DEFINITIONS

"the 2012 Act"—see reg.2.
"benefit"—*ibid.*
"claimant"—*ibid.*
"couple"—see reg.2 and WRA 2012, s.39.
"jobseeker's allowance"—see reg.2.
"universal credit"—*ibid.*

GENERAL NOTE

Sub-para.(3)(aa) applies where a claim for universal credit is made by a person who was previously entitled to an "existing benefit" (namely JSA(IB), ESA(IR), IS, HB and CTC, WTC and, in some circumstances, incapacity benefit and severe disablement allowance: see regs 2(1) and 25(2) of SI 2014/1230). **2.309**

A claim for universal credit must normally be made on the first day for which the claimant wishes to receive it (para.(1)). However, under para.(2), the Secretary of State must extend that time limit by up to one month (but no more) if at least one circumstances in para.(3) applies, or has applied, to the claimant; and, as a result of that circumstance or those circumstances, the claimant could not reasonably have been expected to make the claim earlier. In the case of joint claimants, both must satisfy para.(2) before the time limit can be extended (para.(4)).

In *CP v SSWP (UC)* [2020] UKUT 309 (AAC) Judge Jacobs accepted a concession on behalf of the Secretary of State that, in circumstances where a housing benefit claimant has moved to a new local authority area, a notification from the new authority that housing benefit could no longer be claimed amounted to a 'notification of expiry of benefit' under reg.26(3)(aa), thus enabling backdating of their universal credit claim.

AM v SSWP (UC) [2017] UKUT 131 (AAC) considers what is meant by the official computer system being "inoperative". The claimant had been confused by a question concerning his expected take-home pay (which was relevant to the gateway conditions for universal credit) which had resulted in his being treated as not entitled to universal credit and advised to claim a jobseeker's allowance. Judge Rowland accepted that the question which only allowed either an affirmative or a negative answer was unsatisfactory. The claimant had lost out on two days' benefit and was seeking to have his claim for universal credit back-dated. Judge Rowland concluded that the unsatisfactory nature of the online question was not such as to render the official computer system as inoperative. Consequently, the claimant could not establish a ground for the back-dating of his award of universal credit. **2.310**

Whether the computer system was "inoperative" is a question of fact. An attempt to argue that it was, by reason of heavy traffic at the start of the coronavirus pandemic in March 2020, failed in *NK v SSWP (UC)* [2023] UKUT 65 (AAC).

Submissions to the Court of Appeal in *SSWP v Abdul Miah (by Mashuq Miah)* [2024] EWCA Civ 186 were evidently modified from those to the three-judge panel which had previously heard the case ([2022] UKUT 42 (AAC)). A claim had been made on behalf of the claimant, who had a disability. The claim said nothing about wanting it to start from one month earlier (as reg.26 in its previous form provided for): indeed, there had been no real opportunity to do so. Around 3 months after the DWP had awarded universal credit from the date of claim, the claimant's mother asked for the claim to be backdated. Thus in the Court of Appeal the emphasis shifted to include consideration of ss.8 and 9 of the Social Security Act 1998 and associated parts of the Universal Credit [etc.] (Decisions and Appeals) Regulations 2013 and, in particular, of whether it was possible to revise (i.e. pursuant to the mother's request) a decision on a claim which had been taken and had set the start date without conferring any advantage from reg.26. As Underhill L.J. put it at [49]:

> "It follows from the foregoing that the issue which we have to decide is whether, on the true construction of the relevant provisions, the period covered by a claim for UC is a defining parameter, or (as the majority in the Upper Tribunal put it) a "constitutive part", of the claim such that it cannot be altered, whether by way of revision or appeal, once a determination has been made."

Answering that question in the negative, he observed that the effect of s.1(1) of the Social Security Adjudication Act 1992 is that if a person claims outside the prescribed time, they will not be entitled to benefit. However, it did not follow that the issue of whether a claim had in fact been made in time fell outside normal procedures for determining claims, including those of revision and appeal.

In the context of reg.26, he noted that reg.26 is not "self-executing" i.e. it requires a decision by SSWP in the particular case. The regulation does not impose any express obligation on a claimant seeking to benefit from reg.26 to make an application or request to that effect, but the judge appeared prepared to accept (at [17]) that there must be something to put SSWP on enquiry that it might be a case for the operation of the regulation. While in a reg.26(2) claim there will need to be a determination about whether the specific conditions are satisfied, that did not affect the correct construction of s.1(1) of the 1992 Act; it followed that, like other parts of the determination, the ability to appeal against it, or to seek revision of it was available.

Time within which a claim for personal independence payment is to be made

2.311 **27.** A claim for personal independence payment must be made on the first day of the period in respect of which the claim is made.

DEFINITION

"personal independence payment"—see reg.2.

Time within which a claim for an employment and support allowance is to be made

2.312 **28.** A claim for an employment and support allowance must be made on the first day of the period in respect of which the claim is made or within the period of three months immediately following that day.

DEFINITION

"employment and support allowance"—see reg.2.

Time within which a claim for a jobseeker's allowance is to be made

29.—(1) Subject to paragraphs (2) and (4), a claim for a jobseeker's allowance must be made on the first day of the period in respect of which the claim is made. 2.313

(2) In a case where the claim is not made within the time specified in paragraph (1), the Secretary of State is to extend the time for claiming a jobseeker's allowance, subject to a maximum extension of three months, to the date on which the claim is made, where—

(a) any one or more of the circumstances specified in paragraph (3) applies or has applied to the claimant; and

(b) as a result of that circumstance or those circumstances the claimant could not reasonably have been expected to make the claim earlier.

(3) The circumstances referred to in paragraph (2) are—

(a) the claimant has difficulty communicating because—

(i) the claimant has learning, language or literacy difficulties; or

(ii) the claimant is deaf or blind,

and it was not reasonably practicable for the claimant to obtain assistance from another person to make the claim;

(b) the claimant was caring for a person who is ill or disabled and it was not reasonably practicable for the claimant to obtain assistance from another person to make the claim;

(c) the claimant was given information by an officer of the Department for Work and Pensions which led the claimant to believe that a claim for a jobseeker's allowance would not succeed;

(d) the claimant was given written advice by a solicitor or other professional adviser, a medical practitioner, a local authority or a person working in a Citizens Advice Bureau or agency, which led the claimant to believe that a claim for a jobseeker's allowance would not succeed;

(e) the claimant was required to deal with a domestic emergency affecting the claimant and it was not reasonably practicable for the claimant to obtain assistance from another person to make the claim; or

(f) the claimant was prevented by adverse weather conditions from attending an appropriate office.

(4) In a case where the claim is not made within the time specified in paragraph (1), the prescribed time for claiming a jobseeker's allowance is to be extended, subject to a maximum extension of one month, to the date on which the claim is made, where—

(a) any one or more of the circumstances specified in paragraph (5) applies or has applied to the claimant; and

(b) as a result of that circumstance or those circumstances the claimant could not reasonably have been expected to make the claim earlier.

(5) The circumstances referred to in paragraph (4) are—

(a) the appropriate office where the claimant would be expected to make a claim was closed and alternative arrangements were not available;

(b) the claimant was unable to attend the appropriate office due to difficulties with the claimant's normal mode of transport and there was no reasonable alternative available;

(c) there were adverse postal conditions;

(d) the claimant was previously in receipt of an employment and support allowance and notification of expiry of entitlement to that benefit was not sent to the claimant before the date that the entitlement expired;

(e) the claimant had ceased to be a member of a couple within the period of one month before the claim was made;
(f) during the period of one month before the claim was made a close relative of the claimant had died and for this purpose "close relative" means partner, parent, son, daughter, brother or sister;
(g) the claimant was unable to make telephone contact with the appropriate office where the claimant would be expected to notify an intention of making a claim because the telephone lines to that office were busy or inoperative;
(h) the claimant was unable to make contact by means of an electronic communication used in accordance with Schedule 2 where the claimant would be expected to notify an intention of making a claim because the official computer system was inoperative.

(6) In a case where the time for claiming a jobseeker's allowance is extended under paragraph (2) or (4), the claim is to be treated as made on the first day of the period in respect of which the claim is, by reason of the operation of those paragraphs, timeously made.

DEFINITIONS

"appropriate office"—see reg.2.
"claimant"—*ibid.*
"electronic communication"—*ibid.*
"jobseeker's allowance"—*ibid.*
"official computer system"—*ibid.*
"partner"—*ibid.*

Amendment of claim

2.314 **30.**—(1) A person who has made a claim for benefit may amend it at any time before a determination has been made on the claim by notice in writing received at an appropriate office, by telephone call to a telephone number specified by the Secretary of State or in such other manner as the Secretary of State may decide or accept.

(2) Any claim amended in accordance with paragraph (1) may be treated as if it had been so amended in the first instance.

DEFINITIONS

"benefit"—see reg.2.
"writing"—*ibid.*

Withdrawal of claim

2.315 **31.**—(1) A person who has made a claim for benefit may withdraw it at any time before a determination has been made on it by notice in writing received at an appropriate office, by telephone call to a telephone number specified by the Secretary of State or in such other manner as the Secretary of State may decide or accept.

(2) Any notice of withdrawal given in accordance with paragraph (1) has effect when it is received.

DEFINITION

"appropriate office"—see reg.2.

General Note

See the General Note to the Social Security (Claims and Payments) Regulations 1987 reg.5 which is similarly expressed. 2.316

Advance claim for and award of universal credit 2.317

32.—(1) This regulation applies where—

(a) although a person does not satisfy the conditions of entitlement to universal credit on the date on which a claim is made, the Secretary of State is of the opinion that unless there is a change of circumstances that person will satisfy those conditions for a period beginning on a day not more than one month after the date on which the claim is made; and

(b) the case falls within a class for which Secretary of State accepts advance claims or is a case where Secretary of State is otherwise willing to do so.

(2) The Secretary of State is to treat the claim as if made on the first day of that period.

(3) The Secretary of State may award universal credit accordingly, subject to the requirement that the person satisfies the conditions for entitlement on the first day of that period.

Definition

"universal credit"—see reg.2.

General Note 2.318

Regulation 32 permits claims for universal credit to be made up to one month in advance.

Reclaims of universal credit after nil award due to earnings

[[1]32A.—(1) This regulation applies where— 2.319

(a) a claim is made for universal credit, but no award is made because the condition in section 5(1)(b) or 5(2)(b) of the 2012 Act (condition that the claimant's income, or joint claimants' combined income is such that the amount payable would not be less than the prescribed minimum) is not met; or

(b) entitlement to an award of universal credit ceases because that condition is not met.

(2) The Secretary of State may, subject to any conditions the Secretary of State considers appropriate, treat the claimant (or joint claimants) as making a claim on the first day of each subsequent month, up to a maximum of 5, that would have been an assessment period if an award had been made or, as the case may be, if the award had continued.]

Amendment

1. The Universal Credit (Coronavirus) (Self-employed Claimants and Reclaims) (Amendment) Regulations 2020 (SI 2020/522) (May 21, 2020).

Advance claim for and award of personal independence payment

33.—(1) Where, although a person does not satisfy the requirements for entitlement to personal independence payment on the date on which the claim is made, the Secretary of State is of the opinion that unless there is 2.320

a change of circumstances the person will satisfy those requirements for a period beginning on a day ("the relevant day") not more than 3 months after the date on which the decision on the claim is made, the Secretary of State may award personal independence payment from the relevant day subject to the condition that the person satisfies the requirements for entitlement on the relevant day.

(2) A person who has an award of personal independence payment may make a further claim for personal independence payment during the period of 6 months immediately before the existing award expires.

(3) Where a person makes a claim in accordance with paragraph (2) the Secretary of State may—

(a) treat the claim as if made on the first day after the expiry of the existing award; and

(b) award personal independence payment accordingly, subject to the condition that the person satisfies the requirements for entitlement on that first day after the expiry of the existing award.

DEFINITION

"personal independence payment"—see reg.2.

GENERAL NOTE

2.321 This regulation permits advance awards of a personal independence payment, and also makes provision for renewal claims to be made in advance of the renewal date and which will take effect from that renewal date.

Advance claim for an award of an employment and support allowance or a jobseeker's allowance

2.322 **34.** Where, although a person does not satisfy the requirements of entitlement to an employment and support allowance or a jobseeker's allowance on the date on which a claim is made, the Secretary of State is of the opinion that unless there is a change of circumstances that claimant will satisfy those requirements for a period beginning on a day ("the relevant day") not more than three months after the date on which the claim is made, then the Secretary of State may—

(a) treat the claim as if made for a period beginning with the relevant day; and

(b) award an employment and support allowance or a jobseeker's allowance accordingly, subject to the condition that the person satisfies the requirements for entitlement when those benefits become payable under an award.

DEFINITIONS

"employment and support allowance"—see reg.2.
"jobseeker's allowance"—*ibid.*

Attendance in person

2.323 **35.** Except in a case where regulation 9 of the Personal Independence Payment Regulations applies, every person who makes a claim for benefit, other than a jobseeker's allowance, or any person entitled to benefit, other than a jobseeker's allowance, and any other person by whom, or on whose behalf, payments by way of such a benefit are receivable, must attend at such place and on such days and at such times as the Secretary of State may direct, for the purpose of supplying any information or evidence under regulations 37, 38, 39 and 41, if reasonably so required by the Secretary of State.

DEFINITIONS

"benefit"—see reg.2.
"jobseeker's allowance"—*ibid.*

Duration of awards

36.—(1) A claim for universal credit is to be treated as made for an indefinite period and any award of universal credit on that claim is to be made for an indefinite period. 2.324

(2) The provisions of Schedule 4 are to have effect in relation to claims for a jobseeker's allowance made during periods connected with public holidays.

GENERAL NOTE

Under para.(1), claims for universal credit are treated as made for an indefinite period and any award made is also for an indefinite period. However, this does not prevent the Secretary of State from revising the decision making the award, or from superseding that decision so as to change the award or bring it to an end if there is a subsequent change of circumstances. For revision and supersession of decisions about universal credit see ss.9 and 10 SSA 1998 and regs 5–37 of the Decisions and Appeals Regulations 2013. 2.325

PART 3

EVIDENCE, INFORMATION AND NOTIFICATION OF CHANGES OF CIRCUMSTANCES

Evidence and information in connection with a claim

37.—(1) Subject to regulation 8 of the Personal Independence Payment Regulations, paragraphs (2) and (3) apply to a person who makes a claim for benefit, other than a jobseeker's allowance, or on whose behalf a claim is made. 2.326

(2) The Secretary of State may require the person to supply information or evidence in connection with the claim, or any question arising out of it, as the Secretary of State considers appropriate.

(3) The person must supply the Secretary of State with the information or evidence in such manner as the Secretary of State determines within one month of first being required to do so or such longer period as the Secretary of State considers reasonable.

(4) Where joint claimants have made a claim for universal credit, information relating to that claim may be supplied by the Secretary of State to either or both members of the couple for any purpose connected with the claim.

(5) Where a person is a member of a couple and may make a claim as a single person by virtue of regulation 3(3) (couples) of the Universal Credit Regulations and entitlement to or the amount of any universal credit is or may be affected by the circumstances of their partner, the Secretary of State may require the partner to do any of the following, within one month of being required to do so or such longer period as the Secretary of State may consider reasonable—

(a) to confirm the information given about the partner's circumstances;
(b) to supply information or evidence in connection with the claim, or any question arising out of it, as the Secretary of State may require.

(6) The Secretary of State may require a landlord or a rent officer to supply information or evidence in connection with a claim for universal credit that may include in the calculation of an award an amount in respect of housing costs, and any information or evidence so requested must be supplied within one month of the request or such longer period as the Secretary of State considers reasonable.

(7) Every person providing relevant childcare as defined in regulation 35 of the Universal Credit Regulations, in a case where the calculation of a claimant's award of universal credit may include an amount in respect of childcare costs under regulation 31 of those Regulations, must supply such information or evidence in connection with the claim made by the claimant, or any question arising out of it, as may be required by the Secretary of State, and must do so within one month of being required to do so or such longer period as the Secretary of State may consider reasonable.

(8) In this regulation any reference to a person or joint claimants making a claim for a benefit, other than a jobseeker's allowance, is to be interpreted as including a person or joint claimants in a case where it is not a condition of entitlement to benefit that a claim be made for it.

(9) In this regulation any reference to a claim for a benefit, other than a jobseeker's allowance, is to be interpreted as including a potential award of benefit in a case where it is not a condition of entitlement to benefit that a claim be made for it.

DEFINITIONS

"the Personal Independence Payment Regulations"—see reg.2.
"the Universal Credit Regulations"—*ibid.*
"benefit"—*ibid.*
"claimant"—*ibid.*
"couple"—see reg.2 and WRA 2012 s.39.
"jobseeker's allowance"—see reg.2.
"partner"—*ibid.*
"personal independence payment"—*ibid.*
"universal credit"—see reg.2.

Evidence and information in connection with an award

2.327 **38.**—(1) This regulation, [1 apart from paragraphs (7) and (9)], applies to any person entitled to benefit, other than a jobseeker's allowance, and any other person by whom, or on whose behalf, payments by way of such a benefit are receivable.

(2) Subject to regulation 8 of the Personal Independence Payment Regulations, a person to whom this regulation applies must supply in such manner as the Secretary of State may determine and within the period applicable under regulation 45(4)(a) of the Universal Credit, Personal Independence Payment, Jobseeker's Allowance and Employment and Support Allowance (Decisions and Appeals) Regulations 2013 such information or evidence as the Secretary of State may require for determining whether a decision on the award of benefit should be revised under section 9 of the Social Security Act 1998 or superseded under section 10 of that Act.

(3) A person to whom this regulation applies must supply in such manner and at such times as the Secretary of State may determine such information or evidence as the Secretary of State may require in connection with payment of the benefit awarded.

(4) A person to whom this regulation applies must notify the Secretary of State of any change of circumstances which the person might reasonably be expected to know might affect—

(a) the continuance of entitlement to benefit;
(b) the amount of benefit awarded; or
(c) the payment of benefit,

as soon as reasonably practicable after the change occurs.

(5) A notification of any change of circumstances under paragraph (4) must be given—

(a) in writing or by telephone (unless the Secretary of State determines in any case that notice must be given in a particular way or to accept notice given otherwise than in writing or by telephone); or
(b) in writing if in any class of case the Secretary of State requires written notice (unless the Secretary of State determines in any case to accept notice given otherwise than in writing),

and must be sent or delivered to, or received at, the appropriate office.

(6) Where universal credit has been awarded to joint claimants, information relating to that award may be supplied by the Secretary of State to either or both members of the couple for any purpose connected with that award.

(7) Every person providing relevant childcare as defined in regulation 35 of the Universal Credit Regulations, in a case where the claimant's award of universal credit includes an amount in respect of childcare costs under regulation 31 of those Regulations, must supply such information or evidence in connection with the award, or any question arising out of it, as the Secretary of State may require, and must do so within one month of being required to do so or such longer period as the Secretary of State may consider reasonable.

(8) Where the calculation of an award of universal credit includes, by virtue of regulation 29 of the Universal Credit Regulations, an amount in respect of the fact that a claimant has regular and substantial caring responsibilities for a severely disabled person, the Secretary of State may require a person to whom this regulation applies to furnish a declaration signed by such severely disabled person confirming the particulars respecting the severely disabled person which have been given by that person.

[[1](9) A landlord, in a case where a claimant's award of universal credit includes an amount in respect of housing costs or where the award may be revised or superseded to include such an amount, must supply such information or evidence in connection with the award, or any question arising out of it, as the Secretary of State may require, and must do so within one month of being required to do so or such longer period as the Secretary of State considers reasonable.]

AMENDMENT

1. The Universal Credit (Miscellaneous Amendments) Regulations 2020 (SI 2020/611) reg.3 (July 13, 2020).

DEFINITIONS

"the Universal Credit Regulations"—see reg.2.
"benefit"—*ibid.*
"claimant"—*ibid.*
"jobseeker's allowance"—*ibid.*
"personal independence payment"—*ibid.*
"regular and substantial caring responsibilities for a severely disabled person"—*ibid.*
"universal credit"—*ibid.*
"writing"—*ibid.*

Alternative means of notifying changes of circumstances

2.328 **39.** In such cases and subject to such conditions as the Secretary of State may specify, the duty in regulation 38(4) to notify a change of circumstances may be discharged by notifying the Secretary of State as soon as reasonably practicable—

(a) where the change of circumstances is a birth or death, through a local authority, or a county council in England, by personal attendance at an office specified by that authority or county council, provided the Secretary of State has agreed with that authority or county council for it to facilitate such notification; or
(b) where the change of circumstances is a death, by telephone to a telephone number specified for that purpose by the Secretary of State.

DEFINITION

"local authority"—see reg.2.

Information to be provided to rent officers

2.329 **40.**—(1) The Secretary of State must provide to the rent officer such information as the rent officer may reasonably require to carry out functions under section 122 of the Housing Act 1996.

(2) The information referred to in paragraph (1) may include information required to make a determination under the Rent Officers Order and may include—

(a) the name and address of a universal credit claimant in respect of whom the Secretary of State has applied for a determination;
(b) the amount of any rent (within the meaning of paragraph 2 of Schedule 1 to the Universal Credit Regulations) (meaning of payments in respect of accommodation);
(c) the amount of any service charge payments (within the meaning of paragraph 2 of Schedule 1 to the Universal Credit Regulations);
(d) the number of bedrooms in the accommodation in respect of which a determination is made;
(e) the name and address of a claimant's landlord.

(3) A landlord must provide to the rent officer such information or evidence as the rent officer may reasonably require to make a determination in accordance with the Rent Officers Order and which the rent officer is not able to obtain from the Secretary of State.

(4) The evidence referred to in paragraph (3) may include evidence as to whether a property is let at an Affordable Rent within the meaning in Schedule 2 to the Rent Officers Order.

(5) In this regulation and [1 regulations 37 and 38] "landlord" means any person to whom a claimant or partner is liable to make payments in respect of the occupation of the claimant's accommodation.

(6) In this regulation "the Rent Officers Order" means the Rent Officer (Universal Credit Functions) Order 2013.

AMENDMENT

1. The Universal Credit (Miscellaneous Amendments) Regulations 2020 (SI 2020/611) reg.3(2)(b) (July 13, 2020).

DEFINITIONS

"the Universal Credit Regulations"—see reg.2.
"claimant"—*ibid.*
"universal credit"—*ibid.*

Evidence and information required from pension fund holders

41.—(1) Where a claimant or the claimant's partner is aged not less than 60 and is a member of, or a person deriving entitlement to a pension under a personal pension scheme or an occupational pension scheme, such a person must, where the Secretary of State so requires, furnish the following information— 2.330

(a) the name and address of the pension fund holder;
(b) such other information including any reference or policy number as is needed to enable the personal pension scheme or occupational pension scheme to be identified.

(2) Where the pension fund holder receives from the Secretary of State a request for details concerning the personal pension scheme or occupational pension scheme relating to a person to whom paragraph (1) refers, the pension fund holder must provide the Secretary of State with any information to which the following paragraph refers.

(3) The information to which this paragraph refers is—

(a) where the purchase of an annuity under a personal pension scheme or occupational pension scheme has been deferred, the amount of any income which is being withdrawn from the personal pension scheme or occupational pension scheme;
(b) in the case of—
    (i) a personal pension scheme or occupational pension scheme where income withdrawal is available, the [1 rate of annuity which may have been purchased with the funds held under the scheme]; or
    (ii) a personal pension scheme or occupational pension scheme where income withdrawal is not available, the [1 rate of annuity which might have been purchased with the fund] if the fund were held under a personal pension scheme or occupational pension scheme where income withdrawal was available,

calculated by or on behalf of the pension fund holder by means of tables prepared from time to time by the Government Actuary which are appropriate for this purpose.

(4) In this regulation any reference to a claimant is to be interpreted as including a person in a case where it is not a condition of entitlement to benefit that a claim be made for it.

(5) This regulation does not apply to a person claiming personal independence payment.

(6) In this regulation—

(a) "pension fund holder" means with respect to a personal pension scheme or an occupational pension scheme, the trustees, managers or scheme administrators of the scheme concerned;

(b) "personal pension scheme" means—

(i) a personal pension scheme as defined by section 1 of the Pension Schemes Act 1993(22);

(ii) an annuity contract or trust scheme approved under section 620 or 621 of the Income and Corporation Taxes Act 1988 or a substituted contract within the meaning of section 622(3) of that Act which is treated as having become a registered pension scheme by virtue of paragraph 1(1)(f) of Schedule 36 to the Finance Act 2004;

(iii) a personal pension scheme approved under Chapter 4 of Part 14 of the Income and Corporation Taxes Act 1988 which is treated as having become a registered pension scheme by virtue of paragraph 1(1)(g) of Schedule 36 to the Finance Act 2004;

(c) "occupational pension" means any pension or other periodical payment under an occupational pension scheme but does not include any discretionary payment out of a fund established for relieving hardship in particular cases.

AMENDMENT

1. Social Security (Miscellaneous Amendments No.4) Regulations 2017 (SI 2017/1015) reg.5(3) (November 16, 2017).

DEFINITIONS

"claimant"—see reg.2.
"partner"—*ibid.*

Notification for purposes of sections 111A and 112 of the Administration Act

2.331 **42.** Regulations 43 to 44 below prescribe the person to whom, and manner in which, a change of circumstances must be notified for the purposes of sections 111A(1A) to (1G) and 112(1A) to (1F) of the Administration Act (offences relating to failure to notify a change of circumstances).

DEFINITION

"the Administration Act"—see reg.2.

Notification of changes of circumstances affecting a jobseeker's allowance or an employment and support allowance for purposes of sections 111A and 112 of the Administration Act

2.332 **43.**—(1) Subject to paragraphs (2) and (3), where the benefit affected by the change of circumstances is a jobseeker's allowance or an employment and support allowance, notice must be given to the Secretary of State at the appropriate office—

(a) in writing or by telephone (unless the Secretary of State determines in any case that notice must be in writing or may be given otherwise than in writing or by telephone); or

(b) in writing if in any class of case the Secretary of State requires written notice (unless the Secretary of State determines in any case to accept notice given otherwise than in writing).

(2) Where the notice in writing referred to in paragraph (1) is given or sent by an electronic communication that notice must be given or sent in accordance with the provisions set out in Schedule 2 to these Regulations (electronic communications).

(3) In such cases and subject to such conditions as the Secretary of State may specify, the duty in regulation 38(4) of these Regulations or regulation 31(4) of the Jobseeker's Allowance Regulations to notify a change of circumstances may be discharged by notifying the Secretary of State as soon as reasonably practicable—

(a) where the change of circumstances is a birth or death, through a local authority, or a county council in England, by personal attendance at an office specified by that authority or county council, provided the Secretary of State has agreed with that authority or county council for it to facilitate such notification; or

(b) where the change of circumstances is a death, by telephone to a telephone number specified for that purpose by the Secretary of State.

DEFINITIONS

"the Jobseeker's Allowance Regulations"—see reg.2.
"appropriate office"—*ibid.*
"benefit"—*ibid.*
"electronic communication"—*ibid.*
"employment and support allowance"—*ibid.*
"jobseeker's allowance"—*ibid.*
"writing"—*ibid.*

Notification of changes of circumstances affecting personal independence payment or universal credit for purposes of sections 111A and 112 of the Administration Act

44.—(1) Subject to paragraphs (2) and (3), where the benefit affected by the change of circumstances is personal independence payment or universal credit, notice must be given to the Secretary of State ("S") at the appropriate office— 2.333

(a) in writing or by telephone (unless S determines in any case that notice must be in writing or may be given otherwise than in writing or by telephone); or

(b) in writing if in any class of case S requires written notice (unless S determines in any case to accept notice given otherwise than in writing).

(2) Where the notice in writing referred to in paragraph (1) is given or sent by an electronic communication that notice must be given or sent in accordance with the provisions set out in Schedule 2 to these Regulations (electronic communications).

(3) In such cases and subject to such conditions as the Secretary of State may specify, the duty in regulation 38(4) to notify a change of circumstances

may be discharged by notifying the Secretary of State as soon as reasonably practicable—

(a) where the change of circumstances is a birth or death, through a local authority, or a county council in England, by personal attendance at an office specified by that authority or county council, provided the Secretary of State has agreed with that authority or county council for it to facilitate such notification; or

(b) where the change of circumstances is a death, by telephone to a telephone number specified for that purpose by the Secretary of State.

DEFINITIONS

"the Administration Act"—see reg.2.
"electronic communication"—*ibid.*
"local authority"—*ibid.*
"personal independence payment"—*ibid.*
"universal credit"—*ibid.*
"writing"—*ibid.*

GENERAL NOTE

2.334 SSAA ss.111A(1A) to (1F) and 112(1A) to (1D) create various offences where a person "fails to give a prompt notification of [a change of circumstances] in the prescribed manner to the prescribed person". The main difference between the two sections is that offences under s.111A require proof of dishonesty whereas those under s.112 do not. Regulation 44 provides that the "prescribed person" to whom notice must be given is the Secretary of State and that the "prescribed manner" of giving notice is as set out in paras (1)–(3). The general rule (para.(1)) is that notice may be given by telephone or in writing unless the Secretary of State requires notice to be given in writing. That is subject to the special rules about reporting births and deaths in para.(3). Written notices that are "given or sent by an electronic communication" (i.e., by email and, when the technology permits, online) must satisfy the rules in Sch.2 (para.(2)).

PART 4

PAYMENTS

Time of payment: general provision

2.335 **45.** Subject to the other provisions of this Part, benefit is to be paid in accordance with an award as soon as is reasonably practicable after the award has been made.

DEFINITION

"benefit"—see reg.2.

Direct credit transfer

2.336 **46.**—[1 (1) The Secretary of State may arrange for benefit to be paid by way of direct credit transfer into a bank or other account nominated by the person entitled to benefit, a person acting on their behalf under regulation 57(1) or a person referred to in regulation 57(2).]

(2) A Jobseeker's Allowance or an Employment and Support Allowance are to be paid in accordance with paragraph (1) within seven days of the last day of each successive period of entitlement.

AMENDMENT

1. The Universal Credit and Miscellaneous Amendments (No.2) Regulations 2014 (SI 2014/2888), reg.5(3) (November 26, 2014).

DEFINITIONS

"benefit"—see reg.2.
"partner"—*ibid.*

Payment of universal credit

47.—(1) Universal credit is payable monthly in arrears in respect of each assessment period unless in any case or class of case the Secretary of State arranges otherwise. 2.337

(2) Where universal credit is to be paid in accordance with regulation 46, it is to be paid within seven days of the last day of the assessment period but if it is not possible to pay universal credit within that period of seven days, it is to be paid as soon as reasonably practicable thereafter.

(3) In respect of an award of universal credit which is the subject of an arrangement for payment under regulation 46, the Secretary of State may make a particular payment by credit transfer otherwise than is provided by paragraph (2), if it appears to the Secretary of State appropriate to do so for the purpose of—

(a) paying any arrears of benefit; or
(b) making a payment in respect of a terminal period of an award or for any similar purpose.

(4) Where the Secretary of State has arranged for universal credit to be paid in accordance with regulation 46, joint claimants may nominate a bank or other account into which that benefit is to be paid.

(5) Where joint claimants of universal credit have not nominated a bank or other account into which that benefit is to be paid, the Secretary of State may nominate a bank or other account.

(6) The Secretary of State may, in any case where the Secretary of State considers it is in the interests of—

(a) the claimants;
(b) a child or a qualifying young person for whom one or both of the claimants are responsible; or
(c) a severely disabled person, where the calculation of an award of universal credit includes, by virtue of regulation 29 of the Universal Credit Regulations, an amount in respect of the fact that a claimant has regular and substantial caring responsibilities for that severely disabled person,

arrange that universal credit payable in respect of joint claimants be paid wholly to only one member of the couple or be split between the couple in such proportion as the Secretary of State considers appropriate.

[[2] (6A) The Secretary of State may pay arrears of universal credit in instalments where—

(a) the Secretary of State considers it is necessary for protecting the interests of the claimant, or, in the case of joint claimants, either of the claimants; and

(b) the claimant agrees, or in the case of joint claimants, both claimants agree, that those arrears may be paid in instalments.]

(7) [[1] . . .]

AMENDMENTS

1. The Universal Credit (Persons who have attained state pension credit qualifying age) (Amendment) Regulations 2020 (SI 2020/655) reg.4 (November 25, 2020).

2. The Social Security Benefits (Claims and Payments) (Amendment) Regulations 2021 (SI 2021/1065) reg.3 (October 18, 2021).

DEFINITIONS

"assessment period"—see reg.2 and Universal Credit Regs reg.21.
"benefit"—see reg.2.
"child"—see reg.2 and WRA 2012 s.40.
"couple"—see reg.2 and WRA 2012 s.39.
"employment and support allowance"—see reg.2.
"jobseeker's allowance"—*ibid.*
"qualifying young person"—*ibid.*
"regular and substantial caring responsibilities for a severely disabled person"—*ibid.*
"universal credit"—*ibid.*

GENERAL NOTE

2.338 Regulation 47 contains important rules about the payment of universal credit.

Paragraph (1)

2.339 Universal credit is normally paid monthly in arrears after the end of the relevant assessment period. This is in contrast to the rules for income support, income-based JSA and income-related ESA. The change in policy is linked to the provisions under which earned income for each assessment period is taken to be the amount reported to HMRC by the claimant's (or claimants') employers. Monthly payment in arrears after the end of the assessment period is intended to ensure that no payment is made until after changes in circumstances relating to earned income have been reported and that overpayments will be reduced.

Paragraphs (2) to (5)

2.340 These apply where universal credit is paid by direct transfer under reg.46 which will be the usual method of payment. They are largely administrative. However, the rule in para.(2) that payment by direct transfer must be paid within seven days of the last day of the assessment period or as soon as reasonably practicable thereafter will be important to claimants.

2.341 *Paragraph (6)*

Allows the Secretary of State pay universal credit to one of two joint claimants or to split that payment between them in the circumstances specified. See also reg.58(1).

2.342 *Paragraph (6A)*

For DWP internal guidance, see Advice to Decision Makers Memo 18/21.

2.343 *Paragraph (7)*

Changes of circumstance relating to universal credit normally take effect from the first day of the assessment period in which they occur. Following the revocation of para.(7) with effect from November 25, 2020, a superseding decision made in consequence of person reaching the qualifying age for SPC now takes effect on the first day of the assessment period following that in which that change of circumstances occurs or is expected to occur: see para.26 of Sch.1 to the Universal Credit, Personal Independence Payment, Jobseeker's Allowance and Employment and Support Allowance (Decisions and Appeals) Regulations 2013 as substituted with effect from that date (below).

Payment of personal independence payment

48.—(1) Subject to the following provisions of this regulation and regulation 50, personal independence payment is to be paid at intervals of four weeks in arrears. 2.344

(2) In the case of any person to whom section 82 of the 2012 Act (terminal illness) applies, the Secretary of State may arrange that personal independence payment is to be paid at intervals of one week in advance.

(3) Where the amount of personal independence payment payable is less than £5.00 a week the Secretary of State may arrange that it is to be paid in arrears at such intervals as may be specified not exceeding 12 months.

[[1](4) The Secretary of State may pay arrears of personal independence payment in instalments where—

(a) the Secretary of State considers it is necessary for protecting the interests of the claimant; and

(b) the claimant agrees that those arrears may be paid in instalments.]

[[2](5) The Scottish Ministers may pay arrears of personal independence payment in instalments where—

(a) the Scottish Ministers consider it is necessary for protecting the interests of the claimant, and

(b) the claimant agrees that those arrears may be paid in instalments.]

AMENDMENT

1. The Social Security Benefits (Claims and Payments) (Amendment) Regulations 2021 (SI 2021/1065) reg.3 (October 18, 2021).

2. Social Security (Claims and Payments) (Miscellaneous Amendments) (Scotland) Regulations SSI 2021/305 reg.4 (October 18, 2021).

DEFINITION

"personal independence payment"—see reg.2.

GENERAL NOTE

For DWP internal guidance, see Advice to Decision Makers Memo 18/21. 2.345

As legislative competence for disability benefits (but not for the other benefits covered by these Regulations) has been transferred to the Scottish Parliament, it will be for the Scottish Ministers under subs.(5) to consider whether to pay arrears by instalments. In the case of the other benefits, subs.(4) applies.

Days for payment of personal independence payment

49.—(1) Subject to the following provisions of this regulation, a personal independence payment is payable on the day of the week on which the Secretary of State makes a decision to award that benefit, except that where that decision is made on a Saturday or a Sunday the benefit is to be paid on such day of the week as the Secretary of State may direct in any case. 2.346

(2) The Secretary of State may, in any case or class of case, arrange that personal independence payment or any part of it be paid on any day of the week.

(3) Where personal independence payment is in payment to any person and the day on which it is payable is changed, it is to be paid at a daily rate of 1/7th of the weekly rate in respect of any of the days for which payment would have been made but for that change.

(4) Where there is a change in the amount of any personal independence payment payable, or where entitlement to personal independence payment ends, and these events do not occur on the day of the week referred to in paragraph (1) or (2), personal independence payment is to be paid at a daily rate of 1/7th of the weekly rate.

DEFINITIONS

"benefit"—see reg.2.
"personal independence payment"—*ibid.*

Payment of personal independence payment at a daily rate between periods in hospital or other accommodation

2.347 **50.**—(1) Personal independence payment is to be paid in respect of any person, for any day falling within a period to which paragraph (2) applies, at the daily rate (which is to be equal to 1/7th of the weekly rate) and personal independence payment payable in pursuance of this regulation is to be paid weekly or as the Secretary of State may direct in any case.

(2) This paragraph applies to any period which is not a period of residence—

(a) but which commences immediately following such a period; and
(b) on the first day of which it is expected that, before the expiry of the term of 28 days beginning with that day, the person will commence another period of residence.

(3) Where paragraph (2) applies, the period referred to in that paragraph is to end—

(a) at the expiry of the term of 28 days beginning with the first day of the period referred to in that paragraph; or
(b) if earlier, on the day before the day which is the first day of a period of residence.

(4) In this regulation a "period of residence" means a period of residence where—

(a) the person is a resident of a care home, as defined in section 85(3) of the 2012 Act, and no amount of personal independence payment which is attributable to the daily living component is payable in respect of the person by virtue of regulation 28(1) of the Personal Independence Payment Regulations(29); or
(b) the person is undergoing medical or other treatment as an in-patient at a hospital or similar institution and no amount of personal independence payment which is attributable to the daily living component or the mobility component is payable in respect of the person by virtue of regulation 29 of the Personal Independence Payment Regulations,

and such period is to be deemed to begin on the day after the day on which the person enters the care home, hospital or similar institution and to end on the day before the day on which the person leaves the care home, hospital or similar institution.

DEFINITIONS

"the 2012 Act"—see reg.2.
"the Personal Independence Payment Regulations"—*ibid.*
"personal independence payment"—*ibid.*

Payment of an employment and support allowance

51.—(1) Subject to paragraphs (3) to (8), an employment and support allowance paid in accordance with regulation 46 is to be paid fortnightly in arrears on the day of the week determined in accordance with paragraph (2). **2.348**

(2) The day specified for the purposes of paragraph (1) is the day in column (2) which corresponds to the series of numbers in column (1) which includes the last two digits of the claimant's national insurance number—

(1)	(2)
00 to 19	Monday
20 to 39	Tuesday
40 to 59	Wednesday
60 to 79	Thursday
80 to 99	Friday

(3) The Secretary of State may, in any case or class of case, arrange that the claimant be paid otherwise than fortnightly.

(4) In respect of an award of an employment and support allowance which is the subject of an arrangement for payment under regulation 46, the Secretary of State may make a particular payment by credit transfer otherwise than as provided by paragraph (1), if it appears to the Secretary of State appropriate to do so for the purpose of—

(a) paying any arrears of benefit; or
(b) making a payment in respect of a terminal period of an award or for any similar purpose.

[[1](4A) The Secretary of State may pay arrears of employment and support allowance in instalments where—

(a) the Secretary of State considers it is necessary for protecting the interests of the claimant; and
(b) the claimant agrees that those arrears may be paid in instalments.]

(5) The Secretary of State may, in any case or class of case, arrange that an employment and support allowance be paid on any day of the week and where it is in payment to any person and the day on which it is payable is changed, it is to be paid at a daily rate of 1/7th of the weekly rate in respect of any of the days for which payment would have been made but for that change.

(6) Where the weekly amount of an employment and support allowance is less than £1.00 it may be paid in arrears at intervals of not more than 13 weeks.

(7) Where the weekly amount of an employment and support allowance is less than 10 pence that allowance is not payable.

(8) Where an employment and support allowance is normally payable in arrears and the day on which that benefit is payable by reason of paragraph (2) is affected by office closure, it may for that benefit week be paid wholly

in advance or partly in advance and partly in arrears and on such day as the Secretary of State may direct.

(9) Where under paragraph (8) an employment and support allowance is paid either in advance or partly in advance and partly in arrears it is for any other purposes to be treated as if it were paid in arrears.

(10) For the purposes of paragraph (8), "benefit week" means a period of seven days beginning or ending with such day as the Secretary of State may direct.

(11) For the purposes of paragraph (8), "office closure" means a period during which an appropriate office is closed in connection with a public holiday.

(12) For the purposes of paragraph (11), "public holiday" means—

(a) in England and Wales, Christmas Day, Good Friday or a bank holiday under the Banking and Financial Dealings Act 1971;

(b) in Scotland, a bank holiday under the Banking and Financial Dealings Act 1971 or a local holiday.

AMENDMENT

1. The Social Security Benefits (Claims and Payments) (Amendment) Regulations 2021 (SI 2021/1065) reg.3 (October 18, 2021).

DEFINITIONS

"appropriate office"—see reg.2.
"benefit"—*ibid.*
"claimant"—*ibid.*
"employment and support allowance"—*ibid.*

GENERAL NOTE

2.349 For DWP internal guidance, see Advice to Decision Makers Memo 18/21.

Payment of a jobseeker's allowance

2.350 **52.**—(1) Subject to paragraphs (2) to (4), a jobseeker's allowance paid in accordance with regulation 46 is to be paid fortnightly in arrears unless in any case or class of case the Secretary of State arranges otherwise.

(2) In respect of an award of a jobseeker's allowance which is the subject of an arrangement for payment under regulation 46, the Secretary of State may make a particular payment by credit transfer otherwise than as provided by paragraph (1), if it appears to the Secretary of State appropriate to do so for the purpose of—

(a) paying any arrears of benefit; or

(b) making a payment in respect of a terminal period of an award or for any similar purpose.

[[1](2A) The Secretary of State may pay arrears of jobseeker's allowance in instalments where—

(a) the Secretary of State considers it is necessary for protecting the interests of the claimant; and

(b) the claimant agrees that those arrears may be paid in instalments.]

(3) Where the amount of a jobseeker's allowance is less than £1.00 a week the Secretary of State may direct that it is to be paid at such intervals, not exceeding 13 weeks, as may be specified in the direction.

(4) Where a jobseeker's allowance is normally payable in arrears and the day on which that benefit is normally payable is affected by office closure,

it may for that benefit week be paid wholly in advance or partly in advance and partly in arrears and on such day as the Secretary of State may direct.

(5) Where under paragraph (4) a jobseeker's allowance is paid either in advance or partly in advance and partly in arrears it is for any other purposes to be treated as if it were paid in arrears.

(6) For the purposes of paragraph (4), "benefit week" means a period of seven days ending with a day determined in accordance with the definition of that term in regulation 2(2) (general interpretation) of the Jobseeker's Allowance Regulations.

(7) For the purposes of paragraph (4), "office closure" means a period during which an appropriate office is closed in connection with a public holiday.

(8) For the purposes of paragraph (7), "public holiday" means—

(a) in England and Wales, Christmas Day, Good Friday or a bank holiday under the Banking and Financial Dealings Act 1971;

(b) in Scotland, a bank holiday under the Banking and Financial Dealings Act 1971 or a local holiday.

AMENDMENT

1. The Social Security Benefits (Claims and Payments) (Amendment) Regulations 2021 (SI 2021/1065) (October 18, 2021).

DEFINITIONS

"benefit"—see reg.2.
"jobseeker's allowance"—*ibid.*

GENERAL NOTE

For DWP internal guidance, see Advice to Decision Makers Memo 18/21. 2.351

Fractional amounts of benefit

53. Where the amount of any benefit payable would, but for this regulation, include a fraction of a penny, that fraction is to be disregarded if it is less than half a penny and is otherwise to be treated as a penny. 2.352

DEFINITION

"benefit"—see reg.2.

Payment to persons under age 18

54. Where a benefit is paid to a person under the age of 18, a direct credit transfer under regulation 46 into any such person's account, or the receipt by the person of a payment made by some other means, is sufficient discharge for the Secretary of State. 2.353

Extinguishment of right to payment if payment is not obtained within the prescribed period

55.—(1) The right to payment of any sum by way of benefit is to be extinguished where payment of that sum is not obtained within the period of 12 months from the date on which the right is treated as having arisen. 2.354

(2) For the purposes of this regulation, the right to payment of any sum by way of benefit is to be treated as having arisen—

(a) where notice is given or sent that the sum contained in the notice is ready for collection, on the date of the notice or, if more than one such notice is given or sent, the date of the first such notice;

(b) in relation to any such sum which the Secretary of State has arranged to be paid by means of direct credit transfer in accordance with regulation 46 into a bank or other account, on the due date for payment of the sum or in the case of universal credit on the date of payment of the sum; or

(c) in relation to any such sum to which neither sub-paragraph (a) or (b) applies, on such date as the Secretary of State determines.

(3) The giving or sending of a notice under paragraph (2)(a) is effective for the purposes of that paragraph, even where the sum contained in that notice is more or less than the sum which the person concerned has the right to receive.

(4) Where a question arises whether the right to payment of any sum by way of benefit has been extinguished by the operation of this regulation and the Secretary of State is satisfied that—

(a) the Secretary of State first received written notice requesting payment of that sum after the expiration of 12 months from the date on which the right is treated as having arisen;

(b) from a day within that period of 12 months and continuing until the day the written notice was given, there was good cause for not giving the notice; and

(c) no payment has been made under the provisions of regulation 46 (direct credit transfer),

the period of 12 months is extended to the date on which the Secretary of State decides that question, and this regulation is to apply accordingly as though the right to payment had arisen on that date.

(5) This regulation applies to a person appointed under regulation 57(1) to act on behalf of a claimant or a person referred to in regulation 57(2) as it applies to a claimant.

DEFINITIONS

"benefit"—see reg.2.
"claimant"—*ibid.*

Payments on death

2.355 **56.**—(1) On the death of a person who has made a claim for benefit, the Secretary of State may appoint such person as the Secretary of State thinks fit to proceed with the claim and any related issue of revision, supersession or appeal under the Social Security Act 1998.

(2) Subject to paragraphs (6) and (7), any sum payable by way of benefit which is payable under an award on a claim proceeded with under paragraph (1) may be paid or distributed by the Secretary of State to or amongst persons over the age of 16 claiming as personal representatives, legatees, next of kin or creditors of the deceased and the provisions of regulation 55 (extinguishment of right to payment if payment is not obtained within the prescribed period) are to apply to any such payment or distribution.

(3) Subject to paragraphs (2), (6) and (7), any sum payable by way of benefit to the deceased, payment of which the deceased had not obtained at the date of the deceased's death, may, unless the right to payment was

already extinguished at that date, be paid or distributed to or amongst any persons mentioned in paragraph (2), and regulation 55 is to apply to any such payment or distribution, except that, for the purpose of that regulation, the period of 12 months is to be calculated from the date on which the right to payment of any sum is treated as having arisen in relation to any such person and not from the date on which that right is treated as having arisen in relation to the deceased.

(4) A direct credit transfer under regulation 46 into an account in the name of any person mentioned in paragraph (2), or the receipt by such a person of a payment made by some other means, is sufficient discharge for the Secretary of State for any sum so paid.

(5) Where the Secretary of State is satisfied that any sum payable by way of benefit under paragraph (2) or (3), or part of it, is needed for the well-being of any person under the age of 16, the Secretary of State may obtain sufficient discharge for it by paying the sum or part of it to a person over that age who satisfies the Secretary of State that that person will apply the sum so paid for the well-being of the person under the age of 16.

(6) Paragraphs (2) and (3) are not to apply in any case unless written application for the payment of any sum is made to the Secretary of State within 12 months from the date of the deceased's death or within such longer period as the Secretary of State may allow in any case.

(7) The Secretary of State may dispense with strict proof of the title of any person claiming in accordance with the provisions of this regulation.

(8) In paragraph (2) "next of kin" means—

(a) in England and Wales, the persons who would take beneficially on an intestacy;

(b) in Scotland, the persons entitled to the moveable estate of the deceased on intestacy.

DEFINITION

"benefit"—see reg.2.

PART 5

THIRD PARTIES

Persons unable to act

57.—(1) Where a person ("P1") is, or may be, entitled to benefit (whether or not a claim for benefit has been made by P1 or on P1's behalf) but P1 is unable for the time being to act, the Secretary of State may, if all the conditions in paragraph (2) and the additional conditions in paragraph (3) are met, appoint a person ("P2") to carry out the functions set out in paragraph (4). 2.356

[1(1A) Where a natural person over the age of 18 has been appointed by the Scottish Ministers under a qualifying appointment pursuant to the 2018 Scotland Act in connection with the determination of assistance under section 24 of that Act (whether or not including an appointment to receive assistance on behalf of the individual), the Secretary of State may, if the person agrees, treat that person as if the Secretary of State had appointed that person under paragraph (1).

(1B) In paragraph (1A) a qualifying appointment means—

(a) an appointment made under section 58(1) of the 2018 Scotland Act in a case where section 58(4) of that Act applies, or

(b) an appointment made under section 85B(1) of the 2018 Scotland Act in a case where section 85B(7) of that Act applies.

(1C) In this regulation "the 2018 Scotland Act" means the Social Security (Scotland) Act 2018.]

(2) The conditions are that—

(a) no deputy has been appointed by the Court of Protection under Part 1 of the Mental Capacity Act 2005;

(b) no receiver has been appointed under Part 7 of the Mental Health Act 1983 who is treated as a deputy by virtue of the Mental Capacity Act 2005 with power to claim or receive benefit on P1's behalf;

(c) no attorney with a general power, or a power to claim or receive benefit, has been appointed by P1 under the Powers of Attorney Act 1971, the Enduring Powers of Attorney Act 1985, the Mental Capacity Act 2005 or otherwise; and

(d) in Scotland, P1's estate is not being administered by a judicial factor or any guardian acting or appointed under the Adults with Incapacity (Scotland) Act 2000 who has power to claim or receive benefit on P1's behalf.

(3) The additional conditions are that—

(a) P2 has made a written application to the Secretary of State to be appointed; and

(b) if P2 is a natural person, P2 is over the age of 18.

(4) The functions are exercising on behalf of P1 any right to which P1 may be entitled and receiving and dealing on behalf of P1 with any sums payable to P1.

(5) Anything required by these Regulations to be done by or in relation to P1 may be done by or in relation to P2 or any person mentioned in paragraph (2).

(6) Where a person has been appointed under regulation 82(3) of the Housing Benefit Regulations 2006 by a relevant authority within the meaning of those Regulations to act on behalf of another in relation to a benefit claim or award, the Secretary of State may, if the person so appointed agrees, treat that person as if the Secretary of State had appointed that person under paragraph (1).

(7) A direct credit transfer under regulation 46 into the account of P2 or any person mentioned in paragraph (2), or the receipt by such a person of a payment made by some other means, is sufficient discharge for the Secretary of State for any sum paid.

(8) An appointment under paragraph (1) or (6) comes to an end if—

(a) the Secretary of State at any time revokes it;

(b) P2 resigns P2's office having given one month's notice in writing to the Secretary of State of an intention to do so; or

(c) the Secretary of State is notified that any condition in paragraph (2) is no longer met.

AMENDMENT

1. The Scotland Act 2016 (Social Security) (Consequential Provision) (Miscellaneous Amendment) Regulations 2021 (SI 2021/804) reg.10 (July 26, 2021).

DEFINITION

"benefit"—see reg.2.

GENERAL NOTE

A child claimant of DLA will have had to have an appointee under reg.43(1) of the Social Security (Claims and Payments) Regulations 1987. On conversion to PIP, however, an appointee can only be appointed under this regulation – there is no automatic conversion of the appointee who has acted for the child for DLA purposes: see *P v SSWP (PIP)* [2018] UKUT 359 (AAC). 2.357

Payment to another person on the claimant's behalf

58.—(1) The Secretary of State may direct that universal credit be paid wholly or in part to another person on the claimant's behalf if this appears to the Secretary of State necessary to protect the interests of— 2.358

(a) the claimant;
(b) their partner;
(c) a child or qualifying young person for whom the claimant or their partner or both are responsible; or
(d) a severely disabled person, where the calculation of the award of universal credit includes, by virtue of regulation 29 of the Universal Credit Regulations, an amount in respect of the fact that the claimant has regular and substantial caring responsibilities for that severely disabled person.

(2) The Secretary of State may direct that personal independence payment be paid wholly to another person on the claimant's behalf if this appears to the Secretary of State necessary to protect the interests of the claimant.

DEFINITIONS

"the Universal Credit Regulations"—see reg.2.
"claimant"—*ibid.*
"partner"—*ibid.*
"regular and substantial caring responsibilities for a severely disabled person"—*ibid.*
"universal credit"—*ibid.*

GENERAL NOTE

Paragraph (1)

Universal credit may be paid to third parties in the specified circumstances. 2.359

Direct payment to lender of deductions in respect of interest on secured loans

[1 . . .] 2.360

AMENDMENT

1. Loans for Mortgage Interest Regulations 2017 (SI 2017/725), Sch.5(1), para 8 (April 6, 2018).

GENERAL NOTE

Where, prior to April 6, 2018, an award of universal credit included the housing costs element based on mortgage interest payments, that part of the award was normally paid directly to the lender under the provisions of reg.59 and Sch.5. From that date, UC housing costs for mortgage interest have been replaced with loans (see SI 2017/725) and both reg.59 and Sch.5 have therefore been revoked. 2.361

Deductions which may be made from benefit and paid to third parties

2.362 [[1] **60.** —. . .] deductions may be made from may be made to third parties on behalf of a claimant in accordance with the provisions of Schedule 6 and Schedule 7.

AMENDMENT

1. The Loans for Mortgage Interest Regulations 2017 (SI 2017/725), Sch.5(1), para.8 from April 6, 2018, subject to transitional provisions specified in regs 19, 19A and 20 of those Regulations (as amended).

GENERAL NOTE

2.363 In *R(Blundell and others) v SSWP; R(Day) v SSWP* [2021] EWHC 608 (Admin), a challenge to SSWP's policy in relation to deducting fines from universal credit payments succeeded on the grounds that the policy involved a fettering of discretion (excluding the possibility of a reduction, which was contemplated by the Fines (Deductions from Income Support) Regulations 1992 (SI 1992/2182 as amended)) and an abdication of discretion (by re-directing claimants to the court which had imposed the fine to ask the court to vary it.) The DWP have now amended their guidance so that the default position re deductions for fines is that the minimum deduction (i.e. 5% of the standard allowance) is made: DWP Overpayment Recovery Guide, Appendix 4.

PART 6

MOBILITY COMPONENT OF PERSONAL INDEPENDENCE PAYMENT

Cases where mobility component of personal independence payment not payable

2.364 **61.**—(1) Subject to the following provisions of this regulation, personal independence payment by virtue of entitlement to the mobility component is not payable to any person who would otherwise be entitled to it during any period in respect of which that person has received, or is receiving, any payment—

(a) by way of grant under section 5 of, and paragraph 10 of Schedule 1 to, the National Health Service Act 2006, section 5 of, and paragraph 10 of Schedule 1 to, the National Health Service (Wales) Act 2006 or section 46 of the National Health Service (Scotland) Act 1978 towards the costs of running a private car;

(b) of mobility supplement under—

(i) the Naval, Military and Air Forces etc., (Disablement and Death) Service Pensions Order 2006;

(ii) the Personal Injuries (Civilians) Scheme 1983; or

(iii) the Order referred to in paragraph (i) by virtue of the War Pensions (Naval Auxiliary Personnel) Scheme 1964, the Pensions (Polish Forces) Scheme 1964, the War Pensions (Mercantile Marine) Scheme 1964 or an Order of Her Majesty in relation to the Home Guard dated 21st or 22nd December 1964 or in relation to the Ulster Defence Regiment dated 4th January 1971; or

(c) out of public funds which the Secretary of State is satisfied is analogous to a payment under sub-paragraph (a) or (b).

(2) Paragraph (3) applies where a person in respect of whom personal independence payment is claimed for any period has received any such payment as is referred to in paragraph (1) for a period which, in whole or in part, covers the period for which personal independence payment is claimed.

(3) Such payment referred to in paragraph (1) is to be treated as an aggregate of equal weekly amounts in respect of each week in the period for which it is made and, where in respect of any such week a person is treated as having a weekly amount so calculated which is less than the weekly rate of mobility component of personal independence payment to which, apart from paragraph (1), they would be entitled, any personal independence payment to which that person may be entitled for that week is to be payable at a weekly rate reduced by the weekly amount so calculated.

Payment of personal independence payment on behalf of a claimant (Motability)

62.—(1) This regulation applies where— 2.365

(a) personal independence payment is payable in respect of a claimant by virtue of entitlement to the mobility component at the enhanced rate; and

(b) under arrangements made or negotiated by Motability, an agreement has been entered into by or on behalf of the claimant for the hire or hire-purchase of a vehicle.

(2) Where this regulation applies, the Secretary of State may arrange that any personal independence payment by virtue of entitlement to the mobility component at the enhanced rate be paid in whole or in part on behalf of the claimant in settlement of liability for payments due under the agreement mentioned in paragraph (1).

(3) Subject to regulations 63 and 64, in the case of the hire of a vehicle, an arrangement made by the Secretary of State under paragraph (2) terminates—

(a) where the vehicle is returned to the owner at or before the expiration of the term of hire or any agreed extension of the term of hire, on expiry of the period of the term or extended term;

(b) where the vehicle is retained by or on behalf of the claimant with the owner's consent after the expiration of the term of hire or any agreed extension of the term of hire, on expiry of the period of the term or extended term; or

(c) where the vehicle is retained by or on behalf of the claimant otherwise than with the owner's consent after the expiration of the term of hire or any agreed extension of the term of hire, or its earlier termination, on expiry of whichever is the longer of the following periods—

(i) the period ending with the return of the vehicle to the owner; or

(ii) the period of the term of hire or any agreed extension of the term of hire.

(4) Subject to regulations 63 and 64 in the case of a hire-purchase agreement, an arrangement made by the Secretary of State under paragraph (2) terminates—

(a) on the purchase of the vehicle; or

(b) where the vehicle is returned to, or is repossessed by, the owner under the terms of the agreement before the completion of the purchase, at the end of the original period of the agreement.

(5) In this regulation "Motability" means the company, set up under that name as a charity and originally incorporated under the Companies Act 1985 and subsequently incorporated by Royal Charter.

DEFINITIONS

"claimant"—see reg.2.
"personal independence payment"—*ibid.*

[1 Recovery of expenses

2.366 **62A.**—(1) Paragraph 2 applies where—

(a) an agreement referred to in regulation 62(1)(b) has been entered into; and
(b) a relevant provider is receiving payments of personal independence payment in settlement of liability for payments due under that agreement.

(2) The Secretary of State may require the relevant provider to make payments to meet the reasonable expenses of the Secretary of State in administering the making of the payments of personal independence payment to the relevant provider.

(3) The method by which the expenses under paragraph (2) are to be met is for the Secretary of State to issue an invoice to the relevant provider setting out the expenses that have been incurred and for the relevant provider to pay the sum stated to the Secretary of State.

(4) The first invoice issued by the Secretary of State may recover expenses incurred between 21st July 2016 and the date of the invoice.

(5) Subsequently the Secretary of State may issue invoices no more frequently than annually and only in respect of expenses incurred since the period covered by the previous invoice.

(6) The expenses that the Secretary of State may take into account for the purposes of paragraph (2) include—

(a) the salaries and other costs relating to the employment of staff wholly engaged in the administering of the payments of personal independence payment and where staff have other responsibilities, an apportioned amount of those costs; and
(b) overheads, including rent and other shared costs, relating to those staff.

(7) In determining what expenses were reasonably incurred in administering the making of payments of personal independence payment to a relevant provider, the Secretary of State must have regard to any agreement between the Secretary of State and the relevant provider concerning the level of service to be provided by the Secretary of State in the making of such payments to that relevant provider.]

AMENDMENT

1. The Social Security (Expenses of Paying Sums in Relation to Vehicle Hire) Regulations 2016 (SI 2016/674) reg.5 (July 21, 2016).

Power for the Secretary of State to terminate an arrangement (Motability)

63. The Secretary of State may terminate an arrangement under regulation 62(2) on such date as the Secretary of State decides— 2.367

(a) if requested to do so by the owner of the vehicle to which the arrangement relates; or

(b) if it appears to the Secretary of State that the arrangement is causing undue hardship to the claimant and that it should be terminated earlier than provided for by regulation 62(3) or (4).

Restriction on duration of arrangements by the Secretary of State (Motability)

64. The Secretary of State must terminate an arrangement under regulation 62(2) where the Secretary of State is satisfied that— 2.368

(a) the vehicle to which the arrangement relates has been returned to the owner; and

(b) the expenses of the owner arising out of the hire or hire-purchase agreement have been recovered following the return of the vehicle.

SCHEDULE 1 — POWERS EXERCISED IN MAKING THESE REGULATIONS

1. The following provisions of the Administration Act— 2.369

(a) section 1(1), (1C);

(b) section 5(1)(a), (b), (c), (d), (g), (i), (j), (k), (l), (m), (p), (q), (1A), (2A), (2B), (2C), (3B);

(c) section 7A(2)(b);

(d) section 15A(2);

(e) section 111A(1A)(d), (1B)(d), (1D)(c), (1E)(c);

(f) section 112(1A)(d), (1B)(d), (1C)(c), (1D)(c);

(g) section 189(1) and (5) to (6);

(h) section 191.

2. Paragraph 7A of Schedule 2 to the Abolition of Domestic Rates etc. (Scotland) Act 1987.

3. Paragraph 6 of Schedule 4 to the Local Government Finance Act 1988.

4. Section 24(2)(b), (c) and (d) and section 30 of the Criminal Justice Act 1991.

5. Section 43(2) of the 1991 Act.

6. Paragraphs 1 and 6(2)(b) of Schedule 4 and paragraph 6 of Schedule 8 to, the Local Government Finance Act 1992.

7. Sections 32 and 92 of, and paragraph 3(1)(a), (b), (2)(a), (b) and (c) of Schedule 1 to the 2012 Act.

DEFINITION

"the Administration Act"—see reg.2.

SCHEDULE 2 — ELECTRONIC COMMUNICATIONS

PART 1

USE OF ELECTRONIC COMMUNICATIONS

Use of electronic communications by the Secretary of State

1. The Secretary of State may use an electronic communication in connection with claims for, and awards of, any benefit. 2.370

Conditions for the use of electronic communications by other persons

2.371 2.—(1) A person other than the Secretary of State may use an electronic communication in connection with the matters referred to in paragraph 1 if the conditions specified in sub-paragraphs (2) to (5) are satisfied.

(2) The first condition is that the person is for the time being permitted to use an electronic communication for the purpose in question by an authorisation given by means of a direction of the Secretary of State.

(3) The second condition is that the person uses an approved method of—

(a) authenticating the identity of the sender of the communication where required to do so;

(b) electronic communication;

(c) authenticating any claim or information delivered by means of an electronic communication; and

(d) subject to sub-paragraph (6), submitting any claim or information to the Secretary of State.

(4) The third condition is that any claim or information sent by means of an electronic communication is in an approved form.

(5) The fourth condition is that the person maintains such records as may be specified in a direction given by the Secretary of State.

(6) Where the person uses any method other than the method approved by the Secretary of State of submitting any claim or information, it is to be treated as not having been submitted.

(7) In this paragraph "approved" means approved by means of a direction given by the Secretary of State for the purposes of this Schedule.

Use of intermediaries

2.372 **3.** The Secretary of State may use intermediaries in connection with—

(a) the delivery of any claim or information by means of an electronic communication; and

(b) the authentication or security of anything transmitted by such means,

and may require other persons to use intermediaries in connection with those matters.

PART 2

EVIDENTIAL PROVISIONS

Effect of delivering information by electronic communications

2.373 **4.**—(1) Any claim or information which is delivered by means of an electronic communication is to be treated as having been delivered in the manner or form required by any provision of these Regulations on the day on which the conditions imposed—

(a) by this Schedule; and

(b) by or under an applicable enactment (except to the extent that the condition thereby imposed is incompatible with this Schedule),

are satisfied.

(2) The Secretary of State may, by a direction, determine that any claim or information is to be treated as delivered on a different day (whether earlier or later) from the day specified in sub-paragraph (1).

(3) Any claim or information is not to be taken to have been delivered to an official computer system by means of an electronic communication unless it is accepted by the system to which it is delivered.

Proof of delivery

2.374 **5.**—(1) The use of an approved method of electronic communication is to be presumed, unless the contrary is proved, to have resulted in delivery—

(a) in the case of any claim or information falling to be delivered to the Secretary of State, if the delivery of that claim or information is recorded on an official computer system; or

(b) in the case of any information that falls to be delivered by the Secretary of State, if the despatch of that information is recorded on an official computer system.

(2) The use of an approved method of electronic communication is to be presumed, unless the contrary is proved, not to have resulted in delivery—

(a) in the case of any claim or information falling to be delivered to the Secretary of State, if the delivery of that claim or information is not recorded on an official computer system; or

(b) in the case of information that falls to be delivered by the Secretary of State, if the despatch of that information is not recorded on an official computer system.

(3) The time and date of receipt of any claim or information sent by an approved method of electronic communication is to be presumed, unless the contrary is proved, to be that recorded on an official computer system.

Proof of identity

6.—(1) The identity of— 2.375

(a) the sender of any claim or information delivered by means of an electronic communication to an official computer system; or

(b) the recipient of any claim or information delivered by means of an electronic communication from an official computer system,

is to be presumed, unless the contrary is proved, to be the person whose name is recorded as such on that official computer system.

(2) Any claim or information delivered by an approved method of electronic communication on behalf of another person ("P") is to be deemed to have been delivered by P unless P proves that it was delivered without P's knowledge or connivance.

Proof of content

7. The content of any claim or information sent by means of an electronic communication is to be presumed, unless the contrary is proved, to be that recorded on an official computer system. 2.376

DEFINITIONS

"electronic communication"—see reg.2.
"official computer system"—*ibid.*

GENERAL NOTE

The various steps in Sch.2 are cumulative requirements: *GDC v SSWP (UC)* [2020] UKUT 180 (AAC) at [76]. 2.377

Nothing in Sch.2 (nor elsewhere in these Regulations, nor in the Directions referred to below) makes attending an interview about self-employment part of the process for making a valid electronic claim. Thus, SSWP was in error in "closing" a claim for the claimant's failure to attend one: *PP v SSWP (UC)* [2020] UKUT 109 (AAC).

The Directions of the Secretary of State referred to in Sch.2 (and also in Sch.9ZC of the Social Security (Claims and Payments) Regulations 1987 (SI 1987/1968)) are set out below, as amended; the amending Directions can be found at *https://www.gov.uk/government/publications/the-social-security-electronic-communications-directions* (accessed April 24, 2024). Their legal basis was identified in *GDC* as being ss.8 and 9(5) of the Electronic Communications Act 2000 and s.189 (5A)–(5B) of the Social Security Administration Act 1992.

Rejecting a submission that the Directions provide no approved method for submitting a claim, Judge Wikeley observed in *GDC*:

> "81. First, and fundamentally, I agree with Ms Apps that, reading Direction 4 as a whole, the approved way of submitting a universal credit claim is to use the Secretary of State's approved form on the official website and to follow the method employed by that website. In that context I also accept her argument that references in Direction 4 to 'the method and form set out on the gov.uk website' are sufficiently broad to encompass both what the user can see—the individual questions posed, each of which must be answered before proceeding to the next screen and the next question—as well as what the user cannot see (the coding or programming which underpins the completion and despatch of the online claim

form). As Ms Apps put it, in computing terminology which even I could understand, the form and method include the 'innards' of the Secretary of State's 'official computer system'. Mr Williams argued this involved an unfair and unacceptable lack of transparency—claimants should be able to see each step in the process. I do not consider this affects the construction of the terms of Direction 4. Rather, Mr Williams's point is really a complaint about the information and guidance available more generally about the universal credit scheme and how to claim benefit.

82. Secondly, I consider that Mr Williams's argument assumes a degree of rigour in the drafting of the Secretary of State's Directions which may not be fully justified, not least given the lowly status of such Directions. For example, direction 4(a)(iv) refers to the approved method for 'making the claim', which is sufficiently broadly expressed to include the final step of submitting the claim. I do not read 'making the claim' in this context to be used in contradistinction to, and mutually exclusive to, 'submitting the claim'. It follows, given the digital by default environment, that the old learning about the distinction between a claimant making a claim and the Secretary of State then submitting the claim to an adjudication officer for a decision (see *R(IS) 4/93*) has no place in the universal credit scheme."

The description of the process of claiming online in *GDC* received the approval of the Court of Appeal in *SSWP v Abdul Miah (by Mashuq Miah)* [2024] EWCA Civ 186 at [33].

Social Security

The Social Security (Electronic Communications) Consolidation and Amendment Directions 2011 (as amended)

The Secretary of State for Work and Pensions makes the following Directions in exercise of the powers set out in the Schedule:

Citation, commencement and interpretation

1.—(1) These Directions may be cited as the Social Security (Electronic Communications) Consolidation and Amendment Directions 2011 and they come into force on 23rd January 2012, immediately after the coming into force of the Social Security (Electronic Communications) (No.2) Order 2011.

(2) In these Directions—

"the Claims and Payments Regulations" means the Social Security (Claims and Payments) Regulations 1987;

"relevant benefit" means—

(a) attendance allowance;
(aa) bereavement support payment;
(b) disability living allowance;
(c) council tax benefit;
(d) an employment and support allowance;
(e) housing benefit;
(f) incapacity benefit;
(g) income support;
(h) a jobseeker's allowance;
(hza) maternity allowance;
(ha) personal independence payment;
(i) retirement pension;
(ia) state pension under Part 1 of the Pensions Act 2014;
(j) state pension credit;
(ja) universal credit;
(k) bereavement support payment.

Authorisation

2. A person who, in accordance with paragraph 2 of Schedule 9ZC to the Claims and Payments Regulations or paragraph 2 of Schedule 2 to the Universal Credit, Personal Independence Payment, Jobseeker's Allowance and Employment and Support Allowance (Claims and Payments) Regulations 2013 (electronic communication)—

(a) makes a claim, or provides any certificate, notice, information or evidence in connection with a claim, for the following benefits—
   (i) attendance allowance;
   (ii) carer's allowance;
   (iii) disability living allowance;
   (iv) graduated retirement benefit;
   (v) a jobseeker's allowance;
   (vi) a retirement pension;
   (vii) state pension under Part 1 of the Pensions Act 2014;
   (viii) shared additional pension;
   (ix) universal credit;
   (x) personal independence payment;
   (xi) industrial injuries benefit;
   (xii) an employment and support allowance;
   (xiii) state pension credit;
   (xiv) a social fund funeral payment;
   (xv) a social fund payment in respect of maternity expenses;
   (xvi) maternity allowance.

(b) requests a claim form for attendance allowance or disability living allowance or state pension credit, or a social fund funeral payment, or a social fund payment in respect of maternity expenses, or maternity allowance or bereavement support payment; or

(c) gives a notification of a change of circumstances or provides any certificate, notice information or evidence in relation to carer's allowance, universal credit, industrial injuries benefit, an employment and support allowance, state pension credit, or a social fund funeral payment, or a social fund payment in respect of maternity expenses, or maternity allowance or bereavement support payment or any of the matters mentioned in paragraph 3,

is authorised to do so by means of an electronic communication, provided that the person uses a method and form approved by the Secretary of State for Work and Pensions for that purpose.

Information given electronically: permitted matters

3.—(1) The matters are—

(a) in the case of a relevant benefit, a death;

(b) in the case of attendance allowance, disability living allowance, income support or a jobseeker's allowance, a change of address or a change to the bank or other account into which payments of those benefits are made; and

(c) in the case of a jobseeker's allowance, part-time earnings.

Approved method and form

4. The method and form set out on the gov.uk website or, in the case of a state pension under Part 1 of the Pensions Act 2014, set out on any other website if the Secretary of State for Work and Pensions notifies the person of that other website, at the time of, and for the purposes of, making any claim or request, giving any notification or providing any certificate, notice, information or evidence referred to in paragraph 2 are—

(a) the method approved by the Secretary of State for Work and Pensions for—
   (i) authenticating the identity of the person making the claim or request, giving the notification or providing the certificate, notice, information or evidence;

(ii) electronic communication;
(iii) authenticating the claim, request, notification, certificate, notice, information or evidence delivered;
(iv) making the claim or request, giving the notification or providing the certificate, notice, information or evidence; and

(b) the form approved by the Secretary of State for Work and Pensions in which the claim, request, notification, certificate, notice, information or evidence is to be sent.

Electronic Signatures

5. For the purposes of regulation 1(6) of the Jobseeker's Allowance Regulations 1996, any requirement to provide a signed declaration pursuant to regulation 24(6) of those Regulations may be satisfied by means of an electronic signature provided that the person uses a method established for that purpose by the Secretary of State for Work and Pensions.

Revocations

6. All Directions given by the Secretary of State for Work and Pensions in accordance with paragraph 2 of Schedule 9ZC to the Claims and Payments Regulations prior to these Directions are revoked.

Signed by authority of the Secretary of State for Work and Pensions.

December 2011

Chris Grayling
Minister of State,
Department for Work and Pensions

SCHEDULE

Provisions Conferring Powers Exercised in Making these Directions

regulation 32ZA of, and paragraph 2 of Schedule 9ZC (electronic communication) to, the Claims and Payments Regulations 1987

regulation 1(6) and 24B of the Jobseeker's Allowance Regulations 1996

regulation 74A(2) and (3) of the Council Tax Benefit Regulations 2006

regulation 59A(2) and (3) of the Council Tax Benefit (Persons who have attained the qualifying age for state pension credit) Regulations 2006

regulation 88A(2) and (3) of the Housing Benefit Regulations 2006

regulation 69A(2) and (3) of the Housing Benefit (Persons who have attained the qualifying age for state pension credit) Regulations 2006

SCHEDULE 3 – CONSEQUENTIAL AMENDMENTS

2.378 *AMENDMENTS MADE BY THIS SCHEDULE HAVE BEEN INCORPORATED IN THE REGULATIONS WHICH ARE AMENDED.*

SCHEDULE 4 – SPECIAL PROVISIONS RELATING TO CLAIMS FOR A JOBSEEKER'S ALLOWANCE DURING PERIODS CONNECTED WITH PUBLIC HOLIDAYS [REGULATION 36(2)]

2.379 **1.** In this Schedule and regulation 36(2)—

(a) "public holiday" means—
(i) in England and Wales, Christmas Day, Good Friday or a bank holiday under the Banking and Financial Dealings Act 1971,
(ii) in Scotland, a bank holiday under the Banking and Financial Dealings Act 1971 or a local holiday;

(b) "Christmas and New Year holidays" means—
(i) in England and Wales, the period beginning at the start of Christmas Day and terminating at the end of New Year's Day, or if New Year's Day is a Sunday at the end of 2nd January,

(ii) in Scotland, the period beginning at the start of Christmas Day and terminating at the end of 2nd January, or where New Year's Day is a Saturday or a Sunday terminating at the end of 3rd January;

(c) "Easter Holidays" means the period beginning at the start of Good Friday and terminating at the end of Easter Monday;

(d) "office closure" means a period during which an appropriate office is closed in connection with a public holiday.

2. Where a claim for a jobseeker's allowance is made during any period set out in paragraph 3, the Secretary of State may treat that claim as a claim for a period, to be specified in a decision of the Secretary of State, not exceeding— **2.380**

(a) 35 days after the date of the claim where the claim is made during the period specified in sub-paragraph (a) of paragraph 3; or

(b) 21 days after the date of claim where the claim is made during the period specified in either sub-paragraph (b) or (c) of paragraph 3.

3. For the purposes of paragraph 2 the periods are— **2.381**

(a) in the case of Christmas and New Year holidays, a period beginning with the start of the before the first day of office closure and terminating at the end of the last day of office closure;

(b) in the case of Easter Holidays, a period beginning with the start of the 16th day before the first day of office closure and terminating at the end of the last day of office closure;

(c) in the case of any other public holiday, a period beginning with the start of the 14th day re the first day of office closure and terminating at the end of the last day of office closure.

DEFINITIONS

"appropriate office"—see reg.2.
"jobseeker's allowance"—*ibid.*

SCHEDULE 5 – DIRECT PAYMENT TO LENDER OF DEDUCTIONS IN RESPECT OF INTEREST ON SECURED LOANS [REGULATION 59]

[Revoked by the Loans for Mortgage Interest Regulations 2017 (SI 2017/725) reg.18 and Sch.5, para.8(c) with effect from April 6, 2018] **2.382**

SCHEDULE 6 – DEDUCTIONS FROM BENEFIT AND DIRECT PAYMENT TO THIRD PARTIES [REGULATION 60]

Interpretation

1. [4—(1)] In this Schedule— **2.383**

"assessment period" has the meaning given by regulation 21 (assessment periods) of the Universal Credit Regulations;

"the work allowance" means, in relation to any claimant, the amount applicable to that claimant under regulation 22(2) (deduction of income and work allowance) of the Universal Credit Regulations;

"child element" means, in relation to any claimant, any amount included in the claimant's award of universal credit under regulation 24 (the child element) of the Universal Credit Regulations;

"the Community Charges Regulations" means the Community Charges (Deductions from Income Support) (No.2) Regulations 1990;

"the Community Charges (Scotland) Regulations" means the Community Charges (Deductions from Income Support) (Scotland) Regulations 1989;

"the Council Tax Regulations" means the Council Tax (Deductions from Income Support) Regulations 1993;

"the Fines Regulations" means the Fines (Deductions from Income Support) Regulations 1992;

"standard allowance" means, in relation to any claimant, any amount included in the claimant's award of universal credit under section 9(1) of the 2012 Act;

"water charges" means—

(a) as respects England and Wales, any water and sewerage charges under Chapter 1 of Part 5 of the Water Industry Act 1991;
(b) as respects Scotland, any such charges established by Scottish Water under a charges scheme made under section 29A of the Water Industry (Scotland) Act 2002;

[[4](2) For the purposes of this Schedule, where the relevant percentage of the standard allowance results in a fraction of a penny, that fraction is to be disregarded if it is less than half a penny and otherwise it is to be treated as a penny.]

General

2.384 **2.**—(1) The Secretary of State may deduct an amount from a claimant's award of universal credit and pay that amount to a third party in accordance with the following provisions of this Schedule to discharge (in whole or part) a liability of the claimant to that third party. A payment made to a third party in accordance with this Schedule may be made at such intervals as the Secretary of State may direct.

Limitations applicable to deductions made under this Schedule

2.385 **3.**—(1) The Secretary of State may not deduct an amount from a claimant's award of universal credit under this Schedule and pay that amount to a third party if, in relation to any assessment period, that would—
(a) reduce the amount payable to the claimant to less than one penny; or
(b) result in more than three deductions being made, in relation to that assessment period, under one or more of the provisions mentioned in sub-paragraph (2).

(2) The provisions are—
(a) paragraph 6 (housing costs) of this Schedule;
(b) paragraph 7 (rent and service charges included in rent) of this Schedule;
(c) paragraph 8 (fuel costs) of this Schedule;
(d) paragraph 9 (water charges) of this Schedule;
(e) paragraph 10 (payments in place of payments of child support maintenance) of this Schedule;
(f) paragraph 11 (eligible loans) of this Schedule;
(g) paragraph 12 (integration loans) of this Schedule;
(h) regulation 3 (deductions from income support etc.) of the Community Charges Regulations;
(i) regulation 3 (deductions from income support etc.) of the Community Charges (Scotland) Regulations;
(j) regulation 5 (deduction from debtor's income support etc.) of the Council Tax Regulations; and
(k) regulation 4 (deductions from offender's income support etc.) of the Fines Regulations.

(3) The aggregate amount deducted from a claimant's award of universal credit in relation to any assessment period and paid to a third party under paragraphs 8 (fuel costs) and 9 (water charges) of this Schedule must not, without the claimant's consent, exceed a sum equal to [[4] 25%] of the aggregate of the standard allowance and any child element

Maximum amount

2.386 **4.**—(1) Except as provided for in sub-paragraph (4), the Secretary of State may not deduct an amount from a claimant's award of universal credit under a provision mentioned in paragraph 5(2) of this Schedule if, in relation to any assessment period, that would result in the Secretary of State deducting an amount in excess of [[4] 40%] of the standard allowance ("the maximum amount") from the claimant's award under one or more relevant provisions.

(2) The relevant provisions are—
(a) those mentioned in paragraph 5(2) of this Schedule;
(b) section 26 (higher-level sanctions) of the 2012 Act;
(c) section 27 (other sanctions) of the 2012 Act;
(d) section 71ZG (recovery of payments on account) of the Administration Act(**c**);
(e) section 6B of the Social Security Fraud Act 2001 ("the 2001 Act");
(f) section 7 of the 2001 Act; and
(g) section 9 of the 2001 Act (**c**).

(3) For the purposes of determining whether the maximum amount would be exceeded, no account is to be taken of any liability for continuing need mentioned in—

(a) paragraph 8(4)(b) (fuel costs) of this Schedule; or
(b) paragraph 9(6)(b) or (7)(b)(water charges) of this Schedule.

(4) Subject to paragraph 3 of this Schedule, the Secretary of State may deduct an amount from the claimant's award under paragraph 6 (housing costs), [3 . . .] or paragraph 8 (fuel costs) [3 , or the minimum amount which may be deducted under paragraph 7 (rent and service charges included in rent)] of this Schedule and pay that amount to a third party where the deduction appears to the Secretary of State to be in the claimant's best interests, even though the deduction would result in the maximum amount being exceeded.

Priority as between certain debts

5.—(1) This paragraph applies to a claimant ("C") where, in relation to any assessment period— 2.387

(a) a deduction could otherwise be made from C's award under more than one of the provisions mentioned in sub-paragraph (2); and
(b) the amount of universal credit payable to C in relation to that assessment period is insufficient to enable the Secretary of State to meet all of the liabilities for which in C's case deductions may be made under those provisions or the deduction, were it to be made, would mean that the maximum amount referred to in paragraph 4(1) would be exceeded.

(2) The provisions are—

(a) paragraph 6 (housing costs of this Schedule);
(b) paragraph 7 (rent and service charges included in rent) [3 where the amount of the deduction equals 10% of the standard allowance];
(c) paragraph 8 (fuel costs) of this Schedule;
(d) regulation 3 (deductions from income support etc.) of the Community Charges Regulations, regulation 3 (deductions from income support etc.) of the Community Charges (Scotland) Regulations or (because no such payments are being made in C's case) regulation 5 (deduction from debtor's income support etc.) of the Council Tax Regulations;
(e) regulation 4 (deductions from offender's income support etc.) of the Fines Regulations [9 . . .];
(f) paragraph 9 (water charges) of this Schedule;
(g) paragraph 10 (payments in place of child support maintenance) of this Schedule;
(h) Schedule 7 (deductions from benefit in respect of child support maintenance and payment to persons with care) to these Regulations;
(i) section 78(2) (recovery of social fund awards) of the Administration Act;
(j) section 71ZH(1)(a) or (b) (recovery of hardship payments etc.) of the [5 Administration Act];
(k) section 115A (penalty as alternative to prosecution) of the Administration Act where an overpayment is recoverable from a person by, or due from a person to, the Secretary of State or an authority under or by virtue of section 71 (overpayments – general), section 75 (overpayments of housing benefit) or section 71ZB (recovery of overpayments of certain benefits) of that Act;
(l) section 71 (overpayments – general), section 71ZC (deduction from benefit) or section 75(4) (overpayments of housing benefit) of the Administration Act or an overpayment of working tax credit or child tax credit, where in each case, the overpayment (or part of it) is the result of fraud;
(m) section 115C(4) (incorrect statements etc.) and section 115D(4) (failure to disclose information) of the Administration Act;
(n) section 71 (overpayments – general), section 71ZC (deduction from benefit) or section 75(4) (overpayments of housing benefit) of the Administration Act or an overpayment of working tax credit or child tax credit, where in each case, the overpayment (or part of it) is not the result of fraud;
(o) paragraph 12 (integration loans) of this Schedule;
(p) paragraph 11 (eligible loans) of this Schedule;
[3 (pa) paragraph 7 (rent and service charges included in rent) where the amount of deduction exceeds the minimum amount that may be deducted under that paragraph;]
[9 . . .]

(3) Where this paragraph applies to a claimant, the Secretary of State must make a deduction under any of the provisions mentioned sub-paragraph (2) in accordance with sub-paragraphs (4) and (5).

(4) The Secretary of State must give priority to any such deductions in the order in which they are listed in sub-paragraph (2), with housing costs having the priority.

(5) Where two or more provisions mentioned in any single paragraph of sub-paragraph (2) apply to the claimant, unless the Secretary of State directs otherwise, those deductions have equal priority with each other and the amount of such deductions are to be apportioned accordingly.

(6) For the purposes of sub-paragraph (2)(l) and (n), an overpayment is the result of fraud if, in relation to that overpayment or that part of it, the claimant—

(a) has been found guilty of an offence whether under statute or otherwise;

(b) made an admission after caution of deception or fraud for the purpose of obtaining benefit under the Administration Act, or in the case of a tax credit, under the Tax Credits Act 2002; or

(c) agreed to pay a penalty under section 115A of the Administration Act (penalty as an alternative to prosecution) and the agreement has not been withdrawn.

Housing costs

2.388 **6.**—(1) This paragraph applies where the following condition is met.

(2) The condition is that in any assessment period the claimant is in debt for any item of housing costs which is included in the claimant's award of universal credit under Schedule 5 (housing costs element for owner-occupiers) to the Universal Credit Regulations.

(3) Where this paragraph applies, but subject to sub-paragraph (4), the Secretary of State may, in such cases and circumstances as the Secretary of State may determine, in relation to that assessment period deduct an amount from the claimant's award equal to 5% of the standard allowance in respect of any debt mentioned in sub-paragraph (2) and pay that amount or those amounts to the person to whom any such debt is owed.

(4) Before the Secretary of State may commence (or re-commence) making deductions in respect of any such debt, the claimant's earned income (or in the case of joint claimants their combined earned income) in relation to the previous assessment period must not exceed the work allowance.

(5) [6 . . .]

(6) [6 . . .]

Rent and service charges included in rent

2.389 **7.**—(1) This paragraph applies where all of the following conditions are met.

(2) The first condition is that in any assessment period the claimant—

(a) has an award of universal credit which includes an amount under Schedule 4 (housing costs element for renters) to the Universal Credit Regulations; or

(b) occupies exempt accommodation and has an award of housing benefit under section 130 (housing benefit) of the Contributions and Benefits Act.

(3) The second condition is that the claimant is in debt for any—

(a) rent payments;

(b) service charges which are paid with or as part of the claimant's rent.

(4) The third condition is that the claimant occupies the accommodation to which the debt relates.

(5) Where this paragraph applies, but subject to sub-paragraphs (6) and (7), the Secretary of State may, in such cases and circumstances as the Secretary of State may determine, deduct in relation to that assessment period an amount from the claimant's award [3 which is no less than 10% and no more than 20%] of the standard allowance and pay that amount to the person to whom the debt is owed.

(6) Before the Secretary of State may commence (or re-commence) making deductions in respect of such a debt, the claimant's earned income (or in the case of joint claimants their combined earned income) in relation to the previous assessment period must not exceed the work allowance.

(7) The Secretary of State must stop making such deductions if, in relation to the three assessment periods immediately preceding the date on which the next deduction could otherwise be made, the claimant's earned income (or in the case of joint claimants their combined earned income) equals or exceeds the work allowance.

(8) In this paragraph—

"exempt accommodation" has the meaning given by paragraph 1 of Schedule 1 (interpretation) to the Universal Credit Regulations;

"rent payments" includes any elements included in the claimant's rent which would not fall to be treated as rent under the Housing Benefit Regulations 2006 or as rent payments under the Universal Credit Regulations;

"service charges" includes any items in a charge for services in respect of the accommodation occupied by the claimant which would not fall to be treated as service charges under the Universal Credit Regulations.

Fuel costs

8.—(1) This paragraph applies where the following condition is met. 2.390

(2) The condition is that in any assessment period the claimant is in debt for any [1 fuel item].

(3) Where this paragraph applies, but subject to sub-paragraphs [10(4A), (5) and (6)], the Secretary of State may, in such cases and circumstances as the Secretary of State may determine, deduct in relation to that assessment period the following amounts from the claimant's award and pay them to the person to whom the payment is due.

(4) The amount which may be deducted in respect of any fuel item is—

(a) an amount equal to 5% of the standard allowance; and

(b) an additional amount which the Secretary of State estimates is [10not more than] the average monthly cost necessary to meet the claimant's continuing need for [1 the fuel in respect of which the debt arose, plus such monthly amount as is required to meet any payments required to be made under a green deal plan within the meaning of section 1 of the Energy Act 2011 ("the 2011 Act")], except where current consumption is paid for by other means such as a pre-payment meter.

[10(4A) The Secretary of State may only make deductions under sub-paragraph (4)(b) if—

(a) an application for deductions is made by the person to whom the payment is due; and

(b) except where the application is for a reduction in the amount of a deduction, the claimant consents to the application.]

(5) Before the Secretary of State may commence (or re-commence) making deductions in respect of such a debt, the claimant's earned income (or in the case of joint claimants their combined earned income) in relation to the previous assessment period must not exceed the work allowance.

(6) The Secretary of State must stop making such deductions if, in relation to the three assessment periods immediately preceding the date on which the next deduction could otherwise be made, the claimant's earned income (or in the case of joint claimants their combined earned income) equals or exceeds the work allowance.

(7) As between liabilities for items of gas or electricity, the Secretary of State must give priority to whichever liability the Secretary of State considers it would, having regard to the circumstances and to any requests of the claimant, be appropriate to discharge.

[1 (8) In this paragraph, "fuel item" means –

(a) any charge for mains gas, including for the reconnection of mains gas;

(b) any charge for mains electricity and including any charge for the disconnection and reconnection of mains electricity and including any payments required to be made under a green deal plan within the meaning of section 1 of the 2011 Act.]

Water charges

9.—(1) This paragraph applies where the following condition is met. 2.391

(2) The condition is that in any assessment period the claimant is in debt for water charges, including any charges for reconnection ("the original debt").

(3) Where this paragraph applies, but subject to sub-paragraphs (4) and (5), the Secretary of State may, in such cases and circumstances as the Secretary of State may determine, deduct an amount from the claimant's award in accordance with sub-paragraphs (6) to (8) and pay it to a water undertaker to whom the payment is due or to the person or body authorised to collect water charges for that undertaker.

(4) Before the Secretary of State may commence (or re-commence) making deductions in respect of such a debt, the claimant's earned income (or in the case of joint claimants their combined earned income) in relation to the previous assessment period must not exceed the work allowance.

(5) The Secretary of State must stop making such deductions if, in relation to the three assessment periods immediately preceding the date on which the next deduction could otherwise be made, the claimant's earned income (or in the case of joint claimants their combined earned income) equals or exceeds the work allowance.

(6) Where water charges are determined by means of a water meter, the amount to be deducted under this paragraph in relation to any assessment period is to be—

(a) an amount equal to 5% of the standard allowance towards discharging the original debt; and

(b) an additional amount which the Secretary of State estimates to be the average monthly cost necessary to meet the claimant's continuing need for water consumption.

(7) Where water charges are determined otherwise than by means of a water meter, the amount to be deducted in relation to any assessment period under this paragraph is to be—

(a) the amount referred to in sub-paragraph (6)(a); and

(b) an additional amount equal to the cost necessary to meet the continuing need for water consumption in that assessment period.

(8) Where the claimant is in debt to two water undertakers—

(a) only one amount under sub-paragraph (6)(a) or (7)(a) may be deducted;

(b) a deduction in respect of an original debt for sewerage may only be made after the whole debt in respect of an original debt for water has been paid; and

(c) deductions in respect of continuing charges for both water and for sewerage may be made at the same time.

(9) In this paragraph "water undertaker" means—

(a) in relation to any area in England and Wales, a company holding an appointment as a water undertaker or a sewerage undertaker under the Water Industry Act 1991; or

(b) in relation to any area in Scotland, Scottish Water.

Payments in place of payments of child support maintenance

2.392 **10.**—[7 . . .]

Eligible loans

2.393 **11.**—(1) This paragraph applies where [2 in any assessment period the claimant is in arrears in respect of a loan entered into (whether solely or jointly) with an eligible lender in respect of an eligible loan].

(2) [2 . . .]

(3) [2 . . .]

(4) Where the claimant has an award of universal credit, the Secretary of State may, in such cases and circumstances as the Secretary of State may determine, deduct in relation to the assessment period referred to in sub-paragraph (2) an amount from the claimant's award equal to 5% of the standard allowance and pay that amount to the eligible lender towards discharging the amount owing under the loan agreement.

(5) In a case where the claimant has an award of universal credit but the amount payable to the claimant in relation to that assessment period is insufficient to enable such a deduction to be made, the Secretary of State may instead deduct a weekly amount equal to 5% of the personal allowance for a single claimant aged not less than 25 from any employment and support allowance or jobseeker's allowance awarded to the claimant and pay that amount to the eligible lender.

(6) In a case where the claimant does not have an award of universal credit, but has an award of an employment and support allowance or a jobseeker's allowance, the Secretary of State may deduct a weekly amount equal to 5% of the personal allowance for a single claimant aged not less than 25 from any such award and pay that amount to the eligible lender.

(7) The Secretary of State must not make deductions from a claimant's employment and support allowance or a jobseeker's allowance under this paragraph if that would reduce the amount payable to the claimant to less than 10 pence.

(8) In this paragraph—

"eligible benefit" means—

(a) an employment and support allowance;

(b) a jobseeker's allowance;

(c) universal credit;

"eligible lender" means—

(a) a body registered under section 1 (societies which may be registered) of the Industrial and Provident Societies Act 1965;

(b) a credit union within the meaning of section 1 (registration under the Industrial and Provident Societies Act 1965) of the Credit Unions Act 1979;

(c) a charitable institution within the meaning of section 58(1) (interpretation of Part 2) of the Charities Act 1992;

(d) a body entered on the Scottish Charity Register under section 3 (Scottish Charities Register) of the Charities and Trustee Investment (Scotland) Act 2005;

(e) a community interest company within the meaning of Part 2 of the Companies (Audit, Investigations and Community Enterprise) Act 2004,

which, except for a credit union, [8has permission under the Financial Services and Markets Act 2000 to enter into a contract of the kind mentioned in paragraph 23 or paragraph 23B of Schedule 2 to that Act (credit agreements and contracts for hire of goods)] and which the Secretary of State considers is an appropriate body to which payments on behalf of the claimant may be made in respect of loans made by that body;

"eligible loan" means a loan made by a lender who is, at the time the loan agreement is made, an eligible lender, to a claimant except a loan which—

(a) is secured by a charge or pledge;

(b) is for the purpose of business or self-employment; or

(c) was made by means of a credit card;

"loan agreement" means an agreement between the eligible lender and the claimant in respect of an eligible loan;

"5% of the personal allowance" means 5% of the personal allowance applicable in the claimant's case, rounded up (in any case where that calculation produces a result which is not a multiple of five pence) to the next higher multiple of five pence.

[8(9) The definition of "eligible lender" must be read with—

(a) section 22 of the Financial Services and Markets Act 2000,

(b) any relevant order under that section, and

(c) Schedule 2 to that Act.]

Integration loans

12.—(1) This paragraph applies where [2 the claimant has an integration loan which is recoverable by deductions]. 2.394

(2) [2 . . .]

(3) [2 . . .]

(4) Where this paragraph applies, the amount payable by deductions in any assessment period is to be equal to 5% of the standard allowance.

(5) In this paragraph, "integration loan which is recoverable by deductions" means an integration loan which is made under the Integration Loans for Refugees and Others Regulations 2007 and which is recoverable from the claimant by deductions from the claimant's award of universal credit under regulation 9 of those Regulations.

AMENDMENTS

1. The Social Security (Miscellaneous Amendments) Regulations 2013 (SI 2013/443) reg.10 (April 29, 2013).

2. The Universal Credit and Miscellaneous Amendments Regulations 2014 (SI 2014/597) reg.5 (April 28, 2014).

3. The Universal Credit and Miscellaneous Amendments (No.2) Regulations 2014 (SI 2014/2888) reg.6 (November 26, 2014).

4. The Social Security (Miscellaneous Amendments) (No.2) Regulations 2013 (SI 2013/1508) reg.6 (July 29, 2013).

5. The Universal Credit and Miscellaneous Amendments Regulations 2015 (SI 2015/1754) reg.9 (November 3, 2015).

6. The Loans for Mortgage Interest Regulations 2017 (SI 2017/725), Sch.5(1), para.8 (April 6, 2018), subject to transitional provisions specified in regs 19, 19A and 20 of those Regulations (as amended).

7. The Child Support (Miscellaneous Amendments) Regulations 2019 (SI 2019/1084) reg.7 (July 4, 2019).

8. Financial Services and Markets Act 2000 (Regulated Activities) (Amendment) (No.2) Order 2013 (SI 2013/1881) art.28 and Sch. Para 45 (April 1, 2014).

9. The Fines (Deductions from Income Support) (Miscellaneous Amendments) Regulations 2021 (SI 2021/1077) (October 29, 2021).

10. The Social Security Benefits (Claims and Payments) (Amendment) Regulations 2023 (SI 2023/232) reg.3 (April 1, 2023, in relation to applications for a deduction for a fuel item, or for supersession in relation to a deduction for a fuel item, made on or after that date: reg.1).

DEFINITIONS

"the 1991 Act"—see reg.2.

"the 2012 Act"—*ibid.*

"the Administration Act"—*ibid.*
"assessment period"—see reg.2 and Universal Credit Regs., reg.21.
"benefit"—see reg.2.
"child"—see reg.2 and WRA 2012 s.40.
"claimant"—see reg.2.
"earned income"—see reg.2 and Universal Credit Regs., reg.52.
"employment and support allowance"—see reg.2.
"jobseeker's allowance"—*ibid.*
"universal credit"—*ibid.*
"the Universal Credit Regulations"—*ibid.*

General Note

2.395 For a successful challenge to SSWP's policy regarding deductions from universal credit in respect of court fines, see *R(Blundell and others) v SSWP; R(Day) v SSWP* [2021] EWHC 608 (Admin), annotated under reg.60.

Schedule 7 – Deductions from Benefit in respect of Child Support Maintenance and Payment to Persons with Care [Regulation 60]

Interpretation

2.396 1. In this Schedule—

"beneficiary" means a person who has been awarded a specified benefit;

[1 "fee" means any collection fee under Part 3 of the Child Support Fees Regulations 2014 which is payable by the non-resident parent;]

"maintenance", except in [2 paragraph 3(1)] means child support maintenance which a non-resident parent is liable to pay under the 1991 Act at a flat rate (or would be so liable but for a variation having been agreed to) where that rate applies (or would have applied) because the non-resident parent falls within [2 paragraph 4(1)(a), (b),] (c) or (2) of Schedule 1 to the 1991 Act, and includes such maintenance payable at a transitional rate in accordance with regulations made under section 29(3)(a) of the Child Support, Pensions and Social Security Act 2000;

"person with care" has the same meaning as in section 3 (meaning of certain terms used in this Act) of the 1991 Act;

"specified benefit" means—

(a) an employment and support allowance;
(b) a jobseeker's allowance;
(c) universal credit.

Deductions

2.397 **2.**—(1) Subject to the following provisions of this paragraph and to paragraph 5 (flat rate maintenance), the Secretary of State may deduct from any specified benefit awarded to a beneficiary, an amount equal to the amount of maintenance [1 and any fee] which is payable by the beneficiary and pay the amount deducted to or among the person or persons with care in discharge (in whole or in part) of the liability to pay maintenance [1, and retain any amount deducted in discharge of any liability to pay a fee.].

(2) A deduction [1 for maintenance and fees] may only be made from one specified benefit in respect of the same period.

(3) No amount may be deducted under this Schedule from any employment and support allowance or any jobseeker's allowance awarded to the claimant if that would reduce the amount of the benefit payable to the claimant to less than 10 pence.

(4) No amount may be deducted from any universal credit awarded to the claimant under this Schedule if that would reduce the amount payable to the claimant to less than one penny.

Arrears

2.398 **3.**—(1) [2 . . .] The Secretary of State may deduct the sum of [2 £8.40] per week from any employment and support allowance [2 , jobseeker's allowance or universal credit] which the beneficiary has been awarded and [2 ...] pay the amount deducted to or among the person or persons with care in discharge (in whole or in part) of the beneficiary's liability to pay arrears of maintenance [1 , and retain an amount deducted in discharge of any liability to pay a fee.].

[2(1A) No deduction may be made under sub-paragraph (1) if the beneficiary is liable to pay maintenance.]

(2) [2 . . .]

(3) In sub-paragraph (1) "maintenance" means child support maintenance as defined by section 3(6) of the 1991 Act whether before or after the amendment of the definition of such maintenance by section 1(2)(a) of the Child Support, Pensions and Social Security Act 2000, and includes maintenance payable at a transitional rate in accordance with regulations made under section 29(3)(a) of that Act.

Apportionment

4. Where maintenance is payable to more than one person with care, the amount deducted [1 in respect of maintenance] must be apportioned between the persons with care in accordance with paragraphs 6, 7 and 8 of Schedule 1 (maintenance assessments) to the 1991 Act. **2.399**

Flat rate maintenance

5.—(1) This paragraph applies where the beneficiary and that person's partner are each liable to pay maintenance at a flat rate in accordance with paragraph 4(2) of Schedule 1 to the 1991 Act and either of them has been awarded universal credit (whether as a single claimant or as joint claimants). **2.400**

(2) Where this paragraph applies, an amount not exceeding an amount equal to the flat rate of maintenance [1 and any fee] may be deducted from such an award in respect of the total liability of both partners to pay maintenance [1 and any fee], in the proportions described in regulation 4(3) of the Child Support (Maintenance Calculations and Special Cases) Regulations 2001 or regulation 44(3) of the Child Support Maintenance Calculation Regulations 2012 and must be paid in discharge (in whole or in part) of the respective liabilities to pay maintenance [1 or retained in discharge of any liability to pay a fee.].

Notice

6. Where the Secretary of State commences making deductions under this Schedule, the Secretary of State must notify the beneficiary in writing of the amount and frequency of the deduction and the benefit from which the deduction is made and must give further such notice when there is a change to any of the particulars specified in the notice. **2.401**

AMENDMENTS

1. The Child Support Fees Regulations 2014 (SI 2014/612) reg.15 (August 11, 2014).

2. The Child Support (Miscellaneous Amendments) Regulations 2019 (SI 2019/1084) reg.8 (July 4, 2019).

DEFINITIONS

"the 1991 Act"—see reg.2.
"beneficiary"—see para.(1).
"benefit"—see reg.2.
"child"—see reg.2 and WRA 2012 s.40.
"claimant"—see reg.2.
"employment and support allowance"—*ibid.*
"jobseeker's allowance"—*ibid.*
"maintenance"—see para.(1).
"person with care"—*ibid.*
"specified benefit"—*ibid.*
"universal credit"—see reg.2.

The Social Security and Child Support (Decisions and Appeals) Regulations 1999

(SI 1999/991)

ARRANGEMENT OF REGULATIONS

PART I

GENERAL

PART II

REVISIONS, SUPERSESSIONS AND OTHER MATTERS (SOCIAL SECURITY AND CHILD SUPPORT)

CHAPTER I

REVISIONS

CHAPTER II

SUPERSESSIONS

CHAPTER III

OTHER MATTERS

PART III

SUSPENSION, TERMINATION AND OTHER MATTERS

CHAPTER I

SUSPENSION AND TERMINATION

CHAPTER II

OTHER MATTERS

PART IV

RIGHTS OF APPEAL AND PROCEDURE FOR BRINGING APPEALS

CHAPTER I

GENERAL

General appeals matters not including child support appeals

General appeals matters including child support appeals

PART V

APPEAL TRIBUNALS FOR SOCIAL SECURITY CONTRACTING OUT OF PENSIONS, VACCINE DAMAGE AND CHILD SUPPORT

35.–38. *Revoked.*
38A. Appeals raising issues for decisions by officers of Inland Revenue.
39.–58. *Revoked.*
58A. Appeal to the Upper Tribunal by a partner.

PART VI

REVOCATIONS

59. *Omitted.*

SCHEDULES

Schedule 1 Provisions conferring powers exercised in making these Regulations.
Schedule 2 Decisions against which no appeal lies.
Schedule 3 *Revoked.*
Schedule 3A Date from which superseding decision takes effect where a claimant is in receipt of Income Support or Jobseeker's Allowance.
Schedule 3B Date on which change of circumstances takes effect where claimant entitled to State Pension Credit.
Schedule 3C Date from which change of circumstances takes effect where claimant entitled to Employment and Support Allowance.
Schedule 4 *Omitted.*

Whereas a draft of this Instrument was laid before Parliament in accordance with section 80(1) of the Social Security Act 1998 and approved by resolution of each House of Parliament;

Now, therefore, the Secretary of State for Social Security, in exercise of powers set out in Schedule 1 to this Instrument and of all other powers enabling him in that behalf, with the concurrence of the Lord Chancellor in so far as the Regulations are made under section 6(3) of the Social Security Act 1998, by this Instrument, which contains only regulations made by virtue of, or consequential upon, those provisions of the Social Security Act 1998 and which is made before the end of the period of six months beginning with the coming into force of those provisions, after consultation with the Council on Tribunals in accordance with section 8 of the Tribunals and Inquiries Act 1992, hereby makes the following Regulations:

PART I

GENERAL

Citation, commencement [[28] , application and interpretation]

2.403 **1.**—(1) These Regulations may be cited as the Social Security and Child Support (Decisions and Appeals) Regulations 1999.

(2) These Regulations shall come into force—

(a) in so far as they relate to child support and for the purposes of this regulation and regulation 2 on 1st June, 1999;

(b) in so far as they relate to—

(i) industrial injuries benefit, guardian's allowance and child benefit; and

(ii) a decision made under the Pension Schemes Act 1993 by virtue of section 170(2) of that Act;

on 5th July, 1999;

(c) in so far as they relate to retirement pension, widow's benefit, incapacity benefit, severe disablement allowance and maternity allowance, on 6th September, 1999;

(d) in so far as they relate to [3 working families' tax credit and disabled person's tax credit], on 5th October, 1999;

(e) in so far as they relate to attendance allowance, disability living allowance, invalid care allowance, jobseeker's allowance, credits of contributions or earnings, home responsibilities protection and vaccine damage payments, on 18th October, 1999; and

(f) for all remaining purposes, on 29th November, 1999.

[28 (2A) In so far as these Regulations relate to—

(a) an employment and support allowance payable under the Welfare Reform Act, they apply only in so far as the Act has effect apart from the amendments made by Schedule 3 and Part 1 of Schedule 14 to the Welfare Reform Act 2012 ("the 2012 Act") (removing references to an income-related allowance);

(b) a jobseeker's allowance payable under the Jobseekers Act 1995, they apply only in so far as the Act has effect apart from the amendments made by Part 1 of Schedule 14 to the 2012 Act (removing references to an income-based allowance).

(2B) These Regulations do not apply to universal credit (within the meaning of Part 1 of the Welfare Reform Act 2012) or personal independence payment (within the meaning of Part 4 of that Act).]

(3) In these Regulations, unless the context otherwise requires—

"the Act" means the Social Security Act 1998;

"the 1997 Act" means the Social Security (Recovery of Benefits) Act 1997;

[6 "the Arrears, Interest and Adjustment of Maintenance Assessments Regulations" means the Child Support (Arrears, Interest and Adjustment of Maintenance Assessments) Regulations 1992;]

[10 "assessed income period" is to be construed in accordance with sections 6 and 9 of the State Pension Credit Act;]

"the Claims and Payments Regulations" means the Social Security (Claims and Payments) Regulations 1987;

"appeal" means an appeal to [22 the First-tier Tribunal];

[32 [33 . . .];

"bereavement benefit" means—

[33 (a) bereavement support payment under section 30 of the Pensions Act 2014; or]

(c) a widowed parent's allowance;

[33 . . .]]

[1 "the Board" means the Commissioners [32 for Her Majesty's Revenue and Customs];]

[36 [37 ...]]

"claimant" means—

(a) any person who is a claimant for the purposes of section 191 of the Administration Act [10 section 35(1) of the Jobseekers Act or [18 , section 17(1) of the State Pension Credit Act or section 24(1) of the Welfare Reform Act]] or any other person from whom benefit is alleged to be recoverable; and

(b) any person subject to a decision of [1 an officer of the Board] under the Pension Schemes Act 1993;

[22 . . .]

[21 [27 . . .]]

[32 "contribution-based jobseeker's allowance" means a contribution-based jobseeker's allowance under Part 1 of the Jobseekers Act;]

[18 "contributory employment and support allowance" means a contributory allowance under Part 1 of the Welfare Reform Act;]

[29 "couple" means—

(a) two people who are married to, or civil partners of, each other and are members of the same household; or

(b) two people who are not married to, or civil partners of, each other but are living together [35 as if they were a married couple or civil partners];]

"the date of notification" means—

(a) the date that notification of a decision of the Secretary of State [3 or an officer of the Board] is treated as having been given or sent in accordance with regulation 2(b); [25 . . .]

(b) in the case of a social fund payment arising in accordance with regulations made under section 138(2) of the Contributions and Benefits Act—

(i) the date seven days after the date on which the Secretary of State makes his decision to make a payment to a person to meet expenses for heating;

(ii) where a person collects the instrument of payment at a post office, the date the instrument is collected;

(iii) where an instrument of payment is sent to a post office for collection but is not collected and a replacement instrument is issued, the date on which the replacement instrument is issued; or

(iv) where a person questions his failure to be awarded a payment for expenses for heating, the date on which the notification of the Secretary of State's decision given in response to that question is issued; [25 ; or

(c) where notification of a decision of the Secretary of State is sent by means of an electronic communication (within the meaning given in section 15(1) of the Electronic Communications Act 2000), the date on which the notification is sent.]

[17 "the Deferral of Retirement Pensions etc. Regulations" means the Social Security (Deferral of Retirement Pensions, Shared Additional Pension and Graduated Retirement Benefit) (Miscellaneous Provisions) Regulations 2005;]

[9 "designated authority" means—

(a) the Secretary of State;

(b) a person providing services to the Secretary of State;

(c) a local authority;

(d) a person providing services to, or authorised to exercise any functions of, any such authority.]

[18 "the Employment and Support Allowance Regulations" means the Employment and Support Allowance Regulations 2008;

[24 "failure determination" means a determination by the Secretary of State under regulation 61(2) of the Employment and Support Allowance Regulations or regulation 8(2) of the Employment and Support Allowance (Work-Related Activity) Regulations 2011 that a claimant has failed to satisfy a requirement of regulation 54 of the Employment and Support Allowance Regulations (requirement to take part in a work-focused interview) or regulation 3 of the Employment and Support Allowance (Work-Related Activity) Regulations 2011 (requirement to undertake work-related activity).]

[4 "family" has the same meaning as in section 137 of the Contributions and Benefits Act;]

[22 . . .]

[17 "the Graduated Retirement Benefit Regulations" means the Social Security (Graduated Retirement Benefit) Regulations 2005;]

[18 "income-related employment and support allowance" means an income-related allowance under Part 1 of the Welfare Reform Act;

"the Income Support Regulations" means the Income Support (General) Regulations 1987;

[30 "Income Support Work-Related Activity Regulations" means the Income Support (Work-Related Activity) and Miscellaneous Amendments Regulations 2014;]

"the Jobseeker's Allowance Regulations" means the Jobseeker's Allowance Regulations 1996;

[6 "a joint-claim couple" has the same meaning as in section 1(4) of the Jobseekers Act 1995;

"a joint-claim jobseeker's allowance" has the same meaning as in section 1(4) of the Jobseekers Act 1995;]

[22 . . .]

[18 "'limited capability for work'" has the same meaning as in section 1(4) of the Welfare Reform Act;

[34 "the Loans for Mortgage Interest Regulations" means the Loans for Mortgage Interest Regulations 2017;]

[19 "the Lump Sum Payments Regulations" means the Social Security (Recovery of Benefits) (Lump Sum Payments) Regulations 2008;]

[7 [23 . . .]]

[5 "the Maintenance Calculation Procedure Regulations" means the Child Support (Maintenance Calculation Procedure) Regulations 2000;

"the Maintenance Calculations and Special Cases Regulations" means the Child Support (Maintenance Calculations and Special Cases) Regulations 2000;]

[22 . . .]

[15 . . .]

[8 "official error" means an error made by—

(a) an officer of the Department for Work and Pensions [21 [27 . . .]] or the Board acting as such which no person outside the Department [21 [27 . . .]] or the Inland Revenue caused or to which no person outside the Department [21 [27 . . .]] or the Inland Revenue materially contributed;

(b) a person employed by a designated authority acting on behalf of the authority, which no person outside that authority caused or to which no person outside that authority materially contributed,

but excludes any error of law which is shown to have been an error by virtue of a subsequent decision of [22 the Upper Tribunal] or the court;]

[22 . . .]

[34 "owner-occupier loan payments" means loan payments made under the Loans for Mortgage Interest Regulations;

"owner-occupier payments" has the same meaning as in Part 1 of Schedule 1 to the Loans for Mortgage Interest Regulations.]

[22 . . .]

[22 . . .]

[22 . . .]

[8 "partner" means—

(a) where a person is a member of [16 a couple] the other member of that couple; or

(b) where a person is polygamously married to two or more members of his household, any such member;]

"party to the proceedings" means the Secretary of State [21 [27 . . .]] [3 or, as the case may be, the Board or an officer of the Board,] and any other person—

(a) who is one of the principal parties for the purposes of sections 13 and 14;

(b) who has a right of appeal to [22 the First-tier Tribunal] under section 11(2) of the 1997 Act, section 20 of the Child Support Act [6 . . .] [13, section 2B(6) of the Administration Act] or section 12(2);

[22. . .]

"referral" means a referral of an application for a departure direction to [22 the First-tier Tribunal] under section 28D(1)(b) of the Child Support Act;

[5 "relevant credit" means a credit of contributions or earnings resulting from a decision in accordance with regulations made under section 22(5) of the Contributions and Benefits Act;]

[26 "relevant other child" is to be interpreted by reference to paragraph 10C(2) of Schedule 1 to the Child Support Act];

[6 except where otherwise provided "relevant person" means—

(a) a person with care;

(b) a non-resident parent;

(c) a parent who is treated as a non-resident parent under regulation 8 of the Maintenance Calculations and Special Cases Regulations;

(d) a child, where the application for a maintenance calculation is made by that child under section 7 of the Child Support Act,

in respect of whom a maintenance calculation has been applied for, [22 . . .], or is or has been in force;]

[37 "Scottish disability benefit" means, as the context requires, either of the following benefits—

(a) adult disability payment within the meaning given in regulation 2 of the Disability Assistance for Working Age People (Scotland) Regulations 2022; and

(b) child disability payment within the meaning given in regulation 2 of the Disability Assistance for Children and Young People (Scotland) Regulations 2021;]

[[31] "shared additional pension" means a shared additional pension under section 55A or 55AA of the Contributions and Benefits Act;]

[[10] "state pension credit" means the benefit payable under the State Pension Credit Act;

"State Pension Credit Act" means the State Pension Credit Act 2002;

"State Pension Credit Regulations" means the State Pension Credit Regulations 2002;]

[[3] "tax credit" means working families' tax credit or disabled person's tax credit, construing those terms in accordance with section 1(1) of the Tax Credits Act 1999;]

[[2] "the Transfer Act" means the Social Security Contributions (Transfer of Functions, etc.) Act 1999.]

[[7] "the Variations Regulations" means the Child Support (Variations) Regulations 2000;]

[[18] "'the Welfare Reform Act'" means the Welfare Reform Act 2007;]

[[32] "widowed parent's allowance" means an allowance under section 39A of the Contributions and Benefits Act;]

[[14] "work focused-interview" means an interview in which a person is required to take part in accordance with regulations made under section 2A or 2AA of the Administration Act;]

[[1] (3A) In these Regulations as they relate to any decision made under the Pension Schemes Act 1993 by virtue of section 170(2) of that Act, any reference to the Secretary of State is to be construed as if it were a reference to an officer of the Board.]

(4) In these Regulations, unless the context otherwise requires, a reference—

(a) to a numbered section is to the section of the Act bearing that number;

(b) to a numbered Part is to the Part of these Regulations bearing that number;

(c) to a numbered regulation or Schedule is to the regulation in, or Schedule to, these Regulations bearing that number;

(d) in a regulation or Schedule to a numbered paragraph is to the paragraph in that regulation or Schedule bearing that number;

(e) in a paragraph to a lettered or numbered sub-paragraph is to the sub-paragraph in that paragraph bearing that letter or number.

AMENDMENTS

1. Social Security Contributions (Transfer of Functions, etc.) Act 1999 (Commencement No.2 and Consequential and Transitional Provisions) Order 1999 (SI 1999/1662) art.3(2) (July 5, 1999).

2. Social Security and Child Support (Decisions and Appeals) Amendment (No.3) Regulations 1999 (SI 1999/1670) reg.2(2) (July 5, 1999).

3. Tax Credits (Decisions and Appeals) (Amendment) Regulations 1999 (SI 1999/2570) regs 3 and 4 (October 5, 1999). Note that amendments made by these regulations only have effect with respect to tax credit under the Tax Credits Act 1999 (reg.1(2) of the Amendment Regulations).

4. Social Security and Child Support (Miscellaneous Amendments) Regulations 2000 (SI 2000/1596) reg.14 (June 19, 2000).

5. Social Security Amendment (Joint Claims) Regulations 2001 (SI 2001/518) reg.4(a) (March 19, 2001).

6. Child Support (Decisions and Appeals) (Amendment) Regulations 2000 (SI 2000/3185) reg.2 (various dates as provided in reg.1(1)).

7. Social Security (Breach of Community Order) (Consequential Amendments) Regulations 2001 (SI 2001/1711) reg.2(2)(a) (October 15, 2001).

8. Social Security and Child Support (Decisions and Appeals) (Miscellaneous Amendments) Regulations 2002 (SI 2002/1379) reg.2 (May 20, 2002).

9. Social Security (Jobcentre Plus Interviews) Regulations 2002 (SI 2002/1703) Sch.2 para.6(a) (September 30, 2002).

10. State Pension Credit (Consequential, Transitional and Miscellaneous Provisions) Regulations 2002 (SI 2002/3019) reg.16 (April 7, 2003).

11. Child Benefit and Guardian's Allowance (Decisions and Appeals) Regulations 2003 (SI 2003/916) reg.36 (April 7, 2003). Note that this amendment replaces the words "regulation 27" only so far as the definition relates to child benefit and guardian's allowance. See the annotation to this definition.

12. Social Security and Child Support (Miscellaneous Amendments) Regulations 2003 (SI 2003/1050) reg.3(1) (May 5, 2003).

13. Social Security (Jobcentre Plus Interviews for Partners) Regulations 2003 (SI 2003/1886) reg.15(2) (April 12, 2004).

14. Social Security (Working Neighbourhoods) Regulations 2004 (SI 2004/959) reg.24(2) (April 26, 2004).

15. Social Security, Child Support, and Tax Credits (Decisions and Appeals) Amendment Regulations 2004 (SI 2004/3368) reg.2(2) (December 21, 2004).

16. Civil Partnership (Consequential Amendments) Regulations 2005 (SI 2005/2878) reg.8(2) (December 5, 2005).

17. Social Security (Deferral of Retirement Pensions, Shared Additional Pension and Graduated Retirement Benefit) (Miscellaneous Provisions) Regulations 2005 (SI 2005/2677) reg.9(2) (April 6, 2006).

18. Employment and Support Allowance (Consequential Provisions) (No.2) Regulations 2008 (SI 2008/1554) regs 29 and 30 (July 27, 2008).

19. Social Security (Recovery of Benefits) (Lump Sum Payments) Regulations 2008 (SI 2008/1596) Sch.2 para.1(a) (October 1, 2008).

20. Child Support (Consequential Provisions) Regulations 2008 (SI 2008/2543), reg.4(1) and (2) (October 27, 2008).

21. Child Support (Consequential Provisions) (No.2) Regulations 2008 (SI 2008/2656) reg.4 (November 1, 2008).

22. Tribunals, Courts and Enforcement Act 2007 (Transitional and Consequential Provisions) Order 2008 (SI 2008/2683) Sch.1 paras 95 and 96 (November 3, 2008), subject to a saving under art.3 for reasons explained in the note to ss.5–7 of the Social Security Act 1998.

23. Welfare Reform Act 2009, (Section 26) (Consequential Amendments) Regulations 2010 (SI 2010/424) reg.4(1) and (2) (March 22, 2010).

24. Employment and Support Allowance (Work-Related Activity) Regulations 2011 (SI 2011/1349) reg.21 (June 1, 2011).

25. Social Security (Electronic Communications) Order 2011 (SI 2011/1498) art.5 (June 20, 2011).

26. Child Support (Miscellaneous Amendments) Regulations 2011 (SI 2011/1464) reg.2(1) and (2) (July 4, 2011).

27. Public Bodies (Child Maintenance and Enforcement Commission: Abolition and Transfer of Functions) Order 2012 (SI 2012/2007) art.3(2) and Sch. para.113(1) and (2) (August 1, 2012).

28. Universal Credit, Personal Independence Payment, Jobseeker's Allowance and Employment and Support Allowance (Decisions and Appeals) Regulations

2013 (SI 2013/381) reg.55 (April 8, 2013 in relation to personal independence payment and April 29, 2013 for other purposes).

29. Marriage (Same Sex Couples) Act 2013 (Consequential Provisions) Order 2014 (SI 2014/107) art.2 and Sch.1 para.26 (March 13, 2014, in England and Wales) and Marriage and Civil Partnership (Scotland) Act 2014 and Civil Partnership Act 2004 (Consequential Provisions and Modifications) Order 2014 (SI 2014/3229) Sch.6 para.18 (December 16, 2014, in Scotland).

30. Income Support (Work-Related Activity) and Miscellaneous Amendments Regulations 2014 (SI 2014/1097) reg.12(1) and (2) (April 28, 2014).

31. Pensions Act 2014 (Consequential, Supplementary and Incidental Amendments) Order 2015 (SI 2015/1985) art.18(1) and (2) (April 6, 2016).

32. Social Security (Credits, and Crediting and Treatment of Contributions) (Consequential and Miscellaneous Amendments) Regulations 2016 (SI 2016/1145) reg.4(1) and (2) (January 1, 2017).

33. Pensions Act 2014 (Consequential, Supplementary and Incidental Amendments) Order 2017 (SI 2017/422) art.15(1) and (2) (April 6, 2017, subject to a saving).

34. Loans for Mortgage Interest Regulations 2017 (SI 2017/725) reg.18 and Sch.5 para.11(1) and (2), as amended by the Loans for Mortgage Interest and Social Fund Maternity Grant (Amendment) Regulations 2018 (SI 2018/307) reg.2(11) and (18)(e) (April 6, 2018, subject to a saving).

35. Civil Partnership (Opposite-sex Couples) Regulations 2019 (SI 2019/1458) reg.41(b) and Sch.3 para.54 (December 2, 2019).

36. Social Security (Scotland) Act 2018 (Disability Assistance for Children and Young People) (Consequential Modifications) Order 2021 (SI 2021/786) art.6(1) and (2) (July 26, 2021).

37. Social Security (Disability Assistance for Working Age People) (Consequential Amendments) Order 2022 (SI 2022/177) art.6(1) and (2) (March 21, 2022).

Definitions

"the Child Support Act"—see s.84 of the Social Security Act 1998.

"the Contributions and Benefits Act"—see s.84 of the Social Security Act 1998.

General Note

Paragraphs (2A) and (2B)

These Regulations do not apply to those benefits to which the Universal Credit, Personal Independence Payment, Jobseeker's Allowance and Employment and Support Allowance (Decisions and Appeals) Regulations 2013 apply. Note, however, that that means that these Regulations continue to apply to income-based jobseeker's allowance and income-related and employment and support allowance. They will also continue to apply to contribution-based jobseeker's allowance and contributory employment and support allowance to the extent that those benefits do not fall within the scope of reg.1(3) of the 2013 Regulations after April 29, 2013. **2.404**

Paragraph (3)

The definition of "the Claims and Payments Regulations" is out of sequence due to a drafting error. **2.405**

The definitions of "the Arrears, Interest and Adjustment of Maintenance Assessments Regulations", "the Maintenance Calculation Procedure Regulations", the Maintenance Calculations and Special Cases Regulations", "relevant other child", "relevant person" and "Variations Regulations" are omitted for purposes of cases where child support maintenance is calculated under the scheme introduced by the Child Maintenance and Other Payments Act 2008 (see the Child Support (Meaning of Child and New Calculation Rules) (Consequential and Miscellaneous Amendment) Regulations 2012 (SI 2012/2785), reg.6.). Amendments have also been made to regs 4, 30 and 33 and a number of regulations not included in this volume have been omitted altogether, solely for those purposes. This seems an unnecessarily complicated method of drafting, leaving in force two versions of these Regulations. Since these child support amendments are not relevant to social security cases, this volume takes no account of them.

"the Board"

2.406 Except in regs 3(8H), 11A and 38A, references to the Board are of virtually no practical effect because they are relevant only to decisions in respect of tax credits paid under the Tax Credits Act 1999, which were abolished in 2003. Decisions in respect of child benefit and guardian's allowance are made by HMRC under the Child Benefit and Guardian's Allowance (Decisions and Appeals) Regulations 2003.

"official error"

2.407 The definition of "official error" is important because it is a ground for revision under reg.3, whereas a mistake of fact or law that is not an "official error" is usually a ground of supersession under reg.6, and a supersession is usually effective from a later date than a revision.

Adjudication officers under the pre-1998 Act system of adjudication were "officers of the Department . . . acting as such" and so an error by an adjudication officer can constitute an "official error" (*R(CS) 3/04*, not following *R(I) 5/02*). However, there is no "official error" where an error is made by an authority in its capacity as an employer rather than in its capacity as an administrator of benefits (*EM v Waltham Forest LBC* [2009] UKUT 245 (AAC), *Kingston-Upon-Hull CC v DM (HB)* [2010] UKUT 234 (AAC) (subsequently upheld on appeal without reference to this point)).

Only clear and obvious mistakes amount to errors in this context and a failure to elucidate facts not disclosed by a claimant is unlikely to suffice (*R(SB) 10/91* and *R(SB) 2/93*). However, failing to ask a question on a standard claim form (or otherwise) can amount to an "official error" (*MB v Christchurch BC (HB)* [2014] UKUT 201 (AAC); [2014] AACR 39). There is also no "official error" where a decision is made without investigating a possible discrepancy in the evidence or on incomplete evidence, partly because in such cases a claimant is likely to have contributed to any error (*R(H) 1/04*, *R(H) 2/04*). In *KW v Lancaster CC (HB)* [2011] UKUT 266 (AAC), there was held to be no official error where the substantial cause of the overpayment of housing benefit was the claimant's ex-partner's late payment of child support maintenance, even if the delays involved might have been contributed to by the Child Support Agency not taking enforcement action.

Since it was decided in *CDLA/1707/2005* that a tribunal is entitled to substitute a revision for a supersession or refusal to supersede (see the annotation to s.12(2) of the Social Security Act 1998, above), there have been a number of new decisions on the meaning of "official error". In *CDLA/393/2006*, the Commissioner regarded the adjudication officer's reliance on the claim form without obtaining further evidence as "a failure in the proper standards of administration" but found that the claimant's mother had contributed to the error by the way in which she had completed the claim form. There was therefore no "official error". He said that "in judging what was a material contribution a common sense approach should be taken, rather than a highly refined analysis of causation" and that the way the claim form had been completed should not be seen as merely the setting for the adjudication officer's error.

2.408 This echoes what was said in *R. (Sier) v Cambridge CC Housing Benefit Review Board* [2001] EWCA Civ 1523, the effect of which was summarised in *SN v Hounslow LBC* [2010] UKUT 57 (AAC) (at [19]):

> "The issue before the Court of Appeal was whether a claimant who had obtained a series of benefit overpayments by not disclosing the facts that he had another property (on which he also claimed benefit), and further had ceased to qualify for income support, could avoid recovery on the ground of 'official error' when the DSS, as it then was, had failed to send the authority the usual notification of his income support being stopped.... the Court of Appeal decision emphasises

that the approach to causation in such cases is to be concerned with the practical question of what really caused the overpayments in question to be made. The unanimous (and perhaps not very surprising) conclusion was ... that a claimant who has got benefit by not disclosing relevant facts is not able to turn the case into one of 'overpayment caused by official error' by saying that if only officialdom had been more vigilant he would have been spotted."

In *CH/687/2006*, the claimant was overpaid housing benefit because the amount of her partner's incapacity benefit changed due to the length of time he had been incapable of work. The Deputy Commissioner reviewed the cases and held that there was no official error. Although the local authority had known that the incapacity benefit in payment when the award was made was only short-term incapacity benefit, which would inevitably be replaced by a higher rate if the claimant's partner continued to be incapable of work, the local authority had been entitled to presume that any change in the rate of incapacity benefit would be reported to it. This can therefore be seen as another case where the claimant contributed to the error. In *CPC/206/2005*, the Commissioner stated that the term "official error" is not confined to errors of law but said that it "involves more than merely taking a decision that another decision-maker with the same information would not take". He considered that it would not be helpful further to explain what the term meant. However, he found an official error in the case because "no Secretary of State or decision-maker acting reasonably could have [made the decision under appeal]". That would have been an error of law and it is perhaps difficult to envisage an official error that would not be an error of law in its public law sense (see the annotation to s.11 of the Tribunals Courts and Enforcement Act 2007). An "official error" is not revealed merely because a decision made some time ago in the light of current medical opinion is shown to have been wrong as a result of a change in medical opinion (*R(AF) 5/07*). There will merely have been a mistake of fact justifying supersession.

Generally, notification of a change of circumstances must be made to the office dealing with the relevant benefit and so, if information is not acted on because it has been sent to another office, a claimant will generally have contributed to the error. However, that will not inevitably be the case. In *CH/2567/2007*, the Commissioner had regard to confusing nomenclature (such that even officials got it wrong and the tribunal was confused), the proliferation of correspondence, the repeated notification of the relevant facts to one department that ought to have passed the information to another and the complication of the benefit position (such that the claimant could not reasonably have been expected to realise there had been an overpayment) and he concluded that the claimant had not contributed to the official error involved in one department failing to pass information on to another. 2.409

Generally also, notification of a change of circumstances must be made in writing unless given by telephone (although there are exceptions, see regs 32–32B of the Social Security (Claims and Payments) Regulations 1987). However, even though there had been a duty to make the notification in writing in *West Somerset DC v JA (HB)* [2010] UKUT 190 (AAC), there was "official error" when the claimant gave oral notice of a change of circumstances and the local authority neither acted upon that notification nor informed the claimant that written notice was required. Unusually, none of the notices issued by the local authority that were before the Upper Tribunal had referred to the duty under the legislation relevant to that case to notify a change of circumstances in writing. Had any of them done so, there would presumably have arisen the question whether the requirement to give notice in writing had been waived by the officer receiving the oral notification.

KI v HMRC [2023] UKUT 212 (AAC) "Official error" – failure of the automatic information sharing system between the DWP and HMRC to notify HMRC of an award of DLA did not amount to "official error". *AG v HMRC* [2013] UKUT 530 (AAC); *AM v HMRC (TC)* [2015] UKUT 345 (AAC); *JP v HMRC (TC)* [2013] UKUT 519 (AAC) not wrongly decided. *R. Sier v Cambridge CC HBRB* [2001] EWCA Civ 1523 distinguished. 2.410

The concluding words of the amended definition are imprecise but it is now fairly clear that they apply where the official was acting in accordance with a general Departmental misunderstanding of the law that has been shown to be wrong by a decision of the Upper Tribunal or court that need not itself have directly involved the particular claimant in respect of whom the error was made. The jurisprudential difficulties arising because the Upper Tribunal and courts only declare the law to be as it has always been and because the misunderstanding may not have been shared by anyone outside the Department are familiar ones. However, in *R(P)2/09*, a Tribunal of Commissioners did not dwell on those theoretical problems and gave the words their practical meaning, deciding that there had been no official error where the Department had been shown by a decision of the European Court of Justice to have been misapplying European Community law. The consequence was that the claimant, who had made an application for revision or supersession shortly after the Court's decision, was entitled to have it treated only as an application for supersession effiective from the date the application was made, insofar as she needed to rely on the decision of the Court but could have it treated as an application for revision insofar as she could rely upon domestic legislation. It is not clear whether the Tribunal of Commissioners was referred to reg.7(6), which applies when there has been a "relevant determination" for the purposes of s.27 of the Social Security Act 1998. A decision of the Upper Tribunal or court that shows that there has been an error of law is likely to be such a "relevant determination", so that s.27 has the effect that it is not to be taken into account in any subsequent decision in respect of any period before the date on which the "relevant determination" was made, but reg.7(6) has the effect that it *is* to be taken into account from that date on a supersession on the ground of error of law. (Such a supersession under reg.6(2)(b) (i) is generally possible following such a "relevant determination" precisely because revision for official error is not and so reg.6(3) does not apply.)

The issue was considered in greater depth in *JK v SSWP (DLA)* [2013] UKUT 218 (AAC), where it was pointed out that "the court" is not defined but the judge nonetheless found the term to include the European Court of Justice and further found the restriction implied by the concluding words of the definition of "official error" not to be contrary to European Union law. A decision is not "shown" to be wrong by a decision of a Commissioner if it was plainly wrong on a clear reading of legislation (*BD v SSWP (DLA)* [2013] UKUT 216 (AAC)). Where a decision is wrong both for a reason subsequently revealed by a court and for some other reason, the concluding words of this definition do not prevent the decision from being revised in a way that corrects both errors (*R(P) 2/09* and *BD v SSWP (DLA)*, subject to the effect of s.27 of the 1998 Act). An order made by a Court by consent is not a "decision" for these purposes (*R(FC) 3/98*).

The definition of "official error" does not include errors of tribunals and, in any event, there is no power to revise a decision of a tribunal. Nor is there any power under reg.6 to supersede a decision of a tribunal on the ground of error of law. The consequence is that, where the Secretary of State makes the same official error in a number of cases and some claimants appeal unsuccessfully to the First-tier Tribunal but others do not appeal, it is possible to revise the decisions in order to correct the error in those cases where claimants did not appeal but the error cannot be corrected retrospectively by the Secretary of State in the cases where the claimant did appeal. It was held in *ED v SSWP (DLA)* [2013] UKUT 583 (AAC) that there are sound reasons of principle why the Secretary of State's power to overturn a decision of a tribunal are limited and therefore, even where the official error is a breach of European Union law, this inability to correct the error retrospectively is not itself contrary to European Union law. It is always open to the claimant to make a new claim. It may sometimes also be possible for the claimant to appeal to the Upper Tribunal, so as to correct the error from the date that the earlier decision was effective but that would have involved an impermissible extension of time in *ED*.

"party to the proceedings"

In *CA/1014/1999*, it was held that, where the Secretary of State had decided that an overpayment was recoverable from a claimant but had made no decision in respect of the claimant's appointee, the claimant's appointee was not a "party to the proceedings" against whom the tribunal could make a recoverability decision, even though the appointee had brought the proceedings on behalf of the claimant (and had an express right of appeal under reg.25). However, in *CTC/3543/2004*, the same Commissioner held that, where HMRC had made a decision to the effect that a tax credit was recoverable from both the husband and the wife, the husband was a "party to the proceedings" before the tribunal even though only his wife had appealed (although acting through her husband). **2.411**

Where the Secretary of State has made a decision that an overpayment is recoverable from both a claimant and the claimant's appointee, an appeal brought by the appointee should be treated as an appeal brought on behalf of both the claimant and the appointee unless it is clear that an appeal on behalf of only one of them was intended (*R(A) 2/06*). Even if an appeal by only one of them is intended, *CA/1014/1999* is clearly distinguishable and whichever has not appealed will be a "party to the proceedings", as in *CTC/3543/2004*.

Service of notices or documents

2. Where, by any provision of the Act [3, of the Child Support Act] or of these Regulations— **2.412**

(a) any notice or other document is required to be given or sent [4. . .] to an officer authorised by the Secretary of State [1 or to an officer of the Board], that notice or document shall be treated as having been so given or sent on the day that it is received [4. . .] by an officer authorised by the Secretary of State [1 or by an officer of the Board], as the case may be, and

(b) any notice (including notification of a decision of the Secretary of State [2 or of an officer of the Board] or other document is required to be given or sent to any person other than [4. . .] [1 [4. . .] an officer] authorised by the Secretary of State [1 or an officer of the Board], as the case may be, that notice or document shall, if sent by post to that person's last known address, be treated as having been given or sent on the day that it was posted.

AMENDMENTS

1. Tax Credits (Decisions and Appeals) (Amendment) Regulations 1999 (SI 1999/2570) reg.5 (October 5, 1999). Note that amendments made by these regulations only have effect with respect to tax credit (reg.1(2) of the Amendment Regulations).

2. Tax Credits (Decisions and Appeals) (Amendment) Regulations 2000 (SI 2000/127) reg.2 (February 14, 2000). This amendment has effect with respect only to tax credit (reg.1(2) of the amending Regulations).

3. Child Support (Decisions and Appeals) (Amendment) Regulations 2000 (SI 2000/3185) reg.3 (various dates as provided by reg.1(1)).

4. Tribunals, Courts and Enforcement Act 2007 (Transitional and Consequential Provisions) Order 2008 (SI 2008/2683) Sch.1 paras 95 and 97 (November 3, 2008), subject to a saving under art.3 for reasons explained in the note to ss.5–7 of the Social Security Act 1998.

DEFINITIONS

"the Act"—see reg.1(3).
"the Board"—*ibid.*
"the Child Support Act"—see s.39(1) of the Social Security Act 1998.

GENERAL NOTE

2.413 This regulation re-enacts reg.1(3) of the Social Security (Adjudication) Regulations 1995.

In *R(IB)4/02*, it was held that, where a document had, under reg.53(4) as then in force, to be sent to a chairman or member of a tribunal, para.(a) did not apply. Paragraph (b) applied instead so that the document was sent when posted and not when it was received. Regulation 53(4) has been revoked but the reasoning still holds good when a document must be sent to anyone not mentioned in para.(a). A document may be sent by fax and is received for the purposes of reg.2(a) when it is successfully transmitted to, and received by, a fax machine, irrespective of when it is actually collected from the fax machine *(R(DLA)3/05)*.

In *CG/2973/2004*, the Commissioner had to consider whether the claimant had made a claim for benefit on a certain date. A claim is generally effective only when received. The position is therefore similar to that under reg.2(a), relating to documents to be sent to the Secretary of State. The Commissioner accepted that the claimant had posted a claim form but found that it was more likely to have been lost in the post before it reached the building where it was to be opened than lost in that building or subsequently. Strictly speaking, it was therefore unnecessary for him to consider whether, the claimant having succeeded in showing that the form had been posted, the burden of proving that the letter was lost after arrival at that building rested on her or whether the burden of proving that it was lost before then rested on the Secretary of State. However, having heard full legal argument, he said that the burden would have lain on the claimant to prove delivery so that, if it had been impossible to say where the letter was more likely to have been lost, the claimant would still have failed. He preferred *CIS/306/2003* to *CSIS/48/1992* and *CIS/759/1992*. An appeal against the Commissioner's decision was dismissed (*Levy v Secretary of State for Work and Pensions* [2006] EWCA Civ 890 (reported as *R(G) 2/06*). This decision was distinguished in *R.(Latimer) v Bury Magistrates' Court* [2008] EWHC 2213 (Admin) on the ground that it was based on the statutory language. In the absence of such language, it was held, the appropriate inference to be drawn where it is common ground that a letter has been posted is that it was received, this being a presumption based on the application of common sense rather than a presumption of law.

The "last known address" to which documents must be sent for para.(b) to apply need not be the person's last known *residence* because the concepts are different. Moreover, the sender must consider the address to be reliable and, if he does not, should take reasonable steps to see whether a more reliable one exists (*CCS/2288/2005*). This approach exists to aid the innocent claimant and not the one who has failed to take reasonable steps to keep the relevant authority aware of his whereabouts. Generally, an authority is entitled to rely on a claimant to inform it of any move.

PART II

REVISIONS, SUPERSESSIONS AND OTHER MATTERS SOCIAL SECURITY AND CHILD SUPPORT

CHAPTER I

REVISIONS

Revision of decisions

2.414 **3.**—(1) Subject to the following provisions of this regulation, any decision of the Secretary of State [3 or the Board or an officer of the Board] under section 8 or 10 ("the original decision") may be revised by him [3 or them] if—

[10(a) he or they commence action leading to revision within one month of the date of notification of the original decision; or

(b) an application for a revision is received by the Secretary of State or the Board or an officer of the Board at the appropriate office—

(i) subject to regulation 9A(3), within one month of the date of notification of the original decision;

(ii) where a written statement is requested under [35 paragraph (3)(b) of regulation 3ZA or] paragraph(1)(b) of regulation 28 and is provided within the period specified in head (i), within 14 days of the expiry of that period;

(iii) where a written statement is requested under [35 paragraph (3)(b) of regulation 3ZA or] paragraph(1)(b) of regulation 28 and is provided after the period specified in head (i), within 14 days of the date on which the statement is provided; or

(iv) within such longer period as may be allowed under regulation 4.]

(2) Where the Secretary of State [3 or the Board or an officer of the Board] requires further evidence or information from the applicant in order to consider all the issues raised by an application under paragraph (1)(b) ("the original application"), he [3 or they] shall notify the applicant that further evidence or information is required and the decision may be revised—

(a) where the applicant provides further relevant evidence or information within one month of the date of notification or such longer period of time as the Secretary of State [3 or the Board or an officer of the Board] may allow; or

(b) where the applicant does not provide such evidence or information within the time allowed under sub-paragraph (a), on the basis of the original application.

(3) In the case of a payment out of the social fund in respect of maternity or funeral expenses, a decision under section 8 may be revised where the application is made—

(a) within one month of the date of notification of the decision, or if later

(b) within the time prescribed for claiming such a payment under regulation 19 of, and Schedule 4 to, the Claims and Payments Regulations, or

(c) within such longer period of time as may be allowed under regulation 4.

(4) In the case of a decision made under the Pension Schemes Act 1993 by virtue of section 170(2) of that Act, the decision may be revised at any time by [2 an officer of the Board] where it contains an error.

[10 (4A) Where there is an appeal against an original decision (within the meaning of paragraph (1)) within the time prescribed [21 by Tribunal Procedure Rules], but the appeal has not been determined, the original decision may be revised at any time.]

(5) A decision of the Secretary of State [3 *Board or an officer of the Board*] under section 8 or 10—

(a) [18 except where paragraph (5ZA) applies] which arose from an official error; or

(b) [17 except in a case to which sub-paragraph (c) or (d) applies,] where the decision was made in ignorance of, or was based upon a mistake as to, some material fact and as a result of that ignorance of or mistake as to that fact, the decision was more advantageous to the claimant than it would otherwise have been but for that ignorance or mistake,

[3 *(bb) which was made in ignorance of, or was based on a mistake as to some material fact,*]

(c) [1 [17 subject to subparagraph (d),] where the decision is a disability benefit decision, or is an incapacity benefit decision where there has been an incapacity determination [19 or is an employment and support allowance decision where there has been a limited capability for work determination] (whether before or after the decision), which was made in ignorance of, or was based upon a mistake as to, some material fact in relation to a disability determination embodied in or necessary to the disability benefit decision, [19 , the incapacity determination or the limited capability for work determination], and—

(i) as a result of that ignorance or mistake as to that fact the decision was more advantageous to the claimant than it would otherwise have been but for that ignorance or mistake and,

(ii) the Secretary of State is satisfied that at the time the decision was made the claimant or payee knew or could reasonably have been expected to know of the fact in question and that it was relevant to the decision,]

[17 (d) where the decision [19 is an employment and support allowance decision,] is a disability benefit decision, or is an incapacity benefit decision, which was made in ignorance of, or was based upon a mistake as to, some material fact not in relation to the [19 limited capability for work determination,] incapacity or disability determination embodied in or necessary to [19 the employment and support allowance decision,] the incapacity benefit decision or disability benefit decision, and as a result of that ignorance of, or mistake as to that fact, the decision was more advantageous to the claimant than it would otherwise have been but for the ignorance or mistake,]

may be revised at any time by the Secretary of State [3 *by the Board or an officer of the Board at any time not later than the end of the period of six years immediately following the date of the decision or, where ignorance of the material fact referred to in sub-paragraph (b) was caused by the fraudulent or negligent conduct of the claimant, not later than the end of the period of twenty years immediately following the date of the decision.*]

[18 (5ZA) This paragraph applies where—

(a) the decision which would otherwise fall to be revised is a decision to award a benefit specified in paragraph (5ZB), whether or not the award has already been put in payment;

(b) that award was based on the satisfaction by a person of the contribution conditions, in whole or in part, by virtue of credits of earnings for incapacity for work or approved training in the tax years from 1993–94 to 2007–08;

(c) the official error derives from the failure to transpose correctly information relating to those credits from the Department for Work and Pensions' Pension Strategy Computer System to Her Majesty's Revenue and Customs' computer system (NIRS2) or from related clerical procedures; and

(d) that error has resulted in an award to the claimant which is more advantageous to him than if the error had not been made.

(5ZB) The specified benefits are—

(a) bereavement allowance;

[40 (aa) bereavement support payment under section 30 of the Pensions Act 2014;]
(b) contribution-based jobseeker's allowance;
(c) incapacity benefit;
(d) retirement pension;
(e) widowed mother's allowance;
(f) widowed parent's allowance; [19 . . .]
(g) widow's pension. [19 and
(h) contributory employment and support allowance].

(5ZC) In paragraph (5ZA)(b), "tax year" has the meaning ascribed to it by section 122(1) of the Contributions and Benefits Act.]

[10 (5A) Where—
(a) the Secretary of State or the Board or an officer of the Board, as the case may be, makes a decision under section 8 or 10, or that decision is revised under section 9, in respect of a claim or award ("decision A") and the claimant appeals against decision A;
(b) decision A is superseded or the claimant makes a further claim which is decided ("decision B") after the claimant made the appeal but before the appeal results in a decision by [21 the First-tier Tribunal] ("decision C"); and
(c) the Secretary of State or the Board or an officer of the board, as the case may be, would have made decision B differently if he or they had been aware of decision C at the time he or they made decision B,

decision B may be revised at any time.]

[17 (5B) A decision by the Secretary of State under section 8 or 10 awarding incapacity benefit may be revised at any time if—
(a) it incorporates a determination that the condition in regulation 28(2)(b) of the Social Security (Incapacity for Work) (General) Regulations 1995 (conditions for treating a person as incapable of work until the personal capability assessment is carried out) is satisfied;
(b) the condition referred to in sub-paragraph (a) was not satisfied at the time when the further claim was first determined; and
(c) there is a period before the award which falls to be decided.]

[19 (5C) A decision of the Secretary of State under section 10 made in consequence of a failure determination may be revised at any time if it contained an error to which the claimant did not materially contribute;

[23 ....]]

[29 (5D) A decision by the Secretary of State under section 8 or 10 awarding an employment and support allowance may be revised at any time if—
(a) it incorporates a determination that the conditions in regulation 30 of the Employment and Support Allowance Regulations are satisfied;
(b) the condition referred to in sub-paragraph (a) was not satisfied at the time when the claim was made; and
(c) there is a period before the award which falls to be decided.]

[27 (5E) A decision under section 8 or 10 awarding an employment and support allowance may be revised if—
(a) the decision of the Secretary of State awarding an employment and support allowance was made on the basis that the claimant had made and was pursuing an appeal against a decision of the Secretary of State that the claimant did not have limited capability for work ("the original decision"); and

(b) the appeal to the First-tier Tribunal in relation to the original decision is successful.

(5F) A decision under section 8 or 10 awarding an employment and support allowance may be revised if—

(a) the person's current period of limited capability for work is treated as a continuation of another such period under regulation 145(1) [32 . . .] of the Employment and Support Allowance Regulations; and

(b) regulation 7(1)(b) of those Regulations applies.]

[29 (5G) Where—

(a) a person's entitlement to an employment and support allowance is terminated because of a decision which embodies a determination that the person does not have limited capability for work;

(b) the person appeals that decision to the First-tier Tribunal;

(c) before or after that decision is appealed by the person, that person claims and there is a decision to award–

(i) income support, or

(ii) jobseeker's allowance; and

(d) the decision referred to in sub-paragraph (a) is successfully appealed,

the decision to award income support or jobseeker's allowance may be revised.

(5H) Where—

(a) a conversion decision within the meaning of regulation 5(2)(b) of the Employment and Support Allowance (Transitional Provisions, Housing Benefit and Council Tax Benefit) (Existing Awards) (No. 2) Regulations 2010 (deciding whether an existing award qualifies for conversion) is made in respect of a person;

(b) the person appeals that decision to the First-tier Tribunal;

(c) before or after that decision is appealed by the person, that person claims and there is a decision to award–

(i) income support, or

(ii) jobseeker's allowance; and

(d) the decision referred to in sub-paragraph (a) is successfully appealed,

the decision to award income support or jobseeker's allowance may be revised.]

[31 (5I) Where—

(a) a decision to terminate a person's entitlement to a contributory employment and support allowance is made because of section 1A of the Welfare Reform Act (duration of contributory allowance); and

(b) it is subsequently determined, in relation to the period of entitlement before that decision, that the person had or is treated as having had limited capability for work-related activity,

the decision to terminate that entitlement may be revised.]

[37 (5J) A decision by the Secretary of State under section 8 awarding an employment and support allowance may be revised at any time where—

(a) it is made immediately following the last day of a period for which the claimant was treated as capable of work or as not having limited capability for work under regulation 55ZA of the Jobseeker's Allowance Regulations or regulation 46A of the Jobseeker's Allowance Regulations 2013 (extended period of sickness) and that period lasted 13 weeks; and

(b) it is not a decision which embodies a determination that the claimant is treated as having limited capability for work under regulation 30 of the Employment and Support Allowance Regulations (conditions for treating a claimant as having limited capability for work until a determination about limited capability for work has been made).]

(6) [[33] A decision of the Secretary of State under section 8 or 10 that a jobseeker's allowance is reduced in accordance with section 19 or 19A of the Jobseeker's Act or regulation 69B of the Jobseeker's Allowance Regulations may be revised at anytime by the Secretary of State.]

[[5] (6A) A relevant decision within the meaning of section 2B(2) [[13] or (2A)] of the Administration Act may be revised at any time if it contains an error.]

[[34] (6B) A decision of the Secretary of State under section 8 or 10 awarding a jobseeker's allowance may be revised where the Secretary of State makes a decision under regulation 69B (the period of a reduction under section 19B: claimants ceasing to be available for employment etc.) of the Jobseeker's Allowance Regulations ("the JSA Regulations") that the amount of the award is to be reduced in accordance with regulations 69B and 70 of the JSA Regulations.]

[[9] (7) Where—

(a) the Secretary of State or an officer of the Board makes a decision under section 8 or 10 awarding benefit to a claimant ("the original award"); and
(b) an award of another relevant benefit [[42] or [[43] Scottish disability benefit]] or an increase in the rate of another relevant benefit [[42] or [[43] Scottish disability benefit]] is made to the claimant or a member of his family for a period which includes the date on which the original award took effect,

the Secretary of State or an officer of the Board, as the case may require, may revise the original award.]

[[14] (7ZA) Where—

(a) the Secretary of State makes a decision under section 8 or 10 awarding income support [[23] income-based jobseeker's allowance,] [[19], state pension credit or an income-related employment and support allowance] to a claimant ("the original award");
(b) the claimant has a non-dependant within the meaning of regulation 3 of the Income Support Regulations [[23] , regulation 2 of the Jobseeker's Allowance Regulations] [[19] or regulation 71 of the Employment and Support Allowance Regulations] or a person residing with him within the meaning of paragraph 1(1)(a)(ii), (b)(ii) or (c)(iii) of Schedule I to the State Pension Credit Regulations ("the non-dependant");
(c) but for the non-dependant—
    (i) a severe disability premium would be applicable to the claimant under regulation 17(1)(d) of the Income Support Regulations [[23] , regulation 83(e) or 86A(c) of the Jobseeker's Allowance Regulations] [[19] or regulation 67 of the Employment and Support Allowance Regulations]; or
    (ii) an additional amount would be applicable to the claimant as a severe disabled person under regulation 6(4) of the State Pension Credit Regulations; and
(d) after the original award the non-dependant is awarded benefit which—
    (i) is for a period which includes the date on which the original award took effect; and
    (ii) is such that a severe disability premium becomes applicable to the claimant under paragraph 13(3)(a) of Schedule 2 to the

Income Support Regulations [23, paragraph 15(4)(a) or 20I(3)(a) of Schedule 1 to the Jobseeker's Allowance Regulations] [19 , paragraph 6(4)(a) of Schedule 4 to the Employment and Support Allowance Regulations] or an additional amount for severe disability becomes applicable to him under paragraph 2(2)(a) of Schedule I to the State Pension Credit Regulations,

the Secretary of State may revise the original award.]

[10 (7A) Where a decision as to a claimant's entitlement to a disablement pension under section 103 of the Contributions and Benefits Act is revised by the Secretary of State, or changed on appeal, a decision of the Secretary of State as to the claimant's entitlement to reduced earnings allowance under paragraph 11 or 12 of Schedule 7 to that Act may be revised at any time provided that the revised decision is more advantageous to the claimant than the original decision.]

[14 (7B) A decision under regulation 22A of the Income Support Regulations (reduction in applicable amount where the claimant is appealing against a decision which embodies a determination that he is not incapable of work) may be revised if the appeal is successful [16 or lapses].

(7C) Where a person's entitlement to income support is terminated because of a determination that he is not incapable of work and [16 the decision which embodies that determination is revised or] he subsequently appeals the decision [16 which embodies] that determination and is entitled to income support under regulation 22A of the Income Support Regulations, the decision to terminate entitlement may be revised.]

[23 (7CC) Where—

(a) a person's entitlement to income support is terminated because of a determination that the person is not incapable of work;

(b) the person subsequently claims and is awarded jobseeker's allowance; and

(c) the decision which embodies the determination that the person is not incapable of work is revised or successfully appealed,

the Secretary of State may revise the decisions to terminate income support entitlement and to award jobseeker's allowance.

[36 (7CD) A decision of the Secretary of State under section 10 of the Act made in consequence of a determination under regulation 6(2) of the Income Support Work-Related Activity Regulations that a claimant has [41, without showing good cause,] failed to satisfy a requirement of regulation 2 of those Regulations (requirement to undertake work-related activity) may be revised at any time if it contained an error to which the claimant did not materially contribute.]

[15 (7D) Where—

(a) a person elects for an increase of—

(i) a Category A or Category B retirement pension in accordance with paragraph A1 or 3C of Schedule 5 to the Contributions and Benefits Act (pension increase or lump sum where entitlement to retirement pension is deferred);

(ii) a shared additional pension in accordance with paragraph 1 of Schedule 5A to that Act (pension increase or lump sum where entitlement to shared additional pension is deferred); or, as the case may be,

(iii) graduated retirement benefit in accordance with paragraph 12 or 17 of Schedule 1 to the Graduated Retirement Benefit

Regulations (further provisions replacing section 36(4) of the National Insurance Act 1965: increases of graduated retirement benefit and lump sums);

(b) the Secretary of State decides that the person or his partner is entitled to state pension credit and takes into account the increase of pension or benefit in making or superseding that decision; and

(c) the person's election for an increase is subsequently changed in favour of a lump sum in accordance with regulation 5 of the Deferral of Retirement Pensions etc. Regulations or, as the case may be, paragraph 20D of Schedule 1 to the Graduated Retirement Benefit Regulations,

the Secretary of State may revise the state pension credit decision.

[[38] (7DA) The Secretary of State may revise the state pension credit decision where—

(a) a person chooses under—

(i) section 8(2) of the Pensions Act 2014 (choice of lump sum or survivor's pension under section 9 in certain cases) to be paid a state pension under section 9 of that Act (survivor's pension based on inheritance of deferred old state pension); or

(ii) Regulations made under section 10 of the Pensions Act 2014 (inheritance of graduated retirement benefit) which make provision corresponding or similar to section 8(2) to be paid a state pension under Regulations made under section 10 which make provision corresponding or similar to section 9 of that Act;

(b) the Secretary of State—

(i) decides that the person or their partner is entitled to state pension credit; and

(ii) takes into account the state pension mentioned in sub-paragraph (a) in making or superseding that decision; and

(c) the person's choice for a state pension mentioned in sub-paragraph (a) is subsequently altered in favour of a lump sum in accordance with—

(i) regulation 6 of the State Pension Regulations 2015 (changing a choice of lump sum or survivor's pension); or

(ii) Regulations made under section 10 of the Pensions Act 2014 which make provision corresponding or similar to regulation 6 of the State Pension Regulations 2015.

(7DB) The Secretary of State may revise an award of a state pension under Part 1 of the Pensions Act 2014 where—

(a) the person makes a choice under—

(i) section 8(2) of the Pensions Act 2014; or

(ii) Regulations under section 10 of that Act which make provision corresponding or similar to section 8(2); and

(b) the person subsequently alters their choice in accordance with—

(i) regulation 6 of the State Pension Regulations 2015; or

(ii) Regulations under section 10 of the Pensions Act 2014 which make provision corresponding or similar to regulation 6 of the State Pension Regulations 2015.]

(7E) Where—

(a) a person is awarded a Category A or Category B retirement pension, shared additional pension or, as the case may be, graduated retirement benefit;

(b) an election is made, or treated as made, in respect of the award in accordance with paragraph A1 or 3C of Schedule 5 or paragraph 1 of Schedule 5A to the Contributions and Benefits Act or, as the case may be, in accordance with paragraph 12 or 17 of Schedule 1 to the Graduated Retirement Benefit Regulations; and

(c) the election is subsequently changed in accordance with regulation 5 of the Deferral of Retirement Pensions etc. Regulations or, as the case may be, paragraph 20D of Schedule 1 to the Graduated Retirement Benefit Regulations,

the Secretary of State may revise the award.]

[[30] (7EA) The Secretary of State may revise a decision made under regulation 18(1) that a person ceases to be entitled to a benefit specified in paragraph (7EB).

(7EB) Those benefits are—

(a) a Category A or Category B retirement pension;

(b) a shared additional pension;

(c) graduated retirement benefit;]

[[38] (d) a state pension under Part 1 of the Pensions Act 2014.]

[[16] (7F) A decision under regulation 17(1)(d) of the Income Support Regulations that a person is no longer entitled to a disability premium because of a determination that he is not incapable of work may be revised where the decision which embodies that determination is revised or his appeal against the decision is successful.]

(8) A decision of the Secretary of State [[3] or the Board of an officer of the Board] which is specified in Schedule 2 to the Act or is prescribed in regulation 27 (decisions against which no appeal lies) may be revised at any time.

[[7] (8A) [[24] . . .]]

[[8] (8B) [[25] Where—

(a) a restriction is imposed on a person under section 6B, 7, 8 or 9 of the Social Security Fraud Act 2001 (loss of benefit provisions) as result of the person—

   (i) being convicted of an offence by a court; or

   (ii) agreeing to pay a penalty as an alternative to prosecution under section 115A of the Administration Act or section 109A of the Social Security Administration (Northern Ireland) Act 1992, and

(b) that conviction is quashed or set aside by that or any other court, or the person withdraws his agreement to pay a penalty,

a decision of the Secretary of State made under section 8(1)(a) or made under section 10 in accordance with regulation 6(2)(j) or (k) may be revised at any time.]]

[[20] (8C) A decision made under section 8 or 10 ("the original decision") may be revised at any time—

(a) where, on or after the date of the original decision—

   (i) a late paid contribution is treated as paid under regulation 5 of the Social Security (Crediting and Treatment of Contributions and National Insurance Numbers) Regulations 2001 (treatment of late paid contributions where no consent, connivance or negligence by the primary contributor) on a date which falls on or before the date on which the original decision was made;

   (ii) a direction is given under regulation 6 of those Regulations (treatment of contributions paid late through ignorance or error) that a late contribution shall be treated as paid on a date which falls on or before the date on which the original decision was made; or

(iii) an unpaid contribution is treated as paid under regulation 60 of the Social Security (Contributions) Regulations 2001 (treatment of unpaid contributions where no consent, connivance or negligence by the primary contributor) on a date which falls on or before the date on which the original decision was made; and

(b) where any of paragraphs (i), (ii) or (iii) apply, either an award of benefit would have been made or the amount of benefit awarded would have been different.]

[[22] (8D) A decision made under section 8 or 10 may be revised at any time where, by virtue of regulation 6C (treatment of Class 3 contributions paid under section 13A of the Act) of the Social Security (Crediting and Treatment of Contributions, and National Insurance Numbers) Regulations 2001, a contribution is treated as paid on a date which falls on or before the date on which the decision was made.]

[[39] (8E) A decision in relation to a claim for a contribution-based jobseeker's allowance or a contributory employment and support allowance may be revised at any time where—

(a) on or after the date of the decision a contribution is treated as paid as set out in regulation 7A of the Social Security (Crediting and Treatment of Contributions, and National Insurance Numbers) Regulations 2001 (treatment of Class 2 contributions paid on or before the due date); and

(b) by virtue of the contribution being so treated, the person satisfies the contribution conditions of entitlement listed in column 2 of the table in paragraph (8G) in relation to a contribution-based jobseeker's allowance or a contributory employment and support allowance.

(8F) A decision to award a benefit listed in column 1 of the table in paragraph (8G) may be revised at any time where, on or after the date of the decision—

(a) any of the circumstances set out in paragraph (8H) occur; and

(b) by virtue of the circumstance occurring, the person ceases to satisfy the contribution conditions of entitlement listed in the corresponding entry in column 2 of that table.

(8G) The table referred to in paragraphs (8E) and (8F) is as follows—

1. Benefit	*2. Contribution conditions of entitlement*
Contribution-based jobseeker's allowance	the conditions set out in section 2(1)(a) and (b) of the Jobseekers Act
Contributory employment and support allowance	the first and second conditions set out in paragraphs 1(1) and 2(1) of Schedule 1 to the Welfare Reform Act
[[40] Bereavement support payment under section 30 of the Pensions Act 2014]	[[40] the contribution conditions set out in section 31 of the Pensions Act 2014 (bereavement support payment: contributions and amendments)]
Widowed parent's allowance	the contribution conditions set out in paragraph 5(2) and (3) of Schedule 3 to the Contributions and Benefits Act
[[40] . . .]	[[40] . . .]
Category A or Category B retirement pension under Part II of the Contributions and Benefits Act	the contribution conditions set out in paragraph 5(2) and (3) or, as the case may be, 5A(2) of Schedule 3 to the Contributions and Benefits Act
State pension under Part 1 of the Pensions Act 2014	the conditions of entitlement to a state pension in section 2(1)(b) or, as the case may be, 2(2)(b) or 4(1)(b) and (c) of the Pensions Act 2014

(8H) The circumstances are—

(a) a Class 2 contribution is repaid to a person in consequence of an amendment or correction of the person's relevant profits under section 9ZA or 9ZB of the Taxes Management Act 1970 (amendment or correction of return by taxpayer or officer of the Board); or

(b) a Class 2 contribution is returned to a person under regulation 52 of the Social Security (Contributions) Regulations 2001 (contributions paid in error); or

(c) a Class 1 or Class 2 contribution paid by a person to Her Majesty's Revenue and Customs under section 223 of the Finance Act 2014 (accelerated payment in respect of notice given while tax enquiry is in progress) is repaid to the person.

(8I) A decision to award a benefit specified in paragraph (8K) may be revised at any time where, on or after the date of the decision—

(a) any of the circumstances set out in paragraph (8H) occur; and

(b) by virtue of the circumstances occurring, the decision was more advantageous to the claimant than it would otherwise have been.

(8J) A decision to award a benefit specified in paragraph (8K), or a decision that that benefit is not payable, may be revised at any time where, on or after the date of the decision, a contribution is treated as paid by the relevant day by virtue of regulation 7(1) of the Social Security (Crediting and Treatment of Contributions, and National Insurance Numbers) Regulations 2001 (treatment for the purpose of any contributory benefit of contributions paid under certain provisions relating to the payment and collection of contributions).

(8K) The benefits specified in this paragraph are—

(a) a bereavement benefit;

(b) Category A or Category B retirement pension under Part II of the Contributions and Benefits Act;

(c) a state pension under Part 1 of the Pensions Act 2014.]

[[4] (9) Paragraph (1) shall not apply in respect of—

(a) a relevant change of circumstances which occurred since the decision [[12] had effect] [[14] or, in the case of an advance award under regulation 13, 13A or 13C of the Claims and Payments Regulations, since the decision was made,]or where the Secretary of State has evidence or information which indicates that a relevant change of circumstances will occur; [[19] . . .]

(b) a decision which relates to an attendance allowance or a disability living allowance where the person is terminally ill, within the meaning of section 66(2)(a) of the Contributions and Benefit Act, unless an application for revision which contains an express statement that the person is terminally ill is made either by—

  (i) the person himself; or

  (ii) any other person purporting to act on his behalf whether or not that other person is acting with his knowledge or authority,

but where such an application is received a decision may be so revised notwithstanding that no claim under section 66(1) or, as the case may be, 72(5) or 73(12) of that Act has been made;] [[19] nor

(c) a decision which relates to an employment and support allowance where the claimant is terminally ill, within the meaning of regulation 2(1) of the Employment and Support Allowance Regulations unless the claimant makes an application which contains an express statement that he is terminally ill and where such an application is made, the decision may be revised.".

(10) The Secretary of State [3 or the Board] may treat an application for a supersession as an application for a revision.

(11) In this regulation and regulation 7, "appropriate office" means

(a) the office of the [10 Department for Work and Pensions] the address of which is indicated on the notification of the original decision; or

(b) in the case of a person who has claimed jobseeker's allowance, the office specified by the Secretary of State in accordance with regulation 23 of the Jobseeker's Allowance Regulations [2; or

(c) in the case of a contributions decision which falls within Part II of Schedule 3 to the Act, any National Insurance Contributions office of the Board or any office of the [10 Department for Work and Pensions]; or

(d) in the case of a decision made under the Pension Schemes Act 1993 by virtue of section 170(2) of that Act, any National Insurance Contributions office of the Board;] [3 or

(e) in the case of a person who has claimed working families' tax credit or disabled person's tax credit, a Tax Credits Office, the address of which is indicated on the notification of the original decision;] [5 or

[11(f) in the case of a person who is, or would be, required to take part in a work-focused interview, an office of the Department for Work and Pensions which is designated by the Secretary of State as a Jobcentre Plus Office or an office of a designated authority which displays the **one** logo.]

[39 (12) In this regulation—

"relevant day" has the meaning given in regulation 7(3)(b) of the Social Security (Crediting and Treatment of Contributions, and National Insurance Numbers) Regulations 2001;

"relevant profits" has the meaning given in section 11(3) of the Contributions and Benefits Act.]

[44 (8L) A decision made under section 8 or 10(34) in relation to maternity allowance may be revised at any time where, by virtue of regulation 7(1) of the Social Security (Crediting and Treatment of Contributions, and National Insurance Numbers) Regulations 2001 (treatment for the purpose of any contributory benefit of contributions paid under certain provisions relating to the payment and collection of contributions), a contribution is treated as paid on a date which falls on or before the date on which the decision was made.]

AMENDMENTS

1. Social Security and Child Support (Decisions and Appeals) Amendment (No.2) Regulations 1999 (SI 1999/1623) reg.2 (July 5, 1999).

2. Social Security Contributions (Transfer of Functions, etc.) Act 1999 (Commencement No.2 and Consequential and Transitional Provisions) Order 1999 (SI 1999/1662) art.3(3) (July 5, 1999).

3. Tax Credits (Decisions and Appeals) (Amendment) Regulations 1999 (SI 1999/2570) reg.6 (October 5, 1999). Note that amendments made by these regulations only have effect with respect to tax credit (reg.1(2) of the Amendment Regulations). In the case of para.(5) the amendments are substituted in relation to tax credit; for this reason the substituted words in relation to tax credit are shown in italics.

4. Social Security and Child Support (Decisions and Appeals), Vaccine Damage Payments and Jobseeker's Allowance (Amendment) Regulations 1999 (SI 1999/2677) reg.6 (October 18, 1999).

5. Social Security (Work-focused Interviews) Regulations 2000 (SI 2000/897) reg.16(5) and Sch.6 para.3 (April 3, 2000).

6. Social Security (Joint Claims: Consequential Amendments) Regulations 2000 (SI 2000/1982) reg.5(a) (March 19, 2001).

7. Social Security (Breach of Community Order) (Consequential Amendments) Regulations 2001 (SI 2001/1711) reg.2(2)(b) (October 15, 2001).

8. Social Security (Loss of Benefit) (Consequential Amendments) Regulations 2002 (SI 2002/490) reg.8(a) (April 1, 2002).

9. Social Security (Claims and Payments and Miscellaneous Amendments) Regulations 2002 (SI 2002/428) reg.4(2) (April 2, 2002).

10. Social Security and Child Support (Decisions and Appeals) (Miscellaneous Amendments) Regulations 2002 (SI 2002/1379) reg.3(e) (May 20, 2002).

11. Social Security (Jobcentre Plus Interviews) Regulations 2002 (SI 2002/1703) Sch.2 para.6(b) (September 30, 2002).

12. Social Security and Child Support (Miscellaneous Amendments) Regulations 2003 (SI 2003/1050) reg.3(2) (May 5, 2003).

13. Social Security (Jobcentre Plus Interviews for Partners) Regulations 2003 (SI 2003/1886) reg.15(3) (April 12, 2004).

14. Social Security, Child Support and Tax Credits (Miscellaneous Amendments) Regulations 2005 (SI 2005/337) reg.2(2) (March 18, 2005).

15. Social Security (Deferral of Retirement Pensions, Shared Additional Pension and Graduated Retirement Benefit) (Miscellaneous Provisions) Regulations 2005 (SI 2005/2677) reg.9(3) (April 6, 2006).

16. Social Security (Miscellaneous Amendments) (No.2) Regulations 2006 (SI 2006/832) reg.5(2) (April 10, 2006).

17. Social Security (Miscellaneous Amendments) (No.4) Regulations 2007 (SI 2007/2470) reg.3(2)–(5) (September 24, 2007).

18. Social Security (National Insurance Credits) Amendment Regulations 2007 (SI 2007/2582) reg.3 (October 1, 2007).

19. Employment and Support Allowance (Consequential Provisions) (No.2) Regulations 2008 (SI 2008/1554) regs 29 and 31 (July 27, 2008).

20. Social Security (Miscellaneous Amendments) (No.5) Regulations 2008 (SI 2008/2667) reg.3(1) and (2) (October 30, 2008).

21. Tribunals, Courts and Enforcement Act 2007 (Transitional and Consequential Provisions) Order 2008 (SI 2008/2683) Sch.1 paras 95 and 98 (November 3, 2008).

22. Social Security (Additional Class 3 National Insurance Contributions) Amendment Regulations 2009 (SI 2009/659), reg.2 (April 6, 2009).

23. Social Security (Miscellaneous Amendments) (No.2) Regulations 2009 (SI 2009/1490) reg.3 (July 13, 2009).

24. Welfare Reform Act 2009 (Section 26) (Consequential Amendments) Regulations 2010 (SI 2010/424) reg.4(1) and (3) (March 22, 2010).

25. Social Security (Loss of Benefit) Amendment Regulations 2010 (SI 2010/1160) reg.3(1) and (2) (April 1, 2010).

26. Jobseeker's Allowance (Sanctions for Failure to Attend) Regulations 2010 (SI 2010/509) reg.3(1) and (2) (April 6, 2010).

27. Social Security (Miscellaneous Amendments) (No.3) Regulations 2010 (SI 2010/840) reg.7(1) and (2) (June 28, 2010).

28. Jobseeker's Allowance (Mandatory Work Activity Scheme) Regulations 2011 (SI 2011/688) reg.18(a) (April 25, 2011).

29. Social Security (Miscellaneous Amendments) (No.3) Regulations 2011 (SI 2011/2425) reg.12 (October 31, 2011).

30. Social Security (Suspension of Payment of Benefits and Miscellaneous Amendments) Regulations 2012 (SI 2012/824) reg.4(1) and (2) (April 17, 2012).

31. Employment and Support Allowance (Duration of Contributory Allowance) (Consequential Amendments) Regulations 2012 (SI 2012/913) reg.5 (May 1, 2012).

32. Employment and Support Allowance (Amendment of Linking Rules) Regulations 2012 (SI 2012/919) reg.2 (May 1, 2012).

33. Jobseeker's Allowance (Sanctions) (Amendment) Regulations 2012 (SI 2012/2568) reg.6(1) and (2) (October 22, 2012).

34. Social Security (Miscellaneous Amendments) (No.2) Regulations 2012 (SI 2012/2575) reg.4 (November 5, 2012).

35. Social Security, Child Support, Vaccine Damage and Other Payments (Decisions and Appeals) (Amendment) Regulations 2013 (SI 2013/2380) reg.4(1) and (2) (October 28, 2013).

36. Income Support (Work-Related Activity) and Miscellaneous Amendments Regulations 2014 (SI 2014/1097) reg.12(1) and (3) (April 28, 2014).

37. Jobseeker's Allowance (Extended Period of Sickness) Amendment Regulations 2015 (SI 2015/339) reg.7(1) and (2) (March 30, 2015).

38. Pensions Act 2014 (Consequential, Supplementary and Incidental Amendments) Order 2015 (SI 2015/1985) art.18(1), (3) and (4) (April 6, 2016).

39. Social Security (Credits, and Crediting and Treatment of Contributions) (Consequential and Miscellaneous Amendments) Regulations 2016 (SI 2016/1145) reg.4(1) and (3) (January 1, 2017).

40. Pensions Act 2014 (Consequential, Supplementary and Incidental Amendments) Order 2017 (SI 2017/422) art.15(1) and (3) (April 6, 2017, subject to a saving).

41. Social Security (Miscellaneous Amendments No.4) Regulations 2017 (SI 2017/1015) reg.9 (November 16, 2017).

42. Social Security (Scotland) Act 2018 (Disability Assistance for Children and Young People) (Consequential Modifications) Order 2021 (SI 2021/786) art.6(1) and (3) (July 26, 2021).

43. Social Security (Disability Assistance for Working Age People) (Consequential Amendments) Order 2022 (SI 2022/177) art.6(1) and (3) (March 21, 2022).

44. Social Security (Class 2 National Insurance Contributions Increase of Threshold) Regulations 2022 (SI 2022/1329) reg 8 (December 14, 2022).

DEFINITIONS

"the Administration Act"—see s.84 of the Social Security Act 1998.
"appeal"—see reg.1(3).
"appropriate office"—see para.(11).
"bereavement benefit"—see reg.1(3).
"the Board"—*ibid.*
"claimant"—*ibid.*
"the Claims and Payments Regulations"—*ibid.*
"the Contributions and Benefits Act"—see s.84 of the Social Security Act 1998.
"contribution-based jobseeker's allowance—see reg.1(3).
"contributory employment and support allowance"—*ibid.*
"the date of notification"—*ibid.*
"the Deferral of Retirement Pensions etc. Regulations"—*ibid.*
"designated authority"—*ibid.*
"disability benefit decision"—see reg.7A(1).
"disability determination"—*ibid.*
"employment and support allowance decision"—*ibid.*
"the Employment and Support Allowance Regulations"—see reg.1(3).
"failure determination"—*ibid.*
"family"—*ibid.*
"the Graduated Retirement Benefit Regulations"—*ibid.*
"incapacity benefit decision"—see reg.7A(1).
"incapacity determination"—*ibid.*
"income-related employment and support allowance"—see reg.1(3).
"Income Support Work-Related Activity Regulations"—*ibid.*

"the Jobseekers Act"—see s.84 of the Social Security Act 1998.
"the Jobseeker's Allowance Regulations"—see reg.1(3).
"limited capability for work determination"—see reg.7A(1).
"official error"—See reg.1(3).
"original decision"—see para.(1).
"payee"—see reg.7A(1).
"relevant benefit"—see s.39(1) of the Social Security Act 1998.
"relevant day"—see para.(12).
"relevant profits"—*ibid.*
"Scottish disability benefit"—see reg.1(3).
"tax credit"—*ibid.*
"tax year"–see para.(ZC).
"widowed parent's allowance"—see reg.1(3).
"work-focused interview"—*ibid.*

General Note

2.415 This regulation provides for the circumstances in which a decision may be revised under s.9 of the Social Security Act 1998, whereas reg.6 provides for the circumstances in which a decision may be superseded under s.10. There are three main distinctions between revision and supersession. First, only decisions of the Secretary of State may be revised, whereas not only decisions of the Secretary of State but also decisions of tribunals may be superseded. Secondly, revisions have effect from the date from which the decision being revised was effective (see s.9(3) of the Social Security Act 1998) unless a mistake was made in respect of that date, in which case the correct date is used (reg.5). Supersessions are usually effective from a later date (s.10(5) or reg.7). Thirdly, there is no right of appeal to a tribunal against a decision to revise or not to revise, whereas there is a right of appeal under s.12 against a decision to supersede or not to supersede. Instead, a decision to revise or, in limited circumstances, a decision not to revise, extends the time for appealing against the decision that has been revised (see s.9(5) of the 1998 Act and the annotation to it.

The first and third of these distinctions give rise to considerable problems where there is an appeal to a tribunal and the tribunal considers that a decision expressed as a revision should have been expressed as a supersession or vice versa. These problems were explored by a Tribunal of Commissioners in *R(IB)2/04* and *R(IS)15/04* (see the annotations to s.12 of the 1998 Act and para.(c) in the second column of para.5 of Sch.1 to the Tribunal Procedure (First-tier Tribunal) (Social Entitlement Chamber) Rules 2008). It is arguable that many of the problems are caused by the wide scope of reg.3, which appears to be based on the premise that if it is intended that a new decision should take place from the same date as the decision that is being reconsidered, the new decision must be expressed as a revision rather than a supersession. That approach is unnecessary, as appears to be accepted where it is desired that a new decision given on reconsideration of a decision of a tribunal should take effect from the same date as the original decision, because provision can be made by regulations under s.10(6) for a supersession to take effect from the same date as the decision that has been superseded (see reg.7(5)). If the grounds for revision contained in paras (4) and (5)–(8C) were instead grounds for supersession, many of the problems identified by the Tribunal of Commissioners would be removed. That would leave revision available only for cases where a decision is looked at again within a month or so of its being made or pending an appeal. It is only in those circumstances that the first and third of the distinctions drawn above suggest that revision is more appropriate than supersession.

In addition to the circumstances outlined in this regulation, decisions in respect of advance claims may be revised under regs 13(2), 13A(3) and 13C(3) of the Social Security (Claims and Payments) Regulations 1987 (*R(IB)2/04* at paras 106 and 107). A further power to revise is conferred by s.25(4) of the Social Security Act 1998 in respect of decisions made while a test case is pending before the Upper Tribunal or court.

Note that, for the purpose of the migration of claimants from incapacity benefit to employment and support allowance, regs 6 and 16 of, and Sch.3 to, the Employment and Support Allowance (Transitional Provisions, Housing Benefit and Council Tax Benefit) (Existing Awards) (No.2) Regulations 2010 (SI 2010/1097) applied the 1999 Regulations to conversion decisions, treating a conversion decision as though it were a decision as to entitlement to employment and support allowance made on a claim. See also reg.17 of those Regulations.

Paragraphs (1)–(3)

These allow a decision to be put right "on any ground" where the claimant applies for a revision within one month of the original decision being notified (but note the extension of time permitted where there has been a correction or request for reasons (see para.(1)(b)) or under para.(3)(b) in the case of a social fund payment or under reg.4). They also allow revision where the Secretary of State notices the error within that time. Note that the time for appealing against the original decision runs from the date the decision is revised *or is not revised* following an application under these paragraphs, whether or not the application amounts to a request for "mandatory reconsideration" required under reg.3ZA as a condition of appealing (s.9(5) of the Social Security Act 1998 and r.22(2)(d) and para 5(c) to the Tribunal Procedure (First-tier Tribunal) (Social Entitlement Chamber) Rules 2008), so that a claimant is not prejudiced by seeking a revision before appealing. **2.416**

Paragraph (4A)

This allows the Secretary of State to revise any decision while an appeal is pending in circumstances where it has not been, or could not be, revised under para.(1) or (3). The effect is that the appeal lapses under s.9(6) unless the revised decision is no more advantageous to the appellant than the decision that has been revised (see reg.30). **2.417**

Paragraph (5)

Normally, a decision based on a mistake of law or fact made by the Secretary of State can only be superseded under reg.6(2)(b) unless the error is detected in time to allow revision under paras (1)–(3). Supersession will be effective only from the date the application was made (see s.10(5) of the Social Security Act 1998). Paragraph (5) provides for such a decision to be revised rather than superseded where either there has been an official error or else there has been an overpayment (which might be recoverable under s.71 of the Social Security Administration Act 1992) due to a mistake of fact). In effect, the time limit is removed because revisions generally take effect from the same date as the original decision (see s.9(3) of the Social Security Act 1998). **2.418**

"Official error" is defined in reg.1. In *R(IS)15/04* (subsequently approved by the Court of Appeal in *Beltekian v Westminster CC* [2004] EWCA Civ 1784 (reported as *R(H)8/05*)), the Tribunal of Commissioners noted that a claimant might wish to assert that there were grounds for revision for "official error", whereas a claimant would not wish to rely on para.(5)(b) or (c). Consequently, a claimant might wish to challenge a refusal to revise under para.(5)(a) but, due to there being no right of appeal against a decision under s.9 not to revise and to the time limits for an appeal against the original decision, might be unable to do so save by way of an application for judicial review. The burden of proving that there was an "official error" lies on the claimant where it is he who is applying for revision, but it is for the Secretary of State to produce evidence of the supersession or revision that is in issue before the tribunal (*CH/3439/2004*).

Note that para.(5)(c) protects claimants of disability benefits or incapacity benefits from the full rigour of para.(b) in most cases and effectively prevents there from being a recoverable overpayment where a claimant could not reasonably have known a fact of which the Secretary of State was ignorant, or as to which he made a mistake, or could not reasonably have known that it was relevant. It does not protect the claimant who reasonably did not know that the Secretary of State was ignorant of, or had made a mistake as to, an obviously relevant fact of which he was aware, but that is presumably because in such cases any overpayment is unlikely to be recoverable anyway due to the lack of any misrepresentation or failure to disclose a material fact. More importantly, para.(5)(d) limits the effect of para.(5)(c) so that, where the ignorance or mistake relates to an issue other than the extent of the claimant's incapacity or disability, the general rule in para.(5)(b) applies.

In *AL v SSWP (IB)* [2013] UKUT 476 (AAC), the Upper Tribunal followed *JL v SSWP (DLA)* [2011] UKUT 293 (AAC); [2012] AACR 14, decided in relation to reg.7(2)(c), and held that a decision could not be revised under reg.3(5)(d) in respect of a period before September 24 2007, when that subparagraph was first inserted.

In *JA v SSWP (DLA)* [2014] UKUT 44 (AAC), the judge said that it was not obvious why revision was considered appropriate in the circumstances covered by para.(5), rather than those being grounds for a supersession effective from the same date as the decision being superseded, and he suggested that para.(5) could give rise to practical anomalies and introduced a wholly unnecessary degree of complication into decision-making.

Paragraphs (5ZA)–(5ZC)

2.419 The amendment to para.(5)(a) and the insertion of paras (5ZA)–(5ZC) make it unnecessary to revise decisions awarding the benefits listed in para.(5ZB) made as a result of errors in claimants' favour in transposing information on the Department for Work and Pensions' computer system to HMRC's computer system. The claimants continue to receive the benefits.

Paragraph (5A)

2.420 This enables the Secretary of State to apply a tribunal's decision to any decision made while the appeal was pending, thus making it unnecessary for the claimant to appeal against the further decisions. The paragraph was required because, since the Social Security Act 1998 came into force, it has not been possible to refer to the tribunal questions arising while an appeal is pending or simply not to determine the questions on the basis that the tribunal could deal with all issues down to the date of decision. Although the Tribunal of Commissioners in *R(IS)15/04*, considered that para.(5)(a) was the only part of reg.3, other than paras. (1) to (3) upon which a claimant might wish to rely, it was suggested in *CDLA/3323/2003* that para.(5A) is another provision. The Commissioner held that he was not precluded by "decision B" from making a decision on an appeal from "decision C" that covered the same period as "decision B", in case the Secretary of State declined to revise "decision B" and the claimant was left without any remedy because the time for appealing had expired. He held that "decision B" lapsed in the light of his new award.

Paragraph (5B)

2.421 Regulation 28 of the Social Security (Incapacity for Work) (General) Regulations 1995 provided that a person was to be deemed to satisfy the personal capability assessment before the assessment was carried out if a medical certificate was provided and he or she has not failed a personal capability assessment in the last six months (subject to certain exceptions). In *R(IB) 1/01*, it was held that, where those conditions were not satisfied, the claimant was still entitled to benefit in respect of the claim if he or she subsequently passed the personal capability assessment and, in *R(IB) 8/04*, it was held that a new claim was not necessary once the six months had elapsed. Paragraph (5B) enabled the Secretary of State to revise a decision awarding benefit from a date later than the date of claim (presumably because the claimant had failed a personal capability assessment less than six months before the date of claim but six months before the date from which the award was made) if the claimant subsequently satisfied the personal capability assessment. Since incapacity benefit has now been abolished, this paragraph has effectively been replaced by para.(5D) which applies to employment and support allowance.

Paragraph (5C)

This provides a fairly wide power to revise decisions relating to employment and support allowance that have resulted in sanctions. 2.422

Paragraph (5D)

This paragraph replaces with effect from October 31, 2011 an almost identical paragraph revoked from July 13, 2009, the difference being that subpara.(a) refers to "conditions" in the plural. It is in similar terms to para (5B) and presumably has been made for the same reason after the Secretary of State had second thoughts about the revocation. The explanatory note to the amending regulations suggests that this paragraph enables the Secretary of State "to revise a decision at any time where there is a non-medical change of circumstances relating to an ESA decision". Whatever the true effect is, it is not that broad. 2.423

Paragraph (5E)

When a claimant appeals against a decision of the Secretary of State to the effect that he or she does not have limited capability for work, the claimant is often awarded employment and support allowance at the basic rate while the appeal is pending, without a new claim being made (see reg.3(j) of the Social Security (Claims and Payments) Regulations 1987) and for as long as medical certificates are provided (see reg.30 of the Employment and Support Allowance Regulations 2008 — in Vol.I). If the appeal is unsuccessful, withdrawn, struck out or discontinued, that award is terminated (under reg.147A(5) of the 2008 Regulations). If, however, the appeal is successful, para.(5E) permits the award to be revised, for which purpose any finding of fact embodied in or necessary to the decision of the First-tier Tribunal is to be treated as binding up to the date of any relevant change of circumstances (see reg.147A(6) and (7) of the 2008 Regulations). Revision is necessary because the effect of the First-tier Tribunal's decision will be that the claimant is entitled to include the work-related activity component or support component in addition to the basic rate. Thus, implementation of the decision of the First-tier Tribunal is in practice generally effected through this form of revision rather than more directly. 2.424

Notwithstanding, s.9(3) of the Social Security Act 1998, which provides that a revision is effective from the date the original decision "took, or was to take, effect", a revision under para.(5E) will take effect from the end of the assessment phase in a case where reg.7(38) would have had that effect if the original decision had been favourable to the claimant (*NC v SSWP (ESA)* [2015] UKUT 147 (AAC)).

Paragraph (5F)

The validity of this paragraph was questioned in *SSWP v PT (ESA)* [2011] UKUT 317 (AAC); [2012] AACR 17, although the judge also suggested that it might be validly made under s.9(1) of the Social Security Act 1998 and it is not easy to see why that should not be so. The judge also did not find the paragraph easy to interpret and his decision implicitly raises the question whether it is actually necessary or whether it was inserted as a result of the Department misunderstanding the way the provisions mentioned in it work. 2.425

Paragraphs (5G) and (5H)

These paragraphs are both concerned with the situation that arises where a claimant's appeal against a decision to the effect that there was no entitlement to employment and support allowance is successful but he or she has been awarded income support or jobseeker's allowance while the appeal was pending. They enable the award of income support or jobseeker's allowance to be revised in the light of the successful appeal so as to prevent double entitlement. The benefit already paid under the revised award may be treated as having been paid on account of the award 2.426

of employment and support allowance (see reg.5 of the Social Security (Payments on account, Overpayments and Recovery) Regulations 1988).

Paragraph (5I)

2.427 Section 1A of the Welfare Reform Act 2007 (in Vol.I) has the effect that a person who does not have limited capability for work-related activity ceases to be entitled to contributory employment and support allowance after a year. This paragraph deals with the situation where an award is terminated under that provision while an appeal is pending against the decision that the claimant did not have limited capability for work-related activity and the appeal is subsequently allowed, although it also deals with cases where, after the award was terminated, it is revised or superseded in favour of the claimant from a date before the termination. The paragraph allows the award to be reinstated from the date it was terminated, as well as being increased so as to include the support component.

Paragraphs (6) to (6B)

2.428 These paragraphs are concerned with the revision of decisions to impose sanctions in relation to jobseeker's allowance (para.(6)) or in relation to failures to attend work-focused interviews (para.(6A)) and with the revision of awards following a decision to impose a sanction in relation to jobseeker's allowance (para.(6B)).

In *CJSA/2375/2000*, the claimant was twice disqualified for failing to attend training courses. The second disqualification was for four weeks because there had been the previous disqualification. An appeal against the first disqualification was allowed by a tribunal. The Commissioner, hearing an appeal against a decision by a tribunal dismissing an appeal against the second disqualification, said that the Secretary of State should have revised the second disqualification under the former version of para.(6) following the first tribunal's decision, in order to reduce the period to two weeks. This would more clearly have been appropriate under the new version. The odd use of the single word "anytime" in para.(6) is in the Queen's Printer's version of the amending Regulations.

Paragraph (7)

2.429 There are many instances where an award of benefit affects entitlement to another benefit awarded earlier. If the second award is made in respect of a period which includes the date from which a decision in respect of the first benefit took effect, that earlier decision is revised under this paragraph. If entitlement under the second award arises only after that date, the earlier decision is superseded under reg.6(2)(e) instead. Note that the earlier decision must have resulted in an "award" of benefit. It is suggested that that does not include a refusal of benefit, because the same term is used in sub-para.(b) in relation to the second decision and it is fairly clear that only an increase in entitlement under the second decision, and not a decrease in entitlement, gives rise to a revision under this paragraph. Where a decision in respect of one benefit is affected by a decision in respect of another benefit that is *less* favourable to a claimant, neither this paragraph nor reg.6(2)(e) applies and any consequent revision or supersession must be made under some other provision.

Paragraph (7ZA)

2.430 This enables an award of income support, income-based jobseeker's allowance, employment and support allowance or state pension credit to be revised in circumstances where the award was made while a non-dependant was awaiting determination of a claim for benefit and, as a result of a favourable decision on the non-dependant's claim, the first claimant becomes entitled to a severe disability premium.

Paragraph (7A)

2.431 This enables a decision as to entitlement to reduced earnings allowance to be revised in favour of the claimant following a favourable revision of, or a successful appeal against, a decision in respect of disablement benefit.

Paragraphs (7B) to (7CC)

These paragraphs and para.(7F) date from before the introduction of employment and support allowance, when income support could be claimed on the ground of incapacity for work. Decisions about capacity for work were, in practice, always made in the context of entitlement to incapacity benefit or incapacity "credits". A person who had been entitled to income support on the ground of incapacity for work and was then found not to be incapable of work for the purposes of incapacity benefit or credits was likely to have the award of income support terminated but, if he or she appealed against the incapacity determination, a fresh award of income would be made at a reduced rate until the appeal was determined. These paragraphs had the effect that, if the appeal was unsuccessful or lapsed because the incapacity determination was revised, the income support decision could be revised. Paragraph (7CC) applied if jobseeker's allowance was claimed and awarded while the appeal against the incapacity determination was pending. If the appeal was successful, the termination of income support and the award of jobseeker's allowance could both be revised so that the award of income support could be reinstated in place of the award of jobseeker's allowance. Paragraph (7F) applied if the claimant remained entitled to income support on other grounds (e.g. being a single parent) at a lower rate due to the loss of the disability premium while the appeal against the incapacity determination was pending. Again, there could be a revision of the reduced award of income support if the appeal was successful. 2.432

Paragraph (7CD)

This paragraph gives a wide power to revise a decision under reg.6(2) of the Income Support (Work-Related Activity) and Miscellaneous Amendments Regulations 2014 to the effect that a claimant had not shown good cause for a failure to undertake work-related activity and that was therefore adverse to a claimant. 2.433

Paragraphs (7D) to (7E)

Where entitlement to certain pensions has been deferred or inherited, the claimant may elect to have either an increase in the pension or a lump sum. These paragraphs enable awards of state pension credit and the relevant pensions to be revised following a change in such an election. 2.434

Paragraphs (7EA) and (7EB)

These paragraphs provide a wide power to revise a decision to terminate an award of a retirement or state pension following the suspension of payments. A refusal to exercise the power is not appealable but presumably the power exists partly in case the Department loses contact with a pensioner, so that arrears can be paid when contact is resumed. 2.435

Paragraph (7F)

See the note to paras (7B) to (7CC). 2.436

Paragraph (8)

See the note to reg.6(2)(d). 2.437

Paragraphs (8A) and (8B)

Paragraph (8A) is concerned with the now repealed provisions enabling benefit to be reduced if the claimant had breached a community order imposed by a court. Paragraph (8B) is concerned with the loss of benefit following a conviction or an agreement to pay a penalty in respect of an offence relating to the obtaining of benefit. Both paragraphs enable a decision to be revised if the determination or conviction is set aside or quashed or the agreement to pay a penalty is withdrawn. 2.438

Paragraphs (8C) to (8K)

These paragraphs enable a decision in respect of entitlement to a contributory benefit to be revised if, on or after the date on which the decision was made, it is 2.439

decided either that a contribution should be treated as having been paid before that date or that a contribution that had been paid should be repaid, with the result that the entitlement decision is shown to have been wrong from the outset. Note, however, that reg.4 of the Social Security (Crediting and Treatment of Contributions and National Insurance Numbers) Regulations 2001 has the effect that in some circumstances late paid contributions are treated as having been paid only when they are actually paid, so that if they affect the amount of an award of a bereavement benefit, retirement pension or state pension the award will fall to be superseded under reg.6(2)(sa) rather than being revised, and that it has the effect that in some other circumstances late paid contributions are treated as not having been paid at all.

Paragraph (9)

2.440 On an appeal against a decision as revised, it is not possible for the First-tier Tribunal to have regard to any change of circumstances arising between the date of the original decision and the date of revision (*R(CS) 1/03*). However, it might be arguable, at least in cases where there was evidence of a change of circumstances before the Secretary of State, that a revision decision should be treated as having also been a refusal to supersede the original decision in the light of the change of circumstances and that any appeal following the revision should be treated as being both an appeal against the original decision as revised and the decision not to supersede that decision.

Paragraph (10)

2.441 An application for supersession may be treated as an application for revision. Regulation 6(5) provides that an application for revision may be treated as an application for supersession.

For the powers of the First-tier Tribunal to treat a revision as a refusal to supersede and vice versa, see the note to s.12 of the Social Security Act 1998.

2.442 **[[1] Consideration of revision before appeal**

3ZA. (1) This regulation applies in a case where—

(a) the Secretary of State gives a person written notice of a decision under section 8 or 10 of the Act (whether as originally made or as revised under section 9 of that Act); and

(b) that notice includes a statement to the effect that there is a right of appeal in relation to the decision only if the Secretary of State has considered an application for a revision of the decision.

(2) In a case to which this regulation applies, a person has a right of appeal under section 12(2) of the Act in relation to the decision only if the Secretary of State has considered on an application whether to revise the decision under section 9 of the Act.

(3) The notice referred to in paragraph (1) must inform the person—

(a) of the time limit specified in regulation 3(1) or (3) for making an application for a revision; and

(b) that, where the notice does not include a statement of the reasons for the decision ("written reasons"), he may, within one month of the date of notification of the decision, request that the Secretary of State provide him with written reasons.

(4) Where written reasons are requested under paragraph (3)(b), the Secretary of State must provide them within 14 days of receipt of the request or as soon as practicable afterwards.

(5) Where, as the result of paragraph (2), there is no right of appeal against a decision, the Secretary of State may treat any purported appeal as an application for a revision under section 9 of the Act.]

AMENDMENT

1. Social Security, Child Support, Vaccine Damage and Other Payments (Decisions and Appeals) (Amendment) Regulations 2013 (SI 2013/2380) reg.4(1) and (3) (October 28, 2013).

DEFINITIONS

"the Act"—see reg.1(3).
"appeal" —*ibid.*

GENERAL NOTE

This regulation is made under s.12(3A) and (3B) of the Social Security Act 1998 and it enables the Secretary of State to require a person to apply for a revision before exercising their right of appeal. This is known as "mandatory reconsideration" and harks back to s.33 of the Social Security Administration Act 1992 which had the effect that an appeal relating to attendance allowance or disability living allowance could be brought only following a decision made under s.30 on review. Those provisions were repealed in 1999, when the 1998 Act came into force, and were not re-enacted presumably because requiring a review in all cases created delay that was not justified by improved decision-making and a reduction in the number of appeals. This time, the idea is that the review should be more intensive, with claimants being telephoned to discuss the case, so that evidence is elicited and the decision fully explained and there is an increased likelihood of the right decision being made by the Secretary of State and of claimants only appealing when they have realistic prospects of success. This reduces the need to revise decisions under reg.3(4A) after appeals have been lodged and so it is no longer necessary for appeals to be lodged with the Secretary of State. Instead, they are now lodged with the First-tier Tribunal under r.22 of the Tribunal Procedure (First-tier Tribunal) (Social Entitlement Chamber) Rules 2008. However, note that the regulation applies only where the decision being challenged was made on or after October 28, 2013. 2.443

Note, also, that this regulation applies only where the right of appeal arises under s.12 of the 1998 Act (see para.(2)). Equivalent provision (e.g. reg.9ZB below) is made in respect of some other rights of appeal to the Social Entitlement Chamber of the First-tier Tribunal but by no means all.

Mandatory reconsideration is not uncontroversial. It can cause delay and there is clearly a risk that some claimants with meritorious cases may be dissuaded from appealing by assurances given over the telephone by the Department for Work and Pensions that the challenged decision is right and cannot be revised. A fall in the number of appeals is not an advantage to the extent that it results in wrong decisions being maintained. The Social Security Advisory Committee has considered the impact of "mandatory reconsideration" in a study published in July 2016 (Occasional Paper No.18), which may be found at *https://www.gov.uk/government/publications/government-response-ssac-report-on-decision-making-and-mandatory-reconsideration* (accessed July 2020), together with the Government's responses to its recommendations. 2.444

One possibly unforeseen issue has arisen because reg.30(3) of the Employment and Support Regulations 2008 has the effect that employment and support allowance may be paid while an appeal is pending against a decision that a claimant is not entitled to the allowance because he or she does not have limited capability for work, but not while mandatory reconsideration of such a decision is pending. In that context, the requirement to apply for revision before appealing has been held in *R. (Connor) v Secretary of State for Work and Pensions* [2020] EWHC 1999 (Admin) to amount to a disproportionate interference with the right of access to an independent and impartial tribunal guaranteed by art.6 of the European Convention on Human Rights. The Administrative Court issued a declaration "to the effect that regulation 3ZA of the Decisions and Appeals Regulations is unlawful insofar as it is applied to ESA claimants who would, if pursuing an appeal to the First-tier Tribunal, subject to compliance with the condition at regulation 30(2) of the ESA Regulations, be entitled to receive payment pending appeal pursuant to regulation 30(3)". Consequently, reg.3ZA must be disapplied in such cases (*RR v Secretary of State for Work and Pensions* [2019] UKSC 52; [2019] 1 W.L.R. 6431; [2020] AACR 7 at [29] to [30]—see the end of the note to s.12 of the Tribunals, Courts and Enforcement Act 2007, below) and, presumably, the Secretary of State must cease including statements in accordance with para.(1)(b) in notices of decisions in employment and support allowance cases where reg.30(3) of the 2008 Regulations might lead to employment and support allowance being paid were an appeal to be brought.

Moreover, the legislation is not drafted as clearly as might have been desirable.

Paragraph (1) does not require the Secretary of State to issue a notice complying with subpara.(b) in all cases where the original decision has not already been the subject of reconsideration, although it seems currently to be his policy to do so. Its terms enable the Secretary of State to decide that certain classes of decision, or even individual decisions, should be appealable without the claimant first being obliged to seek reconsideration. Whether he issues a notice complying with subpara.(b) is a matter within his discretion. The regulation does not even expressly forbid the Secretary of State from issuing a notice complying with subpara.(b) when a decision in respect of which such a notice has already been issued has been revised. However, para.03012 in Vol.I of the *Decision Maker's Guide* makes it clear that the policy intention is that: "Once a decision has been subjected to mandatory reconsideration, further dispute rights are not dependent upon a further mandatory reconsideration". The notice issued with the revised decision in those circumstances should be the "notice of the result of mandatory reconsideration", which should be issued in duplicate so that, if the claimant wishes to appeal, they can send one copy to the First-tier Tribunal as required by r.22(4)(a)(i) of the Tribunal Procedure (First-tier Tribunal) (Social Entitlement Chamber) Rules 2008. However, there is scope for confusion if, as sometimes happens, the Secretary of State does not issue a notice in the standard form so that a clerk to the First-tier Tribunal receiving it does not know that there has in fact been consideration of the question whether the challenged decision should be revised and that there is therefore a right of appeal against the decision. A clerk has the power to refuse to admit an appeal if it is not accompanied by a notice of the result of mandatory reconsideration and may well do so if the notice of the decision does not bear the words "mandatory reconsideration" even though a notice without those words may in fact be a "notice of the result of mandatory reconsideration" for the purpose of the Rules. However, a clerk's refusal to admit an appeal should contain a notice that the claimant may ask that the issue be considered afresh by a judge under r.4(3) of the 2008 Rules.

2.445 Where a notice complying with para.(1)(b) is issued, it is para.(2) that operates to restrict the right of appeal. It is to be noted that it does not say under which paragraph of reg.3 any application for revision should be made, although para.(3)(a) clearly anticipates applications being made under reg.3(1) or (3). There are time limits for making applications under those provisions, although time may be extended by the Secretary of State under reg.4. In *R. (CJ) v Secretary of State for Work and Pensions* [2017] UKUT 324 (AAC); [2018] AACR 5, a three-judge panel of the Upper Tribunal held that, when he has refused under reg.4 to extend time for applying for a revision of a decision, the Secretary of State "has considered an application for a revision of the decision" so that there is a right of appeal against the original decision. *A fortiori*, if an application is made late under reg.3(1) or (3) but within the 13-month absolute time limit and the Secretary of State overlooks or fails to deal with the question of lateness and simply considers the merits of the application, the application has been "considered" (*AO v SSWP (CSM)* [2017] UKUT 499 (AAC)). These decisions, which have not been challenged by the Secretary of State, have removed one of the most controversial aspects of mandatory reconsideration as it was originally administered. However, note that HMRC has been given permission to appeal to the Court of Appeal against *AB v HMRC (TC)* [2021] UKUT 328 (AAC), in which the Upper Tribunal applied the approach taken in *CJ* to the similar, but not identical, provisions in ss.21A, 21B and 38(1A) of the Tax Credits Act 2002 (see Vol.IV of this work).

That appeal is due to be heard in December 2023. Where he has not considered the merits of an application for revision before an appeal has been lodged, the Secretary of State will presumably consider whether to revise the decision under reg.3(4A) before writing a response to the appeal. The three-judge panel left open the question whether there is a right of appeal where an application for revision is rejected on the ground that it was made more than 13 months after the original decision (see reg.4(2)(b)) but, in *PH v SSWP (DLA)* [2018] UKUT 404 (AAC); [2019] AACR 14, it has now been held that, in those circumstances, the Secretary of State will not have "considered" an application made under reg.3(1) or (3) and so there is no right of appeal against the original decision.

However, it was also pointed out in *PH* that, as reg.3ZA(2) is not confined to applications made under reg.3(1) and (3), an application for "mandatory reconsideration" might in principle be made under, say, reg.3(5)(a) on the ground of "official error", in respect of which there is no time limit. It was held that the provision under which an application is made is to be determined by considering the substance of the application, rather than its form and that a "spurious" allegation of "official error" would not assist a claimant. In *MW v SSWP (IS)* [2022] UKUT 59 (AAC), however, it was suggested that the First-tier Tribunal would have jurisdiction to determine the appeal only if there had in fact been an official error, rather than (as held in *PH*) whether it was arguable that there was one, because otherwise the time limits and restrictions on revision would be undermined (see *R(IB) 2/04* at [40]). The approach taken in *DB v SSWP (PIP)* [2023] UKUT 95 (AAC) at [76] to [80] is effectively that an official error must be shown to have been material if an appeal is to succeed. In that case, where there was an admitted official error in the Secretary of State's approach to the claimant's case in her original decision and an appeal, which would have been out of time but for a refusal to revise the decision, was brought following the refusal to revise, the case was remitted to the First-tier Tribunal for it to consider whether the official error had caused the Secretary of State to reach the wrong conclusion on the facts and, if so, to give the correct decision.

In both *PH* and *DB*, in which *PH* was followed, the Upper Tribunal recognised that the implication of its analysis is that, in a case where a decision is accompanied by a notice under reg.3ZA(1), and an application for revision is not made until the time limit for making an application under reg.3(1) of (3) has expired and is then made on the ground of "official error", a refusal to revise on that ground has the effect that the time for appealing against the original decision runs from the date the "result of mandatory reconsideration" is issued by virtue of r.22(2)(d)(i) of the Tribunal Procedure (First-tier Tribunal) (Social Entitlement Chamber) Rules 2008. Thus, the constraints imposed by the terms of r.22(2)(d)(ii) and para.5(c) of Sch.1 to the Rules, a predecessor of which was the provision considered in *R(IS) 15/04* (subsequently approved in *Beltekian v Westminster CC* [2004] EWCA Civ 1784 (reported as *R(H) 8/05*)), do not apply. Presumably, though, this only applies if there has been no previous application for "mandatory reconsideration" of the original decision.

It seems odd that a request for reasons under para.(3)(b) has the effect that the usual one-month time limit for applying for a revision under reg.3(1) is automatically extended (see reg.3(1)(b)(ii) and (iii)) whereas there is no equivalent extension of time in relation to applications under reg.3(3). However, the absolute time limit of 13 months is extended in either case (see reg.4(3)(b)).

Paragraph (5) enables the Secretary of State to treat a purported appeal as an application for revision. This would appear to apply whether the appeal is lodged with the Secretary of State in error or whether it is lodged with the First-tier Tribunal and then copied to the Secretary of State, although in the latter case the date of the application for revision is likely to be taken to be the date the appeal was received by the Secretary of State rather than when it was received by the First-tier Tribunal. Note that para.(5) applies only where there is no right of appeal. It will therefore not apply where the original decision was made before October 28, 2013 or was for any other reason not accompanied by a notice of the type mentioned in para.(1). In such a case, the Secretary of State will still be entitled to consider revising the decision under reg.3(4A) but the appeal will have been valid so that the Secretary of State will be obliged to send a response to the appeal to the First-tier Tribunal if the original decision is not revised in the claimant's favour.

Regulation 7 of the Universal Credit, Personal Independence Payment, Jobseeker's Allowance and Employment and Support Allowance (Decisions and Appeals) Regulations 2013 is in the same terms as this regulation. In *PP v SSWP (UC)* [2020] UKUT 109 (AAC), the claimant submitted an appeal by email to the regional office of the First-tier Tribunal (with which he had been in contact in relation to another matter) indicating that he wished to appeal against the Secretary of State's refusal of a claim for universal credit. A judge directed the Secretary of State to produce copies of any decision to refuse the claimant universal credit and any associated mandatory reconsideration notice. The Secretary of State merely sent a copy of an electronic notification to the claimant's universal credit Journal, stating "Your claim has been closed" and "Reason for closure: You didn't book your appointment". The judge directed the claimant to produce a copy of any universal credit mandatory reconsideration notice. The Appellant said that the DWP would not provide him with one but the judge nonetheless refused to admit the appeal without making further enquiries. Before the Upper Tribunal, the Secretary of State conceded that there was no power to refuse a claim for universal credit simply on the ground that the claimant had failed to make an appointment for an interview and that the closure of the claim was technically an appealable decision that the claimant was not entitled to universal credit because he did not satisfy the financial conditions (albeit that one reason for making that finding had been the claimant's failure to book an appointment to discuss his income from self-employment). Moreover, because the only notice of the decision had not included a statement in the terms required by reg.7(1)(b) of the 2013 Regulations, the claimant's right of appeal had not been subject to a condition under reg.7(2) that he first apply for revision. Accordingly, the Upper Tribunal allowed the claimant's appeal, referring as regards the analysis of the nature of the Secretary of State's decision to *R(H) 3/05* at [78] to [80], and directed the First-tier Tribunal to admit the appeal and determine whether the claimant did qualify for universal credit.

2.446 **3A.** *Omitted.*

2.447 **3B.** *Omitted.*

Late application for a revision

2.448 **4.**—(1) The time limit for making an application for a revision specified in regulation 3(1) or (3) [2 or 3A(1)(a)] may be extended where the conditions specified in the following provisions of this regulation are satisfied.

(2) An application for an extension of time shall be made by [2 the relevant person,] the claimant or a person acting on his behalf.

(3) An application shall—

(a) contain particulars of the grounds on which the extension of time is sought and shall contain sufficient details of the decision which it is sought to have revised to enable that decision to be identified; and

(b) be made within 13 months of the date of notification of the decision which it is sought to have revised [3, but if the applicant has requested a statement of the reasons in accordance with [6 regulation 3ZA(3)(b) or] regulation 28(1)(b) the 13 month period shall be extended by—

(i) if the statement is provided within one month of the notification, an additional 14 days; or

(ii) if it is provided after the elapse of a period after the one month ends, the length of that period and an additional 14 days.]

(4) An application for an extension of time shall not be granted unless the applicant satisfies the Secretary of State [5 , the Commission] [1 or the Board or an officer of the Board] that—

(a) it is reasonable to grant the application;

(b) the application for revision has merit [6 , except in a case to which regulation 3ZA or 3B applies.]; and

(c) special circumstances are relevant to the application and as a result of those special circumstances it was not practicable for the application to be made within the time limit specified in regulation 3 [2 or 3A].

(5) In determining whether it is reasonable to grant an application, the Secretary of State [5 , the Commission] [1 or the Board or an officer of the Board] shall have regard to the principle that the greater the amount of time that has elapsed between the expiration of the time specified in regulation 3(1) and (3) [2 and regulation 3A(1)(a)] for applying for a revision and the making of the application for an extension of time, the more compelling should be the special circumstances on which the application is based.

(6) In determining whether it is reasonable to grant the application for an extension of time [6 , except in a case to which regulation 3ZA or 3B applies,], no account shall be taken of the following—

(a) that the applicant or any person acting for him was unaware of or misunderstood the law applicable to his case (including ignorance or misunderstanding of the time limits imposed by these Regulations); or

(b) that [4 the Upper Tribunal] or a court has taken a different view of the law from that previously understood and applied.

(7) An application under this regulation for an extension of time which has been refused may not be renewed.

AMENDMENTS

1. Tax Credits (Decisions and Appeals) (Amendment) Regulations 1999 (SI 1999/2570) reg.7 (October 5, 1999). Note that amendments made by these regulations only have effect with respect to tax credit (reg.1(2) of the Amendment Regulations).

2. Child Support (Decisions and Appeals) (Amendment) Regulations 2000 (SI 2000/3185) reg.6 (various dates as provided by reg.1(1)).

3. Social Security, Child Support and Tax Credits (Miscellaneous Amendments) Regulations 2005 (SI 2005/337) reg.2(3) (March 18, 2005).

4. Tribunals, Courts and Enforcement Act 2007 (Transitional and Consequential Provisions) Order 2008 (SI 2008/2683) Sch.1 paras 95 and 100 (November 3, 2008).

5. Child Support (Miscellaneous Amendments) Regulations 2009 (SI 2009/396) reg.4(1) and (3) (April 6, 2009).

6. Social Security, Child Support, Vaccine Damage and Other Payments (Decisions and Appeals) (Amendment) Regulations 2013 (SI 2013/2380) reg.4(1) and (5) (October 28, 2013).

DEFINITIONS

"the Board"—see reg.1(3).
"claimant"—*ibid.*
"the date of notification"—see reg.1(3).
"relevant person"—*ibid.*

GENERAL NOTE

Amendments made by reg.6 of the Child Support (Meaning of Child and New Calculation Rules) (Consequential and Miscellaneous Amendment) Regulations 2.449

2012 (SI 2012/2785) and effective only for the purpose of certain child support cases are not included in this volume.

Paragraph (1)

2.450 It was held in *R(TC)1/05* that a tribunal did not have jurisdiction to consider whether the Inland Revenue ought, under reg.4, to have extended the time for applying for revision. In that case, the relevant decision was made on April 22, 2002, the claimant sought reconsideration on November 11, 2002 and the Inland Revenue refused to extend the time for applying for revision and therefore refused to revise the decision on November 25, 2002. The claimant appealed. There is no right of appeal against a revision or refusal to revise and so the appeal had to be treated as an appeal against the decision of April 22, 2002. The time for appealing against a decision is not extended under reg.31 when the application for revision is made late and time is not extended under reg.4. In those circumstances (and subject to the possibility that the decision of April 22, 2002 had not been sent to the claimant), the appeal should have been treated as having been late and therefore invalid, unless the tribunal extended the time for appealing. On the facts of *R(TC)1/05*, it made no difference whether the time for applying for revision was extended under reg.4 or whether the time for appealing was extended under reg.31, but the Commissioner pointed out that the test for extending the time for applying for revision is now different from that for extending the time for appealing. He also pointed out that the 13-month absolute time limit for appeals now to be found in rr.22(8)(b) and 23(5) of the Tribunal Procedure (First-tier Tribunal) (Social Entitlement Chamber) Rules 2008 means that in some cases an appeal could be valid only if the time for applying for revision had been extended. It seems regrettable that a tribunal should not have the power to determine whether the Secretary of State ought to have extended time under reg.4, especially as the exercise the Secretary of State is required to perform is not all that simple and a considerable amount of money may turn on it. On the other hand, some of the point of this provision has been removed by the decision in *R.(CJ) v Secretary of State for Work and Pensions* [2017] UKUT 324 (AAC), where a three-judge panel of the Upper Tribunal held that, when he has refused under reg.4(1) to extend time for applying for a revision of a decision, the Secretary of State "has considered an application for a revision of the decision" for the purposes of reg.3ZA(2) so that there is a right of appeal against the original decision even though the Secretary of State has not considered the merits of the application for revision. The three-judge panel left open the question whether there is a right of appeal where an application for revision is rejected under reg.4(2)(b) on the ground that it was made more than 13 months after the original decision but, in *PH v SSWP (DLA)* [2018] UKUT 404 (AAC); [2019] AACR 14, it has now been held that, in those circumstances, the Secretary of State will not have "considered" an application made under reg.3(1) or (3) and so there is no right of appeal against the original decision. In *AB v HMRC (TC)* [2021] UKUT 328 (AAC), the Upper Tribunal applied the approach taken in *CJ* to the similar, but not identical, provisions in ss.21A, 21B and 38(1A) of the Tax Credits Act 2002 (see Vol.IV of this work) but HMRC has been given permission to appeal to the Court of Appeal and the appeal is due to be heard in December 2023.

Paragraphs (4)–(6)

2.451 These paragraphs restrict the Secretary of State's power to extend time when an application for revision under reg.3(1) or (3) is made late but within the absolute 13-month time-limit.

It is important to bear in mind that a refusal to extend time for such an application does not preclude revision under some other paragraph of reg.3, such as reg.3(5)(a) (official error). Nor does it necessarily preclude an appeal against the decision that the claimant wished to have revised. Most importantly, an appeal is not precluded if consideration of the application for revision was required before the claimant had a right of appeal (see reg.3ZA), because the refusal to extend time amounts to consideration of the application (*R.(CJ) v Secretary of State for Work and Pensions* [2017] UKUT 324 (AAC); [2018] AACR 5). If consideration of the application had *not* been required before the claimant had applied for revision, e.g., because the original decision had already been revised in favour of the claimant but the claimant was still dissatisfied and had asked for revision of the revised decision rather than simply appealing, any subsequent appeal would inevitably be late and it would be open to the Secretary of State to object to its admission but the First-tier Tribunal would have the power to direct that time should be extended unless the appeal was eventually brought only after the 13-month absolute time limit had expired (see rule 22(2), (6) and (8) of the Tribunal Procedure (First-tier Tribunal) (Social Entitlement Chamber) Rules 2008).

It is also important to bear in mind that, if the Secretary of State refuses to extend time for an application for revision under reg.3(1) or (3) and is not satisfied that there is any other ground for revision, he may treat the application as being in the alternative an application for supersession (see reg.6(5)) and should consider whether there are grounds for superseding the decision, e.g., on the ground that the original decision was erroneous in point of law, or it was made in ignorance of, or was based upon a mistake as to, some material fact (see reg.6(2)(b)). In that way, clear errors of law or fact should not be perpetuated so as cause a greater loss of benefit than can be regarded as the consequence of making the application late.

In that light, paragraph (4) is not by itself particularly contentious as it merely requires the Secretary of State to approach the issue of extending time in a logical manner, having regard to all the potentially relevant considerations and, in particular, requiring that consideration must be given not only to the merits of the application for revision but also to the cause of the delay. The disapplication of para.(4)(b) in a case to which reg.3ZA applies is perhaps less necessary in the light of *CJ* (see above) than it would otherwise have been, but it does require the Secretary of State to refuse a late application on its merits, rather than refusing to extend time, in any such case where para.(4)(a) and (c) is satisfied.

Paragraph (4)(c) itself requires that there be "special circumstances" making it "not practicable" for the claimant to apply for revision. As Departmental Guidance (para.03076 of Vol.I of the Decision Maker's Guide) recognises, the requirement that there be "special circumstances" does not mean that the claimant's circumstances must be exceptional. Moreover, even though para.(6) appears to be addressed to the para.(4)(a) issue (reasonableness), rather than the para.(4)(c) issue (whether there were "special circumstances"), the existence of para.(6)(a) arguably implies that "practicable" in para.(4)(c) must be construed in the light of *R(S) 3/79* and *R(I) 1/90*, in which it was held that reasonable ignorance of the law or a reasonable mistake as to the law could make it not "practicable" to take action. (In *R(S) 3/79*, reference was made to *Dedman v British Building and Engineering Appliances Ltd* [1974] I.C.R. 53 and *Wall's Meat Co Ltd v Khan* [1979] I.C.R. 52 but it was suggested that, in the social security context, one should focus only on the reasonableness of any ignorance or mistake on the part of the claimant in the light of any advice they received or should have sought, and not on the reasonableness of an advisor's ignorance or mistake.) This is important when para.(6) is disapplied (as it is in a case to which reg.3ZA applies).

Paragraph (5) is also uncontentious as far as it expressly requires that the greater the delay the more compelling the special reasons have to be to make it reasonable to extend time. What is less certain is whether regard may also be had to the strength of the grounds for revision or whether the absence of any mention of it implies that it is not to be regarded as a relevant factor when considering reasonableness.

Paragraph (6) is altogether more contentious. Its disapplication in a case to which reg.3ZA applies may be less important in the light of *CJ* (see above) than it would otherwise be, but does mean that the Secretary of State is not barred from revising a decision in circumstances where, in the event of an appeal, the First-tier Tribunal would probably extend the time for appealing which rather points up the anomaly that can arise where the paragraph does apply. Perhaps the policy behind para.(6)(a) is simply that, if the original decision was not based on an "official error", there should be supersession where there has been a delay in applying for revision due only to a misunderstanding of the law and it is presumed that, following the supersession decision, the claimant will not seek to appeal against the decision that has been superseded.

Paragraph (6)(b) raises all sorts of questions. Does it apply only where, since the decision that the claimant wishes to have revised was made, the Upper Tribunal or a Court has taken a different view from that understood and applied in that decision? Anyway, whose understanding is important? Presumably not the appellant because the view must also be different from that previously "applied". Does it then apply only where the view that was applied was consistent with the understanding of the Department for Work and Pensions as a whole or just of the office where that decision was made? The former seems more likely. Whatever the answers to these questions, it is not easy to see what sub-para.(b) adds to sub-para.(a) in practical terms.

The draftsman of the Public Bodies (Child Maintenance and Enforcement Commission: Abolition and Transfer of Functions) Order 2012 (SI 2012/2007) appears to have overlooked the need to remove the references in paras (4) and (5) to the Commission (i.e. the Child Maintenance and Enforcement Commission) when it was abolished with effect from August 1, 2012, although those Regulations did remove the definition in reg.1(3).

Paragraph (7)

2.452 This prevents repeat out-of-time applications under reg.3(1) or (3) but it does not prevent the claimant from applying for revision under another provision, such as reg.3(5)(a) in respect of which there is no time limit, or from applying for a supersession, although a supersession would almost always be effective from a later date.

Date from which a decision revised under section 9 takes effect

2.453 **5.**—[2 (1)] Where, on a revision under section 9, the Secretary of State [1 or the Board or an officer of the Board] decides that the date from which the decision under section 8 or 10 ("the original decision") took effect was erroneous, the decision under section 9 shall take effect on the date from which the original decision would have taken effect had the error not been made.

[2 (2) Where—

(a) a person attains pensionable age, claims a retirement pension after the prescribed time for claiming and the Secretary of State decides ("the original decision") that he is not entitled because—

(i) in the case of a Category A retirement pension, the person has not satisfied the contribution conditions; or

(ii) in the case of a Category B retirement pension, the person's spouse [3 or civil partner] has not satisfied the contribution conditions;

(b) in accordance with regulation 50A of the Social Security (Contributions) Regulations 2001(Class 3 contributions: tax years 1996–97 to 2001–02) the Board subsequently accepts Class 3 contributions paid after the due date by the claimant or, as the case may be, the spouse [3 or civil partner];

(c) in accordance with regulation 6A of the Social Security (Crediting and Treatment of Contributions, and National Insurance Numbers) Regulations 2001 the contributions are treated as paid on a date earlier than the date on which they were paid; and

(d) the Secretary of State revises the original decision in accordance with regulation 11A(4)(a),

the revised decision shall take effect from—

(i) 1st October 1998; or

(ii) the date on which the claimant attained pensionable age in the case of a Category A pension, or, in the case of a Category

B pension, the date on which the claimant's spouse [3 or civil partner] attained pensionable age,

whichever is later."

AMENDMENTS

1. Tax Credits (Decisions and Appeals) (Amendment) Regulations 1999 (SI 1999/2570) reg.8 (October 5, 1999). Note that amendments made by these regulations only have effect with respect to tax credit (reg.1(2) of the Amendment Regulations).

2. Social Security (Retirement Pensions) Amendment Regulations 2004 (SI 2004/2283) reg.3 (September 27, 2004).

3. Civil Partnership (Consequential Amendments) Regulations 2005 (SI 2005/2878) reg.8(3) (December 5, 2005).

DEFINITION

"the Board"—see reg.1(3).

GENERAL NOTE

These paragraphs provide the exceptions to the general rule in s.9(3) of the Social Security Act 1998 that a revision takes effect from the same date as the original decision that has been revised. **2.454**

Paragraph(1) deals with the obvious case where the effective date of the original decision was wrong.

Paragraph(2) is linked to reg.6(31) and (32) of the Social Security (Claims and Payments) Regulations 1987 and deals with a problem caused by the failure from 1996 to 2003 to inform contributors of deficiencies in their contribution records so that they could pay voluntary Class 3 contributions to make up the deficit. By regulation 50A of the Social Security (Contributions) Regulations 2001, claimants are being allowed to pay their contributions very late. Regulation 6(31) of the 1987 Regulations enables a late claim based on those contributions to be made and this amendment allows an earlier decision disallowing a claim to be revised with effect from October 1, 1998 or the date the claimant or, where appropriate, the claimant's spouse or civil partner reached pensionable age. Without these amendments, the new claim or the revision might be effective from a much later date and that might be unfair because, having discovered about the deficiency, the claimant might have delayed claiming on what was then a correct understanding that there was nothing that could be done about it.

5A. *Omitted.* **2.455**

CHAPTER II

SUPERSESSIONS

Supersession of decisions

6.—(1) Subject to the following provisions of this regulation, for the purposes of section 10, the cases and circumstances in which a decision may be superseded under that section are set out in paragraphs (2) to (4). **2.456**

(2) A decision under section 10 may be made on the Secretary of State's [2 or the Board's] own initiative or on an application made for the purpose on the basis that the decision to be superseded—

(a) is one in respect of which—

(i) there has been a relevant change of circumstances since the decision [11 had effect [15 or, in the case of an advance award under regulation 13, 13A or 13C of the Claims and Payments

Regulations [17 or regulation 146 of the Employment and Support Allowance Regulations], since the decision was made]; or

(ii) it is anticipated that a relevant change of circumstances will occur;

(b) is a decision of the Secretary of State [2 or the Board or an officer of the Board] other than a decision to which sub-paragraph (d) refers and—

(i) the decision was erroneous in point of law, or it was made in ignorance of, or was based upon a mistake as to, some material fact; and

(ii) an application for a supersession was received by the Secretary of State [2 or the Board], or the decision by the Secretary of State [2 or the Board] to act on his [2 or their] own initiative was taken, more than one month after the date of notification of the decision which is to be superseded or after the expiry of such longer period of time as may have been allowed under regulation 4;

[11 (c) is a decision of [19 [25 an appeal tribunal, the First-tier Tribunal, the Upper Tribunal or of a Commissioner]]—

(i) that was made in ignorance of, or was based upon a mistake as to, some material fact; or

(ii) that was made in accordance with section 26(4)(b), in a case where section 26(5) applies;]

(d) is a decision which is specified in Schedule 2 to the Act or is prescribed in regulation 27 (decisions against which no appeal lies); [11 . . .]

[5 (e) is a decision where—

(i) the claimant has been awarded entitlement to a relevant benefit; and

(ii) [9 subsequent to the first day of the period to which that entitlement relates], the claimant or a member of his family becomes entitled to [9 . . .] another relevant benefit [30 or [31 Scottish disability benefit]] or an increase in the rate of another relevant benefit [30 or [31 Scottish disability benefit]];]

[15 (ee) is an original award within the meaning of regulation 3(7ZA) and sub-paragraphs (a) to (c) and (d)(ii) of regulation 3(7ZA) apply but not sub-paragraph (d)(i);]

[3 (f) [26 is a decision that a jobseeker's allowance is payable at the full rate to which the claimant would be entitled in the absence of any reduction where the award is reduced under section 19 of the Jobseekers Act;]]

[24 (fa) [26 is a decision that a jobseeker's allowance is payable at the full rate to which the claimant would be entitled in the absence of any reduction where the award is reduced under section 19A of the Jobseekers Act;]]

[1 (g) is an incapacity benefit decision where there has been an incapacity determination (whether before or after the decision) and where, since the decision was made, the Secretary of State has received medical evidence following an examination in accordance with regulation 8 of the Social Security (Incapacity for Work) (General) Regulations 1995 from a [18 health care professional] referred to in paragraph (1) of that regulation;] [4 [11 . . .]

(h) is one in respect of a person who—

(i) is subsequently the subject of a separate decision or determination as to whether or not he took part in a work-focused interview;

(ii) had been held not to have taken part in a work-focused interview but who had, subsequent to the decision to be superseded, attained the age of 60 or ceased to reside in an area in which there is a requirement to take part in a work-focused interview [13 or, in the case of a partner who was required to take part in a work-focused interview [14 in accordance with regulations made under section 2AA of the Administration Act, ceased to be a partner for the purposes of those regulations or is no longer a partner to whom the requirement to take part in a work-focused interview under those regulations applies];]

[7 (i) [20 . . .]]

[8 (j) is a decision of the Secretary of State that a sanctionable benefit is payable to a claimant where that benefit ceases to be payable or falls to be reduced under section [21 6B,] 7 or 9 of the Social Security Fraud Act 2001 and for this purpose "sanctionable benefit" has the [21 meaning given in section 6A] of that Act;

(k) is a decision of the Secretary of State that a joint-claim jobseeker's allowance is payable where that allowance ceases to be payable or falls to be reduced under section 8 of the Social Security Fraud Act 2001;]

[10 (l) is a relevant decision for the purposes of section 6 of the State Pension Credit Act and—

(i) on making that decision, the Secretary of State specified a period as the assessed income period; and

(ii) that period has ended or is about to end;]

[12 (m) is a relevant decision for the purposes of section 6 of the State Pension Credit Act in a case where—

(i) the information and evidence required under regulation 32(6)(a) of the Claims and Payments Regulations has not been provided in accordance with the time limits set out in regulation 32(6)(c) of those Regulations;

(ii) the Secretary of State was prevented from specifying a new assessed income period under regulation 10(1) of the State Pension Credit Regulations; and

(iii) the information and evidence required under regulation 32(6)(a) of the Claims and Payments Regulations has since been provided;]

[15 (n) is a decision by [19 [25 an appeal tribunal or] the First-tier Tribunal] confirming a decision by the Secretary of State terminating a claimant's entitlement to income support because he no longer falls within the category of person specified in paragraph 7 of Schedule 1B to the Income Support Regulations (persons incapable of work) and a further [19 [25 decision of an appeal tribunal or the First-tier Tribunal]] subsequently determines that he is incapable of work;]

[16 (o) is a decision that a person is entitled to state pension credit and—

(i) the person or his partner makes, or is treated as having made, an election for a lump sum in accordance with—

(aa) paragraph A1 or 3C of Schedule 5 to the Contributions and Benefits Act;

(bb) paragraph 1 of Schedule 5A to that Act; or, as the case may be, (cc) paragraph 12 or 17 of Schedule 1 to the Graduated Retirement Benefit Regulations;

or

(ii) such a lump sum is repaid in consequence of an application to change an election for a lump sum in accordance with regulation 5 of the Deferral of Retirement Pensions etc. Regulations or, as the case may be, paragraph 20D of Schedule 1 to the Graduated Retirement Benefit Regulations;]

[[28] (oa) is a decision that a person is entitled to state pension credit and—

(i) the person—

(aa) chooses under section 8(2) of the Pensions Act 2014, or under Regulations under section 10 of that Act which make provision corresponding or similar to section 8(2), to be paid a lump sum; or

(bb) is entitled to a lump sum under section 8(4) of the Pensions Act 2014, or under Regulations under section 10 of that Act which make provision corresponding or similar to section 8(4), because the person has failed to choose within the period mentioned in section 8(3); or

(ii) such a lump sum is repaid in consequence of an application—

(aa) to alter the choice mentioned in paragraph (i)(aa) in accordance with regulation 6 of the State Pension Regulations 2015 or Regulations made under section 10 of the Pensions Act 2014 which make provision corresponding or similar to regulation 6 of the State Pension Regulations 2015; or

(bb) to make a late choice in accordance with regulation 4(4) of the State Pension Regulations 2015 (when a choice of lump sum or survivor's pension may be made) or Regulations made under section 10 of the Pensions Act 2014 which make provision corresponding or similar to regulation 4(4) of the State Pension Regulations 2015;]

[[17] (p) is a decision awarding employment and support allowance where there has been a failure determination;

(q) is a decision made in consequence of a failure determination where the reduction ceases to have effect under of regulation 64 of the Employment and Support Allowance Regulations;

(r) [[23] is an employment and support allowance decision where, since the decision was made, the Secretary of State has—

(i) received medical evidence from a health care professional approved by the Secretary of State, or

(ii) made a determination that the claimant is to be treated as having limited capability for work in accordance with regulation 20, 25, 26 or 33(2) of the Employment and Support Allowance Regulations;]]

[[18] (s) is a decision where on or after the date on which the decision was made, a late or unpaid contribution is treated as paid under—

(i) regulation 5 of the Social Security (Crediting and Treatment of Contributions and National Insurance Numbers) Regulations 2001 (treatment of late paid contributions where no consent, connivance or negligence by the primary contributor) on a date which falls on or before the date on which the original decision was made;

(ii) regulation 6 of those Regulations (treatment of contributions paid late through ignorance or error) on a date which falls on or before the date on which the original decision was made; or

(iii) regulation 60 of the Social Security (Contributions) Regulations 2001 (treatment of unpaid contributions where no consent, connivance or negligence by the primary contributor) on a date which falls on or before the date on which the original decision was made;]

[[29] (sa) is a decision where on or after the date on which the decision was made, a late contribution is treated as paid by virtue of regulation 4 of the Social Security (Crediting and Treatment of Contributions, and National Insurance Numbers) Regulations 2001 for the purposes of entitlement to—

(i) a bereavement benefit;

(ii) a Category A or Category B retirement pension under Part II of the Contributions and Benefits Act; or

(iii) a state pension under Part 1 of the Pensions Act 2014;]

[[27] (t) is a decision awarding income support where there has been a determination by the Secretary of State under regulation 6(2) of the Income Support Work-Related Activity Regulations that a person has failed to undertake work-related activity;

(u) is a decision made in consequence of a determination by the Secretary of State that a person has failed to undertake work-related activity where a reduction under regulation 8(1) of the Income Support Work-Related Activity Regulations ceases to have effect by virtue of regulation 9 of those Regulations.]

(3) A decision which may be revised under regulation 3 may not be superseded under this regulation except where—

(a) circumstances arise in which the Secretary of State [[2] or the Board or an officer of the Board] may revise that decision under regulation 3; and

(b) further circumstances arise in relation to that decision which are not specified in regulation 3 but are specified in paragraph (2) or (4).

(4) Where the Secretary of State requires [[2] or the Board require] further evidence or information from the applicant in order to consider all the issues raised by an application under paragraph (2) ("the original application"), he [[2] or they] shall notify the applicant that further evidence or information is required and the decision may be superseded—

(a) where the applicant provides further relevant evidence or information within one month of the date of notification or such longer period of time as the Secretary of State [[2] or the Board] may allow; or

(b) where the applicant does not provide such evidence or information within the time allowed under sub-paragraph (a), on the basis of the original application.

(5) The Secretary of State [[2] or the Board] may treat an application for a revision or a notification of a change of circumstances as an application for a supersession.

(6) The following events are not relevant changes of circumstances for the purposes of paragraph (2)—

(a) the repayment of a loan to which regulation 66A of the Income Support Regulations or regulation 136 of the Jobseeker's Allowance

Regulations applies; [[17] , regulation 137 of the Employment and Support Allowance Regulations]

(b) [[15] . . .]

[[3] (c) the fact that a person has become terminally ill, within the meaning of section 66(2)(a) of the Contributions and Benefits Act, unless an application for supersession which contains an express statement that the person is terminally ill is made either by—

(i) the person himself; or

(ii) any other person purporting to act on his behalf whether or not that other person is acting with his knowledge or authority;

and where such an application is received a decision may be so superseded notwithstanding that no claim under section 66(1) or, as the case may be, 72(5) or 73(12) of that Act has been made.]

(7) In paragraph (6)(b), "nursing home" and "residential care home" have the same meanings as they have in regulation 19 of the Income Support Regulations.

[[10] (8) In relation to the assessed income period, the only change of circumstances relevant for the purposes of paragraph (2)(a) is that the assessed income period ends in accordance with section 9(4) of the State Credit Pension Act or the regulations made under section 9(5) of that Act.]

Amendments

1. Social Security and Child Support (Decisions and Appeals) Amendment (No.2) Regulations 1999 (SI 1999/1623) reg.2 (July 5, 1999).

2. Tax Credits (Decisions and Appeals) (Amendment) Regulations 1999 (SI 1999/2570) reg.9 (October 5, 1999). Note that amendments made by these regulations only have effect with respect to tax credit (reg.1(2) of the Amendment Regulations).

3. Social Security and Child Support (Decisions and Appeals), Vaccine Damage Payments and Jobseeker's Allowance (Amendment) Regulations 1999 (SI 1999/2677) reg.7 (October 18, 1999).

4. Social Security (Work-focused Interviews) Regulations 2000 (SI 2000/897) reg.16(5) and Sch.6 para.4 (April 3, 2000).

5. Social Security and Child Support (Miscellaneous Amendments) Regulations 2000 (SI 2000/1596) reg.16 (June 19, 2000).

6. Social Security (Joint Claims: Consequential Amendments) Regulations 2000 (SI 2000/1982) reg.5(b) (March 19, 2001).

7. Social Security (Breach of Community Order) (Consequential Amendments) Regulations 2001 (SI 2001/1711) reg.2(2)(c) (October 15, 2001).

8. Social Security (Loss of Benefit) (Consequential Amendments) Regulations 2002 (SI 2002/490) reg.8(b) (April 1, 2002).

9. Social Security (Claims and Payments and Miscellaneous Amendments) Regulations 2002 (SI 2002/428) reg.4(3) (April 2, 2002).

10. State Pension Credit (Consequential, Transitional and Miscellaneous Provisions) Regulations 2002 (SI 2002/3019) reg.17 (April 7, 2003).

11. Social Security and Child Support (Miscellaneous Amendments) Regulations 2003 (SI 2003/1050) reg.3(3) (May 5, 2003).

12. State Pension Credit (Transitional and Miscellaneous Provisions) Amendment Regulations 2003 (SI 2003/2274) reg.5(2) (October 6, 2003).

13. Social Security (Jobcentre Plus Interviews for Partners) Regulations 2003 (SI 2003/1886) reg.15(4) (April 12, 2004).

14. Social Security (Working Neighbourhoods) Regulations 2004 (SI 2004/959) reg.24(3) (April 26, 2004).

15. Social Security, Child Support and Tax Credits (Miscellaneous Amendments) Regulations 2005 (SI 2005/337) reg.2(4) (March 18, 2005).

16. Social Security (Deferral of Retirement Pensions, Shared Additional Pension and Graduated Retirement Benefit) (Miscellaneous Provisions) Regulations 2005 (SI 2005/2677) reg.9(4) (April 6, 2006).

17. Employment and Support Allowance (Consequential Provisions) (No.2) Regulations 2008 (SI 2008/1554) regs 29 and 32 (July 27, 2008).

18. Social Security (Miscellaneous Amendments) (No.5) Regulations 2008 (SI 2008/2667) reg.3(1) and (3) (October 30, 2008).

19. Tribunals, Courts and Enforcement Act 2007 (Transitional and Consequential Provisions) Order 2008 (SI 2008/2683) Sch.1 paras 95 and 101 (November 3, 2008).

20. Welfare Reform Act 2009 (Section 26) (Consequential Amendments) Regulations 2010 (SI 2010/424) reg.4(1) and (4) (March 22, 2010).

21. Social Security (Loss of Benefit) Amendment Regulations 2010 (SI 2010/1160) reg.3(1) and (3) (April 1, 2010).

22. Jobseeker's Allowance (Sanctions for Failure to Attend) Regulations 2010 (SI 2010/509) reg.3(1) and (3) (April 6, 2010).

23. Social Security (Miscellaneous Amendments) (No.3) Regulations 2010 (SI 2010/840) reg.7(1) and (3) (June 28, 2010).

24. Jobseeker's Allowance (Mandatory Work Activity Scheme) Regulations 2011 (SI 2011/688) reg.18(b) (April 25, 2011).

25. Social Security and Child Support (Supersession of Appeal Decisions) Regulations 2012 (SI 2012/1267) reg.4(1) and (2) (November 3, 2008, the retrospective effect being permitted by s.103(2)(b) of the Welfare Reform Act 2012).

26. Jobseeker's Allowance (Sanctions) (Amendment) Regulations 2012 (SI 2012/2568) reg.6(1) and (3) (October 22, 2012).

27. Income Support (Work-Related Activity) and Miscellaneous Amendments Regulations 2014 (SI 2014/1097) reg.12(1) and (4) (April 28, 2014).

28. Pensions Act 2014 (Consequential, Supplementary and Incidental Amendments) Order 2015 (SI 2015/1985) art.18(1) and (5) (April 6, 2016).

29. Social Security (Credits, and Crediting and Treatment of Contributions) (Consequential and Miscellaneous Amendments) Regulations 2016 (SI 2016/1145) reg.4(1) and (4) (January 1, 2017).

30. Social Security (Scotland) Act 2018 (Disability Assistance for Children and Young People) (Consequential Modifications) Order 2021 (SI 2021/786) art.6(1) and (4) (July 26, 2021).

31. Social Security (Disability Assistance for Working Age People) (Consequential Amendments) Order 2022 (SI 2022/177) art.6(1) and (4) (March 21, 2022).

Definitions

"the Act"—see reg.1(3).
"appeal tribunal"–see s.17(7) of the Social Security Act 1998.
"assessed income period"—*ibid.*
"bereavement benefit"—*ibid.*
"the Board"—*ibid.*
"claimant"—*ibid.*
"Commissioner"–see s.17(7) of the Social Security Act 1998.
"the Contributions and Benefits Act"—see s.84 of the Social Security Act 1998.
"the date of notification"—see reg.1(3).
"the Deferral of Retirement Pensions etc. Regulations"—*ibid.*
"employment and support allowance decision"—see reg.7A(1).
"the Employment and Support Allowance Regulations"—see reg.1(3).
"failure determination"—*ibid.*
"family"—*ibid.*
"the Graduated Retirement Benefit Regulations"—*ibid.*
"health care professional"—see s.39(2) of the Social Security Act 1998.

"incapacity benefit decision"—see reg.7A(1).
"incapacity determination"—*ibid.*
"the Income Support Regulations"—see reg.1(3).
"Income Support Work-Related Activity Regulations"—*ibid.*
"the Jobseekers Act"—see s.84 of the Social Security Act 1998.
"the Jobseeker's Allowance Regulations"—see reg.1(3).
"a joint-claim jobseeker's allowance"—*ibid.*
"nursing home"—see para.(7).
"payee"—see reg.7A(1).
"relevant benefit"—see s.39(1) of the Social Security Act 1998.
"residential care home"—see para.(7).
"Scottish disability benefit"—see reg.1(3).
"State Pension Credit Act"—*ibid.*
"work-focused interview"—*ibid.*

GENERAL NOTE

Paragraph (1)

2.457 This regulation is made under s.10(3) of the Social Security Act 1998.

In *Wood v Secretary of State for Work and Pensions* [2003] EWCA Civ 53 (reported as *R(DLA) 1/03*), the Court of Appeal overruled *R(DLA) 6/02* and held that a decision may be superseded only if one of the conditions in paras (2)–(4) is satisfied. If a claimant has applied for supersession and the conditions are not met, the Secretary of State must refuse to supersede. That is the natural meaning of the provisions but the Tribunal of Commissioners deciding *R(DLA) 6/02* had thought it necessary to give a strained construction to reg.6 because they understood s.12(9) of the 1998 Act precluded an appeal against a refusal to supersede, which would have been unfair. The majority of the Court of Appeal acknowledged that it was difficult to give both reg.6 and s.12(9) a literal construction but they preferred to give an extended construction to s.12(9), holding that there is an appeal against a refusal to supersede, and to take a more literal approach to reg.6, which certainly makes it easier to apply reg.6.

Where a decision is superseded and then the superseding decision is itself superseded, the body making that third decision must be satisfied that there are grounds for superseding the first decision as well as the second decision if the outcome is to be different from that of the first decision (*R(DLA) 1/06*).

It was held by a Tribunal of Commissioners in *R(IB)2/04*, adopting at para.10(4) a suggestion made by Rix L.J. in *Wood*, that the ground of supersession which is found to exist must form the basis of the supersession in the sense that the original decision can only be altered in a way which follows from that ground. This overrules *R(A)1/90*, although no reference was made to that decision by the Tribunal of Commissioners.

However, there is still a question whether the use of the word "may" in paras (1) and (2) means that the Secretary of State need not supersede even if he finds that one of the conditions in paras (2)–(4) is satisfied. In *Wood*, Rix L.J. regarded a superseded decision as an altered decision, which might imply that supersession of an award necessarily implied a change in the claimant's entitlement so that there was no scope for supersession without there being a different outcome. Such an approach would be rather different from that taken in the context of reviews under earlier legislation (see the note to para.(2)(a)(i) below). But, now that it has been established that there is a right of appeal against a refusal to supersede, there is no practical difference between a refusal to supersede and a decision to supersede "at the same rate", at least at the time the decision is given. There may be a difference later to the extent that, if there is a later supersession, the nature of an earlier decision may determine which decision must be superseded but, even then, it is difficult to see how the outcome in terms of entitlement to benefit could be affected. It may well be that there are two or more perfectly acceptable legal analyses, each producing the same practical result and any one of which can properly be applied without the decision-maker erring in law.

There may be no practical difference between a refusal to supersede and a supersession "at the same rate" but, in *CIS/6249/1999*, the Commissioner decided that the Secretary of State had a limited discretion to refuse to supersede even where grounds of supersession existed and any supersession would result in a change in entitlement. Although a power may appear discretionary, there is often a duty to exercise it in a particular way in order that the purpose for which the power is given is not frustrated (*Julius v Lord Bishop of Oxford* (1880) L.R. 5 App. Cas. 214) and therefore the Secretary of State is for practical purposes normally bound to supersede a decision if the conditions for supersession are met and would result in a change of entitlement. However, in *CIS/6249/1999*, there was a competing duty not to abuse power by reviewing an award of income support in respect of a period in the past in circumstances where the claimant would have been unfairly prejudiced. The facts of the case illustrate the operation of the principle. The claimant was an asylum seeker entitled to "urgent cases" payments of income support to which he was not entitled if he had any capital in the form of liquid assets. In October 1995, he had been paid almost £900, representing about 11 weeks' arrears of income support, which he paid into a bank. As long as it remained in his bank, that sum should have disentitled him from income support. In October 1996, he told a visiting officer that he still had £787 but benefit continued in payment until 1998, when a decision was made disentitling him from February 25, 1998. In principle, the claimant had not been entitled to income support from October 1995, but there was no question of the overpayment being recoverable as the Benefits Agency had known he had the money in October 1995. On the other hand, deciding that the claimant had not been entitled to income support throughout the period from October 1995 to February 1998 would have prevented the claimant from being paid any benefit in the future because the claimant would have been unable to show he was entitled to benefit immediately before February 5, 1996 and would have been deprived of the transitional protection given to asylum seekers in receipt of benefit at that date. Had benefit been stopped in October 1995, when it should have been, the claimant would undoubtedly have qualified for benefit again before February 5, 1996. The Commissioner considered that reviewing entitlement before February 25, 1998 would have been so unfair as to be an abuse of power. The same approach would presumably be appropriate in respect of supersession.

CIS/6249/1999 was distinguished (and to some extent its correctness was doubted) **2.458** in *R1/07 (IB)*, where it was held that it was not an abuse of power for a decision to be superseded retrospectively in a case where the claimant had sought advice from the Department for Social Development about working while claiming incapacity benefit but had not been advised that he was required to give notice of any work in writing. The claimant had acted honestly at all times but, as the Commissioner observed, there was no question of the recovery of any overpaid benefit and she considered that any unfairness to the claimant did not outweigh the public interest in ensuring that a correct decision as to entitlement was made. It is not clear from the decision whether the claimant had in fact lost anything to which he would have been entitled had he not received the wrong advice except, presumably, credited contributions during the material period in the past. If a loss of entitlement in the past meant a loss of current entitlement because different contribution years had to be taken into account, that was not recorded. However, the Commissioner did point out that the claimant might have a remedy in the courts if he had suffered any loss.

Although it appears necessary first to determine whether one of the cases in para. (2) applies and then determine what the outcome should be, the two stages need not be kept rigidly apart. In *CDLA/5469/1999*, the Deputy Commissioner pointed out that the fact that a tribunal must, as a first step *in their deliberations*, ask themselves whether there are grounds for supersession does not translate into a rule of practice that the question whether grounds for supersession exist must be treated as a preliminary issue *in the hearing*. In most cases involving ignorance or mistake as to a material fact, he suggests, the tribunal should, after the hearing, first ask itself simply what the facts are that are material to the issue to be decided. Only then should it ask whether the original decision was made in ignorance of any of those facts. If the answer is yes, it can then give its own decision on the basis of the facts found. In *CSDLA/765/2004*, the Commissioner took the opposite approach and suggested that a hearing should initially be restricted to taking evidence relevant to a ground of supersession, but that was not followed in *CSDLA/637/2006*, where the Commissioner said:

> "It is sensible rather that a tribunal hears all the evidence, including what is potentially relevant to current entitlement, but without yet making a final determination with respect to that, in order to compare present circumstances with those which surrounded the original award."

Then, it is generally necessary to consider whether there are grounds for supersession, before making a final decision on entitlement, particularly where the question of entitlement involves an element of judgment. Thus, in *CS v SSWP (DLA)* [2011] UKUT 509 (AAC), the First-tier Tribunal erred in considering whether the claimant was "virtually unable to walk" at the material time without identifying a relevant change of circumstances since the decision being superseded, because that "failed ... to give proper protection to the judgment of the original decision maker".

Nonetheless, it may sometimes be a legitimate inference from a finding that the claimant does not satisfy the conditions of entitlement to benefit that an earlier award was based on a mistake of law or fact or that that there has been a change of circumstances so that the earlier award may be superseded (*CDLA/1820/1998*), although that applies only where no reasonable person could find the conditions of entitlement currently to be satisfied. It is then appropriate to presume that the ground of supersession is the one least unfavourable to the claimant (*Cooke v Secretary of State for Social Security* [2001] EWCA Civ 734 (reported as *R(DLA) 6/01*)). In *CSDLA/637/2006*, however, the Commissioner pointed out that drawing such an inference did not imply that an original award made by a tribunal, as opposed to the Secretary of State, could be superseded, because an error of law is not a ground for superseding a tribunal's decision. She rejected the Secretary of State's contention that it should be presumed that the earlier tribunal had not erred in law and she consequently upheld a decision to the effect that grounds for supersession had not been made out.

The Secretary of State may supersede a decision either on an application or on his own initiative. Where he considers a claimant's application for supersession but reduces entitlement rather than increasing it, he must be treated as having superseded the original decision on his own initiative, rather than on the claimant's application (*R(IB)2/04*, at para.95). That is necessary to avoid the claimant being unfairly prejudiced in respect of the date from which the decision is effective under s.10(5) of the 1998 Act. For the same reason, where a claimant appeals against a decision made on his or her application for supersession and a tribunal makes a decision that is less favourable to the claimant than the decision that is being superseded, the decision will be effective from the date on which it would have been effective if the Secretary of State had acted on his own initiative (*R(IB)2/04*, at para.97). It has been held that if the Secretary of State considers a case on his own motion but decides not to change the award, he is bound nonetheless to issue a decision refusing to revise or supersede the decision, or revising or superseding it "at the same rate" (*CTC/2979/2001*). However, that was doubted in *CDLA/705/2002* and, in *CI/1547/2001*, it was said that the Secretary of State was nearly always bound to issue a decision on a claimant's application but need not do so when considering a case on his own motion. If a decision is given simply in terms of a new award without supersession being mentioned but in circumstances where the new award could be made only on supersession, the defect can be cured by a tribunal giving the decision in the correct form (*R(IB)2/04*, at para.76). However, if the tribunal never discover that the decision should have been a supersession, because they are unaware that there was an award current when the decision was made, the tribunal's decision may well be set aside because it is impossible to infer that circumstances justifying a different outcome on supersession were made out (*CDLA/9/2001*).

Section 10(3) permits regulations to be made prescribing the procedure by which a supersession may be made, but no regulation has been made prescribing the form of an application and the question whether a letter amounts to an application for supersession does not fall within the exclusive jurisdiction of the Secretary of State. A letter providing information about a change of circumstances will often imply a request for supersession (see para.(5)) but not all letters to the Department carry a clear implication to that effect and it may sometimes be difficult to determine whether, in reconsidering a decision, the Secretary of State is acting on his own initiative or in response to an application. This would not matter were it not for the impact the distinction may have on the date from which the application is effective (see s.10(5) of the Social Security Act 1998). It is doubtful whether giving information to a medical advisor during a medical examination amounts to an application for supersession, even though a notification of a change of circumstances may be treated as an application for supersession under para.(5), but the Secretary of State can made a supsersession decision of his own motion when the information is passed to him (*CI/954/2006*).

A final assessment of disablement made under the legislation replaced by the 1998 Act implies that there was no disablement after the end of the award, and so has ongoing effect and requires supersession as well as a new claim for benefit (*R(I) 5/02*), whereas an assessment under the 1998 Act carries no such implication and, after it expires, requires just a new claim. **2.459**

Save in the many instances where reg.7 or Schs 3A–3C provide otherwise, a supersession is effective from the date on which it was made, if the supersession was made on the Secretary of State's own initiative, or on the date of application when the suppression was made on the application of a claimant or other interested person (s.10(5) of the 1998 Act). In *CI/1547/2001*, it was suggested that all appeals against assessment decisions should also be treated as appeals against the consequent entitlement decisions because the provisions for supersession and revision, are too limited, having regard to the dates from which they are effective, to deal satisfactorily with the consequences of a successful appeal on assessment alone. In *CI/954/2006*, the Commissioner made the same point in respect of an application to supersede an assessment of disablement. He also held that, where a person who had been awarded disablement benefit suffered another industrial accident, a claim for disablement benefit in respect of the second accident might have to be treated in the alternative as an application for supersession of the first award and he pointed out that there is an anomolous difference in the extent to which a claim and an application for supersession can be backdated.

Note that payment of benefit may be suspended under reg.16 while consideration is being given to susperseding an award. In a case where payment of attendance allowance was terminated on supersession, because a local authority was paying care home fees, but the claimant was in dispute with a financial adviser and it was possible that money to pay the fees retrospectively would be forthcoming, payment ought merely to have been suspended (*CA/3800/2006; SSWP v DA* [2009] UKUT 214 (ACC)). It made a difference because, if payments were superseded, it was not possible to reinstate them from the date they were terminated by way of a further supersession. Indeed, a three-judge panel in *SSWP v JL (DLA)* [2011] UKUT 293 (AAC); [2012] AACR 14 has held that suspension of payment under reg.16 rather than supersession under reg.6 should normally be the default position where a claimant of attendance allowance or disability allowance first goes into long-term care. **2.460**

However, if payments have been suspended, any supersession decision must deal with the whole period up to the date of the supersession decision. Thus, in *SSWP v NC (ESA)* [2023] UKUT 124 (AAC), where payment of contributory employment and support allowance had been suspended while the claimant was in prison and the Secretary of State did not supersede the award until after the claimant had been released, when she decided only that the claimant had not been entitled to that benefit while in prison, she erred in stating that the claimant could not be entitled to employment and support allowance after his release until he had made a new claim. The judge said at [27]:

> "A person who has a current award of a benefit cannot be expected to, and is neither obliged nor entitled to, make a new claim for the same benefit, even if payments have been suspended."

Even if an award of benefit is a possession within art.1 of Protocol 1 to the European Convention on Human Rights, its removal under the provisions for supersession is not in breach of the Convention (*CDLA/3908/2001*).

For the purpose of the migration of claimants from incapacity benefit to employment and support allowance, regs 6 and 16 of, and Sch.3 to, the Employment and Support Allowance (Transitional Provisions, Housing Benefit and Council Tax Benefit) (Existing Awards) (No.2) Regulations 2010 (SI 2010/1907), apply the 1999 Regulations to conversion decisions, treating a conversion decision as though it were a decision as to entitlement to employment and support allowance made on a claim. For the terms of reg.17 to the 2010 Regulations, see the annotation to reg.3 above. Note that para.(2)(a)(i) is modified by the 2010 Regulatons (see below).

Paragraph (2)

2.461 There is some degree of overlap between the sub-paras (e.g. (a)(i) and (e)) but this is not necessarily a difficulty. In *DS v SSWP (PIP)* [2016] UKUT 538 (AAC); [2017] AACR 19, decided under the equivalent provisions in the Universal Credit, Personal Independence Payment, Jobseeker's Allowance and Employment and Support Allowance (Decisions and Appeals) Regulations 2013, the judge referred to the different dates from which a supersession might be effective under the equivalent of reg.7 or Schs 3A–3C (which provide numerous exceptions to the general rule under s.10(5) that a supersession is effective from the date it is made or the application for it was made) and said:

> "15. ... In my view, all grounds of supersession can apply in so far as the conditions they contain are made out, without any artificial rules to try to make them mutually exclusive. So far as decisions that are advantageous to the claimant go, there is then no difficulty in applying a general principle that the claimant should be able to take the benefit of whatever ground gives the most advantage. So far as decisions that are not advantageous to the claimant are concerned, which will in the great majority of cases be supersessions carried out at the Secretary of State's own initiative, I do not see why the same principle cannot apply. The Secretary of State is entitled to rely on whatever of the grounds of supersession that are made out that result in what he says is the correct position being applied for the longest period."

However, he also held that, if the Secretary of State chose to rely on a simpler and more administratively-convenient ground and was content for the superseding decision to take effect from the date on which it was made rather than from an earlier date that would be more favourable to him, he was entitled to do so, subject to the power of the First-tier Tribunal in the event of an appeal to consider another ground of supersession if its potential application was clearly apparent from the evidence before it.

On the other hand, in *OL v SSWP (ESA)* [2018] UKUT 135 (AAC), it was argued on behalf of the claimant that the general provision applicable to changes of circumstances, reg.6(2)(a), always had to give way to any more specific provision. In that case, a claimant of contributory employment and support allowance had been awarded personal independence payment from October 2013, as a result of which he became entitled also to an income-related employment and support allowance. However, he did not inform those responsible for administering that benefit until November 2016. His case potentially fell within the scope of both reg.6(2)(a)(i) and reg.6(2)(e) and the Secretary of State accepted the claimant's argument and conceded that the latter provision should have been treated as applying to him.

That would have been appropriate even on the analysis adopted in *DS*, because the claimant had drawn the relevant decision-maker's attention to the new award and thereby could be treated as having applied for supersession (see reg.6(5)). The Upper Tribunal agreed with the parties. Because reg.6(2)(e) applied, so did reg.7(7)(a), rather than reg.7(2)(b), and therefore the supersession awarding the income-related allowance was effective from the date in October 2013 from which personal independence payment was awarded, rather than from the date in November 2016 when he notified the employment and support allowance authorities of that award or the date in October 2016 that the First-tier Tribunal had considered relevant.

Paragraph (2)(a)(i)

In *R(I) 56/54* at [28], the Commissioner said: "A relevant change of circumstances postulates that the decision has ceased to be correct". This means that only an award may be superseded on the ground of change of circumstances. A decision that a claimant is not entitled to benefit at all may not be superseded on that ground. Instead, the claimant must make a new claim. This point is now made explicit in s.8(2) of the Social Security Act 1998. *R(I)56/54* also suggests that a change of circumstances is relevant only if it would result in a different "outcome decision". The same approach was taken in *Wood v Secretary of State for Work and Pensions* [2003] EWCA Civ 53 (reported as *R(DLA) 1/03*) but the Court did not refer to *Saker v Secretary of State for Social Services, The Times,* January 16, 1988 (reported as an appendix to *R(I) 2/88*) in which Nicholls L.J. considered what might amount to a "material" fact for the purposes of a provision similar to para. (2)(b)(i) and said that a fact was material "if it was one which, had it been known to the medical board, would have called for serious consideration by the board and might well have affected its decision". On the other hand, in *CIB/2338/2000*, the Commissioner said that the "subtleties based on the *Saker* decision, under which a change may be relevant without justifying a different outcome, have no place in the scheme of adjudication under the 1998 Act" and, in *CIS/3655/2007*, he effectively held that *Saker* no longer applied because the effect of *Wood* is that reg.6 prescribes "outcome criteria" rather than "threshold criteria". In practical terms there is probably nothing to choose between the *Wood* approach and the *Saker* approach because a refusal to supersede has the same effect as a supersession "at the same rate". In other words, properly applied, either approach produces the same outcome, a point acknowledged in *CIS/3655/2007*. However, the *Wood* approach is undoubtedly simpler and, in *CA v SSWP (CSM)* [2020] UKUT 205 (AAC), the Upper Tribunal followed *CIS/3655/2007* and applied it to the provision in child support legislation that is equivalent to reg.6(2)(a)(i). The *Wood* approach has since been applied in the context of housing benefit legislation as well *(NSP v Stoke-on-Trent CC (HB)* [2022] UKUT 86 (AAC)). It was also pointed out in *CA* that, where there have been a number of changes of circumstances, it may be necessary to determine which of them are "material" in the *Wood* sense, in order to identify the date from which the supersession is effective (see reg.7(2) in relation to reg.6(2)(a)(i)). 2.462

A new medical opinion is not itself a change of circumstances but a new medical report may reveal not only a new opinion but also new clinical findings which would show a change of circumstances (*R(IS) 2/97* and *Cooke v Secretary of State for Social Security* [2001] EWCA Civ 734 (reported as *R(DLA) 6/01*)). A lessening of care needs is itself a change of circumstances (*R1/05(DLA)*).

A change of circumstances includes a change in the law due to the coming into force of a statutory provision (*Chief Adjudication Officer v McKiernon* (reported as *R(I) 2/94*)). Any supersession for such a change of circumstances is effective on the date on which the change in legislation had, or takes, effect (reg.7(30) and (30A)). Retrospective legislation may therefore show that the decision being superseded was wrong when it was made and should be superseded under reg.6(2)(b), rather than under reg.6(2)(a)(i). Similarly, a binding decision of the Upper Tribunal or a court on a point of law states the law as it has always been and so is not ordinarily considered to change the law (*In Re Spectrum Plus Ltd* [2005] UKHL 41; [2005] 2

AC 680). This does not create any difficulty where such a decision shows that an earlier decision of the Secretary of State was wrong in law, because the Secretary of State's decision may be superseded under reg.6(2)(b). However, reg.6(2)(b) permits supersession only of decisions of the Secretary of State and it was suggested by the majority in *SSWP v TJ (JSA)* [2015] UKUT 56 (AAC) that, for the purposes of social security adjudication, the making of the binding decision may need to be treated as a change of circumstances affecting the understanding of the law so that a decision of the First-tier Tribunal given before the binding decision was given can be superseded under reg.6(2)(a)(i). Otherwise, where an award of benefit has been made for an indefinite period by the First-tier Tribunal rather than the Secretary of State, it would not be possible to supersede the decision even prospectively so as to give effect to the binding decision from the date it was handed down. (This issue did not actually arise in that case and it was not considered by the Court of Appeal in the subsequent appeal, *Secretary of State for Work and Pensions v Reilly* [2016] EWCA Civ 413; [2017] Q.B. 257; [2017] AACR 14.)

2.463 Although reg.6(2)(a)(i) enables the Secretary of State to supersede a decision on the ground that there has been a change of circumstances "since the decision had effect", a Tribunal of Commissioners has suggested that it would be improper for the Secretary of State to supersede on that ground where the decision being superseded was that of a tribunal and, because the change of circumstances occurred before the decision under appeal and the tribunal was well aware of it, the tribunal could have taken it into account notwithstanding s.12(8)(b) of the Social Security Act 1998 but did not do so (*R(IS) 2/08*). "The Secretary of State should abide by a tribunal's decision in such circumstances." If he considers that the change of circumstances has not properly been taken into account, his remedy is to appeal.

See reg.7(2) for the date from which the supersession is effective.

For the purpose of the migration of claimants from incapacity benefit to employment and support allowance, para.25A(2) of Sch.2 to the Employment and Support Allowance (Transitional Provisions, Housing Benefit and Council Tax Benefit) (Existing Awards) (No.2) Regulations 2010 (SI 2010/1907) ("the 2010 Regulations"), as amended by reg.17(1) and (12) of the Employment and Support Allowance (Transitional Provisions, Housing Benefit and Council Tax Benefit) (Existing Awards) (No.2) (Amendment) Regulations 2010 (SI 2010/2430), provides that, with effect from October 1, 2010, reg.6(2)(a)(i) of the 1999 Regulations is to be read as if for "in the case of an advance award under regulation 13, 13A or 13C of the Claims and Payments Regulations or regulation 146 of the Employment and Support Allowance Regulations" there were substituted "in the cases of an advance award under regulation 13, 13A or 13C of the Claims and Payments Regulations or regulation 146 of the Employment and Support Allowance Regulations or a conversion decision within the meaning of regulation 5(2)(a) of the 2010 Regulations".

Paragraph (2)(a)(ii)

2.464 Section 8(2) of the Social Security Act 1998 provides that, when the Secretary of State makes a decision on a claim, he is precluded from taking account of circumstances not obtaining at the date of his decision. There is no equivalent provision in s.10 in respect of supersessions and this head expressly permits the Secretary of State to anticipate a change of circumstances. This is obviously a useful provision allowing the Secretary of State to act immediately to make the appropriate adjustment when a claimant informs him that his circumstances are about to change. However, it raises some interesting questions. For instance, what ground of supersession would there be if the anticipated change of circumstances did not take place? Perhaps supersession or revision on the ground of mistake of fact would be appropriate? More problematic is that a tribunal is precluded by s.12(8)(b) from having regard to any change of circumstances not obtaining at the date of the Secretary of State's decision and would therefore apparently be bound to ignore the change of circumstances that the Secretary of State had anticipated, even if the tribunal found that the change of circumstances had occurred. It must presumably be inferred that the passage of time is a change of circumstances for the purpose of reg.6(2)(a) even though it is not for the purpose of s.12(8)(b) (*R(DLA) 4/05*). Also, the amendment to this head made in respect of advance awards does not apply to an award made on supersession under this very head so that it might be difficult to supersede a decision in the light of an unanticipated change of circumstances occurring between the date of supersession and the date from which the supersession was effective.

Paragraph (2)(b) and (c)

Paragraph (2)(b)(ii) exists to prevent there from being any overlap between supersession under para.(b) and revision under reg.3(1). A decision ought not to be superseded under sub-paras (b) or (c) so as to produce a different outcome if correcting the error of fact does not itself justify a different decision (*R(IB)2/04*), although, as in cases where para.(a)(i) might apply, it would probably make no practical difference in the long run whether a decision was superseded at the same rate or was not superseded at all. Ignorance or mistake must be as to a primary fact and not merely as to an inference or conclusion of fact. Thus, a decision cannot be superseded simply on the ground that the Secretary of State now takes a different view of the case. "He must go further and assert and prove that the inference might not have been drawn, if the determining authority had not been ignorant of some specific fact of which it could have been aware, or had not been mistaken as to some specific fact which it took into consideration" (*R(I) 3/75*). It may be particularly difficult to show that a tribunal made a mistake of fact if neither party obtained a full statement of reasons and it may be equally difficult to show that a tribunal was ignorant of a material fact if neither party obtained a record of proceedings which would include a note of evidence. In *CDLA/3875/2001* and *CDLA/2115/2003*, the Commissioners commented on the consequence of keeping inadequate records of Secretary of State's decisions. Lack of evidence as to the basis on which an adjudication officer's decision was made had made it impossible for the Secretary of State to point to an error in the decision that he wished to supersede. 2.465

A tribunal should hesitate before superseding the decision of an earlier tribunal for error of fact, where the issue must have been considered by the earlier tribunal if it was doing its job properly (*CDLA/3364/2001*). The tribunal should consider what the consequences may be and should obtain the parties' views. A copy of the statement of the earlier tribunal's reasons should also be obtained if one was issued.

Ignorance of, or a mistake as to, a material fact does not encompass ignorance of, or a mistake as to, the law (*R(G) 3/58*, a decision of a Tribunal of Commissioners). This does not matter where the wrong decision was made by the Secretary of State, because express provision is made in para.(2)(b) for such a decision to be superseded for error of law, but there is no provision in para.(2)(c) for a decision of the First-tier Tribunal or Upper Tribunal to be superseded for error of law. Since the First-tier Tribunal has no greater power than the Secretary of State had when making the decision being appealed, it follows that the First-tier Tribunal cannot make a decision superseding an earlier decision of that tribunal on the ground of error of law (*NH v CMEC* [2009] UKUT 183 (AAC)). However, where a decision of the First-tier Tribunal (or even the Upper Tribunal) is shown only by a subsequent binding decision of the Upper Tribunal or a court to have been wrong in law, there may be grounds for supersession under para.(2)(a)(i) (see *SSWP v TJ (JSA)*, discussed above).

Note that, where a decision of the Secretary of State is superseded under subpara. (b) because it has been shown to have been erroneous in point of law by a decision of the Upper Tribunal or a court involving a different claimant, the supersession may be effective from the date of the decision of the Upper Tribunal or court (see reg.7(6) and (6A)). However, showing that a decision was based on a mistake of law rather than a different understanding of the facts may not be easy (*MP v SSWP (DLA)* [2010] UKUT 130 (AAC)). 2.466

Paragraph (2)(d)

2.467 At first sight, it is difficult to understand how this provision can be effective, given that it overlaps with reg.3(8) and reg.6(3) prevents a decision from being superseded if it can be revised. Presumably, the explanation lies in the date from which it is desired that the decision should be effective. Where it is wished to alter the original decision from the date it was effective or reg.5 applies, revision will be appropriate but, if the original decision is to be altered from some later date determined under s.10(5) of the Social Security Act 1998 or reg.7, supersession will be appropriate. However, if this is correct, it is surprising that it is not made clearer in reg.6(3) or by limiting the scope of reg.3(8).

Paragraph (2)(e)

2.468 The new decision has effect from the date on which entitlement arises to the other benefit or to an increase in the rate of that other benefit (reg.7(7)). If entitlement to the other benefit, or to an increase in the rate of that other benefit, arises on or before the date from which the decision being reconsidered was effective, the decision is revised under reg.3(7) instead of being superseded.

Paragraph (2)(f) and (fa)

2.469 Decisions that jobseeker's allowance be paid at a reduced rate under s.19 or s.19A of the Jobseekers Act 1995 may be revised under reg.3(6).

Paragraph (2)(g)

2.470 With the introduction of employment and support allowance and universal credit, this paragraph has become redundant. It has effectively been replaced by para.(2)(r) in relation to income-related and "old-style" contributory employment and support allowance (i.e., within the scope of reg.1(2A)(a)) and by reg.26 of the Universal Credit, Personal Independence Payment, Jobseeker's Allowance and Employment and Support Allowance (Decisions and Appeals) Regulations 2013 in relation to universal credit and "new style" contributory employment and support allowance.

Paragraph (2)(r)

2.471 Paragraph (2)(r)(i) has the effect that an award of employment and support allowance "embodied in or necessary to which is a determination that a person has or is to be treated as having limited capability for work" (see reg.7A(1)) may be superseded simply on the ground that the Secretary of State has received medical evidence from a health care professional "approved" by him or her. Paragraph (2)(g) had a similar effect for the purposes of incapacity benefit and much of the case law developed in relation to that provision remains relevant to the newer provision. Many determinations under regs. 20, 25 and 26 of the Employment and Support Allowance Regulations, mentioned in para.(2)(r)(ii), which apply to claimants with certain sorts of conditions, undergoing certain sorts of treatment or excluded from work due to contact with infection or contamination, will be based on medical evidence from sources other than approved health care professionals. Reg.33(2) of those Regulations applies to students who are entitled to personal independence payment.

Presumably a healthcare professional will be "approved" for the purposes of para.(2)(r)(i) if approved for the purpose of carrying out examinations under reg.23 of the Employment and Support Allowance Regulations 2008 (see Vol.V of the 2021/22 edition of this work), although the link is not made explicitly in the way that it was in para.(2)(g). Medical evidence from another source may result in supersession under para.(2)(r)(ii) or some other provision altogether, most obviously either para.(2)(a), (b) or (c) on the ground that there has been a change of circumstances or that the decision being superseded was made in ignorance of, or was based on a mistake as to, a material fact.

Like para.(2)(r)(i), para.(2)(g) provided that obtaining a report was in itself grounds for supersession. In *CIB/2338/2000*, it was said that that sub-paragraph was unnecessary because, on a proper understanding of para.(2)(a)(i), it was always possible to identify a relevant change of circumstances in those cases where there was justification for terminating an award. In one sense, that is right. However, it was pointed out that, in the absence of a provision like para.(2)(g), a decision to remove an award following receipt of a medical report could be based either on the ground that there had been a change of circumstances (see para.(2)(a)(i)) or on the ground that benefit should never have been awarded in the first place (see para. (2)(b)). It would at least be theoretically necessary to decide which of those grounds applied and, if there had been a change of circumstances, determine the date of the change, because that would determine the date from which the new decision would be effective which in turn would determine whether there had been any potentially recoverable overpayment. The advantage of superseding a decision under para.(2)(g) was that regard could be had to the new report and any other new evidence, without it being necessary to identify a change of circumstances since, or an error in, the decision being superseded because, in the absence of any specific provision in reg.7, the new decision was effective in either event from the date it was made (s.10(5) of the Social Security Act 1998). The Commissioner said:

> "36. This does not leave claimants exposed to the whim of arbitrary determinations by the Secretary of State or appeal tribunals. In practice, there are three reasons that led to a different assessment under the pre-1998 adjudication scheme: (a) the wrong conclusion was reached on the evidence available at the time of the earlier assessment; (b) there is different evidence now available; (c) there has been a change in the nature or extent of the claimant's disabilities. Those reasons will still exist under the new scheme. They will underlie determinations. What has changed is that it is no longer necessary for the Secretary of State or tribunals to deal with them as an essential legal requirement in determining capacity for work.
>
> 37. Claimants are adequately protected. Determinations by the Secretary of State must be based on relevant evidence and have to be justified on scrutiny by a tribunal on an appeal. Determinations of tribunals have to be made judicially and on a rational evaluation of relevant evidence. They are subject to scrutiny for mistake of law by a Commissioner."

Thus, although it may not be necessary to consider whether there has been a change of circumstances or an error as an essential legal element of the decision itself, it may be necessary to consider those issues as part of the reasoning of the decision and consequently it may be necessary so consider evidence taken into account when the superseded decision was made, particularly if the claimant says his or her condition has not changed since then. See the discussion of *R(M) 1/96* and subsequent cases in the annotation to r.34 of the Tribunal Procedure (First-tier Tribunal) (Social Entitlement Chamber) Rules 2008 as regards the reasons for decision and see the annotation to r.24 of those Rules as regards the duty of the Secretary of State to provide evidence relating to previous decisions and the duty of the First-tier Tribunal to obtain such evidence when it has not been provided. **2.472**

Although the burden of proving grounds for supersession always lies on the person seeking supersession, the burden of proof must be considered in two stages in this sort of case (*CIB/1509/2004*). The Secretary of State must have received the necessary medical evidence following an appropriate medical examination so that, on an appeal, it is plainly for the Secretary of State to produce that evidence but, as he invariably does so, that is not usually a live issue. The second, and more likely to be contentious, stage is considering whether the claimant satisfied the conditions for entitlement to benefit at the date of the Secretary of State's decision. The Commissioner referred to *Kerr v Department for Social Development* [2004] UKHL 23; [2004] 1 W.L.R. 1372 (also reported as an appendix to *R1/04(SF)* (see the annotation to s.3(1) of the Tribunals, Courts and Enforcement Act 2007, where Baroness Hale talked of "a co-operative process of investigation" (at [62]) and said that "it will rarely be necessary to resort to concepts taken from adversarial litigation such as the burden of proof" (at [63]). A tribunal must have regard to all the evidence produced in the investigation and decide the case on the balance of probabilities. The Commissioner followed *CIS/427/1991* in holding that the burden of proof is relevant only: (a) if there is no relevant evidence on an issue (despite an adequate investigation) or (b) if the evidence on the issue is so evenly balanced that it is impossible to determine where the balance of probabilities lies. When superseding a decision on his own initiative, the burden of proof lies on the Secretary of State at both stages so that, in the few cases when it is relevant at the second stage, the case should be decided in favour of the claimant. Normally there is sufficient evidence to enable a tribunal to form a clear view one way or the other.

2.473 In *R(IB) 2/05*, the claimant had twice been referred for medical examinations after being awarded incapacity benefit. On the first occasion he satisfied the personal capability assessment and on the second occasion he did not. Following the second examination, the Secretary of State issued a decision purporting to supersede the original award. The Commissioner declined to rule on a submission that there should have been a supersession decision after the first medical examination because the grounds for supersession under para.(2)(g) are such that it made no difference whether there should already have been a supersession of the original award or even whether there had been a supersession of that award. On any view, there must have been a decision that could properly be superseded under para.(2)(g) and it was unnecessary further to identify the decision. The same reasoning would now apply in relation to para.(2)(r).

In *MC v SSWP (ESA)* [2014] UKUT 125 (AAC); [2014] AACR 35, it was recorded that it was always the Secretary of State's practice to issue a decision following a work capability assessment and inform the claimant that they might appeal if dissatisfied with it. It could be argued that reg.6(2) prescribes circumstances in which a decision *may* be superseded and that, where a claimant has not applied for a supersession and the Secretary of State does not consider that an award need be altered in the light of a medical report, there is no requirement for the Secretary of State to issue any formal decision, far less a decision to supersede, although the claimant should no doubt be informed that, in the light of the result of their recent medical examination, the award will continue as before. Nonetheless, the judge said that the practice seemed desirable and was permissible and, indeed, that it was arguably required. He suggested that, where a decision made under s.10 of the Social Security Act 1998 on the Secretary of State's own initiative makes no difference to the existing award, it might be better to describe it as a decision not to supersede or as a decision to supersede but to replace the original decision with a decision to the same effect, rather than as a refusal to supersede. (There seems no reason why a decision made on the Secretary of State's own initiative not to supersede should not be treated as an appealable decision in the same way as a refusal to supersede following an application made by a claimant (see the note to s.12(9) of the 1998 Act).)

Where a decision is made during the "assessment period" (in broad terms, the first thirteen weeks of a period of entitlement to employment and support allowance), a decision that is adverse to the claimant and results in the termination of an award takes effect immediately but a decision in favour of the claimant takes effect only from the end of the assessment period (see reg.7(38) and (40)), which is the earliest date from which an award may be increased to include the work-related activity component or the support component (see ss.2(2)(a) and (3)(a) and 4(4)(a) and (5)(a) of the Welfare Reform Act 2007 — in Vol.I). In *NC v SSWP (ESA)* [2015] UKUT 147 (AAC), the Secretary of State failed to take account of the temporary effects of an operation undergone by the claimant the day before his decision terminating the claimant's award. The claimant said that those effects had passed after two weeks, which was before the end of the assessment period. The Secretary of State could have terminated the award under para.(2)(a)(ii) from the date that he expected the effects would have passed, rather than terminating it under para (2)(r), but neither the First-tier Tribunal nor the Upper Tribunal could give a decision to that effect because they were precluded by s.12(8)(b) of the Social Security Act 1998 from taking into account a change of circumstances after the date of the Secretary of State's decision.

Paragraph (2)(s)

It is not easy to see when supersession under this subparagraph would be appropriate rather than revision under reg.3(8C), unless the decision being superseded were that of a tribunal. Any supersession is effective from the date on which the late or unpaid contribution is treated as paid (see reg.7(8A)), which, if this subparagraph is to apply at all, must be "on a date which falls on or before the date on which the original decision was made". One wonders whether there has been an error and this subparagraph was intended to apply where the contribution is treated as paid on a date *after* the original decision was made. 2.474

Paragraph (2)(sa)

This paragraph applies where a late paid contribution is treated as paid when it is actually paid, rather than when it should have been paid, and so the supersession is effective accordingly under reg.7(43). See reg.3(8C) to (8K) for circumstances in which the late payment of contributions (or the repayment of contributions) may justify revision. 2.475

Paragraph (3)

This important provision has the effect that revision must be considered before supersession. The exception is arguably unnecessary but it appears to be intended to make clear that, if there are grounds both for revision of a decision (which will usually be effective from the date that the original decision took effect) and for supersession (effective from a later date), the decision may be revised and then, as revised, may also be superseded, with a single composite "stepped" decision being issued. For the First-tier Tribunal's power effectively to substitute a supersession decision for a revision decision but not vice versa, see the note to s.12 of the Social Security Act 1998. 2.476

Paragraph (5)

An application for revision may be treated as an application for supersession. Regulation 3(10) provides that an application for supersession may be treated as an application for revision. For the power of an appeal tribunal to treat a supersession as a refusal to revise and vice versa, see the note to s.12 of the Social Security Act 1998. 2.477

6A. *Omitted.* 2.478

6B. *Omitted.* 2.479

Date from which a decision superseded under section 10 takes effect

7.—[4 (1) This regulation— 2.480

[12 (a) is, except for [14 paragraphs (2)(b) [27 , (bb)] [26 or (be)], (29) and (30)], subject to Schedules 3A [26 , 3B and 3C]; and]

(b) contains exceptions to the provisions of section 10(5) as to the date from which a decision under section 10 which supersedes an earlier decision is to take effect.]

(2) Where a decision under section 10 is made on the ground that there has been, or it is anticipated that there will be, a relevant change of circumstances since the decision [14 had effect] [19 or, in the case of an advance award, since the decision was made], the decision under section 10 shall take effect—

[4 (a) from the date the change occurred or, where the change does not have effect until a later date, from the first date on which such effect occurs where—
(i) the decision is advantageous to the claimant; and
(ii) the change was notified to an appropriate office within one month of the change occurring or within such longer period as may be allowed under regulation 8 for the claimant's failure to notify the change on an earlier date;]
(b) where the decision is advantageous to the claimant and the change was notified to an appropriate office more than one month after the change occurred or after the expiry of any such longer period as may have been allowed under regulation 8—
(i) in the case of a claimant who is in receipt of income support [12, jobseeker's allowance [26, state pension credit or an employment and support allowance] and benefit is paid in arrears, from the beginning of the benefit week in which the notification was made;
(ii) in the case of a claimant who is in receipt of income support [12, jobseeker's allowance [26, state pension credit or an employment and support allowance]] and benefit is paid in advance and the date of notification is the first day of a benefit week from that date and otherwise, from the beginning of the benefit week following the week in which the notification was made; or
(iii) in any other case, the date of notification of the relevant change of circumstances; or
[27 (bb) where the decision is advantageous to the claimant and is made on the Secretary of State's own initiative—
(i) except where paragraph (ii) applies, from the beginning of the benefit week in which the Secretary of State commenced action with a view to supersession; or
(ii) in the case of a claimant who is in receipt of income support, jobseeker's allowance or state pension credit where benefit is paid in advance and the Secretary of State commenced action with a view to supersession on a day which was not the first day of the benefit week, from the beginning of the benefit week following the week in which the Secretary of State commenced such action;
(bc) where—
(i) the claimant is a disabled person or a disabled person's partner;
(ii) the decision is advantageous to the claimant; and
(iii) the decision is made in connection with the cessation of payment of a carer's allowance [49 or carer support payment] relating to that disabled person,

the day after the last day for which carer's allowance [49 or carer support payment] was paid to a person other than the claimant or the claimant's partner;]
[24 (bd) [25 . . .]]
[26 (be) in the case of a claimant who is in receipt of an employment and support allowance and the claimant makes an application which contains an express statement that he is terminally ill within the meaning of regulation 2(1) of the Employment and Support Allowance Regulations, from the date the claimant became terminally ill;]

(c) where the decision is not advantageous to the claimant—

(i) [4 . . .]

[1(ii) in the case of a disability benefit decision, or an incapacity benefit decision where there has been an incapacity determination [29 or an employment and support allowance decision where there has been a limited capability for work determination] (whether before or after the decision), where the Secretary of State is satisfied that in relation to a disability determination embodied in or necessary to the disability benefit decision, or the incapacity determination [29 or an employment and support allowance decision where there has been a limited capability for work determination], the claimant or payee failed to notify an appropriate office of a change of circumstances which regulations under the Administration Act required him to notify, and the claimant or payee, as the case may be, knew or could reasonably have been expected to know that the change of circumstances should have been notified,

(aa) from the date on which the claimant or payee, as the case may be, ought to have notified the change of circumstances, or

(bb) if more than one change has taken place between the date from which the decision to be superseded took effect and the date of the superseding decision, from the date on which the first change ought to have been notified, or

(iii) [22 . . .]

[22(iv) in the case of a disability benefit decision, where the change of circumstances is not in relation to the disability determination embodied in or necessary to the disability benefit decision, from the date of the change; or

(v) in any other case, except in the case of a decision which supersedes a disability benefit decision, from the date of the change.]

[25 (2A) [27 . . .]]

[49 (2B) For the purposes of paragraph (2) "carer support payment" means carer's assistance given in accordance with the Carer's Assistance (Carer Support Payment) (Scotland) Regulations 2023.]

[26 (3) For the purposes of paragraphs (2) and (8) "benefit week" has the same meaning, as the case may be, as in—

(a) regulation 2(1) of the Income Support Regulations;
(b) regulation 1(3) of the Jobseeker's Allowance Regulations;
(c) regulation 1(2) of the State Pension Credit Regulations; or
(d) regulation 2(1) of the Employment and Support Allowance Regulations.]

(4) In paragraph (2) a decision which is to the advantage of the claimant includes a decision specified in regulation 30(2)(a) to (f).

[7 (5) Where the Secretary of State supersedes a decision made by [28[39 an appeal tribunal, the First-tier Tribunal, the Upper Tribunal or a Commissioner]] on the grounds specified in regulation 6(2)(c) [14 (i)] (ignorance of, or mistake as to, a material fact), the decision under section 10 shall take effect, in a case where, as a result of that ignorance of or mistake as to material fact, the decision to be superseded was more advantageous to the claimant than it would otherwise have been and which either—

(a) does not relate to a disability benefit decision or an incapacity benefit decision where there has been an incapacity determination; or

(b) relates to a disability decision or an incapacity benefit decision where there has been an incapacity determination, and the Secretary of State is satisfied that at the time the decision was made the claimant or payee knew or could reasonably have been expected to know of the fact in question and that it was relevant to the decision.

from the date on which the decision of [28[39 an appeal tribunal, the First-tier Tribunal, the Upper Tribunal or a Commissioner]] took, or was to take, effect.]

(6) Any decision made under section 10 in consequence of a decision which is a relevant determination for the purposes of section 27 shall take effect as from the date of the relevant determination.

[19 (6A) Where—

(a) there is a decision which is a relevant determination for the purposes of section 27 and the Secretary of State makes a benefit decision of the kind specified in section 27(1)(b);

(b) there is an appeal against the determination;

(c) after the benefit decision payment is suspended in accordance with regulation 16(1) and (3)(b)(ii); and

(d) on appeal a court, within the meaning of section 27, reverses the determination in whole or in part,

a consequential decision by the Secretary of State under section 10 which supersedes his earlier decision under sub-paragraph (a) shall take effect from the date on which the earlier decision took effect.]

[22 (7) A decision which is superseded in accordance with regulation 6(2)(e) or (ee) shall be superseded—

(a) subject to sub-paragraph (b), from the date on which entitlement arises to the other relevant benefit [47 or [48 Scottish disability benefit]] referred to in regulation 6(2)(e)(ii) or (ee) or to an increase in the rate of that other relevant benefit [47 or [48 Scottish disability benefit]]; or

(b) where the claimant or his partner—

(i) is not a severely disabled person for the purposes of section 135(5) of the Contributions and Benefits Act (the applicable amount) or section 2(7) of the State Pension Credit Act (guarantee credit) [26 or paragraph 6 of Schedule 4 to the Employment and Support Allowance Regulations;]

(ii) by virtue of his having—

(aa) a non-dependant as defined by regulation 3 of the Income Support Regulations [38 , regulation 2 of the Jobseeker's Allowance Regulations] [26 or regulation 71 of the Employment and Support Allowance Regulations]; or

(bb) a person residing with him for the purposes of paragraph 1 of Schedule 1 to the State Pension Credit Regulations whose presence may not be ignored in accordance with paragraph 2 of that Schedule,

at the date the superseded decision would, but for this sub-paragraph, have had effect,

from the date on which the claimant or his partner ceased to have a non-dependant or person residing with him or from the date on which the presence of that person was first ignored.]

[21 (7A) Where a decision is superseded in accordance with regulation 6(2)(o) [44 or (oa)], the superseding decision shall take effect from the day on which a lump sum, or a payment on account of a lump sum, is paid or repaid if that day is the first day of the benefit week but, if it is not, from the next following such day.]

[3 (8) [40 A decision to which regulation 6(2)(f) applies shall take effect from the beginning of the period specified in regulation 69(6) of the Jobseeker's Allowance Regulations.]]

[35 (8ZA) [40 A decision to which regulation 6(2)(fa) applies shall take effect from the beginning of the period specified in regulation 69A(3) of the Jobseeker's Allowance Regulations.]]

[36 (8ZB) [40 . . .]]

[27 (8A) Where a decision is superseded in accordance with regulation 6(2)(s), the superseding decision shall take effect from the date on which the late or unpaid contribution is treated as paid]

[4 (9) [37 Except where paragraph (9A) applies,] a decision relating to attendance allowance or disability living allowance which is advantageous to the claimant and which is made under section 10 on the basis of a relevant change of circumstances shall take effect from—

[14 (a) where the decision is made on the Secretary of State's own initiative—
   (i) the date on which the Secretary of State commenced action with a view to supersession; or
   (ii) subject to paragraph (30), in a case where the relevant circumstances are that there has been a change in the legislation in relation to attendance allowance or disability living allowance, the date on which that change in the legislation had effect;]

(b) where—
   (i) the change is relevant to the question of entitlement to a particular rate of benefit; and
   (ii) the claimant notifies the change before a date one month after he satisfied the conditions of entitlement to that rate or within such longer period as may be allowed under regulation 8,

   the [27 date on which] he satisfied those conditions;

(c) where—
   (i) the change is relevant to the question of whether benefit is payable; and
   (ii) the claimant notifies the change before a date one month after the change or within such longer period as may be allowed under regulation 8,

   the [27 date on which] the change occurred; or

(d) in any other case, the date of the application for the superseding decision.]

[37 (9A) Where—

(a) on or after 8th March 2001, the claimant had an award of attendance allowance, carer's allowance, or the care component of disability living allowance;

(b) the Secretary of State made a superseding decision in accordance with regulation 6(2)(a) to end that award on the ground that there had been, or it was anticipated that there would be, a relevant change of circumstances as a result of the claimant moving, or planning to move, from Great Britain to an EEA state or Switzerland; and

(c) the Secretary of State supersedes that decision in accordance with regulation 6(2)(b)(i) on the ground that it was erroneous in point of law, the superseding decision referred to in sub-paragraph (c) shall take effect from 18th October 2007.]

(10) A decision as to an award of incapacity benefit, which is made under section 10 because section 30B(4) of the Contributions and Benefits Act applies to the claimant, shall take effect as from the date on which he became entitled to the highest rate of the care component of disability living allowance.

(11) A decision as to an award of incapacity benefit or severe disablement allowance, which is made under section 10 because the claimant is to be treated as incapable of work under regulation 10 of the Social Security (Incapacity for Work) (General) Regulations 1995 (certain persons with a severe condition to be treated as incapable of work), shall take effect as from the date he is to be treated as incapable of work.

(12) Where this paragraph applies, a decision under section 10 may be made so as to take effect as from such date not more than eight weeks before—

(a) the application for supersession; or

(b) where no application is made, the date on which the decision under section 10 is made,

as is reasonable in the particular circumstances of the case.

[[46] (12A) Paragraph (12) applies where–

(a) the effect of a decision under section 10 is that owner-occupier loan payments are to be made to a claimant in respect of the claimant's liability to make owner-occupier payments; and

(b) that decision could not have been made earlier because information necessary to make that decision, requested otherwise than in accordance with paragraph 8 of Schedule 4 to the Loans for Mortgage Interest Regulations (provision of information), had not been supplied to the Secretary of State by the lender.

(12B) Where a claimant is receiving owner-occupier loan payments and there is a reduction in the amount owing in connection with a qualifying loan or alternative finance arrangement (within the meaning in Schedule 1 to the Loans for Mortgage Interest Regulations (meaning of owner-occupier payments)), a decision made under section 10 takes effect—

(a) on the first anniversary of the date on which the claimant's liability to make owner-occupier payments was first met by an owner-occupier loan payment; or

(b) where the reduction in the amount owing in connection with a qualifying loan or alternative finance arrangement occurred after the first anniversary of the date referred to in sub-paragraph (a), on the next anniversary of that date following the date of the reduction.

(12C) Where a claimant is receiving owner-occupier loan payments, an insurance payment deduction is made under regulation 14A(1) of the Loans for Mortgage Interest Regulations (insurance payment deduction) in relation to any decision under section 8 or 10 and there is a change in the amount of the owner-occupier payments payable—

(a) on a qualifying loan or alternative finance arrangement (within the meaning in Schedule 1 to the Loans for Mortgage Interest Regulations (meaning of owner-occupier payments)) to which those payments relate; or

(b) on a loan or alternative finance arrangement not so qualifying which is secured on the dwelling occupied as the home to which those payments relate,

a decision under section 10 which is made as a result of that change in the amount of the owner-occupier payments payable shall take effect on whichever of the dates referred to in paragraph (12D) is appropriate in the claimant's case.

(12D) The date on which a decision under section 10 takes effect for the purposes of paragraph (12C) is—

(a) the date on which the claimant's liability to make owner-occupier payments is first met by an owner-occupier loan payment; or

(b) where the change in the amount of the owner-occupier payments payable occurred after the date referred to in sub-paragraph (a), on the date of the next alteration in the standard rate following the date of that change.

(12E) In paragraph (12D), "standard rate" has the same meaning as it has in regulation 13 of the Loans for Mortgage Interest Regulations (standard rate to be applied under regulations 11 and 12).

(12F) Paragraph (12G) applies where—

(a) a claimant is awarded state pension credit;

(b) the claimant or the claimant's partner has reached pensionable age (within the meaning in section 122(1) of the Contributions and Benefits Act);

(c) the claimant is in receipt of owner-occupier loan payments; and

(d) after the date from which sub-paragraph (c) applies—

(i) a non-dependant (within the meaning in regulation 2(1) of the Loans for Mortgage Interest Regulations) begins to reside with the claimant; or

(ii) there has been a change of circumstances in respect of a non-dependant and this reduces the amount of the owner-occupier loan payments.

(12G) Where this paragraph applies, a decision made under section 10 shall take effect—

(a) where there is more than one change of the kind specified in paragraph (12F)(d) in respect of the same non-dependant within the same 26 week period, 26 weeks after the date on which the first such change occurred; and

(b) in any other circumstances, 26 weeks after the date on which a change specified in paragraph (12F)(d) occurred.]

(13) [46 . . .]

(14) [46 . . .]

(15) [46 . . .]

(16) [46 . . .]

(17) [46 . . .]

[12 (17A) [46 . . .]]

[16 (17B) [46 . . .]

(17C) [46 . . .]]

[26 (17D) [46 . . .]

(17E) [46 . . .]

(17F) [46 . . .]

(17G) [46 . . .]]

(17H) Where the decision is superseded in accordance with regulation 6(2)(a)(i) and the relevant circumstances are that the claimant has a non-dependant who has become entitled to main phase employment and support allowance, the superseding decision shall take effect from the date the main phase employment and support allowance is first paid to the non-dependant.]

(18) [[46] . . .]
(19) [[46] . . .]
(20) [[46] . . .]
(21) [[46] . . .]
(22) [[46] . . .]
(23) [[13] [[46] . . .]]
(24) Where—

(a) it has been determined that the amount of a jobseeker's allowance payable to a young person is to be reduced under regulation 63 of the Jobseeker's Allowance Regulations because paragraph (1)(b)(iii), (c), (d), (e) or (f) of that regulation (reduced payments under section 17 of the Jobseekers Act) applied in his case; and
(b) the decision made in consequence of sub-paragraph (a) falls to be superseded by a decision under section 10 because the Secretary of State has subsequently issued a certificate under section 17(4) of the Jobseekers Act with respect to the failure in question,

the decision under section 10 shall take effect as from the same date as the decision made in consequence of sub-paragraph (a) has effect.

[[5] [[17] (25) In a case where a decision ("the first decision") has been made that a person failed without good cause to take part in a work-focused interview, the decision under section 10 shall take effect as from—

(a) the first day of the benefit week to commence for that person following the date of the first decision; or
(b) in a case where a partner has failed without good cause to take part in a work-focused interview [[18] in accordance with regulations made under section 2AA of the Administration Act]—
    (i) the first day of the benefit week to commence for the claimant [[18] (meaning the person who has been awarded benefit within section 2AA(2) of the Administration Act at a higher rate referable to that partner)] following the date of the first decision; or
    (ii) if that date arises five days or less after the day on which the first decision was made, as from the first day of the second benefit week to commence for the claimant following the date of the first decision.]

(26) In paragraph (25), "benefit week" means any period of 7 days corresponding to the week in respect of which the relevant social security benefit is due to be paid.]

[[9] (27) [[31] . . .]]

[[10] (28) A decision to which regulation 6(2)(j) or (k) applies shall take effect from the first day of the disqualification period prescribed for the purposes of section [[32] 6B or] 7 of the Social Security Fraud Act 2001.]

[[12] (29) [[15] Subject to paragraphs (29A) and (29B), a] decision to which regulation 6(2)(1) (state pension credit) refers shall take effect from the day following the day on which the assessed income period ends if that day is the first day of the claimant's benefit week, but if it is not, from the next following such day.]

[[15] (29A) A decision to which regulation 6(2)(l) applies, where—

(a) the decision is advantageous to the claimant; and
(b) the information and evidence required under regulation 32(1) of the Claims and Payments Regulations has not been provided within the period allowed under that regulation,

shall take effect from the day the information and evidence required under that regulation is provided if that day is the first day of the claimant's benefit week, but, if it is not, from the next following such day.

(29B) A decision to which regulation 6(2)(l) applies, where—

(a) the decision is disadvantageous to the claimant; and

(b) the information and evidence required under regulation 32(1) of the Claims and Payments Regulations has not been provided within the period allowed under that regulation,

shall take effect from the day after the period allowed under that regulation expired.

(29C) Except where there is a change of circumstances during the period in which the Secretary of State was prevented from specifying a new assessed income period under regulation 10(1) of the State Pension Credit Regulations, a decision to which regulation 6(2)(m) applies shall take effect from the day on which the information and evidence required under regulation 32(6)(a) of the Claims and Payments Regulations was provided.]

[[14] (30) Where a decision is superseded in accordance with regulation 6(2)(a)(i) and the relevant circumstances are that there has been a change in the legislation in relation to a relevant benefit, the decision under section 10 shall take effect from the date on which that change in the legislation had effect.

[[30] (30A) Where a decision is superseded in accordance with regulation 6(2)(a)(ii) and the relevant change of circumstances is the coming into force of a change in the legislation in relation to a relevant benefit, the decision under section 10 shall take effect from the date on which that change in the legislation takes effect.]

(31) Where a decision is superseded in accordance with regulation 6(2)(a)(ii) and the relevant circumstances are that—

(a) a personal capability assessment has been carried out in the case of a person to whom section 171C(4) of the Contributions and Benefits Act applies; and

(b) the own occupation test remains applicable to him under section 171B(3) of that Act,

the decision under section 10 shall take effect on the day [[27] . . .] on which the own occupation test is no longer applicable to that person.

(32) For the purposes of paragraph (31)—

(a) "personal capability assessment" has the same meaning as in regulation 24 of the Social Security (Incapacity for Work) (General) Regulations 1995;

(b) "own occupation test" has the same meaning as in section 171B(2) of the Contributions and Benefits Act.

(33) A decision to which regulation 6(2)(c)(ii) applies shall take effect from the date on which [[39] the decision of the appeal tribunal, the First-tier Tribunal, the Upper Tribunal or the Commissioner] would have taken effect had it been decided in accordance with the determination of the [[28] Upper Tribunal][[39] or the Commissioner] or the court in the appeal referred to in section 26(1)(b).]

[[19] (34) A decision which supersedes a decision specified in regulation 6(2)(n) shall take effect from the effective date of the Secretary of State's decision to terminate income support which was confirmed by the decision specified in regulation 6(2)(n).]

[26 (35) [41 . . .]

(36) [41 A decision made in accordance with regulation 6(2)(p) shall take effect —

(a) on the first day of the benefit week in which the failure determination was made where, on the date of that determination, the claimant has not been paid an employment and support allowance since the failure to which that determination relates; or

(b) in any other case, on the first day of the benefit week after the end of the benefit week in respect of which the claimant was last paid an employment and support allowance]

(37) A decision made in accordance with regulation 6(2)(q) shall take effect from the first day of the benefit week in which the reduction mentioned in that sub-paragraph ceased to have effect.

(38) [34 A decision made in accordance with regulation 6(2)(r) that embodies a determination that the claimant has—

(a) limited capability for work; or

(b) limited capability for work-related activity; or

(c) limited capability for work and limited capability for work-related activity

which is the first such determination shall take effect from [43 the day after the last day of the relevant period as defined in regulation 4(4) of the Employment and Support Allowance Regulations].]

(39) A decision made in accordance with regulation 6(2)(r), following an application by the claimant, that embodies a determination that the claimant has limited capability for work-related activity shall take effect from the date of the application.]

[34 (40) A decision made in accordance with regulation 6(2)(r) that embodies a determination that the claimant has—

(a) limited capability for work; or

(b) limited capability for work-related activity; or

(c) limited capability for work and limited capability for work-related activity

where regulation 5 of the Employment and Support Allowance Regulations (assessment phase – previous claimants) applies shall take effect from the beginning of the 14th week of the person's continuous period of limited capability for work.]

[42 (41) A decision made in accordance with regulation 6(2)(t) shall take effect from the first day of the next benefit week following the day on which the determination mentioned in that sub-paragraph was made.

(42) A decision made in accordance with regulation 6(2)(u) shall take effect from the first day of the benefit week in which the reduction mentioned in that sub-paragraph ceased to have effect.]

[45 (43) Where the decision is superseded in accordance with regulation 6(2)(sa), the superseding decision shall take effect from the date on which the contributions are treated as paid in accordance with regulation 4(7) of the Social Security (Crediting and Treatment of Contributions, and National Insurance Numbers) Regulations 2001 for the purposes of entitlement to—

(i) a bereavement benefit;

(ii) a Category A or Category B retirement pension under Part II of the Contributions and Benefits Act; or

(iii) a state pension under Part 1 of the Pensions Act 2014.]

AMENDMENTS

1. Social Security and Child Support (Decisions and Appeals) Amendment (No.2) Regulations 1999 (SI 1999/1623) reg.4 (July 5, 1999).

2. Tax Credits (Decisions and Appeals) (Amendment) Regulations 1999 (SI 1999/2570) reg.10 (October 5, 1999). Note that amendments made by these regulations only have effect with respect to tax credit (reg.1(2) of the Amendment Regulations).

3. Social Security and Child Support (Decisions and Appeals), Vaccine Damage Payments and Jobseeker's Allowance (Amendment) Regulations 1999 (SI 1999/2677) reg.8 (October 18, 1999).

4. Social Security Act 1998 (Commencement No.12 and Consequential and Transitional Provisions) Order 1999 (SI 1999/3178) art.3(19) and Sch.19 para.1 (November 29, 1999).

5. Social Security and Child Support (Decisions and Appeals) Amendment Regulations 2000 (SI 2000/119) reg.2 (February 17, 2000).

6. Social Security (Work-focused Interviews) Regulations 2000 (SI 2000/897) reg.16(5) and Sch.6 para.5 (April 3, 2000).

7. Social Security and Child Support (Miscellaneous Amendments) Regulations 2000 (SI 2000/1596) reg.17 (June 19, 2000).

8. Social Security (Joint Claims: Consequential Amendments) Regulations2000 (SI 2000/1982) reg.5(c) (March 19, 2001).

9. Social Security (Breach of Community Order) (Consequential Amendments) Regulations 2001 (SI 2001/1711) reg.2(2)(d) (October 15, 2001).

10. Social Security (Loss of Benefit) (Consequential Amendments) Regulations 2002 (SI 2002/490) reg.8(c) (April 1, 2002).

11. Social Security (Claims and Payments and Miscellaneous Amendments) Regulations 2002 (SI 2002/428) reg.4(4) (April 2, 2002).

12. State Pension Credit (Consequential, Transitional and Miscellaneous Provisions) Regulations 2002 (SI 2002/3019) reg.18 (April 7, 2003).

13. State Pension Credit (Consequential, Transitional and Miscellaneous Provisions) (No.2) Regulations 2002 (SI 2002/3197) reg.6 (April 7, 2003).

14. Social Security and Child Support (Miscellaneous Amendments) Regulations 2003 (SI 2003/1050) reg.3(5) (May 5, 2003).

15. State Pension Credit (Transitional and Miscellaneous Provisions) Amendment Regulations 2003 (SI 2003/2274) reg.5(3) (October 6, 2003).

16. State Pension Credit (Miscellaneous Amendments) Regulations 2004 (SI 2004/647) reg.2 (April 5, 2004).

17. Social Security (Jobcentre Plus Interviews for Partners) Regulations 2003 (SI 2003/1886) reg.15(5) (April 12, 2004).

18. Social Security (Working Neighbourhoods) Regulations 2004 (SI 2004/959) reg.24(4) (April 26, 2004).

19. Social Security, Child Support and Tax Credits (Miscellaneous Amendments) Regulations 2005 (SI 2005/337) reg.2(5) (March 18, 2005).

20. Social Security (Housing Benefit, Council Tax Benefit, State Pension Credit and Miscellaneous Amendments) Regulations 2004 (SI 2004/2327) reg.4 (April 4, 2005).

21. Social Security (Deferral of Retirement Pensions, Shared Additional Pension and Graduated Retirement Benefit) (Miscellaneous Provisions) Regulations 2005 (SI 2005/2677) reg.9(5) (April 6, 2006).

22. Social Security (Miscellaneous Amendments) (No.2) Regulations 2006 (SI 2006/832) reg.5(3) (April 10, 2006).

23. Social Security (Miscellaneous Amendments) (No.3) Regulations 2006 (SI 2006/2377) reg.3(2) (October 2, 2006).

24. Social Security (Miscellaneous Amendments) (No.4) Regulations 2007 (SI 2007/2470) reg.3(6) and (7) (September 24, 2007).

25. Social Security (Miscellaneous Amendments) (No.2) Regulations 2008 (SI 2008/1042) reg.2 (May 19, 2008).

26. Employment and Support Allowance (Consequential Provisions) (No.2) Regulations 2008 (SI 2008/1554) regs 29 and 33 (July 27, 2008).

27. Social Security (Miscellaneous Amendments) (No.5) Regulations 2008 (SI 2008/2667) reg.3(1) and (4) (October 30, 2008).

28. Tribunals, Courts and Enforcement Act 2007 (Transitional and Consequential Provisions) Order 2008 (SI 2008/2683) Sch.1 paras 95 and 104 (November 3, 2008).

29. Social Security (Miscellaneous Amendments) (No.2) Regulations 2009 (SI 2009/1490) reg.3 (July 13, 2009).

30. Social Security (Miscellaneous Amendments) Regulations 2010 (SI 2010/510) reg.4(1) and (2) (March 4, 2010).

31. Welfare Reform Act 2009 (Section 26) (Consequential Amendments) Regulations 2010 (SI 2010/424) reg.4(1) and (5) (March 22, 2010).

32. Social Security (Loss of Benefit) Amendment Regulations 2010 (SI 2010/1160) reg.3(1) and (4) (April 1, 2010).

33. Jobseeker's Allowance (Sanctions for Failure to Attend) Regulations 2010 (SI 2010/509) reg.3(1) and (4) (April 6, 2010).

34. Social Security (Miscellaneous Amendments) (No.3) Regulations 2010 (SI 2010/840) reg.7(1) and (4) (June 28, 2010).

35. Jobseeker's Allowance (Mandatory Work Activity Scheme) Regulations 2011 (SI 2011/688) reg.18(c) (April 25, 2011).

36. Jobseeker's Allowance (Employment, Skills and Enterprise Scheme) Regulations 2011 (SI 2011/917) reg.17 (May 20, 2011).

37. Social Security (Disability Living Allowance, Attendance Allowance and Carer's Allowance) (Miscellaneous Amendments) Regulations 2011 (SI 2011/2426) reg.2 (October 31, 2011).

38. Social Security (Miscellaneous Amendments) Regulations 2012 (SI 2012/757) reg.17 (April 1, 2012).

39. Social Security and Child Support (Supersession of Appeal Decisions) Regulations 2012 (SI 2012/1267) reg.4(1) and (5) (November 3, 2008, the retrospective effect being permitted by s.103(2)(b) of the Welfare Reform Act 2012).

40. Jobseeker's Allowance (Sanctions) (Amendment) Regulations 2012 (SI 2012/2568) reg.6(1) and (4) (October 22, 2012).

41. Employment and Support Allowance (Sanctions) (Amendment) Regulations 2012 (SI 2012/2756) reg.8 (December 3, 2012).

42. Income Support (Work-Related Activity) and Miscellaneous Amendments Regulations 2014 (SI 2014/1097) reg.12(1) and (5) (April 28, 2014).

43. Jobseeker's Allowance (Extended Period of Sickness) Amendment Regulations 2015 (SI 2015/339) reg.7(1) and (3) (March 30, 2015).

44. Pensions Act 2014 (Consequential, Supplementary and Incidental Amendments) Order 2015 (SI 2015/1985) art.18(1) and (6) (April 6, 2016).

45. Social Security (Credits, and Crediting and Treatment of Contributions) (Consequential and Miscellaneous Amendments) Regulations 2016 (SI 2016/1145) reg.4(1) and (5) (January 1, 2017).

46. Loans for Mortgage Interest Regulations 2017 (SI 2017/725) reg.18 and Sch.5 para.11(1) and (3), as amended by the Loans for Mortgage Interest and Social Fund Maternity Grant (Amendment) Regulations 2018 (SI 2018/307) reg.2(11) and (18)(e) (April 6, 2018, subject to a saving – see the annotation to paras (12) to (17G) and (18) to (23), below).

47. Social Security (Scotland) Act 2018 (Disability Assistance for Children and Young People) (Consequential Modifications) Order 2021 (SI 2021/786) art.6(1) and (5) (July 26, 2021).

48. Social Security (Disability Assistance for Working Age People) (Consequential Amendments) Order 2022 (SI 2022/177) art.6(1) and (5) (March 21, 2022).

49. The Carer's Assistance (Carer Support Payment) (Scotland) Regulations 2023 (Consequential Amendments) Order 2023 (SI 2023/1218) art.9 (November 19, 2023).

Definitions

"appeal tribunal"–see s.17(7) of the Social Security Act 1998.
"appropriate office"—see reg.3(11).
"assessed income period"—see reg.1(3).
"bereavement benefit"—*ibid.*
"benefit week"—see para.(3).
"the Board"—see reg.1(3).
"claimant"—*ibid.*
"the Claims and Payments Regulations"—*ibid.*
"Commissioner"–see s.17(7) of the Social Security Act 1998.
"the Contributions and Benefits Act"—see s.84 of the Social Security Act 1998.
"disability benefit decision"—see reg.7A(1).
"disability determination"—*ibid.*
"the Employment and Support Allowance Regulations"—see reg.1(3).
"failure determination"—*ibid.*
"incapacity benefit decision"—See reg.7A(1).
"incapacity determination"—*ibid.*
"the Income Support Regulations"—see reg.1(3).
"the Jobseekers Act"—see s.84 of the Social Security Act 1998.
"the Jobseeker's Allowance Regulations"—see reg.1(3).
"a joint-claim jobseeker's allowance"—*ibid.*
"the Loans for Mortgage Interest Regulations"—*ibid.*
"limited capability for work"—*ibid.*
"owner-occupier loan payments"—*ibid.*
"owner-occupier payments"—*ibid.*
"payee"—see reg.7A(1).
"standard rate"—see paras(17) and (21).
"Scottish disability benefit"—see reg.1(3).
"state pension credit"—*ibid.*
"State Pension Credit Regulations"—*ibid.*
"work-focused interview"—*ibid.*

General Note

This regulation is not quite as complicated as it looks at first sight. As is explained in para.(1), the regulation provides exceptions to the general rule that a supersession decision takes effect from the date it is made or, where applicable, the date the application for supersession was made (s.10(5) of the Social Security Act 1998). The structure of the regulations is as follows: 2.481

Paragraph (1):	Introductory.
Paragraphs (2)–(4):	Supersession for change of circumstances.
Paragraph (5):	Supersession of a tribunal or Commissioner's decision for error of fact.
Paragraphs (6) and 6(A):	Supersession following a test case.
Paragraph (7):	Supersession following an award of another relevant benefit.
Paragraph (7A):	Supersession following a change in election whether to receive an increase in pension or a lump sum following a deferral of pension.
Paragraph (8):	Supersession of an award of jobseeker's allowance following a finding of voluntary unemployment.
Paragraph (8ZA):	Supersession of an award of jobseeker's allowance following the imposition of sanctions for failure to take part in employment schemes.
Paragraph (8A):	Supersession where a late or unpaid contribution has been treated as paid.

Paragraphs (9) and (9A):	Supersession advantageous to claimant of an award of attendance allowance or disability living allowance.
Paragraph (10):	Supersession of an award of short-term incapacity benefit to increase the rate following an award of the highest rate of the care component of disability living allowance.
Paragraph (11):	Supersession of an award of incapacity benefit following a determination that the claimant is to be treated as incapable of work because he or she is suffering from a severe condition.
Paragraphs (12)–(12G):	Supersession of decisions relating to loans for mortgage interest
Paragraphs (13)–(17G):	*Revoked*
Paragraph (17H):	Supersession in an employment and support allowance case where a non-dependant becomes entitled to main phase employment and support allowance.
Paragraphs (18)–(23):	*Revoked*
Paragraph (24):	Supersession in a case where the claimant is a young person and was receiving a reduced amount of jobseeker's allowance on account of failing to complete a course and the Secretary of State has issued a certificate stating that the claimant had good cause for failing to complete the course.
Paragraphs (25) and (26):	Supersession following a determination that the claimant has failed without good cause to take part in a work-focused interview.
Paragraph (27):	Supersession in order to reduce benefit because an offender has breached a community order.
Paragraph (28):	Supersession in order to remove benefit because a person has been convicted of benefit offences.
Paragraphs (29)–(29B):	Supersession in a state pension credit case on the ending of an assessed income period.
Paragraph (29C):	Supersession where late provision of information or evidence has delayed the specification of a new assessed income period.
Paragraphs (30) and (30A):	Supersession following a change in relevant legislation.
Paragraphs (31) and (32):	Supersession following a personal capability assessment carried out before the all work test becomes applicable.
Paragraph (33):	Supersession of a decision determined by a tribunal or Commissioner under s.26 of the Social Security Act 1998 while a test case was pending.
Paragraph (34):	Supersession of a decision of a tribunal in relation to income support where another tribunal has subsequently decided that the claimant is incapable of work.
Paragraphs (35) to (37):	Supersession in an employment and support allowance case where there has been a failure determination.
Paragraphs (38) to (40):	Supersession in an employment and support allowance case following receipt of a new medical opinion.
Paragraphs (41) and (42):	Supersession following a determination that a claimant of income support has failed to undertake work-related activity or to end a reduction made in consequence of such a determination.
Paragraph (43):	Supersession following the late payment of contributions for a bereavement benefit, a retirement pension or a state pension.

Note that Schs 3A, 3B and 3C make further provision in respect of income-related benefits and sometimes, but not always, take precedence over the provisions of this regulation (see para.(1)).

Paragraph (1)

2.482 Section 10(5) of the Social Security Act 1998 provides that a supersession decision takes effect from the date it is made or, where applicable, the date the application for supersession was made. Schedule 3A provides further refinement for income support and jobseeker's allowance cases as do Sch.3B for state pension credit cases and Sch.3C for employment and support allowance cases. Subparagraph (a) has the effect that those Schedules take precedence over most, but not all, of the other paragraphs of this regulation. The exceptions are paras (2)(b) or (bb) (changes of circumstances advantageous to a claimant), (29) (certain decisions relating to state pension credit) or (30) (change of legislation). Where a case is not covered by this regulation or by those schedules, s.10(5) applies.

Paragraph (2)

2.483 Because there is some overlap between reg.6(2)(a) and some other grounds for supersession, e.g., reg.6((2)(e), and there is also some overlap between this paragraph and some other paragraphs in reg.7, it is important to check that no provision more favourable to a claimant applies instead of para.(2) (see *DS v SSWP (PIP)* [2016] UKUT 538 AAC; [2017] AACR 19 and *OL v SSWP (ESA)* [2018] UKUT 135 (AAC), discussed in the note to reg.6(2)).

A supersession on the ground of change of circumstances advantageous to the claimant is effective from the date of the change if the change is notified within a month (or such longer period as is allowed under reg.8) but is otherwise effective only from the date of notification. In *PH v SSWP (DLA)* [2013] UKUT 268 (AAC), it was held that a firmer prognosis amounted to a change of circumstances that could justify a supersession extending an award of disability living allowance but the judge said that it was difficult to see how reg.7(2)(a)(ii) could apply in such a context so that, in order to be effective, any application for supersession would have to be made before the award expired. In practice, a renewal claim would generally be made instead and the issue arose in that case only because the claimant had not made a renewal claim but had successfully appealed against a supersession decision terminating her award prematurely. A claimant who does notify a change of circumstances within one month is entitled to rely on reg.7(2)(a) even if he or she then fails to answer a further question from the Secretary of State within a month (*YZ v SSWP (ESA)* [2016] UKUT 430 (AAC)).

Where the change is not advantageous to the claimant, the supersession is generally effective from the date of change or, in the case of incapacity and disability cases, from the date when the change should have been reported. Presumably, para. (2) does not apply to those attendance allowance and disability living allowance cases where para.(9) applies or, indeed, to any cases where any of paras (10)–(34) applies and the latter provision is in mandatory terms. However, it was suggested in *SK v SSWP (JSA)* [2013] UKUT 138 (AAC) that there may be a mere discretion where para.(12) is concerned, because that provision is expressed in discretionary terms.

2.484 It was pointed out in that case that notifying a change of circumstances or providing information about such a change is not necessarily the same as applying for a supersession, so that any supersession in the light of the information might be on the Secretary of State's initiative and therefore within the scope of subpara.(bb), rather than subpara.(b). It was also held that, where a change of circumstances in fact takes place *after* the date on which the Secretary of State "commenced action with a view to supersession" by asking for information, the change is effective from the date of the change of circumstances.

The inclusion of a reference to a disabled person's partner in head (i) of the new version of reg.7(2)(bc) reverses the effect of *SSWP v JJ* [2009] UKUT 2 (AAC).

See reg.7A for definitions material to para.(2)(c). Regulation 7(2)(c) is concerned to ensure that an appropriate effective date is fixed where the effect of a supersession due to a change of circumstances is that benefit has been overpaid and the overpayment is likely to be recoverable under s.71 of the Social Security Administration Act 1992. (Regulation 3(5)(b) and (c) makes similar provision by way of revision where the original decision was made in ignorance of, or on a mistake as to, a material fact). Section 71(5A) of the 1992 Act provides that an overpayment can generally be recovered only if a decision has properly been given in terms of revision or supersession, a point reiterated in *CIS/4434/2004*. If the decision is in terms of supersession, there will only be an overpayment if the date from which the supersession is effective is before the date on which payment ceased. It is therefore not surprising that the question whether a claimant has "failed to notify" a change of circumstances for the purposes of reg.7(2)(c)(ii) was found in *CDLA/1823/2004* to be similar to the familiar question whether a person has "failed to disclose" a change of circumstances for the purposes of s.71. The Commissioner noted that the phrase "regulations under the Administration Act" refers to reg.32 of the Social Security (Claims and Payments) Regulations 1987, which was considered in some detail in the context of s.71 by the Court of Appeal in *B v Secretary of State for Work and Pensions* [2005] EWCA Civ 929; [2005] 1 W.L.R. 3796 (also reported as *R(IS) 9/06*). He suggested that there will be a failure to notify a change of circumstances if there is a breach of clear and unambiguous instructions, as was the position in *R(IS) 9/06* but that otherwise the issue is likely to be whether the Secretary of State could reasonably have expected the claimant to notify him of the material fact. Determining the question whether reg.7(2)(c)(ii) applies may, therefore, require some evidence as to the instructions given to the claimant. See also *R(A) 2/06*. The practice of dealing with the recovery of overpayments separately from decisions as to entitlement may lead to the same complex issues of fact being considered twice.

2.485 The application of head (ii) is particularly important in relation to attendance allowance, disability living allowance, severe disablement allowance and industrial injuries disablement benefit because heads (ii), (iv) and (v) have the combined effect that supersessions are not retrospective where the change of circumstances relates to a "disability determination" as defined in reg.7A, except where the claimant both was required to notify the change of circumstances and knew or could reasonably have been expected to know that the change of circumstances should be notified. This means that, except where the claimant has clearly been at fault, there is no overpayment and so any question of the recoverability of an overpayment simply does not arise.

The regulation thus includes important safeguards for claimants and, in *SM v SSWP (DLA)* [2021] UKUT 119 (AAC), the Upper Tribunal emphasised the importance of making findings of fact that address the issues raised and, in particular, whether the claimant could reasonably have been expected to know that there had been a change of circumstances that he was under a legal obligation to notify. Even though there was evidence upon which the First-tier Tribunal's decision could properly have found that reg.7(2)(c)(ii) applied, the Upper Tribunal declined to remake the decision on the papers because of the element of judgment involved. The First-tier Tribunal's finding that there had been "some improvement" in the claimant's condition was not by itself sufficiently detailed to justify its decision and the first-tier Tribunal had not made any findings as to the information provided to the claimant about his obligations to disclose changes of circumstances.

The revocation of reg.7(2)(c)(iii) and its replacement with heads (iv) and (v), which contain no exceptions in respect of incapacity determinations, deals with the anomalies revealed in such incapacity benefit cases as *R(IB) 1/05* and *CIB/763/2004*, where there had been changes of circumstances but no failure by the claimant to disclose them (so that head (ii) did not apply) but the Commissioner found that head (iii) did not apply either. Now, any supersession will be effective from the date of the change of circumstances by virtue of head (v). That, of course, will be at least as early as the date applicable under head (ii) and it might seem odd at first sight that a supersession may be effective from an earlier date when there has been no failure to disclose a change of circumstances than where there has been. However, this only acts to the disadvantage of a claimant where a payment of benefit has not already been made. If it has already been made, it will not be recoverable due to the lack of a failure to disclose the change of circumstances. If the payment has not already been made, there are obvious reasons why the supersession should take effect from the date of the change so that only the benefit to which the claimant is properly entitled is paid.

It was held in *SSWP v JL (DLA)* [2011] UKUT 293 (AAC); [2012] AACR 14 that the deletion of reg.7(2)(c)(iii) and the insertion of heads (iv) and (v) were not retrospective and enable a supersession to take effect only from April 10, 2006 or a later date although the amendments can apply where the relevant change of circumstances occurred on an earlier date. The question whether a supersession can take effect from an earlier date must therefore be determined under the legislation in force at that date. **2.486**

There may also still be some difficulties in incapacity cases due to the practice of determining that a person is incapable of work in the contest of "credits" and then relying on that determination when determining entitlement to income support (see reg.10). In *CIB/1599/2005*, the claimant was in receipt of income support on the basis of a decision, made for the purposes of incapacity credits, that he was incapable of work. He failed to inform the social security office that he had taken some casual employment. The Commissioner held that reg.7(2)(c)(ii) did not apply because the claimant was not required by "regulations under the Administration Act" to notify his change of circumstances. Regulation 32 of the Social Security (Claims and Payments) Regulations 1987 applies only to benefit cases and not to "credits" cases. That meant that the "credits" decision could not be superseded with effect from a date before it was made. Given the terms of reg.10, that in turn presumably also limited the scope for superseding the award of income support retrospectively, although the Commissioner expressed no view on that issue.

Paragraph (5)

This provides consistency between, on the one hand, revision and supersession of decisions of the Secretary of State on the ground of error of fact (under regs 3(5) and 6(2)(b)) and, on the other hand, supersession of decisions of tribunals on the ground of error of fact (under reg.6(2)(c)). However, in *JA v SSWP (DLA)* [2014] UKUT 44 (AAC), the judge drew attention to the anomalies that can arise because a decision of the Secretary of State may be altered on revision in the same circumstances as a decision of a tribunal may be altered on supersession and asked whether the distinction was necessary. A decision of a tribunal cannot be revised under s.9 of the Social Security Act 1998 but he said that it was not obvious why the grounds of revision in reg.3(5) were not grounds of supersession to which this paragraph might apply. **2.487**

Paragraph (6)

Where a decision of the Secretary of State is superseded under reg.6(2)(b)(i) because it has been shown to have been erroneous in point of law by a decision of the Upper Tribunal or a court involving a different claimant, the supersession will be effective from the date of the decision of the Upper Tribunal or court. However, showing that a decision was based on a mistake of law rather than a different understanding of the facts may not be easy (*MP v SSWP (DLA)* [2010] UKUT 130 (AAC)). **2.488**

There is a question as to whether para.(6) is compatible with European Union law in a case where an error is revealed by a decision of the Court of Justice of the European Union, because a ruling of that Court is not a determination within the scope of s.27(1) of the Social Security Act 1998, whereas a ruling of a superior

British court is. That question was considered but not answered in *JK v SSWP (DLA)* [2013] UKUT 218 (AAC).

Paragraphs (8) and (8ZA)

2.489 These paragraphs are concerned with the commencement date of a period of reduction in the amount of jobseeker's allowance, imposed where a claimant is considered to be voluntarily unemployed or as a sanction.

Paragraph (9)

2.490 Supersessions of decisions concerning attendance allowance and disability living allowance on the ground of changes of circumstances which are disadvantageous to claimants are dealt with under para.(2)(c). This paragraph deals with supersessions on the grounds of changes of circumstances that are advantageous to the claimant. A claimant is given a month in which to notify the relevant office of the change of circumstances, but *SSWP v DA* [2009] UKUT 214 (AAC) confirms that the month runs from the end of the qualifying period for a higher rate of benefit following a change of circumstances, rather than the date of the change of circumstances itself. It is difficult to envisage a situation in which para.(9)(c) can operate because if the claimant was not entitled to any benefit before the change occurred, a claim would have been appropriate rather than a supersession (*R(I) 56/54* at [28] and see, now, s.8(2) of the Social Security Act 1998). Perhaps its use is envisaged in cases where a claimant becomes terminally ill during the qualifying period, although it is arguable that, even then, a new claim would be appropriate. Paragraph (9)(b) is in terms similar to para.(2)(b) with variations that seem designed merely to take account of the qualifying periods for attendance allowance and disability living allowance and to require the supersession to be effective from the first pay day after the claimant qualifies for the new rate.

Paragraph (9A)

2.491 March 8, 2001 was the date the European Court of Justice decided *Jauch v Pensionsversicherungsanstalt der Arbeiter* (C-215/99) and October 18, 2007 was the date the Court gave a ruling in *Commission of the European Communities v European Parliament and Council of the European Union* (C-299/05) [2007] E.C.R. I–8695, applying principles established in *Jauch*, that had the effect that it was, and had previously been, unlawful for the Secretary of State to terminate an award of attendance allowance, carer's allowance or the care component of disability living allowance on the ground that a person was moving from Great Britain to elsewhere in the European Economic Area or to Switzerland. This paragraph enables a person whose award of one of these benefits was terminated on that ground after the decision in *Jauch* to be re-awarded benefit from the date of the Court's later judgment. It is arguable that "a superseding decision" in subpara.(b) includes a superseding decision made by the Secretary of State that was upheld on an appeal to an appeal tribunal.

Paragraphs (12)–(17G) and (18)–(23)

2.492 These paragraphs are, or were, all concerned with provision for those liable for mortgage interest payments. Paragraphs (12A) to (12G) have been inserted to replace paragraphs (13) to (17G) and (18) to (23). The new provisions apply only in relation to loans for mortgage interest under the Welfare Reform and Work Act 2016, whereas the old provisions applied in cases where the housing costs element of the applicable amount for income-related benefits included an amount in respect of interest on certain loans which were therefore met through the payment of benefit rather than through further loans. The amendments are made with effect from April 6, 2018, but subject to transitional provisions in regs. 19, 19A and 20 of the Loans for Mortgage Interest Regulations 2017 (SI 2017/725). For the revoked paragraphs, see the 2017–18 edition of this work (although note that reg.7(17B)(b) was revoked by reg.4 of the Social Security (Miscellaneous Amendments No.5) Regulations 2017 (SI 2017/1187) with effect from December 1, 2017).

Paragraph (12A) is not predicated on delay by a lender, but simply on the late supply of information for any reason. However, it has been held that the relationship between para.(12) and para.(2) is such that there appears to be a mere discretion to apply para.(12) rather than para.(2) (*SK v SSWP (JSA)* [2013] UKUT 138 (AAC)), although it is arguable that it was intended that the general provision in para.(2) should always give way to the specific provision in para.(12) (see *OL v SSWP (ESA)* [2018] UKUT 135 (AAC), considered in the note to reg.6(2)).

Paragraphs (31) and (32)

With the abolition of incapacity benefit, these paragraphs have become redundant. **2.493**

Paragraphs (38)–(40)

Where a decision is made during the "assessment phase" of employment and support allowance (broadly during the first thirteen weeks of a period of entitlement, but less in some circumstances), a decision that is *adverse* to the claimant and results in the termination of an award takes effect immediately under s.10(5) of the Social Security Act 1998. However, paras (38) and (40) have the effect that a decision *in favour* of the claimant takes effect only from the end of the "assessment phase", because that is the earliest date from which an award may be increased so as to include the work-related activity component or the support component (see ss.2(2)(a) and (3)(a) and 4(4)(a) and (5)(a) of the Welfare Reform Act 2007 — in Vol.I). Paragraph (38) applies in the ordinary case and para.(40) applies where a person ceases to be entitled to employment and support allowance after less than thirteen weeks but becomes entitled again within twelve weeks. **2.494**

The purpose of para.(39) is less clear since it appears merely to duplicate the effect of s.10(5) of the 1998 Act. Perhaps it is thought necessary, for the avoidance of doubt, because grounds given by a claimant for an application for supersession are unlikely to invoke reg.6(2)(r) rather than, say, reg.6(2)(a)(i) or (b) and so the obtaining of the medical evidence justifying supersession under reg.6(2)(r) may have been entirely on the Secretary of State's initiative and, indeed, unrelated to the application made by the claimant.

[1 [4 Definitions for the purposes of Chapters I and II]

7A.—(1) For the purposes of regulations 3(5)(c), 6(2)(g) [56(2)(r)] [2, 7(2)(c) and (5)]— **2.495**

"disability benefit decision" means a decision to award a relevant benefit embodied in or necessary to which is a disability determination,

"disability determination" means—

(a) in the case of a decision as to an award of an attendance allowance or a disability living allowance, whether the person satisfies any of the conditions in section 64, 72(1) or 73(1) to (3), as the case may be, of the Contributions and Benefits Act,

(b) in the case of a decision as to an award of severe disablement allowance, whether the person is disabled for the purpose of section 68 of the Contributions and Benefits Act, or

(c) in the case of a decision as to an award of industrial injuries benefit, whether the existence or extent of any disablement is sufficient for the purposes of section 103 or 108 of the Contributions and Benefits Act or for the benefit to be paid at the rate which was in payment immediately prior to that decision;

[4 "employment and support allowance decision" means a decision to award a relevant benefit or relevant credit embodied in or necessary to which is a determination that a person has or is to be treated as having limited capability for work under Part 1 of the Welfare Reform Act;]

"incapacity benefit decision" means a decision to award a relevant benefit [2 or relevant credit] embodied in or necessary to which is a determination that a person is or is to be treated as incapable of work under Part XIIA of the Contributions and Benefits Act [3 or an award of long term incapacity benefit under regulation 17(1) (transitional awards of long-term incapacity benefit) of the Social Security (Incapacity Benefit) (Transitional) Regulations 1995],

"incapacity determination" means a determination whether a person is incapable of work by applying the [2 personal capability assessment] in regulation 24 of the Social Security (Incapacity for Work) (General) Regulations 1995 or whether a person is to be treated as incapable of work in accordance with regulation 10 (certain persons with a severe condition to be treated as incapable of work) or 27 (exceptional circumstances) of those Regulations, and

[4 "limited capability for work determination" means a determination whether a person has limited capability for work by applying the test of limited capability for work or whether a person is to be treated as having limited capability for work in accordance with regulation 20 of the Employment and Support Allowance Regulations;]

"payee" means a person to whom a benefit referred to in paragraph (a), (b) or (c) of the definition of "disability determination", or a benefit referred to in the definition of "incapacity benefit decision" [4 or "employment and support allowance decision"] is payable.

(2) Where a person's receipt of or entitlement to a benefit ("the first benefit") is a condition of his being entitled to any other benefit, allowance or advantage ("a second benefit") and a decision is revised under regulation 3(5)(c) or a superseding decision is made under regulation 6(2) to which regulation 7(2)(c)(ii) applies, the effect of which is that the first benefit ceases to be payable, or becomes payable at a lower rate than was in payment immediately prior to that revision or supersession, a consequent decision as to his entitlement to the second benefit shall take effect from the date of the change in his entitlement to the first benefit.]

AMENDMENTS

1. Social Security and Child Support (Decisions and Appeals) Amendment (No.2) Regulations 1999 (SI 1999/1623) reg.5 (July 5, 1999).

2. Social Security and Child Support (Miscellaneous Amendments) Regulations 2000 (SI 2000/1596) reg.18 (June 19, 2000).

3. Social Security (Miscellaneous Amendments) (No.4) Regulations 2007 (SI 2007/2470) reg.3(8) (September 24, 2007).

4. Employment and Support Allowance (Consequential Provisions) (No.2) Regulations 2008 (SI 2008/1554) regs 29 and 34 (July 27, 2008).

5. Social Security (Miscellaneous Amendments) (No.3) Regulations 2010 (SI 2010/840) reg.7(1) and (5) (June 28, 2010).

DEFINITIONS

"the Contributions and Benefits Act"—see s.84 of the Social Security Act 1998.
"the Employment and Support Allowance Regulations"—see reg.1(3).
"limited capability for work"—*ibid.*
"relevant benefit"—see s.39(1) of the Social Security Act 1998.
"relevant credit"—see reg.1(3).
"the Welfare Reform Act"—*ibid.*

General Note

"disability determination"

In *CA/2650/2006*, the Commissioner held that the reference to s.64 of the Contributions and Benefits Act (which has a different structure from that in ss. 72 and 73) in head (a) of the definition of "disability determination" refers only to "determinations whether the conditions set out in section 64(2) and (3) were satisfied (and possibly extending to age and non-entitlement to DLA)" and so does not extend to determinations as to residence or presence. 2.496

7B. *Omitted.* 2.497

7C. *Omitted.* 2.498

Effective date for late notifications of change of circumstances

8.—(1) For the purposes of regulation 7(2) [2 and (9)], a longer period of time may be allowed for the notification of a change of circumstances in so far as it affects the effective date of the change where the conditions specified in the following provisions of this regulation are satisfied. 2.499

(2) An application for the purposes of regulation 7(2) [2 or (9)] shall be made by the claimant or a person acting on his behalf.

(3) The application referred to in paragraph (2) shall—

(a) contain particulars of the relevant change of circumstances and the reasons for the failure to notify the change of circumstances on an earlier date; and

[4 (b) be made—

(i) within 13 months of the date the change occurred; or

(ii) in the case of an application for the purposes of regulation 7(9)(b), within 13 months of the date on which the claimant satisfied the conditions of entitlement to the particular rate of benefit.]

(4) An application under this regulation shall not be granted unless the Secretary of State is satisfied [1 or the Board are satisfied] that—

(a) it is reasonable to grant the application;

(b) the change of circumstances notified by the applicant is relevant to the decision which is to be superseded; and

(c) special circumstances are relevant to the application and as a result of those special circumstances it was not practicable for the applicant to notify the change of circumstances within one month of the change occurring.

(5) In determining whether it is reasonable to grant the application, the Secretary of State [1 or the Board] shall have regard to the principle that the greater the amount of time that has elapsed between the date one month after the change of circumstances occurred and the date the application for the purposes of regulation 7(2) [2 or (9)] is made, the more compelling should be the special circumstances on which the application is based.

(6) In determining whether it is reasonable to grant an application, no account shall be taken of the following—

(a) that the applicant or any person acting for him was unaware of, or misunderstood, the law applicable to his case (including ignorance or misunderstanding of the time limits imposed by these Regulations); or

(b) that a [3 the Upper Tribunal] or a court has taken a different view of the law from that previously understood and applied.

(7) An application under this regulation which has been refused may not be renewed.

AMENDMENTS

1. Tax Credits (Decisions and Appeals) (Amendment) Regulations 1999 (SI 1999/2570) reg.11 (October 5, 1999). Note that amendments made by these regulations only have effect with respect to tax credit (reg.1(2) of the Amendment Regulations).

2. Social Security and Child Support (Decisions and Appeals) Amendment Regulations 2000 (SI 2000/119) reg.3 (February 17, 2000).

3. Tribunals, Courts and Enforcement Act 2007 (Transitional and Consequential Provisions) Order 2008 (SI 2008/2683) Sch.1 paras 95 and 106 (November 3, 2008).

4. Social Security (Miscellaneous Amendments) Regulations 2010 (SI 2010/510) reg.4(1) and (3) (March 4, 2010).

DEFINITIONS

"the Board"—see reg.1(3).
"claimant"—*ibid.*

GENERAL NOTE

Paragraph (6)(b)

2.500 See the note to reg.4(6)(b) which is in similar terms.

CHAPTER III

OTHER MATTERS

Certificates of recoverable benefits

2.501 **9.** A certificate of recoverable benefits may be reviewed under section 10 of the 1997 Act where the Secretary of State is satisfied that—

(a) a mistake (whether in computation of the amount specified or otherwise) occurred in the preparation of the certificate;
(b) the benefit recovered from a person who makes a compensation payment (as defined in section 1 of the 1997 Act) is in excess of the amount due to the Secretary of State;
(c) incorrect or insufficient information was supplied to the Secretary of State by the person who applied for the certificate and in consequence the amount of benefit specified in the certificate was less than it would have been had the information supplied been correct or sufficient; or
(d) a ground for appeal is satisfied under section 11 of the 1997 Act.

DEFINITIONS

"the 1997 Act"—see reg.1(3).
"appeal"—*ibid.*

GENERAL NOTE

2.502 These grounds of review are very wide. In *CCR/3391/2005*, the Commissioner suggested that the Secretary of State should always consider reviewing a decision against which an appeal has been brought, so that unnecessary cases did not reach tribunals. Regulation 9(d) may have been drafted with such an approach in mind. A submission to a tribunal would then, in effect, be an explanation for the Secretary of State not reviewing the decision in the light of the grounds of appeal. Where the appellant was the compensator, grounds of appeal were often accompanied by a considerable amount of new evidence obtained in the course of defending the compensation proceedings. Considering a review was, in such circumstances, the first opportunity the Secretary of State had to take such evidence into account. Regulation 9ZB is intended to ensure that a review now takes place *before* any appeal is brought, although it is still possible to review a decision again in the light of any further evidence provided with a notice of appeal.

[1 Review of certificates

9ZA.—(1) A certificate may be reviewed under section 10 of the 1997 Act where the Secretary of State is satisfied that— **2.503**

(a) a mistake (whether in the computation of the amount specified or otherwise) occurred in the preparation of the certificate;

(b) the lump sum payment recovered from a compensator who makes a compensation payment (as defined in section 1A(5) of the 1997 Act) is in excess of the amount due to the Secretary of State;

(c) incorrect or insufficient information was supplied to the Secretary of State by the compensator who applied for the certificate and in consequence the amount of lump sum payment specified in the certificate was less than it would have been had the information supplied been correct or sufficient;

(d) a ground for appeal is satisfied under section 11 of the 1997 Act or an appeal has been made under that section; or

(e) a certificate has been issued and, for any reason, a recoverable lump sum payment was not included in that certificate.

(2) In this regulation and regulations 1(3) in paragraph (b) of the definition of "party to the proceedings", [3 29 [4 . . .]], where applicable—

(a) any reference to the 1997 Act is to be construed so as to include a reference to that Act as applied by regulation 2 of the Lump Sum Payments Regulations and, where applicable, as modified by Schedule 1 to those Regulations;

(b) [2 "certificate" means a certificate of recoverable lump sum payments, including where any of the amounts is nil;]

(c) "lump sum payment" is a payment to which section 1A(2) of the 1997 Act applies;

(d) "P" is to be construed in accordance with regulations 4(1)(a)(i) and 5 of the Lump Sum Payments Regulations.]

AMENDMENTS

1. Social Security (Recovery of Benefits) (Lump Sum Payments) Regulations 2008 (SI 2008/1596) Sch.2 para.1(b) (October 1, 2008).

2. Social Security (Miscellaneous Amendments) (No.3) Regulations 2008 (SI 2008/2365) reg.6(1) and (4) (October 1, 2008).

3. Tribunals, Courts and Enforcement Act 2007 (Transitional and Consequential Provisions) Order 2008 (SI 2008/2683) Sch.1 paras 95 and 107 (November 3, 2008).

4. Social Security, Child Support, Vaccine Damage and Other Payments (Decisions and Appeals) (Amendment) Regulations 2013 (SI 2013/2380) reg.4(1) and (10)(a) (October 28, 2013, subject to a saving).

DEFINITIONS

"the 1997 Act"—see reg.1(3) and para.(2)(a).
"certificate"—see para.(2)(b).
"lump sum payment"—see para.(2)(c).
"P"—see para.(2)(d).

[1 Consideration of review before appeal

2.504 **9ZB.** (1) This regulation applies in a case where—

(a) the Secretary of State has issued a certificate of recoverable benefits or certificate of recoverable lump sum payments; and

(b) that certificate is accompanied by a notice to the effect that there is a right of appeal in relation to the certificate only if the Secretary of State has considered an application for review of the certificate.

(2) In a case to which this regulation applies, a person has a right of appeal under section 11 of the 1997 Act against the certificate only if the Secretary of State has considered an application for review of the certificate under section 10 of that Act.]

AMENDMENT

1. Social Security, Child Support, Vaccine Damage and Other Payments (Decisions and Appeals) (Amendment) Regulations 2013 (SI 2013/2380) reg.4(1) and (6) (October 28, 2013).

DEFINITIONS

"the 1997 Act"—see reg.1(3).
"appeal"—*ibid.*

GENERAL NOTE

2.505 This regulation is made under s.11(2A) and (2B) of the Social Security (Recovery of Benefits) Act 1997 and makes, for appeals under that Act, provision equivalent to reg.3ZA(1) and (2). For the power to treat a purported appeal as an application for review where there is no right of appeal as a result of this provision, see reg.29(6).

[1 Correction of accidental errors

2.506 **9A.**—(1) Accidental errors in a decision of the Secretary of State or an officer of the Board under a relevant enactment within the meaning of section 28(3), or in any record of such a decision, may be corrected by the Secretary of State or an officer of the Board, as the case may be, at any time.

(2) A correction made to, or to the record of, a decision shall be deemed to be part of the decision, or of that record, and the Secretary of State or an officer of the Board shall give a written notice of the correction as soon as practicable to the claimant.

(3) In calculating the time within which an application can be made under regulation 3(1)(b) for a decision to be revised [2. . .] there shall be disregarded any day falling before the day on which notice was given of the decision or to the record thereof under paragraph (2).]

AMENDMENTS

1. Social Security and Child Support (Decisions and Appeals) (Miscellaneous Amendments) Regulations 2002 (SI 2002/1379) reg.4 (May 20, 2002).

2. Tribunals, Courts and Enforcement Act 2007 (Transitional and Consequential Provisions) Order 2008 (SI 2008/2683) Sch.1 paras 95 and 108 (November 3, 2008).

DEFINITIONS

"appeal"—see reg.1(3).
"the Board"—*ibid.*
"claimant"—*ibid.*

[1 Effect of determination as to capacity or capability for work

10.—(1) This regulation applies to a determination whether a person— 2.507
(a) is capable or incapable of work;
(b) is to be treated as capable or incapable of work;
(c) has or does not have limited capability for work; or
(d) is to be treated as having or not having limited capability for work.

(2) A determination (including a determination made following a change of circumstances) as set out in paragraph (1) which is embodied in or necessary to a decision under Chapter II of Part I of the Act or on which such a decision is based shall be conclusive for the purposes of any further decision.]

AMENDMENT

1. Employment and Support Allowance (Consequential Provisions) (No.2) Regulations 2008 (SI 2008/1554) regs 29 and 36 (July 27, 2008).

DEFINITIONS

"the Act"—see reg.1(3).
"limited capability for work"—*ibid.*

GENERAL NOTE

Note that a decision that a person was *not*, or was not to be treated as, incapable of work was not of continuing effect. Consequently, it operated to allow supersession of any award of benefit current at the time it was made but it did not operate so as to prevent a person from making a new claim or a further application for supersession, although he or she might not be entitled to benefit while a new assessment was arranged (*R(IB)1/01* and *R(IB)2/01*). 2.508

Secretary of State to determine certain matters

11. Where, in relation to a determination for any purpose to which Part XIIA of the Contributions and Benefits Act [1 or Part 1 of the Welfare Reform Act] applies, an issue arises as to— 2.509
(a) whether a person is, or is to be treated as, capable or incapable of work in respect of any period; or
[1 (aa) whether a person is, or is to be treated as, having or not having limited capability for work; or]
(b) whether a person is terminally ill,

that issue shall be determined by the Secretary of State, notwithstanding that other matters fall to be determined by another authority.

AMENDMENT

1. Employment and Support Allowance (Consequential Provisions) (No.2) Regulations 2008 (SI 2008/1554) regs 29 and 37 (July 27, 2008).

DEFINITIONS

"the Contributions and Benefits Act"—see s.84 of the Social Security Act 1998.
"limited capability for work"—see reg.1(3).

[1 Issues for decision by officers of Inland Revenue

2.510 **11A.**—(1) Where, on consideration of any claim or other matter, it appears to the Secretary of State that an issue arises which, by virtue of section 8 of the Transfer Act, falls to be decided by an officer of the Board, he shall refer that issue to the Board.

(2) Where—

(a) the Secretary of State has decided any claim or other matter on an assumption of facts—
   (i) as to which there appeared to him to be no dispute, but
   (ii) concerning which, had an issue arisen, that issue would have fallen, by virtue of section 8 of the Transfer Act, to be decided by an officer of the Board; and
(b) an application for revision or an application for supersession [2 or an appeal] is made in relation to the decision of that claim or other matter; and
(c) it appears to the Secretary of State on [2 receipt of the application or appeal] that such an issue arises,

he shall refer that issue to the Board.

(3) Pending the final decision of any issue which has been referred to the Board in accordance with paragraph (1) or (2) above, the Secretary of State may—

(a) determine any other issue arising on consideration of the claim or other matter or, as the case may be, of the application,
(b) seek a preliminary opinion of the Board on the issue referred and decide the claim or other matter or, as the case may be, the application in accordance with that opinion on that issue; or
(c) defer making any decision on the claim or other matter or, as the case may be, the application.

(4) On receipt by the Secretary of State of the final decision of an issue which has been referred to the Board in accordance with paragraph (1) or (2) above, the Secretary of State that—

(a) in a case to which paragraph (3)(b) above applies—
   (i) consider whether the decision ought to be revised under section 9 or superseded under section 10, and
   (ii) if so, revise it, or, as the case may be, make a further decision which supersedes it; or
(b) in a case to which paragraph (3)(a) or (c) above applies, decide the claim or other matter or, as the case may be, the application,

in accordance with the final decision of the issue so referred.

(5) In paragraphs (3) and (4) above "final decision" means the decision of an officer of the Board under section 8 of the Transfer Act or the determination of any appeal in relation to that decision.]

AMENDMENTS

1. Social Security and Child Support (Decisions and Appeals) Amendment (No.3) Regulations 1999 (SI 1999/1623) reg.2(3) (July 5, 1999).

2. Social Security and Child Support (Decisions and Appeals) (Miscellaneous Amendments) Regulations 2002 (SI 2002/1379) reg.5 (May 20, 2002).

DEFINITIONS

"appeal"—see reg.1(3).

"the Board"—*ibid.*

"claim"—by virtue of s.39(2) of the Social Security Act 1998, see s.191 of the Social Security Administration Act 1992.

"final decision"—see para.(5).

"the Transfer Act"—see reg.1(3).

GENERAL NOTE

The Inland Revenue has been merged into HMRC. Some decisions fall to be made by HMRC by virtue of s.170 of the Pensions Schemes Act 1993 (rather than by virtue of s.8 of the Social Security Contributions (Transfer of Functions, etc.) Act 1999) but the Secretary of State may refer to HMRC issues for determination under the 1993 Act notwithstanding that this regulation does not apply (*R(P)1/04*). **2.511**

Decision of the Secretary of State relating to industrial injuries benefit

12.—(1) This regulation applies where, for the purpose of a decision of the Secretary of State relating to a claim for industrial injuries benefit under Part V of the Contributions and Benefits Act an issue to be decided is— **2.512**

(a) the extent of a personal injury for the purposes of section 94 of that Act;

(b) whether the claimant has a disease prescribed for the purposes of section 108 of that Act or the extent of any disablement resulting from such a disease; or

(c) whether the claimant has a disablement for the purposes of section 103 of that Act or the extent of any such disablement.

(2) In connection with making a decision to which this regulation applies, the Secretary of State may refer an issue, together with any relevant evidence or information available to him, including any evidence or information provided by or on behalf of the claimant, to a [1 health care professional approved by the Secretary of State] who has experience in such of the issues specified in paragraph (1) as are relevant to the decision, for such report as appears to the Secretary of State to be necessary for the purpose of providing him with information for use in making the decision.

(3) In making a decision to which this regulation applies, the Secretary of State shall have regard to (among other factors)—

(a) all relevant medical reports provided to him in connection with that decision; and

(b) the experience, in such of the issues specified in paragraph (1) as are relevant to the decision, of any [1 health care professional] who has provided a report, including a [1 health care professional approved by the Secretary of State] who has provided a report following an examination required by the Secretary of State under section 19.

AMENDMENT

1. Social Security (Miscellaneous Amendments) (No.2) Regulations 2007 (SI 2007/1626) reg.4(2) (July 3, 2007).

DEFINITIONS

"claimant"—see reg.1(3).
"health care professional"—see s.39(2) of the Social Security Act 1998.
"industrial injuries benefit"—by virtue of s.39(2) of the Social Security Act 1998, see s.191 of the Social Security Administration Act 1992.
"medical practitioner"—*ibid.*

GENERAL NOTE

2.513 Adjudicating medical authorities have been abolished and so all decisions which an adjudication officer would, or might, have referred to such authorities under the Social Security Administration Act 1992 are now decided by the Secretary of State on the basis of medical advice which, since 2007, may be given by a health care professional other than a doctor. Approved health care professionals receive special training to make an assessment of the disabling effects of an impairment and relate this to the relevant legislation in order to provide advice or reports for those making decisions on behalf of the Secretary of State. Even where a health care professional has not examined a claimant, his or her opinion may be taken into account as evidence, provided the tribunal can identify the factual basis on which the opinion was given. On appeal, para.(3)(b) makes it necessary for a tribunal to know the health care professional's professional qualification and area of expertise (see also *CDLA/2466/2007*).

See s.30 of the Social Security Act 1998 for the effect of an earlier declaration that the claimant has suffered personal injury by accident.

[1 Recrudescence of a prescribed disease

2.514 **12A.**—(1) This regulation applies to a decision made under sections 108 to 110 of the Contributions and Benefits Act where a disease is subsequently treated as a recrudescence under regulation 7 of the Social Security (Industrial Injuries) (Prescribed Diseases) Regulations 1985.

(2) Where this regulation applies Chapter II of Part I of the Act shall apply as if section 8(2) did not apply.]

AMENDMENT

1. Social Security and Child Support (Miscellaneous Amendments) Regulations 2000 (SI 2000/1596) reg.19 (June 19, 2000).

DEFINITION

"the Contributions and Benefits Act"—see s.84 of the Social Security Act 1998.

Income support and social fund determinations on incomplete evidence

2.515 **13.**—(1) [3 Where, for the purpose of a decision under section 8 (decisions by Secretary of State) or 10 (decisions superseding earlier decisions)—

(a) a determination falls to be made by the Secretary of State in respect of a claimant of income support, state pension credit or employment and support allowance as to—
    (i) the amount to be included in an owner-occupier loan payment under regulation 10 of the Loans for Mortgage Interest Regulations (calculation of each loan payment); or

(ii) what housing costs are to be included in the claimant's applicable amount (in the case of income support or employment and support allowance) or the claimant's appropriate minimum guarantee (in the case of state pension credit); and

(b) it appears to the Secretary of State that the Secretary of State is not in possession of all of the evidence or information which is relevant for the purposes of such a determination,

the Secretary of State shall make the determination on the assumption that the amounts to be included in an owner-occupier loan payment, the claimant's applicable amount, or the claimant's appropriate minimum guarantee, as the case may be, are those that can be immediately determined.]

(2) Where, for the purpose of a decision under section 8 or 10—

(a) a determination falls to be made by the Secretary of State as to whether—

(i) in relation to any person, the applicable amount falls to be reduced or disregarded to any extent by virtue of section 126(3) of the Contributions and Benefits Act (persons affected by trade disputes);

(ii) for the purposes of regulation 12 of the Income Support Regulations, a person is by virtue of that regulation to be treated as receiving relevant education; [2 . . .]

(iii) in relation to any claimant, the applicable amount includes severe disability premium by virtue of regulation 17(1)(d) or 18(1)(e), and paragraph 13 of Schedule 2 to, the Income Support Regulations; [2 or

(iv) in relation to any claimant, the applicable amount includes the severe disability premium by virtue of regulation 67(1) or 68(1) of, and paragraph 6 of Schedule 4 to, the Employment and Support Allowance Regulations; and]

(b) it appears to the Secretary of State that he is not in possession of all of the evidence or information which is relevant for the purposes of such a determination,

he shall make the determination on the assumption that the relevant evidence or information which is not in his possession is adverse to the claimant.

[1 (3) Where, for the purposes of a decision under section 8 or 10—

(a) a determination falls to be made by the Secretary of State as to whether a claimant's appropriate minimum guarantee includes an additional amount in accordance with regulation 6(4) of, and paragraph 1 of Schedule I to, the State Pension Credit Regulations; and

(b) it appears to the Secretary of State that he is not in possession of all the evidence or information which is relevant for the purpose of such a determination,

he shall make the determination on the assumption that the relevant evidence or information which is not in his possession is adverse to the claimant.]

AMENDMENTS

1. State Pension Credit (Consequential Transitional and Miscellaneous Provisions) Regulations 2002 (SI 2002/3019) reg.19 (April 7, 2003).

2. Employment and Support Allowance (Consequential Provisions) (No.2) Regulations 2008 (SI 2008/1554) regs 29 and 38 (July 27, 2008).

3. Loans for Mortgage Interest Regulations 2017 (SI 2017/725) reg.18 and Sch.5 para.11(1) and (4), as amended by the Loans for Mortgage Interest and Social Fund Maternity Grant (Amendment) Regulations 2018 (SI 2018/307) reg.2(11) and (18)(e) (April 6, 2018, subject to a saving).

DEFINITIONS

"claimant"—see reg.1(3).
"the Contributions and Benefits Act"—see s.84 of the Social Security Act 1998.
"the Employment and Support Allowance Regulations"—see reg.1(3).
"the Loans for Mortgage Interest Regulations"—*ibid.*
"owner-occupier loan payments"—*ibid.*
"the Income Support Regulations"—*ibid.*
"State Pension Credit Regulations"—*ibid.*

GENERAL NOTE

2.516 The heading of this regulation is now unreliable, as the regulation applies to all income-related benefits (other than housing benefit and universal credit) and to loans for mortgage interest but not to social fund payments. A decision made under this regulation may be revised under reg.3(2) if further evidence favourable to the claimant is provided within a month of the Secretary of State requesting it or such further time as the Secretary of State may allow. If evidence favourable to the claimant is provided later, the decision is likely to be superseded only from the date the evidence was provided.

[1 Retirement pension after period of deferment

2.517 **13A.**—(1) This regulation applies where—
(a) a person claims a Category A or Category B retirement pension, shared additional pension or, as the case may be, graduated retirement benefit;
(b) an election is required by, as the case may be—
(i) paragraph A1 or 3C of Schedule 5 to the Contributions and Benefits Act (pension increase or lump sum where entitlement to retirement pension is deferred);
(ii) paragraph 1 of Schedule 5A to that Act (pension increase or lump sum where entitlement to shared additional pension is deferred); or, as the case may be,
(iii) paragraph 12 or 17 of Schedule 1 to the Graduated Retirement Benefit Regulations (further provisions replacing section 36(4) of the National Insurance Act 1965: increases of graduated retirement benefit and lump sums); and
(c) no election is made when the claim is made.

(2) In the cicumstances specified in paragraph (1) the Secretary of State may decide the claim before any election is made, or is treated as made, for an increase or lump sum.

(3) When an election is made, or is treated as made, the Secretary of State shall revise the decision which he made in pursuance of paragraph (2).]

AMENDMENT

1. Social Security (Deferral of Retirement Pensions, Shared Additional Pension and Graduated Retirement Benefit) (Miscellaneous Provisions) Regulations 2005 (SI 2005/2677) reg.9(6) (April 6, 2006).

DEFINITIONS

"the Contributions and Benefits Act"—see s.84 of the Social Security Act 1998.
"the Graduated Retirement Benefit Regulations"—see reg.1(3).

[1 State pension under Part 1 of the Pensions Act 2014 after period of deferment

13B.—(1) This regulation applies where— 2.518

(a) a person claims a state pension under Part 1 of the Pensions Act 2014;

(b) the person may make a choice under—

(i) section 8(2) of the Pensions Act 2014; or

(ii) Regulations made under section 10 of that Act which make provision corresponding or similar to section 8(2); and

(c) the person does not make such a choice when the claim is made.

(2) The Secretary of State may decide the claim before paragraph (4) applies.

(3) The Secretary of State may revise a decision under paragraph (2) where paragraph (4) applies.

(4) This paragraph applies where the person—

(a) makes a choice mentioned in paragraph (1)(b); or

(b) becomes entitled to a lump sum under section 8(4) of the Pensions Act 2014, or under Regulations made under section 10 of that Act which make provision corresponding or similar to section 8(4), because the person has failed to choose within the period mentioned in section 8(3).]

AMENDMENT

1. Pensions Act 2014 (Consequential, Supplementary and Incidental Amendments) Order 2015 (SI 2015/1985) art.18(1) and (7) (April 6, 2016).

Effect of alteration in the component rates of income support and jobseeker's allowance

14.—(1) Section 159 of the Administration Act (effect of alteration in the component rates of income support) shall not apply to any award of income support in force in favour of a person where there is applicable to that person— 2.519

(a) any amount determined in accordance with regulation 17(2) to (7) of the Income Support Regulations; or

(b) any protected sum determined in accordance with Schedule 3A or 3B of those Regulations; or

(c) any transitional addition, personal expenses addition or special transitional addition applicable under Part II of the Income Support (Transitional) Regulations 1987 (transitional protection).

(2) Where section 159 of the Administration Act does not apply to an award of income support by virtue of paragraph (1), a decision under section 10 may be made in respect of that award for the sole purpose of giving effect to any change made by an order under section 150 of the Administration Act.

(3) Section 159A of the Administration Act (effect of alterations in the component rates of jobseeker's allowance) shall not apply to any award of a jobseeker's allowance in force in favour of a person where there is applicable

to that person any amount determined in accordance with regulations 87 of the Jobseeker's Allowance Regulations.

(4) Where section 159A of the Administration Act does not apply to an award of a jobseeker's allowance by virtue of paragraph (3), a decision under section 10 may be made in respect of that award for the sole purpose of giving effect to any change made by an order under section 150 of the Administration Act.

[1 (5) Section 159B of the Administration Act (effect of alterations affecting state pension credit) shall not apply to any award of state pension credit in favour of a person where in relation to that person the appropriate minimum guarantee includes an amount determined under paragraph 6 of Part III of Schedule I to the State Pension Credit Regulations.

(6) Where section 159B of the Administration Act does not apply to an award of state pension credit by virtue of paragraph (5), a decision under section 10 may be made in respect of that award for the sole purpose of giving effect to any change made to an award under section 150 of the Administration Act.]

AMENDMENT

1. State Pension Credit (Consequential Transitional and Miscellaneous Provisions) Regulations 2002 (SI 2002/3019) reg.20 (April 7, 2003).

DEFINITIONS

"the Administration Act"—see s.84 of the Social Security Act 1998.
"the Income Support Regulations"—see reg.1(3).
"the Jobseeker's Allowance Regulations"—*ibid.*
"state pension credit"—*ibid.*
"State Pension Credit Regulations"—*ibid.*

[1 Termination of award of income support [2 , jobseeker's allowance or employment and support allowance]

2.520 **14A.**—(1) This regulation applies in a case where an award of income support [2 , a jobseeker's allowance or an employment and support allowance] ("the existing benefit") exists in favour of a person and, if that award did not exist and a claim was made by that person or his partner for [2 an employment and support allowance,] a jobseeker's allowance or, as the case may be, income support ("the alternative benefit"), an award of the alternative benefit would be made on that claim.

(2) In a case to which this regulation applies, if a claim for the alternative benefit is made the Secretary of State may bring to an end the award of the existing benefit if he is satisfied that an alternative benefit will be made on that claim.

(3) Where, under paragraph (2), the Secretary of State brings an award of the existing benefit to an end he shall do so with effect from the day immediately preceding the first day on which an award of the alternative benefit takes effect.

(4) Where an award of a jobseeker's allowance is made in accordance with the provisions of this regulation, paragraph 4 of Schedule 1 to the Jobseeker's Act (waiting days) shall not apply.]

[2 (5) Where an award of an employment and support allowance is made in accordance with the provisions of this regulation, paragraph 2 of Schedule 2 to the Welfare Reform Act (waiting days) shall not apply.]

AMENDMENTS

1. Social Security and Child Support (Decisions and Appeals) (Miscellaneous Amendments) Regulations 2002 (SI 2002/1379) reg.6 (May 20, 2002).

2. Employment and Support Allowance (Consequential Provisions) (No.2) Regulations 2008 (SI 2008/1554) regs 29 and 39 (July 27, 2008).

DEFINITIONS

"the alternative benefit"—see para.(1).
"the Jobseekers Act"—see s.84 of the Social Security Act 1998.
"the Welfare Reform Act"—see reg.1(3).

Jobseeker's allowance determinations on incomplete evidence

15. Where, for the purpose of a decision under section 8 or 10— 2.521

(a) a determination falls to be made by the Secretary of State as to whether—
   (i) in relation to any person, the applicable amount falls to be reduced or disregarded to any extent by virtue of section 15 of the Jobseekers Act (persons affected by trade disputes); or
   (ii) for the purposes of regulation 54(2) to (4) of the Jobseeker's Allowance Regulations (relevant education), a person is by virtue of that regulation, to be treated as receiving relevant education; and

(b) it appears to the Secretary of State that he is not in possession of all of the evidence or information which is relevant for the purposes of such a determination.

he shall make the determination on the assumption that the relevant evidence or information which is not in his possession is adverse to the claimant.

DEFINITIONS

"claimant"—see reg.1(3).
"the Jobseekers Act"—see s.84 of the Social Security Act 1998.
"the Jobseeker's Allowance Regulations"—see reg.1(3).

15A.–15D. *Omitted.* 2.522

PART III

SUSPENSION, TERMINATION AND OTHER MATTERS

CHAPTER I

SUSPENSION AND TERMINATION

Suspension in prescribed cases

16.—(1) Subject to paragraph (2), the Secretary of State [1 or the Board] may suspend payment of a relevant benefit, in whole or in part, in the circumstances prescribed in paragraph (3). 2.523

(2) The Secretary of State shall suspend payment of a jobseeker's allowance in the circumstances prescribed in paragraph (3)(a)(i) or (ii) where

the issue or one of the issues is whether a person, who has claimed a jobseeker's allowance, is or was available for employment or whether he is or was actively seeking employment.

(3) The prescribed circumstances are that—

(a) it appears to the Secretary of State [1 or the Board] that—

(i) an issue arises whether the conditions for entitlement to a relevant benefit are or were fulfilled;

(ii) an issue arises whether a decision as to an award of a relevant benefit should be revised under section 9 or superseded under section 10;

(iii) an issue arises whether any amount paid or payable to a person by way of, or in connection with a claim for, a relevant benefit is recoverable under section 71(overpayments), 71A (recovery of jobseeker's allowance: severe hardship cases) or 74 (income support and other payments) of the Administration Act or regulations made under any of those sections; or

(iv) the last address notified to him [1 or them] of a person who is in receipt of a relevant benefit is not the address at which that person is residing; or

(b) an appeal is pending against—

(i) a decision of an [3 the First-tier Tribunal, the Upper Tribunal] or a court;

(ii) a decision given in a different case by [3 the Upper Tribunal] or a court, and it appears to the Secretary of State [1 or the Board] that, if the appeal were to be determined in a particular way, an issue would arise as to whether the award of a relevant benefit (whether the same benefit or not) in the case itself ought to be revised or superseded.

[2(4) For the purposes of section 21(3)(c) an appeal is pending where a decision of [3 the First-tier Tribunal, the Upper Tribunal] or a court has been made and the Secretary of State—

(a) is awaiting receipt of that decision or (in the case of [3 a decision of the First-tier Tribunal]) is considering whether to apply for a statement of the reasons for it, or has applied for such a statement and is awaiting receipt thereof; or

(b) has received that decision or (in the case [3 a decision of the First-tier Tribunal]) the statement of the reasons for it, and is considering whether to apply for [3 permission] to appeal, or where [3 permission] to appeal has been granted, is considering whether to appeal;

and the Secretary of State shall give written notice of his proposal to make a request for a statement of the reasons for a tribunal decision, to apply for leave to appeal, or to appeal, as soon as reasonably practicable.]

AMENDMENTS

1. Tax Credits (Decisions and Appeals) (Amendment) Regulations 1999 (SI 1999/2570) reg.12 (October 5, 1999). Note that amendments made by these regulations only have effect with respect to tax credit under the Tax Credit Act 1999 (reg.1(2) of the Amendment Regulations).

2. Social Security and Child Support (Miscellaneous Amendments) Regulations 2000 (SI 2000/1596) reg.20 (June 19, 2000).

3. Tribunals, Courts and Enforcement Act 2007 (Transitional and Consequential Provisions) Order 2008 (SI 2008/2683) Sch.1 paras 95 and 109 (November 3, 2008).

DEFINITIONS

"the Administration Act"—see s.84 of the Social Security Act 1998.
"the Board"—see reg.1(3).
"relevant benefit"—see s.39(1) of the Social Security Act 1998.

GENERAL NOTE

This regulation provides for the suspension of payments while a question about entitlement is being decided. Entitlement may be terminated under the usual powers of revision or supersession (see regs 3 and 6) or if information is not provided (see reg.18). Regulation 20 provides for the reinstatement of payments where entitlement is not terminated from the beginning of the period of suspension or some earlier date. **2.524**

There is no appeal against a decision to suspend payments under this regulation (see Sch.2 para.24). The claimant is expected to wait until the decision is made as to entitlement. In principle, a suspension is subject to judicial review but, in *R. (Sanneh) v Secretary of State for Work and Pensions* [2012] EWHC 1840 (Admin), an application for judicial review of a decision to suspend benefit while the Secretary of State was pursuing an application for permission to appeal to the Upper Tribunal did not "get off the ground" where "the claimant and her child lived sustainably (though not lavishly)", although it was accepted that in principle a suspension decision could be challenged on "well-recognised grounds such as irrationality". A further application by the same claimant failed when it was conceded that she would never in practice leave the United Kingdom as a result of economic pressure, because she would be eligible to receive support from a local authority under s.17 of the Children Act 1989 which would inevitably prevent her and her daughter facing destitution and homelessness and ensure that neither European Union law nor the European Convention on Human Rights would be breached (*R. (Sanneh) v Secretary of State for Work and Pensions* [2013] EWHC 793 (Admin)).

In *CA/3800/2006*, a claimant entitled to attendance allowance had been paying her own nursing home fees. However, she got into financial difficulties because her money had been badly invested by a financial adviser and the local authority started paying the fees. The claimant was in dispute with her financial adviser and eventually recovered a substantial sum that required her to reimburse the local authority for the fees it had paid. It was held that it had been inappropriate to supersede the award of attendance allowance so as to terminate payment when the local authority started paying the fees because it was impossible to reinstate the payments with effect from the date they had been terminated on a supersession following the reimbursement of the local authority. Instead, because the claimant had been in dispute with her financial adviser, the Secretary of State should merely have suspended payment on the ground that an issue within the scope of reg.16(3)(a)(ii) had arisen. The Commissioner revised the first supersession on the ground of "official error" so that payments could be reinstated from the date they had been stopped. This decision has been followed in *SSWP v DA* [2009] UKUT 214 (AAC) and has been approved by a three-judge panel in *SSWP v JL (DLA)* [2011] UKUT 293 (AAC); [2012] AACR 14. Indeed it was held in the latter case that suspension of payment under reg.16 rather than supersession under reg.6 should normally be the default action where a claimant of attendance allowance or disability allowance goes into long-term care.

Paragraph (1) confers a discretion on the Secretary of State and, where the Secretary of State receives information to the effect that the claimant is being overpaid benefit, the overpayment does not cease to be due to any misrepresentation or failure to disclose by the claimant (so as not to be recoverable under s.71 of the Social Security Administration Act 1992) merely because the Secretary of State does not suspend payments before the claimant is interviewed (*JA v SSWP (DLA)* [2014] UKUT 44 (AAC)).

Provision of information or evidence

2.525 **17.**—(1) This regulation applies where the Secretary of State requires information or evidence for a determination whether a decision awarding a relevant benefit should be—

(a) revised under section 9; or
(b) superseded under section 10.

(2) For the purposes of paragraph (1), the following persons must satisfy the requirements of paragraph (4)—

(a) a person in respect of whom payment of a benefit has been suspended in the circumstances prescribed in regulation 16(3)(a);
(b) a person who has made an application for a decision of the Secretary of State to be revised or superseded;
[[3] (c) a person from whom the Secretary of State requires information or evidence under regulation 32(1) of the Claims and Payments Regulations;
(ca) a person from whom the Secretary of State requires documents, certificates or other evidence under regulation 24(5) or (5A) of the Jobseeker's Allowance Regulations;]
(d) a person who qualifies for income support by virtue of paragraph 7 of Schedule 1B to the Income Support Regulations;
(e) a person whose entitlement to benefit is conditional upon his being, or being treated as, incapable of work;
[[1] (f) a person whose entitlement to an employment and support allowance is conditional on his having, or being treated as having, limited capability for work.]

(3) The Secretary of State shall notify any person to whom paragraph (2) refers of the requirements of this regulation.

(4) A person to whom paragraph (2) refers must either—

(a) supply the information or evidence within—
  [[3] (i) a period of 14 days beginning with the date on which the notification under paragraph (3) was sent to him or such longer period as the Secretary of State allows in that notification; or]
  (ii) such longer period as he satisfies the Secretary of State is necessary in order to enable him to comply with the requirement; or
(b) satisfy the Secretary of State within the [[3] period applicable under"] sub-paragraph (a)(i) that either—
  (i) the information or evidence required of him does not exist; or
  (ii) that it is not possible for him to obtain it.

[[3] (4A) In relation to a person to whom paragraph (2)(ca) refers, paragraph (4)(a)(i) has effect as if for "14 days" there were substituted "7 days".]

(5) The Secretary of State may suspend the payment of a relevant benefit, in whole or in part, to any person to whom paragraph (2)(b) to [[2] (f)] applies who fails to satisfy the requirements of paragraph (4).

(6) In this regulation, "evidence" includes evidence which a person is required to provide in accordance with regulation 2 of the Social Security (Medical Evidence) Regulations 1976.

AMENDMENTS

1. Employment and Support Allowance (Consequential Provisions) (No.2) Regulations 2008 (SI 2008/1554) regs 29 and 40 (July 27, 2008).

2. Social Security (Miscellaneous Amendments) (No.3) Regulations 2010 (SI 2010/840) reg.7(1) and (6) (June 28, 2010).
3. Social Security (Suspension of Payment of Benefits and Miscellaneous Amendments) Regulations 2012 (SI 2012/824) reg.4(1) and (3) (April 17, 2012).

DEFINITIONS

"the Claims and Payments Regulations"—see reg.1(3).
"evidence"—see para.(6).
"the Income Support Regulations"—see reg.1(3).
"limited capability for work"—*ibid.*
"relevant benefit"—see s.39(1) of the Social Security Act 1998.

GENERAL NOTE

A different version of this regulation (reproduced in editions of this work up to 2005) was enacted by reg.13 of the Tax Credits (Decisions and Appeals) (Amendment) Regulations 1999 (SI 1999/2570) with effect from October 5, 1999 in respect of working families' tax credit and disabled person's tax credit, payable under the Tax Credits Act 1999 until 2003. **2.526**

Termination in cases of failure to furnish information or evidence

18.—(1) Subject to paragraphs (2), (3) and (4), the Secretary of State shall decide that where a person— **2.527**

(a) whose benefit has been suspended in accordance with regulation 16 and who subsequently fails to comply with an information requirement made in pursuance of regulation 17; or
(b) whose benefit has been suspended in accordance with regulation 17(5),

that person shall cease to be entitled to that benefit from the date on which payment was suspended except where entitlement to benefit ceases on an earlier date other than under this regulation.

(2) Paragraph (1)(a) shall not apply where not more than one month has elapsed since the information requirement was made in pursuance of regulation 17.

(3) Paragraph (1)(b) shall not apply where not more than one month has elapsed since the first payment was suspended in accordance with regulation 17.

(4) Paragraph (1) shall not apply where benefit has been suspended in part under regulation 16 or, as the case may be, regulation 17.

GENERAL NOTE

A different version of this regulation (reproduced in editions of this work up to 2005) was enacted by reg.13 of the Tax Credits (Decisions and Appeals) (Amendment) Regulations 1999 (SI 1999/2570) with effect from October 5, 1999 in respect of working families' tax credit and disabled person's tax credit, payable under the Tax Credits Act 1999 until 2003. **2.528**

A decision that entitlement has ceased under reg.18(1) will usually be a supersession decision against which an appeal lies (*R(H) 4/08*). A refusal to allow a home visit is not, in itself, a refusal to provide information and there can usually be no termination if the claimant has not been given a deadline under reg.17(3) and (4) by which the information must be provided. Moreover, notwithstanding the exception at the end of para.(1), any termination under reg.18 is effective only from the date of the suspension unless there are alternative grounds for revision or supersession from an earlier date (*CH/2995/2006*). This approach was followed in *GZ v SSWP* [2009] UKUT 93 (AAC), where the Secretary of State discovered in March 2008 that the claimant's partner had been in receipt of working tax credit since February 15, 2008. On April 3, 2008, payment of income-based jobseeker's allowance to the claimant was suspended and he was asked to provide information about his partner's work and receipt of tax credit. He failed to do so and the Secretary of State purported to terminate entitlement from February 15, 2008 under reg.18 solely due to the failure to provide the information requested. The judge, referring to *CH/2995/2006*, pointed out that the question whether the claimant was entitled to benefit before April 3, 2008 depended largely on whether the claimant's partner was actually working, which had not been addressed by the Secretary of State. He therefore substituted a decision to the effect that the termination under reg.18 was effective only from April 3, leaving the Secretary of State to make a further decision in respect of the earlier period if he wished to do so. In *CH v Lewisham LBC (HB)* [2020] UKUT 71 (AAC), the local authority had addressed the factual question whether the claimant had had an income but had purported to rely on an equivalent of reg.18(1)(a) despite terminating the payment from a date earlier than the date from which payments had been suspended. Dismissing the claimant's appeal, the First-tier Tribunal had relied on the same statutory provision and so terminated entitlement from the same date solely on the ground of a failure to comply with an information requirement, albeit not the same one as relied upon by the local authority. The Upper Tribunal set aside the First-tier Tribunal's decision because it had failed to address the underlying factual issue about the claimant's entitlement but, because in this case there was a clear dispute between the parties as to whether the claimant had had the relevant income before the date from which payments had been suspended, remitted the case to the First-tier Tribunal.

In *R(H)1/09*, a claimant of council tax benefit had an annual turnover below £15,000 and so was not required to produce a profit and loss account for tax purposes and had not done so. The local authority had no reason not to believe that he had no such account. It failed to inform the claimant of the council tax benefit provision equivalent to reg.17(4)(b) and did not ask for any alternative evidence when informed by the claimant that he did not have any accounts and that his expenses were simply the same as the previous year. The Deputy Commissioner held that there were no grounds for terminating the award of benefit under the equivalent of reg.18. If the local authority or tribunal had considered that the amount claimed for expenses was unrealistic, they could have asked for further evidence or simply recalculated the claimant's entitlement to council tax benefit on the basis that he had no, or a smaller amount of, expenses.

Note that reg.3(7EA) provides a wide power to revise a decision under this regulation to terminate an award of a retirement or state pension following the suspension of payments.

Suspension and termination for failure to submit to medical examination

2.529 **19.**—(1) Except where regulation 8 of the Social Security (Incapacity for Work) (General) Regulations 1995 [[3] . . .] (where a question arises as to whether a person is capable of work) [[3] or regulation 23 of the Employment and Support Allowance Regulations (where a question arises whether a person has limited capability for work) applies], the Secretary of State [[1]or the Board] may require a person to submit to a medical examination by a [[2] health care professional approved by the Secretary of State] where that person is in receipt of a relevant benefit, and either—

(a) the Secretary of State considers [[1]or the Board consider] it necessary to satisfy himself [[1]or themselves] as to the correctness of the award of the benefit, or of the rate at which it was awarded; or

(b) that person applies for a revision or supersession of the award and the Secretary of State considers [[1] or the Board consider] that the examination is necessary for the purpose of making his [[1] or their] decision.

(2) The Secretary of State [[1] or the Board] may suspend payment of a relevant benefit in whole or in part, to a person who fails, without good cause, on two consecutive occasions to submit to a medical examination in accordance with requirements under paragraph (1) except where entitlement to benefit is suspended on an earlier date other than under this regulation.

(3) Subject to paragraph (4), the Secretary of State [[1] or the Board] may determine that the entitlement to a relevant benefit of a person, in respect of whom payment of such a benefit has been suspended under paragraph (2), shall cease from a date not earlier than the date on which payment was suspended except where entitlement to benefit ceases on an earlier date other than under this regulation.

(4) Paragraph (3) shall not apply where not more than one month has elapsed since the first payment was suspended under paragraph (2).

Amendments

1. Tax Credits (Decisions and Appeals) (Amendment) Regulations 1999 (SI 1999/2570) reg.14 (October 5, 1999). Note that amendments made by these regulations have effect only with respect to tax credit under the Tax Credit Act 1999 (reg.1(2) of the Amendment Regulations).

2. Social Security (Miscellaneous Amendments) (No.2) Regulations 2007 (SI 2007/1626) reg.4(3) (July 3, 2007).

3. Employment and Support Allowance (Consequential Provisions) (No.2) Regulations 2008 (SI 2008/1554) regs 29 and 41 (July 27, 2008).

Definitions

"the Board"—see reg.1(3).

"the Employment and Support Allowance Regulations"—*ibid.*

"health care professional"—see s.39 of the Social Security Act 1998.

"limited capability for work"—see reg.1(3).

"medical examination"—by virtue of s.39(2) of the Social Security Act 1998, see s.191 of the Social Security Administration Act 1992.

"medical practitioner"—*ibid.*

"relevant benefit"—see s.39(1) of the Social Security Act 1998.

General Note

Whereas s.19 of the Social Security Act 1998 provides for the obtaining of a report for the purpose of determining a claim, this regulation provides for the obtaining of a report for the purpose of deciding whether an award should be revised or superseded. In *CDLA/2335/2001*, the claimant's award of disability living allowance was terminated because he had failed to attend two consecutive appointments for medical examinations. The claimant's appeal to a tribunal was dismissed and he appealed to a Commissioner. The Commissioner criticised the submission provided to the tribunal on behalf of the decision-maker, which had failed to include any reference to the statutory provision under which the award had been terminated. The Secretary of State conceded that the relevant provision was reg.19 **2.530** and that the conditions for terminating an award of benefit under para.(3) were not met because, contrary to para.(2), benefit had been suspended before there had been any suggestion that the claimant should attend an appointment for an examination and, contrary to para.(4), more than a month had elapsed since the suspension. The Secretary of State's representative explained that the automated system used to generate decisions was unable to generate a decision in conformity with reg.19 and the decision-maker had used the "least inappropriate" code available. The claimant had said that, following the termination of the award of benefit, he had offered to attend a medical examination but that offer had been rebuffed. The Commissioner observed that a termination under reg.19(3) is effective only until the claimant makes a new claim and that, if the claimant had made such an offer, he should have been told he could make a new claim and that a medical examination would then be arranged.

A decision that entitlement has ceased under reg.19(3) will usually be a supersession decision against which an appeal lies (*R(H) 4/08* and see also para.22 of *CH/2995/2006*). A decision under reg.19(3) cannot be justified merely because there has been a purported suspension under reg.19(2). The conditions for such a suspension must actually have been satisfied (*CDLA/5167/2001*). This will usually involve consideration of whether the claimant had "good cause" for failing to "submit to a medical examination". Presumably those phrases have the same meaning in this regulation as they do in similar provisions, including s.19 of the Social Security Act 1998. See the annotation to that section, in which it is suggested that it does not make any practical difference that reg.19 provides that the Secretary of State may "require" a claimant to attend for and participate in an examination whereas s.19 of the 1998 Act provides for a mere "request" because notice of the appointment must always use "the language of clear and unambiguous mandatory requirement" and that a copy of the notice must be provided by the Secretary of State with the response to any appeal.

The relevance of previous failures to attend medical examinations was considered at some length in *JS v SSWP (ESA)* [2019] UKUT 303 (AAC). As regard cases where good cause for non-attendance had previously been accepted for varying reasons, it was said:

> "17. ... There is no question of changing those decisions, but a later decision-maker may conclude, looking back at the history of the case and taking account of evidence now available, that there has been a pattern of avoidance by the claimant. Even then, it is important to focus on the current failure. The previous conduct may justify careful scrutiny of the current failure, with perhaps a request for supporting evidence. But even a claimant with a lengthy history of failing to attend for what appear, in hindsight, to be highly dubious reasons may still be delayed by inclement weather or have a domestic emergency. And a claimant who has more than one disabling condition may be prevented from attending for different reasons on different occasions."

If the claimant appeals against a decision under reg.19(3) and the Secretary of State concedes that the claimant did have good cause failing to submit to a medical examination and so arranges a new medical examination, the appeal does not immediately lapse (see the annotation to s.9(6) of the Social Security Act 1998, above).

Making of payments which have been suspended

2.531 **20.**—(1) Subject to paragraphs (2) and (3), payment of a benefit suspended in accordance with regulation 16 [1 or 17] shall be made where—

(a) in a case to which regulation 16(2) or (3)(a)(i) to (iii) applies, the Secretary of State is satisfied [2 or the Board are satisfied] that the benefit suspended is properly payable and no outstanding issues remain to be resolved;

(b) in a case to which regulation 16(3)(a)(iv) applies, the Secretary of State is satisfied [2 or the Board are satisfied] that the has [2 or they have] been notified of the address at which the person is residing;

(c) [3 . . .];

(d) [1 in a case to which regulation 17(5) applies, the Secretary of State is satisfied that the benefit is properly payable and the requirements of regulation 17(4) have been satisfied.]

[2 (d) *in a case to which regulation 18(1) applies, the Board are satisfied that the benefit suspended is properly payable and the requirements of regulation 17(2), (4), (5) or (7) have been satisfied.*]

[3 (2) Where regulation 16(3)(b)(i) applies, payment of a benefit suspended shall be made if the Secretary of State—

(a) does not, in the case of a decision of [4 the First-tier Tribunal], apply for a statement of the reasons for that decision within the period [4 specified under Tribunal Procedure Rules];

(b) does not, in the case of a decision of [4 the First-tier Tribunal, the Upper Tribunal] or a court, make an application for [4 permission]to appeal and (where [4 the Upper Tribunal] to appeal is granted) make the appeal within the time prescribed for the making of such applications and appeals;

(c) withdraws an application for [4 permission] to appeal or the appeal; or

(d) is refused [4 permission]to appeal, in circumstances where it is not open to him to renew the application for leave or to make a further application for leave to appeal.

(3) Where regulation 16(3)(b)(ii) applies, payment of a benefit suspended shall be made if the Secretary of State, in relation to the decision of [4 the Upper Tribunal] or the court in a different case—

(a) does not make an application for [4 permission] to appeal and (where [4 permission] to appeal is granted) make the appeal within the time prescribed for the making of such applications and appeals;

(b) withdraws an application for [4 permission] to appeal or the appeal; or

(c) is refused [4 permission] to appeal, in circumstances where it is not open to him to renew the application for [4 permission] or to make a further application for [4 permission] to appeal.]

(4) Payment of benefit which has been suspended in accordance with regulation 19 for failure to submit to a medical examination shall be made where the Secretary of State is satisfied [2 or the Board are satisfied] that it is no longer necessary for the person referred to in that regulation to submit to a medical examination.

AMENDMENTS

1. Social Security and Child Support (Decisions and Appeals) Amendment (No.2) Regulations 1999 (SI 1999/1623) reg.6 (July 5, 1999).

2. Tax Credits (Decisions and Appeals) (Amendment) Regulations 1999 (SI 1999/2570) reg.15 (October 5, 1999). Note that amendments made by these Regulations have effect only with respect to tax credit under the Tax Credit Act 1999 (reg.1(2) of the Amendment Regulations). There are thus two forms of para.(1)(d) as the second form is only substituted for the purposes of tax credit.

3. Social Security and Child Support (Miscellaneous Amendments) Regulations 2000 (SI 2000/1596) reg.21 (June 19, 2000).

4. Tribunals, Courts and Enforcement Act 2007 (Transitional and Consequential Provisions) Order 2008 (SI 2008/2683) Sch.1 paras 95 and 110 (November 3, 2008).

DEFINITIONS

"the Board"—see reg.1(3).
"medical examination"—by virtue of s.39(2) of the Social Security Act 1998, see s.191 of the Social Security Administration Act 1992.

CHAPTER II

OTHER MATTERS

Decisions involving issues that arise on appeal in other cases

2.532 **21.**—(1) For the purposes of section 25(3)(b) (prescribed cases and circumstances in which a decision may be made on a prescribed basis) a case which satisfies the condition in paragraph (2) is a prescribed case.

(2) The condition is that the claimant would be entitled to the benefit to which the decision which falls to be made relates, even if the appeal in the other case referred to in section 25(1)(b) were decided in a way which is the most unfavourable to him.

(3) For the purposes of section 25(3)(b), the prescribed basis on which the Secretary of State [1 or the Board] may make the decision is as if—

(a) the appeal in the other case which is referred to in section 25(1)(b) had already been determined; and
(b) that appeal had been decided in a way which is the most unfavourable to the claimant.

(4) The circumstance prescribed under section 25(5)(c), where an appeal is pending against a decision for the purposes of that section, even though an appeal against the decision has not been brought (or, as the case may be, an application for [2 permission] to appeal against the decision has not been made) but the time for doing so has not yet expired, is where the Secretary of State [1 or the Board—

(a) certifies in writing that he is [1, or certify in writing that they are,] considering appealing against that decision; and
(b) considers [1, or consider,] that, if such an appeal were to be determined in a particular way—
    (i) there would be no entitlement to benefit in a case to which section 25(1)(a) refers; or
    (ii) the appeal would affect the decision in that case in some other way.

AMENDMENTS

1. Tax Credits (Decisions and Appeals) (Amendment) Regulations 1999 (SI 1999/2570) reg.16 (October 5, 1999). Note that amendments made by these regulations only have effect with respect to tax credit under the Tax Credit Act 1999 (reg.1(2) of the Amendment Regulations).

2. Tribunals, Courts and Enforcement Act 2007 (Transitional and Consequential Provisions) Order 2008 (SI 2008/2683) Sch.1 paras 95 and 111 (November 3, 2008).

DEFINITIONS

"the Board"—see reg.1(3).
"claimant"—*ibid.*

Appeals involving issues that arise in other cases

22. The circumstance prescribed under section 26(6)(c), where an appeal is pending against a decision in the case described in section 26(1)(b) even though an appeal against the decision has not been brought (or, as the case may be, an application for [2 permission] to appeal against the decision has not been made) but the time for doing so has not yet expired, is where the Secretary of State [1 or the Board— 2.533

(a) certifies in writing that he is [1, or certify in writing that they are,] considering appealing against that decision; and

(b) considers [1, or consider,] that, if such an appeal were already determined, it would affect the determination of the appeal described in section 26(1)(a).

AMENDMENTS

1. Tax Credits (Decisions and Appeals) (Amendment) Regulations 1999 (SI 1999/2570) reg.17 (October 5, 1999). Note that amendments made by these regulations only have effect with respect to tax credit under the Tax Credit Act 1999 (reg.1(2) of the Amendment Regulations).

2. Tribunals, Courts and Enforcement Act 2007 (Transitional and Consequential Provisions) Order 2008 (SI 2008/2683) Sch.1 paras 95 and 112 (November 3, 2008).

DEFINITION

"the Board"—see reg.1(3).

23. *Omitted.* 2.534

24. *Omitted.* 2.535

PART IV

RIGHTS OF APPEAL AND PROCEDURE FOR BRINGING APPEALS

CHAPTER I

GENERAL

General appeals matters not including child support appeals

Other persons with a right of appeal

25. For the purposes of [3 section 12(2)] [5 but subject to regulation 3ZA,], the following other persons have a right to appeal to [4 the First-tier Tribunal]— 2.536

[2 (ai) any person who has been appointed by the Secretary of State or the Board under regulation 30(1) of the Claims and Payments Regulations (payments on death) to proceed with the claim of a person who has made a claim for benefit and subsequently died;

(aii) any person who is appointed by the Secretary of State to claim benefit on behalf of a deceased person and who claims the benefit under regulation 30(5) and (6) of the Claims and Payments Regulations;

(aiii) any person who is appointed by the Secretary of State to make a claim for reduced earnings allowance or disablement benefit in the name of a person who has died and who claims under regulation 30(6A) and (6B) of the Claims and Payments Regulations;]

(a) any person appointed by the Secretary of State [1 or the Board] under regulation 33(1) of the Claims and Payments Regulations (persons unable to act) to act on behalf of another;

(b) any person claiming attendance allowance or disability living allowance on behalf of another under section 66(2)(b) of the Contributions and Benefits Act or, as the case may be, section 76(3) of that Act (claims on behalf of terminally ill persons);

(c) in relation to a pension scheme, any person who, for the purposes of Part X of the Pension Schemes Act 1993, is an employer, member, trustee or manager by virtue of section 146(8) of that Act.

AMENDMENTS

1. Tax Credits (Decisions and Appeals) (Amendment) Regulations 1999 (SI 1999/2570) reg.18 (October 5, 1999). Note that amendments made by these regulations only have effect with respect to tax credit under the Tax Credit Act 1999 (reg.1(2) of the Amendment Regulations).

2. Social Security and Child Support (Decisions and Appeals) (Miscellaneous Amendments) Regulations 2002 (SI 2002/1379) reg.7 (May 20, 2002).

3. Social Security, Child Support and Tax Credits (Decisions and Appeals) Regulations 2004 (SI 2004/3368) reg.2(3) (December 21, 2004).

4. Tribunals, Courts and Enforcement Act 2007 (Transitional and Consequential Provisions) Order 2008 (SI 2008/2683) Sch.1 paras 95 and 115 (November 3, 2008).

5. (Social Security, Child Support, Vaccine Damage and Other Payments (Decisions and Appeals) (Amendment) Regulations 2013 (SI 2013/2380) reg.4(1) and (7) (October 28, 2013).

DEFINITIONS

"appeal"—see reg.1(3).
"the Board"—see reg.1(3).
"the Claims and Payments Regulations"—*ibid.*
"the Contributions and Benefits Act"—see s.84 of the Social Security Act 1998.

GENERAL NOTE

2.537 In *CA/1014/1999*, an appointee appealed on behalf of a claimant against a decision that an overpayment was recoverable from the claimant. It was held that the tribunal were not entitled to consider whether it was recoverable from the appointee, who was not a "party to the proceedings" as that term is defined in reg.1. However, where an appeal is brought against a decision that an overpayment is recoverable from both the claimant and the appointee, the appeal will generally be regarded as having been brought on behalf of both of them and, even if it is not, both will be parties to the proceedings (*R(A) 2/06*).

Decisions against which an appeal lies

26. [[6] Subject to regulation 3ZA,] an appeal shall lie to [[4] the First-tier Tribunal] against a decision made by the Secretary of State [[1] or an officer of the Board]— 2.538

(a) as to whether a person is entitled to a relevant benefit for which no claim is required by virtue of regulation 3 of the Claims and Payments Regulations; or

(b) as to whether a payment be made out of the social fund to a person to meet expenses for heating by virtue of regulations made under section 138(2) of the Contributions and Benefits Act (payments out of the social fund); [[2] or

(c) under Schedule 6 to the Contributions and Benefits Act (assessment of extent of disablement) in relation to sections 103 (disablement benefit) and 108 (prescribed diseases) of that Act for the purposes of industrial injuries benefit under Part V of that Act;] [[3] or

(d) under section 59 of, and Schedule 7 to, the Welfare Reform and Pensions Act 1999 (couples to make joint-claim for jobseeker's allowance) where one member of the couple is working and the Secretary of State has decided that both members of the couple are not engaged in remunerative work] [[5]; or

(e) under, or by virtue of regulations made under, section 23A (contributions credits for relevant parents or carers) of the Contributions and Benefits Act.]

AMENDMENTS

1. Tax Credits (Decisions and Appeals) (Amendment) Regulations 1999 (SI 1999/2570) reg.19 (October 5, 1999). Note that amendments made by these regulations only have effect with respect to tax credit under the Tax Credit Act 1999 (reg.1(2) of the Amendment Regulations).

2. Social Security and Child Support (Miscellaneous Amendments) Regulations 2000 (SI 2000/1596) reg.22 (June 19, 2000).

3. Social Security Amendment (Joint Claims) Regulations 2001 (SI 2001/518) reg.4(b) (March 19, 2001).

4. Tribunals, Courts and Enforcement Act 2007 (Transitional and Consequential Provisions) Order 2008 (SI 2008/2683) Sch.1 paras 95 and 116 (November 3, 2008).

5. Pensions Act 2007 (Supplementary Provision) Order 2009 (SI 2009/2715) art.2 (April 6, 2010).

6. (Social Security, Child Support, Vaccine Damage and Other Payments (Decisions and Appeals) (Amendment) Regulations 2013 (SI 2013/2380) reg.4(1) and (8) (October 28, 2013).

DEFINITIONS

"appeal"—see reg.1(3).
"the Board"—see reg.1(3).
"the Claims and Payments Regulations"—*ibid.*
"the Contributions and Benefits Act"—see s.84 of the Social Security Act 1998.
"relevant benefit"—see s.89(1) of the Social Security Act 1998.

GENERAL NOTE

Paragraph (c) enables there to be an appeal against an assessment of disablement independently of any appeal against a decision awarding, or refusing to award, 2.539

benefit. This creates difficulties. In *CI/1547/2001*, it was suggested that all appeals against assessment decisions should also be treated as appeals against the consequent entitlement decisions because the provisions for supersession and revision are too limited, having regard to the dates from which they are effective, to deal satisfactorily with the consequences of a successful appeal on assessment alone. For the same reason, an application to supersede an assessment of disablement should generally be treated as also an application to supersede the underlying award (*CI/954/2006*).

A final assessment of disablement made under the legislation replaced by the Social Security Act 1998 Act implies that there was no disablement after the end of the award, and so has ongoing effect and requires supersession of the assessment as well as a new claim for benefit (*R(I) 5/02*). However, an assessment under the 1998 Act carries no such implication and, after it expires, requires just a new claim (*DT v SSWP (II)* [2015] UKUT 509 (AAC)).

Decisions against which no appeal lies

2.540 **27.**—(1) No appeal lies to [1 the First-tier Tribunal] against a decision set out in Schedule 2.

(2) In paragraph (1) and Schedule 2, "decision" includes determinations embodied in or necessary to a decision.

(3) [1 . . .].

AMENDMENT

1. Tribunals, Courts and Enforcement Act 2007 (Transitional and Consequential Provisions) Order 2008 (SI 2008/2683) Sch.1 paras 95 and 117 (November 3, 2008).

DEFINITIONS

"appeal"—see reg.1(3).
"decision"—see para.(2).

GENERAL NOTE

2.541 See note to Sch.2.

Notice of decision against which appeal lies

2.542 **28.**—(1) A person with a right of appeal under the Act or these Regulations against any decision of the Secretary of State [1 or the Board or an officer of the Board] shall—

(a) be given written notice of the decision against which the appeal lies;
(b) be informed that, in a case where that written notice does not include a statement of the reasons for that decision, he may, within one month of the date of notification of that decision, request that the Secretary of State [1 or the Board or an officer of the Board] provide him with a written statement of the reasons for that decision; and
(c) be given written notice of his right of appeal against that decision.

(2) Where a written statement of the reasons for the decision is not included in the written notice of the decision and is requested under paragraph (1)(b), the Secretary of State [1 or the Board or an officer of the Board] shall provide that statement within 14 days of receipt of the request [2 or as soon as practicable afterwards].

AMENDMENTS

1. Tax Credits (Decisions and Appeals) (Amendment) Regulations 1999 (SI 1999/2570) reg.20 (October 5, 1999). Note that amendments made by these regulations only have effect with respect to tax credit under the Tax Credit Act 1999 (reg.1(2) of the Amendment Regulations).

2. Social Security, Child Support and Tax Credits (Miscellaneous Amendments) Regulations 2005 (SI 2005/337) reg.2(6) (March 18, 2005).

DEFINITIONS

"the Act"—see reg.1(3).
"appeal"—*ibid.*
"the Board"—*ibid.*
"the date of notification"—*ibid.*

GENERAL NOTE

Paragraph (1)

There may be circumstances in which a failure to comply with the duties imposed by this regulation may invalidate the decision altogether (see *C3/07-08(IS)*, in which the Deputy Commissioner considered that computer-generated letters could not be reconciled with the statutory provisions for decision-making). The same approach has been taken by the High Court in relation to immigration decisions. Thus, in *R.(E (Russia)) v Secretary of State for the Home Department* [2012] EWCA Civ 357; [2012] 1 W.L.R. 3198, it was held that an immigration decision was invalid when it was accompanied by advice that wrongly stated that the right of appeal against it could be exercised only from outside the United Kingdom. However, in *R(P) 1/04*, it was held that a failure to issue notice of a decision simply had the effect that the time for appealing against the decision did not start to run. The same is true where a decision is issued but it incorrectly tells the claimant that benefit has been awarded for life when it has been awarded only for a limited period. The decision is valid but time for appealing runs from when the claimant is informed of the true nature of the decision (*CDLA/3440/2003*). It is suggested that, where a decision is issued, a failure to provide the information required by sub-para.(c) also has the effect that the decision is valid but that the time for appealing against it does not start to run. If that is so, the time for appealing would run from when the claimant does become aware of his rights. In *C10/07-08(IS)*, a Deputy Commissioner in Northern Ireland has considered, in the context of the Northern Ireland equivalent to s.71(5A) of the Social Security Administration Act 1992 (which provides that a decision cannot usually be made as to whether the overpayment of benefit is recoverable (a "recoverability decision") until the award has been superseded or revised (an "entitlement decision") and an award of the correct amount of entitlement (if any) has been substituted), the effect of a failure to give notice of the entitlement decision before the recoverability decision is made. He held that a failure to give notice of the entitlement decision did not invalidate it or the recoverability decision but that, on an appeal against the recoverability decision, steps should be taken to ensure that there had been no prejudice to the claimant through the failure to give notice of the entitlement decision by, for instance, adjourning so that the claimant could also appeal against the entitlement decision. However, he contemplated that, if prejudice could not otherwise be avoided, it might be necessary to allow the claimant's appeal against the recoverability decision. **2.543**

In child support cases, there is always likely to be prejudice because the interests of a third party entitled to rely on the decision have to be taken into account. In those circumstances, time has been held to run from the date of a decision even though the parties have been misled into thinking they had no right of appeal (*CCS/5515/2002*).

It is arguable that a statement of reasons only counts as such for the purposes of sub-para.(b) if it is adequate but the adequacy of a statement of reasons is very much a matter of judgment and depends on the issues arising in the particular case. A request made under para.(1)(b) extends the time for appealing but, presumably, only if it is properly made and the notice really does not include an adequate statement of reasons. Accordingly, the cautious claimant will treat any purported statement of reasons as being adequate for the purpose and will ensure that the appeal is lodged within the usual one month time limit, even if a fuller explanation is expected in the Secretary of State's submission to the tribunal.

2.544 A failure to refer to the fact that a decision is a supersession can, like most other defects, be cured by a tribunal giving a decision in the proper form (*R(IB)2/04*). On the other hand, if a tribunal does not realise that a decision under appeal was, or should have been, a supersession rather than a decision on a new claim, the tribunal's decision is liable to be set aside if it is impossible to infer that any ground for altering the decision on supersession was made out (*CDLA/9/2001*).

Further particulars required relating to certificate of recoverable benefits [[1] or, as the case may be, recoverable lump sum payments] appeals

2.545 **29.**—(1) [[2] . . .]

(2) [[2] . . .]

(3) [[3] . . .]

(4) [[3] . . .]

(5) [[3] . . .]

(6) [[3] The Secretary of State may treat any—

(a) purported appeal (where, as the result of regulation 9ZB(2) (consideration of review before appeal), there is no right of appeal);

(b) appeal relating to the certificate of recoverable benefits; or

(c) appeal relating to the certificate of recoverable lump sum payments,

as an application for review under section 10 of the 1997 Act.]

AMENDMENTS

1. Social Security (Recovery of Benefits) (Lump Sum Payments) Regulations 2008 (SI 2008/1596) Sch.2 para.1(c), (i) (October 1, 2008).

2. Tribunals, Courts and Enforcement Act 2007 (Transitional and Consequential Provisions) Order 2008 (SI 2008/2683) Sch.1 paras 95 and 118 (November 3, 2008).

3. Social Security, Child Support, Vaccine Damage and Other Payments (Decisions and Appeals) (Amendment) Regulations 2013 (SI 2013/2380) reg.4(1), (9) and (10)(b) (October 28, 2013, save where notice of the certificate of recoverable benefits or recoverable lump sum payments was posted to the appellant's last known address before that date—see reg.8(1) and (3)).

DEFINITIONS

"the 1997 Act"—see reg.1(3).

"appeal"—*ibid.*

GENERAL NOTE

2.546 Paragraphs (3) to (5) made provision for the Secretary of State to obtain particulars omitted from a notice of appeal and they remain in force in respect of appeals relating to certificates issued before October 28, 2013, which must be lodged with the Secretary of State rather than the First-tier Tribunal. When that saving ceases to apply, the heading of the regulation will have become anachronistic.

General appeals matters including child support appeals

Appeal against a decision which has been [2 replaced or] revised

30.—(1) An appeal against a decision of the Secretary of State [5 [6 . . .]] [1 or the Board or an officer of the Board] shall not lapse where the decision [2 is treated as replaced by a decision under section 11 of the Child Support Act by section 28F(5) of that Act, or is revised under section 16 of that Act] or section 9 before the appeal is determined and the decision as [2 replaced or] revised is not more advantageous to the appellant than the decision before it was [2 replaced or] revised. 2.547

(2) Decisions which are more advantageous for the purposes of this regulation include decisions where—

(a) any relevant benefit paid to the appellant is greater or is awarded for a longer period in consequence of the decision made under section 9;

(b) it would have resulted in the amount of relevant benefit in payment being greater but for the operation of any provision of the Administration Act or the Contributions and Benefits Act restricting or suspending the payment of, or disqualifying a claimant from receiving, some or all of the benefit;

(c) as a result of the decision, a denial or disqualification for the receiving of any relevant benefit, is lifted, wholly or in part;

(d) it reverses a decision to pay benefit to a third party;

[3(dd) it reverses a decision under section 29(2) that an accident is not an industrial accident;]

(e) in consequence of the revised decision, benefit paid is not recoverable under section 71, 71A or 74 of the Administration Act or regulations made under any of those sections, or the amount so recoverable is reduced; or

(f) a financial gain accrued or will accrue to the appellant in consequence of the decision.

(3) Where a decision as [2 replaced under section 28F(5) of the Child Support Act, or as revised under section 16 of that Act] or under section 9 is not more advantageous to the appellant than the decision before it was [2 replaced or] revised, the appeal shall be treated as though it had been brought against the decision as [2 replaced or] revised.

(4) The appellant shall have a period of one month from the date of notification of the decision as [2 replaced or] revised to make further representations as to the appeal.

(5) After the expiration of the period specified in paragraph (4), or within that period if the appellant consents in writing, the appeal to the [4 First-tier Tribunal] shall proceed except where, in the light of the further representations from the appellant, the Secretary of State [5 [6 . . .]] [1 or the Board or an officer of the Board] further revises his [1, or revise their,] decision and that decision is more advantageous to the appellant than the decision before it was [2 replaced or] revised.

AMENDMENTS

1. Tax Credits (Decisions and Appeals) (Amendment) Regulations 1999 (SI 1999/2570) reg.21 (October 5, 1999). Note that amendments made by these

regulations only have effect with respect to tax credit under the Tax Credit Act 1999 (reg.1(2) of the Amendment Regulations).

2. Child Support (Decisions and Appeals) (Amendment) Regulations 2000 (SI 2000/3185) reg.11 (various dates as provided by reg.1(1)).

3. Social Security, Child Support and Tax Credits (Miscellaneous Amendments) Regulations 2005 (SI 2005/337) reg.2(7) (March 18, 2005).

4. Tribunals, Courts and Enforcement Act 2007 (Transitional and Consequential Provisions) Order 2008 (SI 2008/2683) Sch.1 paras 95 and 119 (November 3, 2008).

5. Child Support (Miscellaneous Amendments) Regulations 2009 (SI 2009/396) reg.4(1) and (14) (April 6, 2009).

6. Public Bodies (Child Maintenance and Enforcement Commission: Abolition and Transfer of Functions) Order 2012 (SI 2012/2007) art.3(2) and Sch. para.113(1) and (12) (August 1, 2012).

Definitions

"the Administration Act"—see s.84 of the Social Security Act 1998.
"appeal"—see reg.1(3).
"the Board"—*ibid.*
"the Child Support Act"—see s.84 of the Social Security Act 1998.
"the Contributions and Benefits Act"—*ibid.*
"the date of notification"—see reg.1(3).
"relevant benefit"—see s.39(1) of the Social Security Act 1998.

General Note

2.548 Paragraph (1) provides an exception to the general rule that an appeal lapses when the decision under appeal is revised (see s.9(6) of the Social Security Act 1998). It makes it unnecessary for the claimant to submit a fresh appeal where the decision under appeal is replaced by a decision that is no more favourable to the claimant. Paragraph (2), however, makes it clear that a fresh appeal will be required where the new decision is only partially favourable to a claimant as well as when it is wholly favourable but still, in the claimant's view, not satisfactory. On the other hand, in those circumstances, the Secretary of State may decide not to revise the decision if the claimant indicates that he or she would rather the appeal continued, in which case the Secretary of State will invite the First-tier Tribunal to allow the appeal to the extent that she considers right and the claimant will be able to argue for an even more favourable decision (see the annotation to s.9(6) of the Social Security Act 1998, above). Moreover, an appeal does not lapse merely because, on reconsideration, the Secretary of State considers that the claimant scores more points on a work capability assessment but still not enough for entitlement to employment and support allowance (*AJ v SSWP (ESA)* [2014] UKUT 208 (AAC)). In *R(IS) 2/08*, a decision was made in 2003 to the effect that the claimant was not entitled to income support from May 17, 2002. When the claimant appealed, the decision was revised and income support was paid in respect of the period from May 17, 2002 to July 31, 2002. It was held that reg.30(2)(a) did not require the appeal to be treated as having lapsed in respect of the period from August 1, 2002. The Tribunal of Commissioners said—

> ". . . where a period before the date of the original decision is in issue and a revision affects only part of that period, it seems to us that there are many circumstances in which it can be appropriate to regard the decision as being more advantageous to the appellant only in respect of that part of the period and not the remainder of the period. This is particularly so where the Secretary of State knows very well that the revision does not deal with the main issue raise by the appeal and that it would be a waste of time to treat the appeal as having lapsed and to require the appellant to start all over again."

Subparagraph (dd) has effect only in relation to industrial accident declarations made under the now-repealed s.29(2) otherwise than in the course of a claim for benefit. It is probably meant to apply not only to cases where the reversed decision was to the effect that an accident was not an industrial accident but also to cases where it was to the effect that an alleged industrial accident was not an accident at all or did not even take place.

Any dispute as to whether an appeal has lapsed is a question as to the First-tier Tribunal's jurisdiction, upon which the First-tier Tribunal should rule (*GM v SSWP (JSA)* [2014] UKUT 57 (AAC)), presumably either on the Appellant's application for directions for the determination of the case or on the Respondent's application that the case be stuck out. As pointed out in *AI v SSWP (PIP)* [2019] UKUT 103 (AAC), it is a breach of r.8(4) of the Tribunal Procedure (First-tier Tribunal) (Social Entitlement Chamber) Rules 2008 for a case to be struck out on the ground that it has lapsed without the appellant being given an opportunity to object. It was also pointed out in that case that, where a claim is disallowed because a claimant has failed to attend a consultation with a health care professional and, after the claimant has appealed, the Secretary of State accepts that the claimant had good cause for the non-attendance and accordingly arranges another medical consultation, the appeal does not immediately lapse by virtue of that new decision alone as the decision is not by itself a revision that is "more advantageous" to the claimant (see the annotation to s.9(6) of the Social Security Act 1998, above).

Amendments made to this regulation by reg.6 of the Child Support (Meaning of Child and New Calculation Rules) (Consequential and Miscellaneous Amendment) Regulations 2012 (SI 2012/2785) and effective only for the purpose of certain child support cases are not included in this volume. 2.549

30A. *Omitted.* 2.550

31. [1 . . .] 2.551

AMENDMENT

1. Tribunals, Courts and Enforcement Act 2007 (Transitional and Consequential Provisions) Order 2008 (SI 2008/2683) Sch.1 paras 95 and 121 (November 3, 2008).

32. [1 . . .] 2.552

AMENDMENT

1. Social Security, Child Support, Vaccine Damage and Other Payments (Decisions and Appeals) (Amendment) Regulations 2013 (SI 2013/2380) reg.4(1) and (10)(c) (October 28, 2013, subject to a saving—see the note to reg.34).

33. [1 . . .] 2.553

AMENDMENT

1. Social Security, Child Support, Vaccine Damage and Other Payments (Decisions and Appeals) (Amendment) Regulations 2013 (SI 2013/2380) reg.4(1) and (10)(d) (October 28, 2013, subject to a saving—see the note to reg.34).

34. [1 . . .] 2.554

AMENDMENT

1. Social Security, Child Support, Vaccine Damage and Other Payments (Decisions and Appeals) (Amendment) Regulations 2013 (SI 2013/2380) reg.4(1) and (10)(e) (October 28, 2013, subject to savings—see below).

General Note

2.555 The revocation of regs 32–34 does not apply to appeals where notice of the Secretary of State's decision was posted to the appellant's last known address before October 28, 2013 (see reg.8(1) and (3) of the 2013 Amendment Regulations), because such appeals must be lodged with the Secretary of State, rather than the First-tier Tribunal, under r.23 of the Tribunal Procedure (First-tier Tribunal) (Social Entitlement Chamber) Rules 2008. Regulation 32 permitted the Secretary of State to extend the time for appealing and was arguably unnecessary in the light of r.23(4) of the 2008 Rules. Regulation 33 made provision as to the address to which appeals were to be sent and the obtaining by the Secretary of State of particulars omitted from a notice of appeal. Regulation 34 provided for the appointment of a person to act in place of a party to proceedings who had died.

Regulation 34 also remains in force for the limited purpose explained in the note to ss.5–7 of the Social Security Act 1998.

The revocation of reg.34 in other cases arguably leaves a lacuna not yet filled by the 2008 Rules. Although there seems to be no reason why there should not be an appointment under reg.30(1) of the Social Security (Claims and Payments) Regulations 1987 after an appeal relating to a claim for benefit has been lodged, in other cases where an appointment could previously have been made under reg.34 it is likely that an appeal will have to be abated until someone has been appointed to administer the deceased's estate.

Part V

Appeal Tribunals for Social Security Contracting Out of Pensions, Vaccine Damage and Child Support

2.556 **35.–38.** [1 . . .]

Amendment

1. Tribunals, Courts and Enforcement Act 2007 (Transitional and Consequential Provisions) Order 2008 (SI 2008/2683) Sch.1 paras 95 and 124 (November 3, 2008), subject to a saving under art.1(3).

General note

2.557 Except for parts of reg.36, these regulations remain in force in Scotland for the limited purpose explained in the note to ss.5–7 of the Social Security Act 1998.

[1Appeals raising issues for decision by officers of Inland Revenue

2.558 **38A.**—(1) Where, [2 a person has appealed to [3 the First-tier Tribunal and it appears to the First-tier Tribunal,] that an issue arises which, by virtue of section 8 of the Transfer Act, falls to be decided by an officer of the Board, that tribunal [2 [3 . . .] shall—

(a) refer the appeal to the Secretary of State pending the decision of that issue by an officer of the Board; and

(b) require the Secretary of State to refer that issue to the Board;

and the Secretary of State shall refer that issue accordingly.

(2) Pending the final decision of any issue which has been referred to the Board in accordance with paragraph (1) above, the Secretary of State may revise the decision under appeal, or make a further decision superseding

that decision, in accordance with his determination of any issue other than one which has been so referred.

(3) On receipt by the Secretary of State of the final decision of an issue which has been referred in accordance with paragraph (1) above, he shall consider whether the decision under appeal ought to be revised under section 9 or superseded under section 10, and—

(a) if so, revise it or, as the case may be, make a further decision which supersedes it; or

(b) if not, forward the appeal to the [3 First-tier Tribunal] which shall determine the appeal in accordance with the final decision of the issue so referred.

(4) In paragraphs (2) and (3) above, "final decision" has the same meaning as in regulation 11A(3) and (4).]

AMENDMENTS

1. Social Security and Child Support (Decisions and Appeals) Amendment (No.3) Regulations 1999 (SI 1999/1670) reg.2(4) (July 5, 1999).

2. Social Security and Child Support (Decisions and Appeals) (Miscellaneous Amendments) Regulations 2002 (SI 2002/1379) reg.12 (May 20, 2002).

3. Tribunals, Courts and Enforcement Act 2007 (Transitional and Consequential Provisions) Order 2008 (SI 2008/2683) Sch.1 paras 95 and 125 (November 3, 2008).

DEFINITIONS

"appeal"—see reg.1(3).
"the Board"—*ibid.*
"final decision"—by virtue of para.(4), see reg.11A(5).
"the Transfer Act"—see reg.1(3).

GENERAL NOTE

The Inland Revenue has been merged into HMRC. The process envisaged by this regulation has not always worked well, as HMRC has not always made the type of decision required by the First-tier Tribunal or, indeed, any decision at all. The consequence of criticism is that HMRC has now agreed that the First-tier Tribunal (or the Upper Tribunal) may refer cases straight to them and they will then endeavour to deal with them within three months (*SSWP v TB (RP)* [2010] UKUT 88 (AAC); [2010] AACR 38). 2.559

See s.8 of the Social Security Contributions (Transfer of Functions, etc.) Act 1999 and the annotation to it, above, for decisions relating to contributions that fall to be determined by HMRC, including decisions as to the effect of the late payment of contributions on entitlement to benefits. In addition, some decisions fall to be made by HMRC by virtue of s.170 of the Pensions Schemes Act 1993, rather than the 1999 Act, but the Tribunal may refer to HMRC issues for determination under the 1993 Act notwithstanding that this regulation does not apply (*R(P) 1/04*). It might be necessary to adjourn the hearing before the Tribunal while the question was being decided and procedures akin to those laid down in paras (2) and (3) could be followed.

39. – 47. [1 . . .] 2.560

AMENDMENT

1. Tribunals, Courts and Enforcement Act 2007 (Transitional and Consequential Provisions) Order 2008 (SI 2008/2683) Sch.1 paras 95 and 126 (November 3, 2008), subject to a saving under art.1(3).

General note

2.561 Except for regs 41, 44 and 45, these regulations remain in force in Scotland for the limited purpose explained in the note to ss.5–7 of the Social Security Act 1998.

2.562 **48.** [1 . . .]

Amendment

1. Social Security, Child Support and Tax Credits (Decisions and Appeals) Regulations 2004 (SI 2004/3368) reg.2(8) (December 21, 2004).

2.563 **49. – 58.** [1 . . .]

Amendment

1. Tribunals, Courts and Enforcement Act 2007 (Transitional and Consequential Provisions) Order 2008 (SI 2008/2683) Sch.1 paras 95 and 126 (November 3, 2008), subject to a saving under art.1(3).

General note

2.564 Except for regs 50 and 52, these regulations remain in force in Scotland for the limited purpose explained in the note to ss.5–7 of the Social Security Act 1998.

[1 Appeal to [2 the Upper Tribunal] by a partner

2.565 **58A.** A partner within the meaning of section 2AA(7) of the Administration Act (full entitlement to certain benefits conditional on work-focused interview for partner) may appeal to [2 the Upper Tribunal] under section 14 from a decision of [2 the First-tier Tribunal] in respect of a decision specified in section 2B(2A) and (6) of the Administration Act.]

Amendments

1. Social Security, Child Support and Tax Credits (Miscellaneous Amendments) Regulations 2005 (SI 2005/337) reg.2(19) (March 19, 2005).
2. Tribunals, Courts and Enforcement Act 2007 (Transitional and Consequential Provisions) Order 2008 (SI 2008/2683) Sch.1 paras 95 and 127 (November 3, 2008).

Definition

"the Administration Act"—see reg.1(3).

General Note

2.566 This regulation, made under s.14(3)(b) of the Social Security Act 1998, was necessary because a partner does not fall within the term "claimant" in s.14(3)(b). It has presumably been retained lest there be a case where a partner did not have a right of appeal under s.11 of the Tribunals, Courts and Enforcement Act 2007 as a "party".

Part VI

Revocations

2.567 **59.**—*Omitted.*

SCHEDULE 1

PROVISIONS CONFERRING POWERS EXERCISED IN MAKING THESE REGULATIONS 2.568

Column (1) Provision		Column (2) Relevant Amendments
Vaccine Damage Payments Act 1979	Section 4(2) and (3)	The Act, Section 46
Child Support Act 1991	Section 7A(1)	The Act, Section 47
	Section 16(6)	The Act, Section 40
	Section 20(5) and (6)	The Act, Section 42
	Section 28ZA(2)(b) and (4)(c)	The Act, Section 43
	Section 28ZB(6)(c)	The Act, Section 43
	Section 28ZC(7)	The Act, Section 44
	Section 28ZD(1) and (2)	The Act, Section 44
	Section 46B	The Act, Schedule 7, paragraph 44
	Section 51(2)	The Act, Schedule 7, paragraph 46
	Schedule 4A, paragraph 8	The Act, Schedule 7, paragraph 53
Social Security Administration Act 1992	Section 5(1)(hh)	The Act, Section 74
	Section 159	The Act, Schedule 7, paragraph 95
	Section 159A	The Act, Schedule 7, paragraph 96
Pension Schemes Act 1993	Section 170(3)	The Act, Schedule 7, paragraph 131
Social Security (Recovery of Benefits) Act 1997	Section 10	The Act, Schedule 7, paragraph 149
	Section 11(5)	
Social Security Act 1998	Section 6(3)	
	Section 7(6)	
	Section 9(1), (4) and (6)	
	Section 10(3) and (6)	
	Section 11(1)	
	Section 12(2) and (3), (6) and (7)	
	Section 14(10)(a) and (11)	
	Section 16(1) and Schedule 5	
	Section 17	
	Section 18(1)	
	Section 20	
	Section 21(1) to (3)	
	Section 22	
	Section 23	
	Section 24	
	Section 25(3)(b) and (5)(c)	
	Section 26(6)(c)	
	Section 28(1)	
	Section 31(2)	
	Section 79(1) and (3) to (7)	
	Section 84	
	Schedule 1, paragraphs 7, 11 and 12	
	Schedule 2, paragraph 9	
	Schedule 3, paragraphs 1, 4 and 9	

SCHEDULE 2 **Regulation 27**

DECISIONS AGAINST WHICH NO APPEAL LIES

Child benefit

2.569 **1.** A decision of the Secretary of State as to whether an educational establishment be recognised for the purposes of Part IX of the Contributions and Benefits Act.

2. A decision of the Secretary of State to recognise education provided otherwise than at a recognised educational establishment.

3. A decision of the Secretary of State made in accordance with the discretion conferred upon him by the following provisions of the Child Benefit (Residence and Persons Abroad) Regulations 1976—

(a) regulation 2(2)(c)(iii) (decision relating to a child's temporary absence abroad);
(b) regulation 7(3) (certain days of absence abroad disregarded).

4. A decision of the Secretary of State made in accordance with the discretion conferred upon him by regulation 2(1) or (3) of the Child Benefit (General) Regulations 1976 (provisions relating to contributions and expenses in respect of a child).

Claims and payments

2.570 [5 **5.** A decision, being a decision of the Secretary of State unless specified below as a decision of the Board, under the following provisions of the Claims and Payments Regulations—

[8 (a) regulation 4(3) or (3B) (which partner should make a claim for income support or jobseeker's allowance);]
[9 (aa) regulation 4I (which partner should make a claim for an employment and support allowance);]
(b) [8 . . .];
[8 (bb) regulation 4D(7) (which partner should make a claim for state pension credit);]
(c) [8 . . .];
(d) [8 . . .];
(e) [8 . . .];
(f) regulation 7 (decision by the Secretary of State or the Board as to evidence and information required);
(g) regulation 9 and Schedule 1 (decision by the Secretary of State or the board as to interchange of claims with claims for other benefits);
(h) regulation 11 (treating claim for maternity allowance as claim for incapacity benefit [9 or employment and support allowance]);
(i) regulation 15(7) (approving form of particulars required for determination of retirement pension questions in advance of claim);
(j) regulations 20 to 24 (decisions by the Secretary of State or the Board as to the time and manner of payments);
(k) regulation 25(1) (intervals of payment of attendance allowance and disability living allowance where claimant is expected to return to hospital);
(l) regulation 26 (manner and time of payment of income support);
(m) regulation 26A (time and intervals of payment of jobseeker's allowance);
[7 (mm) regulation 26B (payment of state pension credit);]
[9 (mn) regulation 26C (manner and time of payment of employment and support allowance);]
(n) regulation 27(1) and (1A) (decision by the Board as to manner and time of payment of tax credits);
(o) regulation 30 (decision by the Secretary of State or the Board as to claims or payments after death of claimant);
(p) regulation 30A (payment of arrears of joint-claim jobseeker's allowance where nominated person can no longer be traced);
(q) regulation 31 (time and manner of payment of industrial injuries gratuities);
(r) regulation 32 (decision by the Secretary of State or the Board where person unable to act);
(s) regulation 33 (appointments by the Secretary of State or the Board where person unable to act);
(t) regulation 34 (decision by the Secretary of State or the Board as to paying another person on a beneficiaries behalf);

(u) [14 regulation 17(1) (direct payments to qualifying lenders by Secretary of State where specified circumstances met) of the Loans for Mortgage Interest Regulations;]
(v) regulation 35(2) (payment to third person of maternity expenses or expenses for heating in cold weather);
(w) regulation 36 (decision by the Secretary of State or the Board to pay partner as alternative payee);
(x) regulation 38 (decision by the Secretary of State or the Board as to the extinguishment of right to payment of sums by way of benefit where payment not obtained within the prescribed period, except a decision under paragraph (2A) (payment requrested after expiration of prescribed period));
(y) regulations 42 to 46 (mobility component of disability living allowance and disability living allowance for children;
(z) regulation 47(2) and (3) (return of instruments of payment etc. to the Secretary of State or the Board).]

[13 *Schemes that were Contracted-out Pension Schemes*]

6. A decision of the Secretary of State under section 109 of the Pension Schemes Act 1993 or any Order made under it (annual increase of guaranteed minimum pensions). **2.571**

Decisions depending on other cases

7. A decision of the Secretary of State under section 25 or 26 (decisions and appeals depending on other cases). **2.572**

Deductions

8. A decision which falls to be made by the Secretary of State under the Fines (Deductions from Income Support) Regulations 1992, other than [1 a decision whether benefit is sufficient for a deduction to be made]. **2.573**

9.—(1) Except in relation to a decision to which sub-paragraph (2) applies, any decision of the Secretary of State under the Community Charges (Deductions from Income Support) (No.2) Regulations 1990, the Community Charges (Deductions from Income Support) (Scotland) Regulations 1989 or the Council Tax (Deductions from Income Support) Regulations 1993.

(2) This sub-paragraph applies to a decision—
(a) whether there is an outstanding sum due of the amount sought to be deducted;
(b) whether benefit is sufficient for a deduction to be made; and
(c) on the priority to be given to any deduction.

European Community regulations

10. An authorization given by the Secretary of State in accordance with article 22(1) or (1) of Council Regulation (EEC) No.1408/71 [15, as amended from time to time,] on the application of social security schemes to employed persons, to self-employed persons and to members of their families moving within the Community. **2.574**

Expenses

11. A decision of the Secretary of State whether to pay expenses to any person under section 180 of the Administration Act. **2.575**

Guardian's allowance

12. A decision of the Secretary of State relating to the giving of a notice under regulation 5(8) of the Social Security (Guardian's Allowance) Regulations 1975 (children whose surviving parents are in prison or legal custody). **2.576**

Income support

13. A decision of the Secretary of State [3 . . .] made in accordance with paragraph (1) or (2) of regulation 13 (income support and social fund determinations on incomplete evidence). **2.577**

[6 State pension credit

2.578 **13A.** A decision of the Secretary of State made in accordance with paragraph (1) or (3) of regulation 13 in relation to state pension credit (determination on incomplete evidence).]

Industrial injuries benefit

2.579 **14.** A decision of the Secretary of State relating to the question whether—

(a) disablement pension be increased under section 104 of the Contributions and Benefits Act (constant attendance); or

(b) disablement pension be further increased under section 105 of the Contributions and Benefits Act (exceptionally severe disablement);

and if an increase is to be granted or renewed, the period for which and the amount at which it is payable.

15. A decision of the Secretary of State under regulation 2(2) of the Social Security (Industrial Injuries and Diseases) Miscellaneous Provisions Regulations 1986 as to the length of any period of interruption of education which is to be disregarded.

16. A decision of the Secretary of State to approve or not to approve a person undertaking work for the purposes of regulation 17 of the Social Security (General Benefit) Regulations 1982.

17. A decision of the Secretary of State as to how the limitations under Part VI of Schedule 7 to the Contributions and Benefits Act on the benefit payable in respect of any death are to be applied in the circumstances of any case.

Invalid vehicle scheme

2.580 **18.** A decision of the Secretary of State relating to the issue of certificates under regulation 13 of, and Schedule 2 to, the Social Security (Disability Living Allowance) Regulations 1991.

Jobseeker's allowance

2.581 **19.**—(1) A decision of the Secretary of State under Chapter IV of Part II of the Jobseeker's Allowance Regulations as to the day and the time a claimant is to attend at a job centre.

(2) A decision of the Secretary of State as to the day of the week on which a claimant is required to provide a signed declaration under regulation 24(10) of the Jobseeker's Allowance Regulations.

(3) A decision of the Secretary of State [3 . . .] made in accordance with regulation 15 (Jobseeker's allowance determinations on incomplete evidence).

2.582 [10 . . .]

Payments on account, overpayments and recovery

2.583 **20.** A decision of the Secretary of State under the Social Security (Payments on account, Overpayments and Recovery) Regulations 1988, except a decision of the Secretary of State under the following provisions of those Regulations—

(a) [12 . . .]

(b) [12 . . .]

(c) regulation 5 as to the offsetting of a prior payment against a subsequent award;

(d) regulation 11(1) as to whether a payment in excess of entitlement has been credited to a bank or other account;

(e) regulation 13 as to the sums to be deducted in calculating recoverable amounts;

(f) regulation 14(1) as to the treatment of capital to be reduced;

(g) regulation 19 determining a claimant's protected earnings; and

(h) regulation 24 whether a determination as to a claimant's protected earnings is revised or superseded.

[12 **20A.** A decision of the Secretary of State under the Social Security (Payments on Account of Benefit) Regulations 2013 except a decision under regulation 10 of those Regulations.]

Persons abroad

2.584 **21.** A decision of the Secretary of State made under—

(a) regulation 2(1)(a) of the Social Security Benefit (Persons Abroad) Regulations 1975 whether to certify that it is consistent with the proper administration of the

Contributions and Benefits Act that a disqualification under section 113(1)(a) of that Act should not apply;

(b) regulation 9(4) or (5) of those Regulations whether to allow a person to avoid disqualification for receiving benefit during a period of temporary absence from Great Britain longer than that specified in the regulation.

Reciprocal Agreements

22. A decision of the Secretary of State made in accordance with an Order made under section 179 of the Administration Act (reciprocal agreements with countries outside the United Kingdom). **2.585**

Social fund awards

23. A decision of the Secretary of State under section 78 of the Administration Act relating to the recovery of social fund awards. **2.586**

Suspension

24. A decision of the Secretary of State relating to the suspension of a relevant benefit or to the payment of such a benefit which has been suspended under Part III. **2.587**

Up-rating

25. A decision of the Secretary of State relating to the up-rating of benefits under Part X of the Administration Act. **2.588**

[[2] **26.** Any decision treated as a decision of the Secretary of State whether or not to waive or defer a work-focused interview.]

Loss of Benefit

[[4] **27.** [[11] (1) In the circumstances referred to in sub-paragraph (2), a decision of the Secretary of State that a sanctionable benefit as defined in section 6A(1) of the Social Security Fraud Act 2001 is not payable (or is to be reduced) pursuant to section 6B, 7, 8 or 9 of that Act as a result of— **2.589**

(a) a conviction for one or more benefit offences in one set of proceedings;

(b) an agreement to pay a penalty under section 115A of the Administration Act (penalty as alternative to prosecution) or section 109A of the Social Security Administration (Northern Ireland) Act 1992 (the corresponding provision for Northern Ireland) in relation to a benefit offence;

(c) a caution in respect of one or more benefit offences; or

(d) a conviction for one or more benefit offences in each of two sets of proceedings, the later offence or offences being committed within the period of 5 years after the date of any of the convictions for a benefit offence in the earlier proceedings.

(2) The circumstances are that the only ground of appeal is that any of the convictions was erroneous, or that the offender (as defined in section 6B(1) of the Social Security Fraud Act 2001) did not commit the benefit offence in respect of which there has been an agreement to pay a penalty or a caution has been accepted.]]

AMENDMENTS

1. Social Security Act 1998 (Commencement No.12 and Consequential and Transitional Provisions) Order 1999 (SI 1999/3178) art.3(19) and Sch.19 para.2 (November 29, 1999).

2. Social Security (Work-focused Interviews) Regulations 2000 (SI 2000/897), reg.16(5) and Sch.6 para.7 (April 3, 2000).

3. Social Security and Child Support (Miscellaneous Amendments) Regulations 2000 (SI 2000/1596) reg.34 (June 19, 2000).

4. Social Security (Loss of Benefit) Regulations 2001 (SI 2001/4022) reg.21 (April 1, 2002).

5. Social Security and Child Support (Decisions and Appeals) (Miscellaneous Amendments) Regulations 2002 (SI 2002/1379) reg.21 (May 20, 2002).

6. State Pension Credit (Consequential, Transitional and Miscellaneous Provisions) Regulations 2002 (SI 2002/3019) reg.21 (April 7, 2003).

7. State Pension Credit (Decisions and Appeals—Amendments) Regulations 2003 (SI 2003/1581) reg.2 (June 18, 2003).

8. Social Security, Child Support and Tax Credits (Decisions and Appeals) Regulations 2004 (SI 2004/3368) reg.2(9) (December 21, 2004).

9. Employment and Support Allowance (Consequential Provisions) (No.2) Regulations 2008 (SI 2008/1554) regs 29 and 42 (July 27, 2008).

10. Welfare Reform Act 2009 (Section 26) (Consequential Amendments) Regulations 2010 (SI 2010/424) reg.4(1) and (6) (March 22, 2010).

11. Social Security (Loss of Benefit) Amendment Regulations 2010 (SI 2010/1160) reg.3(1) and (5) (April 1, 2010).

12. Social Security (Payment on Account of Benefit) Regulations 2013 (SI 2013/383) reg.21 (April 1, 2013, subject to a saving in respect of interim payments paid under the 1988 Regulations).

13. Pensions Act 2014 (Abolition of Contracting-out for Salary Related Pension Schemes) (Consequential Amendments and Savings) Order 2016 (SI 2016/200) art.15 (April 6, 2016).

14. Loans for Mortgage Interest Regulations 2017 (SI 2017/725) reg.18 and Sch.5 para.11(1) and (5), as amended by the Loans for Mortgage Interest and Social Fund Maternity Grant (Amendment) Regulations 2018 (SI 2018/307) reg.2(11) and (18)(e) (April 6, 2018, subject to a saving).

15. Social Security (Updating of EU References) (Amendment) Regulations 2018 (SI 2018/1084) reg.8 (November 15, 2018).

Definitions

"the Administration Act"—see s.84 of the Social Security Act 1998.
"the Claims and Payments Regulations"—see reg.1(3).
"the Contributions and Benefits Act"—see s.84 of the Social Security Act 1998.
"decision"—see reg.27(2).
"the Jobseeker's Allowance Regulations"—see reg.1(3).
"the Loans for Mortgage Interest Regulations"—*ibid.*
"relevant benefit"—see s.39(1) of the Social Security Act 1998.
"state pension credit"—see reg.1(3).
"work-focused interview"—*ibid.*

General Note

2.590 Before December 21, 2004, para.5(a)–(e) had the effect that decisions under regs 4, 4A, 4D and 6 of the Social Security (Claims and Payments) Regulations 1987 as to whether a claim had been properly made were unappealable and that was also the effect of the original form of para.5 that was replaced from May 20, 2002. Now the only decisions that para.5(a)–(e) makes unappealable are decisions as to which of two partners should make claims where the partners do not agree. The new version of para.5(u) is plainly the result of a drafting error. The previous version referred to reg.34A(1) of the 1987 Regulations and the substitution has been made without regard to the opening words of para.5.

If reg.27 is made under s.12(2) of the Social Security Act 1998, it is arguable that much of Sch.2 to the Regulations is ultra vires, having regard to s.12(3). It is not easy to see why, for instance, a decision of the Secretary of State that an educational establishment be recognised for the purposes of child benefit or to recognise education provided otherwise than at such a recognised establishment (paras 1 and 2 of Sch.2) is not a decision "that relates to the conditions of entitlement" to child benefit, as indeed it may be in child support cases as opposed to child benefit cases (*CF v CMEC (CSM)* [2010] UKUT 39 (AAC)). The fact that a large element of discretion is involved is not material. There is no reason in principle why such a discretion should not be exercised by a tribunal. There may be sound reasons for restricting the rights of appeal in cases where there is a large element of pure discretion (see *TD v SSWP (CSM)* [2013] UKUT 282 (AAC); [2014] AACR 7, holding that judicial review provided an adequate remedy in such cases) and, of course, there was no right of appeal under the old legislation, but it is arguable that neither of those considerations carries much weight against the clear language of s.12(3). On the other hand, it is arguable that reg.27 is made under para.9 of Sch.2 to the Act, which is in much broader terms than s.12. Both regulation-making powers are to be found in Sch.1 to the Regulations. What the point is in having s.12(2) qualified by s.12(3) when there is the broader unqualified power in the same Act is unclear but an argument that a broad power should be regarded as qualified by the scope of the narrower power found little sympathy in *R. v Secretary of State for Social Security, Ex p. Moore, The Times*, March 9, 1993 (but see now *R. (BAPIO Action Ltd) v Secretary of State for the Home Department* [2008] UKHL 27; [2008] 1 A.C. 1003).

The question of the validity of this Schedule has been considered in four Commissioners' decisions without any very clear resolution of these issues. In the first two cases, the Schedule was held to be valid as far as it affected the individual cases, but different grounds were given. In *CJSA/69/2001*, the Commissioner considered that this Schedule was made under s.12(2) of the 1998 Act but held that para.5 was intra vires insofar as it then prohibited any appeal against a decision by the Secretary of State under reg.4 of the Social Security (Claims and Payments) Regulations 1987 that a claim was to be treated as not made until the claimant provided his P45. He pointed out that s.12(3) applies only in respect of a benefit for which a claim has been validly made. However, he declined to determine whether or not the claim *had* been validly made, accepting the submission of the Secretary of State that a right of appeal could arise only after the Secretary of State had decided that a claim had been validly made and that it was beyond the power of a tribunal to consider whether the condition of reg.4(1B)(b) of the 1987 Regulations (or reg.4(1B)(d) which might have been more relevant) was met. It is suggested that an alternative construction of s.12(3) would be that it is necessary for there to be a right of appeal against any decision as to whether or not a claim was valid. *CF/3565/2001*, decided a few days later by a different Commissioner who was apparently unaware of the approach taken in *CJSA/69/2001*, concerned a decision of the Secretary of State not to recognise education provided otherwise than at a recognised educational establishment, which the Commissioner held to fall within para.2 of this Schedule. The Commissioner held that this Schedule was validly made under s.12(1)(a) of, and para.9 of Sch.2 to, the 1998 Act. In fact, as was noted in *CJSA/69/2001*, s.12(1) is not listed in Sch.1 to the Regulations as being a power under which the Regulations were made, doubtless because it does not independently confer any power to make regulations. Curiously, the Commissioner in *CJSA/69/2001* stated that Sch.3 was also not listed in Sch.1 to the Regulations when it is, although it is not clear why the Commissioner mentioned it at all as it is irrelevant. Even more curiously, he did not mention para.9 of Sch.2, which *does* confer the relevant power to make regulations relied upon in *CF/3565/2001* and is also listed in Sch.1 to the Regulations. Equally, the Commissioner deciding *CF/3565/2001* did not consider the argument that the Schedule might have been made under s.12(2) of the 1998 Act. He did however reject a broader argument that the Schedule was ultra vires because it was inconsistent with the European Convention on Human Rights. He held, applying *R. (Alconbury Developments Ltd) v Secretary of State for the Environment, Transport and the Regions* [2001] UKHL 23; [2001] [2003] 2 A.C. 295, that judicial review was an adequate remedy in the case before him, although he left open the question whether the Schedule would be ultra vires for the purposes of other cases.

In *R(IS) 6/04*, the Commissioner again had a challenge to para.5 in its first form **2.591**
and the question was whether an appeal lay against the Secretary of State's decision that the claimant had not complied with the prescribed requirements for making a valid claim. The Commissioner considered it unnecessary to say how the regulation-making power in para.9 of Sch.2 to the Act should be construed or whether para.5 of Sch.2 to the Regulations had been made under that power because he agreed with the construction of s.12 applied in *CJSA/69/2001* so that, even applying the approach

more favourable to the claimant, he considered that para.5 was validly made when the Regulations first came into force. However, he held the absence of a right of appeal to be incompatible with art.6 of the European Convention on Human Rights and so disapplied the paragraph insofar as it was necessary to do so to ensure that a claimant was entitled to appeal against a decision as to whether or when a claim had been validly made in accordance with the prescribed requirements. This restored the position to what it had been before the Social Security Act 1998 had come into force (*R(U) 9/60*). The Secretary of State withdrew an appeal to the Court of Appeal and subsequently amended para.5(a) in order to provide a right of appeal against a decision that a claim had not been validly made. It does not necessarily follow, however, that he accepted that the Commissioner's decision as to the application of art.6 of the Convention was correct. Indeed, in *R(H) 3/05*, leading counsel for one of the claimants acknowledged that the reasoning in *R(IS) 6/04* had been overtaken by that in *Runa Begum v Tower Hamlets London (First Secretary of State intervening)* [2003] UKHL 5; [2003] 2 A.C. 430 in which it was held by the House of Lords that there was no breach of art.6 of the Convention where an appeal from a local authority's decision in respect of their duties to homeless people lay only on a point of law. One possible inference to be drawn from the House of Lords' decision is that judicial review of the unappealable decisions listed in Sch.2 of these Regulations, or the similar provisions relating to housing benefit and council tax benefit in issue in *R(H) 3/05*, is an adequate remedy under the Convention. However, counsel submitted that the House of Lords' conclusion in *Runa Begum*, that there was no unfairness in not having an appeal on a point of fact, was reached against the background of a system of internal review by a different officer of appropriate seniority, whereas, in housing benefit and council tax cases, such system of internal review as there had formerly been had been replaced by an appeal to a tribunal, which is the procedure available in other social security cases. In the absence of as sophisticated a system of review as there was in *Runa Begum*, he argued, there had to be a right of appeal on questions of fact. It was unnecessary for the Tribunal of Commissioners to express a view on that argument and they did not do so. Now that judicial review has adapted so as to be able to include a review of the merits of a decision as well as its legality, where that is required (see *Secretary of State for the Home Department v MB* [2006] EWCA Civ 1140; [2007] Q.B. 415), arguments that it does not provide an adequate remedy for the purposes of the Convention are more difficult to run and they may have become even more so now that is has become possible for judicial review cases to be transferred to the Upper Tribunal (see the note to s.15 of the Tribunals, Courts and Enforcement Act 2007). See, on the other hand, *ZM and AB v HMRC (TC)* [2013] UKUT 547 (AAC); [2014] AACR 17 in which the Upper Tribunal drew a distinction between issues of fact, in respect of which it was held that an appeal did lie under a similar provision in the Tax Credits Act 2002 because judicial review would not in practice be an adequate remedy, and issues of discretion, in which it was held that judicial review was as effective a remedy and an appeal did not lie. In *CI v HMRC (TC)* [2014] UKUT 158 (AAC), the Upper Tribunal declined to draw such a distinction on the ground that it was "over-technical" but, on this approach, much of Sch.2 to the 1999 Regulations would be inconsistent with art.6 of the European Convention on Human Rights and it is suggested that the more subtle approach in *ZM and AB*, which is consistent with *SSWP v AK (CA)* [2014] UKUT 415 (AAC), is to be preferred.

The fourth case in which an ultra vires challenge to Sch.2 was raised is *Campbell v Secretary of State for Work and Pensions* [2005] EWCA Civ 989, where the Court of Appeal agreed with a Tribunal of Commissioners that a decision under the Convention on Social Security between Great Britain and Jamaica was a decision on payability rather than entitlement, because the convention was given force by the Social Security (Jamaica) Order 1997 which was made under s.179 of the Social Security Administration Act 1992. Section 12(3) of the Social Security Act 1998 therefore did not come into play and the decision was unappealable by virtue of para.22 of Sch.2 to the Regulations, read with para.9 of Sch.2 to the Act.

Even if all the exclusions in this Schedule can be legally justified on the ground that judicial review is an adequate remedy, there might be arguments for removing some of them. For instance, the facts of *DB v SSWP (SPC)* [2018] UKUT 46 (AAC) and *RH v SSWP (DLA)* [2018] UKUT 48 (AAC); [2018] AACR 33 raise questions about the manner in which the Secretary of State appoints local authorities to act on behalf of claimants who are said to be unable to act for themselves and it is arguable that the revoking of para.5(s) so as to provide a practical right of appeal in respect of such decisions might encourage a raising of standards, but there are, of course, counter-arguments.

In this Schedule, "decision" includes determinations embodied in or necessary to a decision (see reg.27(2)).

Schedule 3. *Revoked.* 2.592

[1SCHEDULE 3A **Regulation 7(1)(a)**

DATE FROM WHICH SUPERSEDING DECISION TAKES EFFECT WHERE A CLAIMANT IS IN RECEIPT OF INCOME SUPPORT OR JOBSEEKER'S ALLOWANCE.

Income Support

1. Subject to paragraphs 2 to 6, where the amount of income support payable under an award is changed by a superseding decision made on the ground of a change of circumstances, that superseding decision shall take effect— 2.593

(a) where income support is paid in arrears, from the first day of the benefit week in which the relevant change of circumstances occurs or is expected to occur; or

(b) where income support is paid in advance, from the date of the relevant change of circumstances, or the day on which the relevant change of circumstances is expected to occur, if either of those days is the first day of the benefit week and otherwise from the next following such day, and

for the purposes of this paragraph any period of residence in temporary accommodation under arrangements for training made under section 2 of the Employment and Training Act 1973 or section 2 of the Enterprise and New Towns (Scotland) Act 1990 for a period which is expected to last for seven days or less shall not be regarded as a change of circumstances.

2. In the cases set out in paragraph 3, the superseding decision shall take effect from the day on which the relevant change of circumstances occurs or is expected to occur.

3. The cases referred to in paragraph 2 are where—

(a) income support is paid in arrears and entitlement ends, or is expected to end, for a reason other than that the claimant no longer satisfies the provisions of section 124(1)(b) of the Contributions and Benefits Act;

[2(aa) income support is being paid from 8th April 2002 to persons who, immediately before that day, had a preserved right for the purposes of the Income Support Regulations;]

(b) a child or young person referred to in regulation 16(6) of the Income Support Regulations (child in care of local authority or detained in custody) lives, or is expected to live, with the claimant for part only of the benefit week;

(c) [5 . . .]

(d) a person referred to in paragraph 1, 2, 3 or 18 of Schedule 7 to the Income Support Regulations—

  (i) ceases, or is expected to cease, to be a patient; or

  (ii) a member of his family ceases, or is expected to cease, to be a patient, in either case for a period of less than a week;

(e) a person referred to in paragraph 8 of Schedule 7 to the Income Support Regulations—

  (i) ceases to be a prisoner; or

  (ii) becomes a prisoner;

(f) a person to whom section 126 of the Contributions and Benefits Act (trade disputes) applies—

  (i) becomes incapable of work by reason of disease or bodily or mental disablement; or

(ii) enters the maternity period (as defined in section 126(2) of that Act) or the day is known on which that person is expected to enter the maternity period;

(g) during the currency of the claim, a claimant makes a claim for a relevant social security benefit—

(i) the result of which is that his benefit week changes; or

(ii) under regulation 13 of the Claims and Payment Regulations and an award of that benefit on the relevant day for the purposes of that regulation means that his benefit week is expected to change;

[7 (h) regulation 9 of the Social Security (Disability Living Allowance) Regulations 1991 (persons in certain accommodation other than hospitals) applies, or ceases to apply, to the claimant for a period of less than one week [8; or]

(i) regulations under section 86(1) (hospital in-patients) of the Welfare Reform Act 2012 apply, or cease to apply, to the claimant for a period of less than one week.]

4. A superseding decision made in consequence of a payment of income being treated as paid on a particular day under regulation 31(1)(b) [4 (2) or (3)] or 39C(3) of the Income Support Regulations (date on which income is treated as paid) shall take effect from the day on which that payment is treated as paid.

5. Where—

(a) it is decided upon supersession on the ground of a relevant change of circumstances [5 or change specified in paragraph 12 and 13] that the amount of income support is, or is to be, reduced; and

(b) the Secretary of State certifies that it is impracticable for a superseding decision to take effect from the day prescribed in the preceding paragraphs of this Schedule (other than where paragraph 3(g) or 4 applies),

that superseding decision shall take effect—

(i) where the relevant change has occurred, from the first day of the benefit week following that in which that superseding decision is made; or

(ii) where the relevant change is expected to occur, from the first day of the benefit week following that in which that change of circumstances is expected to occur.

6. Where—

(a) a superseding decision ("the former supersession") was made on the ground of a relevant change of circumstances in the cases set out in paragraphs 3(b) to (g); and

(b) that superseding decision is itself superseded by a subsequent decision because the circumstances which gave rise to the former supersession cease to apply ("the second change"),

that subsequent decision shall take effect from the date of the second change.

Jobseeker's Allowance

2.594 **7.** Subject to paragraphs 8 to 11, where a decision in respect of a claim for jobseeker's allowance is superseded on the ground that there has been or there is expected to be, a relevant change of circumstances, the supersession shall take effect from the first day of the benefit week (as defined in regulation 1(3) of the Jobseeker's Allowance Regulations) in which that relevant change of circumstances occurs or is expected to occur.

8. Where the relevant change of circumstances giving rise to the supersession is that—

(a) entitlement to jobseeker's allowance ends, or is expected to end, for a reason other than that the claimant no longer satisfies the provisions of section 3(1)(a) [2 or 3A(1)(a)] of the Jobseekers Act; or

[3 (aa) jobseeker's allowance is being paid from 8th April 2002 to persons who, immediately before that day, had a preserved right for the purposes of the Jobseeker's Allowance Regulations;]

(b) a child or young person who is normally in the care of a local authority or who is detained in custody lives, or is expected to live, with the claimant for a part only of the benefit week; or

(c) [5 . . .]

(d) the partner of the claimant or a member of his family ceases, or is expected to cease, to be a hospital in-patient for a period of less than a week; [2 or,

(e) a joint-claim couple ceases to be [6 couple]],

the supersession shall take effect from the date that the relevant change of circumstances occurs or is expected to occur.

9. Where the relevant change of circumstances giving rise to a supersession is any of those specified in paragraph 8, and, in consequences of those circumstances ceasing to apply, a further superseding decision is made, that further superseding decision shall take effect from the date that those circumstances ceased to apply.

10. Where, under the provisions of regulation 96 or 102C(3) of the Jobseeker's Allowance Regulations, income is treated as paid on a certain date and that payment gives rise, or is expected to give rise, to a relevant change of circumstance resulting in a supersession, that supersession shall take effect from that date.

11. Where a relevant change of circumstances [5 or change specified in paragraphs 12 and 13] occurs which results, or is expected to result, in a reduced award of jobseeker's allowance then, if the Secretary of State is of the opinion that it is impracticable for a supersession to take effect in accordance with [5 paragraph 12 or] the preceding paragraphs of this Schedule, the supersession shall take effect from the first day of the benefit week following that in which the relevant change of circumstances occurs.]

[5Changes other than changes of circumstances

12. Where an amount of income support or jobseeker's allowance payable under an award is changed by a superseding decision specified in paragraph 13 the superseding decision shall take effect— **2.595**

(a) in the case of a change in respect of income support, from the day specified in paragraph 1(a) or (b) for a change of circumstances; and

(b) in the case of a change in respect of jobseeker's allowance, from the day specified in paragraph 7 for a change of circumstances.

13. The following are superseding decisions for the purposes of paragraph 12—

(a) a decision which supersedes a decision specified in regulation 6(2)(b) to (ee); and

(b) a superseding decision which would, but for paragraph 12, take effect from a date specified in regulation 7(5) to (7), (12) to (16), (18) to (20), (22), (24) and (33).]

AMENDMENTS

1. Social Security and Child Support (Miscellaneous Amendments) Regulations 2000 (SI 2000/1596) reg.35 (June 19, 2000).

2. Social Security Amendment (Joint Claim) Regulations 2001 (SI 2001/518) reg.4(c) (March 19, 2001).

3. Social Security Amendment (Residential Care and Nursing Homes) Regulations 2002 (SI 2002/398) reg.3 (April 8, 2002).

4. Social Security (Working Tax Credit and Child Tax Credit) (Consequential Amendments) (No.3) Regulations 2003 (SI 2003/1731) reg.5 (August 8, 2003).

5. Social Security, Child Support and Tax Credits (Miscellaneous Amendments) Regulations 2005 (SI 2005/337) reg.2(21) (March 19, 2005).

6. Civil Partnership (Consequential Amendments) Regulations 2005 (SI 2005/2878) reg.8(4) (December 5, 2005).

7. Social Security (Miscellaneous Amendments) (No.3) Regulations 2006 (SI 2006/2377) reg.3(3) (October 2, 2006).

8. Personal Independence Payment (Supplementary Provisions and Consequential Amendments) Regulations 2013 (SI 2013/388) reg.8 and Sch. para.21 (April 8, 2013).

DEFINITIONS

"the Claims and Payments Regulations"—see reg.1(3).
"the Contributions and Benefits Act"—see s.84 of the Social Security Act 1998.
"the Income Support Regulations"—see reg.1(3).
"the Jobseekers Act"—see s.84 of the Social Security Act 1998.
"the Jobseeker's Allowance Regulations"—see reg.1(3).
"a joint-claim couple"—*ibid.*
"superseding decision"—see para.13.

GENERAL NOTE

Paragraphs 12 and 13 have the effect that any change to an existing award of income support or jobseeker's allowance takes place from the start of a benefit week. However, this does not apply where a change of circumstances is favourable **2.596** to a claimant or is due to a change of legislation, because in such cases reg.7(2)(b) or (bb) or (30) takes precedence over this Schedule (see reg.7(1)(a)). This Schedule takes precedence over all other paragraphs of reg.7.

[1 SCHEDULE 3B

Date on Which Change of Circumstances Takes Effect Where Claimant Entitled to State Pension Credit

2.597 **1.** Where the amount of state pension credit payable under an award is changed by a superseding decision made on the ground that there has been a relevant change of circumstances, that superseding decision shall take effect from the following days—

(a) for the purpose only of determining the day on which an assessed income period begins under section 9 of the State Pension Credit Act, from the day following the day on which the last previous assessed income period ended; and

(b) [6 except as provided in the following paragraphs–

(i) where state pension credit is paid in advance, from the day that change occurs or is expected to occur if either of those days is the first day of a benefit week but if it is not from the next following such day;

(ii) where state pension credit is paid in arrears, from the first day of the benefit week in which that change occurs or is expected to occur.]

[7 **2.** Subject to paragraph 3, where the relevant change is that—

(a) the claimant's income or the income of the claimant's partner (other than deemed income from capital) has changed;

(b) the claimant or the claimant's partner becomes entitled to—

(i) disability living allowance (middle or higher rate care component); or

(ii) attendance allowance; [8 . . .]

[8 (iii) personal independence payment (standard or enhanced rate daily living component under section 78 of the Welfare Reform Act 2012); or]

[9 (iv) armed forces independence payment under the Armed Forces and Resrve Forces (Compensation Scheme) Order 2011; or]

(c) the claimant or the claimant's partner again receives [8 any of the allowances or payments] mentioned in sub-paragraph (b) above immediately after the end of the period specified in paragraph 2A,

the superseding decision shall take effect on the first day of the benefit week in which that change occurs or if that is not practicable in the circumstances of the case, on the first day of the next following benefit week.

2A. A period specified for the purposes of paragraph 2 is a period when the claimant or the claimant's partner is maintained free of charge while undergoing medical or other treatment as an in-patient in—

(a) a hospital or similar institution under—

(i) the National Health Service 2006;

(ii) the National Health Service (Wales) Act 2006; or

(iii) the National Health Service (Scotland) Act 1978; or

(b) a hospital or similar institution maintained or administered by the Defence Council.]

3. Paragraph 2 shall not apply where the only relevant change is that working tax credit under the Tax Credits Act 2002 becomes payable or becomes payable at a higher rate.

4. A superseding decision shall take effect from the day the change of circumstances occurs or is expected to occur if—

(a) the person ceases to be or becomes a prisoner, and for this purpose "prisoner" has the same meaning as in regulation 1(2) of the State Pension Credit Regulations; or

(b) whilst entitled to state pension credit a claimant is awarded another social security benefit and in consequence of that award his benefit week changes or is expected to change.

[2 **5.** In a case where the relevant circumstance is that the claimant ceased to be a patient, if he becomes a patient again in the same benefit week, the superseding decision in respect of ceasing to be a patient shall take effect from the first day of the week in which the change occured.]

6. In paragraph 5, "patient" means a person (other than a prisoner) who is regarded as receiving free in-patient treatment within the meaning of the [4 Social Security (Hospital In-Patients) Regulations 2005.]

[3 **7.** [5 Subject to [6 paragraph 8A], where] an amount of state pension credit payable under an award is changed by a superseding decision specified in paragraph 8 the superseding decision shall take effect from the day specified in paragraph 1(b).

8. The following are superseding decisions for the purposes of paragraph 7—

(a) a decision which supersedes a decision specified in regulation 6(2)(b) to (ee) and (m); and

(b) a superseding decision which would, but for paragraphs 2 and 7, take effect from a date specified in regulation 7(5) to (7), (12) to (16) and (29C).]

[[6] **8A.** Where the relevant change of circumstances is the death of the claimant, the superseding decision shall take effect on the first day of the benefit week next following the date of death.]

[[5] **9.** [[6] . . .]

10. [[6] . . .]

11. In this Schedule, "benefit week" means—

(a) where state pension credit is paid in advance, the period of 7 days beginning on the day on which, in the claimant's case, that benefit is payable;

(b) where state pension credit is paid in arrears, the period of 7 days ending on the day on which, in the claimant's case, that benefit is payable.]

AMENDMENTS

1. State Pension Credit (Consequential, Transitional and Miscellaneous Provisions) Regulations 2002 (SI 2002/3019) reg.22 (April 7, 2003).

2. State Pension Credit (Transitional and Miscellaneous Provisions) Amendment Regulations 2003 (SI 2003/2274) reg.5(4) (October 6, 2003).

3. Social Security (Miscellaneous Amendments) (No.2) Regulations 2006 (SI 2006/832) reg.5(4) (April 10, 2006).

4. Social Security (Miscellaneous Amendments) (No.4) Regulations 2007 (SI 2007/2470) reg.3(9) (September 24, 2007).

5. Social Security (Miscellaneous Amendments) Regulations 2010 (SI 2010/510) reg.4(1) and (4) (March 4, 2010).

6. Social Security (Miscellaneous Amendments) Regulations 2011 (SI 2011/674) reg.8 (April 11, 2011).

7. Social Security (Miscellaneous Amendments) Regulations 2013 (SI 2013/443) reg.5(a) and (c) (April 2, 2013).

8. Social Security (Miscellaneous Amendments) Regulations 2013 (SI 2013/443) reg.5(b) (April 8, 2013).

9. Armed Forces and Reserve Forces Compensation Scheme (Consequential Provisions: Subordinate Legislation) Order 2013 (SI 2013/591) art.7 and Sch. para.15 (April 8, 2013).

DEFINITIONS

"assessed income period"—see reg.1(3).
"benefit week"–see para.(11).
"patient"—see para.6.
"state pension credit"—see reg.1(3).
"State Pension Credit Act"—*ibid.*
"State Pension Credit Regulations"—*ibid.*

GENERAL NOTE

This Schedule takes precedence over reg.7, except where reg.7(2)(b) or (bb), (29) **2.598**
or (30) applies (see reg.7(1)(a)). The misspelling of what should read as "occurred" in para.5 occurs in the Queen's Printer's copy of the statutory instrument.

[[1] SCHEDULE 3C

DATE FROM WHICH CHANGE OF CIRCUMSTANCES TAKES EFFECT WHERE CLAIMANT ENTITLED TO EMPLOYMENT AND SUPPORT ALLOWANCE

1. Subject to paragraphs 2 to 7, where the amount of an employment and support allow- **2.599**
ance payable under an award is changed by a superseding decision made on the ground

of a change of circumstances, that superseding decision shall take effect from the first day of the benefit week in which the relevant change of circumstances occurs or is expected to occur.

2. In the cases set out in paragraph 3, the superseding decision shall take effect from the day on which the relevant change of circumstances occurs or is expected to occur.

3. The cases referred to in paragraph 2 are where—

(a) entitlement ends, or is expected to end, for a reason other than that the claimant no longer satisfies the provisions of paragraph 6(1)(a) of Schedule 1 to the Welfare Reform Act;

(b) a child or young person referred to in regulation 156(6)(d) or (h) of the Employment and Support Allowance Regulations (child in care of local authority or detained in custody) lives, or is expected to live, with the claimant for part only of the benefit week;

(c) a person referred to in paragraph 12 of Schedule 5 to the Employment and Support Allowance Regulations—

(i) ceases, or is expected to cease, to be a patient; or

(ii) a member of the person's family ceases, or is expected to cease, to be a patient, in either case for a period of less than a week;

(d) a person referred to in paragraph 3 of Schedule 5 to the Employment and Support Allowance Regulations—

(i) ceases to be a prisoner; or

(ii) becomes a prisoner;

(e) during the currency of the claim a claimant makes a claim for a relevant social security benefit—

(i) the result of which is that his benefit week changes; or

(ii) in accordance with regulation 13 of the Claims and Payments Regulations and an award of that benefit on the relevant day for the purposes of that regulation means that his benefit week is expected to change.

[[2] (f) regulation 9 of the Social Security (Disability Living Allowance) Regulations 1991 (persons in care homes) applies, or ceases to apply, to the claimant for a period of less than one week; or

(g) regulations under section 85(1) of the Welfare Reform Act 2012 (care home residents) apply, or cease to apply, to the claimant for a period of less than one week.]

4. A superseding decision made in consequence of a payment of income being treated as paid on a particular day under regulation 93 of the Employment and Support Allowance Regulations (date on which income is treated as paid) shall take effect from the day on which that payment is treated as paid.

5. Where—

(a) it is decided upon supersession on the ground of a relevant change of circumstances or change specified in paragraphs 9 and 10 that the amount of an employment and support allowance is, or is to be, reduced; and

(b) the Secretary of State certifies that it is impracticable for a superseding decision to take effect from the day prescribed in paragraph 9 or the preceding paragraphs of this Schedule (other than where paragraph 3(e) or 4 applies),

that superseding decision shall take effect—

(i) where the relevant change has occurred, from the first day of the benefit week following that in which that superseding decision is made; or

(ii) where the relevant change is expected to occur, from the first day of the benefit week following that in which that change of circumstances is expected to occur.

6. Where—

(a) a superseding decision ("the former supersession") was made on the ground of a relevant change of circumstances in the cases set out in paragraph 3(b) to (e); and

(b) that superseding decision is itself superseded by a subsequent decision because the circumstances which gave rise to the former supersession cease to apply ("the second change"),

that subsequent decision shall take effect from the date of the second change.

7. In the case of an employment and support allowance decision where there has been a limited capability for work determination, where—

(a) the Secretary of State is satisfied that, in relation to a limited capability for work determination, the claimant or payee failed to notify an appropriate office of a change of circumstances which regulations under the Administration Act required him to notify; and

(b) the claimant or payee, as the case may be, could reasonably have been expected to know that the change of circumstances should have been notified,

the superseding decision shall take effect—

(i) from the date on which the claimant or payee, as the case may be, ought to have notified the change of circumstances; or

(ii) if more than one change has taken place between the date from which the decision to be superseded took effect and the date of the superseding decision, from the date on which the first change ought to have been notified.

Changes other than changes of circumstances

8. Where— **2.600**

(a) the Secretary of State supersedes a decision made by an appeal tribunal or a Commissioner on the grounds specified in regulation 6(2)(c)(i) (ignorance of, or mistake as to, a material fact);

(b) the decision to be superseded was more advantageous to the claimant because of the ignorance or mistake than it would otherwise have been; and

(c) the material fact—

(i) does not relate to the limited capability for work determination embodied in or necessary to the decision; or

(ii) relates to a limited capability for work determination embodied in or necessary to the decision and the Secretary of State is satisfied that at the time the decision was made the claimant or payee, as the case may be, knew or could reasonably have been expected to know of it and that it was relevant,

the superseding decision shall take effect from the first day of the benefit week in which the decision of the appeal tribunal or the Commissioner took effect or was to take effect.

9. Where an amount of an employment and support allowance payable under an award is changed by a superseding decision specified in paragraph 10 the superseding decision shall take effect from the day specified in paragraph 1 for a change of circumstances.

10. The following are superseding decisions for the purposes of paragraph 9—

(a) a decision which supersedes a decision specified in regulation 6(2)(b) and (d) to (ee); and

(b) a superseding decision which would, but for paragraph 9, take effect from a date specified in regulation 7(6), (7), (12), (13), (17D) to (17F), and (33).]

AMENDMENTS

1. Employment and Support Allowance (Consequential Provisions) (No.2) Regulations 2008 (SI 2008/1554) regs 29 and 43 (July 27, 2008).

2. Social Security (Miscellaneous Amendments) (No.3) Regulations 2013 (SI 2013/2536) reg.8 (October 29, 2013).

Schedules 3D and **4.** *Omitted.* **2.601**

The Universal Credit, Personal Independence Payment, Jobseeker's Allowance and Employment and Support Allowance (Decisions and Appeals) Regulations 2013

(SI 2013/381)

Made *25th February 2013*

Coming into force in accordance with Regulation 1

CONTENTS

PART 1

GENERAL

PART 2

REVISION

CHAPTER 1

REVISION ON ANY GROUND

CHAPTER 2

REVISION ON SPECIFIC GROUNDS

CHAPTER 3

PROCEDURE AND EFFECTIVE DATE

PART 3

SUPERSESSIONS

CHAPTER 1

GROUNDS FOR SUPERSESSION

CHAPTER 2

SUPERSEDING DECISIONS: LIMITATIONS AND PROCEDURE

CHAPTER 3

EFFECTIVE DATES FOR SUPERSESSIONS

PART 4

OTHER MATTERS REALTING TO DECISION-MAKING

PART 5

SUSPENSION

PART 6

TERMINATION

PART 7

APPEALS

SCHEDULES

The Secretary of State makes the following Regulations in exercise of the powers conferred by sections:
– 5(1A), 159D(1) and (6), 189(1), (4) to (6) and section 191 of the Social Security Administration Act 1992;
– 9(1), (4) and (6), 10(3) and (6), 10A, 11(1), 12(2), (3), (3A), (3B), (6) and (7)(b), 16(1), 17, 18(1), 21(1) to (3), 22 and 23, 25(3)(b) and (5)(c), 26(6)(c), 28(1), 31(2), 79(1) and (4) to (7) and 84 of, and paragraph 9 of Schedule 2, paragraphs 1, 4 and 9 of Schedule 3 and Schedule 5 to, the Social Security Act 1998.
A draft of this instrument was laid before and approved by a resolution of each House of Parliament in accordance with section 80(1) of the Social Security Act 1998.
The Social Security Advisory Committee has agreed that the proposals in respect of these Regulations should not be referred to it.

PART 1

GENERAL

Citation, commencement and application

1.—(1) These Regulations may be cited as the Universal Credit, Personal Independence Payment, Jobseeker's Allowance and Employment and Support Allowance (Decisions and Appeals) Regulations 2013. **2.603**

(2) They come into force—

(a) in so far as they relate to personal independence payment and for the purposes of this regulation, on 8th April 2013;

(b) for all remaining purposes, on 29th April 2013.

(3) These Regulations apply in relation to—

(a) an employment and support allowance payable under Part 1 of the 2007 Act as amended by Schedule 3 and Part 1 of Schedule 14 to the 2012 Act (to remove references to an income-related allowance);

(b) a jobseeker's allowance payable under the Jobseekers Act as amended by Part 1 of Schedule 14 to the 2012 Act (to remove references to an income-based allowance);

(c) personal independence payment; and

(d) universal credit.

DEFINITIONS

"the 2007 Act"–see reg.2.
"the 2012 Act"–see reg.2.
"the Jobseekers Act"–see reg.2.
"personal independence payment"–see reg.2.
"universal credit"–see reg.2.

GENERAL NOTE

These Regulations are similar to the Social Security and Child Benefit (Decisions and Appeals) Regulations 1999 but it has been decided to have these separate Regulations for the "working age" benefits introduced by the Welfare Reform Act 2012, including the "new style" contributory employment and support allowance and jobseeker's allowance, rather than further complicate those Regulations, and the opportunity has been taken to simplify the drafting and divide up some of the longer provisions. To avoid duplication, where there is a regulation under the 2013 Regulations that is equivalent to a regulation under 1999 Regulations the notes are not repeated below. **2.604**

Interpretation

2. In these Regulations— **2.605**

"the 1998 Act" means the Social Security Act 1998;

"the 2007 Act" means the Welfare Reform Act 2007;

"the 2012 Act" means the Welfare Reform Act 2012;

"the Administration Act" means the Social Security Administration Act 1992;

"appeal", except where the context otherwise requires, means an appeal to the First-tier Tribunal established under the Tribunals, Courts and Enforcement Act 2007;

"appropriate office" means—

(a) in the case of a contributions decision which falls within Part 2 (contributions decisions) of Schedule 3 (decisions against which an appeal lies) to the 1998 Act, any National Insurance Contributions office of HMRC or any office of the Department for Work and Pensions; or

(b) in any other case, the office of the Department for Work and Pensions, or other place, the address of which is specified on the notification of the original decision referred to in regulation 5(1) (revision on any grounds);

"assessment period" is to be construed in accordance with regulation 21 (assessment periods) of the Universal Credit Regulations;

"benefit" means a benefit or an allowance in relation to which these Regulations apply;

"benefit week" has the same meaning as in—

(a) regulation 2 (interpretation) of the Employment and Support Allowance Regulations 2013 in the case of an employment and support allowance;

(b) regulation 2 (general interpretation) of the Jobseeker's Allowance Regulations 2013, in the case of a jobseeker's allowance;

"child" means a person under the age of 16;

[1 [2 ...]]

"claimant" means—

(a) any person who has claimed—

(i) an employment and support allowance;

(ii) a jobseeker's allowance;

(iii) personal independence payment;

(b) in the case of universal credit, any person who is a claimant for the purposes of section 40 (interpretation) of the 2012 Act; and

(c) any other person from whom an amount of benefit is alleged to be recoverable;

"the Claims and Payments Regulations 2013" means the Universal Credit, Personal Independence Payment, Jobseeker's Allowance and Employment and Support Allowance (Claims and Payments) Regulations 2013;

"the Contributions and Benefits Act" means the Social Security Contributions and Benefits Act 1992;

"the date of notification", in relation to a decision of the Secretary of State, means the date on which the notification of the decision is treated as having been given or sent in accordance with—

(a) regulation 3 (service of documents); or

(b) where the notification is given or sent using an electronic communication, Schedule 2 (electronic communications) to the Claims and Payments Regulations 2013;

"designated authority" means—

(a) the Secretary of State; or

(b) a person providing services to the Secretary of State;

"electronic communication" has the same meaning as in section 15(1) of the Electronic Communications Act 2000;

"employment and support allowance" means an employment and support allowance in relation to which these Regulations apply;

"the Fraud Act" means the Social Security Fraud Act 2001;

"fraud penalty", in relation to any claimant of an employment and support allowance, a jobseeker's allowance or universal credit, means any period during which the provisions of section 6B, 7 or 9 of the Fraud Act apply to the award;

"family" means the claimant's partner and any—

(a) child; or

(b) qualifying young person, within the meaning of regulation 5 (meaning of "qualifying young person") of the Universal Credit Regulations,

who is a member of the same household as the claimant and for whom the either the claimant or their partner is, or both of them are, responsible;

"HMRC" means Her Majesty's Revenue and Customs;

"the Jobseekers Act" means the Jobseekers Act 1995;

"jobseeker's allowance" means a jobseeker's allowance in relation to which these Regulations apply;

"limited capability for work" has the same meaning as in—

(a) section 1(4) of the 2007 Act in relation to an employment and support allowance;

(b) section 37(1) of the 2012 Act in relation to universal credit;

"limited capability for work determination" means—

(a) where the determination relates to an employment and support allowance, a determination whether a person has limited capability for work following a limited capability for work assessment in accordance with regulation 15(1) (determination of limited capability for work) of the Employment and Support Allowance Regulations 2013, or a determination that a person is to be treated as having limited capability for work in accordance with regulation 16 (certain claimants to be treated as having limited capability for work) or 25 (exceptional circumstances) of those Regulations;

(b) where the determination relates to universal credit, a determination whether a person has limited capability for work following a limited capability for work assessment referred to in regulation 39(2) (limited capability for work) of the Universal Credit Regulations, or a determination that a person is to be treated as having limited capability for work in accordance with regulation 39(6) of those Regulations;

"official error" means an error made by—

(a) an officer of the Department for Work and Pensions or HMRC acting as such which was not caused or materially contributed to by any person outside the Department or HMRC;

(b) a person employed by, and acting on behalf of, a designated authority which was not caused or materially contributed to by any person outside that authority,

but excludes any error of law which is shown to have been such by a subsequent decision of the Upper Tribunal, or of the court as defined in section 27(7) of the 1998 Act;

"partner" means one of a couple within the meaning of section 39 (couples) of the 2012 Act;

"personal independence payment" means an allowance payable under Part 4 (personal independence payment) of the 2012 Act;

"relevant benefit" has the same meaning as in Chapter 2 (social security decisions and appeals) of Part 1 (decisions and appeals) of the 1998 Act;

"the Rent Officers Order 2013" means the Rent Officers (Universal Credit Functions) Order 2013;

[2 "Scottish disability benefit" means, as the context requires, either of the following benefits—

(a) adult disability payment within the meaning given in regulation 2 of the Disability Assistance for Working Age People (Scotland) Regulations 2022; and

(b) child disability payment within the meaning given in regulation 2 of the Disability Assistance for Children and Young People (Scotland) Regulations 2021;]

[3 "terminally ill" in relation to a claimant, means that the claimant is suffering from a progressive disease and that death in consequence of that disease can reasonably be [4 expected within 12 months]]

"the Tribunal Procedure Rules" means the Tribunal Procedure (First-tier Tribunal) (Social Entitlement Chamber) Rules 2008;

"the Universal Credit Regulations" means the Universal Credit Regulations 2013;

"universal credit" means the benefit payable under Part 1 (universal credit) of the 2012 Act;

"writing" includes writing produced by means of electronic communications used in accordance with regulation 4 (electronic communications).

AMENDMENTS

1. Social Security (Scotland) Act 2018 (Disability Assistance for Children and Young People) (Consequential Modifications) Order 2021 (SI 2021/786) art.21(1) and (2) (July 26, 2021).

2. Social Security (Disability Assistance for Working Age People) (Consequential Amendments) Order 2022 (SI 2022/177) art.17(1) and (2) (March 21, 2022).

3. Universal Credit and Employment and Support Allowance (Terminal Illness) (Amendment) Regulations 2022 (SI 2022/260) reg.2(4) (April 4, 2022).

4. Social Security (Special Rules for End of Life) Act 2022 s.1(3) (April 3, 2023).

GENERAL NOTE

2.606 For the scope of "official error", see the note to r.1(3) of the Social Security and Child Benefit (Decisions and Appeals) Regulations 1999.

Service of documents

2.607 **3.**—(1) Where, under any provision of these Regulations, any notice or other document is given or sent by post to the Secretary of State, it is to be treated as having been given or sent on the day on which it is received by the Secretary of State.

(2) Where, under any provision of these Regulations, the Secretary of State sends a notice or other document by post to a person's last known address, it is to be treated as having been given or sent on the day on which it was posted.

GENERAL NOTE

2.608 This is equivalent to reg.2 of the Social Security and Child Support (Decisions and Appeals) Regulations 1999. See the note to that provision.

Electronic communications

4. Schedule 2 (electronic communications) to the Claims and Payments Regulations 2013 applies to the delivery of electronic communications to or by the Secretary of State for the purposes of these Regulations in the same manner as it applies to the delivery of electronic communications for the purposes of the Claims and Payments Regulations 2013. **2.609**

DEFINITIONS

"the Claims and Payments Regulations 2013"–see reg.2.
"electronic communication"–see reg.2.

PART 2

REVISION

CHAPTER 1

REVISION ON ANY GROUNDS

Revision on any grounds

5.—(1) Any decision of the Secretary of State under section 8 or 10 of the 1998 Act ("the original decision") may be revised by the Secretary of State if— **2.610**

(a) the Secretary of State commences action leading to the revision within one month of the date of notification of the original decision; or
(b) an application for a revision is received by the Secretary of State at an appropriate office within—
  (i) one month of the date of notification of the original decision (but subject to regulation 38(4)(correction of accidental errors));
  (ii) 14 days of the expiry of that period if a written statement of the reasons for the decision is requested under regulation 7 (consideration of revision before appeal) or regulation 51 (notice of a decision against which an appeal lies) and that statement is provided within the period specified in paragraph (i);
  (iii) 14 days of the date on which that statement was provided if the statement was requested within the period specified in paragraph (i) but was provided after the expiry of that period; or
  (iv) such longer period as may be allowed under regulation 6 (late application for a revision).

(2) Paragraph (1) does not apply—
(a) in respect of a relevant change of circumstances which occurred since the decision had effect or, in the case of an advance award under regulation 32, 33 or 34 of the Claims and Payments Regulations 2013, since the decision was made;
(b) where the Secretary of State has evidence or information which indicates that a relevant change of circumstances will occur;
(c) in respect of a decision which relates to an employment and support allowance or personal independence payment where the claimant is terminally ill, unless the application for a revision contains an express statement that the claimant is terminally ill.

DEFINITIONS

"the 1998 Act"–see reg.2.
"appeal"–see reg.2.
"appropriate office"–see reg.2.
"claimant"–see reg.2.
"the Claims and Payments Regulations 2013"–see reg.2.
"the date of notification"–see reg.2.
"employment and support allowance"–by virtue of reg.2, see reg.1(3)(a).
"personal independence payment"–see reg.2.
"terminally ill"–see reg.2.

GENERAL NOTE

2.611 This regulation is equivalent to reg.3(1) and (9) of the Social Security and Child Support (Decisions and Appeals) Regulations 1999. See the notes to those provisions. The broad power of revision is conferred by s.9 of the Social Security Act 1998 and this regulation is made in exercise of the regulation-making powers conferred by that section.

Late application for a revision

2.612 **6.**—(1) The Secretary of State may extend the time limit specified in regulation 5(1) (revision on any grounds) for making an application for a revision if all of the following conditions are met.

(2) The first condition is that the person wishing to apply for the revision has applied to the Secretary of State at an appropriate office for an extension of time.

(3) The second condition is that the application—

(a) explains why the extension is sought;
(b) contains sufficient details of the decision to which the application relates to enable it to be identified; and
(c) is made within [1 12] months of the latest date by which the application for revision should have been received by the Secretary of State in accordance with regulation 5(1)(b)(i) to (iii).

(4) The third condition is that the Secretary of State is satisfied that it is reasonable to grant the extension.

(5) The fourth condition is that the Secretary of State is satisfied that due to special circumstances it was not practicable for the application for revision to be made within the time limit specified in regulation 5(1)(b)(i) to (iii) (revision on any grounds).

(6) In determining whether it is reasonable to grant an extension of time, the Secretary of State must have regard to the principle that the greater the amount of time that has elapsed between the end of the time limit specified in regulation 5(1)(b)(i) to (iii) (revision on any grounds) and the date of the application, the more compelling should be the special circumstances on which the application is based.

(7) An application under this regulation which has been refused may not be renewed.

AMENDMENT

1. Social Security (Miscellaneous Amendments No.4) Regulations 2017 (SI 2017/1015) reg.16 (November 16, 2017).

DEFINITION

"appropriate office"–see reg.2.

General Note

This regulation is equivalent to reg.4 of the Social Security and Child Support (Decisions and Appeals) Regulations 1999, save that it does not reproduce reg.4(6) which is an unsatisfactory provision restricting the power to extend time. See the note to reg.4(1) of the 1999 Regulations. 2.613

Consideration of revision before appeal

7.—(1) This regulation applies in a case where— 2.614

(a) the Secretary of State gives a person written notice of a decision under section 8 or 10 of the 1998 Act (whether as originally made or as revised under section 9 of that Act); and

(b) that notice includes a statement to the effect that there is a right of appeal in relation to the decision only if the Secretary of State has considered an application for a revision of the decision.

(2) In a case to which this regulation applies, a person has a right of appeal under section 12(2) of the 1998 Act in relation to the decision only if the Secretary of State has considered on an application whether to revise the decision under section 9 of that Act.

(3) The notice referred to in paragraph (1) must inform the person—

(a) of the time limit under regulation 5(1) (revision on any grounds) for making an application for a revision; and

(b) that, where the notice does not include a statement of the reasons for the decision ("written reasons"), the person may, within one month of the date of notification of the decision, request that the Secretary of State provide written reasons.

(4) Where written reasons are requested under paragraph (3)(b), the Secretary of State must provide that statement within 14 days of receipt of the request or as soon as practicable afterwards.

(5) Where, as the result of paragraph (2), there is no right of appeal against a decision, the Secretary of State may treat any purported appeal as an application for a revision under section 9 of the 1998 Act.

Definitions

"the 1998 Act"–see reg.2.
"appeal"–see reg.2.
"the date of notification"–see reg.2.

General Note

This regulation is equivalent to reg.3ZA of the Social Security and Child Support (Decisions and Appeals) Regulations 1999, although this provision came into effect six months earlier. See the note to that provision. *PP v SSWP (UC)* [2020] UKUT 109 (AAC), to which reference is made in that note, was decided against the background of this regulation. Given the similarity between reg.30 of the Employment and Support Allowance Regulations 2008 and reg.26 of the Employment and Support Allowance Regulations 2013 and given also that no distinction was drawn in the case between contributory and income-related employment and support allowances, the effect of *R. (Connor) v Secretary of State for Work and Pensions* [2020] EWHC 1999 (Admin), also mentioned in that note, appears to be that this regulation is unlawful and must be disregarded insofar as it would otherwise be applied to claimants of "new style" employment and support allowance who would, if pursuing an appeal to the First-tier Tribunal, subject to compliance with the condition at reg.26(2) of the 2013 ESA Regulations, be entitled to receive payment pending the appeal pursuant to reg.26(3). 2.615

CHAPTER 2

REVISION ON SPECIFIC GROUNDS

Introduction

2.616 **8.** A decision of the Secretary of State under section 8 or 10 of the 1998 Act may be revised at any time by the Secretary of State in any of the cases and circumstances set out in this Chapter.

DEFINITION

"the 1998 Act"–see reg.2.

GENERAL NOTE

2.617 This Chapter reproduces the relevant provisions of reg.3(4A) to (8K) of the Social Security and Child Support (Decisions and Appeals) Regulations 1999 in a more digestible form. See the beginning of the note to reg.3 of the 1999 Regulations for the differences between revision and supersession, dealt with under regs 22 of 37 of these Regulations. Regulation 32 has the effect that revision takes precedence over supersession where both might otherwise be possible.

Official error, mistake etc.

2.618 **9.** A decision may be revised where the decision—

(a) arose from official error; or
(b) was made in ignorance of, or was based on a mistake as to, some material fact and as a result is more advantageous to a claimant than it would otherwise have been.

DEFINITIONS

"claimant"–see reg.2.
"official error"–see reg.2.

GENERAL NOTE

2.619 This regulation is equivalent to reg.3(5)(a) and (b) of the Social Security and Child Support (Decisions and Appeals) Regulations 1999. See the note to that reg.3(5), and also to reg.1(3) of the 1999 Regulations for the scope of "official error". However, note that the complications of reg.3(5)(c) and (d) have not been reproduced in these Regulations with the result that questions as to whether a claimant could reasonably have been expected to be aware of a material fact or that it was relevant to a decision will arise only in respect of recoverability decisions in respect of personal independence payment under s.71 of the Social Security Administration Act 1992 and will not determine whether a decision as to entitlement to personal independence payment or an employment and support allowance should be revised retrospectively rather than superseded only prospectively.

Paragraph 9(b)

2.620 Evidence that comes to light later, but relates to the time a decision was made, can be used to establish whether a decision was made based on a mistake as to a material fact. In *SSWP v SV* [2023] UKUT 279 (AAC) the Upper Tribunal explained how to apply reg.(9)(b). In this case an award of Universal Credit made following a decision made on 10/03/2020 was revised based on evidence from a witness statement dated 12/04/2022. The Upper Tribunal found that the First-tier Tribunal was wrong to assume that the application of regulation 9(b) depended on the state of the decisionmaker's mind. Regulation 9(b) provides for a decision to be revised where it was made in ignorance of, or was based on a mistake as to, some material fact and as a result is more advantageous to the claimant than it would otherwise have been. As stated at para.17, "It does not matter whether the decision was made by: (a) the Secretary of State acting through an official as decision-maker, who has a mind; or (b) a computer under s.2 of the Social Security Act 1998, which does not have a mind. It does not matter how the mistake came to be made. It could have occurred, for example, because the officer overlooked evidence held by the Department, or because the Department was not aware of the evidence, or because the claimant had deliberately concealed it. In all those cases and others, the decision could be based on a mistake. It is not necessary for the decision to be made by mistake. The power to review is triggered by the mistaken conclusion on a particular fact, not by a flaw in the decision-making process. The decision may have been the only one that could properly have been made on the evidence available at the time. It may only be shown to be mistaken when evidence becomes available later." In other words, while the tribunal must not take account of circumstances that were not obtaining at the decision (s.12(8)(b) of the SSA), later evidence is admissible, provided that it relates to the time of the decision (*R(DLA)* 2/01 and *R(DLA)* 3/01).

Note: the above is about reg.9, in the context of revision for error/mistake about a fact and is therefore restricted to where the decision is consequently more advantageous to the claimant and is in the context of an "any time" revision (i.e: on specific grounds). However, an error/mistake about a fact is also capable of allowing a "late" revision on any grounds under regs 5 and 6. Revision under these rules, although of course time limited to the absolute limit of 13 months from the decision, is possible where the decision was not more advantageous (and in fact was more adverse) because of the mistake/ignorance (e.g.: where the claim neglected to include something about the claimant's housing costs or caring responsibilities, even though they did as a matter of fact exist at the time). Sometimes decision-makers and even First-tier Tribunals consider this is not a ground for such revisions and want to characterise the original decision as not based on an error/mistake about a fact at all. Rather they seek to characterise the claimant's subsequent raising of it as some sort of 'change of circumstances' and so only capable of founding a supersession. It is suggested such an approach is incorrect (see for example the Court of Appeal's recent characterisation of revisions at para.28 of *SSWP v Miah* [2024] EWCA Civ 186).

Decisions against which no appeal lies

10. A decision may be revised where the decision is one which is— **2.621**

(a) specified in Schedule 2 (decisions against which no appeal lies) to the 1998 Act; or

(b) prescribed by regulation 50(2) (decisions which may or may not be appealed).

Definitions

"the 1998 Act"–see reg.2.
"appeal"–see reg.2.

General Note

This regulation is equivalent to reg.3(8) of the Social Security and Child Support (Decisions and Appeals) Regulations 1999. **2.622**

Decisions where there is an appeal

11.—(1) A decision may be revised where there is an appeal against the decision within the time prescribed by the Tribunal Procedure Rules but the appeal has not been decided. **2.623**

(2) Where—

(a) the Secretary of State makes a decision under section 8 or 10 of the 1998 Act or such a decision is revised under section 9(1) of the 1998 Act ("decision A");

(b) the claimant appeals against decision A;

(c) after the appeal has been made, but before it results in a decision by the First-tier Tribunal, the Secretary of State makes another decision ("decision B") which—

(i) supersedes decision A; or

(ii) decides a further claim by the claimant;

(d) after the making of decision B, the First-tier Tribunal makes a decision on the appeal ("decision C"); and

(e) the Secretary of State would have made decision B differently if, at the time, the Secretary of State had been aware of decision C,

the Secretary of State may revise decision B.

DEFINITIONS

"the 1998 Act"–see reg.2.
"appeal"–see reg.2.
"claimant"–see reg.2.
"the Tribunal Procedure Rules"–see reg.2.

GENERAL NOTE

2.624 This regulation is equivalent to reg.3(4A) and (5A) of the Social Security and Child Support (Decisions and Appeals) Regulations 1999. See the note to those provisions. Regulation 7 may result in fewer revisions under reg.11(1) than there might otherwise have been. However, there will still be cases where new evidence is provided during the course of appeal proceedings or where the act of responding to an appeal alerts a decision-maker to an error in the original decision that was missed on revision and so para.(1) is likely to remain useful.

Award of another benefit

2.625 **12.** Where—

(a) the Secretary of State makes a decision to award a benefit to a claimant ("the original award"); and

(b) an award of another relevant benefit [1 or [2 Scottish disability benefit]] or of an increase in the rate of another relevant benefit [1 or [2 Scottish disability benefit]] is made to the claimant or, in the case of universal credit, to a member of their family, for a period which includes the date on which the original award took effect,

the Secretary of State may revise the original award.

AMENDMENTS

1. Social Security (Scotland) Act 2018 (Disability Assistance for Children and Young People) (Consequential Modifications) Order 2021 (SI 2021/786) art.21(1) and (3) (July 26, 2021).

2. Social Security (Disability Assistance for Working Age People) (Consequential Amendments) Order 2022 (SI 2022/177) art.17(1) and (3) (March 21, 2022).

DEFINITIONS

"benefit"–see reg.2.
"claimant"–see reg.2.

"family"–see reg.2.
"relevant benefit"–see reg.2.
"Scottish disability benefit"—see reg.2.
"universal credit"–see reg.2.

GENERAL NOTE

This regulation is equivalent to reg.3(7) of the Social Security and Child Support (Decisions and Appeals) Regulations 1999. See the note to that provision. 2.626

Advance awards etc.

13. A decision pursuant to regulation 32, 33 or 34 of the Claims and Payments Regulations 2013 to make an advance award of benefit may be revised if the conditions for entitlement are found not to have been satisfied at the start of the period for which the claim is treated as having been made. 2.627

DEFINITIONS

"benefit"–see reg.2.
"the Claims and Payments Regulations 2013"–see reg.2.

GENERAL NOTE

Under previous legislation, the power to revise advance awards was to be found in the provisions of the Social Security (Claims and Payments) Regulations 1987 making provision for advance claims and awards (see in particular regs 13(2) and 13A(3)) rather than in reg.3 of the Social Security and Child Support (Decisions and Appeals) Regulations 1999. See the notes to those regulations. It seems that this rule is intended to apply only to advance awards made on initial claims, because specific provision for awards made on renewal claims for personal independence payment is made in reg.18(1). 2.628

Sanctions cases etc.

14.—(1) The following decisions may be revised— 2.629

(a) a decision that the amount of an employment and support allowance is to be reduced by virtue of section 11J(1) (sanctions) of the 2007 Act;
(b) a decision that the amount of a jobseeker's allowance is to be reduced by virtue of section 6J (higher-level sanctions) or 6K(1) (other sanctions) of the Jobseekers Act;
(c) a decision that the amount of universal credit is to be reduced by virtue of section 26(1) (higher-level sanctions) or 27(1) (other sanctions) of the 2012 Act.

(2) A decision under section 6B, 7 or 9 ("the loss of benefit provisions") of the Fraud Act that benefit ceases to be payable or falls to be reduced as a result of the person—

(a) being convicted of an offence; or
(b) agreeing to pay a penalty as an alternative to prosecution,

may be revised where that conviction is quashed or set aside by a court or where the person withdraws the agreement to pay the penalty.

DEFINITIONS

"the 2007 Act"–see reg.2.
"the 2012 Act"–see reg.2.
"benefit"–see reg.2.

"employment and support allowance"–by virtue of reg.2, see reg.1(3)(a).
"the Fraud Act"–see reg.2.
"the Jobseekers Act"–see reg.2.
"jobseeker's allowance"–by virtue of reg.2, see reg.1(3)(b).
"universal credit"–see reg.2.

GENERAL NOTE

2.630 This regulation is equivalent to reg.3(6) and (8B) of the Social Security and Child Support (Decisions and Appeals) Regulations 1999.

The formatting error in the Queen's Printer's version has been corrected here.

Other decisions relating to an employment and support allowance

2.631 **15.**—(1) A decision awarding an employment and support allowance may be revised in any of the following circumstances.

(2) The first circumstance is where—

(a) the decision was made on the basis that the claimant had made and was pursuing an appeal against a decision of the Secretary of State that the claimant did not have limited capability for work ("the original decision"); and

(b) the appeal in relation to the original decision is successful.

(3) The second circumstance is where—

(a) the decision incorporates a determination that the conditions in regulation 26(2) (conditions for treating claimant as having limited capability for work until a determination about limited capability for work has been made) of the Employment and Support Allowance Regulations 2013 are satisfied;

(b) those conditions were not satisfied when the claim was made; and

(c) a decision falls to be made concerning entitlement to that award in respect of a period before the date on which the award took effect.

(4) The third circumstance is where the claimant's current period of limited capability for work is treated as a continuation of another such period under regulation 86 (linking period) of the Employment and Support Allowance Regulations 2013.

[[1] (4A) The fourth circumstance is where the decision—

(a) immediately follows the last day of a period for which the claimant was treated as capable of work or as not having limited capability for work under regulation 55ZA of the Jobseeker's Allowance Regulations or regulation 46A of the Jobseeker's Allowance Regulations 2013 (extended period of sickness) and that period lasted 13 weeks; and

(b) is not a decision which embodies a determination that the person is treated as having limited capability for work under regulation 26 of the Employment and Support Allowance Regulations 2013 (conditions for treating a claimant as having limited capability for work until a determination about limited capability for work has been made).]

(5) A decision terminating a person's entitlement to an employment and support allowance may be revised where—

(a) that entitlement was terminated because of section 1A (duration of contributory allowance) of the 2007 Act; and

(b) it is subsequently determined, in relation to the period of entitlement before that decision, that the person had or is treated as having had limited capability for work-related activity.

AMENDMENT

1. Jobseeker's Allowance (Extended Period of Sickness) Amendment Regulations 2015 (SI 2015/339) reg.8(1) and (2) (March 30, 2015).

DEFINITIONS

"the 2007 Act"–see reg.2.
"appeal"–see reg.2.
"claimant"–see reg.2.
"employment and support allowance"–by virtue of reg.2, see reg.1(3)(a).
"limited capability for work"–see reg.2.

GENERAL NOTE

This regulation is equivalent to reg.3(5D), (5E), (5F), (5I) and (5J) of the Social Security and Child Support (Decisions and Appeals) Regulations 1999. **2.632**

Other decisions relating to a jobseeker's allowance

16.—(1) A decision awarding a jobseeker's allowance may be revised in any of the following circumstances. **2.633**

(2) The first circumstance is where—

(a) the Secretary of State makes a conversion decision (within the meaning of regulation 5(2)(b) of the Employment and Support Allowance (Transitional Provisions, Housing Benefit and Council Tax Benefit) (Existing Awards) (No. 2) Regulations 2010 (deciding whether an existing award qualifies for conversion)) in respect of a person;
(b) the person appeals against that decision;
(c) before or after the appeal is made, there is a decision to award a jobseeker's allowance as the result of a claim being made by that person; and
(d) the appeal in relation to the conversion decision referred to in sub-paragraph (a) is successful.

(3) The second circumstance is where—

(a) a person's entitlement to an employment and support allowance is terminated because of a decision which embodies a determination that the person does not have limited capability for work;
(b) the person appeals against that decision;
(c) before or after the appeal is made, there is a decision to award a jobseeker's allowance as the result of a claim being made by that person; and
(d) the appeal in relation to the termination decision referred to in sub-paragraph (a) is successful.

DEFINITIONS

"appeal"–see reg.2.
"employment and support allowance"–by virtue of reg.2, see reg.1(3)(a).
"jobseeker's allowance"–by virtue of reg.2, see reg.1(3)(b).
"limited capability for work"–see reg.2.

GENERAL NOTE

This regulation is equivalent to reg.3(5G) and (5H) of the Social Security and Child Support (Decisions and Appeals) Regulations 1999. **2.634**

Contributions cases

2.635 **17.**—(1) A decision ("the original decision") may be revised where—

(a) on or after the date of the original decision—

(i) a late paid contribution is treated under regulation 5 (treatment of late paid contributions where no consent, connivance or negligence by the primary contributor) of the Social Security (Crediting and Treatment of Contributions and National Insurance Numbers) Regulations 2001 ("the Crediting Regulations") as paid on a date which falls on or before the date on which the original decision was made;

(ii) a direction is given under regulation 6 (treatment of contributions paid late through ignorance or error) of those Regulations that a late paid contribution is to be treated as paid on a date which falls on or before the date on which the original decision was made; or

(iii) an unpaid contribution is treated under regulation 60 (treatment of unpaid contributions where no consent, connivance or negligence by the primary contributor) of the Social Security (Contributions) Regulations 2001 as paid on a date which falls on or before the date on which the original decision was made; and

(b) either an award of benefit would have been made or the amount of benefit awarded would have been different.

(2) A decision may be revised where, by virtue of regulation 6C (treatment of Class 3 contributions paid under section 13A of the Act) of the Crediting Regulations, a contribution is treated as paid on a date which falls on or before the date on which the decision was made.

[1 (3) A decision in relation to a claim for a jobseeker's allowance or an employment and support allowance may be revised at any time where—

(a) on or after the date of the decision a contribution is treated as paid as set out in regulation 7A of the Social Security (Crediting and Treatment of Contributions, and National Insurance Numbers) Regulations 2001 (treatment of Class 2 contributions paid on or before the due date); and

(b) by virtue of the contribution being so treated, the person satisfies the contribution conditions of entitlement specified in paragraph (6) in relation to that benefit.

(4) A decision to award a jobseeker's allowance or an employment and support allowance may be revised at any time where on or after the date of the decision—

(a) any of the circumstances in paragraph (5) occur; and

(b) by virtue of the circumstance occurring, the person ceases to satisfy the contribution conditions of entitlement specified in paragraph (6) in relation to that benefit.

(5) The circumstances are—

(a) a Class 2 contribution is repaid to a person in consequence of an amendment or correction of the person's relevant profits under section 9ZA or 9ZB of the Taxes Management Act 1970 (amendment or correction of return by taxpayer or officer of the Board);

(b) a Class 2 contribution is returned to a person under regulation 52 of the Social Security (Contributions) Regulations 2001 (contributions paid in error); or

(c) a Class 1 or a Class 2 contribution paid by a person to Her Majesty's Revenue and Customs under section 223 of the Finance Act 2014 (accelerated payment in respect of notice given while tax enquiry is in progress) is repaid to the person.

(6) The contribution conditions of entitlement are—

(a) in relation to a jobseeker's allowance, the conditions set out in section 2(1)(a) and (b) of the Jobseekers Act (the contribution-based conditions); or

(b) in relation to an employment and support allowance, the first and second conditions set out in paragraphs 1(1) and 2(1) of Schedule 1 to the 2007 Act (conditions relating to national insurance).

(7) In this regulation "relevant profits" has the meaning given in section 11(3) of the Contributions and Benefits Act.]

AMENDMENT

1. Social Security (Credits, and Crediting and Treatment of Contributions) (Consequential and Miscellaneous Amendments) Regulations 2016 (SI 2016/1145) reg.4(1) and (5) (January 1, 2017).

DEFINITIONS

"benefit"—see reg.2.
"the Contributions and Benefits Act"—*ibid.*
"the Crediting Regulations"—see para.(1)(a)(i).
"employment and support allowance"—see reg.2.
"the Jobseekers Act"—*ibid.*
"jobseeker's allowance"—*ibid.*
"relevant profits"—see para.(7).

GENERAL NOTE

This regulation is equivalent to reg.3(8C) to (8H) of the Social Security and Child Support (Decisions and Appeals) Regulations 1999. 2.636

Other decisions relating to personal independence payment

18.—(1) Where the Secretary of State makes a decision awarding personal independence payment which takes effect immediately after the expiry of an existing award under regulation 33(3) (advance claim for and award of personal independence payment) of the Claims and Payments Regulations 2013, that decision may be revised if the requirements for entitlement are found not to have been met on the date on which the decision takes effect. 2.637

(2) A decision that personal independence payment is not payable to a person for any period may be revised where—

(a) the Secretary of State determines that the person meets the condition in section 85(2) of the 2012 Act (care home residents where the costs of qualifying services are borne out of local or public funds) on incomplete evidence in accordance with regulation 39(5); and

(b) after that determination is made, any of the costs of the qualifying services are recovered from the person for whom they are provided.

(3) A decision of the Secretary of State made in consequence of a negative determination may be revised at any time if it contains an error to which the claimant did not materially contribute.

DEFINITIONS

"the 2012 Act"–see reg.2.
"claimant"–see reg.2.
"the Claims and Payments Regulations 2013"–see reg.2.
"personal independence payment"–see reg.2.

GENERAL NOTE

Paragraph (1)

2.638 This is equivalent to provision made in respect of disability living allowance in reg.13C(3) of the Social Security (Claims and Payments) Regulations 1987 and permits an award on a continuation claim made in advance of the renewal date to be revised if the conditions of entitlement are not in fact satisfied on the renewal date.

Paragraph (2)

2.639 This is a helpful new provision, enabling the Secretary of State to revise a decision that a personal independence payment is not payable because the costs of accommodation are borne out of public or local funds if part of the costs are subsequently recovered from the claimant. The benefit can then be paid, as it would have been if the claimant had been contributing to the costs from the outset.

Paragraph (3)

2.640 The term "negative determination" is not defined but a footnote to this provision in the Queen's Printer's version of these Regulations refers to s.80(6) of the Welfare Reform Act 2012, where the term is defined solely for the purpose of s.80(5)(a) as—

"a determination that a person does not meet the requirements of—
(a) section 78(1)(a) and (b) or (2)(a) and (b) (daily living component);
(b) section 79(1)(a) to (c) or (2)(a) to (c) (mobility component)."

This does not make it clear whether or not, in these Regulations, the term refers only to such a determination that has been treated as having been made by virtue of regulations made under s.80(5)(a) for breach of a requirement to provide information or evidence or participate in a consultation without a good reason. In fact, regs 8(3) and 9(2) of the Social Security (Personal Independence Payment) Regulations 2013 (see Vol.I) require a "negative determination" to be made where there has been a breach of such requirements without good reason, rather than treating one as having been made. Again, those Regulations do not define the term, but it seems probable that it was intended that at least determinations made under those provisions should fall within the scope of "negative determination" in this regulation and reg.26. The view expressed in *KB v SSWP (PIP)* [2016] UKUT 537 (AAC) is that "negative determination" in these Regulations refers *only* to determinations under regs 8 and 9 of those Regulations.

Such a determination is not a "decision" for the purposes of the Social Security Act 1998; it is given effect through a consequential "outcome" decision under that Act as to the claimant's entitlement to personal independence payment (*OM v SSWP (PIP)* [2017] UKUT 458 (AAC); *AI v SSWP (PIP)* [2019] UKUT 103 (AAC)).

The language of this provision suggests that, for revision under this provision to be appropriate, the "error" must be in the consequential "outcome" decision rather than in the negative determination. Correction of an error in the negative determination would have to be given effect either through revision under another provision (e.g., reg.9(a)) or through supersession.

Other decisions relating to universal credit

2.641 **19.**—(1) Where the Secretary of State has reduced the amount of an award of universal credit as a consequence of regulation 81 (reduction of universal credit) of the Universal Credit Regulations, that decision may be revised.

(2) A decision in relation to universal credit which adopts a determination made under the Rent Officers Order 2013 may be revised at any time in consequence of a rent officer's redetermination made under that Order which resulted in an increase in the amount which represents rent for the purposes of calculating the housing costs element in universal credit.

DEFINITION

"the Rent Officers Order 2013"–see reg.2.
"the Universal Credit Regulations"–see reg.2.
"universal credit"–see reg.2.

CHAPTER 3

PROCEDURE AND EFFECTIVE DATE

Procedure for making an application for a revision

20.—(1) The Secretary of State may treat an application for a supersession under section 10 of the 1998 Act as an application for a revision under section 9 of that Act. **2.642**

(2) The following paragraph applies where the Secretary of State, in order to consider all the issues raised by the application, requires further evidence or information from a person who has applied for a revision ("the applicant").

(3) The Secretary of State must notify the applicant that—

(a) the further evidence or information specified in the notification is required;
(b) if the applicant provides the relevant evidence or information within one month of the date of notification or such longer period as the Secretary of State may allow, the decision may be revised taking such evidence or information into account; and
(c) if the applicant does not provide such evidence or information within that period, the decision may be revised using such evidence or information as was submitted with the application for revision.

DEFINITION

"the 1998 Act"–see reg.2.
"the date of notification"–see reg.2.

GENERAL NOTE

Paragraph (1) is equivalent to reg.3(10) of the Social Security and Child Support (Decisions and Appeals) Regulations 1999. See reg.32(1) below. **2.643**

Effective date of a revision

21. Where, on a revision under section 9 of the 1998 Act, the Secretary of State decides that the date from which the decision under section 8 or 10 of that Act ("the original decision") took effect was wrong, the revision takes effect from the date from which the original decision would have taken effect had the error not been made. **2.644**

DEFINITION

"the 1998 Act"–see reg.2.

General Note

2.645 This regulation is equivalent to reg.5 of the Social Security and Child Support (Decisions and Appeals) Regulations 1999. The general rule in s.9(3) of the Social Security Act 1998 is that a revision takes effect from the same date as the decision being revised. This regulation provides an exception in a case where the decision is being revised, at least in part, precisely because the date from which it was effective was wrong.

Part 3

Supersessions

Chapter 1

Grounds For Supersession

Introduction

2.646 **22.** Subject to regulation 32 (decisions which may not be superseded), the Secretary of State may make a decision under section 10 ("a superseding decision") of the 1998 Act in any of the cases and circumstances set out in this Chapter.

Definition

"the 1998 Act"–see reg.2.

General Note

2.647 This regulation is equivalent to reg.6(1) of the Social Security and Child Support (Decisions and Appeals) Regulations 1999 and the rest of this Chapter reproduces the relevant provisions of reg.6(2) in a more digestible form. See the beginning of the note to reg.3 of the 1999 Regulations for the differences between revision and supersession. Regulation 32 has the effect that revision takes precedence over supersession where both might otherwise be possible. See the note to reg.6(1) of the 1999 Regulations for general observations about supersessions.

Regulation 11 of the Social Security (Personal Independence Payment) Regulations 2013 (see Vol.I) has the effect that the Secretary of State may at any time determine afresh whether a person in receipt of personal independence payment remains unable to carry out daily living activities and mobility activities. In *KB v SSWP (PIP)* [2016] UKUT 537 (AAC), the judge expressed the view, in obiter dicta but nonetheless persuasively, that such a determination did not determine entitlement; any change of entitlement would be determined in a consequential revision or supersession depending on the facts of the case. Moreover, such a determination did not in itself constitute a change of circumstances for the purpose of reg.23 of these Regulations and neither was it a "negative determination" for the purposes of reg.26(2).

Changes of circumstances

2.648 **23.**—(1) The Secretary of State may supersede a decision in respect of which—

(a) there has been a relevant change of circumstances since the decision to be superseded had effect or, in the case of an advance award under regulation 32, 33 or 34 of the Claims and Payments Regulations 2013, since it was made; or

(b) it is expected that a relevant change of circumstances will occur.

(2) The fact that a person has become terminally ill is not a relevant change of circumstances for the purposes of paragraph (1) unless an application for supersession is made which contains an express statement that the person is terminally ill.

DEFINITIONS

"the Claims and Payments Regulations 2013"–see reg.2.
"terminally ill"–see reg.2.

GENERAL NOTE

This is equivalent to reg.6(2)(a) and (6)(c) of the Social Security and Child Support (Decisions and Appeals) Regulations 1999. See the note to reg.6(2)(a) of the 1999 Regulations. The date from which the supersession decision is effective is determined by Sch.1 or, if none of the provisions in the Schedule applies, by s.10(5) of the Social Security Act 1998. A determination under reg.11 of the Social Security (Personal Independence Payment) Regulations 2013 (see Vol.I) does not in itself constitute a change of circumstances for the purpose of this regulation (*KB v SSWP (PIP)* [2016] UKUT 537 (AAC)). Nor does a finding made by a health care practitioner, unless the decision-maker agrees with that finding; thus, it cannot generally be found that there is a ground for supersession under this regulation until the evidence has been assessed (*PV v SSWP (PIP)* [2019] UKUT 82 (AAC)). **2.649**

Error of law, ignorance, mistake etc.

24. A decision of the Secretary of State, other than one to which regulation 25 (decisions against which no appeal lies) refers, may be superseded where— **2.650**

(a) the decision was wrong in law, or was made in ignorance of, or was based on a mistake as to, some material fact; and

(b) an application for a supersession was received, or a decision was taken by the Secretary of State to act on the Secretary of State's own initiative, more than one month after the date of notification of the decision to be superseded or after the expiry of such longer period as may have been allowed under regulation 6 (late application for a revision).

DEFINITIONS

"appeal"–see reg.2.
"the date of notification"–see reg.2.

GENERAL NOTE

This is equivalent to reg.6(2)(b) of the Social Security and Child Support (Decisions and Appeals) Regulations 1999. See the note to that provision. The date from which the supersession decision is effective is determined by reg.35(3) in the case of jobseeker's allowance or employment and support allowance, by reg.35(4) in the case of universal credit and by s.10(5) of the Social Security Act 1998 in the case of personal independence payment. **2.651**

Decisions against which no appeal lies

2.652 **25.** A decision specified in Schedule 2 (decisions against which no appeal lies) to the 1998 Act or prescribed in regulation 50(2) (decisions which may or may not be appealed) may be superseded.

DEFINITIONS

"the 1998 Act"–see reg.2.
"appeal"–see reg.2.

GENERAL NOTE

2.653 This is equivalent to reg.6(2)(d) of the Social Security and Child Support (Decisions and Appeals) Regulations 1999. Like that provision, it is difficult to understand at first sight how it can be effective given that it overlaps with reg.10 and reg.32 prevents a decision from being superseded if it can be revised. See the note to reg.6(2)(d) for a possible explanation. The date from which a supersession under this regulation is effective is determined either under s.10(5) of the Social Security Act 1998 or under reg.35 in the same way as for decisions under reg.24.

Medical evidence and limited capability for work etc.

2.654 **26.**—(1) An employment and support allowance decision, a personal independence payment decision or universal credit decision may be superseded where, since the decision was made, the Secretary of State has—

(a) received medical evidence from a healthcare professional or other person approved by the Secretary of State; or

[1 (b) made a determination that the claimant is to be treated as having—

(i) limited capability for work in accordance with regulation 16, 21, 22 or 29 of the Employment and Support Allowance Regulations 2013; or

(ii) limited capability for work or for work and work-related activity in accordance with Part 5 (capability for work or work-related activity) of the Universal Credit Regulations.]

(2) The decision awarding personal independence payment may be superseded where there has been a negative determination.

(3) In this regulation—

"an employment and support allowance decision", "personal independence payment decision" and "universal credit decision" each has the meaning given in Schedule 1 (effective dates for superseding decisions made on the ground of a change of circumstances);

"healthcare professional" means—

(a) a registered medical practitioner;

(b) a registered nurse; or

(c) an occupational therapist or physiotherapist registered with a regulatory body established by an Order in Council under section 60 (regulation of health professions, social workers, other care workers etc.) of the Health Act 1999.

AMENDMENT

1. Universal Credit and Miscellaneous Amendments Regulations 2014 (SI 2014/597) reg.6 (April 28, 2014).

DEFINITIONS

"claimant"—see reg.2

"employment and support allowance decision"—by virtue of para.(3), see Sch.1 para.11

"healthcare professional"—see para.(3)

"limited capability for work"—see reg.2

"personal independence payment"—see reg.2

"personal independence payment decision"—by virtue of para.(3), see Sch.1 para.19.

"the Universal Credit Regulations"—see reg.2

"universal credit decision"—by virtue of para.(3), see Sch.1 para.30

GENERAL NOTE

Paragraph (1) is equivalent to reg.6(2)(r) of the Social Security and Child Support (Decisions and Appeals) Regulations 1999. See the note to that provision. The date from which the supersession decision is effective is determined by s.10(5) of the Social Security Act 1998 unless it is determined by reg.35(6)–(9). **2.655**

The term "negative determination", used in para.(2) is not defined but, in *KB v SSWP (PIP)* [2016] UKUT 537 (AAC), it was suggested that only a determination under regs 8 or 9 of the Social Security (Personal Independence Payment) Regulations 2013 (see Vol.I), in consequence of a failure to provide information or participate in a consultation, was a "negative determination" and that an adverse determination under reg.11 of those Regulations was not. See the note to reg.18.

In *SF v SSWP (PIP)* [2016] UKUT 481 (AAC), the Upper Tribunal accepted a submission on behalf of the Secretary of State to the effect that supersession under reg.26 was appropriate only as a last resort where there was no other ground of supersession such as change of circumstances under reg.23. However, that view was not accepted in *DS v SSWP (PIP)* [2016] UKUT 538 (AAC); [2017] AACR 19, in which the judge referred to the different dates from which a supersession on the ground of change of circumstances might be effective under Sch.1 (depending on, for instance, whether the supersession was advantageous or not to the claimant and whether and when the claimant might reasonably have been expected to notify the change of circumstances) and said:

> "15. . . . In my view, all grounds of supersession can apply in so far as the conditions they contain are made out, without any artificial rules to try to make them mutually exclusive. So far as decisions that are advantageous to the claimant go, there is then no difficulty in applying a general principle that the claimant should be able to take the benefit of whatever ground gives the most advantage. So far as decisions that are not advantageous to the claimant are concerned, which will in the great majority of cases be supersessions carried out at the Secretary of State's own initiative, I do not see why the same principle cannot apply. The Secretary of State is entitled to rely on whatever of the grounds of supersession that are made out that result in what he says is the correct position being applied for the longest period. But if the Secretary of State chooses to rely on the simpler ground of supersession in regulation 26(1)(a), without going to all the bother of investigating and thinking about what the claimant should or should not have realised needed to be notified in the past, and is content for the superseding decision to take effect from the date on which it is made, I do not see why on appeal a tribunal should be obliged to consider all the elements of regulation 23(1) on relevant change of circumstances first. . . . A tribunal would always retain the discretion under section 12(8)(a) of the Social Security Act 1998 to consider regulation 23(1) in a case in which the Secretary of State has relied only on regulation 26(1)(a) if the potential application of regulation 23(1) is clearly apparent from the evidence before it (which may be different from or more extensive than that before the Secretary of State)."

On the other hand, both judges were agreed that reasons for a decision under reg.26 might need to explain why the decision was different from a previous decision (see *R(M) 1/96* and *R. (Viggers) v Pensions Appeal Tribunal* [2009] EWCA Civ 1321; [2010] AACR 19).

Paragraph (1)(a) therefore authorises a supersession based on an up-to-date health care professional's report on what the Secretary of State calls "planned reviews", without it being necessary for a change of circumstances or an error in the existing award to be proved, provided that the departure from the earlier decision is adequately explained. Thus, when the First-tier Tribunal found that, during the course of an existing award of both components of personal independence payment, the claimant continued to satisfy the conditions of entitlement to the daily living component but did not satisfy the conditions of entitlement to the mobility component, it was entitled to extend the period of the award of the daily living component but it erred in finding that there were no grounds for supersession until the existing award ended. The award of the mobility component should have been terminated from the date of the decision under appeal (*PV v SSWP (PIP)* [2019] UKUT 82 (AAC)).

The relationship between this regulation and reg.11 of the 2013 Regulations has been explained in *BD v SSWP (PIP)* [2020] UKUT 178 (AAC).

Sanctions cases

2.656 **27.**—(1) A decision as to the amount of an award of benefit may be superseded where the amount of that award is to be reduced by virtue of—

(a) section 11J(1) (sanctions) of the 2007 Act;

(b) section 6J(1) (higher-level sanctions) or 6K(1) (other sanctions) of the Jobseekers Act; or

(c) section 26(1) (higher-level sanctions) or 27(1) (other sanctions) of the 2012 Act.

(2) A decision reducing an award of benefit by virtue of any of those provisions may be superseded where the reduction falls to be suspended or terminated.

DEFINITIONS

"the 2007 Act"—see reg.2.
"the 2012 Act"—see reg.2.
"benefit"—see reg.2.
"the Jobseekers Act"—see reg.2.

GENERAL NOTE

2.657 This regulation is equivalent to reg.6(2)(f), (fa), (p) and (q) of the Social Security and Child Support (Decisions and Appeals) Regulations 1999. The date from which the supersession decision is effective is determined by reg.35(10) or (11).

Loss of benefit cases

2.658 **28.** A decision that a benefit is payable to a claimant may be superseded where that benefit ceases to be payable or falls to be reduced by virtue of section 6B, 7 or 9 of the Fraud Act (loss of benefit provisions).

DEFINITIONS

"benefit"—see reg.2.
"claimant"—see reg.2.
"the Fraud Act"—see reg.2.

General Note

This regulation is equivalent to reg.6(2)(i) of the Social Security and Child Support (Decisions and Appeals) Regulations 1999. The date from which the supersession decision is effective is determined by reg.35(12). 2.659

Contributions cases

29. The Secretary of State may supersede a decision ("the original decision") where, on or after the date on which the decision is made, a late or an unpaid contribution is treated as paid under— 2.660

(a) regulation 5 of the Social Security (Crediting and Treatment of Contributions and National Insurance Numbers) Regulations 2001 (treatment of late paid contributions where no consent, connivance or negligence by the primary contributor) on a date which falls on or before the date on which the original decision was made;

(b) regulation 6 of those Regulations (treatment of contributions paid late through ignorance or error) on a date which falls on or before the date on which the original decision was made; or

(c) regulation 60 of the Social Security (Contributions) Regulations 2001 (treatment of unpaid contributions where no consent, connivance or negligence by the primary contributor) on a date which falls on or before the date on which the original decision was made.

General Note

This regulation is equivalent to reg.6(2)(s) of the Social Security and Child Support (Decisions and Appeals) Regulations 1999. The date from which the supersession decision is effective is determined by reg.35(13). 2.661

Housing costs: universal credit

30.—(1) A decision in relation to universal credit which adopts a determination made under the Rent Officers Order 2013 may be superseded where, in consequence of a rent officer's redetermination made in under that Order, the amount which represents rent for the purposes of calculating the housing costs element in universal credit is reduced. 2.662

Definitions

"the Rent Officers Order 2013"—see reg.2.
"universal credit"—see reg.2.

General Note

This regulation is equivalent to reg.7(2)(c) of the Housing Benefit and Council Tax Benefit (Decisions and Appeals) Regulations 2001 (SI 2001/1002). The date from which the supersession decision is effective is determined by reg.35(14). 2.663

Tribunal decisions

31. The Secretary of State may supersede a decision of the First-tier Tribunal or Upper Tribunal which— 2.664

(a) was made in ignorance of, or was based upon a mistake as to, some material fact; or

(b) in a case where section 26(5) (appeals involving issues that arise in other cases) of the 1998 Act applies, was made in accordance with section 26(4)(b) of that Act.

DEFINITIONS

"the 1998 Act"—see reg.2.
"appeal"—see reg.2.

GENERAL NOTE

2.665 This regulation is equivalent to reg.6(2)(c) of the Social Security and Child Support (Decisions and Appeals) Regulations 1999. See the note to that provision.

CHAPTER 2

SUPERSEDING DECISIONS: LIMITATIONS AND PROCEDURE

Decisions which may not be superseded

2.666 **32.** A decision which may be revised under section 9 of the 1998 Act may not be superseded under Chapter 1 of this Part unless—

(a) circumstances arise in which the Secretary of State may revise the decision under Part 2; and
(b) further circumstances arise in relation to that decision which—
   (i) are not set out in that Part; but
   (ii) are set out in Chapter 1 of this Part or are ones where a superseding decision may be made in accordance with regulation 33(3).

DEFINITION

"the 1998 Act"—see reg.2.

GENERAL NOTE

2.667 This regulation is equivalent to reg.6(3) of the Social Security and Child Support (Decisions and Appeals) Regulations 1999.

Procedure for making an application for a supersession

2.668 **33.**—(1) The Secretary of State may treat an application for a revision under section 9 of the 1998 Act, or a notification of a change of circumstances, as an application for a supersession under section 10 of that Act.

(2) The following paragraph applies where the Secretary of State, in order to consider all the issues raised by the application, requires further evidence or information from a person who has applied for a supersession ("the applicant").

(3) The Secretary of State must notify the applicant that—

(a) the further evidence or information specified in the notification is required;
(b) if the applicant provides the relevant evidence or information within one month of the date of notification or such longer period as the Secretary of State may allow, the decision may be superseded taking such information or evidence into account; and
(c) if the applicant does not provide such evidence or information within that period, the decision to be superseded may be superseded taking into account only such evidence or information as was submitted with the application for a supersession.

[[1] (4) In relation to an applicant who is supplying information or evidence of a change of circumstances which is advantageous to the applicant in relation to an award of universal credit, paragraph (3)(b) has effect as if for "one month" there were substituted "14 days".]

AMENDMENT

1. Universal Credit (Miscellaneous Amendments, Saving and Transitional Provision) Regulations 2018 (SI 2018/65) reg.5(1) and (2) (April 11, 2018).

DEFINITIONS

"the 1998 Act"–see reg.2.
"the date of notification"–*ibid.*
"universal credit"—*ibid.*

GENERAL NOTE

This regulation is equivalent to reg.6(4) and (5) of the Social Security and Child Support (Decisions and Appeals) Regulations 1999 although, since para.(4) was introduced from April 11, 2018, the time limit for supplying evidence or information in relation to universal credit has been made much more stringent. The effect of treating a notification of a change of circumstances as an application for supersession may be to make a supersession favourable to a claimant effective from an earlier date than it would be if the Secretary of State were merely to supersede the decision of his own initiative following receipt of the notification. Note that reg.20(1) enables an application for a supersession to be treated as an application for a revision. The aim of these provisions is to ensure that a person is not prejudiced by a failure to use the technically correct language when communicating with the Department. **2.669**

CHAPTER 3

EFFECTIVE DATES FOR SUPERSESSIONS

Introduction

34. This Chapter and Schedule 1 (effective dates for superseding decisions made on the ground of a change of circumstances) contains exceptions to the provisions of section 10(5) of the 1998 Act as to the date from which a decision under section 10 of that Act which supersedes an earlier decision takes effect. **2.670**

DEFINITION

"the 1998 Act"–see reg.2.

GENERAL NOTE

This regulation and reg.35 are equivalent to reg.7 of the Social Security and Child Support (Decisions and Appeals) Regulations 1999, this regulation being equivalent to reg.7(1). Where no provision is made under this Chapter or Sch.1, the supersession will be effective from the date determined under s.10(5) of the Social Security Act 1998. **2.671**

Effective dates: Secretary of State decisions

35.—(1) Schedule 1 (effective dates for superseding decisions made on the ground of a change of circumstances) makes provision for the date from which a superseding decision takes effect where there has been, or it is **2.672**

anticipated that there will be, a relevant change of circumstances since the earlier decision took effect.

(2) This paragraph applies where the Secretary of State supersedes a decision—

(a) on the ground that the decision was wrong in law, or was made in ignorance of, or was based on a mistake as to, some material fact, in accordance with regulation 24 (error of law, ignorance, mistake etc.); or

(b) under regulation 25 (decisions against which no appeal lies).

(3) In a case where paragraph (2) applies and the superseding decision relates to a jobseeker's allowance or an employment and support allowance, the superseding decision takes effect from the first day of the benefit week in which the superseding decision, or where applicable, the application for supersession, was made.

(4) In a case where paragraph (2) applies and the superseding decision relates to universal credit, the superseding decision takes effect from the first day of the assessment period in which the superseding decision, or where applicable, the application for supersession, was made.

(5) A superseding decision made in consequence of a decision which is a relevant determination for the purposes of section 27 of the 1998 Act (restrictions on entitlement to benefit in certain cases of error) takes effect from the date of the relevant determination.

(6) In the case of an employment and support allowance, a superseding decision made in accordance with regulation 26(1) (medical evidence and limited capability for work etc.), following an application by the claimant, that embodies a determination that the claimant has limited capability for work-related activity, takes effect from the date of the application.

(7) In the case of an employment and support allowance, a superseding decision made on the Secretary of State's own initiative in accordance with regulation 26(1) that embodies a determination that the claimant has—

(a) limited capability for work; or

(b) limited capability for work-related activity; or

(c) limited capability for work and limited capability for work-related activity,

takes effect from [[1] the day after the last day of the relevant period as defined in regulation 5(4) of the Employment and Support Allowance Regulations 2013] where the determination is the first such determination.

(8) In the case of an employment and support allowance where regulation 6 of the Employment and Support Allowance Regulations 2013 (assessment phase – previous claimants) applies, a superseding decision made in accordance with regulation 26(1) of these Regulations that embodies a determination that the claimant has—

(a) limited capability for work; or

(b) limited capability for work-related activity; or

(c) limited capability for work and limited capability for work-related activity,

takes effect from the beginning of the 14th week of the claimant's continuous period of limited capability for work.

(9) In the case of universal credit, a superseding decision made in accordance with regulation 26(1) that embodies a determination that the claimant has limited capability for work or limited capability for work and work-related activity takes effect—

(a) in a case to which regulation 28(1) (period for which the LCW or LCWRA element is not to be included) of the Universal Credit Regulations applies, from the beginning of the assessment period specified in that paragraph; or

(b) in any other case, from the beginning of the assessment period in which the decision (if made on the Secretary of State's own initiative) or the application for a supersession was made.

(10) A superseding decision to which regulation 27(1) (sanctions cases: reduction in an award) applies takes effect from the beginning of the period specified in—

(a) regulation 54 of the Employment and Support Allowance Regulations 2013, where the decision relates to the start of a reduction in the amount of an employment and support allowance;

(b) regulation 56 of the Employment and Support Allowance Regulations 2013, where the decision relates to ending the suspension of a such a reduction where a fraud penalty ceases to apply;

(c) regulation 22 of the Jobseeker's Allowance Regulations 2013, where the decision relates to the start of a reduction in the amount of a jobseeker's allowance;

(d) regulation 24 of the Jobseeker's Allowance Regulations 2013, where the decision relates to ending the suspension of such a reduction where a fraud penalty ceases to apply;

(e) regulation 106 of the Universal Credit Regulations, where the decision relates to the start of a reduction in the amount of universal credit;

(f) regulation 108 of the Universal Credit Regulations, where the decision relates to ending the suspension of such a reduction where a fraud penalty ceases to apply.

(11) A superseding decision to which regulation 27(2) (sanctions cases: suspension and termination of a reduction) applies takes effect from the beginning of the period specified in—

(a) regulation 56 of the Employment and Support Allowance Regulations 2013, where the decision relates to the start of a suspension where a fraud penalty applies;

(b) regulation 57 of the Employment and Support Allowance Regulations 2013, where the decision relates to the termination of a reduction in the amount of an employment and support allowance;

(c) regulation 24 of the Jobseeker's Allowance Regulations 2013, where the decision relates to the start of a suspension where a fraud penalty applies;

(d) regulation 25 of the Jobseeker's Allowance Regulations 2013, where the decision relates to the termination of a reduction in the amount of a jobseeker's allowance;

(e) regulation 108 of the Universal Credit Regulations, where the decision relates to the start of a suspension where a fraud penalty applies;

(f) regulation 109 of the Universal Credit Regulations, where the decision relates to the termination of a reduction in the amount of an award of universal credit.

(12) A superseding decision to which regulation 28 (loss of benefit provisions) applies takes effect from the date prescribed for the purposes of section 6B or 7 of the Fraud Act.

(13) Where a decision is superseded in accordance with regulation 29 (contributions cases), the superseding decision takes effect from the date referred to in regulation 29(a), (b) or (c) on which the late or unpaid contribution is treated as paid.

(14) A superseding decision made in consequence of a redetermination in accordance with regulation 30 (housing costs: universal credit) takes effect on the first day of the first assessment period following the day on which that redetermination is received by Secretary of State.

AMENDMENT

1. Jobseeker's Allowance (Extended Period of Sickness) Amendment Regulations 2015 (SI 2015/339) reg.8(1) and (3) (March 30, 2015).

DEFINITIONS

"the 1998 Act"—see reg.2.
"appeal"—see reg.2.
"assessment period"—see reg.2.
"benefit"—see reg.2.
"benefit week"—see reg.2.
"claimant"—see reg.2.
"employment and support allowance"—by virtue of reg.2, see reg.1(3)(a).
"the Fraud Act"—see reg.2.
"jobseeker's allowance"—by virtue of reg.2, see reg.1(3)(b).
"limited capability for work"—see reg.2.
"the Universal Credit Regulations"—see reg.2.
"universal credit"—see reg.2.

GENERAL NOTE

2.673 This regulation is somewhat simpler than reg.7 of the Social Security and Child Support (Decisions and Appeals) Regulations 1999, but this is partly because the provisions equivalent to some of the complicated provisions in reg.7(2) of the 1999 Regulations relating to changes of circumstances are to be found in Sch.1 to these Regulations. The structure is as follows—

Paragraph (1)	Supersession for change of circumstances.
Paragraphs (2)–(4)	Supersession under reg.24 for ignorance or mistake of fact or under reg.25 of an unappealable decision.
Paragraph (5)	Supersession following a test case.
Paragraphs (6)–(8)	Supersession under reg.26 of employment and support allowance decisions related to a limited capability for work or limited capability for work-related activities.
Paragraph (9)	Supersession under reg.26 of universal credit decisions related to a limited capability for work or limited capability for work-related activities.
Paragraphs. (10) and (11)	Supersession under reg.27 relating to reductions imposed as sanctions.
Paragraph (12)	Supersession under reg.28 in order to remove benefit because a person has been convicted of benefit offences.
Paragraph (13)	Supersession under reg.29 following the late payment of contributions.
Paragraph (14)	Supersession under reg.30 of universal credit decisions following a re-determination of housing costs.

Note that the reference only to reg.24 in para.(2)(a) means that paras (3) and (4) do not apply where the supersession is of a tribunal decision and therefore made under reg.31.

Effective dates for superseding decisions where changes notified late

36.—(1) For the purposes of regulation 35(1) (effective dates: Secretary of State decisions) and paragraphs 6, 14 and 21 of Schedule 1 (effective dates for superseding decisions made on the ground of a change of circumstances), the Secretary of State may extend the time allowed for a person ("the applicant") to give notice of a change of circumstances in so far as it affects the effective date of the change if all of the following conditions are met. 2.674

(2) The first condition is that an application is made to the Secretary of State at an appropriate office for an extension of time.

(3) The second condition is that the application—

(a) contains particulars of the change of circumstances and the reasons for the failure to give notice of the change of circumstances on an earlier date; and

(b) is made—

(i) within 13 months of the date on which the change occurred; or

(ii) in the case of personal independence payment where a notification is given under paragraph 15 of Part 2 of Schedule 1 (effective dates for superseding decisions made on the ground of a change of circumstances), within 13 months of the date on which the claimant first satisfied the conditions of entitlement to the particular rate of personal independence payment.

(4) The third condition is that the Secretary of State is satisfied that it is reasonable to grant the extension.

(5) The fourth condition is that the change of circumstances notified by the applicant is relevant to the decision which is to be superseded.

(6) The fifth condition is that the Secretary of State is satisfied that, due to special circumstances, it was not practicable for the applicant to give notice of the change of circumstances within the relevant notification period.

(7) In determining whether it is reasonable to grant an extension of time—

(a) the Secretary of State must have regard to the principle that the greater the amount of time that has elapsed between the end of the relevant notification period and the date of the application, the more compelling should be the special circumstances on which the application is based;

(b) no account must be taken of the fact that the applicant or any person acting for them was unaware of, or misunderstood, the law applicable to the case (including ignorance or misunderstanding of the time limits imposed by these Regulations); and

(c) no account must be taken of the fact that the Upper Tribunal or a court has taken a different view of the law from that previously understood and applied.

(8) An application under this regulation which has been refused may not be renewed.

(9) In this regulation, "the relevant notification period" means—

(a) in the case of universal credit, the assessment period in which the change of circumstances occurs; or

(b) in any other case, a period of one month, beginning with the date on which the change of circumstances occurred.

DEFINITIONS

"appropriate office"–see reg.2.
"assessment period"–see reg.2.
"claimant"–see reg.2.
"personal independence payment"–see reg.2.
"universal credit"–see reg.2.

GENERAL NOTE

2.675 This regulation is equivalent to reg.8 of the Social Security and Child Support (Decisions and Appeals) Regulations 1999.

Effective dates: tribunal cases

2.676 **37.**—(1) This paragraph applies where—

(a) the Secretary of State supersedes a decision of the First-tier Tribunal or the Upper Tribunal on the ground that it is made in ignorance of, or based on a mistake as to, a material fact in accordance with regulation 31(a) (tribunal decisions), and

(b) as a result of that ignorance or mistake, the decision to be superseded was more advantageous to the claimant than it would otherwise have been.

(2) In a case where paragraph (1) applies where the decision relates to—

(a) a jobseeker's allowance;

(b) personal independence payment,

the superseding decision takes effect from the date on which the decision of the First-tier Tribunal or the Upper Tribunal took, or was to take, effect.

(3) In a case where paragraph (1) applies and the decision relates to an employment and support allowance or universal credit where—

(a) the material fact does not relate to a limited capability for work determination embodied in or necessary to the decision; or

(b) the material fact does relate to such a determination and the Secretary of State is satisfied that at the time the decision was made the claimant knew or could reasonably be expected to know of it and that it was relevant,

the superseding decision takes effect from the first day of the benefit week or (as the case may be) the assessment period in which in the Tribunal's decision took or was to take effect.

(4) Where the Secretary of State supersedes a decision of the First-tier Tribunal or the Upper Tribunal in accordance with regulation 31(b) (tribunal decisions), the decision takes effect—

(a) if the decision relates to personal independence payment, from the date on which the decision of the First-tier Tribunal or the Upper Tribunal would have taken effect had it been decided in accordance with the determination of the Upper Tribunal or the court in the appeal referred to in section 26(1)(b) of the 1998 Act;

(b) if the decision relates to a jobseeker's allowance or an employment and support allowance, from the first day of the benefit week in which the Tribunal's decision would have taken effect had it been so decided;

(c) if the decision relates to universal credit, from the first day of the assessment period in which the Tribunal's decision would have taken effect had it been so decided.

(5) Paragraph (6) applies where—

(a) the Upper Tribunal, or the court as defined in section 27(7) (restrictions on entitlement to benefit in certain cases of error) of the 1998 Act, determines an appeal as mentioned in subsection (1)(a) of that section ("the relevant determination");

(b) the Secretary of State makes a decision of the kind specified in subsection (1)(b) of that section;

(c) there is an appeal against the relevant determination;

(d) after the Secretary of State's decision, payment is suspended in accordance with regulation 44 (suspension in prescribed cases); and

(e) on appeal a court, within the meaning of section 27, reverses the relevant determination in whole or part.

(6) A consequential decision by the Secretary of State under section 10 of the 1998 Act which supersedes an earlier decision of the Secretary of State under paragraph (5)(b) takes effect from the date on which the earlier decision took effect.

DEFINITIONS

"the 1998 Act"–see reg.2.
"appeal"–see reg.2.
"assessment period"–see reg.2.
"benefit"–see reg.2.
"benefit week"–see reg.2.
"claimant"–see reg.2.
"employment and support allowance"–by virtue of reg.2, see reg.1(3)(a).
"jobseeker's allowance"–by virtue of reg.2, see reg.1(3)(b).
"limited capability for work determination"–see reg.2.
"personal independence payment"–see reg.2.
"universal credit"–see reg.2.

PART 4

OTHER MATTERS RELATING TO DECISION- MAKING

Correction of accidental errors

38.—(1) An accidental error in a decision of the Secretary of State, or in any record of such a decision, may be corrected by the Secretary of State at any time. **2.677**

(2) Such a correction is to be treated as part of that decision or of that record.

(3) The Secretary of State must give written notice of the correction as soon as practicable to the person to whom the decision was given.

(4) In calculating the time within which an application may be made under regulation 5 (revision on any grounds) for a decision to be revised, no account is to be taken of any day falling before the day on which notice of the correction was given.

GENERAL NOTE

This regulation is equivalent to reg.9A of the Social Security and Child Support (Decisions and Appeals) Regulations 1999. **2.678**

Determinations on incomplete evidence

2.679 **39.**—(1) The following provisions of this regulation apply for the purposes of a decision under section 8 or 10 of the 1998 Act.

(2) Where—

(a) a determination falls to be made by the Secretary of State concerning the matter mentioned in paragraph (3); and

(b) it appears to the Secretary of State that the Secretary of State is not in possession of all of the evidence or information which is relevant for the purposes of the determination,

the Secretary of State must make the determination on the assumption that the relevant evidence or information which is not in the Secretary of State's possession is adverse to the claimant.

(3) The matter is whether, for the purposes of regulation 45 (relevant education) of the Jobseeker's Allowance Regulations 2013 a person is by virtue of that regulation to be treated as receiving relevant education.

(4) Where—

(a) a determination falls to be made by the Secretary of State as to what costs are to be included in claimant's award of universal credit under section 11 (housing costs) of the 2012 Act; and

(b) it appears to the Secretary of State that the Secretary of State is not in possession of all of the evidence or information which is relevant for the purposes of the determination,

the Secretary of State may make the determination on the assumption that the costs to be included in the claimant's award under that section are those that the Secretary of State is able to determine using such evidence or information as is in the Secretary of State's possession.

(5) Where, in the case of personal independence payment—

(a) a determination falls to be made by the Secretary of State as to whether a person meets the condition in section 85(2) (care home residents where the costs of qualifying services are borne out of local or public funds) of the 2012 Act; and

(b) it appears to the Secretary of State that, having made reasonable enquiries, the Secretary of State is not in possession of all of the evidence or information which is or could be relevant for the purposes of the determination,

the Secretary of State may make the determination using such information or evidence as is in the Secretary of State's possession.

DEFINITIONS

"the 1998 Act"–see reg.2.
"the 2012 Act"–see reg.2.
"claimant"–see reg.2.
"personal independence payment"–see reg.2.
"universal credit"–see reg.2.

GENERAL NOTE

2.680 This regulation is equivalent to reg.13 of the Social Security and Child Support (Decisions and Appeals) Regulations 1999.

Determinations as to limited capability for work

40.—(1) Where, in relation to an award of an employment and support allowance, the Secretary of State makes a determination (including a determination made following a change of circumstances) whether a person— 2.681

(a) has or does not have limited capability for work; or

(b) is to be treated as having or not having limited capability for work,

which is embodied in or necessary to a decision under Chapter 2 of Part 1 of the 1998 Act (decisions and appeals) or on which such a decision is based, that determination is to be conclusive for the purposes of any further decision relating to such an allowance.

(2) Paragraph (1) applies to determinations made in relation to universal credit as it applies in the case of an employment and support allowance.

(3) Where, in relation to any purpose for which Part 1 (employment and support allowance) of the 2007 Act or Part 1 (universal credit) of the 2012 Act applies, a determination falls to be made as to whether a person—

(a) is, or is to be treated as, having or not having limited capability for work; or

(b) is terminally ill,

that issue is to be determined by the Secretary of State, notwithstanding the fact that any other matter falls to be determined by another authority.

Definitions

"the 1998 Act"–see reg.2.
"the 2007 Act"–see reg.2.
"the 2012 Act"–see reg.2.
"appeal"–see reg.2.
"employment and support allowance"–by virtue of reg.2, see reg.1(3)(a).
"limited capability for work"–see reg.2.
"terminally ill"–see reg.2.
"universal credit"–see reg.2.

General Note

This regulation is equivalent to regs 10 and 11 of the Social Security and Child Support (Decisions and Appeals) Regulations 1999. 2.682

Effect of alterations affecting universal credit

41.—(1) Subject to paragraph (3), an alteration in the amount of a person's employed earnings (within the meaning of regulation 55(1) of the Universal Credit Regulations) made in accordance with Chapter 2 of Part 6 (earned income) of the Universal Credit Regulations in consequence of information provided to the Secretary of State by HMRC is prescribed for the purposes of section 159D(1)(b)(vi) (effect of alterations affecting universal credit) of the Administration Act. 2.683

(2) For the purposes of this regulation, "alteration" means an increase or decrease in such earnings.

(3) Where the person disputes the figure used in accordance with regulation 55 (employed earnings) of the Universal Credit Regulations to calculate employed earnings in relation to any assessment period, the Secretary of State must—

(a) inform the person that they may request that the Secretary of State gives a decision in relation to the amount of universal credit payable in relation to that assessment period; and
(b) where such a decision is requested, give it within 14 days of receiving the request or as soon as practicable afterwards.

(4) Paragraph (3) does not affect the validity of anything done under section 159D(2) or (3) of the Administration Act in relation to the person's award.

(5) A decision made in accordance with paragraph (3) takes effect on the date on which the alteration under section 159(D)(2) or (3) came into force in relation to the person.

DEFINITIONS

"the Administration Act"–see reg.2.
"assessment period"–see reg.2.
"HMRC"–see reg.2.
"the Universal Credit Regulations"–see reg.2.
"universal credit"–see reg.2.

GENERAL NOTE

2.684 *Paragraph (1)*

This paragraph is made under the power conferred by s.159D(1)(b)(vi) of the Social Security Administration Act 1992. It has the effect that, under s.159D(2), an alteration in the amount of earnings to be taken into account made in consequence of information supplied by HMRC can result in a change in the rate at which universal credit is paid without there being any decision by the Secretary of State. However, it is made subject to para.(3). Whether it adds anything to s.159D(1)(b)(iii) is perhaps debateable.

2.685 *Paragraph (2)*

This paragraph is made under the power conferred by head (d) of the definition of "alteration" in s.159D(6). It may have been thought necessary because the "alteration" mentioned in para.(1) is not of a type covered by heads (a), (b), or (c) of the definition in s.159D(6), but it does not add to the clarity of para.(5).

2.686 *Paragraphs (3) to (5)*

Paragraph (3) is presumably made under the power conferred by the opening words of s.159D(1) because it provides that, where a person disputes the figure used to calculate earnings for the purposes of universal credit, he or she may request that the Secretary of State makes a decision as to the mount of universal credit payable, thus, by implication, disapplying s.159D. Such a decision appears to be appealable (but see the note to para.6 of Sch.2 to the Social Security Act 1998), although a claimant has to go through the rigmarole of first objecting to the figure, then asking for a decision and then applying for mandatory reconsideration, before an appeal may be lodged. Presumably it is hoped that the dispute will be resolved during that process. Where the Secretary of State makes a decision in accordance with this paragraph, reg.61(5) of the Universal Credit Regulations 2013 (see Vol.II) applies so as to enable him either to treat a payment of employed earnings received in one assessment period as paid in a later period or to disregard information received about a payment of employed earnings.

Paragraph (4) ensures that, where a request for a decision by the Secretary of State is made under para.(3), any action taken, or not taken, under s.159D(2) or (3) remains valid until the decision is made.

Paragraph (5) is not well drafted but appears to mean that the Secretary of State's decision takes effect on the same date as that on which the alteration in the amount of employed earnings was originally taken into account through action, or a lack of action, under s.159D(2) or (3).

Issues for HMRC

42.—(1) Where, on consideration of any claim or other matter, it appears to the Secretary of State that an issue arises which, by virtue of section 8 of the Transfer Act, falls to be decided by an officer of HMRC, the Secretary of State must refer that issue to HMRC. **2.687**

(2) Where—

(a) the Secretary of State has decided any claim or other matter on an assumption of facts—

(i) which appeared to the Secretary of State not to be in dispute, but

(ii) concerning which, had an issue arisen, that issue would have fallen, by virtue of section 8 of the Transfer Act, to be decided by HMRC;

(b) an application for a revision or supersession is made, or an appeal is brought, in relation to that claim or other matter; and

(c) it appears to the Secretary of State on receipt of that application or appeal that such an issue arises,

the Secretary of State must refer that issue to HMRC.

(3) Pending the final decision of any issue which has been referred to HMRC in accordance with paragraph (1) or (2), the Secretary of State may—

(a) determine any other issue arising on consideration of the claim, application or other matter,

(b) seek a preliminary opinion from HMRC on the issue referred and decide the claim, application or other matter in accordance with that opinion; or

(c) defer making any decision on the claim, application or other matter.

(4) On receipt by the Secretary of State of the final decision of an issue which has been referred to HMRC under paragraph (1) or (2), the Secretary of State must—

(a) In a case where the Secretary of State made a decision under paragraph (3)(b), decide whether to revise the decision under section 9 of the 1998 Act or to supersede it under section 10 of that Act;

(b) in a case to which paragraph (3)(a) or (c) applies, decide the claim, application or other matter in accordance with the final decision of the issue so referred.

(5) In this regulation—

(a) "final decision" means the decision of HMRC under section 8 (decisions by officers of Board) of the Transfer Act or the determination of any appeal in relation to that decision; and

(b) "the Transfer Act" means the Social Security Contributions (Transfer of Functions, etc.) Act 1999.

DEFINITIONS

"the 1998 Act"–see reg.2.
"appeal"–see reg.2.
"HMRC"–see reg.2.

GENERAL NOTE

This regulation is equivalent to reg.11A of the Social Security and Child Support (Decisions and Appeals) Regulations 1999. **2.688**

Appeals raising issues for HMRC

2.689 **43.**—(1) This regulation applies where—

(a) a person has appealed to the First-tier Tribunal and it appears to the First-tier Tribunal that an issue arises which, by virtue of section 8 of the Transfer Act, falls to be decided by HMRC; and

(b) the tribunal has required the Secretary of State to refer that issue to HMRC.

(2) Pending the final decision of any issue which has been referred to HMRC in accordance with paragraph (1), the Secretary of State may revise the decision under appeal under section 9 of the 1998 Act, or make a further decision under section 10 of that Act superseding that decision, in accordance with the Secretary of State's determination of any issue other than one which has been so referred.

(3) On receipt by the Secretary of State of the final decision of an issue which has been referred to HMRC in accordance with paragraph (1), the Secretary of State must consider whether the decision under appeal ought to be revised or superseded under the 1998 Act, and—

(a) if so, revise it or make a further decision which supersedes it; or

(b) if not, invite the First-tier Tribunal to determine to appeal.

(4) In this regulation, "final decision" and "Transfer Act" have the same meaning as in regulation 42 (issues for HMRC).

Definitions

"the 1998 Act"–see reg.2.
"appeal"–see reg.2.
"HMRC"–see reg.2.

General Note

2.690 This regulation is equivalent to reg.38A of the Social Security and Child Support (Decisions and Appeals) Regulations 1999.

Part 5

Suspension

Suspension in prescribed cases

2.691 **44.**—(1) The Secretary of State may suspend, in whole or part, payment of any benefit to a person ("P") in the circumstances described in paragraph (2).

(2) The circumstances are where—

(a) it appears to the Secretary of State that—

(i) an issue arises whether the conditions for entitlement to the benefit are or were fulfilled;

(ii) an issue arises whether a decision relating to an award of the benefit should be revised under section 9 or superseded under section 10 of the 1998 Act,

(iii) an issue arises whether any amount of benefit paid to P is recoverable under or by virtue of section 71ZB, 71ZG or 71ZH of the Administration Act,

(iv) the last address notified to the Secretary of State of P is not the address at which P resides,

(b) an appeal is pending in P's case against a decision of the First-tier Tribunal, the Upper Tribunal or a court; or

(c) an appeal is pending against a decision given by the Upper Tribunal or a court in a different case and it appears to the Secretary of State that, if the appeal were to be decided in a particular way, an issue would arise as to whether the award of any benefit to P (whether the same benefit or not) ought to be revised or superseded.

(3) For the purposes of section 21(2)(c) (suspension in prescribed circumstances) of the 1998 Act, where an appeal against the decision has not been brought or an application for permission to appeal against the decision has not been made but the time for doing so has not yet expired, an appeal is pending in the circumstances described in paragraph (4).

(4) The circumstances are where a decision of the First-tier Tribunal, the Upper Tribunal or a court has been made and the Secretary of State—

(a) is awaiting receipt of that decision; or

(b) in the case of a decision of the First-tier Tribunal, is considering whether to apply for a statement of reasons for the decision or has applied for such a statement and is awaiting receipt; or

(c) has received that decision or, if it is a decision of the First-tier Tribunal has received the statement of reasons for it, and is considering whether to apply for permission to appeal, or where permission to appeal has been granted, is considering whether to appeal.

(5) Where payment of any benefit is suspended as the result of paragraph (2)(b) or (c), the Secretary of State must, as soon as reasonably practicable, give written notice to P of any proposal to—

(a) request a statement of the reasons for a tribunal decision;

(b) apply for permission to appeal; or

(c) make an appeal.

DEFINITIONS

"the 1998 Act"—see reg.2.
"benefit"—see reg.2.

GENERAL NOTE

This regulation is equivalent to reg.16 of the Social Security and Child Support (Decisions and Appeals) Regulations 1999. 2.692

Provision of information or evidence

45.—(1) This regulation applies where the Secretary of State requires information or evidence from a person mentioned in paragraph (2) ("P") in order to determine whether a decision awarding a benefit should be revised under section 9 of the 1998 Act or superseded under section 10 of that Act. 2.693

(2) The persons are—

(a) a person in respect of whom payment of any benefit has been suspended in the circumstances set out in regulation 44(2)(a) (suspension in prescribed cases);

(b) a person who has made an application for a decision of the Secretary of State to be revised or superseded;

(c) a person from whom the Secretary of State requires information or evidence under regulation 38(2) (evidence and information in connection with an award) of the Claims and Payments Regulations 2013;

(d) a person from whom the Secretary of State requires documents, certificates or other evidence under regulation 31(3) (evidence and information) of the Jobseeker's Allowance Regulations 2013;

(e) a person whose entitlement to an employment and support allowance or universal credit is conditional on their having, or being treated as having, limited capability for work.

(3) The Secretary of State must notify P of the requirements of this regulation.

(4) P must either—

(a) supply the information or evidence within—

(i) a period of 14 days beginning with the date on which the notification under paragraph (3) was given or sent to P or such longer period as the Secretary of State allows in that notification, or

(ii) such longer period as P satisfies the Secretary of State is necessary in order to comply with the requirements, or

(b) satisfy the Secretary of State within the period applicable under sub-paragraph (a)(i) that either—

(i) the information or evidence does not exist, or

(ii) it is not possible for P to obtain it.

(5) In relation to a person to whom paragraph (2)(d) refers, paragraph (4)(a)(i) has effect as if for "14 days" there were substituted "7 days".

(6) The Secretary of State may suspend the payment of a benefit, in whole or part, to any person to whom paragraph (2)(b), (c), (d) or (e) applies who fails to satisfy the requirements of paragraph (4).

(7) In this regulation, "evidence" includes evidence which a person is required to provide in accordance with regulation 2 (evidence of incapacity for work, limited capability for work and confinement) of the Social Security (Medical Evidence) Regulations 1976(3).

DEFINITIONS

"the 1998 Act"–see reg.2.
"the Administration Act"–see reg.2.
"benefit"–see reg.2.
"the Claims and Payments Regulations 2013"–see reg.2.
"employment and support allowance"–by virtue of reg.2, see reg.1(3)(a).
"limited capability for work"–see reg.2.
"universal credit"–see reg.2.

GENERAL NOTE

2.694 This regulation is equivalent to reg.17 of the Social Security and Child Support (Decisions and Appeals) Regulations 1999.

Making of payments which have been suspended

2.695 **46.** The Secretary of State must pay a benefit which has been suspended where—

(a) in a case where regulation 44(2)(a) (suspension in prescribed cases) applies, the Secretary of State is satisfied that the benefit is properly payable and that there are no outstanding issues to be resolved;

(b) in a case to which regulation 45(6) (provision of information or evidence) applies, the Secretary of State is satisfied that the benefit is properly payable and that the requirements of regulation 45(4) have been satisfied;

(c) in a case to which regulation 44(2)(b) (suspension in prescribed cases) applies, the Secretary of State—

(i) does not, in the case of a decision of the First-tier Tribunal, apply for a statement of the reasons for that decision within the period specified under the Tribunal Procedure Rules;

(ii) does not, in the case of a decision of the First-tier Tribunal, the Upper Tribunal or a court, make an application for permission to appeal or (where permission to appeal is granted) make the appeal within the time prescribed for the making of such application or appeal;

(iii) withdraws an application for permission to appeal or withdraws the appeal; or

(iv) is refused permission to appeal, in circumstances where it is not open to the Secretary of State to renew the application for permission or to make a further application for permission to appeal;

(d) in a case to which regulation 44(2)(c) (suspension in prescribed cases) applies, the Secretary of State, in relation to the decision of the Upper Tribunal or a court in a different case—

(i) does not make an application for permission to appeal or (where permission to appeal is granted) make the appeal within the time prescribed for the making of such application or appeal;

(ii) withdraws an application for permission to appeal or withdraws the appeal;

(iii) is refused permission to appeal, in circumstances where it is not open to the Secretary of State to renew the application for permission or to make a further application for permission to appeal.

Definitions

"benefit"—see reg.2.
"the Tribunal Procedure Rules"—see reg.2.

General Note

This regulation is equivalent to reg.20 of the Social Security and Child Support (Decisions and Appeals) Regulations 1999. **2.696**

Part 6

Termination

Termination for failure to furnish information or evidence

47.—(1) This regulation applies where payment of a benefit to a person ("P") has been suspended in full under— **2.697**

(a) regulation 44 (suspension in prescribed cases) and P subsequently fails to comply with a requirement for information or evidence under regulation 45 (provision of information or evidence) and more than one month has elapsed since the requirement was made; or

(b) regulation 45(6) and more than one month has elapsed since the first payment was suspended.

(2) In a case to which this regulation applies, except where entitlement ceases on an earlier date other than under this regulation, the Secretary of State must decide that P ceases to be entitled to that benefit with effect from the date on which the payment of the benefit was suspended.

DEFINITION

"benefit"—see reg.2.

GENERAL NOTE

2.698 This regulation is broadly equivalent to reg.18 of the Social Security and Child Support (Decisions and Appeals) Regulations 1999 but is considerably clearer. A termination is a form of supersession (*R(H) 4/08*) and there is therefore a right of appeal to the First-tier Tribunal under s.12 of the Social Security Act 1998. See the note to reg.18 of the 1999 Regulations for further commentary.

Termination in the case of entitlement to alternative benefits

2.699 **48.**—(1) This paragraph applies where an award of a jobseeker's allowance ("the existing benefit") exists in favour of a person and, if that award did not exist and a claim was made by that person for an employment and support allowance ("the alternative benefit"), an award of the alternative benefit would be made on that claim.

(2) This paragraph applies where an award of an employment and support allowance ("the existing benefit") exists in favour of a person and, if that award did not exist and a claim was made by that person for a jobseeker's allowance ("the alternative benefit"), an award of the alternative benefit would be made on that claim.

(3) In a case where paragraph (1) or (2) applies, if a claim for the alternative benefit is made, the Secretary of State may bring to an end the award of the existing benefit if satisfied that an award of the alternative benefit will be made.

(4) Where the Secretary of State brings an award of the existing benefit to an end under paragraph (3), the Secretary of State must end the award on the day immediately preceding the first day on which an award of the alternative benefit takes effect.

(5) Where an award of a jobseeker's allowance is made in accordance with this regulation, paragraph 4 of Schedule 1 to the Jobseekers Act (waiting days) does not apply.

(6) Where an award of an employment and support allowance is made in accordance with this regulation, paragraph 2 (waiting days) of Schedule 2 (supplementary provisions) to the 2007 Act does not apply.

DEFINITIONS

"the 2007 Act"–see reg.2.

"benefit"–see reg.2.

"employment and support allowance"–by virtue of reg.2, see reg.1(3)(a).

"the Jobseekers Act"–see reg.2.
"jobseeker's allowance"–by virtue of reg.2, see reg.1(3)(b).

General Note

This regulation applies where it is decided that a person entitled to jobseeker's allowance should be entitled to employment and support allowance or vice versa and ensures that there is no gap in entitlement. 2.700

Part 7

Appeals

Other persons with a right of appeal

49. In addition to the claimant, but subject to regulation 7 (consideration of revision before appeal), the following persons have the right of appeal under section 12(2) of the 1998 Act— 2.701

(a) any person appointed by the Secretary of State under regulation 56 (payments on death) of the Claims and Payments Regulations 2013 to proceed with the claim of a person who claimed benefit and subsequently died;
(b) any person appointed by the Secretary of State under regulation 57 (persons unable to act) of those Regulations to act on behalf of another;
(c) any person claiming personal independence payment on behalf of another under section 82(5) of the 2012 Act (terminal illness); and
(d) in the case of a decision under section 71ZB, 71ZG or 71ZH of the Administration Act to recover any amount paid by way of benefit, any person from whom such an amount is recoverable, but only if their rights, duties or obligations are affected by that decision.

Definitions

"the 1998 Act"–see reg.2.
"the 2012 Act"–see reg.2.
"appeal"–see reg.2.
"benefit"–see reg.2.
"claimant"–see reg.2.
"the Claims and Payments Regulations 2013"–see reg.2.
"personal independence payment"–see reg.2.

General Note

This regulation is equivalent to reg.25 of the Social Security and Child Support (Decisions and Appeals) Regulations 1999. 2.702

Decisions which may or may not be appealed

50.—(1) An appeal lies against a decision set out in Schedule 2 (decisions against which an appeal lies). 2.703

(2) No appeal lies against a decision set out in Schedule 3 (decisions against which no appeal lies).

(3) In paragraph (2) and Schedule 3, "decision" includes a determination embodied in or necessary to a decision.

Definition

"appeal"–see reg.2.

General Note

2.704 This regulation is equivalent to regs 26 and 27 of the Social Security and Child Support (Decisions and Appeals) Regulations 1999.

Notice of a decision against which an appeal lies

2.705 **51.**—(1) This regulation applies in the case of a person ("P") who has a right of appeal under the 1998 Act or these Regulations.

(2) The Secretary of State must—

(a) give P written notice of the decision and of the right to appeal against that decision; and

(b) inform P that, where that notice does not include a statement of the reasons for the decision, P may, within one month of the date of notification of that decision, request that the Secretary of State provide a written statement of the reasons for that decision.

(3) If the Secretary of State is requested under paragraph (2)(b) to provide a written statement of reasons, the Secretary of State must provide such a statement within 14 days of the request or as soon as practicable afterwards.

Definitions

"the 1998 Act"–see reg.2.
"appeal"–see reg.2.
"the date of notification"–see reg.2.

General Note

2.706 This regulation is equivalent to reg.28 of the Social Security and Child Support (Decisions and Appeals) Regulations 1999.

Appeals against decisions which have been revised

2.707 **52.**—(1) An appeal against a decision of the Secretary of State does not lapse where—

(a) the decision is revised under section 9 of the 1998 Act before the appeal is decided; and

(b) the decision of the Secretary of State as revised is not more advantageous to the appellant than the decision before it was revised.

(2) In a case to which paragraph (1) applies, the appeal must be treated as though it had been brought against the decision as revised.

(3) The Secretary of State must inform the appellant that they may, within one month of the date of notification of the decision as revised, make further representations as to the appeal.

(4) After the end of that period, or within that period if the appellant consents in writing, the appeal to the First-tier Tribunal must proceed, except where—

(a) the Secretary of State further revises the decision in light of further representations from the appellant; and

(b) that decision is more advantageous to the appellant than the decision before it was revised.

(5) Decisions which are more advantageous for the purpose of this regulation include those where—

(a) the amount of any benefit payable to the appellant is greater, or any benefit is awarded for a longer period, as a result of the decision;

(b) the decision would have resulted in the amount of benefit in payment being greater but for the operation of any provision of the Administration Act or the Contributions and Benefits Act restricting or suspending the payment of, or disqualifying a claimant from receiving, some or all of the benefit;

(c) as a result of the decision, a denial or disqualification for the receipt of any benefit is lifted, wholly or in part;

(d) the decision reverses a decision to pay benefit to a third party instead of to the appellant;

(e) in consequence of the decision, benefit paid is not recoverable under section 71ZB, 71ZG or 71ZH of the Administration Act or regulations made under any of those sections, or the amount so recoverable is reduced; or

(f) a financial gain accrued or will accrue to the appellant in consequence of the decision.

DEFINITIONS

"the 1998 Act"–see reg.2.
"the Administration Act"–see reg.2.
"appeal"–see reg.2.
"benefit"–see reg.2.
"the Contributions and Benefits Act"–see reg.2.
"the date of notification"–see reg.2.
"writing"–see reg.2.

GENERAL NOTE

This regulation is equivalent to reg.30 of the Social Security and Child Support (Decisions and Appeals) Regulations 1999. **2.708**

Where the Secretary of State is minded to revise a decision in the claimant's favour but not to the fullest extent possible, she may give the claimant an opportunity to say whether he or she agrees with the proposed decision or wishes the appeal to continue. If the claimant wishes the appeal to continue, the Secretary of State then does not revise the decision but instead invites the First-tier Tribunal to allow the appeal to the extent that she considers right (see the annotation to s.9(6) of the Social Security Act 1998, above).

Where a claim is disallowed because a claimant has failed to attend a consultation with a health care professional and, after the claimant has appealed, the Secretary of State accepts that the claimant had good cause for the non-attendance and accordingly arranges another consultation, the appeal does not lapse by virtue of that new decision alone as there is no revision and the decision is not "more advantageous" to the claimant for the purposes of this regulation (*AI v SSWP (PIP)* [2019] UKUT 103 (AAC)). See the annotation to s.9(6) of the Social Security Act 1998, above.

Decisions involving issues that arise on appeal in other cases

53.—(1) For the purposes of section 25(3)(b) of the 1998 Act (prescribed cases and circumstances in which a decision may be made on a prescribed basis)— **2.709**

(a) a prescribed case is a case in which the claimant would be entitled to the benefit to which the decision relates, even if the other appeal referred to in section 25(1)(b) of the 1998 Act were decided in a way which is the most unfavourable to the claimant; and

(b) the prescribed basis on which the Secretary of State may make the decision is as if—

(i) the other appeal referred to in section 25(1)(b) of the 1998 Act had already been decided; and

(ii) that appeal had been decided in a way which is the most unfavourable to the claimant.

(2) For the purposes of section 25(5)(c) of the 1998 Act (appeal treated as pending against a decision in a different case, even though an appeal against the decision has not been brought or an application for permission to appeal against the decision has not been made but the time for doing so has not yet expired), the prescribed circumstances are that the Secretary of State—

(a) certifies in writing that the Secretary of State is considering appealing against that decision; and

(b) considers that, if such an appeal were to be decided in a particular way—

(i) there would be no entitlement to benefit in that case; or

(ii) the appeal would affect the decision in that case in some other way.

DEFINITIONS

"the 1998 Act"–see reg.2.
"benefit"–see reg.2.
"claimant"–see reg.2.
"writing"–see reg.2.

GENERAL NOTE

2.710 This regulation is equivalent to reg.21 of the Social Security and Child Support (Decisions and Appeals) Regulations 1999.

Appeals involving issues that arise in other cases

2.711 **54.** For the purposes of section 26(6)(c) of the 1998 Act (appeal is treated as pending against a decision in a different case, even though an appeal against the decision has not been brought or an application for permission to appeal has not been made but the time for doing so has not yet expired) the prescribed circumstances are that the Secretary of State—

(a) certifies in writing that the Secretary of State is considering appealing against that decision; and

(b) considers that, if such an appeal were already decided, it would affect the determination of the appeal referred to in section 26(1)(a) of the 1998 Act.

DEFINITIONS

"the 1998 Act"–see reg.2.
"writing"–see reg.2.

General Note

This regulation is equivalent to reg.22 of the Social Security and Child Support (Decisions and Appeals) Regulations 1999. 2.712

55. *Omitted.* 2.713

Regulation 35

SCHEDULE 1

EFFECTIVE DATES FOR SUPERSEDING DECISIONS MADE ON THE GROUND OF A CHANGE OF CIRCUMSTANCES

PART 1

EMPLOYMENT AND SUPPORT ALLOWANCE AND JOBSEEKER'S ALLOWANCE

1. Subject to the following provisions of this Part and to Part 4, in the case of an employment and support allowance or a jobseeker's allowance, a superseding decision made on the ground of a change of circumstances takes effect from the first day of the benefit week in which the relevant change of circumstances occurs or is expected to occur. 2.714

2. Paragraph 1 does not apply where—

(a) the superseding decision is not advantageous to the claimant; and

(b) there has been an employment and support allowance decision where the Secretary of State is satisfied that, in relation to a limited capability for work determination, the claimant—

(i) failed to notify an appropriate office of a change of circumstances which the claimant was required by regulations under the Administration Act to notify; and

(ii) could not reasonably have been expected to know that the change of circumstances should have been notified.

3. Where a relevant change of circumstances results, or is expected to result, in a reduced award and the Secretary of State is of the opinion that it is impracticable for a superseding decision to take effect from the day set out in paragraph 1, that superseding decision takes effect—

(a) where the relevant change has occurred, from the first day of the benefit week following that in which that superseding decision is made; or

(b) where the relevant change is expected to occur, from the first day of the benefit week following that in which that change of circumstances is expected to occur.

4. Where entitlement ends, or is expected to end, as the result of a change of circumstances, the superseding decision takes effect from the day on which the relevant change of circumstances occurs or is expected to occur.

5. In the case of an employment and support allowance where a person who is subject to—

(a) section 45A or 47 of the Mental Health Act 1983 (power of higher courts to direct hospital admission; removal to hospital of persons serving sentences of imprisonment etc.);

(b) section 59A (hospital direction) of the Criminal Procedure (Scotland) Act 1995; or

(c) section 136 (transfer of prisoners for treatment for mental disorder) of the Mental Health (Care and Treatment) (Scotland) Act 2003,

ceases, or is expected to cease, to be detained in a hospital (as defined in the Act, or the Act of the Scottish Parliament, to which the person is subject) for a period of less than a week, a superseding decision related to that person's departure from, or return to, hospital takes effect from the day on which that change of circumstances occurs or is expected to occur.

6. Where the superseding decision is advantageous to the claimant and the change of circumstances was notified to an appropriate office more than one month after the change occurred or after the expiry of such longer period as may be allowed under regulation 36 (effective dates for superseding decisions where changes notified late), the superseding decision takes effect from the beginning of the benefit week in which the notification was given.

7. In the case of an employment and support allowance decision where the Secretary of State is satisfied that, in relation a limited capability for work determination, the claimant—

(a) failed to notify an appropriate office of a change of circumstances which the claimant was required by regulations under the Administration Act to notify; and

(b) could reasonably have been expected to know that the change of circumstances should have been notified,

the superseding decision takes effect in accordance with paragraph 8.

8. The superseding decision takes effect—

(a) from the date on which the claimant ought to have notified the change of circumstances; or

(b) if more than one change has taken place between the date from which the decision to be superseded took effect and the date of the superseding decision, from the date on which the first change ought to have been notified.

9. In the case of a claimant who makes an application for a supersession which contains an express statement that they are terminally ill, the superseding decision takes effect from the date on which the claimant became terminally ill.

10. Where the superseding decision is advantageous to the claimant and is made on the Secretary of State's own initiative, the decision takes effect from the beginning of the benefit week in which the Secretary of State commenced action with a view to supersession.

11. In this Part—

"employment and support allowance decision" means a decision to award an employment and support allowance embodied in or necessary to which is a determination that the claimant has, or is to be treated as having, limited capability for work;

"week" means a period of 7 days, beginning with midnight between Saturday and Sunday.

PART 2

PERSONAL INDEPENDENCE PAYMENT

2.715 **12.** Subject to the following provisions of this Part and to Part 4, in the case of personal independence payment, a superseding decision made on the ground of a change of circumstances takes effect on the date on which the relevant change of circumstances occurs or is expected to occur.

13. Paragraph 12 does not apply where—

(a) the superseding decision is not advantageous to the claimant; and

(b) there has been a personal independence payment decision where the Secretary of State is satisfied that, in relation to such a decision, the claimant—

(i) failed to notify an appropriate office of a change of circumstances which the claimant was required by regulations under the Administration Act to notify; and

(ii) could not reasonably have been expected to know that the change of circumstances should have been notified.

14. Except in a case where paragraph 15 or 31 applies, where the superseding decision is advantageous to the claimant and the change of circumstances was notified to an appropriate office more than one month after the change occurred or after the expiry of such longer period as may be allowed under regulation 36 (effective dates for superseding decisions where changes notified late), the superseding decision takes effect from the date of notification of the change.

15. Where—

(a) the change is relevant to entitlement to a particular rate of personal independence payment; and

(b) the claimant notifies an appropriate office of the change no later than one month after the date on which they first satisfied the conditions of entitlement to that rate or within such longer period as may be allowed by regulation 36 (effective dates for superseding decisions where changes notified late),

the superseding decision takes effect from the date on which the claimant first satisfied those conditions.

16. Where the Secretary of State is satisfied that, in relation to a personal independence payment decision, the claimant—

(a) failed to notify an appropriate office of a change of circumstances which the claimant was required by regulations under the Administration Act to notify; and

(b) could reasonably have been expected to know that the change of circumstances should have been notified,

the superseding decision takes effect in accordance with paragraph 17.

17. The superseding decision takes effect—

(a) from the date on which the claimant ought to have notified the change of circumstances; or

(b) if more than one change has taken place between the date from which the decision to be superseded took effect and the date of the superseding decision, from the date on which the first change ought to have been notified.

18. Where the superseding decision is advantageous to the claimant and is made on the Secretary of State's own initiative, the decision takes effect from the date on which the Secretary of State commenced action with a view to supersession.

19. In paragraphs 13 and 16, "personal independence payment decision" means a decision to award personal independence payment, embodied in or necessary to which is a determination whether the claimant satisfies any of the requirements in section 78(1) and (2) (daily living component) or section 79(1) and (2) (mobility component) of the 2012 Act.

PART 3

UNIVERSAL CREDIT

20. Subject to the following paragraphs and to Part 4, in the case of universal credit, a superseding decision made on the ground of a change of circumstances takes effect from the first day of the assessment period in which that change occurred or is expected to occur. **2.716**

21. Except in a case to which paragraph 22 or 31 applies, where the superseding decision is advantageous to the claimant and the change of circumstances was notified to an appropriate office after the end of the assessment period in which the change occurred or after the expiry of such longer period as may be allowed under regulation 36 (effective dates for superseding decisions where changes notified late), the superseding decision takes effect from the first day of the assessment period in which the notification was given.

22. In the case of a person to whom regulation 61 (information for calculating earned income) of the Universal Credit Regulations applies, where—

(a) the relevant change of circumstances is that the person's employed earnings are reduced; and

(b) the person provides such information for the purposes of calculating those earnings at such times as the Secretary of State may require,

the superseding decision takes effect from the first day of the assessment period in which that change occurred.

23. In the case of a universal credit decision where the Secretary of State is satisfied that, in relation to a limited capability for work determination, the claimant—

(a) failed to notify an appropriate office of a change of circumstances which the claimant was required by regulations under the Administration Act to notify; and

(b) could reasonably have been expected to know that the change of circumstances should have been notified,

the superseding decision takes effect in accordance with paragraph 24.

24. The superseding decision takes effect—

(a) from the first day of the assessment period in which the claimant ought to have notified the change of circumstances; or

(b) if more than one change has taken place between the date from which the decision to be superseded took effect and the date of the superseding decision, from the first day of the assessment period in which the first change ought to have been notified.

25. Where—

(a) the superseding decision is not advantageous to the claimant; and

(b) there has been a universal credit decision where the Secretary of State is satisfied that, in relation to a limited capability for work determination, the claimant—

(i) failed to notify an appropriate office of a change of circumstances which the claimant was required by regulations under the Administration Act to notify; and

(ii) could not reasonably have been expected to know that the change of circumstances should have been notified,

the superseding decision takes effect on the first day of the assessment period in which the Secretary of State makes that decision.

[2 **26.** Where, in any assessment period, a claimant reaches the qualifying age for state pension credit under the State Pension Credit Act 2002, where claiming as a single person or as a member of a couple to whom regulation 3(2)(a) of the Universal Credit Regulations applies, a superseding decision made in consequence of the person reaching that age takes effect on the first day of the assessment period following that in which the change of circumstances occurs or is expected to occur.]

27. A superseding decision of the Secretary of State to make or to cease making a hardship payment takes effect in accordance with regulation 117 (period of hardship payments) of the Universal Credit Regulations.

28. In the case of a claimant who makes an application for a supersession which contains an express statement that they are terminally ill, the superseding decision takes effect from the first day of the assessment period in which the claimant became terminally ill.

29. Where the superseding decision is advantageous to a claimant and is made on the Secretary of State's own initiative, it takes effect from the first day of the assessment period in which the Secretary of State commenced action with a view to supersession.

30. In this Part, "a universal credit decision" means a decision to award universal credit embodied in or necessary to which is a determination that the claimant has or is to be treated as having limited capability for work.

PART 4

COMMON PROVISIONS

2.717 **31.**—(1) This paragraph applies in relation to an award of personal independence payment or universal credit where the change of circumstances is that the claimant or, in the case of universal credit, a member of their family, becomes entitled to another relevant benefit [3 or [4 Scottish disability benefit]], ceases so to be entitled or the rate of another such benefit [3 or [4 Scottish disability benefit]] alters.

(2) Where this paragraph applies, the superseding decision takes effect from—

(a) where the superseding decision concerns universal credit, the first day of the assessment period in which—

(i) the entitlement to the other benefit [3 or [4 Scottish disability benefit]] arises;

(ii) the entitlement to the other benefit [3 or [4 Scottish disability benefit]] ends; or

(iii) entitlement to a different rate of the other benefit [3 or [4 Scottish disability benefit]] arises;

(b) where the superseding decision concerns personal independence payment, the date on which—

(i) the entitlement to the other benefit arises;

(ii) the entitlement to the other benefit ends; or

(iii) entitlement to a different rate of the other benefit arises.

(3) For the purpose of sub-paragraph (1), where the superseding decision relates to personal independence payment, "relevant benefit" includes any payment made under any of the provisions mentioned in regulation 61(1) (cases where mobility component of personal independence payment not payable) of the Claims and Payments Regulations 2013.

[1 **32.** Where the change of circumstances is that there has been a change in the legislation, the superseding decision takes effect—

(a) in relation to an award of universal credit that exists on the date on which the change in legislation comes into force—

(i) if there is an assessment period for the award that begins on the date on which that change in legislation has effect, from that date; or

(ii) in any other case, from the first day of the next assessment period for the award beginning after the date on which that change had effect;

(b) in any other case, from the date on which that change in the legislation had effect.

33. Where the change of circumstances is the expected coming into force of a change in the legislation, the superseding decision takes effect—

(a) in relation to an award of universal credit that exists on the date on which the change in legislation comes into force—

(i) if there is an assessment period for the award that begins on the date on which that change in legislation has effect, from that date; or

(ii) in any other case, from the first day of the next assessment period for the award beginning after the date on which that change has effect;

(b) in any other case, from the date on which that change in the legislation has effect.]

AMENDMENTS

1. Universal Credit (Miscellaneous Amendments, Saving and Transitional Provision) Regulations 2018 (SI 2018/65) reg.5(1) and (3) (February 14, 2018).

2. Universal Credit (Persons who have attained state pension credit qualifying age) (Amendment) Regulations 2020 (SI 2020/655) reg.5 (November 25, 2020).

3. Social Security (Scotland) Act 2018 (Disability Assistance for Children and Young People) (Consequential Modifications) Order 2021 (SI 2021/786) art.21(1) and (4) (July 26, 2021).

4. Social Security (Disability Assistance for Working Age People) (Consequential Amendments) Order 2022 (SI 2022/177) art.17(1) and (4) (March 21, 2022).

DEFINITIONS

"the 2012 Act"–see reg.2.
"the Administration Act"–see reg.2.
"appropriate office"–see reg.2.
"assessment period"–see reg.2.
"benefit"–see reg.2.
"benefit week"–see reg.2.
"claimant"–see reg.2.
"the Claims and Payments Regulations 2013"–see reg.2.
"the date of notification"–see reg.2.
"employment and support allowance"–by virtue of reg.2, see reg.1(3)(a).
"family"–see reg.2.
"jobseeker's allowance"–by virtue of reg.2, see reg.1(3)(b).
"limited capability for work"–see reg.2.
"limited capability for work determination"–see reg.2.
"personal independence payment"–see reg.2.
"relevant benefit"–see reg.2.
"Scottish disability benefit"—see reg.2.
"terminally ill"–see reg.2.
"the Universal Credit Regulations"–see reg.2.
"universal credit"–see reg.2.

GENERAL NOTE

This schedule is equivalent to Sch.3A and Sch.3B to the Social Security and Child Support (Decisions and Appeals) Regulations 1999 and makes equivalent provision for universal credit. It also makes provision equivalent to some paragraphs of reg.7 of the 1999 Regulations. 2.718

It is arguable that the second amendment to para.31(1) and the amendments to para.31(2)(a) are unnecessary, because the phrases "such benefit" and "the other benefit" might be thought to include Scottish disability benefit as a result of the first amendment to para.31(1). If those amendments are necessary, it is not immediately obvious why para.31(2)(b) has not been amended in the same way as para.31(2)(a), since the Welfare Reform Act 2012 s.77(4) provides that "[a] person is not entitled to personal independence payment while they are entitled to adult disability payment or child disability payment".

Regulation 50(1)

SCHEDULE 2

DECISIONS AGAINST WHICH AN APPEAL LIES

1. A decision as to whether a person is entitled to a benefit for which no claim is required by virtue of regulation 6, 7 or 9(6) and (7) of the Claims and Payments Regulations 2013. 2.719

DEFINITIONS

"appeal"–see reg.2.
"benefit"–see reg.2.
"the Claims and Payments Regulations 2013"–see reg.2.

GENERAL NOTE

This Schedule, read with reg.50(1), is equivalent to reg.26(a) of the Social Security and Child Support (Decisions and Appeals) Regulations 1999. 2.720

Regulation 50(2)

SCHEDULE 3

DECISIONS AGAINST WHICH NO APPEAL LIES

Claims and Payments

2.721 **1.** A decision under any of the following provisions of the Claims and Payments Regulations 2013—

(a) regulation 18 (special provisions where it is certified that a woman is expected to be confined or where she has been confined);
(b) regulation 25 (interchange with claims for other benefits);
(c) regulation 37 (evidence and information in connection with a claim);
(d) regulation 46 (direct credit transfer);
(e) regulation 47 (payment of universal credit);
(f) regulation 48 (payment of personal independence payment);
(g) regulation 49 (days for payment of personal independence payment);
(h) regulation 50(1) (payment of personal independence payment at a daily rate between periods in hospital or other accommodation);
(i) regulation 51 (payment of an employment and support allowance);
(j) regulation 52 (payment of a jobseeker's allowance);
(k) regulation 55, except a decision under paragraph (4) (extinguishment of right to payment if payment is not obtained within the prescribed period);
(l) regulation 56 (payments on death);
(m) regulation 57 (persons unable to act);
(n) regulation 58 (payment to another person on the claimant's behalf);
(o) [1 . . .]
(p) Part 6 (mobility component of personal independence payment).

Other Jobseeker's Allowance Decisions

2.722 **2.** A decision made in accordance with regulation 39(2) (jobseeker's allowance determinations on incomplete evidence) of these Regulations.

Other Decisions relating to Universal Credit

2.723 **3.** A decision in default of a nomination under regulation 21(4) (assessment periods) of the Universal Credit Regulations.

4. A decision in default of an election under regulation 29 (award to include the carer element) of the Universal Credit Regulations.

5. A decision as to the amount of universal credit to which a person is entitled, where it appears to the Secretary of State that the amount is determined by reference to the claimant's entitlement to an increased amount of universal credit in the circumstances referred to in section 160C(2) (implementation of increases in universal credit due to attainment of a particular age) of the Administration Act.

6. So much of a decision as adopts a decision of a rent officer under an order made by virtue of section 122 of the Housing Act 1996 (decisions of rent officers for the purposes of universal credit).

Suspension

2.724 **7.** A decision of the Secretary of State relating to suspending payment of benefit, or to the payment of a benefit which has been suspended, under Part 5 (suspension) of these Regulations.

Decisions Depending on Other Cases

8. A decision of the Secretary of State in accordance with section 25 or 26 of the 1998 Act (decisions and appeals depending on other cases). **2.725**

Expenses

9. A decision of the Secretary of State whether to pay travelling expenses under section 180 of the Administration Act. **2.726**

Deductions

10. A decision of the Secretary of State under the Fines (Deductions from Income Support) Regulations 1992, other than a decision whether benefit is sufficient for a deduction to be made. **2.727**

11. Any decision of the Secretary of State under the Community Charges (Deductions from Income Support) (No. 2) Regulations 1990, the Community Charges (Deductions from Income Support) (Scotland) Regulations 1989 or the Council Tax (Deductions from Income Support) Regulations 1993, except a decision—

(a) whether there is an outstanding sum due of the amount sought to be deducted;
(b) whether benefit is sufficient for the deduction to be made; or
(c) on the priority of the deductions.

Loss of Benefit

12.—(1) In the circumstances referred to in sub-paragraph (2), a decision of the Secretary of State that a sanctionable benefit as defined in section 6A(1) of the Fraud Act is not payable (or is to be reduced) pursuant to section 6B, 7 or 9 of that Act as a result of— **2.728**

(a) a conviction for one or more benefit offences in one set of proceedings;
(b) an agreement to pay a penalty as an alternative to prosecution;
(c) a caution in respect of one or more benefit offences; or
(d) a conviction for one or more benefit offences in each of two sets of proceedings, the later offence or offences being committed within the period of 5 years after the date of any of the convictions for a benefit offence in the earlier proceedings.

(2) The circumstances are that the only ground of appeal is that any of the convictions was erroneous, or that the offender (as defined in section 6B(1) of the Fraud Act) did not commit the benefit offence in respect of which there has been an agreement to pay a penalty or a caution has been accepted.

Payments on Account, Overpayments and Recovery

13. In the case of personal independence payment, a decision of the Secretary of State under the Social Security (Payments on account, Overpayments and Recovery) Regulations 1988, except a decision of the Secretary of State under the following provisions of those Regulations— **2.729**

(a) regulation 5, as to the offsetting of a prior payment against a subsequent award;
(b) regulation 11(1), as to whether a payment in excess of entitlement has been credited to a bank or other account;
(c) regulation 13, as to the sums to be deducted in calculating recoverable amounts.

14. A decision of the Secretary of State under the Social Security (Payments on Account of Benefit) Regulations 2013, except a decision under regulation 10 (bringing payments on account of benefit into account) of those Regulations.

15. A decision of the Secretary of State under the Social Security (Overpayments and Recovery) Regulations 2013, except a decision of the Secretary of State under the following provisions of those Regulations—

(a) regulation 4(3), as to the person from whom an overpayment of a housing payment is recoverable;
(b) regulation 7, as to the treatment of capital to be reduced;
(c) regulation 8, as to the sums to be deducted in calculating recoverable amounts;
(d) regulation 9 (sums to be deducted: change of dwelling).

Reciprocal Agreements

2.730 **16.** A decision of the Secretary of State made in accordance with an Order made under section 179 (reciprocal agreements with countries outside the United Kingdom) of the Administration Act.

European Community Regulations

2.731 **17.** An authorisation given by the Secretary of State in accordance with Article 22(1) or 55(1) of Council Regulation (EEC) No 1408/71[[2], as amended from time to time,] on the application of social security schemes to employed persons, to self-employed persons and to members of their families moving within the European Union.

Up-rating

2.732 **18.** A decision of the Secretary of State relating to the up-rating of benefits under Part 10 (review and alteration of benefits) of the Administration Act.

AMENDMENTS

1. Loans for Mortgage Interest Regulations 2017 (SI 2017/725) reg.18 and Sch.5 para.12, as amended by the Loans for Mortgage Interest and Social Fund Maternity Grant (Amendment) Regulations 2018 (SI 2018/307) reg.2(11) and (18)(e) (April 6, 2018, subject to a saving).

2. Social Security (Updating of EU References) (Amendment) Regulations 2018 (SI 2018/1084) reg.12 (November 15, 2018).

DEFINITIONS

"the 1998 Act"–see reg.2.
"the Administration Act"–see reg.2.
"appeal"–see reg.2.
"assessment period"–see reg.2.
"benefit"–see reg.2.
"claimant"–see reg.2.
"the Claims and Payments Regulations 2013"–see reg.2.
"employment and support allowance"–by virtue of reg.2, see reg.1(3)(a).
"the Fraud Act"–see reg.2.
"jobseeker's allowance"–by virtue of reg.2, see reg.1(3)(b).
"personal independence payment"–see reg.2.
"the Universal Credit Regulations"–see reg.2.
"universal credit"–see reg.2.

GENERAL NOTE

2.733 This Schedule is equivalent to Sch.2 to the Social Security and Child Support (Decisions and Appeals) Regulations 1999. See the note to that Schedule.

The purpose of para.5 is not entirely clear. Not only is it premature, but at first sight it appears unnecessary. Paragraph 24 of Sch.2 to the Welfare Reform Act 2012, which would insert s.160C into the 1992 Act, has not yet been brought into force and presumably the original idea was that, if it were to be, para.50(3) of Sch.2 to the 2012 Act would be brought into force at the same time and that would insert a para.7A into Sch.2 to the Social Security Act 1998 to make much the same provision as para.5 makes. The only difference is that para.5 substitutes "by reference to the claimant's entitlement" for "the recipient's entitlement". Perhaps that is the reason for the inclusion of para.5, as the wording of para.5 may be strictly preferable due partly to the possibility of benefit being paid to someone other than the claimant. On the other hand, it is arguable that the proposed para.7A could be construed to the same effect and no attempt has been made to amend para.7 of Sch.2 to the 1998 Act which uses the same wording as the proposed para.7A.

The Social Security (General Benefit) Regulations 1982

(SI 1982/1408)

ARRANGEMENT OF REGULATIONS

PART I

General

Regs 5-47 and schedules omitted.

The Secretary of State for Social Services, in exercise of the powers conferred upon him by sections 50(4), 56(7), 57(5), 58(3), 60(4) and (7), 61(1), 62(2), 67(1), 68(2), 70(2), 72(1) and (8), 74(1), 81(6), 82(5) and (6), 83(1), 85(1), 86(2) and (5), 90(2), 91(1), 119(3) and (4) and 159(3) of, and paragraphs 2, 3 and 6 of Schedule 8, paragraphs 1 and 8 of Schedule 9 and Schedule 14 of the Social Security Act 1975 and of all other powers enabling him in that behalf, hereby makes the following regulations, which only consolidate the regulation hereby revoked, and which accordingly, by virtue of paragraph 20 of Schedule 3 to the Social Security Act 1980, are not subject to the requirements of section 10 of that Act for prior reference to the Social Security Advisory Committee and, by virtue of section 141(2) and paragraph 12 of Schedule 16 of the Social Security Act 1975, do not require prior reference to the Industrial Injuries Advisory Council:—

PART I

GENERAL

Citation, commencement and application

1.—(1) These regulations may be cited as the Social Security (General Benefit) Regulations 1982 and shall come into operation on 4th November, 1982. 2.735

(2) In these regulations, unless the context otherwise requires—

"the Act" means the Social Security Act 1975;

[[7] . . .]

"the Child Benefit Act" means the Child Benefit Act 1975;

"child benefit" means benefit under Part I of the Child Benefit Act;

[[1] "determining authority" means, as the case may require, the Secretary of State, [[5] the First-tier Tribunal or the Upper Tribunal]

"entitled to child benefit" includes treated as so entitled;

"industrial injuries benefit" means [[2]. . .] disablement benefit and industrial death benefit payable under section 50 of the Act;

"parent" has the meaning assigned to it by section 24(3) of the Child Benefit Act;

[4 "shared additional pension" means a shared additional pension under section 55A [6 or 55AA] of the Social Security Contributions and Benefits Act 1992;]

"standard rate of increase" means the amount specified in Part IV or Part V of Schedule 4 to the Act as the amount of an increase of the benefit in question for an adult dependant;

"the Workmen's Compensation Act" means the Workmen's Compensation Acts 1925 to 1945, or the enactments repealed by the Workmen's Compensation Act 1925 or the enactments repealed by the Workmen's Compensation Act 1906;

and other expressions have the same meanings as in the Act.

(3) Unless the context otherwise requires, any reference in these regulation—

(a) to a numbered section is to the section of the Act bearing that number;

(b) to a numbered regulation is a reference to the regulation bearing that number in these regulations and any reference in a regulation to a numbered paragraph is a reference to the paragraph of that regulation bearing that number.

AMENDMENTS

1. The Social Security Act 1998 (Commencement No.8, and Savings and Consequential and Transitional Provisions) Order 1999 (SI 1999/1958) Sch.5 (July 4, 1999).

2. The Social Security (Abolition of Injury Benefit) (Consequential) Regulations 1983 (SI 1983/186) reg.13 (April 6, 1983).

3. The Social Security (Benefits for Widows and Widowers) (Consequential Amendments) Regulations 2000 (SI 2000/1483) reg.8 (April 9, 2001).

4. The Social Security (Shared Additional Pension) (Miscellaneous Amendments) Regulations 2005 (SI 2005/1551) (July 6, 2005).

5. The Tribunals, Courts and Enforcement Act 2007 (Transitional and Consequential Provisions) Order 2008 (SI 2008/2683) reg.24 (November 3, 2008).

6. The Pensions Act 2014 (Consequential, Supplementary and Incidental Amendments) Order 2015 (SI 2015/1985) art.7 (April 6, 2016).

7. The Pensions Act 2014 (Consequential, Supplementary and Incidental Amendments) Order 2017 (SI 2017/422) art.8 (April 6, 2017).

Exceptions from disqualification for imprisonment etc.

2.736 **2.**—(1) The following provisions of this regulation shall have effect to except benefit from the operation of [section 113(1)(b) of the Social Security Contributions and Benefits Act 1992] which provides that (except where regulations otherwise provide) a person shall be disqualified for receiving any benefit and an increase of benefit shall not be payable in respect of any person as the beneficiary's [8 spouse or civil partner], for any period during which that person is undergoing imprisonment or detention in legal custody (hereinafter in this regulation referred to as "the said provisions").

(2) The said provisions shall not operate to disqualify a person for receiving [1incapacity benefit], [2attendance allowance, disability living allowance], widow's benefit, [11 widowed parent's allowance] child's special allowance, maternity allowance, [7 a shared additional pension] retirement pension of any category, age addition, [3severe disablement allowance],

[4. . .disablement benefit], [5. . .reduced earnings allowance, retirement allowance] or industrial death benefit or to make an increase of benefit not payable in respect of a person as the beneficiary's [8 spouse or civil partner], for any period during which that person is undergoing imprisonment or detention in legal custody in connection with a charge brought or intended to be brought against him in criminal proceedings, or pursuant to any sentence or order for detention made by a court in such proceedings, unless, in relation to him, a penalty is imposed at the conclusion of those proceedings or, in the case of default of payment of a sum adjudged to be paid on conviction, a penalty is imposed in respect of such default.

(3) The said provisions shall not operate to disqualify a person for receiving any benefit (not being a guardian's allowance or death grant), or to make an increase of benefit not payable in respect of a person as the beneficiary's [8 spouse or civil partner], for any period during which that person [10 ("P")] is undergoing detention in legal custody after the conclusion of criminal proceedings if it is a period during which [10 P is detained in a hospital or similar institution in Great Britain as a person suffering from mental disorder unless P satisfies either of the following conditions].

[10 (4) The first condition is that—

(a) P is being detained under section 45A or 47 of the Mental Health Act 1983 (power of higher courts to direct hospital admission; removal to hospital of persons serving sentences of imprisonment etc.); and

(b) in any case where there is in relation to P a release date within the meaning of section 50(3) of that Act, P is being detained on or before the day which the Secretary of State certifies to be that release date.

(4A) The second condition is that P is being detained under—

(a) section 59A of the Criminal Procedure (Scotland) Act 1995 (hospital direction); or

(b) section 136 of the Mental Health (Care and Treatment) (Scotland) Act 2003 (transfer of prisoners for treatment of mental disorder).]

(5) The said provisions shall not operate to disqualify a person for receiving a guardian's allowance or death grant.

[5(6) Subject to paragraph (7), the said provisions shall not operate to disqualify a person for receiving disablement benefit, other than any increase of that benefit, for any period during which he is undergoing imprisonment or detention in legal custody.]

(7) The amount payable by virtue of the last preceding paragraph by way of any disablement pension or pensions in respect of any period, other than a period in respect of which that person is excepted from disqualification by virtue of the provisions of paragraph (3) of this regulation, during which that person is and has continuously been undergoing imprisonment or detention in legal custody, shall not exceed the total amount payable by way of such pension or all such pensions for a period of one year.

(8) For the purposes of this regulation—

(a) "court" means any court in the United Kingdom, the Channel Islands or the Isle of Man or in any place to which the Colonial Prisoners Removal Act 1884 applies [12or the Court Martial, or the Court Martial Appeal Court.]

(b) "hospital or similar institution" means any place (not being a prison, a [13young offender institution], a Borstal institution, a young offenders institution or a remand centre, and not being at or in any such place) in which persons suffering from mental disorder are or may be received for care or treatment;

(c) "penalty" means a sentence of imprisonment, Borstal training or detention under section 53 of the Children and Young Persons Act 1933 or under section 57(3) of the Children and Young Persons (Scotland) Act 1937 or under section 208(3) and 416(4) of the Criminal Proceedings (Scotland) Act 1975 or an order for detention in a [13young offender institution];

(d) in relation to a person who is liable to be detained in Great Britain as a result of any order made under the Colonial Prisoners Removal Act 1884, references to a prison shall be construed as including references to a prison within the meaning of that Act;

(e) [9. . .]

(f) [9. . .]

(g) criminal proceedings against any person shall be deemed to be concluded upon his being found insane in those proceedings so that he cannot be tried or his trial cannot proceed.

(9) Where a person outside Great Britain is undergoing imprisonment or detention in legal custody and, in similar circumstances in Great Britain, he would have been excepted, by the operation of any of the preceding paragraphs of this regulation, from disqualification under the said provisions (referred to in paragraph (1)) for receiving the benefit claimed, he shall not be disqualified for receiving that benefit by reason only of his said imprisonment or detention.

(10) Paragraph (9) applies to increases of benefit not payable under the said provisions as it applied to disqualification for receiving benefit.

AMENDMENTS

1. The Social Security (Incapacity Benefit) (Consequential and Transitional Amendments and Savings) Regulations 1995 (SI 1995/829) reg.16 (April 13, 1995).

2. The Disability Living Allowance and Disability Working Allowance (Consequential Provisions) Regulations 1991 (SI 1991/2742) reg.11 (April 6, 1992).

3. The Social Security (Severe Disablement Allowance) Regulations 1984 (SI 1984/1303) reg.11 (November 29, 1984).

4. The Social Security (Abolition of Injury Benefit) (Consequential) Regulations 1983 (SI 1983/186) reg.13 (April 6, 1983).

5. The Social Security (Industrial Injuries and Diseases) (Miscellaneous Amendments) Regulations 1996 (SI 1996/425) reg.4 (March 24, 1996).

6. The Social Security (Benefits for Widows and Widowers) (Consequential Amendments) Regulations 2000 (SI 2000/1483) reg.6 (April 9, 2001).

7. The Social Security (Shared Additional Pension) (Miscellaneous Amendments) Regulations 2005 (SI 2005/1551) (July 6, 2005).

8. The Social Security (Civil Partnership) (Consequential Amendments) Regulations 2005 (SI 2005/2878) (December 5, 2005).

9. The Social Security (Hospital In-Patients) Regulations 2005 (SI 2005/3360) reg.3 (April 10, 2006).

10. The Social Security (Persons Serving a Sentence of Imprisonment Detained in Hospital) Regulations 2010 (SI 2010/442) reg.2(2) (March 25, 2010).

11. The Pensions Act 2014 (Consequential, Supplementary and Incidental Amendments) Order 2017 (SI 2017/422) art.8 (April 6, 2017).

12. Armed Forces Act 2006 (Consequential Amendments) Order 2009 (SI 2009/2054) Sch.1 (October 31, 2009).

13. Criminal Justice Act 1988 Sch.8 para.1.

DEFINITIONS

"the Act"—reg.1.
"benefit"—C & BA 1992 s.122.
"court"—para.(8)(a).
"Great Britain"—by art.1 of the Union with Scotland Act 1706, this means England, Scotland and Wales.
"hospital or similar institution"—para.(8)(b).
"penalty"—para.(8)(c).
"the said provisions"—para.(1).

GENERAL NOTE

Persons who can bring themselves within the terms of this regulation can escape the disqualification from benefit provided for in s.113(1)(b) of the Contributions and Benefits Act. Different rules apply to different benefits. **2.737**

Under para.(2) the disqualification applies in cases of imprisonment in connection with criminal proceedings where such penalty is imposed at the conclusion of proceedings. Imprisonment outside the exercise of criminal jurisdiction does not disqualify from benefit: *R(S)8/79*. It is now established that "penalty" in this paragraph includes the imposition of a suspended sentence and that a suspended sentence amounts to a sentence of imprisonment: *R(S)1/71*.

Paragraph (3) deals with the transfer of offenders from prison to hospital as mental patients under the mental health legislation. The disqualification in such circumstances exists only for the length of the original sentence: *R(P)2/57* reversing *R(S)9/56*. Provision is made for the Secretary of State to issue a certificate which is conclusive as to the earliest date on which the original sentence would come to an end had the person not been transferred to hospital.

A Commissioner has ruled in *CSS/239/2007* that, without a certificate of the type referred to in reg.2(4) of the General Benefit Regulations, an appellant could not obtain the advantage of the regulation. Paragraphs 8–10 of the decision address questions arising in relation to devolved government in Scotland. **2.738**

A challenge relating to the exclusion from benefits of prisoners transferred to mental hospital under these regulations as being in breach of art.14 of the European Convention when read with art.1 of Protocol No.1 has failed with one exception: see *R. (on the application of EM) v Secretary of State for Work and Pensions* [2009] EWHC 454 (Admin). The excepted class is a small group (there were 45 such persons in detention when the case was decided) of what are described as "technical lifers", namely those, although sentenced to life imprisonment, are treated by the Secretary of State after transfer to hospital as though they had been made the subject of a hospital order under s.37 of the Mental Health Act 1983 and to a restriction order under s.41 of that Act.

Suspension of payment of benefit during imprisonment etc.

3.—(1) Subject to the following provisions of this regulation, the payment to any person of any benefit— **2.739**

(a) which is excepted from the operation of [section 113(1)(b) of the Social Security Contributions and Benefits Act 1992] by virtue of the provisions of regulation 2(2), (5) or (6) or by any of those paragraphs as applied by regulation 2(9); or
(b) which is payable otherwise than in respect of a period during which he is undergoing imprisonment or detention in legal custody;

shall be suspended while that person is undergoing imprisonment or detention in legal custody.

(2) Paragraph (1) shall not operate to require the payment of any benefit to be suspended while the beneficiary is liable to be detained in a hospital or

similar institution as defined in regulation 2(8)(b) during a period for which in his case, benefit to which regulation 2(3) applies is or would be excepted from the operation of the said [section 113(1)] by virtue of the provision of regulation 2(3).

(3) A guardian's allowance or death grant, or any benefit to which paragraph (1)(b) applies may nevertheless be paid while the beneficiary is undergoing imprisonment or detention in legal custody to any person appointed for the purpose by the Secretary of State to receive and deal with any sums payable on behalf of the beneficiary on account of that benefit, and the receipt of any person so appointed shall be a good discharge to the Secretary of State and the National Insurance Fund for any sum so paid.

(4) Where, by virtue of this regulation, payment of benefit under [Part V of the Social Security Contribution and Benefits Act 1992] is suspended for any period, the period of suspension shall not be taken into account in calculating any period under the provisions of regulation 22 of the Social Security (Claims and Payments) Regulations 1979 (extinguishment of right to sums payable by way of benefit which are not obtained within the prescribed time).

Interim payments by way of benefit under the Act

2.740 **4.**—(1) Where, under arrangements made by the Secretary of State with the consent of the Treasury, payment by way of benefit has been made pending determination of a claim for it without due proof of the fulfilment of the relevant conditions or otherwise than in accordance with the provisions of the Act and orders and regulations made under it, the payment so made shall, for the purposes of those provisions, but subject to the following provisions of this regulation, be deemed to be a payment of benefit duly made.

(2) When a claim for benefit in connection with which a payment has been made under arrangements such as are referred to in paragraph (1) above is determined by a determining authority—

(a) if that authority decides that nothing was properly payable by way of the benefit in respect of which the payment was made or that the amount properly payable by way of that benefit was less than the amount of the payment, it may, if appropriate, direct that the whole or part of the overpayment be treated as paid on account of benefit (whether benefit under the Act or the Supplementary Benefits Act 1976) which is properly payable, but subject as aforesaid shall require repayment of the overpayment; and

(b) if that authority decides that the amount properly payable by way of the benefit in respect of which the payment was made equals or exceeds the amount of that payment, it shall treat that payment as paid on account of the benefit properly payable.

(3) Unless before a payment made under arrangements such as are mentioned in paragraph (1) above has been made to a person that person had been informed of the effect of sub-paragraph (a) of paragraph (2) above as it relates to repayment of an overpayment, repayment of an overpayment shall not be required except where the determining authority is satisfied that[1] he, or any person acting for him, has, whether fraudulently or otherwise, misrepresented or failed to disclose any material fact and that the interim payment has been made in consequence of the misrepresentation or failure.]

(4) An overpayment required to be repaid under the provisions of this regulation shall, without prejudice to any other method of recovery, be recoverable by deduction from any benefit then or thereafter payable to the person by whom it is to be repaid or any persons entitled to receive his benefit on his death.

AMENDMENT

1. The Social Security (Payments on account, Overpayment and Recovery) Regulations 1987 (SI 1987/491) reg.19 (April 6, 1987).

GENERAL NOTE

This regulation has not been repealed by the Overpayments Regulations because its provisions will still be needed for cases where the relevant determination was made before April 6, 1987. As time passes the provision will fall into disuse, and will in due course be revoked. **2.741**

The Social Security (Jobcentre Plus Interviews) Regulations 2002

(SI 2002/1703)

ARRANGEMENT OF REGULATIONS

The Secretary of State for Work and Pensions, in exercise of the powers conferred upon him by sections 2A(1), (3) to (6) and (8), 2B(6) and (7), 5(1)(a) and (b), 6(1)(a) and (b), 7A, 189(1), (4) and (5) and 191 of the Social Security Administration Act 1992 and section 68 of, and paragraphs 3(1), 4(4), 6(8), 20(3) and 23(1) of Schedule 7 to, the Child Support,

Pensions and Social Security Act 2000, and of all other powers enabling him in that behalf, after consultation with the Council on Tribunals in accordance with section 8(1) of the Tribunals and Inquiries Act 1992 and in respect of provisions in these Regulations relating to housing benefit and council tax benefit with organisations appearing to him to be representative of the authorities concerned, and after agreement by the Social Security Advisory Committee that proposals in respect of these Regulations should not be referred to it, hereby makes the following Regulations:

Citation and commencement

2.743 **1.** These Regulations may be cited as the Social Security (Jobcentre Plus Interviews) Regulations 2002 and shall come into force on 30th September 2002.

Interpretation and application

2.744 **2.**—(1) In these Regulations, unless the context otherwise requires—

"the 1998 Act" means the Social Security Act 1998;

"benefit week" means any period of seven days corresponding to the week in respect of which the relevant specified benefit is due to be paid;

[3 . . .]

[8 . . .]

"interview" means a work-focused interview with a person who has claimed a specified benefit and which is conducted for any or all of the following purposes—

(a) assessing that person's prospects for existing or future employment (whether paid or voluntary);

(b) assisting or encouraging that person to enhance his prospects of such employment;

(c) identifying activities which that person may undertake to strengthen his existing or future prospects of employment;

(d) identifying current or future employment or training opportunities suitable to that person's needs; and

(e) identifying educational opportunities connected with the existing or future employment prospects or needs of that person;

[3 "lone parent" has the meaning it bears in regulation 2(1) of the Income Support (General) Regulations 1987;]

"officer" means a person who is an officer of, or who is providing services to or exercising functions of, the Secretary of State;

[6 "pensionable age", in the case of a man born before 6th April 1955, means the age when a woman born on the same day as the man would attain pensionable age;]

[3 "relevant benefit" means income support other than income support where one of the following paragraphs of Schedule 1B to the Income Support (General) Regulations 1987 applies—

(a) paragraph 7 (persons incapable of work), or

(b) paragraph 24 or 25 (persons appealing against a decision which embodies a determination that they are not incapable of work);]

[8 "relevant interview" means an interview under these Regulations in relation to the claimant's current award of a specified benefit;]

[3 "specified benefit" means income support, incapacity benefit and severe disablement allowance;]

[3 "specified person" means—

(a) a lone parent, or

(b) a person who claims—

(i) incapacity benefit,

(ii) income support where paragraph 7 (persons incapable of work) of Schedule 1B to the Income Support (General) Regulations 1987 applies,

(iii) income support where paragraph 24 or 25 (persons appealing against a decision which embodies a determination that they are not incapable of work) of Schedule 1B to the Income Support (General) Regulations 1987 applies, or

(iv) severe disablement allowance.]

(2) For the purposes of these Regulations—

(a) a person shall be deemed to be in remunerative work where he is in remunerative work within the meaning prescribed in [4 regulation 6 of the Housing Benefit Regulations 2006]; but

(b) a person shall be deemed not to be in remunerative work where—

(i) he is not in remunerative work in accordance with subparagraph (a) above; or

(ii) he is in remunerative work in accordance with sub-paragraph (a) above and is not entitled to income support but would not be prevented from being entitled to income support solely by being in such work; and

(c) a person shall be deemed to be engaged in part-time work where he is engaged in work for which payment is made but he is not engaged or deemed to be engaged in remunerative work.

[8 (2A) For the purposes of section 2A(2A)(b) of the Social Security Administration Act 1992 and these Regulations, a lone parent is to be treated as responsible for, and a member of the same household as, a child under the age of one only where the lone parent would be treated as being responsible for, and a member of the same household as, such a child under regulations 15 and 16 of the Income Support (General) Regulations 1987, if references in those Regulations to income support were to a specified benefit.]

(3) Except in a case where regulation 16(2) applies [5 . . .] regulations 3 to 15 apply in respect of a person who makes a claim for a specified benefit on or after 30th September 2002 at an office of the Department for Work and Pensions which is designated by the Secretary of State as a Jobcentre Plus Office or at an office of a relevant authority (being a person within section 72(2) of the Welfare Reform and Pensions Act 1999) which displays the **one** logo.

(4) Where a claim for benefit is made by a person ("the appointee") on behalf of another, references in these Regulations to a person claiming benefit shall be treated as a reference to the person on whose behalf the claim is made and not to the appointee.

(5) In these Regulations, unless the context otherwise requires, a reference—

(a) to a numbered regulation is to a regulation in these Regulations bearing that number;

(b) in a regulation to a numbered paragraph or sub-paragraph is to the paragraph or sub-paragraph in that regulation bearing that number;

(c) to a numbered Schedule is to the Schedule to these Regulations bearing that number.

AMENDMENTS

1. The Social Security Amendment (Carer's Allowance) Regulations 2002 (SI 2002/2497) Sch.2 (October 28, 2002).

2. Social Security (Working Neighbourhoods) Regulations 2004 (SI 2004/959) reg.26(2) (April 26, 2004).

3. The Social Security (Work-focused Interviews) Amendment Regulations 2005 (SI 2005/2727) (October 31, 2005).

4. The Housing Benefit and Council Tax Benefit (Consequential Provisions) Regulations 2006 (SI 2006/217) Sch.2 para.21 (March 6, 2006).

5. The Social Security (Working Neighbourhoods) Miscellaneous Amendment Regulations 2006 (SI 2006/909) (April 24, 2006).

6. The Social Security (Work-focused Interviews etc.) (Equalisation of State Pension Age) Amendment Regulations 2010 (SI 2010/563) reg.6(2) (April 6, 2010).

7. Local Education Authorities and Children's Services Authorities (Integration of Functions) (Local and Subordinate Legislation) Order 2010 (SI 2010/1172) Sch.3 para.45 (May 5, 2010).

8. The Social Security (Miscellaneous Amendments) (No.3) Regulations 2011 (SI 2011/2425) reg.14 (October 31, 2011).

Requirement for person claiming a specified benefit to take part in an interview

2.745 **3.**—(1) Subject to regulations 6 to 9, a person who—

[1 (a) either—

(i) makes a claim for a relevant benefit, or

(ii) is entitled to a specified benefit other than a relevant benefit;]

[1 (b) on the day on which he [claims a specified benefit], has attained the age of 16 but has not attained [2 pensionable age]; [4 . . .]

(c) is not in remunerative work, [4 ; and

(d) is not a lone parent who—

(i) makes a claim for or is entitled to income support; and

(ii) falls within paragraph 1 (lone parents) of Schedule 1B (prescribed categories of person) to the Income Support (General) Regulations 1987]

is required to take part in an interview.

(2) An officer shall, except where paragraph (3) applies, conduct the interview.

(3) An officer may, if he considers it appropriate in all the circumstances, arrange for a person who has not attained the age of 18 to attend an interview with [3 such person as the Secretary of State may specify.]

AMENDMENTS

1. The Social Security (Work-focused Interviews) Amendment Regulations 2005 (SI 2005/2727) (October 31, 2005).

2. The Social Security (Work-focused Interviews etc.) (Equalisation of State Pension Age) Amendment Regulations 2010 (SI 2010/563) reg.6(3) (April 6, 2010).

3. The Social Security (Miscellaneous Amendments) (No.3) Regulations 2011 (SI 2011/2425) reg.14 (October 31, 2011).

4. The Social Security (Work-focused Interviews for Lone Parents and Partners) (Amendment) Regulations 2011 (SI 2011/2428) reg.3 (October 31, 2011).

[1 Continuing entitlement to full amount of specified benefit dependent on an interview

4.—(1) This paragraph applies to a person who— 2.746

(a) is not a lone parent who is entitled to income support who falls within paragraph 1 (lone parents) of Schedule 1B (prescribed categories of person) to the Income Support (General) Regulations 1987;

(b) has not attained pensionable age; and

(c) is entitled to a specified benefit.

(2) Subject to regulations 6 to 9, a person to whom paragraph (1) applies is required to take part in an interview as a condition of continuing to be entitled to the full amount of benefit which is payable apart from these Regulations where paragraph (3) and either paragraph (4) or (5) apply.

(3) This paragraph applies to a person who has taken part in a relevant interview or who would have taken part in such an interview but for—

(a) the requirement being waived in accordance with regulation 6; or

(b) the requirement being deferred in accordance with regulation 7.

(4) This paragraph applies to a person when any of the following circumstances arise—

(a) the person's entitlement to carer's allowance [2, or carer support payment under the Carer's Assistance (Carer Support Payment) (Scotland) Regulations 2023,] ceases whilst entitlement to a specified benefit continues;

(b) the person becomes engaged or ceases to be engaged in part-time work;

(c) the person has been undergoing education or training arranged by the officer and that education or training comes to an end; or

(d) the person attains the age of 18 and has not previously taken part in a relevant interview.

(5) This paragraph applies where a person has not been required to take part in a relevant interview for at least 36 months.]

Amendments

1. This regulation inserted by The Social Security (Work-focused Interviews for Lone Parents and Partners) (Amendment) Regulations 2011 (SI 2011/2428) reg.3 (October 31, 2011).

2. The Carer's Assistance (Carer Support Payment) (Scotland) Regulations 2023 (Consequential Amendments) Order 2023 (SI 2023/1218) art.13 (November 19, 2023).

[1 Continuing entitlement to full amount of income support dependent on an interview: lone parents who fall within paragraph 1 of Schedule 1B to the Income Support (General) Regulations 1987

4ZA.—(1) Subject to regulations 4A and 6 to 9, this regulation applies to a lone parent who— 2.747

(a) is entitled to income support;

(b) falls within paragraph 1 (lone parents) of Schedule 1B (prescribed categories of person) to the Income Support (General) Regulations 1987; and

(c) has not attained pensionable age.

(2) A lone parent to whom this regulation applies is required to take part in an interview if the lone parent has not taken part in or been required to take part in a relevant interview.

(3) This paragraph applies to a lone parent to whom this regulation applies who is aged 18 or over and has—

(a) taken part,

(b) failed to take part, or

(c) been treated as taking part,

in a relevant interview.

(4) A lone parent to whom paragraph (3) applies is required to take part in an interview every six months after the date on which the lone parent—

(a) last took part,

(b) last failed to take part, or

(c) was last treated as having taken part,

in a relevant interview.

(5) An officer shall, except where paragraph (6) applies, conduct the interview.

(6) An officer may, if he considers it appropriate in all the circumstances, arrange for a person who has not attained the age of 18 to attend an interview with such person as the Secretary of State may specify.]

AMENDMENT

This regulation inserted by The Social Security (Work-focused Interviews for Lone Parents and Partners) (Amendment) Regulations 2011 (SI 2011/2428) reg.3 (October 31, 2011).

[1 Requirement for certain lone parents to take part in an interview

2.748 **4A.**—(1) This regulation applies to a lone parent who—

(a) [3 is aged 18 or over and] is entitled to income support and is a person to whom paragraph 1 (lone parents) of Schedule 1B to the Income Support (General) Regulations 1987 applies; [5 and]

(b) does not fall within any other paragraph of that Schedule;

(c) [5 . . .]

[5 (2) Subject to regulations 7 to 9, a lone parent to whom this regulation applies is required to take part in one or more interviews as a condition of continuing to be entitled to the full amount of benefit which is payable to him part from these Regulations.]

(3) A lone parent who—

(a) is required to take part in an interview under this regulation, or

(b) has had a requirement to take part in an interview under this regulation waived or deferred,

is not required to take part in an interview under [4 regulation 4ZA] unless this regulation ceases to apply to him.]

AMENDMENTS

1. The Social Security (Lone Parents and Miscellaneous Amendments) Regulations 2008 (SI 2008/3051) reg.8 (November 24, 2008).

2. Social Security (Lone Parents and Miscellaneous Amendments) Regulations 2008 (SI 2008/3051) reg.10 (October 25, 2010).

3. The Social Security (Miscellaneous Amendments) (No.3) Regulations 2011 (SI 2011/2425) reg.14 (October 31, 2011).

4. The Social Security (Work-focused Interviews for Lone Parents and Partners) (Amendment) Regulations 2011 (SI 2011/2428) reg.3 (October 31, 2011).

5. Income Support (Work-Related Activity) and Miscellaneous Amendments Regulations 2014 (SI 2014/1097), reg.14(2) (April 28, 2014).

GENERAL NOTE

Note that Pt 1 of the Schedule to the Social Security (Lone Parents and Miscellaneous Amendments) Regulations 2008 (SI 2008/3051) contains special commencement provision for certain existing claimants. **2.749**

[1 Time when interview is to take place

5.—(1) Where the claimant is not a lone parent entitled to income support who falls within paragraph 1 (lone parents) of Schedule 1B (prescribed categories of person) to the Income Support (General) Regulations 1987, an officer shall arrange for an interview to take place as soon as reasonably practicable after— **2.750**

(a) the expiry of eight weeks after the date the claim for a specified benefit, other than a relevant benefit, is made;
(b) the claim for a relevant benefit is made;
(c) the requirement under regulation 4(2) arises;
(d) in a case where regulation 7(1) applies, the time when that requirement is to apply by virtue of regulation 7(2); or
(e) the requirement to take part in a relevant interview arises, in a case where the requirement to take part in an interview arises because the youngest child a lone parent is responsible for, and a member of the same household as, has attained the age of one.

(2) Where the claimant is a lone parent entitled to income support who falls within paragraph 1 of Schedule 1B to the Income Support (General) Regulations 1987, an officer shall arrange for an interview to take place [2 . . .]—

(a) [2 as soon as reasonably practicable after] the requirement to take part in a relevant interview arises, in a case where the requirement to take part in an interview arises because the youngest child a lone parent is responsible for, and a member of the same household, has attained the age of one;
[2 (aa) in a case where regulation 4A(2) applies, on such a date as may be determined by the officer; or]
(b) in any other case [2 as soon as reasonably practicable after]
  (i) [2 . . .]
  (ii) where regulation 4ZA(2) (first interview) applies [2 . . .], the expiry of 6 months beginning on the date on which the requirement to attend an interview arises;
  (iii) where [2 . . .] regulation 4ZA(3) [2 . . .] (subsequent interviews) applies, the requirement to attend an interview arises; or
  (iv) in a case where regulation 7(1) applies, the time when that requirement is to apply by virtue of regulation 7(2).]

AMENDMENTS

1. This regulation inserted by The Social Security (Work-focused Interviews for Lone Parents and Partners) (Amendment) Regulations 2011 (SI 2011/2428) reg.3 (October 31, 2011).

2. Income Support (Work-Related Activity) and Miscellaneous Amendments Regulations 2014 (SI 2014/1097), reg.14(3) (April 28, 2014).

Waiver of requirement to take part in an interview

2.751 **6.**—(1) [1 Except in a case where a requirement is imposed by virtue of regulation 4A(2), a] requirement imposed by these Regulations to take part in an interview shall not apply where an officer determines that an interview would not—

(a) be of assistance to the person concerned; or

(b) be appropriate in the circumstances.

(2) A person in relation to whom a requirement to take part in an interview has been waived under paragraph (1) shall be treated for the purposes of—

(a) regulation 3,4 [1 or 4ZA]; and

(b) any claim for, or entitlement to, a specified benefit,

as having complied with that requirement.

AMENDMENT

1. Income Support (Work-Related Activity) and Miscellaneous Amendments Regulations 2014 (SI 2014/1097) (April 28, 2014).

Deferment of requirement to take part in an interview

2.752 **7.**—(1) [1 Subject to regulation 8(4)] an officer may determine, in the case of any particular person, that the requirement to take part in an interview shall be deferred at the time the claim is made or the requirement to take part in an interview arises or applies because an interview would not at that time—

(a) be of assistance to that person; or

(b) be appropriate in the circumstances.

(2) Where the officer determines in accordance with paragraph (1) that the requirement to take part in an interview shall be deferred, he shall also determine when that determination is made, the time when the requirement to take part in an interview is to apply in the person's case.

(3) Where a requirement to take part in an interview has been deferred in accordance with paragraph (1), then until—

(a) a determination is made under regulation 6(1);

(b) the person takes part in an interview; or

(c) a relevant decision has been made in relation to that person in accordance with regulation 11(4),

that person shall be treated for the purposes of any claim for, or entitlement to, a specified benefit as having complied with that requirement.

AMENDMENT

1. The Social Security (Work-focused Interviews for Lone Parents and Partners) (Amendment) Regulations 2011 (SI 2011/2428) reg.3 (October 31, 2011).

Exemptions

2.753 **8.**—(1) Subject to paragraph (2), persons who, on the day on which the claim for a specified benefit is made or the requirement to take part in an interview under regulation [5 4 or 4A or 7(2)] arises or applies—

(a) are engaged in remunerative work; or

(b) are claiming, or are entitled to, a jobseeker's allowance, shall be exempt from the requirement to take part in an interview.

(2) Paragraph (1)(b) shall not apply where—

(a) a joint-claim couple (as defined for the purposes of section 1(4) of the Jobseekers Act 1995) have claimed a jobseeker's allowance; and

(b) a member of that couple is a person to whom regulation 3D(1)(c) of the Jobseeker's Allowance Regulations 1996 (further circumstances in which a joint-claim couple may be entitled to a jointclaim jobseeker's allowance) applies.

[[1] (3) A person who, on the day on which the claim for a specified benefit is made or the requirement to take part in an interview under regulation 4 or 7(2) arises or applies is—

(a) required to take part in an interview; or

(b) not required to take part in an interview by virtue of—

(i) a waiver of a requirement; or

(ii) a deferment of an interview,

under the [[4] Social Security (Incapacity Benefit Work-focused Interviews) Regulations 2008.] [[6] . . .] shall be exempt from the requirement to take part in an interview.]

[[6] (4) The requirement to take part in an interview under regulations 3, 4, 4ZA [[7] , 4A] or 7(2) does not apply to a lone parent who is responsible for, and a member of the same household as, a child under the age of one.]

AMENDMENTS

1. The Social Security (Incapacity Benefit Work-focused Interviews) Regulations 2003 (SI 2003/2439) (October 27, 2003).

2. The Social Security (Work-focused Interviews) Amendment Regulations 2005 (SI 2005/2727) (October 31, 2005).

3. The Social Security (Work-focused Interviews for Lone Parents) Amendment Regulations 2007 (SI 2007/1034) (April 30, 2007).

4. The Social Security (Incapacity Benefit Work-focused Interviews) Regulations 2008 (SI 2008/2928) reg.12 (December 15, 2008).

5. The Social Security (Lone Parents and Miscellaneous Amendments) Regulations 2008 (SI 2008/3051) reg.8 (November 24, 2008).

6. The Social Security (Work-focused Interviews for Lone Parents and Partners) (Amendment) Regulations 2011 (SI 2011/2428) reg.3 (October 31, 2011).

7. Income Support (Work-Related Activity) and Miscellaneous Amendments Regulations 2014 (SI 2014/1097), reg.14(5) (April 29, 2014).

Claims for two or more specified benefits

9. A person who would otherwise be required under these Regulations to take part in interviews relating to more than one specified benefit— 2.754

(a) is only required to take part in one interview; and

(b) that interview counts for the purposes of all those benefits.

The interview

10.—(1) The officer shall inform a person who is required to take part in an interview of the place and time of the interview. 2.755

(2) The officer may determine that an interview is to take place in the person's home where it would, in his opinion, be unreasonable to expect that person to attend elsewhere because that person's personal circumstances are such that attending elsewhere would cause him undue inconvenience or endanger his health.

Taking part in an interview

2.756 **11.**—(1) The officer shall determine whether a person has taken part in an interview.

[1 (2) A person who has not taken part in an interview under these Regulations before 31st October 2005 shall be regarded as having taken part in his first interview under these Regulations if—

(a) he attends for the interview at the place and time notified to him by the officer;

(b) where he is a specified person, he participates in discussions with the officer in relation to the specified person's employability, including any action the specified person and the officer agree is reasonable and they are willing to take in order to help the specified person enhance his employment prospects;

(c) he provides answers (where asked) to questions and appropriate information about—

(i) the level to which he has pursued any educational qualifications;

(ii) his employment history;

(iii) any vocational training he has undertaken;

(iv) any skills he has acquired which fit him for employment;

(v) any paid or unpaid employment he is engaged in;

(vi) any medical condition which, in his opinion, puts him at a disadvantage in obtaining employment;

(vii) any caring or childcare responsibilities he has;

(viii) his aspirations for future employment;

(ix) any vocational training or skills which he wishes to undertake or acquire; and

(x) his work related abilities; and

(d) where he is a specified person, he assists the officer in the completion of an action plan which records the matters discussed in relation to sub-paragraph (b) above.

(2A) A person who has taken part in an interview under these Regulations before 31st October 2005 shall be regarded as having taken part in his first interview under these Regulations after 30th October 2005 if—

(a) he attends for the interview at the place and time notified to him by the officer;

(b) where he is a specified person, he participates in discussions with the officer in relation to the specified person's employability, including any action the specified person and the officer agree is reasonable and they are willing to take in order to help the specified person enhance his employment prospects;

(c) he participates in discussions with the officer—

(i) in relation to the person's employability or any progress he might have made towards obtaining employment; and

(ii) in order to consider any of the programmes and support available to help the person obtain employment;

(d) he provides answers (where asked) to questions and appropriate information about—

(i) the content of any report made following his personal capability assessment, insofar as that report relates to the person's capabilities and employability;

and

(ii) his opinion as to the extent to which his medical condition restricts his ability to obtain employment; and

(e) where he is a specified person, he assists the officer in the completion of an action plan which records the matters discussed in relation to sub-paragraph (b) above.

(2B) A person shall be regarded as having taken part in any subsequent interview under these Regulations if—

(a) he attends for the interview at the place and time notified to him by the officer;

(b) he participates in discussions with the officer—

(i) in relation to the person's employability or any progress he might have made towards obtaining employment; and

(ii) in order to consider any of the programmes and support available to help the person obtain employment;

(c) where he is a specified person, he participates in discussions with the officer—

(i) about any action the specified person or the officer might have taken as a result of the matters discussed in relation to paragraphs (2)(b) or (2A)(b) above; and

(ii) about how, if at all, the action plan referred to in paragraphs (2)(d) or (2A)(e) above should be amended;

(d) he provides answers (where asked) to questions and appropriate information about—

(i) the content of any report made following his personal capability assessment, insofar as that report relates to the person's capabilities and employability;

and

(ii) his opinion as to the extent to which his medical condition restricts his ability to obtain employment; and

(e) where he is a specified person, he assists the officer in the completion of any amendment of the action plan referred to in paragraphs (2)(d) or (2A)(e) above in light of the matters discussed in relation to sub-paragraphs (b) and (c) above and the information provided in relation to sub-paragraph (d) above.]

(3) A person who has not attained the age of 18 shall also be regarded as having taken part in an interview if he attends an interview with [2 a person specified by the Secretary of State under regulation 3(3)] at the place and time notified to him by an officer.

(4) Where an officer determines that a person has failed to take part in an interview and good cause has not been shown for that failure within five working days of the [3 date on which the person was notified of his failure to take part in an interview], a relevant decision shall be made for the purposes of section 2B of the Social Security Administration Act 1992.

[3 (5) Where a notice under paragraph (4) is sent by post it is take to have been received on the second working day after it is sent.]

AMENDMENTS

1. The Social Security (Work-focused Interviews) Amendment Regulations 2005 (SI 2005/2727) (October 31, 2005).

2. The Social Security (Miscellaneous Amendments) (No.3) Regulations 2011 (SI 2011/2425) reg.14 (October 31, 2011).

3. Income Support (Work-Related Activity) and Miscellaneous Amendments Regulations 2014 (SI 2014/1097), reg.14(6) (April 29, 2014).

Failure to take part in an interview

2.757 **12.**—(1) A person in respect of whom a relevant decision has been made in accordance with regulation 11(4) shall, subject to paragraph (12), suffer the consequences set out below.

(2) Those consequences are—

(a) where the interview arose in connection with a claim for a [2 relevant benefit], that the person to whom the claim relates is to be regarded as not having made a claim for a [2 relevant benefit];

(b) where an interview which arose in connection with a claim for a [2 relevant benefit] was deferred and benefit became payable by virtue of regulation 7(3), that the person's entitlement to that benefit shall terminate from the first day of the next benefit week following the date on which the relevant decision was made;

(c) where the claimant has an award of benefit and the requirement for the interview arose under regulation [5 4, 4ZA or 4A], [2 or by virtue of the claimant falling within regulation 3(1)(a)(ii),] the claimant's benefit shall be reduced as from the first day of the next benefit week following the day the relevant decision was made, by a sum equal (but subject to paragraphs (3) and (4)) to 20 per cent. of the amount applicable [4. . .] in respect of a single claimant for income support aged not less than 25.

(3) Benefit reduced in accordance with paragraph (2)(c) shall not be reduced below ten pence per week.

(4) Where two or more specified benefits are in payment to a claimant, a deduction made in accordance with this regulation shall be applied, except in a case to which paragraph (5) applies, to the specified benefits in the following order of priority—

(a) income support;

(b) incapacity benefit;

(c) [2. . .];

(d) [2. . .];

(e) severe disablement allowance.

(5) Where the amount of the reduction is greater than some (but not all) of the specified benefits listed in paragraph (4), the reduction shall be made against the first benefit in that list which is the same as, or greater than, the amount of the reduction.

(6) For the purpose of determining whether a specified benefit is the same as, or greater than, the amount of the reduction for the purposes of paragraph (5), ten pence shall be added to the amount of the reduction.

(7) In a case where the whole of the reduction cannot be applied against any one specified benefit because no one benefit is the same as, or greater than, the amount of the reduction, the reduction shall be applied against the first benefit in payment in the list of priorities at paragraph (4) and so on against each benefit in turn until the whole of the reduction is exhausted or, if this is not possible, the whole of the specified benefits are exhausted, subject in each case to ten pence remaining in payment.

(8) [4. . .]

(9) Where a claimant whose benefit has been reduced in accordance with this regulation [6 satisfies a compliance condition], the reduction shall cease to have effect on the first day of the benefit week in which the [6 compliance condition was satisfied].

[6 (9A) In paragraph (9) "compliance condition" means a requirement to—

(a) take part in an interview; or
(b) undertake work-related activity.]

(10) For the avoidance of doubt, a person who is regarded as not having made a claim for any benefit because he failed to take part in an interview shall be required to make a new claim in order to establish entitlement to any specified benefit.

(11) For the purposes of determining the amount of any benefit payable, a claimant shall be treated as receiving the amount of any specified benefit which would have been payable but for a reduction made in accordance with this regulation.

(12) The consequences set out in this regulation shall not apply in the case of a person who brings new facts to the notice of the Secretary of State within one month of the date on which the decision was notified and—

(a) those facts could not reasonably have been brought to the Secretary of State's notice within five working days of the [6 date on which the person was notified of his failure to take part in an interview]; and
(b) those facts show that he had good cause for his failure to take part in the interview.

(13) In paragraphs (2) and (12), the "decision" means the decision that the person failed without good cause to take part in an interview.

AMENDMENTS

1. The Social Security Amendment (Carer's Allowance) Regulations 2002 (SI 2002/2497) Sch.2 (October 28, 2002).

2. The Social Security (Work-focused Interviews) Amendment Regulations 2005 (SI 2005/2727) (October 31, 2005).

3. The Social Security (Lone Parents and Miscellaneous Amendments) Regulations 2008 (SI 2008/3051) reg.8 (November 24, 2008).

4. The Social Security (Miscellaneous Amendments) (No. 3) Regulations 2011 (SI 2011/2425) reg.14 (October 31, 2011).

5. The Social Security (Work-focused Interviews for Lone Parents and Partners) (Amendment) Regulations 2011 (SI 2011/2428) reg.3 (October 31, 2011).

6. Income Support (Work-Related Activity) and Miscellaneous Amendments Regulations 2014 (SI 2014/1097), reg.14(7) (April 28, 2014).

[1 Circumstances where the amount of benefit payable to a claimant is not to be reduced in accordance with regulation 12(2)(c)

12A.—(1) The amount of benefit payable to a claimant is not to be 2.758
reduced in accordance with regulation 12(2)(c) if that amount—

(a) is at the time the relevant decision falls to be made in respect of the current failure, being paid at a reduced rate in accordance with regulation 12(2)(c), regulations 7(3) and 8 of the Social Security (Work-focused Interviews for Lone Parents) and Miscellaneous Amendments Regulations 2000 or regulation 8(1) and (2) of the Income Support (Work-Related Activity) and Miscellaneous Amendments Regulations 2014; and

(b) was last reduced not more than two weeks before the date of the current failure.

(2) In paragraph (1) "current failure" means a failure which may, in the case of a claimant who has an award of benefit, lead to a reduction in benefit under regulation 12(2)(c) in relation to which the Secretary of State has not yet determined whether the amount of benefit payable to the claimant is to be reduced in accordance with that regulation.]

AMENDMENT

1. Inserted by the Income Support (Work-Related Activity) and Miscellaneous Amendments Regulations 2014 (SI 2014/1097), reg.14(8) (April 28, 2014).

Circumstances where regulation 12 does not apply

2.759 **13.** The consequences of a failure to take part in an interview set out in regulation 12 shall not apply where—

(a) he is no longer required to take part in an interview as a condition for continuing to be entitled to the full amount of benefit which is payable apart from these Regulations; or

(b) the person attains [1 pensionable age].

AMENDMENT

1. The Social Security (Work-focused Interviews etc.) (Equalisation of State Pension Age) Amendment Regulations 2010 (SI 2010/563) reg.6(5) (April 6, 2010).

Good cause

2.760 **14.** Matters to be taken into account in determining whether a person has shown good cause for his failure to take part in an interview include—

(a) that the person misunderstood the requirement to take part in the interview due to any learning, language or literacy difficulties of the person or any misleading information given to the person by the officer;

(b) that the person was attending a medical or dental appointment, or accompanying a person for whom the claimant has caring responsibilities to such an appointment, and that it would have been unreasonable, in the circumstances, to rearrange the appointment;

(c) that the person had difficulties with his normal mode of transport and that no reasonable alternative was available;

(d) that the established customs and practices of the religion to which the person belongs prevented him attending on that day or at that time;

(e) that the person was attending an interview with an employer with a view to obtaining employment;

(f) that the person was actually pursuing employment opportunities as a self-employed earner;

(g) that the person or a dependant of his or a person for whom he provides care suffered an accident, sudden illness or relapse of [1 a physical or mental health condition];

(h) that he was attending the funeral of a close friend or relative on the day fixed for the interview;

(i) that a disability from which the person suffers made it impracticable for him to attend at the time fixed for the interview.

AMENDMENT

1. The Social Security (Work-focused Interviews) Amendment Regulations 2005 (SI 2005/2727) (October 31, 2005).

Appeals

15.—(1) This regulation applies to any relevant decision made under regulation 11(4) or any decision under section 10 of the 1998 Act superseding such a decision. 2.761

(2) This regulation applies whether the decision is as originally made or as revised under section 9 of the 1998 Act.

(3) In the case of a decision to which this regulation applies, the person in respect of whom the decision was made shall have a right of appeal under section 12 of the 1998 Act to [1 the First-tier Tribunal].

AMENDMENT

1. The Tribunals, Courts and Enforcement Act 2007 (Transitional and Consequential Provisions) Order 2008 (SI 2008/2683) reg.178 (November 3, 2008).

Revocations and transitional provision

16.—(1) Subject to paragraph (2), the Social Security (Work-focused Interviews) Regulations 2000 ("the 2000 Regulations") and the Social Security (Jobcentre Plus Interviews) Regulations 2001 ("the 2001 Regulations") are hereby revoked to the extent specified in Schedule 1. 2.762

(2) Notwithstanding paragraph (1), both the 2000 Regulations (except for regulations 4, 5 and 12(2)(a) and (b)) and the 2001 Regulations (except for regulations 3 and 11(2)(a) and (b)) [2 . . .] shall continue to apply as if these Regulations had not come into force for the period specified in paragraph (3) in the case of a person who, on the day before the day on which these Regulations come into force, [3—

(a) is a relevant person for the purposes of those Regulations,
(b) is entitled to income support, and
(c) does not fall within paragraph 7, 24 or 25 of Schedule 1B to the Income Support (General) Regulations 1987 (prescribed categories of person).]

(3) The period specified for the purposes of paragraph (2) shall be the period beginning on the day on which these Regulations come to force and ending on the day on which the person—

(a) ceases to be a relevant person for the purposes of the 2000 Regulations or, as the case may be, the 2001 Regulations;
(b) is not entitled to any specified benefit for the purposes of those Regulations; or
(c) attains [4 pensionable age],

whichever shall first occur.

AMENDMENTS

1. Social Security (Working Neighbourhoods) Regulations 2004 (SI 2004/959) reg.26(4) (April 26, 2004).

2. The Social Security (Working Neighbourhoods) Miscellaneous Amendment Regulations 2006 (SI 2006/909) (April 24, 2006).

3. The Social Security (Lone Parents and Miscellaneous Amendments) Regulations 2008 (SI 2008/3051) reg.9 (October 26, 2009).

4. The Social Security (Work-focused Interviews etc.) (Equalisation of State Pension Age) Amendment Regulations 2010 (SI 2010/563) reg.6(6) (April 6, 2010).

GENERAL NOTE

2.763 Regulation 3(3)–(5) of the Social Security (Incapacity Benefit Work-focused Interviews) (Amendment) Regulations 2009 (SI 2009/1541) further provides:

"(3) Regulation 12 (failure to take part in an interview) of the 2000 Regulations and regulation 11 (failure to take part in an interview) of the 2001 Regulations (as saved by regulation 16(2) of the 2002 Regulations) continue to have effect as if the amendment set out in paragraph (2) above had not been made in respect of a person who immediately before 26th October 2009 is—

(a) entitled to a specified benefit as defined in the principal Regulations, and

(b) subject to the consequences specified in regulation 12 of the 2000 Regulations or regulation 11 of the 2001 Regulations.

(4) Any other provisions of the 2000 Regulations and the 2001 Regulations (as saved by regulation 16(2) of the 2002 Regulations, but disregarding the amendment in paragraph (2) above) continue to have effect insofar as it is necessary to give full effect to paragraph (3) above.

(5) For the purposes of regulation 9(8), (9) and (11) (consequences of failure to take part in a work-focused interview) of the principal Regulations, a person referred to in paragraph (3)(a) above is deemed to be subject to the consequences under regulation 9(1) of the principal Regulations; and as from the date on which these Regulations come into force, regulation 12 of the 2000 Regulations and regulation 11 of the 2001 Regulations cease to apply to that person."

Amendments to regulations

2.764 *Omitted.*

2.765 *Schedules 1 and 2 omitted.*

The Social Security (Jobcentre Plus Interviews for Partners) Regulations 2003

GENERAL NOTE

These regulations extend the scheme of work-focused interviews to the partners of claimants, and cover five benefits: income support, income-based jobseeker's allowance, incapacity benefit, severe disablement allowance and carer's allowance. The pattern follows that to be found in the earlier regulations relating to work-focused interviews in other contexts. But those regulations apply only where the claim was made after the commencement date of the regulations where both the partners are between the ages of 18 and 60; these regulations apply whenever benefit is in payment and whenever the claim is through a Jobcentre Plus office. A further distinction is that the interview under these regulations is a once and for all interview without there being provisions for follow-up interviews. Failure to participate results in a deduction equal to 20 per cent of the single adult applicable amount for income support. Both partners have an independent right of appeal, so that both can, in principle, appeal against the same decision.

(SI 2003/1886)

ARRANGEMENT OF REGULATIONS

GENERAL NOTE

Whereas a draft of this instrument was laid before Parliament in accordance with s.190(1) of the Social Security Administration Act 1992 and approved by resolution of each House of Parliament; 2.767

Now, therefore, the Secretary of State for Work and Pensions, in exercise of the powers conferred upon him by ss.2AA(1) and (4)–(7), 2B(6), 189(1) and (4)–(6) and 191 of the Social Security Administration Act 1992 and of all other powers enabling him in that behalf, after consultation with the Council on Tribunals in accordance with s.8(1) of the Tribunals and Inquiries Act 1992, by this instrument, which contains only regulations made by virtue of, or consequential upon, section 2AA of the Social Security Administration Act 1992 and which is made before the end of the period of 6 months beginning with the coming into force of that provision, hereby makes the following Regulations:

Citation and commencement

1. These Regulations may be cited as the Social Security (Jobcentre Plus Interviews for Partners) Regulations 2003 and shall come into force on 12th April 2004. 2.768

Interpretation [4 . . .]

2.—(1) In these Regulations— 2.769

"the 1998 Act" means the Social Security Act 1998;

"benefit week" means any period of seven days corresponding to the week in respect of which the relevant specified benefit is due to be paid;

"claimant" means a claimant of a specified benefit who has a partner to whom these Regulations apply;

[2"couple" means—

(a) two people who are married to, or civil partners of, each other and are members of the same household; or

(b) two people who are not married to, or civil partners of, each other but are living together as if they were a married couple or civil partners;]

"interview" means a work-focused interview with a partner which is conducted for any or all of the following purposes—

(a) assessing the partner's prospects for existing or future employment (whether paid or voluntary);

(b) assisting or encouraging the partner to enhance his prospects of such employment;

(c) identifying activities which the partner may undertake to strengthen his existing or future prospects of employment;

(d) identifying current or future employment or training opportunities suitable to the partner's needs; and

(e) identifying educational opportunities connected with the existing or future employment prospects or needs of the partner;

"officer" means a person who is an officer of, or who is providing services to or exercising functions of, the Secretary of State;

"partner" means a person who is a member of the same couple as the claimant, or, in a case where the claimant has more than one partner, a person who is a partner of the claimant by reason of a polygamous marriage, but only where—

(a) [4 . . .]

(b) both the partner and the claimant have attained the age of 18 but have not attained [5 pensionable age];

[5 "pensionable age", in the case of a man born before 6th April 1955, means the age when a woman born on the same day as the man would attain pensionable age;]

"polygamous marriage" means any marriage during the subsistence of which a party to it is married to more than one person and the ceremony of marriage took place under the law of a country which permits polygamy;

"specified benefit" means a benefit to which section 2AA applies.

[6 (2) For the purposes of these Regulations a person is to be treated as responsible for, and a member of the same household as, a child only where the person would be treated as being responsible for, and a member of the same household as, such a child under regulations 15 and 16 of the Income Support (General) Regulations 1987, if references in those Regulations to income support were to a specified benefit.]

AMENDMENTS

1. Social Security (Working Neighbourhoods) Regulations 2004 (SI 2004/959) reg.27(2) (April 26, 2004).

2. The Civil Partnership (Opposite-sex Couples) Regulations 2019 (SI 2019/1458) Sch.3(2) para.66 (December 2, 2019).

3. The Social Security (Working Neighbourhoods) Miscellaneous Amendment Regulations 2006 (SI 2006/909) (April 24, 2006).

4. The Social Security (Jobcentre Plus Interviews for Partners) Amendment Regulations 2008 (SI 2008/759) (April 28, 2008).

5. The Social Security (Work-focused Interviews etc.) (Equalisation of State Pension Age) Amendment Regulations 2010 (SI 2010/563) reg.7 (April 6, 2010).

6. The Social Security (Work-focused Interviews for Lone Parents and Partners) (Amendment) Regulations 2011 (SI 2011/2428) reg.4 (October 31, 2011).

[1 Partner of a person claiming a specified benefit to take part in an interview

3.—(1) Subject to regulations 5 to 8, a partner to whom this regulation applies is required to take part in an interview as a condition of the claimant continuing to be paid the full amount of a specified benefit which is payable apart from these Regulations. **2.770**

(2) This regulation applies to a partner of a person claiming a specified benefit where—

(a) the claimant has been continuously entitled to a specified benefit for at least 26 weeks;
(b) the claimant has been awarded the benefit at a higher rate referable to the partner;
(c) the benefit is administered from a designated Jobcentre Plus Office; and
(d) the partner has not taken part or been required to take part in an interview under these Regulations.

(3) Where a requirement to take part in an interview arises under this regulation in relation to a particular specified benefit, the requirement also applies in relation to any other specified benefit in payment to the claimant at a higher rate referable to his partner on the date set for the interview and notified to the partner in accordance with regulation 9(1).]

AMENDMENT

1. The Social Security (Jobcentre Plus Interviews for Partners) Amendment Regulations 2008 (SI 2008/759) (April 28, 2008).

[1 Partner of a person claiming jobseeker's allowance to take part in an interview where child or qualifying young person in household

3A.—(1) Subject to regulations 5 to 8, a partner to whom this regulation applies is required to take part in an interview as a condition of the claimant continuing to be paid the full amount of a jobseeker's allowance which is payable apart from these Regulations. **2.771**

(2) This regulation applies to a partner of a person claiming a jobseeker's allowance where—

(a) the claimant or the partner is responsible for a child or qualifying young person who is a member of that person's household;
(b) the claimant has been continuously entitled to a jobseeker's allowance for at least 26 weeks;
(c) the claimant has been awarded that benefit at a higher rate referable to the partner;
(d) the benefit is administered at a designated Jobcentre Plus Office; and
(e) the partner has taken part or failed to take part in an interview under these Regulations.

(3) The requirement to take part in an interview under this regulation arises every six months, on a date to be determined in accordance with paragraphs (4) and (5).

(4) Where the interview referred to in paragraph (2)(e) was on a date before 28th October 2007—

(a) the requirement arises for the first time on 28th April 2008; and
(b) it then arises again every six months after the date on which the partner last took part or failed to take part in an interview.

(5) Where the interview referred to in paragraph (2)(e) was on a date on or after 28th October 2007, the requirement arises every six months after the date on which the partner last took part or failed to take part in an interview.

(6) For the purposes of paragraph (2)(a), "child" and "qualifying young person" are to be construed in accordance with section 142 of the Social Security Contributions and Benefits Act 1992(**5**).

(7) References in paragraphs (2)(e), (4) and (5) to a partner having taken part in an interview are to be construed as including cases where the partner is treated as having taken part in an interview under regulation 5 or 6.]

AMENDMENT

1. The Social Security (Jobcentre Plus Interviews for Partners) Amendment Regulations 2008 (SI 2008/759) (April 28, 2008).

Time when interview is to take place

2.772 **4.** An officer shall arrange for an interview to take place as soon as reasonably practicable after—

(a) the requirement under regulation [1 3 or 3A] arises; or
(b) in a case where regulation 6(1) applies, the time when that requirement is to apply by virtue of regulation 6(2).

AMENDMENT

1. The Social Security (Jobcentre Plus Interviews for Partners) Amendment Regulations 2008 (SI 2008/759) (April 28, 2008).

Waiver of requirement to take part in an interview

2.773 **5.**—(1) A requirement imposed by these Regulations to take part in an interview shall not apply where an officer determines that an interview would not—

(a) be of assistance to the partner concerned; or
(b) be appropriate in the circumstances.

(2) A partner in relation to whom a requirement to take part in an interview has been waived under paragraph (1) shall be treated [1 . . .] as having complied with that requirement.

AMENDMENT

1. The Social Security (Jobcentre Plus Interviews for Partners) Amendment Regulations 2008 (SI 2008/759) (April 28, 2008).

Deferment of requirement to take part in an interview

2.774 **6.**—(1) An officer may determine, in the case of any particular partner, that the requirement to take part in an interview shall be deferred at the time that the requirement to take part in it arises or applies because an interview would not at that time—

(a) be of assistance to the partner concerned; or
(b) be appropriate in the circumstances.

(2) Where the officer determines in accordance with paragraph (1) that the requirement to take part in an interview shall be deferred, he

shall also, when that determination is made, determine the time when the requirement to take part in an interview is to apply in the partner's case.

(3) Where a requirement to take part in an interview has been deferred in accordance with paragraph (1), then until—

(a) a determination is made under regulation 5(1);
(b) the partner takes part in an interview; or
(c) a relevant decision has been made in accordance with regulation 10(3),

the partner shall be treated for the purposes of regulation 3 as having complied with that requirement.

Exemption

[[1] **7.** A partner who, on the day on which the requirement to take part in an interview arises or applies under regulation 3, 3A or 6(2) is— 2.775

(a) in receipt of a specified benefit as a claimant in his own right, or
(b) a member of a couple, one of whom is responsible for, and a member of the same household as, a child under the age of one,

is exempt from the requirement to take part in an interview.]

Amendment

1. This version of reg.7 introduced by The Social Security (Work-focused Interviews for Lone Parents and Partners) (Amendment) Regulations 2011 (SI 2011/2428) reg.4 (October 31, 2011).

Claims for two or more specified benefits

8. A partner who would otherwise be required under these Regulations to take part in interviews relating to more than one specified benefit— 2.776

(a) is only required to take part in one interview during any period where the claimant is in receipt of two or more specified benefits concurrently; and
(b) that interview counts for the purposes of each of those benefits.

The interview

9.—(1) An officer shall inform a partner who is required to take part in an interview of the date, place and time of the interview. 2.777

(2) The officer may determine that an interview is to take place in the partner's home where it would, in his opinion, be unreasonable to expect the partner to attend elsewhere because the partner's personal circumstances are such that attending elsewhere would cause him undue inconvenience or endanger his health.

(3) An officer shall conduct the interview.

Taking part in an interview

10.—(1) The officer shall determine whether a partner has taken part in an interview. 2.778

(2) A partner shall be regarded as having taken part in an interview if and only if—

(a) he attends for the interview at the place and time notified to him by the officer; and

(b) he provides answers (where asked) to questions and appropriate information about—

(i) the level to which he has pursued any educational qualifications;

(ii) his employment history;

(iii) any vocational training he has undertaken;

(iv) any skills he has acquired which fit him for employment;

(v) any paid or unpaid employment he is engaged in;

(vi) any medical condition which, in his opinion, puts him at a disadvantage in obtaining employment; and

(vii) any caring or childcare responsibilities he has.

(3) Where an officer determines that a partner has failed to take part in an interview and good cause has not been shown either by the partner or by the claimant for that failure within five working days of the day on which the interview was to take place, a relevant decision shall be made for the purposes of section 2B of the Social Security Administration Act 1992 and the partner and the claimant shall be notified accordingly.

Failure to take part in an interview

2.779 **11.**—(1) Where a relevant decision has been made in accordance with regulation 10(3), subject to paragraph (11), the specified benefit payable to the claimant in respect of which the requirement for the partner to take part in an interview under regulation [1 3 or 3A] arose shall be reduced, either as from the first day of the next benefit week following the day on which the relevant decision was made, or, if that date arises five days or less after the day on which the relevant decision was made, as from the first day of the second benefit week following the date of the relevant decision.

(2) The deduction made to benefit in accordance with paragraph (1) shall be by a sum equal (but subject to paragraphs (3) and (4)) to 20 per cent. of the amount applicable [3 . . .] in respect of a single claimant for income support aged not less than 25.

(3) Benefit reduced in accordance with paragraph (1) shall not be reduced below ten pence per week.

(4) Where two or more specified benefits are in payment to a claimant, in relation to each of which a requirement for the partner to take part in an interview had arisen under [1 these Regulations], a deduction made in accordance with this regulation shall be applied, except in a case to which paragraph (5) applies, to those benefits in the following order of priority—

(a) an income-based jobseeker's allowance;

[2 (aa) an income-related employment and support allowance under Part 1 of the Welfare Reform Act 2007 (employment and support allowance);]

(b) income support;

(c) incapacity benefit;

(d) severe disablement allowance;

(e) carer's allowance.

(5) Where the amount of the reduction is greater than some (but not all) of those benefits, the reduction shall be made against the first benefit in the list in paragraph (4) which is the same as, or greater than, the amount of the reduction.

(6) For the purpose of determining whether a benefit is the same as, or greater than, the amount of the reduction for the purposes of paragraph (5), ten pence shall be added to the amount of the reduction.

(7) In a case where the whole of the reduction cannot be applied against any one benefit because no one benefit is the same as, or greater than, the amount of the reduction, the reduction shall be applied against the first benefit in the list of priorities at paragraph (4) and so on against each benefit in turn until the whole of the reduction is exhausted or, if this is not possible, the whole of those benefits are exhausted, subject in each case to ten pence remaining in payment.

(8) [3 . . .]

(9) Where the partner of a claimant whose benefit has been reduced in accordance with this regulation subsequently takes part in an interview, the reduction shall cease to have effect on the first day of the benefit week in which the requirement to take part in an interview was met.

(10) For the purposes of determining the amount of any benefit payable, a claimant shall be treated as receiving the amount of any specified benefit which would have been payable but for a reduction made in accordance with this regulation.

(11) Benefit shall not be reduced in accordance with this regulation where the partner or the claimant brings new facts to the notice of the Secretary of State within one month of the date on which the decision that the partner failed without good cause to take part in an interview was notified and—

(a) those facts could not reasonably have been brought to the Secretary of State's notice within five working days of the day on which the interview was to take place; and
(b) those facts show that he had good cause for his failure to take part in the interview.

AMENDMENTS

1. The Social Security (Jobcentre Plus Interviews for Partners) Amendment Regulations 2008 (SI 2008/759) (April 28, 2008).
2. The Employment and Support Allowance (Consequential Provisions) (No.2) Regulations 2008 (SI 2008/1554) reg.71 (October 27, 2008).
3. The Social Security (Miscellaneous Amendments) (No.3) Regulations 2011 (SI 2011/2425) reg.16 (October 31, 2011).

Circumstances where regulation 11 does not apply

12. The reduction of benefit to be made under regulation 11 shall not apply as from the date when a partner who failed to take part in an interview ceases to be a partner for the purposes of these Regulations or is no longer a partner to whom [1 regulation 3 or 3A applies] 2.780

AMENDMENT

1. The Social Security (Jobcentre Plus Interviews for Partners) Amendment Regulations 2008 (SI 2008/759) (April 28, 2008).

Good cause

13. Matters to be taken into account in determining whether the partner or the claimant has shown good cause for the partner's failure to take part in an interview include— 2.781

(a) that the partner misunderstood the requirement to take part in an interview due to any learning, language or literacy difficulties of the partner or any misleading information given to the partner by the officer;

(b) that the partner was attending a medical or dental appointment, or accompanying a person for whom the partner had caring responsibilities to such an appointment, and that it would have been unreasonable, in the circumstances, to rearrange the appointment;
(c) that the partner had difficulties with his normal mode of transport and that no reasonable alternative was available;
(d) that the established customs and practices of the religion to which the partner belongs prevented him attending on that day or at that time;
(e) that the partner was attending an interview with an employer with a view to obtaining employment;
(f) that the partner was actually pursuing employment opportunities as a self-employed earner;
(g) that the partner, claimant or a dependant or a person for whom the partner provides care suffered an accident, sudden illness or relapse of a chronic condition;
(h) that he was attending the funeral of a close friend or relative on the day fixed for the interview;
(i) that a disability from which the partner suffers made it impracticable for him to attend at the time fixed for the interview.

Appeals

2.782 **14.**—(1) This regulation applies to any relevant decision made under regulation 10(3) or any decision under section 10 of the 1998 Act superseding such a decision.

(2) This regulation applies whether the decision is as originally made or as revised under section 9 of the 1998 Act.

(3) In the case of a decision to which this regulation applies, the partner in respect of whom the decision was made and the claimant shall each have a right of appeal under section 12 of the 1998 Act to [1 the First-tier Tribunal]

AMENDMENT

1. The Tribunals, Courts and Enforcement Act 2007 (Transitional and Consequential Provisions) Order 2008 (SI 2008/2683) Sch.1 para.237 (November 3, 2008).

2.783 **15.** *Omitted.*

The Social Security (Loss of Benefit) Regulations 2001

(SI 2001/4022)

2.784 *Made* *18th December 2001*
Coming into force *1st April 2002*

Whereas a draft of this instrument was laid before Parliament in accordance with section 11(3) of the Social Security Fraud Act 2001, section 80(1) of the Social Security Act 1998 and section 5A(3) of the Pensions Appeal Tribunals Act 1943 and approved by resolution of each House of Parliament.

Now, therefore, the Secretary of State, in exercise of the powers conferred by sections 7(3) to (6), 8(3) and (4), 9(2) to (5), 10(1) and (2) and

11(1) of the Social Security Fraud Act 2001, section 189(4) of the Social Security Administration Act 1992, sections 79(4) and 84 of, and paragraph 9 of Schedule 2 to, the Social Security Act 1998 and section 5A(2) of the Pensions Appeal Tribunals Act 1943, and of all other powers enabling him in that behalf, by this Instrument, which is made before the end of the period of 6 months beginning with the coming into force of sections 7 to 13 of the Social Security Fraud Act 2001 and which contains only regulations made by virtue of, or consequential upon, those sections, hereby makes the following Regulations:

PART I

GENERAL

Citation, commencement and interpretation

1.—(1) These Regulations may be cited as the Social Security (Loss of Benefit) Regulations 2001 and shall come into force on 1st April 2002. 2.785

(2) In these Regulations, unless the context otherwise requires—

[[3] "the 2007 Act" means the Welfare Reform Act 2007;

"the 2012 Act" means the Welfare Reform Act 2012;]

"the Act" means the Social Security Fraud Act 2001;

[[3] "the Administration Act" means the Social Security Administration Act 1992;]

[[5] "armed forces independence payment" means armed forces independence payment under the Armed Forces and Reserve Forces Compensation Scheme Order 2011;]

"the Benefits Act" means the Social Security Contributions and Benefits Act 1992;

[[3] "the ESA Regulations" means the Employment and Support Allowance Regulations 2008;]

"the Council Tax Benefit Regulations" means the Council Tax Benefit Regulations 2006;

[[1] "the Council Tax Benefit (State Pension Credit) Regulations" means the Council Tax Benefit (Persons who have attained pensionable age for state pension credit) Regulations 2006;

"the Housing Benefit Regulations" means the Housing Benefit Regulations 2006;

"the Housing Benefit (State Pension Credit) Regulations" means the Housing Benefit (Persons who have attained pensionable age for state pension credit) Regulations 2006;]

"the Income Support Regulations" means the Income Support (General) Regulations 1987;

"the Jobseekers Act" means the Jobseekers Act 1995;

"the Jobseeker's Allowance Regulations" means the Jobseeker's Allowance Regulations 1996;

[[6] "the UC Regulations" means the Universal Credit Regulations 2013;

"assessment period" has the same meaning as in the UC Regulations;]

"claimant" in a regulation means the person claiming the sanctionable benefit referred to in that regulation;

[2 "the determination day" means (subject to paragraph (2A)) the day on which the Secretary of State determines that a restriction under—

(a) section 6B or 7 of the Act would be applicable to the offender were the offender in receipt of a sanctionable benefit;

(b) section 8 of the Act would be applicable to the offender were the offender a member of a joint-claim couple which is in receipt of a joint-claim jobseeker's allowance; or

(c) section 9 of the Act would be applicable to the offender's family member were that member in receipt of income support, jobseeker's allowance, state pension credit, employment and support allowance, housing benefit or council tax benefit;]

"disqualification period" means the period in respect of which the restrictions on payment of a relevant benefit apply in respect of an offender in accordance with section [2 6B(11) or] 7(6) of the Act and shall be interpreted in accordance with [2 regulations 1A and 2]; and

[6 "income-based jobseeker's allowance" means an income-based allowance under the Jobseekers Act as it has effect apart from the amendments made by Part 1 of Schedule 14 to the 2012 Act (to remove references to an income-based allowance);

"income-related employment and support allowance" means an income-related allowance under the Part 1 of the 2007 Act as it has effect apart from the amendments made by Schedule 3 and Part 1 of Schedule 14 to the 2012 Act (to remove references to an income-related allowance);

"joint claimant" means each of joint claimants as defined in section 40 of the 2012 Act;]

"offender" means the person who is subject to the restriction in the payment of his benefit in accordance with section [2 6B or] 7 of the Act.

[2 "pay day" in relation to a sanctionable benefit means the day on which that benefit is due to be paid;

[4 "personal independence payment" means the allowance under Part 4 of the 2012 Act;]

"relevant authority" in relation to housing benefit or council tax benefit means the relevant authority administering the benefit of the offender or the offender's family member.]

[6 "universal credit" means the benefit payable under Part 1 of the 2012 Act.]

[2 (2A) Where, for the purposes of section 6B of the Act, the disqualifying event is an agreement to pay a penalty as referred to in section 6B(1)(b) of the Act, the determination day is the 28th day after the day referred to in the definition of that term in paragraph (2).]

(3) Expressions used in these Regulations which are defined either for the purposes of the Jobseekers Act or for the purposes of the Jobseeker's Allowance Regulations shall, except where the context otherwise requires, have the same meaning as for the purposes of that Act or, as the case may be, those Regulations.

(4) In these Regulations, unless the context otherwise requires, a reference—

(a) to a numbered regulation is to the regulation in these Regulations bearing that number;

(b) in a regulation to a numbered paragraph is to the paragraph in that regulation bearing that number.

AMENDMENTS

1. Housing Benefit and Council Tax Benefit (Consequential Provisions) Regulations 2006 (SI 2006/217) Sch.2 para.20(2) (March 6, 2006).
2. Social Security (Loss of Benefit) Amendment Regulations 2010 (SI 2010/1160) reg.2(1) and (2) (April 1, 2010).
3. Social Security (Loss of Benefit) Amendment Regulations 2013 (SI 2013/385) regs 2 and 3(a), (b) and (c) (April 1, 2013).
4. Social Security (Loss of Benefit) Amendment Regulations 2013 (SI 2013/385) regs 2 and 3(f) (April 8, 2013).
5. Armed Forces and Reserve Forces Compensation Scheme (Consequential Provisions: Subordinate Legislation) Order 2013 (SI 2013/591) art.7 and Sch. para.22(1) and (2) (April 8, 2013).
6. Social Security (Loss of Benefit) (Amendment) Regulations 2013 (SI 2013/385) regs 2 and 3(d), (e) and (g) (April 29, 2013).

[1 Disqualification period: section 6B(11) of the Act

1A.—(1) The first day of the disqualification period for the purposes of section 6B(11) of the Act ("DQ-day") shall be as follows. 2.786

(2) This paragraph applies where on the determination day—
(a) the offender is in receipt of a sanctionable benefit [2 other than a benefit to which paragraph (5A) applies] [3 or universal credit];
(b) the offender is a member of a joint-claim couple which is in receipt of a joint-claim jobseeker's allowance; or
(c) the offender's family member is in receipt of income support, jobseeker's allowance, state pension credit, employment and support allowance, housing benefit or council tax benefit.

(3) Where paragraph (2) applies and paragraph (4) does not apply (but subject to paragraph (7))—
(a) in relation to a sanctionable benefit which is paid in arrears, DQ-day is the day following the first pay day after the end of the period of 28 days beginning with the determination day; and
(b) in relation to a sanctionable benefit which is paid in advance, DQ-day is the first pay day after the end of the period of 28 days beginning with the determination day.

(4) This paragraph applies where on the determination day the offender or (as the case may be) the offender's family member is in receipt of—
(a) either housing benefit or council tax benefit or both of those benefits; and
(b) no other sanctionable benefit.

(5) Where paragraph (4) applies—
(a) in relation to housing benefit or council tax benefit which is paid in arrears, DQ-day is the day following the first pay day after the end of the period of 28 days beginning with the first day after the determination day on which the Secretary of State is notified by the relevant authority that the offender or the offender's family member is in receipt of either housing benefit or council tax benefit (or both of those benefits) or has been awarded either or both of those benefits; and
(b) in relation to housing benefit or council tax benefit which is paid in advance, DQ-day is the first pay day after the end of the period of 28 days beginning with the first day after the determination

day on which the Secretary of State is so notified by the relevant authority.

[2 (5A) This paragraph applies where on the determination day the offender or, as the case may be, the offender's family member is in receipt of a sanctionable benefit which is neither payable wholly in advance nor wholly in arrears and no other sanctionable benefit.]

(6) Where [2 paragraph (5A) applies or where there is no sanctionable benefit payable on the determination day], DQ-day is the first day after the end of the period of 28 days beginning with the determination day.

[3 (6A) Paragraph (6B) applies where, on the determination day, the offender or, as the case may be, the offender's family member is in receipt of universal credit.

(6B) Where this paragraph applies, DQ-day is—

(a) if the first day after the end of the period of 28 days beginning with the determination day is the first day of an assessment period, that day;

(b) if the first day after the end of the period of 28 days beginning with the determination day is not the first day of an assessment period, the first day of the next assessment period after that day.]

(7) Where on the determination day—

(a) paragraph (2) [3 or (6A)] applies in the case of an offender or (as the case may be) the offender's family member, but

(b) that person ceases to be in receipt of a benefit referred to in [3 those paragraphs] before the first day of the disqualification period that would apply by virtue of paragraph (3) [3 or (6B)],

DQ-day is the first day after the end of the period of 28 days beginning with the determination day.]

AMENDMENTS

1. Social Security (Loss of Benefit) Amendment Regulations 2010 (SI 2010/1160) reg.2(1) and (3) (April 1, 2010).

2. Social Security (Loss of Benefit) (Amendment) Regulations 2013 (SI 2013/385) regs 2 and 4(1), (2), (4) and (5) (April 1, 2013).

3. Social Security (Loss of Benefit) (Amendment) Regulations 2013 (SI 2013/385) regs 2 and 4(3), (6) and (7) (April 29, 2013).

[1 Disqualification period: section 7(6) of the Act

2.787 **2.**—(1) The first day of the disqualification period for the purposes of section 7(6) of the Act ("DQ-day") shall be as follows.

(2) This paragraph applies where on the determination day—

(a) the offender is in receipt of a sanctionable benefit [2 other than a benefit to which paragraph (5A) applies] [3 or universal credit];

(b) the offender is a member of a joint-claim couple which is in receipt of a joint-claim jobseeker's allowance; or

(c) the offender's family member is in receipt of income support, jobseeker's allowance, state pension credit, employment and support allowance, housing benefit or council tax benefit.

(3) Where paragraph (2) applies and paragraph (4) does not apply—

(a) in relation to a sanctionable benefit which is paid in arrears, DQ-day is the day following the first pay day after the end of the period of 28 days beginning with the determination day; and

(b) in relation to a sanctionable benefit which is paid in advance, DQ-day is the first pay day after the end of the period of 28 days beginning with the determination day.

(4) This paragraph applies where on the determination day the offender or (as the case may be) the offender's family member is in receipt of—

(a) either housing benefit or council tax benefit or of both of those benefits; and

(b) no other sanctionable benefit.

(5) Where paragraph (4) applies—

(a) in relation to housing benefit or council tax benefit which is paid in arrears, DQ-day is the day following the first pay day after the end of the period of 28 days beginning with the first day after the determination day on which the Secretary of State is notified by the relevant authority that the offender or the offender's family member is in receipt of either housing benefit or council tax benefit (or both of those benefits) or has been awarded either or both of those benefits; and

(b) in relation to housing benefit or council tax benefit which is paid in advance, DQ-day is the first pay day after the end of the period of 28 days beginning with the first day after the determination day on which the Secretary of State is so notified by the relevant authority.

[2 (5A) This paragraph applies where on the determination day the offender or, as the case may be, the offender's family member is in receipt of a sanctionable benefit which is neither payable wholly in advance nor wholly in arrears and no other sanctionable benefit.]

(6) Where [2 paragraph (5A) applies or where there is no sanctionable benefit payable on the determination day], DQ-day is the first day after the end of the period of 28 days beginning with the determination day on which the Secretary of State decides to award—

(a) a sanctionable benefit to the offender;

(b) a joint-claim jobseeker's allowance to a joint-claim couple of which the offender is a member; or

(c) [3 universal credit,] income support, jobseeker's allowance, state pension credit or employment and support allowance to the offender's family member.

[3 (6A) Paragraph (6B) applies where on the determination day, the offender or, as the case may be, the offender's family member is in receipt of universal credit.

(6B) Where this paragraph applies, DQ-day is—

(a) if the first day after the end of the period of 28 days beginning with the determination day is the first day of an assessment period, that day;

(b) if the first day after the end of the period of 28 days beginning with the determination day is not the first day of an assessment period, the first day of the next assessment period after that day.]

(7) For the purposes of the preceding provisions of this regulation [2 but except where paragraph (8) applies], DQ-day is to be no later than 5 years and 28 days after the date of the conviction of the offender for the benefit offence in the later proceedings referred to in section 7(1) of the Act; and section 7(9) of the Act (date of conviction and references to conviction) shall apply for the purposes of this paragraph as it applies for the purposes of section 7 of the Act.]

[2 (8) Where the date of the conviction of the offender for the benefit offence in the later proceedings is on or after 1st April 2013 and on the determination day—

(a) paragraph (2) or (6A) applies in the case of an offender or, as the case may be, an offender's family member; but

(b) that person ceases to be in receipt of a benefit referred to in those paragraphs before the first day of the disqualification period that would apply by virtue of paragraph (3) or (6B),

DQ-day is the first day after the end of the period of 28 days beginning with the determination day.

AMENDMENTS

1. Social Security (Loss of Benefit) Amendment Regulations 2010 (SI 2010/1160) reg.2(1) and (3) (April 1, 2010).

2. Social Security (Loss of Benefit) (Amendment) Regulations 2013 (SI 2013/385) regs 2 and 5(1), (2), (4), (5)(a), (7) and (8) (April 1, 2013).

3. Social Security (Loss of Benefit) (Amendment) Regulations 2013 (SI 2013/385) regs 2 and 5(3), (5)(b) and (6) (April 29, 2013).

[1 Prescribed offences: section 6B(14)(b) of the Act

2.788 **2A.**—(1) Paragraphs (2) to (4) prescribe offences which are relevant offences for the purpose of sections 6B and 7 of the Act where section 6B(14)(b)(i), (ii) or (iii) of the Act applies.

(2) In England and Wales, offences under—

(a) section 8 of the Accessories and Abettors Act 1861;

(b) section 1 of the Criminal Law Act 1977;

(c) section 1, 3, 4 or 5 of the Forgery and Counterfeiting Act 1981;

(d) section 6 or 7 of the Fraud Act 2006; and

(e) section 44, 45 or 46 of the Serious Crime Act 2007.

(3) In England, Wales or Scotland, offences under—

(a) section 182 of the Administration Act;

(b) section 327, 328 or 329 of the Proceeds of Crime Act 2002; and

(c) section 4, 5 or 6 of the Identity Documents Act 2010.

(4) In Scotland—

(a) the common law offences of—

(i) conspiracy to defraud;

(ii) embezzlement;

(iii) fraud;

(iv) fraudulent scheme; and

(v) uttering;

(b) offences under—

(i) section 44 of the Criminal Law (Consolidation) (Scotland) Act 1995;

(ii) section 28 or 30 of the Criminal Justice and Licensing (Scotland) Act 2010 ("the 2010 Act"); and

(c) offences to which section 29 of the 2010 Act (offences aggravated by connection with serious organised crime) applies.

(5) Paragraphs (6) and (7) prescribe offences which are relevant offences for the purpose of sections 6B and 7 of the Act where section 6B(14)(b)(i) or (ii) of the Act applies.

(6) In England and Wales, offences under section 1 of the Fraud Act 2006.

(7) In England, Wales or Scotland, offences under—
(a) section 111A of the Administration Act;
(b) section 35 of the Tax Credits Act 2002.]

AMENDMENT

1. Social Security (Loss of Benefit) (Amendment) Regulations 2013 (SI 2013/385) regs 2 and 6 (April 1, 2013).

PART II

REDUCTIONS

Reduction of income support [1 [3 . . .]]

3.—(1) Subject to paragraphs (2) [2 and (3)], any payment of income support [1 [3 . . .]] which falls to be made to an offender in respect of any week in the disqualification period, or to an offender's family member in respect of any week in the relevant period, shall be reduced— 2.789

(a) where the claimant or a member of his family is pregnant or seriously ill, by a sum equivalent to 20 per cent.;
(b) where the applicable amount of the offender used to calculate that payment of income support has been reduced pursuant to regulation 22A of the Income Support Regulations (appeal against a decision embodying an incapacity for work determination), whether or not the appeal referred to in that regulation is successful, by a sum equivalent to 20 per cent;
(c) in any other case, by a sum equivalent to 40 per cent.,

of the applicable amount of the offender in respect of a single claimant for income support on the first day of the disqualification period or, as the case may be, on the first day of the relevant period, and specified in paragraph 1(1) of Schedule 2 to the Income Support Regulations.

(2) Payment shall not be reduced under paragraph (1) to below 10 pence per week.

(3) A reduction under paragraph (1) shall, if it is not a multiple of 5p, be rounded to the nearest such multiple or, if it is a multiple of 2.5p but not of 5p, to the next lower multiple of 5p.

(4) [2 . . .]

(5) Where the rate of income support [1 [3 . . .]] payable to an offender or an offender's family member changes, the rules set out above for a reduction in the benefit payable shall be applied to the new rate and any adjustment to the reduction shall take effect from the first day of the first benefit week to start after the date of the change.

(6) In this regulation, "benefit week" shall have the same meaning as in regulation of 2(1) of the Income Support Regulations. [1 [3 . . .]]

AMENDMENTS

1. Employment and Support Allowance (Consequential Provisions) (No.2) Regulations 2008 (SI 2008/1554) reg.56(1) and (3) (October 27, 2008).

2. Welfare Reform Act 2009 (Section 26) (Consequential Amendments) Regulations 2010 (SI 2010/424) reg.7(1) and (2) (March 22, 2010).

3. Social Security (Loss of Benefit) (Amendment) Regulations 2013 (SI 2013/385) regs 2 and 7 (April 1, 2013, subject to a saving).

General Note

2.790 For the purposes of these Regulations, reg.16 of, and Sch.3 to, the Employment and Support Allowance (Transitional Provisions, Housing Benefit and Council Tax Benefit) (Existing Awards) (No.2) Regulations 2010 (SI 2010/1907) treat a conversion decision, migrating a claimant from incapacity benefit to employment and support allowance, as though it were a decision as to entitlement to employment and support allowance.

This regulation applied to income-related employment and support allowance from October 27, 2008 until April 1, 2013 and continues to do so by virtue of reg.7(6) of the Social Security (Loss of Benefit) (Amendment) Regulations 2013 (SI 2013/385) in relation to a person whose payment of income-related employment and support allowance was being reduced in accordance with this regulation on April 1, 2013 or where the offence in respect of which income-related employment and support allowance falls to be reduced was committed before that date. In other cases, reg.3ZA now makes provision in respect of income-related employment and support allowance.

[[1] Reduction of income-related employment and support allowance

2.791 **3ZA.**—(1) Subject to paragraphs (4) and (5), any payment of an income-related employment and support allowance which falls to be made to an offender in respect of any week in the disqualification period or to an offender's family member in respect of any week in the relevant period is to be reduced in accordance with paragraph (2).

(2) The amount of the reduction is to be—

(a) where the offender or, as the case may be, the offender's family member, is pregnant or seriously ill, a sum equivalent to 20 per cent.;

(b) where the offender or, as the case may be, the offender's family member is subject to no work-related requirements for the purpose of section 11D of the 2007 Act(1), a sum equivalent to 40 per cent.;

(c) in any other case, a sum equivalent to 100 per cent.,

of the applicable amount for a single claimant specified in paragraph 1(1) of Schedule 4 to the ESA Regulations on the day specified in paragraph (3).

(3) The specified day is—

(a) where a payment to the offender falls to be reduced, on the first day of the disqualification period; or

(b) where a payment to the offender's family member falls to be reduced, on the first day of the relevant period.

(4) Payment must not be reduced under paragraph (2) to below 10 pence per week.

(5) A reduction under paragraph (2) must, if it is not a multiple of 5 pence, be rounded to the nearest such multiple or, if it is a multiple of 2.5 pence but not of 5 pence, to the next lower multiple of 5 pence.

(6) Where the rate of an income-related employment and support allowance payable to an offender or an offender's family member changes, the rules set out above for a reduction in the allowance payable are to be applied to the new rate and any adjustment to the reduction shall take effect from the first day of the first benefit week to start after the date of change.

(7) In paragraph (6), "benefit week" has the same meaning as in regulation 2(1) of the ESA Regulations.]

AMENDMENT

1. Social Security (Loss of Benefit) (Amendment) Regulations 2013 (SI 2013/385) regs 2 and 8 (April 1, 2013).

GENERAL NOTE

Before April 1, 2013, reg.3 provided for the reduction of income-related employment and support allowance. See the note to that regulation. 2.792

[1 Reduction of universal credit

3ZB.–(1) Any payment of universal credit which falls to be made to an offender or an offender's family member ("O") in respect of an assessment period wholly or partly within a disqualification period is to be reduced in accordance with paragraph (2) or (5). 2.793

(2) Except where paragraph (5) applies and subject to paragraphs (6) and (7), the amount of the reduction is to be calculated by multiplying the daily reduction rate by the number of days in the assessment period or, if lower, the number of days in the assessment period to which the reduction is to relate.

(3) The daily reduction rate for the purposes of paragraph (2) is, unless paragraph (4) applies, an amount equal to the amount of the standard allowance applicable to the award multiplied by 12 and divided by 365.

(4) The daily reduction rate for the purposes of paragraph (2) is 40 per cent. of the rate calculated in accordance with paragraph (3) if, at the end of the assessment period—

(a) O, or where O is a joint claimant, the other joint claimant ("J"), falls within section 19 of the 2012 Act (claimant subject no work-related requirements) by virtue of—

(i) subsection (2)(c) of that section (responsible carer for a child under the age of 1), or

(ii) regulation 89(1)(c), (d) or (f) of the UC Regulations (adopter, claimants within 11 weeks before, or 15 weeks after, confinement or responsible foster parent of a child under the age of 1); or

(b) O or, as the case may be, O or J, falls within section 20 of the 2012 Act (claimant subject to work-focused interview only).

(5) Where the disqualification period ends during an assessment period, the amount of the reduction for that assessment period is to be calculated by multiplying the daily reduction rate under paragraph (3) or, as the case may be, paragraph (4) by the number of days in that assessment period which are within the disqualification period.

(6) The amount of the daily reduction rate in paragraphs (3) and (4) is to be rounded down to the nearest 10 pence.

(7) The amount of the reduction under paragraph (2) in respect of any assessment period must not exceed the amount of the standard allowance which is applicable to O in respect of that period.

(8) Where the rate of universal credit payable to O or as the case may be, to O and J, changes, the rules set out above for a reduction in the universal credit payable are to be applied to the new rate and any adjustment to the reduction is to take effect from the first day of the first assessment period to start after the date of the change.

(9) In the case of joint claimants—

(a) each joint claimant is considered individually for the purpose of determining the rate applicable under paragraph (3) or (4); and

(b) half of any applicable rate is applied to each joint claimant accordingly.

(10) In this regulation, "standard allowance" means the allowance of that name, the amount of which is set out in regulation 36 of the UC Regulations.]

AMENDMENT

1. Social Security (Loss of Benefit) (Amendment) Regulations 2013 (SI 2013/385) regs 2 and 9 (April 29, 2013).

[1 Reduction in state pension credit

2.794 **3A.**—(1) Subject to the following provisions of this regulation, state pension credit shall be payable in the case of an offender for any week comprised in the disqualification period or in the case of an offender's family member for any week comprised in the relevant period, as if the rate of benefit were reduced—

(a) where the offender or the offender's family member is pregnant or seriously ill, by 20 per cent. of the relevant sum; or

(b) where sub-paragraph (a) does not apply, by 40 per cent. of the relevant sum.

(2) In paragraph (1), the "relevant sum" is the amount applicable—

(a) except where sub-paragraph (b) applies, in respect of a single claimant aged not less than 25 under paragraph 1(1) of Schedule 2 to the Income Support Regulations; or

(b) if the claimant's family member is the offender and the offender has not attained the age of 25, the amount applicable in respect of a person of the offender's age under paragraph 1(1) of Part I of that Schedule,

on the first day of the disqualification period or, as the case may be, on the first day of the relevant period.

(3) Payment of state pension credit shall not be reduced under this regulation to less than 10 pence per week.

(4) A reduction under paragraph (1) shall, if it is not a multiple of 5 pence, be rounded to the nearest such multiple or, if it is a multiple of 2.5 pence but not of 5 pence, to the next lower multiple of 5 pence.

(5) Where the rate of state pension credit payable to an offender or an offender's family member changes, the rules set out above for a reduction in the credit payable shall be applied to the new rate and any adjustment to the reduction shall take effect from the first day of the first benefit week to start after the date of change.

(6) In paragraph (5), "benefit week" has the same meaning as in regulation 1(2) of the State Pension Credit Regulations 2002.

(7) A person of a prescribed description for the purposes of the definition of "family" in section 137(1) of the Benefits Act as it applies for the purpose of this regulation is—

(a) a person who is an additional spouse for the purposes of section 12(1) of the State Pension Credit Act 2002 (additional spouse in the case of polygamous marriages);

(b) a person [2 who is a qualifying young person for the purposes of section 142(2)] of the Benefits Act.]

AMENDMENTS

1. State Pension Credit Regulations 2002 (SI 2002/1792) reg.25(3) (October 6, 2003).
2. Social Security (Loss of Benefit) (Amendment) Regulations 2013 (SI 2013/385) regs 2 and 10 (April 1, 2013).

Reduction of joint-claim jobseeker's allowance

4. In respect of any part of the disqualification period when section 8(2) of the Act does not apply, the reduced rate of joint-claim jobseeker's allowance payable to the member of that couple who is not the offender shall be— 2.795

(a) in any case in which the member of the couple who is not the offender satisfies the conditions set out in section 2 of the Jobseekers Act (contribution-based conditions), a rate equal to the amount calculated in accordance with section 4(1) of that Act;
(b) in any case where the couple are a couple in hardship for the purposes of regulation 11, a rate equal to the amount calculated in accordance with regulation 16;
(c) in any other case, a rate calculated in accordance with section 4(3A) of the Jobseekers Act save that the applicable amount shall be the amount determined by reference to paragraph 1(1) of Schedule 1 to the Jobseeker's Allowance Regulations as if the member of the couple who is not the offender were a single claimant.

PART III

HARDSHIP

Meaning of "person in hardship"

5.—(1) In this Part of these Regulations, a "person in hardship" means, for the purposes of regulation 6, a person, other than a person to whom paragraph (3) or (4) applies, where— 2.796

(a) she is a single woman who is pregnant and in respect of whom the Secretary of State is satisfied that, unless a jobseeker's allowance is paid, she will suffer hardship;
(b) he is a single person who is responsible for a young person and the Secretary of State is satisfied that, unless a jobseeker's allowance is paid, the young person will suffer hardship;
(c) he is a member of [2 a couple] where—
  [2 (i) at least one member of the couple is a woman who is pregnant; and]
  (ii) the Secretary of State is satisfied that, unless a jobseeker's allowance is paid, the woman will suffer hardship;
(d) he is a member of a polygamous marriage and—
  (i) one member of the marriage is pregnant; and
  (ii) the Secretary of State is satisfied that, unless a jobseeker's allowance is paid, that woman will suffer hardship;
(e) he is a member of [2 a couple] or of a polygamous marriage where—
  (i) one or both members of the couple, or one or more members of the polygamous marriage, are responsible for a child or young person; and

(ii) the Secretary of State is satisfied that, unless a jobseeker's allowance is paid, the child or young person will suffer hardship;

(f) he has an award of a jobseeker's allowance which includes or would, if a claim for a jobseeker's allowance from him were to succeed, have included in his applicable amount a disability premium and the Secretary of State is satisfied that, unless a jobseeker's allowance is paid, the person who would satisfy the conditions of entitlement to that premium would suffer hardship;

(g) he suffers, or his partner suffers, from a chronic medical condition which results in functional capacity being limited or restricted by physical impairment and the Secretary of State is satisfied that—

(i) the suffering has already lasted, or is likely to last, for not less than 26 weeks; and

(ii) unless a jobseeker's allowance is paid to that person, the probability is that the health of the person suffering would, within 2 weeks of the Secretary of State making his decision, decline further than that of a normally healthy adult and that person would suffer hardship;

(h) he does, or his partner does, or in the case of a person who is married to more than one person under a law which permits polygamy, at least one of those persons does, devote a considerable portion of each week to caring for another person who—

(i) is in receipt of an attendance allowance [6 , the care component of disability living allowance at one of the two higher rates prescribed under section 72(4) of the Benefits Act [7 , armed forces independence payment] or the daily living component of personal independence payment at the standard or enhanced rate in accordance with section 78 of the 2012 Act];

(ii) has claimed either attendance allowance [6 , disability living allowance [7 , armed forces independence payment] or personal independence payment], but only for so long as the claim has not been determined, or for 26 weeks from the date of claiming, whichever is the earlier; [6 . . .]

(iii) has claimed either attendance allowance or disability living allowance and has an award of either attendance allowance or the care component of disability living allowance at one of the two higher rates prescribed under section 72(4) of the Benefits Act for a period commencing after the date on which that claim was made; [6 [7 . . .]

(iv) has claimed personal independence payment and has an award of the daily living component of personal independence payment at the standard or enhanced rate in accordance with section 78 of the 2012 Act for a period commencing after the date on which that claim was made;] [7 or

(v) has claimed armed forces independence payment and has an award for a period commencing after the date on which that claim was made,]

and the Secretary of State is satisfied, after taking account of the factors set out in paragraph (5), in so far as they are appropriate to the particular circumstances of the case, that the person providing the care will not be able to continue doing so unless a jobseeker's allowance is paid to the offender;

(i) he is a person or is the partner of a person to whom section 16 of the Jobseekers Act applies by virtue of a direction issued by the Secretary of State, except where the person to whom the direction applies does not satisfy the requirements of section 1(2)(a) to (c) of that Act;

(j) he is a person—

(i) to whom section 3(1)(f)(iii) of the Jobseekers Act (persons under the age of 18) applies, or is the partner of such a person; and

(ii) in respect of whom the Secretary of State is satisfied that the person will, unless a jobseeker's allowance is paid, suffer hardship; or

(k) he is a person—

(i) who, pursuant to the Children Act 1989 [8 or the Social Services and Well-being (Wales) Act 2014], was being looked after by a local authority;

(ii) with whom the local authority had a duty, pursuant to [8 either of those Acts], to take reasonable steps to keep in touch; or

(iii) who, pursuant to [8 either of those Acts], qualified for advice and assistance from a local authority,

but in respect of whom head (i), (ii) or (iii) above, as the case may be, had not applied for a period of 3 years or less as at the date on which he complies with the requirements of regulation 9; and

(iv) who, as at the date on which he complies with the requirements of regulation 9, is under the age of 21.

(2) Except in a case to which paragraph (3) or (4) applies, a person shall, for the purposes of regulation 7, be deemed to be a person in hardship where, after taking account of the factors set out in paragraph (5) in so far as they are appropriate to the particular circumstances of the case, the Secretary of State is satisfied that he or his partner will suffer hardship unless a jobseeker's allowance is paid to him.

(3) In paragraphs (1) and (2), a person shall not be deemed to be a person in hardship—

(a) where he is entitled, or his partner is entitled, to income support or where he or his partner fall within a category of persons prescribed for the purpose of section 124(1)(e) of the Benefits Act; [4or]

(b) during any period in respect of which it has been determined that a jobseeker's allowance is not payable to him pursuant to section [3 8] [5 of the Jobseekers Act (attendance, information and evidence) or that it be reduced pursuant to section 19 or 19A or 19B of that Act (circumstances in which a jobseeker's allowance is reduced)];

(c) [4 . . .]

(4) Paragraph (1)(h) shall not apply in a case where the person being cared for resides in a [1 care home, an Abbeyfield Home or an independent hospital].

(5) Factors which, for the purposes of paragraphs (1) and (2), the Secretary of State is to take into account in determining whether the person is a person in hardship are—

(a) the presence in that person's family of a person who satisfies the requirements for a disability premium specified in paragraphs 13 and 14 of Schedule 1 to the Jobseeker's Allowance Regulations or for a disabled child premium specified in paragraph 16 of that Schedule to those Regulations;

(b) the resources which, without a jobseeker's allowance, are likely to be available to the offender's family, the amount by which these resources fall short of the amount applicable in his case in accordance with regulation 10 (applicable amount in hardship cases), the amount of any resources which may be available to members of the offender's family from any person in the offender's household who is not a member of his family and the length of time for which those factors are likely to persist;

(c) whether there is a substantial risk that essential items, including food, clothing, heating and accommodation, will cease to be available to that person or a member of his family, or will be available at considerably reduced levels and the length of time those factors are likely to persist.

(6) In determining the resources available to that person's family under paragraph (5)(b), any training premium or top-up payment paid pursuant to the Employment and Training Act 1973 shall be disregarded.

[[5] (7) In the preceding paragraphs of this regulation, references to a jobseeker's allowance are to an income-based jobseeker's allowance.]

AMENDMENTS

1. Social Security (Care Homes and Independent Hospitals) Regulations 2005 (SI 2005/2687) reg.15(2) (October 24, 2005).

2. Civil Partnership (Pensions, Social Security and Child Support) (Consequential etc. Provisions) Order 2005 (SI 2005/2877) Sch.3 para.34(2) (December 5, 2005).

3. Social Security (Loss of Benefit) Amendment Regulations 2010 (SI 2010/1160) reg.2(1) and (4) (April 1, 2010).

4. Welfare Reform Act 2009 (Section 26) (Consequential Amendments) Regulations 2010 (SI 2010/424) reg.7(1) and (3) (March 22, 2010).

5. Social Security (Loss of Benefit) (Amendment) Regulations 2013 (SI 2013/385) regs 2 and 11(1), (3) and (4) (April 1, 2013).

6. Social Security (Loss of Benefit) (Amendment) Regulations 2013 (SI 2013/385) regs 2 and 11(1) and (2) (April 8, 2013).

7. Armed Forces and Reserve Forces Compensation Scheme (Consequential Provisions: Subordinate Legislation) Order 2013 (SI 2013/591) art.7 and Sch. para.22(1) and (3) (April 8, 2013).

8. Social Services and Well-being (Wales) Act 2014 and the Regulation and Inspection of Social Care (Wales) Act 2016 (Consequential Amendments) Order 2017 (SI 2017/901) art.8(1) and (2) (November 3, 2017).

Circumstances in which an income-based jobseeker's allowance is payable to a person who is a person in hardship

2.797 **6.**—(1) This regulation applies to a person in hardship within the meaning of regulation 5(1) and is subject to the provisions of regulations 8 and 9.

(2) An income-based jobseeker's allowance shall be payable to a person in hardship even though section [[1] 6B(5) or] 7(2) of the Act prevents payment of a jobseeker's allowance to the offender or section 9 of the Act prevents payment of a jobseeker's allowance to an offender's family member but the allowance shall be payable under this paragraph only if and so long as the claimant satisfies the conditions for entitlement to an income-based jobseeker's allowance.

AMENDMENT

1. Social Security (Loss of Benefit) Amendment Regulations 2010 (SI 2010/1160) reg.2(1) and (5) (April 1, 2010).

Further circumstances in which an income-based jobseeker's allowance is payable to a person who is a person in hardship

7.—(1) This regulation applies to a person in hardship within the meaning of regulation 5(2) and is subject to the provisions of regulations 8 and 9. 2.798

(2) An income-based jobseeker's allowance shall be payable to a person in hardship even though section [1 6B(5) or] 7(2) of the Act prevents payment of a jobseeker's allowance to the offender or section 9 of the Act prevents payment of a jobseeker's allowance to an offender's family member but the allowance shall not be payable under this paragraph—

(a) where the offender is the claimant, in respect of the first 14 days of the disqualification period;

(b) where the offender's family member is the claimant, in respect of the first 14 days of the relevant period,

and shall be payable thereafter only if and so long as the claimant satisfies the conditions for entitlement to an income-based jobseeker's allowance.

AMENDMENT

1. Social Security (Loss of Benefit) Amendment Regulations 2010 (SI 2010/1160) reg.2(1) and (6) (April 1, 2010).

Conditions for payment of income-based jobseeker's allowance

8.—(1) An income-based jobseeker's allowance shall not be payable in accordance with regulation 6 or 7 except where the claimant has— 2.799

(a) furnished on a form approved for the purpose by the Secretary of State or in such other form as he may in any particular case approve, a statement of the circumstances he relies upon to establish entitlement under regulation 5(1) or, as the case may be, 5(2); and

(b) signed the statement.

(2) The completed and signed form shall be delivered by the claimant to such office as the Secretary of State may specify.

Provision of information

9. For the purpose of section [1 6B(7)(b) and] 7(4)(b) of the Act, the offender, and for the purpose of section 9(4)(b) of the Act, the offender or any member of his family, shall provide to the Secretary of State information as to the circumstances of the person alleged to be in hardship. 2.800

AMENDMENT

1. Social Security (Loss of Benefit) Amendment Regulations 2010 (SI 2010/1160) reg.2(1) and (7) (April 1, 2010).

Applicable amount in hardship cases

10.—(1) The weekly applicable amount of a person to whom an income-based jobseeker's allowance is payable in accordance with this Part shall be 2.801

reduced by a sum equivalent to 40 per cent. or, in a case where the claimant or any other member of his family is either pregnant or seriously ill, 20 per cent. of the following amount—

(a) where the claimant is a single claimant aged not less than 18 but less than 25 or a member of a couple or polygamous marriage where one member is aged not less than 18 but less than 25 and the other member or, in the case of a polygamous marriage each other member, is a person under 18 who is not eligible for an income-based jobseeker's allowance under section 3(1)(f)(iii) of the Jobseekers Act or is not subject to a direction under section 16 of that Act, the amount specified in paragraph 1(1)(d) of Schedule 1 to the Jobseeker's Allowance Regulations;

(b) where the claimant is a single claimant aged not less than 25 or a member of a couple or a polygamous marriage (other than a member of a couple or polygamous marriage to whom sub-paragraph (a) applies) at least one of whom is aged not less than 18, the amount specified in paragraph 1(1)(e) of Schedule 1 to the Jobseeker's Allowance Regulations.

(2) A reduction under paragraph (1) shall, if it is not a multiple of 5p, be rounded to the nearest such multiple or, if it is a multiple of 2.5p but not of 5p, to the next lower multiple of 5p.

PART IV

HARDSHIP FOR JOINT-CLAIM COUPLES

Application of Part and meaning of "couple in hardship"

2.802 **11.**—(1) This Part of these Regulations applies in respect of any part of the disqualification period when section 8(2) of the Act would otherwise apply.

(2) In this Part of these Regulations, a "couple in hardship" means, for the purposes of [3 regulation 12], a joint-claim couple, other than a couple to whom paragraph (4) or (5) applies, who are claiming a jointclaim jobseeker's allowance jointly where at least one member of that couple is an offender and where—

(a) [1 care home, an Abbeyfield Home or an independent hospital] and the Secretary of State is satisfied that, unless a joint-claim jobseeker's allowance is paid, she will suffer hardship;

(b) one or both members of the couple are members of a polygamous marriage, one member of the marriage is pregnant and the Secretary of State is satisfied that, unless a joint-claim jobseeker's allowance is paid, she will suffer hardship;

(c) the award of a joint-claim jobseeker's allowance includes, or would, if a claim for a jobseeker's allowance from the couple were to succeed, have included in their applicable amount a disability premium and the Secretary of State is satisfied that, unless a joint-claim jobseeker's allowance is paid, the member of the couple who would have caused the disability premium to be applicable to the couple would suffer hardship;

(d) either member of the couple suffers from a chronic medical condition which results in functional capacity being limited or restricted by physical impairment and the Secretary of State is satisfied that—

(i) the suffering has already lasted or is likely to last, for not less than 26 weeks; and

(ii) unless a joint-claim jobseeker's allowance is paid, the probability is that the health of the person suffering would, within two weeks of the Secretary of State making his decision, decline further than that of a normally healthy adult and the member of the couple who suffers from that condition would suffer hardship;

(e) either member of the couple, or where a member of that couple is married to more than one person under a law which permits polygamy, one member of that marriage, devotes a considerable portion of each week to caring for another person who—

(i) is in receipt of an attendance allowance [4 , the care component of disability living allowance at one of the two higher rates prescribed under section 72(4) of the Benefits Act [5 , armed forces independence payment] or the daily living component of personal independence payment at the standard or enhanced rate in accordance with section 78 of the 2012 Act];

(ii) has claimed either attendance allowance [4 , disability living allowance [5 , armed forces independence payment] or personal independence payment], but only for so long as the claim has not been determined, or for 26 weeks from the date of claiming, whichever is the earlier; [4 . . .]

(iii) has claimed either attendance allowance or disability living allowance and has an award of either attendance allowance or the care component of disability living allowance at one of the two higher rates prescribed under section 72(4) of the Benefits Act for a period commencing after the date on which that claim was made; [4 [5 . . .]

(iv) has claimed personal independence payment and has an award of the daily living component of personal independence payment at the standard or enhanced rate in accordance with section 78 of the 2012 Act for a period commencing after the date on which that claim was made;] [5 or

(v) has claimed armed forces independence payment and has an award for a period commencing after the date on which that claim was made,]

and the Secretary of State is satisfied, after taking account of the factors set out in paragraph (6) in so far as they are appropriate to the particular circumstances of the case, that the person providing the care will not be able to continue doing so unless a joint-claim jobseeker's allowance is paid; or

(f) section 16 of the Jobseekers Act applies to either member of the couple by virtue of a direction issued by the Secretary of State, except where the member of the joint-claim couple to whom the direction applies does not satisfy the requirements of section 1(2)(a) to (c) of that Act;

(g) section 3A(1)(e)(ii) of the Jobseekers Act (member of joint-claim couple under the age of 18) applies to either member of the couple and the Secretary of State is satisfied that unless a jointclaim jobseeker's allowance is paid, the couple will suffer hardship; or

(h) one or both members of the couple is a person—

(i) who, pursuant to the Children Act 1989 [6 or the Social Services and Well-being (Wales) Act 2014], was being looked after by a local authority;

(ii) with whom the local authority had a duty, pursuant to [6 either of those Acts], to take reasonable steps to keep in touch; or

(iii) who, pursuant to [6 either of those Acts], qualified for advice or assistance from a local authority,

but in respect of whom head (i), (ii) or (iii) above, as the case may be, had not applied for a period of 3 years or less as at the date on which the requirements of regulation 15 are complied with; and

(iv) who, as at the date on which the requirements of regulation 15 are complied with, is under the age of 21.

(3) Except in a case to which paragraph (4) or (5) applies, a joint-claim couple shall, for the purposes of [3 regulation 13], be deemed to be a couple in hardship where the Secretary of State is satisfied, after taking account of the factors set out in paragraph (6) in so far as they are appropriate to the particular circumstances of the case, that the couple will suffer hardship unless a joint-claim jobseeker's allowance is paid.

(4) In paragraphs (2) and (3), a joint-claim couple shall not be deemed to be a "couple in hardship"—

(a) where one member of the couple is entitled to income support or falls within a category of persons prescribed for the purposes of section 124(1)(e) of the Benefits Act; or

(b) during a period in respect of which it has been determined that both members of the couple are subject [3 or are treated as subject] to sanctions for the purposes of section [3 8 or] 20A of the Jobseekers Act ([3 attendance, information and evidence;] denial or reduction of joint-claim jobseeker's allowance).

(5) Paragraph (2)(e) shall not apply in a case where the person being cared for resides in a [2 care home, an Abbeyfield Home or an independent hospital].

(6) Factors which, for the purposes of paragraphs (2) and (3), the Secretary of State is to take into account in determining whether a joint-claim couple will suffer hardship are—

(a) the presence in the joint-claim couple of a person who satisfies the requirements for a disability premium specified in paragraphs 20H and 20I of Schedule 1 to the Jobseeker's Allowance Regulations;

(b) the resources which, without a joint-claim jobseeker's allowance, are likely to be available to the joint-claim couple, the amount by which these resources fall short of the amount applicable in their case in accordance with regulation 16 (applicable amount of joint-claim couple in hardship cases), the amount of any resources which may be available to the joint-claim couple from any person in the couple's household who is not a member of the family and the length of time for which those factors are likely to persist;

(c) whether there is a substantial risk that essential items, including food, clothing, heating and accommodation, will cease to be available to the joint-claim couple, or will be available at considerably reduced levels, the hardship that will result and the length of time those factors are likely to persist.

(7) In determining the resources available to the offender's family under paragraph (6)(b), any training premium or top-up payment paid pursuant to the Employment and Training Act 1973 shall be disregarded.

AMENDMENTS

1. Social Security (Care Homes and Independent Hospitals) Regulations 2005 (SI 2005/2687) reg.15(3) (October 24, 2005).

2. Civil Partnership (Pensions, Social Security and Child Support) (Consequential etc. Provisions) Order 2005 (SI 2005/2877) Sch.3 para.34(3) (December 5, 2005).

3. Social Security (Loss of Benefit) Amendment Regulations 2010 (SI 2010/1160) reg.2(1) and (8) (April 1, 2010).

4. Social Security (Loss of Benefit) (Amendment) Regulations 2013 (SI 2013/385) regs 2 and 12 (April 8, 2013).

5. Armed Forces and Reserve Forces Compensation Scheme (Consequential Provisions: Subordinate Legislation) Order 2013 (SI 2013/591) art.7 and Sch. para.22(1) and (4) (April 8, 2013).

6. Social Services and Well-being (Wales) Act 2014 and the Regulation and Inspection of Social Care (Wales) Act 2016 (Consequential Amendments) Order 2017 (SI 2017/901) art.8(1) and (3) (November 3, 2017).

Circumstances in which a joint-claim jobseeker's allowance is payable where a joint-claim couple is a couple in hardship

12.—(1) This regulation applies where a joint-claim couple is a couple in hardship within the meaning of regulation 11(2) and is subject to the provisions of regulations 14 and 15. 2.803

(2) A joint-claim jobseeker's allowance shall be payable to a couple in hardship even though section 8(2) of the Act prevents payment of a joint-claim jobseeker's allowance to the couple or section 8(3) of the Act reduces the amount of a joint-claim jobseeker's allowance payable to the couple but the allowance shall be payable under this paragraph only if and for so long as—

(a) the joint-claim couple satisfy the other conditions of entitlement to a joint-claim jobseeker's allowance; or

(b) one member satisfies those conditions and the other member comes within any paragraph in Schedule A1 to the Jobseeker's Allowance Regulations (categories of members not required to satisfy conditions in section 1(2B)(b) of the Jobseekers Act).

Further circumstances in which a joint-claim jobseeker's allowance is payable to a couple in hardship

13.—(1) This regulation applies to a couple in hardship falling within regulation 11(3) and is subject to the provisions of regulations 14 and 15. 2.804

(2) A joint-claim jobseeker's allowance shall be payable to a couple in hardship even though section 8(2) of the Act prevents payment of a joint-claim jobseeker's allowance to the couple or section 8(3) of the Act reduces the amount of a joint-claim jobseeker's allowance payable to the couple but the allowance—

(a) shall not be payable under this paragraph in respect of the first 14 days of the prescribed period; and

(b) shall be payable thereafter only where the conditions of entitlement to a joint-claim jobseeker's allowance are satisfied or where one member satisfies those conditions and the other member comes within any paragraph in Schedule A1 to the Jobseeker's Allowance Regulations (categories of members not required to satisfy conditions in section 1(2B)(b) of the Jobseekers Act).

Conditions for payment of a joint-claim jobseeker's allowance

2.805 **14.**—(1) A joint-claim jobseeker's allowance shall not be payable in accordance with regulation 12 or 13 except where either member of the couple has—

(a) furnished on a form approved for the purpose by the Secretary of State or in such other form as he may in any particular case approve, a statement of the circumstances he relies upon to establish entitlement under regulation 11(2) or, as the case may be, 11(3); and

(b) signed the statement.

(2) The completed and signed form shall be delivered by a member of the couple to such office as the Secretary of State may specify.

Provision of information

2.806 **15.** For the purposes of section 8(4)(b) of the Act, a member of the couple shall provide to the Secretary of State information as to the circumstances of the alleged hardship of the couple.

Applicable amount of joint-claim couple in hardship cases

2.807 **16.**—(1) The weekly applicable amount of a couple to whom a joint-claim jobseeker's allowance is payable in accordance with this Part shall be reduced by a sum equivalent to 40 per cent. or, in a case where a member of the joint-claim couple is either pregnant or seriously ill or where a member of the joint-claim couple is a member of a polygamous marriage and one of those members is either pregnant or seriously ill, 20 per cent of the following amount—

(a) where one member of the joint-claim couple or of the polygamous marriage is aged not less than 18 but less than 25 and the other member or, in the case of a polygamous marriage, each other member, is a person under 18 to whom section 3A(1 (e)(ii) of the Jobseekers Act applies or is not subject to a direction under section 16 of that Act, the amount specified in paragraph 1(1)(d) of Schedule 1 to the Jobseeker's Allowance Regulations;

(b) where one member of the joint-claim couple or at least one member of the polygamous marriage (other than a member of a couple or polygamous marriage to whom sub-paragraph (a) applies) is aged not less than 18, the amount specified in paragraph 1(1)(e) of Schedule 1 to the Jobseeker's Allowance Regulations.

(2) A reduction under paragraph (1) shall, if it is not a multiple of 5p, be rounded to the nearest such multiple or, if it is a multiple of 2.5p but not of 5p, to the next lower multiple of 5p.

[1 Part 4A

Hardship: Income-Related Employment And Support Allowance

Payment of income-related employment and support allowance to specified persons

16A—(1) Subject to regulation 16B, an income-related employment and support allowance is payable in accordance with the following provisions of this Part to an offender or an offender's family member ("O") where— 2.808

(a) O meets the conditions for entitlement to that allowance;

(b) the amount of the allowance otherwise payable to O is subject to a reduction under regulation 3ZA above or regulation 63 of the ESA Regulations; and

(c) the Secretary of State is satisfied that O, their partner or a child or qualifying young person for whom they are responsible, will be in hardship unless such a payment is made.

(2) The Secretary of State must take the following matters into account in determining whether a person is in hardship for the purpose of paragraph (1)(c)—

(a) whether O's partner or a person in O's family satisfies the requirements for a disability premium specified in paragraphs 6 and 7 of Schedule 4 to the ESA Regulations, or for an element of child tax credit in respect of a child or young person who is disabled or severely disabled within the meaning of regulation 8 of the Child Tax Credit Regulations 2002;

(b) the household's available resources without a payment under paragraph (1), including resources from persons who are not members of the household;

(c) the difference between the available resources and the amount of a payment under paragraph (1) that O would receive;

(d) whether there is a substantial risk that the household will not have access to essential items (including food, clothing, heating and accommodation), or will have access to such essential items at considerably reduced levels, without a payment under paragraph (1); and

(e) the length of time that the factors set out in sub-paragraphs (b) to (d) are likely to continue.

(3) In paragraphs (1) and (2), "partner", "child" and "qualifying young person" have the same meaning as they have in the ESA Regulations.]

Amendment

1. Social Security (Loss of Benefit) (Amendment) Regulations 2013 (SI 2013/385) regs 2 and 13 (April 1, 2013).

[1 Requirements for payments under regulation 16A(1)

16B. The Secretary of State must not make a payment under regulation 16A(1) unless O — 2.809

(a) completes and submits an application in a form approved for the purpose by the Secretary of State, or in such other form as the Secretary of State accepts as sufficient, in such manner as the Secretary of State determines; and

(b) provides such information or evidence relating to the matters specified in regulation 16A(2)(b) to (d) as the Secretary of State may require, in such manner as the Secretary of State determines.]

AMENDMENT

1. Social Security (Loss of Benefit) (Amendment) Regulations 2013 (SI 2013/385) regs 2 and 13 (April 1, 2013).

[1 Amount of payment under regulation 16A(1)

2.810 **16C.**—(1) The amount of a payment under regulation 16A(1) is 60 per cent. of the prescribed amount for a single claimant as set out in paragraph (1)(a) of Part 1 of Schedule 4 to the ESA Regulations.

(2) A payment calculated in accordance with paragraph (1) is to be, if it is not a multiple of 5 pence, rounded to the nearest such multiple or, if it is a multiple of 2.5 pence but not of 5 pence, to the next lower multiple of 5 pence.]

AMENDMENT

1. Social Security (Loss of Benefit) (Amendment) Regulations 2013 (SI 2013/385) regs 2 and 13 (April 1, 2013).

[1 PART 4B

HARDSHIP: UNIVERSAL CREDIT

2.811 Payment of universal credit to specified persons

16D.—(1) Subject to regulation 16E, universal credit is payable in accordance with the following provisions of this Part to an offender or an offender's family member ("O") or where O is a joint claimant, to O and the other joint claimant ("J"), where the Secretary of State is satisfied that they are in hardship.

(2) For the purposes of paragraph (1), O or, as the case may be, O and J must be considered as being in hardship only where—

(a) they meet the conditions for entitlement to universal credit;

(b) they cannot meet their immediate and most basic and essential needs, specified in paragraph (3), or the immediate and most basic and essential needs of a child or qualifying young person for whom O is, or O and J are, responsible only because the amount of their award has been reduced under—

  (i) section 26 or 27 of the 2012 Act by the daily reduction rate determined in accordance with regulation 111 of the UC Regulations; or

  (ii) regulation 3ZB above by the daily reduction rate determined in accordance with paragraph (3) or (4) of that regulation;

(c) they have made every effort to access alternative sources of support to meet, or partially meet, such needs; and

(d) they have made every effort to cease to incur any expenditure which does not relate to such needs.

(3) The needs referred to in paragraph (2) are—
(a) accommodation;
(b) heating;
(c) food;
(d) hygiene.

(4) In paragraph (2)(b), "child" and "qualifying young person" have the same meaning as in Part 1 of the 2012 Act and whether or not O is, or O and J are, responsible for a child or qualifying young person is to be determined in accordance with regulation 4 of the UC Regulations.]

AMENDMENT

1. Social Security (Loss of Benefit) (Amendment) Regulations 2013 (SI 2013/385) regs 2 and 14 (April 29, 2013).

[1 Requirements for payments under regulation 16D(1)

16E. The Secretary of State must not make a payment under regulation 16D(1) unless— 2.812
(a) O completes and submits or, as the case may be, O and J complete and submit, an application in a form approved for the purpose by the Secretary of State, or in such other form as the Secretary of State accepts as sufficient, in such manner as the Secretary of State determines;
(b) O furnishes or, as the case may be, O and J furnish, such information or evidence relating to the matters specified in regulation 16D(2)(b) to (d) as the Secretary of State may require, in such manner as the Secretary of State determines; and
(c) O accepts or, as the case may be O and J accept, that any such payments that are paid are recoverable and may be recovered in accordance with section 71ZH of the Administration Act, except in such cases as the Secretary of State determines otherwise.]

AMENDMENT

1. Social Security (Loss of Benefit) (Amendment) Regulations 2013 (SI 2013/385) regs 2 and 14 (April 29, 2013).

[1 Period in respect of which payments under regulation 16D(1) are to be made

16F. A payment under regulation 16D(1) is to be made in respect of— 2.813
(a) a period which—
(i) begins with the date on which the application under regulation 16E(a) is submitted or, if later, the date on which all of the conditions in regulation 16D(2) are met; and
(ii) ends with the day before the date on which O's, or as the case may be, O and J's next full payment of universal credit for an assessment period is due to be made (or would be made but for a reduction under regulation 3ZB); or
(b) where the period calculated in accordance with paragraph (a) is 7 days or less, that period plus a further period ending with the day

referred to in paragraph (a)(ii) or, if sooner, the last day in respect of which O's, or as the case may be, O and J's award is reduced in accordance with regulation 3ZB.

AMENDMENT

1. Social Security (Loss of Benefit) (Amendment) Regulations 2013 (SI 2013/385) regs 2 and 14 (April 29, 2013).]

[1 The amount of payments under regulation 16D(1)

2.814 **16G.** The amount of a payment under regulation 16D(1) for each day in respect of which such a payment is to be is made is to be determined in accordance with the formula—

$$60\% \text{ of } \left(\frac{A \times 12}{365}\right)$$

where A is equal to the amount of the reduction in the amount of O's award or, as the case may be, the amount of O and J's award, calculated under regulation 3ZB for the assessment period preceding the assessment period in which an application is submitted under regulation 16E(a).]

AMENDMENT

1. Social Security (Loss of Benefit) (Amendment) Regulations 2013 (SI 2013/385) regs 2 and 14 (April 29, 2013).

[1 Recoverability of payments made under regulation 16D(1)

2.815 **16H.** Payments made under regulation 16D(1) are recoverable by virtue of section 71ZH of the Administration Act as if they were hardship payments under regulation 116 of the UC Regulations and for this purpose, regulation 119 of those Regulations applies to payments under regulation 16D(1) as it applies to such hardship payments.]

AMENDMENT

1. Social Security (Loss of Benefit) (Amendment) Regulations 2013 (SI 2013/385) regs 2 and 14 (April 29, 2013).

PART V

HOUSING BENEFIT AND COUNCIL TAX BENEFIT

2.816 **17.** *Omitted.*

2.817 **18.** *Omitted.*

PART VI

DEDUCTIONS FROM BENEFITS AND DISQUALIFYING BENEFITS

Social security benefits not to be sanctionable benefits

19. The following social security benefits are to be treated as a disqualifying benefit but not a sanctionable benefit— **2.818**

(a) constant attendance allowance payable under [1 article 8 of the Naval, Military and Air Forces Etc. (Disablement and Death) Service Pensions Order 2006] ("the Order") or article 14 or 43 of the Personal Injuries (Civilians) Scheme 1983 ("the Scheme");

(b) exceptionally severe disablement allowance payable under [1 article 9 of the Order] or article 15 or 44 of the Scheme;

(c) mobility supplement payable under [1 article 26A] of the Order or article 25A or 48A of the Scheme;

(d) constant attendance allowance and exceptionally severe disablement allowance, payable under sections 104 and 105 respectively of the Benefits Act where a disablement pension is payable under section 103 of that Act; and

(e) [2 bereavement support payment payable under section 30 of the Pensions Act 2014.]

AMENDMENTS

1. Social Security (Loss of Benefit) (Amendment) Regulations 2013 (SI 2013/385) regs 2 and 15 (April 1, 2013).

2. Pensions Act 2014 (Consequential, Supplementary and Incidental Amendments) Order 2017 (SI 2017/422) art.20 (April 6, 2017, subject to a saving).

[1 Benefits to be treated as neither sanctionable nor disqualifying

19A. Each of the following benefits is to be treated as neither a sanctionable benefit nor a disqualifying benefit— **2.819**

(a) statutory adoption pay;

(b) statutory paternity pay;

(c) health in pregnancy grant.]

AMENDMENT

1. Social Security (Loss of Benefit) Amendment Regulations 2010 (SI 2010/1160) reg.2(1) and (11) (April 1, 2010).

Deductions from benefits

20. Any restriction in section [1 6B,] 7, 8 or 9 of the Act shall not apply in relation to payments of benefit to the extent of any deduction from the payments which falls to be made under regulations made under section 5(1)(p) of the Social Security Administration Act 1992 for, or in place of, child support maintenance and for this purpose, "child support maintenance" means such maintenance which is payable under the Child Support Act 1991. **2.820**

AMENDMENT

1. Social Security (Loss of Benefit) Amendment Regulations 2010 (SI 2010/1160) reg.2(1) and (12) (April 1, 2010).

PART VII

OTHER AMENDMENTS

2.821 **21.** *Omitted.*

2.822 **22.** *Omitted.*

The Social Security (Medical Evidence) Regulations 1976

(SI 1976/615)

ARRANGEMENT OF REGULATIONS

The Secretary of State for Social Services, in exercise of powers conferred upon him by section 115(1) of, and Schedule 13 to, the Social Security Act 1975 and of all other powers enabling him in that behalf, after reference to the National Insurance Advisory Committee hereby makes the following regulations:

Citation, commencement, and interpretation

2.824 **1.** (1) These regulations may be cited as the Social Security (Medical Evidence) Regulations 1976, and shall come into operation on 4th October 1976.

(2) In these regulations, unless the context otherwise requires—

"the Act" means the Social Security Act 1975;

[[2] "the Contributions and Benefits Act" means the Social Security Contributions and Benefits Act 1992;]

[4 "the Employment and Support Allowance Regulations" means the Employment and Support Allowance Regulations 2008;]

[5 "limited capability for work" has the meaning—

(a) for the purposes of employment and support allowance, given in section 1(4) of the Welfare Reform Act 2007; and

(b) for the purposes of universal credit, given in section 37 of the Welfare Reform Act 2012;"

"limited capability for work assessment" means the assessment of whether a person has limited capability for work—

(a) for the purposes of old style ESA, under Part 5 of the Employment and Support Allowance Regulations;

(b) for the purposes of new style ESA, under Part 4 of the Employment and Support Allowance Regulations 2013;

(c) for the purposes of universal credit, under Part 5 of the Universal Credit Regulations 2013;]

[3 "personal capability assessment" means the assessment provided for in section 171C of the Contributions and Benefits Act;]

[1 "registered midwife" means a midwife who is registered as a midwife with the Nursing and Midwifery Council under the Nursing and Midwifery Order 2001;]

"doctor" means a registered medical practitioner;

[6 "healthcare professional" means a person, not being the patient, who is—

(a) a registered medical practitioner;

(b) a registered nurse;

(c) a registered occupational therapist or registered physiotherapist;

(d) a registered pharmacist within the meaning of article 3 of the Pharmacy Order 2010;]

"signature" means, in relation to any statement or certificate given in accordance with these regulations, the name by which the person giving that statement or certificate, as the case may be, is usually known (any name other than the surname being either in full or otherwise indicated) written by that person in his own handwriting; and "signed" shall be construed accordingly.

(3) Any reference in these regulations to any provisions made by or contained in any enactment or instrument shall, except in so far as the context otherwise requires, be construed as a reference to that provision as amended or extended by any enactment or instrument and as including a reference to any provision which it re-enacts or replaces, or which may re-enact or replace it, with or without modification.

(4) The rules for the construction of Acts of Parliament contained in the Interpretation Act 1889 shall apply in relation to this instrument and in relation to the revocation effected by it as if this instrument, the regulations revoked by it and regulations revoked by the regulations so revoked were Acts of Parliament, and as if each revocation were a repeal.

[5 (5) For the purposes of the definition of "limited capability for work assessment" in paragraph (2)—

(a) "old style ESA" means an allowance under Part 1 of the Welfare Reform Act 2007 as that Part has effect apart from the amendments made by Schedule 3, and Part 1 of Schedule 14, to the Welfare Reform Act 2012 that remove references to an income-related allowance; and

(b) "new style ESA" means an allowance under Part 1 of the Welfare Reform Act 2007 as amended by the provisions of Schedule 3, and Part 1 of Schedule 14, to the Welfare Reform Act 2012 that remove references to an income-related allowance.]

AMENDMENTS

1. The Nursing and Midwifery Order 2001 (Consequential Amendments) Order 2002 (SI 2002/881) Sch.1 para.1 (April 17, 2002).

2. The Social Security (Medical Evidence) Amendment Regulations 1994 (SI 1994/2975) reg.2 (April 13, 1995).

3. The Social Security (Incapacity for Work) Miscellaneous Amendments Regulations 1999 (SI 1999/3109) reg.5(a) (April 3, 2000).

4. The Employment and Support Allowance (Consequential provisions) (No.2) Regulations 2008 (SI 2008/1554) reg.68 (October 27, 2008).

5. The Universal Credit (Consequential Supplementary, Incidental and Miscellaneous Provisions) Regulations 2013 (SI 2013/630) reg.24 (April 29, 2013).

6. The Social Security (Medical Evidence) and Statutory Sick Pay (Medical Evidence) (Amendment) (No.2) Regulations 2022 (SI 2022/630) reg.2 (July 1, 2022).

Evidence of incapacity for work [8 , limited capability for work] and confinement

2.825 [9 **2.**—(1) Subject to regulation 5 and paragraph (1A) below, where a person claims to be entitled to any benefit, allowance or advantage (other than industrial injuries benefit or statutory sick pay) and entitlement to that benefit, allowance or advantage depends on that person being incapable of work or having limited capability for work, then in respect of each day until that person has been assessed for the purposes of the personal capability assessment or the limited capability for work assessment they shall provide evidence of such incapacity or limited capability by means of a statement given by a [10healthcare professional] in accordance with the rules set out in Part 1 of Schedule 1 to these Regulations.

(1A) Where it would be unreasonable to require a person to provide a statement in accordance with paragraph (1) above that person shall provide such other evidence as may be sufficient to show that they are incapable of work or have limited capability for work so that they should refrain (or should have refrained) from work by reason of some specific disease or bodily or mental disability.]

(2) Every person to whom paragraph (1) applies [2 who has not been assessed for the purposes of the [6 personal capability assessment]] [8 or the limited capability for work assessment] shall, before he returns to work, furnish evidence of the date on which he became fit for work either in accordance with rule 10 of Part 1 of Schedule 1 to these regulations, or by such other means as may be sufficient in the circumstances of the case.

[7 (3) Every woman who claims maternity benefit shall furnish evidence—

(a) where the claims is made in respect of expectation of confinement, that she is pregnant and as to the stage which she has reached in her pregnancy; or

(b) where the claim is made by virtue of the fact of confinement, that she has been confined;

and shall furnish such evidence by means of a maternity certificate given by a doctor or by as registered midwife [not earlier than the beginning of the 20th week before the week in which she is expected to be confined] in accordance with the rules set out in Part I of Schedule 2 to these regulations in the appropriate form set out in Part II of that Schedule or by such other means as may be sufficient in the circumstances of any particular case.]

AMENDMENTS

1. The Social Security (Medical Evidence, Claims and Payments) Amendments Regulations 1982 (SI 1982/699) reg.2 (June 14, 1982).

2. The Social Security (Medical Evidence) Amendment Regulations 1994 (SI 1994/2975) reg.2 (April 13, 1995).

3. The Social Security (Medical Evidence) Amendment Regulations 1992 (SI 1992/2471) reg.3 (March 9, 1992).

4. The Social Security (Incapacity for Work) Miscellaneous Amendments Regulations 1995 (SI 1995/987) reg.4 (April 13, 1995.)

5. The Social Security (Incapacity) Miscellaneous Amendments Regulations 2000 (SI 2000/590) reg.6 (April 3, 2000).

6. The Social Security (Incapacity for Work) Miscellaneous Amendments Regulations 1999 (SI 1999/3109) reg.5(b) (April 3, 2000).

7. The Social Security (Medical Evidence) and Statutory Maternity Pay (Medical Evidence) (Amendment) Regulations 2001 (SI 2001/2931) reg.2 (September 28, 2001).

8. The Employment and Support Allowance (Consequential provisions) (No.2) Regulations 2008 (SI 2008/1554) reg.68 (October 27, 2008).

9. The Social Security (Medical Evidence) and Statutory Sick Pay (Medical Evidence) (Amendment) Regulations 2010 (SI 2010/137) reg.2(2) (April 6, 2010).

10. The Social Security (Medical Evidence) and Statutory Sick Pay (Medical Evidence) (Amendment) (No.2) Regulations 2022 (SI 2022/630) reg.2 (July 1, 2022).

GENERAL NOTE

In *R(15) 8/93,* the Commissioner ruled that the reference in the regulation to "such other means as may be sufficient in the particular circumstances of any particular case" meant that evidence of incapacity need not be in the form of a medical certificate. This means that medical certificates other than in the form set out in the Schedule may be acceptable as well as evidence from the claimant himself or herself (para.14). Whether such evidence is sufficient is a matter for determination by the decision-maker or tribunal. Failure to consider this issue will be an error of law. **2.826**

In *CIB/17533/1996* the Commissioner addressed an issue which was being argued by a number of representatives, namely that there was no jurisdiction to make an all work test determination where the adjudication officer had requested the claimant to obtain the special Form Med. 4 and this form was not available to the adjudication officer when the decision was made. Form Med. 4 is the special form which specifically directs doctors to consider capacity for *all* work in certifying incapacity for work. The Commissioner concludes that "the somewhat legalistic proposition that a decision by an adjudication officer made without a form MED4 is a nullity or is erroneous in law cannot in my view be sustained" (para.8 of Common Appendix).

2.827 *Regulation 3 revoked by the Social Security (Claims and Payments) Regulations 1979 (SI 1979/628) reg.32 (July 9, 1979).*

2.828 *Regulation 4 revoked by the Social Security (Medical Evidence, Claims and Payments) Amendments Regulations 1982 (SI 1982/699) reg.2 (June 14, 1982).*

[1 Self-certificate for first 7 days of a spell of incapacity for work [4 or limited capability for work]

2.829 **5.**—[2 (1) [3 The evidence of incapacity [4 or limited capability for work] required for the purposes of determining entitlement to a benefit, allowance or advantage referred to in regulation 2(1)]—

(a) for a spell of incapacity which lasts for less than 8 days,

(b) in respect of any of the first 7 days of a longer spell of incapacity;

[4 (c) for a period of limited capability for work which lasts less than 8 days; or

(d) in respect of any of the first 7 days of a longer period of limited capability for work,]

may consist of a self certificate instead of a certificate in the form of a statement in writing given by a [5healthcare professional] in accordance with regulation 2(1).

(2) For the purpose of this regulation:—

[4 "self-certificate means either—

(i) a declaration made by the claimant in writing, on a form approved for the purpose by the Secretary of State; or

(ii) where the claim has made a claim for employment and support allowance in accordance with regulation 4G of the Social Security (Claims and Payments) Regulations 1987, an oral declaration by the claimant,

that the claimant has been unfit for work from a date or for a period specified in the declaration and may include a statement that the claimant expects to continue to be unfit for work on days subsequent to the date on which it is made;]

[3 "spell of incapacity" has the meaning given to it by section 171B(3) of the Contributions and Benefits Act.]]

AMENDMENTS

1. The Social Security (Medical Evidence, Claims and Payments) Amendments Regulations 1982 (SI 1982/699) reg.2 (June 14, 1982).

2. The Social Security (Medical Evidence, Claims and Payments) Amendment Regulations 1989 (SI 1989/1686) reg.2 (October 9, 1989).

3. The Social Security (Medical Evidence) Amendment Regulations 1994 (SI 1994/2975) reg.2 (April 13, 1995).

4. The Employment and Support Allowance (Consequential Provisions) (No.2) Regulations 2008 (SI 2008/1554) reg.68 (October 27, 2008).

5. The Social Security (Medical Evidence) and Statutory Sick Pay (Medical Evidence) (Amendment) (No.2) Regulations 2022 (SI 2022/630) reg.2 (July 1, 2022).

[1 SCHEDULE 1 **Regulation 2(1)**

PART 1

RULES

1. In these rules, unless the context otherwise requires— **2.830**

"assessment" means either a consultation between a patient and a [3healthcare professional] which takes place in person or by telephone or a consideration by a doctor of a written report by another [3 healthcare professional] or other health [3 . . .] professional;

"condition" means a specific disease or bodily or mental disability;

[3...]

[3"other health professonal"] means a person (other than a [3 health care professional] and not being the patient) who is [3 . . .], a registered midwife, [3 . . .] or a member of any profession regulated by a body mentioned in section 25(3) of the National Health Service Reform and Health Care Professions Act 2002;

"patient" means the person in respect of whom a statement is given in accordance with these rules.

2. Where a [3 health care professional] issues a statement to a patient in accordance with an obligation arising under a contract, agreement or arrangement under Part 4 of the National Health Service Act 2006 or Part 4 of the National Health Service (Wales) Act 2006 or Part 1 of the National Health Service (Scotland) Act 1978 the [3 health care professional's] statement shall be in a form set out at Part 2 [2 or Part 2A] of this Schedule [2 . . .].

3. Where a [3 health care professional] issues a statement in any case other than in accordance with rule 2, the [3 health care professional's] statement shall be in the form set out in Part 2 [2 or Part 2A] of this Schedule or in a form to like effect [2 . . .].

4. A [3 health care professional's] statement must be based on an assessment made by that [3 health care professional].

5. A [3 health care professional's] statement [2 . . .] shall contain the following particulars—

(a) the patient's name;

(b) the date of the assessment (whether by consultation or consideration of a report as the case may be) on which the [3 health care professional's] statement is based;

(c) the condition in respect of which the [3 health care professional] advises the patient they are not fit for work;

(d) a statement, where the [3 health care professional] considers it appropriate, that the patient may be fit for work;

(e) a statement that the [3 health care professional] will or, as the case may be will not, need to assess the patient's fitness for work again;

(f) the date on which the [3 health care professional's] statement is given;

(g) the address of the [3 health care professional] [2 ; and]

[2 (h) the name of the [3 health care professional] whether in the form of a signature or [3 otherwise; and]]

[3 (i) the profession of the health care professional.]

[2 . . .]

[3 5A. Where the healthcare professional's statement is in the form set out in Part 2 of this Schedule—

(a) the healthcare professional's name shall, irrespective of their profession, be recorded next to the words "doctor's signature";

(b) the healthcare professional's address shall, irrespective of their profession, be recorded next to the words "doctor's address"; and

(c) the healthcare professional shall record their profession within the statement in such place as appears to them to be appropriate.]

6. Subject to rule 8, the condition in respect of which the [3 health care professional] is advising the patient is not fit for work or, as the case may be, which has caused the patient's absence from work shall be specified as precisely as the [3 health care professional's] knowledge of the patient's condition at the time of the assessment permits.

7. Where a [3 health care professional] considers that a patient may be fit for work the [3 health care professional] shall state the reasons for that advice and where this is considered appropriate, the arrangements which the patient might make, with their employer's agreement, to return to work.

8. The condition may be specified less precisely where, in the [3 health care professional's] opinion, disclosure of the precise condition would be prejudicial to the patient's well-being, or to the patient's position with their employer.

9. A [3 health care professional's] statement may be given on a date after the date of the assessment on which it is based, however no further statement shall be furnished in respect of that assessment other than a [3 health care professional's] statement by way of replacement of an original which has been lost, in which case it shall be clearly marked "duplicate".

10. Where, in the [3 health care professional's] opinion, the patient will become fit for work on a day not later than 14 days after the date of the assessment on which the [3 health care professional's] statement is based, the [3 health care professional's] statement shall specify that day.

11. Subject to rules 12 and 13, the [3 health care professional's] statement shall specify the minimum period for which, in the [3 health care professional's] opinion, the patient will not be fit for work or, as the case may be, for which they may be fit for work.

12. The period specified shall begin on the date of the assessment on which the [3 health care professional's] statement is based and shall not exceed 3 months unless the patient has, on the advice of a [3 health care professional], refrained from work for at least 6 months immediately preceding that date.

13. Where—

(a) the patient has been advised by a [3 health care professional] that they are not fit for work and, in consequence, has refrained from work for at least 6 months immediately preceding the date of the assessment on which the [3 health care professional's] statement is based; and

(b) in the [3 health care professional's] opinion, the patient will not be fit for work for the foreseeable future,

instead of specifying a period, the [3 health care professional] may, having regard to the circumstances of the particular case, enter, after the words "case for", the words "an indefinite period".

PART 2

FORM OF [[3]HEALTHCARE PROFESSIONAL'S] STATEMENT 2.831

STATEMENT OF FITNESS FOR WORK
FOR SOCIAL SECURITY OR STATUTORY SICK PAY

Patient's name	Mr, Mrs, Miss, Ms
I assessed your case on:	/ /
and, because of the following condition(s):	
I advise you that:	☐ you are not fit for work. ☐ you may be fit for work taking account of the following advice:

If available, and with your employer's agreement, you may benefit from:

☐ a phased return to work ☐ amended duties
☐ altered hours ☐ workplace adaptations

Comments, including functional effects of your condition(s):

This will be the case for

or from / / to / /

I will/will not need to assess your fitness for work again at the end of this period. (*Please delete as applicable*)

Doctor's signature	
Date of statement	/ /
Doctor's address	

[2]PART 2A

2.832 ALTERNATIVE FORM OF [3HEALTHCARE PROFESSIONAL'S] STATEMENT

STATEMENT OF FITNESS FOR WORK
FOR SOCIAL SECURITY OR STATUTORY SICK PAY

Patient's name — Mr, Mrs, Miss, Ms

I assessed your case on: / /

and, because of the following condition(s):

I advise you that:
☐ you are not fit for work.
☐ you may be fit for work taking account of the following advice:

If available, and with your employer's agreement, you may benefit from:

☐ a phased return to work ☐ amended duties
☐ altered hours ☐ workplace adaptations

Comments, including functional effects of your condition(s):

This will be the case for

or from / / to / /

I will/will not need to assess your fitness for work again at the end of this period.
(*Please delete as applicable*)

Doctor's signature

Date of statement / /

Doctor's address

AMENDMENTS

1. The Social Security (Medical Evidence) and Statutory Sick Pay (Medical Evidence) (Amendment) Regulations 2010 (SI 2010/137) reg.2(3) (April 6, 2010).

2. The Social Security (Medical Evidence) and Statutory Sick Pay (Medical Evidence) (Amendment) Regulations 2022 (SI 2022/298) reg.2 (April 6, 2022).

3. The Social Security (Medical Evidence) and Statutory Sick Pay (Medical Evidence) (Amendment) (No.2) Regulations 2022 (SI 2022/630) reg.2 (July 1, 2022).

SCHEDULES 1A AND 1B *repealed by* The Social Security (Medical Evidence) and Statutory Sick Pay (Medical Evidence) (Amendment) Regulations 2010 (SI 2010/137) reg.2(4) (April 6, 2010). **2.833**

[1]SCHEDULE 2 **Regulation 2(3)**

PART I

RULES

1. In these rules any reference to a woman is a reference to the woman in respect of whom a maternity certificate is given in accordance with these rules. **2.834**

2. A maternity certificate shall be given by a doctor or registered midwife attending the woman and shall not be given by the woman herself.

3. The maternity certificate shall be on a form provided by the Secretary of State for the purpose and the wording shall be that set out in the appropriate part of the form specified in Part II of this Schedule.

4. Every maternity certificate shall be completed in ink or other indelible substance and shall contain the following particulars—

(a) the woman's name;

(b) the week in which the woman is expected to be confined or, if the maternity certificate is given after confinement, the date of that confinement and the date the confinement was expected to take place [2 . . .];

(c) the date of the examination on which the maternity certificate is based;

(d) the date on which the maternity certificate is signed; and

(e) the address of the doctor or where the maternity certificate is signed by a registered midwife the personal identification number given to her by the United Kingdom Central Council for Nursing, Midwifery and Health Visiting ("UKCC") on her registration in Part 10 of the register maintained under section 10 of the Nurses, Midwives and Health Visitors Act 1979 and the expiry date of that registration,

and shall bear opposite the word "Signature", the signature of the person giving the maternity certificate written after there has been entered on the maternity certificate the woman's name and the expected date or, as the case may be, the date of the confinement.

5. After a maternity certificate has been given, no further maternity certificate based on the same examination shall be furnished other than a maternity certificate by way of replacement of an original which has been lost or mislaid, in which case it shall be clearly marked "duplicate".

[2]PART II

FORM OF CERTIFICATE

2.835 **MATERNITY CERTIFICATE**

Please fill in this form in ink

Name of patient

Fill in this part if you are giving the certificate before the confinement
Do not fill this in more [3 than 20 weeks] before the week the baby is expected.

I certify that I examined you on the date were
given below. In my opinion you can expect to have your baby in the week that includes . . . ./. . . . ./. . . . .
. . . ./. . . . ./. . . . .
Week means a period of 7 days starting on a Sunday and ending on a Saturday.

Fill in this part if you are giving the certificate after the confinement.
I certify that I attended you in connection with the birth which took place on

. . . ./. . . . ./. . . . . when you

delivered of a child [ ] children. In my opinion your baby was expected in the week that includes

Date of examination . . . ./. . . . ./. . . . . .

Date of signing . . . ./. . . . ./. . . . .

Signature

Registered midwives

Please give your UKCC Personal Identification Number and the expiry date of your registration with the UKCC.

Doctors
Please stamp your name and address here [4 (unless the form has been stamped, in Wales, by a Local health Board in whose medical performers list you are included or, in Scotland,] by the Health Board in whose primary medical services performers list you are included)] in whose medical list you are included.

AMENDMENTS

1. The Social Security (Medical Evidence) Amendment Regulations 1987 (SI 1987/409) reg.4 (April 6, 1987).
2. The Social Security (Miscellaneous Provisions) Amendment Regulations 1991 (SI 1991/2284) reg.21 (November 1, 1991).
3. General Medical Services and Personal Medical Services Transition and Consequential Provisions Order 2004 (SI 2004/865) Sch.1 (April 1, 2004).
4. The National Treatment Agency (Abolition) and the Health and Social Care Act 2012 (Consequential, Transitional and Saving Provisions) Order 2013 (SI 2013/235) art.11 and Sch.2 Pt.1 para.6(3) (April 1, 2013).

The Social Security (Notification of Change of Circumstances) Regulations 2001

(SI 2001/3252)

Made	*26th September 2001*
Laid before Parliament	*2nd October 2001*
Coming into force	*18th October 2001*

ARRANGEMENT OF REGULATIONS

GENERAL NOTE

Section 16 of the Social Security Fraud Act 2001 (c.11), which came fully into force on October 18, 2001, amends the Administration Act 1992 to create new offences relating to failure to notify a change of circumstances, which affects entitlement to benefit. The requirements of the offences under the amended provisions of the Administration Act (which are not reproduced in Vol.III) are, broadly, fourfold (1) there has been a change of circumstances affecting entitlement to benefit, (2) the change is not excluded by regulations from changes which are required to be notified, (3) the person knows that the change affects entitlement to benefit, and (4) the person dishonestly fails to give a prompt notification in the prescribed manner to the prescribed person. These regulations set out the matter prescribed by the statute for the purposes of the criminal offences. The explanatory note to the regulations indicates that they are intended to mirror the existing requirements prescribed for the purposes of claims and payments under ss.5 and 6 of the Administration Act. The regulations are reproduced here so that those dealing with questions arising in the appeal tribunals and elsewhere in relation to claims for benefit are aware of the existence of these requirements under the criminal law. They may be referred to in overpayment cases. 2.837

The Secretary of State for Work and Pensions, in exercise of the powers conferred on him by ss.111A(1A), (1B), (1D) and (1E), 112(1A) to (1D), 189(1), (3) and (4) and 191 of the Social Security Administration Act 1992 and of all other powers enabling him in that behalf, and after consultation in respect of provisions of these Regulations relating to housing benefit and council tax benefit with organisations appearing to him to be representative of the authorities concerned, by this

Instrument, which is made before the end of the period of six months from the coming into force of s.16 of the Social Security Fraud Act 2001, hereby makes the following Regulations:

Citation and commencement

2.838 **1.** These Regulations may be cited as the Social Security (Notification of Change of Circumstances) Regulations 2001 and shall come into force on 18th October 2001.

Notification for purposes of sections 111A and 112 of the Social Security Administration Act 1992

2.839 **2.** Regulations 3 to 5 below prescribe the person to whom, and manner in which, a change of circumstances must be notified for the purposes of sections 111A(1A) to (1G) and 112(1A) to (1F) of the Social Security Administration Act 1992 (offences relating to failure to notify a change of circumstances).

Change affecting jobseeker's allowance

2.840 **3.**—(1) [2 Subject to [3 paragraphs (1ZA) and(1A),] where the benefit affected by the change of circumstances is a jobseeker's allowance, notice must be given [1 . . .] to the Secretary of State [1 . . .] at the office that the claimant is required to attend in accordance with a notification given to him under regulation 23 of the Jobseeker's Allowance Regulations 1996—

[1 (a) in writing or by telephone (unless the Secretary of State determines in any particular case that notice must be in writing or may be given otherwise than in writing or by telephone); or

(b) in writing if in any class of case he requires written notice (unless he determines in any particular case to accept notice given otherwise than in writing).]

[3 (1ZA) Where the notice in writing referred to in paragraph (1) is given or sent by an electronic communication that notice must be given or sent in accordance with the provisions set out in Schedule 9ZC to the Social Security (Claims and Payments) Regulations 1987 (electronic communication).]

[2 "(1A) In such cases and subject to such conditions as the Secretary of State may specify, notice may be given to the Secretary of State—

(a) where the change of circumstances is a birth or death, through a relevant authority, or a county council in England, by personal attendance at an office specified by that authority or county council, provided the Secretary of State has agreed with that authority or county council for it to facilitate such notification;

(b) where the change of circumstances is a death, by telephone to a telephone number specified for that purpose by the Secretary of State.]

(2) In [2 paragraph (1)] "Secretary of State" includes a person designated as an employment officer by an order made by the Secretary of State under section 8(3) of the Jobseekers Act 1995.

[2 (3) In paragraph (1A) "relevant authority" has the same meaning as in regulation 4(2).]

AMENDMENTS

1. The Social Security (Miscellaneous Amendments) (No.2) Regulations 2006 (SI 2006/832) reg.2 (April 10, 2006).
2. The Social Security (Notification of Changes of Circumstances) Regulations 2010 (SI 2010/444) reg.4(2) (April 5, 2010).
3. The Social Security (Electronic Communications) Order 2011 (SI 2011/1498) reg.6 (June 20, 2011).

Change affecting housing benefit or council tax benefit

4.—[3 (1) Subject to paragraphs (1A) to [4 (1D)], where the benefit affected by the change of circumstances is housing benefit or council tax benefit, notice must be given to the relevant authority at the designated office— 2.841

(a) in writing; or
(b) by telephone—
  (i) where the relevant authority has published a telephone number for that purpose or for the purposes of making a claim unless the authority determines that in any particular case or class of case notification may not be given by telephone; or
  (ii) in any case or class of case where the relevant authority determines that notice may be given by telephone; or
(c) by any other means which the relevant authority agrees to accept in any particular case.]

[2 (1A) In such cases and subject to such conditions as the Secretary of State may specify, notice may be given to the Secretary of State—

(a) where the change of circumstances is a birth or death, through a relevant authority, or a county council in England, by person attendance at an office specified by that authority or county council, provided the Secretary of State has agreed with that authority or county council for it to facilitate such notification; or
(b) where the change of circumstances is a death, by telephone to a telephone number specified for that purpose by the Secretary of State.

(1B) Paragraph (1A) only applies if the authority administering the claimant's housing benefit or council tax benefit agrees with the Secretary of State that notifications may be made in accordance with that paragraph.]

[3 (1C) Notice may be given to the appropriate DWP office by telephone where all the following conditions are met—

(a) the claimant or the claimant's partner is in receipt of income support or a jobseeker's allowance;
(b) the change of circumstances is that the claimant or the claimant's partner starts employment;
(c) as a result of the change, either entitlement to housing benefit or council tax benefit will end, or the amount of benefit will be reduced; and
(d) a telephone number has been provided for this purpose.]

(1D) Where—

(a) the change of circumstances required to be notified is a death; and
(b) the authority administering the claimant's housing benefit or council tax benefit agrees with the Secretary of State that notifications may be made in accordance with paragraph (1A).

Notice in writing may be given or sent to the Secretary of State by an electronic communication in accordance with the provisions set out in Schedule 9ZC to the Social Security (Claims and Payments) Regulation 1987 (electronic communication).

(1E) The provisions set out in that Schedule shall apply to such notice as they apply for the purposes of regulation 32ZA of the Social Security (Claims and Payments) Regulations 1987 (information given electronically).

(2) In this regulation [3 "appropriate DWP office",] [2 "claimant",] "designated office" and "relevant authority" have the same meaning as in the [1 Housing Benefit Regulations 2006, Housing Benefit (Persons who have attained the qualifying age for state pension credit) Regulations 2006, Council Tax Benefit Regulations 2006, and Council Tax Benefit (Persons who have attained the qualifying age for state pension credit) Regulations 2006.]

AMENDMENTS

1. The Housing Benefit and Council Tax Benefit (Consequential Provisions) Regulations 2006 (SI 2006/217) Sch.2 para.9 (March 6, 2006).

2. The Social Security (Notification of Changes of Circumstances) Regulations 2010 (SI 2010/444) reg.4(3) (April 5, 2010).

3. The Housing Benefit and Council Tax Benefit (Miscellaneous Amendments) Regulations 2010 (SI 2010/2449) reg.7 (October 11, 2010).

4. The Social Security (Electronic Communications) (No.2) Order 2011 (SI 2011/2943) reg.3 (January 23, 2012).

Change affecting other benefit payment or advantage

2.842 **5.**—(1) [2 Subject to [5 paragraphs (1ZZA) and (1ZA)] where the benefit or other payment or advantage affected by the change of circumstances is not a jobseeker's allowance, housing benefit or council tax benefit, notice must be given [3 . . .] to the Secretary of State [3 at the appropriate office—

(a) in writing or by telephone (unless the Secretary of State determines in any particular case that notice must be in writing or may be given otherwise than in writing or by telephone); or

(b) in writing if in any class of case he requires written notice (unless he determine in any particular case to accept notice given otherwise than in writing)]

[4 (1ZZA) In such cases and subject to such conditions as the Secretary of State may specify, notice may be given to the Secretary of State—

(a) where the change of circumstances is a birth or death, through a relevant authority, or a county council in England, by personal attendance at an office specified by that authority or county council, provided the Secretary of State has agreed with that authority or county council for it to facilitate such notification; or

(b) where the change of circumstances is a death, by telephone to a telephone number specified for that purpose by the Secretary of State.]

[2 (1ZA) Where this paragraph applies, where the notice in writing referred to in paragraph (1) is given or sent by an electronic communication that notice must be given or sent in accordance with the provisions set out in Schedule 9ZC to the Social Security (Claims and Payments) Regulations 1987 (electronic communication).

[5 (1ZB) Paragraph (1ZA) applies in relation to—
(a) attendance allowance;
(b) carer's allowance;
(c) disability living allowance
(d) an employment and support allowance;
[6 (da) incapacity benefit;]
(e) income support]
[6 (f) retirement pension;
[7 (fa) a state pension under Part 1 of the Pensions Act 2014,]
(g) state pension credit.]

[1 (1A) The reference in paragraph (1) to notice "in writing" includes where that notice relates to child benefit, notice given or sent in accordance with Schedule 9C to the Social Security (Claims and Payments) Regulations 1987 (electronic communication).]

[4 (2) In this regulation—
"the appropriate office" has the same meaning as in the Social Security (Claims and Payments) Regulations 1987;
"relevant authority" has the same meaning as in regulation 4(2).]

AMENDMENTS

1. The Social Security (Electronic Communications) (Child Benefit) Order 2002 (SI 2002/1789) art.8 (October 28, 2002). These regulations are revoked with effect from December 1, 2003 by the Social Security (Electronic Communications) (Carer's Allowance) Order 2003 (SI 2003/2800) reg.4.
2. The Social Security (Electronic Communications) (Carer's Allowance) Order 2003 (SI 2003/2800) reg.3 (December 1, 2003).
3. The Social Security (Notification of Change of Circumstances) Regulations 2003 (SI 2003/3209) reg.3 (January 6, 2004).
4. The Social Security (Notification of Changes of Circumstances) Regulations 2010 (SI 2010/444) reg.4(4) (April 5, 2010).
5. The Social Security (Electronic Communications) Order 2011 (SI 2011/1498) reg.6 (June 20, 2011).
6. The Social Security (Electronic Communications) (No.2) Order 2011 (SI 2011/2943) reg.3 (January 23, 2012).
7. The Pensions Act 2014 (Consequential, Supplementary and Incidental Amendments) Order 2015 (SI 2015/1985) art.23 (April 6, 2016).

The Social Security (Overpayments and Recovery) Regulations 2013

(SI 2013/384)

GENERAL NOTE

These are the "2013 rules" which apply to: 2.843

- recovery of overpayments of universal credit, new-style contribution-based JSA and new-style contribution-based ESA claimed on or after April 29, 2013; and
- recovery of court costs incurred in recovering overpayments, certain advances of universal credit, hardship payments, financial penalties for benefit offences, and civil penalties.

The rules relating to the recovery of overpayments of other benefits are to be found in the Payments on Account etc Regulations at paras 2.914–2.954 below.

The Secretary of State's policy in relation to matters arising under these regulations (among other matters) can be found in the Benefit Overpayment Recovery Guide. It can be found at *https://www.gov.uk/government/publications/benefit-overpayment-recovery-staff-guide* (Accessed April 24, 2024). As stated in the Introduction to the Guide:

> "The Benefit overpayment recovery guide provides a comprehensive overview of the overpayment recovery policy that applies to overpaid Social Security benefit payments, including any associated Civil Penalties or Administrative Penalties. It is not intended however to provide a definitive statement of law and thus should not be seen to replace formal legal advice where appropriate."

PART 1

General

2.844 1. Citation and commencement
2. Interpretation

PART 2

Recoverability

3. Recoverable amount
4. Persons from whom an overpayment may be recovered
5. Circumstances in which a determination need not be reversed, varied, revised or superseded prior to recovery

PART 3

Prevention of duplication of payments

6. Duplication and prescribed income

PART 4

Calculation of recoverable amount of an overpayment

7. Diminution of capital
8. Sums to be deducted
9. Sums to be deducted: change of dwelling

PART 5

The process of recovery

10. Recovery by deduction from benefits
11. Recovery by deduction from universal credit
12. Recovery by deduction from jobseeker's allowance
13. Recovery by deduction from employment and support allowance
14. Recovery by deduction from state pension credit
15. Restrictions on recovery of rent and consequent notifications
16. Offsetting

PART 6

RECOVERY BY DEDUCTION FROM EARNINGS

Parts 7 and 8 omitted.

SCHEDULE 1

EXEMPTION FOR EXISTING MICRO-BUSINESSES AND NEW BUSINESSES

SCHEDULE 2

AMOUNTS TO BE DEDUCTED BY EMPLOYERS

The Secretary of State for Work and Pensions makes the following Regulations in exercise of the powers conferred by sections 71(4), (6)(a) and (b), (8) and (9A) to (9C), 71ZA, 71ZB(2)(b) to (5), 71ZC(1) to (3), 71ZD, 71ZF 71ZG(5), 71ZH(5), 74(2), 75(4), (5)(a) and (8) to (10), 78(2) and (3C) to (3E), 115B(4A), 115C(5), 115D(5), 189(1), (4) to (6) and 191 of the Social Security Administration Act 1992(**1**) ("the Act") and paragraphs 1(1) and 6(b) of Schedule 6 to the Welfare Reform Act 2012. **2.845**

In accordance with section 173(1)(b) of the Act, the Secretary of State has obtained the agreement of the Social Security Advisory Committee that proposals in respect of these Regulations should not be referred to it.

In relation to provisions in these Regulations relating to housing benefit, in accordance with section 176(1) of the Act, consultation has taken place with organisations appearing to the Secretary of State to be representative of the authorities concerned.

PART 1

GENERAL

IN FORCE FROM APRIL 8, 2013

Citation and commencement

1.—(1) These Regulations may be cited as the Social Security (Overpayments and Recovery) Regulations 2013. **2.846**

(2) The following provisions of these Regulations come into force on 8th April 2013—

(a) this Part;

(b) Part 6 and Schedules 1 and 2;

(c) regulation 31 except paragraphs (2)(b), (d), (e) and (g), (4)(b) and (7)(b);
(d) regulation 33(1), (2)(a) and (c) and (3); and
(e) regulation 34(1), (2)(a) and (c) and (3).

(3) All other provisions of these Regulations come into force on 29th April 2013.

Interpretation

2.847 **2.** In these Regulations—

"the Act" means the Social Security Administration Act 1992;
"the 1995 Act" means the Jobseekers Act 1995;
"the 2007 Act" means the Welfare Reform Act 2007;
"the 2012 Act" means the Welfare Reform Act 2012;
"the UC Regulations" means the Universal Credit Regulations 2013;
"the UC etc. Claims and Payments Regulations" means the Universal Credit, Personal Independence Payment, Jobseeker's Allowance and Employment and Support Allowance (Claims and Payments) Regulations 2013;
"assessment period" has the same meaning as in the UC Regulations;
"claimant" means the person who has claimed the benefit concerned;
"couple" has the same meaning as in Part 1 of the 2012 Act;
"employment and support allowance" means an allowance under Part 1 of the 2007 Act as amended by the provisions of Schedule 3, and Part 1 of Schedule 14, to the 2012 Act that remove references to an income-related allowance;
"housing costs" means any amount included in an award of universal credit in respect of rent payments as defined in paragraph 2 of Schedule 1 to the UC Regulations;
"jobseeker's allowance" means an allowance under the 1995 Act as amended by the provisions of Part 1 of Schedule 14 to the 2012 Act that remove references to an income-based allowance;
"liable person" means the person from whom a recoverable amount is recoverable;
"overpayment" means an amount of—
(a) universal credit, jobseeker's allowance or employment and support allowance which may be recovered by the Secretary of State by virtue of section 71ZB(1) of the Act;
[1 . . .]
"overpayment period" means the period over which an overpayment accrues;
"partner" means, where the person being referred to is a member of a couple, the other member of the couple;
"recoverable amount" is to be construed in accordance with regulation 3;
"universal credit" means universal credit under Part 1 of the 2012 Act.

Amendment

1. The Tax Credits (Exercise of Functions) Order 2014 (SI 2014/3280) art.6 (April 1, 2015).

General Note

Article 5(1) of the Exercise of Functions Order provided "The amount specified in a notice…[i.e a notice issued by HMRC concerning an overpayment of tax credit]...is for the purposes of the 2013 Regulations to be treated as if it were an overpayment as defined in reg.2 of those Regulations". So, despite the amendment noted above, which removed an express reference to tax credits, the DWP retained its power to recover overpayments of tax credit, but by a different legal route.

PART 2

RECOVERABILITY

IN FORCE FROM APRIL 29, 2013

Recoverable amounts

3. (1) In these Regulations, "recoverable amount" means— **2.848**

(a) subject to regulations 7 to 9, the amount of any overpayment; and
(b) any other amount recoverable under any provision of the Act specified in paragraph (2).

(2) Those provisions are—

(a) section 71ZE(3) (costs of court action etc.);
(b) section 71ZG (recovery of payments on account);
(c) section 71ZH (recovery of hardship payments);
(d) section 115B(4)(recovery of penalties imposed as an alternative to prosecution);
(e) section 115C(4) (recovery of civil penalties for incorrect statements); and
(f) section 115D(4) (recovery of civil penalties for failure to disclose information).

Persons from whom an overpayment may be recovered

4. (1) The following paragraphs apply for determining the person from whom an overpayment is recoverable in the circumstances specified in those paragraphs. **2.849**

(2) Where the payee is a person appointed under regulation 57 of the UC etc. Claims and Payments Regulations or a person to whom the Secretary of State has directed that payment be made in accordance with regulation 58 of those Regulations, then the overpayment is recoverable from the claimant in addition to the payee.

(3) Where the payee is a person to whom universal credit, jobseeker's allowance or employment and support allowance has been paid pursuant to Schedule 6 to the UC etc. Claims and Payments Regulations (payments to third parties), then, to the extent that the amount paid does not exceed the amount payable to the payee under that Schedule, the overpayment is recoverable from the claimant instead of the payee.

(4) Paragraphs (5) to (7) apply only in relation to overpayments of housing costs.

(5) Where the Secretary of State is satisfied that an overpayment occurred in consequence of any change of dwelling occupied by the claimant as their home, then if the claimant and the payee are not the same person, the overpayment is recoverable from the claimant in addition to the payee.

(6) Where the Secretary of State is satisfied that an overpayment occurred in consequence of a misrepresentation, or a failure to disclose a material fact (in either case, whether fraudulent or otherwise), by any person ("M"),

then, if M and the payee are not the same person, the overpayment is recoverable from M instead of the payee.

(7) Where the Secretary of State is satisfied that an overpayment occurred for a reason other than that mentioned in paragraph (5) or (6), then, except where paragraph (2) or (8) applies in relation to the overpayment, if the claimant and the payee are not the same person, the overpayment is recoverable from the claimant instead of the payee.

(8) This paragraph applies where the overpayment occurred due to the amount of the payment exceeding the amount of housing costs for which the claimant is liable.

(9) In this regulation, "payee" means the person to whom the overpayment has been paid.

Circumstances in which a determination need not be reversed, varied, revised or superseded prior to recovery

2.850 **5.** Section 71ZB(3) of the Act (recoverability of an overpayment dependent on reversal, variation, revision or supersession) does not apply where the circumstances of the overpayment do not provide a basis for the decision pursuant to which the payment was made to be revised under section 9 of the Social Security Act 1998 or superseded under section 10 of that Act.

PART 3

PREVENTION OF DUPLICATION OF PAYMENTS

IN FORCE FROM APRIL 29, 2013

Duplication and prescribed income

2.851 **6.** (1) The income prescribed for the purpose of section 71ZB(5) of the Act (duplication of payments: universal credit) is any income which falls to be taken into account in accordance with Chapters 2 and 3 of Part 6 of the UC Regulations.

(2) The date prescribed for the payment of income for the purpose of that subsection is—

(a) where the payment of income is made in respect of a specific day or period, that day or the first day of that period;

(b) where the payment of income is not so made, the day or first day of the period to which it is fairly attributable.

PART 4

CALCULATION OF RECOVERABLE AMOUNT OF AN OVERPAYMENT

Diminution of capital

2.852 **7.** (1) Paragraph (2) applies where—

(a) there is an overpayment of universal credit which occurred as a consequence of an error relating to the amount of a person's capital; and

(b) the overpayment period is 3 months or more.

(2) Where this paragraph applies, the Secretary of State must, for the purpose only of calculating the recoverable amount of that overpayment—

(a) at the end of the first 3 months of the overpayment period, treat the amount of that capital as having been reduced by the amount of universal credit overpaid during those 3 months;

(b) at the end of each subsequent period of 3 months, if any, of the overpayment period, treat the amount of that capital as having been further reduced by the amount of universal credit overpaid during the immediately preceding 3 months.

(3) Capital is not to be treated as reduced over any period other than 3 months in any circumstances other than those for which paragraph (2) provides.

Sums to be deducted

8. (1) In calculating the recoverable amount of an overpayment of jobseeker's allowance or employment and support allowance, the Secretary of State must deduct the amounts specified in paragraphs (2) and (3). 2.853

(2) Any amount which has been offset under regulation 16.

(3) Any additional amount of universal credit which was not payable to the claimant or their partner under the original or any other determination but which should have been determined to be payable in respect of all or part of the overpayment period to the claimant, or to the claimant and their partner jointly—

(a) on the basis of the claim for universal credit as presented to the Secretary of State;

(b) on the basis of that claim as it would have appeared if any change of circumstances, except a change of the dwelling which the claimant occupies as their home, had been notified at the time that change occurred;

(c) where the overpayment arose by virtue of a misrepresentation or a failure to disclose a material fact, on the basis that that misrepresentation or failure had been remedied prior to the award being made; or

(d) where the overpayment arose by virtue of an error made by, or on behalf of, the Secretary of State, on the basis that that error had not been made.

Sums to be deducted: change of dwelling

9. (1) This regulation applies where an overpayment of housing costs has occurred in the following circumstances— 2.854

(a) the claimant has moved from the dwelling previously occupied as their home ("dwelling A") to another dwelling which they occupy as their home ("dwelling B");

(b) they have been awarded housing costs in respect of dwelling A to which they are not entitled because they are no longer occupying or treated as occupying dwelling A as their home; and

(c) housing costs are payable to the same person in respect of the claimant's occupation of dwelling B as it was paid to in respect of dwelling A.

(2) In calculating the recoverable amount of the overpayment, the Secretary of State may, at his or her discretion, deduct an amount equal to the claimant's entitlement to housing costs for the assessment period in respect of dwelling B for the number of assessment periods equal to the number of assessment periods during which the claimant was overpaid housing costs in respect of dwelling A.

(3) Where a sum has been deducted under paragraph (2), an equivalent sum is to be treated as having been paid in respect of the claimant's entitlement to housing costs in respect of dwelling B for the number of assessment periods equal to the number of assessment periods during which the claimant was overpaid housing costs in respect of dwelling A.

PART 5

THE PROCESS OF RECOVERY

IN FORCE FROM APRIL 29, 2013

Recovery by deduction from benefits

2.855 **10.** (1) Subject to regulations 11 to 14, the Secretary of State may recover a recoverable amount from a liable person by deduction from the benefits specified in paragraph (2) which are payable to them.

(2) Those benefits are—

(a) benefits under Parts 2 to 5 of the Social Security Contributions and Benefits Act 1992;

(b) universal credit;

(c) jobseeker's allowance;

(d) employment and support allowance;

(e) state pension credit payable under the State Pension Credit Act 2002; [1 . . .]

(f) personal independence payment payable under Part 4 of the 2012 Act. [1 ; and]

[1 (g) a state pension under Part 1 of the Pensions Act 2014.]

AMENDMENT

1. The Pensions Act 2014 (Consequential, Supplementary and Incidental Amendments) Order 2015 (SI 2015/1985) art.42 (April 6, 2016).

Recovery by deduction from universal credit

2.856 **11.** (1) The following paragraphs apply where the recoverable amount falls to be recovered by deduction from universal credit payable to the liable person.

(2) Subject to paragraphs (5) to (9), regulation 10 is to apply to the amount of universal credit to which the liable person is presently entitled to the extent that there may be recovered in any one assessment period—

(a) in a case to which paragraph (3) applies, an amount equivalent to not more than [1 40 per cent.] of the appropriate universal credit standard allowance;

(b) in a case to which paragraph (4) applies but paragraph (3) does not apply, an amount equivalent to not more than [1 25 per cent.] of that allowance; and

(c) in any other case, an amount equivalent to not more than [1 15 per cent.] of that allowance.

(3) This paragraph applies where deductions from universal credit are made to recover from the liable person—

(a) the whole or part of an overpayment in respect of which the liable person has—

(i) been found guilty of an offence whether under statute or otherwise;

(ii) made an admission after caution of deception or fraud for the purpose of obtaining benefit under the Act or a tax credit under the Tax Credits Act 2002; or

(iii) agreed to pay a penalty under section 115A of the Act (penalty as an alternative to prosecution) and the agreement has not been withdrawn; or

(b) a payment which is recoverable by virtue of section 71ZH of the Act (hardship payments).

(4) This paragraph applies where amounts are deducted from earned income in an award of universal credit by virtue of regulation 22(1)(b) of the UC Regulations (adjustment to take account of income and amount of earnings disregarded).

(5) Paragraph (2) is subject to paragraphs 4 and 5 of Schedule 6 to the UC etc. Claims and Payments Regulations (payments to third parties).

[[1] (6) For the purpose of paragraph (2), where the relevant percentage of the appropriate universal credit standard allowance results in a fraction of a penny, that fraction is to be disregarded if it is less than half a penny and otherwise it is to be treated as a penny.]

(7) No deduction made under paragraph (2) is to be applied so as to reduce the universal credit in respect of an assessment period to less than 1 penny.

(8) The limitations in paragraph (2) do not apply where the deduction falls to be made from any payment of arrears of universal credit other than any arrears caused by the operation of regulation 46 of the Universal Credit, Personal Independence Payment, Jobseeker's Allowance and Employment and Support Allowance (Decisions and Appeals) Regulations 2013 (making of payments which have been suspended).

(9) The limitations in paragraph (2) do not apply where—

(a) the recoverable amount is an overpayment of housing costs; and

(b) the person from whom that amount falls to be recovered is not the claimant.

(10) In this regulation and in regulation 14, "admission after caution" means—

(a) in England and Wales, an admission after a caution has been administered in accordance with a Code issued under the Police and Criminal Evidence Act 1984;

(b) in Scotland, admission after a caution has been administered, such admission being duly witnessed by two persons.

(11) In paragraph (2), "the appropriate universal credit standard allowance" means the appropriate universal credit standard allowance included in the award of universal credit made to the liable person, or to the liable person and their partner as joint claimants, by virtue of regulation 36 of the UC Regulations.

AMENDMENT

1. The Social Security (Miscellaneous Amendments) (No.2) Regulations 2013 (SI 2013/1508) reg.5 (July 29, 2013).

Recovery by deduction from jobseeker's allowance

2.857 **12.** (1) The following paragraphs apply where the recoverable amount falls to be recovered by deduction from jobseeker's allowance payable to the liable person.

(2) Subject to paragraphs (3) and (4), regulation 10 is to apply to the amount of a jobseeker's allowance to which the liable person is presently entitled to the extent that there may be recovered in respect of any benefit week an amount equivalent to 40 per cent. of the age-related amount applicable to the liable person as specified in regulation 49 of the Jobseeker's Allowance Regulations 2013.

(3) Paragraph (2) is subject to paragraphs 4 and 5 of Schedule 6 to the UC etc. Claims and Payments Regulations (payments to third parties).

(4) Where the amount deductible under paragraph (2) is not a multiple of five pence, it is to be rounded up to the next higher such multiple.

(5) In paragraph (2), "benefit week" has the same meaning as in regulation 2(1) of the Jobseeker's Allowance Regulations 2013.

Recovery by deduction from employment and support allowance

2.858 **13.** (1) The following paragraphs apply where the recoverable amount falls to be recovered by deduction from employment and support allowance payable to the liable person.

(2) Subject to paragraphs (3) and (4), regulation 10 is to apply to the amount of an employment and support allowance to which the liable person is presently entitled to the extent that there may be recovered in respect of any one benefit week an amount equivalent to 40 per cent. of the age-related amount applicable to the liable person as specified in regulation 62(1)(b) of the Employment and Support Allowance Regulations 2013.

(3) Paragraph (2) is subject to paragraphs 4 and 5 of Schedule 6 to the UC etc. Claims and Payments Regulations (payments to third parties).

(4) Where the amount deductible under paragraph (2) is not a multiple of five pence, it is to be rounded up to the next higher such multiple.

(5) In paragraph (2), "benefit week" has the same meaning as in regulation 2 of the Employment and Support Allowance Regulations 2013.

Recovery by deduction from state pension credit

2.859 **14.** (1) The following paragraphs apply where the recoverable amount falls to be recovered by deduction from state pension credit payable to the liable person.

(2) Subject to paragraphs (4) and (5), regulation 10 is to apply to the amount of state pension credit to which the liable person is presently entitled to the extent that there may be recovered in any one benefit week—

(a) in a case to which paragraph (3) applies, an amount equivalent to not more than 5 times 5 per cent. of the standard allowance for a single person aged 25 or over under regulation 36 of the UC Regulations; and

(b) in any other case, an amount equivalent to not more than 3 times 5 per cent. of that allowance.

(3) This paragraph applies where deductions from state pension credit are made to recover from the liable person—

(a) the whole or part of an overpayment in respect of which the liable person has—

(i) been found guilty of an offence whether under statute or otherwise;
(ii) made an admission after caution of deception or fraud for the purpose of obtaining universal credit, jobseeker's allowance or employment and support allowance; or
(iii) agreed to pay a penalty under section 115A of the Act (penalty as an alternative to prosecution) and the agreement has not been withdrawn; or

(b) a payment which is recoverable by virtue of section 71ZH of the Act (hardship payments).

(4) Where the amount deductible under paragraph (2) is not a multiple of five pence, it is to be rounded up to the next higher such multiple.

(5) No deduction made under paragraph (2) is to be applied so as to reduce the state pension credit in respect of a benefit week to less than 10 pence.

(6) In this regulation, "benefit week" has the same meaning as in regulation 2(1) of the State Pension Credit Regulations 2002.

Restrictions on recovery of rent and consequent notifications

15. (1) Paragraph (2) applies where, pursuant to section 71ZC(2)(b) of the Act, an amount of housing costs has been, or falls to be, recovered by deduction from benefit paid to a person ("the landlord") to discharge (in whole or in part) an obligation owed to the landlord by the person on whose behalf the recoverable amount was paid ("the tenant"). **2.860**

(2) Where, in respect of the overpayment of that amount, the landlord has—

(a) been found guilty of an offence whether under statute or otherwise; or
(b) agreed to pay a penalty under section 115A of the Act (penalty as an alternative to prosecution) and the agreement has not been withdrawn,

that obligation is to be taken to be discharged by the amount of the deduction.

(3) In any case to which paragraph (2) applies or will apply when recovery is made, the Secretary of State must notify both the landlord and the tenant—

(a) that the overpayment that it has recovered or that the Secretary of State has determined to recover ("that sum") is, or will be, one to which paragraph (2) applies; and
(b) that the landlord has no right in relation to that sum against the tenant, and that the tenant's obligation to the landlord is to be taken to be discharged by the amount so recovered.

Offsetting

16. (1) Paragraph (2) applies where a person has been paid a sum of benefit under a decision ("the original decision") which is subsequently— **2.861**

(a) revised or further revised;
(b) superseded or further superseded; or
(c) set aside on an appeal.

(2) Any universal credit, jobseeker's allowance or employment and support allowance paid in respect of a period covered by the subsequent decision is to be offset against arrears of entitlement to benefit under that decision and, except to the extent that the universal credit, jobseeker's

allowance or employment and support allowance exceeds the arrears, is to be treated as properly paid on account of them.

(3) Where an amount has been deducted under regulation 8 or 9 (sums to be deducted in calculating recoverable overpayments), an equivalent sum is to be offset against any arrears of entitlement under the subsequent decision except to the extent that the sum exceeds the arrears and is to be treated as properly paid on account of them.

(4) No amount may be offset under paragraph (2) which is an overpayment.

(5) In this regulation, "subsequent decision" means the decision referred to in paragraph (1)(a), (b) or (c) which was taken in relation to the original decision.

PART 6

RECOVERY BY DEDUCTION FROM EARNINGS

IN FORCE FROM APRIL 8, 2013

Interpretation of Part 6

2.862 17.—(1) In this Part—

"appropriate authority", in relation to any recoverable amount, means—

(a) the Secretary of State; or

(b) an authority administering housing benefit if the recoverable amount is recoverable by that authority under section 115B(4)(a), 115C or 115D of the Act,

and where a notice has been issued, "the appropriate authority" means the appropriate authority which issued the notice;

"notice" means a notice issued by an appropriate authority requiring an employer to make deductions from earnings to be paid by the employer to a liable person employed by them and to pay corresponding amounts to that appropriate authority in respect of the recovery of a recoverable amount from the liable person;

"pay-day" in relation to a liable person means an occasion on which earnings are paid to them or the day on which such earnings would normally fall to be paid;

"protected earnings proportion", in relation to a deduction by an employer from a liable person's net earnings, is 60 per cent. of the liable person's net earnings during the period to which the deduction relates, as calculated by the liable person's employer on the relevant pay-day.

(2) In this Part, subject to paragraph (3), "earnings" means any sums payable to a person—

(a) by way of wages or salary (including any fees, bonus, commission, overtime pay or other emoluments payable in addition to wages or salary payable under a contract of service);

(b) by way of pension which is paid with wages or salary (including an annuity in respect of past service, whether or not rendered to the person paying the annuity, and including periodical payments by way of compensation for the loss, abolition or relinquishment, or diminution in the emoluments, of any office or employment); or

(c) by way of statutory sick pay.

(3) "Earnings" does not include—

(a) sums payable by any public department of the Government of Northern Ireland or of a territory outside the United Kingdom;
(b) pay or allowances payable to the liable person as a member of Her Majesty's forces other than pay or allowances payable by their employer to them as a special member of a reserve force (within the meaning of the Reserve Forces Act 1996);
(c) other pensions, allowances or benefit payable under any enactment relating to social security;
(d) pension or allowances payable in respect of disablement or disability;
(e) guaranteed minimum pension within the meaning of the Pension Schemes Act 1993;
(f) working tax credit payable under section 10 of the Tax Credits Act 2002;
(g) sums paid to reimburse expenses wholly and necessarily incurred in the course of the employment.

(4) "Net earnings" means the residue of earnings after deduction of—
(a) income tax;
(b) primary Class I contributions under Part 1 of the Social Security Contributions and Benefits Act 1992;
(c) amounts deductible by way of contributions to a superannuation scheme which provides for the payment of annuities or lump sums—
  (i) to the employee on retirement at a specified age or on becoming incapacitated at some earlier age; or
  (ii) on the employee's death or otherwise, to their personal representative, widow, surviving civil partner, relatives or dependants.

(5) Where these Regulations refer to a notice or notification being given or sent, if sent by post to the last known address of the recipient, it is to be treated as having been given or sent on the day on which it is posted.

Exemption from this Part

18. This Part does not impose any obligation on an employer who is carrying on a business which is— 2.863
(a) a new business; or
(b) an existing micro-business during the exemption period,
and Schedule 1 has effect for the purpose of this regulation.

Notices

19.—(1) A notice must be given or sent to— 2.864
(a) the liable person; and
(b) any employer of the liable person who is to make deductions from the liable person's earnings in accordance with the notice.

(2) A notice must specify—
(a) the full name and address of the liable person;
(b) the name of the employer at whom the notice is directed;
(c) where known, the liable person's place of work, the nature of their work and any staff number, pay roll number or similar identifying number;
(d) the liable person's national insurance number;
[[1] (e) the deduction or rate of deduction to be made in accordance with regulation 20.]
(f) the protected earnings proportion;

(g) the address to which amounts deducted from earnings are to be sent if paid by cheque; and
(h) details of the account into which such amounts are to be transferred if paid by direct credit transfer.

(3) The notice has effect from the next pay-day which falls a minimum of 22 days after the day on which it is given or sent.

(4) References in paragraphs (1) to (3) to a notice include references to a notice as varied in accordance with regulation 25(1).

AMENDMENT

1. The Social Security (Overpayments and Recovery) Amendment Regulations 2015 (SI 2015/499) reg.4 (April 6, 2015).

Amount to be deducted by employer

2.865 **20.**—(1) This regulation applies where an employer has received from an appropriate authority a notice in respect of a liable person in their employment.

(2) Subject to the following provisions of this regulation, the employer must, each pay-day, make a deduction in accordance with paragraph (3) [1 or (38)] from the net earnings which it would otherwise pay to the liable person on that pay-day.

(3) [1 Except where paragraph (3B) applies, the amount to be deducted is—]

(a) where the liable person's earnings are payable weekly, the percentage of their earnings specified in column 2 of Table A in Schedule 2 opposite the band in column 1 of that Table within which their net earnings payable on their pay-day fall;
(b) where the liable person's earnings are payable monthly, the percentage of their earnings specified in column 2 of Table B in that Schedule opposite the band in column 1 of that Table within which their net earnings payable on their pay-day fall; or
(c) a lower amount calculated in the manner specified by the appropriate authority in the notice.

[1 (3A) Paragraph (3B) applies where deductions from earnings are made to recover from the liable person the whole or part of an overpayment in respect of which the liable person has been found guilty of an offence whether under statute or otherwise.

(3B) Where this paragraph applies, the amount to be deducted by the employer is—

(a) where the liable person's earnings are payable weekly, the percentage of their earnings specified in column 2 of Table C in Schedule 2 opposite the band in column 1 of that Table within which their net earnings payable on their pay-day fall;
(b) where the liable person's earnings are payable monthly, the percentage of their earnings specified in column 2 of Table D in Schedule 2 opposite the band in column 1 of that Table within which their net earnings payable on their pay-day fall; or
(c) a lower amount calculated in the manner specified by the appropriate authority in the notice.]

(4) Where any amount calculated under paragraph (3) [1 or (3B)] includes a fraction of a penny, it is to be rounded to the nearest whole penny

with a result of exactly half a penny being rounded down to the nearest whole penny below.

[1 (5) The employer must continue to make deductions in accordance with paragraph (3) or (3B) unless and until—

(a) they are notified by the appropriate authority that the notice—
   (i) has been varied in accordance with regulation 2
   (ii) has been discharged under regulation 26; or
   (iii) has lapsed under regulation 27; or
(b) the employer considers that, as a result of deductions under this regulation, the balance of the recoverable amount which falls to be recovered from the liable person is nil.]

(6) Where, on any pay-day ("the relevant pay-day"), the employer fails to deduct an amount under paragraph (3) [1 or (3B)] or deducts an amount less than the amount specified in that paragraph, the employer must, on the next available pay-day or pay-days, first deduct the amount required to be deducted under paragraph (3) [1 or (3B)] for that pay-day and then the difference between the amount, if any, which was deducted on the relevant pay-day and the amount which should have been deducted on that pay-day.

(7) Where a deduction made in accordance with paragraph (3) [1, or (3B)] or (6) would reduce the amount paid to the liable person below the protected earnings proportion, the employer must deduct only such amount as will result in the employer paying the liable person an amount equal to the protected earnings proportion.

(8) Where, on any pay-day ("the relevant pay-day"), the employer deducts more than the amount required to be deducted under paragraph (3), the employer must, on the next available pay-day or pay-days, deduct only the amount required to be deducted under paragraph (3) [1 or (3B)] less the difference between the amount which was deducted on the relevant pay-day and the amount which should have been deducted on that pay-day.

(9) Where, on any pay-day, an employer makes a deduction from the earnings of a liable person in accordance with the notice, they may also deduct an additional amount not exceeding £1 in respect of their administrative costs and such deduction for administrative costs may reduce the amount which the employer pays to the liable person on that pay-day below the protected earnings proportion.

AMENDMENT

1. The Social Security (Overpayments and Recovery) Amendment Regulations 2015 (SI 2015/499) reg.5 (April 6, 2015).

Employer to notify liable person of deduction

21.—[1 (1) An employer making a deduction from earnings for the purposes of these Regulations must notify the liable person in writing of the amount of the deduction including any amount deducted for administrative costs under regulation 20(9).] 2.866

(2) Such notification must be given or sent not later than the pay-day on which the deduction is made or, where that is impracticable, not later than the following pay-day.

[1 (3) An employer must, within 28 days of receiving a written request from the liable person, provide the liable person with an explanation in writing of how the first amount referred to in paragraph (1) was calculated.]

AMENDMENT

1. The Social Security (Overpayments and Recovery) Amendment Regulations 2015 (SI 2015/499) reg.6 (April 6, 2015).

Payment by employer to the appropriate authority

2.867 **22.**—(1) Amounts deducted by an employer pursuant to regulation 20 (other than any administrative costs deducted under paragraph (9) of that regulation) must be paid by the employer to the appropriate authority by the 19th day of the month following the month in which the deduction is made.

(2) Such payment may be made—

(a) by cheque;

(b) by direct credit transfer; or

(c) by such other method as the appropriate authority may permit.

(3) The employer must keep a record of every amount paid to an appropriate authority pursuant to paragraph (1) and of the employee in respect of whom each such amount was paid.

Information to be provided by the liable person

2.868 **23.**—[1 (1) An employer making a deduction from earnings for the purposes of these Regulations must notify the liable person in writing of the amount of the deduction including any amount deducted for administrative costs under regulation 20(9).]

(2) A notification under paragraph (1)(b) must include the following details—

(a) the name and address of their employer or employers if more than one;

(b) the amount of their earnings or expected earnings; and

(c) their place of work, nature of their work and any staff number, pay roll number or similar identifying number.

Duty of employers and others to notify appropriate authority

2.869 **24.**—(1) In this regulation, "P" means the liable person.

(2) Where a notice is given or sent to a person who is believed to be an employer of P but P is not in that person's employment, that person must notify the appropriate authority of that fact in writing, at the address specified in the notice, within 10 days after the day on which the notice is given or sent.

(3) In paragraphs (4) and (5), "E" means an employer of P.

(4) Where a notice is given or sent to E but E believes that there is no obligation on them under this Part by virtue of regulation 18 and Schedule 1, E must notify the appropriate authority of that fact in writing, at the address specified in the notice, within 10 days after the day on which the notice is given or sent.

(5) Where E is required to make deductions under a notice and P ceases to be in their employment, E must notify the appropriate authority of that fact in writing, at the address specified in the notice, within 10 days after the day on which P ceased to be in their employment.

Power to vary notices

25.—(1) The appropriate authority may vary a notice so as to— 2.870

(a) decrease any amount to be deducted under regulation 20; or

(b) with the agreement of the liable person, increase any such amount but only to the extent that such deductions will result in the employer paying the liable person an amount more than, or equal to, the protected earnings proportion.

(2) Where a notice has been varied and a copy of the notice as varied has been given or sent in accordance with regulation 19(1) and (4), any employer who is liable to make deductions under the notice must comply with the notice as varied from the day it takes effect by virtue of regulation 19(3).

Discharge of notices

26.—(1) The appropriate authority must discharge a notice where the recoverable amount is no longer outstanding. 2.871

(2) The appropriate authority may discharge a notice where—

(a) it appears to them to be defective;

(b) it appears to them that it is ineffective or that some other method of recovering the recoverable amount would be more effective; or

(c) the liable person agrees with the appropriate authority to pay the recoverable amount by another method.

(3) A notice may be considered to be defective for the purpose of paragraph (2)(a) where it does not comply with the requirements of regulation 19(2) and such failure to comply has made it impracticable for an employer to comply with their obligations under these Regulations.

(4) Notification of the discharge of the notice under paragraph (1) or (2) must be given or sent to the liable person and the employer from whom deductions from the liable person's earnings were being made.

(5) Where a notice is discharged by virtue of paragraph (2)(b) or (c), regulation 22 nevertheless applies in respect of any deductions made in respect of the employment but not yet paid to the appropriate authority.

Lapse of notices

27.—(1) Where a liable person in respect of whom deductions are being made in accordance with a notice ceases to be in the employment of an employer, subject to paragraph (2), the notice is to lapse immediately after the pay-day coinciding with, or, if none, the pay-day following, the termination of the employment. 2.872

(2) Where a notice lapses by virtue of paragraph (1), regulation 22 nevertheless applies in respect of any deductions made or to be made in respect of the employment but not yet paid to the appropriate authority.

Crown employment

28. Where a liable person is in the employment of the Crown and a notice is to be sent in respect of that person, then for the purposes of these Regulations— 2.873

(a) the chief officer for the time being of the Department, office or other body in which the liable person is employed is to be treated as having the liable person in their employment (any transfer of the liable person from one Department, office or body to another being treated as a change of employment); and

(b) any earnings paid by the Crown or a minister of the Crown, or out of the public revenue of the United Kingdom, is to be treated as paid by that chief officer.

Priority as between notices and orders requiring deduction from earnings

2.874 **29.**—(1) In this regulation—

"child support order" means a deduction from earnings order under Part 3 of the Child Support (Collection and Enforcement) Regulations 1992(26);

"other deduction order" means an order, other than a child support order, under any other enactment relating to England and Wales which requires deduction from a person's earnings.

(2) Paragraphs (3) to (10) have effect subject to paragraph (11).

(3) Paragraph (4) applies where an employer would otherwise be obliged, on any pay-day, to make deductions from the earnings which it would otherwise pay to the liable person on that pay-day under two or more notices.

[1 (4) Where this paragraph applies, the employer must make deductions under any later notice as if the earnings to which it relates were the residue of the liable person's earnings after the making of any deduction to comply with any earlier notice.]

(5) Paragraph (6) applies where an employer would otherwise be obliged, on any pay-day, to make deductions from the earnings which it would otherwise pay to the liable person on that pay-day, under one or more notices and one or more child support orders.

(6) Where this paragraph applies, the employer must first make deductions under the child support order or orders and then make deductions under the notice or notices.

(7) In England and Wales, paragraph (8) applies where an employer would otherwise be obliged, on any pay-day, to make deductions from the earnings which it would otherwise pay to the liable person on that pay-day, under one or more notices and one or more other deduction orders.

(8) Where this paragraph applies, the employer must—

(a) in a case where there is at least one other deduction order in effect on the first pay-day in respect of which deductions would otherwise be made under the notice, first make deductions under the other deduction order or orders and then under any notice or notices;

(b) in any other case, make deductions under the other deduction order and the notices according to the respective dates on which they were made, disregarding any later notice or order until deductions have been made under the earlier one.

(9) In Scotland, paragraph (10) applies where an employer would otherwise be obliged, on any pay-day, to make deductions from the earnings which it would otherwise pay to the liable person on that pay-day, under one or more notices and one or more diligences against earnings.

(10) Where this paragraph applies, the employer must—

(a) in a case where there is a diligence against earnings in effect on the first pay-day in respect of which deductions would otherwise be made under the notice, first make deductions under any diligence against earnings and then under any notice;

(b) in any other case, make deductions under any notice and then under any diligence against earnings.

(11) An employer may only make deductions under paragraph (4), (6), (8) or (10) up to the extent that such deductions will result in the employer paying the liable person an amount equal to or greater than the protected earnings proportion.

AMENDMENT

1. The Social Security (Overpayments and Recovery) Amendment Regulations 2015 (SI 2015/499) reg.7 (April 6, 2015).

Offences

30. A person who fails to comply with any of the following provisions of this Part is guilty of an offence punishable on summary conviction by a fine not exceeding level 3 on the standard scale— **2.875**

(a) regulation 20(2);
(b) regulation 22(1);
(c) regulation 22(3);
(d) regulation 23.

Regulation 18

SCHEDULE 1

EXEMPTION FOR EXISTING MICRO-BUSINESSES AND NEW BUSINESSES

Micro-businesses

1. A micro-business is a business that has fewer than 10 employees (see paragraphs 6 to 8). **2.876**

Existing micro-businesses

2. An existing micro-business is a business that was a micro-business immediately before 8th April 2013. **2.877**

New businesses

3.—(1) A new business is a business which a person, or a number of persons, ("P") begins to carry on during the period beginning on 8th April 2013 and ending on 31st March 2014. **2.878**

(2) But a business is not a new business if—

(a) P has, at any time during the period of 6 months ending immediately before the date on which P begins to carry on the business, carried on another business consisting of the activities of which the business consists (or most of them); or

(b) P carries on the business as a result of a transfer (within the meaning of sub-paragraph (3)).

(3) P carries on a business as a result of a transfer if P begins to carry on the business on another person ceasing to carry on the activities of which it consists (or most of them) in consequence of arrangements involving P and the other person.

(4) For this purpose, P is to be taken to begin to carry on a business on another person ceasing to carry on such activities if—

(a) P begins to carry on the business otherwise than in partnership on such activities ceasing to be carried on by persons in partnership; or

(b) P is a number of persons in partnership who begin to carry on the business on such activities ceasing to be carried on—

(i) by a person, or a number of persons, otherwise than in partnership;

(ii) by persons in partnership who do not consist only of all the persons who constitute P; or

(iii) partly as mentioned in paragraph (i) and partly as mentioned in paragraph (ii).

(5) P is not to be regarded as beginning to carry on a business for the purposes of sub-paragraph (1) if—

(a) before P begins to carry on the business, P is a party to arrangements under which P may (at any time during the period beginning on 8th April 2013 and ending on 31st March 2014) carry on, as part of the business, activities carried on by any other person; and

(b) the business would have been prevented by sub-paragraph (2)(b) from being a new business if—

(i) P had begun to carry on the activities when beginning to carry on the business; and

(ii) the other person had at that time ceased to carry them on.

(6) "Arrangements" includes an agreement, understanding, scheme, transaction or series of transactions (whether or not legally enforceable).

The exemption period: existing micro-businesses

2.879 4.—(1) This paragraph defines the exemption period in relation to an existing micro-business.

(2) The exemption period starts on 8th April 2013 and ends on the day after a grace period in relation to the business ends, if the grace period is one in which the business grows (see paragraphs 5 and 6).

(3) The following are grace periods in relation to a business for the purposes of this paragraph—

(a) the 6-month period that starts with the first day after 8th April 2013 on which the business has 10 or more employees;

(b) the 6-month period that starts after the end of a grace period (the "earlier grace period") that is not one in which the business grows, in accordance with sub-paragraph (4) or (5).

(4) If the business has 10 or more employees on the day after the end of the earlier grace period, the next grace period starts on that day.

(5) If the business has fewer than 10 employees on that day, the next grace period starts on the next day on which the business has 10 or more employees.

Grace periods in which business grows

2.880 5.—(1) For the purposes of this Schedule, a grace period is one in which a business grows if A is greater than B, where—

(a) A is the number of days in the grace period when the business has 10 or more employees; and

(b) B is the number of days in the grace period when the business has fewer than 10 employees.

Number of employees of a business

6. For the purposes of this Schedule, the number of employees of a business is calculated as follows— 2.881

TH/37.5

where TH is the total number of hours per week for which all the employees of the business are contracted to work.

Employees of a business

7. For the purposes of this Schedule, the employees of a business are the persons who are employed for the purposes of the business in connection with any of the activities of which the business consists. 2.882

Employees

8.—(1) In this Schedule, "employee" means an individual who has entered into, or works under, a contract of employment. 2.883

(2) In sub-paragraph (1) "contract of employment" means a contract of service, whether express or implied, and (if it is express) whether oral or in writing.

Franchises

9. For the purposes of this Schedule, a business that is carried on pursuant to a franchise agreement is treated as part of the business of the franchisor (and not as a separate business carried on by the franchisee). 2.884

Regulation 20(2) [1 and (3B)]

SCHEDULE 2

AMOUNTS TO BE DEDUCTED BY EMPLOYERS

TABLE A: [1 CASES WHERE REGULATION 20(3) APPLIES]

WHERE EARNINGS ARE PAID WEEKLY 2.885

AMOUNT OF NET EARNINGS	DEDUCTION (PER CENT. OF NET EARNINGS)
[1 £100 or less]	Nil
Exceeding £100 but not exceeding £160	3
Exceeding £160 but not exceeding £220	5
Exceeding £220 but not exceeding £270	7
Exceeding £270 but not exceeding £375	11
Exceeding £375 but not exceeding £520	15
Exceeding £520	20

TABLE B: [1 CASES WHERE REGULATION 20(3B) APPLIES]

2.886 **WHERE EARNINGS ARE PAID MONTHLY**

AMOUNT OF NET EARNINGS	DEDUCTION (PER CENT. OF NET EARNINGS)
[1 £430 or less]	Nil
Exceeding £430 but not exceeding £690	3
Exceeding £690 but not exceeding £950	5
Exceeding £950 but not exceeding £1,160	7
Exceeding £1,160 but not exceeding £1,615	11
Exceeding £1,615 but not exceeding £2,240	15
Exceeding £2,240	20

[1 TABLE C: CASES WHERE REGULATION 20(3B) APPLIES

2.887 **WHERE EARNINGS ARE PAID WEEKLY**

AMOUNT OF NET EARNINGS	DEDUCTION (PER CENT. OF NET EARNINGS)
£100 or less	5
Exceeding £100 but not exceeding £160	6
Exceeding £160 but not exceeding £220	10
Exceeding £220 but not exceeding £270	14
Exceeding £270 but not exceeding £375	22
Exceeding £375 but not exceeding £520	30
Exceeding £520	40

TABLE D: CASES WHERE REGULATION 20(3B) APPLIES

2.888 **WHERE EARNINGS ARE PAID WEEKLY**

AMOUNT OF NET EARNINGS	DEDUCTION (PER CENT. OF NET EARNINGS)
£430 or less	5
Exceeding £430 but not exceeding £690	6
Exceeding £690 but not exceeding £950	10
Exceeding £950 but not exceeding £1,160	14

AMOUNT OF NET EARNINGS	DEDUCTION (PER CENT. OF NET EARNINGS)
Exceeding £1,160 but not exceeding £1,615	22
Exceeding £1,615 but not exceeding £2,240	30
Exceeding £2,240	40]

AMENDMENT

1. The Social Security (Overpayments and Recovery) Amendment Regulations 2015 (SI 2015/499) reg.8 (April 6, 2015).

The Social Security (Payments on Account, Overpayments and Recovery) Regulations 1988

(SI 1988/664)

GENERAL NOTE

These regulations relate to "old style" recovery of overpayments. Recovery of overpayments of universal credit, contribution-based JSA, and contribution-based ESA claimed on or after April 29, 2013 (together with certain court costs) are recoverable under the Social Security (Overpayments and Recovery) Regulations 2013 (SI 2013/384) set out at 2.869–2.914 above. Care should be taken to apply the relevant set of regulations to any overpayment in issue. **2.889**

The Secretary of State's policy in relation to maters arising under these regulations (among other matters) can be found in the Benefit Overpayment Recovery Guide, significantly amended with effect from February 9, 2022 and further amended from time to time. It can be found at *https://www.gov.uk/government/publications/benefit-overpayment-recovery-staff-guide* (accessed April 24, 2024). As stated in the Introduction to the Guide:

> "The Benefit overpayment recovery guide provides a comprehensive overview of the overpayment recovery policy that applies to overpaid Social Security benefit payments, including any associated Civil Penalties or Administrative Penalties. It is not intended however to provide a definitive statement of law and thus should not be seen to replace formal legal advice where appropriate."

ARRANGEMENT OF REGULATIONS

PART I

GENERAL

PART II

INTERIM PAYMENTS

PART III

OFFSETTING

PART IV

PREVENTION OF DUPLICATION OF PAYMENTS

PART V

DIRECT CREDIT TRANSFER OVERPAYMENTS

PART VI

REVISION OF DETERMINATION AND CALCULATION OF AMOUNT RECOVERABLE

PART VII

THE PROCESS OF RECOVERY

PART VIII

RECOVERY BY DEDUCTIONS FROM EARNINGS FOLLOWING TRADE DISPUTE

Whereas a draft of the following Regulations was laid before Parliament in accordance with the provisions of section 83(3)(b) of the Social Security Act 1986 and approved by resolution of each House of Parliament.

Now, therefore, the Secretary of State for Social Services, in exercise of the powers conferred upon him by sections 23(8), 27, 51(1)(t) and (u), 53, 83(1), 84(1) and 89 of that Act and all other powers enabling him in that behalf, by this instrument, which contains only regulations made under the sections of the Social Security Act 1986 specified above and provisions consequential on those sections and which is made before the end of a period of 12 months from the commencement of those sections, makes the following Regulations:

PART I

GENERAL

Citation, commencement and interpretation

1.—(1) These regulations may be cited as the Social Security (Payments on account, Overpayments and Recovery) Regulations 1988 and shall come into force on 6th April 1988. **2.891**

(2) In these Regulations, unless the context otherwise requires—

[[13] "the 1995 Act" means the Jobseekers Act 1995;

"the 2007 Act" means the Welfare Reform Act 2007;]

[[13] "the 2012 Act" means the Welfare Reform Act 2012;]

"the Act" means the Social Security Act 1986;

[[10] "the Administration Act" means the Social Security Administration Act 1992;]

[[5] "adjudicating authority" means, as the case may require, the Secretary of State, [[12] the First-tier Tribunal or the Upper Tribunal;]]

"benefit" means [9 a jobseeker's allowance, state pension credit [13 personal independence payment,] [11 , an employment and support allowance] and] any benefit under the Social Security Act 1975 [SSCBA, Parts II to V], [14 , a state pension under Part 1 of the Pensions Act 2014] child benefit, family credit, income support and [1any social fund payment under sections 32(2)(a) and 32(2A) of the Act [SSCBA, section 138(1)(a) and (2)] [3and any incapacity benefit under sections 30A(1) and (5) of the Contributions and Benefits Act]];

[15 . . .]

"bereavement payment" means the sum specified in Part II of Schedule 4 to the Contributions and Benefits Act and referred to in section 36 of that Act;]

[6"the Board" means the Commissioners of Inland Revenue]

"child benefit" means benefit under Part I of the Child Benefit Act 1975 [SSCBA, Part IX];

"the Claims and Payments Regulations" means the Social Security (Claims and Payments) Regulations 1987;

[3"the Contributions and Benefits Act" means the Social Security Contributions and Benefits Act 1992;]

[2"disability living allowance" means a disability living allowance under section 37ZA of the Social Security Act 1975 [SSCBA, s.71];

[7 "disabled person's tax credit" means a disabled person's tax credit under section 129 of the Contributions and Benefits Act and, in relation to things done, or falling to be done, prior to 5th October 1999, shall include a reference to disability working allowance;] [7. . .]

[14 "employment and support allowance" means, for the purposes of Parts 3 to 6, employment and support allowance under Part 1 of the 2007 Act as that Part has effect apart from the amendments made by Schedule 3, and Part 1 of Schedule 14, to the 2012 Act that remove references to an income-related allowance;]

[11 "the Employment and Support Allowance Regulations" means the Employment and Support Allowance Regulations 2008;]

"guardian's allowance" means an allowance under section 38 of the Social Security Act 1975 [SSCBA, s.77];

"income support" means income support under Part II of the Act [SSCBA, Part VII] and includes personal expenses addition, special transitional addition and transitional addition as defined in the Income Support (Transitional) Regulations 1987;

"Income Support Regulations" means the Income Support (General) Regulations 1987;

[14 "jobseeker's allowance" means, for the purposes of Parts 3 to 6, jobseeker's allowance under the 1995 Act as that Act has effect apart from the amendments made by Part 1 of Schedule 14 to the 2012 Act that remove references to an income-based allowance;]

[4 "Jobseeker's Allowance Regulations" means the Jobseeker's Allowance Regulations 1996;]

[13 "personal independence payment" means the allowance under Part 4 of the 2012 Act;]

"severe disablement allowance" means an allowance under section 36 of the Social Security Act 1975 [SSCBA, s.68].

[9 "state pension credit" means the benefit payable under the State Pension Credit Act 2002;

"the State Pension Credit Regulations" means the State Pension Credit Regulations 2002]

[[7] "start notification" means a notification of entitlement to tax credit furnished to an employer by the Board, referred to in section 6(2)(a) of the Tax Credits Act 1999;

"tax credit" means working families' tax credit or disabled person's tax credit;

[[14] "universal credit" means universal credit under Part 1 of the 2012 Act;]

[[11] "the Welfare Reform Act means the Welfare Reform Act 2007;]

"working families' tax credit" means working families' tax credit under section 128 of the Contributions and Benefits Act and, in relation to things done, or falling to be done, prior to 5th October 1999 shall include a reference to family credit.]

(3) Unless the context otherwise requires, any reference in these regulations to a numbered Part or regulation is a reference to the Part or regulation bearing that number in these Regulations and any reference in a regulation to a numbered paragraph is a reference to the paragraph of that regulation bearing that number.

AMENDMENTS

1. The Social Security (Payments on account, Overpayments and Recovery) Amendments Regulations 1989 (SI 1989/136) reg.3 (February 27, 1989).

2. The Disability Living Allowance and Disability Working Allowance (Consequential Provisions) Regulations 1991 (SI 1991/2742) reg.15 (April 6, 1992).

3. The Social Security (Incapacity Benefit) (Consequential and Transitional Amendments and Savings) Regulations 1995 (SI 1995/829) reg.21(2) (April 13, 1995).

4. The Social Security and Child Support (Jobseeker's Allowance) (Consequential Amendments) Regulations 1996 (SI 1996/1345) reg.23(2) (October 7, 1996).

5. The Social Security Act 1998 (Commencement No.12 and Consequential and Transitional Provisions) Order 1999 (SI 1999/3178) Sch.9 para.1 (November 29, 1999).

6. For tax credits purposes only these words substituted by The Tax Credits (Payments on Account, Overpayments and Recovery) (Amendment) Regulations 1999 (SI 1999/2571) reg.3 (October 5, 1999).

7. The Tax Credits (Payments on Account, Overpayments and Recovery) (Amendment) Regulations 1999 (SI 1999/2571) reg.3 (October 5, 1999).

8. The Social Security (Benefits for Widows and Widowers) (Consequential Amendments) Regulations 2000 (SI 2000/1483) reg.10 (April 9, 2001).

9. State Pension Credit (Consequential, Transitional and Miscellaneous Provisions) Regulations 2002 (SI 2002/3019) reg.24 (October 6, 2003).

10. The Social Security, Child Support and Tax Credits (Miscellaneous Amendments) Regulations 2005 (SI 2005/337) reg.10 (March 18, 2005).

11. The Employment and Support Allowance (Consequential Provisions) (No.2) Regulations 2008 (SI 2008/1554) reg.52 (October 27, 2008).

12. The Tribunals, Courts and Enforcement Act 2007 (Transitional and Consequential Provisions) Order 2008 (SI 2008/2683) Sch.1 para.44 (November 3, 2008).

13. The Social Security (Overpayments and Recovery) Regulations 2013 (SI 2013/384) reg.31(2) (April 8, 2013).

14. The Pensions Act 2014 (Consequential, Supplementary and Incidental Amendments) Order 2015 (SI 2015/1985) art.11(2) (April 6, 2016).

15. The Pensions Act 2014 (Consequential, Supplementary and Incidental Amendments) Order 2017 (SI 2017/422) art.13 (April 6, 2017).

Part II

Interim Payments

2.892 Regs 2–4 revoked.

General note

2.893 Regulation 19 of the Social Security (Payments on Account of Benefit) Regulations 2013 (SI 2013/383) revokes Pt II of these Regulations with effect from April 1, 2013, subject to savings in respect of applications for interim payments made before April 1, 2013 and interim payments made pursuant to applications made before April 1, 2013.

Part III

Offsetting

Offsetting prior payment against subsequent award

2.894 **5.**—(1) Subject to [2 paragraphs (1A) [7, (2A) and (6)] and] regulation 6 (exception from offset of recoverable overpayment), any sum paid in respect of a period covered by a subsequent determination in any of the cases set out in paragraph (2) shall be offset against arrears of entitlement under the subsequent determination and, except to the extent that the sum exceeds the arrears, shall be treated as properly paid on account of them.

[2(1A) In paragraph (1) the reference to "any sum paid" shall, in relation to tax credit, include a reference to any amount or calculation of tax credit payable in respect of a period to the date of subsequent determination, which is included in a start notification given by the Board to an employer, and for the payment of which the employer remains responsible.]

(2) Paragraph (1) applies in the following cases—

[6 *Case 1: Payment pursuant to a decision which is revised or superseded, or overturned on appeal*

Where a person has been paid a sum by way of benefit [or by way of a shared additional pension under section 55A [11 or 55AA] of the Social Security Contributions and Benefits Act 1992] pursuant to a decision which is subsequently revised under section 9 of the Social Security Act 1998, superseded under Section 10 of that Act or overturned on appeal.]

Case 2: Award or payment of benefit in lieu

Where a person has been paid a sum by way benefit under the original award and it is subsequently determined, . . ., that another benefit [10 or, as the case may be, universal credit] should be awarded or is payable in lieu of the first.

Case 3: Child benefit and severe disablement allowance

Where either—

(a) a person has been awarded and paid child benefit for a period in respect of which severe disablement allowance [9 , employment and support allowance for those persons with limited capability for work in relation to your in accordance with paragraph 4 of Schedule 1 to the Welfare Reform Act 2007] [4 or incapacity benefit for persons incapacitated in youth in accordance with section 30(A)(1)(b) and (2A) of the Contributions and Benefits Act] is subsequently determined to be payable to the child concerned, or

(b) severe disablement allowance [4 or incapacity benefit for persons incapacitated in youth in accordance with section 30(A)(1)(b) and (2A) of the Contributions and Benefits Act] is awarded and paid for a period in respect of which child benefit is subsequently awarded to someone else, the child concerned in the subsequent determination being the beneficiary of the original award.

Case 4: Increase of benefit for dependant

Where a person has been paid a sum by way of an increase in respect of a dependent person under the original award and it is subsequently determined that that other person is entitled to benefit for that period, or that a third person is entitled to the increase for that period in priority to the beneficiary of the original award.

Case 5: Increase of benefit for partner

Where a person has been paid a sum by way of an increase in respect of a partner (as defined in regulation 2 of the Income Support Regulations) and it is subsequently determined that that other person is entitled to benefit for that period.

[12 Case 6: *Carer Support Payment* Where a person has been paid carer support payment for a period in respect of which any overlapping benefit is subsequently determined to be payable.]

[2 (2A) In paragraph (2), Case 2 shall not apply where either—

(a) the sum paid under the original award, or

(b) the subsequent decision on the revision, supersession or appeal,

referred to in the Case (but not both) is or relates to tax credit.]

[12 (2B) In paragraph (2), for the purposes of Case 6—

"carer support payment" means carer's assistance given in accordance with the Carer's Assistance (Carer Support Payment) (Scotland) Regulations 2023;

"overlapping benefit" means a benefit specified in paragraph (2C).

(2C) The following are overlapping benefits for the purposes of paragraph (2B)—

(a) state pension or retirement pension;
(b) incapacity benefit;
(c) severe disablement allowance;
(d) unemployability supplement that is paid with industrial injuries disablement benefit or war pension;
(e) widowed parent's allowance, widowed mother's allowance or widow's pension, excluding additional pension;
(f) bereavement allowance;
(g) war pension;
(h) maternity allowance;
(i) industrial death benefit;
(j) contribution-based jobseeker's allowance;
(k) contributory employment and support allowance; and
(l) training allowance.

(2D) For the purposes of paragraph (2C)—

"the 2003 Act" means the Income Tax (Earnings and Pensions) Act 2003;

"bereavement allowance" means an allowance referred to in section 39B of the Contributions and Benefits Act, subject to the transitional provisions specified in article 4 of the Pensions Act 2014 (Commencement No. 10) Order 2017;

"contribution-based jobseeker's allowance" means an allowance under the 1995 Act, as amended by the provisions of Part 1 of Schedule 14 to the 2012 Act that remove references to an income-based allowance, and a contribution-based allowance under the 1995 Act, as that Act has effect apart from those provisions;

"contributory employment and support allowance" means an allowance under Part 1 of the 2007 Act, as amended by the provisions of Schedule 3, and Part 1 of Schedule 14, to the 2012 Act that remove references to an income-related allowance, and a contributory allowance under Part 1 of the 2007 Act, as that Part has effect apart from those provisions;

"incapacity benefit" means a benefit referred to in section 30A of the Contributions and Benefits Act;

"industrial death benefit" means a benefit referred to in Part VI of Schedule 7 to the Contributions and Benefits Act;

"maternity allowance" means an allowance referred to in sections 35 and 35B(7) of the Contributions and Benefits Act;

"Personal Injuries Scheme" means any scheme made under the Personal Injuries (Emergency Provisions) Act 1939 or under the Pensions (Navy, Army, Air Force and Mercantile Marine) Act 1939;

"retirement pension" means a pension payable under Part II and Part III of the Contributions and Benefits Act, excluding any additional pension or graduated retirement benefit;

"Service Pensions Instrument" means any instrument described in paragraph (a) or (b) below in so far, but only in so far, as the pensions or other benefits provided by that instrument are not calculated or determined by reference to length of service, namely—

(a) any instrument made in exercise of powers—

(i) referred to in section 12(1) of the Social Security (Miscellaneous Provisions) Act 1977) (pensions or other benefit for disablement or death due to service in the armed forces of the Crown); or

(ii) under section 1 of the Polish Resettlement Act 1947 (pensions and other benefits for disablement or death due to service in certain Polish forces); or

(b) any instrument under which a pension or other benefit may be paid to a person (not being a member of the armed forces of the Crown) out of public funds in respect of death or disablement, wound, injury or disease due to service in any nursing service or other auxiliary service of any of the armed forces of the Crown, or in any other organisation established under the control of the Defence Council or formerly established under the control of the Admiralty, the Army Council or the Air Council;

"state pension" means a pension payable under Part 1 of the Pensions Act 2014;

"training allowance" means an allowance (whether by way of periodical grants or otherwise) payable—

(a) out of public funds by a Government department or by or on behalf of the Secretary of State, Skills Development Scotland, Scottish Enterprise, Highlands and Islands Enterprise or the Welsh Ministers;

(b) to a person ("P") for P's maintenance or in respect of a member of P's family; and

(c) for the period, or part of the period, during which P is following a course of training or instruction provided by, or in pursuance of arrangements made with, that department or approved by that department in relation to P or so provided or approved by or on behalf of the Secretary of State, Skills Development Scotland, Scottish Enterprise, Highlands and Islands Enterprise or the Welsh Ministers,

but it does not include an allowance paid by any Government department to or in respect of P by reason of the fact that P is following a course of full-time education, other than under arrangements made under section 2 of the Employment and Training Act 1973 or section 2 of the Enterprise and New Towns (Scotland) Act 1990, or is training as a teacher;

"unemployability supplement" includes an increase on account of unemployability under any Personal Injuries Scheme or a Service Pensions Instrument;

"war disablement pension" means any retired pay or pension or allowance payable in respect of disablement under an instrument specified in section 639(2) of the 2003 Act;

"war pension" means a war disablement pension, a war widow's pension or a war widower's pension;

"war widow's pension" means any pension or allowance payable to a woman as a widow or surviving civil partner under an instrument specified in section 639(2) of the 2003 Act in respect of the death or disablement of any person;

"war widower's pension" means any pension or allowance payable to a man as a widower or surviving civil partner under an instrument specified in section 639(2) of the 2003 Act in respect of the death or disablement of any person;

"widowed mother's allowance" means an allowance referred to in section 37 of the Contributions and Benefits Act;

"widowed parent's allowance" means an allowance referred to in section 39A of the Contributions and Benefits Act;

"widow's pension" means a pension referred to in section 38 of the Contributions and Benefits Act.]

(3) Where an amount has been deducted under regulation 13(b) (sums to be deducted in calculating recoverable amounts) an equivalent sum shall be offset against any arrears of entitlement of that person under a subsequent award of [5 income support, state pension credit and] [1, or income-based jobseeker's allowance] [8 or an income related employment and support allowance] for the period to which the deducted amount relates.

(4) Where child benefit which has been paid under an award in favour of a person (the original beneficiary) is subsequently awarded to someone else for any week, the benefit shall nevertheless be treated as properly paid if it was received by someone other than the original beneficiary, who—

(a) either had the child living with him or was contributing towards the cost of providing for the child at a weekly rate which was not less than the weekly rate under the original award, and
(b) could have been entitled to child benefit in respect of that child for that week had a claim been made in time.

(5) Any amount which is treated, under paragraph (4), as properly paid shall be deducted from the amount payable to the beneficiary under the subsequent award.

[[7] (6) Subject to regulation 6, any sums under—
(a) Schedule 5 or 5A to the Contributions and Benefits Act (pension increases or lump sum where entitlement to retirement pension or shared additional pension is deferred);
(b) Schedule 1 to the Social Security (Graduated Retirement Benefit) Regulations 2005 (increases or lump sum where entitlement to greaduate retirement benefit is deferred);
[[11] (c) sections 8 or 9 of the Pensions Act 2014; or
(d) Regulations under section 10 of that Act which make provision corresponding or similar to sections 8 or 9 of that Act,]

paid pursuant to a decision which is subsequently revised under section 9 of the Social Security Act 1998, superseded under section 10 of that Act or overturned on appeal, shall be offset against any sums due under the subsequent determination and, except to the extent that the sum exceeds the amount now due, shall be treated as properly paid on account of it.]

AMENDMENTS

1. The Social Security and Child Support (Jobseeker's Allowance) (Consequential Amendments) Regulations 1996 (SI 1996/1345) reg.23(5) and (6) (October 7, 1996).

2. The Tax Credits (Payments on Account, Overpayments and Recovery) (Amendment) Regulations 1999 (SI 1999/2571) reg.7 (October 5, 1999).

3. The Social Security Act 1998 (Commencement No.11 and Transitional Provisions) Order 1999 (SI 1999/2860) Sch.4 (October 18, 1999).

4. The Social Security (Incapacity Benefits) Miscellaneous Amendments Regulations 2000 (SI 2000/3120) reg.5 (April 6, 2001).

5. State Pension Credit (Consequential, Transitional and Miscellaneous Provisions) Regulations 2002 (SI 2002/3019) reg.24 (October 6, 2003).

6. The Social Security (Shared Additional Pension) (Miscellaneous Amendments) Regulations 2005 (SI 2005/1551) (July 6, 2005).

7. The Social Security (Deferral of Retirement Pensions etc.) Regulations 2006 (SI 2006/516) (April 6, 2006).

8. The Employment and Support Allowance (Consequential Provisions) (No.2) Regulations 2008 (SI 2008/1554) reg.52 (October 27, 2008).

9. Social Security (Miscellaneous Amendments) (No.3) Regulations 2010 (SI 2010/840) reg.3 (June 28, 2010).

10. The Social Security (Overpayments and Recovery) Regulations 2013 (SI 2013/384) reg.31(3) (April 29, 2013).

11. The Pensions Act 2014 (Consequential, Supplementary and Incidental Amendments) Order 2015 (SI 2015/1985) art.11(3) (April 6, 2016).

12. The Carer's Assistance (Carer Support Payment) (Scotland) Regulations 2023 (Consequential Amendments) Order 2024 (March 26, 2024).

GENERAL NOTE

2.895 This regulation contains important powers to deal with cases where a subsequent award of one benefit replaces an earlier award of a different benefit. It enables the benefit originally awarded to be treated as paid on account of the benefit subsequently awarded. The circumstances in which the power is available are spelled out in the five cases listed in the regulation. Tribunals may need to refer to this power when the result of their decision is to substitute one benefit for another which has already been awarded.

In *Brown v Secretary of State for Work and Pensions* [2006] EWCA Civ 89, reported as *R(DLA) 2/07*, the Court of Appeal, interpreting reg.5(1) ruled that where payments of disability living allowance had been suspended because there has been an overpayment, and a new decision made, payments subsequently awarded could not be offset against the irrecoverable overpayment, since the amount of payments would vary depending on how long it took for the new decision to be reached.

Exception from offset of recoverable overpayment

6. No amount may be offset under regulation 5(1) which has been determined to be a recoverable overpayment for the purposes of section 53(1) of the Act [SSAA, section 71(1)]. **2.896**

PART IV

PREVENTION OF DUPLICATION OF PAYMENTS

Duplication and prescribed income

7.—[1 (1) For the purposes of section 74(1) of the Social Security Administration Act 1992 ([4 income support, state pension credit and] [6, income-based jobseeker's allowance, income-related employment and support allowance] and other payments), a person's prescribed income is— **2.897**

(a) income required to be taken into account in accordance with Part V of the Income Support Regulations [3or, as the case may be, Part VIII of the Jobseeker's Allowance Regulations] [4 or Part III of the State Pension Credit Regulations] [5 or Part 10 of the Employment and Support Allowance Regulations], except for the income specified in sub-paragraph (b); and]

[2(b) income which, if it were actually paid, would be required to be taken into account in accordance with Chapter VIIA of Part V of the Income Support Regulations [3or, as the case may be, Chapter VIII of Part VIII of the Jobseeker's Allowance Regulations] (child support maintenance); [5 or Chapter 9 of Part 10 to the Employment and Support Allowance Regulations (child support)] but only in so far as it relates to the period beginning with the effective date of the maintenance assessment under which it is payable, as determined in accordance with regulation 30 of the Child Support (Maintenance Assessment Procedure) Regulations 1992, and ending with the first day which is a day specified by the Secretary of State under regulation 4(1) of the Child Support (Collection and Enforcement) Regulations 1992 as being a day on which payment of child support maintenance under that maintenance assessment is due.]

(2) The prescribed date in relation to any payment of income prescribed by [1paragraph (1)(a)] is—

(a) where it is made in respect of a specific day or period, that day or the first day of the period;

(b) where it is not so made, the day or the first day of the period to which it is fairly attributable.

[[2](3) Subject to paragraph (4), the prescribed date in relation to any payment of income prescribed by paragraph (1)(b) is the last day of the maintenance period, determined in accordance with regulation 33 of the Child Support (Maintenance Assessment Procedure) Regulations 1992, to which it relates.

(4) Where the period referred to in paragraph (1)(b) does not consist of a number of complete maintenance periods the prescribed date in relation to income prescribed by that sub-paragraph which relates to any part of that period which is not a complete maintenance period is the last day of that period.]

AMENDMENTS

1. The Social Security (Payments on account, Overpayments and Recovery) Amendment Regulations 1993 (SI 1993/650) reg.2, as amended by The Social Security (Miscellaneous Provisions) Amendment Regulations 1993 (SI 1993/846) reg.4 (April 5, 1993).

2. The Social Security (Payments on account, Overpayments and Recovery) Amendment Regulations 1993 (SI 1993/650) reg.2, as amended by The Social Security (Miscellaneous Provisions) Amendment Regulations 1993 (SI 1993/846) reg.4 (April 5, 1993).

3. The Social Security and Child Support (Jobseeker's Allowance) (Consequential Amendments) Regulations 1996 (SI 1996/1345) reg.23(3) (October 7, 1996).

4. State Pension Credit (Consequential, Transitional and Miscellaneous Provisions) Regulations 2002 (SI 2002/3019) reg.24 (October 6, 2003).

5. The Employment and Support Allowance (Consequential Provisions) (No. 2) Regulations 2008 (SI 2008/1554) reg.52 (October 27, 2008).

6. The Employment and Support Allowance (Miscellaneous Amendments) Regulations 2008 (SI 2008/2428) reg.22 (October 27, 2008).

GENERAL NOTE

2.898 See the notes to s.74(1) of the Administration Act.

Under s.54 of the Child Support Act 1991 "maintenance assessment" means an assessment of maintenance made under that Act, including, except where regulations prescribe otherwise, an interim assessment. Under reg.30 of the Child Support (Maintenance Assessment Procedure) Regulations 1992, the effective date of a new assessment is usually, when the application was made by the person with care of the child, the date on which a maintenance enquiry form was sent to the absent parent or, where the application was made by the absent parent, the date on which an effective maintenance form was received by the Secretary of State. Arrears will inevitably accrue while the assessment is being made. In the meantime income support or income-based JSA can be paid in full to the parent with care. When the arrears are paid, the amount of "overpaid" income support or JSA is recoverable under s.74(1) of the Administration Act.

See the notes to reg.60C of the Income Support (General) Regulations for the interaction with payments of other arrears of child support maintenance, which are excluded from the operation of s.74(1). Note also s.74A of the Administration Act and regs 55A and 60E of the Income Support Regulations and regs 119 and 127 of the Jobseeker's Allowance Regulations.

Duplication and prescribed payments

2.899 **8.**—(1) For the purposes of section [[8] 74(2) of the Administration Act] (recovery of amount of benefit awarded because prescribed payment not made on prescribed date), the payment of any of the following is a prescribed payment—

[12 (za) a state pension under Part 1 of the Pensions Act 2014,]

(a) any benefit under the Social Security Act 1975 [SSCBA, Parts II to V] other than any grant or gratuity or a widow's payment;

[11 (aa) any personal independence payment;]

(b) any child benefit;

[3. . .]

(d) any war disablement pension or war widow's pension which is not in the form of a gratuity and any payment which the Secretary of State accepts as analogous to any such pension;

(e) any allowance paid under the Job Release Act 1977;

(f) any allowance payable by or on behalf of [2Scottish Enterprise Highlands and Islands Enterprise or] [1the Secretary of State] to or in respect of a person for his maintenance for any period during which he is following a course of training or instruction provided or approved by [2Scottish Enterprise Highlands and Islands Enterprise or] [1the Secretary of State]

(g) any payment of benefit under the legislation of any member State [15. . .] concerning the branches of social security mentioned in Article 4(1) of Regulation (EEC) No.1408/71 [14 as amended from time to time,] on the application of social security schemes to employed persons, to self-employed persons and to members of their families moving within the Community, [14 or in Article 3(1) of Regulation (EC) No.883/2004 of the European Parliament and of the Council of 29 April 2004, as amended from time to time, on the coordination of social security systems,] whether or not the benefit has been acquired by virtue of the provisions of [14 either regulation, as amended from time to time;]

[3. . .]

[13 (i) any widowed parent's allowance under section 39A of the Contributions and Benefits Act;]

[8 (j) any contribution-based jobseeker's allowance within the meaning of section 1(4) of the Jobseekers Act.]

[9 (k) payments under the Financial Assistance Scheme Regulations 2005.]

[10 (l) a contributory employment and support allowance.]

(2) The prescribed date, in relation to any payment prescribed by paragraph (1) is the date by which receipt of or entitlement to that benefit would have to be notified to the Secretary of State if it were to be taken into account in determining, whether [5by way of revision or supersession], the amount of or entitlement to [7 income support, [11 universal credit,] a state pension credit] [4, or income-based jobseeker's allowance][10 or income-related employment and support allowance].

AMENDMENTS

1. Employment Act 1989 Sch.5 paras 1 and 4 (November 16, 1989).

2. The Enterprise (Scotland) Consequential Amendments Order 1991 (SI 1991/387) art.14 (April 1, 1991).

3. The Tax Credits (Payments on Account, Overpayments and Recovery) (Amendment) Regulations 1999 (SI 1999/2571) reg.8 (October 5, 1999).

4. The Social Security and Child Support (Jobseeker's Allowance) (Consequential Amendments) Regulations 1996 (SI 1996/1345) reg.23(5) and (6) (October 7, 1996).

5. The Social Security Act 1998 (Commencement No.11 and Transitional Provisions) Order 1999 (SI 1999/2680) Sch.4 (October 18, 1999).

6. The Social Security (Benefits for Widows and Widowers) (Consequential Amendments) Regulations 2000 (SI 2000/1483) reg.10 (April 9, 2001).

7. State Pension Credit (Consequential, Transitional and Miscellaneous Provisions) Regulations 2002 (SI 2002/3019) reg.24 (October 6, 2003).

8. The Social Security, Child Support and Tax Credits (Miscellaneous Amendments) Regulations 2005 (SI 2005/337) reg.10 (March 18, 2005).

9. The Social Security (Payments on Account, Overpayments and Recovery) Amendment Regulations 2005 (SI 2005/3476) (January 19, 2006).

10. The Employment and Support Allowance (Consequential Provisions) (No.2) Regulations 2008 (SI 2008/1554) reg.52 (October 27, 2008).

11. The Social Security (Overpayments and Recovery) Regulations 2013 (SI 2013/384 reg.31(4) (April 29, 2013).

12. The Pensions Act 2014 (Consequential, Supplementary and Incidental Amendments) Order 2015 (SI 2015/1985) art.11(4) (April 6, 2016).

13. The Pensions Act 2014 (Consequential, Supplementary and Incidental Amendments) Order 2017 (SI 2017/422) art.13 (April 6, 2017).

14. The Social Security (Updating of EU References) (Amendment) Regulations 2018 (SI 2018/1084), Schedule, para.7 (November 15, 2018).

15. The Social Security (Amendment) (EU Exit) Regulations 2019 (SI 2019/128) reg.4 and Schedule, para 5) (as applied by European Union (Withdrawal Agreement) Act 2020 Sch.5 para.1(1)) (December 31, 2020). Schedule, para 5 further provides that the amendment "also has effect in relation to regulation 8 as that regulation relates to child benefit and guardian's allowance by virtue of the transitional provision in regulation 44 (recovery of overpayments from awards of child benefit and guardian's allowance) of the Child Benefit and Guardian's Allowance (Administration) Regulations 2003."

General Note

2.900 See the notes to s.74(2) of the Administration Act.

R(IS) 14/94 concerned an overpayment of income support which arose from the award of invalid care allowance. The claimant was an elderly widow, whose daughter was her appointee. Income support was paid to the widow. The daughter was in receipt of invalid care allowance in respect of her mother. Recovery was sought under s.27 of the Social Security Act 1986 (now s.74 of the Administration Act) from the widow.

The claimant argued that the words in reg.8(2) "taken into account" meant that only the claimant's resources and requirements were to be considered. The Commissioner rejects such a narrow reading of the words and says that "the words 'into account' should be given a wide interpretation and in the context include 'take notice of'."

Duplication and maintenance payments

2.901 **9.** For the purposes of section 27(3) of the Act [SSAA, section 74(3)] (recovery of amount of benefit awarded because maintenance payments not made), the following benefits are prescribed—

(a) child benefit;
(b) increase for dependants of any benefit under the Social Security Act 1975 [SSCBA, Parts II to V];
(c) child's special allowance under section 31 of the Social Security Act 1975 [SSCBA, section 56]; and
(d) guardian's allowance.

General Note

2.902 See the notes to s.74(3) of the Administration Act.

Conversion of payments made in a foreign currency

10. [1 (1)] Where a payment of income prescribed by regulation 7(1), or a payment prescribed by regulation 8(1), is made in a currency other than sterling, its value in sterling, for the purposes of section 27 of the Act [SSAA, section 74] and this Part, shall be determined, after conversion by the Bank of England, or by [1any authorised deposit-taker], as the net sterling sum into which it is converted, after any banking charge or commission on the transaction has been deducted. 2.903

[1(2) In this regulation "authorised deposit-taker" means—

(a) a person who has permission under [2Part 4A of that Act] to accept deposits[3.]

[3… .]

(3) Paragraph (2) must be read with—

(a) section 22 of the Financial Services and Markets Act 2000;

(b) any relevant order under that section; and

(c) Schedule 2 to that Act.]

Amendments

1. The Financial Services and Markets Act 2000 (Consequential Amendments and Repeals) Order 2001 (SI 2001/3649) art.389 (December 1, 2001).

2. The Financial Services Act 2012 (Consequential Amendments and Transitional Provisions) Order 2013 (SI 2013/472) art.4 (April 1, 2013).

3. The EEA Passport Rights (Amendment, etc., and Transitional Provisions) (EU Exit) Regulations 2018 (SI 2018/1149) Sch.1(3) para.45 (December 31, 2020).

Part V

Direct Credit Transfer Overpayments

Recovery of overpayments by automated or other direct credit transfer

11.— [4 (A1) This regulation applies only in respect of payments of benefit to which section 71 of the Administration Act applies.] 2.904

(1) [1 Subject to paragraph (4)] where it is determined by the adjudicating authority that a payment in excess of entitlement has been credited to a bank or other account under an arrangement for automated or other direct credit transfer made in accordance with regulation 21 of the Claims and Payments Regulations and that the conditions prescribed by paragraph (2) are satisfied, the excess, or the specified part of it to which the Secretary of State's certificate relates, shall be recoverable under this regulation.

(2) The prescribed conditions for recoverability under paragraph (1) are as follows—

(a) the Secretary of State has certified that the payment in excess of entitlement, or a specified part of it, is materially due to the arrangements for payments to be made by automated or other direct credit transfer; and

[2 (b) notice of the effect to which this regulation would have, in the event of an overpayment, was given to the beneficiary or to a person acting form his—

(i) in writing, where the claim was made in writing; or
(ii) either orally or in writing, where the claim was made by telephone

[3 before the arrangement came into effect.]

(3) Where the arrangement was agreed to before April 6, 1987 the condition prescribed by paragraph (2)(b) need not be satisfied in any case where the application for benefit to be paid by automated or other direct credit transfer contained a statement, or was accompanied by a written statement made by the applicant, which complied with the provisions of regulation 16A(3)(b) and (8) of the Social Security (Claims and Payments) Regulations 1979 or, as the case may be, regulation 7(2)(b) and (6) of the Child Benefit (Claims and Payments) Regulations 1984.

[1 Where the payment mention in paragraph (1) is a payment of tax credit, paragraphs (1) and (2) shall apply with the modifications that—

(a) in paragraph (1) for the words "Secretary of State" there is substituted the words "Board's", and
(b) in paragraph (2) for the words "Secretary of State" there is substituted the word "Board".]

AMENDMENTS

1. The Tax Credits (Payments on Account, Overpayments and Recovery) (Amendment) Regulations 1999 (SI 1999/2571) reg.9 (October 5, 1999).

2. The Social Security (Claims and Payments and Payments on account, Overpayments and Recovery) Amendment Regulations 2005 (SI 2005/34) reg.3 (May 2, 2005).

3. The Social Security (Miscellaneous Amendments) Regulations 2012 (SI 2012/757) reg.16 (April 1, 2012).

4. The Social Security (Overpayments and Recovery) Regulations 2013 (SI 2013/384 reg.31(5) (April 29, 2013).

PART VI

CALCULATION OF AMOUNT RECOVERABLE

Circumstances in which determination need not be revised

2.905 **12.** [2 Section 71(5) or (5A) of the Administration Act] (recoverability dependent on reversal, variation, revision [1 or supersession] of determination) shall not apply where the fact and circumstances of the misrepresentation or non-disclosure do not provide a basis for [1 the decision pursuant to which the payment was made to be revised under section 9 of the Social Security Act 1998 or superseded under section 10 of that Act.]

AMENDMENTS

1. The Social Security Act 1998 (Commencement No.9, and Savings and Consequential and Transitional Provisions) Order 1999 (SI 1999/2422) Sch.8 (September 6, 1999).

2. The Social Security, Child Support and Tax Credits (Miscellaneous Amendments) Regulations 2005 (SI 2005/337) reg.10 (March 18, 2005).

GENERAL NOTE

2.906 See the notes to s.71(5A) of the Administration Act.

Sums to be deducted in calculating recoverable amounts

13.—[6 (1) Subject to paragraphs (1C) and (2), in calculating an amount recoverable under section 71(1) of the Administration Act or under regulation 11 ("the overpayment"), the adjudicating authority must deduct— 2.907

(a) any amount which has been offset under Part 3;

(b) any additional amount of a benefit specified in paragraph (1A) which was not payable under the original, or any other, determination but which should have been determined to be payable in respect of all or part of the overpayment period to the claimant or their partner—

(i) on the basis of the claim as presented to the adjudicating authority; or

(ii) on the basis that any misrepresentation or failure to disclose a material fact had been remedied prior to the award being made.

(1A) The specified benefits are—

(a) universal credit;

(b) income support;

(c) state pension credit;

(d) income-based jobseeker's allowance; and

(e) income-related employment and support allowance.

(1B) In paragraph (1), "overpayment period" means the period over which the overpayment accrued.

(1C) No other deduction is to be made in respect of any other entitlement to benefit which may be, or might have been, determined to exist.]

[2 (2) Paragraph (1) shall apply to tax credit only where both—

(a) The overpayment of benefit referred to in paragraph (1), and

(b) The amount referred to in sub-paragraph (a) of that paragraph,

Are tax credit, and with the modification that sub-paragraph (b) of that paragraph is omitted.]

Amendments

1. The Social Security and Child Support (Jobseeker's Allowance) (Consequential Amendments) Regulations 1996 (SI 1996/1345) reg.23(5) and (6) (October 7, 1996).
2. The Tax Credits (Payments on Account, Overpayments and Recovery) (Amendment) Regulations 1999 (SI 1999/2571) reg.11 (October 5, 1999).
3. State Pension Credit (Consequential, Transitional and Miscellaneous Provisions) Regulations 2002 (SI 2002/3019) reg.24 (October 6, 2003).
4. The Employment and Support Allowance (Consequential Provisions) (No.2) Regulations 2008 (SI 2008/1554) reg.52 (October 27, 2008).
5. The Social Security (Recovery) (Amendment) Regulations 2012 (SI 2012/645) reg.2(1) (April 1, 2012).
6. The Social Security (Overpayments and Recovery) Regulations 2013 (SI 2013/384) reg.31(6) (April 8, 2013).

General Note

See the notes to s.71(1) and (2) of the Administration Act, 1992 for important case law affecting this provision. 2.908

In *CP/5257/1999* the Commissioner interpreted the poorly drafted reg.13 by holding that:

(a) the regulation is not limited to overpayments of income support or income-based jobseeker's allowance, but covers overpaid benefit other than these two benefits; and

(b) the regulation only applies where the benefit sought to be offset is income support or income-based jobseeker's allowance.

In *CIS/1777/2000* a different Commissioner said:

> "[Regulation 13] was amended to include a reference to income-based jobseeker's allowance when that benefit was introduced in 1996. I do not read the provision as authorising the deduction from an overpayment of jobseeker's allowance that would have been paid if a claim for that benefit has been made rather than a claim for income support. Head (i) refers to the claim as presented—the claim as presented was for income support. Head (ii) refers to the claim as it would have appeared if the facts had been correctly represented—if the facts had been correctly known, the claim would have appeared as a claim for income support to which the claimant was not entitled. The claimant might have been advised by the Department of Social Security to make a claim for an income based jobseeker's allowance, but that would have been a different claim—there is no power for the Secretary of State to treat a claim for income support as a claim for income based jobseeker's allowance in the alternative under Schedule 1 to the Social Security (Claims and Payments) Regulations 1987." (See [9]).

The interpretation of the regulation was revisited in *CIS/2291/2001* following the 1999 amendments. The Commissioner concludes:

> "17. Although the wording is particularly obscure for such an important and potentially severe rule, the effect is clear. Anyone who is working or capable of work so as to exclude them from income support must claim jobseeker's allowance. If they do not, and they continue to receive income support, they risk losing both the income support actually received and the jobseeker's allowance they might have received.
> 18. Regulation 13 does not contain any discretion. That rests with the Secretary of State in deciding whether and how to collect any overpayment. No doubt the Secretary of State will take into account whether the public purse has in reality lost the sum claimed as overpaid or some other amount."

> "Regulation 13(1)(b)(ii) requires a hypothetical approach. It requires asking what should have happened if the misrepresentation or, as in this case, failure to disclose had been remedied as soon as possible"

(per Judge Mesher in *KS v SSWP (ESA)* [2019] UKUT 188 (AAC).

In *CDLA/3768/2002,* the Commissioner said:

> "15. . . . the decision maker acting for the Secretary of State [in presenting the case to the tribunal] should first consider whether any amount has been offset under Part III (regulations 5 and 6 of the Social Security (Payments on Account, Overpayments and Recoveries) Regulations 1988. This may call for further enquiry, bearing in mind always that it is for the Secretary of State to meet any problems arising from conflicts of evidence or absence of proof of any relevant issue . . .
> 16. The other issues that regulation 13(1) requires the decision maker and tribunal to identify and deduct is:
>
> > 'any additional amount of income support or income-based jobseeker's allowance which was not payable under the original or any other determination, but which should have been determined to be payable on the basis of the claim as presented to the adjudicating authority or on the basis of the claim as it would have appeared had the misrepresentation or nondisclosure been remedied before the determination'.

I have removed the punctuation for the reasons given in *CIS/2291/2001*. Regulation 13(1) then emphasises that no other deduction shall be made for any other actual or hypothetical entitlement."

In the particular circumstances of the case in *CIS/0546/2008*, a Deputy Commissioner decided that the appellant was entitled to the application of the set off provisions in reg.13 in the context of a claim for income support. Benefit had been stopped when it was established that the appellant and her partner were living together as husband and wife. It appeared that the appellant had not been given the opportunity to elect to make a claim for income support for herself, her partner and the children. In this case, there was a claim for income support affecting the appellant. There was an issue which "should have been determined". This meant that the appellant was entitled to have reg.13 applied to offset all or part of the overpayment which was recoverable from her.

The Administrative Court in *Larusai v Secretary of State for Work and Pensions*, [2003] EWHC 371 (Admin) was called upon to consider the relationship of benefits administered by the Department and tax credits administered by the Board of Inland Revenue in relation to the offsetting of benefits where there are recoverable overpayments of benefits administered by the Department. The claimant had been overpaid income support which was recoverable, but argued that a notional entitlement to working families tax credit should be set off against the overpayment notwithstanding the absence of such a provision in reg.13. The claimant argued that the Secretary of State in exercising his discretion as to the amount of the recoverable overpayment had acted unlawfully in failing to deduct a notional amount of working families tax credit from the overpayment. The decision was never likely to require the Secretary of State to exercise his discretion in the way for which the claimant argued, but the decision is interesting for the way in which the Administrative Court responded to the claimant's arguments: **2.909**

(1) The claimant argued that the Secretary of State's approach in treating tax credits as different from benefits administered by the Department and so precluding any discretionary offset of working families tax credit was irrational. The Court did not accept this, seeing nothing irrational in attempts to change the perception of claimants about the difference between benefits which required a person to be out of work and those which were payable to people in work.

(2) The claimant argued that the policy of the Secretary of State had departed from its own guidelines in pursuing a policy of exercising its discretion only in "exceptional circumstances". The Court concluded that this was a matter of phraseology and did not render the policy unlawful.

(3) The claimant argued that the decision to recover the whole of the overpaid income support without deduction of a notional entitlement to working families tax credit constituted a penal sanction (it appears that the claimant would have been entitled to something in the order of £2,000 by way of working families tax credit). Since the policy in reg.13 was to secure full recovery subject to the specified offsets and since the notional amount of working families tax credit did not constitute a debt by the Department to the claimant, it could not be said that there was anything which could be characterised as a penal sanction; there was no basis for the claimant's argument.

(4) The Court said that an argument based on the Government securing a windfall equal to the notional amount of the working families tax credit was misconceived. It "misrepresents the structural position, as well as the law, to describe this as 'a windfall to the State.'" (See [30].)

(5) The claimant raised the question of hardship resulting from the requirement to repay overpaid benefit. The Court simply notes that the Secretary of State has been provided with full details of the claimant's circumstances, that there

is inevitably an element of hardship when overpaid benefit is recovered, but that it "is not for this court, unless it is satisfied that there has been an unlawful exercise of discretion, to form a view about the financial margins with which this case, or any case, might give rise to." (See [32].)

See also *Department for Work and Pensions v Richards* [2005] EWCA Crim 491.

Public Records Act 1958

2.910 *R(IS) 1/05* gives guidance on the significance of the Public Records Act 1958 to the retention of documents by the Department, and the onus of proof where a claimant asserts that there has been an underpayment of benefit in the past which reduces the amount of a recoverable overpayment. The overpayment at issue in this case had arisen as a result of admitted false statements made by the claimant which resulted in the award of income support. The point of contention was whether the claimant could offset the substantial overpayment by underpayments of benefit in circumstances where many of the relevant documents had long since been destroyed by the Department under its document retention policy.

The requirements of the Public Records Act 1958 were seen as something of a red herring, and the Commissioner has little time for them, noting, "It is difficult to believe that these elaborate procedures [in the 1958 Act] were ever intended to apply to social security claim forms". In fairness, the claimant's representative had abandoned this point in arguing the case before the Commissioner.

The onus of proof in cases such as this was a rather more substantial point, particularly in the light of the House of Lords in *Kerr v Department for Social Development* [2004] UKHL 23. The Commissioner sees no real difference in the views expressed by Lady Hale in *Kerr* and the long-established wisdom that "if a particular matter relates to the qualifying conditions of entitlement it is a claimant who must bear the consequences of ignorance; however, if what is in issue constitute an exception to such conditions, then the Department bears the burden of establishing that factor which operates to disentitled the claimant". (See [43]). The issue which arises under reg.13 is distinct from the recovery of the overpayment; it is not necessarily related to the period which is covered by the s.71 revision or supersession nor to the same benefit the subject of recovery. The Commissioner concludes:

"If, as is trite law, one who submits an initial claim for benefit has the burden of showing that its qualifying conditions are met, it can hardly be the case that one who must pay benefit back because it has been demonstrated that she should never have had it, has an easier task in establishing a similar entitlement to offset against the proven debt. In my judgement, nothing in principle or on account of the statutory language or from the structure of the overpayment scheme or to further its consistency can justify such a departure from what is usual and right." (para.47)

Quarterly diminution of capital

2.911 **14.**—(1) For the purposes of section 53(1) of the Act [SSAA, section 71(1)], where income support, [4 or state pension credit] [2, or income-based jobseeker's allowance] [5, or income-related employment and support allowance] [1, working families' tax credit or disabled person's tax credit] has been overpaid in consequence of a misrepresentation as to the capital a claimant possesses or a failure to disclose its existence, the adjudicating authority shall treat that capital as having been reduced at the end of each quarter from the start of the overpayment period by the amount overpaid by way of income support, [4 or state pension credit] [2, or income based jobseeker's allowance] [5 , or income-related employment and support allowance] [1 working families' tax credit or disabled person's tax credit] within that quarter.

(2) Capital shall not be treated as reduced over any period other than a quarter or in any circumstances other than those for which paragraph (1) provides.

(3) In this regulation—

"a quarter" means a period of 13 weeks starting with the first day on which the overpayment period began and ending on the 90th consecutive day thereafter;

"overpayment period" is a period during which income support [3 or an income based jobseeker's allowance,] [5 , or income-related employment and support allowance] [1 working families' tax credit or disabled person's tax credit] is overpaid in consequence of a misrepresentation as to capital or a failure to disclose its existence.

AMENDMENTS

1. The Tax Credits (Payments on Account, Overpayments and Recovery) (Amendment) Regulations 1999 (SI 1999/2571) reg.12 (October 5, 1999).

2. The Tax Credits (Payments on Account, Overpayments and Recovery) (Amendment) Regulations 1999 (SI 1996/2571) reg.23(5) and (6) (October 7, 1996).

3. The Social Security (Jobseeker's Allowance and Payments on account) (Miscellaneous Amendments) Regulations 1996 (SI 1996/2519) reg.3(2) (October 7, 1996).

4. State Pension Credit (Consequential, Transitional and Miscellaneous Provisions) Regulations 2002 (SI 2002/3019) reg.24 (October 6, 2003).

5. The Employment and Support Allowance (Consequential Provisions) (No.2) Regulations 2008 (SI 2008/1554) reg.52 (October 27, 2008).

GENERAL NOTE

See the notes to s.71(1) and (2) of the Administration Act. 2.912

On the proper interpretation of the rule in reg.14, see *CIS/2570/2007* and *CIS/2365/2007*. See also for a discussion of the proper approach to the application of the diminishing capital rule on successive claims to benefit, *MP v SSWP* [2009] UKUT 193 (AAC).

In *R(IS) 10/08*, the Commissioner effectively holds that capital held by a child should be subject to the diminishing capital rules if an overpayment arises as a result of capital held by a child of the family unit seeking entitlement to income support.

PART VII

THE PROCESS OF RECOVERY

Recovery by deduction from benefits

15.—(1) Subject to regulation 16, where any amount is recoverable under sections 27 or 53(1) of the Act [SSAA, sections 74 or 71(1)], or under these Regulations, that amount shall be recoverable by the Secretary of State from any of the benefits prescribed by the next paragraph, to which the person from whom [1the amount is determined] to be recoverable is entitled. 2.913

(2) The following benefits are prescribed for the purposes of this regulation—

(a) subject to paragraphs (1) and (2) of regulation 16, any benefit under the Social Security Act 1975 [SSCBA, Parts II to V];

[[10](aa) a state pension under Part 1 of the Pensions Act 2014,]

(b) subject to paragraphs (1) and (2) of regulation 16, any child benefit;

(c) [[5]. . .]

(d) subject to regulation 16, any income support [[7] an employment and support allowance] [[6] or state pension credit], [[4]or a jobseeker's allowance].

[[2](e) [[5]. . .];

[[3](f) any incapacity benefit.]

[[8] (g) personal independence payment;]

[[9] (h) universal credit.]

AMENDMENTS

1. The Social Security (Payments on account, Overpayments and Recovery) Amendments Regulations 1988 (SI 1988/688) reg.2(3) (April 11, 1988).

2. The Disability Living Allowance and Disability Working Allowance (Consequential Provisions) Regulations 1991 (SI 1991/2742) reg.15 (April 6, 1992).

3. The Social Security (Incapacity Benefit) (Consequential and Transitional Amendments and Savings) Regulations 1991 (SI 1995/829) reg.21(3) (April 13, 1995).

4. The Social Security (Jobseeker's Allowance and Payments on account) (Miscellaneous Amendments) Regulations 1996 (SI 1996/2519) reg.3(3) (October 7, 1996).

5. The Social Security (Jobseeker's Allowance and Payments on account) (Miscellaneous Amendments) Regulations 1996 (SI 1996/2519) reg.13 (October 5, 1999).

6. State Pension Credit (Consequential, Transitional and Miscellaneous Provisions) Regulations 2002 (SI 2002/3019) reg.24 (October 6, 2003).

7. The Employment and Support Allowance (Consequential Provisions) (No.2) Regulations 2008 (SI 2008/1554) reg.52 (October 27, 2008).

8. The Social Security (Overpayments and Recovery) Regulations 2013 (SI 2013/384) reg.31(7) (April 8, 2013).

9. The Social Security (Overpayment and Recovery Regulations 2013 (SI 2013/384) reg.31(7)(b) (April 29, 2013).

10. The Pensions Act 2014 (Consequential, Supplementary and Incidental Amendments) Order 2015 (SI 2015/1985) art.11(5) (April 6, 2016).

Limitations on deductions from prescribed benefits

2.914 **16.**—(1) Deductions may not be made from entitlement to the benefits prescribed by paragraph (2) except as a means of recovering an overpayment of the benefit from which the deduction is to be made.

(2) The benefits [[1]prescribed] for the purposes of paragraph (1) are guardian's allowance, [[2]. . .] and child benefit.

[[15] (2A) Paragraphs (3) to (7) do not apply where paragraph (7A) applies.]

(3) Regulation 15 shall apply without limitation to any payment of arrears of benefit other than any arrears caused by the operation of [[12] regulation 20 of the Social Security and Child Support (Decisions and Appeals) Regulations 1999 (making of payments which have been suspended)]

(4) Regulation 15 shall apply to the amount of [[5]benefit] to which a person is presently entitled only to the extent that there may [[17] . . .] be recovered in respect of any one benefit week—

(a) in a case to which paragraph (5) applies, not more than the amount there specified; and

(b) in any other case, 3 times 5 per cent of the personal allowance for a single claimant aged not less than 25, that 5 per cent being, where it is not a multiple of 5 pence, rounded to the next higher such multiple.

[6(4A) Paragraph (4) shall apply to the following benefits—

(a) income support;

(b) an income-based jobseeker's allowance;

(c) where, if there was no entitlement to a contribution-based jobseeker's allowance, there would be entitlement to an income-based jobseeker's allowance at the same rate, a contribution-based jobseeker's allowance.]

[11 (d) state pension credit.]

[13 (e) an income-related employment and support allowance;

(f) where, if there was no entitlement to a contributory employment and support allowance, there would be entitlement to an income-related employment and support allowance at the same rate, a contributory employment and support allowance.]

[9 (5) Where a person responsible for the misrepresentation or failure to disclose a material fact has, by reason thereof—

(a) been found guilty of an offence whether under statute or otherwise; or

(b) made an admission after caution of deception or fraud for the purpose of obtaining benefit; or

(c) agreed to pay a penalty under section 115A of the Social Security Administration Act 1992 and the agreement has not been with-drawn,

the amount mentioned in paragraph (4)(a) [17 shall, subject to paragraph (5ZA), be 8 times] 5 per cent. of the personal allowance for a single claimant aged not less than 25, that 5 per cent. being, [14 where it is not a multiple of 5 pence, rounded to the next higher such multiple]]

[17 (5ZA) In a case to which paragraph (5) applies, where deductions fall to be made under Schedule 9 to the Claims and Payments Regulations (payments to third parties), the total of the amount deductible under paragraph (5) and the amount deductible under that Schedule shall not exceed 8 times 5 per cent. of the personal allowance mentioned in paragraph (5).

(5ZB) Paragraph (4)(b) is subject to paragraphs 8 and 9 of Schedule 9 to the Claims and Payments Regulations.]

[6(5A) Regulation 15 shall apply to an amount of a contribution-based jobseeker's allowance, other than a contribution-based jobseeker's allowance to which paragraph (4) applies in accordance with paragraph (4A)(c), to which a person is presently entitled only to the extent that there may, subject to paragraphs 8 and 9 of Schedule 9 to the Claims and Payments Regulations be recovered in respect of any one benefit week a sum equal to one third of the age-related amount applicable to the claimant under section 4(1)(a) of the Jobseekers Act 1995.

(5B) For the purposes of paragraph (5A) where the sum that would otherwise fall to be deducted includes a fraction of a penny, the sum to be deducted shall be rounded down to the nearest whole penny.]

(6) [5 Where—

(a) in the calculation of the income of a person to whom income support is payable, the amount of earnings or other income falling to be taken into account is reduced by paragraphs 4 to 9 of Schedule 8 to the Income Support Regulations (sums to be disregarded in the calculation of earnings) or paragraphs 15 and 16 of Schedule 9 to those

Regulations (sums to be disregarded in the calculation of income other than earnings); or

(b) in the calculation of the income of a person to whom income-based jobseeker's allowance is payable, the amount of earnings or other income falling to be taken into account is reduced by paragraphs 5 to 12 of Schedule 6 to the Jobseeker's Allowance Regulations (sums to be disregarded in the calculation of earnings) or paragraphs 15 and 17 of Schedule 7 to those Regulations (sums to be disregarded in the calculation of income other than earnings),

[11 or

(c) in the calculation of the income of a person to whom state pension credit is payable, the amount of earnings or other income falling to be taken into account is reduced in accordance with paragraph 1 of Schedule 4 (sums to be disregarded in the calculation of income other than capital), or Schedule 6 (sums disregarded from claimant's earnings) to the State Pension Credit Regulations,] [13 or

(d) in the calculation of the income of a person to whom income-related employment and support allowance is payable, the amount of earnings or other income falling to be taken into account is reduced by paragraph 7 of Schedule 7 to the Employment and Support Allowance Regulations (sums to be disregarded in the calculation of earnings) or paragraphs 16 and 17 of Schedule 8 to those Regulations (sums to be disregarded in the calculation of income other than earnings),]

the weekly amount] applicable under paragraph (4) may be increased by not more than half the amount of the reduction, [16 ...].

(7) Regulation 15 shall not be applied to a specified benefit so as to reduce the benefit in any one benefit week to less than 10 pence.

[15 (7A) This paragraph applies where the benefit from which the deduction is to be made under regulation 15 is universal credit.

(7B) Where paragraph (7A) applies, regulation 11 of the Social Security (Overpayments and Recovery) Regulations 2013 applies in relation to those deductions as it applies to deductions from universal credit for the recovery of recoverable amounts under those Regulations.]

(8) In this regulation—

[9 'admission after caution' means—

(i) in England and Wales, an admission after a caution has been administered in accordance with a Code issued under the Police and Criminal Evidence Act 1984;

in Scotland, an admission after a caution has been administered, such admission being duly witnessed by two persons;]

"benefit week" means the week corresponding to the week in respect of which the benefit is paid;

[11 "personal allowance for a single claimant aged not less than 25" means—

(a) in the case of a person who is entitled to [13 an employment and support allowance,] income support or state pension credit, the amount for the time being specified in paragraph 1(1)(e) of column (2) of Schedule 2 to the Income Support Regulations; or

(b) in the case of a person who is entitled to income-based jobseeker's allowance, the amount for the time being specified in paragraph 1(1)(e) of column (2) of Schedule 1 to the Jobseeker's Allowance Regulations;]

"specified benefit" means—

(a) a jobseeker's allowance;

(b) income support when paid alone or together with any incapacity benefit, retirement pension or severe disablement allowance in a combined payment in respect of any period;

(c) if incapacity benefit, retirement pension or severe disablement allowance is paid concurrently with income support in respect of any period but not in a combined payment, income support and such of those benefits as are paid concurrently;

(d) state pension credit when paid alone or together with any retirement pension, incapacity benefit or severe disablement allowance in a combined payment in respect of any period;

(e) if retirement pension, incapacity benefit or severe disablement allowance is paid concurrently with state pension credit in respect of any period but not in a combined payment, state pension credit and such of those benefits as are paid concurrently, but does not include any sum payable by way of child maintenance bonus in accordance with section 10 of the Child Support Act 1995 and the Social Security (Child Maintenance Bonus) Regulations 1996.] [[13] and

(f) an employment and support allowance,]

but does not include any sum payable by way of child maintenance bonus in accordance with section 10 of the Child Support Act 1995 and the Social Security (Child Maintenance Bonus) Regulations 1996.]

AMENDMENTS

1. The Social Security (Payments on account, Overpayments and Recovery) Amendments Regulations 1988 (SI 1988/688) reg.2(4) (April 11, 1988).

2. The Disability Living Allowance and Disability Working Allowance (Consequential Provisions) Regulations 1991 (SI 1991/2742) reg.15 (April 6, 1992).

3. The Social Security (Incapacity Benefit) (Consequential and Transitional Amendments and Savings) Regulations 1995 (SI 1995/829) reg.21(4) (April 13, 1995).

4. The Social Security (Claims and Payments, etc.) Amendment Regulations 1996 (SI 1996/672) reg.4 (April 4, 1996).

5. The Social Security and Child Support (Jobseeker's Allowance) (Consequential Amendments) Regulations 1996 (SI 1996/1345) reg.23(4) (October 7, 1996).

6. The Social Security (Jobseeker's Allowance and Payments on account) (Miscellaneous Amendments) Regulations 1996 (SI 1996/2519) reg.3(4) (October 7, 1996).

7. The Social Security (Child Maintenance Bonus) Regulations 1996 (SI 1996/3195) reg.16(3) (April 7, 1997).

8. The Social Security (Miscellaneous Amendments) Regulations 1997 (SI 1997/454) reg.8(10) (April 6, 1997).

9. The Social Security (Payments on Account, Overpayment and Recovery) Amendment Regulations 2000 (SI 2000/2336) reg.2 (October 2, 2000).

10. The Social Security (Claims and Payments and Miscellaneous Amendments) (No.2) Regulations 2002 (SI 2002/2441) reg.134 (October 23, 2002).

11. State Pension Credit (Consequential, Transitional and Miscellaneous Provisions) Regulations 2002 (SI 2002/3019) reg.24 (October 6, 2003).

12. The Social Security, Child Support and Tax Credits (Miscellaneous Amendments) Regulations 2005 (SI 2005/337) reg.10 (March 18, 2005).

13. The Employment and Support Allowance (Consequential Provisions) (No.2) Regulations 2008 (SI 2008/1554) reg.52 (October 27, 2008).

14. The Social Security (Recovery) (Amendment) Regulations 2012 (SI 2012/645) reg.3(1) (April 1, 2012).

15. The Social Security (Overpayments and Recovery) Regulations 2013 (SI 2013/384) reg.31(8) (April 8, 2013).

16. The Universal Credit, Personal Independence Payment, Jobseeker's Allowance and Employment and Support Allowance (Claims and Payments) Regulations 2013 (SI 2013/380) Sch.3 para.2 (April 29, 2013).

17. The Social Security (Overpayments and Recovery) Amendments Regulations 2015 (SI 2015/499) reg.2 (April 6, 2015).

Recovery from couples

2.915 **17.** In the case of an overpayment of income support [3 or state pension credit] [2, or income-based jobseeker's allowance] [5 or income-related employment and support allowance] [1 ...] to one of [4 a couple], the amount recoverable by deduction, in accordance with regulation 15, may be recovered by deduction from income support [3 or state pension credit] [2, or income-based jobseeker's allowance] [5 or income-related employment and support allowance] [1 ...] payable to either of them, provided that the two of them are [4 a couple] at the date of the deduction.

AMENDMENTS

1. The Tax Credits (Payments on Account, Overpayments and Recovery) (Amendment) Regulations 1999 (SI 1999/2571), reg.14 (October 5, 1999).

2. The Social Security and Child Support (Jobseeker's Allowance) (Consequential Amendments) Regulations 1996 (SI 1996/1345) reg.23(5) and (6) (October 7, 1996).

3. State Pension Credit (Consequential, Transitional and Miscellaneous Provisions) Regulations 2002 (SI 2002/3019) reg.24 (October 6, 2003).

4. The Civil Partnership (Pensions, Social Security and Child Support) (Consequential etc. Provisions) Order 2005 (SI 2005/2877) (December 5, 2005).

5. The Employment and Support Allowance (Consequential Provisions) (No.2) Regulations 2008 (SI 2008/1554) reg.52 (October 27, 2008).

PART VIII

RECOVERY BY DEDUCTIONS FROM EARNINGS FOLLOWING TRADE DISPUTE

Recovery by deductions from earnings

2.916 **18.**—(1) Any sum paid to a person on an award of income support made to him by virtue of section 23(8) of the Act [SSCBA, section 127] (effect of return to work after a trade dispute) shall be recoverable from him in accordance with this Part of these Regulations.

(2) In this Part, unless the context otherwise requires—

"available earnings" means the earnings, including any remuneration paid by or on behalf of an employer to an employee who is for the time being unable to work owing to sickness, which remain payable to a claimant on any pay-day after deduction by his employer of all amounts lawfully deductible by the employer otherwise than by virtue of a deduction notice;

"claimant" means a person to whom an award is made by virtue of section 23(8) of the Act [SSCBA, section 127];

"deduction notice" means a notice under regulation 20 or 25;

"employment" means employment (including employment which has been suspended but not terminated) in remunerative work, and related expressions shall be construed accordingly;

"pay-day" means an occasion on which earnings are paid to a claimant;

"protected earnings" means protected earnings as determined by an adjudicating authority, in accordance with regulation 19(2), under regulation 19(1)(a) or 24;

"recoverable amount" means the amount (determined in accordance with regulation 20(3) or (5) or regulation 25(2)(a)) by reference to which deductions are to be made by an employer from a claimant's earnings by virtue of a deduction notice;

"repaid by the claimant" means paid by the claimant directly to the Secretary of State by way of repayment of income support otherwise recoverable under this Part of these Regulations.

(3) Any notice or other document required or authorised to be given or sent to any person under the provisions of this Part shall be deemed to have been given or sent if it was sent by post to that person in accordance with paragraph (6) of regulation 27 where that regulation applies and, in any other case, at his ordinary or last known address or in the case of an employer at the last place of business where the claimant to which it relates is employed, and if so sent to have been given or sent on the day on which it was posted.

Award and protected earnings

19.—(1) Where an adjudicating authority determines that a person claiming income support is entitled by virtue of section 23(8) of the Act [SSCBA, section 127] (effect of return to work after a trade dispute) and makes an award to him accordingly he shall determine the claimant's protected earnings (that is to say the amount below which his actual earnings must not be reduced by any deduction made under this Part). **2.917**

(2) The adjudicating authority shall include in his decision—

(a) the amount of income support awarded together with a statement that the claimant is a person entitled by virtue of section 23(8) of the Act [SSCBA, section 127] and that accordingly any sum paid to him on that award will be recoverable from him as provided in this Part;
(b) the amount of the claimant's protected earnings, and
(c) a statement of the claimant's duty under regulation 28 (duty to give notice of cessation or resumption of employment).

[[1](3) The protected earnings of the claimant shall be the sum determined by—

(a) taking the sum specified in paragraph (4),
(b) adding the sum specified in paragraph (5), and
(c) subtracting from the result any child benefit which falls to be taken into account in calculating his income for the purposes of Part V of the Income Support Regulations.]

(4) The sum referred to in paragraph (3)(a) shall be the aggregate of the amounts calculated under regulation 17(a) to (d), 18(a) to (e), 20 or 21, as the case may be, of the Income Support Regulations.

(5) The sum referred to in paragraph (3)(b) shall be £27 except where the sum referred to in paragraph (3)(a) includes an amount calculated under regulation 20 in which case the sum shall be £8.00.

AMENDMENT

1. The Social Security (Payments on account, Overpayments and Recovery) Amendments Regulations 1988 (SI 1988/688) reg.2(5) (April 11, 1988).

Service and contents of deduction notices

2.918 **20.**—(1) Where the amount of income support has not already been repaid by the claimant, the Secretary of State shall serve a deduction notice on the employer of the claimant.

(2) A deduction notice shall contain the following particulars—

(a) particulars enabling the employer to identify the claimant;

(b) the recoverable amount;

(c) the claimant's protected earnings as specified in the notification of award.

(3) Subject to paragraph (5) the recoverable amount shall be—

(a) the amount specified in the decision as having been awarded to the claimant by way of income support; reduced by

(b) the amount (if any) which has been repaid by the claimant before the date of the deduction notice.

(4) If a further award relating to the claimant is made the Secretary of State shall cancel the deduction notice (giving written notice of the cancellation to the employer and the claimant) and serve on the employer a further deduction notice.

(5) The recoverable amount to be specified in the further deduction notice shall be the sum of—

(a) the amount determined by applying paragraph (3) to the further award; and

(b) the recoverable amount specified in the cancelled deduction notice less any part of that amount which before the date of the further notice has already been deducted by virtue of the cancelled notice or repaid by the claimant.

Period for which deduction notice has effect

2.919 **21.**—(1) A deduction notice shall come into force when it is served on the employer of the claimant to whom it relates and shall cease to have effect as soon as any of the following conditions is fulfilled—

(a) the notice is cancelled by virtue of regulation 20(4) or paragraph (2) of this regulation;

(b) the claimant ceases to be in the employment of the person on whom the notice was served;

(c) the aggregate of—

(i) any part of the recoverable amount repaid by the claimant on or after the date of the deduction notice, and

(ii) the total amount deducted by virtue of the notice,

reaches the recoverable amount;

(d) there has elapsed a period of 26 weeks beginning with the date of the notice.

(2) The Secretary of State may at any time give a direction in writing cancelling a deduction notice and—

(a) he shall cause a copy of the direction to be served on the employer concerned and on the claimant;

(b) the direction shall take effect when a copy of it is served on the employer concerned.

Effect of deduction notice

22.—(1) Where a deduction notice is in force the following provisions of this regulation shall apply as regards any relevant pay-day. 2.920

(2) Where a claimant's earnings include any bonus, commission or other similar payment which is paid other than on a day on which the remainder of his earnings is paid, then in order to calculate his available earnings for the purposes of this regulation any such bonus, commission or other similar payment shall be treated as being paid to him on the next day of payment of the remainder of his earnings instead of on the day of actual payment.

(3) If on a relevant pay-day a claimant's available earnings—

(a) do not exceed his protected earnings by at least £1, no deduction shall be made;

(b) do exceed his protected earnings by at least £1, his employer shall deduct from the claimant's available earnings one half of the excess over his protected earnings,

so however that where earnings are paid other than weekly the amount of the protected earnings and the figure of £1 shall be adjusted accordingly, in particular—

(c) where earnings are paid monthly, they shall for this purpose be treated as paid every five weeks (and the protected earnings and the figure of £1 accordingly multiplied by five);

(d) where earnings are paid daily, the protected earnings and the figure of £1 shall be divided by five,

and if, in any case to which sub-paragraph (c) or (d) does not apply, there is doubt as to the adjustment to be made this shall be determined by the Secretary of State on the application of the employer or the claimant.

(4) Where on a relevant pay-day earnings are payable to the claimant in respect of more than one pay-day the amount of the protected earnings and the figure of £1 referred to in the preceding paragraph, adjusted where appropriate in accordance with the provisions of that paragraph, shall be multiplied by the number of pay-days to which the earnings relate.

(5) Notwithstanding anything in paragraph (3)—

(a) the employer shall not make a deduction on a relevant pay-day if the claimant satisfies him that up to that day he has not obtained payment of the income support to which the deduction notice relates;

(b) the employer shall not on any relevant pay-day deduct from the claimant's earnings by virtue of the deduction notice an amount greater than the excess of the recoverable amount over the aggregate of all such amounts as, in relation to that notice, are mentioned in regulation 21(1)(c)(i) and (ii); and

(c) where the amount of any deduction which by this regulation the employer is required to make would otherwise include a fraction of 1p, that amount shall be reduced by that fraction.

(6) For the purpose of this regulation "relevant pay-day" means any pay-day beginning with—

(a) the first pay-day falling after the expiration of the period of one month from the date on which the deduction notice comes into force; or

(b) if the employer so chooses, any earlier pay-day after the notice has come into force.

Increase of amount of award on appeal or [1 otherwise]

2.921 **23.** If the amount of the award is increased, whether on appeal or [1 otherwise], this Part shall have effect as if on the date on which the amount of the award was increased—

(a) the amount of the increase was the recoverable amount; and

(b) the claimant's protected earnings [1, where a notice of variation of protected earnings is given under regulation 24, were the earnings stated in the notice]

AMENDMENT

1. The Social Security Act 1998 (Commencement No.12, and Consequential and Transitional Provisions) Order 1999 (SI 1999/3178) Sch.9 (November 29, 1999).

[1 Notice of variation] of protected earnings

2.922 [1 . . .] **24.**—(1) [1 . . .]

[1 (2) The Secretary of State shall give a claimant's employer written notice varying the deduction notice where a decision as to a claimant's protected earnings is revised or superseded.]

(3) Variation of a deduction notice under paragraph (2) shall take effect either from the end of the period of 10 working days beginning with the day on which notice of the variation is given to the employer or, if the employer so chooses, at any earlier time after notice is given.

AMENDMENT

1. The Social Security Act 1998 (Commencement No.12 and Consequential and Transitional Provisions) Order 1999 (SI 1999/3178) Sch.9 (November 29, 1999).

Power to serve further deduction notice on resumption of employment

2.923 **25.**—(1) Where a deduction notice has ceased to have effect by reason of the claimant ceasing to be in the employment of the person on whom the notice was served, the Secretary of State may, if he thinks fit, serve a further deduction notice on any person by whom the claimant is for the time being employed.

(2) Notwithstanding anything in the foregoing provisions of these Regulations, in any such deduction notice—

(a) the recoverable amount shall be equal to the recoverable amount as specified in the previous deduction notice less the aggregate of—

(i) the total of any amounts required to be deducted by virtue of that notice, and

(ii) any additional part of that recoverable amount repaid by the claimant on or after the date of that notice,

or, where this regulation applies in respect of more than one such previous notice, the aggregate of the amounts as so calculated in respect of each such notice;

(b) the amount specified as the claimant's protected earnings shall be the same as that so specified in the last deduction notice relating to him which was previously in force or as subsequently [1 varied].

AMENDMENT

1. The Social Security Act 1998 (Commencement No.12 and Consequential and Transitional Provisions) Order 1999 (SI 1999/3178) Sch.9 (November 29, 1999).

Right of Secretary of State to recover direct from claimant

26. Where [1, at any time, it is not practicable for the Secretary of State] by means of a deduction notice, to effect recovery of the recoverable amount or of so much of that amount as remains to be recovered from the claimant, the amount which remains to be recovered shall, by virtue of this regulation, be recoverable from the claimant by the Secretary of State. **2.924**

AMENDMENT

1. The Social Security Act 1998 (Commencement No.12 and Consequential and Transitional Provisions) Order 1999 (SI 1999/3178) Sch.9 (November 29, 1999).

Duties and liabilities of employers

27.—(1) An employer shall keep a record of the available earnings of each claimant who is an employee in respect of whom a deduction notice is in force and of the payments which he makes in pursuance of the notice. **2.925**

(2) A record of every deduction made by an employer under a deduction notice on any pay-day shall be given or sent by him to the Secretary of State, together with payment of the amount deduced, by not later than the 19th day of the following month.

(3) Where by reason only of the circumstances mentioned in regulation 22(5)(a) the employer makes no deduction from a claimant's weekly earnings on any pay-day he shall within 10 working days after that pay-day give notice of that fact to the Secretary of State.

(4) Where a deduction notice is cancelled by virtue of regulation 20(4) or 21(2) or ceases to have effect by virtue of regulation 21(1) the employer shall within 10 working days after the date on which the notice is cancelled or, as the case may be, ceases to have effect—

(a) return the notice to the Secretary of State and, where regulation 21(1) applies, give notice of the reason for its return;

(b) give notice, in relation to each relevant pay-day (as defined in regulation 22(6)), of the available earnings of the claimant and of any deduction made from those earnings.

(5) If on any pay-day to which regulation 22(3)(b) applies the employer makes no deduction from a claimant's available earnings, or makes a smaller deduction than he was thereby required to make, and in consequence any amount is not deducted while the deduction notice, or any further notice which under regulation 20(4) cancels that notice, has effect—

(a) the amount which is not deducted shall, without prejudice to any other method of recovery from the claimant or otherwise, be recoverable from the employer by the Secretary of State; and

(b) any amount so recovered shall, for the purposes of these Regulations, be deemed to have been repaid by the claimant.

(6) All records and notices to which this regulation applies shall given or sent to the Secretary of State, on a form approved by him, at such office of the [1Department of Social Security] as he may direct.

AMENDMENT

1. The Transfer of Functions (Health and Social Security) Order 1988 (SI 1988/1843) art.3(4) (November 28, 1988).

Claimants to give notice of cessation or resumption of employment

2.926 **28.**—(1) Where a claimant ceases to be in the employment of a person on whom a deduction notice relating to him has been duly served knowing that the full amount of the recoverable amount has not been deducted from his earnings or otherwise recovered by the Secretary of State, he shall give notice within 10 working days to the Secretary of State of his address and of the date of such cessation of employment.

(2) Where on or after such cessation the claimant resumes employment (whether with the same or some other employer) he shall within 10 working days give notice to the Secretary of State of the name of the employer and of the address of his place of employment.

Failure to notify

2.927 **29.** If a person fails to comply with any requirement under regulation 27 or 28 to give notice of any matter to the Secretary of State he shall be guilty of an offence and liable on summary conviction to a fine not exceeding—

(a) for any one offence, level 3 on the standard scale; or

(b) for an offence of continuing any such contravention, £40 for each day on which it is so continued.

[1 PART 8A

RECOVERY BY DEDUCTION FROM EARNINGS: OTHER CASES

Recovery by deduction from earnings: other cases

2.928 **29A.**—(1) Any amount which is recoverable by virtue of section 71(1) or (4), 71ZA or 78(1) of the Administration Act may be recovered by the Secretary of State by deduction from the earnings of the person from whom it is recoverable.

(2) Part 6 of the Social Security (Overpayments and Recovery) Regulations 2013 applies in relation to recovery by deduction from the earnings of a person specified in paragraph (1) by the Secretary of State as it applies to recovery by deduction from the earnings of persons of recoverable amounts under that Part of those Regulations by an appropriate authority.]

AMENDMENT

1. Inserted by The Social Security (Overpayments and Recovery) Regulations 2013 (SI 2013/384) reg.31(9) (April 8, 2013).

The Social Security (Payments on Account of Benefit) Regulations 2013

(SI 2013/383)

COMMENCEMENT: APRIL 1, 2013

PART 1

GENERAL

PART 2

PAYMENTS ON ACCOUNT OF BENEFIT

PART 3

BUDGETING ADVANCES

PART 4

CONSEQUENTIAL AMENDMENTS, REVOCATIONS AND SAVINGS

The Secretary of State for Work and Pensions makes the following Regulations in exercise of the powers conferred by sections 5(1)(r), 189(1), (4) to (6) and 191 of the Social Security Administration Act 1992 and section 84 of, and paragraph 9 of Schedule 2 to, the Social Security Act 1998.

In accordance with section 80(1)(b) of the Social Security Act 1998, a draft of this instrument was laid before Parliament and approved by a resolution of each House of Parliament.

This instrument contains only regulations made by virtue of, or consequential upon, sections 101(1) and 104(1) of the Welfare Reform Act 2012 and is made before the end of the period of 6 months beginning with the coming into force of those sections.

PART 1

GENERAL

Citation and commencement

2.930 **1.**—(1) These Regulations may be cited as the Social Security (Payments on Account of Benefit) Regulations 2013.

(2) They come into force—

(a) for the purposes of this Part and Part 2 (except the provisions specified in paragraph (3)) and Part 4, on 1st April 2013;

(b) for all other purposes, on 29th April 2013.

(3) The specified provisions are—

(a) in regulation 2(1)

(i) the definitions of "the UC etc. Claims and Payments Regulations", "the Universal Credit Regulations" and "universal credit";

(ii) paragraph (a) of the definition of "couple";

(b) regulation 2(2) and (3)(a);

(c) regulation 3(1)(a) and (2)(a)(i) and (b)(i);

(d) regulation 5(3)(a);

(e) regulation 7(2); and

(f) regulation 8(2).

Interpretation

2.931 **2.**—(1) In these Regulations—

"the 1995 Act" means the Jobseekers Act 1995;

"the 2007 Act" means the Welfare Reform Act 2007;

"the 2012 Act" means the Welfare Reform Act 2012;

"the Contributions and Benefits Act" means the Social Security Contributions and Benefits Act 1992;

"the 1988 Regulations" means the Social Security (Payments on account, Overpayments and Recovery) Regulations 1988;

"the Claims and Payments Regulations" means the Social Security (Claims and Payments) Regulations 1987;

"the UC etc. Claims and Payments Regulations" means the Universal Credit, Personal Independence Payment, Jobseeker's Allowance and Employment and Support Allowance (Claims and Payments) Regulations 2013;

"the Universal Credit Regulations" means the Universal Credit Regulations 2013;

"couple"—

(a) where these Regulations apply in relation to universal credit, has the same meaning as in Part 1 of the 2012 Act;

(b) where these Regulations apply in relation to the benefits specified in regulation 3(1)(b) to (f), has the same meaning as in section 137(1) of the Contributions and Benefits Act;

"partner" means, where the person being referred to is a member of a couple, the other member of the couple;

"universal credit" means the benefit under Part 1 of the 2012 Act.

(2) Where these Regulations apply in relation to universal credit, "child" and "qualifying young person" have the same meaning as in Part 1 of the 2012 Act and whether or not a person is responsible for a child or qualifying young person is to be determined in accordance with regulation 4 of the Universal Credit Regulations.

(2) *Omitted.*

(3) In these Regulations, "writing" includes writing produced by means of electronic communications and, where such communications are used by the Secretary of State—

(a) Schedule 2 to the UC etc. Claims and Payments Regulations; or, as the case may be,

(b) Schedule 9ZC to the Claims and Payments Regulations,

has effect in connection with notices required to be given or sent under regulations 8 and 17 as it has effect in connection with claims for, and awards of, any benefit to which those Regulations apply.

PART 2

PAYMENTS ON ACCOUNT OF BENEFIT

Definition of "benefit"

3. (1) In this Part, "benefit" means any of the following— **2.932**

(a) universal credit;

(b) employment and support allowance;

(c) income support;

(d) jobseeker's allowance;

(e) state pension credit;

(f) benefit under Parts 2 to 5 of the Contributions and Benefits Act except attendance allowance [1 , disability living allowance and guardian's allowance].

[2 (g) a state pension under Part 1 of the Pensions Act 2014.]

(2) For the purpose of paragraph (1)—

(a) "employment and support allowance" means an allowance under—

(i) Part 1 of the 2007 Act as amended by Schedule 3, and Part 1 of Schedule 14, to the 2012 Act (to remove references to an income-related allowance); and

(ii) Part 1 of the 2007 Act as it has effect apart from the amendments made by Schedule 3, and Part 1 of Schedule 14, to the 2012 Act;

(b) "jobseeker's allowance" means an allowance under—

(i) the 1995 Act as amended by Part 1 of Schedule 14 to the 2012 Act (to remove references to an income-based allowance); and

(ii) the 1995 Act as it has effect apart from the amendments made by Part 1 of Schedule 14 to the 2012 Act.

AMENDMENTS

1. The Social Security (Miscellaneous Amendments) (No.2) Regulations 2013 (SI 2013/1508) reg.7(2) (July 29, 2013).

2. The Pensions Act 2014 (Consequential, Supplementary and Incidental Amendments) Order 2015 (SI 2015/1985) art.41 (April 6, 2016).

Payments on account of benefit

2.933 **4.**—(1) The Secretary of State may, subject to paragraph (2), make a payment on account of benefit to a person ("A") in accordance with this Part.

(2) Paragraph (1) does not apply pending the determination of an appeal relating to the benefit on account of which the payment would otherwise have been made.

Payment on account of benefit where there is no award of benefit

2.934 **5.**—(1) The Secretary of State may make a payment on account of benefit to A if—

(a) either of paragraphs (2) or (3) applies;

(b) it appears to the Secretary of State likely that the conditions of entitlement for benefit are satisfied [1 (or will be satisfied during the period in respect of which the payment is to be made)]; [...]

(c) the Secretary of State is satisfied that A is in financial need [; and]

[2(d) where the payment on account of benefit is to be on account of universal credit, A has been allocated a national insurance number.]

(2) This paragraph applies where A has made a claim for benefit but the claim has not yet been determined.

(3) This paragraph applies where A is not required to make a claim for benefit by virtue of—

(a) Regulation 6 or 7 of the UC etc. Claims and Payments Regulations (claims not required for entitlement to universal credit or an employment and support allowance in certain cases); or, as the case may be,

(b) regulation 3 of the Claims and Payments Regulations (claims not required for entitlement to benefit in certain cases),

but an award of benefit has not yet been made.

AMENDMENT

1. The Universal Credit and Miscellaneous Amendments (No.2) Regulations 2014 (SI 2014/2888), reg.5(1)(a) (November 26, 2014).

2. The Social Security and Universal Credit (Migration of Tax Credit Claimants and Miscellaneous Amendments) Regulations 2024 (SI 2024/341), reg.6 (April 1, 2024).

GENERAL NOTE

2.935 The amendments made by SI 2024/341 seek to implement the DWP's policy intention that a payment on account should only be made to an individual with a

NINO, to minimise the risk of fraud, which the Court of Appeal's decision in *SSWP v Bui and Onekoya* [2023] EWCA Civ 566, on the unamended legislation, had called into question. The court held that the condition in SSAA s.1(1B)(b) was no different from any other condition and thus that it did not follow that in every case where a claimant for universal credit does not have a NINO, SSWP would be unable to say that it was "likely" that the condition would be satisfied.

Payment on account of benefit where there is an award of benefit

6.—(1) The Secretary of State may make a payment on account of benefit to A if— 2.936

(a) an award of benefit has been made to A;
(b) any of paragraphs (2) to (5) applies; and
(c) the Secretary of State is satisfied that A is in financial need.

(2) This paragraph applies where—

(a) A currently satisfies the conditions of entitlement to that benefit; and
(b) the date on which the first payment of that benefit to A is due to be made in accordance with the award has not yet been reached.

(3) This paragraph applies where—

(a) the first payment of that benefit has been made to A in accordance with the award;
(b) the period in respect of which that payment was made is shorter than the period in respect of which subsequent payments of that benefit are to be made in accordance with that award should entitlement continue; and
(c) the date on which a subsequent payment of that benefit is due to be made to A has not yet been reached.

(4) This paragraph applies where there has been a change of circumstances which would increase the amount of benefit payable under the award and—

(a) the award has not yet been revised or superseded to reflect that change; or
(b) the award has been revised or superseded to reflect that change but the date on which the payment of benefit is due to be made in accordance with the revised or superseded award has not yet been reached.

(5) This paragraph applies where—

(a) A is entitled to a payment of that benefit pursuant to the award; and
(b) it is impracticable to make some or all of that payment on the day on which it is due.

Definition of financial need

7.—(1) A is in financial need for the purposes of regulation 5(1)(c) or 6(1)(c) where the circumstances in regulation 5(2) or (3) or, as the case may be, 6(2), (3), (4) or (5) result in a serious risk of damage to the health or safety of A or any member of their family. 2.937

(2) Where the payment on account of benefit is to be on account of universal credit, the following are members of A's family for the purpose of paragraph (1)—

(a) any child or qualifying young person for whom A is responsible; and
(b) where A is a member of a couple, their partner.

(3) Where the payment on account of benefit is to be on account of a benefit specified in regulation 3(1)(b) to [[1] (g)], for the purpose of

paragraph (1), "family" has the meaning given in section 137(1) of the Contributions and Benefits Act.

AMENDMENT

1. The Pensions Act 2014 (Consequential, Supplementary and Incidental Amendments) Order 2015 (SI 2015/1985) art.41 (April 6, 2016).

Requirement for notice

2.938 8.—(1) The Secretary of State must, on or before making a payment on account of benefit to A, give or send notice in writing to A of their liability—

(a) to have the amount of the payment on account of benefit deducted from subsequent payments of benefit; and

(b) to repay the amount of any payment on account of benefit to the extent that it is not deducted from subsequent payments of benefit.

(2) Where A is a member of a couple and the payment on account of benefit is on account of universal credit, notice in writing must also be given or sent to their partner containing the information referred to in paragraph (1)(a) and (b).

[1 "Payment by direct credit transfer

2.939 **9.** A payment on account of benefit may be paid by way of direct credit transfer into a bank account or other account nominated by A or a person acting on A's behalf.]

AMENDMENT

1. The Universal Credit and Miscellaneous Amendments (No.2) Regulations 2014 (SI 2014/2888), reg.5(1)(b) (November 26, 2014).

Bringing payments on account of benefit into account

2.940 **10.** Where it is practicable to do so, a payment on account of benefit—

(a) which was made in anticipation of an award of benefit, is to be offset by the Secretary of State against the sum payable to A under the award of benefit on account of which it was made;

(b) whether or not made in anticipation of an award, which is not offset under paragraph (a), is to be deducted by the Secretary of State from—

(i) the sum payable to A under the award of benefit on account of which it was made; or

(ii) any sum payable under any subsequent award of that benefit to A.

PART 3

BUDGETING ADVANCES

Payment of budgeting advances

2.941 **11.**—(1) The Secretary of State may make a payment on account of universal credit to a person ("B") in accordance with this Part.

(2) A payment under this Part is to be known as a budgeting advance.

Conditions for payment of budgeting advances

12.—(1) The Secretary of State may make a budgeting advance to B for the purpose of defraying an intermittent expense of B if— 2.942

(a) B makes an application to the Secretary of State for a budgeting advance;
(b) B, or in a case where B is a member of a couple, B or their partner, is in receipt of universal credit;
(c) except where paragraph (2) applies, B or, in a case where B is a member of a couple, B or their partner, has been in receipt of benefit for a continuous period of at least 6 months on the date of the application for a budgeting advance;
(d) the earnings condition in regulation 13 is satisfied; and
(e) the recovery condition in regulation 14 is satisfied.

(2) This paragraph applies where the intermittent expense to be defrayed is necessarily related to B or, in a case where B is a member of a couple, their partner, obtaining or retaining employment.

(3) For the purposes of paragraph (1)(c), "benefit" means—

(a) universal credit;
(b) employment and support allowance;
(c) income support;
(d) jobseeker's allowance; or
(e) state pension credit.

(4) For the purposes of paragraph (3)—

(a) "employment and support allowance" means an income-related allowance under Part 1 of the 2007 Act as it has effect apart from the amendments made by Schedule 3, and Part 1 of Schedule 14, to the 2012 Act (to remove references to an income-related allowance);
(b) "jobseeker's allowance" means an income-based jobseeker's allowance under the 1995 Act as it has effect apart from the amendments made by Part 1 of Schedule 14 to the 2012 Act (to remove references to an income-based allowance).

[[1]13.— Earnings condition

(1) The earnings condition is satisfied— 2.943

(a) in a case where regulation 12(2) (expenses necessarily related to obtaining or retaining employment) does not apply, where paragraph (2) is satisfied;
(b) in a case where regulation 12(2) does apply, where paragraph (4) is satisfied.

(2) This paragraph is satisfied where—

(a) if B is not a member of a couple, B does not have earned income exceeding £2,600, or
(b) if B is a member of a couple, B and their partner jointly do not have earned income exceeding £3,600,

over the relevant period.

(3) In paragraph (2), "the relevant period" means the period covered by the six complete assessment periods preceding the date of the application for the budgeting advance.

(4) This paragraph is satisfied where—

(a) if B is not a member of a couple, B does not have earned inome, or

(b) if B is a member of a couple, B and their partner jointly do not have earned income,

exceeding the permitted amount over the applicable period.

(5) In paragraph (4), "the permitted amount over the applicable period" is to be determined by the formula—

$$N\,x\,(\frac{P}{6})$$

where—

N is the number of complete assessment periods in the applicable period, and

P is—

(i) where sub-paragraph (4)(a) applies, £2,600;

(ii) where sub-paragraph (4)(b) applies, £3,600.

(6) For the purposes of paragraphs (4) and (5), "the applicable period" means—

(a) if there are six or more complete assessment periods immediately preceding the date of the application for the budgeting advance, the period covered by the six complete assessment periods immediately preceding the date of the application for the budgeting advance;

(b) if there are fewer than six complete assessment periods immediately preceding the date of the application for the budgeting advance, the number of complete assessment periods immediately preceding the date of the application for the budgeting advance.

(7) Earned income for each complete assessment period is to be calculated for the purposes of this regulation in accordance with Chapter 2 of Part 6 of the Universal Credit Regulations save that in relation to the earned income of a person who is in gainful self-employment for the purpose of regulation 64 of these Regulations, regulation 62 of those Regulations (minimum income floor) is to be disregarded.

(8) In this regulation, "assessment period" has the meaning given in regulation 21 of the Universal Credit Regulations.]

AMENDMENT

1. Universal Credit and Miscellaneous Amendments Regulations (SI 2015/1754) Pt 1 reg.7 (November 4, 2015).

Recovery condition

2.944 **14.** The recovery condition is satisfied where—

(a) no amount in respect of any budgeting advance previously paid to B or, if B is a member of a couple, B or their partner, remains to be recovered by the Secretary of State; and

(b) taking into account all debts and other liabilities of B or, if B is a member of a couple, of B and their partner, the Secretary of State is satisfied that the budgeting advance can reasonably be expected to be recovered.

Minimum and maximum amounts payable by way of budgeting advance

2.945 **15.**—(1) The minimum amount payable by way of budgeting advance is £100.

(2) Subject to regulation 16(2), the maximum amount payable by way of budgeting advance is—

(a) where B is neither a member of a couple nor responsible for any child or qualifying young person, £348;

(b) where B is a member of a couple but is not responsible for any child or qualifying young person, £464;

(c) where B is responsible for any child or qualifying young person, £812.

Treatment of capital

16.—(1) Where the total of B's capital or, in a case where B is a member of a couple, the total of B's and their partner's capital, exceeds £1,000, the amount of any budgeting advance which may otherwise be paid must be reduced by the amount by which that capital exceeds £1,000. **2.946**

(2) No budgeting advance is payable where, as a result of paragraph (1), the amount of any budgeting advance which would otherwise be payable is reduced to less than £100.

(3) Capital is to be calculated for the purposes of paragraph (1) in accordance with Chapter 1 of Part 6 of the Universal Credit Regulations.

Requirement for notice

17.—(1) The Secretary of State must, on or before making a budgeting advance to B, give or send notice in writing to B of their liability— **2.947**

(a) to have the amount of the budgeting advance deducted from subsequent payments of universal credit; and

(b) to repay the amount of the budgeting advance to the extent that it is not deducted from subsequent payments of universal credit.

(2) Where B is a member of a couple, notice in writing must also be given or sent to their partner containing the information referred to in paragraph (1)(a) and (b).

[[1]18. Payment by direct credit transfer

A budgeting advance may be paid by way of direct credit transfer into a bank account or other account nominated by B or a person acting on B's behalf.] **2.948**

AMENDMENT

1. Universal Credit and Miscellaneous Amendments (No.2) Regulations 2014 (SI 2014/2888) reg.5(1)(c) (November 26, 2014).

PART 4

CONSEQUENTIAL AMENDMENTS, REVOCATIONS AND SAVINGS

Consequential revocation to the 1988 Regulations and savings

19.—(1) Subject to paragraph (2), Part 2 of the 1988 Regulations is revoked. **2.949**

(2) Notwithstanding paragraph (1), Part 2 of the 1988 Regulations is to continue to apply in respect of—

(a) applications for interim payments made before this regulation comes into force; and

(b) interim payments made pursuant to applications referred to in sub-paragraph (a).

Amendments to the Social Security and Child Support (Decisions and Appeals) Regulations 1999 and saving

2.950 **20.**—(1) In Schedule 2 to the Social Security and Child Support (Decisions and Appeals) Regulations 1999 ("the 1999 Regulations")(decisions against which no appeal lies)—

(a) in paragraph 20, subject to paragraph (2), omit sub-paragraphs (a) and (b);

(b) after paragraph 20 insert—

"20A. A decision of the Secretary of State under the Social Security (Payments on Account of Benefit) Regulations 2013 except a decision under regulation 10 of those Regulations.".

(2) Notwithstanding paragraph (1)(a), paragraph 20(a) and (b) of Schedule 2 to the 1999 Regulations is to continue to apply in respect of decisions regarding interim payments referred to in regulation 19(2)(b).

The Social Security (Penalty Notice) Regulations 1997

Arrangement of regulations

The Secretary of State for Social Security, in exercise of the powers conferred by sections 115A(2) (b), 189(1), (3) and (5) and 191 of the Social Security Administration Act 1992, and of all other powers enabling her in that behalf, by this instrument which is made before the end of the period of 6 months beginning with the coming into force of the aforesaid section 115A(2) (b), after consultation with organisations appearing to her to be representative of the authorities concerned, hereby makes the following Regulations:

Citation and commencement

2.952 **1.** These Regulations may be cited as the Social Security (Penalty Notice) Regulations 1997 and shall come into force on 18th December 1997.

Notice

2.953 **2.**—(1) Where the Secretary of State or authority gives to a person a written notice under section 115A(2) of the Social Security Administration Act 1992 [1 "the 1992 Act"], the notice shall contain the information that–

(a) the penalty [1 . . .] applies to an overpayment which is recoverable under section 71, [1 71ZB,] 71A, 75 or 76 of the Social Security Administration Act 1992;

(b) the penalty [1 . . .] applies where it appears to the Secretary of State or authority that the making of the overpayment was attributable to an act or omission by the person and that there are grounds for instituting proceedings for an offence relating to the overpayment;

(c) the penalty is [1 50 per cent of the amount of the overpayment (subject to the maximum and minimum amounts prescribed in section 115A(3) of the 1992 Act] is payable in addition to repayment of the overpayment and is recoverable by the same methods as those by which the overpayment is recoverable;

(d) a person who agrees to pay a penalty may withdraw the agreement within [1 14] days (including the date of the agreement) by notifying the Secretary of State or authority in the manner specified by the Secretary of State or authority; if the person withdraws the agreement, so much of the penalty as has already been recovered shall be repaid and he will no longer be immune from proceedings for an offence;

(e) if it is decided on review or appeal (or in accordance with regulations) that the overpayment is not recoverable or due, so much of the penalty as has already been recovered shall be repaid;

(f) if the amount of the overpayment is revised on review or appeal, except as covered by a new agreement to pay the revised penalty, so much of the penalty as has already been recovered shall be repaid and the person will no longer be immune from proceedings for an offence;

(g) the payment of a penalty does not give the person immunity from prosecution in relation to any other overpayment or any offence not relating to an overpayment.

[1 (1A) Where the Secretary of State or authority gives to a person written notice under section 115A(2) of the 1992 Act in a case to which section 115(1A) of that Act applies, the notice shall contain the information that—

(a) the penalty applies where it appears to the Secretary of State or authority that there are grounds for instituting proceedings against the person for an offence relating to an act or omission on the part of the person in relation to any benefit;

(b) if an overpayment attributable to the act or omission had been made, the overpayment would have been recoverable under section 71, 71ZB, 71A, 75 or 76 of the 1992 Act;

(c) the penalty is £350;

(d) a person who agrees to pay the penalty may withdraw the agreement within 14 days (including the date of the agreement) by notifying the Secretary of State or authority in the manner specified by the Secretary of State or authority; if the person withdraws the agreement, so much of the penalty as has already been recovered shall be repaid and he will no longer be immune from proceedings for an offence;

(e) if it is decided on review or appeal (or in accordance with regulations) that any overpayment attributable to the act or omission would not have been recoverable or due, so much of the penalty as has already been recovered shall be repaid;

(f) the payment of a penalty does not give the person immunity from prosecution in relation to any overpayment or any other offence not relating to an overpayment.]

(2) The notice [1 in either case] shall set out–

(a) the manner specified by the Secretary of State or authority by which the person may agree to pay a penalty;

(b) the manner specified by the Secretary of State or authority by which the person may notify the withdrawal of his agreement to pay a penalty.

AMENDMENT

1. The Social Security (Miscellaneous Amendments) Regulations 2014 (SI 2014/591) reg.5 (April 28, 2014).

GENERAL NOTE

2.954 Regulation 4(5) ofThe Social Security (Miscellaneous Amendments) Regulations 2014 provides that the amendments made by these regulations shall apply "only where the offence in respect of which the notice is given is committed wholly on or after 8th May 2012."

The Social Security (Persons Required to Provide Information) Regulations 2013

(SI 2013/1510)

IN FORCE OCTOBER 1, 2013

ARRANGEMENT OF REGULATIONS

The Secretary of State for Work and Pensions makes the following Regulations in exercise of the powers conferred by sections 109B(2)(ia), 189(1) and (5) and 191 of the Social Security Administration Act 1992.

In accordance with section 176(1) of that Act, the Secretary of State has consulted with organisations appearing to him to be representative of the authorities concerned.

This instrument has not been referred to the Social Security Advisory Committee because it contains only regulations made by virtue of section 110 of the Welfare Reform Act 2012 and is made before the end of the period of 6 months beginning with the coming into force of that section.

Citation and commencement

2.956 **1.**—(1) These Regulations may be cited as the Social Security (Persons Required to Provide Information) Regulations 2013.

(2) They come into force on 1st October 2013.

Persons required to provide information

2.—(1) The following are prescribed as descriptions of persons for the purpose of section 109B(2)(ia) of the Social Security Administration Act 1992 (power of authorised officers to require information)— 2.957

(a) a person who provides relevant childcare;
(b) a person to whom a person in receipt of universal credit ("C") is liable to make rent payments in respect of accommodation which C occupies, or purports to occupy, as their home where C's award of universal credit includes an amount in respect of such payments;
(c) a rent officer to the extent that the information required relates to the rent officer's functions under section 122 of the Housing Act 1996;
(d) a local authority which administers a council tax reduction scheme to the extent that the information required relates to such a scheme.

(2) In this regulation—

(a) "UC Regulations" means the Universal Credit Regulations 2013;
(b) "council tax reduction scheme"—
  (i) in England and Wales, has the meaning given in section 13A(9) of the Local Government Finance Act 1992 and includes a default scheme within the meaning of paragraph 4 of Schedule 1A (or in Wales paragraph 6(1)(e) of Schedule 1B) to that Act; and
  (ii) in Scotland, means a means-tested reduction to an individual's council tax liability in accordance with the Council Tax Reduction (Scotland) Regulations 2012 or the Council Tax Reduction (State Pension Credit) (Scotland) Regulations 2012;
(c) "relevant childcare" has the meaning given in regulation 35 of the UC Regulations;
(d) "rent payments" has the meaning given in paragraph 2 of Schedule 1 to the UC Regulations;
(e) "universal credit" means universal credit under Part 1 of the Welfare Reform Act 2012.

The Social Security Act 1998 (Prescribed Benefits) Regulations 2006

(SI 2006/2529)

Made	*14th September 2006*
Laid before Parliament	*21st September 2006*
Coming into force	*16th October 2006*

The Secretary of State for Work and Pensions makes the following Regulations in exercise of the powers conferred by sections 8(3)(h), 79(1) and 84 of the Social Security Act 1998. 2.958

In accordance with section 173(1)(b) of the Social Security Administration Act 1992, the Secretary of State has obtained the agreement of the Social Security Advisory Committee that proposals in respect of these Regulations need not be referred to it.

Citation and commencement

2.959 **1.** —(1) These Regulations may be cited as the Social Security Act 1998 (Prescribed Benefits) Regulations 2006 and shall come into force on 16th October 2006.

Prescribed benefits

2.960 **2.** The benefits prescribed for the purposes of section 8(3)(h) of the Social Security Act 1998 (decisions by Secretary of State) are—

(a) the following benefits under the Social Security Act 1975—
  - (i) sickness benefit under section 14;
  - (ii) unemployment benefit under section 14;
  - (iii) invalidity pension under section 15;
  - (iv) invalidity allowance under section 16;
  - (v) attendance allowance under section 35; and
  - (vi) mobility allowance under section 37A;

(b) supplementary benefit under the Supplementary Benefit Act 1976.

General Note

2.961 Except for attendance allowance, the benefits listed are benefits that had been abolished before the Social Security Act 1998 Act came into force and are therefore not within the scope of s.8(3)(a) to (g) of that Act. Attendance allowance has presumably been included from an abundance of caution because it is now payable only to people over the age of 65, whereas until 1992 it was payable to younger people.

The need for this provision was revealed by *CDLA/2999/2004*, in which it was held that, because the transitional provision made when the 1998 Act came into force relies on the concept of a "relevant benefit" as defined by s.8(3), there was no power to make a supersession decision under s.10 of the 1998 Act in respect of mobility allowance, with the consequence that an overpayment of mobility allowance could not be recovered under s.71 of the Social Security Administration Act 1992. It is not entirely clear why the scope of s.8(3) of the 1998 Act has not been made precisely the same as the scope of s.71 of the 1992 Act (see para.4(1) of Sch.10 to the 1992 Act) but perhaps it was thought unlikely that any wider prescription would be required in practice. It is doubtful that the omission of the second "s" from the short title of the Supplementary Benefits Act 1976 is significant.

The Employment Protection (Recoupment of [Benefits]) Regulations 1996

(SI 1996/2349)

Made	*10th September 1996*
Laid before Parliament	*11th September 1996*
Coming into force	*7th October 1996*

2.962 The Secretary of State in exercise of the powers conferred on him by section 16 and section 41(4) of the Industrial Tribunals Act 1996, section 58(1) of the Social Security Administration Act 1992, and of all other powers enabling him in that behalf, and after reference to the Social Security Advisory Committee in so far as is required by section 172 of the Social Security Administration Act 1992, and after consultation with the Council on

Tribunals, in so far as is required by section 8 of the Tribunals and Inquiries Act 1992, hereby makes the following Regulations:—

Part I

Introductory

Citation and Commencement

1. These Regulations may be cited as the Employment Protection (Recoupment of [1 Benefits] Regulations 1996 and shall come into force on 7th October 1996. **2.963**

Amendment

1. Universal Credit (Consequential, Supplementary, Incidental and Miscellaneous Provisions) Regulations 2013 (SI 2013/630) reg.50(1) and (3) (April 29, 2013).

General Note

These Regulations began life as the Employment Protection (Recoupment of Jobseeker's Allowance and Income Support) Regulations 1996 and were renamed when they were extended to universal credit, although they had already been extended to income-related (but not contributory) employment and support allowance without a change of name. **2.964**

Interpretation

2.—(1) In these Regulations, unless the context otherwise requires, the following expressions have the meanings hereby assigned to them respectively, that is to say— **2.965**

"the 1992 Act" means the Trade Union and Labour Relations (Consolidation) Act 1992;

"the 1996 Act" means the Employment Rights Act 1996;

"prescribed element" has the meaning assigned to it in Regulation 3 below and the Schedule to these Regulations;

"protected period" has the same meaning as in section 189(5) of the 1992 Act;

"protective award" has the same meaning as in section 189(3) of the 1992 Act;

"recoupable benefit" means any jobseeker's allowance [2 , income-related employment and support allowance] [3 , universal credit] or income support as the case may be, which is recoupable under these Regulations;

"recoupment notice" means a notice under these Regulations;

"Secretary of the Tribunals" means the Secretary of the Central Office of the [1 Employment] Tribunals (England and Wales) or, as the case may require, the Secretary of the Central Office of the [1 Employment] Tribunals (Scotland) for the time being;

[3 "universal credit" means universal credit under Part 1 of the Welfare Reform Act 2012]

(2) In the Schedule to these Regulations references to sections are references to sections of the 1996 Act unless otherwise indicated and references in column 3 of the table to the conclusion of the tribunal proceedings are

references to the conclusion of the proceedings mentioned in the corresponding entry in column 2.

(3) For the purposes of these Regulations (and in particular for the purposes of any calculations to be made by an [1 employment tribunal] as respects the prescribed element) the conclusion of the tribunal proceedings shall be taken to occur—

(a) where the [1 employment tribunal] at the hearing announces the effect of its decision to the parties, on the date on which that announcement is made;

(b) in any other case, on the date on which the decision of the tribunal is sent to the parties.

(4) References to parties in relevant [1 employment tribunal] proceedings shall be taken to include references to persons appearing on behalf of parties in a representative capacity.

(5) References in these Regulations to anything done, or to be done, in, or in consequence of, any tribunal proceedings include references to anything done, or to be done, in, or in consequence of any such proceedings as are in the nature of a review, or re-hearing or a further hearing consequent on an appeal.

AMENDMENTS

1. Employment Rights (Dispute Resolution) Act 1998, s.1(2)(a) (August 1, 1998).

2. Social Security (Miscellaneous Amendments) (No.5) Regulations 2010 (SI 2010/2429) reg.5 (November 1, 2010).

3. Universal Credit (Consequential, Supplementary, Incidental and Miscellaneous Provisions) Regulations 2013 (SI 2013/630) reg.50(1) and (4) (April 29, 2013).

PART II

INDUSTRIAL TRIBUNAL PROCEEDINGS

Application to payments and proceedings

2.966 **3.**—(1) Subject to paragraph (2) below these Regulations apply—

(a) to the payments described in column 1 of the table contained in the Schedule to these Regulations, being, in each case, payments which are the subject of [1 employment tribunal] proceedings of the kind described in the corresponding entry in column 2 and the prescribed element in relation to each such payment is so much of the relevant monetary award as is attributable to the matter described in the corresponding entry in column 3; and

(b) to payments of remuneration in pursuance of a protective award.

(2) The payments to which these Regulations apply by virtue of paragraph (1)(a) above include payments in proceedings under section 192 of the 1992 Act and, accordingly, where an order is made on an employee's complaint under that section, the relevant protective award shall, as respects that employee and to the appropriate extent, be taken to be subsumed in the order made under section 192 so that the provisions of these Regulations relating to monetary awards shall apply to payments under that order to the exclusion of the provisions relating to protective awards, but without prejudice to anything done under the latter in connection with the relevant protective award before the making of the order under section 192.

AMENDMENT

1. Employment Rights (Dispute Resolution) Act 1998 s.1(2)(a) (August 1, 1998).

Duties of the [1 employment tribunals] and of the Secretary of the Tribunals in respect of monetary awards

4.—(1) Where these Regulations apply, no regard shall be had, in assessing the amount of a monetary award, to the amount of any jobseeker's allowance [2 , income-related employment and support allowance] [3 , universal credit] or any income support which may have been paid to or claimed by the employee for a period which coincides with any part of a period to which the prescribed element is attributable. 2.967

(2) Where the [1 employment tribunal] in arriving at a monetary award makes a reduction on account of the employee's contributory fault or on account of any limit imposed by or under the 1992 Act or 1996 Act, a proportionate reduction shall be made in arriving at the amount of the prescribed element.

(3) Subject to the following provisions of this Regulation it shall be the duty of the [1 employment tribunal] to set out in any decision which includes a monetary award the following particulars—

(a) the monetary award;
(b) the amount of the prescribed element, if any;
(c) the dates of the period to which the prescribed element is attributable;
(d) the amount, if any, by which the monetary award exceeds the prescribed element.

(4) Where the [1 employment tribunal] at the hearing announces to the parties the effect of a decision which includes a monetary award it shall inform those parties at the same time of the amount of any prescribed element included in the monetary award and shall explain the effect of Regulations 7 and 8 below in relation to the prescribed element.

(5) Where the [1 employment tribunal] has made such an announcement as is described in paragraph (4) above the Secretary of the Tribunals shall forthwith notify the Secretary of State that the tribunal has decided to make a monetary award including a prescribed element and shall notify him of the particulars set out in paragraph (3) above.

(6) As soon as reasonably practicable after the Secretary of the Tribunals has sent a copy of a decision containing the particulars set out in paragraph (3) above to the parties he shall send a copy of that decision to the Secretary of State.

(7) In addition to containing the particulars required under paragraph (3) above, any such decision as is mentioned in that paragraph shall contain a statement explaining the effect of Regulations 7 and 8 below in relation to the prescribed element.

(8) The requirements of paragraphs (3) to (7) above do not apply where the tribunal is satisfied that in respect of each day falling within the period to which the prescribed element relates the employee has neither received nor claimed jobseeker's allowance [2 , income-related employment and support allowance] [3 , universal credit] or income support.

AMENDMENTS

1. Employment Rights (Dispute Resolution) Act 1998 s.1(2)(a) (August 1, 1998).
2. Social Security (Miscellaneous Amendments) (No.5) Regulations 2010 (SI 2010/2429) reg.5 (November 1, 2010).

3. Universal Credit (Consequential, Supplementary, Incidental and Miscellaneous Provisions) Regulations 2013 (SI 2013/630) reg.50(1) and (5) (April 29, 2013).

Duties of the [1 employment tribunals] and of the Secretary of the Tribunals in respect of protective awards

2.968 **5.** (1) Where, on a complaint under section 189 of the 1992 Act, an [1 employment tribunal]—

(a) at the hearing announces to the parties the effect of a decision to make a protective award; or

(b) (where it has made no such announcement) sends a decision to make such an award to the parties; the Secretary of the Tribunals shall forthwith notify the Secretary of State of the following particulars relating to the award—

(i) where the [1 employment tribunal] has made such an announcement as is described in paragraph (1)(a) above, the date of the hearing or where it has made no such announcement, the date on which the decision was sent to the parties;

(ii) the location of the tribunal;

(iii) the name and address of the employer;

(iv) the description of the employees to whom the award relates; and

(v) the dates of the protected period.

(2)(a) Where an [1 employment tribunal] makes such an announcement as is described in paragraph (1)(a) above in the presence of the employer or his representative it shall advise him of his duties under Regulation 6 below and shall explain the effect of Regulations 7 and 8 below in relation to remuneration under the protective award.

(b) Without prejudice to (a) above any decision of an [1 employment tribunal] to make a protective award under section 189 of the 1992 Act shall contain a statement advising the employer of his duties under Regulation 6 below and an explanation of the effect of Regulations 7 and 8 below in relation to remuneration under the protective award.

AMENDMENT

1. Employment Rights (Dispute Resolution) Act 1998 s.1(2)(a) (August 1, 1998).

Duties of the employer to give information about protective awards

2.969 **6.**—(1) Where an [1 employment tribunal] makes a protective award under section 189 of the 1992 Act against an employer, the employer shall give to the Secretary of State the following information in writing—

(a) the name, address and national insurance number of every employee to whom the award relates; and

(b) the date of termination (or proposed termination) of the employment of each such employee.

(2) Subject to paragraph (3) below the employer shall comply with paragraph (1) above within the period of ten days commencing on the day on which the [1 employment tribunal] at the hearing announces to the parties the effect of a decision to make a protective award or (in the case where no such announcement is made) on the day on which the relevant decision is sent to the parties.

(3) Where, in any case, it is not reasonably practicable for the employer to comply with paragraph (1) above within the period applicable under paragraph (2) above he shall comply as soon as reasonably practicable after the expiration of that period.

AMENDMENT

1. Employment Rights (Dispute Resolution) Act 1998 s.1(2)(a) (August 1, 1998).

PART III

RECOUPMENT OF BENEFIT

Postponement of Awards

7.—(1) This Regulation shall have effect for the purpose of postponing relevant awards in order to enable the Secretary of State to initiate recoupment under Regulation 8 below. 2.970

(2) Accordingly—

(a) so much of the monetary award as consists of the prescribed element;

(b) payment of any remuneration to which an employee would otherwise be entitled under a protective award, shall be treated as stayed (in Scotland, sisted) as respects the relevant employee until—

(i) the Secretary of State has served a recoupment notice on the employer; or

(ii) the Secretary of State has notified the employer in writing that he does not intend to serve a recoupment notice.

(3) The stay or sist under paragraph (2) above is without prejudice to the right of an employee under section 192 of the 1992 Act to present a complaint to an [1 employment tribunal] of his employer's failure to pay remuneration under a protective award and Regulation 3(2) above has effect as respects any such complaint and as respects any order made under section 192(3) of that Act.

AMENDMENT

1. Employment Rights (Dispute Resolution) Act 1998 s.1(2)(a) (August 1, 1998).

Recoupment of Benefit

8.—(1) Recoupment shall be initiated by the Secretary of State serving on the employer a recoupment notice claiming by way of total or partial recoupment of jobseeker's allowance [1 , income-related employment and support allowance] [2 , universal credit] or income support the appropriate amount, computed, as the case may require, under paragraph (2) or (3) below. 2.971

(2) In the case of monetary awards the appropriate amount shall be whichever is the less of the following two sums—

(a) the amount of the prescribed element (less any tax or social security contributions which fall to be deducted therefrom by the employer); or

(b) [2 (i)] the amount paid by way of or paid as on account of jobseeker's allowance [1 , income-related employment and support allowance] or income support to the employee for any period which coincides with any part of the period to which the prescribed element is attributable. [2 ; or

(ii) in the case of an employee entitled to an award of universal credit for any period ("the UC period") which coincides with any part of the period to which the prescribed element is attributable, any amount paid by way of or on account of universal credit for the UC period that would not have been paid if the person's earned income for that period was the same as immediately before the period to which the prescribed element is attributable].

(3) In the case of remuneration under a protective award the appropriate amount shall be whichever is the less of the following two sums—

(a) the amount (less any tax or social security contributions which fall to be deducted therefrom by the employer) accrued due to the employee in respect of so much of the protected period as falls before the date on which the Secretary of State receives from the employer the information required under Regulation 6 above; or

(b) [2 (i)] the amount paid by way of or paid as on account of jobseeker's allowance [1 , income-related employment and support allowance] or income support to the employee for any period which coincides with any part of the protected period falling before the date described in (a) above [2 ; or

(ii) in the case of an employee entitled to an award of universal credit for any period ("the UC period") which coincides with any part of the protected period falling before the date described in (a) above, any amount paid by way of or on account of universal credit for the UC period that would not have been paid if the person's earned income for that period was the same as immediately before the protected period].

(4) A recoupment notice shall be served on the employer by post or otherwise and copies shall likewise be sent to the employee and, if requested, to the Secretary of the Tribunals.

(5) The Secretary of State shall serve a recoupment notice on the employer, or notify the employer that he does not intend to serve such a notice, within the period applicable, as the case may require, under paragraph (6) or (7) below, or as soon as practicable thereafter.

(6) In the case of a monetary award the period shall be—

(a) in any case in which the tribunal at the hearing announces to the parties the effect of its decision as described in Regulation 4(4) above, the period ending 21 days after the conclusion of the hearing or the period ending 9 days after the decision has been sent to the parties, whichever is the later; or

(b) in any other case, the period ending 21 days after the decision has been sent to the parties.

(7) In the case of a protective award the period shall be the period ending 21 days after the Secretary of State has received from the employer the information required under Regulation 6 above.

(8) A recoupment notice served on an employer shall operate as an instruction to the employer to pay, by way of deduction out of the sum due under the award, the recoupable amount to the Secretary of State and it shall be the duty of the employer to comply with the notice. The employer's duty under this paragraph shall not affect his obligation to pay any balance that may be due to the employee under the relevant award.

(9) The duty imposed on the employer by service of the recoupment notice shall not be discharged by payment of the recoupable amount to the employee during the postponement period or thereafter if a recoupment notice is served on the employer during the said period.

(10) Payment by the employer to the Secretary of State under this Regulation shall be a complete discharge in favour of the employer as against the employee in respect of any sum so paid but without prejudice to any rights of the employee under Regulation 10 below.

(11) The recoupable amount shall be recoverable by the Secretary of State from the employer as a debt.

[2 (12) For the purposes of paragraphs (2)(b)(ii) and (3)(b)(ii), "earned income" has the meaning given in regulation 52 of the Universal Credit Regulations 2013.]

AMENDMENTS

1. Social Security (Miscellaneous Amendments) (No.5) Regulations 2010 (SI 2010/2429) reg.5 (November 1, 2010).

2. Universal Credit (Consequential, Supplementary, Incidental and Miscellaneous Provisions) Regulations 2013 (SI 2013/630) reg.50(1) and (6) (April 29, 2013).

GENERAL NOTE

When assessing compensation, an employment tribunal must make a gross award, ignoring any jobseeker's allowance, income-related employment and support allowance, universal credit or income support paid to the employee during the relevant period, (reg.4(1)) and must give the Secretary of State details of the award (regs 4 and 5). The award is then postponed under reg.7 to allow the Secretary of State to recoup under reg.8 from the employer the amount of the relevant benefits paid to the employee during the relevant period. Note that contributory employment and support allowance cannot be recouped. The relevant period is the period in respect of which compensation for loss of pay or arrears of pay is awarded but ends at the date of the employment tribunal's decision if the award covers a period in the future (reg.3 and Sch. and see *Homan v A1 Bacon Co Ltd* [1996] I.C.R. 721). The Secretary of State serves a recoupment notice on the employer who must pay the recoupable amount to the Secretary of State, by way of deduction out of the sum due under the award, and then pay the balance of the award to the employee (reg.8(8)). An employee may give notice to the Secretary of State that he does not accept the amount specified in the recoupment notice (reg.10(1)) and may appeal to the First-tier Tribunal against any decision of the Secretary of State in response to such a notice (reg.10(2B)). 2.972

Order made in secondary proceedings

9.—(1) In the application of any of the above provisions in the case of— 2.973

(a) proceedings for an award under section 192 of the 1992 Act; or
(b) proceedings in the nature of a review, a re-hearing or a further hearing consequent on an appeal,

it shall be the duty of the [1 employment tribunal] or, as the case may require, the Secretary of State, to take the appropriate account of anything done under or in consequence of these Regulations in relation to any award made in the original proceedings.

(2) For the purposes of this Regulation the original proceedings are—

(a) where paragraph (1)(a) above applies the proceedings under section 189 of the 1992 Act; or

(b) where paragraph (1)(b) above applies the proceedings in respect of which the re-hearing, the review or the further hearing consequent on an appeal takes place.

AMENDMENT

1. Employment Rights (Dispute Resolution) Act 1998 s.1(2)(a) (August 1, 1998).

PART IV

DETERMINATION [2 . . .] OF BENEFIT RECOUPED

Provisions relating to determination of amount paid by way of or paid as on account of benefit

2.974 **10.**—(1) Without prejudice to the right of the Secretary of State to recover from an employer the recoupable benefit, an employee on whom a copy of a recoupment notice has been served in accordance with Regulation 8 above may, within 21 days of the date on which such notice was served on him or within such further time as the Secretary of State may for special reasons allow, give notice in writing to the Secretary of State that he does not accept that the amount specified in the recoupment notice in respect of jobseeker's allowance [4 , income-related employment and support allowance] [5 , universal credit] or income support is correct.

[2 (2) Where an employee has given notice in writing to the Secretary of State under paragraph (1) above that he does not accept that an amount specified in the recoupment notice is correct, the Secretary of State shall make a decision as to the amount of jobseeker's allowance [4 , income-related employment and support allowance] [5 , universal credit] or, as the case may be, income support paid in respect of the period to which the prescribed element is attributable or, as appropriate, in respect of so much of the protected period as falls before the date on which the employer complies with Regulation 6 above.

(2A) The Secretary of State may revise either upon application made for the purpose or on his own initiative a decision under paragraph (2) above.

(2B) The employee shall have a right of appeal to [3 the First-tier Tribunal] against a decision of the Secretary of State whether as originally made under paragraph (2) or as revised under paragraph (2A) above.

(2C) The Social Security and Child Support (Decisions and Appeals) Regulations 1999 shall apply for the purposes of paragraphs (2A) and (2B) above as though a decision of the Secretary of State under paragraph (2A) above were made under section 9 of the 1998 Act and any appeal from such a decision were made under section 12 of that Act.

(2D) In this Regulation "the 1998 Act" means the Social Security Act 1998.

(3) Where the Secretary of State recovers too much money from an employer under these Regulations the Secretary of State shall pay to the employee an amount equal to the excess.]

(4) In any case where, after the Secretary of State has recovered from an employer any amount by way of recoupment of benefit, the decision given by the [1 employment tribunal] in consequence of which such recoupment took place is set aside or varied on appeal or on a re-hearing by the

industrial tribunal, the Secretary of State shall make such repayment to the employer or payment to the employee of the whole or part of the amount recovered as he is satisfied should properly be made having regard to the decision given on appeal or re-hearing.

AMENDMENTS

1. Employment Rights (Dispute Resolution) Act 1998 s.1(2)(a) (August 1, 1998).
2. The Social Security Act 1998 (Commencement No.12 and Consequential and Transitional Provisions) Order 1999 (SI 1999/3178) (November 29, 1999).
3. Tribunals, Courts and Enforcement Act 2007 (Transitional and Consequential Provisions Order 2008 (SI 2008/2683) Sch.1 para.73 (November 3, 2008).
4. Social Security (Miscellaneous Amendments) (No.5) Regulations 2010 (SI 2010/2429) reg.5 (November 1, 2010).
5. Universal Credit (Consequential, Supplementary, Incidental and Miscellaneous Provisions) Regulations 2013 (SI 2013/630) reg.50(1) and (7) (April 29, 2013).

GENERAL NOTE

The jurisdiction of the Secretary of State and the tribunal is confined to the question of the amount of jobseeker's allowance, income-related employment and support allowance , universal credit or income support paid in respect of the relevant period. In *R(JSA) 3/03*, it was held that no reduction could be made to the recoupable amount to take account of the loss of tax credits caused by the loss of employment. Presumably the loss of such benefits can be claimed from the employer as a head of compensation (see *Neal v Bingle* [1998] Q.B. 466). 2.975

Revocation and Transition Provision

11. *Omitted.* 2.976

SCHEDULE **Regulation 3**

TABLE RELATING TO MONETARY AWARDS 2.977

Column 1	**Column 2**	**Column 3**
Payment	**Proceedings**	**Matter to which prescribed element is attributable**
1. Guarantee payments under section 28.	1. Complaint under section 34.	1. Any amount found to be due to the employee and ordered to be paid under section 34(3) for a period before the conclusion of the tribunal proceedings.
2. Payments under any collective agreement having regard to which the appropriate Minister has made an exemption order under section 35.	2. Complaint under section 35(4).	2. Any amount found to be due to the employee and ordered to be paid under section 34(3), as applied by section 35(4), for a period before the conclusion of the tribunal proceedings.
3. Payments of remuneration in respect of a period of suspension on medical grounds under section 64 and section 108(2).	3. Complaint under section 70.	3. Any amount found to be due to the employee and ordered to be paid under section 70(3) for a period before the conclusion of the tribunal proceedings.

Column 1	Column 2	Column 3
Payment	**Proceedings**	**Matter to which prescribed element is attributable**
4. Payments of remuneration in respect of a period of suspension on maternity grounds under section 68.	4. Complaint under section 70.	4. Any amount found to be due to the employee and ordered to be paid under section 70(3) for a period before the conclusion of the tribunal proceedings.
5. Payments under an order for reinstatement under section 114(1).	5. Complaint of unfair dismissal under section 111(1).	5. Any amount ordered to be paid under section 114(2)(a) in respect of arrears of pay for a period before the conclusion of the tribunal proceedings.
6. Payments under an order for re-engagement under section 117(8).	6. Complaint of unfair dismissal under section 111(1).	6. Any amount ordered to be paid under section 115(2)(d) in respect of arrears of pay for a period before the conclusion of the tribunal proceedings.
7. Payments under an award of compensation for unfair dismissal in cases falling under section 112(4) (cases where no order for reinstatement or re-engagement has been made).	7. Complaint of unfair dismissal under section 111(1).	7. Any amount ordered to be paid and calculated under section 123 in respect of compensation for loss of wages for a period before the conclusion of the tribunal proceedings.
8. Payments under an award of compensation for unfair dismissal under section 117(3) where reinstatement order not complied with.	8. Proceedings in respect of non-compliance with order.	8. Any amount ordered to be paid and calculated under section 123 in respect of compensation for loss of wages for a period before the conclusion of the tribunal proceedings.
9. Payments under an award of compensation for unfair dismissal under section 117(3) where re-engagement order not complied with.	9. Proceedings in respect of non-compliance with order.	9. Any amount ordered to be paid and calculated under section 123 in respect of compensation for loss of wages for a period before the conclusion of the tribunal proceedings.
10. Payments under an interim order for reinstatement under section 163(4) of the 1992 Act.	10. Proceedings on an application for an order for interim relief under section 161(1) of the 1992 Act.	10. Any amount found to be due to the complainant and ordered to be paid in respect of arrears of pay for the period between the date of termination of employment and the conclusion of the tribunal proceedings.
11. Payments under an interim order for re-engagement under section 163(5)(a) of the 1992 Act.	11. Proceedings on an application for an order for interim relief under section 161(1) of the 1992 Act.	11. Any amount found to be due to the complainant and ordered to be paid in respect of arrears of pay for the period between the date of termination of employment and the conclusion of the tribunal proceedings.

Column 1	Column 2	Column 3
Payment	**Proceedings**	**Matter to which prescribed element is attributable**
12. Payments under an order for the continuation of a contract of employment under section 163(5)(b) of the 1992 Act where employee reasonably refuses re-engagement.	12. Proceedings on an application for an order for interim relief under section 161(1) of the 1992 Act.	12. Any amount found to be due to the complainant and ordered to be paid in respect of arrears of pay for the period between the date of termination of employment and the conclusion of the tribunal proceedings.
13. Payments under an order for the continuation of a contract of employment under section 163(6) of the 1992 Act where employer fails to attend or is unwilling to reinstate or re-engage.	13. Proceedings on an application for an order for interim relief under section 161(1) of the 1992 Act.	13. Any amount found to be due to the complainant and ordered to be paid in respect of arrears of pay for the period between the date of termination of employment and the conclusion of the tribunal proceedings.
14. Payments under an order for the continuation of a contract of employment under sections 166(1) and (2) of the 1992 Act where reinstatement or re-engagement order not complied with.	14. Proceedings in respect of non-compliance with order.	14. Any amount ordered to be paid to the employee by way of compensation under section 166(1)(b) of the 1992 Act for loss of wages for the period between the date of termination of employment and the conclusion of the tribunal proceedings.
15. Payments under an order for compensation under sections 166(3)–(5) of the 1992 Act where order for the continuation of contract of employment not complied with.	15. Proceedings in respect of non-compliance with order.	15. Any amount ordered to be paid to the employee by way of compensation under section 166(3)–(4) of the 1992 Act for loss of wages for the period between the date of termination of employment and the conclusion of the tribunal proceedings.
16. Payments under an order under section 192(3) of the 1992 Act on employer's default in respect of remuneration due to employee under protective award. proceedings.	16. Complaint under section 192(1) of the 1992 Act.	16. Any amount ordered to be paid to the employee in respect of so much of the relevant protected period as falls before the date of the conclusion of the tribunal

The Social Security (Recovery of Benefits) Regulations 1997

(SI 1997/2205)

ARRANGEMENT OF REGULATIONS

The Secretary of State for Social Security, in exercise of the powers conferred by section 189(4), (5) and (6) of the Social Security Administration Act 1992 and sections 4(9), 14(2), (3) and (4), 16(1) and (2), 18, 19, 21(3), 23(1), (2), (5) and (7), 29 and 32 of, and paragraphs 4 and 8 of Schedule 1 to, the Social Security (Recovery of Benefits) Act 1997, and of all other powers enabling her in that behalf, hereby makes the following Regulations:

Citation, commencement and interpretation

2.979 **1.**—(1) These Regulations may be cited as the Social Security (Recovery of Benefits) Regulations 1997 and shall come into force on 6th October 1997.

(2) In these Regulations—

"the 1992 Act" means the Social Security Administration Act 1992;

"the 1997 Act" means the Social Security (Recovery of Benefits) Act 1997;

"commencement day" means the day these Regulations come into force;

"compensator" means a person making a compensation payment;

[1 "Compensation Recovery Unit" means the Compensation Recovery Unit, part of the Department for Work and Pensions, at Wear View House, 1 Eden Street West, Sunderland, SR1 3EY.]

(3) A reference in these Regulations to a numbered section or Schedule is a reference, unless the context otherwise requires, to that section of or Schedule to the 1997 Act.

AMENDMENT

1. The Social Security and Universal Credit (Miscellaneous Amendments) Regulations 2023 (SI 2023/543) reg.2 (June 29, 2023).

DEFINITION

"compensation payment"—see s.1(4) of the Social Security (Recovery of Benefits) Act 1997.

General Note

The Compensation Recovery Unit moved from Washington to Sunderland in June 2023, but its postal address remains: Compensation Recovery Unit, Post Handling Site B, Wolverhampton, WV99 2FR. Its website is: *www.gov.uk/government/collections/cru.* 2.980

Exempted trusts and payments

2.—(1) The following trusts are prescribed for the purposes of paragraph 4 of Schedule 1— 2.981

(a) the Macfarlane Trust established on 10th March 1988 partly out of funds provided by the Secretary of State to the Haemophilia Society for the relief of poverty or distress among those suffering from haemophilia;
(b) the Macfarlane (Special Payments) Trust established on 29th January 1990 partly out of funds provided by the Secretary of State, for the benefit of certain persons suffering from haemophilia;
(c) the Macfarlane (Special Payments) (No.2) Trust established on 3rd May 1991 partly out of funds provided by the Secretary of State, for the benefit of certain persons suffering from haemophilia and other beneficiaries;
(d) the Eileen Trust established on 29th March 1993 out of funds provided by the Secretary of State for the benefit of persons eligible for payment in accordance with its provisions;
[[1](e) a trust established out of funds provided by the Secretary of State in respect of persons who suffered, or who are suffering, from variant Creutzfelt-Jakob disease for the benefit of persons eligible for interim payments in accordance with its provisions;
(f) a trust established out of funds provided by the Secretary of State in respect of persons who suffered, or who are suffering, from variant Creutzfelt-Jakob disease for the benefit of persons eligible for payments, other than interim payments, in accordance with its provisions;]
[[4] (g) the UK Asbestos Trust established on 10th October 2006, for the benefit of certain persons suffering from asbestos-related diseases;
(h) the EL Scheme Trust established on 23rd November 2006, for the benefit of certain persons suffering from asbestos-related diseases.]

(2) The following payments are prescribed for the purposes of paragraph 8 of Schedule 1—

(a) any payment to the extent that it is made—
    (i) in consequence of an action under the Fatal Accidents Act 1976; or
    (ii) in circumstances where, had an action been brought, it would have been brought under that Act;
(b) any payment to the extent that it is made in respect of a liability arising by virtue of section 1 of the Damages (Scotland) Act 1976;
(c) any payment made under the Vaccine Damage Payments Act 1979 to or in respect of the injured person;
(d) any award of compensation made to or in respect of the injured person under the Criminal Injuries Compensation Act 1995 or by the Criminal Injuries Compensation Board under the Criminal Injuries Compensation Scheme 1990 or any earlier scheme;
(e) any compensation payment made by British Coal in accordance with the NCB Pneumoconiosis Compensation Scheme set out in

the Schedule to an agreement made on the 13th September 1974 between the National Coal Board, the National Union of Mine Workers, the National Association of Colliery Overmen Deputies and Shot-firers and the British Association of Colliery Management;

(f) any payment made to the injured person in respect of sensorineural hearing loss where the loss is less than than 50 dB in one or both ears;

(g) any contractual amount paid to an employee by an employer of his in respect of a period of incapacity for work;

(h) any payment made under the National Health Service (Injury Benefits) Regulations 1995 or the National Health Service (Scotland) (Injury Benefits) Regulations 1974;

(i) any payment made by or on behalf of the Secretary of State for the benefit of persons eligible for payment in accordance with the provisions of a scheme established by him on 24th April 1992 or, in Scotland, on 10th April 1992;

[[2] (j) any payment made from the Skipton Fund, the ex-gratia payment scheme administered by the Skipton Fund Limited, incorporated on 25th March 2004, for the benefit of certain persons suffering from hepatitis C and other persons eligible for payments in accordance with the scheme's provisions;]

[[3] (k) any payment made from the London Bombings Relief Charitable Fund, the company limited by guarantee (number 5505072) and registered charity of that name established on 11th July for the purpose of (amongst other things) relieving sickness, disability or financial need of victims (including families or dependants of victims) of the terrorist attacks carried out in London on 7th July 2005;]

[[5] (l) any payment made by MFET Limited, a company limited by guarantee (number 7121661) of that name, established for the purpose in particular of making payments in accordance with arrangements made with the Secretary of State to persons who have acquired HIV as a result of treatment by the NHS with blood or blood products;]

[[6] (m) any payment made from the Caxton Foundation, the charitable trust of that name established on 28th March 2011 out of funds provided by the Secretary of State for the benefit of certain persons suffering from hepatitis C and other persons eligible for payment in accordance with its provisions;]

[[7] (n) any payment made from the Scottish Infected Blood Support Scheme administered by the Common Services Agency (constituted by section 10 of the National Health Service (Scotland) Act 1978);]

[[8] (o) any payment made from a scheme established or approved by the Secretary of State, or trust established with funds provided by the Secretary of State, for the purpose of providing compensation in respect of a person having been infected from contaminated blood products;

(p) any payment made under or by a trust, established for the purpose of giving relief and assistance to disabled persons whose disabilities were caused by the fact that during their mother's pregnancy she had taken a preparation containing the drug known as Thalidomide, and which is approved by the Secretary of State;]

[[9] (q) any payment of victims' payments, or of a lump sum, under the Victims' Payments Regulations 2020;]

[[10] (r) any payment made under the Windrush Compensation Scheme (Expenditure) Act 2020.]

[11 (s) any payment made for the purpose of providing compensation or support in respect of the fire on 14th June 2017 at Grenfell Tower;]

[11 (t) any payment made by the Post Office or the Secretary of State for the purpose of providing compensation or support which is—

(i) in connection with the failings of the Horizon system; or

(ii) otherwise payable following the judgment in Bates and Others v Post Office Ltd ((No. 3) "Common Issues").]

[11 (3) In this Regulation—

the Horizon system" means any version of the computer system used by the Post Office known as Horizon, Horizon Legacy, Horizon Online or HNG-X;

"the Post Office" means Post Office Limited (registered number 02154540).]

AMENDMENTS

1. Social Security Amendment (Capital Disregards and Recovery of Benefits) Regulations 2001 (SI 2001/1118) reg.4 (April 12, 2001).

2. Social Security (Miscellaneous Amendments) (No.2) Regulations 2004 (SI 2004/1141) reg.7 (May 12, 2004).

3. Income-related Benefits (Amendment) (No.2) Regulations 2005 (SI 2005/3391) reg.6 (December 12, 2005).

4. Social Security (Recovery of Benefits) Amendment) Regulations 2007 (SI 2007/357) reg.2 (March 12, 2007).

5. Social Security (Miscellaneous Amendments) (No.2) Regulations 2010 (SI 2010/641) reg.5 (March 11, 2010).

6. Social Security (Miscellaneous Amendments) (No.3) Regulations 2011 (SI 2011/2425) reg.11 (October 31, 2011).

7. Social Security (Scottish Infected Blood Support Scheme) Regulations 2017 (SI 2017/329) reg.2 (April 3, 2017).

8. Social Security (Infected Blood and Thalidomide) Regulations 2017 (SI 2017/870) reg.4 (October 23, 2017).

9. Victims' Payments Regulations 2020 (SI 2020/103) reg.27(1) (May 29, 2020).

10. Social Security (Income and Capital Disregards) (Amendment) Regulations 2021 (SI 2021/1405) reg.9 (January 1, 2022).

11. The Social Security (Income and Capital Disregards) (Amendment) Regulations 2023 (SI 2023/640) reg.9 (July 9, 2023).

DEFINITIONS

"compensation payment"—see s.1(4) of the Social Security (Recovery of Benefits) Act 1997.

"payment"—see s.29 of the Social Security (Recovery of Benefits) Act 1997.

Information to be provided by the compensator

3.—The following information is prescribed for the purposes of section 23(1): **2.982**

(a) the full name and address of the injured person;

(b) where known, the date of birth or national insurance number of that person, or both if both are known;

(c) where the liability arises, or is alleged to arise, in respect of an accident or injury, the date of the accident or injury;

(d) the nature of the accident, injury or disease; and

(e) where known, and where the relevant period may include a period prior to 6th April 1994, whether, at the time of the accident or injury or diagnosis of the disease, the person was employed under a contract of service, and, if he was, the name and address of his employer at that time and the person's payroll number.

DEFINITION

"injured person"—see s.1(4) of the Social Security (Recovery of Benefits) Act 1997.

Information to be provided by the injured person

2.983 **4.** The following information is prescribed for the purposes of section 23(2):

(a) whether the accident, injury or disease resulted from any action taken by another person, or from any failure of another person to act, and, if so, the full name and address of that other person;

(b) whether the injured person has claimed or may claim a compensation payment, and, if so, the full name and address of the person against whom the claim was or may be made;

(c) the amount of any compensation payment and the date on which it was made;

(d) the listed benefits claimed, and for each benefit the date from which it was first claimed and the amount received in the period beginning with that date and ending with the date the information is sent;

(e) in the case of a person who has received statutory sick pay during the relevant period and prior to 6th April 1994, the name and address of any employer who made those payments to him during the relevant period and the dates the employment with that employer began and ended; and

(f) any changes in the medical diagnosis relating to the condition arising from the accident, injury or disease.

DEFINITIONS

"compensation payment"—see s.1(4) of the Social Security (Recovery of Benefits) Act 1997.

"injured person"—*ibid.*

"listed benefit"—see s.29 of the Social Security (Recovery of Benefits) Act 1997.

Information to be provided by the employer

2.984 **5.** The following information is prescribed for the purposes of section 23(5):

(a) the amount of any statutory sick pay the employer has paid to the injured person since the first day of the relevant period and before 6th April 1994;

(b) the date the liability to pay such statutory sick pay first arose and the rate at which it was payable;

(c) the date on which such liability terminated; and

(d) the causes of incapacity for work during any period of entitlement to statutory sick pay during the relevant period and prior to 6th April 1994.

DEFINITION

"injured person"—see s.1(4) of the Social Security (Recovery of Benefits) Act 1997.

Provision of information

6. A person required to give information to the Secretary of State under regulations 3 to 5 shall do so by sending it to the Compensation Recovery Unit not later than 14 days after— 2.985

(a) where he is a person to whom regulation 3 applies, the date on which he receives a claim for compensation from the injured person in respect of the accident, injury or disease;

(b) where he is a person to whom regulation 4 or 5 applies, the date on which the Secretary of State requests the information from him.

DEFINITION

"Compensation Recovery Unit"—see reg. 1(2).

Application for a certificate of recoverable benefits

7.—(1) The following particulars are prescribed for the purposes of section 21(3)(a) (particulars to be included in an application for a certificate of recoverable benefits): 2.986

(a) the full name and address of the injured person;

(b) the date of birth and, where known, the national insurance number of that person;

(c) where the liability arises or is alleged to arise in respect of an accident or injury, the date of the accident or injury;

(d) the nature of the accident, injury or disease;

(e) where the person liable, or alleged to be liable, in respect of the accident, injury or disease, is the employer of the injured person, or has been such an employer, the information prescribed by regulation 5.

(2) An application for a certificate of recoverable benefits is to be treated for the purposes of the 1997 Act as received by the Secretary of State on the day on which it is received by the Compensation Recovery Unit, or if the application is received after normal business hours, or on a day which is not a normal business day at that office, on the next such day.

DEFINITIONS

"the 1997 Act"—see reg. 1(2).
"Compensation Recovery Unit"—*ibid.*
"injured person"—see s. 1(4) of the Social Security (Recovery of Benefits) Act 1997.
"recoverable benefit"—*ibid.*

Payments into court

8.—(1) Subject to the provisions of this regulation, where a party to an action makes a payment into court which, had it been paid directly to another party to the action ("the relevant party"), would have constituted a compensation payment— 2.987

(a) the making of that payment shall be treated for the purposes of the 1997 Act as the making of a compensation payment;

(b) a current certificate of recoverable benefits shall be lodged with the payment; and

(c) where the payment is calculated under section 8, the compensator must give the relevant party the information specified in section 9(1), instead of the person to whom the payment is made.

(2) The liability under section 6(1) to pay an amount equal to the total amount of the recoverable benefits shall not arise until the person making the payment into court has been notified that the whole or any part of the payment into court has been paid out of court to or for the relevant party.

(3) Where a payment into court in satisfaction of his claim is accepted by the relevant party in the initial period, then as respects the compensator in question, the relevant period shall be taken to have ended, if it has not done so already, on the day on which the payment into court (or if there were two or more such payments, the last of them) was made.

(4) Where, after the expiry of the initial period, the payment into court is accepted in satisfaction of the relevant party's claim by consent between the parties, the relevant period shall end, if it has not done so already, on the date on which application to the court for the payment is made.

(5) Where, after the expiry of the initial period, payment out of court is made wholly or partly to or for the relevant party in accordance with an order of the court and in satisfaction of his claim, the relevant period shall end, if it has not done so already, on the date of that order.

(6) In paragraphs (3), (4) and (5), "the initial period" means the period of 21 days after the receipt by the relevant party to the action of notice of the payment into court having been made.

(7) Where a payment into court is paid out wholly to or for the party who made the payment (otherwise than to or for the relevant party to the action) the making of the payment into court shall cease to be regarded as the making of a compensation payment.

(8) A current certificate of recoverable benefits in paragraph (1) means one that is in force as described in section 4(4).

General Note

2.988 See the note to s.16(1) and (2) of the Social Security (Recovery of Benefits) Act 1997, under which this regulation is made.

Reduction of compensation: complex cases

2.989 **9.**—(1) This regulation applies where—

(a) a compensation payment in the form of a lump sum (an "earlier payment") has been made to or in respect of the injured person; and

(b) subsequently another such payment (a "later payment") is made to or in respect of the same injured person in consequence of the same accident, injury or disease.

(2) In determining the liability under section 6(1) arising in connection with the making of the later payment, the amount referred to in that subsection shall be reduced by any amount paid in satisfaction of that liability as it arose in connection with the earlier payment.

(3) Where—

(a) a payment made in satisfaction of the liability under section 6(1) arising in connection with an earlier payment is not reflected in the certificate of recoverable benefits in force at the time of a later payment, and

(b) in consequence, the aggregate of payments made in satisfaction of the liability exceeds what it would have been had that payment been so reflected, the Secretary of State shall pay the compensator who made the later payment an amount equal to the excess.

(4) Where—

(a) a compensator receives a payment under paragraph (3), and

(b) the amount of the compensation payment made by him was calculated under section 8,

then the compensation payment shall be recalculated under section 8, and the compensator shall pay the amount of the increase (if any) to the person to whom the compensation payment was made.

(5) Where both the earlier payment and the later payment are made by the same compensator, he may—

(a) aggregate the gross amounts of the payments made by him;

(b) calculate what would have been the reduction made under section 8(3) if that aggregate amount had been paid at the date of the last payment on the basis that—

(i) so much of the aggregate amount as is attributable to a head of compensation listed in column (1) of Schedule 2 shall be taken to be the part of the gross amount which attributable to that head, and

(ii) the amount of any recoverable benefits shown against any head in column (2) of that Schedule shall be taken to be the amount determined in accordance with the most recent certificate of recoverable benefits;

(c) deduct from that reduction calculated under sub-paragraph (b) the amount of the reduction under section 8(3) from any earlier payment; and

(d) deduct from the latest gross payment the net reduction calculated under sub-paragraph (c) (and accordingly the latest payment may be nil).

(6) Where the Secretary of State is making a refund under paragraph (3), he shall send to the compensator (with the refund) and to the person to whom the compensation payment was made a statement showing—

(a) the total amount that has already been paid by that compensator to the Secretary of State;

(b) the amount that ought to have been paid by that compensator; and

(c) the amount to be repaid to that compensator by the Secretary of State.

(7) Where the reduction of a compensation payment is recalculated by virtue of paragraph (4) or (5) the compensator shall give notice of the calculation to the injured person.

General Note

This regulation is made under ss.18(1)–(3) and 19 of the Social Security (Recovery of Benefits) Act 1997 and is concerned with cases where more than one lump-sum compensation payment is made to a victim in respect of a single accident, injury or disease. (Structured settlements involving periodical payments are dealt with in reg.10). Regulation 9 covers cases where the same compensator makes more than one lump-sum payment and also cases where different compensators make payments because they all contributed to the accident, injury or disease. However, it makes no attempt at apportionment of liability for recoverable benefits between different compensators. It is concerned only to ensure that there is not double recovery and it does not even attempt that in a case where **2.990** benefit has been paid as a result of two different injuries each attributable to a different accident. See *R(CR)2/04* and the note to s.1 of the Act for the way that liability is attributed in such a case. Where two compensators are liable in respect of the same accident, injury or disease, the one making the first compensation payment is likely to have the greater liability to the Secretary of State and must seek a contribution from the other so that they each bear a fair share of the liability for benefits.

Paragraph (2) simply provides that when a second compensation payment is made, the Secretary of State should not recover benefits that were recovered when the earlier payment was made. Paragraph (3) provides for a refund to the compensator if benefits are erroneously recovered for a second time. Paragraph (4) provides that, where the compensator has reduced under s.8 of the Act the amount of compensation paid to the victim (in effect recovering from the victim the benefits that the victim had received and the compensator had to pay to the Secretary of State), he must recalculate the s.8 reduction in the light of a refund under para.(3) and pay the appropriate amount, if any, to the victim. Where the same compensator made both the compensation payments, he may aggregate them for the purpose of recalculating the appropriate s.8 reduction under para.(4) (para.(5)). Paragraphs (6) and (7) require the victim to be told by the Secretary of State about any refund under para.(3) and by the compensator about any recalculation under paras (4) and (5).

Structured settlements

2.991 **10.**—(1) This regulation applies where—

(a) in final settlement of an injured person's claim, an agreement is entered into—

   (i) for the making of periodical payments (whether of an income or capital nature); or

   (ii) for the making of such payments and lump sum payments; and

(b) apart from the provisions of this regulation, those payments would fall to be treated for the purposes of the 1997 Act as compensation payments.

(2) Where this regulation applies, the provisions of the 1997 Act and these Regulations shall be modified in the following way—

(a) the compensator in question shall be taken to have made on that day a single compensation payment;

(b) the relevant period in the case of the compensator in question shall be taken to end (if it has not done so already) on the day of settlement;

(c) payments under the agreement referred to in paragraph (1)(a) shall be taken not to be compensation payments;

(d) paragraphs (5) and (7) of regulation 11 shall not apply.

(3) Where any further payment falls to be made to or in respect of the injured person otherwise than under the agreement in question, paragraph (2) shall be disregarded for the purpose of determining the end of the relevant period in relation to that further payment.

(4) In any case where—

(a) the person making the periodical payments ("the secondary party") does so in pursuance of arrangements entered into with another ("primary party") (as in a case where the primary party purchases an annuity for the injured person from the secondary party), and

(b) apart from those arrangements, the primary party would have been regarded as the compensator,

then for the purposes of the 1997 Act, the primary party shall be regarded as the compensator and the secondary party shall not be so regarded.

(5) In this regulation "the day of settlement" means—

(a) if the agreement referred to in paragraph (1)(a) is approved by a court, the day on which that approval is given; and

(b) in any other case, the day on which the agreement is entered into.

GENERAL NOTE

This regulation is made under s.8(4)–(6) of the Social Security (Recovery of Benefits) Act 1997. **2.992**

Where a final settlement is reached in the form of an agreement that involves the making of periodical payments (whether of a capital or income nature and whether or not they are combined with sum lump sums), the compensator is treated as having made a compensation payment on the day the agreement is reached. That is when the "relevant period" under s.3 of the Act is taken to have ended and when the compensator becomes liable to make a payment to the Secretary of State under s.6. Further payments under the agreement (by whomever they are made (see para.(4)) do not count as compensation payments (para.(2)(c)) but any payments outside it will (para.(3)) and reg.9 will apply to them.

Adjustments

11.—(1) Where the conditions specified in subsection (1) and paragraphs (a) and (b) of subsection (2) of section 14 are satisfied, the Secretary of State shall pay the difference between the amount that has been paid and the amount that ought to have been paid to the compensator. **2.993**

(2) Where the conditions specified in subsection (1) and paragraphs (a) and (b) of subsection (3) of section 14 are satisfied, the compensator shall pay the difference between the total amounts paid and the amount that ought to have been paid to the Secretary of State.

(3) Where the Secretary of State is making a refund under paragraph (1), or demanding payment of a further amount under paragraph (2), he shall send to the compensator (with the refund or demand) and to the person to whom the compensation payment was made a statement showing—

(a) the total amount that has already been paid to the Secretary of State;

(b) the amount that ought to have been paid; and

(c) the difference, and whether a repayment by the Secretary of State or a further payment to him is required.

(4) This paragraph applies where—

(a) the amount of the compensation payment made by the compensator was calculated under section 8; and

(b) the Secretary of State has made a payment under paragraph (1).

(5) Where paragraph (4) applies, the amount of the compensation payment shall be recalculated under section 8 to take account of the fresh certificate of recoverable benefits and the compensator shall pay the amount of the increase (if any) to the person to whom the compensation payment was made.

(6) This paragraph applies where—

(a) the amount of the compensation payment made by the compensator was calculated under section 8;

(b) the compensator has made a payment under paragraph (2); and
(c) the fresh certificate of recoverable benefits issued after the review or appeal was required as a result of the injured person or other person to whom the compensation payment was made supplying to the compensator information knowing it to be incorrect or insufficient with the intent of enhancing the compensation payment calculated under section 8, and the compensator supplying that information to the Secretary of State without knowing it to be incorrect or insufficient.

(7) Where paragraph (6) applies, the compensator may recalculate the compensation payment under section 8 to take account of the fresh certificate of recoverable benefits and may require the repayment to him by the person to whom he made the compensation payment of the difference (if any) between the payment made and the payment as so recalculated.

GENERAL NOTE

2.994 This is a key provision. Paragraphs (1)–(3) simply provide for the appropriate refund or demand for further payment to be made by the Secretary of State following a review or appeal. Of more practical importance are paras (4) and (5) requiring that, where there is a refund, the compensator must recalculate any reduction in a compensation payment made under s.8 of the Social Security (Recovery of Benefits) Act 1997 and pay the amount of any increase in the compensation payment to the claimant. That means that a compensator does not have any practical interest in challenging a certificate for recoverable benefits insofar as he has reduced the claimant's compensation to take account of the benefits (*R(CR) 2/03*). Unfortunately, it appears that these paragraphs are sometimes overlooked even by experienced insurance companies with the result that they retain money due to claimants. Paragraphs (6) and (7) make similar provision for cases where there is a demand for a further payment, only in those circumstances they have the effect that the claimant may have to make a further payment to the compensator. They operate only if the claimant knowingly supplied incorrect, or insufficient, information to the compensator and the compensator innocently passed it on to the Secretary of State.

Transitional provisions

2.995 **12.**—(1) In relation to a compensation payment to which by virtue of section 2 the 1997 Act applies and subject to paragraph (2), a certificate of total benefit issued under Part IV of the 1992 Act shall be treated on or after the commencement date as a certificate of recoverable benefits issued under the 1997 Act and the amount of total benefit treated as that of recoverable benefits.

(2) Paragraph (1) shall not apply to a certificate of total benefit which specifies an amount in respect of disability living allowance without specifying whether that amount was, or is likely to be, paid wholly by way of the care component or the mobility component or (if not wholly one of them) specifying the relevant amount for each component.

[[1](3) Any appeal under section 98 of the 1992 Act made on or after 6th October 1997 which has not been determined before 29th November 1999 shall be referred to an appeal tribunal constituted in accordance with paragraph (31) below.

(3A) Any appeal duly made before 6th October 1997 which has not been referred to a medical appeal tribunal or a social security appeal tribunal shall be referred to and determined by an appeal tribunal constituted in accordance with paragraph (3I) below.

(3B) Any appeal duly made before 6th October 1997 and referred to a medical appeal tribunal shall be determined by an appeal tribunal constituted in accordance with paragraph (3I) below which shall determine all issues.

(3C) Any appeal duly made before 6th October 1997 and referred to a social security appeal tribunal shall be determined by an appeal tribunal which shall consist of a legally qualified panel member and in making its determination, the appeal tribunal shall be bound by any decision of a medical appeal tribunal to which a question under section 98(5) of the 1992 Act was referred.

(3D) An appeal tribunal constituted in accordance with paragraph (3I) below shall completely rehear any appeal made under section 98 of the 1992 Act which stands adjourned immediately before 29th November 1999.

(3E) Where a Commissioner holds that the decision of a medical appeal tribunal or a social security appeal tribunal on an appeal made before 6th October 1997 was erroneous in law and refers the case to an appeal tribunal, that appeal tribunal shall be constituted in accordance with paragraph (3I) below and shall determine all issues in accordance with the Commissioner's direction.

(3F) Regulation 11 of the Social Security (Recoupment) Regulations 1990 ("the 1990 Regulations") and regulation 12 of those Regulations shall have effect in relation to any appeal under section 98 of the 1992 Act made on or after 6th October 1997 with the modification that for the word "chairman" in each place in which it occurs there were substituted the words "legally qualified panel member".

(3G) Regulation 13 of the 1990 Regulations shall have effect in relation to any appeal under section 98 of the 1992 Act made on or after 6th October 1997.

(3H) Any other transitional question arising from an appeal made under section 98 of the 1992 Act in consequence of the coming into force of the Social Security and Child Support (Decisions and Appeals) Regulations 1999 ("the 1999 Regulations") shall be determined by a legally qualified panel member who may for this purpose give such directions consistent with these regulations as are necessary.

(3I) For the purposes of paragraphs (3) to (3B) and (3E) above an appeal tribunal shall be constituted under Chapter I of Part I of the Social Security Act 1998 as though the appeal were made under section 11(1)(b) of the 1997 Act.

(3J) In this regulation, "legally qualified panel member" has the meaning it bears in regulation 1(3) of the 1999 Regulations.]

(4) Paragraph (5) applies where—

(a) an amount has been paid to the Secretary of State under section 82(1)(b) of the 1992 Act,

(b) liability arises on or after the commencement day to make a payment under section 6(1), and

(c) the compensation payments which give rise to the liability to make both payments are to or in respect of the same injured person in consequence of the same accident, injury or disease.

(5) Where this paragraph applies, the liability under section 6 shall be reduced by the payment (or aggregate of the payments, if more than one) described in paragraph (4)(a).

(6) Where—

(a) a payment into court has been made on a date prior to the commencement day but the initial period, as defined in section 93(6) of the 1992 Act, in relation to that payment, expires on or after the commencement day; and

(b) the payment into court is accepted by the other party to the action in the initial period,

that payment into court shall be treated as a compensation payment to which the 1992 Act, and not the 1997 Act, applies.

(7) Where a payment into court has been made prior to the commencement day, remains in court on that day and paragraph (6) does not apply, that payment into court shall be treated as a payment to which the 1997 Act applies, but paragraph (1) (b) and (c) of regulation 8 shall not apply.

AMENDMENT

1. Social Security Act 1998 (Commencement No.12 and Consequential and Transitional Provisions) Order 1999 (SI 1999/3178) art.3(17) and Sch.17 (November 29, 1999).

GENERAL NOTE

2.996 This regulation has been amended in such a way that it now makes transitional provision not only for the coming into force of the Social Security (Recovery of Benefits) Act 1997 but also for the coming into force of the Social Security Act 1998.

The Social Security (Recovery of Benefits) (Lump Sum Payments) Regulations 2008

(SI 2008/1596)

Made	*18th June 2008*
Laid before Parliament	*25th June 2008*
Coming into force	*1st October 2008*

2.997 The Secretary of State for Work and Pensions makes the following Regulations in exercise of the powers conferred by section 189(4) and (6) of the Social Security Administration Act 1992, sections 1A, 14(2), (3) and (4), 18, 19, 21(3), 23(1), (2) and (7) and 29 of, and paragraphs 4 and 8 of Schedule 1 to, the Social Security (Recovery of Benefits) Act 1997, section 79(6) of the Social Security Act 1998 and section 53 of the Child Maintenance and Other Payments Act 2008, which contains only regulations made by virtue of, or consequential on sections 54 and 57(2) of the Child Maintenance and Other Payments Act 2008 and which are made before the end of a period of 6 months beginning with the coming into force of those sections:

PART 1

GENERAL

Citation, commencement and interpretation

1.—(1) These Regulations may be cited as the Social Security (Recovery of Benefits) (Lump Sum Payments) Regulations 2008 and shall come into force on 1st October 2008. 2.998

(2) In these Regulations—

"the Act" means the Social Security (Recovery of Benefits) Act 1997;

[1 "the 2014 Act" means the Mesothelioma Act 2014;]

"compensator" means a person making a compensation payment [1 and includes the scheme administrator who makes a payment in accordance with the Diffuse Mesothelioma Payment Scheme;];

"Compensation Recovery Unit" means the Compensation Recovery Unit part of the Department for Work and Pensions at [2 Wear View House, 1 Eden Street West, Sunderland, SR1 3EY];

[1 "Diffuse Mesothelioma Payment Scheme" means the scheme established by the Diffuse Mesothelioma Payment Scheme Regulations 2014;]

[1 "lump sum payment" means a payment to which any of paragraphs (a) to (d) of section 1A(2) of the Act applies,] except in relation to regulation 18(1)(b);

"recoverable benefits" has the same meaning as in section 1(4)(c) of the Act;

[1 "recoverable lump sum payment"—

(a) in relation to a compensation payment which is a payment under the Diffuse Mesothelioma Payment Scheme, means any specified lump sum payment which is recoverable by virtue of regulation 4A;

(b) in relation to any other description of compensation payment, means any lump sum payment which is recoverable by virtue of regulation 4;

"specified lump sum payment" means a lump sum payment within paragraph (a), (b) or (c) of section 1A(2) of the Act.]

AMENDMENT

1. Social Security (Recovery of Benefits) (Lump Sum Payments) (Amendment) Regulations 2014 (SI 2014/1456) reg.2 and Sch. paras 1 and 2 (July 1, 2014).

2. The Social Security and Universal Credit (Miscellaneous Amendments) Regulations 2023 (SI 2023/543) reg.2 (June 29, 2023).

GENERAL NOTE

The Compensation Recovery Unit moved from Washington to Sunderland in June 2023, but its postal address remains: Compensation Recovery Unit, Post Handling Site B, Wolverhampton, WV99 2FR. Its website is: *www.gov.uk/government/collections/cru*. 2.999

Application of the Act

2.—(1) The provisions of the Act specified in paragraph (2) apply for the purposes of these Regulations with the modifications, where appropriate, prescribed in Schedule 1. 2.1000

(2) The specified provisions are—

(a) section 1(3) (cases in which this Act applies);

(b) sections 10 to 14 (reviews and appeals);
(c) sections 15 and 17 (courts);
(d) sections 18 and 19 (reduction of compensation: complex cases);
(e) sections 20 to 23 (miscellaneous);
(f) sections 26 and 27 (provisions relating to Northern Ireland);
(g) sections 28 to 31 (general);
(h) section 33 (consequential amendments and repeals);
(i) section 34(1) and (3) (short title and extent);
(j) Schedule 1 (compensation payments—exempted payments and power to disregard small payments).

2.1001 3. *Omitted.*

[1 Recovery of lump sum payments from compensation payment made otherwise than under Diffuse Mesothelioma Payment Scheme]

2.1002 **4.**—(1) The Secretary of State may recover the amount of [1 a lump sum payment] where—

(a) a compensation payment in consequence of a disease is made to or in respect of—
  (i) a person ("P"); or
  (ii) a dependant of P,

to whom, or in respect of whom, a lump sum payment has been, or is likely to be, made; and

[1 (ab) the compensation payment is not a payment under the Diffuse Mesothelioma Payment Scheme; and]

(b) the compensation payment is made in consequence of the same disease as the lump sum payment.

[1 (1A) The Secretary of State may also recover the amount of lump sum payments to which section 1A(2)(d) of the Act applies where—

(a) any such payment has been, or is likely to be, made to one or more dependants of P;
(b) by virtue of a notice given under section 3(3) of the 2014 Act, any other dependant of P has ceased to be eligible for a lump sum payment to which section 1A(2)(d) of the Act applies; and
(c) a compensation payment in consequence of P's diffuse mesothelioma is made to that other dependant.]

(2) In paragraph (1), references to a payment made in consequence of a disease—

(a) are references to a payment made by or on behalf of a person who is, or is alleged to be, liable to any extent in respect of the disease; but
(b) do not include references to a payment mentioned in Part 1 of Schedule 1 to the Act.

AMENDMENT

1. Social Security (Recovery of Benefits) (Lump Sum Payments) (Amendment) Regulations 2014 (SI 2014/1456) reg.2 and Sch. paras 1 and 3 (July 1, 2014).

[1 Recovery of specified lump sum payments from compensation payment under Diffuse Mesothelioma Payment Scheme

4A. The Secretary of State may recover the amount of a specified lump sum payment where— 2.1003

(a) a compensation payment in consequence of diffuse mesothelioma is made to or in respect of P, or to a dependant of P, and a lump sum payment has been, or is likely to be, made to P or in respect of P;

(b) that compensation payment is a payment under the Diffuse Mesothelioma Payment Scheme; and

(c) the disease in consequence of which the specified lump sum payment was made is also diffuse mesothelioma.]

AMENDMENT

1. Social Security (Recovery of Benefits) (Lump Sum Payments) (Amendment) Regulations 2014 (SI 2014/1456) reg.2 and Sch. paras 1 and 4 (July 1, 2014).

Application of these Regulations to a dependant of P

5.—(1) Subject to paragraph (2), in these Regulations and any provision of the Act as modified any reference to P is to be construed as if it included a reference to a dependant of P where that dependant is the person to whom, or in respect of whom, a lump sum payment is made. 2.1004

(2) Paragraph (1) does not apply in relation to regulations 4, 10(7) and 12(7) and sections 15 and 23(2) of, and paragraphs 3(a) and 5(1) of Part 1 of Schedule 1 to, the Act.

Compensation payments to which these Regulations apply

6. [1 —(1) Except as stated in paragraph (2),] these Regulations apply in relation to compensation payments made on or after the day on which section 54 of the Child Maintenance and Other Payments Act 2008 comes into force. 2.1005

[1 (2) In any case where—

(a) the lump sum payment falls within section 1A(2)(d) of the Act; or

(b) paragraphs (a) to (c) of regulation 4A apply;

these Regulations apply only in relation to compensation payments which are made on or after 31st March 2014.]

AMENDMENT

1. Social Security (Recovery of Benefits) (Lump Sum Payments) (Amendment) Regulations 2014 (SI 2014/1456) reg.2, Sch. paras 1 and 5 (July 1, 2014).

Exempted trusts and payments

7.—(1) The following trusts are prescribed for the purposes of paragraph 4 of Schedule 1 to the Act— 2.1006

(a) the Macfarlane Trust established on 10th March 1988 partly out of funds provided by the Secretary of State to the Haemophilia Society for the relief of poverty or distress among those suffering from haemophilia;

(b) the Macfarlane (Special Payments) Trust established on 29th January 1990 partly out of funds provided by the Secretary of State, for the benefit of certain persons suffering from haemophilia;

(c) the Macfarlane (Special Payments) (No. 2) Trust established on 3rd May 1991 partly out of funds provided by the Secretary of State, for the benefit of certain persons suffering from haemophilia and other beneficiaries;

(d) the Eileen Trust established on 29th March 1993 out of funds provided by the Secretary of State, for the benefit of persons eligible for payment in accordance with its provisions;

(e) a trust established out of funds provided by the Secretary of State in respect of persons who suffered, or who are suffering, from variant Creutzfeldt-Jakob disease for the benefit of persons eligible for interim payments in accordance with its provisions;

(f) a trust established out of funds provided by the Secretary of State in respect of persons who suffered, or who are suffering, from variant Creutzfeldt-Jakob disease for the benefit of persons eligible for payments, other than interim payments, in accordance with its provisions;

[[1] (g) the UK Asbestos Trust established on 10th October 2006 for the benefit of certain persons suffering from asbestos-related diseases [[4] provided that any payment made in respect of diffuse mesothelioma out of this Trust is not made to or in respect of a person who has received a payment under the Diffuse Mesothelioma Payment Scheme];

(h) the EL Scheme Trust established on 23rd November 2006 for the benefit of certain persons suffering from asbestos-related diseases.]

(2) The following payments are prescribed for the purposes of paragraph 8 of Schedule 1 to the Act—

(a) any payment made under the Vaccine Damage Payments Act 1979 to or in respect of P;

(b) any award of compensation made to or in respect of P under the Criminal Injuries Compensation Act 1995 or by the Criminal Injuries Compensation Board under the Criminal Injuries Compensation Scheme 1990 or any earlier scheme or under the Criminal Injuries Compensation (Northern Ireland) Order 2002;

(c) any payment made to P in respect of sensorineural hearing loss where the loss is less than 50 decibels in one or both ears;

(d) any contractual amount paid to P by an employer of P in respect of a period of incapacity for work;

(e) any payment made under the National Health Service (Injury Benefits) Regulations 1995, the National Health Service (Scotland) (Injury Benefits) Regulations 1998 or the Health and Personal Social Services (Injury Benefits) Regulations (Northern Ireland) 2001;

(f) any payment made by or on behalf of the Secretary of State for the benefit of persons eligible for payment in accordance with the provisions of a scheme established by the Secretary of State on 24th April 1992 or, in Scotland, on 10th April 1992;

(g) any payment made from the Skipton Fund, the ex-gratia payment scheme administered by the Skipton Fund Limited, incorporated on 25th March 2004, for the benefit of certain persons suffering from hepatitis C and other persons eligible for payment in accordance with the scheme's provisions;

(h) any payment made from the London Bombings Relief Charitable Fund, the company limited by guarantee (number 5505072) and registered charity of that name established on 11th July 2005 for the purpose of (amongst other things) relieving sickness, disability or financial need of victims (including families or dependants of victims) of the terrorist attacks carried out in London on 7th July 2005;

[2 (i) any payment made by MFET Limited, a company limited by guarantee (number 7121661) of that name, established for the purpose in particular of making payments in accordance with arrangements made with the Secretary of State to persons who have acquired HIV as a result of treatment by the NHS with blood or blood products;]

[3 (j) any payment made from the Caxton Foundation, the charitable trust of that name established on 28th March 2011 out of funds provided by the Secretary of State for the benefit of certain persons suffering from hepatitis C and other persons eligible for payment in accordance with its provisions;]

[5 (k) any payment made from the Scottish Infected Blood Support Scheme administered by the Common Services Agency (constituted by section 10 of the National Health Service (Scotland) Act 1978);]

[6 (l) any payment made from a scheme established or approved by the Secretary of State, or trust established with funds provided by the Secretary of State, for the purpose of providing compensation in respect of a person having been infected from contaminated blood products;

(m) any payment made under or by a trust, established for the purpose of giving relief and assistance to disabled persons whose disabilities were caused by the fact that during their mother's pregnancy she had taken a preparation containing the drug known as Thalidomide, and which is approved by the Secretary of State;]

[7 (n) any payment of victims' payments, or of a lump sum, under the Victims' Payments Regulations 2020;]

[8 (o) any payment made under the Windrush Compensation Scheme (Expenditure) Act 2020.]

[9 (p) any payment made for the purpose of providing compensation or support in respect of the fire on 14th June 2017 at Grenfell Tower;]

[9 (q) any payment made by the Post Office or the Secretary of State for the purpose of providing compensation or support which is—

(i) in connection with the failings of the Horizon system; or

(ii) otherwise payable following the judgment in Bates and Others v Post Office Ltd ((No. 3) "Common Issues").]

[9 (3) In this regulation—

"the Horizon system" means any version of the computer system used by the Post Office known as Horizon, Horizon Legacy, Horizon Online or HNG-X;

"the Post Office" means Post Office Limited (registered number 02154540).]

AMENDMENTS

1. Social Security (Recovery of Benefits) (Lump Sum Payments) (Amendment) Regulations 2009 (SI 2009/1494) reg.2 (July 13, 2009).

2. Social Security (Miscellaneous Amendments) (No.2) Regulations 2010 (SI 2010/641) reg.13 (March 11, 2010).

3. Social Security (Miscellaneous Amendments) (No.3) Regulations 2011 (SI 2011/2425) reg.24 (October 31, 2011).

4. Social Security (Recovery of Benefits) (Lump Sum Payments) (Amendment) Regulations 2014 (SI 2014/1456) reg.2 and Sch. paras 1 and 6 (July 1, 2014).

5. Social Security (Scottish Infected Blood Support Scheme) Regulations 2017 (SI 2017/329) reg.9 (April 3, 2017).
6. Social Security (Infected Blood and Thalidomide) Regulations 2017 (SI 2017/870) reg.9 (October 23, 2017).
7. Victims' Payments Regulations 2020 (SI 2020/103) reg.27(3) (May 29, 2020).
8. Social Security (Income and Capital Disregards) (Amendment) Regulations 2021 (SI 2021/1405) reg.10 (January 1, 2022).
9. The Social Security (Income and Capital Disregards) (Amendment) Regulations 2023 (SI 2023/640) reg.10 (July 9, 2023).

PART 2

CERTIFICATES

Applications for certificates

2.1007 **8.**—(1) Before making a compensation payment the compensator must apply to the Secretary of State for a certificate.

(2) Where the compensator applies for a certificate, the Secretary of State must—

(a) send to the compensator a written acknowledgment of receipt of the application; and
(b) issue the certificate before the end of the period of 4 weeks.

(3) An application for a certificate is to be treated for the purposes of the Act as received by the Secretary of State on the day on which it is received by the Compensation Recovery Unit, or if the application is received after normal business hours, or on a day which is not a normal business day at that office, on the next such day.

Information contained in certificates

2.1008 **9.**—(1) Subject to paragraph (2), a certificate must specify—

(a) the amounts;
(b) which of the type of payments referred to in section 1A(2) of the Act applies; and
(c) the dates,

of any lump sum payments which have been, or are likely to have been paid.

(2) Where the type of payment is an extra-statutory payment the certificate may specify that type of payment as if it were a payment to which section 1A(2)(a) applies.

[[2] (2A) Where a certificate has been applied for by the scheme administrator, the certificate may contain information which would assist the scheme administrator in making a determination in accordance with the Diffuse Mesothelioma Payment Scheme.]

(3) The Secretary of State may estimate, in such manner as the Secretary of State thinks fit the amount of the lump sum payments specified in the certificate.

(4) Where the Secretary of State issues a certificate, the information contained in that certificate must be provided to—

(a) the person who appears to the Secretary of State to be P; or
(b) any person who the Secretary of State thinks will receive a compensation payment in respect of P.

(5) A person to whom a certificate is issued or who is provided with information under [1 paragraph (4)] is entitled to particulars of the manner in which any amount, type of payment or date specified in the certificate has been determined, if that person applies to the Secretary of State for those particulars.

AMENDMENTS

1. The Social Security (Miscellaneous Amendments) (No.3) Regulations 2008 (SI 2008/2365) reg.6(1) and (2) (October 1, 2008).
2. Social Security (Recovery of Benefits) (Lump Sum Payments) (Amendment) Regulations 2014 (SI 2014/1456) reg.2 and Sch. paras 1 and 7 (July 1, 2014).

PART 3

LIABILITY OF PERSON PAYING COMPENSATION

Liability to pay Secretary of State amount of lump sum payments

10.—(1) A person who makes a compensation payment in any case is liable to pay the Secretary of State an amount equal to the total amount of— 2.1009

(a) in a case to which paragraph (2) applies, the recoverable lump sum payments; or
(b) in a case to which paragraph (3) applies, the compensation payment.

(2) Paragraph (1)(a) applies to a case where—

(a) the compensation payment is equal to, or more than, any recoverable lump sum payments; or
(b) a dependant is a beneficiary of part of a compensation payment made in respect of P, that part of the compensation payment is equal to, or more than, any recoverable lump sum payments which have been made to that dependant.

(3) Paragraph 1(b) applies to a case where—

(a) the compensation payment; or
(b) a dependant is a beneficiary of part of a compensation payment made in respect of P, and recoverable lump sum payments have been made to that dependant, the share of the compensation payment,

[1 is less than the recoverable lump sum payments]

(4) The liability referred to in paragraph (1) arises—

(a) immediately before the compensation payment or, if there is more than one, the first of them is made;
(b) prior to any liability to pay the Secretary of State an amount equal to the total amount of the recoverable benefits payable under section 6 of the Act.

[1 (4A) In any case where recoverable lump sum payments include one or more lump sum payments to which section 1A(2)(d) of the Act applies, the liability referred to in paragraph (1) in respect of those lump sum payments arises prior to any such liability in respect of any other recoverable lump sum payment.]

(5) No amount becomes payable under this regulation before the end of the period of 14 days following the day on which the liability arises.

(6) Subject to paragraph (4), an amount becomes payable under this regulation at the end of the period of 14 days beginning with the day on which a certificate is first issued showing that the amount of recoverable lump sum payment to which it relates has been or is likely to have been paid.

(7) [1 Subject to paragraph (8),] in the case of a lump sum payment which has been made to a dependant of P, this regulation applies only to the extent to which the compensator is making any payment—

(a) (i) under the Fatal Accidents Act 1976;

(ii) to the extent that it is made in respect of a liability arising by virtue of section 1 of the Damages (Scotland) Act 1976; or

(iii) under the Fatal Accidents (Northern Ireland) Order 1977, to that dependant; or

(b) in respect of P, and that dependant is an intended beneficiary of part or all of that payment.

[1 (8) In the case of a lump sum payment to which section 1A(2)(d) of the Act applies which has been made to one or more dependants of P, this regulation also applies to the extent that the compensator is making any of the payments listed in—

(a) paragraph (7)(a), where such a payment is made to another dependant of P who has ceased to be eligible for a lump sum payment to which section 1A(2)(d) of the Act applies by virtue of having given notice under section 3(3) of the 2014 Act;

(b) paragraph (7)(b), where such a dependant is an intended beneficiary of that payment.]

AMENDMENT

1. Social Security (Recovery of Benefits) (Lump Sum Payments) (Amendment) Regulations 2014 (SI 2014/1456) reg.2 and Sch. paras 1 and 8 (July 1, 2014).

Recovery of payment due under regulation 10

2.1010 **11.**—(1) This regulation applies where a compensator has made a compensation payment but—

(a) has not applied for a certificate; or

(b) has not made a payment to the Secretary of State under regulation 10 before the end of the period allowed under that regulation.

(2) The Secretary of State may—

(a) issue the compensator who made the compensation payment with a certificate, if none has been issued; or

(b) issue that compensator with a copy of the certificate or (if more than one has been issued) the most recent one,

and (in either case) issue that compensator with a demand that payment of any amount due under regulation 10 be made immediately.

(3) The Secretary of State may, in accordance with paragraphs (4) and (5), recover the amount for which a demand for payment is made under paragraph (2) from the compensator who made the compensation payment.

(4) If the compensator who made the compensation payment resides or carries on business in England and Wales and a county court so orders, any amount recoverable under paragraph (3) is recoverable by execution issued from the county court or otherwise as if it were payable under an order of that court.

(5) If the compensator who made the payment resides or carries on business in Scotland, any amount recoverable under paragraph (3) may be enforced in like manner as an extract registered decree arbitral bearing a warrant for execution issued by the sheriff court of any sheriffdom in Scotland.

(6) A document bearing a certificate which—

(a) is signed by a person authorised to do so by the Secretary of State; and

(b) states that the document, apart from the certificate, is a record of the amount recoverable under paragraph (3),

is conclusive evidence that that amount is so recoverable.

(7) A certificate under paragraph (6) purporting to be signed by a person authorised to do so by the Secretary of State is to be treated as so signed unless the contrary is proved.

PART 4

REDUCTION OF COMPENSATION PAYMENT

Reduction of compensation payment

12.—(1) [1 Except where regulation 12A applies,] this regulation applies in a case where, in relation to any compensation payment in consequence of a disease made to, or in respect of P, a lump sum payment has been, or is likely to be made to, or in respect of P. 2.1011

(2) In such a case, any claim of a person to receive the compensation payment is to be treated for all purposes as discharged if—

(a) that person is paid the amount (if any) of the compensation payment calculated in accordance with this regulation; and

(b) if the amount of the compensation payment so calculated is nil, that person is given a statement saying so by the compensator who (apart from this regulation) would have paid the gross amount of the compensation payment.

(3) For an award of compensation for which paragraph (1) is satisfied, so much of the gross amount of the compensation payment as is equal to the amount of the lump sum payment is to be reduced (to nil, if necessary) by deducting the amount of the recoverable lump sum payment.

(4) Paragraph (3) is to have effect as if a requirement to reduce a payment by deducting an amount which exceeds that payment were a requirement to reduce that payment to nil.

(5) The amount of the compensation payment calculated in accordance with this regulation is—

(a) the gross amount of the compensation payment;

less

(b) the reductions made under paragraph (3),

(and, accordingly, the amount may be nil).

(6) The reduction specified in paragraph (3) is to be attributed to the heads of compensation in the following order—

(a) damages for non-pecuniary loss;

(b) damages for pecuniary loss,

and, the reduction is to be made before any reduction in respect of recoverable benefits under section 8 of the Act.

(7) [1 Subject to paragraph (8),] where the lump sum payment has been made to a dependant of P, the reduction specified in paragraph (3) may be attributed—

(a) to any damages awarded to that dependant—

(i) under the Fatal Accidents Act 1976;

(ii) to the extent that they are made in respect of a liability arising by virtue of section 1 of the Damages (Scotland) Act 1976; or

(iii) under the Fatal Accidents (Northern Ireland) Order 1977, other than those paid for funeral expenses;

(b) to any part of a compensation payment paid in respect of P, where that dependant is an intended beneficiary of part or all of that compensation.

[1 (8) In the case of a lump sum payment to which section 1A(2)(d) of the Act applies which has been made to one or more dependants of P, this regulation also applies to the extent that the compensator is making any of the payments listed in—

(a) paragraph (7)(a), where such a payment is made to another dependant of P who has ceased to be eligible for a lump sum payment to which section 1A(2)(d) of the Act applies by virtue of having given notice under section 3(3) of the 2014 Act;

(b) paragraph (7)(b), where such a dependant is an intended beneficiary of that payment.]

AMENDMENT

1. Social Security (Recovery of Benefits) (Lump Sum Payments) (Amendment) Regulations 2014 (SI 2014/1456) reg.2 and Sch. paras 1 and 9 (July 1, 2014).

[1 Reduction of compensation payment under Diffuse Mesothelioma Payment Scheme

2.1012 **12A.**—(1) This regulation applies in a case where the compensation payment is a payment under the Diffuse Mesothelioma Payment Scheme.

(2) The gross amount of the compensation payment—

(a) is to be reduced by the amount of the recoverable lump sum payments; and

(b) accordingly, is to be reduced to nil in any case where the amount of the recoverable lump sum payments is equal to or greater than the gross amount of the compensation payment.

(3) The reduction in paragraph (2) is to be made before any reduction in respect of recoverable benefits under section 8A of the Act.

(4) Any claim by a person to receive the compensation payment is to be treated for all purposes as discharged if—

(a) the person is paid the gross amount of the compensation payment less the amount of the recoverable lump sum payments; or

(b) the amount of the recoverable lump sum payments is equal to or greater than the gross amount of the compensation payment and the person is given a statement by the scheme administrator saying that the compensation payment has been reduced to nil.

(5) In the application of paragraph (4) to any case where the compensation payment is to be made to two or more dependants of P, the deduction of the amount of the recoverable lump sum payments is to be made before calculating the amount to be paid to each dependant in accordance with regulation 16(2)(iii) of the Diffuse Mesothelioma Payment Scheme Regulations 2014.]

AMENDMENT

1. Social Security (Recovery of Benefits) (Lump Sum Payments) (Amendment) Regulations 2014 (SI 2014/1456) reg.2 and Sch. paras 1 and 10 (July 1, 2014).

[1 Regulations 12 and 12A]: supplementary

13.—(1) A compensator who makes a compensation payment calculated in accordance with regulation 12 [1 or 12A] must inform the person to whom the payment is made— 2.1013

(a) that the payment has been so calculated; and

(b) of the date for payment by reference to which the calculation has been made.

(2) If the amount of a compensation payment calculated in accordance with regulation 12 [1 or 12A] is nil, a compensator giving a statement saying so is to be treated for the purposes of these Regulations as making a payment within regulation 4(1)(a) [1 or 4A(a) (as the case may be)] on the day on which the statement is given.

(3) Where a compensator—

(a) makes a compensation payment calculated in accordance with regulation 12 [1 or 12A]; and

(b) if the amount of the compensation payment so calculated is nil, gives a statement saying so,

the compensator is to be treated, for the purpose of determining any rights and liabilities in respect of contribution or indemnity, as having paid the gross amount of the compensation payment.

(4) For the purposes of these Regulations—

(a) the gross amount of the compensation payment is the amount of the compensation payment apart from regulation 12 [1 or 12A]; and

(b) the amount of any recoverable lump sum payment is the amount determined in accordance with the certificate.

AMENDMENT

1. Social Security (Recovery of Benefits) (Lump Sum Payments) (Amendment) Regulations 2014 (SI 2014/1456) reg.2 and Sch. paras 1 and 11 (July 1, 2014).

Reduction of compensation: complex cases

14.—(1) This regulation applies where— 2.1014

(a) a compensation payment in the form of a lump sum (an "earlier payment") has been made to or in respect of P; and

(b) subsequently another such payment (a "later payment") is made to or in respect of the same P in consequence of the same disease.

(2) In determining the liability under regulation 10(1) arising in connection with the making of the later payment, the amount referred to in that regulation is to be reduced by any amount paid in satisfaction of that liability as it arose in connection with the earlier payment.

(3) Where—

(a) a payment made in satisfaction of the liability under regulation 10(1) arising in connection with an earlier payment is not reflected in the certificate in force at the time of a later payment; and

(b) in consequence, the aggregate of payments made in satisfaction of the liability exceeds what it would have been had that payment been so reflected,

the Secretary of State is to pay the compensator who made the later payment an amount equal to the excess.

(4) Where—

(a) a compensator receives a payment under paragraph (3); and

(b) the amount of the compensation payment made by that compensator was calculated under regulation 12 [1 or 12A],

then the compensation payment is to be recalculated under regulation 12 [1 or 12A], and the compensator must pay the amount of the increase (if any) to the person to whom the compensation payment was made.

(5) Where both the earlier payment and the later payment are made by the same compensator, that compensator may—

(a) aggregate the gross amounts of the payments made;
(b) calculate what would have been the reduction made under regulation 12(3) if that aggregate amount had been paid at the date of the last payment on the basis that—
  (i) the aggregate amount is to be taken to be the gross amount; and
  (ii) the amount of any recoverable lump sum payment is to be taken to be the amount determined in accordance with the most recent certificate;
(c) deduct from that reduction calculated under sub-paragraph (b) the amount of the reduction under regulation 12(3) from any earlier payment; and
(d) deduct from the latest gross payment the net reduction calculated under sub-paragraph (c) (and accordingly the latest payment may be nil).

(6) Where a refund is made under paragraph (3), the Secretary of State is to send the compensator (with the refund) and the person to whom the compensation payment was made a statement showing—

(a) the total amount that has already been paid by that compensator to the Secretary of State;
(b) the amount that ought to have been paid by that compensator; and
(c) the amount to be repaid to that compensator by the Secretary of State.

(7) Where the reduction of a compensation payment is recalculated by virtue of paragraph (4) or (5) the compensator must give notice of the calculation to P.

AMENDMENT

1. Social Security (Recovery of Benefits) (Lump Sum Payments) (Amendment) Regulations 2014 (SI 2014/1456) reg.2 and Sch. paras 1 and 12 (July 1, 2014).

PART 5

MISCELLANEOUS

Information to be provided by the compensator

2.1015 **15.** The following information is prescribed for the purposes of sections 21(3)(a) and 23(1) of the Act—

(a) the full name and address of P;
(b) where known, the date of birth or national insurance number of P, or both if both are known; and
(c) the nature of the disease.

Information to be provided by P [1 and the scheme administrator]

16. [1 —(1)] The following information is prescribed for the purposes of [1 section 23(2)(a) of the Act]— 2.1016

(a) whether P has claimed or may claim a compensation payment, and if so, the full name and address of the person against whom the claim was or may be made;

(b) the amount of any compensation payment and the date on which it was made;

(c) the amount of the lump sum payment claimed, the type of that payment and the date on which it was paid.

[1 (2) For the purposes of section 23(2)(b) of the Act, the prescribed information is the amount of the lump sum payment falling within section 1A(2)(d) and the date on which it was paid.]

AMENDMENT

1. Social Security (Recovery of Benefits) (Lump Sum Payments) (Amendment) Regulations 2014 (SI 2014/1456) reg.2 and Sch. paras 1 and 13 (July 1, 2014).

Provision of information

17. A person required to give information to the Secretary of State under regulation 15 or 16 is to do so by sending it to the Compensation Recovery Unit not later than 14 days after— 2.1017

(a) where the person is one to whom regulation 15 applies, the date on which the compensator receives a claim for compensation from P in respect of the disease;

(b) where the person is one to whom regulation 16 applies, the date on which the Secretary of State requests the information from P [1 or the scheme administrator, as the case may be].

AMENDMENT

1. Social Security (Recovery of Benefits) (Lump Sum Payments) (Amendment) Regulations 2014 (SI 2014/1456) reg.2 and Sch. paras 1 and 14 (July 1, 2014).

Periodical payments

18.—(1) This regulation applies where in final settlement of P's claim, an agreement is entered into— 2.1018

(a) for the making of periodical payments (whether of an income or capital nature); or

(b) for the making of such payments and lump sum payments,

and, those payments would fall to be treated for the purposes of the Act as compensation payments.

(2) Where this regulation applies—

(a) the compensator in question is to be taken to have made a single compensation payment on the day of settlement;

(b) the total of the payments due to be made under the agreement referred to in paragraph (1) are to be taken to be a compensation payment for the purposes of the Act; and

(c) that single compensation payment is a payment from which lump sum payments may be recovered under these Regulations.

(3) In any case where—

(a) the person making the periodical payments ("the secondary party") does so in pursuance of arrangements entered into with another ("the primary party") (as in a case where the primary party purchases an annuity for P from the secondary party); and
(b) apart from those arrangements, the primary party would have been regarded as the compensator,

then for the purposes of the Act, the primary party is to be regarded as the compensator and the secondary party is not to be so regarded.

(4) In this regulation—

"the day of settlement" means—

(a) if the agreement referred to in paragraph (1) is approved by a court, the day on which that approval is given; and
(b) in any other case, the day on which the agreement is entered into;

"a single compensation payment" means the total amount of the payments due to be made under the agreement referred to in paragraph (1).

Adjustments

2.1019 **19.**—(1) Where the conditions specified in subsection (1) and paragraphs (a) and (b) of subsection (2) of section 14 of the Act are satisfied, the Secretary of State is to pay the difference between the amount that has been paid and the amount that ought to have been paid to the compensator.

(2) Where the conditions specified in subsection (1) and paragraphs (a) and (b) of subsection (3) of section 14 of the Act are satisfied, the compensator is to pay the difference between the amount that has been paid and the amount that ought to have been paid to the Secretary of State.

(3) Where the Secretary of State is making a refund under paragraph (1), or demanding a payment of a further amount under paragraph (2), the Secretary of State is to send to the compensator (with the refund or demand) and to the person to whom the compensation payment was made a statement showing—

(a) the total amount that has already been paid to the Secretary of State;
(b) the amount that ought to have been paid; and
(c) the difference, and whether a repayment by the Secretary of State or a further payment by the compensator to the Secretary of State is required.

(4) This paragraph applies where—

(a) the amount of the compensation payment by the compensator was calculated under regulation 12; and
(b) the Secretary of State has made a payment under paragraph (1).

(5) Where paragraph (4) applies, the amount of the compensation payment is to be recalculated under regulation 12 to take account of the fresh certificate and the compensator must pay the amount of the increase (if any) to the person to whom the compensation payment was made.

[1 (5A) This paragraph applies where—

(a) the amount of the payment made by the compensator was calculated under regulation 12A; and
(b) the Secretary of State has made a payment under paragraph (1).

(5B) Where paragraph (5A) applies, the amount of the compensation payment is to be recalculated under regulation 12A to take account of the fresh certificate and the compensator must pay the amount of the increase (if any) to the applicant as defined by regulation 3 of the Diffuse Mesothelioma Payment Scheme Regulations 2014.]

(6) This paragraph applies where—

(a) the amount of the compensation payment made by the compensator was calculated under regulation 12;

(b) the compensator has made a payment under paragraph (2); and

(c) the fresh certificate issued after the review or appeal was required as a result of P or such other person to whom the compensation payment was made supplying to the compensator information, knowing it to be incorrect or insufficient, with the intent of enhancing the compensation payment calculated under regulation 12, and the compensator supplying that information to the Secretary of State without knowing it to be incorrect or insufficient.

(7) Where paragraph (6) applies, the compensator may recalculate the compensation payment under regulation 12 to take account of the fresh certificate and may require the repayment of the difference (if any) between the payment made and the payment as so recalculated by the person to whom the compensator made the compensation payment.

[1 (8) This paragraph applies where—

(a) the amount of the payment made by the compensator was calculated under regulation 12A; and

(b) the fresh certificate issued after the review or appeal was required as a result of any applicant for payment under the Diffuse Mesothelioma Payment Scheme supplying to the compensator information knowing it to be incorrect or insufficient, and the compensator supplying that information to the Secretary of State without knowing it to be incorrect or insufficient.

(9) Where paragraph (8) applies, the compensator may recalculate the compensation payment under regulation 12A to take account of the fresh certificate and may require the repayment by the applicant responsible for supplying the incorrect or insufficient information of the difference (if any) between the payment made and the payment so recalculated.]

AMENDMENT

1. Social Security (Recovery of Benefits) (Lump Sum Payments) (Amendment) Regulations 2014 (SI 2014/1456) reg.2 and Sch. paras 1 and 15 (July 1, 2014).

SCHEDULE 1

MODIFICATION OF CERTAIN PROVISIONS OF THE ACT

1. This Schedule applies to any case to which regulation 4 [3 or 4A] applies. **2.1020**

2. Where this Schedule applies, section 1 (cases in which this Act applies) is to apply as if in subsection (3), for "Subsection (1)(a)" there were substituted "Section 1A(1)(a)".

3. Where this Schedule applies, section 10 (review of certificates of recoverable benefits) is to apply as if in—

(a) the heading and in subsection (1), there were omitted "of recoverable benefits" in each place it occurs;

(b) subsection (3), for "benefits" there were substituted "lump sum payments, except where that certificate has been reviewed under regulation 9ZA(1)(e) of the Social Security and Child Support (Decisions and Appeals) Regulations 1999 (review of certificates),".

4. Where this Schedule applies, section 11 (appeals against certificates of recoverable benefits) is to apply as if in—

(a) the heading and in subsections (1) and (2)(a), there were omitted "of recoverable benefits" in each place it occurs;
(b) subsection (1)(a), there were omitted ", rate or period";
(c) subsection (1)(b)—
   (i) for "listed benefits" there were substituted "[3 recoverable lump sum payments]";
   (ii) there were omitted "accident, injury or";
(d) subsection (1)(c)—
   (i) for "listed benefits" there were substituted [3 recoverable lump sum payments];
   (ii) for "the injured person during the relevant period" there were substituted "P";
(e) subsection (1)(d), for "1(1)(a)" there were substituted "1A(1)(a)";
(f) subsection (2)(aa) for "section 7(2)(a)" there were substituted "regulation 11(2)(a) of the Lump Sum Payments Regulations";
(g) subsection (2)(b), for "section 8 [3 or 8A]) the injured person" there were substituted "regulation 12 [3 or 12A] of the Lump Sum Payments Regulations) P";
(h) subsection (3), for "section 6" there were substituted "regulation 10 of the Lump Sum Payments Regulations".

5. Where this Schedule applies, section 12 (reference of questions to [2 First-tier Tribunal]) is to apply as if in—

(a) [2 . . .]
(b) subsection (3), there were omitted "accident, injury or";
(c) subsection (4)(a), for "amounts, rates and periods" there were substituted "amount, type and date of payments";
(d) subsections (4)(a) and (c), there were omitted "of recoverable benefits" in each place it occurs.

6. [1 Where this Schedule applies, section 13 (appeal to [2 Upper Tribunal]) is to apply [3 as if in subsection (2)—

(a) in paragraph (b), there were omitted "of recoverable benefits";
(b) in paragraph (bb), for "section 7(2)(a)" there were substituted "regulation 11(2)(a) of the Lump Sum Payments Regulations";
(c) in paragraph (c), for "section 8 or 8A) the injured person" there were substituted "regulation 12 or 12A of the Lump Sum Payments Regulations) P".]]

7. Where this Schedule applies, section 14 (reviews and appeals: supplementary) is to apply as if in—

(a) subsection (1), there were omitted "of recoverable benefits";
(b) subsections (2) and (3), for "section 6" there were substituted "regulation 10 of the Lump Sum Payments Regulations" in each place it occurs;
(c) subsection (4), for "section 8 [3 or 8A]" there were substituted "regulation 12 [3 or 12A] of the Lump Sum Payments Regulations".

8. Where this Schedule applies, for section 15 (court orders) is to apply as if there were substituted—

"15.—(1) This section applies where a court makes an order for a compensation payment to be made in a case where a compensation payment is to be made to a dependant of P—

(a) under the Fatal Accidents Act 1976 (c. 30);
(b) to the extent that it is made in respect of a liability arising by virtue of section 1 of the Damages (Scotland) Act 1976 (c. 13);
(c) under the Fatal Accidents (Northern Ireland) Order 1977 (S.I. 1977/1251 (N.I. 18)); or
(d) in respect of P, where that dependant is an intended beneficiary of part or all of that compensation,

and a lump sum payment has been made to that dependant, unless the order is made with the consent of that dependant and the person by whom the payment is to be made.

(2) The court must specify in the order the amount of the payment made—

(a) under the Fatal Accidents Act 1976;
(b) to the extent that it is made in respect of a liability arising by virtue of section 1 of the Damages (Scotland) Act 1976;
(c) under the Fatal Accidents (Northern Ireland) Order 1977; or
(d) in respect of P, where a dependant of P is an intended beneficiary of part or all of that compensation,

which is attributable to each or any dependant of P who has received a lump sum payment.".

9. Where this Schedule applies, section 17 (benefits irrelevant to assessment of damages) is to apply as if—

(a) in the heading for "benefits" there were substituted "lump sum payments";
(b) there were omitted "accident, injury or";
(c) for "listed benefits" there were substituted "lump sum payments".

10. Where this Schedule applies, section 18 (lump sum and periodical payments) is to apply as if—

(a) in subsection (1)—
   (i) for "the injured person" there were substituted "P";
   (ii) there were omitted "accident, injury or";
(b) in subsection (2), for "section 8" there were substituted "regulation 12 of the Lump Sum Payments Regulations";
(c) for subsection (3) there were substituted—
   "(3) For the purposes of subsection (2), the regulations may provide for—
   (a) the gross amounts of the compensation payments to be aggregated and for the aggregate amount to be the gross amount of the compensation payment for the purposes of regulation 12 of the Lump Sum Payments Regulations; and
   (b) for the amount of any lump sum payment to be taken to be the amount determined in accordance with the most recent certificate.";
(d) in subsection (4), for "the injured person's" there were substituted "P's";
(e) in subsection (5), there were omitted paragraph (a).

11. Where this Schedule applies, section 19 (payments by more than one person) is to apply as if in—

(a) subsection (1)—
   (i) for "injured person" there were substituted "P";
   (ii) there were omitted "accident, injury or";
(b) subsection (2)—
   (i) for "section 6" there were substituted "regulation 10 of the Lump Sum Payments Regulations";
   (ii) for "benefits" there were substituted "lump sum payments";
(c) subsection (3)—
   (i) in paragraph (a), for "benefits" there were substituted "lump sum payments";
   (ii) in paragraph (b), for "section 8 [3 or 8A]" there were substituted "regulation 12 [3 or 12A] of the Lump Sum Payments Regulations".

12. Where this Schedule applies, section 20 (amounts overpaid under section 6) is to apply as if in—

(a) the heading and in subsection (1), for "section 6" there were substituted "regulation 10 of Lump Sum Payments Regulations" in each place it occurs;
(b) subsection (4)(a), for "section 8 [3 or 8A]" there were substituted "regulation 12 [3 or 12A] of the Lump Sum Payments Regulations".

13. Where this Schedule applies, section 21 (compensation payments to be disregarded) is to apply as if in—

(a) subsections (1) and (5)(a), for "sections 6 and 8 [3 or 8A]" there were substituted "regulations 10 and 12 [3 or 12A] of the Lump Sum Payments Regulations" in each place it occurs;
(b) subsection (2)(a), there were omitted "of recoverable benefits";
(c) subsection (3)(a)—
   (i) for "the injured person" there were substituted "P";
   (ii) there were omitted "accident, injury or";
(d) subsection (4), for "section 4" there were substituted "regulation 8 of the Lump Sum Payments Regulations";
(e) subsection (5)(b), for "section 6" there were substituted "regulation 10 of the Lump Sum Payments Regulations".

14. Where this Schedule applies, section 22(1) (liability of insurers) is to apply as if —

(a) in paragraph (a), there were omitted "accident, injury or";
(b) for "section 6" there were substituted "regulation 10 of the Lump Sum Payments Regulations".

15. Where this Schedule applies, section 23 (provision of information) is to apply as if—

(a) in subsection (1), for—
   (i) "any accident, injury or" there were substituted "a";
   (ii) "any person ("the injured person")" there were substituted "P";
   (iii) "the injured person" there were substituted "P";
(b) in subsection (1)(a), there were omitted "accident, injury or";
[3 (ba) after subsection (1)(b) there were inserted—

", and

(c) where the compensation which is sought is a payment under the Diffuse Mesothelioma Payment Scheme, subsection (6A) applies.";

(c) for subsection (2), there were substituted—

"(2) Where P or a dependant of P, receives or claims a lump sum payment which is or is likely to be paid in respect of the disease suffered by P [3 —

(a) the prescribed information about the disease must be given to the Secretary of State by P or a dependant of P, as the case may be;

(b) the prescribed information about any lump sum payment which falls within section 1A(2)(d) must be given to the Secretary of State by the scheme administrator.]

(d) in subsection (3), for "listed benefit" there were substituted "lump sum payment";

(e) in subsection (4)—

(i) for "any accident, injury or" there were substituted "a";

(ii) there were omitted ", or any damage to property,";

(f) there were omitted subsections (5), (6) and (8).

16. Where this Schedule applies, section 26 (residence of the injured person—Northern Ireland) is to apply as if—

(a) in subsections (1)(a) and (b)(i), (2)(a), (b) and (c) and (3)(d)(ii), there were omitted "of recoverable benefits" in each place it occurs;

(b) in subsections (1)(c)(ii) and (2)(c)(i), for "section 6" there were substituted "regulation 10 of the Lump Sum Payments Regulations";

(c) in subsections (1) and (2), for "injured person's address" there were substituted "address of P";

(d) for subsection (3)(a), there were substituted—

"(a) "the address of P" is the address first notified in writing to the person making the payment by or on behalf of P as the residence of P (or if P had died, by or on behalf of the person entitled to receive the compensation payment as the last residence of P),";

(e) in subsection (3)(d)(i) and the heading to this section, for "the injured person" there were substituted "P" in each place it occurs.

17. Where this Schedule applies, section 27 (jurisdiction of courts—Northern Ireland) is to apply as if in—

(a) subsections (1) and (2), for "section 7" there were substituted "regulation 11 of the Lump Sum Payments Regulations" in each place it occurs;

(b) subsection (3)(a)(i), for—

(i) "the injured person" the first time it occurs, there were substituted "P";

(ii) "the injured person or, if he" there were substituted "P or, if P".

18. Where this Schedule applies, section 29 (general interpretation) is to apply as if—

(a) there were omitted the following definitions—

(i) "benefit";

(ii) "compensation scheme for motor accidents";

(iii) "listed benefit";

(b) in the appropriate place, there were inserted the following definitions—

(i) "certificate" means a certificate which includes amounts in respect of recoverable benefits and of recoverable lump sum payments, including where any of those amounts are nil;

(ii) "P" is to be construed in accordance with regulation 5 of the Lump Sum Payments Regulations;

(iii) "recoverable lump sum payments" means any lump sum payments which are recoverable by virtue of regulation 4 [3 or 4A] of the Lump Sum Payments Regulations;

(iv) "the Lump Sum Payments Regulations" means the Social Security (Recovery of Benefits) (Lump Sum Payments) Regulations 2008.

19. Where this Schedule applies, Part 1 of Schedule 1 (compensation payments—exempted payments) is to apply as if—

(a) in paragraph 2 and 3(a), for "the injured person" there were substituted "P" in each place it occurs;

(b) in paragraph 3(a) and (b) there were omitted "accident, injury or" in each place it occurs;

(c) for paragraph 5(1) there were substituted—

"(1) Any payment made to P or a dependant of P by an insurer under the terms of any contract of insurance entered into between P and the insurer before the date on which P or a dependant of P first claims a lump sum payment in consequence of the disease in question suffered by P.";

(d) in paragraph 6 for "an accident, injury or" there were substituted "a".

20. Where this Schedule applies, paragraph 9 of Part 2 of Schedule 1 (compensation payments—power to disregard small payments) is to apply as if in—

(a) sub-paragraph (1), for "sections 6 and 8" there were substituted "regulations 10 and 12 of the Lump Sum Payments Regulations";

(b) sub-paragraph (3)(a)—

(i) for "injured person" there were substituted "P";

(ii) there were omitted "accident, injury or".

AMENDMENTS

1. Social Security (Miscellaneous Amendments) (No.3) Regulations 2008 (SI 2008/2365) reg.6 (October 1, 2008).

2. Tribunals, Courts and Enforcement Act 2007 (Transitional and Consequential Provisions Order 2008 (SI 2008/2683) Sch.1 para.344 (November 3, 2008).

3. Social Security (Recovery of Benefits) (Lump Sum Payments) (Amendment) Regulations 2014 (SI 2014/1456) reg.2 and Sch. paras 1 and 16 (July 1, 2014).

GENERAL NOTE

This Schedule applies, with modifications, a number of the provisions relating to adjudication in the 1997 Act to the recovery of lump sum payments under these Regulations. In particular, ss.9 to 14 of the 1997 Act, relating to reviews and appeals, are applied as modified. In *Aviva Insurance Ltd v SSWP* [2015] UKUT 613 (AAC); [2016] AACR 29, it was accepted that, having regard to *R(CR) 1/02*, a compensator was in principle entitled to argue on an appeal to the First-tier Tribunal that the payment made to the claimant under the Pneumoconiosis etc. (Workers' Compensation) Act 1979 that the Secretary of State now sought to recover ought not to have been made because the Secretary of State had misconstrued the 1979 Act when awarding the payment. However, the argument advanced by the compensator was rejected on its merits. **2.1021**

SCHEDULE 2

Omitted. **2.1022**

The Social Security (Work-focused Interviews for Lone Parents) and Miscellaneous Amendments Regulations 2000

(SI 2000/1926)

ARRANGEMENT OF REGULATIONS

The Secretary of State for Social Security, in exercise of the powers conferred upon him by sections 123(1)(d) and (e) and 137(1) of the Social Security Contributions and Benefits Act 1992 and sectons 2A(1), (3)(b) to (f), (4), (5)(a) and (b), (6), (7) and (8), 2B(2), (6) and (7), 2C, 189(4) to (7A) and 191 of the Social Security Administration Act 1992 and of all other powers enabling him in that behalf, after consultation with the Council on Tribunals in accordance with section 8(1) of the Tribunals and Inquiries Act 1992 and in respect of provisions in these Regulations relating to housing benefit and council tax benefit with organisations appearing to him to be representative of the authorities concerned and after agreement by the Social Security Advisory Committee that proposals in respect of these Regulations should not be referred to it, hereby makes the following Regulations:

Citation, commencement and interpretation

2.1024 **1.**—(1) These Regulations may be cited as the Social Security (Work-focused Interviews for Lone Parents) and Miscellaneous Amendments Regulations 2000.

(2) This Regulation and paragraphs 2 to 5 of Schedule 2 and regulation 10 in so far as it relates to those paragraphs shall come into force on 14th August 2000.

(3) Regulations 2 to 9, paragraph 1 of Schedule 2 and regulation 10 in so far as it relates to that paragraph shall—

(a) come into force on 30th October 2000 in respect of lone parents who on that date—
 (i) live in an area identified in Schedule 1: and
 (ii) are not entitled to income support;
(b) subject to sub-paragraph (a), come into force on 30th April 2001 in respect of lone parents who on that date—
 (i) are not entitled to income support; or
 (ii) are entitled to income support and are not—
  (aa) responsible for; and
  (bb) living in the same household as,
 a child under the age of 13;
(c) subject to the preceding sub-paragraphs, come into force on 1st April 2002 in respect of lone parents who on that date are entitled to income support and are not—
 (i) responsible for; and
 (ii) living in the same household as,
 a child under the age of 9;
(d) subject to the preceding sub-paragraphs, where a lone parent—
 (i) is responsible for and living in the same household as a child whose 13th birthday occurs in the period beginning on 1st May 2001 and ending on 31st March 2002; and

(ii) is not on the date of the 13th birthday responsible for and living in the same household as a younger child,

come into force in respect of that lone parent on the date of that child's 13th birthday;

(e) subject to the preceding sub-paragraphs, where a loneparent—

(i) is responsible for and living in the same household as a child whose 9th birthday occurs in the period beginning on 2nd April 2002 and ending on 6th April 2003; and

(ii) is not on the date of the 9th birthday responsible for and living in the same household as a younger child,

come into force in respect of that lone parent on the date of that child's 9th birthday; and

[1 (f) subject to the preceding sub-paragraphs, come into force on 7th April 2003 in respect of lone parents who on that date are entitled to income support and are not responsible for and living in the same household as a child under the age of 5 years and 3 months;

[3 (g) subject to the preceding sub-paragraphs, come into force on 5th April 2004 in respect of a lone parent who on that date is entitled to income support and is responsible for an living in the same household as a child.]

come into force in respect of that lone parent on the date that child reaches the age of 5 years and 3 months.]

(4) In these Regulations, unless the context otherwise requires—

"the 1998 Act" means the Social Security Act 1998;

"benefit week" means any period of seven days corresponding to the week in respect of which income support is due to be paid;

"lone parent" has the meaning it bears in regulation 2(1) of the Income Support (General) Regulations 1987;

"interview" means a work-focused interview with a lone parent conducted for any or all of the following purposes—

(a) assessing that person's prospects for existing or future employment (whether paid or voluntary);

(b) assisting or encouraging that person to enhance his prospects of such employment;

(c) identifying activities which that person may undertake to strengthen his existing or future prospects of employment;

(d) identifying current or future employment or training opportunities suitable to that person's needs; and

(e) identifying educational opportunities connected with the existing or future employment prospects or needs of that person; and

"officer" means an officer of, or providing services to, the Secretary of State.

[4 "pensionable age", in the case of a man born before 6th April 1955, means the age when a woman born on the same day as the man would attain pensionable age.]

[5 "relevant interview" means an interview under these Regulations in relation to the lone parent's current award of income support.]

(5) In these Regulations, unless the context otherwise requires, a reference—

(a) to a numbered regulation is to a regulation in these Regulations bearing that number;

(b) in a regulation to a numbered paragraph or sub-paragraph is to the paragraph or sub-paragraph in that regulation bearing that number;
(c) to a numbered Schedule is to the Schedule to these Regulations bearing that number.

[[5] (6) For the purposes of section 2A(2A)(b) of the Social Security Administration Act 1992 and these Regulations, a lone parent is to be treated as responsible for, and a member of the same household as, a child under the age of one where the lone parent is treated as being responsible for and a member of the same household as such a child under regulations 15 and 16 of the Income Support (General) Regulations 1987.]

AMENDMENTS

1. The Social Security (Work-focused Interviews for Lone Parents) Amendment Regulations 2002 (SI 2002/670) reg.2 (April 8, 2002).
2. The Social Security (Work-focused Interviews for Lone Parents) Amendment Regulations 2003 (SI 2003/400) reg.2 (April 7, 2003).
3. The Social Security (Miscellaneous Amendments) Regulations 2004 (SI 2004/565) reg.7 (April 5, 2004).
4. The Social Security (Work-focused Interviews etc.) (Equalisation of State Pension Age) Amendment Regulations 2010 (SI 2010/563) reg.4(2) (April 6, 2010).
5. The Social Security (Work-focused Interviews for Lone Parents and Partners) (Amendment) Regulations 2011 (SI 2011/2428) reg.2 (October 31, 2011).

[[1] Requirement for certain lone parents entitled to income support to take part in an interview

2.1025 **2.**—(1) Subject to this regulation and regulations 2ZA and 4 to 6, a lone parent who falls within paragraph 1 (lone parents) of Schedule 1B (prescribed categories of person) to the Income Support (General) Regulations 1987(7) and paragraph (2) or (3) is required to take part in an interview.

(2) A lone parent falls within this paragraph if the lone parent is entitled to income support and has not taken part or been required to take part in a relevant interview.

(3) A lone parent falls within this paragraph if the lone parent has—
(a) taken part;
(b) failed to take part; or
(c) been treated as having taken part,
in a relevant interview.

(4) Where a lone parent falls within paragraph (3) the requirement to take part in an interview arises every six months after the date on which the lone parent—
(a) last took part;
(b) last failed to take part; or
(c) was last treated as having taken part,
in a relevant interview.

(5) Where a determination has been made in relation to a lone parent under regulation 6(1) (waiver) the lone parent is to be treated for the purposes of paragraph (2) of this regulation as if he has not taken part or been required to take part in a relevant interview.]

AMENDMENT

1. This version of the regulation introduced by the Social Security (Work-focused Interviews for Lone Parents and Partners) (Amendment) Regulations 2011 (SI 2011/2428) reg.2 (October 31, 2011).

[1 Requirement for certain lone parents to take part in an interview

2ZA.—(1) This regulation applies to a lone parent if— 2.1026

(a) he is entitled to income support and is a person to whom paragraph 1 (lone parents) of schedule 1B to the Income Support (General) Regulations 1987 applies; [5 and]

(b) no other paragraph of that Schedule applies to him; [5 . . .]

(c) [5 . . .]

[5 (2) Subject to regulations 4 and 5, a lone parent to whom this regulation applies is required to take part in one or more interviews as a condition of continuing to be entitled to the full amount of benefit which is payable to him part from these Regulations.]

AMENDMENTS

1. Inserted by The Social Security (Lone Parents and Miscellaneous Amendments) Regulations 2008 (SI 2008/3051) reg.5 (November 23, 2008).

2. Social Security (Lone Parents and Miscellaneous Amendments) Regulations 2008 (SI 2008/3051) reg.7 (October 25, 2010).

3. The Social Security (Work-focused Interviews for Lone Parents and Partners) (Amendment) Regulations 2011 (SI 2011/2428) reg.2 (October 31, 2011).

4. The Social Security (Lone Parents and Miscellaneous Amendments) Regulations 2012 (SI 2012/874) (May 21, 2012).

5. Income Support (Work-Related Activity) and Miscellaneous Amendments Regulations 2014 (SI 2014/1097), reg.13(2) (April 28, 2014).

GENERAL NOTE

Note that the Schedule to The Social Security (Lone Parents and Miscellaneous Amendments) Regulations 2012 (SI 2012/874) contains special commencement provisions for certain classes of claimant. 2.1027

2A [1 ...] 2.1028

AMENDMENT

1. Omitted under The Social Security (Work-focused Interviews for Lone Parents and Partners) (Amendment) Regulations 2011 (SI 2011/2428) reg.2 (October 31, 2011).

[1 General requirement for lone parents entitled to income support to take part in an interview

2ZB.—(1) Subject to regulations 4 to 6, this regulation applies to a lone parent who does not fall within paragraph 1 (lone parents) of Schedule 1B (prescribed categories of person) to the Income Support (General) Regulations 1987 and is entitled to income support. 2.1029

(2) A lone parent to whom this regulation applies is required to take part in an interview—

(a) where paragraph (3) applies to them; or

(b) where paragraph (4) and either paragraph (5) or (6) applies to them.

(3) This paragraph applies to a lone parent who has not taken part or been required to take part in a relevant interview.

(4) This paragraph applies to a lone parent who has taken part in a relevant interview or who would have taken part in such an interview but for—

(a) the requirement being deferred in accordance with regulation 5, or

(b) the requirement being waived in accordance with regulation 6.

(5) This paragraph applies to a lone parent when any of the following circumstances arise—

(a) the lone parent's entitlement to carer's allowance [2, or carer support payment under the Carer's Assistance (Carer Support Payment) (Scotland) Regulations 2023,] ceases whilst entitlement to income support continues;

(b) the lone parent becomes engaged or ceases to be engaged in part-time work;

(c) the lone parent has been undergoing education or training arranged by an officer and that education or training comes to an end; or

(d) the lone parent attains the age of 18 and has not previously taken part in a relevant interview.

(6) This paragraph applies where a lone parent has not been required to take part in a relevant interview for at least 36 months.]

AMENDMENT

1. Inserted by The Social Security (Work-focused Interviews for Lone Parents and Partners) (Amendment) Regulations 2011 (SI 2011/2428) reg.2 (October 31, 2011).

2. The Carer's Assistance (Carer Support Payment) (Scotland) Regulations 2023 (SI 2023/1218) reg.11 (November 19, 2023).

2.1030 **2B** [1 . . .]

AMENDMENT

1. Omitted under The Social Security (Miscellaneous Amendments) Regulations 2011 (SI 2011/674) reg.9 (April 1 *or* April 4, 2011).

[1 The interview

2.1031 **2C.** —[2 (1) An interview under these Regulations shall take place—

(a) where regulation 2ZA applies, on such date as may be determined by an officer;

(b) in any other case, as soon as is reasonably practicable after the date on which the requirement to take part in the interview arises.]

(2) An officer shall inform the lone parent of the place and time of the interview.

(3) An officer may determine that an interview is to take place in the lone parent's home where it would, in the opinion of the officer, be unreasonable to expect that lone parent to attend elsewhere because that lone parent's personal circumstances are such that attending elsewhere would—

(a) cause him undue inconvenience, or

(b) endanger his health.

AMENDMENTS

1. Inserted by The Social Security (Work-focused Interviews for Lone Parents) Amendment Regulations 2007 (SI 2007/1034) (April 30, 2007).

2. Income Support (Work-Related Activity) and Miscellaneous Amendments Regulations 2014 (SI 2014/1097), reg.13(3) (April 28, 2014).

Taking part in an interview

3.—(1) An officer shall determine whether a lone parent has taken part in an interview. 2.1032

[1 (2) Subject to regulations 5(2) and 6(2), a lone parent who has not taken part in an interview under these Regulations before 31st October 2005 shall be regarded as having taken part in his first interview under these Regulations if—

(a) he attends for the interview at the place and time notified to him by the officer;

(b) he participates in discussions with the officer in relation to the lone parent's employability, including any action the lone parent and the officer agree is reasonable and they are willing to take in order to help the lone parent enhance his employment prospects;

(c) he provides answers (where asked) to questions and appropriate information about—

(i) the level to which he has pursued any educational qualifications;

(ii) his employment history;

(iii) any vocational training he has undertaken;

(iv) any skills he has acquired which fit him for employment;

(v) any paid or unpaid employment he is engaged in;

(vi) any medical condition which, in his opinion, puts him at a disadvantage in obtaining employment;

(vii) any caring or childcare responsibilities he has;

(viii) his aspirations for future employment;

(ix) any vocational training or skills which he wishes to undertake or acquire; and

(x) his work related abilities; and

(d) he assists the officer in the completion of an action plan which records the matters discussed in relation to sub-paragraph (b) above.

(2A) Subject to regulations 5(2) and 6(2), a lone parent who has taken part in an interview under these Regulations before 31st October 2005 shall be regarded as having taken part in his first interview under these Regulations after 30th October 2005 if—

(a) he attends for the interview at the place and time notified to him by the officer;

(b) he participates in discussions with the officer in relation to the lone parent's employability, including any action the lone parent and the officer agree is reasonable and they are willing to take in order to help the lone parent enhance his employment prospects;

(c) he participates in discussions with the officer—

(i) in relation to the lone parent's employability or any progress he might have made towards obtaining employment; and

(ii) in order to consider any of the programmes and support available to help the lone parent obtain employment;

(d) he provides answers (where asked) to questions and appropriate information about—
(i) the content of any report made following his personal capability assessment, insofar as that report relates to the lone parent's capabilities and employability; and
(ii) his opinion as to the extent to which his medical condition restricts his ability to obtain employment; and
(e) he assists the officer in the completion of an action plan which records the matters discussed in relation to sub-paragraph (b) above.

(2B) Subject to regulations 5(2) and 6(2), a lone parent shall be regarded as having taken part in any subsequent interview under these Regulations if—
(a) he attends for the interview at the place and time notified to him by the officer;
(b) he participates in discussions with the officer—
(i) in relation to the lone parent's employability or any progress he might have made towards obtaining employment;
(ii) about any action the lone parent or the officer might have taken as a result of the matters discussed in relation to paragraph (2)(b) or (2A)(b) above;
(iii) about how, if at all, the action plan referred to in paragraphs (2)(d) or (2A)(e) above should be amended; and
(iv) in order to consider any of the programmes and support available to help the lone parent obtain employment;
(c) he provides answers (where asked) to questions and appropriate information about—
(i) the content of any report made following his personal capability assessment, insofar as that report relates to the lone parent's capabilities and employability; and
(ii) his opinion as to the extent to which his medical condition restricts his ability to obtain employment; and
(d) he assists the officer in the completion of any amendment of the action plan referred to in paragraphs (2)(d) or (2A)(e) above in light of the matters discussed in relation to sub-paragraph (b) above and the information provided in relation to sub-paragraph (c) above.]

AMENDMENT

1. The Social Security (Work-focused Interviews) Amendment Regulations 2005 (SI 2005/2727) (October 31, 2005).

[1 Circumstances where requirement to take part in an interview does not apply

2.1033 **4.**—(1) [8 Regulation 2 [9, 2ZA] and 2ZB] shall not apply where the lone parent—
(a) has attained [6 pensionable age];
(b) has not attained the age of 18; or
(c) is—
(i) required to take part in an interview, or
(ii) not required to take part in an interview by virtue of—

(aa) a waiver of a requirement, or

(bb) a deferment of an interview, under the Social Security (Work-focused Interviews) Regulations 2000, the Social Security (Jobcentre Plus Interviews) Regulations 2001, the Social Security (Jobcentre Plus Interviews) Regulations 2002, [3 or the Social Security (Incapacity Benefit Work-focused Interviews) Regulations 2003.]

[8 (1A) [9 Regulation 2 and 2ZA] shall not apply to a lone parent who is treated as responsible for, and a member of the same household as, a child who is under the age of one.]

(2) [2. . .]

[3 (3) [9. . .]

Amendments

1. The Social Security (Work-focused Interviews) Amendment Regulations 2005 (SI 2005/2727) (October 31, 2005).

2. The Social Security (Working Neighbourhoods) Miscellaneous Amendment Regulations 2006 (SI 2006/909) (April 24, 2006).

3. The Social Security (Work-focused Interviews for Lone Parents) Amendment Regulations 2007 (SI 2007/1034) (April 30, 2007).

4. The Social Security (Incapacity Benefit Work-focused Interviews) Regulations 2008 (SI 2008/2928) reg.12 (December 15, 2008).

5. The Social Security (Lone Parents and Miscellaneous Amendments) Regulations 2008 (SI 2008/3051) reg.5 (November 23, 2008).

6. The Social Security (Work-focused Interviews etc.) (Equalisation of State Pension Age) Amendment Regulations 2010 (SI 2010/563) reg.4(3) (April 6, 2010).

7. The Social Security (Miscellaneous Amendments) Regulations 2011 (SI 2011/674) reg.9 (April 1 *or* April 4, 2011).

8. The Social Security (Work-focused Interviews for Lone Parents and Partners) (Amendment) Regulations 2011 (SI 2011/2428) reg.2 (October 31, 2011).

9. Income Support (Work-Related Activity) and Miscellaneous Amendments Regulations 2014 (SI 2014/1097), reg.13(4) (April 28, 2014).

Deferment of requirement to take part in an interview

5.—(1) A requirement by virtue of these Regulations to take part in an interview shall not apply to a person until a date determined by an officer where he determines that an interview would not [1 until] that time be— 2.1034

(a) of assistance to that person; or

(b) appropriate in the circumstances.

(2) Except for the purpose of [2 regulations [4 2, 2ZA and 2A]], where an officer has made a decision under paragraph (1), the person to whom that decision relates shall be treated for the purposes of any claim for, or entitlement to, income suppport as having complied with the requirement to take part in an interview until an officer decides whether that person took part in the interview which had been deferred under paragraph (1).

Amendments

1. The Social Security (Claims and Information and Work-focused Interviews for Lone Parents) Amendment Regulations 2001 (SI 2001/1189) reg.3 (April 23, 2001).

2. The Social Security (Work-focused Interviews) Amendment Regulations 2005 (SI 2005/2727) (October 31, 2005).
3. The Social Security (Lone Parents and Miscellaneous Amendments) Regulations 2008 (SI 2008/3051) reg.5 (November 23, 2008).
4. The Social Security (Miscellaneous Amendments) Regulations 2011 (SI 2011/674) reg.9 (April 1 *or* April 4, 2011).

Waiver

2.1035 **6.**—(1) A requirement imposed by [3 regulations 2(1) and 2ZB(2)] to take part in an interview shall not apply if an officer determines that an interview would not be—

(a) of assistance to the lone parent; or
(b) appropriate in the circumstances.

(2) A person in relation to whom a requirement to take part in an interview has been waived under paragraph (1) shall be treated for the purposes of—

(a) [2 2 [3. . .] and 2A]; and
(b) any claim for, or entitlement to, income support,

as having complied with that requirement.

AMENDMENTS

1. The Social Security (Work-focused Interviews) Amendment Regulations 2005 (SI 2005/2727) (October 31, 2005).
2. The Social Security (Miscellaneous Amendments) Regulations 2011 (SI 2011/674) reg.9 (April 1 *or* April 4, 2011).
3. Income Support (Work-Related Activity) and Miscellaneous Amendments Regulations 2014 (SI 2014/1097), reg.13(5) (April 28, 2014).

Consequence of failure to take part in an interview

2.1036 **7.**—(1) Subject to paragraphs [6 (2), (5) and (5A) and regulations 5 and 6, [5 the consequence specified in paragraph (3) ensues] if a person does not—

(a) take part in any interview when required to do so; and
(b) show good cause for not taking part in an interview before the end of five working days following the [6 date on which the person was notified of his failure to take part in the interview]

[6 (1A) Where a notice under paragraph (1)(b) is sent by post it is taken to have been received on the second working day after it was sent.]

(2) In a case where within one month of the date on which the decision was notified to a lone parent that he failed without good cause to take part in an interview—

(a) he brings new facts to the notice of an officer which could not reasonably have been brought to an officer's notice within five working days of the [6 date on which the person was notified of his failure to take part in the interview]; and
(b) those facts show that he had good cause for his failure to take part in the interview

paragraph (1)(b) shall apply with the modification that for the words "five working days following" there were substituted the words "one month of".

[5 (3) the income support of a lone parent to whom paragraph (1) applies shall be reduced in accordance with regulation 8.]

(4) Where an interview which arose in connection with a claim was deferred and benefit became payable in accordance with regulation 5(2), the person's entitlement to income support shall terminate as from the first day of the next benefit week following the date the decision was made that the person failed without good cause to take part in an interview.

(5) For the purposes of this regulation and regulation 8(1), matters to be taken into account in determining whether a person has shown good cause for his failure to take part in an interview include—

(a) that the lone parent misunderstood the requirement to take part in the interview due to any learning, language or literacy difficulties of the lone parent or any misleading information given to him by an officer;

(b) that the lone parent was attending a medical or dental appointment, or accompanying someone for whom he has caring responsibilities to such an appointment, and that it would be unreasonable, in the circumstances, to have rearranged that appointment;

(c) that the lone parent had difficulties with his normal mode of transport and that no reasonable alternative was available;

(d) that the established customs and practices of the religion to which that lone parent belongs prevented him attending at the time and place for the interview notified to him by an officer;

(e) that the lone parent was attending an interview with an employer with a view to obtaining employment;

(f) that the lone parent was pursuing employment opportunities as a self-employed earner;

(g) that a dependant of the lone parent or someone for whom the lone parent provides care suffered an accident, sudden illness or relapse of [1 a physical or mental health condition];

(h) that the lone parent was attending a funeral of a close friend or relative on the day fixed for the interview; and

(i) that a disability from which the lone parent suffers made it impracticable for him to attend at the time fixed for the interview.

[6 (5A) The amount of income support payable to a person is not to be reduced in accordance with paragraph (3) if that amount—

(a) is, at the time a decision falls to be made in respect of the current failure, being paid at a reduced rate in accordance with paragraph (3) and regulation 8, regulation 12(2)(c) of the Social Security (Jobcentre Plus Interviews) Regulations 2002 or regulation 8(1) and (2) of the Income Support (Work-Related Activity) and Miscellaneous Amendments Regulations 2014; and

(b) was last reduced not more than two weeks before the date of the current failure.

(5B) In paragraph (5A), "current failure" means a failure which may, in the case of a claimant who has an award of income support, lead to a reduction in income support under paragraph (3) and regulation 8 in relation to which the Secretary of State has not yet determined whether the amount of income support payable to the person is to be reduced in accordance with that paragraph and regulation.]

(6) For the avoidance of doubt, a person who is regarded as not having made a claim for income support because he failed to take part in an interview shall be required to make a new claim for income support in order to establish entitlement to that benefit.

AMENDMENTS

1. The Social Security (Work-focused Interviews) Amendment Regulations 2005 (SI 2005/2727) (October 31, 2005).

2. The Social Security (Work-focused Interviews for Lone Parents) Amendment Regulations 2007 (SI 2007/1034) (April 30, 2007).

3. The Social Security (Lone Parents and Miscellaneous Amendments) Regulations 2008 (SI 2008/3051) reg.5 (November 23, 2008).

4. The Social Security (Miscellaneous Amendments) Regulations 2011 (SI 2011/674) reg.9 (April 1 *or* April 4, 2011).

5. The Social Security (Work-focused Interviews for Lone Parents and Partners) (Amendment) Regulations 2011 (SI 2011/2428) reg.2 (October 31, 2011).

6. Income Support (Work-Related Activity) and Miscellaneous Amendments Regulations 2014 (SI 2014/1097), reg.13(6) (April 29, 2014).

Reduction of income support

2.1037 **8.**—(1) Subject to paragraphs (2) and (3), any payment of income support which falls to be made to a person after the date on which an officer decided under these Regulations that that person had not—

(a) taken part; and

(b) shown good cause for not taking part,

in an interview shall be reduced as from the first day of the next benefit week following the date the decision was made, by a sum equal to 20 per cent of the income applicable (specified in Part I of Schedule 2 to the Income Support (General) Regulations 1987) [2 . . .] in respect of a single claimant for income support aged not less than 25.

(2) Payment shall not be reduced under paragraph (1) below 10 pence per week.

(3) A reduction under this regulation shall cease to have effect as regards a person from whichever is the earlier of—

(a) the date on which that person attains [1 pensionable age];

(b) the date on which that person ceased to be a lone parent; [3 . . .]

(c) the first day of the benefit week in which that person [4 satisfies a compliance condition] [3 "and;

(d) the first day of the benefit week in which regulation 4(1A) first applies to that person.]

[4 (4) In paragraph (3)(c), "compliance condition" means a requirement to—

(a) take part in an interview; or

(b) undertake work-related activity.]

AMENDMENTS

1. The Social Security (Work-focused Interviews etc.) (Equalisation of State Pension Age) Amendment Regulations 2010 (SI 2010/563) reg.4(4) (April 6, 2010).

2. The Social Security (Miscellaneous Amendments) (No.3) Regulations 2011 (SI 2011/2425) reg.13 (October 31, 2011).

3. The Social Security (Work-focused Interviews for Lone Parents and Partners) (Amendment) Regulations 2011 (SI 2011/2428) reg.2 (October 31, 2011).

4. Income Support (Work-Related Activity) and Miscellaneous Amendments Regulations 2014 (SI 2014/1097), reg.13(7) (April 29, 2014).

Appeals

9.—(1) This regulation applies to any relevant decision made under these Regulations or any decision under section 10 of the 1998 Act (decisions superseding earlier decisions) superseding such a decision. **2.1038**

(2) This regulation applies—

(a) whether the decision is as originally made or as revised under section 9 of the 1998 Act (revision of decisions); and

(b) as if any decision made, superseded or revised otherwise than by the Secretary of State was a decision made, superseded or revised by him.

(3) In the case of a decision to which this regulation applies, the person in respect of whom the decision was made shall have a right of appeal under section 12 of the 1998 Act [[1] (appeal to First-tier Tribunal) to the First-tier Tribunal]

AMENDMENT

1. The Tribunals, Courts and Enforcement Act 2007 (Transitional and Consequential Provisions) Order 2008 (SI 2008/2683) reg.140 (November 3, 2008).

SCHEDULE 1 **Regulation 1(3)(a)**

AREAS WHERE THESE REGULATIONS COME INTO FORCE ON 30TH OCTOBER 2000 IN RESPECT OF LONE PARENTS WHO ARE NOT ENTITLED TO INCOME SUPPORT **2.1039**

For the purposes of regulation 1(3)(a), the areas are—

(a) the areas of Shropshire County Council and Telford Wrekin District Council; and

(b) the following postcode districts—

DH2 1AA to DH2 1BO
DH2 1XA to DH2 1XQ
DH3 1 and DH3 2
NE8 and NE9
NE10 0
NE10 8 and NE10 9
NE11
NE16 3 to NE16 5
NE16 6NX to NE16 6PE
NE16 8
NE17 7AA to NE17 7HE
NE17 7HG to NE17 7LM
NE17 7TA to NE17 7ZZ
NE21 1
NE21 4 to NE21 6
NE31 1 to NE31 5
NE32 2 to NE32 4
NE33
NE34 0
NE34 6 to NE34 9
NE35 1 and NE35 9
NE36 0 and NE36 1
NE39
NE40 3 to NE40 4
NE42 5 to NE42 6
NE43 7
SR6 7.

(c) The area of Fife Council excluding the following postcode districts—

DD 6 8 and DD 6 9
KY 14 6

KY 16 0
KY 16 9.

AMENDMENT

1. The Social Security (Work-focused Interviews for Lone Parents) Amendment Regulations 2002 (SI 2002/670) reg.2 (April 8, 2002).

2.1040 *Schedule 2 omitted.*

[1 SCHEDULE 3] **Regulation 2B(1)**

2.1041 [2 . . .]

AMENDMENTS

1. Inserted by The Social Security (Work-focused Interviews for Lone Parents) Amendment Regulations 2007 (SI 2007/1034) (April 30, 2007).
2. The Social Security (Miscellaneous Amendments) Regulations 2011 (SI 2011/674) reg.9 (April 1 *or* April 4, 2011).

SECTION B

HMRC-ADMINISTERED BENEFITS

Note

The administration and initial adjudication of claims for child benefit and guardian's allowance are the responsibility of His Majesty's Revenue and Customs but are governed by the Social Security Administration Act 1992 and the Social Security Act 1998. Separate regulations have been made under those Acts for these benefits and they are reproduced in this section. They are naturally similar to, although they do not exactly replicate, the regulations made by the Secretary of State for Work and Pensions that are in Section A above. Where no specific annotation is provided to regulations reproduced in this section, readers are advised to check the annotation of the corresponding provision in Section A.

For equivalent legislation in respect of other HMRC-administered benefits, see Vol.IV.

The Child Benefit and Guardian's Allowance (Administration) Regulations 2003

(SI 2003/492)

Made	*5th March 2003*
Laid before Parliament	*5th March 2003*
Coming into force	*7th April 2003*

ARRANGEMENT OF REGULATIONS

PART I

GENERAL

PART II

CLAIMS AND AWARDS

PART III

PAYMENTS

PART IV

THIRD PARTIES

PART V

OVERPAYMENTS AND RECOVERY

PART VI

REVOCATIONS AND TRANSITIONAL PROVISIONS

SCHEDULE 1

POWERS EXERCISED IN MAKING THESE REGULATIONS

SCHEDULE 2

ELECTRONIC COMMUNICATIONS

PART I GENERAL

PART II GENERAL

PART III EVIDENTIAL PROVISIONS

SCHEDULE 3

REVOCATIONS

The Commissioners of Inland Revenue, in exercise of the powers conferred upon them by the provisions set out in Schedule 1, hereby make the following Regulations:

PART I

GENERAL

Citation, commencement and effect

1.—(1) These Regulations may be cited as the Child Benefit and Guardian's Allowance (Administration) Regulations 2003 and shall come into force on 7th April 2003 immediately after the commencement of section 50 of the Tax Credits Act 2002 for the purposes of entitlement to payment of child benefit and guardian's allowance. **2.1043**

(2) These Regulations have effect only in relation to—

(a) child benefit and guardian's allowance under the Contributions and Benefits Act; and

(b) child benefit and guardian's allowance under the Contributions and Benefits (NI) Act.

Interpretation

2. In these Regulations— **2.1044**

"the adjudicating authority" means—

(a) the Board;

(b) an appeal tribunal constituted under [2 . . .] Chapter 1 of Part 2 of the Social Security (Northern Ireland) Order 1998 or

(c) a Commissioner [2 . . .] to whom an appeal lies under Article 15 of that Order;

[2 (d) the First-tier Tribunal or the Upper Tribunal;]

"the Administration Act" means the Social Security Administration Act 1992;

"the Administration (NI) Act" means the Social Security Administration (Northern Ireland) Act 1992;

[3 "appropriate office" means—

(a) Waterview Park, Washington, Tyne and Wear; or

(b) any other office specified in writing by the Board.]

"the approved form" has the meaning given by regulation 5(1)(a);

"the Board" means the [1 Commissioners for Her Majesty's Revenue and Customs];

"civil partnership" means two people [4 ...] who are civil partners of each other and are neither—(a) separated under a court order, nor (b) separated in circumstances in which the separation is likely to be permanent;

[4 "cohabiting couple" means two people who are not a married couple or in a civil partnership but are living together as if they were married or civil partners;]

"the Contributions and Benefits Act" means the Social Security Contributions and Benefits Act 1992;

"the Contributions and Benefits (NI) Act" means the Social Security Contributions and Benefits (Northern Ireland) Act 1992;

"interim payment" has the meaning given by regulation 22(1);

"married couple" means a man and a woman who are married to each other and are neither—
(a) separated under a court order, nor
(b) separated in circumstances in which the separation is likely to be permanent;

"partner" means a member of a married couple, [4 a civil partnership or a cohabiting couple];

"relevant authority" means—
(a) in relation to child benefit or guardian's allowance under the Contributions and Benefits Act, the Secretary of State or a person providing services to the Secretary of State;
(b) in relation to child benefit or guardian's allowance under the Contributions and Benefits (NI) Act, the Department for Social Development in Northern Ireland or a person providing services to that Department;

[4 . . .]

"writing" includes writing produced by electronic communications used in accordance with Schedule 2.

AMENDMENTS

1. The Child Benefit and Guardian's Allowance (Miscellaneous Amendments) Regulations 2006 (SI 2006/203) (April 10, 2006).

2. The Tribunals, Courts and Enforcement Act 2007 (Transitional and Consequential Provisions) Order 2008 (SI 2008/2683) Sch.1 para.211 (November 3, 2008).

3. The Child Benefit and Guardian's Allowance (Miscellaneous Amendments) Regulations 2009 (SI 2009/3268) reg.3(2) (January 1, 2010).

4. The Civil Partnership (Opposite-sex Couples) Regulations 2019 (SI 2019/1458) reg.41 and Sch.3 para.64 (December 2, 2019).

Use of electronic communications

2.1045 **3.** Schedule 2 (the use of electronic communications) has effect.

Notification for purposes of sections 111A and 112 of the Administration Act and sections 105A and 106 of the Administration (NI) Act

2.1046 **4.**—(1) This regulation prescribes the person to whom, and manner in which, a change of circumstances must be notified for the purposes of sections 111A(1A) to (1G) and 112(1A) to (1F) of the Administration Act and sections 105A(1A) to (1G) and 106(1A) to (1F) of the Administration (NI) Act (offences relating to failure to notify a change of circumstances).

(2) Notice of the change of circumstances must be given to the Board, or, where relevant, a relevant authority, in writing (except where they determine or it determines, in any particular case, that they or it will accept a notice other than in writing) by delivering or sending it to an appropriate office.

PART II

CLAIMS AND AWARDS

Making a claim

2.1047 **5.**—[1 (1) A claim, or an extension of a claim, for child benefit or guardian's allowance must be made—

(a) to the Board, in writing and completed on a form approved or authorised by the Board for the purpose of the claim; or
(b) in such other manner as the Board may decide having regard to all the circumstances.]

(2) The person making the claim must deliver or send it to an appropriate office.

(3) Subject to regulation 10, the claim is made on the date on which it is received by the appropriate office.

AMENDMENT

1. The Child Benefit and Guardian's Allowance (Miscellaneous Amendments) Regulations 2009 (SI 2009/3268) reg.3(3) (January 1, 2010).

Time within which claims to be made

[1 **6.**—(1) The time within which a claim for child benefit or guardian's allowance is to be made is 3 months beginning with any day on which, apart from satisfying the conditions for making the claim, the person making the claim is entitled to the benefit or allowance. 2.1048

(2) Paragraph (1) shall not apply where—
(a) a person has been awarded child benefit or guardian's allowance while he was present and residing in Great Britain, or Northern Ireland;
(b) at a time when payment of the award has not been suspended or terminated (under regulations 18 to 20 of the Child Benefit and Guardian's Allowance (Decisions and Appeals) Regulations 2003 or otherwise), he take up residence in Northern Ireland, or Great Britain as the case may be ("the new country of residence"); and
(c) a new claim for that benefit or allowance is made in the new country of residence, for a period commencing on the later of—
   (i) the date of the change of residence referred to in sub-paragraph (b), or
   (ii) the date on which, apart from satisfying the conditions for making the claim, the person became entitled to the benefit or allowance under the legislation of the new country of residence.]

[2 (d) a person who has claimed asylum and, on or after 6th April 2004, makes a claim for that benefit or allowance and satisfies the following conditions—
   (i) the person is notified that he has been recorded as a refugee by the Secretary of State; and
   (ii) he claims that benefit or allowance within 3 months of receiving that notification.

[3 (e) a person who has been granted section 67 leave makes a claim for that benefit or allowance within three months of receiving notification from the Secretary of State of the grant of that leave.]

(3) In a case falling within paragraph (2)(d) [3 or(2)(e)] the person making the claim shall be treated as having made it on the date when he submitted his claim for asylum.]

[3 (4) In this regulation "section 67 leave" means leave to remain in the United Kingdom granted by the Secretary of State to a person who has been relocated to the United Kingdom pursuant to arrangements made by the Secretary of State under section 67 of the Immigration Act 2016.]

AMENDMENTS

1. The Child Benefit and Guardian's Allowance) (Administration) (Amendment No.3) Regulations 2003 (SI 2003/2107) reg.6 (September 3, 2003).

2. The Child Benefit and Guardian's Allowance (Miscellaneous Amendments) Regulations 2004 (SI 2004/761) reg.2 (April 6, 2004).

3. The Child Benefit, Tax Credits and Childcare Payments (Section 67 Immigration Act 2016 Leave) (Amendment) Regulations 2018 (SI 2018/788) reg.3 (July 20, 2018).

GENERAL NOTE

2.1049 *HMRC v AA (TC and CHB)* [2012] UKUT 121 (AAC) concerned a claimant who was the beneficiary of the decisions of the Administrative Court of April 8, 2008 and April 9, 2009 that the extension of the period before which those subject to immigration control could apply for indefinite leave to remain from four years to five years could not be applied to certain categories of migrants.

The claimant had claimed child benefit on September 3, 2008. He subsequently asked for the award to be backdated to August 28, 2007 on the grounds that following the judicial reviews, he was retrospectively deemed to have indefinite leave to remain from August 28, 2007.

The First-tier Tribunal had applied the provisions in reg.6(2)(d) relating to those who had claimed asylum and been recorded as refugees by analogy to the circumstances presented by the claimant. HMRC appealed to the Upper Tribunal, where the Judge decided that the provisions relating to refugees could not be interpreted to include those in the claimant's circumstances. The limitation in the regulations that the award of child benefit could be backdated for a maximum period of three months applied to the claimant.

In *HMRC v BZ* [2022] UKUT 264 (AAC), the claimant had received a notification dated May 18, 2019 that she had been accepted as having refugee status but which indicated that she could not claim benefits until she had received her Biometric Residence Permit, which only occurred later. Judge Gullick KC held that, while the notification had indeed notified the claimant that she had been recorded as a refugee, the notification of May 18, 2019:

> "was not valid notification of the recording of refugee status for the purpose of Regulation 6(2)(d) of the 2003 Regulations. That is because the notification incorrectly stated that a claim for Child Benefit could not be made until receipt of the BRP. In my judgment, a notification of this sort which contains a statement denying the existence of the very right to claim an entitlement which it would otherwise confer cannot, in this context, be a valid notification. To construe the language of Regulation 6(2)(d) otherwise would, in my judgment, be to ignore its purpose and would be to adopt precisely the sort of 'purely linguistic' approach rejected by Singh LJ in [*R. (on the application of Kaitey) v Secretary of State for the Home Department* [2021] EWCA Civ 1875]."

Evidence and information

2.1050 **7.** [3(1) The Board may require the person making the claim for child benefit or guardian's allowance to supply such information or evidence in connection with the claim, or any questions arising out of it, as the Board considers reasonable.]

(2) A person required under paragraph (1) to furnish [3...] information and evidence must do so—

(a) within one month of being required by the Board to do so; or

(b) within such longer period as the Board may consider reasonable.

[3...]

AMENDMENTS

1. Child Benefit and Guardian's Allowance (Administration) (Amendment) Regulations 2004 (SI 2004/1240) (May 1, 2004).
2. The Child Benefit and Guardian's Allowance (Miscellaneous Amendments) Regulations 2006 (SI 2006/203) (April 10, 2006).
3. The Tax Credits and Child Benefit (Miscellaneous Amendments) Regulations 2023 (SI 2023/179) reg.4 (March 15, 2023).

GENERAL NOTE

This provision would appear to reflect the rather more legalistic approach the Board of Inland Revenue adopt to some issues, since the Department for Work and Pensions never seem to have felt the need for such a provision. 2.1051

Amending claims

8.—(1) A person who has made a claim for child benefit or guardian's allowance may amend it by giving to the Board or a relevant authority notice in writing in accordance with paragraph (2). 2.1052

(2) A notice under paragraph (1) must be delivered or sent to an appropriate office at any time before a determination has been made on the claim.

(3) The Board may treat a claim amended in accordance with this regulation as if it had been so amended when first made.

Withdrawing claims

9.—[1 (1) A person who has made a claim for child benefit or guardian's allowance may withdraw it by giving notice— 2.1053

(a) in writing to the Board,
(b) by telephone to the Board, or
(c) in such other manner as the Board may accept as sufficient in the circumstances of the particular case.]

(2) A notice of withdrawal given in accordance with paragraph [1 (1)(a)] has effect when it is received by an appropriate office.

AMENDMENT

1. The Tax Credits, Child Benefit and Childcare Payments (Miscellaneous Amendments) Regulations 2019 (SI 2019/364) (March 21, 2019).

Defective applications

10.—(1) If an appropriate office receives a defective application, the Board or the relevant authority may refer it back to the person making it or supply him with the approved form for completion. 2.1054

(2) Where—

(a) in accordance with paragraph (1), a defective application has been referred back, or an approved form supplied, to a person; and
(b) a claim is received by an appropriate office—
    (i) within the period of one month beginning with the date on which the defective application was referred back or the approved form was supplied; or
    (ii) within such longer period as the Board may consider reasonable,

the claim shall be treated as having been made on the date on which the appropriate office received the defective application.

(3) "Defective application" means an intended claim which—

(a) is made on an approved form which has not been completed in accordance with the instructions on it; or

(b) is in writing but is not made on the approved form.

Claims for child benefit treated as claims for guardian's allowance and vice versa

2.1055 **11.**—(1) Where it appears to the Board that a person who has made a claim for child benefit in respect of a child [1 or qualifying young person] may be entitled to guardian's allowance in respect of the same child [1 or qualifying young person], the Board may treat, either in the alternative or in addition, the claim as being a claim for guardian's allowance by that person.

(2) Where it appears to the Board that a person who has made a claim for guardian's allowance in respect of a child [1 or qualifying young person] may be entitled to child benefit in respect of the same child [1 or qualifying young person], the Board may treat, either in the alternative or in addition, the claim as being a claim for child benefit by that person.

AMENDMENT

1. The Child Benefit and Guardian's Allowance (Miscellaneous Amendments) Regulations 2006 (SI 2006/203) (April 10, 2006).

Advance claims and awards

2.1056 **12.**—(1) This regulation applies where a person who has made a claim for child benefit or guardian's allowance does not satisfy the requirements for entitlement on the date on which the claim is made.

(2) If the Board are of the opinion that, unless there is a change of circumstances, the person will satisfy those requirements for a period beginning with a date ("the relevant date") not more than 3 months after the date on which the claim is made, they—

(a) may treat the claim as if made for a period beginning with the relevant date; and

(b) may award the benefit or allowance accordingly, subject to the condition that the person satisfies the requirements for entitlement when the benefit or allowance becomes payable under the award.

(3) If the requirements for entitlement are found not to have been satisfied on the relevant date, a decision under paragraph (2)(b) to award benefit may be revised under—

(a) in relation to child benefit and guardian's allowance under the Contributions and Benefits Act, section 9 of the Social Security Act 1998;

(b) in relation to child benefit and guardian's allowance under the Contributions and Benefits (NI) Act, Article 10 the Social Security (Northern Ireland) Order 1998.

Date of entitlement under an award for the purposes of payability

2.1057 **13.**—(1) This regulation applies where child benefit or guardian's allowance is awarded for a period of a week or weeks and the earliest date on which entitlement would commence is not a Monday.

(2) For the purposes of determining the day from which the benefit or allowance is to become payable, entitlement shall be treated as beginning on the Monday next following the earliest date referred to in paragraph (1).

Effective date of change of rate

14. Where a change in the rate of child benefit or guardian's allowance would take effect, but for this regulation, on a day which would not be the appropriate pay day for the benefit or allowance, the change shall take effect from the appropriate pay day next following. **2.1058**

Duration of claims and awards

15.—(1) Subject to paragraphs (2) and (3), a claim for child benefit or guardian's allowance shall be treated as made for an indefinite period and any award shall be made for an indefinite period. **2.1059**

(2) If it would be inappropriate to treat a claim as made and to make an award for an indefinite period (for example, where a relevant change of circumstances is reasonably to be expected in the near future), the claim shall be treated as made for a definite period which is appropriate in the circumstances and any award shall be made for that period.

(3) In any case where benefit or allowance is awarded in respect of days subsequent to the date on which the claim was made, the award shall be subject to the condition that the person by whom the claim was made satisfies the requirements for entitlement.

PART III

PAYMENTS

[[1] Payment by direct credit transfer

16.—(1) Child benefit or guardian's allowance shall be paid in accordance with paragraphs (2) to (6) unless paid in accordance with regulation 17. **2.1060**

(2) Payment of child benefit or guardian's allowance [[3] . . .] shall be made by direct credit transfer into a bank or other account that [[2] the person entitled to the benefit or allowance has] notified to the Board(a) for the purpose of payment of—

(a) a benefit described in section 5(2) of the Social Security Administration Act 1992;

(b) a benefit described in section 5(2) of the Social Security Administration (Northern Ireland Act) 1992; or

(c) a tax credit described in section 1 of the Tax Credits Act 2002, to which that person is entitled.

(3) If a person entitled to child benefit is also entitled to guardian's allowance, the allowance shall be paid into the same bank or other account as that into which the child benefit is paid under this regulation.

(4) The bank account or other account into which the Board may make payment of the allowance or benefit must be—

(a) in the name of—
  (i) the person entitled to the benefit or allowance ("the person"),
  (ii) the person's partner, or
  (iii) a person acting on behalf of the person; or
(b) in the joint names of the person and—
  (i) the person's partner, or
  (ii) a person acting on the person's behalf.

(5) Subject to paragraph (6), the benefit or allowance shall be paid within seven days of the last day of each successive period of entitlement.

(6) The Board may make a particular payment by direct credit transfer otherwise than is provided by paragraph (5) if it appears to them appropriate to do so for the purpose of—
(a) paying any arrears of benefit or allowance, or
(b) making a payment in respect of a terminal period of an award for any similar purpose.]

AMENDMENTS

1. Child Benefit and Guardian's Allowance (Administration) (Amendment) Regulations 2010 (SI 2010/2459) reg.2 (November 1, 2010).

2. Child Benefit and Guardian's Allowance (Administration) (Amendment) Regulations 2016 (SI 2016/681) reg.2 (July 21, 2016).

[1 Payment by other means

2.1061 **17.**—(1) Child benefit or guardian's allowance may be paid by a means other than by direct credit transfer where it appears to the Board to be appropriate to do so in the circumstances of a particular case.

(2) If a person entitled to child benefit is also entitled to guardian's allowance, the allowance shall be paid in the same manner as that in which the child benefit is paid under this regulation.

(3) An instrument of payment issued by the Board pursuant to this regulation shall—
(a) remain the property of the Board, and
(b) be returned immediately to the Board (or such person as the Board may direct) if the person who has the instrument—
  (i) is required to do so by the Board; or
  (ii) ceases to be entitled to any part of the benefit or allowance to which the instrument relates.]

AMENDMENT

1. Child Benefit and Guardian's Allowance (Administration) (Amendment) Regulations 2010 (SI 2010/2459) reg.2 (November 1, 2010).

Time of payment

2.1062 **18.**—(1) Subject to paragraphs (2) to (4), child benefit and guardian's allowance shall be paid in accordance with an award as soon as reasonably practicable after the award has been made.

(2) Child benefit shall be paid—
(a) if a person entitled to it makes an election under regulation 19 or 20, weekly beginning with the first convenient date after the election has been made;

(b) in any other case, in the last week of each successive period of four weeks of the period of entitlement.

(3) Where benefit is paid at four-weekly intervals in accordance with paragraph (2)(b), the Board must arrange for it to be paid weekly if they are satisfied that payment at intervals of four weeks is causing hardship.

(4) If a person who has made a claim for child benefit is also entitled to guardian's allowance, the allowance shall be paid at the same intervals as the child benefit.

(5) The Board must take steps to notify persons to whom child benefit or guardian's allowance is payable of the arrangements they have made for payment in so far as those arrangements affect those persons.

Persons who may elect to have child benefit paid weekly

19.—(1) A person may make an election under this regulation to have child benefit paid weekly if— 2.1063

(a) he is a lone parent; [2 . . .]

(b) he or his partner is receiving—

(i) income support; or

(ii) an income-based allowance payable under Part 1 of the Jobseekers Act 1995 or Part 2 of the Jobseekers (Northern Ireland) Order 1995.

[2 (iii) an income-related employment and support allowance within the meaning in Part 1 of the Welfare Reform Act 2007 or Part 1 of the Welfare Reform Act (Northern Ireland) 2007; or

(iv) a state pension credit within the meaning in the State Pension Credit Act 2002 or the State Pension Credit Act (Northern Ireland) 2002.]

[3 (v) universal credit under Part 1 of the Welfare Reform Act 2012.]

(2) "Lone parent" means a person who has no partner and is entitled to child benefit in respect of a child [1 or qualifying young person] for whom he is responsible.

(3) A person making an election under this regulation—

(a) must furnish, in such manner and at such times as the Board may determine, such certificates, documents, other information or facts as the Board may require which may affect his right to receive payment of the benefit weekly; and

(b) as soon as reasonably practicable after any change of circumstances which he might reasonably be expected to know might affect that right, must notify the Board in writing of that change in accordance with paragraph (4).

(4) A notification under paragraph (3)(b) must be delivered or sent to an appropriate office as regards the Board.

AMENDMENTS

1. The Child Benefit and Guardian's Allowance (Miscellaneous Amendments) Regulations 2006 (SI 2006/203) (April 10, 2006).

2. The Child Benefit and Guardian's Allowance (Miscellaneous Amendments) Regulations 2009 (SI 2009/3268) reg.3(4) (January 1, 2010).

3. The Universal Credit (Consequential Supplementary, Incidental and Miscellaneous Provisions) Regulations 2013 (SI 2013/630) reg.81 (April 29, 2013).

Elections for weekly payment by persons to whom child benefit was payable for a period beginning before and ending after 15th March 1982

2.1064 **20.**—(1) This regulation applies to a person to whom child benefit is payable for an uninterrupted period beginning before and ending after 15th March 1982.

(2) A person to whom this regulation applies may make an election to have the benefit paid weekly after 15th March 1982 if—

(a) he makes it before the end of the period of 26 weeks beginning with the day on which benefit was payable for the first four weeks in respect of which arrangements for four-weekly payment were made;

(b) in the case of benefit under the Contributions and Benefits Act, he was absent from Great Britain on 15th March 1982 for any of the reasons specified in paragraph (3) and he makes the election before the end of the period of 26 weeks beginning with the first week in respect of which benefit became payable to him in Great Britain on his return; or

(c) in the case of benefit under the Contributions and Benefits (NI) Act, he was absent from Northern Ireland on 15th March 1982 for any of the reasons specified in paragraph (3) and he makes the election before the end of the period of 26 weeks beginning with the first week in respect of which benefit became payable to him in Northern Ireland on his return.

(3) The reasons specified in this paragraph are that the person—

(a) was a serving member of the forces;

(b) was the spouse of such a serving member; or

(c) was living with such a serving member as husband or wife.

(4) "Serving member of the forces" means a person, other than one mentioned in Part 2 of Schedule 6 to the Social Security (Contributions) Regulations 2001, who, being over the age of 16 years, is a member of any establishment or organisation specified in Part 1 of that Schedule (being a member who gives full pay service) but does not include any such person while absent on desertion.

Manner of making elections under regulations 19 and 20

2.1065 **21.**—(1) This regulation applies to elections under regulations 19 and 20.

(2) An election—

(a) must be made by notice in writing to the Board; and

(b) must be delivered or sent to an appropriate office as regards the Board.

(3) An election is made on the date on which it is received by the appropriate office.

(4) Where a person has made an election, child benefit is payable weekly so long as—

(a) he remains continually entitled to it; and

(b) in the case of an election under regulation 19, the conditions specified in paragraph (1)(a) or (b) of that regulation continue to be satisfied.

(5) A person who has made an election may cancel it at any time by giving to the Board a notice in writing which must be sent or delivered to an appropriate office as regards the Board.

(6) The Board must give effect to a notice given in accordance with paragraph (5) as soon as reasonably practicable after receiving it.

Interim payments

22.—[1 (1) If the condition in any sub-paragraph of paragraph (1A) is satisfied, the Board may make a payment on account ("an interim payment") of any child benefit or guardian's allowance to which it appears to them that a person— 2.1066

(a) is or may be entitled, were a claim made,

(b) where sub-paragraph (a) of paragraph (1A) applies, would or might be entitled, were a claim made,

(c) where sub-paragraph (b) of that paragraph applies, would or might be entitled, were the national insurance number condition satisfied.

(1A) The conditions are that—

(a) a claim for benefit or allowance has not been made in accordance with these Regulations and it is impracticable for such a claim to be made immediately;

(b) a claim has been made in accordance with these Regulations, the conditions of entitlement are satisfied other than the national insurance number condition, and it is impracticable for that condition to be satisfied immediately;

(c) a claim for the benefit or allowance has been so made but it is impracticable for it, or an application or appeal relating to it, to be determined immediately;

(d) an award of the benefit or allowance has been made but it is impracticable for the person entitled to it to be paid immediately other than by means of an interim payment.]

(2) Paragraph (1) does not apply pending the determination of an appeal [1 . . .].

(3) On or before the making of an interim payment, the Board must give the person to whom payment is to be made notice in writing of his liability under regulations 41 and 42 to have it brought into account and to repay any overpayment.

[1 (4) In this regulation "the national insurance number condition" means the condition imposed—

(a) in Great Britain by section 13(1A) and (1B), of the Administration Act (requirement for claim to be accompanied by details of national insurance number);

(b) in Northern Ireland, by section 11(1A) and (1B) of the Administration (NI) Act.]

AMENDMENT

1. The Child Benefit and Guardian's Allowance (Miscellaneous Amendments) Regulations 2005 (SI 2005/343) reg.8 (March 18, 2005).

Information to be given and changes to be notified

23.—(1) This regulation applies to any person entitled to child benefit or guardian's allowance and any person by whom, or on whose behalf, payments of such benefit or allowance are receivable. 2.1067

(2) A person to whom this regulation applies must furnish in such manner and at such times as the Board may determine such information or evidence as the Board may require for determining whether a decision on an award—

(a) in relation to benefit or allowance under the Contributions and Benefits Act, should be revised under section 9 or superseded under section 10 of the Social Security Act 1998;

(b) in relation to benefit or allowance under the Contributions and Benefits (NI) Act, should be revised under Article 10 or superseded under Article 11 of the Social Security (Northern Ireland) Order 1998.

(3) A person to whom this regulation applies must furnish in such manner and at such times as the Board may determine such information and evidence as the Board may require in connection with the payment of the benefit or allowance.

[[1](3A) Where a person is in receipt of a benefit or allowance by means other than a direct credit transfer, in accordance with regulation 17, that person must, if required, within such time as the Board may determine, provide details of a bank or other account to which payment can be made.]

(4) A person to whom this regulation applies must notify the Board or a relevant authority of any change of circumstances which he might reasonably be expected to know might affect—

(a) the continuance of entitlement to the benefit or allowance; or

(b) the payment of it,

as soon as reasonably practicable after the change occurs.

(5) A notification under paragraph (4)—

(a) must be given by notice in writing or orally; and

(b) must be sent, delivered or given to the appropriate office.

AMENDMENT

1. The Tax Credits and Child Benefit (Miscellaneous Amendments) Regulations 2022 (SI 2022/555).

Fractional amounts of benefit or allowance

2.1068 **24.** Where the amount of any child benefit or guardian's allowance payable includes a fraction of a penny, that fraction—

(a) if it is less than a half, shall be disregarded;

(b) if it is a half or more, shall be treated as a whole penny.

Payments to persons under the age of 18 years

2.1069 **25.** Where a sum of child benefit or guardian's allowance is paid to a person under the age of 18 years (whether on his own behalf or on behalf of another), either of the following is a sufficient discharge to the Board for the sum paid—

(a) a direct credit transfer under [[1] regulation 16] into the person's account;

(b) the receipt by the person of a payment made by some other means.

AMENDMENT

1. Child Benefit and Guardian's Allowance (Administration) (Amendment) Regulations 2010 (SI 2010/2459) reg.2 (November 1, 2010).

Extinguishment of right to payment if payment is not obtained within the prescribed period

26.—[1 (1) A person's right to payment of any sum of child benefit or guardian's allowance shall be extinguished if payment of that sum has not been obtained within 12 months of the issue by the Board of a cheque or other instrument of payment to that person.] 2.1070

(2)–(5) [1 . . .]

(6) This regulation has effect in relation to a person authorised or appointed to act on behalf of a person entitled to child benefit or guardian's allowance in the same manner as it has effect in relation to such a person.

AMENDMENT

1. The Child Benefit and Guardian's Allowance (Miscellaneous Amendments) Regulations 2009 (SI 2009/3268) reg.3(5) (January 1, 2010).

PART IV

THIRD PARTIES

Persons who may act on behalf of those unable to act

27.—(1) Anything required by these regulations to be done by or to any person who is for the time being unable to act may be done by or to— 2.1071

(a) in England and Wales, a receiver appointed by the Court of Protection with power to claim, or, as the case may be, receive, the benefit or allowance on behalf of the person;
(b) in Scotland, [1 guardian acting or appointed under the Adults with Incapacity (Scotland) Act 2000] who is administering the estate of the person;
(c) in Northern Ireland, a controller appointed by the High Court, with power to claim, or, as the case may be, receive, the benefit or allowance on behalf of the person; or
(d) a person appointed under regulation 28(2) to act on behalf of the person.

(2) Where a sum of child benefit or guardian's allowance is paid to a receiver or other person mentioned in paragraph (1)(a), (b), (c) or (d), either of the following is a sufficient discharge to the Board for the sum paid—

(a) a direct credit transfer under [2 regulation 16] into the person's account;
(b) the receipt by the person of a payment made by some other means.

AMENDMENTS

1. The Child Benefit and Guardian's Allowance (Miscellaneous Amendments) Regulations 2005 (SI 2005/343) reg.10 (March 18, 2005).
2. Child Benefit and Guardian's Allowance (Administration) (Amendment) Regulations 2010 (SI 2010/2459) reg.2 (November 1, 2010).

Appointment of persons to act on behalf of those unable to act

28.—(1) This regulation applies where— 2.1072

(a) a person is for the time being unable to act;

(b) the person is, or is alleged to be, entitled to child benefit or guardian's allowance (whether or not a claim for the benefit or allowance has been made by him or on his behalf); and

(c) no receiver or other person mentioned in regulation 27(1)(a), (b) or (c) has been appointed in relation to the person.

(2) The Board may appoint a person who—

(a) has applied in writing to them to act on behalf of the person who is unable to act, and

(b) if a natural person, is over the age of 18 years,

to exercise, on behalf of the person who is unable to act, any right relating to child benefit or guardian's allowance to which that person may be entitled and to receive and deal on his behalf with any sums payable to him in respect of the benefit or allowance.

(3) Where an appointment has been made under paragraph (2)—

(a) the Board may at any time revoke it; and

(b) the person appointed may resign from the appointment after having given one month's notice in writing to the Board of his intention to do so.

(4) An appointment made under paragraph (2) shall terminate when the Board are notified that a receiver or other person mentioned in regulation 27(1)(a), (b) or (c) has been appointed.

Persons who may proceed with a claim made by a person who has died

2.1073 **29.**—(1) The Board may appoint such person as they think fit to proceed with a claim for child benefit or guardian's allowance [[1], and to deal with any issue related to the revision of, supersession of, or appeal in connection with a decision on, that claim] which has been made by a person who has died.

(2) Subject to regulation 32(2), the Board may pay or distribute any sum payable under an award on a claim proceeded with under paragraph (1) to or among—

(a) persons over the age of 16 years claiming as personal representatives, legatees, next of kin or creditors of the person who has died; and

(b) if the person who has died was illegitimate, any other persons over that age.

(3) "Next of kin" means—

(a) in England and Wales, and in Northern Ireland, the persons who would take beneficially on an intestacy;

(b) in Scotland, the persons entitled to the moveable estate of the deceased on intestacy.

(4) Where a sum is paid under paragraph (2) to a person, either of the following is a sufficient discharge to the Board for the sum paid—

(a) a direct credit transfer under [[2] regulation 16] into the person's account;

(b) the receipt by the person of a payment made by some other means.

(5) If the Board consider that a sum or part of a sum which may be paid or distributed under paragraph (2) is needed for the benefit of a person under the age of 16 years, they may obtain a good discharge for that sum

by paying it to a person over that age whom they are satisfied will apply the sum for the benefit of the person under that age.

(6) Regulation 26 (extinguishment of right) applies to a payment or distribution made under paragraph (2).

AMENDMENTS

1. The Child Benefit and Guardian's Allowance (Miscellaneous Amendments) Regulations 2009 (SI 2009/3268) reg.3(5) (January 1, 2010).

2. Child Benefit and Guardian's Allowance (Administration) (Amendment) Regulations 2010 (SI 2010/2459) reg.2 (November 1, 2010).

Persons who may receive payments which a person who has died had not obtained

30.—(1) This regulation applies where a person who has died had not obtained at the date of his death a sum of child benefit or guardian's allowance which was payable to him. 2.1074

(2) Subject to regulation 32(2), the Board may, unless the right to payment had already been extinguished at the date of death, pay or distribute the sum to or amongst the persons mentioned in regulation 29(2)(a) and (b).

(3) Regulation 26 (extinguishment of right) applies to a payment or distribution made under paragraph (2), except that, for the purposes of paragraph (1) of that regulation, the period of 12 months shall be calculated from the date on which the right to payment is treated as having arisen to the person to whom the payment or distribution is made (and not from the date on which that right is treated as having arisen in relation to the person who has died).

Person who may make a claim on behalf of a person who has died

31.—(1) If the conditions specified in paragraph (2) are satisfied, a claim may be made in the name of a person who has died for any child benefit or guardian's allowance to which he would have been entitled if he had claimed it in accordance with these Regulations. 2.1075

(2) Subject to paragraph (3), the following conditions are specified in this paragraph—

(a) within 6 months of the date of death an application must have been made in writing to the Board for a person, whom the Board think fit to be appointed to make the claim, to be so appointed;

(b) a person must have been appointed by the Board to make the claim; and

(c) the person so appointed must have made the claim not more than 6 months after the appointment.

(3) Subject to paragraphs (4) and (5), if the Board certify that to do so would be consistent with the proper administration of the Contributions and Benefits Act, the period of 6 months mentioned in paragraph (2)(a) or (c) shall be extended by such period (not exceeding 6 months) as may be specified in the certificate.

(4) If a certificate given under paragraph (3) specifies a period by which the period of 6 months mentioned in paragraph (2)(a) shall be extended, the period of 6 months mentioned in paragraph (2)(c) shall be shortened by a period corresponding to the period so specified.

(5) No certificate shall be given under paragraph (3) which would enable a claim to be made more than 12 months after the date of death. For the purposes of this paragraph, any period between the date on which the application for a person to be appointed to make the claim is made and the date on which that appointment is made shall be disregarded.

(6) A claim made in accordance with this regulation shall be treated for the purposes of these Regulations as if it had been made on the date of his death by the person who has died.

Regulations 29, 30 and 31: supplementary

2.1076 **32.**—(1) The Board may dispense with strict proof of the title of a person claiming in accordance with regulation 29, 30 or 31.

(2) Neither paragraph (2) of regulation 29 nor paragraph (2) of regulation 30 applies unless written application for payment of the sum under that paragraph is made to the Board within 12 months from the date of death or such longer period as the Board may allow.

Payment to one person on behalf of another

2.1077 **33.**—(1) Subject to paragraph (2), the Board may direct that child benefit or guardian's allowance shall be paid, wholly or in part, to another natural person on behalf of the person entitled to it.

(2) The Board may not make a direction under paragraph (1) unless they are satisfied that it is necessary for protecting the interests of—

(a) the person entitled to the benefit or allowance; or

(b) any child [1 or qualifying young person] in respect of whom the benefit or allowance is payable.

AMENDMENT

1. The Child Benefit and Guardian's Allowance (Miscellaneous Amendments) Regulations 2006 (SI 2006/203) (April 10, 2006).

Payment to partner as alternative payee

2.1078 **34.**—(1) Subject to paragraph (2), where a [1 person with a partner] is entitled to child benefit or guardian's allowance, the Board may make arrangements whereby that benefit or allowance, as well as being payable to the person entitled to it, may, in the alternative, be paid to that person's partner on behalf of that person.

(2) Paragraph (1) does not apply to guardian's allowance where a [1 woman] has elected that the allowance is not to be paid to her husband [1 or male civil partner] in accordance with regulation 10 of the Guardian's Allowance (General) Regulations 2003 (prescribed manner of making an election under section 77(9) of the Contributions and Benefits Act and section 77(9) of the Contributions and Benefits (NI) Act).

AMENDMENTS

1. The Civil Partnership (Opposite-sex Couples) Regulations 2019 (SI 2019/1458) reg.41 and Sch.3 para.64 (December 2, 2019).

PART V

OVERPAYMENTS AND RECOVERY

Recovery of overpayments by direct credit transfer

35.—(1) If the adjudicating authority determines that— 2.1079

(a) a payment of child benefit or guardian's allowance in excess of entitlement has been credited to a bank account or other account under an arrangement for direct credit transfer made in accordance with [1 regulation 16]; and

(b) the conditions specified in paragraph (2) are satisfied,

the excess, or the specified part of it to which the certificate referred to in sub-paragraph (a) of that paragraph relates, shall be recoverable.

(2) The following conditions are specified in this paragraph—

(a) the Board must have certified that the payment in excess of entitlement, or a specified part of it, is materially due to the arrangement for payments to be made by direct credit transfer; and

(b) subject to paragraph (3), notice of the effect which this regulation would have, in the event of an overpayment, must have been given in writing to the person entitled to the benefit or allowance, or to a person acting in his behalf, [1 before the Board made the arrangement for the payment of child benefit or guardian's allowance into that account].

(3) In the case of an arrangement relating to child benefit which was agreed to before 6th April 1987, the condition specified in paragraph (2)(b) need not be satisfied in any case where the application for the benefit to be paid by direct credit transfer contained a statement, or was accompanied by a written statement made by the applicant, which complied with the provisions specified in paragraph (4).

(4) The provisions specified in this paragraph are—

(a) in relation to child benefit under the Contributions and Benefits Act, regulation 7(2)(b) and (6) of the Child Benefit (Claims and Payments) Regulations 1984;

(b) in relation to child benefit under the Contributions and Benefits (NI) Act, regulation 7(2)(b) and (6) of the Child Benefit (Claims and Payments) Regulations (Northern Ireland) 1985.

AMENDMENT

1. Child Benefit and Guardian's Allowance (Administration) (Amendment) Regulations 2010 (SI 2010/2459) reg.2 (November 1, 2010).

Circumstances in which determination need not be reversed, varied, revised or superseded

36.—(1) This regulation applies where, whether fraudulently or otherwise, a person has misrepresented, or failed to disclose, material facts which do not provide a basis for the determination in pursuance of which an amount of child benefit or guardian's allowance was paid— 2.1080

(a) in relation to benefit or allowance under the Contributions and Benefits Act, to be revised under section 9 or superseded under section 10 of the Social Security Act 1998;

(b) in relation to benefit or allowance under the Contributions and Benefits (NI) Act, to be revised under Article 10 or superseded under Article 11 of the Social Security (Northern Ireland) Order 1998.

(2) Where this regulation applies—

(a) in relation to an amount mentioned in paragraph (1) relating to child benefit or guardian's allowance under the Contributions and Benefits Act, neither subsection (5) nor (5A) of section 71 of the Administration Act (recoverability dependent on reversal, variation, revision or supersession of determination) applies;

(b) in relation to an amount mentioned in paragraph (1) relating to child benefit or guardian's allowance under the Contributions and Benefits (NI) Act, neither subsection (5) nor (5A) of section 69 of the Administration (NI) Act (recoverability dependent on reversal, variation, revision or supersession of determination) applies.

Calculating recoverable amounts

2.1081 **37.** Where there has been an overpayment of child benefit or guardian's allowance, in calculating the amounts recoverable under section 71(1) of the Administration Act, section 69(1) of the Administration (NI) Act or regulation 35, the adjudicating authority must deduct any amount which is offset under regulation 38.

Offsetting prior payments of child benefit and guardian's allowance against arrears payable by virtue of a subsequent determination

2.1082 **38.**—(1) Subject to regulation 40, in either of the cases specified in paragraphs (2) and (3)—

(a) a sum of child benefit paid for a period covered by a subsequent determination shall be offset against any arrears of entitlement to the benefit payable for that period by virtue of the subsequent determination;

(b) a sum of guardian's allowance paid for a period covered by a subsequent determination shall be offset against any arrears of entitlement to the allowance payable for that period by virtue of the subsequent determination, and, except to the extent that it exceeds them, the sum so paid shall be treated as properly paid on account of the arrears.

(2) The case specified in this paragraph is where a person has been paid a sum pursuant to a determination which subsequently—

(a) is revised under section 9 or superseded under section 10 of the Social Security Act 1998;

(b) is revised under Article 10 or superseded under Article 11 of the Social Security (Northern Ireland) Order 1998; or

(c) is overturned on appeal.

(3) The case specified in this paragraph is where a person has been paid a sum for a period by way of an increase in respect of a dependent person and it is subsequently determined that—

(a) the dependent person is entitled to the benefit or allowance for that period; or

(b) a third person is entitled to the increase for that period in priority to the person who has been paid.

(4) Where child benefit which has been paid under an award in favour of a person ("the first claimant") is subsequently awarded to another ("the second claimant") for any week, the benefit shall nevertheless be treated as properly paid if it was received by someone (other than the first claimant) who—

(a) had [1 the child or qualifying young person] living with him or was contributing towards the cost of providing for [1 the child or qualifying young person] at a weekly rate which was not less than the weekly rate under the original award; and

(b) could have been entitled to child benefit in respect of [1 that child or qualifying young person] for that week had a claim been made in time.

(5) Any amount which is treated under paragraph (4) as properly paid shall be deducted from the amount payable to the second claimant under the subsequent award.

AMENDMENT

1. The Child Benefit and Guardian's Allowance (Miscellaneous Amendments) Regulations 2006 (SI 2006/203) (April 10, 2006).

Offsetting prior payments of income support or jobseeker's allowance against arrears of child benefit or guardian's allowance payable by virtue of a subsequent determination

39.—(1) This regulation applies where— 2.1083

(a) a person has been paid a sum by way of income support or jobseeker's allowance; and

(b) it is subsequently determined that—

(i) child benefit or guardian's allowance should be awarded or is payable in lieu of the income support or jobseeker's allowance; and

(ii) the income support or jobseeker's allowance was not payable.

(2) Subject to regulation 40, any sum of income support or jobseeker's allowance in respect of the period covered by the subsequent determination—

(a) shall be offset against any arrears of entitlement to the child benefit or guardian's allowance payable for that period by virtue of that determination; and

(b) except to the extent that it exceeds them, the sum so paid shall be treated as properly paid on account of the arrears.

Exception from offset of recoverable overpayment

40. No amount may be offset under regulation 38(1) or 39(2) which has been determined to be a recoverable overpayment for the purposes of section 71(1) of the Administration Act or section 69(1) of the Administration (NI) Act. 2.1084

Bringing interim payments into account

41.—(1) Subject to paragraph (2), if it is practicable to do so— 2.1085

(a) any interim payment made in anticipation of an award of child benefit or guardian's allowance shall be ofset by the adjudicating authority in reduction of the benefit or allowance to be awarded;

(b) any interim payment (whether or not made in anticipation of an award) which is not offset under sub-paragraph (a) shall be deducted by the Board from—

(i) the sum payable under the award of benefit or allowance on account of which the interim payment was made; or

(ii) any sum payable under any subsequent award of the benefit or allowance to the same person.

(2) Paragraph (1) does not apply unless the Board have given the notice required by regulation 22(3).

Recovery of overpaid interim payments

2.1086 **42.**—(1) Subject to paragraph (2), if the adjudicating authority, in the circumstances specified in either of paragraphs (3) and (4), has determined that an interim payment has been overpaid, it shall determine the amount of the overpayment.

(2) Paragraph (1) does not apply unless the Board have given the notice required by regulation 22(3).

(3) The circumstances specified in this paragraph are where an interim payment has been made under regulation 22(1)(a) and (b) and—

(a) the recipient has failed to make a claim in accordance with these Regulations as soon as practicable;

(b) the recipient has made a defective application and the Board have not treated the claim as duly made under regulation 10;

(c) it has been determined that—

(i) there is no entitlement on the claim;

(ii) the entitlement is less than the amount of the interim payment; or

(iii) the benefit or allowance on the claim is not payable; or

(d) the claim has been withdrawn.

(4) The circumstances specified in this paragraph are where an interim payment has been made under regulation 22(1)(c) which exceeds the entitlement under the award of benefit on account of which the interim payment was made.

(5) The amount of any overpayment determined under paragraph (1) shall be recoverable by the Board in the same manner as it would be if it were recoverable under—

(a) in relation to child benefit or guardian's allowance under the Contributions and Benefits Act, section 71(1) of the Administration Act;

(b) in relation to child benefit or guardian's allowance under the Contributions and Benefits (NI) Act, section 69(1) of the Administration (NI) Act.

[1 Recovery of overpayments from awards of child benefit and guardian's allowance

2.1087 **42A.**—(1) Where any amount of child benefit or guardian's allowance is recoverable from a person under—

(a) section 71(1) of the Administration Act,

(b) section 69(1) of the Administration (NI) Act, or
(c) regulation 35(1) or 42(5),

That amount may be recovered by the adjudicating authority from any child benefit or guardian's allowance payable to that person.

(2) For the purposes of paragraph (1), child benefit or guardian's allowance payable includes any payment of arrears of child benefit or guardian's allowance other than a payment of arrears required to be made by regulation 21(1) of the Child Benefit and Guardian's Allowance (Decisions and Appeals) Regulations 2003.]

AMENDMENT

1. Inserted by The Child Benefit and Guardian's Allowance (Administration) (Amendment) Regulations 2012 (SI 2012/1074) reg.3 (May 8, 2012).

PART VI

REVOCATIONS AND TRANSITIONAL PROVISIONS

Revocations

43. The subordinate legislation specified in column (1) of Parts 1 and 2 of Schedule 3, in so far as it relates to child benefit or guardian's allowance, is revoked to the extent mentioned in column (3) of that Schedule. **2.1088**

Transitional provisions

44.—(1) Anything done or commenced under any provision of the instruments revoked by regulation 43, so far as relating to child benefit or guardian's allowance, is to be treated as having been done or as being continued under the corresponding provision of these Regulations. **2.1089**

(2) The revocation by regulation 43 of an instrument which itself revoked an earlier instrument subject to savings does not prevent the continued operation of those savings, in so far as they are capable of continuing to have effect.

(3) "Instrument" includes a Statutory Rule of Northern Ireland.

SCHEDULE 1

Preamble

POWERS EXERCISED IN MAKING THESE REGULATIONS

1. The following provisions of the Administration Act— **2.1090**

(a) section 5(1)(a), (b), (c), (d), (g), (h), (hh), (i), (j), (k), (l), (m), (p), (q) and (r) and (2) (a) and (g);
(b) section 7(1), (2) and (3)(a);
(c) section 71(4), (5), (5A), (6), (7) and (11)(a) and (f);
(d) section 111A(1A), (1B), (1D) and (1E);
(e) section 112(1A) to (1D);
(f) section 189(1), (4), (5) and (6);
(g) section 191.

2. The following provisions of the Administration (NI) Act—
(a) section 5(1)(a), (b), (c), (d), (g), (h), (hh), (i), (j), (k), (l), (m), (n), (q), (r), (s) and (t) and (2)(a) and (g);
(b) section 69(4), (5), (5A), (6), (7) and (11)(a) and (f);
(c) section 105A(1A), (1B), (1D) and (1E);
(d) section 106(1A) to (1D);
(e) section 165(1), (4), (5), (6) and (11A);
(f) section 167(1).

3. Sections 9(1) and 84 of the Social Security Act 1998.

4. Articles 2(2) and 10(1) of the Social Security (Northern Ireland) Order 1998.

5. Sections 132 and 133(1) and (2) of the Finance Act 1999.

6. Sections 50(1) and (2)(b) and (d) and 54(2) of the Tax Credits Act 2002.

Regulation 3

SCHEDULE 2

Electronic Communications

Part I

General

Introduction

2.1091 **1.** This Schedule supersedes the Social Security (Electronic Communications) (Child Benefit) Order 2002 which was made under section 8 of the Electronic Communications Act 2000.

Interpretation

2.1092 **2.**—(1) In this Schedule—
"electronic communications" includes any communications by means of a telecommunication system (within the meaning of the Telecommunications Act 1984);
"official computer system" means a computer system maintained by or on behalf of the Board—
(a) to send or receive information; or
(b) to process or store information.

(2) References in this Schedule to the delivery of information and to information shall be construed in accordance with section 132(8) of the Finance Act 1999.

Scope of this Schedule

2.1093 **3.** This Schedule applies to the delivery of information to or by the Board, the delivery of which is authorised or required by these Regulations.

Part II

General

Use of electronic communications by the Board

2.1094 **4.** The Board may only use electronic communications in connection with the matters referred to in paragraph 3 if—
(a) the recipient has indicated that he consents to the Board using electronic communications in connection with those matters; and
(b) the Board have not been informed that that consent has been withdrawn.

Restrictions on the use of electronic communications by persons other than the Board

2.1095 **5.**—(1) A person other than the Board may only use electronic communications in connection with the matters referred to in paragraph 3 if the conditions specified in subparagraphs (2) to (5) are satisfied.

(2) The first condition is that the person is for the time being permitted to use electronic communications for the purpose in question by an authorisation given by means of a specific or general direction of the Board.

(3) The second condition is that the person uses—
(a) an approved method for authenticating the identity of the sender of the communication;
(b) an approved method of electronic communications; and

(c) an approved method for authenticating any information delivered by means of electronic communications.

(4) The third condition is that any information sent by means of electronic communications is in an approved form (including the manner in which the information is presented).

(5) The fourth condition is that the person maintains such records in written or electronic form as may be specified in a specific or general direction given by the Board.

(6) "Approved" means approved for the purposes of this Schedule, and for the time being, by means of a specific or general direction given by the Board.

Use of intermediaries

6. The Board may use intermediaries in connection with— **2.1096**

(a) the delivery of information by means of electronic communications in connection with the matters referred to in paragraph 3; and

(b) the authentication or security of anything transmitted by any such means, and may require other persons to use intermediaries in connection with those matters.

Part III

Evidential Provisions

Effect of delivering information by means of electronic communications

7.—(1) Information which is delivered by means of electronic communications shall be treated as having been delivered in the manner or form required by any provision of these Regulations if, but only if, all the conditions imposed by— **2.1097**

(a) this Schedule,

(b) any other applicable enactment (except to the extent that the condition thereby imposed is incompatible with this Schedule); and

(c) any specific or general direction given by the Board,

are satisfied.

(2) Information delivered by means of electronic communications shall be treated as having been delivered on the day on which the last of the conditions imposed as mentioned in sub-paragraph (1) is satisfied.

This is subject to the following qualifications.

(3) The Board may by a general or specific direction provide for information to be treated as delivered upon a different date (whether earlier or later) than that given by sub-paragraph (2).

(4) Information shall not be taken to have been delivered to an official computer system by means of electronic communications unless it is accepted by the system to which it is delivered.

Proof of content

8.—(1) A document certified by an officer of the Board to be a printed-out version of any information delivered by means of electronic communications under this Schedule on any occasion shall be evidence, unless the contrary is proved, that that information— **2.1098**

(a) was delivered by means of electronic communications on that occasion; and

(b) constitutes the entirety of what was delivered on that occasion.

(2) A document purporting to be a certificate given in accordance with sub-paragraph (1) shall be presumed to be such a certificate unless the contrary is proved.

Proof of identity of sender or recipient

9. The identity of— **2.1099**

(a) the sender of any information delivered to an official computer system by means of electronic communications under this Schedule, or

(b) the recipient of any information delivered by means of electronic communications from an official computer system,

shall be presumed, unless the contrary is proved, to be the person recorded as such on an official computer system.

Information delivered electronically on another's behalf

10. Any information delivered by an approved method of electronic communications on behalf of any person shall be deemed to have been delivered by him unless he proves that it was delivered without his knowledge or connivance. **2.1100**

Proof of delivery of information

2.1101 **11.**—(1) The use of an authorised method of electronic communications shall be presumed, unless the contrary is proved, to have resulted in the delivery of information—

(a) in the case of information falling to be delivered to the Board, if the delivery of the information has been recorded on an official computer system;

(b) in the case of information falling to be delivered by the Board, if the despatch of the information has been recorded on an official computer system.

(2) The use of an authorised method of electronic communications shall be presumed, unless the contrary is proved, not to have resulted in the delivery of information—

(a) in the case of information falling to be delivered to the Board, if the delivery of the information has not been recorded on an official computer system;

(b) in the case of information falling to be delivered by the Board, if the despatch of the information has not been recorded on an official computer system.

(3) The time of receipt of any information sent by an authorised means of electronic communications shall be presumed, unless the contrary is proved, to be that recorded on an official computer system.

Use of unauthorised means of electronic communications

2.1102 **12.**—(1) Sub-paragraph (2) applies to information which is required to be delivered to the Board in connection with the matters mentioned in paragraph 3.

(2) The use of a means of electronic communications, for the purpose of delivering any information to which this paragraph applies, shall be conclusively presumed not to have resulted in the delivery of that information, unless—

(a) that means of electronic communications is for the time being approved for delivery of information of that kind; and

(b) the sender is approved for the use of that means of electronic communications in relation to information of that kind.

Regulation 43

SCHEDULE 3

REVOCATIONS

PART I

REVOCATIONS APPLICABLE TO GREAT BRITAIN

2.1103 *Omitted*

PART II

REVOCATIONS APPLICABLE TO NORTHERN IRELAND

2.1104 *Omitted*

The Child Benefit and Guardian's Allowance (Administrative Arrangements) Regulations 2003

(SI 2003/494)

Made — *5th March 2003*
Laid before Parliament — *5th March 2003*
Coming into force — *7th April 2003*

ARRANGEMENT OF REGULATIONS

The Commissioners of Inland Revenue, in exercise of the powers conferred upon them by sections 58 and 65(1), (2), (7) and (9) of the Tax Credits Act 2002, hereby make the following Regulations:

Citation and commencement

1. These Regulations may be cited as the Child Benefit and Guardian's Allowance (Administrative Arrangements) Regulations 2003 and shall come into force on 7th April 2003 immediately after the Child Benefit and Guardian's Allowance (Administration) Regulations 2003. **2.1106**

Interpretation

2. In these Regulations— **2.1107**
"the Board" means the [1 Commissioners for Her Majesty's Revenue and Customs];
"defective application" has the meaning given by regulation 10(3) of the principal Regulations;
"the principal Regulations" means the Child Benefit and Guardian's Allowance (Administration) Regulations 2003;
"relevant authority" means—
(a) the Secretary of State;
(b) the Department for Social Development in Northern Ireland; or
(c) a person providing services to the Secretary of State or that Department.

AMENDMENT

1. The Child Benefit and Guardian's Allowance (Miscellaneous Amendments) Regulations 2006 (SI 2006/203) (April 10, 2006).

Provision of information or evidence to relevant authorities

3.—(1) Information or evidence relating to child benefit or guardian's allowance which is held— **2.1108**
(a) by the Board; or
(b) by a person providing services to the Board, in connection with the provision of those services,

may be provided to a relevant authority for the purposes of, or for any purposes connected with, the exercise of that relevant authority's functions under the principal Regulations.

(2) Information or evidence relating to child benefit and guardian's allowance may be provided to a relevant authority by persons other than the Board (whether or not persons by whom claims or notifications relating to child benefit or guardian's allowance are or have been made or given).

Giving of information or advice by relevant authorities

2.1109 **4.** A relevant authority to which a claim or notification is or has been made or given by a person in accordance with the principal Regulations may give information or advice relating to child benefit and guardian's allowance to that person.

Recording, verification and holding, and forwarding, of claims etc. received by relevant authorities

2.1110 **5.**—(1) A relevant authority may record and hold—

(a) claims and notifications received by virtue of the any of the principal Regulations; and

(b) information or evidence received by virtue of regulation 3(2).

(2) Subject to paragraphs (3) and (4), a relevant authority or a person providing services to the Board must forward to the Board such a claim or notification, or such information or evidence, as soon as reasonably practicable after being satisfied that it is complete.

(3) Before forwarding a claim or notification in accordance with paragraph (2), a relevant authority must verify whether the details of the claim or notification are consistent with any details held by it which have been provided in connection with a relevant claim for benefit that relates to—

(a) the person by whom the claim for child benefit or guardian's allowance is or has been made; or

(b) [1 the child or qualifying young person in respect to whom] the child benefit or guardian's allowance is payable.

(4) Before forwarding a claim in accordance with paragraph (2), a relevant authority must verify that—

(a) any national insurance number provided in respect of the person by whom the claim is made exists and has been allocated to that person;

(b) the matters verified in accordance with sub-paragraph (a) accord with—

(i) its own records; or

(ii) in the case of a person providing services to the Secretary of State or the Department for Social Development in Northern Ireland, records held by the Secretary of State or that Department.

(5) Before forwarding a claim in accordance with paragraph (2), a relevant authority may verify the existence of any original document provided by the person making the claim which is required to be returned to him.

(6) If a relevant authority cannot locate any national insurance number in respect of a person by whom such a claim is made, it must forward to the Board or a person providing services to the Board the claim.

(7) "National insurance number" means the national insurance number allocated within the meaning of—

(a) regulation 9 of the Social Security (Crediting and Treatment of Contributions, and National Insurance Numbers) Regulations 2001; or

(b) regulation 9 of the Social Security (Crediting and Treatment of Contributions, and National Insurance Numbers) Regulations (Northern Ireland) 2001.

(8) "Claim for benefit" means a claim for—

(a) a benefit in relation to which—

(i) the Secretary of State has functions under the Social Security Contributions and Benefits Act 1992; or
(ii) the Department for Social Development in Northern Ireland has functions under the Social Security Contributions and Benefits (Northern Ireland) Act 1992; or
(b) a jobseeker's allowance under—
(i) the Jobseekers Act 1995; or
(ii) the Jobseekers (Northern Ireland) Order 1995.
[2 (c) universal credit under Part 1 of the Welfare Reform Act 2012.]

AMENDMENTS

1. The Child Benefit and Guardian's Allowance (Miscellaneous Amendments) Regulations 2006 (SI 2006/203) (April 10, 2006).
2. The Universal Credit (Consequential Supplementary, Incidental and Miscellaneous Provisions) Regulations 2013 (SI 2013/630) reg.82 (April 29, 2013).

The Child Benefit and Guardian's Allowance (Decisions and Appeals) Regulations 2003

(SI 2003/916)

Made — *27th March 2003*
Coming into force — *7th April 2003*

ARRANGEMENT OF REGULATIONS

PART 1

GENERAL

PART 2

REVISION OF DECISIONS

Whereas a draft of this instrument was laid before Parliament in accordance with section 80(1) of the Social Security Act 1998 and Article 75(1A) of the Social Security (Northern Ireland) Order 1998 and approved by resolution of each House of Parliament; 2.1112

Now, therefore, the Commissioners of Inland Revenue, in exercise of the powers conferred upon them by the provisions set out in Schedule 1 and, in accordance with section 8 of the Tribunals and Inquiries Act 1992, after consultation with the Council on Tribunals, hereby make the following Regulations:

PART 1

GENERAL

Citation, commencement and effect

1.—(1) These Regulations may be cited as the Child Benefit and Guardian's Allowance (Decisions and Appeals) Regulations 2003 and shall come into force on 7th April 2003 immediately after the commencement of section 50 of the Tax Credits Act 2002 for the purposes of entitlement to payment of child benefit and guardian's allowance. 2.1113

(2) These Regulations have effect only in relation to—

(a) child benefit and guardian's allowance under the Contributions and Benefits Act; and

(b) child benefit and guardian's allowance under the Contributions and Benefits (NI) Act.

Interpretation

2.—(1) In these Regulations— 2.1114

"the 1998 Act" means the Social Security Act 1998;

"the Administration Act" means the Social Security Administration Act 1992;

"the Administration (NI) Act" means the Social Security Administration (Northern Ireland) Act 1992;

"the Administration Regulations" means the Child Benefit and Guardian's Allowance (Administration) Regulations 2003;

"appeal tribunal" means—

[[1] . . .] in relation to child benefit or guardian's allowance under the Contributions and Benefits (NI) Act, an appeal tribunal constituted under Chapter 1 of Part 2 of the 1998 Order;

[[2] "the appropriate office" [[3] (except in regulation 31)] means—

(a) Waterview Park, Washington, Tyne and Wear; or

(b) any other office specified in writing by the Board.]

"the Board" means the Commissioners of Inland Revenue;

"claimant" means a person who has claimed child benefit or guardian's allowance and includes, in relation to an award or decision, a beneficiary under the award or a person affected by the decision;

"clerk to the appeal tribunal" means—

[[1] . . .] in relation to child benefit or guardian's allowance under the Contributions and Benefits (NI) Act, a clerk assigned to the appeal tribunal in accordance with regulation 37 of the Decisions and Appeals Regulations (NI);

"Commissioner" means—
[1 . . .] in relation to child benefit or guardian's allowance under the Contributions and Benefits (NI) Act, the Chief Social Security Commissioner or any other Social Security Commissioner appointed under the 1998 Order and includes a tribunal of two or more Commissioners constituted under Article 16(7);
"the Contributions and Benefits Act" means the Social Security Contributions and Benefits Act 1992;
"the Contributions and Benefits (NI) Act" means the Social Security Contributions and Benefits (Northern Ireland) Act 1992;
"the Decisions and Appeals Regulations" means the Social Security and Child Support (Decisions and Appeals) Regulations 1999;
"the Decisions and Appeals Regulations (NI)" means the Social Security and Child Support (Decisions and Appeals) Regulations (Northern Ireland) 1999;
"family" has—
(a) in relation to child benefit and guardian's allowance under the Contributions and Benefits Act, the meaning given by section 137 of that Act;
(b) in relation to child benefit and guardian's allowance under the Contributions and Benefits (NI) Act, the meaning given by section 133 of that Act;
"legally qualified panel member" means—
[1 . . .] in relation to child benefit or guardian's allowance under the Contributions and Benefits (NI) Act, a panel member who satisfies the requirements of paragraph 1 of Schedule 2 to the Decisions and Appeals Regulations (NI);
"the Northern Ireland Department" means the Department for Social Development in Northern Ireland;
"the 1998 Order" means the Social Security (Northern Ireland) Order 1998;
"panel" means the panel constituted under [1 . . .] or Article 7;
"panel member" means a person appointed to the panel;
"party to the proceedings" means the Board and any other person who—
(a) is one of the principal parties for the purposes of sections 13 and 14 or Articles 14 and 15; or
(b) has a right of appeal to an appeal tribunal under section 12(2) or Article 13(2);
"relevant benefit" means child tax credit under the Tax Credits Act 2002 and—
(a) in relation to child benefit or guardian's allowance under the Contributions and Benefits Act, any of the benefits mentioned in section 8(3);
(b) in relation to child benefit or guardian's allowance under the Contributions and Benefits (NI) Act, any of the benefits mentioned in Article 9(3);
"superseding decision" has the meaning given by regulation 13(1);
"writing" includes writing produced by electronic communications used in accordance with regulation 4.

(2) In these Regulations—
(a) a reference to a numbered section without more is a reference to the section of the 1998 Act bearing that number;

(b) a reference to a numbered Article without more is a reference to the Article of the 1998 Order bearing that number.

AMENDMENTS

1. Tribunals, Courts and Enforcement Act 2007 (Transitional and Consequential Provisions) Order 2008 (SI 2008/2683) Sch.1 paras 212 and 213 (November 3, 2008).
2. Child Benefit and Guardian's Allowance (Miscellaneous Amendments) Regulations 2009 (SI 2009/3268) reg.4 (January 1, 2010).
3. Tax Credits, Child Benefit and Guardian's Allowance Reviews and Appeals Order 2014 (SI 2014/886) art.5(1) and (2) (April 6, 2014).

GENERAL NOTE

"the Board" **2.1115**

The definition of "the Board" must be read in the light of the Commissioners for Revenue and Customs Act 2005. Section 5(2)(a) vested all the functions of the former Commissioners of Inland Revenue in the Commissioners for Her Majesty's Revenue and Customs and s.4(1) provided that the Commissioners and the officers of Revenue and Customs might together be referred to as Her Majesty's Revenue and Customs.

Service of notices or documents

3.—(1) Where, under any provision of these Regulations— **2.1116**

(a) a notice or other document is required to be given or sent to the clerk to the appeal tribunal or the Board, the notice or document is to be treated as having been so given or sent on the day that it is received by the clerk or the Board;
(b) a notice (including notification of a decision of the Board) or other document is required to be given or sent to any person other than clerk to the appeal tribunal or the Board, the notice or document is, if sent by post to that person's last known address, to be treated as having been given or sent on the day that it was posted.

(2) In these Regulations, "the date of notification", in relation to a decision of the Board, means the date on which notification of the decision is treated under paragraph (1)(b) as having been given or sent.

DEFINITIONS

"the Board"—see reg.2(1).
"clerk to the appeal tribunal"—*ibid.*

GENERAL NOTE

Paragraph (1)

See the note to reg.2 of the Social Security and Child Support (Decisions and Appeals) Regulations 1999 to which this is equivalent. **2.1117**

Paragraph (2)

This has the effect that whenever the phrase "the date of notification" is used in subsequent provisions in these Regulations, it refers to the date on which notification of a decision of the Board is treated under para.(1)(b) as having been given or sent. **2.1118**

Use of electronic communications

2.1119 **4.**—(1) Schedule 2 to the Administration Regulations (the use of electronic communications) applies to the delivery of information to or by the Board which is authorised or required by these Regulations in the same manner as it applies to the delivery of information to or by the Board which is authorised or required by the Administration Regulations.

(2) References in paragraph (1) to the delivery of information shall be construed in accordance with section 132(8) of the Finance Act 1999.

DEFINITIONS

"the Administration Regulations"—see reg.2(1).
"the Board"—*ibid.*

PART 2

REVISION OF DECISIONS

Revision of decisions within a prescribed period or on an application

2.1120 **5.**—(1) Subject to paragraph (3), if the conditions specified in paragraph (2) are satisfied—

(a) a decision under section 8 or 10 may be revised by the Board under section 9; and
(b) a decision under Article 9 or 11 may be revised by them under Article 10.

(2) The conditions specified in this paragraph are that—

(a) the Board commence action leading to the revision within one month of the date of notification of the decision; [1 ...]
(b) subject to regulation 6, an application for the revision [2 , except where the application relates to an anticipatory superseding decision,] was received by the Board at the appropriate office—
 (i) within one month of the date of notification of the decision;
 (ii) if a written statement of the reasons for the decision requested under regulation 26(1)(b) was provided within the period specified in paragraph (i), within 14 days of the expiry of that period; or
 (iii) if such a statement was provided after the period specified in paragraph (i), within 14 days of the date on which the statement was provided [2 ; or
(c) subject to regulation 6 (late applications for revision of decisions), where notification of an anticipatory superseding decision is given, an application for the revision of that decision is received by the Board, at the appropriate office, at any time within the period starting with the date of the notification of the anticipatory superseding decision and ending one month after that decision takes effect in accordance with regulation 16(5) (date as from which superseding decisions take effect).]

(3) Paragraph (1) does not apply in respect of a relevant change of circumstances which occurred since the decision [1 had effect (or, in the case of an advance award under regulation 12 of the Child Benefit and Guardian's Allowance (Administration) Regulations 2003 (advance claims and awards), was made)] or where the Board have evidence or information which indicates that a relevant change of circumstances will occur.

[2 (4) In this regulation "anticipatory superseding decision" means a decision made in accordance with regulation 13(2)(a)(ii) (cases and circumstances in which superseding decisions may be made).]

AMENDMENTS

1. Child Benefit and Guardian's Allowance (Miscellaneous Amendments) Regulations 2005 (SI 2005/343) reg.3 (March 18, 2005).
2. Tax Credits and Child Benefit (Miscellaneous Amendments) Regulations 2023 (SI 2023/179) reg.5(1) and (2) (March 15, 2023).

DEFINITIONS

"the appropriate office"—see reg.2(1).
"the Board"—*ibid.*
"the date of notification"—see reg.3(2).

GENERAL NOTE

This regulation provides for revision of a decision where the Board or the claimant takes action within one month of the date of notification of the decision (or, where an anticipatory superseding decision has been made, either before, or within one month after, it takes effect). It is equivalent to reg.3(1) and (9)(a) of the Social Security and Child Support (Decisions and Appeals) Regulations 1999. The time for making an application may be extended if a request for reasons has been made promptly (para.(2)(b)(ii) and (iii)) or where the conditions of reg.6 are met. The time for appealing against a decision is extended if an application is made for revision, so that the claimant is not prejudiced by first having sought a revision as is now mandatory under s.12(3D) of the Social Security Act 1998 (see reg.28(2)). **2.1121**

Late applications for revision of decisions

6.—(1) The Board may extend the time limits specified in regulation 5(2)(b)(i) to (iii) [2 or (c)] if the first and second conditions are satisfied. **2.1122**

(2) The first condition is that an application for an extension of time must be made to the Board by the claimant or a person acting on his behalf.

(3) The second condition is that the application for the extension of time must—

(a) contain particulars of the grounds on which the extension is sought;
(b) contain sufficient details of the decision which it is sought to have revised so as to enable it to be identified; and
(c) be made within 13 months of the latest date by which the application for revision should have been received by the Board in accordance with regulation 5(2)(b) [2 or (c), as the case may be].

(4) An application for an extension of time must not be granted unless the Board are satisfied that—

(a) it is reasonable to grant it;
(b) the application for revision has merit; and
(c) special circumstances are relevant to the application for an extension of time as a result of which it was not practicable for the application for revision to be made within the time limits specified in regulation 5(2)(b)(i) to (iii).

(5) In determining whether it is reasonable to grant an application for an extension of time, the Board must have regard to the principle that the greater the amount of time that has elapsed between the expiration of the time limits specified in regulation 5(2)(b)(i) to (iii) [2 or (c), as the case

may be] and the making of the application, the more compelling the special circumstances mentioned in paragraph (4)(c) should be.

(6) In determining whether it is reasonable to grant an application for an extension of time, the Board must take no account of the following—

(a) that the applicant or any person acting for him was unaware of, or misunderstood, the law applicable to his case (including being unaware of, or misunderstanding, the time limits imposed by these Regulations); or

(b) that a Commissioner [1 , the Upper Tribunal] or a court has taken a different view of the law from that previously understood and applied.

(7) An application for an extension of time which has been refused may not be renewed.

AMENDMENTS

1. Tribunals, Courts and Enforcement Act 2007 (Transitional and Consequential Provisions) Order 2008 (SI 2008/2683) Sch.1 paras 212 and 214 (November 3, 2008).

2. Tax Credits and Child Benefit (Miscellaneous Amendments) Regulations 2023 (SI 2023/179) reg.5(1) and (3) (March 15, 2023).

DEFINITIONS

"the Board"—see reg.2(1).
"claimant"—*ibid.*
"Commissioner"—*ibid.*

GENERAL NOTE

2.1123 This is equivalent to reg.4 of the Social Security and Child Support (Decisions and Appeals) Regulations 1999.

Procedure for revision of decisions on an application

2.1124 7.—(1) The Board may treat—

(a) an application for a decision under section 10 as an application for a revision under section 9;

(b) an application for a decision under Article 11 as an application for a revision under Article 10.

(2) Paragraph (3) applies where, in order to consider all the issues raised by an application for such a revision, the Board require further evidence or information from the applicant.

(3) Where this paragraph applies, the Board must notify the applicant that further evidence or information is required and—

(a) if the applicant provides relevant further evidence or information within one month of the date of notification or such longer period of time as the Board may allow, the decision may be revised;

(b) if the applicant does not provide such evidence or information within that time, the decision may be revised on the basis of the application.

DEFINITIONS

"the Board"—see reg.2(1).
"the date of notification"—see reg.3(2).

General Note

Paragraph (1)

This is equivalent to reg.3(10) of the Social Security and Child Support (Decisions and Appeals) Regulations 1999 and provides for an application for a superseding decision to be treated as an an application for revision. Regulation 14(1) makes provision for an application for a revision to be treated as an application for superseding decision. **2.1125**

Paragraphs (2) and (3)

These are equivalent to reg.3(2) of the Social Security and Child Support (Decisions and Appeals) Regulations 1999. **2.1126**

Revision of decisions against which there has been an appeal

8.—(1) In the circumstances prescribed by paragraph (2), any of the following decisions may be revised by the Board at any time— **2.1127**

(a) a decision under section 8 or 10;

(b) a decision under Article 9 or 11.

(2) The circumstances prescribed by this paragraph are circumstances where there is an appeal to an appeal tribunal [1 or the First-tier Tribunal] against the decision within the time prescribed by regulation 28, or in a case to which [1 regulations 29 and 29A apply within the time prescribed by those regulations] but the appeal has not been determined.

(3) If—

(a) the Board make one of the following decisions (''the original decision")—

(i) a decision under section 8 or 10 or one under section 9(1) revising such a decision; or

(ii) a decision under Article 9 or 11 or one under Article 10(1) revising such a decision;

(b) the claimant appeals to an appeal tribunal against the original decision;

(c) after the appeal has been made, but before it results in a decision by the appeal tribunal, the Board make a second decision which—

(i) supersedes the original decision in accordance with section 10 or Article 11; or

(ii) decides a further claim for child benefit or guardian's allowance by the claimant; and

(d) the Board would have made their second decision differently if, at the time they made it, they had been aware of the decision subsequently made by the appeal tribunal,

the second decision may be revised by the Board at any time.

Amendment

1. Tribunals, Courts and Enforcement Act 2007 (Transitional and Consequential Provisions) Order 2008 (SI 2008/2683) Sch.1 paras 212 and 215 (November 3, 2008).

Definitions

"appeal tribunal"—see reg.2(1).

"the Board"—*ibid.*

"claimant"—*ibid.*

General Note

2.1128 This is equivalent to reg.3(5A) of the Social Security and Child Support (Decisions and Appeals) Regulations 1999 and enables a decision made while an appeal to a tribunal is pending to be revised in the light of the tribunal's decision.

Revision of decisions against which no appeal lies

2.1129 **9.**—(1) In the case prescribed by paragraph (2), any of the following decisions may be revised by the Board at any time—

(a) a decision under section 8 or 10;

(b) a decision under Article 9 or 11.

(2) The case prescribed by this paragraph is the case of decisions which—

(a) are specified in—

(i) Schedule 2 to the 1998 Act; or

(ii) Schedule 2 to the 1998 Order; or

(b) are prescribed by regulation 25 (decisions against which no appeal lies).

Definition

"the Board"—see reg.2(1).

General Note

2.1130 This is equivalent to reg.3(8) of the Social Security and Child Support (Decisions and Appeals) Regulations 1999.

Revision of decisions arising from official error etc.

2.1131 **10.**—(1) In the circumstances prescribed by paragraph (2), any of the following decisions may be revised by the Board at any time—

(a) a decision under section 8 or 10;

(b) a decision under Article 9 or 11.

(2) The circumstances prescribed by this paragraph are circumstances where the decision—

(a) arose from an official error; or

(b) was made in ignorance of, or was based upon a mistake as to, some material fact and, as a result of that ignorance of, or mistake as to, that fact, is more advantageous to the claimant than it would otherwise have been.

(3) "Official error" means an error made by—

(a) an officer of the Board acting as such, which no person outside the Inland Revenue caused or to which no such person materially contributed; or

(b) a person employed by a person providing services to the Board and acting as such which no other person who was not so employed caused or to which no such other person materially contributed,

but does not include an error of law which is shown to have been an error by virtue of a subsequent decision of a Commissioner [1 , the Upper Tribunal] or the court.

Amendment

1. Tribunals, Courts and Enforcement Act 2007 (Transitional and Consequential Provisions) Order 2008 (SI 2008/2683) Sch.1 paras 212 and 216 (November 3, 2008).

DEFINITIONS

"the Board"—see reg.2(1).
"claimant"—*ibid.*
"Commissioner"—*ibid.*
"Inland Revenue", by virtue of s.39(2) of the Social Security Act 1998, see s.191 of the Social Security Administration Act 1992.
"official error"—see para.(3).

GENERAL NOTE

This is equivalent to reg.3(5) of the Social Security and Child Support (Decisions and Appeals) Regulations 1999. For the interpretation of the definition of "official error", see the note to reg.1(3) of the 1999 Regulations. **2.1132**

Revision of decisions following the award of another relevant benefit

11.—(1) In the circumstances prescribed by paragraph (2), any of the following decisions may be revised by the Board at any time— **2.1133**

(a) a decision under section 8 or 10;
(b) a decision under Article 9 or 11.

(2) The circumstances prescribed by this paragraph are circumstances where—

(a) the decision awards child benefit or guardian's allowance to a person; and
(b) an award of another relevant benefit, or of an increase in the rate of another relevant benefit, is made to that person or a member of his family for a period which includes the date on which the decision took effect.

DEFINITIONS

"the Board"—see reg.2(1).
"family"—*ibid.*
"relevant benefit"—*ibid.*

GENERAL NOTE

This is equivalent to reg.3(7) of the Social Security and Child Support (Decisions and Appeals) Regulations 1999. A decision may be revised where a later decision in respect of a relevant benefit affects entitlement under the earlier decision from the date it took effect. If the later decision affects entitlement under the earlier decision from a later date, the earlier decision is superseded under reg.13(2)(e) instead of being revised. **2.1134**

Date as from which revised decisions take effect

12. If the Board decide that— **2.1135**

(a) on a revision under section 9, the date as from which the decision under section 8 or 10 took effect was erroneous; or
(b) on a revision under Article 10, the date as from which the decision under Article 9 or 11 took effect was erroneous,

the revision shall take effect as from the date from which the decision would have taken effect had the error not been made.

DEFINITION

"the Board"—see reg.2(1).

General Note

2.1136 This is equivalent to reg.5 of the Social Security and Child Support (Decisions and Appeals) Regulations 1999 and provides the exception to the general rule imposed by s.9(3) of the Social Security Act 1998 that a revision is effective from the same date as the decision being revised. The exception is where a ground for the revision is that the effective date of the original decision was wrong.

Part 3

Superseding Decisions

Cases and circumstances in which superseding decisions may be made

2.1137 **13.**—(1) Subject to regulation 15, the Board may make a decision under section 10 or Article 11 ("a superseding decision"), either on their own initiative or on an application received by them at an appropriate office, in any of the cases and circumstances prescribed by paragraph (2).

(2) The cases and circumstances prescribed by this paragraph are cases and circumstances where the decision to be superseded is—

(a) a decision in respect of which—

(i) there has been a relevant change of circumstances since it [1 had effect (or, in the case of an advance award under regulation 12 of the Child Benefit and Guardian's Allowance (Administration) Regulations 2003 (advance claims and awards), was made)]; or

(ii) it is anticipated that there will be such a change;

(b) a decision (other than one to which sub-paragraph (d) refers)—

(i) which was erroneous in point of law, or was made in ignorance of, or was based upon a mistake as to, some material fact; and

(ii) in relation to which an application for a superseding decision was received by the Board, or a decision by the Board to act on their own initiative was taken, more than one month after the date of notification of the decision to be superseded or after the expiry of such longer period of time as may have been allowed under regulation 6;

(c) a decision of an appeal tribunal [2 the First-tier Tribunal, the Upper Tribunal] or a Commissioner which—

(i) was made in ignorance of, or was based upon a mistake as to, some material fact;

(ii) in a case to which subsection (5) of section 26 applies, was dealt with in accordance with subsection (4)(b) of that section; or

(iii) in a case to which paragraph (5) of Article 26 applies, was dealt with in accordance with paragraph (4)(b) of that Article;

(d) a decision—

(i) specified in Schedule 2 to the 1998 Act;

(ii) specified in Schedule 2 to the 1998 Order; or

(iii) prescribed by regulation 25 (decisions against which no appeal lies); or

(e) a decision where—

(i) the claimant has been awarded entitlement to child benefit or guardian's allowance; and

(ii) subsequent to the first day of the period to which that entitlement relates, the claimant or a member of his family becomes entitled to, or to an increase in the rate of, another relevant benefit.

AMENDMENTS

1. Child Benefit and Guardian's Allowance (Miscellaneous Amendments) Regulations 2005 (SI 2005/343) reg.4 (March 18, 2005).

2. Tribunals, Courts and Enforcement Act 2007 (Transitional and Consequential Provisions) Order 2008 (SI 2008/2683) Sch.1 paras 212 and 217 (November 3, 2008).

DEFINITIONS

"appeal tribunal"—see reg.2(1).
"appropriate office"—*ibid.*
"the Board"—*ibid.*
"claimant"—*ibid.*
"Commissioner"—*ibid.*
"the date of notification"—see reg.3(2).
"family"—see reg.2(1).
"relevant benefit"—*ibid.*
"superseding decision"—see para.(1).

GENERAL NOTE

Paragraph (1)

This is equivalent to reg.6(1) of the Social Security and Child Support (Decisions and Appeals) Regulations 1999. See the note to that provision. One difference is the use of the phrase "superseding decision" instead of "supersession" but this seems to be only a matter of style. **2.1138**

Paragraph (2)

This is equivalent to reg.6(2)(a)–(e) of the 1999 Regulations, the other subparagraphs of reg.6(2) of the 1999 regulations not being relevant to child benefit or guardian's allowance. **2.1139**

The context, as well as a comparison with the 1999 Regulations, makes it clear that the "decision" in subpara.(b) refers only to decisions of the Board. Decisions of tribunals and Commissioners fall to be superseded on the ground of ignorance of, or mistake as to, a material fact only under subpara.(c). Subpara.(b)(ii) prevents any overlap with reg.5. In subpara.(d) "decision" also refers only to decisions of the Board, because the relevant decisions do not fall within the jurisdiction of tribunals or Commissioners but, in subparas (a) and (e), "decision" includes decisions of tribunals and Commissioners.

Subparagraph (e) provides for supersession only where the later decision affects entitlement under the earlier decision from a date later than the date from which the earlier decision was effective. If the later decision has effect from the date from which the earlier decision was effective, revision under reg.11 is appropriate if the earlier decision was a decision of the Board. If the earlier decision was a decision of a tribunal or Commissioner, it is not clear that there will always be grounds for supersession, save under subpara.(a)(i), which is unlikely to produce the appropriate degree of backdating.

A superseding decision is effective from the date it is made (s.10(5) of the Social Security Act 1998), save where reg.16 provides otherwise.

See further the note to reg.6 of the 1999 Regulations.

Procedure for making superseding decisions on an application

2.1140 **14.**—(1) The Board may treat—

(a) an application for a revision under section 9 as an application for a decision under section 10;

(b) an application for a revision under Article 10 as an application for a decision under Article 11.

(2) Paragraph (3) applies where, in order to consider all the issues raised by an application for a superseding decision, the Board require further evidence or information from the applicant.

(3) Where this paragraph applies, the Board must notify the applicant that further evidence or information is required and—

(a) if the applicant provides further relevant evidence or information within one month of the date of notification or such longer period of time as the Board may allow, the decision to be superseded may be superseded;

(b) if the applicant does not provide such evidence or information within that period, the decision to be superseded may be superseded on the basis of the application.

DEFINITIONS

"the Board"—see reg.2(1).
"the date of notification"—see reg.3(2).
"superseding decision"—by virtue of reg.2(1), see reg.13(1).

GENERAL NOTE

Paragraph (1)

2.1141 This is equivalent to reg.6(5) of the Social Security and Child Support (Decisions and Appeals) Regulations 1999. It permits an application for revision to be treated as an application for supersession. Regulation 7(1) permits an application for supersession to be treated as an application for revision. See the note to s.12 of the Social Security Act 1998 for a discussion of the question whether, on appeal, a tribunal may treat a superseding decision as a refusal to revise or a revision as a refusal to supersede.

Paragraphs (2) and (3)

2.1142 These are equivalent to reg.6(4) of the 1999 Regulations.

Interaction of revisions and superseding decisions

2.1143 **15.**—(1) This regulation applies to any decision in relation to which circumstances arise in which the decision may be revised under section 9 or Article 10.

(2) A decision to which this regulation applies may not be superseded by a superseding decision unless—

(a) circumstances arise in which the Board may revise the decision in accordance with Part 2;
and

(b) further circumstances arise in relation to the decision which—
  (i) are not specified in any of the regulations in Part 2; but
  (ii) are prescribed by regulation 13(2) or are ones where a superseding decision may be made in accordance with regulation 14(3).

DEFINITIONS

"the Board"—see reg.2(1).
"superseding decision"—by virtue of reg.2(1), see reg.13(1).

GENERAL NOTE

This is equivalent to reg.6(3) of the Social Security and Child Support (Decisions and Appeals) Regulations 1999. **2.1144**

Date as from which superseding decisions take effect

16.—(1) This regulation prescribes cases or circumstances in which a superseding decision shall take effect as from a prescribed date other than the date on which it was made or, where applicable, the date on which the application for it was made. **2.1145**

(2) If a superseding decision is made on the basis that—

(a) there has been a relevant change of circumstances since the decision to be superseded had effect [[1] (or, in the case of an advance award, was made)]; or

(b) it is anticipated there will be such a change,

it shall take effect as from the earliest date prescribed by paragraphs (3) to (8).

(3) In any case where the superseding decision is advantageous to the claimant and notification of the change was given in accordance with any enactment or subordinate legislation under which that notification was required, the date prescribed by this paragraph is—

(a) if the notification was given within one month of the change occurring or such longer period as may be allowed under regulation 17, the date the change occurred or, if later, the first date on which the change has effect; or

(b) if the notification was given after the period mentioned in subparagraph (a), the date of notification of the change.

(4) In any case where the superseding decision is advantageous to the claimant and is made on the Board's own initiative, the date prescribed by this paragraph is the date on which the Board commenced action with a view to the supersession.

(5) In any case where the superseding decision is not advantageous to the claimant, the date prescribed by this paragraph is the date of the change.

(6) Decisions which are advantageous to claimants include those mentioned in regulation 27(5).

(7) If—

(a) the Board supersede a decision made by an appeal tribunal [[2] the First-tier Tribunal, the Upper Tribunal] or a Commissioner in accordance with paragraph (i) of regulation 13(2)(c); and

(b) as a result of the ignorance or mistake referred to in that paragraph, the decision to be superseded was more advantageous to the claimant than it would otherwise have been,

the superseding decision shall take effect as from the date on which the decision of the appeal tribunal or the Commissioner took, or was to take, effect.

(8) If the Board supersede a decision made by an appeal tribunal [[2] the First-tier Tribunal, the Upper Tribunal] or a Commissioner in accordance with paragraph (ii) or (iii) of regulation 13(2)(c), the superseding decision shall take effect as from the date on which it would have taken effect

had it been decided in accordance with the determination of [2 the Upper Tribunal,] the Commissioner or the court in the appeal referred to in section 26(1)(b) or Article 26(1)(b).

(9) If a superseding decision is made in consequence of a decision which is a relevant determination for the purposes of section 27 or Article 27, it shall take effect as from the date of the relevant determination.

[1 (9A) Where—

(a) a Commissioner [2, the Upper Tribunal] or the court determines an appeal as mentioned in section 27(1)(a) or Article 27(1)(a) ("the relevant determination") and the Board make a decision of the kind specified in section 27(1)(b) or Article 27(1)(b);
(b) there is an appeal against the relevant determination;
(c) after the Board's decision, payment is suspended in accordance with regulation 18(1) and (3)(b); and
(d) on appeal the court reverses the relevant determination in whole or in part,

a consequential decision by the Board under section 10 or Article 11 which supersedes the earlier decision referred to in sub-paragraph (a) above shall take effect from the date on which that earlier decision took effect.

In this paragraph "the court" has the meaning given in section 27 or Article 27 (as the case requires).]

(10) If the Board supersede a decision in accordance with subparagraph (e) of regulation 13(2), the superseding decision shall take effect as from the date on which entitlement arises—

(a) to the other relevant benefit referred to in paragraph (ii) of that sub-paragraph; or
(b) to an increase in the rate of that benefit.

AMENDMENTS

1. Child Benefit and Guardian's Allowance (Miscellaneous Amendments) Regulations 2005 (SI 2005/343) reg.5 (March 18, 2005).

2. Tribunals, Courts and Enforcement Act 2007 (Transitional and Consequential Provisions) Order 2008 (SI 2008/2683) Sch.1 paras 212 and 218 (November 3, 2008).

DEFINITIONS

"appeal tribunal"—see reg.2(1).
"the Board"—*ibid.*
"claimant"—*ibid.*
"Commissioner"—*ibid.*
"prescribed"—see s.84 of the Social Security Act 1998.
"relevant benefit"—see reg.2(1).
"superseding decision"—by virtue of reg.2(1), see reg.13(1).

GENERAL NOTE

2.1146 This is equivalent to reg.7(1)–(7) and (33) of the Social Security and Child Support (Decisions and Appeals) Regulations 1999. See the notes to reg.7 of the 1999 Regulations. (The other provisions of reg.7 of the 1999 Regulations have no relevance to child benefit or guardian's allowance.)

Effective date for late notifications of change of circumstances

17.—(1) For the purposes of paragraph (3) of regulation 16, the Board may allow a longer period of time than the period of one month mentioned in sub-paragraph (a) of that paragraph for the notification of a change of circumstances if the first and second conditions are satisfied. **2.1147**

(2) The first condition is that an application for the purposes of regulation 16(3) must be made by the claimant or a person acting on his behalf.

(3) The second condition is that the application for the purposes of regulation 16(3) must—

(a) contain particulars of the relevant change of circumstances and the reasons for the failure to notify the change on an earlier date; and

(b) be made within 13 months of the date on which the change occurred.

(4) An application under this regulation must not be granted unless the Board are satisfied that—

(a) it is reasonable to grant it;

(b) the change of circumstances notified by the applicant is relevant to the decision which is to be superseded; and

(c) special circumstances are relevant to the application as a result of which it was not practicable for the applicant to notify the change of circumstances within one month of the change occurring.

(5) In determining whether it is reasonable to grant an application for the purposes of regulation 16(3), the Board must have regard to the principle that the greater the amount of time that has elapsed between the date one month after the change of circumstances occurred and the date the application is made, the more compelling the special circumstances mentioned in paragraph (4)(c) should be.

(6) In determining whether it is reasonable to grant an application for the purposes of regulation 16(3), the Board must take no account of the following—

(a) that the applicant or any person acting for him was unaware of, or misunderstood, the law applicable to his case (including being unaware of, or misunderstanding, the time limits imposed by these Regulations); or

(b) that a Commissioner [[1], the Upper Tribunal] or a court has taken a different view of the law from that previously understood and applied.

(7) An application for the purposes of regulation 16(3) which has been refused may not be renewed.

AMENDMENT

1. Tribunals, Courts and Enforcement Act 2007 (Transitional and Consequential Provisions) Order 2008 (SI 2008/2683) Sch.1 paras 212 and 219 (November 3, 2008).

DEFINITIONS

"the Board"—see reg.2(1).
"claimant"—*ibid.*
"Commissioner"—*ibid.*

GENERAL NOTE

2.1148 This is equivalent to reg.8 of the Social Security and Child Support (Decisions and Appeals) Regulations 1999.

PART 4

SUSPENSION AND TERMINATION

Suspension in prescribed cases

2.1149 **18.**—(1) The Board may suspend payment of child benefit or guardian's allowance, in whole or in part, in the circumstances prescribed by paragraph (2) or (3).

(2) The circumstances prescribed by this paragraph are circumstances where it appears to the Board that—

(a) an issue arises as to whether the conditions for entitlement to the benefit or allowance are or were fulfilled;

(b) an issue arises as to whether a decision relating to an award of the benefit or allowance should be—
  (i) revised under section 9 or Article 10; or
  (ii) superseded under section 10 or Article 11;

(c) an issue arises as to whether any amount paid or payable to a person by way of, or in connection with a claim for, the benefit or allowance is recoverable under—
  (i) section 71 of the Administration Act;
  (ii) section 69 of the Administration (NI) Act; or
  (iii) regulations made under either of those sections;

(d) the last address notified to them of a person who is in receipt of the benefit or allowance is not the address at which that person is residing; or

(e) the details of a bank account or other account which has been notified to them and to which payment of the benefit or allowance by way of a credit is to be made to a person are incorrect;

[[2] (f) no details of a bank account or other account have been provided by a person who is in receipt of the benefit or allowance by means other than a direct credit transfer and that person has been requested by the Board under regulation 23 of the Child Benefit and Guardian's Allowance (Administration) Regulations 2003 to provide details of an account into which the benefit or allowance can be paid.]

(3) The circumstances prescribed by this paragraph are where—

(a) an appeal is pending against a decision of an appeal tribunal, [[1] the First-tier Tribunal, the Upper Tribunal,] a Commissioner or a court; or

(b) an appeal is pending against a decision given in a different case by a Commissioner [[1] , the Upper Tribunal] or a court (whether or not relating to child benefit or guardian's allowance) and it appears to the Board that, if the appeal were to be determined in a particular way, an issue would arise as to whether the award of child benefit or guardian's allowance should be revised or superseded.

(4) For the purposes of section 21(3)(c) and Article 21(3)(c), the prescribed circumstances are circumstances where an appeal tribunal, [1 the First-tier Tribunal, the Upper Tribunal,] a Commissioner or a court has made a decision and the Board—

(a) are awaiting receipt of the decision or, in the case of an appeal tribunal [1 or First-tier Tribunal] decision, are considering whether to apply for a statement of the reasons for it;
(b) in the case of an appeal tribunal decision, [1 or First-tier Tribunal] have applied for, and are awaiting receipt of, such a statement; or
(c) have received the decision, or, in the case of an appeal tribunal [1 or First-tier Tribunal] decision, such a statement, and are considering—
   (i) whether to apply for leave [1 or permission] to appeal; or
   (ii) where leave [1 or permission] to appeal has been granted, whether to appeal.

(5) In the circumstances prescribed by paragraph (4), the Board must give written notice, as soon as reasonably practicable, to the person in respect of whom payment has been or is to be suspended of their proposal—

(a) to make a request for a statement of the reasons for an appeal tribunal [1 or First-tier Tribunal] decision;
(b) to apply for leave [1 or permission] to appeal; or
(c) to appeal.

AMENDMENTS

1. Tribunals, Courts and Enforcement Act 2007 (Transitional and Consequential Provisions) Order 2008 (SI 2008/2683) Sch.1 paras 212 and 220 (November 3, 2008).

2. Tax Credits and Child Benefit (Miscellaneous Amendments) Regulations 2022 (SI 2022/555) reg.2(1) and (2) (June 9, 2022).

DEFINITIONS

"the Administration Act"—see reg.2(1).
"the Administration (NI) Act"—*ibid.*
"appeal tribunal"—*ibid.*
"the Board"—*ibid.*
"Commissioner"—*ibid.*
"prescribed"—see s.84 of the Social Security Act 1998.

Provision of information or evidence

19.—(1) This regulation applies where the Board require information or evidence for a determination whether a decision awarding child benefit or guardian's allowance should be— 2.1150

(a) revised under section 9 or Article 10; or
(b) superseded under section 10 or Article 11;
[1 (c) suspended under regulation 18.]

(2) A person to whom this paragraph applies must—

(a) supply the information or evidence within—
   (i) the period of one month beginning with the date on which the notification under paragraph (4) was sent to him; or
   (ii) such longer period as he satisfies the Board is necessary in order to enable him to comply with the requirement; or

(b) satisfy the Board within the period of time specified in subparagraph (a)(i) that—
   (i) the information or evidence required of him does not exist; or
   (ii) it is not possible for him to obtain it.

(3) A person to whom paragraph (2) applies is any of the following—
(a) a person in respect of whom payment of the benefit or allowance has been suspended in the circumstances prescribed by regulation 18(2);
(b) a person who has made an application for the decision to be revised or superseded;
(c) a person who fails to comply with the provisions of regulation 23 of the Administration Regulations in so far as they relate to information, facts or evidence required by the Board.

(4) The Board must notify a person to whom paragraph (2) applies of the requirements of that paragraph.

(5) The Board may suspend the payment of benefit or allowance, in whole or in part, to a person falling within paragraph (3)(b) or (c) who fails to satisfy the requirements of paragraph (2).

AMENDMENT

1. Tax Credits and Child Benefit (Miscellaneous Amendments) Regulations 2022 (SI 2022/555) reg.2(1) and (3) (June 9, 2022).

DEFINITIONS

"the Administration Regulations"—see reg.2(1).
"the Board"—*ibid.*

Termination in cases of failure to furnish information or evidence

2.1151 **20.**—(1) Subject to paragraph (3), this regulation applies where—
(a) a person whose benefit or allowance has been suspended under regulation 18 subsequently fails to comply with a requirement for information or evidence under regulation 19 and more than one month has elapsed since the requirement was made; or
(b) a person's benefit or allowance has been suspended under regulation 19(5) and more than one month has elapsed since the first payment was so suspended.

(2) The Board must decide that the person ceases to be entitled to the benefit or allowance from the date on which payment was suspended except where entitlement to the benefit or allowance ceases on an earlier date.

(3) This regulation does not apply where benefit or allowance has been suspended in part under regulation 18 or 19.

DEFINITION

"the Board"—see reg.2(1).

Making of payments which have been suspended

2.1152 **21.**—(1) Payment of benefit or allowance suspended in accordance with regulation 18 or 19 must be made in any of the circumstances prescribed by paragraphs (2) to (5).

(2) The circumstances prescribed by this paragraph are circumstances where—

(a) in a case to which regulation 18(2)(a), (b) or (c) applies, the Board are satisfied that—

(i) the benefit or allowance suspended is properly payable; and

(ii) no outstanding issues remain to be resolved;

(b) in a case to which regulation 18(2)(d) applies, the Board are satisfied that they have been notified of the address at which the person is residing;

(c) in a case to which regulation 18(2)(e) applies, the Board are satisfied that they have been notified of the correct details of the bank account or other account to which payment of the benefit or allowance by way of a credit is to be made to the person.

(3) The circumstances prescribed by this paragraph are circumstances where, in a case to which regulation 18(3)(a) applies, the Board—

(a) in the case of a decision of an appeal tribunal, [1 or the First-tier Tribunal] do not apply for a statement of the reasons for that decision within the period of one month specified in—

(i) in relation to child benefit and guardian's allowance under the Contributions and Benefits Act, regulation 53(4) of the Decisions and Appeals Regulations;

(ii) in relation to child benefit and guardian's allowance under the Contributions and Benefits (NI) Act, regulation 53(4) of the Decisions and Appeals Regulations (NI);

(b) in the case of a decision of an appeal tribunal, [1 First-tier Tribunal, the Upper Tribunal] a Commissioner or a court—

(i) do not make an application for leave [1 or permission] to appeal within the time prescribed for the making of such an application; or

(ii) where leave [1 or permission] to appeal is granted, do not make the appeal within the time prescribed for the making of it;

(c) withdraw an application for leave [1 or permission] to appeal or the appeal; or

(d) are refused leave [1 or permission] to appeal in circumstances where it is not open to them to renew the application, or to make a further application, for such leave [1 or permission].

(4) The circumstances prescribed by this paragraph are circumstances where, in a case to which regulation 18(3)(b) applies, the Board, in relation to the decision of the Commissioner [1 , the Upper Tribunal] or the court in the different case—

(a) do not make an application for leave [1 or permission] to appeal within the time prescribed for the making of such an application;

(b) where leave [1 or permission] to appeal is granted, do not make the appeal within the time prescribed for the making of it;

(c) withdraw an application for leave [1 or permission] to appeal or the appeal; or

(d) are refused leave [1 or permission] to appeal in circumstances where it is not open to them to renew the application, or to make a further application, for such leave [1 or permission].

(5) The circumstances prescribed by this paragraph are circumstances where, in a case to which paragraph (5) of regulation 19 applies, the Board are satisfied that—

(a) the benefit or allowance suspended is properly payable; and
(b) the requirements of paragraph (2) of that regulation have been satisfied.

AMENDMENT

1. Tribunals, Courts and Enforcement Act 2007 (Transitional and Consequential Provisions) Order 2008 (SI 2008/2683) Sch.1 paras 212 and 221 (November 3, 2008).

DEFINITIONS

"appeal tribunal"—see reg.2(1).
"the Board"—*ibid.*
"Commissioner"—*ibid.*
"the Contributions and Benefits Act"—*ibid.*
"the Contributions and Benefits (NI) Act"—*ibid.*
"the Decisions and Appeals Regulations"—*ibid.*
"the Decisions and Appeals (NI) Regulations"—*ibid.*

PART 5

OTHER MATTERS

Decisions involving issues that arise on appeal in other cases

2.1153 **22.**—(1) A case which satisfies the condition specified in paragraph (2) is a prescribed case for the purposes of section 25(3)(b) and Article 25(3)(b) (prescribed cases and circumstances in which a decision may be made on a prescribed basis).

(2) The condition specified in this paragraph is that the claimant would be entitled to the benefit or allowance to which the decision which falls to be made relates, even if the appeal in the other case referred to in section 25(1)(b) or Article 25(1)(b) were decided in a way which is the most unfavourable to him.

(3) For the purposes of subsection (3)(b) of section 25 and paragraph (3)(b) of Article 25, the prescribed basis on which the Board may make the decision is as if—

(a) the appeal in the other case which is referred to in subsection (1)(b) of that section, or paragraph (1)(b) of that Article, had already been determined; and
(b) that appeal had been decided in a way which is the most unfavourable to the claimant.

(4) For the purposes of subsection (5)(c) of section 25 and paragraph (5)(c) of Article 25 (prescribed circumstances in which, for the purposes of the section or the Article, an appeal is pending against a decision), the prescribed circumstances are circumstances where the Board—

(a) certify in writing that they are considering appealing against that decision; and
(b) consider that, if such an appeal were to be determined in a particular way—

(i) there would be no entitlement to the benefit or allowance in a case to which subsection (1)(a) of that section, or paragraph (1)(a) of that Article, refers; or

(ii) the appeal would affect the decision in that case in some other way.

DEFINITIONS

"the Board"—see reg.2(1).
"claimant"—*ibid.*
"prescribed"—see s.84 of the Social Security Act 1998.

Appeals involving issues that arise on appeal in other cases

23. For the purposes of subsection (6)(c) of section 26 and paragraph (6)(c) of Article 26 (prescribed circumstances in which an appeal against a decision which has not been brought, or an application for leave [1 or permission] to appeal has not been made, but the time for so doing has not yet expired, is pending for the purposes of the section or the Article), the prescribed circumstances are circumstances where the Board— 2.1154

(a) certify in writing that they are considering appealing against that decision; and

(b) consider that, if such an appeal were already determined, it would affect the determination of the appeal described in subsection (1)(a) of that section or paragraph (1)(a) of that Article.

AMENDMENT

1. Tribunals, Courts and Enforcement Act 2007 (Transitional and Consequential Provisions) Order 2008 (SI 2008/2683) Sch.1 paras 212 and 222 (November 3, 2008).

DEFINITION

"the Board"—see reg.2(1).

PART 6

RIGHTS OF APPEAL AND PROCEDURE FOR BRINGING APPEALS

Other persons with a right of appeal

24. For the purposes of section 12(2) and Article 13(2), the following persons are prescribed— 2.1155

(a) any person appointed by the Board under regulation 28(1) of the Administration Regulations to act on behalf of another who is unable to act;

(b) any person appointed by the Board under regulation 29(1) of those regulations to proceed with the claim of a person who has made a claim for benefit or allowance and subsequently died;

(c) any person who, having been appointed by the Board under paragraph (2) of regulation 31 of those regulations to claim on behalf of a deceased person, makes a claim in accordance with that regulation.

Definitions

"the Administration Regulations"—see reg.2(1).
"prescribed"—see s.84 of the Social Security Act 1998.

General Note

2.1156 See the note to reg.25 of the Social Security and Child Support (Decisions and Appeals) Regulations 1999.

Decisions against which no appeal lies

2.1157 **25.**—(1) Subject to paragraph (2), for the purposes of section 12(2) and Article 13(2), the decisions set out in Schedule 2 are prescribed as decisions against which no appeal lies to an appeal tribunal [1 or to the First-tier Tribunal].

(2) Paragraph (1) shall not have the effect of prescribing any decision that relates to the conditions of entitlement to child benefit or guardian's allowance for which a claim has been validly made or for which no claim is required.

(3) In this regulation and Schedule 2, "decision" includes any determination embodied in or necessary to a decision.

Amendment

1. Tribunals, Courts and Enforcement Act 2007 (Transitional and Consequential Provisions) Order 2008 (SI 2008/2683) Sch.1 paras 212 and 223 (November 3, 2008).

Definitions

"appeal tribunal"—see reg.2(1).
"prescribed"—see s.84 of the Social Security Act 1998.

General Note

2.1158 Paragraph (2) reiterates what is said in s.12(3) of the Social Security Act 1998. As para.9 of Sch.2 to the Act is not listed among the powers exercised in making these Regulations (see Sch.1), Sch.2 to these Regulations must be made under s.12. For the implication of that, see the note to Sch.2 to the Social Security and Child Support (Decisions and Appeals) Regulations 1999.

Notice of decision against which appeal lies

2.1159 **26.**—(1) A person with a right of appeal under the 1998 Act, the 1998 Order or these Regulations against a decision of the Board must—

(a) be given written notice of the decision against which the appeal lies;
(b) be informed that, in a case where that written notice does not include a statement of the reasons for that decision, he may, within one month of the date of notification of that decision, request that the Board provide him with a written statement of the reasons for that decision; and
(c) be given written notice of his right of appeal against that decision.

(2) If the Board are requested under paragraph (1)(b) to provide a written statement of the reasons for the decision, they [1 shall provide the statement within 14 days of receipt of the request or as soon as practicable afterwards].

Amendment

1. Child Benefit and Guardian's Allowance (Miscellaneous Amendments) Regulations 2005 (SI 2005/343) reg.6 (March 18, 2005).

DEFINITIONS

"the 1998 Act"—see reg.2(1).
"the Board"—*ibid.*
"the 1998 Order"—*ibid.*

GENERAL NOTE

See the note to reg.28 of the Social Security and Child Support (Decisions and Appeals) Regulations 1999. **2.1160**

Appeals against decisions which have been revised

27.—(1) This regulation applies where— **2.1161**
(a) a decision—
(i) under section 8 or 10 is revised under section 9; or
(ii) under Article 9 or 11 is revised under Article 10, before an appeal against that decision is determined; and
(b) the decision as revised is not more advantageous to the appellant than the decision before it was revised.

(2) The appeal shall not lapse and is to be treated as though it had been brought against the decision as revised.

(3) The appellant shall have a period of one month from the date of notification of the decision as revised to make further representations as to the appeal.

(4) After the expiration of the period specified in paragraph (3), or within that period if the appellant consents in writing, the appeal shall proceed unless, in the light of the further representations from the appellant, the Board further revise their decision and that decision is more advantageous to the appellant than the decision before it was revised.

(5) Decisions which are more advantageous to the appellant include those in consequence of which—
(a) child benefit or guardian's allowance paid to him is greater or is awarded for a longer period;
(b) the amount of benefit or allowance in payment would have been greater but for the operation of—
(i) any provision of the Administration Act or the Administration (NI) Act; or
(ii) any provision of the Contributions and Benefits Act, or any provision of the Contributions and Benefits (NI) Act, restricting or suspending the payment of, or disqualifying a claimant from receiving, some or all of the benefit or allowance;
(c) a denial or disqualification for the receiving of benefit or allowance is lifted wholly or in part;
(d) a decision to pay benefit or allowance to a third party is reversed;
(e) benefit or allowance paid is not recoverable under—
(i) section 71 of the Administration Act or section 69 of the Administration (NI) Act; or
(ii) regulations made under either of those sections;
(f) the amount of benefit or allowance paid which is recoverable as mentioned in sub-paragraph (e) is reduced; or
(g) a financial gain accrues or will accrue to the appellant in consequence of the decision.

Definitions

"the Administration Act"—see reg.2(1).
"the Administration (NI) Act"—*ibid.*
"the Board"—*ibid.*
"claimant"—*ibid.*
"the Contributions and Benefits Act"—*ibid.*
"the Contributions and Benefits (NI) Act"—*ibid.*
"the date of notification"—see reg.3(2).
"writing"—see reg.2(1).

General Note

2.1162 Like reg.30 of the Social Security and Child Support (Decisions and Appeals) Regulations 1999, this provides an exception to the general rule that an appeal lapses when the decision under appeal is revised (see s.9(6) of the Social Security Act 1998 and the note to s.9(5)).

2.1163 **28.** *Omitted.*

2.1164 **29.** *Omitted.*

[1 Late appeals to the First-tier Tribunal

2.1165 **29A.** In respect of an appeal to the First-tier Tribunal, the Board may treat a late appeal as made in time in accordance with Tribunal Procedure Rules if the Board is satisfied that it is in the interests of justice, but no appeal shall in any event be brought more than one year after the expiration of the last day for appealing under [2 those rules].

Amendments

1. Tribunals, Courts and Enforcement Act 2007 (Transitional and Consequential Provisions) Order 2008 (SI 2008/2683) Sch.1 paras 212 and 226 (November 3, 2008).

2. Tax Credits, Child Benefit and Guardian's Allowance Reviews and Appeals Order 2014 (SI 2014/886) art.5(1) and (4) (April 6, 2014).

General note

2.1166 This regulation merely serves to narrow the Board's power not to object under r.22(8)(a) of the Tribunal Procedure (First-tier Tribunal (Social Entitlement Chamber) Rules 2008 to a late appeal being admitted by the First-tier Tribunal. The point of it doing so is unclear. The equivalent provision in reg.32 of the Social Security and Child Support (Decisions and Appeals) Regulations 1999 has been revoked. The absolute time limit duplicates r.22(8)(b).

Interests of justice

2.1167 **30.**—(1) For the purposes of paragraph (5)(b) of regulation 29 [1 and regulation 29A], it is not in the interests of justice to grant an application [1 or, as the case may be, treat the appeal as made in time][. . .] unless the panel member is satisfied, or the Board are satisfied, that—

(a) the special circumstances specified in paragraph (2) are relevant [1 . . .]; or
(b) some other special circumstances exist which are wholly exceptional and relevant [1 . . .],

and, as a result of those special circumstances, it was not practicable for the appeal to be brought within the time limit [2 . . .].

(2) The special circumstances specified in this paragraph are that—

(a) the applicant or a partner or dependant of the applicant has died or suffered serious illness;

(b) the applicant is not resident in the United Kingdom; or

(c) normal postal services were disrupted.

(3) "Partner" means—

(a) where a person is a member of a married couple or an unmarried couple, the other member of that couple; or

(b) where a person is polygamously married to two or more members of his household, any such member.

(4) In determining whether it is in the interests of justice to grant an application under regulation 29 [1 or, as the case may be, treat the appeal as made in time under regulation 29A], the panel member or the Board must have regard to the principle that the greater the amount of time that has elapsed between the expiration of the time within which the appeal is to be brought [2 . . .]and the making of the application [1 or, as the case may be, submission of a notice of appeal] the more compelling the special circumstances mentioned in paragraph (1) should be.

(5) In determining whether it is in the interests of justice to grant an application under regulation 29 [1 or, as the case may be, treat the appeal as made in time under regulation 29A], the panel member or the Board must take no account of the following—

(a) that the applicant or any person acting for him was unaware of or misunderstood the law applicable to his case (including ignorance or misunderstanding of the time limits imposed by these Regulations); or

(b) that a Commissioner [1 , the Upper Tribunal] or a court has taken a different view of the law from that previously understood and applied.

AMENDMENTS

1. Tribunals, Courts and Enforcement Act 2007 (Transitional and Consequential Provisions) Order 2008 (SI 2008/2683) Sch.1 paras 212 and 227 (November 3, 2008).

2. Tax Credits, Child Benefit and Guardian's Allowance Reviews and Appeals Order 2014 (SI 2014/886) art.5(1), (5) and (6) (April 6, 2014).

DEFINITIONS

"the Board"—see reg.2(1).
"Commissioner"—*ibid.*
"partner"— see para.(3).

GENERAL NOTE

This is an extraordinarily narrow approach to the interests of justice and appears pointless now that appeals are lodged with the First-tier Tribunal because the First-tier Tribunal has a simple discretionary power, to be exercised judicially of course, to extend time under r.5(3)(a) of the Tribunal Procedure (First-tier Tribunal) (Social Entitlement Chamber) Rules 2008. The equivalent provision in reg.32 of the Social Security and Child Support (Decisions and Appeals) Regulations 1999, upon which this regulation was clearly based, has been revoked. 2.1168

Paragraph (5)

If the claimant is ignorant of the time limit for appealing because the Board has failed to provide the information required by reg.26(1)(c), it is arguable that the notice of decision is defective and time for appealing has not started to run. Otherwise subpara.(a) has 2.1169 the effect that the claimant cannot rely on the Board's failure to provide advice it was legally required to provide, which would be unfair if the First-tier Tribunal's powers were also limited by this regulation. It is not clear whether, for the purposes of subpara.(b), the comparison is with the previous understanding of the whole of HMRC, or a particular office or those giving guidance to decision-makers. Whatever the answer, it is not easy to see what, in practice, subpara.(b) really adds to subpara.(a).

2.1170 **31.** *Omitted.*

2.1171 **32.** *Omitted.*

Death of a party to an appeal

2.1172 **33.**—(1) In any proceedings, on the death of a party to those proceedings (other than a member of the Board), the Board may appoint such person as they think fit to proceed with the appeal in the place of such deceased party.

(2) A grant of probate, confirmation or letters of administration to the estate of the deceased party, whenever taken out, shall have no effect on an appointment made under paragraph (1).

(3) If a person appointed under paragraph (1) has, prior to the date of such appointment, taken any action in relation to the appeal on behalf of the deceased party, the effective date of appointment by the Board shall be the day immediately prior to the first day on which such action was taken.

DEFINITION

"the Board"—see reg.2(1).

GENERAL NOTE

2.1173 This was equivalent to reg.34 of the Social Security and Child Support (Decisions and Appeals) Regulations 1999 which has been revoked.

PART VII

REVOCATIONS, TRANSITIONAL PROVISIONS AND CONSEQUENTIAL AMENDMENTS

Revocations

2.1174 **34.** The following provisions are hereby revoked—

(a) in so far as they relate to child benefit or guardian's allowance under the Contributions and Benefits Act, Parts 2, 3 and 4 of, and Schedule 2 to, the Decisions and Appeals Regulations;

(b) in so far as they relate to child benefit or guardian's allowance under the Contributions and Benefits (NI) Act, Parts 2, 3 and 4 of, and Schedule 1 to, the Decisions and Appeals Regulations (NI).

DEFINITIONS

"the Contributions and Benefits Act"—see reg.2(1).
"the Contributions and Benefits (NI) Act"—*ibid.*
"the Decisions and Appeals Regulations"—*ibid.*
"the decision and Appeals (NI) Regulations"—*ibid.*

Transitional provisions

35. Anything done or commenced under any provision revoked by regulation 34, so far as relating to child benefit or guardian's allowance, is to be treated as having been done or as being continued under the corresponding provision of these Regulations. 2.1175

36. *Omitted.* 2.1176
37. *Omitted.* 2.1177

SCHEDULE 1 **Preamble**

POWERS EXERCISED IN MAKING THESE REGULATIONS

1. Section 5(1)(hh) of the Administration Act. 2.1178
2. Section 5(1)(hh) of the Administration (NI) Act.
3. The following provisions of the 1998 Act—
(a) section 9(1), (4) and (6);
(b) section 10(3) and (6);
(c) section 12(2), (3), (6) and (7);
(d) section 16(1) and paragraphs 1 to 4 and 6 of Schedule 5;
(e) section 21;
(f) section 22;
(g) section 23;
(h) section 25(3)(b) and (5)(c);
(i) section 26(6)(c);
(j) section 79(1), (2A) and (4) to (7);
(k) section 84.
4. The following provisions of the 1998 Order—
(a) Article 2(2);
(b) Article 10(1), (4) and (6);
(c) Article 11(3) and (6);
(d) Article 13(2), (3), (6) and (7);
(e) Article 16(1) and paragraphs 1 to 4 and 6 of Schedule 4;
(f) Article 21;
(g) Article 22;
(h) Article 23;
(i) Article 25(3)(b) and (5)(c);
(j) Article 26(6)(c);
(k) Article 74(1) and (3) to (6).
5. Sections 132 and 133(1) and (2) of the Finance Act 1999.
6. The following provisions of the Tax Credits Act 2002—
(a) section 50(1) and (2)(e) and (f);
(b) section 54(2);
(c) paragraphs 15 and 19 of Schedule 4.

DEFINITIONS

"the 1998 Act"—see reg.2(1).
"the Administration Act"—*ibid.*
"the Administration (NI) Act"—*ibid.*
"the 1998 Order"—*ibid.*

SCHEDULE 2 **Regulation 25**

DECISIONS AGAINST WHICH NO APPEAL LIES

PART I

DECISIONS MADE UNDER PRIMARY LEGISLATION

2.1179 **1.** A decision of the Board whether to recognise, for the purposes of Part 9 of the Contributions and Benefits Act or Part 10 of the Contributions and Benefits (NI) Act—

(a) an educational establishment; or

(b) education provided otherwise than at a recognised educational establishment.

2. A decision of the Board whether to pay expenses to any person under—

(a) sections 180 and 180A of the Administration Act; or

(b) section 156 of the Administration (NI) Act.

3. A decision of the Treasury relating to the up-rating of child benefit or guardian's allowance under—

(a) Part 10 of the Administration Act; or

(b) Part 9 of the Administration (NI) Act.

4. A decision of the Board under—

(a) section 25 or 26; or

(b) Article 25 or 26.

PART II

DECISIONS MADE UNDER SECONDARY LEGISLATION

2.1180 **5.** A decision of the Board relating to—

(a) the suspension of child benefit or allowance under Part 4; or

(b) the payment of such a benefit or allowance which has been so suspended.

6. A decision of the Board under any of the following provisions of the Administration Regulations—

(a) [1 . . .]

(b) regulation 7 (decision as to evidence and information required);

(c) [1 . . .]

(d) regulation 11 (decision as to claims for child benefit treated as claims for guardian's allowance and vice versa);

(e) regulation 18 (decision as to the time of payments);

(f) regulation 19 (decision as to elections to have child benefit paid weekly);

(g) regulation 23 (decision as to information to be given);

(h) regulation 26 (decision as to extinguishment of right to payment if payment is not obtained within the prescribed period) other than a decision under paragraph (5) (decision as to payment request after expiration of prescribed period);

(i) regulation 28 (decision as to appointments where person unable to act);

(j) regulations 29 to 32 (decisions as to claims or payments after death of claimant);

(k) regulation 33 (decision as to paying a person on behalf of another);

(l) regulation 34 (decision as to paying partner as alternative payee);

(m) Part 5 other than a decision under—

(i) regulation 35(1) (decision as to whether a payment in excess of entitlement has been credited to a bank or other account);

(ii) regulation 37 (decision as to the sums to be deducted in calculating recoverable amounts);

(iii) regulation 38 (decision as to the offsetting of a prior payment of child benefit or guardian's allowance against arrears of child benefit or guardian's allowance payable by virtue of a subsequent determination);

(iv) regulation 39 (decision as to the offsetting of a prior payment of income support or jobseeker's allowance against arrears of child benefit or guardian's allowance payable by virtue of a subsequent determination);

(v) regulation 41(1) (decision as to bringing interim payments into account);

(vi) regulation 42(1) (decision as to the overpayment of an interim payment).

7. A decision of the Board made in accordance with the discretion conferred upon them by the following regulations of the Child Benefit (General) Regulations 2003—

(a) regulation 4(1) or (4) (provisions relating to contributions and expenses in respect of a child);

(b) regulation 24(1)(c) or 28(1)(c) (decisions relating to a child's temporary absence abroad).

8. A decision of the Board relating to the giving of a notice under regulation 8(2) of the Guardian's Allowance (General) Regulations 2003 (children whose surviving parents are in prison or legal custody).

9. A decision of the Board made in accordance with an Order made under—

(a) section 179 of the Administration Act (reciprocal agreements with countries outside the United Kingdom); or

(b) section 155 of the Administration (NI) Act (reciprocal agreements with countries outside the United Kingdom).

PART III

OTHER DECISIONS

10. An authorization given by the Board in accordance with Article 22(1) or 55(1) of Council Regulation (EEC) No.1408/71 on the application of social security schemes to employed persons, to self-employed persons and to members of their families moving within the Community. **2.1181**

AMENDMENT

1. Child Benefit and Guardian's Allowance (Decisions and Appeals) (Amendment) Regulations 2004 (SI 2004/3377) reg.2(3) (December 21, 2004).

DEFINITIONS

"the Administration Act"—see reg.2(1).
"the Administration (NI) Act"—*ibid.*
"the Administration Regulations"—*ibid.*
"the Board"—*ibid.*
"the Contributions and Benefits Act"—*ibid.*
"the Contributions and Benefits (NI) Act"—*ibid.*

GENERAL NOTE

See the notes to reg.25 of these Regulations and Sch.2 to the Social Security and Child Support (Decisions and Appeals) Regulations 1999. **2.1182**

PART III

TRIBUNALS

Tribunals, Courts and Enforcement Act 2007

(2007 c.15)

CONTENTS

PART 1

TRIBUNAL JUDICIARY: AND INQUIRIES

CHAPTER 1

TRIBUNAL JUDICIARY: INDEPENDENCE AND SENIOR PRESIDENT

CHAPTER 2

FIRST-TIER TRIBUNAL AND UPPER TRIBUNAL

Establishment

Members and composition of tribunals

Review of decisions and appeals

"Judicial review"

An Act to make provision about tribunals and inquiries; to establish an Administrative Justice and Tribunals Council; to amend the law relating to judicial appointments and appointments to the Law Commission; to amend the law relating to the enforcement of judgments and debts; to make further provision about the management and relief of debt; to make provision protecting cultural objects from seizure or forfeiture in certain circumstances; to amend the law relating to the taking of possession of land affected by compulsory purchase; to alter the powers of the High Court in judicial review applications; and for connected purposes.

[19th July 2007]

PART 1

TRIBUNALS AND INQUIRIES

CHAPTER 1

TRIBUNAL JUDICIARY: INDEPENDENCE AND SENIOR PRESIDENT

1. *Omitted.* 3.2

Senior President of Tribunals

2.—(1) Her Majesty may, on the recommendation of the Lord Chancellor, appoint a person to the office of Senior President of Tribunals. 3.3

(2) Schedule 1 makes further provision about the Senior President of Tribunals and about recommendations for appointment under subsection (1).

(3) A holder of the office of Senior President of Tribunals must, in carrying out the functions of that office, have regard to—

(a) the need for tribunals to be accessible,
(b) the need for proceedings before tribunals—
(i) to be fair, and
(ii) to be handled quickly and efficiently,
(c) the need for members of tribunals to be experts in the subject-matter of, or the law to be applied in, cases in which they decide matters, and
(d) the need to develop innovative methods of resolving disputes that are of a type that may be brought before tribunals.

(4) In subsection (3) "tribunals" means—
(a) the First-tier Tribunal,
(b) the Upper Tribunal,
(c) employment tribunals, [1 and]
(d) the Employment Appeal Tribunal, [1 . . .]
(e) [1 . . .]

AMENDMENT

1. Transfer of Functions of the Asylum and Immigration Tribunal Order 2010 (SI2010/21) Sch.1 paras 36 and 37 (February 15, 2010).

GENERAL NOTE

3.4 Sir Keith Lindblom has been the Senior President of Tribunals since 2020. Like his predecessors, he is a Lord Justice of Appeal (i.e. a judge of the Court of Appeal) in England and Wales, but, in his role as Senior President of Tribunals, he exercises functions throughout the United Kingdom.

Part 4 of Sch.1, which is not reproduced in this work, confers on the Senior President of Tribunals functions in relation to judges and members of relevant tribunals (those listed in subs.(4) and also those tribunals listed in Pts 1–4 of Sch.6 that have not yet been abolished) that are equivalent to the functions the Lord Chief Justice of England and Wales has in relation to judges in the courts under the Constitutional Reform Act 2005. In addition, this Act and other provisions, such as s.15A of the Social Security Act 1998, confer on him a wide variety of functions, which (with a few exceptions) he may delegate to other members of the judiciary or to staff under s.8. By virtue of s.3(4), he presides over both the First-tier Tribunal and the Upper Tribunal.

CHAPTER 2

FIRST-TIER TRIBUNAL AND UPPER TRIBUNAL

Establishment

The First-tier Tribunal and the Upper Tribunal

3.5 **3.**—(1) There is to be a tribunal, known as the First-tier Tribunal, for the purpose of exercising the functions conferred on it under or by virtue of this Act or any other Act.

(2) There is to be a tribunal, known as the Upper Tribunal, for the purpose of exercising the functions conferred on it under or by virtue of this Act or any other Act.

(3) Each of the First-tier Tribunal, and the Upper Tribunal, is to consist of its judges and other members.

(4) The Senior President of Tribunals is to preside over both of the First-tier Tribunal and the Upper Tribunal.

(5) The Upper Tribunal is to be a superior court of record.

General Note

This section came into force on November 3, 2008 when the functions of the appeal tribunals constituted under the Social Security Act 1998 and the Social Security Commissioners appointed under that Act were, subject to one exception (see the note to ss.5–7 of the Social Security Act 1998), transferred to the two new tribunals established under this section. The functions of some other tribunals, outside the scope of this work, were transferred to these new tribunals at the same time (see the Transfer of Tribunal Functions Order 2008) and the functions of many others have been transferred since. **3.6**

The distinction between courts and tribunals is elusive but it can at least be said that, whereas court procedures are largely designed on the assumption that parties will have legal representation even if increasingly frequently they no longer do so, procedures in tribunals dealing with social security cases are designed to make legal representation unnecessary. Nonetheless, tribunals are bound by overarching principles of law, many of which are discussed in the note to this section and elsewhere in this Part of this Volume.

Open justice

One such principle is that of "open justice". Generally, hearings before tribunals are open to the public, but see the annotations to r.30 of the Tribunal Procedure (First-tier Tribunal) (Social Entitlement Chamber) Rules 2008 and r.37 of the Tribunal Procedure (Upper Tribunal) Rules 2008 which permit hearings to be in private and to r.14 of each of those sets of Rules which permit tribunals to make orders prohibiting disclosure or publication of documents or information relating to proceedings. **3.7**

The principle of open justice "is not simply to deter impropriety or sloppiness by the judge hearing the case. It is wider. It is to enable the public to understand and scrutinise the justice system of which the courts are the administrators" (*R. (Guardian News and Media Ltd) v City of Westminster Magistrates' Court (Article 19 intervening)* [2012] EWCA Civ 420; [2013] Q.B. 618 at [79]). One consequence of this is that, in the absence of any contrary legislative provision, non-parties may apply to a tribunal for disclosure of documents in a case.

In the civil courts in England and Wales, C.P.R. r.5.4C permits non-parties to see certain documents in court files. As regards other documents, although the court has the power to allow access, the applicant has no presumed right to be granted it. The approach to be taken was discussed in *Dring v Cape Intermediate Holdings Ltd (Media Lawyers Assoc intervening)* [2019] UKSC 38; [2019] 3 W.L.R. 429 at [42] to [48], the open justice principle having to be balanced against the legitimate interests of any party opposing disclosure. In the Court of Appeal in that case [2018] EWCA Civ 1795; [2019] 1 W.L.R. 479 at [126], it had been held that the principle of open justice was engaged as soon as there was an oral hearing in a case, whether or not the hearing resulted in a decision being made or, alternatively, when a decision was made on the papers. It was not engaged before then. The Supreme Court did not disagree. Where there has been a hearing, "the default position is that the public should be allowed access, not only to the parties' written submissions and arguments, but also to the documents which have been placed before the court and referred to during the hearing", but access to other documents may also be allowed. However, it is always for the person seeking access to explain why it is sought and how granting him or her access will advance the open justice principle. Journalists and, presumably, academic researchers may be better placed than others to demonstrate a good reason for seeking access, but others may also be able to do so.

In *Aria Technology Ltd v HMRC* [2018] UKUT 111 (TC), it was held that, although CPR r.5.4C does not apply in tribunals, it provides useful guidance as to the approach to be taken in relation to documents relating to tribunal proceedings and so suggests that access should be granted to such documents unless there is a reason not to do so. Arguably it only does so as regards the type of documents analogous to those mentioned in CPR r.5.4C but the documents in issue in *Aria Technology* were of that type and the Upper Tribunal may not have intended to go further. It has since been pointed out in *Rotherham MBC v Harron* [2023] UKUT 22 (AAC)—where the Upper Tribunal was not persuaded that the non-party applicant had shown either that he had a good reason for requiring the documents he sought or, since he had not asked the parties for those documents, that it would be proportionate for the Upper Tribunal to be required to provide them—that the decision in *Aria Technology Ltd* must now be read in the light of *Dring* and that there is no equivalent in an appeal to the Upper Tribunal from a decision of the First-tier Tribunal of the "statement of case" mentioned in CPR r.5.4C. It may also be observed that, in *Aria Technology Ltd*, the Upper Tribunal did not consider the impact of s.182 of the Finance Act 1989. That provision, s.50 of the Child Support Act 1991 and s.123 of, and Sch.4 to, the Social Security Administration Act 1992 prohibit staff in His Majesty's Revenue and Customs, the Department for Work and Pensions and His Majesty's Courts and Tribunals Service from publishing information acquired in the course of their employment and which relates to a particular person involved in a tax, child support or social security case. In the light of *Adams v SSWP (CSM)* [2017] UKUT 9 (AAC); [2017] AACR 28, those provisions arguably suggest that citizens are entitled to a reasonable degree of confidentiality as regards to their dealings with certain Government departments, even where there is subsequently litigation, and that documents in tax, child support and social security cases should not routinely be disclosed to non-parties if the parties object. In any event, if a tribunal were minded to allow a non-party access to documents in a social security case, it might be appropriate for it to consider whether any reporting restrictions should be imposed under r.14(1) of the relevant Rules. Indeed, that might be a relevant consideration when conducting the "fact-specific balancing exercise" contemplated by the Supreme Court in *Dring*. It might anyway be necessary to make an order under r.14(1) if disclosure of a document to which reference was made in a public hearing or a decision were to be refused, because the principle of open justice would normally require disclosure of such a document (*Cox v IC* [2018] UKUT 119 (AAC)).

In the light of *Aria Technology Ltd*, the Upper Tribunal decided in *DVLA v IC (Rule 14 Order)* [2020] UKUT 310 (AAC) that a party to proceedings before the First-tier Tribunal required the permission of the tribunal before publishing the tribunal bundle on the internet. Noting that, in the High Court, disclosure of documents was ordered on the basis of an implied undertaking by other parties not to use them for collateral purposes and that there would be practical difficulties in ensuring that personal details contained in bundles were redacted, the Upper Tribunal not only refused permission but also made an order under r.14(1)(a) of the Tribunal Procedure (Upper Tribunal) Rules 2008, prohibiting the party from publishing "the electronic documents and bundles (including the skeleton arguments) provided in accordance with the case management directions for the purposes of these proceedings". See also *Williams v IC* [2021] UKUT 110 (AAC); [2022] 1 W.L.R. 259, where the same approach was taken and the applicant was refused permission to publish tribunal bundles on the internet for the purpose of obtaining representation, on the basis that such publication was not necessary to enable the applicant to obtain representation. In that case, an order under r.14(1) was made prohibiting the publication of the bundles "on the internet or elsewhere by any method" but the applicant was given permission to provide a copy of the bundle to a representative or a person considering whether to be a representative, although it was made clear that the terms of the r.14 order also bound any such person from publishing the documents.

Subsection (1)—the First-tier Tribunal

As explained in the annotation to s.7, the First-tier Tribunal is divided into seven chambers and most social security cases in the First-tier Tribunal are allocated to the Social Entitlement Chamber. The main tribunal administration for such cases is based at five regional centres in England and Wales and one in Scotland, but hearings take place at a large number of venues around Great Britain. More details about the First-tier Tribunal may be found at *https://www.gov.uk/social-security-child-support-tribunal*. Although this First-tier Tribunal exercises jurisdiction in social security cases throughout Great Britain, and therefore in Scotland, there is also an entirely separate First-tier Tribunal for Scotland that exercises jurisdiction in relation to social security benefits provided under Scottish legislation (see Pts XIII and XIV of Vol.IV of this work). **3.8**

The First-tier Tribunal has only the functions conferred upon it by statute. The function of hearing appeals in social security cases is conferred by numerous provisions. The principal one is s.12 of the Social Security Act 1998 and the note to that provision above lists the others. However, in addition to powers conferred by statutory provisions, including Tribunal Procedure Rules, the First-tier Tribunal has such additional powers as may reasonably be implied as being necessary to ensure the attainment of fairness in carrying out its statutory functions (*Lloyd v McMahon* [1987] A.C. 625 and see also the analysis in *Foulser v HMRC* [2013] UKUT 38 (TCC)).

Thus, in *AM (Afghanistan) v Secretary of State for the Home Department* [2017] EWCA Civ 1123, the Court of Appeal has held that, even though it had no express statutory power to do so, the First-tier Tribunal had an implied power to appoint a litigation friend in circumstances where a party lacked capacity to conduct proceedings and such an appointment was required by the common law concept of procedural fairness. For the limited significance of this in social security cases, see the annotation to s.12 of the Social Security Act 1998, above.

Interim relief

The First-tier Tribunal does not generally have a power to grant interim relief while an appeal to it is pending, although it is expressly given such a power in some types of proceedings beyond the scope of this work and it also has power under the Tribunal Procedure (First-tier Tribunal) (Social Entitlement Chamber) Rules 2008 r.5(3)(l) to suspend its own decision pending an appeal to the Upper Tribunal. A submission that, where it does not have a specific statutory power to grant interim relief, it nonetheless could do so was considered to be so unarguable in *DB v Academy Transformation Trust (SEN)* [2022] UKUT 66 (AAC) that permission to appeal to the Upper Tribunal on that ground was refused. At one time it was considered that the High Court had a broad power, in judicial review proceedings, to order a public body to take, or not to take, action pending an appeal to the First-tier Tribunal against one of its decisions. One such case, brought while a special educational needs case was pending before the First-tier Tribunal, was transferred from the High Court to the Upper Tribunal although it was ultimately unsuccessful (*R. (JW) v Learning Trust* [2009] UKUT 197 (AAC); [2010] AACR 11). However, it has now been held that such relief should be granted only if it can be shown both that it is necessary to avoid the appeal being rendered nugatory and that the statutory scheme does not implicitly exclude such relief being given and so would not be undermined (see *R. (ABC Ltd) v Revenue and Customs Commissioners* [2019] UKSC 30; [2019] 1 W.L.R. 4021, and see also *R. (KMI) v Secretary of State for the Home Department)* [2021] EWHC 477 (Admin); [2021] 1 W.L.R. 3081). It is difficult to envisage such an application being successful in a social security context. An application to the First-tier Tribunal for an urgent hearing would generally be more appropriate, both practically and legally. **3.9**

The inquisitorial role and the burden of proof

Proceedings before the First-tier Tribunal in social security cases are intended to be fairly informal. Legal representation is very rare and, in England and Wales, legal aid is not available (except under a pilot scheme running in Manchester and **3.10**

Middlesborough for two years from April 1, 2022, under which up to three hours of advice and assistance, but not representation, may be provided), even for advice about applying to the First-tier Tribunal for permission to appeal to the Upper Tribunal on a point of law, although claimants often have non-lawyer representatives. This context has influenced the case law governing the general approach to be taken to appeals in social security cases.

It has long been recognised that proceedings before tribunals are inquisitorial rather than adversarial and this has been confirmed by the House of Lords in *Kerr v Department for Social Development* [2004] UKHL 23; [2004] 1 W.L.R. 1372 (also reported as an appendix to *R1/04(SF)*), where some of the consequences of this approach were considered. Baroness Hale of Richmond said:

> "61. Ever since the decision of the Divisional Court in *R. v Medical Appeal Tribunal (North Midland Region), Ex p. Hubble* [1958] 2 Q.B. 228, it has been accepted that the process of benefits adjudication is inquisitorial rather than adversarial. Diplock J. as he then was said this of an industrial injury benefit claim at p.240:
>
> > 'A claim by an insured person to benefit under the Act is not truly analogous to a *lis inter partes*. A claim to benefit is a claim to receive money out of the insurance funds . . . Any such claim requires investigation to determine whether any, and if so, what amount of benefit is payable out of the fund. In such an investigation, the minister or insurance officer is not a party adverse to the claimant. If analogy be sought in the other branches of the law, it is to be found in an inquest rather than an action.'
>
> 62. What emerges from all this is a co-operative process of investigation in which both the claimant and the department play their part. The department is the one which knows what questions it needs to ask and what information it needs to have in order to determine whether the conditions of entitlement have been met. The claimant is the one who generally speaking can and must supply that information. But where the information is available to the department rather than the claimant, then the department must take the necessary steps to enable it to be traced.
>
> 63. If that sensible approach is taken, it will rarely be necessary to resort to concepts taken from adversarial litigation such as the burden of proof. The first question will be whether each partner in the process has played their part. If there is still ignorance about a relevant matter then generally speaking it should be determined against the one who has not done all that they reasonably could to discover it. As Mr Commissioner Henty put it in *CIS/5321/1998*: 'a claimant must to the best of his or her ability give such information to the AO as he reasonably can, in default of which a contrary inference can always be drawn.' The same should apply to information which the department can reasonably be expected to discover for itself."

In that particular case the claimant had been unable to tell the department whether either his brother or sister, with whom he had lost contact, was in receipt of relevant benefits. The department could have discovered that information had they had the brother's and sister's dates of birth, which the claimant could have given them but for which the department never asked. It was held that the department could not rely on their failure to ask questions which would have led to the right answer to defeat the claim.

Where all relevant questions have been asked and there are still things unknown, it was held in *Kerr* that it has to be decided who should bear the consequences of the collective ignorance. If the ignorance concerns a matter relevant to conditions of entitlement, the claimant has to bear the consequences but if the ignorance concerns an exception to those conditions, the department must bear the consequences. In *Kerr*, the claimant was prima facie entitled to a funeral payment but would not be entitled if his brother or sister was not receiving benefit or had capital. The ignorance as to whether they were receiving benefit or had capital was therefore ignorance concerning an exception to entitlement and the department had to bear the burden and pay the claim. Lord Hope of Craighead set out, at [16], the following basic principles to be applied where the information available to a decision-maker falls short of what is needed for a clear decision one way or the other.

> "(1) Facts which may reasonably be supposed to be within the claimant's own knowledge are for the claimant to supply at each stage in the inquiry.
> (2) But the claimant must be given a reasonable opportunity to supply them. Knowledge as to the information that is needed to deal with his claim lies with the department, not with him.
> (3) So it is for the department to ask the relevant questions. The claimant is not to be faulted if the relevant questions to show whether or not the claim is excluded by the Regulations were not asked.
> (4) The general rule is that it is for the party who alleges an affirmative to make good his allegation. It is also a general rule that he who desires to take advantage of an exception must bring himself within the provisions of the exception. As Lord Wilberforce observed, exceptions are to be set up by those who rely on them: *Nimmo v Alexander Cowan & Sons Ltd* [1968] A.C. 107, 130."

It is suggested that the tribunal in *Kerr* would not necessarily have been obliged to determine the case in the claimant's favour when the case first came before it. The inquisitorial role of tribunals obliges them to ask questions that the Secretary of State should have asked but has not (*R(IS) 11/99*) and, where a health care professional has failed to ask relevant questions at a medical examination, that may require the First-tier Tribunal to hold an oral hearing even though neither party has asked for one (*MH v SSWP (II)* [2020] UKUT 297 (AAC) at [54], [55] and [57]). It would have been open to the tribunal to ask the claimant whether he knew the dates of birth of his brother and sister and, if the answer was in the affirmative, to give the department the opportunity of investigating the matter further. However, the question whether to adjourn in those circumstances is a matter within the discretion of the tribunal and the department cannot expect always to be given a chance to do something it could perfectly well have done earlier. By the time *Kerr* reached the courts, it was doubtless felt to be a bit late for the department to be making further enquiries. 3.11

Kerr was decided in the context of a claim. It is suggested, however, that it is reasonably clear that, on an appeal against a supersession decision made on the Secretary of State's own initiative, it is the Secretary of State who must bear the burden of ignorance as to whether there are grounds for supersession because it is he who must assert that there are grounds for supersession.

In the light of *Kerr*, it was held in *CIS/213/2004* that, where a question of French law arose when considering a claimant's possible interest in a property in France, it was reasonable to require the Secretary of State to obtain the necessary evidence of French law—questions of foreign law being treated as questions of fact as to which expert witnesses may give evidence (see below). An appeal to the Court of Appeal by the claimant, in which the adequacy of the evidence was challenged, was dismissed (*Martin v Secretary of State for Work and Pensions* [2009] EWCA Civ 1289; [2010] AACR 9).

In *PM v SSWP (IS)* [2014] UKUT 474 (AAC), the claimant was a 19-year old foreign national who had been in care following estrangement from her father and who, the First-tier Tribunal had been told, was too distressed to attend the hearing. Her entitlement to income support depended on whether her father was a "worker" under European Union law at the material time and the Upper Tribunal held that her circumstances required the First-tier Tribunal to obtain the relevant information through the Secretary of State, who could already have obtained the information with a bit more effort. 3.12

The effect of the tribunal having an inquisitorial role was considered by a Tribunal of Commissioners in *R(IS) 17/04*. In 2002, the Secretary of State had superseded awards of benefit from 1988, amounting to some £30,000. The claimant appealed and the

Secretary of State made a written submission and produced a considerable amount of evidence. A tribunal chairman directed that a presenting officer attend the hearing to put the Secretary of State's case. In the event, two investigating officers attended as witnesses but there was no presenting officer and a short adjournment established that none would attend. On the basis that the burden of proof lay on the Secretary of State and that the written material was not sufficient in the light of the specific direction that there be a presenting officer, the tribunal allowed the claimant's appeal without putting to her the Secretary of State's case. The Tribunal of Commissioners held the tribunal to have erred. The written material had been sufficient to raise a case for the claimant to answer and the inquisitorial role of the tribunal required the tribunal "to ascertain and determine the true amount of social security benefit to which the claimant was properly entitled", which, once the tribunal had decided not to adjourn, entailed putting the case raised by the Secretary of State's written material to the claimant and enabling her representative to question the witnesses. The Tribunal of Commissioners rejected a submission that a tribunal could not act fairly if it "descended into the arena" and they referred to another decision of a Tribunal of Commissioners, *R(S) 4/82*, where it was said that it was legitimate for a tribunal to put questions, even probing questions, to a claimant to deal with the obvious points that arose on an appeal. However, questions from a tribunal have to be put carefully and phrased neutrally and a tribunal Judge must avoid the risk described in *Southwark LBC v Kofi-Adu* [2006] EWCA Civ 281 that his descent into the arena "may so hamper his ability properly to evaluate and weigh the evidence before him as to impair his judgment, and may *for that reason* render the trial unfair" (emphasis of the Court of Appeal). See also *Serafin v Malkiewicz (Media Lawyers Association intervening)* [2020] UKSC 23; [2020] 1 W.L.R. 2455, where a judge's questioning of a litigant in person amounted to hostile cross-examination and made the proceedings unfair. In *CS v SSWP (DLA)* [2011] UKUT 509 (AAC), it was held still to be inappropriate for the Secretary of State to include in a response to an appeal a request that the First-tier Tribunal ask the claimant particular questions with a view to removing entitlement from an earlier date than he had done. Rather than asking the First-tier Tribunal to take on a role adverse to the claimant, he should have sent a presenting officer to explore the issues at the hearing, having given the claimant notice of them in the response.

Plainly it is better that the Secretary of State be represented in highly contentious or complex cases and the Tribunal of Commissioners in *R(IS) 17/04* recorded both the Secretary of State's declared policy "to appear by way of a presenting officer at every tribunal hearing where the tribunal had made a direction requiring a presenting officer to attend" and the Secretary of State's acceptance of a recommendation of the National Audit Office that he should himself identify complex cases where spending money on presenting officers might achieve greater financial savings.

3.13 The Tribunal of Commissioners cited with approval *CI/1021/2001*, where it was held that a tribunal is not entitled to rely upon a "failure to discharge the burden of proof as a substitute for a proper enquiry where there is evidence that there is something into which there needs to be an enquiry". A similar approach led a Tribunal of Commissioners in Northern Ireland to hold a tribunal to have erred when, at a "paper hearing", it had incomplete evidence that raised important issues it could not answer and it failed to adjourn in order to give the claimant the opportunity of attending (*R1/02(IB)*). However, it does not follow from *R(IS) 17/04* that decision-making bodies need make no effort to present evidence to a tribunal. In *CTC/2090/2004*, the Board of Inland Revenue failed to provide any evidence to a tribunal on the question whether the claimant or his ex-wife had the main responsibility for their daughter. That was important because it determined which of the parents was entitled to child tax credit. Both of the parents had claimed child tax credit and it had been awarded to the claimant's ex-wife. The Board did not ask for an adjournment and did not even send an officer to the hearing. The tribunal heard evidence from the claimant as to which parent had the main responsibility for the child and allowed his appeal. The Board appealed on the ground that its position was neutral and that as child tax credit could not be awarded to both parents, the tribunal's inquisitorial jurisdiction required it to summons the claimant's ex-wife to provide evidence against the claimant in her interest. The Commissioner gave that argument short shrift. Being neutral did not justify inactivity on the Board's part. In the light of *Kerr*, it had been the Board's duty to investigate the cases of both parents properly and avoid inconsistent decisions, which clearly meant enquiring themselves into the question of which parent had the main responsibility. However, the tribunal's decision would not be binding on the claimant's ex-wife and the tribunal had been entitled to assume that the Board was content for the claimant's appeal to be determined without information being obtained from his ex-wife. In other words, the tribunal's inquisitorial duty in respect of the father's claim had been satisfied by obtaining relevant evidence from him.

What, however, is made plain in *R(IS) 17/04* is that the inquisitorial role of the tribunal is not brought into play only for the purpose of assisting a claimant. A tribunal is part of the machinery for determining the true entitlement of a claimant. It follows that a tribunal is at liberty to follow its own view of a case even if that does not coincide with the view of either the claimant or the Secretary of State (*R. v Deputy Industrial Injuries Commissioner, Ex p. Moore* [1965] 1 Q.B. 456 (C.A.) (also reported as an appendix to *R(I) 4/65*)). Where medical issues arise in a case, a tribunal will often have a medically qualified practitioner among its members. It is entitled to rely on its own medical expertise and will not routinely obtain medical evidence from a claimant's doctor, even if a claimant asks it to do so, although it has power to obtain a medical report in some cases (see r.25(3) of and Sch.2 to the Tribunal Procedure (First-tier Tribunal) (Social Entitlement Chamber) Procedure Rules 2008).

In *SB v HMRC (CHB)* [2013] UKUT 24 (AAC), the First-tier Tribunal was criticised for not acting inquisitorially when it concentrated entirely on the arguments advanced by HMRC based on the documentary evidence and failed to ask the claimant any questions about the more basic point in issue, which was whether she was responsible for her child at the material time. The judge pointed out that there were really only three possibilities: (1) the claimant was responsible for her child; (2) the child was hers but someone else was responsible for her; and (3) the child was not hers at all. Since there was no evidence supporting (2) and (3) and such evidence as there was made them inherently unlikely anyway, the tribunal needed "to step back, take a reality check, and explore whether there was indeed any further evidence supporting (1)". Apart from the evidence the claimant could have given about her care of the child, she had referred in her grounds of appeal to a related tax credit claim and, had the tribunal investigated, it would have discovered that the claim had been allowed by HMRC and that the evidence the claimant was said not to have been provided to HMRC in her child benefit claim had been provided to HMRC in the tax credit claim. This was a fact that the officer dealing with the child benefit claim could have discovered by using internal information systems.

A cautionary point is that the First-tier Tribunal should not rely on the Secretary of State's appeal responses but must consider the terms of the actual decisions letters. In *WK v SSWP and AK (CSM)* [2024] UKUT 7 (AAC) the Upper Tribunal found that the failure to adequately address this issue resulted in outcomes that did not deal with evidential contradictions or enable the appellant to know the case they needed to respond to. It is part of the First-tier Tribunal's inquisitorial role to adequately investigate the Secretary of State's decision-making process so as to correctly determine the decisions under appeal.

However, there are limits to the inquisitorial rule of the First-tier Tribunal. In *JB v SSWP* [2009] UKUT 61 (AAC), the chairman of the appeal tribunal had personally telephoned a doctor's surgery to check the authenticity of documents that had been produced by a claimant. It was held that the chairman had "stopped being a judge and become both an investigator and a witness" and that, as the claimant had already been given an opportunity to prove the authenticity of the documents, the tribunal should either have proceeded on the basis that she had failed to prove their authenticity or have set in motion enquiries by a third person, possibly the tribunal's clerk. On the other hand, it was held in *HI v SSWP (ESA)* [2014] UKUT 238 (AAC) that the First-tier Tribunal had not erred in law in using Google Maps to check the claimant's evidence as to the distance from her home to a supermarket, because a tribunal is entitled to make use of information that it has obtained for itself. However, it did err in law by not putting its finding to the claimant at the hearing because the claimant would have been able to point out that the First-tier Tribunal's estimate of the distance was grossly wrong, either because it had measured the distance between the wrong points or else had misread the scale.

The First-tier Tribunal is generally entitled to accept a concession made by a party against his or her interest without enquiring into it too deeply but care is nonetheless required to avoid accepting submissions made by a party which are contrary to the available evidence or, while appearing to be concessions, in reality assist the party making them (*SB v SSWP (CSM)* [2019] UKUT 375 (AAC)).

Evidence

3.14 Tribunals are not usually bound by the strict rules of evidence applicable in some courts and r.15(2) of the Tribunal Procedure (First-tier Tribunal) (Social Entitlement Chamber) Rules 2008 expressly empowers the First-tier Tribunal to admit evidence that would not be admissible in a civil trial in the United Kingdom or to exclude evidence if, inter alia, it would be unfair to admit it. Subject to questions of unfairness or privilege, the main consideration is simply whether evidence is relevant.

There is no rule that a claimant's own evidence will only be accepted if corroborated (*R(I) 2/51*, considered in detail in *CIS/4022/2007*) but a failure to provide corroborative documents where, if the claimant was telling the truth, such documents would have been readily available to him or her may be relevant and may sometimes even justify the drawing of an adverse inference (see below). In *JS v SSWP (ESA)* [2019] UKUT 303 (AAC) at [12], the Upper Tribunal cautioned against too readily expecting a claimant to be able to produce medical evidence in support of her case, pointing out that an injury might be incapacitating even though it did not require treatment by a doctor and that "doctors do not encourage patients to take up surgery time" in such circumstances.

Kerr is not authority for the proposition that social security authorities are under any obligation to obtain information available to other Government departments or authorities (*Amos v Secretary of State for the Home Department* [2011] EWCA Civ 552; [2011] 1 W.L.R. 2952), at any rate where the claimant can as reasonably be expected to obtain the information. However, it may be arguable that the emphasis in *Kerr* on the duty of the department to cooperate in the investigation of cases has some implications for the standard of evidence that should be expected from the department so far as its own records are concerned. In *R(IS) 11/92*, the Commissioner held that no adverse inference was to be drawn against the department where it had destroyed documents in a general "weeding" programme rather with any specific intention of destroying evidence. However, the three-judge panel in *SSWP v TJ (JSA)* [2015] UKUT 56 (AAC) (in a part of its decision that was not the subject of the appeal to the Court of Appeal in *Secretary of State for Work and Pensions v Reilly* [2016] EWCA Civ 413; [2017] Q.B. 257; [2017] AACR 14) accepted that an intention to destroy evidence is not essential for the drawing of an adverse inference against a spoliator and moreover that the destruction itself need not be deliberate, although it held that it was relevant in the case before it that, although the claimant could no longer remember what documents he had been given, he would at one time have known. A tribunal should probably be slow to disbelieve a claimant who does assert that a document was not received if the department's inability to produce contrary evidence is due to the reckless weeding of documents that should have been seen to be relevant to foreseeable proceedings. Even more is that true when documents have been destroyed while a case has been pending. In *Post Office Counters Ltd v Mahida* [2003] EWCA Civ 1583, the Court of Appeal held a judge to have erred in allowing the Post Office to rely on secondary evidence when the defendant's ability to challenge it had been undermined by the Post Office's own loss or destruction of original documents before proceedings were brought but when proceedings might have been contemplated. In the First-tier Tribunal, there is no rule that a fact can be proved only by the best evidence that might be obtained (*SA v Ealing LBC (HB)* [2012] UKUT 437 (AAC)). Moreover, although certified evidence of a decision of the Secretary of State is conclusive as to the existence of the decision (Social Security Act 1998, s.39ZA), secondary evidence of the terms of a decision is acceptable where there were plainly grounds for a decision that produced the outcome that had been achieved, particularly as the law generally presumes, in the absence of evidence to the contrary, that that which ought to have been done has in fact been done (*CIB/3838/2003*). There is no general duty on the Secretary of State to provide evidence in the form of certified statements, a computer screen print being sufficient to prove that a document has been issued albeit not conclusive (*JM v SSWP (ESA)* [2013] UKUT 234 (AAC); [2014] AACR 5). Similarly, it may be inferred from a record that a document has been "issued" that it was actually posted (*Secretary of State for Work and Pensions v Roach* [2006] EWCA Civ 1746 (reported as *R(CS) 4/07*)). In *CIB/62/2008*, the Commissioner refused leave to appeal because the claimant had delayed making an application for over six months, with the result that the tribunal's file, which would probably have contained evidence that would either have corroborated the claimant's claim that he had asked for an oral hearing and not been granted one or would have contradicted it, had been destroyed. As the claimant was largely to blame for the lack of evidence, the Commissioner held that he would be unable to overcome the presumption that procedures had been properly followed.

In *R(IB) 7/05*, the Commissioner held that it was not necessary for the Secretary of State to follow the certification procedure under s.7 of the the Electronic Communications Act 2000 when there was a challenge to the authenticity of an electronic signature. This approach has also been taken in relation to evidence gathered through surveillance. The conduct of surveillance is governed by the Regulation of Investigatory Powers Act 2000. Evidence gained by illegal surveillance is not inadmissible, although the circumstances in which evidence is obtained illegally may make it of little weight (*CIS/1481/2006*, in which the Commissioner criticised the Department for Work and Pensions for refusing to provide the evidence gathered in the surveillance upon which the reports of the surveillance were based and *BS v SSWP (DLA)* [2016] UKUT 73 (AAC); [2016] AACR 32, where in fact the only flaw was the failure of the Secretary of State to produce the certificate and the First-tier Tribunal was held to have been entitled to accept the presenting officer's evidence that authorisation had been obtained). It is also not necessarily a breach of the rules of natural justice to admit a witness statement from an investigator where the investigator is not present at the hearing and so cannot be questioned, although, if contested, such evidence is clearly likely to be given less weight than evidence that has been tested through cross-examination (*CSIS/21/2008*, permission to appeal against which was refused in *Williamson v SSWP* [2010] CSIH 4) and, particularly where a great deal of money is at stake, the tribunal may require the witnesses to attend, as was done in *R(IS) 17/04*).

A statutory declaration is generally to be given more weight than a simple written statement but, in *SA v SSWP (BB)* [2013] UKUT 436 (AAC); [2014] AACR 20, it was held that the First-tier Tribunal had gone too far in stating that such a declaration should be accepted unless there was "the strongest possible evidence" to the contrary.

If a tribunal directs any body (including an agency of the Department for Work and Pensions) to disclose information in its possession, that body may not rely on the Data Protection Act 2018 to justify ignoring the direction because para.5(2) and (3) of Sch.2 to that Act provides that "the GDPR provisions" listed in para.1 do not apply to personal data "where disclosure of the data is required by an enactment, a rule of law or an order of a court or tribunal" or "where disclosure of the data ... is necessary for the purpose of, or in connection with, legal proceedings (including prospective legal proceedings) ... or ... is otherwise necessary for the purposes of establishing, exercising or defending legal rights", to the extent that the application of those provisions would prevent the controller from making the disclosure. **3.15**

In *CCS/3749/2003*, it was held that a tribunal should refuse to consider any information about proceedings relating to children of a court sitting in private (because

use of the information by a party is potentially a contempt of court) but was entitled to hear evidence about ancillary relief proceedings that had taken in place in private. The distinction arises because it is not a contempt of court to disclose to a tribunal information about proceedings before a court sitting in private unless the case comes within one of the categories specified in s.12(1)(a)–(d) of the Administration of Justice Act 1960, or the court has expressly prohibited publication of the information under s.12(1)(e) of that Act (*AF Noonan Ltd v Bournemouth and Boscombe AFC* [2007] EWCA Civ 848; [2007] 1 W.L.R. 2614). However, evidence disclosed to a court sitting in private may be regarded as confidential and should not usually be disclosed without the permission of the court (*CCS/3749/2003*), although permission is not difficult to obtain if the relevant document really is relevant to an issue before a tribunal (*CCS/1495/2005*). Rule 12.73(1)(c) of the Family Procedure Rules 2010, read with para.2.1 of Practice Direction 12G, makes it unnecessary (subject to a court's direction) for the court's permission to be obtained if a party wishes to disclose information about proceedings relating to children held in private to a tribunal hearing a child support appeal. Rule 9.46 of the Family Procedure Rules 2010, read with Practice Direction 9B, makes similar provision for "information relating to financial remedy proceedings" to be disclosed to a tribunal hearing a child support appeal. No similar provision has been made in respect of social security cases, where the issue is less likely to arise, but, in *CCR/3425/2003*, the Commissioner held that a tribunal did not err in considering medical reports that a compensator seeking to avoid liability under the Social Security (Recovery of Benefits) Act 1997 had obtained in civil proceedings brought by the claimant and had disclosed to the Secretary of State. There was no breach of the Civil Procedure Rules in the compensator relying on the reports before the tribunal and, as regards confidentiality, the Commissioner held that "a person who both claims benefits and seeks compensation must accept that it may be necessary for the Secretary of State to disclose to the compensator medical details obtained in the course of investigating the claimant's entitlement to those benefits and that the Secretary of State may make use of reports disclosed by the compensator when considering the claimant's entitlement to benefits".

On the other hand, in *JC v SSWP (PIP)* [2016] UKUT 533 (AAC) where a representative had obtained 350 pages of medical records and had sent them to the First-tier Tribunal without reading them and therefore without noticing that they included the minutes of a highly sensitive child protection conference, marked "strictly confidential" and with a warning that they should "not be copied or shown, or their contents discussed, with any person without the permission of the child protection co-ordination unit or the court", the Upper Tribunal directed that the representative inform the child protection co-ordination unit of the unauthorised disclosure of child protection information and that the confidential minutes be removed from its file. It said that, in principle, the First-tier Tribunal should have made directions along the same lines. Presumably, if a tribunal discovers that documents are confidential after they have been copied to the parties, it should normally direct the parties to make given at a hearing (including evidence given by videolink or telephone from abroad) arrangements for the copies' destruction.

As regards oral evidence given at a hearing (including evidence given by videolink or telephone from abroad) and the weighing of evidence generally, see the annotation to r.27(1) and (2) of the Tribunal Procedure (First-tier Tribunal) (Social Entitlement Chamber) Rules 2008, below.

Opinion evidence

3.16 Tribunals are not bound by the common law rules of evidence such as, for instance, the rule that evidence of opinion, as opposed to evidence of fact, is usually inadmissible unless given by an expert and so, in *CDLA/2014/2004*, a tribunal erred in refusing to allow a disability consultant to give evidence of his opinion. However, it does not follow that those rules of evidence have no relevance at all. Tribunals have no power to override any privilege of a witness not to give evidence, such as the privilege attaching to solicitor-client communications and the privilege against self-incrimination *(LM v Lewisham LBC (SEN)* [2009] UKUT 2019 (AAC); [2010] AACR 12). Furthermore, the common law rules of evidence may be relevant in the evaluation of evidence because the considerations which have led to the evidence being inadmissible often mean that it has little weight. Thus, in *CDLA/2014/2004*, there might have been good reasons for treating the disability consultant's evidence with caution, but it was wrong to refuse to consider it at all. Similarly, in *Hampshire CC v JP (SEN)* [2009] UKUT 239 (AAC); [2010] AACR 15, the Upper Tribunal held that the weight to be given to an expert's opinion on a matter beyond his or her professional expertise "is likely to be limited and reliance on such an opinion is likely to require some explanation by a tribunal", although the opinion would not be inadmissible in proceedings before a tribunal.

In *R.(RS) v First-tier Tribunal (CIC)* [2012] UKUT 205 (AAC), a three-judge panel held that, in relying on opinion evidence of a police officer as to what had happened during the course of a crime "the tribunal appears to have misconceived – and perhaps abrogated – its duty". It was for the First-tier Tribunal to form a view as to what had happened, rather than relying on the police officer to do so. However, it is suggested that it might have been different had the tribunal properly considered and then adopted the police officer's reasoning. An appeal against the Upper Tribunal's decision was allowed in *R.(RS) v First-tier Tribunal* [2013] EWCA Civ 1040; [2013] AACR 34 but the point that the Upper Tribunal had made about relying on the police officer's opinion on a matter strictly beyond his expertise was not challenged and was accepted as a reason why the case still had to be remitted to the First-tier Tribunal.

Disability consultants are now relied upon not just by claimants but also by the Secretary of State. An "approved disability analyst" may be a doctor but alternatively may be another health care professional who has received special training to make an assessment of the disabling effects of an impairment and relate this to the relevant legislation in order to provide advice or reports for those making decisions on behalf of the Secretary of State (see ss.19 and 39 of the Social Security Act 1998). Even where such analysts have not examined a claimant, their opinions may be taken into account as evidence, provided the tribunal can identify the factual basis on which any opinion was given. It will usually also be necessary for the tribunal to know the professional qualification and areas of expertise of the analyst so that the weight to be attached to any particular aspect of the report may be assessed (*CDLA/2466/2007*).

In *R(DLA) 3/99*, the Commissioner held that it was wrong for a tribunal to accept evidence of an examining medical practitioner on the basis that it must normally prevail over other evidence, even though in practice, once a proper weighing exercise had been carried out without giving an examining medical practitioner's evidence any special weight, the examining medical practitioner's evidence might be accepted in the majority of cases. Equally, a tribunal is not entitled to arrive at a view of the credibility of the claimant and then, as a separate exercise, consider whether that finding might be shifted by the expert evidence available; "The evidence has to be looked at as a whole" (*AJ (Cameroon) v Secretary of State for the Home Department* [2007] EWCA Civ 373). **3.17**

There is no obligation to accept an expert's report merely because there is no opposing expert's report. The First-tier Tribunal must consider the report in the light of such other evidence as there may be, the quality of the reasoning in the report and its own expertise (*R. (CICA) v First-tier Tribunal (CIC)* [2019] UKUT 15 (AAC)). Even where an expert's evidence is found convincing, a tribunal is entitled to accept evidence from a blameless and honest witness that conflicts with it and conclude that, although it cannot identify an error in the expert's evidence, some such error must exist (*Armstrong v First York Ltd* [2005] EWCA Civ 277; [2005] 1 W.L.R. 2751). In *CIB/3074/2003*, the Commissioner suggested that a distinction could be drawn in some cases between the weight to be given to clinical findings of an examining medical officer and the weight to be given to his or her assessment as to the claimant's capabilities in the light of those findings.

"13. In *CIB/15663/1996*, deputy Commissioner Fellner (as she then was) stated that a tribunal was entitled to give full weight to an examining medical officer's findings. A tribunal should of course give full weight to all the evidence, but may often be justified in regarding clinical findings of an examining medical officer as reliable, although even clinical findings should not be regarded as conclusive and may in some cases be displaced by other evidence. However, the impact of any given degree of loss of function will vary from claimant to claimant. In some cases (such as incontinence) a clinical examination will often give very little indication of the extent of impairment of the activities which need to be considered in carrying out the personal capability assessment, although in such cases the examining medical practitioner will often be able to make an informed assessment of the degree of impairment on the basis of the claimant's medical history and other evidence of functional ability. The examining medical officer's choice of a descriptor will therefore generally require the exercise of judgment to a greater or lesser degree, and a tribunal may therefore not necessarily give the same weight to an examining medical officer's choice of descriptors as it does to clinical findings on examination."

Evidence of foreign law

3.18 Conventionally, questions of foreign law are treated as questions of fact, in respect of which expert evidence may be adduced, rather than as questions of law. In the absence of expert evidence, there is a presumption in England and Wales that foreign law is the same as the law of England and Wales. However, that presumption applies only if it is a fair and reasonable assumption to make in a particular case (*Brownlie v FS Cairo (Nile Plaza) LLC* [2021] UKSC 45; [2021] 3 W.L.R. 1011). Otherwise, evidence is required and there will arise the question of which party should be expected to provide it and will bear the consequence of failing to do so. Indeed, in *Soriano v Forensic News LLC* [2021] EWCA Civ 1952; [2022] Q.B. 533, it was pointed out at [62] by Warby LJ, with whom the other members of the Court agreed, that there are cases in which courts have interpreted and applied foreign law without expert evidence and that, generally, modern cases have shown much greater practicality and flexibility in their approach to these conventional principles. Thus, even in the courts, expert evidence is not always necessary when a finding of foreign law is required.

As mentioned above, the Secretary of State's investigatory role was held in *CIS/213/2014* to require him to obtain statements from experts on French law in a social security case where there was a question as to whether the claimant had an interest in a property in France and the circumstances required that question to be answered under French law rather than English law.

However, the First-tier Tribunal may rely on relatively informal evidence, at least if the parties do not dispute its accuracy. In *SSWP v OF (II)* [2011] UKUT 448 (AAC), European law (which was not treated as foreign law to the extent that it was applicable in the United Kingdom) had the effect that industrial injuries benefit was payable under UK law only if the claimant was not entitled to an equivalent benefit under Irish law. The Upper Tribunal, substituting its own decision for that of the First-tier Tribunal, held that it was not necessary to wait for a formal decision by the Irish benefit authorities on a claim, even though one could have been expected under the European implementing legislation (then Council Regulation (EEC) 574/72). It received evidence of Irish law in the form of a leaflet issued by the Irish Department of Social Protection and a statement made by the Irish benefit authorities to the Secretary of State, in the light of which it was common ground between the parties that the claimant was not entitled to a relevant benefit under Irish law.

Child witnesses

3.19 In *R(DLA) 3/06*, the foster parent and appointee of the 12-year old claimant, who was alleged to have learning difficulties and behavioural problems, did not arrange for her to attend the hearing to give oral evidence, despite a summons. The Tribunal of Commissioners said:

> "[W]e consider the approach of the tribunal to the child claimant—in summonsing the child to give evidence, and then in drawing an adverse inference from the fact that she did not attend (despite the view of the local authority, her carer and a clinical psychologist that her attendance might have an adverse effect upon her)—was inappropriate and unlawful as breaching the claimant's right to a fair hearing."

The Tribunal of Commissioners gave general guidance as to the circumstances in which a child's evidence should be heard (see the note to r.27 of the Tribunal Procedure (First-tier Tribunal) (Social Entitlement Chamber) Rules 2008).

Use of the tribunal's own expertise or observations

Even in the courts, a judge is entitled to take a point not advanced by the parties but the Court of Appeal has emphasised that fairness requires that the parties be given an opportunity to comment on the point (*Murphy v Wyatt* [2011] EWCA Civ 408; [2011] 1 W.L.R. 2129). To what extent a party to proceedings may be taken to have waived the right to that opportunity by not attending or being represented at a hearing was not an issue considered by the Court and may depend on the circumstances of the case and the nature of the new issue. However, if the tribunal includes a doctor among its members and the doctor puts a different interpretation on the same clinical findings from that advanced in a report before the tribunal, it may be impossible for the parties or their representatives effectively to comment without seeking medical advice and, therefore, an adjournment may be necessary even if the parties are present (*Evans v Secretary of State for Social Security* (reported as *R(I) 5/94*), *Butterfield v Secretary of State for Defence* [2002] EWHC 2247 (Admin)). In principle, therefore, an adjournment might be necessary where the First-tier Tribunal considers that, if the claimant were as disabled as he or she claimed, he or she would be receiving different treatment, because that is not an issue upon which a claimant can be expected to comment. However, in *MM v SSWP (ESA)* [2018] UKUT 446 (AAC), the Upper Tribunal considered that that would be hopelessly impractical and that, given the differences of view that there may be within the medical profession, the First-tier Tribunal should simply be very cautious about drawing inferences from the treatment received by claimants in the first place. On the facts of the case, it decided that the First-tier Tribunal had erred in basing its decision only on the absence of what it would have regarded as appropriate treatment. Where, however, a non-medical point is raised by a tribunal, it will usually be reasonable to expect the parties or their representatives to comment at the hearing, without any adjournment. This approach also applies where a tribunal makes new findings as a consequence of a medical examination (*MB v DSD (II)* [2010] NICom 133; [2011] AACR 41) or where informal observation of a claimant during a hearing raises an issue in the minds of the tribunal. 3.20

In *Advocate General for Scotland, Petitioner* [2019] CSOH 79; 2019 S.L.T. 1373, the First-tier Tribunal had relied on the expertise of its medically-qualified panel member when construing the word "skull" in the Criminal Injuries Compensation Scheme 2012 and concluding that a fracture of the nasal bones amounted to a fracture of the skull. On an application to the Court of Session for judicial review, the Lord Ordinary said:

> "A Tribunal member is entitled in terms of rule 2(2)(d) [of the Tribunal Procedure (First-tier Tribunal) (Social Entitlement Chamber) Rules 2008] to use appropriate expertise in assisting the Tribunal to understand matters of technical difficulty or complexity. The function of the member with technical expertise is not however to go further and provide evidence. That is the preserve of a witness,

subject to cross examination and in due course evaluation by the Tribunal. In my view if the Tribunal employ the expertise of a member on evidence which is not subject to testing or challenge they transgress the rule that they '... deal with cases fairly and justly'."

It was therefore held that the First-tier Tribunal had erred in relying on the expert member's expertise, that determination of the meaning of a word in a technical sense required evidence and that the First-tier Tribunal had no relevant evidence before it. This approach equates the role of an expert member with that of an assessor such as could be appointed under s.28 and it appears inconsistent with the approach taken in *Evans* and *Butterfield*. The point of having a medically-qualified panel member is to make it unnecessary for a claimant to call medically-qualified witnesses to give oral evidence and be cross-examined. Tribunal members are generally expected to use their expertise in making their own decision in a case and contributing to the decision of the panel as a whole but must, as *Evans* and *Butterfield* make clear, draw the parties' attention to their thinking if it introduces a new issue not covered by the parties' evidence. It is in that way that a tribunal avoids acting unfairly through its use of its own expertise. It is suggested that the First-tier Tribunal's real error in this case was simply in failing to realise that the history of the Scheme and its predecessor pointed clearly to a different construction from the one that it considered most accurately reflected technical medical terminology. That in turn appears to have been at least partly because it failed to give the Criminal Injuries Compensation Authority an opportunity to comment on its reasons for its proposed construction (see the Lord Ordinary's opinion at [24]).

3.21 Where a tribunal observes a claimant acting in a way that seems inconsistent with a claimed level of disability, it has been said that "there is usually no excuse not to put observations to a party, as it can rarely be the case that the perceived inconsistency between a claimant's evidence and what is being observed does not strike any or all of the tribunal members at the time" (*CSDLA/288/2005*). However, it is not necessary for the First-tier Tribunal to put to a party its preliminary views as to the implications of the claimant's demeanour for its assessment of his or her credibility (*CC v SSWP (ESA)* [2019] UKUT 14 (AAC)), not least because it is not generally necessary for it to give reasons for finding that a witness is not believed or is exaggerating (*CIS/4022/2007*; *R3/01 (IB)*). As was said in *JW v SSWP (PIP)* [2019] UKUT 50 (AAC) at [7]:

"It was not for the tribunal to cross-examine the claimant on the evidence that she gave. The task of the tribunal was to assess it."

In any event, in *R(DLA) 8/06*, the Commissioner held that there was not always a duty to put observations to a party where, for instance, the observation merely confirmed a view the tribunal would have formed anyway. In such circumstances, it can be argued that the observation does not really raise a new issue. The Commissioner also held that it was not necessary to explain the legal significance of an observation before obtaining a comment. In any event, it does not follow that a tribunal necessarily errs in law in not putting observations to a claimant even where it would be good practice to do so. As has been pointed out in *CSDLA/463/2007*, if, on appeal, a claimant does not indicate that the opportunity to comment would have led to a comment that might have made a difference to the outcome of the case (whether a suggestion that the observation was inaccurate or a suggestion that the observation was not as significant as the tribunal thought), it is difficult to see that the claimant will have suffered any unfairness. Procedural irregularities do not amount to errors of law unless they result in unfairness or injustice (*R(DLA)3/08*).

Nonetheless, in *ML v SSWP (ESA)* [2012] UKUT 19 (AAC), the First-tier Tribunal was held to have erred in law in going on a site visit, with the claimant and her representative, on the grounds that the Secretary of State, who was not present, had not been asked for his consent, that the purpose of expedition was to test the accuracy of the claimant's evidence rather than better to understand it and that the judge had not continued the record of proceedings after the visit and recorded the claimant's representative's comments made during it. See also *JB v SSWP (ESA)* [2009] UKUT 61 (AAC) and *HI v SSWP (ESA)* [2014] UKUT 238 (AAC), mentioned above.

Relying on decisions of other bodies

The First-tier Tribunal may rely upon, but is not bound by, findings of fact made, or inferentially made, by other bodies, including other social security decision-makers (*GB v Hillingdon LBC (HB)* [2010] UKUT 11 (AAC)), tax inspectors (*R(FC) 1/91*), the former asylum and immigration tribunal (*R (Nahar) v Social Security Commissioners* [2001] EWHC 1049 (Admin), affirmed on a different point [2002] EWCA Civ 859) and courts (*RC v SSWP* [2009] UKUT 62 (AAC) and *DF v Disclosure and Barring Service* [2015] UKUT 199 (AAC)). In *RC v SSWP*, the Upper Tribunal said— 3.22

> "Tribunals must make the best findings they can on the information and evidence available to them. The information may include findings made by previous tribunals and family courts. The significance of those findings will depend on their reliability and relevance. In assessing their reliability, tribunals must consider: (i) the evidence on which they were based; (ii) the nature of the fact-finding process (for example, whether the parent was subject to cross-examination); and (iii) the evidence now available. If there is no evidence to the contrary, tribunals may be entitled to conclude that the findings previously made are sufficient and reliable in the child support context. Whether or not this is so will depend on their relevance in the particular case. In assessing the relevance of previous findings, tribunals must consider: (iv) the facts that are relevant to the issue before the tribunal; (v) the precision with which they have to be found in order to apply the legislation; (vi) whether the previous findings relate, or can be related by other evidence, to the time now in issue; and (vii) the extent to which the issues in the previous proceedings affected the evidence that was obtained or the facts that were found."

That approach is similar to that taken in children cases in the High Court (see *In re E (Children)* [2019] EWCA Civ 1447; [2019] 1 W.L.R. 6765 at [28] and [29] and *Secretary of State for the Home Department v Suffolk CC* [2020] EWCA Civ 731; [2020] Fam 411). It follows that, if a party is arguing that the factual basis stated by another body as the basis of its decision may need to be revisited by the First-tier Tribunal, the evidential and legal basis for such an argument should be fully set out (*ODS v SSWP (UC)* [2019] UKUT 192 (AAC)). If that is not done, the First-tier Tribunal usually need not go behind the other decision, because the correctness of that decision will not be "an issue raised by the appeal" unless other evidence and submissions in the case clearly raise the issue implicitly (see s.12(8)(a) of the Social Security Act 1998).

A conviction is not conclusive evidence of the facts that must necessarily have been found by the criminal court, but it was held in *AM v SSWP (DLA)* [2013] UKUT 94 (AAC) that, in the absence of convincing new evidence, public policy precludes the convicted person from challenging the findings of primary fact lying behind the conviction and the conviction is relevant even if obtained after the decision of the Secretary of State being challenged. However, in *KL v SSWP (DLA)* [2015] UKUT 222 (AAC), it was accepted by the same judge that public policy does not always preclude the convicted person from challenging the findings behind the conviction. It all depends on the circumstances, such as whether the claimant was represented in the criminal proceedings and whether there is new evidence, even if the claimant pleaded guilty. See to the same effect *DF v Disclosure and Barring Service* [2015] UKUT 199 (AAC). However, in *Newcastle CC v LW (HB)* [2013] UKUT 123 (AAC), it was held to be contrary to public policy to allow a person to resile from a plea of guilty in criminal proceedings so as to argue that she had pleaded guilty to a charge of failing to disclose a material fact only to avoid more serious charges relating to mortgage fraud and fraud in relation to "the right to buy". Persons other than a convicted defendant are, of course, never bound by findings made in criminal proceedings.

Adverse inferences

3.23 Where a person fails to produce evidence that he or she could reasonably be expected to produce, it may be justifiable to make findings of fact against that person. The inference is drawn where the likely explanation for the evidence not being produced is that it would be unfavourable to the claimant. Often it can be inferred that it would be sufficient to disentitle the claimant altogether, but that will not always be so. Thus, a claimant's refusal to produce bank statements, or other evidence of the amount of capital or income he or she possessed, may make it appropriate to infer that he or she had capital or income sufficient to disqualify him or her from an income-related benefit at the material date (*R(SB) 34/83*, *R(H) 3/05*). Although in proceedings where the burden of proof is important the drawing of an adverse inference may not be permissible unless there is some other evidence of the material fact, that is not so in proceedings where there is a substantial inquisitorial element such as family proceedings (*Prest v Petrodel Resources Ltd* [2013] UKSC 34; [2013] 2 A.C. 415 at [45]) or social security cases (*SSWP v HS (JSA)* [2016] UKUT 272 (AAC); [2017] AACR 29). However, as made clear in those cases, this is not a licence to engage in pure speculation; regard must be had to the inherent probabilities and to any explanation, even if not a complete justification, offered for the failure to provide the relevant evidence. Thus, save in obvious cases, it may be necessary for reasons to be given for drawing an adverse inference. Indeed, a failure to produce evidence may not be sufficient to justify drawing an adverse inference unless the party concerned has failed to comply with a formal direction or summons issued by the tribunal, perhaps with an express warning that an adverse inference might be drawn in the event of a failure to comply (*R(CS) 6/05*). See also *R. (on the application of Kuzmin) v General Medical Council* [2019] EWHC 2129 (Admin); [2019] 1 W.L.R. 6660, where Hickinbottom L.J. said at [61]:

> "…, whilst emphasising that whether an adverse inference is drawn will be highly dependent upon the facts of the particular case, it seems to me that, generally, no inference will be drawn unless: (i) a prima facie case to answer has been established; (ii) the individual has been given appropriate notice and an appropriate warning that, if he does not give evidence, then such an inference may be drawn; and an opportunity to explain why it would not be reasonable for him to give evidence and, if it is found that he has no reasonable explanation, an opportunity to give evidence; (iii) there is no reasonable explanation for his not giving evidence; and (iv) there are no other circumstances in the particular case which would make it unfair to draw such an inference."

There is a difference between finding there simply to be a lack of evidence and drawing an adverse inference. Thus, *HS* was distinguished in *SSWP v DC (JSA)* [2017] UKUT 464 (AAC); [2018] AACR 16 where, in two separate cases concerning the same claimant, the First-tier Tribunal had directed the Secretary of State to produce evidence and, when he had failed to do so, had relied simply on the lack of evidence rather than drawing an adverse inference. The First-tier Tribunal was held at [33] to be entitled, although not bound, to require strict proof of a matter, whether or not it had expressly been put in issue by a party, rather than relying on the presumption of regularity. On the other hand, it could only rely on a simple lack of evidence if there was no other evidence at all. In one of the two cases, no copy of a letter requiring the claimant to attend an appointment had been provided and, although there was evidence that a letter had been issued requiring the claimant to attend an appointment at a specific time on a particular date, there was no evidence as to what the letter had said as to the place where the claimant should go and so the First-tier Tribunal was entitled to find that it had not been sufficiently clear to be effective. On the other hand, in the other case, the Secretary of State had been unable to provide a letter authorising a company to issue such appointment letters but had nonetheless maintained that it was authorised to issue them. Because authorisation did not need to be in writing, the First-tier Tribunal had erred in finding that there was no evidence at all of authorisation when the company was acting as though authorised and the Secretary of State was asserting that it was authorised.

It is clear from the cases cited that drawing an adverse inference is not a penalty. Drawing an adverse inference is therefore unlikely to be appropriate merely because evidence has been provided late, unless the circumstances justify ignoring the evidence altogether (*CIB/4253/2004*).

In *AP v SSWP (ESA)* [2017] UKUT 304 (AAC), the Upper Tribunal expressed concern at a suggestion that a claimant's refusal to consent to the production of medical records amounted to a breach of a duty to co-operate with the First-tier Tribunal and could justify the drawing of an adverse inference. It referred to the importance that the law attached to the confidentiality of such records and to the fact that a claimant might nonetheless suffer adverse consequences from failing to give consent if the result was to deprive the First-tier Tribunal of evidence favourable to him. It seems that in that case the direction to produce the records had been issued in circumstances where the claimant had not attended a hearing. However, it is arguable that fairness might require the drawing of an adverse inference if the claimant's refusal to produce his medical records prevented a proper evaluation of evidence that might otherwise be in the claimant's favour. The particular circumstances of the case would be important.

The presumption of regularity

In *HS* and *DC*, mentioned above, there were references to the presumption of regularity – in other words, a presumption that that that ought to have been done has in fact been done – although it was also made clear that the First-tier Tribunal was not necessarily obliged to rely on the presumption when entitled to do so. In *VL v SSWP (PC)* [2018] UKUT 403 (AAC), the Upper Tribunal referred to observations of Henderson J. in *Entrust Pension Ltd v Prospect Hospice Ltd* [2012] EWHC 3640 (Ch) that are consistent with that approach. He said: **3.24**

> "38. I now turn to consider whether any assistance can be gained from the presumption of regularity, which is sometimes expressed in the Latin maxim '*Omnia praesumuntur rite esse acta*'. The principal circumstances in which the presumption has been applied appear to be cases where certain formal requirements have to be satisfied, or where due to the lapse of time it would be unreasonable to expect primary evidence to be adduced in order to establish the lawful origin of a proprietary right: see *Halsbury's Laws of England*, 5th edition, volume 20, paragraph 1103 where several examples are given. The presumption is, at least normally, a presumption of fact, not law, and as such it is rebuttable by evidence to the contrary. So viewed, the term 'presumption of fact' is in my judgment something of a misnomer, because such a presumption does not shift the persuasive or evidential burden of proof on the relevant issue, but merely 'describes the readiness of the court to draw certain repeated inferences as a result of common human experience': see *Phipson on Evidence*, 17th edition (2010), paragraph 6-17, and also paragraph 1-17 where it is said that 'Not only are [*presumptions of fact*] always rebuttable, but the trier of fact may refuse to make the usual or natural inference, notwithstanding that there is no rebutting evidence'.
>
> 39. Mr Moeran drew my attention, in this connection, to the judgment of Lindley L.J. in *Harris v Knight* (1890) 15 PD 170 at 179-80, where in relation to the question whether a lost will had been duly executed and attested, he said this:

> 'The maxim, "*Omnia praesumuntur rite esse acta*", is an expression, in a short form, of a reasonable probability, and of the propriety in point of law of acting on such probability. The maxim expresses an inference which may reasonably be drawn when an intention to do some formal act is established; when the evidence is consistent with that intention having been carried into effect in a proper way; but when the actual observance of all due formalities can only be inferred as a matter of probability. The maxim is not wanted where such observance is proved, nor has it any place where such observance is disproved. The maxim only comes into operation where there is no proof one way or the other; but where it is more probable that what was intended to be done was done as it ought to have been done to render it valid; rather than that it was done in some other manner which would defeat the intention proved to exist, and would render what is proved to have been done of no effect.'

This passage appears to suggest that the maxim will be of assistance only where there would otherwise be no proof one way or the other; but since the maxim is also stated to be 'an expression . . . of a reasonable probability' and 'an inference which may reasonably be drawn', I would respectfully question whether it really adds anything to the power which the court anyway has to make a finding of fact on the balance of probabilities based on inferences drawn from circumstantial evidence. But if that is right, the so-called presumption is really no more than a rebuttable statement, founded on common sense and experience, of the inference that it will normally be appropriate to draw in a given situation where primary evidence is lacking.

40. . . . I would not regard the so-called presumption as adding anything, on analysis, to an inference which it would anyway be open to me to draw in the usual way on the balance of probabilities."

Interpreting legislation

3.25 The First-tier Tribunal is bound by decisions of the Upper Tribunal or superior courts on points of law, including the interpretation of legislation (see the note to subs.(2) below under the heading *Precedent*). However, if there is no such authority upon which it may rely, the First-tier Tribunal must interpret the law for itself.

When interpreting the law, any court or tribunal must seek to give effect to the intention of Parliament as expressed by passing the legislation. In the absence of any other relevant considerations, legislation is to be construed literally but sometimes more than one literal interpretation is possible, in which case regard may be had to the likely purpose of the legislation. For instance, it may be appropriate to imply into the legislation a qualification having the effect that it does not apply in some circumstances on the basis that "[t]he legislature intends the language of a statute, or statutory instrument, to be given an informed, rather than a literal meaning" (*Secretary of State for Work and Pensions v Goulding* [2019] EWCA Civ 839 at [23]). Furthermore, where a literal interpretation would produce an absurd result, an entirely non-literal interpretation may be applied. This was the approach taken by Lord Reid in *Luke v Inland Revenue Commissioners* [1963] A.C. 557, although he limited its scope, saying:

> "To apply the words literally is to defeat the obvious intention of the legislation and to produce a wholly unreasonable result. To achieve the obvious intention and produce a reasonable result we must do some violence to the words. ... It is only where the words are absolutely incapable of a construction which will accord with the apparent intention of the provision and will avoid a wholly unreasonable result, that the words of the enactment must prevail."

What is important is that a court or tribunal should not depart from its judicial function of interpretating legislation and usurp the legislative function of Parliament. In *Inco Europe Ltd v First Choice Distribution* [2000] UKHL 15; [2000] 1 W.L.R. 586, Lord Nicholls, with whom the other members of the House agreed, said:

"It has long been established that the role of the courts in construing legislation is not confined to resolving ambiguities in statutory language. The court must be able to correct obvious drafting errors. In suitable cases, in discharging its interpretative function the court will add words, or omit words or substitute words. Some notable instances are given in Professor Sir Rupert Cross' admirable opuscule, *Statutory Interpretation*, 3rd ed., pp. 93-105. He comments, at page 103:

> 'In omitting or inserting words the judge is not really engaged in a hypothetical reconstruction of the intentions of the drafter or the legislature, but is simply making as much sense as he can of the text of the statutory provision read in its appropriate context and within the limits of the judicial role.'

This power is confined to plain cases of drafting mistakes. The courts are ever mindful that their constitutional role in this field is interpretative. They must abstain from any course which might have the appearance of judicial legislation. A statute is expressed in language approved and enacted by the legislature. So the courts exercise considerable caution before adding or omitting or substituting words. Before interpreting a statute in this way the court must be abundantly sure of three matters: (1) the intended purpose of the statute or provision in question; (2) that by inadvertence the draftsman and Parliament failed to give effect to that purpose in the provision in question; and (3) the substance of the provision Parliament would have made, although not necessarily the precise words Parliament would have used, had the error in the Bill been noticed. The third of these conditions is of crucial importance. Otherwise any attempt to determine the meaning of the enactment would cross the boundary between construction and legislation: see Lord Diplock in *Jones v. Wrotham Park Settled Estates* [1980] A.C. 74, 105."

There are innumerable principles of construction to which lawyers refer, many of which are merely guidance, rather than strict rules and many of which are also frequently used, whether consciously or not, by non-lawyers when interpreting everyday non-legal language. Thus, for instance, it can generally be assumed that a word or phrase used in one sense in one part of a piece of legislation is used in the same sense in other parts, but that is not a rigid rule and the context in which it is used in one part may show that it has a different meaning there from the one it has in another part. This is particularly so in lengthy legislation where it is quite possible that more than one draftsman might have been involved in its preparation. Similarly, where a provision contains a list of circumstances in which it applies, the list may be exclusive or merely provide examples and, if the latter, the context may suggest that other circumstances in which the legislation applies must be similar to the examples in the list. In other words, the examples may indicate the type of other cases that Parliament had in mind, rather than merely being used to make it clear that certain common circumstances are included. Another principle is that, generally, "technical words are to be construed in the light of their technical or generally understood meaning" (*Goulding*, see above) but, again, that may depend on the context. Indeed, since the object when construing legislation is to give effect to the apparent intention of Parliament, context is likely to be all-important.

Regard may be had to the history of the legislation and to published background documents indicating its purpose, including reports of the Social Security Advisory Committee and the Industrial Injuries Advisory Council (see ss.170 to 173 of the Social Security Administration Act 1992, above). However, regard is not to be had to what is said in Parliament unless the language of the legislation is ambiguous or obscure or appears to lead to an absurd result, in which case a court or tribunal may take account of a consistent line of statements made in Parliament by Ministers or other promoters of a Bill as to the purpose behind it (together if necessary with such other Parliamentary material as is necessary to understand such statements and their effect) and such statements are clear (*Pepper v Hart* [1992] UKHL 3; [1993] AC 593 and *R. v Secretary of State for the Environment, Transport and the Regions, ex parte Spath Holme Ltd*, [2000] UKHL 61; [2001] 2 A.C. 349). The limitations exist partly because citizens can generally expect legislation to mean what it says and partly because it is not the intention of the Government or other proposer of the Bill—or, more obviously, the understanding of any other speaker in a debate—that is important, but the intention of Parliament as a whole in passing the Bill in the light of the words used in it and such assurances as to its purpose as have authoritatively been given by those responsible for introducing it. See also the further discussion of these issues in *R. (Project for the Registration of Children as British Citizens) v Secretary of State for the Home Department* [2022] UKSC 3; [2022] 2 W.L.R. 343, both at [29] to [31] and in Lady Arden's concurring judgment.

Public policy

3.26 The First-tier Tribunal can also give effect to the overarching principle of law based on public policy that a person should not benefit from his or her own wrong. Legislation may effectively be read as being subject to that rule. Thus, in *R. (Connor) v Chief National Insurance Commissioner* [1981] 1 Q.B. 758, it was held that a claimant who had been convicted of her husband's manslaughter had rightly been refused a widow's allowance, even though she otherwise satisfied the terms of the legislation. That particular issue is now addressed in the Forfeiture Act 1982 (see Part I of this volume), passed partly in the light of that case, but more recently the same principle has been applied in *R v HMRC and Kirklees MBC (CH & CTC)* [2020] UKUT 379 (AAC) to deny housing benefit and tax credits to a person who had fraudulently obtained leave to remain in the United Kingdom—such leave effectively being a condition of the claimant's entitlement to those benefits but not having been revoked at the time when HMRC and the local authority made their decisions.

Legitimate expectation

3.27 The First-tier Tribunal can give effect to a legitimate expectation arising out of Department for Work and Pensions guidance as to the way in which legislation is to be applied in practice (*SB v Oxford CC (HB)* [2014] UKUT 166 (AAC)) but it cannot give effect to any expectation arising out of advice given by a Government Department that is inconsistent with the legislation (*HMRC v Noor* [2013] UKUT 71 (TCC) *Fielder v Harrogate BC* [2020] UKUT 288 (AAC) at [100]). The point that an expectation based on a representation or "promise" made by an official cannot be *legitimate* if giving effect to the representation would prevent the lawful operation of a statutory scheme has been reiterated in *PS v SSWP (CSM)* [2016] UKUT 437 (AAC). The judge added:

> "58. There is, moreover, in my judgment nothing surprising about this conclusion. It has its correlate in the numerous authorities holding similarly that estoppel cannot prevent a statutory duty from being carried out: see *R(CS) 2/97*, *R(P) 1/80*, *R(SB) 1/83*, *R(SB) 4/91* and *R(JSA) 4/04*. Both estoppel and legitimate expectation are based fundamentally on fairness (in the latter as a counter to abuse of power), whether that is procedural fairness or substantive fairness. But neither legal test can, in my judgment, enable fairness to require the Secretary of State to act contrary to duties entrusted to him under an Act of Parliament."

These statements may need to be qualified to some extent, since it is now well established that the doctrine of legitimate expectation in public law can extend to substantive as well as procedural expectations, and can in an appropriate case prevent a public body from applying the law correctly where to do so would give rise to such unfairness as would amount to an abuse of process (*Samarkand Film Partnership (No.3) v Revenue and Customs Commissioners* [2017] EWCA Civ 77; *R. (Hely Hutchinson) v Revenue and Customs Commissioners* [2017] EWCA Civ 1075; [2018] 1 W.L.R. 1682). However, it is doubtful that such an argument can in practice be made in a statutory appeal to the First-tier Tribunal rather than in judicial review proceedings. Moreover, such cases must be regarded as exceptional because it will rarely be arguable that a representation made in published Departmental guidance is so clear and unqualified that a claimant is entitled to rely on it to frustrate the application of the law. In *R. (Ingenious Media Holdings plc) v Revenue and Customs Commissioners* [2015] EWCA Civ 173; [2015] 1

W.L.R. 3183, (subsequently reversed on appeal in *R. (Ingenious Media Holdings plc) v Revenue and Customs Commissioners* [2016] UKSC 54; [2016] 1 W.L.R. 4164, but without reference to this point), Sir Robin Jacob, with whom Tomlinson and Moore-Bick L.JJ. agreed, said of HMRC's *Information Disclosure Guide*:

> "31. This was issued by HMRC mainly but not exclusively for the guidance of its officials. Substantial parts are nonetheless available to the public. However it is elementary that guides of this sort can have no binding effect on the proper construction of a statute. The law is made by Parliament, not pamphlets. Of course a guide by civil servants writing their interpretation of what the law means and how it would apply to particular cases, can in everyday practice be useful. But it is not definitive. It is like a commentary on a statute by an academic: it may be considered by a court as a view of what the statute may mean.
> 32. Such a Guide may even be useful as an aid in considering whether or not a government action was reasonable, should such a question arise. It may also be relevant in considering what might, in circumstances where the question arises, amount to a legitimate expectation as to how a government department may act. But such an expectation has its limits: one cannot really have a legitimate expectation of the meaning of a statute from a pamphlet."

Nor, strictly speaking, can there be a legitimate expectation based on a policy of which the citizen is unaware. However, good administration requires that citizens be treated in accordance with a policy adopted by a Government department unless there are good reasons for not doing so and, in the absence of any reasons for departing from a policy, the courts will require conformity to it where it is favourable to the claimant. Accordingly, a respondent to an appeal to the First-tier Tribunal fails in his or her duty to draw relevant matters to the attention of the tribunal if no mention is made of the favourable policy in the response to the appeal (*Mandalia v Secretary of State for the Home Department* [2015] UKSC 59; [2015] 1 W.L.R. 4546). Moreover, a failure to publish a policy may be unlawful, since non-publication makes it impossible, or at least difficult, for a citizen to make effective representations as to the way the relevant discretion should be exercised (*Lumba v Secretary of State for the Home Department* [2011] UKSC 12; [2012] AC 245, followed in *R. (K) v Secretary of State for Work and Pensions* [2023] EWHC 233 (Admin) where the Court also found that the claimant had had a legitimate expectation that recovery of overpaid universal credit would be waived under a policy that had only been published in part, given unambiguous representations made to her when she had sought clarification of her entitlement in the light of which she had acted to her detriment).

The effect of a decision of the First-tier Tribunal

Unlike decisions of the Upper Tribunal (see below), decisions of the First-tier Tribunal do not create precedents that must be followed in other cases. **3.28** Nonetheless, its decisions are binding on the parties to the proceedings in which they are made and those parties, including the Secretary of State, must give effect to them and obey any directions that are given. In *R. (Majera) v Secretary of State for the Home Department* [2021] UKSC 46; [2022] A.C. 461 at [44], the Supreme Court reiterated the "well established principle of our constitutional law that a court order must be obeyed unless and until it has been set aside or varied by the court (or, conceivably, overruled by legislation)" when deciding that the Secretary of State could not rely on an error in a decision of the First-tier Tribunal's as a defence to a judicial review of her decision not to give effect to it. Her remedy would have been to appeal or otherwise apply for the decision to be set aside. The court referred to Lord Radcliffe's statement in *Smith v East Elloe RDC* [1956] A.C. 736 at 769 that:

> "An order, even if not made in good faith, is still an act capable of legal consequences. It bears no brand of invalidity upon on its forehead. Unless the necessary proceedings are taken at law to establish the cause of invalidity and to get it quashed or otherwise upset, it will remain as effective for its ostensible purpose as the most impeccable of orders."

Moreover, although decisions of the First-tier Tribunal on points of law do not carry any formal precedential value, it would be wrong for the Secretary of State to give effect to decisions adverse to her in the individual cases but to ignore a clear and consistent line of such decisions that she considers to be wrong in law when considering other cases, with the result that claims are refused that would be very likely to succeed on appeal. The proper approach would be to appeal to the Upper Tribunal in order to have the point of law authoritatively established one way or the other, so that all claimants would in future be treated alike—see *R. (Secretary of State for the Home Department) v First-tier Tribunal* [2021] EWHC 1690 (Admin); [2022] 1 W.L.R. 22 at [69]. It may be significant that, in that case, the appropriate remedy had to be through judicial review because there is no right of appeal to the Upper Tribunal in asylum support cases (see the annotation to s.11(5) below)). In social security cases, the Secretary State shares with claimants the advantage of the relatively cheap and informal right of appeal to the Upper Tribunal and she makes appropriate use of it.

Subsection (2)—the Upper Tribunal

3.29 The Upper Tribunal's principal function is hearing appeals on points of law brought under s.11 from decisions of the First-tier Tribunal. In the social security field, it also deals with references of questions arising under s.4 of the Forfeiture Act 1982 and it has a "'judicial review'" jurisdiction (see ss.15–21 of this Act). Although this Upper Tribunal exercises jurisdiction in social security cases throughout Great Britain, and therefore in Scotland, there is also an entirely separate Upper Tribunal for Scotland that exercises jurisdiction in relation to social security benefits provided under Scottish legislation (see Pts XIII and XIV of Vol.IV of this work).

When deciding cases, "an important function of the Upper Tribunal is to develop structured guidance on the use of expressions which are central to the scheme, and so to reduce the risk of inconsistent results by different panels at the First-tier level": (*R. (Jones) v First-tier Tribunal* [2013] UKSC 19; [2013] 2 A.C. 48; [2013] AACR 25).

It is divided into four Chambers (see s.7). Appeals from the Social Entitlement Chamber of the First-tier Tribunal (which includes most social security cases) are allocated to the Administrative Appeals Chamber, which has its main offices in London and Edinburgh, where the social security cases are administered, and other offices in Cardiff and Belfast. Many of its cases are dealt with on paper but hearings take place at its offices and also in Birmingham, Manchester, Leeds and, less often, in other venues.

Legal aid is no longer available for oral advocacy in social security cases before the Upper Tribunal in England and Wales except where there would otherwise be a breach of art.6 of the European Convention on Human Rights or European Union law, but it remains available for advice and written advocacy. Where it appears to the Upper Tribunal to be essential that a claimant be legally represented, it is often able to put the claimant in touch with a pro bono representative. In Scotland, legal aid does remain available, subject to tests of means and merits. In practice, most claimants are unrepresented or have non-lawyer representatives both in England and Wales and in Scotland.

Further information about the Administrative Appeals Chamber and a link to its decided cases (and those of the former Social Security and Child Support Commissioners) are available at *https://www.gov.uk/administrative-appeals-tribunal*.

Precedent

3.30 An important function of the Upper Tribunal is the giving of guidance to the First-tier Tribunal and first-instance decision-makers. It was well established that decisions on matters of legal principle of Social Security Commissioners and Child Support Commissioners in Great Britain were binding on appeal tribunals and the Secretary of State (*R(I) 12/75*). The giving of opinions on matters of law was the reason that Commissioners, and their forerunner, the Umpire appointed under the National Insurance Act 1911, were established and the binding effect of their decisions has been implicitly recognised in statutory provisions (see now ss.25–27 of the Social Security Act 1998). In *Dorset Healthcare NHS Foundation Trust v MH* [2009] UKUT 4 (AAC), a three-judge panel of the Administrative Appeals Chamber of the

Upper Tribunal held that the principles laid down in *R(I) 12/75* should be applied to decisions of the Upper Tribunal. Thus, both decisions of the Upper Tribunal and decisions of Commissioners in Great Britain are binding on the First-tier Tribunal and on the Secretary of State, where the decisions are on matters of legal principle.

Where there are conflicting decisions of the Upper Tribunal or Commissioners, a decision of a three-judge panel of the Upper Tribunal or of a Tribunal of Commissioners in Great Britain (which consisted of three Commissioners) must be followed by the First-tier Tribunal or the Secretary of State in preference to a decision of a single judge or Commissioner (*Dorset Healthcare NHS Foundation Trust v MH* [2009] UKUT 4 (AAC)). Generally, a decision of the Upper Tribunal in a social security, child support, war pension or armed forces compensation case that has been reported in the Administrative Appeals Chamber Reports published by The Stationery Office or a reported decision of a Commissioner should be followed by the First-tier Tribunal or the Secretary of State in preference to an unreported decision, because decisions are reported only if they command the general assent of the majority of the permanent judges of the Administrative Appeals Chamber of the Upper Tribunal or, in the past, the majority of Commissioners (*R(I) 12/75*). However, where a reported decision has been carefully considered in a later, unreported, decision and not followed, that presumption does not apply (*R1/00(FC)*), particularly if the later decision is too recent to have been considered for reporting (*CIB/1205/2005*). Different considerations may apply when considering the relative weight to be given to reported and unreported decisions of the Upper Tribunal in other chambers because the judges themselves have no role in the reporting of the decisions.

However, also note *His Majesty's Revenue and Customs v Secretary of State for Work and Pensions and GS (TC)* [2023] UKUT 9 (AAC) confirms that where there are two previous inconsistent decisions from Upper Tribunal Judges of co-ordinate jurisdiction, as a matter of precedent the second of those decisions should be followed in the absence of cogent reasons to the contrary. See *Re Lune Metal Products Ltd* [2006] EWCA Civ 1720 per Neuberger L.J. at [9]. See too Lord Neuberger in *Willers v Joyce (Re Gubay (deceased) No.2)* [2016] UKSC 44 at [9], Lewison J in *Re Cromptons Leisure Machines Ltd* [2006] EWHC (Ch) 3583, [2007] BCC 214 and HHJ Purle QC in *Re BXL Services* [2012] EWHC 1877 (Ch).

Decisions of Commissioners in Northern Ireland are not strictly binding on the First-tier Tribunal or the Secretary of State in Great Britain but are highly persuasive (*R(SB) 1/90*) and should usually be followed as a matter of comity unless they conflict with a decision of the Upper Tribunal or a Commissioner in Great Britain. Indeed, a decision of a single judge of the Upper Tribunal should be followed in preference even to a decision of a Tribunal of Commissioners in Northern Ireland (*CC v SSWP (ESA)* [2015] UKUT 62 (AAC)). Equally, of course, appeal tribunals and the Department for Social Development in Northern Ireland are not strictly bound by decisions of the Upper Tribunal or Commissioners in Great Britain but will generally follow them (*R1/05(IB)*).

Decisions of superior courts on points of legal principle must be followed by the First-tier Tribunal and the Secretary of State (*R(I) 12/75*), although this may technically be a matter of comity where the decision was made in a different jurisdiction within the United Kingdom (*Marshalls Clay Products Ltd v Caulfield* [2004] EWCA Civ 422; [2004] I.C.R. 1502).

Strictly speaking, it is only that part of a decision of the Upper Tribunal, a **3.31**
Commissioner or a court that amounts to a ruling on a point of law that was expressly or impliedly treated by the judge as a necessary step in reaching his or her conclusion that must be followed. Other comments are "obiter dicta" and are to be regarded as merely persuasive, although the weight to be attached to them depends, as a matter of common sense, on the extent to which the judge or Commissioner intended reliance to be placed on them and on the extent to which they were the subject of argument before the judge or Commissioner. See *R. (Youngsam) v Parole Board* [2019] EWCA Civ 229; [2019] 3 W.L.R. 33 per Leggatt L.J. for an interesting analysis of the approach that an inferior court or tribunal should take when deciding

whether a proposition enunciated in a decision of a superior court is binding on it (although that analysis is itself not binding because the other members of the Court of Appeal considered that the disputed decision of the Supreme Court was too clearly binding on them to require such a detailed consideration of the issue). Indeed, even where a point of legal principle was essential to a decision of the Upper Tribunal or Commissioner, it is not strictly binding if the point was conceded and so the Upper Tribunal or Commissioner was not required to decide it but could merely assume its correctness (*Secretary of State for Work and Pensions v Deane* [2010] EWCA Civ 699; [2011] 1 W.L.R. 743; [2010] AACR 42).

In one case, *CDLA/2288/2007*, it was held that, where a Commissioner has made a decision on a question of fact in the light of detailed medical evidence, that decision is binding on tribunals, unless it can be distinguished or has been overtaken by later medical research which at least casts significant doubt on its accuracy. However, it has been made plain in *MN (Somalia) v Secretary of State for the Home Department* [2014] UKSC 40; [2014] 1 W.L.R. 2064 that, while the Upper Tribunal is entitled to give persuasive guidance on matters of fact, its decisions on factual issues cannot be binding. See also *Swift v Carpenter (Personal Injuries Bar Association intervening)* [2020] EWCA Civ 1295; [2021] 2 W.L.R. 248. The further guidance on severe mental impairment given in *NMcM v SSWP (DLA)* [2014] UKUT 312 (AAC) and the guidance on the assessment of risk when considering the needs for supervision of profoundly deaf claimants given in *KT and SH v Secretary of State for Work and Pensions (PIP)* [2020] UKUT 252 (AAC) must be read in that light, although reasons for any departure from such guidance are likely to be required. Nor can trenchant views expressed by the Upper Tribunal as to the unsuitability of a witness have the binding effect of precluding the First-tier Tribunal from admitting evidence from that witness in another case. The First-tier Tribunal may take such views expressed by the Upper Tribunal into account and may regard them as persuasive but it must make up its own mind in the context of the case before it (*KF v SSD (WP)* [2019] UKUT 154 (AAC)).

Precedent in the Upper Tribunal

3.32 The Upper Tribunal itself generally follows its own decisions on matters of legal principle "in the interests of comity and to secure certainty and avoid confusion". However, it recognises that "a slavish adherence to this could lead to the perpetuation of error", in a jurisdiction where most decisions are given without the assistance of legal submissions by professional representatives acting for the parties, and so a single judge will not follow a decision of another single judge if satisfied that it was wrong (*Dorset Healthcare NHS Foundation Trust v MH* [2009] UKUT 4 (AAC)). Similarly, a three-judge panel will generally follow a decision of another three-judge panel or a decision of a Tribunal of Commissioners but will not do so if satisfied that it was wrong (*R(U) 4/88*). However, a single judge of the Administrative Appeals Chamber will always follow a decision of a three-judge panel (*Dorset Healthcare*). This has the effect that a serious difference of opinion can be resolved by a single judge referring a case to the Chamber President with a view to a three-judge panel being appointed to decide it.

The precise status of a two-judge panel remains uncertain. In the Court of Appeal, a two-judge court is treated in the same way as a three-judge court (*Cave v Robinson Jarvis & Rolf* [2001] EWCA Civ 245; [2002] 1 W.L.R. 581), but, in *IC v Poplar Housing Association* [2020] UKUT 182 (AAC), the Chamber President of the Administrative Appeals Chamber declined to consider herself bound by a decision of a panel comprised of two judges and an expert member, even though the criteria for appointing such a panel were the same as those for appointing a three-judge panel, and her decision has been followed in *Commissioner of the Police of the Metropolis v IC* [2021] UKUT 5 (AAC). In practice, it is very rare for two judges to sit together without an expert member in the Administrative Appeals Chamber and a two-judge panel is unlikely to be appointed on the ground that "the matter involves a question of law of special difficulty or an important point of principle or practice", rather than on the ground that "it is otherwise appropriate" (see the practice statement set out in the annotation to art.3 of the First-tier Tribunal and Upper Tribunal (Composition of Tribunal) Order 2008, below), which may suggest that a decision of a two-judge panel should not carry more precedential weight than a decision of a single judge.

The Upper Tribunal takes the same approach to decisions of other tribunals and courts of equivalent seniority as it takes to its own decisions (*R(IS) 3/08*, where a Commissioner considered a decision of the asylum and immigration tribunal presided over by a senior immigration judge to be of equal status). Decisions of the Employment Appeal Tribunal and the Crown Court and some decisions of county courts and sheriff courts are likely to fall into this category. However, in *TG v SSWP (SPC)* [2015] UKUT 50 (AAC), it was noted that, while the criteria for directing that a case be heard by a three-judge panel are the same in the Immigration and Asylum Chamber of the Upper Tribunal as they are in the Administrative Appeals Chamber, it is not considered that a single judge of the Immigration and Asylum Chamber is bound to follow a decision of a three-judge panel, except in a "starred" or "country guidance" case. Nonetheless, the judge considered that a single judge of the Administrative Appeals Chamber should follow any decision of a three-judge panel in the Asylum and Immigration Chamber "unless there are compelling reasons not to".

In *EC v SSWP (ESA)* [2015] UKUT 618 (AAC), a single judge of the Upper Tribunal concluded that there were compelling reasons for disagreeing with a Tribunal of Social Security Commissioners in Northern Ireland on the ground that he had been provided by the Secretary of State with far more extra-statutory material that it was legitimate to take into account in construing the relevant legislation than the Northern Ireland Department for Social Development had provided to the Tribunal of Commissioners. He considered that he should treat a Tribunal of Commissioners in the same way as he would a three-judge panel of the Upper Tribunal, but it seems doubtful that a single judge would generally feel entitled to disagree with a three-judge panel on such grounds. It is arguable that better reasons why the single judge, being satisfied that the decision of the Tribunal of Commissioners was wrong, was justified in not following it would have been that Northern Ireland decisions are not strictly binding, that it was impossible to convene a judicial panel at that level capable of resolving the different views in a way that was equally authoritative in both jurisdictions and that the difference of legal view was going to be of limited effect because the relevant legislation had already been amended.

The Upper Tribunal is clearly bound by decisions of the High Court or the Outer House of the Court of Session when those courts are exercising their supervisory jurisdiction over the Upper Tribunal (see the note to s.13(8), below). However, where the Upper Tribunal is effectively exercising a jurisdiction formerly exercised by the High Court, it is not bound to follow a decision of a High Court judge exercising that jurisdiction before its transfer to the Upper Tribunal (*Chief Supplementary Benefit Officer v Leary* [1985] 1 W.L.R. 84 (also reported as an appendix to *R(SB) 6/85*); *R(AF) 1/07*). This is true even if the High Court was exercising its supervisory jurisdiction over an inferior tribunal, rather than merely an appellate jurisdiction (*Secretary of State for Justice v RB* [2010] UKUT 454 (AAC); [2012] AACR 31). Moreover, in *Gilchrist v Revenue and Customs Commissioners* [2014] UKUT 169 (TCC); [2015] Ch. 183, it was held that the Upper Tribunal, as a "superior court of record", was not bound by High Court decisions in tax cases, notwithstanding that many High Court decisions were given on appeal from decisions of the special commissioners for income tax whose functions have been transferred to the Upper Tribunal. It was pointed out that many High Court judges now sit regularly in the Tax and Chancery Chamber of the Upper Tribunal and it was said that: "Although of course conceptually possible, it would be surprising if a decision of a High Court judge sitting in the High Court would be binding on a High Court judge sitting in the Upper Tribunal but not if sitting in the High Court". See also *Knightsbridge Pension Fund Trust v Downs* [2017] UKUT 237 (LC), where the Lands Chamber of the Upper Tribunal held that it was not bound by a High Court decision on appeal from a predecessor of the Property Chamber of the First-tier Tribunal. In *Hussain v Waltham Forest LBC* [2019] UKUT 339 (LC); [2020] 1 W.L.R. 2723, the Upper Tribunal, apparently unconsciously although probably not controversially, went a step further and relied on those decisions to hold that it was "well established" that it was not bound by any decision of the High Court other than on judicial review of the Upper Tribunal itself. On the other hand, the status in Scotland of decisions of the Outer House of the Court of Session, which in many, but not all, respects is equivalent to the High Court in England and Wales, has not formally been determined.

However, while it appears from *R(SB) 52/83* that a three-judge panel may be prepared not to follow a decision of a divisional court (i.e. a court of two or more judges of the High Court sitting together), a single judge of the Upper Tribunal will always follow a decision of a divisional court as a matter of judicial comity (*Salisbury Independent Living v Wirral MBC (HB)* [2011] UKUT 44 (AAC); [2012] AACR 37), treating it effectively as though it were a decision of a three-judge panel of the Upper Tribunal.

3.33 Judges of the Upper Tribunal in England and Wales applying the law of England and Wales are bound by decisions of the Court of Appeal and will always, as a matter of comity and practicality, follow decisions of the Inner House of the Court of Session or the Court of Appeal in Northern Ireland that are not in conflict with decisions of the Court of Appeal, although they are not strictly bound by them (*Secretary of State for Work and Pensions v Deane* [2010] EWCA Civ 699). Similarly, Judges of the Upper Tribunal in Scotland applying the law of Scotland are bound by decisions of the Inner House of the Court of Session and, subject to that, will ordinarily follow decisions of the Court of Appeal in England and Wales or the Court of Appeal in Northern Ireland. In *RJ v SSWP (JSA)* [2011] UKUT 477 (AAC); [2012] AACR 28, a judge sitting in Scotland considered that he would be entitled to decline to follow a decision of the Court of Appeal if he was satisfied that it was clearly wrong, but the point did not arise because he did not consider the relevant decision to be wrong at all. Should there ever be a conflict between decisions of the Court of Appeal and the Court of Session, judges in England and Wales would follow the Court of Appeal and judges in Scotland would follow the Inner House of the Court of Session and the Secretary of State's decision-makers would also have to make different decisions depending on which side of the border the cases arose. Presumably steps would be taken, by way of an appeal to the Supreme Court or by legislation, to remove the conflict as rapidly as possible. Commissioners in Northern Ireland are in a similar position, not being strictly bound by either decisions of the Court of Appeal in England and Wales or decisions of the Court of Session (*R 1/05(IB)*).

All Upper Tribunal judges and Commissioners are bound by decisions of the Supreme Court and by decisions of its predecessor, the House of Lords, although, in *Willers v Joyce (No.2)* [2016] UKSC 44; [2018] A.C. 843, it was recorded that the "traditional view in Scotland has been that, subject to some possible exceptions, judgments of the House of Lords in English appeals are at most highly persuasive rather than strictly binding".

The justices of the Supreme Court and their predecessors, the Law Lords, have generally made up the membership of the judicial committee of the Privy Council, which is the final court of appeal for United Kingdom overseas territories and crown dependencies and a number of smaller members, or former members, of the Commonwealth but, even so, its decisions on appeal from overseas courts are not binding in the United Kingdom. Therefore, until recently, a decision of the Court of Appeal had to be followed by the Upper Tribunal in England and Wales even if it had been criticised by the Privy Council (*Re Spectrum Plus Ltd* [2004] EWCA Civ 670; [2004] Ch. 337).

However, in *Willers v Joyce (No.2)*, the Supreme Court has declared that, when deciding that previous authority binding in England and Wales is wrong on a matter of English law, the Privy Council may now direct that courts in England and Wales should treat its decision as representing the law of England and Wales and so, presumably, of Northern Ireland where the common law applies in the same way as it does in England and Wales.

3.34 As with decisions of the Upper Tribunal, strictly speaking, only the reasoning vital to the decision of a court is binding and other comments are not but, where those other comments are made after full argument and expressly for the purpose of giving guidance, they should be followed by the Upper Tribunal except in quite exceptional circumstances (*R(IB) 4/04*). Indeed, a decision of the Court of Appeal deciding a point of principle for the purpose of clarifying the law must be followed, even if that part of the decision is obiter and even if it appears to be inconsistent with previous decisions of the Court of Appeal or the House of Lords (*Sayce v TNT (UK) Ltd* [2011] EWCA Civ 1583; [2012] 1 W.L.R. 1261). Moreover, a considered view on a question of jurisdiction upon which the Court of Appeal had requested argument must be regarded as an essential element of the reasoning of the case and is therefore binding and it is not appropriate for judges in lower courts to say obiter that they consider such a view expressed by the Court of Appeal is wrong (*R. (Nirula) v First-tier Tribunal (Asylum and Immigration Chamber)* [2012] EWCA Civ 1436; [2013] 1 W.L.R. 1090). A decision of the Court of Appeal refusing permission to appeal to that Court is not a full decision for these purposes and, while reasons given by the Court of Appeal for refusing permission are not to be disregarded lightly, their value as precedent must be assessed taking account of all relevant factors, in particular whether the Court heard substantial argument and whether the reasons were given fully (*CCS/2567/1998*, applying *Clark v University of Humberside and Lincolnshire* [2000] 1 W.L.R. 1988, and see also *R(IS) 15/96*).

Decisions of the European Court of Human Rights must be taken into account (Human Rights Act 1998, s.2) but do not take precedence over a binding decision of a domestic court unless the decision of the domestic court predates, and cannot survive, the coming into force of the Human Rights Act 1998 (*Kay v Lambeth LBC* [2006] UKHL 10; [2006] 2 A.C. 465 as explained in *R (RJM) v Secretary of State for Work and Pensions* [2008] UKHL 63; [2009] 1 A.C. 311). The effect of the extensive case law on the duty to "take account" of decisions of the European Court of Human Rights on the interpretation of the ambit of a provision of the Convention itself, as opposed to decisions on how a provision in the Convention is to apply to particular factual circumstances, has been neatly summarised in *R. (Hicks) v Commissioner of Police of the Metropolis* [2014] EWCA Civ 3; [2014] 1 W.L.R. 2152 at [80].

Decisions of the Court of Justice of the European Union (formerly the European Court of Justice) determine European Union law which, while the United Kingdom was a Member State of the European Union and during the "Implementation Period" ending on December 31, 2020, took precedence over domestic law and so such decisions were always binding. Where domestic legislation was inconsistent with European Union legislation or European Union directives having direct effect, tribunals had to disapply the domestic legislation (*R. (Manson) v Ministry of Defence* [2005] EWCA Civ 1678; [2006] I.C.R. 355, *R(JSA) 4/03*). However, while most of that case law has been "retained" and remains binding, more recent decisions are generally not strictly binding but must be taken into account (see ss.4 to 6 of the European Union (Withdrawal) Act 2018 in Part V of this volume, but see the Withdrawal Agreement which arguably requires courts and tribunals to treat a decision of the Court of Justice on the interpretation of the Citizens' Rights provisions of the Agreement as binding).

Subsection (3)

The judges of the First-tier Tribunal include all the legally qualified chairmen of the tribunals whose functions have been transferred to the First-tier Tribunal and the members of the First-tier Tribunal include all the other members of those tribunals. The judges of the Upper Tribunal include the former Social Security Commissioners and Child Support Commissioners and the deputy Commissioners and the former presidents of abolished tribunals. Members of the Upper Tribunal sit with judges hearing appeals from the Disclosure and Barring Service and traffic commissioners and some appeals from the Information Commissioner, which are beyond the scope of this work. There is also a broad power to nominate judges from the courts to sit in the First-tier Tribunal and Upper Tribunal and to assign judges and members of the employment tribunal to chambers of the First-tier Tribunal. For the composition of a tribunal for the purpose of deciding individual cases, see the First-tier Tribunal and Upper Tribunal (Composition of Tribunal) Order 2008. **3.35**

Apart from judges, the members of the First-tier Tribunal hearing social security appeals are either doctors, other people with experience of disability or looking after disabled people or accountants. For the First-tier Tribunal's use of that expertise, see under the heading "*Use of the tribunal's own expertise or observations*", in the annotation to subs.(1). There is no requirement that a medically-qualified member of the First-tier Tribunal should be a specialist in the field of medicine in any particular case before the Tribunal (*ED v SSWP* [2009] UKUT 206 (AAC)). Even in an unusual case, any qualified doctor will usually be able to decide as between competing views (*CSI/146/2003*).

Quite a number of medically qualified tribunal members also work as health care professionals providing reports for use by the Secretary of State when determining claims. In *Gillies v Secretary of State for Work and Pensions* [2006] UKHL 2; [2006] 1 W.L.R. 781 (also reported as *R(DLA) 5/06*), the House of Lords considered whether it was proper for a person who acted as an examining medical practitioner in some cases to sit as a member of a tribunal when reports of other examining medical practitioners were being challenged by claimants. Lord Hope of Craighead pointed out that the "fair-minded and informed observer" by whose standards fairness is to be judged must be taken to be neither complacent nor unduly sensitive or suspicious and to be able distinguish between what is relevant and what is irrelevant and decide what weight should be given to facts that are relevant. He then said:

> "18. ... A fair-minded observer who had considered the facts properly would appreciate that professional detachment and the ability to exercise her own independent judgment on medical issues lay at the heart of [the examining medical practitioner's] relationship with the [Benefits] Agency. He would also appreciate that she was just as capable of exercising those qualities when sitting as a medical member of a disability appeal tribunal. So there is no basis for a finding that there was a reasonable apprehension of bias on the ground that Dr Armstrong had a predisposition to favour the interests of the Benefits Agency... .
>
> "20. ... The fair-minded observer would understand that there was a crucial difference between approaching the issues which the tribunal had to decide with a predisposition in favour of the views of the EMP, and drawing upon her medical knowledge and experience when testing those views against the other evidence. He would appreciate, looking at the matter objectively, that he knowledge and experience could cut both ways as she would be just as well placed to spot the weaknesses in these reports as to spot their strengths. He would have no reason to think, in the absence of other facts indicating the contrary, that she would not apply her medical knowledge and experience in just the same impartial way when she was sitting as a tribunal member as she would when she was acting as an EMP.
>
> 21. ... The observer would appreciate that Dr Armstrong's experience of working as an EMP would be likely to be of benefit to her, and through her to the other tribunal members, when she was evaluating the EMP report. The exercise of her independent judgment, after all, was the function that she was expected to perform as the tribunal's medical member. Her experience in the preparation of these reports was an asset which was available, through her, for the other tribunal members to draw upon when they were considering the whole of the evidence... .
>
> 23. The fact is that the bringing of experience to bear when examining evidence and reaching a decision upon it has nothing to do with bias. The purpose of disqualification on the ground of apparent bias is to preserve the administration of justice from anything that might detract from the basic rules of fairness. One guiding principle is to be found in the concept of independence... . There is no suggestion that that principle was breached in this case. The other principle is to be found in the concept of impartiality—that justice must not only be done but be seen to be done. This too has at its heart the need to maintain public confidence in the integrity of the administration of justice. Impartiality consists in the absence of a predisposition to favour the interests of either side in the dispute. Therein lies the integrity of the adjudication system. But its integrity

is not compromised by the use of specialist knowledge or experience when the judge or tribunal member is examining the evidence."

Lord Rodger of Earlsferry pointed out that the approach adopted on behalf of the claimant in that case might lead to an argument that a member of a tribunal who was disabled should be disqualified on the ground that they would be likely to be partial to the disabled person claiming benefit. He also said that "the position might have been different if there had been any reason to suppose that the [examining medical practitioners] were a close-knit group sharing an esprit de corps". Baroness Hale made a similar point and emphasised that the Tribunal of Commissioners *(CSDLA/1019/1999)* had rejected the suggestion that an examining medical practitioner was a "Benefits Agency doctor" rather than an independent expert adviser. Doctors frequently have to review each others' decisions. She further observed that the Benefits Agency had no particular interest in the outcome of any individual case and was not realistically in a position to influence the doctor's decision one way or the other. Accordingly, the House of Lords held that there was no apparent bias. **3.36**

There is, nonetheless, a difficulty that must arise if some health care professionals sit also as members of tribunals. Inevitably, there will be cases where the report of such a health care professional has to be considered by a panel of the First-tier Tribunal of which the judge or disability qualified member knows the health care professional because he or she has been the medically qualified member of a tribunal on which they have sat on a previous occasion. In *Secretary of State for Work and Pensions v Cunningham*, 2004 S.L.T. 1007 (also reported as *R(DLA) 7/04*) the issue was whether there was apparent bias when a tribunal had to consider a report by an examining medical practitioner who had sat 22 times as a member of a tribunal with the chairman and 14 times with the member of the tribunal with a disability qualification. The Court of Session held that there was an apprehension of bias applying *Lawal v Northern Spirit Ltd* [2003] UKHL 35; [2003] I.C.R. 856, in which the House of Lords held there to have been apparent bias where one party to proceedings before the Employment Appeal Tribunal was represented by a barrister who had previously sat as a part-time judge of that tribunal with the lay members before whom he was appearing. *Cunningham* was cited in argument in *Gillies* but is not mentioned in the speeches of the House of Lords. It is suggested that a case like *Cunningham* turns not on whether health care professionals are "a close-knit group sharing an esprit de corps" but on whether the tribunal is. As a tribunal must work together in a way that health care professionals do not, *Cunningham* can be distinguished from *Gillies* and it is suggested that it is unaffected by the later case. In *Cunningham*, the Court of Session declined to give guidance as to how often a member of a tribunal had to have sat with an examining medical practitioner before there was apparent bias. In *CSDLA/364/2005*, decided before the House of Lords' decision in *Gillies*, it was held that a chairman was disqualified from hearing an appeal if he had sat with the examining medical practitioner only once. However, that decision was not followed in *R(DLA) 3/07* and was subsequently reversed by the Court of Session, without reasons, when the claimant withdrew her opposition to the Secretary of State's appeal. In *R(DLA) 3/07*, the Commissioner referred to *Locabail (UK) Ltd v Bayfield Properties Ltd* [1999] EWCA Civ 3004; [2000] Q.B. 451 in which it was suggested that each case had to be determined on its facts, that any doubts had to be resolved in favour of recusal and that "[t]he greater the passage of time between the event relied on as showing a danger of bias and the case in which the objection is raised, the weaker (other things being equal) the objection will be" but held that there was a reasonable apprehension of bias where the chairman of the tribunal had sat on a tribunal with the health care professionals whose report was being considered on three occasions, the last being three and a half months before the relevant hearing. The practical answer to the problem revealed in these cases is for those responsible for tribunals to ensure that medically qualified tribunal members who are also health care professionals do not sit in the areas where they usually act as health care professionals, so that they only rarely sit with judges and other members who might subsequently have to consider their reports.

Subsection (4)

3.37 In *AEB v Secretary of State for the Home Department* [2022] EWCA Civ 1512, the Court of Appeal was content to adopt the view expressed in *DT v SSWP (II)* [2015] UKUT 509 (AAC) that this subsection provides the Senior President of Tribunals' authority for making Practice Statements. The purpose of Practice Statements "is to provide guidance, both to Tribunal Judges and to Tribunal users, so as to encourage consistency of approach and understanding" (*AEB* at [15]), whereas Practice Directions made under s.23 impose obligations on those to whom they are directed.

Subsection (5)

3.38 The precise significance of the Upper Tribunal being a "superior court of record" remains uncertain. In *R. (Cart) v Upper Tribunal (Public Law Project intervening)* [2011] UKSC 28; [2012] 1 A.C. 663; [2011] AACR 38, Lady Hale said at [43] that being a superior court of record empowered it to set precedent and, in *Addlesee v Dentons Europe LLP* [2019] EWCA Civ 1600; [2019] 3 W.L.R. 1255 at [87], Lewison L.J. said that, because it is a superior court of record, a decision of the Upper Tribunal has a precedential status equivalent to a decision of a High Court judge so as to be binding on a Chancery Master. However, the precedential status of decisions of the former Social Security Commissioners, who were not a superior court of record, had long been recognised as a practical consequence of their appellate status and had been implicitly recognised in statute (see s.27 of the Social Security Act 1998 as originally enacted). In *Advocate General for Scotland v Eba* [2011] UKSC 29; [2012] 1 A.C. 710; [2011] AACR 39, it was pointed out at [16] that "superior court of record" was a term that "is unknown to the law of Scotland and has never been applied to any of the Scottish courts", although it has been applied to other tribunals exercising a jurisdiction throughout Great Britain. The Supreme Court held that, when used in respect of courts in parts of the United Kingdom other than Scotland, the term is used "to indicate a court that keeps a permanent record of its acts and proceedings and has power to punish for contempt". However, it has been felt necessary to give the Upper Tribunal a separate statutory power to punish for contempt in England and Wales and Northern Ireland as well as in Scotland (see s.25). In the end, the use of the term may merely be a declaration of status: it appears to be used where the judges of a tribunal or court include judges of at least the status of High Court judges. (Contrary to what the Supreme Court understood (see *Eba* at [15]), the Transport Tribunal was merely a court of record, like a county court, and not a superior court of record (see Transport Act 1985 Sch.4 para.1).) In any event, it was held in *Cart* and *Eba* that the fact that the Upper Tribunal was a superior court of record did not make it immune from judicial review by, respectively, the High Court or the Court of Session (see the note to s.13(8) below). On the other hand, it has been held that one effect of this subsection is to make it quite clear that the Upper Tribunal must be regarded as a "court" for the purposes of s.42 of the Senior Courts Act 1981 so that, even if a civil proceedings order does not bar a person from bringing proceedings in the First-tier Tribunal without the permission of the High Court, it certainly prevents the person from doing so in the Upper Tribunal (*AO v Shepway DC (HB)* [2013] UKUT 9 (AAC)).

Being a superior court of record would not confer an inherent power to award costs, even if implying such a broad power would not be inconsistent with s.29 (*C7 v Secretary of State for the Home Department* [2023] EWCA Civ 265; [2023] 3 W.L.R. 79).

In *CL (Vietnam) v Secretary of State for the Home Department* [2008] EWCA Civ 1551; [2009] 1 W.L.R. 1873, Sedley L.J. raised the question whether an undertaking given by the Secretary of State to the Asylum and Immigration Tribunal, which was not a superior court of record, was enforceable and had any legal force. Presumably that issue does not arise in relation to the Upper Tribunal in the light of s.3(5), but it might in relation to the First-tier Tribunal.

4. to 6A. *Omitted.* 3.39

Chambers: jurisdiction and Presidents

7.—(1) The Lord Chancellor may, with the concurrence of the Senior President of Tribunals, by order make provision for the organisation of each of the First-tier Tribunal and the Upper Tribunal into a number of chambers. 3.40

(2) There is—

(a) for each chamber of the First-tier Tribunal, and

(b) for each chamber of the Upper Tribunal,

to be a person, or two persons, to preside over that chamber.

[2 (3) A person may at a particular time—

(a) preside over more than one chamber of the First-tier Tribunal;

(b) preside over more than one chamber of the Upper Tribunal;

(c) preside over—

(i) one or more chambers of the First-tier Tribunal, and

(ii) one or more chambers of the Upper Tribunal.]

(4) A person appointed under this section to preside over a chamber is to be known as a Chamber President.

(5) Where two persons are appointed under this section to preside over the same chamber, any reference in an enactment to the Chamber President of the chamber is a reference to a person appointed under this section to preside over the chamber.

(6) The Senior President of Tribunals may (consistently with [2 subsection (2)]) appoint a person who is the Chamber President of a chamber to preside instead, or to preside also, over another chamber.

(7) The [1 Senior President of Tribunals] may (consistently with [2 subsection (2)]) appoint a person who is not a Chamber President to preside over a chamber.

(8) Schedule 4 (eligibility for appointment under subsection (7), appointment of Deputy Chamber Presidents and Acting Chamber Presidents, assignment of judges and other members of the First-tier Tribunal and Upper Tribunal, and further provision about Chamber Presidents and chambers) has effect.

(9) Each of the Lord Chancellor and the Senior President of Tribunals may, with the concurrence of the other, by order—

(a) make provision for the allocation of the First-tier Tribunal's functions between its chambers;

(b) make provision for the allocation of the Upper Tribunal's functions between its chambers;

(c) amend or revoke any order made under this subsection.

Amendments

1. Crime and Courts Act 2013 s.20 and Sch.13 paras 42 and 43 (October 1, 2013).

2. Courts and Tribunals (Judiciary and Functions of Staff) Act 2018 s.1(4) (February 20, 2019).

General Note

The First-tier Tribunal is organised into seven chambers by art.2 of the First-tier Tribunal and Upper Tribunal (Chambers) Order 2010 (SI 2010/2655). By art.6, there are assigned to the Social Entitlement Chamber of the First-tier Tribunal— 3.41

"all functions relating to appeals—

(a) in cases regarding support for asylum seekers, failed asylum seekers, persons designated under section 130 of the Criminal Justice and Immigration Act 2008 or the dependants of any such persons;

(b) in criminal injuries compensation cases;

(c) regarding entitlement to, payments of, or recovery or recoupment of payments of, social security benefits, child support, vaccine damage payment, health in pregnancy grant and tax credits, with the exception of—

(i) appeals under section 11 of the Social Security Contributions (Transfer of Functions, etc.) Act 1999 (appeals against decisions of Her Majesty's Revenue and Customs);

(ii) appeals in respect of employer penalties or employer information penalties (as defined in section 63(11) and (12) of the Tax Credits Act 2002;

(iii) appeals under regulation 28(3) of the Child Trust Funds Regulations 2004;

(d) regarding saving gateway accounts with the exception of appeals against requirements to account for an amount under regulations made under section 14 of the Saving Gateway Accounts Act 2009;

(e) regarding child trust funds with the exception of appeals against requirements to account for an amount under regulations made under section 22(4) Child Trust Funds Act 2004 in relation to section 13 of that Act;

(ea) appealable decisions within the meaning of section 56(3) of the Childcare Payments Act 2014;

(eb) under the Childcare (Free of Charge for Working Parents) (England) Regulations 2022;

(f) regarding payments in consequence of diffuse mesothelioma;

(g) regarding a certificate or waiver decision in relation to NHS charges;

(h) regarding entitlement to be credited with earnings or contributions;

(i) against a decision as to whether an accident was an industrial accident."

The excepted cases mentioned in paras (c), (d) and (e) are assigned to the Tax Chamber under art.7. Note, however, that decisions made by HMRC under arrangements made under s.17 of the 1999 Act do not fall within exception (i) in para.(c) since appeals against such decisions are not brought under s.11 of that Act (*SF v SSWP (HRP)* [2013] UKUT 175 (AAC)). There was a period after the Childcare (Early Years Provision Free of Charge) (Extended Entitlement) Regulations 2016 came into force on December 19, 2016 but before para.(eb) was first introduced with effect from March 6, 2020, during which a number of appeals under the 2016 Regulations were heard in the Social Entitlement Chamber of the First-tier Tribunal. In *HMRC v JS* [2021] UKUT 264 (AAC), that was held to have been wrong because, in the absence of provision in art.6, appeals to the First-tier Tribunal against decisions of HMRC fall to be heard in the Tax Chamber by virtue of art.7(a).

Asylum support cases, falling within the scope of para.(a), were previously determined by adjudicators and criminal injuries compensation cases, falling within the scope of para.(b), were previously determined by the Criminal Injuries Compensation Appeals Panel, both of which were entirely separate from the appeal tribunals that determined social security and child support cases. Although the Social Entitlement Chamber is a single entity in legal terms, its administration still continues to reflect the old divisions, with asylum support appeals and criminal injuries compensation cases (which are outside the scope of this work) being administered separately in central offices while social security and child support cases are administered regionally.

Judge Kate Markus KC is Chamber President of the Social Entitlement Chamber and Judge Greg Sinfield is Chamber President of the Tax Chamber.

The Upper Tribunal is organised into four chambers by art.9. By art.10, there are assigned to the Administrative Appeals Chamber of the Upper Tribunal, inter alia, all appeals against decisions of the Social Entitlement Chamber of the First-tier Tribunal, all references under s.9(5)(b) or under r.7(3) of the Tribunal Procedure (First-tier Tribunal) (Social Entitlement Chamber) Rules 2008 by that Chamber, all determinations and decisions under the Forfeiture Act 1982 and those judicial review cases not expressly allocated to other chambers. Appeals and references from the Tax Chamber of the First-tier Tribunal and some judicial review cases are allocated to the Tax and Chancery Chamber of the Upper Tribunal under art.13. Complex cases transferred from the Tax Chamber of the First-tier Tribunal to the Upper Tribunal are also allocated to the Tax and Chancery Chamber under art.13.

Mrs Justice Williams is Chamber President of the Administrative Appeals Chamber and Mrs Justice Bacon is Chamber President of the Tax and Chancery Chamber.

Article 14 enables the Senior President of Tribunals to resolve any question of doubt as to the chamber to which a case should be allocated and art.15 gives a president of a chamber to which a case is allocated a broad power to transfer a case to another chamber of the same tribunal, with the agreement of that chamber's president.

Senior President of Tribunals: power to delegate

8.—(1) The Senior President of Tribunals may delegate any function he has in his capacity as Senior President of Tribunals— **3.42**

(a) to any judge, or other member, of the Upper Tribunal or First-tier Tribunal;

(b) to staff appointed under section 40(1).

[1 (1A) A function under paragraph 1(1) or 2(1) of Schedule 2 may be delegated under subsection (1) only to a Chamber President of a chamber of the Upper Tribunal.]

(2) Subsection (1) does not apply to functions of the Senior President of Tribunals [1 under any of the following—

section 7(7);
section 7(9);
[2 section 29B;
section 29D;]
paragraph 2(1) of Schedule 3;
paragraph 7(1) of Schedule 3;
paragraph 2 of Schedule 4;
paragraph 5(1) and (3) of Schedule 4;
paragraph 5(5) to (8) of Schedule 4;
paragraph 5A(2)(a) of Schedule 4;
paragraph 5A(3)(a) of Schedule 4;
[2 paragraph 3 of Schedule 5].

(3) A delegation under subsection (1) is not revoked by the delegator's becoming incapacitated.

(4) Any delegation under subsection (1) that is in force immediately before a person ceases to be Senior President of Tribunals continues in force until varied or revoked by a subsequent holder of the office of Senior President of Tribunals.

(5) The delegation under this section of a function shall not prevent the exercise of the function by the Senior President of Tribunals.

AMENDMENTS

1. Crime and Courts Act 2013 s.20 and Sch.13 paras 42 and 44 (October 1, 2013).

2. Courts and Tribunals (Judiciary and Functions of Staff) Act 2018 s.3(1) and Sch. paras 39 and 40 (April 6, 2020).

GENERAL NOTE

3.43 Any function delegated to a Chamber President may be further delegated to another judge or a member of staff, under Sch.4 para.4.

Although that provision has not been amended, it is implicit that it cannot allow a Chamber President further to delegate a function mentioned in subs.(1A) that has been delegated to him or her.

Review of decisions and appeals

Review of decision of First-tier Tribunal

3.44 **9.**—(1) The First-tier Tribunal may review a decision made by it on a matter in a case, other than a decision that is an excluded decision for the purposes of section 11(1) (but see subsection (9)).

(2) The First-tier Tribunal's power under subsection (1) in relation to a decision is exercisable—

(a) of its own initiative, or

(b) on application by a person who for the purposes of section 11(2) has a right of appeal in respect of the decision.

(3) Tribunal Procedure Rules may—

(a) provide that the First-tier Tribunal may not under subsection (1) review (whether of its own initiative or on application under subsection (2)(b)) a decision of a description specified for the purposes of this paragraph in Tribunal Procedure Rules;

(b) provide that the First-tier Tribunal's power under subsection (1) to review a decision of a description specified for the purposes of this paragraph in Tribunal Procedure Rules is exercisable only of the tribunal's own initiative;

(c) provide that an application under subsection (2)(b) that is of a description specified for the purposes of this paragraph in Tribunal Procedure Rules may be made only on grounds specified for the purposes of this paragraph in Tribunal Procedure Rules;

(d) provide, in relation to a decision of a description specified for the purposes of this paragraph in Tribunal Procedure Rules, that the First-tier Tribunal's power under subsection (1) to review the decision of its own initiative is exercisable only on grounds specified for the purposes of this paragraph in Tribunal Procedure Rules.

(4) Where the First-tier Tribunal has under subsection (1) reviewed a decision, the First-tier Tribunal may in the light of the review do any of the following—

(a) correct accidental errors in the decision or in a record of the decision;

(b) amend reasons given for the decision;

(c) set the decision aside.

(5) Where under subsection (4)(c) the First-tier Tribunal sets a decision aside, the First-tier Tribunal must either—

(a) re-decide the matter concerned, or

(b) refer that matter to the Upper Tribunal.

(6) Where a matter is referred to the Upper Tribunal under subsection (5)(b), the Upper Tribunal must re-decide the matter.

(7) Where the Upper Tribunal is under subsection (6) re-deciding a matter, it may make any decision which the First-tier Tribunal could make if the First-tier Tribunal were re-deciding the matter.

(8) Where a tribunal is acting under subsection (5)(a) or (6), it may make such findings of fact as it considers appropriate.

(9) This section has effect as if a decision under subsection (4)(c) to set aside an earlier decision were not an excluded decision for the purposes of section 11(1), but the First-tier Tribunal's only power in the light of a review under subsection (1) of a decision under subsection (4)(c) is the power under subsection (4)(a).

(10) A decision of the First-tier Tribunal may not be reviewed under subsection (1) more than once, and once the First-tier Tribunal has decided that an earlier decision should not be reviewed under subsection (1) it may not then decide to review that earlier decision under that subsection.

(11) Where under this section a decision is set aside and the matter concerned is then re-decided, the decision set aside and the decision made in re-deciding the matter are for the purposes of subsection (10) to be taken to be different decisions.

General Note

This convoluted section replaces s.13(2) of the Social Security Act 1998. Note that s.13(3) of the 1998 Act remains in place. **3.45**

Subsections (1)–(3)

At first sight, this section provides a very broad power to review a decision. However, r.40(2) of the Tribunal Procedure (First-tier Tribunal) (Social Entitlement Chamber) Rules 2008 provides that a decision may be reviewed only where there has been an application for permission to appeal and only if there was an error of law in the decision, so that the circumstances in which there may be a review are similar to those that formerly existed is under s.13(2) of the 1998 Act. (As decisions in respect of criminal injuries compensation and asylum support are excluded decisions, there is no power of review in such cases.) For what amounts to an error of law, see the note to s.11 and, for the general effect of r.40 and its validity, see the note to that rule. **3.46**

Because exercising a power of review requires a finding that there has been an error of law, it is difficult to envisage it being appropriate to review a decision and then take no action, rather than refusing to review it (*VH v Suffolk CC (SEN)* [2010] UKUT 203 (AAC)), unless perhaps the case had ceased to have any practical purpose but there was nevertheless some advantage in simply declaring there to have been an error.

A decision should be reviewed only where it is clearly wrong in law, because otherwise the First-tier Tribunal would be usurping the Upper Tribunal's function of determining appeals on contentious points of law. Nonetheless, there are degrees of clarity and the likelihood of the party in whose favour the original decision was made objecting to the review may be an important consideration when deciding whether a review is appropriate (*R.(RB) v First-tier Tribunal (Review)* [2010] UKUT 160 (AAC); [2010] AACR 41). Claimants are probably more likely in practice to object than the Secretary of State. On the other hand, if a decision is reviewed without first giving a party an opportunity to object, r.40(4) of the 2008 Rules enables the review decision to be set aside if an objection is subsequently received from that party.

There is no general rule that it is inappropriate for a judge to consider whether to review his own decision (*AA v Cheshire and Wirral Partnership NHS Foundation Trust* [2009] UKUT 195 (AAC); [2011] AACR 37). However, in the Social Entitlement Chamber to which social security cases are allocated, para.11 of the Senior President of Tribunals' practice statement on the composition of tribunals (see the note to art.2

of the First-tier Tribunal and Upper Tribunal (Composition of Tribunal) Order 2008, below) requires applications for permission to appeal and reviews to be dealt with by salaried judges, who consequently decide whether to review their own decisions and also those of fee-paid judges sitting in their districts. Apparent attempts by one fee-paid judge to prevent his decisions from being reviewed by purporting to consider whether to review his decisions when they were made were held to be ineffective in *LM v SSWP* [2009] UKUT 185 (AAC) because the effect of r.40(2)(a) of the 2008 Rules is that a power to consider a review under s.9 arises only when an application for permission to appeal is made.

The First-tier Tribunal is entitled to determine the scope of a review and so may review only part of its decision but must then make clear which part is being reviewed (*Point West GR Ltd v Bassi* [2020] EWCA Civ 795 at [25] and [35]).

There is no appeal against a decision to review, or not to review, an earlier decision (see s.11(5)(d)(i)).

Subsection (4)

3.47 Note that, upon a review, the tribunal is not limited to setting aside its decision but may instead correct its decision or amend its reasons.

The power under s.9(4)(a) to correct decisions is distinct from the similar power under r.36 of the Tribunal Procedure (First-tier Tribunal) (Social Entitlement Chamber) Rules 2008, and, in view of subs.(10), it may be important to identify which of the two powers is being exercised. In *GA v SSWP (PIP)* [2017] UKUT 416 (AAC), the Upper Tribunal said that an accidental error was not an error of law so that reg.36 should be used rather than s.9(4)(a), given the effect of r.40(2)(b).

The power under s.9(4)(b) to amend reasons may be useful where the tribunal has simply failed to explain part of its reasoning but there are limits to the extent to which additional reasons may be given. Although the three-judge panel deciding *JS v SSWP (DLA)* [2013] UKUT 100 (AAC); [2013] AACR 30 declined to define "amend", it did state that the power "must not be used to correct defective reasoning or to provide a commentary on the grounds of appeal" and that the amended reasons "must be the reasons that led the tribunal to decide as it did, flawed though they may be, not a later attempt to rationalise the decision". In *SSWP v CM (ESA)* [2012] UKUT 436 (AAC), the Upper Tribunal was sceptical as to whether additional reasons provided on review represented the original reasoning, on the ground that if the First-tier Tribunal had really addressed the more difficult issue in the case dealt with in the additional reasons it was unlikely that it would have mentioned in the original reasons only the easier issue. In both that decision and in *JS v SSWP (DLA)*, the Upper Tribunal said that the power to amend reasons may be exercised only by the presiding judge (or—it was said in the latter case—exceptionally, another member) of the panel that heard the case. However, as noted above, para.11 of the Senior President of Tribunals' practice statement on the composition of tribunals requires reviews to be dealt with by salaried judges. It is difficult for a salaried judge to review a decision where the appropriateness of a review depends on whether or not the reasons of a decision made by a fee-paid judge can be amended satisfactorily. Because the power to amend the reasons for a decision arises only where there has been a review, it is necessary, due to the effect of r.40(1)(b) of the Tribunal Procedure (First-tier Tribunal) (Social Entitlement Chamber) Rules 2008, for the salaried judge to identify an error of law before the case is referred to the fee-paid judge for the reasons to be amended. It might be better if a salaried judge could refer the whole application for permission to appeal and the question of review to the fee-paid judge in such a case. As it is, it may be necessary for the salaried judge at least to leave the fee-paid judge a choice of either amending the reasons or setting the original decision aside. An alternative approach, suggested in *JS v SSWP (DLA)* [2013] UKUT 100 (AAC); [2013] AACR 30, would be for the salaried judge to seek representations from the parties before referring the case to fee-paid judge in which case, as the three-judge panel pointed out, the party not making the application for permission to appeal will be able to consider whether to concede that the decision is erroneous in point of law so that it must be set aside under s.13(3) of the Social Security Act 1998. However, note that r.40(4) of the Tribunal Procedure (First-tier Tribunal) (Social Entitlement Chamber) Rules 2008 enables the First-tier Tribunal to make what is in effect a provisional decision without first obtaining representations on the basis that it may reconsider the decision in the light of representations made afterwards. This may often be a more proportionate approach.

The problems caused by the Practice Statement on the composition of the First-tier Tribunal had been illustrated in *AS v SSWP (ESA)* [2011] UKUT 159 (AAC). The substantive decision had been made by a panel of which the presiding judge was fee-paid. The statement of reasons failed to deal with a certain issue and, upon an application for permission to appeal being received, the salaried judge referred the case to the fee-paid judge who purported to rectify the omission by correcting the statement under r.36 of the Tribunal Procedure (First-tier Tribunal) (Social Entitlement Chamber) Rules 2008. In the light of the correction, the salaried judge refused to review the decision and refused permission to appeal. The Upper Tribunal held that the correction went further than allowed by r.36 (see the annotation to that rule) and that there were no grounds for review because the salaried judge had not been satisfied that there was an error of law. One difficulty, not expressly mentioned by the Upper Tribunal, was that the corrections made by the fee-paid judge could not have been made by the salaried judge under s.9(4)(a) or (b) because the reasons for them were not within his knowledge. He could only have set the decision aside altogether. As it was, the Upper Tribunal declined to take any action on the appeal on the basis that it could have regard to the additional reasons provided by the fee-paid judge, even though she had been wrong to provide them by way of a correction. With those reasons, the decision of the First-tier Tribunal was sound in fact and law. The three-judge panel deciding *JS v SSWP (DLA)* approved that approach. There is no appeal against a decision to take no action or not to take any particular action or to set aside a decision under this subsection (see s.11(5)(d)(ii) and (iii)). However, there appears to be a right of appeal against a decision to correct an error or amend reasons. 3.48

For reasons explained in the annotation to subs.(5)(b), (6) and (7), it is arguable that the power under s.9(4)(c) to set aside a decision should be exercised in a social security case only when the First-tier Tribunal intends to re-decide the case itself under s.9(5)(a).

A discrete part of a decision may be set aside, but it is the decision and not the reasoning that is set aside and it may introduce unforeseen complications if a decision is not set aside in its entirety (*Essex County Council v TB (SEN)* [2014] UKUT 559 (AAC).

Subsections (5)(b), (6) and (7)

A case may be referred to the Upper Tribunal under s.9(5)(b) only if the First-tier Tribunal's decision has been set aside under s.9(4)(c), which, in the light of r.40(2) of the Tribunal Procedure (First-tier Tribunal) (Social Entitlement Chamber) Rules 2008, requires the First-tier Tribunal to be satisfied that there was an error of law in its decision. Therefore, in *LM v HMRC (CHB)* [2016] UKUT 389 (AAC) where the First-tier Tribunal, considering an application for permission to appeal to the Upper Tribunal, said nothing about the merits of the grounds of appeal or about setting aside its decision but merely said that "[t]he matter shall be referred to the Upper Tribunal in accordance with section 9(5)(b) of the Act", the Upper Tribunal treated the First-tier Tribunal as having given permission to appeal, rather than as having referred the case. Reference was made to *JS v SSWP (DLA)* [2013] UKUT 100 (AAC); [2013] AACR 30 which "provides a helpful explanation of the steps needed to be taken in order for a District Tribunal Judge to properly review a First-tier Tribunal's decision, steps which are needed in order to properly 'refer' an appeal to the Upper Tribunal under section 9(5)(b) of the Tribunals, Courts and Enforcement Act 2007". 3.49

Similarly, in *GA v SSWP (PIP)* [2017] UKUT 416 (AAC), the Upper Tribunal found it necessary to treat a reference as a grant of permission to appeal in order to give proper effect to the obvious intention of the First-tier Tribunal. The judge had given permission to appeal on one point and had purported to make a reference on other points without finding there to be a further error of law but simply so that all issues could be decided together. Even more obviously, a case cannot be referred to the Upper Tribunal under s.9(5)(b) when permission to appeal to the Upper Tribunal is being given in respect of the same matter, because a case can be referred under s.9(5)(b) only when the decision of the First-tier Tribunal has been set aside, whereas, by virtue of s.11(5)(e), permission to appeal cannot be given against a decision that *has* been set aside (*HMRC v RS (TC)* [2021] UKUT 310 (AAC)).

Moreover, in *GA*, the Upper Tribunal pointed out that the effect of referring a case to the Upper Tribunal under s.9(5)(b), rather than giving permission to appeal, is to force the Upper Tribunal to re-decide the case under subs.(6), even if that requires it to make fresh findings of fact, and to deprive it of the power to remit the case to the First-tier Tribunal under s.12(2)(b)(i). On an appeal, the Upper Tribunal can decide whether to re-decide the case itself or remit it, having regard to the convenience of the parties as well as its own convenience. It is therefore difficult, given that the power to review a decision arises only when an application for permission to appeal is made, to see that there can ever be an advantage in reviewing a decision in a social security case and then referring the case to the Upper Tribunal, rather than simply giving permission to appeal. (It may be different in some other types of case, for instance in tax cases or information rights cases, where the First-tier Tribunal has a more general power to transfer a complex case to the Upper Tribunal.) This suggests that the power under s.9(4)(c) to set aside a decision on review should be exercised in a social security case only when the First-tier Tribunal intends to re-decide the case itself under s.9(5)(a).

There is no appeal against a decision to refer, or not to refer, a matter to the Upper Tribunal (see s.11(5)(d)(iv)).

Subsection (8)

3.50 This tends to suggest that there need not be a complete rehearing if the reason for a decision being set aside does not vitiate findings made as part of the original decision. If this is so, it may be appropriate in some cases (subject to the views of the parties) for a judge setting aside a decision on the papers to give a new decision straightaway on the basis that it is clear what decision the tribunal should have given on its findings of fact. However, this may be impossible where s.13(3) of the 1998 Act requires the case to be referred to a differently constituted First-tier Tribunal.

Subsection (9)

3.51 Presumably this subsection was included in case the power under para.15(1) of Sch.5 was not fully exercised. It enables a correction of a decision under subs.(4)(c) to set aside a decision.

Subsections (10) and (11)

3.52 If a decision is corrected under subs.(4)(a) or amended reasons are given under subs.(4)(b), there can be no further review of that decision, although there seems no reason why there should not be a correction under the separate power in r.36 of the Tribunal Procedure (First-tier Tribunal) (Social Entitlement Chamber) Rules 2008. The lack of any further power of review makes it particularly important for the parties to have the opportunity to make representations. On the other hand, obtaining representations before reviewing a decision would be time-consuming and cause delay in those cases where the parties were content with the review. Rule 40(4) therefore provides that, if a party has not had an opportunity to make representations before action is taken on a review, it may do so afterwards and ask that the action be set aside. It also provides that parties must be given notice of the right to make such representations where action is taken without the views of the parties being obtained first. In *AM v SSWP* [2009] UKUT 224 (AAC), that was not done.

There can also be no review once there has been a refusal to review. Rule 39(2) has the effect that a tribunal refusing to review a decision will automatically consider whether to grant permission to appeal. The restriction imposed by subs.(10) is unfortunate if two parties apply for a review and the less meritorious application is rejected before the second application is received.

However, where a decision is set aside under subs.(4)(c), a decision substituted for it under subs.(5)(a) is treated as a different decision and may itself be reviewed. It is also the substituted decision against which any appeal must be brought because the decision that has been set aside is an "excluded decision" under s.11(5)(e).

Review of decision of Upper Tribunal

10.—(1) The Upper Tribunal may review a decision made by it on a matter in a case, other than a decision that is an excluded decision for the purposes of section 13(1) (but see subsection (7)). **3.53**

(2) The Upper Tribunal's power under subsection (1) in relation to a decision is exercisable—

(a) of its own initiative, or

(b) on application by a person who for the purposes of section 13(2) has a right of appeal in respect of the decision.

(3) Tribunal Procedure Rules may—

(a) provide that the Upper Tribunal may not under subsection (1) review (whether of its own initiative or on application under subsection (2)(b)) a decision of a description specified for the purposes of this paragraph in Tribunal Procedure Rules;

(b) provide that the Upper Tribunal's power under subsection (1) to review a decision of a description specified for the purposes of this paragraph in Tribunal Procedure Rules is exercisable only of the tribunal's own initiative;

(c) provide that an application under subsection (2)(b) that is of a description specified for the purposes of this paragraph in Tribunal Procedure Rules may be made only on grounds specified for the purposes of this paragraph in Tribunal Procedure Rules;

(d) provide, in relation to a decision of a description specified for the purposes of this paragraph in Tribunal Procedure Rules, that the Upper Tribunal's power under subsection (1) to review the decision of its own initiative is exercisable only on grounds specified for the purposes of this paragraph in Tribunal Procedure Rules.

(4) Where the Upper Tribunal has under subsection (1) reviewed a decision, the Upper Tribunal may in the light of the review do any of the following—

(a) correct accidental errors in the decision or in a record of the decision;

(b) amend reasons given for the decision;

(c) set the decision aside.

(5) Where under subsection (4)(c) the Upper Tribunal sets a decision aside, the Upper Tribunal must re-decide the matter concerned.

(6) Where the Upper Tribunal is acting under subsection (5), it may make such findings of fact as it considers appropriate.

(7) This section has effect as if a decision under subsection (4)(c) to set aside an earlier decision were not an excluded decision for the purposes of section 13(1), but the Upper Tribunal's only power in the light of a review under subsection (1) of a decision under subsection (4)(c) is the power under subsection (4)(a).

(8) A decision of the Upper Tribunal may not be reviewed under subsection (1) more than once, and once the Upper Tribunal has decided that an earlier decision should not be reviewed under subsection (1) it may not then decide to review that earlier decision under that subsection.

(9) Where under this section a decision is set aside and the matter concerned is then re-decided, the decision set aside and the decision made in re-deciding the matter are for the purposes of subsection (8) to be taken to be different decisions.

General Note

3.54 This section is in terms that are very similar to s.9, save that there is no equivalent of s.9(5)(b), (6) and (7). However, the power of review is even more severely curtailed by Tribunal Procedure Rules, being limited to cases where the Upper Tribunal has overlooked a piece of legislation or a binding authority or there has been a binding decision of a superior court since the Upper Tribunal's decision was given (see rr.45(1) and 46 of the Tribunal Procedure (Upper Tribunal) Rules 2008).

It is important to distinguish the powers conferred under s.10(4) from the powers conferred either by s.25 or by Tribunal Procedure Rules. In *R. (Singh) v Secretary of State for the Home Department* [2019] EWCA Civ 1014, the Upper Tribunal had set aside its decision to give permission to apply for judicial review because the decision had been given in breach of the rules of natural justice. The Court of Appeal accepted that it could not have acted under s.10 or under either of rr.6(5) or 43 of the 2008 Rules but held that s.25 had empowered it to set aside the grant of permission.

Right to appeal to Upper Tribunal

3.55 **11.**—(1) For the purposes of subsection (2), the reference to a right of appeal is to a right to appeal to the Upper Tribunal on any point of law arising from a decision made by the First-tier Tribunal other than an excluded decision.

(2) Any party to a case has a right of appeal, subject to subsection (8).

(3) That right may be exercised only with permission (or, in Northern Ireland, leave).

(4) Permission (or leave) may be given by—

(a) the First-tier Tribunal, or

(b) the Upper Tribunal,

on an application by the party.

(5) For the purposes of subsection (1), an "excluded decision" is—

(a) any decision of the First-tier Tribunal on an appeal made in exercise of a right conferred by the Criminal Injuries Compensation Scheme in compliance with section 5(1)(a) of the Criminal Injuries Compensation Act 1995 (appeals against decisions on reviews),

[[1] (aa) any decision of the First-tier Tribunal on an appeal made in exercise of a right conferred by the Victims of Overseas Terrorism Compensation Scheme in compliance with section 52(3) of the Crime and Security Act 2010,]

(b) any decision of the First-tier Tribunal on an appeal under section [[4] section 27(3) or (5), 79(5) or (7) or 111(3) or (5) of the Data Protection Act 2018] (appeals against national security certificate),

(c) any decision of the First-tier Tribunal on an appeal under section 60(1) or (4) of the Freedom of Information Act 2000 (appeals against national security certificate),

[[2] (ca) any decision of the First-tier Tribunal under section 88, 89(3) or 92(3) of the Tax Collection and Management (Wales) Act 2016 (approval for Welsh Revenue Authority to issue certain information notices),

(cb) any decision of the First-tier Tribunal under section 108 of that Act (approval for Welsh Revenue Authority to inspect premises),]

[[3] (cc) any decision of the First-tier Tribunal under section 181E or 181F of that Act (appeals relating to postponement requests),]

(d) a decision of the First-tier Tribunal under section 9—

(i) to review, or not to review, an earlier decision of the tribunal,

(ii) to take no action, or not to take any particular action, in the light of a review of an earlier decision of the tribunal,

(iii) to set aside an earlier decision of the tribunal, or

(iv) to refer, or not to refer, a matter to the Upper Tribunal,

(e) a decision of the First-tier Tribunal that is set aside under section 9 (including a decision set aside after proceedings on an appeal under this section have been begun), or

(f) any decision of the First-tier Tribunal that is of a description specified in an order made by the Lord Chancellor.

(6) A description may be specified under subsection (5)(f) only if—

(a) in the case of a decision of that description, there is a right to appeal to a court, the Upper Tribunal or any other tribunal from the decision and that right is, or includes, something other than a right (however expressed) to appeal on any point of law arising from the decision, or

(b) decisions of that description are made in carrying out a function transferred under section 30 and prior to the transfer of the function under section 30(1) there was no right to appeal from decisions of that description.

(7) Where—

(a) an order under subsection (5)(f) specifies a description of decisions, and

(b) decisions of that description are made in carrying out a function transferred under section 30,

the order must be framed so as to come into force no later than the time when the transfer under section 30 of the function takes effect (but power to revoke the order continues to be exercisable after that time, and power to amend the order continues to be exercisable after that time for the purpose of narrowing the description for the time being specified).

(8) The Lord Chancellor may by order make provision for a person to be treated as being, or to be treated as not being, a party to a case for the purposes of subsection (2).

AMENDMENTS

1. Crime and Security Act 2010 s.48(4) and Sch.2 para.5 (April 8, 2010).

2. Tax Collection and Management (Wales) Act 2016 s.116(1) (January 25, 2018).

3. Tax Collection and Management (Wales) Act 2016 s.118I(1) (as inserted by Land Transaction Tax and Anti-avoidance of Devolved Taxes (Wales) Act 2017 s.76 and Sch.23 para.63) (April 1, 2018).

4. Data Protection Act 2018 s.211 and Sch.19 paras. 130 and 131 (May 25, 2018).

General Note

Subsection (1)

3.56 In *LS v Lambeth LBC (HB)* [2010] UKUT 461 (AAC); [2011] AACR 27, a three-judge panel has decided that there is a right of appeal under s.11 against any decision of the First-tier Tribunal that is not an "excluded decision" (for the meaning of which, see subs.(5)). It was pointed out that, by making an order under subs.(5)(f) and (6)(b), the Lord Chancellor could have preserved the effect of *Morina v SSWP* [2007] EWCA Civ 749; [2007] 1 W.L.R. 3033 (also reported as *R(IS)* 6/07) (in which it was decided that certain interlocutory decisions in social security cases were not "decisions" for the purpose of the right of appeal under s.14 of the Social Security Act 1998) but had not done so.

Nonetheless, interlocutory appeals in respect of decisions made under Tribunal Procedure Rules have not been encouraged. The duty under r.33(2)(c) of the Tribunal Procedure (First-tier Tribunal) (Social Entitlement Chamber) Rules to inform a person of the right of appeal applies only to a decision which finally disposes of all issues in the proceedings and the three-judge panel itself said at [94] that:

> "it will be open to both the First-tier Tribunal and the Upper Tribunal to refuse permission to bring an interlocutory appeal on the ground that it is premature. The circumstances of the individual case must be considered. It is one thing to grant permission for an interlocutory appeal in a case where the final hearing may last for a fortnight. It is another to do so where the final hearing is likely to last about an hour, as is often the case in social security appeals. Moreover, as was suggested in *Dorset Healthcare NHS Foundation Trust v MH* [2009] UKUT 4 (AAC) at [19], where case-management decisions are being challenged, the First-tier Tribunal can treat an application for permission to appeal as an application for a new direction if it is satisfied that the challenged direction is not appropriate."

It must follow that, at least in most social security cases, parties will not be prejudiced by waiting until there has been a final decision in the case and relying on an error in an interlocutory decision as grounds of appeal against the final decision, instead of appealing against the interlocutory decision itself.

See also *Crossland v IC* [2020] UKUT 263 (AAC)) and guidance published for appellants at: *https://www.judiciary.uk/wp-content/uploads/2020/10/UTAAC-Guidance-on-Interim-Appeals-October-2020_.pdf* [Accessed May 9, 2022].

"Point of law"

3.57 An appeal against any other decision lies only on a "point of law". Even though it has been recognised that the Upper Tribunal may have more flexibility in determining what is or is not a point of law than the courts do (*R. (Jones) v First-tier Tribunal* [2013] UKSC 19; [2013] 2 A.C. 48; [2013] AACR 25), judges of the Upper Tribunal may be expected to resist any attempt by an appellant to present an appeal on facts as raising questions of law, even if they have grave doubts about the decision under appeal. No appeal on a question of law should be allowed to be turned into a rehearing of parts of the evidence (*Yeboah v Crofton* [2002] EWCA Civ 794; [2002] I.R.L.R. 634). However, once a judge is satisfied that a decision is erroneous in point of law, he or she is entitled to determine any outstanding questions of fact (see s.12(2)(b)(ii) and (4)).

The Upper Tribunal will give permission to appeal only if there is a realistic prospect of an appeal succeeding, unless there is exceptionally some other good reason to do so: Lord Woolf MR in *Smith v Cosworth Casting Processes Ltd* [1997] 1 W.L.R. 1538.

The meaning of "point of law" was considered by the Court of Appeal in *Nipa Begum v Tower Hamlets LBC* [2000] 1 W.L.R. 306 in a case where a homeless person appealed to the county court under s.204 of the Housing Act 1996 against a decision of a housing authority. An appeal lay "on any point of law arising from" such a decision and the Court of Appeal held that the county court had powers akin to those available on an application for judicial review in the High Court and so could quash a decision on the ground of procedural error, lack of vires, irrationality or inadequacy of reasons as well as for straightforward errors of legal interpretation. However, in *Adesotu v Lewisham LBC (Equality and Human Rights Commission Intervening)* [2019] EWCA Civ 1405; [2019] 1 W.L.R. 5637, the Court of Appeal rejected an argument that it followed that an appeal on a point of law was "a claim for judicial review" for the purposes of s.113(3)(a) of the Equality Act 2010 so as to confer on the appellate body jurisdiction to consider whether there had been a breach of the requirements of that Act.

The approach taken in *Nipa Begum* has been authoritatively reaffirmed by the Court of Appeal in *James v Hertsmere BC* [2020] EWCA Civ 489; [2020] 1 W.L.R. 3606.

In *R(A) 1/72* and *R(IS) 11/99*, Social Security Commissioners had made similar lists of errors that would amount to errors of law, rather than of fact. More recently, in *R(I) 2/06* and *R(DLA) 3/08*, Tribunals of Commissioners have referred to the judgment of the Court of Appeal in *R (Iran) v Secretary of State for the Home Department* [2005] EWCA Civ 982, offering a "brief summary of the points of law that will most often be encountered in practice". These were—

> "(i) Making perverse or irrational findings on a matter or matters that were material to the outcome ('material matters');
> (ii) Failing to give reasons or any adequate reasons for findings on material matters;
> (iii) Failing to take into account and/or resolve conflicts of fact or opinion on material matters;
> (iv) Giving weight to immaterial matters;
> (v) Making a material misdirection of law on any material matter;
> (vi) Committing or permitting a procedural or other irregularity capable of making a material difference to the outcome or the fairness of proceedings;
> (vii) Making a mistake as to a material fact which could be established by objective and uncontentious evidence, where the appellant and/or his advisers were not responsible for the mistake, and where unfairness resulted from the fact that a mistake was made."
>
> "Each of these grounds for detecting any error of law contains the word 'material' (or 'immaterial'). Errors of law of which it can be said that they would have made no difference to the outcome do not matter."

The seven points identified by the Court of Appeal and the issue of "materiality" are considered in more detail below. **3.58**

The meaning of "a point of law" is the same in Scotland as in England and Wales, but there are many different ways of expressing it. In *Murray Group Holdings Ltd v Revenue and Customs Commissioners* [2015] CSIH 77; 2016 S.C. 201, the Inner House of the Court of Session said—

> "[42] Although the concept of appeal on a point of law might seem simple, it has given rise to considerable controversy; indeed in the well-known case of *Edwards* v *Bairstow*, [1956] AC 14, an appeal was taken to the House of Lords to adjudicate upon differences of approach that had developed between the Scottish and English courts. We are of opinion that an appeal on a point of law covers four different categories of case. The first of these categories is appeals on the general law: the content of its rules. In tax appeals these are largely statutory, but the interpretation of a particular statutory provision may be a matter of general law, and tax law also includes a number of general non-statutory rules, such as the redirection principle and the *Ramsay* principle, both of which are relevant to this case. The second category comprises appeals on the application of the law to the facts as found by the First-tier Tribunal. This is in our opinion a clear example of an appeal on a point of law: it is the application of the general rules to particular factual situations that defines the frontiers of a legal rule and thus its practical scope. Furthermore, it is the application of the general rules to particular facts that brings about the development of those rules to meet new situations.

For these reasons we consider that an appeal on the application of the general law to a particular factual situation must be regarded as being on a point of law. This is illustrated by the facts of *Edwards* v *Bairstow*. There the House of Lords, reversing the decisions of the General Commissioners and lower courts, held that a transaction involving the acquisition of spinning plant, dividing it into lots and selling those lots at a profit was an adventure in the nature of trade. In holding otherwise, the Commissioners and the lower courts had misdirected themselves as to the meaning and proper application of the expression "adventure . . . in the nature of trade" found in the relevant taxing statute, the Income Tax Act 1918: see Lord Radcliffe at [1956] AC 36–37.

[43] The third category of appeal on a point of law is where the Tribunal has made a finding "for which there is no evidence or which is inconsistent with the evidence and contradictory of it": *IRC* v *Fraser*, 1942 SC 493, at 497–498, per LP Normand. This runs into a fourth category, comprising cases where the First-tier Tribunal has made a fundamental error in its approach to the case: for example, by asking the wrong question, or by taking account of manifestly irrelevant considerations, or by arriving at a decision that no reasonable tax tribunal could properly reach. In such cases we conceive that the Court of Session and the Upper Tribunal have power to interfere with the decision of the First-tier Tribunal as disclosing an error on a point of law: *Edwards* v *Bairstow*, per Lord Radcliffe at [1956] AC 36."

The Court (whose decision was upheld on appeal to the Supreme Court: *RFC 2012 Plc (formerly The Rangers Football Club Plc) v Advocate General for Scotland* [2017] UKSC 45; [2017] 1 W.L.R. 2767 without reference to these points) also observed that decisions of the First-tier Tribunal relating to tax frequently involve elements of evaluation and judgment and that: "In general, a court, or the Upper Tribunal, should be slow to interfere with the decision of the First-tier Tribunal in cases of this nature." Nonetheless: "It is a matter of degree: the higher the factual component in the evaluative exercise, the slower the court should be to interfere, but correspondingly if the factual component is relatively low and the legal component is high the court may properly interfere."

Although the Court did not draw any distinction between the position of a court and the position of the Upper Tribunal, it is clear that, since one of the reasons why appellate bodies do not interfere is the specialist nature of the First-tier Tribunal, there may be some cases where the Upper Tribunal can properly interfere but an appellate court would not, because the Upper Tribunal may be able to claim as much relevant expertise as the First-tier Tribunal (see below and the annotation to s.13(1) and (2)). This point did not arise for consideration in that case because the Upper Tribunal dismissed the appeal from the First-tier Tribunal and the Court of Session decided that they were both wrong in law.

Challenging findings of fact

3.59 The Court of Appeal's points (i), (iii), (iv) and (vii) and the third and fourth of the Court of Session's points show the limited grounds on which findings of fact may be challenged.

The Court of Appeal emphasised what a demanding concept "perversity" was and so did the Tribunal of Commissioners in *R(I) 2/06*, citing *Murrell v Secretary of State for Social Services* (reported as an appendix to *R(I) 3/84*) in which it was said that an assessment of disablement is perverse only if it is "so wildly wrong that it can be set aside".

In *Yeboah v Crofton* [2002] EWCA Civ 794; [2002] I.R.L.R. 634, Mummery L.J. said that an appeal based on perversity "ought only to succeed where an overwhelming case is made out that the Employment Tribunal reached a decision which no reasonable tribunal, on a proper appreciation of the evidence and the law, would have reached". However, it is clear from the judgment of Irwin J in *British Broadcasting Corporation v Information Commissioner* [2009] EWHC 2348 (Admin) and from the decision of the Court of Appeal in *Department for Work and Pensions v Information Commissioner* [2016] EWCA Civ 758; [2017] 1 W.L.R. 1 that these are merely expressions of the deference that should be paid to the conclusions of a specialist or expert tribunal. In the latter case, Lloyd-Jones L.J. said:

> "34. . . . . Given such expertise in a Tribunal, it is entirely understandable that a reviewing court or Tribunal will be slow to interfere with its findings and evaluation of facts in areas where that expertise has a bearing. This may be regarded not so much as requiring that a different, enhanced standard must be met as an acknowledgement of the reality that an expert Tribunal can normally be expected to apply its expertise in the course of its analysis of facts. It has been described in various ways in the cases. I agree with Irwin J. that the formulation employed by Mummery LJ in *Yeboah* requiring an overwhelming case, may perhaps be the high water mark of this consideration, although the formulation employed by Sir John Donaldson MR in *Murrell* (so wildly wrong as to merit being set aside) would be a close rival."

The other members of the Court agreed with that analysis, although they reached a different conclusion as to the result of the appeal in that particular case. As to the relative expertise of the Upper Tribunal and the First-tier Tribunal, see the observations in *R. (Jones) v First-tier Tribunal* [2013] UKSC 19; [2013] 2 A.C. 48; [2013] AACR 25 and *R. (Hutton) v First-tier Tribunal* [2016] EWCA Civ 1305 to which reference is made in the annotation to s.13(1) and (2) below.

A finding of fact is also perverse if it "was wholly unsupported by any evidence" **3.60** (*Iran*) or it is based on a misunderstanding that "is plain and incontrovertible and where there is no room for difference about it" (*Braintree DC v Thompson* [2005] EWCA Civ 178, a housing benefit case in which the Court of Appeal said that a Deputy Commissioner had not been entitled to substitute his view of the facts for the view of the tribunal). It is particularly difficult to show that a decision is perverse where it required an element of judgment (such as, for instance, whether the claimant was virtually unable to walk). In *Moyna v Secretary of State for Work and Pensions* [2003] UKHL 44, [2003] 1 W.L.R. 1929 (also reported as *R(DLA) 7/03*), Lord Hoffmann, with whom the other members of the House of Lords agreed, said:

> "In any case in which a tribunal has to apply a standard with a greater or lesser degree of imprecision and to take a number of factors into account, there are bound to be cases in which it will be impossible for a reviewing court to say that the tribunal must have erred in deciding the case either way: see *George Mitchell (Chesterhall) Ltd v Finney Lock Seeds Ltd* [1983] 2 A.C. 803, 815–816."

If perversity is not shown, it is usually necessary to show some flaw in the reasoning instead, either because a finding is irrational (i.e. there is something illogical in the reasoning leading to it) or because the tribunal has failed to take into account a relevant matter or has given weight to an irrelevant matter. In order to show that any of these errors has been made, it is necessary to analyse the tribunal's statement of reasons. On the other hand, merely pointing to a different analysis of the evidence from that adopted by the tribunal is not sufficient to show an error of law (*Secretary of State for Work and Pensions v Roach* [2007] EWCA Civ 1746 (reported as *R(CS) 4/07*)). Neither is finding the First-tier Tribunal to have placed too much weight on evidence or a mere disagreement with the First-tier Tribunal's assessment of the evidence, in the absence of a finding that the First-tier Tribunal's decision was irrational (*AE (Iraq) v Secretary of State for the Home Department* [2021] EWCA Civ 948).

One recent decision in which the First-tier Tribunal's reasoning was held to be flawed is *JH v HMRC (TC)* [2015] UKUT 397 (AAC), where the judge said:

> "6. The assessment of the credibility or plausibility of a witness's evidence is primarily a question of fact for the tribunal. In *HK v Secretary of State for the Home*

Department [2006] EWCA Civ 1037 Neuberger LJ said, at [30], that rejection of an account on grounds of implausibility must be done "on reasonably drawn inferences and not simply on conjecture or speculation". In addition, a tribunal may properly draw on its common sense and ability, as practical and informed people, to identify what is or is not plausible.

7. In *Gheisari v Secretary of State for the Home Department* [2004] EWCA Civ 1854 (with which Neuberger LJ agreed) the Court of Appeal emphasised that an account that is unlikely may nonetheless be true, just as a likely account may turn out to be untrue. Faced with an account which a tribunal considers to be improbable, its task is to appraise the evidence and the individual who gave the evidence, and decide whether it is true – *Gheisari* at [12], [13] and [16]. It may not be necessary for a tribunal to carry out a strict two stage test (improbability followed by truth), but:

> 'What would be wrong would be to say . . . . that because evidence is inherently unlikely it inevitably follows that it is wrong. An unlikely description may, upon a consideration of the circumstances as a whole, including the judge's assessments of the witness and any explanations he gives, be a true one.'
>
> (Pill LJ in *Gheisari* at [21])

8. The above discussions were made in the context of asylum appeals, where inherent improbability may be particularly unhelpful because '[m]uch of the evidence is referable to societies with customs and circumstances which are very different from those of which the members of the fact-finding tribunal have any (even second-hand) experience.' (*HK* at [29]). It follows that inherent improbability may be more helpful in cases where the evidence is closer to the experiences of the tribunal, but it will nonetheless only be a component of the overall task which is to decide whether a witness's account did occur not whether it was likely to have occurred. The general approach set out in *HK* and *Gheisari* is apt in cases such as the present. I note that it was followed by the Court of Session Outer House in an appeal concerning a decision relating to the educational needs of a learning disabled child: *G v Argyll and Bute Council* [2008] CSOH 61 at [157].

9. It also follows from this approach that it will generally be inappropriate for a tribunal to appraise evidence by reference to what a reasonable person would have done. The question for the tribunal is what the individual in question is likely to have done, not what some other (hypothetical or actual) person would have done. As both Sedley LJ and Pill LJ said in *Gheisari*, the fact-finder should appraise the person giving the evidence (paragraphs [13] and [21] respectively).

10. Judged by reference to this guidance, the tribunal's decision in the present appeal was made in error of law. The tribunal did not accept the appellant's evidence because it considered that it was improbable. It did so on the basis of what the tribunal would have expected a person in her position to have done, and in one instance the tribunal expressly applied the test of a "reasonable" person in the appellant's position. The tribunal did not, whether as part of a single fact-finding process or by considering the evidence in stages, consider whether the appellant's account was true rather than improbable. Had it done so, the tribunal would have had to consider matters such as the appellant's particular circumstances and her explanation for her actions or those of Mr W, and would have had to assess what it was likely that she or he would have done. Unfortunately, because of the underlying error in the tribunal's approach, in a number of respects it did not ask the appellant to provide an explanation for her actions and choices."

Although tribunals may be found to have erred in the way they have dealt with the evidence before them, Commissioners have pointed out that tribunals cannot be criticised for not taking account of evidence that was not before them at all. In *CDLA/7980/1995*, the Commissioner said that—

> "Finality is another important principle. Parties cannot demand a rehearing simply because, at the original hearing, they failed to adduce the right evidence, failed to ask the right questions or failed to advance the right arguments."

However, the Court of Appeal's point (vii) in the *Iran* case is a limited exception to this approach, derived from *E v Secretary of State for the Home Department* [2004] EWCA Civ 49; [2004] Q.B. 1044 in which the Court of Appeal considered how the general principles for the admission of fresh evidence on appeals, laid down in *Ladd v Marshall* [1954] 1 W.L.R. 1489, should be applied in administrative law cases. The requirements are quite strict: that the evidence that the First-tier Tribunal made a mistake of fact should be "objective and uncontentious", that the mistake should not have been the fault of the relevant party or that party's representative and that the mistake should have caused unfairness. Whether the mistake was the fault of a party or a representative often depends on whether they failed to use "reasonable diligence" in providing evidence to the First-tier Tribunal. Whether the mistake caused unfairness may require consideration of its importance of the mistake to the decision and whether the claimant has an alternative remedy. The context has to be taken into account when considering both these issues. **3.61**

In *DG v SSWP (II)* [2013] UKUT 474 (AAC), it was held that there is no failure of reasonable diligence in obtaining evidence where the evidence was not obtained because the person relying on it had no reason to suppose that the point to which it was directed would be relevant. In that case, the First-tier Tribunal had not believed the claimant when she said that she had broken her wrist and consequently thought she was exaggerating her symptoms. Her appeal to the Upper Tribunal was allowed in the light of x-ray evidence showing clearly that she had broken her wrist.

The Court of Appeal has also warned against undue consideration of a claimant's fault in a social security context. In *Hussain v Secretary of State for Work and Pensions* [2016] EWCA Civ 1428, Bean L.J. with whom Tomlinson and Floyd L.JJ. agreed, said:

> "27. There are cases in which an over strict application of the first principle against a party who appeared without representation, as Mr Hussain did in the First-tier Tribunal, can be contrary to the overriding objective of dealing with cases justly. I prefer, therefore, rather than asking whether a consultant's report could have been obtained with reasonable diligence before the hearing in the FTT, to concentrate on the question of whether it would have been potentially decisive in Mr Hussain's favour or at least have had an important influence on the result of the appeal. . . ."

In that case, the claimant was unsuccessful because the report did not address issues relevant to the case and so did not "call into question" the decision that the First-tier Tribunal had upheld, but an appeal succeeded in *JW v Governing Body of Sinai Jewish Primary School (SEN)* [2019] UKUT 88 (AAC) where the First-tier Tribunal had relied on a statement about the respondent school's financial position, made in the school's response to the claim, that had "been shown not to have been entirely accurate by uncontentious evidence that the Appellants could not reasonably have been expected to find before the hearing of their case by the First-tier Tribunal".

An appeal also succeeded in *PR v SSWP (PIP)* [2021] UKUT 35 (AAC), where the Upper Tribunal accepted that evidence from Google Maps showed that the First-tier Tribunal had erred when assessing the distance that the claimant could walk.

In *SM v SSWP (II)* [2020] UKUT 287 (AAC), the First-tier Tribunal dismissed **3.62** the claimant's appeal on the ground that she could not be suffering from carpal tunnel syndrome because her condition affected her ring finger and the median nerve, which passes through the carpal tunnel, does not, it said, serve the ring finger. On the claimant's further appeal to the Upper Tribunal, the Secretary of State conceded that the appeal should be allowed because the median nerve does in fact serve the ring finger. The judge observed that the *Ladd v Marshall* principles were concerned with the admissibility of evidence in adversarial proceedings, whereas there had been no mention of the median nerve in the evidence before the First-tier Tribunal and the error was entirely that of the First-tier Tribunal, acting inquisitorially with a medical practitioner among its members. He concluded that—

> "45. . . . the *Ladd v Marshall* principles do not apply where, in the exercise of an inquisitorial jurisdiction and enabling role—and/or in reliance on the expertise or experience of a specialist member—a tribunal misdirects itself as to an uncontentious and primary fact on which there was no evidence before it.
>
> 46. Making such an error is simply one of a number of ways in which a tribunal might fail to exercise its inquisitorial jurisdiction and enabling role correctly. The Upper Tribunal is entitled to raise the issue, and either party to the appeal is entitled to seek to prove that the Tribunal has gone astray, by the same mechanisms—including the provision of relevant additional evidence—as would be the case with any other procedural lapse.
>
> 47. By basing its decision in this appeal on the mistaken premise that the Median nerve does not supply the ring finger, the First-tier Tribunal failed to exercise its enabling role correctly. On the contrary, it hindered the proper presentation of the claimant's case by setting up an obstacle of which she was unaware and which had no basis in fact. . ."

The same result could perhaps have been reached on the ground that the First-tier Tribunal's decision was perverse (see above).

Where neither the conditions for the Court of Appeal's point (vii) nor the conditions for the traditional grounds identified in points (i), (iii) and (iv) are met, the only remedy for a mistake of fact made by the First-tier Tribunal is an application for supersession under reg.6(2)(c) of the Social Security and Child Support (Decisions and Appeals) Regulations 1999, reg.13(2)(c) of the Child Benefit and Guardian's Allowance (Decisions and Appeals) Regulations 2003 or reg.31(a) of the Universal Credit, Personal Independence Payment, Jobseeker's Allowance and Employment and Support Allowance (Decisions and Appeals) Regulations 2013. The value of that remedy may be limited by the date from which any such supersession can be effective.

Challenging misdirections of law

3.63 It is much more obvious that a misdirection of law (e.g. the tribunal misunderstanding or overlooking a regulation or making a mistake about the law of property), the Court of Appeal's point (v) in the *Iran* case, is an error of law. It is also a misdirection of law for the First-tier Tribunal to act in excess of its jurisdiction (*Secretary of State for the Home Department v VM (Jamaica)* [2017] EWCA Civ 255) or to rely upon a regulation that is ultra vires (*Foster v Chief Adjudication Officer* [1993] A.C. 754 (also reported as *R(IS) 22/93*)), including on procedural grounds (*Howker v Secretary of State for Work and Pensions* [2002] EWCA Civ 1623 (reported as *R(IB) 3/03*), or has been declared unlawful in judicial review proceedings, provided that the declaration relates to the relevant period (*JN v SSWP (UC)* [2023] UKUT 49 (AAC); [2023] AACR 7).

In *VL v SSWP (IS)* [2011] UKUT 227 (AAC); [2012] AACR 10, it was held that the Upper Tribunal has the power to find subordinate legislation to be invalid not only if it is made beyond the powers conferred by the enabling legislation but also if it conflicts with statutory rights already conferred by other primary legislation. However, it was pointed out that there is only a conflict in cases where there is no other reasonable way to exercise such statutory rights. On one analysis, this is all a question of construction of the enabling power, which can be said to be qualified by the other primary legislation.

It was also reaffirmed in *VL v SSWP (IS)* that the Upper Tribunal may admit arguments under the European Convention on Human Rights notwithstanding that they have not been raised before the First-tier Tribunal. The judge gave short shrift to arguments based on s.12(8)(a) of the Social Security Act 1998 and the practice of the Court of Appeal on appeals from specialist tribunals, pointing out as regards the latter that the Upper Tribunal is itself a specialist tribunal in respect of social security law and probably more so than the First-tier Tribunal which deals mainly with issues of fact and evidence and rarely has the benefit of submissions by legally qualified representatives.

In an appeal brought on human rights grounds, it has been held that the question for an appellate court is not whether a lower court of tribunal has directed itself correctly but whether there has been a breach of the European Convention on Human Rights (*Belfast CC v Miss Behavin' Ltd* [2007] UKHL 19; [2007] 1 W.L.R. 1420). This has to be read in the light of *In re B (a child) (Care Proceedings: Threshold Criteria)* [2013] UKSC 33; [2013] 1 W.L.R. 1911, where Lord Neuberger of Abbotsbury PSC said that "the court system as a whole must fairly determine for itself whether the requirement of proportionality is met, but that does not mean that each court up the appeal chain does so", and see also *R. (Z) Hackney LBC* [2020] UKSC 40; [2020] 1 W.L.R. 4327, although new (e.g., more up-to-date) evidence may be admitted (*R. (Friends of Antique Cultural Treasures Ltd) v Secretary of State for the Environment* [2020] EWCA Civ 649; [2020] 1 W.L.R. 3876). It is necessary for the Upper Tribunal, whether on an appeal under this section or in judicial review proceedings against a decision of the First-tier Tribunal, to be satisfied that there has been a "public law flaw" in the decision of the First-tier Tribunal (*R. (MP) v First-tier Tribunal (CIC)* [2022] UKUT 91 (AAC)), but whether this requires the Upper Tribunal to make its own assessment of proportionality or whether it is confined to considering whether the First-tier Tribunal has properly considered the issue depends on the nature of the case. If the issue is the construction to be put on legislation, including whether subordinate legislation is compatible with the Convention (which was the issue in *MP*), the Upper Tribunal must form its own view, because whether there was an error of law depends on whether the First-tier Tribunal misdirected itself in law and there can only be one correct answer. However, if the issue is whether the First-tier Tribunal has erred on a question of judgement when applying the legislation, rather than construing it, and there might have been two or more permissible answers, the Upper Tribunal must be satisfied that there was some other error of law in the First-tier Tribunal's decision and it is not enough that it would have reached a different conclusion (*PE (Peru) v Secretary of State for the Home Department* [2011] EWCA Civ 274, cited in *MP*, and, more recently, *re H-W (Children)* [2022] UKSC 17; [2022] 1 W.L.R. 3243). This distinction may not be all that important in practice in the social security context because any argument before the First-tier Tribunal is likely to have been fairly limited and so it may be fairly easy to show that it has not had adequate regard to all material considerations. **3.64**

However, there are limits to the extent to which the Upper Tribunal can provide a remedy where subordinate legislation is invalid. It was held in *TS (by TS) v SSWP (DLA)* [2020] UKUT 284 (AAC) that procedural grounds for challenging subordinate legislation in tribunals do not extend to alleged failures of a legislator to comply with the public sector equality duty imposed by s.149(1) of the Equality Act 2010, because s.113 of that Act has the effect of ousting the jurisdiction of tribunals in relation to contraventions of the Act except when the Upper Tribunal is exercising its judicial review jurisdiction or when express provision has been made (e.g., by Sch.17 to the Act which confers jurisdiction on the First-tier Tribunal in relation to disability discrimination in schools).

Moreover, even in a case where a provision in subordinate legislation is held to be invalid either because it is outside the scope of the enabling power or because it is incompatible with the claimant's convention rights, if the claimant's claim depends on part of the relevant instrument being valid and the invalid part is not "substantially severable" from the rest of the instrument, a tribunal or court may be unable to provide a remedy (see the note to s.12 below).

The Upper Tribunal declined to find there to have been an error of law where, on an appeal by the Secretary of State, both parties agreed that there had been a technical error by the First-tier Tribunal in the light of *R(PC) 1/07* but the judge considered that a carefully negotiated settlement reached before *R(PC) 1/07* was decided should not be set at naught, that there was arguably not a "clear error of law" and that the calculation in issue was in any event based on broad brush figures (*SSWP v DL (SPC)* [2013] UKUT 29 (AAC); [2013] AACR 22). The judge considered the alternative approach of finding there to be an error of law but declining to set aside the First-tier Tribunal's decision (see s.12(2)(a)), which would presumably have had the same practical effect, but rejected it.

Inadequate reasons

3.65 The standard of reasoning required from tribunals by the Court of Appeal's point (ii) and the requirement to resolve conflicts (see point (iii)) is considered in detail in the note to r.34 of the Tribunal Procedure (First-tier Tribunal) (Social Entitlement Chamber) Rules 2008. The reasons should be sufficient to avoid "substantial doubt as to whether the [tribunal] erred in law" on any of the other grounds identified in the *Iran* case, but they "need refer only to the main issues in the dispute, not to every consideration" (*South Bucks DC v Porter (No.2)* [2004] UKHL 33; [2004] 1 W.L.R. 1953 at [36]. In the *Iran* case itself, the Court of Appeal referred to *Eagil Trust Co Ltd v Pigott-Brown* [1985] 3 All E.R. 119, 122, where Griffiths L.J. said that, "if it be that the judge has not dealt with a particular argument but it can be seen that there are grounds on which he would have been entitled to reject it, this court should assume that he acted on those grounds unless the appellant can point to convincing reasons leading to a contrary conclusion."

Procedural and other irregularities

3.66 Whether a breach of procedural rules renders a decision invalid or erroneous in point of law is to be determined by considering whether the legislature intended that to be the effect of such a breach (*R(DLA) 3/08*, and *JM v SSWP (ESA)* [2013] UKUT 234; [2014] AACR 5, both citing *R. v Soneji* [2005] UKHL 49; [2006] 1 A.C. 340). Therefore, not every procedural error entitles a party to have a decision set aside on appeal. It largely depends on whether there was any unfairness as a result of the breach. This is point (vi) in the *Iran* case.

The old distinction between "mandatory" and "directory" requirements is no longer regarded as helpful. Instead, it is necessary to consider the language of the legislation and the legislator's intention against the factual situation and seek to do what is just in all the circumstances. This involves considering whether the procedural requirement is satisfied by "substantial" compliance with it and, if so, whether there has in fact been such substantial compliance or whether non-compliance had been waived. If there has not been sufficient compliance and non-compliance has not been waived, consideration should also be given to the intended consequence of non-compliance because it does not necessarily follow from an applicant's failure to comply with a procedural requirement that the application is a nullity (*R. v Secretary of State for the Home Department, Ex p. Jeyeanthan* [2000] 1 W.L.R. 354).

In *North Somerset DC v Honda Motor Europe Ltd* [2010] EWHC 1505 (QB), Burnett J. (as he then was) said:

> "43. It is clear from the analysis in *Soneji* that in any case concerning the consequences of a failure to comply with a statutory time limit, there are potentially two stages in the inquiry. The first is to ask the question identified by Lord Steyn: did Parliament intend total invalidity to result from failure to comply with the statutory requirement? If the answer to that question is 'yes', then no further question arises. Yet if the answer is 'no' a further question arises: despite invalidity not being the inevitable consequence of a failure to comply with a statutory requirement, does it nonetheless have that consequence in the circumstances of the given case and, if so, on what basis? It is at this second stage that the concept of substantial compliance may yet have a bearing on the outcome."

That approach was endorsed and adopted by the Court of Appeal in *Secretary of State for the Home Department v SM (Rwanda)* [2018] EWCA Civ 2770 at [44], where Haddon-Cave L.J. said:

> "... Burnett J's two-stage approach ... , in my view, is applicable in all administrative law cases where questions of statutory construction and validity arise. His two-stage and structured approach has the benefit of (a) giving appropriate primacy to the actual words used by Parliament and (b) ensuring, if necessary, careful consideration is given to the consequences of non-compliance when determining validity."

Consideration must therefore be given to whether the breach of procedural rules might have made any difference to the decision of the tribunal or whether a party to the proceedings has lost anything (such as the opportunity of advancing a particular argument on appeal) as a result of the breach, so that a rehearing is the only way of remedying the breach. For this reason, a breach of a requirement to keep a record of proceedings will render a decision of a tribunal erroneous in point of law if the lack of a record of proceedings makes it difficult to determine whether or not the tribunal has provided an adequate statement of reasons (*R(DLA) 3/08*). On the other hand, a failure to provide any summary of reasons in a decision notice will not render the decision erroneous in point of law because the remedy is to apply for a full statement of reasons (*CIB/4497/1998*). The most commonly relied upon breach is a breach of the statutory duty to give reasons for a decision (see the note to r.34 of the Tribunal Procedure (First-tier Tribunal) (Social Entitlement Chamber) Rules 2008), although this is considered in the *Iran* case to be an entirely separate type of error of law, perhaps because there would be a common law duty to give reasons even if the legislation imposed no duty.

Rules of natural justice

When considering breaches of procedural rules, fairness is judged by reference to the three "rules of natural justice", which are that (a) every party should have a proper opportunity to present his or her case, (b) that there should be no bias and (c) that a decision should be based on the evidence. Even where there is no breach of a statutory provision, breach of the rules of natural justice will amount to at least an irregularity. The scope of the rules is fairly broad but it has nonetheless been suggested that judges ought to express their decisions in terms of the parties' right to a fair hearing under art.6(1) of the European Convention on Human Rights rather than in terms of the rules of natural justice which are apt to be misunderstood (*CJSA/5100/2001* and the linked cases *CIB/2751/2002 and CS/3202/2002*) even if the practical differences are not great. In *CSDLA/773/2004*, the judge disagreed and said that the issue was whether there had been a breach of the rules of natural justice and that any assertion that a convention right had been breached had to be raised as a separate issue. It is suggested that that goes too far in the opposite direction and that, while a tribunal is entitled to focus on the common law questions, those questions must now be considered in the light of art.6 of the Convention. Indeed, the Court of Appeal has doubted that the standard of fairness set by the common law is any weaker than that set by art.6 (*R. (Maftah) v Secretary of State for Foreign and Commonwealth Affairs* [2011] EWCA Civ 350; [2012] Q.B. 477). **3.67**

a) proper opportunity to present their case.

In *R. v Secretary of State for the Home Department, Ex p. Al-Mehdawi* [1990] 1 A.C. **3.68**
876 it was said to be incorrect to state simply that a party to a dispute who has not been heard through no fault of his own has been denied justice. In that case, notice of the hearing had been given to the party's solicitors but they had wrongly addressed their letter telling the party of the hearing. Although the House of Lords accepted that a decision of a tribunal may be erroneous in point of law where the tribunal has been entirely blameless but there had been some fault on the part of the other party, they held that there was no error of law in that case because the solicitors had had notice. Service on a solicitor was also treated as service on a claimant in *Tkachuk v Secretary of State for Work and Pensions* [2007] EWCA Civ 515 (reported as *R(IS) 3/07*). However, in social security cases, notices of hearings and decisions are usually sent both to the claimant and any representative. In *CCS/6302/1999*, a

decision was set aside because a party had not received notice of the appeal due to the Child Support Agency failing to tell the clerk to the tribunal of his change of address. In *CIB/5227/1999*, the claimant simply did not receive the letter from the clerk inviting him to seek an oral hearing and there was no fault on the part of either the tribunal or the Benefits Agency. The Commissioner distinguished *Al-Mehdawi* and did not base his decision to allow the appeal on there having been any fault of anyone (although presumably the failure of the letter to arrive was attributable to someone). He just said that there had been a fundamental unfairness about the proceedings before the tribunal. That was not so in *CIB/4533/1999*, where the claimant's representative had not been sent notice of the hearing but notice was sent to the claimant, who made a mistake about the date and appeared three days late. It was held that the claimant had not been denied a hearing, notwithstanding the lack of notice to his representative, and his appeal to the Commissioner was dismissed.

The rule that a party must have a proper opportunity to present their case is interpreted in a practical sense. Thus, a party was denied that right where he was misled by an official leaflet into thinking that a request for a postponement would be granted without it being necessary to give reasons for the request (*GC v SSWP (ESA)* [2014] UKUT 224 (AAC)) and also where the First-tier Tribunal proceeded to hear a case even though the claimant's representative had been unable to obtain instructions because the claimant was in prison (*JM v SSD (WP)* [2014] UKUT 358 (AAC); [2015] AACR 7). However, it is not necessarily a breach of the rules of natural justice for a tribunal to cite authoritative decisions that were not mentioned during the course of the proceedings before the tribunal. The question is whether the proceedings were unfair and that depends on whether it might reasonably be considered that the case has been decided on a basis that could not have been anticipated by the parties so that they did not have a proper opportunity of addressing the tribunal on the relevant issues (*Sheridan v Stanley Cole (Wainfleet) Ltd* [2003] EWCA Civ 1046; [2003] 4 All E.R. 1181). A judge is not entitled to decide an appeal on a basis contrary to that on which it has been argued without giving the parties an opportunity to comment (*Sayce v TNT (UK) Ltd* [2011] EWCA Civ 1583; [2012] 1 W.L.R. 1261). It is not usually necessary to give a party an opportunity to comment on the tribunal's initial impressions derived from its observations of a party's demeanour or on the inferences it draws from the evidence (*CC v SSWP (ESA)* [2019] UKUT 14 (AAC)), but it may be if they raise a new point that the party could not reasonably have anticipated (*KH (by CH) v SSWP (DLA)* [2022] UKUT 303 (AAC), where the First-tier Tribunal erred in not giving a child's father an opportunity to comment on its thoughts as to how her night-time attention needs might be reduced).

b) bias

3.69 The rule against bias was considered in detail in *Locabail (UK) Ltd v Bayfield Properties Ltd* [1999] EWCA Civ 3004; [2000] Q.B. 451. It has the effect that, where a member of a tribunal has any direct personal interest, apart from the most trivial, in the outcome of proceedings, they are automatically disqualified from hearing the case, irrespective of their knowledge of the interest. In cases where there is no direct personal interest, the question is whether the circumstances would lead a fair-minded and informed observer to conclude that there was a real possibility that the tribunal was biased, in the sense that the tribunal member might unfairly regard with favour or disfavour a party in the proceedings (*Magill v Porter* [2001] UKHL 67; [2002] 2 A.C. 357) and, on appeal, it will be relevant whether the tribunal member knew of the connection with the party because, if he or she did not, no favour or disfavour would have been shown. It was stressed in *CS/1753/2000* that the issue was whether there was a likelihood of bias, not whether there was actual bias. Appearances are therefore important and a decision may be set aside if a tribunal member gives the appearance of having fallen asleep (*Stansbury v Datapulse* [2003] EWCA Civ 1951; [2004] I.C.R. 523) but, in *Locobail* itself, it was stressed that "[t]he mere fact that a judge, earlier in the same case or in a previous case, had commented adversely on a party or witness, or found the evidence of a party or witness to be unreliable, would not without more found a sustainable objection". A judge is not precluded from hearing an appeal merely because he or she refused permission to appeal on the papers before another judge gave permission at a hearing (*Broughal v Walsh Brothers Builders Ltd* [2018] EWCA Civ 1610; [2018] 1 W.L.R. 5781). Judicial continuity may be positively desirable where the same factual issues arise in two separate cases and is permissible provided the tribunal approaches the second case with an open mind. Thus, it is not unlawful for the question whether an overpayment has arisen and is recoverable to be determined by a tribunal with the same constitution as one that has previously decided that the claimant was not entitled to benefit during the period in issue (*R(IS) 1/09*), applying *AMEC Capital Projects Ltd v Whitefriars City Estates Ltd* [2004] EWCA 1418; [2005] 1 All E.R. 723). On the other hand, in *CCS/1876/2006*, the Commissioner made the point that the mere fact that a tribunal chairman is not bound to recuse himself when he has previously decided a case against a party before him does not mean that he is not entitled to arrange for the appeal to be heard by another chairman if he considers it desirable do so in order to strengthen the party's confidence in the fairness of the procedures and if undue expense will not be involved. See also *KU v Bradford MBC* [2009] UKUT 15 (AAC), where the authorities are considered in some detail.

In *Zuma's Choice Pet Products Ltd v Azumi Ltd* [2017] EWCA Civ 2133, it was emphasised that, in considering whether there had been an appearance of bias, it was necessary to consider all of the appellant's allegations together, rather than to consider them individually and conclude that, merely because there was nothing in them individually, there could be nothing in them in combination. It was also held that the fact that a part-time judge was a barrister in the same chambers as an advocate appearing before him did not necessarily give rise to an appearance of bias. In *Lawal v Northern Spirit Ltd* [2003] UKHL 35; [2003] I.C.R. 856, the House of Lords held there to have been apparent bias where a party was represented by a barrister who had previously sat as a part-time judge with lay members of the Employment Appeal Tribunal before whom he was appearing. *Lawal* was followed in *Secretary of State for Work and Pensions v Cunningham* [2004] S.L.T. 1007 (also reported as *R(DLA) 7/04*), where a tribunal had relied on a medical report by an examining medical practitioner with whom two members of the tribunal had sat previously and the Court of Session held there had been apparent bias. On the other hand, in *Gillies v Secretary of State for Work and Pensions* [2006] UKHL 2; [2006] 1 W.L.R. 781, it was held by the House of Lords that there was no appearance of bias merely because a member of a tribunal also acted as an examining medical practitioner for the Secretary of State. (For further discussion of *Cunningham* and *Gillies*, see the note to s.3(3).) A long-standing personal friendship with a witness will also give rise to an appearance of bias and a judge was wrong to take into account the inconvenience to the parties in having to adjourn when he refused to recuse himself. "There was either a real possibility of bias, in which case the judge was disqualified by the principle of judicial impartiality, or there was not, in which case there was no valid objection to trial by him." (*AWG Group Ltd v Morrison* [2006] EWCA Civ 6; [2006] 1 W.L.R. 1163 at [20]). The fact that a judge has recused herself does not necessarily undermine findings of fact made by that judge at an earlier stage of the proceedings: see *W (Children: Reopening/Recusal)* [2020] EWCA Civ 1685, where the judge had recused herself administratively because she had discovered that her son was an acquaintance of a party to the proceedings but had not been aware of that connection when she made her findings of fact. The Court also said that, once the judge had decided to withdraw from the case on the basis of recusal, she should have ensured that the parties were formally notified of her reason for withdrawing.

In *Aspect Windows (Western) Limited v Adam Retter (as representative of the Estate of Mrs C McCorie* [2023] EAT 95 following the promulgation of the decision of the Employment Tribunal arising from a full merits hearing, one of the lay members of the tribunal posted on her LinkedIn page, a link to a report about the decision in the Mail Online. Followers of hers then responded on LinkedIn and she responded to them. The unsuccessful respondent in the employment tribunal appealed on the basis that the LinkedIn posts gave rise to apparent bias against it. Having regard to the particular content of the posts, and applying the guidance in *Magill v Porter* [2001] UKHL 67 and other pertinent authorities, the Employment Appeal Tribunal concluded that, whatever else they might make of the wisdom or appropriateness of posting the link in the first place, the fair-minded and informed observer, having considered the contents of the post, would not in all the circumstances consider that the tribunal member was biased.

Friendship or a past professional relationship with an advocate will not generally give rise to an appearance of bias but a close personal relationship might. The former absolute prohibition on a judge sitting in a case where an advocate is in a close personal relationship with the judge or lives in the judge's household has been removed from the *Guide to Judicial Conduct* for England and Wales and the similar prohibition has been removed from the *Statement of Principles of Judicial Ethics for the Scottish Judiciary*, but clearly it will rarely be appropriate. In *SW v SSWP (IB)* [2010] UKUT 73 (AAC), an argument that there was an appearance of bias was rejected in so far as it was based on the judge knowing the claimant's representative and having previously employed her but was accepted in so far as it was based on the judge having previously been a partner in a solicitors' firm that was still acting for the claimant in respect of a claim for criminal injuries compensation arising out of the same disabilities that gave rise to the claim for incapacity benefit that was before the judge. Moreover, in *RD v SSD (WP)* [2019] UKUT 206 (AAC), it was held that there had been apparent bias where the chairman of a Pensions Appeal Tribunal in Scotland was a solicitor who had been representing the claimant's daughter in a medical negligence case, even though he had been unaware of the connection when the Pensions Appeal Tribunal gave its decision. However, there was no apparent bias where a witness had been the judge's research supervisor at university 30 years earlier (*Resolution Chemicals Ltd v H Lundbeck A/S* [2013] EWCA Civ 1515; [2014] 1 W.L.R. 1943). A judge is not normally assumed to endorse all the views expressed in publications of an organisation of which she or he is a member and so is not to be regarded as tainted by the views of other members of the organisation, provided the organisation's published aims and objectives are in themselves unobjectionable (*Helow v Advocate General for Scotland* [2008] UKHL 62; [2008] 1 W.L.R. 2416).

A party can waive the right to object to the lack of independence of a member of a tribunal but any such waiver must be voluntary, informed and unequivocal (*Millar v Dickson* [2001] UKPC D4; [2002] 1 W.L.R. 1615). However, in *CSDLA/ 444/2002*, it was pointed out, referring to *CS/343/1994* and *CDLA/2050/2002*, that, if objection to the constitution of a tribunal is not taken *before* a hearing, a party does run a substantial risk of being taken to have waived the right to object. It may be relevant whether the claimant was represented or had legal representation. The claimant in *CS/343/1994* was represented (see *KM v SSWP (CSM)* [2019] UKUT 48 at [4]) and in *CDLA/2050/2002* the Commissioner did not need to decide whether or not there had been unfairness and did not so. It was held that the claimant in *CSDLA/444/2002* had not waived the right to object to the members of the tribunal. Although her lay representative had been aware of a relevant decision of a Tribunal of Commissioners on the point, she could not have been expected fully to understand the legal issues involved. The Court of Session did not consider the question of waiver when dismissing the appeal against the Commissioner's decision (*Cunningham* (see above)) but the Commissioner's approach was entirely consistent with that more recently taken by the Court of Appeal when a party delayed asking the judge who had committed him to prison for contempt of court to recuse himself from trying the main actions (*JSC BTA Bank v Ablyazov (No.9)* [2012] EWCA Civ 1551; [2013] 1 W.L.R. 1845).

c) Decision based on the evidence

3.70 Even though there is no breach of the rules of natural justice if a member of a tribunal absents themselves while a witness is giving oral evidence and later returns to participate in the decision, provided the parties have agreed to that procedure and the agreement is voluntary, informed and unequivocal, the First-tier Tribunal is not entitled to adopt such a procedure even with the consent of the parties because to do so would be inconsistent with paragraph 15(6) of Sch.4 to this Act (*Shipton v IC* [2023] UKUT 170 (AAC), distinguishing *R. (Hill) v Institute of Chartered Accountants in England and Wales* [2013] EWCA Civ 555; [2014] 1 W.L.R. 86). What the tribunal should do if a member is unable to be present throughout the hearing is ask the parties whether they give consent under para.15(6) to the case being *decided* in the absence of that member.

A tribunal may legitimately give assistance to the parties by telling them what it thinks of the evidence it has heard so far, but it may not form, or give the impression of having formed, a firm view in favour of one side's credibility when the other side has not yet called its evidence on the relevant point. To do so suggests bias. However, again, where there is such a manifestation of bias, attention should be drawn to it straightaway, because the Upper Tribunal or a court may not look favourably on an allegation of bias if the dissatisfied party has taken his or her chance on the outcome of the case and found it unwelcome (*Amjad v Steadman-Byrne* [2007] EWCA Civ 625; [2007] 1 W.L.R. 2484). Where a member of a tribunal makes it clear through comments or body language that he or she is unimpressed by evidence that is being given, that may be a rational reaction to the evidence even though it may be discourteous or even intemperate. In those circumstances, it does not show that the tribunal member had a closed mind or was biased, with the result that the tribunal's decision is not vitiated (*Ross v Micro Focus Ltd* UKEAT/304/09).

In *MB v Barnet, Enfield and Haringey Mental Health NHS Trust* [2011] UKUT 328 (AAC), a hearing was held to be unfair where, without giving the applicant's counsel an opportunity to comment, the presiding judge effectively told the applicant that his case was hopeless and that he should withdraw it in order to preserve a right to make another application. It was held that, although the judge was trying to be helpful, "he went far too far" and it was suggested that he "could have put the matter more tentatively and helpfully". The Upper Tribunal referred to *R. (S) v Mental Health Review Tribunal* [2002] EWHC 2522 (Admin), where Stanley Burnton J. held that there was an absence of impartiality where a member of a tribunal "expresses himself in such a way as to give rise to a reasonable apprehension that he has a preconceived concluded opinion". However, it seems unlikely that the appeal to the Upper Tribunal in *MB* would have been allowed had the Upper Tribunal not considered that the judge might, on the facts of the case, have been wrong in his assessment of the advantage to the applicant in withdrawing. The case was distinguished in *GB v SW London & St George's Mental Health NHS Trust* [2013] UKUT 58 (AAC) in which it was pointed out that whether unfairness arose from the way in which an indication had been given depended very much on the particular circumstances of the case. A similar approach was taken in *KMN v SSWP (PIP)* [2019] UKUT 42 (AAC), where the Upper Tribunal gave detailed guidance as to the giving of preliminary indications in social security cases, including that it should be made very clear that they are provisional and that the term "offer" should not be used. However, when the claimant had rejected the proposed decision and there had been a full hearing, the First-tier Tribunal had been entitled to change its mind and to make a decision less favourable to the claimant than the one it had originally suggested. Although the Upper Tribunal commented that the claimant might reasonably have thought that, in the light of the terms in which the indication had been given, certain aspects of the case were no longer in issue and that it might therefore have been good practice for the First-tier Tribunal to warn the claimant that it was minded to resile from its indication, it ultimately allowed the claimant's appeal on the ground that the First-tier Tribunal had erred in not adequately explaining why it had changed its mind.

In *JG v Kent and Medway NHS & Social Care Partnership Trust* [2019] UKUT 187 (AAC), the First-tier Tribunal judge presiding at the hearing of the appellant's appeal against his detention under s.3 of the Mental Health Act 1983 informed the parties at the commencement of the hearing that he had accessed the Court of Appeal's judgment dismissing the Crown's appeal against a ruling that the appellant had no case to answer on a charge of murder but said that this would not affect his risk assessment in the case and he had merely accessed the judgment to ascertain the sequence of events prior to the appellant's detention. The appellant, who was legally represented, did not ask the judge to recuse himself and his appeal to the First-tier Tribunal was dismissed. The Upper Tribunal held, first and perhaps controversially, that the judge's research had amounted to a procedural irregularity but, secondly, that "the fair-minded observer would be likely to conclude that there is no real possibility of bias arising from the judge having accessed the Court of Appeal judgment" and it also rejected, as "simply not sustainable", an argument that the judge should be presumed to have been biased because it was to be inferred that he had accessed the judgment in order to bolster the case against the appellant.

In *MH v SSWP (ESA)* [2021] UKUT 90 (AAC), it was held not to be inappropriate for the Secretary of State to inform the First-tier Tribunal of an incident of unacceptable behaviour on the part of a claimant, without the information being revealed to the claimant, because it was relevant to the tribunal's security, but it was a breach of the rules of natural justice for the First-tier Tribunal then to rely on that information as part of its reasons for dismissing the claimant's appeal. As the Upper Tribunal pointed out, this does raise the question whether the information ought in fact to have been included in the Secretary of State's response to the appeal in that case and so shown to the clamant, given that, unusually, it was potentially relevant to the issues in the appeal. Even if not relied upon, it was arguably prejudicial information.

It was stated in *Midland Container Logistics Ltd* [2020] UKUT 5 (AAC) at [50] that "there is no procedural unfairness or lack of transparency in two or more judicial office holders considering together how to approach a particular issue so as to ensure consistency [as regards the imposition of penalties]". On the other hand, in *SW v SSWP (ESA)* [2019] UKUT 415 (AAC), where a case listed for a "paper hearing" was adjourned to give the claimant an opportunity to appear and the same judge sat on both occasions but with different medically-qualified panel members, it was said that "[w]here a judge has discussed the facts with one panel member who is not on the final panel … but actually makes a decision after discussion with a different panel member … then, in the absence of clear evidence to the contrary, it cannot be excluded from possibility that the judge remains influenced by views expressed by the member who did not sit on the final panel, and this is a breach of fair procedure". It was suggested in an earlier edition of this book that the former approach was to be preferred and that it is no more unfair for a judge to discuss a case with a colleague than it is for a judge to carry out legal research in a text book, provided that, if a new point occurs to the judge as a result of the discussions, the parties are given an opportunity to comment on it. However, in *PD v SSWP (PIP)* [2021] UKUT 172 (AAC) at [59] to [60], it was held that that was all very well if what was discussed was a purely legal point, but not if the conversation involved discussing evidence that was not gained in the current proceedings. Where a case is adjourned after oral evidence has been given, it is necessary for a panel to have the same composition or be entirely differently composed, but that is not because the panel will have discussed the case among themselves but because if, say, the judge then sits with a different member on another occasion, he or she may be influenced by having heard evidence that the other member has not heard (*R(U) 3/88; CDLA/2429/2004*). All the members of the tribunal should determine the case on the basis of the same evidence. There is generally no contravention of that principle if the first consideration of the case was entirely on the papers, as it was in *SW*. In *PD*, however, where a case had to be adjourned because the medically-qualified panel member had previously examined the claimant and therefore recused himself but the panel nonetheless formed a view adverse to the claimant and issued directions on that basis, showing that they had discussed the merits of the case and might have been influenced by the medically-qualified member's prior knowledge of the claimant, the judge and other member ought also to have recused themselves so that the adjourned case would be heard by an entirely different panel in accordance with *R(U)* 3/88. In *GT v SSWP (PIP)* [2023] UKUT 58 (AAC), the First-tier Tribunal recorded that the "Duty District Judge (DDJ) was consulted by the Tribunal in order to ensure that the correct decision was made. The DDJ confirmed that the Tribunal could decide, on the balance of probabilities, at what point the symptoms of meningioma manifested and backdate the award accordingly." The Upper Tribunal set the decision aside on the ground that its language "gives the clear impression the First-tier Tribunal was in effect abdicating responsibility for deciding a key issue in the case and contracting out the determination of that issue to the Duty District Judge", in breach of the principle of judicial independence and the rules of natural justice.

Claims that there has been a breach of the rules of natural justice need to be particularised – i.e., the details of what is alleged need to be spelled out clearly – and, if they are, the Upper Tribunal will admit evidence to prove them (*R(M) 1/89*). The need to obtain proper evidence as to what occurred at the hearing from those who were present has been reiterated in *Singh v Secretary of State for the Home Department* [2016] EWCA Civ 492. In particular, the Upper Tribunal will usually obtain statements from members of the First-tier Tribunal, unless the appellant's case is clearly contradicted by, or is adequately supported by, other evidence such as a full record of proceedings (which the Upper Tribunal will be slow to go behind if it contradicts the appellant's case (*CS/343/1994*)) and, even if the allegation appears to be supported by other evidence, the members will be given an opportunity to comment if allegations of personal misconduct are made (*CDLA/5574/2002*). However, where an allegation of unfairness is based entirely on what was said and, perhaps, how it was said, it may be inappropriate to ask for comments if there is a recording or full transcript (*Serafin v Malkiewicz (Media Lawyers Association intervening)* [2020] UKSC 23; [2020] 1 W.L.R. 2455 at [45]). Having listened to a recording in *GJ v SSWP (PIP)* [2022] UKUT 349 (AAC), where it was alleged that questioning by a member of the First-tier Tribunal had been oppressive, the Upper Tribunal concluded that the questioning had, on the contrary, been "in an entirely appropriate inquisitorial style which cannot fairly be described as 'cross-examination' or 'oppressive questioning'".

The materiality of errors

In the *Iran* case, the Court of Appeal stressed the point that only "material" errors of law are important. An error is not material only if the tribunal "would have been *bound* to have reached the same conclusion, notwithstanding the error of law", given findings it made that are not tainted by the error (*Detamu v Secretary of State for the Home Department* [2006] EWCA Civ 604). Errors that would make no difference may be ignored and Commissioners and the Upper Tribunal have often simply dismissed an appeal despite identifying an error of law because the identified error would have made no difference. On the other hand, Commissioners and the Upper Tribunal have frequently set aside decisions on the ground of error of law only to substitute a decision to the same effect as the tribunal's. This is not necessarily inconsistent. It has to be borne in mind that, in social security cases, the Secretary of State has wide, but not unlimited, powers to supersede a decision of a tribunal or a Commissioner on the ground of mistake of fact or change of circumstances and the way in which a decision is expressed may well affect those powers. It may therefore be important for the Upper Tribunal to correct an error made by a tribunal even though the correction has no immediate effect on the amount of benefit payable to the claimant. **3.71**

A decision of the First-tier Tribunal is not invalid or wrong in law merely because it was made under procedural rules that have been held to be invalid on the ground that they were unfair; in such a case, the decision of the First-tier Tribunal will be wrong in law only if the process by which it was reached was unfair in the particular circumstances of the case (*R. (TN (Vietnam)) v Secretary of State for the Home Department* [2021] UKSC 41; [2021] 1 W.L.R. 4902).

Subsection (2)

A "party" is presumably a person who was, or should have been, a party to the proceedings before the First-tier Tribunal. Note that s.13 of the Social Security (Recovery of Benefits) Act 1997 and s.14 of the Social Security Act 1998 make **3.72** additional (and largely unnecessary) provision as to who may appeal to the Upper Tribunal under this section. Subsection (8) permits further provision to be made as to who may or may not exercise the right of appeal. In *Devani v Secretary of State for the Home Department* [2020] EWCA Civ 612; [2020] 1 W.L.R 2613, Underhill L.J., with whom the other members of the Court agreed, said at [27]:

> "I am sure that section 11(2) of the 2007 Act is intended to confer a right of appeal only against some aspect of the actual order of the FTT, and that the phrase 'any party' must be read as referring only to a party who has in that sense lost."

However, in *IC v Moss* [2020] UKUT 174 (AAC), it was held that that sentence should be read as merely a statement of the application of existing principles in a clear case where an appeal by the winner would not be allowed. In other contexts, it may be sufficient for a party to have suffered a practical disadvantage as a result of the decision or its reasoning, even if the decision was not technically adverse to him or her.

A potential witness who is not a "party" cannot challenge by way of an appeal a refusal by the First-tier Tribunal to set aside a summons it has issued. However, the refusal could be challenged in judicial review proceedings and, in England and Wales, the proceedings could be brought in the Upper Tribunal because they would fall within the scope of the practice direction made by the Lord Chief Justice under s.18(6) of this Act (*CB v Suffolk CC (Enforcement Reference)* [2010] UKUT 413 (AAC); [2011] AACR 22). Similarly, it has been held that a person seeking to be added to proceedings is not a "party" until added so that any challenge to a refusal to add him or her must be made by way of an application for judicial review (*Salisbury Independent Living v Wirral BC (HB)* [2011] UKUT 44 (AAC); [2012] AACR 37). On the other hand, a person may be added as a party to proceedings in the First-tier Tribunal after a final decision has been made so as to be enable him or her to appeal (*Razzaq v Charity Commission for England and Wales* [2016] UKUT B46 (TCC)), at least in circumstances where the person could not reasonably have been expected to apply to be added as a party before the decision was made, and in *In re W(A Child) (Care Proceedings: Non-Party Appeal)* [2016] EWCA Civ 1140; [2017] 1 W.L.R., it has been held that witnesses in the High Court who were not formally parties in that Court but had gained the practical status of interveners, were to be regarded as parties entitled to appeal to the Court of Appeal so as to challenge findings made against them. The latter case can perhaps be analysed as a case where, had the case been in a tribunal, the witnesses ought to have been made parties or, alternatively, can perhaps be distinguished on the ground that judicial review was not available as a remedy because it does not lie against the High Court. It was considered in *Pierhead Drinks Ltd v HMRC* [2019] UKUT 7 (TCC), where it was left open whether a witness against whom findings of fact were unfairly made by the First-tier Tribunal might be entitled to bring an appeal. Ultimately it was not necessary for the Upper Tribunal to decide whether the appeal was properly brought because no unfairness was found but it may be noted that there was no consideration of the question whether, had there been unfairness, an adequate remedy could more appropriately have been found through an application for judicial review and therefore whether the Upper Tribunal should simply have treated the appeal as such an application (see ss.15 and 18).

The scope of the right of appeal is largely defined by subs.(1). Note, however, that this right of appeal exists alongside a right of appeal on questions of fact in penalty appeals under paras 2(2) and 4(1) of Sch.2 to the Tax Credits Act 2002 and s.21(10) of the Child Trust Funds Act 2004.

3.73 An appeal will not usually be considered if it has ceased to have any practical importance in the particular case concerned unless there is a good reason for doing so in the public interest because, for instance, there are likely to be a large number of similar cases and the point in issue is a discrete point of statutory construction (*R. v Secretary of State for the Home Department, ex parte Salem* [1999] 1 A.C. 450, *KF v Birmingham & Solihull Mental Health NHS Foundation Trust* [2010] UKUT 185 (AAC); [2011] AACR 3). In *DD v Sussex Partnership NHS Foundation Trust* [2022] UKUT 166 (AAC), which contains a useful survey of the case law on the question of whether appeals that have become academic should still be decided, the fact that the appellant patient had legal representation, which is not always the case in the Upper Tribunal, was one reason given for deciding a point of law that had ceased to be important in that particular case but was likely to arise again in other cases. However, a single ground of appeal that has ceased to be of practical importance in an individual case may be considered where it is related to other grounds of appeal (*Hampshire CC v JP (SEN)* [2009] UKUT 239 (AAC); [2010] AACR 15).

In *Office of Communications v Floe Telecom Limited* [2009] EWCA Civ 47, tribunals were discouraged from giving unnecessary guidance in a case where an appeal was brought against such guidance and the Court of Appeal felt obliged to determine the appeal. It said, at [21]:

> "Specialist tribunals seem to be more prone than ordinary courts to yield to the temptation of generous general advice and guidance. The wish to be helpful to users is understandable. It may even be commendable. But bodies established to adjudicate on disputes are not in the business of giving advisory opinions to litigants or potential litigants. They should take care not to be, or to feel, pressured by the parties or by interveners or by critics to do things which they are not intended, qualified or equipped to do. In general, more harm than good is likely to be done by deciding more than is necessary for the adjudication of the actual dispute".

In *Fish Legal v IC* [2015] UKUT 52 (AAC); [2015] AACR 33, a three-judge panel declined to lay down broad principles that might assist the Information Commissioner and the First-tier Tribunal in other cases. It explained that, while it had tried to be helpful, the nature of the issue before it did not allow it to lay down general principles in the way that had been suggested, it had to act in the context of the case and not write a treatise and it was inappropriate to give the guidance "because guidance must be based either on a wide range of experience, such as the judges of this Chamber have in social security matters, or on detailed evidence covering the scope of the guidance, such as the Immigration and Asylum Chamber receives in its Country Guidance cases". In relation to the matter on which guidance was sought, it had neither the accumulated experience nor the evidence.

However, a lot depends on the context and, in particular, the attitude of the party, usually a public body, at whom the guidance is principally aimed. Guidance that is not strictly necessary to a decision is likely to be mere obiter dicta and is not strictly binding. Indeed, it is often proffered as a suggestion rather than a requirement, where it is a matter of good practice rather than a matter of determination of the law, because it is not open to a judge sitting in a court or tribunal to lay down a mandatory procedure to be complied with in all cases within the course of giving a judgment or decision in an individual case, as that would be to make a practice direction without compliance with the requirements of s.23 (*Bovale Ltd v Secretary of State for Communities and Local Government* [2009] EWCA Civ 171; [2009] 1 W.L.R. 2274). Provided care is taken and a tribunal is appropriately "qualified or equipped", the giving of guidance may be valuable to all concerned. The problem in the *Ofcom* case seems to have been that the guidance was on matters that had been the subject of detailed argument and could not be ignored and yet was unwelcome to the public authority that was expected to apply it. Worse, much of it was wrong.

In *SSWP v LC* [2009] UKUT 153 (AAC), concessions made before the First-tier Tribunal on behalf of the Secretary of State did not prevent the Secretary of State from appealing successfully against the First-tier Tribunal's decision even though the First-tier Tribunal's decision was clearly based on the concessions. That decision was followed in *RJ v HMRC (TC)* [2021] UKUT 40 (AAC) at [136] to [138]. See also the discussion of the practice of appellate courts in the annotation to s.13(3) to (5), below.

Subsections (3) and (4)

3.74 Permission must first be sought from the First-tier Tribunal (r.21(2) of the Tribunal Procedure (Upper Tribunal) Rules 2008), which gives the First-tier Tribunal the opportunity to consider reviewing its decision under s.9 and so remove the necessity for an appeal. Therefore, although the Upper Tribunal may waive the requirement first to apply to the First-tier Tribunal, it will seldom do so unless already seised of the applicant's case and, in particular, will not do so to enable the applicant to defeat an absolute time bar (*MA v SSD* [2009] UKUT 57 (AAC), disagreeing with *HM v SSWP* [2009] UKUT 40 (AAC) on the issue whether there was a power to waive the requirement).

Permission to appeal may be granted on grounds other than those raised by the parties (*Krasniqi v Secretary of State for the Home Department* [2006] EWCA Civ 391). Similarly, unless permission has been expressly refused in respect of some grounds or has otherwise been explicitly granted on limited grounds, a grant of permission is not to be taken as being limited and it is unnecessary for any party to make an application for permission in order to advance new grounds, the Upper Tribunal having adequate case-management powers to avoid unfairness to other parties (*DL-H v Devon Partnership NHS Trust* [2010] UKUT 102 (AAC)). Nonetheless, a judge considering an application for permission to appeal is not bound to trawl through the papers looking for grounds of appeal that have not been advanced by the applicant (*R. (Anayet Begum) v Social Security Commissioner* [2002] EWHC 401 (Admin)). The same approach has been taken in the Court of Session in *Mooney v SSWP*, 2004 S.L.T. 1141 (also reported *sub. nom. Mooney v Social Security Commissioner* as *R(DLA)5/04*). In that case, it was unsuccessfully argued that a Commissioner should have granted leave to appeal on the ground that a tribunal had failed to ask a claimant certain questions. Lord Brodie regarded it as significant that the claimant had failed to aver that the questions would have elicited any favourable evidence and also that the claimant had been represented and his representative had failed to adduce the evidence).

In *RJ v HMRC* [2021] UKUT 40 (AAC); [2021] 1 W.L.R. 3350, it was held at [136] to [140] that HMRC was entitled, on an appeal to the Upper Tribunal, to withdraw a concession of law made before the First-tier Tribunal and that it was unnecessary for HMRC to show that it was just to withdraw the concession. However, it is hard to see why the Upper Tribunal should not be entitled to refuse to allow such a withdrawal in the rare case where it would cause real unfairness due, for instance, to the lateness of the withdrawal (compare the approach taken in the Court of Appeal, discussed in the annotation to s.13(3) to (5), below). It was not suggested that there was that sort of unfairness in *RJ*, and it is perhaps arguable that the case is merely authority for the proposition that the withdrawal of a concession of law will not in itself be regarded as unjust, given the inquisitorial role of the Upper Tribunal and the public interest in public law cases being decided on a correct legal basis.

Permission to appeal may be given even though there is a binding decision of a superior court that will require the Upper Tribunal to dismiss the appeal, if the appellant indicates that he or she intends to appeal against the inevitable decision of the Upper Tribunal with a view to persuading a superior court to take a different view of the law. However, permission should be refused in such a case if the Upper Tribunal considers that there is no prospect of the appellant succeeding in the superior court (*R. (Al Rabbatt) v City of Westminster Magistrates' Court (Attorney General intervening)* [2017] EWHC 1969 (Admin); [2018] 1 W.L.R. 2009, which concerned an application for permission to bring judicial review proceedings but the approach in which seems equally applicable to applications for permission to appeal).

3.75 In the Immigration and Asylum Chamber of the Upper Tribunal, it has been held that subs.(3) requires a respondent to obtain permission to cross-appeal if he or she wishes to challenge a part of the First-tier Tribunal's decision, although such permission is not required in order to raise an issue that the First-tier Tribunal did not address because it was not required to do so due to its decision on another issue or in order to challenge a part of the First-tier Tribunal's decision that did not confer any additional benefit on the respondent in view of its decision on another issue (*SSHD v Smith (appealable decisions; PTA requirements; anonymity)* [2019] UKUT 216 (IAC)). A similar approach was taken in *HMRC v SSE Generation Ltd* [2021] EWCA Civ 105, where the Court of Appeal held the Upper Tribunal to have erred in law in allowing the respondent to argue a point upon which it had been unsuccessful before the First-tier Tribunal but in respect of which it had not obtained permission to appeal, even though the point had been raised in the response to the appeal. Importantly, the Court of Appeal was not referred to r.7(2)(a) of the Tribunal Procedure (Upper Tribunal) Rules 2008 which enables the Upper Tribunal to waive the requirement under r.21(2) to apply to the First-tier Tribunal for permission to appeal before applying to the Upper Tribunal and so it understood the Upper Tribunal not to have had any power to give the respondent permission to appeal in that case. Nonetheless, in the light of the Court of Appeal's decision, it is necessary for permission to appeal expressly to be given to a respondent who wishes to argue that the First-tier Tribunal erred in law in deciding a point against him or her. Rule 24 of the Tribunal Procedure (Upper Tribunal) Regulations 2008 has been amended in the light of that decision, which is discussed further in the annotation to that rule, below.

There is no appeal against a refusal of permission to appeal. Where the First-tier Tribunal refuses permission, the remedy is to apply to the Upper Tribunal. It is not open to the First-tier Tribunal to reconsider its refusal of permission (*R(U) 10/55*) unless there are grounds for the refusal to be set aside under r.37 of the Tribunal Procedure (First-tier Tribunal) (Social Entitlement Chamber) Rules 2008. Where the Upper Tribunal refuses permission, there is no right of appeal because such a decision is an excluded decision under s.13(8)(c). Consequently, there is no power of review under s.9 but it appears from *RC v SSWP* [2009] UKUT 62 (AAC); [2011] AACR 38, [26] that the Upper Tribunal may nonetheless reconsider a refusal of permission to appeal on general principles. In any event, if the conditions of r.43 of the Tribunal Procedure (Upper Tribunal) Rules 2008 are satisfied, a refusal of permission by the Upper Tribunal may be set aside and reconsidered. However, the Upper Tribunal's ultimate decision on a refusal of permission to appeal under s.11(4)(b) is final. In the absence of a right of appeal, judicial review used to lie on limited grounds, but that is now excluded by s.11A.

If the First-tier Tribunal gives permission unlawfully, which is unlikely, the Upper Tribunal must consider afresh whether permission should be given (*Lisle-Mainwaring v Associated Newspapers Ltd* [2018] EWCA Civ 1470; [2018] 1 W.L.R. 4766 at [22]).

Subsections (5)–(7)

Subject to the point made in the note to subs.(2), there is a right of appeal to the Upper Tribunal against all decisions of the Social Entitlement Chamber of the First-tier Tribunal except decisions concerned with criminal injuries compensation (excluded under subs.(5)(a)), certain review decisions (excluded under subs.(5)(d)), decisions set aside on review (excluded under subs.(5)(e)) and decisions concerned with asylum support (excluded by art.2 (a) of the Appeals (Excluded Decisions) Order 2009 (SI 2009/275, as amended), made under subs.(5)(f)). **3.76**

In principle, judicial review will lie where there is no right of appeal and, in the case of decisions excluded under subs.(5)(a) and (d) in England and Wales, applications may be made to the Upper Tribunal (see the note to s.18(6)). However, where decisions are excluded under subs.(5)(d), there will usually be another decision that can be challenged (albeit sometimes made later) or another remedy and so permission to apply for judicial review may be refused if, for instance, an applicant is challenging a review decision and it is considered that he or she should wait for the case to be re-decided (*R. (RB) v First-tier Tribunal (Review)* [2010] UKUT 160 (AAC); [2010] AACR 41).

Note that decisions under section 9(4)(a) and (b) to correct accidental errors or amend reasons are *not* excluded by subs.(5)(d)(ii) and (iii) and so are appealable.

Subsection (5)(e) seems unnecessary.

Subsection (8)

3.77 No relevant order has been made but note that s.13 of the Social Security (Recovery of Benefits) Act 1997, s.14 of the Social Security Act 1998 and legislation concerning housing benefit, council tax benefit and child support maintenance (outside the scope of this work) make further provision as to who may appeal to the Upper Tribunal under this section.

3.78 **[[1]Finality of decisions by Upper Tribunal about permission to appeal**

11A.—(1) Subsections (2) and (3) apply in relation to a decision by the Upper Tribunal to refuse permission (or leave) to appeal further to an application under section 11(4)(b).

(2) The decision is final, and not liable to be questioned or set aside in any other court.

(3) In particular—

(a) the Upper Tribunal is not to be regarded as having exceeded its powers by reason of any error made in reaching the decision;

(b) the supervisory jurisdiction does not extend to, and no application or petition for judicial review may be made or brought in relation to, the decision.

(4) Subsections (2) and (3)do not apply so far as the decision involves or gives rise to any question as to whether—

(a) the Upper Tribunal has or had a valid application before it under section 11(4)(b),

(b) the Upper Tribunal is or was properly constituted for the purpose of dealing with the application, or

(c) the Upper Tribunal is acting or has acted—

(i) in bad faith, or

(ii) in such a procedurally defective way as amounts to a fundamental breach of the principles of natural justice.

(5) Subsections (2) and (3) do not apply so far as provision giving the First-tier Tribunal jurisdiction to make the first-instance decision could (if the Tribunal did not already have that jurisdiction) be made by—

(a) an Act of the Scottish Parliament, or

(b) an Act of the Northern Ireland Assembly the Bill for which would not require the consent of the Secretary of State.

(6) The court of supervisory jurisdiction is not to entertain any application or petition for judicial review in respect of a decision of the First-tier Tribunal that it would not entertain (whether as a matter of law or discretion) in the absence of this section.

(7) In this section—

"decision" includes any purported decision;

"first-instance decision" means the decision in relation to which permission (or leave) to appeal is being sought under section 11(4)(b);

"the supervisory jurisdiction" means the supervisory jurisdiction of—

(a) the High Court, in England and Wales or Northern Ireland, or

(b) the Court of Session, in Scotland,

and "the court of supervisory jurisdiction" is to be read accordingly.]

AMENDMENT

Judicial Review and Courts Act 2022 s.2(1) (July 14, 2022, subject to a saving).

GENERAL NOTE

By virtue of the Judicial Review and Courts Act 2022 Act s.2(2), this section does not apply in relation to a decision (including any purported decision) of the Upper Tribunal made before July 14, 2022. **3.79**

This section reverses the effect of *R. (Cart) v Upper Tribunal (Public Law Project intervening)* [2011] UKSC 28; [2012] 1 A.C. 663; [2011] AACR 38 in relation to England and Wales and *Advocate General for Scotland v Eba* [2011] UKSC 29; [2012] 1 A.C. 710; [2011] AACR 39 in relation to Scotland, in which it had been held that, in the absence of a right of appeal, judicial review lay on limited grounds from a refusal by the Upper Tribunal of permission to appeal under s.11(4)(b). Note, however, that this section does not exclude judicial review of refusals of permission to appeal from bodies other than the First-tier Tribunal, because the right of appeal from such bodies is conferred by other legislation and not by s.11 of this Act.

Nor does this section exclude judicial review in the circumstances mentioned in subs.(4) or, in Scotland or Northern Ireland, subs. (5) or (6).

A challenge to the effectiveness of the ouster of judicial review and an argument that the case fell within the natural justice exception in subs.(4)(c)(ii) both failed in *R. (Oceana) v Upper Tribunal (Immigration and Asylum Chamber)* [2023] EWHC 791 (Admin). As regards the latter point, Saini J said:

> "[33] Crucially, in the present context, Parliament has taken care to require a "fundamental breach" of natural justice before the exception comes into play. That is an important qualification and needs to be given some meaning. Without seeking to be prescriptive, in my judgment that requires a claimant to identify a failure in process which is so grave as to rob the process of any legitimacy. That is a substantial hurdle. When considering whether this hurdle has been surmounted, a court will need to consider the *entire* process, as opposed to focussing on the discrete aspect which is the subject of the claim. The fairness of a process has to be assessed holistically.
>
> [34] Given some of the arguments made by the Claimant, I also need to underline that complaints about the result and the merits of the decision cannot be the subject of the exception. The exception is concerned with failures of *process* and not with disappointing *outcomes*. Parliament has decided that an outcome may in fact be shown to be wrong, but has determined that this is not a basis for allowing a judicial review challenge to be made."

As regards the effectiveness of the ouster, he pointed out at [47] that, in *Cart*, "the Supreme Court expressly acknowledged the right of Parliament to oust or exclude judicial review with the use of clear language".

The effect of the Tribunals, Courts and Enforcement Act 2007 s.11A is therefore to limit the supervisory jurisdiction of the High Court over an Upper Tribunal decision to refuse permission to appeal from a decision of the First-tier Tribunal by setting out, in s.11A(4), exceptions on which the Upper Tribunal decision could be reviewed. The decision in *R. (on the application of LA (Albania)) v Upper Tribunal (Immigration & Asylum Chamber)* [2023] EWCA Civ 1337 states that a mere assertion that one of the s.11A(4) exceptions applied was not sufficient to establish jurisdiction. A genuinely disputable question had to be shown for an applicant's judicial review claim to fall within s.11A(4). The Upper Tribunal had not acted in a procedurally defective way as to amount to a fundamental breach of the principles of natural justice. The Upper Tribunal had refused permission on the papers and addressed all the applicant's grounds of appeal against the First-tier Tribunal's decision, giving reasons why they were unarguable.

In *R. (on the application of LA (Albania)) v Upper Tribunal Immigration and Asylum Chamber and another* [2024] UKSC 53, the Supreme Court refused permission to appeal from the Court of Appeal's decision holding that the post-*Cart* restrictions on Judicial Review of an Upper Tribunal decision refusing permission to appeal are lawful. The Supreme Court makes it plain that it considers those post-*Cart* restrictions are lawful.

Proceedings on appeal to Upper Tribunal

3.80 **12.**—(1) Subsection (2) applies if the Upper Tribunal, in deciding an appeal under section 11, finds that the making of the decision concerned involved the making of an error on a point of law.

(2) The Upper Tribunal—

(a) may (but need not) set aside the decision of the First-tier Tribunal, and

(b) if it does, must either—

(i) remit the case to the First-tier Tribunal with directions for its reconsideration, or

(ii) re-make the decision.

(3) In acting under subsection (2)(b)(i), the Upper Tribunal may also—

(a) direct that the members of the First-tier Tribunal who are chosen to reconsider the case are not to be the same as those who made the decision that has been set aside;

(b) give procedural directions in connection with the reconsideration of the case by the First-tier Tribunal.

(4) In acting under subsection (2)(b)(ii), the Upper Tribunal—

(a) may make any decision which the First-tier Tribunal could make if the First-tier Tribunal were re-making the decision, and

(b) may make such findings of fact as it considers appropriate.

GENERAL NOTE

3.81 Subsection (2)(a) expressly permits the Upper Tribunal to refuse to set aside a decision of the First-tier Tribunal even if it is erroneous in point of law. Certainly courts will generally dismiss an appeal on a point of law where satisfied that the result of decision under appeal was correct even if the decision was otherwise flawed. However, it can be important to substitute a decision based on correct reasoning if there is any possibility of there being a subsequent application for supersession and judges of the Upper Tribunal therefore often set aside a decision only to substitute a decision to the same effect. On the other hand, if there is no point in a case being re-decided even where the decision is flawed and not necessarily correct, the Upper Tribunal will not set it aside but will, in effect, merely declare it to be erroneous in point of law (see *BB v South London and Maudsley NHS Trust* [2009] UKUT 157 (AAC), *Hampshire CC v JP (SEN)* [2009] UKUT 239 (AAC); [2010] AACR 15 and *KF v Birmingham & Solihull Mental Health NHS Foundation Trust* [2010] UKUT 185 (AAC); [2011] AACR 3, all decisions of three-judge panels). This situation is less likely to occur in the social security context.

In *Shipton v IC* [2023] UKUT 170 (AAC), the Upper Tribunal refused to set aside a decision of the First-tier Tribunal where, with the voluntary, informed and unequivocal consent of the parties, a member of the First-tier Tribunal had absented himself from the hearing while witnesses were giving evidence and then had taken part in the decision. Although the procedure was held to be impermissible, the consent of the parties meant there had been no breach of the rules of natural justice, and the Upper Tribunal held that it would have been "quite unreasonable and indeed wholly disproportionate" to set the decision aside. What is reasonable and proportionate must depend on the circumstances of a particular case and a different view might perhaps be taken in at least some social security cases were the issue to arise in that context.

In *ZB v SSWP (CSM)* [2013] UKUT 367 (AAC), it was said that, although a person who had been barred from taking part in proceedings in the First-tier Tribunal was entitled to appeal to the Upper Tribunal against the decision in those proceedings, the fact that they had been so barred might have a bearing on how the Upper Tribunal would exercise its power under s.12(2)(a) to refuse to set aside a decision of the First-tier Tribunal notwithstanding that it has found that the making of the decision involved an error of law. In that case, the Upper Tribunal found that the appellant had not suffered any significant injustice as a result of the First-tier Tribunal's failure to provide a fuller statement of reasons and it declined to set aside the decision. It has been held that, if a case where a party had previously been barred by the First-tier Tribunal is remitted, the party is no longer barred because the proceedings are different (*SL v SSWP (CSM)* [2014] UKUT 128 (AAC)).

Subsection (2)(b) gives the Upper Tribunal a wide discretion as to whether it remits a case to the First-tier Tribunal or re-makes the decision itself. The express power to re-make a decision puts the Upper Tribunal in the same position as its principal predecessor, the Social Security Commissioners, to whom at one time appeals had lain on points of fact as well as law. It is in contrast to the position of the Employment Appeal Tribunal which, it has been held in *Jafri v Lincoln College* [2014] EWCA Civ 449; [2014] I.C.R. 920, is bound to remit a matter when allowing an appeal if the matter is in dispute and more than one outcome is possible, however well placed it might otherwise be to take a decision itself, although a robust approach is taken to whether only one outcome is possible (see *Robinson v Department for Work and Pensions* [2020] EWCA Civ 859). However, although it has a discretion, the Upper Tribunal must provide, at least implicitly, a reason for deciding not to remit. In *AEB v Secretary of State for the Home Department* [2022] EWCA Civ 1512, the Court of Appeal held the Immigration Appeals Chamber of the Upper Tribunal to have erred in law in not remitting a case for rehearing after it had set aside the First-tier Tribunal's decision for errors of law that had resulted in the appellant being denied a fair hearing before that tribunal. It accepted that the Upper Tribunal had a discretion as to whether to remit a case or re-make the decision itself, but considered that reasons were required if the Upper Tribunal decided not to remit and that insufficient reasons had been given. The Court's decision was based partly on a Practice Statement applicable in the Immigration Appeals Chamber of the Upper Tribunal, but the Court also expressed itself in wider terms, pointing out that not remitting a case meant that the losing party would be denied the opportunity of appealing to the Upper Tribunal against a re-made decision, rather than to the Court.

Relevant considerations are likely to be whether there will be a non-legal member of the First-tier Tribunal with relevant expertise and whether a further, or any, hearing is necessary. Thus, where it is unlikely that a claimant will be present or represented at a hearing before the First-tier Tribunal if the case is remitted to it and both parties have made full submissions in writing, the Upper Tribunal is likely to take the view that it should re-make the decision itself (*VB v SSWP* [2008] UKUT 15 (AAC)). The Upper Tribunal's power to re-make the decision itself makes it appropriate to receive evidence and it is likely to wish to have any relevant evidence before it decides whether or not to allow the appeal. "Forcing a party to produce additional evidence only if and when it is required could lead to inefficiency and delay" (*VH v Suffolk CC (SEN)* [2010] UKUT 203 (AAC)). Another reason for not remitting a case might be a need to give guidance on a factual matter in order to promote consistency in decision-making.

It has been held by a three-judge panel of the Immigration and Asylum Chamber of the Upper Tribunal in *VOM v SSHD* [2016] UKUT 410 (IAC) that a right of appeal to the Court of Appeal under s.13 against a decision to set aside a decision of the First-tier Tribunal under s.12(2)(a) does not arise until the Upper Tribunal has disposed of the case under s.12(2)(b). Thus, the Upper Tribunal refused to entertain an application for permission to appeal where, having set aside a decision, it had adjourned proceedings with a view to re-making the decision on a future date. The Court of Appeal did not go that far in *Secretary of State for Work and Pensions v Slavin* [2011] EWCA Civ 1515; [2012] AACR 30 when, in similar circumstances, Richards L.J. said at [37] that "it would have been much better for the judge to determine the outstanding issue so that an appeal to this court, if an appeal had still been necessary, could have been considered by reference to a full set of relevant facts". Indeed, it is hard to see that an appellate court is necessarily less able properly to determine an appeal in those circumstances than it would be if the case had been remitted to the First-tier Tribunal (where it is clear that there is a right of appeal before the decision has been re-made by the First-tier Tribunal—see *AA(Iraq) v Secretary of State for the Home Department* [2017] EWCA Civ 944; [2018] 1 W.L.R. 1083 in which *VOM* was distinguished and *Secretary of State for Work and Pensions v MM* [2019] UKSC 34; 2019 SC (UKSC) 47; [2019] AACR 26) or if there had been a formal direction that the question whether there had been an error of law in the First-tier Tribunal's decision had been taken as a preliminary issue; it is suggested that it rather depends on the circumstances of the particular case and that the approach to be taken to the question whether an application for permission to appeal should be considered before the proceedings have been concluded should be regarded as a matter of practice rather than jurisdiction. In any event, some of the matters relied upon in *VOM* apply only in the Immigration and Asylum Chamber of the Upper Tribunal and not also in the Administrative Appeals Chamber.

In *AW v SSWP (IB)* [2013] UKUT 20 (AAC) the Upper Tribunal left open the question whether, having allowed an appeal against a decision of the First-tier Tribunal not to admit, or to strike out, an appeal made to that Tribunal, it was entitled not only to decide that the appeal to the First-tier Tribunal should be admitted or not struck out but also to determine that appeal. The judge considered that, even if he had the power to do so, he should determine the appeal made to the First-tier Tribunal only if all parties consented to him doing so. One party declined to give consent. Subsection (3)(a) requires a positive direction to be made if is intended that a case that is remitted to the First-tier Tribunal is to be heard by a differently constituted tribunal. Subsection.(3)(b) makes it plain that other procedural directions may be given as well as directions under subs.(2)(b)(i) on the law and under subs.(3)(a) as to the constitution of the tribunal.

The Upper Tribunal should identify outstanding issues of fact or law before referring a case to another tribunal, because otherwise a tribunal is likely to find its role unclear (*Secretary of State for Work and Pensions v Menary-Smith* [2006] EWCA Civ 1751). To like effect, a Tribunal of Commissioners said in *R(IB) 2/07* that it was wrong to suggest that a Commissioner allowing an appeal necessarily had to refer a case to another tribunal, just because no witness had attended to give evidence before the Commissioner and there was a dispute between the parties as to the decision that should be substituted for one that had been set aside. Neither party in that case had suggested there was any material evidence not recorded in the papers or that anything turned on a dispute about that evidence. If the evidence was not in issue, the dispute between the parties was likely to be one of law that a Commissioner should resolve. Similarly, where a tribunal's findings of primary fact are adequate and the reasoning supporting those findings is also adequate, it is wrong to suggest that the Upper Tribunal should refer the case to another tribunal to identify grounds for supersession. The Upper Tribunal can perform that exercise itself under subs.(2)(b)(ii) without making new findings of primary fact (*CDLA/4217/2001*). It was, however, emphasised in *JA (Ghana) v Secretary of State for the Home Department* [2015] EWCA Civ 1031 that remittal will be appropriate if there are issues of credibility or reliability that a party has not had a satisfactory opportunity to address at an oral hearing (e.g., because although there was a hearing before the First-tier Tribunal the relevant findings cannot be relied upon in the light of the First-tier Tribunal's error of law) and it is not convenient for the Upper Tribunal to hold a hearing for the purpose of resolving the issues. Moreover, it was held in that case that, where the Upper Tribunal has made a finding of fact on any issue before remitting a case, the First-tier Tribunal is bound by that finding even if there is no specific direction to that effect. This is consistent with the approach taken in *Kuteh v Secretary of State for Education* [2014] EWCA Civ 1586, where it was held that the Upper Tribunal was bound by a finding made by the Administrative Court when quashing a decision before remitting a case. However, where a case is remitted by the Upper Tribunal to a panel of the First-tier Tribunal that is constituted differently from the panel whose decision has been set aside, the new panel is not entitled to adopt a finding made by the previous panel *only* because the Upper Tribunal has held that particular finding not to be vitiated by any error of law or has not commented on it, although it may adopt the finding for other reasons and must adopt it if directed to do so by the Upper Tribunal (*KK v SSWP (DLA)* [2015] UKUT 417 (AAC)).

See also *Sarkar v Secretary of State for the Home Department* [2014] EWCA Civ 195) in which it was made very plain that, where the error of law does not vitiate a finding of the First-tier Tribunal on a particular issue, the Upper Tribunal may, if it re-makes the decision itself, adopt the finding without considering further evidence or, if it remits the case, issue directions under s.12(2)(b)(i) limiting the scope of the First-tier Tribunal's reconsideration so that it must decide the case on the basis of that finding. In such a case, the Upper Tribunal may even decide to direct that the decision be re-made by the same members who previously decided the case, requiring them to address an issue they had previous failed to consider or to give the reasons they had previously failed to give (*Shah v NHS England* [2013] UKUT 538 (AAC)). However, this will seldom be appropriate or necessary in the social security context, where hearings are generally short and oral evidence from witnesses other than the parties is rare and where it will often be administratively simpler to arrange an entirely new panel rather than reconstitute an earlier one. On the other hand, in the absence of any such practical advantage, it would still be wrong to remit a case to the same panel if that would give rise to "reasonably perceived unfairness to the affected parties" or "damage to the public confidence in the decision making process" (*HCA International Ltd v Competition and Markets Authority* [2015] EWCA Civ 492; [2015] 1 W.L.R. 4341).

Where a case has been remitted to the First-tier Tribunal, the First-tier Tribunal is **3.82** not entitled to decide that the Upper Tribunal had no jurisdiction to give the decision and on that ground refuse to rehear the case. In *Nesbitt's Application* [2013] NIQB 111; [2014] AACR 31, the High Court in Northern Ireland quashed a decision of the President of appeal tribunals who refused to rehear a case that had been remitted by the Chief Social Security Commissioner with a direction that it be reheard. The President had taken the view that the Chief Commissioner had had no jurisdiction to hear the case because the claimant had validly withdrawn his appeal, even though the Chief Commissioner had expressly determined, following an extensive analysis, that the case had not been withdrawn. Treacy J. held that: "Even if the Commissioner had no jurisdiction, it still would not have been open to the [President] to simply reject it and in effect overturn the Commissioner's decision himself. . . . In the absence of adjudication by a court of appropriate jurisdiction on the Commissioner's jurisdiction to hear the appeal his decision remains extant and binding on the [President] regardless of the President's view as to its legality." See also *Rochdale MBC v KW (No.2)* [2015] EWCA Civ 1054; [2016] 1 W.L.R. 198, where it was held that a judge of the Court of Protection had been bound by a consent order of the Court of Appeal and it was futile and inappropriate for him to seek to undermine it by complaining that it was ultra vires or wrong for any other reason.

If a case is referred to a differently constituted tribunal, it is usual for the decision that has been set aside to be included in the papers. That is not inappropriate. Even if their findings of fact cannot be relied upon, issues identified by the first tribunal may well be of assistance to the new tribunal, although it must be careful not to be influenced by the discredited findings (*Swash v Secretary of State for the Home Department* [2006] EWCA Civ 1093; [2007] 1 W.L.R. 1264). There may, however, be special circumstances in which the Upper Tribunal setting the first decision aside considers that the interests of justice require the case to be heard by a tribunal that has not seen that decision and he or she will be able to issue appropriate directions to ensure that that happens (*ibid.*).

If a decision of a tribunal has been superseded while an appeal against it has been pending, it is necessary to consider the effect of the supersession on the appeal or vice versa. If the supersession was under reg.6(2)(c) of the Social Security and Child Support (Decisions and Appeals) Regulations 1999 (ignorance of, or mistake as to, fact), there may be circumstances in which the appeal to the Upper Tribunal should be treated as having lapsed, particularly if the supersession has given the claimant all that he or she seeks on the appeal. Where an appeal, or part of an appeal, has lapsed, it must be struck out under r.8(2) of the Tribunal Procedure (Upper Tribunal) Rules 2008 (*LS v HMRC (TC)* [2017] UKUT 257 (AAC); [2018] AACR 2). If the appeal is not treated as having lapsed and is allowed, the supersession decision is generally allowed to stand, and the decision to be made by the Upper Tribunal or another tribunal following the setting aside of the first tribunal's decision is made in respect of a period ending immediately before the supersession took effect. This approach was held in *R(DLA)2/04* to be justifiable where the parties are content with the outcome of the supersession or where it is plain that supersession would have been appropriate whatever the outcome of the appeal because there had been an obvious change of circumstances or, perhaps, new medical evidence justifying supersession under reg.6(2)(g) of the Social Security and Child Support (Decisions and Appeals) Regulations 1999 in an incapacity benefit case. In *R(DLA)2/04* itself, the claimant had both appealed against and applied for supersession of a decision of a tribunal. The appeal was successful and a Commissioner had referred the case to another tribunal. The application for supersession had failed and the claimant's appeal came before the same tribunal as the remitted appeal. The new tribunal made an award on the remitted appeal and did not limit it on account of the failed supersession application. No award was made on the supersession appeal. On further appeals, the Commissioner held that that was the correct approach where, as in that case, the application for supersession had been under reg.6(2)(c) (error of fact). He advanced three rules:

> "1. An application for supersession that results in a refusal to supersede the original decision does not terminate the period under consideration on an appeal against the original decision.
> 2. Live proceedings arising out of an application for supersession based on ignorance of, or a mistake as to, a material fact lapse when the decision to be superseded is set aside on appeal (provided that there is no further appeal in respect of the original decision).
> 3. Live proceedings arising out of an application for supersession based on a change of circumstances do not lapse when the decision to be superseded is set aside on appeal (but the application may have to be treated as an application for supersession of a different decision or, perhaps, as a new claim, depending on the circumstances)."

3.83 The second and third rules arise because a tribunal a hearing an appeal against the original decision must correct any error of fact in the original decision but, by virtue of s.12(8)(b) of the Social Security Act 1998, must not take account of any subsequent change of circumstances. In *CDLA/3948/2002*, a different Commissioner also held that a supersession of a tribunal's decision became ineffective when the Commissioner set the tribunal's decision aside. Latham L.J. considered that approach to be correct and refused leave to appeal (*Farrington v Secretary of State for Work and Pensions* [2004] EWCA Civ 435).

Where the Upper Tribunal sets aside a decision of a tribunal awarding benefit for a fixed period, the period in issue before the Commissioner or a tribunal to whom the case is remitted is not necessarily limited by the fact that there has been a decision on a renewal claim, although the award on the renewal claim must be treated as having lapsed if an award on the original claim is made in respect of the same period and any benefit paid as a result of the renewal claim must be treated as having been paid on account of the decision eventually made on the earlier claim *(CDLA/3323/2003)*.

The Upper Tribunal has no power to make a declaration of incompatibility under s.4 of the Human Rights Act 1998. In *SH v SSWP (JSA)* [2011] UKUT 428 (AAC), the Judge considered that, there being no other grounds on which the claimant could possibly succeed but it being arguable that the primary legislation in issue was incompatible with the Convention, he should dismiss the appeal before him summarily and grant permission to appeal to the Court of Appeal which can make a declaration of incompatibility. However, he said that the extent to which the Upper Tribunal should enter into the merits of a claimant's contentions in such a case would depend on the particular circumstances of the case. In the case before him, dealing with the arguments would have required the filing of detailed evidence which would ultimately have been unnecessary if the claimant was not minded to take the case to the Court of Appeal due to the risk of an adverse costs order should he lose. In *R. (Kaiyam) v Secretary of State for Justice* [2013] EWCA Civ 1587; [2014] 1 W.L.R. 1208, the Court of Appeal took a similar approach where it was bound by House of Lords authority not to follow subsequent decisions of the European Court of Human Rights. However, in *AB v SSWP (JSA)* [2013] UKUT 288 (AAC) which was another case where the Upper Tribunal considered it unnecessary to consider arguments under the Human Rights Act 1998 because it had no power to make a declaration of incompatibility, the judge declined to grant permission to appeal because, although the case undoubtedly raised a point of principle, he considered that it was best left to the Court of Appeal to decide whether it raised an *important* point of principle or there was some other compelling reason to hear the appeal (see the annotation to s.13(6) and (7)).

A third approach was taken in *PL v SSWP (JSA)* [2016] UKUT 177 (AAC), where the judge decided to consider, and give reasons for rejecting, an argument that primary legislation was incompatible with the Convention and then refused permission to appeal. She took that approach partly because doing so might assist the Court of Appeal if the claimant were to seek permission to appeal but mainly because her view was that the human rights challenge to the legislation was fundamentally flawed and she considered that it might be helpful to the claimant if she were to explain why she had reached that view.

Where a court has made a declaration of incompatibility, a tribunal making a final decision must continue to apply the legislation at it stands, unless and until a remedial order is made under the Human Rights Act 1998 s.10. However, such an order may apply retrospectively. In *JG v SSWP (BB)* [2021] UKUT 194 (AAC), the claimant had appealed to the First-tier Tribunal following a decision of the High Court in Northern Ireland in which a declaration of incompatibility had been made under s.4 of the 1998 Act in respect of legislation equivalent to that applicable in the claimant's case. By the time the claimant's case reached the First-tier Tribunal, the Supreme Court had also made a declaration of incompatibility, but no remedial order under s.10 of the 1998 Act had been made and the First-tier Tribunal dismissed her appeal, applying the unamended legislation. The claimant appealed to the Upper Tribunal and her case was considered at a time when a draft remedial order had been prepared but had not been finalised. The Upper Tribunal said that it was arguable that the First-tier Tribunal should have postponed giving a final decision because a decision on a new claim under legislation as amended by a remedial order that had retrospective effect might be effective from a much later date than a decision made on the original appeal in the light of such an order:

> "Whether that is really necessary in any particular case will depend on the circumstances of the case and it will often not be apparent when the First-tier Tribunal makes its initial decision because it will also depend not only on the remedial action (if any) to be taken but also on what incidental, supplemental or consequential provision is made to make that action effective. It is unlikely that the First-tier Tribunal will be able to anticipate exactly what action will be taken. This case provides a useful illustration."

The Upper Tribunal itself deferred giving a decision until the remedial order had been made and its final terms could be considered.

Although the Upper Tribunal has the power to determine whether subordinate **3.84** legislation is valid insofar as that is necessary for the determination of an appeal (see *Foster v Chief Adjudication Officer* [1993] A.C. 754 (also reported as *R(IS) 22/93*)), there can be a difficulty in providing a remedy if the claimant's claim depends on part of the relevant instrument being valid and the invalid part is not "substantially severable" from the rest of the instrument (i.e., the provision cannot be disapplied without substantially changing the purpose and effect of the legislation, see *Director* *of Public Prosecutions v Hutchinson* [1990] 2 A.C. 783). This is so even if textual severance is possible, the purpose being to avoid judges from trespassing on matters that really fall within the territory of legislators. Thus, in *Attorney-General for Alberta v Attorney-General for Canada* [1947] A.C. 503 at 518, it was said:

> "The real question is whether what remains is so inextricably bound up with the part declared invalid that what remains cannot independently survive or, as has sometimes been put, whether on a fair review of the whole matter it can be assumed that the legislature could have enacted what survives without enacting the part that is ultra vires at all."

That approach was followed in *Independent Jamaica Council for Human Rights (1998) Ltd v Marshall-Burnett* [2005] UKPC 3; [2015] A.C. 356, the consequence being in both cases that primary legislation was struck down *in toto* although only a part of it was unconstitutional.

In *Hutchinson*, Lord Bridge of Harwich who gave the leading speech clearly had that type of approach in mind when, in relation to an earlier case where, without any consideration of severance, an order had been held valid against some people but invalid against others even though textual severance would not have been possible, he held that the decision was justified because substantial severance was possible:

> "In *Daymond v South-West Water Authority* [1976] A.C. 609, the draftsman of the Order had evidently construed the enabling provision as authorising the imposition of charges for sewerage services upon occupiers of property irrespective of whether or not they were connected to sewers. ... But this extension of the scope of the charging power, which, as the majority held, exceeded its proper limit, in no way affected the legislative purpose and effect of the charging power as applied to occupiers of properties which were connected to sewers."

As pointed out by Baroness Hale of Richmond JSC in *Humphreys v Revenue and Customs Commissioners* [2012] UKSC 18; [2012] 1 W.L.R. 1545; [2012] AACR 46, at [34]), similar difficulties can arise in relation to subordinate legislation that is incompatible with a claimant's rights under the European Convention on Human Rights if an invalid provision must be replaced by a new one in order to give the claimant a remedy.

On one analysis, the point is *exactly* the same in both circumstances, because it can be argued that it is generally implicit that enabling powers must be construed so as to permit the making only of subordinate legislation that is compatible with Convention rights. However, cases under the Convention are not usually argued on ultra vires principles, although arguably some could be where severance would be possible. Instead, they are usually argued solely under the Human Rights Act 1998, under which only a person whose Convention rights have been interfered with has a right to a remedy. Therefore, where subordinate legislation has been held to be incompatible with Convention rights, the approach has been to make decisions that are specific to the claimant, rather than to hold the legislation to be invalid for all purposes. In particular, in *Mathieson v Secretary of State for Work and Pensions* [2015] UKSC 47; [2015] 1 W.L.R. 3250; [2015] AACR 19, the Supreme Court was unable to interpret the relevant regulation in a way that was compatible with the claimant's rights but, rather than hold it invalid or issuing a formal declaration (which the Upper Tribunal would have been unable to do), it merely held that the claimant was entitled to benefit, recognising that that would have precedential value in identical cases but also recognising that, on different facts, the regulation might not be incompatible with a claimant's Convention rights. In *RR v Secretary of State for Work and Pensions* [2019] UKSC 52; [2019] 1 W.L.R. 6431; [2020] AACR 7 at [29] to [30], the Supreme Court held that s.6 of the Human Rights Act 1998 required any public authority to take the same approach and so disregard a provision of subordinate legislation that resulted in a breach of a Convention right in any case, provided that it was possible to do so. It would not be possible to do so if it was not clear how the statutory scheme could be applied without the offending provision but, where there was discrimination against a claimant, the authority must "level up" in favour of the claimant even though it would have been open to the legislator to choose between levelling up to the advantage of the claimant or levelling down to the disadvantage of those hitherto treated more favourably. Constitutional proprieties are respected because that choice remains open to the legislator after a decision of a court or tribunal. In other words, if the discrimination is removed, the advantage conferred by the court or tribunal may be withdrawn, subject, of course, to any relevant procedural safeguards that there might be. In *TS (by TS) v SSWP (DLA)* [2020] UKUT 284 (AAC) at [171] to [184], it was pointed out that, when subordinate legislation has been found to have become incompatible with the claimant's Convention rights as the result of an amendment to it, it may be appropriate to disapply the amending instrument rather than the amended one.

Right to appeal to Court of Appeal etc.

13.—(1) For the purposes of subsection (2), the reference to a right of appeal is to a right to appeal to the relevant appellate court on any point of law arising from a decision made by the Upper Tribunal other than an excluded decision. **3.85**

(2) Any party to a case has a right of appeal, subject to subsection (14).

(3) That right may be exercised only with permission (or, in Northern Ireland, leave).

(4) Permission (or leave) may be given by—

(a) the Upper Tribunal, or

(b) the relevant appellate court,

on an application by the party.

(5) An application may be made under subsection (4) to the relevant appellate court only if permission (or leave) has been refused by the Upper Tribunal.

(6) The Lord Chancellor may, as respects an application under subsection (4) that falls within subsection (7) and for which the relevant appellate court is the Court of Appeal in England and Wales or the Court of Appeal in Northern Ireland, by order make provision for permission (or leave) not to be granted on the application unless the Upper Tribunal or (as the case may be) the relevant appellate court considers—

(a) that the proposed appeal would raise some important point of principle or practice, or

(b) that there is some other compelling reason for the relevant appellate court to hear the appeal.

[[1] (6A) Rules of court may make provision for permission not to be granted on an application under subsection (4) to the Court of Session that falls within subsection (7) unless the court considers—

(a) that the proposed appeal would raise some important point of principle[[2] or practice], or

(b) that there is some other compelling reason for the court to hear the appeal.]

(7) An application falls within this subsection if the application is for permission (or leave) to appeal from any decision of the Upper Tribunal on an appeal under section 11.

(8) For the purposes of subsection (1), an "excluded decision" is—

(a) any decision of the Upper Tribunal on an appeal under [[5] section 27(3) or (5), 79(5) or (7) or 111(3) or (5) of the Data Protection Act 2018] (appeals against national security certificate),

(b) any decision of the Upper Tribunal on an appeal under section 60(1) or (4) of the Freedom of Information Act 2000 (appeals against national security certificate),

[[3] (ba) any decision of the Upper Tribunal under section 88, 89(3) or 92(3) of the Tax Collection and Management (Wales) Act 2016 (anaw 6) (approval for Welsh Revenue Authority to issue certain information notices),

(bb) any decision of the Upper Tribunal under section 108 of that Act (approval for Welsh Revenue Authority to inspect premises),]

[[4] (bc) any decision of the Upper Tribunal under section 181E or 181F of that Act (appeals relating to postponement requests),]

(c) any decision of the Upper Tribunal on an application under section 11(4)(b) (application for permission or leave to appeal),

(d) a decision of the Upper Tribunal under section 10—

(i) to review, or not to review, an earlier decision of the tribunal,

(ii) to take no action, or not to take any particular action, in the light of a review of an earlier decision of the tribunal, or

(iii) to set aside an earlier decision of the tribunal,

(e) a decision of the Upper Tribunal that is set aside under section 10 (including a decision set aside after proceedings on an appeal under this section have been begun), or

(f) any decision of the Upper Tribunal that is of a description specified in an order made by the Lord Chancellor.

(9) A description may be specified under subsection (8)(f) only if—

(a) in the case of a decision of that description, there is a right to appeal to a court from the decision and that right is, or includes, something other than a right (however expressed) to appeal on any point of law arising from the decision, or

(b) decisions of that description are made in carrying out a function transferred under section 30 and prior to the transfer of the function under section 30(1) there was no right to appeal from decisions of that description.

(10) Where—

(a) an order under subsection (8)(f) specifies a description of decisions, and

(b) decisions of that description are made in carrying out a function transferred under section 30,

the order must be framed so as to come into force no later than the time when the transfer under section 30 of the function takes effect (but power to revoke the order continues to be exercisable after that time, and power to amend the order continues to be exercisable after that time for the purpose of narrowing the description for the time being specified).

(11) Before the Upper Tribunal decides an application made to it under subsection (4), the Upper Tribunal must specify the court that is to be the relevant appellate court as respects the proposed appeal.

(12) The court to be specified under subsection (11) in relation to a proposed appeal is whichever of the following courts appears to the Upper Tribunal to be the most appropriate—

(a) the Court of Appeal in England and Wales;

(b) the Court of Session;

(c) the Court of Appeal in Northern Ireland.

(13) In this section except subsection (11), "the relevant appellate court", as respects an appeal, means the court specified as respects that appeal by the Upper Tribunal under subsection (11).

(14) The Lord Chancellor may by order make provision for a person to be treated as being, or to be treated as not being, a party to a case for the purposes of subsection (2).

(15) Rules of court may make provision as to the time within which an application under subsection (4) to the relevant appellate court must be made.

AMENDMENTS

1. Crime and Courts Act 2013 s.23 (July 15, 2013).
2. Criminal Justice and Courts Act 2015 s.83(2) (April 13, 2015).
3. Tax Collection and Management (Wales) Act 2016 s.116(2) (January 25, 2018).
4. Tax Collection and Management (Wales) Act 2016 s.118I(2) (as inserted by Land Transaction Tax and Anti-avoidance of Devolved Taxes (Wales) Act 2017 s.76 and Sch.23 para.63) (April 1, 2018).
5. Data Protection Act 2018 s.211 and Sch.19 paras. 130 and 132 (May 25, 2018).

GENERAL NOTE

Subsections (1) and (2)

There is no right of appeal against an "excluded decision", for the meaning of which see subs.(8). There is also no right of appeal against a refusal of permission to appeal to the Upper Tribunal even where such a refusal of permission is not an excluded decision (*Sarfraz v Disclosure and Barring Service* [2015] EWCA Civ 544; [2015] 1 W.L.R. 4441; [2015] AACR 35), although such a refusal of permission may be challenged by way of an application for judicial review without the special procedural restrictions imposed on a challenge to a refusal of permission to appeal from the First-tier Tribunal (see the note to subss.(8) to (10)). There would also be no right of appeal against a ruling of the Upper Tribunal on an issue that did not actually arise in the case in question and was merely intended to give guidance in other cases, because there is no formal jurisdiction to give such a ruling and no party has a sufficient interest in it (*Re X (Court of Protection Practice)* [2015] EWCA Civ 599; [2016] 1 W.L.R. 227). 3.86

For the "relevant appellate court", see subss.(11)–(13).

An appeal lies only on a point of law (for the meaning of which, see the note to s.11(1)) and, where the appeal is against a decision on an appeal under s.11, only if it would raise some important point of principle or practice or there is some other compelling reason for the relevant appellate court to hear the appeal (see the note to subss.(6) and (6A)). Courts are generally reluctant to consider appeals that have ceased to have any practical importance in the particular case concerned, although they may do so if there is a good reason in the public interest (*R. v Secretary of State for the Home Department, ex parte Salem* [1999] 1 A.C. 450).

A "party" is presumably a person who was, or should have been, a party to the proceedings before the Upper Tribunal but see the annotation to s.11(2). Note that s.15 of the Social Security Act 1998 makes additional (and largely unnecessary) provision as to who may appeal from the Upper Tribunal under this section. Subsection (14) permits further provision to be made as to who may or may not exercise the right of appeal.

Where the claimant is the appellant in a social security case, the respondent will be either the Secretary of State for Work and Pensions or His Majesty's Revenue and Customs (*not* the Upper Tribunal). Service should be effected on the Solicitor to the Department for Work and Pensions, Caxton House, Tothill Street, London SW1H 9NA or on General Counsel and Solicitor to HM Revenue and Customs, HM Revenue and Customs, 14 Westfield Avenue, Stratford, London E20 1HZ, as appropriate. 3.87

On an appeal under this section, the Court of Appeal has all the powers of the Upper Tribunal (see the Senior Courts Act 1981 s.15(3) and also CPR r.52.20) and also the powers conferred by s.14. Thus, where an appellant failed to appear and the court considered it inappropriate to determine the appeal in his absence, it struck the appeal out under r.8(3)(b) of the Tribunal Procedure (Upper Tribunal) Rules 2008 and CPR r.52.20, although it expressed its decision in terms of dismissing the appeal (*Leave.EU Group Ltd v Information Commissioner* [2022] EWCA Civ 109).

The court exercises a degree of self-restraint when considering whether a specialist tribunal has got the law wrong (*AH (Sudan) v Secretary of State for the Home Department* [2007] UKHL 49; [2008] 1 A.C. 678, [30]) but less so where the Upper Tribunal has found the First-tier Tribunal to have erred in law on conventional procedural grounds (*AP (Trinidad and Tobago) v Secretary of State for the Home Department* [2011] EWCA Civ 551), although a decision of the Upper Tribunal that a determination by the First-tier Tribunal is inadequately reasoned would be treated with respect by the Court of Appeal (*PK (Congo) v Secretary of State for the Home Department* [2013] EWCA Civ 1500), presumably because the Upper Tribunal considers the adequacy of reasons given by the First-tier Tribunal on a daily basis and effectively sets the standard of reasoning required.

Because appeals from the First-tier Tribunal to the Upper Tribunal and from the Upper Tribunal to an appellate court are both confined to points of law, the issue in an appellate court is often whether the Upper Tribunal was right to find, or not to find, that the First-tier Tribunal erred in law so that the focus, where only conventional public law issues are raised, is simply on whether the First-tier Tribunal erred in law. However, in *R. (Jones) v First-tier Tribunal* [2013] UKSC 19; [2013] 2 A.C. 48; [2013] AACR 25, Lord Hope said—

> "A pragmatic approach should be taken to the dividing line between law and fact, so that the expertise of tribunals at the first-tier and that of the Upper Tribunal can be used to best effect. An appeal court should not venture too readily into this area by classifying issues as issues of law which are really best left for determination by specialist appellate tribunals."

Jones was a case where the Upper Tribunal had rejected a challenge to the decision of the First-tier Tribunal (and in fact did not give any general guidance to promote consistency in decision-making) and the Court of Appeal had overturned its decision but, in a case where the Upper Tribunal has found the First-tier Tribunal to have erred in law and has, under s.12(2)(b)(ii) substituted its own decision for that of the First-tier Tribunal, the implication of it being difficult to decide whether issues are questions of fact or questions of law is that the focus of an appellate court should be on whether the Upper Tribunal's approach was wrong, rather than on whether the First-tier Tribunal's approach was wrong (*per* Lord Carnwath in *Revenue and Customs Commissioners v Pendragon Plc* [2015] UKSC 37; [2015] 1 W.L.R. 2838). Although the Upper Tribunal only had jurisdiction to intervene if the First-tier Tribunal had erred in law, that was not the *main* issue in the case, which had turned on the understanding of a tax law principle and the evaluation of facts in that context rather than on any significant issue of primary fact.

In *R. (MM) v Secretary of State for Work and Pensions* [2013] EWCA Civ 1565; [2016] AACR 11, the Court of Appeal accepted that the Upper Tribunal (Administrative Appeals Chamber) did not have a special expertise in discrimination issues as far as interpretation of the legislation was concerned but its judges were "specialists who are daily dealing with the practices in the social welfare field and are far better equipped than this court to analyse and assess the evidence relating to the particular difficulties which [mental health patients] may face in handling procedures" so that the court would be even more cautious than usual about overturning a finding which was one of mixed law and fact. Similarly, in *Obrey v Secretary of State for Work and Pensions* [2013] EWCA Civ 1584, it was said that "the question whether the indirectly discriminatory effect of a particular rule in the benefits system because it does not distinguish between mental patients and other patients in hospital is, or is not, 'manifestly without reasonable foundation' is very far from being an issue of 'constitutional significance'. On the contrary, it is precisely the kind of issue that is best left for evaluation and judgment by a specialist appellate tribunal with a particular expertise in the field of social security law." In that case, Sullivan L.J. referred to the judgment of Lord Hope in *R. (Jones) v First-tier Tribunal*

However, when the Supreme Court refused permission to appeal, it did so "[w]hile not endorsing the breadth of the Court of Appeal's observations on deference to an expert tribunal on questions of proportionality". Moreover, in *Mathieson v Secretary of State for Work and Pensions* [2015] UKSC 47; [2015] 1 W.L.R. 3250; [2015] AACR 19, the Supreme Court differed from the Upper Tribunal on the question whether social security legislation resulting in unequal treatment was justified because it considered there had been an error of law in the Upper Tribunal's analysis and it had fuller evidence before it. **3.88**

In *R. (Hutton) v First-tier Tribunal* [2016] EWCA Civ 1305, Gross L.J., with whom Rafferty and Floyd L.JJ. agreed, considered the comments of Baroness Hale of Richmond and Lord Hope of Craighead in *AH (Sudan)* and of Lord Hope and Lord Carnwath in *R. (Jones) v First-tier Tribunal* and continued—

"57. Pulling the threads together:

(i) First, this Court should exercise restraint and proceed with caution before interfering with decisions of specialist tribunals. Not only do such tribunals have the expertise which the "ordinary" courts may not have but when a specialised statutory scheme has been entrusted by Parliament to tribunals, the Court should not venture too readily into their field.

(ii) Secondly, if a tribunal decision is clearly based on an error of law, then it must be corrected. This Court should not, however, subject such decisions to inappropriate textual analysis so as to discern an error of law when, on a fair reading of the decision as a whole, none existed. It is probable, as Baroness Hale said, that in understanding and applying the law within their area of expertise, specialist tribunals will have got it right. Moreover, the mere fact that an appellate tribunal or a court would have reached a different conclusion, does not constitute a ground for review or for allowing an appeal.

(iii) Thirdly, it is of the first importance to identify the tribunal of fact, to keep in mind that it and only it will have heard the evidence and to respect its decisions. When determining whether a question was one of "fact" or "law", this Court should have regard to context, as I would respectfully express it ("pragmatism", "expediency" or "policy", *per Jones*), so as to ensure both that decisions of tribunals of fact are given proper weight and to provide scope for specialist appellate tribunals to shape the development of law and practice in their field.

(iv) Fourthly, it is important to note that these authorities not only address the relationship between the courts and specialist appellate tribunals *but also* between specialist first-tier tribunals and appellate tribunals."

In *Secretary of State for Work and Pensions v Robertson* [2015] CSIH 82, the Court of Session held the appeal by the Secretary of State to be incompetent because the Secretary of State had been successful before the Upper Tribunal. Despite his success, the Secretary of State had wished to appeal because, in the course of its decision, the Upper Tribunal had held that a regulation was invalid and the Secretary of State considered that, unless the Court of Session held it to be wrong, he would be bound to follow that finding to the disadvantage of other claimants. The Court of Session held that, because it had not been necessary for the Upper Tribunal to consider whether the regulation was invalid and its finding on that point formed no part of its reason for dismissing the claimant's appeal, the point of law did not arise from the Upper Tribunal's decision. The implication is presumably that the Secretary of State had been wrong to consider that he would be obliged to follow the finding in other cases because it was only *obiter dicta*, although the Court of Session refrained from saying so on the ground that "how the appellant chooses to act is a matter for him".

Normally English and Welsh law is regarded as foreign law in Scotland (and *vice versa*) and so is treated as a matter of fact that has to be proved by evidence. However, where the First-tier Tribunal and Upper Tribunal exercise jurisdiction throughout Great Britain, they are taken to have judicial knowledge of both English and Welsh law and Scots law, wherever they are sitting, so that proof of the law of either part of Great Britain is unnecessary. It follows that, where the Court of Session hears an appeal from the Upper Tribunal in a tax case or social security case, it also is to be taken to have judicial knowledge of English and Welsh law (*Murray Group Holdings Ltd v Revenue and Customs Commissioners* [2015] CSIH 77; 2016 S.C. 201 at [50], upheld on appeal to the Supreme Court but without reference to this point: see *RFC 2012 Plc (formerly The Rangers Football Club Plc) v Advocate General for Scotland* [2017] UKSC 45; [2017] 1 W.L.R. 2767).

It has been held by a three-judge panel of the Immigration and Asylum Chamber of the Upper Tribunal in *VOM v SSHD* [2016] UKUT 410 (IAC) that a right of appeal against a decision of the Upper Tribunal to set aside a decision of the First-tier Tribunal under s.12(2)(a) does not arise until the Upper Tribunal has disposed of the case under s.12(2)(b). However, see the observations on that decision in the annotation to s.12 above.

Subsections (3)–(5)

3.89 Permission to appeal must first be sought from the Upper Tribunal, which gives the Upper Tribunal the opportunity to consider reviewing its decision under s.10 and so remove the necessity for an appeal. If permission is refused by the Upper Tribunal, permission may be sought from the relevant appellate court. It is important for respondents to bear this in mind if they seek not just to resist the appellant's grounds of appeal or to support the Upper Tribunal's decision on a ground that the Upper Tribunal did not consider (which requires the filing of a respondent's notice) but also to argue that the decision should be upheld on a ground that the Upper Tribunal rejected. In those circumstances, there must be a cross-appeal and that requires permission. CPR r.52.13(3) permits such an application to be made in the respondent's notice, although without reference to subs.(5) which appears to require the respondent to seek permission to cross-appeal from the Upper Tribunal in the first instance, even though the case is already pending in the Court of Appeal.

Where a case does not raise an important point of principle or practice, a party is unlikely to be granted permission to appeal on grounds not advanced before the Upper Tribunal if the Upper Tribunal gave a clear opportunity to argue the point by indicating its provisional views (*Secretary of State for Work and Pensions v DH (a child)* [2004] EWCA Civ 16 (reported as *R(DLA) 1/04*)). The Court said that it was "of the utmost value, on an appeal from a specialist tribunal, to have the considered views of the points at issue of that specialist tribunal before testing them on appeal". They were not impressed by the argument that the Commissioner's decision would remain an unfortunate precedent, saying that if the issue was that important it was because there were many similar cases and therefore the Secretary of State would be able to find another case in which to advance his arguments before a Commissioner and, if necessary, the Court.

However, a more relaxed approach is taken where the Upper Tribunal has not given the appellant such an explicit opportunity to address the issue. In *Miskovic v Secretary of State for Work and Pensions* [2011] EWCA Civ 16; [2012] AACR 11, the Court of Appeal rejected an argument, advanced by the Secretary of State, that it was precluded from considering points not argued before the Upper Tribunal and accepted that it could do so, provided it would not be unfair to the other party. This is also the approach of the Court of Session (*Murray Group Holdings Ltd v Revenue and Customs Commissioners* [2015] CSIH 77; 2016 S.C. 201 at [39], upheld on appeal to the Supreme Court (see above) but without reference to this point). The

Court of Appeal also said that it might be reluctant to consider a new point unless all the facts potentially relevant to the correct determination of the point had been found. The public interest in the right decision being made may be material. In *MS (Somalia) v Secretary of State for the Home Department* [2019] EWCA Civ 1345; [2020] Q.B. 364 at [70], the Court of Appeal allowed the appellant Home Secretary to argue that the First-tier Tribunal had failed to apply a statutory presumption in favour of deporting serious criminals on the ground that there was a public interest in such persons being deported when legislation so required. Sometimes, a distinction is drawn between concessions of pure law, which can generally be withdrawn on appeal, and concessions of fact, which generally cannot (e.g., *Glatt v Sinclair* [2013] EWCA Civ 241; [2013] 1 W.L.R. 3602), but that may merely reflect a conventional view that it will not generally be unfair to allow withdrawal of a concession of law but it is more likely to be unfair (and, indeed, inconsistent with the right of appeal where that is limited to points of law) to allow the withdrawal of a concession of fact. Fairness is key, and a grant of permission to appeal is no guarantee that the Court will allow the new point to be taken. Indeed, the fact that permission to appeal has been given by the Court of Appeal itself on a particular point is immaterial if it is a new point that the appellant ought not to be allowed to take on the appeal because taking it would be unfair (*Longfret (UK) Ltd v Revenue and Customs Commissioners* [2020] EWCA Civ 569; [2020] 1 W.L.R. 3809, following *Singh v Dass* [2019] EWCA Civ 360 and *Mullarkey v Broad* [2009] EWCA Civ 2). When deciding whether to allow HMRC to argue new points of EU law on its appeal in *Commissioners for Revenue and Customs v Carrington* [2021] EWCA Civ 174, the Court of Appeal considered (1) the effect of granting such permission on Mrs Carrington; (2) whether the relevant legislation was still relevant; (3) whether there were sufficient findings of fact to enable the court to determine the points of law; (4) whether the new points of law might have a decisive effect on the appeal; and (5) whether, in circumstances where Mrs Carrington had represented herself throughout the proceedings, there would be adequate representation of the opposite case. Permission was given, HMRC having undertaken not to seek repayment of any benefits and to continue making payments of benefits to Mrs Carrington, regardless of the outcome of the appeal, and the Court having adopted HMRC's suggestion that it seek the appointment of an advocate to the Court. However, in a jurisdiction where an appeal lies only on a point of law, which includes a failure to find material facts, and where the Court can remit the matter to a tribunal to make further findings, withdrawal of a concession of fact that is mixed with a concession of law may be justifiable as long as the absence of findings does not make the determination of the point of law too speculative. In any event, if a ground is raised that was not advanced on the appeal before the Upper Tribunal, the Upper Tribunal should consider obtaining the other party's view on it before granting permission (*RH v South London and Maudsley NHS Foundation Trust* [2010] EWCA Civ 1273; [2011] AACR 14). Moreover, if a new point is not raised by an appellant until after the Upper Tribunal has given permission to appeal on some other ground, the appellant must apply to the Court of Appeal for permission to amend the grounds of appeal even if the Upper Tribunal did not expressly limit the grounds on which permission was granted (*Hickey v Secretary of State for Work and Pensions* [2018] EWCA Civ 85).

Where it is necessary for a respondent's notice to be served if a respondent wishes to raise a new point, a failure to comply with the Civil Procedure Rules as regards such notices may result in the Court of Appeal refusing to allow the point to be argued. "The rules are to be complied with by Government litigants in exactly the same way as they are to be complied with by other litigants", even if the consequence is that the point is left open to be taken in other cases so that a finding that a pension scheme involved unlawful discrimination might be effective for the individual appellant alone (*Langford v Secretary of State for Defence* [2019] EWCA Civ 1271; [2020] 1 W.L.R. 537 at [25] and [68]). Arguably, though, if the Secretary of State were minded to maintain his or her position when deciding another case under the scheme, it would be necessary for him or her to draw the claimant's attention to the decision of the court.

A case cannot be said to raise an important point of principle unless the point has not already been established and a party applying for permission to appeal should clearly identify the points of law that are said to raise general points of principle (*Secretary of State for Work and Pensions v Cattrell* [2011] EWCA Civ 572; [2011] AACR 35).

3.90 For the procedure for applying to the Upper Tribunal for permission to appeal, see rr. 44 and 45 of the Tribunal Procedure (Upper Tribunal) Rules 2008. Note that r.44(6)(b) provides that, where the Upper Tribunal refuses to extend the time for applying for permission to appeal, it must refuse permission to appeal, thus satisfying the condition of subs.(5) and reversing the effect of *White v Chief Adjudication Officer* [1986] 2 All E.R. 905 (also reported as an appendix to *R(S) 8/85*). In *White*, it had been held that a Commissioner's refusal to extend time for applying for leave to appeal to the Court of Appeal did not amount to a refusal of leave and was challengeable only by way of a application for judicial review. Now, if permission is refused by the Upper Tribunal on the ground of delay, it is possible for the applicant simply to make an application to the relevant appellant court for permission to appeal, although that court will of course have regard to the delay in applying to the Upper Tribunal. Indeed, at least in England and Wales, the application must include an application to extend time because, where permission to appeal is refused by the Upper Tribunal on the ground that the application to the Upper Tribunal was late, time for appealing to the Court of Appeal runs from the date of the substantive decision of the Upper Tribunal and not from the date of the refusal of permission to appeal (*KM (Bangladesh) v Secretary of State for the Home Department* [2017] EWCA Civ 437).

For the procedure for applying to the Court of Appeal in England and Wales for permission to appeal, see CPR Pt 52. Note that a grant of permission may be set aside by the Court of Appeal under CPR r.52.18, but only "where there is a compelling reason for doing so".

Although both the Upper Tribunal (r.45(5) of the 2008 Rules) and the Court of Appeal (CPR r.52.6(2)) may grant permission to appeal on limited grounds, the Court of Session has no power to do so even if only one ground satisfies the "second appeals test" imposed by rules of court made under subs.(6A) (*HMRC v DCM (Optical Holdings) Ltd* [2019] CSIH 38).

The Upper Tribunal has no express power to grant permission to appeal only on conditions as to costs and it is perhaps doubtful whether it can properly do so. If it does not have the power, it could refuse permission indicating that it is leaving the question of permission to the appellate court so that the imposition of conditions may be considered. If it does impose conditions, any challenge to the conditions by the would-be appellant must be by way of a renewed application to the appellate court for permission to appeal (*R. (Medical Justice) v Secretary of State for the Home Department* [2011] EWCA Civ 269; [2011] 1 W.L.R. 2852). Making a renewed application to the appellate court is also what a would-be appellant must do if he or she fails to comply with any conditions imposed by the Upper Tribunal but still wishes to appeal (*Masri v Consolidated Contractors International Co SAL* [2011] EWCA Civ 898; [2012] 1 W.L.R. 223).

Where the Secretary of State or HMRC seeks permission to appeal in what will be a test case affecting many others, and the proposed respondent is not represented, the appellate court (and the party applying for permission) may wish to take steps with a view to ensuring that the case is properly argued, either by encouraging the respondent to obtain representation or by arranging for the Attorney General to be asked to appoint an advocate to the court. Thus, in *Carrington v Revenue and Customs Commissioners* [2021] EWCA Civ 1724; [2022] 1 W.L.R. 2546 at [17] to [23], it is recorded that HMRC undertook not to apply for costs if it were successful and that the Court suggested that Mrs Carrington seek assistance from Advocate (the Bar Council's pro bono unit). At HMRC's suggestion, the Court also arranged for an advocate to the court to be appointed although, after the advocate had made written submissions, Mrs Carrington obtained pro bono representation and so the Court was able to dispense with further assistance from the advocate.

In November 2020, the Government launched a six-week consultation on *Proposals for reforms to arrangements for obtaining permission to appeal from the Upper Tribunal to the Court of Appeal.* The responses are still being considered.

Subsections (6), (6A) and (7)

The Appeals from the Upper Tribunal to the Court of Appeal Order 2008 (SI 2008/2834) provides that permission to appeal from a decision of the Upper Tribunal to the Court of Appeal may not be given unless one of the conditions set out in subs.(6)(a) and (b) applies. Although the Order does not say so, it can apply only to appeals against decisions of the Upper Tribunal given on appeals under s.11, because subs.(7) limits the order-making power in subs.(6) to such cases (*Clarise Properties Ltd v Rees* [2015] EWCA Civ 1118). Therefore, it does not apply in judicial review proceedings (*R. (Nwankwo) v Secretary of State for the Home Department* [2018] EWCA Civ 5; [2018] 1 W.L.R. 2641). Its effect is duplicated in CPR r.52.7, which makes it clear that the requirement that a second appeal would raise an important point of principle or practice is additional to the test for first appeals which is that the appeal would "have a real prospect of success". If only one of a number of grounds of appeal raises an important point of principle or practice, the Upper Tribunal should carefully consider whether the grant of permission should be limited to that ground (*RH v South London and Maudsley NHS Foundation Trust* [2010] EWCA Civ 1273; [2011] AACR 14). **3.91**

In *PR (Sri Lanka) v Secretary of State for the Home Department* [2011] EWCA Civ 988; [2012] 1 W.L.R. 73, the Court said that, in this context, a point of principle or practice:

> "should be not merely important, but one which calls for attention by the higher courts, specifically the Court of Appeal, rather than being left to be determined within the specialised tribunal system".

It was also held that "compelling" in "some other compelling reason" means legally compelling and indicates that the case must have very high prospects of success. The seriousness of the consequences for the individual or the political importance of the case may be additional grounds but are not by themselves capable of amounting to compelling reasons. Permission was refused in all three cases before the Court. On the other hand, it was held in *JD (Congo) v Secretary of State for the Home Department (Public Law Project intervening)* [2012] EWCA Civ 327; [2012] 1 W.L.R. 3273 that the fact that the Upper Tribunal's decision will have very adverse consequences for the person seeking permission to appeal may, in combination with a strong argument that there has been an error of law, amount to "some other compelling reason" for granting permission to appeal. The point was made that the test is intended to be higher than the ordinary test—a real prospect of success—which is why the argument that there has been an error of law must be "strong". In *MOC v Secretary of State for Work and Pensions* [2022] EWCA Civ 1, the Upper Tribunal had given permission to appeal on the basis that, as the appeal concerned the application of the law to a vulnerable group, it raised "an important point of principle or practice". However, the case ultimately failed on its facts and Singh LJ commented at [74] that it was therefore:

> "... difficult to see how the test for an appeal to this Court could be satisfied, let alone the test for a second appeal. With respect to the UT, this case provides a salutary reminder that, although it has the power to grant permission to appeal, it may be better to leave that question to this Court, which is very familiar with the type of case that will satisfy the second appeal test."

Subsection (6) does not apply to appeals to the Court of Session in Scotland. The Rules of the Court of Session were nonetheless amended in 2008 to limit the grounds upon which permission might be granted by the Court of Session in precisely the same way. In the absence of primary legislation, that amendment was held to be invalid (*KP v Secretary of State for the Home Department* [2012] CSIH 38). Consequently, subs.(6A) was inserted with effect from July 15, 2013 and r.41.57 of the Rules of the Court of Session was promptly made under it, coming into force on August 19, 2013. This purportedly brought the position in Scotland into line with that in England and Wales and Northern Ireland but it was then realised that the words "or practice", which appear in subs.(6)(a), did not appear in subs.(6A)(a) and, accordingly, the rule was amended to omit those words with effect from November 11, 2013. Those words were inserted into subs.(6A)(a) with effect from April 13, 2015, but r.41.57 has not been re-amended in accordance with that amendment. Moreover, r.41.57 does not expressly limit the Upper Tribunal's power to give permission to appeal, although it is arguable that it does so by implication on the basis that, as a matter of comity, the Upper Tribunal ought not to grant permission to appeal to the Court of Session in circumstances where the Court of Session itself could not do so.

That argument was not advanced in either *MCB (Cameroon) v Advocate General for Scotland* [2018] CSIH 6; [2018] SLT 370 or *HMRC v DCM (Optical Holdings) Limited* [2019] CSIH 38), in the latter of which the divergence of the regimes for giving permission in the Upper Tribunal and the Court of Session, both in this regard and as regards the power to give permission on limited grounds, was considered "surprising" and "an area of our procedures which is ripe for review". The Government has consulted on a proposal to legislate to resolve the anomaly.

Subsections (8)–(10)

3.92 Note that subs.(8)(d)(ii) and (iii) does not exclude the right of appeal in respect of decisions made under s.10(4)(a) or (b) to correct accidental errors in earlier decisions or amend reasons. Subsection (8)(e) seems unnecessary. Insofar as it relates to the Upper Tribunal, the Appeals (Excluded Decisions) Order 2009 (SI 2009/275, as amended by SI 2010/41) made under subs.(8)(f) is concerned only with decisions made by the Tax and Chancery Chamber and the Immigration and Asylum Chamber.

In practice, the most important exclusion is the denial of a right of appeal against refusals of permission to appeal to the Upper Tribunal from the First-tier Tribunal (subs.(8)(c)). There is also no right of appeal against a refusal of permission to appeal to the Upper Tribunal from other bodies (*Sarfraz v Disclosure and Barring Service* [2015] EWCA Civ 544; [2015] 1 W.L.R. 4441; [2015] AACR 35) but that is on general policy grounds and not because such a refusal of permission is an excluded decision.

Although an excluded decision may generally be challenged by way of an application to the High Court or Court of Session for judicial review, s.11A now excludes such an application against a refusal of permission to appeal under s.11(4)(b). Where judicial review of an "excluded decision" is still permissible, it is arguable that it is limited to cases that raise some important point of principle or practice or where there is some other compelling reason for the High Court or Court of Session to hear the case (see *R. (Cart) v Upper Tribunal (Public Law Project intervening)* [2011] UKSC 28; [2012] 1 A.C. 663; [2011] AACR 38 in relation to England and Wales and *Advocate General for Scotland v Eba* [2011] UKSC 29; [2012] 1 A.C. 710; [2011] AACR 39 in relation to Scotland, both decided in relation to challenges to refusals of permission to appeal under s.11(4)(b) before s.11A came into force) although, in *Eba* (see that decision at [20]), it appears to have been conceded by counsel for the Government that no such limitation would apply to challenges to decisions excluded under para.(8)(a) or (b) of this section. It is generally inappropriate to order costs against a respondent tribunal in judicial review proceedings unless the tribunal actively resists the challenge to its decision (*R. (Davies) v Birmingham Deputy Coroner* [2004] EWCA Civ 207; [2004] 1 W.L.R. 2739) and it is also likely to be inappropriate to award costs against the interested party if that party has not requested a hearing so as to resist the application although, if the tribunal has a power to award costs, it may be appropriate to direct that the costs of the judicial review proceedings be treated as costs in the tribunal proceedings (*R. (Faqiri) v Upper Tribunal* [2019] EWCA Civ 151; [2019] 1 W.L.R. 4497). In a social security case, where the Upper Tribunal has no power to award costs (see r.10 of the Tribunal Procedure (Upper Tribunal) Rules 2008), it is likely to be appropriate for the High Court simply to make no order for costs if neither the Upper Tribunal nor the interested party has resisted the application.

There was a question as to whether there is any right of appeal against a refusal to set aside an "excluded decision" such as a refusal of permission to appeal. In *Samuda v Secretary of State for Work and Pensions* [2014] EWCA Civ 1, a two-judge court sat to consider an application for permission to appeal, to the Court of Appeal presumably with a view to answering that question. Unfortunately, although the Upper Tribunal had relied on r.43 (see its reasons for refusing permission to appeal as set out in Sir Stanley Burnton's judgment at [6]), the Court seems to have understood that, in considering whether to set aside the refusal of permission, the Upper Tribunal was considering whether to review it under s.10. The Court therefore dismissed the application on the ground that there was no power to review an "excluded decision" (see s.10(1)) and that, in any event, any purported refusal to review would itself be an "excluded decision" under s.13(8)(d). However, r.43 is made under a rule-making power that is not related to s.10, as has now been pointed out in *R. (Singh) v Secretary of State for the Home Department* [2019] EWCA Civ 1014 at [25] and [26], and so the real question was simply whether s.13(8)(c) was to be construed as extending to any refusal to set aside a refusal of permission to appeal under r.43 (or a refusal to make a correction to a refusal of permission to appeal under r.42) in order to give full effect to the legislature's intention. However, arguments to that effect were rejected in *Plecsan v Secretary of State for Work and Pensions* [2023] EWCA Civ 870, where the Court took a literal approach to the legislation and held that a decision refusing to set aside a refusal of permission to appeal was not an excluded decision. A narrow view of the exclusion of a right of appeal has also been taken in the context of analogous legislation relating to appeals from a county court, under which there was no right of appeal to the Court of Appeal from a decision of a circuit judge refusing permission to appeal to himself from a decision of a district judge. It has been held that that does not preclude an appeal against a decision to strike out an application for permission to appeal to a circuit judge and that, in the circumstances of the case, an order drawn as a dismissal of an application for permission to appeal was in fact a striking out of the application so that an appeal lay to the Court of Appeal (*Patel v Mussa* [2015] EWCA Civ 434; [2015] 1 W.L.R. 4788). **3.93**

Subsections (11)–(13)

The Upper Tribunal must specify the relevant appellate court even if it refuses permission to appeal, so that the applicant knows to which court to renew the application. In a social security case, the relevant appellate court will generally be where the claimant lives but there is a considerable element of discretion where there are more than two parties or where the claimant has moved. Relevant considerations are likely to be the convenience of the parties and whether the case raises a point of law where the law may not be the same in all parts of the United Kingdom. **3.94**

The Court of Appeal does not have jurisdiction to hear an appeal where the Upper Tribunal has specified the Court of Session as the relevant appellate court. In *Khurshid v Secretary of State for the Home Department* [2021] EWCA Civ 1515, both the hearing before the First-tier Tribunal and the hearing before the Upper Tribunal had been in Scotland (where the appellant had been living since before bringing his appeal to the First-tier Tribunal) and the Upper Tribunal had specified the Court of Session as the "relevant appellate court". The Court of Appeal accepted, referring to *Tehrani v Secretary of State for the Home Department* [2006] UKHL 47; [2007] 1 A.C. 521, that, had there been exceptional circumstances, it would have been able to reconstitute itself as an administrative court for the purpose of considering an application for judicial review of the Upper Tribunal's decision. However, the appellant's desire to be represented by his English solicitors did not justify such an application when the Court of Session was obviously the relevant appellate court and the Upper Tribunal had specified it as such. It is usual for a judge of the Administrative Appeals Chamber of the Upper Tribunal expressly to specify the relevant appellate court in the body of a grant or refusal of permission to appeal. However, that has not always been so in the Immigration and Asylum Chamber and, in *KP (Pakistan) v Secretary of State for the Home Department* [2019] EWCA Civ 556; [2019] 1 W.L.R. 5631, the Court of Appeal held the Court of Session to have been adequately specified as a result of it merely being named in the heading of the refusal of permission. The result was that the Court of Appeal did not have jurisdiction to consider the appeal before it, notwithstanding that the Court of Appeal itself had given permission after the Upper Tribunal had refused it and that, in breach of r.45(4)(b) of the Tribunal Procedure (Upper Tribunal) Rules 2008, the covering letter sent by the Upper Tribunal with the refusal of permission had explained how a renewed application could be made to the Court of Appeal but had failed to explain how one could be made to the Court of Session.

Subsection (14)

3.95 No relevant order has been made but note that s.13 of the Social Security (Recovery of Benefits) Act 1997, s.14 of the Social Security Act 1998 and legislation concerning housing benefit, council tax benefit and child support maintenance (outside the scope of this work) make further provision as to who may appeal to an appellate court under this section.

Subsection (15)

3.96 In England and Wales, see C.P.R r.52.2 and PD 52D para.3.3, under which the time limit for filing an appellant's notice is now "within 28 days of the date on which notice of the Upper Tribunal's decision on permission to appeal to the Court of Appeal is sent to the appellant". Before October 1, 2012, the time limit for appeals from the Administrative Appeals Chamber was 42 days, which had always been the time limit for appeals from Social Security Commissioners. It was then surprisingly reduced to 21 days until October 1, 2014, when it was increased to the current 28 days to bring it into line with the time limit for appeals from other chambers.

Note, however, that from October 3, 2016 the time limit is only 7 days where the application for permission to appeal follows a refusal by the Upper Tribunal to give permission to appeal against a refusal of permission to bring judicial review proceedings and, if permission to appeal was refused by the Upper Tribunal at a hearing (which is rare in the Administrative Appeals Chamber), it runs from the date of the hearing (CPR r.52.9(3)).

Generally, a successful appellant in the Court of Appeal is entitled to recover their costs of the proceedings in the Court of Appeal, even where an appeal is disposed of by consent (*AL (Albania) v Secretary of State for the Home Department* [2012] EWCA Civ 710; [2012] 1 W.L.R. 2898).

Formerly, Chapter 41 of the Rules of the Court of Session made similar provision in Scotland to that made at the time in England and Wales. The time limit remains 42 days in Scotland but Chapter 41 was rewritten with effect from September 27, 2011 without due regard to the practice of the Upper Tribunal of giving its decisions in writing which has the effect that applications for permission are inevitably made on paper some time after the substantive decision is given. Whereas r.41.26(2) provides that an appeal must be lodged within 42 days of a decision granting permission to appeal being intimated to the appellant, r.41.2(4) provides that an application for permission to appeal must be made within 42 days of the date on which the decision appealed against was intimated to the appellant. Read literally, this would mean that the time for applying to the court expires before the time for applying to the Upper Tribunal. Exactly the same problem had arisen under an earlier version of r.41.2 and had been considered in *Hakim: re Application for Leave to Appeal* [2001] ScotCS 59; 2001 SC 789. The Court of Session took a pragmatic approach and held that the period of 42 days mentioned in the rule should be taken to run from the date of the refusal of leave to appeal by the relevant tribunal, even though that involved "a somewhat forced reading of the statutory provisions and the rules".

Proceedings on appeal to Court of Appeal etc.

14.—(1) Subsection (2) applies if the relevant appellate court, in deciding an appeal under section 13, finds that the making of the decision concerned involved the making of an error on a point of law. 3.97

(2) The relevant appellate court—

(a) may (but need not) set aside the decision of the Upper Tribunal, and

(b) if it does, must either—

(i) remit the case to the Upper Tribunal or, where the decision of the Upper Tribunal was on an appeal or reference from another tribunal or some other person, to the Upper Tribunal or that other tribunal or person, with directions for its reconsideration, or

(ii) re-make the decision.

(3) In acting under subsection (2)(b)(i), the relevant appellate court may also—

(a) direct that the persons who are chosen to reconsider the case are not to be the same as those who—

(i) where the case is remitted to the Upper Tribunal, made the decision of the Upper Tribunal that has been set aside, or

(ii) where the case is remitted to another tribunal or person, made the decision in respect of which the appeal or reference to the Upper Tribunal was made;

(b) give procedural directions in connection with the reconsideration of the case by the Upper Tribunal or other tribunal or person.

(4) In acting under subsection (2)(b)(ii), the relevant appellate court—

(a) may make any decision which the Upper Tribunal could make if the Upper Tribunal were re-making the decision or (as the case may be) which the other tribunal or person could make if that other tribunal or person were re-making the decision, and

(b) may make such findings of fact as it considers appropriate.

(5) Where—

(a) under subsection (2)(b)(i) the relevant appellate court remits a case to the Upper Tribunal, and

(b) the decision set aside under subsection (2)(a) was made by the Upper Tribunal on an appeal or reference from another tribunal or some other person,

the Upper Tribunal may (instead of reconsidering the case itself) remit the case to that other tribunal or person, with the directions given by the relevant appellate court for its reconsideration.

(6) In acting under subsection (5), the Upper Tribunal may also—

(a) direct that the persons who are chosen to reconsider the case are not to be the same as those who made the decision in respect of which the appeal or reference to the Upper Tribunal was made;

(b) give procedural directions in connection with the reconsideration of the case by the other tribunal or person.

(7) In this section "the relevant appellate court", as respects an appeal under section 13, means the court specified as respects that appeal by the Upper Tribunal under section 13(11).

General Note

The Court of Appeal is a creature of statute and has only the powers conferred upon it by legislation. On an appeal from the Upper Tribunal, it has all the powers of 3.98

the Upper Tribunal (Senior Courts Act s.15(3) and also CPR r.52.20), the powers conferred by this section and the power to grant a declaration of incompatibility under s.4 of the Human Rights Act 1998 if it determines that a provision of primary legislation is incompatible with a Convention right. However, it does not have a power to make a declaration of any other type unless the Upper Tribunal had such a power, which it would in judicial review proceedings but not when hearing an appeal from the First-tier Tribunal. In *Humphreys v Revenue and Customs Commissioners* [2012] UKSC 18; [2012] 1 W.L.R. 1545; [2012] AACR 46, Baroness Hale of Richmond JSC observed (at [34]) that it was not obvious how a remedy could be provided on a statutory appeal if it was held that a provision in subordinate legislation should be disapplied because it was inconsistent with the European Convention on Human Rights but it was then necessary to read in an alternative provision in order to overcome the effect of primary legislation that was not in itself incompatible with a Convention right. This highlights a difficulty with the reasoning in *Francis v Secretary of State for Work and Pensions* [2005] EWCA Civ 1303 (also reported as *R(IS) 6/06*), in which the Court of Appeal declined to read additional words into a regulation and instead asserted a power to make a declaration (*not* a declaration of incompatibility), perhaps overlooking the fact that the proceedings before it had not been brought by way of an application for judicial review. In *Burnip v Birmingham CC* [2012] EWCA Civ 629; [2013] AACR 7, decided the day before *Humphreys*, the Court followed *Francis* in granting a declaration. In *Mathieson v Secretary of State for Work and Pensions* [2015] UKSC 47; [2015] 1 W.L.R. 3250; [2015] AACR 19, the Supreme Court was unable to interpret the relevant regulation in a way that was compatible with the claimant's rights and also declined to issue a declaration if, which it did not decide, it had a power to do so when the Court of Appeal had not. It merely disapplied the offending provision and held that the claimant was entitled to benefit, recognising that that would have precedential value in identical cases but also recognising that, on different facts, the regulation might not be incompatible with a claimant's Convention rights. It has now been made clear that any public authority, including a tribunal, must take the same approach (*RR v Secretary of State for Work and Pensions* [2019] UKSC 52; [2019] 1 W.L.R. 6431; [2020] AACR 7--see the note to s.12).

It was made plain in *McAllister v Secretary of State for Work and Pensions*, 2003 S.L.T. 1195 that, before allowing an appeal against a decision of a person or body exercising statutory powers, the Court of Session in Scotland requires to be satisfied that there are proper grounds for doing so. Therefore, a written argument must be submitted, on the basis of which the Court will decide whether the case should be listed for hearing. In England and Wales, the Court of Appeal readily allows appeals by consent, without considering their merits but usually only if satisfied that the parties' consent to allow the appeal is based on apparently competent legal advice and if the parties have advanced plausible reasons to show that the decision of the lower court was wrong. It would not generally do so if, for instance, it was aware that the decision of the lower court had been reported and was causing difficulties. See *Rochdale MBC v KW (No.2)* [2015] EWCA Civ 1054; [2016] 1 W.L.R. 198, where it was held that a judge of the Court of Protection had been bound by a consent order of the Court of Appeal and it was futile and inappropriate for him to seek to undermine it by complaining that it was ultra vires or wrong for any other reason. There have been a number of instances where decisions of Commissioners or the Upper Tribunal have been set aside by the Court of Appeal without the Court considering the merits of the appeal. Although such a decision given by the Court of Appeal is not binding on anyone other than for the purposes of that particular case (*R(FC) 1/97*), it can create difficulties because the decision that has been set aside plainly cannot be regarded as binding either, although the reasoning may still be regarded as persuasive. The law is thus left uncertain.

[1 Appeal to Supreme Court: grant of certificate by Upper Tribunal

14A.—(1) If the Upper Tribunal is satisfied that— 3.99

(a) the conditions in subsection (4) or (5) are fulfilled in relation to the Upper Tribunal's decision in any proceedings, and

(b) as regards that decision, a sufficient case for an appeal to the Supreme Court has been made out to justify an application under section 14B,

the Upper Tribunal may grant a certificate to that effect.

(2) The Upper Tribunal may grant a certificate under this section only on an application made by a party to the proceedings.

(3) The Upper Tribunal may grant a certificate under this section only if the relevant appellate court as regards the proceedings is—

(a) the Court of Appeal in England and Wales, or

(b) the Court of Appeal in Northern Ireland.

(4) The conditions in this subsection are that a point of law of general public importance is involved in the decision of the Upper Tribunal and that point of law is—

(a) a point of law that—

(i) relates wholly or mainly to the construction of an enactment or statutory instrument, and

(ii) has been fully argued in the proceedings and fully considered in the judgment of the Upper Tribunal in the proceedings, or

(b) a point of law—

(i) in respect of which the Upper Tribunal is bound by a decision of the relevant appellate court or the Supreme Court in previous proceedings, and

(ii) that was fully considered in the judgments given by the relevant appellate court or, as the case may be, the Supreme Court in those previous proceedings.

(5) The conditions in this subsection are that a point of law of general public importance is involved in the decision of the Upper Tribunal and that—

(a) the proceedings entail a decision relating to a matter of national importance or consideration of such a matter,

(b) the result of the proceedings is so significant (whether considered on its own or together with other proceedings or likely proceedings) that, in the opinion of the Upper Tribunal, a hearing by the Supreme Court is justified, or

(c) the Upper Tribunal is satisfied that the benefits of earlier consideration by the Supreme Court outweigh the benefits of consideration by the Court of Appeal.

(6) Before the Upper Tribunal decides an application made to it under this section, the Upper Tribunal must specify the court that would be the relevant appellate court if the application were an application for permission (or leave) under section 13.

(7) In this section except subsection (6) and in sections 14B and 14C, "the relevant appellate court", as respects an application, means the court specified as respects that application by the Upper Tribunal under subsection (6).

(8) No appeal lies against the grant or refusal of a certificate under subsection (1).]

AMENDMENT

1. Criminal Justice and Courts Act 2015 s.64 (August 8, 2016).

GENERAL NOTE

3.100 Sections 14A to 14C provide for "leapfrog" appeals straight to the Supreme Court from the Upper Tribunal, thus putting the Upper Tribunal in the same position as the High Court (see ss.12 to 16 of the Administration of Justice Act 1969). Note that, by virtue of s.14A(3), the new sections do not apply if the relevant appellate court would be the Court of Session in Scotland. Section 14C excludes the operation of s.14A in certain types of case.

The circumstances in which the Upper Tribunal might issue a certificate under s.14A will be very rare, particularly where only the conditions of s.14A(4)(a) are satisfied. Note that even where a certificate is issued, the Upper Tribunal may not itself give permission to appeal to the Supreme Court. If the Supreme Court refuses permission, the would-be appellant may appeal to the Court of Appeal. Section 14C(3) provides that a certificate may not be issued under s.14A unless the Upper Tribunal would have given permission to appeal to the Court of Appeal but it does not expressly provide that a certificate is to be taken as the grant of such permission in the event of the Supreme Court refusing permission to appeal to that court.

The first certificate under this section was issued to enable the Supreme Court to decide a case where subs.(4)(b) was satisfied (*RR v Secretary of State for Work and Pensions* [2019] UKSC 52; [2019] 1 W.L.R. 6431; [2020] AACR 7).

[1 Appeal to Supreme Court: permission to appeal

3.101 **14B.—**(1) If the Upper Tribunal grants a certificate under section 14A in relation to any proceedings, a party to those proceedings may apply to the Supreme Court for permission to appeal directly to the Supreme Court.

(2) An application under subsection (1) must be made—

(a) within one month from the date on which that certificate is granted, or

(b) within such time as the Supreme Court may allow in a particular case.

(3) If on such an application it appears to the Supreme Court to be expedient to do so, the Supreme Court may grant permission for such an appeal.

(4) If permission is granted under this section—

(a) no appeal from the decision to which the certificate relates lies to the relevant appellate court, but

(b) an appeal lies from that decision to the Supreme Court.

(5) An application under subsection (1) is to be determined without a hearing.

(6) Subject to subsection (4), no appeal lies to the relevant appellate court from a decision of the Upper Tribunal in respect of which a certificate is granted under section 14A until—

(a) the time within which an application can be made under subsection (1) has expired, and

(b) where such an application is made, that application has been determined in accordance with this section.]

AMENDMENT

1. Criminal Justice and Courts Act 2015 s.64 (August 8, 2016).

[1 Appeal to Supreme Court: exclusions

14C.—(1) No certificate may be granted under section 14A in respect of a decision of the Upper Tribunal in any proceedings where, by virtue of any enactment (other than sections 14A and 14B), no appeal would lie from that decision of the Upper Tribunal to the relevant appellate court, with or without the permission (or leave) of the Upper Tribunal or the relevant appellate court. **3.102**

(2) No certificate may be granted under section 14A in respect of a decision of the Upper Tribunal in any proceedings where, by virtue of any enactment, no appeal would lie from a decision of the relevant appellate court on that decision of the Upper Tribunal to the Supreme Court, with or without the permission (or leave) of the relevant appellate court or the Supreme Court.

(3) Where no appeal would lie to the relevant appellate court from the decision of the Upper Tribunal except with the permission (or leave) of the Upper Tribunal or the relevant appellate court, no certificate may be granted under section 14A in respect of a decision of the Upper Tribunal unless it appears to the Upper Tribunal that it would be a proper case for giving permission (or leave) to appeal to the relevant appellate court.

(4) No certificate may be granted under section 14A in respect of a decision or order of the Upper Tribunal made by it in the exercise of its jurisdiction to punish for contempt.]

AMENDMENT

1. Criminal Justice and Courts Act 2015 s.64 (August 8, 2016).

"Judicial review"

Upper Tribunal's "judicial review" jurisdiction

15.—(1) The Upper Tribunal has power, in cases arising under the law of England and Wales or under the law of Northern Ireland, to grant the following kinds of relief— **3.103**

(a) a mandatory order;
(b) a prohibiting order;
(c) a quashing order;
(d) a declaration;
(e) an injunction.

(2) The power under subsection (1) may be exercised by the Upper Tribunal if—

(a) certain conditions are met (see section 18), or
(b) the tribunal is authorised to proceed even though not all of those conditions are met (see section 19(3) and (4)).

(3) Relief under subsection (1) granted by the Upper Tribunal—

(a) has the same effect as the corresponding relief granted by the High Court on an application for judicial review, and
(b) is enforceable as if it were relief granted by the High Court on an application for judicial review.

(4) In deciding whether to grant relief under subsection (1)(a), (b) or (c), the Upper Tribunal must apply the principles that the High Court would apply in deciding whether to grant that relief on an application for judicial review.

(5) In deciding whether to grant relief under subsection (1)(d) or (e), the Upper Tribunal must—

(a) in cases arising under the law of England and Wales apply the principles that the High Court would apply in deciding whether to grant that relief under section 31(2) of the [1 Senior Courts Act 1981] on an application for judicial review, and

(b) in cases arising under the law of Northern Ireland apply the principles that the High Court would apply in deciding whether to grant that relief on an application for judicial review.

[2 (5A) In cases arising under the law of England and Wales, subsections (2A) and (2B) of section 31 of the Senior Courts Act 1981 apply to the Upper Tribunal when deciding whether to grant relief under subsection (1) as they apply to the High Court when deciding whether to grant relief on an application for judicial review.

(5B) If the tribunal grants relief in reliance on section 31(2B) of the Senior Courts Act 1981 as applied by subsection (5A), the tribunal must certify that the condition in section 31(2B) as so applied is satisfied.]

(6) For the purposes of the application of subsection (3)(a) in relation to cases arising under the law of Northern Ireland—

(a) a mandatory order under subsection (1)(a) shall be taken to correspond to an order of mandamus,

(b) a prohibiting order under subsection (1)(b) shall be taken to correspond to an order of prohibition, and

(c) a quashing order under subsection (1)(c) shall be taken to correspond to an order of certiorari.

AMENDMENTS

1. Constitutional Reform Act 2005 s.59(5) and para.1(2) of Sch.11 (October 1, 2009).

2. Criminal Justice and Courts Act 2015 s.84(4) (August 8, 2016).

GENERAL NOTE

Subsections (1) to (5)

3.104 Sections 15 to 21 introduce the novel concept of a tribunal exercising "judicial review" powers. The provisions are set out in this work because "judicial review" proceedings in relation to the First-tier Tribunal (and perhaps some other "judicial review" proceedings in the social security sphere) are likely to find their way to the Upper Tribunal.

Section 18(6) enables the Lord Chief Justice of England and Wales or the Lord Chief Justice of Northern Ireland to issue a Practice Direction having the effect that cases falling within a specified class will be within the jurisdiction of the Upper Tribunal subject to the other conditions mentioned in s.18 being met. Such cases must be started by making an application for "judicial review" directly to the Upper Tribunal under s.16. If an application is made to the court in such a case, the court will be bound to transfer the case to the Upper Tribunal under s.31A of the Senior Courts Act 1981 or s.25A of the Judicature (Northern Ireland) Act 1978, as the case may be, both those provisions having been inserted into the relevant Acts by s.19 of this Act. Those provisions also permit any case that does not fall within a class specified in a Practice Direction but where other conditions are satisfied to be transferred to the Upper Tribunal on a case-by-case basis. Relevant considerations will include the expertise of the Upper Tribunal in those areas in which it exercises an appellate jurisdiction (including social security law), which might point towards a transfer, and the role and standing of the High Court, which might suggest refusing a transfer in a particularly novel, complex or important case. It is always possible for the High Court to transfer a case with a recommendation that it be heard in the Upper Tribunal by a High Court judge, so as to achieve "the best of both worlds", but, even when a High Court judge is sitting, the Upper Tribunal has no power to make a declaration of incompatibility under s.4 of the Human Rights Act 1998. Another consideration that may be particularly relevant where there is an unrepresented litigant, is the less formal procedure in the Upper Tribunal which permits, for instance, a decision to be made without a hearing. If a case that is not within a specified class is started in the Upper Tribunal in error, the Upper Tribunal must transfer it to the High Court in England and Wales (i.e. the Administrative Court) or the High Court in Northern Ireland, as the case requires, under s.18(3).

By virtue of ss.20 and 21, the position in Scotland is similar, the main difference being that cases cannot be started in the Upper Tribunal.

The Court of Session and the Upper Tribunal may have overlapping jurisdiction **3.105**
in criminal injuries compensation cases having both an English dimension and a Scottish one and a decision has to be made as to where it is more appropriate for a case to be heard, having regard to the facts of the case and its procedural history. In *MB v First-tier Tribunal (CIC)* [2012] UKUT 286 (AAC); [2013] AACR 10 and *NF v First- tier Tribunal (CIC)* [2012] UKUT 287 (AAC); [2013] AACR 11, a three-judge panel considered two cases in both of which the claimant lived in Scotland but the decision of the First-tier Tribunal being challenged had been made on the papers in England. In the first case, the crime causing injury had been committed in England and, in the second case, it had been committed in Scotland. It was held that the Upper Tribunal had jurisdiction in the first case but, in the second case, proceedings were stayed while the applicant made an application to the Court of Session.

Those decisions were considered in *R.(CICA) v First-tier Tribunal (CIC)* [2018] UKUT 439 (AAC); [2019] AACR 18, where the Upper Tribunal held that a case is one "arising under the law of England and Wales" if an application for judicial review is made to the Upper Tribunal on the basis that the High Court of England and Wales would have jurisdiction but for ss.15 to 18. The Upper Tribunal can have no greater jurisdiction than the High Court would have had and, therefore, the Upper Tribunal struck out an application for judicial review seeking a quashing order in respect of a decision of the First-tier Tribunal that had been made in Scotland in a case where all the material events had occurred in Scotland. It did not rule out the possibility that, in the strict sense, the High Court would have had jurisdiction because the First-tier Tribunal was a United Kingdom tribunal that had been exercising powers under legislation applying throughout Great Britain, but, if it did have jurisdiction in that sense, it declined to exercise it (in the same way that it considered the High Court would have done) on the ground that England and Wales was a *forum non conveniens* and so any application should have been brought in the Court of Session. The Upper Tribunal having refused jurisdiction and despite presumably being out of time, the Criminal Injuries Compensation Authority successfully brought judicial review proceedings in the Court of Session (*Advocate General for Scotland, Petitioner* [2019] CSOH 79; 2019 S.L.T. 1373—see the note to s.3(1) above, under the heading *Use of the tribunal's own expertise or observations*).

The main difference between "judicial review" proceedings seeking a "quashing order" or its equivalent in respect of a tribunal decision and an appeal is that the tribunal that made the decision will itself be the respondent in "judicial review" proceedings, although it will seldom take an active part and will usually leave any application to be contested by the "interested party" (who would be the respondent in an appeal). However, another major difference is that, in judicial review proceedings, the Upper Tribunal has a far more limited power to give a final decision rather than remitting the case to the lower tribunal (compare ss.12 and 17). An application for a "mandatory order" or its equivalent might be sought if it was claimed that a tribunal had failed or refused to make a decision and a "prohibiting order" or its equivalent might be sought if it was desired to prevent a tribunal from making a decision.

Generally, though, the same procedural rules that apply to appeals apply also to judicial review proceedings. So do Practice Directions, including *Practice Direction (First-tier and Upper Tribunals: Child, Vulnerable Adults and Sensitive Witnesses)*, below, and so a failure to consider what reasonable adjustments might be needed by a vulnerable claimant may render a decision of the First-tier Tribunal wrong in law (*R (NL) v First-tier Tribunal (CIC)* [2021] UKUT 158 (AAC)).

Subsections (5A) and (5B)

3.106 These subsections do not apply in relation to any case where the application for relief was received by the Upper Tribunal before August 8, 2016 (Criminal Justice and Courts Act 2015 (Commencement No. 4 and Transitional Provisions) Order 2016 (SI 2016/717) art.6).

Nor do they apply to cases where the law of Northern Ireland applies. Perhaps unnecessarily, s.16(3C) to (3F) makes equivalent provision in relation to applications for permission to bring judicial review proceedings in cases under the law of England and Wales.

Subsections (2A) and (2B) were inserted into s.31 of the Senior Courts Act 1981 with effect from April 13, 2015 by s.84(1) of the same Act as inserted subss.(5A) and (5B) into this section and they provide:

"(2A) The High Court—

(a) must refuse to grant relief on an application for judicial review, and

(b) may not make an award under subsection (4) on such an application,

if it appears to the court to be highly likely that the outcome for the applicant would not have been substantially different if the conduct complained of had not occurred.

(2B) The court may disregard the requirements in subsection (2A)(a) and (b) if it considers that it is appropriate to do so for reasons of exceptional public interest."

The reference to "subsection (4)" in s.31(2A)(b) is to the High Court's power to award "damages, restitution or the recovery of a sum due". See s.16(6) of the 2007 Act for the Upper Tribunal's equivalent power and s.16(6A) for provision equivalent to s.31(2A)(b) of the 1981 Act.

Before all these amendments, the High Court and Upper Tribunal generally exercised its discretion to withhold judicial review if satisfied that an error of law had not made a difference to the outcome. However, apart from the fact that s.16(3C)(b) makes it mandatory for the Upper Tribunal to consider the issue where the respondent asks it to do so on an application for permission, the new statutory test is expressed in terms of it being "highly likely" that the outcome would have been "substantially" different. If this is to be a more rigorous test than they previously applied, it will also be more difficult in many cases. As Blake J said in *R. (Logan) v Havering LBC* [2015] EWHC 3193 (Admin) at [59]:

> "In the absence of clear pointers at the time that the flaw was a technical one that made no difference, the court will inevitably be drawn into some degree of speculation or second guessing the decision of the public authority that has the institutional competence to make it."

There is also the question of the extent to which, if the respondent tells the Upper Tribunal that it would have made the same decision irrespective of the claimed error, the Upper Tribunal is entitled to go behind that submission. However, this question will hardly ever arise in practice in the Administrative Appeals Chamber because the respondent in most cases before that Chamber of the Upper Tribunal is the First-tier Tribunal, which seldom takes any part in the proceedings. This, of course, makes s.16(3C)(b) of limited effect too, although if any interested party argues that the claimed error of law would not have made any difference to the outcome the Upper Tribunal would anyway be bound to address the contention in pursuance of its duty to give reasons for its decision.

Application for relief under section 15(1)

16.—(1) This section applies in relation to an application to the Upper Tribunal for relief under section 15(1). 3.107

(2) The application may be made only if permission (or, in a case arising under the law of Northern Ireland, leave) to make it has been obtained from the tribunal.

(3) The tribunal may not grant permission (or leave) to make the application unless it considers that the applicant has a sufficient interest in the matter to which the application relates.

(3A) *Not yet in force.*

(3B) *Not yet in force.*

[1 (3C) In cases arising under the law of England and Wales, when considering whether to grant permission to make the application, the tribunal—

(a) may of its own initiative consider whether the outcome for the applicant would have been substantially different if the conduct complained of had not occurred, and

(b) must consider that question if the respondent asks it to do so.

(3D) In subsection (3C) "the conduct complained of" means the conduct (or alleged conduct) of the respondent that the applicant claims justifies the tribunal in granting relief.

(3E) If, on considering the question mentioned in subsection (3C)(a) and (b), it appears to the tribunal to be highly likely that the outcome for the applicant would not have been substantially different, the tribunal must refuse to grant permission.

(3F) The tribunal may disregard the requirement in subsection (3E) if it considers that it is appropriate to do so for reasons of exceptional public interest.

(3G) If the tribunal grants permission in reliance on subsection (3F), the tribunal must certify that the condition in subsection (3F) is satisfied.]

(4) Subsection (5) applies where the tribunal considers—

(a) that there has been undue delay in making the application, and

(b) that granting the relief sought on the application would be likely to cause substantial hardship to, or substantially prejudice the rights of, any person or would be detrimental to good administration.

(5) The tribunal may—

(a) refuse to grant permission (or leave) for the making of the application;

(b) refuse to grant any relief sought on the application.

(6) The tribunal may award to the applicant damages, restitution or the recovery of a sum due if—

(a) the application includes a claim for such an award arising from any matter to which the application relates, and

(b) the tribunal is satisfied that such an award would have been made by the High Court if the claim had been made in an action begun in the High Court by the applicant at the time of making the application.

[1 (6A) In cases arising under the law of England and Wales, subsections (2A) and (2B) of section 31 of the Senior Courts Act 1981 apply to the Upper Tribunal as regards the making of an award under subsection (6) as they apply to the High Court as regards the making of an award under section 31(4) of the Senior Courts Act 1981.

(6B) If the tribunal makes an award in reliance on section 31(2B) of the Senior Courts Act 1981 as applied by subsection (6A), the tribunal must certify that the condition in section 31(2B) as so applied is satisfied.]

(7) An award under subsection (6) may be enforced as if it were an award of the High Court.

(8) Where—

(a) the tribunal refuses to grant permission (or leave) to apply for relief under section 15(1),

(b) the applicant appeals against that refusal, and

(c) the Court of Appeal grants the permission (or leave),

the Court of Appeal may go on to decide the application for relief under section 15(1).

(9) Subsections (4) and (5) do not prevent Tribunal Procedure Rules from limiting the time within which applications may be made.

AMENDMENT

1. Criminal Justice and Courts Act 2015 s.84(5) and (6) (August 8, 2016).

GENERAL NOTE

3.108 See the annotation to s.15.

For the procedure for applying to the Upper Tribunal for judicial review, see rr.27–33A of the Tribunal Procedure (Upper Tribunal) Rules 2008. Those rules also apply to cases transferred to the Upper Tribunal under s.31A of the Senior Courts Act 1981 s.25A of the Judicature (Northern Ireland) Act 1978 or s.20 of this Act.

Quashing orders under section 15(1): supplementary provision

3.109 **17.**—[1 (A1) In cases arising under the law of England and Wales, section 29A of the Senior Courts Act 1981 applies in relation to a quashing order under section 15(1)(c) of this Act as it applies in relation to a quashing order under section 29 of that Act.]

(1) If the Upper Tribunal makes a quashing order under section 15(1)(c) in respect of a decision, it may in addition—

(a) remit the matter concerned to the court, tribunal or authority that made the decision, with a direction to reconsider the matter and reach a decision in accordance with the findings of the Upper Tribunal, or

(b) substitute its own decision for the decision in question.

(2) The power conferred by subsection (1)(b) is exercisable only if—

(a) the decision in question was made by a court or tribunal,

(b) the [1 quashing order is made] on the ground that there has been an error of law, and

(c) without the error, there would have been only one decision that the court or tribunal could have reached.

(3) Unless the Upper Tribunal otherwise directs, a decision substituted by it under subsection (1)(b) has effect as if it were a decision of the relevant court or tribunal.

AMENDMENTS

1. Judicial Review and Courts Act 2022 s.1(3) (July 14, 2022, subject to a saving).

General Note

Note that the Upper Tribunal has a far more limited power under s.17(1)(b) to substitute a decision for a decision quashed in judicial review proceedings than it does under s.12(2)(b)(ii) to re-make a decision set aside on an appeal. Compare s.12(4) with s.17(2)(c). The limitations were powerfully exposed in *R.(Criminal Injuries Compensation Authority) v First-tier Tribunal (CIC)* [2018] EWCA Civ 1175; [2018] AACR 22, where the Court of Appeal held the Upper Tribunal to have gone too far in holding that, although it had erred in law, the First-tier Tribunal had come to the only conclusion open to it, but the Court of Appeal itself felt that it would be remiss not to say that, although it was obliged to remit the case to the First-tier Tribunal, it considered it likely that the First-tier Tribunal would come to the same view as the Upper Tribunal judge and again decide the case in favour of the claimant. **3.110**

Section 29A of the Senior Courts Act 1981, which is mentioned in subs.(A1) and was inserted into the 1981 Act by the Judicial Review and Courts Act 2022 s.1(1) at the same time as subs.(A1) was inserted into this section, provides that quashing orders may be suspended, that any retrospective effect of a quashing order may be removed or limited and that a quashing order may be made subject to conditions.

Limits of jurisdiction under section 15(1)

18.—(1) This section applies where an application made to the Upper Tribunal seeks (whether or not alone)— **3.111**

(a) relief under section 15(1), or
(b) permission (or, in a case arising under the law of Northern Ireland, leave) to apply for relief under section 15(1).

(2) If Conditions 1 to 4 are met, the tribunal has the function of deciding the application.

(3) If the tribunal does not have the function of deciding the application, it must by order transfer the application to the High Court.

(4) Condition 1 is that the application does not seek anything other than—

(a) relief under section 15(1);
(b) permission (or, in a case arising under the law of Northern Ireland, leave) to apply for relief under section 15(1);
(c) an award under section 16(6);
(d) interest;
(e) costs.

(5) Condition 2 is that the application does not call into question anything done by the Crown Court.

(6) Condition 3 is that the application falls within a class specified for the purposes of this subsection in a direction given in accordance with Part 1 of Schedule 2 to the Constitutional Reform Act 2005.

(7) The power to give directions under subsection (6) includes—

(a) power to vary or revoke directions made in exercise of the power, and
(b) power to make different provision for different purposes.

(8) Condition 4 is that the judge presiding at the hearing of the application is either—

(a) a judge of the High Court or the Court of Appeal in England and Wales or Northern Ireland, or a judge of the Court of Session, or
(b) such other persons as may be agreed from time to time between the Lord Chief Justice, the Lord President, or the Lord Chief Justice of Northern Ireland, as the case may be, and the Senior President of Tribunals.

(9) Where the application is transferred to the High Court under subsection (3)—

(a) the application is to be treated for all purposes as if it—

(i) had been made to the High Court, and

(ii) sought things corresponding to those sought from the tribunal, and

(b) any steps taken, permission (or leave) given or orders made by the tribunal in relation to the application are to be treated as taken, given or made by the High Court.

(10) Rules of court may make provision for the purpose of supplementing subsection (9).

(11) The provision that may be made by Tribunal Procedure Rules about amendment of an application for relief under section 15(1) includes, in particular, provision about amendments that would cause the application to become transferrable under subsection (3).

(12) For the purposes of subsection (9)(a)(ii), in relation to an application transferred to the High Court in Northern Ireland—

(a) an order of mandamus shall be taken to correspond to a mandatory order under section 15(1)(a),

(b) an order of prohibition shall be taken to correspond to a prohibiting order under section 15(1)(b), and

(c) an order of certiorari shall be taken to correspond to a quashing order under section 15(1)(c).

General Note

Subsection (6)

3.112 The Lord Chief Justice of England and Wales has issued *Practice Direction (Upper Tribunal: Judicial Review Jurisdiction)* [2009] 1 W.L.R. 327 specifying the following classes of case:

"(a) Any decision of the First-tier Tribunal on an appeal made in the exercise of a right conferred by the Criminal Injuries Compensation Scheme in compliance with section 5(1) of the Criminal Injuries Compensation Act 1995 (appeals against decisions on review) and

(b) Any decision of the First-tier Tribunal (other than its Immigration and Asylum Chamber) made under Tribunal Procedure Rules or section 9 of the 2007 Act where there is no right of appeal to the Upper Tribunal and that decision is not an excluded decision within paragraph (b), (c), or (f) of section 11(5) of the 2007 Act."

The Practice Direction does not apply where the applicant seeks a declaration of incompatibility under s.4 of the Human Rights Act 1998.

The words in parenthesis in para.(b) were added by another Practice Direction, dated August 21, 2013, which deals comprehensively with judicial review in the Immigration and Asylum Chamber of the Upper Tribunal.

The effect of *LS v Lambeth LBC (HB)* [2010] UKUT 461 (AAC); [2011] AACR 27, in which it was held that an appeal lies against all decisions of the First-tier Tribunal that are not "excluded decisions", appears at first sight to be to limit the scope of para.(b) of the Practice Direction to challenges to decisions excluded from the right of appeal by virtue of s.11(5)(d) and, if it has any practical effect, by s.11(5)(e). However, note that the equivalent provision in Scotland has been interpreted so as to include challenges to procedural omissions as well as to procedural decisions (see the note to s.20(3)).

In practice, the overwhelming majority of judicial review cases brought in the Administrative Appeals Chamber of the Upper Tribunal have been criminal injuries compensation cases within the scope of para.(a) of the Practice Direction. However, applications for judicial review of decisions of the Social Entitlement Chamber of the First-tier Tribunal that fall within the scope of para.(b) are also heard in the Administrative Appeals Chamber of the Upper Tribunal (see art.10(b) of the First-tier Tribunal and Upper Tribunal (Chambers) Order 2010).

Subsection (11)

See r.33A of the Tribunal Procedure (Upper Tribunal) Rules 2008. **3.113**

Transfer of judicial review applications from High Court

19.—(1) *Omitted.* **3.114**

(2) *Omitted.*

(3) Where an application is transferred to the Upper Tribunal under 31A of the [1 Senior Courts Act 1981] or section 25A of the Judicature (Northern Ireland) Act 1978 (transfer from the High Court of judicial review applications)—

(a) the application is to be treated for all purposes as if it—

(i) had been made to the tribunal, and

(ii) sought things corresponding to those sought from the High Court,

(b) the tribunal has the function of deciding the application, even if it does not fall within a class specified under section 18(6), and

(c) any steps taken, permission given, leave given or orders made by the High Court in relation to the application are to be treated as taken, given or made by the tribunal.

(4) Where—

(a) an application for permission is transferred to the Upper Tribunal under section 31A of the [1 Senior Courts Act 1981] and the tribunal grants permission, or

(b) an application for leave is transferred to the Upper Tribunal under section 25A of the Judicature (Northern Ireland) Act 1978 (c. 23) and the tribunal grants leave, the tribunal has the function of deciding any subsequent application brought under the permission or leave, even if the subsequent application does not fall within a class specified under section 18(6).

(5) Tribunal Procedure Rules may make further provision for the purposes of supplementing subsections (3) and (4).

(6) For the purposes of subsection (3)(a)(ii), in relation to an application transferred to the Upper Tribunal under section 25A of the Judicature (Northern Ireland) Act 1978—

(a) a mandatory order under section 15(1)(a) shall be taken to correspond to an order of mandamus,

(b) a prohibiting order under section 15(1)(b) shall be taken to correspond to an order of prohibition, and

(c) a quashing order under section 15(1)(c) shall be taken to correspond to an order of certiorari.

AMENDMENT

1. Constitutional Reform Act 2005 s.59(5) and para.1(2) of Sch.11 (October 1, 2009).

GENERAL NOTE

3.115 Subsections (1) and (2) inserted the sections mentioned in subs.(3) into the 1981 and 1978 Acts respectively. Those provisions effectively require the High Court to transfer cases falling within Conditions 1, 2 and 3 of s.18 to the Upper Tribunal and, as amended, permit the transfer of other cases provided they fall within Conditions 1 and 2 of those conditions. See the note to s.15. For Tribunal Procedure Rules made under subs.(5), see rr.27(1) and (2) and 33A(3) of the Tribunal Procedure (Upper Tribunal) Rules 2008.

Transfer of judicial review applications from the Court of Session

3.116 **20.**—(1) Where an application is made to the supervisory jurisdiction of the Court of Session, the Court—

(a) must, if Conditions 1 [2 and 2 are met, and]

[1 (aa) [2 . . .]]

(b) may, if Conditions 1 [2 and 3] are met, but Condition 2 is not, by order transfer the application to the Upper Tribunal.

(2) Condition 1 is that the application does not seek anything other than an exercise of the supervisory jurisdiction of the Court of Session.

(3) Condition 2 is that the application falls within a class specified for the purposes of this subsection by act of sederunt made with the consent of the Lord Chancellor.

(4) Condition 3 is that the subject matter of the application is not a devolved Scottish matter.

(5) [2 . . .]

[1 (5A) [2 . . .]]

(6) There may not be specified under subsection (3) any class of application which includes an application the subject matter of which is a devolved Scottish matter.

(7) For the purposes of this section, the subject matter of an application is a devolved Scottish matter if it—

(a) concerns the exercise of functions in or as regards Scotland, and

(b) does not relate to a reserved matter within the meaning of the Scotland Act 1998.

(8) In subsection (2), the reference to the exercise of the supervisory jurisdiction of the Court of Session includes a reference to the making of any order in connection with or in consequence of the exercise of that jurisdiction.

AMENDMENTS

1. Borders, Citizenship and Immigration Act 2009 s.53 (August 8, 2011).
2. Crime and Courts Act 2013 s.22(2) (November 1, 2013).

GENERAL NOTE

Subsection (1)

3.117 For the procedure for transfer, see R.C. r.58.7A in relation to mandatory transfers under s.20(1)(a) and r.58(11) in relation to discretionary transfers under s.20(1)(b).

Subsection (3)

3.118 Cases within a class specified under this subsection must be transferred to the Upper Tribunal under s.20(1)(a) if the other condition is satisfied. The Act of Sederunt (Transfer of Judicial Review Applications from the Court of Session)

2008 (SSI 2008/357) specifies "an application which challenges a procedural decision or a procedural ruling of the First-tier Tribunal, established under section 3(1) of the Tribunals, Courts and Enforcement Act 2007". The effect of *LS v Lambeth LBC (HB)* [2010] UKUT 461 (AAC); [2011] AACR 27, in which it was held that an appeal lies against all decisions of the First-tier Tribunal that are not "excluded decisions", appears at first sight to be to limit the scope of the act of sederunt to challenges to decisions excluded from the right of appeal by virtue of s.11(5)(d) and, if it has any practical effect, by s.11(5)(e). However, in *Currie, Petitioner* [2009] CSOH 145; [2010] AACR 8, Lord Hodge interpreted the act of sederunt as extending to procedural omissions or oversights giving rise to unfairness. On the other hand, he said that an application that challenged not only such procedural decisions but also errors of law that were not of a procedural nature did not fall within the terms of the act of sederunt.

Note that criminal injuries compensation cases, which are specified in the practice direction made in England and Wales under s.18(6), are not specified in the act of sederunt in Scotland. Not only are such cases therefore not subject to a mandatory transfer from the Court of Session, they cannot even be transferred on a discretionary basis because criminal injuries compensation is a "devolved Scottish matter" so that "Condition (3)" identified in s.20(4) is not satisfied (*Currie, Petitioner*, above). However, as "Condition 3" need not be met as a condition for a mandatory transfer, there is nothing specific in this Act that would prevent an act of sederunt being made to enable criminal injuries compensation cases to be transferred on a mandatory basis if the other conditions were satisfied.

Note also that even cases within a specified class must be started in the Court of Session because, in relation to Scotland, s.20 does not admit to the possibility of cases being started in the Upper Tribunal as is done in ss.15 and 16 (see, in particular, s.16(1)). In *EF v SSWP* [2009] UKUT 92 (AAC) (reported as *R (IB) 3/09*), an application for judicial review made to the Upper Tribunal in Scotland was therefore held to be incompetent.

[1 Procedural steps where application transferred

20A.—(1) This section applies where the Court of Session transfers an application under section 20(1). 3.119

(2) It is for the Upper Tribunal to determine—

(a) whether the application has been made timeously, and

(b) whether to grant permission for the application to proceed under section 27B of the Court of Session Act 1988 ("the 1988 Act") (requirement for permission).

(3) Accordingly—

(a) the Upper Tribunal has the same powers in relation to the application as the Court of Session would have had in relation to it under sections 27A to 27C of the 1988 Act,

(b) sections 27C and 27D of that Act apply in relation to a decision of the Upper Tribunal under section 27B(1) of that Act as they apply in relation to such a decision of the Court of Session.

(4) The references in section 27C(3) and (4) of the 1988 Act (oral hearings where permission refused) to a different Lord Ordinary from the one who granted or refused permission are to be read as references to different members of the Tribunal from those of whom it was composed when it refused or granted permission.]

Amendment

1. Courts Reform (Scotland) Act 2014 (Consequential Provisions and Modifications) Order 2015 (SI 2015/700) art.7 (September 22, 2015).

General Note

3.120 This section was inserted in consequence of the coming into force of s.89 of the Courts Reform (Scotland) Act 2014 (an Act of the Scottish Parliament), which inserted ss.27A to 27D into the Court of Session Act 1988 and so introduced a requirement that applicants for judicial review in Scotland obtain permission, as in England and Wales. The procedure under ss.27A to 27D, as applied to the Upper Tribunal by this section, is similar to the procedure in the Upper Tribunal in England and Wales, but is not identical. Those sections provide –

"Time limits

27A.—(1) An application to the supervisory jurisdiction of the Court must be made before the end of—

(a) the period of 3 months beginning with the date on which the grounds giving rise to the application first arise, or

(b) such longer period as the Court considers equitable having regard to all the circumstances.

(2) Subsection (1) does not apply to an application to the supervisory jurisdiction of the Court which, by virtue of any enactment, is to be made before the end of a period ending before the period of 3 months mentioned in that subsection (however that first-ending period may be expressed).

Requirement for permission

27B.—(1) No proceedings may be taken in respect of an application to the supervisory jurisdiction of the Court unless the Court has granted permission for the application to proceed.

(2) Subject to subsection (3), the Court may grant permission under subsection (1) for an application to proceed only if it is satisfied that—

(a) the applicant can demonstrate a sufficient interest in the subject matter of the application, and

(b) the application has a real prospect of success.

(3) Where the application relates to a decision of the Upper Tribunal for Scotland in an appeal from the First-tier Tribunal for Scotland under section 46 of the Tribunals (Scotland) Act 2014, the Court may grant permission under subsection (1) for the application to proceed only if it is satisfied that—

(a) the applicant can demonstrate a sufficient interest in the subject matter of the application,

(b) the application has a real prospect of success, and

(c) either—

(i) the application would raise an important point of principle or practice, or

(ii) there is some other compelling reason for allowing the application to proceed.

(4) The Court may grant permission under subsection (1) for an application to proceed—

(a) subject to such conditions as the Court thinks fit,

(b) only on such of the grounds specified in the application as the Court thinks fit.

(5) The Court may decide whether or not to grant permission without an oral hearing having been held.

Oral hearings where permission refused, etc.

27C.—(1) Subsection (2) applies where, in relation to an application to the supervisory jurisdiction of the Court—

(a) the Court—

(i) refuses permission under subsection 27B(1) for the application to proceed, or

(ii) grants permission for the application to proceed subject to conditions or only on particular grounds, and

(b) the Court decides to refuse permission, or grant permission as mentioned in paragraph (a)(ii), without an oral hearing having been held.

(2) The person making the application may, within the period of 7 days beginning with the day on which that decision is made, request a review of the decision at an oral hearing.

(3) A request under subsection (2) must be considered by a different Lord Ordinary from the one who refused permission or granted permission as mentioned in subsection (1)(a)(ii).

(4) Where a request under subsection (2) is granted, the oral hearing must be conducted before a different Lord Ordinary from the one who refused or so granted permission.

(5) At a review following a request under subsection (2), the Court must consider whether to grant permission for the application to proceed; and subsections (2), (3) and (4) of section 27B apply for that purpose.

(6) Section 28 does not apply—

(a) where subsection (2) applies, or

(b) in relation to the refusal of a request made under subsection (2).

Appeals following oral hearings

27D.—(1) Subsection (2) applies where, after an oral hearing to determine whether or not to grant permission for an application to the supervisory jurisdiction of the Court to proceed, the Court—

(a) refuses permission for the application to proceed, or

(b) grants permission for the application to proceed subject to conditions or only on particular grounds.

(2) The person making the application may, within the period of 7 days beginning with the day on which the Court makes its decision, appeal under this section to the Inner House (but may not appeal under any other provision of this Act).

(3) In an appeal under subsection (2), the Inner House must consider whether to grant permission for the application to proceed; and subsections (2), (3) and (4) of section 27B apply for that purpose.

(4) In subsection (1), the reference to an oral hearing is to an oral hearing whether following a request under section 27C(2) or otherwise.".

There has not been any amendment to the Tribunal Procedure (Upper Tribunal) Rules 2008 to reflect this procedure.

Upper Tribunal's "judicial review" jurisdiction: Scotland

21.—(1) The Upper Tribunal has the function of deciding applications transferred to it from the Court of Session under section 20(1). **3.121**

(2) The powers of review of the Upper Tribunal in relation to such applications are the same as the powers of review of the Court of Session in an application to the supervisory jurisdiction of that Court.

(3) In deciding an application by virtue of subsection (1), the Upper Tribunal must apply principles that the Court of Session would apply in deciding an application to the supervisory jurisdiction of that Court.

(4) An order of the Upper Tribunal by virtue of subsection (1)—

(a) has the same effect as the corresponding order granted by the Court of Session on an application to the supervisory jurisdiction of that Court, and

(b) is enforceable as if it were an order so granted by that Court.

(5) Where an application is transferred to the Upper Tribunal by virtue of section 20(1), any steps taken or orders made by the Court of Session in relation to the application (other than the order to transfer the

application under section 20(1)) are to be treated as taken or made by the tribunal.

(6) Tribunal Procedure Rules may make further provision for the purposes of supplementing subsection (5).

GENERAL NOTE

3.122 For the procedure in the Upper Tribunal, see rr.27, 30(2)–(5) and 31–33 of the Tribunal Procedure (Upper Tribunal) Rules 2008.

Miscellaneous

Tribunal Procedure Rules

3.123 **22.**—(1) There are to be rules, to be called "Tribunal Procedure Rules", governing—

(a) the practice and procedure to be followed in the First-tier Tribunal, and

(b) the practice and procedure to be followed in the Upper Tribunal.

(2) Tribunal Procedure Rules are to be made by the Tribunal Procedure Committee.

(3) In Schedule 5—

(a) Part 1 makes further provision about the content of Tribunal Procedure Rules,

(b) Part 2 makes provision about the membership of the Tribunal Procedure Committee,

(c) Part 3 makes provision about the making of Tribunal Procedure Rules by the Committee, and

(d) Part 4 confers power to amend legislation in connection with Tribunal Procedure Rules.

(4) Power to make Tribunal Procedure Rules is to be exercised with a view to securing—

(a) that, in proceedings before the First-tier Tribunal and Upper Tribunal, justice is done,

(b) that the tribunal system is accessible and fair,

(c) that proceedings before the First-tier Tribunal or Upper Tribunal are handled quickly and efficiently,

(d) that the rules are both simple and simply expressed, and

(e) that the rules where appropriate confer on members of the First-tier Tribunal, or Upper Tribunal, responsibility for ensuring that proceedings before the tribunal are handled quickly and efficiently.

(5) In subsection (4)(b) "the tribunal system" means the system for deciding matters within the jurisdiction of the First-tier Tribunal or the Upper Tribunal.

GENERAL NOTE

3.124 This section, and Sch.5, came into force on May 19, 2008. The Tribunal Procedure Committee is similar to the committees that make rules for the courts, being composed mainly of judges and members of tribunals and representatives who appear before tribunals. The Committee is able to keep the Tribunal Procedure Rules under constant review. In the past, some tribunals found it very difficult to get changes made to their rules. Paragraphs 28 and 29 of Sch.5 enable the Lord Chancellor to disallow Rules or require Rules to be made.

There are a number of specific rule-making powers in this Act, not confined to Pt 1 of Sch.5, and in other Acts but they are not to be taken to limit the generality of s.22(1) (see para.1 of Sch.5). The power to make Tribunal Procedure Rules is therefore very wide.

The approach that has been taken is to produce a set of rules for each chamber of the First-tier Tribunal and for the Lands Chamber of the Upper Tribunal and a single set of rules for the other three chambers of the Upper Tribunal. The Tribunal Procedure (First-tier Tribunal) (Social Entitlement Chamber) Rules 2008 and the Tribunal Procedure (Upper Tribunal) Rules 2008 are set out in this volume.

Practice directions

23.—(1) The Senior President of Tribunals may give directions— 3.125

(a) as to the practice and procedure of the First-tier Tribunal;

(b) as to the practice and procedure of the Upper Tribunal.

(2) A Chamber President may give directions as to the practice and procedure of the chamber over which he presides.

(3) A power under this section to give directions includes—

(a) power to vary or revoke directions made in exercise of the power, and

(b) power to make different provision for different purposes (including different provision for different areas).

(4) Directions under subsection (1) may not be given without the approval of the Lord Chancellor.

(5) Directions under subsection (2) may not be given without the approval of—

(a) the Senior President of Tribunals, and

(b) the Lord Chancellor.

(6) Subsections (4) and (5)(b) do not apply to directions to the extent that they consist of guidance about any of the following—

(a) the application or interpretation of the law;

(b) the making of decisions by members of the First-tier Tribunal or Upper Tribunal.

(7) Subsections (4) and (5)(b) do not apply to directions to the extent that they consist of criteria for determining which members of the First-tier Tribunal or Upper Tribunal may be chosen to decide particular categories of matter; but the directions may, to that extent, be given only after consulting the Lord Chancellor.

General Note

Practice Directions are a common feature in courts and have also been used in some tribunals. They may be directed at the parties appearing before the tribunals or to the judges and members of tribunals and the staff of tribunals. This section provides for Practice Directions to be issued by the Senior President of Tribunals (who may delegate that function under s.8) or by a Chamber President. The latter may issue a Practice Direction only with the approval of the Senior President of Tribunals. 3.126

Practice Directions may be used to supplement Tribunal Procedure Rules and a failure by a party to comply with a Practice Direction attracts the same consequences as a failure to comply with a direction given by a tribunal in a particular case (see r.7(2) of the Tribunal Procedure (First-tier Tribunal) (Social Entitlement Chamber) Rules 2008 and r.7(2) of the Tribunal Procedure (Upper Tribunal) Rules 2008). Nonetheless, a Practice Direction cannot override or amend Tribunal Procedure Rules but must, if possible, be interpreted so as to be valid and therefore in a way that is consistent with any such Rules (*EB v Dorset Healthcare NHS Trust* [2020] UKUT 362 (AAC), a decision of a three-judge panel).

Subsections (4) and (5)(b) provide that a Practice Direction may be issued only with the approval of the Lord Chancellor, but those subsections do not apply to the extent that a Practice Direction consists of guidance about the application or interpretation of the law or the making of decisions by judges and other members of tribunals. Practice Directions as to the criteria for deciding which judges and other members may be chosen to decide particular types of case do not require the approval of the Lord Chancellor but do require that he be consulted.

Practice directions relevant to social security cases are set out at the end of this Part of this volume. They are also published at *www.judiciary.uk/guidance-and-resources/*—under "Guidance/resource type", select "Practice Direction".

A practice direction has no legislative force so that, in so far as it contains a statement of law which is wrong, it carries no authority (*In re NY (a child) (Reunite International and others intervening)* [2019] UKSC 49; [2020] A.C. 665 at [38]).

It is not open to a judge sitting in a court or tribunal to lay down a mandatory procedure to be complied with in all cases within the course of giving a judgment or decision in an individual case (*Bovale Ltd v Secretary of State for Communities and Local Government* [2009] EWCA Civ 171; [2009] 1 W.L.R. 2274). That would be to make a practice direction without compliance with the requirements of this section. However, judges do have wide powers under Tribunal Procedure Rules to depart from standard procedures in individual cases or groups of cases. In *R. (KA) v Secretary of State for the Home Department* [2021] EWCA Civ 1040; [2021] 1 W.L.R. 6018, *Bovale* was distinguished, albeit without a concluded view being reached. Whereas in *Bovale* the High Court had purported to lay down a mandatory requirement that was inconsistent with a specific provision of the Civil Procedure Rules, in *KA* the Upper Tribunal had merely indicated that acknowledgments of service filed in judicial review proceedings after the 21-day time limit but within six weeks would be considered when the claim was determined, without the respondent having to apply for an extension of time. Given that the Tribunal Procedure (Upper Tribunal) Rules 2008 r.29 empowered the Upper Tribunal to consider an acknowledgement of service that had been provided late and that the Upper Tribunal had indicated that, although it would generally not determine an application for judicial review until the end of the six-week period, it would consider doing so if asked and if it considered it appropriate, the Upper Tribunal's indication was not inconsistent with the Rules.

Apart from Practice Directions, the Senior President of Tribunals may issue Practice Statements. The distinction between the two was considered in *AEB v Secretary of State for the Home Department* [2022] EWCA Civ 1512, where the Court was content to adopt the view expressed in *DT v SSWP (II)* [2015] UKUT 509 (AAC) that the Senior President of Tribunals' authority for making Practice Statements is derived from s.3(4) of this Act under which he presides over both the First-tier Tribunal and the Upper Tribunal. The purpose of Practice Statements "is to provide guidance, both to Tribunal Judges and to Tribunal users, so as to encourage consistency of approach and understanding" (*AEB* at [15]), whereas Practice Directions made under s.23 impose obligations on those to whom they are directed.

Mediation

3.127 **24.**—(1) A person exercising power to make Tribunal Procedure Rules or give practice directions must, when making provision in relation to mediation, have regard to the following principles—

(a) mediation of matters in dispute between parties to proceedings is to take place only by agreement between those parties;

(b) where parties to proceedings fail to mediate, or where mediation between parties to proceedings fails to resolve disputed matters, the failure is not to affect the outcome of the proceedings.

(2) Practice directions may provide for members to act as mediators in relation to disputed matters in a case that is the subject of proceedings.

(3) The provision that may be made by virtue of subsection (2) includes provision for a member to act as a mediator in relation to disputed matters in a case even though the member has been chosen to decide matters in the case.

(4) Once a member has begun to act as a mediator in relation to a disputed matter in a case that is the subject of proceedings, the member may decide matters in the case only with the consent of the parties.

(5) Staff appointed under section 40(1) may, subject to their terms of appointment, act as mediators in relation to disputed matters in a case that is the subject of proceedings.

(6) In this section—

"member" means a judge or other member of the First-tier Tribunal or a judge or other member of the Upper Tribunal;

"practice direction" means a direction under section 23(1) or (2);

"proceedings" means proceedings before the First-tier Tribunal or proceedings before the Upper Tribunal.

Supplementary powers of Upper Tribunal

25.—(1) In relation to the matters mentioned in subsection (2), the Upper Tribunal— 3.128

(a) has, in England and Wales or in Northern Ireland, the same powers, rights, privileges and authority as the High Court, and

(b) has, in Scotland, the same powers, rights, privileges and authority as the Court of Session.

(2) The matters are—

(a) the attendance and examination of witnesses,

(b) the production and inspection of documents, and

(c) all other matters incidental to the Upper Tribunal's functions.

(3) Subsection (1) shall not be taken—

(a) to limit any power to make Tribunal Procedure Rules;

(b) to be limited by anything in Tribunal Procedure Rules other than an express limitation.

(4) A power, right, privilege or authority conferred in a territory by subsection (1) is available for purposes of proceedings in the Upper Tribunal that take place outside that territory (as well as for purposes of proceedings in the tribunal that take place within that territory).

General Note

The powers of the High Court and the Court of Session include the power to punish a person for contempt of court. Failure to comply with a direction, order, summons or citation issued by a tribunal is a contempt of court but is unlikely to be punishable unless accompanied by a warning (which is a specific requirement in respect of orders, summonses and citations issued under r.16 of either set of Rules). That a tribunal is a "court" for these purposes is clear from *Pickering v Liverpool Daily Post and Echo Newspapers Limited* [1991] 2 A.C. 370. In *MD v SSWP (Enforcement Reference)* [2010] UKUT 202 (AAC); [2011] AACR 5, it was suggested by a three-judge panel that a warning should spell out the penalties that may be imposed for failure to comply. The maximum punishment that may be imposed is a sentence of two years' imprisonment or an unlimited fine (see ss.14 and 15 of the Contempt of Court Act 1981). When a sentence of imprisonment is imposed, consideration should always be given to suspending it and reference to 3.129

that consideration should be included in the reasons for the decision to impose the sentence (*Slade v Slade* [2009] EWCA Civ 748; [2010] 1 W.L.R. 1262). At least in England and Wales, there is also power to sequestrate assets. In view of the seriousness of committal proceedings, it was emphasised in *MD v SSWP (Enforcement Reference)* that it is particularly important that procedural rules are complied with in such proceedings. However, because a failure to comply with procedural requirements does not itself invalidate proceedings, an irregularity might be waived where it could not have caused the alleged contemnor any prejudice or injustice.

The three-judge panel also referred to *M v P (Contempt of Court: Committal Order)* [1993] Fam.167, in which it was held that "(a) the contemnor, (b) the alleged 'victim' of the contempt and (c) other users of the court for whom the maintenance of the authority of the court is of supreme importance" all had interests that justice required the court to take into account in contempt cases. It nonetheless left open the question whether, in *MR v CMEC (No.2)* [2010] UKUT 38 (AAC), another three-judge panel had been correct to state that it was not appropriate for parties other than the alleged contemnor to make submissions in contempt proceedings. In adversarial proceedings, a party may have made an application for the committal. Thus, for instance, in *KJM Superbikes Ltd v Hinton* [2008] EWCA Civ 1280; [2009] 1 W.L.R. 2406, the Court of Appeal considered the circumstances in which a court should entertain an application by a party for the committal of a witness for contempt of court in giving false evidence. See, more recently, *Navigator Equities Ltd & Anor v Deripaska* [2021] EWCA Civ 1799; [2022] 1 WLR 3656, in which general propositions of law in relation to civil contempts are helpfully set out at [82]. In principle, therefore, it is suggested that a party adversely affected by a contempt ought to be permitted to make submissions. On the other hand, in *MD*, the Secretary of State had not wished to make any submissions, which is partly why the three-judge panel did not pursue the question whether he had a right to do so, and there are many circumstances in which no party is, or can show that he or she has been, adversely affected by a contempt of court. In any event, contempt proceedings are rare in social security cases; *MD* appears to be the only example. This is largely because, as suggested in *MD*, it is seldom proportionate in such cases for a tribunal to issue summonses or orders to non-parties that might require to be enforced through the threat of such proceedings and there are other ways of enforcing directions addressed to parties. Thus, non-compliance by a party with a direction to provide evidence will often simply result in adverse findings of fact being made against that party and other serious failures by a party to comply with directions or co-operate with a tribunal may result in that party's case being struck out.

Not only must contempt be proved beyond reasonable doubt but so must any contested facts relevant to a more severe sentence, such as prejudice to other parties or the degree to which there has been subsequent compliance. However, it is for the contemnor to prove, on a balance of probabilities, that a contempt has been purged (see *JSC BTA Bank v Solodchenko (No.2)* [2010] EWHC 2843 (Ch); [2011] 1 W.L.R. 906 in which a number of sentencing principles were considered).

3.130 This section gives the Upper Tribunal power to punish for contempt of court in relation to its own proceedings. Where a person has failed to comply with a requirement to attend at any place for the purpose of giving evidence to the First-tier Tribunal or otherwise to make themselves available to give evidence to the First-tier Tribunal or to swear an oath for in connection with giving evidence in First-tier Tribunal proceedings, that tribunal may refer the case to the Upper Tribunal which may exercise its powers under this section as though the First-tier Tribunal had been the Upper Tribunal (see r.7(3) of the Tribunal Procedure (First-tier Tribunal) (Social Entitlement Chamber) Rules 2008 and r.7(3) and (4) of the Tribunal Procedure (Upper Tribunal) Rules 2008). See the notes to those rules, both generally and in particular for the meaning of the "production ... of documents" in subs. (2)(b). Only the Chamber President (or a person to whom the power is delegated by him) has the power to make a reference from the Social Entitlement Chamber of the First-tier Tribunal to the Upper Tribunal in a social security case (see para.10 of the practice statement set out below in the note to art.2 of the First-tier Tribunal and Upper Tribunal (Composition of Tribunal) Order 2008).

The scope of subs.(2)(c) has been considered in a number of cases. Thus, in *IB v IC* [2011] UKUT 370 (AAC); [2012] AACR 26, it was held that this section did not empower the Upper Tribunal to allow a vexatious litigant subject to a civil proceedings order or an all proceedings order under s.42 of the Senior Courts Act 1981 to bring proceedings before the Upper Tribunal because such a matter was not incidental to the Upper Tribunal's other functions; only the High Court could do so. In *Raftopoulou v HMRC* [2015] UKUT 630 (TCC), it was held that this section did not empower the Upper Tribunal to award *pro bono* costs, which the High Court had the express power to do but (at that time) the Upper Tribunal did not, but in that case there was an appeal and the Court of Appeal left the question open because the point was important but had become academic (*Raftopoulou v Revenue and Customs Commissioners* [2018] EWCA Civ 818; [2019] 1 W.L.R.1528 at [76] and [77]. On the other hand, in *R. (Singh) v Secretary of State for the Home Department* [2019] EWCA Civ 1014, the Court of Appeal held that, because the High Court would have had the power, both under the Civil Procedure Rules and in its inherent jurisdiction, to set aside a grant of permission to apply for judicial review given in breach of the rules of natural justice, the Upper Tribunal could also do so. Leggatt L.J., with whom the other members of the Court agreed, said:

> 17. It is not necessary to decide whether the Upper Tribunal has similar inherent powers to those of the High Court at common law or by virtue of its designation in section 3(5) of the Tribunals, Courts and Enforcement Act 2007 as a "superior court of record" because section 25 of that Act expressly confers such powers on the Upper Tribunal. …
> 18. I see no reason to give section 25 a restrictive interpretation. I agree with the following observations of Mr Martin Rodger QC, Deputy President of the Upper Tribunal (Lands Chamber) in *William Hill Organization Ltd v Crossrail Ltd* [2016] UKUT 275 (LC), para 59:
>
> > "Parliament was obviously aware of the powers of the High Court, both those which are inherent, and those specifically conferred by statute. Section 25 therefore seems to me to be intended to be read literally and applied generally, and to invest the Upper Tribunal with the powers of the High Court in relation to all matters incidental to its functions; the critical limitation in section 25(2)(c) is supplied by the reference to the functions of the Tribunal, and does not depend on the source of the power or the terms in which it has been conferred on the High Court. Parliament could obviously make explicit an intention that the Upper Tribunal was not to possess a particular power, but where it has not done so, and where no express limitation has been imposed by tribunal procedure rules as contemplated by section 25(3)(b), the Upper Tribunal must be taken to have the same powers as the High Court in relation to all matters incidental to its functions."
>
> 19. Pursuant to sections 15 and 16 of the 2007 Act, one of the functions of the Upper Tribunal is to deal with applications for judicial review and, as an aspect of that function, to decide whether or not to grant permission to bring judicial review proceedings. Considering whether to set aside a decision to grant such permission taken in the absence of the respondent and to re-hear the application is a matter incidental to this function. Pursuant to section 25 of the Act, therefore, the Upper Tribunal has the same powers in dealing with the matter as would the High Court. It would be anomalous if the position were otherwise and if the Upper Tribunal, when exercising a judicial review jurisdiction similar to that of the High Court, lacked a power which the High Court has as an essential part of its procedural repertoire to manage its proceedings in a just and effective manner."

First-tier Tribunal and Upper Tribunal: sitting places

3.131 **26.**—Each of the First-tier Tribunal and the Upper Tribunal may decide a case—

(a) in England and Wales,
(b) in Scotland, or
(c) in Northern Ireland,

even though the case arises under the law of a territory other than the one in which the case is decided.

Enforcement

3.132 **27.**—(1) A sum payable in pursuance of a decision of the First-tier Tribunal or Upper Tribunal made in England and Wales—

(a) shall be recoverable as if it were payable under an order of a [1 the county court] in England and Wales;
(b) shall be recoverable as if it were payable under an order of the High Court in England and Wales.

(2) An order for the payment of a sum payable in pursuance of a decision of the First-tier Tribunal or Upper Tribunal made in Scotland (or a copy of such an order certified in accordance with Tribunal Procedure Rules) may be enforced as if it were an extract registered decree arbitral bearing a warrant for execution issued by the sheriff court of any sheriffdom in Scotland.

(3) A sum payable in pursuance of a decision of the First-tier Tribunal or Upper Tribunal made in Northern Ireland—

(a) shall be recoverable as if it were payable under an order of a county court in Northern Ireland;
(b) shall be recoverable as if it were payable under an order of the High Court in Northern Ireland.

(4) This section does not apply to a sum payable in pursuance of—

(a) an award under section 16(6), or
(b) an order by virtue of section 21(1).

(5) The Lord Chancellor may by order make provision for subsection (1) or (3) to apply in relation to a sum of a description specified in the order with the omission of one (but not both) of paragraphs (a) and (b).

(6) Tribunal Procedure Rules—

(a) may make provision as to where, for purposes of this section, a decision is to be taken to be made;
(b) may provide for all or any of subsections (1) to (3) to apply only, or not to apply except, in relation to sums of a description specified in Tribunal Procedure Rules.

AMENDMENT

1. Crime and Courts Act 2013 s.17(5) and Sch.9 para.52 (April 22, 2014).

Assessors

3.133 **28.**—(1) If it appears to the First-tier Tribunal or the Upper Tribunal that a matter before it requires special expertise not otherwise available to it, it may direct that in dealing with that matter it shall have the assistance of a person or persons appearing to it to have relevant knowledge or experience.

(2) The remuneration of a person who gives assistance to either tribunal as mentioned in subsection (1) shall be determined and paid by the Lord Chancellor.

(3) The Lord Chancellor may—

(a) establish panels of persons from which either tribunal may (but need not) select persons to give it assistance as mentioned in subsection (1);

(b) under paragraph (a) establish different panels for different purposes;

(c) after carrying out such consultation as he considers appropriate, appoint persons to a panel established under paragraph (a);

(d) remove a person from such a panel.

Costs or expenses

29.—(1) The costs of and incidental to— 3.134

(a) all proceedings in the First-tier Tribunal, and

(b) all proceedings in the Upper Tribunal,

shall be in the discretion of the Tribunal in which the proceedings take place.

(2) The relevant Tribunal shall have full power to determine by whom and to what extent the costs are to be paid.

(3) Subsections (1) and (2) have effect subject to Tribunal Procedure Rules.

(4) In any proceedings mentioned in subsection (1), the relevant Tribunal may—

(a) disallow, or

(b) (as the case may be) order the legal or other representative concerned to meet,

the whole of any wasted costs or such part of them as may be determined in accordance with Tribunal Procedure Rules.

(5) In subsection (4) "wasted costs" means any costs incurred by a party—

(a) as a result of any improper, unreasonable or negligent act or omission on the part of any legal or other representative or any employee of such a representative, or

(b) which, in the light of any such act or omission occurring after they were incurred, the relevant Tribunal considers it is unreasonable to expect that party to pay.

(6) In this section "legal or other representative", in relation to a party to proceedings, means any person exercising a right of audience or right to conduct the proceedings on his behalf.

(7) In the application of this section in relation to Scotland, any reference in this section to costs is to be read as a reference to expenses.

General Note

Subsections (1)–(3)

Where there is an appeal, any order for costs or expenses, or any failure to make such an order, can generally be a subject of the appeal and so the language of subs. (1) does not preclude the Upper Tribunal from making an order in respect of costs incurred in the First-tier Tribunal. It was held in *Kirkham v IC* [2018] UKUT 65 (AAC) that the Upper Tribunal is also able to make an order in respect of costs incurred in the First-tier Tribunal before the case was transferred to the Upper 3.135

Tribunal from the First-tier Tribunal and the same reasoning would presumably apply where a case was referred to the Upper Tribunal under s.9(5)(b). Moreover, the "power to determine by whom . . . the costs are to be paid" includes a power to order a non-party to pay costs if it is just to do so (*XYZ v Travelers Insurance Co Ltd* [2019] UKSC 48; [2019] 1 W.L.R. 6075, decided on the equivalent wording in s.51(3) of the Senior Courts Act 1981). However, these issues do not arise in social security cases because, subject to the question whether there is a power to make a wasted costs order (considered below), there is no power to award costs at all.

On the other hand, it has been held that subs.(1) does preclude the Upper Tribunal from awarding costs incurred in the Administrative Court, except when judicial review proceedings have been transferred from that Court to the Upper Tribunal. Therefore, where a refusal of the Upper Tribunal to give permission to appeal is successfully challenged by way of an application for judicial review and the case is remitted by the Administrative Court to the Upper Tribunal, the Administrative Court is unable simply to order that the costs of the application for judicial review be treated as costs in the remitted proceedings (and so determined in the light of the outcome of those proceedings). However, this jurisdictional problem can properly be avoided by the Administrative Court transferring the judicial review proceedings to the Upper Tribunal, notwithstanding that the Upper Tribunal is formally the respondent in the proceedings, solely to enable it to make an order for costs in the judicial review proceedings at the same time as it makes an order for costs in the remitted proceedings (*JH (Palestinian Territories) v Secretary of State for the Home Department* [2020] EWCA Civ 919; [2021] 1 W.L.R. 455).

Rule 10 of the Tribunal Procedure (First-tier Tribunal) (Social Entitlement Chamber) Rules 2008 provides that the tribunal "shall not make any order in respect of costs (or, in Scotland, expenses)". By virtue of rr.10(1)(b) and (2) of the Tribunal Procedure (Upper Tribunal) Rules 2008, the same approach applies in the Upper Tribunal to appeals from the Social Entitlement Chamber of the First-tier Tribunal and to cases under the Forfeiture Act 1982.

With effect from June 28, 2022, the Judicial Review and Courts Act 2002 s.48(2) inserted a new s.194A into the Legal Services Act 2007 so as to give the First-tier Tribunal and the Upper Tribunal the same power as courts in England and Wales have under s.194 of the 2007 Act to order a person to make a payment to a prescribed charity where, but for the fact that that a party's representation was provided free of charge, the tribunal would have had the power to order that person to make a payment to that party in respect of the representation. The new power extends across the UK, save where proceedings are within devolved competence (see s.194A(11) and (12)). It has little relevance in social security cases because tribunals generally lack any power to award costs in such cases. However, it may be exercised in other contexts. The charity prescribed under the Legal Services Act 2007 (Prescribed Charity) Order 2008 (SI 2008/2680) (which has effect in relation to s.194A by virtue of s.194C(4)) is the Access to Justice Foundation.

Subsections (4)–(6)

3.136 These subsections provide for a "wasted costs" order to be made against a representative (rather than a party) whose "improper, unreasonable or negligent act or omission" makes it unreasonable for a party to pay costs he or she has incurred. It is not entirely clear whether such orders may be made by the Social Entitlement Chamber or by the Upper Tribunal on appeal from that chamber or in Forfeiture Act cases. The doubt arises because Tribunal Procedure Rules made under subs.(3) may qualify only subss.(1) and (2). If subs.(4) confers a free-standing power to award costs, that power remains available notwithstanding the Tribunal Procedure Rules. However, the better approach may be that subs.(4) merely defines the circumstances in which the broad power in subs.(2) to determine "by whom" costs are to be paid is to be exercised against representatives.

Even if the power is available, it is suggested that it will rarely be possible to use it in the Social Entitlement Chamber. A specially-convened two-judge panel of the Immigration and Asylum Chamber of the First-tier Tribunal, comprised of the Chamber President of the Immigration and Asylum Chamber of the Upper Tribunal sitting with the First-tier Tribunal Chamber President, has held that a wasted costs order may not be imposed on a Home Office presenting officer but may be imposed only on professional advocates, including registered immigration service providers, who may exercise a formal right of audience (*Awuah v SSHD (Wasted Costs Orders – HOPOs – Tribunal Powers)* [2017] UKFTT 555 (IAC)). This decision, while not technically binding, is plainly authoritative. The First-tier Tribunal pointed out that the language of s.29(5) of the 2007 Act is obviously drawn directly from that of s.51(7) of the Senior Courts Act 1981 and it referred to decisions of the courts made under the 1981 Act. It further held that, when Tribunal Procedure Rules (equivalent to r.11 of the Tribunal Procedure (First-tier Tribunal) (Social Entitlement Chamber) Rules 2008) allowed other people to be representatives, they did not thereby confer additional rights of audience for the purposes of s.29(5). In immigration and asylum cases, s.84 of the Immigration and Asylum Act 1999 has the effect that, apart from Government presenting officers, only people who are professional advocates exercising a formal right of audience may provide representation before the First-tier Tribunal or Upper Tribunal "in the course of a business". However, it appears to follow from the decision that, in other types of case, wasted costs orders cannot be imposed on litigants' representatives who are not relevant professional representatives, even if they are paid for their services. Thus. even if there is a power to make a wasted costs order in a social security case, it is probably exercisable only where the representative is a lawyer.

29ZA.–29ZD.*—Expired.* 3.137

GENERAL NOTE

These sections were inserted by way of a temporary modification under s.55 of, and para.2 of Sch.25 to, the Coronavirus Act 2020. The modification was in force from March 25, 2020 until June 28, 2022, when those provisions of the 2020 Act were repealed by the Police, Crime, Sentencing and Courts Act 2022 s.201(2), having been superseded by the Courts Act 2003 Pt 7ZA (Transmission and recording of court and tribunal proceedings), inserted by ss.198 and 199 of the 2022 Act with effect from April 28, 2022. 3.138

[[1] CHAPTER 2A

EXERCISE OF TRIBUNAL FUNCTIONS BY AUTHORISED PERSONS

Meaning of "authorised person" and "judicial office holder"

29A.—In this Chapter— 3.139

"authorised person" means a person authorised under paragraph 3 of Schedule 5 to exercise functions of the First-tier Tribunal or Upper Tribunal;

"judicial office holder" has the meaning given by section 109(4) of the Constitutional Reform Act 2005.]

AMENDMENT

1. Courts and Tribunals (Judiciary and Functions of Staff) Act 2018 s.3(1) and Sch. paras 39 and 41 (January 10, 2020 for regulation-making purposes and April 6, 2020 for all other purposes).

[1 Directions and independence: authorised persons

3.140 **29B.**—(1) The Senior President of Tribunals may give directions to an authorised person.

(2) Apart from such directions, an authorised person exercising a function by virtue of paragraph 3 of Schedule 5 is not subject to the direction of the Lord Chancellor or any other person when exercising the function.

(3) The Senior President of Tribunals may delegate to one or more of the following the Senior President of Tribunals' functions under subsection (1)—

(a) a judicial office holder;

(b) a person appointed under section 2(1) of the Courts Act 2003 or section 40(1) of this Act.

(4) A person to whom functions of the Senior President of Tribunals are delegated under subsection (3)(b) is not subject to the direction of any person other than—

(a) the Senior President of Tribunals, or

(b) a judicial office holder nominated by the Senior President of Tribunals,

when exercising the functions.

(5) Subsections (3) to (5) of section 8 apply to—

(a) a delegation under subsection (3) of this section, and

(b) a nomination under subsection (4) of this section,

as they apply to a delegation under subsection (1) of that section.]

AMENDMENT

1. Courts and Tribunals (Judiciary and Functions of Staff) Act 2018 s.3(1) and Sch. paras 39 and 41 (January 10, 2020 for regulation-making purposes and April 6, 2020 for all other purposes).

GENERAL NOTE

3.141 This section and the three following sections guarantee persons authorised to carry out judicial functions the same independence, immunities and indemnities when acting in that role as judges have.

[1 Protection of authorised persons

3.142 **29C.**—(1) No action lies against an authorised person in respect of what the person does or omits to do—

(a) in the execution of the person's duty as an authorised person exercising, by virtue of paragraph 3 of Schedule 5, functions of a tribunal, and

(b) in relation to a matter within the person's jurisdiction.

(2) An action lies against an authorised person in respect of what the person does or omits to do—

(a) in the purported execution of the person's duty as an authorised person exercising, by virtue of paragraph 3 of Schedule 5, functions of a tribunal, but

(b) in relation to a matter not within the person's jurisdiction,

if, but only if, it is proved that the person acted in bad faith.

(3) If an action is brought in a court in Scotland in circumstances in which subsection (1) or (2) provides that no action lies, the court in which the action is brought—

(a) may, on the application of the defender, dismiss the action, and

(b) if it does so, may find the person bringing the action liable in expenses.

(4) If an action is brought in any other court in circumstances in which subsection (1) or (2) provides that no action lies, the court in which the action is brought—

(a) may, on the application of the defendant, strike out the proceedings in the action, and

(b) if it does so, may if it thinks fit order the person bringing the action to pay costs.]

AMENDMENT

1. Courts and Tribunals (Judiciary and Functions of Staff) Act 2018 s.3(1) and Sch. paras 39 and 41 (January 10, 2020 for regulation-making purposes and April 6, 2020 for all other purposes).

[[1] Costs or expenses in legal proceedings: authorised persons

29D.—(1)A court may not order an authorised person to pay costs in any proceedings in respect of what the person does or omits to do in the execution (or purported execution) of the person's duty as an authorised person exercising, by virtue of paragraph 3 of Schedule 5, a function of a tribunal. **3.143**

(2) But subsection (1) does not apply in relation to any proceedings in which an authorised person—

(a) is being tried for an offence or is appealing against a conviction, or

(b) is proved to have acted in bad faith in respect of the matters giving rise to the proceedings.

(3) A court which is prevented by subsection (1) from ordering an authorised person to pay costs in any proceedings may instead order the Lord Chancellor to make a payment in respect of the costs of a person in the proceedings.

(4) The Lord Chancellor may, after consulting the Senior President of Tribunals, make regulations specifying—

(a) circumstances in which a court must or must not exercise the power conferred on it by subsection (3), and

(b) how the amount of any payment ordered under subsection (3) is to be determined.

(5) The power to make regulations under subsection (4) includes power to make—

(a) any supplementary, incidental or consequential provision, and

(b) any transitory, transitional or saving provision,

which the Lord Chancellor considers necessary or expedient.

(6) The Senior President of Tribunals may delegate the Senior President of Tribunals' functions under subsection (4) to a person who is a judicial office holder.

(7) Subsections (3) to (5) of section 8 apply to a delegation under subsection (6) of this section as they apply to a delegation under subsection (1) of that section.

(8) In the application of this section to Scotland—

(a) references to a court ordering an authorised person to pay costs are to be read as references to a court finding an authorised person liable in expenses, and

(b) the second reference to costs in subsection (3) is to be read as a reference to expenses.]

AMENDMENT

1. Courts and Tribunals (Judiciary and Functions of Staff) Act 2018 s.3(1) and Sch. paras 39 and 41 (January 10, 2020 for regulation-making purposes and April 6, 2020 for all other purposes).

[1 Indemnification of authorised persons

3.144 **29E.**—(1)"Indemnifiable amounts", in relation to an authorised person, means—

(a) costs which the person reasonably incurs in or in connection with proceedings in respect of anything done or omitted to be done in the exercise (or purported exercise) of the person's duty as an authorised person,
(b) costs which the person reasonably incurs in taking steps to dispute a claim which might be made in such proceedings,
(c) damages awarded against the person or costs ordered to be paid by the person in such proceedings, or
(d) sums payable by the person in connection with a reasonable settlement of such proceedings or such a claim.

(2) The Lord Chancellor must indemnify an authorised person in respect of indemnifiable amounts if, in respect of the matters giving rise to the proceedings or claim, the person acted reasonably and in good faith.

(3) The Lord Chancellor may indemnify an authorised person in respect of other indemnifiable amounts unless it is proved, in respect of the matters giving rise to the proceedings or claim, that the person acted in bad faith.

(4) Any question whether, or to what extent, an authorised person is to be indemnified under this section is to be determined by the Lord Chancellor.

(5) The Lord Chancellor may, if an authorised person claiming to be indemnified so requests, make a determination for the purposes of this section with respect to—

(a) costs such as are mentioned in subsection (1)(a) or (b), or
(b) sums such as are mentioned in subsection (1)(d),

before the costs are incurred or the settlement in connection with which the sums are payable is made.

(6) But a determination under subsection (5) before costs are incurred—

(a) is subject to such limitations (if any) as the Lord Chancellor thinks proper and to the subsequent determination of the costs reasonably incurred, and
(b) does not affect any other determination which may fall to be made in connection with the proceedings or claim in question.

(7) In the application of this section to Scotland, references to costs are to be read as references to expenses.]

AMENDMENT

1. Courts and Tribunals (Judiciary and Functions of Staff) Act 2018 s.3(1) and Sch. paras 39 and 41 (January 10, 2020 for regulation-making purposes and April 6, 2020 for all other purposes).

CHAPTERS 3 TO 5

3.145 **30.–45.**—*Omitted.*

CHAPTER 6

SUPPLEMENTARY

46.–48.—*Omitted.* 3.146

Orders and regulations under Part 1: supplemental and procedural provisions

49.—(1) Power— 3.147

(a) of the Lord Chancellor to make an order, or regulations, under this Part,

(b) of the Senior President of Tribunals to make an order under section 7(9), or

(c) of the Scottish Ministers, or the Welsh Ministers, to make an order under paragraph 25(2) of Schedule 7,

is exercisable by statutory instrument.

(2) The Statutory Instruments Act 1946 shall apply in relation to the power to make orders conferred on the Senior President of Tribunals by section 7(9) as if the Senior President of Tribunals were a Minister of the Crown.

(3) Any power mentioned in subsection (1) includes power to make different provision for different purposes.

(4) Without prejudice to the generality of subsection (3), power to make an order under section 30 or 31 includes power to make different provision in relation to England, Scotland, Wales and Northern Ireland respectively.

(5) [1 None of the orders or regulations mentioned in subsection (6) may be made unless a draft of the statutory instrument containing the order or regulations] (whether alone or with other provision) has been laid before, and approved by a resolution of, each House of Parliament.

(6) [1 The orders and regulations] are—

(a) an order under section 11(8), 13(6) or (14), 30, 31(1), 32, 33, 34, 35, 36, 37 or 42(3);

[1 (aa) regulations under section 29D(4);]

(b) an order under paragraph 15 of Schedule 4;

(c) an order under section 42(1)(a) to (d) that provides for fees to be payable in respect of things for which fees have never been payable;

(d) an order under section 31(2), (7) or (9), or paragraph 30(1) of Schedule 5, that contains provision taking the form of an amendment or repeal of an enactment comprised in an Act.

(7) A statutory instrument that—

(a) contains—

   (i) an order mentioned in subsection (8), or

   (ii) regulations under Part 3 of Schedule 9, and

(b) is not subject to any requirement that a draft of the instrument be laid before, and approved by a resolution of, each House of Parliament,

is subject to annulment in pursuance of a resolution of either House of Parliament.

(8) Those orders are—

(a) an order made by the Lord Chancellor under this Part;

(b) an order made by the Senior President of Tribunals under section 7(9).

(9) A statutory instrument that contains an order made by the Scottish Ministers under paragraph 25(2) of Schedule 7 is subject to annulment in pursuance of a resolution of the Scottish Parliament.

(10) A statutory instrument that contains an order made by the Welsh Ministers under paragraph 25(2) of Schedule 7 is subject to annulment in pursuance of a resolution of the National Assembly for Wales.

AMENDMENT

1. Courts and Tribunals (Judiciary and Functions of Staff) Act 2018 s.3(1) and Sch. paras 39 and 42 (January 10, 2020 for regulation-making purposes and April 6, 2020 for all other purposes).

PARTS 2 TO 7

3.148 **50.–143.**—*Omitted.*

PART 8

GENERAL

3.149 **144.**—*Omitted.*

Power to make supplementary or other provision

3.150 **145.**—(1) The Lord Chancellor (or, in relation to Chapter 3 of Part 5 only, the Secretary of State) may by order make any supplementary, incidental, consequential, transitory, transitional or saving provision which he considers necessary or expedient for the purposes of, in consequence of, or for giving full effect to, any provision of this Act.

(2) An order under this section may in particular—

(a) provide for any provision of this Act which comes into force before another to have effect, until that other provision has come into force, with modifications specified in the order;

(b) amend, repeal or revoke any enactment other than one contained in an Act or instrument passed or made after the Session in which this Act is passed.

(3) The amendments that may be made by an order under this section are in addition to those made by or under any other provision of this Act.

(4) An order under this section may make different provision for different purposes.

(5) The power to make an order under this section is exercisable by statutory instrument.

(6) A statutory instrument containing an order under this section, unless it is an order to which subsection (7) applies, is subject to annulment in pursuance of a resolution of either House of Parliament.

(7) No order amending or repealing an enactment contained in an Act may be made under this section unless a draft of the order has been laid before and approved by a resolution of each House of Parliament.

3.151 **146.**—*Omitted.*

Extent

147.—(1) Parts 1, 2 and 6 and this Part extend to England and Wales, Scotland and Northern Ireland. 3.152

(2) The other provisions of this Act extend only to England and Wales.

(3) Subsections (1) and (2) are subject to subsections (4) and (5).

(4) Unless provided otherwise, amendments, repeals and revocations in this Act extend to any part of the United Kingdom to which the provisions amended, repealed or revoked extend.

(5) The following extend also to the Isle of Man—

(a) section 143(1) and (2),

(b) the repeal by this Act of any provision specified in Part 6 of Schedule 23 that extends to the Isle of Man,

(c) sections 145 and 148(5) to (7) so far as relating to—

(i) section 143(1) and (2), and

(ii) the provisions of this Act by which the repeals mentioned in paragraph (b) are effected, and

(d) this section and section 149.

Commencement

148.—(1) Section 60 comes into force at the end of the period of two months beginning with the day on which this Act is passed. 3.153

(2) The provisions of Chapter 3 of Part 5 come into force in accordance with provision made by the Lord Chancellor or the Secretary of State by order.

(3) The provisions of Part 6 come into force, except as provided by subsection (4), in accordance with provision made by the Secretary of State by order.

(4) The provisions of Part 6 come into force, in so far as they extend to Scotland, in accordance with provision made by the Scottish Ministers by order.

(5) The remaining provisions of this Act, except sections 53, 55, 56, 57, 145, 147, 149, this section and Schedule 11, come into force in accordance with provision made by the Lord Chancellor by order.

(6) An order under this section may make different provision for different purposes.

(7) The power to make an order under this section is exercisable by statutory instrument.

Short title

149.—This Act may be cited as the Tribunals, Courts and Enforcement Act 2007. 3.154

Schedules 1 to 3 *Omitted.* 3.155

SCHEDULE 4

CHAMBERS AND CHAMBER PRESIDENTS: FURTHER PROVISION

PART 1

CHAMBER PRESIDENTS: APPOINTMENT, DELEGATION, DEPUTIES AND FURTHER PROVISION

3.156 **1. to 3.** *Omitted.*

Delegation of functions by Chamber Presidents

3.157 **4.** (1) The Chamber President of a chamber of the First-tier Tribunal or Upper Tribunal may delegate any function he has in his capacity as the Chamber President of the chamber—

(a) to any judge, or other member, of either of those tribunals;

(b) to staff appointed under section 40(1).

(2) A delegation under sub-paragraph (1) is not revoked by the delegator's becoming incapacitated.

(3) Any delegation made by a person under sub-paragraph (1) that is in force immediately before the person ceases to be the Chamber President of a chamber continues in force until subsequently varied or revoked by another holder of the office of Chamber President of that chamber.

(4) The delegation under sub-paragraph (1) of a function shall not prevent the exercise of the function by the Chamber President of the chamber concerned.

(5) In this paragraph "delegate" includes further delegate.

3.158 **5. to 8**. *Omitted.*

PART 2

JUDGES AND OTHER MEMBERS OF CHAMBERS: ASSIGNMENT AND JURISDICTION

3.159 **9. to 14.** *Omitted.*

Composition of tribunals

3.160 **15.** (1) The Lord Chancellor must by order make provision, in relation to every matter that may fall to be decided by the First-tier Tribunal or the Upper Tribunal, for determining the number of members of the tribunal who are to decide the matter.

(2) Where an order under sub-paragraph (1) provides for a matter to be decided by a single member of a tribunal, the order—

(a) must make provision for determining whether the matter is to be decided by one of the judges, or by one of the other members, of the tribunal, and

(b) may make provision for determining, if the matter is to be decided by one of the other members of the tribunal, what qualifications (if any) that other member must have.

(3) Where an order under sub-paragraph (1) provides for a matter to be decided by two or more members of a tribunal, the order—

(a) must make provision for determining how many (if any) of those members are to be judges of the tribunal and how many (if any) are to be other members of the tribunal, and

(b) may make provision for determining—

(i) if the matter is to be decided by persons who include one or more of the other members of the tribunal, or

(ii) if the matter is to be decided by two or more of the other members of the tribunal,

what qualifications (if any) that other member or any of those other members must have.

(4) A duty under sub-paragraph (1), (2) or (3) to provide for the determination of anything may be discharged by providing for the thing to be determined by the Senior President of Tribunals, or a Chamber President, in accordance with any provision made under that sub-paragraph.

(5) Power under paragraph (b) of sub-paragraph (2) or (3) to provide for the determination of anything may be exercised by giving, to the Senior President of Tribunals or a Chamber President, power to determine that thing in accordance with any provision made under that paragraph.

(6) Where under sub-paragraphs (1) to (4) a matter is to be decided by two or more members of a tribunal, the matter may, if the parties to the case agree, be decided in the absence of one or more (but not all) of the members chosen to decide the matter.

(7) Where the member, or any of the members, of a tribunal chosen to decide a matter does not have any qualification that he is required to have under sub-paragraphs (2)(b), or (3)(b), and (5), the matter may despite that, if the parties to the case agree, be decided by the chosen member or members.

(8) Before making an order under this paragraph, the Lord Chancellor must consult the Senior President of Tribunals.

(9) In this paragraph "qualification" includes experience.

General Note

Paragraph 15

See the First-tier Tribunal and Upper Tribunal (Composition of Tribunal) Order 2008, below. The Order makes much use of the power in para.15(4) for an order to leave matters of composition to be determined by the Senior President of Tribunals who who has issued practice statements. The relevant practice statements are set out in the notes to the Order. Note that subpara.(6) provides for a case to be determined in the absence of some (but not all!) members of the tribunal, provided the parties agree. However, it does not permit a member of a tribunal to absent themselves from part of the hearing and then take part in deliberations, even with the consent of the parties, although a decision reached in that way in ignorance of the law and with the voluntary, informed and unequivocal consent of the parties will not necessarily be set aside on appeal (*Shipton v IC* [2023] UKUT **3.161**

170 (AAC)). Subparagraph (7) also enables a tribunal to proceed if any of the members of the tribunal does not have the requisite qualifications, provided the parties agree. Thus, if one of the members does not have the relevant qualification, there is a choice between the proceedings being adjourned, the case proceeding without that member and the case proceeding with that member. In this context "member" clearly include a judge, so it would be possible for a hearing to take place without a judge by virtue of either of those paragraphs. However, not only must the parties agree that it is appropriate to proceed but so must the tribunal itself. There are likely to be cases where the lack of the relevant expertise obliges the tribunal to adjourn the proceedings in the interests of justice. Where no-one realises that a member lacks the relevant qualifications, including the member himself or herself, and the tribunal therefore hears the case, the decision of the tribunal is not invalid unless the member deliberately closed his or her eyes to the problem or the lack of relevant qualification has rendered the proceedings unfair (*Coppard v Customs and Excise Commissioners* [2003] EWCA Civ 511; [2003] Q.B. 1428).

SCHEDULE 5

Procedure in First-tier Tribunal and Upper Tribunal

Part 1

Tribunal Procedure Rules

Introductory

3.162 **1.** (1) This Part of this Schedule makes further provision about the content of Tribunal Procedure Rules.

(2) The generality of section 22(1) is not to be taken to be prejudiced by—

(a) the following paragraphs of this Part of this Schedule, or

(b) any other provision (including future provision) authorising or requiring the making of provision by Tribunal Procedure Rules.

(3) In the following paragraphs of this Part of this Schedule "Rules" means Tribunal Procedure Rules.

Concurrent functions

3.163 **2.** Rules may make provision as to who is to decide, or as to how to decide, which of the First-tier Tribunal and Upper Tribunal is to exercise, in relation to any particular matter, a function that is exercisable by the two tribunals on the basis that the question as to which of them is to exercise the function is to be determined by, or under, Rules.

Delegation of functions to staff

3.164 **3.** (1) Rules may provide for functions—

(a) of the First-tier Tribunal, or

(b) of the Upper Tribunal,

to be exercised by staff appointed under section [[2] 2(1) of the Courts Act 2003 or section 40(1) of this Act].

(2) In making provision of the kind mentioned in sub-paragraph (1) in relation to a function, Rules may (in particular)—

(a) provide for the function to be exercisable by a member of staff only if the member of staff is, or is of a description, specified in exercise of a discretion conferred by Rules;

(b) provide for the function to be exercisable by a member of staff only if the member of staff is approved, or is of a description approved, for the purpose by a person specified in Rules.

[[2] (3) A person may exercise functions by virtue of this paragraph only if authorised to do so by the Senior President of Tribunals.

(4) An authorisation under this paragraph—

(a) may be subject to conditions, and

(b) may be varied or revoked by the Senior President of Tribunals at any time.

(5) The Senior President of Tribunals may delegate to one or more of the following the Senior President of Tribunals' functions under the preceding provisions of this paragraph—

(a) a judicial office holder;

(b) a person appointed under section 2(1) of the Courts Act 2003 or section 40(1) of this Act.

(6) A person to whom functions of the Senior President of Tribunals are delegated under sub-paragraph (5)(b) is not subject to the direction of any person other than—

(a) the Senior President of Tribunals, or

(b) a judicial office holder nominated by the Senior President of Tribunals,

when exercising the functions.

(7) Subsections (3) to (5) of section 8 apply to—

(a) a delegation under sub-paragraph (5), and

(b) a nomination under sub-paragraph (6),

as they apply to a delegation under subsection (1) of that section.

(8) In this paragraph—

"function" does not include—

(a) any function so far as its exercise involves authorising a person's committal to prison or arrest;

(b) any function of granting an injunction;

"judicial office holder" has the meaning given by section 109(4) of the Constitutional Reform Act 2005.]

Time limits

4. Rules may make provision for time limits as respects initiating, or taking any step in, proceedings before the First-tier Tribunal or the Upper Tribunal. **3.165**

Repeat applications

5. Rules may make provision restricting the making of fresh applications where a previous application in relation to the same matter has been made. **3.166**

Tribunal acting of its own initiative

6. Rules may make provision about the circumstances in which the First-tier Tribunal, or the Upper Tribunal, may exercise its powers of its own initiative. **3.167**

Hearings

3.168 **7.** Rules may—

(a) make provision for dealing with matters without a hearing;

(b) make provision as respects allowing or requiring a hearing to be in private or as respects allowing or requiring a hearing to be in public.

Proceedings without notice

3.169 **8.** Rules may make provision for proceedings to take place, in circumstances described in Rules, at the request of one party even though the other, or another, party has had no notice.

Representation

3.170 **9.** Rules may make provision conferring additional rights of audience before the First-tier Tribunal or the Upper Tribunal.

Evidence, witnesses and attendance

3.171 **10.** (1) Rules may make provision about evidence (including evidence on oath and administration of oaths).

(2) Rules may modify any rules of evidence provided for elsewhere, so far as they would apply to proceedings before the First-tier Tribunal or Upper Tribunal.

(3) Rules may make provision, where the First-tier Tribunal has required a person—

(a) to attend at any place for the purpose of giving evidence,

(b) otherwise to make himself available to give evidence,

(c) to swear an oath in connection with the giving of evidence,

(d) to give evidence as a witness,

(e) to produce a document, or

(f) to facilitate the inspection of a document or any other thing (including any premises),

for the Upper Tribunal to deal with non-compliance with the requirement as though the requirement had been imposed by the Upper Tribunal.

(4) Rules may make provision for the payment of expenses and allowances to persons giving evidence, producing documents, attending proceedings or required to attend proceedings.

Use of information

3.172 **11.** (1) Rules may make provision for the disclosure or non-disclosure of information received during the course of proceedings before the First-tier Tribunal or Upper Tribunal.

(2) Rules may make provision for imposing reporting restrictions in circumstances described in Rules.

Costs and expenses

3.173 **12.** (1) Rules may make provision for regulating matters relating to costs, or (in Scotland) expenses, of proceedings before the First-tier Tribunal or Upper Tribunal.

(2) The provision mentioned in sub-paragraph (1) includes (in particular)—

(a) provision prescribing scales of costs or expenses;

(b) provision for enabling costs to undergo detailed assessment in England and Wales by [1 the county court] or the High Court;

(c) provision for taxation in Scotland of accounts of expenses by an Auditor of Court;

(d) provision for enabling costs to be taxed in Northern Ireland in a county court or the High Court;

(e) provision for costs or expenses—

(i) not to be allowed in respect of items of a description specified in Rules;

(ii) not to be allowed in proceedings of a description so specified;

(f) provision for other exceptions to either or both of subsections (1) and (2) of section 29.

Set-off and interest

13. (1) Rules may make provision for a party to proceedings to deduct, from amounts payable by him, amounts payable to him. 3.174

(2) Rules may make provision for interest on sums awarded (including provision conferring a discretion or provision in accordance with which interest is to be calculated).

Arbitration

14. Rules may provide for Part 1 of the Arbitration Act 1996 (which extends to England and Wales, and Northern Ireland, but not Scotland) not to apply, or not to apply except so far as is specified in Rules, where the First-tier Tribunal, or Upper Tribunal, acts as arbitrator. 3.175

Correction of errors and setting-aside of decisions on procedural grounds

15. (1) Rules may make provision for the correction of accidental errors in a decision or record of a decision. 3.176

(2) Rules may make provision for the setting aside of a decision in proceedings before the First-tier Tribunal or Upper Tribunal—

(a) where a document relating to the proceedings was not sent to, or was not received at an appropriate time by, a party to the proceedings or a party's representative,

(b) where a document relating to the proceedings was not sent to the First-tier Tribunal or Upper Tribunal at an appropriate time,

(c) where a party to the proceedings, or a party's representative, was not present at a hearing related to the proceedings, or

(d) where there has been any other procedural irregularity in the proceedings.

(3) Sub-paragraphs (1) and (2) shall not be taken to prejudice, or to be prejudiced by, any power to correct errors or set aside decisions that is exercisable apart from rules made by virtue of those sub-paragraphs.

Ancillary powers

16. Rules may confer on the First-tier Tribunal, or the Upper Tribunal, such ancillary powers as are necessary for the proper discharge of its functions. 3.177

Rules may refer to practice directions

3.178 **17.** Rules may, instead of providing for any matter, refer to provision made or to be made about that matter by directions under section 23.

Presumptions

3.179 **18.** Rules may make provision in the form of presumptions (including, in particular, presumptions as to service or notification).

Differential provision

3.180 **19.** Rules may make different provision for different purposes or different areas.

PART 2

3.181 **20.** to **26.**—*Omitted.*

PART 3

MAKING OF TRIBUNAL PROCEDURE RULES BY TRIBUNAL PROCEDURE COMMITTEE

Meaning of "Rules" and "the Committee"

3.182 **27.** In the following provisions of this Part of this Schedule—
"the Committee" means the Tribunal Procedure Committee;
"Rules" means Tribunal Procedure Rules.

Process for making Rules

3.183 **28.** (1) Before the Committee makes Rules, the Committee must—
(a) consult such persons (including such of the Chamber Presidents) as it considers appropriate,
(b) consult the Lord President of the Court of Session if the Rules contain provision relating to proceedings in Scotland, and
(c) meet (unless it is inexpedient to do so).
(2) Rules made by the Committee must be—
(a) signed by a majority of the members of the Committee, and
(b) submitted to the Lord Chancellor.
(3) The Lord Chancellor may allow or disallow Rules so made.
(4) If the Lord Chancellor disallows Rules so made, he must give the Committee written reasons for doing so.
(5) Rules so made and allowed—
(a) come into force on such day as the Lord Chancellor directs, and
(b) are to be contained in a statutory instrument to which the Statutory Instruments Act 1946 applies as if the instrument contained rules made by a Minister of the Crown.
(6) A statutory instrument containing Rules made by the Committee is subject to annulment in pursuance of a resolution of either House of Parliament.

(7) In the case of a member of the Committee appointed under paragraph 24, the terms of his appointment may (in particular) provide that, for the purposes of sub-paragraph (2)(a), he is to count as a member of the Committee only in relation to matters specified in those terms.

[[1] Delegation of functions to staff: reconsideration of decisions

28A. (1) Before making Rules that provide for the exercise of functions of the First-tier Tribunal or Upper Tribunal by authorised persons by virtue of paragraph 3, the Committee must take the following steps in relation to each of the functions in question. 3.184

(2) The Committee must consider whether the Rules should include a right for the parties to proceedings in which a decision is made by an authorised person exercising the function to have the decision reconsidered by a judicial office holder.

(3) If the Committee considers that the rules should include such a right, it must include provision to that effect when it makes the Rules.

(4) If the Committee does not consider that the rules should include such a right, it must inform the Lord Chancellor of—

(a) its decision, and

(b) its reasons for reaching that decision.

(5) In this paragraph "authorised person" and "judicial office holder" have the same meanings as in Chapter 2A of Part 1 of this Act (see section 29A).]

Power of Lord Chancellor to require Rules to be made

29. (1) This paragraph applies if the Lord Chancellor gives the Committee written notice that he thinks it is expedient for Rules to include provision that would achieve a purpose specified in the notice. 3.185

(2) The Committee must make such Rules, in accordance with paragraph 28, as it considers necessary to achieve the specified purpose.

(3) Those Rules must be made—

(a) within such period as may be specified by the Lord Chancellor in the notice, or

(b) if no period is so specified, within a reasonable period after the Lord Chancellor gives the notice to the Committee.

Part 4

Power To Amend Legislation In Connection With Tribunal Procedure Rules

Lord Chancellor's power

30. (1) The Lord Chancellor may by order amend, repeal or revoke any enactment to the extent he considers necessary or desirable— 3.186

(a) in order to facilitate the making of Tribunal Procedure Rules, or

(b) in consequence of—

(i) section 22,

(ii) Part 1 or 3 of this Schedule, or

(iii) Tribunal Procedure Rules.

(2) In this paragraph "enactment" means any enactment whenever passed or made, including an enactment comprised in subordinate legislation (within the meaning of the Interpretation Act 1978).

AMENDMENTS

1. Crime and Courts Act 2013 s.17(5) and Sch.9 para.52 (April 22, 2014).
2. Courts and Tribunals (Judiciary and Functions of Staff) Act 2018 s.3(1) and Sch. paras 39, 43, 44 and 45 (January 10, 2020 for regulation-making purposes and April 6, 2020 for all other purposes).

GENERAL NOTE

Paragraph 1

3.187 The scope of the power to make Tribunal Procedure Rules in s.22(1) is very broad and is not to be treated as limited by any other rule-making power in this Act, including this Schedule, or indeed in any other Act.

Paragraph 3

3.188 The amendments to this paragraph were made at the same time as ss.29A to 29E were inserted into the Act. It is now made clear that the functions delegated are judicial functions. As to the making of rules under this paragraph, see para.28A.

Paragraph 4

3.189 In *JI v HMRC (TC)* [2013] UKUT 199, it was held that, in the light of *Mucelli v Government of Albania* [2009] UKHL 2; [2009] 1 W.L.R. 287, this paragraph did not by itself permit the making of rules that extended time limits laid down in primary legislation. However, in *VK v HMRC (TC)* [2016] UKUT 331 (AAC); [2017] AACR 3, a three-judge panel distinguished *Mucelli* and overruled *JI* and held that the time limit for appeals against tax credit decisions made before April 6, 2014, which was then found in s.39 of the Tax Credits Act 2002, could be extended by Tribunal Procedure Rules made under this paragraph.

Paragraph 10

3.190 See s.25 for the powers of the Upper Tribunal to which reference is made in sub-para.(3).

Paragraph 15

3.191 There is potentially some overlap between Tribunal Procedure Rules made under this paragraph and the power to correct or set aside a decision on a review under s.9 or s.10. However, the circumstances in which a decision may be reviewed are likely to be limited and it is likely to be fairly clear which power should be used.

Note that para.15(2) is broader than s.28(1) of the Social Security Act 1998, which it replaces, as it covers any procedural irregularity (which, at one time, some regulations purporting to be made under s.28 of the 1998 Act did).

Paragraphs 27–29

3.192 The Lord Chancellor may disallow Rules or require particular provision to be made in Rules.

3.193 **Schedules 6–23**: *Omitted.*

The Transfer of Tribunal Functions Order 2008

(SI 2008/2833)

Made	*29th October 2008*
Coming into force	*3rd November 2008*

The Lord Chancellor makes the following Order in exercise of the powers conferred by sections 30(1) and (4), 31(1), (2) and (9), 32(3) and (5), 33(2) and (3), 34(2) and (3), 37(1), 38 and 145 of, and paragraph 30 of Schedule 5 to, the Tribunals, Courts and Enforcement Act 2007. The Scottish Ministers have consented to the making of this order in so far as their consent is required by section 30(7) of that Act. **3.194**

A draft of this Order was laid before Parliament and approved by a resolution of each House of Parliament in accordance with section 49(5) of that Act.

Citation, commencement, interpretation and extent

1.—(1) This Order may be cited as the Transfer of Tribunal Functions Order 2008 and comes into force on 3rd November 2008. **3.195**

(2) A reference in this Order to a Schedule by a number alone is a reference to the Schedule so numbered in this Order.

(3) Subject as follows, this Order extends to England and Wales, Scotland and Northern Ireland.

(4) Except as provided by paragraph (5) or (6), an amendment, repeal or revocation of any enactment by any provision of Schedule 3 extends to the part or parts of the United Kingdom to which the enactment extends.

(5) For the purposes of article 3(3)(a) and (b) the following amendments, repeals and revocations made by the provisions of that Schedule do not extend to Scotland—

(a) paragraphs 145 to 147;
(b) paragraph 150;
(c) paragraph 151(d);
(d) paragraph 152;
(e) paragraph 154;
(f) paragraphs 167 to 173; and
(g) paragraph 228(h), (l), (n) and (r).

(6) The amendments and repeals made by paragraphs 198 to 201 of Schedule 3 do not extend to Scotland.

General Note

The reason for paras (5) and (6) is explained in the note to ss.5–7 of the Social Security Act 1998. **3.196**

2. *Omitted.* **3.197**

Transfer of functions of certain tribunals

3.—(1) Subject to paragraph (3), the functions of the tribunals listed in Table 1 of Schedule 1 are transferred to the First-tier Tribunal. **3.198**

(2) Subject to paragraph (3), the functions of the tribunals listed in Table 2 of Schedule 1 are transferred to the Upper Tribunal.

(3) The following functions are not transferred—

(a) the determination by an appeal tribunal constituted under Chapter 1 of Part 1 of the Social Security Act 1998 of an appeal which is referred to such tribunal by the Scottish Ministers, or the Secretary of State on their behalf, pursuant to section 158 (appeal tribunals) of the Health and Social Care (Community Health and Standards) Act 2003 ("the 2003 Act"); and

(b) the determination by a Social Security Commissioner of an appeal made under section 159 (appeal to social security commissioner) of the 2003 Act against a decision falling within sub-paragraph (a).

General Note

3.199 The reason for para.(3) is explained in the note to ss.5–7 of the Social Security Act 1998.

Abolition of tribunals transferred under section 30(1)

3.200 **4.** The tribunals listed in Table 1 and Table 2 of Schedule 1 are abolished except for—

(a) appeal tribunals constituted under Chapter 1 of Part 1 of the Social Security Act 1998 in respect of Scotland for the purposes of the function described in article 3(3)(a); and

(b) the Social Security Commissioners in respect of Scotland for the purposes of the function described in article 3(3)(b).

General Note

3.201 The reason for the saving is explained in the note to ss.5–7 of the Social Security Act 1998.

3.202 **5. to 8.** *Omitted.*

Minor, consequential and transitional provisions

3.203 **9.**—(1) Schedule 3 contains minor, consequential and supplemental amendments, and repeals and revocations as a consequence of those amendments.

(2) Schedule 4 contains transitional provisions.

SCHEDULE 1

FUNCTIONS TRANSFERRED TO THE FIRST-TIER TRIBUNAL AND UPPER TRIBUNAL

Table 1: Functions transferred to the First-tier Tribunal 3.204

Tribunal	*Enactment*
Adjudicator	Section 5 of the Criminal Injuries Compensation Act 1995
Appeal tribunal	Chapter 1 of Part 1 of the Social Security Act 1998
Asylum Support Adjudicators	Section 102 of the Immigration and Asylum Act 1999
Mental Health Review Tribunal for a region of England	Section 65(1) and (1A)(a) of the Mental Health Act 1983
Pensions Appeal Tribunal in England and Wales	Section 8(2) of the War Pensions (Administrative Provisions) Act 1919 and paragraph 1(1) of the Schedule to the Pensions Appeal Tribunals Act 1943
Special Educational Needs and Disability Tribunal	Section 28H of the Disability Discrimination Act 1995 and section 333 of the Education Act 1996
Tribunal, except in respect of its functions under section 4 of the Safeguarding Vulnerable Groups Act 2004	Section 9 of the Protection of Children Act 1999

Table 2: Functions transferred to the Upper Tribunal 3.205

Tribunal	*Enactment*
Child Support Commissioner	Section 22 of the Child Support Act 1991
Social Security Commissioner	Schedule 4 to the Social Security Act 1998
Tribunal, in respect of its functions under section 4 of the Safeguarding Vulnerable Groups Act 2006	Section 9 of the Protection of Children Act 1999

Schedules 2 and 3. *Omitted.* 3.206

SCHEDULE 4

TRANSITIONAL PROVISIONS

Transitional provisions

1. Subject to article 3(3)(a) any proceedings before a tribunal listed in Table 1 of Schedule 1 which are pending immediately before 3rd November 2008 shall continue on and after 3rd November 2008 as proceedings before the First-tier Tribunal. 3.207

2. Subject to article 3(3)(b) any proceedings before a tribunal listed in Table 2 of Schedule 1 which are pending immediately before 3rd November

2008 shall continue on and after 3rd November 2008 as proceedings before the Upper Tribunal.

3.—(1) The following sub-paragraphs apply where proceedings are continued in the First-tier Tribunal or Upper Tribunal by virtue of paragraph 1 or 2.

(2) Where a hearing began before 3rd November 2008 but was not completed by that date, the First-tier Tribunal or the Upper Tribunal, as the case may be, must be comprised for the continuation of that hearing of the person or persons who began it.

(3) The First-tier Tribunal or Upper Tribunal, as the case may be, may give any direction to ensure that proceedings are dealt with fairly and, in particular, may—

(a) apply any provision in procedural rules which applied to the proceedings before 3rd November 2008; or

(b) disapply provisions of Tribunal Procedure Rules.

(4) In sub-paragraph (3) "procedural rules" means provision (whether called rules or not) regulating practice or procedure before a tribunal.

(5) Any direction or order given or made in proceedings which is in force immediately before 3rd November 2008 remains in force on and after that date as if it were a direction or order of the First-tier Tribunal or Upper Tribunal, as the case may be.

(6) A time period which has started to run before 3rd November 2008 and which has not expired shall continue to apply.

(7) An order for costs may only be made if, and to the extent that, an order could have been made before 3rd November 2008.

4. Subject to article 3(3)(a) and (b) where an appeal lies to a Child Support or Social Security Commissioner from any decision made before 3rd November 2008 by a tribunal listed in Table 1 of Schedule 1, section 11 of the 2007 Act (right to appeal to Upper Tribunal) shall apply as if the decision were a decision made on or after 3rd November 2008 by the First-tier Tribunal.

5. Subject to article 3(3)(b) where an appeal lies to a court from any decision made before 3rd November 2008 by a Child Support or Social Security Commissioner, section 13 of the 2007 Act (right to appeal to Court of Appeal etc.) shall apply as if the decision were a decision made on or after 3rd November 2008 by the Upper Tribunal.

6. Subject to article 3(3)(a) and (b) any case to be remitted by a court on or after 3rd November 2008 in relation to a tribunal listed in Schedule 1 shall be remitted to the First-tier Tribunal or Upper Tribunal as the case may be.

7. *Omitted.*

General Note

3.208 Before November 3, 2008, the time for applying for leave to appeal to a Social Security Commissioner against a decision of an appeal tribunal could not be extended by more than 12 months. No such absolute limit applies to extensions of the time for appealing to the Upper Tribunal against a decision of the First-tier Tribunal. However, where the absolute time limit for appealing against a decision of an appeal tribunal under the old legislation had expired before November 3, 2008, it would give an impermissible retrospective effect to the new legislation to rely on para.4 of this Schedule to extend the time for appealing against that decision (*LS v Lambeth LBC* (HB) [2010] UKUT 461 (AAC), [2011] AACR 27; *ED v SSWP (DLA)* [2013] UKUT 583 (AAC)).

The First-tier Tribunal and Upper Tribunal (Composition of Tribunal) Order 2008

(SI 2008/2835)

Made — *29th October 2008*
Coming into force — *3rd November 2008*

The Lord Chancellor makes the following Order in exercise of the powers conferred by section 145(1) of, and paragraph 15 of Schedule 4 to, the Tribunals, Courts and Enforcement Act 2007. **3.209**

In accordance with paragraph 15(8) of that Act the Lord Chancellor has consulted the Senior President of Tribunals.

In accordance with section 49(5) of that Act a draft of this instrument was laid before Parliament and approved by a resolution of each House of Parliament.

Citation and commencement

1. This Order may be cited as the First-tier Tribunal and Upper Tribunal (Composition of Tribunal) Order 2008 and comes into force on 3rd November 2008. **3.210**

[[1] Interpretation

1A. In this Order— **3.211**

"practice direction" means a direction made under section 23 of the Tribunals, Courts and Enforcement Act 2007 as to the practice and procedure of the First-tier Tribunal or the Upper Tribunal that contains criteria for determining which members of the First-tier Tribunal or Upper Tribunal may be chosen to decide particular categories of matter.]

AMENDMENT

1. First-tier Tribunal and Upper Tribunal (Composition of Tribunal) (Amendment) Order 2018 (SI 2018/606) art.2 (May 18, 2018).

Number of members of the First-tier Tribunal

[[1] **2.**—(1) The number of members of the tribunal who are to decide any matter that falls to be decided by the First-tier Tribunal must be determined by the Senior President of Tribunals in a practice direction in accordance with paragraphs (2) and (3) below. **3.212**

(2) The Senior President of Tribunals must determine whether the tribunal consists of one, two or three members.

(3) The Senior President of Tribunals must have regard to—

(a) the nature of the matter that falls to be decided and the means by which it is to be decided; and

(b) the need for members of tribunals to have particular expertise, skills or knowledge.]

AMENDMENT

1. First-tier Tribunal and Upper Tribunal (Composition of Tribunal) (Amendment) Order 2018 (SI 2018/606) art.3 (May 18, 2018).

General Note

3.213 As is permitted by para.15(4) of Sch.4 to the Tribunals Courts and Enforcement Act 2007, this article leaves it to the Senior President of Tribunals to determine the number of members to determine any particular type of case and the qualifications they must have. It was substituted in 2018 following a public consultation (see *https://www.gov.uk/government/consultations/transforming-our-courts-and-tribunals*) and it no longer requires the Senior President of Tribunals to have regard to the composition of abolished tribunals before their functions were transferred to the First-tier Tribunal, replacing that requirement with a duty to have regard to the nature of the case and the means by which it will be decided. In its consultation paper, the Government had proposed that, if the duty to have regard to the historical position were to be removed, the default composition of both the First-tier Tribunal and the Upper Tribunal should be a single member. However, in the absence of any real argument from the Government to show that that was more appropriate than the historical position, there was a great deal of opposition to the proposal as regards the First-tier Tribunal and the proposal was dropped. Emphasis was instead placed on the need for flexibility.

The substituted article requires the Senior President of Tribunals' determinations to be issued by way of Practice Directions under s.23 of the Tribunals, Courts and Enforcement Act 2007, which require the approval of the Lord Chancellor, whereas previously they had been issued as mere practice statements. By virtue of art.5 of the amending order of 2018, practice statements issued before the Order was made remain in force until replaced by a Practice Direction.

The current Practice Direction on the composition of the First-tier Tribunal was amended following a consultation process in 2023 and is in the following terms-

1. In this Practice Direction:
   (a) "the Composition Order" means the First-tier Tribunal and Upper Tribunal (Composition of Tribunal) Order 2008;
   (b) "the Qualifications Order" means the Qualifications for Appointment of Members to the First-tier Tribunal and Upper Tribunal Order 2008;
   (c) references to numbered rules are to the rules so numbered in the Tribunal Procedure (First-tier Tribunal) (Social Entitlement Chamber) Rules 2008;
   (d) "asylum support case", "criminal injuries compensation case", and "social security and child support case" have the meanings given in rule 1(3).
2. In exercise of the powers conferred by the Composition Order the Senior President of Tribunals, having consulted the Lord Chancellor, makes the following determinations and supplementary provision in relation to matters that fall to be determined by the Social Entitlement Chamber on or after 16 May 2024. These supersede all previous determinations made in respect of the Social Entitlement Chamber, which are set out in:
   a. Practice Statement dated 31 July 2013 on composition of tribunals in social security and child support cases in the Social Entitlement Chamber;
   b. Practice Statement dated 30 October 2008 on composition of tribunals in relation to matters that fall to be decided in criminal injury compensation cases in the Social Entitlement Chamber;
   c. Practice Statement dated 30 October 2008 on composition of tribunals in relation to matters that fall to be decided in asylum support cases in the Social Entitlement Chamber;

   save that the determinations set out in the Practice Statements will continue to apply to cases in which a decision to list the matter for a hearing has been made before 16 May 2024.

3. The number of members of the Tribunal must not exceed three.
4. Paragraphs 5 to 14 below apply to social security and child support cases.
5. Where the appeal relates to:
   (a) an attendance allowance or a disability living allowance under Part III of the Social Security Contributions and Benefits Act 1992; or
   (b) personal independence payment under Part 4 of the Welfare Reform Act 2012;

the Tribunal must, subject to paragraphs 9 to 13, consist of one judge, one other member who is a registered medical practitioner, and one other member who has a disability qualification as set out in article 2(3) of the Qualifications Order.

6. Where the appeal:
   (a) involves the personal capability assessment, as defined in regulation 2(1) of the Social Security (Incapacity for Work) (General) Regulations 1995;
   (b) involves the limited capability for work assessment under Part 5 of the Employment and Support Allowance Regulations 2008, under Part 5 of the Universal Credit Regulations 2013 or under Part 4 of the Employment and Support Allowance Regulations 2013;
   (c) involves the limited capability for work-related activity assessment under Part 6 of the Employment and Support Allowance Regulations 2008, under Part 5 of the Universal Credit Regulations 2013 or under Part 5 of the Employment and Support Allowance Regulations 2013;
   (d) is made under section 11(1)(b) of the Social Security (Recovery of Benefits) Act 1997;
   (e) raises issues relating to severe disablement allowance under section 68 of the Social Security Contributions and Benefits Act 1992 or industrial injuries benefit under Part V of that Act (except for an appeal where the only issue is whether there should be a declaration of an industrial accident under section 29(2) of the Social Security Act 1998);
   (f) is made under section 4 of the Vaccine Damage Payments Act 1979;
   (g) is against a certificate of NHS charges under section 157(1) of the Health and Social Care (Community Health and Standards) Act 2003;
   (h) arises under Part IV of the Child Maintenance and Other Payments Act 2008;

the Tribunal must, subject to paragraphs 8 to 14, consist of one judge and one other member who is a registered medical practitioner.

7. In any other case the Tribunal must consist of one judge.
8. The Chamber President may determine that the Tribunal constituted under paragraph 6 or 7 must also include:
   (a) another member who is an accountant within the meaning of article 2(2)(i) of the Qualifications Order, where the appeal may require the examination of financial accounts;
   (b) an additional other member who is a registered medical practitioner, where the complexity of the medical issues in the appeal so demands;
   (c) such an additional judge or other member as the Chamber President considers appropriate for the purposes of providing further experience for that additional judge or other member or for assisting the Chamber President in the monitoring of standards of decision-making.
9. Where the Chamber President considers, in a particular case, that a matter that would otherwise be decided in accordance with paragraphs 5 or 6 only raises questions of law and the expertise of any of the other members is not 2 necessary to decide the matter, the Chamber President may direct that the Tribunal must consist of one judge, or one judge and any other member whose experience and qualifications are necessary to decide the matter.

10. The powers of the Chamber President referred to in paragraphs 8, 9, 11 and 17 may be delegated to a Regional Tribunal Judge and those referred to in paragraphs 8, 9 and 17 may be delegated to a District Tribunal Judge.
11. A decision, including a decision to give a direction or make an order, made under, or in accordance with, rules 5 to 9, 11, 14 to 19, 25(3), 30, 32, 36, 37 or 41 may be made by a judge, except that a decision made under, or in accordance, with rule 7(3) or rule 5(3)(b) to treat a case as a lead case (whether in accordance with rule 18 (lead cases) or otherwise) must be made by the Chamber President.
12. The determination of an application for permission to appeal under rule 38 and the exercise of the power of review under section 9 of the 2007 Act must be carried out:
    (a) where the judge who constituted or was a member of the Tribunal that made the decision was a fee-paid judge, by a judge who holds or has held salaried judicial office; or
    (b) where the judge who constituted or was a member of the Tribunal that made the decision was a salaried judge, by that judge or, if it would be impracticable or cause undue delay, by another salaried judge,

save that, where the decision is set aside under section 9(4)(c), the matter may only be re-decided under section 9(5)(a) by a Tribunal composed in accordance with paragraph 5, 6 or 7 above.

13. It will be for the presiding member to give any written statement of reasons under rule 34(2).
14. In rule 25(2) (medical and physical examination in appeals under section 12 of the Social Security Act 1998) "an appropriate member" is an other member who is a registered medical practitioner.
15. In criminal injuries compensation cases:
    (a) a decision at a hearing where:
        (i) only the appellant's eligibility under the Criminal Injuries Compensation Scheme is at issue; or
        (ii) the Criminal Injuries Compensation Authority alleges that there are grounds for withholding or reducing an award; may be made by one judge, or one judge and one or two other members, where each other member has any of the qualifications set out in article 2(2)(a)-(d), (f), (i), 2(3), 2(4)(b) or (c) of the Qualifications Order;
    (b) any other matter that falls to be decided at a hearing must be decided by one judge and one or two other members, where each other 3 member has any of the qualifications set out in article 2(2)(a)-(d), (f), (i), 2(3), 2(4)(b) or (c) of the Qualifications Order;
    (c) any matter that falls to be decided otherwise than at a hearing must be made by one judge.
16. Any matter that falls to be decided in an asylum support case must be decided by one judge.
17. In all cases, where the Tribunal consists of a judge and one or two other members, the judge shall be the presiding member. Where the Tribunal comprises more than one judge, the Chamber President (or in a criminal injuries compensation case, the Principal Judge) must select the presiding member. The presiding member may regulate the procedure of the Tribunal.

Sir Keith Lindblom Senior President of Tribunals
2 May 2024

This Practice Direction replaces earlier ones issued in 2008 and 2013. On May 19, 2023 the Senior President of Tribunals announced his decisions on proposed changes to panel composition in various Chambers of the First-tier Tribunal. It was announced that a Practice Direction implementing the changes that had been decided on in respect of the Social Entitlement Chamber (SEC) would be published in due course. The SPT issued the above Practice Direction, which only implements the changes in respect of criminal injuries compensation cases in the SEC. Changes that have been decided on in respect of the SEC will be implemented in due course by means of a further revised Practice Direction.

See para.15(6) and (7) of Sch.4 to the Tribunals, Courts and Enforcement Act 2007 for the power of the First-tier Tribunal to proceed in the absence of a member or with a member who is not appropriately qualified. **3.214**

Until 1999, there was a provision requiring that, where practical, at least one member of a tribunal should be of the same sex as the claimant. Notwithstanding the repeal of that provision, it was said in *CIB/2620/2000*:

> "exceptional cases where the absence of a tribunal member of the same sex as the claimant may inhibit the presentation or understanding of the claimant's case to such an extent that there will be a breach of the requirements of natural justice and of Article 6 of the European Convention on Human Rights if the tribunal is not reconstituted. It is obviously sensible to have a female member of the tribunal, if possible, in a case such as this one; raising as it does sensitive issues relating to a female medical condition. If a claimant specifically raises as an issue the absence from the tribunal of a member of the same sex, it will also be necessary for the tribunal to consider whether there is a real possibility of an injustice if the tribunal is not reconstituted. The repeal of s.46(1) [of the Social Security Administration Act 1992] means that there is no longer a need for the tribunal to consider in every case whether it is practicable for the tribunal to include a member of the same sex as the claimant, but a tribunal will nevertheless be under a duty to raise the matter of its own motion if there is a genuine reason to believe that in the circumstances of the particular case the absence of such a member may lead to injustice."

However, in the case before him, no point had been taken before the tribunal as to the absence of a woman and, although the case was concerned with a female medical condition, the examining medical officer's report was not disputed and the tribunal was not required to investigate any further the effect on the claimant of that condition. Accordingly, a fair-minded and informed observer would not have concluded that there was a real possibility of the hearing having been unfair due to the lack of a woman member of the tribunal and the Commissioner rejected that particular ground of appeal.

In *CB v SSWP (ESA)* [2020] UKUT 15 (AAC), a case where the claimant had expressly asked for an all-female panel, the Upper Tribunal considered the position under the current legislation and, although it was not necessary authoritively to decide the point, accepted that "it 'could not be ruled out that there may be exceptional cases in which fairness requires that every member of the tribunal is of the same sex'—and indeed that the clerk and any presenting officer be female as well".

Paragraph 5 of the Practice Direction–absence of a panel member.

Paragraph 5 requires that for certain appeals a three members panel is required. However, para. 15(6) of Sch.4 to the Tribunals, Courts and Enforcement Act 2007 allows the First-tier Tribunal to sit as a two-person panel in such cases 'if the parties to the case agree'. In *ZY v SSWP (PIP)* [2024] UKUT 163 (AAC) the First-tier Tribunal sat without a disability qualified panel member to decide a PIP appeal. The statement of reasons stated that it considered it was possible to continue to hear and decide the appeal in the absence of one member because the "rules of procedure" enabled it to do so. The Upper Tribunal set aside the decision because the First-tier Tribunal failed to explain why it considered it could decide the appeal with a panel of only two people and because it was unclear that the consent of all the parties, in this appeal in particular the Respondent, was obtained. Whilst it is clear that the Upper Tribunal was correct to set aside the decision it is noted that the Upper Tribunal's attention was not brought to an agreement between HMCTS and the Secretary of State regarding circumstances where the Secretary of State can be taken to have consented to the Tribunal continuing in the absence of one or more member. The agreement states that in circumstances, such as adverse weather conditions, where a) a member is unable at short notice to attend the venue, b) the DWP has already told HMCTS that a presenting officer will not be attending the hearing and c) the appellant (and any representative) agree, the tribunal can hear the appeal in the absence of the member. If a presenting officer is present or due to attend they will be consulted in accordance with r.2(2)(c). This arrangement is set out in Chapter 6 (page.58 para.06372-4) of the "Decision makers' guide: Vol 1: Decision making and appeals: staff guide." The agreement does not refer to "exceptional circumstances". Rather it refers to whether "*it would be sensible to be able to continue with the hearing*". The only example given is adverse weather conditions. It does not refer to travel disruption or sickness as reasons, but neither are excluded. Further, the agreement states that it is a requirement that the "DWP has already told HMCTS that a Presenting Officer will not be attending the hearing." The First-tier Tribunal panel will therefore need to check the available documentation for evidence of consent. However, it is suggested that it can be presumed that the DWP has "already told" HMCTS they are not attending unless there is any indication to the contrary. At the time of writing the agreement is under review.

Paragraphs 5 and 6 of the Practice Direction – registered medical practitioners

3.215 An appeal against a decision that a claimant is to be treated as not having limited capability for work because he or she has failed without good cause to attend a medical examination is not an appeal that "involves the limited capability for work assessment" for the purposes of para.5(b) of the Practice Direction and so a registered medical practitioner should not usually be a member of the First-tier Tribunal in such a case (*CH v SSWP (ESA)* [2017] UKUT 6 (AAC)). It appears that the registered medical practitioner had been present during the hearing, having sat in the previous case and this case having erroneously been listed before a two-person panel, but the judge had recorded that the case was dealt with by him alone. Accordingly, the claimant's appeal to the Upper Tribunal was dismissed. On the other hand, in *TC v SSWP (PIP)* [2017] UKUT 335 (AAC), it was pointed out that the practice statement currently has the effect that, whereas any appeal against a decision that a claimant did not have good cause for failing to attend a medical examination in connection with employment and support allowance is heard by a judge alone, any appeal against a decision that a claimant did not have good cause for failing to attend a medical examination in connection with personal independence payment must be heard by a judge sitting with two members. The facts of that case, where the First-tier Tribunal had not addressed the impact that the claimant's disabilities might have had on his non-attendance, may be thought to illustrate why it might not be bad idea for there to be medically-qualified members sitting on some such cases although others do not turn on medical issues at all. However, following the recent consultation process, the Senior President of Tribunals announced on May 19, 2023 that the position in personal independence payment cases would be brought into line with that in employment and support allowance and universal credit cases.

Section 5 of, and Sch 1 to, the Interpretation Act 1978 provide that, "unless the contrary intention appears",—

> "'Registered medical practitioner' means a fully registered person within the meaning of the Medical Act 1983 who holds a licence to practise under that Act."

However, that definition does not apply in relation to the qualification of registered medical practitioners to sit as members of the First-tier Tribunal because a contrary intention does appear from the relevant legislation. Thus, a challenge by a claimant to the suitability of a registered medical practitioner to sit on the panel determining his case, based partly on the fact that the medical practitioner was not licensed to practise, was rejected by the Upper Tribunal in *DS v SSWP (PIP)* [2016] UKUT 538 (AAC); [2017] AACR 19. The claimant had looked the medical practitioner up on the General Medical Council's website and had discovered that he was registered but did not have a licence to practise and had also been given a warning for conduct some years earlier that did not meet the standards required of a doctor. The Upper Tribunal pointed out that art.2(2)(a) of the Qualifications for Appointment of Members to the First-tier Tribunal and Upper Tribunal Order 2008 (SI 2008/2692) includes "a registered medical practitioner" among those eligible for appointment as a member of the First-tier Tribunal but that art.1(2) defines that term as "a fully registered person within the meaning of the Medical Act 1983 whether or not they hold a licence to practise under that Act". It also held that whether the doctor was a suitable person in general to sit on any particular panel was a matter for the Chamber President or his delegates in making a selection in accordance with the Practice Direction and that, once a selection to a panel had been made, "the Upper Tribunal cannot go behind that selection on the basis of a claimant's or even its own views about the member's suitability". It was noted that no question of bias had been raised in the case.

In any event, there is no obligation on the Chamber President to ensure that a medically qualified tribunal member sitting in any particular case is a specialist in the field of medicine relevant to the case (*ED v SSWP* [2009] UKUT 206 (AAC)). Even if a case is unusual any medical practitioner will ordinarily be able to deal adequately with competing views (*CSI/146/2003*). In *BT v SSW (II)* [2015] UKUT 98 (AAC), the statement of reasons had included a claim that the medically qualified panel member had "a particular expertise in this area", which the claimant challenged. The Upper Tribunal considered the claim to be "both ill-advised and unnecessary" but held that the First-tier Tribunal had been properly constituted and that the claim of specialisation did not have any material effect on its decision. The judge said:

> "18. Reading the statement of reasons, I am uncertain why it was felt necessary to make the point. The statement contains few references to use of the medical member's expertise and such as there are (para 20 – that a medical examination would not assist and para 30 – anticipated healing time) are not phrased in terms that suggest that reliance was being placed on something that only a specialist would know and a registered medical practitioner without such specialism would not. One can imagine, for instance, the position of a panel member who could say something like "In my career as a consultant in X I have conducted more than 200 procedures of the type you have undergone, without ever having noted the consequences you claim". It seems to me that it is only in the latter circumstances that it might be appropriate to mention the specific specialism of the panel member (and fairness would require the particular knowledge to have been put to the parties for comment). . . ."

If a specialist's report is necessary, it is open to the Tribunal to ask the parties to obtain a relevant opinion or to obtain one itself where s.20 of the Social Security Act 1998 applies. **3.216**

It is not inappropriate for a doctor who acts as an examining medical practitioner for an agency of the Department for Work and Pensions also to sit as a tribunal member (*Gillies v Secretary of State for Work and Pensions* [2006] UKHL 2; [2006] 1 W.L.R. 781 (also reported as *R(DLA) 5/06*), but it may be inappropriate for a tribunal judge or a tribunal member with a disability qualification to sit on a tribunal considering a medical report compiled by a doctor with whom they have sat on previous occasions (*Secretary of State for Work and Pensions v Cunningham*, 2004 S.L.T. 1007 (also reported as *R(DLA) 7/04*)). In practice, therefore tribunal members do not sit in areas where they act as health care professionals. See further the notes to ss.3 and 11 of the Tribunals, Courts and Enforcement Act 2007.

The practice of listing employment and support allowance appeals with disability living allowance appeals brought by the same claimant was held to be unlawful by a three-judge panel of the Upper Tribunal, although only by a majority (*MB v SSWP (ESA and DLA)* [2013] UKUT 111 (AAC); [2014] AACR 1). The issue arose because, under paras 5 and 6 of the Practice Direction, a tribunal member with a disability qualification must be a member of a panel hearing a disability living allowance case but is not entitled to be a member of a panel hearing an employment and support allowance case. It was even held unlawful for the cases to be heard consecutively, one immediately after the other, on grounds of principle if the employment and support allowance were held first and on grounds of practicality if the disability living allowance case were heard first. The result seems inconvenient. It may also be noted that, in *Killock v IC* [2021] UKUT 299 (AAC); [2022] AACR 4, the Upper Tribunal saw nothing wrong in three related cases concerning different appellants being heard by it one after another; two which had been transferred from the First-tier Tribunal to the Upper Tribunal being heard by a panel composed of two judges and an expert member and one which was an appeal from the First-tier Tribunal being heard by a panel composed of the two judges, following which a single decision notice and statement of reasons was issued covering all three cases.

Paragraph 8 – additional members

3.217 In *MH v SSWP (II)* [2020] UKUT 297 (AAC), a district tribunal judge had directed that the panel hearing the claimant's appeal should be composed of a judge and two registered medical practitioners. One of the registered medical practitioners was unable to attend due to illness and the First-tier Tribunal, presided over by the same district judge, proceeded to determine the appeal in the absence of that member and the parties who had both not attended the hearing. On appeal, the Secretary of State conceded that the First-tier Tribunal had erred in proceeding in the absence of one of the members hearing the case without obtaining the consent of the parties as required by paragraph 15(6) of Sch.4 to the Tribunals, Courts and Enforcement Act 2007. However, the judge said—

"49. I prefer not to decide these appeals on that basis because I consider it arguable that, even though the district tribunal judge did not in fact issue another direction under the Practice Statement, he could be treated as having done so if there was no unfairness to the claimant and the reasoning process he would have gone through was precisely the same as the reasoning process he did go through. It would be wrong to issue such a direction merely to circumvent paragraph 15(6), but if, as appears to have been the case here, the district tribunal judge was satisfied, having consulted the registered medical practitioner who was present, that the expertise of a consultant neurologist was not in fact necessary for the proper determination of the appeals, it is difficult to see why there should have been unfairness to the claimant when a claimant has no right in the first place to insist on a second registered medical practitioner or a registered medical practitioner having particular expertise. . . ."

Paragraphs 11 and 12 of the Practice Direction – Post-hearing applications

3.218 Where a hearing is concluded subject to calculations being carried out by the Secretary of State and the matter is referred back to the First-tier Tribunal because there is a dispute about the calculations – under what is sometimes called "liberty to apply" – the request to resolve the dispute can best be seen as a post-hearing application for a direction under rules 5 and 6 of the 2008 Rules mentioned in para.10 of the Practice Direction and so may be dealt with by a judge alone even though the main hearing was before a panel composed of a judge and one or two other members (*MQ v SSWP (CSM)* [2017] UKUT 392 (AAC) at [34] to [37]). Whether it is necessary for the judge to be the same one as was a party to the original decision was not an issue that arose in that case and it may depend on whether the principles upon which the calculation is to be made can clearly be discerned from the decision notice and any statement of reasons that has been produced.

One respect in which the Practice Direction is less flexible even than the previous legislation is the requirement in para.12(a) that applications for permission to appeal against decisions made by fee-paid judges *must* be dealt with by salaried judges or former salaried judges as must any reviews. The previous legislation was permissive. The lack of discretion creates difficulties where a salaried judge is faced with an application for permission based on what happened at the hearing or where he or she considers reasons to be inadequate but thinks they could properly be supplemented, because he or she is not able simply to refer the application for permission to appeal to be dealt with by the fee-paid judge. *SE v SSWP* [2009] UKUT 163 (AAC) and *AM v SSWP* [2009] UKUT 224 (AAC) show that the salaried judge must first review the decision, identifying the error of law, before referring the case to the fee-paid judge to take whatever action is appropriate.

Number of members of the Upper Tribunal

3.—(1) The number of members of the tribunal who are to decide any matter that falls to be decided by the Upper Tribunal is one unless determined otherwise under paragraph (2). **3.219**

(2) The tribunal may consist of two or three members if the Senior President of Tribunals so determines [1 in a practice direction].

AMENDMENT

1. First-tier Tribunal and Upper Tribunal (Composition of Tribunal) (Amendment) Order 2018 (SI 2018/606) art.4 (May 18, 2018).

GENERAL NOTE

As is permitted by para.15(4) of Sch.4 to the Tribunals Courts and Enforcement Act 2007, this article leaves it to the Senior President of Tribunals to determine the number of members to determine any particular type of case and the qualifications they must have. The article was amended in 2018 so as to provide that the Senior President of Tribunals' determinations are to be issued by way of practice directions under s.23 of the Tribunals, Courts and Enforcement Act 2007, which require the approval of the Lord Chancellor, whereas previously they had been issued as mere practice statements. By virtue of art.5 of the amending order of 2018, existing practice statements remain in force until a practice direction is made. The practice statement on composition of tribunals in relation to matters that fall to be decided by the Administrative Appeals Chamber of the Upper Tribunal on or after March 26, 2014 is in the following terms— **3.220**

"1. In this Practice Statement;
   a. "the 2007 Act" means the Tribunals, Courts and Enforcement Act 2007;
   b. "the 2008 Order" means the First-tier Tribunal and Upper Tribunal (Composition of Tribunal) Order 2008;
   c. "the 2008 Rules" means the Tribunal Procedure (Upper Tribunal) Rules 2008;
2. In exercise of the powers conferred by the 2008 Order the Senior President of Tribunals makes the following determinations and supplementary provision:—
3. In accordance with articles 3 and 4 of the 2008 Order, any matter that falls to be decided by the Administrative Appeals Chamber of the Upper Tribunal is to be decided by one judge of the Upper Tribunal (or by a Registrar if the Senior President of Tribunals has approved that they may decide the matter) except that—
   a. where the Senior President of Tribunals or the Chamber President considers that the matter involves a question of law of special difficulty or an important point of principle or practice, or that it is otherwise appropriate, the matter is to be decided by two or three judges of the Upper Tribunal;
   b. to e. *Omitted.*
4. to 7. *Omitted*

8. Where more than one member of the Upper Tribunal is to decide a matter, the 'presiding member' for the purposes of article 7 of the 2008 Order and the paragraphs below is—
   a. the senior judge, as determined by the Senior President of Tribunals or Chamber President, if the tribunal is composed under paragraph 3(a), (b)(ii), (c)(ii),(d) or (e)(ii); or
   b. the judge if the tribunal is composed under paragraph 3(b)(i), (c)(i) or (e)(i).
9. Where, under paragraph 3(a), (b), (c), (d) or (e), two or three members of the Upper Tribunal have been chosen to give a decision that will, or may, dispose of proceedings, any ancillary matter that arises before that decision is given may be decided by—
   a. the presiding member; or
   b. by all the members so chosen; or
   c. otherwise than at a hearing, by a judge or Registrar (who the Senior President of Tribunals has approved may decide the matter) nominated by the Chamber President or presiding member.
10. Where the Upper Tribunal has given a decision that disposes of proceedings ('the substantive decision'), any matter decided under, or in accordance with, rule 5(3)(l) or Part 7 of the 2008 Rules or section 10 of the 2007 Act must be decided by the same member or members of the Upper Tribunal as gave the substantive decision.
11. Paragraph 10 does not apply where complying with it would be impractical or would cause undue delay and, in such a case, the matter decided under, or in accordance with, rule 5(3)(l) or Part 7 of the 2008 Rules or section 10 of the 2007 Act must be decided by—
   a. if the substantive decision was given by more than one member of the Upper Tribunal and the presiding member or any other judge from that constitution is available, the members of the Upper Tribunal who gave the substantive decision and are available to decide the matter;
   b. otherwise, another judge of the Upper Tribunal nominated by the Chamber President."

Paragraph 3(a) of the Practice Statement provides for the tribunal to be composed of more than one judge in circumstances where a Tribunal of Commissioners could formerly have been constituted under s.16(7) of the Social Security Act 1998, but there is more flexibility. Two or three judges (as opposed to three or more Commissioners, although the power to appoint more than three Commissioners that existed from 1999 was never exercised) may sit to consider a case raising an important point of principle or practice even if it does not involve a question of law of special difficulty. A three-judge panel may be appointed where there has been disagreement between single judges of the Upper Tribunal. The decision of the three-judge panel will resolve the disagreement because a single judge must always follow a three-judge panel (*Dorset Healthcare NHS Foundation Trust v MH* [2009] UKUT 4 (AAC)). A three-judge panel will generally follow a decision of another three-judge panel or a decision of a Tribunal of Commissioners but will not do so if satisfied that it was wrong (*R(U) 4/88*). The precise status of a decision of a two-judge panel has not yet been determined (see the note to s.3(2) of the Tribunals, Courts and Enforcement Act 2007, under the heading "*Precedent in the Upper Tribunal*").

A two- or three-judge panel may make a decision by a majority, with the presiding judge having a casting vote where there is a two-judge panel (see art.8).

Tribunal consisting of single member

3.221 **4.**—(1) Where a matter is to be decided by a single member of a tribunal, it must be decided by a judge of the tribunal unless paragraph (2) applies.

(2) The matter may be decided by one of the other members of the tribunal if the Senior President of Tribunals so determines.

General Note

3.222 The power to provide for a case to be decided by a single member who is not a judge has not been exercised in relation to social security cases.

Tribunal consisting of two or more members

3.223 **5.** The following articles apply where a matter is to be decided by two or more members of a tribunal.

6. The number of members who are to be judges of the tribunal and the number of members who are to be other members of the tribunal must be determined by the Senior President of Tribunals.

General Note

3.224 See the practice statements set out in the notes to arts 2 and 3.

7. The Senior President of Tribunals must select one of the members (the "presiding member") to chair the tribunal.

General Note

3.225 The function of the Senior President of Tribunals may be delegated (see s.8 of the Tribunals, Courts and Enforcement Act 2007). The Practice Statement relating to the Administrative Appeals Chamber of the Upper Tribunal (see the annotation to art.3) states in para.8 that, where there is more than one judge on a panel, the senior judge will preside but, in other Chambers, including the Social Entitlement Chamber (see para.12 of the Practice Statement set out in the annotation to art.2), it is simply stated that "the Chamber President must select the presiding member". However, there is no need for a specific selection of the presiding member in respect of each panel. The application of a convention that the senior judge presides is sufficient (*HMRC v SDM European Transport Limited* [2016] UKUT 201 (TCC)).

8. If the decision of the tribunal is not unanimous, the decision of the majority is the decision of the tribunal; and the presiding member has a casting vote if the votes are equally divided.

General Note

3.226 Tribunal Procedure Rules do not require that either a decision notice or a statement of reasons should indicate whether a decision was unanimous. Nonetheless, in *SSWP v SS (DLA)* [2010] UKUT 384 (AAC); [2011] AACR 24, it was held that there was a material error of law when a decision notice said that a decision was unanimous but the statement of reasons said it had been reached by a majority, without acknowledging the error. Moreover, the judge said that, although there was generally no duty to include in a statement of reasons the reasons for any dissent, if a decision notice did state that a decision was by a majority, there was a duty to include the reasons of the dissenting member and that the same approach applied if a decision notice stated that a decision was unanimous when in fact it had been reached by a majority. However, in *JD v SSD (WP)* [2014] UKUT 379 (AAC), some doubt was expressed as to whether a failure to give reasons for dissent was an error of law rather than merely being a breach of good practice.

In *PF (Nigeria) v Secretary of State for the Home Department* [2015] EWCA Civ 251; [2015] 1 W.L.R. 5235, it was held that the presiding judge's power to use a casting vote should not be exercised irrespective of the nature and extent of the disagreement between the members of the panel. It could be exercised where there was disagreement as to the law (where the right of appeal on a point of law provides an adequate safeguard), but it should not be exercised where there was disagreement on fundamental issues of primary fact. Instead, the case should be adjourned to be considered by a differently-constituted panel.

The Tribunal Procedure (First-tier Tribunal) (Social Entitlement Chamber) Rules 2008

(SI 2008/2685)

IN FORCE NOVEMBER 3, 2008

CONTENTS

PART 1

INTRODUCTION

PART 3

PROCEEDINGS BEFORE THE TRIBUNAL

CHAPTER 1

BEFORE THE HEARING

CHAPTER 2

HEARINGS

CHAPTER 3

DECISIONS

PART 4

CORRECTING, SETTING ASIDE, REVIEWING AND APPEALING TRIBUNAL DECISIONS

SCHEDULE 1

TIME LIMITS FOR PROVIDING NOTICES OF APPEAL TO THE DECISION MAKER

SCHEDULE 2

ISSUES IN RELATION TO WHICH THE TRIBUNAL MAY REFER A PERSON FOR MEDICAL EXAMINATION UNDER SECTION 20(2) OF THE SOCIAL SECURITY ACT 1998

After consulting in accordance with paragraph 28(1) of Schedule 5 to, the Tribunals, Courts and Enforcement Act 2007, the Tribunal Procedure Committee has made the following Rules in exercise of the powers conferred by sections 20(2) and (3) of the Social Security Act 1998 and sections 9(3), 22 and 29(3) of, and Schedule 5 to, the Tribunals, Courts and Enforcement Act 2007. The Lord Chancellor has allowed the Rules in accordance with paragraph 28(3) of Schedule 5 to the Tribunals, Courts and Enforcement Act 2007.

PART 1

INTRODUCTION

Citation, commencement, application and interpretation

3.228 **1.**—(1) These Rules may be cited as the Tribunal Procedure (First-tier Tribunal) (Social Entitlement Chamber) Rules 2008 and come into force on 3rd November 2008.

(2) [3 These Rules apply to proceedings before the Social Entitlement Chamber of the First-tier Tribunal.]

(3) In these Rules—

"the 2007 Act" means the Tribunals, Courts and Enforcement Act 2007;

"appeal" includes an application under section 19(9) of the Tax Credits Act 2002;

"appellant" means a person who makes an appeal to the Tribunal, or a person substituted as an appellant under rule 9(1) (substitution of parties);

"asylum support case" means proceedings concerning the provision of support for an asylum seeker [1 , a failed asylum seeker or a person designated under s.130 of the Criminal Justice and Immigration Act 2008, or the dependants of any such person]

"criminal injuries compensation case" means proceedings concerning the payment of compensation under a scheme made under the Criminal Injuries Compensation Act 1995 [5 or section 47 of the Crime and Security Act 2010];

"decision maker" means the maker of a decision against which an appeal has been brought;

"dispose of proceedings" includes, unless indicated otherwise, disposing of a part of the proceedings;

"document" means anything in which information is recorded in any form, and an obligation under these Rules to provide or allow access to a document or a copy of a document for any purpose means, unless the Tribunal directs otherwise, an obligation to provide or allow access to such document or copy in a legible form or in a form which can be readily made into a legible form;

"hearing" means an oral hearing and includes a hearing conducted in whole or in part by video link, telephone or other means of instantaneous two-way clcctronic communication;

"legal representative" [2 a person who, for the purposes of the Legal Services Act 2007, is an authorised person in relation to an activity which constitutes the exercise of a right of audience or the conduct of litigation within the meaning of that Act], an advocate or solicitor in Scotland or a barrister or solicitor in Northern Ireland;

"party" means—

(a) a person who is an appellant or respondent in proceedings before the Tribunal;

(b) a person who makes a reference to the Tribunal under section 28D of the Child Support Act 1991;

(c) a person who starts proceedings before the Tribunal under paragraph 3 of Schedule 2 to the Tax Credits Act 2002; or

(d) if the proceedings have been concluded, a person who was a party under paragraph (a), (b) or (c) when the Tribunal finally disposed of all issues in the proceedings;

"practice direction" means a direction given under section 23 of the 2007 Act;

"respondent" means—

(a) in an appeal against a decision, the decision maker and any person other than the appellant who had a right of appeal against the decision;

(b) in a reference under section 28D of the Child Support Act 1991—

(i) the absent parent or non-resident parent;

(ii) the person with care; and

(iii) in Scotland, the child if the child made the application for a departure direction or a variation;

(c) in proceedings under paragraph 3 of Schedule 2 to the Tax Credits Act 2002, a person on whom it is proposed that a penalty be imposed; or [6 . . .]

[6 (cc) an affected party within the meaning of section 61(5) of the Childcare Payments Act 2014, other than an appellant; or

(d) a person substituted or added as a respondent under rule 9 (substitution and addition of parties);

[4 . . .]

"social security and child support case" means any case allocated to the Social Entitlement Chamber [4 of the First-tier Tribunal] except an asylum support case or a criminal injuries compensation case;

"Tribunal" means the First-tier Tribunal.

AMENDMENTS

1. Tribunal Procedure (Amendment) Rules 2009 (SI 2009/274) r.2 (April 1, 2009).

2. Tribunal Procedure (Amendment) Rules 2010 (SI 2010/43) r.3 (January 18, 2010).

3. Tribunal Procedure (Amendment No.3) Rules 2010 (SI 2010/2653) r.5(1) and (2) (November 29, 2010).

4. Tribunal Procedure (Amendment) Rules 2011 (SI 2011/651) r.4(1) and (2) (April 1, 2011).

5. Tribunal Procedure (Amendment) Rules 2013 (SI 2013/477) rr.22 and 23 (April 8, 2013).

6. Tribunal Procedure (Amendment) Rules 2015 (SI 2015/1510) rr.11 and 12 (August 21, 2015).

DEFINITIONS

"the 2007 Act"—see para.(3).

"appellant"—*ibid.*

"asylum support case"—*ibid.*

"criminal injuries compensation case"—*ibid.*

"party"—*ibid.*

"respondent"—*ibid.*

"Tribunal"—*ibid.*

General Note

3.229 By para.(2), these Rules apply to all cases within the Social Entitlement Chamber of the First-tier Tribunal which are those cases formerly dealt with by the appeal tribunals constituted under the Social Security Act 1998, by asylum support adjudicators (known collectively as the "asylum support tribunal") acting under ss.103 and 103A of the Immigration and Asylum Act 1999 and by the adjudicators of the Criminal Injuries Compensation Appeal Panel dealing with cases under schemes made under the Criminal Injuries Compensation Act 1995.

Although there are allocated to the Social Entitlement Chamber a wide variety of cases outside the scope of this work and some that could not properly be called either social security or child support cases, these Rules treat any case within the jurisdiction of the Chamber that is not an asylum support or criminal injuries compensation case as a "social security and child support case".

Note that a "hearing" means an "oral hearing" so that the term "paper hearing" is no longer appropriate for the consideration of a case on the papers. Perhaps "paper determination" will become the commonly used term.

Overriding objective and parties' obligation to co-operate with the Tribunal

3.230 **2.**—(1) The overriding objective of these Rules is to enable the Tribunal to deal with cases fairly and justly.

(2) Dealing with a case fairly and justly includes—

(a) dealing with the case in ways which are proportionate to the importance of the case, the complexity of the issues, the anticipated costs and the resources of the parties;

(b) avoiding unnecessary formality and seeking flexibility in the proceedings;

(c) ensuring, so far as practicable, that the parties are able to participate fully in the proceedings;

(d) using any special expertise of the Tribunal effectively; and

(e) avoiding delay, so far as compatible with proper consideration of the issues.

(3) The Tribunal must seek to give effect to the overriding objective when it—

(a) exercises any power under these Rules; or

(b) interprets any rule or practice direction.

(4) Parties must—

(a) help the Tribunal to further the overriding objective; and

(b) co-operate with the Tribunal generally.

Definitions

"party"—see r.1(3).
"practice direction"—*ibid.*
"Tribunal"—*ibid.*

General Note

3.231 It is nowadays conventional for procedural rules in England and Wales to set out clearly their overriding objective in this manner. The overriding objective of these Rules is rather different from that of the Civil Procedure Rules. There, one object is to ensure, so far as practical, that the parties are on an equal footing. It may be thought that that is not achievable in Citizen v State litigation before tribunals and these Rules do not require it. Instead, they emphasise the need to avoid "unnecessary formality" (see para.(2)(b)) and to promote the "enabling role" of tribunals (see para.(2)(c)) and they do not expressly refer to the resources of the tribunal in the way that the Civil Procedure Rules refer to the resources of the court as a matter to be taken into account when making procedural decisions.

This different emphasis may be important when consideration is being given to enforcing the Rules against unrepresented parties. The approach taken in the courts depends a great deal on the requirement to treat parties equally. Thus, in *Barton v Wright Hassall* [2018] UKSC 12 at [18], Lord Sumption was able to say,

> "The rules provide a framework within which to balance the interest of both sides. That balance is inevitably disturbed if an unrepresented litigant is entitled to greater indulgence in complying with them than his represented opponent."

That may be less true in Citizen v State litigation, although there are other reasons for enforcing rules against a party who happens to be unrepresented.

Perhaps, the key concept is "proportionality" (see para.(2)(a)) which is likely to be relevant in most cases where procedural decisions are being made. Paragraph (2)(b) is also of wide-ranging relevance. It was referred to by the Upper Tribunal in *Sheikh v Care Quality Commission* [2013] UKUT 137 (AAC), in support of the statement that—

> "Where a person makes an inappropriate type of application but an alternative type of application would have been appropriate in order to achieve the purpose desired by the applicant, the First-tier Tribunal should always treat the application as having been made in the appropriate form, unless that would cause any unfairness to any other party. Form should not triumph over substance . . ."

In that case, the First-tier Tribunal was held to have erred in law in not treating a late appeal as an application for the reinstatement of an earlier appeal.

By para.(3), the tribunal is required to "seek to give effect to" the overriding objective when exercising any power under the Rules or interpreting the Rules or a Practice Direction. Note that this does not extend to the exercise of powers under the Tribunals, Courts and Enforcement Act 2007 or other legislation but the principles of the overriding objective might anyway be relevant to the exercise of such powers. By para.(4), parties must help the tribunal to further the overriding objective and co-operate with the tribunal generally and a failure to do so may, in an extreme case, lead to proceedings being struck out under r.8(3)(b).

In *MA v SSWP* [2009] UKUT 211 (AAC), it was said that it was unlikely that the broad principles in r.2 would dictate the decision of a tribunal when considering whether to adjourn a hearing but that the introduction of the principles freed tribunals from the binding effect of earlier case law, although old cases might still be relevant if their principles were compatible with the overriding objective.

Indeed, in *AT v SSWP (ESA)* [2010] UKUT 430 (AAC), it was said that r.2 reinforced a duty to deal with cases fairly and justly that already existed. A failure expressly to refer to r.2 is thus unlikely to be an error of law in itself. Moreover, it was pointed out, while a tribunal must consider those factors in para.(2) that are relevant, the list of relevant factors in the paragraph is not exhaustive and not every listed factor will be relevant in every case. Nonetheless, the Upper Tribunal held the First-tier Tribunal to have erred in failing to consider the duty in r.2(2)(c) to ensure that the parties are able to participate fully in the proceedings when it determined an appeal without adjourning notwithstanding that the claimant had been forced to leave the hearing after 10 minutes through illness *(AM v SSWP (ESA)* [2013] UKUT 563 (AAC)). The Upper Tribunal took the same view in *PM v SSWP (IB)* [2013] UKUT 301 (AAC), where the First-tier Tribunal had decided to proceed in the absence of an agoraphobic claimant who had asked for a domiciliary hearing. In that case, it accepted that the First-tier Tribunal was entitled to have regard to the need to avoid delay but it pointed out that r.2(2)(e) was qualified by the words "so far as compatible with proper consideration of the issues." Rule 2(2)(c) was also considered relevant in *SW v SSWP (DLA)* [2015] UKUT 319 (AAC) and *LO v SSWP (ESA)* [2016] UKUT 10 (AAC); [2016] AACR 31 which were both cases where the First-tier Tribunal had not heard oral evidence from claimants who did not wish to attend a hearing due to health conditions and where it was suggested by the Upper Tribunal that a telephone hearing could have been considered. Similarly, it was invoked in *WA v SSWP (CSM)* [2016] UKUT 86 (AAC), where a party had given fear of her ex-partner as a reason for not attending a child support hearing. Steps that the judge said could be taken included writing to the party to reassure her that intimidation would not be tolerated, holding the hearing by videolink or by telephone, the presence of a security guard in the hearing room, laying out the hearing room in a particular way to create physical separation, the use of screens, staging the parties' entrance and departure from the room, and ensuring that their waiting arrangements minimised the risk of contact.

A somewhat restrictive construction of r.2(2)(d) was applied in *Advocate General for Scotland, Petitioner* [2019] CSOH 79; 2019 S.L.T. 1373 (see the note to s.3 of the Tribunals, Courts and Enforcement Act 2007, above, under the heading *Use of the tribunal's own expertise or observations*).

Rule 2 places obligations on the parties as well as on the First-tier Tribunal itself. Reference was made to it in *JC v SSWP (PIP)* [2016] UKUT 533 (AAC), where it was stated that documents should not be sent to the First-tier Tribunal by a representative if they have not been read, because it is necessary to avoid sending irrelevant or confidential documents. It was also suggested that, where a representative asks a claimant's doctor for a copy of the claimant's medical notes, he or she ought to make a proportionate and focussed request rather than requesting all of the records, because an unfocussed request, and one unlimited in time, increased the risk that irrelevant or confidential documents might be sent to the First-tier Tribunal. In that case, which was concerned with an appeal against a personal independence payment decision made in July 2015, 350 pages of medical records going back to at least 1992 had been obtained and sent to the First-tier Tribunal. While recognising that historic documents may sometimes be relevant, the Upper Tribunal suggested that it might have been appropriate in that case to ask the doctor only for the records from, say, January 1, 2013.

Alternative dispute resolution and arbitration

3.232 **3.**—(1) The Tribunal should seek, where appropriate—

(a) to bring to the attention of the parties the availability of any appropriate alternative procedure for the resolution of the dispute; and

(b) if the parties wish and provided that it is compatible with the overriding objective, to facilitate the use of the procedure.

(2) Part 1 of the Arbitration Act 1996 does not apply to proceedings before the Tribunal.

DEFINITIONS

"party"—see r.1(3).
"Tribunal"—*ibid.*

GENERAL NOTE

3.233 Rule 3(1) applies only if there is an alternative procedure available, which there is not in relation to social security cases. The scope for such schemes is limited by the facts that tribunal proceedings in social security cases are relatively cheap, quick and informal and that the conditions of entitlement often allow for little compromise, which means that alternative methods of dispute resolution normally offer little advantage over tribunal proceedings, particularly as there is now more intensive reconsideration of cases before appeals can be brought (see the note to reg.3ZA of the Social Security and Child Support (Decisions and Appeals) Regulations 1999). However, that is not to say that there are no cases that could be better dealt with outside the tribunal process.

PART 2

GENERAL POWERS AND PROVISIONS

Delegation to staff

4.—(1) Staff appointed under section 40(1) of the 2007 Act (tribunal staff and services) [1 or section 2(1) of the Courts Act 2003 (court officers, staff and services)] may, [1 if authorised by] the Senior President of Tribunals [1 under paragraph 3(3) of Schedule 5 to the 2007 Act] carry out functions of a judicial nature permitted or required to be done by the Tribunal. **3.234**

(2) [1 . . .]

(3) Within 14 days after the date on which the Tribunal sends notice of a decision made by a member of staff under paragraph (1) to a party, that party may apply in writing to the Tribunal for that decision to be considered afresh by a judge.

AMENDMENT

1. Tribunal Procedure (Amendment) Rules 2020 (SI 2020/651) r.3(1) and (2) (July 21, 2020).

DEFINITIONS

"the 2007 Act"—see r.1(3).
"party"—*ibid.*
"Tribunal"—*ibid.*

GENERAL NOTE

The amendments made to this rule are a consequence of those made to the rule-making power in para.3 of Sch.5 to the 2007 Act with effect from April 6, 2020. **3.235**

There is no need to make provision for the delegation of functions of a purely administrative nature and so this rule refers only to functions of a judicial nature. The Senior President of Tribunals has issued a number of practice statements (available at: *http://www.judiciary.gov.uk/publications/*) setting out the delegation of functions to staff in relation to the Social Entitlement Chamber of the First-tier Tribunal. The earliest of the current statements that relates to social security and child support cases delegates limited functions to any member of staff, still often referred to as a clerk, on or after October 1, 2014. The first, and previously the only function that had been delegated, is that of waiving under r.7(2)(a) the requirement that notice of withdrawal under r.17(1)(a) be in writing. This power is usually exercised when a party has informed a clerk over the telephone that he or she wishes to withdraw and has then been told to send in written confirmation but has failed to do so. A further set of functions relates to the question whether a notice of appeal satisfies the requirements set out in r.22(3) and is accompanied by the documents required by r.22(4) or whether a response to an appeal has been submitted within the time limit imposed by r.24(1)(b) or (c). Where a person has failed to comply with those provisions, a clerk may exercise the powers in r.7(2) to waive the requirement or require it to be remedied or may exercise the powers in r.8(1) and (3)(a) to strike the appeal or response out and then reinstate it under r.8(5). The clerk also has the power to give incidental directions and may extend the time for applying for reinstatement. Note that, whereas in relation to appeals the clerk is concerned with the adequacy of the content and not with whether they are in time, the reverse is true in relation to responses. It appears that initially some clerks believed that they had the power to refuse to admit late appeals, although that is plainly not so because the time for appealing is laid down in r.22(2). Clerks still do not have the wide powers to strike out and reinstate cases, to correct decisions and to issue directions that they enjoyed under the Social Security and Child Support (Decisions and Appeals) Regulations 1999 before the First-tier Tribunal was established on November 3, 2008. Note that, except in relation to compliance with r.22(3) and (4) or the time limits in r.24(1)(b) and (c), a clerk cannot even issue a warning that failure to comply with an instruction will, or may, result in a case being struck out; such a warning must be in a direction (see r.8(1) and (3)(a)).

However, the Senior President of Tribunals has now issued practice statements in much more general terms. One, first issued on April 20, 2016 for a period of six months and then renewed on October 19, 2016 for six months, on May 30, 2017 for twelve months from the expiry of the previous one and finally on July 16, 2018 for an indefinite period but "subject to periodic reviews to be led by the Chamber President at intervals agreed by him", authorised "an appropriately trained member of staff ... designated as a 'Tribunal Caseworker' by the Chamber President" to carry out functions. The second, issued on December 1, 2016, for an indefinite period, authorised "a legally qualified member of staff ... designated as a 'Registrar' by the Chamber President" to do so. The third, issued on July 26, 2022, authorises "an appropriately trained member of staff ... designated as a 'Legal Officer' by the Chamber President" to do so. This appears to replace the first one, so that Tribunal Caseworkers have become Legal Officers, although this is not made explicit. In any event, the three practice statements are in virtually identical terms, the last stating:

"Practice Statement authorising Legal Officers to carry out functions of a judicial nature in the First-tier Tribunal (Social Entitlement Chamber)

1. The Senior President of Tribunals hereby authorises any appropriately trained member of staff appointed under section 40(1) of the Tribunals, Courts and Enforcement Act 2007 or section 2(1) of the Courts Act 2003 and designated as a 'Legal Officer' by the Chamber President to carry out the functions of the Tribunal Procedure (First-tier Tribunal) (Social Entitlement Chamber) Rules 2008 set out in paragraph 3 below.
2. A Legal Officer must have been authorised by the Chamber President to exercise those functions. All functions must be exercised under the supervision of a judge and in accordance with guidance issued by the Chamber President.
3. A Legal Officer may make all decisions that a judge assigned to the Social Security and Child Support or Criminal Injuries Compensation jurisdiction may make under the Tribunal Procedure (First-tier Tribunal) (Social Entitlement Chamber) Rules 2008 save those which are substantive final decisions.
4. In accordance with rule 4(3) of the Tribunal Procedure (First-tier Tribunal) (Social Entitlement Chamber) Rules 2008, within 14 days after the date that the Tribunal sends notice of a decision made by a Legal Officer pursuant to an authorisation under paragraph 1 above that party may apply in writing to the Tribunal for the decision to be considered afresh by a judge."

The scope of the delegations under these practice statements is not entirely clear, because at first sight "substantive final decisions" are not decisions that are made under the Rules and it is not obvious that it was envisaged that Tribunal

Caseworkers or Registrars should, for instance, be authorised to give or refuse permission to appeal or to review or set aside "substantive final decisions".

A judge may consider afresh a decision made by a member of staff even if no party makes an application under para.(3) and there may sometimes be a duty to do so. Thus, where a tribunal case worker or registrar has refused to postpone a hearing and the refusal appears inappropriate or at least inadequately reasoned and made without adequate investigation, the judge and members sitting to hear the case should consider afresh whether there should be a postponement before proceeding in the absence of the person who requested the postponement and their failure to do so may lead to the decision of the First-tier Tribunal being set aside (*JC v SSWP (PIP)* [2018] UKUT 110 (AAC); *BV v SSWP (PIP)* [2018] UKUT 444 (AAC); [2019] 1 W.L.R. 3185). In *T v SSWP (ESA)* [2019] UKUT 59 (AAC), it was held that, where a tribunal caseworker had refused a postponement, the First-tier Tribunal had erred in law in proceeding in the claimant's absence before the 14 days for challenging the registrar's decision had elapsed, because the claimant had been deprived of the right to have his application for a postponement considered by a judge. Presumably, therefore, there would not have been an error had the judge and member given proper consideration to the postponement request, effectively considering it afresh and giving reasons for refusing it, when considering under r.31 whether to proceed in the claimant's absence. The First-tier Tribunal had merely recorded that the request had been refused, without considering its merits.

Although para.(3) refers to the "decision" being considered afresh, which is necessary because the decision may have been made otherwise than on a party's application, considering it afresh is to be done as though the provision provided for an appeal, as opposed to a review (*R(KD) v First-tier Tribunal (CIC)* [2018] UKUT 434 (AAC)), so that further information, or a further failure to provide information, may be taken into account. Any other approach would be highly artificial and inconsistent with r.2.

Case management powers

5.—(1) Subject to the provisions of the 2007 Act and any other enactment, the Tribunal may regulate its own procedure. 3.236

(2) The Tribunal may give a direction in relation to the conduct or disposal of proceedings at any time, including a direction amending, suspending or setting aside an earlier direction.

(3) In particular, and without restricting the general powers in paragraphs (1) and (2), the Tribunal may—

(a) extend or shorten the time for complying with any rule, practice direction or direction;

[[1] (aa) [[2] . . .]]

(b) consolidate or hear together two or more sets of proceedings or parts of proceedings raising common issues, or treat a case as a lead case (whether in accordance with rule 18 (lead cases) or otherwise);

(c) permit or require a party to amend a document;

(d) permit or require a party or another person to provide documents, information, evidence or submissions to the Tribunal or a party;

(e) deal with an issue in the proceedings as a preliminary issue;

(f) hold a hearing to consider any matter, including a case management issue;

(g) decide the form of any hearing;

(h) adjourn or postpone a hearing;

(i) require a party to produce a bundle for a hearing;

(j) stay (or, in Scotland, sist) proceedings;

(k) transfer proceedings to another court or tribunal if that other court or tribunal has jurisdiction in relation to the proceedings and—
  (i) because of a change of circumstances since the proceedings were started, the Tribunal no longer has jurisdiction in relation to the proceedings; or
  (ii) the Tribunal considers that the other court or tribunal is a more appropriate forum for the determination of the case; or
(l) suspend the effect of its own decision pending the determination by the Tribunal or the Upper Tribunal of an application for permission to appeal against, and any appeal or review of, that decision.

AMENDMENTS

1. Tribunal Procedure (Amendment No. 4) Rules 2013 (SI 2013/2067) rr.22 and 23 (November 1, 2013).
2. Tribunal Procedure (Amendment) Rules 2015 (SI 2015/1510) rr.11 and 13 (August 21, 2015).

DEFINITIONS

"the 2007 Act"—see r.1(3).
"dispose of proceedings"—*ibid.*
"document"—*ibid.*
"hearing"—*ibid.*
"party"—*ibid.*
"practice direction"—*ibid.*
"Tribunal"—*ibid.*

GENERAL NOTE

Paragraph (1)

3.237 This paragraph, which is in conventional terms, permits the Tribunal to vary the way it handles a case so that the procedure is appropriate to the issues that arise and to the level of representation, if any. See also the note to r.30(5).

In *Foulser v HMRC* [2013] UKUT 38 (TCC), Morgan J. considered that the power to regulate its own procedure would, in an exceptional case where an order barring HMRC from taking any further part in the proceedings was justified but the case did not fall within the scope of rules equivalent to rr.7 and 8 of these Rules, enable the First-tier Tribunal to make the desired order.

Paragraph (2)

3.238 This is in very broad terms and, although para.(3) and r.15(1) set out examples of directions the tribunal may give, they do not restrict the width of the power in this paragraph. The power must, however, be exercised so as to give effect to the overriding objective in r.2 (see r.2(3)). It must also be exercised judicially. A judge is not generally entitled to subvert the decision of a Tribunal to adjourn for a medical report by directing that the case be relisted without the report. On the other hand, if the case is relisted and no point is taken about the absence of the report, the Upper Tribunal may take the view that the final decision is not erroneous in point of law *(CSDLA/866/2002)*. For the consequences of failing to comply with a direction, see r.7.

The procedure for applying for and giving directions is to be found in r.6. Note that, where a direction requires something to be done by a particular day, it must be done by 5pm on that day (r.12(1)) but, if that day is not a working day, the act is done in time if it is done on the next working day (r.12(2)).

In principle, an appeal lies against case management decisions but interlocutory appeals are not encouraged and, particularly in social security cases, permission may be refused on the ground that the appellant should await the final decision, which can then be challenged if the party is dissatisfied with it and a material interlocutory decision was erroneous in point of law (*LS v Lambeth LBC (HB)* [2010] UKUT 461 (AAC); [2011] AACR 27). An application for permission to appeal made to the First-tier Tribunal may also be taken to be an application under r.6(5) for another direction amending, suspending or setting aside the challenged direction (*Dorset Healthcare NHS Foundation Trust v MH* [2009] UKUT 4 (AAC)).

Paragraph (3)(a)

Subparagraph (a) confers a very broad discretion. However, time limits ought to be observed and, in the context of a late application for reconsideration of a refusal of permission to apply for judicial review in an immigration case, the Court of Appeal has said that, under the identical rule in the Tribunal Procedure (Upper Tribunal) Rules 2008, a three stage approach should be adopted by (i) assessing the seriousness and significance of the failure to comply with the time limit, (ii) considering why the default occurred and (iii) evaluating all the circumstances of the case, so as to enable the tribunal to deal justly with the application (*R. (Kigen) v Secretary of State for the Home Department* [2015] EWCA Civ 1286; [2016] 1 W.L.R. 723, following the approach taken in *R. (Hysaj) v Secretary of State for the Home Department* [2014] EWCA Civ 1663; [2015] 1 W.L.R. 2472 in relation to time limits for appealing to the Court of Appeal). It has been held by the Immigration and Asylum Chamber of the Upper Tribunal, when quashing a decision of the First-tier Tribunal to extend time for the Secretary of State to apply for permission to appeal to the Upper Tribunal and its grant of permission, that the same approach should be applied by both the First-tier Tribunal and the Upper Tribunal when considering whether to extend time limits (*R. (Onowu) v First-tier Tribunal* [2016] UKUT 185 (IAC)). However, while accepting that the same three-stage framework should be applied in relation to applications for permission to appeal to the Administrative Appeals Chamber of the Upper Tribunal in social security cases, it has been suggested that the very robust approach taken in immigration and asylum cases to delays attributable to the under-funding and overwork of legal services and public bodies may not be appropriate in social security cases, where proceedings are not so adversarial and legal services may be provided by volunteers (*JP v SSWP* [2017] UKUT 149 (AAC)). See also *Tower Hamlets LBC v Al Ahmed* [2020] EWCA Civ 51; [2020] 1 W.L.R. 1546, although that case turned on there being a different statutory test for extending time under which there was no scope for the three-stage test and all the circumstances, including difficulties in obtaining legal representation and legally aided funding, had to be taken into account when deciding whether there had been "good reason" for the delay. **3.239**

In *R. (CD) v First-tier Tribunal (CIC)* [2010] UKUT 181 (AAC); [2011] AACR 1, the judge declined an invitation to give guidance for future cases where an extension of time for appealing was concerned and, in particular, said that it was not appropriate to have regard to any checklist. In this, he adopted the reasoning of Black J. in *R. (Howes) v Child Support Commissioner* [2007] EWHC 559 (Admin) who said that "the factors that are relevant will be dependent upon the circumstances of the individual case". This approach has also been followed in *Ofsted v AF* [2011] UKUT 72 (AAC); [2011] AACR 32, *IC v PS* [2011] UKUT 94 (AAC) and *R. (YT) v First-tier Tribunal (CIC)* [2013] UKUT 201 (AAC). In *Ofsted v AF*, the judge expressly distinguished *Jurkowska v Hlmad Ltd* [2008] EWCA Civ 231, in which the Court of Appeal had sanctioned the detailed guidance given by the Employment Appeal Tribunal, on the ground that the nature of employment disputes was far more adversarial than disputes between citizens and the State should be. In *R(YT) v First-tier Tribunal (CIC)*, it was held that the fact that delay was due to negligence on the part of solicitors and the claimant might have a cause of action against them was relevant but not determinative. Other relevant factors in that case were the length of the delay, the consequences of the delay, the merits of the case, and the claimant's health and personal circumstances. Both the strength of the case and the reasons for the delay are likely to be relevant factors in most cases (*R. (Birmingham CC) v Birmingham Crown Court* [2009] EWHC 3329 (Admin); [2010] 1 W.L.R. 1287).

Another highly relevant factor in deciding whether to extend time is whether the person concerned acted reasonably. Thus, in *Peters v Sat Katar Limited* [2003] EWCA Civ 943, a person appealing to an employment tribunal who had sent her notice of appeal to the tribunal two weeks before the time limit had acted reasonably in not seeking confirmation from the appeal tribunal that the appeal had been received until nearly four weeks after she had sent it, but only because there was no indication in any of the information and guidance published by the tribunal that told her to contact it if she had not received an acknowledgment within a specified period.

"There is always a balance to be drawn between the length and effects of delay and the merits of the case", see *Pant v Secretary of State for the Home Department* [2003] EWCA Civ 1964, per Carnwath L.J. In that case the Court of Appeal declined to give permission to appeal out of time where the delay, caused principally by the appellant's former solicitors but also by her failure to keep touch with what was going on, had been two and a half years. The Court would have given permission to appeal but for the delay and, before rejecting the application, it assured itself that, although there would be some prejudice to the appellant, she could make another claim which would avoid the worst consequences there would otherwise have been in rejecting her case.

Paragraph (3)(b)

3.240 Although any judge may consolidate or hear together two or more cases, only the Chamber President (or a person to whom he has delegated the power) has the power to treat a social security case as a lead case (see para.10 of the practice statement set out above in the note to art.2 of the First-tier Tribunal and Upper Tribunal (Composition of Tribunal) Order 2008). In *John v IC* [2014] UKUT 444 (AAC), the Upper Tribunal suggested that, where two parties appealed against the same decision, it would be appropriate to direct that the cases be heard together rather than consolidated. It was noted that consolidation had been described in *Zuckerman on Civil Procedure* (3th edn) at para.13.12 as an "arcane process". It has a technical meaning that is arguably inappropriate in appeals to tribunals.

Paragraph (3)(c)

3.241 Sub-paragraph (c) presumably refers to grounds of appeal and other submissions, rather than to evidence, despite the statutory definition.

Paragraph (3)(d)

3.242 Although there is no equivalent here to r.16(3), the principle that a person should not be compelled to produce evidence that he could not be compelled to produce in a court generally applies to privileged documents so that a party should not be directed to produce documents covered by legal advice privilege or litigation privilege (*LM v Lewisham LBC (SEN)* [2009] UKUT 204 (AAC); [2010] AACR 12). On the other hand, it may be arguable that, apart from matters clearly covered by professional privilege, it is open to a judge to direct the disclosure of documents, information or evidence even though privilege or confidentiality could be claimed, placing the burden on the party to claim a right to non-disclosure by making an application under r.6(5) and leaving open the question whether an adverse inference should be drawn.

Where issues of confidentiality potentially arise, it may be appropriate for a party to seek a direction under this paragraph, even though it would be entitled to disclose the documents without one (*Mitchell v Commissioners for Revenue and Customs* [2023] EWCA Civ 261; [2023] Ch. 251).

Resort may be had to the issuing of a formal summons, citation or order under r.16 if a person fails to comply with a direction to produce documents or other evidence under this subparagraph. However, the power to direct a person to provide information or submissions must be exercised proportionately. In *DTM v Ketttering BC (CTB)* [2013] UKUT 625 (AAC), it was held perverse to direct the claimant to inform the tribunal whether he wished his appeal to continue and, if so, whether he wished there to be a hearing, on pain of his case being struck out if he did not reply. The case could have been determined without his response.

This sub-paragraph does not permit the First-tier Tribunal to fulfil its duty to issue its decision to the parties by asking one party to provide copies of the decision and the other information required by r.33(2) to the other parties (*Hyslop v 38/41 CHG Residents Co Ltd* [2017] UKUT 398 (LC)).

Paragraph (3)(f) and (g)

Sub-paragraphs (f) and (g) must be read with rr. 27-30. **3.243**

Paragraph (3)(h)

In sub-para.(h), the distinction between a postponement and an adjournment is that the former occurs before the beginning of the hearing and the latter occurs once the hearing has begun, although an application for an adjournment may be made right at the beginning of a hearing. In *CDLA/3680/1997*, the Commissioner said that "[w]here an application for a postponement is refused—or no reply is received to such an application—it is incumbent on the claimant to take all possible steps to appear, or to have someone appear on his or her behalf, before the tribunal in order to assist the tribunal in considering whether there should be an adjournment". A representative should be ready to argue the case as well as possible if the application for an adjournment is refused. **3.244**

This regulation is concerned only with the postponement or adjournment of oral hearings. There is no express power to adjourn the paper consideration of a case but such a power could be implied (*CDLA/1552/1998*) even without the breadth of r.5(2).

A party seeking a postponement of a hearing is expected to give reasons and in *GC v SSWP (ESA)* [2014] UKUT 224 (AAC) the judge was highly critical of a leaflet produced by Her Majesty's Courts and Tribunals Service that implied that a postponement would be granted on request and failed to tell claimants that they should provide reasons. He set aside a decision made in the claimant's absence after the claimant had informed the First-tier Tribunal that he was unable to attend the hearing but did not explain why, although he did have reasons. But even without misleading leaflets, claimants do not always realise how detailed their reasons need to be and, as pointed out in *BV v SSWP (PIP)* [2018] UKUT 444 (AAC); [2019] 1 W.L.R 3185, they may not realise that reasons given to a clerk over the telephone are not always recorded and so they may not repeat them when told to make a written application. Consequently, fairness may sometimes demand that they be asked for further details before a postponement is refused or that they be told when an application is refused that they may make another application if they provide more detailed reasons. Although time is often short, telephone or email communication are often options.

It is also apparent from *BV* and from *JC v SSWP (PIP)* [2018] UKUT 110 (AAC) that, when a request for a postponement has been refused and the person who requested it fails to appear at the hearing, the way in which the request was made and refused may be relevant when the First-tier Tribunal is considering whether it is in the interests of justice to proceed in that person's absence (see r.31 when it is a party who has not attended). In effect, it may be necessary to reconsider at the hearing the refusal of the postponement, particularly if it appears aberrant or not fully reasoned. Although the refusals in those cases were made by a tribunal caseworker and a registrar respectively, it is difficult to see why it should make any difference that a postponement has been refused by a judge if the refusal appears, perhaps with hindsight and a more detailed knowledge of the case, to have given rise to unfairness. See also the note to r.4 in which it is suggested that, where the postponement was refused by a member of staff and the 14 days allowed under r.4(3) for asking for the decision to be considered afresh by a judge have not elapsed by the time of the hearing, it is likely always to be necessary for the refusal to be considered afresh if the party who asked for the postponement does not appear at the hearing.

3.245 In *CSDLA/90/1998*, the Commissioner was highly critical of a local authority representative who had represented a claimant before a tribunal on an application for an adjournment. The claimant had had a prior engagement and the Commissioner found that the representative had indicated to her that she need not attend the tribunal hearing without asking her why the other engagement should take priority. When the tribunal refused to adjourn the hearing the representative had withdrawn. The Commissioner said that the nature of the other engagement should have been explained to the tribunal, that it was not for a representative to tell a claimant not to attend a hearing (because a tribunal were not bound to grant an adjournment merely because the claimant was not there) and that a representative who wished to withdraw should obtain the leave of the tribunal to do so. The claimant had been entitled to expect her representative to argue her case on the basis of the evidence available to him and doing so would not have prevented him from arguing on appeal that the tribunal had erred in refusing the adjournment.

The power to postpone or adjourn proceedings must not be used arbitrarily or capriciously and, in particular, must not be used in order to defeat the general purpose of the legislation, but otherwise there is a complete discretion so long as it is exercised judicially (*CIS/2292/2000*, citing *Jacobs v Norsalta Ltd* [1977] I.C.R. 189) and in accordance on the overriding objective in r.2(2). Nonetheless, in *CIS/2292/2000*, a tribunal erred in rejecting an application for an adjournment made by the representative of a claimant who was in prison, in circumstances where the claimant's oral evidence had an important part to play.

The overriding objective in r.2(2) may be particularly important where a power to postpone or adjourn a hearing is being considered. It requires a case to be dealt with "in ways that are proportionate to the importance of the case, the complexity of the issues, the anticipated costs and the resources of the parties" and also to the avoidance of delay but only "so far as compatible with proper consideration of the issues". On the other hand, in *MA v SSWP* [2009] UKUT 211 (AAC), it was said that it was unlikely that the broad principles in r.2 would dictate the decision of a tribunal when considering whether to adjourn a hearing but that the introduction of the principles freed tribunals from the binding effect of earlier case law, although old cases might still be relevant if their principles were compatible with the overriding objective. Although whether there should be an adjournment all depends on the facts of a particular case, the judge considered that a tribunal was likely to focus on the questions: (a) what would be the benefit of an adjournment, (b) why was the party asking for the adjournment not ready to proceed, and (c) what impact would an adjournment have on the other party and the operation of the tribunal system. In the case of a request for an adjournment to obtain further evidence, the first of those questions would involve considering what evidence was already before the tribunal, what evidence was likely to be obtained if the proceedings were adjourned, how long it would take to obtain it and whether the tribunal could use its own expertise to compensate for the lack of additional evidence. The judge considered that it would be exceptional for an adjournment that would otherwise be granted to be refused solely on account of the needs of the tribunal system as a whole. In *LO v SSWP (ESA)* [2016] UKUT 10 (AAC); [2016] AACR 31, there arose the question whether, where a claimant states that he or she does not wish to attend a hearing because of disability, a tribunal ought generally to consider whether a telephone hearing would be appropriate. The judge rejected a submission by the Secretary of State that it was unnecessary to do so merely because the claimant had not asked for such a hearing, since it was not the practice of the First-tier Tribunal's administration to inform parties of the possibility of there being a telephone hearing and so claimants could not be expected to ask for one. However, he held that there had been no error of law in the particular case before him. The First-tier Tribunal had given detailed consideration to the question whether there needed to be an adjournment so that the claimant could give evidence and had taken a proportionate approach. Although an offer of a telephone hearing was one possibility that might have been considered, it had not been necessary to do so in that case in order to deal with the issue of adjournment fairly. The claimant might, after all, have declined such an offer. Nonetheless, the implication of the decision is that there may be at least some cases where a failure explicitly to consider whether to offer a telephone hearing will render a decision wrong in law.

In both *CIB/1009/2004* and *CIB/2058/2004*, Commissioners have emphasised that the inquisitorial approach of tribunals is not a complete substitute for representation and have cited *R. v Social Security Commissioner, Ex p. Bibi* (unreported, May 23, 2000) in which Collins J. said that, although there is no absolute right to representation, there is an absolute right to be dealt with fairly and that it was hardly unreasonable for a person to wish to be represented by the particular solicitor with whom she had been dealing. Therefore, a claimant's desire to be represented, or to be represented by a particular person, is a factor that ought to be given proper weight in considering whether or not to grant an adjournment. On the other hand, it is apparent from *DS v SSWP (ESA)* [2019] UKUT 347 (AAC) that the First-tier Tribunal does not necessarily err in refusing to adjourn when a representative fails to appear, even if it wrongly believes that the representative has not contacted the tribunal to say that he would be unable to attend. The Upper Tribunal made no reference to *R. v Social Security Commissioner Ex p. Bibi*, but both the First-tier Tribunal and the Upper Tribunal gave lengthy reasons for their decisions, including references to the procedural history of the case, to the First-tier Tribunal's enabling role and to the written submission from the representative and the further evidence that had been before the First-tier Tribunal. It appears that the Upper Tribunal was simply not persuaded that the presence of the representative could have made any difference to the outcome, given that material and the thorough manner in which the First-tier Tribunal had conducted the hearing and elicited oral evidence, as shown in its statement of reasons. As to the balancing exercise itself, in *CIB/1009/2004* the Commissioner said— 3.246

> "13. A tribunal will always require to be persuaded that an adjournment is necessary—because there is always a potential disadvantage in adjourning a case—but the arguments against an adjournment in tribunal proceedings in a social security case may not be quite the same as those applicable in adversarial proceedings in the courts. In particular, the interests of the parties are not usually as closely balanced. In an ordinary social security case, where the Secretary of State does not provide a representative or have witnesses in attendance, there is very little disadvantage to the Secretary of State in granting the claimant an adjournment. It is usually the claimant himself who suffers the principal disadvantage of delay. If the claimant judges that disadvantage to be less than the disadvantage of proceeding without representation, a tribunal should not too readily substitute its own judgment on the relative weight of those two factors. The main consideration for the tribunal will therefore be whether the adjournment can be justified in the light of the substantial cost of a further hearing and the delay in the determination of another case whose place the adjourned hearing will take. Thus the interests of taxpayers and claimants in general need to be balanced against the interests of the particular appellant.
>
> 14. If the claimant is to blame for need to request an adjournment, his interests are likely to be given correspondingly less weight. A claimant's interests may also be given less weight where his representative's fault has led to the request

for an adjournment. By agreeing to act for a claimant, a representative takes some responsibility for the case and tribunals are entitled to exert pressure on representatives to behave properly. However, in an environment where most representatives are not qualified lawyers and where most claimants are not paying for the services of their representatives, some care must be taken not to cause injustice to a claimant by visiting upon him the sins of his representative. The tribunal's response must be proportionate, having regard to the consequences for the claimant of possibly losing his appeal."

In *CSDLA/90/1998*, the Commissioner also held that, when representation is undertaken by a local authority, the claimant is entitled to be fully represented by the authority until disposal of the appeal and the local authority must, if necessary, arrange representation through their legal department in order to avoid a postponement or an adjournment of a hearing. In *CIB/1009/2004*, the Commissioner disagreed with that approach and said that a local authority was entitled to limit the power of representatives to call upon other resources of the authority when a particular representative was unavailable due to illness. However, he went on to say that a representative should make reasonable efforts to secure alternative representation, even if that meant cancelling some other appointments, and that that implied that a request for an adjournment due to the non-availability of a representative should contain a clear indication that consideration had been given to the possibility of someone else representing the claimant. In the absence of such an explanation, the tribunal might be entitled to infer that the reasonable efforts had not been made to find alternative representation. However, a failure by a representing authority to make reasonable efforts to secure alternative representation should not have led to a refusal of an adjournment, when further efforts might not have made any difference, the claimant himself was blameless, a lot of money was at stake and the case was not straightforward so that an experienced representative might have assisted the tribunal to reach a conclusion favourable to the claimant.

In *Evans v Secretary of State for Social Security* (reported as *R(I)5/94*), a medical appeal tribunal disagreed with the opinions of two consultants. The Court of Appeal held that, where a tribunal proposed to put a different interpretation on the same clinical findings from that put by another expert, "fairness points to the need for an adjournment so that, where possible, the tribunal's provisional view can be brought to the attention of the claimant's own advisers". A similar approach has been taken by Park J. when hearing an appeal from a Pensions Appeal Tribunal (*Butterfield v Secretary of State for Defence* [2002] EWHC 2247 (Admin)). He said that, when a medically qualified member of a tribunal is the only person present with specialist medical knowledge and he perceives a possible medical objection to the claimant's case that has not been pointed out before, he must draw it to the claimant's attention and it may be necessary to offer the claimant an adjournment so that he has a realistic opportunity to consider the point "however inconvenient and irksome that may be". This makes clear what was probably meant in *Evans*. There need not always be an adjournment but the tribunal's provisional view should be put to the claimant and the claimant should expressly be *offered* an adjournment. See also *MB v DSD (II)* [2010] NICom 133; [2011] AACR 41, where an appeal tribunal made new findings as a consequence of a medical examination and it was held that fairness required the claimant to have an opportunity to comment on those findings after the examination.

3.247 There is no general rule that an appeal to a tribunal should be postponed while related criminal proceedings are pending (*Mote v Secretary of State for Work and Pensions* [2007] EWCA Civ 1324 (reported as *R(IS) 4/08*)). The wishes of the parties will be relevant but will not be determinative. Often a claimant will not wish an appeal to be heard while criminal proceedings are pending lest anything he says at the tribunal hearing is used against him in the criminal trial. However, another claimant may prefer an appeal to be heard first because a finding that he or she was entitled to benefit is likely to undermine a prosecution for obtaining the same benefit by deception.

Adjournments are sometimes necessary because a member of the tribunal is obliged to stand down to avoid an appearance of bias (see the annotation to s.11 of the Tribunals, Courts and Enforcement Act 2007). In *CCS/1876/2006*, the Commissioner suggested that there might be occasions when it was prudent for a member of a tribunal to stand down in order to strengthen a party's confidence in the fairness of the procedures, even if there was no strict legal duty to do so, but he did acknowledge that the expense of an adjournment had to be kept in mind.

Adjournments are also sometimes necessary in order to obtain further evidence and particularly evidence of previous awards of benefit. Thus, there may arise on an appeal to the Upper Tribunal the question whether the First-tier Tribunal erred in law in failing to adjourn to obtain further evidence or in failing to give reasons for not doing so. In such cases, it may be relevant how the case was argued before the First-tier Tribunal, particularly if the claimant was represented. In *AG v SSWP (ESA)* [2017] UKUT 413 (AAC), the judge said—

> "7. . . . I see no reason why, generally speaking, a tribunal ought not to be able to rely upon the absence of an adjournment request in order for further evidence to be obtained where a claimant has an experienced representative in the field of welfare benefits law. But it may well be good practice for a tribunal, where it thinks such an application could reasonably and sensibly be made, to query with the representative whether or not doing so has been considered. . . ."

A failure to adopt such "good practice" is unlikely in itself to render a decision wrong in law. In both *MH v SSWP (ESA)* [2018] UKUT 194 (AAC) and *MC v SSWP (ESA)* [2018] UKUT 391 (AAC), concerned with employment and support allowance, representatives had referred to successful claims to personal independence payment but had not requested adjournments for the purpose of obtaining the evidence on which personal independence payment had been awarded. Arguments that the First-tier Tribunal should have adjourned of its own volition to obtain that evidence were rejected given the other evidence that was before it in each case. Indeed, it is arguable that, whether or not a claimant was represented, the real question is simply whether obtaining the evidence was so necessary in the interests of justice that the First-tier Tribunal erred in law in not obtaining it of its own volition (see the annotation to r.24 as regards evidence of previous awards that ought to be provided by the respondent). It is clearly difficult for an experienced representative to argue that evidence ought to have been obtained if he or she did not suggest it at the time, but whether or not there has been a request for an adjournment may be more directly relevant to the question whether the First-tier Tribunal was under a duty to explain in its reasons why it did not adjourn (see the annotation to r.34). In any event, even though the "good practice" may not essential, following it might reduce the likelihood of the First-tier Tribunal falling into error in borderline cases.

It was held in *LJT v SSWP (PIP)* [2019] UKUT 21 (AAC) that, when adjourning a case, the First-tier Tribunal is not entitled to bind itself by saying that "the appeal must proceed when next listed", although it may indicate in less dogmatic terms that it considers that, absent a particularly compelling reason, the case should not be further adjourned. It was further pointed out that, when deciding whether or not to postpone or adjourn a case, it was wrong to consider merely the length of such delay as there had been in the past: it was necessary to consider the reasons for the delay and upon whose application or initiative earlier directions for postponement or adjournment had been made. It was liable to be unfair to hold against a party asking for a further adjournment, delay caused by earlier applications made by another party or caused by decisions made by the First-tier Tribunal on its own initiative. It is also relevant whether earlier applications by the same party were obviously based on good grounds. In this case, part of the delay was due to the First-tier Tribunal having adjourned on an earlier occasion in order to obtain a copy of the claimant's GP records without, it appeared, having considered first taking evidence from the claimant that might have made the adjournment unnecessary.

At a hearing following an adjournment, the tribunal may be constituted by one or more members who sat on the earlier tribunal and one or more who did not, if no evidence was taken before the adjournment. If evidence was taken before the adjournment, the tribunal should generally be either entirely the same or entirely differently constituted and, in the latter case, must have a complete rehearing, although it is entitled to accept the recorded evidence of a witness who gave evidence at the first hearing provided the rules of natural justice are not infringed (*R(U) 3/88*).

3.248 In fact current practice requires a judge to indicate whether any evidence has been heard at an adjourned hearing and, if it has, the clerk will always arrange for the tribunal to consist either of entirely the same members or entirely different members. This avoids the risk of subconscious bias being carried over from one hearing to the other or of a member remembering evidence from the first hearing that does not appear in the record of proceedings (see *CDLA/2429/2004*).

In *SW v SSWP (ESA)* [2019] UKUT 415 (AAC), where a case listed for a "paper hearing" was adjourned to give the claimant an opportunity to appear and the same judge sat on both occasions but with different medically-qualified panel members, it was said that "[w]here a judge has discussed the facts with one panel member who is not on the final panel ... but actually makes a decision after discussion with a different panel member ... then, in the absence of clear evidence to the contrary, it cannot be excluded from possibility that the judge remains influenced by views expressed by the member who did not sit on the final panel, and this is a breach of fair procedure", but this is debateable (see the note to s.11 of the Tribunals, Courts and Enforcement Act 2007, above, under the heading *Procedural and other irregularities*).

A judge should not subvert a decision of a tribunal to adjourn for a medical report by immediately directing that the case be relisted without the report (*CSDLA/866/2002*).

An unfair refusal to adjourn may make the final decision of the tribunal erroneous in point of law so that an appeal may be brought against that final decision (*R. v Medical Appeal Tribunal (Midland Region) Ex p. Carrarini* [1966] 1 W.L.R. 883 (also reported as an appendix to *R(I) 13/65*); *LS v Lambeth LBC (HB)* [2010] UKUT 461 (AAC); [2011] AACR 27).

A refusal to adjourn was an issue in *CM/449/1990*, where the claim was made on behalf of a child with severe learning difficulties. His mother had written as soon as she was given notice of the hearing to apply for an adjournment on the ground that her son was away in short-term care. The tribunal refused the adjournment and dismissed the appeal, saying that they were not prepared to grant it "due to the high incidence of requests for adjournments". The Commissioner allowed the claimant's appeal on the ground that no reasonable tribunal could have refused the request for an adjournment and also on the ground that the tribunal had based their decision entirely on a wholly irrelevant consideration. It may be arguable that the Commissioner went too far in holding that the prevalence of requests for adjournments can never be a factor to be taken into account in considering such a request, but even if that is right, such a consideration cannot prevail without any regard at all being had to the particular facts and circumstances of the individual case. More recently, a refusal by the First-tier Tribunal to adjourn on the ground, among others, that "it was not in the habit" of adjourning so that a police officer could produce documents that were in dispute, was set aside on the ground that it was unfair in the circumstances of the case (*R. (YR) v First-tier Tribunal (CIC)* [2010] UKUT 204 (AAC)).

A refusal to adjourn should be recorded in the record of proceedings (*R(DLA) 3/08*) and it is desirable for a brief reason for the refusal to be included either in the record of proceedings or in the statement of reasons for the tribunal's decision (*Carpenter v Secretary of State for Work and Pensions* [2003] EWCA Civ 33 (also reported as *R(IB) 6/03*)), although a failure in either of these respects will not necessarily render a tribunal's decision erroneous in point of law. It will, however, do so if the decision appears aberrant without reasons (*R. (Birmingham CC) v Birmingham Crown Court* [2009] EWHC 3329 (Admin); [2010] 1 W.L.R. 1302).

Paragraph (3)(i)

The inability of the First-tier Tribunal to award costs in social security cases means that it is important that it considers upon whom the financial burden of preparing a bundle is placed. If it wishes the costs to be shared, it should direct both parties to prepare it. See *Eclipse Film Partners No.35 LLP v Revenue and Customs Commissioners (No.2)* [2016] UKSC 24; [2016] 1 W.L.R. 1939. **3.249**

Paragraph (3)(k)

Sub-paragraph (k) applies only where the First-tier Tribunal had jurisdiction at the time the proceedings were begun. Otherwise, the Tribunal is required to strike the proceedings out under r.8(2). Rule 5(3)(k)(i) applies where the First-tier Tribunal loses jurisdiction and r.5(3)(k)(ii) applies only where the First-tier Tribunal and another tribunal have concurrent jurisdiction (which may be the case in some circumstances where a person moves to or from Northern Ireland). **3.250**

Paragraph (3)(l)

Sub-paragraph (l) permits the effect of a decision to be suspended pending an appeal to the Upper Tribunal. There is no provision enabling the First-tier Tribunal to suspend a decision pending an appeal to it and an argument that the First-tier Tribunal nonetheless has such a power was considered to be so unarguable in *DB v Academy Transformation Trust (SEN)* [2022] UKUT 66 (AAC) that permission to appeal to the Upper Tribunal on the point was refused. Whether judicial review proceedings could be brought in the Administrative Court or the Court of Session to achieve a suspension pending an appeal seems doubtful (see the note to the Tribunals, Courts and Enforcement 2008 s.3(1), above, under the heading "*Interim relief*"). **3.251**

Giving tribunals power to suspend a decision pending an appeal to an appellate tribunal is consistent with the approach taken in the courts, where an appellate court has been held to have an inherent jurisdiction to suspend a decision while an appeal is pending (*Admiral Taverns (Cygnet) Ltd v Daniel* [2008] EWCA Civ 1501; [2009] 1 W.L.R. 2192). However, it is usually unnecessary for the Tribunal to suspend a decision in a social security case concerned with entitlement, due to the Secretary of State's power to suspend payments under, for instance, reg.16 of the Social Security and Child Support (Decisions and Appeals) Regulations 1999 (see, in particular, reg.16(3)(b)(i) and (4)). In the past, the Secretary of State has generally not taken action to recover an overpayment while an appeal against a decision that the overpayment is recoverable is pending but he could now take the view that an appeal does not require him to stay his hand unless the Tribunal so directs under this provision, which would not necessarily be appropriate as a matter of course and could in any event presumably be limited to part of its decision. The power to suspend the effect of a decision may also be useful in appeals under the Social Security (Recovery of Benefits) Act 1997, because s.14 of that Act and the regulations made under it completely fail to deal with the consequences of a successful appeal to the Upper Tribunal. There is no automatic right to a suspension in any particular case. In *Carmarthenshire CC v MW (SEN)* [2010] UKUT 348 (AAC); [2011] AACR 17, which was concerned with the Upper Tribunal's power to suspend the effect of a decision of the First-tier Tribunal, it was held that there has to be balancing exercise, taking into account the practical consequences of suspending the decision on one side and the practical consequences of not doing so on the other. The chances of the appeal succeeding would be relevant but it was doubted whether a good prospect of the appeal succeeding could operate as a threshold condition, particularly in a case of urgency where the grounds of appeal might not have been formulated.

The First-tier Tribunal is entitled to suspend the effect of its own decision pending its determination of an application for permission to appeal and then, having considered the merits of the application and refused permission to appeal, may refuse to continue the suspension pending a renewed application to the Upper Tribunal (*Cabinet Office v IC* [2016] UKUT 476 (AAC)). In such circumstances, the would-be appellant may make an application to the Upper Tribunal for a further suspension.

3.252 **5A.** *Expired.*

AMENDMENT

1. Tribunal Procedure (Coronavirus) (Amendment) Rules 2020 (SI 2020/416) r.4(1) and (2) (April 10, 2020).

GENERAL NOTE

3.253 This coronavirus temporary rule was in force from April 10, 2020 to September 25, 2022.

Procedure for applying for and giving directions

3.254 **6.**—(1) The Tribunal may give a direction on the application of one or more of the parties or on its own initiative.

(2) An application for a direction may be made—

(a) by sending or delivering a written application to the Tribunal; or

(b) orally during the course of a hearing.

(3) An application for a direction must include the reason for making that application.

(4) Unless the Tribunal considers that there is good reason not to do so, the Tribunal must send written notice of any direction to every party and to any other person affected by the direction.

(5) If a party or any other person sent notice of the direction under paragraph (4) wishes to challenge a direction which the Tribunal has given, they may do so by applying for another direction which amends, suspends or sets aside the first direction.

DEFINITIONS

"hearing"—see r.1(3).
"party"—*ibid.*
"Tribunal"—*ibid.*

GENERAL NOTE

3.255 There is no requirement that a person be given the opportunity to make representations before a direction is given. Plainly it is to be expected that such an opportunity would be given where a direction is to be given at a hearing but in other cases, where an application is made in writing or the tribunal proposes to issue a direction on its own initiative, it is often simpler and more proportionate to make the direction and then see whether anyone objects. If a direction is given and a party or other person affected objects to it, the remedy is to apply for another direction amending, suspending or setting aside the first direction (see para.(5)).

In *Dorset Healthcare NHS Foundation Trust v MH* [2009] UKUT 4 (AAC), the Upper Tribunal emphasised the desirability of the First-tier Tribunal considering whether to vary a direction, either on its own initiative under r.5(3) or on an application under r.6(5), before contemplating granting permission to appeal, at least in a case where the original direction was made without the benefit of full argument. It was held in *R. (Spahiu) v Secretary of State for the Home Department* [2018] EWCA

Civ 2604; [2019] 1 W.L.R. 1297 that there is no distinction between case management directions and case management decisions and so any decision made in the exercise of case management powers may be amended or set aside under r.6(5). The view expressed in that case (at [48] and [49]) that the equivalent provision relating to the Upper Tribunal provided a form of review under s.10 of the Tribunals, Courts and Enforcement Act 2007 (equivalent to s.9 in the First-tier Tribunal) so that a decision may only be reviewed once (see ss.9(10) and 10(8)) is inconsistent with the approach taken in *R. (Singh) v Secretary of State for the Home Department* [2019] 1 W.L.R. 1014 at [26] and, as Coulson L.J. who gave the lead judgment in *Spahiu* was also a member of the Court in *Singh*, should presumably no longer be considered to be correct.

There is no general duty to give reasons for decisions that do not "dispose of proceedings" (see r.34) but reasons may nonetheless be required for an interlocutory decision that would appear aberrant without reasons (*R. (Birmingham CC) v Birmingham Crown Court* [2009] EWHC 3329 (Admin); [2010] 1 W.L.R. 1287).

Failure to comply with rules etc.

7.—(1) An irregularity resulting from a failure to comply with any requirement in these Rules, a practice direction or a direction, does not of itself render void the proceedings or any step taken in the proceedings. **3.256**

(2) If a party has failed to comply with a requirement in these Rules, a practice direction or a direction, the Tribunal may take such action as it considers just, which may include—

(a) waiving the requirement;
(b) requiring the failure to be remedied;
(c) exercising its power under rule 8 (striking out a party's case); or
(d) exercising its power under paragraph (3).

(3) The Tribunal may refer to the Upper Tribunal, and ask the Upper Tribunal to exercise its power under section 25 of the 2007 Act in relation to, any failure by a person to comply with a requirement imposed by the Tribunal—

(a) to attend at any place for the purpose of giving evidence;
(b) otherwise to make themselves available to give evidence;
(c) to swear an oath in connection with the giving of evidence;
(d) to give evidence as a witness;
(e) to produce a document; or
(f) to facilitate the inspection of a document or any other thing (including any premises).

DEFINITIONS

"the 2007 Act"—see r.1(3).
"document"—*ibid.*
"party"—*ibid.*
"practice direction"—*ibid.*
"Tribunal"—*ibid.*

GENERAL NOTE

Paragraph (1)

This is an important provision which enables a tribunal to overlook an immaterial breach of the requirements of any rule, practice direction or direction. Although para.(2) is concerned with the consequences of a party failing to comply with a requirement, it appears to be implicit in para.(1) that a failure by the tribunal itself **3.257** to comply with a requirement can be waived, provided of course that that does not result in undue unfairness to a party. Note, however, that it does not deal with a breach of any statutory requirement other than one contained in the Rules.

Paragraph (2)

3.258 This sets out the possible procedural consequences of a party failing to comply with a requirement of the Rules, a practice direction or a direction. However, there can be other consequences. Thus, for instance, a failure to comply with a direction to provide evidence may simply lead to the case being heard without the evidence, which will usually be to the disadvantage of the person who failed to provide the evidence. Whether it is appropriate to draw an adverse inference from a failure to provide evidence will depend on the circumstances (*CCS/3757/2004* and see also the note to s.3(1) of the Tribunals, Courts and Enforcement Act 2007).

The powers to strike out a case or refer it to the Upper Tribunal may be used only if an appropriate warning has been given (see r.8(3)(a) and the note to para.(3) of this rule).

The powers in subparas (a), (b) and (c) may be exercised by a clerk where a notice of appeal does not satisfy the requirements set out in r.22(3) or is not accompanied by the documents required by r.22(4) and the power to waive an irregularity under subpara.(a) may be exercised by a clerk where a party has given notice of withdrawal under r.17(1)(a) orally but not in writing (see the note to r.4).

Paragraph (3)

3.259 This enables a breach of a requirement to give evidence or produce or make available a document to be referred to the Upper Tribunal with a view to the Upper Tribunal punishing the person for contempt of court (with a term of imprisonment of up to two years and an unlimited fine) under s.25 of the Tribunals' Courts and Enforcement Act 2007, as applied by r.7(4) of the Tribunal Procedure (Upper Tribunal) Rules 2008. In *CB v Suffolk CC (Enforcement Reference)* [2010] UKUT 413 (AAC); [2011] AACR 22, the Upper Tribunal fined a witness £500 for ignoring a summons issued by the Health, Education and Social Care Chamber of the First-tier Tribunal and, under s.16(3) of the Contempt of Court Act 1981, specified a term of imprisonment of seven days to be served if the fine was not paid within the time allowed. The Upper Tribunal emphasised that, if a person thought that a summons was inappropriate, the proper course of action was to ask the First-tier Tribunal to set it aside (see r.16(4)(a)) and, if that failed, to apply to the Upper Tribunal for judicial review to quash the summons. Simply ignoring a summons was not a legitimate course of action. In *BO v Care Quality Commission (Enforcement Reference)* [2013] UKUT 53 (AAC), a fine of £100, with an alternative of two days imprisonment, was imposed in another case where a summons had been ignored.

It has been held that a response to an appeal required under r.24(1) to (3), which is primarily a submission, is not a "document" within the scope of r.7(3)(e), although the documents that ought to accompany it by virtue of r.24(4) would be (*AP v HMRC (Enforcement Reference)* [2014] UKUT 182 (AAC); [2014] AACR 37). However, it is arguable that the better view, although one that would produce the same result where a decision-maker failed to provide a response to an appeal, is that a written submission is a "document" but that a person cannot "produce" a document that does not exist. In other words, in this context "produce" means "provide" rather than "create". In social security cases, a reference under para.(3) may only be made by the Chamber President (see the Practice Statement on the composition of the First-tier Tribunal in social security and child support cases set out above in the note to art.2 of the First-tier Tribunal and Upper Tribunal (Composition of Tribunals) Order 2008) or a judge to whom he has delegated that function (see para.4 of Sch.4 to the 2007 Act) and is likely to be made only as a matter of last resort. In *MD v SSWP (Enforcement Reference)* [2010] UKUT 202

(AAC); [2011] AACR 5, a three-judge panel said that, before a reference is made, the First-tier Tribunal should be satisfied that all the procedural requirements have been met and, in particular, that any summons, citation or order under r.16 was sent to the correct address and included an appropriate warning and, in the case of a summons or citation, was accompanied by an offer to pay expenses. It would be inappropriate to rely on r.7(1) if there might be any prejudice or injustice to the contemnor. The three-judge panel also suggested that, before making a reference, the First-tier Tribunal should give an alleged contemnor an opportunity to explain their conduct so that it could consider whether the matter did indeed warrant a reference. The implication may be that, even where the relevant direction is not made under r.16, it should contain a warning as to the possible effect of breaching it if the First-tier Tribunal is contemplating a reference in that event.

Paragraph (3)(c) must be read subject to s.5 of the Oaths Act 1978, which permits a person who objects to being sworn to make a solemn affirmation instead.

Striking out a party's case

8.—(1) The proceedings, or the appropriate part of them, will automatically be struck out if the appellant has failed to comply with a direction that stated that failure by a party to comply with the direction would lead to the striking out of the proceedings or that part of them. 3.260

(2) The Tribunal must strike out the whole or a part of the proceedings if the Tribunal—

(a) does not have jurisdiction in relation to the proceedings or that part of them; and

(b) does not exercise its power under rule 5(3)(k)(i) (transfer to another court or tribunal) in relation to the proceedings or that part of them.

(3) The Tribunal may strike out the whole or a part of the proceedings if—

(a) the appellant has failed to comply with a direction which stated that failure by the appellant to comply with the direction could lead to the striking out of the proceedings or part of them;

(b) the appellant has failed to co-operate with the Tribunal to such an extent that the Tribunal cannot deal with the proceedings fairly and justly; or

(c) the Tribunal considers there is no reasonable prospect of the appellant's case, or part of it, succeeding.

(4) The Tribunal may not strike out the whole or a part of the proceedings under paragraph (2) or (3)(b) or (c) without first giving the appellant an opportunity to make representations in relation to the proposed striking out.

(5) If the proceedings, or part of them, have been struck out under paragraph (1) or (3)(a), the appellant may apply for the proceedings, or part of them, to be reinstated.

(6) An application under paragraph (5) must be made in writing and received by the Tribunal within 1 month after the date on which the Tribunal sent notification of the striking out to the appellant.

(7) This rule applies to a respondent as it applies to an appellant except that—

(a) a reference to the striking out of the proceedings is to be read as a reference to the barring of the respondent from taking further part in the proceedings; and

(b) a reference to an application for the reinstatement of proceedings which have been struck out is to be read as a reference to an application for the lifting of the bar on the respondent from taking further part in the proceedings.

(8) If a respondent has been barred from taking further part in proceedings under this rule and that bar has not been lifted, the Tribunal need not consider any response or other submission made by that respondent [1 and may summarily determine any or all issues against that respondent].

AMENDMENT

1. Tribunal Procedure (Amendment No.3) Rules 2010 (SI 2010/2653) r.5(1) and (3) (November 29, 2010).

DEFINITIONS

"appellant"—see r.1(3).
"party"—*ibid.*
"respondent"—*ibid.*
"Tribunal"—*ibid.*

GENERAL NOTE

3.261 Note that, although paras (1)–(6) are expressed in terms of striking out proceedings brought by the appellant, by virtue of paras (7) and (8) they also provide for barring a respondent from taking further part in the proceedings. A decision to strike out proceedings is one that "disposes of proceedings" so that the parties are entitled to ask for a statement of reasons if one is not supplied with the decision (see r.34). It is suggested that a respondent who has been barred from taking a further part in proceedings is also entitled to a statement of reasons for the barring.

The powers to strike an appeal out under paras (1) or (3)(a) and then reinstate it under para.(5) may be exercised by a clerk where a notice of appeal does not satisfy the requirements set out in r.22(3) or is not accompanied by the documents required by r.22(4). A clerk may also bar a respondent from taking part in proceedings if a response is not submitted within the time required by r.24(1)(b) or (c). See the note to r.4.

A decision to strike out an appeal under paras (2) or (3) may be made without an oral hearing (see r.27(3)) and the usual reason for the Secretary of State or HMRC applying for the striking out of a social security appeal will be to avoid the cost of a hearing or of preparing a full response with all the accompanying documents. However, there are many occasions when it is appropriate for there to be an oral hearing of a strike-out application so that oral representations may be made. In the social security context, an oral hearing is likely to defeat the purpose of an application under r.8(3)(c) but that is not so in areas of law where an oral hearing of an appeal can take several days. See the note to para.(3) for the need to ensure that striking a case out without a hearing does not result in unfairness.

Paragraph (1)

3.262 This provides for an automatic strike out where a person has failed to comply with a direction that carried a warning that, unless there was compliance, the case "will" be struck out. No further exercise of judicial discretion is required for the strike-out to take effect provided that it is clear that there has not been compliance. It is important to distinguish this paragraph from para.(3)(a), which provides for a case to be struck out for failure to comply with a direction that carried a warning that if there was no compliance the case "may" be struck out. In the latter case, there needs to be a judicial decision exercising the power to strike out. Because a strike out under para.(1) is automatic, there can be no effective appeal against it. However, it is possible to apply for reinstatement under paras (5) and (6) and then, if necessary, to appeal against a refusal to reinstate the appeal. An alternative approach would be to appeal against the earlier direction insofar as it stated that failure to comply with it would lead to the appeal being struck out (as was done in *Salisbury Independent Living v Wirral MBC (HB)* [2011] UKUT 44 (AAC); [2012] AACR 37).

In *DTM v Ketttering BC (CTB)* [2013] UKUT 625 (AAC), it was held that, because a judge had issued a direction stating that a failure to comply with it "will lead to the striking out of the appeal without any further procedure under rule 8(1) of the Tribunal Procedure (First-tier Tribunal (Social Entitlement Chamber) Rules 2008" and the result of non-compliance was that the appeal was indeed struck out, the First-tier Tribunal no longer had jurisdiction to hear the appeal in the absence of reinstatement under para.(5). The Upper Tribunal substituted its own decision, first reinstating the appeal against the local authority's decision and then determining it.

The direction in that case had actually been given because the claimant had not returned the enquiry form issued by the First-tier Tribunal, asking him whether he wished to withdraw his appeal and, if not, whether he wished there to be an oral hearing. The direction had required the claimant to state within 14 days of the date of the direction whether he wished his appeal to continue. In fact, the direction was not posted to the claimant for a week and the claimant replied to the direction by returning the enquiry form so that it arrived nearly a week after the deadline. The Upper Tribunal said that it had been irrational to issue the direction at all because the failure to return the enquiry form did not prevent the First-tier Tribunal from determining the appeal and, indeed, the failure to return it would have entitled the First-tier Tribunal to determine the appeal without a hearing if it considered that not to be inappropriate (see r.27(1)). The inquisitorial role of the First-tier Tribunal and the overriding objective both pointed towards determining the appeal one way or another, rather than issuing a direction that included words having the effect that non-compliance would lead automatically to striking it out.

Standard form directions issued in the name of a judge but without any consideration by a judge or registrar cannot amount to directions for the purpose of this paragraph. Moreover, a statement that, if a party "does not comply with the direction and fails without reasonable explanation to [do so] shall be automatically barred" does not amount to a statement that failure by a party to comply with the direction "would lead to the striking out of the proceedings" for the purposes of this paragraph. Thus, when the party did offer an explanation for non-compliance, it had to be considered and so a further standard form notice, issued in the name of a judge but without judicial consideration and simply informing the party that it was automatically barred but could apply for reinstatement, was also invalid and the party had not been validly barred at all (*Enfield LBC v NH (SEN)* [2019] UKUT 1 (AAC); [2019] AACR 19).

Paragraph (2)

This replaces reg.46(1)(a) of the Social Security and Child Support (Decisions and Appeals) Regulations 1999. However, it is not limited to cases excluded from the scope of s.12 of the Social Security Act 1998 by virtue of Sch.2 to that Act or Sch.2 to the 1999 Regulations. Moreover, unlike Reg.46, its terms are mandatory, so that a final decision to the effect that the tribunal lacks jurisdiction must always be in the form of a decision to strike out the appeal. Most importantly, whereas in *Morina v Secretary of State for Work and Pensions* [2007] EWCA Civ 749; [2007] 1 W.L.R. 3033 (also reported as *R(IS) 6/07*) the Court of Appeal held that that there was no right of appeal under s.14 of the Social Security Act 1998 against a decision under reg.46(1)(a), in *LS v Lambeth LBC (HB)* [2010] UKUT 461 (AAC); [2011] AACR 27 it has been held that there is a right of appeal against any decision of the **3.263**

First-tier Tribunal (other than an "excluded decision" within the scope of s.11(5) of the Tribunals, Courts and Enforcement Act 2007).

Where an appeal has lapsed because the decision under appeal was made under s.16 of the Tax Credits Act 2002 and has been replaced by a decision under s.18, it must be struck out under this provision (*LS v HMRC (TC)* [2017] UKUT 257 (AAC); [2018] AACR 2). Arguably, the same approach should be taken where the decision under appeal was made under s.8 or s.10 of the Social Security Act 1998 and has been revised under s.9 to the advantage of the appellant so that s.9(6) applies, but in practice files are closed administratively unless the appellant objects when informed that the appeal has lapsed.

In *AW v Essex CC (SEN)* [2010] UKUT 74 (AAC); [2010] AACR 35 (subsequently reversed by the Court of Appeal without reference to this point), it was emphasised that there was a distinction between the equivalent of para.(2) in the Tribunal Procedure (First-tier Tribunal) (Health, Education and Social Care Chamber) Rules 2008 (SI 2008/2699) and the equivalent of para.(3)(c). It is appropriate to use the latter provision, which is discretionary, where a case appears hopeless but is nonetheless one that the First-tier Tribunal has jurisdiction to consider. Similarly, in *DC v Bromley LBC (HB)* [2018] UKUT 416 (AAC), it was held at [59] that, generally, "any application that a case be struck out because the law is clear should be made under rule 8(3)(c) . . ., rather than under rule 8(2)".

By virtue of para.(4), a party must be given an opportunity to make representations before his or her case is struck out and there will be some cases where justice requires there to be a hearing, notwithstanding r.27(3).

Paragraph (3)

3.264 Striking out under para.(3) is discretionary and must be proportionate (see r.2(2)(a) and (3)) so that, where a case is being struck out under sub-para.(a) or (b), regard must be had to both the culpability of the party whose case is being struck out and the amount at stake on the appeal. This point was made in *Alpha Rocks Solicitors v Alade* [2015] EWCA Civ 685; [2015] 1 W.L.R. 4534 in relation to ordinary civil proceedings. The Court of Appeal also held that a judge considering on the papers whether to strike out a case should avoid conducting a mini-trial and should not determine issues of credibility "where oral evidence at least *might* have put a different complexion on the allegations made" (emphasis of the Court).

Rule 27(3) permits the Tribunal to strike out a case without a hearing but, by virtue of para.(4), a party must be given an opportunity to make representations before his or her case is struck out under sub-para.(b) or (c). Where an effective opportunity to make representations would require a hearing, it is likely to be simpler and fairer to determine the appeal in the ordinary way instead of striking it out. Thus sub-paras (b) and (c) should probably be used only in clear and obvious cases.

There is no right to make representations before a case is struck out under subpara.(a); instead there is a right to apply for reinstatement after the event, by virtue of paras (5) and (6). In *Camden LBC v FG (SEN)* [2010] UKUT 249 (AAC), it was suggested that case management directions directed to a respondent and containing a warning that a failure to comply with them might result in the First-tier Tribunal's use of its powers to strike out a case under r.8 ought to have referred specifically to the equivalents of paras (3)(a), (7) and (8) of this rule and that an order under the equivalent of r.8(3)(a) addressed to a respondent ought to have referred to the equivalent of para.(7) and also to the equivalent of paras (5) and (6). However, in the particular case, the failure was not important because the respondent did protest and its letter was in fact treated as an application for reinstatement under paras (5) and (6).

3.265 In *AP v SSWP (ESA)* [2017] UKUT 304 (AAC), the Upper Tribunal expressed concern at a suggestion that a claimant's refusal to consent to the production of medical records amounted to a breach of a duty to co-operate with the First-tier Tribunal and could justify striking the case out under sub-para.(b) or the drawing of an adverse inference. It referred to the importance that the law attached to the confidentiality of such records. Clearly there could be no objection to the case being decided adversely to a claimant in those circumstances if the other evidence was not sufficient to satisfy the First-tier Tribunal to decide the case in his or her favour. Whether fairness might require either drawing an adverse inference or striking the case out if the claimant's refusal to produce his medical records prevented a proper evaluation of evidence that might otherwise be in the claimant's favour would no doubt depend on the circumstances of the case.

Sub-paragraph (c) reintroduces a power to strike a case out where it has no reasonable prospect of success. It includes the power to strike out a case for "abuse of process" (*Shiner v Revenue and Customs Commissioners* [2018] EWCA Civ 31; [2018] 1 W.L.R. 2812), but this will rarely be relevant in a social security context. The "appellant's case" is not the same as the "grounds on which the appellant relies" in r.22(3)(f) or r.23(6)(e) and so the First-tier Tribunal must look beyond the appellant's formal grounds of appeal and consider whether there are any other obvious grounds that might have a reasonable prospect of success (*HJ v IC* [2016] UKUT 82 (AAC); [2016] AACR 33). An equivalent power in reg.48 of the 1999 Regs was revoked in 2004.

The main, perhaps only, reason why the Secretary of State or HMRC might make an application under sub-para.(c) in a social security case is that it is thought appropriate that the case be determined without a hearing. Whether or not an opportunity to have an oral hearing is required for compliance with the European Convention on Human Rights in a social security case depends on whether or not any oral evidence might make any difference to the outcome (*Fexler v Sweden* ECHR Application No. 36801/06). The judge must still address the issue in the appeal when considering whether to strike a case out under sub-para.(c), but may do so summarily, having given the appellant an opportunity to make representations. In *HMRC v Fairford Group plc (in liquidation)* [2014] UKUT 329 (TCC), the Upper Tribunal said:

> "The First-tier Tribunal must decide whether there is a realistic, as opposed to a fanciful (in the sense of being entirely without substance) prospect of succeeding on the issue at a full hearing. ... The tribunal must avoid conducting a 'mini-trial'. ... [T]he strike out procedure is to deal with cases that are not fit for a full hearing at all."

The advantages of this procedure may not be insignificant in financial terms, given that not only are the costs of a hearing saved but also a case may be struck out by a judge alone without other members. However, striking out a case under sub-para.(c) will clearly not be appropriate where there is a dispute as regards which either oral evidence or the expertise of specialist members might be required. Thus, it was inappropriate to exercise the power to strike out an appeal on the ground that it had no prospect of success so as to deny an appellant an oral hearing in a case where there were disputed issues of fact (*AW v IC* [2013] UKUT 30 (AAC)) or a discretion had to be exercised in respect of which oral representations might have been made (*R. (AM) v First-tier Tribunal (CIC)* [2013] UKUT 333 (AAC)). Striking a case out without an oral hearing was also held to be inappropriate when it amounted to a breach of an unqualified promise in guidance notes that there would be an oral hearing of the appeal (*AM v IC* [2014] UKUT 239 (AAC)). Thus, in a social security case, striking a case out without an oral hearing is likely to be most appropriate where there is a clear statutory bar to entitlement, such as a time limit or age limit, which the claimant cannot satisfy. **3.266**

An application by a respondent for the striking out of an appeal under sub-para. (c) should be copied to the claimant and be accompanied by a full response that complies with r.24 unless that would clearly be disproportionate, so that the First-tier Tribunal has all the material necessary to enable it properly to decide whether the appeal has no reasonable prospect of success, the claimant is able to make effective representations and the appeal is ready for determination if it is not struck out (*JT v HMRC (TC)* [2015] UKUT 81 (AAC)).

Paragraphs (5) and (6)

3.267 These paragraphs apply only to cases struck out under para.(1) or (3)(a). In other cases, the Tribunal must give the party an opportunity to make representations *before* a case is struck out. In *Synergy Child Services Ltd v Ofsted* [2009] UKUT 125 (AAC), the Upper Tribunal allowed an appeal against a refusal to reinstate a struck-out appeal under the equivalent provisions in the Tribunal Procedure (First-tier Tribunal) (Health, Education and Social Care Chamber) Rules 2008 (SI 2008/2699) and held that, when considering whether to reinstate an appeal, "a Tribunal should have regard to the broad justice of the case, in the light of all the circumstances obtaining at the time the application for reinstatement is being considered". Nonetheless, it said that "[w]here there has been flagrant disobedience by a party, belated compliance or a change of circumstances making compliance irrelevant will not always require a Tribunal to reinstate an appeal".

The need to enforce orders in the courts has been emphasised in *Thevarajah v Riordan* [2015] UKSC 78; [2016] 1 W.L.R. 76, a decision in respect of relief from sanction (in the form of barring the defendant from defending the claim), where it was held that belated compliance with an "unless" order equivalent to the type of direction mentioned in r.8(1) could not amount to a change of circumstances justifying relief unless accompanied by other facts. While cases on time-limits and sanctions in the Civil Procedure Rules do not apply directly, tribunals should generally follow a similar approach (*BPP Holdings v Commissioners for Her Majesty's Revenue and Customs* [2017] UKSC 55; [2017] 1 W.L.R. 2945, where it was held that the Upper Tribunal had erred in allowing an appeal from a decision of the Tax Chamber of the First-tier Tribunal to bar HMRC from further participation in the taxpayer's appeal in a case where it had not only failed to comply with the order to file replies to certain requests by providing replies that were manifestly inadequate but had also failed to remedy the breach for several months, subsequently pleading a lack of resources but having failed to seek a variation of the order).

Where an application for reinstatement has been refused, the party can make another application. This may be justified where, for instance, the first application was rejected in ignorance of a material fact or compelling evidence or where there has been a material change of circumstances (*R.(BD) v First-tier Tribunal (CIC)* [2013] UKUT 332 (AAC)).

In *Camden LBC v FG (SEN)* [2010] UKUT 249 (AAC), the decision refusing to lift a bar on a respondent was communicated by telephone initially and then it appears that a letter was sent, "pp'd" on behalf of the judge. The Upper Tribunal recommended that such a decision should be in the form of an order signed by the judge and that it ought to draw attention to the right to make an application under the equivalent of Pt 4 of these Rules, although such notice does not appear to be mandatory where barring a respondent does not dispose of all issues in the proceedings (see r.33). As noted above, it was also suggested that an order under the equivalent of r.8(3)(a) (or, inferentially, perhaps r.8(1)) addressed to a respondent ought to refer to the right to make an application under paras (5) and (6). These comments were endorsed in *JP v SSWP (ESA)* [2016] UKUT 48 (AAC), where it was said also that not only was it desirable that judicial decisions be conveyed to the parties in a form that showed that they had been made by a judge but that it was also desirable that they should state by which judge and when they were made.

Paragraphs (7) and (8)

3.268 Now that para.(8) has been amended, it is clear that the effect of barring a respondent is to allow the First-tier Tribunal summarily to determine a case, or part of a case, against a respondent, so that barring a respondent can have the same effect as striking out an appellant. Simply striking out a respondent's case would not always be appropriate because it is not always obvious what decision should be put in the place of the one that has been challenged. Sometimes it might be appropriate simply to decide a case in the appellant's favour to the greatest permissible extent. Sometimes it might be appropriate merely to hold a hearing in the absence of the respondent.

In *ZB v SSWP (CSM)* [2013] UKUT 367 (AAC), it was held that a person barred under para.(7) from taking further part in proceedings nonetheless does not lose the right to appeal and is therefore also entitled to a statement of reasons. However, the fact that a person has been barred from taking further part in the proceedings so that the First-tier Tribunal is entitled to determine issues against him or her summarily has a bearing on how much detail is required in the statement of reasons and on how the Upper Tribunal exercises its power under s.12(2)(a) of the Tribunals, Courts and Enforcement Act 2007 not to set aside the First-tier Tribunal's decision even if it is satisfied that it is wrong in law. Presumably, it might therefore also be a reason for refusing permission to appeal in a case notwithstanding that there is an arguable point of law. In *ZB* itself, the First-tier Tribunal had in fact largely explained its decision in the decision notice and, although the Upper Tribunal held that the First-tier Tribunal had erred in law in refusing to provide a fuller statement of reasons, the Upper Tribunal refused to set aside the First-tier Tribunal's decision because it considered it to be unlikely that the First-tier Tribunal had erred in its approach to the case and it was therefore not satisfied that the appellant had suffered any significant injustice.

In *SL v SSWP (CSM)* [2014] UKUT 128 (AAC), it was pointed out that barring a person from taking any *further* part in proceedings and determining a case summarily did not entitle the First-tier Tribunal to ignore evidence already provided. The First-tier Tribunal was still required "to act rationally on material of probative value in making its decision", giving proper consideration to submissions made and taking account of evidence submitted, albeit that it could "deal with the respondent's case rather more briefly than would otherwise be required." Perhaps more controversially, it was also held that, if the Upper Tribunal allowed an appeal and remitted the case to the First-tier Tribunal, a bar imposed before the First-tier Tribunal made its first decision no longer applied because the remitted case amounted to different "proceedings". If the bar was properly imposed, it is not obvious why that should necessarily be the case just because an appeal on a different issue had been successful although it might well be appropriate to reconsider whether the bar should continue if the reason for the bar has been remedied. In *CW v SSWP (CSM)* [2014] UKUT 290 (AAC), it was held that a bar comes to an end when a decision disposing of all issues in the proceedings is issued. This is arguably inconsistent with *ZB* because, if a bar has come to an end, there is no reason why it should affect the Upper Tribunal's approach to the case if the Upper Tribunal is satisfied that there was an error of law.

Referring a case to the Upper Tribunal under r.7(3) provides an alternative to barring if it is necessary for evidence to be provided and the drawing of adverse inferences is not appropriate. In the days before these remedies were available, resort could be had to judicial review if the Secretary of State was in default. **3.269**

In *R.(Davies) v Commissioners' Office* [2008] EWHC 334 (Admin), Black J. declared irrational the Secretary of State's refusal to comply with a tribunal's directions to disclose evidence. She said that the only proper course for the Secretary of State, if he objected to directions, was to return to the tribunal and seek a variation. See now r.6(5), although there would now also be the possibility of appealing against the directions. The same point was forcefully made by the Court of Appeal in *BPP Holdings v Commissioners for Her Majesty's Revenue and Customs* ([2016] EWCA Civ 121; [2016] 1 W.L.R. 1915 at [43] (subsequently upheld on appeal to the Supreme Court – see above) in relation to HMRC's failure to comply with an order of the First-tier Tribunal. See also *R. (Majera) v Secretary of State for the Home Department* [2021] UKSC 46; [2021] 3 W.L.R. 1075, where the Supreme Court has reiterated at [44] the fundamental point that a Secretary of State is not entitled to disregard a decision of the First-tier Tribunal even if he or she considers it to be wrong in law. In that case, the remedy would have been to apply for permission to appeal:

> "It is a well-established principle of our constitutional law that a court order must be obeyed unless and until it has been set aside or varied by the court (or, conceivably, overruled by legislation)."

Substitution and addition of parties

3.270 **9.**—(1) The Tribunal may give a direction substituting a party if—

(a) the wrong person has been named as a party; or

(b) the substitution has become necessary because of a change in circumstances since the start of proceedings.

(2) The Tribunal may give a direction adding a person to the proceedings as a respondent.

(3) If the Tribunal gives a direction under paragraph (1) or (2) it may give such consequential directions as it considers appropriate.

DEFINITIONS

"party"—see r.1(3).
"respondent"—*ibid.*
"Tribunal"—*ibid.*

GENERAL NOTE

Paragraph (2)

3.271 A person joined as a respondent becomes a party and acquires all the rights of a party, including the right to require there to be a hearing, the right to obtain a statement of reasons and the right to apply for permission to appeal. A person claiming to be affected by a decision, despite not having automatically been a party to the proceedings, and wishing to appeal may even apply to be added as a respondent after the decision has been made (*Razzaq v Charity Commission for England and Wales* [2016] UKUT 546 (TCC)). However, a person whose application to be added as a respondent is refused is not a party and so has no right of appeal under s.11 of the Tribunals, Courts and Enforcement Act 2007, although a challenge to the refusal may be made by way of an application to the Upper Tribunal for judicial review (*Salisbury Independent Living v Wirral BC (HB)* [2011] UKUT 44 (AAC); [2012] AACR 37).

The possibility of using the power to add parties as a means of avoiding injustice may sometimes impose upon the First-tier Tribunal a duty to invite a person to be added as a party, although a person should not be added without their consent unless the law requires it, as to which the question whether or not their rights or interests may be affected by the proceedings is likely to be an important, and often determinative, consideration (*IC v Spiers* [2022] UKUT 93 (AAC)).

However, given the wide scope of the definition of "respondent" in r.1(3), it will seldom be necessary to add a party as a respondent in a social security case because a person with an interest in a decision under appeal will usually have had a right of appeal against it and so will automatically be a respondent. However, it may be necessary to add as a respondent a person from whom an overpayment might be recoverable instead of the appellant if he or she is not already one (*DBH v West Lindsey DC (HB)* [2021] UKUT 256 (AAC)). This will be necessary where the Secretary of State has not made a decision in respect of all those from whom an overpayment might be recoverable, which would automatically have made them all parties to any appeal. In the past, there were at least two other types of cases where non-parties were invited to attend hearings. The injured person would sometimes be invited to attend a hearing of an appeal under the Social Security (Recovery of Benefits) Act 1997 brought by a compensator even though there had been no deduction under s.8 of that Act so that the injured person had no right of appeal and no direct interest in the case. A person in receipt of widow's benefit would sometimes be invited to attend a hearing of an appeal against a refusal to award another woman widow's benefit based on contributions paid by the same man where there was a possibility that there might have been polygamous marriages. In both cases, the reason for inviting the non-party was that success by the appellant might logically lead to an award of benefit to the non-party being revised or superseded. The problem was, that, in the unfortunate absence of any power in the Secretary of State to refer the question of revision or supersession to a tribunal, any decision on the first appeal was not binding in relation to the revision or supersession. It would be unfair for it to be binding without the question properly being referred and the non-party being given a clear indication of the grounds upon which there might be revision or supersession. However, if a person is added as a party and has all the rights of a party and is made properly aware of the issues, there is no reason in principle why the decision to which they are a party should not be binding on them unless, in a case to which it applies, s.17(2) of the Social Security Act 1998 (or the equivalent provisions relating to housing benefit and child support) necessarily carries a contrary implication.

Section 17(2) does not now apply to tax credit cases (see the note to that section). **3.272**

Therefore, in *CM v HMRC (TC)* [2014] UKUT 272 (AAC), the Upper Tribunal suggested that, where there were competing claims for child tax credit, the second claimant could be added as a party to an appeal by the first claimant, against their will if necessary, on the basis that the decision would then be binding on both claimants. In that case, the claimant who had been awarded child tax credit had been invited to attend the hearing of the other claimant's appeal by the First-tier Tribunal but was not added as a party. The other claimant's appeal was successful. The Upper Tribunal dismissed the first claimant's appeal against the First-tier Tribunal's decision on the ground that, not being a party, he had no right to bring it but pointed out that he was also not bound by the decision and would have a separate right of appeal if HMRC terminated his entitlement. The suggestion that one claimant should be joined as a party to an appeal by a competing claimant was made against that background and it was expressly acknowledged that there was no point in joining a person as a party unless HMRC might be in a position to make a separate decision on that person's claim in the light of the First-tier Tribunal's decision (which HMRC seems to have thought it could not on the facts of that case).

However, in *GC v HMRC (CHB)* [2018] UKUT 223 (AAC), it was suggested that, where there were competing claims for child benefit and one claimant had appealed, not only should the other claimant be made a party to the appeal but also his or her right to child benefit would then be determined in that appeal. The Upper Tribunal did not fully analyse how that could be achieved, but it presumably had in mind that, if the previously unsuccessful claimant's appeal were allowed, the other claimant would, as a party, be bound by the findings (although no consideration was given to any implication of s.17(2) of the Social Security Act 1998) and his or her award could be revised or superseded in the light of those findings. Whether or not there would, in those circumstances, be a period of double payment in the period before HMRC made its new decision would depend on whether the award was either revised or else superseded in circumstances where the supersession had retrospective effect and, if either, whether any resulting overpayment was recoverable. The child's father had been awarded child benefit when the mother's award was terminated. She successfully appealed against the termination and the father then appealed to the Upper Tribunal. In this case, rather than dismissing the appeal as was done in *CM*, the Upper Tribunal joined the mother to the proceedings and then allowed the father's appeal on the ground that not making him a party to the mother's appeal had been a breach of the rules of natural justice. (If it had had any doubt about the propriety of allowing the appeal when the father had not been a party to the proceedings before the First-tier Tribunal or at the time of lodging the appeal, the Upper Tribunal could probably have achieved the same result by treating the father as having made an application for judicial review.) The implication of the decision appears to be that the First-tier Tribunal has a *duty* to join a competing claimant to a child benefit appeal, rather than having a mere power to do so, at least if it is minded to allow the appeal.

No power to award costs

3.273 **10.** The Tribunal may not make any order in respect of costs (or, in Scotland, expenses).

DEFINITION

"Tribunal"—see r.1(3).

GENERAL NOTE

3.274 See the note to s.29 to the Tribunals, Courts and Enforcement Act 2007.

Representatives

3.275 **11.**—(1) A party may appoint a representative (whether a legal representative or not) to represent that party in the proceedings.

(2) Subject to paragraph (3), if a party appoints a representative, that party (or the representative if the representative is a legal representative) must send or deliver to the Tribunal written notice of the representative's name and address.

(3) In a case to which rule 23 (cases in which the notice of appeal is to be sent to the decision maker) applies, if the appellant (or the appellant's representative if the representative is a legal representative) provides written notification of the appellant's representative's name and address to the decision maker before the decision maker provides its response to the Tribunal, the appellant need not take any further steps in order to comply with paragraph (2).

(4) If the Tribunal receives notice that a party has appointed a representative under paragraph (2), it must send a copy of that notice to each other party.

(5) Anything permitted or required to be done by a party under these Rules, a practice direction or a direction may be done by the representative of that party, except signing a witness statement.

(6) A person who receives due notice of the appointment of a representative—

(a) must provide to the representative any document which is required to be provided to the represented party, and need not provide that document to the represented party; and

(b) may assume that the representative is and remains authorised as such until they receive written notification that this is not so from the representative or the represented party.

(7) At a hearing a party may be accompanied by another person whose name and address has not been notified under paragraph (2) or (3) but who, with the permission of the Tribunal, may act as a representative or otherwise assist in presenting the party's case at the hearing.

(8) Paragraphs (2) to (6) do not apply to a person who accompanies a party under paragraph (7).

DEFINITIONS

"appeal"—see r.1(3).
"appellant"—*ibid.*
"decision maker"—*ibid.*
"document"—*ibid.*
"hearing"—*ibid.*
"legal representative"—*ibid.*
"party"—*ibid.*
"practice direction"—*ibid.*
"Tribunal"—*ibid.*

GENERAL NOTE

Paragraph (1)

A party has a right to be represented by any person (subject to their proper behaviour). Thus, under earlier legislation, a chairman erred in refusing to hear submissions by what he described as a "McKenzie friend" and it was an error of law for him to insist that the claimant specify at the beginning of the hearing whether the person accompanying her was going to act as a representative in the conventional sense (*CS/1753/2000*). In *CDLA/2462/2003*, the Commissioner reiterated the point that representatives may also be witnesses. **3.276**

> "8. Tribunals operate less formally than courts. They do not operate rights of audience. They allow, of course, professional legal representation. But they also allow lay representation and assistance from anyone whom the claimant wishes to assist in presenting a case to a tribunal. Given that breadth of representation, it is inevitable that the roles of representative and witness cannot be separated in the way that they would in a court. The same person may wish to put the claimant's case and give evidence in support of that case. The tribunal must take care to distinguish evidence from representation so that the former's provenance is known and can be the subject of questioning by the tribunal and other parties. But, subject to the practicalities of the way in which the taking of evidence is handled, there is no objection in principle to the same person acting in different capacities as a witness and as a representative. Nor is there any reason in principle why the probative value of evidence should depend upon whether or not it came from a representative.
>
> . . .
>
> 13. I emphasise that I am concerned here with a representative who wanted to give evidence from his own knowledge. I am not concerned with the different circumstance of a representative who wants to make a statement of the claimant's evidence to the appeal tribunal. Some tribunals refuse a representative the chance to do this. They insist on hearing the evidence from the claimant, allowing the representative to supplement the tribunal's questions to ensure that all the evidence is elicited from the claimant. That is a matter that is within the chairman's control of the procedure under regulation 49(1) [now r.5(1)]. Nothing I have written above affects the use of that power by [a] chairman to control the way that the claimant's own evidence is presented."

In *PM v SSWP (IS)* [2014] UKUT 474 (AAC), the judge expressed surprise that the First-tier Tribunal had not been prepared to accept evidence from the claimant's representative in a case where the claimant was a 19-year old foreign national who had been in care following estrangement from her father and who, the First-tier Tribunal had been told, was too distressed to attend the hearing. The First-tier Tribunal had said that only statements of fact made by representatives as to matters within their own personal knowledge were evidence. The Upper Tribunal referred to *PL v Walsall MBC* [2009] UKUT 27 (AAC), a case where an assertion of a local authority's submission-writer, supported by computer printouts, was held to be sufficient evidence to prove that certain decisions had been made, because the fact that the evidence was not of matters within the submission-writer's personal knowledge merely made it hearsay which might affect its probative worth but did not make it inadmissible. (That statements of fact in a representative's written submission, including the Secretary of State's response to an appeal, may amount to evidence has been reiterated in *AS v SSWP (CA)* [2015] UKUT 592 (AAC); [2016] AACR 22.) The evidence in *PM* had been as to the claimant's father's last known address and place of work, which the Upper Tribunal commented "was likely to prove an uncontroversial issue capable of objective verification and not one where there was any risk of the evidence being compromised if it was mediated through a representative". Similarly, the First-tier Tribunal is entitled to accept evidence given by a presenting officer from his or her knowledge of the relevant files (*BS v SSWP (DLA)* [2016] UKUT 73 (AAC); [2016] AACR 32).

In *JF v SSWP (DLA)* [2012] UKUT 335 (AAC) a claimant complained that a person accompanying her was told not to speak on her behalf. The Upper Tribunal commented that there was no record of the First-tier Tribunal having received any evidence from the companion and that "if someone who has accompanied a claimant wishes to speak, . . . the First-tier Tribunal should remember that that person may well be able to give material evidence and, unless the claimant objects, it should give him or her an opportunity to do so, even if not immediately, and it should then make a note of the evidence as it would evidence from the claimant". It was similarly accepted in *SK v SSWP (ESA)* [2014] UKUT 141 (AAC) that representatives may be able to give useful evidence.

3.277 It does not follow that a claimant is always entitled to an adjournment for the purpose of being represented but, if an adjournment is refused, it has to be recognised that the claimant may be disadvantaged unless, of course, the First-tier Tribunal is minded to allow the claimant's appeal anyway. In particular, where a claimant has mental health problems and asks for a postponement or adjournment for the purposes of obtaining representation, the First-tier Tribunal must consider whether the adjournment may be a reasonable adjustment required under the Equality Act 2010 to enable the claimant to overcome a disadvantage suffered as a result of a disability (*DC v SSWP (ESA)* [2014] UKUT 218 (AAC)).

The possible conflict of interest where a person employed by a local authority represents a claimant in a housing benefit case where the same local authority is a party was considered in *CSHC/729/2003*. The Commissioner commended the practice of the representative concerned in drawing claimants' attention to the potential conflict. The Commissioner reserved the question whether he or a tribunal had any power to prevent a representative chosen by a claimant from acting. It is suggested that, in the absence of misconduct by the representative, there is no such power, although the Tribunal could ensure that the claimant had made an informed choice.

No provision is made in these Rules for parties who lack capacity to conduct their own cases or to appoint a representative. However, reg.25 of the Social Security and Child Support (Decisions and Appeals) Regulations 1999, reg.24 of the Child Benefit and Guardian's Allowance (Decisions and Appeals) Regulations 2003 and reg.49 of the Universal Credit, Personal Independence Payment, Jobseeker's Allowance and Employment and Support Allowance (Decisions and Appeals) Regulations 2013 provide that those appointed by the Secretary of State to act on behalf of claimants or their estates in relation to claims may appeal and so presumably they have all the powers of appellants. It may also be implicit that those who have a legal right to claim or receive benefits as executors, deputies appointed by the Court of Protection or, in Scotland, judicial factors or other guardians also have a right to appeal in relation to those benefits, although, in *AMA v Greater Manchester West Mental Health NHS Foundation Trust* [2015] UKUT 36 (AAC); [2015] AACR 30 it was held that appointment as a deputy by the Court of Protection does not necessarily entitle the deputy to act in tribunal proceedings on behalf of the patient; it depends on the terms of the Court's order.

If it is necessary to do so in order to secure a person's right to a fair hearing, the First-tier Tribunal may appoint a litigation friend, notwithstanding the lack of any express statutory power to do so (*AM (Afghanistan) v Secretary of State for the Home Department* [2017] EWCA Civ 1123). However, that will rarely be required in social security cases (see the note to s.12(2) of the Social Security Act 1998, above).

An appointee or litigation friend may appoint a representative under this rule.

Paragraphs (2)–(6)

These paragraphs provide for the formal appointment of a representative. Notice must be given to the Tribunal (para.(2)) unless an appellant has already given notice to the decision-maker before the decision-maker has sent the response to the appeal to the Tribunal (para.(3)), in which case the decision-maker must inform the Tribunal of the name and address of the appellant's representative (see r.24(4)(c)). A formally appointed representative may act on behalf of the party in all respects (except to sign a witness statement) and should be sent any documents that would otherwise be sent to the party (paras (5) and (6)(a)). However, it is presumably possible for the Tribunal to exclude a representative from a hearing under r.30(5) without excluding the party. **3.278**

In *MP v SSWP (DLA)* [2010] UKUT 103 (AAC), the claimant had solicitors acting for her. As required by r.23(2), they had sent the notice of appeal to the Secretary of State who had duly informed the Tribunals Service that they were acting, as anticipated by para.(3). However, the Tribunals Service sent an "enquiry form", asking whether a hearing was wanted, only to the claimant, who completed it wrongly. It was held that there had been no breach of r.11(6)(a) because the "enquiry form" was not a document "which is required to be provided", but the judge questioned whether it was sensible not to send a copy to the solicitors and observed that r.11(6)(b) would have permitted it to be sent only to the solicitors.

Paragraphs (7) and (8)

These paragraphs enable a party who is present at a hearing to be represented or assisted at the hearing by any person, without there having been any formal notice of appointment. Although the Tribunal's permission is required, it is suggested that, unless r.30(5) applies, it will only exceptionally be appropriate for the Tribunal to refuse permission, particularly as the party need only provide a written notice under para.(2) in order to avoid the need for permission. Without a written notice of appointment, a person who acts as a representative at a hearing has no rights as a representative outside the hearing. Obviously, a written notice may be provided at the hearing so that the person becomes entitled to act as a full representative thereafter. **3.279**

Calculating time

12.—(1) Except in asylum support cases, an act required by these Rules, a practice direction or a direction to be done on or by a particular day must be done by 5pm on that day. **3.280**

(2) If the time specified by these Rules, a practice direction or a direction for doing any act ends on a day other than a working day, the act is done in time if it is done on the next working day.

(3) In this rule "working day" means any day except a Saturday or Sunday, Christmas Day, Good Friday or a bank holiday under section 1 of the Banking and Financial Dealings Act 1971.

DEFINITIONS

"asylum support case"—see r.1(3).
"practice direction"—*ibid.*
"working day"—see para.(3).

General Note

Paragraph (3)

3.281 Christmas Day and Good Friday are holidays under the common law in England, Wales and Northern Ireland, rather than being bank holidays, which is why they are specifically mentioned in this paragraph. The following days are bank holidays in England, Wales and Northern Ireland, either because they are mentioned in Sch.1 to the 1971 Act or by virtue of Royal proclamations under s.1(2) and (3) of that Act: New Year's Day, Easter Monday, the first Monday in May, the last Monday in May, the last Monday in August, and December 26. In Northern Ireland, there are additional bank holidays on March 17 (St Patrick's Day), by virtue of Sch.1 to the 1971 Act, and July 12 (the anniversary of the Battle of the Boyne), by virtue of a proclamation by the Secretary of State for Northern Ireland under s.1(5) of that Act. Where a bank holiday would otherwise fall on a Saturday or Sunday, the following Monday (and Tuesday, where December 26 is on a Sunday) is substituted. Additional bank holidays may be announced by Royal proclamation and so may variations. Thus, there was an additional bank holiday on April 29, 2011 on the occasion of Prince William's wedding and, in 2012, the late May bank holiday was put back to 4 June and there was an additional bank holiday on 5 June to celebrate the Queen's Diamond Jubilee.

Scotland has different bank holidays under the 1971 Act but they are not always observed as public holidays as there is a tradition of observing various local public holidays or institutional holidays instead of, or occasionally as well as, bank holidays. The statutory bank holidays, including those announced by Royal proclamation, are New Year's Day, January 2, Good Friday, the first Monday in May, the last Monday in May, the first Monday in August, November 30 (St Andrew's Day), Christmas Day and December 26. Where a bank holiday would otherwise fall on a Saturday or Sunday the following Monday (or Tuesday, where January 2 or December 26 is on a Sunday), is substituted. These, subject to variations or additions announced by Royal proclamation, are the relevant days for the purposes of this rule although Royal Mail does in fact operate on November 30. November 30 is a comparatively recent addition to the list and, where it is observed as a holiday, it is often in place of one of the other bank holidays. Ironically, the clearing banks in Scotland observe the English bank holidays so that they are open on January 2, the first Monday in August and November 30 but are closed on Easter Monday and the last Monday in August.

The relevant days to be treated as bank holidays will depend on the part of the United Kingdom in which the "act"—which will be the receipt of a document where the Rules provide that a document must be received by the Tribunal or a party within a specified time—must be performed. No specific provision is made in respect of local holidays or other causes of postal delays where a party lives outside the United Kingdom but the general power to extend time under r.5(3)(a) may be invoked.

Sending and delivery of documents

3.282 **13.**—(1) Any document to be provided to the Tribunal under these Rules, a practice direction or a direction must be—

(a) sent by pre-paid post or delivered by hand to the address specified for the proceedings;

(b) sent by fax to the number specified for the proceedings; or

(c) sent or delivered by such other method as the Tribunal may permit or direct.

(2) Subject to paragraph (3), if a party provides a fax number, email address or other details for the electronic transmission of documents to them, that party must accept delivery of documents by that method.

(3) If a party informs the Tribunal and all other parties that a particular form of communication (other than pre-paid post or delivery by hand)

should not be used to provide documents to that party, that form of communication must not be so used.

(4) If the Tribunal or a party sends a document to a party or the Tribunal by email or any other electronic means of communication, the recipient may request that the sender provide a hard copy of the document to the recipient. The recipient must make such a request as soon as reasonably practicable after receiving the document electronically.

(5) The Tribunal and each party may assume that the address provided by a party or its representative is and remains the address to which documents should be sent or delivered until receiving written notification to the contrary.

DEFINITIONS

"document"—see r.1(3).
"party"—*ibid.*
"practice direction"—*ibid.*
"Tribunal"—*ibid.*

GENERAL NOTE

In these Rules, a party is usually required to provide, or send, a document so that it is *received* by a certain date. See r.12 for the calculation of time. 3.283

A document may be sent by fax and, in *R(DLA) 3/05*, it was held that a fax is received when it is successfully transmitted to, and received by, a fax machine, irrespective of whether anyone actually collects it from the machine. Furthermore, the faxed request for a statement of reasons in that case was received by the clerk to the appeal tribunal when received at the tribunal venue, even though the clerk did not visit that venue until some days later. The Commissioner said that it would have been different if the venue had been a casual venue, such as local authority premises. Here, it was a dedicated venue and the fax number had been given to representatives precisely to enable them to communicate with the clerk. There was nothing in any document issued with the decision notice to indicate that the request for a statement of reasons had to be addressed to a different place.

Where documents are sent by the Tribunal to a party under these Rules, the important date is usually the date they are *sent*. However, a decision of the Tribunal may be set aside under r.37 if it is accepted that notice of hearing or a direction was not in fact received by a party even though it was properly posted. In *R(SB) 55/83*, it was held that a setting aside under what is now r.37 was the *only* remedy in these circumstances, but Commissioners later declined to follow that decision and held that an appeal will lie if a decision is not set aside (*CCS/6302/1999*, *CIB/303/1999*), while endorsing the view expressed in *R(SB) 19/83* that an application for a setting aside is to be preferred. Rule 41 permits the First-tier Tribunal to treat an application for permission to appeal as an application for a setting aside.

Paragraph (1)

When sending documents to the Tribunal, fax may always be used if available but email may be used only if the Tribunal has specifically said so. 3.284

However, in a guidance note dated March 17, 2016, the Chamber President of the Social Entitlement Chamber of the First-tier Tribunal has permitted the delivery of documents to the Tribunal by electronic means by any party in a social security or child support case who has indicated his or her consent to receiving communications by electronic means. Moreover, would-be appellants are now invited to submit appeals online in most social security cases, although not in vaccine damage payment cases, child support cases or against decisions made by HMRC (see *https://www.gov.uk/appeal-benefit-decision/submit-appeal*).

Paragraphs (2) and (3)

3.285 When sending documents to a party, any available method of communication may be used unless the party has specifically said that fax or email may not be used. Any address or number given may be assumed to be still in use until notice to the contrary is given (see para.(5)).

Paragraph (4)

3.286 This paragraph enables a party or the Tribunal to require a hard copy of a faxed or emailed document to be provided even though the fax or email delivery may have been sufficient for the purpose of complying with a time limit. It might be used, for instance, where a fax is poorly reproduced or where printing a large email attachment would be unduly onerous. Note that it is not necessary to provide a hard copy of a fax or email unless requested to do so. However, where a time limit runs to the date a document is received, it might be wise to send a hard copy if there is any reason to doubt that the document will be received electronically even if sent.

Use of documents and information

3.287 **14.**—(1) The Tribunal may make an order prohibiting the disclosure or publication of—

(a) specified documents or information relating to the proceedings; or
(b) any matter likely to lead members of the public to identify any person whom the Tribunal considers should not be identified.

(2) The Tribunal may give a direction prohibiting the disclosure of a document or information to a person if—

(a) the Tribunal is satisfied that such disclosure would be likely to cause that person or some other person serious harm; and
(b) the Tribunal is satisfied, having regard to the interests of justice, that it is proportionate to give such a direction.

(3) If a party ("the first party") considers that the Tribunal should give a direction under paragraph (2) prohibiting the disclosure of a document or information to another party ("the second party"), the first party must—

(a) exclude the relevant document or information from any documents that will be provided to the second party; and
(b) provide to the Tribunal the excluded document or information, and the reason for its exclusion, so that the Tribunal may decide whether the document or information should be disclosed to the second party or should be the subject of a direction under paragraph (2).

(4) The Tribunal must conduct proceedings as appropriate in order to give effect to a direction given under paragraph (2).

(5) If the Tribunal gives a direction under paragraph (2) which prevents disclosure to a party who has appointed a representative, the Tribunal may give a direction that the documents or information be disclosed to that representative if the Tribunal is satisfied that—

(a) disclosure to the representative would be in the interests of the party; and
(b) the representative will act in accordance with paragraph (6).

(6) Documents or information disclosed to a representative in accordance with a direction under paragraph (5) must not be disclosed either directly or indirectly to any other person without the Tribunal's consent.

DEFINITIONS

"document"—see r.1(3).
"party"—*ibid.*
"Tribunal"—*ibid.*

GENERAL NOTE

Paragraph (1)

An order under this paragraph may be directed to an individual and be concerned only with an individual document (e.g. prohibiting an appellant from disclosing to someone else a document disclosed to the appellant by the respondent) or it may be directed to the public in general and effectively amount to a reporting restriction. Hearings of social security cases are usually attended only by those immediately interested in them but most hearings are, in principle, open to the public, including the press (see r.30). It is difficult to envisage it being appropriate to prohibit the publication of any information at all about a hearing held in public but it might often be appropriate to make an order prohibiting the publishing of information that may lead to a child or vulnerable adult being identified if there would otherwise be any serious risk of such publication. It will generally be necessary properly to balance the right of one person to respect of his or her private life under art.8 of the European Convention on Human Rights and the right of another person to freedom of expression under art.10 (see *Re British Broadcasting Corporation* [2009] UKHL 34; [2010] 1 A.C. 145, where it is noteworthy that, although the House of Lords discharged an anonymity order so as to permit the BBC to broadcast an acquitted defendant's name, it saw no need to mention his name itself). See also *In re M (A Patient) (Court of Protection: Reporting Restrictions)* [2011] EWHC 1197 (Fam); [2012] 1 W.L.R. 287. It was made clear in *Re a Teacher (Rule 14 Order)* [2023] UKUT 39 (AAC); [2023] AACR 6 that an order under rule 14(1)(b) only restricts the identification of any relevant person as a person connected with the proceedings before the First-tier Tribunal and that, therefore, it does not affect the publication of other information about the person, provided that the form and content of such publication does not allow the person to be linked to the proceedings. 3.288

Orders under r.14(1) are not likely to be appropriate in the social security context very often, but in *TD v SSWP (PIP)* [2020] UKUT 283 (AAC), there arose the question of redacting parts of a document submitted by the Secretary of State as proof of authorisation of surveillance under the Regulation of Investigatory Powers Act 2000. The Secretary of State's representative had handed up at the hearing an unredacted copy of the authorisation, marked "For Judge only". It was suggested that, if the Secretary of State wished any part of the evidence to be withheld from the claimant, her representative should be ready to provide a redacted copy so that the claimant at least could see that, and it was held that any issue over the extent of any redactions should be determined by the whole tribunal. No reference was made to the relevant Practice Statement on the composition of tribunals (see the annotation to art.2 of the First-tier Tribunal and Upper Tribunal (Composition of Tribunal) Order 2008, above) but, although para.5 of that Practice Statement is made subject to para.10, the latter merely provides that a decision under r.14 "may" be made by a judge alone. It is clearly generally appropriate, as the Upper Tribunal held, for important case-management decisions made at a hearing that are likely to affect the panel's decision to be determined by the whole panel. In *DVLA v IC (Rule 14 Order)* [2020] UKUT 310 (AAC), the Upper Tribunal held that, as in courts, documents and information which are disclosed in a tribunal case are subject to an implied undertaking that they will not be used other than for the purposes of that particular case. Accordingly, while a litigant can show them to a legal advisor, he or she cannot publish them on the Internet, even for the purpose of soliciting advice, without permission. Again, this is unlikely often to be an issue in social security cases, although it might be in child support cases. In the circumstances of the particular case, the

Upper Tribunal made an order under the equivalent r.14 of the Tribunal Procedure (Upper Tribunal) Rules 2008, prohibiting the second respondent from publishing the electronic documents and bundles (including the skeleton arguments) provided in accordance with case management directions issued by the Upper Tribunal.

The existence of the powers conferred by this paragraph is a factor to be borne in mind when deciding under r.30(3) whether a hearing should be in private or in public, which requires consideration of the terms of art.6(1). Preventing the publication of parties' names may be appropriate even if a hearing is in public or the press are admitted to a private hearing (*L v L (Ancillary Relief Proceedings: Anonymity)* [2015] EWHC 2621 (Fam); [2016] 1 W.L.R. 1259).

A breach of an order made under this paragraph is a contempt of court. However, it can be enforced only through an application for committal made to the High Court or, in Scotland, the Court of Session.

An order made during proceedings may be varied after the proceedings have ended (*Abbasi v Newcastle-upon-Tyne Hospitals NHS Foundation Trust* [2021] EWHC 1699 (Fam); [2022] 2 W.L.R. 465). A non-party may apply for a variation of an order under para.(1) without applying to be made a party to the proceedings. This was done in *Re X (Reporting restriction order: Variation)* [2015] UKUT 380 (AAC); [2016] AACR 6, where a local authority that had not been a party to proceedings before the Upper Tribunal was aware of them and of an order that had been made under r.14(1) of the Tribunal Procedure (Upper Tribunal) Rules 2008 and sought permission to disclose information relating to the proceedings to the police. Applying guidance given by the Court of Appeal in relation to care proceedings in *Re C (A Minor) (Care Proceedings: Disclosure)* [1997] Fam 76, the order prohibiting publication of any matter likely to lead members of the public to identify certain adults and children was varied so as to permit disclosure of the decision of the Upper Tribunal and the identities of individuals mentioned in it to the police and other relevant bodies for the limited purposes of investigating criminal offences, bringing prosecutions and protecting any child or vulnerable adult. However, if a non-party wishes to challenge the decision on such an application, he or she may need to apply to be added as a party so as to be able to appeal under s.11 of the Tribunals, Courts and Enforcement Act 2007.

A non-party may apply to a tribunal for access to documents that are in the tribunal's file (see the discussion of "open justice" at the beginning of the note to s.3 of the Tribunals, Courts and Enforcement Act 2007, above).

Paragraphs (2)–(6)

3.289 These paragraphs replace reg.42 of the Social Security and Child Support (Decisions and Appeals) Regulations 1999, although they are not limited to medical advice or evidence. It is suggested that "serious harm" merely means harm that would be sufficiently serious to justify what would otherwise be a breach of the right to a fair hearing guaranteed by art.6 of the European Convention on Human Rights. In effect, the application of this rule requires a person's art.8 rights to be balanced against his or her art.6 rights. In *RM v St Andrew's Healthcare* [2010] UKUT 119 (AAC), a case concerned with the equivalent provision in the Tribunal Procedure (First-tier Tribunal) (Health, Education and Social Care Chamber) Rules 2008 (SI 2008/2699), very substantial weight was given to the art.6 right to a fair hearing in the light of *Secretary of State for the Home Department v AF (No.3)* [2009] UKHL 28; [2010] 2 A.C. 269, but both those cases were concerned with the deprivation of a person's liberty and it is suggested that, in social security cases where less is at stake, the need to avoid serious harm may more often justify non-disclosure, although it will still be very rare. Although "Courts have shown an aversion to permitting counsel to see or hear evidence which he is not at liberty to disclose to his client" (*Browning v Information Commissioner* [2014] EWCA Civ 1050), they will do so where necessary, particularly where it is necessary to protect children and vulnerable adults. However, the consent of the representative to the procedure is always necessary (*C v C (Court of Protection: Disclosure)* [2014] EWHC 131 (Fam);

[2014] 1 W.L.R. 2731). In *RM v St Andrew's Healthcare*, the judge also made the point that any order for non-disclosure ought to identify the information that is not to be disclosed, rather than, or as well as, specific documents. The disadvantage of referring only to specific documents is that the information may, unknown to the tribunal, also be contained in other documents that are not covered by the order. A similar balancing exercise was required under the former legislation even before the Human Rights Act 1998 came into effect (*CDLA/1347/1999*, disagreeing with the absolutist view expressed in *CSDLA/5/1995* that "no adverserial dispute should be decided against a party on the basis of evidence not disclosed to them unless that party has been given sufficient indication of the gist of that evidence to give them a proper opportunity to put forward their case"). Provided the risk of serious harm to the claimant is properly balanced against his or her right to a fair hearing, there is unlikely to be a breach of the European Convention on Human Rights, particularly if the claimant has a representative to whom disclosure has been made (see *R. (Roberts) v Parole Board* [2005] UKHL 45; [2005] 2 A.C. 738). This balancing exercise requires the nature of the feared "serious harm" to be clearly identified (*M v ABM University Health Board* [2018] UKUT 120 (AAC) at [87]).

Note the power in r.30(5)(c) to exclude a person from a hearing, and the power in r.33(2) not to provide a full statement of reasons, in order to give effect to a direction under para.(2). In *CDLA/1347/1999*, it was suggested that, if a tribunal was minded to reveal evidence that had been withheld on medical advice, it might be prudent to give the medical advisor the opportunity of justifying the advice before revealing the evidence. The Commissioner also agreed with a suggestion that, if reasons for a decision were being given, withheld evidence should be referred to in a supplementary statement of reasons given to the Secretary of State (and the claimant's representative if the evidence had been revealed to him or her) but not given to the claimant. That would have the effect that, in the event of an appeal, the Upper Tribunal would know how the evidence had been approached. See, now, *Davies v IC* [2019] UKUT 185 (AAC); [2019] 1 W.L.R. 6641; [2020] AACR 2) and the *Practice Direction: Closed Judgments* which is set out at the end of this Part of this volume.

In most cases concerning attendance allowance or disability living allowance, this rule will not give rise to great problems because evidence that a claimant is seriously ill, which is the sort of evidence that would normally be withheld, is evidence that is likely to assist the claimant rather than the reverse. It is in cases concerning disablement benefit, where causation is often in issue, that the problem arises most acutely. There, if a tribunal are satisifed that evidence should be withheld but would be likely to be contested by a claimant if he or she knew of it, it is suggested that they should take care to ensure that it is properly tested by, for example, obtaining a second opinion. If proceedings cannot properly be adversarial, they must be truly inquisitorial. Indeed, if there were contradictory evidence and the claimant would be likely to contest the withheld evidence, a tribunal might well be particularly slow to conclude that this rule should be applied and might choose either to disclose the evidence or else to disregard it. However, it is clear from *In re A (Forced Marriage: Special Advocates)* [2010] EWHC 2438 (Fam); [2012] Fam 102 that a case may sometimes properly be determined by a judge on the basis of information that has not been disclosed to a party and that the appointment of a special advocate in such a case is necessary only if there is something that a special advocate could do that it would not be appropriate for the judge to do.

In *Dorset Healthcare NHS Foundation Trust v MH* [2009] UKUT 4 (AAC), it was **3.290**
made clear that serious harm was not the only ground upon which disclosure of documents may be withheld. In that case, documents were withheld from a patient on the ground of confidentiality but it was not suggested that the tribunal should see the withheld documents. It is doubtful that a tribunal could properly have regard to evidence that had not been disclosed to a party in any circumstances other than those contemplated in this rule unless, perhaps, a legally qualified representative acting for the party was prepared to consent to it doing so despite not being able to obtain the informed consent of the party.

A challenge to the validity of r.13(2) to (8) of the Tribunal Procedure (First-Tier Tribunal) (Immigration and Asylum Chamber) Rules 2014 (SI 2014/ 2604), equivalent to r.14(2) to (6) of these Rules, was rejected in *R. (Immigration Law Practitioners Association) v Tribunal Procedure Committee* [2016] EWHC 218 (Admin) broadly on the basis that the provisions were not inherently unfair, even though it was difficult to see how they could properly be used in that context.

Evidence and submissions

3.291 **15.**—(1) Without restriction on the general powers in rule 5(1) and (2) (case management powers), the Tribunal may give directions as to—

(a) issues on which it requires evidence or submissions;
(b) the nature of the evidence or submissions it requires;
(c) whether the parties are permitted or required to provide expert evidence;
(d) any limit on the number of witnesses whose evidence a party may put forward, whether in relation to a particular issue or generally;
(e) the manner in which any evidence or submissions are to be provided, which may include a direction for them to be given—
 (i) orally at a hearing; or
 (ii) by written submissions or witness statement; and
(f) the time at which any evidence or submissions are to be provided.

(2) The Tribunal may—

(a) admit evidence whether or not—
 (i) the evidence would be admissible in a civil trial in the United Kingdom; or
 (ii) the evidence was available to a previous decision maker; or
(b) exclude evidence that would otherwise be admissible where—
 (i) the evidence was not provided within the time allowed by a direction or a practice direction;
 (ii) the evidence was otherwise provided in a manner that did not comply with a direction or a practice direction; or
 (iii) it would otherwise be unfair to admit the evidence.

(3) The Tribunal may consent to a witness giving, or require any witness to give, evidence on oath, and may administer an oath for that purpose.

DEFINITIONS

"decision maker"—see r.1(3).
"hearing"—*ibid.*
"party"—*ibid.*
"practice direction"—*ibid.*
"Tribunal"—*ibid.*

GENERAL NOTE

Paragraph (1)

3.292 Rule 6 makes the necessary procedural provision. Trenchant views expressed by the Upper Tribunal as to the unsuitability of an expert witness cannot have the binding effect of precluding the First-tier Tribunal from admitting evidence from that witness in another case. The First-tier Tribunal may take such views expressed by the Upper Tribunal into account and may regard them as persuasive but it must make up its own mind whether to admit the evidence in the case before it (*KF v SSD (WP)* [2019] UKUT 154 (AAC)).

Paragraph (2)

Paragraph (2)(a) makes explicit powers to admit evidence that were formerly implicit. Note that the Tribunal merely has a power to admit evidence that would be inadmissible in a civil trial and it cannot override any privilege of a witness not to give evidence (see the note to s.3(1) of the Tribunal, Courts and Enforcement Act 2007). Beyond that, the main consideration will simply be whether the evidence is relevant. **3.293**

Paragraph (2)(b) enables evidence to be excluded. If evidence is relevant, it is not inadmissible just because it is confidential to a third party, and so it can be excluded only under r.15(2)(b) (*NSP v Stoke-on-Trent CC (HB)* [2020] UKUT 311 (AAC) at [74] to [78]). This power, like all other powers under the Rules, must be exercised so as to give effect to the overriding objective in r.2. Evidence may be admitted in whole or in part and for some purposes but not others (*Pensions Regulator v Hermes Parcelnet Ltd* [2021] UKUT 20 (AAC) at [19], a case that was really concerned about the extent to which a tribunal may rely on findings made by another tribunal—see the note to s.3(1) of the Tribunals, Courts and Enforcement Act 2007). It will rarely be proportionate to exclude relevant evidence simply because it is provided late, unless some prejudice would be suffered by another party or the delay makes it more difficult for the tribunal to consider the evidence. See *CIB/4253/2004* and also *Nottinghamshire and City of Nottingham Fire Authority v Gladman Commercial Properties Ltd (Nottingham CC, Part 20 defendant)* [2011] EWHC 1918 (Ch); [2011] 1 W.L.R. 3235, in which Peter Smith J. said that:

> "[a] decision to exclude a late amendment or witness statement where there is no identifiable prejudice that cannot be addressed can lead to unfairness in the trial procedure and it is essential that the courts ensure that the overriding objective is followed and all parties have a full and fair hearing consistent with that approach."

He held that the person seeking to introduce the evidence does not have a heavy onus merely because it is late and that lateness is only one factor and all factors should be considered.

A claimant's transcript of his recording of a health care professional's consultation was held in *JB v SSWP (PIP)* [2019] UKUT 179 (AAC) to be admissible evidence for the purpose of resolving any dispute as to what took place in the consultation, even if the recording had been made covertly. The claimant had provided a copy of the recording as well as the transcript, so that the accuracy of the latter could be verified.

Paragraph (3)

This makes explicit that the Tribunal may consent to evidence being given on oath where it is the witness or a party who wishes that to be done. In practice, it is fairly rare for evidence to be given on oath in social security cases. **3.294**

By virtue of s.5 of the Oaths Act 1978, any person who objects to being sworn shall be permitted to make his or her solemn affirmation instead of taking an oath. In England, Wales and Northern Ireland, a Christian or Jew usually swears an oath with the New Testament, or, in the case of a Jew, the Old Testament, in his or her uplifted hand (*ibid.*, s.1(1)) but if the person desires to swear without holding the Bible but "with uplifted hand in the form and manner in which an oath is usually administered in Scotland", he or she must be permitted to do so (s.3). In the case of a person who is neither a Christian not a Jew, the oath shall be administered in any lawful manner (*ibid.*, s.1(3)), but such a person may prefer to affirm.

Summoning or citation of witnesses and orders to answer questions or produce documents

3.295 **16.**—(1) On the application of a party or on its own initiative, the Tribunal may—

(a) by summons (or, in Scotland, citation) require any person to attend as a witness at a hearing at the time and place specified in the summons or citation; or

(b) order any person to answer any questions or produce any documents in that person's possession or control which relate to any issue in the proceedings.

(2) A summons or citation under paragraph (1)(a) must—

(a) give the person required to attend 14 days' notice of the hearing or such shorter period as the Tribunal may direct; and

(b) where the person is not a party, make provision for the person's necessary expenses of attendance to be paid, and state who is to pay them.

(3) No person may be compelled to give any evidence or produce any document that the person could not be compelled to give or produce on a trial of an action in a court of law in the part of the United Kingdom where the proceedings are due to be determined.

(4) A summons, citation or order under this rule must—

(a) state that the person on whom the requirement is imposed may apply to the Tribunal to vary or set aside the summons, citation or order, if they have not had an opportunity to object to it; and

(b) state the consequences of failure to comply with the summons, citation or order.

DEFINITIONS

"document"—see r.1(3).
"hearing"—*ibid.*
"party"—*ibid.*
"Tribunal"—*ibid.*

GENERAL NOTE

3.296 This rule includes a power to order the production of documents without requiring attendance at a hearing. A failure to comply with a summons, citation or order under this rule is a contempt of court that may be referred to the Upper Tribunal under r.7(3). The Upper Tribunal has the power to impose a term of imprisonment not exceeding two years and an unlimited fine. In *MD v SSWP (Enforcement Reference)* [2010] UKUT 202 (AAC); [2011] AACR 5, a three-judge panel said that, before a reference is made, the First-tier Tribunal should be satisfied that all the procedural requirements had been met and, in particular, that any summons, citation or order was sent to the correct address and included an appropriate warning and, in the case of a summons or citation, was accompanied by an offer to pay expenses. It is unlikely to be appropriate to waive any such requirements, unless it was clear that there was no prejudice or injustice to the alleged contemnor in doing so.

The three-judge panel also made it clear that the First-tier Tribunal should consider whether attendance is really required before issuing a summons. In that case a doctor had been directed to provide a copy of his patient's medical notes. When he failed to do so, he was summoned to attend a hearing. The Upper Tribunal commented that it was unclear why he had been summoned under s.16(1)(a) instead of being formally ordered under r.16(1)(b) to produce the records and that "an order to compel a practising doctor to attend a hearing should not be made without a very compelling reason for doing so". Nonetheless, it has been made clear in *CB v Suffolk*

County Council (Enforcement Reference) [2010] UKUT 413 (AAC); [2011] AACR 22 that it is wrong to draw the impression from *MD v SSWP (Enforcement Reference)* "that a person on whom a witness summons has been served can simply sit back, await any reference to the Upper Tribunal and only then argue that the witness summons was not appropriately issued". An application may be made to the First-tier Tribunal for a summons to be set aside (see para.(4)(a)) and a refusal to set it aside may be challenged by way of an application to the Upper Tribunal for judicial review. If a summons is not successfully challenged, it must be obeyed. In that case, the Upper Tribunal fined a witness £500 for failing to comply with a summons issued by the Health, Education and Social Care Chamber of the First-tier Tribunal.

More controversially, when commenting on the First-tier Tribunal's failure to comply with the requirement under r.16(2)(b) to "make provision for the person's necessary expenses of attendance to be paid", it was said in *MD v SSWP (Enforcement Reference)* that "[a] witness such as a doctor who is ordered to attend a hearing may clearly incur very considerable expenses". That is plainly a material consideration when deciding whether it is proportionate to issue a summons but, in *CB v Suffolk CC (Enforcement Reference)*, it was held that the scheme of expenses for witnesses operated by the Tribunals Service, which was the same as that for jurors and covered travel expenses and loss of earnings up to a fixed limit, was sufficient for compliance with r.16(2)(b) and that it was not necessary to compensate for all financial loss.

In *Camden LBC v FG (SEN)* [2010] UKUT 249 (AAC), it was suggested that a summons should be signed by a judge "rather than being pp'd (as happened here) on his or her behalf", but the summons in that case was nonetheless held valid. The importance of conveying judicial documents to the parties in a form that shows not only that they have been made by a judge but also by which judge and when they were made has been emphasised in *JP v SSWP (ESA)* [2016] UKUT 48 (AAC).

This rule does not permit the First-tier Tribunal to issue a summons to a person **3.297**
outside the UK with a view to it being served outside the UK, but there are cases where it may be appropriate to issue a summons so that it may be served personally on a potential witness if he or she visits the UK (*Clavis Liberty Fund 1 LP v Revenue and Customs Commissioners* [2015] UKUT 72 (TCC); [2015] 1 W.L.R. 2949).

A Practice Direction dated 24 February 2015 in respect of Witness Summonses and Orders to Produce Documents has been issued by the Chamber President of the Tax Chamber of the First-tier Tribunal. Although not of direct application in the Social Entitlement Chamber, it contains useful guidance as to the desirability of making a prior request to a witness to attend before applying for a summons, the need for the First-tier Tribunal to be satisfied as to the relevance of the evidence sought, the information to be included in a summons of order, the desirability of a summoned witness providing a witness statement, the rights of parties to approach a summoned witness and the scope and amount of "necessary expenses for attendance" of a witness. It is published at: *https://www.judiciary.gov.uk/publications/first-tier-tribunal-tax-chamber-practice-direction-witness-summonses-and-orders-to-produce-documents/*. In *FN v SSWP (UC)* [2022] UKUT 77 (AAC), the claimant understood that she needed to obtain evidence from either her estranged husband, against whom she had obtained a non-molestation injunction, or through the Secretary of State. The husband declined to co-operate with the claimant through her social worker and, on data protection grounds, the Secretary of State declined to provide the evidence before making her decision although, after the claimant had appealed, she said that she would provide it if the First-tier Tribunal made an order to that effect. The First-tier Tribunal refused to make an order against the husband, even when the background of domestic violence was explained, on the ground that the claimant should first approach him through solicitors, but it eventually made one against the Secretary of State, which was ignored. Having allowed the claimant's appeal on other grounds, the Upper Tribunal judge acknowledged that making an order under r.16 should not be a first resort but commented that it seemed to him "that, speaking generally, in the context of domestic violence and a non-molestation injunction there may realistically be limitations on what a party can be expected to achieve on their own initiative, even with a degree of support, and that in such circumstances the FtT's power to make an order under r.16 of the FtT's Rules may be a useful tool for enabling DWP's data protection issues to be overcome and enabling justice to be done". He may have had in mind the cost of instructing solicitors.

Withdrawal

3.298 **17.**—(1) Subject to paragraph (2), a party may give notice of the withdrawal of its case, or any part of it—

(a) [1 . . .] by sending or delivering to the Tribunal a written notice of withdrawal; or

(b) orally at a hearing.

(2) In the circumstances described in paragraph (3), a notice of withdrawal will not take effect unless the Tribunal consents to the withdrawal.

(3) The circumstances referred to in paragraph (2) are where a party gives notice of withdrawal—

(a) [1 . . .] in a criminal injuries compensation case; [1 . . .]

(b) [1 in a social security and child support case where the tribunal has directed that notice of withdrawal shall take effect only with the Tribunal's consent; or

(c) at a hearing.]

[2 (4) An application for a withdrawn case to be reinstated may be made by—

(a) the party who withdrew the case;

(b) where an appeal in a social security and child support case has been withdrawn, a respondent.

(5) An application under paragraph (4) must be made in writing and be received by the Tribunal within 1 month after the earlier of—

(a) the date on which the applicant was sent notice under paragraph (6) that the withdrawal had taken effect; or

(b) if the applicant was present at the hearing when the case was withdrawn orally under paragraph (1)(b), the date of that hearing.]

(6) The Tribunal must notify each party in writing [1 that a withdrawal has taken effect] under this rule.

AMENDMENTS

1. Tribunal Procedure (Amendment) Rules 2013 (SI 2013/477) rr.22 and 24 (April 8, 2013).

2. Tribunal Procedure (Amendment) Rules 2015 (SI 2015/1510) rr.11 and 14 (August 21, 2015).

DEFINITIONS

"criminal injuries compensation case"—see r.1(3).
"hearing"—*ibid.*
"party"—*ibid.*
"respondent"—*ibid.*
"social security and child support case"—*ibid.*
"Tribunal"—*ibid.*

GENERAL NOTE

3.299 Paragraphs (1) and (6) replace reg.40 of the Social Security and Child Support (Decisions and Appeals) Regulations 1999. However, there are differences. First, this applies to the withdrawal of a respondent's case as well as to an appeal or reference.

Secondly, paras (2) and (3) have the effect that a case cannot be withdrawn without the consent of the Tribunal where a judge has directed that consent is necessary or at a hearing. Thirdly, para.(4)(a) allows a party who has withdrawn a case to apply for it to be reinstated, avoiding the difficulty that arose in *Rydqvist v Secretary of State for Work and Pensions* [2002] EWCA Civ 947; [2002] 1 W.L.R. 3343. Clearly any possible prejudice to the respondent will be highly relevant when the Tribunal is considering whether to permit the case to be reinstated. The existence of the one-month time limit for an application for reinstatement may suggest that an application should be granted if made within that period unless there is a clear reason for not doing so, such as the previous conduct of the party, obvious lack of merit in the case or prejudice to another party.

The right to withdraw part of a case does not enable a claimant to prevent the First-tier Tribunal from adjudicating on part of a decision of the Secretary of State that is favourable to them (*AE v SSWP (ESA)* [2014] UKUT 5 (AAC); [2014] AACR 23). This was because the claimant's "case" was that the unfavourable part of the Secretary of State's was wrong. In the context of that case, the Upper Tribunal held that the First-tier Tribunal was bound in law to consider the other part of the Secretary of State's decision but that would not usually be so due to the effect of s.12(8)(a) of the Social Security Act 1998. In any event, to the extent that support for part of a decision of the Secretary of State might be part of a claimant's case, withdrawal of that part of the case would be an invitation to adjudicate on the issue rather than the reverse. A challenge to part of a decision of the Secretary of State can clearly be withdrawn under this rule but s.12(8)(a) has the effect that the First-tier Tribunal would usually still have the power to consider that part of the decision if it thought it necessary to do so. Therefore, there may not be much point in formally withdrawing only part of a case in the social security context.

The requirement that a notice of withdrawal must be in writing unless given at a hearing may be waived and, indeed, a clerk may waive the requirement (see the note to r.4).

In *WM v SSWP (DLA)* [2015] UKUT 642 (AAC), the Upper Tribunal made it **3.300**
plain that, since the amendments to r.17(1)(a) and (3) in 2013, a withdrawal of a social security or child support case made otherwise than at a hearing is automatically effective unless the First-tier Tribunal has given a direction under para.(3)(b) and that, where a hearing is adjourned, a notice of withdrawal given during the period of the adjournment is not given "at a hearing" for the purposes of para.(3)(c). The judge also held that "rising to eat lunch . . . does not constitute a formal adjournment of the proceedings" and so does not interrupt the hearing for the purposes of this rule; it is only adjournment from one day to another that interrupts a hearing. In the circumstances of that case, the First-tier Tribunal had no power to decline to accept the withdrawal and so had no jurisdiction to make a decision on the appeal that was less favourable to the claimant than the Secretary of State's decision. The First-tier Tribunal has been discouraged by the Upper Tribunal in *PD v SSWP (PIP)* [2021] UKUT 172 (AAC) at [65] to [82] from preventing withdrawals of ordinary two-party social security appeals. It was pointed out that, generally, respondents have adequate powers of revision or supersession and so rarely need an appeal to be continued and that, in any event, a respondent may now apply for a withdrawn appeal to be reinstated under para.(4), if that is really necessary. The judge accepted that sometimes it might be desirable to prevent a claimant from withdrawing against his or her best interests and that there might be other cases where preventing a withdrawal could be justified. However,

> "[71] ... the considerable pressure on judicial resources and the resulting increase in the waiting times for other claimants, favours allowing appellants who make an informed decision to withdraw their appeals to do so with a minimum of formality.
>
> [72.] As far as giving a direction simply because an appeal has gone part-heard is concerned, why should a claimant who, having attended a hearing, realises for the first time that her appeal lacks merit, have obstacles placed in her way if she wishes to withdraw it?"

In that particular case, the First-tier Tribunal had not suggested that it was minded to make a decision less favourable than the one under appeal and it did not ultimately do so, with the result that the Upper Tribunal was unable to discern any legitimate reason for preventing the claimant from withdrawing her appeal.

3.301 The party who withdrew the case does not have an automatic right to reinstatement under para.4(a), even if the application is made within the month allowed under para.(5) without an extension of time being given under r.5(3)(a). Relevant considerations include the circumstances of the withdrawal, the reasons given for the application for reinstatement and the amount at stake (*JS v South London and Maudsley NHS Foundation Trust* [2019] UKUT 172 (AAC); [2020] AACR 1).

Paragraph (4)(b) now enables a respondent (who might be the decision-maker but might be a third party where, for instance, there has been a joint claim or the case concerns child support maintenance) to object to the withdrawal of a social security or child support appeal by applying for it to be reinstated. A respondent might wish to do so where he or she might be unfairly prejudiced by having to make a new application for supersession or lodge a new appeal or make a new decision, as the case might be, due to the limits on the backdating of supersession decisions and the time limits for appeals. Making such an application for supersession, lodging an appeal or making a decision would usually have been unnecessary while the other proceedings were effective. Thus, the decision-maker may wish to apply for a withdrawn appeal to be reinstated if it appears (e.g., in the light of evidence that emerged in the appeal proceedings before the appeal was withdrawn or in the light of an observation by the First-tier Tribunal) that the decision that was the subject of the appeal was too generous to the claimant but it cannot be revised or superseded with effect from a sufficiently early date. However, it is suggested that the conduct of all parties may be relevant and that an appeal should not necessarily be reinstated if the decision-maker was clearly at fault in making the original decision and the claimant was blameless: in other words, it is suggested that the First-tier Tribunal should consider whether reinstatement would be fair in all the circumstances of the case. It is also suggested that reinstatement will seldom be desirable where the decision-maker could achieve the same result by revising the original decision against which the claimant would then have a fresh right of appeal.

An appeal that has been reinstated cannot be withdrawn again (*FI v SSWP (CSM)* [2020] UKUT 173 (AAC)). However, if all parties were to agree that the appeal should be dismissed, it is perhaps unlikely that the First-tier Tribunal would decide otherwise.

Lead cases

3.302 **18.**—(1) This rule applies if—

(a) two or more cases have been started before the Tribunal;

(b) in each such case the Tribunal has not made a decision disposing of the proceedings; and

(c) the cases give rise to common or related issues of fact or law.

(2) The Tribunal may give a direction—

(a) specifying one or more cases falling under paragraph (1) as a lead case or lead cases; and

(b) staying (or, in Scotland, sisting) the other cases falling under paragraph (1) ("the related cases").

(3) When the Tribunal makes a decision in respect of the common or related issues—

(a) the Tribunal must send a copy of that decision to each party in each of the related cases; and

(b) subject to paragraph (4), that decision shall be binding on each of those parties.

(4) Within 1 month after the date on which the Tribunal sent a copy of the decision to a party under paragraph (3)(a), that party may apply in writing for a direction that the decision does not apply to, and is not binding on the parties to, a particular related case.

(5) The Tribunal must give directions in respect of cases which are stayed or sisted under paragraph (2)(b), providing for the disposal of or further directions in those cases.

(6) If the lead case or cases lapse or are withdrawn before the Tribunal makes a decision in respect of the common or related issues, the Tribunal must give directions as to—

(a) whether another case or other cases are to be specified as a lead case or lead cases; and

(b) whether any direction affecting the related cases should be set aside or amended.

Definitions

"dispose of proceedings"—see r.1(3).
"party"—*ibid.*
"Tribunal"—*ibid.*

General Note

The effect of this rule could be achieved through case management directions under r.5 but the rule provides an off-the-peg process for dealing with cases raising common or related issues of fact or law. It need not be used if a different process appears more appropriate. If it is used, one or more lead cases are selected and are then treated as binding on the other cases unless, within one month of being sent a copy of the decision in the lead cases, a party in another case objects. Presumably "decision" in para.(3) must include the reasons for the decision. Paragraph (4) appears to allow an objection either on the ground that the lead case is distinguishable and does not apply for that reason or on the ground that the party simply wishes to challenge the decision in the lead case and have his or her case dealt with separately, possibly with a view to appealing. The likelihood of objections on that latter ground may be a reason for not applying this rule in the first place but it would be unfair if parties who were separately represented could not elect to have their own cases decided individually. Note that only the Chamber President (or a person to whom the power is delegated by her) has the power to treat a social security case as a lead case (see para.10 of the practice statement set out above in the note to art.2 of the First-tier Tribunal and Upper Tribunal (Composition of Tribunal) Order 2008). 3.303

Where common issues of law arise in social security cases, s.26 of the Social Security Act 1998 may provide an alternative procedure.

[1 Confidentiality in social security and child support cases

19. — (1) Paragraph (4) applies to— 3.304

(a) proceedings under the Child Support Act 1991 in the circumstances described in paragraph (2), other than an appeal against a reduced benefit decision (as defined in section 46(10)(b) of the Child Support Act 1991, as that section had effect prior to the commencement of section 15(b) of the Child Maintenance and Other Payments Act 2008);

(b) proceedings where the parties to the appeal include former joint claimants who are no longer living together in the circumstances described in paragraph (3).

(2) The circumstances referred to in paragraph (1)(a) are that the absent parent, non-resident parent or person with care would like their address or the address of the child to be kept confidential and has given notice to that effect—

(a) in the notice of appeal or when notifying the Secretary of State or the Tribunal of any subsequent change of address; or

(b) within 14 days after an enquiry is made by the recipient of the notice of appeal or the notification referred to in sub-paragraph (a).

(3) The circumstances referred to in paragraph (1)(b) are that one of the former joint claimants would like their address to be kept confidential and has given notice to that effect—

(a) in the notice of appeal or when notifying the decision maker or the tribunal of any subsequent change of address; or

(b) within 14 days after an enquiry is made by the recipient of the notice of appeal or the notification referred to in sub-paragraph (a).

(4) Where this paragraph applies, the Secretary of State or other decision maker and the Tribunal must take appropriate steps to secure the confidentiality of the address and of any information which could reasonably be expected to enable a person to identify the address, to the extent that the address or that information is not already known to each other party.

(5) In this rule—

"absent parent", "non-resident parent" and "person with care" have the meanings set out in section 3 of the Child Support Act 1991;

"joint claimants" means the persons who made a joint claim for a jobseeker's allowance under the Jobseekers Act 1995, a tax credit under the Tax Credits Act 2002 or in relation to whom an award of universal credit is made under Part 1 of the Welfare Reform Act 2012.]

AMENDMENT

1. Tribunal Procedure (Amendment No.3) Rules 2014 (SI 2014/2128) rr.33 to 35 (October 20, 2014).

DEFINITIONS

"absent parent"—see para.(7).
"appeal"—see r.1(3).
"joint claimants"—see para.(7).
"non-resident parent"—*ibid.*
"parent with care"—*ibid.*
"party"—see r.1(3).
"Tribunal"—*ibid.*

GENERAL NOTE

3.305 This rule applies to child support cases and those social security cases in which it is most likely that former partners will both be parties. It is open to the First-tier Tribunal to exercise its case-management powers under r.5 so as to make provision for confidentiality in other types of case should that be appropriate. See also the powers exercisable under r.14.

3.306 **20.**—*Omitted.*

Expenses in social security and child support cases

21.—(1) This rule applies only to social security and child support cases. 3.307

(2) The Secretary of State may pay such travelling and other allowances (including compensation for loss of remunerative time) as the Secretary of State may determine to any person required to attend a hearing in proceedings under section 20 of the Child Support Act 1991, section 12 of the Social Security Act 1998 or paragraph 6 of Schedule 7 to the Child Support, Pensions and Social Security Act 2000.

DEFINITIONS

"hearing"—see r.1(3).
"social security and child support case"—*ibid.*

GENERAL NOTE

This rule reproduces the effect of para.4(1)(a) of Sch.1 to the Social Security Act 1998. (Paragraph 4(1)(b) is replaced by a new s.20A.) It suffers from the same defect as the old provision, which is that it does not apply to all social security cases in which claimants might be required to attend hearings, although in practice the Tribunals Service seems never to have refused to pay expenses to those not within the scope of the old provision (e.g. an injured person appealing under s.11 of the Social Security (Recovery of Benefits) Act 1997). 3.308

The rule is also unsatisfactory because it seems unlikely that para.10(4) of Sch.5 to the Tribunals, Courts and Enforcement Act 2007 envisages Rules that give the Secretary of State the power to determine what expenses are to be paid, although it is perhaps more appropriate that the power to determine the level of payment should lie with the Secretary of State rather than the Tribunal Procedure Committee.

PART 3

PROCEEDINGS BEFORE THE TRIBUNAL

CHAPTER 1

BEFORE THE HEARING

Cases in which the notice of appeal is to be sent to the Tribunal

22.—(1) [1 This rule applies to all cases except those to which— 3.309

(a) rule 23 (cases in which the notice of appeal is to be sent to the decision maker), or
(b) rule 26 (social security and child support cases started by reference or information in writing),

applies.]

(2) An appellant must start proceedings by sending or delivering a notice of appeal to the Tribunal so that it is received—

(a) in asylum support cases, within 3 days after the date on which the appellant received written notice of the decision being challenged;
(b) in criminal injuries compensation cases, within 90 days after the date of the decision being challenged;

[1 (c) in appeals under the Vaccine Damage Payments Act 1979, at any time;
(d) in other cases—

(i) if mandatory reconsideration applies, within 1 month after the date on which the appellant was sent notice of the result of mandatory reconsideration;

(ii) if mandatory reconsideration does not apply, within the time specified in Schedule 1 to these Rules [3 (time limits for providing notices of appeal in social security and child support cases where mandatory reconsideration does not apply)].

(3) The notice of appeal must be in English or Welsh, must be signed by the appellant and must state—

(a) the name and address of the appellant;

(b) the name and address of the appellant's representative (if any);

(c) an address where documents for the appellant may be sent or delivered;

(d) the name and address of any respondent [1 other than the decision maker];

(e) [1 . . .]; and

(f) the grounds on which the appellant relies.

(4) The appellant must provide with the notice of appeal—

(a) [1 a copy of—

(i) the notice of the result of mandatory reconsideration, in any social security and child support case to which mandatory reconsideration applies;

(ii) the decision being challenged, in any other case;]

(b) any statement of reasons for that decision that the appellant has [1 . . .; and]

(c) any documents in support of the appellant's case which have not been supplied to the respondent; [1 . . .]

(d) [1 . . .].

(5) In asylum support cases the notice of appeal must also—

(a) state whether the appellant will require an interpreter at any hearing, and if so for which language or dialect; and

(b) state whether the appellant intends to attend or be represented at any hearing.

(6) If the appellant provides the notice of appeal to the Tribunal later than the time required by paragraph (2) or by an extension of time allowed under rule 5(3)(a) [2 . . .] (power to extend time)—

(a) the notice of appeal must include a request for an extension of time and the reason why the notice of appeal was not provided in time; and

(b) [1 subject to paragraph (8)] unless the Tribunal extends time for the notice of appeal under rule 5(3)(a) [2 . . .] (power to extend time) the Tribunal must not admit the notice of appeal.

(7) The Tribunal must send a copy of the notice of appeal and any accompanying documents to each other party—

(a) in asylum support cases, on the day that the Tribunal receives the notice of appeal, or (if that is not reasonably practicable) as soon as reasonably practicable on the following day;

(b) in [1 all other] cases, as soon as reasonably practicable after the Tribunal receives the notice of appeal.

[3 (7A) [4 His Majesty's] Revenue and Customs must, upon receipt of the notice of appeal from the Tribunal under the Childcare Payments Act 2014, inform the Tribunal whether there are any affected parties within the meaning of section 61(5) of that Act other than the appellant and, if so, provide their names and addresses.]

[1 (8) Where an appeal in a social security and child support case is not made within the time specified in paragraph (2)—

(a) it will be treated as having been made in time, unless the Tribunal directs otherwise, if it is made within not more than 12 months of the time specified and neither the decision maker nor any other respondent objects;

(b) the time for bringing the appeal may not be extended under rule 5(3)(a) by more than 12 months.

[3 (9) For the purposes of this rule, mandatory reconsideration applies where—

(a) the notice of the decision being challenged includes a statement to the effect that there is a right of appeal in relation to the decision only if the decision-maker has considered an application for the revision, reversal, review or reconsideration (as the case may be) of the decision being challenged; or

(b) the appeal is brought against a decision made by [4 His Majesty's] Revenue and Customs.]]

AMENDMENTS

1. Tribunal Procedure (Amendment) Rules 2013 (SI 2013/477) rr.22 and 25 (April 8, 2013).

2. Tribunal Procedure (Amendment) Rules 2014 (SI 2014/514) rr.21 and 22 (April 6, 2014).

3. Tribunal Procedure (Amendment) Rules 2015 (SI 2015/1510) rr.11 and 15 (August 21, 2015).

4. Tribunal Procedure (Amendment) Rules 2023 (SI 2023/327) r.2 (April 6, 2023).

DEFINITIONS

"appellant"–see r.1(3).
"asylum support case"–*ibid.*
"criminal injuries compensation case–*ibid.*
"decision maker"–*ibid.*
"document"–*ibid.*
"hearing"–*ibid.*
"mandatory reconsideration"–see para.(9).
"party"–see r.1(3).
"respondent"–*ibid.*
"social security and child support case"–*ibid.*
"Tribunal"–*ibid.*

GENERAL NOTE

Paragraphs (1) and (2)

Until April 8, 2013, notice of appeal in social security cases was always sent to the decision-maker under r.23. Now, all decisions except those made by local authorities in respect of housing benefit (or the abolished council tax benefit) inform claimants that an appeal should be sent to the First-tier Tribunal. This has been the case in relation to all decisions made by the Secretary of State since October 28, 2013 and in relation to decisions made by HMRC since April 6, 2014. **3.310**

Paragraphs (3) and (4)

3.311 It is now possible to submit an appeal online in most social security cases, although not in vaccine damage payment cases, child support cases or against decisions made by HMRC (see *https://www.gov.uk/appeal-benefit-decision/submit-appeal*). When doing so, the requirement to send the mandatory reconsideration notice so as to comply with r.22(4)(a)(i) is waived but appellants need to provide a reference number from it instead.

There are also standard paper appeal forms produced by His Majesty's Courts and Tribunals Service: SSCS1 is the appropriate form for appeals against most decisions within the scope of this work but there are separate forms for appeals against decisions under the Social Security (Recovery of Benefits) Act 1997 (SSCS3), decisions of HMRC (SSCS5), decisions of the Scheme Administrator for the Diffuse Mesothelioma Payment Scheme (SSCS6) and decisions relating to vaccine damage payments (SSCS7). There are Welsh versions of all the forms. As at August 2023, the forms may all be found at *https://www.gov.uk/government/collections/social-security-and-child-support-forms*. Clicking on SSCS1 produces a link to the online forms as well.

It is not legally necessary to complete one of these forms, provided that the relevant information required by para.(3) is given with the notice of appeal. However, completing the form ensures that appellants have provided all the correct information and, indeed, also the information mentioned in para.(5) that is not strictly required in social security and child support cases. An extra copy of a mandatory reconsideration decision is issued to claimants and others so that they can retain one copy while complying with para.(4)(a)(i). Sending that document is likely to be particularly important because it will enable the First-tier Tribunal to identify the relevant office to which the decision maker's copy of the notice of appeal should be sent under para.(7). Claimants are not expected to identify that office in the notice itself (see para.(3)(d)).

The precise address to which paper appeals should be sent depends on where the appellant lives. For England and Wales, they should be sent to HMCTS Benefit Appeals, PO Box 12626, Harlow CM20 9QF and, for Scotland, they should be sent to HMCTS SSCS Appeals Centre, PO Box 13150, Harlow CM20 9TT. Clerks at those centres may enforce the requirements of paras (3) and (4) or may waive them (see the note to r.4). It is intended that a copy of the notice of appeal and any accompanying documents should be sent by the First-tier Tribunal to the decision maker and any other respondent within five days at the most. The decision maker will then be expected to provide a response under r.24.

3.312 A typed name can amount to a signature when it has been adopted by the person concerned through his or her signing another document or taking some other active step in an appeal (*R(DLA) 2/98*). So can a name on an email (*Hudson v Hathaway* [2022] EWCA Civ 1648; [2023] 2 WLR 1227) and, of course, a name on an electronic form. In *CIB/460/2003*, the claimant's mother, who had not been appointed to act on behalf of the claimant, signed the appeal. No-one had objected and the claimant himself had signed a form issued by the clerk, asking him, among other things, whether he wanted to withdraw his appeal. He had said "no". The Commissioner rejected a submission made on behalf of the Secretary of State to the effect that the appeal was not valid.

Under r.11(5), a notice of appeal may be signed by a representative provided that written notice of the appointment of the representative is given to the First-tier Tribunal under r.11(2) or (3). In *CO v Havering LBC (HB)* [2015] UKUT 28 (AAC), a notice of appeal was held valid even though it was signed by the claimant's solicitor rather than by the claimant personally and the solicitor had not provided the claimant's written authority to act as her representative so that r.11(5) did not apply. (A copy of the notice countersigned by the claimant was received only after the absolute time limit for appealing had expired.) The judge left open the question whether a notice of appeal signed by a representative who neither had written authority nor was not under a professional obligation to act only on instructions should be treated as having been signed by the appellant. However, even if the signature of such a representative does not amount to the appellant's signature, it is arguable in the light of *R(DLA) 2/98* and

CIB/460/2003 that the requirement that the notice be signed personally can be waived under r.7 if the real appellant has subsequently adopted the appeal.

In *CS v SSWP (DLA)* [2011] UKUT 509 (AAC), it was accepted that the First-tier Tribunal had been right to treat an appeal against an entitlement decision as being also an appeal against a related recoverability decision. It is therefore clear that the details provided for the purpose of complying with para.(6)(d) are not to be regarded as conclusive as to the decision being challenged. See also *SSD v CM (WP)* [2017] UKUT 8 (AAC); [2017] AACR 27.

Paragraph (6)

Giving the reason for delay assists the decision-maker in deciding whether or not to object to a late appeal being treated as made in time under para.(8)(a). It seems unlikely that a failure to comply with this paragraph would be held to render a late appeal invalid; rather it merely increases the likelihood of the decision-maker objecting to the appeal being admitted. **3.313**

Paragraph (8)(b) makes it clear that the time for appealing cannot be extended under r.5(3)(a) by more than 12 months.

Paragraph (8)

Subparagraph (a) reverses the effect of *R(TC) 1/05*, in which it was held that an appeal tribunal did not have jurisdiction to hear a late appeal where express consideration had not been given to extending the time for appealing. **3.314**

Subparagraph (b) imposes an absolute time limit but it has been held that an absolute time limit must be read as being subject to the First-tier Tribunal's discretion so far as that is necessary to avoid a breach of art.6 of the European Convention on Human Rights. Thus, in a really exceptional case, where the appellant has done everything possible to act within time, an appeal lodged after this absolute time limit could be admitted (*Pomiechowski v District Court of Legnica, Poland* [2012] UKSC 20; [2012] 1 W.L.R. 1604). The strictness of this test was emphasised in *Adesina v Nursing and Midwifery Council* [2013] EWCA Civ 818; [2013] 1 W.L.R. 3156, cited in *KK v Sheffield CC (CTB)* [2015] UKUT 0367 (AAC). Fault on the part of a representative, including a solicitor, is not necessarily to be attributed to a party who personally has done all he or she could (*Public Prosecutors Office, Athens v O'Connor* [2022] UKSC 4; [2022] 1 W.L.R. 903).

Having such an absolute time limit prohibiting the bringing of appeals more than a year late is not in itself incompatible with the European Convention on Human Rights (*Denson v Secretary of State for Work and Pensions* [2004] EWCA Civ 462 (reported as *R(CS) 4/04*). Nonetheless, it can work injustice, particularly in a case where an unrepresented claimant has been challenging the wrong decision and nobody tells him or her until it is too late which decision it is that must be challenged if he or she is to succeed in obtaining the benefit sought.

In *RS v SSD* [2008] UKUT 1 (AAC); R(AF) 1/09, it was held that the fact that a Pensions Appeal Tribunal had erroneously admitted an appeal that ought not to have been admitted because it was too late did not oblige the Tribunal to determine the appeal. Instead, it was obliged to decline jurisdiction which, under these Rules, would have required it to strike the appeal out under r.8(2). That general approach was not adopted by the majority of the three-judge panel in *LS v Lambeth LBC (HB)* [2010] UKUT 461 (AAC); [2011] AACR 27, but that decision was decided partly under old procedural rules and the procedural history of the case was unusual. Under these Rules, an extension of time is regarded as a case-management direction under r.5(3)(a), so that, even if the simple approach taken in *RS* is not appropriate, an extension that ought not to have been granted should presumably be set aside under r.6(5).

In *KD v SSWP* [2021] UKUT 329 (AAC) the Appellant's notice of appeal was lodged about 22 months after the one month time limit for making an appeal. The First-tier Tribunal decided it could not admit the late appeal and struck it out without requesting a response from the DWP. The Upper Tribunal found that the

First-tier Tribunal had erred in law because a) it failed to provide adequate reasons as to for the conclusion that the case was not exceptional b) failed to comply with rule 8(4) of the Tribunal Procedural Rules because the Appellant was not put properly on notice as to the basis of the proposed striking out, amounting to a breach of the principles of natural justice and c) erred in law by failing to consider whether it could properly admit appeals in respect of four earlier decisions on the Appellant's claim to disablement benefit (and especially the level of the disablement assessment arrived at in each decision). The jurisdictional decision on whether appeals can be treated as being in time is one that only the First-tier Tribunal can take.

In *MZ v SSWP* (UC) [2022] UKUT 292 (AAC) the First-tier Tribunal had also struck out the appeal on the basis that it was outside the 13 month time limit. The appellant was waiting on Department of Work and Pensions to award Universal Credit to the appellant in light of her settled status in the UK and requested updates on multiple occasions within the 13-month time limit, but DWP had seemingly failed to action this in a timely manner. This raised questions as to whether the actions (or omissions) of the Department and/or the Job Centre materially contribute to the reasons why the appeal was lodged late. This might have a bearing on whether the circumstances were truly exceptional. The Upper Tribunal found that the First-tier Tribunal had erred in law because it failed to exercise its discretion in considering whether it was appropriate to hold an oral hearing of the application for permission to appeal in which to assess whether the circumstances are exceptional.

A very detailed analysis of these and other cases is to be found in *GJ v SSWP* (PIP) [2022] UKUT 340 (AAC). The appeal was clearly late, but the history was complicated. The claimant had been refused a Personal Independence Payment in 2017. That decision was not changed following a Department of Work and Pensions "Legal Entitlements and Administrative Practices (LEAP) review. The claimant's appeal to the First-tier Tribunal was struck out as being outside the 13 month time limit. The Upper Tribunal reviewed the case law and also referred to the decision in *Rakoczy v General Medical Council* [2022] EWHC 890 (Admin), which recognised that refusing a late appeal must not impair the very essence of the right to appeal in order to protect human rights. However, the case also recognised that "a case would need to be very exceptional indeed in order to benefit from the *Adesina* principle". The Upper Tribunal concluded that had it had referenced *Rakoczy* when deciding *MZ v SSWP (UC)* it might have put stronger emphasis on the "truly exceptional" nature of what was required. The Upper Tribunal unsurprisingly, concluded that the scope for extending the absolute time limit so as to avoid a breach of the European Convention on Human Rights "...is very narrowly drawn indee...*Adesina* is about the right of access to the justice system and can only apply if the effect of a time limit is to restrict or reduce the access left to the individual in such a way or to such an extent that the very essence of the right is impaired".

Paragraph (9)

3.315 From October 28, 2013, the Secretary of State has been empowered to issue a notice within the scope of para.(9) in all cases where he is the decision-maker and did not already have that power, so that the would-be appellant is bound to apply for a revision or equivalent reconsideration before exercising a right of appeal (see regs 3ZA, 3B and 9ZB of the Social Security and Child Support (Decisions and Appeals) Regulations 1999, reg.11A of the Vaccine Damage Payments Regulations 1979, reg.4B of the Mesothelioma Lump Sum Payments (Claims and Reconsiderations) Regulations 2008 and new provisions in child support legislation beyond the scope of this work, as well as reg.7 of the Universal Credit, Personal Independence Payment, Jobseeker's Allowance and Employment and Support Allowance (Decisions and Appeals) Regulations 2013 which had been in force since earlier in 2013). There is no provision for mandatory reconsideration in relation to the recovery of NHS charges, although appeals in those cases are among those now sent to the First-tier Tribunal. In contrast, s.12(3D) of the Social Security Act 1998 (in relation to child benefit and guardian's allowance), s.38(1A) to (1C) of the Tax Credits Act 2002 and s.56(2) of the Childcare Payments Act 2014 ensure that there is *always* a requirement to seek a revision or review before appealing against a decision made by HMRC (except decisions under the Child Trust Funds Act 2004, to which r.23 applies).

In *PP v SSWP (UC)* [2020] UKUT 109 (AAC), the claimant submitted an appeal by email to the regional office of the First-tier Tribunal (with which he had been in contact in relation to another matter) indicating that he wished to appeal against the Secretary of State's refusal of a claim for universal credit. A judge directed the Secretary of State to produce copies of any decision to refuse the claimant universal credit and any associated mandatory reconsideration notice. The Secretary of State merely sent a copy of an electronic notification to the claimant's universal credit Journal, stating "Your claim has been closed" and "Reason for closure: You didn't book your appointment". The judge directed the claimant to produce a copy of any universal credit mandatory reconsideration notice. The Appellant said that the DWP would not provide him with one but the judge nonetheless, without making further enquiries, refused to admit the appeal on the ground that the claimant had not provided a notice of the result of mandatory reconsideration as required by r.22(4)(a)(i). Before the Upper Tribunal, the Secretary of State conceded that there was no power to refuse a claim for universal credit simply on the ground that the claimant had failed to make an appointment for an interview and that the closure of the claim was technically an appealable decision that the claimant was not entitled to universal credit because he did not satisfy the financial conditions (albeit that one reason for making that finding had been the claimant's failure to book an appointment to discuss his income from self-employment). Moreover, because the only notice of the decision had not included a statement in the terms required by reg.7(1)(b) of the 2013 Regulations and para.(9)(a) of this rule, the claimant's right of appeal had not been subject to a condition under reg.7(2) that he first apply for revision and so mandatory reconsideration did not apply for the purposes of this rule and the claimant had not been required to provide a notice of the result of mandatory reconsideration. Accordingly, the Upper Tribunal allowed the claimant's appeal, referring as regards the analysis of the nature of the Secretary of State's decision to *R(H) 3/05* at [78] to [80], and directed the First-tier Tribunal to admit the appeal and determine whether the claimant did qualify for universal credit.

Paragraph 9(b) 3.316

There is an exception to the requirement for mandatory reconsideration in some appeals against a decision made by His Majesty's Revenues and Customs. This is because of the Court of Appeal decision in *Commissioners for HMRC v Arrbab* [2024] EWCA Civ 16. The Court of Appeal found that s.38(1A) of the Tax Credits Act 2002 was ultra vires the enabling legislation and should be treated as struck out. This means that, whilst a claimant can still ask for a review of a decision, seeking a review is no longer a precondition of the right of appeal. It is important to be clear that this case only concerns Tax Credit appeals and not all HMRC appeals. Appeals about Child Benefit and Guardians Allowance are governed by S12 (3D) of the Social Security Act 1998 and Regs 3, 3ZA and 4 of the Social Security and Child Support (Decisions and Appeals) Regulations 1999 and are therefore not affected. His Majesty's Revenue and Customs has stated that it will not be appealing the Court of Appeal's decision. There is an obvious inconsistency between r.22(9)(b) and the Court of Appeal's decision, in that mandatory reconsideration does not apply to an appeal against a Tax Credit decision by HMRC. It appears (para.78) that the Court of Appeal considered that r.22(9)(b) could survive its decision but with respect to the Court of Appeal, in its present form, a Tax Credit decision would fall within r.22(9)(b) and so the time limit would be that within r.22(d)(i) and the appellant would be required to send the notice of the result of the MR in accordance with r.22(4). Therefore, until the Tribunal Rules are changed, it might be that the First Tier Tribunal will have to disapply/

waive r.22(9)(b) in light of the decision, for the rules and the Act as interpreted by the Court of Appeal to be workable.

The decision in *Commissioners for HMRC v Arrbab* also has implications for late appeals against Tax Credit decisions. The main issue is about appeals made outside the 'absolute' 13-month time limit, as those made within that period are, in the light of *Arrbab*, not rendered problematic merely by not having been preceded by an HMRC review. It is suggested that a late Tax Credit appeal should be admitted on the grounds that the time limit has not actually started to run, as long as, on the facts, the claimant has been materially disadvantaged (i.e by being misled about their rights) in making an on-time appeal. Whether a particular claimant has been materially misled must of course depend on the facts. But in the Tax Credits context, where a claimant seeking to challenge a decision was refused a mandatory reconsideration and told that they did not have the right of appeal against that, it is suggested that they will have been materially misled, will have a right of appeal and that the appeal should be regarded as being made on time on the basis that the time limit has not started to run.

It is suggested that there could also be a ECHR context here too. The ECHR has authority to the effect that appeal time limits as limitations on the art.6 right of access to a Tribunal need to be sufficiently clear not to render access to the Tribunal excessively difficult or impossible (see cases such as *De Geouffre de la Pradelle v France*, Application No. 12964/87 at para.34 and *Bellet v France* Application No. 23805/94 at para.38). Even if it was considered (contrary to the argument above) that the time limits in r.22 did start to run in such cases, so that the appeal is made outside the 'absolute' time limit, it is arguable that an Article 6 ECHR compliant approach requires the consideration of whether or not there are very exceptional reasons for such lateness, such that the appeal should still be admitted. There is authority (for example *Adesina)* that in such a case, where the claimant has done everything they could to appeal in time, it will be necessary to admit the appeal in order to protect the Article 6 right to a fair hearing. Arguably, in the light of *Arrbab*, a claimant refused an MR and told that they could not appeal could at least potentially constitute such a case.

The sole function of parts of r.22 is to set the primary time-limit for bringing an appeal. So another (and perhaps more straight forward) approach to the issue is that because a Tax Credit appeal will only be brought outside the primary time-limit if (a) a notice of a mandatory reconsideration has been sent and (b) the appeal is started more than one month after it was sent, an appeal against a tax credit decision in relation to which HMRC has never sent a notice of mandatory reconsideration will always be in-time. This approach appears to be consistent with emphasised words in para.78 of *Arrbab*.

Cases in which the notice of appeal is to be sent to the decision maker

3.317 **23.**—(1) [3 This rule applies to [5 appeals under paragraph 6 of Schedule 7 to the Child Support, Pensions and Social Security Act 2000 (housing benefit and council tax benefit: revisions and appeals) or under section 22 of the Child Trust Funds Act 2004].]

(2) An appellant must start proceedings by sending or delivering a notice of appeal to the decision maker so that it is received [5 [6 ...]—

- (a) in a housing benefit or council tax benefit case [6, no later than the latest of]—
  - (i) one month after the date on which notice of the decision being challenged was sent to the appellant;
  - (ii) if a written statement of reasons for the decision was requested within that month, 14 days after the later of—
    - (aa) the end of that month; or

(ab) the date on which the written statement of reasons was provided; or

(iii) if the appellant made an application for revision of the decision under regulation 4(1)(a) of the Housing Benefit and Council Tax Benefit (Decisions and Appeals) Regulations 2001 and that application was unsuccessful, one month after the date on which notice that the decision would not be revised was sent to the appellant;

(b) in an appeal under section 22 of the Child Trust Funds Act 2004, the period of 30 days specified in section 23(1) of that Act].]

(3) If the appellant provides the notice of appeal to the decision maker later than the time required by [5 paragraph (2)(a)] the notice of appeal must include the reason why the notice of appeal was not provided in time.

(4) Subject to paragraph (5), where an appeal is not made within the time specified in [5 paragraph (2)], it will be treated as having been made in time [2 if neither the decision maker nor any other respondent objects].

(5) No appeal may be made more than 12 months after the time specified in [5 paragraph (2)].

(6) The notice of appeal must be in English or Welsh, must be signed by the appellant and must state—

(a) the name and address of the appellant;

(b) the name and address of the appellant's representative (if any);

(c) an address where documents for the appellant may be sent or delivered;

(d) details of the decision being appealed; and

(e) the grounds on which the appellant relies.

(7) The decision maker must refer the case to the Tribunal immediately if—

(a) the appeal has been made after the time specified in [5 paragraph (2)] and the decision maker [2 or any other respondent] objects to it being treated as having been made in time; or

(b) the decision maker considers that the appeal has been made more than 12 months after the time specified in [5 paragraph (2)].

[1 (8) Notwithstanding rule 5(3)(a) [4 [5 . . .]] (case management powers) and rule 7(2) (failure to comply with rules etc.), the Tribunal must not extend the time limit in paragraph (5).]

Amendments

1. Tribunal Procedure (Amendment No.2) Rules 2009 (SI 2009/1975) rr.2 and 3 (September 1, 2009).

2. Tribunal Procedure (Amendment) Rules 2012 (SI 2012/500) r.4 (April 6, 2012).

3. Tribunal Procedure (Amendment) Rules 2013 (SI 2013/477) rr.22 and 26 (April 8, 2013).

4. Tribunal Procedure (Amendment No. 4) Rules 2013 (SI 2013/2067) rr.22 and 26 (November 1, 2013).

5. Tribunal Procedure (Amendment) Rules 2015 (SI 2015/1510) rr.11 and 16 (August 21, 2015).

6. Tribunal Procedure (Amendment No.2) Rules 2018 (SI 2018/1053) r.2 (October 13, 2018).

DEFINITIONS

"appeal"—see r.1(3).
"appellant"—*ibid.*
"decision maker"—*ibid.*
"social security and child support case"—*ibid.*
"Tribunal"—*ibid.*

GENERAL NOTE

Paragraph (1)

3.318 Until April 8, 2013, this rule applied to all social security and child support cases except those within the scope of r.26. However, for most practical purposes it now applies only to appeals against decisions by local authorities concerning housing benefit (or the abolished council tax benefit). Technically, it also applies to appeals against decisions under the Child Trust Funds Act 2004 (see Vol.IV) (which are now probably only a theoretical possibility) and to very late appeals against decisions made by HMRC before April 6, 2014. Rule 18 of the Rules that made the 2015 amendments provides that the amendments to r.23 of, and the substitution of Sch.1 to, the 2008 Rules "have no effect in relation to any appeal against a decision made before 6th April 2014 where the decision maker was Her Majesty's Revenue and Customs". This saving makes explicit what would probably be the position anyway: any such appeal must be referred to the First-tier Tribunal which will refuse to admit it on the ground that it is irremediably out of time (unless to do so would be a breach of the European Convention on Human Rights—see the annotation to r.22(8)).

Paragraphs (2)–(8)

3.319 See the annotations to r.22(3)–(8) and para.5 of Sch.1, which make similar provision albeit not in the same order.

Responses and replies

3.320 **24.**—[1 (1) When a decision maker receives a copy of a notice of appeal from the Tribunal under rule 22(7), the decision maker must send or deliver a response to the Tribunal—

(a) in asylum support cases, so that it is received within 3 days after the date on which the Tribunal received the notice of appeal;
(b) in—
 (i) criminal injuries compensation cases, or
 (ii) appeals under the Child Support Act 1991,
 within 42 days after the date on which the decision maker received the copy of the notice of appeal; and
(c) in other cases, within 28 days after the date on which the decision maker received the copy of the notice of appeal.

(1A) Where a decision maker receives a notice of appeal from an appellant under rule 23(2), the decision maker must send or deliver a response to the Tribunal so that it is received as soon as reasonably practicable after the decision maker received the notice of appeal.]

(2) The response must state—

(a) the name and address of the decision maker;
(b) the name and address of the decision maker's representative (if any);
(c) an address where documents for the decision maker may be sent or delivered;

(d) the names and addresses of any other respondents and their representatives (if any);

(e) whether the decision maker opposes the appellant's case and, if so, any grounds for such opposition which are not set out in any documents which are before the Tribunal; and

(f) any further information or documents required by a practice direction or direction.

(3) The response may include a submission as to whether it would be appropriate for the case to be disposed of without a hearing.

(4) The decision maker must provide with the response—

(a) a copy of any written record of the decision under challenge, and any statement of reasons for that decision, if they were not sent with the notice of appeal;

(b) copies of all documents relevant to the case in the decision maker's possession, unless a practice direction or direction states otherwise; and

(c) in cases to which rule 23 (cases in which the notice of appeal is to be sent to the decision maker) applies, a copy of the notice of appeal, any documents provided by the appellant with the notice of appeal and (if they have not otherwise been provided to the Tribunal) the name and address of the appellant's representative (if any).

(5) The decision maker must provide a copy of the response and any accompanying documents to each other party at the same time as it provides the response to the Tribunal.

(6) The appellant and any other respondent may make a written submission and supply further documents in reply to the decision maker's response.

(7) Any submission or further documents under paragraph (6) must be provided to the Tribunal within 1 month after the date on which the decision maker sent the response to the party providing the reply, and the Tribunal must send a copy to each other party.

AMENDMENT

1. Tribunal Procedure (Amendment) Rules 2013 rr.22 and 27(a), as amended by the Tribunal Procedure (Amendment No.3) Rules 2014 (SI 2014/2128) rr.36–37 (October 1, 2014).

DEFINITIONS

"appeal"—see r.1(3).
"appellant"—*ibid.*
"asylum support case"—*ibid.*
"criminal injuries compensation case"—*ibid.*
"decision maker"—*ibid.*
"document"—*ibid.*
"hearing"—*ibid.*
"party"—*ibid.*
"practice direction"—*ibid.*
"respondent"—*ibid.*
"Tribunal"—*ibid.*

GENERAL NOTE

Paragraphs (1)–(5)

These paragraphs make express provision for the decision-maker's response to an appeal, as to which the Social Security and Child Support (Decisions and 3.321

Appeals) Regulations 1999 were curiously silent. Originally, they made no provision for any precise time limit in social security and child support cases. In part this was because some time could be taken investigating points raised in the grounds of appeal and deciding whether to revise the decision being challenged under reg.3(4A) of the 1999 Regulations, which would cause the appeal to lapse under s.9(6) of the Social Security Act 1998. With the introduction of "mandatory reconsideration", requiring consideration to be given to revision *before* an appeal is made, that justification for the lack of a time limit evaporated. The new para.(1) imposes time limits within which responses to appeals must be provided by the Secretary of State or HMRC in social security and child support cases where there has been direct lodgement or mandatory reconsideration. These are six weeks from the date that the Secretary of State received a copy of the notice of appeal from the First-tier Tribunal in child support cases and four weeks in other cases. (There were already time limits in asylum support and criminal injuries compensation cases.) Clerks have been given the power to waive the time limit or to strike out a respondent's case for failing to comply with it (see the annotation to r.4 above).

Paragraph (1A) applies to housing benefit cases and the few remaining other cases where the appeal was sent directly to the decision-maker and mandatory reconsideration did not apply. It does not impose a time limit, maintaining the status quo and giving the decision-maker a substantial opportunity to consider whether to revise the decision being challenged before submitting a response.

In *IS v Craven DC (HB)* [2013] UKUT 9 (AAC), the Upper Tribunal said that a response to an appeal:

> "needs to (i) set out accurately what the outcome decision under appeal is, (ii) summarise the relevant facts (with page references to pages in the appeal bundle), (iii) set out or incorporate the appellant's grounds of appeal, (iv) set out the relevant law (both statutory and caselaw), (v) explain why on the facts and the law the decision under appeal was made and is justified, and is not wrong for any of the reasons suggested in the appeal, and (vi) have attached to it all relevant evidence in the local authority's possession."

A response is directed to both the appellant and the First-tier Tribunal. In *LH v SSWP (PIP)* [2018] UKUT 57 (AAC), there was some consideration of the extent to which a response need "set out the relevant law" and, although the Upper Tribunal was critical of a response that did not set out the descriptors in a personal independence payment case, it did not go as far as to say that the response was unlawful and allowed the claimant's appeal on another ground. However, the response is often the only information given to the claimant as to the legal issues in the case (although some information may have been incorporated into notices of decisions and so can be incorporated into a response by reference) and, in *MT v SSWP (IS)* [2010] UKUT 382 (AAC), it was held that there was an error of law where, as the Secretary of State's representative conceded:

> "the appeals process may well have run its entire course without the claimant ever [being] told that there was a regulation that governs the diminishment of capital for overpayment purposes".

It was recorded in *TM v SSWP (PIP)* [2019] UKUT 204 (AAC) that the Secretary of State had produced a new template for responses to appeals in personal independence payment cases, which included references to the law and listed the descriptors and thus appeared to meet the concerns raised in *LH*, but in *TM* itself the response had been even less satisfactory than in *LH* because the website addresses intended to enable the appellant to find the relevant legislation were incorrect.

As in *IS*, it was suggested in *SSWP v G (VDP)* [2015] UKUT 321 (AAC); [2017] AACR 20 at [146] that a response should do something to help the First-tier Tribunal get to grips with the evidence by summarising it, particularly where there is a very large volume of evidence. A response also needs to engage with the grounds of appeal so that, for instance, if a claimant specifically argues that she was incapable of work-related activity at the time of the Secretary of State's decision, r.24(2)(e) requires the Secretary of State to explain why the relevant statutory provision is not satisfied on the facts of the case and that carries with it a need to set out, in those cases where there was an arguable risk to a claimant in being required to engage in some forms of work-related activity, the range or type of work-related activity which the claimant might be expected to undertake in the relevant area and to explain why there would be no substantial risk to the claimant's health if he or she were found not to have limited capability for work-related activity (*MN v SSWP (ESA)* [2013] UKUT 262 (AAC); [2014] AACR 6, as read in the light of *IM v SSWP (ESA)* [2014] UKUT 412 (AAC); [2015] AACR 10 and, in relation to "Jobcentre Plus Offers", *KC v SSWP (ESA)* [2017] UKUT 94 (AAC)). Indeed, even in relation to an appeal against a decision that the claimant did not have limited capability for work, it is helpful if a response includes information about the range of work-related activity available in the relevant area so as to enable the First-tier Tribunal, should it allow the appeal, fairly to go on and consider whether the claimant had limited capability for work-related activity (see *IM*).

A Tribunal of Commissioners in Northern Ireland held in *JC v DSD (IB)* [2011] NICom 177; [2014] AACR 30 that, in an incapacity benefit case, the Department for Social Development should list details of all previous assessment determinations within the current claim, which the Department had said "should be straightforward in most cases . . . from computer records", but that the assessments themselves need only be provided "in a limited class of case, where there is an assertion that there has been no change in the claimant's condition, and where the evidence associated with the previous adjudication history is relevant to that submission or, for example, where the claimant's medical condition, and the evidence associated with the previous adjudication history assists in the assessment of the claimant's overall capacity". No reference was made to that decision in *ST v SSWP (ESA)* [2012] UKUT 469 (AAC), in which it was held that, in employment and support allowance cases, the Secretary of State should send with the response any copy of the report of a previous medical examination that is in his possession in a case where the claimant appeals on the ground that their condition is no better than when the previous examination was "passed", because the previous report will necessarily be relevant in the absence of a material supervening event (such as a change in the law or a surgical operation). Even when it is not clear that such a report is relevant, the response should at least inform the First-tier Tribunal whether there are previous reports in the Secretary of State's possession that *might* be relevant. 3.322

In *FN v SSWP (ESA)* [2015] UKUT 670 (AAC); [2016] AACR 24, a three-judge panel broadly agreed with both those decisions but stressed that the previous adjudication history and associated evidence is not always relevant to the case under consideration and that, even if the Secretary of State has not produced all the information and evidence that he should have produced with his response to an appeal, it does not necessarily follow that the First-tier Tribunal will err in proceeding in the absence of the evidence. It said –

> "79. . . . We can envisage a situation where a First-tier Tribunal considers that it has sufficient relevant evidence before it to determine the issues arising in the appeal without the requirement to call for evidence which is missing because the Secretary of State has failed in his duty to provide it.
> 80. . . . Our view is that the first choice for the tribunal should not be to adjourn but to get on with the task of determining the issues arising in the appeal when satisfied that it has the necessary relevant evidence before it. It might be the case that having weighed and assessed the appellant's oral evidence, the tribunal might be satisfied that the evidence is credible, should be accepted and the appeal be allowed. . . ."

It is suggested that the question for the First-tier Tribunal is not just whether it has sufficient evidence to enable it to determine the issues before it but whether it has sufficient evidence to do so *fairly* in a case where the evidence before it suggests a decision adverse to the claimant. This may involve an assessment of the probable helpfulness to the claimant of evidence that the Secretary of State could produce but has not produced. Even if the First-tier Tribunal reasonably decides to proceed in the absence of previous medical reports that it considers the Secretary of State should have produced, it is arguable that, if it decides the case against the claimant, its decision may be set aside for inadvertent procedural error (either under r.37 or on review or appeal) if it transpires that the reports that should have been produced would substantially have supported the claimant's case. In *JL v SSWP (ESA)* [2018] UKUT 94 (AAC), the Upper Tribunal declined to apply a literal construction to the words "assertion that there has been no change" in *JC* in a case where the inference to be drawn form a claimant's submissions was that she was arguing that there had been no significant change in her condition arising out of an accident she had suffered ten years previously and for which she was still receiving treatment. "An expert tribunal will understand that some conditions heal; others do not."

Following *JC* and *FN*, the Department for Work and Pensions issued internal instructions to the effect that, in appeals against decisions superseding awards of employment and support allowance, the First-tier Tribunal was to be provided with a decision-making chronology and history with relevant reports if they were available (see *RP v SSWP (ESA)* [2020] UKUT 148 (AAC)).

3.323 The decisions in *JC* and *FN* were considered in some detail and followed in *CH v SSWP (PIP)* [2018] UKUT 330 (AAC); [2019] AACR 11, where the question arose whether evidence relating to previous assessments in respect of disability living allowance were potentially relevant on a claim for that allowance's successor, personal independence payment just as, in *FN*, there had been the question whether evidence relating to earlier assessments in respect of incapacity benefit were potentially relevant when considering entitlement to that benefit's successor, employment and support allowance. The Upper Tribunal declined an invitation to specify areas of overlap, but did offer the following guidance—

> "48. First, although in *FN* at [83] the Upper Tribunal said that overlap between the substantive criteria was only an example of when past evidence might be relevant, it is difficult to envisage in what other circumstances DLA evidence would be relevant. . . . .
>
> 49. Second, as is clear from the case law to which I have referred, DLA evidence will not be relevant where the claimant's condition has since improved.
>
> 50. Third, DLA evidence could not assist where the claimant's case in the PIP appeal is inconsistent with the particular PIP descriptor being applicable. Thus, where the evidence of the claimant in the example at paragraph 15 is that he or she is able to walk over 50 metres at 1.5 times normal walking speed, DLA evidence relating to a previous award of the HRMC will not be relevant.
>
> 51. Fourth, it is highly unlikely that evidence other than the medical evidence from the DLA claim could be relevant to a subsequent PIP claim. Other evidence, such as what the claimant said in the DLA claim form, can be repeated for the purpose of the PIP claim if thought relevant. Previous statements by the claimant are unlikely to assist as to credibility as such statements are just as likely to show consistent misrepresentation or exaggeration as they are to show truth or accuracy.
>
> 52. Fifth, the age of the evidence is likely to affect its relevance but on occasions even quite old evidence may assist, for example where there is reason to doubt the PIP evidence or it is incomplete. Older evidence may also assist where variability is in issue (see *JC* at [50(viii)]). It is not appropriate to specify a particular age beyond which DLA evidence will not assist although, in general, relevance is likely to decrease with age. Whether it does assist in any particular case is a matter for the First-tier Tribunal's judgment.
>
> 53. Sixth, an indefinite award of DLA would have been based on the prognosis given at that time but that prognosis is unlikely to provide assistance at the time

of a PIP decision when there is a reliable up-to-date assessment of the claimant's actual condition.

54. Finally, PIP assessments may not be as reliable as the Secretary of State would like to have the Tribunal believe (see paragraphs 25-27). It is the tribunal's task to decide what weight to afford the PIP evidence. Medical evidence relating to a previous DLA award may assist in evaluating the quality of the PIP assessment."

As to the duty of the Secretary of State to attach evidence to responses, the Upper Tribunal noted that the Secretary of State's policy, which had not always been followed in practice, was that disability living allowance evidence would be included where the claimant has asked for it to be taken into account, but where the claimant has not asked, the appeal submission would inform the tribunal only of that fact and the level and date of the last disability living allowance award in a transfer case. The information provided to the tribunal did not state what disability living allowance evidence was in the Secretary of State's possession including whether there was an examining medical practitioner's report, nor were copies provided. The Judge said—

"57. . . . In the light of the decisions in *JC* and *FN*, I consider that, even if the claimant does not ask for the DLA evidence to be taken into account, the Secretary of State's duty means that she should consider whether DLA evidence in her possession is relevant to the PIP appeal, taking into account the guidance in these Reasons, and should provide to the tribunal the relevant evidence which is in her possession. It would usually be sufficient for the Secretary of State to consider the medical evidence that was available for the most recent determination. I do not consider that it would be unduly onerous for the Secretary of State to do this. I acknowledge that it is not my role to mandate the Secretary of State's performance of her duties, but I note that the Secretary of State has indicated that she will be addressing her procedures in the light of this decision and so I suggest that as a matter of good practice she could consider taking on board my observations."

As to the First-tier Tribunal's duty to obtain evidence where the Secretary of State did not provide it, the Judge said—

"59. As was made clear in *JC* and *FN* the tribunal is not required as a matter of law to consider DLA evidence on a PIP appeal if the evidence is not relevant (*JC* at [50(vi)] and *FN* [79]). Moreover, a tribunal will not always err in law in determining an appeal without all relevant evidence (*FN* at [78] and [79]). The question is whether the evidence is necessary fairly to determine the appeal. Thus, at [84] the Upper Tribunal said:

'a First-tier Tribunal is entitled to call on what evidence it considers relevant to the proper determination of the issues arising in the appeal' (emphasis added)

60. In disability appeals there is frequently relevant evidence, such as GP records, which is not before the tribunal. There is no general requirement on the tribunal to obtain such evidence. It is for the tribunal to decide whether it is proportionate to do so, consistently with the overriding objective. The position has been put succinctly by Judge Nicholas Paines QC in *GC v SSWP (ESA)* [2014] UKUT 174 (AAC):

'34. Tribunals are often faced with cases in which categories of information that might be helpful to the tribunal are not in their papers. For example, they may or may not have a claimant's GP records; the claimant may have been to a specialist for treatment, but the papers do not contain any report from the specialist; the claimant may not have been examined on behalf of the DWP by an examining medical practitioner; or, as here, an ability similar to the ability at issue before the tribunal may have been adjudicated on for the purposes of another social security benefit, but the papers are not before the tribunal. Other examples can no doubt be proffered. In all these situations, it seems to me, the tribunal has a discretion, to be exercised judicially, as to whether they adjourn with a view to obtaining the further material.

35. In exercising that discretion, the tribunal will balance the competing factors, which include: the wishes of the claimant, particularly if represented; the delay to the proceedings before it; the amplitude of the evidence already before it; the likely relevance or helpfulness, so far as it can be judged, of the missing material, etc.'

61. Ultimately it is for the First-tier Tribunal to make its own judgment whether DLA evidence may be relevant and whether to call for it in a PIP appeal. In accordance with the decisions in *JC* and *FN*, and without setting down any hard and fast rules, the following guidance should assist in deciding whether to call for the relevant evidence.

62. First and most obviously, it must reasonably be considered that the DLA evidence would be relevant to the PIP decision as discussed above. At a minimum this will depend on there being relevant overlapping criteria in issue and a plausible case that the claimant's condition has not improved.

63. Second, even if the DLA evidence is likely to be relevant on the above basis, the First-tier Tribunal will not be required to obtain that evidence if it is satisfied that the PIP evidence is reliable and sufficient to enable it to determine whether the PIP criteria which are in issue are satisfied.

64. Third, if the First-tier Tribunal considers that the PIP evidence is insufficient or if it has cause to doubt the reliability of the PIP evidence, it should consider obtaining potentially relevant DLA evidence.

65. Fourth, if the First-tier Tribunal decides that the appellant is not credible and so making false or exaggerated claims about their difficulties, that may make it unnecessary to call for the DLA evidence. However, the tribunal might also consider whether the DLA evidence could assist in assessing the appellant's credibility where that is called in to question.

66. Fifth, if the claimant relies on the DLA award, the tribunal must address the argument made – see the discussion in *KW* v *SSWP (ESA)* [2018] UKUT 216 (AAC) – but it is a matter for the tribunal to determine whether to obtain the DLA evidence.

67. If the DWP's processes work, the question whether the tribunal should obtain the DLA evidence should only arise where the claimant did not ask for it to be taken into account and the Secretary of State has decided that it is not relevant. It is not consistent with the tribunal's investigative and enabling role simply to leave matters there. The claimant may not have appreciated that DLA evidence may be relevant, and the Secretary of State does not have the last word on relevance. But how is the First-tier Tribunal to go about the task of deciding whether to call for the DLA evidence where it does not know what DLA evidence there is? In the light of what the tribunal knows about the level and date of the last DLA award, it will be able to make a judgment as to whether there is any question of DLA evidence being potentially relevant and, in particular, whether any overlapping criteria are likely to be in issue. If they are not, it need not consider further whether to obtain that evidence. But if there is a possibility of the DLA evidence being relevant, then the tribunal ought to consider whether to obtain it.

68. Where an appeal is determined in the absence of the claimant it would only be in very obvious cases that the tribunal might consider obtaining the DLA evidence, for instance where there is a clear and substantial inconsistency between the PIP assessment and a recent DLA award. If the claimant is present, the tribunal can explore matters further if it appears that the DLA evidence may be relevant. It could find out more about the basis for the award, whether there was a medical examination, what other medical evidence there was, and why the

claimant did not ask for the DLA evidence to be taken into account. It is for the tribunal to decide what inquiries to make but I give these examples to show that they can be made quickly and easily at a hearing and do not impose an undue burden on the tribunal.

69. In summary, the tribunal need only consider whether to obtain the DLA evidence if it has decided that it is or may be relevant. There is no question of it being required to obtain it simply to see what else there is. Even where the tribunal decides that the DLA evidence would be relevant, it may decide to determine the appeal without obtaining it. But it must consider whether to do so and take into account the range of relevant considerations, as explained in *GC*, and with due regard to the restraint to be exercised as urged by the Upper Tribunal in *FN* at [80]. Finally, where the question whether to seek DLA evidence has arisen and the tribunal decides to proceed without it, the duty on the tribunal to act judicially means that an appropriate explanation should be given. In most cases a brief explanation will suffice."

In *SE v SSWP (PIP) (Final decision)* [2021] UKUT 79 (AAC), it was said:

"Bearing in mind that ESA (and the equivalent provisions in relation to universal credit) examine a number of activities testing mental, cognitive and intellectual function (and accordingly, simple cognitive tests generally form part of the assessment), it is entirely possible that an assessment carried out for the purposes of the work capability assessment will yield useful evidence in the context of assessing whether people with learning disabilities can score points under activities 8 and/or 10 for PIP, even though the activities under the two benefits are different. Both claimant representatives and the Secretary of State in the exercise of her responsibilities under rule 24(4) of the FtT rules to provide 'all documents relevant to the case in the decision maker's possession' may need to bear this in mind."

Notwithstanding what was said in *CH* at [67], where a claimant was represented **3.324**
before the First-tier Tribunal, it may be difficult for him or her to argue on an appeal to the Upper Tribunal that evidence relating to previous assessments ought to have been obtained if the representative did not make such a suggestion at the time (see the annotation to r.5(3)(h)).

Moreover, evidence relating to previous assessments obviously cannot be provided if the Secretary of State has not kept it. Evidence of the Department for Work and Pensions' retention policy for documents in disability cases was recorded in *GD v SSWP (PIP)* [2017] UKUT 415 (AAC) as follows—

"a. PIP Reassessment Claimants are asked at outset if they want the DWP to include their DLA medical evidence when considering the PIP claim. Where DLA medical evidence is used, then that evidence will be attached to the claimants PIP file and marked as supporting that PIP decision. This will be kept for at least 2 years if the PIP decision was a disallowance, or longer if the decision was an award. If there has been no request from the claimant to use their DLA medical evidence for their PIP claim then the old DLA evidence will be destroyed 3 months after the DLA decision has terminated. The PIP retention period is 24 months if the evidence is no longer classified as supporting. Once the DLA evidence has been included as part of the PIP claim it will have the same retention as any other PIP supporting document.

b. There is a departmental policy regarding document and data retention. However, benefits decide what fits their circumstances as documents can be retained for longer/shorter if there is a valid business need e.g. DLA is roughly 14 months for documents but PIP is 24 months due to the potential linking provision of Regulation 15 of the Social Security (Personal Independence Payment) Regulations 2013, but is consistent within each benefit.

c. . . . . Normally the DLA File is destroyed 14 months after it ceases to support an existing award. This period starts from 7 months after termination of award. The computer record will keep for 7 months and then close. The paper file will then be destroyed 14 months after that. However if any of that DLA evidence has been considered within the PIP claim then that evidence will support the PIP decision and it will be kept for as long as the PIP decision is current and 2 years after the PIP is no longer current.
d. If the DLA medical evidence has been used to consider the PIP claim then this will be included in the evidence bundle sent to the tribunal."

However, in *CH (by TH) v SSWP (PIP)* [2020] UKUT 70 (AAC), it appeared that the practice outlined there had not been followed and the judge said at [17] that, if the issue continues to arise, tribunals should probe whether what was said in *GD* "is accurate in relation to the particular time which the case before them concerns and its application to that case".

There may be instances where evidence can be provided even though the retention policy suggests that the documents should have been destroyed, but generally regard should clearly be had to the policy when consideration is being given by the First-tier Tribunal to directing the Secretary of State to provide evidence relating to former claims.

Because good administration requires that citizens be treated in accordance with a policy adopted by a Government department unless there are good reasons for not doing so, a respondent to an appeal to the First-tier Tribunal fails in his or her duty to draw relevant matters to the attention of the tribunal if no mention is made of a policy favourable to the appellant in the response to the appeal (*Mandalia v Secretary of State for the Home Department* [2015] UKSC 59; [2015] 1 W.L.R. 4546). This is relevant where the decision under appeal involved exercising an element of discretion or at least judgment and there is published guidance as to how the discretion or judgment should be exercised. It is presumably not necessary to refer to the policy document itself if the submission is in accordance with it, but a decision of the First-tier Tribunal may well be set aside if the First-tier Tribunal makes a decision that is adverse to a claimant but is inconsistent with a published policy unless a good reason for departing from the policy has been given (see, for instance, *SB v Oxford CC (HB)* [2014] UKUT 166 (AAC)).

3.325 In *TM v HMRC (TC)* [2013] UKUT 444 (AAC), HMRC did not send a copy of its response to the claimant, as required by para.(5), because it was not sure that the claimant was still living at the address it held for him and it was concerned about data protection issues. It sent a copy of the response to the First-tier Tribunal with a covering letter asking for directions. The First-tier Tribunal overlooked that request and heard the appeal without the claimant having seen the response. The Upper Tribunal doubted whether the data protection concern was well-founded, given s.35(1) of the Data Protection Act 1998 which exempts data from non-disclosure if "disclosure is required by or under any enactment, by any rule of law or by order of the court". The Upper Tribunal's decision appears to suggest that HMRC should either have withheld the response from the First-tier Tribunal until it had obtained directions or else it should have sent the response to the claimant notwithstanding its concerns. However, it is not clear why the Upper Tribunal apparently thought it was wrong for the HMRC to enclose a copy of the response with its request for directions, although it may have thought that the request for directions would probably not have been overlooked if the response had not been sent with it.

In *JT v HMTC (TC)* [2015] UKUT 81 (AAC), HMRC applied for the striking out of the claimant's appeal but did not send a copy of the application to the claimant. The First-tier Tribunal overlooked the nature of the application and treated it as a response to the appeal, which it heard and dismissed in the claimant's absence. The Upper Tribunal suggested that an application by a respondent for the striking out of an appeal under r.8(3)(c) should be copied to the claimant and be accompanied by a full response that complies with r.24 unless that would clearly be disproportionate, so as to ensure that the First-tier Tribunal has all the material necessary to enable it properly to decide whether the appeal has no reasonable prospect of success, the claimant is able to make effective representations and the appeal is ready for determination if it is not struck out.

In *FI v HMRC (CHB)* [2018] UKUT 226 (AAC), HMRC failed to include with its response copies of letters sent by the claimant on the ground that, although they indicated that the claimant might be self-employed they did not, in its view, show on the balance of probabilities that she was. The Upper Tribunal set aside the First-tier Tribunal's decision on the ground that the letters should have been included because they were relevant and it was not for HMRC to usurp the role of the tribunal. The Upper Tribunal held that that was so notwithstanding that the claimant could have provided the documents and that in *FN v SSWP (ESA)* [2015] UKUT 670 (AAC); [2016] AACR 24, it had been held that not every breach of r.24 would result in a decision of the First-tier Tribunal being held to be wrong in law.

In *John v IC* [2014] UKUT 444 (AAC), the Upper Tribunal rejected an argument that a respondent was required to cross-appeal or submit a respondent's notice if disagreeing with a decision being challenged on appeal to the First-tier Tribunal. It was held that new issues could be raised in a response and, referring to *Birkett v Department for the Environment, Food and Rural Affairs* [2011] EWCA Civ 1606, that the First-tier Tribunal could exercise its case-management powers to prevent unfairness to an appellant.

The term "document" used in r.24(4)(b) is defined in r.1(3) so as to include recordings of telephone calls and so HMRC, which records calls to its Helpline and retains them for five years, had failed to comply with the provision when it had failed to provide with its response transcripts of highly relevant telephone conversations (*AG v HMRC (TC)* [2013] UKUT 530 (AAC)).

However, statements of fact in the Secretary of State's response to an appeal may amount to evidence and the absence of supporting documentary evidence is not always fatal. In *AS v SSWP (CA)* [2015] UKUT 592 (AAC); [2016] AACR 22, the claimant said that he had telephoned the Carer's Allowance Unit and informed it of his employment and earnings. It was stated in the Secretary of State's response that no record of such a conversation could be found. The Upper Tribunal considered the significance of such statements in responses, saying—

> "The critical issue is what weight is to be attached to them, and that is for the First-tier Tribunal to assess. The blander or broader the statement, the less weight it might be given. However in this case there was a specific evidential statement made in the appeal response that a full search of the CA Unit's clerical records had been made and in my judgment that evidence was entitled to be given weight. The particular weight to be attached to it was a matter for the fact-finding tribunal to evaluate as part of its fact-finding jurisdiction, and does not here give rise to any error of law."

In particular, it was held that there was no rule of law requiring the Secretary of State to produce evidence as to his system for recording telephone conversations.

Similarly, in *BS v SSWP (DLA)* [2016] UKUT 73 (AAC); [2016] AACR 32, the failure of the Secretary of State to produce a document proving authorisation of surveillance under the Regulation of Investigatory Powers Act 2000 was remedied by the First-tier Tribunal's acceptance of oral evidence from the presenting officer that there had been the requisite authorisation in the particular case. It was suggested in *TD v SSWP (PIP)* [2020] UKUT 283 (AAC) that any challenge to evidence requiring proof of authorisation under the 2000 Act ought generally to be raised in advance so that the necessary evidence can be produced either before or at the hearing. It was also suggested that, if the Secretary of State wished any part of the evidence to be withheld from the claimant, her representative should be ready to provide a redacted copy of the evidence so that the claimant at least could see that.

Any issue over the extent of any redactions could then be considered by the First-tier Tribunal under r.14.

Indeed, in any case where an appellant is dissatisfied with the disclosure of documents with a response, he or she may apply for a direction under r.5(3)(d) for the disclosure by the respondent of further documents. When the First-tier Tribunal is considering an application for such a direction, there is no presumption that the respondent's expressed view of what is "relevant" for the purposes of r.24(4)(b) must be accepted unless there are clear grounds to for believing the contrary (*SSD v LA (AFCS)* [2011] UKUT 391 (AAC)).

Paragraphs (6) and (7)

3.326 These paragraphs make express provision for other parties to reply to the decision-makers response. Again, the 1999 Regs made no such provision but in practice parties were given the opportunity when asked whether they wanted a hearing. A one-month time limit is now provided, but that may be regarded as a minimum period that must be given to the parties before a case is determined and it will seldom be proportionate to refuse to accept a late submission or evidence unless another party would be unduly affected by the delay, particularly where there is to be an oral hearing at which submissions and new evidence can be expected whether or not written notice has been given.

Following receipt of an appeal, the First-tier Tribunal sends the appellant and any third party an "enquiry form" asking whether they want an oral hearing and whether they have any further evidence to submit. In *MP v SSWP (DLA)* [2010] UKUT 103 (AAC), a paper hearing took place within a week of the Tribunals Service (and, presumably the claimant's representative) receiving the Secretary of State's response and of the "enquiry form" being sent out. It was held that there had been a breach of the rules of natural justice, as the claimant's solicitors had further evidence to send and the claimant had not had the month allowed by subs.(7) in which to send it. The judge said that the First-tier Tribunal had also clearly been wrong to hold that there were no grounds, in those circumstances, for setting the decision aside under r.37. Current practice is for the "enquiry form" to ask the parties to send any further submission or evidence within 28 days of them receiving the response from the decision maker (which in practice gives them the the statutory month).

Medical and physical examination in appeals under section 12 of the Social Security Act 1998

3.327 **25.**—(1) This rule applies only to appeals under section 12 of the Social Security Act 1998.

(2) At a hearing an appropriate member of the Tribunal may carry out a physical examination of a person if the case relates to—

(a) the extent of that person's disablement and its assessment in accordance with section 68(6) of and Schedule 6 to, or section 103 of, the Social Security Contributions and Benefits Act 1992; or

(b) diseases or injuries prescribed for the purpose of section 108 of that Act.

(3) If an issue which falls within Schedule 2 to these Rules (issues in relation to which the Tribunal may refer a person for medical examination) is raised in an appeal, the Tribunal may exercise its power under section 20 of the Social Security Act 1998 to refer a person to a health care professional approved by the Secretary of State for—

(a) the examination of that person; and

(b) the production of a report on the condition of that person.

(4) Neither paragraph (2) nor paragraph (3) entitles the Tribunal to require a person to undergo a physical test for the purpose of determining whether that person is unable to walk or virtually unable to do so.

DEFINITIONS

"hearing"—see r.1(3).
"Tribunal"—*ibid.*

GENERAL NOTE

Paragraph (2)

For the meaning of "physical examination", see the note to s.20(3) of the Social Security Act 1998. The "appropriate member" will be a registered medical practitioner (see para.14 of the practice statement reproduced above in the note to art.2 of the First-tier Tribunal and Upper Tribunal (Composition of Tribunal) Order 2008). **3.328**

These are the *only* circumstances in which a person may be examined on an appeal under s.12 of the 1998 Act (see s.20(3)). However, the limitation does not apply in other cases, such as appeals under the Social Security (Recovery of Benefits) Act 1997.

Where the Tribunal has the power to examine a claimant it need not do so if it considers that an examination is unnecessary. It is not always necessary to carry out a physical examination in order to assess functional loss. It may be better in some cases simply to question the claimant about the practical effects of an injury. However, if not minded to conduct a physical examination in a case where one is permissible, it is good practice for the Tribunal to state as much during the course of the hearing so that the claimant has an opportunity to make representation on the point (*R(I) 10/62, CI/3384/2006*). Whether a failure to do so renders a decision liable to be set aside on appeal is likely to depend on the circumstances and, in particular, whether the claimant can show that an examination might have led to a different outcome.

Chaperones

Examinations are possible only where there is a separate room available for them. **3.329**
The General Medical Council has stringent conditions on the conduct of intimate examinations. This is set out in The GMC Guidance (Intimate Examinations and Chaperones). In particular, a doctor conducting an intimate examination (which can include physical touching) must offer a chaperone to the appellant. The Guidance states that, "Intimate examinations can be embarrassing or distressing for patients and whenever you examine a patient you should be sensitive to what they may think of as intimate. This is likely to include examinations of breasts, genitalia and rectum, but could also include any examination where it is necessary to touch or even be close to the patient."

His Majesty's Courts and Tribunals Service should provide a medical assistant to act as Chaperone. In the First-tier Tribunal where a chaperone is not present a family member, judge or clerk are not considered to be appropriate chaperones. If a trained medical chaperone is not present, then it would be unwise for the medical member to conduct an examination. If a complaint is made where no medical chaperone was present, the GMC would have to investigate the complaint. In the event that there is no medical chaperone booked and it is deemed necessary to conduct an examination, the First-tier Tribunal is likely to consider it necessary to adjourn the hearing.

In *MB v DSD (II)* [2010] NICom 133; [2011] AACR 41, it was held that, where a tribunal makes new findings of significance in consequence of a medical examination, fairness may require all parties to the proceedings to have an opportunity to comment on those findings, even if that sometimes involves an adjournment to allow the claimant to seek advice. See also *Evans v Secretary of State for Social Services* (reported as *R(I) 5/94*).

Paragraph (4)

3.330 This paragraph applies to examinations within para.(3) as well as those within para.(2). It must be presumed to do so by prescribing a "condition" under s.20(2) of the Social Security Act 1998 and thereby extending the limitation imposed by s.20(3)(b), which is otherwise confined to what may be done "at a hearing".

Social security and child support cases started by reference or information in writing

3.331 **26.**—(1) This rule applies to proceedings under section 28D of the Child Support Act 1991 and paragraph 3 of Schedule 2 to the Tax Credits Act 2002.

(2) A person starting proceedings under section 28D of the Child Support Act 1991 must send or deliver a written reference to the Tribunal.

(3) A person starting proceedings under paragraph 3 of Schedule 2 to the Tax Credits Act 2002 must send or deliver an information in writing to the Tribunal.

(4) The reference or the information in writing must include—

(a) an address where documents for the person starting proceedings may be sent or delivered;

(b) the names and addresses of the respondents and their representatives (if any); and

(c) a submission on the issues that arise for determination by the Tribunal.

(5) Unless a practice direction or direction states otherwise, the person starting proceedings must also provide a copy of each document in their possession which is relevant to the proceedings.

(6) Subject to any obligation under rule 19(3) (confidentiality in child support cases), the person starting proceedings must provide a copy of the written reference or the information in writing and any accompanying documents to each respondent at the same time as they provide the written reference or the information in writing to the Tribunal.

(7) Each respondent may send or deliver to the Tribunal a written submission and any further relevant documents within one month of the date on which the person starting proceedings sent a copy of the written reference or the information in writing to that respondent.

DEFINITIONS

"document"—see r.1(3).
"practice direction"—*ibid.*
"respondent"—*ibid.*
"social security and child support case"—*ibid.*
"Tribunal"—*ibid.*

GENERAL NOTE

3.332 This rule makes specific provision for certain child support cases initiated by the Secretary of State and tax credit penalty cases initiated by HMRC. Paragraph (7) provides for responses by respondents. A one-month time limit is provided, but that may be regarded as a minimum period that must be given to the respondents before a case is determined and it will seldom be proportionate to refuse to accept a late submission or evidence unless another party would be unduly affected by the delay, particularly where there is to be an oral hearing at which submissions and new evidence can be expected whether or not written notice has been given.

CHAPTER 2

HEARINGS

Decision with or without a hearing

27.—(1) Subject to the following paragraphs, the Tribunal must hold a hearing before making a decision which disposes of proceedings unless— 3.333

(a) each party has consented to, or has not objected to, the matter being decided without a hearing; and

(b) the Tribunal considers that it is able to decide the matter without a hearing.

(2) This rule does not apply to decisions under Part 4.

(3) The Tribunal may in any event dispose of proceedings without a hearing under rule 8 (striking out a party's case).

(4) In a criminal injuries compensation case—

(a) the Tribunal may make a decision which disposes of proceedings without a hearing; and

(b) subject to paragraph (5), if the Tribunal makes a decision which disposes of proceedings without a hearing, any party may make a written application to the Tribunal for the decision to be reconsidered at a hearing.

(5) An application under paragraph (4)(b) may not be made in relation to a decision—

(a) not to extend a time limit;

(b) not to set aside a previous decision;

(c) not to allow an appeal against a decision not to extend a time limit; or

(d) not to allow an appeal against a decision not to reopen a case.

(6) An application under paragraph (4)(b) must be received within 1 month after the date on which the Tribunal sent notice of the decision to the party making the application.

DEFINITIONS

"criminal injuries compensation case"—see r.1(3).
"dispose of proceedings"—*ibid.*
"hearing"—*ibid.*
"party"—*ibid.*
"Tribunal"—*ibid.*

GENERAL NOTE

Paragraphs (1) and (2)

Paragraph (1) applies where the decision to be made will be one "which disposes of proceedings". It is primarily concerned with the final substantive decision on an 3.334

appeal or reference but, were it not for para.(3), it would also apply to decisions to strike out proceedings. Paragraph (2) makes it clear that it does not apply to decisions relating to reviews and permission to appeal to the Upper Tribunal. It is less clear whether it applies to a decision whether or not to extend the time for appealing to the First-tier Tribunal. On one view, a decision not to extend time disposes of proceedings but the better argument may be that it merely prevents the proceedings from being started. However, even where this rule does not require there to be a hearing, it may be appropriate for the Tribunal to direct one under r.5(3)(f). See the annotations to paras (4)–(6), below, but the overriding objective in r.2 requires that a proportionate approach be taken.

The paragraph has the effect that, where it applies, there must be a hearing if any party wants one. The Secretary of State or HMRC will say whether or not they want a hearing when submitting a response (see r.24(3)), reference or information. The Tribunal asks the other parties whether or not they want a hearing by sending them a form to return. If there is no reply, the party may be taken to have "not objected to the matter being decided without a hearing." In effect, therefore, these paragraphs replace reg.39 of the Social Security and Child Support (Decisions and Appeals) Regulations 1999. However, note that the legislation no longer refers to an approved form on which a party was required to indicate whether or not he wished to have a hearing, so that the basis for the decision in *R3/04(IB)* has been removed, and that the provision in reg.46(1)(d) for simply striking proceedings out if the approved form was not returned by a party has not been re-enacted. Now, a case cannot be struck out for failure to return a form unless the Tribunal has directed the form be returned and has warned the party that being struck out will, or may, be the consequence of not complying with the direction (see r.8(1) and (3)(a)). In *R3/04(IB)*, the requirement to issue an approved form to a party was held to be the reason why a clerk to a tribunal could not rely on an indication in the appellant's letter of appeal that a hearing was not wanted. There may still be reasons why reliance should not be placed on such an indication, not the least of which is that the appellant is unlikely to have been aware of the precise case against him or her before receiving the response to the appeal.

Where a joint claim is made, both claimants are parties. If only one of them has appealed, the other is a respondent as a person who had a right of appeal (see the definition of "respondent" in r.1(3)). Consequently, there should be a hearing unless both have consented to the case being determined on the papers. This is important where they have separated since making the claim, as in *PD v HMRC (TC)* [2010] UKUT 159 (AAC).

In *LM v SSWP (ESA)* [2020] UKUT 41 (AAC), there was held to have been a breach of this rule where the claimant had asked for a hearing and the First-tier Tribunal, having looked at the papers in the case, allowed the claimant's appeal without a hearing to the extent of deciding that she had limited capability for work, on the ground that to do so was proportionate, avoided delay and was in the interest of justice and therefore in accordance with the overriding objective in r.2. A breach of r.27 might have been immaterial if the claimant had been awarded everything that she could possibly have obtained on her appeal but the Upper Tribunal pointed out that that was not so in this case, particularly as the claimant had previously been found to have had limited capability for work-related activity and so had been entitled to more than the First-tier Tribunal had awarded her. What the First-tier Tribunal could properly have done was to indicate its preliminary view of the merits of the case and invited the claimant to withdraw her request for a hearing if she was content to accept a decision being made in the terms suggested.

In *CF v SSWP (CSM)* [2022] UKUT 271 (AAC), a hearing took place, following which the judge issued directions requiring further evidence to be provided. Another judge then, without the parties having consented to the case being decided without a hearing and without them having been provided with the judge's note of what was said at the first hearing, decided it on the papers, having regard to the fact the parties had had the opportunity to attend a hearing "and taking account of the factors in the overriding objective, including the delay from the date of decision, the need for finality in appeals, proportionality and the issues in the case". The decision was unsurprisingly set aside by the Upper Tribunal on the ground that, although the condition in r.27(1)(b) might have been satisfied, the condition in r.27(1)(a) clearly was not. This is not to say that, following a hearing, the First-tier Tribunal may never issue directions requiring further evidence and then decide the case without a further hearing, but the hearing must have been complete except as regards the further evidence, the decision must be made by the judge or panel who had heard the case and the parties must generally have agreed to make any further representations in writing rather than orally (*CF* at [24]). There may perhaps be cases where the additional evidence merely confirms what had already been said and there is clearly nothing further that the losing party could have said about it at a hearing, but a decision is liable to be set aside if a party subsequently shows that a hearing might conceivably have made a difference.

Where a claimant asks for a paper determination and asks for it not to take place until a certain date because further evidence will be provided, the tribunal must either wait until that date or inform the claimant that it will not do so (*CDLA/792/2006*). It will seldom be appropriate not to wait for evidence unless the time requested is unreasonably long or there has been previous delay on the part of the claimant. Rule 24(7) implies that an appellant should have at least a month from being issued with a response to an appeal in which to provide further evidence. However, it was said in *EZ v SSWP (ESA)* [2013] UKUT 644 (AAC) that an open-ended statement that evidence would be provided at some time did not require the First-tier Tribunal to wait forever and parties and representatives had as much of a duty to keep the First-tier Tribunal informed as to when they expected to be able to provide evidence as the tribunal's staff did to impose deadlines. **3.335**

Taking part in a hearing before a tribunal does not breach an extended civil restraint order imposed on a vexatious litigant by a county court and where a claimant asked that his case be decided on the papers because he feared he would be in breach of such an order and his requests for information on the issue had been ignored by both the county court and the Tribunals Service, there had been a breach of the rules of natural justice (*JW v SSWP* [2009] UKUT 198 (AAC)).

There are many cases where a claimant really has no realistic prospects of success unless he or she attends an oral hearing and gives evidence. Even though claimants are advised in general terms that the chances of success may be greater at an oral hearing, it may be thought that the mere fact that they are offered the choice will suggest to many that a paper hearing is a not a foolish option. In *CDLA/1347/1999*, it was said that, if a tribunal considering an appeal on the papers was wholly unable to do justice without there being an oral hearing, it ought to adjourn the proceedings, and direct that there be one but that, otherwise, a tribunal was generally entitled to take the view that a claimant who had rejected the option of an oral hearing having had notice of the issues in the case had had an adequate opportunity to put his case and had lost the chance of strengthening it by giving oral evidence. In considering whether a claimant has had an adequate opportunity to state his or her case in writing, it will be necessary to consider what information has been provided to the claimant. In *LH v SSWP (PIP)* [2018] UKUT 57 (AAC), it was observed that, if, as was then usually the case, the respondent had not explained to the claimant what the descriptors relating to personal independence payment were and why they were relevant, it might have been unreasonable to have expected the claimant to have realised what the issues in her case really were so that she could adduce relevant evidence and argument. Even if such a lack of information does not lead to the conclusion that there should be a hearing, it might be necessary to ensure that the claimant is provided with the relevant information and a further opportunity to make submissions before proceeding without one.

In *R1/02(IB)*, a Tribunal of Commissioners in Northern Ireland set aside a decision of a tribunal who did not adjourn in the face of incomplete evidence raising questions that they could not answer. Having enough evidence to decide a case in favour of a claimant is likely to be a good reason for not holding a hearing if neither party has asked for one, but the facts that the First-tier Tribunal had enough evidence to be "able to decide the matter without a hearing" and had "adequate information to come to a reasoned decision" were not regarded as sufficient by themselves in *FY v SSWP (ESA)* [2017] UKUT 501 (AAC), where the decision was adverse to a claimant who had a range of health problems and had been in receipt of the relevant benefit for some four years. In *CIS/4248/2001*, the Commissioner held that an oral hearing should have been directed in a case where an apparently unrepresented claimant had opted for a paper hearing of an appeal against a decision that income support amounting to some £10,000 had been overpaid and was recoverable from her, in circumstances where the claimant had put forward a case that was tenable if she was believed.

> "A very great deal of money was at stake. Oral evidence would have assisted the tribunal's assessment of honesty, which was central to the case. She had not, as far as could be seen, had the benefit of advice from anyone with experience of tribunals. Those are all factors that suggest that justice required an oral hearing in this case."

3.336 At one time, there was a standard "record of proceedings" for "paper hearings" in which a judge ticked boxes to confirm not only that the claimant had made such an election but also that the chairman was satisfied that a hearing was not required. Now that that form is no longer used, it may be necessary for a judge to explain why the case was dealt with on the papers and without an adjournment if asked to provide a statement of reasons for the decision. Rule 27(1)(b) expressly requires the First-tier Tribunal to be satisfied that it is able to decide the matter without a hearing. In *MH v Pembrokeshire CC (HB)* [2010] UKUT 28 (AAC), the First-tier Tribunal declined to accept a claimant's assertion that he suffered from a mental disorder, saying that he had not produced medical evidence and had elected a paper hearing. The decision was set aside by the Upper Tribunal because the First-tier Tribunal had given no indication that it had considered adjourning. The judge drew attention to the overriding objective in r.2. No one had told the claimant that he needed to produce medical evidence or ask for a hearing. However, it is clear from *AT v SSWP (ESA)* [2010] UKUT 430 (AAC), in which *MH* was distinguished, that a failure expressly to refer to the overriding objective is unlikely to be an error of law in itself and, while a tribunal must consider those factors in para.(2) that are relevant, not every factor will be relevant in every case.

In *MM v SSWP (ESA)* [2011] 334 (AAC), it was held that the First-tier Tribunal ought to have explained why it considered that para.(1)(b) was satisfied so that no oral hearing was necessary and that a mere reference to the overriding objective in r.2 would not be sufficient if obvious factors pointed the other way. It does not necessarily follow from these cases that reasons must always be given for not holding an oral hearing, but they may be illustrative of the point made in *R. v Higher Education Funding Council, Ex p. Institute of Dental Surgery* [1994] 1 W.L.R. 242, at 263, that, even if there is no general duty to give reasons for interlocutory decisions, a decision is liable to be set aside on the ground of failure to give reasons if, in the absence of reasons, it appears aberrant.

In *DG v SSWP (ESA)* [2010] UKUT 409 (AAC), a decision made on the papers was set aside where a mentally ill claimant had not sought a hearing after being given advice from the jobcentre that he need not do anything, which was held to have been misleading when the claimant had not been made aware of the consequences of the choice.

On the other hand, in *KP v Hertfordshire CC (SEN)* [2010] UKUT 119 (AAC), the Upper Tribunal was not persuaded that there was any duty to hold a hearing of a directions application when no request for a hearing had been made.

On a paper determination, or indeed any hearing not attended by a claimant, it will always be an error of law for a tribunal to remove an award that has already been made unless the claimant has been given specific notice (in the sense of being focussed on their own particular case) that this is under consideration (*CDLA/1480/2006*).

There is a continuing duty to consider whether it is in the interests of justice to proceed with a hearing in a party's absence so that, if in the course of considering a case on the papers issues emerge that cannot really be dealt with fairly in the absence of the party, an initial decision not to direct a hearing may have to be reconsidered (*KO v SSWP (ESA)* [2013] UKUT 544 (AAC)).

When a decision is set aside by the Upper Tribunal and referred to another tribunal, it is the invariable practice to hold an oral hearing. However, in *CIB/4193/2003*, the Commissioner noted that that was not the practice where a decision was set aside by a legally qualified panel member under s.13 of the Social Security Act 1998 and he suggested that claimants should be given a fresh opportunity to ask for an oral hearing. He commented that some claimants might reassess their prospects of success "on a paper determination" once they had lost a case and had to apply for leave to appeal. On the facts of the case, he held that there had been a breach of the rules of natural justice because the claimant had been inadvertently misled into not asking for the oral hearing she wanted.

In *LO v SSWP (ESA)* [2016] UKUT 10 (AAC); [2016] AACR 31, there arose the question whether, where an unrepresented claimant states that he or she does not wish to attend a hearing because of disability, a tribunal ought generally to consider whether a telephone hearing would be appropriate. The judge rejected a submission by the Secretary of State that it was unnecessary to do so merely because the claimant had not asked for such a hearing, since it was not the practice of the First-tier Tribunal's administration to inform parties of the possibility of there being a telephone hearing and so claimants could not be expected to ask for one. However, he held that there had been no error of law in the particular case before him. The First-tier Tribunal had given detailed consideration to the question whether there needed to be an adjournment so that the claimant could give evidence and had taken a proportionate approach. Although an offer of a telephone hearing was one possibility that might have been considered, it had not been necessary to do so in that case in order to deal with the issue of adjournment fairly. The claimant might, after all, have declined such an offer. Nonetheless, the implication of the decision is that there may be at least some cases where a failure explicitly to consider whether to offer a telephone hearing will render a decision wrong in law. See also *JM v SSWP (PIP)* [2018] UKUT 108 (AAC), where a claimant had said she wanted a case to be decided without a hearing because she had an unpredictable medical condition and it was held that express consideration should have been given to offering her a telephone hearing, given that the information provided to her had not mentioned such a possibility.

In *DT v SSWP (UC)* [2019] UKUT 268 (AAC), a decision of the First-tier Tribunal made without a hearing was set aside where the claimant had made it clear that she was asking for the case to be decided on the papers only because she had regular medical appointments and the First-tier Tribunal had made no effort to arrange a hearing on a date she could manage.

Where a claimant's response to a listing questionnaire is equivocal because, for instance, the claimant indicates that a decision on the papers would be preferred but then says that he or she is available to attend at any time, the First-tier Tribunal should, unless directing an oral hearing, either contact the claimant to resolve the ambiguity or at least address the equivocation in the decision notice or any statement of reasons (see *RA v SSWP (II)* [2021] UKUT 148 (AAC)) so that, if the claimant's intention was misunderstood and he or she complains, the decision can be set aside under r.37.

Vulnerable adults and children

3.337 Similarly, in *WA v SSWP (CSM)* [2016] UKUT 86 (AAC), a tribunal had erred in proceeding in the absence of a party who had given fear of her ex-partner as a reason for not attending a child support hearing, without at least considering writing to her to stress that everyone has the right to attend a hearing without fear of intimidation and that the tribunal would not tolerate any attempt by one party to intimidate the other. The judge stated that "[a]ny such communication should record that it is given on a neutral basis; that is without making a finding as to whether any allegations made are accepted" and he pointed out that in some cases it might be necessary to seek the views of one parent before writing to the other. Other steps that he suggested could be taken in such a case included a hearing by video link or the "presence of a security guard in the hearing room, attendance by telephone link, laying out the hearing room in a particular way to create physical separation or possibly use of screens if available, staging the parties' entrance and departure from the room, and their waiting arrangements, to minimise proximity".

Guidance as to reasonable adjustments that may need to be made at a hearing where a litigant suffers from Asperger's syndrome may be derived from *Rackham v New Professionals Ltd* UKEAT/0110/15/LA and *Galo v Bombardier Aerospace UK* [2016] NICA 25. In *CH v SSWP (JSA) (No.2)* [2018] UKUT 320 (AAC), the Upper Tribunal made adjustments to its normal hearing procedure to meet the reasonable needs of an appellant with reading (and related difficulties with memory, concentration and information processing) and difficulties with interpersonal interactions. These were allowing a 15-minute break after each 45 minutes, allowing the appellant to record the proceedings (subject to the usual condition that the recording not be published in any format), allowing another person to read parts of the appellant's speaking note and switching off all fluorescent ceiling lighting. The judge gave detailed reasons for making these adjustments. As to the importance of considering whether to make reasonable adjustments and the consequences of not doing so, see *Practice Direction (First-tier and Upper Tribunals: Child, Vulnerable Adults and Sensitive Witnesses)*, below, and the annotation to it.

In *R(DLA) 3/06*, the Tribunal of Commissioners allowed an appeal against a decision of a tribunal who had drawn an adverse inference against a 12-year old claimant, alleged to have learning difficulties and behavioural problems, because her foster parent and appointee had failed to arrange for her to give evidence to the tribunal despite a summons. The Tribunal of Commissioners gave the following general guidance about child witnesses.

"(i) A tribunal should have proper regard to the wishes of a child of sufficiently mature years and understanding who wishes to give evidence in a DLA claim made on his behalf. However, a tribunal should be very cautious before requiring any child to give evidence, and should only call for a child to give evidence if it is satisfied that a just decision cannot otherwise be made. Before reaching such a conclusion, the tribunal should consider first all the other available evidence, and then ask itself whether any necessary additional evidence can be obtained from another source, for example, a health visitor, social worker, teacher, family member or friend, to avoid the need for the child to be called at all.

(ii) In any event, a tribunal should be very slow to exercise its power to require a child to give evidence if that child's parent or carer takes the view that for the child to give evidence may be detrimental to the child's welfare, particularly if there is evidence from a competent professional that to do so might be harmful. It would be wholly exceptional for it to be appropriate for a tribunal to call a child in such circumstances.

(iii) Even if it is those representing the child, rather than the tribunal, who wish the child to give evidence, as *Brown v Secretary of State for the Home Department* (LTA 97/6885/J) indicates, a tribunal has power to disallow the child from giving evidence if it is against the child's interests to do so. If it is proposed that the child gives evidence, the tribunal must consider whether it is in that child's interests to do so.

(iv) The tribunal should bear in mind that the mere presence of a child at a hearing is unlikely to give a reliable indication of the effect of a child's disability in normal circumstances.

(v) Where a decision is taken to call a child to give evidence, after submissions from interested persons (including the parents or carers of the child) a tribunal should give consideration to precisely how that evidence will be taken, so that the interests and welfare of the child are maintained, giving any directions that are appropriate. In doing so the tribunal will bear in mind that a child may perceive what is said at a tribunal hearing very differently from an adult. It will be necessary for the tribunal to identify any matters that the child ought not to hear (e.g. it will not generally be appropriate for a child to hear criticism of those responsible for his or her care) and questions that the child ought not to be asked (e.g. it will not generally be appropriate to question a child about his or her own care needs).

(vi) In addition, where a child is to be called to give evidence, the tribunal will need to give consideration to practical matters such as the geography of the hearing room, having an appropriate adult in close attendance, whether any of the tribunal (including the chairman) should be selected because of experience in dealing with child witnesses and even (in appropriate cases) taking such steps as taking the child's evidence by video link if available, giving directions where appropriate."

See again, *Practice Direction (First-tier and Upper Tribunals: Child, Vulnerable Adults and Sensitive Witnesses)*, below. However, although care must be taken when considering whether to hear evidence from a child, there can be no presumption against a child giving evidence and regard must be had to the fairness of the proceedings as well as the interests of the child (*In re W (Children) (Family Proceedings: Evidence)* [2010] UKSC 12; [2010] 1 W.L.R. 701). Indeed, in *JP v SSWP (DLA)* [2014] UKUT 275 (AAC); [2015] AACR 2, the judge pointed out that *In re W* had been decided after *R(DLA) 3/06* and the making of the Practice Direction and he said that para.5 of the Practice Direction was inconsistent with the decision of the Supreme Court in saying that a tribunal *must* decline to hear evidence from a child if it would prejudice the child's welfare. In 2014, the then Senior President of Tribunals announced that he would revise the Practice Direction but, in *AM (Afghanistan) v Secretary of State for the Home Department* [2017] EWCA Civ 1123 at [30], Ryder SPT, with whom Underhill and Gross L.JJ. agreed, said that it must be followed. **3.338**

In the 1990s, domiciliary hearings were still fairly common and it was said in *CI/4093/1999* that "[i]f in fact the claimant cannot reasonably be expected to come to the tribunal, then the tribunal must offer to come to the claimant." However, it was pointed out in *KO v SSWP (ESA)* [2013] UKUT 544 (AAC) that that decision was of some antiquity. The judge said—

> "Matters have moved on during that time in respect of the desirability of holding domiciliary hearings. It is rare that they are either appropriate or necessary. Enquiries may need to be made as to how an appellant attends other appointments, such as hospital visits. Few people are totally housebound, and it may be that an appellant can attend if transport is provided. If the issue has not become apparent prior to the date the scheduled hearing those enquiries should be made as early as possible on that day in a telephone call to the appellant's home by the clerk at the venue as the case may be able to proceed as listed or later in the day if a taxi could be arranged, or an adjournment may be necessary so that a taxi could be provided on another occasion. If other methods of transport (such as a private ambulance) are under consideration, or if it is thought that the tribunal venue itself may be unsuitable and another venue, whether a hearing centre or a local community facility may be preferable, or, unusually that the issue of a domiciliary visit does arise, the tribunal will want to adjourn the case for the attention of the local District Tribunal Judge who will know about local options and facilities,

and who may direct medical evidence as to the nature of the difficulties in order to assess suitability."

In *DB v Secretary of State for Work and Pensions (DLA)* [2016] UKUT 205 (AAC), the same judge reiterated the point that a difficulty in getting around does not necessarily justify a domiciliary hearing and made the point that technology including telephony can enable a person to participate in a hearing without actually attending (see the definition of "hearing" in r.1(3), which allows hearings to take place by telephone or video, which have both become much more commonly used since the Covid-19 pandemic). She rejected a submission on behalf of the Secretary of State that the First-tier Tribunal was not required to consider obtaining medical records or directing a domiciliary hearing or other steps to facilitate participation unless an application was made, but continued:

> "45. That does not mean that a tribunal must initiate such enquiries in every case; it need not treat litigants who are unrepresented as if they invariably needed help and guidance. The tribunal process does not consist of the hearing alone. The administrative arm provides information and options to an appellant at the outset and where there is no contra indication in the case papers the tribunal can rely upon the choices a litigant has made. Many appellants do not want to be present at a hearing; they are used to decisions in respect of benefit matters being made without their oral input and are happy to make their points on paper. That is a legitimate position to adopt; it does not necessarily indicate that the person does not know any better, but the tribunal must be alert to the possibility of a genuine lack of understanding of the possibilities. . . ."

The respondent has as much right to ask for a hearing as an appellant and, where an appellant does not want to attend a hearing or is unable to do so due to being abroad, there is no unfairness merely because the respondent is represented at the hearing and the appellant neither attends nor is represented (*FY v SSWP (RP)* [2018] UKUT 146 (AAC)), although there may be occasions, particularly where a claimant is unable to attend a hearing and has not just chosen not to do so, when the raising of a new point during the hearing may require an adjournment so that the claimant can address it.

The tribunal has considerable latitude in deciding how a hearing will be conducted but it must be fair. If the rules of natural justice (which effectively guarantee a fair hearing) are broken, the decision of the tribunal is liable to be set aside on appeal on the ground that it is erroneous in point of law. See further the annotation to s.11 of the Tribunals, Courts and Enforcement Act 2007.

Telephone, video and hybrid hearings

3.339 Remote hearings, in which at least some of, and usually all of, the parties, witnesses and members of the First-tier Tribunal participated by telephone or video link, became common from mid-2020 as a result of the Covid-19 pandemic but, from October 2021, there was a general move back towards having face-to-face hearings. Nonetheless, now that the First-tier Tribunal has been provided with the technology and has become experienced in using it, it has become recognised that remote hearings may often be a more suitable way of conducting proceedings than face-to-face hearings, particularly when parties would prefer a remote hearing or find it more convenient. Thus, a significant proportion of cases are still listed on the basis that at least some of the parties or witnesses will participate by telephone or videolink. However, even when that is so, the general rule since October 2021 has been that hearings are conducted from a tribunal venue, with panels sitting together, save in exceptional or unavoidable circumstances including where to do so would pose an unacceptable risk to a person's health or wellbeing or where there is not a suitable hearing room or adequate equipment at a venue for use by the judge or panel.

Novel practical issues can arise in remote hearings. For instance, if the judge mutes an appellant because he or she interrupts other witnesses, fairness may demand that the appellant be asked after each other witness has given evidence whether he or she has heard the evidence properly, particularly in a hearing in which some participants have had technical difficulties.

In *JS v Wirral MBC (HB)* [2021] UKUT 219 (AAC), an appeal was listed for a determination on the papers because the appellant had said on his listing enquiry form that he did not want a hearing. Given the background to the case and the obvious importance of the appellant giving oral evidence if he was serious about pursuing his appeal, the First-tier Tribunal drew the inference that the appellant had something to hide. However, the listing enquiry form had been sent to the tribunal in April 2020, during the first national lockdown to combat the Covid-19 pandemic, and it emerged during the appellant's appeal to the Upper Tribunal that he had been "shielding" at the time. Moreover, the form did not at that time offer appellants a remote hearing in which they could participate by telephone or videolink, rather than a face-to-face hearing. In those circumstances, the Upper Tribunal held that it had been unfair to decide the appeal on the papers.

On the other hand, in *TC v Islington LBC (SEN)* [2021] UKUT 196 (AAC), the Upper Tribunal rejected an appeal brought on the ground that one of the appellants and another witness had been unable to participate properly in a remote hearing due to their hearing disabilities. The decision turned on the particular facts of the case. The Upper Tribunal was satisfied that the First-tier Tribunal had properly considered how the giving of their evidence could be facilitated and neither of them had indicated during the hearing that they were having difficulty. Moreover, on analysis, there was very little objective evidence to suggest that the presentation of the appellants' case was materially impeded by the relevant appellant's hearing impairment. On the contrary, their dissatisfaction with the way the hearing had unfolded reflected choices that they had made during the hearing rather than failures of communication due to hearing disabilities:

> "That they chose to focus on certain, strongly-held, key points to the exclusion of others was a decision in the admittedly difficult context for litigants in person of a tribunal hearing. That, having received the FtT's reasons for its decision, they wished they had argued it differently is an experience that will be shared by many litigants, whether or not they have a hearing impairment."

Oral evidence given at a hearing

In *R. (SS) v Secretary of State for the Home Department* [2018] EWCA Civ 1391), **3.340**
the Court of Appeal warned of the danger of drawing a conclusion from a witness's demeanour as to the likelihood that the witness is telling the truth and said:

> "40. This is not to say that judges (or jurors) lack the ability to tell whether witnesses are lying. Still less does it follow that there is no value in oral evidence. But research confirms that people do not in fact generally rely on demeanour to detect deception but on the fact that liars are more likely to tell stories that are illogical, implausible, internally inconsistent and contain fewer details than persons telling the truth: see Minzner, 'Detecting Lies Using Demeanor, Bias and Context' (2008) 29 Cardozo LR 2557. One of the main potential benefits of cross-examination is that skilful questioning can expose inconsistencies in false stories.
>
> 41. No doubt it is impossible, and perhaps undesirable, to ignore altogether the impression created by the demeanour of a witness giving evidence. But to attach any significant weight to such impressions in assessing credibility risks making judgments which at best have no rational basis and at worst reflect conscious or unconscious biases and prejudices. One of the most important qualities expected of a judge is that they will strive to avoid being influenced by personal biases and prejudices in their decision-making. That requires eschewing judgments based on the appearance of a witness or on their tone, manner or other aspects of their behaviour in answering questions. Rather than attempting to assess whether

testimony is truthful from the manner in which it is given, the only objective and reliable approach is to focus on the content of the testimony and to consider whether it is consistent with other evidence (including evidence of what the witness has said on other occasions) and with known or probable facts."

This perhaps tends to suggest that, while remote hearings can make communication between participants more difficult, they should not make it more difficult to assess credibility, and other advantages to parties, such as not having to travel long distances, may outweigh the disadvantages.

For a decision considering a number of the authorities on credibility and the Upper Tribunal's reluctance to interfere with a decision of the First-tier Tribunal that was based on its carefully reasoned assessment of oral evidence, see *NN v HMRC (TC)* [2019] UKUT 386 (AAC).

A tribunal is entitled to take account of all that it sees and hears at a hearing but if it sees something that appears important, fairness generally requires that the party concerned should be given an opportunity of commenting on what the tribunal has seen. In *R(DLA) 8/06*, the Commissioner cautioned tribunals against giving too much weight to observations of a claimant's apparent well-being that might be unrepresentative and so be unreliable as evidence of his health generally. Giving a claimant an opportunity to comment enables the claimant to put the observation into a broader context. However, the Commissioner also pointed out that, where an observation merely confirms a conclusion that the tribunal would have reached anyway, a failure to invite the claimant to comment on it will not render the decision erroneous in point of law although, unless a judge makes clear what significance a recorded observation had in the tribunal's reasoning when he or she is writing the statement of reasons, it is likely to be assumed that it must have had an effect on the decision. The Commissioner also made clear that a judge does not have to ask precise questions amounting to a cross-examination of the claimant but can ask an open question that gives a claimant the opportunity to comment. He said—

"... .the chairman did not point out to the claimant the significance of the observations that the tribunal had made. But the claimant must have realised this. He had presented his claim on the basis of pain and exhaustion and the observations were clearly directly relevant to that."

What is important is whether, taking the hearing as a whole, the claimant has an adequate opportunity to address the issues raised by any significant observations. It is not usually necessary to give a party an opportunity to comment on the tribunal's initial impressions derived from its observations of a party's demeanour or on the inferences it draws from the evidence (*CC v SSWP (ESA)* [2019] UKUT 14 (AAC)), but it may be if they raise a new point that the party could not reasonably have anticipated (*KH (by CH) v SSWP (DLA)* [2022] UKUT 303 (AAC), where the First-tier Tribunal erred in not giving a child's father an opportunity to comment on its thoughts as to how her night-time attention needs might be reduced). See, further, the note to s.3(1) of the Tribunals, Courts and Enforcement Act 2007.

Representatives in social security cases are often in a position to give evidence from their own knowledge and it has on several occasions been said that they should not be stopped from doing so (see the note to r.11(1)). However, it was pointed out in *JE v SSWP (PIP)* [2020] UKUT 17 (AAC) that, where two members of a representative organisation attend a hearing and one has evidence to give, they ought to make that clear at the outset.

Taking evidence from overseas

3.341 The possibility of a tribunal hearing evidence by video link or telephone from a witness who is in another country raises sensitive issues. In *SSHD v Agbabiaka (evidence from abroad, Nare guidance)* [2021] UKUT 286 (IAC), the Upper Tribunal noted that there had "long been an understanding among Nation States that one

State should not seek to exercise the powers of its courts within the territory of another, without having the permission of that other State to do so". The opinion of the Foreign, Commonwealth and Development Office ("FCDO") was that the provision of written evidence from abroad was not affected by that convention and neither was the provision of oral submissions. The Upper Tribunal regarded that opinion as determinative, although it pointed out at [24] that the dividing line between submissions and oral evidence may in practice not be an easy one to hold, particularly where a litigant does not have legal representation. However, a court or tribunal ought not to take oral evidence from abroad unless the relevant country has given permission because, otherwise, there is a risk of damaging the United Kingdom's diplomatic relationship with the other country.

What emerged in *Agbabiaka* was that, although the FCDO maintained a list of countries that had given permission for oral evidence to be taken from a witness in their territory, the checks on which it was based had been confined only to evidence in "civil and commercial proceedings", which was interpreted by the FCDO as not including administrative proceedings before tribunals (which would include not only immigration and asylum cases but also social security cases in the First-tier Tribunal and Upper Tribunal) or criminal proceedings. This lacuna had been recognised in June 2021 and the FCDO proposed to initiate similar checks from November 2021 so as to identify countries that were content to give permission for oral evidence to be taken from witnesses in administrative proceedings before tribunals and criminal proceedings. Meanwhile, tribunals had to stop receiving oral evidence from abroad in social security (and many other) cases. Now, if a party wishes to give evidence, or to call another witness to give evidence, from abroad, he or she should inform the First-tier Tribunal in advance so that the First-tier Tribunal's administration has time to contact the FCDO's "Taking of Evidence Unit" and obtain confirmation that the taking of oral evidence from the relevant country is permissible. The guidance in *Agbabiaka* states that:

> "1. There is an understanding among Nation States that one State should not seek to exercise the powers of its courts within the territory of another, without having the permission of that other State to do so. Any breach of that understanding by a court or tribunal in the United Kingdom risks damaging this country's relationship with other States with which it has diplomatic relations and is, thus, contrary to the public interest. The potential damage includes harm to the interests of justice.
> 2. The position of the Secretary of State for Foreign, Commonwealth and Development Affairs is that it is accordingly necessary for there to be permission from such a foreign State (whether on an individual or general basis) before oral evidence can be taken from that State by a court or tribunal in the United Kingdom. Such permission is not considered necessary in the case of written evidence or oral submissions.
> 3. Henceforth, it will be for the party to proceedings before the First-tier Tribunal who is seeking to have oral evidence given from abroad to make the necessary enquiries with the Taking of Evidence Unit (ToE) of the Foreign, Commonwealth and Development Office (FCDO), in order to ascertain whether the government of the foreign State has any objection to the giving of evidence to the Tribunal from its territory.
> 4. The First-tier Tribunal will need to be informed at an early stage of the wish to give evidence from abroad. The party concerned will need to give the Tribunal an indication of the nature of the proposed evidence (which need not, at this stage, be in the form of a witness statement).
> 5. The Tribunal's duty to seek to give effect to the overriding objective may require it, in particular, to consider alternatives to the giving of oral evidence where (for example) there are delays in the FCDO obtaining an answer from the foreign State. Each case will need to be considered on its merits.
> 6. The experience gained by the First-tier Tribunal in hearing oral evidence given

in the United Kingdom by remote means during the Covid-19 pandemic is such that there should no longer be a general requirement for such evidence to be given from another court or tribunal hearing centre.
7. The guidance given by the Upper Tribunal in Nare (evidence by electronic means) Zimbabwe [2011] UKUT 00443 (IAC) is amended to the above extent."

From 7 April 2022 His Majesty's Courts and Tribunals Service have assumed responsibility for contacting the ToE Unit on behalf of any party who has notified the tribunal that they propose to rely upon oral evidence from a person overseas.

If it becomes apparent at a hearing that a party or witness is joining from overseas and that the ToE Unit has not confirmed whether the state has given permission, the tribunal will consider the overriding objective (rule 2), and either a) adjourn the appeal with appropriate directions for making enquiries of the ToE Unit; or might b) decide the appeal.

It is suggested that although a party who is overseas may not give oral evidence in such circumstances, it would be permissible for them to make brief submissions about whether the tribunal should adjourn and the directions that might be made. Relevant factors may include the relevance and significance of the oral evidence, whether the party has failed to respond to directions asking them to inform the tribunal whether they wish to give oral evidence from overseas, and delay.

A further complication has arisen because it appears that, where a country has given permission to take evidence via video or telephone, this may be limited to nationals and residents of that country only. This means that those people just visiting (temporary visitors) may not be permitted to give evidence in any event. Clarification is being sought from FCDO but in the meantime it should be assumed that any permission given does not extend to temporary visitors.

However, although the First-tier Tribunal should try to ensure that it does not receive evidence from abroad without the consent of the relevant country's government, it does not err in law merely because it receives evidence without that consent. In *Raza v Secretary of State for the Home Department* [2023] EWCA Civ 29, Elizabeth Laing LJ, with whom the other members of the Court agreed, said at [76]:

> "The primary question for this Court is whether there is any provision or rule of domestic law which shows that the FtT hearing was unlawful and a nullity. There is none. The [Nationality, Immigration and Asylum Act 2002] expressly requires some appeals to be made from, and some to be continued from, abroad. The 2002 Act does not provide that the lawfulness of such appeals depends on any condition, such as the obtaining of permission from a foreign state. The Rules assume that a hearing can be conducted partly by video link. The Rules do not provide for any further conditions in relation to the taking of evidence from abroad. Neither Nare nor *Agbabiaka* suggests that the taking of video evidence from abroad without the permission of the state concerned is unlawful, or that it makes the hearing a nullity. *Agbabiaka* suggests that such a hearing might be contrary to the public interest because of its potential to damage international relations, and, thus contrary to the interests of justice, but that is a different point. I accept Mr Kovats's submission that the sanctions for such conduct are diplomatic, not legal."

Permission is not required where persons wish to give oral evidence by video or telephone from England, Scotland, Wales, Northern Ireland, the Isle of Man, the Channel Islands, or from British Overseas Territories. Nor is there any requirement to seek permission from the tribunal in relation to documentary evidence or the production of a written witness statement or written evidence from abroad. This means, subject to the Tribunal Procedural Rules, that a party may rely upon written submissions, or written evidence that has been supplied by an individual who is situated within the territory of another state without needing to establish to the satisfaction of the tribunal that there is no legal or diplomatic barrier to their doing so.

Interpreters

HMCTS should provide an official interpreter if given notice of the requirement. However, in the absence of an official interpreter, a tribunal may use an unofficial one, provided it is satisfied that the proposed interpreter has an adequate command of both languages and knows what is required—i.e. a translation in both directions rather than a precis and with no comments. In *ZO v SSWP (IB)* [2010] UKUT 143 (AAC), it was said: **3.342**

> "4. It is preferable to have an independent interpreter rather than a relative acting as interpreter, but there is no absolute rule that only an independent interpreter will do. Indeed, in giving guidance on this issue, the First-tier Tribunal Bench Book states that the use of 'a relative acting as an interpreter is permissible provided that he understands what is required, i.e. that he should simply translate the questions accurately and relay to the tribunal the answers given by the appellant in his own words without comment or explanation. This is sometimes difficult to get across, and particularly in cases where credibility is in issue it may be preferable to adjourn with a direction ... However, each case must be considered on its merits and there is certainly no rule which requires a tribunal to adjourn for an official interpreter, and a tribunal could be criticised for adjourning if there is a relative or friend willing and able to undertake the task'."

In that case, the official interpreter failed to attend the hearing but the claimant was accompanied by her son who spoke good English and offered to interpret. The First-tier Tribunal erred in informing the claimant that, if she wanted a hearing there would have to be adjournment and that otherwise her case would be decided on the papers. It should have considered whether the claimant's son understood what was required and so would have been an adequate interpreter. Reference was made to *ZO* in *AS v SSWP (ESA)* [2019] UKUT 261 (AAC), where the First-tier Tribunal did allow a friend of the claimant to interpret but was held to have erred in failing to record in its statement of reasons whether the friend was instructed how to undertake the task correctly and whether she interpreted so that the accuracy of interpretation of the questions and the answers could safely be relied upon. That should no doubt be done and it may be wise for a judge to record that it has been done but, arguably, the Upper Tribunal should have applied the presumption of regularity and presumed that it had been done unless there was evidence to the contrary.

In *DS v SSWP (ESA)* [2013] UKUT 572 (AAC), it was accepted that there had been a procedural irregularity in the proceedings before the First-tier Tribunal because the claimant's request that an interpreter be provided at his hearing was mislaid by the tribunal's administration and so not considered by a judge. However, it was held that no unfairness had resulted because the claimant had in fact been able to communicate effectively. In reaching that conclusion, the Upper Tribunal did not merely rely upon the First-tier Tribunal having recorded that the claimant had been "able to make himself understood as he attended the medical and the tribunal hearing and gave evidence by himself and had no problems in communicating" but, having made the point that "[o]ne must surely be alive to the possibility that a combination of not wishing to lose face and not wishing to challenge the tribunal's authority might create the impression of good communication skills" and that "[i]t is also possible that some nuances may have been lost", it also considered the detailed record of proceedings and statement of reasons, which enabled it to be satisfied both that the claimant's allegations that the tribunal had misunderstood him had not been made out and that the claimant had understood the questions put to him by the tribunal. In *BF v SSWP (PIP)* [2019] UKUT 420 (AAC) on the other hand, there was not that evidence of an ability to communicate well. The claimant had requested that there be an interpreter for a hearing and it is not clear from the Upper Tribunal's decision whether there had been. In the event, the claimant refused to go into the hearing room, but there were nonetheless issues before the Upper Tribunal as to whether the health care professional's report was flawed because there had not been an interpreter and whether there had been adequate communication between the claimant and the clerk to the tribunal. The judge pointed out that the claimant had used an interpreter for an NHS consultation and said that "it was not for the First-tier Tribunal to substitute its own judgment of how fluent and confident the appellant was in English for the purposes of legal proceedings".

There is not necessarily a conflict between the decisions. Both judges were alert to the danger of too readily assuming from an ability to speak and understand some English that a claimant is sufficiently fluent to be able to participate properly in tribunal proceedings. However, there was clear evidence as to the claimant's ability to communicate effectively in *DS*, but apparently not in *BF*. Thus, a judge may decide that a person can have, or has had, a fair hearing without an interpreter, but must have an evidential basis for doing so.

Record of proceedings

3.343 There is no statutory duty upon the presiding tribunal judge to keep a record of proceedings before the First-tier Tribunal. However, there is a general duty to do so (see *R.(AW) v First-tier Tribunal (CIC)* [2013] UKUT 350 (AAC)) and, in any event, the Senior President of Tribunals issued a Practice Statement dated October 30, 2008 which more or less replicated the Social Security and Child Support (Decisions and Appeals) Regulations 1999 reg.55. That Practice Statement has now been replaced by *Practice Statement: Record of Proceedings in Social Security and Child Support Cases in the Social Entitlement Chamber on or after 31 March 2022*, which is in very similar terms but extends the time for which a record of proceedings must be kept from six months to 18 months, which is what it had been until 1999. It provides:

"1. In this Practice Statement—
   a. a rule referred to by number means that rule in the Tribunal Procedure (First-tier Tribunal) Social Entitlement Chamber) Rules 2008;
   b. 'social security and child support case' has the meaning given in rule 1(3).
2. A record of the proceedings at a hearing in a social security and child support case must be made by the presiding member, or in the case of a Tribunal composed of only one member, by that member.
3. The record must be sufficient to indicate any evidence taken and submissions made and any procedural applications, and may be in such medium as the member may determine.
4. The Tribunal must preserve—
   a. the record of proceedings;
   b. the decision notice; and
   c. any written reasons for the Tribunal's decision

   for the period specified in paragraph 5.
5. The specified period is 18 months from the date of—
   a. the decision made by the Tribunal;
   b. any written reasons for the Tribunal's decision;
   c. any correction under rule 36;
   d. any refusal to set aside a decision under rule 37; or
   e. any determination of an application for permission to appeal against the decision,

   or until the date on which those documents are sent to the Upper Tribunal in connection with an appeal against the decision or an application for permission to appeal, if that occurs within the 18 months.

6. Any party to the proceedings may within the time specified in paragraph 5 apply in writing for a copy of the record of proceedings and a copy must be supplied to him."

Proceedings are now generally recorded digitally. In *MK v SSWP (II)* [2014] UKUT 323 (AAC), it was said that, in those circumstances, the recording was the record of proceedings so that it could not be argued that the record was inadequate on the basis of omissions in the judge's note. The Upper Tribunal also said that, in those circumstances, the judge's note was personal and so not disclosable in any circumstances, referring to *R. (McIntyre) v Parole Board* [2013] EWHC 1969 (Admin), in which the Administrative Court drew a clear distinction between a record of proceedings and other notes made by a judge that are confidential and should not be disclosed. In *R. (AW) v First-tier Tribunal (CIC)* [2013] UKUT 350 (AAC), it had been suggested that the confidentiality of the judge's note could be waived in the interests of efficiency given the cost of obtaining a transcript of a recording or the length of time it takes an appellate judge to listen to a recording. However, it is noteworthy that the new Practice Statement, like the previous one, places the duty to make the record of proceedings on the "presiding member", who is always a judge (see the note to the First-tier Tribunal and Upper Tribunal (Composition of Tribunal) Order 2008 art.2, above) and that it makes no reference to recordings made by, or on behalf of, HMCTS. It may therefore be arguable in the Upper Tribunal that the presiding judge is required to maintain a record of proceedings, notwithstanding that there is also a recording, and that such a record is, in accordance with *McIntyre*, to be distinguished from any confidential notes. There being such a duty would reflect the practical advantage of having a readily and cheaply available note in addition to the recording. The reference to "such medium as the member may determine" in para.3 would enable that to be done either in an electronic format or in a handwritten document that could then be scanned and added to electronic case documents.

"It is entirely proper and reasonable for a judge who is determining a permission application to consult the official record of proceedings and to decide (without further recourse to the parties) whether that record corroborates an assertion in the grounds of appeal", particularly as a party may ask for a copy of the recording (*R. (Oceana) v Upper Tribunal (Immigration and Asylum Chamber)* [2023] EWHC 791 (Admin) at [39] to [41]).

Although parties are routinely given copies of the recording, a person will generally also be entitled to an official transcript of public proceedings, presumably taken from the recording, provided that he or she is prepared to pay for it (*Kirkham v IC* [2019] UKUT 381 (AAC) and see, further, the annotation to *Practice Direction (Upper Tribunal: Transcripts of Proceedings)*, below. It may be noted that, having obtained both the recording and the transcript, Mr Kirkham asked the judge to provide a copy of her notes. She refused, relying on *McIntyre*, and the Upper Tribunal refused Mr Kirkham permission to appeal, rejecting arguments that *McIntyre* had been wrongly decided or did not apply to tribunals (*Kirkham v IC (Record of Proceedings)* [2020] UKUT 336(AAC)).

A recording of a hearing is a court record falling within the scope of s.32 of the Freedom of Information Act 2000 and any question whether the Practice Statement applies or it should be disclosed to someone not entitled to it under the Practice Statement is a matter for the tribunal and not for the Information Commissioner (*Edem v IC* [2015] UKUT 210 (AAC)).

Paragraph 3 of the Practice Statement confirms that the "record of proceedings" is a note of the evidence taken, and the submissions and any procedural applications made, at the hearing, as was held in *R(DLA) 3/08*. The reference to evidence and submissions is often taken to refer to the oral evidence and submissions but it probably extends to at least a record of the written evidence and submissions before the First-tier Tribunal which may in turn imply a duty on someone to keep a copy of those documents. In practice, HMCTS usually keeps the whole file (whether in a physical form or electronically) for the requisite period, which complies with the duty imposed however the Practice Statement is construed.

This, together with the duty to keep the other documents mentioned in para.4, usually makes it unnecessary for a person appealing, or seeking permission to appeal, to the Upper Tribunal to supply copies of such documents with the appeal or application, because the Upper Tribunal automatically obtains them from the First-tier Tribunal. During the period from 1999 to 2022, when the First-tier Tribunal was obliged to keep those documents only for six months, a person bringing a very late appeal or application for permission to appeal sometimes found it necessary to supply such documents to support the appeal or application. In *CIB/62/2008*, a claimant who had not kept those documents and made an application to a tribunal chairman for leave to appeal more than six months late, with the consequence that the tribunal's file had been destroyed, was refused leave to appeal by both the chairman and a Commissioner. The latter held that the claimant's assertion that he had asked for an oral hearing of his appeal before the tribunal which had been refused would not be enough to overcome the presumption that the tribunal proceedings had been properly conducted, when the claimant's own delay had resulted in the probable destruction of the evidence that would either have supported or contradicted his assertion.

The duty imposed by para.6 to provide a party with a copy of the record of proceedings is a duty to provide one that is intelligible or capable of being made intelligible to the party. However, one obvious remedy when a provided record is illegible is simply to ask the clerk to obtain and provide a legible copy. A failure to comply with the duty to provide an intelligible record will render the tribunal's decision erroneous in point of law only if, in a particular case, the consequence is a real possibility of unfairness or injustice (*R(DLA) 3/08*). Thus, in *CB v SSWP (ESA)* [2014] UKUT 545 (AAC), it was stated that "the duration of a hearing must be recorded to demonstrate that the hearing did not begin before the notified time and was of sufficient length to allow the parties to put forward their cases", but the failure to record the duration of the hearing in that case was only a material error because it meant that there was no indication of the period for which the First- tier Tribunal had found that the claimant had sat without discomfort and so the relevance of the finding was unclear on the claimant's appeal to the Upper Tribunal.

The extent to which a lack of a record of proceedings results in unfairness or injustice may turn on the extent to which the deficiency can be made good by obtaining evidence as to what happened or was said at a hearing from the parties or the First-tier Tribunal. Where an appeal is based on what happened at a hearing, the Upper Tribunal will be slow to go behind a full record of proceedings (*CS/343/1994*) but will admit evidence if it is necessary to do so where a full and particularised allegation is made that the conduct of the hearing led to a breach of the rules of natural justice (*R(M) 1/89*). The Upper Tribunal may obtain statements from those present at the hearing, including the members of the First-tier Tribunal, but it will not be necessary to obtain statements from members of the First-tier Tribunal if the appellant's case is supported by other evidence, such as the record of proceedings and the statement of reasons, unless the case involves an allegation of personal misconduct that it would be unfair to find proved without the person concerned having had the opportunity of commenting (*CDLA/5574/2002*). The need to obtain proper evidence as to what occurred at the hearing has been reiterated in *Singh v Secretary of State for the Home Department* [2016] EWCA Civ 492.

3.344 However, it is not just in cases where procedural impropriety is alleged that a record of proceedings is an important document. Because a statement of reasons ought to deal with the principal points raised by the parties but the First-tier Tribunal is not always required to consider points that have not been explicitly raised, and because the First-tier Tribunal generally has an investigatory role, the record of proceedings may be an important document in a case where it is suggested that the statement of reasons is inadequate or that the First-tier Tribunal failed to ask questions about a particular issue. On the other hand, an incomplete record may be supplemented by other evidence. In *CH/2484/2006*, the Deputy Commissioner said:

> "I appreciate that a record of proceedings is not a complete verbatim note and that it is possible for points to be omitted, but if an appellant to the Commissioner wishes to base a submission on the overlooking of evidence or submissions and the evidence or submission are not recorded in the record, it seems to me to be necessary as a general rule for it to equip itself with evidence (such as a statement by someone who was present) that that piece of evidence or submission was in fact made. It should also raise the matter with the other side in advance, so as to avoid surprise and facilitate agreement on the position if possible."

In that case, the local authority was the appellant. Where a claimant is an appellant and the Secretary of State was not present at the hearing before the tribunal, the Secretary of State will not be in a position to dispute a statement by the claimant as to what occurred at that hearing. As suggested above, it will be open to the Upper Tribunal to seek the views of the First-tier Tribunal, but it will not be obliged to do so.

Paragraph (3)

Where a strike-out decision is made without a hearing, care has to be taken to ensure that the effect is not that the claimant is improperly deprived of a hearing of their appeal (*O'T v Immigration Services Commissioner* [2019] UKUT 6 (AAC) and see the note to r.8(3)). In a criminal injuries compensation case, a party whose case has been struck out without a hearing may apply for the decision to be reconsidered at a hearing under para.(4)(b) (*R. (NT) v First-tier Tribunal (CIC)* [2013] UKUT 357 (AAC)). **3.345**

Paragraphs (4)–(6)

Rule 27(4)(b) gives a claimant a right to apply for a hearing in a criminal injuries compensation case where the case has been struck out without a hearing in accordance with para.(3) (*R. (NT) v First-tier Tribunal (CIC)* [2013] UKUT 357 (AAC)). **3.346**

The word "extend" in r.27(5)(c) does not include "waive" (*JM v Advocate General for Scotland* [2013] CSOH 169).

It is not obligatory to determine a case falling within para.(5) without a hearing and it is well-established that procedural fairness may require a person to be offered an oral hearing where legislation does not provide an absolute right to one. Relevant factors were identified in *R. (Osborne) v Parole Board* [2013] UKSC 61; [2014] 1 A.C. 1115 of which the first, and perhaps the most relevant in the social security context, is "where facts which appear . . . to be important are in dispute, or where a significant explanation or mitigation is advanced which needs to be heard orally in order fairly to determine its credibility". In some cases it may also be necessary to provide reasons for refusing an oral hearing (*R. (VAA) v First-tier Tribunal* [2010] UKUT 36 (AAC)). In *R. (AG) v First-tier Tribunal (CIC)* [2013] UKUT 357 (AAC), the Upper Tribunal held that it was not appropriate for the First-tier Tribunal to challenge the honesty or integrity of a claimant where an oral hearing has been refused and that reasons for refusing a hearing need to refer to the specific facts of the case in issue and not just "a standard (or perhaps pro forma) list of reasons". In *R. (TG) v First-tier Tribunal (CIC)* [2013] UKUT 366 (AAC), the Upper Tribunal said that—

> "The particular factors in this case which should have prompted the First-tier Tribunal to offer the applicant the opportunity to have an oral hearing include the complexity of the factual background (including the applicant's complaints about the nature of the investigation, her very lengthy (if not always accurate)

analysis of the case, her belief that the investigation was bungled, the police complaint investigation, and the continuing trouble between the two families) and the applicant's obvious difficulties in keeping to the most relevant matters when expressing herself in writing."

Entitlement to attend a hearing

3.347 **28.** Subject to rule 30(5) (exclusion of a person from a hearing), each party to proceedings is entitled to attend a hearing.

DEFINITIONS

"hearing"—see r.1(3).
"party"—*ibid.*

GENERAL NOTE

3.348 This makes it plain that, except where r.30(5) applies, a party may always attend a hearing even when the hearing is in private. By virtue of r.11(5) a properly appointed representative also has a right to attend a hearing, whether or not the party does so. By virtue of r.11(7), a party who attends hearing may be accompanied by a person acting as a representative or assistant.

In *TA v SSWP (PIP)* [2018] UKUT 26 (AAC), the decision of the First-tier Tribunal was set aside where the hearing had taken place 90 miles from the appellant's home although there were several closer hearing centres. She had originally asked for the decision to be made on the papers and the case had, perfectly properly in the light of that request, been listed at a distant venue rather than the one nearest her home. However, the First-tier Tribunal adjourned so that she could attend but then, unaccountably, directed that the case be listed at the same venue. When the claimant protested, the case was listed even further away from her home. The Upper Tribunal pointed out that the claimant, who had been injured in a road traffic accident and said she was nervous about using public transport, was entitled to attend a hearing. Although she had originally asked for her case to be decided on the papers, she was entitled to change her mind in the light of the First-tier Tribunal's adjournment, which had been given for precisely to enable to do so. Something very similar happened in *TB v SSD (WP)* [2014] UKUT 357 (AAC) and in *FJ v SSWP (PIP)* [2019] UKUT 27 (AAC). It would appear that in none of these cases had the panel deciding the case considered the case's history before deciding to proceed in the appellant's absence.

Notice of hearings

3.349 **29.**—(1) The Tribunal must give each party entitled to attend a hearing reasonable notice of the time and place of the hearing (including any adjourned or postponed hearing) and any changes to the time and place of the hearing.

(2) The period of notice under paragraph (1) must be at least 14 days except that—

(a) in an asylum support case the Tribunal must give at least 1 day's and not more than 5 days' notice; and
(b) the Tribunal may give shorter notice—
  (i) with the parties' consent; or
  (ii) in urgent or exceptional circumstances.

DEFINITIONS

"asylum support case"—see r.1(3).
"hearing"—*ibid.*

"party"—*ibid.*
"Tribunal"—*ibid.*

GENERAL NOTE

Where a joint claim is made, both claimants are parties. If only one of them has appealed, the other is a respondent as a person who had a right of appeal (see the definition of "respondent" in r.1(3)). Consequently, both should be notified of a hearing. A failure to do so is unlikely to be of practical importance if the claimants are still living together but it may be important where they have separated, as in *PD v HMRC (TC)* [2010] UKUT 159 (AAC). 3.350

As the terms of para.(1) make clear, the requirement to give 14 days' notice applies where the time of a hearing is changed, just as much as it applies to a change of date. Occasionally, this may be important. In *MB v SSWP (PIP)* [2020] UKUT 296 (AAC), the claimant received a telephone message on her answer phone on the evening before her hearing, telling her that the time had been changed from 2 pm to 10 am. She had been intending to be accompanied to the hearing by her sister, but because of the late change of time her sister had been unable to change her work schedule. The claimant could nonetheless have waived the right to notice, but the Upper Tribunal said that "the FtT would have to take great care to ensure that a claimant, who may have felt they had little option but to attend, was giving genuine and informed consent" to the hearing taking place at a new time, despite the short notice, and was not satisfied that it had done so.

See also GK v SSWP [2016] UKUT 465 (AAC) a tribunal's case management decision to hear an appeal at an earlier time on the scheduled day must be guided by the overriding objective.

Public and private hearings

30.—(1) Subject to the following paragraphs, all hearings must be held in public. 3.351

(2) A hearing in a criminal injuries compensation case must be held in private unless—

(a) the appellant has consented to the hearing being held in public; and
(b) the Tribunal considers that it is in the interests of justice for the hearing to be held in public.

(3) The Tribunal may give a direction that a hearing, or part of it, is to be held in private.

[[1] (3A) *Expired.*

(4) Where a hearing, or part of it, is to be held in private, the Tribunal may determine who is permitted to attend the hearing or part of it.

(5) The Tribunal may give a direction excluding from any hearing, or part of it—

(a) any person whose conduct the Tribunal considers is disrupting or is likely to disrupt the hearing;
(b) any person whose presence the Tribunal considers is likely to prevent another person from giving evidence or making submissions freely;
(c) any person who the Tribunal considers should be excluded in order to give effect to a direction under rule 14(2) (withholding information likely to cause harm); or
(d) any person where the purpose of the hearing would be defeated by the attendance of that person.

(6) The Tribunal may give a direction excluding a witness from a hearing until that witness gives evidence.

AMENDMENT

1. Tribunal Procedure (Coronavirus) (Amendment) Rules 2020 (SI 2020/416) r.4(1) and (3) (April 10, 2020). This temporary paragraph expired on September 25, 2022.

DEFINITIONS

"appellant"—see r.1(3).
"criminal injuries compensation case"—*ibid.*
"hearing"—*ibid.*
"Tribunal"—*ibid.*

GENERAL NOTE

Paragraphs (1) and (2)

3.352 Paragraph (1) expresses the general rule, which is that hearings should usually be in public. Paragraph (2), which applies only to criminal injuries compensation cases, is anomalous but continues the previous practice in such cases.

A hearing is in public, notwithstanding the lack of any publication of a list of cases, if it takes place within reasonable office hours at a publicly recognised court or tribunal hearing centre (*DF v SSWP (ESA)* [2015] UKUT 143 (AAC)), provided that there is no barrier (such as a locked door) to prevent access by a member of the public wishing to drop in to see how the hearing is being conducted (*Storer v British Gas Plc* [2000] 1 W.L.R. 1237 (CA)). Thus, usually, a hearing by telephone will only be in public if the judge is in an accessible hearing room and the telephone is on loudspeaker. Remote hearings obviously have a practical effect on the general public's ability to observe hearings in accordance with the principle of open justice. However, the Courts Act 2003 ss.85A and 85B (inserted by the Police, Crime, Sentencing and Courts Act 2022 ss.198 and 199 with effect from April 28, 2022) and the Remote Observation and Recording (Courts and Tribunals) Regulations 2022 (SI 2022/705), made under s.85A, allow people to observe proceedings that are transmitted to them, either to "designated live-streaming premises" or to a more limited audience of people who have first identified themselves to the tribunal (or to someone acting on its behalf). Most tribunal cases are not transmitted to designated live-streaming premises and so, when a tribunal case is heard remotely, it will not usually be possible for members of the public to observe it unless the tribunal is made aware that they wish to do so. The legislation does not expressly require all transmission to be live, so it appears that recordings made under s.85A(6) of the 2003 Act may be transmitted after the event to those who have a good enough reason for wishing to watch, or listen to, the proceedings. See also, guidance on the making of directions under s.85A(2) that has been issued by the Lord Chief Justice and Senior President of Tribunals and is published at [2022] 1 W.L.R. 3538 and at *https://www.judiciary.uk/guidance-and-resources/practice-guidance-on-remote-observation-of-hearings-new-powers/*.

The fact that a hearing is in public does not necessarily mean that it can be recorded by members of the public. In an unpublished decision dated August 8, 2011, the First-tier Tribunal sitting in Exeter refused to allow the BBC to bring recording equipment into a hearing. The BBC wished to be able to broadcast part of the proceedings as part of a Radio 4 documentary programme about the personal capability assessment for incapacity benefit. The First-tier Tribunal considered *Attorney General v British Broadcasting Corporation* [1981] AC 303 and concluded that the tribunal was a "court" for the purposes of s.9 of the Contempt of Court Act 1981. Although s.9(1)(a) of that Act permits a person to "use in court, or bring into court for use, any tape recorder or other instrument for recording sound" provided he or she has the permission of the court, s.9(1)(b) makes it always a contempt of court to:

"publish a recording of legal proceedings made by means of any such instrument, or any recording derived directly or indirectly form it, by playing it in the hearing of the public or any section of the public".

The tribunal or court has no power to give permission for a sound recording of proceedings to be broadcast to the public by the BBC. The First-tier Tribunal therefore refused permission to bring any equipment capable of recording sound, including mobile telephones, into the hearing because part of the reason for making a recording would be so that parts of it could be broadcast. It was further pointed out that the ban on broadcasting also applied to any CD of the proceedings that might be provided by the tribunal to the claimant as a record of the proceedings (see the note to r.27).

Equally, the fact that a hearing is in private does not mean that it is a contempt of court to disclose or publish information about the proceedings, unless an order restricting disclosure or publication has been made under r.14(1) (see s.12 of the Administration of Justice Act 1960, considered in *R. (BD) v First-tier Tribunal (CIC)* [2013] UKUT 332 (AAC)).

Paragraph 3

Paragraph (3) enables the Tribunal to direct that a particular case be heard in private, either in whole or in part. In practice, this does not arise as a live issue in social security cases very often because it is very rare for members of the general public to attend hearings. The issue perhaps arises primarily where one party is accompanied by a large number of people and there arises the question whether it is appropriate for them all to attend the hearing. Directing that a hearing be in private enables the numbers to be regulated under para.(4). **3.353**

The Rules give no guidance as to how it is to be decided whether or not a hearing is to be in private. Regulation 49(6) of the Social Security and Child Support (Decisions and Appeals) Regulations 1999 provided that a hearing could be in private only—

"(a) in the interests of national security, morals, public order or children;

(b) for the protection of the private or family life of one or more parties to the proceedings; or

(c) in special circumstances, because publicity would prejudice the interests of justice."

The language was based on art.6(1) of the European Convention on Human Rights, but art.6 is concerned with the right of *a party* to a public hearing. Consequently, as far as art.6 is concerned, a party may waive that right (*Schuler-Zgraggen v Switzerland*, judgment of June 24, 1993, Series A, No.263; (1993) 16 E.H.R.R. 405, at [58]) and consent to a hearing being in private even if those grounds are not made out. Regulation 49(6) did not permit such a waiver. The reason for that may have been that there are other interests in there being a public hearing, not the least of which is the right of the public to see how justice is administered, which includes the right of the press to comment on the administration of justice. That right, too, may require the approach formerly taken in reg.49(6), although the need to protect the private or family life of people other than the parties (e.g. witnesses and people who might be mentioned in evidence) may need to be taken into account so reg.49(6)(b) may have been too narrowly drawn.

However, where the press are not present and where the parties wish a hearing to be in private so that the number of people present may be limited to avoid a timid claimant from being overwhelmed and unable properly to present his or her case, it may be open to a Tribunal to direct that the hearing be in private even if the conditions of the former reg.49(6) are not met, simply on the ground that the interests of justice require that the claimant should be enabled to put his or her case effectively (see r.2(2)(c)). **3.354**

In all of this, it should not be forgotten that concerns about publicity can be met by the imposition of appropriate reporting restrictions under r.14(1). Generally, it will be preferable for the Tribunal to impose reporting restrictions rather than holding a hearing in private if the reporting restrictions will achieve all that is necessary. On the other hand, if there is a legitimate press interest in a case but a good reason for excluding the general public, it would be possible to admit the press to a hearing held in private under para.(4) (*Independent News and Media Ltd v A* [2010] EWCA Civ 343; [2010] 1 W.L.R. 2262) while, if necessary, prohibiting the publication of the names of the parties (*L v L (Ancillary Relief Proceedings: Anonymity)* [2015] EWHC 2621 (Fam); [2016] 1 W.L.R. 1259).

Even in the courts, it is recognised that the confidential nature of documents that must be considered at a hearing may sometimes justify holding the hearing in private (see, for instance, *Eurasian Natural Resources Corporation Ltd v Dechert LLP* [2014] EWHC 3389 (Ch); [2015] 1 W.L.R. 4621).

3.355 In *CIB/2751/2002 and CS/3202/2002*, the Commissioner considered how domiciliary hearings might be affected by the former reg.49(6). He suggested that it might be possible to hold a public hearing near a claimant's home rather than actually in it. Given that few people other than those invited by the parties ever watch tribunal hearings, the problems raised may be more theoretical than real but the legislation does require them to be addressed. The answer may be that, where a domiciliary hearing in a claimant's home is necessary, it will usually be justifiable to hold the hearing in private in order to protect the claimant's private or family life. Presumably a claimant who has asked for a domiciliary hearing can be taken to have waived his rights to privacy to the extent necessary to allow the hearing to take place with other parties being present.

In *KM v SSWP (CSM)* [2019] UKUT 48 (AAC) it was made plain that it was not appropriate for a clerk to decide who should be present at a hearing and to tell people accompanying parties that they can only be present throughout the hearing if they are there for moral support, rather than as witnesses, unless the judge or panel has specifically so. In that case, a party's daughter had attended to support the party's case by giving evidence and it was indicated by the clerk that she should stay in the waiting room. Because the party did not specifically say during the hearing that she wished her daughter to give evidence, the effect of what the clerk said was that the judge did not know that there was a potential witness in the building. As the party had been unrepresented, it was held that unfairness had resulted.

Paragraph (4)

3.356 If a case is to be heard in private, the tribunal has a broad power to determine who may attend it. However, certain people have a right to attend a hearing even if it is in private. By r.28, a party always has a right to be present (subject to r.30(5)) and, the consequence is that, by virtue of r.11(5), so does a properly appointed representative whether the party attends or not. Where a party does attend, he or she may be accompanied by a person acting either as a representative or merely as an assistant (see r.11(7)). Plainly relevant witnesses must be allowed to attend for the purpose of giving evidence.

Beyond that, it is all a matter of discretion, there being no equivalent to reg.49(9) of the 1999 Regulations. It is likely to be desirable for the clerk or usher to be present and also a judge or Chamber President or the Senior President of Tribunals monitoring the tribunal. It is also likely to be appropriate to allow a claimant to be accompanied by a friend or relative even if he or she is there only for moral support and is not providing any actual assistance. As to others, it is suggested that, where a person has a reason for attending other than mere curiosity, the views of the parties should be ascertained and taken into account. In practice, parties seldom object to a person being present if they are made aware of a good reason for his or her presence. It will therefore generally be appropriate to allow people undergoing training to attend, whether the person is a member of the decision-maker's staff, a new judge or member of the Tribunal or a trainee lawyer shadowing the judge.

A journalist may also have a legitimate reason for being present and consideration may need to be given to the question whether reporting restrictions imposed under r.14(1) will provide adequate protection for the parties and other vulnerable people. See the note to that rule.

Paragraph (5)

This paragraph allows any person who would otherwise be entitled to attend a hearing to be excluded, where that is necessary on one of the specified grounds. Plainly the power to exclude a party or representative should be exercised only where there is absolutely no practical alternative. See *R. (Secretary of State for the Home Department) v Inner West London Assistant Deputy Coroner* [2010] EWHC 3098 (Admin); [2011] 1 W.L.R. 2564 for the importance attached to the rights of parties and representatives to be present at hearings. In relation to sub-para.(b), it would be desirable to consider whether alternative methods of giving evidence (e.g. by videolink or from behind a screen) would achieve the necessary effect and be practical. **3.357**

In *WS v SSWP (IB)* [2012] UKUT 202 (AAC), there was evidence in the documents that the claimant was prone to violence and habitually carried a lock knife. The First-tier Tribunal, having discussed the matter with his representative, declined to allow the claimant into the hearing unless he consented to be searched. He did not consent to be searched and so the hearing took place in his absence. The First-tier Tribunal considered that the claimant was absent through his own choice and that view was not challenged. The Upper Tribunal observed that the situation was not covered by r.30(5)(a) because it could not be said that the claimant was "likely to disrupt the hearing" but suggested that it could have relied on the power in r.5(1) to "regulate its own procedure", provided it did not breach art.6 of the European Convention on Human Rights. There would, it considered, not have been a breach of art.6 in the circumstances that arose.

Now, under s.53 of the Courts Act 2003, as applied and modified by art.3 of the Tribunal Security Order 2014 (SI 2014/786), tribunal security officers may exclude members of the public from a tribunal building or part of a tribunal building if the person refuses to be searched under s.52 or to surrender an article if asked to do so under s.54 or for the purposes of enabling tribunal business to be carried on without interference or delay, maintaining order or securing the safety of any person in the tribunal building and may remove any person from a tribunal room at the request of a judge, and they may use reasonable force for those purposes. Section 53 was considered in *R. (O'Connor) v Aldershot Magistrates' Court* [2016] EWHC 2792 (Admin); [2017] 1 W.L.R. 2833. It was held that, where there is a dispute as to whether the conditions for exclusion are satisfied or there is room for such a dispute (e.g., because it is proposed in advance to exclude a particular category of person), the matter should be referred to a judge or justice of the peace who will be the final arbiter. Moreover, where it is proposed to exclude a group of people, fairness may require that one of them should be able to make representations before a final decision is made. However, wrongly excluding people from a hearing does not necessarily have the effect that the hearing is not in public, although it may have that effect and thus invalidate the proceedings.

Paragraph (6)

Whether witnesses should be excluded from a hearing until they give evidence depends very much on the circumstances of the case. There is often a fear that dishonest witnesses will tailor their evidence so that it fits with other evidence in the case if they hear that evidence before giving their own. Evidence can often be stronger if it is consistent without the witnesses having had the opportunity of hearing each other's answers to questions. On the other hand, witnesses can often usefully comment on other evidence and can pick up points not mentioned by other witnesses, which is important in social security cases, where parties are seldom represented by lawyers and there is rarely any proper examination-in-chief **3.358** or cross-examination. Indeed, a representative may often be a witness (see the note to r.11(1)). The Tribunal is given a broad discretion as to how to approach a case. If it intends to exclude witnesses from a hearing, it is suggested it should take the same approach to the witnesses of all parties lest it give the impression of having formed a view that the witnesses of one party only are suspected of dishonesty.

3.359 **30A.** *Expired.*

GENERAL NOTE

3.360 This coronavirus temporary rule was in force from April 10, 2020 to September 25, 2022.

Hearings in a party's absence

3.361 **31.** If a party fails to attend a hearing the Tribunal may proceed with the hearing if the Tribunal—

(a) is satisfied that the party has been notified of the hearing or that reasonable steps have been taken to notify the party of the hearing; and

(b) considers that it is in the interests of justice to proceed with the hearing.

DEFINITIONS

"hearing"—see r.1(3).
"party"—*ibid.*
"Tribunal"—*ibid.*

GENERAL NOTE

3.362 Where the First-tier Tribunal is composed of more than one member, the decision whether or not to proceed in a party's absence is a matter for the whole tribunal and not just the judge (*RK v SSWP (ESA)* [2018] UKUT 436 (AAC)).

It was unsurprisingly held in *LJT v SSWP (PIP)* (2019) UKUT 21 (AAC) that, when granting a request for a postponement but saying that the case "must proceed" on the next occasion, the First-tier Tribunal cannot be taken to have issued a direction that is binding on the panel considering the case on the next occasion should the claimant fail to appear. Even if the direction were in theory binding, it could be set aside under r.6(5). It is also clear from *LJT* that, although a history of postponements and adjournments may be relevant when deciding whether to proceed in a claimant's absence, it is unfair to hold against a claimant a previous adjournment that was clearly not the claimant's fault.

In *Cooke v Glenrose Fish Co* [2004] I.C.R. 1188, the Employment Appeal Tribunal suggested that an employment tribunal should always at least consider telephoning an appellant who has failed to appear before proceeding in his absence and should ordinarily do so where there was an indication that the appellant had been intending to appear at the hearing because, for instance, solicitors were on the record. An oversight can then be rectified. However, the Employment Appeal Tribunal also held that employment tribunals were entitled to take a robust approach and generally to proceed to hear cases where there was an unexplained absence, because any injustice could be put right on review. The provision in these Rules equivalent to a review would be r.37, which permits the setting aside of a decision where a party or his representative was not present at a hearing. The Employment Appeal Tribunal remarked that "it would appear to be a necessary concomitant of the more stringent attitude encouraged by [the President] that there be the less stringent attitude on a review if a party who has not attended comes forward with a genuine and full explanation and shows that the original hearing was not one from which he deliberately absented himself".

In *PS v SSWP (ESA)* [2017] UKUT 55 (AAC), it was stressed that it did not follow from *Cooke* that the First-tier Tribunal must, as a matter of law, always consider whether to telephone an appellant in the event of an unexplained absence from a hearing in the Social Entitlement Chamber, both for practical reasons and because the decisions in such cases are very fact-specific. In particular, there is usually far less inconvenience to other people in a social security decision being set aside if it subsequently turns out that there was a good reason for the non-attendance than there is in an employment tribunal case. On the other hand, where a case in which some £20,000 was at stake had been listed for an all-day hearing, involving presenting officers from two government departments, the claimant should have been telephoned (*KD v SSWP (ESA and IS)*; *KD v HMRC (TC)* [2020] UKUT 9 (AAC)). 3.363

SA v SSWP (PIP) [2017] UKUT 224 (AAC) is a good example of the concomitant approach in *Cooke*. The First-tier Tribunal disbelieved the Appellant's account of a fall which meant she could not attend the hearing. However, the fall was clearly corroborated by the internal clerical record, which had not been checked by the Tribunal. The Upper Tribunal found that there was a breach of natural justice to go ahead with hearing in Appellant's absence in such circumstances.

Where a claimant sent a message to a representative to say she would not be attending a hearing and wished the tribunal to proceed in her absence and the representative made no application for an adjournment, a Commissioner declined to hold the tribunal to have erred in not adjourning (*CSIB/404/2005*). However, he set the tribunal's decision aside for failure to deal adequately with questions concerning the claimant's mental health, even though it was difficult to see how the tribunal could have allowed the claimant's appeal on the evidence before it. That may suggest that, where the claimant's presence is required to establish the facts and the non-attendance might have been attributable, at least in part, to the claimant's mental health, a tribunal really should consider whether an adjournment would be in the interests of justice, just as they would if the claimant had not asked for a hearing (see the annotation to r.27). Of course, a tribunal is entitled to take into account the fact that the claimant has asked for a hearing and then failed to attend it in considering whether justice requires an adjournment and whether attendance in the future is likely.

Compliance with the conditions of r.31 does not prevent the setting aside of the tribunal's decision under r.37 on the ground that a party or representative was not present at the hearing, if it is just to do so (*KH v SSWP (CSM)* [2012] UKUT 329 (AAC)). Indeed, the existence of r.37 enables the First-tier Tribunal to take a more robust approach under r.31. It follows that compliance with r.31 also does not prevent a decision being set aside on review or appeal on the ground that there has been a breach of the rules of natural justice if it turns out that the First-tier Tribunal drew the wrong conclusions from the evidence available to it. In *GJ v SSWP (CSM)* [2012] UKUT 447 (AAC) it was observed on the absent party's appeal: "The issue is whether Mr J had a fair hearing. It is not whether the tribunal reasonably believed that he did." In *KH v SSWP (CSM)* the Upper Tribunal also approved the statement in *R(SB) 19/83*—

> "As a practical matter it is the duty of the appeal tribunal when a claimant does not attend and is not represented on the appeal to ask the tribunal clerk if the claimant has been properly notified of the hearing .... And the record of proceedings should show that this has been done or (where this is the case) how otherwise the tribunal was satisfied that the absent claimant was notified of the hearing."

The Upper Tribunal also emphasised the importance of the First-tier Tribunal showing, at least if a statement of reasons is requested, that the relevant factors have been considered and weighed up. It suggested that best practice would be for an explanation to be included (contemporaneously) in the record of proceedings. 3.364

Deciding whether to proceed in the absence of a party will involve consideration of many of the issues that are relevant to deciding whether there should be a hearing where no party has asked for one (see the note to r.27). Whether or not the absent party asked for a hearing in the first place may be relevant, although the possibility of a person who asked for a hearing having changed his or her mind must not be overlooked.

Where a party fails to attend a hearing after being refused a postponement, it may be necessary, when considering whether it is the interests of justice to proceed in the party's absence, effectively to reconsider at the hearing the refusal of the postponement, particularly if it appears aberrant or not fully reasoned (*JC v SSWP (PIP)* [2018] UKUT 110 (AAC); *BV v SSWP (PIP)* [2018] UKUT 444 (AAC); [2019] 1 W.L.R. 3185 and see the note to r.5(3)(h)). See also the note to r.4 in which it is suggested that, where the postponement was refused by a member of staff and the 14 days allowed under r.4(3) for asking for the decision to be considered afresh by a judge have not elapsed by the time of the hearing, it is likely always to be necessary for the refusal to be considered afresh if the party who asked for the postponement does not appear at the hearing.

The First-tier Tribunal has been held to have erred in failing to consider the duty in r.2(2)(c) to ensure that the parties are able to participate fully in the proceedings when it decided to proceed in the absence of an agoraphobic claimant who had asked for a domiciliary hearing (*PM v SSWP (IB)* [2013] UKUT 301 (AAC)) and when it determined an appeal without adjourning notwithstanding that the claimant had been forced to leave the hearing through illness (*AM v SSWP (ESA)* [2013] UKUT 563 (AAC); *HP v SSWP (PIP)* [2019] UKUT 36 (AAC)). In *SW v SSWP (DLA)* [2015] UKUT 319 (AAC), the Upper Tribunal referred not only to r.2(2)(c) but also to the Senior President of Tribunals' *Practice Direction (First-tier and Upper Tribunals: Children, Vulnerable Adults and Sensitive Witnesses)* (see below) and said that the First-tier Tribunal should have had regard to that Practice Direction in a case where the claimant had explained why she found it stressful to be around other people and had asked whether the First-tier Tribunal could telephone her on the day of the hearing if it had any questions. However, failing to refer to the Practice Direction in a case where a party is vulnerable is not necessarily an error of law, not least because the Tribunal Procedure Rules, common law and the European Convention on Human Rights all require the First-tier Tribunal to have regard to substantially the same considerations as the Practice Direction (*JH(S) v SSWP (ESA)* [2015] UKUT 567 (AAC)).

3.365 There is a continuing duty to consider whether it is in the interests of justice to proceed with a hearing in a party's absence so that, if in the course of considering a case in the absence of a party issues emerge that cannot really be dealt with fairly in the absence of the party, an initial decision to proceed in the parties' absence may have to be reconsidered (*KO v SSWP (ESA)* [2013] UKUT 544 (AAC)). Similarly, where a claimant attends a hearing but is unable to continue participating in it due to illness, consideration must be given to adjourning rather than simply deciding the case on the basis of the evidence and arguments already received (see *AM* and *HP*, above) and, indeed, unless the claimant has positively agreed to there being no adjournment or the First-tier Tribunal is satisfied that the hearing has effectively finished, an adjournment may be required for proper compliance with rr.27(1) and 28. The raising of a new issue that the absent party could not have expected may also require reconsideration of a decision to proceed in his or her absence. On the other hand, it is not always unfair for the Tribunal to take a new point when deciding a case in a party's avoidable absence. In *AB v SSWP (CSM)* [2021] UKUT 129 (AAC), the absent party had not given details of the commitment that he had said prevented him from attending the hearing and it should have been apparent to him from directions previously issued by the First-tier Tribunal that it did not regard its jurisdiction to be limited to the points raised in the grounds of appeal. Moreover, as the Upper Tribunal said at [92]:

> "One cannot always know from the papers that are circulated in advance quite how the other parent's case will be put and what evidence will be given. Absenting oneself from the hearing always runs the risk that of depriving oneself of the opportunity to answer any unexpected evidence or address additional issues."

Moreover, there can still be a duty to consider whether a hearing is required in the interests of justice even after a decision has been reached. In *AK v HMRC (TC)* [2016] UKUT 98 (AAC), the claimant had arrived 35 minutes late for a hearing listed for 1½ hours before the First-tier Tribunal, which by then had already decided to dismiss her appeal against HMRC's decision that, in the absence of almost any other evidence, it was to be inferred from a credit reference agency's reports that she had been living with a man as his wife. There was no indication that the First-tier Tribunal had considered re-opening the case (by setting aside its decision if the decision notice had been signed and, if necessary, adjourning the hearing) or that it had ascertained the reason for the claimant's lateness or balanced that against the amount at stake in the appeal, which was over £8,600. Moreover, the claimant's oral evidence was likely to be particularly important because HMRC had not interviewed her before making its decision. The Upper Tribunal held that, in the absence of any adequate reasoning, the First-tier Tribunal's failure to consider, or reconsider, the claimant's case when she arrived appeared aberrant and so rendered its substantive decision wrong in law.

It may be a relevant consideration when deciding whether to proceed in a claimant's absence that a the Secretary of State or a health care professional has failed to ask relevant questions so that the First-tier Tribunal needs to do so—see *MH v SSWP (II)* [2020] UKUT 297 (AAC) at [55]. In that case, the First-tier Tribunal gave as one reason for proceeding in the claimant's absence that "this was an appeal where the Tribunal has specifically directed that it should proceed by way of an oral hearing where the claimant might attend for the purposes of being examined and in order that the Tribunal might obtain a detailed medical and work history" but the Upper Tribunal could find no indication that the claimant had been told that that was why an oral hearing had been directed.

In *GL v Elysium Healthcare Hospital* [2020] UKUT 308 (AAC), the patient was self-isolating during the Covid-19 pandemic, within a flat that he shared with another patient. He was allowed to participate in the hearing before the First-tier Tribunal by telephone but he declined to do so because he was anxious about being overheard by his flat-mate. The First-tier Tribunal refused an application for an adjournment and decided to proceed in his absence on the ground that "in the current difficult climate the hearing was fair and the patient had been given the opportunity to participate and it was largely due to his anxiety that he was unable to do so." The Upper Tribunal allowed the patient's appeal because the First-tier Tribunal had not adequately considered either whether his fear about being overheard was reasonable or whether his anxiety was genuine. It had approached the question of an adjournment on the basis that the patient's concern was the mode of hearing, rather than the possibility of being overheard. That the hearing was by telephone was merely part of the context.

Chapter 3

Decisions

Consent orders

32.—(1) The Tribunal may, at the request of the parties but only if it considers it appropriate, make a consent order disposing of the proceedings and making such other appropriate provision as the parties have agreed. **3.366**

(2) Notwithstanding any other provision of these Rules, the Tribunal need not hold a hearing before making an order under paragraph (1), or provide reasons for the order.

DEFINITIONS

"hearing"—see r.1(3).
"party"—*ibid.*
"Tribunal"—*ibid.*

GENERAL NOTE

3.367 A consent order, which necessarily involves a decision by the First-tier Tribunal that it is "appropriate", is a decision that may be set aside under r.37 or on a review or appeal (*R.(LR) v First-tier Tribunal* [2012] UKUT 213 (AAC)). However, consent orders have little place in social security cases before the First-tier Tribunal because decision-makers generally have the power to revise the decision under appeal, which causes the appeal to lapse (see, for instance, s.9(1) and (6) of the Social Security Act 1998 and reg.3(4A) of the Social Security and Child Support (Decisions and Appeals) Regulations 1999).

Notice of decisions

3.368 **33.**—(1) The Tribunal may give a decision orally at a hearing.

(2) Subject to rule 14(2) (withholding information likely to cause harm), the Tribunal must provide to each party as soon as reasonably practicable after making [[1] a decision (other than a decision under Part 4) which finally disposes of all issues in the proceedings or of a preliminary issue dealt with following a direction under rule 5(3)(e)]—

(a) a decision notice stating the Tribunal's decision;
(b) where appropriate, notification of the right to apply for a written statement of reasons under rule 34(3); and
(c) notification of any right of appeal against the decision and the time within which, and the manner in which, such right of appeal may be exercised.

(3) In asylum support cases the notice and notifications required by paragraph (2) must be provided at the hearing or sent on the day that the decision is made.

AMENDMENT

1. Tribunal Procedure (Amendment) Rules 2013 (SI 2013/477) rr.22 and 28 (April 8, 2013).

DEFINITIONS

"asylum support case"—see r.1(3).
"hearing"—*ibid.*
"party"—*ibid.*
"Tribunal"—*ibid.*

GENERAL NOTE

Paragraph (1)

3.369 It is common practice to give a decision orally. It used to be considered that such a decision was not effective until written notice of it was given although, if the First-tier Tribunal did change its mind, it was usually required to invite further submissions (*SK (Sri Lanka) v Secretary of State for the Home Department* [2008] EWCA Civ 495, *R(I) 14/71, SSD v PY (WP)* [2012] UKUT 116 (AAC); [2012] AACR 44). However, in *Patel v Secretary of State for the Home Department* [2015] EWCA Civ 1175, the Court of Appeal held that a tribunal had no power to change a decision after it had been given orally. It said that the rule in the courts that a decision could be amended until an order was drawn up did not apply in tribunals where there is simply a decision and no distinction between a judgment and an order, it being relevant that there was an express power to give "a decision" orally. The Court's decision was given in the context of the Upper Tribunal's powers and it appears not to have been referred to the power of the Upper Tribunal to set aside decisions (equivalent to r.37 of these Rules), which might have been relevant in that case and which is entirely separate from the power of review that it did consider (see *R. (Singh) v Secretary of State for the Home Department* [2019] EWCA Civ 1014), but that does not undermine the main thrust of its reasoning which appears equally applicable to the First-tier Tribunal (although the distinction between a decision notice and reasons is clearer in the First-tier Tribunal than in the Upper Tribunal). This issue may not matter a great deal in social security cases in the First-tier Tribunal because decision notices are usually given to the parties before they leave the hearing venue so that there is not much opportunity for a change of mind.

However, the decision in *Patel v SSHD* [2015] EWCA Civ 1175 was applied in *KK v SSWP (PIP)* [2023] UKUT 151 (AAC). In this case the First-tier Tribunal had announced one decision at the end of the substantive hearing and then changed its mind after further discussion with the Appellant and announced a different decision. The Upper Tribunal found that the First-tier Tribunal had erred in law by changing its decision after it had been promulgated orally at the end of the hearing.

Paragraph (2)

It is not entirely clear whether "finally disposes of all issues in the proceedings" means something different from "disposes of proceedings" (see the note to r.27 above). 3.370

It is usual practice for decision notices to bear the names and judicial titles of the judge and members of the First-tier Tribunal, as would be the case in the civil courts in England and Wales under CPR r.40.2(1), but there is no requirement that a decision be signed (*Leighton v IC (No.2)* [2020] UKUT 23 (AAC)).

Although a decision may be made by a majority where the Tribunal is composed of more than one member (see art.8 of the First-tier Tribunal and Upper Tribunal (Composition of Tribunal) Order 2008), there is no express duty to record, in the decision notice, the reasons of the dissenting member of the Tribunal, or even to record in the notice that the decision was reached by a majority. This is because Reg. 53(5) of the Social Security and Child Support (Decisions and Appeals) Regulations 1999 was not re-enacted in the 2008 Rules. See also Rule 34 below. However, if a statement is made as to whether a decision was unanimous, it must be accurate. In *SSWP v SS (DLA)* [2010] UKUT 384 (AAC); [2011] AACR 24, it was held that there was a material error of law when a decision notice said that a decision was unanimous but the statement of reasons said it had been reached by a majority, without acknowledging any error.

Where the Secretary of State's decision is defective in form but the tribunal agrees with its substance, it is not necessary for the tribunal to reformulate the Secretary of State's decision in the tribunal's decision notice unless the decision as expressed by the Secretary of State is wrong in some *material* respect (e.g. it states an incorrect ground of supersession) or there is likely to be some practical benefit to the claimant or to the adjudication process in future in reformulating the decision (*R(IB)2/04*, para.82). On the other hand, attempting to reformulate the decision may serve to focus the tribunal's mind on the correct issues and so it may have a value. Where a statement of reasons is requested under r.34(3), the statement should explain what the decision under appeal should have been even if the decision notice does not.

Where an appeal is against an "outcome decision" expressed in terms of a claimant's entitlement to benefit, a decision notice "should make it absolutely clear whether the tribunal has made an outcome decision (subject, in some cases, to the precise amount being calculated by the Secretary of State) or has remitted the final decision on entitlement to the Secretary of State" (*R(IS) 2/08*). 3.371

There is no requirement that a decision notice include any reasons at all but there is nothing forbidding a judge from including brief reasons in the decision notice and it is suggested that it may often good practice to do so (although differing views have been expressed by Commissioners on this issue, see *CIB/4497/1998* and *CSDLA/551/1999*). Apart from anything else, an unsuccessful party is more likely to ask for a statement of reasons under r.34 if no reasons at all are given for a decision, especially if it arises at a paper determination. Moreover, there are cases where the issue determined by the tribunal is almost bound to arise again and it is then helpful to all concerned if some indication of the First-tier Tribunal's reasoning is included in a decision notice if it will not otherwise be obvious to a person who did not attend the hearing. Thus, it was observed in *MW v SSWP (II)* [2011] UKUT 465 (AAC) that it was unfortunate that previous appeal tribunals allowing appeals by the claimant and making provisional assessments of disablement had not recorded at least a brief reason for rejecting the Secretary of State's submissions, given that the making of a provisional assessment necessarily meant that at least one further assessment would have to be made by the Secretary of State. However, it was not suggested that there was a positive duty to give reasons in such a case in the absence of a request by either party.

Nonetheless, in cases concerned with medical assessments for employment and support allowance, personal independence payment or universal credit, in respect of which a person's entitlement to benefit depends on the number of points scored in respect of prescribed descriptors, the general practice is for a decision notice to record the descriptors in respect of which it has been found that the claimant scored points. In *CP v SSWP (PIP)* [2016] UKUT 444 (AAC), it was stated that, while it was quite proper for the First-tier Tribunal, having concluded that the claimant scored sufficient points for the maximum amount of benefit, not to consider any further descriptors that might have been put in issue, it would be good practice in such a case for the decision notice to state that, given that the points added by the tribunal result in the maximum possible award, it has not been necessary to consider whether further points are merited, so as to avoid misapprehension particularly if a supersession of the award were to be contemplated.

There being no duty to include any reasons at all in a decision notice, where some reasons are given but are inadequate, the consequence is not to render the tribunal's decision erroneous in point of law. The remedy is to apply for a proper statement of reasons under r.34(3) (*CIB/4497/1998*). Such a statement cures any inadequacy in reasons given in a decision notice (*CSDLA/531/2000, CIS/2345/2001*). However, if the reasons in the full statement are inconsistent with the reasons given in a decision notice, the decision of the tribunal will be set aside as erroneous in point of law (*CCR/3396/2000, CIS/2345/2001, SSWP v C O'N (ESA)* [2018] UKUT 80 (AAC), *JC v SSWP (PIP)* [2019] UKUT 181 (AAC)). In criminal injuries compensation cases, the First-tier Tribunal has had a practice of giving fairly detailed hand-written summary reasons on the decision notice but recording that they are not the full reasons and informing the claimant of the right to ask for full reasons. The Upper Tribunal was critical of a failure of the First-tier Tribunal to provide a full statement of reasons when asked to provide a legible copy of the summary reasons even though, treating them as full reasons, the Upper Tribunal was still able to reject the claimant's challenge to their adequacy (*R. (MC) v First-tier Tribunal (CIC)* [2014] UKUT 544 (AAC)).

Reasons for decisions

3.372 **34.**—(1) In asylum support cases the Tribunal must send a written statement of reasons for a decision which disposes of proceedings (except a decision under Part 4) to each party—

(a) if the case is decided at a hearing, within 3 days after the hearing; or

(b) if the case is decided without a hearing, on the day that the decision is made.

(2) In all other cases the Tribunal may give reasons for a decision which disposes of proceedings (except a decision under Part 4)—

(a) orally at a hearing; or

(b) in a written statement of reasons to each party.

(3) Unless the Tribunal has already provided a written statement of reasons under paragraph (2)(b), a party may make a written application to the Tribunal for such statement following a decision [1 which finally disposes of—

(a) all issues in the proceedings; or

(b) a preliminary issue dealt with following a direction under rule 5(3)(e).]

(4) An application under paragraph (3) must be received within 1 month of the date on which the Tribunal sent or otherwise provided to the party a decision notice relating to the decision [1 . . .]

(5) If a party makes an application in accordance with paragraphs (3) and (4) the Tribunal must, subject to rule 14(2) (withholding information likely to cause harm), send a written statement of reasons to each party within 1 month of the date on which it received the application or as soon as reasonably practicable after the end of that period.

Amendment

1. Tribunal Procedure (Amendment) Rules 2013 (SI 2013/477) rr.22 and 29 (April 8, 2013).

Definitions

"asylum support case"—see r.1(3).
"dispose of proceedings"—*ibid.*
"hearing"—*ibid.*
"party"—*ibid.*
"Tribunal"—*ibid.*

General Note

Practice Direction from the Senior President of Tribunals: Reasons for decisions

Much has been said about what needs to be included in a written statement of reasons. The following pages provide information covering various issues that would need to be dealt with in a statement, if relevant to the particular appeal. However, it is suggested that the starting point for any written statement is now the Senior President of Tribunal Guidance which states:

1. This Practice Direction states basic and important principles on the giving of written reasons for decisions in the First-tier Tribunal. It is of general application throughout the First-tier Tribunal. It relates to the whole range of substantive and procedural decision-making in the Tribunal, by both judges and non-legal members. Accordingly, it must always be read and applied having regard to the particular nature of the decision in question and the particular circumstances in which that decision is made.
2. The procedure rules applying in the First-tier Tribunal specify circumstances in which the Tribunal must provide written reasons for its decision. Whilst many decisions are subject to an express requirement for written reasons to be given for them, some are not. In some circumstances

written reasons are mandatory only upon request by a party. In every case the Tribunal must be alert to the type of decision it is making and to the relevant requirements of the rules on the giving of reasons, if any such requirements are engaged. It is important to recognise that the giving of reasons may be required in the interests of justice even if not mandated by the rules.

3. In some cases or jurisdictions the Tribunal will be able to give its decision at, or soon after, the conclusion of a hearing by providing a notice of decision and/or by stating its reasons orally.
4. Modern ways of working, facilitated by digital processes, will generally enable greater efficiencies in the work of the tribunals, including the logistics of decision-making. Full use should be made of any tools and techniques that are available to assist in the swift production of decisions.
5. Where reasons are given, they must always be adequate, clear, appropriately concise, and focused upon the principal controversial issues on which the outcome of the case has turned. To be adequate, the reasons for a judicial decision must explain to the parties why they have won and lost[1]. The reasons must enable the reader to understand why the matter was decided as it was and what conclusions were reached on the main issues in dispute [2]. They must always enable an appellate body to understand why the decision was reached, so that it is able to assess whether the decision involved the making of an error on a point of law [3]. These fundamental principles apply to the tribunals as well as to the courts.
6. Providing adequate reasons does not usually require the First-tier Tribunal to identify all of the evidence relied upon in reaching its findings of fact, to elaborate at length its conclusions on any issue of law, or to express every step of its reasoning. The reasons provided for any decision should be proportionate, not only to the resources of the Tribunal, but to the significance and complexity of the issues that have to be decided. Reasons need refer only to the main issues and evidence in dispute, and explain how those issues essential to the Tribunal's conclusion have been resolved [4].
7. Stating reasons at any greater length than is necessary in the particular case is not in the interests of justice. To do so is an inefficient use of judicial time, does not assist either the parties or an appellate court or tribunal [5], and is therefore inconsistent with the overriding objective. Providing concise reasons is to be encouraged. Adequate reasons for a substantive decision may often be short. In some cases a few succinct paragraphs will suffice. For a procedural decision the reasons required will usually be shorter.
8. Judges and members in the First-tier Tribunal should expect that the Upper Tribunal will approach its own decisions on appeal in accordance with the well settled principle that appellate tribunals exercise appropriate restraint when considering a challenge to a decision based on the adequacy of reasons [6]. As the Court of Appeal has emphasised, a realistic and reasonably benevolent approach will be taken such that decisions under appeal will be read fairly and not hypercritically [7].
9. As an expert tribunal, the First-tier Tribunal will generally be taken to be aware of the relevant authorities within the jurisdiction being exercised, and to be applying those cases without the need to refer to them specifically, unless it is clear from the language of the decision that they have failed to do so [8]. The Upper Tribunal will not readily assume that a tribunal has misdirected itself merely because every step in its reasoning is not fully set out in its decision [9]. Thus, a challenge based on the adequacy of reasons should only succeed when the appellate body cannot understand the Tribunal's thought process in making material findings [10].
10. This Practice Direction is made by the Senior President of Tribunals without the approval of the Lord Chancellor under section 23(6) of the Tribunals, Courts and Enforcement Act 2007, on the basis that it consists solely of

guidance about the application or interpretation of the law, and the making of decisions by judges and members in the First-tier Tribunal.

Sir Keith Lindblom

Senior President of Tribunals

4 June 2024

[1] *English v Emery Reimbold* [2002] EWCA Civ 605 at [16]

[2] *South Bucks v Porter* [2004] UKHL 33 at [36]

[3] *Flannery v Halifax Estate Agencies Ltd [*2000] 1 WLR 377 (CA)

[4] *SSHD v TC* [2023] UKUT 164 (IAC) Annex para 8

[5] e.g. *Jones v Jones* [2011] EWCA Civ 41 at [3]

[6] TC Annex para 13

[7] *DPP v Greenberg* [2021] EWCA Civ 672 at [57]

[8] *TC Annex* para 12; *Yalcin v SSHD* [2024] EWCA Civ 74 at [50-51]; *Ullah v SSHD* [2024] EWCA Civ 201 at [26]

[9] *TC Annex* para 13

[10] *HJ (Afghanistan) v SSHD* [2017] EWCA Civ 2716; *R (Iran) v SSHD* [2005] EWCA Civ 982

What impact the Practice Statement will have when the Upper Tribunal considers an application for permission to appeal which includes a challenge to the adequacy of the First-tier Tribunal's written statement of reasons remains to be seen.

Paragraphs (2)–(5)

These paragraphs replace reg.53(4) of the Social Security and Child Support (Decisions and Appeals) Regulations 1999 but add two refinements. The first is to make it clear that reasons may be given orally but that a written statement may subsequently be requested. The second is to impose a time limit, albeit not absolute, within which a tribunal must provide a statement of reasons. Whether a tribunal would be found to have erred in law because reasons were not provided "as soon as reasonably practicable" after the standard one month in circumstances where delay would not previously have been sufficient to vitiate the decision remains to be seen. Practically speaking it is unlikely that this issue will fall to be decided by the Upper Tribunal. This is because a delay in a statement of reasons being provided will have been dealt with by the First-Tier Tribunal ensuring that action is taken to chase the judge for the statement (which could result in a complaint of misconduct) or because there would have been a Rule 37 procedural set aside. 3.373

A refusal to adjourn is not a "decision" for which a statement of reasons may be required under this rule, although an unexplained refusal to adjourn may make a final decision erroneous in point of law unless an explanation that is not perverse may be inferred from the circumstances (*Carpenter v Secretary of State for Work and Pensions* [2003] EWCA Civ 33 (reported as *R(IB) 6/03*)). Indeed, although a duty to give reasons under this rule applies only to decisions that dispose of proceedings, there is a common-law duty to give reasons for any decision that would appear aberrant without reasons (*R. (Birmingham CC) v Birmingham Crown Court* [2009] EWHC 3329 (Admin); [2010] 1 W.L.R. 1287), referred to in *SA v Ealing LBC (HB)* [2012] UKUT 437 (AAC)). However, the effect of not providing reasons for an apparently aberrant interlocutory decision for which reasons are not required by this rule may, in practice, be that the decision will be set aside on the ground of perversity rather than explicitly on the ground that no reasons have been given.

MT v SSWP ((IS) [2010] UKUT 382 (AAC) is perhaps an example of this. The First-tier Tribunal was held to have erred in law in failing to give reasons for proceeding with a hearing in the absence of a presenting officer when a judge had earlier directed the attendance of a presenting officer on the basis that such attendance was "essential", but it may be significant that its failure to explain why the presence was no longer regarded as "essential" was compounded by the inadequacy of the Secretary of State's submission and the First-tier Tribunal's failure to explain to the claimant at the hearing what the case against him really was. In the absence of any such apparent irrationality in an interlocutory decision and therefore of any duty to provide reasons at all, summary reasons will be adequate (*KP v Hertfordshire CC (SEN)* [2010] UKUT 233 (AAC)).

A judge's power to write a statement of reasons survives the termination of his or her appointment as a judge. The statement must at least be adopted by the judge (or possibly another member) of the tribunal who heard the appeal. Therefore a statement written by a regional chairman in the erroneous belief that it could not be written by the chairman who heard the appeal because her appointment had come to an end, was not valid (*CIS/2132/1998*).

In *R. (Sturton) v Social Security Commissioner* [2007] EWHC 2957 (Admin), the decision notice was not sent on the day of the hearing to a party who had not been present at the hearing, even though the notice stated that it had been sent then, so that, when that party subsequently obtained a copy and made an application for a statement of reasons within a month of the copy actually being sent to him, the application was in time.

3.374 It is usually an error of law to fail to issue a statement of reasons when a request is made within the prescribed time. An application for permission to appeal received within that time is treated as a request for such a statement (r.38(7)). In both *R(IS) 11/99* and *R3/02(IB)*, it is stated that there are occasions when an error of law can be demonstrated without there being a statement of reasons—*MC v SSWP (CSM)* [2020] UKUT 157 (AAC) is a recent example of an appeal being allowed in such circumstances (because the digital record of proceedings was sufficient to show that evidence had been wrongly excluded)—although it is obviously not possible to challenge a tribunal's decision on the grounds of inadequacy of reasoning in circumstances where there is no written statement of reasons and no duty to provide one. Furthermore, a tribunal's decision will not be erroneous in law for breach of the duty imposed by this rule if the decision notice issued under r.33(2)(a) in fact contains all that would be required in a full statement of reasons *(R(IS) 11/99)*, or if the two documents read together provide an adequate statement between them (*CIS/2345/2001*).

Long decisions need to be properly organised. In *Jasim v Secretary of State for the Home Department* [2006] EWCA Civ 342, the Court of Appeal commented on the "unmanageable length" of some paragraphs in a decision of the Asylum and Immigration Tribunal, one of which ran for almost three pages of single-spaced type. It was suggested that the use of shorter paragraphs, with sub-paragraphs and cross-headings where appropriate, was a useful aid not just to the reader but also to the writer.

Standard form decisions have been frowned upon in *CI/5199/1998* and *CIB/4497/1998*, not on grounds of principle but because they tend to be used not only when appropriate but also when the circumstances of the case make it inappropriate.

3.375 In *Peters v Sat Katar Limited* [2003] EWCA Civ 943, the use of standard recitals as reasons revealed that no regard whatsoever had been had to the particular circumstances of a case where the exercise of a discretion required all the circumstances to be taken into account.

Including in a statement of reasons a "protective essay", emphasising that the standard of reasoning that is required is adequacy rather than perfection and therefore designed impermissibly to discourage a party from appealing, has been described as "an invitation to appellate judges to scrutinise the statement in greater depth" because it inevitably betrays a lack of confidence on the part of the judge writing the statement in the quality of his or her own reasoning and raises the question whether "other parts of the statement are merely a form of words designed to protect the decision from scrutiny, rather than an explanation of the actual reasoning that led to the decision" (*CH v SSWP (PIP)* [2020] UKUT 19 (AAC) at [44] and [45]).

This rule includes no express duty to record the tribunal's findings but it is necessary to record a tribunal's findings on any matters in dispute as part of the explanation for its decision (*R(I) 4/02* and also *R2/01(IB)*, a decision of a Tribunal of Commissioners in Northern Ireland). Indeed, it has been said in *Evans v Secretary of State for Social Services* (reported as *R(I)5/94*) that there are occasions when a record of the tribunal's findings provides a complete explanation for the decision.

Reasons for interlocutory decisions

Whether reasons are needed for an interlocutory decision is likely to depend on the context. Although an appeal lies against interlocutory decisions (*LS v Lambeth LBC (HB)* [2010] UKUT 461 (AAC); [2011] AACR 27), there is no statutory requirement under r.34 to give reasons for decisions that do not finally dispose of all issues in the proceedings and no general common law requirement to do so either, although a decision may be set aside on the ground of a failure to provide reasons if a discretion has been exercised in a particularly unusual manner (*Jones v Governing Body of Burdett Coutts School* [1999] I.C.R. 38, 47) or the decision appears aberrant (*R. v Higher Education Funding Council, Ex p. Institute of Dental Surgery* [1994] 1 W.L.R. 242 at 263). 3.376

Where reasons for interlocutory decisions are requested, they are sometimes conveyed in a letter signed by the clerk to the tribunal. This is not improper, provided that the reasons are those of the tribunal (*R. v Stoke CC, Ex p. Highgate Projects* (1993) 26 H.L.R. 551) and, indeed, it would not necessarily be improper for a clerk to assist in the drafting of reasons (*Virdi v Law Society (Solicitors Disciplinary Tribunal intervening)* [2010] EWCA Civ 100 ; [2010] 1 W.L.R. 2840).

For the need to give reasons for deciding a case without a hearing, see the annotation to r.27(4)–(6) above.

Inconsistency

In *Sandhu v Secretary of State for Work and Pensions* [2010] EWCA Civ 962, the Court of Appeal held reasons to be flawed for inconsistency when at one point the First-tier Tribunal said that it accepted that the claimant could not put any weight on his right leg and then at another point it found he could walk with crutches. (Using crutches to mobilise without putting weight on one leg is not walking.) 3.377

In *CDLA/1807/2003*, the tribunal chairman produced two statements of reasons for the tribunal's decision, the second because he had forgotten he had already written a statement. The reasons differed. The Commissioner commented that the reasons should be a statement of the *tribunal's* reasons and not the chairman's later rationalisation of the conclusion reached by the tribunal and that at least one of the statements plainly did not accurately reflect the tribunal's reasons. He set aside the tribunal's decision. Inexplicable inconsistency between the decision notice and the statement of reasons led to appeals being allowed in *CCR/3396/2000, CIS/2345/2001, SSWP v C O'N (ESA)* [2018] UKUT 80 (AAC) and *JC v SSWP (PIP)* [2019] UKUT 181 (AAC).

Majority decisions

Although there is no express duty to record, in the decision notice, the reasons of a dissenting member of the Tribunal where a decision is made by a majority (see Rule 33 above) it is generally considered to be at least good practice that it is recorded in the statement of reasons. In *SSWP v SS (DLA)* [2010] UKUT 384 (AAC); [2011] AACR 24, it was held that there is no duty to record whether or not a decision is unanimous but there was nonetheless a material error of law when a decision notice said that a decision was unanimous and the statement of reasons said it had been reached by a majority, without acknowledging any error. Moreover, the judge said that, if a decision notice *did* state that a decision was 3.378

by a majority, there was a duty to include the reasons of the dissenting member and that the same approach applied if a decision notice stated that a decision was unanimous when in fact it had been reached by a majority. However, in *JD v SSD (WP)* [2014] UKUT 379 (AAC), some doubt was expressed as to whether a failure to give reasons for dissent was an error of law rather than merely being a breach of good practice. In *R. (CICA) v First-tier Tribunal (CIC)* [2019] UKUT 15 (AAC), it was suggested that the point might be "relatively academic" and might not add anything to a general challenge to the adequacy of the First-tier Tribunal's reasoning:

> "If the reasoning of the majority is otherwise impeccable, it is difficult to see why failing to provide reasons for a dissent should make the decision materially wrong in law. On the other hand, where the adequacy of reasoning is debatable, which implies that disagreement might not have been unreasonable, a failure to indicate the grounds of dissent may amount to a failure to explain why the majority disagreed with the dissentient and therefore a failure to address a material issue in the case and that may tip the balance in favour of quashing the decision. This is particularly likely to be so where, as here, there is an argument before the First-tier Tribunal as to the significance of a medical report and it is the medically qualified panel member who dissents."

Cases where evidence has been withheld from a party

3.379 If there is a closed procedure under which evidence is withheld from a party, the First-tier Tribunal must nonetheless provide full reasons for its decision, even if that can only be done by providing closed reasons that are also withheld from that party but will be available to other parties and to the Upper Tribunal in the event of an appeal (*Davies v IC* [2019] UKUT 185 (AAC); [2019] 1 W.L.R. 6641; [2020] AACR 2).

Adequate reasons

3.380 The inadequacy of statements of reasons is probably the most common ground upon which decisions are set aside by the Upper Tribunal.

In *Re Poyser and Mills' Arbitration* [1964] 2 Q.B. 467, 478, Megaw J. said:

> "Parliament provided that reasons shall be given, and in my view that must be read as meaning that proper, adequate reasons must be given. The reasons that are set out must be reasons that will not only be intelligible, but which deal with the substantial points that have been raised."

In *R(A) 1/72*, the Chief Commissioner, considering an appeal from a delegated medical practitioner acting on behalf of the Attendance Allowance Board, said:

> "The obligation to give reasons for the decision in [a case involving a conflict of evidence] imports a requirement to do more than only to state the conclusion, and for the determining authority to state that on the evidence the authority is not satisfied that the statutory conditions are met, does no more than this. It affords no guide to the selective process by which the evidence has been accepted, rejected, weighed or considered, or the reasons for any of these things. It is not, of course, obligatory thus to deal with every piece of evidence or to over elaborate, but in an administrative quasi-judicial decision the minimum requirement must at least be that the claimant, looking at the decision should be able to discern on the face of it the reasons why the evidence has failed to satisfy the authority. For the purpose of the regulation which requires the reasons for the review decision to be set out, a decision based, and only based, on a conclusion that the total effect of the evidence fails to satisfy, without reasons given for reaching that conclusion, will in many cases be no adequate decision at all."

In *R. (Asha Foundation) v Millennium Commission* [2003] EWCA Civ 66 (*The Times*, January 24, 2003), the Court of Appeal considered the approach Sedley J. had taken in *R. v Higher Education Funding Council, Ex p. Institute of Dental Surgery* [1994] 1 W.L.R. 242 to the question of whether there was a duty to give any reasons at all and held that, where there is a duty to give reasons, the same approach should be taken to the question whether reasons were adequate. Sedley J.'s approach required the balancing of a number of considerations, which might vary from case to case. He said:

> "The giving of reasons may among other things concentrate the decision-maker's mind on the right questions; demonstrate to the recipient that this is so; show that the issues have been conscientiously addressed and how the result has been reached or alternatively alert the recipient to a justiciable flaw in the process.
>
> On the other side of the argument, it may place an undue burden on decision-makers; demand an appearance of unanimity where there is diversity; call for the articulation of sometimes inexpressible value judgments; and offer an invitation to the captious to comb the reasons for previously unsuspected grounds of challenge."

In *KMN v SSWP (PIP)* [2019] UKUT 42 (AAC), it was held that, where the First-tier Tribunal has given an indication as to the decision it is minded to give and the suggestion is rejected by the claimant with the result that there is a full hearing, it is entitled to change its mind and make a decision less favourable to the claimant than the one it had previously suggested but it must then give reasons for its change of mind. The Upper Tribunal also pointed out that the claimant might reasonably have thought that, in the light of the terms in which the indication had been given in that case, certain aspects of the case were no longer in issue and that it might therefore have been good practice for the First-tier Tribunal to warn the claimant that it was minded to resile from its indication. Had that practice been followed, the First-tier Tribunal would probably have addressed the issue in its reasons. Indeed, many Upper Tribunal cases decided on the basis of inadequate reasons reflect a procedural defect in the proceedings before the First-tier Tribunal or at least the possibility of such a defect or a failure to ask appropriate questions.

Thus, in *RT v SSWP (PIP)* [2019] UKUT 207 (AAC); [2020] AACR 4, it was held that the overwhelming majority of appellants in social security cases are, strictly speaking, vulnerable adults for the purpose of *Practice Direction (First-tier and Upper Tribunals: Child, Vulnerable Adults and Sensitive Witnesses)* and that, in the light of *AM (Afghanistan) v Secretary of State for the Home Department* [2017] EWCA Civ 1123, it was necessary for the First-tier Tribunal to indicate in its reasons for decision whether it had followed that Practice Direction, although in many cases a failure to refer to the point in its reasons would not be a material error of law because it would be obvious that no special provision need be made for the claimant. It would however, be a material error in any case where the claimant or any other witness might have required reasonable adjustments to the First-tier Tribunal's usual practice (see the annotation to the Practice Direction, below). Similarly, although stating that a party has made a concession of fact may be a perfectly adequate explanation for accepting that fact, further reasoning may be required if the concession appears to be contrary to other available evidence or if what is expressed as a concession is in reality an assertion in the interests of the party making it (*SB v SSWP (CSM)* [2019] UKUT 375 (AAC)).

In *KH (dec'd) by AMH v SSWP (IIDB)* [2021] UKUT 189 (AAC), the claimant's response to the decision of the First-tier Tribunal was to submit a medical report contradicting its key finding. When writing the statement of reasons for the tribunal's decision, the judge included a paragraph in which he said that that evidence was "unlikely" to have affected the tribunal's findings. The Upper Tribunal criticised that paragraph, because "it is not the function of a statement of reasons to discuss and dismiss evidence that the Tribunal did not take into account when reaching its decision". What, on the other hand, the First-tier Tribunal could, and should, have done was treat the submission of the medical report as an application for the setting aside of the decision under r.37. However, the Upper Tribunal was not prepared to find the relevant paragraph of the reasons showed that such a deemed application for setting aside would have been unsuccessful and that the First-tier Tribunal's error was therefore immaterial, both because the relevant paragraph had only said that the new evidence was "unlikely" to have made any difference and because the First-tier Tribunal judge had apparently not consulted the medically-qualified member of the tribunal before expressing that view.

Lying/dishonesty

3.381 Reasons should not suggest that the First-tier Tribunal has become side-tracked by an issue that may not be relevant. The fact that a witness has lied on one occasion does not necessarily mean that the whole of his or her evidence is unreliable (*SSWP v AM (IS)* [2010] UKUT 428 (AAC) at [26]; *MW v Leeds CC (HB)* [2018] UKUT 319 (AAC) at [8]). Nor does dishonesty within the proceedings before the Tribunal. In *VS v SSWP (ESA)* [2017] UKUT 274 (AAC), the First-tier Tribunal was criticised for giving the impression that it was more interested in investigating and condemning the claimant's behaviour in concealing an adverse psychological report than in whether she actually had limited capability for work. On the other hand, repeated references to a claimant's dishonesty in a statement of reasons may be justified, as in *MH v SSWP (PIP)* [2022] UKUT 248 (AAC) where the Upper Tribunal said at [25]:

> "... this was not a case like *VS* where it appears the FtT had become rather fixated upon one particular aspect of the appeal and the damage to credibility that it thought that had caused. The FtT, in the case now before me, did properly apply its adverse credibility conclusions. Its frequent references to the lack of credibility, when explaining and justifying its conclusion with respect to each activity in issue, was perhaps unnecessarily repetitive ... but on my reading what it was doing was simply stressing its disbelief with respect to each compartmentalised consideration of each activity for the sake of thoroughness."

A Tribunal of Commissioners in Northern Ireland has held in *R 3/01 (IB)* that there is no universal obligation on a tribunal to explain an assessment of credibility. It will usually be sufficient to say that a witness is not believed or is exaggerating. It is the decision that has to be explained. A tribunal is not obliged to give reasons for its reasons. There may be situations when a further explanation will be required but the only standard is that the reasons should explain the decision. Much the same approach has been taken in Great Britain, the authorities being analysed in *CIS/4022/2007*.

Extent of reasons on matters of judgement

3.382 It was acknowledged in *Baron v Secretary of State for Social Services* (reported as an appendix to *R(M) 6/86*) that there are limits to the extent to which a tribunal can be expected to give reasons for decisions on matters of judgment, such as the distance a claimant could walk without having to stop or the extent of breathlessness and pain which caused him to stop. See also *DC v SSWP* [2009] UKUT 45 (AAC) where the Upper Tribunal said that precise findings as to the distance a person can walk and the time taken are unrealistic and that the First-tier Tribunal should not attempt to make more precise findings than are really justified by the evidence. Assessments of disablement also give rise to difficult judgments. In *CI/636/1993*, the Commissioner said:

> "Whether or how far the duty in law to give reasons for their decision extends beyond saying that the particular percentage arrived at is in the medical judgment of the tribunal a fair one on these particular facts must depend on the nature

of the individual case and the issues that have been raised in it. It seems to me that the position is correctly summarised by the Commissioner in *R(I) 30/61* at paragraph 8: there may well be cases where a mere statement that the tribunal makes an assessment at a particular percentage is in itself a sufficient record, since it implies that they think that is a fair assessment; but in other cases findings of fact and an explanation of reasons will be needed to show that evidence they have accepted or rejected as justifying the making of a smaller or larger assessment, since otherwise the claimant will be left guessing as to the basis on which the decision has been arrived at. And in a case where specific submissions backed with expert medical evidence have been addressed to them on the basis of assessment to be used, it will normally be an error of law for the tribunal simply to state their conclusion in the form of a percentage without making it clear to what extent and for what reasons they are accepting or rejecting the suggested basis, since they will not have carried out the general duty to give reasons on a material issue raised before them: see *R(I) 18/61*, para.13."

In many cases it will be obvious from a finding as to the claimant's loss of faculty what the resulting disablement must have been but in others it is necessary for a tribunal to make specific findings as to the resulting disabilities (*CI/343/1988*). In *CI/1802/2001*, it was again stressed that a decision assessing the extent of a claimant's disablement is likely to be inadequate if the tribunal have not explained the factual basis of their decision.

"This can often be simply expressed. In many cases it will be enough to say that the evidence given by the claimant about the effect of a particular accident or disease on his or her daily life has been accepted. In some cases, where the claimant's evidence is for some reason found to be unreliable, it may be that the tribunal will state that it felt able to accept only those disabilities which in its expert opinion were likely to flow from problems disclosed on clinical examination. Other cases may need more detail."

However, where a tribunal assesses disablement for the purpose of determining entitlement to disablement benefit and the claimant is not suffering from an injury specified in Sch.2 to the Social Security (General Benefit) Regulations 1982, it is not necessary for the statement of reasons to refer to the prescribed degrees of disablement set against the injuries in that Schedule even though reg.11(8) of those Regulations suggests that the Schedule may act as a general guide to the assessment of disablement (*R(I) 1/04*). See, also, the decision of the Tribunal of Commissioners in *R(I) 2/06*, where the same approach was taken and *CI/1802/2001* was approved. Those were cases involving relatively low assessments. It may be more important to have regard to the Schedule where higher assessments are concerned, but provided that clear findings of fact are recorded and the First-tier Tribunal addresses any specific arguments raised as to the level of the assessment, the Upper Tribunal is unlikely to interfere with its judgment on the ground that its reasoning is inadequate even if it does not expressly refer to the Schedule (*DS v SSD (WP)* [2016] UKUT 51 (AAC)).

Treatment of Health Care Professional Reports

Resorting to describing a Benefits Agency Medical Service doctor as "independent" as a reason for preferring his evidence to medical evidence obtained on behalf **3.383** of the claimant was described as "irrational" in *CIB/563/2001*, given that the Benefits Agency Medical Service doctor was trained and paid by one of the parties to the proceedings, although it may be noted that the Court of Appeal in Northern Ireland made the same "error" in *O'Neill v Department for Communities* [2018] NICA 29 at [40]. Presumably, the tribunal and the Court both wished merely to emphasise the professional expertise of the doctor or disability analyst, although the distinction between independence and professionalism is important in some cases. In any event, in *CIB/563/2001*, the tribunal's simple reliance on the independence of the Benefits Agency Medical Service doctor was inadequate because the doctor acting on behalf of the claimant had recorded different clinical findings and there was no suggestion that he did not conduct a full examination or failed to take account of the claimant's history. Similarly, in *CS v SSWP (ESA)* [2018] UKUT 106 (AAC) it was held to be unfair to take into account as a reason for rejecting a claimant's evidence the fact that he had not made a formal complaint against the health care professional, particularly as the claimant had learning difficulties and a mental illness. Nor was it a sufficient ground in that case for rejecting medical evidence as to the effects of the claimant's mental health issues or learning difficulties that the doctor had acquired information from the claimant and his parents. There was no indication that the doctor was merely repeating information and not offering his or her own opinion in the light not only of the information but also professional judgement.

Dealing with descriptors (the all work test and PIP)

3.384 In *R3/01(IB)*, the Tribunal of Commissioners also held that a tribunal must record their findings on every descriptor of the all work test that is in issue and those raised by clear implication but that there is no universal rule that individual reasons must be given for the selection of a particular descriptor. The reasons given must explain why the tribunal reached the decision they did but need not always explain why it did not reach any different conclusion. However, it is suggested that there *is* a need to explain why a *specific* contention advanced by a party has not been accepted, at least where the contention is a major part of that party's case. It was said in *Flannery v Halifax Estate Agencies Ltd* [2001] 1 W.L.R. 377, CA, that, where there is expert evidence and analysis advanced by both parties, a statement of reasons must "enter into the issues" in order to explain why the unsuccessful party's evidence has failed to prevail. This was applied in *BB v South London and Maudsley NHS Trust* [2009] UKUT 159 (AAC) and *Hampshire CC v JP (SEN)* [2009] UKUT 239 (AAC); [2010] AACR 13. However, in *English v Emery Reimbold & Strick Ltd.* [2002] ECWA Civ 605; [2002] 1 W.L.R. 2409, the Court of Appeal sought to discourage the "cottage industry" of applications inspired by *Flannery* and followed *Eagil Trust Co Ltd v Pigott-Brown* [1985] 3 All E.R. 119, 122 in which Griffiths L.J. had stressed that there was no duty on a judge in giving his reasons to deal with every argument presented to him. The Court also said that, while a judge will often need to refer to a piece of evidence or to a submission which he has accepted or rejected, provided the reference is clear, it may be unnecessary to detail, or even summarise, the evidence or submission in question.

> "The essential requirement is that the terms of the judgment should enable the parties and any appellate tribunal readily to analyse the reasoning that was essential to the Judge's decision."

It will therefore not be an error of law for the First-tier Tribunal not to mention lesser arguments on a particular issue, provided that there were grounds on which they could properly have been rejected and it can be assumed that the First-tier Tribunal acted on those grounds (*AS (Iran) v Secretary of State for the Home Department* [2017] EWCA Civ 1539).

However, the First-tier Tribunal must address the principal arguments that were rejected and therefore, where the First-tier Tribunal rejects an argument that an earlier award of the same, or a different, benefit is relevant, it should give reasons for doing so (*CH v SSWP (PIP)* [2018] UKUT 330 (AAC); [2019] AACR 11 at [66]). However, even if it does not expressly address the argument, it will not err in law if, in a case where there was no evidence of the basis of the previous award, the necessary implication of its findings and reasoning is that either it disagreed with the previous assessment in the light of the evidence before it or it found that there had been a material improvement in the claimant's condition (*VH v SSWP (ESA)* [2018] UKUT 290 (AAC)). Similarly, the Upper Tribunal held reasoning to be inadequate where it provided reasons that addressed the terms of the descriptors for personal independence payment but failed to address in respect of many of them the more general, but potentially relevant, arguments that the claimant had advanced in relation to pain and tiredness (*MM v SSWP (PIP)* [2018] UKUT 93 (AAC)).

Concessions

The First-tier Tribunal is not usually obliged to explain why it has accepted a concession, but is likely to be obliged to explain why it has *not* accepted one, particularly if it appears that it may have overlooked it (*LH v SSWP (PIP)* [2022] UKUT 32 (AAC)). **3.385**

Burden of proof

Where a tribunal has rejected a claimant's account as to how he came by an injury, it is not bound to make any finding as to how he did come by it, where that would be no more than speculation (*AJ (Cameroon) v Secretary of State for the Home Department* [2007] EWCA Civ 373). However, there will, of course, be cases where a tribunal's finding that the injury was due to a different cause is the explanation for rejecting the claimant's case. In *CCS/1626/2002*, the Commissioner said that a person could hardly complain about the adequacy of findings of fact or reasoning lying behind an estimate of income when the need to make an estimate was due to that person's failure to provide better evidence. In *R(I) 3/03*, a Tribunal of Commissioners criticised the Secretary of State for supporting, by reference to an occasional infelicitous word in a statement of reasons, an unrealistic argument advanced by a claimant to the effect that a tribunal had overlooked a basic proposition of law. They said that there are some propositions of law, such as the nature of the civil burden and standard of proof, that are of such fundamental importance in the work of tribunals that it is almost inconceivable that tribunals will have overlooked them and that it should therefore be assumed that they have understood them unless there is something to show otherwise in the substance of what a tribunal has decided. **3.386**

Guidance on medical case

Specific guidance as to the approach to be taken in medical cases before tribunals has been given by the Court of Appeal in *Evans v Secretary of State for Social Services* (reported as *R(I) 5/94*) where it was said: **3.387**

> "1. The decision should record the medical question or questions which the tribunal is required to answer. Provided the questions are set out and the answers are directed to the questions it should then be possible for the parties to know the issues to which the tribunal have addressed themselves.
> 2. In cases where the tribunal have medically examined the claimant they should record their findings. These findings by themselves may be sufficient to demonstrate the reason why they have reached a particular conclusion.
> 3. Where, however, the clinical findings do not point to some obvious diagnosis it may be necessary to give a short explanation as to why they have made one diagnosis rather than another. Such an explanation will be important in cases where the tribunal's diagnosis differs from a reasoned diagnosis of another qualified practitioner who has examined the claimant on an earlier occasion.
> 4. A decision on a question of causation may pose particular difficulties when one is examining the adequacy of the reasons for a decision. In some cases it may be sufficient for the tribunal to record that it was not satisfied that the present condition was caused by the relevant trauma. Where, however, a claimant has previously been in receipt of some benefit or allowance (particularly if paid over a long period of time) and there is no question of malingering or bad faith then . . . the tribunal should go further than merely to state a conclusion. If one accepts that the underlying principle is fairness the claimant should be given some explanation, which may be very short, to enable him or his advisors to know where the break in causation has been found. Thus it may well be that the claimant will wish

> to reapply and for this purpose fairness requires that, if possible, he should be told why his claim has failed."

That was in the context of decisions of a medical appeal tribunal who had jurisdiction in respect of certain issues only, including the "medical questions" in respect of mobility allowance and the "disablement questions" in respect of disablement benefit. The reference to "the medical question or questions" must be read against that background and must therefore be taken to refer to the *legal* issues as much as the medical issues in a case.

In *DW v SSWP (II)* [2022] UKUT 183 (AAC), the Upper Tribunal considered the extent to which the First-tier Tribunal, when it includes a registered medical practitioner among its members, is required to give reasons for any medical opinion that it expresses:

> "17. In courts, medical expertise is provided by witnesses who are entitled to give opinion evidence. If there is a dispute as to the evidence, the witnesses may be required to give reasons for their opinions and the court is then required to consider that reasoning. As was said in *Flannery v Halifax Estate Agencies Ltd* [1999] EWCA Civ 811; [2000] 1 WLR 377 at 382B – '... where the dispute involves something in the nature of an intellectual exchange, with reasons and analysis advanced on either side, the judge must enter into the issues canvassed before him and explain why he prefers one case over the other.' Otherwise, the court may simply rely on the opinion offered. Where a tribunal includes a registered medical practitioner as a member and so has its own expertise, it is required to give reasons for its conclusion but is generally entitled to rely on its own expertise. I do not accept that the First-tier Tribunal is obliged to give reasons for its reasons in the absence of reasoned evidence that contradicts its opinion. It may be that, on an appeal to the Upper Tribunal, a party is entitled to adduce evidence for the purpose of showing that there is a contradictory body of medical opinion and that, in the circumstances of a particular case, the First-tier Tribunal's reliance on its unexplained opinion is inadequate, but that has not been done here as regards Mr Rogers' paragraph 88 point. On the contrary, he readily accepts that '[w]hat the Tribunal states may be correct'."

In *MM v SSWP (ESA)* [2018] UKUT 446 (AAC), the Upper Tribunal considered that, given the differences of view that there may be within the medical profession, the First-tier Tribunal should be very cautious about drawing inferences from the treatment received by claimants. On the facts of the case, it decided that the First-tier Tribunal had erred in basing its decision only on the absence of what it would have regarded as appropriate treatment had the claimant been as disabled as she said it was. Had it given additional reasons for doubting the claimant's account, it might not have been found to have erred in law.

In *CDLA/5419/1999*, it is pointed out that the fact that a claimant is unsuccessful does not always imply rejection of the medical evidence advanced by him or her. In that case, the claimant's doctor said that the claimant required attention but he did not specify how much. The tribunal accepted that the claimant required some attention but found that it was not sufficient to qualify for disability living allowance. The Commissioner said that the doctor's evidence had therefore not supported the element of the claimant's case upon which she failed and that, in the circumstances of the case, there had been no duty to refer to the doctor's evidence at all. In *HL v SSWP (DLA)* [2011] UKUT 183 (AAC), the Upper Tribunal said:

> "All too often, judges present the tribunal's reasons as if the tribunal had a choice between accepting the evidence of the GP or of the examining medical practitioner. There may be cases where that is so, but in many cases the reports each have their strengths and each their limitations as an assessment of the

claimant's disablement. In those cases, what a proper analysis usually requires is for the tribunal to show a balance between the value that can be distilled from each report and its limitations."

A similar point has been made by a Tribunal of Commissioners in Northern Ireland (*R2/04(DLA)*) and by the Court of Appeal in Northern Ireland (*Quinn v Department for Social Development* [2004] NICA 22). In the former case, however, the Tribunal of Commissioners added that, "where it is evident that the claimant attaches great significance to a letter or report, it may be prudent for a tribunal to say, briefly, that it has read the document but derived no assistance from it" and it may be helpful to say why if the relevance or value of the evidence is likely to be controversial.

In *R(M) 1/96*, the Commissioner held that the fact of a previous award does not raise any presumption in the claimant's favour or result in the need for consistency having to be treated as a separate issue on a renewal claim. However, he said that the requirement for a tribunal to give reasons for its decision means that it is usually necessary for a tribunal to explain why it is not renewing a previous award, unless that is obvious from their findings. The same approach applied where a person had been in receipt of employment and support allowance for seven years following a serious accident in respect of which she was still receiving treatment and there was no obvious evidence of improvement (*JL v SSWP (ESA)* [2018] UKUT 94 (AAC)) and also where the award of personal independence payment being challenged was at first sight factually inconsistent with earlier awards of disability living allowance over many years to which the claimant had pointed in support of his case (*YM v SSWP (PIP)* [2018] UKUT 18 (AAC)). The approach was also applied by the Court of Appeal in Northern Ireland in *Quinn* although the Court held that, in the circumstances of that particular case, there had been no need for the tribunal to refer to a medical report obtained for the purpose of determining the previous claim. More generally, the mere fact that another tribunal has given more detailed reasons when considering the same issue does not render the briefer reasons of a second tribunal inadequate, particularly when they are based on a clear finding of credibility (*SSWP v AM (IS)* [2010] UKUT 428 (AAC)). On the other hand, where an award for one period is markedly different from an award made in respect of an immediately subsequent period, it may be necessary to explain the difference even though the assessment in respect of the later period would not be binding on it (*R. (Viggers) v Pensions Appeal Tribunal* [2009] EWCA Civ 1321; [2010] AACR 19, in which Ward L.J. said (at [22]): "It is elementary for the principle of public law that there should be, as far as possible, consistency in administrative decisions.") However, Etherton L.J. said (at [26]) that it "would have been sufficient for the Tribunal to say that, having had regard to an having taken into account the 40% assessment, nonetheless in the light of the all the evidence before it and the members' expertise it concluded that the assessment should be that of 6-14% for the earlier period". Perhaps the reality is that, if a tribunal does in fact have regard to an earlier award and is obliged expressly to mention that fact, its other reasoning will generally show, at least implicitly, that it either thought the award in respect of the later period was too generous or that it considered there had been a change of circumstances. However, it is suggested that the parties should be told which of those two possibilities the tribunal had in mind.

Where the First-tier Tribunal finds that a claimant does not score sufficient points under Sch.2 to the Employment and Support Allowance Regulations 2008 for entitlement to employment and support allowance, it will normally be necessary for it also to refer expressly to reg.29(2)(b) in order to show that that provision has not been overlooked. However, the extent to which reasons need be given for not finding that provision to apply depends very much on the circumstances of the case (*NS v SSWP (ESA)* [2014] UKUT 115 (AAC); [2014] AACR 33). It is likely to be necessary to give specific reasons where the First-tier Tribunal has disagreed fundamentally with the appellant about the effects of their condition (*ibid.*) or where the claimant has scored a substantial number of points under mental health descriptors (*AJ v SSWP (ESA)* [2014] UKUT 208 (AAC)). On the other hand, where a represented claimant advances a case in very general terms and presents no evidence of a substantial risk, specific reasons are less likely to be required (*JK v SSWP (ESA)* [2014] UKUT 140 (AAC); [2014] AACR 34).

In *Baron v Secretary of State for Social Services* (reported as an appendix to *R(M) 6/86*), it was said that:

> "The overriding test must always be: is the tribunal providing both parties with the materials which will enable them to know that the tribunal has made no error of law in reaching its findings of fact?"

The approach taken in social security cases is not very different from that taken in other areas of public law. In the context of planning, Lord Brown of Eaton-under-Heywood summarised the effect of case law in *South Bucks DC v Porter (No.2)* [2004] UKHL 33 [2004] 1 W.L.R. 1953 (at [36]):

> "The reasons for a decision must be intelligible and they must be adequate. They must enable the reader to understand why the matter was decided as it was and what conclusions were reached on the 'principal important controversial issues', disclosing how any issue of law or fact was resolved. Reasons can be briefly stated, the degree of particularity required depending entirely on the nature of the issues falling for decision. The reasoning must not give rise to a substantial doubt as to whether the decision-maker erred in law, for example by misunderstanding some relevant policy or some other important matter or by failing to reach a rational decision on relevant grounds. But such adverse inference will not readily be drawn. The reasons need refer only to the main issues in the dispute, not to every material consideration. They should enable disappointed developers to assess their prospects of obtaining some alternative development permission, or, as the case may be, their unsuccessful opponents to understand how the policy or approach underlying the grant of permission may impact upon future such applications. Decision letters [which contain statements of reasons] must be read in a straightforward manner, recognising that they are addressed to parties well aware of the issues involved and the arguments advanced. A reasons challenge will only succeed if the party aggrieved can satisfy the court that he has genuinely been substantially prejudiced by the failure to provide an adequately reasoned decision".

In *R(DLA)3/08*, a Tribunal of Commissioners adopted that passage and said that it applied equally to social security cases. Reference to it was also made in *DS v SSWP (ESA)* [2019] UKUT 347 (AAC), where, before reviewing the authorities in both Scotland and England and Wales, the judge said:

> "6. … The procedure before the tribunal is deliberately designed to be different from procedures in many courts; it is a simple and quick procedure, designed not to be over-complicated at all levels.
> 7. In my opinion, it is not in keeping with this approach for judges in the First-tier be held to an excessively high standard in statements of reasons …"

Even when reasons are plainly flawed, a decision will not necessarily be set aside. Referring to a decision of a reviewing officer as to whether a homeless person had a priority need for housing, Lord Neuberger said in *Holmes-Moorhouse v Richmond upon Thames LBC* [2009] UKHL 7; [2009] 1 W.L.R. 413—

> ". . . a decision can often survive despite the existence of an error in the reasoning advanced to support it. For example, sometimes the error is irrelevant to the outcome; sometimes it is too trivial (objectively, or in the eyes of the decision-maker) to affect the outcome; sometimes it is obvious from the rest of the reasoning, read as a whole, that the decision would have been the same

notwithstanding the error; sometimes, there is more than one reason for the conclusion, and the error only undermines one of the reasons; sometimes, the decision is the only one which could rationally have been reached. In all such cases, the error should not (save, perhaps, in wholly exceptional circumstances) justify the decision being quashed."

The European Court of Human Rights has taken much the same approach as the United Kingdom's courts. In *Hirvisari v Finland* 2001, it was said:

> "Although Article 6(1) obliges courts to give reasons for their decisions, it cannot be understood as requiring a detailed answer to every argument. Thus, in dismissing an appeal, an appellate court may, in principle, simply endorse the reasons for the lower court's decision . . . A lower court or authority in turn must give such reasons as to enable the parties to make effective use of any existing rights of appeal."

Indeed, where a decision-maker has given good reasons for a decision, and there was not a specific challenge to that part of the decision, a tribunal may well be presumed to have adopted the reasoning. On the other hand, where a decision-maker had not given reasons for superseding a decision so as to substitute a fixed rate award for an indefinite one, the First-tier Tribunal's failure to give reasons for that change led to its decision being quashed even though the claimant's grounds of appeal to the First-tier Tribunal had not specifically challenged that aspect of the decision (*GT v SSWP (PIP)* [2019] UKUT 30 (AAC)).

Delay

In *R(IS) 5/04*, it was held that a delay in providing reasons did not necessarily render a decision erroneous in point of law. The Commissioner said that a delay in providing reasons may itself amount to a breach of art.6 of the European Convention on Human Rights (although, if the tribunal's decision was not flawed in any other respect, the remedy for such a breach would presumably be an award of damages by a court) and she also held that a delay may be relevant on an appeal because it may indicate that the reasons are unreliable. However, in the particular case before her, where the statement of reasons had been requested on July 1, 2002 and was not sent to the parties until October 29, 2002, the Commissioner found there to have been no error of law. In *R(DLA)3/08*, the Tribunal of Commissioners observed that *R(IS)5/04* appeared to be consistent with *Bangs v Connex South Eastern Ltd* [2005] EWCA Civ 14, in which it was held that there had been no error of law despite the fact that a decision of an employment tribunal was not promulgated until a year after the hearing ended. Delay may give rise to the state's liability to pay compensation to the victim of the delay but, where an appeal against the tribunal's decision lies only on a point of law, the Court of Appeal held that it was not enough to claim that the decision is "unsafe" because of the delay. However, that was before the time limit in para.(5) was introduced and, in any event, there may be exceptional cases in which unreasonable delay in promulgating a decision can properly be treated as a serious procedural error or material irregularity giving rise to a question of law if there is a real risk that, due to the delayed decision, the party complaining was deprived of the substance of his right to a fair trial under art.6 of the Convention. It is necessary to consider whether the delay has caused the tribunal to misremember any of the oral evidence or to fail to deal with a material point (*R. (SS) v Secretary of State for the Home Department* [2018] EWCA Civ 1391). Effectively, therefore, delay is merely a factor to be borne in mind when assessing the adequacy of a statement of reasons. In *Bond v Dunster Properties Ltd* [2011] EWCA Civ 455, a delay of 22 months was not sufficient to make findings of fact unsafe. **3.388**

Supplementing reasons

3.389 It was recommended by the Court of Appeal in *English v Emery Reimbold & Strick Ltd* [2002] EWCA Civ 605; [2002] 1 W.L.R. 2409 that, where an application for permission to appeal to the Court of Appeal was made to the High Court on the ground that its reasons were inadequate, it should consider giving additional reasons and that, where such an application for permission to appeal was made to the Court of Appeal on the ground that the High Court's reasons were inadequate, the Court of Appeal should consider inviting the High Court to provide additional reasons. Lord Phillips MR, giving the judgment of the Court, said:

> "[24] We are not greatly attracted by the suggestion that a judge who has given inadequate reasons should be invited to have a second bite at the cherry. But we are much less attracted at the prospect of expensive appellate proceedings on the ground of lack of reasons. Where the judge who has heard the evidence has based a rational decision on it, the successful party will suffer an injustice if that decision is appealed, let alone set aside, simply because the judge has not included in his judgment adequate reasons for his decision. The appellate court will not be in as good a position to substitute its decision, should it decide that this course is viable, while an appeal followed by a rehearing will involve a hideous waste of costs."

In *VK v Norfolk CC* [2004] EWHC 2921 (Admin), it was held that it was not appropriate for the High Court, when hearing a statutory appeal from the Special Educational Needs and Disability Tribunal, to invite that Tribunal to supplement its reasons, unless what was sought was "merely elucidatory". However, in *Barke v SEETEC Business Technology Centre Ltd* [2005] EWCA Civ 578; [2005] I.C.R. 1373, the Court of Appeal held to be lawful the practice of the Employment Appeal Tribunal, developed in the light of *English*, of sifting the appeals before it and, in appropriate cases, inviting the employment tribunal to clarify or supplement its reasons. In doing so, it rejected at [23] to [28] an argument that such an invitation would be futile because, under its procedural rules, the employment tribunal was "functus officio" after it had given reasons for its decision and had no power to supplement them.

The rules of the First-tier Tribunal do not appear to be materially different from those that then applied to employment tribunals (which the High Court in *VK* had distinguished from those applying to the Special Educational Needs and Disability Tribunal). Nonetheless, the Upper Tribunal has said on several occasions that the First-tier Tribunal should not supplement its reasons on its own initiative when giving or refusing permission to appeal in a social security, or similar, case, although it arguably remains unclear whether they might be accepted in some circumstances.

3.390 In *CA/4297/2004*, an appeal tribunal had dismissed an appeal against the disallowance of a renewal claim for attendance allowance. When the appellant applied for permission to appeal, the application was dealt with by a different chairman who asked the chairman who had presided at the hearing to provide further reasons if he could do so. Having earlier referred to the difficulty there would be "in securing that the subsequent statement of reasons was truly that of the whole tribunal and not that of the chairman alone", the Commissioner distinguished *Barke* on the ground that balancing the considerations identified in *English* in a social security case favoured not giving a chairman "another bite at the cherry". He said at [22]:

> "Most (although not all) appeals to the Commissioner (after the grant of leave) are decided speedily without oral hearings and on the basis of relatively brief written submissions. If the case is sent back to the tribunal any waste of costs will be relatively limited and certainly not 'hideous'. A chairman considering an application for leave to appeal who is unhappy with the reasons given by the tribunal can set the decision aside and refer it under section 13(2) [of the Social

Security Act 1998, the forerunner of the power of review under section 9 of the Tribunals, Courts and Enforcement Act 2007] without even troubling the Commissioner, and this procedure is relatively efficient in resource terms."

Accordingly, he appears to have decided that the additional reasons should not have been given and to have accepted that the original reasons were inadequate, although the precise basis on which the appeal was allowed is obscure because he did not expressly reject the Secretary of State's argument (recorded at [9]) that the original reasons were in fact adequate.

The principle in *R. (on the application of Bancoult) v Secretary of State for Foreign and Commonwealth Affairs* [2007] EWCA Civ 498, which held that "in principle a decision maker who gives one set of reasons cannot, when challenged, come up with another set" was referred to in *GS v Secretary of State for Work & Pensions* [2024] UKUT 4 (AAC) in which the Upper Tribunal found that First-tier Tribunal's failure to mention evidence taken during hearing in its statement of reasons for decision, and later reliance on that evidence when refusing permission to appeal, amounted to error of law. The claimant had appealed against a work capability assessment decision under universal credit. He requested a statement of reasons for the Tribunal's decision. The statement recorded that the claimant's wife had attended the hearing but did not mention that she had given any oral evidence at the hearing. The claimant asked for permission to appeal to the Upper Tribunal. The judge that had presided over the First-tier Tribunal refused the application, giving reasons including that the claimant's wife's oral evidence had been taken into account when the tribunal refused his appeal, and that it had found that his wife's oral evidence was unreliable. The Upper Tribunal found that a) the First-tier Tribunal's reasons for its decision recorded that the appellant's wife attended the hearing but made no mention of her giving evidence. From those reasons, the Appellant could not know whether his wife's evidence was accepted or rejected and, if rejected, why, b) the judge who determined the claimant's application for permission to appeal to the Upper Tribunal acted alone, which meant that since the reasons given for the tribunal's dismissal of the appeal made no mention of the wife's evidence, it could not be certain that the reasons given by the judge at the permission stage were, in fact, the reasons of the panel that dismissed the appeal (the panel consisted of the judge and a medical member) and c) the reasons given at the permission stage fall foul of *R. (on the application of Bancoult) v Secretary of State for Foreign and Commonwealth Affairs* [2007] EWCA Civ 498, they were essentially new reasons that formed no part of the First-tier Tribunal's' earlier explanation of why it dismissed the appellant's appeal against the Secretary of State's decision.

In *CAF/2150/2007*, a Commissioner deciding an appeal from a Pensions Appeal Tribunal—brought under different legislation but nonetheless an appeal with similarities to social security appeals—held uncontroversially that the Tribunal's usual practice of giving brief reasons initially and then giving more detailed reasons if leave to appeal was sought was wrong. However, he appears to have accepted that additional reasons could sometimes be given. What he said was:

> "When an application for leave to appeal is made, it may be appropriate to comment on the grounds. However, it is not the occasion to provide additional reasons that the tribunal had when it made the decision but did not disclose to the parties at the time. On those occasions when it is permissible and proper to provide additional reasons, they must be those of the tribunal as a whole and not those of the chairman."

If additional reasons are sometimes acceptable, it is not entirely clear why they should *never* be given when giving or refusing permission to appeal and it is arguable that the second sentence of the above passage should be read in the light of the Commissioner's disapproval of what had become a general practice. Moreover, in *CT v SSD* [2009] UKUT 167 (AAC), the Upper Tribunal accepted that it might sometimes be appropriate for the Upper Tribunal to exercise its apparent power under r.5(3)(n) of the Tribunal Procedure (Upper Tribunal) Rules 2008 to direct the First-tier Tribunal to supplement its reasons before an application for permission to appeal was determined by the Upper Tribunal. If that is so, it is difficult to see why the First-tier Tribunal should never provide such supplementary reasons on its own initiative. In practice, though, the Upper Tribunal does not exercise any power it may have to direct or invite the First-tier Tribunal to provide supplementary reasons (see the note to r.5(3)(n) of the Tribunal Procedure (Upper Tribunal) Rules 2008).

More recently, in *Cabinet Office v IC* [2020] UKUT 140 (AAC), an appeal from the General Regulatory Chamber of the First-tier Tribunal, the Upper Tribunal has again held that the First-tier Tribunal has no power to supplement its reasons when refusing permission to appeal. However, its reasoning at [26] and [27] is different from that in *CA/4296/2004* and is arguably inconsistent with what was said in *Barke* at [23] to [28]. Counsel do not appear to have drawn the judge's attention to *Barke* at all.

It appears clear from these decisions that the Upper Tribunal is at best sceptical about the value and appropriateness of additional reasons. However, it also seems reasonably clear, in the light of *VK*, that a judge of the First-tier Tribunal may at least elucidate the tribunal's original reasoning and, in the light of *Barke*, that the provision of additional reasons would not be inconsistent with the Rules. Indeed, reasons for refusing permission to appeal may legitimately include points of law whether or not they formed part of the First-tier Tribunal's original reasoning. It is the reliability, or the perception of reliability, of additional findings of fact or other reasoning on issues of fact that is the problem, particularly if the judge stating them was not the only member of the tribunal that heard the case, and there is force in the point made in *CA/4297/2004* that, on balance, the provision of supplementary reasons is generally undesirable in the social security context. If a judge does give further reasons in the light of *CAF/2150/2007* and *CT v SSD* [2009] UKUT 167 (AAC), and there is nonetheless an appeal, it will be for the Upper Tribunal to consider whether to take them into account. Even if it concludes that they ought not to have been given and finds the First-tier Tribunal to have erred in law, it may adopt them when deciding how to dispose of the case (see *CAF/2150/2007* and *AS v SSWP (ESA)* [2011] UKUT 159 (AAC), although it may be arguable that it would have been more appropriate to have set the First-tier Tribunal's decisions aside in those cases and remade them to the same effect, rather than refusing to set them aside—see the note to s.12 of the Tribunals, Courts and Enforcement Act 2007).

PART 4

CORRECTING, SETTING ASIDE, REVIEWING AND APPEALING TRIBUNAL DECISIONS

Interpretation

3.391 **35.** In this Part—

"appeal" means the exercise of a right of appeal—

(a) under paragraph 2(2) or 4(1) of Schedule 2 to the Tax Credits Act 2002;

(b) under section 21(10) of the Child Trust Funds Act 2004; or

(c) on a point of law under section 11 of the 2007 Act; and

"review" means the review of a decision by the Tribunal under section 9 of the 2007 Act.

DEFINITIONS

"the 2007 Act"—see r.1(3).
"Tribunal"—*ibid.*

GENERAL NOTE

The references to the Tax Credits Act 2002 and the Child Trust Funds Act 2004 are to appeals against decisions in penalty cases, where rights of appeal, which are not confined to points of law, remain in force alongside the right of appeal under s.11 of the Tribunals, Courts and Enforcement Act 2007. 3.392

Clerical mistakes and accidental slips or omissions

36. The Tribunal may at any time correct any clerical mistake or other accidental slip or omission in a decision, direction or any document produced by it, by— 3.393

(a) sending notification of the amended decision or direction, or a copy of the amended document, to all parties; and
(b) making any necessary amendment to any information published in relation to the decision, direction or document.

DEFINITIONS

"document"—see r.1(3).
"party"—*ibid.*
"Tribunal"—*ibid.*

GENERAL NOTE

Rule 36 allows correction only of accidental errors, "such as a typing mistake or misspelling of a name or an omission about which both sides if asked, would agree" (*CI/3887/1999*). It cannot be used to remove an error of law on an issue central to an appeal. If a judge realises, after a decision has been issued, that there is an obvious and fundamental error of law in the decision, a party may be invited to apply for permission to appeal so that the decision may be reviewed and a rehearing directed (*Camden LBC v YV* [2012] UKUT 190 (AAC); [2013] AACR 2). 3.394

In *AS v SSWP (ESA)* [2011] UKUT 159, the Upper Tribunal said:

> "16. Rule 36 is by its contents a species of slip rule and should be interpreted in accordance with the nature of that type of provision. As such, it deals with matters that were in the judge's mind when writing but for some reason did not find their way onto the page. Typical examples are the typing error that produces the wrong date or a momentary lapse of concentration that results in the word 'not' being omitted. The rule does not cover matters that the judge had planned to mention but forgot to include. Obviously, it is difficult for the Upper Tribunal to know what was in the judge's mind, but the extent of the changes are an indication. It is difficult to classify the omission of a total of nine lines of explanation as in the same category of mistake as a typing error or a momentary lapse of concentration. For that reason, I decide that the changes made by the presiding judge were not authorised by rule 36."

Nonetheless, the Upper Tribunal then went on to rely upon those reasons when refusing to set aside the First-tier Tribunal's decision. That approach was approved by a three-judge panel in *JS v SSWP (DLA)* [2013] UKUT 100 (AAC) although it declined to rely on additional reasons itself. Also, in *CG v SSWP (DLA)* [2011] UKUT 453 (AAC), the Upper Tribunal judge declined to rely on the nine additional paragraphs added to a 10-paragraph decision in order to refute grounds of appeal, when the reasoning was inadequate even with the additional reasons. Moreover, in *AS (Afghanistan) v Secretary of State for the Home Department* [2019] EWCA Civ 208; [2019] 1 W.L.R. 3065, while it was accepted that the power to correct a mistake under a rule like this extended to a mistake in a statement of reasons as well as a mistake in a decision notice and that it extended to errors of expression but not errors of substance, the Court of Appeal held that it was not appropriate for the power to be exercised in a case where there was a real doubt as to whether the mistake was a mere error of expression rather than an error of substance. It rejected a suggestion that the tribunal should be given an opportunity to explain which it was, because there would be a perception of unfairness. Presumably, the same perception of unfairness could arise from refusing to set aside a decision on the basis of additional reasons, as was done in *AS v SSWP (ESA)*, but the particular facts of a case are likely to be important. However, a correction may completely reverse the effect of a decision, e.g. where the First-tier Tribunal has said that it dismissed an appeal but meant to allow it or where the word "not" has been accidentally omitted (*Devani v Secretary of State for the Home Department* [2020] EWCA Civ 612; [2020] 1 W.L.R 2613 at [23] and [24]).

3.395 A written decision is only effective when it is sent out (*R(I) 14/74*, *SK (Sri Lanka) v Secretary of State for the Home Department* [2008] EWCA Civ 495, *SSD v PY (WP)* [2012] UKUT 116 (AAC); [2012] AACR 44, *re L (Children) (Preliminary Finding: Power to Reverse)* [2013] UKSC 8; [2013] 1 W.L.R. 634). Until then, it may be altered informally. However, a decision given orally is effective when it is announced and so cannot subsequently be changed informally (*Patel v Secretary of State for the Home Department* [2015] EWCA Civ 1175, but note that it was pointed out in *R. (Singh) v Secretary of State for the Home Department* [2019] EWCA Civ 1014 that the Court was not referred to all the ways in which a decision may be corrected or set aside formally).

A refusal to correct an acknowledged error of fact in reasons for a decision on the ground that it is not a mere slip may imply that the decision was based on a significant misapprehension of the facts and must be set aside (*Space Airconditioning plc v Guy* [2012] EWCA Civ 1664; [2013] 1 W.L.R. 1293).

A correction no longer automatically extends time limits. Note that a separate power to correct a decision arises on review (see s.9(4)(a) of the Tribunals, Courts and Enforcement Act 2007).

Setting aside a decision which disposes of proceedings

3.396 **37.**—(1) The Tribunal may set aside a decision which disposes of proceedings, or part of such a decision, and re-make the decision, or the relevant part of it, if—

(a) the Tribunal considers that it is in the interests of justice to do so; and
(b) one or more of the conditions in paragraph (2) are satisfied.

(2) The conditions are—

(a) a document relating to the proceedings was not sent to, or was not received at an appropriate time by, a party or a party's representative;
(b) a document relating to the proceedings was not sent to the Tribunal at an appropriate time;
(c) a party, or a party's representative, was not present at a hearing related to the proceedings; or
(d) there has been some other procedural irregularity in the proceedings.

(3) A party applying for a decision, or part of a decision, to be set aside under paragraph (1) must make a written application to the Tribunal so that it is received no later than 1 month after the date on which the Tribunal sent notice of the decision to the party.

DEFINITIONS

"dispose of proceedings"—see r.1(3).
"document"—*ibid.*

"hearing"—*ibid.*
"party"—*ibid.*
"Tribunal"—*ibid.*

General Note

The one-month time limit for making an application may be extended under r.5(3)(a). It has been said that an application of some sort is required because the First-tier Tribunal has no power to set aside a decision of its own motion, although it may invite an application from the adversely affected party if it perceives that there may otherwise have been an injustice (*MA v SSWP (PIP)* [2020] UKUT 172 (AAC)). However, in *KH (dec'd) by AMH v SSWP (IIDB)* [2021] UKUT 189 (AAC), the judge expressed some doubt about the correctness of that view but said that it in any event applied only where the applicant had made an unequivocal application for something and r.41 did not empower the First-tier Tribunal to treat that application as being also, or instead, an application for the setting aside of a decision. Where, as in *KH*, the applicant had sent a document to the First-tier Tribunal but had not made a clear application, the issue was simply whether the document should be interpreted as an application for the setting aside of a decision. In that case, the claimant had provided medical evidence dating from before the First-tier Tribunal's decision that directly contradicted a crucial finding of the First-tier Tribunal, and it was held that the First-tier Tribunal should have treated the submission of that document as an application for the setting aside of the decision on the ground that "a document relating to the proceedings was not sent to the Tribunal at an appropriate time". 3.397

Note that a separate power to set aside a decision arises on review (see s.9(4)(c) of the Tribunals, Courts and Enforcement Act 2007). There is also a broad power under r.6(5) to set aside case management decisions.

Until a written decision is issued in writing to the parties, it may be recalled without recourse to a formal setting aside under this rule or s.9 of the 2007 Act. However, a decision given orally is effective when it is announced and so cannot subsequently be changed informally (*Patel v Secretary of State for the Home Department* [2015] EWCA Civ 1175, but note that it was pointed out in *R. (Singh) v Secretary of State for the Home Department* [2019] EWCA Civ 1014 that the Court was not referred to all the ways in which a decision may be corrected or set aside formally, including the equivalent of this rule). If a claimant merely arrives late after an appeal has been heard but while the other party is still present, there is no reason why, if the parties agree or do not have a good reason for disagreeing and if there is time, the tribunal not should simply start again (*CJ v SSWP (IS)* [2013] UKUT 131(AAC), *AK v HMRC (TC)* [2016] UKUT 98 (AAC)) but, if the decision has been given orally or if a decision notice has been handed to any party, it will be necessary formally to set the first decision aside before rehearing the case.

Setting aside under r.37 is appropriate where a claimant has not received notice of a hearing that has been properly sent (*R(SB) 19/83*). In *R(SB) 55/83*, it was held that that was the only remedy available to a claimant in those circumstances and that there was no basis upon which a Commissioner could allow an appeal. That approach has been rejected in *CDLA/5413/1999* where it is held that a decision of a tribunal is erroneous in law where notice of a hearing has not been received by a party even though there may have been no breach of the rules of natural justice by the tribunal. See also *CIB/303/1999* and, more recently, *KH v SSWP (CSM)* [2012] UKUT 329 (AAC) in which the Upper Tribunal referred to the clear, albeit obiter, statement in *R(SB) 22/83* that the jurisdiction to set aside on appeal a tribunal's decision on the ground of a breach of the rules of natural justice was additional to the power conferred on the lower tribunal to set aside its decisions. Although the First-tier Tribunal had refused to set aside the decision made in the appellant's absence because it found as a fact that he had had notice of the hearing, the Upper Tribunal did not regard 3.398

itself as bound by that finding and allowed the appeal on the ground that the appellant had not received notice of the hearing and his presence might have made a difference to the outcome. Moreover, it is now apparent that even the Court of Appeal does not regard a failure to apply for the setting aside of a decision of a lower court where that would have been appropriate to be an absolute bar to an appeal (*Williams v Hinton* [2011] EWCA Civ 1123). In *CIB/5227/1999*, it was pointed out that it was necessary to explain fully the circumstances of the case when making an application for a decision to be set aside. In that case, as in *CDLA/5413/1999*, the reason that the claimant had not received notice of the hearing was that none had been sent because the claimant had not received the clerk's direction requiring him to state whether he wished there to be an oral hearing.

In *CSB/15394/1996* and *CSB/574/1997*, a tribunal refused to set aside a decision on the ground that the claimant's case for the setting aside amounted to an allegation that there had been a breach of the rules of natural justice which was an error of law so that an appeal to a Commissioner was the appropriate course for the claimant to take. The Commissioner hearing the appeal disagreed with that approach. He pointed out that most grounds for setting aside would also be proper grounds for appeal and that the forerunner of this rule existed to provide an expeditious alternative to an appeal. On the other hand, in *CSDLA/303/1998*, the Commissioner held that a claimant was not entitled to raise by way of appeal an issue of fact determined under the forerunner of this rule. The tribunal considering the application for setting aside had found as a fact that a fax allegedly sent to the Independent Tribunal Service had not in fact been sent. The Commissioner held that that question of fact could not be considered on an appeal because "there could be no question of unfairness arising as the claimant had been provided with the remedy of seeking set aside". It is not recorded whether or not the claimant was offered an oral hearing of the application for setting aside, which would have been unusual. It may still be arguable that a finding made on such an application without an oral hearing is not sufficient to remove the Upper Tribunal's jurisdiction to consider the same issue on an appeal.

In *CG/2973/2004*, the Commissioner held a tribunal decision to be erroneous in point of law because medical evidence sent by the claimant in support of an application for an adjournment had not been received by the tribunal. He also held that the fact that the claimant had unsuccessfully tried to have the decision set aside on the same ground did not prevent her from taking the point on appeal to a Commissioner. He observed that the chairman who had refused to set the decision aside had done so on the basis that her presence could not have made any difference to the outcome of her hearing. The case is therefore distinguishable from *CSDLA/303/1998*. The fact that the applicant's presence would not have made any difference is a matter that can legitimately be taken into account when considering whether "to set the decision aside is in the interests of justice" and it would also be relevant to the question whether there had been a breach of the rules of natural justice, but the Commissioner disagreed with the chairman's view of the possible importance of the claimant's evidence.

3.399 An appeal against *CG/2973/2004* was dismissed by the Court of Appeal (*Levy v Secretary of State for Work and Pensions* [2006] EWCA Civ 890 (reported as *R(G) 2/06*)), but the relevance of the claimant's application under the forerunner of r.37 was not the subject of argument in the Court of Appeal.

Paragraph (1)(a) specifically provides that, even where the conditions of para.2 are satisfied, a decision need be set aside only if it is "in the interests of justice to do so". This is consistent with the European Convention on Human Rights. Under the Convention, a person who did not receive notice of a hearing is not entitled as of right to have the decision set aside, unless he has a real prospect of success on a rehearing (*Akram v Adam* [2004] EWCA Civ 1601; [2005] 1 W.L.R. 2762).

Tribunals are entitled to take a robust approach to the non-appearance of parties and to proceed to hear cases in their absence, but a necessary concomitant of such a robust approach must be a greater preparedness to set aside decisions under r.37(2)(c) (*Cooke v Glenrose Fish Co* [2004] I.C.R. 1188, *GA v Southwark LBC (HB)* [2013] UKUT 170 (AAC)).

The principle of taking a robust approach to set aside decisions is illustrated in *Herman v Information Commissioner and the Chief Constable of Kent Police* [2023] UKUT 240 (AAC). The Upper Tribunal was dealing with an appeal concerning Rule 41 of The Tribunal Procedure (First-tier Tribunal) (General Regulatory Chamber) Rules 2009, which is in the same terms as Rule 37. On October 11, 2017 the First-tier Tribunal had proceeded to determine and refuse the Appellant's Freedom of Information Act 2000 application in their absence and on the mistaken understanding that the Appellant had refused to attend the hearing. Over four years later, on February 20, 2022, the Appellant made an application to appeal the decision. On August 31, 2022 the First-tier Tribunal extended time to admit the application but refused to set aside the Tribunal's decision of October 17, 2017. The Upper Tribunal found that the overall error of the First-tier Tribunal was in failing to weigh in its consideration the central importance of an Appellant being able to attend the oral hearing of their appeal. That was plainly a significant factor in determining where the 'interests of justice' lay. The error of law the First-tier Tribunal made in its refusal to set aside decision was to concentrate solely on the underlying merits of the appeal and in not having any, or any sufficient, regard to the Appellant's absence from the hearing and why that was so. The Upper Tribunal noted that there had not been any application before the First-tier Tribunal that the merits of the appeal were so poor that the appeal should have been struck out. Therefore, the First-tier Tribunal was required to hold and oral hearing and the Appellant had been entitled to attend. The Upper Tribunal referred to para.9 of *MK v SSWP (ESA)* [2018] UKUT 33 (AAC), which references the relevant cases that establish a concomitant between proceeding in an Appellant's absence and being prepared to set aside. Dealing with the issue of delay it is noted that the First-tier Tribunal's decision to admit the application of 20 February 2022 was not challenged and had not been set aside and so remained in place. That decision of the First-tier Tribunal was therefore binding in the First-tier Tribunal proceedings and so binds the Upper Tribunal equally in remaking the First-tier Tribunal decision whether to set aside the October 17, 2017 First-tier Tribunal's decision (see *R. (on the application of Majera) v SSHD* [2021] UKSC 46 [2022] AC 461).

A similar sentiment was expressed in *MP v SSWP (DLA)* [2010] UKUT 103 (AAC) where a claimant was not given the month prescribed by r.24(7) for submitting a reply to a decision-maker's response so that medical evidence held by her representative was not submitted before the appeal was determined on the papers. The First-tier Tribunal refused to set aside its decision on the ground that no element of r.37(2) was satisfied. The Upper Tribunal held that there was a right of appeal against the refusal to set aside and that the case had fallen within both para.(2)(b) and para.(2)(d) but in any event he held there to have been a breach of the rules of natural justice and he set aside the substantive decision as well.

Indeed, even where a tribunal has proceeded in the absence of a party after a judge has refused an application for postponement or adjournment, it is permissible to set the decision aside under r.37. In *Family Channel Ltd v Fatima* [2020] EWCA Civ 824; [2020] 1 W.L.R. 5104, decided under the equivalent provision in C.P.R. r.39.3(3), it was held that that provision justified "a less draconian approach" than was required on an application for an adjournment so that it did not matter that the medical evidence on the setting-aside application was much the same as it had been on the application for adjournment. However, it is arguable that both the C.P.R. provision and r.37 merely require that the issue of fairness be reconsidered afresh on a setting-aside application, with the benefit of hindsight and perhaps a better appreciation of all the circumstances. Either approach supports the point made in *KO v SSWP (ESA)* [2013] UKUT 544 (AAC) that a decision to proceed in the absence of a party needs to be kept under review throughout the hearing (see the annotation to r.27). **3.400**

In principle, a decision should not be set aside without giving the other party an opportunity of commenting on the application, either before the decision is set aside or afterwards, on the basis that the setting aside may itself be set aside (*GA v Southwark LBC (HB)* [2013] UKUT 170 (AAC)). This is particularly important where a public authority is applying for the decision to be set aside. It is less important where a claimant is the applicant only because many public authorities are prepared to waive their right to have an opportunity to comment on the ground that it is not a good use of resources. In *GA v Southwark LBC (HB)*, the local authority telephoned the First-tier Tribunal 10 minutes after the hearing of the claimant's appeal was due to start and asked for a postponement. The appeal was against a decision to the effect that some £22,000 in housing benefit and council tax benefit had been overpaid to her and was recoverable. The judge refused the request for a postponement and allowed the claimant's appeal in a decision that did not disclose any error of law. The local authority promptly asked for the decision to be set aside and, four months later, a judge did set the decision aside without the claimant having been given any notice of the setting aside application. The Upper Tribunal allowed the claimant's appeal against the setting aside decision on the ground that she had not been given an opportunity to make representations. It substituted its own decision refusing to set aside the appeal decision on the ground that it was not in the interests of justice to do so because the local authority had not been frank as to its reason for not attending the original hearing, the claimant had had no notice of the setting aside application for four months and, while the local authority had an arguable case on the facts, it could not be said that it was likely to be successful if the substantive appeal were reheard.

Where there has been a breach of natural justice that does not fall within the scope of r.37 and an application under this rule has been rejected for that reason, the judge should consider reviewing the decision if an application for permission to appeal is submitted (*CDLA/792/2006*).

If a case is reheard by a differently constituted tribunal, it is usual for the decision that has been set aside to be included in the papers. That is not inappropriate. Even if their findings of fact cannot be relied upon, issues identified by the first tribunal may well be of assistance to the new tribunal, although it must be careful not to be influenced by the discredited findings (*Swash v Secretary of State for the Home Department* [2006] EWCA Civ 1093; [2007] 1 W.L.R. 1264). There may, however, be special circumstances in which the judge setting the first decision aside considers that the interests of justice require the case to be heard by a tribunal that has not seen that decision and he or she will be able to issue appropriate directions to ensure that that happens (*ibid*).

Application for permission to appeal

3.401 **38.**—(1) This rule does not apply to asylum support cases or criminal injuries compensation cases.

(2) A person seeking permission to appeal must make a written application to the Tribunal for permission to appeal.

(3) An application under paragraph (2) must be sent or delivered to the Tribunal so that it is received no later than 1 month after the latest of the dates that the Tribunal sends to the person making the application—

[[1](za) the relevant decision notice;]

(a) written reasons for the decision; [[1], if the decision disposes of—
   (i) all issues in the proceedings; or
   (ii) subject to paragraph (3A), a preliminary issue dealt with following a direction under rule 5(3)(e);]

(b) notification of amended reasons for, or correction of, the decision following a review; or

(c) notification that an application for the decision to be set aside has been unsuccessful.

[[1] (3A) The Tribunal may direct that the 1 month within which a party may send or deliver an application for permission to appeal against a decision that disposes of a preliminary issue shall run from the date of the decision that disposes of all issues in the proceedings.]

(4) The date in paragraph (3)(c) applies only if the application for the decision to be set aside was made within the time stipulated in rule 37 (setting aside a decision which disposes of proceedings) or any extension of that time granted by the Tribunal.

(5) If the person seeking permission to appeal sends or delivers the application to the Tribunal later than the time required by paragraph (3) or by any extension of time under rule 5(3)(a) (power to extend time)—

(a) the application must include a request for an extension of time and the reason why the application was not provided in time; and

(b) unless the Tribunal extends time for the application under rule 5(3)(a) (power to extend time) the Tribunal must not admit the application.

(6) An application under paragraph (2) must—

(a) identify the decision of the Tribunal to which it relates;

(b) identify the alleged error or errors of law in the decision; and

(c) state the result the party making the application is seeking.

(7) If a person makes an application under paragraph (2) [1 in respect of a decision that disposes of proceedings or of a preliminary issue dealt with following a direction under rule 5(3)(e)] when the Tribunal has not given a written statement of reasons for its decision—

(a) if no application for a written statement of reasons has been made to the Tribunal, the application for permission must be treated as such an application;

(b) unless the Tribunal decides to give permission and directs that this sub-paragraph does not apply, the application is not to be treated as an application for permission to appeal; and

(c) if an application for a written statement of reasons has been, or is, refused because of a delay in making the application, the Tribunal must only admit the application for permission if the Tribunal considers that it is in the interests of justice to do so.

AMENDMENT

1. Tribunal Procedure (Amendment) Rules 2013 (SI 2013/477) rr.22 and 30 (April 8, 2013).

DEFINITIONS

"appeal"—see r.35.
"asylum support case"—see r.1(3).
"criminal injuries compensation case"—*ibid.*
"dispose of proceedings"—*ibid.*
"party"—*ibid.*
"Tribunal"—*ibid.*

GENERAL NOTE

Paragraphs (3) and (3A)

Where there is no duty to provide a statement of reasons because the decision is purely interlocutory and neither disposes of the proceedings nor is a decision on a preliminary issue following a direction explicitly directing that the issue be dealt with as a preliminary point, the time for appealing runs from the date of the decision itself. Where a decision is given on a preliminary issue, the First-tier Tribunal can decide whether the time for appealing should run from the final decision disposing of all other issues in the case or from the date of the decision on the preliminary issue itself. Which of the courses of action is appropriate will depend a great deal on the circumstances of the individual case. **3.402**

Paragraph (5)

3.403 There is no longer an absolute time limit on applications. Previously an application could not be accepted if it was more than a year late. It is still unlikely that permission would be given where there had been such a delay but it is not inconceivable in, say, a case where an unrepresented claimant has been actively challenging some other decision and has not been told that success in that challenge depended on a successful appeal against the decision of the Tribunal.

Rule 5(3)(a) does not expressly require "special reasons" to be shown for an extension of time, as was the position under reg.58 of the Social Security and Child Support (Decisions and Appeals) Regulations 1999, but it is suggested that this may not make any difference because "[t]he concept of special reasons [was] a broad and flexible one" (*R. (Howes) v Social Security Commissioner* [2007] EWHC 559 (Admin)). The reasons for delay were never the only relevant factor (*R(M) 1/87*, applying the approach of the Court of Appeal in *R. v Secretary of State for the Home Department Ex p. Mehta* [1975] 1 W.L.R. 1087). That the merits of the case are also relevant has been confirmed in *R. (Birmingham CC) v Birmingham Crown Court* [2009] EWHC 3329 (Admin); [2010] 1 W.L.R. 1287.

In *CCS/2064/1999*, it was suggested that relevant factors included the strength of the grounds of appeal, the amount of money involved, whether the decision affected current entitlement, whether there was an adequate alternative remedy, the difficulties that the lapse of time might create for making any further findings of fact and the way in which the parties had conducted the case, including their respective contributions to delay. However, in *R. (Howes) v Social Security Commissioner* [2007] EWHC 559 (Admin), Black J., in rejecting an argument that deciding whether there were special reasons required consideration of the factors listed in CPR r.3.9, also disapproved of judge-made lists of relevant considerations and said that "the factors that are relevant will be dependent upon the circumstances of the individual case". The amount of delay is likely to be relevant in most cases but, in *CSDLA/71/1999*, the Commissioner made it plain that "special reasons" for admitting a late application for leave to appeal would not necessarily be found merely because the application was made only two or three days late, even if the applicant had an arguable case on the merits. In that case, the applicant was not helped by the fact that the original explanation for the delay advanced by his representative turned out not to be true and the Commissioner refused leave to appeal. See further the annotation to r.5(3)(a).

It should be noted that the legal consequence of a decision of the First-tier Tribunal to refuse to admit a late application for permission to appeal under rule 38(5)(b) (because time was not extended for the late application to be treated as if it had been made in time) is that the Upper Tribunal can only admit the renewed application for permission to appeal for consideration by the Upper Tribunal if (a) the application to the Upper Tribunal explains why the application for permission to appeal was made late to the First-tier Tribunal, and (b) it is in the interests of justice to admit the application (Rule 21(7) of the Tribunal Procedure (Upper Tribunal) Rules 2008.

Paragraph (7)

3.404 Although the circumstances in which a person can demonstrate an error of law in the absence of a statement of reasons are limited, they are not negligible (see *R(IS) 11/99*). This paragraph makes provision for cases where there is no statement of reasons, either because no application has previously been made or because a statement of reasons has been refused. If there has not already been an application for a statement of reasons, the application for permission to appeal is treated as such an application either instead of, or if it so directs under sub-para.(b), as well as an application for permission to appeal. Sub-paragraph (b) applies only if the Tribunal decides to give permission to appeal either at the same time as issuing a statement of reasons or despite the refusal of such a statement. Where the Tribunal would refuse permission to appeal or would review its decision, it must give the applicant another opportunity to apply for permission to appeal in the light of its decision whether or not to issue a statement of reasons.

However, it is arguable that sub-para.(b) does not prevent the Tribunal from treating the application as an application for a correction or setting aside (see r.41).

Sub-paragraph (c) (unlike sub-paras (a) and (b)) applies whether or not there has been a previous application for a statement of reasons. It has the effect of treating the delay in applying for a statement of reasons (which is the only ground upon which a statement of reasons may be refused) in the same way as delay in applying for permission to appeal. The application for permission will not be admitted unless the Tribunal is persuaded that it is in the interests of justice to admit it despite the delay, just as, under para.(5)(b), a late application for permission will not be admitted unless it is in the interests of justice to extend the time for making the application.

In *WO'C v SSWP (CCS)* [2020] UKUT 34 (AAC), it was held that, where a person applied for permission to appeal without having previously applied for a statement of reasons and so that the application was treated as an application for a statement of reasons under para.(a), the application ceased to be an application for permission unless permission to appeal was given and para.(b) was disapplied, with the result that the First-tier Tribunal had no power to refuse permission to appeal until the applicant submitted a new application because s.11(4) of the Tribunals, Courts and Enforcement Act 2008 required there to be such an application. Accordingly, particularly as the judge had not purported to determine an application for permission to appeal, the letter sent to the applicant by the tribunal staff telling him that he could make an application to the Upper Tribunal for permission to appeal was wrong. It should have advised him that he could make a new application to the First-tier Tribunal.

Indeed, it seems to be a common misunderstanding of the First-tier Tribunal's administration that an appellant who has been refused a statement of reasons due to delay is not entitled to apply for permission to appeal. In *SB v SSWP (PIP)* [2020] UKUT 198 (AAC), it had gone as far as rejecting the application for permission to appeal without referring it to a judge. Unsurprisingly, that was held to have been unlawful. Notwithstanding what had apparently happened in that case, in *HMRC v AD (CHB)* [2020] UKUT 353 (AAC) the Upper Tribunal was prepared to presume that HMRC's application to the First-tier Tribunal for permission to appeal had been considered by a judge—perhaps, due to the Covid-19 pandemic, the judge did not have access to the First-tier Tribunal's file to check whether that was so—but he said that a copy of the judge's determination should have been sent to the parties.

Tribunal's consideration of application for permission to appeal

39.—(1) On receiving an application for permission to appeal the Tribunal must first consider, taking into account the overriding objective in rule 2, whether to review the decision in accordance with rule 40 (review of a decision). 3.405

(2) If the Tribunal decides not to review the decision, or reviews the decision and decides to take no action in relation to the decision, or part of it, the Tribunal must consider whether to give permission to appeal in relation to the decision or that part of it.

(3) The Tribunal must send a record of its decision to the parties as soon as practicable.

(4) If the Tribunal refuses permission to appeal it must send with the record of its decision—

(a) a statement of its reasons for such refusal; and

(b) notification of the right to make an application to the Upper Tribunal for permission to appeal and the time within which, and the method by which, such application must be made.

(5) The Tribunal may give permission to appeal on limited grounds, but must comply with paragraph (4) in relation to any grounds on which it has refused permission.

DEFINITIONS

"appeal"—see r.35.
"party"—see r.1(3).
"review"—see r.35.
"Tribunal"—see r.1(3).

GENERAL NOTE

3.406 The Senior President of Tribunals has issued a Practice Statement which has the effect of replacing reg.58(6) of the Social Security and Child Support (Decisions and Appeals) Regulations 1999 so that, as before, applications for permission to appeal are considered by salaried judges where the decision was made by, or by a tribunal presided over by, a fee-paid judge (see para.11 of the *Practice Statement on the composition of the tribunals in social security and child support cases in the Social Entitlement Chamber* set out above in the note to art.2 of the First-tier Tribunal and Upper Tribunal (Composition of Tribunal) Order 2008).

There is no requirement to obtain observations from parties other than the applicant and it is suggested that it is unnecessary to do so unless the Tribunal is contemplating reviewing the decision that is being challenged and, even then, it will not always be necessary to do so because a dissatisfied party may apply for the new decision to be set aside (see r.40(4)). This is because it is recognised that, where issues of law are concerned, generally "there may be little that the successful party can say in opposition to an application for permission to appeal" *Global Energy Horizons Corp v Gray* [2020] EWCA Civ 1668; [2021] 1 W.L.R. 2264 at [495].

Paragraphs (1) and (2)

3.407 Before deciding whether or not to grant permission to appeal, the Tribunal must first decide whether or not to review the decision under s.9 of the Tribunals, Courts and Enforcement Act 2007, as limited by r.40. A decision may be reviewed if it is erroneous in point of law (see r.40(2)(b)). However, it does not follow that the effect of r.39(1) is that a decision must be reviewed if it is erroneous in point of law. A decision should be reviewed only if there is a "clear" error of law and regard should also be had to whether the point is contentious, because the First-tier Tribunal must not usurp the Upper Tribunal's function of determining appeals on contentious points of law and because reviewing decisions where there is a dispute between the parties as to the law may cause delay rather than reducing it, which is the point of the power of review (*R. (RB) v First-tier Tribunal (Review)* [2010] UKUT 160 (AAC); [2010] AACR 41). Therefore, the First-tier Tribunal may decide not to review a decision simply because it considers that it should instead grant permission to appeal.

It was held in *R. (Oceana) v Upper Tribunal (Immigration and Asylum Chamber)* [2023] EWHC 791 (Admin) at [39] to [41] that it is "entirely proper and reasonable for a judge who is determining a permission application to consult the official record of proceedings and to decide (without further recourse to the parties) whether that record corroborates an assertion in the grounds of appeal".

Paragraph (4)

3.408 Reasons for refusing permission to appeal can usually be very brief and will often simply be that the application does not raise any point of law. Reasons can be valuable in persuading an applicant not to make an application to the Upper Tribunal in a hopeless case or in alerting the applicant of the need to rewrite the grounds. If an application raises allegations about the conduct of the Tribunal, it is likely to be desirable to make it clear whether the Tribunal disputes the accuracy of the allegations.

Paragraph (5)

3.409 Except where some grounds advanced are completely misconceived, it may not be helpful to grant a party without a legal representative permission to appeal on limited grounds, because doing so can make an appeal to the Upper Tribunal more complicated and the Upper Tribunal itself generally makes observations and issues directions before any response to an appeal is required, thus focussing the parties' attention on the more important issues. Where a party is represented by a lawyer used to formal pleading, other considerations may apply.

It was said in the 2011/12 edition of this work that "the Upper Tribunal exercises an investigatory approach to appeals and so is not confined by the grounds of appeal or the grounds of permission". However, in *AW v SSWP (IB)* [2012] UKUT 104 (AAC), it was held that that was unsound and that, while the Upper Tribunal is not confined to the grounds of appeal in an ordinary case, it is restricted by specific limitations in a grant of permission to appeal. Otherwise, there is no point in the limitations. In that case, the First-tier Tribunal had failed to comply with the duty imposed by para.(5) to inform the claimant of her right to apply to the Upper Tribunal for permission to appeal on those grounds on which permission had been refused by the First-tier Tribunal and the claimant had not made such an application. Presumably the Upper Tribunal Judge could have invited her to do so had he thought there was anything in the grounds, which he did not.

A judge giving permission to appeal on limited grounds must say so clearly in the decision itself and not merely in the reasons for the decision; otherwise there is a risk that the decision will be treated by the Upper Tribunal as a grant of unlimited permission (*Safi v Secretary of State for the Home Department* [2018] UKUT 388 (IAC)).

Review of a decision

40.—(1) This rule does not apply to asylum support cases or criminal injuries compensation cases. 3.410

(2) The Tribunal may only undertake a review of a decision—

(a) pursuant to rule 39(1) (review on an application for permission to appeal); and

(b) if it is satisfied that there was an error of law in the decision.

(3) The Tribunal must notify the parties in writing of the outcome of any review, and of any right of appeal in relation to the outcome.

(4) If the Tribunal takes any action in relation to a decision following a review without first giving every party an opportunity to make representations, the notice under paragraph (3) must state that any party that did not have an opportunity to make representations may apply for such action to be set aside and for the decision to be reviewed again.

Definitions

"appeal"—see r.35.
"asylum support case"—see r.1(3).
"criminal injuries compensation case"—*ibid.*
"party"—*ibid.*
"review"—see r.35.
"Tribunal—see r.1(3).

General Note

Paragraph (2)

The power of review arises under s.9(1) of the Tribunals, Courts and Enforcement Act 2007. 3.411

Section 9(2) provides for the power of review to be exercised either on the tribunal's initiative or on an application, but s.9(3)(b) enables rules to provide that it is exercisable only on the Tribunal's own initiative. In *JS v Kingston upon Hull CC (HB)* [2014] UKUT 43 (AAC), it was held that para.(2)(a), providing that a decision may be reviewed only on an application for permission to appeal, was not validly made under s.9(3) of the Tribunals, Courts and Enforcement Act 2007, although it was valid under the more general rule-making powers under that Act. The Upper Tribunal considered that the subparagraph had the effect that the First-tier Tribunal was prevented from reviewing a decision on its own initiative. However, it is arguable that it merely limits the circumstances in which the First-tier Tribunal may review a decision on its own initiative, since an application for permission to appeal does not necessarily imply an application for review (even though it may always be treated as one under r.41). Making a rule imposing such a limitation is not expressly authorised by s.9(3). However, although the First-tier Tribunal is not entitled to consider reviewing its decision before an application for permission to appeal is made (*LM v SSWP* [2009] UKUT 185 (AAC)), it can always invite an application for permission to appeal and so the limitation is of little practical importance. The main effect of para.(2)(a) is simply to prevent sequential applications for review and for permission to appeal. The real problem in *JS* was that the review was to the advantage of the local authority but the claimant did not accept that the original decision was wrong. It may be noted that, in *R. (TN (Vietnam)) v First-tier Tribunal* [2018] EWHC 3546; [2019] 1 W.L.R. 2675, the Administrative Court rejected an argument that the equivalent provision in r.35 of the Tribunal Procedure (First-tier Tribunal) (Immigration and Asylum Chamber) Rules 2014 (SI 2014/2604) was invalid because it purported entirely to remove the First-tier Tribunal's power under s.9(2) to review decisions on its own initiative.

Paragraph (2)(b), made under s.9(3)(d), limits the ground of review to an error of law. Since appeals under s.11 lie only on points of law, a review therefore provides a way of avoiding an appeal where the appeal would plainly be allowed. For what amounts to an error law for the purposes of para.(2)(b), see the note to s.11. Note that the production of "objective and uncontentious" evidence showing a mistake of fact that has caused unfairness may be sufficient to show an error of law if a lack of reasonable diligence was not the reason for the evidence not being produced before the decision was made. In *DG v SSWP (II)* [2013] UKUT 474 (AAC) there was held to be an error of law when x-ray evidence showed that the First-tier Tribunal's finding that the claimant had not broken her wrist was wrong. There was no lack of reasonable diligence because the claimant could not have expected that she would be disbelieved on that point. Thus it may occasionally be appropriate to review a decision where that decision has prompted the claimant to produce more evidence.

3.412 See s.9(4), (5) and (8) for the powers of the Tribunal on review. These powers are wider than they were under s.13(2) of the Social Security Act 1998 and the similar provisions relating to housing benefit, council tax benefit and child support, which s.9, as limited by this rule, replaces. Note, however, that s.13(3) of the 1998 Act remains in place.

The power of review under s.9 is to be exercised only if there is a "clear" error of law (*R. (RB) v First-tier Tribunal (Review)* [2010] UKUT 160 (AAC); [2010] AACR 41). Because the power to review a decision arises only when an error of law has been identified, it is wrong to refer to the process of considering whether there is an error of law as a review (*VH v Suffolk CC (SEN)* [2010] UKUT 203 (AAC)).

In *SE v SSWP* [2009] UKUT 163 (AAC) and *AM v SSWP* [2009] UKUT 224 (AAC) the Upper Tribunal has also pointed out that, by virtue of subpara.(b), the First-tier Tribunal is not entitled to amend its reasons under s.9(4)(b) of the Tribunals, Courts and Enforcement Act 2007 before it has identified a point of law and it has stressed the importance of the First-tier Tribunal giving parties an opportunity to make representations either before any review or afterwards by way of an application under r.40(4) for the review decision to be set aside.

Paragraph (3)

3.413 Section 11(5)(d) of the 2007 Act has the effect that there is no right of appeal against a decision whether or not to review a decision, to take no action on a review, to set aside a decision on a review or to refer, or not refer, a matter to the Upper

Tribunal on review. However, that is because there is always another decision that may be the subject of an appeal. Where the Tribunal refuses to review a decision or reviews it but takes no action, the Tribunal must consider whether to give permission to appeal against the original decision. Where the tribunal reviews a decision and either takes action itself or refers it to the Upper Tribunal to be redecided, there will be a right to apply for permission to appeal against the new decision.

Where a decision is reviewed without all the parties having had the opportunity to make representations, notice must also be given of the right to apply for the new decision to be set aside (see para.(4)).

There is no express duty to give reasons for a review but it will generally be helpful to give some indication for the benefit of the parties and both the judge and any other members whose decision has been set aside and for those who must re-decide the case if that is not done by the reviewing judge straightaway. However, since a decision should be reviewed only where there is a clear error of law, reasons can usually be short and "[o]ften a single sentence is sufficient, where, for instance, all that needs to be done is to draw attention to an overlooked authority or statutory provision or to agree with a ground of appeal" *(R. (RB) v First-tier Tribunal (Review)* [2010] UKUT 160 (AAC); [2010] AACR 41).

Paragraph (4)

The clear implication of this paragraph is that the Tribunal may either obtain submissions from the parties other than the applicant before reviewing a case or review the case first and then wait to see whether any of the other parties objects. Plainly the second of those approaches may lead to a quicker decision and less work where there is no objection to the review. In *R. (RB) v First-tier Tribunal (Review)* [2010] UKUT 160 (AAC); [2010] AACR 41, it was pointed out that para.(4) enables the First-tier Tribunal to take a robust approach to the question whether a perceived error of law is clear enough to justify a review. However, it was also said that regard had to be had to the likelihood of the previously successful party objecting to the review. In the social security context, where many claimants are unrepresented and might not object in circumstances where a represented party would, some care needs to be taken before decisions are reviewed adversely to them and it may sometimes be preferable to obtain representations before making a review decision rather than afterwards. The Secretary of State, on the other hand, is not only less likely to object but may also positively welcome not being asked to make representations in cases that seem clear to a tribunal judge. If submissions are obtained and all the parties assert that the decision is erroneous in point of law, the Tribunal will be obliged to set the decision aside in those cases where s.13(3) of the Social Security Act 1998 (or an equivalent provision in legislation beyond the scope of this work) applies. 3.414

In *SSWP v CM (ESA)* [2012] UKUT 436 (AAC) it has been suggested that the words "the decision to be reviewed again" should be read as "alternative action to be taken", because s.9(10) of the Tribunals, Courts and Enforcement Act 2007 does not allow a second review of a decision. However, this may not be a necessary construction. It might be argued that, if a review decision is set aside in circumstances where a party had not had an opportunity to make representations then it should be treated as never having taken place so as not to prohibit what would otherwise be a second review.

Power to treat an application as a different type of application

41. The Tribunal may treat an application for a decision to be corrected, set aside or reviewed, or for permission to appeal against a decision, as an application for any other one of those things. 3.415

DEFINITIONS

"appeal"—see r.35.
"review"—*ibid.*
"Tribunal"—see r.1(3).

General Note

3.416 In *WO'C v SSWP (CCS)* [2020] UKUT 34 (AAC), it was held that, although r.41 did not provide for an application for a decision to be set aside to be treated as an application for a statement of reasons for the decision, it was nonetheless permissible for the First-tier Tribunal to do so but that the First-tier Tribunal had not erred in law in not doing so on the facts of the case because the relevant email could be read solely as a set aside application, rather than as demonstrating a wish to contest the substantive decision even if that application did not succeed.

[1 SCHEDULE 1 rule 22

Time Limits for providing notices of appeal in social security and child support cases where mandatory reconsideration does not apply

3.417

	Type of proceedings	*Time for providing notice of appeal*
1	Appeal against a certification of NHS charges under section 157(1) of the Health and Social Care (Community Health and Standards) Act 2003	(a) 3 months after the latest of— (i) the date on the certificate; (ii) the date on which the compensation payment was made; (iii) if the certificate has been reviewed, the date the certificate was confirmed or a fresh certificate was issued; or (iv) the date of any agreement to treat an earlier compensation payment as having been made in final discharge of a claim made by or in respect of an injured person and arising out of the injury or death; or (b) if the person to whom the certificate has been issued makes an application under section 157(4) of the Health and Social Care (Community Health and Standards) Act 2003, one month after— (i) the date of the decision on that application; or (ii) if the person appeals against that decision under section 157(6) of that Act, the date on which the appeal is decided or withdrawn.
2	Appeal against a waiver decision under section 157(6) of the Health and Social Care (Community Health and Standards) Act 2003	One month after the date of the decision.
3	Appeal against a certificate of NHS charges under section 7 of the Road Traffic (NHS Charges) Act 1999	3 months after the latest of— (a) the date on which the liability under section 1(2) of the Road Traffic (NHS Charges) Act 1999 was discharged; (b) if the certificate has been reviewed, the date the certificate was confirmed or a fresh certificate was issued; or (c) the date of any agreement to treat an earlier compensation payment as having

	Type of proceedings	*Time for providing notice of appeal*
		been made in final discharge of a claim made by or in respect of a traffic casualty and arising out of the injury or death.
4	Appeal against a certificate of recoverable benefits under section 11 of the Social Security (Recovery of Benefits) Act 1997	One month after the latest of— (a) the date on which any payment to the Secretary of State required under section 6 of the Social Security (Recovery of Benefits) Act 1997 was made; (b) if the certificate has been reviewed, the date the certificate was confirmed or a fresh certificate was issued; (c) the date of any agreement to treat an earlier compensation payment as having been made in final discharge of a claim made by or in respect of an injured person and arising out of the accident, injury or disease.
5	Cases other than those listed above	The latest of— (a) one month after the date on which notice of the decision being challenged was sent to the appellant; (b) if a written statement of reasons for the decision was requested within that month, 14 days after the later of— (i) the end of that month; or (ii) the date on which the written statement of reasons was provided; (c) if the appellant made an application for the revision of the decision under— (i) regulation 17(1)(a) of the Child Support (Maintenance Assessment Procedure) Regulations 1992; (ii) regulation 3(1) or (3) or 3A(1)(a) of the Social Security and Child Support (Decisions and Appeals) Regulations 1999; (iii) regulation 14(1)(a) of the Child Support Maintenance Calculation Regulations 2012; or (iv) regulation 5 of the Universal Credit, Personal Independence Payment, Jobseeker's Allowance and Employment and Support Allowance (Decisions and Appeals) Regulations 2013, and the application was unsuccessful, one month after the date on which notice that the decision would not be revised was sent to the appellant.]

AMENDMENT

1. Tribunal Procedure (Amendment) Rules 2015 (SI 2015/1510) rr.11 and 17 and Sch. (August 21, 2015).

DEFINITIONS

"appeal"—see r.1(3).
"appellant"—*ibid.*

GENERAL NOTE

3.418 Originally, Sch.1 applied just for the purposes of r.23 but, from April 2013 (i.e. during the transition to direct lodgement), it applied to both r.22 and r.23. Now, the time limits for r.23 have been incorporated into that rule and this Schedule applies only in the few cases where a notice of appeal in a social security or child support appeal must be sent to the First-tier Tribunal under r.22 but there is no requirement to apply for reconsideration before lodging the appeal.

The first three paragraphs deal with cases concerned with the recovery of NHS charges, which are beyond the scope of this work but where the legislation makes no provision for mandatory reconsideration. Paragraphs 4 and 5 deal with other social security and child support cases where there is no mandatory reconsideration. This will usually be because the Secretary of State has, either by accident or design, not provided the requisite notice with the decision being challenged (see, in relation to social security cases, regs 3ZA(1) and 9ZB(1) of the Social Security and Child Support (Decisions and Appeals) Regulations 1999 and reg.7 of the Universal Credit, Personal Independence Payment, Jobseeker's Allowance and Employment and Support Allowance (Decisions and Appeals) Regulations 2013).

In addition to the re-ordering of the paragraphs and the deletion of those that are now unnecessary, there have been substantive amendments to what is now head (c) in the second column of para.5. First, a reference to the 2013 Regulations has been added, while the reference to housing benefit and council tax benefit legislation has been moved to r.23(2)(a)(iii). Secondly, each of the references to child support legislation is now to sub-para.(a) of para.(1) of the relevant provision, rather than just to para.(1). This gives statutory effect to *AS v SSWP (CSM)* [2012] UKUT 448 (AAC); [2013] AACR 18 and explicitly brings child support cases into line with social security cases so that the time for appealing is automatically extended where there has been an unsuccessful revision only if the application for revision was made within one month (or any longer period allowed by the Secretary of State) of the decision being challenged. A similar amendment has been made in what is now r.23(2)(a)(iii).

The consequence of this, as pointed out by a Tribunal of Commissioners in *R(IS)15/04* (subsequently approved by the Court of Appeal in *Beltekian v Westminster CC* [2004] EWCA Civ 1784 (reported as *R(H)8/05*), is that there is no way of challenging a refusal to revise in a social security case, if it is too late to appeal against the original decision, other than by way of an application for judicial review. This is most unsatisfactory. The Tribunal pointed out that claimants would not wish to apply for revision under reg.3(5) of the 1999 Regulations except on the ground of "official error" because the other grounds for revision result in decisions less favourable to the claimant than the decision that has been revised. However, claimants might well apply for revision under other paragraphs in reg.3 and so the problem is not confined to "official error" cases. On the other hand, the significance of this restriction has been reduced as a result of the introduction of "mandatory reconsideration" (see the note to s.12 of the Social Security Act 1998, under the heading "*Can supersession decisions be substituted for revision decisions and vice versa?*").

Where it is still possible to appeal against the original decision following a refusal to revise, the Tribunal held in *R(IB)2/04* (at para.39) that the appeal can succeed only if it can be shown that the decision should have been revised. Otherwise, as was pointed out in *CCS/5515/2002*, late appeals could easily be brought by making entirely unmeritorious applications for revision.

Rule 18 of Tribunal Procedure (Amendment) Rules 2015 provides that the amendments to r.23 and the substitution of this Schedule "have no effect in relation to any appeal against a decision made before 6th April 2014 where the decision maker was Her Majesty's Revenue and Customs". This ensures that any such appeal must be referred to the First-tier Tribunal which will refuse to admit it on the ground that it is irremediably out of time (unless to do so would be a breach of the European Convention on Human Rights—see the annotation to r.22(8)).

Rule 25(3)

SCHEDULE 2

ISSUES IN RELATION TO WHICH THE TRIBUNAL MAY REFER A PERSON FOR MEDICAL EXAMINATION UNDER SECTION 20(2) OF THE SOCIAL SECURITY ACT 1998

An issue falls within this Schedule if the issue— 3.419

(a) is whether the claimant satisfies the conditions for entitlement to—
  (i) an attendance allowance specified in section 64 and 65(1) of the Social Security Contributions and Benefits Act 1992;
  (ii) severe disablement allowance under section 68 of that Act;
  (iii) the care component of a disability living allowance specified in section 72(1) and (2) of that Act;
  (iv) the mobility component of a disability living allowance specified in section 73(1), (8) and (9) of that Act; [1 . . .]
  (v) a disabled person's tax credit specified in section 129(1)(b) of that Act;
  [1 (vi) the daily living component of personal independence payment specified in section 78 of the Welfare Reform Act 2012; or
  (vii) the mobility component of personal independence payment specified in section 79 of the Welfare Reform Act 2012.]
(b) relates to the period throughout which the claimant is likely to satisfy the conditions for entitlement to an attendance allowance or a disability living allowance;
(c) is the rate at which an attendance allowance is payable;
(d) is the rate at which the care component or the mobility component of a disability living allowance is payable;
(e) is whether a person is incapable of work for the purposes of the Social Security Contributions and Benefits Act 1992;
(f) relates to the extent of a person's disablement and its assessment in accordance with Schedule 6 to the Social Security Contributions and Benefits Act 1992;
(g) is whether the claimant suffers a loss of physical or mental faculty as a result of the relevant accident for the purposes of section 103 of the Social Security Contributions and Benefits Act 1992;
(h) relates to any payment arising under, or by virtue of a scheme having effect under, section 111 of, and Schedule 8 to, the Social Security Contributions and Benefits Act 1992 (workmen's compensation);
(i) is whether a person has limited capability for work or work-related activity for the purposes of the Welfare Reform Act 2007;
[1 (j) is the rate at which the daily living component or mobility component of personal independence payment is payable.]

AMENDMENT

1. Tribunal Procedure (Amendment) Rules 2013 (SI 2013/477) rr.22 and 32 (April 8, 2013).

DEFINITION

"Tribunal"—see r.1(3).

The Tribunal Procedure (Upper Tribunal) Rules 2008

(SI 2008/2698)

In force November 3, 2008

Contents

Part 1

Introduction

Part 2

General Powers and Provisions

Part 3

Procedure for cases in the Upper Tribunal

22A. *Omitted.*
23. Notice of appeal
24. Response to the notice of appeal
25. Appellant's reply
26. References under the Forfeiture Act 1982
26A. Cases transferred or referred to the Upper Tribunal, applications made directly to the Upper Tribunal, cases where an offence has been certified and proceedings without notice to a respondent.
26B. *Omitted.*
26C. *Omitted.*

PART 4

JUDICIAL REVIEW PROCEEDINGS IN THE UPPER TRIBUNAL

27. Application of this Part to judicial review proceedings transferred to the Upper Tribunal
28. Applications for permission to bring judicial review proceedings
28A. *Omitted.*
29. Acknowledgment of service
30. Decision on permission or summary dismissal, and reconsideration of permission or summary dismissal at a hearing
31. Responses
32. Applicant seeking to rely on additional grounds
35. Right to make representations
33A. Amendments and additional grounds resulting in transfer of proceedings to the High Court in England and Wales

PART 5

HEARINGS

34. Decision with or without a hearing
35. Entitlement to attend a hearing
36. Notice of hearings
36A. *Omitted.*
37. Public and private hearings
37A. *Expired.*
38. Hearings in a party's absence

PART 6

DECISIONS

39. Consent orders
40. Decisions
40A. *Revoked.*

PART 7

CORRECTING, SETTING ASIDE, REVIEWING AND APPEALING DECISIONS OF THE UPPER TRIBUNAL

After consulting in accordance with paragraph 28(1) of Schedule 5 to, the Tribunals, Courts and Enforcement Act 2007 the Tribunal Procedure Committee has made the following Rules in exercise of the power conferred by sections 10(3), 16(9), 22 and 29(3) and (4) of, and Schedule 5 to, that Act.

The Lord Chancellor has allowed the Rules in accordance with paragraph 28(3) of Schedule 5 to the Tribunals, Courts and Enforcement Act 2007.

PART 1

INTRODUCTION

Citation, commencement, application and interpretation

3.421 **1.**—(1) These Rules may be cited as the Tribunal Procedure (Upper Tribunal) Rules 2008 and come into force on 3rd November 2008.

(2) These Rules apply to proceedings before the Upper Tribunal [[2] except proceedings in the Lands Chamber].

(3) In these Rules—

"the 2007 Act" means the Tribunals, Courts and Enforcement Act 2007;

[[1] "appellant" means—

(a) a person who makes an appeal, or applies for permission to appeal, to the Upper Tribunal;

(b) in proceedings transferred or referred to the Upper Tribunal from the First-tier Tribunal, a person who started the proceedings in the First-tier Tribunal; or

(c) a person substituted as an appellant under rule 9(1) (substitution and addition of parties);]

[[5] "applicant" means—

(a) a person who applies for permission to bring, or does bring, judicial review proceedings before the Upper Tribunal and, in judicial review proceedings transferred to the Upper Tribunal from a court, includes a person who was a claimant or petitioner in the proceedings immediately before they were transferred; or

(b) a person who refers a financial services case [[11] or a wholesale energy case] to the Upper Tribunal;]

[2 "appropriate national authority" means, in relation to an appeal, the Secretary of State, the Scottish Ministers [8, the Department of the Environment in Northern Ireland] or the Welsh Ministers, as the case may be;]

[4 "asylum case" means proceedings before the Upper Tribunal on appeal against a decision in proceedings under section 82, 83 or 83A of the Nationality, Immigration and Asylum Act 2002 in which a person claims that removal from, or a requirement to leave, the United Kingdom would breach the United Kingdom's obligations under the Convention relating to the Status of Refugees done at Geneva on 28 July 1951 and the Protocol to the Convention;]

[8 "authorised person" means—

(a) an examiner appointed by the Secretary of State under section 66A of the Road Traffic Act 1988;

(b) an examiner appointed by the Department of the Environment in Northern Ireland under Article 74 of the Road Traffic (Northern Ireland) Order 1995; or

(c) any person authorised in writing by the Department of the Environment in Northern Ireland for the purposes of the Goods Vehicles (Licensing of Operators) Act (Northern Ireland) 2010;

and includes a person acting under the direction of such an examiner or other authorised person, who has detained the vehicle to which an appeal relates;]]

[1 . . .]

[12 "disability discrimination in schools case" means proceedings concerning discrimination in the education of a child or young person or related matters;]

"dispose of proceedings" includes, unless indicated otherwise, disposing of a part of the proceedings;

"document" means anything in which information is recorded in any form, and an obligation under these Rules or any practice direction or direction to provide or allow access to a document or a copy of a document for any purpose means, unless the Upper Tribunal directs otherwise, an obligation to provide or allow access to such document or copy in a legible form or in a form which can be readily made into a legible form;

[19 . . .]

[15 "financial sanctions case" means an appeal to the Upper Tribunal under section 147(6) of the Policing and Crime Act 2017;]

[5 "financial services case" means a reference to the Upper Tribunal in respect of—

(a) [9 a decision of the Financial Conduct Authority;

(aa) a decision of the Prudential Regulation Authority;]

(b) a decision of the Bank of England;

(c) a decision of the Pensions Regulator; [11 . . .]

(d) a decision of a person relating to the assessment of any compensation or consideration under the Banking (Special Provisions) Act 2008 or the Banking Act 2009;] [6 or]

[6 (e) any determination, calculation or dispute which may be referred to the Upper Tribunal under the Financial Services and Markets Act 2000 (Contribution to Costs of Special Resolution Regime) Regulations 2010 (and in these Rules a decision in respect of which a reference has been made to the Upper Tribunal in a financial services case includes any such determination, calculation or, except for the purposes of rule 5(5), dispute relating to the making of payments under the Regulations).]

[7 [10...]]

"hearing" means an oral hearing and includes a hearing conducted in whole or in part by video link, telephone or other means of instantaneous two-way electronic communication;

[4 "immigration case" means proceedings before the Upper Tribunal on appeal against a decision in proceedings under section 40A of the British Nationality Act 1981, section 82 of the Nationality, Immigration and Asylum Act 2002, [18 ...] [20 ...] [19 [20 ...] or the Immigration (Citizens' Rights Appeals) (EU Exit) Regulations 2020] that are not an asylum case [18 [19 ...]];]

[10 "immigration judicial review proceedings" means judicial review proceedings which are designated as an immigration matter—

(a) in a direction made in accordance with Part 1 of Schedule 2 to the Constitutional Reform Act 2005 specifying a class of case for the purposes of section 18(6) of the 2007 Act; or

(b) in an order of the High Court in England and Wales made under section 31A(3) of the Senior Courts Act 1981, transferring to the Upper Tribunal an application of a kind described in section 31A(1) of that Act;]

"interested party" means—

(a) a person who is directly affected by the outcome sought in judicial review proceedings, and has been named as an interested party under rule 28 or 29 (judicial review), or has been substituted or added as an interested party under rule 9 [5 (addition, substitution and removal of parties)] [5. . .]

(b) in judicial review proceedings transferred to the Upper Tribunal under section 25A(2) or (3) of the Judicature (Northern Ireland) Act 1978 or section 31A(2) or (3) of the [2A Senior Courts Act 1981], a person who was an interested party in the proceedings immediately before they were transferred to the Upper Tribunal; [5 [17. . .]]

[5 (c) in a financial services case [11 or a wholesale energy case], any person other than the applicant who could have referred the case to the Upper Tribunal and who has been added or substituted as an interested party under rule 9 (addition, substitution and removal of parties);

[15 (d) in a financial sanctions case, any person other than the appellant upon whom the Treasury has imposed a monetary penalty under Part 8 of the Policing and Crime Act 2017 in connection with the same matters as led to the decision that is the subject of the appeal and who has been added or substituted as an interested party under rule 9 (addition, substitution and removal of parties);] [17 and]

[17 (e) in a trade remedies case, any person other than the appellant who could have appealed to the Upper Tribunal and who has been added or substituted as an interested party under rule 9 (addition, substitution and removal of parties);]

"judicial review proceedings" means proceedings within the jurisdiction of the Upper Tribunal pursuant to section 15 or 21 of the 2007 Act, whether such proceedings are started in the Upper Tribunal or transferred to the Upper Tribunal;

[1 . . .]

"mental health case" means proceedings before the Upper Tribunal on appeal against a decision in proceedings under the Mental Health Act 1983 or paragraph 5(2) of the Schedule to the Repatriation of Prisoners Act 1984;

[3 "national security certificate appeal" means an appeal under section 28 of the Data Protection Act 1998 [16, sections 27, 79 or 111 of the Data Protection Act 2018] or section 60 of the Freedom of Information Act 2000 (including that section as applied and modified by regulation 18 of the Environmental Information Regulations 2004);]

"party" means a person who is an appellant, an applicant, a respondent or an interested party in proceedings before the Upper Tribunal, a person who has referred a question [5 or matter] to the Upper Tribunal or, if the proceedings have been concluded, a person who was an appellant, an applicant, a respondent or an interested party when the [10 Upper] Tribunal finally disposed of all issues in the proceedings;

"permission" includes leave in cases arising under the law of Northern Ireland;

"practice direction" means a direction given under section 23 of the 2007 Act;

[14 "QCS Board" means a Board constituted under Part 2 of the Transport Act 2000;

"quality contracts scheme" has the meaning provided for in section 124(3) (quality contracts scheme) of the Transport Act 2000;

"quality contracts scheme case" means proceedings in the Upper Tribunal under Part 2 of the Transport Act 2000;]

[5 "reference", in a financial services case, includes an appeal;]

[3 "relevant minister" means the Minister or designated person responsible for the signing of the certificate to which a national security certificate appeal relates;]

"respondent" means—

(a) in an appeal, or application for permission to appeal, against a decision of another tribunal, any person other than the appellant who—
  - (i) was a party before that other tribunal;
  - (ii) [1. . .] or
  - (iii) otherwise has a right of appeal against the decision of the other tribunal and has given notice to the Upper Tribunal that they wish to be a party to the appeal;

[16 (b) in any other any other application for permission to appeal, or any other appeal except a road transport case, the person who made the decision that has been challenged;]

(c) in judicial review proceedings—
  - (i) in proceedings started in the Upper Tribunal, the person named by the applicant as the respondent;
  - (ii) in proceedings transferred to the Upper Tribunal under section 25A(2) or (3) of the Judicature (Northern Ireland) Act 1978 or section 31A(2) or (3) of the [2A Senior Courts Act 1981], a person who was a defendant in the proceedings immediately before they were transferred;

(iii) in proceedings transferred to the Upper Tribunal under section 20(1) of the 2007 Act, a person to whom intimation of the petition was made before the proceedings were transferred, or to whom the Upper Tribunal has required intimation to be made;

[[1] (ca) in proceedings transferred or referred to the Upper Tribunal from the First-tier Tribunal, a person who was a respondent in the proceedings in the First-tier Tribunal;]

(d) in a reference under the Forfeiture Act 1982, the person whose eligibility for a benefit or advantage is in issue; [[5] . . .]

[[5](da) [[9] in a financial services case—

(i) where the case is a multiple regulator case, both the primary and secondary regulator as defined in Schedule 3 to these rules (but subject to the operation of paragraph 4A(3) of that Schedule);

(ii) where the case is a single regulator case, the maker of the decision in respect of which a reference has been made; or]]

[[11] (db) in a wholesale energy case, in relation to Great Britain, the Gas and Electricity Markets Authority or, in relation to Northern Ireland, the Northern Ireland Authority for Utility Regulation; or]

(e) a person substituted or added as a respondent under rule 9 (substitution and addition of parties);

[[8] [[17] "road transport case" means an appeal against a decision of—

(a) a traffic commissioner, other than an appeal pursuant to—

(i) section 6F of the Transport Act 1985, or

(ii) section 123T of the Transport Act 2000, or

(b) the Department of the Environment in Northern Ireland;]]

[[1] . . .]

[[12] "special educational needs case" means proceedings concerning the education of a child or young person who has or may have special educational needs, including proceedings relating to—

(a) an EHC needs assessment within the meaning of section 36(2) of the Children and Families Act 2014; [[14] . . .]

[[14](aa) a detained person's EHC needs assessment within the meaning of section 70(5) of the Children and Families Act 2014; or]

(b) an EHC plan within the meaning of section 37(2) of that Act,

of such a child or young person;]

[[2] "tribunal" does not include a traffic commissioner;]

[[17] "TRA" means the Trade Remedies Authority;

"trade remedies case" means an appeal pursuant to the Trade Remedies (Reconsideration and Appeals) (EU Exit) Regulations 2019 against a decision made by the TRA or a determination of the Secretary of State;]

[[11] "wholesale energy case" means a reference to the Upper Tribunal in respect of a decision of—

(a) in relation to Great Britain, the Gas and Electricity Markets Authority under the Electricity and Gas (Market Integrity and Transparency) (Enforcement etc.) Regulations 2013; or

(b) in relation to Northern Ireland, the Northern Ireland Authority for Utility Regulation under the Electricity and Gas (Market Integrity and Transparency) (Enforcement etc.) Regulations (Northern Ireland) 2013;]

"working day" means any day except a Saturday or Sunday, Christmas Day, Good Friday or a bank holiday under section 1 of the Banking and Financial Dealings Act 1971.

[[12] "young person" means, in relation to a special educational needs case or a disability discrimination in schools case, a person over compulsory school age but under 25.]

AMENDMENTS

1. Tribunal Procedure (Amendment) Rules 2009 (SI 2009/274) r.5 (April 1, 2009).

2. Tribunal Procedure (Amendment No.2) Rules 2009 (SI 2009/1975) rr.7 and 8 (September 1, 2009).

2A. Constitutional Reform Act 2005 s.59(5) and para.1(2) of Sch.11 (October 1, 2009).

3. Tribunal Procedure (Amendment) Rules 2010 (SI 2010/43) rr.5 and 6 (January 18, 2010).

4. Tribunal Procedure (Amendment No.2) Rules 2010 (SI 2010/44) rr.2 and 3 (February 15, 2010).

5. Tribunal Procedure (Upper Tribunal) (Amendment) Rules 2010 (SI 2010/747) rr.2 and 4 (April 6, 2010).

6. Tribunal Procedure (Amendment) Rules 2011 (SI 2011/651) r.8(1) and (2) (April 1, 2011).

7. Tribunal Procedure (Upper Tribunal) (Amendment) Rules 2011 (SI 2011/2343) rr.2 and 4 (October 17, 2011).

8. Tribunal Procedure (Amendment No.2) Rules 2012 (SI 2012/1363) rr.4 and 5 (July 1, 2012).

9. Tribunal Procedure (Amendment No.2) Rules 2013 (SI 2013/606) r.2(1) and (2) (April 1, 2013).

10. Tribunal Procedure (Amendment No. 4) Rules 2013 (SI 2013/2067) rr.2 and 4 (November 1, 2013).

11. Tribunal Procedure (Amendment) Rules 2014 (SI 2014/514) rr.2 and 4 (April 6, 2014).

12. Tribunal Procedure (Amendment No.3) Rules 2014 (SI 2014/2128) rr.2 and 4(a), (c) and (d) (September 1, 2014).

13. Tribunal Procedure (Amendment No.3) Rules 2014 (SI 2014/2128) rr.2 and 4(b) (October 20, 2014).

14. Tribunal Procedure (Amendment) Rules 2015 (SI 2015/1510) rr.2 and 3 (August 21, 2015).

15. Tribunal Procedure (Amendment) Rules 2017 (SI 2017/723) rr.5 and 7 (July 23, 2017).

16. Tribunal Procedure (Amendment No.2) Rules 2018 (SI 2018/1053) r.3(1) and (2) (October 13, 2018).

17. Tribunal Procedure (Amendment) Rules 2019 (SI 2019/925) r.2(1) and (2) (June 3, 2019, subject to a saving).

18. Immigration (Citizens' Rights Appeals) (EU Exit) Regulations 2020 (2020/61) Sch.4 para.5(1) and (2) (January 31, 2020).

19. Tribunal Procedure (Amendment) Rules 2020 (SI 2020/651) r.5(1) and (2) (July 21, 2020).

20. Immigration and Social Security Co-ordination (EU Withdrawal) Act 2020 (Consequential, Saving, Transitional and Transitory Provisions) (EU Exit) Regulations 2020 (SI 2020/1309) reg.33 (December 31, 2020, subject to a saving).

DEFINITIONS

"the 2007 Act"—see para.(3).
"appellant"—*ibid.*
"applicant"—*ibid.*

"interested party"—*ibid.*
"judicial review proceedings"—*ibid.*
"party"—*ibid.*
"permission"—*ibid.*
"practice direction"—*ibid.*
"respondent"—*ibid.*

GENERAL NOTE

3.422 The Upper Tribunal has jurisdiction in some "judicial review proceedings", by virtue of ss.15–21 of the Tribunals, Courts and Enforcement Act 2007. Note that the terms "applicant" and "interested party" are used only in relation to such cases and certain financial service cases outside the scope of this work. A person applying for permission to appeal *to* the Upper Tribunal is included within the term "appellant" and in all cases other than judicial review proceedings, every party other than the appellant or person making a reference is a "respondent". A person applying for a decision to be set aside or for permission to appeal *from* the Upper Tribunal is referred to in the Rules merely as "a party applying for . . . " or "a person seeking . . . ".

For the meaning of "bank holiday" in the definition of "working day", see the note to r.12(3) of the Tribunal Procedure (First-tier Tribunal) (Social Entitlement Chamber) Rules 2008, above.

Overriding objective and parties' obligation to co-operate with the Upper Tribunal

3.423 **2.**—(1) The overriding objective of these Rules is to enable the Upper Tribunal to deal with cases fairly and justly.

(2) Dealing with a case fairly and justly includes—

(a) dealing with the case in ways which are proportionate to the importance of the case, the complexity of the issues, the anticipated costs and the resources of the parties;
(b) avoiding unnecessary formality and seeking flexibility in the proceedings;
(c) ensuring, so far as practicable, that the parties are able to participate fully in the proceedings;
(d) using any special expertise of the Upper Tribunal effectively; and
(e) avoiding delay, so far as compatible with proper consideration of the issues.

(3) The Upper Tribunal must seek to give effect to the overriding objective when it—

(a) exercises any power under these Rules; or
(b) interprets any rule or practice direction.

(4) Parties must—

(a) help the Upper Tribunal to further the overriding objective; and
(b) co-operate with the Upper Tribunal generally.

DEFINITIONS

"party"—see r.1(3).
"practice direction"—*ibid.*

GENERAL NOTE

3.424 See the note to r.2 of the Tribunal Procedure (First-tier Tribunal) (Social Entitlement Chamber) Rules 2008, above.

Alternative dispute resolution and arbitration

3.—(1) The Upper Tribunal should seek, where appropriate— 3.425

(a) to bring to the attention of the parties the availability of any appropriate alternative procedure for the resolution of the dispute; and

(b) if the parties wish and provided that it is compatible with the overriding objective, to facilitate the use of the procedure.

(2) Part 1 of the Arbitration Act 1996 does not apply to proceedings before the Upper Tribunal.

Definition

"party"—see r.1(3).

General Note

Rule 3(1) applies only if there is an alternative procedure available and none currently is. Such a procedure would be useful only where the Upper Tribunal was concerned with a complicated issue of fact, which is very seldom the position in a social security case. 3.426

Part 2

General Powers and Provisions

Delegation to staff

4.—(1) Staff appointed under section 40(1) of the 2007 Act (tribunal staff and services) [1 or section 2(1) of the Courts Act 2003 (court officers, staff and services)] may, [1 if authorised by] the Senior President of Tribunals [1 under paragraph 3(3) of Schedule 5 to the 2007 Act] carry out functions of a judicial nature permitted or required to be done by the Upper Tribunal. 3.427

(2) [1 . . .]

(3) Within 14 days after the date on which the Upper Tribunal sends notice of a decision made by a member of staff under paragraph (1) to a party, that party may apply in writing to the Upper Tribunal for that decision to be considered afresh by a judge.

Amendment

1. Tribunal Procedure (Amendment) Rules 2020 (SI 2020/651) r.5(1) and (3) (July 21, 2020).

Definitions

"the 2007 Act"—see r.1(3).
"party"—*ibid.*

General Note

The amendments made to this rule are a consequence of those made to the rule-making power in para.3 of Sch.5 to the 2007 Act with effect from April 6, 2020. 3.428

There is no need to make provision for the delegation of functions of a purely administrative nature and so this rule refers only to functions of a judicial nature. The Senior President of Tribunals has issued a Practice Statement (available at:

http://www.judiciary.gov.uk/publications) recording his approval of the delegation of certain functions to legally qualified members of staff of the Upper Tribunal, known as Registrars. The functions that are delegated are—

(a) exercising any case management powers under r.5 except—
   (i) extending time under r.5(3)(a) in relation to the time limits for appeals referred to in rr.21(3) and (6), 22(5), 23(2) and (5) and 44(3), (4) and (6) or in relation to the time limits for judicial review proceedings referred to in rr.28(2), (3) and (7) and 30(5);
   (ii) suspending a decision under r.5(3)(l) or (m);
   (iii) requiring a tribunal to provide reasons for its decision under r.5(3)(n);
(b) dealing with irregularities under r.7(2) (except taking action under r.7(2)(d) or (4));
(c) striking out under r.8(1) or (3)(a) and reinstating proceedings under r.8(5);
(d) giving directions substituting or adding parties under r.9;
(e) summarily assessing costs under r.10(8)(a);
(f) making orders prohibiting disclosure or publication of documents and information under r.14;
(g) giving directions in relation to evidence and submissions under r.15(1);
(h) summoning (or, in Scotland, citing) witnesses and issuing orders to persons to answer questions and produce documents under r.16; and
(i) giving consent to withdraw a case and reinstating a case under r.17.

Case management powers

3.429 **5.**—(1) Subject to the provisions of the 2007 Act and any other enactment, the Upper Tribunal may regulate its own procedure.

(2) The Upper Tribunal may give a direction in relation to the conduct or disposal of proceedings at any time, including a direction amending, suspending or setting aside an earlier direction.

(3) In particular, and without restricting the general powers in paragraphs (1) and (2), the Upper Tribunal may—

(a) extend or shorten the time for complying with any rule, practice direction or direction;
(b) consolidate or hear together two or more sets of proceedings or parts of proceedings raising common issues, or treat a case as a lead case;
(c) permit or require a party to amend a document;
(d) permit or require a party or another person to provide documents, information, evidence or submissions to the Upper Tribunal or a party;
(e) deal with an issue in the proceedings as a preliminary issue;
(f) hold a hearing to consider any matter, including a case management issue;
(g) decide the form of any hearing;
(h) adjourn or postpone a hearing;
(i) require a party to produce a bundle for a hearing;
(j) stay (or, in Scotland, sist) proceedings;
(k) transfer proceedings to another court or tribunal if that other court or tribunal has jurisdiction in relation to the proceedings and—
   (i) because of a change of circumstances since the proceedings were started, the Upper Tribunal no longer has jurisdiction in relation to the proceedings; or
   (ii) the Upper Tribunal considers that the other court or tribunal is a more appropriate forum for the determination of the case;
(l) suspend the effect of its own decision pending an appeal or review of that decision;

(m) in an appeal, or an application for permission to appeal, against the decision of another tribunal, suspend the effect of that decision pending the determination of the application for permission to appeal, and any appeal;

(n) [[1] require any person, body or other tribunal whose decision is the subject of proceedings before the Upper Tribunal to provide reasons for the decision, or other information or documents in relation to the decision or any proceedings before that person, body or tribunal.]

[[2] (4) [[7] . . .]]

[[3] (5) In a financial services case, the Upper Tribunal may direct that the effect of the decision in respect of which the reference has been made is to be suspended pending the determination of the reference, if it is satisfied that to do so would not prejudice—

(a) the interests of any persons (whether consumers, investors or otherwise) intended to be protected by that notice; [[4] . . .]

(b) the smooth operation or integrity of any market intended to be protected by that notice; [[4] or]

[[4] (c) the stability of the financial system of the United Kingdom.]

[[6] (5A) In a financial sanctions case, the Upper Tribunal may direct that the payment of a monetary penalty that is the subject of an appeal be suspended pending the determination of the appeal or its withdrawal.]

(6) Paragraph (5) does not apply in the case of a reference in respect of a decision of the Pensions Regulator.]

[[5] (7) In a wholesale energy case, the Upper Tribunal may direct that the effect of the decision in respect of which the reference has been made is to be suspended pending the determination of the reference.]

Amendments

1. Tribunal Procedure (Amendment No.2) Rules 2009 (SI 2009/1975) rr.7 and 9 (September 1, 2009).

2. Tribunal Procedure (Amendment No.2) Rules 2010 (SI 2010/44) rr.2 and 4 (February 15, 2010).

3. Tribunal Procedure (Upper Tribunal) (Amendment) Rules 2010 (SI 2010/747) rr.2 and 5 (April 6, 2010).

4. Tribunal Procedure (Amendment No.2) Rules 2013 (SI 2013/606) r.2(1) and (3) (April 1, 2013).

5. Tribunal Procedure (Amendment) Rules 2014 (SI 2014/514) rr.2 and 4 (April 6, 2014).

6. Tribunal Procedure (Amendment) Rules 2017 (SI 2017/723) rr.5 and 8 (July 23, 2017).

7. Tribunal Procedure (Amendment) Rules 2020 (SI 2020/651) r.5(1) and (4) (July 21, 2020).

Definitions

"the 2007 Act"—see r.1(3).
"dispose of proceedings"—*ibid.*
"document"—*ibid.*
"financial sanctions case"—*ibid.*
"financial services case"—*ibid.*
"hearing" *ibid.*
"party"—*ibid.*
"permission"—*ibid.*
"practice direction"—*ibid.*
"wholesale energy case"—*ibid.*

General Note

Paragraph (2)

3.430 This is in very broad terms and, although para.(3) and r.15(1) set out examples of directions the Upper Tribunal may give, they do not restrict the width of the power in this paragraph. The power must, however, be exercised so as to give effect to the overriding objective in r.2 (see r.2(3)). The procedure for applying for and giving directions is to be found in r.6. Note that, where a direction requires something to be done by a particular day, it must be done by 5pm on that day (r.12(1)) but, if that day is not a working day, the act is done in time if it is done on the next working day (r.12(2)).

Paragraph (3)

3.431 Sub-paragraph (a) is in very broad terms. See the note to r.5(3)(a) of the Tribunal Procedure (First-tier Tribunal) (Social Entitlement Chamber) Rules 2008, above.

Sub-paragraph (c) presumably refers to grounds of appeal and other submissions, rather than to evidence.

Sub-paragraphs (f), (g) and (h) must be read with rr.34–37. See also the note to r.5(3)(f), (g) and (h) of the Tribunal Procedure (First-tier Tribunal) (Social Entitlement Chamber) Rules 2008, above.

When making a direction for the preparation of a bundle under sub-para.(i) in a case where there is no power, or only a limited power, to award costs, it is important that the Upper Tribunal considers upon whom the financial burden of preparing a bundle should be placed. If it wishes the cost to be shared, it should direct both parties to prepare it. See *Eclipse Film Partners No.35 LLP v Revenue and Customs Commissioners (No.2)* [2016] UKSC 24; [2016] 1 W.L.R. 1939.

Sub-paragraph (k) applies only where the Upper Tribunal had jurisdiction at the time the proceedings were begun. Otherwise, the Tribunal is required to strike the proceedings out under r.8(2). Rule 5(3)(k)(i) applies where the Upper Tribunal loses jurisdiction and r.5(3)(k)(ii) applies only where the Upper Tribunal and another tribunal have concurrent jurisdiction (which may be the case in some circumstances where a person moves to or from Northern Ireland).

3.432 Sub-paragraphs (l) and (m) permit the effect of a decision to be suspended pending an appeal from or to the Upper Tribunal. The power to suspend the effect of its own decision conferred by sub-para.(l) does not extend to suspending its precedential effect on other claims pending an appeal (*SSD v AD and MM (No.2)* [2009] UKUT 69 (AAC)), but in social security cases such an extended power is unnecessary in the light of s.25 (and s.26) of the Social Security Act 1998. The First-tier Tribunal also has power to suspend the effect of its decision pending an appeal to the Upper Tribunal (see r.5(3)(l) of the Tribunal Procedure (First-tier Tribunal) (Social Entitlement Chamber) Rules 2008 and so the power in sub-para.(m) is most likely to be invoked where the First-tier Tribunal has refused to suspend the effect of its own decision. It is usually unnecessary to suspend a decision in a social security case concerned with entitlement, due to the Secretary of State's power to suspend payments under reg.16 of the Social Security and Child Support (Decisions and Appeals) Regulations 1999 or reg.44 of the Universal Credit, Personal Independence Payment, Jobseeker's Allowance and Employment and Support Allowance (Decisions and Appeals) Regulations 2013. In the past, the Secretary of State has generally not taken action to recover an overpayment while an appeal against a decision that the overpayment is recoverable is pending but he could now take the view that an appeal does not require him to stay his hand unless the tribunal so directs under this provision, which would not necessarily be appropriate as a matter of course and could in any event presumably be limited to part of its decision. The power to suspend the effect of a decision may also be useful in appeals against decisions under the Social Security (Recovery of Benefits) Act 1997, because s.14 of that Act and the regulations made under it completely fail to deal with the consequences of a successful appeal to the Upper Tribunal or an appellate court. In *Carmarthenshire CC v MW (SEN)* [2010] UKUT 348 (AAC); [2011] AACR 17, it was held that r.5(3)(m) required a balancing exercise, taking into account the practical consequences of suspending the decision on one side and the practical consequences of not doing so on the other. The chances of the appeal succeeding would be relevant but it was doubted whether a good prospect of the appeal succeeding could operate as a threshold condition, particularly in a case of urgency where the grounds of appeal might not have been formulated.

In *Cabinet Office v IC* [2016] UKUT 476 (AAC), the Upper Tribunal continued a suspension of the effect of the First-tier Tribunal's decision for 23 days after issue of his refusal of permission to appeal from that decision, in case the Cabinet Office wished to apply for permission to bring judicial review proceedings. The period was calculated by adding 7 days to the 16-day time limit for applying for judicial review, so as to give the Cabinet Office time to get any application for a further suspension before a judge in the Administrative Court if it wished to do so. It is not clear whether the judge read "review" in r.5(3)(l) as including judicial review or read "appeal" in both that provision and r.5(3)(m) as including an application for judicial review or whether, acting outside the Rules, he exercised an implied power.

Sub-paragraph (n) permits the Upper Tribunal to direct the First-tier Tribunal, among others, to provide reasons for a decision that is the subject of an appeal or judicial review proceedings. As the First-tier Tribunal is, in any event, under a statutory duty to provide reasons for those of its decisions that dispose of proceedings (see, in relation to social security cases, r.34 of the Tribunal Procedure (First-tier Tribunal (Social Entitlement Chamber) Rules 2008), sub-para.(n) has generally been taken to permit the Upper Tribunal to require the First-tier Tribunal to supplement reasons that it has already given (see *CT v SSD* [2009] UKUT 167 (AAC)), although perhaps another reading of the provision would be that it is intended to have effect only where there is no other statutory duty on the First-tier Tribunal, or other relevant body, to provide reasons. The precise scope of the sub-paragraph is probably academic given that, even in the absence of sub-para.(n), the Upper Tribunal appears to have the power to invite the First-tier Tribunal to give further reasons were it to consider it appropriate to do so.

This emerges from a series of decisions of the higher courts in different contexts. In the context of appeals to the Court of Appeal from the High Court following lengthy trials, it was recommended by the Court of Appeal in *English v Emery Reimbold & Strick Ltd* [2002] EWCA Civ 605; [2002] 1 W.L.R. 2409 that, where an application for permission to appeal to the Court of Appeal was made to the High Court on the ground that its reasons were inadequate, it should consider giving additional reasons and that, where such an application for permission to appeal was made to the Court of Appeal on the ground that the High Court's reasons were inadequate, the Court of Appeal should consider inviting the High Court to provide additional reasons. Lord Phillips MR, giving the judgment of the Court said:

> "[24] We are not greatly attracted by the suggestion that a judge who has given inadequate reasons should be invited to have a second bite at the cherry. But we are much less attracted at the prospect of expensive appellate proceedings on the ground of lack of reasons. Where the judge who has heard the evidence has based a rational decision on it, the successful party will suffer an injustice if that decision is appealed, let alone set aside, simply because the judge has not included in his judgment adequate reasons for his decision. The appellate court will not be in as good a position to substitute its decision, should it decide that this course is viable, while an appeal followed by a rehearing will involve a hideous waste of costs."

(Moreover, of course, the additional costs payable by the losing party would have been caused by an error of the court to which it had not contributed.) In *VK v Norfolk CC* [2004] EWHC 2921 (Admin), a statutory appeal to the High Court from the Special Educational Needs and Disability Tribunal, the respondent submitted that, in the light of *English*, the High Court should, having found the Tribunal's reasons to be inadequate, remit the case to the Tribunal to enable it to supplement the reasons. Although the High Court had no express power to direct the Tribunal to do that, Stanley Burnton J accepted at [69] to [80] that he could nonetheless adjourn and *invite* the Tribunal to supplement its reasons, in the expectation that it would do so. Nevertheless, he refused to follow that course and said that it would never be appropriate to follow it in the type of appeal that was before him unless what was sought was "merely elucidatory". He distinguished *English* on two grounds: first, that, in *VK*, the Tribunal was required by its procedural rules to provide reasons at the same time as its written decision and that allowing it to supplement its reasons would be inconsistent with that requirement and, secondly, that there was no permission stage in the type of appeal before him, whereas *English* envisaged reasons being supplemented at that stage and so before the substantive hearing of an appeal. He also referred to the need for speed and finality in cases concerned with a child's education. Meanwhile, the approach suggested in *English* had been followed by the Employment Appeal Tribunal who had adopted a practice of sifting appeals before they were heard and, in appropriate cases, inviting the employment tribunal to clarify or supplement its reasons. In *VK*, Stanley Burnton J pointed out that, unlike the Tribunal with which he was concerned, employment tribunals were not obliged to provide their reasons at the same time as their decisions.

The Employment Appeal Tribunal's practice was specifically considered and upheld by the Court of Appeal in *Barke v SEETEC Business Technology Centre Ltd* [2005] EWCA Civ 578; [2005] I.C.R. 1373. The Court decided that the Employment Appeal Tribunal, like the Tribunal in *VK*, had no express power to direct an employment tribunal to clarify or supplement its reasons but it agreed with Stanley Burnton J that it nonetheless was entitled to invite it to do so. In so deciding, it rejected at [23] to [28] an argument that such an invitation would be futile because, under its procedural rules, the employment tribunal was "functus officio" after it had given reasons for its decision and had no power to supplement them. It recognised that it would not always be appropriate to issue such an invitation if, for example "the inadequacy of reasoning is on its face so fundamental that there is a real risk that supplementary reasons will be reconstructions of proper reasons, rather than the unexplained actual reasons for the decision". It also said that the Employment Appeal Tribunal "should always be alive to the danger that an employment tribunal might tailor its response to a request for explanations or further reasons (usually subconsciously rather than deliberately) so as to put the decision in the best possible light". In *Hatungimana v Secretary of State for the Home Department* [2006] EWCA Civ 231, the Court of Appeal declined to apply *Barke* on an appeal from the Asylum and Immigration Tribunal, stressing that the procedural rules of that tribunal were different from those governing employment tribunals.

However, the procedural rules applicable to the appeal tribunals and Commissioners formerly constituted under the Social Security Act 1998 and since replaced by, respectively, the First-tier Tribunal and the Upper Tribunal do not appear to have been materially distinguishable from the procedural rules applicable to employment tribunals and the Employment Appeal Tribunal. Nor do the present rules applicable in the First-tier Tribunal and the Upper Tribunal. Accordingly, it appears that, strictly speaking, the Upper Tribunal would have the same power to invite the First-tier Tribunal to clarify or supplement its reasons as the Court of Appeal found that the Employment Appeal Tribunal had in *Barke*, even if it did not have any power of direction conferred by r.5(3)(n).

Nonetheless, the Upper Tribunal has very seldom, and possibly never, exercised the power to direct, or invite, the First-tier Tribunal to provide supplementary reasons in social security cases. The reasons for this appear to be essentially practical. In *CT v SSD* [2009] UKUT 167 (AAC), the Upper Tribunal said, obiter, that, although it might be appropriate, under r.5(3)(n), to ask a First-tier Tribunal to supplement its reasons before an application for permission to appeal was determined by the Upper Tribunal, it would generally be inappropriate to do so at a later stage in the proceedings before the Upper Tribunal because the passage of time would have made it difficult for the First-tier Tribunal to give further reasons and its recollection would not be reliable. Even at the application stage, a considerable amount of time may have passed since the First-tier Tribunal's decision, although that may lessen with the electronic submission and transfer of documents. Moreover, as pointed out in *CA/4297/2004*, a balancing exercise of the type that led to the conclusion in *English* that allowing the High Court to supplement its reasons was the lesser of two evils, may lead to the same conclusion in relation to employment tribunals but does not generally do so in relation to tribunals hearing social security cases. Proceedings in social security cases in the First-tier Tribunal, where the parties hardly ever have legal representation and where hearings typically last for about an hour, sometimes less than that and rarely for more than two hours are not comparable to High Court trials or many employment tribunal cases that can last for days and in which huge amounts of costs may be run up. Furthermore, obtaining supplementary reasons causes delay and can be time-consuming in itself and may in the end not even result in the original decision being upheld. In the Upper Tribunal, social security cases are typically decided on the papers and the First-tier Tribunal usually hears remitted cases fairly promptly. Therefore, even in terms simply of judicial time and the tribunals' administrative costs, there may be no saving through seeking supplementary reasons in social security cases. Once one brings into account unease about the First-tier Tribunal getting "a second bite at the cherry", the risk identified in *Barke* that supplemental reasons may not reflect the First-tier Tribunal's original reasoning and difficulties that there may be in expecting unrepresented claimants to deal with arguments about supplementary reasons in proceedings largely conducted on paper, it is perhaps not surprising that the Upper Tribunal appears to have concluded that, at least generally, it is not worthwhile for it to give the First-tier Tribunal an opportunity to clarify or supplement its reasons in social security cases.

As to the question whether the First-tier Tribunal may supplement its reasons on its own initiative, see the note to r.34 of the Tribunal Procedure (First-tier Tribunal) (Social Entitlement Chamber) Rules 2008, above.

5A. *Expired.* **3.433**

General Note

This coronavirus temporary rule was in force from April 10, 2020 to September 25, 2022. **3.434**

Procedure for applying for and giving directions

6.—(1) The Upper Tribunal may give a direction on the application of one or more of the parties or on its own initiative. **3.435**

(2) An application for a direction may be made—

(a) by sending or delivering a written application to the Upper Tribunal; or

(b) orally during the course of a hearing.

(3) An application for a direction must include the reason for making that application.

(4) Unless the Upper Tribunal considers that there is good reason not to do so, the Upper Tribunal must send written notice of any direction to every party and to any other person affected by the direction.

(5) If a party or any other person sent notice of the direction under paragraph (4) wishes to challenge a direction which the Upper Tribunal has given, they may do so by applying for another direction which amends, suspends or sets aside the first direction.

DEFINITIONS

"hearing"—see r.1(3).
"party"—*ibid.*

GENERAL NOTE

3.436 See the note to r.6 of the Tribunal Procedure (First-tier Tribunal) (Social Entitlement Chamber) Rules 2008, above.

Failure to comply with rules etc.

3.437 7.—(1) An irregularity resulting from a failure to comply with any requirement in these Rules, a practice direction or a direction, does not of itself render void the proceedings or any step taken in the proceedings.

(2) If a party has failed to comply with a requirement in these Rules, a practice direction or a direction, the Upper Tribunal may take such action as it considers just, which may include—

(a) waiving the requirement;
(b) requiring the failure to be remedied;
(c) exercising its power under rule 8 (striking out a party's case); or
(d) except in [1 a mental health case, an asylum case or an immigration case], restricting a party's participation in the proceedings.

(3) Paragraph (4) applies where the First-tier Tribunal has referred to the Upper Tribunal a failure by a person to comply with a requirement imposed by the First-tier Tribunal—

(a) to attend at any place for the purpose of giving evidence;
(b) otherwise to make themselves available to give evidence;
(c) to swear an oath in connection with the giving of evidence;
(d) to give evidence as a witness;
(e) to produce a document; or
(f) to facilitate the inspection of a document or any other thing (including any premises).

(4) The Upper Tribunal may exercise its power under section 25 of the 2007 Act (supplementary powers of the Upper Tribunal) in relation to such non-compliance as if the requirement had been imposed by the Upper Tribunal.

AMENDMENT

1. Tribunal Procedure (Amendment No.2) Rules 2010 (SI 2010/44) rr.2 and 5 (February 15, 2010).

DEFINITIONS

"the 2007 Act"—see r.1(3).
"asylum case"—*ibid.*
"document"—*ibid.*
"immigration case"—*ibid.*
"mental health case"—*ibid.*
"party"—*ibid.*
"practice direction"—*ibid.*

General Note

Paragraphs (1) and (2)(a) enable the Upper Tribunal to overlook a breach of a rule, practice direction or direction. On the other hand, under para.2(c), such a breach can lead to a case being struck out under r.8, provided an appropriate warning has been given. Alternatively, the Upper Tribunal may exercise its powers under s.25 of the Tribunals, Courts and Enforcement Act 2007 to punish the person for contempt of court (with a term of imprisonment of up to two years and an unlimited fine). Paragraph (1) may imply a greater power of waiver than exists in para.(2)(a), because an irregularity may be the fault of a lower tribunal (see the examples in the note to r.21(2)) or of the Upper Tribunal, rather than of a party, and it may be too late to remedy it. **3.438**

Paragraphs (3) and (4) are concerned with cases where the First-tier Tribunal refers a case to the Upper Tribunal because there has been non-compliance with a summons, order or direction issued by that tribunal in connection with the attendance or examination of witnesses or the production or inspection of documents. They are made under para.10 of Sch.5 to the 2007 Act. A referral is necessary because the First-tier Tribunal does not have its own power to punish for contempt. The impression given by the three-judge panel decisions in *PA v CMEC* [2009] UKUT 283 (AAC), *MR v CMEC* [2009] UKUT 284 (AAC) and *MR v CMEC No.1* [2009] UKUT 285 (AAC) that, on a reference by the First-tier Tribunal for breach of a direction to produce evidence, it was necessary for the Upper Tribunal to make its own direction to produce evidence before it could punish the defaulter for contempt of court has been corrected in the subsequent three-judge panel decision of *MD v SSWP (Enforcement Reference)* [2010] UKUT 202 (AAC); [2011] AACR 5, where it was explained that the Upper Tribunal made its own direction in *MR v CMEC No.1* [2009] UKUT 285 (AAC) because that course was, as a matter of discretion, the course which the Upper Tribunal considered appropriate in all the circumstances. It was expressly stated that it "was not because the exercise of the Upper Tribunal's powers was in any way conditional upon the making of a further order". In *CB v Suffolk CC (Enforcement Reference)* [2010] UKUT 413 (AAC); [2011] AACR 22, the Upper Tribunal fined a witness £500 for failing to comply with a summons issued by the Health, Education and Social Care Chamber of the First-tier Tribunal. See also *BO v Care Quality Commission (Enforcement Reference)* [2013] UKUT 53 (AAC), where a fine of £100 was imposed for non-compliance with a summons.

Paragraph (3)(c) must be read subject to s.5 of the Oaths Act 1978, which permits a person who objects to being sworn to make a solemn affirmation instead.

Striking out a party's case

8.—[2 (1A) Except for paragraph (2), this rule does not apply to an asylum case or an immigration case.] **3.439**

[3 (1) The proceedings, or the appropriate part of them, will automatically be struck out—

(a) if the appellant or applicant has failed to comply with a direction that stated that failure by the appellant or applicant to comply with the direction would lead to the striking out of the proceedings or part of them; or

[4(b) in immigration judicial review proceedings, when a fee has not been paid, as required, in respect of an application under rule 30(4) or upon the grant of permission.]

(2) The Upper Tribunal must strike out the whole or a part of the proceedings if the Upper Tribunal—

(a) does not have jurisdiction in relation to the proceedings or that part of them; and

(b) does not exercise its power under rule 5(3)(k)(i) (transfer to another court or tribunal) in relation to the proceedings or that part of them.

(3) The Upper Tribunal may strike out the whole or a part of the proceedings if—

(a) the appellant or applicant has failed to comply with a direction which stated that failure by the appellant or applicant to comply with the direction could lead to the striking out of the proceedings or part of them;

(b) the appellant or applicant has failed to co-operate with the Upper Tribunal to such an extent that the Upper Tribunal cannot deal with the proceedings fairly and justly; or

(c) in proceedings which are not an appeal from the decision of another tribunal or judicial review proceedings, the Upper Tribunal considers there is no reasonable prospect of the appellant's or the applicant's case, or part of it, succeeding.

(4) The Upper Tribunal may not strike out the whole or a part of the proceedings under paragraph (2) or (3)(b) or (c) without first giving the appellant or applicant an opportunity to make representations in relation to the proposed striking out.

(5) If the proceedings have been struck out under paragraph (1) or (3)(a), the appellant or applicant may apply for the proceedings, or part of them, to be reinstated.

(6) An application under paragraph (5) must be made in writing and received by the Upper Tribunal within 1 month after the date on which the Upper Tribunal sent notification of the striking out to the appellant or applicant.

(7) This rule applies to a respondent [1 or an interested party] as it applies to an appellant or applicant except that—

(a) a reference to the striking out of the proceedings is to be read as a reference to the barring of the respondent [1 or an interested party] from taking further part in the proceedings; and

(b) a reference to an application for the reinstatement of proceedings which have been struck out is to be read as a reference to an application for the lifting of the bar on the respondent [1 or an interested party] from taking further part in the proceedings.

(8) If a respondent [1 or an interested party] has been barred from taking further part in proceedings under this rule and that bar has not been lifted, the Upper Tribunal need not consider any response or other submission made by that respondent [1 or interested party, and may summarily determine any or all issues against that respondent or interested party].

AMENDMENTS

1. Tribunal Procedure (Amendment) Rules 2009 (SI 2009/274) r.6 (April 1, 2009).

2. Tribunal Procedure (Amendment No.2) Rules 2010 (SI 2010/44) rr.2 and 6 (February 15, 2010).

3. Tribunal Procedure (Upper Tribunal) (Amendment) Rules 2011 (SI 2011/2343) rr.2 and 5 (October 17, 2011).

4. Tribunal Procedure (Amendment No. 4) Rules 2013 (SI 2013/2067) rr.2 and 5 (November 1, 2013).

DEFINITIONS

"appellant"—see r.1(3).
"applicant"—*ibid.*
"asylum case" – *ibid.*
"immigration case" – *ibid.*
"immigration judicial review proceedings"—*ibid.*
"interested party"—*ibid.*
"party"—*ibid.*
"respondent"—*ibid.*

GENERAL NOTE

Note that, although paras (1)–(6) are expressed in terms of striking out proceedings brought by the appellant, by virtue of paras (7) and (8) they also provide for barring a respondent from taking further part in the proceedings. 3.440

See the annotations to the equivalent provisions in r.8 of the Tribunal Procedure (First-tier Tribunal) (Social Entitlement Chamber) Rules 2008. However, there are some minor differences.

Registrars may issue directions warning parties that their cases will, or may, be struck out if they do not comply and they may exercise the powers to strike out proceedings (or, presumably, bar respondents) under paras (1) and (3)(a) and to reinstate proceedings (or, presumably, lift a bar) under para.(5). They do not have the power to strike proceedings out under paras (2), (3)(b) or (3(c). See the annotation to r.4.

Sub-paragraph (1)(b) applies only to "immigration judicial review proceedings" and therefore is not relevant to social security cases. Fees are not payable in social security cases.

Sub-paragraph (2) applies not only where the Upper Tribunal lacks jurisdiction in the strict sense but also where it declines jurisdiction on *forum non conveniens* grounds (*R. (CICA) v First-tier Tribunal (CIC)* [2018] UKUT 439 (AAC); [2019] AACR 18 where the Upper Tribunal may have had jurisdiction in the strict sense to determine the application for judicial review but, if so, the Court of Session was nonetheless clearly and distinctly the more appropriate forum).

In *LS v HMRC (TC)* [2017] UKUT 257 (AAC); [2018] AACR 2, it was held that, where a decision under s.16 of the Tax Credits Act 2002 against which an appeal has been brought lapses as the result of a subsequent decision made under s.18, any appeal to the First-tier Tribunal should be struck out under r.8(2) Tribunal Procedure (First-tier Tribunal) (Social Entitlement Chamber) Rules 2008 on the ground that the First-tier Tribunal no longer has jurisdiction in relation to the proceedings. However, it was also held that the making of a s.18 decision did not require the Upper Tribunal similarly to strike out a case under para.(2) of this regulation and that the Upper Tribunal had jurisdiction under s.11 of the Tribunals. Courts and Enforcement Act 2007 to set aside a decision of the First-tier Tribunal given on an appeal against a s.16 decision notwithstanding that a s.18 decision had been made, irrespective of whether the s.18 decision was made before or after the First-tier Tribunal's decision.

The Upper Tribunal's decision as to its own jurisdiction is probably not controversial in a case where the s.18 decision was made before the First-tier Tribunal's decision, since the Upper Tribunal would otherwise be unable to correct a failure by the First-tier Tribunal to strike out the appeal before it. However, it is not obvious why an appeal to the Upper Tribunal should not lapse where a subsequent decision renders the First-tier Tribunal's decision, and the question whether it erred in law, entirely academic, and why the Upper Tribunal should not then be under the same obligation to strike the case out as the First-tier Tribunal is when an appeal to it has lapsed. Striking an appeal out need not always be done summarily and need not prevent the Upper Tribunal from expressing a view on the merits of the First-tier Tribunal's decision if it considers it desirable to do so. 3.441

This point is not of a great deal of practical importance, given that the Upper Tribunal in *LS* did accept that, when a s.18 decision had been given, any decision of the Upper Tribunal on an appeal from a decision of the First-tier Tribunal under s.16 would be of only academic interest between the parties. In one of the cases before it, in which a s.18 decision had been made since the First-tier Tribunal's decision and it found the First-tier Tribunal to have erred in law, the Upper Tribunal merely set aside the First-tier Tribunal's decision and neither remitted the case nor re-made the decision. However, the Upper Tribunal's decision does require all such appeals to be determined once permission has been given (unless they are withdrawn), albeit that a fairly summary determination may be possible in many cases. This is because there is no power to strike an appeal from the First-tier Tribunal out under r.8(3)(c) for lack of prospects of success.

Indeed, sub-para.(3)(c) has little application to social security cases because it does not apply to appeals from the First-tier Tribunal or judicial review proceedings (presumably because the permission requirement makes it unnecessary in the case of appellants and applicants and there is little advantage in barring respondents in such cases) and there is no appellant or applicant in a reference under the Forfeiture Act 1982 (*SSWP v LK (RP)* [2019] UKUT 421 (AAC) at [53] to [60]). On the other hand, in the absence (then) of a power to certify an application for permission to appeal as being totally without merit so as prevent it being renewed orally when it has been refused on the papers in those jurisdictions where that may be done (see r.22(3) and (4)), the Upper Tribunal has exercised its power to strike out a renewed application for permission when satisfied that it had no arguable merit and that the applicant had "had more than her day in court at the FTT" (*Gaskin v IC* [2016] UKUT 382 (AAC)). More recently, applications for permission to appeal and for permission to apply for judicial review were struck out without oral hearings in *Crossland v IC* [2020] UKUT 263 (AAC) and *Crossland v IC* [2020] UKUT 264 (AAC), the former being a decision of the Chamber President of the Administrative Appeals Chamber of the Upper Tribunal. In both cases, the applicant was seeking permission to appeal against case-management decisions of the First-tier Tribunal and the judges emphasised the limited circumstances in which the Upper Tribunal would interfere with interlocutory decisions of the First-tier Tribunal and considered that the applications for permission to appeal had no merit. See further the note to r.8(3) of the Tribunal Procedure (First-tier Tribunal) (Social Entitlement Chamber) Rules 2008.

[1 Addition, substitution and removal of parties

3.442 **9.**—(1) The Upper Tribunal may give a direction adding, substituting or removing a party as an appellant, a respondent or an interested party.

(2) If the Upper Tribunal gives a direction under paragraph (1) it may give such consequential directions as it considers appropriate.

(3) A person who is not a party may apply to the Upper Tribunal to be added or substituted as a party.

(4) If a person who is entitled to be a party to proceedings by virtue of another enactment applies to be added as a party, and any conditions applicable to that entitlement have been satisfied, the Upper Tribunal must give a direction adding that person as a respondent or, if appropriate, as an appellant.]

[2 (5) In an asylum case, the United Kingdom Representative of the United Nations High Commissioner for Refugees ("the United Kingdom Representative") may give notice to the Upper Tribunal that the United Kingdom Representative wishes to participate in the proceedings.

(6) If the United Kingdom Representative gives notice under paragraph (5)—

(i) the United Kingdom Representative is entitled to participate in any hearing; and
(ii) all documents which are required to be sent or delivered to parties must be sent or delivered to the United Kingdom Representative.]

AMENDMENTS

1. Tribunal Procedure (Amendment No.2) Rules 2009 (SI 2009/1975) rr.7 and 10 (September 1, 2009).
2. Tribunal Procedure (Amendment No.2) Rules 2010 (SI 2010/44) rr.2 and 7 (February 15, 2010).

DEFINITIONS

"appellant" – *ibid.*
"asylum case" – *ibid.*
"interested party" – *ibid.*
"party"—*ibid.*
"respondent"—*ibid.*

GENERAL NOTE

See the note to r.9 of the Tribunal Procedure (First-tier Tribunal) (Social Entitlement Chamber) Rules 2008, above. This rule does not permit the substitution of an applicant in judicial review proceedings. 3.443

[1 Orders for costs

10.—(1) The Upper Tribunal may not make an order in respect of costs (or, in Scotland, expenses) in proceedings [2 transferred or referred by, or on appeal from] another tribunal except – 3.444
[3 (aa) in a national security certificate appeal, to the extent permitted by paragraph (1A);]
(a) in proceedings [2 transferred by, or on appeal from] from the Tax Chamber of the First-tier Tribunal; or
(b) to the extent and in the circumstances that the other tribunal had the power to make an order in respect of costs (or, in Scotland, expenses).

[3 (1A) In a national security certificate appeal—
(a) the Upper Tribunal may make an order in respect of costs or expenses in the circumstances described at paragraph (3)(c) and (d);
(b) if the appeal is against a certificate, the Upper Tribunal may make an order in respect of costs or expenses against the relevant Minister and in favour of the appellant if the Upper Tribunal allows the appeal and quashes the certificate to any extent or the Minister withdraws the certificate;
(c) if the appeal is against the application of a certificate, the Upper Tribunal may make an order in respect of costs or expenses—
  (i) against the appellant and in favour of any other party if the Upper Tribunal dismisses the appeal to any extent; or
  (ii) in favour of the appellant and against any other party if the Upper Tribunal allows the appeal to any extent.]

(2) The Upper Tribunal may not make an order in respect of costs or expenses under section 4 of the Forfeiture Act 1982.

(3) In other proceedings, the Upper Tribunal may not make an order in respect of costs or expenses except—

(a) in judicial review proceedings;
(b) [[2]. . .];
(c) under section 29(4) of the 2007 Act (wasted costs) [[5] and costs incurred in applying for such costs]; [[4]. . .]
(d) if the Upper Tribunal considers that a party or its representative has acted unreasonably in bringing, defending or conducting the proceedings; [[4] [[8] ...]
(e) if, in a financial services case [[7] or a wholesale energy case], the Upper Tribunal considers that the decision in respect of which the reference was made was unreasonable] [[8] or
(f) if, in a financial sanctions case, the Upper Tribunal considers that the decision to impose or uphold a monetary penalty in respect of which the appeal was made was unreasonable;]

(4) The Upper Tribunal may make an order for costs (or, in Scotland, expenses) on an application or on its own initiative.

(5) A person making an application for an order for costs or expenses must—

(a) send or deliver a written application to the Upper Tribunal and to the person against whom it is proposed that the order be made; and
(b) send or deliver with the application a schedule of the costs or expenses claimed sufficient to allow summary assessment of such costs or expenses by the Upper Tribunal.

(6) An application for an order for costs or expenses may be made at any time during the proceedings but may not be made later than 1 month after the date on which the Upper Tribunal sends—

(a) a decision notice recording the decision which finally disposes of all issues in the proceedings; or
(b) [[5] notice under rule 17(5) that a withdrawal which ends the proceedings has taken effect.]

(7) The Upper Tribunal may not make an order for costs or expenses against a person (the "paying person") without first—

(a) giving that person an opportunity to make representations; and
(b) if the paying person is an individual and the order is to be made under paragraph (3)(a), (b) or (d), considering that person's financial means.

(8) The amount of costs or expenses to be paid under an order under this rule may be ascertained by—

(a) summary assessment by the Upper Tribunal;
(b) agreement of a specified sum by the paying person and the person entitled to receive the costs or expenses ("the receiving person"); or
(c) assessment of the whole or a specified part of the costs or expenses [[5], including the costs or expenses of the assessment,] incurred by the receiving person, if not agreed.

(9) Following an order for assessment under paragraph (8)(c), the paying person or the receiving person may apply—

(a) in England and Wales, to the High Court or the Costs Office of the Supreme Court (as specified in the order) for a detailed assessment of the costs on the standard basis or, if specified in the order, on the indemnity basis; and the Civil Procedure Rules 1998 shall apply, with necessary modifications, to that application and assessment as if the proceedings in the tribunal had been proceedings in a court to which the Civil Procedure Rules 1998 apply;

(b) in Scotland, to the Auditor of the Court of Session for the taxation of the expenses according to the fees payable in that court; or

(c) in Northern Ireland, to the Taxing Office of the High Court of Northern Ireland for taxation on the standard basis or, if specified in the order, on the indemnity basis.]

[5 (10) Upon making an order for the assessment of costs, the [6 Upper] Tribunal may order an amount to be paid on account before the costs or expenses are assessed.]

AMENDMENTS

1. Tribunal Procedure (Amendment) Rules 2009 (SI 2009/274) r.7 (April 1, 2009).

2. Tribunal Procedure (Amendment No.2) Rules 2009 (SI 2009/1975) rr.7 and 10 (September 1, 2009).

3. Tribunal Procedure (Amendment) Rules 2010 (SI 2010/43) rr.5 and 7 (January 18, 2010).

4. Tribunal Procedure (Upper Tribunal) (Amendment) Rules 2010 (SI 2010/747), rr.2 and 6 (April 6, 2010).

5. Tribunal Procedure (Amendment) Rules 2013 (SI 2013/477) rr.49–53 (April 1, 2013).

6. Tribunal Procedure (Amendment No. 4) Rules 2013 (SI 2013/2067) rr.2 and 6 (November 1, 2013).

7. Tribunal Procedure (Amendment) Rules 2014 (SI 2014/514) rr.2 and 6 (April 6, 2014).

8. Tribunal Procedure (Amendment) Rules 2017 (SI 2017/723) rr.5 and 9 (July 23, 2017).

DEFINITIONS

"the 2007 Act"—see r.1(3).
"financial sanctions case"—*ibid.*
"financial services case"—*ibid.*
"national security certificate appeal"—*ibid.*
"party"—*ibid.*
"relevant Minister"—*ibid.*
"wholesale energy case"—*ibid.*

GENERAL NOTE

The effect of para.(1)(b) is that there is no power to award costs in social security cases on appeal from the First-tier Tribunal, because the First-tier Tribunal has no power to award costs in such cases (see r.10 of the Tribunal Procedure (First-tier Tribunal) (Social Entitlement Chamber) Rules 2008, above), but see the note to s.29 of the Tribunals, Courts and Enforcement Act 2007 where it is suggested that it is just arguable that the Upper Tribunal has a power to make a wasted costs order against a lawyer acting for a party in such an appeal. There was no application for a wasted costs order in *AM v SSWP (JSA and IS)* [2019] UKUT 361 (AAC) and the Upper Tribunal had no difficulty in rejecting, at [22] to [28], the application for costs against the Secretary of State made in that case. Paragraph (2) has the effect that there is no power to award costs in cases under the Forfeiture Act 1982. 3.445

In many appeals from the Health, Education and Social Care Chamber, the General Regulatory Chamber, the Immigration and Asylum Chamber (since October 20, 2014) and the Tax Chamber of the First-tier Tribunal, the Upper Tribunal has a power to award costs if a party of its representative has acted unreasonably in bringing, defending or conducting the proceedings. It is clear that the fact that proceedings are unsuccessful does not mean that it was unreasonable to bring them (*Buckinghamshire CC v ST (SEN)* [2013] UKUT 468 (AAC); *DK v NHS England* [2014] UKUT 171 (AAC)). Conduct in the making of the decision being challenged is not relevant (*Distinctive Care Ltd v Revenue and Customs* [2019] EWCA Civ 1010), save where Tribunal Procedure Rules make specific provision.

Paragraph (3) leaves the general discretion to award costs in judicial review proceedings entirely unfettered. However, in *R.(LR) v First-tier Tribunal (HESC)* (Costs) [2013] UKUT 294 (AAC); [2013] AACR 27, a three-judge panel presided over by the Senior President of Tribunals has decided that in cases within the exclusive jurisdiction of the Administrative Appeals Chamber of the Upper Tribunal (as opposed to cases transferred to it by the High Court on a discretionary basis) where the respondent is a tribunal, the Upper Tribunal should not make an order for costs where the First-tier Tribunal would not have been able to do so. Thus the powers of the Upper Tribunal to award costs in judicial review proceedings against a tribunal are, at least for most practical purposes, the same as its powers on an appeal from that tribunal under para.(1)(b). This approach was followed in judicial review proceedings in a criminal injuries compensation case in *R.(H) v First-tier Tribunal (CIC)* [2014] UKUT 338 (AAC). However, the judge seems to have overlooked the fact that there is no power to award costs at all in the Social Entitlement Chamber of the First-tier Tribunal so, although he made no order for costs, he did so after considering whether the interested party had acted reasonably in resisting the applicant's case. In *R(MM and DM) v SSWP (Costs)* [2015] UKUT 566 (AAC); [2016] AACR 12, a three-judge panel has held that, in judicial review cases transferred to the Upper Tribunal from the High Court, costs are to be awarded in accordance with the principles that would be applied in the High Court. These may be found in the *Administrative Court Judicial Review Guide*, published in October each year by His Majesty's Courts and Tribunals Service and available online.

Note that, notwithstanding the terms of s.29(1) of the 2007 Act, the Upper Tribunal has power to award costs incurred in judicial review proceedings in the Administrative Court where that court has transferred the proceedings to the Upper Tribunal. On the other hand, where a refusal of the Upper Tribunal to give permission to appeal from a decision of the First-tier Tribunal is successfully challenged by way of an application for judicial review and the case is remitted by the Administrative Court to the Upper Tribunal, the Administrative Court is unable simply to order that the costs of the application for judicial review be treated as costs in the remitted proceedings (and so determined in the light of the outcome of those proceedings). However, it has been held that this jurisdictional problem can properly be avoided by the Administrative Court transferring the judicial review proceedings to the Upper Tribunal, notwithstanding that the Upper Tribunal is formally the respondent in the proceedings, solely to enable it to make an order for costs in the judicial review proceedings at the same time as it makes an order for costs in the remitted proceedings (*JH (Palestinian Territories) v Secretary of State for the Home Department* [2020] EWCA Civ 919; [2021] 1 W.L.R. 455).

Nonetheless, the Upper Tribunal is not always obliged to follow the practice of the High Court. In *Mann v Transport for London* [2018] EWCA Civ 1520; [2018] 1 W.L.R. 5104, it was held that, as r.10 does not contain provisions analogous to CPR r.36, the Upper Tribunal is not obliged to award costs on an indemnity basis in circumstances where a party has failed to "better" an offer of settlement and a court would award costs on such a basis.

3.446 For a case on wasted costs in the Immigration and Asylum Chamber of the Upper Tribunal, see *Okondu v Secretary of State for the Home Department* [2014] UKUT

377 (IAC), in which it was held that it was not necessarily improper, unreasonable or negligent to advance an unarguable case. In *Awuah v SSHD (Wasted Costs Orders – HOPOs – Tribunal Powers)* [2017] UKFTT 555 (IAC), it has been held that there is no power to make wasted costs orders against representatives who are not professional advocates (see, above, the note to s.29 of the Tribunals, Courts and Enforcement Act 2007). Further guidance relating to wasted costs that is likely to be as relevant in the Administrative Appeals Chamber of the Upper Tribunal as it is in immigration and asylum cases has been given by the Chamber President of the Immigration and Asylum Chamber of the Upper Tribunal, sitting as a judge of the First-tier Tribunal, in *Cancino (costs – First-tier Tribunal – new powers)* [2015] UKFTT 59 (IAC). See also *Presidential Guidance Note No.2 of 2018*, published online.

Notwithstanding the lack of specific provision in this rule, it has been held that the Upper Tribunal has the same power to make protective costs orders, costs capping orders and orders limiting costs in appeals as the High Court has. See *Drummond v HMRC* [2016] UKUT 221 (TCC), where it was said—

> "In exercising the same powers as the High Court to make a PCO, CCO or ACO, I take it as axiomatic that the UT should look to the same rules and criteria that govern the High Court when it exercises those powers, bearing in mind that the UT is governed by the UT Rules and especially the overriding objective in those rules and not the CPR. Whether to make such an order is a matter for the UT, in its discretion, to decide based on its evaluation of the circumstances of the case."

Since June 28, 2022, the Legal Services Act 2007 s.1494A (inserted by the Judicial Review and Courts Act 2002 s.48(2)) has given the Upper Tribunal the same power as courts in England and Wales have under s.194 of the 2007 Act to order a person to make a payment to a prescribed charity where, but for the fact that that a party's representation was provided free of charge, the Upper Tribunal would have had the power to order that person to make a payment to that party in respect of the representation. The new power extends across the UK, save where proceedings are within devolved competence (see s.194A(11) and (12)). It has little relevance in social security cases, because tribunals generally lack any power to award costs in such cases. However, it may be exercised in other contexts. The charity prescribed under the Legal Services Act 2007 (Prescribed Charity) Order 2008 (SI 2008/2680) (which has effect in relation to s.194A by virtue of s.194C(4)) is the Access to Justice Foundation.

Where there is no power, or only a limited power, to award costs, it is important that, when directing under r.5(3)(i) that a party should prepare a bundle for a hearing, the Upper Tribunal considers upon whom the financial burden of preparing it should be placed. If it wishes the cost to be shared by two parties, it should direct them both to prepare it. See *Eclipse Film Partners No 35 LLP v Revenue and Customs Commissioners (No 2)* [2016] UKSC 24; [2016] 1 W.L.R. 1939.

Section 73(14) of the Social Security Contributions and Benefits Act 1992 requires that the mobility component of disability living allowance be disregarded when assessing a party's means under para.(7)(b) (*Brace v IC* [2019] UKUT 305 (AAC)). That section does not appear to have a counterpart in the legislation relating to personal independence payment.

For a detailed decision on the assessment of costs, see *JW v Wirral MBC (SEN)* [2021] UKUT 70 (AAC).

Representatives

11.—(1) [5 Subject to paragraph (5A),] a party may appoint a representative (whether a legal representative or not) to represent that party in the proceedings. [4 save that a party in an asylum or immigration case may not 3.447

be represented by any person prohibited from representing by section 84 of the Immigration and Asylum Act 1999]

(2) If a party appoints a representative, that party (or the representative if the representative is a legal representative) must send or deliver to the Upper Tribunal [1 . . .] written notice of the representative's name and address.

[1 (2A) If the Upper Tribunal receives notice that a party has appointed a representative under paragraph (2), it must send a copy of that notice to each other party.]

(3) Anything permitted or required to be done by a party under these Rules, a practice direction or a direction may be done by the representative of that party, except signing a witness statement.

(4) A person who receives due notice of the appointment of a representative—

(a) must provide to the representative any document which is required to be provided to the represented party, and need not provide that document to the represented party; and

(b) may assume that the representative is and remains authorised as such until they receive written notification that this is not so from the representative or the represented party.

(5) [5 Subject to paragraph (5B),] at a hearing a party may be accompanied by another person whose name and address has not been notified under paragraph (2) but who, subject to paragraph (8) and with the permission of the Upper Tribunal, may act as a representative or otherwise assist in presenting the party's case at the hearing.

[5 (5A) In [6 immigration judicial review] proceedings, a party may appoint as a representative only a person authorised under the Legal Services Act 2007 to undertake the conduct of litigation in the High Court.

(5B) At a hearing of [6 immigration judicial review] proceedings, rights of audience before the Upper Tribunal are restricted to persons authorised to exercise those rights in the High Court under the Legal Services Act 2007.]

(6) Paragraphs (2) to (4) do not apply to a person who accompanies a party under paragraph (5).

(7) In a mental health case if the patient has not appointed a representative the Upper Tribunal may appoint a legal representative for the patient where—

(a) the patient has stated that they do not wish to conduct their own case or that they wish to be represented; or

(b) the patient lacks the capacity to appoint a representative but the Upper Tribunal believes that it is in the patient's best interests for the patient to be represented.

(8) In a mental health case a party may not appoint as a representative, or be represented or assisted at a hearing by—

(a) a person liable to be detained or subject to guardianship or after-care under supervision, or who is a community patient, under the Mental Health Act 1983; or

(b) a person receiving treatment for mental disorder at the same hospital [2 or] home as the patient.

[1 (9) In this rule "legal representative" means [3 a person who, for the purposes of the Legal Services Act 2007, is an authorised person in relation to an activity which constitutes the exercise of a right of audience or the conduct of litigaton within the meaning of that Act,] [4 a qualified person as defined in section 84(2) of the Immigration and Asylum Act 1999,], an advocate or solicitor in Scotland or a barrister or solicitor in Northern Ireland.]

[4 (10) In an asylum case or an immigration case, an appellant's representative before the First-tier Tribunal will be treated as that party's representative before the Upper Tribunal, unless the Upper Tribunal receives notice–

(a) of a new representative under paragraph (2) of this rule; or

(b) from the appellant stating that they are n longer represented.]

AMENDMENTS

1. Tribunal Procedure (Amendment) Rules 2009 (SI 2009/274) r.6 (April 1, 2009).

2. Tribunal Procedure (Amendment No.2) Rules 2009 (SI 2009/1975) rr.7 and 12 (September 1, 2009).

3. Tribunal Procedure (Amendment) Rules 2010 (SI 2010/43) rr.5 and 8 (January 18, 2010).

4. Tribunal Procedure (Amendment No.2) Rules 2010 (SI 2010/44) rr.2 and 8 (February 15, 2010).

3. Tribunal Procedure (Upper Tribunal) (Amendment) Rules 2011 (SI 2011/2343) rr.2 and 6 (October 17, 2011).

5. Tribunal Procedure (Amendment No. 4) Rules 2013 (SI 2013/2067) rr.2 and 7 (November 1, 2013).

DEFINITIONS

"asylum case"—see r.1(3).
"document"—*ibid.*
"hearing"—*ibid.*
"immigration case"—*ibid.*
"immigration judicial review proceedings"—*ibid.*
"legal representative"—see para.(9).
"mental health case"—see r.1(3).
"party"—*ibid.*
"permission"—*ibid.*
"practice direction"—*ibid.*

GENERAL NOTE

See the note to r.11(1) of the Tribunal Procedure (First-tier Tribunal) (Social Entitlement) Rules 2008. **3.448**

Paragraphs (2)–(4)

These paragraphs provide for the formal appointment of a representative who may then act on behalf of the party in all respects (except to sign a witness statement) and should be sent any documents that would otherwise be sent to the party. However, it is presumably possible for the Upper Tribunal to exclude a representative from a hearing under r.37(4) without excluding the party. **3.449**

Note that representatives, other than solicitors, barristers and advocates, are expected to provide written authority to act, signed by the party. In *CSDLA/2/2001*, two different representatives, each purporting to act on behalf of the same claimant, lodged separate applications for leave to appeal. The Commissioner said that a representative should obtain a fresh mandate from a claimant before sending what would now be an application for permission to appeal to the Upper Tribunal, rather than relying on a mandate obtained before a hearing before a lower tribunal. That would show that the representative had discussed the case with the claimant and had obtained specific instructions to apply for permission to appeal.

Paragraphs (5) and (6)

3.450 These paragraphs enable a party who is present at a hearing of a social security case to be represented or assisted at the hearing by any person, without there having been any formal notice of appointment. Although the Tribunal's permission is required, it is suggested that, unless r.37(4) applies, it will only exceptionally be appropriate for the Upper Tribunal to refuse permission, particularly as the party need only provide a written notice under para.(2) in order to avoid the need for permission. Without a written notice of appointment, a person who acts as a representative at a hearing has no rights as a representative outside the hearing. Obviously, a written notice may be provided at the hearing so that the person becomes entitled to act as a full representative thereafter.

Paragraphs (7) and (8)

3.451 These paragraphs do not apply to social security cases.

Calculating time

3.452 **12.**—(1) An act required by these Rules, a practice direction or a direction to be done on or by a particular day must be done by 5pm on that day.

(2) If the time specified by these Rules, a practice direction or a direction for doing any act ends on a day other than a working day, the act is done in time if it is done on the next working day.

(3) In a special educational needs case or a disability discrimination in schools case, the following days must not be counted when calculating the time by which an act must be done—

(a) 25th December to 1st January inclusive; and

(b) any day in August.

[[2] (3A) In an asylum case or an immigration case, when calculating the time by which an act must be done, in addition to the days specified in the definition of "working days" in rule 1 (interpretation), the following days must also not be counted as working days—

(a) 27th to 31st December inclusive; [[4] . . .]

(b) [[4] . . .]]

(4) Paragraph (3) [[2] or (3A)] does not apply where the Upper Tribunal directs that an act must be done by or on a specified date.

[[1] (5) [[3] . . .]]

AMENDMENTS

1. Tribunal Procedure (Amendment) Rules 2009 (SI 2009/274) r.9 (April 1, 2009).

2. Tribunal Procedure (Amendment No.2) Rules 2010 (SI 2010/44) rr.2 and 9 (February 15, 2010).

3. Tribunal Procedure (Amendment No.3) Rules 2014 (SI 2014/2128) rr.2 and 6(b) (September 1, 2014).

4. Tribunal Procedure (Amendment No.3) Rules 2014 (SI 2014/2128) rr.2 and 6(a) (October 20, 2014).

DEFINITIONS

"asylum case"—see r.1(3).

"disability discrimination in schools case"—*ibid.*

"immigration case"—*ibid.*

"practice direction"—*ibid.*

"special educational needs case"—*ibid.*

"working day"—*ibid.*

Sending and delivery of documents

13.—(1) [5 Subject to paragraph (1A),] any document to be provided to the Upper Tribunal under these Rules, a practice direction or a direction must be— 3.453

(a) sent by pre-paid post or [1 by document exchange, or delivered by hand] to the address specified for the proceedings;

(b) sent by fax to the number specified for the proceedings; [5 ...]

[5(ba) uploaded to the Upper Tribunal's secure portal; or]

(c) sent or delivered by such other method as the Upper Tribunal may permit or direct.

[5 (1A) A practice direction may specify for any document subject to paragraph (1)—

(a) the requirements that must be fulfilled for it to be uploaded to the Upper Tribunal's secure portal; and

(b) for any specified category of party in any specified category of case, that it must be so uploaded to the Upper Tribunal's secure portal.]

(2) Subject to [5 paragraphs (2A) and (3)], if a party provides a fax number, email address or other details for the electronic transmission of documents to them [5 (including transmission through the Upper Tribunal's secure portal)], that party must accept delivery of documents by that method.

[5 (2A) A party is required to accept delivery of documents through the Upper Tribunal's secure portal only if the document is sent through that portal to that party by the Upper Tribunal.]

(3) If a party informs the Upper Tribunal and all other parties that a particular form of communication, other than pre-paid post or delivery by hand, should not be used to provide documents to that party, that form of communication must not be so used.

(4) If the Upper Tribunal or a party sends a document to a party or the Upper Tribunal by email or any other electronic means of communication [5 (including transmission through the Upper Tribunal's secure portal)], the recipient may request that the sender provide a hard copy of the document to the recipient. The recipient must make such a request as soon as reasonably practicable after receiving the document electronically.

(5) The Upper Tribunal and each party may assume that the address provided by a party or its representative is and remains the address to which documents should be sent or delivered until receiving written notification to the contrary.

[2 (6) Subject to paragraph (7), if a document submitted to the Upper Tribunal is not written in English, it must be accompanied by an English Translation.

(7) In proceedings that are in Wales or have a connection with Wales, a document or translation may be submitted to the [3 Upper] Tribunal in Welsh.]

[4 (8) In judicial review proceedings, unless the contrary is proved, a document sent by first class post will be deemed to be provided or received on the second working day after it was posted.]

AMENDMENTS

1. Tribunal Procedure (Amendment) Rules 2009 (SI 2009/274) r.10 (April 1, 2009).

2. Tribunal Procedure (Amendment No.2) Rules 2010 (SI 2010/44) rr.2 and 10 (February 15, 2010).
3. Tribunal Procedure (Amendment No. 4) Rules 2013 (SI 2013/2067) rr.2 and 8 (November 1, 2013).
4. Tribunal Procedure (Amendment) Rules 2022 (SI 2022/312) r.3(1) and (2) (April 6, 2022).
5. Tribunal Procedure (Amendment) Rules 2023 (SI 2023/327) r.5 (April 6, 2023).

DEFINITIONS

"asylum case"—see r.1(3).
"document"—*ibid.*
"immigration case"—*ibid.*
"judicial review proceedings"—*ibid.*
"party"—*ibid.*
"practice direction"—*ibid.*

GENERAL NOTE

3.454 See the note to r.13 of the Tribunal Procedure (First-tier Tribunal) (Social Entitlement Chamber) Rules 2008, above.

The Administrative Appeals Chamber of the Upper Tribunal generally permits documents to be submitted by email and, even before the 2023 amendments to this rule, it permitted documents to be filed online through CE-File, as to which the Chamber President has issued the following guidance (published at *https://www.judiciary.uk/wp-content/uploads/2022/04/UT-AAC-CE-File-Guidance-Note-1.pdf*).

"Upper Tribunal Administrative Appeals Chamber
Note for Users
Electronic Filing of Documents Online: CE-File

1. CE-File is the online system for filing documents electronically at the Upper Tribunal Administrative Appeals Chamber ('the Tribunal'). It is also a database that enables Tribunal users to access their cases.
2. It is now a permitted method for sending and delivering documents to the Tribunal for the purpose of rule 13(1)(c) of the Tribunal Procedure (Upper Tribunal) Rules 2008 (SI 2008/2698, 'the Upper Tribunal Rules').
3. Since CE-File became operational for internal purposes in August 2021, all new applications and appeals (other than in Scotland) have been assigned a CE-File reference number in the format UA-yyyy-xxxxxx-zzz (where yyyy is the year, xxxxxx represents the file number and zzz a suffix indicating the subject matter). Appeals in Scotland are assigned a reference number in the format: UA-yyyy- SCO-xxxxxx-zzz.
4. For proceedings commenced on or after 7 March 2022, any party or their representative may use CE-File to make applications and appeals and provide documents to the Tribunal. To do so, they must first register, as is explained at [9] below. Parties and representatives may also use it in other proceedings where the Tribunal has provided a CE-File reference in the format UA-yyyy-xxxxxx-zzz.
5. Professional representatives are strongly encouraged to use CE-File to commence new cases or deliver documents to the Tribunal. In due course, its use may become mandatory so professional representatives are encouraged to familiarise themselves with the system as soon as possible.
6. Litigants in person (unrepresented parties) may also use CE-File, but the Tribunal will continue to accept documents from all users by post, DX, fax, email or by hand. As use of CE-File relies on scanned documents, unrepresented users

may prefer to continue to use other methods e.g. post and will not be disadvantaged by doing so.

7. CE-File has size limits. Parties or representatives may use CE-File to lodge electronic bundles if the size limit (currently 50MB) allows but, if it is appropriate in any particular case to lodge a larger bundle, they will need to use other means (e.g. the Tribunal's Document Upload Centre) to file the bundle.

8. It remains the case that fees are not payable in proceedings in the Tribunal.

Registering for and using CE-File

9. To use CE-File, users must first register as an E-Filer. This will allow users to file documents electronically. To register or log in and file a document using CE-File, a party or representative should follow these 4 steps:

(a) access the CE-File website address: *https://efile.cefile-app.com/login*;

(b) log on to an existing account or register for an account by following the 'Register as an E-Filer' link at the bottom of the landing page;

(c) enter details of a new case or use the details of an existing case (select 'Upper Tribunal (Administrative Appeals Chamber)' from the 'Courts' menu and then select whether this is a filing for a 'New Case' or an 'Existing Case');

(d) upload the appropriate document (explain what is being filed and upload the claim/application form or documents in Microsoft Word or PDF format).

Once a filing in a new case is accepted, a case number will be created and users will be notified of it in CE-File and via email. In CE-File this will appear in the top right corner of the screen.

DAME JUDITH FARBEY DBE
CHAMBER PRESIDENT
11 April 2022"

Use of documents and information

14.—(1) The Upper Tribunal may make an order prohibiting the disclosure or publication of— 3.455

(a) specified documents or information relating to the proceedings; or

(b) any matter likely to lead members of the public to identify any person whom the Upper Tribunal considers should not be identified.

(2) The Upper Tribunal may give a direction prohibiting the disclosure of a document or information to a person if—

(a) the Upper Tribunal is satisfied that such disclosure would be likely to cause that person or some other person serious harm; and

(b) the Upper Tribunal is satisfied, having regard to the interests of justice, that it is proportionate to give such a direction.

(3) If a party ("the first party") considers that the Upper Tribunal should give a direction under paragraph (2) prohibiting the disclosure of a document or information to another party ("the second party"), the first party must—

(a) exclude the relevant document or information from any documents that will be provided to the second party; and

(b) provide to the Upper Tribunal the excluded document or information, and the reason for its exclusion, so that the Upper Tribunal may decide whether the document or information should be disclosed to the second party or should be the subject of a direction under paragraph (2).

(4) [[1] . . .]

(5) If the Upper Tribunal gives a direction under paragraph (2) which prevents disclosure to a party who has appointed a representative, the Upper Tribunal may give a direction that the documents or information be disclosed to that representative if the Upper Tribunal is satisfied that—

(a) disclosure to the representative would be in the interests of the party; and

(b) the representative will act in accordance with paragraph (6).

(6) Documents or information disclosed to a representative in accordance with a direction under paragraph (5) must not be disclosed either directly or indirectly to any other person without the Upper Tribunal's consent.

(7) Unless the Upper Tribunal gives a direction to the contrary, information about mental health cases and the names of any persons concerned in such cases must not be made public.

[[1] (8) The Upper Tribunal may, on its own initiative or on the application of a party, give a direction that certain documents or information must or may be disclosed to the Upper Tribunal on the basis that the Upper Tribunal will not disclose such documents or information to other persons, or specified other persons.

[[2] (8A) In a trade remedies case, the Upper Tribunal may give a direction under paragraph (8) if the Upper Tribunal is satisfied that—

(a) where such documents or information have been supplied to the TRA, the TRA is treating such documents or information as confidential in accordance with—

(i) regulation 45 of the Trade Remedies (Dumping and Subsidisation) (EU Exit) Regulations 2019;

(ii) regulation 16 of the Trade Remedies (Increase in Imports Causing Serious Injury to UK Producers) (EU Exit) Regulations 2019; or

(iii) regulation 5 of the Trade Remedies (Reconsideration and Appeals) (EU Exit) Regulations 2019; or

(b) where such documents or information have not been supplied to the TRA, if such documents or information were to be supplied to the TRA in accordance with regulation 5 of the Trade Remedies (Reconsideration and Appeals) (EU Exit) Regulations 2019, the TRA would be entitled to treat such documents or information as confidential in accordance with that regulation,

and the Upper Tribunal is not precluded from considering such documents or information in making its decision in the case.]

(9) A party making an application for a direction under paragraph (8) may withhold the relevant documents or information from other parties until the Upper Tribunal has granted or refused the application.

(10) In a case involving matters relating to national security, the Upper Tribunal must ensure that information is not disclosed contrary to the interests of national security.

(11) The Upper Tribunal must conduct proceedings and record its decision and reasons appropriately so as not to undermine the effect of an order made under paragraph (1), a direction given under paragraph (2) or (8) or the duty imposed by paragraph (10).]

AMENDMENTS

1. Tribunal Procedure (Amendment No.2) Rules 2009 (SI 2009/1975) rr.7 and 13 (September 1, 2009).

2. Tribunal Procedure (Amendment) Rules 2019 (SI 2019/925) r.2(1) and (3) (June 3, 2019, subject to a saving).

DEFINITIONS

"document"—see r.1(3).
"mental health case"—*ibid.*
"party"—*ibid.*
"TRA"—*ibid.*
"trade remedies case"—*ibid.*

GENERAL NOTE

Paragraph (1)

See the note to r.14(1) of the Tribunal Procedure (First-tier Tribunal) (Social Entitlement Chamber) Rules 2008, above. **3.456**

Note para.(11), which requires the Upper Tribunal to conduct its proceedings and record its decisions and reasons appropriately so as not to undermine the effect of its order.

A breach of an order made under this paragraph is a contempt of court and may be punished by the Upper Tribunal under s.25 of the Tribunals, Courts and Enforcement Act 2007 by a term of imprisonment not exceeding two years and an unlimited fine.

The Administrative Appeals Chamber of the Upper Tribunal has a general practice of anonymising decisions in social security and child support cases and in some other types of case, when publishing them (other than to the parties) or when referring to them, but this does not amount to the making of orders under r.14(1). Unless a specific order is made, claimants or others who know about the cases are not subject to any reporting restrictions and, indeed, claimants may ask that their cases are not anonymised (*Adams v SSWP (CSM)* [2017] UKUT 9 (AAC); [2017] AACR 28). However, staff in the Department for Work and Pensions, His Majesty's Revenue and Customs and His Majesty's Courts and Tribunals Service are prohibited from publishing information acquired in the course of their employment and which relates to a particular person involved in a tax, child support or social security case (Finance Act 1989 s.182; Child Support Act 1991 s.50; Social Security Administration Act 1992 s.123 and Sch.4). **3.457**

For the Administrative Appeal Chamber's approach to a request for anonymity in a non-social security case where anonymisation is not usual, see *D v IC* [2018] UKUT 441 (AAC). That decision was upheld by the Court of Appeal in *Moss v Information Commissioner* [2020] EWCA Civ 580, which includes a useful summary of the relevant case law.

Paragraphs (2)–(6)

See the note to r.14(2)–(6) of the Tribunal Procedure (First-tier Tribunal) (Social Entitlement Chamber) Rules 2008, above. Note para.(11), which requires the Upper Tribunal to conduct its proceedings and record its decisions and reasons appropriately so as not to undermine the effect of its direction. Particularly relevant will be the power in r.37(4)(c) to exclude a person from a hearing, and the power in r.40(2) not to provide a full decision, in order to give effect to a direction under para.(2). **3.458**

Paragraph (7)

This paragraph does not apply to social security cases and, in applying to *all* information, appears anomalous. **3.459**

Paragraphs (8)–(10)

3.460 Although these paragraphs are broadly expressed, they are unlikely to be relevant in social security cases.

Paragraph (11)

3.461 See, in particular, rr.37(4)(c) and 40(3), empowering the Upper Tribunal to exclude a person from proceedings and to record its decision and reasons so as to comply with this duty. Reporting restrictions under para.(1) may also be necessary in order to back up a direction under para.(2).

Evidence and submissions

3.462 **15.**—(1) Without restriction on the general powers in rule 5(1) and (2) (case management powers), the Upper Tribunal may give directions as to—

(a) issues on which it requires evidence or submissions;
(b) the nature of the evidence or submissions it requires;
(c) whether the parties are permitted or required to provide expert evidence, and if so whether the parties must jointly appoint a single expert to provide such evidence;
(d) any limit on the number of witnesses whose evidence a party may put forward, whether in relation to a particular issue or generally;
(e) the manner in which any evidence or submissions are to be provided, which may include a direction for them to be given—
  (i) orally at a hearing; or
  (ii) by written submissions or witness statement; and
(f) the time at which any evidence or submissions are to be provided.

(2) The Upper Tribunal may—

(a) admit evidence whether or not—
  (i) the evidence would be admissible in a civil trial in the United Kingdom; or
  (ii) the evidence was available to a previous decision maker; or
(b) exclude evidence that would otherwise be admissible where—
  (i) the evidence was not provided within the time allowed by a direction or a practice direction;
  (ii) the evidence was otherwise provided in a manner that did not comply with a direction or a practice direction; or
  (iii) it would otherwise be unfair to admit the evidence.

[[1] (2A) In an asylum case or an immigration case—

(a) if a party wishes the Upper Tribunal to consider evidence that was not before the First-tier Tribunal, that party must send or deliver a notice to the Upper Tribunal and any other party—
  (i) indicating the nature of the evidence; and
  (ii) explaining why it was not submitted to the First-tier Tribunal; and
(b) when considering whether to admit evidence that was not before the First-tier Tribunal, the Upper Tribunal must have regard to whether there has been unreasonable delay in producing that evidence.]

(3) The Upper Tribunal may consent to a witness giving, or require any witness to give, evidence on oath, and may administer an oath for that pur-pose.

AMENDMENT

1. Tribunal Procedure (Amendment No.2) Rules 2010 (SI 2010/44) rr.2 and 11 (February 15, 2010).

DEFINITIONS

"asylum case"—see r.1(3).
"hearing"—*ibid.*
"immigration case"—*ibid.*
"party"—*ibid.*
"practice direction"—*ibid.*

GENERAL NOTE

See the note to r.15 of the Tribunal Procedure (First-tier Tribunal) (Social Entitlement Chamber) Rules 2008, above. **3.463**

In *PR v SSWP (PIP)* [2021] UKUT 35 (AAC), the Upper Tribunal considered the criteria for admitting evidence for the purpose of proving that the First-tier Tribunal had made an error of fact that amounted to an error of law (see the annotation to s.11 of the Tribunals, Courts and Enforcement Act 2007, above) and concluded that the strict approach taken in *Ladd v Marshall* [1954] 1 W.L.R. 1489 was not appropriate.

Summoning or citation of witnesses and orders to answer questions or produce documents

16.—(1) On the application of a party or on its own initiative, the Upper Tribunal may— **3.464**

(a) by summons (or, in Scotland, citation) require any person to attend as a witness at a hearing at the time and place specified in the summons or citation; or
(b) order any person to answer any questions or produce any documents in that person's possession or control which relate to any issue in the proceedings.

(2) A summons or citation under paragraph (1)(a) must—

(a) give the person required to attend 14 days' notice of the hearing or such shorter period as the Upper Tribunal may direct; and
(b) where the person is not a party, make provision for the person's necessary expenses of attendance to be paid, and state who is to pay them.

(3) No person may be compelled to give any evidence or produce any document that the person could not be compelled to give or produce on a trial of an action in a court of law in the part of the United Kingdom where the proceedings are due to be determined.

[[1] (4) A person who receives a summons, citation or order may apply to the Upper Tribunal for it to be varied or set aside if they did not have an opportunity to object to it before it was made or issued.

(5) A person making an application under paragraph (4) must do so as soon as reasonably practicable after receiving notice of the summons, citation or order.

(6) A summons, citation or order under this rule must—

(a) state that the person on whom the requirement is imposed may apply to the Upper Tribunal to vary or set aside the summons, citation or order, if they did not have an opportunity to object to it before it was made or issued; and

(b) state the consequences of failure to comply with the summons, citation or order.]

AMENDMENT

1. Tribunal Procedure (Amendment) Rules 2009 (SI 2009/274) r.11 (April 1, 2009).

DEFINITIONS

"document"—see r.1(3).
"hearing"—*ibid.*
"party"—*ibid.*

GENERAL NOTE

3.465 This rule includes a power to order the production of documents without requiring attendance at a hearing. A failure to comply with a summons, citation or order under this rule is a contempt of court that may be punished by the Upper Tribunal with a term of imprisonment not exceeding two years and an unlimited fine under s.25 of the Tribunals, Courts and Enforcement Act 2007. In *MD v SSWP (Enforcement Reference)* [2010] UKUT 202 (AAC); [2011] AACR 5, a three-judge panel suggested that, when committal for contempt is being considered, a failure to comply with any of the procedural requirements is unlikely to be overlooked, unless it was clear that there was no prejudice or injustice to the alleged contemnor in doing so. It also suggested that a warning such as is required by r.16(6)(b) should be in explicit terms, referring to the possibility of imprisonment or a fine.

More controversially, when commenting on a failure to "make provision for the person's necessary expenses of attendance to be paid" (see r.16(2)(b)), it said that "[a] witness such as a doctor who is ordered to attend a hearing may clearly incur very considerable expenses". That is plainly a material consideration when deciding whether it is proportionate to issue a summons at all but it is not clear that r.16(2)(b) requires the payment of anything other than travel and subsistence expenses. Since then, it has been held by another three-judge panel in *CB v Suffolk CC (Enforcement Reference)* [2010] UKUT 202 (AAC); [2011] AACR 22 that the scheme of expenses for witnesses operated by the Tribunals Service, which was the same as that for jurors and covered travel expenses and loss of earnings up to a fixed limit, was sufficient for compliance with r.16(2)(b) and that it was not necessary to compensate for all financial loss.

Withdrawal

3.466 **17.**—(1) Subject to paragraph (2), a party may give notice of the withdrawal of its case, or any part of it—

(a) [2 . . .] by sending or delivering to the Upper Tribunal a written notice of withdrawal; or

(b) orally at a hearing.

(2) Notice of withdrawal will not take effect unless the Upper Tribunal consents to the withdrawal except in relation to an application for permission to appeal.

(3) A party which has withdrawn its case may apply to the Upper Tribunal for the case to be reinstated.

(4) An application under paragraph (3) must be made in writing and be received by the Upper Tribunal within 1 month after—

(a) the date on which the Upper Tribunal received the notice under paragraph (1)(a); or

(b) the date of the hearing at which the case was withdrawn orally under paragraph (1)(b).

(5) The Upper Tribunal must notify each party in writing [2 that a withdrawal has taken effect]under this rule.

[1 (6) Paragraph (3) does not apply to a financial services case other than a reference against a penalty.]

AMENDMENTS

1. Tribunal Procedure (Upper Tribunal) (Amendment) Rules 2010 (SI 2010/747) rr.2 and 7 (April 6, 2010).

2. Tribunal Procedure (Amendment) Rules 2013 (SI 2013/477) rr.49 and 54 (April 1, 2013).

DEFINITIONS

"financial service case"—see r.1(3).
"hearing"—*ibid.*
"party"—*ibid.*
"permission"—*ibid.*

GENERAL NOTE

This rule replaces reg.26 of the Social Security Commissioners (Procedure) Regulations 1999 but it applies to the withdrawal of a respondent's case as well as to the case of an appellant or person making a reference. The existence of the one-month time limit for an application for reinstatement, which did not exist in the old provision, may suggest that an application should be granted if made within that period unless there is a clear reason for not doing so, such as the previous conduct of the party, obvious lack of merit in the case or prejudice to another party. **3.467**

17A. *Omitted.* **3.468**

Notice of funding of legal services

18. If a party is granted funding of legal services at any time, that party must as soon as practicable— **3.469**

(a) (i) if [1 civil legal services (within the meaning of section 8 of the Legal Aid, Sentencing and Punishment of Offenders Act 2012) are provided under arrangements made for the purposes of Part 1 of that Act or by] the Northern Ireland Legal Services Commission, send a copy of the [1 certificate or] funding notice to the Upper Tribunal; or

(ii) if funding is granted by the Scottish Legal Aid Board, send a copy of the legal aid certificate to the Upper Tribunal; and

(b) notify every other party in writing that funding has been granted.

AMENDMENT

1. Tribunal Procedure (Amendment) Rules 2013 (SI 2013/477) rr.49 and 55 (April 1, 2013).

DEFINITION

"party"—see r.1(3).

General Note

3.470 Public funding is rare in social security cases but it is helpful for a judge to know whether a party is funded if he or she is considering directing the party to produce a submission or a bundle of documents.

It will also be relevant in judicial review proceedings and other proceedings where the Upper Tribunal has the power to award costs.

[1 Confidentiality in social security and child support cases

3.471 **19.**—(1) Paragraph (4) applies to an appeal against a decision of the First-tier Tribunal—

(a) in proceedings under the Child Support Act 1991 in the circumstances described in paragraph (2), other than an appeal against a reduced benefit decision (as defined in section 46(10)(b) of the Child Support Act 1991, as that section had effect prior to the commencement of section 15(b) of the Child Maintenance and Other Payments Act 2008); or

(b) in proceedings where the parties to the appeal include former joint claimants who are no longer living together in the circumstances described in paragraph (3).

(2) The circumstances referred to in paragraph (1)(a) are that—

(a) in the proceedings in the First-tier Tribunal in respect of which the appeal has been brought, there was an obligation to keep a person's address confidential; or

(b) an absent parent, non-resident parent or person with care would like their address or the address of the child to be kept confidential and has given notice to that effect to the Upper Tribunal—

(i) in an application for permission to appeal or notice of appeal;

(ii) within 1 month after an enquiry by the Upper Tribunal; or

(iii) when notifying any subsequent change of address after proceedings have been started.

(3 The circumstances referred to in paragraph (1)(b) are that—

(a) in the proceedings in the First-tier Tribunal in respect of which the appeal has been brought, there was an obligation to keep a person's address confidential; or

(b) one of the former joint claimants would like their address to be kept confidential and has given notice to that effect to the Upper Tribunal—

(i) in an application for permission to appeal or notice of appeal;

(ii) within 1 month after an enquiry by the Upper Tribunal; or

(iii) when notifying any subsequent change of address after proceedings have been started.

(4) Where this paragraph applies, the Secretary of State or other decision maker and the Upper Tribunal must take appropriate steps to secure the confidentiality of the address and of any information which could reasonably be expected to enable a person to identify the address, to the extent that the address or that information is not already known to each other party.

(5) In this rule—

"absent parent", "non-resident parent" and "person with care" have the meanings set out in section 3 of the Child Support Act 1991;

"joint claimants" means the persons who made a joint claim for a jobseeker's allowance under the Jobseekers Act 1995, a tax credit under the Tax Credits Act 2002 or in relation to whom an award of universal credit is made under Part 1 of the Welfare Reform Act 2012.]

Amendment

1. Tribunal Procedure (Amendment No.3) Rules 2014 (SI 2014/2128) rr.2 and 7 (October 20, 2014).

Definitions

"absent parent"—see para.(5).
"joint claimants"—*ibid.*
"non-resident parent"—*ibid.*
"party"—see r.1(3).
"permission"—*ibid.*
"person with care" —see para.(5).

Power to pay expenses and allowances

20.—(1) In proceedings brought under section 4 of the Safeguarding Vulnerable Groups Act 2006 [1. . .], the Secretary of State may pay such allowances for the purpose of or in connection with the attendance of persons at hearings as the Secretary of State may, with the consent of the Treasury, determine. 3.472

(2) Paragraph (3) applies to proceedings on appeal from a decision of—

(a) the First-tier Tribunal in proceedings under the Child Support Act 1991, section 12 of the Social Security Act 1998 or paragraph 6 of Schedule 7 to the Child Support, Pensions and Social Security Act 2000;

(b) the First-tier Tribunal in a war pensions and armed forces case (as defined in the Tribunal Procedure (First-tier Tribunal) (War Pensions and Armed Forces Compensation Chamber) Rules 2008); or

(c) a Pensions Appeal Tribunal for Scotland or Northern Ireland.

(3) The Lord Chancellor (or, in Scotland, the Secretary of State) may pay to any person who attends any hearing such travelling and other allowances, including compensation for loss of remunerative time, as the Lord Chancellor (or, in Scotland, the Secretary of State) may determine.

Amendment

1. Tribunal Procedure (Amendment) Rules 2009 (SI 2009/274) r.12 (April 1, 2009).

Definitions

"hearing"—see r.1(3).
"judicial review proceedings"—*ibid.*

General Note

Paragraph (1) does not apply to social security cases. Paragraphs (2) and (3) reproduce the effect of para.3 of Sch.4 to the Social Security Act 1998. Paragraph (2) suffers from the same defect as the old provision, which is that it does not apply to all social security cases in which claimants might be required to attend hearings, although in practice HM Courts and Tribunals Service seems never to have refused to pay expenses to those not within the scope of the old provision (e.g. an injured 3.473

person appealing against a decision under the Social Security (Recovery of Benefits) Act 1997).

The rule is also unsatisfactory because it seems unlikely that para.10(4) of Sch.5 to the Tribunals, Courts and Enforcement Act 2007 envisages Rules that give the Secretary of State the power to determine what expenses are to be paid, although it is perhaps more appropriate that the power should lie with the Secretary of State than with the Tribunal Procedure Committee.

3.474 **20A.** *Omitted.*
20B. *Omitted.*

PART 3

[PROCEDURE FOR CASES IN] THE UPPER TRIBUNAL

Application to the Upper Tribunal for permission to appeal

3.475 **21.**—(1) [1 . . .]

[6 (1A) This rule does not apply to an application for permission to appeal to the Upper Tribunal if such application is made under rule 24 (response to notice of appeal).]

(2) A person may apply to the Upper Tribunal for permission to appeal to the Upper Tribunal against a decision of another tribunal only if—

(a) they have made an application for permission to appeal to the tribunal which made the decision challenged; and

(b) that application has been refused or has not been admitted [3 or has been granted only on limited grounds.]

(3) An application for permission to appeal must be made in writing and received by the Upper Tribunal no later than—

(a) in the case of an application under section 4 of the Safeguarding Vulnerable Groups Act 2006, 3 months after the date on which written notice of the decision being challenged was sent to the appellant; [2 . . .

(aa) [5 in an asylum case or an immigration case where the appellant is in the United Kingdom at the time that the application is made, 14 days after the date on which notice of the First-tier Tribunal's refusal of permission was sent to the appellant;]

(ab) [4 . . .] or]

(b) otherwise, a month after the date on which the tribunal that made the decision under challenge sent notice of its refusal of permission to appeal, or refusal to admit the application for permission to appeal, to the appellant.

[2 (3A) [4. . .]]

(4) The application must state—

(a) the name and address of the appellant;

(b) the name and address of the representative (if any) of the appellant;

(c) an address where documents for the appellant may be sent or delivered;

(d) details (including the full reference) of the decision challenged;

(e) the grounds on which the appellant relies; and

(f) whether the appellant wants the application to be dealt with at a hearing.

(5) The appellant must provide with the application a copy of—

(a) any written record of the decision being challenged;

(b) any separate written statement of reasons for that decision; and

(c) if the application is for permission to appeal against a decision of another tribunal, the notice of refusal of permission to appeal, or notice of refusal to admit the application for permission to appeal, from that other tribunal.

(6) If the appellant provides the application to the Upper Tribunal later than the time required by paragraph (3) or by an extension of time allowed under rule 5(3)(a) (power to extend time)—

(a) the application must include a request for an extension of time and the reason why the application was not provided in time; and

(b) unless the Upper Tribunal extends time for the application under rule 5(3)(a) (power to extend time) the Upper Tribunal must not admit the application.

(7) If the appellant makes an application to the Upper Tribunal for permission to appeal against the decision of another tribunal, and that other tribunal refused to admit the appellant's application for permission to appeal because the application for permission or for a written statement of reasons was not made in time—

(a) the application to the Upper Tribunal for permission to appeal must include the reason why the application to the other tribunal for permission to appeal or for a written statement of reasons, as the case may be, was not made in time; and

(b) the Upper Tribunal must only admit the application if the Upper Tribunal considers that it is in the interests of justice for it to do so.

[[3] (8) In this rule, a reference to notice of a refusal of permission to appeal is to be taken to include a reference to notice of a grant of permission to appeal on limited grounds.]

AMENDMENTS

1. Tribunal Procedure (Amendment No.2) Rules 2009 (SI 2009/1975) rr.7 and 15 (September 1, 2009).

2. Tribunal Procedure (Amendment No.2) Rules 2010 (SI 2010/44) rr.2 and 13 (February 15, 2010).

3. Tribunal Procedure (Amendment) Rules 2014 (SI 2014/514) rr.2 and 7 (April 6, 2014).

4. Tribunal Procedure (Amendment No.3) Rules 2014 (SI 2014/2128) rr.2 and 8 (October 20, 2014).

5. Tribunal Procedure (Amendment) Rules 2020 (SI 2020/651) r.5(1) and (6) (July 21, 2020).

6. Tribunal Procedure (Amendment) Rules 2022 (SI 2022/312) r.3(1) and (3) (April 6, 2022).

DEFINITIONS

"appellant"—see r.1(3).
"asylum case"—see r.1(3).
"document"—*ibid.*
"hearing"—*ibid.*

"immigration case"—*ibid.*
"permission"—*ibid.*

General Note

3.476 This replaces regs 9 and 10 of the Social Security Commissioners (Procedure) Regulations 1999 but without the absolute time limit of 13 months and without any express duty on a public authority to notify a claimant that it has made an application.

Paragraph (2)

3.477 Paragraph (2) has given rise to some difficulties. Generally, it will be enforced because an application to the First-tier Tribunal gives it the opportunity to review its decision but there are circumstances where the existence of an irregularity emerges only after a case has apparently been properly brought before the Upper Tribunal or where the Upper Tribunal wishes to give permission in a case related to another one already before it or the applicant has been misadvised by the First-tier Tribunal. In such cases waiving the requirement to apply to the lower tribunal for permission may be sensible.

In *HM v SSWP* [2009] UKUT 40 (AAC), the claimant applied to what was then an appeal tribunal for leave to appeal but was then wrongly told that leave had been granted when in fact no decision had been made. The Upper Tribunal held it had no jurisdiction to consider the appeal, referring to *CSCS/4/2008*, where a Commissioner had said that a breach of the similar requirement in reg.9(1) of the Social Security Commissioners (Procedure) Regulations 1999 had not been the sort of irregularity that could be waived. However, in *MA v SSD* [2009] UKUT 57 (AAC), another judge disagreed with that approach and held that, as the requirement to obtain a ruling from the First-tier Tribunal was imposed by the Rules rather than by primary legislation, it could be waived under r.7(2)(a). He did not in fact waive it in that case, where a chairman of a Pensions Appeal Tribunal had purported to grant leave to appeal but had done so unlawfully because the application had been made more than 13 months late, in breach of the absolute time-limit that then applied. The Upper Tribunal judge took the view that the Secretary of State should not have the advantage of the time bar removed retrospectively. If the irregularity was on the part of the Pensions Appeal Tribunal rather then the appellant, it is arguable that the power of waiver arose by implication under r.7(1) rather than expressly under r.7(2)(a) (see the note to r.7), although it is also arguable both that the material irregularity lay in the applicant making her application late and that r.21(2) imposes on an appellant a duty to obtain a valid decision so that the appellant is in any event in breach if the decision is invalid.

Nonetheless, whatever detailed criticism might be made of the reasoning of that decision, it was followed in *ZN v Redbridge LBC (HB)* [2013] UKUT 503 (AAC) insofar as it was held that a failure to obtain a ruling from the First-tier Tribunal may be waived and that proposition is no longer in doubt.

The same view has been taken in the Immigration and Asylum Chamber of the Upper Tribunal when the First-tier Tribunal refused to consider the application made to it (*Ved v SSHD* [2014] UKUT 150 (IAC)).

However, in *SSHD v Smith (appealable decisions; PTA requirements; anonymity)* [2019] UKUT 216 (IAC) at [54], it was said that "[t]he Upper Tribunal is very unlikely to be sympathetic to a request that it should invoke rule 7(2)(a), where a person who could and should have applied for permission to appeal to the First-tier Tribunal against an adverse decision of that body seeks to challenge that adverse decision only after the other party has been given permission to appeal against a decision in the same proceedings which was in favour of the first-mentioned person". (See the note to s.11(3) and (4) of the Tribunals, Courts and Enforcement Act 2007, above, for the limited circumstances in which it may be necessary to obtain permission to cross-appeal.)

In *WO'C v SSWP (CSM)* [2020] UKUT 34 (AAC), the Upper Tribunal declined to waive the irregularity under r.7(2)(b)—in circumstances explained in the note to reg.38(7) of the Tribunal Procedure (First-tier Tribunal) (Social Entitlement Chamber Rules 2008—in view of delay on the part of the applicant at an earlier stage in the proceedings. The Upper Tribunal could presumably have considered the reasons for the delay itself as part of its consideration of whether or not to waive the irregularity but there was no evidence on that point before it so that the applicant would have had to be given a specific opportunity to make representations on that issue. He was therefore left to make a late application to the First-tier Tribunal for permission to appeal in the ordinary way.

Paragraphs (3)–(7)

Note that, under para.(3), the application must now be *received* by the Upper Tribunal within the time limit. The power to extend time is no longer limited to cases where there are "special reasons" but that may not make much difference in practice because the same considerations are likely to be relevant (see the note to r.38(5) of the Tribunal Procedure (First-tier Tribunal) (Social Entitlement Chamber) Rules 2008, above). Paragraph (7) makes it clear that, where an application for permission made to the First-tier Tribunal was made late but nonetheless accepted, there is no need for the Upper Tribunal to consider that delay (giving effect to *CIB/4791/2001*). Paragraph (7) also makes specific provision for cases where there is no statement of the First-tier Tribunal's reasons due to delay in applying for one. The word "any" in para.(5)(b) has the effect that there is no longer an irregularity just because no statement of reasons is submitted in such a case. However, it remains difficult to demonstrate an error of law without a statement of reasons and, in particular, the First-tier Tribunal's decision cannot be challenged on the ground of inadequacy of reasons in the absence of either such a statement or a duty to provide one (*R(IS) 11/99*). 3.478

If there is a question as to whether the proceedings before the First-tier Tribunal were fair and it is not answered by the recording of the hearing or the First-tier Tribunal's statement of reasons, it is likely to be necessary for the parties to produce adequate evidence to support their arguments. Mere assertions based on second- or third-hand hearsay are unlikely to be sufficient (*Singh v Secretary of State for the Home Department* [2016] EWCA Civ 492; *AA v Bristol CC* [2023] UKUT 52 (AAC)).

Decision in relation to permission to appeal

22.—(1) [4 [5 [8 If the Upper Tribunal refuses permission to appeal [3 or refuses to admit a late application for permission], it must send written notice of the refusal and of the reasons for the refusal to the appellant. 3.479

(2) If the Upper Tribunal gives permission to appeal—

(a) the Upper Tribunal must send written notice of the permission, and of the reasons for any limitations or conditions on such permission, to each party;

(b) subject to any direction by the Upper Tribunal, the application for permission to appeal stands as the notice of appeal and the Upper Tribunal must send to each respondent a copy of the application for permission to appeal and any documents provided with it by the appellant; and

(c) the Upper Tribunal may, with the consent of the appellant and each respondent, determine the appeal without obtaining any further response.

[1 (3) Paragraph (4) applies where the Upper Tribunal, without a hearing, determines an application for permission to appeal—

(a) against a decision of—

(i) the Tax Chamber of the First-tier Tribunal;

(ii) the Health, Education and Social Care Chamber of the First-tier Tribunal;

[2 (iia) the General Regulatory Chamber of the First-tier Tribunal;]
[3 (iib) [6 ...]]
(iii) the Mental Health Review Tribunal for Wales; or
(iv) the Special Educational Needs Tribunal for Wales; or
(b) under section 4 of the Safeguarding Vulnerable Groups Act 2006.]

(4) [7 Subject to paragraph (4A),] in the circumstances set out at paragraph (3) the appellant may apply for the decision to be reconsidered at a hearing if the Upper Tribunal—

(a) refuses permission to appeal [3 or refuses to admit a late application for permission]; or
(b) gives permission to appeal on limited grounds or subject to conditions.

[7 (4A) Where the Upper Tribunal considers the whole or part of an application to be totally without merit, it shall record that fact in its decision notice and, in those circumstances, the person seeking permission may not request the decision or part of the decision (as the case may be) to be reconsidered at a hearing.]

(5) An application under paragraph (4) must be made in writing and received by the Upper Tribunal within 14 days after the date on which the Upper Tribunal sent written notice of its decision regarding the application to the appellant.

Amendments

1. Tribunal Procedure (Amendment) Rules 2009 (SI 2009/274) r.14 (April 1, 2009).
2. Tribunal Procedure (Amendment No.2) Rules 2009 (SI 2009/1975) rr.7 and 16 (September 1, 2009).
3. Tribunal Procedure (Amendment) Rules 2014 (SI 2014/514) rr.2 and 8 (April 6, 2014).
4. Tribunal Procedure (Amendment No.2) Rules 2014 (SI 2014/1505) rr.2 and 3 (June 30, 2014).
5. Tribunal Procedure (Amendment No.3) Rules 2014 (SI 2014/2128) rr.2 and 9 (October 20, 2014).
6. Tribunal Procedure (Amendment) Rules 2018 (SI 2018/511) r.3 (April 23, 2018).
7. Tribunal Procedure (Amendment) Rules 2022 (SI 2022/312) r.3(1) and (4) (April 6, 2022).
8. The Tribunal Procedure (Amendment No. 2) Rules 2023 (SI 2023/1280) article 3 (December 25 2023).

Definitions

"appellant"—see r.1(3).
"document"—*ibid.*
"hearing"—*ibid.*
"party"—*ibid.*
"permission"—*ibid.*
"respondent"—*ibid.*

General Note

Paragraph (2)

3.480 Generally, applications for permission to appeal are considered without notice to the respondent and, when permission to appeal is granted by the Upper Tribunal, the application stands as the appeal and is sent to the respondent. In social security cases, the Upper Tribunal will have obtained the First-tier Tribunal's file to assist it determine the application and that will form the basis of the bundle of documents sent to the respondent (and to the appellant). The next stage in the proceedings will simply be for the respondent to submit a response under r.24. This is the effect of para.(2)(b).

However, where the respondent has had notice of the application and made submissions on it, it is possible to seek the consent of both parties to the appeal being determined without any further response. This is the effect of para.(2)(c).

It was held in *R. (Oceana) v Upper Tribunal (Immigration and Asylum Chamber)* [2023] EWHC 791 (Admin) at [39] to [41] that it is "entirely proper and reasonable for a judge who is determining a permission application to consult the official record of proceedings and to decide (without further recourse to the parties) whether that record corroborates an assertion in the grounds of appeal".

There is no specific provision for adding grounds of appeal after permission has been given, in cases where the grant of permission has not been expressly limited. In these circumstances, the Upper Tribunal has a broad discretionary power to admit a new ground, which it should exercise in accordance with the overriding objective in r.2 (*Bramley Ferry Supplies v HMRC* [2017] UKUT 214 (TCC)). In practice, the Administrative Appeals Chamber of the Upper Tribunal does not usually take a strict approach in social security cases, unless a very significant delay in raising a new point is liable to create unfairness towards the other party.

In *Patel v Secretary of State for the Home Department* [2015] EWCA Civ 1175, the Court of Appeal held that a tribunal had no power informally to change a decision after it had been given orally. It said that the rule in the courts that a decision could be amended until an order was drawn up did not apply in tribunals where there is simply a decision and no distinction between a judgment and an order, it being relevant that there was an express power in r.40(1) to give a decision orally. Therefore, when a judge had said that he was granting permission to appeal, he could not later during the hearing consider whether he should refuse to admit the application for permission because it was late. In *R. (Singh) v Secretary of State for the Home Department* [2019] EWCA Civ 1014, it was pointed out that the Court in *Patel* had not been referred to all the ways in which a decision of the Upper Tribunal may be changed formally. Rule 43 was not relevant in either case, because it allows for the setting aside of a refusal of permission to appeal or to apply for judicial review but not of a grant of permission, but in *Singh* the Court of Appeal held that permission to apply for judicial review given in breach of the rules of natural justice could be set aside because, under s.25 of the Tribunals, Courts and Enforcement Act, the Upper Tribunal had the same powers as the High Court. However, the main thrust of the decision in *Patel* is not undermined by its failure to appreciate all the ways in which a decision of the Upper Tribunal may formally be changed or set aside.

Paragraphs (3)–(5)

These paragraphs do not apply to social security cases on appeal from the Social Entitlement Chamber of the First-tier Tribunal. If the person applying for permission to appeal wants an oral hearing in a social security case, it is necessary to say so in the application for permission (see r.21(4)(f)). **3.481**

If permission to appeal is given to appeal on reconsideration at a hearing under para.(4), the judge who refused permission to appeal on the papers is not precluded from hearing the appeal (*Broughal v Walsh Brothers Builders Ltd* [2018] EWCA Civ 1610); [2018] 1 W.L.R. 5781).

Paragraph (4A) is similar to r.30(4A)—see the annotation thereto. Until it was added in 2022, there was no power to certify an application for permission to appeal as being totally without merit so as prevent it being renewed orally when it has been refused on the papers, but the Upper Tribunal occasionally struck out a renewed application under r.8(3)(c) when satisfied that it had no arguable merit and that the applicant had "had more than her day in court at the FTT" (*Gaskin v IC* [2016]

UKUT 382 (AAC)) or the application related to a case-management decision of the First-tier Tribunal and had no reasonable prospect of success (*Crossland v IC* [2020] UKUT 263 (AAC)). For a decision applying the new power and considering some of the authorities as to how it should be exercised, see *Fraser v IC (TWM)* [2022] UKUT 328 (AAC).

3.482 **22A.** *Omitted.*

Notice of appeal

3.483 **23.**—(1) [1 This rule applies—

(a) to proceedings on appeal to the Upper Tribunal for which permission to appeal is not required, except proceedings to which rule 26A [3 [6, 26B or 26C]] applies;

(b) if another tribunal has given permission for a party to appeal to the Upper Tribunal; or

(c) subject to any other direction by the Upper Tribunal, if the Upper Tribunal has given permission to appeal and has given a direction that the application for permission to appeal does not stand as the notice of appeal.

[2 (1A) In an asylum case or an immigration case in which the First-tier Tribunal has given permission to appeal, subject to any direction of the First-tier Tribunal or the Upper Tribunal, the application for permission to appeal sent or delivered to the First-tier Tribunal stands as the notice of appeal and accordingly paragraphs (2) to (6) of this rule do not apply.]

(2) The appellant must provide a notice of appeal to the Upper Tribunal so that it is received within 1 month after—

(a) the date that the tribunal that gave permission to appeal sent notice of such permission to the appellant; or

[5 (b) if permission to appeal is not required, the date on which notice of decision to which the appeal relates—

(i) was sent to the appellant; [7 ...]

(ii) in a quality contracts scheme case, if the notice was not sent to the appellant, the date on which the notice was published in a newspaper in accordance with the requirement of section 125 (notice and consultation requirements) of the Transport Act 2000 [7 or]]]

[7 (iii) in a trade remedies case—

(aa) where the appeal is against a decision made by the TRA and notice is required to be published in accordance with the Trade Remedies (Reconsideration and Appeals) (EU Exit) Regulations 2019, the date of such publication or (if later) when the notice comes into effect;

(bb) where the appeal is against a decision made by the TRA and no notice is required to be published in accordance with the Trade Remedies (Reconsideration and Appeals) (EU Exit) Regulations 2019, the date on which the appellant is notified of the decision, or

(cc) where the appeal is against a determination of the Secretary of State under the Taxation (Cross-border Trade) Act 2018, the Trade Remedies (Dumping and Subsidisation) (EU Exit) Regulations 2019, the Trade Remedies (Increase in Imports Causing Serious Injury to UK Producers)

(EU Exit) Regulations 2019 or the Trade Remedies (Reconsideration and Appeals) (EU Exit) Regulations 2019 (as the case may be), the date on which the notice is published in accordance with the relevant provision or (if later) when the notice comes into effect;]

(3) The notice of appeal must include the information listed in rule 21(4)(a) to (e) (content of the application for permission to appeal) and, where the Upper Tribunal has given permission to appeal, the Upper Tribunal's case reference.

(4) If another tribunal has granted permission to appeal, the appellant must provide with the notice of appeal a copy of—

(a) any written record of the decision being challenged;
(b) any separate written statement of reasons for that decision; and
(c) the notice of permission to appeal.

(5) If the appellant provides the notice of appeal to the Upper Tribunal later than the time required by paragraph (2) or by an extension of time allowed under rule 5(3)(a) (power to extend time)—

(a) the notice of appeal must include a request for an extension of time and the reason why the notice was not provided in time; and
(b) unless the Upper Tribunal extends time for the notice of appeal under rule 5(3)(a) (power to extend time) the Upper Tribunal must not admit the notice of appeal.

[1 (6) When the Upper Tribunal receives the notice of appeal it must send a copy of the notice and any accompanying documents—

(a) to each respondent; [7 ...]
(b) [4 in a road transport case, to—
 (i) the decision maker;
 (ii) the appropriate national authority; and
 (iii) in a case relating to the detention of a vehicle, the authorised person [7 or]]]

[7 (c) in an appeal against a decision of a traffic commissioner pursuant to section 6F of the Transport Act 1985 or section 123T of the Transport Act 2000, to—
 (i) the respondent, and
 (ii) the traffic commissioner who was the decision maker.

(6A) In a case to which paragraph (6)(c) applies, the Upper Tribunal must at the same time require such commissioner to—

(a) send or deliver to the Upper Tribunal (within such time as the Upper Tribunal may specify)—
 (i) a copy of any written record of the decision under challenge, and any statement of reasons for that decision, and
 (ii) copies of all documents relevant to the case in such commissioner's possession, and
(b) provide copies of such documents to each other party at the same time as they are provided to the Upper Tribunal.]

[5 (7) Paragraph (6)(a) does not apply in a quality contracts scheme case, in respect of which Schedule A1 makes alternative and further provision.]

AMENDMENTS

1. Tribunal Procedure (Amendment No.2) Rules 2009 (SI 2009/1975) rr.7 and 17 (September 1, 2009).

2. Tribunal Procedure (Amendment No.2) Rules 2010 (SI 2010/44) rr.2 and 14 (February 15, 2010).
3. Tribunal Procedure (Upper Tribunal) (Amendment) Rules 2010 (SI 2010/747) rr.2 and 8 (April 6, 2010).
4. Tribunal Procedure (Amendment No.2) Rules 2012 (SI 2012/1363 rr.4 and 7 (July 1, 2012).
5. Tribunal Procedure (Amendment) Rules 2015 (SI 2015/1510) rr.2 and 4 (August 21, 2015).
6. Tribunal Procedure (Amendment) Rules 2017 (SI 2017/723) rr.5 and 10 (July 23, 2017).
7. Tribunal Procedure (Amendment) Rules 2019 (SI 2019/925) r.2(1) and (4) (June 3, 2019, subject to a saving).

DEFINITIONS

"appellant"—see r.1(3).
"appropriate national authority"—*ibid.*
"asylum case—*ibid.*
"authorised person"—*ibid.*
"document"—*ibid.*
"immigration case"—*ibid.*
"party"—*ibid.*
"permission"—*ibid.*
"quality contracts scheme case"—*ibid.*
"respondent"—*ibid.*
"road transport case"—*ibid.*
"TRA"—*ibid.*
"trade remedies case"—*ibid.*

GENERAL NOTE

Paragraph (1)

3.484 Because r.22(2)(b) has the effect that an application for permission to appeal in a social security case almost invariably stands as an appeal where the Upper Tribunal has granted permission, this rule generally applies only where the First-tier Tribunal has granted permission to appeal.

Where the First-tier Tribunal has given permission to appeal on limited grounds, only those grounds may be advanced in the notice of appeal and, if it is wished to add other grounds, an application for permission to appeal on those additional grounds must be made to the Upper Tribunal. In other cases, the grounds of appeal need not be limited to the grounds put before the First-tier Tribunal. Once the notice of appeal has been lodged, the Upper Tribunal has a broad discretionary power to admit a new ground, which it should exercise in accordance with the overriding objective in r.2 (*Bramley Ferry Supplies v HMRC* [2017] UKUT 214 (TCC)). In practice, the Administrative Appeals Chamber of the Upper Tribunal does not generally take a strict approach in social security cases, unless either the First-tier Tribunal expressly limited the grounds of appeal, which is rare, or a very significant delay in raising a new point is liable to create unfairness towards the other party.

Paragraph (5)

3.485 See the note to r.38(5) of the Tribunal Procedure (First-tier Tribunal) (Social Entitlement Chamber) Rules 2008, above.

Paragraph (6)

3.486 In practice in social security cases, the Upper Tribunal obtains the First-tier Tribunal's file and constructs its own bundle of documents.

Response to the notice of appeal

24.—[2 [7 (1) This rule and rule 25 do not apply to— 3.487

(a) a road transport case, in respect of which Schedule 1 makes alternative provision; or

(b) a financial sanctions case in respect of which Schedule 4 makes alternative provision.]

(1A) Subject to any direction given by the Upper Tribunal, a respondent may [9 , and if paragraph (1B) applies must,] provide a response to a notice of appeal.]

[9 (1B) In the case of an appeal against the decision of another tribunal, a respondent must provide a response to a notice of appeal if the respondent—

(a) wishes the Upper Tribunal to uphold the decision for reasons other than those given by the tribunal; or

(b) relies on any grounds on which the respondent was unsuccessful in the proceedings which are the subject of the appeal.

(1C) If paragraph (1B) applies, to the extent that the respondent needs any permission, including permission to appeal to the Upper Tribunal, the response must include an application to the Upper Tribunal for such permission.]

(2) Any response provided under paragraph [3 (1A)] must be in writing and must be sent or delivered to the Upper Tribunal so that it is received—

[4 (a) if an application for permission to appeal stands as the notice of appeal, no later than one month after the date on which the respondent was sent notice that permission to appeal had been granted;

(aa) [8 . . .]

[6 (ab) in a quality contracts scheme case, no later than 1 month after the date on which a copy of the notice of appeal is sent to the respondent;] [8 or]

(b) in any other case, no later than 1 month after the date on which the Upper Tribunal sent a copy of the notice of appeal to the respondent.

(3) The response must state—

(a) the name and address of the respondent;

(b) the name and address of the representative (if any) of the respondent;

(c) an address where documents for the respondent may be sent or delivered;

(d) whether the respondent opposes the appeal;

(e) the grounds on which the respondent relies, including [2 (in the case of an appeal against another tribunal)] any grounds [9 —

(i) to uphold the decision for reasons other than those given by the tribunal; or

(ii) on which the respondent was unsuccessful in the proceedings which are the subject of the appeal;]

[9 (ea) the reasons why any permission applied for under paragraph (1C) should be given; and]

(f) whether the respondent wants the case to be dealt with at a hearing.

(4) If the respondent provides the response to the Upper Tribunal later than the time required by paragraph (2) or by an extension of time allowed under rule 5(3)(a) (power to extend time), the response must include a

request for an extension of time and the reason why the [1 response] was not provided in time.

(5) When the Upper Tribunal receives the response it must send a copy of the response and any accompanying documents to the appellant and each other party.

[6 (6) Paragraph (5) does not apply in a quality contracts scheme case, in respect of which Schedule A1 makes alternative and further provision.]

AMENDMENTS

1. Tribunal Procedure (Amendment) Rules 2009 (SI 2009/274) r.15 (April 1, 2009).

2. Tribunal Procedure (Amendment No.2) Rules 2009 (SI 2009/1975) rr.7 and 18 (September 1, 2009).

3. Tribunal Procedure (Amendment) Rules 2010 (SI 2010/43) rr.5 and 9 (January 18, 2010).

4. Tribunal Procedure (Amendment No.2) Rules 2010 (SI 2010/44) rr.2 and 15 (February 15, 2010).

5. Tribunal Procedure (Amendment No.2) Rules 2012 (SI 2012/1363) rr.4 and 8 (July 1, 2012).

6. Tribunal Procedure (Amendment) Rules 2015 (SI 2015/1510) rr.2 and 5 (August 21, 2015).

7. Tribunal Procedure (Amendment) Rules 2017 (SI 2017/723) rr.5 and 11 (July 23, 2017).

8. Tribunal Procedure (Amendment) Rules 2020 (SI 2020/651) r.5(1) and (8) (July 21, 2020).

9. Tribunal Procedure (Amendment) Rules 2022 (SI 2022/312) r.3(1) and (5) (April 6, 2022).

DEFINITIONS

"appellant"—see r.1(3).
"document"—*ibid.*
"financial sanctions case"—*ibid.*
"hearing"—*ibid.*
"party"—*ibid.*
"permission"—*ibid.*
"quality contracts scheme case"— *ibid.*
"respondent"—*ibid.*
"road transport case"—*ibid.*

GENERAL NOTE

3.488 If there is more than one respondent, this rule has the effect that they must make simultaneous responses unless the Upper Tribunal directs otherwise. In practice, it nearly always directs sequential responses from the respondents with the appellant replying after the last respondent has had an opportunity to respond to the appeal.

The amendment made in 2022 to para.(3)(e) is not well drafted but it can be seen what was meant.

The 2022 amendments to this rule were made in response to decisions of the Court of Appeal in *Devani v Secretary of State for the Home Department* [2020] EWCA Civ 612; [2020] 1 W.L.R. 2613 and *HMRC v SSE Generation Ltd* [2021] EWCA Civ 105 and have considerably complicated it.

In the former case, it was held at [31] and [34] that, although para.(1A) was then in entirely discretionary terms, there was an obligation to submit a response in cases where respondents wished to rely on grounds on which they had been unsuccessful before the First-tier Tribunal or, more generally, where it was necessary in the interests of fairness and in accordance with the over-riding objective to put the tribunal and appellant on notice of a point that the respondent wished to raise.

In the latter case, the Tax and Chancery Chamber of the Upper Tribunal was held to have erred in law in allowing SSE to argue a point upon which it had been unsuccessful before the First-tier Tribunal but in respect of which it had not obtained permission to appeal under the Tribunals, Courts and Enforcement Act 2007 s.11(3), even though it had raised the point in the response to the appeal and the Upper Tribunal had been satisfied that there was no unfairness to HMRC. The practice in the Administrative Appeals Chamber of the Upper Tribunal, where it is comparatively rare for permission to appeal to be given on limited grounds, had previously been to allow a respondent to raise any new issue in his or her response to the appeal, just as the appellant could raise new issues in his or her grounds of appeal, as long as no unfairness was caused to any other party. The Court of Appeal's reasoning is not altogether satisfactory.

There are two important elements in the reasoning. First, it accepted a concession by leading counsel for the respondent as to the Upper Tribunal's power to give permission to appeal. Secondly, it took a narrow approach to r.24(3)(e), which then required a response to state "the grounds on which the respondent relies, including (in the case of an appeal against the decision of another tribunal) any grounds on which the respondent was unsuccessful in the proceedings which are the subject of the appeal, but intends to rely in the appeal". Rose LJ (with whom David Richards and Popplewell LJJ agreed) said at [77]:

> "SSE did not seek permission to appeal from the FTT and Mr Peacock accepts that they could not have sought permission from the Upper Tribunal without first having made an unsuccessful application to the FTT. I agree with HMRC's submission that rule 24(3)(f) [sic] cannot obviate the need for permission set out in section 11 TCEA. The grounds referred to there are the grounds on which the party relies in its character as a respondent to appeal. Certainly if the respondent succeeded on an issue before the FTT because the FTT accepted one of a number of arguments while rejecting other arguments for the same result, the respondent can raise those unsuccessful arguments if its success is challenged on appeal by the opposing party. But the respondent cannot raise an issue which it lost before the FTT unless it obtains permission to appeal for itself."

SSE's concession that the Upper Tribunal could not have given permission to appeal because there had been no application to the First-tier Tribunal was based on r.21(2), but it overlooked the Upper Tribunal's power to waive the requirement imposed by r.21(2) under r.7(2)(a). SSE had instead submitted that HMRC's concern that a broad interpretation of r.24(3)(e) would entitle a respondent to re-run every issue on which it lost before the FTT without the filter of the permission stage could be met through the Upper Tribunal's case management powers under r.5, as applied in accordance with the overriding objective in r.2.

The court acknowledged the practical difficulties facing respondents—although it may only have had in mind legally-represented parties in tax cases and not also unrepresented parties in social security cases—and noted that C.P.R. r.52.13 allows a respondent to an appeal in the courts to seek permission to appeal within a response to an appeal. It also referred to the "venerable principle" that the task of the First-tier Tribunal and the Upper Tribunal is to arrive at the collection of the correct amount of tax (see *Investec Asset Finance Plc v HMRC* [2020] EWCA Civ 579 at [60] and [100]). However, in the light of the respondent's concession that the Upper Tribunal could not give permission to appeal, it considered itself driven, as a matter of statutory construction, to the conclusion it reached.

In the absence of the concession, it might perhaps have reached a different decision, given the Upper Tribunal's clear finding that there was no unfairness to HMRC in allowing the respondent's argument to be advanced before it. It is noteworthy that, in *SSHD v Smith (appealable decisions; PTA requirements; anonymity: Belgium)* [2019] UKUT 216 (IAC), where the Upper Tribunal reached a similar conclusion to the Court of Appeal's, the Upper Tribunal expressly referred to the possibility of waiver under r.7(2) although, in the immigration and asylum context, **3.489** it did not envisage the Upper Tribunal being sympathetic where a person "could and should" have applied to the First-tier Tribunal. Rule 7(2)(a) would have enabled the Upper Tribunal to achieve the same effect as could have been achieved by an appellate court under C.P.R. r.52.13. The problem with the court's decision is that it made a jurisdictional point out of an issue where there was arguably an element of discretion. The amendments to the Rules do not avoid the need to seek permission, which arguably would have been impermissible, and they make it explicit, but the insertion of r.21(1A) makes it plain that the Upper Tribunal can give permission notwithstanding that there has been no application to the First-tier Tribunal. Thus, if the Upper Tribunal notices that an application for permission is required, it can clearly invite the respondent to make one. If it overlooks the point, an appellate court may now be prepared to treat it as having given permission if its failure to do so has not caused unfairness.

If there is a dispute as to whether the proceedings before the First-tier Tribunal were conducted fairly and it is not answered by the recording of the hearing or the First-tier Tribunal's statement of reasons, it is likely to be necessary for the respondent to produce adequate evidence to support his or her arguments. Mere assertions based on second- or third-hand hearsay are unlikely to be sufficient (*Singh v Secretary of State for the Home Departmen*t [2016] EWCA Civ 492; *AA v Bristol CC* [2023] UKUT 52 (AAC)).

Appellant's reply

3.490 **25.**—(1) Subject to any direction given by the Upper Tribunal, the appellant may provide a reply to any response provided under rule 24 (response to the notice of appeal).

(2) [1 Subject to paragraph (2A), any] reply provided under paragraph (1) must be in writing and must be sent or delivered to the Upper Tribunal so that it is received within one month after the date on which the Upper Tribunal sent a copy of the response to the appellant.

[1 (2A) [3 In an asylum case or an immigration case, the time limit in paragraph (2) is one month after the date on which the Upper Tribunal sent a copy of the response to the appellant, or five days before the hearing of the appeal, whichever is the earlier.]

[2 (2B) In a quality contracts scheme case, the time limit in paragraph (2) is 1 month from the date on which the respondent sent a copy of the response to the appellant.]

(3) When the Upper Tribunal receives the reply it must send a copy of the reply and any accompanying documents to each respondent.

[2 (4) Paragraph (3) does not apply in a quality contracts scheme case, in respect of which Schedule A1 makes alternative and further provision.]

AMENDMENTS

1. Tribunal Procedure (Amendment No.2) Rules 2010 (SI 2010/44) rr.2 and 16 (February 15, 2010).

2. Tribunal Procedure (Amendment) Rules 2015 (SI 2015/1510) rr.2 and 6 (August 21, 2015).

3. Tribunal Procedure (Amendment) Rules 2020 (SI 2020/651) r.5(1) and (9) (July 21, 2020).

DEFINITIONS

"appellant"—see r.1(3).
"asylum case"—*ibid.*
"document"—*ibid.*

"immigration case"—*ibid.*
"quality contracts scheme case"—*ibid.*
"respondent"—*ibid.*

GENERAL NOTE

This rule is expressly made subject to a direction by the Upper Tribunal. Where it appears to a judge granting permission to appeal that there is an obvious error in a decision of the First-tier Tribunal, it is common for the judge to direct simultaneous observations from all parties in order to speed up the process. 3.491

References under the Forfeiture Act 1982

26.—(1) If a question arises which is required to be determined by the Upper Tribunal under section 4 of the Forfeiture Act 1982, the person to whom the application for the relevant benefit or advantage has been made must refer the question to the Upper Tribunal. 3.492

(2) The reference must be in writing and must include—

(a) a statement of the question for determination;

(b) a statement of the relevant facts;

(c) the grounds upon which the reference is made; and

(d) an address for sending documents to the person making the reference and each respondent.

(3) When the Upper Tribunal receives the reference it must send a copy of the reference and any accompanying documents to each respondent.

(4) Rules 24 (response to the notice of appeal) and 25 (appellant's reply) apply to a reference made under this rule as if it were a notice of appeal.

DEFINITIONS

"document"—see r.1(3).
"respondent"—*ibid.*

GENERAL NOTE

This rule is made under s.4(2) of the Forfeiture Act 1982. As to the duty to make a reference under this rule, see the annotation to s.4(1) of that Act, above. 3.493

[1 Cases transferred or referred to the Upper Tribunal, applications made directly to the Upper Tribunal [5 , cases where an offence has been certified] and proceedings without notice to a respondent

26A.—(1) [2 Paragraphs (2) and (3) apply to— 3.494

(a) a case transferred or referred to the Upper Tribunal from the First-tier Tribunal; [5 ...]

(b) a case, other than an appeal or a case to which rule 26 (references under the Forfeiture Act 1982) applies, which is started by an application made directly to the Upper Tribunal [5 or]]

[5 (c) a case where an offence has been certified to the Upper Tribunal.]

(2) In a case to which this paragraph applies—

(a) the Upper Tribunal must give directions as to the procedure to be followed in the consideration and disposal of the proceedings; [4 ...]

[4 (aa) in a reference under [6 section 325 or 326 of the Charities Act 2011], the Upper Tribunal may give directions providing for an application to join the proceedings as a party and the time within which it may be made; and]

(b) the preceding rules in this Part will only apply to the proceedings to the extent provided for by such directions.

(3) If a case or matter to which this paragraph applies is to be determined without notice to or the involvement of a respondent—

(a) any provision in these Rules requiring a document to be provided by or to a respondent; and

(b) any other provision in these Rules permitting a respondent to participate in the proceedings

does not apply to that case or matter.]

[3 (4) Schedule 2 makes further provision for national security certificate appeals transferred to the Upper Tribunal.]

Amendments

1. Tribunal Procedure (Amendment) Rules 2009 (SI 2009/274) r.16 (April 1, 2009).

2. Tribunal Procedure (Amendment No.2) Rules 2009 (SI 2009/1975) rr.7 and 19 (September 1, 2009).

3. Tribunal Procedure (Amendment) Rules 2010 (SI 2010/43) rr.5 and 10 (January 18, 2010).

4. Tribunal Procedure (Amendment) Rules 2012 (SI 2012/500) r.5 (April 6, 2012).

5. Tribunal Procedure (Amendment) Rules 2019 (SI 2019/925) r.2(1) and (5) (June 3, 2019, subject to a saving).

6. Tribunal Procedure (Amendment No.2) Rules 2022 (SI 2022/1030) r.5(1) and (3) (November 1, 2022).

Definition

"national security certificate appeal"—see r.1(3).

General Note

3.495 This rule makes provision for cases other than appeals and references within the scope of r.26 by effectively leaving it to the Upper Tribunal to give case management directions on a case-by-case basis. It has no application to social security cases, except where a case is referred to the Upper Tribunal under s.9(5)(b) of the Tribunals, Courts and Enforcement Act 2007 or r.7(3) of the Tribunal Procedure (First-tier Tribunal) (Social Entitlement Chamber) Rules 2008.

3.496 **26B.** *Omitted.*

3.497 **26C.** *Omitted.*

Part 4

Judicial Review Proceedings in the Upper Tribunal

Application of this Part to judicial review proceedings transferred to the Upper Tribunal

3.498 **27.**—(1) When a court transfers judicial review proceedings to the Upper Tribunal, the Upper Tribunal—

(a) must notify each party in writing that the proceedings have been transferred to the Upper Tribunal; and

(b) must give directions as to the future conduct of the proceedings.

(2) The directions given under paragraph (1)(b) may modify or disapply for the purposes of the proceedings any of the provisions of the following rules in this Part.

(3) In proceedings transferred from the Court of Session under section 20(1) of the 2007 Act, the directions given under paragraph (1)(b) must—

(a) if the Court of Session did not make a first order specifying the required intimation, service and advertisement of the petition, state the Upper Tribunal's requirements in relation to those matters;

(b) state whether the Upper Tribunal will consider summary dismissal of the proceedings; and

(c) where necessary, modify or disapply provisions relating to permission in the following rules in this Part.

Definitions

"the 2007 Act"—see r.1(3).
"judicial review proceedings"—*ibid.*
"party"—*ibid.*
"permission"—*ibid.*

General Note

This rule applies to judicial review proceedings transferred from a court, as opposed to proceedings started in the Upper Tribunal. Because cases may be transferred at any stage of the proceedings, the Upper Tribunal is given a broad power to give directions as to how the case will proceed and how much of rr.28–33 need apply to the case. At the time these Rules were made, rr. 28 and 29 could not apply to cases transferred by the Court of Session, because there was no requirement to obtain permission to apply for judicial review in Scotland. Instead, the Upper Tribunal could hold a preliminary hearing to consider whether summary dismissal of the proceedings was appropriate, which would be equivalent to a first hearing in the Court of Session and had much the same effect as considering whether to refuse permission to apply for judicial review. Hence para.(3)(b) and r.30(2) and (3)(b). Now there is a requirement for permission (see s.20A of the Tribunals, Courts and Enforcement Act 2007 and the note to that section) but it appears not to have been thought necessary to amend these Rules. **3.499**

Applications for permission to bring judicial review proceedings

28.—(1) A person seeking permission to bring judicial review proceedings before the Upper Tribunal under section 16 of the 2007 Act must make a written application to the Upper Tribunal for such permission. **3.500**

(2) Subject to paragraph (3), an application under paragraph (1) must be made promptly and, unless any other enactment specifies a shorter time limit, must be sent or delivered to the Upper Tribunal so that it is received no later than 3 months after the date of the decision [1, action or omission] to which the application relates.

(3) An application for permission to bring judicial review proceedings challenging a decision of the First-tier Tribunal may be made later than the time required by paragraph (2) if it is made within 1 month after the date on which the First-tier Tribunal sent—

(a) written reasons for the decision; or

(b) notification that an application for the decision to be set aside has been unsuccessful, provided that that application was made in time.

(4) The application must state—

(a) the name and address of the applicant, the respondent and any other person whom the applicant considers to be an interested party;

(b) the name and address of the applicant's representative (if any);

(c) an address where documents for the applicant may be sent or delivered;

(d) details of the decision challenged (including the date, the full reference and the identity of the decision maker);

(e) that the application is for permission to bring judicial review proceedings;

(f) the outcome that the applicant is seeking; and

(g) the facts and grounds on which the applicant relies.

(5) If the application relates to proceedings in a court or tribunal, the application must name as an interested party each party to those proceedings who is not the applicant or a respondent.

(6) The applicant must send with the application—

(a) a copy of any written record of the decision in the applicant's possession or control; and

(b) copies of any other documents in the applicant's possession or control on which the applicant intends to rely.

(7) If the applicant provides the application to the Upper Tribunal later than the time required by paragraph (2) or (3) or by an extension of time allowed under rule 5(3)(a) (power to extend time)—

(a) the application must include a request for an extension of time and the reason why the application was not provided in time; and

(b) unless the Upper Tribunal extends time for the application under rule 5(3)(a) (power to extend time) the Upper Tribunal must not admit the application.

(8) [[2] Except where rule 28A(2)(a) (special provisions for [[3] immigration judicial review] proceedings) applies,] when the Upper Tribunal receives the application it must send a copy of the application and any accompanying documents to each person named in the application as a respondent or interested party.

AMENDMENTS

1. Tribunal Procedure (Amendment) Rules 2009 (SI 2009/274) r.17 (April 1, 2009).

2. Tribunal Procedure (Upper Tribunal) (Amendment) Rules 2011 (SI 2011/2343) rr.2 and 7 (October 17, 2011).

3. Tribunal Procedure (Amendment No. 4) Rules 2013 (SI 2013/2067) rr.2 and 10 (November 1, 2013).

DEFINITIONS

"the 2007 Act"—see r.1(3).
"applicant"—*ibid.*
"document"—*ibid.*
"immigration judicial review proceedings"—*ibid.*
"interested party"—*ibid.*

"judicial review proceedings"—*ibid.*
"party"—*ibid.*
"permission"—*ibid.*
"respondent"—*ibid.*

GENERAL NOTE

This rule applies to judicial review proceedings started in the Upper Tribunal (see the notes to ss.15 and 18 of the Tribunals, Courts and Enforcement Act 2007). Rule 9 gives the Upper Tribunal wide power to substitute the correct parties and add additional parties where the applicant fails to identify the correct respondent and interested party. Where, as will currently always be the case in the Administrative Appeals Chamber, the decision being challenged is a decision of the First-tier Tribunal, the respondent will be the First-tier Tribunal and the parties to the case before the First-tier Tribunal, other than the applicant, will be interested parties. **3.501**

Paragraph (3) provides for the extension of the three-month time limit in para.(2) but does not interfere with the requirement in para.(2) that an application be made "promptly" so that, where statements of reasons were provided over three years after the decision in one case and over 18 months after the decision in another, applications that could have been made without statements of reasons were held to be late even though made within a month of the statement of reasons being provided (*R. (CICA) v First-tier Tribunal (CIC)* [2015] UKUT 299 (AAC); *R. (CICA) v First-tier Tribunal (CIC)* [2015] UKUT 371 (AAC)).

In *R. (Spahiu) v Secretary of State for the Home Department* [2018] EWCA Civ 2604; [2019] 1 W.L.R. 1297, the Court of Appeal decided that the Civil Procedure Rules applied by analogy to judicial review proceedings in the Upper Tribunal so that a party could amend a statement of facts and grounds without permission before it was "served", by which it appears to have meant before it was received by the parties after being sent to them under para.(8). As that paragraph provides that the Upper Tribunal, rather than the applicant, must send a copy of the application to the other parties, it might previously have been thought that the Rules actually required permission to be given under r.5(3)(c) for any amendment after the application had been sent to the Upper Tribunal. In any event, the Court held that a decision to allow an amendment to a statement of facts and grounds was a case management direction that could itself be amended or set aside under r.6(5). Curiously, it considered (at [48] and [49]) that r.6(5) provided for a form of review under s.10 of the Tribunals, Courts and Enforcement Act 2007, but that approach is inconsistent with the approach taken in *R. (Singh) v Secretary of State for the Home Department* [2019] EWCA Civ 1014 where, at [26], it is made clear that r.6(5) is not related to s.10. It may be noted that Coulson L.J., who gave the lead judgment in *Spahiu*, was also a member of the Court in *Singh* and the analysis in the latter case is clearly to be preferred. The view expressed in *Spahiu* that the Civil Procedure Rules apply by analogy to judicial review proceedings in the Upper Tribunal may suggest that in the light of *R. (Good Law Project Ltd) v Secretary of State for Health and Social Care* [2022] EWCA Civ 355; [2022] 1 W.L.R. 2339, a particularly strict approach must be taken to whether an application under r.28 has been made in time and that time should not be extended unless the applicant took all reasonable steps to comply with r.28 but was unable to do so.

28A. *Omitted.* **3.502**

Acknowledgment of service

29.—(1) A person who is sent [3 or provided with] a copy of an application for permission under rule 28(8) (application for permission to bring judicial review proceedings) [3 or rule 28A(2)(a) (special provisions for [4 immigration judicial review] proceedings)] and wishes to take part in **3.503**

the proceedings must [3 provide] to the Upper Tribunal an acknowledgment of service so that it is received no later than 21 days after the date on which the Upper Tribunal sent [3, or in [4 immigration judicial review] proceedings the applicant provided,] a copy of the application to that person.

(2) An acknowledgment of service under paragraph (1) must be in writing and state—

(a) whether the person intends to [1 support or] oppose the application for permission;

(b) their grounds for any [1 support or] opposition under sub-paragraph (a), or any other submission or information which they consider may assist the Upper Tribunal; and

(c) the name and address of any other person not named in the application as a respondent or interested party whom the person providing the acknowledgment considers to be an interested party.

[3 (2A) In [4 immigration judicial review] proceedings, a person who provides an acknowledgement of service under paragraph (1) must also provide a copy to—

(a) the applicant; and

(b) any other person named in the application under rule 28(4)(a) or acknowledgement of service under paragraph (2)(c)

no later than the time specified in paragraph (1).]

(3) A person who is sent [3 or provided with] a copy of an application for permission under rule 28(8) [3 or 28A(2)(a)] but does not provide an acknowledgment of service [3 to the Upper Tribunal] may not take part in the application for permission [2 unless allowed to do so by the Upper Tribunal], but may take part in the subsequent proceedings if the application is successful.

AMENDMENTS

1. Tribunal Procedure (Amendment) Rules 2009 (SI 2009/274) r.18 (April 1, 2009).

2. Tribunal Procedure (Amendment) Rules 2011 (SI 2011/651) r.8(1) and (3) (April 1, 2011).

3. Tribunal Procedure (Upper Tribunal) (Amendment) Rules 2011 (SI 2011/2343) rr.2 and 9 (October 17, 2011).

4. Tribunal Procedure (Amendment No. 4) Rules 2013 (SI 2013/2067) rr.2 and 12 (November 1, 2013).

DEFINITIONS

"immigration judicial review proceedings"—see r.1(3).
"interested party"—*ibid.*
"judicial review proceedings"—*ibid.*
"party"—*ibid.*
"permission"—*ibid.*
"respondent"—*ibid.*

GENERAL NOTE

3.504 This rule is based on the procedure in the Administrative Court in England and Wales under CPR rr.54.8 and 54.9. The respondent, i.e. the First-tier Tribunal whose decision is being challenged, will only rarely take part in proceedings, so that it will fall to the interested parties to decide whether or not to oppose the application, just as it does on an appeal. Although the 21-day time limit is drawn from the procedure in the Court, it is reduced for most purposes to 21 days from the date that an application is *sent*, rather than from when it is served, for consistency with most other time limits in situations where the Upper Tribunal, rather than a party, sends a document. However, in immigration judicial review cases, time runs from the date that the application is "provided" by the applicant and it was held in *R. (Sutharsan) v SSHD* [2019] UKUT 217 (IAC) that, in that particular context, consistency with the procedure in the Administrative Court was intended and that that required that "a copy application which is sent by post is deemed to have been provided on the second business day after it was posted, unless the contrary is proved". As a consequence of that decision, r.13(8) was introduced. It provides that, in all judicial review cases, "unless the contrary is proved, a document sent by first class post will be deemed to be provided or received on the second working day after it was posted".

The way that r.29 operates was analysed in detail in *R. (KA) v Secretary of State for the Home Department* [2021] EWCA Civ 1040; [2021] 1 W.L.R. 6018.

Decision on permission or summary dismissal, and reconsideration of permission or summary dismissal at a hearing

30.—(1) The Upper Tribunal must send to the applicant, each respondent and any other person who provided an acknowledgment of service to the Upper Tribunal, and may send to any other person who may have an interest in the proceedings, written notice of— **3.505**

(a) its decision in relation to the application for permission; and

[3 (b) the reasons for any—

(i) refusal of the application or refusal to admit the late application, or

(ii) limitations or conditions on permission.]

(2) In proceedings transferred from the Court of Session under section 20(1) of the 2007 Act, where the Upper Tribunal has considered whether summarily to dismiss of the proceedings, the Upper Tribunal must send to the applicant and each respondent, and may send to any other person who may have an interest in the proceedings, written notice of—

(a) its decision in relation to the summary dismissal of proceedings; and

(b) the reasons for any decision summarily to dismiss part or all of the proceedings, or any limitations or conditions on the continuation of such proceedings.

(3) Paragraph (4) applies where the Upper Tribunal, without a hearing—

[3 (a) determines an application for permission to bring judicial review proceedings by—

(i) refusing permission or refusing to admit the late application, or

(ii) giving permission on limited grounds or subject to conditions];

(b) in proceedings transferred from the Court of Session, summarily dismisses part or all of the proceedings, or imposes any limitations or conditions on the continuation of such proceedings.

(4) [2 Subject to paragraph (4A), in] the circumstances specified in paragraph (3) the applicant may apply for the decision to be reconsidered at a hearing.

[2 (4A) Where the Upper Tribunal refuses permission to bring immigration judicial review proceedings [3 or refuses to admit a late application for permission to bring such proceedings] and considers the application to be totally without merit, it shall record that fact in its decision notice and, in those circumstances, the applicant may not request the decision to be reconsidered at a hearing.]

(5) An application under paragraph (4) must be made in writing and must be sent or delivered to the Upper Tribunal so that it is received within 14 days [[1] , or in [[2] immigration judicial review] proceedings 9 days,] after the date on which the Upper Tribunal sent written notice of its decision regarding the application to the applicant.

AMENDMENTS

1. Tribunal Procedure (Upper Tribunal) (Amendment) Rules 2011 (SI 2011/2343) rr.2 and 10 (October 17, 2011).

2. Tribunal Procedure (Amendment No. 4) Rules 2013 (SI 2013/2067) rr.2 and 13 (November 1, 2013).

3. Tribunal Procedure (Amendment) Rules 2014 (SI 2014/514) rr.2 and 11 (April 6, 2014).

DEFINITIONS

"the 2007 Act"—see r.1(3).
"applicant"—*ibid.*
"immigration judicial review proceedings"—*ibid.*
"hearing"—*ibid.*
"judicial review proceedings"—*ibid.*
"permission"—*ibid.*
"respondent"—*ibid.*

GENERAL NOTE

3.506 This rule is based on the procedure in the Administrative Court in England and Wales under CPR rr.54.10–54.12. An application for permission to apply for judicial review that is refused, or is only partially successful, on paper may be renewed at an oral hearing under paras (3)(a) and (4). Dismissal of judicial review proceedings at a first hearing under RC r.58.9 was the equivalent in Scotland of a refusal of permission to apply for judicial review in England and Wales or Northern Ireland and so equivalent provision for summary dismissal by the Upper Tribunal is made in paras (3)(b) and (4). However, there is now a requirement for permission in Scotland by virtue of s.20A of the Tribunals, Courts and Enforcement Act 2007. This rule has not been amended, perhaps because it is considered unnecessary to do so in view of the terms of s.20A itself.

For the purposes of para.(4A), which does not apply to social security cases, a claim for judicial review may be "totally without merit" if it is bound to fail, even if it is not abusive or vexatious (*R. (Grace) v Secretary of State for the Home Department* [2014] EWCA Civ 1091; [2014] 1 W.L.R. 3432).

In *R. (Wasif) v Secretary of State for the Home Department (Practice Note)* [2016] EWCA Civ 82; [2016] 1 W.L.R. 2793, the Court of Appeal has said that the question is essentially whether there is any prospect of a judge being persuaded to grant permission following an oral hearing, bearing in mind that one purpose of a hearing would be to give the claimant an opportunity to address issues that may not have been anticipated in the original grounds. The Court also said that, while reasons for refusing permission that are given in summary form are acceptable when the applicant has the right to renew the application, where certification is made care is needed to ensure that all the applicant's points are identified and addressed. Reasons for certification should be separate from reasons for refusing permission, since the tests are not the same. Finally, the Court said that certification of a case as totally without merit is not appealable as such; any appeal must be against the refusal of permission.

The right to apply under r.30(4) for reconsideration at a hearing when permission has been refused on the papers makes it inappropriate to seek permission to appeal to the Court of Appeal against a refusal of permission on the papers (*R. (MD Afghanistan) v Secretary of State for the Home Department* [2012] EWCA Civ 194; [2012] 1 W.L.R. 2422). An application for permission to appeal is therefore likely to be treated as an application for reconsideration.

In *R. (Kigen) v Secretary of State for the Home Department* [2015] EWCA Civ 1286, [2016] 1 W.L.R. 723, the Court of Appeal gave guidance as to the approach to be taken to extending time under r.5(3)(a) for making an application for reconsideration. Following the approach taken in *R. (Hysaj) v Secretary of State for the Home Department* [2014] EWCA Civ 1663; [2015] 1 W.L.R. 2472 in relation to time limits for appealing to the Court of Appeal, it said that a three-stage approach should be adopted by (i) assessing the seriousness and significance of the failure to comply with the time limit, (ii) considering why the default occurred and (iii) evaluating all the circumstances of the case, so as to enable the tribunal to deal justly with the application.

Responses

31.—(1) Any person to whom the Upper Tribunal has sent notice of the grant of permission under rule 30(1) (notification of decision on permission), and who wishes to contest the application or support it on additional grounds, must provide detailed grounds for contesting or supporting the application to the Upper Tribunal. **3.507**

(2) Any detailed grounds must be provided in writing and must be sent or delivered to the Upper Tribunal so that they are received not more than 35 days after the Upper Tribunal sent notice of the grant of permission under rule 30(1).

Definition

"permission"—see r.1(3).

General Note

This rule, including the 35-day time limit, is based on the procedure in the Administrative Court in England and Wales under CPR r.54.14(a). **3.508**

Applicant seeking to rely on additional grounds

32. The applicant may not rely on any grounds, other than those grounds on which the applicant obtained permission for the judicial review proceedings, without the consent of the Upper Tribunal. **3.509**

Definitions

"applicant"—see r.1(3).
"judicial review proceedings"—*ibid.*
"permission"—*ibid.*

General Note

This rule is based on the procedure in the Administrative Court in England and Wales under CPR r.54.15. **3.510**

Right to make representations

3.511 **33.** Each party and, with the permission of the Upper Tribunal, any other person, may—

(a) submit evidence, except at the hearing of an application for permission;

(b) make representations at any hearing which they are entitled to attend; and

(c) make written representations in relation to a decision to be made without a hearing.

DEFINITIONS

"hearing"—see r.1(3).
"party"—*ibid.*
"permission"—*ibid.*

GENERAL NOTE

3.512 This rule is based on the procedure in the Administrative Court in England and Wales under CPR rr.54.14(b) and 54, 17.

[1 Amendments and additional grounds resulting in transfer of proceedings to the High Court in England and Wales

3.513 **33A.**—(1) This rule applies only to judicial review proceedings arising under the law of England and Wales.

(2) In relation to such proceedings—

(a) the powers of the Upper Tribunal to permit or require amendments under rule 5(3)(c) extend to amendments which would, once in place, give rise to an obligation or power to transfer the proceedings to the High Court in England and Wales under section 18(3) of the 2007 Act or paragraph (3);

(b) except with the permission of the Upper Tribunal, additional grounds may not be advanced, whether by an applicant or otherwise, if they would give rise to an obligation or power to transfer the proceedings to the High Court in England and Wales under section 18(3) of the 2007 Act or paragraph (3).

(3) Where the High Court in England and Wales has transferred judicial review proceedings to the Upper Tribunal under any power or duty and subsequently the proceedings are amended or any party advances additional grounds—

(a) if the proceedings in their present form could not have been transferred to the Upper Tribunal under the relevant power or duty had they been in that form at the time of the transfer, the Upper Tribunal must transfer the proceedings back to the High Court in England and Wales;

(b) subject to sub-paragraph (a), where the proceedings were transferred to the Upper Tribunal under section 31A(3) of the Senior Courts Act 1981 (power to transfer judicial review proceedings to the Upper Tribunal), the Upper Tribunal may transfer proceedings back to the High Court in England and Wales if it appears just and convenient to do so.]

Amendment

1. Tribunal Procedure (Upper Tribunal) (Amendment) Rules 2011 (SI 2011/2343) rr.2 and 11 (October 17, 2011).

Definitions

"applicant"—see r.1(3).
"judicial review proceedings—*ibid.*
"party"—*ibid.*

General Note

The Upper Tribunal has only a limited jurisdiction to hear judicial review proceedings (see ss.15–21 of the Tribunals, Courts and Enforcement Act 2007, set out in the main work). Rule 33A makes provision for cases where amendments to such proceedings might make it appropriate for the Upper Tribunal to transfer the case to the High Court in England and Wales, even where the High Court has originally transferred the case to the Upper Tribunal. No equivalent provision has been made in respect of Scotland or Northern Ireland but, so far, there have not been any judicial review proceedings in the Upper Tribunal in those parts of the United Kingdom. There may be some cases where it is appropriate to split the proceedings and transfer to the High Court only that part not within the jurisdiction of the Upper Tribunal but in other cases it will be preferable to keep the proceedings together and, if the Upper Tribunal does not have jurisdiction in respect of part of them, transfer the whole proceedings to the High Court. Alternatively, para.(2)(b) enables the Upper Tribunal to refuse to permit an amendment that might require proceedings to be transferred to the High Court, which would leave the party seeking the amendment to consider bringing separate proceedings in the High Court. **3.514**

The background to this rule was explained in detail in *R. (B) v Secretary of State for the Home Department* [2016] UKUT 182 (IAC) by Walker J., who was chairman of the Tribunal Procedure Committee when the rule was introduced. The parties had agreed that judicial review proceedings that had been transferred to the Upper Tribunal should be transferred back to the High Court so that it could consider an application for permission to amend the claim to add a claim for a declaration of incompatibility under s.4 of the Human Rights Act 1998. Walker J. pointed out that that was inappropriate in the light of this rule and that the proper procedure was to make the application for permission to amend to the Upper Tribunal, with the proceedings being transferred to the High Court only if the amendment were allowed. On reflection, the parties agreed that such an application would be premature.

Part 5

Hearings

Decision with or without a hearing

34.—(1) Subject to [1 paragraphs (2) and (3)], the Upper Tribunal may make any decision without a hearing. **3.515**

(2) The Upper Tribunal must have regard to any view expressed by a party when deciding whether to hold a hearing to consider any matter, and the form of any such hearing.

[1 (3) In immigration judicial review proceedings, the Upper Tribunal must hold a hearing before making a decision which disposes of proceedings.

(4) Paragraph (3) does not affect the power of the Upper Tribunal to—

(a) strike out a party's case, pursuant to rule 8(1)(b) or 8(2);

(b) consent to withdrawal, pursuant to rule 17;

(c) determine an application for permission to bring judicial review proceedings, pursuant to rule 30; or

(d) make a consent order disposing of proceedings, pursuant to rule 39,

without a hearing.]

Amendment

1. Tribunal Procedure (Amendment No. 4) Rules 2013 (SI 2013/2067) rr.2 and 14 (November 1, 2013).

Definitions

"hearing"—see r.1(3).

"immigration judicial review proceedings"—*ibid.*

"party"—*ibid.*

General Note

3.516 The European Convention on Human Rights does not require a second-tier tribunal such as the Upper Tribunal to hold an oral hearing where there has been an opportunity to have an oral hearing before the First-tier Tribunal (*Hoppe v Germany* [2003] F.L.R. 384, *Fexler v Sweden* ECtHR Application No. 36801/06). At common law a case can be determined without an oral hearing unless that would be unfair because, for instance, oral evidence is required (*R. (O'Connell) v Parole Board* [2007] EWHC 2591 (Admin); [2008] 1 W.L.R 979) or the case is complex (*R. (Thompson) v Law Society* [2004] EWCA Civ 167; [2004] 1 W.L.R. 2522). It is suggested that the Upper Tribunal is entitled to refuse a request for an oral hearing where oral evidence would be irrelevant and there is no reason to suppose that oral argument could make any difference to the outcome.

A judge who is minded to reject a claimant's appeal despite the fact that it has been supported by the Secretary of State is not bound to direct an oral hearing if no request for a hearing has been made despite an opportunity having been given (*Miller v Secretary of State for Work and Pensions*, 2002 G.W.D. 25–861, IH).

This rule replaces reg.23 of the Social Security Commissioners (Procedure) Regulations 1999. Regulation 23(2) specifically stated that, where a request for a hearing was made by a party, "the Commissioner shall grant the request unless he is satisfied that the proceedings can properly be determined without a hearing" but the absence of a similar provision in this rule may well make no difference because a refusal of a request for a hearing must be for a good reason. In practice, requests by unrepresented claimants are often refused because the judge is prepared to decide the case in favour of the claimant or because they are made specifically for the purpose of giving evidence in circumstances where the appeal lies on a point of law in respect of which it is clear the claimant will be unable to provide any assistance. It will normally be appropriate to give a written reason for refusing a request for an oral hearing (see r.40(4)). A direction as to whether there will be a hearing falls within the scope of r.5 (see r.5(3)(f)) and so the provisions of r.6 apply. A person applying for permission to appeal to the Upper Tribunal should indicate whether he or she wants the application to be determined at a hearing (see r.21(4)(f)), which is particularly important in social security cases where there is no right to renew orally an application refused on paper. A respondent should indicate whether or not he or she wishes there to be an oral hearing when submitting a response to an appeal or reference (see r.24(3)(f)) and the appellant is usually asked by the Upper Tribunal to do so when replying, although there is no specific provision to that effect in r.25.

In *CH v SSWP (JSA) (No.2)* [2018] UKUT 320 (AAC), the Upper Tribunal made adjustments to its normal hearing procedure to meet the reasonable needs of an appellant with reading (and related difficulties with memory, concentration and information processing) and difficulties with interpersonal interactions. These were allowing a 15-minute break after each 45 minutes, allowing the appellant to record the proceedings (subject to the usual condition that the recording not be published in any format), allowing another person to read parts of the appellant's speaking note and switching off all fluorescent ceiling lighting. The judge gave detailed reasons for making these adjustments. **3.517**

Before oral hearings, lawyers conventionally submit skeleton arguments, outlining the submissions that are to be made, but there is no need to do that in the Upper Tribunal if the arguments have already been adequately set out in written submissions as parts of grounds of appeal, responses or replies. If skeleton arguments are to be submitted, that should be done in good time, particularly if another party does not have legal representation (*R(IS) 2/08* at [56] to [60], *NA v SSWP (ESA)* [2018] UKUT 399 (AAC) at [4] to [8]).

Entitlement to attend a hearing

35.—(1) Subject to rule 37(4) (exclusion of a person from a hearing), each party is entitled to attend a hearing. **3.518**

[1 (2) In a national security certificate appeal the relevant Minister is entitled to attend any hearing.]

AMENDMENT

1. Tribunal Procedure (Amendment) Rules 2010 (SI 2010/43) rr.5 and 11 (January 18, 2010).

DEFINITIONS

"hearing"—see r.1(3).
"national security certificate appeal"—*ibid.*
"party"—*ibid.*
"relevant Minister"—*ibid.*

GENERAL NOTE

This rule makes it plain that, except where r.37(4) applies, a party may always attend a hearing even when the hearing is in private. By virtue of r.11(3) a properly appointed representative also has a right to attend a hearing, whether or not the party does so. By virtue of r.11(5), a party who attends a hearing may be accompanied by a person acting as a representative or assistant. **3.519**

Notice of hearings

36.—(1) The Upper Tribunal must give each party entitled to attend a hearing reasonable notice of the time and place of the hearing (including any adjourned or postponed hearing) and any change to the time and place of the hearing. **3.520**

(2) The period of notice under paragraph (1) must be at least 14 days except that—

(a) in applications for permission to bring judicial review proceedings, the period of notice must be at least 2 working days; [1 [2 . . .]]

(aa) [1 (aa) [2 . . .]]

(b) [1 [2 . . .]]] the Upper Tribunal may give shorter notice—

(i) with the parties' consent; or

(ii) in urgent or exceptional cases.

AMENDMENTS

1. Tribunal Procedure (Amendment) (No.2) Rules 2010 (SI 2010/44) rr.2 and 17 (February 15, 2010).

2. Tribunal Procedure (Amendment) Rules 2020 (SI 2020/651) r.5(1) and (10) (July 21, 2020).

DEFINITIONS

"hearing"—*ibid.*
"judicial review proceedings"—*ibid.*
"party"—*ibid.*
"permission"—*ibid.*
"working day"—*ibid.*

3.521 **36A.** [1 ...]

AMENDMENT

1. Tribunal Procedure (Amendment) Rules 2021 (SI 2021/322) r.2 (April 6, 2021).

Public and private hearings

3.522 **37.**—(1) Subject to the following paragraphs, all hearings must be held in public.

(2) The Upper Tribunal may give a direction that a hearing, or part of it, is to be held in private.

[5 (2ZA) *Expired.*]

[3 (2A) In a national security certificate appeal, the Upper Tribunal must have regard to its duty under rule 14(10) (no disclosure of information contrary to the interests of national security) when considering whether to give a direction that a hearing, or part of it, is to be held in private.]

(3) Where a hearing, or part of it, is to be held in private, the Upper Tribunal may determine who is entitled to attend the hearing or part of it.

(4) The Upper Tribunal may give a direction excluding from any hearing, or part of it—

(a) any person whose conduct the Upper Tribunal considers is disrupting or is likely to disrupt the hearing;

(b) any person whose presence the Upper Tribunal considers is likely to prevent another person from giving evidence or making submissions freely;

(c) any person who the Upper Tribunal considers should be excluded in order to give effect to [2 the requirement at rule 14(11) (prevention of disclosure or publication of documents and information)]; or

(d) any person where the purpose of the hearing would be defeated by the attendance of that person [1 ; or

(e) a person under [4 18, other than a young person who is a party in a special educational needs case or a disability discrimination in schools case].]

(5) The Upper Tribunal may give a direction excluding a witness from a hearing until that witness gives evidence.

AMENDMENTS

1. Tribunal Procedure (Amendment) Rules 2009 (SI 2009/274) r.19 (April 1, 2009).

2. Tribunal Procedure (Amendment No.2) Rules 2009 (SI 2009/1975) regs 7 and 20 (September 1, 2009).

3. Tribunal Procedure (Amendment) Rules 2010 (SI 2010/43) regs 5 and 12 (January 18, 2010).

4. Tribunal Procedure (Amendment No.3) Rules 2014 (SI 2014/2128) rr.2 and 13 (September 1, 2014).

5. Tribunal Procedure (Coronavirus) (Amendment) Rules 2020 (SI 2020/416) r.5(1) and (3) (April 10, 2020). This temporary paragraph expired on September 25, 2022.

DEFINITIONS

"disability discrimination in schools case"—see r.1(3).
"hearing"—*ibid.*
"national security certificate appeal"—*ibid.*
"special educational needs case" —*ibid.*
"young person" —*ibid.*

GENERAL NOTE

Paragraphs (1) and (2)

These paragraphs replace reg.24(5) of the Social Security Commissioners (Procedure) Regulations 1999. Paragraph (1) expresses the general rule, which is that hearings should usually be in public. Paragraph (2) enables the Upper Tribunal to direct that a particular case be heard in private, either in whole or in part. Although it does not specifically provide that a hearing may take place in public only for "special reasons", as reg.24(5) did, the same considerations will still apply. See the notes to r.30(1) and (3) of the Tribunal Procedure (First-tier Tribunal) (Social Entitlement Chamber) Rules 2008 for the meaning of "in public" and considerations relevant to a decision to hold a hearing in private. As in the First-tier Tribunal, this does not arise as a live issue very often because it is very rare for members of the general public to attend hearings. Where someone does attend, concerns raised by a party can often be met by the imposition of appropriate reporting restrictions under r.14(1). Hearings of the Upper Tribunal are usually recorded. Such a recording is a document for the purposes of s.32 of the Freedom of Information Act 2000 and so the question whether it should be disclosed to any person is a matter for the Upper Tribunal and not for the Information Commissioner (*Edem v IC* [2015] UKUT 210 (AAC)). 3.523

Paragraph (3)

If a case is to be heard in private, the tribunal has a broad power to determine who may attend it. However, certain people have a right to attend a hearing even if it is in private. By r.35, a party always has a right to be present (subject to r.37(4)) and, the consequence is that, by virtue of r.11(3), so does a properly appointed representative whether the party attends or not. Where a party does attend, he or she may be accompanied by a person acting either as a representative or merely as an assistant 3.524

(see r.11(5)). Plainly relevant witnesses must be allowed to attend for the purpose of giving evidence.

Beyond that, it is all a matter of discretion, as it was under reg.24(6)(g) of the Social Security Commissioners (Procedure) Regulations 1999. See the note to r.30(4) of the Tribunal Procedure (First-tier Tribunal) (Social Entitlement Chamber) Rules 2008, above.

Paragraphs (4) and (5)

3.525 See the notes to r.30(5) and (6) of the Tribunal Procedure (First-tier Tribunal) (Social Entitlement Chamber) Rules 2008, above, but note that a power to exclude children has been added.

3.526 **37A.** *Expired.*

General Note

3.527 This coronavirus temporary rule was in force from April 10, 2020 to September 25, 2022.

Hearings in a party's absence

3.528 **38.** If a party fails to attend a hearing, the Upper Tribunal may proceed with the hearing if the Upper Tribunal—

(a) is satisfied that the party has been notified of the hearing or that reasonable steps have been taken to notify the party of the hearing; and

(b) considers that it is in the interests of justice to proceed with the hearing.

Definitions

"hearing"—see r.1(3).
"party"—*ibid.*

General Note

3.529 See the note to r.31 of the Tribunal Procedure (First-tier Tribunal) (Social Entitlement Chamber) Rules 2008, above.

Part 6

Decisions

Consent orders

3.530 **39.**—(1) The Upper Tribunal may, at the request of the parties but only if it considers it appropriate, make a consent order disposing of the proceedings and making such other appropriate provision as the parties have agreed.

(2) Notwithstanding any other provision of these Rules, the [2 Upper] Tribunal need not hold a hearing before making an order under paragraph (1)[1 . . .].

AMENDMENTS

1. Tribunal Procedure (Amendment) Rules 2009 (SI 2009/274) r.20 (April 1, 2009).

2.Tribunal Procedure (Amendment No. 4) Rules 2013 (SI 2013/2067) rr.2 and 15 (November 1, 2013).

DEFINITIONS

"hearing"—see r.1(3).
"party"—*ibid.*

GENERAL NOTE

This rule may not have a great deal of relevance to social security cases because it is concerned with cases where there needs to be an "order" and where "other appropriate provision" may need to be made and it applies only "at the request of the parties". Where the parties are agreed as to the outcome of a social security case before the Upper Tribunal, it is usually sufficient for the judge to give a decision to that effect under r.40, which may be given without reasons if the parties consent. 3.531

Indeed, in *TG v SSD* [2009] UKUT 282 (AAC), the Upper Tribunal pointed out that a draft consent order whereby the claimant agreed that an appeal would be dismissed but the Secretary of State agreed to make a more favourable decision was unsound because dismissal of the appeal would leave the lower tribunal's decision in existence. It was necessary for the appeal to be allowed and for the Upper Tribunal to exercise the lower tribunal's power to remit the case to the Secretary of State.

Decisions

40.—(1) The Upper Tribunal may give a decision orally at a hearing. 3.532

[6 (1A) Subject to paragraph (1B), in immigration judicial review proceedings, a decision which disposes of proceedings shall be given at a hearing.

(1B) Paragraph (1A) does not affect the power of the Upper Tribunal to—

(a) strike out a party's case, pursuant to rule 8(1)(b) or 8(2);
(b) consent to withdrawal, pursuant to rule 17;
(c) determine an application for permission to bring judicial review proceedings, pursuant to rule 30; or
(d) make a consent order disposing of proceedings, pursuant to rule 39,

without a hearing.]

(2) [1 . . .] [4 Except where [7 rule 22 (decision in relation to permission to appeal) applies,] the Upper Tribunal must provide to each party as soon as reasonably practicable after making [5 a decision (other than a decision under Part 7) which finally disposes of all issues in the proceedings or of a preliminary issue dealt with following a direction under r.5(3)(e)]—

(a) a decision notice stating the [5 Upper] Tribunal's decision; and
(b) notification of any rights of review or appeal against the decision and the time and manner in which such rights of review or appeal may be exercised.

(3) [1 Subject to rule [2 14(11) (prevention of disclosure or publication of documents and information)],] the Upper Tribunal must provide written reasons for its decision with a decision notice provided under paragraph (2)(a) unless—

(a) the decision was made with the consent of the parties; or
(b) the parties have consented to the Upper Tribunal not giving written reasons.

(4) The [2 Upper] Tribunal may provide written reasons for any decision to which paragraph (2) does not apply.

[3 (5) In a national security certificate appeal, when the Upper Tribunal provides a notice or reasons to the parties under this rule, it must also provide the notice or reasons to the relevant Minister and the Information Commissioner, if they are not parties.

AMENDMENTS

1. Tribunal Procedure (Amendment) Rules 2009 (SI 2009/274) r.21 (April 1, 2009).

2. Tribunal Procedure (Amendment No.2) Rules 2009 (SI 2009/1975) rr.7 and 21 (September 1, 2009).

3. Tribunal Procedure (Amendment) Rules 2010 (SI 2010/43) rr.5 and 13 (January 18, 2010).

4. Tribunal Procedure (Amendment No.2) Rules 2010 (SI 2010/44) rr.2 and 19 (February 15, 2010).

5. Tribunal Procedure (Amendment) Rules 2013 (SI 2013/477) rr.49 and 56 (April 1, 2013).

6. Tribunal Procedure (Amendment No. 4) Rules 2013 (SI 2013/2067) rr.2 and 16 (November 1, 2013).

7. Tribunal Procedure (Amendment No.3) Rules 2014 (SI 2014/2128) rr.2 and 14 (October 20, 2014).

DEFINITIONS

"asylum case"—see r.1(3).
"hearing"—*ibid.*
"immigration judicial review proceedings"—*ibid.*
"national security certificate appeal"—*ibid.*
"party"—*ibid.*
"relevant minister"—*ibid.*

GENERAL NOTE

3.533 See the notes to rr.33 and 34 of the Tribunal Procedure (First-tier Tribunal) (Social Entitlement Chamber) Rules 2008, above. Presumably the clause "finally disposes of all issues in the proceedings" includes a decision to strike proceedings out under r.8 but does not include a refusal of permission to appeal, a refusal of permission to apply for judicial review or summary dismissal of judicial review proceedings, in respect of all of which specific provision is made (see rr.22(1), 30(1)(b) and 30(2)(b)). In any event, it is usually good practice to provide reasons for any decision (where they may not be obvious to the parties adversely affected by the decision) and para.(4) makes specific provision for that to be done.

A decision given by consent without reasons has effect in the particular proceedings in which it is made but is not binding authority in any other case. Therefore, the Secretary of State was wrong to rely upon directions given in such a case when making a written submission to a Social Security Commissioner (*CSDLA/101/2000*). See also the note to r.39 above.

3.534 **40A.** *Revoked*

PART 7

CORRECTING, SETTING ASIDE, REVIEWING AND APPEALING DECISIONS OF THE UPPER TRIBUNAL

Interpretation

41. In this Part— 3.535

"appeal" [1 ,except in rule 44(2) (application for permission to appeal),] means the exercise of a right of appeal under section 13 of the 2007 Act; and

"review" means the review of a decision by the Upper Tribunal under section 10 of the 2007 Act.

AMENDMENT

1. Tribunal Procedure (Amendment) Rules 2009 (SI 2009/274) r.22 (April 1, 2009).

DEFINITION

"the 2007 Act"—see r.1(3).

Clerical mistakes and accidental slips or omissions

42. The Upper Tribunal may at any time correct any clerical mistake or other accidental slip or omission in a decision or record of a decision by— 3.536

(a) sending notification of the amended decision, or a copy of the amended record, to all parties; and

(b) making any necessary amendment to any information published in relation to the decision or record.

DEFINITION

"party"—see r.1(3).

GENERAL NOTE

See the note to r.36 of the Tribunal Procedure (First-tier Tribunal) (Social Entitlement Chamber) Rules 2008, above. Note that a separate power to correct a decision arises on review (see s.10(4)(a) of the Tribunals, Courts and Enforcement Act 2007). 3.537

Setting aside a decision which disposes of proceedings

43.—(1) The Upper Tribunal may set aside a decision which disposes of proceedings, or part of such a decision, and re-make the decision or the relevant part of it, if— 3.538

(a) the Upper Tribunal considers that it is in the interests of justice to do so; and

(b) one or more of the conditions in paragraph (2) are satisfied.

(2) The conditions are—

(a) a document relating to the proceedings was not sent to, or was not received at an appropriate time by, a party or a party's representative;

(b) a document relating to the proceedings was not sent to the Upper Tribunal at an appropriate time;
(c) a party, or a party's representative, was not present at a hearing related to the proceedings; or
(d) there has been some other procedural irregularity in the proceedings.

(3) [1 Except where paragraph (4) applies,] a party applying for a decision, or part of a decision, to be set aside under paragraph (1) must make a written application to the Upper Tribunal so that it is received no later than 1 month after the date on which the [2 Upper] Tribunal sent notice of the decision to the party.

[1 (4) In an asylum case or an immigration case, the written application referred to in paragraph (3) must be sent or delivered so that it is received by the Upper Tribunal—

(a) where the person who appealed to the First-tier Tribunal is in the United Kingdom at the time that the application is made, no later than twelve days after the date on which the Upper Tribunal or, as the case may be in an asylum case, the Secretary of State for the Home Department, sent notice of the decision to the party making the application; or
(b) where the person who appealed to the First-tier Tribunal is outside the United Kingdom at the time that the application is made, no later than thirty eight days after the date on which the Upper Tribunal sent notice of the decision to the party making the application.

(5) Where a notice of decision is sent electronically or delivered personally, the time limits in paragraph (4) are ten working days.]

AMENDMENTS

1. Tribunal Procedure (Amendment No.2) Rules 2010 (SI 2010/44) rr.2 and 21 (February 15, 2010).

2. Tribunal Procedure (Amendment No. 4) Rules 2013 (SI 2013/2067) rr.2 and 17 (November 1, 2013).

DEFINITIONS

"asylum case"—see r.1(3).
"dispose of proceedings"—*ibid.*
"document"—*ibid.*
"hearing"—*ibid.*
"immigration case"—*ibid.*
"party"—*ibid.*

GENERAL NOTE

3.539 See the note to r.37 of the Tribunal Procedure (First-tier Tribunal) (Social Entitlement Chamber) Rules 2008, above. The one-month time limit for making an application may be extended under r.5(3)(a). Note that a separate power to set aside a decision arises on review (see s.10(4)(c) of the 2007 Act).

Since, procedural irregularities in the proceedings before the First-tier Tribunal would be relevant to the decision of the Upper Tribunal whether to give permission to appeal or allow an appeal, r.43 is concerned only with procedural irregularities in the proceedings before the Upper Tribunal and so an application under r.43 is not an opportunity to challenge the Upper Tribunal's decision as to whether there was, or arguably was, an irregularity in the proceedings before the First-tier Tribunal (*SK v SSWP (AA)* [2016] UKUT 529 (AAC); [2017] AACR 25) (approved on this point by the Court of Appeal in *Plescan v Secretary of State for Work and Pensions* [2023] EWCA Civ 870 at [16]). It is also limited to the procedure before the Upper Tribunal and does not cover how the First-tier Tribunal handled the case. It may, however, be possible to conceive of a case in which an irregularity in the proceedings before the Upper Tribunal was caused by an irregularity in the proceedings before the First-tier Tribunal (e.g., a document going astray in the proceedings in the First-tier Tribunal that therefore was not before the Upper Tribunal when it should have been). In such a case, the Upper Tribunal's decision might be set aside if the irregularity came to light only after that decision was given.

Although this rule allows for the setting aside of a refusal of permission to appeal, it does not permit the setting aside of a grant of permission to appeal because such a decision is not one that "disposes of proceedings". However, in *R. (Singh) v Secretary of State for the Home Department* [2019] EWCA Civ 1014, it was held that permission to apply for judicial review given in breach of the rules of natural justice could be set aside because, under s.25 of the Tribunals, Courts and Enforcement Act, the Upper Tribunal had the same powers as the High Court and the High Court would have been able to set aside a grant of permission in such circumstances.

In *DJ (Pakistan) v Secretary of State for the Home Department* [2022] EWCA Civ 1057; [2022] 1 W.L.R. 5381, the Court of Appeal held that a decision of the Immigration and Asylum Chamber of the Upper Tribunal under r.43 could not be the subject of an appeal to the Court of Appeal. However, although there was considerable discussion in Macur LJ's judgment as to whether it should be necessary to appeal against an r.43 decision rather than the substantive decision that has not been set aside or that has been substituted for a decision that has been set aside, the basis of the Court's decision was actually that the r.43 decision, in that case, was an "excluded decision" within the scope of the Appeals (Excluded Decisions) Order 2009 (SI 2009/275) art.3(m), made under the Tribunals, Courts and Enforcement Act 2007 s.13(8)(f), which applies only to certain types of decision in chambers of the Upper Tribunal other than the Administrative Appeals Chamber. Accordingly, the Court's decision has no relevance to social security cases in the Administrative Appeals Chamber, save that some of the reasoning may suggest that, when an application for permission to appeal against an r.43 decision is made in such a case, consideration should be given to whether it might be better directed at a relevant substantive decision. *DJ (Pakistan)* was accordingly distinguished in *Plecsan v Secretary of State for Work and Pensions* [2023] EWCA Civ 870, where the Court took a literal approach to the legislation and held the Tribunals, Courts and Enforcement Act 2007 s.13 conferred jurisdiction on the Court of Appeal to consider an appeal against a decision of the Upper Tribunal refusing to set aside under r.43 its earlier decision refusing permission to appeal to the Upper Tribunal against a decision of the First-tier Tribunal. This was not an excluded decision. The appeal would not be an appeal against the refusal of permission; it would be an appeal against the refusal to set aside.

Application for permission to appeal

44.—(1) [5 Subject to [5 paragraphs (4A) and (4B)],] a person seeking permission to appeal must make a written application to the Upper Tribunal for permission to appeal. 3.540

(2) Paragraph (3) applies to an application under paragraph (1) in respect of a decision—

(a) on an appeal against a decision in a social security and child support case (as defined in the Tribunal Procedure (First-tier Tribunal) (Social Entitlement Chamber) Rules 2008);

(b) on an appeal against a decision in proceedings in the War Pensions and Armed Forces Compensation Chamber of the First-tier Tribunal); [1 . . .]

[1 (ba) on an appeal against a decision of a Pensions Appeal Tribunal for Scotland or Northern Ireland; or]

(c) in proceedings under the Forfeiture Act 1982.

(3) Where this paragraph applies, the application must be sent or delivered to the Upper Tribunal so that it is received within 3 months after the date on which the Upper Tribunal sent to the person making the application—

(a) written notice of the decision;

(b) notification of amended reasons for, or correction of, the decision following a review; or

(c) notification that an application for the decision to be set aside has been unsuccessful.

[2 (3A) An application under paragraph (1) in respect of a decision in an asylum case or an immigration case must be sent or delivered to the Upper Tribunal so that it is received within the appropriate period after the Upper Tribunal or, as the case may be in an asylum case, the Secretary of State for the Home Department, sent any of the documents in paragraph (3) to the party making the application.

(3B) The appropriate period referred to in paragraph (3A) is as follows—

(a) where the person who appealed to the First-tier Tribunal is in the United Kingdom at the time that the application is made—

(i) [4 twelve working days]; or

(ii) if the party making the application is in detention under the Immigration Acts, seven working days; and

(b) where the person who appealed to the First-tier Tribunal is outside the United Kingdom at the time that the application is made, thirty eight days.

(3C) Where a notice of decision is sent electronically or delivered personally, the time limits in paragraph (3B) are—

(a) in sub-paragraph (a)(i), ten working days;

(b) in sub-paragraph (a)(ii), five working days; and

(c) in sub-paragraph (b), ten working days.]

[3 (3D) An application under paragraph (1) in respect of a decision in a financial services case must be sent or delivered to the Upper Tribunal so that it is received within 14 days after the date on which the Upper Tribunal sent to the person making the application—

(a) written notice of the decision;

(b) notification of amended reasons for, or correction of, the decision following a review; or

(c) notification that an application for the decision to be set aside has been unsuccessful.]

(4) Where paragraph (3) [2 [3 , (3A) [6 , (3D) or (4C)]]] does not apply, an application under paragraph (1) must be sent or delivered to the Upper Tribunal so that it is received within 1 month after the latest of the dates on which the Upper Tribunal sent to the person making the application—

(a) written reasons for the decision;

(b) notification of amended reasons for, or correction of, the decision following a review; or

(c) notification that an application for the decision to be set aside has been unsuccessful.

[5 (4A) [6 Where a decision that disposes of immigration judicial review proceedings is given at a hearing, a party may apply at that hearing for permission to appeal, and the Upper Tribunal must consider at the hearing whether to give or refuse permission to appeal.]]

[6 (4B) Where a decision that disposes of immigration judicial review proceedings is given at a hearing and no application for permission to appeal is made at that hearing—

(a) the Upper Tribunal must nonetheless consider at the hearing whether to give or refuse permission to appeal; and

(b) if permission to appeal is given to a party, it shall be deemed for the purposes of section 13(4) of the 2007 Act to be given on application by that party.

(4C) Where a decision that disposes of immigration judicial review proceedings is given pursuant to rule 30 and the Upper Tribunal records under rule 30(4A) that the application is totally without merit, an application under paragraph (1) must be sent or delivered to the Upper Tribunal so that it is received within 7 days after the later of the dates on which the Upper Tribunal sent to the applicant—

(a) written reasons for the decision; or

(b) notification of amended reasons for, or correction of, the decision following a review.]

(5) The date in paragraph (3)(c) or (4)(c) applies only if the application for the decision to be set aside was made within the time stipulated in rule 43 (setting aside a decision which disposes of proceedings) or any extension of that time granted by the Upper Tribunal.

(6) If the person seeking permission to appeal provides the application to the Upper Tribunal later than the time required by paragraph (3) [2, (3A)] [3 , (3D)] or (4), or by any extension of time under rule 5(3)(a) (power to extend time)—

(a) the application must include a request for an extension of time and the reason why the application notice was not provided in time; and

(b) unless the Upper Tribunal extends time for the application under rule 5(3)(a) (power to extend time) the Upper Tribunal must refuse the application.

(7) An application under paragraph (1) [5 or (4A)(a)] must—

(a) identify the decision of the [6 Upper] Tribunal to which it relates;

(b) identify the alleged error or errors of law in the decision; and

(c) state the result the party making the application is seeking.

AMENDMENTS

1. Tribunal Procedure (Amendment) Rules 2009 (SI 2009/274) r.23 (April 1, 2009).

2. Tribunal Procedure (Amendment) (No.2) Rules 2010 (SI 2010/44) rr.2 and 22 (February 15, 2010).

3. Tribunal Procedure (Upper Tribunal) (Amendment) Rules 2010 (SI 2010/747) rr.2 and 10 (April 6, 2010).

4. Tribunal Procedure (Amendment) Rules 2011 (SI 2011/651) r.8(1) and (4) (April 1, 2011).

5. Tribunal Procedure (Upper Tribunal) (Amendment) Rules 2012 (SI 2012/2890) rr.2 and 3 (December 11, 2012).

6. Tribunal Procedure (Amendment No. 4) Rules 2013 (SI 2013/2067) rr.2 and 18 (November 1, 2013).

DEFINITIONS

"appeal"—see r.41.
"asylum case"—see r.1(3).
"dispose of proceedings"—*ibid.*
"financial services case"—*ibid.*
"immigration case"—*ibid.*
"immigration judicial review proceedings"—*ibid.*
"judicial review proceedings"—*ibid.*
"party"—*ibid.*
"permission"—*ibid.*
"working day"—*ibid.*

GENERAL NOTE

3.541 Paragraph (3), which prescribes a three-month time limit, applies to social security cases and is more favourable than paras (3A)–(4), which apply to other types of case. This generous time-limit existed under the earlier legislation because it is commonly only at this stage that parties, including the Secretary of State, HMRC and local authorities, first seek legal advice.

Paragraph (4A) was introduced in response to comments by the Court of Appeal in *R. (NB (Algeria)) v Secretary of State for the Home Department* [2012] EWCA Civ 1050. It does not apply to social security cases in the Administrative Appeals Chamber.

Note that para.(6)(b) uses the word "refuse", from which it follows that a decision by the Upper Tribunal not to extend the time for applying for permission to appeal does not prevent the applicant from applying to the appellate court for permission, although the appellate court will, of course, have regard to the delay in applying to the Upper Tribunal. This is because the condition in s.13(5) of the Tribunals, Courts and Enforcement Act 2007 (that permission have been "refused" by the Upper Tribunal before an application may be made to the appellate court) will have been satisfied. Thus, the effect of *White v Chief Adjudication Officer* [1986] 2 All E.R. 905 (also reported as an appendix to *R(S) 8/85*) has at last been reversed. In *White*, it had been held that a Commissioner's refusal to extend time for applying for leave to appeal to the Court of Appeal did not amount to a refusal of leave to appeal and was challengeable only by way of an application for judicial review.

Upper Tribunal's consideration of application for permission to appeal

3.542 **45.**—(1) On receiving an application for permission to appeal the Upper Tribunal may review the decision in accordance with rule 46 (review of a decision), but may only do so if—

(a) when making the decision the Upper Tribunal overlooked a legislative provision or binding authority which could have had a material effect on the decision; or
(b) since the Upper Tribunal's decision, a court has made a decision which is binding on the Upper Tribunal and which, had it been made before the Upper Tribunal's decision, could have had a material effect on the decision.

(2) If the Upper Tribunal decides not to review the decision, or reviews the decision and decides to take no action in relation to the decision or part of it, the Upper Tribunal must consider whether to give permission to appeal in relation to the decision or that part of it.

(3) The Upper Tribunal must [1 provide] a record of its decision to the parties as soon as practicable.

(4) If the Upper Tribunal refuses permission to appeal it must [1 provide] with the record of its decision—

(a) a statement of its reasons for such refusal; and

(b) notification of the right to make an application to the relevant appellate court for permission to appeal and the time within which, and the method by which, such application must be made.

(5) The Upper Tribunal may give permission to appeal on limited grounds, but must comply with paragraph (4) in relation to any grounds on which it has refused permission.

AMENDMENT

1. Tribunal Procedure (Amendment No. 4) Rules 2013 (SI 2013/2067) rr.2 and 19 (November 1, 2013).

DEFINITIONS

"appeal"—see r.41.
"permission"—see r.1(3).
"party"—*ibid.*
"review"—see r.41.

GENERAL NOTE

Paragraphs (1) and (2)

Before deciding whether or not to grant permission to appeal, the Upper Tribunal must first decide whether or not to review the decision under s.10 of the Tribunals, Courts and Enforcement Act 2007, as limited by para.(1). A decision may be reviewed only if the judge overlooked an important piece of legislation or case law or superior court has since made a decision that suggests that the decision of the Upper Tribunal was wrong. An example of the Upper Tribunal having overlooked a legislative provision may be seen in *Wychavon DC v EM (HB)* [2012] UKUT 12 (AAC); [2012] AACR 41, a housing benefit case concerned with a mentally disabled claimant's liability to pay rent. The judge had overlooked s.7 of the Mental Capacity Act 2005 and a decision of the Court of Appeal dealing with the law in relation to the supply of necessaries, consideration of which led him to review his previous decision in favour of the local authority and to decide the case against it. The word "could" is used in both subparas (a) and (b) of para.(1), which perhaps suggests that the Upper Tribunal might set aside a decision before hearing full argument rather than obtaining representations before deciding whether or not the decision should be reviewed. 3.543

It is not usually necessary to obtain the views of opposing parties to an application for permission to appeal on a point of law, but the Upper Tribunal should consider doing so if a ground is raised that was not advanced on the appeal before it (*RH v South London and Maudsley NHS Foundation Trust* [2010] EWCA Civ 1273; [2011] AACR 14). Moreover, in *Global Energy Horizons Corp v Gray* [2020] EWCA Civ 1668; [2021] 1 W.L.R. 2264 at [495] the Court of Appeal observed that:

> "While on many matters, including generally issues of law, there may be little that the successful party can say in opposition to an application for permission to appeal, we do not share the view that the same applies where detailed findings of fact in a complex case are challenged, and that goes as much for applications to this court as to the court below."

Paragraph (4)

3.544 Reasons for refusing permission to appeal can usually be very brief and will often simply be that the application does not raise any point of law or does not raise an important point of principle and practice, as required by the Order made under s.13(6) of the 2007 Act (see the note to that provision), or that a new point of law would not have persuaded the judge to reach a different conclusion. Reasons can be valuable in persuading an applicant not to make an application to the appellate court in a hopeless case. If an application raises allegations about the conduct of the Upper Tribunal, it is likely to assist the court if the Upper Tribunal makes it clear whether it disputes the accuracy of the allegations.

Review of a decision

3.545 **46.**—(1) [1 The Upper Tribunal may only undertake a review of a decision pursuant to rule 45(1) (review on an application for permission to appeal).]

(2) The Upper Tribunal must notify the parties in writing of the outcome of any review and of any rights of review or appeal in relation to the outcome.

(3) If the Upper Tribunal decides to take any action in relation to a decision following a review without first giving every party an opportunity to make representations, the notice under paragraph (2) must state that any party that did not have an opportunity to make representations may apply for such action to be set aside and for the decision to be reviewed again.

AMENDMENT

1. Tribunal Procedure (Upper Tribunal) (Amendment) Rules 2011 (SI 2011/2343) rr.2 and 12 (October 17, 2011).

DEFINITIONS

"appeal"—see r.41.
"party"—see r.1(3).
"review"—see r.41.

GENERAL NOTE

Paragraph (1)

3.546 The power of review arises under s.10(1) of the Tribunals, Courts and Enforcement Act 2007. Section 10(2) provides for the power to be exercised either on the tribunal's initiative or on an application but s.10(3)(b) enables rules to provide that it is exercisable only on the Upper Tribunal's own initiative. That is what para. (1) of this rule does. A party may not make a free-standing application for a review (although if he or she does, the Upper Tribunal can, under r.48, treat it as an application for permission to appeal) but the Upper Tribunal may review a decision on its own initiative once there has been an application for permission to appeal. Rule 45(1), made under s.10(3)(d), limits the ground of review to cases where the Upper Tribunal overlooked a legislative provision or binding authority or there has since been a new binding authority. Since appeals under s.13 lie only on points of law, a review therefore provides a way of avoiding an appeal where the appeal would plainly be allowed or where the Upper Tribunal ought to deal with an overlooked issue before the question of permission to appeal is considered. See s.10(4), (5) and (6) for the powers of the Upper Tribunal on review.

Paragraph (2)

Section 13(8)(d) has the effect that there is no right of appeal against a decision whether or not to review a decision, to take no action on a review, to set aside a decision on a review or to refer, or not refer, a matter to the Upper Tribunal on review. However, that is because there is always another decision that may be the subject of an appeal. Where the Upper Tribunal refuses to review a decision or reviews it but takes no action or merely amends its reasons, the Upper Tribunal must consider whether to give permission to appeal against the original decision. Where the tribunal reviews a decision and re-decides the case, there will be a right to apply for permission to appeal against the new decision. **3.547**

Where a decision is reviewed without all the parties having had the opportunity to make representations, notice must also be given of the right to apply for the new decision to be set aside (see para.(3)).

Paragraph (3)

The clear implication of this paragraph is that the Upper Tribunal may either obtain submissions from the parties other than the applicant before reviewing a case or review the case first and then wait to see whether any of the other parties objects. Plainly the second of those approaches may lead to a quicker decision and less work where there is no objection to the review. However, it is suggested that that approach is appropriate only where both the ground of review and the appropriate decision are very clear. **3.548**

[1 Setting aside] a decision in proceedings under the Forfeiture Act 1982

47.—(1) A person who referred a question to the Upper Tribunal under rule 26 (references under the Forfeiture Act 1982) must refer the Upper Tribunal's previous decision in relation to the question to the Upper Tribunal if they— **3.549**

(a) consider that the decision should be [1 set aside and re-made under this rule]; or

(b) have received a written application for the decision to be [1 set aside and re-made under this rule] from the person to whom the decision related.

(2) The Upper Tribunal may [1 set aside the decision, either in whole or in part, and re-make it] if—

(a) [1 ...];

(b) the decision was made in ignorance of, or was based on a mistake as to, some material fact; or

(c) there has been a relevant change in circumstances since the decision was made.

[1 (3) Rule 26(2) to (4), Parts 5 and 6 and this Part apply to a reference under this rule as they apply to a reference under rule 26(1).]

AMENDMENT

1. Tribunal Procedure (Upper Tribunal) (Amendment) Rules 2011 (SI 2011/2343) rr.2 and 13 (October 17, 2011).

GENERAL NOTE

Wide grounds for setting aside a decision are provided for in cases under the Forfeiture Act 1982, where the Upper Tribunal is the primary fact-finding body and there is no other mechanism for dealing with errors of fact that might have been **3.550** made. This rule largely reproduces the effect of reg.15(2) and (3) of the Social Security Commissioners (Procedure) Regulations 1999. The effect of para.(4) of reg.15 has not been reproduced and it is therefore merely left implicit that the Upper Tribunal may determine the date from which a new decision takes effect.

[1 Power to treat an application as a different type of application

3.551 **48.** The [2 Upper] Tribunal may treat an application for a decision to be corrected, set aside or reviewed, or for permission to appeal against a decision, as an application for any other one of those things.]

AMENDMENTS

1. Tribunal Procedure (Amendment No.3) Rules 2010 (SI 2010/2653) r.8 (November 29, 2010).

2. Tribunal Procedure (Amendment No. 4) Rules 2013 (SI 2013/2067) rr.2 and 20 (November 1, 2013).

DEFINITIONS

"appeal"—see r.41.
"review"—*ibid.*

3.552 **Schedules A1 to 4.** *Omitted.*

PRACTICE DIRECTIONS

Practice Direction (First-Tier And Upper Tribunals: Child, Vulnerable Adult And Sensitive Witnesses)

3.553 1. In this Practice Direction:

a. "child" means a person who has not attained the age of 18;
b. "vulnerable adult" has the same meaning as in the Safeguarding Vulnerable Groups Act 2006;
c. "sensitive witness" means an adult witness where the quality of evidence given by the witness is likely to be diminished by reason of fear or distress on the part of the witness in connection with giving evidence in the case.

Circumstances under which a child, vulnerable adult or sensitive witness may give evidence

3.554 2. A child, vulnerable adult or sensitive witness will only be required to attend as a witness and give evidence at a hearing where the Tribunal determines that the evidence is necessary to enable the fair hearing of the case and their welfare would not be prejudiced by doing so.

3. In determining whether it is necessary for a child, vulnerable adult or sensitive witness to give evidence to enable the fair hearing of a case the Tribunal should have regard to all the available evidence and any representations made by the parties.

4. In determining whether the welfare of the child, vulnerable adult or sensitive witness would be prejudiced it may be appropriate for the Tribunal to invite submissions from interested persons, such as a child's parents.

5. The Tribunal may decline to issue a witness summons under the Tribunal Procedure Rules or to permit a child, vulnerable adult or sensitive witness to give evidence where it is satisfied that the evidence is not necessary to enable the fair hearing of the case and must decline to do so where the witness's welfare would be prejudiced by them giving evidence.

Manner in which evidence is given

6. The Tribunal must consider how to facilitate the giving of any evidence by a child, vulnerable adult or sensitive witness. **3.555**
7. It may be appropriate for the Tribunal to direct that the evidence should be given by telephone, video link or other means directed by the Tribunal, or to direct that a person be appointed for the purpose of the hearing who has the appropriate skills or experience in facilitating the giving of evidence by a child, vulnerable adult or sensitive witness.
8. This Practice Direction is made by the Senior President of Tribunals with the agreement of the Lord Chancellor. It is made in the exercise of powers conferred by the Tribunals, Courts and Enforcement Act 2007.

LORD JUSTICE CARNWATH
Senior President of Tribunals
30 October 2008

GENERAL NOTE

On July 29, 2014, the then Senior President of Tribunals announced that, in light of *JP v SSWP (DLA)* [2014] UKUT 275 (AAC); [2015] AACR 2 in which it was said that para.5 of this Practice Direction was inconsistent with *In re W (Children) (Family Proceedings: Evidence)* [2010] UKSC 12; [2010] 1 W.L.R. 701, this Practice Direction would be revised and brought into line with developments in the law. See the note to r.27 of the Tribunal Procedure (First-tier Tribunal) (Social Entitlement Chamber) Rules 2008. However, in *AM (Afghanistan) v Secretary of State for the Home Department* [2017] EWCA Civ 1123 at [30], Ryder SPT, with whom Underhill and Gross L.JJ. agreed, said that it must be followed, without making any reference to those cases. **3.556**

For the relevance of this Practice Direction to deciding whether to proceed with a hearing in a party's absence, see the annotation to r.31 of those Rules.

In *RT v SSWP (PIP)* [2019] UKUT 207 (AAC); [2020] AACR 4, it was held that the reference to the Safeguarding Vulnerable Groups Act 2006 had to be read as a reference to that Act as in force at the time the Practice Direction was made on 30 October 2008, with the result that the overwhelming majority of appellants in social security cases are, strictly speaking, vulnerable adults for the purpose of the Practice Direction. Moreover, in the light of *AM (Afghanistan)*, it was necessary for the First-tier Tribunal to indicate in its reasons for decision whether it had followed the Practice Direction, although in many cases a failure to do so would not be a material error of law because it would be obvious that no special provision need be made for the claimant. In *RT* itself, where the claimant had been diagnosed as having an Autistic Spectrum Condition together with depression, anxiety and agoraphobia, it was held that the First-tier Tribunal *had* either made a material error of law by failing to follow the Practice Direction or, if it had had regard to it, by failing to record that it had done so and to explain its apparent decision that no special arrangements were appropriate in the light of it. That case was followed in *JE v SSWP (PIP)* [2020] UKUT 17 (AAC) where it was reiterated that claimants' representatives ought to draw a tribunal's attention to any requirement that the claimant had for special provision and, at [18], that in a borderline case a failure to do so may have the effect that the First-tier Tribunal does not err in law in not recognising the issue itself. It was also considered in *AA and BA v A Local Authority (SEN)* [2021] UKUT 54 (AAC), where the Upper Tribunal again emphasised that any failure to follow the Practice Direction had to be material if it was to amount to an error of law and refused permission to appeal because, although there might have been shortcomings in the First-tier Tribunal's making of appropriate adjustments, it was not arguable that they made any material difference to the evidence that was given by the witnesses.

Judges may reasonably differ as to the measures required to enable a party to participate in any particular case and so such disagreement does not necessarily demonstrate an error of law (*RR v SSWP (CSM)* [2022] UKUT 7 (AAC)). However, where one judge has positively directed that certain measures should be taken, another judge should not take a different approach without a good reason and, if no reason is given and none is readily apparent, doing so might be regarded as wrong in law (see *CSDLA/866/2002*, although that case was concerned with the obtaining of a medical report rather than the making of reasonable adjustments to enable a person to participate in a hearing). There is no obligation on a tribunal proactively to manage a case so as to enable a disabled person to participate in proceedings if that person has been barred from doing so under the Tribunal Procedure (First-tier Tribunal) (Social Entitlement Chamber) Rules 2008 r.8 or the Tribunal Procedure (Upper Tribunal) Rules 2008 r.8 but nonetheless attends the hearing (*Hirachand v Hirachand* [2021] EWCA Civ 1498; [2022] 1 W.L.R. 1162).

Practice Direction (First-Tier And Upper Tribunals: Use Of The Welsh Language In Tribunals In Wales)

General

3.557 1. The purpose of this Practice Direction is to reflect the principle of the Welsh Language Act 1993 that in the administration of justice in Wales, the English and Welsh languages should be treated on a basis of equality.

2. In this Practice Direction "Welsh case" means a case which is before the Tribunal in which all "individual parties" are resident in Wales or which has been classified as a Welsh case by the Tribunal. An "individual party" is a party other than a Government Department or Agency. Where not all of the "individual parties" are resident in Wales the Tribunal will decide whether the case should be classified as a Welsh case or not.

Use of the Welsh language

3.558 3. In a Welsh case the Welsh language may be used by any party or witnesses or in any document placed before the Tribunal or (subject to the listing provisions below) at any hearing.

Listing

3.559 4. Unless it is not reasonably practicable to do so a party, or their representative, must inform the Tribunal 21 days before any hearing in a

Welsh case that the Welsh language will be used by the party, their representative, any witness to be called by that party or in any document to be produced by the party.

5. Where the proceedings are on appeal to the Upper Tribunal and the Welsh language was used in the Tribunal below, the Tribunal Manager must make arrangements for the continued use of the Welsh language in the proceedings before the Upper Tribunal.
6. Where practicable, a hearing in which the Welsh language is to be used must be listed before a Welsh speaking Tribunal and, where translation facilities are needed, at a venue with simultaneous translation facilities.

Interpreters

7. Whenever an interpreter is needed to translate evidence from English into Welsh or from Welsh into English, the Tribunal Manager in whose tribunal the case is to be heard must ensure that the attendance is secured of an interpreter whose name is included in the list of approved interpreters. **3.560**

Witnesses

8. When a witness in a case in which the Welsh language may be used is required to give evidence on oath or affirmation the Tribunal must inform the witness that they may be sworn or affirm in Welsh or English as they wish. **3.561**
9. This Practice Direction is made by the Senior President of Tribunals with the agreement of the Lord Chancellor. It is made in the exercise of powers conferred by the Tribunals, Courts and Enforcement Act 2007.

LORD JUSTICE CARNWATH
Senior President of Tribunals
30 October 2008

Practice Direction (Upper Tribunal: Transcripts Of Proceedings)

1. At any hearing where the proceedings are recorded such recordings must be preserved by the Tribunal for six months from the date of the hearing to which the recording relates, and any party to the proceedings may, within that period, apply in writing for a transcript and a transcript must be supplied to that party. **3.562**
2. If a transcript is supplied to a party under paragraph 1, that party must pay for the production and supply of the transcript unless they have applied in writing for, and the Tribunal has given, a direction that the transcript be produced and supplied at public expense.
3. The Tribunal may direct a transcript be supplied at public expense if satisfied that:
   a. a recording of the relevant proceedings is in existence; and
   b. the party making the application;
      i. has applied, or intends to apply, for permission to challenge the Upper Tribunal's decision in another court and has reasonable grounds for bringing or intending to challenge that decision; or

ii. has been granted permission to challenge the Upper Tribunal's decision and has brought, or intends to bring, such proceedings; or
iii. is a respondent to any such challenge to a decision of the Upper Tribunal in another court; and

c. the transcript is necessary for the purpose of challenging the Upper Tribunal's decision; and
d. the party's financial circumstances are such that that party cannot afford to pay for the transcript from their own income or funds.

4. Any transcript of proceedings directed to be supplied at public expense must be restricted to that part of the proceedings necessary for the purposes of any such challenge.
5. For the purposes of considering an application for a transcript at public expense, the Tribunal may give directions, for example, requiring the party to disclose details of their financial circumstances.
6. This Practice Direction is made by the Senior President of Tribunals with the agreement of the Lord Chancellor. It is made in the exercise of powers conferred by the Tribunals, Courts and Enforcement Act 2007.

LORD JUSTICE CARNWATH
Senior President of Tribunals
30 October 2008

GENERAL NOTE

3.563 This Practice Direction has the effect that anyone may ask for a transcript of a recording of proceedings but will have to pay for it, except in the circumstances listed in para.3. It is to be noted that the right to a transcript is not a right to a copy of the recording. In relation to the courts, *Practice Direction (Audio Recordings of Proceedings: Access)* [2014] 1 W.L.R. 632 makes it clear that "there is generally no right, either for a party or non-party, to listen to or receive a copy of . . . a recording [so as] to minimise the risk of misuse of . . . recordings". That Practice Direction makes provision for a person who has obtained a copy of the official transcript to apply for permission to listen to or receive a recording, although it also makes clear that permission will be granted "only in exceptional circumstances, for example where there is cogent evidence that the official transcript may have been wrongly transcribed." However, in both the First-tier Tribunal and the Upper Tribunal, recordings are frequently provided to parties because it is simpler and cheaper for both the party and the tribunal than providing a transcript, although only with a warning that broadcasting it is likely to be punished as a contempt of court.

This Practice Direction applies only to the Upper Tribunal, being merely a continuation of a practice statement of the former Chief Social Security Commissioner, but it has been held that the First-tier Tribunal has no power to refuse to provide an official transcript of public proceedings, if the person seeking it is prepared to pay for it, and that it is irrelevant that a recording has already been provided to that person (*Kirkham v IC* [2019] UKUT 381 (AAC)).

Practice Direction: Closed Judgments

3.564 1. This Practice Direction applies to any Court of Tribunal giving a "closed" judgment following a closed material procedure, whether pursuant to the provisions of Part 1 of the Justice and Security Act 2013, in the High Court, the Divisional Court or the Court of Appeal;

in proceedings in relation to Terrorism Prevention and Investigation Measures; in any Tribunal established under the Tribunals, Courts and Enforcements Act 2007 (save for the Employment Tribunal and the Employment Appeals Tribunal) and in any appeals therefrom.

2. A single printed copy and an electronic copy of each closed judgment and any related open judgment must be lodged with the RCJ Senior Information Officer within 14 days of being delivered or handed down, for consideration for inclusion in the library of closed judgments now established in the Royal Courts of Justice.
3. If it is decided to retain the judgment in the library, the relevant judge(s) or tribunal judge(s) will be informed. If the judgment is not to be retained, it will be disposed of securely.
4. Both printed and electronic judgments must at all times be maintained under secure handling provisions as set down in *Closed Judgments Library – Security Guidance* of 2017, a copy of which can be obtained from the RCJ Senior Information Officer.
5. Any questions should be directed in the first instance to the RCJ Senior Information Officer, telephone 020 7947 7939, email – RCJinfomanagement@justice.gov.uk.
6. This Practice Direction is made under the procedure set out in Part 1 of Schedule 2 to the Constitutional Reform Act 2005 and under Civil Procedure Act 1997, section 5, Courts Act 2003, sections 74 and 81 in respect of the Courts of England and Wales. It is made under the procedure set out in Tribunals, Courts and Enforcement Act 2007, section 23, in respect of the First-tier and Upper Tribunals. It is made by the Lord Chief Justice and Senior President of Tribunals with the approval of the Lord Chancellor.

LORD BURNETT OF MALDON CJ
SIR ERNEST RYDER SP
14 January 2019

PART IV

HUMAN RIGHTS LAW

Human Rights Act 1998

(1998 c.42)

ARRANGEMENT OF SECTIONS

Introduction **4.1**

GENERAL NOTE

4.2 This Act has been described as "the first historic step . . . towards a constitutional Bill of Rights" (A. Lester, and D. Pannick (eds), *Human Rights Law and Practice* (Butterworths: London, 1999), para.1.44. It followed a Labour consultation paper of December 1996 entitled *Bringing Rights Home*, a manifesto commitment by the Labour Party in 1997, and an October 1997 White Paper entitled *Rights Brought Home: The Human Rights Bill*, Cmnd.3782.

The Act entered into force on October 2, 2000: The Human Rights Act 1998 (Commencement No.2) Order 2000 (SI 2000/1851). The commencement of each section is noted in the annotation to each section.

The UK has been a party to the European Convention on Human Rights since September 23, 1953 and has recognised the right of individual petition under the Convention continuously since January 14, 1966. Until this Act come into force, rights accruing for individuals under the Convention could not be invoked directly to determine whether they have been victims of a violation of the rights protected by the Convention. Individuals within the jurisdiction could only use the "ordinary" law of the land to secure their rights. If they believed that these have been denied them by the state or a part of the state, and they have sought redress under the national legal order (exhausted domestic remedies in the language of the Convention), they have been able to make an application to the Commission of Human Rights (prior to November 1, 1998) and direct to the Court of Human Rights (from November 1, 1998) claiming to be victims of a violation of one of the rights protected. If the application is admitted, then the Court of Human Rights may adjudicate on the issue. Decisions of the Court may be consulted at *http://www.hudoc.echr.coe.int*. The United Kingdom is not a signatory to Protocol No.16, which came into force on August 1, 2018 and allows the highest court in a State to seek a non-binding advisory opinion from the Court.

The Convention organs, which are part of the Council of Europe, are located in Strasbourg; they should not be confused with the institutions of the European Union. The Court of Justice of the European Union is located in Luxembourg.

Introduction

The Convention Rights

1.—(1) In this Act "the Convention rights" means the rights and fundamental freedoms set out in— **4.3**

(a) Articles 2 to 12 and 14 of the Convention,
(b) Articles 1 to 3 of the First Protocol, and
[[2] (c) Article 1 of the Thirteenth Protocol,]

as read with Articles 16 to 18 of the Convention.

(2) Those Articles are to have effect for the purposes of this Act subject to any designated derogation or reservation (as to which see sections 14 and 15).

(3) The Articles are set out in Schedule 1.

(4) The [[1] Secretary of State] may by order make such amendments to this Act as he considers appropriate to reflect the effect, in relation to the United Kingdom, of a protocol.

(5) In subsection (4) "protocol" means a protocol to the Convention—

(a) which the United Kingdom has ratified; or
(b) which the United Kingdom has signed with a view to ratification.

(6) No amendment may be made by an order under subsection (4) so as to come into force before the protocol concerned is in force in relation to the United Kingdom.

COMMENCEMENT

October 2, 2000: the Human Rights Act 1998 (Commencement No.2) Order 2000 (SI 2000/1851). **4.4**

AMENDMENTS

1. The Secretary of State for Constitutional Affairs Order 2003 (SI 2003/1887) (August 19, 2003).

2. Human Rights Act 1998 (Amendment) Order 2004 (SI 2004/1574) (June 22, 2004).

GENERAL NOTE

The Preamble to the Act describes its objective as to give "further effect" to the rights and freedoms guaranteed by the European Convention on Human Rights. The further effect given to the rights encompassed by the Act is their effect within the national legal order, so that they can be invoked directly in proceedings before United Kingdom courts and tribunals. This is the scheme of incorporation adopted for the United Kingdom. The late former President of the Court has expressed the advantages of incorporation as follows, **4.5**

> "It has in fact two advantages: it provides the national court with the possibility of taking account of the Convention and the Strasbourg case-law to resolve the dispute before it, and at the same time it gives the European organs an opportunity to discover the views of the national courts regarding the interpretation of the Convention and its application to a specific set of circumstances. The dialogue

> which thus develops between those who are called upon to apply the Convention on the domestic level and those who must do so on the European level is crucial for an effective protection of the rights guaranteed under the Convention." (Rolv Ryssdal, Speech at the ceremony for the 40th anniversary of the European Convention on Human Rights at Trieste, 18 December 1990, Council of Europe document Court (90) 318, 2.)

Convention rights are defined in subs.(1) as arts 2–12 and 14 of the Convention itself, together with certain articles of the First and Sixth Protocols as read with arts 16–18 of the Convention. These articles are set out in Sch.1. Their effect is subject to the terms of any derogation under art.15 of the Convention or any reservation filed by the UK Government. Derogations are governed in more detail by s.14, and reservations by s.15; any current derogations and reservations are set out in Sch.3. The Secretary of State is given power to amend the Act to give effect to rights contained in protocols to the Convention which have not yet been ratified by the UK.

Convention rights as defined in s.1 do not include art.1 which provides that parties to the Convention "shall secure to everyone within their jurisdiction the rights and freedoms" set out in arts 2–18 of the Convention. Nor do they include art.13 which gives a right to an effective remedy in the following terms:

> "Everyone whose rights and freedoms as set forth in this Convention are violated shall have an effective remedy before a national authority notwithstanding that the violation has been committed by persons acting in an official capacity."

The incorporation of art.1 among Convention rights named by the Act is probably not necessary since the purpose of the Act is to give effect to Convention rights within the national legal order. However, it should be noted that the rights given by the Convention are not linked in any way to the nationality of an individual; they are guaranteed to all within the UK's jurisdiction. This differs from many rights given by EU law where the beneficiaries are nationals of the Member States of the European Union.

4.6 The failure to include art.13 among the Convention rights may be more problematic, though the Lord Chancellor stoutly argued that its inclusion was not necessary because the Act gives effect "to Article 13 by establishing a scheme under which Convention rights can be raised before out domestic courts": HL Vol.583 col.475 (November 18, 1997). In the Commons, the Home Secretary made a similar point. There is apparently some concern that inclusion of the article might lead all manner of courts and tribunals to "invent" new remedies for violation of Convention rights. The Act is cautious on the issue of remedies where a violation is found: see commentary to s.8. However, both the Lord Chancellor and the Home Secretary conceded that in considering any question of remedies, courts or tribunals may have regard to the terms of art.13 under s.2 of the Act. However, situations may arise where the scheme of the Act arguably does not offer an effective remedy for the violation, though it should be noted that the nature and scope of the effectiveness of the remedy required under art.13 has hardly been touched on in the Strasbourg case law.

An example might help to illustrate the possible lacuna. Suppose a claimant before an appeal tribunal succeeds in persuading the tribunal that there has been an excessive delay in giving judgment on an appeal; this would constitute a violation of art.6(1) ECHR. In this type of case, the Court of Human Rights has often awarded some compensation for the delay, but an appeal tribunal has no power to award compensation, or interest on late benefit. This would leave the individual without a remedy unless the mere statement that there was a violation was considered sufficient in the circumstances of the case. Any claim for compensation would have to be the subject of separate (and wholly novel) proceedings in a different forum. It is at least arguable that making a person in this position go to two judicial bodies for a remedy for the same violation is a failure to provide an effective remedy.

In *Kelly v SSWP* [2024] EWCA Civ 613, the exclusion of art.13 from "the Convention rights" was among the reasons why it would be inappropriate for the court to make a declaration of incompatibility in respect of the past discrimination experienced by Ms Kelly, because "the HRA is itself a carefully crafted remedial scheme" (at [87]), with attributes which Elisabeth Laing J went on to set out. See further 4.30.

Interpretation of Convention rights

2.—(1) A court or tribunal determining a question which has arisen in connection with a Convention right must take into account any— 4.7

(a) judgment, decision, declaration or advisory opinion of the European Court of Human Rights,

(b) opinion of the Commission given in a report adopted under Article 31 of the Convention,

(c) decision of the Commission in connection with Article 26 or 27(2) of the Convention, or

(d) decision of the Committee of Ministers taken under Article 46 of the Convention,

whenever made or given, so far as, in the opinion of the court or tribunal, it is relevant to the proceedings in which that question has arisen.

(2) Evidence of any judgment, decision, declaration or opinion of which account may have to be taken under this section is to be given in proceedings before any court or tribunal in such manner as may be provided by rules.

(3) In this section "rules" means rules of court or, in the case of proceedings before a tribunal, rules made for the purposes of this section—

(a) by [1 . . .] [2 the Lord Chancellor or] the Secretary of State, in relation to any proceedings outside Scotland;

(b) by the Secretary of State, in relation to proceedings in Scotland; or

(c) by a Northern Ireland department, in relation to proceedings before a tribunal in Northern Ireland—

(i) which deals with transferred matters; and

(ii) for which no rules made under paragraph (a) are in force.

Commencement

October 2, 2000: The Human Rights Act 1998 (Commencement No.2) Order 2000 (SI 2000/1851). 4.8

Amendments

1. The Secretary of State for Constitutional Affairs Order 2003 (SI 2003/1887) (August 19, 2003).

2. The Transfer of Functions (Lord Chancellor and Secretary of State) Order 2005 (SI 2005/3429) (January 12, 2006).

General Note

Introduction

This section requires courts and tribunals to have regard to the Strasbourg case law, past, present and future, in deciding any question relating to a Convention right. Note that the Strasbourg case law is not binding. There are two reasons for this. First, it will not always be easy to transplant directly the point being made by the Strasbourg organ where the case involves the complexities of other legal systems. Secondly, the Convention sets a minimum standard; one possibly dramatic effect of incorporation is that the United Kingdom authorities will 4.9

set a higher standard than the common European standard which is set by the Strasbourg organs.

The section refers to dispositions of three Strasbourg organs: the Commission, the Court and the Committee of Ministers, reflecting previous structures in Strasbourg as well as the current one.

The post-1998 system of protection

4.10 Protocol 11 amended the Convention to make provision for a wholly judicial system of determination of applications. From November 1, 1998 a new permanent Court was established, to handle both the admissibility and merits phases of application. The Court is also charged with seeking to secure friendly settlement of matters before it. Individual applications are made to the Court under art.34 and individuals have full standing before it.

Significant further changes were made by Protocol No.14, which took effect from June 1, 2010. It introduced no changes to the Convention rights listed in the Schedule to the Human Rights Act 1998, but made significant changes to the admissibility rules, to the way in which the Strasbourg Court works, and to the potential sanctions for failure by a respondent State to comply with a judgment of the Strasbourg Court.

The Court has long operated with a substantial backlog of cases and in June 2009 adopted a prioritisation policy, which was subsequently amended in May 2017 and again in early 2021.

4.11 The May 2017 version, which appears below, has now been amended to split category IV into a higher and lower category. Category IV is likely to be of particular relevance in the social security context as it is into that category which viable claims under art.14/A1P1 appear likely to fall.

I. Urgent applications (in particular risk to life or health of the applicant, the applicant deprived of liberty as a direct consequence of the alleged violation of his or her Convention rights, other circumstances linked to the personal or family situation of the applicant, particularly where the well-being of a child is at issue, application of Rule 39 of the Rules of Court)

II. Applications raising questions capable of having an impact on the effectiveness of the Convention system (in particular a structural or endemic situation that the Court has not yet examined, pilot-judgment procedure) or applications raising an important question of general interest (in particular a serious question capable of having major implications for domestic legal systems or for the European system)

III. Applications which on their face raise as main complaints issues under Articles 2, 3, 4 or 5 § 1 of the Convention ("core rights"), irrespective of whether they are repetitive, and which have given rise to direct threats to the physical integrity and dignity of human beings

IV. Potentially well-founded applications based on other Articles

V. Applications raising issues already dealt with in a pilot/leading judgment ("well established case-law cases")

VI. Applications identified as giving rise to a problem of admissibility

VII. Applications which are manifestly inadmissible

Following the 2021 initiative, some category IV cases will be identified as "impact cases" and will receive more expeditious case-processing. The criteria for an "impact case" are that the conclusion of the case might lead to a change or clarification of international or domestic legislation or practice; the case touches upon moral or social issues; the case deals with an emerging or otherwise significant human rights issue. If any of these criteria are met, the Court may take into account whether the case has had significant media coverage domestically and/or is politically sensitive.

Protocol No.15 entered into force on August 1, 2021. It amends the Preamble to the Convention, which now includes a reference to the subsidiarity principle and to the margin of appreciation doctrine. The six month time-limit for submitting an application to the Court after the final national decision has been reduced to four months, starting from February 1, 2022. Among other changes, when considering the admissibility criterion of "significant disadvantage", the second condition, namely that a case which has not been duly considered by a domestic tribunal cannot be rejected, has been deleted.

Admissibility

The criteria flow from the terms of arts 34 and 35 and involve the consideration of the following questions: **4.12**

1. Can the applicant claim to be a victim?
2. Is the defendant State a party to the Convention?
3. Have domestic remedies been exhausted?
4. Is the application filed within the six-month time-limit?
5. Is the application signed?
6. Has the application been brought before?
7. Is the application compatible with the Convention?
8. Is the application manifestly ill-founded?
9. Is there an abuse of the right of petition?

Additionally, the Court is required to declare an application inadmissible if it considers that:

> "the applicant has not suffered a significant disadvantage, unless respect for human rights as defined in the Convention and the Protocols thereto requires an examination of the application on the merits and provided that no case may be rejected on this ground which has not been duly considered by a domestic tribunal."

There is no definition of "significant disadvantage". Respect for human rights may nevertheless justify consideration of the application, but the former additional safeguard, that the application of Convention rights to the claim must have been considered before the national courts or tribunals has been removed by Protocol No.15.

Composition and jurisdiction

Single judge formations of the Court are able to declare an application inadmissible in clear-cut cases where the application is wholly without merit: see arts 26 and 27. If the application is not declared inadmissible, it is forwarded to a committee or to a chamber for further examination. **4.13**

Three judge formations (committees) may invite the judge sitting in respect of the defendant state to replace one of their number, if not already a member of the committee. Committees are able to make judgments on the merits in clear-cut cases where the case-law on the interpretation of the Convention is well settled: art.28. They will also deal "to the extent possible" with non-impact category IV cases.

Matters not dealt with under arts 27 and 28 are allocated to a chamber of seven judges. The chamber will consider the written arguments of the parties, investigate the material facts if these are in contention, and hear oral argument. This stage of the proceedings concludes with a decision whether the complaint is admissible and whether a friendly settlement is possible. There follows a consideration of the merits. The admissibility and merits phases may exceptionally be joined: art.29.

Certain cases of special difficulty may be relinquished by a chamber to a Grand Chamber of 17 judges: art.30. It is also possible for any party to a judgment of a chamber to request referral of the judgment to a Grand Chamber. In such cases, a panel of five judges of the Grand Chamber decides whether or not to accept the request. Many such requests are denied. **4.14**

With effect from October 18, 2021, the Court amended its Rules of Court, in particular with regard to the composition of, and organisation of the proceedings of, the Grand Chamber. Further amendments were made with effect from March 3, 2023 addressing third-party interventions. The Court's Rules have now been further amended, up to and including March 28, 2024. They may be found at https://www.echr.coe.int/documents/d/echr/Rules_Court_ENG. In October 2023, the main change made was the introduction of a new procedure to deal with highly sensitive documents. Changes in January 2024 include a change in the formal requirements for starting an application, while in March 2024 changes were made to rule 39, concerning interim measures.

In relation to the execution of judgments, the Committee of Ministers may request an interpretation of a final judgment for the purpose of facilitating the supervision of its execution: art.46(3). Where the Committee of Ministers considers that a state is refusing to abide by a final judgment of the Court, it may refer to the Court the question whether that state has failed to fulfil its obligation under art.46(1). If the Court finds a violation of that obligation, it shall refer it back to the Committee of Ministers for consideration of the measures to be taken: art.46(4) and (5).

Which authorities are the most important?

4.15 Though the section requires courts and tribunals to have regard to authorities from all three Strasbourg organs, but there can be little doubt that the most important are the judgments of the Court of Human Rights.

Too great a reliance should not be placed on decisions on admissibility of any antiquity, since these have not always been fully reasoned and where the decision is to declare an application inadmissible are, by definition, not based on any comprehensive consideration of the merits. Furthermore the volume of such decisions has been such that the quality of the reasoning in admissibility decisions can be opaque. How much can be learned from a decision which outlines some facts as asserted in the application and then decides that the application is "manifestly ill-founded"? In many cases no observations had been sought from the respondent government.

Authorities on the interpretation of the concept of a "victim" of a violation of the Convention may be particularly persuasive, because of the drafting of s.7(7): see commentary to that section. The same view is taken of the concept of "just satisfaction" in s.8(3): see commentary to that section.

The relationship between Strasbourg judgments and national judgments

4.16 The task of the domestic courts is that of "keeping pace with the Strasbourg jurisprudence as it develops over time, neither more nor less": *R(Ullah) v Special Adjudicator* [2004] 2 A.C. 323.

Kay v Lambeth LBC, Leeds CC v Price [2006] UKHL 10, [2006] 2 A.C. 465 provides guidance for courts and tribunals when faced with a judgment of the Court of Human Rights which conflicts with an earlier binding authority of a national court. Both Justice and Liberty were permitted to intervene in the case. The Court rejected the argument that a lower court could depart from what would otherwise be a binding precedent of a higher court where there was a later judgment of the Court of Human Rights which was clearly inconsistent with the judgment of the higher court. The effect of the House of Lords ruling is that the development of case law will be influenced by the judgments of the Court of Human Rights, but that legal certainty can only be maintained if conflicts between decisions of the Court of Human Rights and those of national courts are determined within the hierarchy of courts in the national legal order.

In *R. (on the application of RJM) v Secretary of State for Work and Pensions,* [2008] UKHL 63, the House of Lords addressed the questions touched on in *Kay.* Lord Neuberger said:

> "64. Where the Court of Appeal considers that an earlier decision of this House, which would otherwise be binding on it, may be, or even is clearly, inconsistent with a subsequent decision of the ECtHR, then (absent wholly exceptional circumstances) the court should faithfully follow the decision of the House, and leave it to your Lordships to decide whether to modify or reverse its earlier decision. To hold otherwise would be to go against what Lord Bingham decided. As a matter of principle, it should be for this House, not for the Court of Appeal, to determine whether one of its earlier decisions has been overtaken by a decision of

the ECtHR. As a matter of practice, as the recent decision of this House in *Animal Defenders* [2008] 2 WLR 781 shows, decisions of the ECtHR are not always followed as literally as some might expect. As to what would constitute exceptional circumstances, I cannot do better than to refer back to the exceptional features which Lord Bingham identified as justifying the Court of Appeal's approach in *East Berkshire* [2004] QB 558: see *Kay* [2006] 2 AC 465, para 45."

But the position in relation to the Court of Appeal's respect for its own previous decisions is different:

"65. When it comes to its own previous decisions, I consider that different considerations apply. It is clear from what was said in *Young* [1944] KB 718 that the Court of Appeal is freer to depart from its earlier decisions than from those of this House: a decision of this House could not, I think, be held by the Court of Appeal to have been arrived at per incuriam. Further, more recent jurisprudence suggests that the concept of per incuriam in this context has been interpreted rather generously—see the discussion in the judgment of Lloyd L.J. in *Desnousse v Newham London Borough Council* [2006] EWCA Civ 547, [2006] QB 831, paras 71 to 75.

66. The principle promulgated in *Young* [1944] KB 718 was, of course, laid down at a time when there were no international courts whose decisions had the domestic force which decisions of the ECtHR now have, following the passing of the 1998 Act, and in particular section 2(1)(a). In my judgment, the law in areas such as that of precedent should be free to develop, albeit in a principled and cautious fashion, to take into account such changes. Accordingly, I would hold that, where it concludes that one of its previous decisions is inconsistent with a subsequent decision of the ECtHR, the Court of Appeal should be free (but not obliged) to depart from that decision."

Legislation

Interpretation of legislation

3.—(1) So far as it is possible to do so, primary legislation and subordinate legislation must be read and given effect in a way which is compatible with the Convention rights. **4.17**

(2) This section—

(a) applies to primary legislation and subordinate legislation whenever enacted;

(b) does not affect the validity, continuing operation or enforcement of any incompatible primary legislation; and

(c) does not affect the validity, continuing operation or enforcement of any incompatible subordinate legislation if (disregarding any possibility of revocation) primary legislation prevents removal of the incompatibility.

COMMENCEMENT

October 2, 2000: The Human Rights Act 1998 (Commencement No.2) Order 2000 (SI 2000/1851). **4.18**

GENERAL NOTE

There is a powerful principle of statutory interpretation here: so far as it is *possible* to do so, primary and secondary legislation whenever enacted *must* be read in a way which is compatible with Convention rights whenever a question of Convention rights is in issue. The requirement applies to all users of the legislation; it does not apply solely to courts and tribunals, nor does it require that a public authority (see s.6) is a party to the issue raised. **4.19**

The principle is clearly mandatory and strongly so. A judge writing in a journal has said that the section creates a rebuttable presumption in favour of an interpretation consistent with Convention rights: Lord Steyn, "Incorporation and Devolution—A Few Reflections on the Changing Scene" [1998] E.H.R.L.R. 153, 155.

However, where primary legislation cannot be read compatibly with Convention rights, then a court or tribunal does not have the power to strike down or ignore the incompatible primary legislation. Certain courts may, however, declare the legislation incompatible with Convention rights. This preserves the sovereignty of Parliament and is one of the clever features of the Act that have enabled it to fit into the constitutional traditions of the UK.

Where secondary legislation cannot be read compatibly with Convention rights, two possibilities will arise. First, if the incompatibility of the secondary legislation is required by the primary legislation under which it is made, then the status of the secondary legislation is the same as that of incompatible primary legislation. Its validity, continuing operation and enforcement are unaffected. But if the incompatibility is not required by the primary legislation, then it cannot be said to be within the powers of the primary legislation under which it is enacted, and the orthodox view, now re-affirmed by the Supreme Court in *RR v SSWP* [2019] UKSC 52; [2020] AACR 7, has been that any court or tribunal (and seemingly anyone called on to interpret that legislation) can disregard it: its validity, continuing operation and enforcement will be affected.

To some extent, this obligation to force an interpretation from a statutory provision was not entirely new, since European Union law (when applicable in the UK) requires legislation implementing the requirements of EU law to be read, so far as it is possible to do so, in a manner which achieves the objectives of the treaties: see the view taken in the House of Lords in *Webb v EMO Air Cargo (UK) Ltd* [1992] 2 All E.R. 929.

The application of the rule of interpretation in s.3 has now been the subject of comment in the highest courts of the United Kingdom.

4.20 The distinction between interpretation and legislation had been made by Lord Woolf C.J., in the Court of Appeal in *Poplar Housing and Regeneration Community Association Ltd v Donoghue* [2002] Q.B. 48,

> "It is difficult to overestimate the importance of section 3. It applies to legislation passed both before and after the Human Rights Act 1998 came into force. Subject to the section not requiring the court to go beyond what is possible, it is mandatory in its terms. . . . Now, when section 3 applies, the courts have to adjust their traditional role in relation to interpretation so as to give effect to the direction contained in section 3. It is as though legislation which predates the Human Rights Act 1998 and conflicts with the Convention has to be treated as being subsequently amended to incorporate the language of section 3. . . . Section 3 does not entitle the court to *legislate* (its task is still one of *interpretation*, but interpretation in accordance with the direction contained in section 3. . . .
>
> The most difficult task which courts face is distinguishing between legislation and interpretation. Here practical experience of seeking to apply section 3 will provide the best guide. However, if it is necessary in order to obtain compliance to radically alter the effect of the legislation this will be an indication that more than interpretation is involved."

In *R. v A (Complainant's Sexual History) (No.2)* [2002] A.C. 45, the House of Lords has commented on the effect of the obligation in s.3 in the context of the interpretation of s.41 of the Youth Justice and Criminal Evidence Act 1999 in relation to the evidence which may be adduced in rape trials. Lord Steyn said,

> ". . . the interpretative obligation under section 3 is a strong one. It applies even if there is no ambiguity in the language in the sense of the language being capable of two different meanings. It is an emphatic adjuration by the legislature . . . Section 3 places a duty on the court to strive to find a possible interpretation

compatible with Convention rights. Under ordinary methods of interpretation a court may depart from the language of the statute to avoid absurd consequences: section 3 goes much further. . . . Section 3 . . . requires a court to find an interpretation compatible with Convention rights if it is possible to do so. . . . In accordance with the will of Parliament as reflected in section 3 it will sometimes be necessary to adopt an interpretation which linguistically may appear strained. The techniques to be used will not only involve the reading down of express language in a statute but also the implication of provisions. A declaration of incompatibility is a measure of last resort. It must be avoided unless it is plainly impossible to do so."

Lord Hope of Craighead said,

"The rule of construction which section 3 lays down is quite unlike any previous rule of statutory interpretation. There is no need to identify an ambiguity or absurdity. Compatibility with Convention rights is the sole guiding principle. That is the paramount object which the rule seeks to achieve. But the rule is only a rule of interpretation. It does not entitle the judges to act as legislators."

The court also endorsed the distinction between interpretation and legislation identifed by Lord Woolf C.J. in the *Poplar Housing* case. 4.21

This point was also reiterated by the House of Lords in *Re S (FC); Re S and Re W* [2002] 2 All E.R. 192, where Lord Nicholls said,

"In applying section 3 courts must be ever mindful of this outer limit. The Human Rights Act reserves the amendment of primary legislation to Parliament. By this means the Act seeks to preserve parliamentary sovereignty. The Act maintains the constitutional boundary. Interpretation of statutes is a matter for the courts; the enactment of statutes, and the amendment of statutes, are matters for Parliament. . . . The area of real difficulty lies in identifying the limits of interpretation in a particular case. . . . For present purposes it is sufficient to say that a meaning which departs substantially from a fundamental feature of an Act of Parliament is likely to have crossed the boundary between interpretation and amendment. This is especially so where the departure has important practical repercussions which the court is not equipped to evaluate. In such a case the overall contextual setting may leave no scope for rendering the statutory provision Convention compliant by legitimate use of the process of interpretation."

In *Ghaidan v Godin-Mendoza*, [2004] UKHL 30, the House of Lords ruled that the policy reasons for giving a statutory tenancy to the survivor of a cohabiting heterosexual couple applied equally to the survivor of a cohabiting homosexual couple. In so holding, they interpreted paras.2 and 3 of Sch.1 to the Rent Act 1977 to secure compatibility with Convention rights. This avoided less favourable treatment of homosexual couples in the enjoyment of their Convention rights under art.8 ECHR which could not be objectively justified.

The case is important for its re-affirmation of the approach which should be adopted in reading and giving effect to primary and subordinate legislation in a way which is compatible with Convention rights. Significantly, the judges in the House of Lords did not attempt to write words into or delete words from the statutory provisions in issue, preferring simply to indicate what the substantive effect of those provisions should be (see opinion of Lord Nicholls at [35]). The task of interpretation under s.3 required courts, if necessary, to depart from the unambiguous meaning of a legislative provision in order to ensure respect for Convention rights. Lord Steyn said that declarations of incompatibility under s.4 were remedies of last resort, and that s.3 represents the principal remedial measure. Lord Steyn also indicated that there had been a tendency to concentrate too much on linguistic features of particular legislative provisions; what was required was a broad purposive approach concentrating on the Convention right in issue. Lord Rodger said, 4.22

"123. Attaching decisive importance to the precise adjustments required to the language of any particular provision would reduce the exercise envisaged by s.3(1) to a game where the outcome would depend in part on the particular turn of phrase chosen by the draftsman and in part on the skill of the court in devising brief formulae to make the provision compatible with Convention rights. The statute book is the work of many different hands in different parliaments over hundreds of years and, even today, two different draftsmen might choose different language to express the same proposition. In enacting s.3(1), it cannot have been the intention of parliament to place those asserting their rights at the mercy of the linguistic choices of the individual who happened to draft the provision in question. What matters is not so much the particular phraseology chosen by the draftsman as the substance of the measure which Parliament has enacted in those words. Equally, it cannot have been the intention of Parliament to place a premium on the skill of those called on to think up a neat way round the draftsman's language. Parliament was not out to devise an entertaining parlour game for lawyers, but, so far as possible, to make legislation operate compatibly with Convention rights. This means concentrating on matters of substance, rather than on matters of mere language.

124. Sometimes it may be possible to isolate a particular phrase which causes the difficulty and to read in words that modify it so as to remove the incompatibility. Or else the court may read in words that qualify the provision as a whole. At other times the appropriate solution may be to read down the provision so that it falls to be given effect in a way that is compatible with the Convention rights in question. In other cases the easiest solution may be to put the offending part of the provision into different words which convey the meaning that will be compatible with those rights. The preferred technique will depend on the particular provision and also, in reality, on the person doing the interpreting. This does not matter since they are simply different means of achieving the same substantive result. However, precisely because s.3(1) is to be operated by many others besides the courts, and because it is concerned with interpreting and not with amending the offending provision, it respectfully seems to me that it would be going too far to insist that those using the section to interpret legislation should match the standards to be expected of a parliamentary draftsman amending the provision: *cf. R. v Lambert* [2002] 2 A.C. 545 at 585, para.80, *per* Lord Hope of Craighead. It is enough that the interpretation placed on the provision should be clear, however it may be expressed and whatever the precise means adopted to achieve it."

The proper approach to the application of s.3 would appear in the light of all the authorities to involve a number of steps. First, it is necessary to identify the legislative provision which it is argued breaches Convention rights: see *R. v A (No.2)* [2002] A.C. 45. Then consideration should be given to whether that provision involves a breach of Convention rights: see *Poplar Housing and Regeneration Community Association Ltd v Donoghue* [2002] Q.B. 48. If there is, then a s.3 interpretation is needed and the focus here should be on compatibility with the Convention right. This can be achieved by reading in Convention rights, that is, by implying words in the legislative provision to secure compatibility with Convention rights; or by reading down, that is, by applying a narrower interpretation in order to secure compatibility. But it is not necessary to specify the precise rewording of the provision: see *Ghaidan v Godin-Mendoza* above.

The limits of interpretation are reached where the required construction conflicts with the express words of a legislative provision: see *R. (Anderson) v Secretary of State for the Home Department* [2003] 1 A.C. 837. The same conclusion will be reached if there is a conflict with the legislative provision by necessary implication. Finally, the limits of construction are reached when the construction placed on the provision alters the statutory scheme in a fundamental way.

In *R(G) 2/04*, the Commissioner, following the decision of the Court of Appeal in *R. (Hooper) v Secretary of State for Work and Pensions* [2003] 1 W.L.R 2623 in this respect—which was not in issue in the appeal to the House of Lords—decided that the words of the statute admitted of only one interpretation. The effect of this was to preclude a man from claiming widow's benefit in respect of a spouse who died before April 9, 2001. See annotations to art.14 ECHR for more detail on this line of cases.

In *AR v SSWP (BB)* [2020] UKUT 165 (AAC) a three-judge panel declined to hold that the word "spouse" in s.39A SSCBA could be read so as to include a bereaved party to a Muslim *Nikah* which had not complied with the law of England and Wales in relation to marriage. The "grain" of the legislation was to make provision for bereaved parties to marriages which were so compliant and thus s.3 did not offer a route to remedy the breach of the claimant's human rights which the Secretary of State accepted there was.

The orthodox view as to the powers and duties of the First-tier Tribunal and Upper Tribunal when considering an appeal where secondary legislation breaches the Convention was challenged by the majority decision of the Court of Appeal in *SSWP v Carmichael and Sefton Council* [2018] EWCA Civ 548; [2018] 1 W.L.R. 3429 but was subsequently re-affirmed by the Supreme Court in *RR v SSWP* [2019] UKSC 52; [2020] AACR 7. The former case concerned how effect was to be given to the judgment of the Supreme Court in the original *Carmichael* case, which had held in judicial review proceedings that because of Mrs Carmichael's "transparent medical need for an additional bedroom", the application to her husband's claim of the so-called "bedroom tax" legislation had involved a breach of art.14, taken with art.8. 4.23

On his statutory appeal, the First-tier Tribunal had earlier found in Mr Carmichael's favour by reading words into the relevant provisions of the Housing Benefit Regulations 2006, a process which on subsequent appeal it was common ground had been impermissible. A three-judge panel of the Upper Tribunal ruled that, in order to avoid a breach of s.6(1) of the Act, Mr Carmichael's housing benefit was to be calculated without making a deduction for the additional bedroom required because of Mrs Carmichael's needs.

The Upper Tribunal had placed reliance on authorities including the Supreme Court's decision in *Mathieson v SSWP* [2015] UKSC 47; [2015]1 W.L.R. 3250. In that case the child claimant's disability living allowance had been suspended during a prolonged in-patient stay in hospital in accordance with the secondary legislation then applicable, which the Supreme Court concluded constituted a breach of art.14 taken with A1P1. The Supreme Court ruled that the First-tier Tribunal "should have substituted a decision that Cameron was entitled to continued payment of DLA with effect from October 6, 2010 to the date from which payment of it was reinstated."

SSWP appealed against the Upper Tribunal's decision on grounds including that it had been wrong to find that it and the First-tier Tribunal had the power to devise solutions to Convention violations which involve the provision of benefit under conditions different from those provided for by the legislative scheme governing the benefit in question. SSWP's argument was (a) that the approach of both tribunals to s.3 had involved an impermissible re-writing of the legislation; (b) neither had the power to make a declaration of incompatibility and this was not a case for one in any event; (c) s.8 provides that damages may be awarded for acts that are unlawful by virtue of the Act, but does not extend existing powers of courts and tribunals; and (d) the Upper Tribunal ought merely to have declared the regulation incompatible and left a remedy (damages) to the courts. 4.24

The majority (Sir Brian Leveson PQBD and Flaux L.J.) agreed. They sought to confine *Mathieson* to being a case "turning on its own particular facts", in which "their Lordships [did] not appear to have considered any constitutional implications of the remedy they adopted" and considered that it did not "[reflect] a consistent line of authority." *Foster v Chef Adjudication Officer* [1993] A.C. 754, the authority for the proposition that tribunals may disapply unlawful secondary legislation in order to arrive at a decision that was not erroneous on a point of law, was distinguished on a basis which is not entirely clear. In particular, whether the regulation is unlawful because it is in excess of the regulation-making power for some other reason or is unlawful for Convention incompatibility does not self-evidently affect why the ability to disapply it should exist.

In a powerful dissent Leggatt L.J. set out why the Act in his view does authorise, indeed require, tribunals to disapply, in a particular case, a regulation to the extent that it is not Convention-compliant. He relies on *Foster* and on s.7 of the Act, under which a victim of the unlawful act may "rely on the Convention right or rights concerned in any legal proceedings". When seen against other authorities, in his view *Mathieson* is part of a consistent line of authority. In any event, the case is indistinguishable and, even if it stood alone, would have to be applied.

4.25 *SSWP v Carmichael and Sefton Council* was distinguished in *JT v First-tier Tribunal, Criminal Injuries Compensation Authority and Equality and Human Rights Commission* [2018] EWCA Civ 1735, holding in essence that the prohibition on disapplication identified in *Carmichael* related only to situations where it was not possible to identify a particular offending provision in the relevant secondary legislation.

The Upper Tribunal issued a leap-frog certificate under ss.14A to 14C of the Tribunals, Courts and Enforcement Act 2007 in *Secretary of State for Work and Pensions v (1) DL and (2) RR (HB)* [2018] UKUT 355 (AAC), a case in which the Upper Tribunal was bound by *Carmichael.* In *RR v SSWP* [2019] UKSC 52, the Supreme Court allowed the claimant's appeal, holding that there was nothing unconstitutional about a court or tribunal disapplying a provision of subordinate legislation which would otherwise result in their acting incompatibly with a Convention right, where it is necessary to do so in order to comply with the Human Rights Act. There was a clear distinction between primary legislation which was incompatible and subordinate legislation: see ss.3(2) and 6(2). A similar Order was made to that made by the Upper Tribunal in the second *Carmichael* case (see 4.23).

TS v SSWP; EK v SSWP (DLA) [2020] UKUT 284 (AAC) illustrates the need to focus on precisely what provision of subordinate legislation a court or tribunal needs to disapply. The case concerned the "past presence" rules for disability living allowance. Previously, the relevant statutory instrument had required a claimant to have been present in Great Britain for 26 weeks out of the preceding 52. That was then amended, so as to require past presence for 104 weeks out of the preceding 156. The child claimants successfully argued their human rights had been breached, but did so on the footing that it was the increase from 26/52 weeks to 104/156 weeks that represented the breach. Consequently, it was not the legislation as amended which fell to be disapplied, but the subordinate legislation which had effected the increase and so it was the requirement for 26 weeks out of 52 which fell to be applied to their claims (rather than no past presence test at all).

Declaration of incompatibility

4.26 **4.**—(1) Subsection (2) applies in any proceedings in which a court determines whether a provision of primary legislation is compatible with a Convention right.

(2) If the court is satisfied that the provision is incompatible with a Convention right, it may make a declaration of that incompatibility.

(3) Subsection (4) applies in any proceedings in which a court determines whether a provision of subordinate legislation, made in the exercise of a power conferred by primary legislation, is compatible with a Convention right.

(4) If the court is satisfied—

(a) that the provision is incompatible with a Convention right, and

(b) that (disregarding any possibility of revocation) the primary legislation concerned prevents removal of the incompatibility,

it may make a declaration of that incompatibility.

(5) In this section "court" means—

(a) [2 the Supreme Court;]

(b) the Judicial Committee of the Privy Council;

(c) [3 Court Martial Appeal Court;]

(d) in Scotland, the High Court of Justiciary sitting otherwise than as a trial court or the Court of Session;

(e) in England and Wales or Northern Ireland, the High Court or the Court of Appeal.

[1 (f) the Court of Protection, in any matter being dealt with by the President of the Family Division, the [4 Chancellor of the High Court] or a puisne judge of the High Court.]

(6) A declaration under this section ("a declaration of incompatibility")—

(a) does not affect the validity, continuing operation or enforcement of the provision in respect of which it is given; and

(b) is not binding on the parties to the proceedings in which it is made.

COMMENCEMENT

October 2, 2000: The Human Rights Act 1998 (Commencement No.2) Order 2000 (SI 2000/1851). **4.27**

AMENDMENTS

1. Mental Capacity Act 2005 Sch.6 para.43 (October 1, 2007).
2. Constitutional Reform Act 2005 Sch.9(1) para.66(2) (October 1, 2009).
3. Armed Forces Act 2006 Sch.16 para.156 (October 31, 2009).
4. Crime and Courts Act 2013 Sch.14(3) para.5(5) (October 1, 2013).

GENERAL NOTE

This section gives certain courts power to make declarations of incompatibility where primary or secondary legislation cannot be read compatibly with Convention rights. It is a discretionary power available to the higher courts only. It arises in any proceedings; there is again no requirement that one of the parties is a public authority. Neither First-tier Tribunals nor the Upper Tribunal have the power to make declarations of incompatibility. **4.28**

It is perhaps unfortunate that the only routes to declarations of incompatibility in the social security jurisdiction are appeal from the Upper Tribunal to the Court of Appeal, or taking judicial review proceedings in the High Court against a decision of a First-tier Tribunal or the Upper Tribunal, where judicial review lies against the Upper Tribunal.

In *R(IS)12/04*, the Commissioner concludes that a tribunal's lack of power to make a declaration of incompatibility is not a good reason for not dealing fully with human rights issues raised before tribunals. The Commissioner notes that in some circumstances, tribunals do have the power to declare subordinate legislation to have been invalidly made. The tribunal's reasons were found to be inadequate because they had dismissed detailed human rights arguments on the basis that they could not make a declaration of incompatibility under s.4.

A judge of the Upper Tribunal gave more developed guidance on how either a First-tier Tribunal or the Upper Tribunal should proceed when faced with a case where the only possible remedy for a claimant would be a declaration of incompatibility. *SH v SSWP (JSA)* [2011] UKUT 428 (AAC) concerned an appeal by a claimant who had been refused a jobseeker's allowance on the grounds that he did not meet the contribution conditions. He argued that there was discrimination contrary to art.14 ECHR as between those who were employed and paid Class 1 contributions and those who had formerly been self-employed whose Class 2 and 4 contributions did not count towards building an entitlement to a contribution-based jobseeker's allowance. The judge took the view that he was faced with a case where, were he to accept the contentions of the appellant, the only possible remedy available would be a declaration of incompatibility under s.4, which it was not within the competence of the Upper Tribunal to make. That was the position here, since the contribution conditions are set out in primary legislation in terms which are "far too clear to permit any other interpretation." (At [16].) In these circumstances, after reviewing the authorities, the judge provided guidance on how the Upper Tribunal (or indeed a First-tier Tribunal in the same situation) should proceed in the following terms:

> "21. The extent to which it is appropriate for the Upper Tribunal, in a case where the only possible remedy would be a declaration of incompatibility, to enter into the merits of the claimant's contentions that legislation infringes the Convention must in my judgment depend on the circumstances of the particular case. In the present case full consideration of the justification argument is likely to require evidence from the Secretary of State. I see no point in my making directions for the filing of such evidence, with a view to my expressing an opinion on whether the alleged discrimination is justified, when (a) the Claimant may not be prepared to incur the risk of liability for costs which would be involved in appealing to the Court of Appeal, and (b) the Court of Appeal might hold that the claim fails in any event for want of a sufficient 'personal characteristic'. It does not seem to me that there is any point in my purporting to decide points which are arguable, when I would have no jurisdiction to grant any remedy. I therefore dismiss the appeal without further ado.
>
> 22. Nor would I presently be inclined to give permission to appeal to the Court of Appeal, were the Claimant to make an application for permission. It seems to me that it should be left for the Court of Appeal to decide whether it is appropriate for it to entertain the case, and what directions for the filing of evidence by the Secretary of State should be made. However, if the Claimant wishes to apply for permission, he should make the application, and I will formally consider and decide it."

4.29 Judge Wikeley has followed *SH v SSWP (JSA)* [2011] UKUT 428 (AAC) in *AB v SSWP (JSA)* [2013] UKUT 288 (AAC). He found that tribunal did not err in law when it found that the claimant could not succeed before it in an argument that the abatement rule under which occupational pension payments were taken into account in determining entitlement to contribution-based jobseeker's allowance constituted indirect discrimination which could not be justified.

In *PL v SSWP (JSA)* [2016] UKUT 177 (AAC), Judge Markus QC considered that the discrimination grounds before her were "fundamentally flawed" and that it might assist the claimant if she explained why. Alternatively, if the claimant were nonetheless to take the matter to the Court of Appeal, such an explanation might assist that court by way of "jurisprudential spadework and analysis" (citing *AB*). This may perhaps be seen as an application of the "circumstances of the case" approach favoured by Judge Turnbull in *SH*.

The effect of a declaration of incompatibility is not to declare the legislation invalid, inoperative or unenforceable, and so does not give rise to any claim for damages for breach of the Human Rights Act: *Re K: A Child*, Court of Appeal, November 15, 2000 [2001] 2 All E.R. 719. The impeached provision will continue in full force and effect pending any amendment. The effect of a declaration of incompatibility is to put the Government on notice of the incompatibility. The Government may then choose to take the remedial action provided for in s.10 of and Sch.2 to the Act.

On July 10, 2003, the House of Lords ruled on the appeal in *Wilson v Secretary of State for Trade and Industry* [2003] UKHL 40. They reversed the decision of the Court of Appeal to make a declaration of incompatibility in respect of s.127 of the Consumer Credit Act 1974.

Wilson had borrowed £5,000 from First County Trust on the security of her BMW 318 convertible. The loan agreement added a £250 document fee to the £5,000 loan, thus mis-stating the amount of the loan as £5,250. In 1999 Wilson issued a claim in the county court, inter alia, for a declaration that the loan agreement was unenforceable because it did not contain all the prescribed terms. The county court ruled in the lender's favour, but this was reversed in the Court of Appeal, but adjourned to enable Convention rights arguments to be considered. The Secretary of State argued that the Court had no power to make a declaration of incompatibility because the agreement pre-dated October 2, 2000, the date the Human Rights Act 1998 entered into force. However, the Court said that the act which violated Convention rights was not the agreement but any order of the Court making the loan agreement unenforceable. They went on to make a declaration of incompatibility. **4.30**

The House of Lords has ruled that the Human Rights Act 1998 is not to be applied retrospectively, and so there was no jurisdiction in the Court of Appeal to make the declaration of incompatibility. A statute concerned with Convention rights could not render acts unlawful which were lawful when they were undertaken, since this would impose retrospective liability.

Lord Hobhouse in *Wilson* indicated, seemingly obiter, (at [127]) that "If the legislation in question has been amended or repealed no question of a declaration under s.4 can arise". In *HM and MK v SSWP* [2023] UKUT 15 (AAC), the Upper Tribunal, carrying out "jurisprudential spadework and analysis" on a claim of discrimination brought by two claimants without children who had been refused bereavement benefits following the death of their partners (with whom they had not entered into a marriage or civil partnership), rejected claims of discrimination on the grounds of marital status and of gender. As regards discrimination on the ground of sexual orientation, the claimants had been in a similar position to the couple in *Steinfeld* [2018] UKSC 32, who had wished to formalise their relationship otherwise than by getting married. At the time in question, same-sex couples had the choice between marriage and civil partnership, a choice that was not open to heterosexual couples. SSWP's position was that given that a declaration of incompatibility had been made in *Steinfeld* and acted upon by Parliament, the remedy of a declaration of incompatibility would be unavailable, as it would amount to calling into question proceedings in Parliament. The Upper Tribunal, with some diffidence given that it has no jurisdiction to make a declaration of incompatibility anyway and therefore obiter but in deference to the arguments put to it, applied Lord Hobhouse's dictum in the absence of any other authority, while recognising some of the difficulties to which it might give rise.

On appeal to the Court of Appeal (*Kelly v SSWP* [2024] EWCA Civ 613), it was the availability of a remedy under s.4 that was the exclusive focus of attention, other challenges to the Upper Tribunal's decision having been abandoned. It was common ground before the Court of Appeal that Lord Hobhouse's dicta were both persuasive and correct. However, it was submitted that, because of certain transitional provisions relating to bereavement benefit of at best marginal continuing relevance, Ms Kelly was nonetheless entitled to seek a declaration of incompatibility.

Ms Kelly's appeal failed because she was held in a different position from her chosen comparators to whom, because of the transitional provisions, the legislation continued to apply, and any difference in treatment was justified.

Having so concluded, the Court then went on to consider whether, if it was wrong in the foregoing, it would be appropriate to exercise its power to make a declaration of incompatibility. It was held that it would not be because:

(a) "To make a further declaration of incompatibility in relation to two statutory provisions which are clinging onto the statute book, if at all, by the slenderest of threads, would not be an appropriate use of the power, when, in substance, Parliament and the Secretary of State are aware of the real past incompatibility [i.e. the same as in *Steinfeld*] which underlies this complaint, and have remedied it" (at [83]).

(b) There were analogies with the discrimination identified in *Re McLaughlin* [2018] UKSC 48 and in *Jackson v SSWP* [2020] EWHC 183 (Admin), which had been considered by Parliament when making the subsequent Remedial Order. That had given Parliament the opportunity to consider whether to give a retrospective remedy for discrimination in similar circumstances. It would be inappropriate to make a declaration, the only purpose of which could be to encourage the Government and Parliament to reconsider that decision (at [84], read together with [95]).

(c) The scheme of the HRA is such that a declaration of incompatibility would be unlikely to prompt a legislative response of the kind Ms Kelly sought. Article 13 (the right to an effective remedy) is not one of the "Convention rights" for the purposes of the HRA. Those include encouraging those who construe legislation to construe it compatibly with Convention rights (s.3); to bring a legislative incompatibility to the attention of Parliament and the executive (s.4) and to encourage public authorities not to act incompatibly with Convention rights (s.6). The HRA does not give a general right to compensation for past unlawful acts and it was not evident to the court that Ms Kelly would have had any right in the social security context to compensation for a past breach of her Convention rights (at [86]–[91]).

4.31 In its admissibility decision of June 18, 2002 in *Hobbs v United Kingdom* (App.63684/00), the Court of Human Rights ruled that a declaration of incompatibility is not an effective remedy within the meaning of art.35 of the Convention for the purpose of the rule requiring an applicant to exhaust domestic remedies. The Court rejected the Government's invitation to reconsider this position in its admissibility decision of March 16, 2004 in *Walker v United Kingdom* (App.37212/02). The Court was strongly influenced by the fact that a declaration of incompatibility was not binding on the parties.

This view has been confirmed by the Grand Chamber of the Strasbourg Court in *Burden v United Kingdom* (App.13378/05), judgment of April 28, 2008, at [40]–[44].

Right of Crown to intervene

4.32 **5.**—(1) Where a court is considering whether to make a declaration of incompatibility, the Crown is entitled to notice in accordance with rules of court.

(2) In any case to which subsection (1) applies—

(a) a Minister of the Crown (or a person nominated by him),

(b) a member of the Scottish Executive,

(c) a Northern Ireland Minister,

(d) a Northern Ireland department,

is entitled, on giving notice in accordance with rules of court, to be joined as a party to the proceedings.

(3) Notice under subsection (2) may be given at any time during the proceedings.

(4) A person who has been made a party to criminal proceedings (other than in Scotland) as the result of a notice under subsection (2) may, with leave, appeal to the [1 Supreme Court] against any declaration of incompatibility made in the proceedings.

(5) In subsection (4)—
"criminal proceedings" includes all proceedings before the [2 Courts-Martial Appeal Court]; and
"leave" means leave granted by the court making the declaration of incompatibility or by the [1 Supreme Court].

COMMENCEMENT

October 2, 2000: The Human Rights Act 1998 (Commencement No.2) Order 2000 (SI 2000/1851). **4.33**

AMENDMENTS

1. Constitutional Reform Act 2005 Sch.9(1) para.66(3) (October 1, 2009).
2. Armed Forces Act 2006 Sch.16 para.156 (October 31, 2009).

Public authorities

Acts of public authorities

6.—(1) It is unlawful for a public authority to act in a way which is incompatible with a Convention right. **4.34**

(2) Subsection (1) does not apply to an act if—
(a) as the result of one or more provisions of primary legislation, the authority could not have acted differently; or
(b) in the case of one or more provisions of, or made under, primary legislation which cannot be read or given effect in a way which is compatible with the Convention rights, the authority was acting so as to give effect to or enforce those provisions.

(3) In this section "public authority" includes—
(a) a court or tribunal, and
(b) any person certain of whose functions are functions of a public nature,
but does not include either House of Parliament or a person exercising functions in connection with proceedings in Parliament.

(4) [1 . . .].

(5) In relation to a particular act, a person is not a public authority by virtue only of subsection (3)(b) if the nature of the act is private.

(6) "An act" includes a failure to act but does not include a failure to—
(a) introduce in, or lay before, Parliament a proposal for legislation; or
(b) make any primary legislation or remedial order.

COMMENCEMENT

October 2, 2000: The Human Rights Act 1998 (Commencement No.2) Order 2000 (SI 2000/1851). **4.35**

AMENDMENT

1. Constitutional Reform Act 2005, Sch.18(5) para.1 (October 1, 2009).

GENERAL NOTE

The obligation in s.6(1) is at the heart of the scheme of incorporation in the Act. It could be said that all the other provisions flow from the requirement that public **4.36** authorities of any kind act compatibly with Convention rights. Note that there is a "defence" in s.6(2) where there was a statutory requirement to act in a particular manner. Here there will, of course, be an incompatibility between the statutory provision and Convention rights.

The key concept in the section is that of a public authority. This includes courts and tribunals, but not either House of Parliament, and is extended to "any person certain of whose functions are functions of a public nature" The difficult two words become very difficult 12 words. Only "certain" of the authority's functions need be of a public nature, and there is no liability in respect of the exercise of their functions of a private nature.

The question of what constitutes a public authority is reminiscent of the definitional problem of determining what are "emanations of the State" for the purposes of the horizontal application of EC Directives. The test is certainly not the same, but the same difficulties will arise in determining those institutions at the margins of State power which constitute public authorities. The definition will require judicial interpretation, but it is clearly a functional test.

4.37 There is, however, no doubt that the Department and all its constituent parts constitute public authorities, as, of course, do the tribunals and other judicial bodies. All must act compatibly with Convention rights. This means that they must take up obvious Convention points even if they are not raised by the parties, since otherwise they would be acting unlawfully by acting in a manner which is not compatible with Convention rights.

In *Poplar Housing and Regeneration Community Association Ltd v Donoghue* [2002] Q.B. 48, the Court of Appeal provided some useful guidance on the definition of the notion of a public authority as defined in the section. The definition is to be given a generous interpretation. Hybrid bodies which exercised both public and private functions were public authorities only in relation to acts of a public nature and not acts of a private nature. But the fact that a public regulatory body supervised a body did not necessarily indicate that any act subject to supervision was an act of a public nature.

On the concept of "public authority" for the purposes of this Act, see also *Parochial Church Council of the Parish of Aston Cantlow and Wilmcote with Billesley, Warwickshire v Wallbank* [2004] 1 A.C. 546; [2003] UKHL 37; [2003] 3 W.L.R. 283; and *Hampshire CC v Beer t/a Hammer Trout Farm* [2003] EWCA Civ 1056; [2004] 1 W.L.R. 233.

4.38 In the *Aston Cantlow* case, Lord Nicholls said,

> "12. What, then, is the touchstone to be used in deciding whether a function is public for this purpose? Clearly there is no single test of universal application. There cannot be, given the diverse nature of governmental functions and the variety of means by which these functions are discharged today. Factors to be taken into account include the extent to which in carrying out the relevant function the body is publicly funded, or is exercising statutory powers, or is taking the place of central government or local authorities, or is providing a public service."

The duty of courts to act compatibly and precedent

4.39 In *Leeds CC v Price* [2006] UKHL 10, the House of Lords ruled that in almost all cases where there is a conflict between authorities of the Court of Human Rights in Strasbourg and of a superior court in the United Kingdom, an inferior court or tribunal in the United Kingdom should follow the decision of the national court. That is a controversial proposition, but the rule may well not apply if the point at issue is not in dispute between the parties. So, for example, in *Esfandiari* [2006] EWCA Civ 282, reported as *R(IS) 11/06*, neither party contested the proposition that all benefits count as possessions following the decision of the Court of Human Rights in *Stec,* even though an earlier Court of Appeal decision has ruled that means-tested benefits cannot be treated as "possessions" for the purpose of art.1 of Protocol 1. This may simply be an illustration of the Court of Appeal not regarding the House of Lords ruling as applying to them, or, perhaps rather more likely, that there was recent and specific Strasbourg authority on the point. There is certainly authority that in such circumstances, any court or tribunal should not lightly depart from germane Strasbourg case law: see *Attorney General's reference No 4 of 2002* [2004] UKHL 43, at [33]; and *Anderson* [2002] UKHL 46, at [17]–[18].

See further annotations to s.2.

Section 6(2)

The proper interpretation of subs.(2) is discussed in the judgment of the House of Lords in *Hooper* [2005] UKHL 29: see [2]–[6], [41]–[52], [62]–[83], [91]–[96], and [101]–[126]. **4.40**

In July 2008, the House of Lords again considered this aspect of the Act in *Doherty v Birmingham CC* [2008] UKHL 57 in a case which concerned the obtaining of a possession order against a traveller under a procedure which it was argued would breach art.8 of the Convention (on which see *Connors v United Kingdom,* (App.66746/01) May 24 2004, (2005) 40 EHRR 9; and *McCann v United Kingdom,* (App.19009/04) May 13, 2008). In the course of their deliberations, the House gives detailed consideration to the circumstances in which a breach of the Act will be avoided because of the operation of s.6(2)(b). The position adopted in earlier cases was re-affirmed. The House confirmed that three distinct situations can arise under the provision. The first is where a decision to exercise or not to exercise a power that is given in primary legislation would inevitably give rise to a violation of Convention rights. The second is at the opposite end of the spectrum where no statutory provision concerns the exercise of discretion by a public body which acts in violation of Convention rights; such action will be unlawful under s.6(1) because s.6(2)(b) cannot apply. The third situation is said to lie in the middle:

> "This is where the act or omission takes place within the context of a scheme which primary legislation has laid down that gives general powers, such as powers of management, to a public authority. . . . The answer to the question whether or not s.6(2)(b) applies will depend on the extent to which the act or omission can be said to give effect to any of the provisions of the scheme that is to be found in the statutes." (At [39], per Lord Hope of Craighead.)

The House has indicated that there are two possible gateways by which a violation of Convention rights might be addressed in such situations. The first gateway provides two possibilities. The first is that the use of the interpretative obligation in s.3 results in an interpretation which avoids the violation which is alleged. The second is that the interpretative obligation does not help, but that a court of sufficient seniority can give a declaration of incompatibility under s.4 which results in a remedial order under s.10. The second gateway involves an argument that the public authority whose decision is challenged has made an improper use of its powers; this route offers a procedural protection in that the court will consider whether the public authority acted unreasonably in the *Wednesbury* sense in taking the action that it did (See [52]–[55]).

For how the duty may fall to be applied by tribunals, see the decision of the Supreme Court in *RR v SSWP* [2019] UKSC 52, discussed under s.3.

Proceedings

7.—(1) A person who claims that a public authority has acted (or proposes to act) in a way which is made unlawful by section 6(1) may— **4.41**

(a) bring proceedings against the authority under this Act in the appropriate court or tribunal, or

(b) rely on the Convention right or rights concerned in any legal proceedings,

but only if he is (or would be) a victim of the unlawful act.

(2) In subsection (1)(a) "appropriate court or tribunal" means such court or tribunal as may be determined in accordance with rules; and proceedings against an authority include a counterclaim or similar proceeding.

(3) If the proceedings are brought on an application for judicial review, the applicant is to be taken to have a sufficient interest in relation to the unlawful act only if he is, or would be, a victim of that act.

(4) If the proceedings are made by way of a petition for judicial review in Scotland, the applicant shall be taken to have title and interest to sue in relation to the unlawful act only if he is, or would be, a victim of that act.

(5) Proceedings under subsection (1)(a) must be brought before the end of—

(a) the period of one year beginning with the date on which the act complained of took place; or

(b) such longer period as the court or tribunal considers equitable having regard to all the circumstances,

but that is subject to any rule imposing a stricter time limit in relation to the procedure in question.

(6) In subsection (1)(b) "legal proceedings" includes—

(a) proceedings brought by or at the instigation of a public authority; and

(b) an appeal against the decision of a court or tribunal.

(7) For the purposes of this section, a person is a victim of an unlawful act only if he would be a victim for the purposes of Article 34 of the Convention if proceedings were brought in the European Court of Human Rights in respect of that act.

(8) Nothing in this Act creates a criminal offence.

(9) In this section "rules" means—

(a) in relation to proceedings before a court or tribunal outside Scotland, rules made by [[1] . . .] [[2] the Lord Chancellor or] the Secretary of State for the purposes of this section or rules of court,

(b) in relation to proceedings before a court or tribunal in Scotland, rules made by the Secretary of State for those purposes,

(c) in relation to proceedings before a tribunal in Northern Ireland—

   (i) which deals with transferred matters; and

   (ii) for which no rules made under paragraph (a) are in force, rules made by a Northern Ireland department for those purposes,

and includes provision made by order under section 1 of the Courts and Legal Services Act 1990.

(10) In making rules, regard must be had to section 9.

(11) The Minister who has power to make rules in relation to a particular tribunal may, to the extent he considers it necessary to ensure that the tribunal can provide an appropriate remedy in relation to an act (or proposed act) of a public authority which is (or would be) unlawful as a result of section 6(1), by order add to—

(a) the relief or remedies which the tribunal may grant; or

(b) the grounds on which it may grant any of them.

(12) An order made under subsection (11) may contain such incidental, supplemental, consequential or transitional provision as the Minister making it considers appropriate.

(13) "The Minister" includes the Northern Ireland department concerned.

COMMENCEMENT

October 2, 2000: The Human Rights Act 1998 (Commencement No.2) Order 2000 (SI 2000/1851). **4.42**

AMENDMENTS

1. The Secretary of State for Constitutional Affairs Order 2003 (SI 2003/1887) (August 19, 2003).

2. The Transfer of Functions (Lord Chancellor and Secretary of State) Order 2005 (SI 2005/3429) (January 12, 2006).

GENERAL NOTE

Introduction

This section is full of difficulty. A person who believes that a public authority **4.43** has acted unlawfully by not acting in a manner compatible with Convention rights may bring proceedings under s.7. Such a person must under subs.(7) show that they would be a victim for the purposes of art.34 of the Convention if proceedings were brought before the Court of Human Rights in respect of the allegedly unlawful act.

The section refers to at least three different types of proceedings: (1) the so-called new "constitutional tort" under subs.(1)(a); (2) judicial review under subs.(3); and (3) "any legal proceedings" in subs.(1)(b).

Standing to raise the complaint: the victim requirement

Under subs.(7) which applies to the whole section, only a person who can show **4.44** that they would fall within the victim requirement under art.34 of the Convention has standing to complain of the unlawful act by the public authority. The concept of "victim" is a particular concept under Convention case law, and for this reason the interpretative requirement to have regard to Convention case law must be particularly strong since otherwise the specific reference to art.34 in subs.(7) would be otiose. Article 34 has replaced art.25 in the original version of the Convention prior to its amendment by Protocol 11.

Fortunately, the Strasbourg authorities—and here admissibility decisions of the Commission under the "old" system of protection (see commentary to s.2) will be particularly useful—have been generous in the matter of standing to make an application under the Convention.

The term "person" under the Convention (*personne physique* in the French text) clearly refers only to natural persons, but the Commission has accepted applications from corporate and unincorporated bodies whose rights under the Convention have been violated. So complaints have been accepted from companies, partnerships, trades unions, churches, political parties, and numerous other types of institution. It would seem that only public bodies themselves are excluded from the possibility of making an individual petition. Furthermore, there are no restrictions on grounds of nationality, residence or any other status.

Standing has been extended to representative complaints, for example, by parents **4.45** on behalf of children where that is appropriate, though there is no age limit for making an application: App.10929/84 *Nielsen v Denmark* (1986) 46 D.R. 55 and App.22920/93 *MB v United Kingdom* (1994) 77-A D.R. 42. Equally, there is no bar to application by persons under a disability: App.1572/62 *X v Austria* (1962) 5 Yearbook 238.

Associations have no standing to bring actions in a representative capacity: App.10581/83 *Norris and National Gay Federation v Ireland* (1984) 44 D.R. 132, though if they provide evidence that they are acting on behalf of specified individuals, the application may be accepted: App.10983/84 *Confédération des Syndicats médicaux français et Fédération nationale des Infirmiers v France* (1986) 47 D.R. 225.

In some cases potential victims may make an application, such as in cases where covert surveillance might take place without any notification of the possibility to the individual: *Klass v Germany*, judgment of September 6, 1978, Series A No.28; (1979–80) 2 E.H.R.R. 214.

4.46 The Commission and the Court will not, however, countenance an application in the abstract as a means of testing the compatibility of provisions of a national legal order: App.9297/81 *X Association v Sweden* (1982) 28 D.R. 204. Drawing the distinction between potential victims and claims in the abstract is not always easy: see App.10039/82 *Leigh v United Kingdom* (1984) 38 D.R. 74.

In *Director General of Fair Trading v Proprietary Association of Great Britain*, Court of Appeal, July 26, 2001 [2001] EWCA Civ 1217 (sometimes referred to as *Re medicaments (No.4))*, the Court of Appeal made some passing, and inconclusive comments on the nature of the "victim requirement" under s.7. The Court expressly avoided dealing with the possible distinction between interest groups which are really associations of interested individuals which might be regarded as a group of individuals each of whom may be regarded as a victim and broader representative groups (examples given are Amnesty International or the Joint Council for the Welfare of Immigrants) which have special expertise but who cannot be classified as a collection of victims. The Court simply stated that each case must be decided in its own context.

Note the discussion of the victim requirement (particularly victim status and retrospectivity) in the judgment of the House of Lords in *Hooper* [2005] UKHL 29: see [53]–[59].

SSWP v Sister IS and Sister KM [2009] UKUT 200 (AAC) concerned claims by nuns for state pension credit, which were refused on the grounds that they were members of a religious order who are fully maintained by that order. It was argued that the exclusionary provision breached art.14 read with art.1 of Protocol 1. The three-judge panel dismissed this argument relying on Sedley L.J.'s reasoning in *Langley v Bradford MBC*, reported as *R(H) 6/05*, that a housing benefit claimant was not a victim under the Human Rights Act 1998, because the discriminatory effect of a provision could be removed without conferring any advantage on her. The three-judge panel said (at [33]) that it was "possible to remove any element of religious discrimination (if there is one) by removing the reference to religion". It followed that the claimants could not establish that they were victims within s.7(1)(b).

In *Taylor v Department for Communities* [2022] NICA 21, the Court of Appeal in Northern Ireland dismissed an appeal by the claimant who had brought judicial review proceedings based on art.14 in relation to his housing benefit, primarily on the ground that he was not a "victim". The Court observed:

> "[19] In *Senator Lines GMBH v Austria and Others* [2006] 21 BHRC 640 the Grand Chamber of the ECtHR, in determining whether the particular application was admissible, reflected on the concept of "*potential victim.*" Referring to concrete examples in its jurisprudence, the court recalled one case where an alien's removal had been ordered but not enforced and another where a law prohibiting homosexual acts was capable of being, but had not been, applied to a certain category of the population which included the applicant. The judgment continues, at page 11:
>
> > 'However, for an applicant to be able to claim to be a *victim* in such a situation *he must produce reasonable and convincing evidence of the likelihood that a violation affecting him personally will occur; mere suspicion or conjecture is insufficient …*' (emphasis added)

[20] In *Burden v United Kingdom* (2008) 24 BHRC 709 (App.13378/05) the applicants were elderly unmarried sisters. They owned a house in their joint names worth £875,000. Each had made a will leaving all her property to the other. By ss 3, 3A and 4 of the Inheritance Tax Act 1984 inheritance tax of 40% would be levied upon the death of each. The government contested the admissibility of the application on the grounds that the applicants could not claim to be 'victims' of any violation (under article 34 ECHR) as the complaint was prospective and hypothetical, given that no liability to inheritance tax had actually accrued and might never accrue.

[21] Rejecting his argument, the Grand Chamber reasoned and concluded as follows. In order to be able to lodge a petition in pursuance of article 34, a person, non-governmental organisation or group of individuals had to be able to claim to be *the victim* of a violation of the convention rights. In order to claim to be a victim of a violation, a person had to be directly affected by the impugned measure. The ECHR did not, therefore, envisage the bringing of an *actio popularis* for the interpretation of the rights set out therein or permit individuals to complain about a provision of national law simply because they considered, without having been directly affected by it, that it might contravene the convention. It was, however, open to a person to contend that a law violated his rights, in the absence of an individual measure of implementation, if he was required either to modify his conduct or risk being prosecuted or if he was a member of a class of people *at "real risk"* of being directly affected by the legislation. Given their age, the wills they had made and the value of the property each owned, the applicants had established that there was a real risk that, in the not too distant future, one of them would be required to pay substantial inheritance tax on the property inherited from her sister. Accordingly, both were directly affected by the impugned legislation and thus had victim status.

[22] Plainly a vague or fanciful possibility of a future Convention violation will not suffice. In short, "*risk*" in this context denotes *real risk*. This requires, per *Senator Lines*, a reasonable and convincing evidential foundation."

Subsection (1)(a): the new constitutional tort

A person who can show that they meet the victim test may bring proceedings against the authority "in the appropriate court or tribunal". This is to be determined in accordance with rules to be made, outside Scotland, by the Lord Chancellor or the Secretary of State. The Civil Procedure Rules simply map this action onto the existing division of responsibilities between the county courts and the High Court. **4.47**

The time limits for such an action are, however, specified in subs.(5). The action is to be brought within one year of the date on which the act complained of took place or such longer period as the court or tribunal considers equitable having regard to all the circumstances. There is a proviso that both the one year time limit and any extension of it is to be without prejudice to any rule imposing a stricter time limit "in relation to the procedure in question." An example would be judicial review where the normal time limit is three months unless this is extended by the court. However, where an action is brought under a procedure with a longer limitation period, it would seem that the longer limitation period will apply; such proceedings would not, however, arise under subs.(1)(a) but presumably under subs.(1)(b).

Under s.9(1), where the unlawful act of which the applicant complains is a judicial act, it is stated that proceedings under s.7(1)(a) may be brought only by exercising a right of appeal, seeking judicial review against those bodies susceptible to judicial review, or "in such other forum as may be prescribed by rules."

Judicial review: subss. (3) and (4)

4.48 Where the proceedings are by way of judicial review on the grounds that a public authority has acted unlawfully, the normal sufficient interest test of standing (which would permit action by a representative body or a pressure group) is replaced by a test that the applicant must satisfy the victim test in subs.(7).

Raising Convention rights in any legal proceedings: subs. (1) (b)

4.49 Convention rights may be raised in any legal proceedings, provided that the person can show that they would be a victim under art.34 of the Convention. So a person bringing proceedings on a well-established cause of action can raise his or her Convention rights at any time. Indeed, the court or tribunal is under a duty by virtue of s.6(1) to take obvious Convention points since they are under a duty to act in a manner compatible with the Convention.

Apart from judicial review claims (which may be important if a person is seeking the possibility of a money remedy), Convention rights are most likely to be raised in the course of appeals to the First-tier Tribunal and the Upper Tribunal. The commentary to the Convention rights set out in Sch.1 gives some indication of the sorts of issues which might be raised under them.

In *CSIB/973/1999* a Scottish Commissioner warns of the need for responsible resort to the taking of human rights points. He complains of a point which was "in the nature of a wrap up omnibus ground of appeal placed before the Commissioners no doubt in the hope that there was something in the point." The Commissioner regrets the absence of rules setting out the manner in which human rights points are to be taken before the Commissioners. He goes on to indicate the content of those rules; this might assist those contemplating raising human rights points before both tribunals and Commissioners. The provision of the Convention which it is argued has been breached should be identified, together with the remedy sought in respect of the breach. The legal principles and authorities relied on and any error of law by the tribunal which it is asserted were made consequent on the breach should also be identified. Such points should be taken on proper notice so that both parties can research them and focus on them in their arguments to the adjudicating body. That is, no doubt, good advice, but the duty in s.6(1) on public authorities to act compatibly with Convention rights means that adjudicating bodies must themselves consider obvious points arising under the Convention even if they are not raised by the parties.

4.50 In *R(IS) 12/04* the Commissioner reminds tribunals of the need to address fully arguments based on Convention rights in the following terms,

> "13. Finally, it is necessary to consider the adequacy of the tribunal's reasons. I agree with the Secretary of State that a tribunal's lack of any power to make a declaration of incompatibility is not a good reason for not dealing fully with Human Rights issues, particularly since a tribunal may have power in some cases to declare subordinate legislation to have been invalidly made-see *Chief Adjudication Officer v Foster* [1993] 1 All E.R. 705. The claimant in this appeal clearly went to considerable trouble to set out his arguments under the Human Rights Act clearly and comprehensively in response to the chairman's direction, and I consider that he was entitled to a much fuller explanation of the tribunal's reasons for rejecting his arguments than the very short passage at the end of the statement of reasons set out above. The reasons for the tribunal's rejection of the claimant's discrimination arguments are not apparent from the statement, and I therefore consider that, in all the circumstances, the tribunal's reasons were inadequate."

The Court of Appeal in *R. (on the application of Hooper, Withey, Naylor and Martin v Secretary of State for Work and Pensions* [2003] EWCA Civ 813 addresses at [29]–[46] the question of when a person becomes a victim within the meaning of s.7, and did not find the application of Strasbourg case law to be satisfactory. The Strasbourg authorities appeared to provide that only when a man has made a claim to a benefit is he in a position to complain that he is not being treated in the same way as a woman, and so, only then, would become a victim for the purposes of art.34 of the Convention. The Court of Appeal describes as "unattractive" an argument raised by the United Kingdom Government before the Court of Human Rights in *White v United Kingdom* (App.53134/99), admissibility decision of June 7, 2001, that the claimant was not a victim because he had not claimed on the official form, notwithstanding that this was designed specifically for widows. Differing from the views expressed by Moses J. in the court below, the Court of Appeal concludes that it is not necessary for the claim to be made in writing in order to constitute the applicant as a victim for the purpose of asserting his Convention rights. The Court of Appeal says, ". . . we can see no reason in principle why an oral claim, made and rejected, should not suffice to constitute a claim." Note, however, that the oral claim is not a perfected claim for the purposes of the Claims and Payments Regulations, simply for the purposes of giving a person standing to claim Convention rights as a victim of a violation of those rights. This aspect of the Court of Appeal's decision was accepted by the House of Lords, [2005] UKHL 29.

Section 7A omitted. **4.51**

Judicial remedies

8.—(1) In relation to any act (or proposed act) of a public authority which the court finds is (or would be) unlawful, it may grant such relief or remedy, or make such order, within its powers as it considers just and appropriate. **4.52**

(2) But damages may be awarded only by a court which has power to award damages, or to order the payment of compensation, in civil proceedings.

(3) No award of damages is to be made unless, taking account of all the circumstances of the case, including—

(a) any other relief or remedy granted, or order made, in relation to the act in question (by that or any other court), and

(b) the consequences of any decision (of that or any other court) in respect of that act,

the court is satisfied that the award is necessary to afford just satisfaction to the person in whose favour it is made.

(4) In determining—

(a) whether to award damages, or

(b) the amount of an award,

the court must take into account the principles applied by the European Court of Human Rights in relation to the award of compensation under Article 41 of the Convention.

(5) A public authority against which damages are awarded is to be treated—

(a) in Scotland, for the purposes of section 3 of the Law Reform (Miscellaneous Provisions) (Scotland) Act 1940 as if the award were made in an action of damages in which the authority has been found liable in respect of loss or damage to the person to whom the award is made;

(b) for the purposes of the Civil Liability (Contribution) Act 1978 as liable in respect of damage suffered by the person to whom the award is made.

(6) In this section—

"court" includes a tribunal;

"damages" means damages for an unlawful act of a public authority; and

"unlawful" means unlawful under section 6(1).

COMMENCEMENT

4.53 October 2, 2000: The Human Rights Act 1998 (Commencement No.2) Order 2000 (SI 2000/1851).

GENERAL NOTE

4.54 Section 8(1) grants a broad competence, but the nature of the remedies available will vary according to the forum. The relief, remedy or order open to the court or tribunal must be one already within its powers: see *R(T) v Chief Constable of Greater Manchester Police* [2014] UKSC 35; [2015] A.C. 49 at [63]. So the Act gives no new competence to decision-making bodies to provide a remedy for a violation of a Convention right. The decision not to extend the powers of all courts and tribunals to include new remedies for violations of Convention rights was apparently motivated by a concern that there would be an explosion of damages awards in this area across a wide range of decision-making bodies. This was the same concern which led to the exclusion of art.13 of the Convention from the incorporated rights. There is, accordingly, a wide but not unlimited range of remedies available for breaches of Convention rights.

The drafting of s.8 reveals a concern that damages for violations of Convention rights should be contained. Section 8(2) provides that damages for an unlawful act of a public authority under the Act may be awarded only by a court (or tribunal) which has power to award damages, or to order the payment of compensation, in civil proceedings. Furthermore, damages, though not the remedy of last resort, are circumscribed since they are not to be made unless the court is satisfied that the award is necessary to afford just satisfaction to the person in whose favour the award is made, having regard to all the circumstances of the case, and in particular any other remedy or relief granted and the consequences of any decision in respect of the breach of Convention rights: subs.(3). As noted above, decisions about the award of damages and the amount of damages are to be informed by reference to the case law of the Court of Human Rights in awarding just satisfaction.

A number of observations need to be made about the structure of s.8. It assumes that the range of remedies currently available to United Kingdom courts will be adequate to remedy breaches of Convention rights. It seeks to discourage an explosion of damages awards. The Lord Chancellor indicated that the intent was to match the awards victims would get if they received just satisfaction under art.41: HL Vol.582 col.1232, November 3, 1997. It establishes a system in which the luck of the forum will determine whether duplication of litigation will be needed to secure a money remedy. A good example would be an appeal heard by an appeal tribunal, which has no power to award damages, and it has been established that it has no power to award interest on the late payment of benefit; This undoubtedly follows from the reasoning of the Social Security Commissioner in *R(FC)2/90*; see also the decision of the Court of Justice in *R. v Secretary of State for Social Security; Ex p. Sutton* [1997] E.C.R. I-2163; [1997] 2 C.M.L.R. 382. Nor it seems would any other court. Yet the Court of Human Rights has awarded interest on the late payment of benefit: *Schuler-Zgraggen v Switzerland*, judgment of June 24, 1993, Series A, No.263; (1993) 16 E.H.R.R. 405. In the early days of Community law, an action for a declaration was one means of securing a judicial statement of an entitlement under Community law. This would seem to be the only route open within the national legal order to a victim who had only received social security benefit to which he or she was entitled some years late and who wished to raise the claim for interest on the late payment. Otherwise, such a person would have to raise the complaint that no interest was available before the Court in Strasbourg.

4.55 Perhaps the most pertinent point to make is that the deference to the provisions of the Convention on just satisfaction in the national legislation is misplaced. The provisions in art.41 of the Convention on affording just satisfaction are a safety net where the national legal order does not offer full compensation for the breach of the Convention.

The starting point is that the national legal order should determine what remedies are appropriate for breaches of the Convention. Such an obligation flows from art.13 of the Convention. Indeed, it could be argued that the effect of s.8 replicates the failures of earlier years to recognise what was demanded by the Convention. It assumes that the current panoply of remedies available in the national legal order meets the requirements of the Convention. It also reveals a deep anxiety about damages as a remedy for breach of a Convention right.

The potential gap in remedies available can, however, be cured under the rule-making power in s.7(11) and (12) which enables additional powers to be given to tribunals to add to the remedies open to them, and to define the grounds on which any additional remedies may be granted.

Where the act complained of is a judicial act, damages as a remedy is limited to compensation for unlawful detention awarded in accordance with art.5(5): s.9(3). 4.56

In *CSIS/460/2002,* the Commissioner makes some comments on the nature of remedies for a violation of Convention rights in the context of an argument that one remedy could be to order a permanent stay of the proceedings. The Commissioner concludes,

> "A tribunal has no power to impose a permanent stay of an appeal. There is no express statutory provision nor can one be implied by virtue of necessity. Mr Orr drew an analogy with an appeal abating. However that derives from a principle of common law and is not a stay by a court or tribunal. Where an appellant dies before the determination of the appeal, the appeal is not terminated by that fact. However, unless and until there is an appointment of someone to proceed with the appeal or there is a personal representative, then no-one is legally competent to take the appeal forward. In such circumstances, the appeal is considered as automatically 'abated', by which is meant suspended. It can nevertheless be revived by the appropriate procedure. Any statement by a tribunal or a Commissioner that an appeal has been abated is thus for clarification only. Abatement is therefore very different from the power to grant a permanent stay. Such a concept could in any event give no advantage to the respondent as it would leave outstanding the adverse decision. The Secretary of State is not legally obliged to contine the customary suspension of recovery procedures and would have no reason to do so if the appeal is permanently stayed." (para.49)

See also discussion of remedies in *Dyer v Watson* [2002] 4 All E.R. 1, especially the analysis by Lord Millett at [128]–[133].

Judicial acts

9.—(1) Proceedings under section 7(1)(a) in respect of a judicial act may be brought only 4.57

(a) by exercising a right of appeal;

(b) on an application (in Scotland a petition) for judicial review; or

(c) in such other forum as may be prescribed by rules.

(2) That does not affect any rule of law which prevents a court from being the subject of judicial review.

[[2] (3) In proceedings under this Act in respect of a judicial act done in good faith, damages may not be awarded otherwise than

(a) to compensate a person to the extent required by Article 5(5) of the Convention, or

(b) to compensate a person for a judicial act that is incompatible with Article 6 of the Convention in circumstances where the person is detained and, but for the incompatibility, the person would not have been detained or would not have been detained for so long.]

(4) An award of damages permitted by subsection (3) is to be made against the Crown; but no award may be made unless the appropriate person, if not a party to the proceedings, is joined.

(5) In this section—

"appropriate person" means the Minister responsible for the court concerned, or a person or government department nominated by him;

"court" includes a tribunal;

"judge" includes a member of a tribunal, a justice of the peace [[1] (or, in Northern Ireland, a lay magistrate)] and a clerk or other officer entitled to exercise the jurisdiction of a court;

"judicial act" means a judicial act of a court and includes an act done on the instructions, or on behalf, of a judge; and

"rules" has the same meaning as in section 7(9).

COMMENCEMENT

4.58 October 2, 2000: The Human Rights Act 1998 (Commencement No.2) Order 2000 (SI 2000/1851).

AMENDMENTS

1. The Justice (Northern Ireland) Act 2002 (Commencement No.8) Order 2005 SR 2005/109 art.2 Sch. (April 1, 2005).

2. The Human Rights Act 1998 (Remedial) Order 2020 (SI 2020/1160) (October 21, 2020). The amendment applies in relation to judicial acts occurring before (as well as those occurring after) the commencement date.

Remedial action

Power to take remedial action

4.59 **10.**—(1) This section applies if—

(a) a provision of legislation has been declared under section 4 to be incompatible with a Convention right and, if an appeal lies—
   (i) all persons who may appeal have stated in writing that they do not intend to do so;
   (ii) the time for bringing an appeal has expired and no appeal has been brought within that time; or
   (iii) an appeal brought within that time has been determined or abandoned; or

(b) it appears to a Minister of the Crown or Her Majesty in Council that, having regard to a finding of the European Court of Human Rights made after the coming into force of this section in proceedings against the United Kingdom, a provision of legislation is incompatible with an obligation of the United Kingdom arising from the Convention.

(2) If a Minister of the Crown considers that there are compelling reasons for proceeding under this section, he may by order make such amendments to the legislation as he considers necessary to remove the incompatibility.

(3) If, in the case of subordinate legislation, a Minister of the Crown considers—

(a) that it is necessary to amend the primary legislation under which the subordinate legislation in question was made, in order to enable the incompatibility to be removed, and

(b) that there are compelling reasons for proceeding under this section,

he may by order make such amendments to the primary legislation as he considers necessary.

(4) This section also applies where the provision in question is in subordinate legislation and has been quashed, or declared invalid, by reason of incompatibility with a Convention right and the Minister proposes to proceed under paragraph 2(b) of Schedule 2.

(5) If the legislation is an Order in Council, the power conferred by subsection (2) or (3) is exercisable by Her Majesty in Council.

(6) In this section "legislation" does not include a Measure of the Church Assembly or of the General Synod of the Church of England.

(7) Schedule 2 makes further provision about remedial orders.

COMMENCEMENT

October 2, 2000: The Human Rights Act 1998 (Commencement No.2) Order 2000 (SI 2000/1851). **4.60**

GENERAL NOTE

This section and Sch.2 make provision for a fast-track Parliamentary procedure to respond to a declaration of incompatibility by a court. **4.61**

Other rights and proceedings

Safeguard for existing human rights

11.—A person's reliance on a Convention right does not restrict— **4.62**

(a) any other right or freedom conferred on him by or under any law having effect in any part of the United Kingdom; or

(b) his right to make any claim or bring any proceedings which he could make or bring apart from sections 7 to 9.

COMMENCEMENT

October 2, 2000: The Human Rights Act 1998 (Commencement No.2) Order 2000 (SI 2000/1851). **4.63**

GENERAL NOTE

The rights given to persons under s.7 to complain of unlawful acts by public authorities in acting in a manner incompatible with the Convention does not limit in any way existing rights under UK law. The new rights are additional to existing rights and not in substitution for them. **4.64**

Freedom of expression

12.—(1) This section applies if a court is considering whether to grant any relief which, if granted, might affect the exercise of the Convention right to freedom of expression. **4.65**

(2) If the person against whom the application for relief is made ("the respondent") is neither present nor represented, no such relief is to be granted unless the court is satisfied—

(a) that the applicant has taken all practicable steps to notify the respondent; or

(b) that there are compelling reasons why the respondent should not be notified.

(3) No such relief is to be granted so as to restrain publication before trial unless the court is satisfied that the applicant is likely to establish that publication should not be allowed.

(4) The court must have particular regard to the importance of the Convention right to freedom of expression and, where the proceedings relate to material which the respondent claims, or which appears to the court, to be journalistic, literary or artistic material (or to conduct connected with such material), to—

(a) the extent to which—

(i) the material has, or is about to, become available to the public; or

(ii) it is, or would be, in the public interest for the material to be published;

(b) any relevant privacy code.

(5) In this section—

"court" includes a tribunal; and

"relief" includes any remedy or order (other than in criminal proceedings).

COMMENCEMENT

4.66 October 2, 2000: The Human Rights Act 1998 (Commencement No.2) Order 2000 (SI 2000/1851).

GENERAL NOTE

4.67 This section is a response to concerns expressed by media interests that the Act would limit freedom of expression by giving priority to the development of privacy under art.8 of the Convention. The effect of the section was reviewed in *PJS v News Group Newspapers Ltd* [2016] UKSC 26.

Freedom of thought, conscience and religion

4.68 **13.**—(1) If a court's determination of any question arising under this Act might affect the exercise by a religious organisation (itself or its members collectively) of the Convention right to freedom of thought, conscience and religion, it must have particular regard to the importance of that right.

(2) In this section "court" includes a tribunal.

COMMENCEMENT

4.69 October 2, 2000: The Human Rights Act 1998 (Commencement No.2) Order 2000 (SI 2000/1851).

GENERAL NOTE

4.70 This section was included in response to concerns expressed on behalf of religious groups that priority would be given to other provisions of the Convention than the provision on freedom of religion in art.9 and that churches would find themselves being required in the name of human rights to do things contrary to their tenets. The Strasbourg case law, in any event, makes it clear that a balance has to be struck between the pluralism of a modern democratic society and respect for religious and personal beliefs.

Derogations and reservations

Derogations

14.—(1) In this Act "designated derogation" means— 4.71

[. . .[1]] any derogation by the United Kingdom from an Article of the Convention, or of any protocol to the Convention, which is designated for the purposes of this Act in an order made by the Secretary of State.

(2) [. . .[1]].

(3) If a designated derogation is amended or replaced it ceases to be a designated derogation.

(4) But subsection (3) does not prevent the [[2] Secretary of State] from exercising his power under subsection (1)[. . .[1]] to make a fresh designation order in respect of the Article concerned.

(5) The [[2] Secretary of State] must by order make such amendments to Schedule 3 as he considers appropriate to reflect—

(a) any designation order; or

(b) the effect of subsection (3).

(6) A designation order may be made in anticipation of the making by the United Kingdom of a proposed derogation.

Commencement

October 2, 2000: The Human Rights Act 1998 (Commencement No.2) Order 2000 (SI 2000/1851). 4.72

Amendments

1. The Human Rights Act (Amendment) Order 2001 (SI 2001/1216) art.2 (April 1, 2001).

2. The Secretary of State for Constitutional Affairs Order 2003 (SI 2003/1887) (August 19, 2003).

Reservations

15.—(1) In this Act "designated reservation" means— 4.73

(a) the United Kingdom's reservation to Article 2 of the First Protocol to the Convention; and

(b) any other reservation by the United Kingdom to an Article of the Convention, or of any protocol to the Convention, which is designated for the purposes of this Act in an order made by the Secretary of State.

(2) The text of the reservation referred to in subsection (1)(a) is set out in Part II of Schedule 3.

(3) If a designated reservation is withdrawn wholly or in part it ceases to be a designated reservation.

(4) But subsection (3) does not prevent the [[1] Secretary of State] from exercising his power under subsection (1)(b) to make a fresh designation order in respect of the Article concerned.

(5) The [[1] Secretary of State] must by order make such amendments to this Act as he considers appropriate to reflect—

(a) any designation order; or

(b) the effect of subsection (3).

COMMENCEMENT

4.74 October 2, 2000: The Human Rights Act 1998 (Commencement No.2) Order 2000 (SI 2000/1851).

AMENDMENT

1. The Secretary of State for Constitutional Affairs Order 2003 (SI 2003/1887) (August 19, 2003).

Period for which designated derogations have effect

4.75 **16.**—(1) If it has not already been withdrawn by the United Kingdom, a designated derogation ceases to have effect for the purposes of this Act—

[. . .[1]] at the end of the period of five years beginning with the date on which the order designating it was made.

(2) At any time before the period—

(a) fixed by subsection (1) [. . .[1]], or

(b) extended by an order under this subsection,

comes to an end, the [[2] Secretary of State] may by order extend it by a further period of five years.

(3) An order under section 14(1)[. . .[1]] ceases to have effect at the end of the period for consideration, unless a resolution has been passed by each House approving the order.

(4) Subsection (3) does not affect—

(a) anything done in reliance on the order; or

(b) the power to make a fresh order under section 14(1)[. . .[1]].

(5) In subsection (3) "period for consideration" means the period of forty days beginning with the day on which the order was made.

(6) In calculating the period for consideration, no account is to be taken of any time during which—

(a) Parliament is dissolved or prorogued; or

(b) both Houses are adjourned for more than four days.

(7) If a designated derogation is withdrawn by the United Kingdom, the [[2] Secretary of State] must by order make such amendments to this Act as he considers are required to reflect that withdrawal.

COMMENCEMENT

4.76 October 2, 2000: The Human Rights Act 1998 (Commencement No.2) Order 2000 (SI 2000/1851).

AMENDMENTS

1. The Human Rights Act (Amendment) Order 2001 (SI 2001/1216) art.3 (April 1, 2001).

2. The Secretary of State for Constitutional Affairs Order 2003 (SI 2003/1887) (August 19, 2003).

Periodic review of designated reservations

4.77 **17.**—(1) The appropriate Minister must review the designated reservation referred to in section 15(1)(a)—

(a) before the end of the period of five years beginning with the date on which section 1(2) came into force; and

(b) if that designation is still in force, before the end of the period of five years beginning with the date on which the last report relating to it was laid under subsection (3).

(2) The appropriate Minister must review each of the other designated reservations (if any)—

(a) before the end of the period of five years beginning with the date on which the order designating the reservation first came into force; and

(b) if the designation is still in force, before the end of the period of five years beginning with the date on which the last report relating to it was laid under subsection (3).

(3) The Minister conducting a review under this section must prepare a report on the result of the review and lay a copy of it before each House of Parliament.

COMMENCEMENT

October 2, 2000: The Human Rights Act 1998 (Commencement No.2) Order 2000 (SI 2000/1851). **4.78**

Judges of the European Court of Human Rights

Section 18 omitted. **4.79**

Parliamentary procedure

Statements of compatibility

19.—(1) A Minister of the Crown in charge of a Bill in either House of Parliament must, before Second Reading of the Bill— **4.80**

(a) make a statement to the effect that in his view the provisions of the Bill are compatible with the Convention rights ("a statement of compatibility"); or

(b) make a statement to the effect that although he is unable to make a statement of compatibility the government nevertheless wishes the House to proceed with the Bill.

(2) The statement must be in writing and be published in such manner as the Minister making it considers appropriate.

COMMENCEMENT

Section 19 entered into force on November 24, 1998: (SI 1998/2882). **4.81**

GENERAL NOTE

Part of the scheme of the Act is to require improved pre-legislative scrutiny of legislation to ensure its compliance with Convention rights. The use of the section to date has been disappointing, since no reasoning is publicly available to elaborate a simple Ministerial statement that the provisions of a Bill are compatible with Convention rights. **4.82**

Reviews carried out by the Parliamentary Joint Committee on Human Rights are rather more rigorous.

4.83 *Section 20 omitted.*

Interpretation, etc.

4.84 **21.**—(1) In this Act—

"amend" includes repeal and apply (with or without modifications);

"the appropriate Minister" means the Minister of the Crown having charge of the appropriate authorised government department (within the meaning of the Crown Proceedings Act 1947);

"the Commission" means the European Commission of Human Rights;

"the Convention" means the Convention for the Protection of Human Rights and Fundamental Freedoms, agreed by the Council of Europe at Rome on 4th November 1950 as it has effect for the time being in relation to the United Kingdom;

"declaration of incompatibility" means a declaration under section 4;

"Minister of the Crown" has the same meaning as in the Ministers of the Crown Act 1975;

"Northern Ireland Minister" includes the First Minister and the deputy First Minister in Northern Ireland;

"primary legislation" means any—

(a) public general Act;
(b) local and personal Act;
(c) private Act;
(d) Measure of the Church Assembly;
(e) Measure of the General Synod of the Church of England;
(f) Order in Council—
 (i) made in exercise of Her Majesty's Royal Prerogative;
 (ii) made under section 38(1)(a) of the Northern Ireland Constitution Act 1973 or the corresponding provision of the Northern Ireland Act 1998; or
 (iii) amending an Act of a kind mentioned in paragraph (a), (b) or (c);

and includes an order or other instrument made under primary legislation (otherwise than by the [2 Welsh Ministers, the First Minister for Wales, the Counsel General to the Welsh [4 . . .] Government], a member of the Scottish Executive, a Northern Ireland Minister or a Northern Ireland department) to the extent to which it operates to bring one or more provisions of that legislation into force or amends any primary legislation;

"the First Protocol" means the protocol to the Convention agreed at Paris on March 20 1952;

[1. . .]

"the Eleventh Protocol" means the protocol to the Convention (restructuring the control machinery established by the Convention) agreed at Strasbourg on May 11 1994;

[1 "the Thirteenth Protocol" means the protocol to the Convention (concerning the abolition of the death penalty in all circumstances agreed at Vilnius on 3rd May 2002;]

"remedial order" means an order under section 10;

"subordinate legislation" means any—

(a) Order in Council other than one—

(i) made in exercise of Her Majesty's Royal Prerogative;

(ii) made under section 38(1)(a) of the Northern Ireland Constitution Act 1973 or the corresponding provision of the Northern Ireland Act 1998; or

(iii) amending an Act of a kind mentioned in the definition of primary legislation;

(b) Act of the Scottish Parliament;

[2 (ba) Measure of the National Assembly for Wales;

(bb) Act of the National Assembly for Wales;]

(c) Act of the Parliament of Northern Ireland;

(d) Measure of the Assembly established under section 1 of the Northern Ireland Assembly Act 1973;

(e) Act of the Northern Ireland Assembly;

(f) order, rules, regulations, scheme, warrant, byelaw or other instrument made under primary legislation (except to the extent to which it operates to bring one or more provisions of that legislation into force or amends any primary legislation);

(g) order, rules, regulations, scheme, warrant, byelaw or other instrument made under legislation mentioned in paragraph (b), (c), (d) or (e) or made under an Order in Council applying only to Northern Ireland;

(h) order, rules, regulations, scheme, warrant, byelaw or other instrument made by a member of the Scottish Executive, [2 Welsh Ministers, the First Minister for Wales, the Counsel General to the Welsh [2 . . .] Government,] a Northern Ireland Minister or a Northern Ireland department in exercise of prerogative or other executive functions of Her Majesty which are exercisable by such a person on behalf of Her Majesty;

"transferred matters" has the same meaning as in the Northern Ireland Act 1998; and

"tribunal" means any tribunal in which legal proceedings may be brought.

(2) The references in paragraphs (b) and (c) of section 2(1) to Articles are to Articles of the Convention as they had effect immediately before the coming into force of the Eleventh Protocol.

(3) The reference in paragraph (d) of section 2(1) to Article 46 includes a reference to Articles 32 and 54 of the Convention as they had effect immediately before the coming into force of the Eleventh Protocol.

(4) The references in section 2(1) to a report or decision of the Commission or a decision of the Committee of Ministers include references to a report or decision made as provided by paragraphs 3, 4 and 6 of Article 5 of the Eleventh Protocol (transitional provisions).

(5) [3 . . .]

COMMENCEMENT

Section 21(5) entered into force on November 9, 1998. The remainder of the section entered into force on October 2, 2000: The Human Rights Act 1998 (Commencement No.2) Order 2000 (SI 2000/1851). **4.85**

AMENDMENTS

1. Human Rights Act 1998 (Amendment) Order 2004 (SI 2004/1574) art.2(2) (June 22, 2004).

2. Government of Wales Act 2006 Sch.10 para.56 (May 3, 2007 immediately after the ordinary election as specified in 2006 c.32 s.161(1); May 25, 2007 immediately after the end of the initial period for purposes of functions of the Welsh Ministers, the First Minister, the Counsel General and the Assembly Commission and in relation to the Auditor General and the Comptroller and Auditor General as specified in 2006 c.32 s.161(4)-(5)).

3. Armed Forces Act 2006 Sch.17 para.1 (October 31, 2009).

4. Wales Act 2014 s.4(2)(a) (February 17, 2015).

General Note

4.86 As regards the status for the purposes of this Act of "retained direct principal EU legislation" and "retained direct minor EU legislation" (now respectively known, following the Retained EU Law (Revocation and Reform) Act 2023, as "assimilated direct principal legislation" and "assimilated direct minor legislation") following the United Kingdom's withdrawal from the European Union, see the European Union (Withdrawal) Act 2018, Sch.8, para.30.

Short title, commencement, application and extent

4.87 **22.**—(1) This Act may be cited as the Human Rights Act 1998.

(2) Sections 18, 20 and 21(5) and this section come into force on the passing of this Act.

(3) The other provisions of this Act come into force on such day as the Secretary of State may by order appoint; and different days may be appointed for different purposes.

(4) Paragraph (b) of subsection (1) of section 7 applies to proceedings brought by or at the instigation of a public authority whenever the act in question took place; but otherwise that subsection does not apply to an act taking place before the coming into force of that section.

(4A) *Omitted.*

(5) This Act binds the Crown.

(6) This Act extends to Northern Ireland.

(7) [1 ...]

Amendment

1. Armed Forces Act 2006 Sch.17 para.1 (October 31, 2009).

General Note

4.88 This section entered into force on November 9, 1998.

Subsection (4) provides that the lawfulness of an act of a public authority may be called into question in proceedings under s.7(1)(b) (any legal proceedings in which Convention rights are raised) whenever that act took place if those proceedings are begun by a public authority. In other words, it has a retrospective effect in this regard, but if the proceedings are brought other than by a public authority, no complaint can be made about an act of a public authority prior to the entry into force of s.7(1)(b).

The issue of the possible retrospective application of the Human Rights Act 1998 in the context of tribunal decisions would appear to have been laid to rest; the position is neatly summarised in *R(IS)3/02*, where the Commissioner concludes:

> "The effect and interaction of sections 3, 6, 7 and 22 of the Human Rights Act in relation to appeals from inferior tribunal decisions given before 2 October 2000 was much debated before me but the argument that Mr Cox [of Counsel] sought to advance in this appeal, that the 1998 Act had a retrospective effect extending even to turning past lawful decisions of courts and tribunals into unlawful ones in United Kingdom law from 2 October 2000 and to obliging appellate courts

to reverse the effect retrospectively from that date onwards, has now conclusively been shown to be untenable: see *R v Lambert* [2001] 3 W.L.R. 206, affirming what was said by Sir Andrew Morritt V-C in *Wilson v First County Trust Ltd (No.2)* [2001] 3 W.L.R. 42, 51; and cf also the recent decision of the Tribunal of Scots Commissioners in case *CSDLA 1019/99*." (At para.15.)

For the now unlikely, but not impossible, situation where Convention rights prior to October 2, 2000 fall to be considered, see *CDLA/1338/2001*, *R(IS)6/04*, *CSIS/460/2002*, and *CCS/1306/2001*. The latter summarises at para.22 the case law on the extent to which Convention rights can be relied upon prior to October 2, 2000. **4.89**

Schedules

Schedule 1

The Articles

Part I

The Convention

Rights and Freedoms

Article 2—Right to life

1. Everyone's right to life shall be protected by law. No one shall be deprived of his life intentionally save in the execution of a sentence of a court following his conviction of a crime for which this penalty is provided by law. **4.90**

2. Deprivation of life shall not be regarded as inflicted in contravention of this Article when it results from the use of force which is no more than absolutely necessary:

(a) in defence of any person from unlawful violence;
(b) in order to effect a lawful arrest or to prevent the escape of a person lawfully detained;
(c) in action lawfully taken for the purpose of quelling a riot or insurrection.

General Note

This article is unlikely to have much relevance in the social security jurisdiction. It is not a vehicle for arguing for a particular allocation of resources by the state. So arguments that without the payment of benefit, a person's life will be at risk and so the state cannot be said to be protecting by law everyone's right to life are destined to fail. This would appear to follow from those cases where the relatives of murder victims have sought to argue that the police failed to protect the victim: App.9837/82 *M v United Kingdom and Ireland* (1986) 47 D.R. 27. **4.91**

For an (unsuccessful) attempt to rely on breach of art.2 where the claimant had committed suicide having experienced benefit problems resulting in the withdrawal of her ESA award, see *Dove v HM Assistant Coroner for Teesside and Hartlepool, Rahman and SSWP* [2021] EWHC 2511 (Admin), discussed in the 2021–22 edition of Vol.V and, where applicable, the updating material in Vol.II of this year's edition, in the annotation to the Employment and Support Allowance Regulations 2008 (SI 2008/794) reg.24. The Divisional Court's decision has been overturned by the Court of Appeal, though not on this aspect: [2023] EWCA 289.

Article 3—Prohibition of torture

No one shall be subjected to torture or to inhuman or degrading treatment or punishment. **4.92**

General Note

This article is concerned with conduct which attains a minimum level of severity. It is not concerned with anything which a person might find degrading. See e.g. **4.93**

MSS v Belgium and Greece (2011) 53 EHRR 2 at [219]. The effect of setting a high threshold is that trivial complaints, and even activity which is considered undesirable or illegal, will not fall within the scope of the article unless they cause sufficiently serious suffering or humiliation to the victim. The assessment of seriousness is relative. Relevant factors include the duration of the treatment, its physical and mental effects, and the sex, age, and state of health of the victim: see *MSS* at [219]. But it should also be remembered that the Convention is a "living instrument" whose standards are not set in stone; it receives a living interpretation and must be considered in the light of present day circumstances.

It follows that arguments, for example, that a medical examination in connection with a benefit claim was felt to be degrading or inhuman by the claimant will fall well below the threshold required to engage this article even where the doctor behaves improperly.

In *R. (on the application of Joanne Reynolds) v Secretary of State for Work and Pensions*, judgment of March 7, 2002, [2002] EWHC 426, it was argued that a failure to pay the claimant more than £41.35 per week by way of social security constituted degrading treatment. Wilson J. gives this argument short shrift, pointing out that "Article 3 proscribes ill-treatment of a depth which the level of payment to Ms Reynolds wholly fails to reach."

4.94 In *Secretary of State for the Home Department v Limbuela, Tesema and Adam* [2005] UKHL 66, the House of Lords upheld the courts below in holding that the refusal to provide State support for three asylum seekers, who had not applied for asylum within three days of their arrival in the United Kingdom under s.55 of the Nationality, Immigration and Asylum Act 2002, engaged their Convention rights under art.3. Lord Hope noted that the relevant domestic legal regime

> "removes from asylum-seekers the ability to fend for themselves by earning money while they remain in that category. They cannot seek employment for at last 12 months, and resort to self-employment too is prohibited" (at [56]).

Lord Bingham at [7] said that:

> "Treatment is inhuman or degrading if, to a seriously detrimental extent, it denies the most basic needs of any human being. As in all article 3 cases, the treatment, to be proscribed, must achieve a minimum standard of severity, and I would accept that in a context such as this, not involving the deliberate infliction of pain or suffering, the threshold is a high one. A general public duty to house the homeless or provide for the destitute cannot be spelled out of article 3. But I have no doubt that the threshold may be crossed if a late applicant with no means and no alternative sources of support, unable to support himself, is, by the deliberate action of the state, denied shelter, food or the most basic necessities of life."

An attempt to rely on art.3 in the light of *Limbuela* failed in the High Court of Northern Ireland in *An application by Tadeusz Stach for judicial review* [2018] NIQB 93. Mr Stach, who had been street homeless, sought to challenge the exclusion of EU national jobseekers who did not hold "worker" status from housing benefit following the amendments made to the relevant Northern Ireland legislation in 2014. Girvan J. distinguished *Limbuela*, noting at [37] that whereas asylum seekers such as those in *Limbuela* could not return to their own country, EU nationals could return to their own Member State and (citing Lord Hope in *Patmalniece v SSWP* [2011] UKSC 11 at [80]), the "basic principle of community law that persons who depend on social assistance will be taken care of in their own member state." He noted that EU jobseekers were not deprived of all benefits as they were still able to access job-seekers allowance (as Mr Stach had done until he failed the "Genuine Prospects of Work" test). He noted that "EU jobseekers are voluntary residents in the country who must take the country's benefits system as they find it." He noted the range of public and voluntary provision in Northern Ireland available to provide assistance to homeless EU jobseekers and finally that there was no indication that

Mr Stach had sought to bring to the attention of the authorities that he was facing street homelessness, thus one of the triggers for intervention referred to in *Limbuela* was not made out. In *Stach v Department for Social Development and the Department for Work and Pensions* [2020] NICA 4, the Court of Appeal in Northern Ireland, following an extensive review of *Limbuela* and other authorities, dismissed Mr Stach's art.3 appeal. A challenge under art.14 also failed: see below.

Article 4—Prohibition of slavery and forced labour

1. No one shall be held in slavery or servitude. 4.95

2. No one shall be required to perform forced or compulsory labour.

3. For the purpose of this Article the term "forced or compulsory labour" shall not include:

(a) any work required to be done in the ordinary course of detention imposed according to the provisions of Article 5 of this Convention or during conditional release from such detention;

(b) any service of a military character or, in case of conscientious objectors in countries where they are recognised, service exacted instead of compulsory military service;

(c) any service exacted in case of an emergency or calamity threatening the life or well-being of the community;

(d) any work or service which forms part of normal civic obligations.

General Note

Being required to be available for work as a condition of entitlement to benefit will not constitute forced or compulsory labour. 4.96

The applicant, in *Stummer v Austria* (App 37452/06), Judgment of the Grand Chamber of July 7, 2011, sought to argue that a requirement to work in prison without affiliation to the old-age pension system could no longer be regarded as "work required to be done in the ordinary course of detention." The Grand Chamber disagreed noting a lack of European consensus on this issue. Such practice as there was did not warrant the interpretation for which the applicant argued.

In joined decisions *CSJSA/495/2007* and *CJSA/505/2007*, the Commissioner dismissed as unarguable a complaint by an appellant that the requirements of the New Deal programme with its obligation to participate in an intensive activity period employment programme constituted a modern form of slavery.

The fourth issue determined by the Supreme Court in *R (on the application of Reilly) v SSWP* [2013] UKSC 68 was whether the conditionality requirements for entitlement to jobseeker's allowance involving participation in work or work-related activity constituted forced labour under art.4. The Supreme Court after consideration of the key Strasbourg authorities concluded that they did not.

Article 5—Right to liberty and security

1. Everyone has the right to liberty and security of person. No one shall be deprived of his liberty save in the following cases and in accordance with a procedure prescribed by law: 4.97

(a) the lawful detention of a person after conviction by a competent court;

(b) the lawful arrest or detention of a person for non-compliance with the lawful order of a court or in order to secure the fulfilment of any obligation prescribed by law;

(c) the lawful arrest or detention of a person effected for the purpose of bringing him before the competent legal authority on reasonable suspicion of having committed an offence or when it is reasonably considered necessary to prevent his committing an offence or fleeing after having done so;

(d) the detention of a minor by lawful order for the purpose of educational supervision or his lawful detention for the purpose of bringing him before the competent legal authority;

(e) the lawful detention of persons for the prevention of the spreading of infectious diseases, of persons of unsound mind, alcoholics or drug addicts or vagrants;

(f) the lawful arrest or detention of a person to prevent his effecting an unauthorised entry into the country or of a person against whom action is being taken with a view to deportation or extradition.

2. Everyone who is arrested shall be informed promptly, in a language which he understands, of the reasons for his arrest and of any charge against him.

3. Everyone arrested or detained in accordance with the provisions of paragraph 1 (c) of this Article shall be brought promptly before a judge or other officer authorised by law to exercise judicial power and shall be entitled to trial within a reasonable time or to release pending trial. Release may be conditioned by guarantees to appear for trial.

4. Everyone who is deprived of his liberty by arrest or detention shall be entitled to take proceedings by which the lawfulness of his detention shall be decided speedily by a court and his release ordered if the detention is not lawful.

5. Everyone who has been the victim of arrest or detention in contravention of the provisions of this Article shall have an enforceable right to compensation.

GENERAL NOTE

4.98 There are two parts to the protections afforded by art.5. First, it prohibits detention save in the exhaustive list of circumstances listed in para.(1). Secondly, it offers a set of procedural guarantees for those detained. Though the article refers to liberty and security of the person, the Strasbourg organs have not treated liberty and security as different concepts; there is no authority for arguing that security of the person refers to physical integrity independent of liberty. The article has little application in the field of social security.

Article 6—Right to a fair trial

4.99 **1.** In the determination of his civil rights and obligations or of any criminal charge against him, everyone is entitled to a fair and public hearing within a reasonable time by an independent and impartial tribunal established by law. Judgment shall be pronounced publicly but the press and public may be excluded from all or part of the trial in the interest of morals, public order or national security in a democratic society, where the interests of juveniles or the protection of the private life of the parties so require, or to the extent strictly necessary in the opinion of the court in special circumstances where publicity would prejudice the interests of justice.

2. Everyone charged with a criminal offence shall be presumed innocent until proved guilty according to law.

3. Everyone charged with a criminal offence has the following minimum rights:

(a) to be informed promptly, in a language which he understands and in detail, of the nature and cause of the accusation against him;
(b) to have adequate time and facilities for the preparation of his defence;
(c) to defend himself in person or through legal assistance of his own choosing or, if he has not sufficient means to pay for legal assistance, to be given it free when the interests of justice so require;
(d) to examine or have examined witnesses against him and to obtain the attendance and examination of witnesses on his behalf under the same conditions as witnesses against him;
(e) to have the free assistance of an interpreter if he cannot understand or speak the language used in court.

GENERAL NOTE

The structure of these annotations

4.100 Introductory remarks: (para.4.101)

Does the adjudication of social security disputes involve the determination of civil rights and obligations?: (para.4.102)

The application of art.6 to appeal proceedings: (para.4.103)

The right of access to a court: (para.4.105)

An overview of the requirements of fair trial under art.6: (para.4.108)

Equality of arms: (para.4.109)

A judicial process: (para.4.110)

Appearance in person: (para.4.111)

Effective participation: (para.4.112)

A reasoned decision: (para.4.113)

An independent and impartial tribunal established by law: (para.4.114)

A public hearing: (para.4.115)

A public judgment: (para.4.116)

Judgment in a reasonable time: (para.4.117)

Criminal charges: (para.4.120)

Introductory remarks

Article 6 is central to the scheme of protection in the Convention, and has generated the largest number of applications and judgments. Article 6 is an omnibus provision which contains a blueprint for what constitutes a fair trial. Although it has generated an extensive case law, there are few areas where the adjudication of social security disputes presents concerns about compatibility with the requirements of art.6. This is because the rules of procedure applicable to both First-tier Tribunals and the Upper Tribunal contain provisions which effectively guarantee the rights enshrined in art.6. There is also a long tradition of respect for a broadly construed notion of natural justice in the tribunals. Nevertheless, there are issues to be considered, and there is no cause for complacency in ensuring that those before the tribunals get a fair trial within the ambit of art.6. **4.101**

There have been statements by Commissioners and judges of the Upper Tribunal recognising the significance of art.6. In *CJSA/5100/2001,* a case not long after the entry into force of the Human Rights Act 1998, one Commissioner noted:

> "5. I choose to explain my decision in terms of the claimant's Convention right to a fair hearing under article 6(1) of the European Convention on Human Rights and Fundamental Freedoms. In particular, I rely on the equality of arms principle that has developed in the jurisprudence of the Strasbourg authorities as part of that right. It requires that the procedure followed by the tribunal must strike a fair balance between the parties so that none is at a disadvantage as against the others. . .
>
> 6. I could, no doubt, have reached the same conclusion under domestic principles of natural justice. However, the Human Rights Act 1998 provides a convenient opportunity for Commissioners to rebase their decisions on procedural fairness in fresh terms. In my view, this would be desirable. I am sure that tribunals are familiar with the principles of natural justice. However, increasingly the cases that come to me suggest that they are not applying them. If there is a common theme in those cases, it is that the tribunal has not provided a procedural balance between the parties. The introduction of the language of balance would provide a touchstone for tribunals."

See also comments in *CIB/2751/2002,* and *DG v SSWP (ESA)* [2010] UKUT 409 (AAC).

In *R. (on the application of Thompson) v The Law Society* [2002] EWCA Civ 167. Clarke L.J., delivering the judgment of the Court of Appeal with which his colleagues agreed, summarised the proper approach to issues of fair trial as follows:

> "The key point as a matter of principle is that the question whether the procedure satisfies article 6(1), where there is a determination of civil rights and obligations, must be answered by reference to the whole process. The question in each case is whether the process involves a court or courts having 'full jurisdiction to deal with the case as the nature of the decision requires'. There may be cases in which a public and oral hearing is required at first instances and other cases where it is

not, just as there may be cases in which the potential availability of judicial review will not be sufficient to avoid a breach of article 6(1)".

What follows presents some observations on the structure and content of art.6, and how its provisions apply in the First-tier Tribunal and the Upper Tribunal.

Does the adjudication of social security disputes involve the determination of civil rights and obligations?

4.102 Article 6 is concerned with the determination of civil rights and obligations, and of criminal charges (see further below on criminal charges). Initially there was some uncertainty as to whether art.6 covered proceedings of an administrative nature, since it had been argued that the concept of civil rights and obligations concerned only disputes having a private law character. It is, however, now firmly established that art.6 does cover social security adjudication, whether or not the benefit is contributory or non-contributory: *Feldbrugge v The Netherlands,* Series A No.99; (1986) 8 E.H.R.R. 425; *Deumeland v Germany,* Series A No.120; (1986) 8 E.H.R.R. 448; and *Salesi v Italy,* Series A No.257-E; (1998) 26 E.H.R.R. 187. The Strasbourg Court recapitulated its case-law in *Schuler-Zgraggen v Switzerland,* Series A No.263; (1993) 16 E.H.R.R. 405, where it said:

> "... the development in the law that was initiated by [the] judgments [in *Feldbrugge* and *Deumeland*] and the principle of equality of treatment warrant taking the view that today the general rule is that Article 6(1) does apply in the field of social insurance, including even welfare assistance." (at [46].)

See also *Schouten and Meldrum v The Netherlands,* Series A No.304; (1994) 19 E.H.R.R. 432.

In *Stevens and Knight v United Kingdom* (App.28918/85), decision of September 9, 1998, the Commission, in an admissibility decision, simply ignored arguments that the determination of claims to sickness benefit, statutory sick pay and invalidity benefit did not constitute the determination of civil rights and obligations.

Numerous national authorities have adopted the approach taken by the Strasbourg Court: see, for example, *CDLA/5413/1999.* In *Wood v Secretary of State for Work and Pensions* [2003] EWCA Civ 53 (see [24]) (reported as *R(DLA) 1/03*) the Secretary of State made a concession (quite unnecessary in the light of the Strasbourg authorities) which would appear to mean that all social security appeals involve the determination of civil rights and obligations and so attract the protection of art.6. See also *R(IS) 6/04,* but note para.68 of *R(H) 3/05.*

In a housing case, *Begum v Tower Hamlets LBC* [2003] UKHL 5, the House of Lords also took a broad view of what constitutes the determination of civil rights and obligations (without making any definitive ruling on what does and does not fall within this formulation in art.6) and went on to make a number of pertinent comments on what constitutes independence and impartiality for the purposes of the article. A decision by a rehousing manager employed by a local authority reviewing a decision to offer a particular property to the applicant was held not to constitute an "independent and impartial tribunal" for the purposes of art.6, but a determination on review by the county court "on any point of law arising from the decision", even one which did not permit the making of fresh findings of fact, did meet the requirements of art.6.

The application of art.6 to appeal proceedings

4.103 The initial decision made by a decision maker does not attract the protection of art.6, since there must be a dispute—*contestation* in French—before art.6 bites. Thus, the first instance adjudication of social security disputes arises in proceedings before the First-tier Tribunal. But does art.6 also apply to appeals from decisions of the First-tier Tribunal?

Article 6 does not require Contracting States to have a system of appeals from decisions at first instance in civil cases: *De Cubber v Belgium*, Series A No.86; (1985) 7 E.H.R.R. 236, at [32], but if the state does provide a system of appeals, it too must comply with the guarantees to be found in art.6(1): *Fejde v Sweden*, Series A No.212-C; (1994) 17 E.H.R.R. 14, at [32]. It follows that a defect at first instance might be corrected at the appellate stage of the proceedings. Where there is an appeal, the requirement to exhaust domestic remedies before a complaint can be made under the Convention means that it must be used, and it will then be the totality of the domestic proceedings which is considered by the Strasbourg Court. It will always be necessary to look at the character of the appellate proceedings to determine the extent to which they are able to remedy any deficiency at first instance.

A fair appeal is unlikely to be able to correct a defect arising from a structural problem in the first instance court or tribunal which results in its not being an independent and impartial tribunal: *De Cubber v Belgium*, Series A No.86; (1985) 7 E.H.R.R. 236, at [33]. There is a suggestion that the quashing by an appeal court on the specific ground that the first instance court or tribunal was not independent and impartial might have cured the defect, but this could amount to recognition that there was no right to a court in the particular instance. This is a right which the Strasbourg Court has read into art.6 (see below).

There has been an ongoing debate in English law concerning the adequacy 4.104
of judicial review as a remedy for what might be regarded as an earlier breach of Convention rights. The decision in *Albert and Le Compte v Belgium* (1983) 5 E.H.R.R. 533 made clear that even if the body taking the decision did not itself meet the requirements of art.6, it was sufficient if it was "subject to subsequent control by a judicial body that has full jurisdiction and does provide the guarantees of Article 6(1)." Lord Hoffmann noted in *R v Secretary of State for the Environment Ex parte Alconbury Developments Ltd* [2001] UKHL 23 that, in the phrase quoted above:

> "'full jurisdiction' does not mean full decision-making power. It means full jurisdiction to deal with the case as the nature of the decision requires."

In *CTC/0031/2006* the Commissioner considered this question in the context of an appeal concerning the backdating of a claim to Child Tax Credit. The Commissioner dismissed the appeal on the grounds that the acceptance of a "manner" of claiming is an administrative act involving the exercise of discretion. Accordingly, judicial review was an adequate remedy and there was no basis for the argument that art.6 required the recognition of a right to appeal to a tribunal on this question. The case was followed in *SG v HMRC (TC)* [2011] UKUT 199 (AAC).

However, in *Tsfayo v United Kingdom* (2009) 48 E.H.R.R. 18; [2006] ECHR 1158, the issue was whether the claimant had "good cause" for not having claimed earlier. The statutory test did not express it in terms of the subjective opinion of the decision-maker. The Court held that art.6 required an appeal to a tribunal with full-fact finding jurisdiction and that judicial review would not provide a sufficient alternative. At para.45 the Court indicated that:

> "The Court considers that the decision-making process in the present case was significantly different. In *Bryan, Runa Begum* and the other cases cited at [43] above, the issues to be determined required a measure of professional knowledge or experience and the exercise of administrative discretion pursuant to wider policy aims. In contrast, in the instant case, the HBRB was deciding a simple question of fact, namely whether there was 'good cause' for the applicant's delay in making a claim . . ."

Tsfayo was applied to a different aspect of the tax credit claiming process in *ZM v HMRC* [2013] UKUT 547(AAC); [2014] AACR 17. The judge viewed the relevant aspect of the claiming process as a "simple question of fact", like that in *Tsfayo*, and held judicial review to be an inadequate alternative for art.6 purposes.

The right of access to a court

4.105 The Strasbourg Court has recognised that art.6 must contain a right of access to a court for the determination of a particular issue. So the prohibition (at the time) in English Prison Rules on bringing a defamation action against a prison officer, who was alleged to have accused the prisoner wrongly of having assaulted him, violated this right: *Golder v United Kingdom*, Series A No.18; (1979–80) 1 E.H.R.R. 524. A similar conclusion was reached in a case originating from Ireland where there was no procedure by which a father could challenge a decision of the authorities placing his daughter for adoption: *Keegan v Ireland*, Series A No.290; (1994) 18 E.H.R.R. 342. Over-zealous application of procedural rules may fall foul of the article, as also may an over-formalistic approach, as in *Dos Santos Calado v Portugal* (App.55997/14), where the Constitutional Court had rejected the application by the claimant in a dispute concerning the amount of her retirement pension on the ground that she had cited the wrong sub-paragraph of the legislation under which she sought to apply. In *Kuznetsov v Russia* (App.24970/08) time for appealing against a decision had stared to run before the applicant had been informed of it and his attempt to appeal late had been rejected inter alia because he had not made a formal application for an extension of time. Unduly burdensome costs regimes, to the detriment of those in dispute with the State, may also constitute a restriction on the right of access to a court: *Zustović v Croatia* (App.27903/15). In an extreme case, art.6 may even require the FtT to admit an appeal lodged after the absolute time limit imposed by r.22(8) of its rules of procedure: see the commentary on that provision at para.3.314.

The right might even include a right to some sort of representation in order to make the right effective. In *Airey v Ireland*, Series A No.32; (1979–80) 2 E.H.R.R. 305, the applicant had been unable to find a lawyer to act for her because of her financial position and the absence of legal aid. She needed a separation order to protect her from her husband who was prone to violence towards her. The procedure was complex and not such as could be managed effectively by a litigant in person. The Court concluded that, in such circumstances, art.6 requires the provision of legal assistance where "such assistance proves indispensable for an effective access to court" (at [26]). The case is sometimes wrongly read too sweepingly as imposing an obligation on the state to have a legal aid scheme, at least for complex litigation. The judgment is rather more limited; it will be necessary to look at the nature of the right being protected by the litigation, what is at stake for the applicant, and the complexity of the procedure before the particular decision-making body in making a judgment as to whether art.6 requires a state to provide legal assistance.

In *CJSA/5101/2001* the claimant sought to rely on the *Airey* case to ground an entitlement to legal representation. The Commissioner stated:

> "The claimant has no right to legal representation under British law in a social security case, and the European Convention on Human Rights does not give him that right. I have no power under British law to grant him legal representation and the European Convention on Human Rights, again does not give me that power." (at para.9.)

Though undoubtedly correct in the circumstances of the case before him, it is not entirely inconceivable that a set of circumstances might arise in which the *Airey* test would require the provision legal assistance and possibly legal representation in order to satisfy the requirements of art.6.

4.106 Following the passing of the Legal Aid, Sentencing and Punishment of Offenders Act 2012, the availability of legally aided advice, assistance and representation for social security adjudication is severely limited, although there was a late concession by the Government which has resulted in legal advice and assistance being available following a refusal of permission to appeal to the Upper Tribunal by the First-tier Tribunal, which encompasses advice and assistance on appeals (as they must be) on a point of law to the Upper Tribunal, and thereafter to the Court of Appeal and Supreme Court. The only possibility for legal aid for representation (as distinct from advice and assistance) would appear to be those situations in which the requirements of the Legal Aid, Sentencing and Punishment of Offenders Act 2012, s.10 are met. Section 10 provides:

"**10. Exceptional cases**

(1) Civil legal services other than services described in Part 1 of Schedule 1 are to be available to an individual under this Part if subsection (2) or (4) is satisfied.

(2) This subsection is satisfied where the Director—

(a) has made an exceptional case determination in relation to the individual and the services, and

(b) has determined that the individual qualifies for the services in accordance with this Part,

(and has not withdrawn either determination).

(3) For the purposes of subsection (2), an exceptional case determination is a determination—

(a) that it is necessary to make the services available to the individual under this Part because failure to do so would be a breach of—

(i) the individual's Convention rights (within the meaning of the Human Rights Act 1998), or

(ii) any rights of the individual to the provision of legal services that are retained enforceable EU rights, or

(b) that it is appropriate to do so, in the particular circumstances of the case, having regard to any risk that failure to do so would be such a breach.

(4) This subsection is satisfied where—

(a) the services consist of advocacy in proceedings at an inquest under the Coroners Act 1988 into the death of a member of the individual's family,

(b) the Director has made a wider public interest determination in relation to the individual and the inquest, and

(c) the Director has determined that the individual qualifies for the services in accordance with this Part,

(and neither determination has been withdrawn).

(5) For the purposes of subsection (4), a wider public interest determination is a determination that, in the particular circumstances of the case, the provision of advocacy under this Part for the individual for the purposes of the inquest is likely to produce significant benefits for a class of person, other than the individual and the members of the individual's family.

(6) For the purposes of this section an individual is a member of another individual's family if—

(a) they are relatives (whether of the full blood or half blood or by marriage or civil partnership),

(b) they are cohabitants (as defined in Part 4 of the Family Law Act 1996), or

(c) one has parental responsibility for the other."

See also the Civil Legal Aid (Preliminary Proceedings) Regulations 2013 (SI 2013/265), and the *Lord Chancellor's Exceptional Funding Guidance (Non-Inquests)*.

The Upper Tribunal has on occasion been critical of the refusal of legal aid: see, for example, *JC v SSWP (ESA)* [2014] UKUT 352 (AAC); [2015] AACR 6 at para.63.

There are separate provisions relating to judicial review proceedings under which advice, assistance and representation may be available.

Civil legal aid in Scotland is the province of the Scottish Civil Legal Aid Board *http://www.slab.org.uk* and the availability of both advice and assistance, and 4.107

representation, appears to be significantly more generous than the provision in England and Wales.

Part of the decision of the Tribunal of Commissioners in *CIB/3645/2002* concerned an argument that the absence of a right of appeal in the social security legislation contravened the claimant's rights under art.6. The Tribunal of Commissioners ruled that the decision that the claimant was, or was not, permanently incapacitated for work at the time of leaving Great Britain for Jamaica concerned the payability of benefit while the claimant was in Jamaica rather his entitlement to the benefit. The decision was accordingly not within the scope of the Social Security Act 1998, s.12(3). Furthermore art.6 was not relevant because art.6 had "no part to play in the ambit of substantive rights, as opposed to procedural rights." (at para.43), since art.13(2) of the Social Security (Jamaica) Order 1997 (SI 1997/871) provided a subjective test, under which the Secretary of State determined whether benefit was to continue to be payable abroad where he considered the claimant likely to be permanently incapacitated for work on leaving Great Britain. The Tribunal of Commissioners indicates that it has not come to this decision lightly and adds a rider in para.54 of its decision:

> "Finally, we should make clear that our decision is limited to the issues before us. On the basis of the decision of Mr Commissioner Howell Q.C. in *CIB/3654/2002* [this appears to be an erroneous reference, which should be to *CIS/540/2002*, now reported as *R(IS) 6/04*], it may be arguable that that the Human Rights Act and Art.6 of the European Convention may require rights of appeal to be granted against decisions under reciprocal agreement provisions in respect of which rights of appeal had existed previously. There may also be other cases in which it may be arguable that para.22 of Sch.2 of the Decisions and Appeals Regulations does not restrict certain rights of appeal without deciding whether the provision is ultra vires (as found in *CIB/3586/2000* (starred decision 15/00)). We express no view on the correctness of those decisions."

The appeal against this decision was dismissed by the Court of Appeal: *Campbell v SSWP* [2005] EWCA Civ. 989.

In relation to the impact of art.6 on the requirement for revision before appealing in an ESA case, see *R. (Connor) v Secretary of State for Work and Pensions* [2020] EWHC 1999 (Admin) noted at para.2.444.

An overview of the requirements of fair trial under art.6

4.108 The Strasbourg organs have indicated that art.6(1) demands not only an overall requirement of a fair hearing but also the presence of specific features in order for there to be a fair trial. The overall requirement has been summarised as follows:

> "The effect of Article 6(1) is, inter alia, to place the 'tribunal' under a duty to conduct a proper examination of the submissions, arguments and evidence adduced by the parties, without prejudice to its assessment of whether they are relevant to its decision." (*Kraska v Switzerland*, Series A No.254-B; (1994) 18 E.H.R.R. 188, at [30]).

It is important that the general requirements for a fair trial are appreciated, since they continue to be developed in specific circumstances by the Strasbourg Court. Certain of the requirements are of a general nature, whereas others are more specifically stated in art.6. This over-riding requirement of fairness reflects five inherent requirements for a fair trial and four explicit requirements set out in art.6.

The inherent requirements are: (a) *égalité des armes*, or "equality of arms"; (b) a judicial process; (c) a right to appearance in person; (d) a right to effective participation; and (e) a right to a reasoned decision.

The explicit rights are to: (a) an independent and impartial tribunal established by law; (b) a public hearing; (c) a public judgment; and (d) judgment in a reasonable time.

Each of these nine ingredients of the fair trial will now be considered.

Equality of arms

4.109 Equality of arms is an inelegant translation of *égalité des armes.* An idiomatic translation is more helpful, namely procedural equality. In national law, this has long been an inherent aspect of natural justice. Procedural equality requires that each party has a broadly equal opportunity to present a case in circumstances which do not place one of the parties as a substantial disadvantage as regards the opposing party (see e.g. *Dombo Beheer BV v The Netherlands*, Series A No.274-A; (1994) 18 E.H.R.R. 213, at [33] and *Steel and Morris v United Kingdom* (App.68416/01 at [59]).

In an expansive reading of the Strasbourg case law, the Commissioner in *CDLA/2748/2002* draws on specific case-law relating to criminal proceedings in art.6(3)(e) on the provision of interpretation and translation to suggest that art.6 requires that effective and efficient interpretation and translation is a feature of tribunal adjudication where the claimant needs this. He says that "a failure of interpretation must therefore affect the fairness of the tribunal hearing." (para.11).

FY v SSWP (RP) [2018] UKUT 146 (AAC) raised an interesting point in connection with equality of arms. Rule 27 of the First-tier Tribunal's rules of procedure requires it to hold a hearing unless each party has consented to, or not objected to, the matter being decided without a hearing and the FtT considers it is able to decide the matter without a hearing. The claimant, who lived in Canada, wanted his appeal decided on the papers. The DWP, after some prevarication, decided they wanted an oral hearing, which under r.27 they were entitled to. The claimant, in no position to attend a hearing in person from Canada, submitted that the rule would only be ECHR complaint if it were read without the part which enabled one party to insist on an oral hearing. After a review of ECHR caselaw, Judge Wikeley observed:

> "52. I am not persuaded that the imbalance of power in the Tribunal setting is such that there is necessarily an inequality of arms for the purposes of Article 6(1) ECHR. I do not doubt that in general terms the State may start with an institutional advantage in many types of tribunal proceedings. . . .
>
> 53. However, the working out of the principle of equality of arms means that one must consider both the general and the particular context. At the general level, the Tribunal's inquisitorial ethos and enabling role, already noted, has been specifically developed to act as a counterweight to the State's institutional advantage. At the level of the particular, there is simply no evidence in this case that the Appellant was put at any material disadvantage whatsoever. The Tribunal's record of proceedings shows that the hearing lasted for approximately 15 minutes. There is no suggestion that the Department's representative made any new points at the oral hearing. Rather, the record of proceedings simply notes the presenting officer's submission. . . .
>
> 54. This submission was no more than a resumé of the Department's much more extensive written response on the Appellant's appeal. The reality was that this was a case which, although it led to an oral hearing, was effectively decided on the basis of the parties' detailed written submissions – as in fact the Appellant had wanted."

For this and other reasons the submission that there was inequality of arms was rejected.

A judicial process

4.110 A judicial process requires each side to have the opportunity to have knowledge of and comment on the observations filed or evidence adduced by the opposing party: *Ruiz-Mateos v Spain*, Series A No.262; (1993) 16 E.H.R.R. 505, at [63]. Non-disclosure of material by one side to the other is likely to give rise to violations of this feature of a fair trial, as might issues of the circumstances in which evidence was acquired. In *Feldbrugge v The Netherlands,* Series A No.99; (1986) 8 E.H.R.R. 425, the applicant complained that she had not had a proper opportunity to present her case. The Court found that the proceedings before the President of the Appeals Board "were not attended to a sufficient degree, by one of the principal guarantees of a judicial procedure" (at [44]) in that, although the applicant had been afforded the opportunity to comment on her condition during the medical examinations, she was neither able to present oral argument nor to file written pleadings before the President of the Appeals Board; nor was she able to consult the two reports of the consultants and to formulate objections to them.

Appearance in person

4.111 Can a trial be fair if there is no right of appearance in person? The Strasbourg Court has considered in some detail the importance of a right to appearance in person in *Elo v Finland* (App.30742), judgment of September 26, 2006. The case concerned accident compensation and it was held that written submissions were sufficient to meet the requirements of a fair trial. The Court considers that the "question is whether hearing oral evidence from the applicant and the doctors treating him could have produced anything relevant and decisive which was not already encompassed in the written evidence and submissions." In the circumstances of this case, the Court concluded that oral evidence would have added little to the written submissions. The Strasbourg Court has adopted a distinctly pragmatic approach to this aspect of art.6, as it has to some other rights forming part of the article.

Effective participation

4.112 Mere presence at a trial may not be sufficient. There must also be an ability to participate in the proceedings in an effective manner. The principal authority relates to the treatment of juveniles in the criminal process: *T v United Kingdom* (App.24724/94) and *V v United Kingdom* (App.24888/94), (2000) 30 E.H.R.R. 121; and *SC v United Kingdom* (App.60958/00), (2005) 40 E.H.R.R. 226.

In *Schuler-Zgraggen v Switzerland,* Series A No.263; (1993) 16 E.H.R.R. 405, (which was principally concerned with the right to a public hearing) the applicant had not availed herself of the opportunity to request a hearing, but nevertheless complained that the proceedings were unfair because the Federal Insurance Court had not ordered a hearing of its own motion. The Court accepted the arguments of the Government that purely written proceedings did not in the circumstances of this case prejudice the interests of the litigant. It was accepted that a written procedure would offer advantages of efficiency and speed which might be jeopardised if oral hearings became the rule. The Court ruled:

> "The Court reiterates that the public character of court hearings constitutes a fundamental principle enshrined in Article 6(1). Admittedly, neither the letter nor the spirit of this provision prevents a person from waiving of his own free will, either expressly or tacitly, the entitlement to have his case heard in public, but any such waiver must be made in an unequivocal manner and must not run counter to any important public interest." (at [58].)

The possibility of holding "paper hearings" before the First-tier Tribunal is unlikely to generate any possibility of a lack of fairness (either in relation to appearance in person or effective participation) under art.6 for a number of reasons. Firstly, an appellant always has the opportunity to request an oral hearing. Furthermore, in all cases, r.27 (decision with or without a hearing) of the First-tier Tribunal's rules of procedure requires the tribunal, regardless of the wishes of the parties, always to consider whether it is able to decide the appeal without an oral hearing. The decisions of the Upper Tribunal on the proper application of r.27 discussed in the annotations to that rule (paras 3.334–3.346) show that art.6 considerations are at the heart of the requirement to show that the rule has been considered in cases where the tribunal proceeds in the absence of the parties. See also *FY v SSWP (RP)*, discussed at para.4.109.

A reasoned decision

The requirement for a reasoned decision is regarded as implicit in the notion of a fair trial. The level of reasoning need not be detailed. If a court or tribunal gives reasons, then the requirement for a reasoned decision is prima facie met, but a decision which on its face shows that it was made on a basis not open to the judge cannot be said to be a reasoned decision (see *De Moor v Belgium*, Series A No.292-A; (1994) 18 E.H.R.R. 372). For a case in which a violation of art.6 was found because of the inadequacy of the reasons for rejecting certain medical evidence in a social security context, see *H.A.L. v Finland* (App.38267/97), judgment of January 27, 2004. A failure to address in the Court's reasons a significant point raised by the applicant was found to be a breach of the article in *Uche v Switzerland* (App.12211/09). **4.113**

The use of short-form decisions in tribunals is unlikely to fall foul of this provision, since a party is entitled to a full statement of reasons on application within one month of the day on which the decision notice was notified to the parties. Decisions of the Upper Tribunal are given in full, except a decision made with the consent of the parties to set aside a tribunal decision and remit the case for a rehearing by the tribunal, or otherwise to dispose of the appeal.

An independent and impartial tribunal established by law

The requirement that there is an independent and impartial tribunal established by law includes a subjective and an objective element. The subjective test involves an enquiry into whether the particular judge in the case was actually biased, or lacking in independence or impartiality. Propriety will be presumed in the absence of specific evidence of bias. The objective test involves determination of whether the court or tribunal offers guarantees sufficient to exclude any legitimate doubt about its impartiality or independence. This can include both specific difficulties caused by certain persons being involved in particular decisions, as well as what might be called structural problems with the forum for the resolution of the dispute. The failure to disclose at the outset of proceedings the blood tie between the presiding judge and his son, who worked for the firm representing one of the parties, was held to be a breach in *Koulias v Cyprus* (App.48781/12). Disclosure was seen as an important procedural safeguard to provide adequate guarantees for objective and subjective impartiality. A good example of structural problems can be found in the English courts-martial cases, which have determined that the role (at the time) of the convening officer in the management of the prosecution case conflicted with his role as convenor of the court-martial, in particular his appointment of its members (who were subordinate in rank to himself and fell within his chain of command) (see *Findlay v United Kingdom* (App.22107/93), (1997) 24 E.H.R.R. 221; and *Coyne v United Kingdom* (App.25942/94), *The Times*, October 24, 1997, ECHR. **4.114**

Tsfayo v United Kingdom (App.60860/00), (2009) 48 E.H.R.R. 457 found a violation of art.6 was found on the grounds that the (now abolished) Housing Benefit Review Board was not an independent and impartial tribunal. However, the comments in the case on the relationship between appeals and other remedies are of considerable significance.

The issue of an independent and impartial tribunal raises the question of bias by one or more members of the court or tribunal. This has provided to be a contentious issue in relation, in particular, to the medical members of certain social security tribunals. This issue is considered in detail in the annotations to the Tribunals, Courts and Enforcement Act 2007 s.3 (see above at 3.35–3.36) and that material is not repeated here.

A public hearing

Publicity is seen as one of the guarantees of the fairness of a trial, but the requirement for hearings to be in public is surrounded by a substantial list of circumstances in which the presumption of public hearings is displaced. It is now also **4.115** clear that interlocutory matters do not have to be in public. So the Commission has rejected a complaint that interlocutory proceedings before a High Court Master in Chambers without elaborating its reasons violated art.6: *X v United Kingdom* (App.3860/68), (1970) 30 CD 70. A similar view would almost certainly be taken of proceedings for permission to appeal. As already noted, a written procedure may suffice provided that there are proper opportunities for requesting or ordering an oral hearing.

In *DF v SSWP* [2015] UKUT 143 (AAC), Judge Gamble held that lack of pre-publication of the hearing lists for scheduled appeal hearings did not breach the requirements for a public hearing in art.6. Judge Gamble said:

> "25. . . . . The minimum requirement of a public hearing, in my view, is that it takes place within reasonable office hours and at a publicly recognised court or tribunal hearing centre. That is so even if no pre-publicity of listed cases is available unless that can be shown in any case to be a stratagem to deprive a claimant of a public hearing. . . . ."

A public judgment

4.116 Article 6(1), on its face, requires that judgment is pronounced publicly, and this requirement is not expressed to be subject to the list of limitations which apply to a public trial. The leading case is *Pretto v Italy*, Series A No.71; (1984) 6 E.H.R.R. 182, and adopts a pragmatic view to the right. The Court seems to have been very accommodating to a wide range of practice in this regard among the Contracting States, indicating that the form of publicity to be given to a judgment is to be assessed in the light of special features of particular proceedings. It certainly appears to be the case that nothing more than the formal disposition need be announced publicly, and it seems that the public availability of the outcome is as important as the matter being read out in open court. So in the *Pretto* case, the availability of the disposition in the court registry was considered to meet the requirements for public pronouncement of the judgment.

Judgment in a reasonable time

4.117 Article 6(1) provides that litigants are entitled to judgment in a reasonable time. Complaints of violations of this requirement have been the single most numerous sort of alleged violation of the Convention. Such cases have rarely involved the United Kingdom (but see *Robins v United Kingdom*, (1998) 26 E.H.R.R. 527).

For a pithy statement of how the courts and tribunals of England and Wales deal with the requirement that judgment be given within a reasonable time, see *Bond v Dunster Properties Ltd* [2011] EWCA Civ 455, at [1]–[6].

Though the case law is voluminous, the principles can be stated quite simply. The first task is to determine the period or periods in issue, before moving on to consider the reasonableness of the length of the proceedings. The period in issue will include any appellate proceedings. In forming judgments on the reasonableness of the length of the proceedings, the following factors are relevant: the complexity of the case, the behaviour of the applicant, the conduct of the judicial authorities, and what is at stake for the applicant: see, among other cases, *Frydlender v France* (App.30979/96). However, backlogs of judicial business are not a defence to unreasonable delays. In *Deumeland v Germany,* Series A No.120; (1986) 8 E.H.R.R. 448, the period in issue was ten years, seven months and three weeks from the application to the Berlin Social Security Court to the rejection of the application to the Bundesverfassungsgericht. The claim to benefit involved a straightforward factual issue involving no great legal complexity, but the behaviour of Klaus Deumeland had protracted the proceedings. Detailed examination of the progress of the case through the various courts showed that the case had lain dormant before the Berlin Social Security Court for significant periods, and the period taken to resolve the second set of proceedings before the appellate body was excessive. There was a violation of the right to judgment within a reasonable time, but it is significant that the Court also finds that the mere declaration of a violation was in the circumstances of the case considered to be adequate just satisfaction under what is now art.41 of the Convention. A delay of a little over six years in *Salesi v Italy*, Series A No.257-E; (1998) 26 E.H.R.R. 187, was also found to constitute a violation of art.6(1) and it mattered not that her case concerned welfare assistance rather than, as in *Deumeland*, social insurance. The reasonableness of the time taken to give judgment must be determined in each case in the light of its own particular circumstances. The Court considers special diligence is necessary in pension disputes: *Pejčić v Serbia* (App.34799/07).

Somorjai v Hungary (App.60934/13) involved resolving a factual dispute to enable Regulation 1408/71/EEC to be applied correctly and a challenge to the Hungarian legislation limiting the period for which a claimant was entitled to arrears of pension following revision for official error. The litigation took seven years, without fault on the art of Mr Somorjai but equally without any finding that the case had been dormant before any of the courts or other public bodies concerned. Unlike in *Deumeland*, a modest sum was awarded by way of just satisfaction. **4.118**

On the remedies for a breach of the right, see the judgment of the Grand Chamber in *Scordino v Italy (No.1)* (App.36813/97), (2007) 45 E.H.R.R. 207.

The issue of judgment within a reasonable time in the social security context was raised in *R(IS) 1/04*, where the claimant argued that the (it should be said not wholly unusual) lengthy period before an overpayment decision was taken meant that there was a breach of art.6. An overpayment decision was made on October 14, 2000 in respect of an overpayment which had arisen in 1994 and 1995. The Commissioner concludes that for the purposes of the measurement of time in the context of a complaint that judgment has not been given within a reasonable time, time started running on October 14, 2000, since it was at that point that a dispute arose; a different Commissioner in *R(IS) 2/04* takes the same view at para.20. That was enough to dispose of the point since a tribunal determined the appeal in May 2001 which was manifestly within a reasonable time. The claimant had also sought to suggest that overpayment decisions were in the nature of criminal charges. The Commissioner, after careful consideration of the authorities, concludes that overpayment decisions involve the determination of civil rights and obligations and not the determination of a criminal charge (see [12]–[17]).

See also *CIS/4220/2002*, which draws on the decision of the Court in *Dyer v Watson* [2002] 4 All E.R. 1.

In *AS v SSWP (CA)* [2015] UKUT 592 (AAC); [2016] AACR 22, Judge Wright considered how a First-tier Tribunal should deal with an established claim that there has not been judgment in a reasonable time contrary to art.6 ECHR. The issue of delay arose in the following circumstances. The Secretary of State made an entitlement decision on September 4, 2004 in respect of non-entitlement to carer's allowance arising from April 16, 2001. But it was not until January 5, 2007 that an overpayment decision was made. There was then a further five-year delay before a letter which was dated April 11, 2007 was accepted as an appeal against the overpayment decision. The tribunal's decision was made in May 2014. In considering at paras 49-56 how the tribunal should have responded to this issue, Judge Wright assumes that the delays would amount to a failure to give judgment in a reasonable time in breach of Article 6 of the European Convention. He concludes that it will usually be the case that a tribunal must proceed to determine the appeal notwithstanding the delay, and cannot simply not proceed on the grounds that there has been an unreasonable delay. The person affected must seek a remedy elsewhere in the form of compensation, and the tribunal has no power to award compensation: see *Cocchiarella v Italy* (App.64886/01) Judgment of Grand Chamber of March 29, 2006.

In *Bullerwell v United Kingdom* (App.48013/99), (2003) 36 E.H.R.R. CD 76, the **4.119**
Strasbourg Court ruled as inadmissible a complaint that judgment was not given in a reasonable time in an industrial injuries benefit case which involved four hearings by a medical appeal tribunal, three appeals to the Commissioner, and an application

for judicial review which resulted in an unsuccessful appeal to the Court of Appeal. The outcome is unsurprising even though the first appeal was lodged in July 1991 and the trail of litigation ended in July 1998 when the House of Lords refused a petition for leave to appeal the refusal of leave to apply for judicial review. The Court applies its tried and tested methodology of considering the complexity of the case, the parties' conduct and that of the competent authorities, and the importance of what was at stake for the applicant in the litigation. There is nothing significant in the decision but it is an excellent example of the approach of the Court to admissibility of complaints and contains a detailed and fair analysis of the course of these lengthy proceedings.

In its admissibility decision of April 8, 2003 in *Wingrave v United Kingdom* (App.40029/02), the Strasbourg Court had declared inadmissible part of the claim (relating (1) to a breach of contract claim, (2) to the requirement to make a new claim at age 65 for disability living allowance, and (3) concerning the quality of her representation) but adjourned the issue concerning the length of the proceedings. The appeal had been twice remitted for rehearing by the Commissioners and had taken nearly five years to conclude. By a decision of May 18, 2004, the Court declared this aspect of the complaint admissible, but a friendly settlement was subsequently reached under which the applicant's executors received from the respondent State an ex gratia payment of £4,500: decision of November 29, 2005.

In *CDLA/1761/2002* the claimant raised an art.6 issue in relation to the delay (of about six months) in producing the written statement of reasons for the tribunal's decision. The Commissioner did not need to address the argument in full, but rightly notes that art.6 is concerned with the overall length of the proceedings and not with delays in relation to specific parts of the process.

Criminal charges

4.120 A question arises as to whether proceedings for penalty additions to overpayments, and of possible penalty proceedings under the tax credits legislation, as well as determinations of the Upper Tribunal under the Forfeiture Act of 1982, constitute the determination of criminal charges under art.6 and so attract the additional protections for such matters in the article.

The concept of a criminal charge is an autonomous one under the Convention, and so it is not the classification of the matter under national law which is determinative of the issue. National classification is not, however, wholly irrelevant since the Strasbourg organs have always regarded as a criminal charge something so considered by national law.

In other cases the following factors have been taken into account in making the determination: the nature of the "offence", the severity of the sanction imposed having regard in particular to any loss of liberty since this is a principal characteristic of criminal liability: see *Engel v The Netherlands*, Series A No.22; (1979–80) 1 E.H.R.R. 647. Having regard to this case and to the judgment of the Court in *Ravnsborg v Sweden* Series A No.283-B; (1994) 18 E.H.R.R. 38, it is argued that such proceedings would not constitute the determination of a criminal charge. The essence of the penalty provision is civil rather than criminal in nature.

However, in *King v United Kingdom* (App 13881/02), judgment of November 16, 2004, which concerned a penalty determination in relation to tax liabilities, the Strasbourg Court found a violation of art.6(1) on grounds of delay and characterised the penalty proceedings as criminal charges. The question of their classification is, however, not argued in the judgment. The United Kingdom government seems to have accepted that the proceedings did involve a criminal charge. The classification would not matter where the sole issue is delay, but could, in other circumstances, be a matter of importance since criminal charges attract additional protections under art.6. An example would be an entitlement to free legal assistance under art.6(3)(c) where the interests of justice demand this.

Article 7—No punishment without law

1. No one shall be held guilty of any criminal offence on account of any act or omission which did not constitute a criminal offence under national or international law at the time when it was committed. Nor shall a heavier penalty be imposed than the one that was applicable at the time the criminal offence was committed. **4.121**

2. This Article shall not prejudice the trial and punishment of any person for any act or omission which, at the time when it was committed, was criminal according to the general principles of law recognised by civilised nations.

Article 8—Right to respect for private and family life

1. Everyone has the right to respect for his private and family life, his home and his correspondence. **4.122**

2. There shall be no interference by a public authority with the exercise of this right except such as is in accordance with the law and is necessary in a democratic society in the interests of national security, public safety or the economic well-being of the country, for the prevention of disorder or crime, for the protection of health or morals, or for the protection of the rights and freedoms of others.

General Note

Introduction

Article 8 is one of the most open-ended provisions of the Convention and is not yet fully developed in its scope. The concept of private life is very wide and not easily contained within a single comprehensive definition. The protection of private life (as distinct from family life) under art.8 can now be organised under a number of headings: **4.123**

- freedom from interference with physical and psychological integrity, which includes interference with the person, searches of property, surveillance and interception of communications, and the dissemination of images;
- the collection, storage and use of personal information;
- freedom to develop one's identity, which includes discovering information about childhood and parenthood, aspects of the use of names, transsexuality, and cultural identity;
- a right to personal autonomy, which includes sexual preference, and the establishment of a settled circle of friends, and respect for decisions in relation to health and medical treatment;
- the protection of one's living environment;
- protection of the home; and
- protection of correspondence.

Like the series of articles which follows, the rights given in para.(1) are limited by the exceptions listed in para.(2). If there is an interference with one of the rights protected in the first paragraph, then it will be necessary to see whether this is justified under the limitations in the second paragraph. Here the Strasbourg organs have consistently required the interference to be: (1) for one of the specified reasons; (2) in accordance with law; (3) necessary in a democratic society; and (4) proportionate in the sense that there is no other way of protecting the recognised interest which constitutes a lesser interference with the right.

Benefit, family life and private life

Article 8 of the Convention guarantees respect private life, home and correspondence, for family life, subject to the limitation contained in the article. Family life encompasses ties between near relatives, which certainly extends to children, parents and grandparents, though it is unclear how far it includes relationships **4.124** between siblings, aunts and uncles. In general the Strasbourg organs have preferred relationships in the vertical line to those in the horizontal line.

The Government's response to the Supreme Court's decision in *R(Steinfeld and Keidan) v Secretary of State for International Development* [2018] UKSC 32 making a declaration of incompatibility (based on art.14 taken with art.8) in respect of the exclusion of heterosexual couples from the Civil Partnership Act 2004 was the Civil Partnerships, Marriages and Deaths (Registration etc.) Act 2019. The Civil Partnership (Opposite-sex Couples) Regulations 2019 (SI 2019/1458), in force from December 2, 2019, make it possible for heterosexual couples, who are otherwise eligible, to enter into a civil partnership. The Regulations amend an extensive range of social security (and other) legislation. Reference should be made to the notes in respect of specific provisions for the detail.

R(SC and others) v SSWP and others [2021] UKSC 26 concerned the introduction of (broadly) a two-child limit on the number of children for whom child tax credit and universal credit would be paid, where a third or subsequent child is born on or after April 6, 2017. The claimants sought to argue that the measure breached arts 8 and 12; further that art.14 was breached when taken together with art.8 and/or A1P1. The challenge failed. Further discussion can be found under each of the articles concerned.

4.125 When the case had been in the Court of Appeal, in relation to art.8 (and art.12) Leggatt L.J., giving the judgment of the Court, noted at [29] that "The root difficulty facing the claimant's case is that the Convention is not aimed at securing social and economic rights". At [30]-[31] he observed that art.8 had never been held to impose an obligation on the state to have in place any positive programme of financial support for private or family life and that attempts to argue otherwise, as in *Petrovic v Austria* (2001) 33 EHRR 14, had "met with short shrift". He noted that where the European Court of Human Rights had held that the Convention imposed obligations on the state to make socio-economic provision for basic material needs, it had done so by reference to art.3.

A submission that the aim of the legislation was to influence recipients of child tax credit to have smaller families and was incompatible with respect for their dignity failed before the Court as it previously had below. The most that could be said on the evidence was that the legislative intention was that recipients of child tax credit would have to decide whether or not to have more than two children in the knowledge that their income derived from child tax credit would not increase in consequence. Nor was there any evidence to support a submission, put forward as a further reason why art.8 was breached, that the integration of third and subsequent children into their families was damaged as a result of the measure.

It is clear from the decision of the Court of Appeal and House of Lords in *R. (on the application of Hooper, Withey, Naylor and Martin) v Secretary of State for Work and Pensions,* [2003] EWCA Civ 813, and [2005] UKHL 29, that benefits for widows and widowers fall within the ambit of art.8. However, income support and income-based jobseeker's allowance schemes do not, according to the Court of Appeal, *per se* engage art.8: see *Carson and Reynolds v Secretary of State for Work and Pensions,* [2003] EWCA Civ 797.

4.126 In *C1/05-06 (WB)*, *C2/05-06 (WB)*, and *C3/05-06 (WB)*, a Commissioner in Northern Ireland concluded that an absolute three months time limit for claiming widow's benefit does not violate art.8. She said,

> "17. . . . . I am doubtful that the three month time limit for claiming a benefit can in any way be linked to or have a "meaningful connection" with an Article 8 right in the absence of any Article 14 discrimination. However, even if a link exists, it is too tenuous to be within the ambit of the right. The right is not to the benefit but to the respect set out in Article 8. The time limit in no way violates that respect."

In *CP/1183/2007* the Commissioner dismisses in short form the possibility of arguing that differential state retirement ages for men and women can constitute a violation of art.8 when read in conjunction with art.14.

CM v SSWP (DLA) [2013] UKUT 27 concerned a human rights challenge to the hospital rules under which DLA ceased to be payable for a child under 16 once that child had been in hospital for 84 days. The Judge found that art.8 did not apply. Family life continued during the long period in hospital of a very sick three-year-old child, albeit with additional difficulties. The Upper Tribunal decision was reversed by the Supreme Court as *Cameron Mathieson, a deceased child (by his father Craig Mathieson) v SSWP* [2015] UKSC 47, [2015] AACR 19 on the basis that there was a breach of art.14 with art.1 of protocol 1 and art.8 did not need to be considered further.

A challenge under art.8 to the DWP's data retention policies in respect of transsexuals failed in *R(C) v SSWP* [2017] UKSC 72. Whilst the policies were considered an interference with the right of those affected by them to respect for their private lives, the need to retain historic data in order to calculate entitlement to state retirement pension and to counter fraud were accepted as legitimate aims and the Supreme Court concluded that the DWP's policies were proportionate ways of implementing them. Further, any discrimination there might be under art.14 was justified. **4.127**

In *CJSA/935/1999* the Commissioner made some *obiter* comments on the rights of transsexuals to respect for their identity. The issue had arisen in the context of a claim that the use of the national insurance number in a jobseeker's agreement enabled the claimant's gender at birth to be identified. The decision contains a useful overview of some leading decisions in this area both under European Union law and under the European Convention on Human Rights.

For a summary of the position of transsexuals in the light of decisions of the Strasbourg Court, see the opinions of the House of Lords in *Bellinger v Bellinger* [2003] UKHL 21 (April 10, 2003).

But note the decision of the Court of Human Rights in *Grant v United Kingdom* (App.32570/03), Judgment of May 23, 2006, which concerned a male-to-female transsexual who had been refused a pension on reaching the age of 60. Initial failures to secure the pension before reaching the age of 65 were reopened following the grant of a gender recognition certificate under the Gender Recognition Act 2004. Grant succeeded in securing a judgment that the United Kingdom was in breach of art.8 E.C.H.R. from July 2002 when the Court of Human Rights handed down its decision in *Goodwin v United Kingdom* (2002) 35 E.H.R.R. 447.

In *Jivan v Romania* (App.62250/19), the Court found a breach of art.8 in the State's failure (including on the part of the appeal court) adequately to assess the degree of disability of an older man. The Court's reasoning is somewhat brief, but suggests that the State may have focussed on the main presenting medical issue (a partial amputation) to the exclusion of a wider range of medical and social factors. It observed: **4.128**

> "The Court reiterates that a wide margin is usually allowed to the State under the Convention in issues of general policy, including social, economic, and healthcare policies (see, for instance, *McDonald*, cited above, § 54, with further references). However, if a restriction on fundamental rights applies to a particularly vulnerable group in society that has suffered considerable discrimination in the past, such as persons with disabilities, or elderly dependent people, then the State's margin of appreciation is substantially narrower and it must have very weighty reasons for the restrictions in question (see *Guberina v. Croatia*, 23682/13, § 73, 22 March 2016, in the context of discrimination of a physically disabled child; *Alajos Kiss v. Hungary*, 38832/06, § 42, 20 May 2010, in the context of the restriction of a mentally disabled person's right to vote; and *Cînța v. Romania*, 3891/19, § 41, 18 February 2020, in the context of the restriction of a mentally ill parent's right to contact with his child)."

In *Beeler v Switzerland* (App.78630/12) (Grand Chamber), the Strasbourg Court has reviewed existing authorities on when benefits issues may fall within the ambit of art.8. The issue arose acutely in the case, as Switzerland has not ratified Protocol

1, so a claim based on art.14 could only succeed if taken together with art.8. The Court observed:

> "66. An analysis of the case-law summarised above indicates that the Court has not always been entirely consistent in defining the factors leading it to find that complaints concerning social welfare benefits fell within the ambit of Article 8 of the Convention.
>
> 67. The Court notes at the outset that all financial benefits generally have a certain effect on the way in which the family life of the person concerned is managed, although that fact alone is not sufficient to bring them within the ambit of Article 8. Otherwise, all welfare benefits would fall within the ambit of that Article, an approach which would be excessive.
>
> 68. It is therefore necessary for the Court to clarify the relevant criteria in order to specify, or indeed to circumscribe, what falls within the ambit of Article 8 in the sphere of welfare benefits.
>
> 69. It can also be seen from the case-law summarised above that in the field of social welfare benefits, the sphere of protection of Article 1 of Protocol No. 1 and that of Article 8 of the Convention intersect and overlap, although the interests secured under those Articles are different. In determining which complaints fall within the ambit of Article 8, the Court must redress the inconsistencies noted under Article 8, particularly when read in conjunction with Article 14 of the Convention ... .
>
> It follows that the Court can no longer simply accept either a legal presumption to the effect that in providing the benefit in question, the State is displaying its support and respect for family life (see the case-law cited in paragraph 65 above), or a hypothetical causal link whereby it ascertains whether the grant of a particular benefit is "liable to affect the way in which family life is organised" (see the case-law cited in paragraph 64 above).
>
> 70. In the Court's view, the Grand Chamber judgment in *Konstantin Markin* [(App.30078/06) (Grand Chamber)] should be taken as the main reference point here:
>
> > '*(i) On whether Article 14 taken in conjunction with Article 8 is applicable*
> >
> > 129. The Court must determine at the outset whether the facts of the case fall within the scope of Article 8 and hence of Article 14 of the Convention. It has repeatedly held that Article 14 of the Convention is pertinent if "the subject matter of the disadvantage ... constitutes one of the modalities of the exercise of a right guaranteed ...", or if the contested measures are 'linked to the exercise of a right guaranteed
> >
> > ... For Article 14 to be applicable, it is enough for the facts of the case to fall within the ambit of one or more of the provisions of the Convention (see *Thlimmenos v. Greece* [GC], App.34369/97, § 40, ECHR 2000-IV; *E.B. v. France*, cited above, §§47–48; and *Fretté v. France*, App.336515/97, §31, ECHR 2002-I, with further references.
> >
> > 130. It is true that Article 8 does not include a right to parental leave or impose any positive obligation on States to provide parental-leave allowances. At the same time, by enabling one of the parents to stay at home to look after the children, parental *leave* and_related *allowances* promote family life and *necessarily affect the way in which it is organised* [emphasis added *in original*]. Parental leave and parental allowances therefore come within the scope of Article 8 of the Convention. It follows that Article 14, taken together with Article 8, is applicable. Accordingly, if a State does decide to create a parental-leave scheme, it must do so in a manner which is compatible with Article 14 of the Convention (see *Petrovic*, cited above, §§ 26–29).'
>
> 71. In the context of *Konstantin Markin*, the applicability of Article 14 of the Convention in conjunction with Article 8 stemmed from the fact that the parental

leave and the corresponding allowance had '*necessarily affect[ed] the way in which [family life was] organised*' (compare and contrast the approach followed in the cases referred to in paragraphs 64 and 65 above), both measures having been aimed at enabling one of the parents to remain at home to look after the children (in this case, infants). Thus, a close link between the allowance associated with parental leave and the enjoyment of family life was considered necessary.
72. Accordingly, for Article 14 of the Convention to be applicable in this specific context, the subject matter of the alleged disadvantage must constitute one of the modalities of exercising the right to respect for family life as guaranteed by Article 8 of the Convention, in the sense that the measures seek to promote family life and necessarily affect the way in which it is organised. The Court considers that a range of factors are relevant for determining the nature of the benefit in question and that they should be examined as a whole. These will include, in particular: the aim of the benefit, as determined by the Court in the light of the legislation concerned; the criteria for awarding, calculating and terminating the benefit as set forth in the relevant statutory provisions; the effects on the way in which family life is organised, as envisaged by the legislation; and the practical repercussions of the benefit, given the applicant's individual circumstances and family life throughout the period during which the benefit is paid."

Surveillance in social security cases

In *R(DLA) 4/02* the claimant argued that covert filming of the claimant in public places by the Department violated her Convention rights under art.8. The Commissioner did not agree having regard to the balance which had to be struck between the interests of the individual and those of the community as a whole. In claiming benefit, the claimant had necessarily accepted a degree of interference with her private life. The covert filming had been limited to activities in public and was brief. The information gathered was used only for the purposes of considering the claimant's continuing entitlement to the benefit she had claimed. **4.129**

In *CIS/1481/2006* which is excoriating about the behaviour of officers of the Department in the matter before him, and critical of the tribunal's approach to the case, a Commissioner has provided very useful guidance on issues concerning the use of surveillance techniques to support decision-making in the Department. In particular, there is the most helpful guidance about the application of the Regulation of Investigatory Powers Act 2000 (RIPA) to surveillance by the Department. Such action is, of course, frequently attacked as a violation of art.8 ECHR. The Commissioner summarises a detailed section of his decision as follows:

"50. More generally, where there is a challenge under Article 8 of the European Convention against evidence produced by the Secretary of State, or the conduct or results of surveillance are otherwise challenged before an appeal tribunal, RIPA now provides effective answers. If the Secretary of State provides the tribunal and the claimant with a copy of the application and authorisation for the surveillance, and it is clear that the authorisation covers the surveillance, then the tribunal will usually need to take matters no further. The tribunal may properly take the view that the Secretary of State can rely fully on the evidence obtained from the surveillance without further investigation by itself. If the claimant has continuing or other concerns, then he or she may take them to the investigatory powers tribunal. With that in mind, I suggest that the Secretary of State should, in cases such as this, produce the proper documentation about surveillance to an appellant and the tribunal together with the evidence from the surveillance on which the Secretary of State seeks to rely."

CIS/1481/2006 has been followed in *DG v SSWP (DLA)* [2011] UKUT 14 (AAC), at paras 43–47.

For observations by the Court of Appeal on the issue of surveillance, see *Jones v University of Warwick* [2003] 1 W.L.R. 954.

Article 9—Freedom of thought, conscience and religion

4.130 **1.** Everyone has the right to freedom of thought, conscience and religion; this right includes freedom to change his religion or belief and freedom, either alone or in community with others and in public or private, to manifest his religion or belief, in worship, teaching, practice and observance.

2. Freedom to manifest one's religion or beliefs shall be subject only to such limitations as are prescribed by law and are necessary in a democratic society in the interests of public safety, for the protection of public order, health or morals, or for the protection of the rights and freedoms of others.

GENERAL NOTE

4.131 Reliance on this article to avoid the normal requirements, for example, to pay national insurance contributions are most unlikely to succeed. The Commission has held that a Dutch system of old-age pension insurance, alleged to interfere with the religious duty of caring for old people, did not violate the article: App.1497/62, *Reformed Church of X v The Netherlands* (1962) 5 Y.B. 286; and App.2065/63, *X v The Netherlands* (1965) 8 Y.B. 266.

In *SC v SSWP* at first instance ([2018] EWHC 864 (Admin)), Ouseley J. dismissed any role for art.9 (paras 80 and 95), observing that it does not require public welfare support for the consequences of the exercise of the freedoms it confers. The point does not appear to have been pursued in the subsequent appeal.

Article 10—Freedom of expression

4.132 **1.** Everyone has the right to freedom of expression. This right shall include freedom to hold opinions and to receive and impart information and ideas without interference by public authority and regardless of frontiers. This Article shall not prevent States from requiring the licensing of broadcasting, television or cinema enterprises.

2. The exercise of these freedoms, since it carries with it duties and responsibilities, may be subject to such formalities, conditions, restrictions or penalties as are prescribed by law and are necessary in a democratic society, in the interests of national security, territorial integrity or public safety, for the prevention of disorder or crime, for the protection of health or morals, for the protection of the reputation or rights of others, for preventing the disclosure of information received in confidence, or for maintaining the authority and impartiality of the judiciary.

Article 11—Freedom of assembly and association

4.133 **1.** Everyone has the right to freedom of peaceful assembly and to freedom of association with others, including the right to form and to join trade unions for the protection of his interests.

2. No restrictions shall be placed on the exercise of these rights other than such as are prescribed by law and are necessary in a democratic society in the interests of national security or public safety, for the prevention of disorder or crime, for the protection of health or morals or for the protection of the rights and freedoms of others. This Article shall not prevent the imposition of lawful restrictions on the exercise of these rights by members of the armed forces, of the police or of the administration of the State.

Article 12—Right to marry

4.134 Men and women of marriageable age have the right to marry and to found a family, according to the national laws governing the exercise of this right.

GENERAL NOTE

4.135 *SC* (as to which see art.8 above) provides a rare example of this article being considered in a social security context. The Supreme Court dismissed the application for the same reasons it had dismissed the art.8 claim. It noted that according to the Strasbourg court, the article only protects the right to found a family within marriage: *Goodwin v UK* (2002) 35 E.H.R.R. 18. That was not the case on the evidence. Further, art.12 does not impose an obligation on the state to provide the material means to found a family: *Cannatella v Switzerland* (App.25928/94, April 11, 1996).

Article 14—Prohibition of discrimination

The enjoyment of the rights and freedoms set forth in this Convention shall be secured without discrimination on any ground such as sex, race, colour, language, religion, political or other opinion, national or social origin, association with a national minority, property, birth or other status. 4.136

GENERAL NOTE

The structure of these annotations 4.137

The general structure of art.14

Article 14 prohibits discrimination on the grounds of sex, race, colour, language, religion, political or other opinion, national or social origin, association with a national minority, property, birth or other status. Discrimination can be either direct or indirect: *DH v Czech Republic* (App.57325/00), November 13, 2007 [Grand Chamber]. A difference in treatment may also arise where a claimant can show that a "neutrally formulated measure affects a disproportionate number of members of a group of persons sharing a characteristic which is alleged to be the ground of discrimination, so as to give rise to a presumption of indirect discrimination" (per Lord Reid in *SC* after reviewing *DH v Czech Republic* (2007) E.H.R.R. 3 and other authorities.) Once that point is reached, the burden shifts to the state to show the indirect difference in treatment is not discriminatory. Note however the suggestion, referred to by Lord Reid at [62] but which he did not find it necessary to address, that indirect discrimination may be confined to the "suspect grounds" (see below). 4.138

The protection of art.14 is only applicable in relation to the enjoyment of the rights and freedoms set forth in the Convention. It is the linking of art.14 with another article of the Convention which gives it substance. In order to have effect, it does not have to be shown that there is a violation of the substantive article, merely that the alleged discrimination operates in a field which is covered by the protections afforded by those provisions. Indeed the practice of the Strasbourg Court has been to decline to consider art.14 in conjunction with another article if they find a violation of that article on its face, unless the essence of the complaint is discrimination. The article has proved to be a fruitful source of complaints in social security cases. However, the position of the Strasbourg Court is now well established in relation to complaints of violations of the prohibition of discrimination in the social security context. Since most challenges relate to economic and social policy choices, it has proved relatively easy for states to show that those choices are reasonably and objectively justified.

The Strasbourg approach to art.14 in the social security context

4.139 The Strasbourg approach to the determination of complaints raising art.14 issues is threefold:

(1) Does the complaint of discrimination fall within the sphere or ambit of a protected right?
(2) Can the applicants can properly compare themselves with a class of persons who are treated more favourably?
(3) Can the difference in treatment be reasonably and objectively justified and is it proportionate to its aim?

Nearly all social security cases fall within the scope of art.1 of Protocol 1 (the right to property) following the admissibility decision in the *Stec* case: see below.

In relation to the second issue, the court has, over time, referred to the comparators as being, or not being, in "similar situations" (*Marckx v Belgium* (App.6833/74), June 13, 1979, Series A, No. 31, (1979–80) 2 E.H.R.R. 330, [32]) or in "relevantly similar situations" (*Burden v United Kingdom,* (App.13378/05), April 29, 2008 [Grand Chamber], [60]), or in "analogous situations" (*Stubbings v United Kingdom* (Apps 22083/93 and 22095/93), October 22, 1996, (1997) 23 E.H.R.R. 213, [71]). The phrase "relevantly similar situations" appears to be the currently favoured formulation. Additionally, the right not to be discriminated against in the enjoyment of rights falling within the scope of the Convention will be violated where contracting parties fail to treat persons in different situations differently without any objective and reasonable justification for doing so. This has come to be known as the *Thlimmenos* principle from the case of *Thlimmenos v Greece*, (App.34369/97), April 6, 2000, (2001) 31 E.H.R.R. 411. See also *Guberina v Croatia* (2018) 66 E.H.R.R. 11.

The third question is whether the treatment can be justified. The court has made it clear that art.14 is concerned with arbitrary discrimination and so there will only be a breach of art.14 if there is no objective or reasonable justification.

Article 14 enumerates certain grounds upon which the prohibition of discrimination is based (such as sex, race, language, and religion) but also leaves the list open by referring to "other status". Where the differential treatment is:

- between men and women (*Konstantin Markin v Russia* (App.30078/06) [Grand Chamber] at [127]);
- on grounds of nationality (*Gaygusuz v Austria* (App.17371/90), September 16, 1996, (1997) 23 E.H.R.R. 364, [42]);
- on grounds of race (*Timishev v Russia,*(Apps. 55762/00 and 55974/00), December 13, 2005, (2007) 44 E.H.R.R. 37, [58]);
- on grounds of religion (*Hoffmann v Austria* (App.12875/87), June 23, 1993, Series A, No. 255–C, (1994) 17 E.H.R.R. 293, [36]);
- on grounds of legitimacy (*Inze v Austria,* (App.8695/79), October 28, 1987, Series A, No. 126, (1988) 10 E.H.R.R. 394, [41]);
- on grounds of sexual orientation (*E.B. v France,* (App.43546/02), January 22, 2008 [Grand Chamber], [93]); (*Beizaras and Levickas v Lithuania* (App.41288/15) at [114]);
- On grounds of ethnic origin (*DH v Czech Republic* (App.57325/11 [Grand Chamber] at [176]); and
- On grounds of disability (*Guberina v Croatia* (App.23682/130 at [73]).

(the so-called "suspect" grounds), very weighty reasons are required to justify the differential treatment.

The Court has indicated in *Šaltinyte v Lithuania* (App.32934/19), Decision of October 26, 2021, that discrimination on grounds of age "has not, to date" been suggested to require "very weighty reasons".

Where the basis for the difference of treatment is grounds of sex or race, the contracting parties enjoy no margin of appreciation and will find it exceedingly difficult to establish objective and reasonable justification.

It follows that the nature of the justification presented will vary with the nature of the differential treatment in issue. While it will be reasonably easy for a contracting party to show that a difference of treatment pursues a legitimate aim, the case law suggests that meeting the test of objective and reasonable justification will vary according to the circumstances of each case. The test is tied in with the margin of appreciation.

The Strasbourg Court's approach to social security cases is typified by the decision of the Grand Chamber in *Stummer v Austria* (App.37452/02), Judgment of July 7, 2011. The case concerned a complaint by a prisoner that he was the victim of discrimination since as a working prisoner he was not affiliated to the old-age pension system and so was deprived of a pension. **4.140**

The court first considered whether the complaint was one within the scope of the rights protected by the Convention. This was easy to answer, since the Grand Chamber in its admissibility decision in *Stec v United Kingdom* (Apps No 65731/01 and 65900/01) Decision of September 5, 2005, (2005) 41 E.H.R.R. SE295, held that art.1 of Protocol 1 applied to welfare benefits in general for which a contracting party had provided, whether conditional or not on the payment of contributions. The court had said that art.1 of Protocol 1 does not include a right to receive a social security payment, although where a state creates entitlement to a benefit, it must do so in a manner which is compatible with art.14. The full effect of the *Stec* admissibility decision has been accepted by the House of Lords in *R. (on the application of RJM) v Secretary of State for Work and Pensions* [2008] UKHL 63, where Lord Neuberger says:

> "31. . . . I recognise that the admissibility decision in Stec represents a departure from the principle normally applied to claims which rely on A1P1. However, Stec . . . was a carefully considered decision, in which the relevant authorities and principles were fully canvassed, and where the Grand Chamber of the ECtHR came to a clear conclusion, which was expressly intended to be generally applied by national courts. Accordingly, it seems to me that it would require the most exceptional circumstances before any national court should refuse to apply the decision."

The Strasbourg Court defines discrimination as treating people in a relevantly similar situation differently without an objective and reasonable justification. In order to establish objective and reasonable justification, the state imposing the measure is required to show that the differential treatment pursues a legitimate aim and that there is a reasonable relationship of proportionality between the means employed and the aim sought to be realised (*Stummer*, at [87]). So, when considering art.14, it is best to start by considering differential treatment and only to use the term "discrimination" when that differential treatment cannot be objectively and reasonably justified or shown to be proportionate.

It is very significant that the court has held that, where general measures of economic or social strategy are in issue (and where the differential treatment is not related to the specially protected groups), a wide margin of appreciation (or discretion) is allowed to the state. In such cases, the court will not find a violation unless the measure in issue can be regarded as "manifestly without reasonable foundation." (*Stummer*, at [89].)

Note, however, that in *JD and A v United Kingdom* (Apps 32949/17 and 34614/17) a seven-judge chamber of the ECtHR, giving judgment on October 24, 2019, held at [88]–[89] that the "manifestly without reasonable foundation" test is limited to transitional measures forming part of a scheme carried out in order to correct an inequality. A subsequent attempt by the United Kingdom to have the case referred to the Grand Chamber proved unsuccessful. The decision subsequently was among those considered by the Supreme Court in *SC* in its review of the "manifestly without reasonable foundation" test.

In the *Stummer* case the grounds of different treatment related to a matter of "other status"; the comparison was between working prisoners and employees not in prison. These groups were regarded as appropriate comparators, which meant that the different treatment required justification. The court considered that the Austrian government had shown a legitimate aim in its different treatment in the following terms "preserving the economic efficiency and overall consistency of the old-age pension system by excluding from benefits persons who have not made meaningful contributions" (*Stummer,* at [98]). The court gave lengthy consideration to the question of whether the difference in treatment was proportionate and concluded that it was. It could not be said that the Austrian approach was manifestly without reasonable foundation, and so there was no violation of art.14 read with art.1 of Protocol 1.

In *Belli and Arquier-Martinez v Switzerland* (App.65550/13) Ms Belli, who lived in Brasil with her mother and step-father, was seeking to challenge the habitual residence conditon imposed by Swiss law for receipt of certain non-contributory disability benefits. Ms Belli was disabled from birth and she argued that the "other status" arose because, unlike people who had become disabled later in life as the result of illness or accident, she had never been able to make the social security contributions which would have led to a contributory benefit which she could have exported. The Court accepted this, but then went on to hold that the difference in treatment was justified in the circumstances of the case and notably by reference to the need to maintain the social solidarity which underpins the payment of non-contributory benefits by imposing a habitual residence condition.

For a decision in which the Strasbourg Court held in a case of discrimination on the ground of nationality that the necessary "weighty reasons" existed, see *Savickis v Latvia* (App.49270/11) (Grand Chamber).

A complaint that a time-limited (4 years) reduction (of between 0% and 19%) had been made to pensions as part of national austerity measures has recently even been rejected as manifestly ill-founded in *Žegarac and Others v Serbia* (App.54805/15).

Some judgments of the Strasbourg Court in social security cases involving the United Kingdom

4.141 The long-awaited judgment of the Court of Human Rights in *Runkee and White v United Kingdom* (Apps 42949/98 and 53134/99) was handed down on May 10, 2007. This finally resolved the position in relation to the litigation concerning widowers' entitlements under the legislation in force prior to April 9, 2001. The court ruled that there was no violation of art.14 taken in conjunction with art.1 of Protocol 1 in connection with non-entitlement to a widow's pension but that there was a violation of art.14 taken in conjunction with art.1 of Protocol 1 concerning non-entitlement to a widow's payment.

See *Hobbs, Richard, Walsh and Geen v United Kingdom* (Apps 63684/00, 63475/00, 63484/00 and 63468/00), November 14, 2006, for the corresponding decision to that in *Runkee and White* in relation to widow's bereavement allowance in which a violation of art.14 taken with art.1 of Protocol 1 was found.

Following the judgment of the House of Lords in *R. v Secretary of State for Work and Pensions, ex parte Carson, R. v Secretary of State for Work and Pensions, ex parte Reynolds* [2005] UKHL 37, ruling that there was no breach of art.14 in relation to the rules on the uprating of pensions to certain pensioners living overseas, application was made to the Strasbourg Court. The Chamber judgment of November 4, 2008 was referred to the Grand Chamber, which delivered judgment in *Carson v United Kingdom*, (App.42184/05) on March 16, 2010. The Grand Chamber ruled by 11 votes to six that the United Kingdom was not in violation of art.14 when read in conjunction with art.1 of Protocol 1. The Strasbourg Court noted that, in order for an issue to arise under art.14, there had to be a difference in the treatment of persons in relevantly similar situations. The judgment of the court did not consider that it sufficed for the applicants to have paid National Insurance contributions in the United Kingdom to place them in a relevantly similar position to all other pensioners, regardless of their country of residence. The applicants were accordingly not in a relevantly similar situation with the group with whom they sought to compare themselves.

Nor did the judgment of the court consider that the applicants were in a relevantly similar position to pensioners living in countries with which the United Kingdom had concluded a bilateral agreement providing for up-rating. Those living in reciprocal agreement countries were treated differently from those living elsewhere because an agreement had been entered into; and an agreement had been entered into because the United Kingdom considered it to be in its interests. In that connection, states clearly had a right under international law to conclude bilateral social security treaties and indeed this was the preferred method used by the Member States of the Council of Europe to secure reciprocity of welfare benefits. If entering into bilateral arrangements in the social security sphere obliged a state to confer the same advantages on all those living in all other countries, the right of states to enter into reciprocal agreements and their interest in so doing would effectively be undermined. **4.142**

In *X and others v Ireland* (Apps 23851/20 and 24360/20), the application failed, insofar as it related to art.14 with A1P1 (it was held not to fall within the ambit of art.8), because the applicants could not establish that they were in a relevantly similar position to those who did receive Irish child benefit. They had applied at a time when they had not yet been granted the right of residence in Ireland (though they were some months afterwards). They were not in a similar position to those who had the right of residence. More generally, the Court observed:

> "96. The subject-matter at issue in this case is entitlement to a universal (i.e., non-means tested) statutory social welfare benefit payable to all parents who satisfy the eligibility criteria, including the criterion of residence, which has a legal element (right to reside) and a factual element (habitual residence).
>
> 97. In its case-law the Court has noted that "the essentially national character of the social security system is itself recognised in the relevant international instruments" (*Carson and Others v. the United Kingdom* [GC], no. 42184/05, § 85, ECHR 2010). While the issue in that particular case was quite different, namely whether it was discriminatory to exclude from the uprating of the State pension those pensioners who were resident in third countries that had not concluded social security agreements with the United Kingdom, the point made about the essentially national character of social security systems is of broader application. This is also reflected in the fact that, under the European Social Charter States, may require not just residence but also a prescribed period of residence (see paragraph 53 above) before granting non-contributory benefits to those entitled to equal treatment in relation to social security.
>
> 98. As for the purpose of the impugned measure, this can be described as defining the category of persons who may claim child benefit. While the applicants complain of the exclusionary effect for them, during the period in question, of the criterion of lawful residence, the Court observes that this criterion is a necessary corollary of the essentially national character of social security systems, as outlined above. Moreover, it can be said that this criterion has an inclusionary effect inasmuch as it broadens entitlement to child benefit so as to include not just Irish nationals or those benefitting from specific forms of residence (such as EU nationals exercising freedom of movement), but the entire resident population.

> Both Supreme Court judgments emphasised the neutral and non-discriminatory nature of the criterion of lawful residence, and its effect of making a wide range of people resident in the State on various bases equally eligible for the benefit sought (see paragraphs 28-30 and 36-38 above).
>
> 99. Turning to the context, the Court observes that the general context of this case is that of immigration policy. In this respect, the Court has often affirmed that a State is entitled, as a matter of well-established international law and subject to its treaty obligations, to control the entry of non-nationals into its territory and their residence there (see among many authorities *Jeunesse*, cited above, § 100). In addition to this general context, the applicants' particular context should also be considered. Each of them claimed child benefit at a time when their personal immigration status had yet to be determined, and when their essential material needs were being met through the system of direct provision. Their immigration status changed with the grant of residence rights within a relatively short time – a matter of months in each case. Leaving aside the payment in their particular cases of the benefit claimed following the judgment of the Court of Appeal, which was subsequently overturned, with this change of legal status came immediate entitlement to child benefit, which they began to receive from that point in time onwards.
>
> 100. In view of the above, the Court is unable to find that the legal and factual elements characterising the applicants' situation at the time they first applied for child benefit, considered in their totality and in context, were such as to place them in a relevantly similar situation to persons who already had the status of legal resident in Ireland. As stated above (see paragraph 67 above), the conditions for receipt of a social welfare benefit that comes within the ambit of Article 1 of Protocol No. 1 must be compatible with Article 14 of the Convention. That presupposes, however, that the requirement of comparability is met by the claimant, which it has not been by the present applicants."

The substantive issue in *Stec v United Kingdom* (Apps 65731/01 and 65900/01) April 12, 2006 [Grand Chamber], (2006) 43 E.H.R.R. 47, related to the impact of differential state pensionable ages on entitlement to a reduced earnings allowance. The court found no violation, accepting that the process of equalising pensionable age for men and women was legitimate, and it was not prepared to criticise the government for not beginning the process sooner.

In *Pearson v United Kingdom* (App.8374/03), August 22, 2006, the Strasbourg Court ruled that the differential age for entitlement to a state retirement pension of 65 for a man and 60 for a woman was objectively justifiable. The court refers to its decision in the *Stec* case (citing [61]–[65]) in finding that the differential state pensionable ages are within the state's margin of appreciation and that it cannot be criticised for not having moved earlier towards equalisation of the pension age for men and women (which will be reached in 2020).

4.143 In *Susan Richardson v United Kingdom* (App.26252/08), Decision of April 10, 2012, the applicant complained that the deferral of payment of a state retirement pension for those born after April 1950 until the age of 65 (for those born before April 1950 the pension was payable from the age of 60) amounted to a violation of art.14 read with art.1 of Protocol 1. The Strasbourg Court declared the application manifestly ill-founded on the grounds that changes as to pensionable age fall within the margin of appreciation of a state and could not be questioned provided that it is shown that the changes are in the general interest, are reasonable, and do not amount to a total loss of pension entitlement (see [24]).

On the same day, the judgment in *Walker v United Kingdom,* (App.37212/02) was delivered. This concerned the requirement for a man to pay national insurance contributions beyond the age of 60 when the liability of a woman ceases. For exactly the same reasons as given in *Pearson,* the Strasbourg Court finds that there is no violation of art.14 read in conjunction with art.1 of Protocol 1.

The same conclusion was also reached in *Barrow v United Kingdom* (App.42735/02), August 22, 2006, in a complaint concerning a woman who suffered a reduction in benefit at the age of 60 where her long-term incapacity benefit was replaced with the state retirement pension. She complained that such a reduction would not arise for a man, for whom the transition would not arise until he reached state pensionable age of 65.

In *B v United Kingdom* (App.36571/06), Judgment of February 14, 2012, (reported as [2012] AACR 39) the Court of Human Rights considered that differential treatment of: (a) persons who did not have the capacity to understand the obligation to report, and (b) persons who did have this capacity, could be justified as pursuing the legitimate aim of "ensuring the smooth operation of the welfare system and the facilitation of the recovery of overpaid benefits" (see [59]) which was reasonably and objectively justifiable. Nor did the contested provision breach the requirement of proportionality: public authorities should not be prevented from correcting mistakes—even their own—in the award of benefits and to hold otherwise would result in the unjust enrichment of the benefit recipient. There were safeguards in the United Kingdom system and no interest was charged on overpaid benefit which was recovered.

In *JD and A v United Kingdom* (Apps 32949/17 and 34614/17) a seven-judge chamber of the ECtHR giving judgment on October 24, 2019 held at [88]–[89] that the "manifestly without reasonable foundation" test is limited to transitional measures forming part of a scheme carried out in order to correct an inequality. A subsequent attempt by the United Kingdom to have the case referred to the Grand Chamber proved unsuccessful.

National authorities on "status"

Some national case law (referred to in detail in earlier editions of this work) suggested that art.14 was only concerned with differential treatment where the basis of comparison was a "personal characteristic". That is no longer so central to the protection provided by art.14 and must in any event be interpreted broadly, the alternative (if opaque) formulation of an "identifiable characteristic" sometimes being adopted. **4.144**

The opinions of the House of Lords in *Carson and Reynolds* [2005] UKHL 37 at [13] and [53]–[54], confirmed the importance of identifying a personal characteristic but also indicated that this is to be interpreted broadly so that it does not simply encompass something a person is born with. So in *Francis v Secretary of State for Work and Pensions* [2005] EWCA Civ 1303, reported as *R(IS) 6/06* the Court of Appeal affirmed the need to identify a personal characteristic but indicated that this need not be immutable and can be the result of the exercise of choice.

AL (Serbia) v Secretary of State for the Home Department; R (on the application of Rudi) v Secretary of State for the Home Department, [2008] UKHL 42, contains a very helpful discussion by Baroness Hale of aspects of art.14 at [20]–[35]. This stresses that Strasbourg case law does not place great emphasis on the identification of an exact comparator, rather asking whether differences in otherwise similar situations justify a different treatment. It is also hinted that too much attention has been focused on the notion of "personal characteristic" which is not central to the Strasbourg case law, although clearly differences based on such matters as sex, race or ethnic origin will require very weighty reasons if they are not to be condemned as violations of art.14. See also the discussion in *R. (on the application of RJM) v Secretary of State for Work and Pensions* [2008] UKHL 63.

The approach advocated in the *AL (Serbia)* case was followed in *TW v SSWP (PIP)* [2017] UKUT 25 (AAC), which is a decision of a three-judge panel considering whether the transitional regulations relating to conversion from disability living allowance to personal independence payment are discriminatory and invalid. Rather than determine whether those moving from disability living allowance to personal independence payment and those who were making a wholly new claim to a personal independence payment were in an analogous position, the Upper Tribunal focused on whether the claimed difference in treatment could be justified **4.145** since "arguments on justification may well demonstrate that a claimed comparator is not in a truly analogous position, and therefore that the difference in treatment is not actually due to a personal or other identifiable characteristic of the claimant at all ..." ([45]). The Upper Tribunal concluded that the transitional regulations were neither discriminatory nor ultra vires. The decision was upheld by the Court of Appeal: [2019] EWCA Civ 15; [2019] AACR 15.

The courts have latterly shown themselves ready to recognise a variety of forms of "other status". The Supreme Court in *R. (Stott) v Secretary of State for Justice* [2018] UKSC 59; [2018] 3 W.L.R. 1831 indicated that, while the allegedly discriminatory treatment cannot itself be a status, there is no requirement that a status must have social or legal significance outside the context of the legislation and apart from the fact that it is the ground on which the allegedly discriminatory treatment is based. It is not an objection that the relevant status is given precise definition and significance by the legislation which uses it as a ground for treating people differently.

However, in *R. v Docherty* [2016] UKSC 62; [2017] 1 W.L.R. 181, the defendant complained that there was discrimination against him on the grounds of having been made subject to a harsher sentencing regime that had latterly been introduced, in effect submitting that an Act of Parliament should have been applied to him after Royal Assent but before its provisions had been brought into effect by commencement order. This was rejected, Lord Hughes, giving the judgment of the Court, observing at [63] that:

> "Assuming for the sake of argument that status as a prisoner subject to a particular regime can in some circumstances amount to sufficient status to bring article 14 into question (*Clift v UK* [2010] ECHR 1106), it cannot do so if the suggested status is defined entirely by the alleged discrimination."

In *Simawi v LB Haringey* [2019] EWCA Civ 1770, the Court of Appeal analysed *Stott* and *Docherty*, concluding at [41]:

> "The observations of all the justices in *Stott* were *obiter*; because (with the exception of Lord Carnwath) they all decided that Mr Stott satisfied the 'independent existence condition'. As Lady Black said, the 'independent existence condition' lives on in *Docherty*. *Docherty* was a decision of the Supreme Court in which *Clift v United Kingdom* was considered. The decision that Mr Docherty did not have 'other status' because 'the suggested status is defined entirely by the alleged discrimination' was part of the *ratio* of the decision. *Stott* does not depart from *Docherty* in that respect. It therefore binds us."

The principles are not always easy to apply.

In *Mathieson v SSWP* [2015] UKSC 47, the Supreme Court had no great difficulty in concluding that the child claimant, as a severely disabled child in need of in-patient hospital treatment extending beyond 84 days, had a status falling within the grounds of discrimination prohibited by art.14.

Of the various forms of "status" that were under consideration by the Court of Appeal in *SC*, being a woman or being a child indisputably constituted a "status".

4.146 Defining the various possible statuses was relevant to the remainder of the art.14 analysis and the area of dispute was around what status, if any, a child affected by the two-child rule might have. Having reviewed the authorities and concluded "that a status need not be innate or an inherent aspect of an individual's personality but may be a feature of a person's circumstances or living situation on which a legal consequence depends", Leggatt L.J. held (at [76]) that "being a member of a household or family unit which contains more than two children, or being a child member of such a household, can without difficulty be regarded as an 'other status' for the purpose of article 14." The Supreme Court agreed: [2021] UKSC 26 at [69]–[72].

However, the requirement for the difference in treatment to be based on an identifiable "status" remains. In *R(T) v SSWP* [2022] EWHC 351 (Admin), the claimants, who were in receipt of a variety of "legacy" benefits, complained that the £20 weekly temporary uplift to universal credit introduced as a response to the Covid-19 pandemic had not been extended to those in receipt of legacy benefits. Among their grounds were that there had been direct discrimination against those in receipt of such benefits. At [24] Swift J rejected this, observing:

> "There is no meaningful difference between the other status relied on—being a person in receipt of a legacy benefit—and the less favourable treatment alleged, namely the failure to raise the amount paid as personal allowance to persons in receipt of a legacy benefit."

That complaint was in substance a public law challenge on conventional grounds, rather than correctly to be viewed as a discrimination claim. (He did, however, go on to consider the issue of justification, for the purposes of the direct discrimination claim and also for the purposes of a claim of indirect discrimination, based on disability (as to which he saw no problem over "status")). The claimant's appeal to the Court of Appeal (on other grounds) was dismissed: [2023] EWCA Civ 24.

Similarly, a formulation of a discrimination claim that the claimant had been discriminated against on the ground of his inability to meet the eligibility conditions of the Criminal Injuries Compensation Scheme 2012 was rejected in *MP v FtT and CICA* [2022] UKUT 91 (AAC). An appeal to the Court of Appeal (on other grounds) was rejected in *R (Peiris) v First-tier Tribunal* [2023] EWCA Civ 1527.

R(SC) v SSWP

The decision of a unanimous seven judge Supreme Court in *R (SC and others) v SSWP* [2021] UKSC 26 contains an extensive review of earlier authorities, including some of its own decisions, some of which now have to be read in the light of what is said about them in *SC*. In particular, the Court examined three questions of general importance relevant to the issue of justification under art.14, namely **4.147**

(a) the correct approach to unincorporated international law (such as the UN Convention on the Rights of the Child) – though it should be noted that this is now the subject of the United Nations Convention on the Rights of the Child (incorporation) (Scotland) Act 2024 (partially commenced at the time of writing);
(b) whether the proposition that the court will respect the policy choice of the executive or the legislature unless it is "manifestly without reasonable foundation" accurately reflects the approach of the Strasbourg court. This included consideration of the latter's decision in *JD and A v United Kingdom* (Apps 32949/17 and 34614/17); and
(c) the use which can be made of Parliamentary debates and other Parliamentary material when considering whether primary legislation is compatible with Convention rights.

Each is examined in turn.

In the social security context the point arises most frequently in relation to the United Nations Convention on the Rights of the Child (UNCRC) but is equally applicable to, for instance, the United Nations Convention on the Rights of Persons with Disabilities. The UNCRC had played an increasingly prominent part in a number of decisions up to and including Supreme Court level, among them *SG v SSWP* [2015] UKSC 16, *Mathieson v SSWP* [2015] UKSC 47 and *DA v SSWP* [2019] UKSC 21. In *SC*, Lord Reed reiterates that treaties are not contracts which domestic courts can enforce and that an unincorporated treaty does not form part of the law of the UK: see *JH Rayner (Mincing Lane) Ltd v Department of Trade and Industry* [1990] 2 AC 418. That is unaffected by the Human Rights Act, save insofar as it gives domestic effect to the European Convention on Human Rights. Following a review (at [80]-[82]) of the Strasbourg authorities, Lord Reed concludes (at [84]) that they provide no basis for any departure from the rule that domestic courts cannot determine whether the UK **4.148** has violated its obligations under unincorporated international treaties. Cases such as *X v Austria* (2013) 57 E.H.R.R. 14 and *EB v France* (2008) 47 E.H.R.R. 21 do not use the UNCRC as a yardstick for assessing whether there has been a breach of the Convention; they do, however, indicate that in a case under art.14 together with art.8, the best interests of the child are a relevant consideration.

On turning to the domestic decisions, Lord Reed points out that the majority in *SG* had concluded that an argument based on art.3.1 of the UNCRC was irrelevant. Lord Carnwath's conclusion that there had been a breach of art.3.1 was obiter.

Turning to *Mathieson*, Lord Reed indicates at [91] that the remarks of Lord Wilson, giving a judgment with which the majority of the court agreed, about international law should not be regarded as forming part of the ratio of the decision and must also be regarded as having been made per incuriam. Lord Reed continued:

> "what Lord Wilson took from the unincorporated international treaties was that the Secretary of State had been under a duty to treat the best interests of children as a primary consideration before making the legislation. There could have been no objection if he had instead treated the best interests of children as a relevant factor in the court's assessment of whether the differential treatment resulting from the legislation was justified under article 14 of the Convention: an approach which could have been taken directly from article 14 taken together with article 8 as interpreted in *X v Austria* and other cases."

While the difference on a conceptual level is evident, one may perhaps question how great the difference in practice between the two approaches is likely to be.

In *DA*, Lord Wilson had observed that "a foundation for the decision [not to exempt the relevant category of children from the cap] not made in substantial compliance with article 3.1 might well be manifestly unreasonable". Lord Carnwath (with whom Lord Hughes and Lord Reed expressed agreement) agreed that the "best interests" principle at art.3.1 of the UNCRC was "potentially relevant". Lord Reed concludes at [96] that "it does not appear to me that Lord Wilson's remarks about the UNCRC formed part of the essential grounds of the decision."

4.149 The proposition that the court will respect the policy choice of the executive or the legislature in relation to general measures of economic or social strategy in the context of welfare benefits has its domestic source in *Humphreys v HMRC* [2012] UKSC 18. The decision of the Strasbourg court in JD, in particular, raised whether that test should continue to be followed. Lord Reed's judgment contains a wide-ranging and detailed examination of the Strasbourg court's approach, summed up at [115] and [116]:

> "115. In summary, therefore, the court's approach to justification generally is a matter of some complexity, as a number of factors affecting the width of the margin of appreciation can arise from "the circumstances, the subject matter and its background". Notwithstanding that complexity, some general points can be identified.
>
>> (1) One is that the court distinguishes between differences of treatment on certain grounds, discussed in paras 100-113 above, which for the reasons explained are regarded as especially serious and therefore call, in principle, for a strict test of justification (or, in the case of differences in treatment on the ground of race or ethnic origin, have been said to be incapable of justification), and differences of treatment on other grounds, which are in principle the subject of less intensive review.
>>
>> (2) Another, repeated in many of the judgments already cited, sometimes alongside a statement that "very weighty reasons" must be shown, is that a wide margin is usually allowed to the state when it comes to general measures of economic or social strategy. That was said, for example, in *Ponomaryov*, para 52, in relation to state provision of education; in *Schalk*, para 97, in relation to the legal recognition of same-sex relationships; in *Biao v Denmark*, para 93, in relation to the grant of residence permits; in *Guberina*, para 73, in relation to taxation; in *Bah v United Kingdom*, para

37, in relation to the provision of social housing; in *Stummer v Austria*, para 89, in relation to the provision of a state retirement pension; and in *Yiğit v Turkey*, para 70, in relation to a widow's pension. In some of these cases, the width of the margin of appreciation available in principle was reflected in the statement that the court "will generally respect the legislature's policy choice unless it is 'manifestly without reasonable foundation'": see *Bah*, para 37, and *Stummer*, para 89.

(3) A third is that the width of the margin of appreciation can be affected to a considerable extent by the existence, or absence, of common standards among the contracting states: see *Petrovic* and *Markin*.

(4) A fourth, linked to the third, is that a wide margin of appreciation is in principle available, even where there is differential treatment based on one of the so-called suspect grounds, where the state is taking steps to eliminate a historical inequality over a transitional period. Similarly, in areas of evolving rights, where there is no established consensus, a wide margin has been allowed in the timing of legislative changes: see *Inze v Austria*, *Schalk* and *Stummer v Austria*.

(5) Finally, there may be a wide variety of other factors which bear on the width of the margin of appreciation in particular circumstances. The point is illustrated by such cases as *MS v Germany*, *Ponomaryov* and *Eweida v United Kingdom*.

116. As the cases demonstrate, more than one of those points may be relevant in the circumstances of a particular case, and, unless one factor is of overriding significance, it is then necessary for the court to make a balanced overall assessment."

Lord Reed notes how the phrase "manifestly without reasonable foundation" appears to have first been used in *Stec* (2006) 43 E.H.R.R. 74. Following a review of the ensuing caselaw, he concludes at [129]:

"129. Up to this point, the cases from *Stec* onwards concerned with welfare benefits and pensions can be seen to have generally followed a consistent approach. Although that approach is far from mechanical, the points noted in para 115 above can readily be discerned.

(1) In relation to the first point, the court has consistently differentiated between cases where "suspect" and "non-suspect" grounds of differential treatment have been in issue.

(2) In relation to the second point, the court has almost always recognised the general appropriateness of a wide margin in relation to general measures of economic or social strategy, reflected in the context of welfare benefits, pensions and social housing by the "manifestly without reasonable foundation" formulation.

(3) In relation to the third point, the relevance of the existence or absence of common standards is evident from such cases as *Stec*, *Tomás* and *Stummer*.

(4) In relation to the fourth point, the relevance of the measure in question forming part of arrangements intended to eliminate an historical inequality over time appears from *Stec*, *Runkee*, *Andrle* and *British Gurkha*.

(5) In relation to the fifth point, the potential relevance of other circumstances is illustrated by *Muñoz Díaz v Spain* 50 E.H.R.R. 49, where the court attached importance to the conduct of the domestic authorities in creating a legitimate expectation that the applicant would receive favourable treatment."

As to *JD*, in detailed analysis at [121]-[142], Lord Reed notes in particular the recent case of *Jurčič v Croatia* [2021] IRLR 511, which treats *JD*

"as establishing merely that cases concerning transitional measures designed to correct historical inequalities form an exception to a general principle that,

> notwithstanding that a wide margin, reflected by the "manifestly without reasonable foundation" formulation, is generally appropriate in the field of welfare benefits, a stricter approach, calling for "very weighty reasons", is appropriate where a difference in treatment is based on sex."

Turning to domestic authorities, Lord Reed notes that in *Humphreys*, only a limited range of authority was cited, not including cases concerned with non-transitional measures and a "suspect" ground – which was what *Humphreys* concerned. Key points are at [151]:

a. The "manifestly without reasonable foundation" formulation does not express a pass/fail test, the application of which will necessarily be determinative of the outcome. Other factors may also be relevant.

b. The Strasbourg requirement for "very weighty reasons" to be shown where suspect grounds are in issue is not superseded in such cases by the "manifestly without reasonable foundation" test. Instead, the degree of deference usually appropriate in relation to social or economic policy choices may have to be taken into account in assessing whether "very weighty reasons" have been shown. Therefore, having reviewed domestic authorities applying the *Humphreys* approach, such as *SG v SSWP*, *MA v SSWP* and *DA v SSWP*, Lord Reed concludes at [158]:

> "Nevertheless, it is appropriate that the approach which this court has adopted since *Humphreys* should be modified in order to reflect the nuanced nature of the judgment which is required, following the jurisprudence of the European court. In the light of that jurisprudence as it currently stands, it remains the position that a low intensity of review is generally appropriate, other things being equal, in cases concerned with judgments of social and economic policy in the field of welfare benefits and pensions, so that the judgment of the executive or legislature will generally be respected unless it is manifestly without reasonable foundation. Nevertheless, the intensity of the court's scrutiny can be influenced by a wide range of factors, depending on the circumstances of the particular case, as indeed it would be if the court were applying the domestic test of reasonableness rather than the Convention test of proportionality. In particular, very weighty reasons will usually have to be shown, and the intensity of review will usually be correspondingly high, if a difference in treatment on a "suspect" ground is to be justified. Those grounds, as currently recognised, are discussed in paras 101-113 above; but, as I have explained, they may develop over time as the approach of the European court evolves. But other factors can sometimes lower the intensity of review even where a suspect ground is in issue, as cases such as *Schalk*, *Eweida* and *Tomás* illustrate, besides the cases concerned with "transitional measures", such as *Stec*, *Runkee* and *British Gurkha*. Equally, even where there is no "suspect" ground, there may be factors which call for a stricter standard of review than might otherwise be necessary, such as the impact of a measure on the best interests of children."

4.150 In a section of his judgment addressing some constitutional fundamentals, Lord Reed recalls the context of the doctrine of Parliamentary privilege, underpinned as it is by the principle of the separation of powers. He notes that Government and Parliament are separate and therefore that the Government's reasons for promoting legislation cannot be treated as necessarily explaining why Parliament chose to enact it. He notes the nature of the political process and (at [171]) that "the courts have to be careful not to undermine Parliament's performance of its functions by requiring it, or encouraging it, to confirm to a judicial model of rationality". He notes that "[T]he intention of Parliament or (otherwise put) the object or aim of legislation, is an essentially legal construct, rather than something which can be discovered by an empirical investigation." Accordingly he observes that considerable care has to be taken when considering the use of Parliamentary materials in connection with the Human Rights Act. It may however be legitimate to refer to parliamentary debates and other Parliamentary material (citing Lord Nicholls in *Wilson v First County Trust Ltd (No 2)* [2003] UKHL 40; [2004] 1 AC 816, though noting the cautions Lord Nicholls expressed.)

As to the weight that should be given to Parliament's judgement, relevant factors (at [180]) may include the subject-matter of the legislation and whether it is relatively recent or dates from an age with different values. If Parliament has made its own judgement, the court is more inclined to accept it, out of respect for democratic decision-making. It would however be contrary to both authority and statute to undertake a critical assessment of Parliamentary debates and the courts must not treat the absence or poverty of debate in Parliament as a reason supporting a finding of incompatibility.

National authorities on art.14 read with art.1 of Protocol 1 in relation to specific benefits

The growth in human rights challenges to particular aspects of domestic social security legislation has grown substantially in recent years. Most are based on art.14 with art.1 of Protocol 1. This part of the Commentary has been re-ordered so as to group the challenges by the broad types of benefit or issue concerned (see 4.135 for an index of sub-headings). All of the decisions, insofar as they rely on any of the matters canvassed in 4.146, should now be read subject to the decision in *SC*. 4.151

Note that notwithstanding the difficulties which the lack of a NI number may cause a prospective benefit claimant (see Social Security Administration Act 1009 s.1(1A) and (1B)), the administrative process by which NI numbers are allocated does not fall within the ambit of either art.8 or art.1 of Protocol 1 to the European Convention on Human Rights: *R(BK) v SSWP* [2023] EWHC 378 (Admin).

(a) "Bedroom Tax"

Put briefly, the Housing Benefit Regulations 2006 (SI 2006/213) (as amended) provided that housing benefit would be paid according to a formula which required deductions to be made where the claimant's home contained more bedrooms than the legislation deemed to be needed, applying a table of the categories of person entitled to a bedroom. The impact of the legislation was mitigated by a scheme of Discretionary Housing Payments, considered by SSWP to provide a flexible vehicle for responding to need. A number of human rights-based challenges were made by individuals contending that the legislation should not apply to them in view of their disability or other circumstances. 4.152

The appeals against the decisions of the Upper Tribunal in *Burnip* [2011] UKUT 23, *Trengrove* [2011] UKUT 172 and *Gorry* [2011] UKUT 198 were consolidated before the Court of Appeal: *Burnip v Birmingham CC and SSWP*; *Trengrove v Walsall MC and SSWP*; and *Gorry v Wiltshire Council and SSWP*; *EHRC intervening* [2012] EWCA Civ 629, reported as [2013] AACR 7. *Burnip* and *Trengrove* concerned disabled individuals who required 24-hour care and therefore needed an additional bedroom for their carer, while *Gorry* concerned two disabled daughters who each required their own bedroom because of their disabilities, when girls of the same age without their disabilities would normally be able to share a bedroom. The appeals concerned the absence in the housing benefit rules of provisions allowing more than one bedroom where the beneficiary had a disability which either precluded their sharing a bedroom with a sibling or required a carer to live in. The challenge sought to establish that there was a positive obligation to treat those in different circumstances differently. The decision is an important authority on the concept of positive obligations under art.14 in the context of social security entitlements. Maurice Kay L.J. said:

> "17. On behalf of the Secretary of State, Mr Tim Eicke QC submits that the *Thlimmenos* principle is not as wide as is suggested. He submits that there is no example of the courts applying *Thlimmenos* so as to require a state to take positive steps to allocate a greater share of public resources to a particular person or group. The limited instances in which the principle has been invoked concern

exclusionary rules (as in *Thlimmenos* itself and *AM (Somalia)).*

18. Whilst it is true that there has been a conspicuous lack of cases post-*Thlimmenos* in which a positive obligation to allocate resources has been established, I am not persuaded that it is because of a legal no-go area. I accept that it is incumbent upon a court to approach such an issue with caution and to consider with care any explanation which is proffered by the public authority for the discrimination. However, this arises more at the stage of justification than at the earlier stage of considering whether discrimination has been established. I can see no warrant for imposing a *prior* limitation on the *Thlimmenos* principle. To do so would be to depart from the emphasis in Article 14 cases which, as Baroness Hale demonstrated in *AL (Serbia)* (at paragraph 25), is 'to concentrate on the reasons for the difference in treatment and whether they amount to an objective and reasonable justification'. I would apply the same approach to a *Thlimmenos* failure to treat differently persons whose situations are significantly different."

In allowing all three appeals in a unanimous decision, the Court of Appeal considered that there is a prima facie case of discrimination in the failure to treat the situations of disabled and non-disabled people differently and that the Secretary of State could not justify that difference in treatment. The circumstances of two of the appellants had, by the time of the judgment, been resolved by amendments to the housing benefit regulations but that of the third (Gorry) had not, and further amendments to the regulations were required (see SI 2013/2828).

Further challenges were made by others and on appeal to the Supreme Court were heard together and a single judgment was given as *R. (on the application of Carmichael and Rourke) (formerly known as MA and others) v SSWP* [2016] UKSC 58; [2017] AACR 9.

4.153 In the case previously known as *MA* (but also involving Carmichael) the Court of Appeal ([2014] EWCA Civ 13) had dismissed the claimants' challenge that there was unlawful treatment of them on the grounds of disability. In *Rutherford*, another of the cases heard in the Supreme Court, a differently constituted Court of Appeal ([2016] EWCA Civ 29) ruled that the two children with disabilities in the Gorry family were in the same situation as Mr Burnip (above) had been, in needing an extra bedroom for a carer because of his disability, and that the discriminatory treatment of them was manifestly without reasonable foundation.

Addressing the various appeals, Lord Toulson rejected the notion that "weighty reasons" for justification were required where discrimination was on the grounds of disability and re-affirmed the applicability of the "manifestly without reasonable foundation" test. Reliance by the court on that test in the face of a direct attack upon it should now be read subject to the judgment in *SC* at [97]-[162]. He further held that the Court of Appeal in *MA* had not erred in applying the test, in that it was proper to take into account the availability of the Discretionary Housing Payment mechanism when considering justification. He did, however, carve out from his remarks the situation of those with a "transparent medical need for an additional bedroom" (such as Mr Burnip and the children in the Gorry family had been in the earlier cases and Mrs Carmichael and the Rutherford family were in the cases before him), with the consequence that those claimants succeeded, but the others whose cases were considered in the appeal did not.

The issues involved in giving effect to the Supreme Court's decision in Mr Carmichael's favour in the context of his statutory benefit appeal were addressed in *SSWP v Carmichael and Sefton Council* [2018] EWCA Civ 548, discussed under s.3 of the Act above, but the decision of the majority in the Court of Appeal in that case no longer represents good law, following the decision of the Supreme Court in *RR v SSWP* [2019] UKSC 52; [2020] AACR 7.

A challenge by a disabled young adult to being restricted to the one bedroom shared accommodation rate was rejected in *CM v Bradford MDC and SSWP* [2020] UKUT 285.

(b) Benefit cap/Two child limit 4.154

A challenge to the benefit cap which had initially been introduced by the Welfare Reform Act 2012 failed in the Court of Appeal in *R(SG) v SSWP* [2014] EWCA Civ 156. Although the cap had a disproportionate impact on women, its imposition was not manifestly without reasonable foundation; the government objective of changing what was described as a welfare dependency culture was a legitimate aim of the measure. The Supreme Court, by a majority of 3 to 2, in *R(SG) v Secretary of State* [2015] UKSC 16, upheld the judgment of the Court of Appeal in ruling that the benefit cap was not unlawful. Though concerns were expressed by three judges that the benefit cap was not compatible with duties of the United Kingdom under the United Nations Convention on the Rights of the Child (UNCRC), that Convention was, however, not incorporated into UK law and so could not be relied on in making a case that there was unlawful discrimination on grounds of sex under art.14 ECHR. That view has now been reiterated in *SC* (above). Reliance by the majority on the "manifestly without reasonable foundation" test should now be understood in the light of the judgment in *SC* at [97]-[162].

In *R(DA) v SSWP* [2018] EWCA Civ 504, a challenge was brought to the benefit cap, as reduced from its previous level by the Welfare Reform and Work Act 2016. Those discriminated against were said to be single parents of children aged under two and those children. The Court of Appeal by a majority (Sir Brian Leveson PQBD and Sir Patrick Elias; McCombe L.J. dissenting) held that there was no discrimination against that cohort of parents and that (while it gave it some consideration) the issue of justification did not strictly arise. As regards the children, the court considered that their inclusion did not add anything of substance to the discrimination claims brought by their parents. In particular, their claims did not engage art.3 of the UNCRC any more than did the claims of the children in *SG*. The case was heard by the Supreme Court ([2019] UKSC 21) together with *R(DS) v SSWP*, which was leapfrogging from the High Court. The Supreme Court dismissed the claimants' appeals by a 5:2 majority. Lord Wilson, giving the principal judgment for the majority, saw the complaint in both cases in essence as being one of *Thlimmenos* discrimination, i.e. that the situations of the claimants in both cases were relevantly different from others to whom the cap has been applied and so, subject to justification, they should have been treated differently. At [55] he noted that:

> "This court has been proceeding down two different paths in its search for the proper test by which to assess the justification under article 14 for an economic measure introduced by the democratically empowered arms of the state. In retrospect this duality has been unhelpful."

The issue arising from recent cases had been whether the question whether the measure in question established a fair balance between all the interests in play did, or did not, fall to be assessed in the welfare benefits context by reference to the "manifestly without reasonable foundation" test. At [65] he accepts that it does.

As to the relevance of the UNCRC, he concludes that in the case of all the claimants (i.e. parents and children), the court was required to assess whether the setting of the benefit cap breached the Convention. His conclusion "by a narrow margin" ([87]) was that it did not. His remarks on the UNCRC now have to be understood in the light of Lord Reed's judgment in *SC* (at [96]).

As to justification, while the position of the claimants in *DA* (where the children had been aged under two when proceedings began) was stronger than that of those in *DS*, where the children were older, it nonetheless failed. He observed ([88]): 4.155

> "The appellants have not entered any substantial challenge to the government's belief that there are better long-term outcomes for children who live in households in which an adult works. The belief may not represent the surest foundation for the similarity of treatment in relation to the cap; but it is a reasonable

foundation, in particular when accompanied by provision for DHPs which are intended on a bespoke basis to address, and which on the evidence are just about adequate in addressing, particular hardship which the similarity of treatment may cause."

Lord Carnwath and Lord Hodge were troubled by whether the claimants had sufficient "status" for the purpose of an art.14 claim but proceeded on an assumption that they did. Both agreed with Lord Wilson as to the applicability of the "manifestly without reasonable foundation" test (and also as to the applicability of the UNCRC). As to that test, however, Lord Kerr dissented while Lady Hale (dissenting overall) expressed the view ([152]) that the court might need to return to the question in the future. Her dissent however was based ([132]) on the application of the principle of justification to the facts. *SC* notes at [156] that as *DA* "did not concern "suspect" grounds of differential treatment, the difference between that reasoning and the more nuanced reasoning of the European Court did not affect the court's decision." Had it been necessary to do so, Lord Kerr ([196]) would have found that there had been a breach of art.3 of the UNCRC. As to this, see the discussion of *SC* above.

The Welfare Reform and Work Act 2016 also imposed a limit of two on the number of children in respect of whom child tax credit and universal credit is payable. The limit applies, with a few exceptions, to all children born after April 6, 2017. In the challenge to that limit in *SC*, the claimants' case made it through to the final hurdle of whether there was an "objective and reasonable justification" for certain of the differences in treatment to which the measure gives rise. The differences of treatment which survived were those of indirect discrimination against women and discrimination against children living in households containing more than two children. As to the former, discrimination on the grounds of gender requires "very weighty reasons". However, the object of the legislation, seen to be that of protecting the economic well-being of the country, was a legitimate one. It was inevitable that this would affect more women than men because more women than men are bringing up children. No way had been suggested of how the legitimate aim could be achieved without affecting a greater number of women than men. As to whether the inevitable impact on women outweighed the importance of achieving the aims pursued, Parliament had decided that it did not and there was no basis on which the court could properly conclude otherwise. As to discrimination against children living in households containing more than two children, that was not a ground calling for "very weighty reasons". Parliament's assessment had to be treated with the greatest respect but the best interests of children was also relevant. At [205]-[207] Lord Reed addressed the various objections, concluding that the assessment of proportionality came down to whether Parliament made the right judgement. There were no legal standards for determining where the balance should be struck: democratically elected institutions were in a far better position to reflect a collective sense of what is fair and affordable or of where the balance of fairness lies. In the circumstances in which it was passed "the democratic credentials of the measure could not be stronger."

4.156 *(c) Bereavement*

On August 30, 2018, the Supreme Court gave judgment in *Siobhan McLaughlin* [2018] UKSC 48. The difference in treatment between unmarried and married partners in their ability to access widowed parent's allowance was held to be lacking in justification and so a breach of art.14 read with art.8 and/or A1P1. Lady Hale, giving the majority judgment, observed at [39] that:

"The allowance exists because of the responsibilities of the deceased and the survivor towards their children. Those responsibilities are the same whether or not they are married to or in a civil partnership with one another. The purpose of the allowance is to diminish the financial loss caused to families with children by the death of a parent. That loss is the same whether or not the parents are married to or in a civil partnership with one another."

The declaration of incompatibility does not provide those in Ms McLaughlin's position with an immediate remedy. An attempt to secure a remedy via a broader reading of the word "spouse" in s.39A SSCBA failed in *AR v SSWP (BB)* [2020] UKUT 165 (AAC).

R (Jackson) v SSWP [2020] EWHC 183 (Admin) similarly resulted in a declaration of incompatibility being made, in respect of the higher rate of bereavement support payment for an unmarried surviving partner with children.

On 28 July 2020, the Minister announced to Parliament the intention to make a remedial order under s.10 of the Human Rights Act 1998 to address the breach of human rights found to have occurred in cases such as *McLaughlin* and *Jackson*. That would in principle be capable of conferring rights retrospectively: see 1998 Act, Sch.2, para.1(1)(b). For a discussion of the interaction of the order when in draft with the social security decision process, see *JG v SSWP (BB)* [2021] UKUT 194 (AAC). An amended order was laid before Parliament and the Bereavement Benefits (Remedial) Order 2023 (SI 2023/132) came into force on February 9, 2023.

In *Secretary of State for Work and Pensions v Akhtar* [2021] EWCA Civ 1353, the Court of Appeal reversed the Upper Tribunal's decision in *NA v SSWP (BB)* [2019] UKUT 144 (AAC). Following a detailed review of the treatment of polygamous marriages for social security purposes, concluding that the Social Security and Family Allowances (Polygamous Marriages) Regulations 1975 (SI 1975/561) applied only to polygamous marriages that were valid under English law, the Court of Appeal held that in relation to bereavement payment, people who have contracted a marriage which is valid under English law and those who have not are not in an analogous position, alternatively the difference in treatment created by the legislation is justified. Consequently, save to the extent already identified by the Supreme Court in relation to widowed parent's allowance in *Re McLaughlin's Application for Judicial Review* [2018] UKSC 48, the claimant's case on human rights grounds likewise failed.

In *HM and MK v SSWP* [2023] UKUT 15 (AAC), the Upper Tribunal, carrying out "jurisprudential spadework and analysis" on a claim of discrimination brought by two claimants without children who had been refused bereavement benefits following the death of their partners (with whom they had not entered into a marriage or civil partnership), rejected claims of discrimination on the grounds of marital status and of gender. It considered that it was bound by *SSWP v Akhtar* to hold that the claimants were not in an analogous position to those who had entered into a legally valid marriage or civil partnership. While the statistical evidence showed that the effects of the legislative provisions excluding unmarried partners were experienced by a greater number of women than men, applying the approach in *SC*, the indirect discrimination was justified. A challenge to these aspects of the Upper Tribunal's decision was abandoned in *Kelly v SSWP* [2024] EWCA Civ 613. For the issues with regard to remedy in relation to the further ground of discrimination on the ground of sexual orientation, see under s.4 of the Act (above). The Court of Appeal which, unlike the Upper Tribunal, had the jurisdiction to make a declaration of incompatibility, declined to do so.

O'Donnell v Department for Communities [2020] NICA 36 concerned a claim for bereavement support payment by the husband whose late wife had, throughout her working life (as the court was at pains to emphasise), been unable to work on account of congenital disability and so to satisfy the contribution conditions for the benefit, which required actual payment of a modest level of contributions. The court held that the failure to differentiate between the respective situations of such a person and of a person who, though able to work, had not done so, constituted *Thlimmenos* discrimination and failed the test of justification. The court read wording into the Northern Ireland equivalent of s.30(1)(d) of the Pensions Act 2014 treating the contribution condition as having been met where the deceased was unable to comply with it throughout her working life due to disability. Although **4.157** the decision does not ultimately turn on it, the case highlights how the Northern Ireland equivalent of what is primary legislation in Great Britain may constitute secondary legislation, being made under the Northern Ireland Act 1998, something which may significantly affect the remedy available under the Human Rights Act.

The decision in *O'Donnell v Department for Communities* was considered in *R. (Jwanczuk) v SSWP* [2022] EWHC 2298 (Admin). The judge was not bound by the decision of the Court of Appeal in Northern Ireland and considered the matter afresh, ultimately reaching a similar result. The Court of Appeal dismissed the Secretary of State's appeal; however, he has been given permission to appeal by the Supreme Court.

Lennon v Department for Social Development [2020] NICA 15 concerned the Northern Ireland equivalents of s.39A (4) and (5) SSCBA. Under those provisions, if a claimant and a person who they were not married to, or in a civil partnership with, were living together as a married couple, widowed parent's allowance was not payable, while entitlement was lost if the claimant married or formed a civil partnership. The Court of Appeal in Northern Ireland held that a household consisting of a single parent and a child was not in an analogous situation with a household with two adults and a child. Further, the provision was in any event justified. The aim of ensuring that finite funds were deployed to whom, and when, they were most needed was a legitimate one. The court saw widowed parent's allowance as:

> "an earnings-replacement benefit, designed to replace lost earnings of a spouse which could not be replaced by the survivor by virtue of their particular difficulties in accessing the labour market due to childcare responsibilities. Where the claimant cohabits or remarries, payment ends as the surviving spouse has another adult with whom he or she can share the financial burden and from whom they might expect some financial support. The aim of sections 39A(4) and 39A(5)(b) is therefore to ensure public funding is allocated as effectively as possible, in line with the purpose of WPA."

The court considered that the means were proportionate and that the State was entitled to adopt a broad-brush approach.

For a case examining the consequences of bereavement in the context of transition from tax credits to universal credit, see *RJ v HMRC; HMRC v RJ* [2021] UKUT 40 under *Universal Credit* (below).

4.158 *(d) Disability (see also Hospitalisation and other payability issues, below)*

In *R. (on the application of RJM) v Secretary of State for Work and Pensions* [2008] UKHL 63, the House of Lords ruled that a question of entitlement to a disability premium as part of income support falls within the ambit of art.1 of Protocol 1 such that art.14 is engaged. The House went on to conclude that homelessness was a status within art.14 but that the differential treatment could be justified.

In *Stevenson v SSWP* [2017] EWCA Civ 2123; [2018] AACR 17, the Court of Appeal held that the failure, when the maximum amount for disabled homeowners in respect of which mortgage interest was payable for income support purposes was increased in 2009 from £100,000 to £200,000 for new claimants, to make provision for those who were in receipt of income support before the relevant implementation date, was not manifestly without reasonable foundation.

In *NT v SSWP* [2009] UKUT 37 (AAC), the judge ruled that the age cut-off of 65 for entitlement to the mobility component of a disability living allowance was a matter within the margin of appreciation of the United Kingdom. Consideration of the justification for the choice to legislate an age cut- off date simply required the Secretary of State to provide a rational explanation for the policy of the law in this case. The Secretary of State had, in the consideration of the judge, met that obligation.

In *Worley v SSWP* [2019] EWCA Civ 15; [2019] AACR 15, the Court of Appeal upheld the decision of a three-judge panel ([2017] UKUT 25) which had found to be justified the difference of treatment which was occasioned by the detailed transitional arrangements, to the disadvantage of those such as the claimant who had been in receipt of DLA and who stood to gain from the transfer to Personal Independence Payment, compared with new claimants of PIP.

In *R(RF) v SSWP* [2017] EWHC 3375 (Admin); [2018] AACR 13, the exclusion by the Social Security (Personal Independence Payment) (Amendment) Regulations 2017 (SI 2017/194) from certain of the descriptors for PIP mobility activity 1 of those whose difficulty arose from psychological distress was struck down, applying the "manifestly without reasonable foundation" test on the grounds inter alia that it failed all limbs of the test established by *Huang v Secretary of State for the Home Department* [2007] 2 A.C. 167 and *Bank Mellat v HM Treasury (No.2)* [2014] A.C. 700, namely that: **4.159**

(i) the objective of the measure is sufficiently important to justify the limitation of a protected right; and
(ii) the measure is rationally connected to that objective; and
(iii) a less intrusive measure could not have been used without unacceptably compromising the achievement of the objective; and
(iv) when balancing the severity of the measure's effects on the rights of the persons to whom it applies against the importance of the objective, to the extent that the measure will contribute to its achievement, the former outweighs the latter.

Mostyn J. observed ([59]) that "The wish to save nearly £1 billion a year at the expense of those with mental health impairments is not a reasonable foundation for passing this measure". He indicated that his conclusion was fortified by reference to art.19 of the United Nations Convention on the Rights of Persons with Disabilities ("Living independently and being included in the community.")

On January 19, 2018 in a written statement (HCWS414) the Secretary of State indicated that the Government would not appeal against *RF* and would implement the judgment in *MH v SSWP* [2016] UKUT 531 which SI 2017/194 had sought to reverse. A written answer dated January 29, 2018 by the Minister for Disabled People, Health and Work sets out the detail.

In *Re Cox's Judicial Review* [2021] NICA 46, the Court of Appeal in Northern Ireland reversed the High Court's decision ([2020] NIQB 53) which had held that, in order to be eligible for universal credit and personal independence payment automatically and immediately on the ground of terminal illness a person had to demonstrate that their death could reasonably be expected within 6 months, was manifestly without reasonable foundation. **4.160**

The Court of Appeal indicated that it derived "considerable assistance" from Lord Reed's judgment in *SC* (which had not been available at first instance), citing specifically [125], [161] and [162], concluding that:

> "[74] In this area of welfare benefits substantial weight is generally accorded to the primary decision maker. We do not accept that this is a case in which the difference of treatment is based on a suspect ground such as sex or religion. We accept that a relatively strict approach has been taken in cases concerned with persons with disabilities in order to foster their full participation and integration in society. That objective is honoured in this case by the application process based on need. This is not a case where the applicant has been excluded from the benefit.
> [75] The legislature has been involved in a detailed consideration of where to draw the line in this welfare benefit in 1990 and 2010. There has been continuing review of that decision since 2018. The Minister intends to submit a further proposed amendment to the Northern Ireland Assembly which will provide an opportunity for debate and reflection by the legislature. This is an area where considerable weight should be given to the views of the primary decision maker. These choices are for the political process and not for the courts."

The case is one of a number of telling examples of the effect of *SC* on the law in this area.

A challenge to the rule that when a claimant has received a Loan for Mortgage Interest, it is immediately due and repayable when the property is sold was brought by people with severe disabilities, arguing that applying the rule to them involved *Thlimmenos* discrimination. The challenge failed: *R (Vincent) v SSWP* [2020] EWHC 1976 (Admin).

A challenge based on discrimination on the ground of age brought by a claimant who was severely sight impaired but who was already over the age of 65 when the Regulations were introduced which enabled a person with such impairment to qualify for the higher rate mobility component of disability living allowance failed in *JA-K v SSWP (DLA)* [2017] UKUT 420 (AAC); [2018] 1 W.L.R. 2657 (see [76]–[78].

A challenge to the Social Security (Personal Independence Payment) (Amendment) Regulations 2017 (SI 2017/194) to the extent that they made amendments relating to activity 3 following the Upper Tribunal's decision in *SSWP v LB (PIP)* [2016] UKUT 0530 (AAC) failed in *CK and JM v SSWP* [2022] UKUT 122 (AAC).

4.161 *(e) Family issues (see also Bedroom Tax/Two Child limit, above)*

In *Humphreys v HMRC* [2012] UKSC 18, the Supreme Court upheld the courts below, holding that the payment of child tax credit to the principal carer does not breach art.14 when read with art.1 of Protocol No.1, since any discrimination against the secondary carer is objectively justified. The reasons for so concluding can be found at [22]–[33].

In *VL v SSWP (IS)* [2011] UKUT 227, the Upper Tribunal judge ruled that the removal of income support from lone parents whose children had reached the age of 12 did not constitute discrimination on grounds of sex, since the Secretary of State had provided a rational explanation for the policy of the law and the methods of achieving the objectives of the policy are proportionate.

In *JH v HMRC (CHB)* [2015] UKUT 479 (AAC); [2016] AACR 15, Judge Levenson disapplied the provisions of reg.3(3) of the Child Benefit (General) Regulations 2006 (SI 2006/223) as being in breach of art.14 when read with art.1 of Protocol 1 in refusing child benefit in respect of an 18-year old on the autistic spectrum ("the young person") who was being educated at home under arrangements funded by the local authority. The preclusion of benefit in such cases where the home schooling had not started before the young person was 16 years of age amounted to a difference of treatment which required justification if it was not to be unlawful discrimination. No justification was found for the difference in treatment in relation to the age when home schooling started, and this was accepted by HMRC.

In *R (Taylor Moore) v SSWP* [2020] EWHC 2287 (Admin), Swift J rejected a claim that the difference in how statutory maternity pay and maternity allowance were taken into account for universal credit purposes breached art.14. While the former counted as earned income, attracting the application of a taper, while the latter did not, the difference was held to be justified by a range of practical considerations linked to the universal credit system, prominent among which were the close links between statutory maternity pay and the Real Time Information system used by HMRC and the DWP.

In *SK and LL v SSWP (IS)* [2020] UKUT 145 (AAC) the "first child only" rule in the regulations governing Sure Start Maternity Grant was found to be discriminatory against two categories of claimant.

4.162 *(f) Hospitalisation and other payability issues*

Cameron Mathieson, a deceased child (by his father Craig Mathieson) v SSWP [2015] UKSC 47; [2015] AACR 19 concerned a challenge to the hospital rules under which DLA ceased to be payable for a child under 16 once that child had been in hospital for 84 days. The challenge arose in the context of the care provided by parents of a very sick three-year-old who was in hospital for more than 84 days and in respect of whom payment of DLA was withdrawn. The Supreme Court unanimously allowed the appeal. The Supreme Court acknowledged that in the area of welfare benefits a court will not interfere with policy choices unless the resulting rule was manifestly without reasonable foundation. Bright-line rules will not be invalidated merely because there are some hard cases which fall on the wrong side of it. In this case, however, the evidence before the Supreme Court showed that the claimant's circumstances were not a hard case but were typical of difficulties the whole class would face. Provision by the State for children in hospital did not remove the needs for which DLA provided, and so the stated objective of avoiding double provision was not made out and the rule was manifestly without reasonable foundation. The Supreme Court considered the conclusion in harmony with the provisions of the UN Convention on the Rights of the Child and the UN Convention on the Rights of Persons with Disabilities (as to which, see now the discussion of *SC* at 4.148). The Supreme Court did not, however, strike down the provisions for the suspension of disability living allowance, leaving it to the Secretary of State to determine what measures now needed to be taken to remedy the violation of human rights which arose as a result of the 84 day rule.

The Court of Appeal in *Obrey, Snodgrass and Shadforth v SSWP* [2013] EWCA Civ 1584 dismissed an appeal against the decision in *SSWP and Warwick DC v OB, JS and JS (CTB)* [2012] UKUT 489 (AAC) which held that the provisions of the housing benefit legislation which causes entitlement to cease after persons have been in hospital for 52 weeks, though indirectly discriminatory in respect of those with a mental illness, was capable of objective justification since the "bright line" provision was a policy matter not "manifestly without reasonable foundation".

In *ML v SSWP (DLA)* [2016] UKUT 323 (AAC); [2017] AACR 2, the suspension of the care component while the claimant was in a residential care home was held not to amount to unlawful discrimination. There was justification because, on the evidence in this case, unlike that before the Supreme Court in *Mathieson*, there would be double provision, the need to avoid which justified the suspension. **4.163**

In *MH v SSWP (PIP)* [2017] UKUT 424 (AAC); [2018] AACR 15, Judge Lane rejected a challenge to the rules restricting payment of personal independence payment to hospital in-patients alleging that they discriminated against such patients compared with care home residents and/or those living at home. The judge did not accept that either provided a valid comparison but that if she was wrong in that, the discrimination would in any event be justified.

An appeal, relying on *Mathieson*, against the DLA payability rules when it was an adult with learning difficulties who was the hospitalised claimant failed in *MOC (by MG) v SSWP (DLA)* [2020] UKUT 134 (AAC), the judge accepting that evidence about the need for relatives to provide care for the claimant in hospital fell well short of that which had been before the Supreme Court in *Mathieson*. A further appeal was dismissed by the Court of Appeal in *MOC (by his litigation friend MG) v Secretary of State for Work and Pensions* [2022] EWCA Civ 1, in particular because, in a claim of indirect discrimination, the alleged disproportionate effect on a certain group was not proved.

A challenge relating to the exclusion from benefits of prisoners transferred to mental hospital under the Social Security (Hospital In-Patients) Regulations 2005 (SI 2005/3360) as being in breach of art.14 when read with art.1 of Protocol 1 failed with one exception: see *R. (on the application of EM) v Secretary of State for Work and Pensions* [2009] EWHC 454 (Admin). The excepted class is a small group (there were 45 such persons in detention when the case was decided) of what are described as "technical lifers", namely those, although sentenced to life imprisonment, are treated by the Secretary of State after transfer to hospital as though they had been made the subject of a hospital order under s.37 of the Mental Health Act 1983 and to a restriction order under s.41 of that Act.

(g) Migration, residence **4.164**

In *Esfandiari v Secretary of State for Work and Pensions* [2006] EWCA Civ 282; *R(IS) 11/06*, the Court of Appeal considered whether the funeral payments provisions which restrict the payment of funeral expenses where the funeral is held in the United Kingdom (or in certain cases another country within the European Economic Area) are compatible with the European Convention. The court was unanimous in concluding that this was not a case of discrimination at all but even if those migrants who wished to bury relatives in their country of origin were a group, then any differential treatment could easily be justified as matters where the state enjoyed a wide margin of appreciation is setting its policy. The Court of Appeal regards the different outcome in EU law as arising because of the special rights which migrant workers are accorded under what is now the EU Treaty.

In *Couronne v Secretary of State for Work and Pensions, Bontemps v Secretary of State for Work and Pensions* [2006] EWHC 1514 (Admin), it was argued that the refusal to award jobseekers allowance to British Citizens arriving from Mauritius (whose parents had been displaced from the Chagos Islands) constituted discrimination in breach of art.14 when read with art.8 and/or art.1 of Protocol 1. It was argued, inter alia, that the comparator group (British Citizens of Irish ethnic origin) are exempt from the habitual residence test, whereas the claimants were not. The habitual residence test was regarded as a legitimate one aimed at protecting the social security system from claims by those with no genuine connection with the United Kingdom. The decision of the Administrative Court was upheld by the Court of Appeal at [2007] EWCA Civ 1086.

The Supreme Court in *R(HC) v SSWP* [2017] UKSC 73 dismissed a fall-back claim based on art.14 of the ECHR, taken with A1P1 or art.8, on the basis that the Government's evidenced reasons for not providing support to *Zambrano* carers, including the objectives of reducing costs by allocating benefits to those with the greatest connection with this country, of encouraging immigrants here unlawfully to regularise their stay, of encouraging third country nationals wishing to have children here to ensure that they had sufficient resources to support themselves and their children, and of reducing "benefit tourism" could not be said to be manifestly without reasonable foundation.

4.165 In *Stach v Department for Social Development and Department for Work and Pensions* [2020] NICA 4, the Court of Appeal in Northern Ireland dismissed a challenge to the exclusion of EU national jobseekers who did not hold "worker" status from housing benefit following the amendments made to the relevant Northern Ireland legislation in 2014. Among the grounds was a breach of art.14 read with art.1 of Protocol 1. The court relied heavily on *DA*, of which it said:

> "*DA* represents the most comprehensive recent exposition by the Supreme Court of the correct approach to art.14 ECHR cases, providing welcome clarity on certain important issues. In the context of the instant proceedings its most arresting feature is the unequivocal espousal by the majority of the 'manifestly without reasonable foundation' test in the determination of the issue of justification in art.14 cases. The decision also makes a contribution to the frequently challenging issues of 'other status' and comparators. There is much learning in the five judgments delivered."

In this human rights-based challenge the court also relied extensively on key domestic authorities in relation to EU law, notably *Mirga v SSWP* [2016] UKSC 1 and *Patmalniece v SSWP* [2011] UKSC 11 en route to its conclusion that:

> "93. The several principles and provisions of EU law highlighted throughout this judgment combine to fortify and justify the foundation upon which the impugned statutory provision rests. The protection of the resources of the host Member State concerned, the UK, is legitimate. The desire to prevent exploitation of the welfare benefits of the host Member State is equally legitimate. So too the imperative of promoting social integration. EU law specifically permits the provision of differing treatment in the realm of social assistance to nationals of the host Member State (on the one hand) and nationals of other Member States who are not economically or socially integrated in the host Member State (on the other). The latter group includes migrant EU citizen jobseekers. The host Member State

can lawfully deny social assistance to the migrant EU citizen jobseeker (and others) during the initial period of residence of three months and for longer in certain circumstances. Furthermore it is a basic principle of EU law that those in need of social assistance will receive the appropriate care in their own Member State. Juxtaposing the broader legal framework in tandem with the policy justification proffered by the respondent Departments, we consider that the impugned statutory provision has a solid foundation which comfortably exceeds the merely rational, tenable or reasonable. It plainly satisfies the test of manifestly without reasonable foundation. While we consider that it also satisfies other more intrusive formulations of the proportionality/justification test, we observe that the Appellant's case was not put in this way. To summarise, the proportionality of the impugned statutory provision is clearly demonstrated."

These observations must now be read subject to *SC*.

In *TS v SSWP (DLA); EK v SSWP (DLA)* [2020] UKUT 284 (AAC), the Upper Tribunal held that the increase in the "Past Presence Test" required for eligibility for disability living allowance from 26 weeks out of 52 to 104 weeks out of 156 breached art.14 in respect of two children who had lived abroad with their families before returning to the United Kingdom. The judge had additional and differing evidence from that which had been before the Upper Tribunal in *FM v SSWP (DLA)* [2017] UKUT 380; [2019] AACR 8, which he declined to follow. The case also contains a lengthy consideration of whether on a statutory appeal the First-tier Tribunal and Upper Tribunal have jurisdiction to consider an alleged breach of the Public Sector Equality Duty in s.149 of the Equality Act 2010, concluding that they do not.

(h) Pensions and pension credit **4.166**

The saga of the Government's response to the discrimination between men and women which occurred in relation to benefits for widows and widowers was considered by the House of Lords in *R. v Secretary of State for Work and Pensions Ex p. Hooper* [2005] UKHL 29 and is discussed in some detail in earlier editions of this work. The matter is now largely of historical interest.

The challenge brought by women to the transitional provisions aimed at raising and equalising, as between men and women, the state pension age has failed in the Divisional Court ([2019] EWHC 2552) and in the Court of Appeal: *Delve and Glynn v SSWP* [2020] EWCA Civ 1199. As regards age discrimination, the Divisional Court had held, following *Ackermann v Germany* (2006) 42 E.H.R.R. SE1 and other decisions of the Strasbourg Court to similar effect, it was not possible to claim equal treatment "in time" between different generations of pensioners. Indeed, at [52] the court doubted whether the generations were in comparable situations at all. If they were, however, the legislation was not "manifestly without reasonable foundation" and thus a claim of discrimination on the ground of age was rejected. The Court of Appeal distanced itself from the Divisional Court's conclusion regarding the *Ackermann* line of cases but was in agreement that the measure was in any event not manifestly without reasonable foundation. As regards the claim of indirect discrimination on the ground of gender, this too was dismissed by the Court of Appeal, which concluded that there was no sufficient causal link between the withdrawal of the state pension from women in the age group 60 to 65 and the disadvantage caused to that group.

A challenge to the exclusion of mixed-age couples from pension credit failed in *R (Prichard) v SSWP* [2020] EWHC 1495 (Admin).

In *GM v SSWP (RP)* [2022] UKUT 85 (AAC), a challenge brought by a pensioner who was unable to access a Category B pension from as early a date as she might otherwise have been able to, because of the effects of SSAA 1992 s.1 and the Social Security (Claims and Payments) Regulations 1987 (SI 1987/1968) regs 3(1)(cb) and 19 failed. If it was seen as a *Thlimmenos* challenge, she could not point to a similarity of treatment with persons in relevantly different situations. In any event, it was a challenge to primary legislation (SSAA s.1), which could not be read down to accommodate the claimant's submission without departing from the "grain" of the legislation (see the General Note on Human Rights Act 1998 s.3), while the Upper Tribunal had no power to make a declaration of incompatibility. A claim of direct discrimination failed because the claimant and her claimed comparator were subject to different legal regimes (because of the date of the legislative change which the case concerned) and thus not in a relevantly similar situation; but if, contrary to that, they were, the difference in treatment was justified in the light of the detailed evidence as to the operational factors which had led to, and enabled, the legislative change.

For a challenge to the rules on claiming a winter fuel payment said to result from the differential ages of entitlement to state pension, see *JE v Secretary of State for Work and Pensions (SF)* [2022] UKUT 12, discussed under "Other benefits" below.

4.167 *(i) Universal credit*

Article 14 has been at the centre of a series of challenges in respect of the transitional arrangements to universal credit, which have come before the Court of Appeal. In *R(TP), AR and SXC v SSWP* [2020] EWCA Civ 37, the court considered together appeals by the Secretary of State against the two decisions of the Administrative Court set out immediately below, dismissing both.

In *R(TP and AR) v SSWP* [2018] EWHC 1474 (Admin), the failure of the universal credit legislation to make provision for the needs of those who under predecessor benefits would have qualified for the severe disability and enhanced disability premiums was held not to involve differential treatment or, if it did, it was justified. A claim of discrimination as between those who had carers and those who did not was rejected on the ground that the treatment was justified. However, the operation of the transitional arrangements, under which a person formerly entitled to those premiums would have to apply for universal credit if he or she moved to a new housing authority area (when those moving within the same housing authority area would not) and on doing so would not receive any transitional protection to compensate for the loss of income to which the loss of the premiums significantly contributed, was held by Lewis J. ([88]) to be manifestly without reasonable foundation and not to strike a fair balance.

TP and AR found themselves back in the Administrative Court in *R(TP, AR and SXC) v SSWP* [2019] EWHC 1116 (Admin). Once again it was the receipt of severe disability premium under the legacy benefit regime which was the essential background. The Secretary of State in the formulation of policy had made a distinction between "natural migrants" (who were to transfer to universal credit following a change of circumstances) and "managed migrants" who experienced no change of circumstances but who migrated following a notice requiring them to do so. The baseline position was that managed migrants would receive transitional protection but natural migrants would not. However, the regulations which were impugned in the present case (parts of the Universal Credit (Transitional Provisions) (SDP Gateway) Amendment Regulations 2019 (SI 2019/10); and the (proposed) Universal Credit (Managed Migration Pilot and Miscellaneous Amendments) Regulations 2019) sought to ensure that from January 16, 2019 no further claimants in receipt of severe disablement premium would be treated as "natural migrants" (even if they were to experience a change of circumstances) but as "managed migrants". The upshot would be that such people would have transitional protection ensuring they were not worse off as the result of the migration to universal credit. Those who had migrated before January 16, 2019 (such as the claimants in the case) would still not benefit from such protection, but would receive additional flat rate payments which left them around £100 per month worse off.

4.168 Swift J. maintained a rigorous focus on what had to be justified, namely the difference in treatment between the two groups. The point was that the Secretary of State had decided to make provision, but in different ways for the two groups. Much of the Secretary of State's attempted justification was rejected as not being directed to justifying that difference in treatment. The offending parts of the regulations failed to strike a proportionate balance with the interests of the pre-16/1/2019 natural migrant group and the proposed flat-rate payments to natural migrants were quashed.

An attempt by SXC to secure compensation failed: *R(SXC) v SSWP* [2019] EWHC 2774 (Admin).

TP and AR returned to the Administrative Court a further time in *R (TP and AR) v SSWP* [2022] EWHC 123 (Admin). The challenge was to the failure in regulations to provide transitional payments to compensate "natural migrants" to universal credit for the loss of enhanced disability premium and the reduction as a result of universal credit's lower rate for a disabled child compared with the child tax credit scheme. Holgate J held that, even applying a low intensity of review or allowing a wide margin of appreciation, SSWP had failed to justify the differential treatment. The case is notable, inter alia, as one where discrimination has been found despite the generally cautionary tenor of the judgment in *SC*. SSWP has been refused permission to appeal to the Court of Appeal.

In *SSWP v JA* [2024] UKUT 52 (AAC), Judge Church drew heavily on *TP and AR* in holding that there was discrimination against a claimant who has migrated from a legacy benefit to universal credit when they move from a type of accommodation funded by a local authority by way of housing benefit (in this case, specified accommodation) and which does not attract the housing costs element of universal credit, to another type of accommodation (in this case, mainstream rented accommodation), which is funded by the housing costs element of universal credit. As Judge Church put it at [92]:

> "the calculation that was made upon the relevant change of circumstances (the Claimant moving from specified to mainstream accommodation) took into account her new entitlement (i.e. to the Housing Costs Element of Universal Credit in the amount of £366.37 per month) but it ignored what she had lost in terms of her entitlement to Housing Benefit (in the amount of £613.12 per month). This resulted in the Claimant losing the entirety of her £285 per month Transitional Element of Universal Credit in one fell swoop."

In *TD and AD v SSWP and another* [2019] EWHC 462 (Admin), a challenge was brought by two claimants whose entitlement under the pre-universal credit benefits regime had wrongly been terminated. The effect of such termination, however, was to subject them to the universal credit regime, to their financial disadvantage. No transitional protection was made in respect of them. Once they were within the universal credit regime, under the Universal Credit (Transitional Provisions) Regulations 2014 (SI 2014/1230), there was no going back. May J. somewhat reluctantly came to the conclusion (at [77]–[80]) that (in particular) the detailed consideration which the position of claimants in such a situation had received in the run-up to making the legislation and the decision to withhold transitional protection as a matter of policy meant that it could not be said to be "manifestly without reasonable foundation".

In *R (TD, AD and Reynolds) v SSWP* [2020] EWCA Civ 618, the Court of Appeal allowed the claimants' appeal, concluding that May J had erred in law by treating the question of justification not as a question which she herself had to decide but as one which required adequate consideration by the Secretary of State. The court went on to hold that the difference in treatment was manifestly disproportionate in its impact on the claimants having regard to the legitimate aim which the Secretary of State sought to achieve. It was therefore manifestly without reasonable foundation. **4.169**

In *R(Parkin) v SSWP* [2019] EWHC 2356 (Admin), a claimant in poorly-remunerated self-employment failed in an attempt to establish that the "minimum income floor" in universal credit unlawfully discriminated against her as a self-employed person in comparison with those who were employed. Elisabeth Laing J was prepared to accept that self-employment was a status for art.14 purposes but not that the employed and the self-employed were in relevantly analogous circumstances. The judge considered that in any event, the difference in treatment was not manifestly without reasonable foundation.

For a discussion of the differential treatment of statutory maternity pay and maternity allowance for universal credit purposes, see the *Taylor Moore* case, noted under "Family issues", above.

A challenge to the formulae used for converting weekly housing costs into monthly figures for universal credit purposes, which was capable of creating a limited disadvantage to weekly tenants in some instances, failed in *R (Sheena Caine) v SSWP* [2020] EWHC 2482 (Admin). There were sound administrative aims behind the formulae and the differences to which they might lead were small even in those instances where they did arise.

4.170 In *SSWP v Salvato* [2021] EWCA Civ 1482, the Court of Appeal allowed the Secretary of State's appeal against the decision of the Administrative Court ([2021] EWHC 102 (Admin)). The challenge was to the "proof of payment" rule – that childcare costs would not be covered by universal credit if there was merely a liability to pay them; rather, they had to have been actually paid, something which on the evidence claimants, who were more likely to be female, found difficult to do. This was to be contrasted with the housing costs element, which universal credit would cover if there was a liability to meet them. There was a notably developed evidential base. The Court of Appeal acknowledged that there was force in the Secretary of State's argument that, because "the Proof of Payment Rule was not concerned with a condition of entitlement to a particular welfare benefit or an element of it, but with the mechanism and timing of payment of an element of the benefit to which the claimant was entitled in principle", the case might more appropriately be regarded as falling within art.14 with art.8 (rather than with A1P1), but nothing turned on that. Turning to whether indirect discrimination could be established, the Court recalled that:

> "As a starting point, it is well-established that a *prima facie* case of indirect discrimination can be established without adducing direct statistical evidence of the number of people with a protected status who are adversely affected by the impugned rule: see the approach taken by the Grand Chamber of the ECtHR in *DH* ... above) at [188]–[193]. In that case, the statistical evidence relied upon by the claimants was undisputed. The respondent (the Czech government) submitted that it was 'insufficiently conclusive', and the court accepted that 'it may not have been entirely reliable'. On the other hand, the respondent had produced no statistical evidence to contradict it. Irrespective of its flaws, the claimant's evidence was found to be sufficiently reliable for the purpose of making out a *prima facie* case of indirect discrimination; it illustrated a trend from which it was possible to infer that the number of Roma children in special schools was disproportionately high, even though the exact percentage was difficult to establish."

This was the preliminary to close consideration of the unusually detailed evidence in *Salvato*, the Court concluding "not without some hesitation" that the judge below had been entitled to conclude that the evidence raised was "just" sufficient to raise a prima facie case of indirect discrimination.

The Court of Appeal referred closely to *SC*, holding that the discrimination which was involved could be justified and that the route adopted was not irrational. The approach of the judge below had focussed on the wrong issue ([92]) and had led him to apply a greater degree of intensity of review than was actually warranted ([99]).

In *RJ v HMRC; HMRC v RJ* [2021] UKUT 40 the claimant had been a party to a joint claim for child tax credit. His wife died, with the consequence that the joint claim was terminated. Because of the transition to universal credit, he was required to claim that instead, a benefit for which he was ineligible because he had received a life insurance payout. Judge West held that the claimant was not in an analogous situation to a married or cohabiting couple; rather, he was being treated differently as a single claimant rather than a joint claimant. The judge observed (at [106]):

> "It is not appropriate to say that any replacement benefit system must replicate features and definitions used in the former system and, if it does not do so, then to seek to argue that the new system includes differential treatment within the meaning of Article 14 as the new system treats people in a certain (and illegitimate) way when, under the previous and replaced system, they would have been treated in a different way."

Further, however the matter was analysed, it concerned a general measure of economic or social strategy and the State should be accorded a wide margin of appreciation. If there was differential treatment of people in an analogous situation, it was in any event justified.

In *PR v SSWP* [2023] UKUT 290 (AAC) the sole issue was whether the disadvantage experienced by the claimant fell within the ambit of A1P1 at all, SSWP conceding that if it did, the difference in treatment could not be justified. The case concerned reg.28 of the Universal Credit Regulations, which stipulates that an award of universal credit is not to include the Limited Capability for Work Related Activity element for what is in effect a three month waiting period. Although there are exceptions to that rule, the claimant's circumstances (in which her age was a key factor) did not fall within them. SSWP sought to argue that the rule in issue was not a condition of entitlement but a matter relating to the mechanism and timing of payment, relying on obiter remarks of Andrews LJ in *Salvato* (as to which, see para.4.170) and submitting that *Stec* could as a result be distinguished. Judge Wright noted that *Salvato* was a case which plainly did relate to the mechanism and timing of payment, whereas the provision before him had the effect of depriving the claimant of entitlement for the three month waiting period. Consequently, the offending parts of reg.28 had to be disapplied.

(j) Other benefits 4.171

SSWP v Sister IS and Sister KM, [2009] UKUT 200 (AAC) concerned claims by nuns for state pension credit, which were refused on the grounds that they were members of a religious order who are fully maintained by that order. See the discussion under s.7 of the Act.

In *CM v SSWP* [2009] UKUT 43 (AAC), the judge ruled that denial of income support to a pregnant student nurse intercalating a period of study was objectively and reasonably justified.

In *Faith Stewart v SSWP* [2011] EWCA Civ 907; [2012] AACR 9 the Secretary of State conceded that the rules on the eligibility of prisoners to funeral payments under the social fund constituted indirect discrimination against prisoners but argued successfully (on different grounds than those taken before the Upper Tribunal) that such discrimination was justified. This was based upon the objectives of the scheme to provide a quick and simple test of eligibility enabling payments to be made without delay, coupled with the complexity of any means-tested approach applicable to prisoners which would be likely to impact upon other groups and to be subject to complaints from those other groups that they were the victims of unlawful discrimination.

In *R(T) v SSWP* [2022] EWHC 351 (Admin), the claimants, who were in receipt of a variety of "legacy" benefits, complained that the £20 weekly temporary uplift to universal credit introduced as a response to the Covid-19 pandemic had not been extended to those in receipt of such benefits. Swift J rejected a submission on behalf of the Secretary of State that no valid comparison could be drawn between those in receipt of different benefits. However, he held that the difference in treatment was justified. He observed that:

> "31. The central question raised by the Claimants' discrimination claims is whether it was lawful for the Secretary of State to direct her attention to the

position of new benefits claimants—all of whom would have made claims for Universal Credit. I consider that she was. New benefits claimants would need to adjust to a loss in income. They would be affected differently to persons already claiming benefits. Given the objective pursued by the 2020 Regulations and the circumstances in which the decision to make those Regulations was made, legal scrutiny of the decision to make the 2020 Regulations must allow the Secretary of State a degree of latitude. All this being so, the distinction between the legacy benefits personal allowances and the Universal Credit standard allowance, consequent on the 2020 Regulations, rested on sufficient reason."

Considering the position of those in receipt of legacy benefits, he observed:

> "34. The Claimants' submissions focus on the low level of income replacement provided by any of ESA, IS and JSA. In absolute terms the amounts paid are low. It is obvious that any person required to rely only on that level of income will suffer hardship. I also accept that in the context of the pandemic it is likely that it may have been more difficult still to meet basic expenses from that level of income. However, these matters are distinct from the justification advanced by the Secretary of State for the decision to make the 2020 Regulations."

The judge noted it was relevant that one formulation of the discrimination claim was on the basis of disability (a so-called "suspect ground") and also that that claim was one of indirect discrimination. The judge concluded:

> "38. In considering the case before me I have in mind what was said by Lord Reed at paragraph 162 of his judgment in *SC*. All legislation draws lines differentiating between different classes or persons. Any court adjudicating on a discrimination challenge must be astute to identify the permissible limit of political discretion. The circumstances in which the decisions to make the 2020 Regulations were taken and for that matter also, the decisions in November 2020 at the time of the annual up-rating, and in March 2021 when the 2021 Regulations were made, were exceptional. Each decision was an exercise of political judgment on aspects of a programme of measures designed to achieve macroeconomic objectives at a time of major national disruption. The 2020 Regulations adopted in pursuit of that programme, drew a broad distinction between Universal Credit and legacy benefits when deciding to provide additional support to persons who lost employment or income because of the pandemic and thereby came within the range of state means-tested benefits for the first time. With the benefit of hindsight it may well be possible to pick holes in the strict logic of the decisions taken. But in the circumstances of this case, where the decision challenged (the 2020 Regulations) was a temporary measure addressing a situation which the government was entitled to regard as one of national emergency, a sensible margin of discretion must be permitted. Even accounting for the fact that the Claimants' indirect discrimination case is a claim on grounds of disability, I am satisfied that the reasons relied on by the Secretary of State to explain the decision to make the 2020 Regulations provide a sufficient justification. The justification provided is sufficient to answer each of the discrimination claims the Claimants advance."

4.172 On appeal to the Court of Appeal ([2023] EWCA Civ 24), the sole issue was whether Swift J, when considering the discrimination issue had confined himself to considering the question of justification at the time the uplift was originally implemented (March 2020), rather than on the evidence at the time of proceedings before him (November 2021), contrary to *Wilson v First County Trust* [2003] UKHL 40. By then, evidence was available of the impact on those on legacy benefits and further decisions had been taken, including in March 2021 a decision to continue the uplift for universal credit claimants (but not others) for a further six months.

The Court of Appeal dismissed the appeal, holding:

"54. Although he did not spell it out, the judge's acceptance of Ms Parker's evidence necessarily involved an inference that the anti-poverty goal the appellants say the measure was intended to achieve was rejected. That rendered the evidence from the appellants' witnesses, which assumed that the reduction of poverty was the goal of the measure, irrelevant. Instead, the judge accepted the SSWP's broad focus on the position of new UC claimants, adjusting to a sudden loss in income in the pandemic and thereby affected differently to existing benefit claimants. He also accepted that although the 2020 Regulations made no attempt to distinguish between new and existing UC claimants and so benefited a group of people who fell outside the SSWP's objective, distinguishing between these two groups of UC claimants would have given rise to technical difficulties, particularly in the urgent circumstances that presented. Moreover, the across-the-board change to UC could be implemented safely and swiftly, allowing for support to be provided to the greatest number of people in the shortest possible time. It was also capable of being easily and simply presented to the public.

55. Significantly, the judge recognised that in absolute terms the amounts paid by way of legacy benefits were low and it was obvious that any person required to rely on that level of income replacement provided by legacy benefits would suffer hardship and would find it more difficult to meet basic living expenses during the pandemic. However, given that the SSWP's policy rationale was not to alleviate poverty or financial hardship faced in consequence of the pandemic, he regarded this as a different matter and distinct from the SSWP's justification for the decision to make the 2020 Regulations. In other words, applying an uplift to legacy benefits would not have furthered the SSWP's policy objectives in March 2020. In any event, nor would it have been operationally feasible without significant risk to the delivery of legacy benefits.

56. It is plain from paragraph 38 that the judge did not treat the question of justification as one that simply required adequate consideration by the SSWP, as Mr Burton appeared to suggest in reply. The judge treated it as a question which he had to decide himself, having regard to the policy rationale advanced by the SSWP and the prevailing circumstances. The judge found that the SSWP's broad policy rationale and reasons for making and extending the UC uplift without also making a corresponding uplift in the legacy benefit amounts payable, were sufficient justification for each decision in this case. As Lord Reed explained, justification is an expression of the proportionality principle: the question is whether a difference of treatment pursues a legitimate aim, and whether there is a reasonable relationship of proportionality between the legitimate aim sought to be realised and the means employed.

57. In making his assessment the judge rightly recognised that the decisions in this case involved complex social and political judgments and difficult socio-economic choices. The measures introduced were temporary, designed to address a situation reasonably regarded as a national emergency. The assessment made by the judge having regard to all the circumstances of this case was that the difference in treatment was proportionate in its impact on the disabled legacy benefit claimants having regard to the legitimate aims which the SSWP sought to achieve. There was no error in that approach.

58. For the reasons I have given, the appellants' criticisms of the judge's approach based on a policy objective of alleviating poverty that required the accurate identification of those suffering the greatest financial deprivation or most increased hardship (namely that faced by disabled legacy benefit claimants), cannot found any arguable basis for concluding that Swift J erred in law. The evidence advanced in support of the appellants' case, while compelling on its own terms, was not relevant to the SSWP's broad policy objective or rationale, and the judge cannot be criticised for regarding it as directed to a distinct and different point.

59. Furthermore, the judge expressly addressed the ongoing nature of the decision-making process: see for example, paragraphs 30, 36 and 37 of his judgment. His conclusions in those paragraphs (and in paragraph 38) reflected his

evaluation of the SSWP's evidence as to the reasons for the successive decisions made '*throughout the relevant period*' not to apply the uplift to recipients of legacy benefits. Many of the factors that informed the decision in March 2020 inevitably informed the decision in March 2021 as the judge found. Taking it in stages, he found that the SSWP reasonably concluded that there was nothing to justify a change in policy in November 2020: the course of the pandemic remained unpredictable, and at that stage it was anticipated that the 2020 Regulations would expire in March 2021 without extension. By March 2021 when the decision was taken to extend the UC uplift for a further six months, lockdown measures had been reimposed and the pandemic impacts continued to be felt, justifying the need for continued support for the UC cohort. For the same reasons as those relied on in March 2020, the SSWP decided not to apply an equivalent uplift to legacy benefits: to do so would not fulfil the government's primary objective, and it would not have been operationally feasible to do so at that point.

60. It is plain from these paragraphs and the judgment read as a whole, that the judge understood that the challenge was to the 2021 Regulations. The 2021 Regulations (and the decisions underlying them) could not be considered in a vacuum. He had to consider what happened in March 2020 given the evidence in the case, and the fact that the measure was introduced and renewed in changing circumstances but with a broad rationale and social policy objective that remained unchanged. In my judgment, the judge made no error and *Wilson No 2* does not dictate that he should have adopted a different approach."

In *JE v Secretary of State for Work and Pensions (SF)* [2022] UKUT 12 (AAC), the claimant argued that he had been discriminated against because the differential in the ages when state pension could be claimed between men and women meant that he needed to make a claim for winter fuel payment each year, when a woman of the same age, who by then would have been in receipt of state pension, would have been eligible for, and probably benefited from, the discretion enjoyed by the Secretary of State under the Social Fund Winter Fuel Payment Regulations 2000 (SI 2000/729) to make an award without a claim to those in receipt of specified benefits (including state pension). The appeal failed, as they were not in an analogous position ([44]–[47]) and any difference in treatment was in any case justified, in particular because the exercise of the Secretary of State's discretion to make a winter fuel payment without a claim needed to be based upon something—the DWP's records of existing receipt of one of the specified benefits.

Article 14 in conjunction with art.8

4.173 For the important recent decision of the Strasbourg Court concerning the ambit of art.8 in the social security context, *Beeler v Switzerland* (App.78630/12) (Grand Chamber), see under art.8 above. The cases discussed below should now be considered with regard to what is said in *Beeler*. In an early example of the Strasbourg Court applying *Beeler*, in *X and others v Ireland* (Apps 23851/20 and 24360/20), it held that Irish child benefit (which appears to have similarities to UK child benefit) did not have as its intended purpose "to promote family life and affect the way in which it was organised" and the Court was unable to conclude that the benefit, given its statutory basis, nature and purpose, represented a modality of the applicants' exercising of their right to respect for family life.

A number of art.14 claims have also made use of art.8 on family and private life but since the admissibility decision in *Stec,* it has been more usual simply to rely on art.14 read with art.1 of Protocol 1.

However, as noted in *SC* in the Court of Appeal at [52]:

"relying on article 14 in conjunction with A1P1 focuses on the proprietary interest, or "possession", of the person entitled to claim child tax credit – that is, the parent – rather than on the rights of the child in respect of whom the benefit is claimed. That focus is potentially relevant to whether there is an objective and reasonable justification for the difference in treatment of which the claimants complain. It therefore may be important to the claimants' case, which emphasises the rights and interests of the children affected by the measure, to establish that the two child limit also falls within the ambit of article 8." (In the event however, the claim based on art.14 with art.8 fared no better than the claim based on art.14 with A1P1.)

The Supreme Court at [41] likewise held that the adult appellants' case fell within the ambit of art.8.

However, complaints under art.14 in conjunction with art.8 have been raised in relation to widow's benefits: see *Willis v United Kingdom* (App.36042/97), June 11, 2002, [2002] 35 E.H.R.R. 21; *Runkee and White v United Kingdom* (Apps 42949/98 and 53134/99), Judgments of May 10, 2007); *Thomas v United Kingdom* (App.63701/00), July 17, 2008; and to state pensions: *Carson v United Kingdom* (App.42184/05), November 4, 2008. In all these cases, the Strasbourg Court examined the case using the link to property rights rather than the link to private and family life in art.8.

In national proceedings, there have been cases arguing that the housing benefit scheme and child support falls within the sphere of application of art.8. However, the complex discussions in both the Court of Appeal and the House of Lords which arose in *Secretary of State for Work and Pensions v M; Langley v Bradford Metropolitan DC and Secretary of State for Work and Pensions* [2004] EWCA Civ 1343; and *Secretary of State for Work and Pensions v M* [2006] UKHL 11 would not now be necessary in relation to the housing benefit scheme and probably also the child support system, since art.1 of Protocol 1 would be regarded as engaged following the *Stec* decision.

It may, however, be appropriate to rely on art.8 where the case concerns questions of mechanics and timing of benefit rather than the conditions of entitlement to it: see the discussion in *SSWP v Salvato* (annotated under art.14 read with art.1 of Protocol 1, above).

In *Francis v Secretary of State for Work and Pensions* [2005] EWCA Civ 1303 (the **4.174**
appeal against *CIS/1965/2003*, reported as *R(IS) 6/06)*, the Court of Appeal found that the refusal to award a maternity grant constituted discrimination contrary to art.14 of the Convention. The Secretary of State had conceded that the circumstances presented by Ms Francis engaged art.8 of the Convention. Ms Francis argued that her situation as a person with a residence order in respect of a child born to her sister was analogous to that of an adopter under the Adoption Act 1976. There was no objective justification for the difference in treatment.

In *R(P) 2/06* a Tribunal of Commissioners concluded that the United Kingdom rules preventing the payment of widows' benefits to widows of polygamous marriages in the circumstances of the cases before them did not fall foul of the prohibition of discrimination in art.14 when read with art.8. The Tribunal of Commissioners was unanimous as to the outcome, although one Commissioner's line of reasoning differs from that of his two colleagues.

Article 8 was raised (as well as art.1 of Protocol 1) in *R (SG) v SSWP* [2014] EWCA Civ 156, the challenge to the "benefit cap" measures. The Court of Appeal accepted that art.8 was engaged but determined the point on the same grounds as the claims which linked art.1 of Protocol 1 to the art. 14 prohibition.

An application by Siobhan McLaughlin for Judicial Review [2016] NICA 53 failed in the Northern Ireland Court of Appeal on the basis of art.14, taken with art.8, as it likewise had on art.14 and A1P1 but succeeded on further appeal to the Supreme Court ([2018] UKSC 48): see para.4.132.

In *R(RF) v SSWP* [2017] EWHC 3375 (Admin); [2018] AACR 13, the exclusion **4.175**
from certain of the descriptors for PIP mobility activity 1 of those whose difficulty arose from psychological distress (see 4.122) was held to engage art.8 as well as art.1 of Protocol 1, but this does not appear to have affected the outcome.

In *R(Steinfeld and Keidan) v Secretary of State for International Development* [2018] UKSC 32 the Supreme Court made a declaration of incompatibility (based on art.14 taken with art.8) in respect of the exclusion of heterosexual couples from the Civil Partnership Act 2004. Legislation has since followed: the Civil Partnerships, Marriages and Deaths (Registration etc.) Act 2019 and the

Civil Partnership (Opposite-sex couples) Regulations 2019 (SI 2019/1458) make it possible for heterosexual couples, who are otherwise eligible, to enter into a civil partnership. For discussion of the possible impact on subsequent claims of discrimination on the same ground of the fact that legislation has already been made in response to a declaration of incompatibility, see the General Note on s.4.

Article 8 is also raised in the two benefit cap cases, *R(DA) v SSWP* and *R(DS) v SSWP*. In their judgments ([2019] UKSC 21), all of the justices found that the cases fell within the ambit of art.8. For further discussion of the cases, see 4.150.

In *R(Parkin) v SSWP* [2019] EWHC 2356 (Admin), the judge was prepared ([91]) to assume that the subject matter of the disadvantage experienced by the self-employed claimant due to the operation of the minimum income floor fell within the ambit of art.8, because universal credit "has components designed in part to meet (at least in part) costs of housing and the costs of being responsible for a child or for children".

Article 16—Restrictions on political activity of aliens

4.176 Nothing in Articles 10, 11 and 14 shall be regarded as preventing the High Contracting Parties from imposing restrictions on the political activity of aliens.

Article 17—Prohibition of abuse of rights

4.177 Nothing in this Convention may be interpreted as implying for any State, group or person any right to engage in any activity or perform any act aimed at the destruction of any of the rights and freedoms set forth herein or at their limitation to a greater extent than is provided for in the Convention.

Article 18—Limitation on use of restrictions on rights

4.178 The restrictions permitted under this Convention to the said rights and freedoms shall not be applied for any purpose other than those for which they have been prescribed.

PART II

THE FIRST PROTOCOL

Article 1—Protection of property

4.179 Every natural or legal person is entitled to the peaceful enjoyment of his possessions. No one shall be deprived of his possessions except in the public interest and subject to the conditions provided for by law and by the general principles of international law. The preceding provisions shall not, however, in any way impair the right of a State to enforce such laws as it deems necessary to control the use of property in accordance with the general interest or to secure the payment of taxes or other contributions or penalties.

GENERAL NOTE

Introduction

4.180 The protection of property rights as human rights presents particular problems, and it is therefore not surprising that agreement could not be reached on their inclusion in the Convention as originally drafted. A right to property is included in art.1 of Protocol 1, but its content is broadly framed and the permissible restrictions are broad in scope.

Though drafted rather differently, the structure of the provision is similar to that found in arts 8–11. There is a general right to peaceful enjoyment of possessions. Interferences can, however, be justified on the conditions set out in the article which include references both to the "public interest" and the "general interest"; this is the test of proportionality that pervades the Convention's consideration of interferences and requires the balancing of the interests of the individual against the collective interest.

The Court has repeatedly said that the article comprises three distinct rules: *Sporrong and Lönnroth v Sweden*, (Apps 7151-2/75), September 23, 1982, Series

A, No. 52, (1983) 5 E.H.R.R. 35, at [61]. See *Jahn v Germany* (Apps 46720/99, 72203/01 and 72552/01), June 30, 2005 [Grand Chamber], (2006) 42 E.H.R.R. 49, ECHR 2005-VI, at [78]; and *Hutten-Czapska v Poland* (App.35014/97), June 19, 2006 [Grand Chamber], (2007) 45 E.H.R.R. 52, ECHR 2006-VIII, at [157]. First, everyone is entitled to peaceful enjoyment of their possessions. Secondly, deprivation of possessions is subject to certain conditions. Finally, contracting parties are entitled to control the use of property where it is in the general interest. But these are not distinct rules, since the second and third rules relate to interferences with the peaceful enjoyment of possessions which may be justified in the general interest.

Once it has been established that the applicant has an interest which can be classified as a possession, the general approach of the Strasbourg Court is to consider first whether there has been a deprivation of possessions, followed by consideration of whether there has been a control of the use of possessions, since these are matters specifically dealt with by the article. Only if there has been neither deprivation of possessions nor a control of their use does the Court consider, as a separate issue, whether there has been some other interference with the peaceful enjoyment of possessions. Such interferences will, however, only be unlawful if they are not in the general interest. In its case law, the Court has brought together the tests it applies in relation to deprivations, the control of the use of property, and to other interferences with property, so that the questions the Court will ask in each of these circumstances raise essentially the same issues. **4.181**

Possessions have been defined in broad terms by both the Commission and the Court. In this context, it is worth noting that the French text of the Convention uses the term "*biens*" which connotes a very broad range of property rights. The term has an autonomous meaning; it extends beyond physical goods, and covers a wide range of rights and interests which may be classified as assets.

In *Beeler v Switzerland* (App.78630/12) (Grand Chamber) the Strasbourg Court took the opportunity to review existing authority, observing:

> "[T]he Court observes that its case-law has now taken on sufficient maturity and stability for it to give a clear definition of the threshold required for the applicability of Article 1 of Protocol No.1, including in the sphere of social welfare benefits. It should be reiterated in this connection that that Article does not create a right to acquire property or to receive a pension of a particular amount. Its protection applies only to existing possessions and, under certain circumstances, to the 'legitimate expectation' of obtaining an asset; for the recognition of a possession consisting in a legitimate expectation, the applicant must have an assertable right which may not fall short of a sufficiently established, substantive proprietary interest under the national law (see *Bélané Nagy*, cited above, §§ 74–79).
>
> 58. Thus, where the applicant does not satisfy, or ceases to satisfy, the legal conditions laid down in domestic law for entitlement to any particular form of benefits or pension, there is no interference with the rights under Article 1 of Protocol No 1 if the conditions had changed before the applicant became eligible for the benefit in question. Where the suspension or diminution of a pension was not due to any changes in the applicant's own circumstances, but to changes in the law or its implementation, this may result in an interference with the rights under Article 1 of Protocol No.1. Accordingly, where the domestic legal conditions for entitlement to any particular form of benefits or pension have changed and where, as a result, the person concerned no longer fully satisfies them, a careful consideration of the individual circumstances of the case—in particular, the nature of the change in the conditions—may be warranted in order to verify the existence of a sufficiently established, substantive proprietary interest under the national law (ibid., §§ 86–89)."

Social security payments and pensions

4.182 Entitlements arising under pension and social security schemes have proved difficult to classify; the position was for some time unclear. A distinction had been drawn in the case law between benefits which were paid on the basis of contributions, and those which were paid without reference to contributions. But the case law did not always seem to maintain this distinction. However, the admissibility decision of the Grand Chamber in the *Stec* case (*Stec v United Kingdom* (Apps 65731/01 and 65900/01), Decision of July 6, 2005 [Grand Chamber], (2005) 41 E.H.R.R. SE18) has clarified matters.

An example of the ambiguity caused by the earlier case law can be found in the *Gaygusuz* case (*Gaygusuz v Austria* (App.17371/90), September 16, 1996, (1997) 23 E.H.R.R. 364). Gaygusuz was a Turkish national who had worked in Austria, where he had paid contributions under the Austrian social security scheme. He had experienced periods of unemployment and periods when he was unfit for work. He applied for an advance on his retirement pension as a form of emergency assistance, but was refused because he was not an Austrian national. He complained that there had been a violation of art.14 when read in conjunction with art.1 of Protocol 1. The first question was whether the substance of the claim was a matter within the scope of the article, since otherwise art.14 could not be brought into play. Both the Commission and the Court concluded that the article was applicable but for different reasons. The Commission concluded that the article was brought into play because the obligation to pay "taxes or other contributions" falls within its field of application. The Court, however, concluded that the link with the obligation to pay taxes or other contributions was not required. That was sufficient to engage the anti-discrimination provision in art.14 and to find a violation since the discrimination between nationals and non-nationals was blatant. The Court took the same approach in the *Koua Poirrez* case (*Koua Poirrez v France* (App.40892/98), September 30, 2003, (2005) 40 E.H.R.R. 12, at [37]).

In the *Stec* case, the Grand Chamber accepted that the *Gaygusuz* case was ambiguous on the significance of contributions in bringing a claim within the scope of art.1 of Protocol 1 for the purpose of claiming discriminatory treatment which breached art.14 of the Convention. The Grand Chamber lays down a new approach which is to be applied in future cases, relying on an interpretation which renders the rights in the Convention practical and effective rather than theoretical and illusory. The Grand Chamber also referred to the Court's case law under art.6 which had brought disputes concerned all forms of social security within the scope of that article. The Court concluded that, whenever persons can assert a right to a welfare benefit under national law, art.1 of Protocol 1 applies. The Court goes on to note that the bringing of social security fairly and squarely within the scope of art.1 of Protocol 1 does not create any right to acquire property. However, if a Contracting Party does create rights to social security benefits, the benefit schemes must be operated in a manner which is compatible with the prohibition of discrimination set out in art.14.

4.183 Attempts have been made to argue that the suspension of retirement pension for those serving terms of imprisonment breached the property rights in art.1 of Protocol 1, but the applications were declared inadmissible (Apps 27004/95, *Josef Szrabjer v United Kingdom*, and 27011/95, *Walter Clarke v United Kingdom*, Decisions of October 23, 1997) and invalidity benefit (App.27537/95, *George Carlin v United Kingdom*, Decision of December 3, 1997). The public interest was served by avoiding a situation in which prisoners enjoyed the advantage of accumulating a lump sum by receiving a State benefit without any outgoing living expenses. Arguments based on discrimination between prisoners and non-prisoners were dismissed as a comparison of two different factual situations. Other comparisons were also found to be without merit. See also discussion of benefits for widowers in the commentary on art.14 above. For a Grand Chamber judgment which considered the entitlement of those working in prison to affiliation to the old-age pension system, see *Stummer v Austria* (App.37452/02), Judgment of July 7, 2011.

In *Čakarević v Croatia* (App.48921/13) action to recover overpaid unemployment benefit, when the applicant was unemployed, in poor health and without income and had never been informed that unemployment benefit was time-limited and when the wrongful continuance of it was the State's fault, was held to breach A1P1.

In *CP/4762/2001* the Commissioner found that the provisions under which a person became entitled to a retirement pension normally with effect from the Monday following their 65th birthday gives rise to no Convention issue either under art.1 of Protocol 1, nor under that provision when read in conjunctions with art.14

In *CP/0281/2002*, the Commissioner ruled that there was no breach of art.1 of Protocol 1 as a consequence of the requirement under the Pension Schemes Act 1993 that any additional pension is reduced by the amount of any guaranteed minimum pension payable to a person.

In *R. (Smith) v Secretary of State for Defence and Secretary of State for Work and Pensions* [2004] EWHC 1797 (Admin), Wilson J. held that a non-contributory pension under the Armed Forces Pension Scheme was a possession within the ambit of art.1 of Protocol 1. This extended to the spouse of the pension holder following the making of a pension-sharing order. However, art.1 of Protocol 1 does not guarantee a right to a pension of a particular amount, nor payment from a particular time.

In *R(P) 1/06*, the Commissioner ruled that the three months' time limit on the backdating of a claim for retirement pension did not constitute a deprivation of property contrary to art.1 of Protocol 1. Nor was there any question of a claim based on discrimination by reading art.14 together with art.1 of Protocol 1.

In *R1/07 (IB)* a Commissioner in Northern Ireland said: **4.184**

> "15. I consider there is no merit in the submission based on art.1 of Protocol 1. There is no inbuilt Convention right to any State benefit. A State is not obliged to provide benefit. The right to benefit only arises when the conditions therefore (which are provided under domestic legislation) are satisfied. In this case they were not so satisfied. The claimant was not entitled to the benefit because he worked and his work did not fall within the categories of exempt work. The basic rule in relation to IB is that those who work are not entitled to it. The benefit is, after all, an incapacity for work benefit. There are exceptions to this basic rule but they relate only to certain categories of work. The relevant category here includes that the work be work of which the required notice is given. Working on the assumption that the domestic law requirement of written notice within 42 days is valid, there is no entitlement to IB if work is done which does not come within an exempt category. art.1 of Protocol 1 is not therefore invoked, there being no property to enjoy. The claimant is not being asked to repay benefit incorrectly paid. His benefit entitlement is merely being determined according to the applicable statutory conditions of entitlement."

Notwithstanding the claimant's inability to meet domestic conditions of entitlement, there was found to be a breach of A1P1 in *Valverde Digon v Spain* (App.22386/19) The applicant's partner died in July 2014, three days after their civil partnership had been registered. The requirement to register civil partnerships at least two years prior to the death of one of the partners in order to be eligible for a survivor's pension had entered into force only three months prior to the death. On her claim for a survivor's pension, the domestic courts had stated that a partnership had to be registered two years prior to the death of the deceased partner. Similar issues arose, with a similar result, in *Domenech Aradilla and Rodríguez González v Spain* (Apps 32667/19 and 30807/20).

See also annotations to art.14.

Article 2—Right to education

4.185 No person shall be denied the right to education. In the exercise of any functions which it assumes in relation to education and to teaching, the State shall respect the right of parents to ensure such education and teaching in conformity with their own religious and philosophical convictions.

GENERAL NOTE

4.186 The full scope of this right is yet to be determined. The existing case law is mainly concerned with primary education, but the Commission has not ruled out the application of the provision to higher education (see, for example, *Sulak v Turkey* (1996) 84 D.R. 101). The confused state of the exclusion of students in full-time higher education from entitlement to most social security benefits might well leave the United Kingdom exposed to challenge under this provision. On the assumption that the provision applies to higher education, it could be argued that students are currently required to abandon their courses completely in order to become eligible for certain social security benefits with the result that they lose entitlement to the balance of finance to support their studies if they wish to return to their courses later on. This could be argued to operate to deny them the right to an education.

In *R(Douglas) v North Tyneside MBC and Secretary of State for Education and Skills* [2003] EWCA Civ 1847; [2004] 1 W.L.R. 2363 the Court of Appeal ruled that tertiary education falls within the ambit of art.2 of Protocol 1. The Court of Appeal held that, although there was no European or domestic authority establishing clearly that tertiary education falls within the ambit of art.2 of Protocol 1, the Convention was a living instrument and the number of adults in higher education had grown. There was no principle that the article applied only to earlier stages of education, and so tertiary education falls within the ambit of the article. The court went on to hold that the funding arrangements for students, from which Mr Douglas was excluded by reason of his age, did not involve denying anyone the right to education, although if the funding arrangements had been specifically designed to discriminate against a particular category of person that might have been another matter, for then the arrangements could be said to be necessarily concerned with the right to education.

Douglas was applied in *CM v SSWP* [2009] UKUT 43 (AAC); *R(IS) 7/09.*

Article 3—Right to free elections

4.187 The High Contracting Parties undertake to hold free elections at reasonable intervals by secret ballot, under conditions which will ensure the free expression of the opinion of the people in the choice of the legislature.

PART III

ARTICLE 1 OF THE THIRTEENTH PROTOCOL

Omitted (concerns the abolition of the death penalty).

SCHEDULE 2

REMEDIAL ORDERS

Orders

4.188 **1.** (1) A remedial order may—

(a) contain such incidental, supplemental, consequential or transitional provision as the person making it considers appropriate;

(b) be made so as to have effect from a date earlier than that on which it is made;

(c) make provision for the delegation of specific functions;

(d) make different provision for different cases.

(2) The power conferred by sub-paragraph (1)(a) includes—

(a) power to amend primary legislation (including primary legislation other than that which contains the incompatible provision); and

(b) power to amend or revoke subordinate legislation (including subordinate legislation other than that which contains the incompatible provision).

(3) A remedial order may be made so as to have the same extent as the legislation which it affects.

(4) No person is to be guilty of an offence solely as a result of the retrospective effect of a remedial order.

Procedure

2. No remedial order may be made unless— **4.189**

(a) a draft of the order has been approved by a resolution of each House of Parliament made after the end of the period of 60 days beginning with the day on which the draft was laid; or

(b) it is declared in the order that it appears to the person making it that, because of the urgency of the matter, it is necessary to make the order without a draft being so approved.

Orders laid in draft

3. (1) No draft may be laid under paragraph 2(a) unless— **4.190**

(a) the person proposing to make the order has laid before Parliament a document which contains a draft of the proposed order and the required information; and

(b) the period of 60 days, beginning with the day on which the document required by this sub-paragraph was laid, has ended.

(2) If representations have been made during that period, the draft laid under paragraph 2(a) must be accompanied by a statement containing—

(a) a summary of the representations; and

(b) if, as a result of the representations, the proposed order has been changed, details of the changes.

Urgent cases

4. (1) If a remedial order ("the original order") is made without being approved **4.191**
in draft, the person making it must lay it before Parliament, accompanied by the required information, after it is made.

(2) If representations have been made during the period of 60 days beginning with the day on which the original order was made, the person making it must (after the end of that period) lay before Parliament a statement containing—

(a) a summary of the representations; and

(b) if, as a result of the representations, he considers it appropriate to make changes to the original order, details of the changes.

(3) If sub-paragraph (2)(b) applies, the person making the statement must—

(a) make a further remedial order replacing the original order; and

(b) lay the replacement order before Parliament.

(4) If, at the end of the period of 120 days beginning with the day on which the original order was made, a resolution has not been passed by each House approving the original or replacement order, the order ceases to have effect (but without that affecting anything previously done under either order or the power to make a fresh remedial order).

Definitions

4.192 **5.** In this Schedule—

"representations" means representations about a remedial order (or proposed remedial order) made to the person making (or proposing to make) it and includes any relevant Parliamentary report or resolution; and

"required information" means—

(a) an explanation of the incompatibility which the order (or proposed order) seeks to remove, including particulars of the relevant declaration, finding or order; and

(b) a statement of the reasons for proceeding under section 10 and for making an order in those terms.

Calculating periods

4.193 **6.** In calculating any period for the purposes of this Schedule, no account is to be taken of any time during which—

(a) Parliament is dissolved or prorogued; or

(b) both Houses are adjourned for more than four days.

[[1]**7.** (1) This paragraph applies in relation to–

(a) any remedial order made, and any draft of such an order proposed to be made,–

(i) by the Scottish Ministers; or

(ii) within devolved competence (within the meaning of the Scotland Act 1998) by Her Majesty in Council; and

(b) any document or statement to be laid in connection with such an order (or proposed order).

(2) This Schedule has effect in relation to any such order (or proposed order), document or statement subject to the following modifications.

(3) Any reference to Parliament, each House of Parliament or both Houses of Parliament shall be construed as a reference to the Scottish Parliament.

(4) Paragraph 6 does not apply and instead, in calculating any period for the purposes of this Schedule, no account is to be taken of any time during which the Scottish Parliament is dissolved or is in recess for more than four days.]

AMENDMENT

1. The Scotland Act 1998 (Consequential Modifications) Order 2000 (SI 2000/2040) art.2, Sch. Pt. I para. 21 (July 27, 2000).

GENERAL NOTE

4.194 What can be done by an order under this Schedule may be of some importance when considering remedies in cases where a breach of the Convention is claimed. Examples in the social security context may be found in the Bereavement Benefits (Remedial) Order 2023 (SI 2023/134) and in the Jobseekers (Back to Work Schemes) Act 2013 (Remedial) Order 2020 (SI 1085/2020), addressing the issues raised by *Reilly and Hewstone v SSWP* [2016] EWCA Civ 413; [2017] AACR 14. More generally, there is the Human Rights Act 1988 (Remedial) Order 2020 passed to remedy a deficiency identified by the Strasbourg court in *Hammerton v UK* (App.6287/10): see s.9 of the 1998 Act.

For an interim decision examining the interplay between a previous draft of the Bereavement Benefits (Remedial) Order and social security decision-taking processes, see *JG v SSWP (BB)* [2021] UKUT 194 (AAC).

SCHEDULE 3

DEROGATION AND RESERVATION

[. . .] 4.195

PART II

RESERVATION

4.196 At the time of signing the present (First) Protocol, I declare that, in view of certain provisions of the Education Acts in the United Kingdom, the principle affirmed in the second sentence of Article 2 is accepted by the United Kingdom only so far as it is compatible with the provision of efficient instruction and training, and the avoidance of unreasonable public expenditure.

Dated March 20, 1952. Made by the United Kingdom Permanent Representative to the Council of Europe.

GENERAL NOTE

4.197 The derogations of 1988 and 1989 in respect of art.5(3) of the Convention were withdrawn by the Government on February 26, 2001. The amendments to the Act were made by The Human Rights Act (Amendment) Order 2001 (SI 2001/1216) which entered into force on April 1, 2001.

The derogation contained in the Human Rights Act (Designated Derogation) Order 2001 (SI 2001/3644) in force from November 13, 2001 contained derogations from the provisions of art.5(1) to permit the detention of foreign nationals in the United Kingdom under the Anti-terrorism, Crime and Security Act 2001. That derogation has been withdrawn and effect is given to its withdrawal by the repeal of Pt I of Sch.3 to the Human Rights Act 1998 by the Human Rights Act 1998 (Amendment) Order 2005 (SI 2005/1071) with effect from April 8, 2005.

Schedule 4 omitted. 4.198

PART V

THE EUROPEAN DIMENSION

United Kingdom Withdrawal from the European Union

On December 31, 2020, the "implementation period" in connection with the United Kingdom's withdrawal from the European Union came to an end. A consequence of that was that the operation of EU law, which had been in large measure preserved during that period by s.1A of the European Union (Withdrawal) Act 2018, ceased. The relevance of matters of EU law is now determined by domestic legislation. Sections 2 to 7C of the European Union (Withdrawal) Act 2018 made provision, important in structural terms, concerning the ongoing status of, and interpretation (ss.6 and 7C and see also Schedule 1, para. 5 and Schedule 8, paras. 1-2A) to be given to, various forms of EU law and domestic legislation associated with it. Subsequently, the Retained EU Law (Revocation and Reform) Act 2023 (REULRRA) set out to remove the special features which EU law had in the UK legal system. This resulted in substantial amendment to the 2018 Act, including abolition in UK law of the principle of the supremacy of EU law and of the applicability of general principles of EU law.

In the social security context the impact of the more general provisions is likely to be secondary in many cases to the express provision made by Part 2 of the Withdrawal Agreement in respect of Citizens' Rights. Part 2 addresses the preservation of limited rights associated with the exercise of freedom of movement before the end of the implementation period and also social security co-ordination issues. The content of Part 2 does not mirror, but borrows substantially from, Directive 2004/38 (the Citizenship Directive) and follows Regulation 883/2004 and the implementing regulation, Regulation 987/2009. Caselaw on these provisions will remain relevant for a considerable time to come. Rights which under the Withdrawal Agreement are intended to be directly enforceable are given effect in domestic law by s.7A of the 2018 Act. This remains the case after REULRRA.

While (subject to transitional provisions) it is no longer generally possible for a UK court or tribunal to make a new reference to the Court of Justice of the European Union under art.267 TFEU, express provision is made by the Withdrawal Agreement for such references to be possible in relation to Part 2 for (broadly) an 8 year period.

It may be critical in certain cases to determine whether or not a person falls within the scope of Part 2 of the Withdrawal Agreement, as for those who do not, the legal environment has significantly altered. Rights of free movement are abolished by the Immigration and Social Security Co-ordination (EU Withdrawal) Act 2020, with the intention that immigration from EU member States (other than Ireland, in respect of which the Common Travel Area assumes greater importance) is to be governed by the Immigration Rules. Matters of social security co-ordination in such cases are intended to be addressed via the Protocol on Social Security Co-ordination which forms part of the Trade and Co-operation Agreement concluded between the European Union and the United Kingdom on December 24, 2020. Although the Protocol in many respects follows closely Regulation 883/2004, there are significant differences, in particular in the exclusion of long-term care benefits and family benefits from the Protocol's coverage. Annex VII to the Protocol contains implementing provisions, which closely, though not exactly, follow Regulation 987/2009 (the implementing regulation for Regulation 883/2004).

The UK Government's increasing reliance on domestic legislation included the creation of "EU settled status" under Appendix EU of the Immigration Rules, which took full effect from March 30, 2019. Such leave was granted with a relatively light touch and those who were able to establish a continuous qualifying period of residence of five years and were granted settled status in consequence are able to rely on that status as a sufficient right to reside for benefit purposes following the Social Security (Income-related Benefits) (Updating and Amendment) (EU Exit) Regulations 2019 (SI 2019/872) and the Child Benefit and Child Tax Credit (Amendment) (EU Exit) Regulations 2019 (SI 2019/867). Both sets of Regulations have been in force since May 7, 2019 and are incorporated in the text in other volumes relating to the benefits concerned.

The position of those granted only "pre-settled" status (because they could not at the time demonstrate the five-year period above) is more complex. Under the legislation as it stands relating to the various benefits, the right to reside conferred by a grant of pre-settled status was excluded from being a qualifying right to reside for benefit purposes, with the consequence that such people were required to establish a right to reside under the existing categories (i.e. as a worker, self-employed person, self-sufficient person etc.) However, on 18 December 2020 in *Fratila and Another v SSWP* [2020] EWCA Civ 1741 the Court of Appeal held that that exclusion contravened established EU case law. There are likely to be those with pre-settled status whose benefit claims will have been refused on the basis of the domestic legislation, or who were deterred from applying because of it. On February 22, 2021 the Secretary of State was given permission to appeal against the Court of Appeal's decision. The appeal to the Supreme Court was stayed, apparently pending the outcome of the preliminary reference made, just before the end of the implementation period for UK withdrawal from the EU, by an appeal tribunal in Northern Ireland. On July 15, 2021, the CJEU gave judgment in *CG v Department for Communities* (C-709/20). It held that art.24 of Directive 2004/38/EC did not preclude measures which excluded from social assistance people who did not have sufficient resources (nor other lawful basis of residence under EU law) but where the state had nonetheless granted a right of residence under national law (i.e. pre-settled status). However, it was incumbent on the state to ensure there was no violation of the fundamental rights of the claimant and her children under arts 1,7 and 24 of the Charter. For this purpose, all sources of assistance under national law could be taken into account. When *Fratila* returned to the Supreme Court, the Court ([2021] UKSC 53) applied *CG* in relation to pre-settled status, but refused to allow an argument based on the provisions of the Charter to be raised, as the point had not been taken below. The implications of the CJEU's reference to the Charter were considered by the Upper Tribunal in *SSWP v AT (UC)* [2022] UKUT 330 (AAC), upholding the FtT's decision that the claimant could rely on the Charter in her circumstances. SSWP's appeal was dismissed by the Court of Appeal ([2023] EWCA Civ 1307) and permission to appeal to the Supreme Court has been refused. It remains to be determined whether there are those whose nationality and/or immigration status differs from those of AT (or differed at the end of the implementation period) who can nonetheless potentially take advantage of that judgment. DMG Memo 5/24 sets out the DWP's view as to how *AT* should be implemented, including expressing the Department's view as to categories of people to whom the decision does not apply.

The nature of the rights conferred by pre-settled status has been examined in cases outside the social security context: *R. (Independent Monitoring Authority for the Citizens' Rights Agreements) v SSHD* [2023] 1 W.L.R. 817 and a series of cases concerning eligibility for housing assistance of which one, *Fertré v Vale of White Horse DC* [2024] EWHC 1754 (KB), has been at High Court level. Both authorities in essence take the view that pre-settled status is (as put in *Fertré* at [72]) "no more than the gateway or passport to the potential acquisition of a particular right at the relevant time."

Mention should be made of the temporary provision made by The Citizens' Rights (Application Deadline and Temporary Protection) (EU Exit) Regulations 2020 (SI 2020/1209) which preserved the ability to rely on a modified form of the Immigration (European Economic Area Regulations 2016 until 30 June 2021, in order to cater for those at that point yet to make their application for settled status or whose applications had not yet been determined and also of the Immigration and Social Security Co-ordination (EU Withdrawal) Act 2020 (Consequential Saving, Transitional and Transitory Provisions) (EU Exit) Regulations 2020 (SI 2020/1309). The savings provisions in the latter are concerned with (a) deportation and exclusion orders and (b) continuing parts of the 2016 Regulations to allow in-time applications which had been made under those Regulations to be decided upon. See the 2021–22 edition of Vol.V and, where applicable, the updating material in Vol.II of this year's edition for the domestic legislation. There have been limited provisions for extra-statutory payment for a short period to categories of those who had not applied for, or been granted, settled or pre-settled status by the 30 June 2021 deadline and policy (primarily Advice to Decision Makers Circular 19.21) encouraged a "pragmatic approach".

European Union (Withdrawal) Act 2018

(2018 c.16)

ARRANGEMENT OF SECTIONS REPRODUCED

Preamble

SCHEDULES

An Act to repeal the European Communities Act 1972 and make other provision in connection with the withdrawal of the United Kingdom from the EU.

[26th June 2018]

Repeal of the European Communities Act 1972

1. The European Communities Act 1972 is repealed on exit day. **5.2**

GENERAL NOTE

This was, but is no longer, subject to s.1A, which preserved the effect of the 1972 Act in modified form during the implementation period ending on December 31, 2020 ("IP completion day"). **5.3**

Saving for ECA for implementation period

5.4 [1**1A.** [2...]

(5) Subsections (1) to (4) are repealed on IP completion day.

(6) In this Act—

"the implementation period" means the transition or implementation period provided for by Part 4 of the withdrawal agreement and beginning with exit day and ending on IP completion day;

"IP completion day" (and related expressions) have the same meaning as in the European Union (Withdrawal Agreement) Act 2020 (see section 39(1) to (5) of that Act);

"withdrawal agreement" has the same meaning as in that Act (see section 39(1) and (6) of that Act).

(7) In this Act—

(a) references to the European Communities Act 1972 are to be read, so far as the context permits or requires, as being or (as the case may be) including references to that Act as it continues to have effect by virtue of subsections (2) to (4) above, and

(b) references to any Part of the withdrawal agreement or the EEA EFTA separation agreement include references to any other provisions of that agreement so far as applying to that Part.]

AMENDMENTS

1. European Union (Withdrawal Agreement) Act 2020 s.1 (January 31, 2020).
2. European Union (Withdrawal) Act 2018 s.1A(5) (December 31, 2020).

DEFINITIONS

"domestic law": see s.20(1).
"exit day": see s.20(1).
"IP completion day" see the European Union (Withdrawal Agreement) Act 2020, s.39(1).
"Minister of the Crown": s.20(1).
"withdrawal agreement" means "the agreement between the United Kingdom and the EU under Article 50(2) of the Treaty on European Union which sets out the arrangements for the United Kingdom's withdrawal from the EU (as that agreement is modified from time to time in accordance with any provision of it)" (2020 Act, s.39(1)). Section 39(6) of the 2020 Act is not relevant to social security.

GENERAL NOTE

5.5 By Sch.8 para.37A the repeal of section 1A(1) to (4) by section 1A(5) and the repeal of section 1B(1) to (5) by section 1B(6) do not prevent an enactment to which section 2 applies from continuing to be read, on and after IP completion day and by virtue of section 2, in accordance with section 1B(3) or (4).

[1Saving for EU-derived domestic legislation for implementation period

5.6 **1B.** [2...]

(6) Subsections (1) to (5) are repealed on IP completion day.

(7) In this Act "EU-derived domestic legislation" means any enactment so far as—

(a) made under section 2(2) of, or paragraph 1A of Schedule 2 to, the European Communities Act 1972,

(b) passed or made, or operating, for a purpose mentioned in section 2(2)(a) or (b) of that Act,

(c) relating to—

(i) anything which falls within paragraph (a) or (b), or

(ii) any rights, powers, liabilities, obligations, restrictions, remedies or procedures which are recognised and available in domestic law by virtue of section 2(1) of the European Communities Act 1972, or

(d) relating otherwise to the EU or the EEA,

but does not include any enactment contained in the European Communities Act 1972 or any enactment contained in this Act or the European Union (Withdrawal Agreement) Act 2020 or in regulations made under this Act or the Act of 2020.]

AMENDMENTS

1. European Union (Withdrawal Agreement) Act 2020 s.1 (January 31, 2020).
2. European Union (Withdrawal) Act 2018 s.1B(6) (December 31, 2020).

DEFINITIONS

"domestic law": see s.20(1).
"the EEA": see s.20(1).
"enactment": see s.20(1).
"EU entity": see s.20(1).
"exit day": see s.20(1).
"withdrawal agreement": see s.1A(6).

GENERAL NOTE

By Sch.8 para.37A the repeal of s.1A(1) to (4) by s.1A(5) and the repeal of s.1B(1) to (5) by s.1B(6) do not prevent an enactment to which s.2 applies from continuing to be read, on and after IP completion day and by virtue of s.2, in accordance with s.1B(3) or (4). 5.7

Saving for EU-derived domestic legislation

2. (1) EU-derived domestic legislation, as it has effect in domestic law immediately before [1IP completion day], continues to have effect in domestic law on and after [1IP completion day]. 5.8

[2...]

(3) This section is subject to section 5 and Schedule 1 (exceptions to savings and incorporation) [3 and section 5A (savings and incorporation: supplementary)].

AMENDMENTS

1. European Union (Withdrawal Agreement) Act 2020 s.25(1)(a) (December 31, 2020) (SI 2020/1622, reg.5(d)).
2. European Union (Withdrawal Agreement) Act 2020 s.25(1)(b) (December 31, 2020) (SI 2020/1622, reg.5(d)).
3. European Union (Withdrawal Agreement) Act 2020 s.25(1)(c) (December 31, 2020) (SI 2020/1622, reg.5(d)).

DEFINITIONS

"domestic law": see s.20(1).
"EU-derived domestic legislation": see s.1B(7).
"IP completion day": see the European Union (Withdrawal Agreement) Act 2020, s.39(1).

General Note

5.9 By Sch 8 para.37A the repeal of s.1A(1) to (4) by s.1A(5) and the repeal of s.1B(1) to (5) by s.1B(6) do not prevent an enactment to which s.2 applies from continuing to be read, on and after IP completion day and by virtue of s.2, in accordance with section 1B(3) or (4).

Incorporation of direct EU legislation

5.10 **3.** (1) Direct EU legislation, so far as operative immediately before [[1]IP completion day], forms part of domestic law on and after [[1]IP completion day].

(2) In this Act "direct EU legislation" means—

(a) any EU regulation, EU decision or EU tertiary legislation, as it has effect in EU law immediately before [[2]IP completion day] and so far as—

[[3](ai) it is applicable to and in the United Kingdom by virtue of Part 4 of the withdrawal agreement,

(bi) it neither has effect nor is to have effect by virtue of section 7A or 7B,]

(i) it is not an exempt EU instrument (for which see section 20(1) and Schedule 6) [[4]and],

[[5]...]

(iii) its effect is not reproduced in an enactment to which section 2(1) applies,

(b) any Annex to the EEA agreement, as it has effect in EU law immediately before [[6]IP completion day] and so far as—

[[7](ai) it is applicable to and in the United Kingdom by virtue of Part 4 of the withdrawal agreement,

(bi) it neither has effect nor is to have effect by virtue of section 7A or 7B,]

(i) it refers to, or contains adaptations of, anything falling within paragraph (a), and

(ii) its effect is not reproduced in an enactment to which section 2(1) applies, or

(c) Protocol 1 to the EEA agreement (which contains horizontal adaptations that apply in relation to EU instruments referred to in the Annexes to that agreement), as it has effect in EU law immediately before [[8]IP completion day and so far as—] [[8]

(i) it is applicable to and in the United Kingdom by virtue of Part 4 of the withdrawal agreement, and

(ii) it neither has effect nor is to have effect by virtue of section 7A or 7B.]

(3) For the purposes of this Act, any direct EU legislation is operative immediately before [[9]IP completion day] if—

(a) in the case of anything which comes into force at a particular time and is stated to apply from a later time, it is in force and applies immediately before [[9]IP completion day],

(b) in the case of a decision which specifies to whom it is addressed, it has been notified to that person before [[9]IP completion day], and

(c) in any other case, it is in force immediately before [[9]IP completion day].

(4) This section—

(a) brings into domestic law any direct EU legislation only in the form of the English language version of that legislation, and
(b) does not apply to any such legislation for which there is no such version,

but paragraph (a) does not affect the use of the other language versions of that legislation for the purposes of interpreting it.

(5) This section is subject to section 5 and Schedule 1 (exceptions to savings and incorporation) [10and section 5A (savings and incorporation: supplementary)].

AMENDMENTS

1. European Union (Withdrawal Agreement) Act 2020 s.25(2)(a) (December 31, 2020) (SI 2020/1622, reg.5(d)).
2. European Union (Withdrawal Agreement) Act 2020 s.25(2)(b)(i) (December 31, 2020) (SI 2020/1622, reg.5(d)).
3. European Union (Withdrawal Agreement) Act 2020 s.25(2)(b)(ii) (December 31, 2020) (SI 2020/1622, reg.5(d)).
4. European Union (Withdrawal Agreement) Act 2020 s.25(2)(b)(iii) (December 31, 2020) (SI 2020/1622, reg.5(d)).
5. European Union (Withdrawal Agreement) Act 2020 s.25(2)(b)(iv) (December 31, 2020) (SI 2020/1622, reg.5(d)).
6. European Union (Withdrawal Agreement) Act 2020 s.25(2)(c)(i) (December 31, 2020) (SI 2020/1622, reg.5(d)).
7. European Union (Withdrawal Agreement) Act 2020 s.25(2)(c)(ii) (December 31, 2020) (SI 2020/1622, reg.5(d)).
8. European Union (Withdrawal Agreement) Act 2020 s.25(2)(d) (December 31, 2020) (SI 2020/1622, reg.5(d)).
9. European Union (Withdrawal Agreement) Act 2020 s.25(2)(e) (December 31, 2020) (SI 2020/1622 reg.5(d)).
10. European Union (Withdrawal Agreement) Act 2020 s.25(2)(f) (December 31, 2020) (SI 2020/1622, reg.5(d)).

DEFINITIONS

"direct EU legislation": see s.3(2).
"domestic law": see s.20(1).
"EEA agreement": Schedule 1 to the Interpretation Act 1978.
"EU decision": see s.20(1).
"EU regulation": see s.20(1).
"EU tertiary legislation": see s.20(1).
"exempt EU instrument": see s.20(1).
"IP completion day": see the European Union (Withdrawal Agreement) Act 2020, s.39(1).
"withdrawal agreement": see s.1A(6).

GENERAL NOTE

For the interpretation of references within materials forming part of domestic law by virtue of this section, see Sch.8 paras 1-2A. **5.11**

For an early post-Brexit case on the status of an EU regulation, see *Lipton v BA City Flyer Ltd* [2021] EWCA Civ 454 at [52]-[84]. An appeal to the Supreme Court is pending, but it appears not on this issue.

Saving for rights etc. under section 2(1) of the ECA

4. *[1 Repealed]* **5.12**

Amendment

1. REULRRA s.2 (January 1, 2024).

Exceptions to savings and incorporation

5.13 **5.**—[[2](A1) The principle of the supremacy of EU law is not part of domestic law. This applies after the end of 2023, in relation to any enactment or rule of law (whenever passed or made).

(A2) Any provision of [[4]assimilated direct legislation]—

(a) must, so far as possible, be read and given effect in a way which is compatible with all domestic enactments, and

(b) is subject to all domestic enactments, so far as it is incompatible with them.

(A3) Subsection (A2) is subject to—

(a) section 186 of the Data Protection Act 2018 (data subject's rights and other prohibitions and restrictions);

(b) regulations under section 7(1) of the Retained EU Law (Revocation and Reform) Act 2023.]

[[2]...]

[[3](A4) No general principle of EU law is part of domestic law after the end of 2023.]

(4) The Charter of Fundamental Rights is not part of domestic law on or after [[1]IP completion day].

[[3]...]

(6) Schedule 1 (which makes further provision about exceptions to savings and incorporation) has effect.

[[1](7) Subsections [[2](A1)] to (6) and Schedule 1 are subject to relevant separation agreement law (for which see section 7C).]

[[2](8) In this section "domestic enactment" means an enactment other than one consisting of [[4] assimilated direct legislation.]]

Amendment

1. European Union (Withdrawal Agreement) Act 2020 s.25(4)(a) (December 31, 2020) (SI 2020/1622, reg.5(d)).
2. REULRRA s.3 (January 1, 2024).
3. REULRRA s.4 (January 1, 2024).
4. REULRRA Sch.2, para.8 (January 1, 2024).

Definitions

"Charter of Fundamental Rights: see s.20(1).
"domestic law": see s.20(1).
"enactment": see s.20(1).
"IP completion day": see the European Union (Withdrawal Agreement) Act 2020 s.39(1).
"modification": see s.20(1) for "modify" and related expressions.

General Note

5.14 Sch 8 para.39 contains important transitional provisions concerning the disapplication of the Charter of Fundamental Rights. For the text of the Charter and commentary upon it, see earlier editions of this volume.

Section 5(A1) and the repeal of the former s.5(2) seek to effect a fundamental change in the status of EU law in relation, in particular, to domestic legislation passed or made before exit day and decisions such as *R (Open Rights Group) v*

SSHD [2021] EWCA Civ 800 noted in earlier editions of this work must be read subject to this amendment and are now of essentially historical interest.

In *SSWP v AT (UC)* [2022] UKUT 330, AT had moved to the UK exercising her rights under art.21 TFEU and had been granted pre-settled status before the end of the Brexit implementation period and claimed universal credit after it. The case was an appeal against the decision of the First-tier Tribunal, which had relied on the now repealed s.5(5) to apply the principles of the Charter as "fundamental rights or principles which exist irrespective of the Charter". However, on appeal, neither party sought to uphold this reasoning. A three-judge panel nonetheless held that the Charter did apply, relying principally on s.7A of this Act and arts 4 and 13 of the Withdrawal Agreement. The Court of Appeal dismissed the Secretary of State's appeal: [2023] EWCA Civ 1307. The Supreme Court has refused permission to appeal. 5.15

[1Savings and incorporation: supplementary

5A. The fact that anything which continues to be, or forms part of, domestic law on or after IP completion day by virtue of section 2 [2 or 3] has an effect immediately before IP completion day which is time-limited by reference to the implementation period does not prevent it from having an indefinite effect on and after IP completion day by virtue of section 2 [2 or 3].] 5.16

AMENDMENT

1. European Union (Withdrawal Agreement) Act 2020 s.25(5) (December 31, 2020) (SI 2020/1622 reg.5(d)).

2. Retained EU Law (Revocation and Reform) Act 2023 (Consequential Amendment) Regulations (SI 2023/1424) Sch.1 para.89 (January 1, 2024).

DEFINITIONS

"domestic law": see s.20(1)

"IP completion day": see the European Union (Withdrawal Agreement) Act 2020 s.39(1)

"implementation period": see s.1A(6)

Interpretation of [7 assimilated] law

6.—(1) A court or tribunal— 5.17

(a) is not bound by any principles laid down, or any decisions made, on or after [1IP completion day] by the European Court, and

(b) cannot refer any matter to the European Court on or after [1IP completion day].

(2) Subject to this and subsections (3) to (6), a court or tribunal may have regard to anything done on or after [1IP completion day] by the European Court, another EU entity or the EU so far as it is relevant to any matter before the court or tribunal.

(3) Any question as to the validity, meaning or effect of any [7 assimilated law] is to be decided, so far as that law is unmodified on or after [1IP completion day] and so far as they are relevant to it—

(a) in accordance with any [7 assimilated] case law [6...], and

(b) having regard (among other things) to the limits, immediately before [1IP completion day], of EU competences.

(4) But—

(a) the Supreme Court is not bound by any [7 assimilated] EU case law,

(b) the High Court of Justiciary is not bound by any [7 assimilated] EU case law when—

(i) sitting as a court of appeal otherwise than in relation to a compatibility issue (within the meaning given by section 288ZA(2) of the Criminal Procedure (Scotland) Act 1995) or a devolution issue (within the meaning given by paragraph 1 of Schedule 6 to the Scotland Act 1998), or

(ii) sitting on a reference under section 123(1) of the Criminal Procedure (Scotland) Act 1995, [2...]

[2(ba) a relevant court or relevant tribunal is not bound by any [7 assimilated] EU case law so far as is provided for by regulations under subsection (5A), and]

(c) no court or tribunal is bound by any [7 assimilated] domestic case law that it would not otherwise be bound by.

(5) In deciding whether to depart from any [7 assimilated] EU case law [3 by virtue of subsection (4)(a) or (b)], the Supreme Court or the High Court of Justiciary must apply the same test as it would apply in deciding whether to depart from its own case law.

[4(5A) A Minister of the Crown may by regulations provide for—

(a) a court or tribunal to be a relevant court or (as the case may be) a relevant tribunal for the purposes of this section,

(b) the extent to which, or circumstances in which, a relevant court or relevant tribunal is not to be bound by retained EU case law,

(c) the test which a relevant court or relevant tribunal must apply in deciding whether to depart from any retained EU case law, or

(d) considerations which are to be relevant to—

(i) the Supreme Court or the High Court of Justiciary in applying the test mentioned in subsection (5), or

(ii) a relevant court or relevant tribunal in applying any test provided for by virtue of paragraph (c) above.

(5B) Regulations under subsection (5A) may (among other things) provide for—

(a) the High Court of Justiciary to be a relevant court when sitting otherwise than as mentioned in subsection (4)(b)(i) and (ii),

(b) the extent to which, or circumstances in which, a relevant court or relevant tribunal not being bound by retained EU case law includes (or does not include) that court or tribunal not being bound by retained domestic case law which relates to retained EU case law,

(c) other matters arising in relation to retained domestic case law which relates to retained EU case law (including by making provision of a kind which could be made in relation to retained EU case law), or

(d) the test mentioned in paragraph (c) of subsection (5A) or the considerations mentioned in paragraph (d) of that subsection to be determined (whether with or without the consent of a Minister of the Crown) by a person mentioned in subsection (5C)(a) to (e) or by more than one of those persons acting jointly.

(5C) Before making regulations under subsection (5A), a Minister of the Crown must consult—

(a) the President of the Supreme Court,

(b) the Lord Chief Justice of England and Wales,

(c) the Lord President of the Court of Session,

(d) the Lord Chief Justice of Northern Ireland,

(e) the Senior President of Tribunals, and
(f) such other persons as the Minister of the Crown considers appropriate.

(5D) No regulations may be made under subsection (5A) after IP completion day.]

(6) Subsection (3) does not prevent the validity, meaning or effect of any [7 assimilated] law which has been modified on or after [1IP completion day] from being decided as provided for in that subsection if doing so is consistent with the intention of the modifications.

[5(6A) Subsections (1) to (6) are subject to relevant separation agreement law (for which see section 7C).]

(7) In this Act—

[7"assimilated case law" means—
(a) assimilated domestic case law, and
(b) assimilated EU case law;

"assimilated domestic case law" means any principles laid down by, and any decisions of, a court or tribunal in the United Kingdom, as they have effect immediately before IP completion day and so far as they—
(a) relate to anything to which section 2 or 3 applies, and
(b) are not excluded by section 5 or Schedule 1,
(as those principles and decisions are modified by or under this Act or by other domestic law from time to time);

"assimilated EU case law" means any principles laid down by, and any decisions of, the European Court, as they have effect in EU law immediately before IP completion day and so far as they—
(a) relate to anything to which section 2 or 3 applies, and
(b) are not excluded by section 5 or Schedule 1,
(as those principles and decisions are modified by or under this Act or by other domestic law from time to time);

"assimilated law" means anything which, on or after IP completion day, continues to be, or forms part of, domestic law by virtue of section 2 or 3 or subsection (3) or (6) above (as that body of law is added to or otherwise modified by or under this Act or by other domestic law from time to time).]

[6...]

[7...]

AMENDMENTS

1. European Union (Withdrawal Agreement) Act 2020 s.26(1)(a) (January 31, 2020 for limited purposes; December 31, 2020 otherwise) (SI 2020/1622, reg.5(e)).

2. European Union (Withdrawal Agreement) Act 2020 s.26(1)(b) (December 31, 2020) (SI 2020/1622, reg.5(e)).

3. European Union (Withdrawal Agreement) Act 2020 s.26(1)(c) (December 31, 2020) (SI 2020/1622, reg.5(e)).

4. European Union (Withdrawal Agreement) Act 2020 s.26(1)(d) (May 19, 2020) (SI 2020/518, reg 2(l)).

5. European Union (Withdrawal Agreement) Act 2020 s.26(1)(e) (December 31, 2020) (SI 2020/1622, reg.5(e)).

6. REULRRA s.4 (January 1, 2024).

7. REULRRA Sch.2(8) (January 1, 2024).

Definitions

In addition to the definitions set out in s.6(7), note the following:
"European Court": see Schedule 1 to the Interpretation Act 1978.
"EU entity": see s.20(1).
"the EU": see Schedule 1 to the Interpretation Act 1978.
"IP completion day": see the European Union (Withdrawal Agreement) Act 2020, s.39(1).
"Minister of the Crown": see s.20(1).
"tribunal": see s.20(1).
"unmodified": see s.20(1) for "modify" and related expressions.

General Note

5.18 Section 6(1)(a) has to be read subject to arts 4, 86 and 89 of the Withdrawal Agreement so far as rulings made in cases pending at the end of the implementation period are concerned: *HMRC v Perfect* [2022] EWCA Civ 330.

Despite what s.6(1)(b) says, art.157 of the Withdrawal Agreement does allow references to be made to the CJEU in relation to the Citizens' Rights provisions.

The regulations under s.6(5A) are the European Union (Withdrawal) Act 2018 (Relevant Court) (Retained EU Case Law) Regulations 2020 (SI 2020/1525) which provide as follows:

5.19 The Secretary of State makes these Regulations in exercise of the powers conferred by section 6(5A)(a), (b) and (c) and (5B)(a) of the European Union (Withdrawal) Act 2018

In accordance with section 6(5C) of that Act, the Secretary of State has carried out the necessary consultations.

In accordance with paragraph 9A of Schedule 7 to that Act, a draft of this instrument has been laid before, and approved by a resolution of, each House of Parliament.

Citation and commencement

1. These Regulations may be cited as the European Union (Withdrawal) Act 2018 (Relevant Court) (Retained EU Case Law) Regulations 2020 and come into force on IP completion day.

Interpretation

2. In these Regulations—

"the 2018 Act" means the European Union (Withdrawal) Act 2018;

"post-transition case law" means any principles laid down by, and any decisions of, a court or tribunal in the United Kingdom, as they have effect on or after IP completion day.

Relevant courts

3. For the purposes of section 6 of the 2018 Act, each of the following is a relevant court—

(a) the Court Martial Appeal Court,

(b) the Court of Appeal in England and Wales,

(c) the Inner House of the Court of Session,

(d) the High Court of Justiciary when sitting as a court of appeal in relation to a compatibility issue (within the meaning given by section 288ZA(2) of the Criminal Procedure (Scotland)Act 1995) or a devolution issue (within the meaning given by paragraph 1 of Schedule 6to the Scotland Act 1998),

(e) the court for hearing appeals under section 57(1)(b) of the Representation of the People Act 1983,

(f) the Lands Valuation Appeal Court, and

(g) the Court of Appeal in Northern Ireland.

Extent to which a relevant court is not bound by retained EU case law

4.—(1) A relevant court is not bound by any retained EU case law except as provided in paragraph (2).

(2) A relevant court is bound by retained EU case law so far as there is post-transition case law which modifies or applies that retained EU case law and which is binding on the relevant court.

Test to be applied

5. In deciding whether to depart from any retained EU case law by virtue of section 6(4)(ba) of the 2018 Act and these Regulations, a relevant court must apply the same test as the Supreme Court would apply in deciding whether to depart from the case law of the Supreme Court.

At the date at which the law in this volume is stated, sections 6A–6C (to be introduced by REULRRA s.6) are not yet in force. They are due to come into force on October 1, 2024: see SI 2024/714.

[[1]6D. Incompatibility orders

(1) This section applies if a court or tribunal decides, in the course of any proceedings—

(a) that a provision of retained direct EU legislation is incompatible with, and by virtue of section 5(A2)(b) subject to, any domestic enactment, or

(b) that a domestic enactment is incompatible with, and by virtue of section 7(1) of the Retained EU Law (Revocation and Reform) Act 2023 subject to, a provision of retained direct EU legislation.

(2) The court or tribunal must make an order (an "incompatibility order") to that effect (in addition to any exercise of other powers that it may have in relation to the proceedings).

(3) An incompatibility order may (among other things)—

(a) set out the effect of the relevant provision in its operation in relation to that particular case;

(b) delay the coming into force of the order;

(c) remove or limit any effect of the operation of the relevant provision before the coming into force of the order.

(4) Provision included in an incompatibility order may be made subject to conditions.

(5) In this section—

"domestic enactment" has the same meaning as in section 5 of this Act;

"the relevant provision" means section 5(A2)(b) of this Act or section 7(1) of the Retained EU Law (Revocation and Reform) Act 2023 (as the case may be).]

AMENDMENT

1. REULRRA s.8 (January 1, 2024).

Status of [[7] assimilated] law

7.—(1) Anything which— 5.20

(a) was, immediately before exit day, primary legislation of a particular kind, subordinate legislation of a particular kind or another enactment of a particular kind, and

(b) continues to be domestic law on and after exit day by virtue of [[1]section 1A(2) or 1B(2)],

continues to be domestic law as an enactment of the same kind.

[[2](1A) Anything which—

(a) was, immediately before IP completion day, primary legislation of a particular kind, subordinate legislation of a particular kind or another enactment of a particular kind, and

(b) continues to be domestic law on and after IP completion day by virtue of section 2,

continues to be domestic law as an enactment of the same kind.]

[[8](4A) [[7]Assimilated direct] legislation [[10]...] may only be modified by—

(a) primary legislation, or

(b) subordinate legislation so far as it is made under a power which permits such a modification by virtue of—

(i) paragraph 3, 8(3), 11A, 11B or 12(3) of Schedule 8,

(ii) any other provision made by or under this Act,

(iii) any provision made by or under an Act of Parliament passed before, and in the same Session as, this Act, or

(iv) any provision made on or after the passing of this Act by or under primary legislation.]

(5) For other provisions about the status of [[7] assimilated] law, see—

(a) section 5[[6](A1) to (A3)] [[3]and (7)] (status of [[7] assimilated] law in relation to other enactments or rules of law),

(b) section 6 (status of [[7] assimilated] case law [[11]...],

[[4](ba) section 7C (status of case law of European Court etc. in relation to [[7] assimilated] law which is relevant separation agreement law),]

(c) section 15(2) and Part 2 of Schedule 5 (status of [[7] assimilated law] for the purposes of the rules of evidence),

[[9](d) paragraph 16 of Schedule 8 (information about Scottish instruments which amend or revoke subordinate legislation under section 2(2) of the European Communities Act 1972),]

(e) paragraphs 19 and 20 of that Schedule (status of certain [[7] assimilated direct] EU legislation for the purposes of the Interpretation Act 1978), and

(f) paragraph 30 of that Schedule (status of [[7] assimilated direct] EU legislation for the purposes of the Human Rights Act 1998).

[[7]...]

AMENDMENTS

1. European Union (Withdrawal Agreement) Act 2020 Sch.5(2) para.40(2) (January 31, 2020).

2. European Union (Withdrawal Agreement) Act 2020 Sch.5(2) para.40(3) (December 31, 2020) (SI 2020/1622, reg.5(j)).

3. European Union (Withdrawal Agreement) Act 2020 Sch.5(2) para.40(4)(a) (December 31, 2020) (SI 2020/1622, reg.5(j)).

4. European Union (Withdrawal Agreement) Act 2020 Sch.5(2) para.40(4)(b) (December 31, 2020) (SI 2020/1622, reg.5(j)).

5. European Union (Withdrawal Agreement) Act 2020 Sch.5(2) para.40(5) (January 31, 2020).

6. REULRRA s.3 (January 1, 2024).

7. REULRRA Sch.2 para.8 (January 1, 2024).

8. REULRRA Sch.3 para.13 (June 29, 2023).

9. REULRRA s.10(2) (June 29, 2023).

10. Retained EU Law (Revocation and Reform) Act 2023 (Consequential Amendment) Regulations (SI 2023/1424) Sch.1 para.89 (January 1, 2024).
11. REULRRA s.4 (January 1, 2024).

DEFINITIONS

"domestic law": see s.20(1).
"EEA agreement": see Sch.1 to the Interpretation Act 1978.
"enactment": see s.20(1).
"European Court": see Sch.1 to the Interpretation Act 1978.
"exit day": see s.20(1) to (5).
"IP completion day": see.s.1A(6).
"modify": see s.20(1).
"primary legislation": see s.20(1).
"assimilated case law": see s.6(7).
"assimilated direct legislation": see s.20(1).
"assimilated direct minor legislation": see s.20(1).
"assimilated direct principal legislation": see s.20(1).
"assimilated law": see s.6(7).
"retained general principles of EU law": see s.6(7).
"subordinate legislation": see s.20(1).

[[1]General implementation of remainder of withdrawal agreement 5.21

7A.—(1) Subsection (2) applies to—
(a) all such rights, powers, liabilities, obligations and restrictions from time to time created or arising by or under the withdrawal agreement, and
(b) all such remedies and procedures from time to time provided for by or under the withdrawal agreement,

as in accordance with the withdrawal agreement are without further enactment to be given legal effect or used in the United Kingdom.

(2) The rights, powers, liabilities, obligations, restrictions, remedies and procedures concerned are to be—
(a) recognised and available in domestic law, and
(b) enforced, allowed and followed accordingly.

(3) Every enactment (including an enactment contained in this Act) is to be read and has effect subject to subsection (2).

(3A) *Omitted*

(4) This section does not apply in relation to Part 4 of the withdrawal agreement so far as section 2(1) of the European Communities Act 1972 applies in relation to that Part.

(5) See also (among other things)—
(a) Part 3 of the European Union (Withdrawal Agreement) Act 2020 (further provision about citizens' rights),
(b) *omitted,*
(c) section 7C of this Act (interpretation of law relating to withdrawal agreement etc.),
(d) – (f) *omitted*

AMENDMENT

1. European Union (Withdrawal Agreement) Act 2020 s.5 (January 31, 2020).

DEFINITIONS

"domestic law": see s.20(1)
"enactment": see s.20(1)
"European Communities Act 1972": see s.1A(7)(a)
"withdrawal agreement": see s.1A(6)

GENERAL NOTE

5.22 The role of s.7A in meaning that judgments, whenever delivered, by the CJEU on references made by UK courts and tribunals before the end of 2020 are binding in the UK is explained by the Court of Appeal in *HMRC v Perfect* [2022] EWCA Civ 330:

> "The fact that section 7A speaks of aspects of the Withdrawal Agreement being given legal effect 'without further enactment' cannot imply that, wherever domestic legislation is requisite for the Withdrawal Agreement to be effective within the United Kingdom, the provision does not operate."

The section creates, in respect of the matters derived from the Withdrawal Agreement listed in s.7A(1), a "conduit pipe", similar to the effect previously given by s.2 of the European Communities Act 1972: *SSWP v AT* [2022] UKUT 330 at [67]–[69] and see further *SSWP v AT* [2023] EWCA Civ 1307 at [60]–[62].

[[1]General implementation of EEA EFTA and Swiss agreements

5.23 **7B.** (1) Subsection (2) applies to all such rights, powers, liabilities, obligations, restrictions, remedies and procedures as-

(a) would from time to time be created or arise, or (in the case of remedies or procedures) be provided for, by or under the EEA EFTA separation agreement or the Swiss citizens' rights agreement, and
(b) would, in accordance with Article 4(1) of the withdrawal agreement, be required to be given legal effect or used in the United Kingdom without further enactment,

if that Article were to apply in relation to the EEA EFTA separation agreement and the Swiss citizens' rights agreement, those agreements were part of EU law and the relevant EEA states and Switzerland were member States.

(2) The rights, powers, liabilities, obligations, restrictions, remedies and procedures concerned are to be—

(a) recognised and available in domestic law, and
(b) enforced, allowed and followed accordingly.

(3) Every enactment (other than section 7A but otherwise including an enactment contained in this Act) is to be read and has effect subject to subsection (2).

(4) See also (among other things)—

(a) Part 3 of the European Union (Withdrawal Agreement) Act 2020 (further provision about citizens' rights),
(b) section 7C of this Act (interpretation of law relating to the EEA EFTA separation agreement and the Swiss citizens' rights agreement etc.),
(c) section 8B of this Act (power in connection with certain other separation issues), and
(d) Part 1B of Schedule 2 to this Act (powers involving devolved authorities in connection with certain other separation issues).

(5) In this section "the relevant EEA states" means Norway, Iceland and Liechtenstein.

(6) In this Act "EEA EFTA separation agreement" and "Swiss citizens' rights agreement" have the same meanings as in the European Union (Withdrawal Agreement) Act 2020 (see section 39(1) of that Act).]

AMENDMENT

1. European Union (Withdrawal Agreement) Act 2020 s.5 (January 31, 2020).

DEFINITIONS

"devolved authority": see s.20(1).

"domestic law": see s.20(1).

"EEA EFTA separation agreement" means (as modified from time to time in accordance with any provision of it) the Agreement on arrangements between Iceland, the Principality of Liechtenstein, the Kingdom of Norway and the United Kingdom of Great Britain and Northern Ireland following the withdrawal of the United Kingdom from the European Union, the EEA Agreement and other agreements applicable between the United Kingdom and the EEA EFTA States by virtue of the United Kingdom's membership of the European Union": European Union (Withdrawal Agreement) Act 2020 s.39(1).

"enactment": see s.20(1).

"Swiss citizens' rights agreement" means (as modified from time to time in accordance with any provision of it) the Agreement signed at Bern on 25 February 2019 between the United Kingdom of Great Britain and Northern Ireland and the Swiss Confederation on citizens' rights following the withdrawal of the United Kingdom from—

(a) the European Union, and

(b) the free movement of persons agreement,

so far as the Agreement operates for the purposes of the case where 'specified date' for the purposes of that Agreement has the meaning given in Article 2(b)(ii) of that Agreement": European Union (Withdrawal Agreement) Act 2020 s.39(1).

GENERAL NOTE

The EEA EFTA separation agreement and Swiss citizens' rights agreement are not included in this volume for reasons of space. They may respectively be found at *https://www.gov.uk/government/publications/eea-efta-separation-agreement-and-explainer* and *https://www.gov.uk/government/publications/swiss-citizens-rights-agreement-and-explainer* [both accessed May 5, 2024]. **5.24**

A Convention on Social Security Coordination between Iceland, Liechtenstein, Norway and the UK was signed on 30 June, 2023 and implemented by SI 2023/1060. It is in force from January 1, 2024.

[1Interpretation of relevant separation agreement law

7C.—(1) Any question as to the validity, meaning or effect of any relevant separation agreement law is to be decided, so far as they are applicable— **5.25**

(a) in accordance with the withdrawal agreement, the EEA EFTA separation agreement and the Swiss citizens' rights agreement, and

(b) having regard (among other things) to the desirability of ensuring that, where one of those agreements makes provision which corresponds to provision made by another of those agreements, the effect of relevant separation agreement law in relation to the matters dealt with by the corresponding provision in each agreement is consistent.

(2) See (among other things)—

(a) Article 4 of the withdrawal agreement (methods and principles relating to the effect, the implementation and the application of the agreement),

(b) Articles 158 and 160 of the withdrawal agreement (jurisdiction of the European Court in relation to Part 2 and certain provisions of Part 5 of the agreement),

(c) *omitted*,

(d) Article 4 of the EEA EFTA separation agreement (methods and principles relating to the effect, the implementation and the application of the agreement), and

(e) Article 4 of the Swiss citizens' rights agreement (methods and principles relating to the effect, the implementation and the application of the agreement).

(3) In this Act "relevant separation agreement law" means—

(a) any of the following provisions or anything which is domestic law by virtue of any of them—

(i) section 7A, 7B, 8B or 8C or Part 1B or 1C of Schedule 2 or this section, or

(ii) Part 3, or section 20, of the European Union (Withdrawal Agreement) Act 2020 (citizens' rights and financial provision), or

(b) anything not falling within paragraph (a) so far as it is domestic law for the purposes of, or otherwise within the scope of—

(i) the withdrawal agreement (other than Part 4 of that agreement),

(ii) the EEA EFTA separation agreement, or

(iii) the Swiss citizens' rights agreement,

as that body of law is added to or otherwise modified by or under this Act or by other domestic law from time to time.]

Amendment

1. European Union (Withdrawal Agreement) Act 2020 s.26(2) (January 31, 2020).

Definitions

"domestic law": see s.20(1).

"EEA EFTA separation agreement" and "Swiss citizens' rights agreement": see Definitions to s.7B.

"relevant separation agreement law": see s.7C(3).

"withdrawal agreement": see s.1A(6).

General Note

5.26 For the text of "the EEA EFTA separation agreement" and "Swiss citizens' rights agreement, see General Note to s.7B.

Dealing with deficiencies arising from withdrawal

5.27 **8.**—(1) A Minister of the Crown may by regulations make such provision as the Minister considers appropriate to prevent, remedy or mitigate—

(a) any failure of retained EU law to operate effectively, or

(b) any other deficiency in retained EU law,

arising from the withdrawal of the United Kingdom from the EU.

(2) Deficiencies in retained EU law are where the Minister considers that retained EU law—

(a) contains anything which has no practical application in relation to the United Kingdom or any part of it or is otherwise redundant or substantially redundant,

(b) confers functions on, or in relation to, EU entities which no longer have functions in that respect under EU law in relation to the United Kingdom or any part of it,

(c) makes provision for, or in connection with, reciprocal arrangements between—

(i) the United Kingdom or any part of it or a public authority in the United Kingdom, and

(ii) the EU, an EU entity, a member State or a public authority in a member State,

which no longer exist or are no longer appropriate,

(d) makes provision for, or in connection with, other arrangements which—

(i) involve the EU, an EU entity, a member State or a public authority in a member State, or

(ii) are otherwise dependent upon the United Kingdom's membership of the EU [[1]or Part 4 of the withdrawal agreement],

and which no longer exist or are no longer appropriate,

(e) makes provision for, or in connection with, any reciprocal or other arrangements not falling within paragraph (c) or (d) which no longer exist, or are no longer appropriate, as a result of the United Kingdom ceasing to be a party to any of the EU Treaties [[2]or as a result of either the end of the implementation period or any other effect of the withdrawal agreement],

[[3](ea) is not clear in its effect as a result of the operation of any provision of sections 2 to 6 or Schedule 1,]

(f) does not contain any functions or restrictions which—

(i) were in an EU directive and in force immediately before [[4]IP completion day] (including any power to make EU tertiary legislation), and

(ii) it is appropriate to retain, or

(g) contains EU references which are no longer appropriate.

(3) There is also a deficiency in retained EU law where the Minister considers that there is—

(a) anything in retained EU law which is of a similar kind to any deficiency which falls within subsection (2), or

(b) a deficiency in retained EU law of a kind described, or provided for, in regulations made by a Minister of the Crown.

(4) But retained EU law is not deficient merely because it does not contain any modification of EU law which is adopted or notified, comes into force or only applies on or after [[5]IP completion day].

(5) Regulations under subsection (1) may make any provision that could be made by an Act of Parliament.

(6) Regulations under subsection (1) may (among other things) provide for functions of EU entities or public authorities in member States (including making an instrument of a legislative character or providing funding) to be—

(a) exercisable instead by a public authority (whether or not established for the purpose) in the United Kingdom, or

(b) replaced, abolished or otherwise modified.

(7) But regulations under subsection (1) may not—

(a) impose or increase taxation or fees,

(b) make retrospective provision,

(c) create a relevant criminal offence,

(d) establish a public authority,

[6...]

(f) amend, repeal or revoke the Human Rights Act 1998 or any subordinate legislation made under it, or

(g) amend or repeal the Scotland Act 1998, the Government of Wales Act 2006 or the Northern Ireland Act 1998 (unless the regulations are made by virtue of paragraph 21(b) of Schedule 7 to this Act or are amending or repealing any provision of those Acts which modifies another enactment).

(8) No regulations may be made under this section after the end of the period of two years beginning with [7IP completion day].

(9) [8The reference in subsection (1) to a failure or other deficiency arising from the withdrawal of the United Kingdom from the EU includes a reference to any failure or other deficiency arising from—

(a) any aspect of that withdrawal, including (among other things)—

(i) the end of the implementation period, or

(ii) any other effect of the withdrawal agreement, or

(b) that withdrawal, or any such aspect of it, taken together with the operation of any provision, or the interaction between any provisions, made by or under this Act [9or the European Union (Withdrawal Agreement) Act 2020].]

AMENDMENTS

1. European Union (Withdrawal Agreement) Act 2020 s.27(2)(a) (January 31, 2020).

2. European Union (Withdrawal Agreement) Act 2020 s.27(2)(b) (January 31, 2020).

3. European Union (Withdrawal Agreement) Act 2020 s.27(2)(c) (January 31, 2020).

4. European Union (Withdrawal Agreement) Act 2020 s.27(2)(d) (January 31, 2020).

5. European Union (Withdrawal Agreement) Act 2020 s.27(3) (January 31, 2020).

6. European Union (Withdrawal Agreement) Act 2020 s.27(4) (January 31, 2020).

7. European Union (Withdrawal Agreement) Act 2020 s.27(5) (January 31, 2020).

8. European Union (Withdrawal Agreement) Act 2020 s.27(6)(a) (January 31, 2020).

9. European Union (Withdrawal Agreement) Act 2020 s.27(6)(b) (January 31, 2020).

DEFINITIONS

"assimilated law": see s.6(7).

"the EU": see Schedule 1 to the Interpretation Act 1978.

"EU directive": see s.20(1).

"EU entity": see s.20(1).

"EU references": see s.20(1).

"EU tertiary legislation": see s.20(1).
"EU Treaties": see Sch.1 to the Interpretation Act 1978
"implementation period": see s.1A(6).
"IP completion day": see s.1A(6).
"member State": see s.20(1) and Sch.1 tot the Interpretation Act 1978.
"Minister of the Crown": see s.20(1).
"modification": see, via "modify", s.20(1).
"public authority": see s.20(1).
"public authority in the United Kingdom": see s.20(8).
"withdrawal agreement": see s.1A(6).

GENERAL NOTE

Regulations made under this section include, in relation to social security, the Cessation of EU Law Relating to Prohibitions on Grounds of Nationality and Free Movement of Persons Regulations 2022 (SI 2022/1240) (in force from November 29, 2022). The text is set out at paras 5.108–5.116. In summary, the Regulations sought to guard against EU provisions relating to the matters referred to in the title of the Regulations (in particular arts 18, 21 and 45 TFEU) having any continuing effect in the UK via the (in any event since repealed) s.4(1) of the Act. They also amend Regulation 492/2011.

[[1]Supplementary power in connection with implementation period

8A. (1) A Minister of the Crown may by regulations— 5.28

(a) provide for other modifications for the purposes of section 1B(3)(f)(i) (whether applying in all cases or particular cases or descriptions of case),
(b) provide for subsection (3) or (4) of section 1B not to apply to any extent in particular cases or descriptions of case,
(c) make different provision in particular cases or descriptions of case to that made by subsection (3) or (4) of that section,
(d) modify any enactment contained in this Act in consequence of any repeal made by section 1A(5) or 1B(6), or
(e) make such provision not falling within paragraph (a), (b), (c) or (d) as the Minister considers appropriate for any purpose of, or otherwise in connection with, Part 4 of the withdrawal agreement.

(2) The power to make regulations under subsection (1) may (among other things) be exercised by modifying any provision made by or under an enactment.

(3) In subsection (2) "enactment" does not include primary legislation passed or made after IP completion day.

(4) No regulations may be made under subsection (1) after the end of the period of two years beginning with IP completion day.]

AMENDMENT

1. European Union (Withdrawal Agreement) Act 2020 s.3 (January 23, 2020).

DEFINITIONS

"enactment": see s.20(1).
"Minister of the Crown": see s.20(1).
"modifications"/"modifying": see s.20(1).
"withdrawal agreement": see s.1A(6).

General Note

5.29 Schedule 2 (not reproduced) confers powers to make regulations involving devolved authorities which correspond to the powers conferred by ss.8 to 8C.

Interpretation

5.30 **20.**—(1) In this Act—

[17"assimilated direct legislation" means any direct EU legislation which forms part of domestic law by virtue of section 3 (as modified by or under this Act or by other domestic law from time to time, and including any instruments made under it on or after IP completion day);

"assimilated direct minor legislation" means any assimilated direct legislation which is not assimilated direct principal legislation;

"assimilated direct principal legislation" means—

(a) any EU regulation so far as it—
 (i) forms part of domestic law on and after IP completion day by virtue of section 3, and
 (ii) was not EU tertiary legislation immediately before IP completion day, or

(b) any Annex to the EEA agreement so far as it—
 (i) forms part of domestic law on and after IP completion day by virtue of section 3, and
 (ii) refers to, or contains adaptations of, any EU regulation so far as it falls within paragraph (a),

(as modified by or under this Act or by other domestic law from time to time);]

"Charter of Fundamental Rights" means the Charter of Fundamental Rights of the European Union of 7 December 2000, as adopted at Strasbourg on 12 December 2007;

[1"Commons sitting day" means a day on which the House of Commons is sitting (and a day is only a day on which the House of Commons is sitting if the House begins to sit on that day);

"devolved authority" means—

(a) the Scottish Ministers,
(b) the Welsh Ministers, or
(c) a Northern Ireland department;

"domestic law" means—

(a) in [2sections 3, 7A and 7B], the law of England and Wales, Scotland and Northern Ireland, and
(b) in any other case, the law of England and Wales, Scotland or Northern Ireland;

"the EEA" means the European Economic Area;

"enactment" means an enactment whenever passed or made and includes—

(a) an enactment contained in any Order in Council, order, rules, regulations, scheme, warrant, byelaw or other instrument made under an Act,
(b) an enactment contained in any Order in Council made in exercise of Her Majesty's Prerogative,
(c) an enactment contained in, or in an instrument made under, an Act of the Scottish Parliament,

(d) an enactment contained in, or in an instrument made under, a Measure or Act of the National Assembly for Wales,
(e) an enactment contained in, or in an instrument made under, Northern Ireland legislation,
(f) an enactment contained in any instrument made by a member of the Scottish Government, the Welsh Ministers, the First Minister for Wales, the Counsel General to the Welsh Government, a Northern Ireland Minister, the First Minister in Northern Ireland, the deputy First Minister in Northern Ireland or a Northern Ireland department in exercise of prerogative or other executive functions of Her Majesty which are exercisable by such a person on behalf of Her Majesty,
(g) an enactment contained in, or in an instrument made under, a Measure of the Church Assembly or of the General Synod of the Church of England, and
(h) except in [[3]sections 1B and 7] or where there is otherwise a contrary intention, any [[17] assimilated direct] legislation;

"EU decision" means—
(a) a decision within the meaning of Article 288 of the Treaty on the Functioning of the European Union, or
(b) a decision under former Article 34(2)(c) of the Treaty on European Union;

"EU directive" means a directive within the meaning of Article 288 of the Treaty on the Functioning of the European Union;

"EU entity" means an EU institution or any office, body or agency of the EU;

"EU reference" means—
(a) any reference to the EU, an EU entity or a member State,
(b) any reference to an EU directive or any other EU law, or
(c) any other reference which relates to the EU;

"EU regulation" means a regulation within the meaning of Article 288 of the Treaty on the Functioning of the European Union;

"EU tertiary legislation" means—
(a) any provision made under—
  (i) an EU regulation,
  (ii) a decision within the meaning of Article 288 of the Treaty on the Functioning of the European Union, or
  (iii) an EU directive,

by virtue of Article 290 or 291(2) of the Treaty on the Functioning of the European Union or former Article 202 of the Treaty establishing the European Community, or
(b) any measure adopted in accordance with former Article 34(2)(c) of the Treaty on European Union to implement decisions under former Article 34(2)(c),

but does not include any such provision or measure which is an EU directive;

"exempt EU instrument" means anything which is an exempt EU instrument by virtue of Schedule 6;

[[4]"exit day" means [[5]31 January 2020] at 11.00 p.m. (and see subsections (2) to (5));]

[[16]"future relationship agreement" has the same meaning as in the European Union (Future Relationship) Act 2020 (see section 37 of that Act);]

[6"Joint Committee" means the Joint Committee established by Article 164(1) of the withdrawal agreement;

"Lords sitting day" means a day on which the House of Lords is sitting (and a day is only a day on which the House of Lords is sitting if the House begins to sit on that day);]

"member State" (except in the definitions of "direct EU legislation" and "EU reference") does not include the United Kingdom;

"Minister of the Crown" has the same meaning as in the Ministers of the Crown Act 1975 and also includes the Commissioners for Her Majesty's Revenue and Customs;

"modify" includes amend, repeal or revoke (and related expressions are to be read accordingly);

"Northern Ireland devolved authority" means the First Minister and deputy First Minister in Northern Ireland acting jointly, a Northern Ireland Minister or a Northern Ireland department;

"primary legislation" means—

(a) an Act of Parliament,

(b) an Act of the Scottish Parliament,

(c) a Measure or Act of the National Assembly for Wales, or

(d) Northern Ireland legislation;

"public authority" means a public authority within the meaning of section 6 of the Human Rights Act 1998;

[7"ratify", whether in relation to the withdrawal agreement or otherwise, has the same meaning as it does for the purposes of Part 2 of the Constitutional Reform and Governance Act 2010 in relation to a treaty (see section 25 of that Act);]

"relevant criminal offence" means an offence for which an individual who has reached the age of 18 (or, in relation to Scotland or Northern Ireland, 21) is capable of being sentenced to imprisonment for a term of more than 2 years (ignoring any enactment prohibiting or restricting the imprisonment of individuals who have no previous convictions);

[17...]

"retrospective provision", in relation to provision made by regulations, means provision taking effect from a date earlier than the date on which the regulations are made;

"subordinate legislation" means—

(a) any Order in Council, order, rules, regulations, scheme, warrant, byelaw or other instrument made under any Act, or

(b) any instrument made under an Act of the Scottish Parliament, Northern Ireland legislation or a Measure or Act of the National Assembly for Wales,

and (except in section 7 or Schedule 2 or where there is a contrary intention) includes any Order in Council, order, rules, regulations, scheme, warrant, byelaw or other instrument made on or after [9IP completion day] under any [17 assimilated direct] legislation;

"tribunal" means any tribunal in which legal proceedings may be brought;

"Wales" and "Welsh zone" have the same meaning as in the Government of Wales Act 2006 (see section 158 of that Act) [10.]

[10...]

(2) In this [11Act references to before, after or on exit day, or to beginning with exit day, are to be read as references to before, after or at 11.00 p.m.

on [12 31 January 2020] or (as the case may be) to beginning with 11.00 p.m. on that day.]]

(3)–(5) *omitted*

[14 (5A) In this Act references to anything which continues to be domestic law by virtue of section 1B(2) include—

(a) references to anything to which section 1B(2) applies which continues to be domestic law on or after exit day (whether or not it would have done so irrespective of that provision), and

(b) references to anything which continues to be domestic law on or after exit day by virtue of section 1B(2) (as that body of law is added to or otherwise modified by or under this Act or by other domestic law from time to time).]

(6) In this Act references to anything which continues to be domestic law by virtue of section 2 include references to anything to which subsection (1) of that section applies which continues to be domestic law on or after [15 IP completion day] (whether or not it would have done so irrespective of that section).

[18 ...]

(8) References in this Act (however expressed) to a public authority in the United Kingdom include references to a public authority in any part of the United Kingdom.

(9) References in this Act to former Article 34(2)(c) of the Treaty on European Union are references to that Article as it had effect at any time before the coming into force of the Treaty of Lisbon.

(10) *omitted*

AMENDMENTS

1. European Union (Withdrawal Agreement) Act 2020 Sch.5 para.44(2)(a) (January 23, 2020).

2. European Union (Withdrawal Agreement) Act 2020 Sch.5 para.44(2)(b) (January 31, 2020).

3. European Union (Withdrawal Agreement) Act 2020 Sch.5 para.44(2)(c) (January 31, 2020).

4. The European Union (Withdrawal) Act 2018 (Exit Day) (Amendment) (No.2) Regulations 2019 (SI 2019/859) reg.2(2) (April 11, 2019).

5. The European Union (Withdrawal) Act 2018 (Exit Day) (Amendment) (No.3) Regulations 2019 (SI 2019/1423) reg.2(2) (October 30, 2019).

6. European Union (Withdrawal Agreement) Act 2020 Sch.5 para.44(2)(d) (January 23, 2020).

7. European Union (Withdrawal Agreement) Act 2020 Sch.5 para.66 (January 23, 2020).

8. European Union (Withdrawal Agreement) Act 2020 Sch.5 para.44(2)(f) (January 31, 2020).

9. European Union (Withdrawal Agreement) Act 2020 Sch.5 para.44(2)(g) (January 31, 2020).

10. European Union (Withdrawal Agreement) Act 2020 Sch.5 para.44(2)(h) (January 31, 2020).

11. The European Union (Withdrawal) Act 2018 (Exit Day) (Amendment) (No.2) Regulations 2019 (SI 2019/859) reg.2(3) (April 11, 2019).

12. The European Union (Withdrawal) Act 2018 (Exit Day) (Amendment) (No.3) Regulations 2019 (SI 2019/1423) reg. 2(3) (October 30, 2019).

13. European Union (Withdrawal) (No.2) Act 2019 s.4(1) with saving in s.4(2) (September 9, 2019).

14. European Union (Withdrawal Agreement) Act 2020 Sch.5 para.44(3) (January 23, 2020).
15. European Union (Withdrawal Agreement) Act 2020 Sch.5 para.44(4) (January 31, 2020).
16. European Union (Future Relationship) Act 2020 s.39 and Sch.6 para.6 (December 31, 2020).
17. REULRRA Sch.2 para.8(9) (January 1, 2024).
18. Retained EU Law (Revocation and Reform) Act 2023 (Consequential Amendment) Regulations (SI 2023/1424) Sch.1 para.89 (January 1, 2024).

Index of defined expressions

5.31 **21.**—(1) In this Act, the expressions listed in the left-hand column have the meaning given by, or are to be interpreted in accordance with, the provisions listed in the right-hand column.

Expression	*Provision*
[[1]Anything which continues to be domestic law by virtue of section 1B(2)	Section 20(5A)]
Anything which continues to be domestic law by virtue of section 2	Section 20(6)
[[15]...]	
Article (in relation to the Treaty on European Union or the Treaty on the Functioning of the European Union)	Section 20(10)
[[14]Assimilated case law	Section 6(7)
Assimilated direct legislation	Section 20(1)
Assimilated direct minor legislation	Section 20(1)
Assimilated direct principal legislation	Section 20(1)
Assimilated domestic case law	Section 6(7)
Assimilated EU case law	Section 6(7)
Assimilated law	Section 6(7)]
Charter of Fundamental Rights	Section 20(1)
[[2]Commons sitting day	Section 20(1)]
Devolved authority	Section 20(1)
Direct EU legislation	Section 3(2)
Domestic law	Section 20(1)
The EEA	Section 20(1)
EEA agreement	Schedule 1 to the Interpretation Act 1978
[[3]EEA EFTA separation agreement	Section 7B(6)]
Enactment	Section 20(1)
The EU	Schedule 1 to the Interpretation Act 1978
EU decision	Section 20(1)
[[4]EU-derived domestic legislation	Section 1B(7)]
EU directive	Section 20(1)
EU entity	Section 20(1)
EU institution	Schedule 1 to the Interpretation Act 1978
EU instrument	Schedule 1 to the Interpretation Act 1978

Euratom Treaty	Schedule 1 to the Interpretation Act 1978
EU reference	Section 20(1)
EU regulation	Section 20(1)
[5European Communities Act 1972	Section 1A(7)(a)]
European Court	Schedule 1 to the Interpretation Act 1978
EU tertiary legislation	Section 20(1)
EU Treaties	Schedule 1 to the Interpretation Act 1978
Exempt EU instrument	Section 20(1)
Exit day (and related expressions)	Section 20(1) to (5)
Former Article 34(2)(c) of Treaty on European Union	Section 20(9)
[12Future relationship agreement	Section 20(1)]
[6Implementation period	Section 1A(6)
IP completion day (and related expressions)	Section 1A(6)
Joint Committee	Section 20(1)
Lords sitting day	Section 20(1)]
Member State	Section 20(1) and Schedule 1 to the Interpretation Act 1978
Minister of the Crown	Section 20(1)
Modify (and related expressions)	Section 20(1)
Northern Ireland devolved authority	Section 20(1)
Operative (in relation to direct EU legislation)	Section 3(3)
[7Part (of withdrawal agreement or EEA EFTA separation agreement)	Section 1A(7)(b)]
Primary legislation	Section 20(1)
Public authority	Section 20(1)
Public authority in the United Kingdom (however expressed)	Section 20(8)
[8Qualifying Northern Ireland goods	Section 8C(6)
Ratify	Section 20(1)]
Relevant criminal offence	Section 20(1) (and paragraph 44 of Schedule 8)
[9Relevant separation agreement law	Section 7C(3)]
[14...]	
[13...]	
Retrospective provision	Section 20(1)
Subordinate legislation	Section 20(1)
[10Swiss citizens' rights agreement	Section 7B(6)]
Tribunal	Section 20(1)
Wales	Section 20(1)
Welsh zone	Section 20(1)
Withdrawal agreement	[11Section 1A(6)]

(2) See paragraph 22 of Schedule 8 for amendments made by this Act to Schedule 1 to the Interpretation Act 1978.

AMENDMENTS

1. European Union (Withdrawal Agreement) Act 2020 s.42(7) (January 31, 2020).
2. European Union (Withdrawal Agreement) Act 2020 s.42(7), Sch.5 para.45(b) (January 31, 2020).
3. European Union (Withdrawal Agreement) Act 2020 s.42(7), Sch.5 para.45(c) (January 31, 2020).
4. European Union (Withdrawal Agreement) Act 2020 s.42(7), Sch.5 para.45(d) (January 31, 2020).
5. European Union (Withdrawal Agreement) Act 2020 s.42(7), Sch.5 para.45(e) (January 31, 2020).
6. European Union (Withdrawal Agreement) Act 2020 s.42(7), Sch.5 para.45(f) (January 31, 2020).
7. European Union (Withdrawal Agreement) Act 2020 s.42(7), Sch.5 para.45(g) (January 31, 2020).
8. European Union (Withdrawal Agreement) Act 2020 s.42(7), Sch.5 para.45(h) (January 31, 2020).
9. European Union (Withdrawal Agreement) Act 2020 s.42(7), Sch.5 para.45(i) (January 31, 2020).
10. European Union (Withdrawal Agreement) Act 2020 s.42(7), Sch.5 para.45(j) (January 31, 2020).
11. European Union (Withdrawal Agreement) Act 2020 s.42(7), Sch.5 para.45(k) (January 31, 2020).
12. European Union (Future Relationship) Act 2020 s.39 and Sch.6 para.7 (December 31, 2020).
13. REULRRA s.4 (January 1, 2024).
14. REULRRA Sch.8 para.10 (January 1, 2024).
15. Retained EU Law (Revocation and Reform) Act 2023 (Consequential Amendment) Regulations (SI 2023/1424) Sch.1 para.89 (January 1, 2024).

Consequential and transitional provision

5.32 **23.** (1) A Minister of the Crown may by regulations make such provision as the Minister considers appropriate in consequence of this Act.

(2) The power to make regulations under subsection (1) may (among other things) be exercised by modifying any provision made by or under an enactment.

(3) In subsection (2) "enactment" does not include primary legislation passed or made after [[1]IP completion day].

(4) No regulations may be made under subsection (1) after the end of the period of 10 years beginning with [[2]IP completion day].

(5) Parts 1 and 2 of Schedule 8 (which contain consequential provision) have effect.

(6) A Minister of the Crown may by regulations make such transitional, transitory or saving provision as the Minister considers appropriate in connection with the coming into force of any provision of this Act (including its operation in connection with exit day [[3]or IP completion day]).

(7) Parts 3 and 4 of Schedule 8 (which contain transitional, transitory and saving provision) have effect.

(8) The enactments mentioned in Schedule 9 (which contains repeals not made elsewhere in this Act) are repealed to the extent specified.

AMENDMENTS

1. European Union (Withdrawal Agreement) Act 2020 s.42(7), Sch.5 para.46(2) (January 31, 2020).
2. European Union (Withdrawal Agreement) Act 2020 s.42(7), Sch.5 para.46(3) (January 31, 2020).
3. European Union (Withdrawal Agreement) Act 2020 s.42(7), Sch.5 para.46(4) (January 31, 2020).

DEFINITIONS

"Minister of the Crown": see s.20(1)

GENERAL NOTE

Selected paragraphs of Schedule 8 are included below. Schedule 9 is not reproduced in this volume. **5.33**

Extent

24.—(1) Subject to subsections (2) and (3), this Act extends to England and Wales, Scotland and Northern Ireland. **5.34**

(2) Any provision of this Act which amends or repeals an enactment has the same extent as the enactment amended or repealed.

(3) [*omitted*]

DEFINITION

"enactment": see s.20(1) .

Commencement and short title

25.—(1) The following provisions— **5.35**

(a) sections 8 to 11 (including Schedule 2),
(b) paragraphs 4, 5, 21(2)(b), 48(b), 51(2)(c) and (d) and (4) of Schedule 3 (and section 12(8) and (12) so far as relating to those paragraphs),
(c) sections 13 and 14 (including Schedule 4),
(d) sections 16 to 18,
(e) sections 20 to 22 (including Schedules 6 and 7),
(f) section 23(1) to (4) and (6),
(g) paragraph 41(10), 43 and 44 of Schedule 8 (and section 23(7) so far as relating to those paragraphs),
(h) section 24, and
(i) this section,

come into force on the day on which this Act is passed.

(2), (3) [*omitted*]

(4) The provisions of this Act, so far as they are not brought into force by subsections (1) to (3), come into force on such day as a Minister of the Crown may by regulations appoint; and different days may be appointed for different purposes.

(5) This Act may be cited as the European Union (Withdrawal) Act 2018.

DEFINITIONS

"Minister of the Crown": see s.20(1).

General Note

5.36 The commencement of this Act was complex, reflecting its 2018 origins and the evolving political landscape which eventually resulted in the European Union (Withdrawal Agreement) Act 2020, which made very substantial amendments to the 2018 Act, some of them temporary in nature to provide for the implementation period between "exit day" and "IP completion day" and others with longer term effect from IP completion day.

The following commencement orders have been made in respect of the 2018 Act:

European Union (Withdrawal) Act 2018 (Commencement and Transitional Provisions) Regulations 2018/808;

European Union (Withdrawal) Act 2018 (Commencement No. 2) Regulations 2019/399;

European Union (Withdrawal) Act 2018 (Commencement No. 3) Regulations 2019/1077;

European Union (Withdrawal) Act 2018 (Commencement No. 4) Regulations 2019/1198;

European Union (Withdrawal) Act 2018 (Commencement No. 5, Transitional Provisions and Amendment) Regulations 2020/74;

European Union (Withdrawal) Act 2018 and European Union (Withdrawal Agreement) Act 2020 (Commencement, Transitional and Savings Provisions) Regulations 2020/1622;

and the following in respect of the 2020 Act:

European Union (Withdrawal Agreement) Act 2020 (Commencement No. 1) Regulations 2020/75;

European Union (Withdrawal Agreement) Act 2020 (Commencement No. 2) Regulations 2020/317;

European Union (Withdrawal Agreement) Act 2020 (Commencement No. 3) Regulations 2020/518;

European Union (Withdrawal) Act 2018 and European Union (Withdrawal Agreement) Act 2020 (Commencement, Transitional and Savings Provisions) Regulations 2020/1622.

SCHEDULES

SCHEDULE 1

Further Provision About Exceptions to Savings and Incorporation

Challenges to validity of [9 assimilated] law

5.37 **1.** (1) There is no right in domestic law on or after [1IP completion day] to challenge any [9 assimilated] law on the basis that, immediately before [1IP completion day], an EU instrument was invalid.

(2) Sub-paragraph (1) does not apply so far as—

(a) the European Court has decided before [1IP completion day] that the instrument is invalid, or

(b) the challenge is of a kind described, or provided for, in regulations made by a Minister of the Crown.

(3) Regulations under sub-paragraph (2)(b) may (among other things) provide for a challenge which would otherwise have been against an EU institution to be against a public authority in the United Kingdom.

5.38 [8...]

Rule in Francovich

4. There is no right in domestic law on or after [[4]IP completion day] to damages in accordance with the rule in *Francovich*. 5.39

Interpretation

5. (1) References in section 5 and this Schedule to the principle of the supremacy of EU law, the Charter of Fundamental Rights, any general principle of EU law or the rule in *Francovich* are to be read as references to that principle, Charter or rule so far as it would otherwise continue to be, or form part of, domestic law on or after [[5]IP completion day] [[6]by virtue of section 2, 3, 4 or 6(3) or (6) and otherwise in accordance with this Act]. 5.40

[[7]...]

Amendments

1. European Union (Withdrawal Agreement) Act 2020 s.25(6)(a) (January 31, 2020 for limited purposes; otherwise December 31, 2020) (SI 2020/1622 reg.3(k)).
2. European Union (Withdrawal Agreement) Act 2020 s.25(6)(a) (substitution came into force on January 31, 2020 but only takes effect on December 31, 2020) (SI 2020/1622 reg. 3(k)).
3. European Union (Withdrawal Agreement) Act 2020 s.25(6)(a) (substitution came into force on January 31, 2020 but only takes effect on December 31, 2020) (SI 2020/1622 reg. 3(k))
4. European Union (Withdrawal Agreement) Act 2020 s.25(6)(a) (substitution came into force on January 31, 2020 but only takes effect on December 31, 2020) (SI 2020/1622 reg. 3(k)).
5. European Union (Withdrawal Agreement) Act 2020 c. 1 Pt 4 s.25(6)(a) (substitution came into force on January 31, 2020 but only takes effect on December 31, 2020) (SI 2020/1622 reg. 3(k))
6. European Union (Withdrawal Agreement) Act 2020 Pt 4 s.25(6)(b) (December 31, 2020) (SI 2020/1622 reg. 5(d)).
7. REULRRA s.3 (January 1, 2024).
8. REULRRA s.4 (January 1, 2024).
9. REULRRA Sch.8 para.11 (January 1, 2024).

General Note

Note that Sch.8, para.39 contains important transitional provisions qualifying the application of paras 1 and 4, though now subject to subsequent legislative changes. A helpful summary of the effect of a number of those transitional provisions (albeit conditioned by the matter before the Court, a *Francovich* claim) is provided by *Jersey Choice Ltd v Her Majesty's Treasury* [2021] EWCA Civ 1941 at [20]–[24]. 5.41

On appeal to the Supreme Court, the parties agreed, and the Court was prepared to accept, that the summary was an accurate statement of the law as it then stood, but the Court emphasised that the law being applied was no longer the current law in the United Kingdom: [2024] UKSC 5 at [26].

Additionally, a limited exception to Sch.1, para.1 is provided by the Challenges to Validity of EU Instruments (EU Exit) Regulations 2019 SI 2019/673.

SCHEDULE 5

Publication and Rules of Evidence

(Selected provisions)

Questions as to meaning of EU law

5.42 **3.** (1) Where it is necessary [[1]in legal proceedings] to decide a question as to—

(a) the meaning or effect in EU law of any of the EU Treaties or any other treaty relating to the EU, or

(b) the validity, meaning or effect in EU law of any EU instrument,

the question is to be treated [[2]...] as a question of law.

(2) In this paragraph—

[[3]...]

"treaty" includes—

(a) any international agreement, and

(b) any protocol or annex to a treaty or international agreement.

Power to make provision about judicial notice and admissibility

5.43 **4.** (1) A Minister of the Crown may by regulations—

(a) make provision enabling or requiring judicial notice to be taken of a relevant matter, or

(b) provide for the admissibility in any legal proceedings of specified evidence of—

(i) a relevant matter, or

(ii) instruments or documents issued by or in the custody of an EU entity.

(2) Regulations under sub-paragraph (1)(b) may provide that evidence is admissible only where specified conditions are met (for example, conditions as to certification of documents).

(3) Regulations under this paragraph may modify any provision made by or under an enactment.

(4) In sub-paragraph (3) "enactment" does not include primary legislation passed or made after [[4]IP completion day].

(5) For the purposes of this paragraph each of the following is a "relevant matter"—

[[7](a) assimilated law]

(b) EU law,

(c) the EEA agreement, [[5]...]

[[5](ca) the EEA EFTA separation agreement,

(cb) the Swiss citizens' rights agreement,

(cc) the withdrawal agreement, and]

(d) anything which is specified in the regulations and which relates to a matter mentioned in paragraph (a), (b) [[6], (c), (ca), (cb) or (cc)].

Amendments

1. European Union (Withdrawal Agreement) Act 2020 Sch.5(2) para.48(3)(a)(i) (December 31, 2020) (SI 2020/1622 reg.5(j)).

2. European Union (Withdrawal Agreement) Act 2020 Sch.5(2) para.48(3)(a)(ii) (December 31, 2020) (SI 2020/1622 reg.5(j)).
3. European Union (Withdrawal Agreement) Act 2020 Sch.5(2) para.48(3)(b) (December 31, 2020) (SI 2020/1622 reg.5(j)).
4. European Union (Withdrawal Agreement) Act 2020 Sch.5(2) para.48(4)(a) (January 31, 2020).
5. European Union (Withdrawal Agreement) Act 2020 Sch.5(2) para.48(4)(b)(i) (January 31, 2020).
6. European Union (Withdrawal Agreement) Act 2020 Sch.5(2) para.48(4)(b) (ii) (January 31, 2020).
7. REULRRA Sch.8 para.13 (January 1, 2024).

SCHEDULE 8

CONSEQUENTIAL, TRANSITIONAL, TRANSITORY AND SAVING PROVISION

(SELECTED PROVISIONS)

PART 1 GENERAL CONSEQUENTIAL PROVISION

Existing ambulatory references to [3 assimilated direct] legislation

1. (1) Any reference [1so far as it], immediately before [2IP completion day]— 5.44
(a) exists in—
(i) any enactment,
(ii) any EU regulation, EU decision, EU tertiary legislation or provision of the EEA agreement which is to form part of domestic law by virtue of section 3, or
(iii) any document relating to anything falling within sub-paragraph (i) or (ii), and
(b) is a reference to (as it has effect from time to time) any EU regulation, EU decision, EU tertiary legislation or provision of the EEA agreement which is to form part of domestic law by virtue of section 3,

is to be read, on or after [2IP completion day], as a reference to the EU regulation, EU decision, EU tertiary legislation or provision of the EEA agreement as it forms part of domestic law by virtue of section 3 and, unless the contrary intention appears, as modified by domestic law from time to time.

(2) Sub-paragraph (1) does not apply to any reference [1so far as it] forms part of a power to make, confirm or approve subordinate legislation so far as the power to make the subordinate legislation—
(a) continues to be part of domestic law by virtue of section 2, and
(b) is subject to a procedure before Parliament, the Scottish Parliament, the National Assembly for Wales or the Northern Ireland Assembly.

(3) Sub-paragraphs (1) and (2) are subject to any other provision made by or under this Act or any other enactment.

AMENDMENTS

1. European Union Withdrawal (Consequential Modifications) (EU Exit) Regulations SI 2020/1447 reg.3(2)(a) (December 31, 2020).

2. European Union (Withdrawal Agreement) Act 2020 Sch.5(2) para.54(2) (December 31, 2020.

3. REULRRA Sch.8 para.15 (January 1, 2024).

GENERAL NOTE

5.45 See also:

(a) the modifications of the effect of provisions within paras 1–2A contained in European Union (Withdrawal) Act 2018 and European Union (Withdrawal Agreement) Act 2020 (Commencement, Transitional and Savings Provisions) Regulations 2020 (SI 2020/1622) reg.19; and

(b) Interpretation Act 1978 s.20 (as amended with effect from December 31, 2020) which materially provides:

"(2A) Where—

(a) an Act passed on or after IP completion day refers to any treaty relating to the EU or any instrument or other document of an EU entity, and

(b) the treaty, instrument or document has effect by virtue of section 7A or 7B of the European Union (Withdrawal) Act 2018 (general implementation of remainder of EU withdrawal agreement etc.), the reference, unless the contrary intention appears and so far as required for the purposes of relevant separation agreement law, is a reference to the treaty, instrument or document as it so has effect (including, so far as so required, as it has effect from time to time).

(3) Subject to subsection (2A), where an Act passed on or after IP completion day refers to any EU regulation, EU decision, EU tertiary legislation or provision of the EEA agreement, the reference, unless the contrary intention appears, is a reference to the EU regulation, EU decision, EU tertiary legislation or provision of the EEA agreement as it forms part of domestic law by virtue of section 3 of the European Union (Withdrawal) Act 2018 or section 1 of the Direct Payments to Farmers (Legislative Continuity) Act 2020.

(4) Subsection (3) does not determine any question as to whether the reference is to be read as a reference to the EU regulation, EU decision, EU tertiary legislation or provision of the EEA agreement as modified by domestic law (and, accordingly, is without prejudice to subsection (2)).

(5) Any expression in subsection (3) or (4) which is defined in the European Union (Withdrawal) Act 2018 has the same meaning in the subsection concerned as in that Act."

Paragraphs (1)–(2A) are concerned with legislation made before IP completion day, while the Interpretation Act s.20 deals with references in provisions made on or after that date.

[[1]Existing ambulatory references to relevant separation agreement law

5.46 **1A.**—(1) Any reference which, immediately before IP completion day—

(a) exists in—

(i) any enactment,

(ii) any EU regulation, EU decision, EU tertiary legislation or provision of the EEA agreement which is to form part of domestic law by virtue of section 3, or

(iii) any document relating to anything falling within sub-paragraph (i) or (ii), and

(b) is a reference to (as it has effect from time to time) any of the EU Treaties, any EU instrument or any other document of an EU entity,

is, if the treaty, instrument or document has effect on or after IP completion day by virtue of section 7A or 7B and so far as required for the purposes of relevant separation agreement law, to be read on or after that day as, or including, a reference to the treaty, instrument or document as it so has effect (including, so far as so required, as it has effect from time to time).

(2) In sub-paragraph (1) "treaty" includes any international agreement (and any protocol or annex to a treaty or international agreement).

(3) Sub-paragraphs (1) and (2) are subject to any other provision made by or under this Act or any other enactment.]

General Note

See General Note to para.1. **5.47**

Other existing ambulatory references

2. (1) Any reference [1so far as it]— **5.48**

(a) exists, immediately before [2IP completion day], in—

(i) any enactment,

(ii) any EU regulation, EU decision, EU tertiary legislation or provision of the EEA agreement which is to form part of domestic law by virtue of section 3, or

(iii) any document relating to anything falling within sub-paragraph (i) or (ii),

(b) is not a reference to which paragraph 1(1) applies, and

(c) is, immediately before [2IP completion day], a reference to (as it has effect from time to time) any of the EU Treaties, any EU instrument or any other document of an EU entity,

is to be read, on or after [2IP completion day], as a reference to the EU Treaty, instrument or document as it has effect immediately before [F6IP completion day].

(2) Sub-paragraph (1) does not apply to any reference [1so far as it] forms part of a power to make, confirm or approve subordinate legislation so far as the power to make the subordinate legislation—

(a) continues to be part of domestic law by virtue of section 2, and

(b) is subject to a procedure before Parliament, the Scottish Parliament, the National Assembly for Wales or the Northern Ireland Assembly.

[2(2A) Sub-paragraph (1) does not apply so far as any reference forms part of relevant separation agreement law.]

(3) Sub-paragraphs (1) [2to (2A)] are subject to any other provision made by or under this Act or any other enactment.

Amendments

1. European Union Withdrawal (Consequential Modifications) (EU Exit) Regulations 2020 (SI 2020/1447) reg.3(2)(c) (December 31, 2020).

2. European Union (Withdrawal Agreement) Act 2020 Sch.5(2) para.54(3) (December 31, 2020).

GENERAL NOTE

5.49 See General Note to para.1.

Existing non-ambulatory references

5.50 [[1]**2A.**(1) Any reference which, immediately before IP completion day—

(a) exists in—

(i) any enactment, or

(ii) any EU regulation, EU decision, EU tertiary legislation or provision of the EEA agreement which is to form part of domestic law by virtue of section 3, and

(b) is a reference to any of the EU Treaties, any EU instrument or any other document of an EU entity as it has effect at a particular time which is earlier than IP completion day,

is to be read, on or after IP completion day, in accordance with one or more of subparagraphs (2) to (4).

(2) If the treaty, instrument or document has effect by virtue of section 7A or 7B on or after IP completion day and so far as required for the purposes of relevant separation agreement law, the reference is to be read on or after that day as, or as including, a reference to the treaty, instrument or document as it so has effect (including, so far as so required, as it has effect from time to time).

(3) So far as—

(a) the reference is a reference to—

(i) any EU regulation, EU decision or EU tertiary legislation,

(ii) any provision of the EEA agreement, or

(iii) any part of anything falling within sub-paragraph (i) or (ii),

(b) what has been referred to ("the subject law") is to form part of domestic law by virtue of section 3 [...*omitted*]

(c) there has been no relevant modification of the subject law after the particular time and before IP completion day [...*omitted*],

the reference is to be read, on or after IP completion day, as a reference to the subject law as it forms part of domestic law by virtue of section 3 [... *omitted*]

(4) So far as the reference is not to be read in accordance with sub-paragraphs (2) and (3), the reference is to be read, on or after IP completion day, as a reference to the treaty, instrument or document as it had effect in EU law at the particular time.

(5) Sub-paragraph (3) does not determine whether, where the subject law is modified by domestic law on or after IP completion day, the reference is to be read as a reference to the subject law as modified; [...*omitted*].

(6) This paragraph is subject to any provision made by or under this Act or any other enactment.

[(6A) *omitted*]

(7) In this paragraph—

"relevant modification" means any modification in EU law which—

(a) is to form part of domestic law by virtue of section 3 [...*omitted*] and

(b) would, if the reference were to the subject law as modified, result in an alteration to the effect of the reference (ignoring any alteration which is irrelevant in the context concerned);

"the subject law" has the meaning given by sub-paragraph (3)(b);
"treaty" includes any international agreement (and any protocol or annex to a treaty or international agreement).]

GENERAL NOTE

See General Note to para.1. 5.51

PART 2

SPECIFIC CONSEQUENTIAL PROVISION

Human Rights Act 1998

30. (1) This paragraph has effect for the purposes of the Human Rights Act 1998. 5.52

(2) Any [1 assimilated direct principal] legislation is to be treated as primary legislation.

(3) Any [1 assimilated direct minor] legislation is to be treated as primary legislation so far as it amends any primary legislation but otherwise is to be treated as subordinate legislation.

(4) In this paragraph "amend", "primary legislation" and "subordinate legislation" have the same meaning as in the Human Rights Act 1998.

AMENDMENT

1. REULRRA Sch.8 para.15 (January 1, 2024).

PART 3

GENERAL TRANSITIONAL, TRANSITORY OR SAVING PROVISION

[1 **36A.** (1) Anything done— 5.53

(a) in connection with anything which continues to be domestic law by virtue of section 1A(2) or 1B(2), or
(b) for a purpose mentioned in section 2(2)(a) or (b) of the European Communities Act 1972 or otherwise related to the EU or the EEA,

if in force or effective immediately before exit day, continues to be in force or effective on and after exit day.

(2) Anything done—

(a) in connection with anything which continues to be domestic law by virtue of section 1A(2) or 1B(2), or
(b) for a purpose mentioned in section 2(2)(a) or (b) of the European Communities Act 1972 or otherwise related to the EU or the EEA,

which, immediately before exit day, is in the process of being done continues to be done on and after exit day.

(3) Sub-paragraphs (1) and (2) are subject to—
(a) sections 1 to 1B and the withdrawal of the United Kingdom from the EU,
(b) any provision made under section 23(6) of this Act or section 41(5) of the European Union (Withdrawal Agreement) Act 2020, and
(c) any other provision made by or under this Act, the European Union (Withdrawal Agreement) Act 2020 or any other enactment.

(4) References in this paragraph to anything done include references to anything omitted to be done.]

AMENDMENT

1. European Union (Withdrawal Agreement) Act 2020 Sch.5(2) para.55(2) (January 31, 2020)

Continuation of existing acts etc.

5.54 **37.**(1) Anything done—
(a) in connection with anything which continues to be, or forms part of, domestic law by virtue of section 2, 3, 4 or 6(3) or (6), or
(b) for a purpose mentioned in section 2(2)(a) or (b) of the European Communities Act 1972 or otherwise related to the EU or the EEA,

if in force or effective immediately before [1 IP completion day], continues to be in force or effective on and after [1 IP completion day].

(2) Anything done—
(a) in connection with anything which continues to be, or forms part of, domestic law by virtue of section 2, 3, 4 or 6(3) or (6), or
(b) for a purpose mentioned in section 2(2)(a) or (b) of the European Communities Act 1972 or otherwise related to the EU or the EEA,

which, immediately before [1 IP completion day], is in the process of being done continues to be done on and after [1 IP completion day].

(3) Sub-paragraphs (1) and (2) are subject to—
(a) [1sections 1 to 1B] and the withdrawal of the United Kingdom from the EU,
(b) sections 2 to [1 7B] and Schedule 1,
(c) any provision made under section 23(6) [1of this Act or section 41(5) of the European Union (Withdrawal Agreement) Act 2020], and
(d) any other provision made by or under this Act [1, the European Union (Withdrawal Agreement) Act 2020] or any other enactment.

(4) References in this paragraph to anything done include references to anything omitted to be done.

AMENDMENTS

1. European Union (Withdrawal Agreement) Act 2020 Sch.5 para.55(3) (December 31, 2020).

PART 4

SPECIFIC TRANSITIONAL, TRANSITORY AND SAVING PROVISION

[2**37A.** The repeal of section 1A(1) to (4) by section 1A(5) and the repeal of section 1B(1) to (5) by section 1B(6) do not prevent an enactment to which section 2 applies from continuing to be read, on and after IP completion day and by virtue of section 2, in accordance with section 1B(3) or (4).] 5.55

38. Section 4(2)(b) does not apply in relation to any rights, powers, liabilities, obligations, restrictions, remedies or procedures so far as they are of a kind recognised by a court or tribunal in the United Kingdom in a case decided on or after [3IP completion day] but begun before [3IP completion day] (whether or not as an essential part of the decision in the case).

39. (1) Subject as follows and subject to [4relevant separation agreement law (for which see section 7C) and] any provision made by regulations under [5section 23(6) of this Act or section 41(5) of the European Union (Withdrawal Agreement) Act 2020, section 5(4) and paragraphs [7 1 and 4] of Schedule 1] apply in relation to anything occurring before [6IP completion day] (as well as anything occurring on or after [6IP completion day]).

(2) Section 5(4) and paragraphs [7 1 and 4] of Schedule 1 do not affect any decision of a court or tribunal made before [4IP completion day].

(3) Section 5(4) and [7 paragraph] 4 of Schedule 1 do not apply in relation to any proceedings begun, but not finally decided, before a court or tribunal in the United Kingdom before [6IP completion day].

(4) Paragraphs [7 1 and 4] of Schedule 1 do not apply in relation to any conduct which occurred before [6IP completion day] which gives rise to any criminal liability.

[7...]

(7) Paragraph 4 of Schedule 1 does not apply in relation to any proceedings begun within the period of two years beginning with [6IP completion day] so far as the proceedings relate to anything which occurred before [6IP completion day].

AMENDMENTS

1. European Union Withdrawal (Consequential Modifications) (EU Exit) Regulations 2020 (SI 2020/1447), reg.3 (December 31, 2020).
2. European Union (Withdrawal Agreement) Act 2020 Sch.5(2) para.56(3) (December 31, 2020) (SI 2020/1622 reg.5(j)).
3. European Union (Withdrawal Agreement) Act 2020 Sch.5(2) para.56(4) (December 31, 2020) (SI 2020/1622 reg.5(j)).
4. European Union (Withdrawal Agreement) Act 2020 Sch.5(2) para.56(5)(b)(i) (December 31, 2020) (SI 2020/1622, reg.5(j)).
5. European Union (Withdrawal Agreement) Act 2020 Sch.5(2) para.56(5)(b)(ii) (December 31, 2020) (SI 2020/1622, reg.5(j)).
6. European Union (Withdrawal Agreement) Act 2020 Sch.5(2) para.56(5)(a) (SI 2020/1622, reg.5(j)).
7. REULRRA s.4(7) (January 1, 2024).

General Note

5.56 Paragraphs (1), (2) and (2A): note para.19 of the European Union (Withdrawal) Act 2018 and European Union (Withdrawal Agreement) Act 2020 (Commencement, Transitional and Savings Provisions) Regulations 2020 (SI 2020/1622) which provides:

"(1) Paragraphs 1 and 2A(3) of Schedule 8 to EU(W)A 2018 do not apply to any reading on or after IP completion day of a reference so far as the reference relates to a time before IP completion day (unless a contrary intention appears in relation to the reference concerned).

(2) Paragraph 2 of that Schedule does not apply to any reading on or after IP completion day of a reference so far as the reference relates to a time before IP completion day which is earlier than immediately before IP completion day (unless a contrary intention appears in relation to the reference concerned)."

Paragraph 39: Subject to ensuing legislative changes a helpful summary of the effect of a number of those transitional provisions (albeit conditioned by the matter before the Court, a *Francovich* claim) is provided by *Jersey Choice Ltd v Her Majesty's Treasury* [2021] EWCA Civ 1941 at [20]–[24]. On appeal to the Supreme Court, the parties agreed, and the Court was prepared to accept, that the summary was an accurate statement of the law as it then stood, but the Court emphasised that the law being applied was no longer the current law in the United Kingdom: [2024] UKSC 5 at [26].

European Union (Withdrawal Agreement) Act 2020

(2020 c.1)

Arrangement Of Sections Reproduced

(For ss.7-9, see the 2021–22 edition of Vol. V and, where applicable, the updating material in Vol. II of this year's edition)

5.58 **Co-ordination of social security systems**

13. (1) An appropriate authority may by regulations make such provision as the authority considers appropriate—

(a) to implement Title III of Part 2 of the withdrawal agreement (coordination of social security systems),

(b) to supplement the effect of section 7A of the European Union (Withdrawal) Act 2018 in relation to that Title, or
(c) otherwise for the purposes of dealing with matters arising out of, or related to, that Title (including matters arising by virtue of section 7A of that Act and that Title).

(2) An appropriate authority may by regulations make such provision as the authority considers appropriate—
(a) to implement Title III of Part 2 of the EEA EFTA separation agreement (co-ordination of social security systems),
(b) to supplement the effect of section 7B of the European Union (Withdrawal) Act 2018 in relation to that Title, or
(c) otherwise for the purposes of dealing with matters arising out of, or related to, that Title (including matters arising by virtue of section 7B of that Act and that Title).

(3) An appropriate authority may by regulations make such provision as the authority considers appropriate—
(a) to implement social security co-ordination provisions of the Swiss citizens' rights agreement,
(b) to supplement the effect of section 7B of the European Union (Withdrawal) Act 2018 in relation to those provisions, or
(c) otherwise for the purposes of dealing with matters arising out of, or related to, those provisions (including matters arising by virtue of section 7B of that Act and those provisions).

(4) For the purposes of subsection (3) the following are "social security co-ordination provisions" of the Swiss citizens' rights agreement—
(a) Part 3 of that agreement (co-ordination of social security systems);
(b) Article 23(4) of that agreement as regards social security co-ordination.

(5) The power to make regulations under subsection (1), (2) or (3) may (among other things) be exercised by modifying any provision made by or under an enactment.

(6) In this section, "appropriate authority" means—
(a) a Minister of the Crown,
(b) a devolved authority, or
(c) a Minister of the Crown acting jointly with a devolved authority.

(7) Schedule 1 contains further provision about the power of devolved authorities to make regulations under this section.

DEFINITIONS

"EEA EFTA separation agreement": s.39.
"enactment": s.39.
"Minister of the Crown": s.39.
"modifying": s.39 .
"Swiss citizens' rights agreement": s.39.

GENERAL NOTE

For interpretation of references to parts of legal instruments, see s.17(4). **5.59**

Non-discrimination, equal treatment and rights of workers etc.

14. (1) An appropriate authority may by regulations make such provision as the authority considers appropriate for the purpose of implementing any of the following provisions of the withdrawal agreement— **5.60**

(a) Article 12 (prohibition of discrimination on grounds of nationality);
(b) Article 23 (right to equal treatment);
(c) Articles 24(1) and 25(1) (rights of workers and the self-employed);
(d) Articles 24(3) and 25(3) (rights of employed or self-employed frontier workers) as regards rights enjoyed as workers.

(2) An appropriate authority may by regulations make such provision as the authority considers appropriate for the purpose of implementing any of the following provisions of the EEA EFTA separation agreement—

(a) Article 11 (prohibition of discrimination on grounds of nationality);
(b) Article 22 (right to equal treatment);
(c) Articles 23(1) and 24(1) (rights of workers and the self-employed);
(d) Articles 23(3) and 24(3) (rights of employed or self-employed frontier workers) as regards rights enjoyed as workers.

(3) An appropriate authority may by regulations make such provision as the authority considers appropriate for the purpose of implementing any of the following provisions of the Swiss citizens' rights agreement—

(a) Article 7 (prohibition of discrimination on grounds of nationality);
(b) Article 18 (right to take up employment etc.);
(c) Article 19 (rights of employed or self-employed persons etc.);
(d) Article 20(1) (rights of frontier workers);
(e) Article 23(1) (rights of persons providing services).

(4) If the appropriate authority considers it appropriate, regulations under subsection (1), (2) or (3) relating to the implementation of a provision mentioned in that subsection, may be made so as to apply both to—

(a) persons to whom the provision in question applies, and
(b) persons to whom that provision does not apply but who may be granted leave to enter or remain in the United Kingdom by virtue of residence scheme immigration rules, whether or not they have been granted such leave (see section 17).

(5) The power to make regulations under subsection (1), (2) or (3) may (among other things) be exercised by modifying any provision made by or under an enactment.

(6) In this section, "appropriate authority" means—

(a) a Minister of the Crown,
(b) a devolved authority, or
(c) a Minister of the Crown acting jointly with a devolved authority.

(7) Schedule 1 contains further provision about the power of devolved authorities to make regulations under this section.

DEFINITIONS

"EEA EFTA separation agreement": s.39.
"leave to enter or remain": s.17.
"residence scheme immigration rules": s.17.
"Swiss citizens' rights agreement": s.39.
"withdrawal agreement": s.39.

Independent Monitoring Authority for the Citizens' Rights Agreements

5.61 **15.** (1) A body corporate called the Independent Monitoring Authority for the Citizens' Rights Agreements is established.

(2) In this Part that body is referred to as "the IMA" .

(3) Schedule 2 contains provision relating to the IMA (including provisions about the IMA's constitution and functions).

GENERAL NOTE

For the Practice Statement requiring the IMA to be served with proceedings in the courts which raise the application of the Citizens' Rights Agreements, see 5.130. The Practice Statement does not apply to proceedings in the tribunals.

Regulations: supplementary

16. (1) In sections 7, 8, 9 and 14— 5.62

(a) a power to make provision for the purpose of implementing a provision of the withdrawal agreement includes power to make provision to supplement the effect of section 7A of the European Union (Withdrawal) Act 2018 in relation to that provision of the agreement,

(b) a power to make provision for the purpose of implementing a provision of the EEA EFTA separation agreement includes power to make provision to supplement the effect of section 7B of that Act in relation to that provision of the agreement, and

(c) a power to make provision for the purpose of implementing a provision of the Swiss citizens' rights agreement includes power to make provision to supplement the effect of section 7B of that Act in relation to that provision of the agreement.

(2) The conferral of a power on a Minister of the Crown under section 7, 8, 9 or 11 does not affect the extent of any power of a devolved authority under section 12, 13 or 14 which overlaps with a power under section 7, 8, 9 or 11 by virtue of section 17(4).

(3) Regulations under this Part may not provide for the conferral of functions (including the conferral of a discretion) on, or the delegation of functions to, a person who is not a public authority (but may so provide if the person is a public authority).

(4) In subsection (3), "public authority" means a person who exercises functions of a public nature.

DEFINITIONS

"devolved authority": s.39.
"EEA EFTA separation agreement": s.39.
"Minister of the Crown": s.39.
"Swiss citizens' rights agreement": s.39.
"withdrawal agreement": s.39.

Interpretation: Part 3

17. (1) In this Part, "residence scheme immigration rules" means— 5.63

(a) Appendix EU to the immigration rules except those rules, or changes to that Appendix, which are identified in the immigration rules as not having effect in connection with the residence scheme that operates in connection with the withdrawal of the United Kingdom from the EU, and

(b) any other immigration rules which are identified in the immigration rules as having effect in connection with the withdrawal of the United Kingdom from the EU.

(2) In this Part, "relevant entry clearance immigration rules" means any immigration rules which are identified in the immigration rules as having effect in connection with the granting of entry clearance for the purposes of acquiring leave to enter or remain in the United Kingdom by virtue of residence scheme immigration rules.

(3) In this Part, references to having leave to enter or remain in the United Kingdom granted by virtue of residence scheme immigration rules include references to having such leave granted by virtue of those rules before this section comes into force.

(4) In this Part, a reference to a Chapter, Title, Part or other provision of the withdrawal agreement, EEA EFTA separation agreement or Swiss citizens' rights agreement includes a reference to—

(a) any other provision of the agreement in question so far as relating to that Chapter, Title, Part or other provision, and

(b) any provision of EU law which is applied by, or referred to in, that Chapter, Title, Part or other provision (to the extent of the application or reference).

(5) In this Part—

"entry clearance" has the meaning given by section 33(1) of the Immigration Act 1971 (interpretation);

"immigration rules" has the same meaning as in the Immigration Act 1971.

Repeal of unnecessary or spent enactments

General Note

5.64 Section 36 repeals a number of provisions of the European Union (Withdrawal) Act 2018 and the European Union (Withdrawal) Act 2019. They are only of historic interest and are not reproduced here.

Parliamentary sovereignty

5.65 **38.** (1) It is recognised that the Parliament of the United Kingdom is sovereign.

(2) In particular, its sovereignty subsists notwithstanding—

(a) directly applicable or directly effective EU law continuing to be recognised and available in domestic law by virtue of section 1A or 1B of the European Union (Withdrawal) Act 2018 (savings of existing law for the implementation period),

(b) section 7A of that Act (other directly applicable or directly effective aspects of the withdrawal agreement),

(c) section 7B of that Act (deemed direct applicability or direct effect in relation to the EEA EFTA separation agreement and the Swiss citizens' rights agreement), and

(d) section 7C of that Act (interpretation of law relating to the withdrawal agreement (other than the implementation period), the EEA EFTA separation agreement and the Swiss citizens' rights agreement).

(3) Accordingly, nothing in this Act derogates from the sovereignty of the Parliament of the United Kingdom.

DEFINITIONS

"EEA EFTA separation agreement": s.39
"Swiss citizens' rights agreement": s.39
"withdrawal agreement": s.39

Interpretation

39. (1) In this Act— 5.66

"devolved authority" means—

(a) the Scottish Ministers,
(b) the Welsh Ministers, or
(c) a Northern Ireland department;

"EEA EFTA separation agreement" means (as modified from time to time in accordance with any provision of it) the Agreement on arrangements between Iceland, the Principality of Liechtenstein, the Kingdom of Norway and the United Kingdom of Great Britain and Northern Ireland following the withdrawal of the United Kingdom from the European Union, the EEA Agreement and other agreements applicable between the United Kingdom and the EEA EFTA States by virtue of the United Kingdom's membership of the European Union;

"enactment" means an enactment whenever passed or made and includes—

(a) an enactment contained in any Order in Council, order, rules, regulations, scheme, warrant, byelaw or other instrument made under an Act of Parliament,
(b) an enactment contained in any Order in Council made in exercise of Her Majesty's Prerogative,
(c) an enactment contained in, or in an instrument made under, an Act of the Scottish Parliament,
(d) an enactment contained in, or in an instrument made under, a Measure or Act of the National Assembly for Wales,
(e) an enactment contained in, or in an instrument made under, Northern Ireland legislation,
(f) an enactment contained in any instrument made by a member of the Scottish Government, the Welsh Ministers, the First Minister for Wales, the Counsel General to the Welsh Government, a Northern Ireland Minister, the First Minister in Northern Ireland, the deputy First Minister in Northern Ireland or a Northern Ireland department in exercise of prerogative or other executive functions of Her Majesty which are exercisable by such a person on behalf of Her Majesty,
(g) an enactment contained in, or in an instrument made under, a Measure of the Church Assembly or of the General Synod of the Church of England, and
(h) any retained direct EU legislation;

"IP completion day" means 31 December 2020 at 11.00 p.m (and see subsections (2) to (5));

"Minister of the Crown" has the same meaning as in the Ministers of the Crown Act 1975 and also includes the Commissioners for Her Majesty's Revenue and Customs;

"modify" includes amend, repeal or revoke (and related expressions are to be read accordingly);

"primary legislation" means—

(a) an Act of Parliament,
(b) an Act of the Scottish Parliament,
(c) a Measure or Act of the National Assembly for Wales, or
(d) Northern Ireland legislation;

"subordinate legislation" means any Order in Council, order, rules, regulations, scheme, warrant, byelaw or other instrument made under any primary legislation;

"Swiss citizens' rights agreement" means (as modified from time to time in accordance with any provision of it) the Agreement signed at Bern on 25 February 2019 between the United Kingdom of Great Britain and Northern Ireland and the Swiss Confederation on citizens' rights following the withdrawal of the United Kingdom from—
(a) the European Union, and
(b) the free movement of persons agreement,

so far as the Agreement operates for the purposes of the case where "specified date" for the purposes of that Agreement has the meaning given in Article 2(b)(ii) of that Agreement;

"withdrawal agreement" means the agreement between the United Kingdom and the EU under Article 50(2) of the Treaty on European Union which sets out the arrangements for the United Kingdom's withdrawal from the EU (as that agreement is modified from time to time in accordance with any provision of it).

(2) In this Act references to before, after or on IP completion day, or to beginning with IP completion day, are to be read as references to before, after or at 11.00 p.m. on 31 December 2020 or (as the case may be) to beginning with 11.00 p.m. on that day.

(3) Subsection (4) applies if, by virtue of any change to EU summer-time arrangements, the transition or implementation period provided for by Part 4 of the withdrawal agreement is to end on a day or time which is different from that specified in the definition of "IP completion day" in subsection (1).

(4) A Minister of the Crown may by regulations—
(a) amend the definition of "IP completion day" in subsection (1) to ensure that the day and time specified in the definition are the day and time that the transition or implementation period provided for by Part 4 of the withdrawal agreement is to end, and
(b) amend subsection (2) in consequence of any such amendment.

(5) In subsection (3) "EU summer-time arrangements" means the arrangements provided for by Directive 2000/84/EC of the European Parliament and of the Council of 19 January 2001 on summer-time arrangements.

(6) In this Act any reference to an Article of the Treaty on European Union includes a reference to that Article as applied by Article 106a of the Euratom Treaty.

Regulations

5.67 **40.** Schedule 4 contains provision about regulations under this Act (including provision about procedure).

GENERAL NOTE

5.68 In the interests of saving space, Sch.4 is not reproduced

Consequential and transitional provision etc.

41. (1) A Minister of the Crown may by regulations make such provision as the Minister considers appropriate in consequence of this Act. 5.69

(2) The power to make regulations under subsection (1) may (among other things) be exercised by modifying any provision made by or under an enactment.

(3) In subsection (2) "enactment" does not include primary legislation passed or made after IP completion day.

(4) Parts 1 and 2 of Schedule 5 contain minor and consequential provision.

(5) A Minister of the Crown may by regulations make such transitional, transitory or saving provision as the Minister considers appropriate in connection with the coming into force of any provision of this Act (including its operation in connection with exit day or IP completion day).

(6) Part 3 of Schedule 5 contains transitional, transitory and saving provision.

Definitions

"enactment": s.39 (but note s.41(3)).
"IP completion day": s.39.
"Minister of the Crown": s.39.

General Note

In the interests of saving space, Sch.5 is in general not reproduced, but the following provision should be noted: 5.70

1. (1) Any provision in subordinate legislation made before exit day under—

(a) any provision of the European Union (Withdrawal) Act 2018 (or any provision made under any such provision), or

(b) any other enactment,

which provides, by reference to exit day (however expressed), for all or part of that or any other subordinate legislation to come into force immediately before exit day, on exit day or at any time after exit day is to be read instead as providing for the subordinate legislation or (as the case may be) the part to come into force immediately before IP completion day, on IP completion day or (as the case may be) at the time concerned after IP completion day.

(2) Sub-paragraph (1) does not apply so far as it is expressly disapplied by the subordinate legislation that provides as mentioned in that sub-paragraph.

(3) An appropriate authority may by regulations—

(a) provide for sub-paragraph (1) not to apply to any extent in particular cases or descriptions of case, or

(b) make different provision in particular cases or descriptions of case to that made by sub-paragraph (1).

(4) But see paragraph 2 for further provision about the power of a devolved authority acting alone to make regulations under sub-paragraph (3).

(5) No regulations may be made under sub-paragraph (3) after the end of the period of one year beginning with IP completion day.

(6) In this paragraph "appropriate authority" means—

(a) a Minister of the Crown,

(b) a devolved authority, or

(c) a Minister of the Crown acting jointly with a devolved authority.

Extent, commencement and short title

5.71 **42.** (1) Subject to subsections (2) to (5), this Act extends to England and Wales, Scotland and Northern Ireland.

(2) Any provision of this Act which amends or repeals an enactment has the same extent as the enactment amended or repealed.

(3) Accordingly, section 1 (but not section 2) also extends to the Isle of Man, the Channel Islands and Gibraltar.

(4) The power in section 36 of the Immigration Act 1971 or (as the case may be) section 60(4) of the UK Borders Act 2007 may be exercised so as to extend (with or without modifications) to the Isle of Man or any of the Channel Islands the modifications made to that Act by section 10 above.

(5) Paragraphs 1 and 2 of Schedule 5, so far as they relate to the modification of any provision in subordinate legislation which extends outside England and Wales, Scotland and Northern Ireland, also extend there.

(6) The following provisions—

(a) sections 3 and 4,

(b) sections 11, 16 and 17,

(c) sections 20, 29 and 31 to 40 (including Schedule 4),

(d) section 41(1) to (3) and (5),

(e) the following provisions of Schedule 5—

(i) paragraphs 1(3) to (6) and 2,

(ii) paragraph 3(2) to (8),

(iii) paragraph 4,

(iv) paragraphs 5 and 7(a) and (b),

(v) paragraphs 8 and 12(a) and (b),

(vi) paragraphs 17, 20, 22, 24, 27 and 31,

(vii) paragraphs 32, 36(a) and (b) and 37(b) and (c),

(viii) paragraphs 38, 41(1) and (3)(a),42,44(1),(2)(a),(d) and (e) and (3),47(1), (2), (4) and (6)and 50,

(ix) paragraphs 51 and 56(1) and(7)(b) for the purposes of making regulations under section 8A of, of Part 1A of Schedule 2 to, the European Union (Withdrawal) Act 2018,

(x) paragraphs 52(1) and (3) to (7) and 53(1) to (4), (6), (7) (a), (8)(a) and (9) to (13),

(xi) paragraph 56(1) and (6)(b) to (d), and

(xii) paragraphs 65 to 68,

(and section 41(4) and (6) so far as relating to any provision so far as it falls within any of sub-paragraphs (i) to (xii)), and

(f) this section,

come into force on the day on which this Act is passed.

(7) The provisions of this Act, so far as they are not brought into force by subsection (6), come into force on such day as a Minister of the Crown may by regulations appoint; and different days may be appointed for different purposes.

(8) This Act may be cited as the European Union (Withdrawal Agreement) Act 2020.

DEFINITIONS

"Minister of the Crown": s.39.

General Note

For the issues around the commencement of this Act and the European Union (Withdrawal) Act 2018 and a list of the relevant commencement orders, see the General Note to the 2018 Act, s.25. 5.72

Immigration and Social Security Co-ordination (EU Withdrawal) Act 2020

(2020 c.20)

Arrangement Of Sections Reproduced

Schedules:

Power to modify retained direct EU legislation relating to social security co-ordination

6. (1) An appropriate authority may by regulations modify the retained direct EU legislation mentioned in subsection (2). 5.74

(2) The retained direct EU legislation is—

(a) Regulation (EC) No 883/2004 of the European Parliament and of the Council on the co-ordination of social security systems;

(b) Regulation (EC) No 987/2009 of the European Parliament and of the Council laying down the procedure for implementing Regulation (EC) No 883/2004;

(c) Regulation (EEC) No 1408/71 on the application of social security schemes to employed persons, to self-employed persons and to members of their families moving within the Community;

(d) Regulation (EEC) No 574/72 fixing the procedure for implementing Regulation (EEC) No 1408/71;

(e) Regulation (EC) No 859/2003 extending Regulation (EEC) No 1408/71 to nationals of non-EU Member Countries.

(3) The power to make regulations under subsection (1) includes power—

(a) to make different provision for different categories of person to whom they apply (and the categories may be defined by reference to a person's date of arrival in the United Kingdom, their immigration status, their nationality or otherwise);

(b) otherwise to make different provision for different purposes;

(c) to make supplementary, incidental, consequential, transitional, transitory or saving provision;

(d) to provide for a person to exercise a discretion in dealing with any matter.

(4) The power to make provision mentioned in subsection (3)(c) includes power to modify—

(a) any provision made by primary legislation passed before, or in the same Session as, this Act;

(b) any provision made under primary legislation before, or in the same Session as, this Act is passed;
(c) retained direct EU legislation which is not mentioned in subsection (2).

[[1]...]

(7) In this section, "appropriate authority" means—
(a) the Secretary of State or the Treasury,
(b) a Northern Ireland department, or
(c) a Minister of the Crown acting jointly with a Northern Ireland department.

(8) Schedule 2 contains further provision about the power to make regulations under this section.

(9) Schedule 3 contains provision about the making of regulations under this section.

AMENDMENTS

1. Retained EU Law (Revocation and Reform) Act 2023 (Consequential Amendment) Regulations (SI 2023/1424) Sch.1 para.92 (January 1, 2024).

DEFINITIONS

By s.7:
"domestic law" means the law of England and Wales, Scotland or Northern Ireland;
"Minister of the Crown" has the same meaning as in the Ministers of the Crown Act 1975 and also includes the Commissioners for Her Majesty's Revenue and Customs;
"modify" includes amend, repeal or revoke (and related expressions are to be read accordingly);
"primary legislation" means—
(a) an Act of Parliament;
(b) an Act of the Scottish Parliament;
(c) an Act or Measure of Senedd Cymru;
(d) Northern Ireland legislation.

GENERAL NOTE

5.75 Regulations made under the power conferred by this section are the Social Security Co-ordination (Revocation of Retained Direct EU Legislation and Related Amendments) (EU Exit) Regulations 2020 (SI 2020/1508), discussed below in the Updating Notes to the various EU instruments concerned at 5.163–5.164.

SCHEDULE 2

FURTHER PROVISION ABOUT THE SCOPE OF THE POWER UNDER SECTION 6

GENERAL NOTE

5.76 The Schedule contains detailed provisions relating to procedure where the interests of the legislature in Scotland or Northern Ireland are involved under the respective devolution settlements. It is not reproduced here to save space.

SCHEDULE 3

Regulations Under Section 6

PART 1

Statutory Instruments

1. Any power to make regulations under section 6— **5.77**

(a) so far as exercisable by the Secretary of State or the Treasury, or by a Minister of the Crown acting jointly with a Northern Ireland department, is exercisable by statutory instrument, and

(b) so far as exercisable by a Northern Ireland department (other than when acting jointly with a Minister of the Crown), is exercisable by statutory rule for the purposes of the Statutory Rules (Northern Ireland) Order 1979 (SI 1979/1573 (NI 12)) (and not by statutory instrument).

PART 2

SCRUTINY OF REGULATIONS UNDER SECTION 6

Scrutiny where sole exercise

2. (1) A statutory instrument containing regulations of the Secretary of State or the Treasury under section 6 may not be made unless a draft of the instrument has been laid before, and approved by a resolution of, each House of Parliament. **5.78**

(2) Regulations of a Northern Ireland department under section 6 may not be made unless a draft of the regulations has been laid before, and approved by a resolution of, the Northern Ireland Assembly.

(3) This paragraph does not apply to regulations to which paragraph 3 applies (Minister of the Crown and a Northern Ireland department acting jointly).

Scrutiny where joint exercise

3. Regulations under section 6 of a Minister of the Crown acting jointly with a Northern Ireland department may not be made unless— **5.79**

(a) a draft of the statutory instrument containing those regulations has been laid before, and approved by a resolution of, each House of Parliament, and

(b) a draft of the regulations has been laid before, and approved by a resolution of, the Northern Ireland Assembly.

Combination of instruments

4. (1) Sub-paragraph (2) applies to a statutory instrument containing regulations under section 6 which is subject to a procedure before Parliament for the approval of the instrument in draft before it is made. **5.80**

(2) The statutory instrument may also include regulations under another Act which are made by statutory instrument which is subject to a procedure before Parliament that provides for the annulment of the instrument after it has been made.

(3) Where regulations are included as mentioned in sub-paragraph (2), the procedure applicable to the statutory instrument—

(a) is the procedure mentioned in sub-paragraph (1), and

(b) is not the procedure mentioned in sub-paragraph (2).

(4) Sub-paragraphs (1) to (3) apply in relation to a statutory rule as they apply in relation to a statutory instrument but as if—

(a) the references to Parliament were references to the Northern Ireland Assembly, and

(b) the reference to another Act in sub-paragraph (2) included Northern Ireland legislation.

(5) Sub-paragraphs (1) to (3) apply in relation to a statutory instrument containing regulations under section 6 which is subject to a procedure before the Northern Ireland Assembly as well as a procedure before Parliament as they apply to a statutory instrument containing regulations under section 6 which is subject to a procedure before Parliament but as if the references to Parliament were references to Parliament and the Northern Ireland Assembly.

(6) This paragraph does not prevent the inclusion of other regulations in a statutory instrument or statutory rule which contains regulations under section 6 (and, accordingly, references in this Schedule to an instrument containing regulations are to be read as references to an instrument containing (whether alone or with other provision) regulations).

The European Union (Future Relationship) Act 2020

(2020 c.29)

5.81 **Social security co-ordination**

26. (1) The following provisions of the Trade and Cooperation Agreement, in its English language version, form part of domestic law on and after the relevant day—

(a) the SSC Protocol;

(b) [1 Title I of Heading 4 of Part 2 (Trade, Transport, Fisheries and Other Arrangements);]

(c) Articles [1 6 and 775], so far as applying to the SSC Protocol.

(2) Any enactment has effect on and after the relevant day with such modifications as—

(a) are required in consequence of subsection (1) or otherwise for the purposes of implementing the provisions mentioned in that subsection, and

(b) are capable of being ascertained from those provisions or otherwise from the Trade and Cooperation Agreement.

(3) Subsections (1) and (2)—

(a) are subject to any equivalent or other provision—

(i) which (whether before, on or after the relevant day) is made by or under this Act or any other enactment or otherwise forms part of domestic law, and

(ii) which is for the purposes of (or has the effect of) implementing to any extent the Trade and Cooperation Agreement or any other future relationship agreement, and

(b) do not limit the scope of any power which is capable of being exercised to make any such provision.

(4) The references to the Trade and Cooperation Agreement in—

(a) subsections (1) and (2), and

(b) the definition of "the SSC Protocol" in subsection (5),

are (except as provided in that definition) references to the agreement as it has effect on the relevant day.

(5) In this section—

"domestic law" means— (a) in subsection (1), the law of England and Wales, Scotland and Northern Ireland, and (b) in subsection (3)(a)(i), the law of England and Wales, Scotland or Northern Ireland; "relevant day", in relation to any provision mentioned in subsection (1) or any aspect of it, means—

(a) so far as the provision or aspect concerned is provisionally applied before it comes into force, the time and day from which the provisional application applies, and

(b) so far as the provision or aspect concerned is not provisionally applied before it comes into force, the time and day when it comes into force;

"the SSC Protocol" means the Protocol on Social Security Coordination contained in the Trade and Cooperation Agreement, as that protocol is modified or supplemented from time to time in accordance with Article SSC.11(6), Article SSC.11(8) or Article SSC.68 of that protocol;

and references to the purposes of (or having the effect of) implementing an agreement (or any provision of an agreement) include references to the purposes of (or having the effect of) making provision consequential on any such implementation.

Amendments

1. European Union (Future Relationship) Act 2020 (References to the Trade and Cooperation Agreement) Regulations 2021 (SI 2021/884) reg.2 and Schedule (July 24, 2021).

General Note

For the text of the Protocol on Social Security Coordination, see para.5.196 below. **5.82**

For discussion of the implications of the more general implementing provisions (s.29), see *Lipton v BA City Flyer Ltd* [2021] EWCA Civ 454 at [77]-[82]. While the general (s.29) may be expected to yield to the specific (s.26), the sections have a similarity of approach and Green L.J.'s observations may be of assistance in the s.26 context.

Retained EU Law (Revocation and Reform) Act 2023

(2023 c.28)

General Note

The *Explanatory Notes* (TSO) state the purpose of the Act as being "to enable the amendment of retained EU law and to remove the special features it has in the UK legal system". This has resulted in extensive changes to the European Union (Withdrawal) Act 2018, where numerous changes in terminology emphasise this theme. The Act contains a miscellany of provisions, not all of which are likely to affect social security. It is important to note that the effects of ss.7A and 7B of the 2018 Act, which give effect respectively to obligations derived from the Withdrawal Agreement (including the Citizens' Rights provisions) and from the EEA EFTA Separation Agreement and Swiss citizens' rights Agreement are left unchanged by this Act. That said, on a more general level, the abolition of the supremacy of EU law (s.3) and of the applicability of general principles of EU law (s.4) are noteworthy. It is further intended to create an environment where courts and tribunals may be more ready to depart from decisions of the CJEU (s.6), although not all the amendments made by that section are in force at the time of writing. An issue which had a high political profile during the passage of the Bill was that of "sunsetting" legislation, but the resulting list of "sunsetted" legislation contains nothing of relevance to social security. The Act also contains wide-ranging powers to restate, revoke, replace and update retained EU law. **5.83**

Arrangement of sections reproduced

Preamble

Schedules are not reproduced. While Sch.1 contains a lengthy list of legislative provisions which are subject to the "sunset" effected by s.1, none of them addresses matters which are the subject of the present volume.

An Act to revoke certain retained EU law; to make provision relating to the interpretation of retained EU law and to its relationship with other law; to make provision relating to powers to modify retained EU law; to enable the restatement, replacement or updating of certain retained EU law; to enable the updating of restatements and replacement provision; to abolish the business impact target; and for connected purposes.

[29th June 2023]

5.84 **Sunset of EU-derived subordinate legislation and retained direct EU legislation**

1.—(1) Legislation listed in Schedule 1 is revoked at the end of 2023, to the extent specified there.

(2) In that Schedule—

(a) Part 1 lists subordinate legislation;

(b) Part 2 lists retained direct EU legislation.

(3) The revocation of an instrument, or a provision of an instrument, by subsection (1) does not affect an amendment made by the instrument or provision to any other enactment.

(4) Subsection (1) does not apply to anything specified in regulations made by a relevant national authority.

(5) No regulations may be made under subsection (4) after 31 October 2023.

General Note

5.85 Regulations under subs.(4) are the Retained EU Law (Revocation and Reform) Act 2023 (Revocation and Sunset Disapplication) Regulations 2023 (SI 2023/1143). As no social security measure is within the sunset, there is no relevant question of disapplication for the purposes of this Volume.

Sunset of retained EU rights, powers, liabilities etc. 5.86

2.—(1) Section 4 of the European Union (Withdrawal) Act 2018 (saving for rights, powers, liabilities etc under section 2(1) of the European Communities Act 1972) is repealed at the end of 2023.

(2) Accordingly, anything which, immediately before the end of 2023, is retained EU law by virtue of that section is not recognised or available in domestic law at or after that time (and, accordingly, is not to be enforced, allowed or followed).

Abolition of supremacy of EU law 5.87

Section 3 makes amendments to other legislation, which are noted there.

Abolition of general principles of EU law 5.88

Section 4 makes amendments to other legislation, which are noted there.

"Assimilated law" 5.89

5.—(1) As regards all times after the end of 2023, the things listed in the left-hand column are to be known by the names in the right-hand column.

At or before the end of 2023	After the end of 2023
Retained EU law	Assimilated law
Retained case law	Assimilated case law
Retained direct EU legislation	Assimilated direct legislation
Retained direct minor EU legislation	Assimilated direct minor legislation
Retained direct principal EU legislation	Assimilated direct principal
Retained domestic case law	Assimilated domestic case law
Retained EU case law	Assimilated EU case law
Retained EU obligation	Assimilated obligation

...

(2) Accordingly, as regards all times at or before the end of 2023, the things listed in the right-hand column continue to be known by the names in the left-hand column.

(3) *The sub-section makes amendments to other legislation which are noted there as appropriate.*

(4) A reference in an enactment to a thing in the left-hand column of the table in subsection (1) is to be read, as regards all times after the end of 2023, as a reference to the thing by its name in the right-hand column.

(5) Subsection (4) does not apply to any title of an enactment (including any provision about how an enactment may be cited) or any reference to a title of an enactment.

(6) The provision that may be made by regulations under section 19 (power to make consequential provision) in consequence of subsection (1) of this section includes, in particular—

(a) provision adding entries to the table in subsection (1) for things which relate to the things for which there are entries in the table (and adding definitions for those things to subsection (7));
(b) provision amending an enactment in consequence of the name of a thing being changed by subsection (1) (including by virtue of regulations under section 19).

(7) In this section—

"retained case law", "retained domestic case law" and "retained EU case law" have the meaning given by section 6(7) of the European Union (Withdrawal) Act 2018 (as it has effect on the day on which this Act is passed);

"retained EU law", "retained direct EU legislation", "retained direct minor EU legislation", "retained direct principal EU legislation" and "retained EU obligation" have the meaning given by Schedule 1 to the Interpretation Act 1978 (as it has effect on the day on which this Act is passed);

...[omitted].

GENERAL NOTE

5.90 Subsection (1) appears to be intended as a declaratory statement: actual amendments to the text of, for instance, the European Union (Withdrawal) Act 2018 to give effect to the change in terminology are made elsewhere e.g. in Sch.2 of this Act. This work only changes the terminology where there has been legislative amendment to do so.

5.91 **Compatibility**

7.—(1) A relevant national authority may by regulations provide that subsection (2) applies (and section 5(A2) of the European Union (Withdrawal) Act 2018 does not apply) to the relationship between—

(a) any domestic enactment specified in the regulations, and
(b) any provision of [[1]assimilated direct] legislation so specified.

(2) Where this subsection applies, the domestic enactment specified under subsection (1)(a)—

(a) must, so far as possible, be read and given effect in a way which is compatible with the provision of [[1]assimilated direct] legislation specified under subsection (1)(b), and
(b) is subject to that provision of [[1]assimilated direct] legislation so far as it is incompatible with it.

(3) Regulations under subsection (1) may make provision by modifying any enactment.

(4) No regulations may be made under subsection (1) after 23 June 2026.

(5) In this section "domestic enactment" has the same meaning as in section 5 of the European Union (Withdrawal) Act 2018.

AMENDMENT

1. REULRRA Sch. 2 para.11 (January 1, 2024).

5.92 **Incompatibility orders**

Section 8 introduces a s.6D to the EU (Withdrawal) Act 2018 and is shown there.

Scope of powers 5.93

Section 9 makes amendments to parts of Schedule 8 to the EU (Withdrawal) Act 2018, in particular as to the scope of regulation-making powers, and of Schedule 3, which are not within the scope of this volume.

Procedural requirements 5.94

With one exception, noted in the text where it occurs, the amendments made by section 10 are outside the scope of this volume.

Power to restate retained EU law 5.95

11.—(1) A relevant national authority may by regulations restate, to any extent, any secondary retained EU law.

(2) In this Act "secondary retained EU law" means—

(a) any retained EU law that is not primary legislation;

(b) any retained EU law that is primary legislation the text of which was inserted by subordinate legislation.

(3) A restatement is not retained EU law.

(4) Any effect which is produced in relation to the thing being restated by virtue of the retained EU law mentioned in subsection (5) does not apply in relation to the restatement.

(5) The retained EU law referred to in subsection (4) is—

(a) the principle of the supremacy of EU law,

(b) retained general principles of EU law, and

(c) anything which is retained EU law by virtue of section or 6(3) or (6) of the European Union (Withdrawal) Act 2018.

(6) But a restatement may, if the relevant authority considers it appropriate, itself produce an effect that is equivalent to an effect referred to in subsection (4).

(7) No regulations may be made under this section after the end of 2023.

(8) In this section—

"restatement": references to restatement, in relation to anything which is retained EU law by virtue of section 4 or 6(3) or (6) of the European Union (Withdrawal) Act 2018, include codification;

"retained general principles of EU law" the meaning given by section 6(7) of the European Union (Withdrawal) Act 2018.

Power to restate assimilated law or reproduce sunsetted retained EU rights, powers, liabilities etc 5.96

12.—(1) A relevant national authority may by regulations restate, to any extent, any secondary assimilated law.

(2) In this Act "secondary assimilated law" means—

(a) any assimilated law that is not primary legislation;

(b) any assimilated law that is primary legislation the text of which was inserted by subordinate legislation.

(3) A restatement is not assimilated law.

(4) Any effect which is produced in relation to the thing being restated by virtue of anything that is assimilated law by virtue of section 6(3) or (6) of the European Union (Withdrawal) Act 2018 does not apply in relation to the restatement.

(5) But a restatement may, if the relevant national authority considers it appropriate, itself produce an effect that is equivalent to an effect referred to in subsection (4).

(6) A restatement may also, if the relevant national authority considers it appropriate, produce an effect that is equivalent to an effect within subsection (7).

(7) An effect is within this subsection if it would, but for sections 2 to 4, be produced in relation to the thing being restated by virtue of—

(a) the principle of the supremacy of EU law,
(b) retained general principles of EU law, or
(c) anything which was retained EU law by virtue of section 4 of the European Union (Withdrawal) Act 2018.

(8) A relevant national authority may by regulations reproduce, to any extent, the effect that anything which was retained EU law by virtue of section 4 or 6(3) or (6) of European Union (Withdrawal) Act 2018 would have, but for sections 2 to 4 of this Act.

(9) No regulations may be made under this section after 23 June 2026.

(10) In this section—

"restatement": references to restatement, in relation to anything which is assimilated law by virtue of section 6(3) or (6) of the European Union (Withdrawal) Act 2018, include codification;

"retained general principles of EU law" has the meaning that was given by section 6(7) of the European Union (Withdrawal) Act 2018 immediately before the end of 2023.

5.97 **Powers to restate or reproduce: general**

13.—(1) This section applies for the purposes of sections 11 and 12.

(2) A restatement may use words or concepts that are different from those used in the law being restated.

(3) A restatement may make any change which the relevant national authority considers appropriate for one or more of the following purposes—

(a) resolving ambiguities;
(b) removing doubts or anomalies;
(c) facilitating improvement in the clarity or accessibility of the law (including by omitting anything which is legally unnecessary).

(4) Regulations under section 11 or 12—

(a) may make provision about the relationship between what is restated and a relevant enactment specified in the regulations, but
(b) subject to that, may not make express provision about the relationship between what is restated and other enactments.

(5) Regulations under section 11 or 12 may not codify or reproduce the principle of the supremacy of EU law or a retained general principle of EU law.

(6) Nothing in subsection (5)—

(a) prevents regulations under section 11 or 12 from codifying or reproducing, in relation to a particular enactment, an effect equivalent to an effect which is produced, or would but for sections 2 to 4 be produced, in relation to the enactment by virtue of the principle of supremacy of EU law or retained general principles of EU law, or
(b) prevents regulations under section 11 or 12 which codify or reproduce anything which is or was retained EU law by virtue of section

4 of the European Union (Withdrawal) Act 2018 from producing an effect equivalent to an effect which is produced, or would but for sections 2 to 4 be produced, in relation to that thing by virtue of the principle of supremacy of EU law or retained general principles of EU law.

(7) The provision that may be made by regulations under section 11 or 12may be made by modifying any enactment.

(8) In sections 11 and 12, references to producing an effect that is equivalent to another effect are to doing so by express provision or otherwise.

(9) In subsection (4)(a) "relevant enactment" means—

(a) if the provision made by the regulations is made by modifying [1assimilated direct] legislation, any [[1]assimilated direct] legislation;

(b) otherwise, any domestic enactment (as defined by section 5 of the European Union (Withdrawal) Act 2018).

(10) In subsections (5) and (6) "retained general principles of EU law" has the same meaning as in section 11 or 12 (as the case may be).

(11) In this section "restatement"—

(a) in relation to section 11, has the same meaning as in that section;

(b) in relation to section 12, has the same meaning as in that section but also includes reproduction;

and similar references are to be read accordingly.

AMENDMENTS

1. REULRRA Sch.2, para.11 (January 1, 2024).

Powers to revoke or replace 5.98

14.—(1) A relevant national authority may by regulations revoke any secondary retained EU law without replacing it.

(2) A relevant national authority may by regulations revoke any secondary retained EU law and replace it with such provision as the relevant national authority considers to be appropriate and to achieve the same or similar objectives.

(3) A relevant national authority may by regulations revoke any secondary retained EU law and make such alternative provision as the relevant national authority considers appropriate.

(4) Regulations under subsection (2) or (3)—

(a) may confer a power to make subordinate legislation that corresponds or is similar to a power to make subordinate legislation conferred by secondary retained EU law revoked by the regulations (and may not otherwise confer a power to make subordinate legislation);

(b) subject to that, may confer functions (including discretions) on any person;

(c) may create a criminal offence that corresponds or is similar to a criminal offence created by secondary retained EU law revoked by the regulations (and may not otherwise create a criminal offence);

(d) may provide for the imposition of monetary penalties in cases that correspond or are similar to cases in which secondary retained EU law revoked by the regulations enables monetary penalties to be imposed (and may not otherwise provide for the imposition of monetary penalties);

(e) may provide for the charging of fees;
(f) may not—
(i) impose taxation;
(ii) establish a public authority.

(5) No provision may be made by a relevant national authority under this section in relation to a particular subject area unless the relevant national authority considers that the overall effect of the changes made by it under this section (including changes made previously) in relation to that subject area does not increase the regulatory burden.

(6) For the purposes of subsection (5), the creation of a voluntary scheme is not to be regarded as increasing the regulatory burden.

(7) The provision that may be made by regulations under this section may be made by modifying any secondary retained EU law.

(8) Any provision made by virtue of this section is not retained EU law.

(9) No regulations may be made under this section after 23 June 2026.

(10) In this section—

"burden" includes (among other things)—
(a) a financial cost;
(b) an administrative inconvenience;
(c) an obstacle to trade or innovation;
(d) an obstacle to efficiency, productivity or profitability;
(e) a sanction (criminal or otherwise) which affects the carrying on of any lawful activity;

"revoke"—
(a) includes repeal, and
(b) in relation to anything which is retained EU law by virtue of section 4 of the European Union (Withdrawal) Act 2018, means provide that it is not recognised or available in domestic law (and, accordingly, not to be enforced, allowed or followed);

"secondary retained EU law": references to secondary retained EU law are to be read after the end of 2023 as references to secondary assimilated law.

(11) In subsection (8) the reference to retained EU law is to be read after the end of 2023 as a reference to assimilated law.

General Note

5.99 Relevant Regulations made under this section are the Retained EU Law (Revocation and Reform) Act 2023 (Revocation and Sunset Disapplication) Regulations 2023 (SI 2023/1143). The Regulations, seemingly by way of tidying up, revoke the Immigration (European Economic Area) and Accession (Amendment) Regulations 2004 (SI 2004/1236), the Accession (Immigration and Worker Authorisation) (Amendment) Regulations 2007 (SI 2007/475) and the Accession (Worker Authorisation and Worker Registration) (Amendment) Regulations 2009 (SI 2009/2426).

5.100 **Power to update**

15.—(1) A relevant national authority may by regulations make such modifications of any secondary retained EU law, or of any provision made by virtue of section 11, 12 or 14, as the relevant national authority considers appropriate to take account of—
(a) changes in technology, or
(b) developments in scientific understanding.

(2) In subsection (1), the reference to secondary retained EU law is to be read after the end of 2023 as a reference to secondary assimilated law.

Sections 16–18: omitted **5.101**

Consequential provision **5.102**

19.—(1) A relevant national authority may by regulations make such provision as the relevant national authority considers appropriate in consequence of this Act.

(2) The provision referred to in subsection (1) includes provision modifying any enactment, including this Act.

General Note

Regulations made under this section are the Retained EU Law (Revocation and Reform) Act 2023 (Consequential Amendment) Regulations (SI 2023/1424). Amendments made by these regulations are noted in the text where relevant. **5.103**

Regulations: general **5.104**

20.—(1) A power to make regulations under this Act includes power to make—

(a) different provision for different purposes or areas;

(b) supplementary, incidental, consequential, transitional, transitory or saving provision (including provision modifying any enactment, including this Act).

(2) Schedule 4 contains restrictions on the powers of devolved authorities to make regulations under this Act.

(3) Schedule 5 contains provision about the procedure for making regulations under this Act.

(4) A prohibition in this Act on making regulations after any particular time does not affect the continuation in force of regulations made before that time.

(5) ... *[omitted]*.

[Schedules 4 and 5 are not reproduced for reasons of space.]

Interpretation **5.105**

21.—(1) In this Act—

"assimilated law" has the meaning given by section 5(1);

"devolved authority" means—

(a) the Scottish Ministers,

(b) the Welsh Ministers, or

(c) a Northern Ireland department;

"domestic law" means the law of England and Wales, Scotland or Northern Ireland;

"enactment" means—

(a) an enactment (whenever passed or made) contained in, or in an instrument made under, any primary legislation, or

(b) any [[1]assimilated direct] legislation;

"Minister of the Crown" has the same meaning as in the Ministers of the Crown Act 1975 and also includes the Commissioners for His Majesty's Revenue and Customs;

"modify" includes amend, repeal or revoke (and related expressions are to be read accordingly);

"Northern Ireland devolved authority" means—

(a) the First Minister and deputy First Minister acting jointly,

(b) a Northern Ireland Minister, or

(c) a Northern Ireland department;

"primary legislation" means—

(a) an Act of Parliament,

(b) an Act of the Scottish Parliament,

(c) an Act or Measure of Senedd Cymru, or

(d) Northern Ireland legislation;

"relevant national authority" means—

(a) a Minister of the Crown,

(b) a devolved authority, or

(c) a Minister of the Crown acting jointly with one or more devolved authorities;

"secondary assimilated law" has the meaning given by section 12(2);

"secondary retained EU law" has the meaning given by section 11(2);

"subordinate legislation" means—

(a) an instrument (other than an instrument that is Northern Ireland legislation) made under any primary legislation, or

(b) an instrument made on or after IP completion day under any [1assimilated direct] legislation.

(2) In this Act—

(a) references to an instrument made under an Act include in particular any Order in Council, order, rules, regulations, scheme, warrant or byelaw made under an Act;

(b) references to an instrument made under any [1assimialated direct] legislation include in particular any Order in Council, order, rules, regulations, scheme, warrant or byelaw made under any [1assimilated direct] legislation.

(3) In this Act references to anything which is retained EU law by virtue of section 4 of the European Union (Withdrawal) Act 2018 include references to any modifications, made on or after IP completion day, of the rights, powers, liabilities, obligations, restrictions, remedies or procedures concerned.

AMENDMENTS

1. REULRRA Sch.2, para.11 (January 1, 2024).

5.106 **Commencement, transitional and savings**

22.—(1) The following provisions come into force on the day on which this Act is passed—

(a) sections 1 and 2;

(b) section 5(1), (2) and (4) to (7);

(c) section 7;

(d) sections 9 to 17 and Schedule 3;

(e) sections 19 to 21, this section, section 23 and Schedules 4 and 5.

(2) Section 18 comes into force at the end of the period of two months beginning with the day on which this Act is passed.

(3) The other provisions of this Act come into force on such day as a Minister of the Crown may by regulations appoint.

(4) A relevant national authority may by regulations make such transitional, transitory or saving provision as the relevant national authority considers appropriate in connection with—

(a) the coming into force of any provision of this Act,

(b) the revocation of anything by section 1, or

(c) anything ceasing to be recognised or available in domestic law (and, accordingly, ceasing to be enforced, allowed or followed) as a result of section 2.

(5) Sections 2, 3 and 4 do not apply in relation to anything occurring before the end of 2023.

(6) The amendments made by Schedule 2 do not apply as regards any time at or before the end of 2023.

Extent and short title 5.107

23.—(1) Subject to subsection (2), this Act extends to England and Wales, Scotland and Northern Ireland.

(2) Any amendment, repeal or revocation made by this Act has the same extent within the United Kingdom as the provision to which it relates.

(3) This Act may be cited as the Retained EU Law (Revocation and Reform) Act 2023.

The Cessation of EU Law Relating to Prohibitions on Grounds of Nationality and Free Movement of Persons Regulations 2022

SI 2022/1240
Made 28th November 2022

The Secretary of State, in exercise of the powers conferred by section 8(1) of, and paragraph 21 of Schedule 7 to, the European Union (Withdrawal) Act 2018 makes the following Regulations.

In accordance with paragraph 1(3) of Schedule 7 to that Act, a draft of this instrument has been laid before Parliament and approved by a resolution of each House of Parliament.

1.—Citation, commencement and interpretation 5.108

(1) These Regulations may be cited as the Cessation of EU Law Relating to Prohibitions on Grounds of Nationality and Free Movement of Persons Regulations 2022.

(2) These Regulations come into force on the day after the day on which they are made.

(3) In these Regulations, "relevant matters" are the matters set out in the Schedule.

(4) Nothing in these Regulations is to be construed as implying in any respect the continued application, recognition or availability in domestic law of—

(a) the prohibitions ref erred to in regulation 2;

(b) the rights, powers, liabilities, obligations, restrictions, remedies and procedures referred to in regulation 3; or

(c) Article 7(2) of Regulation (EU) No 492/2011 of the European Parliament and of the Council of 5th April 2011 on freedom of movement for workers within the Union.

5.109 **2. Cessation of prohibitions on grounds of nationality**

The prohibitions on the grounds of nationality which—

(a) continue by virtue of section 4(1) of the European Union (Withdrawal) Act 2018; and

(b) are derived from—

(i) Article 18 of the Treaty on the Functioning of the European Union;

(ii) Article 4 of the EEA Agreement; and

(iii) Article 2 of the Agreement between the European Community and its Member States and the Swiss Confederation on the free movement of persons signed at Brussels on 21st June 1999,

so far as they relate to relevant matters, cease to be recognised and available in domestic law (and to be enforced, allowed and followed accordingly).

5.110 **3. Cessation of free movement of persons**

Any rights, powers, liabilities, obligations, restrictions, remedies and procedures which—

(a) continue by virtue of section 4(1) of the European Union (Withdrawal) Act 2018; and

(b) are derived (directly or indirectly) from—

(i) Article 21 or 45 of the Treaty on the Functioning of the European Union;

(ii) Article 28 or 29 of the EEA Agreement; or

(iii) Articles 3(6), 9(2), (3) and (6), and 15 of Annex 1 to the Agreement between the European Community and its Member States and the Swiss Confederation on the free movement of persons signed at Brussels on 21st June 1999,

so far as they relate to relevant matters, cease to be recognised and available in domestic law (and to be enforced, allowed and followed accordingly).

5.111 **4. Amendment of Regulation (EU) No 492/2011**

(1) Regulation (EU) No 492/2011 of the European Parliament and of the Council of 5th April 2011 on freedom of movement for workers within the Union is amended as follows.

(2) In Article 7—

(a) after paragraph 2, insert—

"2A.

Paragraphs 1 and 2 do not apply in relation to the matters set out in the Schedule to the Cessation of EU Law Relating to Prohibitions on Grounds of Nationality and Free Movement of Persons Regulations 2022 (relevant matters).";

(b) omit paragraph 3.

(3) Omit Articles 9 and 10.

Signed by authority of the Secretary of State for Work and Pensions
Guy Opperman
Minister of State Department for Work and Pensions
28th November 2022

SCHEDULE

RELEVANT MATTERS

1.—Social security and statutory payments 5.112

(1) Social security, including—

(a) any scheme providing financial assistance to or in respect of individuals, in particular providing such assistance to or in respect of individuals—
   (i) who qualify by reason of old age, survivorship, bereavement, disability, sickness, incapacity, injury, unemployment, maternity, paternity, the care they provide to other individuals or having responsibility for other individuals;
   (ii) who qualify by reason of low income; or
   (iii) in relation to their housing costs; and

(b) tax credits under Part 1 of the Tax Credits Act 2002.

(2) The following payments under the following Parts of the Social Security Contributions and Benefits Act 1992—

(a) statutory adoption pay under Part 12ZB;
(b) statutory maternity pay under Part 12;
(c) statutory parental bereavement pay under Part 12ZD;
(d) statutory paternity pay under Part 12ZA;
(e) statutory shared parental pay under Part 12ZC; and
(f) statutory sick pay under Part 11.

(3) Sub-paragraph (2) is without prejudice to sub-paragraph (1).

2.—Social assistance 5.113

(1) Social assistance, within the meaning of Directive 2004/38/EC of the European Parliament and of the Council of 29th April 2004 on the right of citizens of the Union and their family members to move and reside freely within the territory of the Member States ("the Directive").

(2) The reference in subparagraph (1) to the Directive includes a reference to the case law of the Court of Justice of the European Union which interprets the concept of social assistance.

3.—Housing 5.114

(1) Housing, including—

(a) any accommodation provided to homeless persons; and
(b) mobile homes.

(2) "Mobile home" means caravan, motor vehicle, boat or other movable structure designed or adapted for human habitation, but does not include—

(a) any railway rolling stock which is for the time being on rails forming part of a railway system; or
(b) any tent.

4. Education, training and apprenticeships 5.115

Education, training and apprenticeships, including—

(a) social and physical training (including the promotion of the development of young children);

(b) vocational training (including that which helps people prepare for, obtain and retain employment);
(c) the charging of fees in connection with education and training; and
(d) the provision of financial assistance or financial resources in connection with education, training or apprenticeships.

5.116 **5.—Childcare, employer-supported childcare and the childcare payment scheme, etc.**

(1) Childcare, including—
(a) the provision of childcare free of charge; and
(b) the provision of financial assistance or financial resources in connection with the provision of childcare, including—
(i) childcare vouchers, within the meaning given in section 84 of the Income Tax (Earnings and Pensions) Act 2003 ("the 2003 Act"), or a scheme to which section 270A of that Act applies;
(ii) a scheme to which section 318 of the 2003 Act applies (employer-provided childcare);
(iii) a scheme to which section 318A of the 2003 Act applies (employer-contracted childcare);
(iv) a scheme under section 1 of the Childcare Payments Act 2014 (childcare payment scheme).

(2) "Childcare", for the purposes of this paragraph, means any form of care for a child but does not include—
(a) any form of health care for a child;
(b) care provided for a child if the care—
(i) is provided in any of the following establishments as part of the establishment's activities—
(aa) a children's home;
(bb) a care home;
(cc) a hospital in which the child is a patient;
(dd) a residential family centre; and
(ii) is so provided by the person carrying on the establishment or a person employed by the establishment (including a person who is employed under a contract of services); or
(c) care provided for a child who is detained in—
(i) a young offender institution;
(ii) a secure training college; or
(iii) a secure college.

(3) In this paragraph—

"care home", "children's home" and "residential family centre" have the same meaning as in the Care Standards Act 2000;

"child" means a person under the age of 18, except for the purposes of sub-paragraph (1)(b)(i) to (iv);

"hospital" has the meaning given by section 275 of the National Health Service Act 2006.

Extracts from the Agreement on the withdrawal of the United Kingdom of Great Britain and Northern Ireland from the European Union and the European Atomic Energy Community

(The full text may be found in OJ 2019/C 3841/01 or at *https://www.legislation.gov.uk/eut/withdrawal-agreement/contents/adopted* [Accessed May 7, 2024]

As to the approach to be adopted in interpreting the Withdrawal Agreement, see *R. (on the application of Independent Monitoring Authority for the Citizens' Rights Agreements) v Secretary of State for the Home Department* [2022] EWHC 3274 (Admin) at [64]: **5.117**

> "This claim is about the interpretation of the WA. The WA is an international treaty. As such, the relevant interpretative principles are those contained in the Vienna Convention on the Law of Treaties 1969; in particular, Articles 31 (general rule of interpretation) and 32 (supplementary means of interpretation). Article 31(1) provides that a treaty is to be interpreted in good faith in accordance with the ordinary meaning to be given to the terms of the treaty, in their context and in the light of the treaty's object and purpose. That is an essentially objective exercise."

The approach is amplified at [131]:

> "Article 4(3) of the WA provides that 'the provisions of this Agreement referring to Union law or to concepts or provisions thereof shall be interpreted and applied in accordance with the methods and general principles of Union law'. To that extent, the fact that the United Kingdom has left the EU does not mean EU legal concepts must be ignored; indeed, the contrary is the case. Otherwise, however, EU legal concepts such as free movement are not to be imported into, or inferred from, the WA, except insofar as that may be necessary in order to comply with the general rule of interpretation in Article 31 of the Vienna Convention."

Preamble

THE EUROPEAN UNION ... AND THE UNITED KINGDOM OF GREAT BRITAIN AND NORTHERN IRELAND, **5.118**

CONSIDERING that on 29 March 2017 the United Kingdom of Great Britain and Northern Ireland ("United Kingdom"), following the outcome of a referendum held in the United Kingdom and its sovereign decision to leave the European Union, notified its intention to withdraw from the European Union ("Union") ... in accordance with Article 50 of the Treaty on European Union ("TEU"), ...,

WISHING to set out the arrangements for the withdrawal of the United Kingdom from the Union ..., taking account of the framework for their future relationship,

Extracts from the Agreement on the withdrawal of the United Kingdom

NOTING the guidelines of 29 April and 15 December 2017 and of 23 March 2018 provided by the European Council in the light of which the Union is to conclude the Agreement setting out the arrangements for the withdrawal of the United Kingdom from the Union ...,

RECALLING that, pursuant to Article 50 TEU, … , and subject to the arrangements laid down in this Agreement, the law of the Union … in its entirety ceases to apply to the United Kingdom from the date of entry into force of this Agreement,

STRESSING that the objective of this Agreement is to ensure an orderly withdrawal of the United Kingdom from the Union … ,

RECOGNISING that it is necessary to provide reciprocal protection for Union citizens and for United Kingdom nationals, as well as their respective family members, where they have exercised free movement rights before a date set in this Agreement, and to ensure that their rights under this Agreement are enforceable and based on the principle of non-discrimination; recognising also that rights deriving from periods of social security insurance should be protected,

RESOLVED to ensure an orderly withdrawal through various separation provisions aiming to prevent disruption and to provide legal certainty to citizens and economic operators as well as to judicial and administrative authorities in the Union and in the United Kingdom, while not excluding the possibility of relevant separation provisions being superseded by the agreement(s) on the future relationship,

CONSIDERING that it is in the interest of both the Union and the United Kingdom to determine a transition or implementation period during which—notwithstanding all consequences of the United Kingdom's withdrawal from the Union as regards the United Kingdom's participation in the institutions, bodies, offices and agencies of the Union, in particular the end, on the date of entry into force of this Agreement, of the mandates of all members of institutions, bodies and agencies of the Union nominated, appointed or elected in relation to the United Kingdom's membership of the Union—Union law, including international agreements, should be applicable to and in the United Kingdom, and, as a general rule, with the same effect as regards the Member States, in order to avoid disruption in the period during which the agreement(s) on the future relationship will be negotiated,

RECOGNISING that, even if Union law will be applicable to and in the United Kingdom during the transition period, the specificities of the United Kingdom as a State having withdrawn from the Union mean that it will be important for the United Kingdom to be able to take steps to prepare and establish new international arrangements of its own, including in areas of Union exclusive competence, provided such agreements do not enter into force or apply during that period, unless so authorised by the Union,

…

CONSIDERING that in order to guarantee the correct interpretation and application of this Agreement and compliance with the obligations under this Agreement, it is essential to establish provisions ensuring overall governance, in particular binding dispute-settlement and enforcement rules that fully respect the autonomy of the respective legal orders of the Union and of the United Kingdom as well as the United Kingdom's status as a third country,

…

UNDERLINING that this Agreement is founded on an overall balance of benefits, rights and obligations for the Union and the United Kingdom,

NOTING that in parallel with this Agreement, the Parties have made a Political Declaration setting out the framework for the future relationship between the European Union and the United Kingdom of Great Britain and Northern Ireland,

CONSIDERING that there is a need for both the United Kingdom and the Union to take all necessary steps to begin as soon as possible from the date of entry into force of this Agreement, the formal negotiations of one or several agreements governing their future relationship with a view to ensuring that, to the extent possible, those agreements apply from the end of the transition period,

HAVE AGREED AS FOLLOWS:

Part One

Common Provisions

Article 1

Objective

This Agreement sets out the arrangements for the withdrawal of the United Kingdom of Great Britain and Northern Ireland ("United Kingdom") from the European Union ("Union") … . 5.119

Article 2

Definitions

For the purposes of this Agreement, the following definitions shall apply: 5.120

(a) "Union law" means:
  (i) the Treaty on European Union ("TEU"), the Treaty on the Functioning of the European Union ("TFEU") and the Treaty establishing the European Atomic Energy Community ("Euratom Treaty"), as amended or supplemented, as well as the Treaties of Accession and the Charter of Fundamental Rights of the European Union, together referred to as "the Treaties";
  (ii) the general principles of the Union's law;
  (iii) the acts adopted by the institutions, bodies, offices or agencies of the Union;
  (iv) the international agreements to which the Union is party and the international agreements concluded by the Member States acting on behalf of the Union;
  (v) the agreements between Member States entered into in their capacity as Member States of the Union;
  (vi) acts of the Representatives of the Governments of the Member States meeting within the European Council or the Council of the European Union ("Council");
  (vii) the declarations made in the context of intergovernmental conferences which adopted the Treaties;

(b) "Member States" means the Kingdom of Belgium, the Republic of Bulgaria, the Czech Republic, the Kingdom of Denmark, the Federal Republic of Germany, the Republic of Estonia, Ireland, the Hellenic

Republic, the Kingdom of Spain, the French Republic, the Republic of Croatia, the Italian Republic, the Republic of Cyprus, the Republic of Latvia, the Republic of Lithuania, the Grand Duchy of Luxembourg, Hungary, the Republic of Malta, the Kingdom of the Netherlands, the Republic of Austria, the Republic of Poland, the Portuguese Republic, Romania, the Republic of Slovenia, the Slovak Republic, the Republic of Finland and the Kingdom of Sweden;

(c) "Union citizen" means any person holding the nationality of a Member State;

(d) "United Kingdom national" means a national of the United Kingdom, as defined in the New Declaration by the Government of the United Kingdom of Great Britain and Northern Ireland of 31 December 1982 on the definition of the term "nationals" together with Declaration No 63 annexed to the Final Act of the intergovernmental conference which adopted the Treaty of Lisbon;

(e) "transition period" means the period provided in Article 126;

(f) "day" means a calendar day, unless otherwise provided in this Agreement or in provisions of Union law made applicable by this Agreement.

Article 3

Territorial scope

5.121 1. Unless otherwise provided in this Agreement or in Union law made applicable by this Agreement, any reference in this Agreement to the United Kingdom or its territory shall be understood as referring to: (a) the United Kingdom; (b) Gibraltar, to the extent that Union law was applicable to it before the date of entry into force of this Agreement; (c) the Channel Islands and the Isle of Man, to the extent that Union law was applicable to them before the date of entry into force of this Agreement; (d) the Sovereign Base Areas of Akrotiri and Dhekelia in Cyprus, to the extent necessary to ensure the implementation of the arrangements set out in the Protocol on the Sovereign Base Areas of the United Kingdom of Great Britain and Northern Ireland in Cyprus annexed to the Act concerning the conditions of accession of the Czech Republic, the Republic of Estonia, the Republic of Cyprus, the Republic of Latvia, the Republic of Lithuania, the Republic of Hungary, the Republic of Malta, the Republic of Poland, the Republic of Slovenia and the Slovak Republic to the European Union; (e) the overseas countries and territories listed in Annex II to the TFEU having special relations with the United Kingdom, where the provisions of this Agreement relate to the special arrangements for the association of the overseas countries and territories with the Union.

2. Unless otherwise provided in this Agreement or in Union law made applicable by this Agreement, any reference in this Agreement to Member States, or their territory, shall be understood as covering the territories of the Member States to which the Treaties apply as provided in Article 355 TFEU.

Article 4

Methods and principles relating to the effect, the implementation and the application of this Agreement

1. The provisions of this Agreement and the provisions of Union law made applicable by this Agreement shall produce in respect of and in the United Kingdom the same legal effects as those which they produce within the Union and its Member States. Accordingly, legal or natural persons shall in particular be able to rely directly on the provisions contained or referred to in this Agreement which meet the conditions for direct effect under Union law. **5.122**

2. The United Kingdom shall ensure compliance with paragraph 1, including as regards the required powers of its judicial and administrative authorities to disapply inconsistent or incompatible domestic provisions, through domestic primary legislation.

3. The provisions of this Agreement referring to Union law or to concepts or provisions thereof shall be interpreted and applied in accordance with the methods and general principles of Union law.

4. The provisions of this Agreement referring to Union law or to concepts or provisions thereof shall in their implementation and application be interpreted in conformity with the relevant case law of the Court of Justice of the European Union handed down before the end of the transition period.

5. In the interpretation and application of this Agreement, the United Kingdom's judicial and administrative authorities shall have due regard to relevant case law of the Court of Justice of the European Union handed down after the end of the transition period.

General Note

Art.4(1) applies in relation to the Withdrawal Agreement the concept of direct effect familiar from EU law. It refers to the content of a rule and describes its capacity to give rise to rights for individuals which they can plead before national courts, and which national courts must recognise. Just as it is the case that not every provision of national law gives rise to rights for individuals, so too it is the case that not every provision of European Union law (nor of the Withdrawal Agreement) gives rise to direct effect. It is necessary to consider the scope and wording of any provision in order to determine whether it is capable of giving rise to direct effect. the requirements for direct effect are that the rule in question is sufficiently clear and precise and is unconditional. **5.123**

The "domestic primary legislation" which the UK is required by art.4(2) to put in place to ensure compliance with art.4(1) is European Union (Withdrawal) Act 2018, s.7A.

As the definition of "Union law" in art.2 includes the Charter, it was among the "methods and general principles of Union law" for the purposes of art.4(3) Accordingly, the "methods" in accordance with which the provisions of the Withdrawal Agreement were to be interpreted and applied include those of the Charter (*SSWP v AT* [2022] UKUT 330 at [105]); *CG* had established that the UK was implementing or acting in the scope of EU law (art.21 TFEU) when it had granted CG a domestic law right of residence (Pre-settled status) and the same applied to AT: *SSWP v AT* at [106]. The Court of Appeal took a generally similar approach in dismissing the Secretary of State's appeal: [2023] EWCA Civ 1307.

Article 5

Good faith

5.124 The Union and the United Kingdom shall, in full mutual respect and good faith, assist each other in carrying out tasks which flow from this Agreement. They shall take all appropriate measures, whether general or particular, to ensure fulfilment of the obligations arising from this Agreement and shall refrain from any measures which could jeopardise the attainment of the objectives of this Agreement. This Article is without prejudice to the application of Union law pursuant to this Agreement, in particular the principle of sincere cooperation.

Article 6

References to Union law

5.125 1. With the exception of Parts Four and Five, unless otherwise provided in this Agreement all references in this Agreement to Union law shall be understood as references to Union law, including as amended or replaced, as applicable on the last day of the transition period.

2. Where in this Agreement reference is made to Union acts or provisions thereof, such reference shall, where relevant, be understood to include a reference to Union law or provisions thereof that, although replaced or superseded by the act referred to, continue to apply in accordance with that act.

3. For the purposes of this Agreement, references to provisions of Union law made applicable by this Agreement shall be understood to include references to the relevant Union acts supplementing or implementing those provisions.

Article 7

References to the Union and to Member States

5.126 1. For the purposes of this Agreement, all references to Member States and competent authorities of Member States in provisions of Union law made applicable by this Agreement shall be understood as including the United Kingdom and its competent authorities, except as regards: (a) the nomination, appointment or election of members of the institutions, bodies, offices and agencies of the Union, as well as the participation in the decision-making and the attendance in the meetings of the institutions; (b) the participation in the decision-making and governance of the bodies, offices and agencies of the Union; (c) the attendance in the meetings of the committees referred to in Article 3(2) of Regulation (EU) No 182/2011 of the European Parliament and of the Council, of Commission expert groups or of other similar entities, or in the meetings of expert groups or similar entities of bodies, offices and agencies of the Union, unless otherwise provided in this Agreement.

2. …

Article 8

Access to networks, information systems and databases

Unless otherwise provided in this Agreement, at the end of the transition period the United Kingdom shall cease to be entitled to access any network, any information system and any database established on the basis of Union law. The United Kingdom shall take appropriate measures to ensure that it does not access a network, information system or database which it is no longer entitled to access. **5.127**

General Note

By way of derogation, art.34 provides for the United Kingdom to take part in the Electronic Exchange of Social Security Information (EESSI). **5.128**

Part Two

Citizens' Rights

General Note

Following the end of the implementation/transition period for the Withdrawal Agreement on 31 December 2020, Part Two is now in force. In general terms it provides for continuing rights to reside for those who exercised rights of free movement before the end of the transition period and their families on a basis which, though not identical to that of Directive 2004/38/EC, has many references to it. In respect of people within the scope of Part Two, provision is made for ongoing equal treatment and for the continuance of rights under Regulation (EU) No 492/2011. **5.129**

Title III of Part Two (arts 30–36) makes provision for the ongoing application of Regulations (EC) No 883/2004 and (EC) No 987/2009 to the persons covered by the Title, namely United Kingdom nationals who at the end of the transition period are subject to the legislation of a Member State or who reside in a Member State and are subject to the legislation of the United Kingdom and (in each case) their family members and survivors; and vice versa in respect of Union Citizens. Title III also makes provision for those who, though not falling within the above, have accumulated rights in the United Kingdom and a Member State as the result of previous periods of activity in the Member State. The United Kingdom has the status of observer in the Administrative Commission, whose decisions listed in Annex I to the Withdrawal Agreement continue to apply.

Art.4 of the Withdrawal Agreement envisages that the Citizens' Rights provisions will produce the same effects in the United Kingdom as in the Member States. References to Union law are to be interpreted in conformity with the caselaw of the CJEU handed down before the end of the transition period. In respect of caselaw handed down thereafter, the UK's judicial and administrative authorities are to have "due regard" to it (art.4(5)). Considerations of space preclude including the various items of EU legislation and the commentary on them, for which reference should be made to the 2020-21 edition of this work. However, each is the subject of a note below updating the relevant commentary.

Art.158 provides the opportunity for courts and tribunals in the United Kingdom to request the CJEU to give a preliminary ruling concerning the interpretation of Part Two in cases which commence at first instance within (in general) 8 years of the transition period. Art.159 provides for the creation of an independent authority in the United Kingdom to monitor the implementation and application of Part Two. The text of arts 158 and 159 follows the text of Part Two below. **5.130**

Detailed Guidance to staff on the application of Part Two, prepared jointly by the DWP, HMRC and the Department of Health and Social Care may be found at *https://www.gov.uk/government/publications/social-security-arrangements-between-the-uk-and-the-eu-from-1-january-2021-staff-guide* (accessed May 5, 2024).

Monitoring of the implementation and application of Part Two is the responsibility of the Independent Monitoring Authority (IMA) under art.159. In the courts, a Practice Direction requires notice of proceedings to be given to the IMA.

Practice Direction – claims relating to EU and EEA EFTA citizens' rights under part 2 of the Withdrawal Agreement and part 2 of the EEA EFTA separation agreement

Introduction

1.1 The international treaties governing the United Kingdom's withdrawal from the European Union (the Withdrawal Agreement and the EEA EFTA Separation Agreement), provide for certain rights including— (a) residency rights, (b) the right to work and be self-employed, (c) recognition of certain professional qualifications, (d) the right to co-ordination of social security, and (e) rights of non-discrimination on the grounds of nationality and equal treatment.

Scope and Interpretation

1.2 This Practice Direction applies to any proceedings in which a citizens' rights issue arises.

1.3 A 'citizens' rights issue' is an issue relating to rights arising under— (a) Part 2 of the Withdrawal Agreement; or (b) Part 2 of the EEA EFTA Separation Agreement.

Notice of proceedings

2.1 When a party serves a statement of case which raises a citizens' rights issue, that party must send a copy of the statement of case to the IMA at the same time.

2.2 Notice under paragraph 2.1 should be sent either – (a) by email; or (b) in hard copy to—The Independent Monitoring Authority for the Citizens' Rights Agreements, 3rd Floor, Civic Centre, Oystermouth Road, Swansea SA1 3SN.

2.3 In the event of non-compliance with paragraphs 2.1 and 2.2—(a) the court will consider whether any order should be made or any step taken; but (b) any such order or step must not involve any sanction (including any stay, dismissal or striking out) or costs penalty or other costs order against the relevant or other party.

While the Civil Procedure Rules (and so Practice Directions associated with them) do not apply to the tribunals and there is no equivalent Practice Direction for tribunals at the time of writing, it would be open to a tribunal to serve the IMA so as to provide it with an opportunity to apply to be joined if it so wished.

TITLE I

GENERAL PROVISIONS

Article 9

5.131 **Definitions**

For the purposes of this Part, and without prejudice to Title III, the following definitions shall apply:

(a) "family members" means the following persons, irrespective of their nationality, who fall within the personal scope provided for in Article 10 of this Agreement:
   (i) family members of Union citizens or family members of United Kingdom nationals as defined in point (2) of Article 2 of Directive 2004/38/EC of the European Parliament and of the Council;
   (ii) persons other than those defined in Article 3(2) of Directive 2004/38/EC whose presence is required by Union citizens or United Kingdom nationals in order not to deprive those Union citizens or United Kingdom nationals of a right of residence granted by this Part;
(b) "frontier workers" means Union citizens or United Kingdom nationals who pursue an economic activity in accordance with Article 45 or 49 TFEU in one or more States in which they do not reside;
(c) "host State" means:
   (i) in respect of Union citizens and their family members, the United Kingdom, if they exercised their right of residence there in accordance with Union law before the end of the transition period and continue to reside there thereafter;
   (ii) in respect of United Kingdom nationals and their family members, the Member State in which they exercised their right of residence in accordance with Union law before the end of the transition period and in which they continue to reside thereafter;
(d) "State of work" means:
   (i) in respect of Union citizens, the United Kingdom, if they pursued an economic activity as frontier workers there before the end of the transition period and continue to do so thereafter;
   (ii) in respect of United Kingdom nationals, a Member State in which they pursued an economic activity as frontier workers before the end of the transition period and in which they continue to do so thereafter;
(e) "rights of custody" means rights of custody within the meaning of point (9) of Article 2 of Council Regulation (EC) No 2201/2003, including rights of custody acquired by judgment, by operation of law or by an agreement having legal effect.

General Note

Council Regulation (EC) No 2201/2003 of 27 November 2003 concerning jurisdiction and the recognition and enforcement of judgments in matrimonial matters and the matters of parental responsibility, available at *https://eur-lex.europa.eu/legal-content/EN/TXT/?uri=celex%3A32003R2201* (Accessed May 1, 2023). **5.132**

Article 10

Personal scope

1. Without prejudice to Title III, this Part shall apply to the following persons: **5.133**
(a) Union citizens who exercised their right to reside in the United Kingdom in accordance with Union law before the end of the transition period and continue to reside there thereafter;

(b) United Kingdom nationals who exercised their right to reside in a Member State in accordance with Union law before the end of the transition period and continue to reside there thereafter;

(c) Union citizens who exercised their right as frontier workers in the United Kingdom in accordance with Union law before the end of the transition period and continue to do so thereafter;

(d) United Kingdom nationals who exercised their right as frontier workers in one or more Member States in accordance with Union law before the end of the transition period and continue to do so thereafter;

(e) family members of the persons referred to in points (a) to (d), provided that they fulfil one of the following conditions:

(i) they resided in the host State in accordance with Union law before the end of the transition period and continue to reside there thereafter;

(ii) they were directly related to a person referred to in points (a) to (d) and resided outside the host State before the end of the transition period, provided that they fulfil the conditions set out in point (2) of Article 2 of Directive 2004/38/EC at the time they seek residence under this Part in order to join the person referred to in points (a) to (d) of this paragraph;

(iii) they were born to, or legally adopted by, persons referred to in points (a) to (d) after the end of the transition period, whether inside or outside the host State, and fulfil the conditions set out in point (2)(c) of Article 2 of Directive 2004/38/EC at the time they seek residence under this Part in order to join the person referred to in points (a) to (d) of this paragraph and fulfil one of the following conditions:

– both parents are persons referred to in points (a) to (d);

– one parent is a person referred to in points (a) to (d) and the other is a national of the host State; or

– one parent is a person referred to in points (a) to (d) and has sole or joint rights of custody of the child, in accordance with the applicable rules of family law of a Member State or of the United Kingdom, including applicable rules of private international law under which rights of custody established under the law of a third State are recognised in the Member State or in the United Kingdom, in particular as regards the best interests of the child, and without prejudice to the normal operation of such applicable rules of private international law;

(f) family members who resided in the host State in accordance with Articles 12 and 13, Article 16(2) and Articles 17 and 18 of Directive 2004/38/EC before the end of the transition period and continue to reside there thereafter.

2. Persons falling under points (a) and (b) of Article 3(2) of Directive 2004/38/EC whose residence was facilitated by the host State in accordance with its national legislation before the end of the transition period in accordance with Article 3(2) of that Directive shall retain their right of residence in the host State in accordance with this Part, provided that they continue to reside in the host State thereafter. The notion of rights of custody is to be interpreted in accordance with point (9) of Article 2 of Regulation (EC) No 2201/2003. Therefore, it covers rights of custody acquired by judgment, by operation of law or by an agreement having legal effect.

3. Paragraph 2 shall also apply to persons falling under points (a) and (b) of Article 3(2) of Directive 2004/38/EC who have applied for facilitation of entry and residence before the end of the transition period, and whose residence is being facilitated by the host State in accordance with its national legislation thereafter.

4. Without prejudice to any right to residence which the persons concerned may have in their own right, the host State shall, in accordance with its national legislation and in accordance with point (b) of Article 3(2) of Directive 2004/38/EC, facilitate entry and residence for the partner with whom the person referred to in points (a) to (d) of paragraph 1 of this Article has a durable relationship, duly attested, where that partner resided outside the host State before the end of the transition period, provided that the relationship was durable before the end of the transition period and continues at the time the partner seeks residence under this Part.

5. In the cases referred to in paragraphs 3 and 4, the host State shall undertake an extensive examination of the personal circumstances of the persons concerned and shall justify any denial of entry or residence to such persons.

General Note

ADM Memo 19/21 and DMG Memo 14/21 emphasise that those claimants who fall within the scope of art.10 will retain their entitlement to benefits if they have made a claim before the end of the "grace period" of June 30, 2021 for applying for settled status which has not yet been determined (or is under appeal). **5.134**

The personal scope, as set out in this article, may be of vital importance and should be checked carefully as the article can have surprising results in some cases. Among questions being brought before the courts and tribunals are what quality of residence paragraph 1(a) envisages in referring to those "who exercised their right to reside in the United Kingdom in accordance with Union law before the end of the transition period" and when it must be shown and the quality of residence required when they "continue to reside there thereafter." The position of third country national family members may also come to be examined.

Article 11

Continuity of residence

Continuity of residence for the purposes of Articles 9 and 10 shall not be affected by absences as referred to in Article 15(2). **5.135**

The right of permanent residence acquired under Directive 2004/38/EC before the end of the transition period shall not be treated as lost through absence from the host State for a period specified in Article 15(3).

Article 12

Non-discrimination

Within the scope of this Part, and without prejudice to any special provisions contained therein, any discrimination on grounds of nationality within the meaning of the first subparagraph of Article 18 TFEU shall be prohibited in the host State and the State of work in respect of the persons referred to in Article 10 of this Agreement. **5.136**

Title II

Rights And Obligations

Chapter 1

Rights Related To Residence, Residence Documents

Article 13

Residence rights

5.137 1. Union citizens and United Kingdom nationals shall have the right to reside in the host State under the limitations and conditions as set out in Articles 21, 45 or 49 TFEU and in Article 6(1), points (a), (b) or (c) of Article 7(1), Article 7(3), Article 14, Article 16(1) or Article 17(1) of Directive 2004/38/EC.

2. Family members who are either Union citizens or United Kingdom nationals shall have the right to reside in the host State as set out in Article 21 TFEU and in Article 6(1), point (d) of Article 7(1), Article 12(1) or (3), Article 13(1), Article 14, Article 16(1) or Article 17(3) and (4) of Directive 2004/38/EC, subject to the limitations and conditions set out in those provisions.

3. Family members who are neither Union citizens nor United Kingdom nationals shall have the right to reside in the host State under Article 21 TFEU and as set out in Article 6(2), Article 7(2), Article 12(2) or (3), Article 13(2), Article 14, Article 16(2), Article 17(3) or (4) or Article 18 of Directive 2004/38/EC, subject to the limitations and conditions set out in those provisions.

4. The host State may not impose any limitations or conditions for obtaining, retaining or losing residence rights on the persons referred to in paragraphs 1, 2 and 3, other than those provided for in this Title. There shall be no discretion in applying the limitations and conditions provided for in this Title, other than in favour of the person concerned.

General Note

5.138 In *SSWP v AT* [2022] UKUT 330, SSWP submitted that art.13(1) created a unique type of right ("sui generis"), subject to the limitations and conditions referred to in the article, but not the right under art.21 TFEU on which AT had relied to move to the UK (as had the claimant in *CG v Department for Communities* (C-709/20)). The argument was rejected at [96]–[102], the panel concluding:

> "What AT retained, after the end of the transition period, was that part of her bundle of Article 21 TFEU rights which entitled her to continue to reside in the UK. CG shows that that right continues to generate legal effects even when the residence does not comply with the conditions in the [Citizens' Rights Directive], at least for those who have a right of residence granted under national law." [at 102]

A similar argument on behalf of the Secretary of State was rejected by the Court of Appeal: see *SSWP v AT* [2023] EWCA Civ 1307 at [93] – [95]. The Supreme Court has refused permission to appeal.

The rights created by art.13 are rights of residence in the host state. They do not confer a right to move to other states. Thus in *R. (on the application of Independent Monitoring Authority for the Citizens' Rights Agreements) v Secretary of State for the Home Department* [2022] EWHC 3274 (Admin) at [133], Lane J noted that it was not in dispute that the rights in art.13 were not free movement rights, notwithstanding they contain limitations and conditions set out in the Directive.

Article 13

The *Independent Monitoring Authority* case also considers the "limitations or conditions" contemplated by art.13(4), the judge holding that the requirement for a person with pre-settled status to make a further application in order to obtain settled status was in breach.

The place, if any, under the article of rights conferred by a grant of pre-settled status is among the questions under consideration by courts and tribunals.

Most recently at the time of writing, *Fertré v Vale of White Horse DC* [2024] EWHC 1754 (KB) has held at [72] that pre-settled status is "no more than the gateway or passport to the potential acquisition of a particular right at the relevant time." Article 13(4) is capable of operating so as to enable SSHD to apply less onerous conditions when granting pre-settled status, but it does not operate to expand the rights conferred by Title II: *Fertré* at [80]–[90].

Article 14

Right of exit and of entry

1. Union citizens and United Kingdom nationals, their respective family members, and other persons, who reside in the territory of the host State in accordance with the conditions set out in this Title shall have the right to leave the host State and the right to enter it, as set out in Article 4(1) and the first subparagraph of Article 5(1) of Directive 2004/38/EC, with a valid passport or national identity card in the case of Union citizens and United Kingdom nationals, and with a valid passport in the case of their respective family members and other persons who are not Union citizens or United Kingdom nationals. 5.139

Five years after the end of the transition period, the host State may decide no longer to accept national identity cards for the purposes of entry to or exit from its territory if such cards do not include a chip that complies with the applicable International Civil Aviation Organisation standards related to biometric identification.

2. No exit visa, entry visa or equivalent formality shall be required of holders of a valid document issued in accordance with Article 18 or 26.

3. Where the host State requires family members who join the Union citizen or United Kingdom national after the end of the transition period to have an entry visa, the host State shall grant such persons every facility to obtain the necessary visas. Such visas shall be issued free of charge as soon as possible, and on the basis of an accelerated procedure.

Article 15

Right of permanent residence

1. Union citizens and United Kingdom nationals, and their respective family members, who have resided legally in the host State in accordance with Union law for a continuous period of 5 years or for the period specified in Article 17 of Directive 2004/38/EC, shall have the right to reside permanently in the host State under the conditions set out in Articles 16, 17 and 18 of Directive 2004/38/EC. Periods of legal residence or work in accordance with Union law before and after the end of the transition period shall be included in the calculation of the qualifying period necessary for acquisition of the right of permanent residence. 5.140

2. Continuity of residence for the purposes of acquisition of the right of permanent residence shall be determined in accordance with Article 16(3) and Article 21 of Directive 2004/38/EC.

3. Once acquired, the right of permanent residence shall be lost only through absence from the host State for a period exceeding 5 consecutive years.

General Note

5.141 The stipulation in art.15(3) of a 5-year period of absence before the right of permanent residence is lost is more generous than the period (2 years) applicable under art.16 of the Directive.

For consideration of the lawfulness of the procedural steps associated with an application for settled status, see the discussion of the *Independent Monitoring Authority* case under art.18.

Article 16

Accumulation of periods

5.142 Union citizens and United Kingdom nationals, and their respective family members, who before the end of the transition period resided legally in the host State in accordance with the conditions of Article 7 of Directive 2004/38/EC for a period of less than 5 years, shall have the right to acquire the right to reside permanently under the conditions set out in Article 15 of this Agreement once they have completed the necessary periods of residence. Periods of legal residence or work in accordance with Union law before and after the end of the transition period shall be included in the calculation of the qualifying period necessary for acquisition of the right of permanent residence.

Article 17

Status and changes

5.143 1. The right of Union citizens and United Kingdom nationals, and their respective family members, to rely directly on this Part shall not be affected when they change status, for example between student, worker, self-employed person and economically inactive person. Persons who, at the end of the transition period, enjoy a right of residence in their capacity as family members of Union citizens or United Kingdom nationals, cannot become persons referred to in points (a) to (d) of Article 10(1).

2. The rights provided for in this Title for the family members who are dependants of Union citizens or United Kingdom nationals before the end of the transition period, shall be maintained even after they cease to be dependants.

General Note

Article 17(2) may provide important protection for family members in the event that their dependency ends.

Article 18

Issuance of residence documents

5.144 1. The host State may require Union citizens or United Kingdom nationals, their respective family members and other persons, who reside in its territory in accordance with the conditions set out in this Title, to apply for a new residence status which confers the rights under this Title and a document evidencing such status which may be in a digital form.

Applying for such a residence status shall be subject to the following conditions:

(a) the purpose of the application procedure shall be to verify whether the applicant is entitled to the residence rights set out in this Title. Where that is the case, the applicant shall have a right to be granted the residence status and the document evidencing that status;

(b) the deadline for submitting the application shall not be less than 6 months from the end of the transition period, for persons residing in the host State before the end of the transition period. For persons who have the right to commence residence after the end of the transition period in the host State in accordance with this Title, the deadline for submitting the application shall be 3 months after their arrival or the expiry of the deadline referred to in the first subparagraph, whichever is later.

A certificate of application for the residence status shall be issued immediately;

(c) the deadline for submitting the application referred to in point (b) shall be extended automatically by 1 year where the Union has notified the United Kingdom, or the United Kingdom has notified the Union, that technical problems prevent the host State either from registering the application or from issuing the certificate of application referred to in point (b). The host State shall publish that notification and shall provide appropriate public information for the persons concerned in good time;

(d) where the deadline for submitting the application referred to in point (b) is not respected by the persons concerned, the competent authorities shall assess all the circumstances and reasons for not respecting the deadline and shall allow those persons to submit an application within a reasonable further period of time if there are reasonable grounds for the failure to respect the deadline;

(e) the host State shall ensure that any administrative procedures for applications are smooth, transparent and simple, and that any unnecessary administrative burdens are avoided;

(f) application forms shall be short, simple, user friendly and adapted to the context of this Agreement; applications made by families at the same time shall be considered together;

(g) the document evidencing the status shall be issued free of charge or for a charge not exceeding that imposed on citizens or nationals of the host State for the issuing of similar documents;

(h) persons who, before the end of the transition period, hold a valid permanent residence document issued under Article 19 or 20 of Directive 2004/38/EC or hold a valid domestic immigration document conferring a permanent right to reside in the host State, shall have the right to exchange that document within the period referred to in point (b) of this paragraph for a new residence document upon application after a verification of their identity, a criminality and security check in accordance with point (p) of this paragraph and confirmation of their ongoing residence; such new residence documents shall be issued free of charge;

(i) the identity of the applicants shall be verified through the presentation of a valid passport or national identity card for Union citizens and United Kingdom nationals, and through the presentation of a valid passport for their respective family members and other persons who are not Union citizens or United Kingdom nationals; the acceptance of such identity documents shall not be made conditional upon any criteria other than that of the validity of the document. Where the identity document is retained by the competent authorities of the host State while the application is pending, the host State shall return that document upon application without delay, before the decision on the application has been taken;

(j) supporting documents other than identity documents, such as civil status documents, may be submitted in copy. Originals of supporting documents may be required only in specific cases where there is a reasonable doubt as to the authenticity of the supporting documents submitted;

(k) the host State may only require Union citizens and United Kingdom nationals to present, in addition to the identity documents referred to in point (i) of this paragraph, the following supporting documents as referred to in Article 8(3) of Directive 2004/38/EC:

  (i) where they reside in the host State in accordance with point (a) of Article 7(1) of Directive 2004/38/EC as workers or self-employed, a confirmation of engagement from the employer or a certificate of employment, or proof that they are self-employed;

  (ii) where they reside in the host State in accordance with point (b) of Article 7(1) of Directive 2004/38/EC as economically inactive persons, evidence that they have sufficient resources for themselves and their family members not to become a burden on the social assistance system of the host State during their period of residence and that they have comprehensive sickness insurance cover in the host State; or

  (iii) where they reside in the host State in accordance with point (c) of Article 7(1) of Directive 2004/38/EC as students, proof of enrolment at an establishment accredited or financed by the host State on the basis of its legislation or administrative practice, proof of comprehensive sickness insurance cover, and a declaration or equivalent means of proof, that they have sufficient resources for themselves and their family members not to become a burden on the social assistance system of the host State during their period of residence. The host State may not require such declarations to refer to any specific amount of resources.

With regard to the condition of sufficient resources, Article 8(4) of Directive 2004/38/EC shall apply;

(l) the host State may only require family members who fall under point (e)(i) of Article 10(1) or Article 10(2) or (3) of this Agreement and who reside in the host State in accordance with point (d) of Article 7(1) or Article 7(2) of Directive 2004/38/EC to present, in addition to the identity documents referred to in point (i) of this paragraph, the following supporting documents as referred to in Article 8(5) or 10(2) of Directive 2004/38/EC:

  (i) a document attesting to the existence of a family relationship or registered partnership;

(ii) the registration certificate or, in the absence of a registration system, any other proof that the Union citizen or the United Kingdom national with whom they reside actually resides in the host State;

(iii) for direct descendants who are under the age of 21 or who are dependants and dependent direct relatives in the ascending line, and for those of the spouse or registered partner, documentary evidence that the conditions set out in point (c) or (d) of Article 2(2) of Directive 2004/38/EC are fulfilled;

(iv) for the persons referred to in Article 10(2) or (3) of this Agreement, a document issued by the relevant authority in the host State in accordance with Article 3(2) of Directive 2004/38/EC.

With regard to the condition of sufficient resources as concerns family members who are themselves Union citizens or United Kingdom nationals, Article 8(4) of Directive 2004/38/EC shall apply;

(m) the host State may only require family members who fall under point (e)(ii) of Article 10(1) or Article 10(4) of this Agreement to present, in addition to the identity documents referred to in point (i) of this paragraph, the following supporting documents as referred to in Articles 8(5) and 10(2) of Directive 2004/38/EC:

(i) a document attesting to the existence of a family relationship or of a registered partnership;

(ii) the registration certificate or, in the absence of a registration system, any other proof of residence in the host State of the Union citizen or of the United Kingdom nationals whom they are joining in the host State;

(iii) for spouses or registered partners, a document attesting to the existence of a family relationship or a registered partnership before the end of the transition period;

(iv) for direct descendants who are under the age of 21 or who are dependants and dependent direct relatives in the ascending line and those of the spouse or registered partner, documentary evidence that they were related to Union citizens or United Kingdom nationals before the end of the transition period and fulfil the conditions set out in point (c) or (d) of Article 2(2) of Directive 2004/38/EC relating to age or dependence;

(v) for the persons referred to in Article 10(4) of this Agreement, proof that a durable relationship with Union citizens or United Kingdom nationals existed before the end of the transition period and continues to exist thereafter;

(n) for cases other than those set out in points (k), (l) and (m), the host State shall not require applicants to present supporting documents that go beyond what is strictly necessary and proportionate to provide evidence that the conditions relating to the right of residence under this Title have been fulfilled;

(o) the competent authorities of the host State shall help the applicants to prove their eligibility and to avoid any errors or omissions in their applications; they shall give the applicants the opportunity to furnish supplementary evidence and to correct any deficiencies, errors or omissions;

(p) criminality and security checks may be carried out systematically on applicants, with the exclusive aim of verifying whether the restrictions set out in Article 20 of this Agreement may be applicable. For that purpose, applicants may be required to declare past criminal convictions which appear in their criminal record in accordance with the law of the State of conviction at the time of the application. The host State may, if it considers this essential, apply the procedure set out in Article 27(3) of Directive 2004/38/EC with respect to enquiries to other States regarding previous criminal records;

(q) the new residence document shall include a statement that it has been issued in accordance with this Agreement;

(r) the applicant shall have access to judicial and, where appropriate, administrative redress procedures in the host State against any decision refusing to grant the residence status. The redress procedures shall allow for an examination of the legality of the decision, as well as of the facts and circumstances on which the proposed decision is based. Such redress procedures shall ensure that the decision is not disproportionate.

2. During the period referred to in point (b) of paragraph 1 of this Article and its possible one-year extension under point (c) of that paragraph, all rights provided for in this Part shall be deemed to apply to Union citizens or United Kingdom nationals, their respective family members, and other persons residing in the host State, in accordance with the conditions and subject to the restrictions set out in Article 20.

3. Pending a final decision by the competent authorities on any application referred to in paragraph 1, and pending a final judgment handed down in case of judicial redress sought against any rejection of such application by the competent administrative authorities, all rights provided for in this Part shall be deemed to apply to the applicant, including Article 21 on safeguards and right of appeal, subject to the conditions set out in Article 20(4).

4. Where a host State has chosen not to require Union citizens or United Kingdom nationals, their family members, and other persons, residing in its territory in accordance with the conditions set out in this Title, to apply for the new residence status referred to in paragraph 1 as a condition for legal residence, those eligible for residence rights under this Title shall have the right to receive, in accordance with the conditions set out in Directive 2004/38/EC, a residence document, which may be in a digital form, that includes a statement that it has been issued in accordance with this Agreement.

General Note

5.145 ADM Memo 19/21 and DMG Memo 14/21 emphasise that claimants who fall within the scope of art.10 who have failed to submit their application for settled status before the end of the "grace period" on June 30, 2021 may be protected by art.18 if they have reasonable grounds (as determined by the Home Office by the issue of a "certificate of application") for submitting their application for settled status late.

For those who have been in the UK for five years, the decision in *R. (on the application of Independent Monitoring Authority for the Citizens' Rights Agreements) v Secretary of State for the Home Department* [2022] EWHC 3274 (Admin) may be relevant. The decision holds that the requirement for a person with pre-settled status to make a further application in order to obtain settled status is unlawful and at [192] that:

> "Properly interpreted, the WA means that the rights conferred by the grant of new residence status under Article 18 to those who do not, at that point, have a right

of permanent residence, includes the right to reside permanently in the United Kingdom, pursuant to Article 15, once the five-year period has been satisfied (subject to the conditions mentioned in Article 15(1))."

Fertré suggests that there should be a degree of consistency between the approaches of art.18(1) (sometimes termed "constitutive") and art.18(4) ("declaratory") and thus that it remains necessary for a person with pre-settled status to be able to point to other rights under the Citizens' Rights provisions at the time when the issue arises.

The scope of the deeming effected by art.18(3) is likely to require consideration by courts and tribunals.

Article 19

Issuance of residence documents during the transition period

1. During the transition period, a host State may allow applications for a residence status or residence document as referred to in Article 18(1) and (4) to be made voluntarily from the date of entry into force of this Agreement. 5.146

2. Decisions to accept or refuse such applications shall be taken in accordance with Article 18(1) and (4). Decisions under Article 18(1) shall have no effect until after the end of the transition period.

3. If an application under Article 18(1) is accepted before the end of the transition period, the host State may not withdraw the decision granting the residence status before the end of the transition period on any grounds other than those set out in Chapter VI and Article 35 of Directive 2004/38/EC.

4. If an application is refused before the end of the transition period, the applicant may apply again at any time before the expiry of the period set out in point (b) of Article 18(1).

5. Without prejudice to paragraph 4, the redress procedures under point (r) of Article 18(1) shall be available from the date of any decision to refuse an application referred to in paragraph 2 of this Article.

Article 20

Restrictions of the rights of residence and entry

1. The conduct of Union citizens or United Kingdom nationals, their family members, and other persons, who exercise rights under this Title, where that conduct occurred before the end of the transition period, shall be considered in accordance with Chapter VI of Directive 2004/38/EC. 5.147

2. The conduct of Union citizens or United Kingdom nationals, their family members, and other persons, who exercise rights under this Title, where that conduct occurred after the end of the transition period, may constitute grounds for restricting the right of residence by the host State or the right of entry in the State of work in accordance with national legislation.

3. The host State or the State of work may adopt the necessary measures to refuse, terminate or withdraw any right conferred by this Title in the case of the abuse of those rights or fraud, as set out in Article 35 of Directive 2004/38/EC. Such measures shall be subject to the procedural safeguards provided for in Article 21 of this Agreement.

4. The host State or the State of work may remove applicants who submitted fraudulent or abusive applications from its territory under the

conditions set out in Directive 2004/38/EC, in particular Articles 31 and 35 thereof, even before a final judgment has been handed down in the case of judicial redress sought against any rejection of such an application.

Article 21

Safeguards and right of appeal

5.148 The safeguards set out in Article 15 and Chapter VI of Directive 2004/38/EC shall apply in respect of any decision by the host State that restricts residence rights of the persons referred to in Article 10 of this Agreement.

Article 22

Related rights

5.149 In accordance with Article 23 of Directive 2004/38/EC, irrespective of nationality, the family members of a Union citizen or United Kingdom national who have the right of residence or the right of permanent residence in the host State or the State of work shall be entitled to take up employment or self-employment there.

Article 23

Equal treatment

5.150 1. In accordance with Article 24 of Directive 2004/38/EC, subject to the specific provisions provided for in this Title and Titles I and IV of this Part, all Union citizens or United Kingdom nationals residing on the basis of this Agreement in the territory of the host State shall enjoy equal treatment with the nationals of that State within the scope of this Part. The benefit of this right shall be extended to those family members of Union citizens or United Kingdom nationals who have the right of residence or permanent residence.

2. By way of derogation from paragraph 1, the host State shall not be obliged to confer entitlement to social assistance during periods of residence on the basis of Article 6 or point (b) of Article 14(4) of Directive 2004/38/EC, nor shall it be obliged, prior to a person's acquisition of the right of permanent residence in accordance with Article 15 of this Agreement, to grant maintenance aid for studies, including vocational training, consisting in student grants or student loans to persons other than workers, self-employed persons, persons who retain such status or to members of their families.

General Note

Among the issues under consideration by courts and tribunals are what constitutes "residing on the basis of this Agreement" for the purposes of this article and whether it is subject (mutatis mutandis) to the authorities which apply to Article 24 of the Directive itself, which limit reliance on that Article to those who have a right of residence under the Directive: see C-333/13 *Dano*. *Fertré* at [76] holds that it is.

CHAPTER 2

RIGHTS OF WORKERS AND SELF-EMPLOYED PERSONS

Article 24

Rights of workers

1. Subject to the limitations set out in Article 45(3) and (4) TFEU, workers in the host State and frontier workers in the State or States of work shall enjoy the rights guaranteed by Article 45 TFEU and the rights granted by Regulation (EU) No 492/2011 of the European Parliament and of the Council. These rights include: **5.151**

(a) the right not to be discriminated against on grounds of nationality as regards employment, remuneration and other conditions of work and employment;
(b) the right to take up and pursue an activity in accordance with the rules applicable to the nationals of the host State or the State of work;
(c) the right to assistance afforded by the employment offices of the host State or the State of work as offered to own nationals;
(d) the right to equal treatment in respect of conditions of employment and work, in particular as regards remuneration, dismissal and in case of unemployment, reinstatement or re-employment;
(e) the right to social and tax advantages;
(f) collective rights;
(g) the rights and benefits accorded to national workers in matters of housing;
(h) the right for their children to be admitted to the general educational, apprenticeship and vocational training courses under the same conditions as the nationals of the host State or the State of work, if such children are residing in the territory where the worker works.

2. Where a direct descendant of a worker who has ceased to reside in the host State is in education in that State, the primary carer for that descendant shall have the right to reside in that State until the descendant reaches the age of majority, and after the age of majority if that descendant continues to need the presence and care of the primary carer in order to pursue and complete his or her education.

3. Employed frontier workers shall enjoy the right to enter and exit the State of work in accordance with Article 14 of this Agreement and shall retain the rights they enjoyed as workers there, provided they are in one of the circumstances set out in points (a), (b), (c) and (d) of Article 7(3) of Directive 2004/38/EC, even where they do not move their residence to the State of work.

Article 25

Rights of self-employed persons

1. Subject to the limitations set out in Articles 51 and 52 TFEU, self-employed persons in the host State and self-employed frontier workers in the State or States of work shall enjoy the rights guaranteed by Articles 49 and 55 TFEU. These rights include: **5.152**

(a) the right to take up and pursue activities as self-employed persons and to set up and manage undertakings under the conditions laid down by the host State for its own nationals, as set out in Article 49 TFEU;
(b) the rights as set out in points (c) to (h) of Article 24(1) of this Agreement.

2. Article 24(2) shall apply to direct descendants of self-employed workers.

3. Article 24(3) shall apply to self-employed frontier workers.

Article 26

Issuance of a document identifying frontier workers' rights

5.153 The State of work may require Union citizens and United Kingdom nationals who have rights as frontier workers under this Title to apply for a document certifying that they have such rights under this Title. Such Union citizens and United Kingdom nationals shall have the right to be issued with such a document.

CHAPTER 3

PROFESSIONAL QUALIFICATIONS

5.154 Arts 27-29 *omitted*

TITLE III

COORDINATION OF SOCIAL SECURITY SYSTEMS

Article 30

Persons covered

5.155 1. This Title shall apply to the following persons:
(a) Union citizens who are subject to the legislation of the United Kingdom at the end of the transition period, as well as their family members and survivors;
(b) United Kingdom nationals who are subject to the legislation of a Member State at the end of the transition period, as well as their family members and survivors;
(c) Union citizens who reside in the United Kingdom and are subject to the legislation of a Member State at the end of the transition period, as well as their family members and survivors;
(d) United Kingdom nationals who reside in a Member State, and are subject to the legislation of the United Kingdom at the end of the transition period, as well as their family members and survivors;
(e) persons who do not fall within points (a) to (d) but are:
    (i) Union citizens who pursue an activity as an employed or self-employed person in the United Kingdom at the end of the transition period, and who, based on Title II of Regulation (EC)

No 883/2004 of the European Parliament and of the Council, are subject to the legislation of a Member State, as well as their family members and survivors; or

(ii) United Kingdom nationals who pursue an activity as an employed or self-employed person in one or more Member States at the end of the transition period, and who, based on Title II of Regulation (EC) No 883/2004, are subject to the legislation of the United Kingdom, as well as their family members and survivors;

(f) stateless persons and refugees, residing in a Member State or in the United Kingdom, who are in one of the situations described in points (a) to (e), as well as their family members and survivors;

(g) nationals of third countries, as well as members of their families and survivors, who are in one of the situations described in points (a) to (e), provided that they fulfil the conditions of Council Regulation (EC) No 859/2003.

2. The persons referred to in paragraph 1 shall be covered for as long as they continue without interruption to be in one of the situations set out in that paragraph involving both a Member State and the United Kingdom at the same time.

3. This Title shall also apply to persons who do not, or who no longer, fall within points (a) to (e) of paragraph 1 of this Article but who fall within Article 10 of this Agreement, as well as their family members and survivors.

4. The persons referred to in paragraph 3 shall be covered for as long as they continue to have a right to reside in the host State under Article 13 of this Agreement, or a right to work in their State of work under Article 24 or 25 of this Agreement.

5. Where this Article refers to family members and survivors, those persons shall be covered by this Title only to the extent that they derive rights and obligations in that capacity under Regulation (EC) No 883/2004.

Article 31

Social security coordination rules

1. The rules and objectives set out in Article 48 TFEU, Regulation (EC) No 883/2004 and Regulation (EC) No 987/2009 of the European Parliament and of the Council shall apply to the persons covered by this Title. 5.156

The Union and the United Kingdom shall take due account of the Decisions and Recommendations of the Administrative Commission for the Coordination of Social Security Systems attached to the European Commission, set up under Regulation (EC) No 883/2004 ("Administrative Commission") listed in Part I of Annex I to this Agreement.

2. By way of derogation from Article 9 of this Agreement, for the purposes of this Title, the definitions in Article 1 of Regulation (EC) No 883/2004 shall apply.

3. With regard to nationals of third countries who fulfil the conditions of Regulation (EC) No 859/2003, as well as their family members

or survivors within the scope of this Title, the references to Regulation (EC) No 883/2004 and Regulation (EC) No 987/2009 in this Title shall be understood as references to Council Regulation (EEC) No 1408/71 and Council Regulation (EEC) No 574/72 respectively. References to specific provisions of Regulation (EC) No 883/2004 and Regulation (EC) No 987/2009 shall be understood as references to the corresponding provisions of Regulation (EEC) No 1408/71 and Regulation (EEC) No 574/72.

General Note

5.157 Article 48 of the Treaty on the Functioning of the European Union provides for the co-ordination of social security rules in the Member States in order to minimise a potential barrier to the free movement of workers. The previous history of free movement between Member States and the United Kingdom and the ongoing Trade and Co-operation Agreement have resulted in co-ordination mechanisms like the Citizens' Rights provisions of the Withdrawal Agreement and the Protocol on Social Security Co-ordination which adopt a very similar approach. Co-ordination requires co-operation to provide interchange between different national social security systems. The Luxembourg Court has frequently drawn attention to the distinction between harmonisation and co-ordination and noted that the substantive and procedural difference between national social security systems of the Member States remain unaffected by what is now art.48 and its secondary legislation: *Stewart v SSWP* (C-503/09) at [75] to [76]. But it has also been established that those exercising the right of freedom of movement should not lose advantages in the field of social security; this has come to be known as the *Petroni* principle: *Petroni* (24/75) [1975] E.C.R. 1149, at [13]. In *JM v SSWP (HRP) and another* [2018] UKUT 2 (AAC) the application of such principles defeated a claim for home responsibilities protection for a period when the claimant had been bringing up children in the Netherlands rather than the UK and in receipt of Dutch child benefit rather than, as domestic legislation required, UK child benefit. The consequential disadvantage for her was that she could only receive a pension in respect of such years under Dutch law at a later age than she could have done under UK law if the Dutch child-raising years had been taken into account. As Judge Wikeley put it:

> "a move to another member state "may, depending on the case, be more or less advantageous or disadvantageous for the person concerned, according to the combination of national rules applicable pursuant to Regulation No 1408/71" (see C-208/07 *von Chamier-Glisczinski v Deutsche Angestellten-Krankenkasse*)."

Three general principles emerge from the complex rules of co-ordination which can be found in Reg. 883/2004 and the case law and are likely to figure solely under the Withdrawal Agreement and the Protocol:

1. A national of a Member State or the UK is not to be disqualified from entitlement to benefits on the grounds of nationality or on a change of country or residence within the European Union.
2. A national of a Member State or the UK may become entitled to a benefit by having contributions or qualifying periods of employment or residence in one Member State aggregated with those arising in another Member State.
3. A national of a Member State or the UK should not be better off in relation to entitlement to benefits by reason of his or her exercise of rights to move freely between Member States or the UK.

The Preamble to regulations can be an important aid to its interpretation. A number of important points from the Preamble to Regulation 883/2004 can be identified. The regulation is concerned only with the co-ordination of different social security systems. This regulation is a natural successor to Regulation 1408/71 and retains the principles established in that regulation, but updates them in the light of the case-law of the Luxembourg Court, and provides for the co-ordination of certain additional benefits. At a number of points, the Preamble stresses the application of the principle of proportionality in this field. **5.158**

Regulation 883/2004 is based upon six key principles:

(1) In respect of any claim to benefit, the beneficiary is subject to the social security system of one country alone. This will generally, but by no means always, be the Member State where the person is working at the material time.

(2) All those covered by the co-ordinating rules are subject to the same rights and obligations as nationals of the competent Member State. This is the principle of equal treatment.

(3) Periods of insurance, employment, self-employment and residence accrued in different Member States may be added together where this is necessary to meet the conditions of entitlement to a benefit. This is known as the principle of aggregation.

(4) Subject to considerable limitations which should be strictly construed, benefits to which title has been acquired in one Member State may be taken to another Member State. This is the principle of the exportability of benefits.

(5) The legal effects of entitlement in one Member State, and the facts upon which that entitlement is based must be recognised in other Member States. This is the principle of the assimilation of legal effects and facts (now spelled out in art.5.)

(6) Member States undertake to co-operate in the administration of the co-ordinating rules in the regulation. This can be regarded as the duty of co-operation.

The regulation has to be interpreted in accordance with general principles of law, including the principle of certainty and the requirement that there must be no disproportionate effect on the predictability and effectiveness of the Regulation: *Hudzinski v Agentur für Arbeit Wesel-Familienkasse* (C-611/10 and 612/10) [2012] 3 C.M.L.R. 23, considered in some detail in *IG v SSWP (AA)* [2016] UKUT 176 (AAC); [2016] AACR 41 at paras.27-42.

Co-ordination not harmonisation

The regulation, like its predecessors, is concerned with the co-ordination of social security schemes and not with the harmonization of the social security laws of the Member States. The Luxembourg Court has consistently stressed this distinction in its judgments on provisions of Regulation 1408/71. So, for example, in *Hervein and Lorthiois* (C-393 and C-394/99) [2002] E.C.R. I-2829, the Court said: **5.159**

> ". . . the system put in place by Regulation No 1408/71 is merely a system of coordination. . . .
> . . . it . . . does not follow from [arts 39 and 43 of the Treaty] that, in the absence of harmonisation of the social security legislation, neutrality as regard the complexity, for the persons concerned, of the administration of their social security cover will be guaranteed in all circumstances" (paras 52 and 58).

In *Jörn Petersen* (C-228/07) [2008] E.C.R.1–6989 the Luxembourg Court said:

> "... Regulation 1408/71 does not set up a common scheme of social security, but allows different social security schemes to exist and its sole objective is to ensure the coordination of those schemes (Case 21/87 *Borowitz* [1988] ECR 3715, paragraph 23, and Case C-331/06 *Chuck* [2008] ECR I-0000, paragraph 27)". (See [41].)

The purpose of the regulation is to build bridges in order to connect different social security schemes so that those moving within the Union are not disadvantaged as a result of exercising their rights of free movement. However, notwithstanding this important distinction between co-ordination and harmonisation, there are certainly adaptive pressures on Member States as a result of the requirements of co-ordination of benefit schemes which tend to pull Member State policy closer together. So there are limits to the freedom of action of the Member States in relation to their national social security rules. In *Kalsbeek* (100/63) [1964] E.C.R. 565, the Luxembourg Court said:

> "Article 51 [now art.48 TFEU] ... cannot allow [national] regulations to fall short of the objectives which it sets, which are intended to favour freedom of movement for worker and which would be incompatible with any reduction in their rights". (At 574.)

5.160 That requirement needs to be read in the context of a statement in a later judgment in *Salgado Alonso* (C-306/03) [2005] E.C.R. I-705:

> "It should be recalled that the Court has consistently held that Member States remain competent to define the conditions for granting a social security benefit, even if they make them more strict, provided that the conditions adopted do not give rise to overt or disguised discrimination between Community workers ..." (At [27].)

However, States are not free to make provision when they are not the competent State for a particular class of benefit: C-302/84 *Ten Holder* [1986] ECR 1821 at para.21. Exceptions are permitted on two conditions: "if there are specific and particularly close connecting factors between the territory of that State and the situation at issue, on condition that the predictability and effectiveness of the application of the coordination rules ... are not disproportionately affected": see *Ministerstvo práce a sociálinch věcí v B* (Case C-394/13) at para.28.

The requirement that workers should not lose advantages in the field of social security has come to be known as "the Petroni principle"; in *Petroni* (24/75) [1975] E.C.R. 1149, the Luxembourg Court said:

> "The aim of Articles 48 to 51 [now art.45 to 48 TFEU] would not be attained if, as a consequence of the exercise of their right to freedom of movement, workers were to lose advantages in the field of social security guaranteed them in any event by the laws of a single Member State". (At [13].)

In *ES v SSWP (PIP)* [2024] UKUT 13 (AAC), the claimant could not meet the "past presence" test in reg.16 of the Social Security (Personal Independence Payment) Regulations 2013. However, reg.22 disapplied that test where "a relevant EU Regulation applies" and certain other conditions are met. Regulation 883/2004 is a "relevant EU Regulation" for this purpose. Judge Jacobs notes that art.31 does not provide that Regulation 883/2004 itself applies, which "would be inappropriate in a withdrawal agreement". Rather, it provides for the "rules and objectives" of Regulation 883/2004 to apply and that was sufficient to bring the claimant within reg.22 of the PIP Regulations.

Article 32

Special situations covered

1. The following rules shall apply in the following situations to the extent set out in this Article, insofar as they relate to persons not or no longer covered by Article 30: 5.161

(a) the following persons shall be covered by this Title for the purposes of reliance on and aggregation of periods of insurance, employment, self-employment or residence, including rights and obligations deriving from such periods in accordance with Regulation (EC) No 883/2004:

(i) Union citizens, as well as stateless persons and refugees residing in a Member State and nationals of third countries who fulfil the conditions of Regulation (EC) No 859/2003, who have been subject to the legislation of the United Kingdom before the end of the transition period, as well as their family members and survivors;

(ii) United Kingdom nationals, as well as stateless persons and refugees residing in the United Kingdom and nationals of third countries who fulfil the conditions of Regulation (EC) No 859/2003, who have been subject to the legislation of a Member State before the end of the transition period, as well as their family members and survivors; for the purposes of the aggregation of periods, periods completed both before and after the end of the transition period shall be taken into account in accordance with Regulation (EC) No 883/2004;

(b) the rules set out in Articles 20 and 27 of Regulation (EC) No 883/2004 shall continue to apply to persons who, before the end of the transition period, had requested authorisation to receive a course of planned health care treatment pursuant to Regulation (EC) No 883/2004, until the end of the treatment. The corresponding reimbursement procedures shall also apply even after the treatment ends. Such persons and the accompanying persons shall enjoy the right to enter and exit the State of treatment in accordance with Article 14, mutatis mutandis;

(c) the rules set out in Articles 19 and 27 of Regulation (EC) No 883/2004 shall continue to apply to persons who are covered by Regulation (EC) No 883/2004 and who are on a stay at the end of the transition period in a Member State or the United Kingdom, until the end of their stay. The corresponding reimbursement procedures shall also apply even after the stay or treatment ends;

(d) the rules set out in Articles 67, 68 and 69 of Regulation (EC) No 883/2004 shall continue to apply, for as long as the conditions are fulfilled, to awards of family benefits to which there is entitlement at the end of the transition period for the following persons:

(i) Union citizens, stateless persons and refugees residing in a Member State as well as nationals of third countries who fulfil the conditions of Regulation (EC) No 859/2003 and reside in a Member State, who are subject to the legislation of a Member

State and have family members residing in the United Kingdom at the end of the transition period;

(ii) United Kingdom nationals, as well as stateless persons and refugees residing in the United Kingdom and nationals of third countries who fulfil the conditions of Regulation (EC) No 859/2003 and reside in the United Kingdom, who are subject to the legislation of the United Kingdom and have family members residing in a Member State at the end of the transition period;

(e) in the situations set out in point (d)(i) and (ii) of this paragraph, for any persons who have rights as family members at the end of the transition period under Regulation (EC) No 883/2004, such as derived rights for sickness benefits in kind, that Regulation and the corresponding provisions of Regulation (EC) No 987/2009 shall continue to apply for as long as the conditions provided therein are fulfilled.

2. The provisions of Chapter 1 of Title III of Regulation (EC) No 883/2004 as regards sickness benefits shall apply to persons receiving benefits under point (a) of paragraph 1 of this Article. This paragraph shall apply mutatis mutandis as regards family benefits based on Articles 67, 68 and 69 of Regulation (EC) No 883/2004.

Article 33

Nationals of Iceland, Liechtenstein, Norway and Switzerland

5.162 1. The provisions of this Title applicable to Union citizens shall apply to nationals of Iceland, the Principality of Liechtenstein, the Kingdom of Norway, and the Swiss Confederation provided that:

(a) Iceland, the Principality of Liechtenstein, the Kingdom of Norway, and the Swiss Confederation, as applicable, have concluded and apply corresponding agreements with the United Kingdom which apply to Union citizens; and

(b) Iceland, the Principality of Liechtenstein, the Kingdom of Norway, and the Swiss Confederation, as applicable, have concluded and apply corresponding agreements with the Union which apply to United Kingdom nationals.

2. Upon notification from the United Kingdom and from the Union of the date of entry into force of the agreements referred to in paragraph 1 of this Article, the Joint Committee established by Article 164 ("Joint Committee") shall set the date from which the provisions of this Title shall apply to the nationals of Iceland, the Principality of Liechtenstein, the Kingdom of Norway, and the Swiss Confederation, as applicable.

Article 34

Administrative cooperation

5.163 1. By way of derogation from Articles 7 and 128(1), as of the date of entry into force of this Agreement, the United Kingdom shall have the status of observer in the Administrative Commission. It may, where the items on the agenda relating to this Title concern the United Kingdom, send a representative, to be present in an advisory capacity, to the meetings of the Administrative Commission and to the meetings of the bodies referred to in Articles 73 and 74 of Regulation (EC) No 883/2004 where such items are discussed.

2. By way of derogation from Article 8, the United Kingdom shall take part in the Electronic Exchange of Social Security Information (EESSI) and bear the related costs.

Article 35

Reimbursement, recovery and offsetting

The provisions of Regulations (EC) No 883/2004 and (EC) No 987/2009 on reimbursement, recovery and offsetting shall continue to apply in relation to events, insofar as they relate to persons not covered by Article 30, that: 5.164

(a) occurred before the end of the transition period; or
(b) occur after the end of the transition period and relate to persons who were covered by Articles 30 or 32 when the event occurred.

Article 36

Development of law and adaptations of Union acts

1. Where Regulations (EC) No 883/2004 and (EC) No 987/2009 are amended or replaced after the end of the transition period, references to those Regulations in this Agreement shall be understood as referring to those Regulations as amended or replaced, in accordance with the acts listed in Part II of Annex I to this Agreement. 5.165

The Joint Committee shall revise Part II of Annex I to this Agreement and align it to any act amending or replacing Regulations (EC) No 883/2004 and (EC) No 987/2009 as soon as such act is adopted by the Union. To that end, the Union shall, as soon as possible after adoption, inform the United Kingdom within the Joint Committee of any act amending or replacing those Regulations.

2. By way of derogation from the second subparagraph of paragraph 1, the Joint Committee shall assess the effects of an act amending or replacing Regulations (EC) No 883/2004 and (EC) No 987/2009 where that act:

(a) amends or replaces the matters covered by Article 3 of Regulation (EC) No 883/2004; or
(b) makes a cash benefit exportable where that cash benefit was non-exportable under Regulation (EC) No 883/2004 at the end of the transition period, or makes a cash benefit non-exportable, where that cash benefit was exportable at the end of the transition period; or
(c) makes a cash benefit exportable for an unlimited period of time, where that cash benefit was exportable only for a limited period of time under Regulation (EC) No 883/2004 at the end of the transition period, or makes a cash benefit exportable only for a limited period of time, where that cash benefit was exportable for

an unlimited period of time under that Regulation at the end of the transition period. In making its assessment, the Joint Committee shall consider in good faith the scale of the changes referred to in the first subparagraph of this paragraph, as well as the importance of the continued good functioning of Regulations (EC) No 883/2004 and (EC) No 987/2009 between the Union and the United Kingdom and the importance of there being a competent State in relation to individuals within the scope of Regulation (EC) No 883/2004.

If the Joint Committee so decides within 6 months from receiving the information given by the Union pursuant to paragraph 1, Part II of Annex I to this Agreement shall not be aligned to the act referred to in the first subparagraph of this paragraph.

For the purposes of this paragraph:

(a) "exportable" means payable under Regulation (EC) No 883/2004 to or in relation to a person residing in a Member State or in the United Kingdom if the institution responsible for providing the benefit is not situated there; "non-exportable" shall be interpreted accordingly; and

(b) "exportable for an unlimited period of time" means exportable for as long as the conditions giving rise to the entitlements are met.

3. Regulations (EC) No 883/2004 and (EC) No 987/2009 shall, for the purposes of this Agreement, be understood as comprising the adaptations listed in Part III of Annex I to this Agreement. As soon as possible after the adoption of any changes in domestic provisions of relevance to Part III of Annex I to this Agreement, the United Kingdom shall inform the Union thereof within the Joint Committee.

4. The Decisions and Recommendations of the Administrative Commission shall, for the purposes of this Agreement, be understood as comprising the decisions and recommendations listed in Part I of Annex I. The Joint Committee shall amend Part I of Annex I to reflect any new Decision or Recommendation adopted by the Administrative Commission. To that end, as soon as possible after adoption of decisions and recommendations of the Administrative Commission, the Union shall inform the United Kingdom thereof within the Joint Committee. Such amendments shall be made by the Joint Committee on a proposal of the Union or the United Kingdom.

Title IV

Other Provisions

Article 37

Publicity

5.166 The Member States and the United Kingdom shall disseminate information concerning the rights and obligations of persons covered by this Part, in particular by means of awareness-raising campaigns conducted, as appropriate, through national and local media and other means of communication.

Article 38

More favourable provisions

1. This Part shall not affect any laws, regulations or administrative provisions applicable in a host State or a State of work which would be more favourable to the persons concerned. This paragraph shall not apply to Title III. 5.167

2. Article 12 and Article 23(1) shall be without prejudice to the Common Travel Area arrangements between the United Kingdom and Ireland as regards more favourable treatment which may result from these arrangements for the persons concerned.

Article 39

Life-long protection

The persons covered by this Part shall enjoy the rights provided for in the relevant Titles of this Part for their lifetime, unless they cease to meet the conditions set out in those Titles. 5.168

TITLE X

UNION JUDICIAL AND ADMINISTRATIVE PROCEDURES

CHAPTER 1

JUDICIAL PROCEDURES

Article 86

Pending cases before the Court of Justice of the European Union

1. The Court of Justice of the European Union shall continue to have jurisdiction in any proceedings brought by or against the United Kingdom before the end of the transition period. Such jurisdiction shall apply to all stages of proceedings, including appeal proceedings before the Court of Justice and proceedings before the General Court where the case is referred back to the General Court. 5.169

2. The Court of Justice of the European Union shall continue to have jurisdiction to give preliminary rulings on requests from courts and tribunals of the United Kingdom made before the end of the transition period.

3. For the purposes of this Chapter, proceedings shall be considered as having been brought before the Court of Justice of the European Union, and requests for preliminary rulings shall be considered as having been made, at the moment at which the document initiating the proceedings has been registered by the registry of the Court of Justice or the General Court, as the case may be.

Article 87

New cases before the Court of Justice

5.170 1. If the European Commission considers that the United Kingdom has failed to fulfil an obligation under the Treaties or under Part Four of this Agreement before the end of the transition period, the European Commission may, within 4 years after the end of the transition period, bring the matter before the Court of Justice of the European Union in accordance with the requirements laid down in Article 258 TFEU or the second subparagraph of Article 108(2) TFEU, as the case may be. The Court of Justice of the European Union shall have jurisdiction over such cases.

2. If the United Kingdom does not comply with a decision referred to in Article 95(1) of this Agreement, or fails to give legal effect in the United Kingdom's legal order to a decision, as referred to in that provision, that was addressed to a natural or legal person residing or established in the United Kingdom, the European Commission may, within 4 years from the date of the decision concerned, bring the matter to the Court of Justice of the European Union in accordance with the requirements laid down in Article 258 TFEU or the second subparagraph of Article 108(2) TFEU, as the case may be. The Court of Justice of the European Union shall have jurisdiction over such cases.

3. In deciding to bring matters under this Article, the European Commission shall apply the same principles in respect of the United Kingdom as in respect of any Member State.

Article 88

Procedural rules

5.171 The provisions of Union law governing the procedure before the Court of Justice of the European Union shall apply in respect of the proceedings and requests for preliminary rulings referred to in this Title.

Article 89

Binding force and enforceability of judgments and orders

5.172 1. Judgments and orders of the Court of Justice of the European Union handed down before the end of the transition period, as well as such judgments and orders handed down after the end of the transition period in proceedings referred to in Articles 86 and 87, shall have binding force in their entirety on and in the United Kingdom.

2. If, in a judgment referred to in paragraph 1, the Court of Justice of the European Union finds that the United Kingdom has failed to fulfil an obligation under the Treaties or this Agreement, the United Kingdom shall take the necessary measures to comply with that judgment.

3. Articles 280 and 299 TFEU shall apply in the United Kingdom in respect of the enforcement of the judgments and orders of the Court of Justice of the European Union referred to in paragraph 1 of this Article.

Article 90

Right to intervene and participate in the procedure

Until the judgments and orders of the Court of Justice of the European Union in all proceedings and requests for preliminary rulings referred to in Article 86 have become final, the United Kingdom may intervene in the same way as a Member State or, in the cases brought before the Court of Justice of the European Union in accordance with Article 267 TFEU, participate in the procedure before the Court of Justice of the European Union in the same way as a Member State. During that period, the Registrar of the Court of Justice of the European Union shall notify the United Kingdom, at the same time and in the same manner as the Member States, of any case referred to the Court of Justice of the European Union for a preliminary ruling by a court or tribunal of a Member State. 5.173

Part Four

Transition

Article 126

Transition period

There shall be a transition or implementation period, which shall start on the date of entry into force of this Agreement and end on 31 December 2020. 5.174

Article 127

Scope of the transition

1. Unless otherwise provided in this Agreement, Union law shall be applicable to and in the United Kingdom during the transition period … 5.175

…

3. During the transition period, the Union law applicable pursuant to paragraph 1 shall produce in respect of and in the United Kingdom the same legal effects as those which it produces within the Union and its Member States, and shall be interpreted and applied in accordance with the same methods and general principles as those applicable within the Union.

...

6. Unless otherwise provided in this Agreement, during the transition period, any reference to Member States in the Union law applicable pursuant to paragraph 1, including as implemented and applied by Member States, shall be understood as including the United Kingdom.

...

Article 131

Supervision and enforcement

5.176 During the transition period, the institutions, bodies, offices and agencies of the Union shall have the powers conferred upon them by Union law in relation to the United Kingdom and to natural and legal persons residing or established in the United Kingdom. In particular, the Court of Justice of the European Union shall have jurisdiction as provided for in the Treaties.

The first paragraph shall also apply during the transition period as regards the interpretation and application of this Agreement.

PART SIX

INSTITUTIONAL AND FINAL PROVISIONS

TITLE I

CONSISTENT INTERPRETATION AND APPLICATION

Article 158

References to the Court of Justice of the European Union concerning Part Two

5.177 1. Where, in a case which commenced at first instance within 8 years from the end of the transition period before a court or tribunal in the United Kingdom, a question is raised concerning the interpretation of Part Two of this Agreement, and where that court or tribunal considers that a decision on that question is necessary to enable it to give judgment in that case, that court or tribunal may request the Court of Justice of the European Union to give a preliminary ruling on that question. However, where the subject matter of the case before the court or tribunal in the United Kingdom is a decision on an application made pursuant to Article 18(1) or (4) or pursuant to Article 19, a request for a preliminary ruling may be made only where the case commenced at first instance within a period of 8 years from the date from which Article 19 applies.

2. The Court of Justice of the European Union shall have jurisdiction to give preliminary rulings on requests pursuant to paragraph 1. The legal effects in the United Kingdom of such preliminary rulings shall be the same as the legal effects of preliminary rulings given pursuant to Article 267 TFEU in the Union and its Member States.

3. In the event that the Joint Committee adopts a decision under Article 132(1), the period of eight years referred to in the second subparagraph of paragraph 1 shall be automatically extended by the corresponding number of months by which the transition period is extended.

General Note

Any national court or tribunal can refer questions on the interpretation of Part Two (Citizens' Rights) to the Court of Justice under this article. Given the terms of art.4 of the Withdrawal Agreement, the objective of the procedure continues to be a partnership between national courts and tribunals and the Luxembourg Court to ensure the uniform application in all Member States of Part Two. **5.178**

The effect of a court or tribunal seeking a ruling is that the national proceedings stand adjourned pending the receipt of the ruling of the Luxembourg Court. The case is then relisted for determination before the national court or tribunal in the light of the ruling of the Luxembourg Court on the point of referred. The Luxembourg Court is careful not to determine the point arising under national law.

Distilling a considerable body of case law and adding points specific to the social security jurisdictions, the following factors are likely to be relevant in the determination by a First-tier Tribunal or the Upper Tribunal of the exercise of the discretion to refer questions to the Luxembourg Court, namely whether: **5.179**

1. a serious point of interpretation of Part Two arises in the case which has been fully argued by the parties;
2. the relevant facts have been found or are substantially agreed;
3. the point of law will be substantially determinative of the case;
4. there is any European Union authority precisely or closely in point;
5. there is any national authority addressing the point of European Union law; and
6. it seems certain that at some stage in the life of the case, it will have to be referred to the Luxembourg Court.

However, the requirement that a decision on the issue be "necessary to enable [the court or tribunal] to give judgment in that case" will need to be met, just as it was in relation to references under TFEU art.267 (as to which, see *Eli Lilly and Co v Genentech Inc* (C-239/19) and *London Steam-Ship Owners' Mutual Insurance Assoc Ltd v Spain (The Prestige)* [2022] EWCA Civ 238).

The expense and delay caused by an inappropriate reference will be issues every adjudicating body will consider. The factors set out above are consistent with European Union law on the exercise of the discretion to refer. The absence of full argument on the European Union law point—from both the claimant and the Secretary of State—(and full argument is likely to be rare in First-tier Tribunals) suggests that caution should be the order of the day before the First-tier Tribunals. On the other hand, tribunals should not be inhibited from making a reference if the relevant facts have been found, if the point has been fully argued, if the tribunal concludes that the appeal turns on the proper interpretation of Part Two, if there is no relevant authority which suggests that the question of interpretation is free from doubt, and if it seems certain that at some stage a reference will need to be made to resolve the question. It is probably fair to say that such circumstances will not be commonplace in the First-tier Tribunals.

CJEU Press Release No.96/18, June 29, 2018 announced that, from July 1, 2018, all requests for preliminary rulings involving natural persons will be anonymised and replaced with initials and any additional elements likely to permit identification will be removed: *https://curia.europa.eu/jcms/Jo2_7052/en/?annee=2018* [accessed June 14, 2022]. Press Release No.1/23, January 9, 2023, announced that, in order to make it easier to identify anonymised cases, from 1 January 2023, all new anonymised cases involving proceedings between natural persons (whose names have, since 1 July 2018, been replaced with initials for reasons relating to the protection of personal data) or proceedings between natural persons and legal persons that do not have a distinctive name, would be allocated a fictional name suggested by a computerised automatic name generator: see *https://curia.europa.eu/jcms/upload/docs/application/pdf/2023-01/cp230001en.pdf* [Accessed May 5, 2024]. It is assumed similar approaches will be followed in regards to art.158.

The adjudicating body is responsible for drafting the questions it wishes to refer. The question should be couched in terms which pose a general question of law rather than the specific issues raised in the case. The questions should be self-contained and self-explanatory, since they will be notified to the Commission, Council and the Member States under art.20 of the Statute of the Court. Those so notified may choose within two months of the notification to submit written observations on the questions raised.

5.180 By virtue of art.158(2), a ruling given by the Luxembourg Court is binding on the national court or tribunal as to the interpretation of the measure in question. It will also bind future courts or tribunals determining similar questions.

The Luxembourg Court's Recommendations to national courts and tribunals, in relation to the initiation of preliminary ruling proceedings were published in [2019] OJ C 380/01 (November 8, 2019) and can be accessed at *https://eur-lex.europa.eu/legal-content/EN/TXT/?uri=CELEX%3A32019H1108%2801%29&qid=1715098627206* [accessed May 7, 2024]. They would seem equally applicable to references under art.158.

Article 159

Monitoring of the implementation and application of Part Two

5.181 1. In the United Kingdom, the implementation and application of Part Two shall be monitored by an independent authority (the "Authority") which shall have powers equivalent to those of the European Commission acting under the Treaties to conduct inquiries on its own initiative concerning alleged breaches of Part Two by the administrative authorities of the United Kingdom and to receive complaints from Union citizens and their family members for the purposes of conducting such inquiries. The Authority shall also have the right, following such complaints, to bring a legal action before a competent court or tribunal in the United Kingdom in an appropriate judicial procedure with a view to seeking an adequate remedy.

2. The European Commission and the Authority shall each annually inform the specialised Committee on citizens' rights referred to in point (a) of Article 165(1) on the implementation and application of Part Two in the

Union and in the United Kingdom, respectively. The information provided shall, in particular, cover measures taken to implement or comply with Part Two and the number and nature of complaints received.

3. The Joint Committee shall assess, no earlier than 8 years after the end of the transition period, the functioning of the Authority. Following such assessment, it may decide, in good faith, pursuant to point (f) of Article 164(4) and Article 166, that the United Kingdom may abolish the Authority.

General Note

For discussion of the Practice Direction which applies to cases in the courts raising issues relating to rights under Part Two, see the annotation to the General Note to Part Two (above). 5.182

Title IV

Final Provisions

Article 185

Entry into force and application

This Agreement shall enter into force on one of the following dates, whichever is the earliest: (a) the day following the end of the period provided for in Article 50(3) TEU, as extended by the European Council in agreement with the United Kingdom, provided that, prior to that date, the depositary of this Agreement has received the written notifications by the Union and the United Kingdom regarding the completion of the necessary internal procedures; (b) the first day of the month following the receipt by the depositary of this Agreement of the last of the written notifications referred to in point (a). 5.183

...

Parts Two and Three, with the exception of Article 19, Article 34(1), Article 44, and Article 96(1), ..., shall apply as from the end of the transition period.

...

Updating of commentary on EU law measures

The following sections should be read together with the commentary on the EU instrument concerned in the 2020–21 edition of this work, which these sections update. The reasons for this approach are explained in the introductory note on United Kingdom Withdrawal from the European Union at the beginning of this Part. The dates of more recent decisions of the CJEU have been added. See European Union (Withdrawal) Act 2018 s.6 for the approach to decisions delivered on or after the end of the Brexit implementation period. 5.184

5.185

Treaty on the Functioning of the European Union

(Updating commentary to be read together with 2020–21 edition, paras 3.90–3.149)

Para(s). in 2020–21 edition	**Updating commentary**
3.92–3.93	*Art.18 TFEU* The CJEU held that the existence of the more specific non-discrimination provision in art.24 of Directive 2004/38 did not supplant art.18 TFEU which could accordingly be relied upon where a person's right to reside arose otherwise than under the Directive (in that case via art.10 of Regulation 492/2011): see *Krefeld* (C–181/19) Judgment of October 6, 2020. An appeal by the Secretary of State to the Supreme Court against the decision of the Court of Appeal in *R. (Fratila and Tanase) v SSWP* [2020] EWCA Civ 1741 was initially stayed pending the outcome of the reference to the CJEU by an appeal tribunal in Northern Ireland in *CG v Department for Communities* (C-709/20). The CJEU held that the situation was governed by the more specific art.24 of Directive 2004/38/EC rather than by art.18 TFEU and that art.24 did not confer a right to equal treatment where the right to reside was conferred by domestic law, more generously than EU law, such as was the case in relation to pre-settled status. The CJEU also held (at [84]–[92]) that arts 1, 7 and 24 of the EU Charter provided a baseline below which a Member State could not allow a person's circumstances to fall. In *SSWP v Fratila and Tanase* [2021] UKSC 53, the Supreme Court subsequently allowed the Secretary of State's appeal, following the decision of the CJEU in *CG v Department for Communities* to the extent of holding that as the claimants did not have a right to reside under Directive 2004/38, they could not rely on the EU principle of non-discrimination on the ground of nationality. Fratila and Tanase were not permitted by the Supreme Court to run an argument based on the EU Charter, as it had not been taken earlier in the case. It has, however, been run, successfully in *SSWP v AT* [2023] EWCA Civ 1307, discussed further below.
3.95–3.101	In *X v Staatssecretaris van Justitie en Veiligheid* (June 22, 2023) the Court considered the claim to a derivative right brought by the third country national mother of a Dutch national child who had never resided in the Netherlands and who had ben brought up in Thailand by his grandmother. The Court, while emphasising that the benefits of citizenship of the Union were intended to be as available to a minor as to anyone else, concluded that Art.20 did not confer a right on the mother where it was not possible to conclude that the child would exercise their rights by entering and residing with her in the Netherlands. The case contains a useful review of the principles applying to the grant of a derivative right.
3.108–3.110	*Art.21 TFEU* Where a former *Chen* child had acquired a right of permanent residence and remained a minor, her primary carer was judged to have a right of residence in order to give "useful effect" to the child's rights: *FE v HMRC (CHB)* [2022] UKUT 4 (AAC). In *Sandwell MBC v KK and SSWP (HB)* [2022] UKUT 123 (AAC), Judge Wright applied *Krefeld* (above) to hold that the Immigration (European Economic Area) Regulations 2016 (SI 2016/1052) reg.16(1)(a) did not preclude a jobseeker from relying on a derivative right under Regulation 492/2011 art.10.

Para(s). in 2020–21 edition	Updating commentary
	For the continuing relevance under EU law (where it applies or is otherwise relevant) of *Martinez Sala, Grzelczyk* and *Trojani* (see paras 3.109–3.110 of the 2020/21 edition), see the discussion of *Krefeld* in relation to art.18 TFEU above. In *SSWP v AT (UC)* [2022] UKUT 330, SSWP submitted that art.13(1) created a unique type of right ("sui generis"), subject to the limitations and conditions referred to in the article, but not the right under art.21 TFEU on which AT had relied to move to the UK (as had the claimant in *CG v Department for Communities* (C-709/20)). The argument was rejected at [96]–[102], the panel concluding: "What AT retained, after the end of the transition period, was that part of her bundle of Article 21 TFEU rights which entitled her to continue to reside in the UK. CG shows that that right continues to generate legal effects even when the residence does not comply with the conditions in the [Citizens' Rights Directive], at least for those who have a right of residence granted under national law." [at 102] A similar argument on behalf of the Secretary of State was rejected by the Court of Appeal: see *SSWP v AT* [2023] EWCA Civ 1307 at [93]–[95].
3.120–3.129	*Art.45 TFEU* For those outside the scope of Part Two of the Withdrawal Agreement, any ability there might otherwise have been to rely after December 31, 2020 on art.45 via s.4 of the European Union (Withdrawal) Act 2018 is likely to be excluded by the sweeping provision in Immigration and Social Security Co-ordination (EU Withdrawal) Act 2020, s.1 and Sch.1, para 6.
3.126	*Art.45 TFEU – Work seekers* In *GMA v État Belge* (C-710/19) the CJEU reiterated that, in accordance with *Antonissen*, workseekers had to be given a reasonable time to apprise themselves of offers of employment corresponding to their vocational qualifications. See also under art.14(4)(b) of Directive 2004/38.
3.132–3.134	*Art.49 TFEU – Right of Establishment* While art.13(1) of the Withdrawal Agreement preserves the ability to rely on art.49 for those within the scope of the Agreement, any ability which might otherwise have existed for others to rely on this Article after December 31, 2020 via s.4 of the European Union (Withdrawal) Act 2018 has been removed by the Freedom of Establishment and Free Movement of Services (EU Exit) Regulations 2019/1401.
3.133	In *N v HMRC (CHB)* [2021] 28, Judge Mitchell held that characteristics (1) and (3) in *Jany* presuppose that there has been an agreement as to remuneration. As such an element is lacking in the way in which a street musician performs and obtains funds, he could not be self-employed.
3.135–3.136	*Art.56 – Services* Any ability which might otherwise have existed to rely on this Article after December 31, 2020 via s.4 of the European Union (Withdrawal) Act 2018 has been removed by the Freedom of Establishment and Free Movement of Services (EU Exit) Regulations 2019/1401.

5.186

Charter of Fundamental Rights of the European Union (Updating commentary to be read together with 2020–21 edition, paras 3.150 to 3.212)

Para(s) in 2020–21 edition	**Updating commentary**
3.152	*Art. 1—Human dignity* In *CG v Department for Communities* (C-709/20) (which related to a decision before the end of the Brexit transition period) the CJEU had relied on arts 1,7 and 24 of the Charter to hold that the claimant who had moved in the exercise of her right under art.21 TFEU and had then been granted Pre-settled status could not be refused universal credit without the State ensuring that she could nevertheless live with her children in dignified conditions. In *SSWP v AT (UC)* [2022] UKUT 330, a three-judge panel of the Upper Tribunal applied *CG* to a decision which post-dated the end of the transition period. It held that where *CG* was applicable, as in the case before it, an individualised assessment was required: [111]–[118]. It explained what art.1 required by reference to the decisions of the CJEU in *Jawo v Germany* (C-136/17) and *Haqbin v Federaal Agentschap voor de opvang van asielzoekers* (C-233/18), concluding at [125] that: "… [The] range of matters with which Article 1 is concerned, albeit strictly limited, extends to the provision of support for a person's 'most basic needs'. These will no doubt vary from person to person, though typically they will include housing (which we take as including a basic level of heating adequate for a person's health), food, clothing and hygiene. *Haqbin* also shows that the state may breach its obligations under Article 1 if a person lacks these things even for a very limited time, though it is right to note that the applicant in that case, as an unaccompanied minor asylum-seeker, was particularly vulnerable. In cases where a person is deprived of the means to meet his most basic needs for a very short time, the question whether Article 1 is breached will be sensitive to contextual matters of this kind." The Secretary of State's appeal was dismissed: see *SSWP v AT* [2023] EWCA Civ 1307. The Court of Appeal reviewed the scope of the concept of "dignity" at [32]–[36] and at [104]–[113] rejected an argument by SSWP that Art.1 had no greater effect than does Art.4 (or Art.3 of the ECHR). SSWP's criticisms of the First-tier Tribunal's findings of fact and resulting conclusion, and the Upper Tribunal's endorsement of them, were dismissed at [170]–[176]. Green LJ does add "an important caveat or word of caution" at [177]–[179] that exploring the concept of "dignity" in any greater detail, or its interaction with other rights conferred by the Charter or ECHR, will have to await other cases. The Supreme Court has refused permission to appeal.
3.159	*Art. 7—Respect for private and family life- General Note* The article was referred to, with art.24, in both *CG v Department for Communities* (C-709/20) and *SSWP v AT (UC)* [2022] UKUT 330, but both were very much ancillary to art.1 in the respective decisions. See under art.1 for more detail.
3.177	*Art. 24—The Rights of the Child—General Note* The article was referred to, with art.7, in both *CG v Department for Communities* (C-709/20) and *SSWP v AT (UC)* [2022] UKUT 330, but both were very much ancillary to art.1 in the respective decisions. See under art.1 for more detail.

Regulation (EU) No.492/2011 of the European Parliament and of the Council of 5 April 2011 on freedom of movement for workers within the Union 5.187

(Updating commentary to be read together with 2020-21 edition, paras 3.213–3.233.)

Para(s) in 2020-21 edition	**Updating commentary**
	For those covered by Part Two of the Withdrawal Agreement, art.24 preserves the ability to rely on this Regulation. For others, Immigration and Social Security Co-ordination (EU Withdrawal) Act 2020 Schedule, para.4 (introduced by s.1) provides: "Retained direct EU legislation 4(1) Article 1 of the Workers Regulation is omitted. (2) Articles 2 to 10 of the Workers Regulation cease to apply so far as— (a) they are inconsistent with any provision made by or under the Immigration Acts (including, and as amended by, this Act), or (b) they are otherwise capable of affecting the interpretation, application or operation of any such provision. (3) In this paragraph, "the Workers Regulation" means Regulation (EU) No 492/2011 of the European Parliament and of the Council of 5 April 2011 on freedom of movement for workers within the Union." "Retained direct EU legislation" is known as "Assimilated direct legislation" with effect from January 1, 2024.
3.215–3.222	*Art.7* With effect from November 29, 2022, The Cessation of EU Law Relating to Prohibitions on Grounds of Nationality and Free Movement of Persons Regulations 2022 (SI 2022/1240) reg.4: inserts the following as a new para.2A: "Paragraphs 1 and 2 do not apply in relation to the matters set out in the Schedule to The Cessation of EU Law Relating to Prohibitions on Grounds of Nationality and Free Movement of Persons Regulations 2022 (relevant matters)." and omits para.3 from art.7. The text of the Regulations is set out at paras 5.83–5.91. The "relevant matters" in the Schedule appear to be designed to catch anything to do with social security or social assistance.
3.223–3.225	*Art.9* With effect from November 29, 2022, the Cessation of EU Law Relating to Prohibitions on Grounds of Nationality and Free Movement of Persons Regulations 2022 (SI 2022/1240) reg.4 omits art.9.
3.226–3.230	*Art.10* With effect from November 29, 2022, the Cessation of EU Law Relating to Prohibitions on Grounds of Nationality and Free Movement of Persons Regulations 2022 (SI 2022/1240) reg.4 omits art.10.
3.230	The Court (Decision of October 6, 2020) followed the Advocate General on this point in *Jobcenter Krefeld*. In *Sandwell MBC v KK and SSWP (HB)* [2022] UKUT 123 (AAC), Judge Wright applied *Krefeld* to hold that the Immigration (European Economic Area) Regulations 2016 (SI 2016/1052) reg.16(1)(a) does not preclude a jobseeker from relying on a derivative right under Regulation 492/2011 art.10.

5.188 Regulation (EU) No 492/2011 of the European Parliament and of the Council of 5 April 2011 on freedom of movement of workers within the Union

(Updating commentary to be read together with 2020-21 edition, paras 3.213–3.233)

Para(s) in 2020–21 edition	Updating commentary
3.217	For those outside the scope of Part Two of the Withdrawal Agreement, there is likely no longer to be any ability to rely on the Regulation: Immigration and Social Security Co-ordination (EU Withdrawal) Act 2020, Schedule1 para 4 provides: "Articles 2 to 10 of the Workers Regulation cease to apply so far as— (a) they are inconsistent with any provision made by or under the Immigration Acts (including, and as amended by, this Act), or (b) they are otherwise capable of affecting the interpretation, application or operation of any such provision." For those within the scope of the Withdrawal Agreement, see its arts 12 and 23 for non-discrimination provisions likely to be interpreted so as to confer similar protections to those previously afforded by the Regulation.
3.217-3.221	The availability of a social assistance benefit to a dependent family member of a worker constitutes a "social advantage" for the migrant worker and cannot be refused where it would be granted to a worker who was a national of the host Member State: *GV v Chief Appeals Officer* (C-488/21) (December 21, 2023).

5.189 Directive 2004/38/EC of the European Parliament and of the Council of 29 April 2004 on the right of citizens of the Union and their family members to move and reside freely within the territory of the Member States amending Regulation (EEC) No 1612/68 and repealing Directives 64/221/EEC, 68/360/EEC, 72/194/EEC, 73/148/EEC, 75/34/EEC, 75/35/EEC, 90/364/EEC, 90/365/EEC and 93/96/EEC

(Updating commentary to be read together with 2020-21 edition, paras 3.234–3.335)

Para(s) in 2020–21 edition	Updating commentary
3.234	For those outside the scope of Part Two of the Withdrawal Agreement, any ability there might otherwise have been to rely after December 31, 2020 on the Directive via s.4 of the European Union (Withdrawal) Act 2018 is likely to be excluded by the sweeping provision in Immigration and Social Security Co-ordination (EU Withdrawal) Act 2020, s.1 and Sch.1, para 6. For those within the the scope of Part Two, the content of the Part does not entirely mirror, but borrows substantially from, the Directive. As regards the interpretation of Part Two where it adopts provisions from the Directive, note art.4 of the Withdrawal Agreement (see para.5.88) as well as the provisions of domestic law referred to in the General Note concerning United Kingdom Withdrawal from the European Union (at the beginning of this Part of this volume).

Para(s) in 2020–21 edition	Updating commentary
3.238	*Art.2(2)(d)—family members* A reference to the CJEU has been made in *XXX v État belge* (C-607/21) asking the following questions: In the context of the examination of the concept of a dependant for the purposes of art.2(2)(d) … should account be taken of the situation of an applicant who is already in the territory of the State in which the sponsor is established? If the answer to the first question is in the affirmative, should an applicant who is lawfully in the territory of that State be treated differently from an applicant who is there unlawfully? Is art.2(2)(d) … to be interpreted as meaning that, in order to be regarded as a dependant and thus to fall within the definition of "family member" referred to in that provision, a direct relative in the ascending line [may] rely on a situation of real material dependence in the country of origin established by documents which, at the time of lodging the application for a residence card as a family member of a Union citizen, were, however, issued several years previously, on the ground that the departure from the country of origin and the lodging of the application for a residence card in the host Member State did not occur at the same time? If the answer to the third question is in the negative, what are the criteria for assessing the situation of material dependence of an applicant seeking to join a European citizen or his or her partner, as a relative in the ascending line, without having been able to obtain a residence permit on the basis of an application lodged immediately after his or her departure from the country of origin?
3.238	*Art.2(2)(d)—family members* In *GV v Chief Appeals Officer* (C-488/21) (December 21, 2023) the CJEU, noting that the Court had not previously been asked to consider the conditions for retaining a right based on dependency (rather than those for acquiring it) made clear that such a right is retained as long as the person remains dependent on the worker concerned, until the point where the dependent qualifies for a right under art.16 of the Directive on the basis of five years' continuous residence.
3.238	*Art.2(2)(d)—family members* In *ZK and MS v Minister for Justice and Equality* (C-248/22), the High Court of Ireland has asked whether Council Directive 2004/38/EC prohibits the simultaneous conferral of derived rights of residence on the estranged spouse and the de facto, durable partner of a European Union citizen lawfully exercising his right of free movement as a worker under the Directive.
3.244–3.249	*Art.3(2)(a)—beneficiaries* In *SRS and AA v Minister for Justice and Equality* (C-22/21) (September 15, 2022; text rectified October 28, 2022), the Court held: "Point (a) of the first subparagraph of Article 3(2) of Directive 2004/38/EC … must be interpreted as meaning that the concept of 'any other family members who are members of the household of the Union citizen having the primary right of residence', mentioned in that provision, refers to persons who have a relationship of dependence with that citizen, based on close and stable personal ties, forged within the same household, in the context of a shared domestic life going beyond a mere temporary cohabitation entered into for reasons of pure convenience."

Para(s) in 2020–21 edition	Updating commentary
3.249	The CJEU followed its decision in *Lounes* (C-165/16) in *GV v Chief Appeals Officer* (C-488/21) (December 21, 2023). GV, a Romanian national, was dependent on her daughter, AC. AC was also a Romanian national but had additionally acquired Irish citizenship while working in Ireland. GV had appealed against the refusal of disability allowance, which is a "special non-contributory cash benefit". The Court held that because Directive 2004/38 only governs the conditions of entry and residence in a Member State other than that of which a person is a national, from the moment of AC's naturalisation the Directive no longer applied. However, the need to make effective the rights conferred by arts 21 and 45 TFEU meant that a family member of a worker who having exercised their right of freedom of movement acquires the nationality of the host Member State was entitled to a derived right of residence on terms no stricter than those of the Directive.
3.254	*Art. 6—right of residence for up to three months* In *S v Familienkasse Niedersachsen-Bremen der Bundesagentur für Arbeit* (C-411/20) (August 1, 2022), the claimant was able to rely on her rights under art.6 during the first three months to claim German family benefits. These did not amount to "social assistance" for the purposes of the Directive and so the provisions of art.24, which would otherwise have permitted Germany to refuse the benefits concerned, did not apply.
3.255	*Art. 7 – self-employed persons* In *N v HMRC (CHB)* [2021] UKUT 28 (AAC), Judge Mitchell held that, to the extent the two cases might be in conflict, whether there was self-employment for the purposes of art.7 fell to be examined by reference to the tests in *Jany* (C-268/99) rather than those in the social security coordination case of *van Roosdalen* (300/84). Characteristics (1) and (3) in *Jany* presuppose that there has been an agreement as to remuneration. As such an element is lacking in the way in which a street musician performs and obtains funds, he could not be self-employed.
3.271–3.276	*Art. 7—right of residence for more than three months—self-sufficiency* For a domestic case applying *S v Familienkasse Niedersachsen-Bremen der Bundesagentur für Arbeit* (C-411/20) (August 1, 2022) in an unusual context, see *SSWP v WV (UC)* [2023] UKUT 112 (AAC). The male claimant, a Belgian national, had married a British woman who was in receipt of "legacy" means-tested benefits and disability benefits. When the claimant moved in with her, he was supported from the benefits payable to her, together with the carer's allowance he successfully claimed. The Upper Tribunal held that the line of cases from *Chen* (C-200/02) to *Bajratari* (C-93/18) precluded consideration of the source of resources a claimant had (as long as they were not social assistance payable in respect of the claimant themselves: see C-333/13 *Dano v Jobcenter Leipzig* at [80]). The claimant's receipt of carer's allowance, which SSWP conceded is not "social assistance" for the purposes of the Directive, had the paradoxical effect that the amount of "social assistance" (understood as in *Brey* and as more recently reiterated in the *S* case) payable in respect of the couple was less than had been payable to the female claimant when single. In those circumstances, the male claimant was able to establish that he had had sufficient resources for the purposes of art.7(1)(b) up to the time when the couple moved to a new local authority area and consequently had to claim universal credit instead of legacy benefits. He was entitled to a *Brey*-style assessment of whether he had become an unreasonable burden on the social assistance system of the UK, the Upper Tribunal concluding that he had not. As a result, the couple's joint claim was to be paid at the couple rate rather than the single person's rate which would have been applicable had one partner lacked the right to reside. Permission to appeal has been given by the Court of Appeal.

Para(s) in 2020–21 edition	**Updating commentary**
3.277–3.278	*Art.7 – Comprehensive Sickness Insurance* A state is permitted to levy a proportionate charge for access to its publicly funded healthcare system by a person who is exercising a right of residence under art.7(1)(b): see *A v Latvijas Republikas Veselības ministrija* (C-535/19) (July 15, 2021). The area of comprehensive sickness insurance cover, a perennial problem for students and those claiming to be self-sufficient (and, in the latter case, their families), was addressed by the CJEU in *VI v HMRC* (C-247/20) (decision of March 10, 2022). A reference to the CJEU by the Appeal Tribunal in Northern Ireland had asked the following questions: (1) "Is a child EEA Permanent Resident required to maintain Comprehensive Sickness Insurance in order to maintain a right to reside, as s/he would as a self-sufficient person, pursuant to Regulation 4(1) of the 2016 Regulations? (2) Is the requirement, pursuant to reg.4(3)(b) ofThe Immigration (European Economic Area) Regulations 2016 (that Comprehensive Sickness Insurance cover in the United Kingdom is only satisfied for a student or self-sufficient person, with regard to reg.16(2)(b)(ii) of The Immigration (European Economic Area) Regulations 2016, if such cover extends to both that person and all their relevant family members), illegal under EU law in light of Article 7(1) of Directive 2004/381 and the jurisprudence of the Court of Justice of the European Union in paragraph 70 of *Teixeira (*C–480/08)? (3) Following the decision in paragraph 53 of *Ahmad v Secretary of State for the Home Department* [2014] EWCA Civ 988, are the Common Travel Area reciprocal arrangements in place regarding Health Insurance cover between the United Kingdom and the Republic of Ireland considered 'reciprocal arrangements' and therefore constitute Comprehensive Sickness Insurance for the purposes of Regulation 4(1) of the [Immigration (European Economic Area) Regulations 2016]?" In an Opinion of September 30, 2021, Advocate General Hogan referred to the express wording within art.16(1) and proposed that the first of the three questions be answered in the negative. As regards the second question, he noted that VI had not claimed the case fell within Regulation 492/2011 art.10, which was the successor of the provision which had been in issue in *Teixeira* and suggested that art.7 of the Directive had to be taken as it stood. At [56]–[64] the Advocate General included some remarks on whether reliance on a publicly funded health system could amount to comprehensive sickness insurance cover (CSIC), although this was not the question put by the referring court. Having raised the point, he recognised that this was not the case in which to attempt to answer it definitively. The Advocate General's observations did not however stop the Court. Having first reaffirmed that the Directive expressly made clear that a right of permanent residence is not subject to conditions (thus answering question 1), it turned to dealing with an earlier period, before the child had acquired a right of permanent residence and also lacked CSIC, at any rate in any form recognised before the decision in the present case. The Court first grappled with the degree of ambiguity in the English text as to whether CSIC was required not only for the person claiming the primary right to reside but also for their family members (as defined), concluding that it was. In *VI*, the child was an Irish national (cf. *Zhu and Chen* (C-200/02)) and VI's right arose as primary carer of a *Chen* child. Such a person is not thereby a "family member" for the purposes of Directive 2004/38 but the Court applied by analogy the requirement for a family member to have CSIC to the primary carer. Thus it was that the question arose whether the entitlement of VI and her son to treatment under the NHS during the relevant period amounted to CSIC.

Para(s) in 2020–21 edition	Updating commentary
	The Court, building on the Latvian case cited above held: "69. In that regard, it must be recalled that, although the host Member State may, subject to compliance with the principle of proportionality, make affiliation to its public sickness insurance system of an economically inactive Union citizen, residing in its territory on the basis of Article 7(1)(b) of Directive 2004/38, subject to conditions intended to ensure that that citizen does not become an unreasonable burden on the public finances of that Member State, such as the conclusion or maintaining, by that citizen, of comprehensive private sickness insurance enabling the reimbursement to that Member State of the health expenses it has incurred for that citizen's benefit, or the payment, by that citizen, of a contribution to that Member State's public sickness insurance system (judgment of 15 July 2021, *A (Public health care)*, C535/19, EU:C:2021:595 at [59]), the fact remains that, once a Union citizen is affiliated to such a public sickness insurance system in the host Member State, he or she has comprehensive sickness insurance within the meaning of Article 7(1)(b). 70. Furthermore, in a situation, such as that in the main proceedings, in which the economically inactive Union citizen at issue is a child, one of whose parents, a third-country national, has worked and was subject to tax in the host State during the period at issue, it would be disproportionate to deny that child and the parent who is his or her primary carer a right of residence, under Article 7(1)(b) of Directive 2004/38, on the sole ground that, during that period, they were affiliated free of charge to the public sickness insurance system of that State. It cannot be considered that that affiliation free of charge constitutes, in such circumstances, an unreasonable burden on the public finances of that State." It did not regard *Teixeira* as relevant. In *FE v HMRC (CHB)* [2022] UKUT 4 (AAC), the Upper Tribunal reached a similar conclusion in relation to question 1, while the Court of Appeal, in the days before a right of permanent residence was created by the Directive, reached a similar conclusion to the CJEU on whether a primary carer of a *Chen* child was themselves required to have CSIC in *W v Secretary of State for the Home Department* [2006] EWCA Civ 1494. In the light of *VI*, SSWP accepted that a history of apparent affiliation to the NHS was sufficient in *WH v Powys CC and SSWP (HB)* [2022] UKUT 203. Those looking forward to a ruling by the CJEU on the Common Travel Area arrangements (an area surprisingly rarely tested in the courts and tribunals) will have been disappointed, however. The CJEU in *VI* declined to deal with it on the basis that it had not been given enough information and on that issue the reference had failed to comply with relevant procedural requirements of the Court.
3.290	*Art.13—retention of the right of residence by family members in the event of divorce (etc.)* The Court of Appeal's decision in *Balogun v SSHD* [2023] EWCA Civ 414 contains a useful review of the law in this area. Balogun, a third country national married to a French national, was working when divorce proceedings were begun. One month later he was imprisoned. The Court held that he needed to meet the relevant art.13(2) condition when the divorce was finalised (not when divorce proceedings were initiated) and that he lost his ability to do so (by virtue of being a worker) when he was imprisoned. He was unable in this context to rely on the decision in *Orfanopoulos v Land Baden-Württemberg* (C-482/01) which (in different circumstances) had indicated that a person who had been registered as part of the labour force did not cease to be part of the labour force when in prison provided he returned to work within a reasonable period after his release.

Para(s) in 2020–21 edition	Updating commentary
3.290	In its decision of September 2, 2021, the CJEU held that none of the matters raised by the referring court in *X v Belgian State* (C-930-19) called into question the validity of art.13(2). In *AT v LB Hillingdon and SSWP (HB)* [2023] UKUT 149 (AAC), SSWP conceded that "the drafting of regulation 10(5) of the EEA Regulations does not fully transpose the retained right to reside in the UK conferred by article 13(2)(a) of the Directive on a family member of a third country national following the dissolution of a marriage between the third country national and an EEA citizen who was exercising treaty rights in the UK. The terms of the EEA Regulations, as drafted, cover only the third country national who was a party to the marriage, whereas the terms of article 13(2)(a) protect the third country national family members of the Union citizen."
3.291	*Art.14—retention of the right of residence* In *GMA v État Belge* (C-710/19) the CJEU appears to have confirmed (at [33]) what has been accepted in the UK to be the case, that art.14(4)(b) applies to jobseekers generally and not merely those who entered the host Member State in order to seek work. The Court reaffirms that a 6-month period to look for work does not appear in principle to be insufficient (at [42]). The period runs from when the person registered as a jobseeker ([37]). During that period, while a Member State may require the jobseeker to seek employment, it cannot require the person concerned to demonstrate a genuine chance of being engaged (at [44]-[45]). The Court was also asked to rule on the relevance of post-decision offers of employment in the face of a statutory limitation to facts at the date of decision (presumably a Belgian equivalent of s.12(8)(b) of SSA 1998) but, as Belgium had unlawfully imposed a requirement to demonstrate a genuine chance of being engaged on GMA during the first 6 months of his jobseeking, the Court did not need to answer it.
3.296	*Art.16—right of permanent residence-eligibility-general rule* In *VI v HMRC* (C-247/20), the CJEU reiterated the notion that, as the wording of art.16 provides, a right of permanent residence once obtained is not subject to complying with the conditions of art.7.
3.316	*Art.24—equal treatment* The Court (Decision of October 6, 2020) followed the Advocate General on this point in *Jobcenter Krefeld*. In *Sandwell MBC v KK and SSWP (HB)* [2022] UKUT 123 (AAC), Judge Wright applied *Krefeld* to hold that the Immigration (European Economic Area) Regulations 2016 (SI 2016/1052) reg.16(1)(a) does not preclude a jobseeker from relying on a derivative right under Regulation 492/2011 art.10. In *CG v Department for Communities* (C-709/20) (July 15, 2021), the CJEU addressed: "whether Article 24 of Directive 2004/38 must be interpreted as precluding legislation of a host Member State which excludes from social assistance economically inactive Union citizens who do not have sufficient resources and to whom that State has granted, on the basis of national law, a temporary right of residence, where those benefits are guaranteed to nationals of the Member State concerned who are in the same situation",

Para(s) in 2020–21 edition	Updating commentary
3.316	relying on C-333/13 to answer the question in the negative. The CJEU further ruled that in a case such as the one before them where art.24 was unavailable to the claimant, the claimant might nonetheless have a degree of protection from arts 1, 7 and 24 of the EU Charter. The claimants in *SSWP v Fratila and Tanase* [2021] UKSC 53 were not permitted by the Supreme Court to argue that point. However, in *SSWP v AT (UC)* [2022] UKUT 330 a three-judge panel of the Upper Tribunal upheld the ability of the claimant to rely on the Charter. For further details, see the discussion of art.1 of the Charter, above. The Secretary of State's appeal to the Court of Appeal has been dismissed ([2023] EWCA Civ 1307) and the Supreme Court has refused permission to appeal. *S v Familienkasse Niedersachsen-Bremen der Bundesagentur fur Arbeit* (C-411/20) (August 1, 2022) confirms that the initial right of residence under art.6 is nonetheless a right under the Directive and a Member State can only derogate from the principle of equal treatment to the extent that art.24 provides. In permitting such derogation in respect of "social assistance" it does not permit derogation in respect of benefits not falling within the Court's concept of social assistance, explained in *Pensionsversicherungsanstalt v Brey* (C-140/12) at [61]: "Accordingly, that concept must be interpreted as covering all assistance introduced by the public authorities, whether at national, regional or local level, that can be claimed by an individual who does not have resources sufficient to meet his own basic needs and the needs of his family and who, by reason of that fact, may become a burden on the public finances of the host Member State during his period of residence which could have consequences for the overall level of assistance which may be granted by that State (see, to that effect, *Bidar*, paragraph 56; *Eind*, paragraph 29; and *Förster*, paragraph 48; see also, by analogy, Case C-578/08 *Chakroun* [2010] ECR I-1839, paragraph 46, and *Kamberaj*, paragraph 91)."

Regulation (EC) No. 883/2004 of the European Parliament and of the Council of 29 April 2004 on the coordination of social security systems 5.190

(Updating commentary to be read together with 2020-21 edition, paras 3.336–3.551)

Para(s) in 2020–21 edition	Updating commentary
3.336	*General Note* Following the expiry on December 31, 2020 of the implementation period for the UK's withdrawal from the EU, Regulation 883/2004 has a somewhat complex status. As regards those who fall within the scope of art.30 of the Withdrawal Agreement or within one of the special circumstances addressed in art.32, it continues to apply via art.31. Note should be taken of the modifications for which the Withdrawal Agreement provides, including those in Annex I, Part 2 (although, curiously, most of these were already within the Regulation as it previously stood). The position with regard to the implementing regulation, Regulation 987/2009, is similar. Provisions in the Withdrawal Agreement, which are intended to be directly enforceable, take effect in domestic law via s.7A of the European Union (Withdrawal) Act 2018. However, Regulation 883/2004 in its own right (i.e. divorced from its underpinning by the Withdrawal Agreement), which would otherwise have constituted "retained direct EU legislation" (or as it is now termed "assimilated direct legislation") under s.3 of the 2018 Act is repealed, subject to very limited savings, by the Social Security Co-ordination (Revocation of Retained Direct EU Legislation and Related Amendments) (EU Exit) Regulations 2020/1508. (The same also applies to its predecessor, Regulation 1408/71 and its implementing Regulation 574/72.) Equivalent provision is made in relation to devolved benefits in Scotland by Scottish SI 2020/399. Those not in a position to rely on the Withdrawal Agreement will in consequence be reliant on the Protocol on Social Security Co-ordination which forms part of the Trade and Co-operation Agreement concluded between the European Union and the United Kingdom on December 24, 2020: see para.5.158. It forms part of domestic law by virtue of the European Union (Future Relationship) Act 2020 s.26, the effect of which remains to be explored (though see the General Note to that section). Irish nationals enjoy a special position because of the Common Travel Area and the Convention on Social Security between the UK and Ireland: see *https://www.gov.uk/government/publications/memorandum-of-understanding-between-the-uk-and-ireland-on-the-cta* (accessed May 7, 2024) and the Social Security (Ireland) Order 2019 (SI 2019/622) (not reproduced in this volume for reasons of space), which has the Convention in its Schedule.
3.338–3.339	*General Note—application of Regulation 883/04 to Iceland, Liechtenstein, Norway and Switzerland* The Citizens Rights' Agreements between the UK and Switzerland and the UK and Iceland, Liechtenstein and Norway are part of domestic law by virtue of European Union (Withdrawal) Act 2018 s.7B. See the General Note to that section for further detail.
3.349	*Art.1(c)—definition of "insured person"* The Court of Appeal allowed the claimant's appeal in *Harrington v SSWP* [2023] EWCA Civ 433. See the discussion under art.11, with which the applicability of arts 1(c)(p) and (q) is inextricably linked.
3.351	In relation to *Harrington v SSWP* see above.

Para(s) in 2020–21 edition	**Updating commentary**
3.354	*Art.1(z)—definition of "family benefit"* The Court of Appeal, having permitted HMRC to raise arguments not raised below, has reversed the decision of the Upper Tribunal in *WC v HMRC (CHB)* [2019] UKUT 289 (AAC): see *HMRC v Carrington* [2021] EWCA Civ 1724.
3.363	*Art.3—matters covered* Art.3(1)(a) has been held in *A v Latvijas Republikas Veselības ministrija* (C-535/19) (July 15, 2021) at [38] to mean that "medical care, financed by the state, which is granted without any individual and discretionary assessment of personal needs, to persons falling within the categories of recipients defined by national legislation, constitutes "sickness benefits" within the meaning of [art.3], this falling within the scope of [the Regulation]".
3.364	Previous editions of this work had referred to the "abundantly clear" "willingness of the Luxembourg Court to unravel national benefit structures", exemplified by the decisions in *Commission v European Parliament and Council* (C-299/05) and *Bartlett, Ramos and Taylor v SSWP* (C-537/09). On a domestic level, however, in *Michaela Simkova v SSWP* [2024] EWCA Civ 419, the Court of Appeal has taken the view that the CJEU's decision rested on the fact that the benefit in question (DLA) had two separate components under national law, both of which could be discretely claimed and give rise to stand-alone entitlements. There was, therefore, no general principle that elements of a benefit could be severed. By contrast *Vera Hoecks v Centre Public d'Aide Sociale de Kalmthout* (Case 122/84) was authority for the proposition that composite, blended social benefit schemes fell outside the scope of Regulation 1408/71 and remained good law under Regulation 883/2004. In *Simkova*, the claimant, who was resident in Great Britain and a claimant of universal credit, sought to argue that the child element of the UC calculation could be severed and that, so severed, it would constitute a "family benefit". Her teenage son lived outside the UK and on her case, that element would be exportable. Both because of the view the Court of Appeal took of the above authorities and following consideration of the legislative context and purpose of Regulation 883/2004, her case failed. The court placed particular weight on the "central premise underlying the legislation … that it amounts to a regime of coordination and not harmonisation and does not (save in certain limited respects) fetter the discretion of Member States as to the configuration of their social welfare systems). Disaggregation, as sought by the claimant, would be inconsistent with that premise and, as it "would be a controversial and complex policy, would in the court's view have been set out comprehensively and explicitly, were it to exist at all". The court considered the matter to be clear and not to require a reference to the CJEU under art.158 of the Withdrawal Agreement.

Para(s) in 2020–21 edition	**Updating commentary**
3.367–3.371	*Art.4—equality of treatment* In *S v Familienkasse Niedersachsen-Bremen der Bundesagentur für Arbeit* (C-411/20) (August 1, 2022) the CJEU held at [61]: "Regulation No 883/2004 does not contain any provision which would allow the host Member State of a Union citizen, who is a national of another Member State lawfully resident in the first Member State, to operate, in the light of the fact that that citizen is economically inactive, a difference in treatment between that citizen and its own nationals as regards the conditions for the grant of 'family benefits' within the meaning of Article 3(1)(j) of that regulation, read in conjunction with Article 1(z) thereof. Accordingly, Article 4 of that regulation precludes a measure which applies such a difference in treatment." It would, however, be necessary for a claimant to have established that they were habitually resident.
3.379	*Art.7—waiving of residence rules* Adjusting the amount of family benefits payable to recipients who live in another Member State to reflect the differing cost of living there is precluded by art.7: see *Commission v Austria* (C-328/20) (June 16, 2022). The Court of Appeal, having permitted HMRC to raise arguments not raised below, has reversed the decision of the Upper Tribunal in *WC v HMRC (CHB)* [2019] UKUT 289 (AAC): see *HMRC v Carrington* [2021] EWCA Civ 1724.
3.390	*Art.11—determination of the legislation applicable-general rules* A telling example, consistent with principle, is provided by *A v Latvijas Republikas Veselības ministrija* (C-535/19) (July 15, 2021). The CJEU reiterated that the provision is intended not only to prevent the concurrent application of a number of legislative systems to a given situation but also to ensure that persons covered by the Regulation are not left without social security cover because there is no legislation which is applicable to them. It is not as such intended to lay down the conditions governing the existence of a right to social security benefits (at [46] and [47]). However, states cannot opt out of art.11(3)(e) where it applies. Accordingly, an Italian citizen who had left Italy and was no longer entitled to healthcare there, and who had moved to Latvia as a self-sufficient person in order to be with his Latvian wife and their children, had the right to affiliate to the Latvian public sickness insurance system. That was however subject the right of the Latvian authorities to levy a proportionate charge: as A was there on the basis of self-sufficiency under art.7(1)(b) of Directive 2004/38/EC, the requirement to maintain comprehensive sickness insurance cover under that provision would be rendered redundant if he were to be entitled to free access.
3.391	For a case examining the position under art.11(3) (a) and (e) of an aid worker employed to work outside the EU by an undertaking in the EU, see *QY v Finanzamt Österreich* (C-372/20) (November 25, 2021).

Para(s) in 2020–21 edition	**Updating commentary**
3.391–3.395	In *Harrington v SSWP* [2023] EWCA Civ 433; [2023] AACR 8 the issue, put shortly, was whether the child claimant of the care component of DLA, who was resident in the UK and who fulfilled the conditions of entitlement under UK law, could rely on her residence rather than be dependent on rights as the family member of her father, who was self-employed and living in Belgium. Whether the claimant was an "insured person" turned on whether the UK was the competent state. In her own right, the claimant fell within art.11(3)(e), which would make the UK the competent state. However, art.21 makes provision for cash benefits to be paid to an insured person (such as the claimant's father was, in Belgium—for him, the competent state) and to members of their family even though the latter resided in a state other than the competent state. So it came down to which should prevail: the claimant's entitlement in her own right (from the UK) or her entitlement as the family member of her father (from Belgium). The case went off to the Administrative Commission established under Title IV of the Regulation ([24]–[30] of Lewis LJ's judgment provide a rare view of the processes of that body) but its decision was inconclusive. The background to the matter was the policy aim, reflected in art.11 and in recital 45, that the legislation of only one State should be applicable to a person. Lewis LJ concluded that the wording and purpose of art.21 indicated that it did not operate as a rule of priority (he contrasted other regulations which did). Rather, its purpose was to protect family members from losing entitlement to benefits when they resided in a different Member State from the insured person. This view was consistent with the history of the provision, with the policy aim of promoting freedom of movement of workers and the self-employed and with the nature of a non-contributory benefit payable to assist with care costs, which when costs might differ from State to State would most sensibly be linked with the costs in the state where the claimant resides. The general rule that priority is given to the State of economic activity is capable of being displaced. In *SP v Department for Communities (PIP)* [2023] NiCom23, the claimant was able to rely on art.11(3)(e) to claim personal independence payment from the UK, her state of residence, despite being in receipt of an invalidity pension from the Republic of Ireland, exported in reliance on art.7. The invalidity pension did not bring her within any of limbs (a) to (d) of art.11(3). Further, following *Konevod v SSWP* [2020] EWCA Civ 809 and *Harrington v SSWP* [2023] EWCA Civ 433; art.11(3) was not displaced by the rules of Title III.
3.416	*Art.21—cash benefits* *AH v SSWP (DLA)* has now been appealed to the Court of Appeal as *Harrington v SSWP* [2023] EWCA Civ 433, where the Court discusses the wording and purpose of art.21. See the note under art.11 above.
3.432	*Art.32—prioritisation of the right to benefits in kind* There is no equivalent rule to reg.32 dealing with matters of priority in relation to cash sickness benefits: see the discussion of *Harrington v SSWP* [2023] EWCA Civ 433 under art.11 above.

Para(s) in 2020–21 edition	Updating commentary
3.461	*Art.52—award of benefits* In *SC v Zakład Ubezpieczeń Społecznych I Oddział w Warszawie* (C-866/19) (October 21, 2021), the CJEU held that art.52(1)(b) must be interpreted as meaning that, for the purposes of determining the limit which non-contribution periods may not exceed in relation to contribution periods, as provided for by the national legislation, the competent institution of the Member State concerned must take into consideration, when calculating the theoretical amount of the benefit referred to in point (i) of that provision, all the periods of insurance, including those periods of insurance completed under the legislation of other Member States, whereas the calculation of the actual amount of the benefit referred to in point (ii) of that provision is made having regard solely to the periods of insurance completed under the legislation of the Member State concerned.
3.483	*Art.65—unemployed persons who resided in a Member State other than the competent State* In *K v Raad van bestuur van het Uitvoeringsinstituut werknemersverzekeringen* (C-285/20) (September 30, 2021) [2022] P.T.S.R. 250 the Court held that art.65(2) and (5) had to be interpreted as applying to a situation in which, before being wholly unemployed, the person concerned resided in a Member State other than the competent Member State and was not actually employed but was on sick leave and received, on that basis, sickness benefits paid by the competent Member State, provided, however, that, in accordance with the national law of the competent Member State, entitlement to such benefits is treated in the same way as the pursuit of an activity as an employed person. The Court further held that those provisions must be interpreted as meaning that the reasons, in particular of a family nature, for which the person concerned has transferred his or her residence to a Member State other than the competent Member State do not have to be taken into account for the purposes of applying those provisions. Key to the Court's decision was art.1(a), which defines the concept of "activity as an employed person" as being "any activity or equivalent situation treated as such for the purposes of the social security legislation of the Member State in which such activity or equivalent situation exists".
3.490–3.491	*Art.67—members of the family residing in another Member State* As art.67 is a specific application in the context of family benefits of the more general principle in art.7, the breach of the former involved in adjusting family benefits by reference to the Member State of residence of the recipient likewise involves a breach of the latter: *Commission v Austria* (C-328/20) (June 16, 2022). The position of a person in receipt of pensions from two Member States was considered in *DN v Finanzamt Österreich* (C-199/21) (October 13, 2022), the Court concluding that: "The second sentence of Article 67 of Regulation No 883/2004 must be interpreted as meaning that, where a person is in receipt of pensions in two Member States, that person is entitled to family benefits in accordance with the legislation of those two Member States. Where the receipt of such benefits in one of those Member States is precluded pursuant to the national legislation, the priority rules referred to in Article 68(1) and (2) of that regulation do not apply." An attempt to argue that the child element of universal credit was severable from the rest of the award (with a view to arguing that the severed element constituted a "family benefit" so as to be payable in respect of a child residing outside the UK) failed in *Michaela Simkova v SSWP* [2024] EWCA Civ 419. For fuller discussion of the case, see 3.364.

Para(s) in 2020–21 edition	Updating commentary
3.493	*Art.68—priority rules in the event of overlapping* The Court of Appeal, having permitted HMRC to raise arguments not raised below, has reversed the decision of the Upper Tribunal in *WC v HMRC (CHB)* [2019] UKUT 289 (AAC): see *HMRC v Carrington* [2021] EWCA Civ 1724.
3.496	*Art.68(3)—priority rules in the event of overlapping* *QY v Finanzamt Österreich* (C-372/20) (November 25, 2021) held that Regulation 883/2004 art.68(3)(a) and Regulation 987/2009 art.60(2) and (3) are to be interpreted as being mutually binding on the institution of the Member State with primary competence and the institution of the Member State with secondary competence, such that the applicant for family benefits must submit only one application to only one of those institutions and that it is then for those two institutions to deal with that application jointly.
3.510–3.511	*Art.72—tasks of the Administrative Commission—General Note* Article 36(4) of the Withdrawal Agreement provides a list of the Decisions of the Administrative Commission for the purposes of the Withdrawal Agreement. There is provision for the list to be modified.
3.523	*Art.81—claims declarations or appeals* In *FS v Chief Appeals Officer* (C-3/21) (September 29, 2022), the Court held: 1. Article 81 of Regulation 883/2004 of the European Parliament and of the Council of 29 April 2004 on the coordination of social security systems must be interpreted as meaning that the concept of "claim" in that article refers only to an application made by a person who has exercised his or her right to freedom of movement to the authorities of a Member State which is not competent under the conflict rules laid down by that regulation. Therefore, that concept does not include either the initial application made under the legislation of a Member State by a person who has not yet exercised his or her right to freedom of movement or the periodic payment, by the authorities of that Member State, of a benefit normally payable, at the time of that payment, by another Member State. 2. EU law, and in particular the principle of effectiveness, does not preclude the application of national legislation which makes the retroactive effect of an application for child benefit subject to a limitation period of 12 months, since that period does not render practically impossible or excessively difficult the exercise by the migrant workers concerned of the rights conferred by Regulation 883/2004.
3.539	*Annex II—Provisions of conventions which remain in force and which, where applicable, are restricted to the persons covered thereby* Annex I of the Withdrawal Agreement purports to add provisions to this Annex which, however, it appears already formed part of the Regulation as amended.
3.540	*Annex III—Restriction of rights to benefits in kind for members of the family of a frontier worker* The United Kingdom has been added to Annex III for the purposes of the Withdrawal Agreement by Annex I of the latter.
3.543	*Annex VI—Identification of Type A legislation which should be subject to special coordination* Annex I of the Withdrawal Agreement purports to add provisions to this Annex which, however, it appears already formed part of the Regulation as amended.

Para(s) in 2020–21 edition	**Updating commentary**
3.545–3.546	*Annex VIII—Cases in which the pro rata calculation shall be waived or shall not apply* Annex I of the Withdrawal Agreement purports to add provisions to both Part 1 and Part 2 of this Annex which, however, it appears already formed part of the Regulation as amended.
3.550	*Annex X—Special non-contributory cash benefits* Annex I of the Withdrawal Agreement purports to add provisions to this Annex which, however, it appears already formed part of the Regulation as amended.
3.551	*Annex XI—Special provisions for the application of the legislation of the Member States* Annex I of the Withdrawal Agreement purports to add provisions to this Annex which, however, it appears already formed part of the Regulation as amended.

Regulation (EC) No. 987/2009 of the European Parliament and of the Council of 16 September 2009 laying down the procedure for implementing Regulation (EC) No 883/2004 on the coordination of social security systems (Text with relevance for the EEA and for Switzerland) 5.191

(Updating commentary to be read together with 2020-21 edition, paras 3.552–3.685)

Para(s) in 2020-21 edition	**Updating commentary**
3.552	*General Note* Following the expiry on December 31, 2020 of the implementation period for the UK's withdrawal from the EU, Regulation 987/2009, like Regulation 883/2004 which it implements, has a somewhat complex status. As regards those who fall within the scope of art.30 of the Withdrawal Agreement or within one of the special circumstances addressed in art.32, it continues to apply via art.31. Note should be taken of the modifications for which the Withdrawal Agreement provides, including those in Annex I, Part 2 (although, curiously, most of these were already within the Regulation as it previously stood). Provisions in the Withdrawal Agreement, which are intended to be directly enforceable, take effect in domestic law via s.7A of the European Union (Withdrawal) Act 2018. However, Regulation 987/2009 in its own right (i.e. divorced from its underpinning by the Withdrawal Agreement), which would otherwise have constituted "retained direct EU legislation" (or as it is now termed "assimilated direct legislation") under s.3 of the 2018 Act is repealed, subject to very limited savings, by the Social Security Co-ordination (Revocation of Retained Direct EU Legislation and Related Amendments) (EU Exit) Regulations 2020/1508. (The same also applies to the predecessor regulations, Regulation 1408/71 and its Regulation 574/72.) Equivalent provision is made in relation to devolved benefits in Scotland by Scottish SI 2020/399. Those not in a position to rely on the Withdrawal Agreement will in consequence be reliant on the Protocol on Social Security Co-ordination which forms part of the Trade and Co-operation Agreement concluded between the European Union and the United Kingdom on December 24, 2020: see para.5.147. It forms part of domestic law by virtue of the European Union (Future Relationship) Act 2020 s.26, the effect of which remains to be explored (though see the General Note to that section).

Para(s) in 2020-21 edition	**Updating commentary**
3.617	For an instance of where reliance on art.21 TFEU assisted in having child-raising periods in another Member State taken into account where the terms of art.44(2) cannot be complied with, see *CC v Pensionsversicherungsanstalt* (C-570) (7 July 2022)
3.638	*Art.60(2) and (3)—procedure for applying Articles 67 and 68 of the basic Regulation* *QY v Finanzamt Österreich* (C-372/20) (November 25, 2021) held that Regulation 883/2004 art.68(3)(a) and art.60(2) and (3) of this Regulation are to be interpreted as being mutually binding on the institution of the Member State with primary competence and the institution of the Member State with secondary competence, such that the applicant for family benefits must submit only one application to only one of those institutions and that it is then for those two institutions to deal with that application jointly.
3.676	*Annex 1—Implementing provisions for bilateral agreements remaining in force and new bilateral implementing agreements* Annex I of the Withdrawal Agreement purports to add provisions to this Annex most, but not all, of which, however, it appears already formed part of the Regulation as amended.
3.678	*Annex 3—Member states claiming the reimbursement of the cost of benefits in kind on the basis of fixed amounts* Annex I of the Withdrawal Agreement purports to add the United Kingdom to this Annex but it appears it already was under the Regulation as previously amended.

5.192

Regulation (EC) No. 859/2003 of 14 May 2003 extending the provisions of Regulation (EEC) No 1408/71 and Regulation (EEC) No 574/72 to nationals of third countries who are not already covered by those provisions solely on the ground of their nationality

(Updating commentary to be read together with 2020-21 edition, paras 3.686–3.693)

Para(s) in 2020-21 edition	**Updating commentary**
3.685	*General Note* Following the expiry on December 31, 2020 of the implementation period for the UK's withdrawal from the EU, third country nationals fulfilling the conditions of Regulation 859/2003 and members of their families and survivors are entitled to rely on Part Two of the Withdrawal Agreement if they meet the other qualifying conditions for doing so. Apart from that, the Regulation, which would otherwise have constituted "retained direct EU legislation" (or as it is now termed "assimilated direct legislation") under European Union (Withdrawal) Act 2018 s.3, is repealed, subject to very limited savings, by the Social Security Co-ordination (Revocation of Retained Direct EU Legislation and Related Amendments) (EU Exit) Regulations 2020/1508.

Directive 79/7/EC of 19 December 1978 on the progressive implementation of the principle of equal treatment for men and women in matters of social security 5.193

(Updating commentary to be read together with 2020-21 edition, paras 3.694–3.724)

Para(s) in 2020-21 edition	Updating commentary
3.695	*General Note* Directly enforceable rights under a Directive will unless excluded by the legislature be capable of being enforced via European Union (Withdrawal) Act 2018 s.4. Additionally, art.2 and Annex 1 of the Ireland/Northern Ireland Protocol to the Withdrawal Agreement entrench various provisions against discrimination, of which this Directive is one. The legislation establishing a general principle of parity between the social security systems of Great Britain and Northern Ireland (see Northern Ireland Act 1998 s.87) bolsters the likelihood that the provisions of the Directive will continue to be applied in Great Britain also.

Extracts from the Trade and Cooperation Agreement

Article 8: Committees

1. The following Committees are hereby established: 5.194

...

(p) the Specialised Committee on Social Security Coordination, which addresses matters covered by Heading Four of Part Two and the Protocol on Social Security Co-ordination;

HEADING FOUR: SOCIAL SECURITY COORDINATION AND VISAS FOR SHORT-TERM VISITS

TITLE I:

SOCIAL SECURITY COORDINATION

Article 488: Overview 5.195

Member States and the United Kingdom shall coordinate their social security systems in accordance with the Protocol on Social Security Coordination, in order to secure the social security entitlements of the persons covered therein.

Article 489: Legally residing

1. The Protocol on Social Security Coordination shall apply to persons legally residing in a Member State or the United Kingdom.

2. Paragraph 1 of this Article shall not affect entitlements to cash benefits which relate to previous periods of legal residence of persons covered by Article SSC.2 [Persons covered] of the Protocol on Social Security Coordination.

Article 490: Cross border situations

1. The Protocol on Social Security Coordination only applies to situations arising between one or more Member States and the United Kingdom.

2. The Protocol on Social Security Coordination shall not apply to persons whose situations are confined in all respects either to the United Kingdom, or to the Member States.

PROTOCOL ON SOCIAL SECURITY COORDINATION

GENERAL NOTE

5.196 The Protocol, which forms part of the EU-UK Trade and Co-operation Agreement concluded on December 24, 2020, derives its force in domestic law from s.26 of the European Union (Future Relationship) Act 2020 (see para.5.81). While that section incorporates the Protocol into domestic law, its sweeping approach leaves open, at least for now, a number of questions concerning the enforceability of individual provisions.

The text of the Trade and Cooperation Agreement, including the Protocol on Social Security Coordination, was re-published in amended form (Official Journal L149/10 of April 30, 2021). There were changes to the numbering of the Agreement and a host of minor changes (by way of correction of typographical errors and other tidying up) to the Protocol. The text here follows the amended version, save that the titles of cross-referenced provisions have been added in square brackets to assist navigation.

Those who are within scope of the Citizens' Rights part of the Withdrawal Agreement will wish to explore its provisions in relation to social security co-ordination. It presently appears that the two schemes exist in parallel. While the Citizens' Rights provisions directly apply (in modified form) Regulation 883/2004 and its implementing Regulation 987/2009, the Protocol very closely follows—often with beneficial tweaks to the drafting—those Regulations, decisions on which will continue to be influential via the provisions of the European Union (Withdrawal) Act 2018. For such decisions, see the commentary on those instruments in the 2020-21 edition, the updating material at paras 5.190 and 5.191 of this edition and the General Note to art.31 of the Withdrawal Agreement at para.5.157.

TITLE I:

GENERAL PROVISIONS

Article SSC.1: Definitions

5.197 For the purposes of this Protocol, the following definitions apply:

(a) "activity as an employed person" means any activity or equivalent situation treated as such for the purposes of the social security legislation of the State in which such activity or equivalent situation exists;

(b) "activity as a self-employed person" means any activity or equivalent situation treated as such for the purposes of the social security legislation of the State in which such activity or equivalent situation exists;

(c) "assisted reproduction services" means any medical, surgical or obstetric services provided for the purpose of assisting a person to carry a child;

(d) "benefits in kind" means:
  (i) for the purposes of Chapter 1 [Sickness, maternity and equivalent paternity benefits] of Title III, benefits in kind provided for under the legislation of a State which are intended to supply, make available, pay directly or reimburse the cost of medical care and products and services ancillary to that care;
  (ii) for the purposes of Chapter 2 [Accidents at work and occupational diseases] of Title III, all benefits in kind relating to accidents at work and occupational diseases as defined in point (i) and provided for under the States' accidents at work and occupational diseases schemes;

(e) "child-raising period" refers to any period which is credited under the pension legislation of a State or which provides a supplement to a pension explicitly for the reason that a person has raised a child, irrespective of the method used to calculate those periods and whether they accrue during the time of child-raising or are acknowledged retroactively;

(f) "civil servant" means a person considered to be such or treated as such by the State to which the administration employing them is subject;

(g) "competent authority" means, in respect of each State, the Minister, Ministers or other equivalent authority responsible for social security schemes throughout or in any part of the State in question;

(h) "competent institution" means:
  (i) the institution with which the person concerned is insured at the time of the application for benefit; or
  (ii) the institution from which the person concerned is or would be entitled to benefits if that person or a member or members of their family resided in the State in which the institution is situated; or
  (iii) the institution designated by the competent authority of the State concerned; or
  (iv) in the case of a scheme relating to an employer's obligations in respect of the benefits set out in Article SSC.3(1) [Matters covered], either the employer or the insurer involved or, in default thereof, the body or authority designated by the competent authority of the State concerned;

(i) "competent State" means the State in which the competent institution is situated;

(j) "death grant" means any one-off payment in the event of death, excluding the lump-sum benefits referred to in point (w);

(k) "family benefit" means all benefits in kind or in cash intended to meet family expenses;

(l) "frontier worker" means any person pursuing an activity as an employed or self-employed person in a State and who resides in another State to which that person returns as a rule daily or at least once a week;

(m) "home base" means the place from where the crew member normally starts and ends a duty period or a series of duty periods, and where, under normal conditions, the operator/airline is not responsible for the accommodation of the crew member concerned;

(n) "institution" means, in respect of each State, the body or authority responsible for applying all or part of the legislation;

(o) "institution of the place of residence" and "institution of the place of stay" mean, respectively, the institution which is competent to provide benefits in the place where the person concerned resides and the institution which is competent to provide benefits in the place where the person concerned is staying, in accordance with the legislation administered by that institution or, where no such institution exists, the institution designated by the competent authority of the State concerned;

(p) "insured person", in relation to the social security branches covered by Chapters 1 [Sickness, maternity and equivalent paternity benefits] and 3 [Death grants] of Title III [Special provisions concerning the various categories of benefits], means any person satisfying the conditions required under the legislation of the State competent under Title II [Determination of the legislation applicable] in order to have the right to benefits, taking into account the provisions of this Protocol;

(q) "legislation" means, in respect of each State, laws, regulations and other statutory provisions and all other implementing measures relating to the social security branches covered by Article SSC.3(1), but excludes contractual provisions other than those which serve to implement an insurance obligation arising from the laws and regulations referred to in this point or which have been the subject of a decision by the public authorities which makes them obligatory or extends their scope, provided that the State concerned makes a declaration to that effect, notified to the Specialised Committee on Social Security Coordination. The European Union shall publish such a declaration in the Official Journal of the European Union;

(r) "long-term care benefit" means a benefit in kind or in cash the purpose of which is to address the care needs of a person who, on account of impairment, requires considerable assistance, including but not limited to assistance from another person or persons to carry out essential activities of daily living for an extended period of time in order to support their personal autonomy; this includes benefits granted for the same purpose to a person providing such assistance;

(s) "member of the family" means:

 (i) (A) any person defined or recognised as a member of the family or designated as a member of the household by the legislation under which benefits are provided;

 (B) with regard to benefits in kind pursuant to Chapter 1 [Sickness, maternity and equivalent paternity benefits] of Title III [Special provisions concerning the various categories of benefits], any person defined or recognised as a member of the family or designated as a member of the household by the legislation of the State in which that person resides;

 (ii) if the legislation of a State which is applicable under point (i) does not make a distinction between the members of the family and other persons to whom it is applicable, the spouse, minor children, and dependent children who have reached the age of majority shall be considered members of the family;

(iii) if, under the legislation which is applicable under points (i) and (ii), a person is considered a member of the family or member of the household only if that person lives in the same household as the insured person or pensioner, this condition shall be considered satisfied if the person in question is mainly dependent on the insured person or pensioner;

(t) "period of employment" or "period of self-employment" mean periods so defined or recognised by the legislation under which they were completed, and all periods treated as such, where they are regarded by that legislation as equivalent to periods of employment or to periods of self-employment;

(u) "period of insurance" means periods of contribution, employment or self-employment as defined or recognised as periods of insurance by the legislation under which they were completed or considered as completed, and all periods treated as such, where they are regarded by that legislation as equivalent to periods of insurance;

(v) "period of residence" means periods so defined or recognised by the legislation under which they were completed or considered as completed;

(w) "pension" covers not only pensions but also lump-sum benefits which can be substituted for them and payments in the form of reimbursement of contributions and, subject to the provisions of Title III [Special provisions concerning the various categories of benefits], revaluation increases or supplementary allowances;

(x) "pre-retirement benefit" means all cash benefits, other than an unemployment benefit or an early old-age benefit, provided from a specified age to workers who have reduced, ceased or suspended their remunerative activities until the age at which they qualify for an old-age pension or an early retirement pension, the receipt of which is not conditional upon the person concerned being available to the employment services of the competent State; "early old-age benefit" means a benefit provided before the normal pension entitlement age is reached and which either continues to be provided once the said age is reached or is replaced by another old-age benefit;

(y) "refugee" has the meaning assigned to it in Article 1 of the Convention relating to the Status of Refugees, signed in Geneva on 28 July 1951;

(z) "registered office or place of business" means the registered office or place of business where the essential decisions of the undertaking are adopted and where the functions of its central administration are carried out;

(aa) "residence" means the place where a person habitually resides;

(bb) "special non-contributory cash benefits" means those non-contributory cash benefits which:

(i) are intended to provide either:

(A) supplementary, substitute or ancillary cover against the risks covered by the branches of social security referred to in Article SSC.3(1) [Matters covered], and which guarantee the persons concerned a minimum subsistence income having regard to the economic and social situation in the State concerned; or

(B) solely specific protection for the disabled, closely linked to the said person's social environment in the State concerned, and

(ii) where the financing exclusively derives from compulsory taxation intended to cover general public expenditure and the conditions for providing and for calculating the benefits are not dependent on any contribution in respect of the beneficiary. However, benefits provided to supplement a contributory benefit shall not be considered to be contributory benefits for this reason alone;

(cc) "special scheme for civil servants" means any social security scheme which is different from the general social security scheme applicable to employed persons in the State concerned and to which all, or certain categories of, civil servants are directly subject;

(dd) "stateless person" has the meaning assigned to it in Article 1 of the Convention relating to the Status of Stateless Persons, signed in New York on 28 September 1954;

(ee) "stay" means temporary residence.

General Note

5.198 Corresponding provision of Regulation 883/2004: art.1.

The extent to which the Protocol draws on the techniques of Regulation 883/2004 is immediately evident from these definitions. The concept of a "child-raising period" is new and is addressed in art.SSC.44. "Long-term care benefits" is a term referring to a category of benefits listed in Annex SSC-1 and excluded from the Protocol by art.SSC.4. For the remainder, reference should be made to the 2020-21 edition and to the update at para.5.163. Note that the list of special non-contributory cash benefits at annex SSC-1 now includes the mobility component of personal independence payment and a variety of Scottish benefits.

Article SSC.2: Persons covered

5.199 This Protocol shall apply to persons, including stateless persons and refugees, who are or have been subject to the legislation of one or more States, as well as to the members of their families and their survivors.

General Note

5.200 Corresponding provision of Regulation 883/2004: art.2. The definition simplifies the equivalent definition in the Regulation.

Article SSC.3: Matters covered

5.201 1. This Protocol applies to the following branches of social security:

(a) sickness benefits;
(b) maternity and equivalent paternity benefits;
(c) invalidity benefits;
(d) old-age benefits;
(e) survivors' benefits;
(f) benefits in respect of accidents at work and occupational diseases;

(g) death grants;
(h) unemployment benefits;
(i) pre-retirement benefits.

2. Unless otherwise provided for in Annex SSC-6 [Special provisions for the application of the legislation of the Member States and of the United Kingdom], this Protocol applies to general and special social security schemes, whether contributory or non-contributory, and to schemes relating to the obligations of an employer or ship-owner.

3. The provisions of Title III [Special provisions concerning the various categories of benefits] do not, however, affect the legislative provisions of any State concerning a ship-owner's obligations.

4. This Protocol does not apply to:

(a) special non-contributory cash benefits which are listed in Part 1 [Special non-contributory cash benefits] of Annex SSC-1 [Certain benefits in cash to which this Protocol shall not apply];
(b) social and medical assistance;
(c) benefits in relation to which a State assumes the liability for damages to persons and provides for compensation, such as those for victims of war and military action or their consequences; victims of crime, assassination or terrorist acts; victims of damage occasioned by agents of the State in the course of their duties; or victims who have suffered a disadvantage for political or religious reasons or for reasons of descent;
(d) long-term care benefits which are listed in Part 2 [Long-term care benefits] of Annex SSC-1 [Certain benefits in cash to which this Protocol shall not apply];
(e) assisted reproduction services;
(f) payments which are connected to a branch of social security listed in paragraph 1 and which are:
    (i) paid to meet expenses for heating in cold weather; and
    (ii) listed in Part 3 [Payments which are connected to a branch of social security listed in Article SSC.3(1) [Matters covered] and which are paid to meet expenses for heating in cold weather (point (f) of Article SSC.3(4) [Matters covered]] of Annex SSC-1 [Certain benefits in cash to which this Protocol shall not apply];
(g) family benefits.

General Note

Corresponding provision of Regulation 883/2004: art.3. The coverage is different from that in the Regulation. Unlike the Regulation, it does not apply to, among others, special non-contributory cash benefits and family benefits. The treatment of special non-contributory cash benefits under art.70 of the Regulation may mean that there is little practical difference in the result, but the exclusion of family benefits (so there is no equivalent to Chapter 8 of the Regulation) appears significant. So also is the exclusion of "long-term care benefits", listed in Annex SSC-1 as including attendance allowance, the care component of disability living allowance, the daily living component of personal independence payment and carer's allowance. 5.202

Article SSC.4: Non-discrimination between Member States

5.203 1. Social security coordination arrangements established in this Protocol shall be based on the principle of non-discrimination between the Member States.

2. This Article is without prejudice to any arrangements made between the United Kingdom and Ireland concerning the Common Travel Area.

GENERAL NOTE

5.204 The article is directed to how the United Kingdom must treat Member States (equally); hence the need for the derogation in art.4(2).

Article SSC.5: Equality of treatment

5.205 1. Unless otherwise provided for in this Protocol, as regards the branches of social security covered by Article SSC.3(1) [Matters covered], persons to whom this Protocol applies shall enjoy the same benefits and be subject to the same obligations under the legislation of any State as the nationals thereof.

2. This provision does not apply to the matters referred to in Article SSC.3(4) [Matters covered].

GENERAL NOTE

5.206 Within the scope of the benefits covered, this mirrors art.4 of Regulation 883/2004.

Article SSC.6 : Equal treatment of benefits, income, facts or events

5.207 Unless otherwise provided for in this Protocol, the States shall ensure the application of the principle of equal treatment of benefits, income, facts or events in the following manner:

(a) where, under the legislation of the competent State, the receipt of social security benefits and other income has certain legal effects, the relevant provisions of that legislation shall also apply to the receipt of equivalent benefits acquired under the legislation of another State or to income acquired in another State;

(b) where, under the legislation of the competent State, legal effects are attributed to the occurrence of certain facts or events, that State shall take account of like facts or events that have occurred in any other State as though they had taken place in its own territory.

GENERAL NOTE

5.208 Corresponding provision of Regulation 883/2004: art.5.

Article SSC.7: Aggregation of periods

Unless otherwise provided for in this Protocol, the competent institution of a State shall, to the extent necessary, take into account periods of insurance, employment, self-employment or residence completed under the legislation of any other State as though they were periods completed under the legislation which it applies, where its legislation makes conditional upon the completion of periods of insurance, employment, self-employment or residence: 5.209

(a) the acquisition, retention, duration or recovery of the right to benefits;
(b) the coverage by legislation; or
(c) the access to or the exemption from compulsory, optional continued or voluntary insurance.

General Note

This is a re-ordering of art.6 of Regulation 883/2004. 5.210

Article SSC.8: Waiving of residence rules

The States shall ensure the application of the principle of exportability of cash benefits in accordance with points (a) and (b): 5.211

(a) Cash benefits payable under the legislation of a State or under this Protocol shall not be subject to any reduction, amendment, suspension, withdrawal or confiscation on account of the fact that the beneficiary or the members of their family reside in a State other than that in which the institution responsible for providing benefits is situated.
(b) Point (a) does not apply to the cash benefits covered by points (c) and (h) of Article SSC.3(1) [Matters covered].

General Note

This narrows the scope of the equivalent (art.7) in Regulation 883/2004. Art. SSC 8(b) excludes invalidity benefits and unemployment benefits from its scope. 5.212

Article SSC.9: Preventing of overlapping of benefits

Unless otherwise provided, this Protocol shall neither confer nor maintain the right to several benefits of the same kind for one and the same period of compulsory insurance. 5.213

General Note

Corresponding provision of Regulation 883/2004: art.10. 5.214

Title II: Determination of the Legislation Applicable

Article SSC.10: General rules

5.215 1. Persons to whom this Protocol applies shall be subject to the legislation of a single State only. Such legislation shall be determined in accordance with this Title.

2. For the purposes of this Title, persons receiving cash benefits because or as a consequence of their activity as an employed or self-employed person shall be considered to be pursuing the said activity. This shall not apply to invalidity, old-age or survivors' pensions or to pensions in respect of accidents at work or occupational diseases or to sickness benefits in cash covering treatment for an unlimited period.

3. Subject to Articles SSC.11 [Detached workers], SSC.12 [Pursuit of activities in two or more States] and SSC.13 [Voluntary insurance or optional continued insurance]:

(a) a person pursuing an activity as an employed or self-employed person in a State shall be subject to the legislation of that State;
(b) a civil servant shall be subject to the legislation of the State to which the administration employing them is subject;
(c) any other person to whom points (a) and (b) do not apply shall be subject to the legislation of the State of residence, without prejudice to other provisions of this Protocol guaranteeing them benefits under the legislation of one or more other States.

4. For the purposes of this Title, an activity as an employed or self-employed person normally pursued on board a vessel at sea flying the flag of a State shall be deemed to be an activity pursued in the said State. However, a person employed on board a vessel flying the flag of a State and remunerated for such activity by an undertaking or a person whose registered office or place of business is in another State shall be subject to the legislation of the latter State if that person resides in that State. The undertaking or person paying the remuneration shall be considered as the employer for the purposes of the said legislation.

5. An activity as a flight crew or cabin crew member performing air passenger or freight services shall be deemed to be an activity pursued in the State where the home base is located.

General Note

5.216 The structure and technique of art. SSC10 follow closely those employed by art.11 of Regulation 883/2004.

Article SSC.11: Detached workers

5.217 1. By way of derogation from Article SSC.10(3) [General rules] and as a transitional measure in relation to the situation that existed before the entry into force of this Agreement, the following rules as regards the applicable legislation apply between the Member States listed in Category A of Annex SSC-8 [Transitional provisions regarding the application of Article SSC.11] and the United Kingdom:

(a) a person who pursues an activity as an employed person in a State for an employer which normally carries out its activities there and who is sent by that employer to another State to perform work on that employer's behalf shall continue to be subject to the legislation of the first State, provided that:
   (i) the duration of such work does not exceed 24 months; and
   (ii) that person is not sent to replace another detached worker.

(b) a person who normally pursues an activity as a self-employed person in a State who goes to pursue a similar activity in another State shall continue to be subject to the legislation of the first State, provided that the anticipated duration of such activity does not exceed 24 months.

2. By the date of entry into force of this Agreement, the Union shall notify the United Kingdom which of the following categories each Member State falls under:

(a) Category A: The Member State has notified the Union that it wishes to derogate from Article SSC.10 [General rules] in accordance with this Article;
(b) Category B: The Member State has notified the Union that it does not wish to derogate from Article SSC.10 [General rules]; or
(c) Category C: The Member State has not indicated whether it wishes to derogate from Article SSC.10 [General rules].

3. The document referred to in paragraph 2 shall become the content of Annex SSC-8 [Transitional provisions regarding the application of Article SSC.11] on the date of entry into force of this Agreement.

4. For Member States which are listed in Category A on the date of entry into force of this Agreement, points (a) and (b) of paragraph 1 shall apply.

5. For Member States which are listed in Category C on the date of entry into force of this Agreement, points (a) and (b) of paragraph 1 shall apply as though that Member State was listed in Category A for one month after the date of entry into force of this Agreement. The Specialised Committee on Social Security Coordination shall move a Member State from Category C to Category A if the Union notifies the Specialised Committee on Social Security Coordination that that Member State wishes to be so moved.

6. A month after the date of entry into force of this Agreement, Categories B and C will cease to exist. The Parties shall publish an updated Annex SSC-8 [Transitional provisions regarding the application of Article SSC.11] as soon as possible thereafter. For the purpose of paragraph 1, Annex SSC-8 will be considered as containing only Category A Member States as from the date of that publication.

7. Where a person is in a situation referred to in paragraph 1 involving a Category C Member State before the publication of an updated Annex SSC-8 [Transitional provisions regarding the application of Article SSC.11] in accordance with paragraph 6, paragraph 1 shall continue to apply to that person for the duration of their activities under paragraph 1.

8. The Union shall notify the Specialised Committee on Social Security Coordination if a Member State wishes to be removed from Category A of Annex SSC-8 [Transitional provisions regarding the application of Article SSC.11] and the Specialised Committee on Social Security Coordination shall, at the request of the Union, remove that Member State from Category A of Annex SSC-8. The Parties shall publish an updated Annex SSC-8

which shall apply as from the first day of the second month following the receipt of the request by the Specialised Committee on Social Security Coordination.

9. Where a person is in a situation referred to in paragraph 1 before the publication of an updated Annex SSC-8 [Transitional provisions regarding the application of Article SSC.11] in accordance with paragraph 8, paragraph 1 shall continue to apply to that person for the duration of that person's activities under paragraph 1.

General Note

5.218 This surprisingly detailed article provides for the possibility of continuation, on a transitional basis, of the rules applicable to posted workers under art.12 of Regulation 883/2004.

Article SSC.12: Pursuit of activities in two or more States

5.219 1. A person who normally pursues an activity as an employed person in one or more Member States as well as in the United Kingdom shall be subject to:

(a) the legislation of the State of residence if that person pursues a substantial part of their activity in that State; or

(b) if that person does not pursue a substantial part of their activity in the State of residence:

(i) the legislation of the State in which the registered office or place of business of the undertaking or employer is situated if that person is employed by one undertaking or employer; or

(ii) the legislation of the State in which the registered office or place of business of the undertakings or employers is situated if that person is employed by two or more undertakings or employers which have their registered office or place of business in only one State; or

(iii) the legislation of the State in which the registered office or place of business of the undertaking or employer is situated other than the State of residence if that person is employed by two or more undertakings or employers, which have their registered office or place of business in a Member State and the United Kingdom, one of which is the State of residence; or

(iv) the legislation of the State of residence if that person is employed by two or more undertakings or employers, at least two of which have their registered office or place of business in different States other than the State of residence.

2. A person who normally pursues an activity as a self-employed person in one or more Member States as well as in the United Kingdom shall be subject to:

(a) the legislation of the State of residence if that person pursues a substantial part of their activity in that State; or

(b) the legislation of the State in which the centre of interest of their activities is situated, if that person does not reside in one of the States in which that person pursues a substantial part of their activity.

3. A person who normally pursues an activity as an employed person and an activity as a self-employed person in two or more States shall be subject to the legislation of the State in which that person pursues an activity as an employed person or, if that person pursues such an activity in two or more States, to the legislation determined in accordance with paragraph 1.

4. A person who is employed as a civil servant by a State and who pursues an activity as an employed person or as a self-employed person in one or more other States shall be subject to the legislation of the State to which the administration employing that person is subject.

5. A person who normally pursues an activity as an employed person in two or more Member States (and not in the United Kingdom) shall be subject to the legislation of the United Kingdom if that person does not pursue a substantial part of that activity in the State of residence and that person:

(a) is employed by one or more undertakings or employers, all of which have their registered office or place of business in the United Kingdom;
(b) resides in a Member State and is employed by two or more undertakings or employers, all of which have their registered office or place of business in the United Kingdom and the Member State of residence;
(c) resides in the United Kingdom and is employed by two or more undertakings or employers, at least two of which have their registered office or place of business in different Member States; or
(d) resides in the United Kingdom and is employed by one or more undertakings or employers, none of which have a registered office or place of business in another State.

6. A person who normally pursues an activity as a self-employed person in two or more Member States (and not in the United Kingdom), without pursuing a substantial part of that activity in the State of residence, shall be subject to the legislation of the United Kingdom if the centre of interest of their activity is situated in the United Kingdom.

7. Paragraph 6 shall not apply in the case of a person who normally pursues an activity as an employed person and as a self-employed person in two or more Member States.

General Note

While this in many respects follows closely art.13 of Regulation 883/2004, special provisions have been introduced at art.SSC12(5) and (6). 5.220

Article SSC.13: Voluntary insurance or optional continued insurance

1. Articles SSC.10 [General rules], SSC.11 [Detached workers] and SSC.12 [Pursuit of activities in two or more States] do not apply to voluntary insurance or to optional continued insurance unless, in respect of one of the branches referred to in Article SSC.3, [Matters covered] only a voluntary scheme of insurance exists in a State. 5.221

2. Where, by virtue of the legislation of a State, the person concerned is subject to compulsory insurance in that State, that person may not be

subject to a voluntary insurance scheme or an optional continued insurance scheme in another State. In all other cases in which, for a given branch, there is a choice between several voluntary insurance schemes or optional continued insurance schemes, the person concerned shall join only the scheme of their choice.

3. However, in respect of invalidity, old-age and survivors' benefits, the person concerned may join the voluntary or optional continued insurance scheme of a State, even if that person is compulsorily subject to the legislation of another State, provided that that person has been subject, at some stage in his or her career, to the legislation of the first State because or as a consequence of an activity as an employed or self-employed person and if such overlapping is explicitly or implicitly allowed under the legislation of the first State.

4. Where the legislation of a State makes admission to voluntary insurance or optional continued insurance conditional upon residence in that State or upon previous activity as an employed or self-employed person, point (b) of Article SSC.6 [Equal treatment of benefits, income, facts or events] shall apply only to persons who have been subject, at some earlier stage, to the legislation of that State on the basis of an activity as an employed or self-employed person.

Article SSC.14: Obligations of the employer

5.222 1. An employer who has its registered office or place of business outside the competent State shall fulfil all the obligations laid down by the legislation applicable to its employees, notably the obligation to pay the contributions provided for by that legislation, as if it had its registered office or place of business in the competent State.

2. An employer who does not have a place of business in the State whose legislation is applicable and the employee may agree that the latter may fulfil the employer's obligations on its behalf as regards the payment of contributions without prejudice to the employer's underlying obligations. The employer shall send notice of such an arrangement to the competent institution of that State.

General Note

5.223 This provision is new.

Title III: Special Provisions Concerning the Various Categories of Benefits

Chapter 1: Sickness, Maternity and Equivalent Paternity Benefits

General Note

Once again, the structure closely mirrors Title III of Regulation 883/2004. 5.224

Section 1: Insured persons and members of their families except pensioners and members of their families

Article SSC.15: Residence in a State other than the competent State

An insured person or members of their family who reside in a State other than the competent State shall receive in the State of residence benefits in kind provided, on behalf of the competent institution, by the institution of the place of residence, in accordance with the legislation it applies, as though the persons concerned were insured under the said legislation. 5.225

General Note

Corresponding provision of Regulation 883/2004: art.17. 5.226

Article SSC.16: Stay in the competent State when residence is in another State – special rules for the members of the families of frontier workers

1. Unless otherwise provided for by paragraph 2, the insured person and the members of their family referred to in Article SSC.15 [Residence in a State other than the competent State] shall also be entitled to benefits in kind while staying in the competent State. The benefits in kind shall be provided by the competent institution and at its own expense, in accordance with the legislation it applies, as though the persons concerned resided in that State. 5.227

2. The members of the family of a frontier worker shall be entitled to benefits in kind during their stay in the competent State.

Where the competent State is listed in Annex SSC-2 [Restriction of rights to benefits in kind for members of the family of a frontier worker] however, the members of the family of a frontier worker who reside in the same State as the frontier worker shall be entitled to benefits in kind in the competent State only under the conditions laid down in Article SSC.17(1) [Stay outside the competent State].

General Note

Corresponding provision of Regulation 883/2004: art.18. 5.228

Article SSC.17: Stay outside the competent State

5.229 1. Unless otherwise provided for by paragraph 2, an insured person and the members of their family staying in a State other than the competent State shall be entitled to benefits in kind, provided on behalf of the competent institution by the institution of the place of stay in accordance with the legislation it applies, as though the persons concerned were insured under that legislation, where:

(a) the benefits in kind become necessary on medical grounds during their stay, in the opinion of the provider of the benefits in kind, taking into account the nature of the benefits and the expected length of the stay;

(b) the person did not travel to that State with the purpose of receiving the benefits in kind, unless the person is a passenger or member of the crew on a vessel or aircraft travelling to that State and the benefits in kind became necessary on medical grounds during the voyage or flight; and

(c) a valid entitlement document is presented in accordance with Article SSCI.22(1) [Stay in a State other than the competent State] of Annex SSC-7 [Implementing Part].

2. Appendix SSCI-2 [Entitlement document] to Annex SSC-7 [Implementing Part] lists benefits in kind which, in order to be provided during a stay in another State, require for practical reasons a prior agreement between the person concerned and the institution providing the care.

General Note

5.230 Art.SSC17 makes some changes from the approach of art.19 of Regulation 883/2004, by introducing the opinion of the provider of benefits in kind as the apparently determinative factor and by introducing conditions that travel be not for the purpose of receiving benefits in kind (as to which see art.SSC18) and that a valid entitlement document be presented.

Article SSC.18: Travel with the purpose of receiving benefits in kind – authorisation to receive appropriate treatment outside the State of residence

5.231 1. Unless otherwise provided for in this Protocol, an insured person travelling to another State with the purpose of receiving benefits in kind during the stay shall seek authorisation from the competent institution.

2. An insured person who is authorised by the competent institution to go to another State with the purpose of receiving the treatment appropriate to their condition shall receive the benefits in kind provided, on behalf of the competent institution, by the institution of the place of stay, in accordance with the legislation it applies, as though that person were insured under the said legislation. The authorisation shall be accorded where the treatment in question is among the benefits provided for by the legislation in the State where the person concerned resides and where that person cannot be given such treatment within a time limit which is medically justifiable, taking into account their current state of health and the probable course of their illness.

3. Paragraphs 1 and 2 apply mutatis mutandis to the members of the family of an insured person.

4. If the members of the family of an insured person reside in a State other than the State in which the insured person resides, and this State has opted for reimbursement on the basis of fixed amounts, the cost of the benefits in kind referred to in paragraph 2 shall be borne by the institution of the place of residence of the members of the family. In this case, for the purposes of paragraph 1, the institution of the place of residence of the members of the family shall be considered to be the competent institution.

GENERAL NOTE

Corresponding provision of Regulation 883/2004: art.20. 5.232

Article SSC.19: Cash benefits

1. An insured person and members of their family residing or staying in a State other than the competent State shall be entitled to cash benefits provided by the competent institution in accordance with the legislation it applies. By agreement between the competent institution and the institution of the place of residence or stay, such benefits may, however, be provided by the institution of the place of residence or stay at the expense of the competent institution in accordance with the legislation of the competent State. 5.233

2. The competent institution of a State whose legislation stipulates that the calculation of cash benefits shall be based on average income or on an average contribution basis shall determine such average income or average contribution basis exclusively by reference to the incomes confirmed as having been paid, or contribution bases applied, during the periods completed under the said legislation.

3. The competent institution of a State whose legislation provides that the calculation of cash benefits shall be based on standard income shall take into account exclusively the standard income or, where appropriate, the average of standard incomes for the periods completed under the said legislation.

4. Paragraphs 2 and 3 shall apply mutatis mutandis to cases where the legislation applied by the competent institution lays down a specific reference period which corresponds in the case in question either wholly or partly to the periods which the person concerned has completed under the legislation of one or more other States.

GENERAL NOTE

Corresponding provision of Regulation 883/2004: art.21. 5.234

Article SSC.20: Pension claimants

1. An insured person who, on making a claim for a pension, or during the investigation thereof, ceases to be entitled to benefits in kind under the legislation of the State last competent, shall remain entitled to benefits in kind under the legislation of the State in which that person resides, provided 5.235

that the pension claimant satisfies the insurance conditions of the legislation of the State referred to in paragraph 2. The right to benefits in kind in the State of residence shall also apply to the members of the family of the pension claimant.

2. The benefits in kind shall be chargeable to the institution of the State which, in the event of a pension being awarded, would become competent under Articles SSC.21 [Right to benefits in kind under the legislation of the State of residence], SSC.22 [No right to benefits in kind under the legislation of the State of residence] and SSC.23 [Pensions under the legislation of one or more States other than the State of residence, where there is a right to benefits in kind in the latter State].

General Note

5.236 Corresponding provision of Regulation 883/2004: art.22.

Section 2: Special provisions for pensioners and members of their families

Article SSC.21: Right to benefits in kind under the legislation of the State of residence

5.237 A person who receives a pension or pensions under the legislation of two or more States, of which one is the State of residence, and who is entitled to benefits in kind under the legislation of that State, shall, with the members of their family, receive such benefits in kind from and at the expense of the institution of the place of residence, as though that person were a pensioner whose pension was payable solely under the legislation of that State.

General Note

5.238 Corresponding provision of Regulation 883/2004: art.23.

Article SSC.22: No right to benefits in kind under the legislation of the State of residence

5.239 1. A person who:

(a) resides in a State;
(b) receives a pension or pensions under the legislation of one or more States; and
(c) is not entitled to benefits in kind under the legislation of the State of residence,

shall nevertheless receive such benefits for themselves and the members of their family, insofar as the pensioner would be entitled to them under the legislation of the State competent in respect of their pension or at least one of the States competent, if that person resided in that State. The benefits in kind shall be provided at the expense of the institution referred to in paragraph 2 by the institution of the place of residence, as though the person concerned were entitled to a pension and entitled to benefits in kind under the legislation of that State.

2. In the cases covered by paragraph 1, the cost of the benefits in kind shall be borne by the institution as determined in accordance with the following rules:

(a) where the pensioner is treated as if he or she were entitled to benefits in kind under the legislation of one State, the cost of those benefits shall be borne by the competent institution of that State;

(b) where the pensioner is treated as if he or she were entitled to benefits in kind under the legislation of two or more States, the cost of those benefits shall be borne by the competent institution of the State to whose legislation the person has been subject for the longest period of time;

(c) if the application of the rule in point (b) would result in several institutions being responsible for the cost of those benefits, the cost shall be borne by the competent institution of the State to whose legislation the pensioner was last subject.

General Note

This closely follows art.24 of Regulation 883/2004, though with less opaque drafting. **5.240**

Article SSC.23: Pensions under the legislation of one or more States other than the State of residence, where there is a right to benefits in kind in the latter State

Where a person receiving a pension or pensions under the legislation of one or more States resides in a State under whose legislation the right to receive benefits in kind is not subject to conditions of insurance, or conditions of activity as an employed or self-employed person, and that person does not receive a pension from the State of residence, the cost of benefits in kind provided to them and to members of their family shall be borne by the institution of one of the States competent in respect of the person's pensions determined in accordance with Article SSC.22(2) [No right to benefits in kind under the legislation of the State of residence], to the extent that the person and the members of their family would be entitled to such benefits if they resided in that State. **5.241**

General Note

Corresponding provision of Regulation 883/2004: art.25. **5.242**

Article SSC.24: Residence of members of the family in a State other than the one in which the pensioner resides

Where a person: **5.243**

(a) receives a pension or pensions under the legislation of one or more States; and

(b) resides in a State other than the one in which members of his or her family reside,

those members of that person's family shall be entitled to receive benefits in kind from the institution of the place of their residence in accordance with the legislation it applies insofar as the pensioner is entitled to benefits in kind under the legislation of a State. The costs shall be borne by the competent institution responsible for the costs of the benefits in kind provided to the pensioner in their State of residence.

General Note

5.244 This is a slightly recast form of art. 26 of Regulation 883/2004

Article SSC.25: Stay of the pensioner or the members of their family in a State other than the State of residence – stay in the competent State – authorisation for appropriate treatment outside the State of residence

5.245 1. Article SSC.17 [Stay outside the competent State] applies mutatis mutandis to:

(a) a person receiving a pension or pensions under the legislation of one or more States and who is entitled to benefits in kind under the legislation of one of the States which provide their pension(s);
(b) the members of their family, who are staying in a State other than the one in which they reside.

2. Article SSC.16(1) [Stay in the competent State when residence is in another State—special rules for the members of the families of frontier workers] applies mutatis mutandis to the persons described in paragraph 1 when they stay in the State in which is situated the competent institution responsible for the cost of the benefits in kind provided to the pensioner in his or her State of residence and that State has opted for this and is listed in Annex SSC-3 [More rights for pensioners returning to the competent State].

3. Article SSC.18 [Travel with the purpose of receiving benefits in kind—authorisation to receive appropriate treatment outside the State of residence] applies mutatis mutandis to a pensioner or members of his or her family who are staying in a State other than the one in which they reside with the purpose of receiving in that State the treatment appropriate to their condition.

4. Unless otherwise provided for by paragraph 5, the cost of the benefits in kind referred to in paragraphs 1 to 3 shall be borne by the competent institution responsible for the cost of benefits in kind provided to the pensioner in their State of residence.

5. The cost of the benefits in kind referred to in paragraph 3 shall be borne by the institution of the place of residence of the pensioner or of the members of their family, if these persons reside in a State which has opted for reimbursement on the basis of fixed amounts. In these cases, for the purposes of paragraph 3, the institution of the place of residence of the pensioner or of the members of their family shall be considered to be the competent institution.

General Note

5.246 This reflects, with minor drafting changes, art.27 of Regulation 883/2004.

Article SSC.26

Article SSC.26: Cash benefits for pensioners

1. Cash benefits shall be paid to a person receiving a pension or pensions under the legislation of one or more States by the competent institution of the State in which is situated the competent institution responsible for the cost of benefits in kind provided to the pensioner in their State of residence. Article SSC.19 [Cash benefits] applies mutatis mutandis. 5.247

2. Paragraph 1 also applies to the members of a pensioner's family.

GENERAL NOTE

Corresponding provision of Regulation 883/2004: art.29. 5.248

Article SSC.27: Contributions by pensioners

1. The institution of a State which is responsible under the legislation it applies for making deductions in respect of contributions for sickness, maternity and equivalent paternity benefits, may request and recover such deductions, calculated in accordance with the legislation it applies, only to the extent that the cost of the benefits pursuant to Articles SSC.21 [Right to benefits in kind under the legislation of the State of residence] to SSC.24 [Residence of members of the family in a State other than the one in which the pensioner resides] is to be borne by an institution of that State. 5.249

2. Where, in the cases referred to in Article SSC.23 [Pensions under the legislation of one or more States other than the State of residence, where there is a right to benefits in kind in the latter State], the acquisition of sickness, maternity and equivalent paternity benefits is subject to the payment of contributions or similar payments under the legislation of a State in which the pensioner concerned resides, these contributions shall not be payable by virtue of such residence.

GENERAL NOTE

Corresponding provision of Regulation 883/2004: art.30 5.250

Section 3: Common provisions

Article SSC.28: General provisions

Articles SSC.21 [Right to benefits in kind under the legislation of the State of residence] to SSC.27 [Contributions by pensioners] do not apply to a pensioner or the members of the pensioner's family who are entitled to benefits under the legislation of a State on the basis of an activity as an employed or self-employed person. In such a case, the person concerned shall be subject, for the purposes of this Chapter, to Articles SSC.15 [Residence in a State other than the competent State] to SSC.19 [Cash benefits]. 5.251

General Note

5.252 Corresponding provision of Regulation 883/2004: art.31.

Article SSC.29: Prioritising of the right to benefits in kind – special rule for the right of members of the family to benefits in the State of residence

5.253 1. Unless otherwise provided for by paragraphs 2 and 3, where a member of the family has an independent right to benefits in kind based on the legislation of a State or on this Chapter such right shall take priority over a derivative right to benefits in kind for members of the family.

2. Unless otherwise provided for by paragraph 3, where the independent right in the State of residence exists directly and solely on the basis of the residence of the person concerned in that State, a derivative right to benefits in kind shall take priority over the independent right.

3. Notwithstanding paragraphs 1 and 2, benefits in kind shall be provided to the members of the family of an insured person at the expense of the competent institution in the State in which they reside, where:

(a) those members of the family reside in a State under whose legislation the right to benefits in kind is not subject to conditions of insurance or activity as an employed or self-employed person; and
(b) the spouse or the person caring for the children of the insured person pursues an activity as an employed or self-employed person in that State, or receives a pension from that State on the basis of an activity as an employed or self-employed person.

General Note

5.254 This is a re-drafting of art.32 of Regulation 883/2004.

Article SSC.30: Reimbursements between institutions

5.255 1. The benefits in kind provided by the institution of a State on behalf of the institution of another State under this Chapter shall give rise to full reimbursement.

2. The reimbursements referred to in paragraph 1 shall be determined and effected in accordance with the arrangements set out in Annex SSC-7 [Implementing Part], either on production of proof of actual expenditure, or on the basis of fixed amounts for States whose legal or administrative structures are such that the use of reimbursement on the basis of actual expenditure is not appropriate.

3. The States, and their competent authorities, may provide for other methods of reimbursement or waive all reimbursement between the institutions coming under their jurisdiction.

General Note

5.256 Corresponding provision of Regulation 883/2004: art.35.

Chapter 2: Benefits in Respect of Accidents at Work and Occupational Diseases

Article SSC.31: Right to benefits in kind and in cash

1. Without prejudice to any more favourable provisions in paragraphs 2 and 3 of this Article, Articles SSC.15 [Residence in a State other than the competent State], SSC.16(1) [Stay in the competent State when residence is in another State – special rules for the members of the families of frontier workers], SSC.17(1) [Stay outside the competent State] and SSC.18(1) [Travel with the purpose of receiving benefits in kind – authorisation to receive appropriate treatment outside the State of residence] also apply to benefits relating to accidents at work or occupational diseases. 5.257

2. A person who has sustained an accident at work or has contracted an occupational disease and who resides or stays in a State other than the competent State shall be entitled to the special benefits in kind of the scheme covering accidents at work and occupational diseases provided, on behalf of the competent institution, by the institution of the place of residence or stay in accordance with the legislation which it applies, as though that person were insured under that legislation.

3. The competent institution may not refuse to grant the authorisation provided for in Article SSC.18(1) [Travel with the purpose of receiving benefits in kind – authorisation to receive appropriate treatment outside the State of residence] to a person who has sustained an accident at work or who has contracted an occupational disease and is entitled to benefits chargeable to that institution, where the treatment appropriate to his or her condition cannot be given in the State in which that person resides within a time limit which is medically justifiable, taking into account that person's current state of health and the probable course of the illness.

4. Article SSC.19 [Cash benefits] also applies to benefits falling within this Chapter.

General Note

Corresponding provision of Regulation 883/2004: art.36. 5.258

Article SSC.32: Costs of transport

1. The competent institution of a State whose legislation provides for meeting the costs of transporting a person who has sustained an accident at work or is suffering from an occupational disease, either to their place of residence or to a hospital, shall meet such costs to the corresponding place in the State where the person resides, provided that that institution gives prior authorisation for such transport, duly taking into account the reasons justifying it. Such authorisation shall not be required in the case of a frontier worker. 5.259

2. The competent institution of a State whose legislation provides for meeting the costs of transporting the body of a person killed in an accident at work to the place of burial shall, in accordance with the legislation it applies, meet such costs to the corresponding place in the State where the person was residing at the time of the accident.

General Note

5.260 Corresponding provision of Regulation 883/2004: art.37.

Article SSC.33: Benefits for an occupational disease where the person suffering from such a disease has been exposed to the same risk in several States

5.261 When a person who has contracted an occupational disease has, under the legislation of two or more States, pursued an activity which by its nature is likely to cause the said disease, the benefits that that person or his or her survivors may claim shall be provided exclusively under the legislation of the last of those States whose conditions are satisfied.

General Note

5.262 Corresponding provision of Regulation 883/2004: art.38.

Article SSC.34: Aggravation of an occupational disease

5.263 In the event of aggravation of an occupational disease for which a person suffering from such a disease has received or is receiving benefits under the legislation of a State, the following rules shall apply:

(a) if the person concerned, while in receipt of benefits, has not pursued, under the legislation of another State, an activity as an employed or self-employed person likely to cause or aggravate the disease in question, the competent institution of the first State shall bear the cost of the benefits under the provisions of the legislation which it applies, taking into account the aggravation;
(b) if the person concerned, while in receipt of benefits, has pursued such an activity under the legislation of another State, the competent institution of the first State shall bear the cost of the benefits under the legislation it applies without taking the aggravation into account. The competent institution of the second State shall grant a supplement to the person concerned, the amount of which shall be equal to the difference between the amount of benefits due after the aggravation and the amount which would have been due prior to the aggravation under the legislation it applies, if the disease in question had occurred under the legislation of that State;
(c) the rules concerning reduction, suspension or withdrawal laid down by the legislation of a State shall not be invoked against persons receiving benefits provided by institutions of two States in accordance with point (b).

General Note

5.264 Corresponding provision of Regulation 883/2004: art.39.

Article SSC.35: Rules for taking into account the special features of certain legislation

5.265 1. If there is no insurance against accidents at work or occupational diseases in the State in which the person concerned resides or stays, or if such insurance exists but there is no institution responsible for providing benefits in kind, those benefits shall be provided by the institution of the place of residence or stay responsible for providing benefits in kind in the event of sickness.

2. If there is no insurance against accidents at work or occupational diseases in the competent State, the provisions of this Chapter concerning benefits in kind shall nevertheless be applied to a person who is entitled to those benefits in the event of sickness, maternity or equivalent paternity under the legislation of that State if that person sustains an accident at work or suffers from an occupational disease during a residence or stay in another State. Costs shall be borne by the institution that is competent for the benefits in kind under the legislation of the competent State.

3. Article SSC.6 [Equal treatment of benefits, income, facts or events] applies to the competent institution in a State as regards the equivalence of accidents at work and occupational diseases which either have occurred or have been confirmed subsequently under the legislation of another State when assessing the degree of incapacity, the right to benefits or the amount thereof, on condition that:

(a) no compensation is due in respect of an accident at work or an occupational disease which had occurred or had been confirmed previously under the legislation it applies; and
(b) no compensation is due in respect of an accident at work or an occupational disease which had occurred or had been confirmed subsequently, under the legislation of the other State under which the accident at work or the occupational disease had occurred or been confirmed.

General Note

Corresponding provision of Regulation 883/2004: art.40. **5.266**

Article SSC.36: Reimbursements between institutions

1. Article SSC.30 [Reimbursements between institutions] also applies to **5.267** benefits falling within this Chapter, and reimbursement shall be made on the basis of actual costs.

2. The States, or their competent authorities, may provide for other methods of reimbursement or waive all reimbursement between the institutions under their jurisdiction.

General Note

Corresponding provision of Regulation 883/2004: art.41. **5.268**

Chapter 3: Death Grants

Article SSC.37: Right to grants where death occurs in, or where the person entitled resides in, a State other than the competent one

1. When an insured person or a member of their family dies in a State **5.269** other than the competent State, the death shall be deemed to have occurred in the competent State.

2. The competent institution shall be obliged to provide death grants payable under the legislation it applies, even if the person entitled resides in a State other than the competent State.

3. Paragraphs 1 and 2 shall also apply when the death is the result of an accident at work or an occupational disease.

General Note

5.270 Corresponding provision of Regulation 883/2004: art.42.

Article SSC.38: Provision of benefits in the event of the death of a pensioner

5.271 1. In the event of the death of a pensioner who was entitled to a pension under the legislation of one State, or to pensions under the legislations of two or more States, when that pensioner was residing in a State other than that of the institution responsible for the cost of benefits in kind provided under Articles SSC.22 [No right to benefits in kind under the legislation of the State of residence] and SSC.23 [Pensions under the legislation of one or more States other than the State of residence, where there is a right to benefits in kind in the latter State], the death grants payable under the legislation administered by that institution shall be provided at its own expense as though the pensioner had been residing at the time of their death in the State in which that institution is situated.

2. Paragraph 1 applies mutatis mutandis to the members of the family of a pensioner.

General Note

5.272 Corresponding provision of Regulation 883/2004: art.43.

Chapter 4: Invalidity Benefits

Article SSC.39: Calculation of invalidity benefits

5.273 Without prejudice to Article SSC.7 [Aggregation of periods], where, under the legislation of the State competent under Title II [Determination of the legislation applicable] of this Protocol, the amount of invalidity benefits is dependent on the duration of the periods of insurance, employment, self-employment or residence, the competent State is not required to take into account any such periods completed under the legislation of another State for the purposes of calculating the amount of invalidity benefit payable.

General Note

5.274 This is a considerable simplification compared with the rules regarding "Type A" and "Type B" schemes to be found in arts 44 and 46 of Regulation 883/2004, although the interaction with art.SSC.7 may give rise to some uncertainty.

Article SSC.40: Special provisions on aggregation of periods

5.275 The competent institution of a State whose legislation makes the acquisition, retention or recovery of the right to benefits conditional upon the completion of periods of insurance or residence shall, where necessary, apply Article SSC.46 [Special provisions on aggregation of periods] mutatis mutandis.

GENERAL NOTE

Corresponding provision of Regulation 883/2004: art.45. 5.276

Article SSC.41: Aggravation of invalidity

In the case of aggravation of an invalidity for which a person is receiving benefits under the legislation of a State in accordance with this Protocol, the benefit shall continue to be provided in accordance with this Chapter, taking the aggravation into account. 5.277

GENERAL NOTE

Removal of the "Type A"/"Type B" approach has resulted in a simplification compared with Regulation 883/2004, art.47. 5.278

Article SSC.42: Conversion of invalidity benefits into old-age benefits

1. Where provided for in the legislation of the State paying invalidity benefit in accordance with this Protocol, invalidity benefits shall be converted into old-age benefits under the conditions laid down by the legislation under which they are provided and in accordance with Chapter 5 of Title III [Old-age and survivors' pensions]. 5.279

2. Where a person receiving invalidity benefits can establish a claim to old-age benefits under the legislation of one or more other States, in accordance with Article SSC.45 [General provisions], any institution which is responsible for providing invalidity benefits under the legislation of a State shall continue to provide such a person with the invalidity benefits to which he or she is entitled under the legislation it applies until paragraph 1 becomes applicable in respect of that institution, or otherwise for as long as the person concerned satisfies the conditions for such benefits.

GENERAL NOTE

Removal of the "Type A"/"Type B" approach has resulted in a simplif[illegible]ion compared with R[illegible] 5.280

Article SSC.43: Special provisions for civil servants

Articles SSC.7 [Aggregation of periods], SSC.39 [Calculation of invalidity benefits], SSC.41 [Aggravation of invalidity], SSC.42 [Conversion of invalidity benefits into old-age benefits] and Article SSC.55(2) and (3) [Special provisions for civil servants] apply mutatis mutandis to persons covered by a special scheme for civil servants. 5.281

GENERAL NOTE

Corresponding provision of Regulation 883/2004: art.49.

5.282

Chapter 5: Old-Age and Survivors' Pensions

Article SSC.44: Taking into account child-raising periods

5.283 1. Where, under the legislation of the State which is competent under Title II [Determination of the legislation applicable], no child-raising period is taken into account, the institution of the State whose legislation, according to Title II [Determination of the legislation applicable], was applicable to the person concerned on the grounds that he or she was pursuing an activity as an employed or self-employed person at the date when, under that legislation, the child-raising period started to be taken into account for the child concerned, shall remain responsible for taking into account that period as a child-raising period under its own legislation, as if such child-raising took place in its own territory.

2. Paragraph 1 shall not apply if the person concerned is, or becomes, subject to the legislation of another State due to the pursuit of an employed or self-employed activity.

General Note

5.284 This provision, not found in Regulation 883/2004, seeks to ensure that a "child-raising period" (as defined) can for social security purposes be attributed to a State rather than risking falling into a void between States.

Article SSC.45: General provisions

5.285 1. All the competent institutions shall determine entitlement to benefit, under all the legislations of the States to which the person concerned has been subject, when a request for award has been submitted, unless the person concerned expressly requests deferment of the award of old-age benefits under the legislation of one or more States.

2. If at a given moment the person concerned does not satisfy, or no longer satisfies, the conditions laid down by all the legislations of the States to which that person has been subject, the institutions applying legislation the conditions of which have been satisfied shall not take into account, when performing the calculation in accordance with point (a) or (b) of Article SSC.47(1) [Award of benefits], the [illegible] legislation the conditions of [illegible] satisfied, wh[illegible]is gives rise to a lower [illegible]

3. Paragraph 2 [illegible] apply mutatis mutandis when the p[illegible] has expressly request[illegible] [illegible]ment of the award of old-age benefits.

4. A new calculation sha[illegible] [illegible]erformed automatically as and when the conditions to be fulfilled under the [illegible]er legislations are satisfied or when a person requests the award of an old-age benefit deferred in accordance with paragraph 1, unless the periods completed under the other legislations have already been taken into account by virtue of paragraph 2 or 3.

General Note

5.286 Corresponding provision of Regulation 883/2004: art.50.

Article SSC.46: Special provisions on aggregation of periods

1. Where the legislation of a State makes the granting of certain benefits conditional upon the periods of insurance having been completed only in a specific activity as an employed or self-employed person or in an occupation which is subject to a special scheme for employed or self-employed persons, the competent institution of that State shall take into account periods completed under the legislation of other States only if completed under a corresponding scheme or, failing that, in the same occupation, or where appropriate, in the same activity as an employed or self-employed person. 5.287

If, account having been taken of the periods thus completed, the person concerned does not satisfy the conditions for receipt of the benefits of a special scheme, these periods shall be taken into account for the purposes of providing the benefits of the general scheme or, failing that, of the scheme applicable to manual or clerical workers, as the case may be, provided that the person concerned had been affiliated to one or other of those schemes.

2. The periods of insurance completed under a special scheme of a State shall be taken into account for the purposes of providing the benefits of the general scheme or, failing that, of the scheme applicable to manual or clerical workers, as the case may be, of another State, provided that the person concerned had been affiliated to one or other of those schemes, even if those periods have already been taken into account in the latter State under a special scheme.

3. Where the legislation or specific scheme of a State makes the acquisition, retention or recovery of the right to benefits conditional upon the person concerned being insured at the time of the materialisation of the risk, this condition shall be regarded as having been satisfied if that person has been previously insured under the legislation or specific scheme of that State and is, at the time of the materialisation of the risk, insured under the legislation of another State for the same risk or, failing that, if a benefit is due under the legislation of another State for the same risk. The latter condition shall, however, be deemed to be fulfilled in the cases referred to in Article SSC.52 [Periods of insurance or residence of less than one year].

General Note

Corresponding provision of Regulation 883/2004: art.51. 5.288

Article SSC.47: Award of benefits

1. The competent institution shall calculate the amount of the benefit that would be due: 5.289

(a) under the legislation it applies, only where the conditions for entitlement to benefits have been satisfied exclusively under national law (independent benefit);

(b) by calculating a theoretical amount and subsequently an actual amount (pro rata benefit), as follows:

   (i) the theoretical amount of the benefit is equal to the benefit which the person concerned could claim if all the periods of insurance and/or of residence which have been completed under the legislations of the other States had been completed under the legislation it applies on the date of the award of the benefit. If, under this legislation, the amount does not depend on the duration of the periods completed, that amount shall be regarded as being the theoretical amount;

(ii) the competent institution shall then establish the actual amount of the pro rata benefit by applying to the theoretical amount the ratio between the duration of the periods completed before materialisation of the risk under the legislation it applies and the total duration of the periods completed before materialisation of the risk under the legislations of all the States concerned.

2. Where appropriate, the competent institution shall apply, to the amount calculated in accordance with points (a) and (b) of paragraph 1, all the rules relating to reduction, suspension or withdrawal, under the legislation it applies, within the limits provided for by Articles SSC.48 [Rules to prevent overlapping], SSC.49 [Overlapping of benefits of the same kind] and SSC.50 [Overlapping of benefits of a different kind].

3. The person concerned shall be entitled to receive from the competent institution of each State the higher of the amounts calculated in accordance with points (a) and (b) of paragraph 1.

4. Where the calculation pursuant to point (a) of paragraph 1 in one State invariably results in the independent benefit being equal to or higher than the pro rata benefit, calculated in accordance with point (b) of paragraph 1, the competent institution shall waive the pro rata calculation, provided that:

(a) such a situation is set out in Part 1 of Annex SSC-4 [Cases in which the pro rata calculation shall be waived or shall not apply];

(b) no legislation containing rules against overlapping, as referred to in Articles SSC.49 [Overlapping of benefits of the same kind] and SSC.50 [Overlapping of benefits of a different kind], is applicable unless the conditions laid down in Article SSC.50(2) are fulfilled; and

(c) Article SSC.52 [Periods of insurance or residence of less than one year] is not applicable in relation to periods completed under the legislation of another State in the specific circumstances of the case.

5. Notwithstanding paragraphs 1, 2 and 3, the pro rata calculation shall not apply to schemes providing benefits in respect of which periods of time are of no relevance to the calculation, subject to such schemes being listed in Part 2 of Annex SSC-4 [Cases in which the pro rata calculation shall be waived or shall not apply]. In such cases, the person concerned shall be entitled to the benefit calculated in accordance with the legislation of the State concerned.

General Note

5.290 Corresponding provision of Regulation 883/2004: art.52.

Article SSC.48: Rules to prevent overlapping

5.291 1. Any overlapping of old-age and survivors' benefits calculated or provided on the basis of periods of insurance or residence completed by the same person shall be considered to be overlapping of benefits of the same kind.

2. Overlapping of benefits which cannot be considered to be of the same kind within the meaning of paragraph 1 shall be considered to be overlapping of benefits of a different kind.

3. The following provisions shall be applicable for the purposes of rules to prevent overlapping laid down by the legislation of a State in the case of overlapping of a benefit in respect of old age or survivors with a benefit of the same kind or a benefit of a different kind or with other income:

(a) the competent institution shall take into account the benefits or incomes acquired in another State only where the legislation it applies provides for benefits or income acquired abroad to be taken into account;

(b) the competent institution shall take into account the amount of benefits to be paid by another State before deduction of tax, social security contributions and other individual levies or deductions, unless the legislation it applies provides for the application of rules to prevent overlapping after such deductions, under the conditions and the procedures laid down in Annex SSC-7 [Implementing Part];

(c) the competent institution shall not take into account the amount of benefits acquired under the legislation of another State on the basis of voluntary insurance or continued optional insurance;

(d) if a single State applies rules to prevent overlapping because the person concerned receives benefits of the same or of a different kind under the legislation of other States or income acquired in other States, the benefit due may be reduced solely by the amount of such benefits or such income.

General Note

Corresponding provision of Regulation 883/2004: art.53. **5.292**

Article SSC.49: Overlapping of benefits of the same kind

1. Where benefits of the same kind due under the legislation of two or more States overlap, the rules to prevent overlapping laid down by the legislation of a State shall not be applicable to a pro rata benefit. **5.293**

2. The rules to prevent overlapping shall apply to an independent benefit only if the benefit concerned is:

(a) a benefit the amount of which does not depend on the duration of periods of insurance or residence; or

(b) a benefit the amount of which is determined on the basis of a credited period deemed to have been completed between the date on which the risk materialised and a later date, overlapping with:

  (i) a benefit of the same type, except where an agreement has been concluded between two or more States to avoid the same credited period being taken into account more than once; or

  (ii) a benefit referred to in point (a).

The benefits and agreements referred to in points (a) and (b) are listed in Annex SSC-5 [Benefits and agreements which allow the application of Article SSC.49 [Overlapping of benefits of the same kind]].

General Note

5.294 Corresponding provision of Regulation 883/2004: art.54.

Article SSC.50: Overlapping of benefits of a different kind

5.295 1. If the receipt of benefits of a different kind or other income requires the application of the rules to prevent overlapping provided for by the legislation of the States concerned regarding:

(a) two or more independent benefits, the competent institutions shall divide the amounts of the benefit or benefits or other income, as they have been taken into account, by the number of benefits subject to the said rules;

however, the application of this point cannot deprive the person concerned of their status as a pensioner for the purposes of the other chapters of this Title under the conditions and the procedures laid down in Annex SSC-7 [Implementing Part];

(b) one or more pro rata benefits, the competent institutions shall take into account the benefit or benefits or other income and all the elements stipulated for applying the rules to prevent overlapping as a function of the ratio between the periods of insurance and/or residence established for the calculation referred to in point (b)(ii) of Article SSC.47(1) [Award of benefits];

(c) one or more independent benefits and one or more pro rata benefits, the competent institutions shall apply mutatis mutandis point (a) as regards independent benefits and point (b) as regards pro-rata benefits.

2. The competent institution shall not apply the division stipulated in respect of independent benefits, if the legislation it applies provides for account to be taken of benefits of a different kind or other income and all other elements for calculating part of their amount determined as a function of the ratio between periods of insurance or residence referred to in point (b)(ii) of Article SSC.47(1) [Award of benefits].

3. Paragraphs 1 and 2 shall apply mutatis mutandis where the legislation of one or more States provides that a right to a benefit cannot be acquired in the case where the person concerned is in receipt of a benefit of a different kind, payable under the legislation of another State, or of other income.

General Note

5.296 Corresponding provision of Regulation 883/2004: art.55.

Article SSC.51: Additional provisions for the calculation of benefits

5.297 1. For the calculation of the theoretical and pro rata amounts referred to in point (b) of Article SSC.47(1) [Award of benefits], the following rules apply:

(a) where the total length of the periods of insurance and/or residence completed before the risk materialised under the legislations of all the States concerned is longer than the maximum period required by the legislation of one of these States for receipt of full benefit, the competent institution of that State shall take into account this maximum period instead of the total length of the periods completed; this method of calculation shall not result in the imposition on that institution of the cost of a benefit greater than the full benefit provided for by the legislation it applies. This provision shall not apply to benefits the amount of which does not depend on the length of insurance;

(b) the procedure for taking into account overlapping periods is laid down in Annex SSC-7 [Implementing Part];

(c) if the legislation of a State provides that the benefits are to be calculated on the basis of incomes, contributions, bases of contributions, increases, earnings, other amounts or a combination of more than one of them (average, proportional, fixed or credited), the competent institution shall:

(i) determine the basis for calculation of the benefits in accordance only with periods of insurance completed under the legislation it applies;

(ii) use, in order to determine the amount to be calculated in accordance with the periods of insurance and/or residence completed under the legislation of the other States, the same elements determined or recorded for the periods of insurance completed under the legislation it applies;

where necessary in accordance with the procedures laid down in Annex SSC-6 [Special provisions for the application of the legislation of the Member States and of the United Kingdom] for the State concerned;

(d) in the event that point (c) is not applicable because the legislation of a State provides for the benefit to be calculated on the basis of elements other than periods of insurance or residence which are not linked to time, the competent institution shall take into account, in respect of each period of insurance or residence completed under the legislation of any other State, the amount of the capital accrued, the capital which is considered as having been accrued or any other element for the calculation under the legislation it administers divided by the corresponding units of periods in the pension scheme concerned.

2. The provisions of the legislation of a State concerning the revalorisation of the elements taken into account for the calculation of benefits shall apply, as appropriate, to the elements to be taken into account by the competent institution of that State, in accordance with paragraph 1, in respect of the periods of insurance or residence completed under the legislation of other States.

General Note

Corresponding provision of Regulation 883/2004: art.56. **5.298**

Article SSC.52: Periods of insurance or residence of less than one year

1. Notwithstanding point (b) of Article SSC.47(1) [Award of benefits], the institution of a State shall not be required to provide benefits in respect of periods completed under the legislation it applies which are taken into account when the risk materialises, if: **5.299**

(a) the duration of the said periods is less than one year, and

(b) taking only these periods into account no right to benefit is acquired under that legislation.

For the purposes of this Article, 'periods' shall mean all periods of insurance, employment, self-employment or residence which either qualify for, or directly increase, the benefit concerned.

2. The competent institution of each of the States concerned shall take into account the periods referred to in paragraph 1, for the purposes of point (b)(i) of Article SSC.47(1) [Award of benefits].

3. If the effect of applying paragraph 1 would be to relieve all the institutions of the States concerned of their obligations, benefits shall be provided exclusively under the legislation of the last of those States whose conditions are satisfied, as if all the periods of insurance and residence completed and taken into account in accordance with Articles SSC.7 [Aggregation of periods] and SSC.46(1) and (2) [Special provisions on aggregation of periods] had been completed under the legislation of that State.

4. This Article does not apply to schemes listed in Part 2 [Cases in which Article 47(5) applies] of Annex SSC-4 [Cases in which the pro rata calculation shall be waived or shall not apply].

General Note

5.300 Corresponding provision of Regulation 883/2004: art.57.

Article SSC.53: Award of a supplement

5.301 1. A recipient of benefits to whom this Chapter applies may not, in the State of residence and under whose legislation a benefit is payable to them, be provided with a benefit which is less than the minimum benefit fixed by that legislation for a period of insurance or residence equal to all the periods taken into account for the payment in accordance with this Chapter.

2. The competent institution of that State shall pay them throughout the period of their residence in its territory a supplement equal to the difference between the total of the benefits due under this Chapter and the amount of the minimum benefit.

General Note

5.302 Corresponding provision of Regulation 883/2004: art.58.

Article SSC.54: Recalculation and revaluation of benefits

5.303 1. If the method for determining benefits or the rules for calculating benefits are altered under the legislation of a State, or if the personal situation of the person concerned undergoes a relevant change which, under that legislation, would lead to an adjustment of the amount of the benefit, a recalculation shall be carried out in accordance with Article SSC.47 [Award of benefits].

2. On the other hand, if, by reason of an increase in the cost of living or changes in the level of income or other grounds for adjustment, the benefits of the State concerned are altered by a percentage or fixed amount, such percentage or fixed amount shall be applied directly to the benefits determined in accordance with Article SSC.47 [Award of benefits], without the need for a recalculation.

General Note

Corresponding provision of Regulation 883/2004: art.59. 5.304

Article SSC.55: Special provisions for civil servants

1. Articles SSC.7 [Aggregation of periods] and SSC.45 [General provisions], SSC.46(3) [Special provisions on aggregation of periods] and Article SSC.47 [Award of benefits] to SSC.54 [Recalculation and revaluation of benefits] apply mutatis mutandis to persons covered by a special scheme for civil servants. 5.305

2. However, if the legislation of a competent State makes the acquisition, liquidation, retention or recovery of the right to benefits under a special scheme for civil servants subject to the condition that all periods of insurance be completed under one or more special schemes for civil servants in that State, or be regarded by the legislation of that State as equivalent to such periods, the competent institution of that State shall take into account only the periods which can be recognised under the legislation it applies.

If, account having been taken of the periods thus completed, the person concerned does not satisfy the conditions for the receipt of these benefits, these periods shall be taken into account for the award of benefits under the general scheme or, failing that, the scheme applicable to manual or clerical workers, as the case may be.

3. Where, under the legislation of a State, benefits under a special scheme for civil servants are calculated on the basis of the last salary or salaries received during a reference period, the competent institution of that State shall take into account, for the purposes of the calculation, only those salaries, duly revalued, which were received during the period or periods for which the person concerned was subject to that legislation.

General Note

Corresponding provision of Regulation 883/2004: art.60. 5.306

Chapter 6: Unemployment Benefits

Article SSC.56: Special provisions on aggregation of periods of insurance, employment or self-employment

1. The competent institution of a State whose legislation makes the acquisition, retention, recovery or duration of the right to benefits conditional upon the completion of either periods of insurance, employment or self-employment shall, to the extent necessary, take into account periods of insurance, employment or self-employment completed under the legislation of any other State as though they were completed under the legislation it applies. 5.307

However, when the applicable legislation makes the right to benefits conditional on the completion of periods of insurance, the periods of employment or self-employment completed under the legislation of another State shall not be taken into account unless such periods would have been considered to be periods of insurance had they been completed in accordance with the applicable legislation.

2. The application of paragraph 1 of this Article shall be conditional on the person concerned having the most recently completed, in accordance with the legislation under which the benefits are claimed:

(a) periods of insurance, if that legislation requires periods of insurance,
(b) periods of employment, if that legislation requires periods of employment, or
(c) periods of self-employment, if that legislation requires periods of self-employment.

General Note

5.308 Corresponding provision of Regulation 883/2004: art.61.

Article SSC.57: Calculation of unemployment benefits

5.309 1. Where the calculation of unemployment benefits is based on the amount of the previous salary or professional income of the person concerned, the competent State shall take into account the salary or professional income received by the person concerned based exclusively on their last activity as an employed or self-employed person under the legislation of the competent State.

2. Where the legislation applied by the competent State provides for a specific reference period for the determination of the salary or professional income used to calculate the amount of benefit, and the person concerned was subject to the legislation of another State for all or part of that reference period, the competent State shall only take into account the salary or professional income received during their last activity as an employed or self-employed person under that legislation.

General Note

5.310 The article departs from the corresponding provision of Regulation 883/2004 (art.62) in part by way of re-drafting and in part because art.65 of the Regulation, which concerns situations in which the claimant was residing, during their last period of work, in a country other than the competent State, finds no place in the Protocol.

Chapter 7: Pre-Retirement Benefits

Article SSC.58: Benefits

5.311 When the applicable legislation makes the right to pre-retirement benefits conditional on the completion of periods of insurance, of employment or of self-employment, Article SSC.7 [Aggregation of periods] shall not apply.

General Note

5.312 Corresponding provision of Regulation 883/2004: art.66.

Title IV: Miscellaneous Provisions

Article SSC.59: Cooperation

5.313 1. The competent authorities of the States shall notify the Specialised Committee on Social Security Coordination of any changes to their legislation as regards the branches of social security covered by Article SSC.3 [Matters covered] which are relevant to or may affect the implementation of this Protocol.

2. Unless this Protocol requires such information to be notified to the Specialised Committee on Social Security Coordination, the competent authorities of the States shall communicate to each other measures taken to implement this Protocol that are not notified under paragraph 1 and that are relevant for the implementation of the Protocol.

3. For the purposes of this Protocol, the authorities and institutions of the States shall lend one another their good offices and act as though implementing their own legislation. The administrative assistance given by the said authorities and institutions shall, as a rule, be free of charge. However, the Specialised Committee on Social Security Coordination shall establish the nature of reimbursable expenses and the limits above which their reimbursement is due.

4. The authorities and institutions of the States may, for the purposes of this Protocol, communicate directly with one another and with the persons involved or their representatives.

5. The institutions and persons covered by this Protocol shall have a duty of mutual information and cooperation to ensure the correct implementation of this Protocol.

The institutions, in accordance with the principle of good administration, shall respond to all queries within a reasonable period of time and shall in this connection provide the persons concerned with any information required for exercising the rights conferred on them by this Protocol.

The persons concerned must inform the institutions of the competent State and of the State of residence as soon as possible of any change in their personal or family situation which affects their right to benefits under this Protocol.

6. Failure to respect the obligation of information referred to in the third subparagraph of paragraph 5 may result in the application of proportionate measures in accordance with national law. Nevertheless, these measures shall be equivalent to those applicable to similar situations under domestic law and shall not make it impossible or excessively difficult in practice for claimants to exercise the rights conferred on them by this Protocol.

7. In the event of difficulties in the interpretation or application of this Protocol which could jeopardise the rights of a person covered by it, the institution of the competent State or of the State of residence of the person concerned, shall contact the institution(s) of the State(s) concerned. If a solution cannot be found within a reasonable period, a Party may request to hold consultations in the framework of the Specialised Committee on Social Security Coordination.

8. The authorities, institutions and tribunals of one State may not reject applications or other documents submitted to them on the grounds that they are written in an official language of the Union, including in English.

GENERAL NOTE

Corresponding provision of Regulation 883/2004: art.76, albeit the mechanisms naturally now reflect the Protocol. **5.314**

Article SSC.60: Data processing

5.315 1. The States shall progressively use new technologies for the exchange, access and processing of the data required to apply this Protocol.

2. Each State shall be responsible for managing its own part of the data-processing services.

3. An electronic document sent or issued by an institution in conformity with the Protocol and Annex SSC-7 [Implementing Part] may not be rejected by any authority or institution of another State on the grounds that it was received by electronic means, once the receiving institution has declared that it can receive electronic documents. Reproduction and recording of such documents shall be presumed to be a correct and accurate reproduction of the original document or representation of the information it relates to, unless there is proof to the contrary.

4. An electronic document shall be considered valid if the computer system on which the document is recorded contains the safeguards necessary in order to prevent any alteration, disclosure or unauthorised access to the recording. It shall at any time be possible to reproduce the recorded information in an immediately readable form.

General Note

5.316 Corresponding provision of Regulation 883/2004: art.78.

Article SSC.61: Exemptions

5.317 1. Any exemption from or reduction of taxes, stamp duty, notarial or registration fees provided for under the legislation of one State in respect of certificates or documents required to be produced in application of the legislation of that State shall be extended to similar certificates or documents required to be produced in application of the legislation of another State or of this Protocol.

2. All statements, documents and certificates of any kind whatsoever required to be produced in application of this Protocol shall be exempt from authentication by diplomatic or consular authorities.

General Note

5.318 Corresponding provision of Regulation 883/2004: art.80.

Article SSC.62: Claims, declarations or appeals

5.319 Any claim, declaration or appeal which should have been submitted, in application of the legislation of one State, within a specified period to an authority, institution or tribunal of that State shall be admissible if it is submitted within the same period to a corresponding authority, institution or tribunal of another State. In such a case, the authority, institution or tribunal receiving the claim, declaration or appeal shall forward it without delay to the competent authority, institution or tribunal of the former State either directly or through the competent authorities of the States concerned. The date on which such claims, declarations or appeals were submitted to the authority, institution or tribunal of the second State shall be considered as the date of their submission to the competent authority, institution or tribunal.

General Note

Corresponding provision of Regulation 883/2004: art.81. 5.320

Article SSC.63: Medical examinations

1. Medical examinations provided for by the legislation of one State may be carried out, at the request of the competent institution, in the territory of another State, by the institution of the place of stay or residence of the person entitled to benefits, under the conditions laid down in Annex SSC-7 [Implementing Part] or agreed between the competent authorities of the States concerned. 5.321

2. Medical examinations carried out under the conditions laid down in paragraph 1 shall be considered as having been carried out in the territory of the competent State.

General Note

Corresponding provision of Regulation 883/2004: art.82. Art.SSC.63(2) is new. 5.322

Article SSC.64: Collection of contributions and recovery of benefits

1. Collection of contributions due to an institution of one State and recovery of benefits provided by the institution of one State but not due, may be effected in another State in accordance with the procedures and with the guarantees and privileges applicable to the collection of contributions due to the corresponding institution of the latter and the recovery of benefits provided by it but not due. 5.323

2. Enforceable decisions of the judicial and administrative authorities relating to the collection of contributions, interest and any other charges or to the recovery of benefits provided but not due under the legislation of one State shall be recognised and enforced at the request of the competent institution in another State within the limits and in accordance with the procedures laid down by the legislation and any other procedures applicable to similar decisions of the latter. Such decisions shall be declared enforceable in that State insofar as the legislation and any other procedures of that State so require.

3. Claims of an institution of one State shall in enforcement, bankruptcy or settlement proceedings in another State enjoy the same privileges as the legislation that the latter accords to claims of the same kind.

4. The procedure for implementing this Article, including costs reimbursement, shall be governed by Annex SSC-7 [Implementing Part] or, where necessary and as a complementary measure, by means of agreements between the States.

General Note

Corresponding provision of Regulation 883/2004: art.84. 5.324

Article SSC.65: Rights of institutions

5.325 1. If a person receives benefits under the legislation of a State in respect of an injury resulting from events occurring in another State, any rights of the institution responsible for providing benefits against a third party liable to provide compensation for the injury shall be governed by the following rules:

(a) where the institution responsible for providing benefits is, under the legislation it applies, subrogated to the rights which the beneficiary has against the third party, such subrogation shall be recognised by each State;

(b) where the institution responsible for providing benefits has a direct right against the third party, each State shall recognise such rights.

2. If a person receives benefits under the legislation of one State in respect of an injury resulting from events occurring in another State, the provisions of the said legislation which determine the cases in which the civil liability of employers or of their employees is to be excluded shall apply with regard to the said person or to the competent institution.

Paragraph 1 shall also apply to any rights of the institution responsible for providing benefits against employers or their employees in cases where their liability is not excluded.

3. Where, in accordance with Articles SSC.30(3) [Reimbursements between institutions] or 36(2) [Reimbursements between institutions], two or more States or their competent authorities have concluded an agreement to waive reimbursement between institutions under their jurisdiction, or, where reimbursement does not depend on the amount of benefits actually provided, any rights arising against a liable third party shall be governed by the following rules:

(a) where the institution of the State of residence or stay grants benefits to a person in respect of an injury sustained in its territory, that institution, in accordance with the provisions of the legislation it applies, shall exercise the right to subrogation or direct action against the third party liable to provide compensation for the injury;

(b) for the application of (a):

  (i) the person receiving benefits shall be deemed to be insured with the institution of the place of residence or stay, and

  (ii) that institution shall be deemed to be the institution responsible for providing benefits;

(c) paragraphs 1 and 2 shall remain applicable in respect of any benefits not covered by the waiver agreement or a reimbursement which does not depend on the amount of benefits actually provided.

General Note

5.326 Corresponding provision of Regulation 883/2004: art.85.

Article SSC.66: Implementation of legislation

5.327 Special provisions for implementing the legislation of a certain State are referred to in Annex SSC-6 [Special provisions for the application of the legislation of the Member States and of the United Kingdom to the Protocol].

General Note

Just as in the case of Regulation 883/2004 (art.83 and Annex XI) there is an Annex of special provisions which will require checking in individual cases. **5.328**

Title V: Final Provisions

Article SSC.67: Protection of individual rights

1. The Parties shall ensure in accordance with their domestic legal orders that the provisions of the Protocol on Social Security Coordination have the force of law, either directly or through domestic legislation giving effect to these provisions, so that legal or natural persons can invoke those provisions before domestic courts, tribunals and administrative authorities. **5.329**

2. The Parties shall ensure the means for legal and natural persons to effectively protect their rights under this Protocol, such as the possibility to address complaints to administrative bodies or to bring legal action before a competent court or tribunal in an appropriate judicial procedure, in order to seek an adequate and timely remedy.

General Note

See European Union (Future Relationship) Act 2020 s.26 at para.5.81. **5.330**

Article SSC.68: Amendments

The Specialised Committee on Social Security Coordination may amend the Annexes and Appendices to this Protocol. **5.331**

Article SSC.69: Termination of this Protocol

Without prejudice to Article 779 of this Agreement [Termination], each Party may at any moment terminate this Protocol, by written notification through diplomatic channels. In that event, this Protocol shall cease to be in force on the first day of the ninth month following the date of notification. **5.332**

Article SSC.70: Sunset clause

1. This Protocol shall cease to apply fifteen years after the entry into force of this Agreement. **5.333**

2. Not less than 12 months before this Protocol ceases to apply in accordance with paragraph 1, either Party shall notify the other Party of its wish to enter into negotiations with a view to concluding an updated Protocol.

Article SSC.71: Post-termination arrangements

When this Protocol ceases to apply pursuant to Article SSC.69 [Termination of this Protocol], Article SSC.70 [Sunset clause] or Article **5.334**

779 of this Agreement [Termination], the rights of insured persons regarding entitlements which are based on periods completed or facts or events that occurred before this Protocol ceases to apply shall be retained. The Partnership Council may lay down additional arrangements setting out appropriate consequential and transitional arrangements in good time before this Protocol ceases to apply.

Annex SCC-1: Certain Benefits in Cash to Which the Protocol Shall Not Apply

Part 1

Special non-contributory cash benefits
(Point (a) of Article SSC.3(4) of this Protocol [Matters covered])

5.335 (i) UNITED KINGDOM

(a) State Pension Credit (State Pension Credit Act 2002 and State Pension Credit Act (Northern Ireland) 2002);
(b) Income-based allowances for jobseekers (Jobseekers Act 1995 and Jobseekers (Northern Ireland) Order 1995);
(c) Disability Living Allowance, mobility component (Social Security Contributions and Benefits Act 1992 and Social Security Contributions and Benefits (Northern Ireland) Act 1992);
(d) Personal Independence Payment, mobility component (Welfare Reform Act 2012 (Part 4) and Welfare Reform (Northern Ireland) Order 2015 (Part 5));
(e) Employment and Support Allowance Income-related (Welfare Reform Act 2007 and Welfare Reform Act (Northern Ireland) 2007);
(f) Best Start Foods payment (Welfare Foods (Best Start Foods) (Scotland) Regulations 2019 (SSI 2019/193));
(g) Best Start Grants (pregnancy and baby grant, early learning grant, school-age grant) (The Early Years Assistance (Best Start Grants) (Scotland) Regulations 2018 (SSI 2018/370));
(h) Funeral Support Payment (Funeral Expense Assistance (Scotland) Regulations 2019 (SSI 2019/292)).

(ii) MEMBER STATES

AUSTRIA

Compensatory supplement (Federal Act of 9 September 1955 on General Social Insurance—ASVG, Federal Act of 11 October 1978 on Social insurance for persons engaged in trade and commerce—GSVG and Federal Act of 11 October 1978 on Social insurance for farmers—BSVG).

BELGIUM

(a) Income replacement allowance (Law of 27 February 1987);
(b) Guaranteed income for elderly persons (Law of 22 March 2001).

BULGARIA

Social Pension for old age (Article 89 of the Social Insurance Code).

CYPRUS

(a) Social Pension (Social Pension Law of 1995 (Law 25(I)/95), as amended);

(b) Severe motor disability allowance (Council of Ministers' Decisions Nos 38210 of 16 October 1992, 41370 of 1 August 1994, 46183 of 11 June 1997 and 53675 of 16 May 2001);

(c) Special grant to blind persons (Special Grants Law of 1996 (Law 77(I)/96), as amended).

CZECH REPUBLIC

Social allowance (State Social Support Act No.117/1995 Sb.).

DENMARK

Accommodation expenses for pensioners (Law on individual accommodation assistance, consolidated by Law No.204 of 29 March 1995).

ESTONIA

(a) Disabled adult allowance (Social Benefits for Disabled Persons Act of 27 January 1999);

(b) State unemployment allowance (Labour Market Services and Support Act of 29 September 2005).

FINLAND

(a) Housing allowance for pensioners (Act concerning the Housing Allowance for pensioners, 571/2007);

(b) Labour market support (Act on Unemployment Benefits 1290/2002);

(c) Special assistance for immigrants (Act on Special Assistance for Immigrants, 1192/2002).

FRANCE

(a) Supplementary allowances of:

  (i) the Special Invalidity Fund; and

  (ii) the Old Age Solidarity Fund in respect of acquired rights (Law of 30 June 1956, codified in Book VIII of the Social Security Code);

(b) Disabled adults' allowance (Law of 30 June 1975, codified in Book VIII of the Social Security Code);

(c) Special allowance (Law of 10 July 1952, codified in Book VIII of the Social Security Code) in respect of acquired rights;

(d) Old-age solidarity allowance (ordinance of 24 June 2004, codified in Book VIII of the Social Security Code) as of 1 January 2006.

GERMANY

(a) Basic subsistence income for the elderly and for persons with reduced earning capacity under Chapter 4 of Book XII of the Social Code;

(b) Benefits to cover subsistence costs under the basic provision for jobseekers unless, with respect to these benefits, the eligibility requirements for a temporary supplement following receipt of unemployment benefit (Article 24(1) of Book II of the Social Code) are fulfilled.

GREECE

Special benefits for the elderly (Law 1296/82).

HUNGARY

(a) Invalidity annuity (Decree No.83/1987 (XII 27) of the Council of Ministers on Invalidity Annuity);
(b) Non-contributory old age allowance (Act III of 1993 on Social Administration and Social Benefits);
(c) Transport allowance (Government Decree No.164/1995 (XII 27) on Transport Allowances for Persons with Severe Physical Handicap).

IRELAND

(a) Jobseekers' allowance (Social Welfare Consolidation Act 2005, Part 3, Chapter 2);
(b) State pension (non-contributory) (Social Welfare Consolidation Act 2005, Part 3, Chapter 4);
(c) Widow's (non-contributory) pension and widower's (non-contributory) pension (Social Welfare Consolidation Act 2005, Part 3, Chapter 6);
(d) Disability allowance (Social Welfare Consolidation Act 2005, Part 3, Chapter 10);
(e) Mobility allowance (Health Act 1970, Section 61);
(f) Blind pension (Social Welfare Consolidation Act 2005, Part 3, Chapter 5).

ITALY

(a) Social pensions for persons without means (Law No.153 of 30 April 1969);
(b) Pensions and allowances for the civilian disabled or invalids (Laws No.118 of 30 March 1971, No.18 of 11 February 1980 and No 508 of 21 November 1988);
(c) Pensions and allowances for the deaf and dumb (Laws No.381 of 26 May 1970 and No.508 of 21 November 1988);
(d) Pensions and allowances for the civilian blind (Laws No.382 of 27 May 1970 and No.508 of 21 November 1988);
(e) Benefits supplementing the minimum pensions (Laws No.218 of 4 April 1952, No.638 of 11 November 1983 and No.407 of 29 December 1990);
(f) Benefits supplementing disability allowances (Law No.222 of 12 June 1984);
(g) Social allowance (Law No.335 of 8 August 1995);
(h) Social increase (Article 1(1) and (12) of Law No.544 of 29 December 1988 and successive amendments).

LATVIA

(a) State Social Security Benefit (Law on State Social Benefits of 1 January 2003);
(b) Allowance for the compensation of transportation expenses for disabled persons with restricted mobility (Law on State Social Benefits of 1 January 2003).

LITHUANIA

(a) Social assistance pension (Law of 2005 on State Social Assistance Benefits, Article 5);

(b) Relief compensation (Law of 2005 on State Social Assistance Benefits, Article 15);

(c) Transport compensation for the disabled who have mobility problems (Law of 2000 on Transport Compensation, Article 7).

LUXEMBOURG

Income for the seriously disabled (Article 1(2), Law of 12 September 2003), with the exception of persons recognised as being disabled workers and employed on the mainstream labour market or in a sheltered environment.

MALTA

(a) Supplementary allowance (Section 73 of the Social Security Act (Cap.318) 1987);

(b) Age pension (Social Security Act (Cap.318) 1987).

NETHERLANDS

(a) Work and Employment Support for Disabled Young Persons Act of 24 April 1997 (Wet Wajong).

(b) Supplementary Benefits Act of 6 November 1986 (TW).

POLAND

Social pension (Act of 27 June 2003 on social pensions).

PORTUGAL

(a) Non-contributory State old-age and invalidity pension (Decree-Law No.464/80 of 13 October 1980);

(b) Non-contributory widowhood pension (Regulatory Decree No.52/81 of 11 November 1981);

(c) Solidarity supplement for the elderly (Decree—Law No.232/2005 of 29 December 2005, amended by Decree—Law No.236/2006 of 11 December 2006).

SLOVAKIA

(a) Adjustment awarded before 1 January 2004 to pensions constituting the sole source of income;

(b) Social pension which has been awarded before 1 January 2004.

SLOVENIA

(a) State pension (Pension and Disability Insurance Act of 23 December 1999);

(b) Income support for pensioners (Pension and Disability Insurance Act of 23 December 1999);

(c) Maintenance allowance (Pension and Disability Insurance Act of 23 December 1999).

SPAIN

(a) Minimum income guarantee (Law No.13/82 of 7 April 1982);

(b) Cash benefits to assist the elderly and invalids unable to work (Royal Decree No.2620/81 of 24 July 1981):
   (i) Non-contributory invalidity and retirement pensions as provided for in Chapter II of Title VI of the Consolidated Text of the General Law on Social Security, approved by Royal Legislative Decree No.8/2015 of 30 October 2015; and
   (ii) the benefits which supplement the above pensions, as provided for in the legislation of the Comunidades Autonómas, where such supplements guarantee a minimum subsistence income having regard to the economic and social situation in the Comunidades Autonómas concerned;

(c) Allowances to promote mobility and to compensate for transport costs (Law No.13/1982 of 7 April 1982).

SWEDEN

(a) Housing supplements for persons receiving a pension (Law 2001:761);
(b) Financial support for the elderly (Law 2001:853).

Part 2
Long-term care benefits
(Point (d) of Article SSC.3(4) of this Protocol)

(i) UNITED KINGDOM

(a) Attendance Allowance (Social Security Contributions and Benefits Act 1992, Social Security (Attendance Allowance) Regulations 1991, Social Security Contributions and Benefits (Northern Ireland) Act 1992 and Social Security (Attendance Allowance) Regulations (Northern Ireland) 1992);
(b) Carer's Allowance (Social Security Contributions and Benefits Act 1992, The Social Security (Invalid Care Allowance) Regulations 1976, Social Security Contributions and Benefits (Northern Ireland) Act 1992) and The Social Security (Invalid Care Allowance) Regulations 1976 (Northern Ireland);
(c) Disability Living Allowance, care component (Social Security Contributions and Benefits Act 1992, Social Security (Disability Living Allowance) Regulations 1991, Social Security Contributions and Benefits (Northern Ireland) Act 1992 and Social Security (Disability Living Allowance) Regulations (Northern Ireland) 1992);
(d) Personal Independence Payment, daily living component (Welfare Reform Act 2012 (Part 4), Social Security (Personal Independence Payment) Regulations 2013, Personal Independence Payment (Transitional Provisions) Regulations 2013, Personal Independence Payment (Transitional Provisions) (Amendment) Regulations 2019, Welfare Reform (Northern Ireland) Order 2015 (Part 5), Personal Independence Payment Regulations (Northern Ireland) 2016, Personal Independence Payment (Transitional Provisions) Regulations (Northern Ireland) 2016 and Personal Independence Payment (Transitional Provisions) (Amendment) Regulations (Northern Ireland) 2019;

(e) Carer's Allowance Supplement (The Social Security (Scotland) Act 2018);
(f) Young Carer's Grant (The Carer's Assistance (Young Carer Grants) (Scotland) Regulations 2020 (as amended)).

(ii) MEMBER STATES

AUSTRIA
(a) Federal Long-term care allowance Act (Bundespflegegeldgesetz, BPGG), original version BGBl. No.110/1993, last amendment BGBl- I No.100/2016.
(b) Regulation on the staging of the Federal long-term care allowance (Einstufungsverordnung zum Bundespflegegeldgesetz (EinstV)).
(c) Regulation of the Federal minister for Labour, Social affairs and Consumer protection on needs assessments of care for children and young people in accordance with the Federal Nursing Care Act. (Bundespflegegeldgesetz, Kinder-EinstV).
(d) Numerous applicable statutory bases, e.g. Agreement between the Federal Government and the Länder on joint measures for persons in need of care. Social Assistance Acts and Disability Acts of the Länder.
(e) Care Fund Law (Pflegefondsgesetz, PFG), Original version: Official Journal (BGBI. I) No.57/2011.
(f) Care Services Statistics Ordinance 2012 (Pflegedienstleistungsstatistik-Verordnung 2012).
(g) Support for the 24-hour care: Federal Long-term care allowance Act (Bundespflegegeldgesetz, BPGG).
(h) Guidelines for the support of the 24-hour care (§ 21b of the Federal Long-term care allowance Act (Bundespflegegeldgesetz)).
(i) Guidelines for granting benefits to support caring family members (§ 21a of the Federal Long-term care allowance Act (Bundespflegegeldgesetz)).
(j) Care recourse interdiction.
(k) Federal Act on a specific supplement due to the abolition of access to funds when housing people in inpatient care facilities.
(l) Federal Act on a specific supplement due to the abolition of access to funds when housing people in inpatient care facilities for 2019 and 2020, BGBl. I No.95/2019.

BELGIUM
(a) Health Care and Sickness Benefit Compulsory Insurance Act (Loi relative à l'assurance obligatoire soins de santé et indemnités/Wet betreffende de verplichte verzekering voor geneeskundige verzorging en uitkeringen), coordinated on 14 July 1994.
(b) Act of 27 February 1987 on allowances for persons with disabilities (Loi relative aux allocations aux personnes handicapées/Wet betreffende de tegemoetkomingen aan gehandicapten).
(c) Flemish social protection (Vlaamse sociale bescherming): Decree of the Flemish Parliament of 18 May 2018 on the organisation of

Flemish social protection (Decreet houdende Vlaamse sociale bescherming/) and Orders of the Flemish government of 30 November 2018.

(d) Walloon Code for Social Action and Health (Code wallon de l'Action sociale et de la Santé), decretal part. Part 1, book IIIter, instituted by Decree of 8 November 2018.

(e) Walloon Regulatory Code for Social Action and Health, part I/1 instituted by Walloon Government Decree of 21 December 2018.

(f) Decree of 13 December 2018 on offers to elderly or dependent persons as well as on palliative care (Dekret über die Angebote für Senioren und Personen mit Unterstützungsbedarf sowie über die Palliativpflege).

(g) Decree of 4 June 2007 on psychiatric nursing homes (Dekret über die psychiatrischen Pflegewohnheime).

(h) Government Decree of 20 June 2017 on mobility aids (Erlass über die Mobilitätshilfen).

(i) Decree of 13 December 2016 on the establishment of a German Community Office for self-determined life (Dekret zur Schaffung einer Dienststelle der Deutschsprachigen Gemeinschaft für selbstbestimmtes Leben).

(j) Royal Decree of 5 March 1990 on the allowance for assistance to the elderly (Arrêté royal du 5 mars 1990 relatif à l'allocation pour l'aide aux personnes âgées).

(k) Government Decree of 19 December 2019 on transitional arrangements relating to the procedure for obtaining a prior authorization or an approval for the coverage or the sharing of costs of long-term rehabilitation abroad (Erlass der Regierung zur übergansweisen Regelung des Verfahrens zur Erlangung einer Vorabgeehmigung oder Zustimmung zwecks Kostenübernahme oder Kostenbeteiligung für eine Langzeitrehabilitation im Ausland).

(l) Order of 21 December 2018 on Brussels health insurance bodies in the field of health care and assistance to people (Ordonnance du 21 décembre 2018 relative aux organismes assureurs bruxellois dans le domaine des soins de santé et de l'aide aux personnes).

(m) Cooperation between federated entities.

(n) Cooperation agreement of 31 December 2018 between the Flemish Community, the Walloon Region, the French Community Commission, the Joint Community Commission and the German-speaking Community concerning mobility aids.

(o) Cooperation agreement of 31 December 2018 between the Flemish Community, the Walloon Region, the French Community, the Joint Community Commission, the French Community Commission and the German-speaking Community concerning the financing of care when using care institutions located outside the limits of the federated entity.

BULGARIA

(a) Social Insurance Code (Кодекс за социално осигуряване), 1999 title amended 2003.

(b) Law on Social Assistance (Закон за социално подпомагане), 1998.

(c) Regulation on the Implementation of the Law on Social Assistance (Правилник за прилагане на Закона за социално подпомагане), 1998.
(d) Law on Integration of People with Disabilities 2019 (Закон за хората с увреждания), 2019.
(e) Personal Assistance Act 2019 (Закон за личната помощ) 2019 which entered into force on 1 September 2019.
(f) Regulation on the Implementation of the Law on Integration of People with Disabilities (Правилник за прилагане на Закона за интеграция на хората с увреждания), 2004.
(g) Ordinance on the medical expertise (Наредба за медицинската експертиза) 2010.
(h) Tariff of the Fees for Social Services Financed by the State Budget (Тарифа за таксите засоциални услуги, финансирани от държавния бюджет), 2003.

CROATIA
(a) Social Welfare Act (Zakon o socijalnoj skrbi) of 2013, OJ No.157/13, 152/14, 99/15, 52/16, 16/17, 130/17 and 98/19)
(b) Foster Families Act (Zakon o udomiteljstvu) OJ No.90/11 and 78/12, as amended.
(c) Ordinance on minimum requirements for delivery of social services (Pravilnik o minimalnim uvjetima za pružanje socijalnih usluga) of 2014, OJ No.40/14 and 66/15.
(d) Ordinance on participation and method of payment of beneficiaries in the maintenance costs of accommodation outside the family (Pravilnik o sudjelovanju i načinu plaćanja korisnika I drugih obveznika uzdržavanja u troškovima smještaja izvan vlastite obitelji) of 1998, OJ No.112/98 and 05/02, as amended.
(e) Ordinance on the content and manner of keeping records of individuals who are professionally engaged in social services delivery as a profession (Pravilnik o sadržaju I načinu vođenja evidencije fizičkih osoba koje profesionalno pružaju socijalne usluge) of 2015, OJ No.66/15.

CYPRUS
(a) Social Welfare Services (Υπηρεσίες Κοινωνικής Ευημερίας).
(b) The Guaranteed Minimum Income and in General the Social Benefits (Emergency Needs and Care Needs) Regulations and Decrees as they are amended or superseded. Homes for the Elderly and Disabled Persons Laws (Οι περί Στεγών για Ηλικιωμένους και Αναπήρους Νόμοι) of 1991–2011.[L.222/91 and L.65(I)/2011].
(c) Adult Day-Care Centres Laws (Οι περί Κέντρων Ενηλίκων Νόμοι) (L.38(I)/1997 and L.64(I)/2011).
(d) State Aid Scheme, under the Regulation 360/2012 for the provision of services of general economic interest (De minimis) [Σχέδιο Κρατικών Ενισχύσεων Ησσονος Σημασίας, βαση του Κανονισμού 360/2012 για την παροχή υπηρεσιών γενικού οικονομικού συμφέροντος].
(e) Welfare Benefits Administration Service (Υπηρεσία Διαχείρισης Επιδομάτων Πρόνοιας).
(f) The Guaranteed Minimum Income and generally for Welfare Benefits Law of 2014 as it is amended or superseded.

(g) The Guaranteed Minimum Income and generally for Welfare Benefits Regulations and Decrees as they are amended or superseded.

CZECH REPUBLIC

(a) Act. No.108/2006 on social services (Zákon o sociálních službách).
(b) Act No.372/2011 on Health Services (Zákon o zdravotních službách).
(c) Act No.48/1997 on Public Health Insurance (Zákon o veřejném zdravotním pojištění).

DENMARK

(a) Consolidated Act No.988 of 17 August 2017 on Social Services (om social service).
(b) Consolidated Act No.119 of 1 February 2019 on Social Housing (om almene boliger).

ESTONIA

Social Welfare Act (Sotsiaalhoolekande seadus) 2016.

FINLAND

(a) Services and Assistance for the Disabled Act (Laki vammaisuuden perusteella järjestettävistä palveluista ja tukitoimista) of 3 April 1987.
(b) Act on Supporting the Functional Capacity of the Ageing Population and on Social and Health Care Services for Older People (Laki ikääntyneen väestön toimintakyvyn tukemisesta sekä iäkkäiden sosiaali- ja terveyspalveluista) of 28 December 2012.
(c) Social Welfare Act (Sosiaalihuoltolaki) of 30 December 2014.
(d) Health Care Act (Terveydenhuoltolaki) of 30 December 2010.
(e) Primary Health Care Act (Kansanterveyslaki) of 28 January 1972.
(f) Act on Informal Care Support (Laki omaishoidon tuesta) of 2 December 2005.
(g) Family Care Act (Perhehoitolaki) of 20 March 2015.

FRANCE

(a) Supplement for a third party (majoration pour tierce personne, MTP): Articles L.341-4 and L.355-1 of the Social Security Code (Code de la sécurité sociale).
(b) Supplementary benefit for recourse to a third party (prestation complémentaire pour recours à tierce personne): Article L.434-2 of the Social Security Code.
(c) Special education supplement for a disabled child (complément d'allocation d'éducation de l'enfant handicapé): Article L.541-1 of the Social Security Code.
(d) Disability compensation allowance (prestation de compensation du handicap, PCH): Articles L.245-1 to L.245-14 of the Social action and Family Code (Code de l'action sociale et des familles).
(e) Allowance for loss of autonomy (allocation personnalisée d'autonomie, APA): Articles L.232-1 to L.232-28 of the Social action and Family Code (Code de l'action sociale et des familles).

GERMANY

(a) Long-term care insurance (Pflegeversicherung):

(b) Social long-term care insurance for persons insured under statutory sickness insurance and private compulsory long-term care insurance for persons insured under private sickness insurance: Social CodeSozialgesetzbuch, Book XI (SGB XI), last amended by Article 2 of the Act of 21 December 2019 (BGBl. I p.2913).

GREECE

(a) Law No.1140/1981, as amended.

(b) Legislative Decree No.162/73 and Joint Ministerial Decision No.Π4β/5814/1997.

(c) Ministerial Decision No.Π1γ/ΑΓΠ/οικ.14963 of 9 October 2001.

(d) Law No.4025/2011.

(e) Law No.4109/2013.

(f) Law No.4199/2013 art. 127.

(g) Law No.4368/2016 art. 334.

(h) Law No.4483/2017 art. 153.

(i) Law No.498/1-11-2018, arts 28, 30 and 31, for the "Unified Health Benefits Regulation" of the National Service Provider Organization Health (EOPYY).

HUNGARY

(a) Long-term care services providing personal social care (social services):

(b) Act III of 1993 on Social Administration and Social Assistance (törvény a szociális igazgatásról és szociális ellátásokról) supplemented by Government and Ministerial decrees.

IRELAND

(a) Health Act 1970 (No.1 of 1970).

(b) Nursing Homes Support Scheme Act 2009 (No.15 of 2009).

(c) Social Welfare Consolidation Act 2005.

(d) Constant Attendance Allowance.

(e) Carer's Benefit.

(f) Carer's Allowance.

(g) Carer's Support Grant.

(h) Domiciliary Care Allowance.

ITALY

(a) Law No.118 of 30 March 1971 on civilian invalidity benefits (Legge 30 Marzo 1971, n.118 - Conversione in Legge del D.L. 30 gennaio 1971, n.5 e nuove norme in favore dei mutilati ed invalidi civili).

(b) Law No.18 of 11 February 1980 on Constant attendance allowance (Legge 11 Febbraio 1980, n.18 - Indennità di accompagnamento agli invalidi civili totalmente inabili).

(c) Law No.104 of 5 February 1992, Article 33 (Framework law on disability) (Legge 5 Febbraio 1992, n.104 - Legge-quadro per l'assistenza, l'integrazione sociale e i diritti delle persone handicappate).

(d) Legislative Decree No.112 of 31 March 1998 on the transfer of legislative tasks and administrative competences from the State to the Regions and local entities (Decreto Legislativo 31 Marzo 1998, n.112 - Conferimento di funzioni e compiti amministrativi dello Stato alle regioni ed agli enti locali, in attuazione del capo I della Legge 15 Marzo 1997, n.59).
(e) Regulation (CE) 883/04 on social security coordination of the European Parliament and Council (Regolamento (CE) 883 del 29 aprile 2004 del Parlamento Europeo e del Consiglio, relativo al coordinamento dei sistemi di sicurezza sociale - SNCB – art.70 and Annex X).
(f) Law No.183 of 4 November 2010, Article 24, modifying the rules regarding the permits for the assistance to disabled persons in difficult situations (Legge n.183 del 4 Novembre 2010, art.24 - Modifiche alla disciplina in materia di permessi per l'assistenza a portatori di handicap in situazione di gravità).
(g) Law No.147 of 27 December 2013 containing provisions for drawing up the annual and pluri-annual budget of the State - Stability Law 2014 (Disposizioni per la formazione del bilancio annuale e pluriennale dello Stato - Legge di stabilità 2014).

LATVIA

(a) Law on Social Services and Social Assistance (Sociālo pakalpojumu un sociālās palīdzības likums) 31/10/2002.
(b) Medical Treatment Law (Ārstniecības likums) 12/06/1997.
(c) Law on Patient Rights (Pacientu tiesību likums) 30/12/2009
(d) Regulations of the Cabinet of Ministers No.555 on Health care organisation and payment procedure (Ministru kabineta 2018. gada 28.augusta noteikumi Nr.555 "Veselības aprūpes pakalpojumu organizēšanas un samaksas kārtība") 28/08/2018.
(e) Regulations of the Cabinet of Ministers No.275 on Procedures for Payment of Social Care and Social Rehabilitation Services and the Procedures for Covering Service Costs from a Local Government Budget (Ministru kabineta 2003.gada 27.maija noteikumi Nr.275 "Sociālās aprūpes un sociālās rehabilitācijas pakalpojumu samaksas kārtība un kārtība, kādā pakalpojuma izmaksas tiek segtas no pašvaldības budžeta") 27/05/2003.
(f) Regulations of the Cabinet of Ministers No.138 on Receiving of Social Services and Social Assistance (Ministru kabineta 2019.gada 2.aprīļa noteikumi Nr 138 "Noteiku mi par sociālo pakalpojumu un sociālās palīdzības saņemšanu") 02/04/2019.

LITHUANIA

(a) Law on Target compensations (Tikslinių kompensacijų įstatymas) of 29 June 2016 (No.XII-2507).
(b) Law on Social Services (Socialinių paslaugų įstatymas) of 19 January 2006 (No.X-493).
(c) Law on Health Insurance (Sveikatos draudimo įstatymas) of 21 May 1996 (No.I-1343).
(d) Law on Healthcare system (Sveikatos sistemos įstatymas) of 19 July 1994 (No.I-552).

(e) Law on Health Care Institutions (Sveikatos priežiūros įstaigų įstatymas) of 6 June 1996 (No.I-1367).

LUXEMBOURG

Law of 19 June 1998 introducing the dependency insurance, amended by the Law of 23 December 2005 and the Law of 29 August 2017.

MALTA

(a) Social Security Act (Att dwar is-Sigurta' Socjali) (Cap. 318).
(b) Subsidiary Legislation 318.19: State-Owned Institutions and Hostels Rates Regulations (Regolamenti dwar it-Trasferiment ta' Fondi għal Hostels Statali Indikati).
(c) Subsidiary Legislation 318.17: Transfer of Funds (Government Financed Beds) Regulations (Regolamenti dwar it-Trasferiment ta' Fondi għal Sodod Iffinanzjati mill-Gvern).
(d) Subsidiary Legislation 318.13: State Financed Residential Services Rates Regulations (Regolamenti dwar Rati għal Servizzi Residenzjali Finanzjali mill-Istat).

THE NETHERLANDS

Long term care act (Wet langdurige zorg (WLZ)), Law of 3 December 2014.

POLAND

(a) Law on Health Care Services financed from Public Means (Ustawa o świadczeniach opieki drowotnej finansowanych ze środków publicznych) of 27 August 2004.
(b) Law on Social Assistance (Ustawa o pomocy społecznej) of 12 March 2004.
(c) Law on Family Benefits (Ustawa o świadczeniach rodzinnych) of 28 November 2003.
(d) Law on Social Pension (Ustawa o rencie socjalnej) of 27 June 2003.
(e) Law on Social Insurance Fund Pensions (Ustawa o emeryturach i rentach z Funduszu Ubezpieczeń Społecznych) of 17 December 1998.
(f) Law on Vocational and Social Rehabilitation and Employment of Disabled Persons (Ustawa o rehabilitacji zawodowej i społecznej oraz zatrudnianiu osób niepełnosprawnych) of 27 August 1997.
(g) Law on support for pregnant women and their families "For life" (Ustawa o wsparciu kobiet w ciąży i rodzin "Za życiem") of 4 November 2016.
(h) Law on supplementary benefit for persons unable to live independently (Ustawa o świadczeniu uzupełniającym dla osób niezdolnych do samodzielnej egzystencji) of 31 July 2019.

PORTUGAL

(a) Social insurance and guaranteeing sufficient resources.
(b) Statutory Decree 265/99 of 14 July 1999 on the long-term care supplement (complemento por dependência), as amended on several occasions.

(c) Act 90/2009 of 31 August 2009 on the special protection system in case of disability (regime especial de proteção na invalidez), re-published in consolidated version by Statutory Decree 246/2015 of 20 October 2015, amended.
(d) Social security system and National Health Service.
(e) Statutory Decree 101/06 of 6 June 2006 on the National network of integrated continuing care (rede de cuidados continuados integrados), re-published in a consolidated version in Statutory Decree 136/2015 of 28 July 2015.
(f) Decree-Law No.8/2010 of 28 January 2010, amended and republished by Decree-Law No.22/2011 of 10 February 2011 on the creation of units and teams for integrated continuous care in mental health (unidades e equipas de cuidados continuados integrados de saúde mental).
(g) Decree No.343/.2015 of 12 October 2015 on standards governing hospital and ambulatory paediatric care as well as the discharge management teams and the paediatric care teams within the framework of the national network of long-term integrated care (condições de instalação e funcionamento das unidades de internamento de cuidados integrados pediátricos e de ambulatório pediátricas, bem como as condições a que devem obedecer as equipas de gestão de altas e as equipas de cuidados continuados integrados destinadas a cuidados pediátricos da Rede Nacional de Cuidados Continuados Integrados).
(h) Law No.6/2009 of 6 September on the status of informal carer (Estatuto do cuidador informal).

ROMANIA

(a) Law 17 of 6 March 2000 on Social Assistance of Senior Persons (Legea privind asistența socială a persoanelor vârstnice), with subsequent amendments.
(b) Law 448 of 6 December 2006 on Protection and Promotion of the Rights of Persons with Disability (Legea privind protecția și promovarea drepturilor persoanelor cu handicap), with subsequent amendments.
(c) Social Assistance Law (Legea asistenței sociale) No. 292 of 20 December 2011.

SLOVAKIA

(a) Law on Social Services (Zákon o sociálnych službách) No.448/2008.
(b) Law on Financial Benefits for Compensation of Disabled Persons (Zákon o peňažných príspevkoch na kompenzáciu ťažkého zdravotného postihnutia) No.447/2008.
(c) Law on Health Care and Services Related to Health Care (Zákon o zdravotnej starostlivosti a službách súvisiacich s poskytovaním zdravotnej starostlivosti) No.576/2004.
(d) Law on Health Care Providers, Medical Workers and Professional Medical Associations (Zákon o poskytovateľoch zdravotnej starostlivosti, zdravotníckych pracovníkoch a stavovských organizáciách v zdravotníctve) No.578/2004.

(e) Law on Subsistence Minimum (Zákon o životnom minime) No.601/2003.
(f) Law on Family (Zákon o rodine) No.36/2005.
(g) Law on Social and legal protection of children and social guardianship (Zákon o sociálno-právnej ochrane detí a sociálnej kuratele) No.305/2005.
(h) Law on Social Work (Zákon o sociálnej práci) No.219/2014.

SLOVENIA

No specific law related to long-term care. Long-term care benefits are included in the following acts:

(a) Pension and Disability Insurance Act (Zakon o pokojninskem in invalidskem zavarovanju) (Official Gazette of the Republic of Slovenia, No.96/2012, and subsequent amendments).
(b) Financial Social Assistance Act (Zakon o socialno vartsvenih prejemkih) (Official Gazette of the Republic of Slovenia, No.61/2010, and subsequent amendments).
(c) Exercise of Rights to Public Funds Act (Zakon o uveljavljanju pravic iz javnih sredstev) (Official Gazette of the Republic of Slovenia, No.62/2010, and subsequent amendments).
(d) Social Protection Act (Zakon o socialnem varstvu) (Official Gazette of the Republic of Slovenia, No.3/2004—official consolidated text, and subsequent amendments).
(e) Parental Care and Family Benefits Act (Zakon o starševskem varstvu in družinskih prejemkih) (Official Gazette of the Republic of Slovenia, No.110/2006—official consolidated text, and subsequent amendments).
(f) Mentally and Physically Handicapped Persons Act (Zakon o družbenem varstvu duševno in telesno prizadetih oseb) (Official Gazette of the Republic of Slovenia, No.41/83, and subsequent amendments).
(g) Health Care and Health Insurance Act (Zakon o zdravstvenem varstvu in zdravstvenem zavarovanju) (Official Gazette of the Republic of Slovenia, No.72/2006—official consolidated text, and subsequent amendments).
(h) War Veterans Act (Zakon o vojnih veteranih) (Official Gazette of the Republic of Slovenia, No.59/06 official consolidated text, and subsequent amendments)
(i) War Disability Act (Zakon o vojnih invalidih) (Official Gazette of the Republic of Slovenia, No.63/59 official consolidated text, and subsequent amendments)
(j) Fiscal Balance Act (Zakon za uravnoteženje javnih finance (ZUJF)) (Official Gazette of the Republic of Slovenia, No.40/2012, and subsequent amendments).
(k) Act Regulating Adjustments of Transfers to Individuals and Households in the Republic of Slovenia (Zakon o usklajevanju transferjev posameznikom in gospodinjstvom v Republiki Sloveniji) (Official Gazette of the Republic of Slovenia, No.114/2006—official consolidated text, and subsequent amendments).

SPAIN

(a) Law No.39/2006 on the Promotion of Personal Autonomy and Assistance to persons in situations of dependence of 14 December 2006, as amended.
(b) Ministerial Order of 15 April 1969.
(c) Royal Decree No. 1300/95 of 21 July 1995, as amended.
(d) Royal Decree No. 1647/97 of 31 October 1997, as amended.

SWEDEN

(a) Social Services Act (Socialtjänstlagen (2001:453)) of 2001.
(b) The Health Care Act (Hälso- och sjukvårdslag (2017:30)) of 2017.

Part 3: Payments which are connected to a branch of social security listed in Article SSC.3(1) [Matters covered] of the Protocol and which are paid to meet expenses for heating in cold weather (point (f) of Article SSC.3(4)[Matters covered] of the Protocol).

(i) UNITED KINGDOM

5.336 Winter Fuel Payment (Social Security Contributions and Benefits Act 1992, Social Fund Winter Fuel Payment Regulations 2000, Social Security Contributions and Benefits (Northern Ireland) Act 1992 and Social Fund Winter Fuel Payment Regulations (Northern Ireland) 2000).

(ii) MEMBER STATES

DENMARK

(a) Act on Social and state pensions, LBK no. 983 of 23/09/2019
(b) Regulations on social and state pensions, BEK no. 1602 of 27/12/2019.

ANNEX SSC-2: RESTRICTION OF RIGHTS TO BENEFITS IN KIND FOR MEMBERS OF THE FAMILY OF A FRONTIER WORKER

5.337 (referred to in Article SSC.16(2)[Stay in the competent State when residence is in another State – special rules for the members of the families of frontier workers])
CROATIA
DENMARK
IRELAND
FINLAND
SWEDEN
UNITED KINGDOM

ANNEX SSC-3: MORE RIGHTS FOR PENSIONERS RETURNING TO THE COMPETENT STATE

(Article SSC.25(2) [Stay of the pensioner or the members of their family in a State other than the State of residence – stay in the competent State – authorisation for appropriate treatment outside the State of residence]) **5.338**

AUSTRIA
BELGIUM
BULGARIA
CYPRUS
CZECH REPUBLIC
FRANCE
GERMANY
GREECE
HUNGARY
LUXEMBOURG
THE NETHERLANDS
POLAND
SLOVENIA
SPAIN
SWEDEN

ANNEX SSC-4: CASES IN WHICH THE PRO RATA CALCULATION SHALL BE WAIVED OR SHALL NOT APPLY

(Articles SSC.47(4) and 47(5) [Award of benefits] of this Protocol)

PART 1: CASES IN WHICH THE PRO RATA CALCULATION SHALL BE WAIVED PURSUANT TO ARTICLE SSC.47(4) [AWARD OF BENEFITS]

AUSTRIA

(a) All applications for benefits under the Federal Act of 9 September 1955 on General Social Insurance—ASVG, the Federal Act of 11 October 1978 on social insurance for self-employed persons engaged in trade and commerce—GSVG, the Federal Act of 11 October 1978 on social insurance for self-employed farmers—BSVG and the Federal Act of 30 November 1978 on social insurance for the self-employed in the liberal professions (FSVG); **5.339**

(b) All applications for survivors' pensions based on a pension account pursuant to the General Pensions Act (APG) of 18 November 2004, with the exception of cases under Part 2;

(c) All applications for survivors' pensions of the Austrian Provincial Chambers of Physicians (Landesärztekammer) based on basic provision (basic and any supplementary benefit, or basic pension);

(d) All applications for survivors' support from the pension fund of the Austrian Chamber of Veterinary Surgeons;

(e) All applications for benefits from widows and orphans pensions according to the statutes of the welfare institutions of the Austrian bar associations, Part A;

(f) All applications for benefits under the Notary Insurance Act of 3 February 1972—NVG 1972.

CYPRUS

All applications for old age, widow's and widower's pensions.

DENMARK

All applications for pensions referred to in the law on social pensions, except for pensions mentioned in Annex SSC-5 [Benefits and Agreements which allow the application of Article SSC.49 [Overlapping of benefits of the same kind]] to this Protocol.

IRELAND

All applications for state pension (transition), state pension (contributory), widow's (contributory) pension and widower's (contributory) pension.

LATVIA

All applications for survivor's pensions (Law on State pensions of 1 January 1996; Law on State funded pensions of 1 July 2001).

LITHUANIA

All applications for State social insurance survivor's pensions calculated on the basis of the basic amount of survivor's pension (Law on State Social Insurance Pensions).

NETHERLANDS

All applications for old-age pensions under the law on general old-age insurance (AOW).

POLAND

All applications for old-age under the defined benefits scheme and survivors' pensions, except for the cases where the totalised periods of insurance completed under the legislation of more than one country are equal to or longer than 20 years for women and 25 years for men but the national periods of insurance are inferior to these limits (and not less than 15 years for women and 20 years for men), and the calculation is made under Articles 27 and 28 of the Act of 17 December 1998 (OJ 2015, item 748).

PORTUGAL

All applications for old-age and survivors' pension claims, except for the cases where the totalised periods of insurance completed under the legislation of more than one country are equal to or longer than 21 calendar years but the national periods of insurance are equal or inferior to 20 years, and the calculation is made under Articles 32 and 33 of Decree-Law No.187/2007 of 10 May 2007.

SLOVAKIA

(a) All applications for survivors' pension (widow's pension, widower's and orphan's pension) calculated according to the legislation in force before 1 January 2004, the amount of which is derived from a pension formerly paid to the deceased;

(b) All applications for pensions calculated pursuant to Act No.461/2003 Coll. on social security as amended.

SWEDEN

(a) Applications for an old-age pension in the form of a guaranteed pension (Chapters 66 and 67 of the Social Insurance Code).
(b) Applications for an old-age pension in the form of a supplementary pension (Chapter 63 of the Social Insurance Code).

UNITED KINGDOM

All applications for retirement pension, state pension pursuant to Part 1 of the Pensions Act 2014, widows' and bereavement benefits, with the exception of those for which during a tax year beginning on or after 6 April 1975:

(i) the party concerned had completed periods of insurance, employment or residence under the legislation of the United Kingdom and a Member State; and one (or more) of the tax years was not considered a qualifying year within the meaning of the legislation of the United Kingdom;
(ii) the periods of insurance completed under the legislation in force in the United Kingdom for the periods prior to 5 July 1948 would be taken into account for the purposes of point (b) of Article SSC.47(1) of this Protocol by application of the periods of insurance, employment or residence under the legislation of a Member State.

All applications for additional pension pursuant to the Social Security Contributions and Benefits Act 1992, section 44, and the Social Security Contributions and Benefits (Northern Ireland) Act 1992, section 44.

PART 2
CASES IN WHICH ARTICLE SSC.47(5) APPLIES 5.340

AUSTRIA

(a) Old-age pensions and survivor's pensions derived thereof based on a pension account pursuant to the General Pensions Act (APG) of 18 November 2004;
(b) Compulsory allowances under Article 41 of the Federal Law of 28 December 2001, BGBl I Nr. 154 on the general salary fund of Austrian pharmacists (Pharmazeutische Gehaltskasse für Österreich);
(c) Retirement and early retirement pensions of the Austrian Provincial Chambers of Physicians based on basic provision (basic and any supplementary benefit, or basic pension), and all pension benefits of the Austrian Provincial Chambers of Physicians based on additional provision (additional or individual pension);
(d) Old-age support from the pension fund of the Austrian Chamber of Veterinary Surgeons;
(e) Benefits according to the statutes of the welfare institutions of the Austrian bar associations, Parts A and B, with the exception

of applications for benefits from widows' and orphans' pensions according to the statutes of the welfare institutions of the Austrian bar associations, Part A;

(f) Benefits by the welfare institutions of the Federal Chamber of Architects and Consulting Engineers under the Austrian Civil Engineers' Chamber Act (Ziviltechnikerkammergesetz) 1993 and the statutes of the welfare institutions, with the exception of benefits on grounds of survivors' benefits deriving from the last-named benefits;

(g) Benefits according to the statute of the welfare institution of the Federal Chamber of Professional Accountants and Tax Advisors under the Austrian Professional Accountants and Tax Advisors' Act (Wirtschaftstreuhandberufsgesetz).

BULGARIA

Old age pensions from the Supplementary Compulsory Pension Insurance, under Part II, Title II, of the Social Insurance Code.

CROATIA

Pensions from the compulsory insurance scheme based on the individual capitalised savings according to the Compulsory and Voluntary Pension Funds Act (OG 49/99, as amended) and the Act on Pension Insurance Companies and Payment of Pensions Based on Individual Capitalised Savings (OG 106/99, as amended), except in the cases provided by Articles 47 and 48 of the Compulsory and Voluntary Pension Funds Act and survivor's pension).

CZECH REPUBLIC

Pensions paid from the Second Pillar scheme established by Act No.426/2011 Coll., on pension savings.

DENMARK

(a) Personal pensions;

(b) Benefits in the event of death (accrued based on contributions to Arbejdsmarkedets Tillægspension related to the time before 1 January 2002);

(c) Benefits in the event of death (accrued based on contributions to Arbejdsmarkedets Tillægspension related to the time after 1 January 2002) referred to in the Consolidated Act on Labour Market Supplementary Pension (Arbejdsmarkedets Tillægspension) 942:2009.

ESTONIA

Mandatory funded old-age pension scheme.

FRANCE

Basic or supplementary schemes in which old-age benefits are calculated on the basis of retirement points.

HUNGARY

Pension benefits based on membership of private pension funds.

LATVIA

Old-age pensions (Law on State pensions of 1 January 1996; Law on State funded pensions of 1 July 2001).

POLAND

Old-age pensions under the defined contribution scheme.

PORTUGAL

Supplementary pensions granted pursuant to Decree-Law No.26/2008 of 22 February 2008 (public capitalisation scheme).

SLOVAKIA

Mandatory old-age pension saving.

SLOVENIA

Pension from compulsory supplementary pension insurance.

SWEDEN

Old-age pension in the form of an income pension and a premium pension (Chapters 62 and 64 of the Social Insurance Code).

UNITED KINGDOM

Graduated retirement benefits paid pursuant to the National Insurance Act 1965, sections 36 and 37, and the National Insurance Act (Northern Ireland) 1966, sections 35 and 36.

ANNEX SSC-5: BENEFITS AND AGREEMENTS WHICH ALLOW THE APPLICATION OF ARTICLE SSC.49

[Overlapping of benefits of the same kind]

I. Benefits referred to in point (a) of Article SSC.49(2) [Overlapping of benefits of the same kind] of the Protocol, the amount of which is independent of the length of periods of insurance or residence completed 5.341

DENMARK

The full Danish national old-age pension acquired after 10 years' residence by persons who will have been awarded a pension by 1 October 1989

FINLAND

National pensions and spouse's pensions determined according to the transitional rules and awarded prior to 1 January 1994 (Act on Enforcement of the National Pensions Act, 569/2007)

The additional amount of child's pension when calculating independent benefit according to the National Pension Act (the National Pension Act, 568/2007)

FRANCE

Widower's or widow's invalidity pension under the general social security system or under the agricultural workers scheme where it is calculated on the basis of the deceased spouse's invalidity pension settled in accordance with point (a) of Article SSC.47(1) [Award of benefits].

GREECE

Benefits under Law No.4169/1961 relating to the agricultural insurance scheme (OGA).

NETHERLANDS

General Surviving Relatives Act of 21 December 1995 (ANW).

The Work and Income according to Labour Capacity Act of 10 November 2005 (WIA).

SPAIN

Survivors' pensions granted under the general and special schemes, with the exception of the Special Scheme for Civil Servants.

SWEDEN

Income-related sickness compensation and income-related activity compensation (Chapter 34 of the Social Insurance Code).

Guaranteed pension and guaranteed compensation which replaced the full state pensions provided under the legislation on the state pension which applied before 1 January 1993, and the full state pension awarded under the transitional rules of the legislation applying from that date.

5.342 II. Benefits referred to in point (b) of Article SSC.49(2) [Overlapping of benefits of the same kind] of this Protocol, the amount of which is determined by reference to a credited period deemed to have been completed between the date on which the risk materialised and a later date.

FINLAND

Employment pensions for which account is taken of future periods according to the national legislation.

GERMANY

Survivors' pensions, for which account is taken of a supplementary period.

Old-age pensions, for which account is taken of a supplementary period already acquired.

ITALY

Italian pensions for total incapacity for work (inabilità).

LATVIA

Survivors' pension calculated on the basis of assumed insurance periods (Article 23(8) of the Law on State Pensions of 1 January 1996).

LITHUANIA

(a) State social insurance work incapacity pensions, paid under the Law on State Social Insurance Pensions.

(b) State social insurance survivors' and orphans' pensions, calculated on the basis of the work incapacity pension of the deceased under the Law on State Social Insurance Pensions.

LUXEMBOURG
Survivors' pensions.

SLOVAKIA
Slovak survivors' pension derived from the invalidity pension.

SPAIN
The pensions for retirement under the Special Scheme for Civil Servants due under Title I of the consolidated text of the Law on State Pensioners if at the time of materialisation of the risk the beneficiary was an active civil servant or treated as such; death and survivors' (widows'/widowers', orphans' and parents') pensions due under Title I of the consolidated text of the Law on State Pensioners if at the time of death the civil servant was active or treated as such.

SWEDEN
Sickness compensation and activity compensation in the form of guarantee compensation (Chapter 35 of the Social Insurance Code).
Survivors' pension calculated on the basis of credited insurance periods (Chapters 76–85 of the Social Insurance Code).

III. Agreements referred to in point (b)(i) of Article SSC.49(2) [Overlapping of benefits of the same kind] of this Protocol intended to prevent the same credited period being taken into account two or more times: 5.343

The Social Security Agreement of 28 April 1997 between the Republic of Finland and the Federal Republic of Germany.

The Social Security Agreement of 10 November 2000 between the Republic of Finland and the Grand Duchy of Luxembourg.

Nordic Convention on social security of 18 August 2003.

ANNEX SSC-6: SPECIAL PROVISIONS FOR THE APPLICATION OF THE LEGISLATION OF THE MEMBER STATES AND OF THE UNITED KINGDOM

(Article SSC.3(2), Article SSC.51(1) and Article SSC.66)

AUSTRIA 5.344

1. For the purpose of acquiring periods in the pension insurance, attendance at a school or comparable educational establishment in another State shall be regarded as equivalent to attendance at a school or educational establishment pursuant to Articles 227(1)(1) and 228(1)(3) of the Allgemeines Sozialversicherungsgesetz (ASVG) (General Social Security Act), Article 116(7) of the Gewerbliches Sozialversicherungsgesetz (GSVG) (Federal Act on Social Insurance for Persons engaged in Trade and Commerce) and Article 107(7) of the Bauern-Sozialversicherungsgesetz (BSVG) (Social Security Act for Farmers), when the person concerned was

subject at some time to Austrian legislation on the grounds that he pursued an activity as an employed or self-employed person, and the special contributions provided for under Article 227(3) of the ASVG, Article 116(9) of the GSVG and Article 107(9) of the BSGV for the purchase of such periods of education, are paid.

2. For the calculation of the pro rata benefit referred to in point (b) of Article SSC.47(1) [Award of benefits] of this Protocol, special increments for contributions for supplementary insurance and the miners' supplementary benefit under Austrian legislation shall be disregarded. In those cases the pro rata benefit calculated without those contributions shall, if appropriate, be increased by unreduced special increments for contributions for supplementary insurance and the miners' supplementary benefit.

3. Where pursuant to Article SSC.7 [Aggregation of periods] of this Protocol substitute periods under an Austrian pension insurance scheme have been completed but cannot form a basis for calculation pursuant to Articles 238 and 239 of the ASVG, Articles 122 and 123 of the GSVG and Articles 113 and 114 of the BSVG, the calculation basis for periods of childcare pursuant to Article 239 of the ASVG, Article 123 of the GSVG and Article 114 of the BSVG shall be used.

BULGARIA

Article 33(1) of the Bulgarian Health Insurance Act applies to all persons for whom Bulgaria is the competent Member State under Chapter 1 [Sickness, maternity and equivalent paternity benefits] of Title III [Special provisions concerning the various categories of benefits] of this Protocol.

CYPRUS

For the purpose of applying the provisions of Articles SSC.7 [Aggregation of periods], SSC.46 [Special provisions on aggregation of periods] and SSC.56 [Special provisions on aggregation of periods of insurance, employment or self-employment] of this Protocol, for any period commencing on or after 6 October 1980, a week of insurance under the legislation of the Republic of Cyprus is determined by dividing the total insurable earnings for the relevant period by the weekly amount of the basic insurable earnings applicable in the relevant contribution year, provided that the number of weeks so determined shall not exceed the number of calendar weeks in the relevant period.

CZECH REPUBLIC

For the purposes of defining members of the family in accordance with point (s) of Article SSC.1 [Definitions] of this Protocol, "spouse" includes registered partners as defined in the Czech act No.115/2006 Coll., on registered partnership.

DENMARK

1. (a) For the purpose of calculating the pension under the "lov om social pension" (Social Pension Act), periods of activity as an employed or self-employed person completed under Danish legislation by a frontier worker or a worker who has gone to Denmark to do work of a seasonal nature are

regarded as periods of residence completed in Denmark by the surviving spouse in so far as, during those periods, the surviving spouse was linked to the abovementioned worker by marriage without separation from bed and board or de facto separation on grounds of incompatibility, and provided that, during those periods, the spouse resided in the territory of another State. For the purposes of this point, "work of a seasonal nature" means work which, being dependent on the succession of the seasons, automatically recurs each year.

(b) For the purpose of calculating the pension under the "lov om social pension" (Social Pension Act), periods of activity as an employed or self-employed person completed under Danish legislation before 1 January 1984 by a person to whom point (a) does not apply shall be regarded as periods of residence completed in Denmark by the surviving spouse, in so far as, during those periods, the surviving spouse was linked to that person by marriage without separation from bed and board or de facto separation on grounds of incompatibility, and provided that, during those periods, the spouse resided in the territory of another State.

(c) Periods to be taken into account under points (a) and (b) shall not be taken into consideration if they coincide with the periods taken into account for the calculation of the pension due to the person concerned under the legislation on compulsory insurance of another State, or with the periods during which the person concerned received a pension under such legislation. Those periods shall, however, be taken into consideration if the annual amount of the said pension is less than half the basic amount of the social pension.

2. (a) Notwithstanding the provisions of Article SSC.7 [Aggregation of periods] of this Protocol, persons who have not been gainfully employed in one or more States are entitled to a Danish social pension only if they have been, or have previously been, permanent residents of Denmark for at least 3 years, subject to the age limits prescribed by Danish legislation. Subject to Article SSC.5 [Equality of treatment] of this Protocol, Article SSC.8 [Waiving of residence rules] of this Protocol does not apply to a Danish social pension to which entitlement has been acquired by such persons.

(b) The provisions referred to in point (a) do not apply to Danish social pension entitlement for the members of the family of persons who are or have been gainfully employed in Denmark, or for students or the members of their families.

3. The temporary benefit for unemployed persons who have been admitted to the ledighedsydelse (flexible job scheme) (Law No.455 of 10 June 1997) is covered by Chapter 6 [Unemployment benefits] of Title III [Special provisions concerning the various categories of benefits] of this Protocol.

4. Where the beneficiary of a Danish social pension is also entitled to a survivor's pension from another State, those pensions for the implementation of Danish legislation shall be regarded as benefits of the same kind within the meaning of Article SSC.48(1) [Rules to prevent overlapping], subject to the condition, however, that the person whose periods of insurance or of residence serve as the basis for the calculation of the survivor's pension had also acquired a right to a Danish social pension.

ESTONIA

For the purpose of calculating parental benefits, periods of employment in States other than Estonia shall be considered to be based on the same average amount of Social Tax as paid during the periods of employment in Estonia with which they are aggregated. If during the reference year the person has been employed only in other States, the calculation of the benefit shall be considered to be based on the average Social Tax paid in Estonia between the reference year and the maternity leave.

FINLAND

1. For the purposes of determining entitlement and of calculating the amount of the Finnish national pension under Articles SSC.47 [Award of benefits], SSC.48 [Rules to prevent overlapping] and SSC.49 [Overlapping of benefits of the same kind] of this Protocol, pensions acquired under the legislation of another State are treated in the same way as pensions acquired under Finnish legislation.

2. When applying point (b)(i) of Article SSC.47(1) [Award of benefits] of this Protocol for the purpose of calculating earnings for the credited period under Finnish legislation on earnings-related pensions, where an individual has pension insurance periods based on activity as an employed or self-employed person in another State for part of the reference period under Finnish legislation, the earnings for the credited period shall be equivalent to the sum of earnings obtained during the part of the reference period in Finland, divided by the number of months for which there were insurance periods in Finland during the reference period.

FRANCE

1. For persons receiving benefits in kind in France pursuant to Article SSC.15 [Residence in a State other than the competent State] or SSC.24 [Residence of members of the family in a State other than the one in which the pensioner resides] of this Protocol who are resident in the French departments of Haut-Rhin, Bas-Rhin or Moselle, benefits in kind provided on behalf of the institution of another State which is responsible for bearing their cost include benefits provided by both the general sickness insurance scheme and the obligatory supplementary local sickness insurance scheme of Alsace-Moselle.

2. French legislation applicable to a person engaged, or formerly engaged, in an activity as an employed or self-employed person for the application of Chapter 5 [Old-age and survivors' pensions] of Title III [Special provisions concerning the various categories of benefits] of this Protocol includes both the basic old-age insurance scheme(s) and the supplementary retirement scheme(s) to which the person concerned was subject.

GERMANY

1. Notwithstanding point (a) of Article SSC.6 [Equal treatment of benefits, income, facts or events] of this Protocol and point 1 of Article 5(4) of the Sozialgesetzbuch VI (Volume VI of the Social Code), a person who receives a full old-age pension under the legislation of another State may request to be compulsorily insured under the German pension insurance scheme.

2. Notwithstanding point (a) of Article SSC.6 [Equal treatment of benefits, income, facts or events] of this Protocol and Article 7 of the Sozialgesetzbuch VI (Volume VI of the Social Code), a person who is compulsorily insured in another State, or receives an old-age pension under the legislation of another State may join the voluntary insurance scheme in Germany.

3. For the purpose of granting cash benefits under §47(1) of SGB V, §47(1) of SGB VII and §200(2) of the Reichsversicherungsordnung to insured persons who live in another State, German insurance schemes calculate net pay, which is used to assess benefits, as if the insured person lived in Germany, unless the insured person requests an assessment on the basis of the net pay which he actually receives.

4. Nationals of other States whose place of residence or usual abode is outside Germany and who fulfil the general conditions of the German pension insurance scheme may pay voluntary contributions only if they had been voluntarily or compulsorily insured in the German pension insurance scheme at some time previously; this also applies to stateless persons and refugees whose place of residence or usual abode is in another State.

5. The pauschale Anrechnungszeit (fixed credit period) pursuant to Article 253 of the Sozialgesetzbuch VI (Volume VI of the Social Code) shall be determined exclusively with reference to German periods.

6. In cases where the German pension legislation, in force on 31 December 1991, is applicable for the recalculation of a pension, only the German legislation applies for the purposes of crediting German Ersatzzeiten (substitute periods).

7. The German legislation on accidents at work and occupational diseases to be compensated for under the law governing foreign pensions and on benefits for insurance periods which can be credited under the law governing foreign pensions in the territories named in paragraph 1(2)(3) of the Act on affairs of displaced persons and refugees (Bundesvertriebenengesetz) continues to apply within the scope of application of this Protocol, notwithstanding the provisions of paragraph 2 of the Act on foreign pensions (Fremdrentengesetz).

8. For the calculation of the theoretical amount referred to in point (b) (i) of Article SSC.47(1) [Award of benefits] of this Protocol, in pension schemes for liberal professions, the competent institution shall take as a basis, in respect of each of the years of insurance completed under the legislation of any other State, the average annual pension entitlement acquired during the period of membership of the competent institution through the payment of contributions.

GREECE

1. Law No.1469/84 concerning voluntary affiliation to the pension insurance scheme for Greek nationals and foreign nationals of Greek origin is applicable to nationals of other States, stateless persons and refugees, where the persons concerned, regardless of their place of residence or stay, have at some time in the past been compulsorily or voluntarily affiliated to the Greek pension insurance scheme.

2 Notwithstanding point (a) of Article SSC.6 [Equal treatment of benefits, income, facts or events] of this Protocol and Article 34 of Law 1140/1981, a person who receives a pension in respect of accidents at

work or occupational diseases under the legislation of another State may request to be compulsorily insured under the legislation applied by OGA, to the extent that they pursue an activity falling within the scope of that legislation.

IRELAND

1. Notwithstanding Article SSC.19(2) [Cash benefits] and Article SSC.57 [Calculation of unemployment benefits] of this Protocol, for the purposes of calculating the prescribed reckonable weekly earnings of an insured person for the grant of sickness or unemployment benefit under Irish legislation, an amount equal to the average weekly wage of employed persons in the relevant prescribed year shall be credited to that insured person in respect of each week of activity as an employed person under the legislation of another State during that prescribed year.

MALTA

Special provisions for civil servants

(a) Solely for the purposes of the application of Articles SSC.43 [Special provisions for civil servants] and SSC.55 [Special provisions for civil servants] of this Protocol, persons employed under the Malta Armed Forces Act (Chapter 220 of the Laws of Malta), the Police Act (Chapter 164 of the Laws of Malta) and the Prisons Act (Chapter 260 of the Laws of Malta) shall be treated as civil servants.

(b) Pensions payable under the above Acts and under the Pensions Ordinance (Chapter 93 of the Laws of Malta) shall, solely for the purposes of point (cc) of Article SSC.1 [Definitions] of this Protocol, be considered as "special schemes for civil servants".

NETHERLANDS

1. Health care insurance

(a) As regards entitlement to benefits in kind under Dutch legislation, persons entitled to benefits in kind for the purpose of the implementation of Chapters 1 [Sickness, maternity and equivalent paternity benefits] and 2 [Benefits in respect of accidents at work and occupational diseases] of Title III of this Protocol shall mean:

    (i) persons who, under Article 2 of the Zorgverzekeringswet (Health Care Insurance Act), are obliged to take out insurance under a health care insurer; and

    (ii) in so far as they are not already included under point (i), members of the family of active military personnel who are living in another State and persons who are resident in another State and who, under this Protocol, are entitled to health care in their state of residence, the costs being borne by the Netherlands.

(b) The persons referred to in point 1(a)(i) must, in accordance with the provisions of the Zorgverzekeringswet (Health Care Insurance Act), take out insurance with a health care insurer, and the persons referred to in point 1(a)(ii) must register with the College voor zorgverzekeringen (Health Care Insurance Board).

(c) The provisions of the Zorgverzekeringswet (Health Care Insurance Act) and the Algemene Wet Bijzondere Ziektekosten (General Act on

Exceptional Medical Expenses) concerning liability for the payment of contributions shall apply to the persons referred to in point (a) and the members of their families. In respect of members of the family, the contributions shall be levied on the person from whom the right to health care is derived with the exception of the members of the family of military personnel living in another State, who shall be levied directly.

(d) The provisions of the Zorgverzekeringswet (Health Care Insurance Act) concerning late insurance shall apply mutatis mutandis in the event of late registration with the College voor zorgverzekeringen (Health Care Insurance Board) in respect of the persons referred to in point (a)(ii).

(e) Persons entitled to benefits in kind by virtue of the legislation of a State other than the Netherlands who reside in the Netherlands or stay temporarily in the Netherlands shall be entitled to benefits in kind in accordance with the policy offered to insured persons in the Netherlands by the institution of the place of residence or the place of stay, taking into account Article 11(1), (2) and (3) and Article 19(1) of the Zorgverzekeringswet (Health Care Insurance Act), as well as to benefits in kind provided for by the Algemene Wet Bijzondere Ziektekosten (General Act on Exceptional Medical Expenses).

(f) For the purposes of Articles SSC.21 to SSC.27 of this Protocol, the following benefits, in addition to pensions covered by Chapters 4 [Invalidity benefits] and 5 [Old-age and surivivors' pensions] of Title III [Special provision concerning the various categories of benefits] of this Protocol, shall be treated as pensions due under Dutch legislation:
   - pensions awarded under the Law of 6 January 1966 on pensions for civil servants and their survivors (Algemene burgerlijke pensioenwet) (Netherlands Civil Service Pensions Act),
   - pensions awarded under the Law of 6 October 1966 on pensions for military personnel and their survivors (Algemene militaire pensioenwet) (Military Pensions Act),
   - benefits for incapacity for work awarded under the Law of 7 June 1972 on benefits for incapacity for work for military personnel (Wetarbeidsongeschiktheidsvoorziening militairen) (Military Personnel Incapacity for Work Act),
   - pensions awarded under the Law of 15 February 1967 on pensions for employees of the NV Nederlandse Spoorwegen (Dutch Railway Company) and their survivors (Spoorwegpensioenwet) (Railway Pensions Act),
   - pensions awarded under the Reglement Dienstvoorwaarden Nederlandse Spoorwegen (governing conditions of employment of the Netherlands Railway Company),
   - benefits awarded to retired persons before reaching the pensionable age of 65 years under a pension designed to provide income for former employed persons in their old age, or benefits provided in the event of premature exit from the labour market under a scheme set up by the state or by an industrial agreement for persons aged 55 or over,
   - benefits awarded to military personnel and civil servants under a scheme applicable in the event of redundancy, superannuation and early retirement.

(g) For the purposes of Article SSC.16(1) [Stay in the competent State when residence is in another State—special rules for the members of the families of frontier workers]of this Protocol, the persons referred to in point (a)(ii) of this paragraph who stay temporarily in the Netherlands shall be entitled to benefits in kind in accordance with the policy offered to insured persons in the Netherlands by the institution of the place of stay, taking into account Article 11(1), (2) and (3) and Article 19(1) of the Zorgverzekeringswet (Health Care Insurance Act), as well as to benefits in kind provided for by the Algemene Wet Bijzondere Ziektekosten (General Act on Exceptional Medical Expenses).

2. Application of the Algemene Ouderdomswet (AOW) (General Old Age Pensions Act)

(a) The reduction referred to in Article 13(1) of the AOW (General Old Age Pensions Act) shall not be applied for calendar years before 1 January 1957 during which a recipient not satisfying the conditions for having such years treated as periods of insurance:
- resided in the Netherlands between the ages of 15 and 65,
- while residing in another State, worked in the Netherlands for an employer established in the Netherlands, or
- worked in another State during periods regarded as periods of insurance under the Dutch social security system.

By way of derogation from Article 7 of the AOW, anyone who resided or worked in the Netherlands in accordance with the above conditions only prior to 1 January 1957 shall also be regarded as being entitled to a pension.

(b) The reduction referred to in Article 13(1) of the AOW shall not apply to calendar years prior to 2 August 1989 during which a person, between the ages of 15 and 65, who is or was married was not insured under the above legislation, while being resident in the territory of a State other than the Netherlands, if these calendar years coincide with periods of insurance completed by the person's spouse under the above legislation or with calendar years to be taken into account under point 2(a), provided that the couple's marriage subsisted during that time.

By way of derogation from Article 7 of the AOW, such a person shall be regarded as being entitled to a pension.

(c) The reduction referred to in Article 13(2) of the AOW shall not apply to calendar years before 1 January 1957 during which a pensioner's spouse who fails to satisfy the conditions for having such years treated as periods of insurance:
- resided in the Netherlands between the ages of 15 and 65, or
- while residing in another State, worked in the Netherlands for an employer established in the Netherlands, or
- worked in another State during periods regarded as periods of insurance under the Netherlands social security system.

(d) The reduction referred to in Article 13(2) of the AOW shall not apply to calendar years prior to 2 August 1989 during which a pensioner's spouse resident in a State other than the Netherlands, between the ages of 15 and 65, was not insured under the AOW, if those calendar years coincide with periods of insurance completed by the pensioner under that legislation or with calendar years to be taken into account under point 2(a), provided that the couple's marriage subsisted during that time.

(e) Points 2(a), 2(b), 2(c) and 2(d) shall not apply to periods which coincide with:

- periods which may be taken into account for calculating pension rights under the old-age insurance legislation of a State other than the Netherlands, or
- periods for which the person concerned has drawn an old-age pension under such legislation.

Periods of voluntary insurance under the system of another State shall not be taken into account for the purposes of this point.

(f) Points 2(a), 2(b), 2(c) and 2(d) shall apply only if the person concerned has resided in one or more States for 6 years after the age of 59 and only for such time as that person is resident in one of those States.

(g) By way of derogation from Chapter IV of the AOW, anyone resident in a State other than the Netherlands whose spouse is covered by compulsory insurance under that legislation shall be authorised to take out voluntary insurance under that legislation for periods during which the spouse is compulsorily insured.

This authorisation shall not cease where the spouse's compulsory insurance is terminated as a result of their death and where the survivor receives only a pension under the Algemene nabestaandenwet (General Surviving Relatives Act).

In any event, the authorisation in respect of voluntary insurance ceases on the date on which the person reaches the age of 65.

The contribution to be paid for voluntary insurance shall be set in accordance with the provisions relating to the determination of the contribution for voluntary insurance under the AOW. However, if the voluntary insurance follows on from a period of insurance as referred to in point 2(b), the contribution shall be set in accordance with the provisions relating to the determination of the contribution for compulsory insurance under the AOW, with the income to be taken into account being deemed to have been received in the Netherlands.

(h) The authorisation referred to in point 2(g) shall not be granted to anyone insured under another State's legislation on pensions or survivors' benefits.

(i) Anyone wishing to take out voluntary insurance under point 2(g) shall be required to apply for it to the Social Insurance Bank (Sociale Verzekeringsbank) not later than 1 year after the date on which the conditions for participation are fulfilled.

3. Application of the Algemene nabestaandenwet (ANW) (General Surviving Relatives Act)

(a) Where the surviving spouse is entitled to a survivor's pension under the ANW (General Surviving Relatives Act) pursuant to Article SSC.46(3) of this Protocol, that pension shall be calculated in accordance with point (b) of Article SSC.47(1) [Award of benefits] of this Protocol.

For the application of these provisions, periods of insurance prior to 1 October 1959 shall also be regarded as periods of insurance completed under Dutch legislation if during those periods the insured person, after the age of 15:

- resided in the Netherlands; or
- while resident in another State, worked in the Netherlands for an employer established in the Netherlands; or
- worked in another State during periods regarded as periods of insurance under the Dutch social security system.

(b) Account shall not be taken of the periods to be taken into consideration under point 3(a) which coincide with periods of compulsory insurance completed under the legislation of another State in respect of survivor's pensions.

(c) For the purposes of point (b) of Article SSC.47(1) [Award of benefits] of this Protocol, only periods of insurance completed under Dutch legislation after the age of 15 shall be taken into account as periods of insurance.

(d) By way of derogation from Article 63a(1) of the ANW, a person resident in a State other than the Netherlands whose spouse is compulsorily insured under the ANW shall be authorised to take out voluntary insurance under the ANW provided that such insurance has already begun by the date of application of this Protocol, but only for periods during which the spouse is compulsorily insured.

That authorisation shall cease as from the date of termination of the spouse's compulsory insurance under the ANW, unless the spouse's compulsory insurance is terminated as a result of their death and where the survivor only receives a pension under the ANW.

In any event, the authorisation in respect of voluntary insurance ceases on the date on which the person reaches the age of 65.

The contribution to be paid for voluntary insurance shall be set in accordance with the provisions relating to the determination of contributions for voluntary insurance under the ANW. However, if the voluntary insurance follows on from a period of insurance as referred to in point 2(b), the contribution shall be set in accordance with the provisions relating to the determination of contributions for compulsory insurance under the ANW, with the income to be taken into account being deemed to have been received in the Netherlands.

4. Application of Dutch legislation relating to incapacity for work

In calculating benefits under either the WAO, WIA or the WAZ, the Netherlands institutions shall take account of:

- periods of paid employment, and periods treated as such, completed in the Netherlands before 1 July 1967,
- periods of insurance completed under the WAO,
- periods of insurance completed by the person concerned, after the age of 15, under the Algemene Arbeidsongeschiktheidswet (General Act on Incapacity for Work), in so far as they do not coincide with the periods of insurance completed under the WAO,
- periods of insurance completed under the WAZ,
- periods of insurance completed under the WIA.

SPAIN

1. For the purpose of implementing point (1)(b) of Article SSC.47(1) [Award of benefits] of this Protocol, the years which the worker lacks to reach the pensionable or compulsory retirement age as stipulated under Article 31(4) of the consolidated version of the Ley de Clases Pasivas del Estado (Law on State Pensioners) shall be taken into account as actual years of service to the State only if at the time of the event in respect of which death pensions are due, the beneficiary was covered by Spain's special scheme for civil servants or was performing an activity assimilated under the scheme, or if, at the time of the event in respect of which the pensions are due, the beneficiary was performing an activity that would have required the person concerned to be included under the State's special scheme for civil servants, the armed forces or the judiciary, had the activity been performed in Spain.

2. (a) Under point (c) of Article SSC.51(1) [Additional provisions for the calculation of benefits], the calculation of the theoretical Spanish benefit shall be carried out on the basis of the actual contributions of the person during the years immediately preceding payment of the last contribution to Spanish social security. Where, in the calculation of the basic amount for the pension, periods of insurance and/or residence under the legislation of other States have to be taken into account, the contribution basis in Spain which is closest in time to the reference periods shall be used for those periods, taking into account the development of the retail price index.

(b) The amount of the pension obtained shall be increased by the amount of the increases and revaluations calculated for each subsequent year for pensions of the same nature.

3. Periods completed in other States which must be calculated in the special scheme for civil servants, the armed forces and the judicial administration, will be treated in the same way, for the purposes of Article SSC.51 [Additional provisions for the calculation of benefits] of this Protocol, as the periods closest in time covered as a civil servant in Spain.

4. The additional amounts based on age referred to in the Second Transitional Provision of the General Law on Social Security shall be applicable to all beneficiaries under this Protocol who have contributions to their name under the Spanish legislation prior to 1 January 1967; it shall not be possible, by application of Article SSC.6 [Equal treatment of benefits, income, facts or events] of this Protocol, to treat periods of insurance credited in another State prior to 1 January 1967 as being the same as contributions paid in Spain, solely for the purposes of this Protocol. The date corresponding to 1 January 1967 shall be 1 August 1970 for the Special Scheme for Seafarers and 1 April 1969 for the Special Social Security Scheme for Coal Mining.

SWEDEN

1. The provisions of this Protocol on the aggregation of insurance periods and periods of residence shall not apply to the transitional provisions in the Swedish legislation on entitlement to guarantee pension for persons born in or before 1937 who have been resident in Sweden for a specified period before applying for a pension (Act 2000:798).

2. For the purpose of calculating income for notional income-related sickness compensation and income-related activity compensation in accordance

with Chapter 8 of the Lag (1962:381) om allmän försäkring (the National Insurance Act), the following shall apply:

(a) where the insured person, during the reference period, has also been subject to the legislation of one or more other States on account of activity as an employed or self-employed person, income in the State(s) concerned shall be deemed to be equivalent to the insured person's average gross income in Sweden during the part of the reference period in Sweden, calculated by dividing the earnings in Sweden by the number of years over which those earnings accrued.

3. (a) For the purpose of calculating notional pension assets for income-based survivor's pension (Act 2000:461), if the requirement in Swedish legislation for pension entitlement in respect of at least three out of the 5 calendar years immediately preceding the insured person's death (reference period) is not met, account shall also be taken of insurance periods completed in other States as if they had been completed in Sweden. Insurance periods in other States shall be regarded as based on the average Swedish pension base. If the person concerned has only 1 year in Sweden with a pension base, each insurance period in another State shall be regarded as constituting the same amount.

(b) For the purpose of calculating notional pension credits for widows' pensions relating to deaths on or after 1 January 2003, if the requirement in Swedish legislation for pension credits in respect of at least two out of the 4 years immediately preceding the insured person's death (reference period) is not met and insurance periods were completed in another State during the reference period, those years shall be regarded as being based on the same pension credits as the Swedish year.

UNITED KINGDOM

1. Where, in accordance with United Kingdom legislation, a person may be entitled to a retirement pension if:

(a) the contributions of a former spouse are taken into account as if they were that person's own contributions; or

(b) the relevant contribution conditions are satisfied by that person's spouse or former spouse, then provided, in each case, that the spouse or former spouse is or had been exercising an activity as an employed or self-employed person, and had been subject to the legislation of two or more States, the provisions of Chapter 5 [Old-age and survivors' pensions] ofTitle III [Special provisions concerning the various categories of benefits] of this Protocol shall apply in order to determine entitlement under United Kingdom legislation. In that case, references in Articles SSC.44 to SSC.55 of this Protocol to "periods of insurance" shall be construed as references to periods of insurance completed by:

   (i) a spouse or former spouse where a claim is made by:
      - a married woman, or
      - a person whose marriage has terminated otherwise than by the death of the spouse; or

   (ii) a former spouse, where a claim is made by:
      - a widower who immediately before pensionable age is not entitled to a widowed parent's allowance, or

- a widow who immediately before pensionable age is not entitled to a widowed mother's allowance, widowed parent's allowance or widow's pension, or who is only entitled to an age-related widow's pension calculated pursuant to point (b) of Article SSC.47(1) [Award of benefits] of this Protocol, and for this purpose "age related widow's pension" means a widow's pension payable at a reduced rate in accordance with section 39(4) of the Social Security Contributions and Benefits Act 1992.

2. For the purposes of Article SSC.8 [Waiving of residence rules] of this Protocol in the case of old-age or survivors' cash benefits, pensions for accidents at work or occupational diseases and death grants, any beneficiary under United Kingdom legislation who is staying in the territory of another State shall, during that stay, be considered as if they resided in the territory of that other State.

3. (1) For the purpose of calculating an earnings factor in order to determine entitlement to benefits under United Kingdom legislation, for each week of activity as an employed person under the legislation of a Member State, and which commenced during the relevant income tax year within the meaning of United Kingdom legislation, the person concerned shall be deemed to have paid contributions as an employed earner, or have earnings on which contributions have been paid, on the basis of earnings equivalent to two-thirds of that year's upper earnings limit.

(2) For the purposes of point (b) of Article SSC.47(1) [Award of benefits] of this Protocol, where:

(a) in any income tax year starting on or after 6 April 1975, a person carrying out activity as an employed person has completed periods of insurance, employment or residence exclusively in a Member State, and the application of point (1) of this paragraph results in that year being counted as a qualifying year within the meaning of United Kingdom legislation for the purposes of point (b)(i) of Article SSC.47(1) of this Protocol, they shall be deemed to have been insured for 52 weeks in that year in that Member State;

(b) any income tax year starting on or after 6 April 1975 does not count as a qualifying year within the meaning of United Kingdom legislation for the purposes of point (b)(i) of Article SSC.47(1) of this Protocol, any periods of insurance, employment or residence completed in that year shall be disregarded.

(3) For the purpose of converting an earnings factor into periods of insurance, the earnings factor achieved in the relevant income tax year within the meaning of United Kingdom legislation shall be divided by that year's lower earnings limit. The result shall be expressed as a whole number, any remaining fraction being ignored. The figure so calculated shall be treated as representing the number of weeks of insurance completed under United Kingdom legislation during that year, provided that such figure shall not exceed the number of weeks during which in that year the person was subject to that legislation.

ANNEX SSC-7: IMPLEMENTING PART

General Note

5.345 The provisions of this Annex perform in relation to the Protocol, a similar role to that performed in relation to Regulation 883/2004 by its implementing regulation, Regulation 987/2009, whose provisions the Annex closely follows.

Title I: General Provisions

Chapter 1

Article SSCI.1: Definitions

5.346 1. For the purposes of this Annex, the definitions set out in Article SSC.1 of this Protocol [Definitions] apply.

2. In addition to the definitions referred to in paragraph 1:

(a) "access point" means an entity providing:

  (i) an electronic contact point;

  (ii) automatic routing based on the address; and

  (iii) intelligent routing based on software that enables automatic checking and routing (for example, an artificial intelligence application) or human intervention;

(b) "liaison body" means any body designated by the competent authority of a State for one or more of the branches of social security referred to in Article SSC.3 [Matters covered] of this Protocol to respond to requests for information and assistance for the purposes of the application of this Protocol and of this Annex and which has to fulfil the tasks assigned to it under Title IV [Financial provisions] of this Annex;

(c) "document" means a set of data, irrespective of the medium used, structured in such a way that it can be exchanged electronically and which must be communicated in order to enable the operation of the Protocol and this Annex;

(d) "Structured Electronic Document" means any structured document in a format designed for the electronic exchange of information between States;

(e) "transmission by electronic means" means the transmission of data using electronic equipment for the processing (including digital compression) of data and employing wires, radio transmission, optical technologies or any other electromagnetic means;

(f) "fraud" means any deliberate act or deliberate omission to act, carried out with the intention to either:

  (i) receive social security benefits, or enable another person to receive social security benefits, when the conditions of entitlement to such benefits under the law of the State(s) concerned or the Protocol are not met; or

  (ii) avoid paying social security contributions, or enable another person to avoid paying social security contributions, when such contributions are required under the law of the State(s) concerned or this Protocol.

Article SSCI.1

General Note

Corresponding provision of Regulation 987/2009: art.1 5.347

Chapter 2: Provisions Concerning Cooperation and Exchanges of Data

Article SSCI.2: Scope and rules for exchanges between institutions

1. For the purposes of this Annex, exchanges between authorities of the States and institutions and persons covered by this Protocol shall be based on the principles of public service, efficiency, active assistance, rapid delivery and accessibility, including e-accessibility, in particular for the disabled and the elderly. 5.348

2. The institutions shall without delay provide or exchange all data necessary for establishing and determining the rights and obligations of persons to whom this Protocol applies. Such data shall be transferred between the States directly by the institutions themselves or indirectly via the liaison bodies.

3. Where a person has mistakenly submitted information, documents or claims to an institution in the territory of a State other than that in which the institution designated, in accordance with this Annex, is situated, the information, documents or claims shall be resubmitted without delay by the former institution to the institution designated in accordance with this Annex, indicating the date on which they were initially submitted. That date shall be binding on the latter institution. The institutions of the States shall not, however, be held liable, or be deemed to have taken a decision by virtue of their failure to act as a result of the late transmission of information, documents or claims by States' institutions.

4. Where data are transferred indirectly via the liaison body of the State of destination, time limits for responding to claims shall start from the date when that liaison body received the claim, as if it had been received by the institution in that State.

General Note

Corresponding provision of Regulation 987/2009: art.2. 5.349

Article SSCI.3: Scope and rules for exchanges between the persons concerned and institutions

1. The States shall ensure that the necessary information is made available to the persons concerned in order to inform them of the provisions introduced by this Protocol and this Annex to enable them to assert their rights. They shall also provide for user-friendly services. 5.350

2. Persons to whom this Protocol applies shall be required to forward to the relevant institution the information, documents or supporting evidence necessary to establish their situation or that of their families, to establish or

maintain their rights and obligations and to determine the applicable legislation and their obligations under it.

3. To the extent necessary for the application of this Protocol and this Annex, the relevant institutions shall forward the information and issue the documents to the persons concerned without delay and in all cases within any time limits specified under the legislation of the State in question.

The relevant institution shall notify the claimant residing or staying in another State of its decision directly or through the liaison body of the State of residence or stay. When refusing the benefits, it shall also indicate the reasons for refusal, the remedies and periods allowed for appeals. A copy of this decision shall be sent to other involved institutions.

General Note

5.351 Corresponding provision of Regulation 987/2009: art.3.

Article SSCI.4: Forms, documents and methods of exchanging data

5.352 1. Subject to Article SSCI.75 [Interim provisions for forms and documents] and Appendix SSCI-2 [Entitlement document], the structure, content and format of forms and documents issued on behalf of the States for the purposes of implementing this Protocol shall be agreed by the Specialised Committee on Social Security Coordination.

2. The transmission of data between the institutions or the liaison bodies may, subject to the approval of the Specialised Committee on Social Security Coordination, be carried out via the Electronic Exchange of Social Security Information. To the extent the forms and documents referred to in paragraph 1 are exchanged via the Electronic Exchange of Social Security Information, they shall respect the rules applicable to that system.

Where the transmission of data between institutions or the liaison bodies is not carried out via the Electronic Exchange of Social Security Information, the relevant institutions and liaison bodies shall use the arrangements appropriate to each case, and favour the use of electronic means as far as possible.

3. In their communications with the persons concerned, the relevant institutions shall use the arrangements appropriate to each case, and favour the use of electronic means as far as possible.

General Note

5.353 Corresponding provision of Regulation 987/2009: art.4, which art.SSCI.4 adapts for the new context.

Article SSCI.5: Legal value of documents and supporting evidence issued in another State

5.354 1. Documents issued by the institution of a State and showing the position of a person for the purposes of the application of this Protocol and this Annex, and supporting evidence on the basis of which the documents have been issued, shall be accepted by the institutions of the other States for as long as they have not been withdrawn or declared to be invalid by the State in which they were issued.

2. Where there is doubt about the validity of a document or the accuracy of the facts on which the particulars contained therein are based, the institution of the State that receives the document shall ask the issuing institution for the necessary clarification and, where appropriate, the withdrawal of that document. The issuing institution shall reconsider the grounds for issuing the document and, if necessary, withdraw it.

3. Pursuant to paragraph 2, where there is doubt about the information provided by the persons concerned, the validity of a document or supporting evidence or the accuracy of the facts on which the particulars contained therein are based, the institution of the place of stay or residence shall, insofar as this is possible, at the request of the competent institution, proceed to the necessary verification of this information or document.

4. Where no agreement is reached between the institutions concerned, the matter may be brought before the Specialised Committee on Social Security Coordination by the competent authorities no earlier than one month following the date on which the institution that received the document submitted its request. The Specialised Committee on Social Security Coordination shall endeavour to reconcile the points of view within six months of the date on which the matter was brought before it.

General Note

Corresponding provision of Regulation 987/2009: art.5. **5.355**

Article SSCI.6 : Provisional application of legislation and provisional granting of benefits

1. Unless otherwise provided for in this Annex, where there is a difference of views between the institutions or authorities of two or more States concerning the determination of the applicable legislation, the person concerned shall be made provisionally subject to the legislation of one of those States, the order of priority being determined as follows: **5.356**

(a) the legislation of the State where the person actually pursues their employment or self-employment, if the employment or self-employment is pursued in only one State;
(b) the legislation of the State of residence if the person concerned pursues employment or self-employment in two or more States and performs part of their activity or activities in the State of residence, or if the person concerned is neither employed nor self-employed;
(c) in all other cases, the legislation of the State the application of which was first requested if the person pursues an activity, or activities, in two or more States.

2. Where there is a difference of views between the institutions or authorities of two or more States about which institution should provide the benefits in cash or in kind, the person concerned who could claim benefits if there was no dispute shall be entitled, on a provisional basis,

to the benefits provided for by the legislation applied by the institution of that person's place of residence or, if that person does not reside on the territory of one of the States concerned, to the benefits provided for by the legislation applied by the institution to which the request was first submitted.

3. Where no agreement is reached between the institutions or authorities concerned, the matter may be brought before the Specialised Committee on Social Security Coordination by a Party no earlier than one month after the date on which the difference of views, as referred to in paragraph 1 or 2 arose. The Specialised Committee on Social Security Coordination shall seek to reconcile the points of view within six months of the date on which the matter was brought before it.

4. Where it is established either that the applicable legislation is not that of the State of provisional membership, or the institution which granted the benefits on a provisional basis was not the competent institution, the institution identified as being competent shall be deemed retroactively to have been so, as if that difference of views had not existed, at the latest from either the date of provisional membership or of the first provisional granting of the benefits concerned.

5. If necessary, the institution identified as being competent and the institution which provisionally paid the cash benefits or provisionally received contributions shall settle the financial situation of the person concerned as regards contributions and cash benefits paid provisionally, where appropriate, in accordance with Chapter 2 of Title IV [Recovery of benefits provided but not due, recovery of provisional payments and contributions, offsetting and assistance with recovery] of this Annex.

Benefits in kind granted provisionally by an institution in accordance with paragraph 2 shall be reimbursed by the competent institution in accordance with Title IV [Financial provisions] of this Annex.

General Note

5.357 Corresponding provision of Regulation 987/2009: art.5.

Article SSCI.7: Provisional calculation of benefits and contributions

5.358 1. Unless otherwise provided for in this Annex, where a person is eligible for a benefit, or is liable to pay a contribution in accordance with this Protocol, and the competent institution does not have all the information concerning the situation in another State which is necessary to calculate definitively the amount of that benefit or contribution, that institution shall, on request of the person concerned, award this benefit or calculate this contribution on a provisional basis, if such a calculation is possible on the basis of the information at the disposal of that institution.

2. The benefit or the contribution concerned shall be recalculated once all the necessary supporting evidence or documents are provided to the institution concerned.

General Note

5.359 Corresponding provision of Regulation 987/2009: art.7.

Chapter 3: Other General Provisions for the Application of this Protocol

Article SSCI.8: Other procedures between authorities and institutions

1. Two or more States, or their competent authorities, may agree procedures other than those provided for by this Annex, provided that such procedures do not adversely affect the rights or obligations of the persons concerned. 5.360

2. Any agreements concluded to this end shall be notified to the Specialised Committee on Social Security Coordination and listed in the Appendix SSCI-1 [Implementing provisions for bilateral agreements remaining in force and new bilateral implementing agreements].

3. Provisions contained in implementing agreements concluded between two or more States with the same purpose as, or which are similar to, those referred to in paragraph 2, which are in force on the day preceding the entry into force of this Agreement, shall continue to apply, for the purposes of relations between those States, provided they are also included in Appendix SSCI-1 [Implementing provisions for bilateral agreements remaining in force and new bilateral implementing agreements] to this Protocol.

General Note

Corresponding provision of Regulation 987/2009: art.9. 5.361

Article SSCI.9: Prevention of overlapping of benefits

Notwithstanding other provisions in this Protocol, when benefits due under the legislation of two or more States are mutually reduced, suspended or withdrawn, any amounts that would not be paid in the event of strict application of the rules concerning reduction, suspension or withdrawal laid down by the legislation of the State concerned shall be divided by the number of benefits subjected to reduction, suspension or withdrawal. 5.362

General Note

Corresponding provision of Regulation 987/2009: art.10. 5.363

Article SSCI.10: Elements for determining residence

1. Where there is a difference of views between the institutions of two or more States about the determination of the residence of a person to whom this Protocol applies, these institutions shall establish by common agreement the centre of interests of the person concerned, based on an overall assessment of all available information relating to relevant facts, which may include, as appropriate: 5.364

(a) the duration and continuity of presence on the territory of the States concerned;

(b) that person's situation, including:
  - (i) the nature and the specific characteristics of any activity pursued, in particular the place where such activity is habitually pursued, the stability of the activity, and the duration of any work contract;
  - (ii) that person's family status and family ties;
  - (iii) the exercise of any non-remunerated activity;
  - (iv) in the case of students, the source of that student's income;
  - (v) that person's housing situation, in particular how permanent it is;
  - (vi) the State in which that person is deemed to reside for taxation purposes.

2. Where the consideration of the various criteria based on relevant facts as set out in paragraph 1 does not lead to agreement between the institutions concerned, the person's intention, as it appears from such facts and circumstances, especially the reasons that led the person to move, shall be considered to be decisive for establishing that person's actual place of residence.

3. The centre of interest of a student who goes to another State to pursue a full time course of study shall not be considered as being in the State of study for the entire duration of the course of study in that State, without prejudice to the possibility of rebutting this presumption.

4. Paragraph 3 applies mutatis mutandis to the family members of the student.

GENERAL NOTE

5.365 Corresponding provision of Regulation 987/2009: art.11. Paras 3 and 4 of art. SSCI 10 are new.

Article SSCI.11: Aggregation of periods

5.366 1. For the purposes of applying Article SSC.7 [Aggregation of periods] the competent institution shall contact the institutions of the States to whose legislation the person concerned has also been subject in order to determine all the periods completed under their legislation.

2. The respective periods of insurance, employment, self-employment or residence completed under the legislation of a State shall be added to those completed under the legislation of any other State, insofar as necessary for the purposes of applying Article SSC.7 [Aggregation of periods], provided that these periods do not overlap.

3. Where a period of insurance or residence which is completed in accordance with compulsory insurance under the legislation of a State coincides with a period of insurance completed on the basis of voluntary insurance or continued optional insurance under the legislation of another State, only the period completed on the basis of compulsory insurance shall be taken into account.

4. Where a period of insurance or residence other than an equivalent period completed under the legislation of a State coincides with an equivalent period on the basis of the legislation of another State, only the period other than an equivalent period shall be taken into account.

5. Any period regarded as equivalent under the legislation of two or more States shall be taken into account only by the institution of the State to whose legislation the person concerned was last compulsorily subject before that period. In the event that the person concerned was not compulsorily subject to the legislation of a State before that period, the latter shall be taken into account by the institution of the State to whose legislation the person concerned was compulsorily subject for the first time after that period.

6. In the event that the time in which certain periods of insurance or residence were completed under the legislation of a State cannot be determined precisely, it shall be presumed that these periods do not overlap with periods of insurance or residence completed under the legislation of another State, and account shall be taken thereof, where advantageous to the person concerned, insofar as they can reasonably be taken into consideration.

General Note

Corresponding provision of Regulation 987/2009: art.12. **5.367**

Article SSCI.12: Rules for conversion of periods

1. Where periods completed under the legislation of a State are expressed in units different from those provided for by the legislation of another State, the conversion needed for the purpose of aggregation under Article SSC.7 [Aggregation of periods] shall be carried out under the following rules: **5.368**

(a) the period to be used as the basis for the conversion shall be that communicated by the institution of the State under whose legislation the period was completed;

(b) in the case of schemes where the periods are expressed in days the conversion from days to other units, and vice versa, as well as between different schemes based on days shall be calculated according to the following table:

Scheme based on	1 day corresponds to	1 week corresponds to	1 month corresponds to	1 quarter corresponds to	Maximum of days in one calendar year
5 days	9 hours	5 days	22 days	66 days	264 days
6 days	8 hours	6 days	26 days	78 days	312 days
7 days	6 hours	7 days	30 days	90 days	360 days

(c) in the case of schemes where the periods are expressed in units other than days,

(i) three months or 13 weeks shall be equivalent to one quarter, and vice versa;

(ii) one year shall be equivalent to four quarters, 12 months or 52 weeks, and vice versa;

(iii) for the conversion of weeks into months, and vice versa, weeks and months shall be converted into days in accordance with the conversion rules for the schemes based on six days in the table in point (b);

(d) in the case of periods expressed in fractions, those figures shall be converted into the next smaller integer unit applying the rules laid down in points (b) and (c). Fractions of years shall be converted into months unless the scheme involved is based on quarters;

(e) if the conversion under this paragraph results in a fraction of a unit, the next higher integer unit shall be taken as the result of the conversion under this paragraph.

2. The application of paragraph 1 shall not have the effect of producing, for the total sum of the periods completed during one calendar year, a total exceeding the number of days indicated in the last column in the table in point (b) of paragraph 1, 52 weeks, 12 months or four quarters.

If the periods to be converted correspond to the maximum annual amount of periods under the legislation of the State in which they have been completed, the application of paragraph 1 shall not result within one calendar year in periods that are shorter than the possible maximum annual amount of periods provided under the legislation concerned.

3. The conversion shall be carried out either in one single operation covering all those periods which were communicated as an aggregate, or for each year, if the periods were communicated on a year-by-year basis.

4. Where an institution communicates periods expressed in days, it shall at the same time indicate whether the scheme it administers is based on five days, six days or seven days.

General Note

5.369 Corresponding provision of Regulation 987/2009: art.13.

TITLE II: DETERMINATION OF THE LEGISLATION APPLICABLE

Article SSCI.13: Details relating to Articles SSC.11 [Detached workers] and SSC.12 [Pursuit of activities in two or more States] of the Protocol

5.370 1. For the purposes of the application of point (a) of Article SSC.11(1) [Detached workers], a "person who pursues an activity as an employed person in a State for an employer which normally carries out its activities there and who is sent by that employer to another State" shall include a person who is recruited with a view to being sent to another State, provided that, immediately before the start of that person's employment, the person concerned is already subject to the legislation of the State in which their employer is established.

2. For the purposes of the application of point (a) of Article SSC.11(1) [Detached workers] of this Protocol, the words "which normally carries out its activities there" shall refer to an employer that ordinarily performs substantial activities, other than purely internal management activities, in

the territory of the State in which it is established, taking account of all criteria characterising the activities carried out by the undertaking in question. The relevant criteria must be suited to the specific characteristics of each employer and the real nature of the activities carried out.

3. For the purposes of the application of point (b) of Article SSC.11(1) of this Protocol [Detached workers], the words "who normally pursues an activity as a self-employed person" shall refer to a person who habitually carries out substantial activities in the territory of the State in which that person is established. In particular, that person must have already pursued their activity for some time before the date when they wish to take advantage of the provisions of that Article and, during any period of temporary activity in another State, must continue to fulfil, in the State where they are established, the requirements for the pursuit of their activity in order to be able to pursue it on their return.

4. For the purposes of the application of point (b) of Article SSC.11(1) of this Protocol [Detached workers], the criterion for determining whether the activity that a self-employed person goes to pursue in another State is "similar" to the self-employed activity normally pursued shall be that of the actual nature of the activity, rather than of the designation of employed or self-employed activity that may be given to this activity by the other State.

5. For the purposes of the application of Article SSC.12(1) and (5) [Pursuit of activities in two or more States] of this Protocol, a person who "normally pursues an activity as an employed person" in "one or more Member States as well as the United Kingdom", or in "two or more Member States" respectively, shall refer to a person who simultaneously, or in alternation, for the same undertaking or employer or for various undertakings or employers, exercises one or more separate activities in such States.

6. For the purposes of Article SSC.12(1) and (5) [Pursuit of activities in two or more States] of this Protocol, an employed flight crew or cabin crew member normally pursuing air passenger or freight services in two or more States shall be subject to the legislation of the State where the home base, as defined in Article SSC.1 [Definitions] of this Protocol, is located.

7. Marginal activities shall be disregarded for the purposes of determining the applicable legislation under Article SSC.12 [Pursuit of activities in two or more States] of this Protocol. Article SSCI.15 [Procedure for the application of Article SSC.12] of this Annex shall apply to all cases under this Article.

8. For the purposes of the application of Article SSC.12(2) and (6) [Pursuit of activities in two or more States] of this Protocol, a person who "normally pursues an activity as a self-employed person" in "one or more Member States as well as the United Kingdom", or in "two or more Member States respectively", shall refer, in particular, to a person who simultaneously or in alternation pursues one or more separate self-employed activities, irrespective of the nature of those activities, in such States.

9. For the purposes of distinguishing the activities under paragraphs 5 and 8 of this Article from the situations described in Article SSC.11(1) [Detached workers] of this Protocol, the duration of the activity in one or more States (whether it is permanent or of an ad hoc or temporary nature) shall be decisive. For these purposes, an overall assessment shall be made of all the relevant facts including, in particular, in the case of an employed person, the place of work as defined in the employment contract.

10. For the purposes of the application of Article SSC.12(1) (2), (5) and (6) [Pursuit of activities in two or more States] of this Protocol, a "substantial part of employed or self-employed activity" pursued in a State shall mean a quantitatively substantial part of all the activities of the employed or self-employed person pursued there, without this necessarily being the major part of those activities.

11. To determine whether a substantial part of the activities is pursued in a State, the following indicative criteria shall be taken into account:

(a) in the case of an employed activity, the working time or the remuneration; and

(b) in the case of a self-employed activity, the turnover, working time, number of services rendered or income.

In the framework of an overall assessment, a share of less than 25% in respect of the criteria mentioned above shall be an indicator that a substantial part of the activities is not being pursued in the relevant State.

12. For the purposes of the application of point (b) of Article SSC.12(2) [Pursuit of activities in two or more States] of this Protocol, the "centre of interest" of the activities of a self-employed person shall be determined by taking account of all the aspects of that person's occupational activities, notably the place where the person's fixed and permanent place of business is located, the habitual nature or the duration of the activities pursued, the number of services rendered, and the intention of the person concerned as revealed by all the circumstances.

13. For the determination of the applicable legislation under paragraphs 10, 11 and 12, the institutions concerned shall take into account the situation projected for the following 12 calendar months.

14. If a person pursues his or her activity as an employed person in two or more States on behalf of an employer established outside the territory of the States, and if this person resides in a State without pursuing substantial activity there, they shall be subject to the legislation of the State of residence.

General Note

5.371 Corresponding provision of Regulation 987/2009: art.14.

Article SSCI.14: Procedures for the application of point (b) of Article SSC.10(3), Article SSC.10(4) [General rules] and Article SSC.11 [Detached workers] of the Protocol (on the provision of information to the institutions concerned)

5.372 1. Unless otherwise provided for by Article SSCI.15 [Procedure for the application of Article SSC.12] of this Annex, where a person pursues their activity outside the competent State, the employer or, in the case of a person who does not pursue an activity as an employed person, the person concerned shall inform the competent institution of the State whose legislation is applicable thereof, whenever possible in advance. That institution shall issue the attestation referred to in Article SSCI.16(2) [Provision of information to persons concerned and employers] of this Annex to the person concerned and shall without delay make information concerning the legislation applicable to that person, pursuant to point (b) of Article SSC.10(3) [General rules] or Article SSC.11 [Detached workers] of this

Protocol, available to the institution designated by the competent authority of the State in which the activity is pursued.

2. An employer within the meaning of Article SSC.10(4) [General rules] of this Protocol who has an employee on board a vessel flying the flag of another State shall inform the competent institution of the State whose legislation is applicable thereof whenever possible in advance. That institution shall, without delay, make information concerning the legislation applicable to this person concerned, pursuant to Article SSC.10(4) [General rules] of this Protocol, available to the institution designated by the competent authority of the State whose flag, the vessel on which the employee is to perform the activity, is flying.

General Note

Corresponding provision of Regulation 987/2009: art.15. 5.373

Article SSCI.15: Procedure for the application of Article SSC.12 [Pursuit of activities in two or more States] of this Protocol

1. A person who pursues activities in two or more States, or where Article SSC.12(5) or (6) [Pursuit of activities in two or more States] applies, shall inform the institution designated by the competent authority of the State of residence thereof. 5.374

2. The designated institution of the place of residence shall without delay determine the legislation applicable to the person concerned, having regard to Article SSC.12 [Pursuit of activities in two or more States] of this Protocol and Article SSCI.13 [Details relating to Articles SSC.11 [Detached workers] of this Annex. That initial determination shall be provisional. The institution shall inform the designated institutions of each State in which an activity is pursued of its provisional determination.

3. The provisional determination of the applicable legislation, as provided for in paragraph 2, shall become definitive within two months of the institutions designated by the competent authorities of the State(s) concerned being informed of it, in accordance with paragraph 2, unless the legislation has already been definitively determined on the basis of paragraph 4, or at least one of the institutions concerned informs the institution designated by the competent authority of the State of residence by the end of this two-month period that it cannot yet accept the determination or that it takes a different view on this.

4. Where uncertainty about the determination of the applicable legislation requires contacts between the institutions or authorities of two or more States, at the request of one or more of the institutions designated by the competent authorities of the State(s) concerned, or of the competent authorities themselves, the legislation applicable to the person concerned shall be determined by common agreement, having regard to Article SSC.12 [Pursuit of activities in two or more States] of this Protocol and the relevant provisions of Article SSCI.13 [Details relating to Articles SSC.11 [Detached workers] of this Annex.

Where there is a difference of views between the institutions or competent authorities concerned, those bodies shall seek agreement in accordance with the conditions set out above and Article SSCI.6 [Provisional application of legislation and provisional granting of benefits] shall apply.

5. The competent institution of the State whose legislation is determined to be applicable either provisionally or definitively shall without delay inform the person concerned.

6. If the person concerned fails to provide the information referred to in paragraph 1, this Article shall be applied at the initiative of the institution designated by the competent authority of the State of residence as soon as it is appraised of that person's situation, possibly via another institution concerned.

General Note

5.375 Corresponding provision of Regulation 987/2009: art.16.

Article SSCI.16: Provision of information to persons concerned and employers

5.376 1. The competent institution of the State whose legislation becomes applicable pursuant to Title II [Determination of the legislation applicable] of this Protocol shall inform the person concerned and, where appropriate, their employer(s) of the obligations laid down in that legislation. It shall provide them with the necessary assistance to complete the formalities required by that legislation.

2. At the request of the person concerned or of the employer, the competent institution of the State whose legislation is applicable pursuant to Title II [Determination of the legislation applicable] shall provide an attestation that such legislation is applicable and shall indicate, where appropriate, until what date and under what conditions.

General Note

5.377 Corresponding provision of Regulation 987/2009: art.19.

Article SSCI.17: Cooperation between institutions

5.378 1. The relevant institutions shall communicate to the competent institution of the State whose legislation is applicable to a person pursuant to Title II [Determination of the legislation applicable] of this Protocol the necessary information required to establish the date on which that legislation becomes applicable and the contributions which that person and his or her employer(s) are liable to pay under that legislation.

2. The competent institution of the State whose legislation becomes applicable to a person pursuant to Title II [Determination of the legislation applicable] of this Protocol shall make the information indicating the date on which the application of that legislation takes effect available to the institution designated by the competent authority of the State to whose legislation that person was last subject.

General Note

5.379 Corresponding provision of Regulation 987/2009: art.20.

Article SSCI.18: Cooperation in case of doubts about the validity of issued documents concerning the applicable legislation

1. Where there is doubt about the validity of a document showing the position of the person for the purposes of the applicable legislation or the accuracy of the facts on which the document is based, the institution of the State that receives the document shall ask the issuing institution for the necessary clarification and, where appropriate, the withdrawal or rectification of that document. The requesting institution shall substantiate its request and provide the relevant supporting documentation that gave rise to the request. 5.380

2. When receiving such a request, the issuing institution shall reconsider the grounds for issuing the document and, where an error is detected, withdraw it or rectify it within 30 working days from the receipt of the request. The withdrawal or rectification shall have retroactive effect. However, in cases where there is a risk of disproportionate outcome, and in particular, of the loss of status as an insured person for the whole or part of the relevant period in the State(s) concerned, the States shall consider a more proportionate arrangement in such case. When the available evidence permits the issuing institution to find that the applicant of the document has committed fraud, it shall withdraw or rectify the document without delay and with retroactive effect.

General Note

There is no corresponding provision in Regulation 987/2009. 5.381

Title III: Special Provisions Concerning the Various Categories of Benefits

Chapter 1: Sickness, Maternity and Equivalent Paternity Benefits

Article SSCI.19: General implementing provisions

1. The competent authorities or institutions shall ensure that any necessary information is made available to insured persons regarding the procedures and conditions for the granting of benefits in kind where such benefits are received in the territory of a State other than that of the competent institution. 5.382

2. Notwithstanding point (a) of Article SSC.6 [Equal treatment of benefits, income, facts or events] of this Protocol, a State may become responsible for the cost of benefits in accordance with Article SSC.20 [Pension claimants] of this Protocol only if, either the insured person has made a claim for a pension under the legislation of that State, or in accordance with Articles SSC.21 [Right to benefits in kind under the legislation of the State of residence] to SSC.27 [Contributions by pensioners] of this Protocol, they receive a pension under the legislation of that State.

General Note

Corresponding provision of Regulation 987/2009: art.22. 5.383

Article SSCI.20: Regime applicable in the event of the existence of more than one regime in the State of residence or stay

5.384 If the legislation of the State of residence or stay comprises more than one scheme of sickness, maternity and paternity insurance for more than one category of insured persons, the provisions applicable under Articles SSC.15 [Residence in a State other than the competent State], SSC.17(1) [Stay outside the competent State], SSC.18 [Travel with the purpose of receiving benefits in kind – authorisation to receive appropriate treatment outside the State of residence], SSC.20 [Pension claimants], SSC.22 [No right to benefits in kind under the legislation of the State of residence] and SSC.24 [Residence of members of the family in a State other than the one in which the pensioner resides] of this Protocol shall be those of the legislation on the general scheme for employed persons.

General Note

5.385 Corresponding provision of Regulation 987/2009: art.23.

Article SSCI.21: Residence in a State other than the competent State

Procedure and scope of right

5.386 1. For the purposes of the application of Article SSC.15 [Residence in a State other than the competent State], of this Protocol, the insured person or members of that person's family shall be obliged to register promptly with the institution of the place of residence. Their right to benefits in kind in the State of residence shall be certified by a document issued by the competent institution upon request of the insured person or upon request of the institution of the place of residence.

2. The document referred to in paragraph 1 shall remain valid until the competent institution informs the institution of the place of residence of its cancellation.

The institution of the place of residence shall inform the competent institution of any registration under paragraph 1 and of any change or cancellation of that registration.

3. This Article applies mutatis mutandis to the persons referred to in Articles SSC.20 [Pension claimants], SSC.22 [No right to benefits in kind under the legislation of the State of residence], SSC.23 [Pensions under the legislation of one or more States other than the State of residence, where there is a right to benefits in kind in the latter State] and SSC.24 [Residence of members of the family in a State other than the one in which the pensioner resides] of this Protocol.

Reimbursement

5.387 4. Where a person or the members of that person's family:

(a) have been issued with the document referred to in paragraph 1;

(b) have registered that document with the institution of the place of residence in accordance with paragraph 1; and

(c) a health fee has been paid by or on behalf of the person or members of their family to the State of residence as part of an application for a permit to enter, stay, work or reside in that State,

that person or members of that person's family may apply to the institution of the State of residence for reimbursement (in whole or part, as the case may be) of the health fee paid.

5. Where a claim is made in accordance with paragraph 1, the institution of the State of residence shall determine that claim within three calendar months, starting on the day the claim was received, and shall make any reimbursement in accordance with this Article.

6. Where the period of validity of the document referred to in paragraph 1 is less than the period of time in respect of which the health fee has been paid, the amount reimbursed shall not exceed that portion of the health fee which corresponds to the period for which the document had been issued.

7. Where the health fee was paid by another person on behalf of a person to whom this Article applies, reimbursement may be made to that other person.

General Note

Corresponding provision of Regulation 987/2009: art.24. Paragraphs 4 to 7 have no equivalent. **5.388**

Article SSCI.22: Stay in a State other than the competent State

Procedure and scope of right

1. For the purposes of the application of Article SSC.17 [Stay outside the competent State] of this Protocol, the insured person shall present to the health care provider in the State of stay an entitlement document issued by the competent institution indicating his entitlement to benefits in kind. If the insured person does not have such a document, the institution of the place of stay, upon request or if otherwise necessary, shall contact the competent institution in order to obtain one. **5.389**

2. That document shall indicate that the insured person is entitled to benefits in kind under the conditions laid down in Article SSC.17 [Stay outside the competent State] of this Protocol on the same terms as those applicable to persons insured under the legislation of the State of stay, and shall satisfy the requirements in Appendix SSCI-2.

3. The benefits in kind referred to in Article SSC.17(1) [Stay outside the competent State] of this Protocol shall refer to the benefits in kind which are provided in the State of stay, in accordance with its legislation, and which become necessary on medical grounds with a view to preventing an insured person from being forced to return, before the end of the planned duration of stay, to the competent State to obtain the necessary treatment.

Procedure and arrangements for meeting the costs and providing reimbursement of benefits in kind

5.390 4. If the insured person has actually borne the costs of all or part of the benefits in kind provided within the framework of Article SSC.17 [Stay outside the competent State] of this Protocol and if the legislation applied by the institution of the place of stay enables reimbursement of those costs to an insured person, they may send an application for reimbursement to the institution of the place of stay. In that case, that institution shall reimburse directly to that person the amount of the costs corresponding to those benefits within the limits of and under the conditions of the reimbursement rates laid down in its legislation.

5. If the reimbursement of such costs has not been requested directly from the institution of the place of stay, the costs incurred shall be reimbursed to the person concerned by the competent institution in accordance with the reimbursement rates administered by the institution of the place of stay or the amounts which would have been subject to reimbursement to the institution of the place of stay, if Article SSCI.47 [Principles] had applied in the case concerned.

The institution of the place of stay shall provide the competent institution, upon request, with all necessary information about these rates or amounts.

6. By way of derogation from paragraph 5, the competent institution may undertake the reimbursement of the costs incurred within the limits of and under the conditions of the reimbursement rates laid down in its legislation, provided that the insured person has agreed to this provision being applied to them.

7. If the legislation of the State of stay does not provide for reimbursement pursuant to paragraphs 4 and 5 in the case concerned, the competent institution may reimburse the costs within the limits of and under the conditions of the reimbursement rates laid down in its legislation, without the agreement of the insured person.

8. The reimbursement to the insured person shall not, in any event, exceed the amount of costs actually incurred by them.

9. In the case of substantial expenditure, the competent institution may pay the insured person an appropriate advance as soon as that person submits the application for reimbursement to it.

Family Members

5.391 10. Paragraphs 1 to 9 apply mutatis mutandis to the members of the family of the insured person.

Reimbursement for students

11. Where a person:

5.392 (a) holds a valid entitlement document referred to in Appendix SSCI-2 issued by the competent institution;

(b) has been accepted by a higher education institution in a State other than the competent State ("State of study") to pursue a full-time course of study leading to a higher education qualification recognised by that State, including diplomas, certificates or doctoral degrees at a higher education institution, which may cover a preparatory course prior to such education, in accordance with national law, or compulsory training;

(c) does not exercise, or has not exercised, an activity as an employed or self-employed person in the State of study during the period to which the health fee relates; and

(d) a health fee has been paid by or on behalf of that person to the State of study as part of an application for a permit to enter, stay or reside for the purposes of pursuing a full-time course of study in that State;

that person may apply to the institution of the State of study for reimbursement (in whole or part, as the case may be) of the health fee paid.

12. Where a claim is made in accordance with paragraph 11, the institution of the State of study shall process and settle that claim within a reasonable period but not later than six calendar months starting on the day the claim was received and make any reimbursement in accordance with this Article.

13. Where the period of validity of the entitlement document referred to in point (a) of paragraph 11 is less than the period of time in respect of which the health fee has been paid, the amount of the health fee reimbursed shall be the amount paid which corresponds to the period of validity of that document.

14. Where the health fee was paid by another person on behalf of a person to whom this Article applies, reimbursement may be made to that other person.

15. Paragraphs 11 to 14 apply mutatis mutandis to the members of the family of that person.

16. This Article shall enter into force 12 months after the date of entry into force of this Agreement.

17. A person who satisfied the conditions in paragraph 11 in the period between the entry into force of this Agreement and the date specified in paragraph 16 may, upon the entry into force of this Article, make a claim for reimbursement under paragraph 11 in relation to that period.

18. By way of derogation from Article SSC.5(1) [Equality of treatment], charges may be imposed by the State of study in accordance with its national law in respect of benefits in kind that do not fulfil the criteria set out in point (a) of Article SSC.17(1) [Stay outside the competent State] and which are provided to a person in respect of whom reimbursement has been made during that person's stay for the period to which that reimbursement relates.

General Note

Corresponding provision of Regulation 987/2009: art.25. Paras.11 to 18 are new. 5.393

Article SSCI.23: Scheduled treatment

Authorisation procedure

1. For the purposes of the application of Article SSC.18(1) [Travel with the purpose of receiving benefits in kind – authorisation to receive appropriate treatment outside the State of residence] of this Protocol, the insured person shall present a document issued by the competent institution to the institution of the place of stay. For the purposes of this Article, the competent institution shall mean the institution which bears the cost of the 5.394

scheduled treatment; in the cases referred to in Articles SSC.18(4) [Travel with the purpose of receiving benefits in kind – authorisation to receive appropriate treatment outside the State of residence] and SSC.25(5) [Stay of the pensioner or the members of their family in a State other than the State of residence – stay in the competent State – authorisation for appropriate treatment outside the State of residence] of this Protocol, in which the benefits in kind provided in the State of residence are reimbursed on the basis of fixed amounts, the competent institution shall mean the institution of the place of residence.

2. If an insured person does not reside in the competent State, they shall request authorisation from the institution of the place of residence, which shall forward it to the competent institution without delay.

In that event, the institution of the place of residence shall certify in a statement whether the conditions set out in the second sentence of Article SSC.18(2) [Travel with the purpose of receiving benefits in kind – authorisation to receive appropriate treatment outside the State of residence] of this Protocol are met in the State of residence.

The competent institution may refuse to grant the requested authorisation only if, in accordance with the assessment of the institution of the place of residence, the conditions set out in the second sentence of Article SSC.18(2) [Travel with the purpose of receiving benefits in kind – authorisation to receive appropriate treatment outside the State of residence] of this Protocol are not met in the State of residence of the insured person, or if the same treatment can be provided in the competent State itself, within a time-limit which is medically justifiable, taking into account the current state of health and the probable course of illness of the person concerned.

The competent institution shall inform the institution of the place of residence of its decision.

In the absence of a reply within the deadlines set by its national legislation, the authorisation shall be considered to have been granted by the competent institution.

3. If an insured person who does not reside in the competent Party is in need of urgent vitally necessary treatment, and the authorisation cannot be refused in accordance with the second sentence of Article SSC.18(2) [Travel with the purpose of receiving benefits in kind – authorisation to receive appropriate treatment outside the State of residence] of this Protocol, the authorisation shall be granted by the institution of the place of residence on behalf of the competent institution, which shall be immediately informed by the institution of the place of residence.

The competent institution shall accept the findings and the treatment options of the doctors approved by the institution of the place of residence that issues the authorisation, concerning the need for urgent vitally necessary treatment.

4. At any time during the procedure granting the authorisation, the competent institution shall retain the right to have the insured person examined by a doctor of its own choice in the Party of stay or residence.

5. The institution of the place of stay shall, without prejudice to any decision regarding authorisation, inform the competent institution if it appears medically appropriate to supplement the treatment covered by the existing authorisation.

Meeting the cost of benefits in kind incurred by the insured person

6. Without prejudice to paragraph 7, Article SSCI.22(4) and (5) [Stay in a State other than the competent State] apply mutatis mutandis. **5.395**

7. If the insured person has actually borne all or part of the costs for the authorised medical treatment themselves and the costs which the competent institution is obliged to reimburse to the institution of the place of stay or to the insured person according to paragraph 6 (actual cost) are lower than the costs which it would have had to assume for the same treatment in the competent State (notional cost), the competent institution shall reimburse, upon request, the cost of treatment incurred by the insured person up to the amount by which the notional cost exceeds the actual cost. The reimbursed sum may not, however, exceed the costs actually incurred by the insured person and may take account of the amount which the insured person would have had to pay if the treatment had been delivered in the competent State.

Meeting the costs of travel and stay as part of scheduled treatment

8. Where the national legislation of the competent institution provides for the reimbursement of the costs of travel and stay which are inseparable from the treatment of the insured person, such costs for the person concerned and, if necessary, for a person who must accompany them, shall be assumed by this institution when an authorisation is granted in the case of treatment in another State. **5.396**

Family members

9. Paragraphs 1 to 8 apply mutatis mutandis to the members of the family of the insured person. **5.397**

General Note

Corresponding provision of Regulation 987/2009: art.26. **5.398**

Article SSCI.24: Cash benefits relating to incapacity for work in the event of stay or residence in a State other than the competent State

Procedure to be followed by the insured person

1. If the legislation of the competent State requires that the insured person presents a certificate in order to be entitled to cash benefits relating to incapacity for work pursuant to Article SSC.19(1) [Cash benefits] of this Protocol, the insured person shall ask the doctor of the State of residence who established that person's state of health to certify his or her incapacity for work and its probable duration. **5.399**

2. The insured person shall send the certificate to the competent institution within the time limit laid down by the legislation of the competent State.

3. Where the doctors providing treatment in the State of residence do not issue certificates of incapacity for work, and where such certificates are required under the legislation of the competent State, the person concerned shall apply directly to the institution of the place of residence. That

institution shall immediately arrange for a medical assessment of the person's incapacity for work and for the certificate referred to in paragraph 1 to be drawn up. The certificate shall be forwarded to the competent institution forthwith.

4. The forwarding of the document referred to in paragraphs 1, 2 and 3 shall not exempt the insured person from fulfilling the obligations provided for by the applicable legislation, in particular with regard to that person's employer. Where appropriate, the employer or the competent institution may call upon the employee to participate in activities designed to promote and assist his or her return to employment.

Procedure to be followed by the institution of the State of residence

5.400 5. At the request of the competent institution, the institution of the place of residence shall carry out any necessary administrative checks or medical examinations of the person concerned in accordance with the legislation applied by this latter institution. The report of the examining doctor concerning, in particular, the probable duration of the incapacity for work, shall be forwarded without delay by the institution of the place of residence to the competent institution.

Procedure to be followed by the competent institution

5.401 6. The competent institution shall reserve the right to have the insured person examined by a doctor of its choice.

7. Without prejudice to the second sentence of Article SSC.19(1) [Cash benefits] of this Protocol, the competent institution shall pay the cash benefits directly to the person concerned and shall, where necessary, inform the institution of the place of residence thereof.

8. For the purposes of the application of Article SSC.19(1) [Cash benefits] of this Protocol, the particulars of the certificate of incapacity for work of an insured person drawn up in another State on the basis of the medical findings of the examining doctor or institution shall have the same legal value as a certificate drawn up in the competent State.

9. If the competent institution refuses the cash benefits, it shall notify its decision to the insured person and at the same time to the institution of the place of residence.

Procedure in the event of a stay in a State other than the competent State

5.402 10. Paragraphs 1 to 9 apply mutatis mutandis when the insured person stays in a State other than the competent State.

General Note

5.403 Corresponding provision of Regulation 987/2009: art.27.

Article SSCI.25: Contributions by pensioners

5.404 If a person receives a pension from more than one State, the amount of contributions deducted from all the pensions paid shall, under no circumstances, be greater than the amount deducted in respect of a person who receives the same amount of pension from the competent State.

General Note

Corresponding provision of Regulation 987/2009: art.30. 5.405

Article SSCI.26: Special implementing measures

1. When a person or a group of persons are exempted upon request from compulsory sickness insurance and such persons are thus not covered by a sickness insurance scheme to which this Protocol applies, the institution of a State shall not, solely because of this exemption, become responsible for bearing the costs of benefits in kind or in cash provided to such persons or to a member of their family under Articles SSC.15–SCC.30 of this Protocol. 5.406

2. When the persons referred to in paragraph 1 and the members of their families reside in a State where the right to receive benefits in kind is not subject to conditions of insurance, or of activity as an employed or self-employed person, they shall be liable to pay the full costs of benefits in kind provided in their State of residence.

General Note

Corresponding provision of Regulation 987/2009: art.32. 5.407

Chapter 2: Benefits in Respect of Accidents at Work and Occupational Diseases

Article SSCI.27: Right to benefits in kind and in cash in the event of residence or stay in a State other than the competent State

1. For the purposes of the application of Article SSC.31 [Right to benefits in kind and in cash] of this Protocol, the procedures laid down in Articles SSCI.21 [Residence in a State other than the competent State] to SSCI.24 [Cash benefits relating to incapacity for work in the event of stay or residence in a State other than the competent State] of this Annex apply mutatis mutandis. 5.408

2. When providing special benefits in kind in connection with accidents at work and occupational diseases under the national legislation of the State of stay or residence, the institution of that State shall without delay inform the competent institution.

General Note

Corresponding provision of Regulation 987/2009: art.33. 5.409

Article SSCI.28: Procedure in the event of an accident at work or occupational disease which occurs in a State other than the competent State

1. If an accident at work occurs or an occupational disease is diagnosed for the first time in a State other than the competent State, the declaration 5.410

or notification of the accident at work or the occupational disease, where the declaration or notification exists under national legislation, shall be carried out in accordance with the legislation of the competent State, without prejudice, where appropriate, to any other applicable legal provisions in force in the State in which the accident at work occurred or in which the first medical diagnosis of the occupational disease was made, which remain applicable in such cases. The declaration or notification shall be addressed to the competent institution.

2. The institution of the State in the territory of which the accident at work occurred or in which the occupational disease was first diagnosed, shall notify the competent institution of medical certificates drawn up in the territory of that State.

3. Where, as a result of an accident while travelling to or from work which occurs in the territory of a State other than the competent State, an inquiry is necessary in the territory of the first State in order to determine any entitlement to relevant benefits, a person may be appointed for that purpose by the competent institution, which shall inform the authorities of that State. The institutions shall cooperate with each other in order to assess all relevant information and to consult the reports and any other documents relating to the accident.

4. Following treatment, a detailed report accompanied by medical certificates relating to the permanent consequences of the accident or disease, in particular the injured person's present state and the recovery or stabilisation of injuries, shall be sent upon request of the competent institution. The relevant fees shall be paid by the institution of the place of residence or of stay, where appropriate, at the rate applied by that institution to the charge of the competent institution.

5. At the request of the institution of the place of residence or stay, where appropriate, the competent institution shall notify it of the decision setting the date for the recovery or stabilisation of injuries and, where appropriate, the decision concerning the granting of a pension.

General Note

5.411 Corresponding provision of Regulation 987/2009: art.34.

Article SSCI.29: Disputes concerning the occupational nature of the accident or disease

5.412 1. Where the competent institution disputes the application of the legislation relating to accidents at work or occupational diseases under Article SSC.31(2) [Right to benefits in kind and in cash] of this Protocol, it shall without delay inform the institution of the place of residence or stay which provided the benefits in kind, which will then be considered as sickness insurance benefits.

2. When a final decision has been taken on that subject, the competent institution shall, without delay, inform the institution of the place of residence or stay which provided the benefits in kind.

Where an accident at work or occupational disease is not established, benefits in kind shall continue to be provided as sickness benefits if the person concerned is entitled to them.

Article SSCI.29

Where an accident at work or occupational disease is established, sickness benefits in kind provided to the person concerned shall be considered as accident at work or occupational disease benefits from the date on which the accident at work occurred or the occupational disease was first medically diagnosed.

3. The second subparagraph of Article SSCI.6(5) [Provisional application of legislation and provisional granting of benefits] of this Annex applies mutatis mutandis.

General Note

Corresponding provision of Regulation 987/2009: art.35. 5.413

Article SSCI.30: Procedure in the event of exposure to the risk of an occupational disease in two or more States

1. In the case referred to in Article SSC.33 [Benefits for an occupational disease where the person suffering from such a disease has been exposed to the same risk in several States] of this Protocol, the declaration or notification of the occupational disease shall be sent to the competent institution for occupational diseases of the last State under the legislation of which the person concerned pursued an activity likely to cause that disease. 5.414

When the institution to which the declaration or notification was sent establishes that an activity likely to cause the occupational disease in question was last pursued under the legislation of another State, it shall send the declaration or notification and all accompanying certificates to the equivalent institution in that State.

2. Where the institution of the last State under the legislation of which the person concerned pursued an activity likely to cause the occupational disease in question establishes that the person concerned or his survivors do not meet the requirements of that legislation, inter alia, because the person concerned had never pursued in that State an activity which caused the occupational disease or because that State does not recognise the occupational nature of the disease, that institution shall forward without delay the declaration or notification and all accompanying certificates, including the findings and reports of medical examinations performed by the first institution to the institution of the previous State under the legislation of which the person concerned pursued an activity likely to cause the occupational disease in question.

3. Where appropriate, the institutions shall reiterate the procedure set out in paragraph 2 going back as far as the equivalent institution in the State under whose legislation the person concerned first pursued an activity likely to cause the occupational disease in question.

General Note

Corresponding provision of Regulation 987/2009: art.36. 5.415

Article SSCI.31: Exchange of information between institutions and advance payments in the event of an appeal against rejection

5.416 1. In the event of an appeal against a decision to refuse benefits taken by the institution of a State under the legislation of which the person concerned pursued an activity likely to cause the occupational disease in question, that institution shall inform the institution to which the declaration or notification was sent, in accordance with the procedure provided for in Article SSCI.30(2) [Procedure in the event of exposure to the risk of an occupational disease in two or more States], and shall subsequently inform it when a final decision is reached.

2. Where a person is entitled to benefits under the legislation applied by the institution to which the declaration or notification was sent, that institution shall make the advance payments, the amount of which shall be determined, where appropriate, after consulting the institution which made the decision against which the appeal was lodged, and in such a way that overpayments are avoided. The latter institution shall reimburse the advance payments made if, as a result of the appeal, it is obliged to provide those benefits. That amount will then be deducted from the benefits due to the person concerned, in accordance with the procedure provided for in Articles SSCI.56 [Benefits received unduly] and 57 [Provisionally paid benefits in cash or contributions].

3. The second subparagraph of Article SSCI.6(5) [Provisional application of legislation and provisional granting of benefits] applies mutatis mutandis.

General Note

5.417 Corresponding provision of Regulation 987/2009: art.37.

Article SSCI.32: Aggravation of an occupational disease

5.418 In the cases covered by Article SSC.34 [Aggravation of an occupational disease] of this Protocol, the claimant must provide the institution in the State from which they are claiming entitlement to benefits with details concerning benefits previously granted for the occupational disease in question. That institution may contact any other previously competent institution in order to obtain the information it considers necessary.

General Note

5.419 Corresponding provision of Regulation 987/2009: art.38.

Article SSCI.33: Assessment of the degree of incapacity in the event of occupational accidents or diseases which occurred previously or subsequently

5.420 Where a previous or subsequent incapacity for work was caused by an accident which occurred when the person concerned was subject to the legislation of a State which makes no distinction according to the origin of the incapacity to work, the competent institution or the body designated by the competent authority of the State in question shall:

(a) upon request by the competent institution of another State, provide information concerning the degree of the previous or subsequent incapacity for work, and where possible, information making it possible to determine whether the incapacity is the result of an accident at work within the meaning of the legislation applied by the institution in the other State;

(b) take into account the degree of incapacity caused by these previous or subsequent cases when determining the right to benefits and the amount, in accordance with the applicable legislation.

General Note

Corresponding provision of Regulation 987/2009: art.39. 5.421

Article SSCI.34: Submission and investigation of claims for pensions or supplementary allowances

In order to receive a pension or supplementary allowance under the legislation of a State, the person concerned or their survivors residing in the territory of another State shall submit, where appropriate, a claim either to the competent institution or to the institution of the place of residence, which shall send it to the competent institution. 5.422

The claim shall contain the information required under the legislation applied by the competent institution.

General Note

Corresponding provision of Regulation 987/2009: art.40. 5.423

CHAPTER 3: DEATH GRANTS

Article SSCI.35: Claim for death grants

For the purposes of applying Articles SSC.37 [Right to grants where death occurs in a State other than the competent one] and SSC.38 [Provision of benefits in the event of the death of a pensioner] of this Protocol, the claim for death grants shall be sent either to the competent institution or to the institution of the claimant's place of residence, which shall send it to the competent institution. 5.424

The claim shall contain the information required under the legislation applied by the competent institution.

General Note

Corresponding provision of Regulation 987/2009: art.42. 5.425

CHAPTER 4: INVALIDITY BENEFITS AND OLD-AGE AND SURVIVORS' PENSIONS

Article SSCI.36: Additional provisions for the calculation of the benefit

5.426 1. For the purposes of calculating the theoretical amount and the actual amount of the benefit in accordance with point (b) of Article SSC.47(1) [Award of benefits] of this Protocol, the rules provided for in Article SSCI.11(3), (4), (5) and (6) [Aggregation of periods] of this Annex apply.

2. Where periods of voluntary or optional continued insurance have not been taken into account under Article SSC.11(3)[Aggregation of periods] of this Annex, the institution of the State under whose legislation those periods were completed shall calculate the amount corresponding to those periods under the legislation it applies. The actual amount of the benefit, calculated in accordance with point (b) of Article SSC.47(1) [Award of benefits] of this Protocol, shall be increased by the amount corresponding to periods of voluntary or optional continued insurance.

3. The institution of each State shall calculate, under the legislation it applies, the amount due corresponding to periods of voluntary or optional continued insurance which, under point (c) of Article SSC.48(3) [Rules to prevent overlapping] of the Protocol, shall not be subject to the another *(sic)* State's rules relating to withdrawal, reduction or suspension.

Where the legislation applied by the competent institution does not allow it to determine this amount directly, on the grounds that that legislation allocates different values to insurance periods, a notional amount may be established. The Specialised Committee on Social Security Coordination shall lay down the detailed arrangements for the determination of that notional amount.

General Note

5.427 Corresponding provision of Regulation 987/2009: art.43.

Article SSCI.37: Claims for benefits

Submission of claims for old-age and survivors' pensions

5.428 1. The claimant shall submit a claim to the institution of his place of residence or to the institution of the last State whose legislation was applicable. If the person concerned was not, at any time, subject to the legislation applied by the institution of the place of residence, that institution shall forward the claim to the institution of the last State whose legislation was applicable.

2. The date of submission of the claim shall apply in all the institutions concerned.

3. By way of derogation from paragraph 2, if the claimant does not, despite having been asked to do so, notify the fact that he or she has been employed or has resided in other States, the date on which the claimant completes his or her initial claim or submits a new claim for his or her missing periods of

employment or/and residence in a State shall be considered as the date of submission of the claim to the institution applying the legislation in question, subject to more favourable provisions of that legislation.

General Note

Corresponding provision of Regulation 987/2009: art.45 paras 4 to 6. 5.429

Article SSCI.38: Certificates and information to be submitted with the claim by the claimant

1. The claim shall be submitted by the claimant in accordance with the provisions of the legislation applied by the institution referred to in Article SSCI.37(1) [Claims for benefits], and be accompanied by the supporting documents required by that legislation. In particular, the claimant shall supply all available relevant information and supporting documents relating to periods of insurance (institutions, identification numbers), employment (employers) or self-employment (nature and place of activity) and residence (addresses) which may have been completed under other legislation, as well as the length of those periods. 5.430

2. Where, in accordance with Article SSC.45(1) [General Provisions] of this Protocol, the claimant requests deferment of the award of old-age benefits under the legislation of one or more States, the claimant shall state that in their claim and specify under which legislation the deferment is requested. In order to enable the claimant to exercise that right, the institutions concerned shall, upon the request of the claimant, notify them of all the information available to them so that he or she can assess the consequences of concurrent or successive awards of benefits which they might claim.

3. Should the claimant withdraw a claim for benefits provided for under the legislation of a particular State, that withdrawal shall not be considered as a concurrent withdrawal of claims for benefits under the legislation of another State.

General Note

Corresponding provision of Regulation 987/2009: art.46. 5.431

Article SSCI.39: Investigation of claims by the institutions concerned

Contact institution

1. The institution to which the claim for benefits is submitted or forwarded in accordance with Article SSCI.37(1) [Claims for benefits] shall be referred to hereinafter as the "contact institution". The institution of the place of residence shall not be referred to as the contact institution if the person concerned has not, at any time, been subject to the legislation which that institution applies. 5.432

In addition to investigating the claim for benefits under the legislation which it applies, this institution shall, in its capacity as contact institution, promote the exchange of data, the communication of decisions and the operations necessary for the investigation of the claim by the institutions concerned, and supply the claimant, upon request, with any information relevant to the aspects of the investigation which arise under this Protocol, and keep the claimant informed of its progress.

Investigation of claims for old-age and survivors pensions

5.433 2. The contact institution shall, without delay, send claims for benefits and all the documents which it has available and, where appropriate, the relevant documents supplied by the claimant to all the institutions in question so that they can all start the investigation of the claim concurrently. The contact institution shall notify the other institutions of periods of insurance or residence subject to its legislation. It shall also indicate which documents shall be submitted at a later date and supplement the claim as soon as possible.

3. Each of the institutions in question shall notify the contact institution and the other institutions in question, as soon as possible, of the periods of insurance or residence subject to their legislation.

4. Each of the institutions in question shall calculate the amount of benefits in accordance with Article SSC.47 [Award of benefits] of this Protocol and shall notify the contact institution and the other institutions concerned of its decision, of the amount of benefits due and of any information required for the purposes of Articles SSC.48 [Rules to prevent overlapping] to SSC.50 [Overlapping of benefits of a different kind] of this Protocol.

5. Should an institution establish, on the basis of the information referred to in paragraphs 2 and 3 of this Article, that Article SSC.52(2) or (3) [Periods of insurance or residence of less than one year] of this Protocol is applicable, it shall inform the contact institution and the other institutions concerned.

General Note

5.434 Corresponding provision of Regulation 987/2009: art.47 paras 1 and 4 to 7.

Article SSCI.40: Notification of decisions to the claimant

5.435 1. Each institution shall notify the claimant of the decision it has taken in accordance with the applicable legislation. Each decision shall specify the remedies and periods allowed for appeals. Once the contact institution has been notified of all decisions taken by each institution, it shall send the claimant and the other institutions concerned a summary of those decisions. A model summary shall be drawn up by the Specialised Committee on Social Security Coordination. The summary shall be sent to the claimant in the language of the institution or, at the request of the claimant, in any language of their choice, including English, recognised as an official language of the Union.

2. Where it appears to the claimant following receipt of the summary that his or her rights may have been adversely affected by the interaction of decisions taken by two or more institutions, the claimant shall have the right to a review of the decisions by the institutions concerned within the time limits laid down in the respective national legislation. The time limits

shall commence on the date of receipt of the summary. The claimant shall be notified of the result of the review in writing.

GENERAL NOTE

Corresponding provision of Regulation 987/2009: art.48. **5.436**

Article SSCI.41: Determination of the degree of invalidity

Each institution shall, in accordance with its legislation, have the possibility of having the claimant examined by a medical doctor or other expert of its choice to determine the degree of invalidity. However, the institution of a State shall take into consideration documents, medical reports and administrative information collected by the institution of any other State as if they had been drawn up in its own territory. **5.437**

GENERAL NOTE

Corresponding provision of Regulation 987/2009: art.49 para.2. **5.438**

Article SSCI.42: Provisional instalments and advance payment of a benefit

1. Notwithstanding Article SSCI.7 [Provisional calculation of benefits and contributions] of this Annex, any institution which establishes, while investigating a claim for benefits, that the claimant is entitled to an independent benefit under the applicable legislation, in accordance with point (a) of Article SSC.47(1) [Award of benefits] of this Protocol, shall pay that benefit without delay. That payment shall be considered provisional if the amount might be affected by the result of the claim investigation procedure. **5.439**

2. Whenever it is evident from the information available that the claimant is entitled to a payment from an institution under point (b) of Article SSC.47(1) [Award of benefits] of this Protocol, that institution shall make an advance payment, the amount of which shall be as close as possible to the amount which will probably be paid under point (b) of Article SSC.47(1) [Award of benefits] of this Protocol.

3. Each institution which is obliged to pay the provisional benefits or advance payment under paragraphs 1 or 2 shall inform the claimant without delay, specifically drawing the claimant's attention to the provisional nature of the measure and any rights of appeal in accordance with its legislation.

GENERAL NOTE

Corresponding provision of Regulation 987/2009: art.50. **5.440**

Article SSCI.43: New calculation of benefits

5.441 1. Where there is a new calculation of benefits in accordance with Articles SSC.45(4) [General provisions] and SSC.54(1) [Recalculation and revaluation of benefits] of this Protocol, Article SSCI.42 [Provisional instalments and advance payment of a benefit] of this Annex shall be applicable mutatis mutandis.

2. Where there is a new calculation, withdrawal or suspension of the benefit, the institution which took the decision shall inform the person concerned without delay and shall inform each of the institutions in respect of which the person concerned has an entitlement.

General Note

5.442 Corresponding provision of Regulation 987/2009: art.51.

Article SSCI.44: Measures intended to accelerate the pension calculation process

5.443 1. In order to facilitate and accelerate the investigation of claims and the payment of benefits, the institutions to whose legislation a person has been subject shall:

(a) exchange with or make available to institutions of other States the elements for identifying persons who change from one applicable national legislation to another, and together ensure that those identification elements are retained and correspond, or, failing that, provide those persons with the means to access their identification elements directly;
(b) sufficiently in advance of the minimum age for commencing pension rights or before an age to be determined by national legislation, exchange with or make available to the person concerned and to institutions of other States information (periods completed or other important elements) on the pension entitlements of persons who have changed from one applicable legislation to another or, failing that, inform those persons of, or provide them with, the means of familiarising themselves with their prospective benefit entitlement.

2. For the purposes of paragraph 1, the Specialised Committee on Social Security Coordination shall determine the elements of information to be exchanged or made available and shall establish the appropriate procedures and mechanisms, taking account of the characteristics, administrative and technical organisation, and the technological means at the disposal of national pension schemes. The Specialised Committee on Social Security Coordination shall ensure the implementation of those pension schemes by organising a follow-up to the measures taken and their application.

3. For the purposes of paragraph 1, the institution in the first State where a person is allocated a Personal Identification Number (PIN) for the purposes of social security administration should be provided with the information referred to in this Article.

General Note

5.444 Corresponding provision of Regulation 987/2009: art.52.

Article SSCI.45

Article SSCI.45: Coordination measures in the States

1. Without prejudice to Article SSC.46 [Special provisions on aggregation of periods] of this Protocol, where national legislation includes rules for determining this institution responsible or the scheme applicable or for designating periods of insurance to a specific scheme, those rules shall be applied, taking into account only periods of insurance completed under the legislation of the State concerned. **5.445**

2. Where national legislation includes rules for the coordination of special schemes for civil servants and the general scheme for employed persons, those rules shall not be affected by the provisions of this Protocol and of this Annex.

General Note

Corresponding provision of Regulation 987/2009: art.53. **5.446**

Chapter 5: Unemployment Benefits

Article SSCI.46: Aggregation of periods and calculation of benefits

1. Article SSCI.11(1) [Aggregation of periods] of this Annex applies mutatis mutandis to Article SSC.56 [Special provisions on aggregation of periods of insurance, employment or self-employment] of this Protocol. Without prejudice to the underlying obligations of the institutions involved, the person concerned may submit to the competent institution a document issued by the institution of the State to whose legislation they were subject in respect of that person's last activity as an employed or self-employed person specifying the periods completed under that legislation. **5.447**

2. For the purposes of applying Article SSC.57 [Calculation of unemployment benefits] of this Protocol, the competent institution of a State whose legislation provides that the calculation of benefits varies with the number of members of the family shall also take into account the members of the family of the person concerned residing in another State as if they resided in the competent State. This provision shall not apply where, in the State of residence of members of the family, another person is entitled to unemployment benefits calculated on the basis of the number of members of the family.

General Note

Corresponding provision of Regulation 987/2009: art.54, paras 1 and 3. **5.448**

Title IV: Financial Provisions

Chapter 1: Reimbursement of the Cost of Benefits in Application of Article SSC.30 [Reimbursements Between Institutions] and

ARTICLE SSC.36 [REIMBURSEMENTS BETWEEN INSTITUTIONS] OF THIS PROTOCOL

5.449 Articles SSCI.47 – SSCl.54 *omitted*

CHAPTER 2: RECOVERY OF BENEFITS PROVIDED BUT NOT DUE, RECOVERY OF PROVISIONAL PAYMENTS AND CONTRIBUTIONS, OFFSETTING AND ASSISTANCE WITH RECOVERY

Section 1: Principles

Article SSCI.55: Common provisions

5.450 For the purposes of applying Article SSC.64 [Collection of contributions and recovery of benefits] of this Protocol and within the framework defined therein, the recovery of claims shall, wherever possible, be by way of offsetting either between the institutions of the Member State concerned and of the United Kingdom, or vis-à-vis the natural or legal person concerned in accordance with Articles SSCI.56 [Benefits received unduly] to SSCI.58 [Costs relating to offsetting] of this Annex. If it is not possible to recover all or any of the claim via this offsetting procedure, the remainder of the amount due shall be recovered in accordance with Articles SSCI.59 [Definitions and common provisions] to SSCI.69 [Costs related to recovery] of this Annex.

GENERAL NOTE

5.451 Corresponding provision of Regulation 987/2009: art.71.

Section 2: Offsetting

Article SSCI.56: Benefits received unduly

5.452 1. If the institution of a State has paid undue benefits to a person, that institution may, within the terms and limits laid down in the legislation it applies, request the institution of the State responsible for paying benefits to the person concerned to deduct the undue amount from arrears or on-going payments owed to the person concerned regardless of the social security branch under which the benefit is paid. The institution of the latter State shall deduct the amount concerned subject to the conditions and limits applying to this kind of offsetting procedure in accordance with the legislation it applies in the same way as if it had made the overpayments itself, and shall transfer the amount deducted to the institution that has paid undue benefits.

2. By way of derogation from paragraph 1, if, when awarding or reviewing benefits in respect of invalidity benefits, old-age and survivors' pensions pursuant to Chapters 3 [Death grants] and 4 [Invalidity benefits] of Title III [Special provisions concerning the various categories of benefits]

of this Protocol, the institution of a State has paid to a person benefits of undue sum, that institution may request the institution of the State responsible for the payment of corresponding benefits to the person concerned to deduct the amount overpaid from the arrears payable to the person concerned. After the latter institution has informed the institution that has paid an undue sum of these arrears, the institution which has paid the undue sum shall within two months communicate the amount of the undue sum. If the institution which is due to pay arrears receives that communication within the deadline it shall transfer the amount deducted to the institution which has paid undue sums. If the deadline expires, that institution shall without delay pay out the arrears to the person concerned.

3. If a person has received social welfare assistance in one State during a period in which they were entitled to benefits under the legislation of another State, the body which provided the assistance may, if it is legally entitled to reclaim the benefits due to the person concerned, request the institution of any other State responsible for paying benefits in favour of the person concerned to deduct the amount of assistance paid from the amounts which that State pays to the person concerned.

This provision applies mutatis mutandis to any family member of a person concerned who has received assistance in the territory of a State during a period in which the insured person was entitled to benefits under the legislation of another State in respect of that family member.

The institution of a State which has paid an undue amount of assistance shall send a statement of the amount due to the institution of the other State, which shall then deduct the amount, subject to the conditions and limits laid down for this kind of offsetting procedure in accordance with the legislation it applies, and transfer the amount without delay to the institution that has paid the undue amount.

General Note

Corresponding provision of Regulation 987/2009: art.72. **5.453**

Article SSCI.57: Provisionally paid benefits in cash or contributions

1. For the purposes of applying Article SSCI.6 [Provisional application of legislation and provisional granting of benefits], at the latest three months after the applicable legislation has been determined or the institution responsible for paying the benefits has been identified, the institution which provisionally paid the cash benefits shall draw up a statement of the amount provisionally paid and shall send it to the institution identified as being competent. **5.454**

The institution identified as being competent for paying the benefits shall deduct the amount due in respect of the provisional payment from the arrears of the corresponding benefits it owes to the person concerned and shall without delay transfer the amount deducted to the institution which provisionally paid the cash benefits.

If the amount of provisionally paid benefits exceeds the amount of arrears, or if arrears do not exist, the institution identified as being competent shall deduct this amount from ongoing payments subject to the conditions and limits applying to this kind of offsetting procedure under the legislation it applies, and without delay transfer the amount deducted to the institution which provisionally paid the cash benefits.

2. The institution which has provisionally received contributions from a legal or natural person shall not reimburse the amounts in question to the person who paid them until it has ascertained from the institution identified as being competent the sums due to it under Article SSCI.6(4) [Provisional application of legislation and provisional granting of benefits].

Upon request of the institution identified as being competent, which shall be made at the latest three months after the applicable legislation has been determined, the institution that has provisionally received contributions shall transfer them to the institution identified as being competent for that period for the purpose of settling the situation concerning the contributions owed by the legal or natural person to it. The contributions transferred shall be retroactively deemed as having been paid to the institution identified as being competent.

If the amount of provisionally paid contributions exceeds the amount the legal or natural person owes to the institution identified as being competent, the institution which provisionally received contributions shall reimburse the amount in excess to the legal or natural person concerned.

General Note

5.455 Corresponding provision of Regulation 987/2009: art.73.

Article SSCI.58: Costs related to offsetting

5.456 No costs are payable where the debt is recovered via the offsetting procedure provided for in Articles SSCI.56 [Benefits received unduly] and SSCI.57 [Provisionally paid benefits in cash or contributions].

General Note

5.457 Corresponding provision of Regulation 987/2009: art.74.

Section 3: Recovery

Article SSCI.59: Definitions and common provisions

5.458 1. For the purposes of this Section:

- "claim" means all claims relating to contributions or to benefits paid or provided unduly, including interest, fines, administrative penalties and all other charges and costs connected with the claim in accordance with the legislation of the State making the claim;
- "applicant party" means, in respect of each State, any institution which makes a request for information, notification or recovery concerning a claim as defined above;
- "requested party" means, in respect of each State, any institution to which a request for information, notification or recovery can be made.

2. Requests and any related communications between the States shall, in general, be addressed via designated institutions.

3. Practical implementation measures, including, among others, those related to Article SSCI.4 [Forms, documents and methods of exchanging data], and to setting a minimum threshold for the amounts for which a request for recovery can be made, shall be taken by the Specialised Committee on Social Security Coordination.

General Note

Corresponding provision of Regulation 987/2009: art.75. **5.459**

Article SSCI.60: Requests for information

1. At the request of the applicant party, the requested party shall provide any information which would be useful to the applicant party in the recovery of its claim. **5.460**

2. In order to obtain that information, the requested party shall make use of the powers provided for under the laws, regulations or administrative practices applying to the recovery of similar claims arising in its own State. The request for information shall indicate the name, last known address, and any other relevant information relating to the identification of the legal or natural person concerned to whom the information to be provided relates and the nature and amount of the claim in respect of which the request is made.

3. The requested party shall not be obliged to supply information:

(a) which it would not be able to obtain for the purpose of recovering similar claims arising in its own territory;

(b) which would disclose any commercial, industrial or professional secrets; or

(c) the disclosure of which would be liable to prejudice the security of or be contrary to the public policy of a State.

4. The requested party shall inform the applicant party of the grounds for refusing a request for information.

General Note

Corresponding provision of Regulation 987/2009: art.76. **5.461**

Article SSCI.61: Notification

1. The requested party shall, at the request of the applicant party, and in accordance with the rules in force for the notification of similar instruments or decisions in its own territory, notify the addressee of all instruments and decisions, including those of a judicial nature, which come from the State of the applicant party and which relate to a claim or to its recovery. **5.462**

2. The request for notification shall indicate the name, address and any other relevant information relating to the identification of the addressee concerned to which the applicant party normally has access, the nature and the subject of the instrument or decision to be notified and, if necessary the

name, address and any other relevant information relating to the identification of the debtor and the claim to which the instrument or decision relates, and any other useful information.

3. The requested party shall without delay inform the applicant party of the action taken on its request for notification and, particularly, of the date on which the decision or instrument was forwarded to the addressee.

General Note

5.463 Corresponding provision of Regulation 987/2009: art.77.

Article SSCI.62: Request for recovery

5.464 1. At the request of the applicant party, the requested party shall recover claims that are the subject of an instrument permitting enforcement issued by the applicant party to the extent permitted by and in accordance with the laws and administrative practices in force in the State of the requested party.

2. The applicant party may only make a request for recovery if:

(a) it also provides to the requested party an official or certified copy of the instrument permitting enforcement of the claim in the State of the applicant party, except in cases where Article SSCI.64(3) [Payment arrangements and deadline] is applied;

(b) the claim or instrument permitting its enforcement are not contested in its own State;

(c) it has, in its own State, applied appropriate recovery procedures available to it on the basis of the instrument referred to in paragraph 1, and the measures taken will not result in the payment in full of the claim;

(d) the period of limitation according to its own legislation has not expired.

3. The request for recovery shall indicate:

(a) the name, address and any other relevant information relating to the identification of the natural or legal person concerned or to the identification of any third party holding that person's assets;

(b) the name, address and any other relevant information relating to the identification of the applicant party;

(c) a reference to the instrument permitting its enforcement, issued in the State of the applicant party;

(d) the nature and amount of the claim, including the principal, interest, fines, administrative penalties and all other charges and costs due indicated in the currencies of the State(s) of the applicant and requested parties;

(e) the date of notification of the instrument to the addressee by the applicant party or by the requested party;

(f) the date from which and the period during which enforcement is possible under the laws in force in the State of the applicant party;

(g) any other relevant information.

4. The request for recovery shall also contain a declaration by the applicant party confirming that the conditions laid down in paragraph 2 have been fulfilled.

5. The applicant party shall forward to the requested party any relevant information relating to the matter which gave rise to the request for recovery, as soon as this comes to its knowledge.

General Note

Corresponding provision of Regulation 987/2009: art.78. Para. 2(d) has been added. **5.465**

Article SSCI.63: Instrument permitting enforcement of recovery

1. In accordance with Article SSC.64(2) [Collection of contributions and recovery of benefits] of this Protocol, the instrument permitting enforcement of the claim shall be directly recognised and treated automatically as an instrument permitting the enforcement of a claim of the State of the requested party. **5.466**

2. Notwithstanding paragraph 1, the instrument permitting enforcement of the claim may, where appropriate and in accordance with the provisions in force in the State of the requested party, be accepted as, recognised as, supplemented with, or replaced by an instrument authorising enforcement in the territory of that State.

Within three months of the date of receipt of the request for recovery, the State(s) shall endeavour to complete the acceptance, recognition, supplementing or replacement, except in cases where the third subparagraph of this paragraph applies. States may not refuse to complete these actions where the instrument permitting enforcement is properly drawn up. The requested party shall inform the applicant party of the grounds for exceeding the three-month period.

If any of these actions should give rise to a dispute in connection with the claim or the instrument permitting enforcement issued by the applicant party, Article SSCI.65 [Contestation concerning the claim or the instrument permitting enforcement of its recovery and contestation concerning enforcement measures] shall apply.

General Note

Corresponding provision of Regulation 987/2009: art.79. **5.467**

Article SSCI.64: Payment arrangements and deadline

1. Claims shall be recovered in the currency of the State of the requested party. The entire amount of the claim that is recovered by the requested party shall be remitted by the requested party to the applicant party. **5.468**

2. The requested party may, where the laws, regulations or administrative provisions in force in its own State so permit, and after consulting the applicant party, allow the debtor time to pay or authorise payment by instalment. Any interest charged by the requested party in respect of such extra time to pay shall also be remitted to the applicant party.

3. From the date on which the instrument permitting enforcement of the recovery of the claim has been directly recognised in accordance with Article SSCI.63(1) [Instrument permitting enforcement of recovery], or accepted, recognised, supplemented or replaced in accordance with Article SSCI.63(2) [Instrument permitting enforcement of recovery], interest shall be charged for late payment under the laws, regulations and administrative

provisions in force in the State of the requested party and shall also be remitted to the applicant party.

General Note

5.469 Corresponding provision of Regulation 987/2009: art.80.

Article SSCI.65: Contestation concerning the claim or the instrument permitting enforcement of its recovery and contestation concerning enforcement measures

5.470 1. If, in the course of the recovery procedure, the claim or the instrument permitting its enforcement issued in the State of the applicant party are contested by an interested party, the action shall be brought by this party before the appropriate authorities of the State of the applicant party, in accordance with the laws in force in that State. The applicant party shall without delay notify the requested party of this action. The interested party may also inform the requested party of the action.

2. As soon as the requested party has received the notification or information referred to in paragraph 1 either from the applicant party or from the interested party, it shall suspend the enforcement procedure pending the decision of the appropriate authority in the matter, unless the applicant party requests otherwise in accordance with the second subparagraph of this paragraph. Should the requested party deem it necessary, and without prejudice to Article SSCI.68 [Precautionary measures], it may take precautionary measures to guarantee recovery insofar as the laws or regulations in force in its own State allow such action for similar claims.

Notwithstanding the first subparagraph, the applicant party may, in accordance with the laws, regulations and administrative practices in force in its own State, request the requested party to recover a contested claim, insofar as the relevant laws, regulations and administrative practices in force in the requested party's State allow such action. If the result of the contestation is subsequently favourable to the debtor, the applicant party shall be liable for the reimbursement of any sums recovered, together with any compensation due, in accordance with the legislation in force in the requested party's State.

3. Where the contestation concerns enforcement measures taken in the State of the requested party, the action shall be brought before the appropriate authority of that State in accordance with its laws and regulations.

4. Where the appropriate authority before which the action is brought in accordance with paragraph 1 is a judicial or administrative tribunal, the decision of that tribunal, insofar as it is favourable to the applicant party and permits recovery of the claim in the State of the applicant party, shall constitute the "instrument permitting enforcement" within the meaning of Articles SSCI.62 [Request for recovery] and SSCI.63 [Instrument permitting enforcement of recovery] and the recovery of the claim shall proceed on the basis of that decision.

General Note

5.471 Corresponding provision of Regulation 987/2009: art.81.

Article SSCI.66: Limits applying to assistance

1. The requested party shall not be obliged: **5.472**

(a) to grant the assistance provided for in Articles SSCI.62 [Request for recovery] to SSCI.65 [Contestation concerning the claim or the instrument permitting enforcement of its recovery and contestation concerning enforcement measures], if recovery of the claim would, because of the situation of the debtor, create serious economic or social difficulties in the State of the requested party, insofar as the laws, regulations or administrative practices in force in the State of the requested party allow such action for similar national claims;

(b) to grant the assistance provided for in Articles SSCI.60 [Request for information] to SSCI.65 [Contestation concerning the claim or the instrument permitting enforcement of its recovery and contestation concerning enforcement measures], if the initial request under Articles SSCI.60 [Request for information] to SSCI.62 [Request for recovery] applies to claims more than five years old, dating from the moment the instrument permitting the recovery was established in accordance with the laws, regulations or administrative practices in force in the State of the applicant party at the date of the request. However, if the claim or instrument is contested, the time limit begins from the moment that the State of the applicant party establishes that the claim or the enforcement order permitting recovery may no longer be contested.

2. The requested party shall inform the applicant party of the grounds for refusing a request for assistance.

General Note

Corresponding provision of Regulation 987/2009: art.82. **5.473**

Article SSCI.67: Periods of limitation

1. Questions concerning periods of limitation shall be governed as follows: **5.474**

(a) by the laws in force in the State of the applicant party, insofar as they concern the claim or the instrument permitting its enforcement; and

(b) by the laws in force in the State of the requested party, insofar as they concern enforcement measures in the requested State.

Periods of limitation according to the laws in force in the State of the requested party shall start from the date of direct recognition or from the date of acceptance, recognition, supplementing or replacement in accordance with Article SSCI.63 [Instrument permitting enforcement of recovery].

2. Steps taken in the recovery of claims by the requested party in pursuance of a request for assistance, which, if they had been carried out by the applicant party, would have had the effect of suspending or interrupting the period of limitation according to the laws in force in the State of the applicant party, shall be deemed to have been taken in the latter, insofar as that effect is concerned.

General Note

5.475 Corresponding provision of Regulation 987/2009: art.83.

Article SSCI.68: Precautionary measures

5.476 Upon reasoned request by the applicant party, the requested party shall take precautionary measures to ensure recovery of a claim insofar as the laws and regulations in force in the State of the requested party so permit.

For the purposes of implementing the first paragraph, the provisions and procedures laid down in Articles SSCI.62 [Request for recovery], SSCI.63 [Instrument permitting enforcement of recovery], SSCI.65 [Contestation concerning the claim or the instrument permitting enforcement of its recovery and contestation concerning enforcement measures] and SSCI.66 [Limits applying to assistance] of this Annex apply mutatis mutandis.

General Note

5.477 Corresponding provision of Regulation 987/2009: art.84.

Article SSCI.69: Costs related to recovery

5.478 1. The requested party shall recover from the natural or legal person concerned and retain any costs linked to recovery which it incurs, in accordance with the laws and regulations of the State of the requested party that apply to similar claims.

2. Mutual assistance afforded under this Section shall, as a rule, be free of charge. However, where recovery poses a specific problem or concerns a very large amount in costs, the applicant and the requested parties may agree on reimbursement arrangements specific to the cases in question.

The State of the applicant party shall remain liable to the State of the requested party for any costs and any losses incurred as a result of actions held to be unfounded, as far as either the substance of the claim or the validity of the instrument issued by the applicant party is concerned.

General Note

5.479 Corresponding provision of Regulation 987/2009: art.85.

Title V: Miscellaneous, Transitional and Final Provisions

Article SSCI.70: Medical examination and administrative checks

5.480 1. Without prejudice to other provisions, where a recipient or a claimant of benefits, or a member of that person's family, is staying or residing within the territory of a State other than that in which the debtor institution is located, the medical examination shall be carried out, at the request of that institution, by the institution of the beneficiary's place of stay or residence in accordance with the procedures laid down by the legislation applied by that institution.

Article SSCI.70

The debtor institution shall inform the institution of the place of stay or residence of any special requirements, if necessary, to be followed and points to be covered by the medical examination.

2. The institution of the place of stay or residence shall forward a report to the debtor institution that requested the medical examination. This institution shall be bound by the findings of the institution of the place of stay or residence.

The debtor institution shall reserve the right to have the beneficiary examined by a doctor of its choice. However, the beneficiary may be asked to return to the State of the debtor institution only if that beneficiary is able to make the journey without prejudice to that person's health and the cost of travel and accommodation is paid for by the debtor institution.

3. Where a recipient or a claimant of benefits, or a member of that person's family, is staying or residing in the territory of a State other than that in which the debtor institution is located, the administrative check shall, at the request of the debtor institution, be performed by the institution of the beneficiary's place of stay or residence.

Paragraph 2 shall also apply in this case.

4. As an exception to the principle of free-of-charge mutual administrative cooperation in Article SSC.59(3) [Cooperation] of this Protocol, the effective amount of the expenses of the checks referred to in paragraphs 1 to 3 shall be refunded to the institution which was requested to carry them out by the debtor institution which requested them.

GENERAL NOTE

Corresponding provision of Regulation 987/2009: art.87. paras 1-3 and 6. 5.481

Article SSCI.71: Notifications

1. The States shall notify the Specialised Committee on Social Security Coordination of the details of the bodies and entities defined in Article SSC.1 [Definitions] of the Protocol and points (a) and (b) of Article SSCI.1(2) [Definitions] of this Annex, and of the institutions designated in accordance with this Annex. 5.482

2. The bodies specified in paragraph 1 shall be provided with an electronic identity in the form of an identification code and electronic address.

3. The Specialised Committee on Social Security Coordination shall establish the structure, content and detailed arrangements, including the common format and model, for notification of the details specified in paragraph 1.

4. For the purposes of implementing this Protocol, the United Kingdom may take part in the Electronic Exchange of Social Security Information and bear the related costs.

5. The States shall be responsible for keeping the information specified in paragraph 1 up to date.

GENERAL NOTE

Corresponding provision of Regulation 987/2009: art.88. 5.483

Article SSCI.72: Information

5.484 The Specialised Committee on Social Security Coordination shall prepare the information needed to ensure that the parties concerned are aware of their rights and the administrative formalities required in order to assert them. This information shall, where possible, be disseminated electronically via publication online on sites accessible to the public. The Specialised Committee on Social Security Coordination shall ensure that the information is regularly updated and monitor the quality of services provided to customers.

General Note

5.485 Corresponding provision of Regulation 987/2009: art.89.

Article SSCI.73: Currency conversion

5.486 For the purposes of this Protocol and this Annex, the exchange rate between two currencies shall be the reference rate published by the financial institution designated for this purpose by the Specialised Committee on Social Security Coordination. The date to be taken into account for determining the exchange rate shall be fixed by the Specialised Committee on Social Security Coordination.

General Note

5.487 Corresponding provision of Regulation 987/2009: art.90.

Article SSCI.74: Implementing provisions

5.488 The Specialised Committee on Social Security Coordination may adopt further guidance on the implementation of this Protocol and of this Annex.

Article SSCI.75: Interim provisions for forms and documents

5.489 1. For an interim period, the end date of which shall be agreed by the Specialised Committee on Social Security Coordination, all forms and documents issued by the competent institutions in the format used immediately before this Protocol comes into force shall be valid for the purposes of implementing this Protocol and, where appropriate, shall continue to be used for the exchange of information between competent institutions. All such forms and documents issued before and during that interim period shall be valid until their expiry or cancellation.

2. The forms and documents valid in accordance with paragraph 1 include:

(a) European Health Insurance Cards issued on behalf of the United Kingdom, which shall be valid entitlement documents for the purposes of Article SSC.17 [Stay outside the competent State], and Article SSC.25(1) [Stay of the pensioner or the members of their family in a State other than the State of residence – stay in the competent State – authorisation for appropriate treatment outside the State of residence] of this Protocol and SSCI.22 [Stay in a State other than the competent State] of this Annex; and

(b) Portable documents which certify a person's social security situation as required to give effect to the Protocol.

Appendix SSCI-1: Administrative Arrangements Between Two or More States (Referred to in Article SSCI.8 Of This Annex)

BELGIUM — UNITED KINGDOM

The Exchange of Letters of 4 May and 14 June 1976 regarding Article 105(2) of Regulation (EEC) No 574/72 (waiving of reimbursement of the costs of administrative checks and medical examinations) **5.490**

The Exchange of Letters of 18 January and 14 March 1977 regarding Article 36(3) of Regulation (EEC) No 1408/71 (arrangement for reimbursement or waiving of reimbursement of the costs of benefits in kind provided under the terms of Chapter 1 of Title III of Regulation (EEC) No 1408/71) as amended by the Exchange of Letters of 4 May and 23 July 1982 (agreement for reimbursement of costs incurred under Article 22(1)(a) of Regulation (EEC) No 1408/71)

DENMARK — UNITED KINGDOM

The Exchange of Letters of 30 March and 19 April 1977 as modified by an Exchange of Letters of 8 November 1989 and of 10 January 1990 on agreement of waiving of reimbursement of the costs of benefits in kind and administrative checks and medical examinations

ESTONIA — UNITED KINGDOM

The Arrangement finalised on 29 March 2006 between the Competent Authorities of the Republic of Estonia and of the United Kingdom under Article 36(3) and 63(3) of Regulation (EEC) No 1408/71 establishing other methods of reimbursement of the costs of benefits in kind provided under Regulation (EC) No 883/2004 by both countries with effect from 1 May 2004

FINLAND — UNITED KINGDOM

The Exchange of Letters 1 and 20 June 1995 concerning Article 36(3) and 63(3) of Regulation (EEC) No 1408/71 (reimbursement or waiving of reimbursement of the cost of benefits in kind) and Article 105(2) of Regulation (EEC) 574/72 (waiving of reimbursement of the cost of administrative checks and medical examinations)

FRANCE — UNITED KINGDOM

The Exchange of Letters of 25 March and 28 April 1997 regarding Article 105(2) of Regulation (EEC) No 574/72 (waiving of reimbursement of the costs of administrative checks and medical examinations)

The Agreement of 8 December 1998 on the specific methods of determining the amounts to be reimbursed for benefits in kind pursuant to Regulations (EEC) No 1408/71 and (EEC) No 574/72

HUNGARY — UNITED KINGDOM

The Arrangement finalised on 1 November 2005 between the Competent Authorities of the Republic of Hungary and of the United Kingdom under Article 35(3) and 41(2) of Regulation (EEC) No 883/2004 establishing other methods of reimbursement of the costs of benefits in kind provided under that Regulation by both countries with effect from 1 May 2004

IRELAND — UNITED KINGDOM

The Exchange of Letters of 9 July 1975 regarding Article 36(3) and 63(3) of Regulation (EEC) No 1408/71 (arrangement for reimbursement or waiving of reimbursement of the costs of benefits in kind provided under the terms of Chapter 1 or 4 of Title III of Regulation (EEC) No 1408/71) and Article 105(2) of Regulation (EEC) No 574/72 (waiving of reimbursement of the costs of administrative checks and medical examinations)

ITALY — UNITED KINGDOM

The Arrangement signed on 15 December 2005 between the Competent Authorities of the Italian Republic and of the United Kingdom under Article 36(3) and 63(3) of Regulation (EEC) No 1408/71 establishing other methods of reimbursement of the costs of benefits in kind provided under Regulation (EC) No 883/2004 by both countries with effect from 1 January 2005

LUXEMBOURG — UNITED KINGDOM

The Exchange of Letters of 18 December 1975 and 20 January 1976 regarding Article 105(2) of Regulation (EEC) No 574/72 (waiving of reimbursement of the costs entailed in administrative checks and medical examinations referred to in Article 105 of Regulation (EEC) No 574/72)

MALTA — UNITED KINGDOM

The Arrangement finalised on 17 January 2007 between the Competent Authorities of Malta and of the United Kingdom under Article 35(3) and 41(2) of Regulation (EEC) No 883/2004 establishing other methods of reimbursement of the costs of benefits in kind provided under that Regulation by both countries with effect from 1 May 2004

NETHERLANDS — UNITED KINGDOM

The second sentence of Article 3 of the Administrative Arrangement of 12 June 1956 on the implementation of the Convention of 11 August 1954

PORTUGAL — UNITED KINGDOM

The Arrangement of 8 June 2004 establishing other methods of reimbursement of the costs of benefits in kind provided by both countries with effect from 1 January 2003

SPAIN — UNITED KINGDOM

The Agreement of 18 June 1999 on the reimbursement of costs for benefits in kind granted pursuant to the provisions of Regulations (EEC) No 1408/71 and (EEC) No 574/72

SWEDEN — UNITED KINGDOM

The Arrangement of 15 April 1997 concerning Article 36(3) and Article 63(3) of Regulation (EEC) No 1408/71 (reimbursement or waiving of reimbursement of the cost of benefits in kind) and Article 105(2) of Regulation (EEC) No 574/72 (waiving of refunds of the costs of administrative checks and medical examinations)

APPENDIX SSCI-2

ENTITLEMENT DOCUMENT

(Article SSC.17 [Stay outside the competent State], and Article SSC.25(1) [Stay of the pensioner or the members of their family in a State other than the State of residence – stay in the competent State – authorisation for appropriate treatment outside the State of residence] of this Protocol and SSCI.22 [Stay in a State other than the competent State] of this Annex. **5.491**

1. Entitlement documents issued for the purposes of Article SSC.17 [Stay outside the competent State] and Article SSC.25(1) [Stay of the pensioner or the members of their family in a State other than the State of residence – stay in the competent State – authorisation for appropriate treatment outside the State of residence] of this Protocol by the competent institutions of Member States shall comply with Decision No S2 of 12 June 2009 of the Administrative Commission concerning the technical specifications of the European Health Insurance Card.

2. Entitlement documents issued for the purposes of Article SSC.17 [Stay outside the competent State] and Article SSC.25(1) [Stay of the pensioner or the members of their family in a State other than the State of residence – stay in the competent State – authorisation for appropriate treatment outside the State of residence] by the competent institutions of the United Kingdom shall contain the following data:

(a) surname and forename of the document holder;
(b) personal identification number of the document holder;
(c) date of birth of the document holder;
(d) expiry date of the document;
(e) the code “UK” in lieu of the ISO code of the United Kingdom;
(f) identification number and acronym of the United Kingdom institution issuing the document;
(g) logical number of the document;
(h) in the case of a provisional document, the date of issue and date of delivery of the document, and the signature and stamp of the United Kingdom institution.

3. The technical specifications of entitlement documents issued by the United Kingdom shall be notified without delay to the Specialised Committee on Social Security Coordination in order to facilitate the acceptance of the respective documents by institutions of the Member States providing the benefits in kind.

Benefits in Kind Requiring Prior Agreement

5.492 (Article SSC.17 [Stay outside the competent State] and Article SSC.25(1) [Stay of the pensioner or the members of their family in a State other than the State of residence – stay in the competent State – authorisation for appropriate treatment outside the State of residence] of this Protocol)

1. The benefits in kind to be provided under Article SSC.17 [Stay outside the competent State] and Article SSC.25(1) [Stay of the pensioner or the members of their family in a State other than the State of residence – stay in the competent State – authorisation for appropriate treatment outside the State of residence] of this Protocol shall include benefits provided in conjunction with chronic or existing illnesses as well as in conjunction with pregnancy and childbirth.

2. Benefits in kind, including those in conjunction with chronic or existing illnesses or in conjunction with childbirth, are not covered by these provisions when the objective of the stay in another State is to receive these treatments.

3. Any vital medical treatment which is only accessible in a specialised medical unit or given by specialised staff or equipment must be subject to a prior agreement between the insured person and the unit providing the treatment in order to ensure that the treatment is available during the insured person's stay in a State other than the competent State or the one of residence.

4. A non-exhaustive list of the treatments which fulfil these criteria is the following:

(a) kidney dialysis;
(b) oxygen therapy;
(c) special asthma treatment;
(d) echocardiography in case of chronic autoimmune diseases;
(e) chemotherapy.

Appendix SSCI-3 States Claiming the Reimbursement of the Cost of Benefits in Kind on the Basis of Fixed Amounts

(Referred to in Article SSCI.48(1) [Identification of the State(s) Concerned] of this Annex

5.493 IRELAND
SPAIN
CYPRUS
PORTUGAL

SWEDEN
UNITED KINGDOM

Annex SSC-8: Transitional Provisions Regarding the Application of Article SSC.11

[Detached Workers]

Member states 5.494

INDEX

This index has been prepared using Sweet and Maxwell's Legal Taxonomy. Main index entries conform to keywords provided by the Legal Taxonomy except where references to specific documents or non-standard terms (denoted by quotation marks) have been included. These keywords provide a means of identifying similar concepts in other Sweet & Maxwell publications and online services to which keywords from the Legal Taxonomy have been applied. Readers may find some minor differences between terms used in the text and those which appear in the index. Suggestions to *sweetandmaxwell.taxonomy@thomson.com.*

(All references are to paragraph number)